SELECTED COMMERCIAL STATUTES

FOR PAYMENT SYSTEMS COURSES

2019 Edition

Advisory Panel

CAROL L. CHOMSKY
Professor of Law
University of Minnesota Law School

CHRISTINA L. KUNZ
Professor Emerita
Mitchell Hamline School of Law

ELIZABETH R. SCHILTZ
Herrick Professor of Law
University of St. Thomas School of Law

CHARLES J. TABB
Mildred Van Voorhis Jones Chair in Law
University of Illinois College of Law

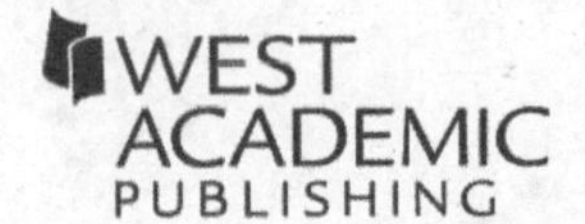

444 Cedar Street, Suite 700
St. Paul, MN 55101
1-877-888-1330

Printed in the United States of America

ISBN: 978-1-68467-009-3

PREFACE

As commercial law professors who use statutory law supplements in our own classes, the four of us on the Advisory Panel welcome the opportunity to continue shaping this mainstay of commercial law teaching to serve the evolving needs of students and teachers. Although the statutes and codes included in the volume are available electronically, a one-volume annotatable hard-copy resource remains a valuable tool for teaching and learning the provisions. From our experience updating the compilation each year, we also know the amount of work involved in creating a usable reference tool, making the continued publication of the statutory law supplements a worthwhile endeavor.

Our goal is to offer a set of supplements that will meet the needs of the teachers of most commercial law subjects. We reconsider decisions on content each year, so we hope that you will let us know how this version served you. We thank faculty who provided feedback in the survey we conducted in early 2019, the results of which are reflected in our decisions about what to include or omit in this year's volumes.

In 2019, West Academic is publishing a comprehensive statutory supplement (a useful tool for students taking more than one commercial law course) as well as abridged volumes appropriate for use in courses on secured transactions, sales and contracts, or payment systems. The materials in each volume reflect changes through the dates noted for each provision. We have indicated where to find changes in law adopted after those dates. Where we have identified typographical errors and outdated cross-references, we have included corrections in square brackets and italics, e.g., [*unrevised Article 1*].

As we determine what to include or exclude from the comprehensive supplement and how to maximize the usability of the volume, we are constrained by publishing parameters that limit the volume's maximum size, so page thickness, margin size, and font size must be chosen to avoid increasing the size of the comprehensive volume. The price of the book must also stay competitive and within the reach of law students; dividing the comprehensive supplement into multiple volumes to make it less bulky to use (as has been suggested to us) would result in increased cost. While the comprehensive supplement necessarily remains long and somewhat bulky, the abridged volumes are slimmer and more transportable. This year, we trimmed from each of the abridged volumes material we think is not used by most teachers of the targeted subjects to make them more practical for students who do not need a volume for multiple courses.

With these constraints in mind and based on our own judgments and discussions with other commercial law professors, we made the following selection decisions:

- The volumes contain the current Uniform Commercial Code (UCC), reflecting all amendments and revisions adopted by the American Law Institute (ALI) and the Uniform Law Commission (ULC) and thus dated 2019. The comprehensive volume contains the entire UCC. The abridged volumes omit portions of the UCC not typically taught in the targeted courses to make those volumes slimmer for easier handling.

- Where appropriate, the volumes also contain older versions of UCC Articles still in transition. For that reason, the comprehensive and Payments volumes include both the 1990 version of and the 2002 amendments to Articles 3 and 4, because those three different versions are in effect across enacting jurisdictions. The Sales and Contracts volume contains the 2000 version of Article 1 because so many older Article 2 cases contain references to that unrevised version.

- We have not included in any of the volumes the 2003 amendments to Articles 2 and 2A, except those made as part of the Article 7 revisions, because they were withdrawn by the ULC and the ALI in May 2011. The amendments are available on Westlaw for historical reference.

- Professors differ widely on which international sources they teach, if any. We omit some suggested sources (for instance, the ICC's Incoterms) because copyright permission fees would make the book too expensive. Some less frequently used international sources (for instance,

UNIDROIT and UNCITRAL) are readily available online and should be accessed there, to keep the book less expensive and less unwieldy for its users. For online access to those materials, see:

www.uncitral.org
www.unidroit.org
www.iccwbo.org

- These statutory supplements cannot include the wide variety of material treated in consumer law classes without becoming too bulky for other use. The supplements will nonetheless be adequate for use with consumer law books that have incorporated much of the non-commercial law material directly into their texts.
- We have included links to, rather than full text of, lengthy material previously incorporated that we think is used infrequently (Regulation CC Commentary and Official Interpretations of Regulation E) to reduce the length of the volume without sacrificing critical content.
- For teachers who cover bankruptcy topics in their commercial law courses, the comprehensive supplement and the Secured Transactions volume include the bankruptcy statute; the comprehensive volume also includes the bankruptcy rules. For the bankruptcy forms, we refer the user to a site for electronic access, where the forms may be completed electronically and are updated to reflect any changes made in the annual revision cycle.

Advisory Panel:

Prof. Carol L. Chomsky, University of Minnesota Law School, Minneapolis, MN
Prof. Emerita Christina L. Kunz, Mitchell Hamline School of Law, St. Paul, MN
Prof. Elizabeth R. Schiltz, University of St. Thomas School of Law, Minneapolis, MN
Prof. Charles J. Tabb, University of Illinois College of Law, Champaign, IL

April 2019

STUDENT GUIDE: HOW TO USE THE UCC

The Uniform Commercial Code (UCC) was first promulgated in the 1950s and has been widely enacted throughout the United States. The UCC is not a static product, however. The Permanent Editorial Board for the Uniform Commercial Code, composed of members from the American Law Institute (ALI) and the Uniform Law Commission (ULC), advises its member organizations on further changes needed in the UCC and prepares commentaries to interpret its provisions.

In the years since first adoption of the UCC, additional Articles expanded coverage into emerging areas of law (Article 2A on leases of goods in 1987, Article 4A on funds transfers in 1989). Articles were deleted if no longer necessary in light of modern commercial realities (Article 6 on bulk sales in 1989). Articles were revised to modernize the law (Article 3 on negotiable instruments and Article 4 on bank deposits and collections in 1990, Article 8 on investment securities in 1994, Article 5 on letters of credit in 1995, Article 9 on secured transactions in 1998, Article 1 containing definitions and rules applicable throughout the UCC in 2001, Article 7 on documents of title in 2003). Regular consideration of amendments has kept the UCC current with new developments in commercial practices, including concerns related to electronic commerce and consumer protection.

While most revisions and amendments are adopted by many or all jurisdictions, not all revisions are successful or lasting. In 2003, a set of amendments to Article 2 (sales) and Article 2A (leases) was approved by ALI and ULC, but the amendments were withdrawn from the Official Text in 2011 after no state legislatures adopted them. The withdrawn amendments are not included in this volume, although they remain of historical interest.

To effectively use the UCC in this volume, you should be aware of the following choices about the substance and format:

- The American Law Institute (ALI) and the Uniform Law Commission (ULC, formerly known as the National Conference of Commissioners on Uniform State Laws) has promulgated the Official Text of the Uniform Commercial Code in a series of enactments, followed by subsequent modifications that may take the form of changes to individual sections or redrafts of a whole Article. When referring to such modifications, we use the terms "amended" or "amendment" to refer to changes in language of individual sections. We use the term "revised" or "revision" to refer to a rewrite of an entire UCC Article.
- The comprehensive volume contains the entire UCC. The abridged volumes contain only the Articles of the UCC generally used in the related courses. All of the Articles contained in each volume are the current versions, reflecting all amendments and revisions adopted by the ALI and ULC, and thus dated 2019. Older versions of Articles are included if they are still in use in some jurisdictions or the older version is referenced in many judicial opinions that are likely to be used in teaching.
- The first page of each Article of the UCC indicates the history of adoption of the Article and its amendments and shows where in the appendices to find earlier versions, revisions, and amendments, if included.
- Commentaries written by the PEB [Permanent Editorial Board of the UCC] are included in an Appendix to the UCC. The comprehensive volume contains all the commentaries except those that have been superseded by subsequent revisions to the UCC. The abridged volumes contain only the commentaries typically covered in the related courses.

For additional source material on the history of the adoption of UCC sections, see

www.ali.org
www.uniformlaws.org

The Uniform Law Commission website (*www.uniformlaws.org*) contains information on pending legislation and enactments of each Article of the UCC.

TABLE OF CONTENTS

UNIFORM COMMERCIAL CODE*

The American Law Institute
and the
Uniform Law Commission

UNIFORM COMMERCIAL CODE (2019)

Articles 1, 3, 4, 4A, 5, and 7.

ARTICLE 1. GENERAL PROVISIONS

PART 1. GENERAL PROVISIONS

PART 2. GENERAL DEFINITIONS AND PRINCIPLES OF INTERPRETATION

PART 3. TERRITORIAL APPLICABILITY AND GENERAL RULES

* * *

ARTICLE 3. NEGOTIABLE INSTRUMENTS

PART 1. GENERAL PROVISIONS AND DEFINITIONS

PART 3. EXECUTION OF SENDER'S PAYMENT ORDER BY RECEIVING BANK

PART 4. PAYMENT

PART 5. MISCELLANEOUS PROVISIONS

ARTICLE 5. LETTERS OF CREDIT

* * *

UNIFORM COMMERCIAL CODE

ARTICLE 7. DOCUMENTS OF TITLE

PART 1. GENERAL

PART 2. WAREHOUSE RECEIPTS: SPECIAL PROVISIONS

PART 3. BILLS OF LADING: SPECIAL PROVISIONS

PART 4. WAREHOUSE RECEIPTS AND BILLS OF LADING: GENERAL OBLIGATIONS

PART 5. WAREHOUSE RECEIPTS AND BILLS OF LADING: NEGOTIATION AND TRANSFER

UCC ARTICLE 1 (2019)

GENERAL PROVISIONS

Article 1 was revised in 2001 and amended in 2017 and 2018.

In 2018, the ALI and ULC approved amendments to UCC Articles 1, 3, 8, and 9, to assist in development and storage of electronic residential mortgage notes, in concert with the proposed federal National Electronic Mortgage Note Repository Act. The Prefatory Note to those UCC amendments says that "the plan is to seek enactment in the states only if and when the federal Repository Act is adopted." As of the date of publication of this volume, the federal Repository Act has not been enacted, so the amendments are not included here. Further information is available at ali.org and uniformlaws.org.

UNIFORM COMMERCIAL CODE

National Conference of Commissioners on Uniform State Laws

DRAFTING COMMITTEE TO REVISE UNIFORM COMMERCIAL CODE ARTICLE 1—GENERAL PROVISIONS

Boris Auerbach, Wyoming, Ohio, *Chair*
Marion W. Benfield, Jr., New Braunfels, Texas
Amelia H. Boss, Philadelphia, Pennsylvania, *The American Law Institute Representative*
James C. McKay, Jr., Washington, DC, *Committee on Style Liaison*
H. Kathleen Patchel, Indianapolis, Indiana, *National Conference Associate Reporter*
Curtis R. Reitz, Philadelphia, Pennsylvania
Carlyle C. Ring, Jr., Washington, DC, *Enactment Plan Coordinator*
James J. White, Ann Arbor, Michigan
Neil B. Cohen, Brooklyn, New York, *Reporter*

EX OFFICIO

John L. McClaugherty, Charleston, West Virginia, *NCUSSL President*
Robert J. Tennessen, Minneapolis, Minnesota, *NCUSSL Division Chair*

AMERICAN BAR ASSOCIATION ADVISORS

Harry C. Sigman, Los Angeles, California, *Advisor*
Richard R. Goldberg, Philadelphia, Pennsylvania, *Real Property, Probate & Trust Law Section Advisor*
William J. Woodward, Jr., Philadelphia, Pennsylvania, *Business Law Section Advisor*

EXECUTIVE DIRECTOR

Fred H. Miller, Norman, Oklahoma, *NCUSSL Executive Director*
William J. Pierce, Ann Arbor, Michigan, *NCUSSL Executive Director Emeritus*

Article 1 Concordance

Unrevised	Revised
1–101	1–101
1–102(1, 2)	1–103
1–102(3, 4)	1–302
1–102(5)	1–106
1–103	1–103
1–104	1–104
1–105	1–301
1–106	1–305
1–107	1–306
1–108	1–105
1–109	1–107
1–201(25, 26, 27)	1–202
1–201(37)	1–201(b)(35), 1–203
1–201(44)	1–204
1–201 (all other)	1–201
1–202	1–307
1–203	1–304
1–204(1)	1–302
1–204(2, 3)	1–205
1–205	1–303
1–206	deleted
1–207	1–308

PART 1

GENERAL PROVISIONS

§ 1–101. Short Titles.

(a) This [Act] may be cited as the Uniform Commercial Code.

(b) This article may be cited as Uniform Commercial Code-General Provisions.

Official Comment

Source: Former Section 1–101.

Changes from former law: Subsection (b) is new. It is added in order to make the structure of Article 1 parallel with that of the other articles of the Uniform Commercial Code.

1. Each other article of the Uniform Commercial Code (except Articles 10 and 11) may also be cited by its own short title. See Sections 2–101, 2A–101, 3–101, 4–101, 4A–101, 5–101, 6–101, 7–101, 8–101, and 9–101.

§ 1–102. Scope of Article.

This article applies to a transaction to the extent that it is governed by another article of [the Uniform Commercial Code].

Official Comment

Source: New.

1. This section is intended to resolve confusion that has occasionally arisen as to the applicability of the substantive rules in this article. This section makes clear what has always been the case—the rules in Article 1 apply to transactions to the extent that those transactions are governed by one of the other articles of the Uniform Commercial Code. See also Comment 1 to Section 1–301.

§ 1–103. Construction of [Uniform Commercial Code] to Promote Its Purposes and Policies; Applicability of Supplemental Principles of Law.

(a) [The Uniform Commercial Code] must be liberally construed and applied to promote its underlying purposes and policies, which are:

(1) to simplify, clarify, and modernize the law governing commercial transactions;

(2) to permit the continued expansion of commercial practices through custom, usage, and agreement of the parties; and

(3) to make uniform the law among the various jurisdictions.

(b) Unless displaced by the particular provisions of [the Uniform Commercial Code], the principles of law and equity, including the law merchant and the law relative to capacity to contract, principal and agent, estoppel, fraud, misrepresentation, duress, coercion, mistake, bankruptcy, and other validating or invalidating cause supplement its provisions.

Official Comment

Source: Former Section 1–102 (1)–(2); Former Section 1–103.

Changes from former law: This section is derived from subsections (1) and (2) of former Section 1–102 and from former Section 1–103. Subsection (a) of this section combines subsections (1) and (2) of former Section 1–102. Except for changing the form of reference to the Uniform Commercial Code and minor stylistic changes, its language is the same as subsections (1) and (2) of former Section 1–102. Except for changing the form of reference to the Uniform Commercial Code and minor stylistic changes, subsection (b) of this section is identical to former Section 1–103. The provisions have been combined in this section to reflect the interrelationship between them.

1. The Uniform Commercial Code is drawn to provide flexibility so that, since it is intended to be a semi-permanent and infrequently-amended piece of legislation, it will provide its own machinery for expansion of commercial practices. It is intended to make it possible for the law embodied in the Uniform Commercial Code to be applied by the courts in the light of unforeseen and new circumstances and practices. The proper construction of the Uniform Commercial Code requires, of course, that its interpretation and application be limited to its reason.

Even prior to the enactment of the Uniform Commercial Code, courts were careful to keep broad acts from being hampered in their effects by later acts of limited scope. See *Pacific Wool Growers v. Draper & Co.*, 158 Or. 1, 73 P.2d 1391 (1937), and compare Section 1–104. The courts have often recognized that the policies embodied in an act are applicable in reason to subject-matter that was not expressly included in the language of the act, *Commercial Nat. Bank of New Orleans v. Canal-Louisiana Bank & Trust Co.*, 239 U.S. 520, 36 S.Ct. 194, 60 L.Ed. 417 (1916) (bona fide purchase policy of Uniform Warehouse Receipts Act extended to case not covered but of equivalent nature), and did the same where reason and policy so required, even where the subject-matter had been intentionally excluded from the act in general. *Agar v. Orda*, 264 N.Y. 248, 190 N.E. 479 (1934) (Uniform Sales Act change in seller's remedies applied to contract for sale of choses in action even though the general coverage of that Act was intentionally limited to goods "other than things in action.") They implemented a statutory policy with liberal and useful remedies not provided in the statutory text. They disregarded a statutory limitation of remedy where the reason of the limitation did not apply. *Fiterman v. J. N. Johnson & Co.*, 156 Minn. 201, 194 N.W. 399 (1923) (requirement of return of the goods as a condition to rescission for breach of warranty; also, partial rescission allowed). Nothing in the Uniform Commercial Code stands in the way of the continuance of such action by the courts.

The Uniform Commercial Code should be construed in accordance with its underlying purposes and policies. The text of each section should be read in the light of the purpose and policy of the rule or principle in question, as also of the Uniform Commercial Code as a whole, and the application of the language should be construed narrowly or broadly, as the case may be, in conformity with the purposes and policies involved.

2. **Applicability of supplemental principles of law.** Subsection (b) states the basic relationship of the Uniform Commercial Code to supplemental bodies of law. The Uniform Commercial Code was drafted against the backdrop of existing bodies of law, including the common law and equity, and relies on those bodies of law to supplement it provisions in many important ways. At the same time, the Uniform Commercial Code is the primary source of commercial law rules in areas that it governs, and its rules represent choices made by its drafters and the enacting legislatures about the appropriate policies to be furthered in the transactions it covers. Therefore, while principles of common law and equity may *supplement* provisions of the Uniform Commercial Code, they may not be used to *supplant* its provisions, or the purposes and policies those provisions reflect, unless a specific provision of the Uniform Commercial Code provides otherwise. In the absence of such a provision, the Uniform Commercial Code preempts principles of common law and equity that are inconsistent with either its provisions or its purposes and policies.

The language of subsection (b) is intended to reflect both the concept of supplementation and the concept of preemption. Some courts, however, had difficulty in applying the identical language of former Section 1–103 to determine when other law appropriately may be applied to supplement the Uniform Commercial Code, and when that law has been displaced by the Code. Some decisions applied other law in situations in which that application, while not inconsistent with the text of any particular provision of the Uniform Commercial Code, clearly was inconsistent with the underlying purposes and policies reflected in the relevant provisions of the Code. *See, e.g., Sheerbonnet, Ltd. v. American Express Bank, Ltd.*, 951 F. Supp. 403 (S.D.N.Y. 1995). In part, this difficulty arose from Comment 1 to former Section 1–103, which stated that "this section indicates the continued applicability to commercial contracts of all supplemental bodies of law except insofar as they are explicitly displaced by this Act." The "explicitly displaced" language of that Comment did not accurately reflect the proper scope of Uniform Commercial Code preemption, which extends to displacement of other law that is inconsistent with the purposes and policies of the Uniform Commercial Code, as well as with its text.

3. **Application of subsection (b) to statutes.** The primary focus of Section 1–103 is on the relationship between the Uniform Commercial Code and principles of common law and equity as developed by the courts. State law, however, increasingly is statutory. Not only are there a growing number of state statutes addressing specific issues that come within the scope of the Uniform Commercial Code, but in some States many general principles of common law and equity have been codified. When the other law relating to a matter within the scope of the Uniform Commercial Code is a statute, the principles of subsection (b) remain relevant to the court's analysis of the relationship between that statute and the Uniform Commercial Code, but other principles of statutory interpretation that specifically address the interrelationship between statutes will be relevant as well. In some situations, the principles of subsection (b) still will be determinative. For example, the mere fact that an equitable

principle is stated in statutory form rather than in judicial decisions should not change the court's analysis of whether the principle can be used to supplement the Uniform Commercial Code—under subsection (b), equitable principles may supplement provisions of the Uniform Commercial Code only if they are consistent with the purposes and policies of the Uniform Commercial Code as well as its text. In other situations, however, other interpretive principles addressing the interrelationship between statutes may lead the court to conclude that the other statute is controlling, even though it conflicts with the Uniform Commercial Code. This, for example, would be the result in a situation where the other statute was specifically intended to provide additional protection to a class of individuals engaging in transactions covered by the Uniform Commercial Code.

4. **Listing not exclusive.** The list of sources of supplemental law in subsection (b) is intended to be merely illustrative of the other law that may supplement the Uniform Commercial Code, and is not exclusive. No listing could be exhaustive. Further, the fact that a particular section of the Uniform Commercial Code makes express reference to other law is not intended to suggest the negation of the general application of the principles of subsection (b). Note also that the word "bankruptcy" in subsection (b), continuing the use of that word from former Section 1–103, should be understood not as a specific reference to federal bankruptcy law but, rather as a reference to general principles of insolvency, whether under federal or state law.

§ 1–104. Construction Against Implied Repeal.

[The Uniform Commercial Code] being a general act intended as a unified coverage of its subject matter, no part of it shall be deemed to be impliedly repealed by subsequent legislation if such construction can reasonably be avoided.

Official Comment

Source: Former Section 1–104.

Changes from former law: Except for changing the form of reference to the Uniform Commercial Code, this section is identical to former Section 1–104.

1. This section embodies the policy that an act that bears evidence of carefully considered permanent regulative intention should not lightly be regarded as impliedly repealed by subsequent legislation. The Uniform Commercial Code, carefully integrated and intended as a uniform codification of permanent character covering an entire "field" of law, is to be regarded as particularly resistant to implied repeal.

§ 1–105. Severability.

If any provision or clause of [the Uniform Commercial Code] or its application to any person or circumstance is held invalid, the invalidity does not affect other provisions or applications of [the Uniform Commercial Code] which can be given effect without the invalid provision or application, and to this end the provisions of [the Uniform Commercial Code] are severable.

Official Comment

Source: Former Section 1–108.

Changes from former law: Except for changing the form of reference to the Uniform Commercial Code, this section is identical to former Section 1–108.

1. This is the model severability section recommended by the National Conference of Commissioners on Uniform State Laws for inclusion in all acts of extensive scope.

§ 1–106. Use of Singular and Plural; Gender.

In [the Uniform Commercial Code], unless the statutory context otherwise requires:

(1) words in the singular number include the plural, and those in the plural include the singular; and

(2) words of any gender also refer to any other gender.

Official Comment

Source: Former Section 1–102(5). See also 1 U.S.C. Section 1.

Changes from former law: Other than minor stylistic changes, this section is identical to former Section 1–102(5).

1. This section makes it clear that the use of singular or plural in the text of the Uniform Commercial Code is generally only a matter of drafting style—singular words may be applied in the plural, and plural words may be applied in the singular. Only when it is clear from the statutory context that the use of the singular or plural does not include the other is this rule inapplicable. *See, e.g.,* Section 9–322.

§ 1–107. Section Captions.

Section captions are part of [the Uniform Commercial Code].

Official Comment

Source: Former Section 1–109.

Changes from former law: None.

1. Section captions are a part of the text of the Uniform Commercial Code, and not mere surplusage. This is not the case, however, with respect to subsection headings appearing in Article 9. See Comment 3 to Section 9–101 ("subsection headings are not a part of the official text itself and have not been approved by the sponsors.").

§ 1–108. Relation to Electronic Signatures in Global and National Commerce Act.

This article modifies, limits, and supersedes the Federal Electronic Signatures in Global and National Commerce Act, 15 U.S.C. § 7001 *et seq.*, except that nothing in this article modifies, limits, or supersedes section 7001(c) of that act or authorizes electronic delivery of any of the notices described in section 7003(b) of that Act.

Official Comment

Source: New

1. The federal Electronic Signatures in Global and National Commerce Act, 15 U.S.C. Section 7001 *et seq.* became effective in 2000. Section 102(a) of that Act provides that a State statute may modify, limit, or supersede the provisions of section 101 of that Act with respect to state law if such statute, *inter alia,* specifies the alternative procedures or requirements for the use or acceptance (or both) of electronic records or electronic signatures to establish the legal effect, validity, or enforceability of contracts or other records, and (i) such alternative procedures or requirements are consistent with Titles I and II of that Act, (ii) such alternative procedures or requirements do not require, or accord greater legal status or effect to, the implementation or application of a specific technology or technical specification for performing the functions of creating, storing, generating, receiving, communicating, or authenticating electronic records or electronic signatures; and (iii) if enacted or adopted after the date of the enactment of that Act, makes specific reference to that Act. Article 1 fulfills the first two of those three criteria; this Section fulfills the third criterion listed above.

2. As stated in this section, however, Article 1 does not modify, limit, or supersede Section 101(c) of the Electronic Signatures in Global and National Commerce Act (requiring affirmative consent from a consumer to electronic delivery of transactional disclosures that are required by state law to be in writing); nor does it authorize electronic delivery of any of the notices described in Section 103(b) of that Act.

PART 2

GENERAL DEFINITIONS AND PRINCIPLES OF INTERPRETATION

§ 1–201. General Definitions.

(a) Unless the context otherwise requires, words or phrases defined in this section, or in the additional definitions contained in other articles of [the Uniform Commercial Code] that apply to particular articles or parts thereof, have the meanings stated.

(b) Subject to definitions contained in other articles of [the Uniform Commercial Code] that apply to particular articles or parts thereof:

(1) "Action", in the sense of a judicial proceeding, includes recoupment, counterclaim, set-off, suit in equity, and any other proceeding in which rights are determined.

(2) "Aggrieved party" means a party entitled to pursue a remedy.

(3) "Agreement", as distinguished from "contract", means the bargain of the parties in fact, as found in their language or inferred from other circumstances, including course of performance, course of dealing, or usage of trade as provided in Section 1–303.

(4) "Bank" means a person engaged in the business of banking and includes a savings bank, savings and loan association, credit union, and trust company.

(5) "Bearer" means a person in control of a negotiable electronic document of title or a person in possession of a negotiable instrument, negotiable tangible document of title, or certificated security that is payable to bearer or indorsed in blank.

(6) "Bill of lading" means a document of title evidencing the receipt of goods for shipment issued by a person engaged in the business of directly or indirectly transporting or forwarding goods. The term does not include a warehouse receipt.

(7) "Branch" includes a separately incorporated foreign branch of a bank.

(8) "Burden of establishing" a fact means the burden of persuading the trier of fact that the existence of the fact is more probable than its nonexistence.

(9) "Buyer in ordinary course of business" means a person that buys goods in good faith, without knowledge that the sale violates the rights of another person in the goods, and in the ordinary course from a person, other than a pawnbroker, in the business of selling goods of that kind. A person buys goods in the ordinary course if the sale to the person comports with the usual or customary practices in the kind of business in which the seller is engaged or with the seller's own usual or customary practices. A person that sells oil, gas, or other minerals at the wellhead or minehead is a person in the business of selling goods of that kind. A buyer in ordinary course of business may buy for cash, by exchange of other property, or on secured or unsecured credit, and may acquire goods or documents of title under a preexisting contract for sale. Only a buyer that takes possession of the goods or has a right to recover the goods from the seller under Article 2 may be a buyer in ordinary course of business. "Buyer in ordinary course of business" does not include a person that acquires goods in a transfer in bulk or as security for or in total or partial satisfaction of a money debt.

(10) "Conspicuous", with reference to a term, means so written, displayed, or presented that a reasonable person against which it is to operate ought to have noticed it. Whether a term is "conspicuous" or not is a decision for the court. Conspicuous terms include the following:

(A) a heading in capitals equal to or greater in size than the surrounding text, or in contrasting type, font, or color to the surrounding text of the same or lesser size; and

(B) language in the body of a record or display in larger type than the surrounding text, or in contrasting type, font, or color to the surrounding text of the same size, or set off from surrounding text of the same size by symbols or other marks that call attention to the language.

(11) "Consumer" means an individual who enters into a transaction primarily for personal, family, or household purposes.

(12) "Contract", as distinguished from "agreement", means the total legal obligation that results from the parties' agreement as determined by [the Uniform Commercial Code] as supplemented by any other applicable laws.

(13) "Creditor" includes a general creditor, a secured creditor, a lien creditor, and any representative of creditors, including an assignee for the benefit of creditors, a trustee in bankruptcy, a receiver in equity, and an executor or administrator of an insolvent debtor's or assignor's estate.

(14) "Defendant" includes a person in the position of defendant in a counterclaim, cross-claim, or third-party claim.

(15) "Delivery", with respect to an electronic document of title means voluntary transfer of control and with respect to an instrument, a tangible document of title, or chattel paper, means voluntary transfer of possession.

(16) "Document of title" means a record (i) that in the regular course of business or financing is treated as adequately evidencing that the person in possession or control of the record is entitled to receive, control, hold, and dispose of the record and the goods the record covers and (ii) that purports to be issued by or addressed to a bailee and to cover goods in the bailee's possession which are either identified or are fungible portions of an identified mass. The term includes a bill of lading, transport document, dock warrant, dock receipt, warehouse receipt, and order for delivery of goods. An electronic document of title means a document of title evidenced by a record consisting of information stored in an electronic medium. A tangible document of title means a document of title evidenced by a record consisting of information that is inscribed on a tangible medium.

(17) "Fault" means a default, breach, or wrongful act or omission.

(18) "Fungible goods" means:

(A) goods of which any unit, by nature or usage of trade, is the equivalent of any other like unit; or

(B) goods that by agreement are treated as equivalent.

(19) "Genuine" means free of forgery or counterfeiting.

(20) "Good faith," except as otherwise provided in Article 5, means honesty in fact and the observance of reasonable commercial standards of fair dealing.

(21) "Holder" means:

(A) the person in possession of a negotiable instrument that is payable either to bearer or to an identified person that is the person in possession;

(B) the person in possession of a negotiable tangible document of title if the goods are deliverable either to bearer or to the order of the person in possession; or

(C) the person in control of a negotiable electronic document of title.

(22) "Insolvency proceeding" includes an assignment for the benefit of creditors or other proceeding intended to liquidate or rehabilitate the estate of the person involved.

(23) "Insolvent" means:

(A) having generally ceased to pay debts in the ordinary course of business other than as a result of bona fide dispute;

(B) being unable to pay debts as they become due; or

(C) being insolvent within the meaning of federal bankruptcy law.

(24) "Money" means a medium of exchange currently authorized or adopted by a domestic or foreign government. The term includes a monetary unit of account established by an intergovernmental organization or by agreement between two or more countries.

(25) "Organization" means a person other than an individual.

(26) "Party", as distinguished from "third party", means a person that has engaged in a transaction or made an agreement subject to [the Uniform Commercial Code].

(27) "Person" means an individual, corporation, business trust, estate, trust, partnership, limited liability company, association, joint venture, government, governmental subdivision, agency, or instrumentality, public corporation, or any other legal or commercial entity.

(28) "Present value" means the amount as of a date certain of one or more sums payable in the future, discounted to the date certain by use of either an interest rate specified by the parties if that rate is not manifestly unreasonable at the time the transaction is entered into or, if an interest rate is

not so specified, a commercially reasonable rate that takes into account the facts and circumstances at the time the transaction is entered into.

(29) "Purchase" means taking by sale, lease, discount, negotiation, mortgage, pledge, lien, security interest, issue or reissue, gift, or any other voluntary transaction creating an interest in property.

(30) "Purchaser" means a person that takes by purchase.

(31) "Record" means information that is inscribed on a tangible medium or that is stored in an electronic or other medium and is retrievable in perceivable form.

(32) "Remedy" means any remedial right to which an aggrieved party is entitled with or without resort to a tribunal.

(33) "Representative" means a person empowered to act for another, including an agent, an officer of a corporation or association, and a trustee, executor, or administrator of an estate.

(34) "Right" includes remedy.

(35) "Security interest" means an interest in personal property or fixtures which secures payment or performance of an obligation. "Security interest" includes any interest of a consignor and a buyer of accounts, chattel paper, a payment intangible, or a promissory note in a transaction that is subject to Article 9. "Security interest" does not include the special property interest of a buyer of goods on identification of those goods to a contract for sale under Section 2–401, but a buyer may also acquire a "security interest" by complying with Article 9. Except as otherwise provided in Section 2–505, the right of a seller or lessor of goods under Article 2 or 2A to retain or acquire possession of the goods is not a "security interest", but a seller or lessor may also acquire a "security interest" by complying with Article 9. The retention or reservation of title by a seller of goods notwithstanding shipment or delivery to the buyer under Section 2–401 is limited in effect to a reservation of a "security interest." Whether a transaction in the form of a lease creates a "security interest" is determined pursuant to Section 1–203.

(36) "Send" in connection with a writing, record, or notice means:

(A) to deposit in the mail or deliver for transmission by any other usual means of communication with postage or cost of transmission provided for and properly addressed and, in the case of an instrument, to an address specified thereon or otherwise agreed, or if there be none to any address reasonable under the circumstances; or

(B) in any other way to cause to be received any record or notice within the time it would have arrived if properly sent.

(37) "Signed" includes using any symbol executed or adopted with present intention to adopt or accept a writing.

(38) "State" means a State of the United States, the District of Columbia, Puerto Rico, the United States Virgin Islands, or any territory or insular possession subject to the jurisdiction of the United States.

(39) "Surety" includes a guarantor or other secondary obligor.

(40) "Term" means a portion of an agreement that relates to a particular matter.

(41) "Unauthorized signature" means a signature made without actual, implied, or apparent authority. The term includes a forgery.

(42) "Warehouse receipt" means a document of title issued by a person engaged in the business of storing goods for hire.

(43) "Writing" includes printing, typewriting, or any other intentional reduction to tangible form. "Written" has a corresponding meaning.

As amended in 2003.

Official Comment

Source: Former Section 1–201.

Changes from former law: In order to make it clear that all definitions in the Uniform Commercial Code (not just those appearing in Article 1, as stated in former Section 1–201, but also those appearing in other Articles) do not apply if the context otherwise requires, a new subsection (a) to that effect has been added, and the definitions now appear in subsection (b). The reference in subsection (a) to the "context" is intended to refer to the context in which the defined term is used in the Uniform Commercial Code. In other words, the definition applies whenever the defined term is used unless the context in which the defined term is used in the statute indicates that the term was not used in its defined sense. Consider, for example, Sections 3–103(a)(9) [*version before 2002 revision*] (defining "promise," in relevant part, as "a written undertaking to pay money signed by the person undertaking to pay") and 3–303(a)(1) (indicating that an instrument is issued or transferred for value if "the instrument is issued or transferred for a promise of performance, to the extent that the promise has been performed"). It is clear from the statutory context of the use of the word "promise" in Section 3–303(a)(1) that the term was not used in the sense of its definition in Section 3–103(a)(9) [*version before 2002 revision*]. Thus, the Section 3–103(a)(9) [*version before 2002 revision*] definition should not be used to give meaning to the word "promise" in Section 3–303(a).

Some definitions in former Section 1–201 have been reformulated as substantive provisions and have been moved to other sections. See Sections 1–202 (explicating concepts of notice and knowledge formerly addressed in Sections 1–201(25)–(27)), 1–204 (determining when a person gives value for rights, replacing the definition of "value" in former Section 1–201(44)), and 1–206 (addressing the meaning of presumptions, replacing the definitions of "presumption" and "presumed" in former Section 1–201(31)). Similarly, the portion of the definition of "security interest" in former Section 1–201(37) which explained the difference between a security interest and a lease has been relocated to Section 1–203.

Two definitions in former Section 1–201 have been deleted. The definition of "honor" in former Section 1–201(21) has been moved to Section 2–103(1)(b), inasmuch as the definition only applies to the use of the word in Article 2. [*Note from West Advisory Panel: This sentence appears to be in error because, although "honor" was deleted from Article 1, no conforming amendment to Section 2–103(1) was made as part of the Article 1 revision.*] The definition of "telegram" in former Section 1–201(41) has been deleted because that word no longer appears in the definition of "conspicuous."

Other than minor stylistic changes and renumbering, the remaining definitions in this section are as in former Article 1 except as noted below.

1. "Action." Unchanged from former Section 1–201, which was derived from similar definitions in Section 191, Uniform Negotiable Instruments Law; Section 76, Uniform Sales Act; Section 58, Uniform Warehouse Receipts Act; Section 53, Uniform Bills of Lading Act.

2. "Aggrieved party." Unchanged from former Section 1–201.

3. "Agreement." Derived from former Section 1–201. As used in the Uniform Commercial Code the word is intended to include full recognition of usage of trade, course of dealing, course of performance and the surrounding circumstances as effective parts thereof, and of any agreement permitted under the provisions of the Uniform Commercial Code to displace a stated rule of law. Whether an agreement has legal consequences is determined by applicable provisions of the Uniform Commercial Code and, to the extent provided in Section 1–103, by the law of contracts.

4. "Bank." Derived from Section 4A–104.

5. "Bearer." Unchanged, except in one respect, from former section 1–201, which was derived from Section 191, Uniform Negotiable Instruments Law. The term bearer applies to negotiable documents of title and has been broadened to include a person in control of an electronic negotiable document of title. Control of an electronic document of title is defined in Article 7 (Section 7–106).

6. "Bill of Lading." Derived from former Section 1–201. The reference to, and definition of, an "airbill" has been deleted as no longer necessary. A bill of lading is one type of document of title as defined in subsection (16). This definition should be read in conjunction with the definition of carrier in Article 7 (Section 7–102).

7. "Branch." Unchanged from former Section 1–201.

8. "Burden of establishing a fact." Unchanged from former Section 1–201.

9. "Buyer in ordinary course of business." Except for minor stylistic changes, identical to former Section 1–201 (as amended in conjunction with the 1999 revisions to Article 9). The major significance of the phrase lies in Section 2–403 and in the Article on Secured Transactions (Article 9).

The first sentence of paragraph (9) makes clear that a buyer from a pawnbroker cannot be a buyer in ordinary course of business. The second sentence explains what it means to buy "in the ordinary course." The penultimate sentence prevents a buyer that does not have the right to possession as against the seller from being a buyer in ordinary course of business. Concerning when a buyer obtains possessory rights, see Sections 2–502 and 2–716. However, the penultimate sentence is not intended to affect a buyer's status as a buyer in ordinary course of business in cases (such as a "drop shipment") involving delivery by the seller to a person buying from the buyer or a donee from the buyer. The requirement relates to whether *as against the seller* the buyer or one taking through the buyer has possessory rights.

10. "Conspicuous." Derived from former Section 1–201(10). This definition states the general standard that to be conspicuous a term ought to be noticed by a reasonable person. Whether a term is conspicuous is an issue for the court. Subparagraphs (A) and (B) set out several methods for making a term conspicuous. Requiring that a term be conspicuous blends a notice function (the term ought to be noticed) and a planning function (giving guidance to the party relying on the term regarding how that result can be achieved). Although these paragraphs indicate some of the methods for making a term attention-calling, the test is whether attention can reasonably be expected to be called to it. The statutory language should not be construed to permit a result that is inconsistent with that test.

11. "Consumer." Derived from Section 9–102(a)(25).

12. "Contract." Except for minor stylistic changes, identical to former Section 1–201.

13. "Creditor." Unchanged from former Section 1–201.

14. "Defendant." Except for minor stylistic changes, identical to former Section 1–201, which was derived from Section 76, Uniform Sales Act.

15. "Delivery." Derived from former Section 1–201. The reference to certificated securities has been deleted in light of the more specific treatment of the matter in Section 8–301. The definition has been revised to accommodate electronic documents of title. Control of an electronic document of title is defined in Article 7 (Section 7–106).

16. "Document of title." Derived from former Section 1–201, which was derived from Section 76, Uniform Sales Act. This definition makes explicit that the obligation or designation of a third party as "bailee" is essential to a document of title and clearly rejects any such result as obtained in *Hixson v. Ward*, 254 Ill.App. 505 (1929), which treated a conditional sales contract as a document of title. Also the definition is left open so that new types of documents may be included, including documents which gain commercial recognition in the international arena. See UNCITRAL Draft Instrument on the Carriage of Goods By Sea. It is unforeseeable what documents may one day serve the essential purpose now filled by warehouse receipts and bills of lading. The definition is stated in terms of the function of the documents with the intention that any document which gains commercial recognition as accomplishing the desired result shall be included within its scope. Fungible goods are adequately identified within the language of the definition by identification of the mass of which they are a part.

Dock warrants were within the Sales Act definition of document of title apparently for the purpose of recognizing a valid tender by means of such paper. In current commercial practice a dock warrant or receipt is a kind of interim certificate issued by shipping companies upon delivery of the goods at the dock, entitling a designated person to be issued a bill of lading. The receipt itself is invariably nonnegotiable in form although it may indicate that a negotiable bill is to be forthcoming. Such a document is not within the general compass of the definition, although trade usage may in some cases entitle such paper to be treated as a document of title. If the dock receipt actually represents a storage obligation undertaken by the shipping company, then it is a warehouse receipt within this Section regardless of the name given to the instrument.

The goods must be "described," but the description may be by marks or labels and may be qualified in such a way as to disclaim personal knowledge of the issuer regarding contents or condition. However, baggage and parcel checks and similar "tokens" of storage which identify stored goods only as those received in exchange for the token are not covered by this Article. The definition is broad enough to include an airway bill.

A document of title may be either tangible or electronic. Tangible documents of title should be construed to mean traditional paper documents. Electronic documents of title are documents that are stored in an electronic medium instead of in tangible form. The concept of an electronic medium should be construed liberally to include electronic, digital, magnetic, optical, electromagnetic, or any other current or similar emerging technologies. As to reissuing a document of title in an alternative medium, see Article 7, Section 7–105. Control for electronic documents of title is defined in Article 7 (Section 7–106).

17. "Fault." Derived from former Section 1–201. "Default" has been added to the list of events constituting fault.

18. "Fungible goods." Derived from former Section 1–201. References to securities have been deleted because Article 8 no longer uses the term "fungible" to describe securities. Accordingly, this provision now defines the concept only in the context of goods.

19. "Genuine." Unchanged from former Section 1–201.

20. "Good faith." Former Section 1–201(19) defined "good faith" simply as honesty in fact; the definition contained no element of commercial reasonableness. Initially, that definition applied throughout the Code with only one exception. Former Section 2–103(1)(b) provided that "in that Article . . . good faith in the case of a merchant means honesty in fact and the observance of reasonable commercial standards of fair dealing in the trade." This alternative definition was limited in applicability though, because it applied only to transactions within the scope of Article 2 and it applied only to merchants.

Over time, however, amendments to the Uniform Commercial Code brought the Article 2 merchant concept of good faith (subjective honesty and objective commercial reasonableness) into other Articles. First, Article 2A explicitly incorporated the Article 2 standard. See Section 2A–103(7). [*Note from West Advisory Panel: This provision appears in § 2A–103(3).*] Then, other Articles broadened the applicability of that standard by adopting it for all parties rather than just for merchants. *See, e.g.,* Sections 3–103(a)(4) [*version before 2002 revision*], 4A–105(a)(6), 7–102(a)(6), 8–102(a)(10), and 9–102(a)(43). Finally, Articles 2 and 2A were amended so as to apply the standard to non-merchants as well as merchants. See Sections 2–103(1)(j), 2A–103(1)(m) [*withdrawn 2003 Amendments to Articles 2 and 2A*]. All of these definitions are comprised of two elements—honesty in fact *and* the observance of reasonable commercial standards of fair dealing. Only revised Article 5 defines "good faith" solely in terms of subjective honesty, and only Article 6 (in the few states that have not chosen to delete the Article) is without a definition of good faith. (It should be noted that, while revised Article 6 did not define good faith, Comment 2 to revised Section 6–102 states that "this Article adopts the definition of 'good faith' in Article 1 in all cases, even when the buyer is a merchant.")

Thus, the definition of "good faith" in this section merely confirms what has been the case for a number of years as Articles of the UCC have been amended or revised—the obligation of "good faith," applicable in each Article, is to be interpreted in the context of all Articles except for Article 5 as including both the subjective element of honesty in fact and the objective element of the observance of reasonable commercial standards of fair dealing. As a result, both the subjective and objective elements are part of the standard of "good faith," whether that obligation is specifically referenced in another Article of the Code (other than Article 5) or is provided by this Article.

Of course, as noted in the statutory text, the definition of "good faith" in this section does not apply when the narrower definition of "good faith" in revised Article 5 is applicable.

As noted above, the definition of "good faith" in this section requires not only honesty in fact but also "observance of reasonable commercial standards of fair dealing." Although "fair dealing" is a broad term that must be defined in context, it is clear that it is concerned with the fairness of conduct rather than the care with which an act is performed. This is an entirely different concept than whether a party exercised ordinary care in conducting a transaction. Both concepts are to be determined in the light of reasonable commercial standards, but those standards in each case are directed to different aspects of commercial conduct. See e.g., Sections 3–103(a)(9) [*version before 2002 revision*] and 4–104(c) and Comment 4 to Section 3–103.

21. "Holder." Derived from former Section 1–201. The definition has been reorganized for clarity and amended to provide for electronic negotiable documents of title.

22. "Insolvency proceedings." Unchanged from former Section 1–201.

23. "Insolvent." Derived from former Section 1–201. The three tests of insolvency—"generally ceased to pay debts in the ordinary course of business other than as a result of a bona fide dispute as to them," "unable to pay debts as they become due," and "insolvent within the meaning of the federal bankruptcy law"—are expressly set up as alternative tests and must be approached from a commercial standpoint.

24. "Money." Substantively identical to former Section 1–201. The test is that of sanction of government, whether by authorization before issue or adoption afterward, which recognizes the circulating medium as a part of the official currency of that government. The narrow view that money is limited to legal tender is rejected.

25. "Organization." The former definition of this word has been replaced with the standard definition used in acts prepared by the National Conference of Commissioners on Uniform State Laws.

26. "Party." Substantively identical to former Section 1–201. Mention of a party includes, of course, a person acting through an agent. However, where an agent comes into opposition or contrast to the principal, particular account is taken of that situation.

27. "Person." The former definition of this word has been replaced with the standard definition used in acts prepared by the National Conference of Commissioners on Uniform State Laws.

28. "Present value." This definition was formerly contained within the definition of "security interest" in former Section 1–201(37).

29. "Purchase." Derived from former Section 1–201. The form of definition has been changed from "includes" to "means."

30. "Purchaser." Unchanged from former Section 1–201.

31. "Record." Derived from Section 9–102(a)(69).

32. "Remedy." Unchanged from former Section 1–201. The purpose is to make it clear that both remedy and right (as defined) include those remedial rights of "self help" which are among the most important bodies of rights under the Uniform Commercial Code, remedial rights being those to which an aggrieved party may resort on its own.

33. "Representative." Derived from former Section 1–201. Reorganized, and form changed from "includes" to "means."

34. "Right." Except for minor stylistic changes, identical to former Section 1–201.

35. "Security Interest." The definition is the first paragraph of the definition of "security interest" in former Section 1–201, with minor stylistic changes. The remaining portion of that definition has been moved to Section 1–203. Note that, because of the scope of Article 9, the term includes the interest of certain outright buyers of certain kinds of property.

36. "Send." Derived from former Section 1–201. Compare "notifies".

37. "Signed." Derived from former Section 1–201. Former Section 1–201 referred to "intention to authenticate"; because other articles now use the term "authenticate," the language has been changed to "intention to adopt or accept." The latter formulation is derived from the definition of "authenticate" in Section 9–102(a)(7). This provision refers only to writings, because the term "signed," as used in some articles, refers only to writings. This provision also makes it clear that, as the term "signed" is used in the Uniform Commercial Code, a complete signature is not necessary. The symbol may be printed, stamped or written; it may be by initials or by thumbprint. It may be on any part of the document and in appropriate cases may be found in a billhead or letterhead. No catalog of possible situations can be complete and the court must use common sense and commercial experience in passing upon these matters. The question always is whether the symbol was executed or adopted by the party with present intention to adopt or accept the writing.

38. "State." This is the standard definition of the term used in acts prepared by the National Conference of Commissioners on Uniform State Laws.

39. "Surety." This definition makes it clear that "surety" includes all secondary obligors, not just those whose obligation refers to the person obligated as a surety. As to the nature of secondary obligations generally, see Restatement (Third), Suretyship and Guaranty Section 1 (1996).

40. "Term." Unchanged from former Section 1–201.

41. "Unauthorized signature." Unchanged from former Section 1–201.

42. "Warehouse receipt." Derived from former Section 1–201, which was derived from Section 76(1), Uniform Sales Act; Section 1, Uniform Warehouse Receipts Act. Receipts issued by a field warehouse are included, provided the warehouseman and the depositor of the goods are different persons. The definition makes clear that the receipt must qualify as a document of title under subsection (16).

43. "Written" or "writing." Unchanged from former Section 1–201.

As amended in 2003 and 2005.

§ 1–202. Notice; Knowledge.

(a) Subject to subsection (f), a person has "notice" of a fact if the person:

(1) has actual knowledge of it;

(2) has received a notice or notification of it; or

(3) from all the facts and circumstances known to the person at the time in question, has reason to know that it exists.

(b) "Knowledge" means actual knowledge. "Knows" has a corresponding meaning.

(c) "Discover", "learn", or words of similar import refer to knowledge rather than to reason to know.

(d) A person "notifies" or "gives" a notice or notification to another person by taking such steps as may be reasonably required to inform the other person in ordinary course, whether or not the other person actually comes to know of it.

(e) Subject to subsection (f), a person "receives" a notice or notification when:

(1) it comes to that person's attention; or

(2) it is duly delivered in a form reasonable under the circumstances at the place of business through which the contract was made or at another location held out by that person as the place for receipt of such communications.

(f) Notice, knowledge, or a notice or notification received by an organization is effective for a particular transaction from the time it is brought to the attention of the individual conducting that transaction and, in any event, from the time it would have been brought to the individual's attention if the organization had exercised due diligence. An organization exercises due diligence if it maintains reasonable routines for communicating significant information to the person conducting the transaction and there is reasonable compliance with the routines. Due diligence does not require an individual acting for the organization to communicate information unless the communication is part of the individual's regular duties or the individual has reason to know of the transaction and that the transaction would be materially affected by the information.

Official Comment

Source: Derived from former Section 1–201(25)–(27).

Changes from former law: These provisions are substantive rather than purely definitional. Accordingly, they have been relocated from Section 1–201 to this section. The reference to the "forgotten notice" doctrine has been deleted.

1. Under subsection (a), a person has notice of a fact when, *inter alia*, the person has received a notification of the fact in question.

2. As provided in subsection (d), the word "notifies" is used when the essential fact is the proper dispatch of the notice, not its receipt. Compare "Send." When the essential fact is the other party's receipt of the notice, that is stated. Subsection (e) states when a notification is received.

3. Subsection (f) makes clear that notice, knowledge, or a notification, although "received," for instance, by a clerk in Department A of an organization, is effective for a transaction conducted in Department B only from the time when it was or should have been communicated to the individual conducting that transaction.

§ 1–203. Lease Distinguished From Security Interest.

(a) Whether a transaction in the form of a lease creates a lease or security interest is determined by the facts of each case.

(b) A transaction in the form of a lease creates a security interest if the consideration that the lessee is to pay the lessor for the right to possession and use of the goods is an obligation for the term of the lease and is not subject to termination by the lessee, and:

(1) the original term of the lease is equal to or greater than the remaining economic life of the goods;

(2) the lessee is bound to renew the lease for the remaining economic life of the goods or is bound to become the owner of the goods;

(3) the lessee has an option to renew the lease for the remaining economic life of the goods for no additional consideration or for nominal additional consideration upon compliance with the lease agreement; or

(4) the lessee has an option to become the owner of the goods for no additional consideration or for nominal additional consideration upon compliance with the lease agreement.

(c) A transaction in the form of a lease does not create a security interest merely because:

(1) the present value of the consideration the lessee is obligated to pay the lessor for the right to possession and use of the goods is substantially equal to or is greater than the fair market value of the goods at the time the lease is entered into;

(2) the lessee assumes risk of loss of the goods;

(3) the lessee agrees to pay, with respect to the goods, taxes, insurance, filing, recording, or registration fees, or service or maintenance costs;

(4) the lessee has an option to renew the lease or to become the owner of the goods;

(5) the lessee has an option to renew the lease for a fixed rent that is equal to or greater than the reasonably predictable fair market rent for the use of the goods for the term of the renewal at the time the option is to be performed; or

(6) the lessee has an option to become the owner of the goods for a fixed price that is equal to or greater than the reasonably predictable fair market value of the goods at the time the option is to be performed.

(d) Additional consideration is nominal if it is less than the lessee's reasonably predictable cost of performing under the lease agreement if the option is not exercised. Additional consideration is not nominal if:

(1) when the option to renew the lease is granted to the lessee, the rent is stated to be the fair market rent for the use of the goods for the term of the renewal determined at the time the option is to be performed; or

(2) when the option to become the owner of the goods is granted to the lessee, the price is stated to be the fair market value of the goods determined at the time the option is to be performed.

(e) The "remaining economic life of the goods" and "reasonably predictable" fair market rent, fair market value, or cost of performing under the lease agreement must be determined with reference to the facts and circumstances at the time the transaction is entered into.

Official Comment

Source: Former Section 1–201(37).

Changes from former law: This section is substantively identical to those portions of former Section 1–201(37) that distinguished "true" leases from security interests, except that the definition of "present value" formerly embedded in Section 1–201(37) has been placed in Section 1–201(28) [*unrevised Article 1; see Concordance, p. 12*].

1. An interest in personal property or fixtures which secures payment or performance of an obligation is a "security interest." See Section 1–201(37) [*unrevised Article 1; see Concordance, p. 12*]. Security interests are sometimes created by transactions in the form of leases. Because it can be difficult to distinguish leases that create security interests from those that do not, this section provides rules that govern the determination of whether a transaction in the form of a lease creates a security interest.

2. One of the reasons it was decided to codify the law with respect to leases was to resolve an issue that created considerable confusion in the courts: what is a lease? The confusion existed, in part, due to the last two sentences of the definition of security interest in the 1978 Official Text of the Act, Section 1–201(37). The confusion was compounded by the rather considerable change in the federal, state and local tax laws and accounting rules as they relate to leases of goods. The answer is important because the definition of lease determines not only the rights and remedies of the parties to the lease but also those of third parties. If a transaction creates a lease and not a security interest, the lessee's interest in the goods is limited to its leasehold estate; the residual interest in the goods belongs to the lessor. This has significant implications to the lessee's creditors. "On common law theory, the lessor, since he has not parted with title, is entitled to full protection against the lessee's creditors and trustee in bankruptcy. . . ." 1 G. Gilmore, *Security Interests in Personal Property* Section 3.6, at 76 (1965).

Under pre-UCC chattel security law there was generally no requirement that the lessor file the lease, a financing statement, or the like, to enforce the lease agreement against the lessee or any third party; the Article on Secured Transactions (Article 9) did not change the common law in that respect. Coogan, *Leasing and the Uniform Commercial Code*, in Equipment Leasing—Leveraged Leasing 681, 700 n.25, 729 n.80 (2d ed. 1980). The Article on Leases (Article 2A) did not change the law in that respect, except for leases of fixtures. Section 2A–309. An examination of the common law will not provide an adequate answer to the question of what is a lease. The definition of security interest in Section 1–201(37) of the 1978 Official Text of the Act provided that the Article on Secured Transactions (Article 9) governs security interests disguised as leases, *i.e.*, leases intended as security; however, the definition became vague and outmoded.

Lease is defined in Article 2A as a transfer of the right to possession and use of goods for a term, in return for consideration. Section 2A–103(1)(j). The definition continues by stating that the retention or creation of a security interest is not a lease. Thus, the task of sharpening the line between true leases and security interests disguised as leases continues to be a function of this Article.

This section begins where Section 1–201(35) [*should be 1-201(b)(35)*] leaves off. It draws a sharper line between leases and security interests disguised as leases to create greater certainty in commercial transactions.

Prior to enactment of the rules now codified in this section, the 1978 Official Text of Section 1–201(37) provided that whether a lease was intended as security (*i.e.*, a security interest disguised as a lease) was to be determined from the facts of each case; however, (a) the inclusion of an option to purchase did not itself make the lease one intended for security, and (b) an agreement that upon compliance with the terms of the lease the lessee would become, or had the option to become, the owner of the property for no additional consideration, or for a nominal consideration, did make the lease one intended for security.

Reference to the intent of the parties to create a lease or security interest led to unfortunate results. In discovering intent, courts relied upon factors that were thought to be more consistent with sales or loans than leases. Most of these criteria, however, were as applicable to true leases as to security interests. Examples include the typical net lease provisions, a purported lessor's lack of storage facilities or its character as a financing party rather than a dealer in goods. Accordingly, this section contains no reference to the parties' intent.

Subsections (a) and (b) were originally taken from Section 1(2) of the Uniform Conditional Sales Act (act withdrawn 1943), modified to reflect current leasing practice. Thus, reference to the case law prior to the incorporation of those concepts in this article will provide a useful source of precedent. Gilmore, *Security Law, Formalism and Article 9*, 47 Neb.L.Rev. 659, 671 (1968). Whether a transaction creates a lease or a security interest continues to be determined by the facts of each case. Subsection (b) further provides that a transaction creates a security interest if the lessee has an obligation to continue paying consideration for the term of the lease, if the obligation is not terminable by the lessee (thus correcting early statutory gloss, *e.g.*, *In re Royer's Bakery, Inc.*, 1 U.C.C. Rep.Serv. (Callaghan) 342 (Bankr.E.D.Pa. 1963)) and if one of four additional tests is met. The first of these four tests, subparagraph (1), is that the original lease term is equal to or greater than the remaining economic life of the goods. The second of these tests, subparagraph (2), is that the lessee is either bound to renew the lease for the remaining economic life of the goods or to become the owner of the goods. *In re Gehrke Enters.*, 1 Bankr. 647, 651–52 (Bankr.W.D.Wis. 1979). The third of these tests, subparagraph (3), is whether the lessee has an option to renew the lease for the remaining economic life of the goods for no additional consideration or for nominal additional consideration, which is defined later in this section. *In re Celeryvale Transp.*, 44 Bankr. 1007, 1014–15 (Bankr.E.D.Tenn. 1984). The fourth of these tests, subparagraph (4), is whether the lessee has an option to become the owner of the goods for no additional consideration or for nominal additional consideration. All of these tests focus on economics, not the intent of the parties. *In re Berge*, 32 Bankr. 370, 371–73 (Bankr.W.D.Wis. 1983).

The focus on economics is reinforced by subsection (c). It states that a transaction does not create a security interest merely because the transaction has certain characteristics listed therein. Subparagraph (1) has no statutory derivative; it states that a full payout lease does not *per se* create a security interest. *Rushton v. Shea*, 419 F.Supp. 1349, 1365 (D.Del. 1976). Subparagraphs (2) and (3) provide the same regarding the provisions of the typical net lease. *Compare All-States Leasing Co. v. Ochs*, 42 Or.App. 319, 600 P.2d 899 (Ct.App. 1979), *with In re Tillery*, 571 F.2d 1361 (5th Cir. 1978). Subparagraph (4) restates and expands the provisions of the 1978 Official Text of Section 1–201(37) to make clear that the option can be to buy or renew. Subparagraphs (5) and (6) treat fixed price options and provide that fair market value must be determined at the time the transaction is entered into. *Compare Arnold Mach. Co. v. Balls*, 624 P.2d 678 (Utah 1981), *with Aoki v. Shepherd Mach. Co.*, 665 F.2d 941 (9th Cir. 1982).

The relationship of subsection (b) to subsection (c) deserves to be explored. The fixed price purchase option provides a useful example. A fixed price purchase option in a lease does not of itself create a security interest. This is particularly true if the fixed price is equal to or greater than the reasonably predictable fair market value of the goods at the time the option is to be performed. A security interest is created only if the option price is nominal and the conditions stated in the introduction to the second paragraph of this subsection are met. There is a set of purchase options whose fixed price is less than fair market value but greater than nominal that must be determined on the facts of each case to ascertain whether the transaction in which the option is included creates a lease or a security interest.

It was possible to provide for various other permutations and combinations with respect to options to purchase and renew. For example, this section could have stated a rule to govern the facts of *In re Marhoefer Packing Co.*, 674 F.2d 1139 (7th Cir. 1982). This was not done because it would unnecessarily complicate the definition. Further development of this rule is left to the courts.

Subsections (d) and (e) provide definitions and rules of construction.

§ 1–204. Value.

Except as otherwise provided in Articles 3, 4, [and] 5, [and 6], a person gives value for rights if the person acquires them:

(1) in return for a binding commitment to extend credit or for the extension of immediately available credit, whether or not drawn upon and whether or not a charge-back is provided for in the event of difficulties in collection;

(2) as security for, or in total or partial satisfaction of, a preexisting claim;

(3) by accepting delivery under a preexisting contract for purchase; or

(4) in return for any consideration sufficient to support a simple contract.

Official Comment

Source: Former Section 1–201(44).

Changes from former law: Unchanged from former Section 1–201, which was derived from Sections 25, 26, 27, 191, Uniform Negotiable Instruments Law; Section 76, Uniform Sales Act; Section 53, Uniform Bills of Lading Act; Section 58, Uniform Warehouse Receipts Act; Section 22(1), Uniform Stock Transfer Act; Section 1, Uniform Trust Receipts Act. These provisions are substantive rather than purely definitional. Accordingly, they have been relocated from former Section 1–201 to this section.

1. All the Uniform Acts in the commercial law field (except the Uniform Conditional Sales Act) have carried definitions of "value." All those definitions provided that value was any consideration sufficient to support a simple contract, including the taking of property in satisfaction of or as security for a pre-existing claim. Subsections (1), (2), and (4) in substance continue the definitions of "value" in the earlier acts. Subsection (3) makes explicit that "value" is also given in a third situation: where a buyer by taking delivery under a pre-existing contract converts a contingent into a fixed obligation.

This definition is not applicable to Articles 3 and 4, but the express inclusion of immediately available credit as value follows the separate definitions in those Articles. See Sections 4–208, 4–209, 3–303. A bank or other financing agency which in good faith makes advances against property held as collateral becomes a bona fide purchaser of that property even though provision may be made for charge-back in case of trouble. Checking credit is "immediately available" within the meaning of this section if the bank would be subject to an action for slander of credit in case checks drawn against the credit were dishonored, and when a charge-back is not discretionary with the bank, but may only be made when difficulties in collection arise in connection with the specific transaction involved.

§ 1-205. Reasonable Time; Seasonableness.

(a) Whether a time for taking an action required by [the Uniform Commercial Code] is reasonable depends on the nature, purpose, and circumstances of the action.

(b) An action is taken seasonably if it is taken at or within the time agreed or, if no time is agreed, at or within a reasonable time.

Official Comment

Source: Former Section 1-204(2)-(3).

Changes from former law: This section is derived from subsections (2) and (3) of former Section 1-204. Subsection (1) of that section is now incorporated in Section 1-302(b).

1. Subsection (a) makes it clear that requirements that actions be taken within a "reasonable" time are to be applied in the transactional context of the particular action.

2. Under subsection (b), the agreement that fixes the time need not be part of the main agreement, but may occur separately. Notice also that under the definition of "agreement" (Section 1-201) the circumstances of the transaction, including course of dealing or usages of trade or course of performance may be material. On the question what is a reasonable time these matters will often be important.

§ 1-206. Presumptions.

Whenever [the Uniform Commercial Code] creates a "presumption" with respect to a fact, or provides that a fact is "presumed," the trier of fact must find the existence of the fact unless and until evidence is introduced that supports a finding of its nonexistence.

Legislative Note: Former Section 1-206, a Statute of Frauds for sales of "kinds of personal property not otherwise covered," has been deleted. The other articles of the Uniform Commercial Code make individual determinations as to requirements for memorializing transactions within their scope, so that the primary effect of former Section 1-206 was to impose a writing requirement on sales transactions not otherwise governed by the UCC. Deletion of former Section 1-206 does not constitute a recommendation to legislatures as to whether such sales transactions should be covered by a Statute of Frauds; rather, it reflects a determination that there is no need for uniform commercial law to resolve that issue.

Official Comment

Source: Former Section 1-201(31).

Changes from former law. None, other than stylistic changes.

1. Several sections of the Uniform Commercial Code state that there is a "presumption" as to a certain fact, or that the fact is "presumed." This section, derived from the definition appearing in former Section 1-201(31), indicates the effect of those provisions on the proof process.

PART 3

TERRITORIAL APPLICABILITY AND GENERAL RULES

§ 1-301. Territorial Applicability; Parties' Power to Choose Applicable Law.

(a) Except as otherwise provided in this section, when a transaction bears a reasonable relation to this state and also to another state or nation the parties may agree that the law either of this state or of such other state or nation shall govern their rights and duties.

(b) In the absence of an agreement effective under subsection (a), and except as provided in subsection (c), [the Uniform Commercial Code] applies to transactions bearing an appropriate relation to this state.

(c) If one of the following provisions of [the Uniform Commercial Code] specifies the applicable law, that provision governs and a contrary agreement is effective only to the extent permitted by the law so specified:

(1) Section 2–402;

(2) Sections 2A–105 and 2A–106;

(3) Section 4–102;

(4) Section 4A–507;

(5) Section 5–116;

[(6) Section 6–103;]

(7) Section 8–110;

(8) Sections 9–301 through 9–307.

As amended in 2008.

Official Comment

Source: Former Section 1–105.

Changes from former law: This section is substantively identical to former Section 1–105. Changes in language are stylistic only.

1. Subsection (a) states affirmatively the right of the parties to a multi-state transaction or a transaction involving foreign trade to choose their own law. That right is subject to the firm rules stated in the sections listed in subsection (c), and is limited to jurisdictions to which the transaction bears a "reasonable relation." In general, the test of "reasonable relation" is similar to that laid down by the Supreme Court in *Seeman v. Philadelphia Warehouse Co.*, 274 U.S. 403, 47 S.Ct. 626, 71 L.Ed. 1123 (1927). Ordinarily the law chosen must be that of a jurisdiction where a significant enough portion of the making or performance of the contract is to occur or occurs. But an agreement as to choice of law may sometimes take effect as a shorthand expression of the intent of the parties as to matters governed by their agreement, even though the transaction has no significant contact with the jurisdiction chosen.

2. Where there is no agreement as to the governing law, the Act is applicable to any transaction having an "appropriate" relation to any state which enacts it. Of course, the Act applies to any transaction which takes place in its entirety in a state which has enacted the Act. But the mere fact that suit is brought in a state does not make it appropriate to apply the substantive law of that state. Cases where a relation to the enacting state is not "appropriate" include, for example, those where the parties have clearly contracted on the basis of some other law, as where the law of the place of contracting and the law of the place of contemplated performance are the same and are contrary to the law under the Code.

3. Where a transaction has significant contacts with a state which has enacted the Act and also with other jurisdictions, the question what relation is "appropriate" is left to judicial decision. In deciding that question, the court is not strictly bound by precedents established in other contexts. Thus a conflict-of-laws decision refusing to apply a purely local statute or rule of law to a particular multi-state transaction may not be valid precedent for refusal to apply the Code in an analogous situation. Application of the Code in such circumstances may be justified by its comprehensiveness, by the policy of uniformity, and by the fact that it is in large part a reformulation and restatement of the law merchant and of the understanding of a business community which transcends state and even national boundaries. *Compare Global Commerce Corp. v. Clark-Babbitt Industries, Inc.*, 239 F.2d 716, 719 (2d Cir. 1956). In particular, where a transaction is governed in large part by the Code, application of another law to some detail of performance because of an accident of geography may violate the commercial understanding of the parties.

4. Subsection (c) spells out essential limitations on the parties' right to choose the applicable law. Especially in Article 9 parties taking a security interest or asked to extend credit which may be subject to a security interest must have sure ways to find out whether and where to file and where to look for possible existing filings.

5. Sections 9–301 through 9–307 should be consulted as to the rules for perfection of security interests and agricultural liens and the effect of perfection and nonperfection and priority. In transactions to which the Hague Securities Convention applies, the requirements for foreclosure and the like, the characterization of a

transfer as being outright or by way of security, and certain other issues will generally be governed by the law specified in the account agreement. See PEB Commentary No. 19, dated April 11, 2017.

6. This section is subject to Section 1–102, which states the scope of Article 1. As that section indicates, the rules of Article 1, including this section, apply to a transaction to the extent that transaction is governed by one of the other Articles of the Uniform Commercial Code.

As amended in 2008 and 2017.

§ 1–302. Variation by Agreement.

(a) Except as otherwise provided in subsection (b) or elsewhere in [the Uniform Commercial Code], the effect of provisions of [the Uniform Commercial Code] may be varied by agreement.

(b) The obligations of good faith, diligence, reasonableness, and care prescribed by [the Uniform Commercial Code] may not be disclaimed by agreement. The parties, by agreement, may determine the standards by which the performance of those obligations is to be measured if those standards are not manifestly unreasonable. Whenever [the Uniform Commercial Code] requires an action to be taken within a reasonable time, a time that is not manifestly unreasonable may be fixed by agreement.

(c) The presence in certain provisions of [the Uniform Commercial Code] of the phrase "unless otherwise agreed", or words of similar import, does not imply that the effect of other provisions may not be varied by agreement under this section.

Official Comment

Source: Former Sections 1–102(3)–(4) and 1–204(1).

Changes: This section combines the rules from subsections (3) and (4) of former Section 1–102 and subsection (1) of former Section 1–204. No substantive changes are made.

1. Subsection (a) states affirmatively at the outset that freedom of contract is a principle of the Uniform Commercial Code: "the effect" of its provisions may be varied by "agreement." The meaning of the statute itself must be found in its text, including its definitions, and in appropriate extrinsic aids; it cannot be varied by agreement. But the Uniform Commercial Code seeks to avoid the type of interference with evolutionary growth found in pre-Code cases such as *Manhattan Co. v. Morgan*, 242 N.Y. 38, 150 N.E. 594 (1926). Thus, private parties cannot make an instrument negotiable within the meaning of Article 3 except as provided in Section 3–104; nor can they change the meaning of such terms as "bona fide purchaser," "holder in due course," or "due negotiation," as used in the Uniform Commercial Code. But an agreement can change the legal consequences that would otherwise flow from the provisions of the Uniform Commercial Code. "Agreement" here includes the effect given to course of dealing, usage of trade and course of performance by Sections 1–201 and 1–303; the effect of an agreement on the rights of third parties is left to specific provisions of the Uniform Commercial Code and to supplementary principles applicable under Section 1–103. The rights of third parties under Section 9–317 when a security interest is unperfected, for example, cannot be destroyed by a clause in the security agreement.

This principle of freedom of contract is subject to specific exceptions found elsewhere in the Uniform Commercial Code and to the general exception stated here. The specific exceptions vary in explicitness: the statute of frauds found in Section 2–201, for example, does not explicitly preclude oral waiver of the requirement of a writing, but a fair reading denies enforcement to such a waiver as part of the "contract" made unenforceable; Section 9–602, on the other hand, is a quite explicit limitation on freedom of contract. Under the exception for "the obligations of good faith, diligence, reasonableness and care prescribed by [the Uniform Commercial Code]," provisions of the Uniform Commercial Code prescribing such obligations are not to be disclaimed. However, the section also recognizes the prevailing practice of having agreements set forth standards by which due diligence is measured and explicitly provides that, in the absence of a showing that the standards manifestly are unreasonable, the agreement controls. In this connection, Section 1–303 incorporating into the agreement prior course of dealing and usages of trade is of particular importance.

Subsection (b) also recognizes that nothing is stronger evidence of a reasonable time than the fixing of such time by a fair agreement between the parties. However, provision is made for disregarding a clause which whether by inadvertence or overreaching fixes a time so unreasonable that it amounts to eliminating all remedy under the contract. The parties are not required to fix the most reasonable time but may fix any time which is not obviously unfair as judged by the time of contracting.

2. An agreement that varies the effect of provisions of the Uniform Commercial Code may do so by stating the rules that will govern in lieu of the provisions varied. Alternatively, the parties may vary the effect of such provisions by stating that their relationship will be governed by recognized bodies of rules or principles applicable to commercial transactions. Such bodies of rules or principles may include, for example, those that are promulgated by intergovernmental authorities such as UNCITRAL or UNIDROIT (*see, e.g.*, UNIDROIT Principles of International Commercial Contracts), or non-legal codes such as trade codes.

3. Subsection (c) is intended to make it clear that, as a matter of drafting, phrases such as "unless otherwise agreed" have been used to avoid controversy as to whether the subject matter of a particular section does or does not fall within the exceptions to subsection (b), but absence of such words contains no negative implication since under subsection (b) the general and residual rule is that the effect of all provisions of the Uniform Commercial Code may be varied by agreement.

§ 1–303. Course of Performance, Course of Dealing, and Usage of Trade.

(a) A "course of performance" is a sequence of conduct between the parties to a particular transaction that exists if:

(1) the agreement of the parties with respect to the transaction involves repeated occasions for performance by a party; and

(2) the other party, with knowledge of the nature of the performance and opportunity for objection to it, accepts the performance or acquiesces in it without objection.

(b) A "course of dealing" is a sequence of conduct concerning previous transactions between the parties to a particular transaction that is fairly to be regarded as establishing a common basis of understanding for interpreting their expressions and other conduct.

(c) A "usage of trade" is any practice or method of dealing having such regularity of observance in a place, vocation, or trade as to justify an expectation that it will be observed with respect to the transaction in question. The existence and scope of such a usage must be proved as facts. If it is established that such a usage is embodied in a trade code or similar record, the interpretation of the record is a question of law.

(d) A course of performance or course of dealing between the parties or usage of trade in the vocation or trade in which they are engaged or of which they are or should be aware is relevant in ascertaining the meaning of the parties' agreement, may give particular meaning to specific terms of the agreement, and may supplement or qualify the terms of the agreement. A usage of trade applicable in the place in which part of the performance under the agreement is to occur may be so utilized as to that part of the performance.

(e) Except as otherwise provided in subsection (f), the express terms of an agreement and any applicable course of performance, course of dealing, or usage of trade must be construed whenever reasonable as consistent with each other. If such a construction is unreasonable:

(1) express terms prevail over course of performance, course of dealing, and usage of trade;

(2) course of performance prevails over course of dealing and usage of trade; and

(3) course of dealing prevails over usage of trade.

(f) Subject to Section 2–209 and Section 2A–208, a course of performance is relevant to show a waiver or modification of any term inconsistent with the course of performance.

(g) Evidence of a relevant usage of trade offered by one party is not admissible unless that party has given the other party notice that the court finds sufficient to prevent unfair surprise to the other party.

Official Comment

Source: Former Sections 1–205, 2–208, and Section 2A–207.

Changes from former law: This section integrates the "course of performance" concept from Articles 2 and 2A into the principles of former Section 1–205, which deals with course of dealing and usage of trade. In so doing, the section slightly modifies the articulation of the course of performance rules to fit more comfortably with the approach and structure of former Section 1–205. There are also slight modifications to be more consistent with the definition of "agreement" in former Section 1–201(3). It should be noted that a course of performance that might otherwise establish a defense to the obligation of a party to a negotiable instrument is not available as a defense against a holder in due course who took the instrument without notice of that course of performance.

1. The Uniform Commercial Code rejects both the "lay-dictionary" and the "conveyancer's" reading of a commercial agreement. Instead the meaning of the agreement of the parties is to be determined by the language used by them and by their action, read and interpreted in the light of commercial practices and other surrounding circumstances. The measure and background for interpretation are set by the commercial context, which may explain and supplement even the language of a formal or final writing.

2. "Course of dealing," as defined in subsection (b), is restricted, literally, to a sequence of conduct between the parties previous to the agreement. A sequence of conduct after or under the agreement, however, is a "course of performance." "Course of dealing" may enter the agreement either by explicit provisions of the agreement or by tacit recognition.

3. The Uniform Commercial Code deals with "usage of trade" as a factor in reaching the commercial meaning of the agreement that the parties have made. The language used is to be interpreted as meaning what it may fairly be expected to mean to parties involved in the particular commercial transaction in a given locality or in a given vocation or trade. By adopting in this context the term "usage of trade," the Uniform Commercial Code expresses its intent to reject those cases which see evidence of "custom" as representing an effort to displace or negate "established rules of law." A distinction is to be drawn between mandatory rules of law such as the Statute of Frauds provisions of Article 2 on Sales whose very office is to control and restrict the actions of the parties, and which cannot be abrogated by agreement, or by a usage of trade, and those rules of law (such as those in Part 3 of Article 2 on Sales) which fill in points which the parties have not considered and in fact agreed upon. The latter rules hold "unless otherwise agreed" but yield to the contrary agreement of the parties. Part of the agreement of the parties to which such rules yield is to be sought for in the usages of trade which furnish the background and give particular meaning to the language used, and are the framework of common understanding controlling any general rules of law which hold only when there is no such understanding.

4. A usage of trade under subsection (c) must have the "regularity of observance" specified. The ancient English tests for "custom" are abandoned in this connection. Therefore, it is not required that a usage of trade be "ancient or immemorial," "universal," or the like. Under the requirement of subsection (c) full recognition is thus available for new usages and for usages currently observed by the great majority of decent dealers, even though dissidents ready to cut corners do not agree. There is room also for proper recognition of usage agreed upon by merchants in trade codes.

5. The policies of the Uniform Commercial Code controlling explicit unconscionable contracts and clauses (Sections 1–304, 2–302) apply to implicit clauses that rest on usage of trade and carry forward the policy underlying the ancient requirement that a custom or usage must be "reasonable." However, the emphasis is shifted. The very fact of commercial acceptance makes out a *prima facie* case that the usage is reasonable, and the burden is no longer on the usage to establish itself as being reasonable. But the anciently established policing of usage by the courts is continued to the extent necessary to cope with the situation arising if an unconscionable or dishonest practice should become standard.

6. Subsection (d), giving the prescribed effect to usages of which the parties "are or should be aware," reinforces the provision of subsection (c) requiring not universality but only the described "regularity of observance" of the practice or method. This subsection also reinforces the point of subsection (c) that such usages may be either general to trade or particular to a special branch of trade.

7. Although the definition of "agreement" in Section 1–201 includes the elements of course of performance, course of dealing, and usage of trade, the fact that express reference is made in some sections to those elements is not to be construed as carrying a contrary intent or implication elsewhere. Compare Section 1–302(c).

8. In cases of a well established line of usage varying from the general rules of the Uniform Commercial Code where the precise amount of the variation has not been worked out into a single standard, the party relying on the usage is entitled, in any event, to the minimum variation demonstrated. The whole is not to be disregarded because no particular line of detail has been established. In case a dominant pattern has been fairly evidenced, the party relying on the usage is entitled under this section to go to the trier of fact on the question of whether such dominant pattern has been incorporated into the agreement.

9. Subsection (g) is intended to insure that this Act's liberal recognition of the needs of commerce in regard to usage of trade shall not be made into an instrument of abuse.

§ 1–304. Obligation of Good Faith.

Every contract or duty within [the Uniform Commercial Code] imposes an obligation of good faith in its performance and enforcement.

Official Comment

Source: Former Section 1–203.

Changes from former law: Except for changing the form of reference to the Uniform Commercial Code, this section is identical to former Section 1–203.

1. This section sets forth a basic principle running throughout the Uniform Commercial Code. The principle is that in commercial transactions good faith is required in the performance and enforcement of all agreements or duties. While this duty is explicitly stated in some provisions of the Uniform Commercial Code, the applicability of the duty is broader than merely these situations and applies generally, as stated in this section, to the performance or enforcement of every contract or duty within this Act. It is further implemented by Section 1–303 on course of dealing, course of performance, and usage of trade. This section does not support an independent cause of action for failure to perform or enforce in good faith. Rather, this section means that a failure to perform or enforce, in good faith, a specific duty or obligation under the contract, constitutes a breach of that contract or makes unavailable, under the particular circumstances, a remedial right or power. This distinction makes it clear that the doctrine of good faith merely directs a court towards interpreting contracts within the commercial context in which they are created, performed, and enforced, and does not create a separate duty of fairness and reasonableness which can be independently breached.

2. "Performance and enforcement" of contracts and duties within the Uniform Commercial Code include the exercise of rights created by the Uniform Commercial Code.

§ 1–305. Remedies to Be Liberally Administered.

(a) The remedies provided by [the Uniform Commercial Code] must be liberally administered to the end that the aggrieved party may be put in as good a position as if the other party had fully performed but neither consequential or special damages nor penal damages may be had except as specifically provided in [the Uniform Commercial Code] or by other rule of law.

(b) Any right or obligation declared by [the Uniform Commercial Code] is enforceable by action unless the provision declaring it specifies a different and limited effect.

Official Comment

Source: Former Section 1–106.

Changes from former law: Other than changes in the form of reference to the Uniform Commercial Code, this section is identical to former Section 1–106.

1. Subsection (a) is intended to effect three propositions. The first is to negate the possibility of unduly narrow or technical interpretation of remedial provisions by providing that the remedies in the Uniform Commercial Code are to be liberally administered to the end stated in this section. The second is to make it clear that compensatory damages are limited to compensation. They do not include consequential or special damages, or penal damages; and the Uniform Commercial Code elsewhere makes it clear that damages must be minimized. Cf. Sections 1–304, 2–706(1), and 2–712(2). The third purpose of subsection (a) is to reject any doctrine that damages must be calculable with mathematical accuracy. Compensatory damages are often at best approximate: they have to be proved with whatever definiteness and accuracy the facts permit, but no more. Cf. Section 2–204(3).

2. Under subsection (b), any right or obligation described in the Uniform Commercial Code is enforceable by action, even though no remedy may be expressly provided, unless a particular provision specifies a different and limited effect. Whether specific performance or other equitable relief is available is determined not by this section but by specific provisions and by supplementary principles. Cf. Sections 1–103, 2–716.

3. "Consequential" or "special" damages and "penal" damages are not defined in the Uniform Commercial Code; rather, these terms are used in the sense in which they are used outside the Uniform Commercial Code.

§ 1–306. Waiver or Renunciation of Claim or Right After Breach.

A claim or right arising out of an alleged breach may be discharged in whole or in part without consideration by agreement of the aggrieved party in an authenticated record.

Official Comment

Source: Former Section 1–107.

Changes from former law: This section changes former law in two respects. First, former Section 1–107, requiring the "delivery" of a "written waiver or renunciation" merges the separate concepts of the aggrieved party's agreement to forego rights and the manifestation of that agreement. This section separates those concepts, and explicitly requires *agreement* of the aggrieved party. Second, the revised section reflects developments in electronic commerce by providing for memorialization in an authenticated record. In this context, a party may "authenticate" a record by (i) signing a record that is a writing or (ii) attaching to or logically associating with a record that is not a writing an electronic sound, symbol or process with the present intent to adopt or accept the record. See Sections 1–201(b)(37) and 9–102(a)(7).

1. This section makes consideration unnecessary to the effective renunciation or waiver of rights or claims arising out of an alleged breach of a commercial contract where the agreement effecting such renunciation is memorialized in a record authenticated by the aggrieved party. Its provisions, however, must be read in conjunction with the section imposing an obligation of good faith. (Section 1–304).

§ 1–307. Prima Facie Evidence by Third-Party Documents.

A document in due form purporting to be a bill of lading, policy or certificate of insurance, official weigher's or inspector's certificate, consular invoice, or any other document authorized or required by the contract to be issued by a third party is prima facie evidence of its own authenticity and genuineness and of the facts stated in the document by the third party.

Official Comment

Source: Former Section 1–202.

Changes from former law: Except for minor stylistic changes, this Section is identical to former Section 1–202.

1. This section supplies judicial recognition for documents that are relied upon as trustworthy by commercial parties.

2. This section is concerned only with documents that have been given a preferred status by the parties themselves who have required their procurement in the agreement, and for this reason the applicability of the section is limited to actions arising out of the contract that authorized or required the document. The list of documents is intended to be illustrative and not exclusive.

3. The provisions of this section go no further than establishing the documents in question as prima facie evidence and leave to the court the ultimate determination of the facts where the accuracy or authenticity of the documents is questioned. In this connection the section calls for a commercially reasonable interpretation.

4. Documents governed by this section need not be writings if records in another medium are generally relied upon in the context.

§ 1–308. Performance or Acceptance Under Reservation of Rights.

(a) A party that with explicit reservation of rights performs or promises performance or assents to performance in a manner demanded or offered by the other party does not thereby prejudice the rights reserved. Such words as "without prejudice," "under protest," or the like are sufficient.

(b) Subsection (a) does not apply to an accord and satisfaction.

Official Comment

Source: Former Section 1–207.

Changes from former law: This section is identical to former Section 1–207.

1. This section provides machinery for the continuation of performance along the lines contemplated by the contract despite a pending dispute, by adopting the mercantile device of going ahead with delivery, acceptance,

or payment "without prejudice," "under protest," "under reserve," "with reservation of all our rights," and the like. All of these phrases completely reserve all rights within the meaning of this section. The section therefore contemplates that limited as well as general reservations and acceptance by a party may be made "subject to satisfaction of our purchaser," "subject to acceptance by our customers," or the like.

2. This section does not add any new requirement of language of reservation where not already required by law, but merely provides a specific measure on which a party can rely as that party makes or concurs in any interim adjustment in the course of performance. It does not affect or impair the provisions of this Act such as those under which the buyer's remedies for defect survive acceptance without being expressly claimed if notice of the defects is given within a reasonable time. Nor does it disturb the policy of those cases which restrict the effect of a waiver of a defect to reasonable limits under the circumstances, even though no such reservation is expressed.

The section is not addressed to the creation or loss of remedies in the ordinary course of performance but rather to a method of procedure where one party is claiming as of right something which the other believes to be unwarranted.

3. Subsection (b) states that this section does not apply to an accord and satisfaction. Section 3–311 governs if an accord and satisfaction is attempted by tender of a negotiable instrument as stated in that section. If Section 3–311 does not apply, the issue of whether an accord and satisfaction has been effected is determined by the law of contract. Whether or not Section 3–311 applies, this section has no application to an accord and satisfaction.

§ 1–309. Option to Accelerate at Will.

A term providing that one party or that party's successor in interest may accelerate payment or performance or require collateral or additional collateral "at will" or when the party "deems itself insecure," or words of similar import, means that the party has power to do so only if that party in good faith believes that the prospect of payment or performance is impaired. The burden of establishing lack of good faith is on the party against which the power has been exercised.

Official Comment

Source: Former Section 1–208.

Changes from former law: Except for minor stylistic changes, this section is identical to former Section 1–208.

1. The common use of acceleration clauses in many transactions governed by the Uniform Commercial Code, including sales of goods on credit, notes payable at a definite time, and secured transactions, raises an issue as to the effect to be given to a clause that seemingly grants the power to accelerate at the whim and caprice of one party. This section is intended to make clear that despite language that might be so construed and which further might be held to make the agreement void as against public policy or to make the contract illusory or too indefinite for enforcement, the option is to be exercised only in the good faith belief that the prospect of payment or performance is impaired.

Obviously this section has no application to demand instruments or obligations whose very nature permits call at any time with or without reason. This section applies only to an obligation of payment or performance which in the first instance is due at a future date.

§ 1–310. Subordinated Obligations.

An obligation may be issued as subordinated to performance of another obligation of the person obligated, or a creditor may subordinate its right to performance of an obligation by agreement with either the person obligated or another creditor of the person obligated. Subordination does not create a security interest as against either the common debtor or a subordinated creditor.

Official Comment

Source: Former Section 1–209.

Changes from former law: This section is substantively identical to former Section 1–209. The language in that section stating that it "shall be construed as declaring the law as it existed prior to the enactment of this section and not as modifying it" has been deleted.

1. Billions of dollars of subordinated debt are held by the public and by institutional investors. Commonly, the subordinated debt is subordinated on issue or acquisition and is evidenced by an investment security or by a

negotiable or non-negotiable note. Debt is also sometimes subordinated after it arises, either by agreement between the subordinating creditor and the debtor, by agreement between two creditors of the same debtor, or by agreement of all three parties. The subordinated creditor may be a stockholder or other "insider" interested in the common debtor; the subordinated debt may consist of accounts or other rights to payment not evidenced by any instrument. All such cases are included in the terms "subordinated obligation," "subordination," and "subordinated creditor."

2. Subordination agreements are enforceable between the parties as contracts; and in the bankruptcy of the common debtor dividends otherwise payable to the subordinated creditor are turned over to the superior creditor. This "turn-over" practice has on occasion been explained in terms of "equitable lien," "equitable assignment," or "constructive trust," but whatever the label the practice is essentially an equitable remedy and does not mean that there is a transaction "that creates a security interest in personal property . . . by contract" or a "sale of accounts, chattel paper, payment intangibles, or promissory notes" within the meaning of Section 9–109. On the other hand, nothing in this section prevents one creditor from assigning his rights to another creditor of the same debtor in such a way as to create a security interest within Article 9, where the parties so intend.

3. The enforcement of subordination agreements is largely left to supplementary principles under Section 1–103. If the subordinated debt is evidenced by a certificated security, Section 8–202(a) authorizes enforcement against purchasers on terms stated or referred to on the security certificate. If the fact of subordination is noted on a negotiable instrument, a holder under Sections 3–302 and 3–306 is subject to the term because notice precludes him from taking free of the subordination. Sections 3–302(3)(a) [*unrevised Article 3 (Appendix A)*], 3–306, and 8–317 [*unrevised Article 8*] severely limit the rights of levying creditors of a subordinated creditor in such cases.

UCC ARTICLE 3 (2019)

NEGOTIABLE INSTRUMENTS

Article 3 was revised in 1990 and amended in 2002 and 2018.

Pre-1990 Article 3..Appendix B
2002 amendments ....Appendix C

In 2018, the ALI and ULC approved amendments to UCC Articles 1, 3, 8, and 9, to assist in development and storage of electronic residential mortgage notes, in concert with the proposed federal National Electronic Mortgage Note Repository Act. The Prefatory Note to those UCC amendments says that "the plan is to seek enactment in the states only if and when the federal Repository Act is adopted." As of the date of publication of this volume, the federal Repository Act has not been enacted, so the amendments are not included here. Further information is available at ali.org and uniformlaws.org.

PART 1. GENERAL PROVISIONS AND DEFINITIONS

PART 2. NEGOTIATION, TRANSFER, AND INDORSEMENT

PART 3. ENFORCEMENT OF INSTRUMENTS

PART 4. LIABILITY OF PARTIES

PART 5. DISHONOR

PART 6. DISCHARGE AND PAYMENT

ARTICLE 3 (2019)

National Conference of Commissioners on Uniform State Laws (1990)

REPORTERS

Robert L. Jordan, Los Angeles, California
William D. Warren, Los Angeles, California

DRAFTING COMMITTEE

CO-CHAIRMEN

Robert Haydock, Jr., Boston, Massachusetts
Carlyle C. Ring, Jr., Alexandria, Virginia

MEMBERS

Boris Auerbach, Cincinnati, Ohio
William M. Burke, Los Angeles, California
William E. Hogan, New York, New York
Charles W. Joiner, Ann Arbor, Michigan
Frederick H. Miller, Norman, Oklahoma
Donald J. Rapson, Livingston, New Jersey, *The American Law Institute Representative*
Lawrence J. Bugge, Madison, Wisconsin, *President (Member Ex Officio)*
Neal Ossen, Hartford, Connecticut, *Chairman, Division C (Member Ex Officio)*

REVIEW COMMITTEE

CHAIRMAN

Frank F. Jestrab, Chevy Chase, Maryland

MEMBERS

Rupert R. Bullivant, Portland, Oregon
Michael Franck, Lansing, Michigan

CONSULTANT

Fairfax Leary, Jr., Villanova, Pennsylvania

ADVISORS

Thomas C. Baxter, Jr., *Federal Reserve Bank of New York*
Roland E. Brandel, *American Bar Association*
Leon P. Ciferni, *National Westminster Bank USA*
William B. Davenport, *American Bar Association, Section of Business Law, Ad Hoc Committee on Payment Systems*
Carl Felsenfeld, *Association of the Bar of the City of New York*
Thomas J. Greco, *American Bankers Association*
Oliver I. Ireland, *Board of Governors of Federal Reserve System*
John R.H. Kimball, *Federal Reserve Bank of Boston*
John F. Lee, *New York Clearing House Association*
Norman R. Nelson, *New York Clearing House Association*
Ernest T. Patrikis, *Federal Reserve Bank of New York*
Anne B. Pope, *National Corporate Cash Management Association*
Paul S. Turner, *Occidental Petroleum Corporation and National Corporate Cash Management Association*
Stanley M. Walker, *Exxon Company, U.S.A. and National Corporate Cash Management Association*

ADDITIONAL PARTICIPANTS

Henry N. Dyhouse, *U.S. Central Credit Union*
Robert Egan, *Chemical Bank*
Paul T. Even, *National Gypsum Company*
James Foorman, *First Chicago Corporation*
J. Kevin French, *Exxon Company, U.S.A.*

UNIFORM COMMERCIAL CODE

Richard M. Gottlieb, *Manufacturers Hanover Trust Company*
Douglas E. Harris, *Morgan Guaranty Trust Company of New York*
Arthur L. Herold, *National Corporate Cash Management Association*
Shirley Holder, *Atlantic Richfield Company*
Paul E. Homrighausen, *Bankers Clearing House Association and National Automated Clearing House Association*
Gail M. Inaba, *Morgan Guaranty Trust Company of New York*
Richard P. Kessler, Jr., *Credit Union National Association*
James W. Kopp, *Shell Oil Company*
Donald R. Lawrence, *Citibank N.A.*
Robert M. MacAllister, *Chase Manhattan Bank NA*
Thomas E. Montgomery, *California Bankers Association*
W. Robert Moore, *American Bankers Association*
Samuel Newman, *Manufacturers Hanover Trust Company*
Nena Nodge, *National Corporate Cash Management Association*
Robert J. Pisapia, *Occidental Petroleum Corporation*
Deborah S. Prutzman, *Arnold & Porter*
James S. Rogers, Professor of Law, Newton, Massachusetts
Robert M. Rosenblith, *Manufacturers Hanover Trust Company*
Jamileh Soufan, *American General Corporation*
Irma Villarreal, *Aon Corporation*

PREFATORY NOTE

Revised Article 3 (with miscellaneous and conforming amendments to Articles 1 and 4) is a companion undertaking to Article 4A on funds transfers. Both efforts were undertaken for the purpose of accommodating modern technologies and practices in payment systems and with respect to negotiable instruments. Both efforts were drafted by the same committee over essentially the same period of time. The work on Article 4A was accorded priority and completed in 1989, and revised Article 3 was completed in 1990.

Revised Article 3 may, not inappropriately, be regarded as the latest effort in the progressive codification of the common law of negotiable instruments that began with the English Bills of Exchange Act enacted by Parliament in 1882. The Uniform Negotiable Instruments Law was promulgated by the Conference in 1896, and it in turn was reorganized and modernized by original Article 3—Commercial Paper as part of the Uniform Commercial Code jointly promulgated in 1952 by the Conference and the American Law Institute. Revised Article 3 in 1990 modernizes, reorganizes and clarifies the law.

Purpose of Drafting Effort

The original Articles 3 and 4 and their predecessors were based upon a paper payment system. Literally, there has been an explosion in the volume of paper to process since Articles 3 and 4 were first promulgated. In the early '50s, around 7 billion checks were processed annually. Correctly anticipating an increase in check volume as the result of a retail approach taken by bankers at that time, the American Bankers Association in 1954 placed a team on a research and development project to identify the most efficient method of processing checks mechanically. The eminently successful MICR line technology was the result. Upon its implementation, checks were processed at high rates of speed. In major part as a result of this technology, a seven-fold explosion in check volume has occurred between the '50s and 1988. In 1988, the Federal Reserve estimated check volume at 48 billion written annually. In 1987, Congress enacted the Expedited Funds Availability Act, and the Federal Reserve Board implemented it in 1988 with Regulation CC. Regulation CC covers many aspects of the forward check collection process and all aspects of the return process.

Present Articles 3 and 4, written for a paper-based system, do not adequately address the issues of responsibility and liability as they relate to modern technologies now employed and the procedures required by the current volume of checks and by the "Expedited Funds Availability Act" and Regulation CC. While agreements among parties to particular transactions have provided some relief, such stop-gap measures are no longer adequate.

In addition, practices have developed which are not easily accommodated within existing Article 3. For example, variable rate notes were unknown when Article 3 first was promulgated; they are common today. Questions about the "cash equivalency" of cashier's checks and money orders have arisen as banks have sought to raise defenses to the payment of these instruments.

The revision of Article 3 and Article 4 to update, improve and maintain the viability of it is necessary to accommodate these changing practices and modern technologies, the needs of a rapidly expanding national and international economy, the requirement for more rapid funds availability, and the need for more clarity and certainty. Absent such an update, further Federal preemption of state law may likely occur.

Uniformity is Essential

Traditionally, the legal structures for payments have been regulated by state law through the Uniform Commercial Code. In recent years, however, the Federal government has established regulations for credit and debit cards, and for the availability of funds in a way that regulates much of the check collection process.

With respect to wholesale funds transfers, on an average day two trillion dollars is transferred. Article 4A of the UCC promulgated in 1989 provides the governing comprehensive rules. In 1990, 12 states enacted Article 4A including California, New York and Illinois. In 1991, Article 4A has been introduced in the legislatures of most of the other states, and it is anticipated that most, if not all, will enact Article 4A uniformly. Within a short time, perhaps by 1992, the law of wholesale funds transfers should be uniform throughout the 50 states.

The law for payments through checks and which governs other negotiable instruments similarly should be uniform and up-to-date, either through state enactments or Federal preemption. Otherwise, checks as a viable payment system in international and national transactions will be severely hampered and the utility of other negotiable instruments impaired.

Process of Achieving Uniformity

The essence of uniform law revision is to obtain a sufficient consensus and balance among the interests of the various participants so that universal and uniform adoption by the legislatures of all 50 states may be achieved. As is the practice of the Conference, announcement of the drafting undertaking for Articles 3, 4 and 4A was widely circulated in 1985. Anyone who so requested, received notice of all meetings and was invited to attend. Upon request, names were put on a mailing list to receive copies of drafts as they progressed. In addition, the American Bar Association Ad Hoc Committee on Payments Systems closely followed the work of the Conference and widely circulated the drafts.

The Drafting Committee had 3 or 4 meetings each year and, by August 1990, had held 20 meetings. The drafting meetings began on Friday morning and ended on Sunday at noon. All the meetings were well attended, and the average attendance was 50 or more. The discussion of the drafts was open for comment by all those who attended. In addition, the reporters received a substantial amount of comment and suggestions by written and other communications between meetings of the drafting committee. The work product was read line for line at the annual meetings of the Conference three different years. In addition, the American Law Institute circulated the drafts two or three times to its entire membership. The ALI consultative group also held a meeting to comment and make suggestions on the draft. In addition, progress reports were published annually in *The Business Lawyer* from 1985 through 1990.

The consensus, balance and quality achieved in this lengthy deliberative process is a product not only of the fine work of the reporters and the drafting committee, but also the faithful and energetic participation of the advisors and participants in the drafting meetings. The advisors representing a variety of interests were:

Thomas C. Baxter, Jr., Federal Reserve Bank of New York
Roland E. Brandel, American Bar Association
Leon P. Ciferni, National Westminster Bank USA
William B. Davenport, American Bar Association, Section of Business Law, Ad Hoc Committee on Payment Systems
Carl Felsenfeld, Association of the Bar of the City of New York
Thomas J. Greco, American Bankers Association
Oliver I. Ireland, Board of Governors of Federal Reserve System

UNIFORM COMMERCIAL CODE

John R. H. Kimball, Federal Reserve Bank of Boston
John F. Lee, New York Clearing House Association
Norman R. Nelson, New York Clearing House Association
Ernest T. Patrikis, Federal Reserve Bank of New York
Anne B. Pope, National Corporate Cash Management Association
Paul S. Turner, Occidental Petroleum Corporation and National Corporate Cash Management Association
Stanley M. Walker, Exxon Company, U.S.A. and National Corporate Cash Management Association

Other participants who regularly attended drafting meetings were:

Henry N. Dyhouse, U.S. Central Credit Union
Robert Egan, Chemical Bank
Paul T. Even, National Gypsum Corporation
James Foorman, First Chicago Corporation
J. Kevin French, Exxon Company, U.S.A.
Richard M. Gottlieb, Manufacturers Hanover Trust Company
Douglas E. Harris, National Corporate Cash Management Association
Arthur L. Herold, National Corporate Cash Management Association
Shirley Holder, Atlantic Richfield Company
Paul E. Homrighausen, Bankers Clearing House Association
Gail M. Inaba, Morgan Guaranty Trust Company of New York
Richard P. Kessler, Jr., Credit Union National Association
James W. Kopp, Shell Oil Company
Donald R. Lawrence, Citibank, N.A.
Robert M. McAllister, Chase Manhattan Bank, N.A.
Thomas E. Montgomery, California Bankers Association
W. Robert Moore, American Bankers Association
Samuel Newman, Manufacturers Hanover Trust Company
Nena Nodge, National Corporate Cash Management Association
Robert J. Pisapia, Occidental Petroleum Corporation
Deborah S. Prutzman, Arnold & Porter
James S. Rogers, Professor of Law, Newton, Massachusetts
Robert M. Rosenblith, Manufacturers Hanover Trust Company
Jamileh Soufan, American General Corporation
Irma Villarreal, Aon Corporation

Balance Achieved

The consensus reflected in Revised Article 3 and in the conforming amendments to Articles 1 and 4 is supported by the participants from the banking community, the users, and the Federal regulators because it reflects a balance that each interest can reasonably embrace. Some of the benefits of the Revision include:

A. Benefits in the Public Interest

Certainty—Revised Articles 3 and 4 remove numerous uncertainties that exist in the current provisions and thus reduce risk to the payment system and allow appropriate planning by its users and operators.

Speed and Reliability—The Revision removes impediments to the use of automation, and better conforms to Regulation CC to expedite the availability of funds to customers and to reduce risks to banks.

Lower Costs—The Revision by providing for modern technologies, lowers costs to banks and thus to their customers.

Reduced Litigation—By clarification of troublesome issues, and by the provisions of Sections 3–404 through 3–406 which reform rules for allocation of loss from forgeries and alterations, the Revision should significantly reduce litigation.

B. Benefits to Users

"Good Faith"—The definition of good faith under Sections 3–103(a)(4) and 4–104(c) is expanded to include observance of reasonable commercial standards of fair dealing. This objective standard for good faith applies to the performance of all duties and obligations established under Articles 3 and 4.

Fiduciary Provisions—Section 3–307 protects drawers and persons owed a fiduciary responsibility by imposing stricter standards for obtaining holder in due course rights by a person dealing with the defaulting agent or fiduciary. It also spells out the circumstances under which a person receiving funds has notice of a breach of fiduciary duty, and resulting liability.

Accord and Satisfaction—Under Section 3–311 payees can avoid the unintentional accord and satisfaction by returning the funds or by giving a notice that requires checks to be sent to a particular office where such proposals can be handled. On the other hand, the drawer of a full settlement check is protected from the instrument being indorsed with protest and thus losing the money and being liable on the balance of the claim.

Cashier's Checks—Section 3–411 and related provisions considerably improve the acceptability of bank obligations like cashier's checks as cash equivalents by providing disincentives to wrongful dishonor, such as the possible recovery of consequential damages.

Indorser Liability—Section 3–415 gives more time to hold a check before the user loses indorser liability.

Reporting Forgeries—Section 4–406 increases the outside time a customer has to report forged checks or alterations to thirty days. It also requires a bank truncating checks to retain the item or the capacity to furnish legible copies for seven years.

Individual Agent and Corporate Liability—Section 3–402, as to corporate instruments signed by agents without adequate indication and representation, (except as against a holder in due course), allows a representative to show the parties did not intend individual liability. It affords full protection to the agent that signs a corporate check, even though the check does not show representative status. Also, Section 3–403(b) makes it clear that a signature of an organization is considered unauthorized if more than one signature is required and it is missing.

Direct Suits—Section 3–420 allows a person whose indorsement is forged to sue the depositary bank directly, rather than each drawee of the checks involved.

C. Benefits to the Banking Community

Certainty—Section 3–104 and related provisions clarify what types of contracts are within Article 3 and how they are to be treated, thus promoting certainty of legal rules and reducing litigation costs and risks. Checks that may omit "words of negotiability" are included as fully negotiable; confusion over travelers checks is eliminated; variable rate instruments are included; and there is clarification of the impact of the FTC "Holder" Rule, clarification of the ability of parties to an instrument that is not included in Article 3 to contract for the application of its rules to their contract; and clarification of ordinary money orders as checks rather than bank obligations.

"Ordinary Care"—In Sections 3–103(a)(7) and 4–104(c), ordinary care is defined, making clear that financial institutions taking checks for processing or for payment by automated means need not manually handle each instrument if that is consistent with the institution's procedures and the procedures used do not vary unreasonably from the general usage of banks. This clarification is designed to accommodate and facilitate efficiency, thus lowering costs and lowering expedited funds availability risks. The definition of ordinary care relates to those specific instances in the Code where the standard of ordinary care is set forth.

Statute of Limitations—Sections 3–118 and 4–111 include statutory periods of limitations which will make the law uniform rather than leaving the topic to widely varying state laws.

Employee Fraud—Section 3–405 expands a per se negligence rule to the case of an indorsement forged by an employee whose duties involve handling checks. It also covers that of a faithless employee who supplies a name and then forges the indorsement, but does not require a precise match between the name of the payee and the indorsement.

UNIFORM COMMERCIAL CODE

Bank Definition—The definition of bank is expanded for the purposes of Articles 3 and 4 to clearly include savings and loans and credit unions so that their checks are directly governed by the Code. Section 4–104 clarifies that checks drawn on credit lines are subject to the rules for checks drawn on deposit accounts.

Truncation—Section 4–110 authorizes electronic presentment of items and related provisions remove impediments to truncation. Truncation will reduce risks from mandated funds availability and improve the check collection process. Section 4–406 allows an institution the benefit of its provisions even though it does not return the checks due to truncation. If both the customer and the institution fail to use ordinary care, a comparative negligence standard is used rather than placing the full loss on the institution.

Table of Disposition of Sections in Former Article 3

The reference to a section in Revised Article 3 is to the section that refers to the issue addressed by the section in Former Article 3. If there is no comparable section in Revised Article 3 to a section in Former Article 3, that fact is indicated by the word "Omitted."

Former Article 3 Section	Revised Article 3 or 4 Section
3–101	3–101
3–102(1)(a)	3–105(a)
3–102(1)(b)	3–103(a)(6)
3–102(1)(c)	3–103(a)(9)
3–102(1)(d)	Omitted. See Comment 2 to 3–414.
3–102(1)(e)	3–104(b)
3–102(2)	3–103(b)
3–102(3)	3–103(c)
3–102(4)	3–103(d)
3–103(1)	3–102(a)
3–103(2)	3–102(b)
3–104(1)	3–104(a)
3–104(2)(a)	3–104(e)
3–104(2)(b)	3–104(f)
3–104(2)(c)	3–104(j)
3–104(2)(d)	3–104(e)
3–104(3)	Omitted.
3–105(1)(a)	3–106(a)
3–105(1)(b)	Omitted. See Comment 1 to 3–106.
3–105(1)(c)	Omitted. See Comment 1 to 3–106.
3–105(1)(d)	Omitted. See Comment 1 to 3–106.
3–105(1)(e)	Omitted. See Comment 1 to 3–106.
3–105(1)(f)	3–106(b)(ii)
3–105(1)(g)	3–106(b)(ii)
3–105(1)(h)	3–106(b)(ii)
3–105(2)(a)	3–106(a)(ii)
3–105(2)(b)	3–106(b)(ii)
3–106(1)	3–104(a)
3–106(2)	Omitted.
3–107(1)	Omitted. See Comment to 3–107.
3–107(2)	3–107
3–108	3–108(a)
3–109(1)	3–108(b)
3–109(2)	Omitted.
3–110(1)	3–109(b)
3–110(1)(a)	Omitted.
3–110(1)(b)	Omitted.
3–110(1)(c)	Omitted.

	ARTICLE 3 (2019)
3–110(1)(d)	3–110(d)
3–110(1)(e)	3–110(c)(2)(i)
3–110(1)(f)	3–110(c)(2)(iv)
3–110(1)(g)	Omitted.
3–110(2)	Omitted.
3–110(3)	3–109(b)
3–111(a)	3–109(a)(1)
3–111(b)	3–109(a)(1)
3–111(c)	3–109(a)(3) and 3–205(b)
3–112(1)(a)	Omitted.
3–112(1)(b)	3–104(a)(3)(i)
3–112(1)(c)	3–104(a)(3)(i)
3–112(1)(d)	3–104(a)(3)(ii)
3–112(1)(e)	3–104(a)(3)(iii)
3–112(1)(f)	3–311
3–112(1)(g)	Omitted.
3–112(2)	Omitted.
3–113	Omitted.
3–114(1)	Omitted. See Comment to 3–113.
3–114(2)	3–113(a)
3–114(3)	Omitted. See Comment to 3–113.
3–115	3–115
3–116(a)	3–110(d)
3–116(b)	3–110(d)
3–117(a)	3–110(c)(2)(ii)
3–117(b)	3–110(c)(2)(i)
3–117(c)	Omitted.
3–118(a)	3–104(e) and 3–103(a)(6)
3–118(b)	3–114
3–118(c)	3–114
3–118(d)	3–112
3–118(e)	3–116(a)
3–118(f)	Omitted.
3–119	3–117 and 3–106(a) and (b)
3–120	4–106(a)
3–121	4–106(b)
3–122	Omitted. See Comment 1 to 3–118.
3–201(1)	3–203(b)
3–201(2)	3–204(c)
3–201(3)	3–203(c)
3–202(1)	3–201(a)
3–202(2)	3–204(a)
3–202(3)	3–203(d)
3–202(4)	Omitted.
3–203	3–204(d)
3–204(1)	3–205(a)
3–204(2)	3–205(b)
3–204(3)	3–205(c)
3–205	Omitted.
3–206(1)	3–206(a)
3–206(2)	3–206(c)(4) and (d)
3–206(3)	3–206(b), (c), and (e)
3–206(4)	3–206(d) and (e)
3–207(1)(a)	3–202(a)(i)
3–207(1)(b)	3–202(a)(ii)
3–207(1)(c)	3–202(a)(iii)

3–207(1)(d)	3–202(a)(iii)
3–207(2)	3–202(b)
3–208	3–207
3–301	Omitted. See Comment to 3–301.
3–302(1)	3–302(a)
3–302(2)	Omitted. See Comment 4 to 3–302.
3–302(3)(a)	3–302(c)(i)
3–302(3)(b)	3–302(c)(iii)
3–302(3)(c)	3–302(c)(ii)
3–302(4)	3–302(e)
3–303(a)	3–303(a)(1) and (2)
3–303(b)	3–303(a)(3)
3–303(c)	3–303(a)(4) and (5)
3–304(1)(a)	3–302(a)(1)
3–304(1)(b)	Omitted.
3–304(2)	3–307(b)
3–304(3)(a)	3–302(a)(2)(iii); 3–304(b)(1)
3–304(3)(b)	3–304(b)(3)
3–304(3)(c)	3–304(a)(1), (2) and (3)
3–304(4)(a)	Omitted.
3–304(4)(b)	Omitted.
3–304(4)(c)	Omitted.
3–304(4)(d)	Omitted.
3–304(4)(e)	3–307
3–304(4)(f)	3–304(c)
3–304(5)	3–302(b)
3–304(6)	Omitted.
3–305(1)	3–306
3–305(2)(a)	3–305(a)(1)(i)
3–305(2)(b)	3–305(a)(1)(ii)
3–305(2)(c)	3–305(a)(1)(iii)
3–305(2)(d)	3–305(a)(1)(iv)
3–305(2)(e)	3–601(b)
3–306(a)	3–306
3–306(b)	3–305(a)(2)
3–306(c)	3–305(a)(2); 3–303(b); 3–105(b)
3–306(d)	3–305(c)
3–307(1)(a)	3–308(a)
3–307(1)(b)	3–308(a)
3–307(2)	3–308(b)
3–307(3)	3–308(b)
3–401(1)	3–401(a)
3–401(2)	3–401(b)
3–402	3–204(a)
3–403(1)	3–402(a)
3–403(2)(a)	3–402(b)(2)
3–403(2)(b)	3–402(b)(2)
3–403(3)	3–402(b)(1)
3–404(1)	3–403(a)
3–404(2)	3–403(a)
3–405(1)(a)	3–404(a)
3–405(1)(b)	3–404(b)(i)
3–405(1)(c)	3–405
3–405(2)	3–403(c)
3–406	3–406
3–407(1)(a)	3–407(a)(i)

3–407(1)(b)	3–407(a)(ii)
3–407(1)(c)	3–407(a)(i)
3–407(2)(a)	3–407(b)
3–407(2)(b)	3–407(b)
3–407(3)	3–407(c)
3–408	3–303(b)
3–409(1)	3–408
3–409(2)	Omitted. See Comment 1 to 3–408.
3–410(1)	3–409(a)
3–410(2)	3–409(b)
3–410(3)	3–409(c)
3–411(1)	3–409(d); 3–414(c); 3–415(d)
3–411(2)	3–409(d)
3–411(3)	Omitted.
3–412(1)	3–410(a)
3–412(2)	3–410(b)
3–412(3)	3–410(c)
3–413(1)	3–412; 3–413(a)
3–413(2)	3–414(b) and (e)
3–413(3)	Omitted.
3–414(1)	3–415(a) and (b)
3–414(2)	Omitted.
3–415(1)	3–419(a)
3–415(2)	3–419(b)
3–415(3)	Omitted. See 3–605(h)
3–415(4)	3–419(c)
3–415(5)	3–419(e)
3–416(1)	Omitted.
3–416(2)	3–419(d)
3–416(3)	Omitted.
3–416(4)	3–419(c)
3–416(5)	Omitted.
3–416(6)	Omitted.
3–417(1)	3–417
3–417(2)	3–416
3–417(3)	Omitted.
3–417(4)	Omitted.
3–418	3–418
3–419(1)	3–420(a)
3–419(2)	3–420(b)
3–419(3)	3–420(c)
3–419(4)	3–206(c)(4) and (d)
3–501(1)(a)	3–414(b); 3–502(b)(3) and (4)
3–501(1)(b)	3–415(a); 3–502(a)(1) and (2); 3–502(b), (c), (d) and (e)
3–501(1)(c)	3–414(f); 3–415(e)
3–501(2)(a)	3–503(a)
3–501(2)(b)	Omitted. See Comment 2 to 3–414.
3–501(3)	Omitted. See Comment to 3–505.
3–501(4)	Omitted.
3–502(1)(a)	3–415(e)
3–502(1)(b)	3–414(f)
3–502(2)	Omitted. See Comment to 3–505.
3–503	Omitted. See Comment to 3–502.
3–504(1)	3–501(a)
3–504(2)(a)	3–501(b)(1)
3–504(2)(b)	3–501(b)(1)

3–504(2)(c)	3–501(b)(1); 3–111
3–504(3)(a)	3–501(b)(1)
3–504(3)(b)	Omitted.
3–504(4)	3–501(b)(1)
3–504(5)	Omitted.
3–505(1)(a)	3–501(b)(2)(i)
3–505(1)(b)	3–501(b)(2)(ii)
3–505(1)(c)	Omitted.
3–505(1)(d)	3–501(b)(2)(iii)
3–505(2)	Omitted.
3–506(1)	Omitted.
3–506(2)	Omitted.
3–507(1)	3–502
3–507(2)	Omitted.
3–507(3)	3–501(b)(3)(i)
3–507(4)	Omitted.
3–508(1)	3–503(b)
3–508(2)	3–503(c)
3–508(3)	3–503(b)
3–508(4)	Omitted.
3–508(5)	Omitted.
3–508(6)	Omitted.
3–508(7)	Omitted.
3–508(8)	3–503(b)
3–509(1)	3–505(b)
3–509(2)	3–505(b)
3–509(3)	3–505(b)
3–509(4)	Omitted.
3–509(5)	Omitted.
3–510(a)	3–505(a)(1)
3–510(b)	3–505(a)(2)
3–510(c)	3–505(a)(3)
3–511(1)	Omitted.
3–511(2)(a)	3–504(a)(iv)
3–511(2)(b)	3–504(a)(ii), (iv), and (v); 3–504(b)
3–511(2)(c)	3–504(a)(i)
3–511(3)(a)	3–504(a)(ii)
3–511(3)(b)	3–504(a)(ii)
3–511(4)	3–502(f)
3–511(5)	Omitted.
3–511(6)	Omitted.
3–601(1)	3–601(a)
3–601(2)	3–601(a)
3–601(3)	Omitted.
3–602	3–601(b)
3–603(1)	3–602(a) and (b)
3–603(1)(a)	3–602(b)(2)
3–603(1)(b)	Omitted. See 3–206(c)(3).
3–603(2)	Omitted.
3–604(1)	3–603(c)
3–604(2)	3–603(b)
3–604(3)	3–603(c)
3–605(1)(a)	3–604(a)(i)
3–605(1)(b)	3–604(a)(ii)
3–605(2)	3–604(b)
3–606(1)(a)	3–605(b) and (c)

PART 1

GENERAL PROVISIONS AND DEFINITIONS

§ 3–101. Short Title.

This Article may be cited as Uniform Commercial Code—Negotiable Instruments.

§ 3–102. Subject Matter.

(a) This Article applies to negotiable instruments. It does not apply to money, to payment orders governed by Article 4A, or to securities governed by Article 8.

(b) If there is conflict between this Article and Article 4 or 9, Articles 4 and 9 govern.

(c) Regulations of the Board of Governors of the Federal Reserve System and operating circulars of the Federal Reserve Banks supersede any inconsistent provision of this Article to the extent of the inconsistency.

Official Comment

1. Former Article 3 had no provision affirmatively stating its scope. Former Section 3–103 was a limitation on scope. In revised Article 3, Section 3–102 states that Article 3 applies to "negotiable instruments," defined in Section 3–104. Section 3–104(b) also defines the term "instrument" as a synonym for "negotiable instrument." In most places Article 3 uses the shorter term "instrument." This follows the convention used in former Article 3.

2. The reference in former Section 3–103(1) to "documents of title" is omitted as superfluous because these documents contain no promise to pay money. The definition of "payment order" in Section 4A–103(a)(1)(iii) excludes drafts which are governed by Article 3. Section 3–102(a) makes clear that a payment order governed by Article 4A is not governed by Article 3. Thus, Article 3 and Article 4A are mutually exclusive.

Article 8 states in Section 8–103(d) that "A writing that is a security certificate is governed by this Article and not by Article 3, even though it also meets the requirements of that Article." Section 3–102(a) conforms to this provision. With respect to some promises or orders to pay money, there may be a question whether the promise or order is an instrument under Section 3–104(a) or a certificated security under Section 8–102(a)(4) and (15). Whether a writing is covered by Article 3 or Article 8 has important consequences. Among other things, under Section 8–207, the issuer of a certificated security may treat the registered owner as the owner for all purposes until the presentment for registration of a transfer. The issuer of a negotiable instrument, on the other hand, may discharge its obligation to pay the instrument only by paying a person entitled to enforce under Section 3–301. There are also important consequences to an indorser. An indorser of a security does not undertake the issuer's obligation or make any warranty that the issuer will honor the underlying obligation, while an indorser of a negotiable instrument becomes secondarily liable on the underlying obligation.

Ordinarily the distinction between instruments and certificated securities in non-bearer form should be relatively clear. A certificated security under Article 8 must be in registered form (Section 8–102(a)(13)) so that it can be registered on the issuer's records. By contrast, registration plays no part in Article 3. The distinction between an instrument and a certificated security in bearer form may be somewhat more difficult and will generally lie in the economic functions of the two writings. Ordinarily, negotiable instruments under Article 3 will be separate and distinct instruments, while certificated securities under Article 8 will be either one of a class or series or by their terms divisible into a class or series (Section 8–102(a)(15)(ii)). Thus, a promissory note in bearer form could come under either Article 3 if it were simply an individual note, or under Article 8 if it were one of a series of notes or divisible into a series. An additional distinction is whether the instrument is of the type commonly dealt in on securities exchanges or markets or commonly recognized as a medium for investment (Section 8–102(a)(15)(iii)). Thus, a check written in bearer form (i.e., a check made payable to "cash") would not be a certificated security within Article 8 of the Uniform Commercial Code.

Occasionally, a particular writing may fit the definition of both a negotiable instrument under Article 3 and of an investment security under Article 8. In such cases, the instrument is subject exclusively to the requirements of Article 8. Section 8–103(d) and Section 3–102(a).

3. Although the terms of Article 3 apply to transactions by Federal Reserve Banks, federal preemption would make ineffective any Article 3 provision that conflicts with federal law. The activities of the Federal Reserve Banks are governed by regulations of the Federal Reserve Board and by operating circulars issued by the Reserve Banks themselves. In some instances, the operating circulars are issued pursuant to a Federal Reserve Board regulation. In other cases, the Reserve Bank issues the operating circular under its own authority under the Federal Reserve Act, subject to review by the Federal Reserve Board. Section 3–102(c) states that Federal Reserve Board regulations and operating circulars of the Federal Reserve Banks supersede any inconsistent provision of Article 3 to the extent of the inconsistency. Federal Reserve Board regulations, being valid exercises of regulatory authority pursuant to a federal statute, take precedence over state law if there is an inconsistency. *Childs v. Federal Reserve Bank of Dallas*, 719 F.2d 812 (5th Cir. 1983), reh. den. 724 F.2d 127 (5th Cir. 1984). Section 3–102(c) treats operating circulars as having the same effect whether issued under the Reserve Bank's own authority or under a Federal Reserve Board regulation. Federal statutes may also preempt Article 3. For example, the Expedited Funds Availability Act, 12 U.S.C. § 4001 et seq., provides that the Act and the regulations issued pursuant to the Act supersede any inconsistent provisions of the UCC. 12 U.S.C. § 4007(b).

4. In *Clearfield Trust Co. v. United States*, 318 U.S. 363 (1943), the Court held that if the United States is a party to an instrument, its rights and duties are governed by federal common law in the absence of a specific federal statute or regulation. In *United States v. Kimbell Foods, Inc.*, 440 U.S. 715 (1979), the Court stated a three-pronged test to ascertain whether the federal common-law rule should follow the state rule. In most instances courts under the *Kimbell* test have shown a willingness to adopt UCC rules in formulating federal common law on the subject. In *Kimbell* the Court adopted the priorities rules of Article 9.

5. In 1989 the United Nations Commission on International Trade Law completed a Convention on International Bills of Exchange and International Promissory Notes. If the United States becomes a party to this Convention, the Convention will preempt state law with respect to international bills and notes governed by the Convention. Thus, an international bill of exchange or promissory note that meets the definition of instrument in Section 3–104 will not be governed by Article 3 if it is governed by the Convention. That Convention applies only to bills and notes that indicate on their face that they involve cross-border transactions. It does not apply at all to checks. Convention Articles 1(3), 2(1), 2(2). Moreover, because it applies only if the bill or note specifically calls for application of the Convention, Convention Article 1, there is little chance that the Convention will apply accidentally to a transaction that the parties intended to be governed by this Article.

As amended in 1995 and 2002.

§ 3–103. Definitions.

(a) In this Article:

(1) "Acceptor" means a drawee who has accepted a draft.

(2) "Consumer account" means an account established by an individual primarily for personal, family, or household purposes.

(3) "Consumer transaction" means a transaction in which an individual incurs an obligation primarily for personal, family, or household purposes.

(4) "Drawee" means a person ordered in a draft to make payment.

(5) "Drawer" means a person who signs or is identified in a draft as a person ordering payment.

(6) ["Good faith" means honesty in fact and the observance of reasonable commercial standards of fair dealing.] [*Note from West Advisory Panel: This subsection will be deleted if the jurisdiction adopts the definition of good faith in revised Article 1 (2001).*]

(7) "Maker" means a person who signs or is identified in a note as a person undertaking to pay.

(8) "Order" means a written instruction to pay money signed by the person giving the instruction. The instruction may be addressed to any person, including the person giving the instruction, or to one or more persons jointly or in the alternative but not in succession. An authorization to pay is not an order unless the person authorized to pay is also instructed to pay.

(9) "Ordinary care" in the case of a person engaged in business means observance of reasonable commercial standards, prevailing in the area in which the person is located, with respect to the business in which the person is engaged. In the case of a bank that takes an instrument for processing for collection or payment by automated means, reasonable commercial standards do not require the bank to examine the instrument if the failure to examine does not violate the bank's prescribed procedures and the bank's procedures do not vary unreasonably from general banking usage not disapproved by this Article or Article 4.

(10) "Party" means a party to an instrument.

(11) "Principal obligor," with respect to an instrument, means the accommodated party or any other party to the instrument against whom a secondary obligor has recourse under this article.

(12) "Promise" means a written undertaking to pay money signed by the person undertaking to pay. An acknowledgment of an obligation by the obligor is not a promise unless the obligor also undertakes to pay the obligation.

(13) "Prove" with respect to a fact means to meet the burden of establishing the fact (Section 1–201(b)(8)).

(14) ["Record" means information that is inscribed on a tangible medium or that is stored in an electronic or other medium and is retrievable in perceivable form.]

(15) "Remitter" means a person who purchases an instrument from its issuer if the instrument is payable to an identified person other than the purchaser.

(16) "Remotely-created consumer item" means an item drawn on a consumer account, which is not created by the payor bank and does not bear a handwritten signature purporting to be the signature of the drawer.

(17) "Secondary obligor," with respect to an instrument, means (a) an indorser or an accommodation party, (b) a drawer having the obligation described in Section 3–414(d), or (c) any other party to the instrument that has recourse against another party to the instrument pursuant to Section 3–116(b).

(b) Other definitions applying to this Article and the sections in which they appear are:

"Acceptance" Section 3–409
"Accommodated party" Section 3–419
"Accommodation party" Section 3–419
"Account" Section 4–104
"Alteration" Section 3–407
"Anomalous indorsement" Section 3–205
"Blank indorsement" Section 3–205
"Cashier's check" Section 3–104
"Certificate of deposit" Section 3–104
"Certified check" Section 3–409
"Check" Section 3–104
"Consideration" Section 3–303

"Draft" Section 3–104
"Holder in due course" Section 3–302
"Incomplete instrument" Section 3–115
"Indorsement" Section 3–204
"Indorser" Section 3–204
"Instrument" Section 3–104
"Issue" Section 3–105
"Issuer" Section 3–105
"Negotiable instrument" Section 3–104
"Negotiation" Section 3–201
"Note" Section 3–104
"Payable at a definite time" Section 3–108
"Payable on demand" Section 3–108
"Payable to bearer" Section 3–109
"Payable to order" Section 3–109
"Payment" Section 3–602
"Person entitled to enforce" Section 3–301
"Presentment" Section 3–501
"Reacquisition" Section 3–207
"Special indorsement" Section 3–205
"Teller's check" Section 3–104
"Transfer of instrument" Section 3–203
"Traveler's check" Section 3–104
"Value" Section 3–303

(c) The following definitions in other Articles apply to this Article:

"Banking day" Section 4–104
"Clearing house" Section 4–104
"Collecting bank" Section 4–105
"Depositary bank" Section 4–105
"Documentary draft" Section 4–104
"Intermediary bank" Section 4–105
"Item" Section 4–104
"Payor bank" Section 4–105
"Suspends payments" Section 4–104

(d) In addition, Article 1 contains general definitions and principles of construction and interpretation applicable throughout this Article.

Legislative Note. A jurisdiction that enacts this statute that has not yet enacted the revised version of UCC Article 1 should add to Section 3–103 the definition of "good faith" that appears in the official version of Section 1–201(b)(20) and the definition of "record" that appears in the official version of Section 1–201(b)(31). Sections 3–103(a)(6) and (14) are reserved for that purpose. A jurisdiction that already has adopted or simultaneously adopts the revised Article 1 should not add those definitions, but should leave those numbers "reserved." If jurisdictions follow the numbering suggested here, the subsections will have the same numbering in all jurisdictions that have adopted these amendments (whether they have or have not adopted the revised version of UCC Article 1).

As amended in 2001 and 2002.

Official Comment

1. Subsection (a) defines some common terms used throughout the Article that were not defined by former Article 3 and adds the definitions of "order" and "promise" found in former Section 3–102(1)(b) and (c).

2. The definition of "order" includes an instruction given by the signer to itself. The most common example of this kind of order is a cashier's check: a draft with respect to which the drawer and drawee are the same bank or branches of the same bank. Former Section 3–118(a) treated a cashier's check as a note. It stated "a draft drawn on the drawer is effective as a note." Although it is technically more correct to treat a cashier's check as a promise by the issuing bank to pay rather than an order to pay, a cashier's check is in the form of a check and it is normally

referred to as a check. Thus, revised Article 3 follows banking practice in referring to a cashier's check as both a draft and a check rather than a note. Some insurance companies also follow the practice of issuing drafts in which the drawer draws on itself and makes the draft payable at or through a bank. These instruments are also treated as drafts. The obligation of the drawer of a cashier's check or other draft drawn on the drawer is stated in Section 3–412.

An order may be addressed to more than one person as drawee either jointly or in the alternative. The authorization of alternative drawees follows former Section 3–102(1)(b) and recognizes the practice of drawers, such as corporations issuing dividend checks, who for commercial convenience name a number of drawees, usually in different parts of the country. Section 3–501(b)(1) provides that presentment may be made to any one of multiple drawees. Drawees in succession are not permitted because the holder should not be required to make more than one presentment. Dishonor by any drawee named in the draft entitles the holder to rights of recourse against the drawer or indorsers.

3. The last sentence of subsection (a)(12) is intended to make it clear that an I.O.U. or other written acknowledgment of indebtedness is not a note unless there is also an undertaking to pay the obligation.

4. This Article now uses the broadened definition of good faith in revised Article 1. The definition requires not only honesty in fact but also "observance of reasonable commercial standards of fair dealing." Although fair dealing is a broad term that must be defined in context, it is clear that it is concerned with the fairness of conduct rather than the care with which an act is performed. Failure to exercise ordinary care in conducting a transaction is an entirely different concept than failure to deal fairly in conducting the transaction. Both fair dealing and ordinary care, which is defined in Section 3–103(a)(9), are to be judged in the light of reasonable commercial standards, but those standards in each case are directed to different aspects of commercial conduct.

5. Subsection (a)(9) is a definition of ordinary care which is applicable not only to Article 3 but to Article 4 as well. See Section 4–104(c). The general rule is stated in the first sentence of subsection (a)(9) and it applies both to banks and to persons engaged in businesses other than banking. Ordinary care means observance of reasonable commercial standards of the relevant businesses prevailing in the area in which the person is located. The second sentence of subsection (a)(9) is a particular rule limited to the duty of a bank to examine an instrument taken by a bank for processing for collection or payment by automated means. This particular rule applies primarily to Section 4–406 and it is discussed in Comment 4 to that section. Nothing in Section 3–103(a)(9) is intended to prevent a customer from proving that the procedures followed by a bank are unreasonable, arbitrary, or unfair.

6. The definition of consumer account includes a joint account established by more than one individual. See Section 1–106(1) [*unrevised Article 1; see Concordance, p. 12*].

As amended in 2001 and 2002.

§ 3–104. Negotiable Instrument.

(a) Except as provided in subsections (c) and (d), "negotiable instrument" means an unconditional promise or order to pay a fixed amount of money, with or without interest or other charges described in the promise or order, if it:

(1) is payable to bearer or to order at the time it is issued or first comes into possession of a holder;

(2) is payable on demand or at a definite time; and

(3) does not state any other undertaking or instruction by the person promising or ordering payment to do any act in addition to the payment of money, but the promise or order may contain (i) an undertaking or power to give, maintain, or protect collateral to secure payment, (ii) an authorization or power to the holder to confess judgment or realize on or dispose of collateral, or (iii) a waiver of the benefit of any law intended for the advantage or protection of an obligor.

(b) "Instrument" means a negotiable instrument.

(c) An order that meets all of the requirements of subsection (a), except paragraph (1), and otherwise falls within the definition of "check" in subsection (f) is a negotiable instrument and a check.

(d) A promise or order other than a check is not an instrument if, at the time it is issued or first comes into possession of a holder, it contains a conspicuous statement, however expressed, to the effect that the promise or order is not negotiable or is not an instrument governed by this Article.

(e) An instrument is a "note" if it is a promise and is a "draft" if it is an order. If an instrument falls within the definition of both "note" and "draft," a person entitled to enforce the instrument may treat it as either.

(f) "Check" means (i) a draft, other than a documentary draft, payable on demand and drawn on a bank or (ii) a cashier's check or teller's check. An instrument may be a check even though it is described on its face by another term, such as "money order."

(g) "Cashier's check" means a draft with respect to which the drawer and drawee are the same bank or branches of the same bank.

(h) "Teller's check" means a draft drawn by a bank (i) on another bank, or (ii) payable at or through a bank.

(i) "Traveler's check" means an instrument that (i) is payable on demand, (ii) is drawn on or payable at or through a bank, (iii) is designated by the term "traveler's check" or by a substantially similar term, and (iv) requires, as a condition to payment, a countersignature by a person whose specimen signature appears on the instrument.

(j) "Certificate of deposit" means an instrument containing an acknowledgment by a bank that a sum of money has been received by the bank and a promise by the bank to repay the sum of money. A certificate of deposit is a note of the bank.

Official Comment

1. The definition of "negotiable instrument" defines the scope of Article 3 since Section 3-102 states: "This Article applies to negotiable instruments." The definition in Section 3-104(a) incorporates other definitions in Article 3. An instrument is either a "promise," defined in Section 3-103(a)(12), or "order," defined in Section 3-103(a)(8). A promise is a written undertaking to pay money signed by the person undertaking to pay. An order is a written instruction to pay money signed by the person giving the instruction. Thus, the term "negotiable instrument" is limited to a signed writing that orders or promises payment of money. "Money" is defined in Section 1-201(24) [*unrevised Article 1; see Concordance, p. 12*] and is not limited to United States dollars. It also includes a medium of exchange established by a foreign government or monetary units of account established by an intergovernmental organization or by agreement between two or more nations. Five other requirements are stated in Section 3-104(a): First, the promise or order must be "unconditional." The quoted term is explained in Section 3-106. Second, the amount of money must be "a fixed amount . . . with or without interest or other charges described in the promise or order." Section 3-112(b) relates to "interest." Third, the promise or order must be "payable to bearer or to order." The quoted phrase is explained in Section 3-109. An exception to this requirement is stated in subsection (c). Fourth, the promise or order must be payable "on demand or at a definite time." The quoted phrase is explained in Section 3-108. Fifth, the promise or order may not state "any other undertaking or instruction by the person promising or ordering payment to do any act in addition to the payment of money" with three exceptions. The quoted phrase is based on the first sentence of N.I.L. Section 5 which is the precursor of "no other promise, order, obligation or power given by the maker or drawer" appearing in former Section 3-104(1)(b). The words "instruction" and "undertaking" are used instead of "order" and "promise" that are used in the N.I.L. formulation because the latter words are defined terms that include only orders or promises to pay money. The three exceptions stated in Section 3-104(a)(3) are based on and are intended to have the same meaning as former Section 3-112(1)(b), (c), (d), and (e), as well as N.I.L. § 5(1), (2), and (3). Subsection (b) states that "instrument" means a "negotiable instrument." This follows former Section 3-102(1)(e) which treated the two terms as synonymous.

2. Unless subsection (c) applies, the effect of subsection (a)(1) and Section 3-102(a) is to exclude from Article 3 any promise or order that is not payable to bearer or to order. There is no provision in revised Article 3 that is comparable to former Section 3-805. The comment to former Section 3-805 states that the typical example of a writing covered by that section is a check reading "Pay John Doe." Such a check was governed by former Article 3 but there could not be a holder in due course of the check. Under Section 3-104(c) such a check is governed by revised Article 3 and there can be a holder in due course of the check. But subsection (c) applies only to checks. The comment to former Section 3-805 does not state any example other than the check to illustrate that section. Subsection (c) is based on the belief that it is good policy to treat checks, which are payment instruments, as negotiable instruments whether or not they contain the words "to the order of". These words are almost always pre-printed on the check form. Occasionally the drawer of a check may strike out these words before issuing the check. In the past some credit unions used check forms that did not contain the quoted words. Such check forms may still be in use but they are no longer common. Absence of the quoted words can easily be overlooked and

should not affect the rights of holders who may pay money or give credit for a check without being aware that it is not in the conventional form.

Total exclusion from Article 3 of other promises or orders that are not payable to bearer or to order serves a useful purpose. It provides a simple device to clearly exclude a writing that does not fit the pattern of typical negotiable instruments and which is not intended to be a negotiable instrument. If a writing could be an instrument despite the absence of "to order" or "to bearer" language and a dispute arises with respect to the writing, it might be argued that the writing is a negotiable instrument because the other requirements of subsection (a) are somehow met. Even if the argument is eventually found to be without merit it can be used as a litigation ploy. Words making a promise or order payable to bearer or to order are the most distinguishing feature of a negotiable instrument and such words are frequently referred to as "words of negotiability." Article 3 is not meant to apply to contracts for the sale of goods or services or the sale or lease of real property or similar writings that may contain a promise to pay money. The use of words of negotiability in such contracts would be an aberration. Absence of the words precludes any argument that such contracts might be negotiable instruments.

An order or promise that is excluded from Article 3 because of the requirements of Section 3–104(a) may nevertheless be similar to a negotiable instrument in many respects. Although such a writing cannot be made a negotiable instrument within Article 3 by contract or conduct of its parties, nothing in Section 3–104 or in Section 3–102 is intended to mean that in a particular case involving such a writing a court could not arrive at a result similar to the result that would follow if the writing were a negotiable instrument. For example, a court might find that the obligor with respect to a promise that does not fall within Section 3–104(a) is precluded from asserting a defense against a bona fide purchaser. The preclusion could be based on estoppel or ordinary principles of contract. It does not depend upon the law of negotiable instruments. An example is stated in the paragraph following Case # 2 in Comment 4 to Section 3–302.

Moreover, consistent with the principle stated in Section 1–102(2)(b) [*unrevised Article 1; see Concordance, p. 12*], the immediate parties to an order or promise that is not an instrument may provide by agreement that one or more of the provisions of Article 3 determine their rights and obligations under the writing. Upholding the parties' choice is not inconsistent with Article 3. Such an agreement may bind a transferee of the writing if the transferee has notice of it or the agreement arises from usage of trade and the agreement does not violate other law or public policy. An example of such an agreement is a provision that a transferee of the writing has the rights of a holder in due course stated in Article 3 if the transferee took rights under the writing in good faith, for value, and without notice of a claim or defense.

Even without an agreement of the parties to an order or promise that is not an instrument, it may be appropriate, consistent with the principles stated in Section 1–102(2) [*unrevised Article 1; see Concordance, p. 12*], for a court to apply one or more provisions of Article 3 to the writing by analogy, taking into account the expectations of the parties and the differences between the writing and an instrument governed by Article 3. Whether such application is appropriate depends upon the facts of each case.

3. Subsection (d) allows exclusion from Article 3 of a writing that would otherwise be an instrument under subsection (a) by a statement to the effect that the writing is not negotiable or is not governed by Article 3. For example, a promissory note can be stamped with the legend NOT NEGOTIABLE. The effect under subsection (d) is not only to negate the possibility of a holder in due course, but to prevent the writing from being a negotiable instrument for any purpose. Subsection (d) does not, however, apply to a check. If a writing is excluded from Article 3 by subsection (d), a court could, nevertheless, apply Article 3 principles to it by analogy as stated in Comment 2.

4. Instruments are divided into two general categories: drafts and notes. A draft is an instrument that is an order. A note is an instrument that is a promise. Section 3–104(e). The term "bill of exchange" is not used in Article 3. It is generally understood to be a synonym for the term "draft." Subsections (f) through (j) define particular instruments that fall within the categories of draft and note. The term "draft," defined in subsection (e), includes a "check" which is defined in subsection (f). "Check" includes a share draft drawn on a credit union payable through a bank because the definition of bank (Section 4–105) includes credit unions. However, a draft drawn on an insurance company payable through a bank is not a check because it is not drawn on a bank. "Money orders" are sold both by banks and non-banks. They vary in form and their form determines how they are treated in Article 3. The most common form of money order sold by banks is that of an ordinary check drawn by the purchaser except that the amount is machine impressed. That kind of money order is a check under Article 3 and is subject to a stop order by the purchaser-drawer as in the case of ordinary checks. The seller bank is the drawee and has no obligation to a holder to pay the money order. If a money order falls within the definition of a teller's check, the rules applicable to teller's checks apply. Postal money orders are subject to federal law. "Teller's check" is separately defined in subsection (h). A teller's check is always drawn by a bank and is usually drawn on another bank. In some cases a teller's check is drawn on a nonbank but is made payable at or through a bank. Article 3

treats both types of teller's check identically, and both are included in the definition of "check." A cashier's check, defined in subsection (g), is also included in the definition of "check." Traveler's checks are issued both by banks and nonbanks and may be in the form of a note or draft. Subsection (i) states the essential characteristics of a traveler's check. The requirement that the instrument be "drawn on or payable at or through a bank" may be satisfied without words on the instrument that identify a bank as drawee or paying agent so long as the instrument bears an appropriate routing number that identifies a bank as paying agent.

The definitions in Regulation CC § 229.2 of the terms "check," "cashier's check," "teller's check," and "traveler's check" are different from the definitions of those terms in Article 3.

Certificates of deposit are treated in former Article 3 as a separate type of instrument. In revised Article 3, Section 3-104(j) treats them as notes.

5. There are some differences between the requirements of Article 3 and the requirements included in Article 3 of the Convention on International Bills of Exchange and International Promissory Notes. Most obviously, the Convention does not include the limitation on extraneous undertakings set forth in Section 3-104(a)(3), and does not permit documents payable to bearer that would be permissible under Section 3-104(a)(1) and Section 3-109. See Convention Article 3. In most respects, however, the requirements of Section 3-104 and Article 3 of the Convention are quite similar.

As amended in 2002.

§ 3-105. Issue of Instrument.

(a) "Issue" means the first delivery of an instrument by the maker or drawer, whether to a holder or nonholder, for the purpose of giving rights on the instrument to any person.

(b) An unissued instrument, or an unissued incomplete instrument that is completed, is binding on the maker or drawer, but nonissuance is a defense. An instrument that is conditionally issued or is issued for a special purpose is binding on the maker or drawer, but failure of the condition or special purpose to be fulfilled is a defense.

(c) "Issuer" applies to issued and unissued instruments and means a maker or drawer of an instrument.

Official Comment

1. Under former Section 3-102(1)(a) "issue" was defined as the first delivery to a "holder or a remitter" but the term "remitter" was neither defined nor otherwise used. In revised Article 3, Section 3-105(a) defines "issue" more broadly to include the first delivery to anyone by the drawer or maker for the purpose of giving rights to anyone on the instrument. "Delivery" with respect to instruments is defined in Section 1-201(14) [*unrevised Article 1; see Concordance, p. 12*] as meaning "voluntary transfer of possession."

2. Subsection (b) continues the rule that nonissuance, conditional issuance or issuance for a special purpose is a defense of the maker or drawer of an instrument. Thus, the defense can be asserted against a person other than a holder in due course. The same rule applies to nonissuance of an incomplete instrument later completed.

3. Subsection (c) defines "issuer" to include the signer of an unissued instrument for convenience of reference in the statute.

§ 3-106. Unconditional Promise or Order.

(a) Except as provided in this section, for the purposes of Section 3-104(a), a promise or order is unconditional unless it states (i) an express condition to payment, (ii) that the promise or order is subject to or governed by another record, or (iii) that rights or obligations with respect to the promise or order are stated in another record. A reference to another record does not of itself make the promise or order conditional.

(b) A promise or order is not made conditional (i) by a reference to another record for a statement of rights with respect to collateral, prepayment, or acceleration, or (ii) because payment is limited to resort to a particular fund or source.

(c) If a promise or order requires, as a condition to payment, a countersignature by a person whose specimen signature appears on the promise or order, the condition does not make the promise or order conditional for the purposes of Section 3–104(a). If the person whose specimen signature appears on an instrument fails to countersign the instrument, the failure to countersign is a defense to the obligation of the issuer, but the failure does not prevent a transferee of the instrument from becoming a holder of the instrument.

(d) If a promise or order at the time it is issued or first comes into possession of a holder contains a statement, required by applicable statutory or administrative law, to the effect that the rights of a holder or transferee are subject to claims or defenses that the issuer could assert against the original payee, the promise or order is not thereby made conditional for the purposes of Section 3–104(a); but if the promise or order is an instrument, there cannot be a holder in due course of the instrument.

As amended in 2002.

Official Comment

1. This provision replaces former Section 3–105. Its purpose is to define when a promise or order fulfills the requirement in Section 3–104(a) that it be an "unconditional" promise or order to pay. Under Section 3–106(a) a promise or order is deemed to be unconditional unless one of the two tests of the subsection make the promise or order conditional. If the promise or order states an express condition to payment, the promise or order is not an instrument. For example, a promise states, "I promise to pay $100,000 to the order of John Doe if he conveys title to Blackacre to me." The promise is not an instrument because there is an express condition to payment. However, suppose a promise states, "In consideration of John Doe's promise to convey title to Blackacre I promise to pay $100,000 to the order of John Doe." That promise can be an instrument if Section 3–104 is otherwise satisfied. Although the recital of the executory promise of Doe to convey Blackacre might be read as an implied condition that the promise be performed, the condition is not an express condition as required by Section 3–106(a)(i). This result is consistent with former Section 3–105(1)(a) and (b). Former Section 3–105(1)(b) is not repeated in Section 3–106 because it is not necessary. It is an example of an implied condition. Former Section 3–105(1)(d), (e), and (f) and the first clause of former Section 3–105(1)(c) are other examples of implied conditions. They are not repeated in Section 3–106 because they are not necessary. The law is not changed.

Section 3–106(a)(ii) and (iii) carry forward the substance of former Section 3–105(2)(a). The only change is the use of "writing" instead of "agreement" and a broadening of the language that can result in conditionality. For example, a promissory note is not an instrument defined by Section 3–104 if it contains any of the following statements: 1. "This note is subject to a contract of sale dated April 1, 1990 between the payee and maker of this note." 2. "This note is subject to a loan and security agreement dated April 1, 1990 between the payee and maker of this note." 3. "Rights and obligations of the parties with respect to this note are stated in an agreement dated April 1, 1990 between the payee and maker of this note." It is not relevant whether any condition to payment is or is not stated in the writing to which reference is made. The rationale is that the holder of a negotiable instrument should not be required to examine another document to determine rights with respect to payment. But subsection (b)(i) permits reference to a separate writing for information with respect to collateral, prepayment, or acceleration.

Many notes issued in commercial transactions are secured by collateral, are subject to acceleration in the event of default, or are subject to prepayment. A statement of rights and obligations concerning collateral, prepayment, or acceleration does not prevent the note from being an instrument if the statement is in the note itself. See Section 3–104(a)(3) and Section 3–108(b). In some cases it may be convenient not to include a statement concerning collateral, prepayment, or acceleration in the note, but rather to refer to an accompanying loan agreement, security agreement or mortgage for that statement. Subsection (b)(i) allows a reference to the appropriate writing for a statement of these rights. For example, a note would not be made conditional by the following statement: "This note is secured by a security interest in collateral described in a security agreement dated April 1, 1990 between the payee and maker of this note. Rights and obligations with respect to the collateral are [stated in] [governed by] the security agreement." The bracketed words are alternatives, either of which complies.

Subsection (b)(ii) addresses the issues covered by former Section 3–105(1)(f), (g), and (h) and Section 3–105(2)(b). Under Section 3–106(a) a promise or order is not made conditional because payment is limited to payment from a particular source or fund. This reverses the result of former Section 3–105(2)(b). There is no cogent reason why the general credit of a legal entity must be pledged to have a negotiable instrument. Market forces determine the marketability of instruments of this kind. If potential buyers don't want promises or orders that are payable only from a particular source or fund, they won't take them, but Article 3 should apply.

2. Subsection (c) applies to traveler's checks or other instruments that may require a countersignature. Although the requirement of a countersignature is a condition to the obligation to pay, traveler's checks are treated in the commercial world as money substitutes and therefore should be governed by Article 3. The first sentence of subsection (c) allows a traveler's check to meet the definition of instrument by stating that the countersignature condition does not make it conditional for the purposes of Section 3–104. The second sentence states the effect of a failure to meet the condition. Suppose a thief steals a traveler's check and cashes it by skillfully imitating the specimen signature so that the countersignature appears to be authentic. The countersignature is for the purpose of identification of the owner of the instrument. It is not an indorsement. Subsection (c) provides that the failure of the owner to countersign does not prevent a transferee from becoming a holder. Thus, the merchant or bank that cashed the traveler's check becomes a holder when the traveler's check is taken. The forged countersignature is a defense to the obligation of the issuer to pay the instrument, and is included in defenses under Section 3–305(a)(2). These defenses may not be asserted against a holder in due course. Whether a holder has notice of the defense is a factual question. If the countersignature is a very bad forgery, there may be notice. But if the merchant or bank cashed a traveler's check and the countersignature appeared to be similar to the specimen signature, there might not be notice that the countersignature was forged. Thus, the merchant or bank could be a holder in due course.

3. Subsection (d) concerns the effect of a statement to the effect that the rights of a holder or transferee are subject to claims and defenses that the issuer could assert against the original payee. The subsection applies only if the statement is required by statutory or administrative law. The prime example is the Federal Trade Commission Rule (16 C.F.R. Part 433) preserving consumers' claims and defenses in consumer credit sales. The intent of the FTC rule is to make it impossible for there to be a holder in due course of a note bearing the FTC legend and undoubtedly that is the result. But, under former Article 3, the legend may also have had the unintended effect of making the note conditional, thus excluding the note from former Article 3 altogether. Subsection (d) is designed to make it possible to preclude the possibility of a holder in due course without excluding the instrument from Article 3. Most of the provisions of Article 3 are not affected by the holder-in-due-course doctrine and there is no reason why Article 3 should not apply to a note bearing the FTC legend if holder-in-due-course rights are not involved. Under subsection (d) the statement does not make the note conditional. If the note otherwise meets the requirements of Section 3–104(a) it is a negotiable instrument for all purposes except that there cannot be a holder in due course of the note. No particular form of legend or statement is required by subsection (d). The form of a particular legend or statement may be determined by the other statute or administrative law. For example, the FTC legend required in a note taken by the seller in a consumer sale of goods or services is tailored to that particular transaction and therefore uses language that is somewhat different from that stated in subsection (d), but the difference in expression does not affect the essential similarity of the message conveyed. The effect of the FTC legend is to make the rights of a holder or transferee subject to claims or defenses that the issuer could assert against the original payee of the note.

§ 3–107. Instrument Payable in Foreign Money.

Unless the instrument otherwise provides, an instrument that states the amount payable in foreign money may be paid in the foreign money or in an equivalent amount in dollars calculated by using the current bank-offered spot rate at the place of payment for the purchase of dollars on the day on which the instrument is paid.

Official Comment

The definition of instrument in Section 3–104 requires that the promise or order be payable in "money." That term is defined in Section 1–201(24) [*unrevised Article 1; see Concordance, p. 12*] and is not limited to United States dollars. Section 3–107 states than an instrument payable in foreign money may be paid in dollars if the instrument does not prohibit it. It also states a conversion rate which applies in the absence of a different conversion rate stated in the instrument. The reference in former Section 3–107(1) to instruments payable in "currency" or "current funds" has been dropped as superfluous.

§ 3–108. Payable on Demand or at Definite Time.

(a) A promise or order is "payable on demand" if it (i) states that it is payable on demand or at sight, or otherwise indicates that it is payable at the will of the holder, or (ii) does not state any time of payment.

(b) A promise or order is "payable at a definite time" if it is payable on elapse of a definite period of time after sight or acceptance or at a fixed date or dates or at a time or times readily ascertainable at the time the promise or order is issued, subject to rights of (i) prepayment, (ii) acceleration, (iii) extension at the option of the holder, or (iv) extension to a further definite time at the option of the maker or acceptor or automatically upon or after a specified act or event.

(c) If an instrument, payable at a fixed date, is also payable upon demand made before the fixed date, the instrument is payable on demand until the fixed date and, if demand for payment is not made before that date, becomes payable at a definite time on the fixed date.

Official Comment

This section is a restatement of former Section 3–108 and Section 3–109. Subsection (b) broadens former Section 3–109 somewhat by providing that a definite time includes a time readily ascertainable at the time the promise or order is issued. Subsection (b)(iii) and (iv) restates former Section 3–109(1)(d). It adopts the generally accepted rule that a clause providing for extension at the option of the holder, even without a time limit, does not affect negotiability since the holder is given only a right which the holder would have without the clause. If the extension is to be at the option of the maker or acceptor or is to be automatic, a definite time limit must be stated or the time of payment remains uncertain and the order or promise is not a negotiable instrument. If a definite time limit is stated, the effect upon certainty of time of payment is the same as if the instrument were made payable at the ultimate date with a term providing for acceleration.

§ 3–109. Payable to Bearer or to Order.

(a) A promise or order is payable to bearer if it:

(1) states that it is payable to bearer or to the order of bearer or otherwise indicates that the person in possession of the promise or order is entitled to payment;

(2) does not state a payee; or

(3) states that it is payable to or to the order of cash or otherwise indicates that it is not payable to an identified person.

(b) A promise or order that is not payable to bearer is payable to order if it is payable (i) to the order of an identified person or (ii) to an identified person or order. A promise or order that is payable to order is payable to the identified person.

(c) An instrument payable to bearer may become payable to an identified person if it is specially indorsed pursuant to Section 3–205(a). An instrument payable to an identified person may become payable to bearer if it is indorsed in blank pursuant to Section 3–205(b).

Official Comment

1. Under Section 3–104(a), a promise or order cannot be an instrument unless the instrument is payable to bearer or to order when it is issued or unless Section 3–104(c) applies. The terms "payable to bearer" and "payable to order" are defined in Section 3–109. The quoted terms are also relevant in determining how an instrument is negotiated. If the instrument is payable to bearer it can be negotiated by delivery alone. Section 3–201(b). An instrument that is payable to an identified person cannot be negotiated without the indorsement of the identified person. Section 3–201(b). An instrument payable to order is payable to an identified person. Section 3–109(b). Thus, an instrument payable to order requires the indorsement of the person to whose order the instrument is payable.

2. Subsection (a) states when an instrument is payable to bearer. An instrument is payable to bearer if it states that it is payable to bearer, but some instruments use ambiguous terms. For example, check forms usually have the words "to the order of" printed at the beginning of the line to be filled in for the name of the payee. If the drawer writes in the word "bearer" or "cash," the check reads "to the order of bearer" or "to the order of cash." In each case the check is payable to bearer. Sometimes the drawer will write the name of the payee "John Doe" but will add the words "or bearer." In that case the check is payable to bearer. Subsection (a). Under subsection (b), if an instrument is payable to bearer it can't be payable to order. This is different from former Section 3–110(3). An instrument that purports to be payable both to order and bearer states contradictory terms. A transferee of the instrument should be able to rely on the bearer term and acquire rights as a holder without obtaining the indorsement of the identified payee. An instrument is also payable to bearer if it does not state a payee. Instruments that do not state a payee are in most cases incomplete instruments. In some cases the drawer of a check may deliver or mail it to the person to be paid without filling in the line for the name of the payee. Under subsection (a) the check is payable to bearer when it is sent or delivered. It is also an incomplete instrument. This case is discussed in Comment 2 to Section 3–115. Subsection (a)(3) contains the words "otherwise indicates that it

is not payable to an identified person." The quoted words are meant to cover uncommon cases in which an instrument indicates that it is not meant to be payable to a specific person. Such an instrument is treated like a check payable to "cash." The quoted words are not meant to apply to an instrument stating that it is payable to an identified person such as "ABC Corporation" if ABC Corporation is a nonexistent company. Although the holder of the check cannot be the nonexistent company, the instrument is not payable to bearer. Negotiation of such an instrument is governed by Section 3–404(b).

§ 3–110. Identification of Person to Whom Instrument Is Payable.

(a) The person to whom an instrument is initially payable is determined by the intent of the person, whether or not authorized, signing as, or in the name or behalf of, the issuer of the instrument. The instrument is payable to the person intended by the signer even if that person is identified in the instrument by a name or other identification that is not that of the intended person. If more than one person signs in the name or behalf of the issuer of an instrument and all the signers do not intend the same person as payee, the instrument is payable to any person intended by one or more of the signers.

(b) If the signature of the issuer of an instrument is made by automated means, such as a check-writing machine, the payee of the instrument is determined by the intent of the person who supplied the name or identification of the payee, whether or not authorized to do so.

(c) A person to whom an instrument is payable may be identified in any way, including by name, identifying number, office, or account number. For the purpose of determining the holder of an instrument, the following rules apply:

(1) If an instrument is payable to an account and the account is identified only by number, the instrument is payable to the person to whom the account is payable. If an instrument is payable to an account identified by number and by the name of a person, the instrument is payable to the named person, whether or not that person is the owner of the account identified by number.

(2) If an instrument is payable to:

(i) a trust, an estate, or a person described as trustee or representative of a trust or estate, the instrument is payable to the trustee, the representative, or a successor of either, whether or not the beneficiary or estate is also named;

(ii) a person described as agent or similar representative of a named or identified person, the instrument is payable to the represented person, the representative, or a successor of the representative;

(iii) a fund or organization that is not a legal entity, the instrument is payable to a representative of the members of the fund or organization; or

(iv) an office or to a person described as holding an office, the instrument is payable to the named person, the incumbent of the office, or a successor to the incumbent.

(d) If an instrument is payable to two or more persons alternatively, it is payable to any of them and may be negotiated, discharged, or enforced by any or all of them in possession of the instrument. If an instrument is payable to two or more persons not alternatively, it is payable to all of them and may be negotiated, discharged, or enforced only by all of them. If an instrument payable to two or more persons is ambiguous as to whether it is payable to the persons alternatively, the instrument is payable to the persons alternatively.

Official Comment

1. Section 3–110 states rules for determining the identity of the person to whom an instrument is initially payable if the instrument is payable to an identified person. This issue usually arises in a dispute over the validity of an indorsement in the name of the payee. Subsection (a) states the general rule that the person to whom an instrument is payable is determined by the intent of "the person, whether or not authorized, signing as, or in the name or behalf of, the issuer of the instrument." "Issuer" means the maker or drawer of the instrument. Section 3–105(c). If X signs a check as drawer of a check on X's account, the intent of X controls. If X, as President of Corporation, signs a check as President in behalf of Corporation as drawer, the intent of X controls. If X forges Y's signature as drawer of a check, the intent of X also controls. Under Section 3–103(a)(5), Y is referred to as the drawer of the check because the signing of Y's name identifies Y as the drawer. But since Y's signature was forged

Y has no liability as drawer (Section 3–403(a)) unless some other provision of Article 3 or Article 4 makes Y liable. Since X, even though unauthorized, signed in the name of Y as issuer, the intent of X determines to whom the check is payable.

In the case of a check payable to "John Smith," since there are many people in the world named "John Smith" it is not possible to identify the payee of the check unless there is some further identification or the intention of the drawer is determined. Name alone is sufficient under subsection (a), but the intention of the drawer determines which John Smith is the person to whom the check is payable. The same issue is presented in cases of misdescriptions of the payee. The drawer intends to pay a person known to the drawer as John Smith. In fact that person's name is James Smith or John Jones or some other entirely different name. If the check identifies the payee as John Smith, it is nevertheless payable to the person intended by the drawer. That person may indorse the check in either the name John Smith or the person's correct name or in both names. Section 3–204(d). The intent of the drawer is also controlling in fictitious payee cases. Section 3–404(b). The last sentence of subsection (a) refers to rare cases in which the signature of an organization requires more than one signature and the persons signing on behalf of the organization do not all intend the same person as payee. Any person intended by a signer for the organization is the payee and an indorsement by that person is an effective indorsement.

Subsection (b) recognizes the fact that in a large number of cases there is no human signer of an instrument because the instrument, usually a check, is produced by automated means such as a check-writing machine. In that case, the relevant intent is that of the person who supplied the name of the payee. In most cases that person is an employee of the drawer, but in some cases the person could be an outsider who is committing a fraud by introducing names of payees of checks into the system that produces the checks. A check-writing machine is likely to be operated by means of a computer in which is stored information as to name and address of the payee and the amount of the check. Access to the computer may allow production of fraudulent checks without knowledge of the organization that is the issuer of the check. Section 3–404(b) is also concerned with this issue. See Case # 4 in Comment 2 to Section 3–404.

2. Subsection (c) allows the payee to be identified in any way including the various ways stated. Subsection (c)(1) relates to instruments payable to bank accounts. In some cases the account might be identified by name and number, and the name and number might refer to different persons. For example, a check is payable to "X Corporation Account No. 12345 in Bank of Podunk." Under the last sentence of subsection (c)(1), this check is payable to X Corporation and can be negotiated by X Corporation even if Account No. 12345 is some other person's account or the check is not deposited in that account. In other cases the payee is identified by an account number and the name of the owner of the account is not stated. For example, Debtor pays Creditor by issuing a check drawn on Payor Bank. The check is payable to a bank account owned by Creditor but identified only by number. Under the first sentence of subsection (c)(1) the check is payable to Creditor and, under Section 1–201(20) [*unrevised Article 1; see Concordance, p. 12*], Creditor becomes the holder when the check is delivered. Under Section 3–201(b), further negotiation of the check requires the indorsement of Creditor. But under Section 4–205(a), if the check is taken by a depositary bank for collection, the bank may become a holder without the indorsement. Under Section 3–102(b), provisions of Article 4 prevail over those of Article 3. The depositary bank warrants that the amount of the check was credited to the payee's account.

3. Subsection (c)(2) replaces former Section 3–117 and subsection (1)(e), (f), and (g) of former Section 3–110. This provision merely determines who can deal with an instrument as a holder. It does not determine ownership of the instrument or its proceeds. Subsection (c)(2)(i) covers trusts and estates. If the instrument is payable to the trust or estate or to the trustee or representative of the trust or estate, the instrument is payable to the trustee or representative or any successor. Under subsection (c)(2)(ii), if the instrument states that it is payable to Doe, President of X Corporation, either Doe or X Corporation can be holder of the instrument. Subsection (c)(2)(iii) concerns informal organizations that are not legal entities such as unincorporated clubs and the like. Any representative of the members of the organization can act as holder. Subsection (c)(2)(iv) applies principally to instruments payable to public offices such as a check payable to County Tax Collector.

4. Subsection (d) replaces former Section 3–116. An instrument payable to X or Y is governed by the first sentence of subsection (d). An instrument payable to X and Y is governed by the second sentence of subsection (d). If an instrument is payable to X or Y, either is the payee and if either is in possession that person is the holder and the person entitled to enforce the instrument. Section 3–301. If an instrument is payable to X and Y, neither X nor Y acting alone is the person to whom the instrument is payable. Neither person, acting alone, can be the holder of the instrument. The instrument is "payable to an identified person." The "identified person" is X and Y acting jointly. Section 3–109(b) and Section 1–102(5)(a) [*unrevised Article 1; see Concordance, p. 12*]. Thus, under Section 1–201(20) [*unrevised Article 1; see Concordance, p. 12*] X or Y, acting alone, cannot be the holder or the

person entitled to enforce or negotiate the instrument because neither, acting alone, is the identified person stated in the instrument.

The third sentence of subsection (d) is directed to cases in which it is not clear whether an instrument is payable to multiple payees alternatively. In the case of ambiguity persons dealing with the instrument should be able to rely on the indorsement of a single payee. For example, an instrument payable to X and/or Y is treated like an instrument payable to X or Y.

§ 3-111. Place of Payment.

Except as otherwise provided for items in Article 4, an instrument is payable at the place of payment stated in the instrument. If no place of payment is stated, an instrument is payable at the address of the drawee or maker stated in the instrument. If no address is stated, the place of payment is the place of business of the drawee or maker. If a drawee or maker has more than one place of business, the place of payment is any place of business of the drawee or maker chosen by the person entitled to enforce the instrument. If the drawee or maker has no place of business, the place of payment is the residence of the drawee or maker.

Official Comment

If an instrument is payable at a bank in the United States, Section 3-501(b)(1) states that presentment must be made at the place of payment, i.e. the bank. The place of presentment of a check is governed by Regulation CC § 229.36.

§ 3-112. Interest.

(a) Unless otherwise provided in the instrument, (i) an instrument is not payable with interest, and (ii) interest on an interest-bearing instrument is payable from the date of the instrument.

(b) Interest may be stated in an instrument as a fixed or variable amount of money or it may be expressed as a fixed or variable rate or rates. The amount or rate of interest may be stated or described in the instrument in any manner and may require reference to information not contained in the instrument. If an instrument provides for interest, but the amount of interest payable cannot be ascertained from the description, interest is payable at the judgment rate in effect at the place of payment of the instrument and at the time interest first accrues.

Official Comment

1. Under Section 3-104(a) the requirement of a "fixed amount" applies only to principal. The amount of interest payable is that described in the instrument. If the description of interest in the instrument does not allow for the amount of interest to be ascertained, interest is payable at the judgment rate. Hence, if an instrument calls for interest, the amount of interest will always be determinable. If a variable rate of interest is prescribed, the amount of interest is ascertainable by reference to the formula or index described or referred to in the instrument. The last sentence of subsection (b) replaces subsection (d) of former Section 3-118.

2. The purpose of subsection (b) is to clarify the meaning of "interest" in the introductory clause of Section 3-104(a). It is not intended to validate a provision for interest in an instrument if that provision violates other law.

§ 3-113. Date of Instrument.

(a) An instrument may be antedated or postdated. The date stated determines the time of payment if the instrument is payable at a fixed period after date. Except as provided in Section 4-401(c), an instrument payable on demand is not payable before the date of the instrument.

(b) If an instrument is undated, its date is the date of its issue or, in the case of an unissued instrument, the date it first comes into possession of a holder.

Official Comment

This section replaces former Section 3-114. Subsections (1) and (3) of former Section 3-114 are deleted as unnecessary. Section 3-113(a) is based in part on subsection (2) of former Section 3-114. The rule that a demand instrument is not payable before the date of the instrument is subject to Section 4-401(c) which allows the payor bank to pay a postdated check unless the drawer has notified the bank of the postdating pursuant to a procedure prescribed in that subsection. With respect to an undated instrument, the date is the date of issue.

§ 3–114. Contradictory Terms of Instrument.

If an instrument contains contradictory terms, typewritten terms prevail over printed terms, handwritten terms prevail over both, and words prevail over numbers.

Official Comment

Section 3–114 replaces subsections (b) and (c) of former Section 3–118.

§ 3–115. Incomplete Instrument.

(a) "Incomplete instrument" means a signed writing, whether or not issued by the signer, the contents of which show at the time of signing that it is incomplete but that the signer intended it to be completed by the addition of words or numbers.

(b) Subject to subsection (c), if an incomplete instrument is an instrument under Section 3–104, it may be enforced according to its terms if it is not completed, or according to its terms as augmented by completion. If an incomplete instrument is not an instrument under Section 3–104, but, after completion, the requirements of Section 3–104 are met, the instrument may be enforced according to its terms as augmented by completion.

(c) If words or numbers are added to an incomplete instrument without authority of the signer, there is an alteration of the incomplete instrument under Section 3-407.

(d) The burden of establishing that words or numbers were added to an incomplete instrument without authority of the signer is on the person asserting the lack of authority.

Official Comment

1. This section generally carries forward the rules set out in former Section 3–115. The term "incomplete instrument" applies both to an "instrument," i.e. a writing meeting all the requirements of Section 3–104, and to a writing intended to be an instrument that is signed but lacks some element of an instrument. The test in both cases is whether the contents show that it is incomplete and that the signer intended that additional words or numbers be added.

2. If an incomplete instrument meets the requirements of Section 3–104 and is not completed it may be enforced in accordance with its terms. Suppose, in the following two cases, that a note delivered to the payee is incomplete solely because a space on the pre-printed note form for the due date is not filled in:

Case # 1. If the incomplete instrument is never completed, the note is payable on demand. Section 3–108(a)(ii). However, if the payee and the maker agreed to a due date, the maker may have a defense under Section 3–117 if demand for payment is made before the due date agreed to by the parties.

Case # 2. If the payee completes the note by filling in the due date agreed to by the parties, the note is payable on the due date stated. However, if the due date filled in was not the date agreed to by the parties there is an alteration of the note. Section 3–407 governs the case.

Suppose Debtor pays Creditor by giving Creditor a check on which the space for the name of the payee is left blank. The check is an instrument but it is incomplete. The check is enforceable in its incomplete form and it is payable to bearer because it does not state a payee. Section 3–109(a)(2). Thus, Creditor is a holder of the check. Normally in this kind of case Creditor would simply fill in the space with Creditor's name. When that occurs the check becomes payable to the Creditor.

3. In some cases the incomplete instrument does not meet the requirements of Section 3–104. An example is a check with the amount not filled in. The check cannot be enforced until the amount is filled in. If the payee fills in an amount authorized by the drawer the check meets the requirements of Section 3–104 and is enforceable as completed. If the payee fills in an unauthorized amount there is an alteration of the check and Section 3–407 applies.

4. Section 3-302(a)(1) also bears on the problem of incomplete instruments. Under that section a person cannot be a holder in due course of the instrument if it is so incomplete as to call into question its validity. Subsection (d) of Section 3–115 is based on the last clause of subsection (2) of former Section 3–115.

§ 3–116. Joint and Several Liability; Contribution.

(a) Except as otherwise provided in the instrument, two or more persons who have the same liability on an instrument as makers, drawers, acceptors, indorsers who indorse as joint payees, or anomalous indorsers are jointly and severally liable in the capacity in which they sign.

(b) Except as provided in Section 3–419(f) or by agreement of the affected parties, a party having joint and several liability who pays the instrument is entitled to receive from any party having the same joint and several liability contribution in accordance with applicable law.

As amended in 2002.

Official Comment

1. Subsection (a) replaces subsection (e) of former Section 3–118. Subsection (b) states contribution rights of parties with joint and several liability by referring to applicable law. But subsection (b) is subject to Section 3–419(f). If one of the parties with joint and several liability is an accommodation party and the other is the accommodated party, Section 3–419(f) applies. Because one of the joint and several obligors may have recourse against the other joint and several obligor under subsection (b), each party that is jointly and severally liable under subsection (a) is a secondary obligor in part and a principal obligor in part, as those terms are defined in Section 3–103(a). Accordingly, Section 3–605 determines the effect of a release, an extension of time, or a modification of the obligation of one of the joint and several obligors, as well as the effect of an impairment of collateral provided by one of those obligors.

2. Indorsers normally do not have joint and several liability. Rather, an earlier indorser has liability to a later indorser. But indorsers can have joint and several liability in two cases. If an instrument is payable to two payees jointly, both payees must indorse. The indorsement is a joint indorsement and the indorsers have joint and several liability and subsection (b) applies. The other case is that of two or more anomalous indorsers. The term is defined in Section 3–205(d). An anomalous indorsement normally indicates that the indorser signed as an accommodation party. If more than one accommodation party indorses a note as an accommodation to the maker, the indorsers have joint and several liability and subsection (b) applies.

As amended in 2002.

§ 3–117. Other Agreements Affecting Instrument.

Subject to applicable law regarding exclusion of proof of contemporaneous or previous agreements, the obligation of a party to an instrument to pay the instrument may be modified, supplemented, or nullified by a separate agreement of the obligor and a person entitled to enforce the instrument, if the instrument is issued or the obligation is incurred in reliance on the agreement or as part of the same transaction giving rise to the agreement. To the extent an obligation is modified, supplemented, or nullified by an agreement under this section, the agreement is a defense to the obligation.

Official Comment

1. The separate agreement might be a security agreement or mortgage or it might be an agreement that contradicts the terms of the instrument. For example, a person may be induced to sign an instrument under an agreement that the signer will not be liable on the instrument unless certain conditions are met. Suppose X requested credit from Creditor who is willing to give the credit only if an acceptable accommodation party will sign the note of X as co-maker. Y agrees to sign as co-maker on the condition that Creditor also obtain the signature of Z as co-maker. Creditor agrees and Y signs as co-maker with X. Creditor fails to obtain the signature of Z on the note. Under Sections 3–412 and 3–419(b), Y is obliged to pay the note, but Section 3–117 applies. In this case, the agreement modifies the terms of the note by stating a condition to the obligation of Y to pay the note. This case is essentially similar to a case in which a maker of a note is induced to sign the note by fraud of the holder. Although the agreement that Y not be liable on the note unless Z also signs may not have been fraudulently made, a subsequent attempt by Creditor to require Y to pay the note in violation of the agreement is a bad faith act. Section 3–117, in treating the agreement as a defense, allows Y to assert the agreement against Creditor, but the defense would not be good against a subsequent holder in due course of the note that took it without notice of the agreement. If there cannot be a holder in due course because of Section 3–106(d), a subsequent holder that took the note in good faith, for value and without knowledge of the agreement would not be able to enforce the liability of Y. This result is consistent with the risk that a holder not in due course takes with respect to fraud in inducing issuance of an instrument.

2. The effect of merger or integration clauses to the effect that a writing is intended to be the complete and exclusive statement of the terms of the agreement or that the agreement is not subject to conditions is left to the supplementary law of the jurisdiction pursuant to Section 1–103. Thus, in the case discussed in Comment 1, whether Y is permitted to prove the condition to Y's obligation to pay the note is determined by that law. Moreover, nothing in this section is intended to validate an agreement which is fraudulent or void as against public policy, as in the case of a note given to deceive a bank examiner.

§ 3–118. Statute of Limitations.

(a) Except as provided in subsection (e), an action to enforce the obligation of a party to pay a note payable at a definite time must be commenced within six years after the due date or dates stated in the note or, if a due date is accelerated, within six years after the accelerated due date.

(b) Except as provided in subsection (d) or (e), if demand for payment is made to the maker of a note payable on demand, an action to enforce the obligation of a party to pay the note must be commenced within six years after the demand. If no demand for payment is made to the maker, an action to enforce the note is barred if neither principal nor interest on the note has been paid for a continuous period of 10 years.

(c) Except as provided in subsection (d), an action to enforce the obligation of a party to an unaccepted draft to pay the draft must be commenced within three years after dishonor of the draft or 10 years after the date of the draft, whichever period expires first.

(d) An action to enforce the obligation of the acceptor of a certified check or the issuer of a teller's check, cashier's check, or traveler's check must be commenced within three years after demand for payment is made to the acceptor or issuer, as the case may be.

(e) An action to enforce the obligation of a party to a certificate of deposit to pay the instrument must be commenced within six years after demand for payment is made to the maker, but if the instrument states a due date and the maker is not required to pay before that date, the six-year period begins when a demand for payment is in effect and the due date has passed.

(f) An action to enforce the obligation of a party to pay an accepted draft, other than a certified check, must be commenced (i) within six years after the due date or dates stated in the draft or acceptance if the obligation of the acceptor is payable at a definite time, or (ii) within six years after the date of the acceptance if the obligation of the acceptor is payable on demand.

(g) Unless governed by other law regarding claims for indemnity or contribution, an action (i) for conversion of an instrument, for money had and received, or like action based on conversion, (ii) for breach of warranty, or (iii) to enforce an obligation, duty, or right arising under this Article and not governed by this section must be commenced within three years after the [cause of action] accrues.

Official Comment

1. Section 3–118 differs from former Section 3–122, which states when a cause of action accrues on an instrument. Section 3–118 does not define when a cause of action accrues. Accrual of a cause of action is stated in other sections of Article 3 such as those that state the various obligations of parties to an instrument. The only purpose of Section 3–118 is to define the time within which an action to enforce an obligation, duty, or right arising under Article 3 must be commenced. Section 3–118 does not attempt to state all rules with respect to a statute of limitations. For example, the circumstances under which the running of a limitations period may be tolled is left to other law pursuant to Section 1–103.

2. The first six subsections apply to actions to enforce an obligation of any party to an instrument to pay the instrument. This changes present law in that indorsers who may become liable on an instrument after issue are subject to a period of limitations running from the same date as that of the maker or drawer. Subsections (a) and (b) apply to notes. If the note is payable at a definite time, a six-year limitations period starts at the due date of the note, subject to prior acceleration. If the note is payable on demand, there are two limitations periods. Although a note payable on demand could theoretically be called a day after it was issued, the normal expectation of the parties is that the note will remain outstanding until there is some reason to call it. If the law provides that the limitations period does not start until demand is made, the cause of action to enforce it may never be barred. On the other hand, if the limitations period starts when demand for payment may be made, i.e. at any time after the note was issued, the payee of a note on which interest or portions of principal are being paid could lose the right to enforce the note even though it was treated as a continuing obligation by the parties. Some demand notes

are not enforced because the payee has forgiven the debt. This is particularly true in family and other noncommercial transactions. A demand note found after the death of the payee may be presented for payment many years after it was issued. The maker may be a relative and it may be difficult to determine whether the note represents a real or a forgiven debt. Subsection (b) is designed to bar notes that no longer represent a claim to payment and to require reasonably prompt action to enforce notes on which there is default. If a demand for payment is made to the maker, a six-year limitations period starts to run when demand is made. The second sentence of subsection (b) bars an action to enforce a demand note if no demand has been made on the note and no payment of interest or principal has been made for a continuous period of 10 years. This covers the case of a note that does not bear interest or a case in which interest due on the note has not been paid. This kind of case is likely to be a family transaction in which a failure to demand payment may indicate that the holder did not intend to enforce the obligation but neglected to destroy the note. A limitations period that bars stale claims in this kind of case is appropriate if the period is relatively long.

3. Subsection (c) applies primarily to personal uncertified checks. Checks are payment instruments rather than credit instruments. The limitations period expires three years after the date of dishonor or 10 years after the date of the check, whichever is earlier. Teller's checks, cashier's checks, certified checks, and traveler's checks are treated differently under subsection (d) because they are commonly treated as cash equivalents. A great delay in presenting a cashier's check for payment in most cases will occur because the check was mislaid during that period. The person to whom traveler's checks are issued may hold them indefinitely as a safe form of cash for use in an emergency. There is no compelling reason for barring the claim of the owner of the cashier's check or traveler's check. Under subsection (d) the claim is never barred because the three-year limitations period does not start to run until demand for payment is made. The limitations period in subsection (d) in effect applies only to cases in which there is a dispute about the legitimacy of the claim of the person demanding payment.

4. Subsection (e) covers certificates of deposit. The limitations period of six years doesn't start to run until the depositor demands payment. Most certificates of deposit are payable on demand even if they state a due date. The effect of a demand for payment before maturity is usually that the bank will pay, but that a penalty will be assessed against the depositor in the form of a reduction in the amount of interest that is paid. Subsection (e) also provides for cases in which the bank has no obligation to pay until the due date. In that case the limitations period doesn't start to run until there is a demand for payment in effect and the due date has passed.

5. Subsection (f) applies to accepted drafts other than certified checks. When a draft is accepted it is in effect turned into a note of the acceptor. In almost all cases the acceptor will agree to pay at a definite time. Subsection (f) states that in that case the six-year limitations period starts to run on the due date. In the rare case in which the obligation of the acceptor is payable on demand, the six-year limitations period starts to run at the date of the acceptance.

6. Subsection (g) covers warranty and conversion cases and other actions to enforce obligations or rights arising under Article 3. A three-year period is stated and subsection (g) follows general law in stating that the period runs from the time the cause of action accrues. Since the traditional term "cause of action" may have been replaced in some states by "claim for relief" or some equivalent term, the words "cause of action" have been bracketed to indicate that the words may be replaced by an appropriate substitute to conform to local practice.

7. One of the most significant differences between this Article and the Convention on International Bills of Exchange and International Promissory Notes is that the statute of limitation under the Convention generally is only four years, rather than the six years provided by this section. See Convention Article 84.

As amended in 2002.

§ 3–119. Notice of Right to Defend Action.

In an action for breach of an obligation for which a third person is answerable over pursuant to this Article or Article 4, the defendant may give the third person notice of the litigation in a record, and the person notified may then give similar notice to any other person who is answerable over. If the notice states (i) that the person notified may come in and defend and (ii) that failure to do so will bind the person notified in an action later brought by the person giving the notice as to any determination of fact common to the two litigations, the person notified is so bound unless after seasonable receipt of the notice the person notified does come in and defend.

As amended in 2002.

Official Comment

This section is a restatement of former Section 3–803.

PART 2

NEGOTIATION, TRANSFER, AND INDORSEMENT

§ 3–201. Negotiation.

(a) "Negotiation" means a transfer of possession, whether voluntary or involuntary, of an instrument by a person other than the issuer to a person who thereby becomes its holder.

(b) Except for negotiation by a remitter, if an instrument is payable to an identified person, negotiation requires transfer of possession of the instrument and its indorsement by the holder. If an instrument is payable to bearer, it may be negotiated by transfer of possession alone.

Official Comment

1. Subsections (a) and (b) are based in part on subsection (1) of former Section 3–202. A person can become holder of an instrument when the instrument is issued to that person, or the status of holder can arise as the result of an event that occurs after issuance. "Negotiation" is the term used in Article 3 to describe this post-issuance event. Normally, negotiation occurs as the result of a voluntary transfer of possession of an instrument by a holder to another person who becomes the holder as a result of the transfer. Negotiation always requires a change in possession of the instrument because nobody can be a holder without possessing the instrument, either directly or through an agent. But in some cases the transfer of possession is involuntary and in some cases the person transferring possession is not a holder. In defining "negotiation" former Section 3–202(1) used the word "transfer," an undefined term, and "delivery," defined in Section 1–201(14) [*unrevised Article 1; see Concordance, p. 12*] to mean voluntary change of possession. Instead, subsections (a) and (b) use the term "transfer of possession" and, subsection (a) states that negotiation can occur by an involuntary transfer of possession. For example, if an instrument is payable to bearer and it is stolen by Thief or is found by Finder, Thief or Finder becomes the holder of the instrument when possession is obtained. In this case there is an involuntary transfer of possession that results in negotiation to Thief or Finder.

2. In most cases negotiation occurs by a transfer of possession by a holder or remitter. Remitter transactions usually involve a cashier's or teller's check. For example, Buyer buys goods from Seller and pays for them with a cashier's check of Bank that Buyer buys from Bank. The check is issued by Bank when it is delivered to Buyer, regardless of whether the check is payable to Buyer or to Seller. Section 3–105(a). If the check is payable to Buyer, negotiation to Seller is done by delivery of the check to Seller after it is indorsed by Buyer. It is more common, however, that the check when issued will be payable to Seller. In that case Buyer is referred to as the "remitter." Section 3–103(a)(15). The remitter, although not a party to the check, is the owner of the check until ownership is transferred to Seller by delivery. This transfer is a negotiation because Seller becomes the holder of the check when Seller obtains possession. In some cases Seller may have acted fraudulently in obtaining possession of the check. In those cases Buyer may be entitled to rescind the transfer to Seller because of the fraud and assert a claim of ownership to the check under Section 3–306 against Seller or a subsequent transferee of the check. Section 3–202(b) provides for rescission of negotiation, and that provision applies to rescission by a remitter as well as by a holder.

3. Other sections of Article 3 may modify the rule stated in the first sentence of subsection (b). See for example, Sections 3–404, 3–405 and 3–406.

§ 3–202. Negotiation Subject to Rescission.

(a) Negotiation is effective even if obtained (i) from an infant, a corporation exceeding its powers, or a person without capacity, (ii) by fraud, duress, or mistake, or (iii) in breach of duty or as part of an illegal transaction.

(b) To the extent permitted by other law, negotiation may be rescinded or may be subject to other remedies, but those remedies may not be asserted against a subsequent holder in due course or a person paying the instrument in good faith and without knowledge of facts that are a basis for rescission or other remedy.

Official Comment

1. This section is based on former Section 3-207. Subsection (2) of former Section 3-207 prohibited rescission of a negotiation against holders in due course. Subsection (b) of Section 3-202 extends this protection to payor banks.

2. Subsection (a) applies even though the lack of capacity or the illegality, is of a character which goes to the essence of the transaction and makes it entirely void. It is inherent in the character of negotiable instruments that any person in possession of an instrument which by its terms is payable to that person or to bearer is a holder and may be dealt with by anyone as a holder. The principle finds its most extreme application in the well settled rule that a holder in due course may take the instrument even from a thief and be protected against the claim of the rightful owner. The policy of subsection (a) is that any person to whom an instrument is negotiated is a holder until the instrument has been recovered from that person's possession. The remedy of a person with a claim to an instrument is to recover the instrument by replevin or otherwise; to impound it or to enjoin its enforcement, collection or negotiation; to recover its proceeds from the holder; or to intervene in any action brought by the holder against the obligor. As provided in Section 3-305(c), the claim of the claimant is not a defense to the obligor unless the claimant defends the action.

3. There can be no rescission or other remedy against a holder in due course or a person who pays in good faith and without notice, even though the prior negotiation may have been fraudulent or illegal in its essence and entirely void. As against any other party the claimant may have any remedy permitted by law. This section is not intended to specify what that remedy may be, or to prevent any court from imposing conditions or limitations such as prompt action or return of the consideration received. All such questions are left to the law of the particular jurisdiction. Section 3-202 gives no right that would not otherwise exist. The section is intended to mean that any remedies afforded by other law are cut off only by a holder in due course.

§ 3-203. Transfer of Instrument; Rights Acquired by Transfer.

(a) An instrument is transferred when it is delivered by a person other than its issuer for the purpose of giving to the person receiving delivery the right to enforce the instrument.

(b) Transfer of an instrument, whether or not the transfer is a negotiation, vests in the transferee any right of the transferor to enforce the instrument, including any right as a holder in due course, but the transferee cannot acquire rights of a holder in due course by a transfer, directly or indirectly, from a holder in due course if the transferee engaged in fraud or illegality affecting the instrument.

(c) Unless otherwise agreed, if an instrument is transferred for value and the transferee does not become a holder because of lack of indorsement by the transferor, the transferee has a specifically enforceable right to the unqualified indorsement of the transferor, but negotiation of the instrument does not occur until the indorsement is made.

(d) If a transferor purports to transfer less than the entire instrument, negotiation of the instrument does not occur. The transferee obtains no rights under this Article and has only the rights of a partial assignee.

Official Comment

1. Section 3-203 is based on former Section 3-201 which stated that a transferee received such rights as the transferor had. The former section was confusing because some rights of the transferor are not vested in the transferee unless the transfer is a negotiation. For example, a transferee that did not become the holder could not negotiate the instrument, a right that the transferor had. Former Section 3-201 did not define "transfer." Subsection (a) defines transfer by limiting it to cases in which possession of the instrument is delivered for the purpose of giving to the person receiving delivery the right to enforce the instrument.

Although transfer of an instrument might mean in a particular case that title to the instrument passes to the transferee, that result does not follow in all cases. The right to enforce an instrument and ownership of the instrument are two different concepts. A thief who steals a check payable to bearer becomes the holder of the check and a person entitled to enforce it, but does not become the owner of the check. If the thief transfers the check to a purchaser the transferee obtains the right to enforce the check. If the purchaser is not a holder in due course, the owner's claim to the check may be asserted against the purchaser. Ownership rights in instruments may be determined by principles of the law of property, independent of Article 3, which do not depend upon whether the instrument was transferred under Section 3-203. Moreover, a person who has an ownership right in an instrument might not be a person entitled to enforce the instrument. For example, suppose X is the owner and holder of an instrument payable to X. X sells the instrument to Y but is unable to deliver immediate possession to Y. Instead, X signs a document conveying all of X's right, title, and interest in the instrument to Y. Although the document may be effective to give Y a claim to ownership of the instrument, Y is not a person entitled to enforce the instrument until Y obtains possession of the instrument. No transfer of the instrument occurs under Section 3–203(a) until it is delivered to Y.

An instrument is a reified right to payment. The right is represented by the instrument itself. The right to payment is transferred by delivery of possession of the instrument "by a person other than its issuer for the purpose of giving to the person receiving delivery the right to enforce the instrument." The quoted phrase excludes issue of an instrument, defined in Section 3–105, and cases in which a delivery of possession is for some purpose other than transfer of the right to enforce. For example, if a check is presented for payment by delivering the check to the drawee, no transfer of the check to the drawee occurs because there is no intent to give the drawee the right to enforce the check.

2. Subsection (b) states that transfer vests in the transferee any right of the transferor to enforce the instrument "including any right as a holder in due course." If the transferee is not a holder because the transferor did not indorse, the transferee is nevertheless a person entitled to enforce the instrument under Section 3–301 if the transferor was a holder at the time of transfer. Although the transferee is not a holder, under subsection (b) the transferee obtained the rights of the transferor as holder. Because the transferee's rights are derivative of the transferor's rights, those rights must be proved. Because the transferee is not a holder, there is no presumption under Section 3–308 that the transferee, by producing the instrument, is entitled to payment. The instrument, by its terms, is not payable to the transferee and the transferee must account for possession of the unindorsed instrument by proving the transaction through which the transferee acquired it. Proof of a transfer to the transferee by a holder is proof that the transferee has acquired the rights of a holder. At that point the transferee is entitled to the presumption under Section 3–308.

Under subsection (b) a holder in due course that transfers an instrument transfers those rights as a holder in due course to the purchaser. The policy is to assure the holder in due course a free market for the instrument. There is one exception to this rule stated in the concluding clause of subsection (b). A person who is party to fraud or illegality affecting the instrument is not permitted to wash the instrument clean by passing it into the hands of a holder in due course and then repurchasing it.

3. Subsection (c) applies only to a transfer for value. It applies only if the instrument is payable to order or specially indorsed to the transferor. The transferee acquires, in the absence of a contrary agreement, the specifically enforceable right to the indorsement of the transferor. Unless otherwise agreed, it is a right to the general indorsement of the transferor with full liability as indorser, rather than to an indorsement without recourse. The question may arise if the transferee has paid in advance and the indorsement is omitted fraudulently or through oversight. A transferor who is willing to indorse only without recourse or unwilling to indorse at all should make those intentions clear before transfer. The agreement of the transferee to take less than an unqualified indorsement need not be an express one, and the understanding may be implied from conduct, from past practice, or from the circumstances of the transaction. Subsection (c) provides that there is no negotiation of the instrument until the indorsement by the transferor is made. Until that time the transferee does not become a holder, and if earlier notice of a defense or claim is received, the transferee does not qualify as a holder in due course under Section 3–302.

4. The operation of Section 3–203 is illustrated by the following cases. In each case Payee, by fraud, induced Maker to issue a note to Payee. The fraud is a defense to the obligation of Maker to pay the note under Section 3–305(a)(2).

Case # 1. Payee negotiated the note to X who took as a holder in due course. After the instrument became overdue X negotiated the note to Y who had notice of the fraud. Y succeeds to X's rights as a holder in due course and takes free of Maker's defense of fraud.

Case # 2. Payee negotiated the note to X who took as a holder in due course. Payee then repurchased the note from X. Payee does not succeed to X's rights as a holder in due course and is subject to Maker's defense of fraud.

Case # 3. Payee negotiated the note to X who took as a holder in due course. X sold the note to Purchaser who received possession. The note, however, was indorsed to X and X failed to indorse it. Purchaser is a person entitled to enforce the instrument under Section 3–301 and succeeds to the rights of X as holder in due course. Purchaser is not a holder, however, and under Section 3–308 Purchaser will have to prove the transaction with X under which the rights of X as holder in due course were acquired.

Case # 4. Payee sold the note to Purchaser who took for value, in good faith and without notice of the defense of Maker. Purchaser received possession of the note but Payee neglected to indorse it. Purchaser became a person entitled to enforce the instrument but did not become the holder because of the missing indorsement. If Purchaser received notice of the defense of Maker before obtaining the indorsement of Payee, Purchaser cannot become a holder in due course because at the time notice was received the note had not been negotiated to Purchaser. If indorsement by Payee was made after Purchaser received notice, Purchaser had notice of the defense when it became the holder.

5. Subsection (d) restates former Section 3-202(3). The cause of action on an instrument cannot be split. Any indorsement which purports to convey to any party less than the entire amount of the instrument is not effective for negotiation. This is true of either "Pay A one-half," or "Pay A two-thirds and B one-third." Neither A nor B becomes a holder. On the other hand an indorsement reading merely "Pay A and B" is effective, since it transfers the entire cause of action to A and B as tenants in common. An indorsement purporting to convey less than the entire instrument does, however, operate as a partial assignment of the cause of action. Subsection (d) makes no attempt to state the legal effect of such an assignment, which is left to other law. A partial assignee of an instrument has rights only to the extent the applicable law gives rights, either at law or in equity, to a partial assignee.

6. The rules for transferring instruments set out in this section are similar to the rules in Article 13 of the Convention on International Bills of Exchange and International Promissory Notes.

As amended in 2002.

§ 3-204. Indorsement.

(a) "Indorsement" means a signature, other than that of a signer as maker, drawer, or acceptor, that alone or accompanied by other words is made on an instrument for the purpose of (i) negotiating the instrument, (ii) restricting payment of the instrument, or (iii) incurring indorser's liability on the instrument, but regardless of the intent of the signer, a signature and its accompanying words is an indorsement unless the accompanying words, terms of the instrument, place of the signature, or other circumstances unambiguously indicate that the signature was made for a purpose other than indorsement. For the purpose of determining whether a signature is made on an instrument, a paper affixed to the instrument is a part of the instrument.

(b) "Indorser" means a person who makes an indorsement.

(c) For the purpose of determining whether the transferee of an instrument is a holder, an indorsement that transfers a security interest in the instrument is effective as an unqualified indorsement of the instrument.

(d) If an instrument is payable to a holder under a name that is not the name of the holder, indorsement may be made by the holder in the name stated in the instrument or in the holder's name or both, but signature in both names may be required by a person paying or taking the instrument for value or collection.

Official Comment

1. Subsection (a) is a definition of "indorsement," a term which was not defined in former Article 3. Indorsement is defined in terms of the purpose of the signature. If a blank or special indorsement is made to give rights as a holder to a transferee the indorsement is made for the purpose of negotiating the instrument. Subsection (a)(i). If the holder of a check has an account in the drawee bank and wants to be sure that payment of the check will be made by credit to the holder's account, the holder can indorse the check by signing the holder's name with the accompanying words "for deposit only" before presenting the check for payment to the drawee bank. In that case the purpose of the quoted words is to restrict payment of the instrument. Subsection (a)(ii). If X wants to guarantee payment of a note signed by Y as maker, X can do so by signing X's name to the back of the note as an indorsement. This indorsement is known as an anomalous indorsement (Section 3-205(d)) and is made for the purpose of incurring indorser's liability on the note. Subsection (a)(iii). In some cases an indorsement may serve more than one purpose. For example, if the holder of a check deposits it to the holder's account in a depositary bank for collection and indorses the check by signing the holder's name with the accompanying words "for deposit only" the purpose of the indorsement is both to negotiate the check to the depositary bank and to restrict payment of the check.

The "but" clause of the first sentence of subsection (a) elaborates on former Section 3–402. In some cases it may not be clear whether a signature was meant to be that of an indorser, a party to the instrument in some other capacity such as drawer, maker or acceptor, or a person who was not signing as a party. The general rule is that a signature is an indorsement if the instrument does not indicate an unambiguous intent of the signer not to sign as an indorser. Intent may be determined by words accompanying the signature, the place of signature, or other circumstances. For example, suppose a depositary bank gives cash for a check properly indorsed by the payee. The bank requires the payee's employee to sign the back of the check as evidence that the employee received the cash. If the signature consists only of the initials of the employee it is not reasonable to assume that it was meant to be an indorsement. If there was a full signature but accompanying words indicated that it was meant as a receipt for the cash given for the check, it is not an indorsement. If the signature is not qualified in any way and appears in the place normally used for indorsements, it may be an indorsement even though the signer intended the signature to be a receipt. To take another example, suppose the drawee of a draft signs the draft on the back in the space usually used for indorsements. No words accompany the signature. Since the drawee has no reason to sign a draft unless the intent is to accept the draft, the signature is effective as an acceptance. Custom and usage may be used to determine intent. For example, by long-established custom and usage, a signature in the lower right hand corner of an instrument indicates an intent to sign as the maker of a note or the drawer of a draft. Any similar clear indication of an intent to sign in some other capacity or for some other purpose may establish that a signature is not an indorsement. For example, if the owner of a traveler's check countersigns the check in the process of negotiating it, the countersignature is not an indorsement. The countersignature is a condition to the issuer's obligation to pay and its purpose is to provide a means of verifying the identify *[should be "identity"]* of the person negotiating the traveler's check by allowing comparison of the specimen signature and the countersignature. The countersignature is not necessary for negotiation and the signer does not incur indorser's liability. See Comment 2 to Section 3–106.

The last sentence of subsection (a) is based on subsection (2) of former Section 3–202. An indorsement on an allonge is valid even though there is sufficient space on the instrument for an indorsement.

2. Assume that Payee indorses a note to Creditor as security for a debt. Under subsection (b) of Section 3–203 Creditor takes Payee's rights to enforce or transfer the instrument subject to the limitations imposed by Article 9. Subsection (c) of Section 3–204 makes clear that Payee's indorsement to Creditor, even though it mentions creation of a security interest, is an unqualified indorsement that gives to Creditor the right to enforce the note as its holder.

3. Subsection (d) is a restatement of former Section 3–203. Section 3–110(a) states that an instrument is payable to the person intended by the person signing as or in the name or behalf of the issuer even if that person is identified by a name that is not the true name of the person. In some cases the name used in the instrument is a misspelling of the correct name and in some cases the two names may be entirely different. The payee may indorse in the name used in the instrument, in the payee's correct name, or in both. In each case the indorsement is effective. But because an indorsement in a name different from that used in the instrument may raise a question about its validity and an indorsement in a name that is not the correct name of the payee may raise a problem of identifying the indorser, the accepted commercial practice is to indorse in both names. Subsection (d) allows a person paying or taking the instrument for value or collection to require indorsement in both names.

§ 3–205. Special Indorsement; Blank Indorsement; Anomalous Indorsement.

(a) If an indorsement is made by the holder of an instrument, whether payable to an identified person or payable to bearer, and the indorsement identifies a person to whom it makes the instrument payable, it is a "special indorsement." When specially indorsed, an instrument becomes payable to the identified person and may be negotiated only by the indorsement of that person. The principles stated in Section 3–110 apply to special indorsements.

(b) If an indorsement is made by the holder of an instrument and it is not a special indorsement, it is a "blank indorsement." When indorsed in blank, an instrument becomes payable to bearer and may be negotiated by transfer of possession alone until specially indorsed.

(c) The holder may convert a blank indorsement that consists only of a signature into a special indorsement by writing, above the signature of the indorser, words identifying the person to whom the instrument is made payable.

(d) "Anomalous indorsement" means an indorsement made by a person who is not the holder of the instrument. An anomalous indorsement does not affect the manner in which the instrument may be negotiated.

Official Comment

1. Subsection (a) is based on subsection (1) of former Section 3–204. It states the test of a special indorsement to be whether the indorsement identifies a person to whom the instrument is payable. Section 3–110 states rules for identifying the payee of an instrument. Section 3–205(a) incorporates the principles stated in Section 3–110 in identifying an indorsee. The language of Section 3–110 refers to language used by the issuer of the instrument. When that section is used with respect to an indorsement, Section 3–110 must be read as referring to the language used by the indorser.

2. Subsection (b) is based on subsection (2) of former Section 3–204. An indorsement made by the holder is either a special or blank indorsement. If the indorsement is made by a holder and is not a special indorsement, it is a blank indorsement. For example, the holder of an instrument, intending to make a special indorsement, writes the words "Pay to the order of" without completing the indorsement by writing the name of the indorsee. The holder's signature appears under the quoted words. The indorsement is not a special indorsement because it does not identify a person to whom it makes the instrument payable. Since it is not a special indorsement it is a blank indorsement and the instrument is payable to bearer. The result is analogous to that of a check in which the name of the payee is left blank by the drawer. In that case the check is payable to bearer. See the last paragraphs of Comment 2 to Section 3–115.

A blank indorsement is usually the signature of the indorser on the back of the instrument without other words. Subsection (c) is based on subsection (3) of former Section 3–204. A "restrictive indorsement" described in Section 3–206 can be either a blank indorsement or a special indorsement. "Pay to T, in trust for B" is a restrictive indorsement. It is also a special indorsement because it identifies T as the person to whom the instrument is payable. "For deposit only" followed by the signature of the payee of a check is a restrictive indorsement. It is also a blank indorsement because it does not identify the person to whom the instrument is payable.

3. The only effect of an "anomalous indorsement," defined in subsection (d), is to make the signer liable on the instrument as an indorser. Such an indorsement is normally made by an accommodation party. Section 3–419.

4. Articles 14 and 16 of the Convention on International Bills of Exchange and International Promissory Notes includes similar rules for blank and special indorsements.

As amended in 2002.

§ 3-206. Restrictive Indorsement.

(a) An indorsement limiting payment to a particular person or otherwise prohibiting further transfer or negotiation of the instrument is not effective to prevent further transfer or negotiation of the instrument.

(b) An indorsement stating a condition to the right of the indorsee to receive payment does not affect the right of the indorsee to enforce the instrument. A person paying the instrument or taking it for value or collection may disregard the condition, and the rights and liabilities of that person are not affected by whether the condition has been fulfilled.

(c) If an instrument bears an indorsement (i) described in Section 4–201(b), or (ii) in blank or to a particular bank using the words "for deposit," "for collection," or other words indicating a purpose of having the instrument collected by a bank for the indorser or for a particular account, the following rules apply:

(1) A person, other than a bank, who purchases the instrument when so indorsed converts the instrument unless the amount paid for the instrument is received by the indorser or applied consistently with the indorsement.

(2) A depositary bank that purchases the instrument or takes it for collection when so indorsed converts the instrument unless the amount paid by the bank with respect to the instrument is received by the indorser or applied consistently with the indorsement.

(3) A payor bank that is also the depositary bank or that takes the instrument for immediate payment over the counter from a person other than a collecting bank converts the instrument

unless the proceeds of the instrument are received by the indorser or applied consistently with the indorsement.

(4) Except as otherwise provided in paragraph (3), a payor bank or intermediary bank may disregard the indorsement and is not liable if the proceeds of the instrument are not received by the indorser or applied consistently with the indorsement.

(d) Except for an indorsement covered by subsection (c), if an instrument bears an indorsement using words to the effect that payment is to be made to the indorsee as agent, trustee, or other fiduciary for the benefit of the indorser or another person, the following rules apply:

(1) Unless there is notice of breach of fiduciary duty as provided in Section 3-307, a person who purchases the instrument from the indorsee or takes the instrument from the indorsee for collection or payment may pay the proceeds of payment or the value given for the instrument to the indorsee without regard to whether the indorsee violates a fiduciary duty to the indorser.

(2) A subsequent transferee of the instrument or person who pays the instrument is neither given notice nor otherwise affected by the restriction in the indorsement unless the transferee or payor knows that the fiduciary dealt with the instrument or its proceeds in breach of fiduciary duty.

(e) The presence on an instrument of an indorsement to which this section applies does not prevent a purchaser of the instrument from becoming a holder in due course of the instrument unless the purchaser is a converter under subsection (c) or has notice or knowledge of breach of fiduciary duty as stated in subsection (d).

(f) In an action to enforce the obligation of a party to pay the instrument, the obligor has a defense if payment would violate an indorsement to which this section applies and the payment is not permitted by this section.

Official Comment

1. This section replaces former Sections 3-205 and 3-206 and clarifies the law of restrictive indorsements.

2. Subsection (a) provides that an indorsement that purports to limit further transfer or negotiation is ineffective to prevent further transfer or negotiation. If a payee indorses "Pay A only," A may negotiate the instrument to subsequent holders who may ignore the restriction on the indorsement. Subsection (b) provides that an indorsement that states a condition to the right of a holder to receive payment is ineffective to condition payment. Thus if a payee indorses "Pay A if A ships goods complying with our contract," the right of A to enforce the instrument is not affected by the condition. In the case of a note, the obligation of the maker to pay A is not affected by the indorsement. In the case of a check, the drawee can pay A without regard to the condition, and if the check is dishonored the drawer is liable to pay A. If the check was negotiated by the payee to A in return for a promise to perform a contract and the promise was not kept, the payee would have a defense or counterclaim against A if the check were dishonored and A sued the payee as indorser, but the payee would have that defense or counterclaim whether or not the condition to the right of A was expressed in the indorsement. Former Section 3-206 treated a conditional indorsement like indorsements for deposit or collection. In revised Article 3, Section 3-206(b) rejects that approach and makes the conditional indorsement ineffective with respect to parties other than the indorser and indorsee. Since the indorsements referred to in subsections (a) and (b) are not effective as restrictive indorsements, they are no longer described as restrictive indorsements.

3. The great majority of restrictive indorsements are those that fall within subsection (c) which continues previous law. The depositary bank or the payor bank, if it takes the check for immediate payment over the counter, must act consistently with the indorsement, but an intermediary bank or payor bank that takes the check from a collecting bank is not affected by the indorsement. Any other person is also bound by the indorsement. For example, suppose a check is payable to X, who indorses in blank but writes above the signature the words "For deposit only." The check is stolen and is cashed at a grocery store by the thief. The grocery store indorses the check and deposits it in Depositary Bank. The account of the grocery store is credited and the check is forwarded to Payor Bank which pays the check. Under subsection (c), the grocery store and Depositary Bank are converters of the check because X did not receive the amount paid for the check. Payor Bank and any intermediary bank in the collection process are not liable to X. This Article does not displace the law of waiver as it may apply to restrictive indorsements. The circumstances under which a restrictive indorsement may be waived by the person who made it is not determined by this Article.

4. Subsection (d) replaces subsection (4) of former Section 3-206. Suppose Payee indorses a check "Pay to T in trust for B." T indorses in blank and delivers it to (a) Holder for value; (b) Depositary Bank for collection; or (c) Payor Bank for payment. In each case these takers can safely pay T so long as they have no notice under Section 3-307 of any breach of fiduciary duty that T may be committing. For example, under subsection (b) [Previous incorrect cross reference corrected by Permanent Editorial Board action November 1992] of Section 3-307 these takers have notice of a breach of trust if the check was taken in any transaction known by the taker to be for T's personal benefit. Subsequent transferees of the check from Holder or Depositary Bank are not affected by the restriction unless they have knowledge that T dealt with the check in breach of trust.

5. Subsection (f) allows a restrictive indorsement to be used as a defense by a person obliged to pay the instrument if that person would be liable for paying in violation of the indorsement.

§ 3-207. Reacquisition.

Reacquisition of an instrument occurs if it is transferred to a former holder, by negotiation or otherwise. A former holder who reacquires the instrument may cancel indorsements made after the reacquirer first became a holder of the instrument. If the cancellation causes the instrument to be payable to the reacquirer or to bearer, the reacquirer may negotiate the instrument. An indorser whose indorsement is canceled is discharged, and the discharge is effective against any subsequent holder.

Official Comment

Section 3-207 restates former Section 3-208. Reacquisition refers to cases in which a former holder reacquires the instrument either by negotiation from the present holder or by a transfer other than negotiation. If the reacquisition is by negotiation, the former holder reacquires the status of holder. Although Section 3-207 allows the holder to cancel all indorsements made after the holder first acquired holder status, cancellation is not necessary. Status of holder is not affected whether or not cancellation is made. But if the reacquisition is not the result of negotiation the former holder can obtain holder status only by striking the former holder's indorsement and any subsequent indorsements. The latter case is an exception to the general rule that if an instrument is payable to an identified person, the indorsement of that person is necessary to allow a subsequent transferee to obtain the status of holder. Reacquisition without indorsement by the person to whom the instrument is payable is illustrated by two examples:

Case # 1. X, a former holder, buys the instrument from Y, the present holder. Y delivers the instrument to X but fails to indorse it. Negotiation does not occur because the transfer of possession did not result in X's becoming holder. Section 3-201(a). The instrument by its terms is payable to Y, not to X. But X can obtain the status of holder by striking X's indorsement and all subsequent indorsements. When these indorsements are struck, the instrument by its terms is payable either to X or to bearer, depending upon how X originally became holder. In either case X becomes holder. Section 1-201(20) [*unrevised Article 1; see Concordance, p. 12*].

Case # 2. X, the holder of an instrument payable to X, negotiates it to Y by special indorsement. The negotiation is part of an underlying transaction between X and Y. The underlying transaction is rescinded by agreement of X and Y, and Y returns the instrument without Y's indorsement. The analysis is the same as that in Case # 1. X can obtain holder status by cancelling X's indorsement to Y.

In Case # 1 and Case # 2, X acquired ownership of the instrument after reacquisition, but X's title was clouded because the instrument by its terms was not payable to X. Normally, X can remedy the problem by obtaining Y's indorsement, but in some cases X may not be able to conveniently obtain that indorsement. Section 3-207 is a rule of convenience which relieves X of the burden of obtaining an indorsement that serves no substantive purpose. The effect of cancellation of any indorsement under Section 3-207 is to nullify it. Thus, the person whose indorsement is canceled is relieved of indorser's liability. Since cancellation is notice of discharge, discharge is effective even with respect to the rights of a holder in due course. Sections 3-601 and 3-604.

PART 3

ENFORCEMENT OF INSTRUMENTS

§ 3-301. Person Entitled to Enforce Instrument.

"Person entitled to enforce" an instrument means (i) the holder of the instrument, (ii) a nonholder in possession of the instrument who has the rights of a holder, or (iii) a person not in possession of the instrument who is entitled to enforce the instrument pursuant to Section 3–309 or 3–418(d). A person may be a person entitled to enforce the instrument even though the person is not the owner of the instrument or is in wrongful possession of the instrument.

Official Comment

This section replaces former Section 3–301 that stated the rights of a holder. The rights stated in former Section 3–301 to transfer, negotiate, enforce, or discharge an instrument are stated in other sections of Article 3. In revised Article 3, Section 3–301 defines "person entitled to enforce" an instrument. The definition recognizes that enforcement is not limited to holders. The quoted phrase includes a person enforcing a lost or stolen instrument. Section 3–309. It also includes a person in possession of an instrument who is not a holder. A nonholder in possession of an instrument includes a person that acquired rights of a holder by subrogation or under Section 3–203(a). It also includes both a remitter that has received an instrument from the issuer but has not yet transferred or negotiated the instrument to another person and also any other person who under applicable law is a successor to the holder or otherwise acquires the holder's rights.

As amended in 2002.

§ 3–302. Holder in Due Course.

(a) Subject to subsection (c) and Section 3–106(d), "holder in due course" means the holder of an instrument if:

(1) the instrument when issued or negotiated to the holder does not bear such apparent evidence of forgery or alteration or is not otherwise so irregular or incomplete as to call into question its authenticity; and

(2) the holder took the instrument (i) for value, (ii) in good faith, (iii) without notice that the instrument is overdue or has been dishonored or that there is an uncured default with respect to payment of another instrument issued as part of the same series, (iv) without notice that the instrument contains an unauthorized signature or has been altered, (v) without notice of any claim to the instrument described in Section 3–306, and (vi) without notice that any party has a defense or claim in recoupment described in Section 3–305(a).

(b) Notice of discharge of a party, other than discharge in an insolvency proceeding, is not notice of a defense under subsection (a), but discharge is effective against a person who became a holder in due course with notice of the discharge. Public filing or recording of a document does not of itself constitute notice of a defense, claim in recoupment, or claim to the instrument.

(c) Except to the extent a transferor or predecessor in interest has rights as a holder in due course, a person does not acquire rights of a holder in due course of an instrument taken (i) by legal process or by purchase in an execution, bankruptcy, or creditor's sale or similar proceeding, (ii) by purchase as part of a bulk transaction not in ordinary course of business of the transferor, or (iii) as the successor in interest to an estate or other organization.

(d) If, under Section 3–303(a)(1), the promise of performance that is the consideration for an instrument has been partially performed, the holder may assert rights as a holder in due course of the instrument only to the fraction of the amount payable under the instrument equal to the value of the partial performance divided by the value of the promised performance.

(e) If (i) the person entitled to enforce an instrument has only a security interest in the instrument and (ii) the person obliged to pay the instrument has a defense, claim in recoupment, or claim to the instrument that may be asserted against the person who granted the security interest, the person entitled to enforce the instrument may assert rights as a holder in due course only to an amount payable under the instrument which, at the time of enforcement of the instrument, does not exceed the amount of the unpaid obligation secured.

(f) To be effective, notice must be received at a time and in a manner that gives a reasonable opportunity to act on it.

(g) This section is subject to any law limiting status as a holder in due course in particular classes of transactions.

Official Comment

1. Subsection (a)(1) is a return to the N.I.L. rule that the taker of an irregular or incomplete instrument is not a person the law should protect against defenses of the obligor or claims of prior owners. This reflects a policy choice against extending the holder in due course doctrine to an instrument that is so incomplete or irregular "as to call into question its authenticity." The term "authenticity" is used to make it clear that the irregularity or incompleteness must indicate that the instrument may not be what it purports to be. Persons who purchase or pay such instruments should do so at their own risk. Under subsection (1) of former Section 3–304, irregularity or incompleteness gave a purchaser notice of a claim or defense. But it was not clear from that provision whether the claim or defense had to be related to the irregularity or incomplete aspect of the instrument. This ambiguity is not present in subsection (a)(1).

2. Subsection (a)(2) restates subsection (1) of former Section 3–302. Section 3–305(a) makes a distinction between defenses to the obligation to pay an instrument and claims in recoupment by the maker or drawer that may be asserted to reduce the amount payable on the instrument. Because of this distinction, which was not made in former Article 3, the reference in subsection (a)(2)(vi) is to both a defense and a claim in recoupment. Notice of forgery or alteration is stated separately because forgery and alteration are not technically defenses under subsection (a) of Section 3–305.

3. Discharge is also separately treated in the first sentence of subsection (b). Except for discharge in an insolvency proceeding, which is specifically stated to be a real defense in Section 3–305(a)(1), discharge is not expressed in Article 3 as a defense and is not included in Section 3–305(a)(2). Discharge is effective against anybody except a person having rights of a holder in due course who took the instrument without notice of the discharge. Notice of discharge does not disqualify a person from becoming a holder in due course. For example, a check certified after it is negotiated by the payee may subsequently be negotiated to a holder. If the holder had notice that the certification occurred after negotiation by the payee, the holder necessarily had notice of the discharge of the payee as indorser. Section 3–415(d). Notice of that discharge does not prevent the holder from becoming a holder in due course, but the discharge is effective against the holder. Section 3–601(b). Notice of a defense under Section 3–305(a)(1) of a maker, drawer or acceptor based on a bankruptcy discharge is different. There is no reason to give holder in due course status to a person with notice of that defense. The second sentence of subsection (b) is from former Section 3–304(5).

4. Professor Britton in his treatise *Bills and Notes* 309 (1961) stated: "A substantial number of decisions before the [N.I.L.] indicates that at common law there was nothing in the position of the payee as such which made it impossible for him to be a holder in due course." The courts were divided, however, about whether the payee of an instrument could be a holder in due course under the N.I.L. Some courts read N.I.L. § 52(4) to mean that a person could be a holder in due course only if the instrument was "negotiated" to that person. N.I.L. § 30 stated that "an instrument is negotiated when it is transferred from one person to another in such manner as to constitute the transferee the holder thereof." Normally, an instrument is "issued" to the payee; it is not transferred to the payee. N.I.L. § 191 defined "issue" as the "first delivery of the instrument . . . to a person who takes it as a holder." Thus, some courts concluded that the payee never could be a holder in due course. Other courts concluded that there was no evidence that the N.I.L. was intended to change the common law rule that the payee could be a holder in due course. Professor Britton states on p. 318: "The typical situations which raise the [issue] are those where the defense of a maker is interposed because of fraud by a [maker who is] principal debtor . . . against a surety co-maker, or where the defense of fraud by a purchasing remitter is interposed by the drawer of the instrument against the good faith purchasing payee."

Former Section 3–302(2) stated: "A payee may be a holder in due course." This provision was intended to resolve the split of authority under the N.I.L. It made clear that there was no intent to change the common-law rule that allowed a payee to become a holder in due course. See Comment 2 to former Section 3–302. But there was no need to put subsection (2) in former Section 3–302 because the split in authority under the N.I.L. was caused by the particular wording of N.I.L. § 52(4). The troublesome language in that section was not repeated in former Article 3 nor is it repeated in revised Article 3. Former Section 3–302(2) has been omitted in revised Article 3 because it is surplusage and may be misleading. The payee of an instrument can be a holder in due course, but use of the holder-in-due-course doctrine by the payee of an instrument is not the normal situation.

The primary importance of the concept of holder in due course is with respect to assertion of defenses or claims in recoupment (Section 3–305) and of claims to the instrument (Section 3–306). The holder-in-due-course doctrine assumes the following case as typical. Obligor issues a note or check to Obligee. Obligor is the maker of the note or drawer of the check. Obligee is the payee. Obligor has some defense to Obligor's obligation to pay the instrument. For example, Obligor issued the instrument for goods that Obligee promised to deliver. Obligee never delivered the goods. The failure of Obligee to deliver the goods is a defense. Section 3–303(b). Although Obligor has a defense against Obligee, if the instrument is negotiated to Holder and the requirements of subsection (a) are met, Holder may enforce the instrument against Obligor free of the defense. Section 3–305(b). In the typical case the holder in due course is not the payee of the instrument. Rather, the holder in due course is an immediate or remote transferee of the payee. If Obligor in our example is the only obligor on the check or note, the holder-in-due-course doctrine is irrelevant in determining rights between Obligor and Obligee with respect to the instrument.

But in a small percentage of cases it is appropriate to allow the payee of an instrument to assert rights as a holder in due course. The cases are like those referred to in the quotation from Professor Britton referred to above, or other cases in which conduct of some third party is the basis of the defense of the issuer of the instrument. The following are examples:

Case # 1. Buyer pays for goods bought from Seller by giving to Seller a cashier's check bought from Bank. Bank has a defense to its obligation to pay the check because Buyer bought the check from Bank with a check known to be drawn on an account with insufficient funds to cover the check. If Bank issued the check to Buyer as payee and Buyer indorsed it over to Seller, it is clear that Seller can be a holder in due course taking free of the defense if Seller had no notice of the defense. Seller is a transferee of the check. There is no good reason why Seller's position should be any different if Bank drew the check to the order of Seller as payee. In that case, when Buyer took delivery of the check from Bank, Buyer became the owner of the check even though Buyer was not the holder. Buyer was a remitter. Section 3–103(a)(15). At that point nobody was the holder. When Buyer delivered the check to Seller, ownership of the check was transferred to Seller who also became the holder. This is a negotiation. Section 3–201. The rights of Seller should not be affected by the fact that in one case the negotiation to Seller was by a holder and in the other case the negotiation was by a remitter. Moreover, it should be irrelevant whether Bank delivered the check to Buyer and Buyer delivered it to Seller or whether Bank delivered it directly to Seller. In either case Seller can be a holder in due course that takes free of Bank's defense.

Case # 2. X fraudulently induces Y to join X in a spurious venture to purchase a business. The purchase is to be financed by a bank loan for part of the price. Bank lends money to X and Y by deposit in a joint account of X and Y who sign a note payable to Bank for the amount of the loan. X then withdraws the money from the joint account and absconds. Bank acted in good faith and without notice of the fraud of X against Y. Bank is payee of the note executed by Y, but its right to enforce the note against Y should not be affected by the fact that Y was induced to execute the note by the fraud of X. Bank can be a holder in due course that takes free of the defense of Y. Case # 2 is similar to Case # 1. In each case the payee of the instrument has given value to the person committing the fraud in exchange for the obligation of the person against whom the fraud was committed. In each case the payee was not party to the fraud and had no notice of it.

Suppose in Case # 2 that the note does not meet the requirements of Section 3–104(a) and thus is not a negotiable instrument covered by Article 3. In that case, Bank cannot be a holder in due course but the result should be the same. Bank's rights are determined by general principles of contract law. Restatement Second, Contracts § 164(2) governs the case. If Y is induced to enter into a contract with Bank by a fraudulent misrepresentation by X, the contract is voidable by Y unless Bank "in good faith and without reason to know of the misrepresentation either gives value or relies materially on the transaction." Comment e to § 164(2) states:

> "This is the same principle that protects an innocent person who purchases goods or commercial paper in good faith, without notice and for value from one who obtained them from the original owner by a misrepresentation. See Uniform Commercial Code §§ 2–403(1), 3–305. In the cases that fall within [§ 164(2)], however, the innocent person deals directly with the recipient of the misrepresentation, which is made by one not a party to the contract."

The same result follows in Case # 2 if Y had been induced to sign the note as an accommodation party (Section 3–419). If Y signs as co-maker of a note for the benefit of X, Y is a surety with respect to the obligation of X to pay the note but is liable as maker of the note to pay Bank. Section 3–419(b). If Bank is a holder in due course, the fraud of X cannot be asserted against Bank under Section 3–305(b). But the result is the same without resort to holder-in-due-course doctrine. If the note is not a negotiable instrument governed by Article 3, general rules of suretyship apply. Restatement, Security § 119 states that the surety (Y) cannot assert a defense against the creditor (Bank) based on the fraud of the principal (X) if the creditor "without knowledge of the fraud . . . extended credit to the principal on the security of the surety's promise . . . ." The underlying principle of § 119 is the same as that of § 164(2) of Restatement Second, Contracts.

Case # 3. Corporation draws a check payable to Bank. The check is given to an officer of Corporation who is instructed to deliver it to Bank in payment of a debt owed by Corporation to Bank. Instead, the officer, intending to defraud Corporation, delivers the check to Bank in payment of the officer's personal debt, or the check is delivered to Bank for deposit to the officer's personal account. If Bank obtains payment of the check, Bank has received funds of Corporation which have been used for the personal benefit of the officer. Corporation in this case will assert a claim to the proceeds of the check against Bank. If Bank was a holder in due course of the check it took the check free of Corporation's claim. Section 3-306. The issue in this case is whether Bank had notice of the claim when it took the check. If Bank knew that the officer was a fiduciary with respect to the check, the issue is governed by Section 3-307.

Case # 4. Employer, who owed money to X, signed a blank check and delivered it to Secretary with instructions to complete the check by typing in X's name and the amount owed to X. Secretary fraudulently completed the check by typing in the name of Y, a creditor to whom Secretary owed money. Secretary then delivered the check to Y in payment of Secretary's debt. Y obtained payment of the check. This case is similar to Case # 3. Since Secretary was authorized to complete the check, Employer is bound by Secretary's act in making the check payable to Y. The drawee bank properly paid the check. Y received funds of Employer which were used for the personal benefit of Secretary. Employer asserts a claim to these funds against Y. If Y is a holder in due course, Y takes free of the claim. Whether Y is a holder in due course depends upon whether Y had notice of Employer's claim.

5. Subsection (c) is based on former Section 3-302(3). Like former Section 3-302(3), subsection (c) is intended to state existing case law. It covers a few situations in which the purchaser takes an instrument under unusual circumstances. The purchaser is treated as a successor in interest to the prior holder and can acquire no better rights. But if the prior holder was a holder in due course, the purchaser obtains rights of a holder in due course.

Subsection (c) applies to a purchaser in an execution sale or sale in bankruptcy. It applies equally to an attaching creditor or any other person who acquires the instrument by legal process or to a representative, such as an executor, administrator, receiver or assignee for the benefit of creditors, who takes the instrument as part of an estate. Subsection (c) applies to bulk purchases lying outside of the ordinary course of business of the seller. For example, it applies to the purchase by one bank of a substantial part of the paper held by another bank which is threatened with insolvency and seeking to liquidate its assets. Subsection (c) would also apply when a new partnership takes over for value all of the assets of an old one after a new member has entered the firm, or to a reorganized or consolidated corporation taking over the assets of a predecessor.

In the absence of controlling state law to the contrary, subsection (c) applies to a sale by a state bank commissioner of the assets of an insolvent bank. However, subsection (c) may be preempted by federal law if the Federal Deposit Insurance Corporation takes over an insolvent bank. Under the governing federal law, the FDIC and similar financial institution insurers are given holder in due course status and that status is also acquired by their assignees under the shelter doctrine.

6. Subsections (d) and (e) clarify two matters not specifically addressed by former Article 3:

Case # 5. Payee negotiates a $1,000 note to Holder who agrees to pay $900 for it. After paying $500, Holder learns that Payee defrauded Maker in the transaction giving rise to the note. Under subsection (d) Holder may assert rights as a holder in due course to the extent of $555.55 ($500 ÷ $900 = .555 × $1,000 = $555.55). This formula rewards Holder with a ratable portion of the bargained for profit.

Case # 6. Payee negotiates a note of Maker for $1,000 to Holder as security for payment of Payee's debt to Holder of $600. Maker has a defense which is good against Payee but of which Holder has no notice. Subsection (e) applies. Holder may assert rights as a holder in due course only to the extent of $600. Payee does not get the benefit of the holder-in-due-course status of Holder. With respect to $400 of the note, Maker may assert any rights that Maker has against Payee. A different result follows if the payee of a note negotiated it to a person who took it as a holder in due course and that person pledged the note as security for a debt. Because the defense cannot be asserted against the pledgor, the pledgee can assert rights as a holder in due course for the full amount of the note for the benefit of both the pledgor and the pledgee.

7. There is a large body of state statutory and case law restricting the use of the holder in due course doctrine in consumer transactions as well as some business transactions that raise similar issues. Subsection (g) subordinates Article 3 to that law and any other similar law that may evolve in the future. Section 3-106(d) also relates to statutory or administrative law intended to restrict use of the holder-in-due-course doctrine. See Comment 3 to Section 3-106.

8. The status of holder in due course resembles the status of protected holder under Article 29 of the Convention on International Bills of Exchange and International Promissory Notes. The requirements for being a protected holder under Article 29 generally track those of Section 3–302.

As amended in 2002.

§ 3–303. Value and Consideration.

(a) An instrument is issued or transferred for value if:

(1) the instrument is issued or transferred for a promise of performance, to the extent the promise has been performed;

(2) the transferee acquires a security interest or other lien in the instrument other than a lien obtained by judicial proceeding;

(3) the instrument is issued or transferred as payment of, or as security for, an antecedent claim against any person, whether or not the claim is due;

(4) the instrument is issued or transferred in exchange for a negotiable instrument; or

(5) the instrument is issued or transferred in exchange for the incurring of an irrevocable obligation to a third party by the person taking the instrument.

(b) "Consideration" means any consideration sufficient to support a simple contract. The drawer or maker of an instrument has a defense if the instrument is issued without consideration. If an instrument is issued for a promise of performance, the issuer has a defense to the extent performance of the promise is due and the promise has not been performed. If an instrument is issued for value as stated in subsection (a), the instrument is also issued for consideration.

Official Comment

1. Subsection (a) is a restatement of former Section 3–303 and subsection (b) replaces former Section 3–408. The distinction between value and consideration in Article 3 is a very fine one. Whether an instrument is taken for value is relevant to the issue of whether a holder is a holder in due course. If an instrument is not issued for consideration the issuer has a defense to the obligation to pay the instrument. Consideration is defined in subsection (b) as "any consideration sufficient to support a simple contract." The definition of value in Section 1–201(44) [*unrevised Article 1; see Concordance, p. 12*], which doesn't apply to Article 3, includes "any consideration sufficient to support a simple contract." Thus, outside Article 3, anything that is consideration is also value. A different rule applies in Article 3. Subsection (b) of Section 3–303 states that if an instrument is issued for value it is also issued for consideration.

Case # 1. X owes Y $1,000. The debt is not represented by a note. Later X issues a note to Y for the debt. Under subsection (a)(3) X's note is issued for value. Under subsection (b) the note is also issued for consideration whether or not, under contract law, Y is deemed to have given consideration for the note.

Case # 2. X issues a check to Y in consideration of Y's promise to perform services in the future. Although the executory promise is consideration for issuance of the check it is value only to the extent the promise is performed. Subsection (a)(1).

Case # 3. X issues a note to Y in consideration of Y's promise to perform services. If at the due date of the note Y's performance is not yet due, Y may enforce the note because it was issued for consideration. But if at the due date of the note, Y's performance is due and has not been performed, X has a defense. Subsection (b).

2. Subsection (a), which defines value, has primary importance in cases in which the issue is whether the holder of an instrument is a holder in due course and particularly to cases in which the issuer of the instrument has a defense to the instrument. Suppose Buyer and Seller signed a contract on April 1 for the sale of goods to be delivered on May 1. Payment of 50% of the price of the goods was due upon signing of the contract. On April 1 Buyer delivered to Seller a check in the amount due under the contract. The check was drawn by X to Buyer as payee and was indorsed to Seller. When the check was presented for payment to the drawee on April 2, it was dishonored because X had stopped payment. At that time Seller had not taken any action to perform the contract with Buyer. If X has a defense on the check, the defense can be asserted against Seller who is not a holder in due course because Seller did not give value for the check. Subsection (a)(1). The policy basis for subsection (a)(1) is that the holder who gives an executory promise of performance will not suffer an out-of-pocket loss to the extent

the executory promise is unperformed at the time the holder learns of dishonor of the instrument. When Seller took delivery of the check on April 1, Buyer's obligation to pay 50% of the price on that date was suspended, but when the check was dishonored on April 2 the obligation revived. Section 3–310(b). If payment for goods is due at or before delivery and the buyer fails to make the payment, the seller is excused from performing the promise to deliver the goods. Section 2–703. Thus, Seller is protected from an out-of-pocket loss even if the check is not enforceable. Holder-in-due-course status is not necessary to protect Seller.

3. Subsection (a)(2) equates value with the obtaining of a security interest or a nonjudicial lien in the instrument. The term "security interest" covers Article 9 cases in which an instrument is taken as collateral as well as bank collection cases in which a bank acquires a security interest under Section 4–210. The acquisition of a common-law or statutory banker's lien is also value under subsection (a)(2). An attaching creditor or other person who acquires a lien by judicial proceedings does not give value for the purposes of subsection (a)(2).

4. Subsection (a)(3) follows former Section 3–303(b) in providing that the holder takes for value if the instrument is taken in payment of or as security for an antecedent claim, even though there is no extension of time or other concession, and whether or not the claim is due. Subsection (a)(3) applies to any claim against any person; there is no requirement that the claim arise out of contract. In particular the provision is intended to apply to an instrument given in payment of or as security for the debt of a third person, even though no concession is made in return.

5. Subsection (a)(4) and (5) restate former Section 3–303(c). They state generally recognized exceptions to the rule that an executory promise is not value. A negotiable instrument is value because it carries the possibility of negotiation to a holder in due course, after which the party who gives it is obliged to pay. The same reasoning applies to any irrevocable commitment to a third person, such as a letter of credit issued when an instrument is taken.

6. The term "promise" in paragraph (a)(1) is used in the phrase "promise of performance" and for that reason does not have the specialized meaning given that term in Section 3–103(a)(12). See Section 1–201 ("Changes from Former Law"). No inference should be drawn from the decision to use the phrase "promise of performance," although the phrase does include the word "promise," which has the specialized definition set forth in Section 3–103. Indeed, that is true even though "undertaking" is used instead of "promise" in Section 3–104(a)(3). See Section 3–104 comment 1 (explaining the use of the term "undertaking" in Section 3–104 to avoid use of the defined term "promise").

As amended in 2002.

§ 3–304. Overdue Instrument.

(a) An instrument payable on demand becomes overdue at the earliest of the following times:

(1) on the day after the day demand for payment is duly made;

(2) if the instrument is a check, 90 days after its date; or

(3) if the instrument is not a check, when the instrument has been outstanding for a period of time after its date which is unreasonably long under the circumstances of the particular case in light of the nature of the instrument and usage of the trade.

(b) With respect to an instrument payable at a definite time the following rules apply:

(1) If the principal is payable in installments and a due date has not been accelerated, the instrument becomes overdue upon default under the instrument for nonpayment of an installment, and the instrument remains overdue until the default is cured.

(2) If the principal is not payable in installments and the due date has not been accelerated, the instrument becomes overdue on the day after the due date.

(3) If a due date with respect to principal has been accelerated, the instrument becomes overdue on the day after the accelerated due date.

(c) Unless the due date of principal has been accelerated, an instrument does not become overdue if there is default in payment of interest but no default in payment of principal.

Official Comment

1. To be a holder in due course, one must take without notice that an instrument is overdue. Section 3–302(a)(2)(iii). Section 3–304 replaces subsection (3) of former Section 3–304. For the sake of clarity it treats demand and time instruments separately. Subsection (a) applies to demand instruments. A check becomes stale after 90 days.

Under former Section 3–304(3)(c), a holder that took a demand note had notice that it was overdue if it was taken "more than a reasonable length of time after its issue." In substitution for this test, subsection (a)(3) requires the trier of fact to look at both the circumstances of the particular case and the nature of the instrument and trade usage. Whether a demand note is stale may vary a great deal depending on the facts of the particular case.

2. Subsections (b) and (c) cover time instruments. They follow the distinction made under former Article 3 between defaults in payment of principal and interest. In subsection (b) installment instruments and single payment instruments are treated separately. If an installment is late, the instrument is overdue until the default is cured.

§ 3–305. Defenses and Claims in Recoupment.

(a) Except as otherwise provided in this section, the right to enforce the obligation of a party to pay an instrument is subject to the following:

(1) a defense of the obligor based on (i) infancy of the obligor to the extent it is a defense to a simple contract, (ii) duress, lack of legal capacity, or illegality of the transaction which, under other law, nullifies the obligation of the obligor, (iii) fraud that induced the obligor to sign the instrument with neither knowledge nor reasonable opportunity to learn of its character or its essential terms, or (iv) discharge of the obligor in insolvency proceedings;

(2) a defense of the obligor stated in another section of this Article or a defense of the obligor that would be available if the person entitled to enforce the instrument were enforcing a right to payment under a simple contract; and

(3) a claim in recoupment of the obligor against the original payee of the instrument if the claim arose from the transaction that gave rise to the instrument; but the claim of the obligor may be asserted against a transferee of the instrument only to reduce the amount owing on the instrument at the time the action is brought.

(b) The right of a holder in due course to enforce the obligation of a party to pay the instrument is subject to defenses of the obligor stated in subsection (a)(1), but is not subject to defenses of the obligor stated in subsection (a)(2) or claims in recoupment stated in subsection (a)(3) against a person other than the holder.

(c) Except as stated in subsection (d), in an action to enforce the obligation of a party to pay the instrument, the obligor may not assert against the person entitled to enforce the instrument a defense, claim in recoupment, or claim to the instrument (Section 3–306) of another person, but the other person's claim to the instrument may be asserted by the obligor if the other person is joined in the action and personally asserts the claim against the person entitled to enforce the instrument. An obligor is not obliged to pay the instrument if the person seeking enforcement of the instrument does not have rights of a holder in due course and the obligor proves that the instrument is a lost or stolen instrument.

(d) In an action to enforce the obligation of an accommodation party to pay an instrument, the accommodation party may assert against the person entitled to enforce the instrument any defense or claim in recoupment under subsection (a) that the accommodated party could assert against the person entitled to enforce the instrument, except the defenses of discharge in insolvency proceedings, infancy, and lack of legal capacity.

(e) In a consumer transaction, if law other than this article requires that an instrument include a statement to the effect that the rights of a holder or transferee are subject to a claim or defense that the issuer could assert against the original payee, and the instrument does not include such a statement:

(1) the instrument has the same effect as if the instrument included such a statement;

(2) the issuer may assert against the holder or transferee all claims and defenses that would have been available if the instrument included such a statement; and

(3) the extent to which claims may be asserted against the holder or transferee is determined as if the instrument included such a statement.

(f) This section is subject to law other than this article that establishes a different rule for consumer transactions.

Legislative Note: If a consumer protection law in this state addresses the same issue as subsection (g), it should be examined for consistency with subsection (g) and, if inconsistent, should be amended. [Note from West Advisory Panel: So in original; should be (e).]

As amended in 2002.

Official Comment

1. Subsection (a) states the defenses to the obligation of a party to pay the instrument. Subsection (a)(1) states the "real defenses" that may be asserted against any person entitled to enforce the instrument.

Subsection (a)(1)(i) allows assertion of the defense of infancy against a holder in due course, even though the effect of the defense is to render the instrument voidable but not void. The policy is one of protection of the infant even at the expense of occasional loss to an innocent purchaser. No attempt is made to state when infancy is available as a defense or the conditions under which it may be asserted. In some jurisdictions it is held that an infant cannot rescind the transaction or set up the defense unless the holder is restored to the position held before the instrument was taken which, in the case of a holder in due course, is normally impossible. In other states an infant who has misrepresented age may be estopped to assert infancy. Such questions are left to other law, as an integral part of the policy of each state as to the protection of infants.

Subsection (a)(1)(ii) covers mental incompetence, guardianship, ultra vires acts or lack of corporate capacity to do business, or any other incapacity apart from infancy. Such incapacity is largely statutory. Its existence and effect is left to the law of each state. If under the state law the effect is to render the obligation of the instrument entirely null and void, the defense may be asserted against a holder in due course. If the effect is merely to render the obligation voidable at the election of the obligor, the defense is cut off.

Duress, which is also covered by subsection (a)(ii), is a matter of degree. An instrument signed at the point of a gun is void, even in the hands of a holder in due course. One signed under threat to prosecute the son of the maker for theft may be merely voidable, so that the defense is cut off. Illegality is most frequently a matter of gambling or usury, but may arise in other forms under a variety of statutes. The statutes differ in their provisions and the interpretations given them. They are primarily a matter of local concern and local policy. All such matters are therefore left to the local law. If under that law the effect of the duress or the illegality is to make the obligation entirely null and void, the defense may be asserted against a holder in due course. Otherwise it is cut off.

Subsection (a)(1)(iii) refers to "real" or "essential" fraud, sometimes called fraud in the essence or fraud in the factum, as effective against a holder in due course. The common illustration is that of the maker who is tricked into signing a note in the belief that it is merely a receipt or some other document. The theory of the defense is that the signature on the instrument is ineffective because the signer did not intend to sign such an instrument at all. Under this provision the defense extends to an instrument signed with knowledge that it is a negotiable instrument, but without knowledge of its essential terms. The test of the defense is that of excusable ignorance of the contents of the writing signed. The party must not only have been in ignorance, but must also have had no reasonable opportunity to obtain knowledge. In determining what is a reasonable opportunity all relevant factors are to be taken into account, including the intelligence, education, business experience, and ability to read or understand English of the signer. Also relevant is the nature of the representations that were made, whether the signer had good reason to rely on the representations or to have confidence in the person making them, the presence or absence of any third person who might read or explain the instrument to the signer, or any other possibility of obtaining independent information, and the apparent necessity, or lack of it, for acting without delay. Unless the misrepresentation meets this test, the defense is cut off by a holder in due course.

Subsection (a)(1)(iv) states specifically that the defense of discharge in insolvency proceedings is not cut off when the instrument is purchased by a holder in due course. "Insolvency proceedings" is defined in Section 1–201(22) [*unrevised Article 1; see Concordance, p. 12*], and it includes bankruptcy whether or not the debtor is insolvent. Subsection (2)(e) of former Section 3–305 is omitted. The substance of that provision is stated in Section 3–601(b).

2. Subsection (a)(2) states other defenses that, pursuant to subsection (b), are cut off by a holder in due course. These defenses comprise those specifically stated in Article 3 and those based on common law contract principles. Article 3 defenses are nonissuance of the instrument, conditional issuance, and issuance for a special purpose (Section 3–105(b)); failure to countersign a traveler's check (Section 3–106(c)); modification of the obligation by a separate agreement (Section 3–117); payment that violates a restrictive indorsement (Section 3–206(f)); instruments issued without consideration or for which promised performance has not been given (Section 3–303(b)), and breach of warranty when a draft is accepted (Section 3–417(b)). The most prevalent common law defenses are fraud, misrepresentation or mistake in the issuance of the instrument. In most cases the holder in due course will be an immediate or remote transferee of the payee of the instrument. In most cases the holder-in-due-course doctrine is irrelevant if defenses are being asserted against the payee of the instrument, but in a small number of cases the payee of the instrument may be a holder in due course. Those cases are discussed in Comment 4 to Section 3–302.

Assume Buyer issues a note to Seller in payment of the price of goods that Seller fraudulently promises to deliver but which are never delivered. Seller negotiates the note to Holder who has no notice of the fraud. If Holder is a holder in due course, Holder is not subject to Buyer's defense of fraud. But in some cases an original party to the instrument is a holder in due course. For example, Buyer fraudulently induces Bank to issue a cashier's check to the order of Seller. The check is delivered by Bank to Seller, who has no notice of the fraud. Seller can be a holder in due course and can take the check free of Bank's defense of fraud. This case is discussed as Case # 1 in Comment 4 to Section 3–302. Former Section 3–305 stated that a holder in due course takes free of defenses of "any party to the instrument with whom the holder has not dealt." The meaning of this language was not at all clear and if read literally could have produced the wrong result. In the hypothetical case, it could be argued that Seller "dealt" with Bank because Bank delivered the check to Seller. But it is clear that Seller should take free of Bank's defense against Buyer regardless of whether Seller took delivery of the check from Buyer or from Bank. The quoted language is not included in Section 3–305. It is not necessary. If Buyer issues an instrument to Seller and Buyer has a defense against Seller, that defense can obviously be asserted. Buyer and Seller are the only people involved. The holder-in-due-course doctrine has no relevance. The doctrine applies only to cases in which more than two parties are involved. Its essence is that the holder in due course does not have to suffer the consequences of a defense of the obligor on the instrument that arose from an occurrence with a third party.

3. Subsection (a)(3) is concerned with claims in recoupment which can be illustrated by the following example. Buyer issues a note to the order of Seller in exchange for a promise of Seller to deliver specified equipment. If Seller fails to deliver the equipment or delivers equipment that is rightfully rejected, Buyer has a defense to the note because the performance that was the consideration for the note was not rendered. Section 3–303(b). This defense is included in Section 3–305(a)(2). That defense can always be asserted against Seller. This result is the same as that reached under former Section 3–408.

But suppose Seller delivered the promised equipment and it was accepted by Buyer. The equipment, however, was defective. Buyer retained the equipment and incurred expenses with respect to its repair. In this case, Buyer does not have a defense under Section 3–303(b). Seller delivered the equipment and the equipment was accepted. Under Article 2, Buyer is obliged to pay the price of the equipment which is represented by the note. But Buyer may have a claim against Seller for breach of warranty. If Buyer has a warranty claim, the claim may be asserted against Seller as a counterclaim or as a claim in recoupment to reduce the amount owing on the note. It is not relevant whether Seller is or is not a holder in due course of the note or whether Seller knew or had notice that Buyer had the warranty claim. It is obvious that holder-in-due-course doctrine cannot be used to allow Seller to cut off a warranty claim that Buyer has against Seller. Subsection (b) specifically covers this point by stating that a holder in due course is not subject to a "claim in recoupment . . . against a person other than the holder."

Suppose Seller negotiates the note to Holder. If Holder had notice of Buyer's warranty claim at the time the note was negotiated to Holder, Holder is not a holder in due course (Section 3–302(a)(2)(iv)) and Buyer may assert the claim against Holder (Section 3–305(a)(3)) but only as a claim in recoupment, i.e. to reduce the amount owed on the note. If the warranty claim is $1,000 and the unpaid note is $10,000, Buyer owes $9,000 to Holder. If the warranty claim is more than the unpaid amount of the note, Buyer owes nothing to Holder, but Buyer cannot recover the unpaid amount of the warranty claim from Holder. If Buyer had already partially paid the note, Buyer is not entitled to recover the amounts paid. The claim can be used only as an offset to amounts owing on the note. If Holder had no notice of Buyer's claim and otherwise qualifies as a holder in due course, Buyer may not assert the claim against Holder. Section 3–305(b).

The result under Section 3–305 is consistent with the result reached under former Article 3, but the rules for reaching the result are stated differently. Under former Article 3 Buyer could assert rights against Holder only if Holder was not a holder in due course, and Holder's status depended upon whether Holder had notice of a defense by Buyer. Courts have held that Holder had that notice if Holder had notice of Buyer's warranty claim. The rationale under former Article 3 was "failure of consideration." This rationale does not distinguish between cases in which the seller fails to perform and those in which the buyer accepts the performance of seller but makes a claim against the seller because the performance is faulty. The term "failure of consideration" is subject to varying interpretations and is not used in Article 3. The use of the term "claim in recoupment" in Section 3-305(a)(3) is a more precise statement of the nature of Buyer's right against Holder. The use of the term does not change the law because the treatment of a defense under subsection (a)(2) and a claim in recoupment under subsection (a)(3) is essentially the same.

Under former Article 3, case law was divided on the issue of the extent to which an obligor on a note could assert against a transferee who is not a holder in due course a debt or other claim that the obligor had against the original payee of the instrument. Some courts limited claims to those that arose in the transaction that gave rise to the note. This is the approach taken in Section 3-305(a)(3). Other courts allowed the obligor on the note to use any debt or other claim, no matter how unrelated to the note, to offset the amount owed on the note. Under current judicial authority and non-UCC statutory law, there will be many cases in which a transferee of a note arising from a sale transaction will not qualify as a holder in due course. For example, applicable law may require the use of a note to which there cannot be a holder in due course. See Section 3-106(d) and Comment 3 to Section 3-106. It is reasonable to provide that the buyer should not be denied the right to assert claims arising out of the sale transaction. Subsection (a)(3) is based on the belief that it is not reasonable to require the transferee to bear the risk that wholly unrelated claims may also be asserted. The determination of whether a claim arose from the transaction that gave rise to the instrument is determined by law other than this Article and thus may vary as local law varies.

4. Subsection (c) concerns claims and defenses of a person other than the obligor on the instrument. It applies principally to cases in which an obligation is paid with the instrument of a third person. For example, Buyer buys goods from Seller and negotiates to Seller a cashier's check issued by Bank in payment of the price. Shortly after delivering the check to Seller, Buyer learns that Seller had defrauded Buyer in the sale transaction. Seller may enforce the check against Bank even though Seller is not a holder in due course. Bank has no defense to its obligation to pay the check and it may not assert defenses, claims in recoupment, or claims to the instrument of Buyer, except to the extent permitted by the "but" clause of the first sentence of subsection (c). Buyer may have a claim to the instrument under Section 3-306 based on a right to rescind the negotiation to Seller because of Seller's fraud. Section 3-202(b) and Comment 2 to Section 3-201. Bank cannot assert that claim unless Buyer is joined in the action in which Seller is trying to enforce payment of the check. In that case Bank may pay the amount of the check into court and the court will decide whether that amount belongs to Buyer or Seller. The last sentence of subsection (c) allows the issuer of an instrument such as a cashier's check to refuse payment in the rare case in which the issuer can prove that the instrument is a lost or stolen instrument and the person seeking enforcement does not have rights of a holder in due course.

5. Subsection (d) applies to instruments signed for accommodation (Section 3-419) and this subsection equates the obligation of the accommodation party to that of the accommodated party. The accommodation party can assert whatever defense or claim the accommodated party had against the person enforcing the instrument. The only exceptions are discharge in bankruptcy, infancy and lack of capacity. The same rule does not apply to an indorsement by a holder of the instrument in negotiating the instrument. The indorser, as transferor, makes a warranty to the indorsee, as transferee, that no defense or claim in recoupment is good against the indorser. Section 3-416(a)(4). Thus, if the indorsee sues the indorser because of dishonor of the instrument, the indorser may not assert the defense or claim in recoupment of the maker or drawer against the indorsee.

Section 3-305(d) must be read in conjunction with Section 3-605, which provides rules (usually referred to as suretyship defenses) for determining when the obligation of an accommodation party is discharged, in whole or in part, because of some act or omission of a person entitled to enforce the instrument. To the extent a rule stated in Section 3-605 is inconsistent with Section 3-305(d), the Section 3-605 rule governs. For example, Section 3-605(a) provides rules for determining when and to what extent a discharge of the accommodated party under Section 3-604 will discharge the accommodation party. As explained in Comment 2 to Section 3-605, discharge of the accommodated party is normally part of a settlement under which the holder of a note accepts partial payment from an accommodated party who is financially unable to pay the entire amount of the note. If the holder then brings an action against the accommodation party to recover the remaining unpaid amount of the note, the accommodation party cannot use Section 3-305(d) to nullify Section 3-605(a) by asserting the discharge of the accommodated party as a defense. On the other hand, suppose the accommodated party is a buyer of goods who issued the note to the seller who took the note for the buyer's obligation to pay for the goods. Suppose the buyer has a claim for breach of warranty with respect to the goods against the seller and the warranty claim may be asserted against the holder of the note. The warranty claim is a claim in recoupment. If the holder and the accommodated party reach a settlement under which the holder accepts payment less than the amount of the note in full satisfaction of the note and the warranty claim, the accommodation party could defend an action on the note by the holder by asserting the accord and satisfaction under Section 3–305(d). There is no conflict with Section 3–605(a) because that provision is not intended to apply to settlement of disputed claims.

6. Subsection (e) is added to clarify the treatment of an instrument that omits the notice currently required by the Federal Trade Commission Rule related to certain consumer credit sales and consumer purchase money loans (16 C.F.R. Part 433). This subsection adopts the view that the instrument should be treated as if the language required by the FTC Rule were present. It is based on the language describing that rule in Section 3–106(d) and the analogous provision in Section 9–404(d).

7. Subsection (f) is modeled on Sections 9–403(e) and 9–404(c). It ensures that Section 3–305 is interpreted to accommodate relevant consumer-protection laws. The absence of such a provision from other sections in Article 3 should not justify any inference about the meaning of those sections.

8. Articles 28 and 30 of the Convention on International Bills of Exchange and International Promissory Notes includes a similar dichotomy, with a narrower group of defenses available against a protected holder under Articles 28(1) and 30 than are available under Article 28(2) against a holder that is not a protected holder.

As amended in 1994 and 2002.

§ 3–306. Claims to an Instrument.

A person taking an instrument, other than a person having rights of a holder in due course, is subject to a claim of a property or possessory right in the instrument or its proceeds, including a claim to rescind a negotiation and to recover the instrument or its proceeds. A person having rights of a holder in due course takes free of the claim to the instrument.

Official Comment

This section expands on the reference to "claims to" the instrument mentioned in former Sections 3–305 and 3–306. Claims covered by the section include not only claims to ownership but also any other claim of a property or possessory right. It includes the claim to a lien or the claim of a person in rightful possession of an instrument who was wrongfully deprived of possession. Also included is a claim based on Section 3–202(b) for rescission of a negotiation of the instrument by the claimant. Claims to an instrument under Section 3–306 are different from claims in recoupment referred to in Section 3–305(a)(3). The rule of this section is similar to the rule of Article 30(2) of the Convention on International Bills of Exchange and International Promissory Notes.

As amended in 2002.

§ 3–307. Notice of Breach of Fiduciary Duty.

(a) In this section:

(1) "Fiduciary" means an agent, trustee, partner, corporate officer or director, or other representative owing a fiduciary duty with respect to an instrument.

(2) "Represented person" means the principal, beneficiary, partnership, corporation, or other person to whom the duty stated in paragraph (1) is owed.

(b) If (i) an instrument is taken from a fiduciary for payment or collection or for value, (ii) the taker has knowledge of the fiduciary status of the fiduciary, and (iii) the represented person makes a claim to the instrument or its proceeds on the basis that the transaction of the fiduciary is a breach of fiduciary duty, the following rules apply:

(1) Notice of breach of fiduciary duty by the fiduciary is notice of the claim of the represented person.

(2) In the case of an instrument payable to the represented person or the fiduciary as such, the taker has notice of the breach of fiduciary duty if the instrument is (i) taken in payment of or as security for a debt known by the taker to be the personal debt of the fiduciary, (ii) taken in a transaction known by the taker to be for the personal benefit of the fiduciary, or (iii) deposited to an account other than an account of the fiduciary, as such, or an account of the represented person.

(3) If an instrument is issued by the represented person or the fiduciary as such, and made payable to the fiduciary personally, the taker does not have notice of the breach of fiduciary duty unless the taker knows of the breach of fiduciary duty.

(4) If an instrument is issued by the represented person or the fiduciary as such, to the taker as payee, the taker has notice of the breach of fiduciary duty if the instrument is (i) taken in payment of or as security for a debt known by the taker to be the personal debt of the fiduciary, (ii) taken in a transaction known by the taker to be for the personal benefit of the fiduciary, or (iii) deposited to an account other than an account of the fiduciary, as such, or an account of the represented person.

Official Comment

1. This section states rules for determining when a person who has taken an instrument from a fiduciary has notice of a breach of fiduciary duty that occurs as a result of the transaction with the fiduciary. Former Section 3-304(2) and (4)(e) related to this issue, but those provisions were unclear in their meaning. Section 3-307 is intended to clarify the law by stating rules that comprehensively cover the issue of when the taker of an instrument has notice of breach of a fiduciary duty and thus notice of a claim to the instrument or its proceeds.

2. Subsection (a) defines the terms "fiduciary" and "represented person" and the introductory paragraph of subsection (b) describes the transaction to which the section applies. The basic scenario is one in which the fiduciary in effect embezzles money of the represented person by applying the proceeds of an instrument that belongs to the represented person to the personal use of the fiduciary. The person dealing with the fiduciary may be a depositary bank that takes the instrument for collection or a bank or other person that pays value for the instrument. The section also covers a transaction in which an instrument is presented for payment to a payor bank that pays the instrument by giving value to the fiduciary. Subsections (b)(2), (3), and (4) state rules for determining when the person dealing with the fiduciary has notice of breach of fiduciary duty. Subsection (b)(1) states that notice of breach of fiduciary duty is notice of the represented person's claim to the instrument or its proceeds.

Under Section 3-306, a person taking an instrument is subject to a claim to the instrument or its proceeds, unless the taker has rights of a holder in due course. Under Section 3-302(a)(2)(v), the taker cannot be a holder in due course if the instrument was taken with notice of a claim under Section 3-306. Section 3-307 applies to cases in which a represented person is asserting a claim because a breach of fiduciary duty resulted in a misapplication of the proceeds of an instrument. The claim of the represented person is a claim described in Section 3-306. Section 3-307 states rules for determining when a person taking an instrument has notice of the claim which will prevent assertion of rights as a holder in due course. It also states rules for determining when a payor bank pays an instrument with notice of breach of fiduciary duty.

Section 3-307(b) applies only if the person dealing with the fiduciary "has knowledge of the fiduciary status of the fiduciary." Notice which does not amount to knowledge is not enough to cause Section 3-307 to apply. "Knowledge" is defined in Section 1-201(25) [*unrevised Article 1; see Concordance, p. 12*]. In most cases, the "taker" referred to in Section 3-307 will be a bank or other organization. Knowledge of an organization is determined by the rules stated in Section 1-201(27) [*unrevised Article 1; see Concordance, p. 12*]. In many cases, the individual who receives and processes an instrument on behalf of the organization that is the taker of the instrument "for payment or collection or for value" is a clerk who has no knowledge of any fiduciary status of the person from whom the instrument is received. In such cases, Section 3-307 doesn't apply because, under Section 1-201(27) [*unrevised Article 1; see Concordance, p. 12*], knowledge of the organization is determined by the knowledge of the "individual conducting that transaction," i.e. the clerk who receives and processes the instrument. Furthermore, paragraphs (2) and (4) each require that the person acting for the organization have knowledge of facts that indicate a breach of fiduciary duty. In the case of an instrument taken for deposit to an account, the knowledge is found in the fact that the deposit is made to an account other than that of the represented person or a fiduciary account for benefit of that person. In other cases the person acting for the organization must know that the instrument is taken in payment or as security for a personal debt of the fiduciary or for the personal benefit of the fiduciary. For example, if the instrument is being used to buy goods or services, the person acting for the organization must know that the goods or services are for the personal benefit of the fiduciary. The requirement that the taker have knowledge rather than notice is meant to limit Section 3-307 to relatively uncommon cases in which the person who deals with the fiduciary knows all the relevant facts: the fiduciary status and that the proceeds of the instrument are being used for the personal debt or benefit of the fiduciary or are being paid to an account that is not an account of the represented person or of the fiduciary, as such. Mere notice of these facts is not enough to put the taker on notice of the breach of fiduciary duty and does not give rise to any duty of investigation by the taker.

3. Subsection (b)(2) applies to instruments payable to the represented person or the fiduciary as such. For example, a check payable to Corporation is indorsed in the name of Corporation by Doe as its President. Doe gives the check to Bank as partial repayment of a personal loan that Bank had made to Doe. The check was indorsed either in blank or to Bank. Bank collects the check and applies the proceeds to reduce the amount owed on Doe's loan. If the person acting for Bank in the transaction knows that Doe is a fiduciary and that the check is being used to pay a personal obligation of Doe, subsection (b)(2) applies. If Corporation has a claim to the proceeds of the check because the use of the check by Doe was a breach of fiduciary duty, Bank has notice of the claim and did not take the check as a holder in due course. The same result follows if Doe had indorsed the check to himself before giving it to Bank. Subsection (b)(2) follows Uniform Fiduciaries Act § 4 in providing that if the instrument is payable to the fiduciary, as such, or to the represented person, the taker has notice of a claim if the instrument is negotiated for the fiduciary's personal debt. If fiduciary funds are deposited to a personal account of the fiduciary or to an account that is not an account of the represented person or of the fiduciary, as such, there is a split of authority concerning whether the bank is on notice of a breach of fiduciary duty. Subsection (b)(2)(iii) states that the bank is given notice of breach of fiduciary duty because of the deposit. The Uniform Fiduciaries Act § 9 states that the bank is not on notice unless it has knowledge of facts that makes its receipt of the deposit an act of bad faith.

The rationale of subsection (b)(2) is that it is not normal for an instrument payable to the represented person or the fiduciary, as such, to be used for the personal benefit of the fiduciary. It is likely that such use reflects an unlawful use of the proceeds of the instrument. If the fiduciary is entitled to compensation from the represented person for services rendered or for expenses incurred by the fiduciary the normal mode of payment is by a check drawn on the fiduciary account to the order of the fiduciary.

4. Subsection (b)(3) is based on Uniform Fiduciaries Act § 6 and applies when the instrument is drawn by the represented person or the fiduciary as such to the fiduciary personally. The term "personally" is used as it is used in the Uniform Fiduciaries Act to mean that the instrument is payable to the payee as an individual and not as a fiduciary. For example, Doe as President of Corporation writes a check on Corporation's account to the order of Doe personally. The check is then indorsed over to Bank as in Comment 3. In this case there is no notice of breach of fiduciary duty because there is nothing unusual about the transaction. Corporation may have owed Doe money for salary, reimbursement for expenses incurred for the benefit of Corporation, or for any other reason. If Doe is authorized to write checks on behalf of Corporation to pay debts of Corporation, the check is a normal way of paying a debt owed to Doe. Bank may assume that Doe may use the instrument for his personal benefit.

5. Subsection (b)(4) can be illustrated by a hypothetical case. Corporation draws a check payable to an organization. X, an officer or employee of Corporation, delivers the check to a person acting for the organization. The person signing the check on behalf of Corporation is X or another person. If the person acting for the organization in the transaction knows that X is a fiduciary, the organization is on notice of a claim by Corporation if it takes the instrument under the same circumstances stated in subsection (b)(2). If the organization is a bank and the check is taken in repayment of a personal loan of the bank to X, the case is like the case discussed in Comment 3. It is unusual for Corporation, the represented person, to pay a personal debt of Doe by issuing a check to the bank. It is more likely that the use of the check by Doe reflects an unlawful use of the proceeds of the check. The same analysis applies if the check is made payable to an organization in payment of goods or services. If the person acting for the organization knew of the fiduciary status of X and that the goods or services were for X's personal benefit, the organization is on notice of a claim by Corporation to the proceeds of the check. See the discussion in the last paragraph of Comment 2.

§ 3–308. Proof of Signatures and Status as Holder in Due Course.

(a) In an action with respect to an instrument, the authenticity of, and authority to make, each signature on the instrument is admitted unless specifically denied in the pleadings. If the validity of a signature is denied in the pleadings, the burden of establishing validity is on the person claiming validity, but the signature is presumed to be authentic and authorized unless the action is to enforce the liability of the purported signer and the signer is dead or incompetent at the time of trial of the issue of validity of the signature. If an action to enforce the instrument is brought against a person as the undisclosed principal of a person who signed the instrument as a party to the instrument, the plaintiff has the burden of establishing that the defendant is liable on the instrument as a represented person under Section 3–402(a).

(b) If the validity of signatures is admitted or proved and there is compliance with subsection (a), a plaintiff producing the instrument is entitled to payment if the plaintiff proves entitlement to enforce the instrument under Section 3–301, unless the defendant proves a defense or claim in recoupment. If a defense or claim in recoupment is proved, the right to payment of the plaintiff is subject to the defense or claim, except to the extent the plaintiff proves that the plaintiff has rights of a holder in due course which are not subject to the defense or claim.

Official Comment

1. Section 3–308 is a modification of former Section 3–307. The first two sentences of subsection (a) are a restatement of former Section 3–307(1). The purpose of the requirement of a specific denial in the pleadings is to give the plaintiff notice of the defendant's claim of forgery or lack of authority as to the particular signature, and to afford the plaintiff an opportunity to investigate and obtain evidence. If local rules of pleading permit, the denial may be on information and belief, or it may be a denial of knowledge or information sufficient to form a belief. It need not be under oath unless the local statutes or rules require verification. In the absence of such specific denial the signature stands admitted, and is not in issue. Nothing in this section is intended, however, to prevent amendment of the pleading in a proper case.

The question of the burden of establishing the signature arises only when it has been put in issue by specific denial. "Burden of establishing" is defined in Section 1–201. The burden is on the party claiming under the signature, but the signature is presumed to be authentic and authorized except as stated in the second sentence of subsection (a). "Presumed" is defined in Section 1–201 [*unrevised Article 1; see Concordance, p. 12*] and means that until some evidence is introduced which would support a finding that the signature is forged or unauthorized, the plaintiff is not required to prove that it is valid. The presumption rests upon the fact that in ordinary experience forged or unauthorized signatures are very uncommon, and normally any evidence is within the control of, or more accessible to, the defendant. The defendant is therefore required to make some sufficient showing of the grounds for the denial before the plaintiff is required to introduce evidence. The defendant's evidence need not be sufficient to require a directed verdict, but it must be enough to support the denial by permitting a finding in the defendant's favor. Until introduction of such evidence the presumption requires a finding for the plaintiff. Once such evidence is introduced the burden of establishing the signature by a preponderance of the total evidence is on the plaintiff. The presumption does not arise if the action is to enforce the obligation of a purported signer who has died or become incompetent before the evidence is required, and so is disabled from obtaining or introducing it. "Action" is defined in Section 1–201 and includes a claim asserted against the estate of a deceased or an incompetent.

The last sentence of subsection (a) is a new provision that is necessary to take into account Section 3–402(a) that allows an undisclosed principal to be liable on an instrument signed by an authorized representative. In that case the person enforcing the instrument must prove that the undisclosed principal is liable.

2. Subsection (b) restates former Section 3–307(2) and (3). Once signatures are proved or admitted a holder, by mere production of the instrument, proves "entitlement to enforce the instrument" because under Section 3–301 a holder is a person entitled to enforce the instrument. Any other person in possession of an instrument may recover only if that person has the rights of a holder. Section 3–301. That person must prove a transfer giving that person such rights under Section 3–203(b) or that such rights were obtained by subrogation or succession.

If a plaintiff producing the instrument proves entitlement to enforce the instrument, either as a holder or a person with rights of a holder, the plaintiff is entitled to recovery unless the defendant proves a defense or claim in recoupment. Until proof of a defense or claim in recoupment is made, the issue as to whether the plaintiff has rights of a holder in due course does not arise. In the absence of a defense or claim in recoupment, any person entitled to enforce the instrument is entitled to recover. If a defense or claim in recoupment is proved, the plaintiff may seek to cut off the defense or claim in recoupment by proving that the plaintiff is a holder in due course or that the plaintiff has rights of a holder in due course under Section 3–203(b) or by subrogation or succession. All elements of Section 3–302(a) must be proved.

Nothing in this section is intended to say that the plaintiff must necessarily prove rights as a holder in due course. The plaintiff may elect to introduce no further evidence, in which case a verdict may be directed for the plaintiff or the defendant, or the issue of the defense or claim in recoupment may be left to the trier of fact, according to the weight and sufficiency of the defendant's evidence. The plaintiff may elect to rebut the defense or claim in recoupment by proof to the contrary, in which case a verdict may be directed for either party or the issue may be for the trier of fact. Subsection (b) means only that if the plaintiff claims the rights of a holder in due course against the defense or claim in recoupment, the plaintiff has the burden of proof on that issue.

§ 3–309. Enforcement of Lost, Destroyed, or Stolen Instrument.

(a) A person not in possession of an instrument is entitled to enforce the instrument if:

(1) the person seeking to enforce the instrument:

(A) was entitled to enforce the instrument when loss of possession occurred; or

(B) has directly or indirectly acquired ownership of the instrument from a person who was entitled to enforce the instrument when loss of possession occurred;

(2) the loss of possession was not the result of a transfer by the person or a lawful seizure; and

(3) the person cannot reasonably obtain possession of the instrument because the instrument was destroyed, its whereabouts cannot be determined, or it is in the wrongful possession of an unknown person or a person that cannot be found or is not amenable to service of process.

(b) A person seeking enforcement of an instrument under subsection (a) must prove the terms of the instrument and the person's right to enforce the instrument. If that proof is made, Section 3–308 applies to the case as if the person seeking enforcement had produced the instrument. The court may not enter judgment in favor of the person seeking enforcement unless it finds that the person required to pay the instrument is adequately protected against loss that might occur by reason of a claim by another person to enforce the instrument. Adequate protection may be provided by any reasonable means.

As amended in 2002.

Official Comment

1. Section 3–309 is a modification of former Section 3–804. The rights stated are those of "a person entitled to enforce the instrument" at the time of loss rather than those of an "owner" as in former Section 3–804. Under subsection (b), judgment to enforce the instrument cannot be given unless the court finds that the defendant will be adequately protected against a claim to the instrument by a holder that may appear at some later time. The court is given discretion in determining how adequate protection is to be assured. Former Section 3–804 allowed the court to "require security indemnifying the defendant against loss." Under Section 3–309 adequate protection is a flexible concept. For example, there is substantial risk that a holder in due course may make a demand for payment if the instrument was payable to bearer when it was lost or stolen. On the other hand if the instrument was payable to the person who lost the instrument and that person did not indorse the instrument, no other person could be a holder of the instrument. In some cases there is risk of loss only if there is doubt about whether the facts alleged by the person who lost the instrument are true. Thus, the type of adequate protection that is reasonable in the circumstances may depend on the degree of certainty about the facts in the case.

2. Subsection (a) is intended to reject the result in *Dennis Joslin Co. v. Robinson Broadcasting Corp.*, 977 F. Supp. 491 (D.D.C. 1997). A transferee of a lost instrument need prove only that its transferor was entitled to enforce, not that the transferee was in possession at the time the instrument was lost. The protections of subsection (a) should also be available when instruments are lost during transit, because whatever the precise status of ownership at the point of loss, either the sender or the receiver ordinarily would have been entitled to enforce the instrument during the course of transit. The amendments to subsection (a) are not intended to alter in any way the rules that apply to the preservation of checks in connection with truncation or any other expedited method of check collection or processing.

3. A security interest may attach to the right of a person not in possession of an instrument to enforce the instrument. Although the secured party may not be the owner of the instrument, the secured party may nevertheless be entitled to exercise its debtor's right to enforce the instrument by resorting to its collection rights under the circumstances described in Section 9–607. This section does not address whether the person required to pay the instrument owes any duty to a secured party that is not itself the owner of the instrument.

As amended in 2002.

§ 3–310. Effect of Instrument on Obligation for Which Taken.

(a) Unless otherwise agreed, if a certified check, cashier's check, or teller's check is taken for an obligation, the obligation is discharged to the same extent discharge would result if an amount of money equal to the amount of the instrument were taken in payment of the obligation. Discharge of the obligation does not affect any liability that the obligor may have as an indorser of the instrument.

(b) Unless otherwise agreed and except as provided in subsection (a), if a note or an uncertified check is taken for an obligation, the obligation is suspended to the same extent the obligation would be discharged if an amount of money equal to the amount of the instrument were taken, and the following rules apply:

(1) In the case of an uncertified check, suspension of the obligation continues until dishonor of the check or until it is paid or certified. Payment or certification of the check results in discharge of the obligation to the extent of the amount of the check.

(2) In the case of a note, suspension of the obligation continues until dishonor of the note or until it is paid. Payment of the note results in discharge of the obligation to the extent of the payment.

(3) Except as provided in paragraph (4), if the check or note is dishonored and the obligee of the obligation for which the instrument was taken is the person entitled to enforce the instrument, the obligee may enforce either the instrument or the obligation. In the case of an instrument of a third person which is negotiated to the obligee by the obligor, discharge of the obligor on the instrument also discharges the obligation.

(4) If the person entitled to enforce the instrument taken for an obligation is a person other than the obligee, the obligee may not enforce the obligation to the extent the obligation is suspended. If the obligee is the person entitled to enforce the instrument but no longer has possession of it because it was lost, stolen, or destroyed, the obligation may not be enforced to the extent of the amount payable on the instrument, and to that extent the obligee's rights against the obligor are limited to enforcement of the instrument.

(c) If an instrument other than one described in subsection (a) or (b) is taken for an obligation, the effect is (i) that stated in subsection (a) if the instrument is one on which a bank is liable as maker or acceptor, or (ii) that stated in subsection (b) in any other case.

Official Comment

1. Section 3-310 is a modification of former Section 3-802. As a practical matter, application of former Section 3-802 was limited to cases in which a check or a note was given for an obligation. Subsections (a) and (b) of Section 3-310 are therefore stated in terms of checks and notes in the interests of clarity. Subsection (c) covers the rare cases in which some other instrument is given to pay an obligation.

2. Subsection (a) deals with the case in which a certified check, cashier's check or teller's check is given in payment of an obligation. In that case the obligation is discharged unless there is an agreement to the contrary. Subsection (a) drops the exception in former Section 3-802 for cases in which there is a right of recourse on the instrument against the obligor. Under former Section 3-802(1)(a) the obligation was not discharged if there was a right of recourse on the instrument against the obligor. Subsection (a) changes this result. The underlying obligation is discharged, but any right of recourse on the instrument is preserved.

3. Subsection (b) concerns cases in which an uncertified check or a note is taken for an obligation. The typical case is that in which a buyer pays for goods or services by giving the seller the buyer's personal check, or in which the buyer signs a note for the purchase price. Subsection (b) also applies to the uncommon cases in which a check or note of a third person is given in payment of the obligation. Subsection (b) preserves the rule under former Section 3-802(1)(b) that the buyer's obligation to pay the price is suspended, but subsection (b) spells out the effect more precisely. If the check or note is dishonored, the seller may sue on either the dishonored instrument or the contract of sale if the seller has possession of the instrument and is the person entitled to enforce it. If the right to enforce the instrument is held by somebody other than the seller, the seller can't enforce the right to payment of the price under the sales contract because that right is represented by the instrument which is enforceable by somebody else. Thus, if the seller sold the note or the check to a holder and has not reacquired it after dishonor, the only right that survives is the right to enforce the instrument. What that means is that even though the suspension of the obligation may end upon dishonor under paragraph (b)(1), the obligation is not revived in the circumstances described in paragraph (b)(4).

The last sentence of subsection (b)(3) applies to cases in which an instrument of another person is indorsed over to the obligee in payment of the obligation. For example, Buyer delivers an uncertified personal check of X payable to the order of Buyer to Seller in payment of the price of goods. Buyer indorses the check over to Seller. Buyer is liable on the check as indorser. If Seller neglects to present the check for payment or to deposit it for collection within 30 days of the indorsement, Buyer's liability as indorser is discharged. Section 3-415(e). Under the last sentence of Section 3-310(b)(3) Buyer is also discharged on the obligation to pay for the goods.

4. There was uncertainty concerning the applicability of former Section 3–802 to the case in which the check given for the obligation was stolen from the payee, the payee's signature was forged, and the forger obtained payment. The last sentence of subsection (b)(4) addresses this issue. If the payor bank pays a holder, the drawer is discharged on the underlying obligation because the check was paid. Subsection (b)(1). If the payor bank pays a person not entitled to enforce the instrument, as in the hypothetical case, the suspension of the underlying obligation continues because the check has not been paid. Section 3–602(a). The payee's cause of action is against the depositary bank or payor bank in conversion under Section 3–420 or against the drawer under Section 3–309. In the latter case, the drawer's obligation under Section 3–414(b) is triggered by dishonor which occurs because the check is unpaid. Presentment for payment to the drawee is excused under Section 3–504(a)(i) and, under Section 3–502(e), dishonor occurs without presentment if the check is not paid. The payee cannot merely ignore the instrument and sue the drawer on the underlying contract. This would impose on the drawer the risk that the check when stolen was indorsed in blank or to bearer.

A similar analysis applies with respect to lost instruments that have not been paid. If a creditor takes a check of the debtor in payment of an obligation, the obligation is suspended under the introductory paragraph of subsection (b). If the creditor then loses the check, what are the creditor's rights? The creditor can request the debtor to issue a new check and in many cases, the debtor will issue a replacement check after stopping payment on the lost check. In that case both the debtor and creditor are protected. But the debtor is not obliged to issue a new check. If the debtor refuses to issue a replacement check, the last sentence of subsection (b)(4) applies. The creditor may not enforce the obligation of debtor for which the check was taken. The creditor may assert only rights on the check. The creditor can proceed under Section 3–309 to enforce the obligation of the debtor, as drawer, to pay the check.

5. Subsection (c) deals with rare cases in which other instruments are taken for obligations. If a bank is the obligor on the instrument, subsection (a) applies and the obligation is discharged. In any other case subsection (b) applies.

As amended in 2002.

§ 3–311. Accord and Satisfaction by Use of Instrument.

(a) If a person against whom a claim is asserted proves that (i) that person in good faith tendered an instrument to the claimant as full satisfaction of the claim, (ii) the amount of the claim was unliquidated or subject to a bona fide dispute, and (iii) the claimant obtained payment of the instrument, the following subsections apply.

(b) Unless subsection (c) applies, the claim is discharged if the person against whom the claim is asserted proves that the instrument or an accompanying written communication contained a conspicuous statement to the effect that the instrument was tendered as full satisfaction of the claim.

(c) Subject to subsection (d), a claim is not discharged under subsection (b) if either of the following applies:

(1) The claimant, if an organization, proves that (i) within a reasonable time before the tender, the claimant sent a conspicuous statement to the person against whom the claim is asserted that communications concerning disputed debts, including an instrument tendered as full satisfaction of a debt, are to be sent to a designated person, office, or place, and (ii) the instrument or accompanying communication was not received by that designated person, office, or place.

(2) The claimant, whether or not an organization, proves that within 90 days after payment of the instrument, the claimant tendered repayment of the amount of the instrument to the person against whom the claim is asserted. This paragraph does not apply if the claimant is an organization that sent a statement complying with paragraph (1)(i).

(d) A claim is discharged if the person against whom the claim is asserted proves that within a reasonable time before collection of the instrument was initiated, the claimant, or an agent of the claimant having direct responsibility with respect to the disputed obligation, knew that the instrument was tendered in full satisfaction of the claim.

Official Comment

1. This section deals with an informal method of dispute resolution carried out by use of a negotiable instrument. In the typical case there is a dispute concerning the amount that is owed on a claim.

Case # 1. The claim is for the price of goods or services sold to a consumer who asserts that he or she is not obliged to pay the full price for which the consumer was billed because of a defect or breach of warranty with respect to the goods or services.

Case # 2. A claim is made on an insurance policy. The insurance company alleges that it is not liable under the policy for the amount of the claim.

In either case the person against whom the claim is asserted may attempt an accord and satisfaction of the disputed claim by tendering a check to the claimant for some amount less than the full amount claimed by the claimant. A statement will be included on the check or in a communication accompanying the check to the effect that the check is offered as full payment or full satisfaction of the claim. Frequently, there is also a statement to the effect that obtaining payment of the check is an agreement by the claimant to a settlement of the dispute for the amount tendered. Before enactment of revised Article 3, the case law was in conflict over the question of whether obtaining payment of the check had the effect of an agreement to the settlement proposed by the debtor. This issue was governed by a common law rule, but some courts hold that the common law was modified by former Section 1–207 which they interpreted as applying to full settlement checks.

2. Comment d. to Restatement of Contracts, Section 281 discusses the full satisfaction check and the applicable common law rule. In a case like Case # 1, the buyer can propose a settlement of the disputed bill by a clear notation on the check indicating that the check is tendered as full satisfaction of the bill. Under the common law rule the seller, by obtaining payment of the check accepts the offer of compromise by the buyer. The result is the same if the seller adds a notation to the check indicating that the check is accepted under protest or in only partial satisfaction of the claim. Under the common law rule the seller can refuse the check or can accept it subject to the condition stated by the buyer, but the seller can't accept the check and refuse to be bound by the condition. The rule applies only to an unliquidated claim or a claim disputed in good faith by the buyer. The dispute in the courts was whether Section 1–207 [*unrevised Article 1; see Concordance, p. 12*] changed the common law rule. The Restatement states that section "need not be read as changing this well-established rule."

3. As part of the revision of Article 3, Section 1–207 [*unrevised Article 1; see Concordance, p. 12*] has been amended to add subsection (2) stating that Section 1–207 [*unrevised Article 1; see Concordance, p. 12*] "does not apply to an accord and satisfaction." Because of that amendment and revised Article 3, Section 3–311 governs full satisfaction checks. Section 3–311 follows the common law rule with some minor variations to reflect modern business conditions. In cases covered by Section 3–311 there will often be an individual on one side of the dispute and a business organization on the other. This section is not designed to favor either the individual or the business organization. In Case # 1 the person seeking the accord and satisfaction is an individual. In Case # 2 the person seeking the accord and satisfaction is an insurance company. Section 3–311 is based on a belief that the common law rule produces a fair result and that informal dispute resolution by full satisfaction checks should be encouraged.

4. Subsection (a) states three requirements for application of Section 3–311. "Good faith" in subsection (a)(i) is defined in Section 3–103(a)(6) as not only honesty in fact, but the observance of reasonable commercial standards of fair dealing. The meaning of "fair dealing" will depend upon the facts in the particular case. For example, suppose an insurer tenders a check in settlement of a claim for personal injury in an accident clearly covered by the insurance policy. The claimant is necessitous and the amount of the check is very small in relationship to the extent of the injury and the amount recoverable under the policy. If the trier of fact determines that the insurer was taking unfair advantage of the claimant, an accord and satisfaction would not result from payment of the check because of the absence of good faith by the insurer in making the tender. Another example of lack of good faith is found in the practice of some business debtors in routinely printing full satisfaction language on their check stocks so that all or a large part of the debts of the debtor are paid by checks bearing the full satisfaction language, whether or not there is any dispute with the creditor. Under such a practice the claimant cannot be sure whether a tender in full satisfaction is or is not being made. Use of a check on which full satisfaction language was affixed routinely pursuant to such a business practice may prevent an accord and satisfaction on the ground that the check was not tendered in good faith under subsection (a)(i).

Section 3–311 does not apply to cases in which the debt is a liquidated amount and not subject to a bona fide dispute. Subsection (a)(ii). Other law applies to cases in which a debtor is seeking discharge of such a debt by paying less than the amount owed. For the purpose of subsection (a)(iii) obtaining acceptance of a check is considered to be obtaining payment of the check.

The person seeking the accord and satisfaction must prove that the requirements of subsection (a) are met. If that person also proves that the statement required by subsection (b) was given, the claim is discharged unless subsection (c) applies. Normally the statement required by subsection (b) is written on the check. Thus, the canceled check can be used to prove the statement as well as the fact that the claimant obtained payment of the check. Subsection (b) requires a "conspicuous" statement that the instrument was tendered in full satisfaction of the claim. "Conspicuous" is defined in Section 1–201(10) [*unrevised Article 1; see Concordance, p. 12*]. The statement is conspicuous if "it is so written that a reasonable person against whom it is to operate ought to have noticed it." If the claimant can reasonably be expected to examine the check, almost any statement on the check should be noticed and is therefore conspicuous. In cases in which the claimant is an individual the claimant will receive the check and will normally indorse it. Since the statement concerning tender in full satisfaction normally will appear above the space provided for the claimant's indorsement of the check, the claimant "ought to have noticed" the statement.

5. Subsection (c)(1) is a limitation on subsection (b) in cases in which the claimant is an organization. It is designed to protect the claimant against inadvertent accord and satisfaction. If the claimant is an organization payment of the check might be obtained without notice to the personnel of the organization concerned with the disputed claim. Some business organizations have claims against very large numbers of customers. Examples are department stores, public utilities and the like. These claims are normally paid by checks sent by customers to a designated office at which clerks employed by the claimant or a bank acting for the claimant process the checks and record the amounts paid. If the processing office is not designed to deal with communications extraneous to recording the amount of the check and the account number of the customer, payment of a full satisfaction check can easily be obtained without knowledge by the claimant of the existence of the full satisfaction statement. This is particularly true if the statement is written on the reverse side of the check in the area in which indorsements are usually written. Normally, the clerks of the claimant have no reason to look at the reverse side of checks. Indorsement by the claimant normally is done by mechanical means or there may be no indorsement at all. Section 4–205(a). Subsection (c)(1) allows the claimant to protect itself by advising customers by a conspicuous statement that communications regarding disputed debts must be sent to a particular person, office, or place. The statement must be given to the customer within a reasonable time before the tender is made. This requirement is designed to assure that the customer has reasonable notice that the full satisfaction check must be sent to a particular place. The reasonable time requirement could be satisfied by a notice on the billing statement sent to the customer. If the full satisfaction check is sent to the designated destination and the check is paid, the claim is discharged. If the claimant proves that the check was not received at the designated destination the claim is not discharged unless subsection (d) applies.

6. Subsection (c)(2) is also designed to prevent inadvertent accord and satisfaction. It can be used by a claimant other than an organization or by a claimant as an alternative to subsection (c)(1). Some organizations may be reluctant to use subsection (c)(1) because it may result in confusion of customers that causes checks to be routinely sent to the special designated person, office, or place. Thus, much of the benefit of rapid processing of checks may be lost. An organization that chooses not to send a notice complying with subsection (c)(1)(i) may prevent an inadvertent accord and satisfaction by complying with subsection (c)(2). If the claimant discovers that it has obtained payment of a full satisfaction check, it may prevent an accord and satisfaction if, within 90 days of the payment of the check, the claimant tenders repayment of the amount of the check to the person against whom the claim is asserted.

7. Subsection (c) is subject to subsection (d). If a person against whom a claim is asserted proves that the claimant obtained payment of a check known to have been tendered in full satisfaction of the claim by "the claimant or an agent of the claimant having direct responsibility with respect to the disputed obligation," the claim is discharged even if (i) the check was not sent to the person, office, or place required by a notice complying with subsection (c)(1), or (ii) the claimant tendered repayment of the amount of the check in compliance with subsection (c)(2).

A claimant knows that a check was tendered in full satisfaction of a claim when the claimant "has actual knowledge" of that fact. Section 1–201(25) [*unrevised Article 1; see Concordance, p. 12*]. Under Section 1–201(27) [*unrevised Article 1; see Concordance, p. 12*], if the claimant is an organization, it has knowledge that a check was tendered in full satisfaction of the claim when that fact is

> "brought to the attention of the individual conducting that transaction, and in any event when it would have been brought to his attention if the organization had exercised due diligence. An organization exercises due diligence if it maintains reasonable routines for communicating significant information to the person conducting the transaction and there is reasonable compliance with the routines. Due diligence does not require an individual acting for the organization to communicate information unless such communication is part of his regular duties or unless he has reason to know of the transaction and that the transaction would be materially affected by the information."

With respect to an attempted accord and satisfaction the "individual conducting that transaction" is an employee or other agent of the organization having direct responsibility with respect to the dispute. For example, if the check and communication are received by a collection agency acting for the claimant to collect the disputed claim, obtaining payment of the check will result in an accord and satisfaction even if the claimant gave notice, pursuant to subsection (c)(1), that full satisfaction checks be sent to some other office. Similarly, if a customer asserting a claim for breach of warranty with respect to defective goods purchased in a retail outlet of a large chain store delivers the full satisfaction check to the manager of the retail outlet at which the goods were purchased, obtaining payment of the check will also result in an accord and satisfaction. On the other hand, if the check is mailed to the chief executive officer of the chain store subsection (d) would probably not be satisfied. The chief executive officer of a large corporation may have general responsibility for operations of the company, but does not normally have direct responsibility for resolving a small disputed bill to a customer. A check for a relatively small amount mailed to a high executive officer of a large organization is not likely to receive the executive's personal attention. Rather, the check would normally be routinely sent to the appropriate office for deposit and credit to the customer's account. If the check does receive the personal attention of the high executive officer and the officer is aware of the full-satisfaction language, collection of the check will result in an accord and satisfaction because subsection (d) applies. In this case the officer has assumed direct responsibility with respect to the disputed transaction.

If a full satisfaction check is sent to a lock box or other office processing checks sent to the claimant, it is irrelevant whether the clerk processing the check did or did not see the statement that the check was tendered as full satisfaction of the claim. Knowledge of the clerk is not imputed to the organization because the clerk has no responsibility with respect to an accord and satisfaction. Moreover, there is no failure of "due diligence" under Section 1-201(27) [*unrevised Article 1; see Concordance, p. 12*] if the claimant does not require its clerks to look for full satisfaction statements on checks or accompanying communications. Nor is there any duty of the claimant to assign that duty to its clerks. Section 3-311(c) is intended to allow a claimant to avoid an inadvertent accord and satisfaction by complying with either subsection (c)(1) or (2) without burdening the check-processing operation with extraneous and wasteful additional duties.

8. In some cases the disputed claim may have been assigned to a finance company or bank as part of a financing arrangement with respect to accounts receivable. If the account debtor was notified of the assignment, the claimant is the assignee of the account receivable and the "agent of the claimant" in subsection (d) refers to an agent of the assignee.

§ 3-312. Lost, Destroyed, or Stolen Cashier's Check, Teller's Check, or Certified Check.

(a) In this section:

(1) "Check" means a cashier's check, teller's check, or certified check.

(2) "Claimant" means a person who claims the right to receive the amount of a cashier's check, teller's check, or certified check that was lost, destroyed, or stolen.

(3) "Declaration of loss" means a statement, made in a record under penalty of perjury, to the effect that (i) the declarer lost possession of a check, (ii) the declarer is the drawer or payee of the check, in the case of a certified check, or the remitter or payee of the check, in the case of a cashier's check or teller's check, (iii) the loss of possession was not the result of a transfer by the declarer or a lawful seizure, and (iv) the declarer cannot reasonably obtain possession of the check because the check was destroyed, its whereabouts cannot be determined, or it is in the wrongful possession of an unknown person or a person that cannot be found or is not amenable to service of process.

(4) "Obligated bank" means the issuer of a cashier's check or teller's check or the acceptor of a certified check.

(b) A claimant may assert a claim to the amount of a check by a communication to the obligated bank describing the check with reasonable certainty and requesting payment of the amount of the check, if (i) the claimant is the drawer or payee of a certified check or the remitter or payee of a cashier's check or teller's check, (ii) the communication contains or is accompanied by a declaration of loss of the claimant with respect to the check, (iii) the communication is received at a time and in a manner affording the bank a reasonable time to act on it before the check is paid, and (iv) the claimant provides reasonable identification if requested by the obligated bank. Delivery of a declaration of loss is a warranty of the truth of the statements made in the declaration. If a claim is asserted in compliance with this subsection, the following rules apply:

(1) The claim becomes enforceable at the later of (i) the time the claim is asserted, or (ii) the 90th day following the date of the check, in the case of a cashier's check or teller's check, or the 90th day following the date of the acceptance, in the case of a certified check.

(2) Until the claim becomes enforceable, it has no legal effect and the obligated bank may pay the check or, in the case of a teller's check, may permit the drawee to pay the check. Payment to a person entitled to enforce the check discharges all liability of the obligated bank with respect to the check.

(3) If the claim becomes enforceable before the check is presented for payment, the obligated bank is not obliged to pay the check.

(4) When the claim becomes enforceable, the obligated bank becomes obliged to pay the amount of the check to the claimant if payment of the check has not been made to a person entitled to enforce the check. Subject to Section 4–302(a)(1), payment to the claimant discharges all liability of the obligated bank with respect to the check.

(c) If the obligated bank pays the amount of a check to a claimant under subsection (b)(4) and the check is presented for payment by a person having rights of a holder in due course, the claimant is obliged to (i) refund the payment to the obligated bank if the check is paid, or (ii) pay the amount of the check to the person having rights of a holder in due course if the check is dishonored.

(d) If a claimant has the right to assert a claim under subsection (b) and is also a person entitled to enforce a cashier's check, teller's check, or certified check which is lost, destroyed, or stolen, the claimant may assert rights with respect to the check either under this section or Section 3–309.

As added in 1991 and amended in 2002.

Official Comment

1. This section applies to cases in which a cashier's check, teller's check, or certified check is lost, destroyed, or stolen. In one typical case a customer of a bank closes his or her account and takes a cashier's check or teller's check of the bank as payment of the amount of the account. The customer may be moving to a new area and the check is to be used to open a bank account in that area. In such a case the check will normally be payable to the customer. In another typical case a cashier's check or teller's check is bought from a bank for the purpose of paying some obligation of the buyer of the check. In such a case the check may be made payable to the customer and then negotiated to the creditor by indorsement. But often, the payee of the check is the creditor. In the latter case the customer is a remitter. The section covers loss of the check by either the remitter or the payee. The section also covers loss of a certified check by either the drawer or payee.

Under Section 3–309 a person seeking to enforce a lost, destroyed, or stolen cashier's check or teller's check may be required by the court to give adequate protection to the issuing bank against loss that might occur by reason of the claim by another person to enforce the check. This might require the posting of an expensive bond for the amount of the check. The purpose of Section 3–312 is to offer a person who loses such a check a means of getting refund of the amount of the check within a reasonable period of time without the expense of posting a bond and with full protection of the obligated bank.

2. A claim to the amount of a lost, destroyed, or stolen cashier's check, teller's check, or certified check may be made under subsection (b) if the following requirements of that subsection are met. First, a claim may be asserted only by the drawer or payee of a certified check or the remitter or payee of a cashier's check or teller's check. An indorsee of a check is not covered because the indorsee is not an original party to the check or a remitter. Limitation to an original party or remitter gives the obligated bank the ability to determine, at the time it becomes obligated on the check, the identity of the person or persons who can assert a claim with respect to the check. The bank is not faced with having to determine the rights of some person who was not a party to the check at that time or with whom the bank had not dealt. If a cashier's check is issued to the order of the person who purchased it from the bank and that person indorses it over to a third person who loses the check, the third person may assert rights to enforce the check under Section 3–309 but has no rights under Section 3–312.

Second, the claim must be asserted by a communication to the obligated bank describing the check with reasonable certainty and requesting payment of the amount of the check. "Obligated bank" is defined in subsection (a)(4). Third, the communication must be received in time to allow the obligated bank to act on the claim before the check is paid, and the claimant must provide reasonable identification if requested. Subsections (b)(iii) and (iv). Fourth, the communication must contain or be accompanied by a declaration of loss described in subsection (b). This declaration is an affidavit or other writing made under penalty of perjury alleging the loss, destruction, or theft of the check and stating that the declarer is a person entitled to assert a claim, i.e. the drawer or payee of a certified check or the remitter or payee of a cashier's check or teller's check.

A claimant who delivers a declaration of loss makes a warranty of the truth of the statements made in the declaration. The warranty is made to the obligated bank and anybody who has a right to enforce the check. If the declaration of loss falsely alleges loss of a cashier's check that did not in fact occur, a holder of the check who was unable to obtain payment because subsection (b)(3) and (4) caused the obligated bank to dishonor the check would have a cause of action against the declarer for breach of warranty.

The obligated bank may not impose additional requirements on the claimant to assert a claim under subsection (b). For example, the obligated bank may not require the posting of a bond or other form of security. Section 3–312(b) states the procedure for asserting claims covered by the section. Thus, procedures that may be stated in other law for stating claims to property do not apply and are displaced within the meaning of Section 1–103.

3. A claim asserted under subsection (b) does not have any legal effect, however, until the date it becomes enforceable, which cannot be earlier than 90 days after the date of a cashier's check or teller's check or 90 days after the date of acceptance of a certified check. Thus, if a lost check is presented for payment within the 90-day period, the bank may pay a person entitled to enforce the check without regard to the claim and is discharged of all liability with respect to the check. This ensures the continued utility of cashier's checks, teller's checks, and certified checks as cash equivalents. Virtually all such checks are presented for payment within 90 days.

If the claim becomes enforceable and payment has not been made to a person entitled to enforce the check, the bank becomes obligated to pay the amount of the check to the claimant. Subsection (b)(4). When the bank becomes obligated to pay the amount of the check to the claimant, the bank is relieved of its obligation to pay the check. Subsection (b)(3). Thus, any person entitled to enforce the check, including even a holder in due course, loses the right to enforce the check after a claim under subsection (b) becomes enforceable.

If the obligated bank pays the claimant under subsection (b)(4), the bank is discharged of all liability with respect to the check. The only exception is the unlikely case in which the obligated bank subsequently incurs liability under Section 4–302(a)(1) with respect to the check. For example, Obligated Bank is the issuer of a cashier's check and, after a claim becomes enforceable, it pays the claimant under subsection (b)(4). Later the check is presented to Obligated Bank for payment over the counter. Under subsection (b)(3), Obligated Bank is not obliged to pay the check and may dishonor the check by returning it to the person who presented it for payment. But the normal rules of check collection are not affected by Section 3–312. If Obligated Bank retains the check beyond midnight of the day of presentment without settling for it, it becomes accountable for the amount of the check under Section 4–302(a)(1) even though it had no obligation to pay the check.

An obligated bank that pays the amount of a check to a claimant under subsection (b)(4) is discharged of all liability on the check so long as the assertion of the claim meets the requirements of subsection (b) discussed in Comment 2. This is important in cases of fraudulent declarations of loss. For example, if the claimant falsely alleges a loss that in fact did not occur, the bank, subject to Section 1–203 [*unrevised Article 1; see Concordance, p. 12*], may rely on the declaration of loss. On the other hand, a claim may be asserted only by a person described in subsection (b)(i). Thus, the bank is discharged under subsection (a)(4) only if it pays such a person. Although it is highly unlikely, it is possible that more than one person could assert a claim under subsection (b) to the amount of a check. Such a case could occur if one of the claimants makes a false declaration of loss. The obligated bank is not required to determine whether a claimant who complies with subsection (b) is acting wrongfully. The bank may utilize procedures outside this Article, such as interpleader, under which the conflicting claims may be adjudicated.

Although it is unlikely that a lost check would be presented for payment after the claimant was paid by the bank under subsection (b)(4), it is possible for it to happen. Suppose the declaration of loss by the claimant fraudulently alleged a loss that in fact did not occur. If the claimant negotiated the check, presentment for payment would occur shortly after negotiation in almost all cases. Thus, a fraudulent declaration of loss is not likely to occur unless the check is negotiated after the 90-day period has already expired or shortly before expiration. In such a case the holder of the check, who may not have noticed the date of the check, is not entitled to payment from the obligated bank if the check is presented for payment after the claim becomes enforceable. Subsection (b)(3). The remedy of the holder who is denied payment in that case is an action against the claimant under subsection (c) if the holder is a holder in due course, or for breach of warranty under subsection (b). The holder would also have common law remedies against the claimant under the law of restitution or fraud.

4. The following cases illustrate the operation of Section 3–312:

Case # 1. Obligated Bank (OB) certified a check drawn by its customer, Drawer (D), payable to Payee (P). Two days after the check was certified, D lost the check and then asserted a claim pursuant to subsection (b). The check had not been presented for payment when D's claim became enforceable 90 days after the check was certified. Under subsection (b)(4), at the time D's claim became enforceable OB became obliged to pay D the amount of the check. If the check is later presented for payment, OB may refuse to pay the check and has no obligation to anyone to pay the check. Any obligation owed by D to P, for which the check was intended as payment, is unaffected because the check was never delivered to P.

Case # 2. Obligated Bank (OB) issued a teller's check to Remitter (R) payable to Payee (P). R delivered the check to P in payment of an obligation. P lost the check and then asserted a claim pursuant to subsection (b). To carry out P's order, OB issued an order pursuant to Section 4–403(a) to the drawee of the teller's check to stop payment of the check effective on the 90th day after the date of the teller's check. The check was not presented for payment. On the 90th day after the date of the teller's check P's claim becomes enforceable and OB becomes obliged to pay P the amount of the check. As in Case # 1, OB has no further liability with respect to the check to anyone. When R delivered the check to P, R's underlying obligation to P was discharged under Section 3–310. Thus, R suffered no loss. Since P received the amount of the check, P also suffered no loss except with respect to the delay in receiving the amount of the check.

Case # 3. Obligated Bank (OB) issued a cashier's check to its customer, Payee (P). Two days after issue, the check was stolen from P who then asserted a claim pursuant to subsection (b). Ten days after issue, the check was deposited by X in an account in Depositary Bank (DB). X had found the check and forged the indorsement of P. DB promptly presented the check to OB and obtained payment on behalf of X. On the 90th day after the date of the check P's claim becomes enforceable and P is entitled to receive the amount of the check from OB. Subsection (b)(4). Although the check was presented for payment before P's claim becomes enforceable, OB is not discharged. Because of the forged indorsement X was not a holder and neither was DB. Thus, neither is a person entitled to enforce the check (Section 3–301) and OB is not discharged under Section 3–602(a). Thus, under subsection (b)(4), because OB did not pay a person entitled to enforce the check, OB must pay P. OB's remedy is against DB for breach of warranty under Section 4–208(a)(1). As an alternative to the remedy under Section 3–312, P could recover from DB for conversion under Section 3–420(a).

Case # 4. Obligated Bank (OB) issued a cashier's check to its customer, Payee (P). P made an unrestricted blank indorsement of the check and mailed the check to P's bank for deposit to P's account. The check was never received by P's bank. When P discovered the loss, P asserted a claim pursuant to subsection (b). X found the check and deposited it in X's account in Depositary Bank (DB) after indorsing the check. DB presented the check for payment before the end of the 90-day period after its date. OB paid the check. Because of the unrestricted blank indorsement by P, X became a holder of the check. DB also became a holder. Since the check was paid before P's claim became enforceable and payment was made to a person entitled to enforce the check, OB is discharged of all liability with respect to the check. Subsection (b)(2). Thus, P is not entitled to payment from OB. Subsection (b)(4) doesn't apply.

Case # 5. Obligated Bank (OB) issued a cashier's check to its customer, Payee (P). P made an unrestricted blank indorsement of the check and mailed the check to P's bank for deposit to P's account. The check was never received by P's bank. When P discovered the loss, P asserted a claim pursuant to subsection (b). At the end of the 90-day period after the date of the check, OB paid the amount of the check to P under subsection (b)(4). X then found the check and deposited it to X's account in Depositary Bank (DB). DB presented the check to OB for payment. OB is not obliged to pay the check. Subsection (b)(4). If OB dishonors the check, DB's remedy is to charge back X's account. Section 4–214(a). Although P, as an indorser, would normally have liability to DB under Section 3–415(a) because the check was dishonored, P is released from that liability under Section 3–415(e) because collection of the check was initiated more than 30 days after the indorsement. DB has a remedy only against X. A depositary bank that takes a cashier's check that cannot be presented for payment before expiration of the 90-day period after its date is on notice that the check might not be paid because of the possibility of a claim asserted under subsection (b) which would excuse the issuer of the check from paying the check. Thus, the depositary bank cannot safely release funds with respect to the check until it has assurance that the check has been paid. DB cannot be a holder in due course of the check because it took the check when the check was overdue. Section 3–304(a)(2). Thus, DB has no action against P under subsection (c).

Case # 6. Obligated Bank (OB) issued a cashier's check payable to bearer and delivered it to its customer, Remitter (R). R held the check for 90 days and then wrongfully asserted a claim to the amount of the check under subsection (b). The declaration of loss fraudulently stated that the check was lost. R received payment from OB under subsection (b)(4). R then negotiated the check to X for value. X presented the check to OB for payment. Although OB, under subsection (b)(2), was not obliged to pay the check, OB paid X by mistake. OB's teller did not notice that the check was more than 90 days old and was not aware that OB was not obliged to pay the check. If X took the check in good faith, OB may not recover from X. Section 3–418(c). OB's remedy is to recover from R for fraud or for breach of warranty in making a false declaration of loss. Subsection (b).

As amended in 2004.

PART 4

LIABILITY OF PARTIES

§ 3–401. Signature.

(a) A person is not liable on an instrument unless (i) the person signed the instrument, or (ii) the person is represented by an agent or representative who signed the instrument and the signature is binding on the represented person under Section 3–402.

(b) A signature may be made (i) manually or by means of a device or machine, and (ii) by the use of any name, including a trade or assumed name, or by a word, mark, or symbol executed or adopted by a person with present intention to authenticate a writing.

Official Comment

1. Obligation on an instrument depends on a signature that is binding on the obligor. The signature may be made by the obligor personally or by an agent authorized to act for the obligor. Signature by agents is covered by Section 3–402. It is not necessary that the name of the obligor appear on the instrument, so long as there is a signature that binds the obligor. Signature includes an indorsement.

2. A signature may be handwritten, typed, printed or made in any other manner. It need not be subscribed, and may appear in the body of the instrument, as in the case of "I, John Doe, promise to pay . . ." without any other signature. It may be made by mark, or even by thumbprint. It may be made in any name, including any trade name or assumed name, however false and fictitious, which is adopted for the purpose. Parol evidence is admissible to identify the signer, and when the signer is identified the signature is effective. Indorsement in a name other than that of the indorser is governed by Section 3–204(d).

This section is not intended to affect any other law requiring a signature by mark to be witnessed, or any signature to be otherwise authenticated, or requiring any form of proof.

§ 3–402. Signature by Representative.

(a) If a person acting, or purporting to act, as a representative signs an instrument by signing either the name of the represented person or the name of the signer, the represented person is bound by the signature to the same extent the represented person would be bound if the signature were on a simple contract. If the represented person is bound, the signature of the representative is the "authorized signature of the represented person" and the represented person is liable on the instrument, whether or not identified in the instrument.

(b) If a representative signs the name of the representative to an instrument and the signature is an authorized signature of the represented person, the following rules apply:

(1) If the form of the signature shows unambiguously that the signature is made on behalf of the represented person who is identified in the instrument, the representative is not liable on the instrument.

(2) Subject to subsection (c), if (i) the form of the signature does not show unambiguously that the signature is made in a representative capacity or (ii) the represented person is not identified in the instrument, the representative is liable on the instrument to a holder in due course that took the instrument without notice that the representative was not intended to be liable on the instrument. With respect to any other person, the representative is liable on the instrument

unless the representative proves that the original parties did not intend the representative to be liable on the instrument.

(c) If a representative signs the name of the representative as drawer of a check without indication of the representative status and the check is payable from an account of the represented person who is identified on the check, the signer is not liable on the check if the signature is an authorized signature of the represented person.

Official Comment

1. Subsection (a) states when the represented person is bound on an instrument if the instrument is signed by a representative. If under the law of agency the represented person would be bound by the act of the representative in signing either the name of the represented person or that of the representative, the signature is the authorized signature of the represented person. Former Section 3–401(1) stated that "no person is liable on an instrument unless his signature appears thereon." This was interpreted as meaning that an undisclosed principal is not liable on an instrument. This interpretation provided an exception to ordinary agency law that binds an undisclosed principal on a simple contract.

It is questionable whether this exception was justified by the language of former Article 3 and there is no apparent policy justification for it. The exception is rejected by subsection (a) which returns to ordinary rules of agency. If P, the principal, authorized A, the agent, to borrow money on P's behalf and A signed A's name to a note without disclosing that the signature was on behalf of P, A is liable on the instrument. But if the person entitled to enforce the note can also prove that P authorized A to sign on P's behalf, why shouldn't P also be liable on the instrument? To recognize the liability of P takes nothing away from the utility of negotiable instruments. Furthermore, imposing liability on P has the merit of making it impossible to have an instrument on which nobody is liable even though it was authorized by P. That result could occur under former Section 3–401(1) if an authorized agent signed "as agent" but the note did not identify the principal. If the dispute was between the agent and the payee of the note, the agent could escape liability on the note by proving that the agent and the payee did not intend that the agent be liable on the note when the note was issued. Former Section 3–403(2)(b). Under the prevailing interpretation of former Section 3–401(1), the principal was not liable on the note under former 3–401(1) because the principal's name did not appear on the note. Thus, nobody was liable on the note even though all parties knew that the note was signed by the agent on behalf of the principal. Under Section 3–402(a) the principal would be liable on the note.

2. Subsection (b) concerns the question of when an agent who signs an instrument on behalf of a principal is bound on the instrument. The approach followed by former Section 3–403 was to specify the form of signature that imposed or avoided liability. This approach was unsatisfactory. There are many ways in which there can be ambiguity about a signature. It is better to state a general rule. Subsection (b)(1) states that if the form of the signature unambiguously shows that it is made on behalf of an identified represented person (for example, "P, by A, Treasurer") the agent is not liable. This is a workable standard for a court to apply. Subsection (b)(2) partly changes former Section 3–403(2). Subsection (b)(2) relates to cases in which the agent signs on behalf of a principal but the form of the signature does not fall within subsection (b)(1). The following cases are illustrative. In each case John Doe is the authorized agent of Richard Roe and John Doe signs a note on behalf of Richard Roe. In each case the intention of the original parties to the instrument is that Roe is to be liable on the instrument but Doe is not to be liable.

Case # 1. Doe signs "John Doe" without indicating in the note that Doe is signing as agent. The note does not identify Richard Roe as the represented person.

Case # 2. Doe signs "John Doe, Agent" but the note does not identify Richard Roe as the represented person.

Case # 3. The name "Richard Roe" is written on the note and immediately below that name Doe signs "John Doe" without indicating that Doe signed as agent.

In each case Doe is liable on the instrument to a holder in due course without notice that Doe was not intended to be liable. In none of the cases does Doe's signature unambiguously show that Doe was signing as agent for an identified principal. A holder in due course should be able to resolve any ambiguity against Doe.

But the situation is different if a holder in due course is not involved. In each case Roe is liable on the note. Subsection (a). If the original parties to the note did not intend that Doe also be liable, imposing liability on Doe is a windfall to the person enforcing the note. Under subsection (b)(2) Doe is prima facie liable because his signature appears on the note and the form of the signature does not unambiguously refute personal liability. But

Doe can escape liability by proving that the original parties did not intend that he be liable on the note. This is a change from former Section 3-403(2)(a).

A number of cases under former Article 3 involved situations in which an agent signed the agent's name to a note, without qualification and without naming the person represented, intending to bind the principal but not the agent. The agent attempted to prove that the other party had the same intention. Some of these cases involved mistake, and in some there was evidence that the agent may have been deceived into signing in that manner. In some of the cases the court refused to allow proof of the intention of the parties and imposed liability on the agent based on former Section 3-403(2)(a) even though both parties to the instrument may have intended that the agent not be liable. Subsection (b)(2) changes the result of those cases, and is consistent with Section 3-117 which allows oral or written agreements to modify or nullify apparent obligations on the instrument.

Former Section 3-403 spoke of the represented person being "named" in the instrument. Section 3-402 speaks of the represented person being "identified" in the instrument. This change in terminology is intended to reject decisions under former Section 3-403(2) requiring that the instrument state the legal name of the represented person.

3. Subsection (c) is directed at the check cases. It states that if the check identifies the represented person the agent who signs on the signature line does not have to indicate agency status. Virtually all checks used today are in personalized form which identify the person on whose account the check is drawn. In this case, nobody is deceived into thinking that the person signing the check is meant to be liable. This subsection is meant to overrule cases decided under former Article 3 such as Griffin v. Ellinger, 538 S.W.2d 97 (Texas 1976).

§ 3-403. Unauthorized Signature.

(a) Unless otherwise provided in this Article or Article 4, an unauthorized signature is ineffective except as the signature of the unauthorized signer in favor of a person who in good faith pays the instrument or takes it for value. An unauthorized signature may be ratified for all purposes of this Article.

(b) If the signature of more than one person is required to constitute the authorized signature of an organization, the signature of the organization is unauthorized if one of the required signatures is lacking.

(c) The civil or criminal liability of a person who makes an unauthorized signature is not affected by any provision of this Article which makes the unauthorized signature effective for the purposes of this Article.

Official Comment

1. "Unauthorized" signature is defined in Section 1-201(43) [*unrevised Article 1; see Concordance, p. 12*] as one that includes a forgery as well as a signature made by one exceeding actual or apparent authority. Former Section 3-404(1) stated that an unauthorized signature was inoperative as the signature of the person whose name was signed unless that person "is precluded from denying it." Under former Section 3-406 if negligence by the person whose name was signed contributed to an unauthorized signature, that person "is precluded from asserting the . . . lack of authority." Both of these sections were applied to cases in which a forged signature appeared on an instrument and the person asserting rights on the instrument alleged that the negligence of the purported signer contributed to the forgery. Since the standards for liability between the two sections differ, the overlap between the sections caused confusion. Section 3-403(a) deals with the problem by removing the preclusion language that appeared in former Section 3-404.

2. The except clause of the first sentence of subsection (a) states the generally accepted rule that the unauthorized signature, while it is wholly inoperative as that of the person whose name is signed, is effective to impose liability upon the signer or to transfer any rights that the signer may have in the instrument. The signer's liability is not in damages for breach of warranty of authority, but is full liability on the instrument in the capacity in which the signer signed. It is, however, limited to parties who take or pay the instrument in good faith; and one who knows that the signature is unauthorized cannot recover from the signer on the instrument.

3. The last sentence of subsection (a) allows an unauthorized signature to be ratified. Ratification is a retroactive adoption of the unauthorized signature by the person whose name is signed and may be found from conduct as well as from express statements. For example, it may be found from the retention of benefits received in the transaction with knowledge of the unauthorized signature. Although the forger is not an agent, ratification is governed by the rules and principles applicable to ratification of unauthorized acts of an agent.

Ratification is effective for all purposes of this Article. The unauthorized signature becomes valid so far as its effect as a signature is concerned. Although the ratification may relieve the signer of liability on the instrument, it does not of itself relieve the signer of liability to the person whose name is signed. It does not in any way affect the criminal law. No policy of the criminal law prevents a person whose name is forged to assume liability to others on the instrument by ratifying the forgery, but the ratification cannot affect the rights of the state. While the ratification may be taken into account with other relevant facts in determining punishment, it does not relieve the signer of criminal liability.

4. Subsection (b) clarifies the meaning of "unauthorized" in cases in which an instrument contains less than all of the signatures that are required as authority to pay a check. Judicial authority was split on the issue whether the one-year notice period under former Section 4–406(4) (now Section 4–406(f)) barred a customer's suit against a payor bank that paid a check containing less than all of the signatures required by the customer to authorize payment of the check. Some cases took the view that if a customer required that a check contain the signatures of both A and B to authorize payment and only A signed, there was no unauthorized signature within the meaning of that term in former Section 4–406(4) because A's signature was neither unauthorized nor forged. The other cases correctly pointed out that it was the customer's signature at issue and not that of A; hence, the customer's signature was unauthorized if all signatures required to authorize payment of the check were not on the check. Subsection (b) follows the latter line of cases. The same analysis applies if A forged the signature of B. Because the forgery is not effective as a signature of B, the required signature of B is lacking.

Subsection (b) refers to "the authorized signature of an organization." The definition of "organization" in Section 1–201(28) [*unrevised Article 1; see Concordance, p. 12*] is very broad. It covers not only commercial entities but also "two or more persons having a joint or common interest." Hence subsection (b) would apply when a husband and wife are both required to sign an instrument.

§ 3–404. Impostors; Fictitious Payees.

(a) If an impostor, by use of the mails or otherwise, induces the issuer of an instrument to issue the instrument to the impostor, or to a person acting in concert with the impostor, by impersonating the payee of the instrument or a person authorized to act for the payee, an indorsement of the instrument by any person in the name of the payee is effective as the indorsement of the payee in favor of a person who, in good faith, pays the instrument or takes it for value or for collection.

(b) If (i) a person whose intent determines to whom an instrument is payable (Section 3–110(a) or (b)) does not intend the person identified as payee to have any interest in the instrument, or (ii) the person identified as payee of an instrument is a fictitious person, the following rules apply until the instrument is negotiated by special indorsement:

(1) Any person in possession of the instrument is its holder.

(2) An indorsement by any person in the name of the payee stated in the instrument is effective as the indorsement of the payee in favor of a person who, in good faith, pays the instrument or takes it for value or for collection.

(c) Under subsection (a) or (b), an indorsement is made in the name of a payee if (i) it is made in a name substantially similar to that of the payee or (ii) the instrument, whether or not indorsed, is deposited in a depositary bank to an account in a name substantially similar to that of the payee.

(d) With respect to an instrument to which subsection (a) or (b) applies, if a person paying the instrument or taking it for value or for collection fails to exercise ordinary care in paying or taking the instrument and that failure substantially contributes to loss resulting from payment of the instrument, the person bearing the loss may recover from the person failing to exercise ordinary care to the extent the failure to exercise ordinary care contributed to the loss.

Official Comment

1. Under former Article 3, the impostor cases were governed by former Section 3–405(1)(a) and the fictitious payee cases were governed by Section 3–405(1)(b). Section 3–404 replaces former Section 3–405(1)(a) and (b) and modifies the previous law in some respects. Former Section 3–405 was read by some courts to require that the indorsement be in the exact name of the named payee. Revised Article 3 rejects this result. Section 3–404(c) requires only that the indorsement be made in a name "substantially similar" to that of the payee. Subsection (c) also recognizes the fact that checks may be deposited without indorsement. Section 4–205(a).

Subsection (a) changes the former law in a case in which the impostor is impersonating an agent. Under former Section 3–405(1)(a), if Impostor impersonated Smith and induced the drawer to draw a check to the order of Smith, Impostor could negotiate the check. If Impostor impersonated Smith, the president of Smith Corporation, and the check was payable to the order of Smith Corporation, the section did not apply. See the last paragraph of Comment 2 to former Section 3–405. In revised Article 3, Section 3–404(a) gives Impostor the power to negotiate the check in both cases.

2. Subsection (b) is based in part on former Section 3–405(1)(b) and in part on N.I.L. § 9(3). It covers cases in which an instrument is payable to a fictitious or nonexisting person and to cases in which the payee is a real person but the drawer or maker does not intend the payee to have any interest in the instrument. Subsection (b) applies to any instrument, but its primary importance is with respect to checks of corporations and other organizations. It also applies to forged check cases. The following cases illustrate subsection (b):

Case # 1. Treasurer is authorized to draw checks in behalf of Corporation. Treasurer fraudulently draws a check of Corporation payable to Supplier Co., a non-existent company. Subsection (b) applies because Supplier Co. is a fictitious person and because Treasurer did not intend Supplier Co. to have any interest in the check. Under subsection (b)(1) Treasurer, as the person in possession of the check, becomes the holder of the check. Treasurer indorses the check in the name "Supplier Co." and deposits it in Depositary Bank. Under subsection (b)(2) and (c)(i), the indorsement is effective to make Depositary Bank the holder and therefore a person entitled to enforce the instrument. Section 3–301.

Case # 2. Same facts as Case # 1 except that Supplier Co. is an actual company that does business with Corporation. If Treasurer intended to steal the check when the check was drawn, the result in Case # 2 is the same as the result in Case # 1. Subsection (b) applies because Treasurer did not intend Supplier Co. to have any interest in the check. It does not make any difference whether Supplier Co. was or was not a creditor of Corporation when the check was drawn. If Treasurer did not decide to steal the check until after the check was drawn, the case is covered by Section 3–405 rather than Section 3–404(b), but the result is the same. See Case # 6 in Comment 3 to Section 3–405.

Case # 3. Checks of Corporation must be signed by two officers. President and Treasurer both sign a check of Corporation payable to Supplier Co., a company that does business with Corporation from time to time but to which Corporation does not owe any money. Treasurer knows that no money is owed to Supplier Co. and does not intend that Supplier Co. have any interest in the check. President believes that money is owed to Supplier Co. Treasurer obtains possession of the check after it is signed. Subsection (b) applies because Treasurer is "a person whose intent determines to whom an instrument is payable" and Treasurer does not intend Supplier Co. to have any interest in the check. Treasurer becomes the holder of the check and may negotiate it by indorsing it in the name "Supplier Co."

Case # 4. Checks of Corporation are signed by a check-writing machine. Names of payees of checks produced by the machine are determined by information entered into the computer that operates the machine. Thief, a person who is not an employee or other agent of Corporation, obtains access to the computer and causes the check-writing machine to produce a check payable to Supplier Co., a non-existent company. Subsection (b)(ii) applies. Thief then obtains possession of the check. At that point Thief becomes the holder of the check because Thief is the person in possession of the instrument. Subsection (b)(1). Under Section 3–301 Thief, as holder, is the "person entitled to enforce the instrument" even though Thief does not have title to the check and is in wrongful possession of it. Thief indorses the check in the name "Supplier Co." and deposits it in an account in Depositary Bank which Thief opened in the name "Supplier Co." Depositary Bank takes the check in good faith and credits the "Supplier Co." account. Under subsection (b)(2) and (c)(i), the indorsement is effective. Depositary Bank becomes the holder and the person entitled to enforce the check. The check is presented to the drawee bank for payment and payment is made. Thief then withdraws the credit to the account. Although the check was issued without authority given by Corporation, the drawee bank is entitled to pay the check and charge Corporation's account if there was an agreement with Corporation allowing the bank to debit Corporation's account for payment of checks produced by the check-writing machine whether or not authorized. The indorsement is also effective if Supplier Co. is a real person. In that case subsection (b)(i) applies. Under Section 3–110(b) Thief is the person whose intent determines to whom the check is payable, and Thief did not intend Supplier Co. to have any interest in the check. When the drawee bank pays the check, there is no breach of warranty under Section 3–417(a)(1) or 4–208(a)(1) because Depositary Bank was a person entitled to enforce the check when it was forwarded for payment.

Case # 5. Thief, who is not an employee or agent of Corporation, steals check forms of Corporation. John Doe is president of Corporation and is authorized to sign checks on behalf of Corporation as drawer. Thief draws a check in the name of Corporation as drawer by forging the signature of Doe. Thief makes the check payable to the order of Supplier Co. with the intention of stealing it. Whether Supplier Co. is a fictitious person or a real person, Thief becomes the holder of the check and the person entitled to enforce it. The analysis is the same as that in Case # 4. Thief deposits the check in an account in Depositary Bank which Thief opened in the name "Supplier Co." Thief either indorses the check in a name other than "Supplier Co." or does not indorse the check at all. Under Section 4–205(a) a depositary bank may become holder of a check deposited to the account of a customer if the customer was a holder, whether or not the customer indorses. Subsection (c)(ii) treats deposit to an account in a name substantially similar to that of the payee as the equivalent of indorsement in the name of the payee. Thus, the deposit is an effective indorsement of the check. Depositary Bank becomes the holder of the check and the person entitled to enforce the check. If the check is paid by the drawee bank, there is no breach of warranty under Section 3–417(a)(1) or 4–208(a)(1) because Depositary Bank was a person entitled to enforce the check when it was forwarded for payment and, unless Depositary Bank knew about the forgery of Doe's signature, there is no breach of warranty under Section 3–417(a)(3) or 4–208(a)(3). Because the check was a forged check the drawee bank is not entitled to charge Corporation's account unless Section 3–406 or Section 4–406 applies.

3. In cases governed by subsection (a) the dispute will normally be between the drawer of the check that was obtained by the impostor and the drawee bank that paid it. The drawer is precluded from obtaining recredit of the drawer's account by arguing that the check was paid on a forged indorsement so long as the drawee bank acted in good faith in paying the check. Cases governed by subsection (b) are illustrated by Cases # 1 through # 5 in Comment 2. In Cases # 1, # 2, and # 3 there is no forgery of the check, thus the drawer of the check takes the loss if there is no lack of good faith by the banks involved. Cases # 4 and # 5 are forged check cases. Depositary Bank is entitled to retain the proceeds of the check if it didn't know about the forgery. Under Section 3–418 the drawee bank is not entitled to recover from Depositary Bank on the basis of payment by mistake because Depositary Bank took the check in good faith and gave value for the check when the credit given for the check was withdrawn. And there is no breach of warranty under Section 3–417(a)(1) or (3) or 4–208(a)(1) or (3). Unless Section 3–406 applies the loss is taken by the drawee bank if a forged check is paid, and that is the result in Case # 5. In Case # 4 the loss is taken by Corporation, the drawer, because an agreement between Corporation and the drawee bank allowed the bank to debit Corporation's account despite the unauthorized use of the check-writing machine.

If a check payable to an impostor, fictitious payee, or payee not intended to have an interest in the check is paid, the effect of subsections (a) and (b) is to place the loss on the drawer of the check rather than on the drawee or the depositary bank that took the check for collection. Cases governed by subsection (a) always involve fraud, and fraud is almost always involved in cases governed by subsection (b). The drawer is in the best position to avoid the fraud and thus should take the loss. This is true in Case # 1, Case # 2, and Case # 3. But in some cases the person taking the check might have detected the fraud and thus have prevented the loss by the exercise of ordinary care. In those cases, if that person failed to exercise ordinary care, it is reasonable that that person bear loss to the extent the failure contributed to the loss. Subsection (d) is intended to reach that result. It allows the person who suffers loss as a result of payment of the check to recover from the person who failed to exercise ordinary care. In Case # 1, Case # 2, and Case # 3, the person suffering the loss is Corporation, the drawer of the check. In each case the most likely defendant is the depositary bank that took the check and failed to exercise ordinary care. In those cases, the drawer has a cause of action against the offending bank to recover a portion of the loss. The amount of loss to be allocated to each party is left to the trier of fact. Ordinary care is defined in Section 3–103(a)(9). An example of the type of conduct by a depositary bank that could give rise to recovery under subsection (d) is discussed in Comment 4 to Section 3–405. That comment addresses the last sentence of Section 3–405(b) which is similar to Section 3–404(d).

In Case # 1, Case # 2, and Case # 3, there was no forgery of the drawer's signature. But cases involving checks payable to a fictitious payee or a payee not intended to have an interest in the check are often forged check cases as well. Examples are Case # 4 and Case # 5. Normally, the loss in forged check cases is on the drawee bank that paid the check. Case # 5 is an example. In Case # 4 the risk with respect to the forgery is shifted to the drawer because of the agreement between the drawer and the drawee bank. The doctrine that prevents a drawee bank from recovering payment with respect to a forged check if the payment was made to a person who took the check for value and in good faith is incorporated into Section 3–418 and Sections 3–417(a)(3) and 4–208(a)(3). This doctrine is based on the assumption that the depositary bank normally has no way of detecting the forgery because the drawer is not that bank's customer. On the other hand, the drawee bank, at least in some cases, may be able to detect the forgery by comparing the signature on the check with the specimen signature that the drawee has on file. But in some forged check cases the depositary bank is in a position to detect the fraud. Those cases typically involve a check payable to a fictitious payee or a payee not intended to have an interest in the check. Subsection (d) applies to those cases. If the depositary bank failed to exercise ordinary care and the failure substantially contributed to the loss, the drawer in Case # 4 or the drawee bank in Case # 5 has a cause of action against the depositary bank under subsection (d). Comment 4 to Section 3–405 can be used as a guide to the type of conduct that could give rise to recovery under Section 3–404(d).

§ 3–405. Employer's Responsibility for Fraudulent Indorsement by Employee.

(a) In this section:

(1) "Employee" includes an independent contractor and employee of an independent contractor retained by the employer.

(2) "Fraudulent indorsement" means (i) in the case of an instrument payable to the employer, a forged indorsement purporting to be that of the employer, or (ii) in the case of an instrument with respect to which the employer is the issuer, a forged indorsement purporting to be that of the person identified as payee.

(3) "Responsibility" with respect to instruments means authority (i) to sign or indorse instruments on behalf of the employer, (ii) to process instruments received by the employer for bookkeeping purposes, for deposit to an account, or for other disposition, (iii) to prepare or process instruments for issue in the name of the employer, (iv) to supply information determining the names or addresses of payees of instruments to be issued in the name of the employer, (v) to control the disposition of instruments to be issued in the name of the employer, or (vi) to act otherwise with respect to instruments in a responsible capacity. "Responsibility" does not include authority that merely allows an employee to have access to instruments or blank or incomplete instrument forms that are being stored or transported or are part of incoming or outgoing mail, or similar access.

(b) For the purpose of determining the rights and liabilities of a person who, in good faith, pays an instrument or takes it for value or for collection, if an employer entrusted an employee with responsibility with respect to the instrument and the employee or a person acting in concert with the employee makes a fraudulent indorsement of the instrument, the indorsement is effective as the indorsement of the person to whom the instrument is payable if it is made in the name of that person. If the person paying the instrument or taking it for value or for collection fails to exercise ordinary care in paying or taking the instrument and that failure substantially contributes to loss resulting from the fraud, the person bearing the loss may recover from the person failing to exercise ordinary care to the extent the failure to exercise ordinary care contributed to the loss.

(c) Under subsection (b), an indorsement is made in the name of the person to whom an instrument is payable if (i) it is made in a name substantially similar to the name of that person or (ii) the instrument, whether or not indorsed, is deposited in a depositary bank to an account in a name substantially similar to the name of that person.

Official Comment

1. Section 3–405 is addressed to fraudulent indorsements made by an employee with respect to instruments with respect to which the employer has given responsibility to the employee. It covers two categories of fraudulent indorsements: indorsements made in the name of the employer to instruments payable to the employer and indorsements made in the name of payees of instruments issued by the employer. This section applies to instruments generally but normally the instrument will be a check. Section 3–405 adopts the principle that the risk of loss for fraudulent indorsements by employees who are entrusted with responsibility with respect to checks should fall on the employer rather than the bank that takes the check or pays it, if the bank was not negligent in the transaction. Section 3–405 is based on the belief that the employer is in a far better position to avoid the loss by care in choosing employees, in supervising them, and in adopting other measures to prevent forged indorsements on instruments payable to the employer or fraud in the issuance of instruments in the name of the employer. If the bank failed to exercise ordinary care, subsection (b) allows the employer to shift loss to the bank to the extent the bank's failure to exercise ordinary care contributed to the loss. "Ordinary care" is defined in Section 3–103(a)(9). The provision applies regardless of whether the employer is negligent.

The first category of cases governed by Section 3–405 are those involving indorsements made in the name of payees of instruments issued by the employer. In this category, Section 3–405 includes cases that were covered by former Section 3–405(1)(c). The scope of Section 3–405 in revised Article 3 is, however, somewhat wider. It covers some cases not covered by former Section 3–405(1)(c) in which the entrusted employee makes a forged indorsement to a check drawn by the employer. An example is Case # 6 in Comment 3. Moreover, a larger group of employees is included in revised Section 3–405. The key provision is the definition of "responsibility" in subsection (a)(1) which identifies the kind of responsibility delegated to an employee which will cause the employer to take responsibility for the fraudulent acts of that employee. An employer can insure this risk by employee fidelity bonds.

The second category of cases governed by Section 3–405—fraudulent indorsements of the name of the employer to instruments payable to the employer—were covered in former Article 3 by Section 3–406. Under former Section 3–406, the employer took the loss only if negligence of the employer could be proved. Under revised Article 3, Section 3–406 need not be used with respect to forgeries of the employer's indorsement. Section 3–405 imposes the loss on the employer without proof of negligence.

2. With respect to cases governed by former Section 3–405(1)(c), Section 3–405 is more favorable to employers in one respect. The bank was entitled to the preclusion provided by former Section 3–405(1)(c) if it took the check in good faith. The fact that the bank acted negligently did not shift the loss to the bank so long as the bank acted in good faith. Under revised Section 3–405 the loss may be recovered from the bank to the extent the failure of the bank to exercise ordinary care contributed to the loss.

3. Section 3–404(b) and Section 3–405 both apply to cases of employee fraud. Section 3–404(b) is not limited to cases of employee fraud, but most of the cases to which it applies will be cases of employee fraud. The following cases illustrate the application of Section 3–405. In each case it is assumed that the bank that took the check acted in good faith and was not negligent.

Case # 1. Janitor, an employee of Employer, steals a check for a very large amount payable to Employer after finding it on a desk in one of Employer's offices. Janitor forges Employer's indorsement on the check and obtains payment. Since Janitor was not entrusted with "responsibility" with respect to the check, Section 3–405 does not apply. Section 3–406 might apply to this case. The issue would be whether Employer was negligent in safeguarding the check. If not, Employer could assert that the indorsement was forged and bring an action for conversion against the depositary or payor bank under Section 3–420.

Case # 2. X is Treasurer of Corporation and is authorized to write checks on behalf of Corporation by signing X's name as Treasurer. X draws a check in the name of Corporation and signs X's name as Treasurer. The check is made payable to X. X then indorses the check and obtains payment. Assume that Corporation did not owe any money to X and did not authorize X to write the check. Although the writing of the check was not authorized, Corporation is bound as drawer of the check because X had authority to sign checks on behalf of Corporation. This result follows from agency law and Section 3–402(a). Section 3–405 does not apply in this case because there is no forged indorsement. X was payee of the check so the indorsement is valid. Section 3–110(a).

Case # 3. The duties of Employee, a bookkeeper, include posting the amounts of checks payable to Employer to the accounts of the drawers of the checks. Employee steals a check payable to Employer which was entrusted to Employee and forges Employer's indorsement. The check is deposited by Employee to an account in Depositary Bank which Employee opened in the same name as Employer, and the check is honored by the drawee bank. The indorsement is effective as Employer's indorsement because Employee's duties include processing checks for bookkeeping purposes. Thus, Employee is entrusted with "responsibility" with respect to the check. Neither Depositary Bank nor the drawee bank is liable to Employer for conversion of the check. The same result follows if Employee deposited the check in the account in Depositary Bank without indorsement. Section 4–205(a). Under subsection (c) deposit in a depositary bank in an account in a name substantially similar to that of Employer is the equivalent of an indorsement in the name of Employer.

Case # 4. Employee's duties include stamping Employer's unrestricted blank indorsement on checks received by Employer and depositing them in Employer's bank account. After stamping Employer's unrestricted blank indorsement on a check, Employee steals the check and deposits it in Employee's personal bank account. Section 3–405 doesn't apply because there is no forged indorsement. Employee is authorized by Employer to indorse Employer's checks. The fraud by Employee is not the indorsement but rather the theft of the indorsed check. Whether Employer has a cause of action against the bank in which the check was deposited is determined by whether the bank had notice of the breach of fiduciary duty by Employee. The issue is determined under Section 3–307.

Case # 5. The computer that controls Employer's check-writing machine was programmed to cause a check to be issued to Supplier Co. to which money was owed by Employer. The address of Supplier Co. was included in the information in the computer. Employee is an accounts payable clerk whose duties include entering information into the computer. Employee fraudulently changed the address of Supplier Co. in the computer data bank to an address of Employee. The check was subsequently produced by the check-writing machine and mailed to the address that Employee had entered into the computer. Employee obtained possession of the check, indorsed it in the name of Supplier Co, and deposited it to an account in Depositary

Bank which Employee opened in the name "Supplier Co." The check was honored by the drawee bank. The indorsement is effective under Section 3–405(b) because Employee's duties allowed Employee to supply information determining the address of the payee of the check. An employee that is entrusted with duties that enable the employee to determine the address to which a check is to be sent controls the disposition of the check and facilitates forgery of the indorsement. The employer is held responsible. The drawee may debit the account of Employer for the amount of the check. There is no breach of warranty by Depositary Bank under Section 3–417(a)(1) or 4–208(a)(1).

Case # 6. Treasurer is authorized to draw checks in behalf of Corporation. Treasurer draws a check of Corporation payable to Supplier Co., a company that sold goods to Corporation. The check was issued to pay the price of these goods. At the time the check was signed Treasurer had no intention of stealing the check. Later, Treasurer stole the check, indorsed it in the name "Supplier Co." and obtained payment by depositing it to an account in Depositary Bank which Treasurer opened in the name "Supplier Co.". The indorsement is effective under Section 3–405(b). Section 3–404(b) does not apply to this case.

Case # 7. Checks of Corporation are signed by Treasurer in behalf of Corporation as drawer. Clerk's duties include the preparation of checks for issue by Corporation. Clerk prepares a check payable to the order of Supplier Co. for Treasurer's signature. Clerk fraudulently informs Treasurer that the check is needed to pay a debt owed to Supplier Co, a company that does business with Corporation. No money is owed to Supplier Co. and Clerk intends to steal the check. Treasurer signs it and returns it to Clerk for mailing. Clerk does not indorse the check but deposits it to an account in Depositary Bank which Clerk opened in the name "Supplier Co.". The check is honored by the drawee bank. Section 3–404(b)(i) does not apply to this case because Clerk, under Section 3–110(a), is not the person whose intent determines to whom the check is payable. But Section 3–405 does apply and it treats the deposit by Clerk as an effective indorsement by Clerk because Clerk was entrusted with responsibility with respect to the check. If Supplier Co. is a fictitious person Section 3–404(b)(ii) applies. But the result is the same. Clerk's deposit is treated as an effective indorsement of the check whether Supplier Co. is a fictitious or a real person or whether money was or was not owing to Supplier Co. The drawee bank may debit the account of Corporation for the amount of the check and there is no breach of warranty by Depositary Bank under Section 3–417(1)(a).

4. The last sentence of subsection (b) is similar to subsection (d) of Section 3–404 which is discussed in Comment 3 to Section 3–404. In Case # 5, Case # 6, or Case # 7 the depositary bank may have failed to exercise ordinary care when it allowed the employee to open an account in the name "Supplier Co.," to deposit checks payable to "Supplier Co." in that account, or to withdraw funds from that account that were proceeds of checks payable to Supplier Co. Failure to exercise ordinary care is to be determined in the context of all the facts relating to the bank's conduct with respect to the bank's collection of the check. If the trier of fact finds that there was such a failure and that the failure substantially contributed to loss, it could find the depositary bank liable to the extent the failure contributed to the loss. The last sentence of subsection (b) can be illustrated by an example. Suppose in Case # 5 that the check is not payable to an obscure "Supplier Co." but rather to a well-known national corporation. In addition, the check is for a very large amount of money. Before depositing the check, Employee opens an account in Depositary Bank in the name of the corporation and states to the person conducting the transaction for the bank that Employee is manager of a new office being opened by the corporation. Depositary Bank opens the account without requiring Employee to produce any resolutions of the corporation's board of directors or other evidence of authorization of Employee to act for the corporation. A few days later, the check is deposited, the account is credited, and the check is presented for payment. After Depositary Bank receives payment, it allows Employee to withdraw the credit by a wire transfer to an account in a bank in a foreign country. The trier of fact could find that Depositary Bank did not exercise ordinary care and that the failure to exercise ordinary care contributed to the loss suffered by Employer. The trier of fact could allow recovery by Employer from Depositary Bank for all or part of the loss suffered by Employer.

As amended in 2005.

§ 3–406. Negligence Contributing to Forged Signature or Alteration of Instrument.

(a) A person whose failure to exercise ordinary care substantially contributes to an alteration of an instrument or to the making of a forged signature on an instrument is precluded from asserting the alteration or the forgery against a person who, in good faith, pays the instrument or takes it for value or for collection.

(b) Under subsection (a), if the person asserting the preclusion fails to exercise ordinary care in paying or taking the instrument and that failure substantially contributes to loss, the loss is allocated between the person precluded and the person asserting the preclusion according to the extent to which the failure of each to exercise ordinary care contributed to the loss.

(c) Under subsection (a), the burden of proving failure to exercise ordinary care is on the person asserting the preclusion. Under subsection (b), the burden of proving failure to exercise ordinary care is on the person precluded.

Official Comment

1. Section 3–406(a) is based on former Section 3–406. With respect to alteration, Section 3–406 adopts the doctrine of *Young v. Grote*, 4 Bing. 253 (1827), which held that a drawer who so negligently draws an instrument as to facilitate its material alteration is liable to a drawee who pays the altered instrument in good faith. Under Section 3–406 the doctrine is expanded to apply not only to drafts but to all instruments. It includes in the protected class any "person who, in good faith, pays the instrument or takes it for value or for collection." Section 3–406 rejects decisions holding that the maker of a note owes no duty of care to the holder because at the time the instrument is issued there is no contract between them. By issuing the instrument and "setting it afloat upon a sea of strangers" the maker or drawer voluntarily enters into a relation with later holders which justifies imposition of a duty of care. In this respect an instrument so negligently drawn as to facilitate alteration does not differ in principle from an instrument containing blanks which may be filled. Under Section 3–407 a person paying an altered instrument or taking it for value, in good faith and without notice of the alteration may enforce rights with respect to the instrument according to its original terms. If negligence of the obligor substantially contributes to an alteration, this section gives the holder or the payor the alternative right to treat the altered instrument as though it had been issued in the altered form.

No attempt is made to define particular conduct that will constitute "failure to exercise ordinary care [that] substantially contributes to an alteration." Rather, "ordinary care" is defined in Section 3–103(a)(9) in general terms. The question is left to the court or the jury for decision in the light of the circumstances in the particular case including reasonable commercial standards that may apply.

Section 3–406 does not make the negligent party liable in tort for damages resulting from the alteration. If the negligent party is estopped from asserting the alteration the person taking the instrument is fully protected because the taker can treat the instrument as having been issued in the altered form.

2. Section 3–406 applies equally to a failure to exercise ordinary care that substantially contributes to the making of a forged signature on an instrument. Section 3–406 refers to "forged signature" rather than "unauthorized signature" that appeared in former Section 3–406 because it more accurately describes the scope of the provision. Unauthorized signature is a broader concept that includes not only forgery but also the signature of an agent which does not bind the principal under the law of agency. The agency cases are resolved independently under agency law. Section 3–406 is not necessary in those cases.

The "substantially contributes" test of former Section 3–406 is continued in this section in preference to a "direct and proximate cause" test. The "substantially contributes" test is meant to be less stringent than a "direct and proximate cause" test. Under the less stringent test the preclusion should be easier to establish. Conduct "substantially contributes" to a material alteration or forged signature if it is a contributing cause of the alteration or signature and a substantial factor in bringing it about. The analysis of "substantially contributes" in former Section 3–406 by the court in *Thompson Maple Products v. Citizens National Bank of Corry*, 234 A.2d 32 (Pa.Super.Ct. 1967), states what is intended by the use of the same words in revised Section 3–406(b). Since Section 3–404(d) and Section 3–405(b) also use the words "substantially contributes" the analysis of these words also applies to those provisions.

3. The following cases illustrate the kind of conduct that can be the basis of a preclusion under Section 3–406(a):

Case # 1. Employer signs checks drawn on Employer's account by use of a rubber stamp of Employer's signature. Employer keeps the rubber stamp along with Employer's personalized blank check forms in an unlocked desk drawer. An unauthorized person fraudulently uses the check forms to write checks on Employer's account. The checks are signed by use of the rubber stamp. If Employer demands that Employer's account in the drawee bank be recredited because the forged check was not properly payable, the drawee bank may defend by asserting that Employer is precluded from asserting the forgery. The trier of fact could find that Employer failed to exercise ordinary care to safeguard the rubber stamp and the check forms and that the failure substantially contributed to the forgery of Employer's signature by the unauthorized use of the rubber stamp.

Case # 2. An insurance company draws a check to the order of Sarah Smith in payment of a claim of a policyholder, Sarah Smith, who lives in Alabama. The insurance company also has a policyholder with the same name who lives in Illinois. By mistake, the insurance company mails the check to the Illinois Sarah Smith who indorses the check and obtains payment. Because the payee of the check is the Alabama Sarah Smith, the indorsement by the Illinois Sarah Smith is a forged indorsement. Section 3–110(a). The trier of fact could find that the insurance company failed to exercise ordinary care when it mailed the check to the wrong person and that the failure substantially contributed to the making of the forged indorsement. In that event the insurance company could be precluded from asserting the forged indorsement against the drawee bank that honored the check.

Case # 3. A company writes a check for $10. The figure "10" and the word "ten" are typewritten in the appropriate spaces on the check form. A large blank space is left after the figure and the word. The payee of the check, using a typewriter with a typeface similar to that used on the check, writes the word "thousand" after the word "ten" and a comma and three zeros after the figure "10". The drawee bank in good faith pays $10,000 when the check is presented for payment and debits the account of the drawer in that amount. The trier of fact could find that the drawer failed to exercise ordinary care in writing the check and that the failure substantially contributed to the alteration. In that case the drawer is precluded from asserting the alteration against the drawee if the check was paid in good faith.

4. Subsection (b) differs from former Section 3–406 in that it adopts a concept of comparative negligence. If the person precluded under subsection (a) proves that the person asserting the preclusion failed to exercise ordinary care and that failure substantially contributed to the loss, the loss may be allocated between the two parties on a comparative negligence basis. In the case of a forged indorsement the litigation is usually between the payee of the check and the depositary bank that took the check for collection. An example is a case like Case # 1 of Comment 3 to Section 3–405. If the trier of fact finds that Employer failed to exercise ordinary care in safeguarding the check and that the failure substantially contributed to the making of the forged indorsement, subsection (a) of Section 3–406 applies. If Employer brings an action for conversion against the depositary bank that took the checks from the forger, the depositary bank could assert the preclusion under subsection (a). But suppose the forger opened an account in the depositary bank in a name identical to that of Employer, the payee of the check, and then deposited the check in the account. Subsection (b) may apply. There may be an issue whether the depositary bank should have been alerted to possible fraud when a new account was opened for a corporation shortly before a very large check payable to a payee with the same name is deposited. Circumstances surrounding the opening of the account may have suggested that the corporation to which the check was payable may not be the same as the corporation for which the account was opened. If the trier of fact finds that collecting the check under these circumstances was a failure to exercise ordinary care, it could allocate the loss between the depositary bank and Employer, the payee.

§ 3–407. Alteration.

(a) "Alteration" means (i) an unauthorized change in an instrument that purports to modify in any respect the obligation of a party, or (ii) an unauthorized addition of words or numbers or other change to an incomplete instrument relating to the obligation of a party.

(b) Except as provided in subsection (c), an alteration fraudulently made discharges a party whose obligation is affected by the alteration unless that party assents or is precluded from asserting the alteration. No other alteration discharges a party, and the instrument may be enforced according to its original terms.

(c) A payor bank or drawee paying a fraudulently altered instrument or a person taking it for value, in good faith and without notice of the alteration, may enforce rights with respect to the instrument (i) according to its original terms, or (ii) in the case of an incomplete instrument altered by unauthorized completion, according to its terms as completed.

Official Comment

1. This provision restates former Section 3–407. Former Section 3–407 defined a "material" alteration as any alteration that changes the contract of the parties in any respect. Revised Section 3–407 refers to such a change as an alteration. As under subsection (2) of former Section 3–407, discharge because of alteration occurs only in the case of an alteration fraudulently made. There is no discharge if a blank is filled in the honest belief that it is authorized or if a change is made with a benevolent motive such as a desire to give the obligor the benefit of a lower interest rate. Changes favorable to the obligor are unlikely to be made with any fraudulent intent, but if such an intent is found the alteration may operate as a discharge.

Discharge is a personal defense of the party whose obligation is modified and anyone whose obligation is not affected is not discharged. But if an alteration discharges a party there is also discharge of any party having a right of recourse against the discharged party because the obligation of the party with the right of recourse is affected by the alteration. Assent to the alteration given before or after it is made will prevent the party from asserting the discharge. The phrase "or is precluded from asserting the alteration" in subsection (b) recognizes the possibility of an estoppel or other ground barring the defense which does not rest on assent.

2. Under subsection (c) a person paying a fraudulently altered instrument or taking it for value, in good faith and without notice of the alteration, is not affected by a discharge under subsection (b). The person paying or taking the instrument may assert rights with respect to the instrument according to its original terms or, in the case of an incomplete instrument that is altered by unauthorized completion, according to its terms as completed. If blanks are filled or an incomplete instrument is otherwise completed, subsection (c) places the loss upon the party who left the instrument incomplete by permitting enforcement in its completed form. This result is intended even though the instrument was stolen from the issuer and completed after the theft.

§ 3–408. Drawee Not Liable on Unaccepted Draft.

A check or other draft does not of itself operate as an assignment of funds in the hands of the drawee available for its payment, and the drawee is not liable on the instrument until the drawee accepts it.

Official Comment

1. This section is a restatement of former Section 3–409(1). Subsection (2) of former Section 3–409 is deleted as misleading and superfluous. Comment 3 says of subsection (2): "It is intended to make it clear that this section does not in any way affect any liability which may arise apart from the instrument." In reality subsection (2) did not make anything clear and was a source of confusion. If all it meant was that a bank that has not certified a check may engage in other conduct that might make it liable to a holder, it stated the obvious and was superfluous. Section 1–103 is adequate to cover those cases.

2. Liability with respect to drafts may arise under other law. For example, Section 4–302 imposes liability on a payor bank for late return of an item.

§ 3–409. Acceptance of Draft; Certified Check.

(a) "Acceptance" means the drawee's signed agreement to pay a draft as presented. It must be written on the draft and may consist of the drawee's signature alone. Acceptance may be made at any time and becomes effective when notification pursuant to instructions is given or the accepted draft is delivered for the purpose of giving rights on the acceptance to any person.

(b) A draft may be accepted although it has not been signed by the drawer, is otherwise incomplete, is overdue, or has been dishonored.

(c) If a draft is payable at a fixed period after sight and the acceptor fails to date the acceptance, the holder may complete the acceptance by supplying a date in good faith.

(d) "Certified check" means a check accepted by the bank on which it is drawn. Acceptance may be made as stated in subsection (a) or by a writing on the check which indicates that the check is certified. The drawee of a check has no obligation to certify the check, and refusal to certify is not dishonor of the check.

Official Comment

1. The first three subsections of Section 3–409 are a restatement of former Section 3–410. Subsection (d) adds a definition of certified check which is a type of accepted draft.

2. Subsection (a) states the generally recognized rule that the mere signature of the drawee on the instrument is a sufficient acceptance. Customarily the signature is written vertically across the face of the instrument, but since the drawee has no reason to sign for any other purpose a signature in any other place, even on the back of the instrument, is sufficient. It need not be accompanied by such words as "Accepted," "Certified," or "Good." It must not, however, bear any words indicating an intent to refuse to honor the draft. The last sentence of subsection (a) states the generally recognized rule that an acceptance written on the draft takes effect when the drawee notifies the holder or gives notice according to instructions.

3. The purpose of subsection (c) is to provide a definite date of payment if none appears on the instrument. An undated acceptance of a draft payable "thirty days after sight" is incomplete. Unless the acceptor writes in a

different date the holder is authorized to complete the acceptance according to the terms of the draft by supplying a date of acceptance. Any date supplied by the holder is effective if made in good faith.

4. The last sentence of subsection (d) states the generally recognized rule that in the absence of agreement a bank is under no obligation to certify a check. A check is a demand instrument calling for payment rather than acceptance. The bank may be liable for breach of any agreement with the drawer, the holder, or any other person by which it undertakes to certify. Its liability is not on the instrument, since the drawee is not so liable until acceptance. Section 3–408. Any liability is for breach of the separate agreement.

§ 3–410. Acceptance Varying Draft.

(a) If the terms of a drawee's acceptance vary from the terms of the draft as presented, the holder may refuse the acceptance and treat the draft as dishonored. In that case, the drawee may cancel the acceptance.

(b) The terms of a draft are not varied by an acceptance to pay at a particular bank or place in the United States, unless the acceptance states that the draft is to be paid only at that bank or place.

(c) If the holder assents to an acceptance varying the terms of a draft, the obligation of each drawer and indorser that does not expressly assent to the acceptance is discharged.

Official Comment

1. This section is a restatement of former Section 3–412. It applies to conditional acceptances, acceptances for part of the amount, acceptances to pay at a different time from that required by the draft, or to the acceptance of less than all of the drawees. It applies to any other engagement changing the essential terms of the draft. If the drawee makes a varied acceptance the holder may either reject it or assent to it. The holder may reject by insisting on acceptance of the draft as presented. Refusal by the drawee to accept the draft as presented is dishonor. In that event the drawee is not bound by the varied acceptance and is entitled to have it canceled.

If the holder assents to the varied acceptance, the drawee's obligation as acceptor is according to the terms of the varied acceptance. Under subsection (c) the effect of the holder's assent is to discharge any drawer or indorser who does not also assent. The assent of the drawer or indorser must be affirmatively expressed. Mere failure to object within a reasonable time is not assent which will prevent the discharge.

2. Under subsection (b) an acceptance does not vary from the terms of the draft if it provides for payment at any particular bank or place in the United States unless the acceptance states that the draft is to be paid only at such bank or place. Section 3–501(b)(1) states that if an instrument is payable at a bank in the United States presentment must be made at the place of payment (Section 3–111) which in this case is at the designated bank.

§ 3–411. Refusal to Pay Cashier's Checks, Teller's Checks, and Certified Checks.

(a) In this section, "obligated bank" means the acceptor of a certified check or the issuer of a cashier's check or teller's check bought from the issuer.

(b) If the obligated bank wrongfully (i) refuses to pay a cashier's check or certified check, (ii) stops payment of a teller's check, or (iii) refuses to pay a dishonored teller's check, the person asserting the right to enforce the check is entitled to compensation for expenses and loss of interest resulting from the nonpayment and may recover consequential damages if the obligated bank refuses to pay after receiving notice of particular circumstances giving rise to the damages.

(c) Expenses or consequential damages under subsection (b) are not recoverable if the refusal of the obligated bank to pay occurs because (i) the bank suspends payments, (ii) the obligated bank asserts a claim or defense of the bank that it has reasonable grounds to believe is available against the person entitled to enforce the instrument, (iii) the obligated bank has a reasonable doubt whether the person demanding payment is the person entitled to enforce the instrument, or (iv) payment is prohibited by law.

Official Comment

1. In some cases a creditor may require that the debt be paid by an obligation of a bank. The debtor may comply by obtaining certification of the debtor's check, but more frequently the debtor buys from a bank a cashier's check or teller's check payable to the creditor. The check is taken by the creditor as a cash equivalent on the assumption that the bank will pay the check. Sometimes, the debtor wants to retract payment by inducing the obligated bank not to pay. The typical case involves a dispute between the parties to the transaction in which the

check is given in payment. In the case of a certified check or cashier's check, the bank can safely pay the holder of the check despite notice that there may be an adverse claim to the check (Section 3–602). It is also clear that the bank that sells a teller's check has no duty to order the bank on which it is drawn not to pay it. A debtor using any of these types of checks has no right to stop payment. Nevertheless, some banks will refuse payment as an accommodation to a customer. Section 3–411 is designed to discourage this practice.

2. The term "obligated bank" refers to the issuer of the cashier's check or teller's check and the acceptor of the certified check. If the obligated bank wrongfully refuses to pay, it is liable to pay for expenses and loss of interest resulting from the refusal to pay. There is no express provision for attorney's fees, but attorney's fees are not meant to be necessarily excluded. They could be granted because they fit within the language "expenses . . . resulting from the nonpayment." In addition the bank may be liable to pay consequential damages if it has notice of the particular circumstances giving rise to the damages.

3. Subsection (c) provides that expenses or consequential damages are not recoverable if the refusal to pay is because of the reasons stated. The purpose is to limit that recovery to cases in which the bank refuses to pay even though its obligation to pay is clear and it is able to pay. Subsection (b) applies only if the refusal to honor the check is wrongful. If the bank is not obliged to pay there is no recovery. The bank may assert any claim or defense that it has, but normally the bank would not have a claim or defense. In the usual case it is a remitter that is asserting a claim to the check on the basis of a rescission of negotiation to the payee under Section 3–202. See Comment 2 to Section 3–201. The bank can assert that claim if there is compliance with Section 3–305(c), but the bank is not protected from damages under subsection (b) if the claim of the remitter is not upheld. In that case, the bank is insulated from damages only if payment is enjoined under Section 3–602(b)(1). Subsection (c)(iii) refers to cases in which the bank may have a reasonable doubt about the identity of the person demanding payment. For example, a cashier's check is payable to "Supplier Co." The person in possession of the check presents it for payment over the counter and claims to be an officer of Supplier Co. The bank may refuse payment until it has been given adequate proof that the presentment in fact is being made for Supplier Co., the person entitled to enforce the check.

§ 3–412. Obligation of Issuer of Note or Cashier's Check.

The issuer of a note or cashier's check or other draft drawn on the drawer is obliged to pay the instrument (i) according to its terms at the time it was issued or, if not issued, at the time it first came into possession of a holder, or (ii) if the issuer signed an incomplete instrument, according to its terms when completed, to the extent stated in Sections 3–115 and 3–407. The obligation is owed to a person entitled to enforce the instrument or to an indorser who paid the instrument under Section 3–415.

Official Comment

1. The obligations of the maker, acceptor, drawer, and indorser are stated in four separate sections. Section 3–412 states the obligation of the maker of a note and is consistent with former Section 3–413(1). Section 3–412 also applies to the issuer of a cashier's check or other draft drawn on the drawer. Under former Section 3–118(a), since a cashier's check or other draft drawn on the drawer was "effective as a note," the drawer was liable under former Section 3–413(1) as a maker. Under Sections 3–103(a)(8) and 3–104(f) a cashier's check or other draft drawn on the drawer is treated as a draft to reflect common commercial usage, but the liability of the drawer is stated by Section 3–412 as being the same as that of the maker of a note rather than that of the drawer of a draft. Thus, Section 3–412 does not in substance change former law.

2. Under Section 3–105(b) nonissuance of either a complete or incomplete instrument is a defense by a maker or drawer against a person that is not a holder in due course.

3. The obligation of the maker may be modified in the case of alteration if, under Section 3–406, the maker is precluded from asserting the alteration.

4. The rule of this section is similar to the rule of Article 39 of the Convention on International Bills of Exchange and International Promissory Notes.

As amended in 2002.

§ 3–413. Obligation of Acceptor.

(a) The acceptor of a draft is obliged to pay the draft (i) according to its terms at the time it was accepted, even though the acceptance states that the draft is payable "as originally drawn" or equivalent terms, (ii) if the acceptance varies the terms of the draft, according to the terms of the draft as varied, or

(iii) if the acceptance is of a draft that is an incomplete instrument, according to its terms when completed, to the extent stated in Sections 3–115 and 3–407. The obligation is owed to a person entitled to enforce the draft or to the drawer or an indorser who paid the draft under Section 3–414 or 3–415.

(b) If the certification of a check or other acceptance of a draft states the amount certified or accepted, the obligation of the acceptor is that amount. If (i) the certification or acceptance does not state an amount, (ii) the amount of the instrument is subsequently raised, and (iii) the instrument is then negotiated to a holder in due course, the obligation of the acceptor is the amount of the instrument at the time it was taken by the holder in due course.

Official Comment

Subsection (a) is consistent with former Section 3–413(1). Subsection (b) has primary importance with respect to certified checks. It protects the holder in due course of a certified check that was altered after certification and before negotiation to the holder in due course. A bank can avoid liability for the altered amount by stating on the check the amount the bank agrees to pay. The subsection applies to other accepted drafts as well. The rule of this section is similar to the rule of Articles 41 of the Convention on International Bills of Exchange and International Promissory Notes. Articles 42 and 43 of the Convention include more detailed rules that in many respects do not have parallels in this Article.

As amended in 2002.

§ 3–414. Obligation of Drawer.

(a) This section does not apply to cashier's checks or other drafts drawn on the drawer.

(b) If an unaccepted draft is dishonored, the drawer is obliged to pay the draft (i) according to its terms at the time it was issued or, if not issued, at the time it first came into possession of a holder, or (ii) if the drawer signed an incomplete instrument, according to its terms when completed, to the extent stated in Sections 3–115 and 3–407. The obligation is owed to a person entitled to enforce the draft or to an indorser who paid the draft under Section 3–415.

(c) If a draft is accepted by a bank, the drawer is discharged, regardless of when or by whom acceptance was obtained.

(d) If a draft is accepted and the acceptor is not a bank, the obligation of the drawer to pay the draft if the draft is dishonored by the acceptor is the same as the obligation of an indorser under Section 3–415(a) and (c).

(e) If a draft states that it is drawn "without recourse" or otherwise disclaims liability of the drawer to pay the draft, the drawer is not liable under subsection (b) to pay the draft if the draft is not a check. A disclaimer of the liability stated in subsection (b) is not effective if the draft is a check.

(f) If (i) a check is not presented for payment or given to a depositary bank for collection within 30 days after its date, (ii) the drawee suspends payments after expiration of the 30-day period without paying the check, and (iii) because of the suspension of payments, the drawer is deprived of funds maintained with the drawee to cover payment of the check, the drawer to the extent deprived of funds may discharge its obligation to pay the check by assigning to the person entitled to enforce the check the rights of the drawer against the drawee with respect to the funds.

Official Comment

1. Subsection (a) excludes cashier's checks because the obligation of the issuer of a cashier's check is stated in Section 3–412.

2. Subsection (b) states the obligation of the drawer on an unaccepted draft. It replaces former Section 3–413(2). The requirement under former Article 3 of notice of dishonor or protest has been eliminated. Under revised Article 3, notice of dishonor is necessary only with respect to indorser's liability. The liability of the drawer of an unaccepted draft is treated as a primary liability. Under former Section 3–102(1)(d) the term "secondary party" was used to refer to a drawer or indorser. The quoted term is not used in revised Article 3. The effect of a draft drawn without recourse is stated in subsection (e).

3. Under subsection (c) the drawer is discharged of liability on a draft accepted by a bank regardless of when acceptance was obtained. This changes former Section 3–411(1) which provided that the drawer is

discharged only if the holder obtains acceptance. Holders that have a bank obligation do not normally rely on the drawer to guarantee the bank's solvency. A holder can obtain protection against the insolvency of a bank acceptor by a specific guaranty of payment by the drawer or by obtaining an indorsement by the drawer. Section 3–205(d).

4. Subsection (d) states the liability of the drawer if a draft is accepted by a drawee other than a bank and the acceptor dishonors. The drawer of an unaccepted draft is the only party liable on the instrument. The drawee has no liability on the draft. Section 3–408. When the draft is accepted, the obligations change. The drawee, as acceptor, becomes primarily liable and the drawer's liability is that of a person secondarily liable as a guarantor of payment. The drawer's liability is identical to that of an indorser, and subsection (d) states the drawer's liability that way. The drawer is liable to pay the person entitled to enforce the draft or any indorser that pays pursuant to Section 3–415. The drawer in this case is discharged if notice of dishonor is required by Section 3–503 and is not given in compliance with that section. A drawer that pays has a right of recourse against the acceptor. Section 3–413(a).

5. Subsection (e) does not permit the drawer of a check to avoid liability under subsection (b) by drawing the check without recourse. There is no legitimate purpose served by issuing a check on which nobody is liable. Drawing without recourse is effective to disclaim liability of the drawer if the draft is not a check. Suppose, in a documentary sale, Seller draws a draft on Buyer for the price of goods shipped to Buyer. The draft is payable upon delivery to the drawee of an order bill of lading covering the goods. Seller delivers the draft with the bill of lading to Finance Company that is named as payee of the draft. If Seller draws without recourse Finance Company takes the risk that Buyer will dishonor. If Buyer dishonors, Finance Company has no recourse against Seller but it can obtain reimbursement by selling the goods which it controls through the bill of lading.

6. Subsection (f) is derived from former Section 3–502(1)(b). It is designed to protect the drawer of a check against loss resulting from suspension of payments by the drawee bank when the holder of the check delays collection of the check. For example, X writes a check payable to Y for $1,000. The check is covered by funds in X's account in the drawee bank. Y delays initiation of collection of the check for more than 30 days after the date of the check. The drawee bank suspends payments after the 30-day period and before the check is presented for payment. If the $1,000 of funds in X's account have not been withdrawn, X has a claim for those funds against the drawee bank and, if subsection (e) were not in effect, X would be liable to Y on the check because the check was dishonored. Section 3–502(e). If the suspension of payments by the drawee bank will result in payment to X of less than the full amount of the $1,000 in the account or if there is a significant delay in payment to X, X will suffer a loss which would not have been suffered if Y had promptly initiated collection of the check. In most cases, X will not suffer any loss because of the existence of federal bank deposit insurance that covers accounts up to $100,000. Thus, subsection (e) has relatively little importance. There might be some cases, however, in which the account is not fully insured because it exceeds $100,000 or because the account doesn't qualify for deposit insurance. Subsection (f) retains the phrase "deprived of funds maintained with the drawee" appearing in former Section 3–502(1)(b). The quoted phrase applies if the suspension of payments by the drawee prevents the drawer from receiving the benefit of funds which would have paid the check if the holder had been timely in initiating collection. Thus, any significant delay in obtaining full payment of the funds is a deprivation of funds. The drawer can discharge drawer's liability by assigning rights against the drawee with respect to the funds to the holder.

7. The obligation of the drawer under this section is similar to the obligation of the drawer under Article 38 of the Convention on International Bills of Exchange and International Promissory Notes.

As amended in 2002.

§ 3–415. Obligation of Indorser.

(a) Subject to subsections (b), (c), (d), (e) and to Section 3–419(d), if an instrument is dishonored, an indorser is obliged to pay the amount due on the instrument (i) according to the terms of the instrument at the time it was indorsed, or (ii) if the indorser indorsed an incomplete instrument, according to its terms when completed, to the extent stated in Sections 3–115 and 3–407. The obligation of the indorser is owed to a person entitled to enforce the instrument or to a subsequent indorser who paid the instrument under this section.

(b) If an indorsement states that it is made "without recourse" or otherwise disclaims liability of the indorser, the indorser is not liable under subsection (a) to pay the instrument.

(c) If notice of dishonor of an instrument is required by Section 3–503 and notice of dishonor complying with that section is not given to an indorser, the liability of the indorser under subsection (a) is discharged.

(d) If a draft is accepted by a bank after an indorsement is made, the liability of the indorser under subsection (a) is discharged.

(e) If an indorser of a check is liable under subsection (a) and the check is not presented for payment, or given to a depositary bank for collection, within 30 days after the day the indorsement was made, the liability of the indorser under subsection (a) is discharged.

As amended in 1993.

Official Comment

1. Subsections (a) and (b) restate the substance of former Section 3-414(1). Subsection (2) of former Section 3-414 has been dropped because it is superfluous. Although notice of dishonor is not mentioned in subsection (a), it must be given in some cases to charge an indorser. It is covered in subsection (c). Regulation CC § 229.35(b) provides that a bank handling a check for collection or return is liable to a bank that subsequently handles the check to the extent the latter bank does not receive payment for the check. This liability applies whether or not the bank incurring the liability indorsed the check.

2. Section 3-503 states when notice of dishonor is required and how it must be given. If required notice of dishonor is not given in compliance with Section 3-503, subsection (c) of Section 3-415 states that the effect is to discharge the indorser's obligation.

3. Subsection (d) is similar in effect to Section 3-414(c) if the draft is accepted by a bank after the indorsement is made. See Comment 3 to Section 3-414. If a draft is accepted by a bank before the indorsement is made, the indorser incurs the obligation stated in subsection (a).

4. Subsection (e) modifies former Sections 3-503(2)(b) and 3-502(1)(a) by stating a 30-day rather than a seven-day period, and stating it as an absolute rather than a presumptive period.

5. As stated in subsection (a), the obligation of an indorser to pay the amount due on the instrument is generally owed not only to a person entitled to enforce the instrument but also to a subsequent indorser who paid the instrument. But if the prior indorser and the subsequent indorser are both anomalous indorsers, this rule does not apply. In that case, Section 3-116 applies. Under Section 3-116(a), the anomalous indorsers are jointly and severally liable and if either pays the instrument the indorser who pays has a right of contribution against the other. Section 3-116(b). The right to contribution in Section 3-116(b) is subject to "agreement of the affected parties." Suppose the subsequent indorser can prove an agreement with the prior indorser under which the prior indorser agreed to treat the subsequent indorser as a guarantor of the obligation of the prior indorser. Rights of the two indorsers between themselves would be governed by the agreement. Under suretyship law, the subsequent indorser under such an agreement is referred to as a sub-surety. Under the agreement, if the subsequent indorser pays the instrument there is a right to reimbursement from the prior indorser; if the prior indorser pays the instrument, there is no right of recourse against the subsequent indorser. See PEB Commentary No. 11, dated February 10, 1994.

6. The rule of this section is similar to the rule of Article 44 of the Convention on International Bills of Exchange and International Promissory Notes.

As amended in 1994 and 2002.

§ 3-416. Transfer Warranties.

(a) A person who transfers an instrument for consideration warrants to the transferee and, if the transfer is by indorsement, to any subsequent transferee that:

(1) the warrantor is a person entitled to enforce the instrument;

(2) all signatures on the instrument are authentic and authorized;

(3) the instrument has not been altered;

(4) the instrument is not subject to a defense or claim in recoupment of any party which can be asserted against the warrantor;

(5) the warrantor has no knowledge of any insolvency proceeding commenced with respect to the maker or acceptor or, in the case of an unaccepted draft, the drawer; and

(6) with respect to a remotely-created consumer item, that the person on whose account the item is drawn authorized the issuance of the item in the amount for which the item is drawn.

(b) A person to whom the warranties under subsection (a) are made and who took the instrument in good faith may recover from the warrantor as damages for breach of warranty an amount equal to the loss suffered as a result of the breach, but not more than the amount of the instrument plus expenses and loss of interest incurred as a result of the breach.

(c) The warranties stated in subsection (a) cannot be disclaimed with respect to checks. Unless notice of a claim for breach of warranty is given to the warrantor within 30 days after the claimant has reason to know of the breach and the identity of the warrantor, the liability of the warrantor under subsection (b) is discharged to the extent of any loss caused by the delay in giving notice of the claim.

(d) A [cause of action] for breach of warranty under this section accrues when the claimant has reason to know of the breach.

As amended in 2002.

Official Comment

1. Subsection (a) is taken from subsection (2) of former Section 3–417. Subsections (3) and (4) of former Section 3–417 are deleted. Warranties under subsection (a) in favor of the immediate transferee apply to all persons who transfer an instrument for consideration whether or not the transfer is accompanied by indorsement. Any consideration sufficient to support a simple contract will support those warranties. If there is an indorsement the warranty runs with the instrument and the remote holder may sue the indorser-warrantor directly and thus avoid a multiplicity of suits.

2. Since the purpose of transfer (Section 3–203(a)) is to give the transferee the right to enforce the instrument, subsection (a)(1) is a warranty that the transferor is a person entitled to enforce the instrument (Section 3–301). Under Section 3–203(b) transfer gives the transferee any right of the transferor to enforce the instrument. Subsection (a)(1) is in effect a warranty that there are no unauthorized or missing indorsements that prevent the transferor from making the transferee a person entitled to enforce the instrument.

3. The rationale of subsection (a)(4) is that the transferee does not undertake to buy an instrument that is not enforceable in whole or in part, unless there is a contrary agreement. Even if the transferee takes as a holder in due course who takes free of the defense or claim in recoupment, the warranty gives the transferee the option of proceeding against the transferor rather than litigating with the obligor on the instrument the issue of the holder-in-due-course status of the transferee. Subsection (3) of former Section 3–417 which limits this warranty is deleted. The rationale is that while the purpose of a "no recourse" indorsement is to avoid a guaranty of payment, the indorsement does not clearly indicate an intent to disclaim warranties.

4. Under subsection (a)(5) the transferor does not warrant against difficulties of collection, impairment of the credit of the obligor or even insolvency. The transferee is expected to determine such questions before taking the obligation. If insolvency proceedings as defined in Section 1–201(22) [*unrevised Article 1; see Concordance, p. 12*] have been instituted against the party who is expected to pay and the transferor knows it, the concealment of that fact amounts to a fraud upon the transferee, and the warranty against knowledge of such proceedings is provided accordingly.

5. Transfer warranties may be disclaimed with respect to any instrument except a check. Between the immediate parties disclaimer may be made by agreement. In the case of an indorser, disclaimer of transferor's liability, to be effective, must appear in the indorsement with words such as "without warranties" or some other specific reference to warranties. But in the case of a check, subsection (c) of Section 3–416 provides that transfer warranties cannot be disclaimed at all. In the check collection process the banking system relies on these warranties.

6. Subsection (b) states the measure of damages for breach of warranty. There is no express provision for attorney's fees, but attorney's fees are not meant to be necessarily excluded. They could be granted because they fit within the phrase "expenses . . . incurred as a result of the breach." The intention is to leave to other state law the issue as to when attorney's fees are recoverable.

7. Since the traditional term "cause of action" may have been replaced in some states by "claim for relief" or some equivalent term, the words "cause of action" in subsection (d) have been bracketed to indicate that the words may be replaced by an appropriate substitute to conform to local practice.

8. Subsection (a)(6) is based on a number of nonuniform amendments designed to address concerns about certain kinds of check fraud. The provision implements a limited rejection of *Price v. Neal*, 97 Eng. Rep. 871 (K.B. 1762), so that in certain circumstances (those involving remotely-created consumer items) the payor bank can use a warranty claim to absolve itself of responsibility for honoring an unauthorized item. The provision rests on the premise that monitoring by depositary banks can control this type of fraud more effectively than any practices readily available to payor banks. The provision expressly includes both the case in which the consumer does not authorize the item at all and also the case in which the consumer authorizes the item but in an amount different from the amount in which the item is drawn. Similar provisions appear in Sections 3–417, 4–207, and 4–208.

The provision supplements applicable federal law, which requires telemarketers who submit instruments for payment to obtain the customer's "express verifiable authorization," which may be either in writing or tape recorded and must be made available upon request to the customer's bank. Federal Trade Commission's Telemarketing Sales Rule, 16 C.F.R. § 310.3(a)(3), implementing the Telemarketing and Consumer Fraud and Abuse Prevention Act, 15 U.S.C. §§ 6101–6108. Some states also have consumer-protection laws governing authorization of instruments in telemarketing transactions. *See, e.g.*, 9 Vt. Stat. Ann. § 2464.

9. Article 45 of the Convention on International Bills of Exchange and International Promissory Notes includes warranties that are similar (except for the warranty in subsection (a)(6)).

As amended in 2002.

§ 3–417. Presentment Warranties.

(a) If an unaccepted draft is presented to the drawee for payment or acceptance and the drawee pays or accepts the draft, (i) the person obtaining payment or acceptance, at the time of presentment, and (ii) a previous transferor of the draft, at the time of transfer, warrant to the drawee making payment or accepting the draft in good faith that:

(1) the warrantor is, or was, at the time the warrantor transferred the draft, a person entitled to enforce the draft or authorized to obtain payment or acceptance of the draft on behalf of a person entitled to enforce the draft;

(2) the draft has not been altered;

(3) the warrantor has no knowledge that the signature of the drawer of the draft is unauthorized; and

(4) with respect to any remotely-created consumer item, that the person on whose account the item is drawn authorized the issuance of the item in the amount for which the item is drawn.

(b) A drawee making payment may recover from any warrantor damages for breach of warranty equal to the amount paid by the drawee less the amount the drawee received or is entitled to receive from the drawer because of the payment. In addition, the drawee is entitled to compensation for expenses and loss of interest resulting from the breach. The right of the drawee to recover damages under this subsection is not affected by any failure of the drawee to exercise ordinary care in making payment. If the drawee accepts the draft, breach of warranty is a defense to the obligation of the acceptor. If the acceptor makes payment with respect to the draft, the acceptor is entitled to recover from any warrantor for breach of warranty the amounts stated in this subsection.

(c) If a drawee asserts a claim for breach of warranty under subsection (a) based on an unauthorized indorsement of the draft or an alteration of the draft, the warrantor may defend by proving that the indorsement is effective under Section 3–404 or 3–405 or the drawer is precluded under Section 3–406 or 4–406 from asserting against the drawee the unauthorized indorsement or alteration.

(d) If (i) a dishonored draft is presented for payment to the drawer or an indorser or (ii) any other instrument is presented for payment to a party obliged to pay the instrument, and (iii) payment is received, the following rules apply:

(1) The person obtaining payment and a prior transferor of the instrument warrant to the person making payment in good faith that the warrantor is, or was, at the time the warrantor transferred the instrument, a person entitled to enforce the instrument or authorized to obtain payment on behalf of a person entitled to enforce the instrument.

(2) The person making payment may recover from any warrantor for breach of warranty an amount equal to the amount paid plus expenses and loss of interest resulting from the breach.

(e) The warranties stated in subsections (a) and (d) cannot be disclaimed with respect to checks. Unless notice of a claim for breach of warranty is given to the warrantor within 30 days after the claimant has reason to know of the breach and the identity of the warrantor, the liability of the warrantor under subsection (b) or (d) is discharged to the extent of any loss caused by the delay in giving notice of the claim.

(f) A [cause of action] for breach of warranty under this section accrues when the claimant has reason to know of the breach.

As amended in 2002.

Official Comment

1. This section replaces subsection (1) of former Section 3–417. The former provision was difficult to understand because it purported to state in one subsection all warranties given to any person paying any instrument. The result was a provision replete with exceptions that could not be readily understood except after close scrutiny of the language. In revised Section 3–417, presentment warranties made to drawees of uncertified checks and other unaccepted drafts are stated in subsection (a). All other presentment warranties are stated in subsection (d).

2. Subsection (a) states three warranties. Subsection (a)(1) in effect is a warranty that there are no unauthorized or missing indorsements. "Person entitled to enforce" is defined in Section 3–301. Subsection (a)(2) is a warranty that there is no alteration. Subsection (a)(3) is a warranty of no knowledge that there is a forged drawer's signature. Subsection (a) states that the warranties are made to the drawee and subsections (b) and (c) identify the drawee as the person entitled to recover for breach of warranty. There is no warranty made to the drawer under subsection (a) when presentment is made to the drawee. Warranty to the drawer is governed by subsection (d) and that applies only when presentment for payment is made to the drawer with respect to a dishonored draft. In *Sun 'N Sand, Inc. v. United California Bank*, 582 P.2d 920 (Cal. 1978), the court held that under former Section 3–417(1) a warranty was made to the drawer of a check when the check was presented to the drawee for payment. The result in that case is rejected.

3. Subsection (a)(1) retains the rule that the drawee does not admit the authenticity of indorsements and subsection (a)(3) retains the rule of *Price v. Neal*, 3 Burr. 1354 (1762), that the drawee takes the risk that the drawer's signature is unauthorized unless the person presenting the draft has knowledge that the drawer's signature is unauthorized. Under subsection (a)(3) the warranty of no knowledge that the drawer's signature is unauthorized is also given by prior transferors of the draft.

4. Subsection (d) applies to presentment for payment in all cases not covered by subsection (a). It applies to presentment of notes and accepted drafts to any party obliged to pay the instrument, including an indorser, and to presentment of dishonored drafts if made to the drawer or an indorser. In cases covered by subsection (d), there is only one warranty and it is the same as that stated in subsection (a)(1). There are no warranties comparable to subsections (a)(2) and (a)(3) because they are appropriate only in the case of presentment to the drawee of an unaccepted draft. With respect to presentment of an accepted draft to the acceptor, there is no warranty with respect to alteration or knowledge that the signature of the drawer is unauthorized. Those warranties were made to the drawee when the draft was presented for acceptance (Section 3–417(a)(2) and (3)) and breach of that warranty is a defense to the obligation of the drawee as acceptor to pay the draft. If the drawee pays the accepted draft the drawee may recover the payment from any warrantor who was in breach of warranty when the draft was accepted. Section 3–417(b). Thus, there is no necessity for these warranties to be repeated when the accepted draft is presented for payment. Former Section 3–417(1)(b)(iii) and (c)(iii) are not included in revised Section 3–417 because they are unnecessary. Former Section 3–417(1)(c)(iv) is not included because it is also unnecessary. The acceptor should know what the terms of the draft were at the time acceptance was made.

If presentment is made to the drawer or maker, there is no necessity for a warranty concerning the signature of that person or with respect to alteration. If presentment is made to an indorser, the indorser had itself warranted authenticity of signatures and that the instrument was not altered. Section 3–416(a)(2) and (3).

5. The measure of damages for breach of warranty under subsection (a) is stated in subsection (b). There is no express provision for attorney's fees, but attorney's fees are not meant to be necessarily excluded. They could be granted because they fit within the language "expenses . . . resulting from the breach." Subsection (b) provides that the right of the drawee to recover for breach of warranty is not affected by a failure of the drawee to exercise

ordinary care in paying the draft. This provision follows the result reached under former Article 3 in *Hartford Accident & Indemnity Co. v. First Pennsylvania Bank*, 859 F.2d 295 (3d Cir. 1988).

6. Subsection (c) applies to checks and other unaccepted drafts. It gives to the warrantor the benefit of rights that the drawee has against the drawer under Section 3–404, 3–405, 3–406, or 4–406. If the drawer's conduct contributed to a loss from forgery or alteration, the drawee should not be allowed to shift the loss from the drawer to the warrantor.

7. The first sentence of subsection (e) recognizes that checks are normally paid by automated means and that payor banks rely on warranties in making payment. Thus, it is not appropriate to allow disclaimer or warranties appearing on checks that normally will not be examined by the payor bank. The second sentence requires a breach of warranty claim to be asserted within 30 days after the drawee learns of the breach and the identity of the warrantor.

8. Since the traditional term "cause of action" may have been replaced in some states by "claim for relief" or some equivalent term, the words "cause of action" in subsection (f) have been bracketed to indicate that the words may be replaced by an appropriate substitute to conform to local practice.

9. For discussion of subsection (a)(4), see Comment 8 to Section 3–416.

As amended in 2002.

§ 3–418. Payment or Acceptance by Mistake.

(a) Except as provided in subsection (c), if the drawee of a draft pays or accepts the draft and the drawee acted on the mistaken belief that (i) payment of the draft had not been stopped pursuant to Section 4–403 or (ii) the signature of the drawer of the draft was authorized, the drawee may recover the amount of the draft from the person to whom or for whose benefit payment was made or, in the case of acceptance, may revoke the acceptance. Rights of the drawee under this subsection are not affected by failure of the drawee to exercise ordinary care in paying or accepting the draft.

(b) Except as provided in subsection (c), if an instrument has been paid or accepted by mistake and the case is not covered by subsection (a), the person paying or accepting may, to the extent permitted by the law governing mistake and restitution, (i) recover the payment from the person to whom or for whose benefit payment was made or (ii) in the case of acceptance, may revoke the acceptance.

(c) The remedies provided by subsection (a) or (b) may not be asserted against a person who took the instrument in good faith and for value or who in good faith changed position in reliance on the payment or acceptance. This subsection does not limit remedies provided by Section 3–417 or 4–407.

(d) Notwithstanding Section 4–215, if an instrument is paid or accepted by mistake and the payor or acceptor recovers payment or revokes acceptance under subsection (a) or (b), the instrument is deemed not to have been paid or accepted and is treated as dishonored, and the person from whom payment is recovered has rights as a person entitled to enforce the dishonored instrument.

Official Comment

1. This section covers payment or acceptance by mistake and replaces former Section 3–418. Under former Article 3, the remedy of a drawee that paid or accepted a draft by mistake was based on the law of mistake and restitution, but that remedy was not specifically stated. It was provided by Section 1–103. Former Section 3–418 was simply a limitation on the unstated remedy under the law of mistake and restitution. Under revised Article 3, Section 3–418 specifically states the right of restitution in subsections (a) and (b). Subsection (a) allows restitution in the two most common cases in which the problem is presented: payment or acceptance of forged checks and checks on which the drawer has stopped payment. If the drawee acted under a mistaken belief that the check was not forged or had not been stopped, the drawee is entitled to recover the funds paid or to revoke the acceptance whether or not the drawee acted negligently. But in each case, by virtue of subsection (c), the drawee loses the remedy if the person receiving payment or acceptance was a person who took the check in good faith and for value or who in good faith changed position in reliance on the payment or acceptance. Subsections (a) and (c) are consistent with former Section 3–418 and the rule of *Price v. Neal.* The result in the two cases covered by subsection (a) is that the drawee in most cases will not have a remedy against the person paid because there is usually a person who took the check in good faith and for value or who in good faith changed position in reliance on the payment or acceptance.

2. If a check has been paid by mistake and the payee receiving payment did not give value for the check or did not change position in reliance on the payment, the drawee bank is entitled to recover the amount of the check under subsection (a) regardless of how the check was paid. The drawee bank normally pays a check by a credit to an account of the collecting bank that presents the check for payment. The payee of the check normally receives the payment by a credit to the payee's account in the depositary bank. But in some cases the payee of the check may have received payment directly from the drawee bank by presenting the check for payment over the counter. In those cases the payee is entitled to receive cash, but the payee may prefer another form of payment such as a cashier's check or teller's check issued by the drawee bank. Suppose Seller contracted to sell goods to Buyer. The contract provided for immediate payment by Buyer and delivery of the goods 20 days after payment. Buyer paid by mailing a check for $10,000 drawn on Bank payable to Seller. The next day Buyer gave a stop payment order to Bank with respect to the check Buyer had mailed to Seller. A few days later Seller presented Buyer's check to Bank for payment over the counter and requested a cashier's check as payment. Bank issued and delivered a cashier's check for $10,000 payable to Seller. The teller failed to discover Buyer's stop order. The next day Bank discovered the mistake and immediately advised Seller of the facts. Seller refused to return the cashier's check and did not deliver any goods to Buyer.

Under Section 4–215, Buyer's check was paid by Bank at the time it delivered its cashier's check to Seller. See Comment 3 to Section 4–215. Bank is obliged to pay the cashier's check and has no defense to that obligation. The cashier's check was issued for consideration because it was issued in payment of Buyer's check. Although Bank has no defense on its cashier's check it may have a right to recover $10,000, the amount of Buyer's check, from Seller under Section 3–418(a). Bank paid Buyer's check by mistake. Seller did not give value for Buyer's check because the promise to deliver goods to Buyer was never performed. Section 3–303(a)(1). And, on these facts, Seller did not change position in reliance on the payment of Buyer's check. Thus, the first sentence of Section 3–418(c) does not apply and Seller is obliged to return $10,000 to Bank. Bank is obliged to pay the cashier's check but it has a counterclaim against Seller based on its rights under Section 3–418(a). This claim can be asserted against Seller, but it cannot be asserted against some other person with rights of a holder in due course of the cashier's check. A person without rights of a holder in due course of the cashier's check would take subject to Bank's claim against Seller because it is a claim in recoupment. Section 3–305(a)(3).

If Bank recovers from Seller under Section 3–418(a), the payment of Buyer's check is treated as unpaid and dishonored. Section 3–418(d). One consequence is that Seller may enforce Buyer's obligation as drawer to pay the check. Section 3–414. Another consequence is that Seller's rights against Buyer on the contract of sale are also preserved. Under Section 3–310(b) Buyer's obligation to pay for the goods was suspended when Seller took Buyer's check and remains suspended until the check is either dishonored or paid. Under Section ~~3–310(b)(2)~~ 3–310(b)(1) [Previous incorrect cross reference corrected by Permanent Editorial Board action November 1992] the obligation is discharged when the check is paid. Since Section 3–418(d) treats Buyer's check as unpaid and dishonored, Buyer's obligation is not discharged and suspension of the obligation terminates. Under Section 3–310(b)(3), Seller may enforce either the contract of sale or the check subject to defenses and claims of Buyer.

If Seller had released the goods to Buyer before learning about the stop order, Bank would have no recovery against Seller under Section 3–418(a) because Seller in that case gave value for Buyer's check. Section 3–418(c). In this case Bank's sole remedy is under Section 4–407 by subrogation.

3. Subsection (b) covers cases of payment or acceptance by mistake that are not covered by subsection (a). It directs courts to deal with those cases under the law governing mistake and restitution. Perhaps the most important class of cases that falls under subsection (b), because it is not covered by subsection (a), is that of payment by the drawee bank of a check with respect to which the bank has no duty to the drawer to pay either because the drawer has no account with the bank or because available funds in the drawer's account are not sufficient to cover the amount of the check. With respect to such a case, under Restatement of Restitution § 29, if the bank paid because of a mistaken belief that there were available funds in the drawer's account sufficient to cover the amount of the check, the bank is entitled to restitution. But § 29 is subject to Restatement of Restitution § 33 which denies restitution if the holder of the check receiving payment paid value in good faith for the check and had no reason to know that the check was paid by mistake when payment was received.

The result in some cases is clear. For example, suppose Father gives Daughter a check for $10,000 as a birthday gift. The check is drawn on Bank in which both Father and Daughter have accounts. Daughter deposits the check in her account in Bank. An employee of Bank, acting under the belief that there were available funds in Father's account to cover the check, caused Daughter's account to be credited for $10,000. In fact, Father's account was overdrawn and Father did not have overdraft privileges. Since Daughter received the check gratuitously there is clear unjust enrichment if she is allowed to keep the $10,000 and Bank is unable to obtain reimbursement from Father. Thus, Bank should be permitted to reverse the credit to Daughter's account. But this case is not typical.

In most cases the remedy of restitution will not be available because the person receiving payment of the check will have given value for it in good faith.

In some cases, however, it may not be clear whether a drawee bank should have a right of restitution. For example, a check-kiting scheme may involve a large number of checks drawn on a number of different banks in which the drawer's credit balances are based on uncollected funds represented by fraudulently drawn checks. No attempt is made in Section 3–418 to state rules for determining the conflicting claims of the various banks that may be victimized by such a scheme. Rather, such cases are better resolved on the basis of general principles of law and the particular facts presented in the litigation.

4. The right of the drawee to recover a payment or to revoke an acceptance under Section 3–418 is not affected by the rules under Article 4 that determine when an item is paid. Even though a payor bank may have paid an item under Section 4–215, it may have a right to recover the payment under Section 3–418. *National Savings & Trust Co. v. Park Corp.*, 722 F.2d 1303 (6th Cir. 1983), cert. denied, 466 U.S. 939 (1984), correctly states the law on the issue under former Article 3. Revised Article 3 does not change the previous law.

§ 3–419. Instruments Signed for Accommodation.

(a) If an instrument is issued for value given for the benefit of a party to the instrument ("accommodated party") and another party to the instrument ("accommodation party") signs the instrument for the purpose of incurring liability on the instrument without being a direct beneficiary of the value given for the instrument, the instrument is signed by the accommodation party "for accommodation."

(b) An accommodation party may sign the instrument as maker, drawer, acceptor, or indorser and, subject to subsection (d), is obliged to pay the instrument in the capacity in which the accommodation party signs. The obligation of an accommodation party may be enforced notwithstanding any statute of frauds and whether or not the accommodation party receives consideration for the accommodation.

(c) A person signing an instrument is presumed to be an accommodation party and there is notice that the instrument is signed for accommodation if the signature is an anomalous indorsement or is accompanied by words indicating that the signer is acting as surety or guarantor with respect to the obligation of another party to the instrument. Except as provided in Section 3–605, the obligation of an accommodation party to pay the instrument is not affected by the fact that the person enforcing the obligation had notice when the instrument was taken by that person that the accommodation party signed the instrument for accommodation.

(d) If the signature of a party to an instrument is accompanied by words indicating unambiguously that the party is guaranteeing collection rather than payment of the obligation of another party to the instrument, the signer is obliged to pay the amount due on the instrument to a person entitled to enforce the instrument only if (i) execution of judgment against the other party has been returned unsatisfied, (ii) the other party is insolvent or in an insolvency proceeding, (iii) the other party cannot be served with process, or (iv) it is otherwise apparent that payment cannot be obtained from the other party.

(e) If the signature of a party to an instrument is accompanied by words indicating that the party guarantees payment or the signer signs the instrument as an accommodation party in some other manner that does not unambiguously indicate an intention to guarantee collection rather than payment, the signer is obliged to pay the amount due on the instrument to a person entitled to enforce the instrument in the same circumstances as the accommodated party would be obliged, without prior resort to the accommodated party by the person entitled to enforce the instrument.

(f) An accommodation party who pays the instrument is entitled to reimbursement from the accommodated party and is entitled to enforce the instrument against the accommodated party. In proper circumstances, an accommodation party may obtain relief that requires the accommodated party to perform its obligations on the instrument. An accommodated party that pays the instrument has no right of recourse against, and is not entitled to contribution from, an accommodation party.

As amended in 2002.

Official Comment

1. Section 3–419 replaces former Section 3–415 and 3–416. An accommodation party is a person who signs an instrument to benefit the accommodated party either by signing at the time value is obtained by the accommodated party or later, and who is not a direct beneficiary of the value obtained. An accommodation party

will usually be a co-maker or anomalous indorser. Subsection (a) distinguishes between direct and indirect benefit. For example, if X cosigns a note of Corporation that is given for a loan to Corporation, X is an accommodation party if no part of the loan was paid to X or for X's direct benefit. This is true even though X may receive indirect benefit from the loan because X is employed by Corporation or is a stockholder of Corporation, or even if X is the sole stockholder so long as Corporation and X are recognized as separate entities.

2. It does not matter whether an accommodation party signs gratuitously either at the time the instrument is issued or after the instrument is in the possession of a holder. Subsection (b) of Section 3–419 takes the view stated in Comment 3 to former Section 3–415 that there need be no consideration running to the accommodation party: "The obligation of the accommodation party is supported by any consideration for which the instrument is taken before it is due. Subsection (2) is intended to change occasional decisions holding that there is no sufficient consideration where an accommodation party signs a note after it is in the hands of a holder who has given value. The [accommodation] party is liable to the holder in such a case even though there is no extension of time or other concession."

3. As stated in Comment 1, whether a person is an accommodation party is a question of fact. But it is almost always the case that a co-maker who signs with words of guaranty after the signature is an accommodation party. The same is true of an anomalous indorser. In either case a person taking the instrument is put on notice of the accommodation status of the co-maker or indorser. This is relevant to Section 3–605(e). But, under subsection (c), signing with words of guaranty or as an anomalous indorser also creates a presumption that the signer is an accommodation party. A party challenging accommodation party status would have to rebut this presumption by producing evidence that the signer was in fact a direct beneficiary of the value given for the instrument.

An accommodation party is always a surety. A surety who is not a party to the instrument, however, is not an accommodation party. For example, if M issues a note payable to the order of P, and S signs a separate contract in which S agrees to pay P the amount of the instrument if it is dishonored, S is a surety but is not an accommodation party. In such a case, S's rights and duties are determined under the general law of suretyship. In unusual cases two parties to an instrument may have a surety relationship that is not governed by Article 3 because the requirements of Section 3–419(a) are not met. In those cases the general law of suretyship applies to the relationship. See PEB Commentary No. 11, dated February 10, 1994.

4. Subsection (b) states that an accommodation party is liable on the instrument in the capacity in which the party signed the instrument. In most cases that capacity will be either that of a maker or indorser of a note. But subsection (d) provides a limitation on subsection (b). If the signature of the accommodation party is accompanied by words indicating unambiguously that the party is guaranteeing collection rather than payment of the instrument, liability is limited to that stated in subsection (d), which is based on former Section 3–416(2).

Former Article 3 was confusing because the obligation of a guarantor was covered both in Section 3–415 and in Section 3–416. The latter section suggested that a signature accompanied by words of guaranty created an obligation distinct from that of an accommodation party. Revised Article 3 eliminates that confusion by stating in Section 3–419 the obligation of a person who uses words of guaranty. Portions of former Section 3–416 are preserved. Former Section 3–416(2) is reflected in Section 3–419(d) and former Section 3–416(4) is reflected in Section 3–419(c). Words added to an anomalous indorsement indicating that payment of the instrument is guaranteed by the indorser do not change the liability of the indorser as stated in Section 3–415. This is a change from former Section 3–416(5). See PEB Commentary No. 11, dated February 10, 1994.

5. Subsection (e) like former Section 3–415(5), provides that an accommodation party that pays the instrument is entitled to enforce the instrument against the accommodated party. Since the accommodation party that pays the instrument is entitled to enforce the instrument against the accommodated party, the accommodation party also obtains rights to any security interest or other collateral that secures payment of the instrument. Subsection (e) also provides that an accommodation party that pays the instrument is entitled to reimbursement from the accommodated party. See PEB Commentary No. 11, dated February 10, 1994.

6. In occasional cases, the accommodation party might pay the instrument even though the accommodated party had a defense to its obligation that was available to the accommodation party under Section 3–305(d). In such cases, the accommodation party's right to reimbursement may conflict with the accommodated party's right to raise its defense. For example, suppose the accommodation party pays the instrument without being aware of the defense. In that case the accommodation party should be entitled to reimbursement. Suppose the accommodation party paid the instrument with knowledge of the defense. In that case, to the extent of the defense, reimbursement ordinarily would not be justified, but under some circumstances reimbursement may be justified

depending upon the facts of the case. The resolution of this conflict is left to the general law of suretyship. Section 1–103. See PEB Commentary No. 11, dated February 10, 1994.

7. Section 3–419, along with Section 3–116(a) and (b), Section 3–305(d) and Section 3–605, provides rules governing the rights of accommodation parties. In addition, except to the extent that it is displaced by provisions of this Article, the general law of suretyship also applies to the rights of accommodation parties. Section 1–103. See PEB Commentary No. 11, dated February 10, 1994.

As amended in 1994 and 2002.

§ 3–420. Conversion of Instrument.

(a) The law applicable to conversion of personal property applies to instruments. An instrument is also converted if it is taken by transfer, other than a negotiation, from a person not entitled to enforce the instrument or a bank makes or obtains payment with respect to the instrument for a person not entitled to enforce the instrument or receive payment. An action for conversion of an instrument may not be brought by (i) the issuer or acceptor of the instrument or (ii) a payee or indorsee who did not receive delivery of the instrument either directly or through delivery to an agent or a co-payee.

(b) In an action under subsection (a), the measure of liability is presumed to be the amount payable on the instrument, but recovery may not exceed the amount of the plaintiff's interest in the instrument.

(c) A representative, other than a depositary bank, who has in good faith dealt with an instrument or its proceeds on behalf of one who was not the person entitled to enforce the instrument is not liable in conversion to that person beyond the amount of any proceeds that it has not paid out.

Official Comment

1. Section 3–420 is a modification of former Section 3–419. The first sentence of Section 3–420(a) states a general rule that the law of conversion applicable to personal property also applies to instruments. Paragraphs (a) and (b) of former Section 3–419(1) are deleted as inappropriate in cases of noncash items that may be delivered for acceptance or payment in collection letters that contain varying instructions as to what to do in the event of nonpayment on the day of delivery. It is better to allow such cases to be governed by the general law of conversion that would address the issue of when, under the circumstances prevailing, the presenter's right to possession has been denied. The second sentence of Section 3–420(a) states that an instrument is converted if it is taken by transfer other than a negotiation from a person not entitled to enforce the instrument or taken for collection or payment from a person not entitled to enforce the instrument or receive payment. This covers cases in which a depositary or payor bank takes an instrument bearing a forged indorsement. It also covers cases in which an instrument is payable to two persons and the two persons are not alternative payees, e.g. a check payable to John and Jane Doe. Under Section 3–110(d) the check can be negotiated or enforced only by both persons acting jointly. Thus, neither payee acting without the consent of the other, is a person entitled to enforce the instrument. If John indorses the check and Jane does not, the indorsement is not effective to allow negotiation of the check. If Depositary Bank takes the check for deposit to John's account, Depositary Bank is liable to Jane for conversion of the check if she did not consent to the transaction. John, acting alone, is not the person entitled to enforce the check because John is not the holder of the check. Section 3–110(d) and Comment 4 to Section 3–110. Depositary Bank does not get any greater rights under Section 4–205(1). If it acted for John as its customer, it did not become holder of the check under that provision because John, its customer, was not a holder.

Under former Article 3, the cases were divided on the issue of whether the drawer of a check with a forged indorsement can assert rights against a depositary bank that took the check. The last sentence of Section 3–420(a) resolves the conflict by following the rule stated in *Stone & Webster Engineering Corp. v. First National Bank & Trust Co.*, 184 N.E.2d 358 (Mass. 1962). There is no reason why a drawer should have an action in conversion. The check represents an obligation of the drawer rather than property of the drawer. The drawer has an adequate remedy against the payor bank for recredit of the drawer's account for unauthorized payment of the check.

There was also a split of authority under former Article 3 on the issue of whether a payee who never received the instrument is a proper plaintiff in a conversion action. The typical case was one in which a check was stolen from the drawer or in which the check was mailed to an address different from that of the payee and was stolen after it arrived at that address. The thief forged the indorsement of the payee and obtained payment by depositing the check to an account in a depositary bank. The issue was whether the payee could bring an action in conversion against the depositary bank or the drawee bank. In revised Article 3, under the last sentence of Section 3–420(a), the payee has no conversion action because the check was never delivered to the payee. Until delivery, the payee does not have any interest in the check. The payee never became the holder of the check nor a person entitled to enforce the check. Section 3–301. Nor is the payee injured by the fraud. Normally the drawer of a check intends to pay an obligation owed to the payee. But if the check is never delivered to the payee, the obligation owed to the payee is not affected. If the check falls into the hands of a thief who obtains payment after forging the signature of the payee as an indorsement, the obligation owed to the payee continues to exist after the thief receives payment. Since the payee's right to enforce the underlying obligation is unaffected by the fraud of the thief, there is no reason to give any additional remedy to the payee. The drawer of the check has no conversion remedy, but the drawee is not entitled to charge the drawer's account when the drawee wrongfully honored the check. The remedy of the drawee is against the depositary bank for breach of warranty under Section 3–417(a)(1) or 4–208(a)(1). The loss will fall on the person who gave value to the thief for the check.

The situation is different if the check is delivered to the payee. If the check is taken for an obligation owed to the payee, the last sentence of Section 3–310(b)(4) provides that the obligation may not be enforced to the extent of the amount of the check. The payee's rights are restricted to enforcement of the payee's rights in the instrument. In this event the payee is injured by the theft and has a cause of action for conversion.

The payee receives delivery when the check comes into the payee's possession, as for example when it is put into the payee's mailbox. Delivery to an agent is delivery to the payee. If a check is payable to more than one payee, delivery to one of the payees is deemed to be delivery to all of the payees. Occasionally, the person asserting a conversion cause of action is an indorsee rather than the original payee. If the check is stolen before the check can be delivered to the indorsee and the indorsee's indorsement is forged, the analysis is similar. For example, a check is payable to the order of A. A indorses it to B and puts it into an envelope addressed to B. The envelope is never delivered to B. Rather, Thief steals the envelope, forges B's indorsement to the check and obtains payment. Because the check was never delivered to B, the indorsee, B has no cause of action for conversion, but A does have such an action. A is the owner of the check. B never obtained rights in the check. If A intended to negotiate the check to B in payment of an obligation, that obligation was not affected by the conduct of Thief. B can enforce that obligation. Thief stole A's property not B's.

2. Subsection (2) of former Section 3–419 is amended because it is not clear why the former law distinguished between the liability of the drawee and that of other converters. Why should there be a conclusive presumption that the liability is face amount if a drawee refuses to pay or return an instrument or makes payment on a forged indorsement, while the liability of a maker who does the same thing is only presumed to be the face amount? Moreover, it was not clear under former Section 3–419(2) what face amount meant. If a note for $10,000 is payable in a year at 10% interest, it is common to refer to $10,000 as the face amount, but if the note is converted the loss to the owner also includes the loss of interest. In revised Article 3, Section 3–420(b), by referring to "amount payable on the instrument," allows the full amount due under the instrument to be recovered.

The "but" clause in subsection (b) addresses the problem of conversion actions in multiple payee checks. Section 3–110(d) states that an instrument cannot be enforced unless all payees join in the action. But an action for conversion might be brought by a payee having no interest or a limited interest in the proceeds of the check. This clause prevents such a plaintiff from receiving a windfall. An example is a check payable to a building contractor and a supplier of building material. The check is not payable to the payees alternatively. Section 3–110(d). The check is delivered to the contractor by the owner of the building. Suppose the contractor forges supplier's signature as an indorsement of the check and receives the entire proceeds of the check. The supplier should not, without qualification, be able to recover the entire amount of the check from the bank that converted the check. Depending upon the contract between the contractor and the supplier, the amount of the check may be due entirely to the contractor, in which case there should be no recovery, entirely to the supplier, in which case recovery should be for the entire amount, or part may be due to one and the rest to the other, in which case recovery should be limited to the amount due to the supplier.

3. Subsection (3) of former Section 3–419 drew criticism from the courts, that saw no reason why a depositary bank should have the defense stated in the subsection. See *Knesz v. Central Jersey Bank & Trust Co.*, 477 A.2d 806 (N.J. 1984). The depositary bank is ultimately liable in the case of a forged indorsement check because of its warranty to the payor bank under Section 4–208(a)(1) and it is usually the most convenient defendant in cases involving multiple checks drawn on different banks. There is no basis for requiring the owner of the check to bring multiple actions against the various payor banks and to require those banks to assert warranty rights against the depositary bank. In revised Article 3, the defense provided by Section 3–420(c) is limited to collecting banks other than the depositary bank. If suit is brought against both the payor bank and the depositary bank, the owner, of course, is entitled to but one recovery.

PART 5

DISHONOR

§ 3–501. Presentment.

(a) "Presentment" means a demand made by or on behalf of a person entitled to enforce an instrument (i) to pay the instrument made to the drawee or a party obliged to pay the instrument or, in the case of a note or accepted draft payable at a bank, to the bank, or (ii) to accept a draft made to the drawee.

(b) The following rules are subject to Article 4, agreement of the parties, and clearing-house rules and the like:

(1) Presentment may be made at the place of payment of the instrument and must be made at the place of payment if the instrument is payable at a bank in the United States; may be made by any commercially reasonable means, including an oral, written, or electronic communication; is effective when the demand for payment or acceptance is received by the person to whom presentment is made; and is effective if made to any one of two or more makers, acceptors, drawees, or other payors.

(2) Upon demand of the person to whom presentment is made, the person making presentment must (i) exhibit the instrument, (ii) give reasonable identification and, if presentment is made on behalf of another person, reasonable evidence of authority to do so, and (iii) sign a receipt on the instrument for any payment made or surrender the instrument if full payment is made.

(3) Without dishonoring the instrument, the party to whom presentment is made may (i) return the instrument for lack of a necessary indorsement, or (ii) refuse payment or acceptance for failure of the presentment to comply with the terms of the instrument, an agreement of the parties, or other applicable law or rule.

(4) The party to whom presentment is made may treat presentment as occurring on the next business day after the day of presentment if the party to whom presentment is made has established a cut-off hour not earlier than 2 p.m. for the receipt and processing of instruments presented for payment or acceptance and presentment is made after the cut-off hour.

Official Comment

Subsection (a) defines presentment. Subsection (b)(1) states the place and manner of presentment. Electronic presentment is authorized. The communication of the demand for payment or acceptance is effective when received. Subsection (b)(2) restates former Section 3–505. Subsection (b)(2)(i) allows the person to whom presentment is made to require exhibition of the instrument, unless the parties have agreed otherwise as in an electronic presentment agreement. Former Section 3–507(3) is the antecedent of subsection (b)(3)(i). Since a payor must decide whether to pay or accept on the day of presentment, subsection (b)(4) allows the payor to set a cut-off hour for receipt of instruments presented.

§ 3–502. Dishonor.

(a) Dishonor of a note is governed by the following rules:

(1) If the note is payable on demand, the note is dishonored if presentment is duly made to the maker and the note is not paid on the day of presentment.

(2) If the note is not payable on demand and is payable at or through a bank or the terms of the note require presentment, the note is dishonored if presentment is duly made and the note is not paid on the day it becomes payable or the day of presentment, whichever is later.

(3) If the note is not payable on demand and paragraph (2) does not apply, the note is dishonored if it is not paid on the day it becomes payable.

(b) Dishonor of an unaccepted draft other than a documentary draft is governed by the following rules:

(1) If a check is duly presented for payment to the payor bank otherwise than for immediate payment over the counter, the check is dishonored if the payor bank makes timely return of the check or sends timely notice of dishonor or nonpayment under Section 4-301 or 4-302, or becomes accountable for the amount of the check under Section 4-302.

(2) If a draft is payable on demand and paragraph (1) does not apply, the draft is dishonored if presentment for payment is duly made to the drawee and the draft is not paid on the day of presentment.

(3) If a draft is payable on a date stated in the draft, the draft is dishonored if (i) presentment for payment is duly made to the drawee and payment is not made on the day the draft becomes payable or the day of presentment, whichever is later, or (ii) presentment for acceptance is duly made before the day the draft becomes payable and the draft is not accepted on the day of presentment.

(4) If a draft is payable on elapse of a period of time after sight or acceptance, the draft is dishonored if presentment for acceptance is duly made and the draft is not accepted on the day of presentment.

(c) Dishonor of an unaccepted documentary draft occurs according to the rules stated in subsection (b)(2), (3), and (4), except that payment or acceptance may be delayed without dishonor until no later than the close of the third business day of the drawee following the day on which payment or acceptance is required by those paragraphs.

(d) Dishonor of an accepted draft is governed by the following rules:

(1) If the draft is payable on demand, the draft is dishonored if presentment for payment is duly made to the acceptor and the draft is not paid on the day of presentment.

(2) If the draft is not payable on demand, the draft is dishonored if presentment for payment is duly made to the acceptor and payment is not made on the day it becomes payable or the day of presentment, whichever is later.

(e) In any case in which presentment is otherwise required for dishonor under this section and presentment is excused under Section 3-504, dishonor occurs without presentment if the instrument is not duly accepted or paid.

(f) If a draft is dishonored because timely acceptance of the draft was not made and the person entitled to demand acceptance consents to a late acceptance, from the time of acceptance the draft is treated as never having been dishonored.

Official Comment

1. Section 3-415 provides that an indorser is obliged to pay an instrument if the instrument is dishonored and is discharged if the indorser is entitled to notice of dishonor and notice is not given. Under Section 3-414, the drawer is obliged to pay an unaccepted draft if it is dishonored. The drawer, however, is not entitled to notice of dishonor except to the extent required in a case governed by Section 3-414(d). Part 5 tells when an instrument is dishonored (Section 3-502) and what it means to give notice of dishonor (Section 3-503). Often dishonor does not occur until presentment (Section 3-501), and frequently presentment and notice of dishonor are excused (Section 3-504).

2. In the great majority of cases presentment and notice of dishonor are waived with respect to notes. In most cases a formal demand for payment to the maker of the note is not contemplated. Rather, the maker is expected to send payment to the holder of the note on the date or dates on which payment is due. If payment is not made when due, the holder usually makes a demand for payment, but in the normal case in which presentment is waived, demand is irrelevant and the holder can proceed against indorsers when payment is not received. Under former Article 3, in the small minority of cases in which presentment and dishonor were not waived with respect to notes, the indorser was discharged from liability (former Section 3-502(1)(a)) unless the holder made presentment to the maker on the exact day the note was due (former Section 3-503(1)(c)) and gave notice of dishonor to the indorser before midnight of the third business day after dishonor (former Section 3-508(2)). These provisions are omitted from Revised Article 3 as inconsistent with practice which seldom involves face-to-face dealings.

3. Subsection (a) applies to notes. Subsection (a)(1) applies to notes payable on demand. Dishonor requires presentment, and dishonor occurs if payment is not made on the day of presentment. There is no change from previous Article 3. Subsection (a)(2) applies to notes payable at a definite time if the note is payable at or through a bank or, by its terms, presentment is required. Dishonor requires presentment, and dishonor occurs if payment is not made on the due date or the day of presentment if presentment is made after the due date. Subsection (a)(3) applies to all other notes. If the note is not paid on its due date it is dishonored. This allows holders to collect notes in ways that make sense commercially without having to be concerned about a formal presentment on a given day.

4. Subsection (b) applies to unaccepted drafts other than documentary drafts. Subsection (b)(1) applies to checks. Except for checks presented for immediate payment over the counter, which are covered by subsection (b)(2), dishonor occurs according to rules stated in Article 4. Those rules contemplate four separate situations that warrant discussion. The first two situations arise in the normal course of affairs, in which the drawee bank makes settlement for the amount of the check to the presenting bank. In the first situation, the drawee bank under Section 4–301 recovers this settlement if it returns the check by its midnight deadline (Section 4–104). In that case the check is not paid and dishonor occurs under Section 3–502(b)(1). The second situation arises if the drawee bank has made such a settlement and does not return the check or give notice of dishonor or nonpayment within the midnight deadline. In that case, the settlement becomes final payment of the check under Section 4–215. Because the drawee bank already has paid such an item, it cannot be "accountable" for the item under the terms of Section 4–302(a)(1). Thus, no dishonor occurs regardless of whether the drawee bank retains the check indefinitely or for some reason returns the check after its midnight deadline.

The third and fourth situations arise less commonly, in cases in which the drawee bank does not settle for the check when it is received. Under Section 4–302 if the drawee bank is not also the depositary bank and retains the check without settling for it beyond midnight of the day it is presented for payment, the bank at that point becomes "accountable" for the amount of the check, i.e., it is obliged to pay the amount of the check. If the drawee bank is also the depositary bank, the bank becomes accountable for the amount of the check if the bank does not pay the check or return it or send notice of dishonor by its midnight deadline. Hence, if the drawee bank is also the depositary bank and does not either settle for the check when it is received (a settlement that would ripen into final payment if the drawee bank failed to take action to recover the settlement by its midnight deadline) or return the check or an appropriate notice by its midnight deadline, the drawee bank will become accountable for the amount of the check under Section 4–302. Thus, in all cases in which the drawee bank becomes accountable under Section 4–302, the check has not been paid (either by a settlement that became unrecoverable or otherwise) and thus, under Section 3–502(b)(1), the check is dishonored.

The fact that a bank that is accountable for the amount of the check under Section 4–302 is obliged to pay the check does not mean that the check has been paid. Indeed, because each of the paragraphs of Section 4–302(b) is limited by its terms to situations in which a bank has not paid the item, a drawee bank will be accountable under Section 4–302 only in situations in which it has not previously paid the check. Section 3–502(b)(1) reflects the view that a person presenting a check is entitled to payment, not just the ability to hold the drawee accountable under Section 4–302. If that payment is not made in a timely manner, the check is dishonored.

Regulation CC Section 229.36(d) provides that settlement between banks for the forward collection of checks is final. The relationship of that section to Articles 3 and 4 is discussed in the Commentary to that section.

Subsection (b)(2) applies to demand drafts other than those governed by subsection (b)(1). It covers checks presented for immediate payment over the counter and demand drafts other than checks. Dishonor occurs if presentment for payment is made and payment is not made on the day of presentment.

Subsection (b)(3) and (4) applies to time drafts. An unaccepted time draft differs from a time note. The maker of a note knows that the note has been issued, but the drawee of a draft may not know that a draft has been drawn on it. Thus, with respect to drafts, presentment for payment or acceptance is required. Subsection (b)(3) applies to drafts payable on a date stated in the draft. Dishonor occurs if presentment for payment is made and payment is not made on the day the draft becomes payable or the day of presentment if presentment is made after the due date. The holder of an unaccepted draft payable on a stated date has the option of presenting the draft for acceptance before the day the draft becomes payable to establish whether the drawee is willing to assume liability by accepting. Under subsection (b)(3)(ii) dishonor occurs when the draft is presented and not accepted. Subsection (b)(4) applies to unaccepted drafts payable on elapse of a period of time after sight or acceptance. If the draft is payable 30 days after sight, the draft must be presented for acceptance to start the running of the 30-day period. Dishonor occurs if it is not accepted. The rules in subsection (b)(3) and (4) follow former Section 3–501(1)(a).

5. Subsection (c) gives drawees an extended period to pay documentary drafts because of the time that may be needed to examine the documents. The period prescribed is that given by Section 5–112 in cases in which a letter of credit is involved.

6. Subsection (d) governs accepted drafts. If the acceptor's obligation is to pay on demand the rule, stated in subsection (d)(1), is the same as for that of a demand note stated in subsection (a)(1). If the acceptor's obligation is to pay at a definite time the rule, stated in subsection (d)(2), is the same as that of a time note payable at a bank stated in subsection (b)(2).

7. Subsection (e) is a limitation on subsection (a)(1) and (2), subsection (b), subsection (c), and subsection (d). Each of those provisions states dishonor as occurring after presentment. If presentment is excused under Section 3–504, dishonor occurs under those provisions without presentment if the instrument is not duly accepted or paid.

8. Under subsection (b)(3)(ii) and (4) if a draft is presented for acceptance and the draft is not accepted on the day of presentment, there is dishonor. But after dishonor, the holder may consent to late acceptance. In that case, under subsection (f), the late acceptance cures the dishonor. The draft is treated as never having been dishonored. If the draft is subsequently presented for payment and payment is refused dishonor occurs at that time.

As amended in 2002.

§ 3–503. Notice of Dishonor.

(a) The obligation of an indorser stated in Section 3–415(a) and the obligation of a drawer stated in Section 3–414(d) may not be enforced unless (i) the indorser or drawer is given notice of dishonor of the instrument complying with this section or (ii) notice of dishonor is excused under Section 3–504(b).

(b) Notice of dishonor may be given by any person; may be given by any commercially reasonable means, including an oral, written, or electronic communication; and is sufficient if it reasonably identifies the instrument and indicates that the instrument has been dishonored or has not been paid or accepted. Return of an instrument given to a bank for collection is sufficient notice of dishonor.

(c) Subject to Section 3–504(c), with respect to an instrument taken for collection by a collecting bank, notice of dishonor must be given (i) by the bank before midnight of the next banking day following the banking day on which the bank receives notice of dishonor of the instrument, or (ii) by any other person within 30 days following the day on which the person receives notice of dishonor. With respect to any other instrument, notice of dishonor must be given within 30 days following the day on which dishonor occurs.

Official Comment

1. Subsection (a) is consistent with former Section 3–501(2)(a), but notice of dishonor is no longer relevant to the liability of a drawer except for the case of a draft accepted by an acceptor other than a bank. Comments 2 and 4 to Section 3–414. There is no reason why drawers should be discharged on instruments they draw until payment or acceptance. They are entitled to have the instrument presented to the drawee and dishonored (Section 3–414(b)) before they are liable to pay, but no notice of dishonor need be made to them as a condition of liability. Subsection (b), which states how notice of dishonor is given, is based on former Section 3–508(3).

2. Subsection (c) replaces former Section 3–508(2). It differs from that section in that it provides a 30-day period for a person other than a collecting bank to give notice of dishonor rather than the three-day period allowed in former Article 3. Delay in giving notice of dishonor may be excused under Section 3–504(c).

§ 3–504. Excused Presentment and Notice of Dishonor.

(a) Presentment for payment or acceptance of an instrument is excused if (i) the person entitled to present the instrument cannot with reasonable diligence make presentment, (ii) the maker or acceptor has repudiated an obligation to pay the instrument or is dead or in insolvency proceedings, (iii) by the terms of the instrument presentment is not necessary to enforce the obligation of indorsers or the drawer, (iv) the drawer or indorser whose obligation is being enforced has waived presentment or otherwise has no reason to expect or right to require that the instrument be paid or accepted, or (v) the drawer instructed the drawee not to pay or accept the draft or the drawee was not obligated to the drawer to pay the draft.

(b) Notice of dishonor is excused if (i) by the terms of the instrument notice of dishonor is not necessary to enforce the obligation of a party to pay the instrument, or (ii) the party whose obligation is being enforced waived notice of dishonor. A waiver of presentment is also a waiver of notice of dishonor.

(c) Delay in giving notice of dishonor is excused if the delay was caused by circumstances beyond the control of the person giving the notice and the person giving the notice exercised reasonable diligence after the cause of the delay ceased to operate.

Official Comment

Section 3-504 is largely a restatement of former Section 3-511. Subsection (4) of former Section 3-511 is replaced by Section 3-502(f).

§ 3-505. Evidence of Dishonor.

(a) The following are admissible as evidence and create a presumption of dishonor and of any notice of dishonor stated:

(1) a document regular in form as provided in subsection (b) which purports to be a protest;

(2) a purported stamp or writing of the drawee, payor bank, or presenting bank on or accompanying the instrument stating that acceptance or payment has been refused unless reasons for the refusal are stated and the reasons are not consistent with dishonor;

(3) a book or record of the drawee, payor bank, or collecting bank, kept in the usual course of business which shows dishonor, even if there is no evidence of who made the entry.

(b) A protest is a certificate of dishonor made by a United States consul or vice consul, or a notary public or other person authorized to administer oaths by the law of the place where dishonor occurs. It may be made upon information satisfactory to that person. The protest must identify the instrument and certify either that presentment has been made or, if not made, the reason why it was not made, and that the instrument has been dishonored by nonacceptance or nonpayment. The protest may also certify that notice of dishonor has been given to some or all parties.

Official Comment

Protest is no longer mandatory and must be requested by the holder. Even if requested, protest is not a condition to the liability of indorsers or drawers. Protest is a service provided by the banking system to establish that dishonor has occurred. Like other services provided by the banking system, it will be available if market incentives, inter-bank agreements, or governmental regulations require it, but liabilities of parties no longer rest on it. Protest may be a requirement for liability on international drafts governed by foreign law which this Article cannot affect.

PART 6

DISCHARGE AND PAYMENT

§ 3-601. Discharge and Effect of Discharge.

(a) The obligation of a party to pay the instrument is discharged as stated in this Article or by an act or agreement with the party which would discharge an obligation to pay money under a simple contract.

(b) Discharge of the obligation of a party is not effective against a person acquiring rights of a holder in due course of the instrument without notice of the discharge.

Official Comment

Subsection (a) replaces subsections (1) and (2) of former Section 3-601. Subsection (b) restates former Section 3-602. Notice of discharge is not treated as notice of a defense that prevents holder in due course status. Section 3-302(b). Discharge is effective against a holder in due course only if the holder had notice of the discharge when holder in due course status was acquired. For example, if an instrument bearing a canceled indorsement is taken by a holder, the holder has notice that the indorser has been discharged. Thus, the discharge is effective against the holder even if the holder is a holder in due course.

§ 3–602. Payment.

(a) Subject to subsection (e), an instrument is paid to the extent payment is made by or on behalf of a party obliged to pay the instrument, and to a person entitled to enforce the instrument.

(b) Subject to subsection (e), a note is paid to the extent payment is made by or on behalf of a party obliged to pay the note to a person that formerly was entitled to enforce the note only if at the time of the payment the party obliged to pay has not received adequate notification that the note has been transferred and that payment is to be made to the transferee. A notification is adequate only if it is signed by the transferor or the transferee; reasonably identifies the transferred note; and provides an address at which payments subsequently are to be made. Upon request, a transferee shall seasonably furnish reasonable proof that the note has been transferred. Unless the transferee complies with the request, a payment to the person that formerly was entitled to enforce the note is effective for purposes of subsection (c) even if the party obliged to pay the note has received a notification under this paragraph.

(c) Subject to subsection (e), to the extent of a payment under subsections (a) and (b), the obligation of the party obliged to pay the instrument is discharged even though payment is made with knowledge of a claim to the instrument under Section 3–306 by another person.

(d) Subject to subsection (e), a transferee, or any party that has acquired rights in the instrument directly or indirectly from a transferee, including any such party that has rights as a holder in due course, is deemed to have notice of any payment that is made under subsection (b) after the date that the note is transferred to the transferee but before the party obliged to pay the note receives adequate notification of the transfer.

(e) The obligation of a party to pay the instrument is not discharged under subsections (a) through (d) if:

(1) a claim to the instrument under Section 3–306 is enforceable against the party receiving payment and (i) payment is made with knowledge by the payor that payment is prohibited by injunction or similar process of a court of competent jurisdiction, or (ii) in the case of an instrument other than a cashier's check, teller's check, or certified check, the party making payment accepted, from the person having a claim to the instrument, indemnity against loss resulting from refusal to pay the person entitled to enforce the instrument; or

(2) the person making payment knows that the instrument is a stolen instrument and pays a person it knows is in wrongful possession of the instrument.

(f) As used in this section, "signed," with respect to a record that is not a writing, includes the attachment to or logical association with the record of an electronic symbol, sound, or process with the present intent to adopt or accept the record.

As amended in 2002.

Official Comment

1. This section replaces former Section 3–603(1). The phrase "claim to the instrument" in subsection (a) means, by reference to Section 3–306, a claim of ownership or possession and not a claim in recoupment. Subsection (e)(1)(ii) is added to conform to Section 3–411. Section 3–411 is intended to discourage an obligated bank from refusing payment of a cashier's check, certified check or dishonored teller's check at the request of a claimant to the check who provided the bank with indemnity against loss. See Comment 1 to Section 3–411. An obligated bank that refuses payment under those circumstances not only remains liable on the check but may also be liable to the holder of the check for consequential damages. Section 3–602(e)(1)(ii) and Section 3–411, read together, change the rule of former Section 3–603(1) with respect to the obligation of the obligated bank on the check. Payment to the holder of a cashier's check, teller's check, or certified check discharges the obligation of the obligated bank on the check to both the holder and the claimant even though indemnity has been given by the person asserting the claim. If the obligated bank pays the check in violation of an agreement with the claimant in connection with the indemnity agreement, any liability that the bank may have for violation of the agreement is not governed by Article 3, but is left to other law. This section continues the rule that the obligor is not discharged on the instrument if payment is made in violation of an injunction against payment. See Section 3–411(c)(iv).

2. Subsection (a) covers payments made in a traditional manner, to the person entitled to enforce the instrument. Subsection (b), which provides an alternative method of payment, deals with the situation in which a

person entitled to enforce the instrument transfers the instrument without giving notice to parties obligated to pay the instrument. If that happens and one of those parties subsequently makes a payment to the transferor, the payment is effective even though it is not made to the person entitled to enforce the instrument. Unlike the earlier version of Section 3–602, this rule is consistent with Section 9–406(a), Restatement of Mortgages § 5.5, and Restatement of Contracts § 338(1).

3. In determining the party to whom a payment is made for purposes of this section, courts should look to traditional rules of agency. Thus, if the original payee of a note transfers ownership of the note to a third party but continues to service the obligation, the law of agency might treat payments made to the original payee as payments made to the third party.

4. Subsection (d) assures that the discharge provided by subsection (c) is effective against the transferee and those whose rights derive from the transferee. By deeming those persons to have notice of any payment made under subsection (b), subsection (d) gives those persons "notice of the discharge" within the meaning of Section 3–302(b). Accordingly, the discharge is effective against those persons, even if any of them has the rights of a holder in due course. Compare Section 3–601(b). The deemed notice provided by subsection (d) does not, however, prevent a person from becoming or acquiring the rights of, a holder in due course. See Section 3–302(b). Thus, such a person does not become subject to other defenses described in Section 3–305(a)(2), claims in recoupment described in Section 3–305(a)(3), or claims to the instrument under Section 3–306. A transferee can prevent payment to the transferor from discharging the obligation on the note by assuring that each person who is obligated on the note receives adequate notification pursuant to subsection (b) prior to making a payment.

As amended in 2002 and 2003.

§ 3–603. Tender of Payment.

(a) If tender of payment of an obligation to pay an instrument is made to a person entitled to enforce the instrument, the effect of tender is governed by principles of law applicable to tender of payment under a simple contract.

(b) If tender of payment of an obligation to pay an instrument is made to a person entitled to enforce the instrument and the tender is refused, there is discharge, to the extent of the amount of the tender, of the obligation of an indorser or accommodation party having a right of recourse with respect to the obligation to which the tender relates.

(c) If tender of payment of an amount due on an instrument is made to a person entitled to enforce the instrument, the obligation of the obligor to pay interest after the due date on the amount tendered is discharged. If presentment is required with respect to an instrument and the obligor is able and ready to pay on the due date at every place of payment stated in the instrument, the obligor is deemed to have made tender of payment on the due date to the person entitled to enforce the instrument.

Official Comment

Section 3–603 replaces former Section 3–604. Subsection (a) generally incorporates the law of tender of payment applicable to simple contracts. Subsections (b) and (c) state particular rules. Subsection (b) replaces former Section 3–604(2). Under subsection (b) refusal of a tender of payment discharges any indorser or accommodation party having a right of recourse against the party making the tender. Subsection (c) replaces former Section 3–604(1) and (3).

§ 3–604. Discharge by Cancellation or Renunciation.

(a) A person entitled to enforce an instrument, with or without consideration, may discharge the obligation of a party to pay the instrument (i) by an intentional voluntary act, such as surrender of the instrument to the party, destruction, mutilation, or cancellation of the instrument, cancellation or striking out of the party's signature, or the addition of words to the instrument indicating discharge, or (ii) by agreeing not to sue or otherwise renouncing rights against the party by a signed record.

(b) Cancellation or striking out of an indorsement pursuant to subsection (a) does not affect the status and rights of a party derived from the indorsement.

(c) In this section, "signed," with respect to a record that is not a writing, includes the attachment to or logical association with the record of an electronic symbol, sound, or process with the present intent to adopt or accept the record.

As amended in 2002.

Official Comment

Section 3–604 replaces former Section 3–605.

§ 3–605. Discharge of Secondary Obligors.

(a) If a person entitled to enforce an instrument releases the obligation of a principal obligor in whole or in part, and another party to the instrument is a secondary obligor with respect to the obligation of that principal obligor, the following rules apply:

(1) Any obligations of the principal obligor to the secondary obligor with respect to any previous payment by the secondary obligor are not affected. Unless the terms of the release preserve the secondary obligor's recourse, the principal obligor is discharged, to the extent of the release, from any other duties to the secondary obligor under this article.

(2) Unless the terms of the release provide that the person entitled to enforce the instrument retains the right to enforce the instrument against the secondary obligor, the secondary obligor is discharged to the same extent as the principal obligor from any unperformed portion of its obligation on the instrument. If the instrument is a check and the obligation of the secondary obligor is based on an indorsement of the check, the secondary obligor is discharged without regard to the language or circumstances of the discharge or other release.

(3) If the secondary obligor is not discharged under paragraph (2), the secondary obligor is discharged to the extent of the value of the consideration for the release, and to the extent that the release would otherwise cause the secondary obligor a loss.

(b) If a person entitled to enforce an instrument grants a principal obligor an extension of the time at which one or more payments are due on the instrument and another party to the instrument is a secondary obligor with respect to the obligation of that principal obligor, the following rules apply:

(1) Any obligations of the principal obligor to the secondary obligor with respect to any previous payment by the secondary obligor are not affected. Unless the terms of the extension preserve the secondary obligor's recourse, the extension correspondingly extends the time for performance of any other duties owed to the secondary obligor by the principal obligor under this article.

(2) The secondary obligor is discharged to the extent that the extension would otherwise cause the secondary obligor a loss.

(3) To the extent that the secondary obligor is not discharged under paragraph (2), the secondary obligor may perform its obligations to a person entitled to enforce the instrument as if the time for payment had not been extended or, unless the terms of the extension provide that the person entitled to enforce the instrument retains the right to enforce the instrument against the secondary obligor as if the time for payment had not been extended, treat the time for performance of its obligations as having been extended correspondingly.

(c) If a person entitled to enforce an instrument agrees, with or without consideration, to a modification of the obligation of a principal obligor other than a complete or partial release or an extension of the due date and another party to the instrument is a secondary obligor with respect to the obligation of that principal obligor, the following rules apply:

(1) Any obligations of the principal obligor to the secondary obligor with respect to any previous payment by the secondary obligor are not affected. The modification correspondingly modifies any other duties owed to the secondary obligor by the principal obligor under this article.

(2) The secondary obligor is discharged from any unperformed portion of its obligation to the extent that the modification would otherwise cause the secondary obligor a loss.

(3) To the extent that the secondary obligor is not discharged under paragraph (2), the secondary obligor may satisfy its obligation on the instrument as if the modification had not occurred, or treat its obligation on the instrument as having been modified correspondingly.

(d) If the obligation of a principal obligor is secured by an interest in collateral, another party to the instrument is a secondary obligor with respect to that obligation, and a person entitled to enforce the instrument impairs the value of the interest in collateral, the obligation of the secondary obligor is discharged to the extent of the impairment. The value of an interest in collateral is impaired to the extent the value of the interest is reduced to an amount less than the amount of the recourse of the secondary obligor, or the reduction in value of the interest causes an increase in the amount by which the amount of the recourse exceeds the value of the interest. For purposes of this subsection, impairing the value of an interest in collateral includes failure to obtain or maintain perfection or recordation of the interest in collateral, release of collateral without substitution of collateral of equal value or equivalent reduction of the underlying obligation, failure to perform a duty to preserve the value of collateral owed, under Article 9 or other law, to a debtor or other person secondarily liable, and failure to comply with applicable law in disposing of or otherwise enforcing the interest in collateral.

(e) A secondary obligor is not discharged under subsections (a)(3), (b), (c), or (d) unless the person entitled to enforce the instrument knows that the person is a secondary obligor or has notice under Section 3-419(c) that the instrument was signed for accommodation.

(f) A secondary obligor is not discharged under this section if the secondary obligor consents to the event or conduct that is the basis of the discharge, or the instrument or a separate agreement of the party provides for waiver of discharge under this section specifically or by general language indicating that parties waive defenses based on suretyship or impairment of collateral. Unless the circumstances indicate otherwise, consent by the principal obligor to an act that would lead to a discharge under this section constitutes consent to that act by the secondary obligor if the secondary obligor controls the principal obligor or deals with the person entitled to enforce the instrument on behalf of the principal obligor.

(g) A release or extension preserves a secondary obligor's recourse if the terms of the release or extension provide that:

(1) the person entitled to enforce the instrument retains the right to enforce the instrument against the secondary obligor; and

(2) the recourse of the secondary obligor continues as if the release or extension had not been granted.

(h) Except as otherwise provided in subsection (i), a secondary obligor asserting discharge under this section has the burden of persuasion both with respect to the occurrence of the acts alleged to harm the secondary obligor and loss or prejudice caused by those acts.

(i) If the secondary obligor demonstrates prejudice caused by an impairment of its recourse, and the circumstances of the case indicate that the amount of loss is not reasonably susceptible of calculation or requires proof of facts that are not ascertainable, it is presumed that the act impairing recourse caused a loss or impairment equal to the liability of the secondary obligor on the instrument. In that event, the burden of persuasion as to any lesser amount of the loss is on the person entitled to enforce the instrument.

As amended in 2002.

Official Comment

1. This section contains rules that are applicable when a secondary obligor (as defined in Section 3-103(a)(17)) is a party to an instrument. These rules essentially parallel modern interpretations of the law of suretyship and guaranty that apply when a secondary obligor is not a party to an instrument. See generally Restatement of the Law, Third, Suretyship and Guaranty (1996). Of course, the rules in this section do not resolve all possible issues concerning the rights and duties of the parties. In the event that a situation is presented that is not resolved by this section (or the other related sections of this Article), the resolution may be provided by the general law of suretyship because, pursuant to Section 1-103, that law is applicable unless displaced by provisions of this Act.

2. Like the law of suretyship and guaranty, Section 3-605 provides secondary obligors with defenses that are not available to other parties to instruments. The general operation of Section 3-605, and its relationship to the law of suretyship and guaranty, can be illustrated by an example. Bank agrees to lend $10,000 to Borrower,

but only if Backer also is liable for repayment of the loan. The parties could consummate that transaction in three different ways. First, if Borrower and Backer incurred those obligations with contracts not governed by this Article (such as a note that is not an instrument for purposes of this Article), the general law of suretyship and guaranty would be applicable. Under modern nomenclature, Bank is the "obligee," Borrower is the "principal obligor," and Backer is the "secondary obligor." See Restatement of Suretyship and Guaranty § 1. Then assume that Bank and Borrower agree to a modification of their rights and obligations after the note is signed. For example, they might agree that Borrower may repay the loan at some date after the due date, or that Borrower may discharge its repayment obligation by paying Bank $3,000 rather than $10,000. Alternatively, suppose that Bank releases collateral that Borrower has given to secure the loan. Under the law of suretyship and guaranty, the secondary obligor may be discharged under certain circumstances if these modifications of the obligations between Bank (the obligee) and Borrower (the principal obligor) are made without the consent of Backer (the secondary obligor). The rights that the secondary obligor has to a discharge of its liability in such cases commonly are referred to as suretyship defenses. The extent of the discharge depends upon the particular circumstances. See Restatement of Suretyship and Guaranty §§ 37, 39–44.

A second possibility is that the parties might decide to evidence the loan by a negotiable instrument. In that scenario, Borrower signs a note under which Borrower is obliged to pay $10,000 to the order of Bank on a due date stated in the note. Backer becomes liable for the repayment obligation by signing the note as a co-maker or indorser. In either case the note is signed for accommodation, Backer is an accommodation party, and Borrower is the accommodated party. See Section 3–419 (describing the obligations of accommodation parties). For purposes of Section 3–605, Backer is also a "secondary obligor" and Borrower is a "principal obligor," as those terms are defined in Section 3–103. Because Backer is a party to the instrument, its rights to a discharge based on any modification of obligations between Bank and Borrower are governed by Section 3–605 rather than by the general law of suretyship and guaranty. Within Section 3–605, subsection (a) describes the consequences of a release of Borrower, subsection (b) describes the consequences of an extension of time, and subsection (c) describes the consequences of other modifications.

The third possibility is that Borrower would use an instrument governed by this Article to evidence its repayment obligation, but Backer's obligation would be created in some way other than by becoming party to that instrument. In that case, Backer's rights are determined by suretyship and guaranty law rather than by this Article. See Comment 3 to Section 3–419.

A person also can acquire secondary liability without having been a secondary obligor at the time that the principal obligation was created. For example, a transferee of real or personal property that assumes the obligation of the transferor as maker of a note secured by the property becomes by operation of law a principal obligor, with the transferor becoming a secondary obligor. Restatement of Suretyship and Guaranty § 2(e); Restatement of Mortgages § 5.1. Article 3 does not determine the effect of the release of the transferee in that case because the assuming transferee is not a "party" to the instrument as defined in Section 3–103(a)(10). Section 3–605(a) does not apply then because the holder has not discharged the obligation of a "principal obligor," a term defined in Section 3–103(a)(11). Thus, the resolution of that question is governed by the law of suretyship. See Restatement of Suretyship and Guaranty § 39.

3. Section 3–605 is not, however, limited to the conventional situation of the accommodation party discussed in Comment 2. It also applies in four other situations. First, it applies to indorsers of notes who are not accommodation parties. Unless an indorser signs without recourse, the indorser's liability under Section 3–415(a) is functionally similar to that of a guarantor of payment. For example, if Bank in the second hypothetical discussed in Comment 2 indorsed the note and transferred it to Second Bank, Bank is liable to Second Bank in the event of dishonor of the note by Borrower. Section 3–415(a). Because of that secondary liability as indorser, Bank qualifies as a "secondary obligor" under Section 3–103(a)(17) and has the same rights under Section 3–605 as an accommodation party.

Second, a similar analysis applies to the drawer of a draft that is accepted by a party that is not a bank. Under Section 3–414(d), that drawer has liability on the same terms as an indorser under Section 3–415(a). Thus, the drawer in that case is a "secondary obligor" under Section 3–103(a)(17) and has rights under Section 3–605 to that extent.

Third, a similar principle justifies application of Section 3–605 to persons who indorse a check. Assume that Drawer draws a check to the order of Payee. Payee then indorses the check and transfers it to Transferee. If Transferee presents the check and it is dishonored, Transferee may recover from Drawer under Section 3–414 or Payee under Section 3–415. Because of that secondary liability as an indorser, Payee is a secondary obligor under Section 3–103(a)(17). Drawer is a "principal obligor" under Section 3–103(a)(11). As noted in Comment 4, below, however, Section 3–605(a)(3) will discharge indorsers of checks in some cases in which other secondary obligors will not be discharged by this section.

Fourth, this section also deals with the rights of co-makers of instruments, even when those co-makers do not qualify as accommodation parties. The co-makers' rights of contribution under Section 3–116 make each co-maker a secondary obligor to the extent of that right of contribution.

4. Subsection (a) is based on Restatement of Suretyship and Guaranty § 39. It addresses the effects of a release of the principal obligor by the person entitled to enforce the instrument. Paragraph (a)(1) governs the effect of that release on the principal obligor's duties to the secondary obligor; paragraphs (a)(2) and (a)(3) govern the effect of that release on the secondary obligor's duties to the person entitled to enforce the instrument.

With respect to the duties of the principal obligor, the release of course cannot affect obligations of the principal obligor with respect to payments that the secondary obligor already has made. But with respect to future payments by the secondary obligor, paragraph (a)(1) (based on Restatement of Suretyship and Guaranty § 39(a)) provides that the principal obligor is discharged, to the extent of the release, from any other duties to the secondary obligor. That rule is appropriate because otherwise the discharge granted to the principal obligor would be illusory: it would have obtained a release from a person entitled to enforce that instrument, but it would be directly liable for the same sum to the secondary obligor if the secondary obligor later complied with its secondary obligation to pay the instrument. This discharge does not occur, though, if the terms of the release effect a "preservation of recourse" as described in subsection (g). See Comment 10, below.

The discharge under paragraph (a)(1) of the principal obligor's duties to the secondary obligor is broad, applying to all duties under this article. This includes not only the principal obligor's liability as a party to an instrument (as a maker, drawer or indorser under Sections 3–412 through 3–415) but also obligations under Sections 3–116 and 3–419.

Paragraph (a)(2) is based closely on Restatement of Suretyship and Guaranty § 39(b). It articulates a default rule that the release of a principal obligor also discharges the secondary obligor, to the extent of the release granted to the principal obligor, from any unperformed portion of its obligation on the instrument. The discharge of the secondary obligor under paragraph (a)(2) is phrased more narrowly than the discharge of the principal obligor is phrased under paragraph (a)(1) because, unlike principal obligors, the only obligations of secondary obligors in Article 3 are "on the instrument" as makers or indorsers.

The parties can opt out of that rule by including a contrary statement in the terms of the release. The provision does not contemplate that any "magic words" are necessary. Thus, discharge of the secondary obligor under paragraph (a)(2) is avoided not only if the terms of the release track the statutory language (e.g., the person entitled to enforce the instrument "retains the right to enforce the instrument" against the secondary obligor), or if the terms of the release effect a preservation of recourse under subsection (g), but also if the terms of the release include a simple statement that the parties intend to "release the principal obligor but not the secondary obligor" or that the person entitled to enforce the instrument "reserves its rights" against the secondary obligor. At the same time, because paragraph (a)(2) refers to the "terms of the release," extrinsic circumstances cannot be used to establish that the parties intended the secondary obligor to remain obligated. If a release of the principal obligor includes such a provision, the secondary obligor is, nonetheless, discharged to the extent of the consideration that is paid for the release; that consideration is treated as a payment in partial satisfaction of the instrument.

Notwithstanding language in the release that prevents discharge of the secondary obligor under paragraph (a)(2), paragraph (a)(3) discharges the secondary obligor from its obligation to a person entitled to enforce the instrument to the extent that the release otherwise would cause the secondary obligor a loss. The rationale for that provision is that a release of the principal obligor changes the economic risk for which the secondary obligor contracted. This risk may be increased in two ways. First, by releasing the principal obligor, the person entitled to enforce the instrument has eliminated the likelihood of future payments by the principal obligor that would lessen the obligation of the secondary obligor. Second, unless the release effects a preservation of the secondary obligor's recourse, the release eliminates the secondary obligor's claims against the principal obligor with respect to any future payment by the secondary obligor. The discharge provided by this paragraph prevents that increased risk from causing the secondary obligor a loss. Moreover, permitting releases to be negotiated between the principal obligor and the person entitled to enforce the instrument without regard to the consequences to the secondary obligor would create an undue risk of opportunistic behavior by the obligee and principal obligor. That concern is lessened, and the discharge is not provided by paragraph (a)(3), if the secondary obligor has consented to the release or is deemed to have consented to it under subsection (f) (which presumes consent by a secondary obligor to actions taken by a principal obligor if the secondary obligor controls the principal obligor or deals with the person entitled to enforce the instrument on behalf of the principal obligor). See Comment 9, below.

Subsection (a) (and Restatement Section 39(b), the concepts of which it follows quite closely) is designed to facilitate negotiated workouts between a creditor and a principal obligor, so long as they are not at the expense of a secondary obligor who has not consented to the arrangement (either specifically or by waiving its rights to discharge under this section). Thus, for example, the provision facilitates an arrangement in which the principal obligor pays some portion of a guaranteed obligation, the person entitled to enforce the instrument grants a release to the principal obligor in exchange for that payment, and the person entitled to enforce the instrument pursues the secondary obligor for the remainder of the obligation. Under paragraph (a)(2), the person entitled to enforce the instrument may pursue the secondary obligor despite the release of the principal obligor so long as the terms of the release provide for this result. Under paragraph (a)(3), though, the secondary obligor will be protected against any loss it might suffer by reason of that release (if the secondary obligor has not waived discharge under subsection (f)). It should be noted that the obligee may be able to minimize the risk of such loss (and, thus, of the secondary obligor's discharge) by giving the secondary obligor prompt notice of the release even though such notice is not required.

The foregoing principles are illustrated by the following cases:

Case # 1. D borrows $1000 from C. The repayment obligation is evidenced by a note issued by D, payable to the order of C. S is an accommodation indorser of the note. As the due date of the note approaches, it becomes obvious that D cannot pay the full amount of the note and may soon be facing bankruptcy. C, in order to collect as much as possible from D and lessen the need to seek recovery from S, agrees to release D from its obligation under the note in exchange for $100 in cash. The agreement to release D is silent as to the effect of the release on S. Pursuant to Section 3–605(a)(2), the release of D discharges S from its obligations to C on the note.

Case # 2. Same facts as Case 1, except that the terms of the release provide that C retains its rights to enforce the instrument against S. D is discharged from its obligations to S pursuant to Section 3–605(a)(1), but S is not discharged from its obligations to C pursuant to Section 3–605(a)(2). However, if S could have recovered from D any sum it paid to C (had D not been discharged from its obligation to S), S has been harmed by the release and is discharged pursuant to Section 3–605(a)(3) to the extent of that harm.

Case # 3. Same facts as Case 1, except that the terms of the release provide that C retains its rights to enforce the instrument against S and that S retains its recourse against D. Under subsection (g), the release effects a preservation of recourse. Thus, S is not discharged from its obligations to C pursuant to Section 3–605(a)(2) and D is not discharged from its obligations to S pursuant to Section 3–605(a)(1). Because S's claims against D are preserved, S will not suffer the kind of loss described in Case 2. If no other loss is suffered by S as a result of the release, S is not discharged pursuant to this section.

Case # 4. Same facts as Case 3, except that D had made arrangements to work at a second job in order to earn the money to fulfill its obligations on the note. When C released D, however, D canceled the plans for the second job. While S still retains its recourse against D, S may be discharged from its obligation under the instrument to the extent that D's decision to forgo the second job causes S a loss because forgoing the job renders D unable to fulfill its obligations to S under Section 3–419.

Subsection (a) reflects a change from former Section 3–605(b), which provided categorically that the release of a principal obligor by the person entitled to enforce the instrument did not discharge a secondary obligor's obligation on the instrument and assumed that the release also did not discharge the principal obligor's obligations to the secondary obligor under Section 3–419. The rule under subsection (a) is much closer to the policy of the Restatement of Suretyship and Guaranty than was former Section 3–605(b). The change, however, is likely to affect only a narrow category of cases. First, as discussed above, Section 3–605 applies only to transactions in which the payment obligation is represented by a negotiable instrument, and, within that set of transactions, only to those transactions in which the secondary obligation is incurred by indorsement or cosigning, not to transactions that involve a separate document of guaranty. See Comment 2, above. Second, as provided in subsection (f), secondary obligors cannot obtain a discharge under subsection (a) in any transaction in which they have consented to the challenged conduct. Thus, subsection (a) will not apply to any transaction that includes a provision waiving suretyship defenses (a provision that is almost universally included in commercial loan documentation) or to any transaction in which the creditor obtains the consent of the secondary obligor at the time of the release.

The principal way in which subsection (a) goes beyond the policy of Restatement § 39 is with respect to the liability of indorsers of checks. Specifically, the last sentence of paragraph (a)(2) provides that a release of a principal obligor grants a complete discharge to the indorser of a check, without requiring the indorser to prove harm. In that particular context, it seems likely that continuing responsibility for the indorser often would be so inconsistent with the expectations of the parties as to create a windfall for the creditor and an unfair surprise for the indorser. Thus, the statute implements a simple rule that grants a complete discharge. The creditor, of course, can avoid that rule by contracting with the secondary obligor for a different result at the time that the creditor grants the release to the principal obligor.

5. Subsection (b) is based on Restatement of Suretyship and Guaranty § 40 and relates to extensions of the due date of the instrument. An extension of time to pay a note is often beneficial to the secondary obligor because the additional time may enable the principal obligor to obtain the funds to pay the instrument. In some cases, however, the extension may cause loss to the secondary obligor, particularly if deterioration of the financial condition of the principal obligor reduces the amount that the secondary obligor is able to recover on its right of recourse when default occurs. For example, suppose that the instrument is an installment note and the principal debtor is temporarily short of funds to pay a monthly installment. The payee agrees to extend the due date of the installment for a month or two to allow the debtor to pay when funds are available. Paragraph (b)(2) provides that an extension of time results in a discharge of the secondary obligor, but only to the extent that the secondary obligor proves that the extension caused loss. See subsection (h) (discussing the burden of proof under Section 3–605). Thus, if the extension is for a long period, the secondary obligor might be able to prove that during the period of extension the principal obligor became insolvent, reducing the value of the right of recourse of the secondary obligor. In such a case, paragraph (b)(2) discharges the secondary obligor to the extent of that harm. Although not required to notify the secondary obligor of the extension, the payee can minimize the risk of loss by the secondary obligor by giving the secondary obligor prompt notice of the extension; prompt notice can enhance the likelihood that the secondary obligor's right of recourse can remain valuable, and thus can limit the likelihood that the secondary obligor will suffer a loss because of the extension. See Restatement of Suretyship and Guaranty Section 38 comment b.

If the secondary obligor is not discharged under paragraph (b)(2) (either because it would not suffer a loss by reason of the extension or because it has waived its right to discharge pursuant to subsection (f)), it is important to understand the effect of the extension on the rights and obligations of the secondary obligor. Consider the following cases:

Case # 5. A borrows money from Lender and issues a note payable to the order of Lender that is due on April 1, 2002. B signs the note for accommodation at the request of Lender. B signed the note either as co-maker or as an anomalous indorser. In either case Lender subsequently makes an agreement with A extending the due date of A's obligation to pay the note to July 1, 2002. In either case B did not agree to the extension, and the extension did not address Lender's rights against B. Under paragraph (b)(1), A's obligations to B under this article are also extended to July 1, 2002. Under paragraph (b)(3), if B is not discharged, B may treat its obligations to Lender as also extended, or may pay the instrument on the original due date.

Case # 6. Same facts as Case 5, except that the extension agreement includes a statement that the Lender retains its right to enforce the note against B on its original terms. Under paragraph (b)(3), B is liable on the original due date, but under paragraph (b)(1), A's obligations to B under Section 3–419 are not due until July 1, 2002.

Case # 7. Same facts as Case 5, except that the extension agreement includes a statement that the Lender retains its right to enforce the note against B on its original terms and B retains its recourse against A as though no extension had been granted. Under paragraph (b)(3), B is liable on the original due date. Under paragraph (b)(1), A's obligations to B under Section 3–419 are not extended.

Under section 3–605(b), the results in Case 5 and Case 7 are identical to the results that follow from the law of suretyship and guaranty. See Restatement of Suretyship and Guaranty § 40. The situation in Case 6 is not specifically addressed in the Restatement, but the resolution in this Section is consistent with the concepts of suretyship and guaranty law as reflected in the Restatement. If the secondary obligor is called upon to pay on the due date, it may be difficult to quantify the extent to which the extension has impaired the right of recourse of the secondary obligor at that time. Still, the secondary obligor does have a right to make a claim against the obligee at that time. As a practical matter a suit making such a claim should establish the facts relevant to the extent of the impairment. See Restatement of Suretyship and Guaranty § 37(4).

As a practical matter, an extension of the due date will normally occur only when the principal obligor is unable to pay on the due date. The interest of the secondary obligor normally is to acquiesce in the willingness of the person entitled to enforce the instrument to wait for payment from the principal obligor rather than to pay right away and rely on an action against the principal obligor that may have little or no value. But in unusual cases the secondary obligor may prefer to pay the holder on the original due date so as to avoid continuing accrual of interest. In such cases, the secondary obligor may do so. See paragraph (b)(3). If the terms of the extension provide that the person entitled to enforce the instrument retains its right to enforce the instrument against the secondary obligor on the original due date, though, those terms are effective and the secondary obligor may not delay payment until the extended due date. Unless the extension agreement effects a preservation of recourse, however, the secondary obligor may not proceed against the principal obligor under Section 3–419 until the extended due date. See paragraph (b)(1). To the extent that delay causes loss to the secondary obligor it is discharged under paragraph (b)(2).

Even in those cases in which a secondary obligor does not have a duty to pay the instrument on the original due date, it always has the right to pay the instrument on that date, and perhaps minimize its loss by doing so. The secondary obligor is not precluded, however, from asserting its rights to discharge under Section 3–605(b)(2) if it does not exercise that option. The critical issue is whether the extension caused the secondary obligor a loss by increasing the difference between its cost of performing its obligation on the instrument and the amount recoverable from the principal obligor under this Article. The decision by the secondary obligor not to exercise its option to pay on the original due date may, under the circumstances, be a factor to be considered in the determination of that issue, especially if the secondary obligor has been given prompt notice of the extension (as discussed above).

6. Subsection (c) is based on Restatement of Suretyship and Guaranty § 41. It is a residual provision, which applies to modifications of the obligation of the principal obligor that are not covered by subsections (a) and (b). Under subsection (c)(1), a modification of the obligation of the principal obligor on the instrument (other than a release covered by subsection (a) or an extension of the due date covered by subsection (b)), will correspondingly modify the duties of the principal obligor to the secondary obligor. Under subsection (c)(2), such a modification also will result in discharge of the secondary obligor to the extent the modification causes loss to the secondary obligor. To the extent that the secondary obligor is not discharged and the obligation changes the amount of money payable on the instrument, or the timing of such payment, subsection (c)(3) provides the secondary obligor with a choice: it may satisfy its obligation on the instrument as if the modification had not occurred, or it may treat its obligation to pay the instrument as having been modified in a manner corresponding to the modification of the principal obligor's obligation.

The following cases illustrate the application of subsection (c):

Case # 8. Corporation borrows money from Lender and issues a note payable to Lender. X signs the note as an accommodation party for Corporation. The note refers to a loan agreement under which the note was issued, which states various events of default that allow Lender to accelerate the due date of the note. Among the events of default are breach of covenants not to incur debt beyond specified limits and not to engage in any line of business substantially different from that currently carried on by Corporation. Without consent of X, Lender agrees to modify the covenants to allow Corporation to enter into a new line of business that X considers to be risky, and to incur debt beyond the limits specified in the loan agreement to finance the new venture. This modification discharges X to the extent that the modification otherwise would cause X a loss.

Case # 9. Corporation borrows money from Lender and issues a note payable to Lender in the amount of $100,000. X signs the note as an accommodation party for Corporation. The note calls for 60 equal monthly payments of interest and principal. Before the first payment is made, Corporation and Lender agree to modify the note by changing the repayment schedule to require four annual payments of interest only, followed by a fifth payment of interest and the entire $100,000 principal balance. To the extent that the modification does not discharge X, X has the option of fulfilling its obligation on the note in accordance with the original terms or the modified terms.

7. Subsection (d) is based on Restatement of Suretyship and Guaranty § 42 and deals with the discharge of secondary obligors by impairment of collateral. The last sentence of subsection (d) states four common examples of what is meant by impairment. Because it uses the term "includes," the provision allows a court to find impairment in other cases as well. There is extensive case law on impairment of collateral. The secondary obligor is discharged to the extent that the secondary obligor proves that impairment was caused by a person entitled to enforce the instrument. For example, assume that the payee of a secured note fails to perfect the security interest. The collateral is owned by the principal obligor who subsequently files in bankruptcy. As a result of the failure to perfect, the security interest is not enforceable in bankruptcy. If the payee were to obtain payment from the secondary obligor, the secondary obligor would be subrogated to the payee's security interest in the collateral under Section 3–419 and general principles of suretyship law. See Restatement of Suretyship and Guaranty § 28(1)(c). In this situation, though, the value of the security interest is impaired completely because the security interest is unenforceable. Thus, the secondary obligor is discharged from its obligation on the note to the extent of that impairment. If the value of the collateral impaired is as much or more than the amount of the note, and if

there will be no recovery on the note as an unsecured claim, there is a complete discharge. Subsection (d) applies whether the collateral is personalty or realty, whenever the obligation in question is in the form of a negotiable instrument.

8. Subsection (e) is based on the former Section 3-605(h). The requirement of knowledge in the first clause is consistent with Section 9-628. The requirement of notice in the second clause is consistent with Section 3-419(c).

9. The importance of the suretyship defenses provided in Section 3-605 is greatly diminished by the fact that the right to discharge can be waived as provided in subsection (f). The waiver can be effectuated by a provision in the instrument or in a separate agreement. It is standard practice to include such a waiver of suretyship defenses in notes prepared by financial institutions or other commercial creditors. Thus, Section 3-605 will result in the discharge of an accommodation party on a note only in the occasional case in which the note does not include such a waiver clause and the person entitled to enforce the note nevertheless takes actions that would give rise to a discharge under this section without obtaining the consent of the secondary obligor.

Because subsection (f) by its terms applies only to a discharge "under this section," subsection (f) does not operate to waive a defense created by other law (such as the law governing enforcement of security interests under Article 9) that cannot be waived under that law. See, e.g., Section 9-602.

The last sentence of subsection (f) creates an inference of consent on the part of the secondary obligor whenever the secondary obligor controls the principal obligor or deals with the creditor on behalf of the principal obligor. That sentence is based on Restatement of Suretyship and Guaranty § 48(2).

10. Subsection (g) explains the criteria for determining whether the terms of a release or extension preserve the secondary obligor's recourse, a concept of importance in the application of subsections (a) and (b). First, the terms of the release or extension must provide that the person entitled to enforce the instrument retains the right to enforce the instrument against the secondary obligor. Second, the terms of the release or extension must provide that the recourse of the secondary obligor against the principal obligor continues as though the release or extension had not been granted. Those requirements are drawn from Restatement of Suretyship and Guaranty § 38.

11. Subsections (h) and (i) articulate rules for the burden of persuasion under Section 3-605. Those rules are based on Restatement of Suretyship and Guaranty § 49.

As amended in 2002.

UCC ARTICLE 4 (2019)

BANK DEPOSITS AND COLLECTIONS

Article 4 was revised in 1990 and amended in 2002 by the same drafting committees that promulgated the 1990 revision and the 2002 amendments to UCC Article 3.

PART 1. GENERAL PROVISIONS AND DEFINITIONS

PART 2. COLLECTION OF ITEMS: DEPOSITARY AND COLLECTING BANKS

PART 3. COLLECTION OF ITEMS: PAYOR BANKS

PART 1

GENERAL PROVISIONS AND DEFINITIONS

§ 4–101. Short Title.

This Article may be cited as Uniform Commercial Code—Bank Deposits and Collections.

As amended in 1990.

Official Comment

1. The great number of checks handled by banks and the country-wide nature of the bank collection process require uniformity in the law of bank collections. There is needed a uniform statement of the principal rules of the bank collection process with ample provision for flexibility to meet the needs of the large volume handled and the changing needs and conditions that are bound to come with the years. This Article meets that need.

2. In 1950 at the time Article 4 was drafted, 6.7 billion checks were written annually. By the time of the 1990 revision of Article 4 annual volume was estimated by the American Bankers Association to be about 50 billion checks. The banking system could not have coped with this increase in check volume had it not developed in the late 1950s and early 1960s an automated system for check collection based on encoding checks with machine-readable information by Magnetic Ink Character Recognition (MICR). An important goal of the 1990 revision of Article 4 is to promote the efficiency of the check collection process by making the provisions of Article 4 more compatible with the needs of an automated system and, by doing so, increase the speed and lower the cost of check collection for those who write and receive checks. An additional goal of the 1990 revision of Article 4 is to remove any statutory barriers in the Article to the ultimate adoption of programs allowing the presentment of checks to payor banks by electronic transmission of information captured from the MICR line on the checks. The potential of these programs for saving the time and expense of transporting the huge volume of checks from depositary to payor banks is evident.

3. Article 4 defines rights between parties with respect to bank deposits and collections. It is not a regulatory statute. It does not regulate the terms of the bank-customer agreement, nor does it prescribe what constraints different jurisdictions may wish to impose on that relationship in the interest of consumer protection. The revisions in Article 4 are intended to create a legal framework that accommodates automation and truncation for the benefit of all bank customers. This may raise consumer problems which enacting jurisdictions may wish to address in individual legislation. For example, with respect to Section 4–401(c), jurisdictions may wish to examine their unfair and deceptive practices laws to determine whether they are adequate to protect drawers who postdate

checks from unscrupulous practices that may arise on the part of persons who induce drawers to issue postdated checks in the erroneous belief that the checks will not be immediately payable. Another example arises from the fact that under various truncation plans customers will no longer receive their cancelled checks and will no longer have the cancelled check to prove payment. Individual legislation might provide that a copy of a bank statement along with a copy of the check is prima facie evidence of payment.

§ 4–102. Applicability.

(a) To the extent that items within this Article are also within Articles 3 and 8, they are subject to those Articles. If there is conflict, this Article governs Article 3, but Article 8 governs this Article.

(b) The liability of a bank for action or non-action with respect to an item handled by it for purposes of presentment, payment, or collection is governed by the law of the place where the bank is located. In the case of action or non-action by or at a branch or separate office of a bank, its liability is governed by the law of the place where the branch or separate office is located.

As amended in 1990.

Official Comment

1. The rules of Article 3 governing negotiable instruments, their transfer, and the contracts of the parties thereto apply to the items collected through banking channels wherever no specific provision is found in this Article. In the case of conflict, this Article governs. See Section 3–102(b).

Bonds and like instruments constituting investment securities under Article 8 may also be handled by banks for collection purposes. Various sections of Article 8 prescribe rules of transfer some of which (see ~~Sections 8–304 and 8–306~~ Sections 8–108 and 8–304) [Amendments approved by the Permanent Editorial Board for Uniform Commercial Code November 4, 1995] may conflict with provisions of this Article (Sections 4–205, 4–207, and 4–208). In the case of conflict, Article 8 governs.

Section 4–210 deals specifically with overlapping problems and possible conflicts between this Article and Article 9. However, similar reconciling provisions are not necessary in the case of Articles 5 and 7. Sections 4–301 and 4–302 are consistent with Section 5–112 [*unrevised Article 5*]. In the case of Article 7 documents of title frequently accompany items but they are not themselves items. See Section 4–104(a)(9).

In *Clearfield Trust Co. v. United States*, 318 U.S. 363 (1943), the Court held that if the United States is a party to an instrument, its rights and duties are governed by federal common law in the absence of a specific federal statute or regulation. In *United States v. Kimbell Foods, Inc.*, 440 U.S. 715 (1979), the Court stated a three-pronged test to ascertain whether the federal common-law rule should follow the state rule. In most instances courts under the *Kimbell* test have shown a willingness to adopt UCC rules in formulating federal common law on the subject. In *Kimbell* the Court adopted the priorities rules of Article 9.

In addition, applicable federal law may supersede provisions of this Article. One federal law that does so is the Expedited Funds Availability Act, 12 U.S.C. § 4001 et seq., and its implementing Regulation CC, 12 CFR Pt. 229. In some instances this law is alluded to in the statute, e.g., Section 4–215(e) and (f). In other instances, although not referred to in this Article, the provisions of the EFAA and Regulation CC control with respect to checks. For example, except between the depositary bank and its customer, all settlements are final and not provisional (Regulation CC, Section 229.36(d)), and the midnight deadline may be extended (Regulation CC, Section 229.30(c)). The comments to this Article suggest in most instances the relevant Regulation CC provisions.

2. Subsection (b) is designed to state a workable rule for the solution of otherwise vexatious problems of the conflicts of laws:

a. The routine and mechanical nature of bank collections makes it imperative that one law govern the activities of one office of a bank. The requirement found in some cases that to hold an indorser notice must be given in accordance with the law of the place of indorsement, since that method of notice became an implied term of the indorser's contract, is more theoretical than practical.

b. Adoption of what is in essence a tort theory of the conflict of laws is consistent with the general theory of this Article that the basic duty of a collecting bank is one of good faith and the exercise of ordinary care. Justification lies in the fact that, in using an ambulatory instrument, the drawer, payee, and indorsers must know that action will be taken with respect to it in other jurisdictions. This is especially pertinent with respect to the law of the place of payment.

c. The phrase "action or non-action with respect to any item handled by it for purposes of presentment, payment, or collection" is intended to make the conflicts rule of subsection (b) apply from the inception of the collection process of an item through all phases of deposit, forwarding, presentment, payment and remittance or credit of proceeds. Specifically the subsection applies to the initial act of a depositary bank in receiving an item and to the incidents of such receipt. The conflicts rule of *Weissman v. Banque De Bruxelles*, 254 N.Y. 488, 173 N.E. 835 (1930), is rejected. The subsection applies to questions of possible vicarious liability of a bank for action or non-action of sub-agents (see Section 4–202(c)), and tests these questions by the law of the state of the location of the bank which uses the sub-agent. The conflicts rule of *St. Nicholas Bank of New York v. State Nat. Bank*, 128 N.Y. 26, 27 N.E. 849, 13 L.R.A. 241 (1891), is rejected. The subsection applies to action or non-action of a payor bank in connection with handling an item (see Sections 4–215(a), 4–301, 4–302, 4–303) as well as action or non-action of a collecting bank (Sections 4–201 through 4–216); to action or non-action of a bank which suspends payment or is affected by another bank suspending payment (Section 4–216); to action or non-action of a bank with respect to an item under the rule of Part 4 of Article 4.

d. In a case in which subsection (b) makes this Article applicable, Section 4–103(a) leaves open the possibility of an agreement with respect to applicable law. This freedom of agreement follows the general policy of Section 1–105 [*unrevised Article 1; see Concordance, p. 12*].

§ 4–103. Variation by Agreement; Measure of Damages; Action Constituting Ordinary Care.

(a) The effect of the provisions of this Article may be varied by agreement, but the parties to the agreement cannot disclaim a bank's responsibility for its lack of good faith or failure to exercise ordinary care or limit the measure of damages for the lack or failure. However, the parties may determine by agreement the standards by which the bank's responsibility is to be measured if those standards are not manifestly unreasonable.

(b) Federal Reserve regulations and operating circulars, clearing-house rules, and the like have the effect of agreements under subsection (a), whether or not specifically assented to by all parties interested in items handled.

(c) Action or non-action approved by this Article or pursuant to Federal Reserve regulations or operating circulars is the exercise of ordinary care and, in the absence of special instructions, action or non-action consistent with clearing-house rules and the like or with a general banking usage not disapproved by this Article, is prima facie the exercise of ordinary care.

(d) The specification or approval of certain procedures by this Article is not disapproval of other procedures that may be reasonable under the circumstances.

(e) The measure of damages for failure to exercise ordinary care in handling an item is the amount of the item reduced by an amount that could not have been realized by the exercise of ordinary care. If there is also bad faith it includes any other damages the party suffered as a proximate consequence.

As amended in 1990.

Official Comment

1. Section 1–102 states the general principles and rules for variation of the effect of this Act by agreement and the limitations to this power. Section 4–103 states the specific rules for variation of Article 4 by agreement and also certain standards of ordinary care. In view of the technical complexity of the field of bank collections, the enormous number of items handled by banks, the certainty that there will be variations from the normal in each day's work in each bank, the certainty of changing conditions and the possibility of developing improved methods of collection to speed the process, it would be unwise to freeze present methods of operation by mandatory statutory rules. This section, therefore, permits within wide limits variation of the effect of provisions of the Article by agreement.

2. Subsection (a) confers blanket power to vary all provisions of the Article by agreements of the ordinary kind. The agreements may not disclaim a bank's responsibility for its own lack of good faith or failure to exercise ordinary care and may not limit the measure of damages for the lack or failure, but this subsection like Section 1–102(3) [*unrevised Article 1; see Concordance, p. 12*] approves the practice of parties determining by agreement the standards by which the responsibility is to be measured. In the absence of a showing that the standards manifestly are unreasonable, the agreement controls. Owners of items and other interested parties are not affected by

agreements under this subsection unless they are parties to the agreement or are bound by adoption, ratification, estoppel or the like.

As here used "agreement" has the meaning given to it by Section 1-201(3) [*unrevised Article 1; see Concordance, p. 12*]. The agreement may be direct, as between the owner and the depositary bank; or indirect, as in the case in which the owner authorizes a particular type of procedure and any bank in the collection chain acts pursuant to such authorization. It may be with respect to a single item; or to all items handled for a particular customer, e.g., a general agreement between the depositary bank and the customer at the time a deposit account is opened. Legends on deposit tickets, collection letters and acknowledgments of items, coupled with action by the affected party constituting acceptance, adoption, ratification, estoppel or the like, are agreements if they meet the tests of the definition of "agreement." See Section 1-201(3) [*unrevised Article 1; see Concordance, p. 12*]. *First Nat. Bank of Denver v. Federal Reserve Bank*, 6 F.2d 339 (8th Cir. 1925) (deposit slip); *Jefferson County Bldg. Ass'n v. Southern Bank & Trust Co.*, 225 Ala. 25, 142 So. 66 (1932) (signature card and deposit slip); *Semingson v. Stock Yards Nat. Bank*, 162 Minn. 424, 203 N.W. 412 (1925) (passbook); *Farmers State Bank v. Union Nat. Bank*, 42 N.D. 449, 454, 173 N.W. 789, 790 (1919) (acknowledgment of receipt of item).

3. Subsection (a) (subject to its limitations with respect to good faith and ordinary care) goes far to meet the requirements of flexibility. However, it does not by itself confer fully effective flexibility. Since it is recognized that banks handle a great number of items every business day and that the parties interested in each item include the owner of the item, the drawer (if it is a check), all nonbank indorsers, the payor bank and from one to five or more collecting banks, it is obvious that it is impossible, practically, to obtain direct agreements from all of these parties on all items. In total, the interested parties constitute virtually every adult person and business organization in the United States. On the other hand they may become bound to agreements on the principle that collecting banks acting as agents have authority to make binding agreements with respect to items being handled. This conclusion was assumed but was not flatly decided in *Federal Reserve Bank of Richmond v. Malloy*, 264 U.S. 160, at 167, 44 S.Ct. 296, at 298, 68 L.Ed. 617, 31 A.L.R. 1261 (1924).

To meet this problem subsection (b) provides that official or quasi-official rules of collection, that is Federal Reserve regulations and operating circulars, clearing-house rules, and the like, have the effect of agreements under subsection (a), whether or not specifically assented to by all parties interested in items handled. Consequently, such official or quasi-official rules may, standing by themselves but subject to the good faith and ordinary care limitations, vary the effect of the provisions of Article 4.

Federal Reserve regulations. Various sections of the Federal Reserve Act (12 U.S.C. § 221 et seq.) authorize the Board of Governors of the Federal Reserve System to direct the Federal Reserve banks to exercise bank collection functions. For example, Section 16 (12 U.S.C. § 248(*o*)) authorizes the Board to require each Federal Reserve bank to exercise the functions of a clearing house for its members and Section 13 (12 U.S.C. § 342) authorizes each Federal Reserve bank to receive deposits from nonmember banks solely for the purposes of exchange or of collection. Under this statutory authorization the Board has issued Regulation J (Subpart A—Collection of Checks and Other Items). Under the supremacy clause of the Constitution, federal regulations prevail over state statutes. Moreover, the Expedited Funds Availability Act, 12 U.S.C. Section 4007(b) provides that the Act and Regulation CC, 12 CFR 229, supersede "any provision of the law of any State, including the Uniform Commercial Code as in effect in such State, which is inconsistent with this chapter or such regulations." See Comment 1 to Section 4-102.

Federal Reserve operating circulars. The regulations of the Federal Reserve Board authorize the Federal Reserve banks to promulgate operating circulars covering operating details. Regulation J, for example, provides that "Each Reserve Bank shall receive and handle items in accordance with this subpart, and shall issue operating circulars governing the details of its handling of items and other matters deemed appropriate by the Reserve Bank." This Article recognizes that "operating circulars" issued pursuant to the regulations and concerned with operating details as appropriate may, within their proper sphere, vary the effect of the Article.

Clearing-House Rules. Local clearing houses have long issued rules governing the details of clearing; hours of clearing, media of remittance, time for return of mis-sent items and the like. The case law has recognized these rules, within their proper sphere, as binding on affected parties and as appropriate sources for the courts to look to in filling out details of bank collection law. Subsection (b) in recognizing clearing-house rules as a means of preserving flexibility continues the sensible approach indicated in the cases. Included in the term "clearing houses" are county and regional clearing houses as well as those within a single city or town. There is, of course, no intention of authorizing a local clearing house or a group of clearing houses to rewrite the basic law generally. The term "clearing-house rules" should be understood in the light of functions the clearing houses have exercised in the past.

And the like. This phrase is to be construed in the light of the foregoing. "Federal Reserve regulations and operating circulars" cover rules and regulations issued by public or quasi-public agencies under statutory authority. "Clearing-house rules" cover rules issued by a group of banks which have associated themselves to perform through a clearing house some of their collection, payment and clearing functions. Other agencies or associations of this kind may be established in the future whose rules and regulations could be appropriately looked on as constituting means of avoiding absolute statutory rigidity. The phrase "and the like" leaves open possibilities for future development. An agreement between a number of banks or even all the banks in an area simply because they are banks, would not of itself, by virtue of the phrase "and the like," meet the purposes and objectives of subsection (b).

4. Under this Article banks come under the general obligations of the use of good faith and the exercise of ordinary care. "Good faith" is defined in Section 1-201(b)(20). The term "ordinary care" is defined in Section 3-103(a)(9). These definitions are made to apply to Article 4 by Section 4-104(c). Section 4-202 states respects in which collecting banks must use ordinary care. Subsection (c) of Section 4-103 provides that action or non-action approved by the Article or pursuant to Federal Reserve regulations or operating circulars constitutes the exercise of ordinary care. Federal Reserve regulations and operating circulars constitute an affirmative standard of ordinary care equally with the provisions of Article 4 itself.

Subsection (c) further provides that, absent special instructions, action or non-action consistent with clearing-house rules and the like or with a general banking usage not disapproved by the Article, prima facie constitutes the exercise of ordinary care. Clearing-house rules and the phrase "and the like" have the significance set forth above in these Comments. The term "general banking usage" is not defined but should be taken to mean a general usage common to banks in the area concerned. See Section 1-205(2) [*unrevised Article 1; see Concordance, p. 12*]. In a case in which the adjective "general" is used, the intention is to require a usage broader than a mere practice between two or three banks but it is not intended to require a usage broader than a mere practice between two or three banks but it is not intended to require anything as broad as a country-wide usage. A usage followed generally throughout a state, a substantial portion of a state, a metropolitan area or the like would certainly be sufficient. Consistently with the principle of Section 1-205(3) [*unrevised Article 1; see Concordance, p. 12*], action or non-action consistent with clearing-house rules or the like or with banking usages prima facie constitutes the exercise of ordinary care. However, the phrase "in the absence of special instructions" affords owners of items an opportunity to prescribe other standards and although there may be no direct supervision or control of clearing houses or banking usages by official supervisory authorities, the confirmation of ordinary care by compliance with these standards is prima facie only, thus conferring on the courts the ultimate power to determine ordinary care in any case in which it should appear desirable to do so. The prima facie rule does, however, impose on the party contesting the standards to establish that they are unreasonable, arbitrary or unfair as used by the particular bank.

5. Subsection (d), in line with the flexible approach required for the bank collection process is designed to make clear that a novel procedure adopted by a bank is not to be considered unreasonable merely because that procedure is not specifically contemplated by this Article or by agreement, or because it has not yet been generally accepted as a bank usage. Changing conditions constantly call for new procedures and someone has to use the new procedure first. If this procedure is found to be reasonable under the circumstances, provided, of course, that it is not inconsistent with any provision of the Article or other law or agreement, the bank which has followed the new procedure should not be found to have failed in the exercise of ordinary care.

6. Subsection (e) sets forth a rule for determining the measure of damages for failure to exercise ordinary care which, under subsection (a), cannot be limited by agreement. In the absence of bad faith the maximum recovery is the amount of the item concerned. The term "bad faith" is not defined; the connotation is the absence of good faith (Section 3-103). When it is established that some part or all of the item could not have been collected even by the use of ordinary care the recovery is reduced by the amount that would have been in any event uncollectible. This limitation on recovery follows the case law. Finally, if bad faith is established the rule opens to allow the recovery of other damages, whose "proximateness" is to be tested by the ordinary rules applied in comparable cases. Of course, it continues to be as necessary under subsection (e) as it has been under ordinary common law principles that, before the damage rule of the subsection becomes operative, liability of the bank and some loss to the customer or owner must be established.

As amended in 2002.

§ 4–104. Definitions and Index of Definitions.

(a) In this Article, unless the context otherwise requires:

(1) "Account" means any deposit or credit account with a bank, including a demand, time, savings, passbook, share draft, or like account, other than an account evidenced by a certificate of deposit;

(2) "Afternoon" means the period of a day between noon and midnight;

(3) "Banking day" means the part of a day on which a bank is open to the public for carrying on substantially all of its banking functions;

(4) "Clearing house" means an association of banks or other payors regularly clearing items;

(5) "Customer" means a person having an account with a bank or for whom a bank has agreed to collect items, including a bank that maintains an account at another bank;

(6) "Documentary draft" means a draft to be presented for acceptance or payment if specified documents, certificated securities (Section 8–102) or instructions for uncertificated securities (Section 8–102), or other certificates, statements, or the like are to be received by the drawee or other payor before acceptance or payment of the draft;

(7) "Draft" means a draft as defined in Section 3–104 or an item, other than an instrument, that is an order;

(8) "Drawee" means a person ordered in a draft to make payment;

(9) "Item" means an instrument or a promise or order to pay money handled by a bank for collection or payment. The term does not include a payment order governed by Article 4A or a credit or debit card slip;

(10) "Midnight deadline" with respect to a bank is midnight on its next banking day following the banking day on which it receives the relevant item or notice or from which the time for taking action commences to run, whichever is later;

(11) "Settle" means to pay in cash, by clearing-house settlement, in a charge or credit or by remittance, or otherwise as agreed. A settlement may be either provisional or final;

(12) "Suspends payments" with respect to a bank means that it has been closed by order of the supervisory authorities, that a public officer has been appointed to take it over, or that it ceases or refuses to make payments in the ordinary course of business.

(b) Other definitions applying to this Article and the sections in which they appear are:

"Agreement for electronic presentment" Section 4–110.
"Collecting bank" Section 4–105.
"Depositary bank" Section 4–105.
"Intermediary bank" Section 4–105.
"Payor bank" Section 4–105.
"Presenting bank" Section 4–105.
"Presentment notice" Section 4–110.

(c) "Control" as provided in Section 7–106 and the following definitions in other Articles apply to this Article:

"Acceptance" Section 3–409.
"Alteration" Section 3–407.
"Cashier's check" Section 3–104.
"Certificate of deposit" Section 3–104.
"Certified check" Section 3–409.
"Check" Section 3–104.
["Good Faith" Section 3–103.] [*Note from West Advisory Panel: The definition of good faith in § 3–103 will be deleted if the jurisdiction adopts the definition of good faith in revised Article 1.*]
"Holder in due course" Section 3–302.
"Instrument" Section 3–104.

"Notice of dishonor" Section 3–503.
"Order" Section 3–103.
"Ordinary care" Section 3–103.
"Person entitled to enforce" Section 3–301.
"Presentment" Section 3–501.
"Promise" Section 3–103.
"Prove" Section 3–103.
"Record" Section 3–103.
"Remotely-Created consumer item" Section 3–103.
"Teller's check" Section 3–104.
"Unauthorized signature" Section 3–403.

(d) In addition, Article 1 contains general definitions and principles of construction and interpretation applicable throughout this Article.

As amended in 1990, 1994, 2001, 2002 and 2003.

Official Comment

1. Paragraph (a)(1): "Account" is defined to include both asset accounts in which a customer has deposited money and accounts from which a customer may draw on a line of credit. The limiting factor is that the account must be in a bank.

2. Paragraph (a)(3): "Banking day." Under this definition that part of a business day when a bank is open only for limited functions, e.g., to receive deposits and cash checks, but with loan, bookkeeping and other departments closed, is not part of a banking day.

3. Paragraph (a)(4): "Clearing house." Occasionally express companies, governmental agencies and other nonbanks deal directly with a clearing house; hence the definition does not limit the term to an association of banks.

4. Paragraph (a)(5): "Customer." It is to be noted that this term includes a bank carrying an account with another bank as well as the more typical nonbank customer or depositor.

5. Paragraph (a)(6): "Documentary draft" applies even though the documents do not accompany the draft but are to be received by the drawee or other payor before acceptance or payment of the draft. Documents may be either in electronic or tangible form. See Article 5, Section 5–102, Comment 2 and Article 1, Section 1–201 (definition of "document of title").

6. Paragraph (a)(7): "Draft" is defined in Section 3–104 as a form of instrument. Since Article 4 applies to items that may not fall within the definition of instrument, the term is defined here to include an item that is a written order to pay money, even though the item may not qualify as an instrument. The term "order" is defined in Section 3–103.

7. Paragraph (a)(8): "Drawee" is defined in Section 3–103 in terms of an Article 3 draft which is a form of instrument. Here "drawee" is defined in terms of an Article 4 draft which includes items that may not be instruments.

8. Paragraph (a)(9): "Item" is defined broadly to include an instrument, as defined in Section 3–104, as well as promises or orders that may not be within the definition of "instrument." The terms "promise" and "order" are defined in Section 3–103. A promise is a written undertaking to pay money. An order is a written instruction to pay money. But see Section 4–110(c). Since bonds and other investment securities under Article 8 may be within the term "instrument" or "promise," they are items and when handled by banks for collection are subject to this Article. See Comment 1 to Section 4–102. The functional limitation on the meaning of this term is the willingness of the banking system to handle the instrument, undertaking or instruction for collection or payment.

9. Paragraph (a)(10): "Midnight deadline." The use of this phrase is an example of the more mechanical approach used in this Article. Midnight is selected as a termination point or time limit to obtain greater uniformity and definiteness than would be possible from other possible terminating points, such as the close of the banking day or business day.

10. Paragraph (a)(11): The term "settle" has substantial importance throughout Article 4. In the American Bankers Association Bank Collection Code, in deferred posting statutes, in Federal Reserve regulations and operating circulars, in clearing-house rules, in agreements between banks and customers and in legends on deposit tickets and collection letters, there is repeated reference to "conditional" or "provisional" credits or payments. Tied

in with this concept of creditors or payments being in some way tentative, has been a related but somewhat different problem as to when an item is "paid" or "finally paid" either to determine the relative priority of the item as against attachments, stop-payment orders and the like or in insolvency situations. There has been extensive litigation in the various states on these problems. To a substantial extent the confusion, the litigation and even the resulting court decisions fail to take into account that in the collection process some debits or credits are provisional or tentative and others are final and that very many debits or credits are provisional or tentative for awhile but later become final. Similarly, some cases fail to recognize that within a single bank, particularly a payor bank, each item goes through a series of processes and that in a payor bank most of these processes are preliminary to the basic act of payment or "final payment."

The term "settle" is used as a convenient term to characterize a broad variety of conditional, provisional, tentative and also final payments of items. Such a comprehensive term is needed because it is frequently difficult or unnecessary to determine whether a particular action is tentative or final or when a particular credit shifts from the tentative class to the final class. Therefore, its use throughout the Article indicates that in that particular context it is unnecessary or unwise to determine whether the debit or the credit or the payment is tentative or final. However, if qualified by the adjective "provisional" its tentative nature is intended, and if qualified by the adjective "final" its permanent nature is intended.

Examples of the various types of settlement contemplated by the term include payments in cash; the efficient but somewhat complicated process of payment through the adjustment and offsetting of balances through clearing houses; debit or credit entries in accounts between banks; the forwarding of various types of remittance instruments, sometimes to cover a particular item but more frequently to cover an entire group of items received on a particular day.

11. Paragraph (a)(12): "Suspends payments." This term is designed to afford an objective test to determine when a bank is no longer operating as a part of the banking system.

As amended in 2003.

§ 4–105. Definitions of Types of Banks.

In this Article:

(1) ["Bank" means a person engaged in the business of banking, including a savings bank, savings and loan association, credit union, or trust company;]

(2) "Depositary bank" means the first bank to take an item even though it is also the payor bank, unless the item is presented for immediate payment over the counter;

(3) "Payor bank" means a bank that is the drawee of a draft;

(4) "Intermediary bank" means a bank to which an item is transferred in course of collection except the depositary or payor bank;

(5) "Collecting bank" means a bank handling an item for collection except the payor bank;

(6) "Presenting bank" means a bank presenting an item except a payor bank.

Legislative Note: A jurisdiction that enacts this statute that has not yet enacted the revised version of UCC Article 1 should leave the definition of "Bank" in Section 4–105(1). Section 4–105(1) is reserved for that purpose. A jurisdiction that has adopted or simultaneously adopts the revised Article 1 should delete the definition of "Bank" from Section 4–105(1), but should leave those numbers "reserved." If jurisdictions follow the numbering suggested here, the subsections will have the same numbering in all jurisdictions that have adopted these amendments (whether they have or have not adopted the revised version of UCC Article 1). In either case, they should change the title of the section, as indicated in these revisions, so that all jurisdictions will have the same title for the section.

As amended in 1990 and 2002.

Official Comment

1. The definitions in general exclude a bank to which an item is issued, as this bank does not take by transfer except in the particular case covered in which the item is issued to a payee for collection, as in the case in which a corporation is transferring balances from one account to another. Thus, the definition of "depositary bank"

does not include the bank to which a check is made payable if a check is given in payment of a mortgage. This bank has the status of a payee under Article 3 on Negotiable Instruments and not that of a collecting bank.

2. Paragraph (1): "Bank" is defined in Section 1-201(4) [*unrevised Article 1; see Concordance, p. 12*] as meaning "any person engaged in the business of banking." The definition in paragraph (1) makes clear that "bank" includes savings banks, savings and loan associations, credit unions and trust companies, in addition to the commercial banks commonly denoted by use of the term "bank."

3. Paragraph (2): A bank that takes an "on us" item for collection, for application to a customer's loan, or first handles the item for other reasons is a depositary bank even though it is also the payor bank. However, if the holder presents the item for immediate payment over the counter, the payor bank is not a depositary bank.

4. Paragraph (3): The definition of "payor bank" is clarified by use of the term "drawee." That term is defined in Section 4-104 as meaning "a person ordered in a draft to make payment." An "order" is defined in Section 3-103 as meaning "a written instruction to pay money. . . . An authorization to pay is not an order unless the person authorized to pay is also instructed to pay." The definition of order is incorporated into Article 4 by Section 4-104(c). Thus a payor bank is one instructed to pay in the item. A bank does not become a payor bank by being merely authorized to pay or by being given an instruction to pay not contained in the item.

5. Paragraph (4): The term "intermediary bank" includes the last bank in the collection process if the drawee is not a bank. Usually the last bank is also a presenting bank.

§ 4-106. Payable Through or Payable at Bank: Collecting Bank.

(a) If an item states that it is "payable through" a bank identified in the item, (i) the item designates the bank as a collecting bank and does not by itself authorize the bank to pay the item, and (ii) the item may be presented for payment only by or through the bank.

ALTERNATIVE A

(b) If an item states that it is "payable at" a bank identified in the item, the item is equivalent to a draft drawn on the bank.

ALTERNATIVE B

(b) If an item states that it is "payable at" a bank identified in the item, (i) the item designates the bank as a collecting bank and does not by itself authorize the bank to pay the item, and (ii) the item may be presented for payment only by or through the bank.

(c) If a draft names a nonbank drawee and it is unclear whether a bank named in the draft is a co-drawee or a collecting bank, the bank is a collecting bank.

As added in 1990.

Official Comment

1. This section replaces former Sections 3-120 and 3-121. Some items are made "payable through" a particular bank. Subsection (a) states that such language makes the bank a collecting bank and not a payor bank. An item identifying a "payable through" bank can be presented for payment to the drawee only by the "payable through" bank. The item cannot be presented to the drawee over the counter for immediate payment or by a collecting bank other than the "payable through" bank.

2. Subsection (b) retains the alternative approach of the present law. Under Alternative A a note payable at a bank is the equivalent of a draft drawn on the bank and the midnight deadline provisions of Sections 4-301 and 4-302 apply. Under Alternative B a "payable at" bank is in the same position as a "payable through" bank under subsection (a).

3. Subsection (c) rejects the view of some cases that a bank named below the name of a drawee is itself a drawee. The commercial understanding is that this bank is a collecting bank and is not accountable under Section 4-302 for holding an item beyond its deadline. The liability of the bank is governed by Sections 4-202(a) and 4-103(e).

§ 4–107. Separate Office of Bank.

A branch or separate office of a bank is a separate bank for the purpose of computing the time within which and determining the place at or to which action may be taken or notices or orders shall be given under this Article and under Article 3.

As amended in 1962 and 1990.

Official Comment

1. A rule with respect to the status of a branch or separate office of a bank as a part of any statute on bank collections is highly desirable if not absolutely necessary. However, practices in the operations of branches and separate offices vary substantially in the different states and it has not been possible to find any single rule that is logically correct, fair in all situations and workable under all different types of practices. The decision not to draft the section with greater specificity leaves to the courts the resolution of the issues arising under this section on the basis of the facts of each case.

2. In many states and for many purposes a branch or separate office of the bank should be treated as a separate bank. Many branches function as separate banks in the handling and payment of items and require time for doing so similar to that of a separate bank. This is particularly true if branch banking is permitted throughout a state or in different towns and cities. Similarly, if there is this separate functioning a particular branch or separate office is the only proper place for various types of action to be taken or orders or notices to be given. Examples include the drawing of a check on a particular branch by a customer whose account is carried at that branch; the presentment of that same check at that branch; the issuance of an order to the branch to stop payment on the check.

3. Section 1 of the American Bankers Association Bank Collection Code provided simply: "A branch or office of any such bank shall be deemed a bank." Although this rule appears to be brief and simple, as applied to particular sections of the ABA Code it produces illogical and, in some cases, unreasonable results. For example, under Section 11 of the ABA Code it seems anomalous for one branch of a bank to have charged an item to the account of the drawer and another branch to have the power to elect to treat the item as dishonored. Similar logical problems would flow from applying the same rule to Article 4. Warranties by one branch to another branch under Sections 4–207 and 4–208 (each considered a separate bank) do not make sense.

4. Assuming that it is not desirable to make each branch a separate bank for all purposes, this section provides that a branch or separate office is a separate bank for certain purposes. In so doing the single legal entity of the bank as a whole is preserved, thereby carrying with it the liability of the institution as a whole on such obligations as it may be under. On the other hand, in cases in which the Article provides a number of time limits for different types of action by banks, if a branch functions as a separate bank, it should have the time limits available to a separate bank. Similarly if in its relations to customers a branch functions as a separate bank, notices and orders with respect to accounts of customers of the branch should be given at the branch. For example, whether a branch has notice sufficient to affect its status as a holder in due course of an item taken by it should depend upon what notice that branch has received with respect to the item. Similarly the receipt of a stop-payment order at one branch should not be notice to another branch so as to impair the right of the second branch to be a holder in due course of the item, although in circumstances in which ordinary care requires the communication of a notice or order to the proper branch of a bank, the notice or order would be effective at the proper branch from the time it was or should have been received. See Section 1–201(27) [*unrevised Article 1; see Concordance, p. 12*].

5. The bracketed language ("maintaining its own deposit ledger") in former Section 4–106 is deleted. Today banks keep records on customer accounts by electronic data storage. This has led most banks with branches to centralize to some degree their record keeping. The place where records are kept has little meaning if the information is electronically stored and is instantly retrievable at all branches of the bank. Hence, the inference to be drawn from the deletion of the bracketed language is that where record keeping is done is no longer an important factor in determining whether a branch is a separate bank.

§ 4–108. Time of Receipt of Items.

(a) For the purpose of allowing time to process items, prove balances, and make the necessary entries on its books to determine its position for the day, a bank may fix an afternoon hour of 2 P.M. or later as a cutoff hour for the handling of money and items and the making of entries on its books.

(b) An item or deposit of money received on any day after a cutoff hour so fixed or after the close of the banking day may be treated as being received at the opening of the next banking day.

As amended in 1990.

Official Comment

1. Each of the huge volume of checks processed each day must go through a series of accounting procedures that consume time. Many banks have found it necessary to establish a cutoff hour to allow time for these procedures to be completed within the time limits imposed by Article 4. Subsection (a) approves a cutoff hour of this type provided it is not earlier than 2 P.M. Subsection (b) provides that if such a cutoff hour is fixed, items received after the cutoff hour may be treated as being received at the opening of the next banking day. If the number of items received either through the mail or over the counter tends to taper off radically as the afternoon hours progress, a 2 P.M. cutoff hour does not involve a large portion of the items received but at the same time permits a bank using such a cutoff hour to leave its doors open later in the afternoon without forcing into the evening the completion of its settling and proving process.

2. The provision in subsection (b) that items or deposits received after the close of the banking day may be treated as received at the opening of the next banking day is important in cases in which a bank closes at twelve or one o'clock, e.g., on a Saturday, but continues to receive some items by mail or over the counter if, for example, it opens Saturday evening for the limited purpose of receiving deposits and cashing checks.

§ 4-109. Delays.

(a) Unless otherwise instructed, a collecting bank in a good faith effort to secure payment of a specific item drawn on a payor other than a bank, and with or without the approval of any person involved, may waive, modify, or extend time limits imposed or permitted by this [Act] for a period not exceeding two additional banking days without discharge of drawers or indorsers or liability to its transferor or a prior party.

(b) Delay by a collecting bank or payor bank beyond time limits prescribed or permitted by this [Act] or by instructions is excused if (i) the delay is caused by interruption of communication or computer facilities, suspension of payments by another bank, war, emergency conditions, failure of equipment, or other circumstances beyond the control of the bank, and (ii) the bank exercises such diligence as the circumstances require.

As amended in 1990.

Official Comment

1. Sections 4-202(b), 4-214, 4-301, and 4-302 prescribe various time limits for the handling of items. These are the limits of time within which a bank, in fulfillment of its obligation to exercise ordinary care, must handle items entrusted to it for collection or payment. Under Section 4-103 they may be varied by agreement or by Federal Reserve regulations or operating circular, clearing-house rules, or the like. Subsection (a) permits a very limited extension of these time limits. It authorizes a collecting bank to take additional time in attempting to collect drafts drawn on nonbank payors with or without the approval of any interested party. The right of a collecting bank to waive time limits under subsection (a) does not apply to checks. The two-day extension can only be granted in a good faith effort to secure payment and only with respect to specific items. It cannot be exercised if the customer instructs otherwise. Thus limited the escape provision should afford a limited degree of flexibility in special cases but should not interfere with the overall requirement and objective of speedy collections.

2. An extension granted under subsection (a) is without discharge of drawers or indorsers. It therefore extends the times for presentment or payment as specified in Article 3.

3. Subsection (b) is another escape clause from time limits. This clause operates not only with respect to time limits imposed by the Article itself but also time limits imposed by special instructions, by agreement or by Federal regulations or operating circulars, clearing-house rules or the like. The latter time limits are "permitted" by the Code. For example, a payor bank that fails to make timely return of a dishonored item may be accountable for the amount of the item. Subsection (b) excuses a bank from this liability when its failure to meet its midnight deadline resulted from, for example, a computer breakdown that was beyond the control of the bank, so long as the bank exercised the degree of diligence that the circumstances required. In *Port City State Bank v. American National Bank*, 486 F.2d 196 (10th Cir. 1973), the court held that a bank exercised sufficient diligence to be excused under this subsection. If delay is sought to be excused under this subsection, the bank has the burden of proof on

the issue of whether it exercised "such diligence as the circumstances require." The subsection is consistent with Regulation CC, Section 229.38(e).

§ 4–110. Electronic Presentment.

(a) "Agreement for electronic presentment" means an agreement, clearing-house rule, or Federal Reserve regulation or operating circular, providing that presentment of an item may be made by transmission of an image of an item or information describing the item ("presentment notice") rather than delivery of the item itself. The agreement may provide for procedures governing retention, presentment, payment, dishonor, and other matters concerning items subject to the agreement.

(b) Presentment of an item pursuant to an agreement for presentment is made when the presentment notice is received.

(c) If presentment is made by presentment notice, a reference to "item" or "check" in this Article means the presentment notice unless the context otherwise indicates.

As added in 1990.

Official Comment

1. "An agreement for electronic presentment" refers to an agreement under which presentment may be made to a payor bank by a presentment notice rather than by presentment of the item. Under imaging technology now under development, the presentment notice might be an image of the item. The electronic presentment agreement may provide that the item may be retained by a depositary bank, other collecting bank, or even a customer of the depositary bank, or it may provide that the item will follow the presentment notice. The identifying characteristic of an electronic presentment agreement is that presentment occurs when the presentment notice is received. "An agreement for electronic presentment" does not refer to the common case of retention of items by payor banks because the item itself is presented to the payor bank in these cases. Payor bank check retention is a matter of agreement between payor banks and their customers. Provisions on payor bank check retention are found in Section 4–406(b).

2. The assumptions under which the electronic presentment amendments are based are as follows: No bank will participate in an electronic presentment program without an agreement. These agreements may be either bilateral (Section 4–103(a)), under which two banks that frequently do business with each other may agree to depositary bank check retention, or multilateral (Section 4–103(b)), in which large segments of the banking industry may participate in such a program. In the latter case, federal or other uniform regulatory standards would likely supply the substance of the electronic presentment agreement, the application of which could be triggered by the use of some form of identifier on the item. Regulation CC, Section 229.36(c) authorizes truncation agreements but forbids them from extending return times or otherwise varying requirements of the part of Regulation CC governing check collection without the agreement of all parties interested in the check. For instance, an extension of return time could damage a depositary bank which must make funds available to its customers under mandatory availability schedules. The Expedited Funds Availability Act, 12 U.S.C. Section 4008(b)(2), directs the Federal Reserve Board to consider requiring that banks provide for check truncation.

3. The parties affected by an agreement for electronic presentment, with the exception of the customer, can be expected to protect themselves. For example, the payor bank can probably be expected to limit its risk of loss from drawer forgery by limiting the dollar amount of eligible items (Federal Reserve program), by reconcilement agreements (ABA Safekeeping program), by insurance (credit union share draft program), or by other means. Because agreements will exist, only minimal amendments are needed to make clear that the UCC does not prohibit electronic presentment.

§ 4–111. Statute of Limitations.

An action to enforce an obligation, duty, or right arising under this Article must be commenced within three years after the [cause of action] accrues.

As added in 1990.

Official Comment

This section conforms to the period of limitations set by Section 3–118(g) for actions for breach of warranty and to enforce other obligations, duties or rights arising under Article 3. Bracketing "cause of action" recognizes that some states use a different term, such as "claim for relief."

PART 2

COLLECTION OF ITEMS: DEPOSITARY AND COLLECTING BANKS

§ 4-201. Status of Collecting Bank as Agent and Provisional Status of Credits; Applicability of Article; Item Indorsed "Pay Any Bank".

(a) Unless a contrary intent clearly appears and before the time that a settlement given by a collecting bank for an item is or becomes final, the bank, with respect to an item, is an agent or sub-agent of the owner of the item and any settlement given for the item is provisional. This provision applies regardless of the form of indorsement or lack of indorsement and even though credit given for the item is subject to immediate withdrawal as of right or is in fact withdrawn; but the continuance of ownership of an item by its owner and any rights of the owner to proceeds of the item are subject to rights of a collecting bank, such as those resulting from outstanding advances on the item and rights of recoupment or setoff. If an item is handled by banks for purposes of presentment, payment, collection, or return, the relevant provisions of this Article apply even though action of the parties clearly establishes that a particular bank has purchased the item and is the owner of it.

(b) After an item has been indorsed with the words "pay any bank" or the like, only a bank may acquire the rights of a holder until the item has been:

(1) returned to the customer initiating collection; or

(2) specially indorsed by a bank to a person who is not a bank.

As amended in 1990.

Official Comment

1. This section states certain basic rules of the bank collection process. One basic rule, appearing in the last sentence of subsection (a), is that, to the extent applicable, the provisions of the Article govern without regard to whether a bank handling an item owns the item or is an agent for collection. Historically, much time has been spent and effort expended in determining or attempting to determine whether a bank was a purchaser of an item or merely an agent for collection. See discussion of this subject and cases cited in 11 A.L.R. 1043, 16 A.L.R. 1084, 42 A.L.R. 492, 68 A.L.R. 725, 99 A.L.R. 486. See also Section 4 of the American Bankers Association Bank Collection Code. The general approach of Article 4, similar to that of other articles, is to provide, within reasonable limits, rules or answers to major problems known to exist in the bank collection process without regard to questions of status and ownership but to keep general principles such as status and ownership available to cover residual areas not covered by specific rules. In line with this approach, the last sentence of subsection (a) says in effect that Article 4 applies to practically every item moving through banks for the purpose of presentment, payment or collection.

2. Within this general rule of broad coverage, the first two sentences of subsection (a) state a rule of agency status. "Unless a contrary intent clearly appears" the status of a collecting bank is that of an agent or sub-agent for the owner of the item. Although as indicated in Comment 1 it is much less important under Article 4 to determine status than has been the case heretofore, status may have importance in some residual areas not covered by specific rules. Further, since status has been considered so important in the past, to omit all reference to it might cause confusion. The status of agency "applies regardless of the form of indorsement or lack of indorsement and even though credit given for the item is subject to immediate withdrawal as of right or is in fact withdrawn." Thus questions heretofore litigated as to whether ordinary indorsements "for deposit," "for collection" or in blank have the effect of creating an agency status or a purchase, no longer have significance in varying the prima facie rule of agency. Similarly, the nature of the credit given for an item or whether it is subject to immediate withdrawal as of right or is in fact withdrawn, does not alter the agency status. See A.L.R. references supra in Comment 1.

A contrary intent can change agency status but this must be clear. An example of a clear contrary intent would be if collateral papers established or the item bore a legend stating that the item was sold absolutely to the depositary bank.

3. The prima facie agency status of collecting banks is consistent with prevailing law and practice today. Section 2 of the American Bankers Association Bank Collection Code so provided. Legends on deposit tickets,

collection letters and acknowledgments of items and Federal Reserve operating circulars consistently so provide. The status is consistent with rights of charge-back (Section 4–214 and Section 11 of the ABA Code) and risk of loss in the event of insolvency (Section 4–216 and Section 13 of the ABA Code). The right of charge-back with respect to checks is limited by Regulation CC, Section 226.36(d).

4. Affirmative statement of a prima facie agency status for collecting banks requires certain limitations and qualifications. Under current practices substantially all bank collections sooner or later merge into bank credits, at least if collection is effected. Usually, this takes place within a few days of the initiation of collection. An intermediary bank receives final collection and evidences the result of its collection by a "credit" on its books to the depositary bank. The depositary bank evidences the results of its collection by a "credit" in the account of its customer. As used in these instances the term "credit" clearly indicates a debtor-creditor relationship. At some stage in the bank collection process the agency status of a collecting bank changes to that of debtor, a debtor of its customer. Usually at about the same time it also becomes a creditor for the amount of the item, a creditor of some intermediary, payor or other bank. Thus the collection is completed, all agency aspects are terminated and the identity of the item has become completely merged in bank accounts, that of the customer with the depositary bank and that of one bank with another.

Although Section 4–215(a) provides that an item is finally paid when the payor bank takes or fails to take certain action with respect to the item, the final payment of the item may or may not result in the simultaneous final settlement for the item in the case of all prior parties. If a series of provisional debits and credits for the item have been entered in accounts between banks, the final payment of the item by the payor bank may result in the automatic firming up of all these provisional debits and credits under Section 4–215(c), and the consequent receipt of final settlement for the item by each collecting bank and the customer of the depositary bank simultaneously with such action of the payor bank. However, if the payor bank or some intermediary bank accounts for the item with a remittance draft, the next prior bank usually does not receive final settlement for the item until the remittance draft finally clears. See Section 4–213(c). The first sentence of subsection (a) provides that the agency status of a collecting bank (whether intermediary or depositary) continues until the settlement given by it for the item is or becomes final. In the case of the series of provisional credits covered by Section 4–215(c), this could be simultaneously with the final payment of the item by the payor bank. In cases in which remittance drafts are used or in straight noncash collections, this would not be until the times specified in Sections 4–213(c) and 4–215(d). With respect to checks Regulation CC Sections 229.31(c), 229.32(b) and 229.36(d) provide that all settlements between banks are final in both the forward collection and return of checks.

Under Section 4–213(a) settlements for items may be made by any means agreed to by the parties. Since it is impossible to contemplate all the kinds of settlements that will be utilized, no attempt is made in Article 4 to provide when settlement is final in all cases. The guiding principle is that settlements should be final when the presenting person has received usable funds. Section 4–213(c) and (d) and Section 4–215(c) provide when final settlement occurs with respect to certain kinds of settlement, but these provisions are not intended to be exclusive.

A number of practical results flow from the rule continuing the agency status of a collecting bank until its settlement for the item is or becomes final, some of which are specifically set forth in this Article. One is that risk of loss continues in the owner of the item rather than the agent bank. See Section 4–214. Offsetting rights favorable to the owner are that pending such final settlement, the owner has the preference rights of Section 4–216 and the direct rights of Section 4–302 against the payor bank. It also follows from this rule that the dollar limitations of Federal Deposit Insurance are measured by the claim of the owner of the item rather than that of the collecting bank. With respect to checks, rights of the parties in insolvency are determined by Regulation CC Section 229.39 and the liability of a bank handling a check to a subsequent bank that does not receive payment because of suspension of payments by another bank is stated in Regulation CC Section 229.35(b).

5. In those cases in which some period of time elapses between the final payment of the item by the payor bank and the time that the settlement of the collecting bank is or becomes final, e.g., if the payor bank or an intermediary bank accounts for the item with a remittance draft or in straight noncash collections, the continuance of the agency status of the collecting bank necessarily carries with it the continuance of the owner's status as principal. The second sentence of subsection (a) provides that whatever rights the owner has to proceeds of the item are subject to the rights of collecting banks for outstanding advances on the item and other valid rights, if any. The rule provides a sound rule to govern cases of attempted attachment of proceeds of a non-cash item in the hands of the payor bank as property of the absent owner. If a collecting bank has made an advance on an item which is still outstanding, its right to obtain reimbursement for this advance should be superior to the rights of the owner to the proceeds or to the rights of a creditor of the owner. An intentional crediting of proceeds of an item to the account of a prior bank known to be insolvent, for the purpose of acquiring a right of setoff, would not produce a valid setoff. See 8 Zollman, *Banks and Banking* (1936) Sec. 5443.

6. This section and Article 4 as a whole represent an intentional abandonment of the approach to bank collection problems appearing in Section 4 of the American Bankers Association Bank Collection Code. Because the tremendous volume of items handled makes impossible the examination by all banks of all indorsements on all items and thus in fact this examination is not made, except perhaps by depositary banks, it is unrealistic to base the rights and duties of all banks in the collection chain on variations in the form of indorsements. It is anomalous to provide throughout the ABA Code that the prima facie status of collecting banks is that of agent or sub-agent but in Section 4 to provide that subsequent holders (sub-agents) shall have the right to rely on the presumption that the bank of deposit (the primary agent) is the owner of the item. It is unrealistic, particularly in this background, to base rights and duties on status of agent or owner. Thus Section 4–201 makes the pertinent provisions of Article 4 applicable to substantially all items handled by banks for presentment, payment or collection, recognizes the prima facie status of most banks as agents, and then seeks to state appropriate limits and some attributes to the general rules so expressed.

7. Subsection (b) protects the ownership rights with respect to an item indorsed "pay any bank or banker" or in similar terms of a customer initiating collection or of any bank acquiring a security interest under Section 4–210, in the event the item is subsequently acquired under improper circumstances by a person who is not a bank and transferred by that person to another person, whether or not a bank. Upon return to the customer initiating collection of an item so indorsed, the indorsement may be cancelled (Section 3–207). A bank holding an item so indorsed may transfer the item out of banking channels by special indorsement; however, under Section 4–103(e), the bank would be liable to the owner of the item for any loss resulting therefrom if the transfer had been made in bad faith or with lack of ordinary care. If briefer and more simple forms of bank indorsements are developed under Section 4–206 (e.g., the use of bank transit numbers in lieu of present lengthy forms of bank indorsements), a depositary bank having the transit number "X100" could make subsection (b) operative by indorsements such as "Pay any bank—X100." Regulation CC Section 229.35(c) states the effect of an indorsement on a check by a bank.

§ 4–202. Responsibility for Collection or Return; When Action Timely.

(a) A collecting bank must exercise ordinary care in:

(1) presenting an item or sending it for presentment;

(2) sending notice of dishonor or nonpayment or returning an item other than a documentary draft to the bank's transferor after learning that the item has not been paid or accepted, as the case may be;

(3) settling for an item when the bank receives final settlement; and

(4) notifying its transferor of any loss or delay in transit within a reasonable time after discovery thereof.

(b) A collecting bank exercises ordinary care under subsection (a) by taking proper action before its midnight deadline following receipt of an item, notice, or settlement. Taking proper action within a reasonably longer time may constitute the exercise of ordinary care, but the bank has the burden of establishing timeliness.

(c) Subject to subsection (a)(1), a bank is not liable for the insolvency, neglect, misconduct, mistake, or default of another bank or person or for loss or destruction of an item in the possession of others or in transit.

As amended in 1990.

Official Comment

1. Subsection (a) states the basic responsibilities of a collecting bank. Of course, under Section 1–203 [*unrevised Article 1; see Concordance, p. 12*] a collecting bank is subject to the standard requirement of good faith. By subsection (a) it must also use ordinary care in the exercise of its basic collection tasks. By Section 4–103(a) neither requirement may be disclaimed.

2. If the bank makes presentment itself, subsection (a)(1) requires ordinary care with respect both to the time and manner of presentment. (Sections 3–501 and 4–212.) If it forwards the item to be presented the subsection requires ordinary care with respect to routing (Section 4–204), and also in the selection of intermediary banks or other agents.

3. Subsection (a) describes types of basic action with respect to which a collecting bank must use ordinary care. Subsection (b) deals with the time for taking action. It first prescribes the general standard for timely action, namely, for items received on Monday, proper action (such as forwarding or presenting) on Monday or Tuesday is timely. Although under current "production line" operations banks customarily move items along on regular schedules substantially briefer than two days, the subsection states an outside time within which a bank may know it has taken timely action. To provide flexibility from this standard norm, the subsection further states that action within a reasonably longer time may be timely but the bank has the burden of proof. In the case of time items, action after the midnight deadline, but sufficiently in advance of maturity for proper presentation, is a clear example of a "reasonably longer time" that is timely. The standard of requiring action not later than Tuesday in the case of Monday items is also subject to possibilities of variation under the general provisions of Section 4–103, or under the special provisions regarding time of receipt of items (Section 4–108), and regarding delays (Section 4–109). This subsection (b) deals only with collecting banks. The time limits applicable to payor banks appear in Sections 4–301 and 4–302.

4. At common law the so-called New York collection rule subjected the initial collecting bank to liability for the actions of subsequent banks in the collection chain; the so-called Massachusetts rule was that each bank, subject to the duty of selecting proper intermediaries, was liable only for its own negligence. Subsection (c) adopts the Massachusetts rule. But since this is stated to be subject to subsection (a)(1) a collecting bank remains responsible for using ordinary care in selecting properly qualified intermediary banks and agents and in giving proper instructions to them. Regulation CC Section 229.36(d) states the liability of a bank during the forward collection of checks.

§ 4–203. Effect of Instructions.

Subject to Article 3 concerning conversion of instruments (Section 3–420) and restrictive indorsements (Section 3–206), only a collecting bank's transferor can give instructions that affect the bank or constitute notice to it, and a collecting bank is not liable to prior parties for any action taken pursuant to the instructions or in accordance with any agreement with its transferor.

As amended in 1990.

Official Comment

This section adopts a "chain of command" theory which renders it unnecessary for an intermediary or collecting bank to determine whether its transferor is "authorized" to give the instructions. Equally the bank is not put on notice of any "revocation of authority" or "lack of authority" by notice received from any other person. The desirability of speed in the collection process and the fact that, by reason of advances made, the transferor may have the paramount interest in the item requires the rule.

The section is made subject to the provisions of Article 3 concerning conversion of instruments (Section 3–420) and restrictive indorsements (Section 3–206). Of course instructions from or an agreement with its transferor does not relieve a collecting bank of its general obligation to exercise good faith and ordinary care. See Section 4–103(a). If in any particular case a bank has exercised good faith and ordinary care and is relieved of responsibility by reason of instructions of or an agreement with its transferor, the owner of the item may still have a remedy for loss against the transferor (another bank) if such transferor has given wrongful instructions.

The rules of the section are applied only to collecting banks. Payor banks always have the problem of making proper payment of an item; whether such payment is proper should be based upon all of the rules of Articles 3 and 4 and all of the facts of any particular case, and should not be dependent exclusively upon instructions from or an agreement with a person presenting the item.

§ 4–204. Methods of Sending and Presenting; Sending Directly to Payor Bank.

(a) A collecting bank shall send items by a reasonably prompt method, taking into consideration relevant instructions, the nature of the item, the number of those items on hand, the cost of collection involved, and the method generally used by it or others to present those items.

(b) A collecting bank may send:

(1) an item directly to the payor bank;

(2) an item to a nonbank payor if authorized by its transferor; and

(3) an item other than documentary drafts to a nonbank payor, if authorized by Federal Reserve regulation or operating circular, clearing-house rule, or the like.

(c) Presentment may be made by a presenting bank at a place where the payor bank or other payor has requested that presentment be made.

As amended in 1962 and 1990.

Official Comment

1. Subsection (a) prescribes the general standards applicable to proper sending or forwarding of items. Because of the many types of methods available and the desirability of preserving flexibility any attempt to prescribe limited or precise methods is avoided.

2. Subsection (b)(1) codifies the practice of direct mail, express, messenger or like presentment to payor banks. The practice is now country-wide and is justified by the need for speed, the general responsibility of banks, Federal Deposit Insurance protection and other reasons.

3. Full approval of the practice of direct sending is limited to cases in which a bank is a payor. Since nonbank drawees or payors may be of unknown responsibility, substantial risks may be attached to placing in their hands the instruments calling for payments from them. This is obviously so in the case of documentary drafts. However, in some cities practices have long existed under clearing-house procedures to forward certain types of items to certain nonbank payors. Examples include insurance loss drafts drawn by field agents on home offices. For the purpose of leaving the door open to legitimate practices of this kind, subsection (b)(3) affirmatively approves direct sending of any item other than documentary drafts to any nonbank payor, if authorized by Federal Reserve regulation or operating circular, clearing-house rule or the like.

On the other hand subsection (b)(2) approves sending any item directly to a nonbank payor if authorized by a collecting bank's transferor. This permits special instructions or agreements out of the norm and is consistent with the "chain of command" theory of Section 4-203. However, if a transferor other than the owner of the item, e.g., a prior collecting bank, authorizes a direct sending to a nonbank payor, such transferor assumes responsibility for the propriety or impropriety of such authorization.

4. Section 3-501(b) provides where presentment may be made. This provision is expressly subject to Article 4. Section 4-204(c) specifically approves presentment by a presenting bank at any place requested by the payor bank or other payor. The time when a check is received by a payor bank for presentment is governed by Regulation CC Section 229.36(b).

§ 4-205. Depositary Bank Holder of Unindorsed Item.

If a customer delivers an item to a depositary bank for collection:

(1) the depositary bank becomes a holder of the item at the time it receives the item for collection if the customer at the time of delivery was a holder of the item, whether or not the customer indorses the item, and, if the bank satisfies the other requirements of Section 3-302, it is a holder in due course; and

(2) the depositary bank warrants to collecting banks, the payor bank or other payor, and the drawer that the amount of the item was paid to the customer or deposited to the customer's account.

As amended in 1990.

Official Comment

Section 3-201(b) provides that negotiation of an instrument payable to order requires indorsement by the holder. The rule of former Section 4-205(1) was that the depositary bank may supply a missing indorsement of its customer unless the item contains the words "payee's indorsement required" or the like. The cases have differed on the status of the depositary bank as a holder if it fails to supply its customer's indorsement. *Marine Midland Bank, N.A. v. Price, Miller, Evans & Flowers*, 446 N.Y.S.2d 797 (N.Y.App.Div. 4th Dept. 1981), *rev'd*, 455 N.Y.S.2d 565 (N.Y. 1982). It is common practice for depositary banks to receive unindorsed checks under so-called "lock-box" agreements from customers who receive a high volume of checks. No function would be served by requiring a depositary bank to run these items through a machine that would supply the customer's indorsement except to afford the drawer and the subsequent banks evidence that the proceeds of the item reached the customer's account. Paragraph (1) provides that the depositary bank becomes a holder when it takes the item for deposit if the depositor is a holder. Whether it supplies the customer's indorsement is immaterial. Paragraph (2) satisfies the need for a receipt of funds by the depositary bank by imposing on that bank a warranty that it paid the customer or deposited the item to the customer's account. This warranty runs not only to collecting banks and to the payor bank or nonbank drawee but also to the drawer, affording protection to these parties that the depositary bank received the item and applied it to the benefit of the holder.

§ 4–206. Transfer Between Banks.

Any agreed method that identifies the transferor bank is sufficient for the item's further transfer to another bank.

As amended in 1990.

Official Comment

This section is designed to permit the simplest possible form of transfer from one bank to another, once an item gets in the bank collection chain, provided only identity of the transferor bank is preserved. This is important for tracing purposes and if recourse is necessary. However, since the responsibilities of the various banks appear in the Article it becomes unnecessary to have liability or responsibility depend on more formal indorsements. Simplicity in the form of transfer is conducive to speed. If the transfer is between banks, this section takes the place of the more formal requirements of Section 3–201.

§ 4–207. Transfer Warranties.

(a) A customer or collecting bank that transfers an item and receives a settlement or other consideration warrants to the transferee and to any subsequent collecting bank that:

(1) the warrantor is a person entitled to enforce the item;

(2) all signatures on the item are authentic and authorized;

(3) the item has not been altered;

(4) the item is not subject to a defense or claim in recoupment (Section 3–305(a)) of any party that can be asserted against the warrantor;

(5) the warrantor has no knowledge of any insolvency proceeding commenced with respect to the maker or acceptor or, in the case of an unaccepted draft, the drawer; and

(6) with respect to any remotely-created consumer item, that the person on whose account the item is drawn authorized the issuance of the item in the amount for which the item is drawn.

(b) If an item is dishonored, a customer or collecting bank transferring the item and receiving settlement or other consideration is obliged to pay the amount due on the item (i) according to the terms of the item at the time it was transferred, or (ii) if the transfer was of an incomplete item, according to its terms when completed as stated in Sections 3–115 and 3–407. The obligation of a transferor is owed to the transferee and to any subsequent collecting bank that takes the item in good faith. A transferor cannot disclaim its obligation under this subsection by an indorsement stating that it is made "without recourse" or otherwise disclaiming liability.

(c) A person to whom the warranties under subsection (a) are made and who took the item in good faith may recover from the warrantor as damages for breach of warranty an amount equal to the loss suffered as a result of the breach, but not more than the amount of the item plus expenses and loss of interest incurred as a result of the breach.

(d) The warranties stated in subsection (a) cannot be disclaimed with respect to checks. Unless notice of a claim for breach of warranty is given to the warrantor within 30 days after the claimant has reason to know of the breach and the identity of the warrantor, the warrantor is discharged to the extent of any loss caused by the delay in giving notice of the claim.

(e) A cause of action for breach of warranty under this section accrues when the claimant has reason to know of the breach.

As added in 1990 and amended in 2002.

Official Comment

1. Except for subsection (b), this section conforms to Section 3–416 and extends its coverage to items. The substance of this section is discussed in the Comment to Section 3–416. Subsection (b) provides that customers or collecting banks that transfer items, whether by indorsement or not, undertake to pay the item if the item is dishonored. This obligation cannot be disclaimed by a "without recourse" indorsement or otherwise. With respect to checks, Regulation CC Section 229.34 states the warranties made by paying and returning banks.

2. For an explanation of subsection (a)(6), see comment 8 to Section 3–416.

As amended in 2002.

§ 4–208. Presentment Warranties.

(a) If an unaccepted draft is presented to the drawee for payment or acceptance and the drawee pays or accepts the draft, (i) the person obtaining payment or acceptance, at the time of presentment, and (ii) a previous transferor of the draft, at the time of transfer, warrant to the drawee that pays or accepts the draft in good faith that:

(1) the warrantor is, or was, at the time the warrantor transferred the draft, a person entitled to enforce the draft or authorized to obtain payment or acceptance of the draft on behalf of a person entitled to enforce the draft;

(2) the draft has not been altered;

(3) the warrantor has no knowledge that the signature of the purported drawer of the draft is unauthorized; and

(4) with respect to any remotely-created consumer item, that the person on whose account the item is drawn authorized the issuance of the item in the amount for which the item is drawn.

(b) A drawee making payment may recover from a warrantor damages for breach of warranty equal to the amount paid by the drawee less the amount the drawee received or is entitled to receive from the drawer because of the payment. In addition, the drawee is entitled to compensation for expenses and loss of interest resulting from the breach. The right of the drawee to recover damages under this subsection is not affected by any failure of the drawee to exercise ordinary care in making payment. If the drawee accepts the draft (i) breach of warranty is a defense to the obligation of the acceptor, and (ii) if the acceptor makes payment with respect to the draft, the acceptor is entitled to recover from a warrantor for breach of warranty the amounts stated in this subsection.

(c) If a drawee asserts a claim for breach of warranty under subsection (a) based on an unauthorized indorsement of the draft or an alteration of the draft, the warrantor may defend by proving that the indorsement is effective under Section 3–404 or 3–405 or the drawer is precluded under Section 3–406 or 4–406 from asserting against the drawee the unauthorized indorsement or alteration.

(d) If (i) a dishonored draft is presented for payment to the drawer or an indorser or (ii) any other item is presented for payment to a party obliged to pay the item, and the item is paid, the person obtaining payment and a prior transferor of the item warrant to the person making payment in good faith that the warrantor is, or was, at the time the warrantor transferred the item, a person entitled to enforce the item or authorized to obtain payment on behalf of a person entitled to enforce the item. The person making payment may recover from any warrantor for breach of warranty an amount equal to the amount paid plus expenses and loss of interest resulting from the breach.

(e) The warranties stated in subsections (a) and (d) cannot be disclaimed with respect to checks. Unless notice of a claim for breach of warranty is given to the warrantor within 30 days after the claimant has reason to know of the breach and the identity of the warrantor, the warrantor is discharged to the extent of any loss caused by the delay in giving notice of the claim.

(f) A cause of action for breach of warranty under this section accrues when the claimant has reason to know of the breach.

As added in 1990 and amended in 2002.

Official Comment

1. This section conforms to Section 3–417 and extends its coverage to items. The substance of this section is discussed in the Comment to Section 3–417. "Draft" is defined in Section 4–104 as including an item that is an order to pay so as to make clear that the term "draft" in Article 4 may include items that are not instruments within Section 3–104.

2. For an explanation of subsection (a)(4), see comment 8 to Section 3–416.

As amended in 2002.

§ 4–209. Encoding and Retention Warranties.

(a) A person who encodes information on or with respect to an item after issue warrants to any subsequent collecting bank and to the payor bank or other payor that the information is correctly encoded. If the customer of a depositary bank encodes, that bank also makes the warranty.

(b) A person who undertakes to retain an item pursuant to an agreement for electronic presentment warrants to any subsequent collecting bank and to the payor bank or other payor that retention and presentment of the item comply with the agreement. If a customer of a depositary bank undertakes to retain an item, that bank also makes this warranty.

(c) A person to whom warranties are made under this section and who took the item in good faith may recover from the warrantor as damages for breach of warranty an amount equal to the loss suffered as a result of the breach, plus expenses and loss of interest incurred as a result of the breach.

As added in 1990.

Official Comment

1. Encoding and retention warranties are included in Article 4 because they are unique to the bank collection process. These warranties are breached only by the person doing the encoding or retaining the item and not by subsequent banks handling the item. Encoding and check retention may be done by customers who are payees of a large volume of checks; hence, this section imposes warranties on customers as well as banks. If a customer encodes or retains, the depositary bank is also liable for any breach of this warranty.

2. A misencoding of the amount on the MICR line is not an alteration under Section 3–407(a) which defines alteration as changing the contract of the parties. If a drawer wrote a check for $2,500 and the depositary bank encoded $25,000 on the MICR line, the payor bank could debit the drawer's account for only $2,500. This subsection would allow the payor bank to hold the depositary bank liable for the amount paid out over $2,500 without first pursuing the person who received payment. Intervening collecting banks would not be liable to the payor bank for the depositary bank's error. If a drawer wrote a check for $25,000 and the depositary bank encoded $2,500, the payor bank becomes liable for the full amount of the check. The payor bank's rights against the depositary bank depend on whether the payor bank has suffered a loss. Since the payor bank can debit the drawer's account for $25,000, the payor bank has a loss only to the extent that the drawer's account is less than the full amount of the check. There is no requirement that the payor bank pursue collection against the drawer beyond the amount in the drawer's account as a condition to the payor bank's action against the depositary bank for breach of warranty. See *Georgia Railroad Bank & Trust Co. v. First National Bank & Trust*, 229 S.E.2d 482 (Ga.App. 1976), aff'd, 235 S.E.2d 1 (Ga. 1977), and *First National Bank of Boston v. Fidelity Bank, National Association*, 724 F.Supp. 1168 (E.D.Pa. 1989).

3. A person retaining items under an electronic presentment agreement (Section 4–110) warrants that it has complied with the terms of the agreement regarding its possession of the item and its sending a proper presentment notice. If the keeper is a customer, its depositary bank also makes this warranty.

§ 4–210. Security Interest of Collecting Bank in Items, Accompanying Documents and Proceeds.

(a) A collecting bank has a security interest in an item and any accompanying documents or the proceeds of either:

(1) in case of an item deposited in an account, to the extent to which credit given for the item has been withdrawn or applied;

(2) in case of an item for which it has given credit available for withdrawal as of right, to the extent of the credit given, whether or not the credit is drawn upon or there is a right of charge-back; or

(3) if it makes an advance on or against the item.

(b) If credit given for several items received at one time or pursuant to a single agreement is withdrawn or applied in part, the security interest remains upon all the items, any accompanying documents or the proceeds of either. For the purpose of this section, credits first given are first withdrawn.

(c) Receipt by a collecting bank of a final settlement for an item is a realization on its security interest in the item, accompanying documents, and proceeds. So long as the bank does not receive final settlement for the item or give up possession of the item or possession or control of the accompanying documents for purposes other than collection, the security interest continues to that extent and is subject to Article 9, but:

(1) no security agreement is necessary to make the security interest enforceable (Section 9–203(b)(3)(A));

(2) no filing is required to perfect the security interest; and

(3) the security interest has priority over conflicting perfected security interests in the item, accompanying documents, or proceeds.

As amended in 1999 and 2003.

Official Comment

1. Subsection (a) states a rational rule for the interest of a bank in an item. The customer of the depositary bank is normally the owner of the item and the several collecting banks are agents of the customer (Section 4–201). A collecting agent may properly make advances on the security of paper held for collection, and acquires at common law a possessory lien for these advances. Subsection (a) applies an analogous principle to a bank in the collection chain which extends credit on items in the course of collection. The bank has a security interest to the extent stated in this section. To the extent of its security interest it is a holder for value (Sections 3–303, 4–211) and a holder in due course if it satisfies the other requirements for that status (Section 3–302). Subsection (a) does not derogate from the banker's general common law lien or right of setoff against indebtedness owing in deposit accounts. See Section 1–103. Rather subsection (a) specifically implements and extends the principle as a part of the bank collection process.

2. Subsection (b) spreads the security interest of the bank over all items in a single deposit or received under a single agreement and a single giving of credit. It also adopts the "first-in, first-out" rule.

3. Collection statistics establish that the vast majority of items handled for collection are in fact collected. The first sentence of subsection (c) reflects the fact that in the normal case the bank's security interest is self-liquidating. The remainder of the subsection correlates the security interest with the provisions of Article 9, particularly for use in the cases of noncollection in which the security interest may be important.

§ 4–211. When Bank Gives Value for Purposes of Holder in Due Course.

For purposes of determining its status as a holder in due course, a bank has given value to the extent it has a security interest in an item, if the bank otherwise complies with the requirements of Section 3–302 on what constitutes a holder in due course.

As amended in 1990.

Official Comment

The section completes the thought of the previous section and makes clear that a security interest in an item is "value" for the purpose of determining the holder's status as a holder in due course. The provision is in accord with the prior law (N.I.L. Section 27) and with Article 3 (Section 3–303). The section does not prescribe a security interest under Section 4–210 as a test of "value" generally because the meaning of "value" under other Articles is adequately defined in Section 1–201 [*unrevised Article 1; see Concordance, p. 12*].

§ 4–212. Presentment by Notice of Item Not Payable by, Through, or at Bank; Liability of Drawer or Indorser.

(a) Unless otherwise instructed, a collecting bank may present an item not payable by, through, or at a bank by sending to the party to accept or pay a record providing notice that the bank holds the item for acceptance or payment. The notice must be sent in time to be received on or before the day when presentment is due and the bank must meet any requirement of the party to accept or pay under Section 3–501 by the close of the bank's next banking day after it knows of the requirement.

(b) If presentment is made by notice and payment, acceptance, or request for compliance with a requirement under Section 3–501 is not received by the close of business on the day after maturity or, in the case of demand items, by the close of business on the third banking day after notice was sent, the presenting bank may treat the item as dishonored and charge any drawer or indorser by sending it notice of the facts.

As amended in 1990 and 2002.

Official Comment

1. This section codifies a practice extensively followed in presentation of trade acceptances and documentary and other drafts drawn on nonbank payors. It imposes a duty on the payor to respond to the notice of the item if the item is not to be considered dishonored. Notice of such a dishonor charges drawers and indorsers. Presentment under this section is good presentment under Article 3. See Section 3–501.

2. A drawee not receiving notice is not, of course, liable to the drawer for wrongful dishonor.

3. A bank so presenting an instrument must be sufficiently close to the drawee to be able to exhibit the instrument on the day it is requested to do so or the next business day at the latest.

§ 4–213. Medium and Time of Settlement by Bank.

(a) With respect to settlement by a bank, the medium and time of settlement may be prescribed by Federal Reserve regulations or circulars, clearing-house rules, and the like, or agreement. In the absence of such prescription:

(1) the medium of settlement is cash or credit to an account in a Federal Reserve bank of or specified by the person to receive settlement; and

(2) the time of settlement, is:

(i) with respect to tender of settlement by cash, a cashier's check, or teller's check, when the cash or check is sent or delivered;

(ii) with respect to tender of settlement by credit in an account in a Federal Reserve Bank, when the credit is made;

(iii) with respect to tender of settlement by a credit or debit to an account in a bank, when the credit or debit is made or, in the case of tender of settlement by authority to charge an account, when the authority is sent or delivered; or

(iv) with respect to tender of settlement by a funds transfer, when payment is made pursuant to Section 4A–406(a) to the person receiving settlement.

(b) If the tender of settlement is not by a medium authorized by subsection (a) or the time of settlement is not fixed by subsection (a), no settlement occurs until the tender of settlement is accepted by the person receiving settlement.

(c) If settlement for an item is made by cashier's check or teller's check and the person receiving settlement, before its midnight deadline:

(1) presents or forwards the check for collection, settlement is final when the check is finally paid; or

(2) fails to present or forward the check for collection, settlement is final at the midnight deadline of the person receiving settlement.

(d) If settlement for an item is made by giving authority to charge the account of the bank giving settlement in the bank receiving settlement, settlement is final when the charge is made by the bank receiving settlement if there are funds available in the account for the amount of the item.

As amended in 1990.

Official Comment

1. Subsection (a) sets forth the medium of settlement that the person receiving settlement must accept. In nearly all cases the medium of settlement will be determined by agreement or by Federal Reserve regulations and circulars, clearing-house rules, and the like. In the absence of regulations, rules or agreement, the person receiving settlement may demand cash or credit in a Federal Reserve bank. If the person receiving settlement does not have an account in a Federal Reserve bank, it may specify the account of another bank in a Federal Reserve bank. In the unusual case in which there is no agreement on the medium of settlement and the bank making settlement tenders settlement other than cash or Federal Reserve bank credit, no settlement has occurred under subsection (b) unless the person receiving settlement accepts the settlement tendered. For example, if a payor bank, without agreement, tenders a teller's check, the bank receiving the settlement may reject the check and return it to the payor bank or it may accept the check as settlement.

2. In several provisions of Article 4 the time that a settlement occurs is relevant. Subsection (a) sets out a general rule that the time of settlement, like the means of settlement, may be prescribed by agreement. In the absence of agreement, the time of settlement for tender of the common agreed media of settlement is that set out in subsection (a)(2). The time of settlement by cash, cashier's or teller's check or authority to charge an account is the time the cash, check or authority is sent, unless presentment is over the counter in which case settlement occurs upon delivery to the presenter. If there is no agreement on the time of settlement and the tender of settlement is not made by one of the media set out in subsection (a), under subsection (b) the time of settlement is the time the settlement is accepted by the person receiving settlement.

3. Subsections (c) and (d) are special provisions for settlement by remittance drafts and authority to charge an account in the bank receiving settlement. The relationship between final settlement and final payment under Section 4–215 is addressed in subsection (b) of Section 4–215. With respect to settlement by cashier's checks or teller's checks, other than in response to over-the-counter presentment, the bank receiving settlement can keep the risk that the check will not be paid on the bank tendering the check in settlement by acting to initiate collection of the check within the midnight deadline of the bank receiving settlement. If the bank fails to initiate settlement before its midnight deadline, final settlement occurs at the midnight deadline, and the bank receiving settlement assumes the risk that the check will not be paid. If there is no agreement that permits the bank tendering settlement to tender a cashier's or teller's check, subsection (b) allows the bank receiving the check to reject it, and, if it does, no settlement occurs. However, if the bank accepts the check, settlement occurs and the time of final settlement is governed by subsection (c).

With respect to settlement by tender of authority to charge the account of the bank making settlement in the bank receiving settlement, subsection (d) provides that final settlement does not take place until the account charged has available funds to cover the amount of the item. If there is no agreement that permits the bank tendering settlement to tender an authority to charge an account as settlement, subsection (b) allows the bank receiving the tender to reject it. However, if the bank accepts the authority, settlement occurs and the time of final settlement is governed by subsection (d).

§ 4–214. Right of Charge-Back or Refund; Liability of Collecting Bank; Return of Item.

(a) If a collecting bank has made provisional settlement with its customer for an item and fails by reason of dishonor, suspension of payments by a bank, or otherwise to receive settlement for the item which is or becomes final, the bank may revoke the settlement given by it, charge back the amount of any credit given for the item to its customer's account, or obtain refund from its customer, whether or not it is able to return the item, if by its midnight deadline or within a longer reasonable time after it learns the facts it returns the item or sends notification of the facts. If the return or notice is delayed beyond the bank's midnight deadline or a longer reasonable time after it learns the facts, the bank may revoke the settlement, charge back the credit, or obtain refund from its customer, but it is liable for any loss resulting from the delay. These rights to revoke, charge back, and obtain refund terminate if and when a settlement for the item received by the bank is or becomes final.

(b) A collecting bank returns an item when it is sent or delivered to the bank's customer or transferor or pursuant to its instructions.

(c) A depositary bank that is also the payor may charge back the amount of an item to its customer's account or obtain refund in accordance with the section governing return of an item received by a payor bank for credit on its books (Section 4–301).

(d) The right to charge back is not affected by:

(1) previous use of a credit given for the item; or

(2) failure by any bank to exercise ordinary care with respect to the item, but a bank so failing remains liable.

(e) A failure to charge back or claim refund does not affect other rights of the bank against the customer or any other party.

(f) If credit is given in dollars as the equivalent of the value of an item payable in foreign money, the dollar amount of any charge-back or refund must be calculated on the basis of the bank-offered spot rate for the foreign money prevailing on the day when the person entitled to the charge-back or refund learns that it will not receive payment in ordinary course.

As amended in 1990.

Official Comment

1. Under current bank practice, in a major portion of cases banks make provisional settlement for items when they are first received and then await subsequent determination of whether the item will be finally paid. This is the principal characteristic of what are referred to in banking parlance as "cash items." Statistically, this practice of settling provisionally first and then awaiting final payment is justified because the vast majority of such cash items are finally paid, with the result that in this great preponderance of cases it becomes unnecessary for the banks making the provisional settlements to make any further entries. In due course the provisional settlements become final simply with the lapse of time. However, in those cases in which the item being collected is not finally paid or if for various reasons the bank making the provisional settlement does not itself receive final payment, provision is made in subsection (a) for the reversal of the provisional settlements, charge-back of provisional credits and the right to obtain refund.

2. Various causes of a bank's not receiving final payment, with the resulting right of charge-back or refund, are stated or suggested in subsection (a). These include dishonor of the original item; dishonor of a remittance instrument given for it; reversal of a provisional credit for the item; suspension of payments by another bank. The causes stated are illustrative; the right of charge-back or refund is stated to exist whether the failure to receive final payment in ordinary course arises through one of them "or otherwise."

3. The right of charge-back or refund exists if a collecting bank has made a provisional settlement for an item with its customer but terminates if and when a settlement received by the bank for the item is or becomes final. If the bank fails to receive such a final settlement the right of charge-back or refund must be exercised promptly after the bank learns the facts. The right exists (if so promptly exercised) whether or not the bank is able to return the item. The second sentence of subsection (a) adopts the view of *Appliance Buyers Credit Corp. v. Prospect National Bank*, 708 F.2d 290 (7th Cir. 1983), that if the midnight deadline for returning an item or giving notice is not met, a collecting bank loses its rights only to the extent of damages for any loss resulting from the delay.

4. Subsection (b) states when an item is returned by a collecting bank. Regulation CC, Section 229.31 preempts this subsection with respect to checks by allowing direct return to the depositary bank. Because a returned check may follow a different path than in forward collection, settlement given for the check is final and not provisional except as between the depositary bank and its customer. Regulation CC Section 229.36(d). See also Regulations CC Sections 229.31(c) and 229.32(b). Thus owing to the federal preemption, this subsection applies only to noncheck items.

5. The rule of subsection (d) relating to charge-back (as distinguished from claim for refund) applies irrespective of the cause of the nonpayment, and of the person ultimately liable for nonpayment. Thus charge-back is permitted even if nonpayment results from the depositary bank's own negligence. Any other rule would result in litigation based upon a claim for wrongful dishonor of other checks of the customer, with potential damages far in excess of the amount of the item. Any other rule would require a bank to determine difficult questions of fact. The customer's protection is found in the general obligation of good faith (Sections 1–203 [*unrevised Article 1; see Concordance, p. 12*] and 4–103). If bad faith is established the customer's recovery "includes other damages, if any, suffered by the party as a proximate consequence" (Section 4–103(e); see also Section 4–402).

6. It is clear that the charge-back does not relieve the bank from any liability for failure to exercise ordinary care in handling the item. The measure of damages for such failure is stated in Section 4-103(e).

7. Subsection (f) states a rule fixing the time for determining the rate of exchange if there is a charge-back or refund of a credit given in dollars for an item payable in a foreign currency. Compare Section 3-107. Fixing such a rule is desirable to avoid disputes. If in any case the parties wish to fix a different time for determining the rate of exchange, they may do so by agreement.

§ 4-215. Final Payment of Item by Payor Bank; When Provisional Debits and Credits Become Final; When Certain Credits Become Available for Withdrawal.

(a) An item is finally paid by a payor bank when the bank has first done any of the following:

(1) paid the item in cash;

(2) settled for the item without having a right to revoke the settlement under statute, clearing-house rule, or agreement; or

(3) made a provisional settlement for the item and failed to revoke the settlement in the time and manner permitted by statute, clearing-house rule, or agreement.

(b) If provisional settlement for an item does not become final, the item is not finally paid.

(c) If provisional settlement for an item between the presenting and payor banks is made through a clearing house or by debits or credits in an account between them, then to the extent that provisional debits or credits for the item are entered in accounts between the presenting and payor banks or between the presenting and successive prior collecting banks seriatim, they become final upon final payment of the item by the payor bank.

(d) If a collecting bank receives a settlement for an item which is or becomes final, the bank is accountable to its customer for the amount of the item and any provisional credit given for the item in an account with its customer becomes final.

(e) Subject to (i) applicable law stating a time for availability of funds and (ii) any right of the bank to apply the credit to an obligation of the customer, credit given by a bank for an item in a customer's account becomes available for withdrawal as of right:

(1) if the bank has received a provisional settlement for the item, when the settlement becomes final and the bank has had a reasonable time to receive return of the item and the item has not been received within that time;

(2) if the bank is both the depositary bank and the payor bank, and the item is finally paid, at the opening of the bank's second banking day following receipt of the item.

(f) Subject to applicable law stating a time for availability of funds and any right of a bank to apply a deposit to an obligation of the depositor, a deposit of money becomes available for withdrawal as of right at the opening of the bank's next banking day after receipt of the deposit.

As amended in 1990.

Official Comment

1. By the definition and use of the term "settle" (Section 4-104(a)(11)) this Article recognizes that various debits or credits, remittances, settlements or payments given for an item may be either provisional or final, that settlements sometimes are provisional and sometimes are final and sometimes are provisional for awhile but later become final. Subsection (a) defines when settlement for an item constitutes final payment.

Final payment of an item is important for a number of reasons. It is one of several factors determining the relative priorities between items and notices, stop-payment orders, legal process and setoffs (Section 4-303). It is the "end of the line" in the collection process and the "turn around" point commencing the return flow of proceeds. It is the point at which many provisional settlements become final. See Section 4-215(c). Final payment of an item by the payor bank fixes preferential rights under Section 4-216.

2. If an item being collected moves through several states, e.g., is deposited for collection in California, moves through two or three California banks to the Federal Reserve Bank of San Francisco, to the Federal Reserve Bank of Boston, to a payor bank in Maine, the collection process involves the eastward journey of the item from

California to Maine and the westward journey of the proceeds from Maine to California. Subsection (a) recognizes that final payment does not take place, in this hypothetical case, on the journey of the item eastward. It also adopts the view that neither does final payment occur on the journey westward because what in fact is journeying westward are *proceeds* of the item.

3. Traditionally and under various decisions payment in cash of an item by a payor bank has been considered final payment. Subsection (a)(1) recognizes and provides that payment of an item in cash by a payor bank is final payment.

4. Section 4–104(a)(11) defines "settle" as meaning "to pay in cash, by clearing-house settlement, in a charge or credit or by remittance, or otherwise as agreed. A settlement may be either provisional or final." Subsection (a)(2) of Section 4–215 provides that an item is finally paid by a payor bank when the bank has "settled for the item without having a right to revoke the settlement under statute, clearing-house rule or agreement." Former subsection (1)(b) is modified by subsection (a)(2) to make clear that a payor bank cannot make settlement provisional by unilaterally reserving a right to revoke the settlement. The right must come from a statute (e.g., Section 4–301), clearing-house rule or other agreement. Subsection (a)(2) provides in effect that if the payor bank finally settles for an item this constitutes final payment of the item. The subsection operates if nothing has occurred and no situation exists making the settlement provisional. If under statute, clearing-house rule or agreement, a right of revocation of the settlement exists, the settlement is provisional. Conversely, if there is an absence of a right to revoke under statute, clearing-house rule or agreement, the settlement is final and such final settlement constitutes final payment of the item.

A primary example of a statutory right on the part of the payor bank to revoke a settlement is the right to revoke conferred by Section 4–301. The underlying theory and reason for deferred posting statutes (Section 4–301) is to require a settlement on the date of receipt of an item but to keep that settlement provisional with the right to revoke prior to the midnight deadline. In any case in which Section 4–301 is applicable, any settlement by the payor bank is provisional solely by virtue of the statute, subsection (a)(2) of Section 4–215 does not operate, and such provisional settlement does not constitute final payment of the item. With respect to checks, Regulation CC Section 229.36(d) provides that settlement between banks for the forward collection of checks is final. The relationship of this provision to Article 4 is discussed in the Commentary to that section.

A second important example of a right to revoke a settlement is that arising under clearing-house rules. It is very common for clearing-house rules to provide that items exchanged and settled for in a clearing (e.g., before 10:00 a.m. on Monday) may be returned and the settlements revoked up to but not later than 2:00 p.m. on the same day (Monday) or under deferred posting at some hour on the next business day (e.g., 2:00 p.m. Tuesday). Under this type of rule the Monday morning settlement is provisional and being provisional does not constitute a final payment of the item.

An example of an agreement allowing the payor bank to revoke a settlement is a case in which the payor bank is also the depositary bank and has signed a receipt or duplicate deposit ticket or has made an entry in a passbook acknowledging receipt, for credit to the account of A, of a check drawn on it by B. If the receipt, deposit ticket, passbook or other agreement with A is to the effect that any credit so entered is provisional and may be revoked pending the time required by the payor bank to process the item to determine if it is in good form and there are funds to cover it, the agreement keeps the receipt or credit provisional and avoids its being either final settlement or final payment.

The most important application of subsection (a)(2) is that in which presentment of an item has been made over the counter for immediate payment. In this case Section 4–301(a) does not apply to make the settlement provisional, and final payment has occurred unless a rule or agreement provides otherwise.

5. Former Section 4–213(1)(c) provided that final payment occurred when the payor bank completed the "process of posting." The term was defined in former Section 4–109. In the present Article, Section 4–109 has been deleted and the process-of-posting test has been abandoned in Section 4–215(a) for determining when final payment is made. Difficulties in determining when the events described in former Section 4–109 take place make the process-of-posting test unsuitable for a system of automated check collection or electronic presentment.

6. The last sentence of former Section 4–213(1) is deleted as an unnecessary source of confusion. Initially the view that payor bank may be accountable for, that is, liable for the amount of, an item that it has already paid seems incongruous. This is particularly true in the light of the language formerly found in Section 4–302 stating that the payor bank can defend against liability for accountability by showing that it has already settled for the item. But, at least with respect to former Section 4–213(1)(c), such a provision was needed because under the process-of-posting test a payor bank may have paid an item without settling for it. Now that Article 4 has

abandoned the process-of-posting test, the sentence is no longer needed. If the payor bank has neither paid the item nor returned it within its midnight deadline, the payor bank is accountable under Section 4-302.

7. Subsection (a)(3) covers the situation in which the payor bank makes a provisional settlement for an item, and this settlement becomes final at a later time by reason of the failure of the payor bank to revoke it in the time and manner permitted by statute, clearing-house rule or agreement. An example of this type of situation is the clearing-house settlement referred to in Comment 4. In the illustration there given if the time limit for the return of items received in the Monday morning clearing is 2:00 p.m. on Tuesday and the provisional settlement has not been revoked at that time in a manner permitted by the clearing-house rules, the provisional settlement made on Monday morning becomes final at 2:00 p.m. on Tuesday. Subsection (a)(3) provides specifically that in this situation the item is finally paid at 2:00 p.m. Tuesday. If on the other hand a payor bank receives an item in the mail on Monday and makes some provisional settlement for the item on Monday, it has until midnight on Tuesday to return the item or give notice and revoke any settlement under Section 4-301. In this situation subsection (a)(3) of Section 4-215 provides that if the provisional settlement made on Monday is not revoked before midnight on Tuesday as permitted by Section 4-301, the item is finally paid at midnight on Tuesday. With respect to checks, Regulation CC Section 229.30(c) allows an extension of the midnight deadline under certain circumstances. If a bank does not expeditiously return a check liability may accrue under Regulation CC Section 229.38. For the relationship of that liability to responsibility under this Article, see Regulation CC Sections 229.30 and 229.38.

8. Subsection (b) relates final settlement to final payment under Section 4-215. For example, if a payor bank makes provisional settlement for an item by sending a cashier's or teller's check and that settlement fails to become final under Section 4-213(c), subsection (b) provides that final payment has not occurred. If the item is not paid, the drawer remains liable, and under Section 4-302(a) the payor bank is accountable unless it has returned the item before its midnight deadline. In this regard, subsection (b) is an exception to subsection (a)(3). Even if the payor bank has not returned an item by its midnight deadline there is still no final payment if provisional settlement had been made and settlement failed to become final. However, if presentment of the item was over the counter for immediate payment, final payment has occurred under Section 4-215(a)(2). Subsection (b) does not apply because the settlement was not provisional. Section 4-301(a). In this case the presenting person, often the payee of the item, has the right to demand cash or the cash equivalent of federal reserve credit. If the presenting person accepts another medium of settlement such as a cashier's or teller's check, the presenting person takes the risk that the payor bank may fail to pay a cashier's check because of insolvency or that the drawee of a teller's check may dishonor it.

9. Subsection (c) states the country-wide usage that when the item is finally paid by the payor bank under subsection (a) this final payment automatically without further action "firms up" other provisional settlements made for it. However, the subsection makes clear that this "firming up" occurs only if the settlement between the presenting and payor banks was made either through a clearing house or by debits and credits in accounts between them. It does not take place if the payor bank remits for the item by sending some form of remittance instrument. Further, the "firming up" continues only to the extent that provisional debits and credits are entered seriatim in accounts between banks which are successive to the presenting bank. The automatic "firming up" is broken at any time that any collecting bank remits for the item by sending a remittance draft, because final payment to the remittee then usually depends upon final payment of the remittance draft.

10. Subsection (d) states the general rule that if a collecting bank receives settlement for an item which is or becomes final, the bank is accountable to its customer for the amount of the item. One means of accounting is to remit to its customer the amount it has received on the item. If previously it gave to its customer a provisional credit for the item in an account its receipt of final settlement for the item "firms up" this provisional credit and makes it final. When this credit given by it so becomes final, in the usual case its agency status terminates and it becomes a debtor to its customer for the amount of the item. See Section 4-201(a). If the accounting is by a remittance instrument or authorization to charge further time will usually be required to complete its accounting (Section 4-213).

11. Subsection (e) states when certain credits given by a bank to its customer become available for withdrawal as of right. Subsection (e)(1) deals with the situation in which a bank has given a credit (usually provisional) for an item to its customer and in turn has received a provisional settlement for the item from an intermediary or payor bank to which it has forwarded the item. In this situation before the provisional credit entered by the collecting bank in the account of its customer becomes available for withdrawal as of right, it is not only necessary that the provisional settlement received by the bank for the item becomes final but also that the collecting bank has a reasonable time to receive return of the item and the item has not been received within that time. How much time is "reasonable" for these purposes will of course depend on the distance the item has to travel

and the number of banks through which it must pass (having in mind not only travel time by regular lines of transmission but also the successive midnight deadlines of the several banks) and other pertinent facts. Also, if the provisional settlement received is some form of a remittance instrument or authorization to charge, the "reasonable" time depends on the identity and location of the payor of the remittance instrument, the means for clearing such instrument, and other pertinent facts. With respect to checks Regulation CC Sections 229.10–229.13 or similar applicable state law (Section 229.20) control. This is also time for the situation described in Comment 12.

12. Subsection (e)(2) deals with the situation of a bank that is both a depositary bank and a payor bank. The subsection recognizes that if A and B are both customers of a depositary-payor bank and A deposits B's check on the depositary-payor in A's account on Monday, time must be allowed to permit the check under the deferred posting rules of Section 4–301 to reach the bookkeeper for B's account at some time on Tuesday, and, if there are insufficient funds in B's account, to reverse or charge back the provisional credit in A's account. Consequently this provisional credit in A's account does not become available for withdrawal as of right until the opening of business on Wednesday. If it is determined on Tuesday that there are insufficient funds in B's account to pay the check, the credit to A's account can be reversed on Tuesday. On the other hand if the item is in fact paid on Tuesday, the rule of subsection (e)(2) is desirable to avoid uncertainty and possible disputes between the bank and its customer as to exactly what hour within the day the credit is available.

§ 4–216. Insolvency and Preference.

(a) If an item is in or comes into the possession of a payor or collecting bank that suspends payment and the item has not been finally paid, the item must be returned by the receiver, trustee, or agent in charge of the closed bank to the presenting bank or the closed bank's customer.

(b) If a payor bank finally pays an item and suspends payments without making a settlement for the item with its customer or the presenting bank which settlement is or becomes final, the owner of the item has a preferred claim against the payor bank.

(c) If a payor bank gives or a collecting bank gives or receives a provisional settlement for an item and thereafter suspends payments, the suspension does not prevent or interfere with the settlement's becoming final if the finality occurs automatically upon the lapse of certain time or the happening of certain events.

(d) If a collecting bank receives from subsequent parties settlement for an item, which settlement is or becomes final and the bank suspends payments without making a settlement for the item with its customer which settlement is or becomes final, the owner of the item has a preferred claim against the collecting bank.

As amended in 1990.

Official Comment

1. The underlying purpose of the provisions of this section is not to confer upon banks, holders of items or anyone else preferential positions in the event of bank failures over general depositors or any other creditors of the failed banks. The purpose is to fix as definitely as possible the cut-off point of time for the completion or cessation of the collection process in the case of items that happen to be in the process at the time a particular bank suspends payments. It must be remembered that in bank collections as a whole and in the handling of items by an individual bank, items go through a whole series of processes. It must also be remembered that at any particular point of time a particular bank (at least one of any size) is functioning as a depositary bank for some items, as an intermediary bank for others, as a presenting bank for still others and as a payor bank for still others, and that when it suspends payments it will have close to its normal load of items working through its various processes. For the convenience of receivers, owners of items, banks, and in fact substantially everyone concerned, it is recognized that at the particular moment of time that a bank suspends payment, a certain portion of the items being handled by it have progressed far enough in the bank collection process that it is preferable to permit them to continue the remaining distance, rather than to send them back and reverse the many entries that have been made or the steps that have been taken with respect to them. Therefore, having this background and these purposes in mind, the section states what items must be turned backward at the moment suspension intervenes and what items have progressed far enough that the collection process with respect to them continues, with the resulting necessary statement of rights of various parties flowing from this prescription of the cut-off time.

2. The rules stated are similar to those stated in the American Bankers Association Bank Collection Code, but with the abandonment of any theory of trust. On the other hand, some law previous to this Act may be relevant. See Note, *Uniform Commercial Code: Stopping Payment of an Item Deposited with an Insolvent Depositary Bank*, 40 Okla.L.Rev. 689 (1987). Although for practical purposes Federal Deposit Insurance affects materially the result of bank failures on holders of items and banks, no attempt is made to vary the rules of the section by reason of such insurance.

3. It is recognized that in view of *Jennings v. United States Fidelity & Guaranty Co.*, 294 U.S. 216, 55 S.Ct. 394, 79 L.Ed. 869, 99 A.L.R. 1248 (1935), amendment of the National Bank Act would be necessary to have this section apply to national banks. But there is no reason why it should not apply to others. See Section 1–108 [*unrevised Article 1; see Concordance, p. 12*].

PART 3

COLLECTION OF ITEMS: PAYOR BANKS

§ 4–301. Deferred Posting; Recovery of Payment by Return of Items; Time of Dishonor; Return of Items by Payor Bank.

(a) If a payor bank settles for a demand item other than a documentary draft presented otherwise than for immediate payment over the counter before midnight of the banking day of receipt, the payor bank may revoke the settlement and recover the settlement if, before it has made final payment and before its midnight deadline, it

(1) returns the item;

(2) returns an image of the item, if the party to which the return is made has entered into an agreement to accept an image as a return of the item and the image is returned in accordance with that agreement; or

(3) sends a record providing notice of dishonor or nonpayment if the item is unavailable for return.

(b) If a demand item is received by a payor bank for credit on its books, it may return the item or send notice of dishonor and may revoke any credit given or recover the amount thereof withdrawn by its customer, if it acts within the time limit and in the manner specified in subsection (a).

(c) Unless previous notice of dishonor has been sent, an item is dishonored at the time when for purposes of dishonor it is returned or notice sent in accordance with this section.

(d) An item is returned:

(1) as to an item presented through a clearing house, when it is delivered to the presenting or last collecting bank or to the clearing house or is sent or delivered in accordance with clearing-house rules; or

(2) in all other cases, when it is sent or delivered to the bank's customer or transferor or pursuant to instructions.

As amended in 1990 and 2002.

Official Comment

1. The term "deferred posting" appears in the caption of Section 4–301. This refers to the practice permitted by statute in most of the states before the UCC under which a payor bank receives items on one day but does not post the items to the customer's account until the next day. Items dishonored were then returned after the posting on the day after receipt. Under Section 4–301 the concept of "deferred posting" merely allows a payor bank that has settled for an item on the day of receipt to return a dishonored item on the next day before its midnight deadline, without regard to when the item was actually posted. With respect to checks Regulation CC Section 229.30(c) extends the midnight deadline under the UCC under certain circumstances. See the Commentary to Regulation CC Section 229.38(d) on the relationship between the UCC and Regulation CC on settlement.

2. The function of this section is to provide the circumstances under which a payor bank that has made timely settlement for an item may return the item and revoke the settlement so that it may recover any settlement made. These circumstances are: (1) the item must be a demand item other than a documentary draft; (2) the item

must be presented otherwise than for immediate payment over the counter; and (3) the payor bank must return the item (or give notice if the item is unavailable for return) before its midnight deadline and before it has paid the item. With respect to checks, see Regulation CC Section 229.31(f) on notice in lieu of return and Regulation CC Section 229.33 as to the different requirement of notice of nonpayment. An instance of when an item may be unavailable for return arises under a collecting bank check retention plan under which presentment is made by a presentment notice and the item is retained by the collecting bank. Section 4–215(a)(2) provides that final payment occurs if the payor bank has settled for an item without a right to revoke the settlement under statute, clearing-house rule or agreement. In any case in which Section 4–301(a) is applicable, the payor bank has a right to revoke the settlement by statute; therefore, Section 4–215(a)(2) is inoperable, and the settlement is provisional. Hence, if the settlement is not over the counter and the payor bank settles in a manner that does not constitute final payment, the payor bank can revoke the settlement by returning the item before its midnight deadline.

3. The relationship of Section 4–301(a) to final settlement and final payment under Section 4–215 is illustrated by the following case. Depositary Bank sends by mail an item to Payor Bank with instructions to settle by remitting a teller's check drawn on a bank in the city where Depositary Bank is located. Payor Bank sends the teller's check on the day the item was presented. Having made timely settlement, under the deferred posting provisions of Section 4–301(a), Payor Bank may revoke that settlement by returning the item before its midnight deadline. If it fails to return the item before its midnight deadline, it has finally paid the item if the bank on which the teller's check was drawn honors the check. But if the teller's check is dishonored there has been no final settlement under Section 4–213(c) and no final payment under Section 4–215(b). Since the Payor Bank has neither paid the item nor made timely return, it is accountable for the item under Section 4–302(a).

4. The time limits for action imposed by subsection (a) are adopted by subsection (b) for cases in which the payor bank is also the depositary bank, but in this case the requirement of a settlement on the day of receipt is omitted.

5. Subsection (c) fixes a base point from which to measure the time within which notice of dishonor must be given. See Section 3–503.

6. Subsection (d) leaves banks free to agree upon the manner of returning items but establishes a precise time when an item is "returned." For definition of "sent" as used in paragraphs (1) and (2) see Section 1–201(38) [*unrevised Article 1; see Concordance, p. 12*]. Obviously the subsection assumes that the item has not been "finally paid" under Section 4–215(a). If it has been, this provision has no operation.

7. The fact that an item has been paid under proposed Section 4–215 does not preclude the payor bank from asserting rights of restitution or revocation under Section 3–418. *National Savings and Trust Co. v. Park Corp.*, 722 F.2d 1303 (6th Cir. 1983), cert. denied, 466 U.S. 939 (1984), is the correct interpretation of the present law on this issue.

8. Paragraph (a)(2) is designed to facilitate electronic check-processing by authorizing the payor bank to return an image of the item instead of the actual item. It applies only when the payor bank and the party to which the return has been made have agreed that the payor bank can make such a return and when the return complies with the agreement. The purpose of the paragraph is to prevent third parties (such as the depositor of the check) from contending that the payor bank missed its midnight deadline because it failed to return the actual item in a timely manner. If the payor bank missed its midnight deadline, payment would have become final under Section 4–215 and the depositary bank would have lost its right of chargeback under Section 4–214. Of course, the depositary bank might enter into an agreement with its depositor to resolve that problem, but it is not clear that agreements by banks with their customers can resolve all such issues. In any event, paragraph (a)(2) should eliminate the need for such agreements. The provision rests on the premise that it is inappropriate to penalize a payor bank simply because it returns the actual item a few business days after the midnight deadline of the payor bank sent notice before that deadline to a collecting bank that had agreed to accept such notices.

Nothing in paragraph (a)(2) authorizes the payor bank to destroy the check.

As amended in 2002.

§ 4–302. Payor Bank's Responsibility for Late Return of Item.

(a) If an item is presented to and received by a payor bank, the bank is accountable for the amount of:

(1) a demand item, other than a documentary draft, whether properly payable or not, if the bank, in any case in which it is not also the depositary bank, retains the item beyond midnight of the

banking day of receipt without settling for it or, whether or not it is also the depositary bank, does not pay or return the item or send notice of dishonor until after its midnight deadline; or

(2) any other properly payable item unless, within the time allowed for acceptance or payment of that item, the bank either accepts or pays the item or returns it and accompanying documents.

(b) The liability of a payor bank to pay an item pursuant to subsection (a) is subject to defenses based on breach of a presentment warranty (Section 4-208) or proof that the person seeking enforcement of the liability presented or transferred the item for the purpose of defrauding the payor bank.

As amended in 1990.

Official Comment

1. Subsection (a)(1) continues the former law distinguishing between cases in which the payor bank is not also the depositary bank and those in which the payor bank is also the depositary bank ("on us" items). For "on us" items the payor bank is accountable if it retains the item beyond its midnight deadline without settling for it. If the payor bank is not the depositary bank it is accountable if it retains the item beyond midnight of the banking day of receipt without settling for it. It may avoid accountability either by settling for the item on the day of receipt and returning the item before its midnight deadline under Section 4-301 or by returning the item on the day of receipt. This rule is consistent with the deferred posting practice authorized by Section 4-301 which allows the payor bank to make provisional settlement for an item on the day of receipt and to revoke that settlement by returning the item on the next day. With respect to checks, Regulation CC Section 229.36(d) provides that settlements between banks for forward collection of checks are final when made. See the Commentary on that provision for its effect on the UCC.

2. If the settlement given by the payor bank does not become final, there has been no payment under Section 4-215(b), and the payor bank giving the failed settlement is accountable under subsection (a)(1) of Section 4-302. For instance, the payor bank makes provisional settlement by sending a teller's check that is dishonored. In such a case settlement is not final under Section 4-213(c) and no payment occurs under Section 4-215(b). Payor bank is accountable on the item. The general principle is that unless settlement provides the presenting bank with usable funds, settlement has failed and the payor bank is accountable for the amount of the item. On the other hand, if the payor bank makes a settlement for the item that becomes final under Section 4-215, the item has been paid and thus the payor bank is not accountable for the item under this Section.

3. Subsection (b) is an elaboration of the deleted introductory language of former Section 4-302: "In the absence of a valid defense such as breach of a presentment warranty (subsection (1) of Section 4-207), settlement effected or the like. . . ." A payor bank can defend an action against it based on accountability by showing that the item contained a forged indorsement or a fraudulent alteration. Subsection (b) drops the ambiguous "or the like" language and provides that the payor bank may also raise the defense of fraud. Decisions that hold an accountable bank's liability to be "absolute" are rejected. A payor bank that makes a late return of an item should not be liable to a defrauder operating a check kiting scheme. In *Bank of Leumi Trust Co. v. Bally's Park Place Inc.*, 528 F.Supp. 349 (S.D.N.Y. 1981), and *American National Bank v. Foodbasket*, 497 P.2d 546 (Wyo. 1972), banks that were accountable under Section 4-302 for missing their midnight deadline were successful in defending against parties who initiated collection knowing that the check would not be paid. The "settlement effected" language is deleted as unnecessary. If a payor bank is accountable for an item it is liable to pay it. If it has made final payment for an item, it is no longer accountable for the item.

As amended in 2002.

§ 4-303. When Items Subject to Notice, Stop-Payment Order, Legal Process, or Setoff; Order in Which Items May Be Charged or Certified.

(a) Any knowledge, notice, or stop-payment order received by, legal process served upon, or setoff exercised by a payor bank comes too late to terminate, suspend, or modify the bank's right or duty to pay an item or to charge its customer's account for the item if the knowledge, notice, stop-payment order, or legal process is received or served and a reasonable time for the bank to act thereon expires or the setoff is exercised after the earliest of the following:

(1) the bank accepts or certifies the item;

(2) the bank pays the item in cash;

(3) the bank settles for the item without having a right to revoke the settlement under statute, clearing-house rule, or agreement;

(4) the bank becomes accountable for the amount of the item under Section 4–302 dealing with the payor bank's responsibility for late return of items; or

(5) with respect to checks, a cutoff hour no earlier than one hour after the opening of the next banking day after the banking day on which the bank received the check and no later than the close of that next banking day or, if no cutoff hour is fixed, the close of the next banking day after the banking day on which the bank received the check.

(b) Subject to subsection (a), items may be accepted, paid, certified, or charged to the indicated account of its customer in any order.

As amended in 1990.

Official Comment

1. While a payor bank is processing an item presented for payment, it may receive knowledge or a legal notice affecting the item, such as knowledge or a notice that the drawer has filed a petition in bankruptcy or made an assignment for the benefit of creditors; may receive an order of the drawer stopping payment on the item; may have served on it an attachment of the account of the drawer; or the bank itself may exercise a right of setoff against the drawer's account. Each of these events affects the account of the drawer and may eliminate or freeze all or part of whatever balance is available to pay the item. Subsection (a) states the rule for determining the relative priorities between these various legal events and the item.

2. The rule is that if any one of several things has been done to the item or if it has reached any one of several stages in its processing at the time the knowledge, notice, stop-payment order or legal process is received or served and a reasonable time for the bank to act thereon expires or the setoff is exercised, the knowledge, notice, stop-payment order, legal process or setoff comes too late, the item has priority and a charge to the customer's account may be made and is effective. With respect to the effect of the customer's bankruptcy, the bank's rights are governed by Bankruptcy Code Section 542(c) which codifies the result of *Bank of Marin v. England*, 385 U.S. 99 (1966). Section 4–405 applies to the death or incompetence of the customer.

3. Once a payor bank has accepted or certified an item or has paid the item in cash, the event has occurred that determines priorities between the item and the various legal events usually described as the "four legals." Paragraphs (1) and (2) of subsection (a) so provide. If a payor bank settles for an item presented over the counter for immediate payment by a cashier's check or teller's check which the presenting person agrees to accept, paragraph (3) of subsection (a) would control and the event determining priority has occurred. Because presentment was over the counter, Section 4–301(a) does not apply to give the payor bank the statutory right to revoke the settlement. Thus the requirements of paragraph (3) have been met unless a clearing-house rule or agreement of the parties provides otherwise.

4. In the usual case settlement for checks is by entries in bank accounts. Since the process-of-posting test has been abandoned as inappropriate for automated check collection, the determining event for priorities is a given hour on the day after the item is received. (Paragraph (5) of subsection (a).) The hour may be fixed by the bank no earlier than one hour after the opening on the next banking day after the bank received the check and no later than the close of that banking day. If an item is received after the payor bank's regular Section 4–108 cutoff hour, it is treated as received the next banking day. If a bank receives an item after its regular cutoff hour on Monday and an attachment is levied at noon on Tuesday, the attachment is prior to the item if the bank had not before that hour taken the action described in paragraphs (1), (2), and (3) of subsection (a). The Commentary to Regulation CC Section 229.36(d) explains that even though settlement by a paying bank for a check is final for Regulation CC purposes, the paying bank's right to return the check before its midnight deadline under the UCC is not affected.

5. Another event conferring priority for an item and a charge to the customer's account based upon the item is stated by the language "become accountable for the amount of the item under Section 4–302 dealing with the payor bank's responsibility for late return of items." Expiration of the deadline under Section 4–302 with resulting accountability by the payor bank for the amount of the item, establishes priority of the item over notices, stop-payment orders, legal process or setoff.

6. In the case of knowledge, notice, stop-payment orders and legal process the effective time for determining whether they were received too late to affect the payment of an item and a charge to the customer's account by reason of such payment, is receipt plus a reasonable time for the bank to act on any of these

communications. Usually a relatively short time is required to communicate to the accounting department advice of one of these events but certainly some time is necessary. Compare Sections 1–201(27) [*unrevised Article 1; see Concordance, p. 12*] and 4–403. In the case of setoff the effective time is when the setoff is actually made.

7. As between one item and another no priority rule is stated. This is justified because of the impossibility of stating a rule that would be fair in all cases, having in mind the almost infinite number of combinations of large and small checks in relation to the available balance on hand in the drawer's account; the possible methods of receipt; and other variables. Further, the drawer has drawn all the checks, the drawer should have funds available to meet all of them and has no basis for urging one should be paid before another; and the holders have no direct right against the payor bank in any event, unless of course, the bank has accepted, certified or finally paid a particular item, or has become liable for it under Section 4–302. Under subsection (b) the bank has the right to pay items for which it is itself liable ahead of those for which it is not.

PART 4

RELATIONSHIP BETWEEN PAYOR BANK AND ITS CUSTOMER

§ 4–401. When Bank May Charge Customer's Account.

(a) A bank may charge against the account of a customer an item that is properly payable from the account even though the charge creates an overdraft. An item is properly payable if it is authorized by the customer and is in accordance with any agreement between the customer and bank.

(b) A customer is not liable for the amount of an overdraft if the customer neither signed the item nor benefited from the proceeds of the item.

(c) A bank may charge against the account of a customer a check that is otherwise properly payable from the account, even though payment was made before the date of the check, unless the customer has given notice to the bank of the postdating describing the check with reasonable certainty. The notice is effective for the period stated in Section 4–403(b) for stop-payment orders, and must be received at such time and in such manner as to afford the bank a reasonable opportunity to act on it before the bank takes any action with respect to the check described in Section 4–303. If a bank charges against the account of a customer a check before the date stated in the notice of postdating, the bank is liable for damages for the loss resulting from its act. The loss may include damages for dishonor of subsequent items under Section 4–402.

(d) A bank that in good faith makes payment to a holder may charge the indicated account of its customer according to:

(1) the original terms of the altered item; or

(2) the terms of the completed item, even though the bank knows the item has been completed unless the bank has notice that the completion was improper.

As amended in 1990.

Official Comment

1. An item is properly payable from a customer's account if the customer has authorized the payment and the payment does not violate any agreement that may exist between the bank and its customer. For an example of a payment held to violate an agreement with a customer, see *Torrance National Bank v. Enesco Federal Credit Union*, 285 P.2d 737 (Cal.App. 1955). An item drawn for more than the amount of a customer's account may be properly payable. Thus under subsection (a) a bank may charge the customer's account for an item even though payment results in an overdraft. An item containing a forged drawer's signature or forged indorsement is not properly payable. Concern has arisen whether a bank may require a customer to execute a stop-payment order when the customer notifies the bank of the loss of an unindorsed or specially indorsed check. Since such a check cannot be properly payable from the customer's account, it is inappropriate for a bank to require stop-payment order in such a case.

2. Subsection (b) adopts the view of case authority holding that if there is more than one customer who can draw on an account, the nonsigning customer is not liable for an overdraft unless that person benefits from the proceeds of the item.

3. Subsection (c) is added because the automated check collection system cannot accommodate postdated checks. A check is usually paid upon presentment without respect to the date of the check. Under the former law, if a payor bank paid a postdated check before its stated date, it could not charge the customer's account because the check was not "properly payable." Hence, the bank might have been liable for wrongfully dishonoring subsequent checks of the drawer that would have been paid had the postdated check not been prematurely paid. Under subsection (c) a customer wishing to postdate a check must notify the payor bank of its postdating in time to allow the bank to act on the customer's notice before the bank has to commit itself to pay the check. If the bank fails to act on the customer's timely notice, it may be liable for damages for the resulting loss which may include damages for dishonor of subsequent items. This Act does not regulate fees that banks charge their customers for a notice of postdating or other services covered by the Act, but under principles of law such as unconscionability or good faith and fair dealing, courts have reviewed fees and the bank's exercise of a discretion to set fees. *Perdue v. Crocker National Bank*, 38 Cal.3d 913 (1985) (unconscionability); *Best v. United Bank of Oregon*, 739 P.2d 554, 562–566 (1987) (good faith and fair dealing). In addition, Section 1–203 [*unrevised Article 1; see Concordance, p. 12*] provides that every contract or duty within this Act imposes an obligation of good faith in its performance or enforcement.

4. Section 3–407(c) states that a payor bank or drawee which pays a fraudulently altered instrument in good faith and without notice of the alteration may enforce rights with respect to the instrument according to its original terms or, in the case of an incomplete instrument altered by unauthorized completion, according to its terms as completed. Section 4–401(d) follows the rule stated in Section 3–407(c) by applying it to an altered item and allows the bank to enforce rights with respect to the altered item by charging the customer's account.

§ 4–402. Bank's Liability to Customer for Wrongful Dishonor; Time of Determining Insufficiency of Account.

(a) Except as otherwise provided in this Article, a payor bank wrongfully dishonors an item if it dishonors an item that is properly payable, but a bank may dishonor an item that would create an overdraft unless it has agreed to pay the overdraft.

(b) A payor bank is liable to its customer for damages proximately caused by the wrongful dishonor of an item. Liability is limited to actual damages proved and may include damages for an arrest or prosecution of the customer or other consequential damages. Whether any consequential damages are proximately caused by the wrongful dishonor is a question of fact to be determined in each case.

(c) A payor bank's determination of the customer's account balance on which a decision to dishonor for insufficiency of available funds is based may be made at any time between the time the item is received by the payor bank and the time that the payor bank returns the item or gives notice in lieu of return, and no more than one determination need be made. If, at the election of the payor bank, a subsequent balance determination is made for the purpose of reevaluating the bank's decision to dishonor the item, the account balance at that time is determinative of whether a dishonor for insufficiency of available funds is wrongful.

As amended in 1990.

Official Comment

1. Subsection (a) states positively what has been assumed under the original Article: that if a bank fails to honor a properly payable item it may be liable to its customer for wrongful dishonor. Under subsection (b) the payor bank's wrongful dishonor of an item gives rise to a statutory cause of action. Damages may include consequential damages. Confusion has resulted from the attempts of courts to reconcile the first and second sentences of former Section 4–402. The second sentence implied that the bank was liable for some form of damages other than those proximately caused by the dishonor if the dishonor was other than by mistake. But nothing in the section described what these noncompensatory damages might be. Some courts have held that in distinguishing between mistaken dishonors and nonmistaken dishonors, the so-called "trader" rule has been retained that allowed a "merchant or trader" to recover substantial damages for wrongful dishonor without proof of damages actually suffered. Comment 3 to former Section 4–402 indicated that this was not the intent of the drafters. White & Summers, Uniform Commercial Code, Section 18–4 (1988), states: "The negative implication is that when wrongful dishonors occur not 'through mistake' but willfully, the court may impose damages greater than 'actual damages'. . . . Certainly the reference to 'mistake' in the second sentence of 4–402 invites a court to

adopt the relevant pre-Code distinction." Subsection (b) by deleting the reference to mistake in the second sentence precludes any inference that Section 4–402 retains the "trader" rule. Whether a bank is liable for noncompensatory damages, such as punitive damages, must be decided by Section 1–103 and Section 1–106 [*unrevised Article 1; see Concordance, p. 12*] ("by other rule of law").

2. Wrongful dishonor is different from "failure to exercise ordinary care in handling an item," and the measure of damages is that stated in this section, not that stated in Section 4–103(e). By the same token, if a dishonor comes within this section, the measure of damages of this section applies and not another measure of damages. If the wrongful refusal of the beneficiary's bank to make funds available from a funds transfer causes the beneficiary's check to be dishonored, no specific guidance is given as to whether recovery is under this section or Article 4A. In each case this issue must be viewed in its factual context, and it was thought unwise to seek to establish certainty at the cost of fairness.

3. The second and third sentences of subsection (b) reject decisions holding that as a matter of law the dishonor of a check is not the "proximate cause" of the arrest and prosecution of the customer and leave to determination in each case as a question of fact whether the dishonor is or may be the "proximate cause."

4. Banks commonly determine whether there are sufficient funds in an account to pay an item after the close of banking hours on the day of presentment when they post debit and credit items to the account. The determination is made on the basis of credits available for withdrawal as of right or made available for withdrawal by the bank as an accommodation to its customer. When it is determined that payment of the item would overdraw the account, the item may be returned at any time before the bank's midnight deadline the following day. Before the item is returned new credits that are withdrawable as of right may have been added to the account. Subsection (c) eliminates uncertainty under Article 4 as to whether the failure to make a second determination before the item is returned on the day following presentment is a wrongful dishonor if new credits were added to the account on that day that would have covered the amount of the check.

5. Section 4–402 has been construed to preclude an action for wrongful dishonor by a plaintiff other than the bank's customer. *Loucks v. Albuquerque National Bank*, 418 P.2d 191 (N.Mex. 1966). Some courts have allowed a plaintiff other than the customer to sue when the customer is a business entity that is one and the same with the individual or individuals operating it. *Murdaugh Volkswagen, Inc. v. First National Bank*, 801 F.2d 719 (4th Cir. 1986) and *Karsh v. American City Bank*, 113 Cal.App.3d 419, 169 Cal.Rptr. 851 (1980). However, where the wrongful dishonor impugns the reputation of an operator of the business, the issue is not merely, as the court in *Koger v. East First National Bank*, 443 So.2d 141 (Fla.App. 1983), put it, one of a literal versus a liberal interpretation of Section 4–402. Rather the issue is whether the statutory cause of action in Section 4–402 displaces, in accordance with Section 1–103, any cause of action that existed at common law in a person who is not the customer whose reputation was damaged. See *Marcum v. Security Trust and Savings Co.*, 221 Ala. 419, 129 So. 74 (1930). While Section 4–402 should not be interpreted to displace the latter cause of action, the section itself gives no cause of action to other than a "customer," however that definition is construed, and thus confers no cause of action on the holder of a dishonored item. *First American National Bank v. Commerce Union Bank*, 692 S.W.2d 642 (Tenn.App. 1985).

§ 4–403. Customer's Right to Stop Payment; Burden of Proof of Loss.

(a) A customer or any person authorized to draw on the account if there is more than one person may stop payment of any item drawn on the customer's account or close the account by an order to the bank describing the item or account with reasonable certainty received at a time and in a manner that affords the bank a reasonable opportunity to act on it before any action by the bank with respect to the item described in Section 4–303. If the signature of more than one person is required to draw on an account, any of these persons may stop payment or close the account.

(b) A stop-payment order is effective for six months, but it lapses after 14 calendar days if the original order was oral and was not confirmed in a record within that period. A stop-payment order may be renewed for additional six-month periods by a record given to the bank within a period during which the stop-payment order is effective.

(c) The burden of establishing the fact and amount of loss resulting from the payment of an item contrary to a stop-payment order or order to close an account is on the customer. The loss from payment of an item contrary to a stop-payment order may include damages for dishonor of subsequent items under Section 4–402.

As amended in 1990 and 2002.

Official Comment

1. The position taken by this section is that stopping payment or closing an account is a service which depositors expect and are entitled to receive from banks notwithstanding its difficulty, inconvenience and expense. The inevitable occasional losses through failure to stop or close should be borne by the banks as a cost of the business of banking.

2. Subsection (a) follows the decisions holding that a payee or indorsee has no right to stop payment. This is consistent with the provision governing payment or satisfaction. See Section 3–602. The sole exception to this rule is found in Section 4–405 on payment after notice of death, by which any person claiming an interest in the account can stop payment.

3. Payment is commonly stopped only on checks; but the right to stop payment is not limited to checks, and extends to any item payable by any bank. If the maker of a note payable at a bank is in a position analogous to that of a drawer (Section 4–106) the maker may stop payment of the note. By analogy the rule extends to drawees other than banks.

4. A cashier's check or teller's check purchased by a customer whose account is debited in payment for the check is not a check drawn on the customer's account within the meaning of subsection (a); hence, a customer purchasing a cashier's check or teller's check has no right to stop payment of such a check under subsection (a). If a bank issuing a cashier's check or teller's check refuses to pay the check as an accommodation to its customer or for other reasons, its liability on the check is governed by Section 3–411. There is no right to stop payment after certification of a check or other acceptance of a draft, and this is true no matter who procures the certification. See Sections 3–411 and 4–303. The acceptance is the drawee's own engagement to pay, and it is not required to impair its credit by refusing payment for the convenience of the drawer.

5. Subsection (a) makes clear that if there is more than one person authorized to draw on a customer's account any one of them can stop payment of any check drawn on the account or can order the account closed. Moreover, if there is a customer, such as a corporation, that requires its checks to bear the signatures of more than one person, any of these persons may stop payment on a check. In describing the item, the customer, in the absence of a contrary agreement, must meet the standard of what information allows the bank under the technology then existing to identify the item with reasonable certainty.

6. Under subsection (b), a stop-payment order is effective after the order, whether written or oral, is received by the bank and the bank has a reasonable opportunity to act on it. If the order is written it remains in effect for six months from that time. If the order is oral it lapses after 14 days unless there is written confirmation. If there is written confirmation within the 14-day period, the six-month period dates from the giving of the oral order. A stop-payment order may be renewed any number of times by written notice given during a six-month period while a stop order is in effect. A new stop-payment order may be given after a six-month period expires, but such a notice takes effect from the date given. When a stop-payment order expires it is as though the order had never been given, and the payor bank may pay the item in good faith under Section 4–404 even though a stop-payment order had once been given.

7. A payment in violation of an effective direction to stop payment is an improper payment, even though it is made by mistake or inadvertence. Any agreement to the contrary is invalid under Section 4–103(a) if in paying the item over the stop-payment order the bank has failed to exercise ordinary care. An agreement to the contrary which is imposed upon a customer as part of a standard form contract would have to be evaluated in the light of the general obligation of good faith. Sections 1–203 [*unrevised Article 1; see Concordance, p. 12*] and 4–104(c). The drawee is, however, entitled to subrogation to prevent unjust enrichment (Section 4–407); retains common law defenses, e.g., that by conduct in recognizing the payment the customer has ratified the bank's action in paying over a stop-payment order (Section 1–103); and retains common law rights, e.g., to recover money paid under a mistake under Section 3–418. It has sometimes been said that payment cannot be stopped against a holder in due course, but the statement is inaccurate. The payment can be stopped but the drawer remains liable on the instrument to the holder in due course (Sections 3–305, 3–414) and the drawee, if it pays, becomes subrogated to the rights of the holder in due course against the drawer. Section 4–407. The relationship between Sections 4–403 and 4–407 is discussed in the comments to Section 4–407. Any defenses available against a holder in due course remain available to the drawer, but other defenses are cut off to the same extent as if the holder were bringing the action.

§ 4–404. Bank Not Obliged to Pay Check More Than Six Months Old.

A bank is under no obligation to a customer having a checking account to pay a check, other than a certified check, which is presented more than six months after its date, but it may charge its customer's account for a payment made thereafter in good faith.

Official Comment

This section incorporates a type of statute that had been adopted in 26 jurisdictions before the Code. The time limit is set at six months because banking and commercial practice regards a check outstanding for longer than that period as stale, and a bank will normally not pay such a check without consulting the depositor. It is therefore not required to do so, but is given the option to pay because it may be in a position to know, as in the case of dividend checks, that the drawer wants payment made.

Certified checks are excluded from the section because they are the primary obligation of the certifying bank (Sections 3–409 and 3–413). The obligation runs directly to the holder of the check. The customer's account was presumably charged when the check was certified.

§ 4–405. Death or Incompetence of Customer.

(a) A payor or collecting bank's authority to accept, pay, or collect an item or to account for proceeds of its collection, if otherwise effective, is not rendered ineffective by incompetence of a customer of either bank existing at the time the item is issued or its collection is undertaken if the bank does not know of an adjudication of incompetence. Neither death nor incompetence of a customer revokes the authority to accept, pay, collect, or account until the bank knows of the fact of death or of an adjudication of incompetence and has reasonable opportunity to act on it.

(b) Even with knowledge, a bank may for 10 days after the date of death pay or certify checks drawn on or before that date unless ordered to stop payment by a person claiming an interest in the account.

As amended in 1990.

Official Comment

1. Subsection (a) follows existing decisions holding that a drawee (payor) bank is not liable for the payment of a check before it has notice of the death or incompetence of the drawer. The justice and necessity of the rule are obvious. A check is an order to pay which the bank must obey under penalty of possible liability for dishonor. Further, with the tremendous volume of items handled any rule that required banks to verify the continued life and competency of drawers would be completely unworkable.

One or both of these same reasons apply to other phases of the bank collection and payment process and the rule is made wide enough to apply to these other phases. It applies to all kinds of "items"; to "customers" who own items as well as "customers" who draw or make them; to the function of collecting items as well as the function of accepting or paying them; to the carrying out of instructions to account for proceeds even though these may involve transfers to third parties; to depositary and intermediary banks as well as payor banks; and to incompetency existing at the time of the issuance of an item or the commencement of the collection or payment process as well as to incompetency occurring thereafter. Further, the requirement of actual knowledge makes inapplicable the rule of some cases that an adjudication of incompetency is constructive notice to all the world because obviously it is as impossible for banks to keep posted on such adjudications (in the absence of actual knowledge) as it is to keep posted as to death of immediate or remote customers.

2. Subsection (b) provides a limited period after death during which a bank may continue to pay checks (as distinguished from other items) even though it has notice. The purpose of the provision, as of the existing statutes, is to permit holders of checks drawn and issued shortly before death to cash them without the necessity of filing a claim in probate. The justification is that these checks normally are given in immediate payment of an obligation, that there is almost never any reason why they should not be paid, and that filing in probate is a useless formality, burdensome to the holder, the executor, the court and the bank.

This section does not prevent an executor or administrator from recovering the payment from the holder of the check. It is not intended to affect the validity of any gift causa mortis or other transfer in contemplation of death, but merely to relieve the bank of liability for the payment.

3. Any surviving relative, creditor or other person who claims an interest in the account may give a direction to the bank not to pay checks, or not to pay a particular check. Such notice has the same effect as a

direction to stop payment. The bank has no responsibility to determine the validity of the claim or even whether it is "colorable." But obviously anyone who has an interest in the estate, including the person named as executor in a will, even if the will has not yet been admitted to probate, is entitled to claim an interest in the account.

§ 4–406. Customer's Duty to Discover and Report Unauthorized Signature or Alteration.

(a) A bank that sends or makes available to a customer a statement of account showing payment of items for the account shall either return or make available to the customer the items paid or provide information in the statement of account sufficient to allow the customer reasonably to identify the items paid. The statement of account provides sufficient information if the item is described by item number, amount, and date of payment.

(b) If the items are not returned to the customer, the person retaining the items shall either retain the items or, if the items are destroyed, maintain the capacity to furnish legible copies of the items until the expiration of seven years after receipt of the items. A customer may request an item from the bank that paid the item, and that bank must provide in a reasonable time either the item or, if the item has been destroyed or is not otherwise obtainable, a legible copy of the item.

(c) If a bank sends or makes available a statement of account or items pursuant to subsection (a), the customer must exercise reasonable promptness in examining the statement or the items to determine whether any payment was not authorized because of an alteration of an item or because a purported signature by or on behalf of the customer was not authorized. If, based on the statement or items provided, the customer should reasonably have discovered the unauthorized payment, the customer must promptly notify the bank of the relevant facts.

(d) If the bank proves that the customer failed, with respect to an item, to comply with the duties imposed on the customer by subsection (c), the customer is precluded from asserting against the bank:

(1) the customer's unauthorized signature or any alteration on the item, if the bank also proves that it suffered a loss by reason of the failure; and

(2) the customer's unauthorized signature or alteration by the same wrongdoer on any other item paid in good faith by the bank if the payment was made before the bank received notice from the customer of the unauthorized signature or alteration and after the customer had been afforded a reasonable period of time, not exceeding 30 days, in which to examine the item or statement of account and notify the bank.

(e) If subsection (d) applies and the customer proves that the bank failed to exercise ordinary care in paying the item and that the failure substantially contributed to loss, the loss is allocated between the customer precluded and the bank asserting the preclusion according to the extent to which the failure of the customer to comply with subsection (c) and the failure of the bank to exercise ordinary care contributed to the loss. If the customer proves that the bank did not pay the item in good faith, the preclusion under subsection (d) does not apply.

(f) Without regard to care or lack of care of either the customer or the bank, a customer who does not within one year after the statement or items are made available to the customer (subsection (a)) discover and report the customer's unauthorized signature on or any alteration on the item is precluded from asserting against the bank the unauthorized signature or alteration. If there is a preclusion under this subsection, the payor bank may not recover for breach of warranty under Section 4–208 with respect to the unauthorized signature or alteration to which the preclusion applies.

As amended in 1990.

Revised Official Comment

1. Under subsection (a), if a bank that has paid a check or other item for the account of a customer makes available to the customer a statement of account showing payment of the item, the bank must either return the item to the customer or provide a description of the item sufficient to allow the customer to identify it. Under subsection (c), the customer has a duty to exercise reasonable promptness in examining the statement or the returned item to discover any unauthorized signature of the customer or any alteration and to promptly notify the bank if the customer should reasonably have discovered the unauthorized signature or alteration.

The duty stated in subsection (c) becomes operative only if the "bank sends or makes available a statement of account or items pursuant to subsection (a)." A bank is not under a duty to send a statement of account or the paid items to the customer; but, if it does not do so, the customer does not have any duties under subsection (c).

Under subsection (a), a statement of account must provide information "sufficient to allow the customer reasonably to identify the items paid." If the bank supplies its customer with an image of the paid item, it complies with this standard. But a safe harbor rule is provided. The bank complies with the standard of providing "sufficient information" if "the item is described by item number, amount, and date of payment." This means that the customer's duties under subsection (c) are triggered if the bank sends a statement of account complying with the safe harbor rule without returning the paid items. A bank does not have to return the paid items unless it has agreed with the customer to do so. Whether there is such an agreement depends upon the particular circumstances. See Section 1-201(3) [*unrevised Article 1; see Concordance, p. 12*]. If the bank elects to provide the minimum information that is "sufficient" under subsection (a) and, as a consequence, the customer could not "reasonably have discovered the unauthorized payment," there is no preclusion under subsection (d). If the customer made a record of the issued checks on the check stub or carbonized copies furnished by the bank in the checkbook, the customer should usually be able to verify the paid items shown on the statement of account and discover any unauthorized or altered checks. But there could be exceptional circumstances. For example, if a check is altered by changing the name of the payee, the customer could not normally detect the fraud unless the customer is given the paid check or the statement of account discloses the name of the payee of the altered check. If the customer could not "reasonably have discovered the unauthorized payment" under subsection (c) there would not be a preclusion under subsection (d).

The safe harbor provided by subsection (a) serves to permit a bank, based on the state of existing technology, to trigger the customer's duties under subsection (c) by providing a "statement of account showing payment of items" without having to return the paid items, in any case in which the bank has not agreed with the customer to return the paid items. The safe harbor does not, however, preclude a customer under subsection (d) from asserting its unauthorized signature or an alteration against a bank in those circumstances in which under subsection (c) the customer should not "reasonably have discovered the unauthorized payment." Whether the customer has failed to comply with its duties under subsection (c) is determined on a case-by-case basis.

The provision in subsection (a) that a statement of account contains "sufficient information if the item is described by item number, amount, and date of payment" is based upon the existing state of technology. This information was chosen because it can be obtained by the bank's computer from the check's MICR line without examination of the items involved. The other two items of information that the customer would normally want to know—the name of the payee and the date of the item—cannot currently be obtained from the MICR line. The safe harbor rule is important in determining the feasibility of payor or collecting bank check retention plans. A customer who keeps a record of checks written, e.g., on the check stubs or carbonized copies of the checks supplied by the bank in the checkbook, will usually have sufficient information to identify the items on the basis of item number, amount, and date of payment. But customers who do not utilize these record-keeping methods may not. The policy decision is that accommodating customers who do not keep adequate records is not as desirable as accommodating customers who keep more careful records. This policy results in less cost to the check collection system and thus to all customers of the system. It is expected that technological advances such as image processing may make it possible for banks to give customers more information in the future in a manner that is fully compatible with automation or truncation systems. At that time the Permanent Editorial Board may wish to make recommendations for an amendment revising the safe harbor requirements in the light of those advances.

2. Subsection (d) states the consequences of a failure by the customer to perform its duty under subsection (c) to report an alteration or the customer's unauthorized signature. Subsection (d)(1) applies to the unauthorized payment of the item to which the duty to report under subsection (c) applies. If the bank proves that the customer "should reasonably have discovered the unauthorized payment" (See Comment 1) and did not notify the bank, the customer is precluded from asserting against the bank the alteration or the customer's unauthorized signature if the bank proves that it suffered a loss as a result of the failure of the customer to perform its subsection (c) duty. Subsection (d)(2) applies to cases in which the customer fails to report an unauthorized signature or alteration with respect to an item in breach of the subsection (c) duty (See Comment 1) and the bank subsequently pays other items of the customer with respect to which there is an alteration or unauthorized signature of the customer and the same wrongdoer is involved. If the payment of the subsequent items occurred after the customer has had a reasonable time (not exceeding 30 days) to report with respect to the first item and before the bank received notice of the unauthorized signature or alteration of the first item, the customer is precluded from asserting the alteration or unauthorized signature with respect to the subsequent items.

If the customer is precluded in a single or multiple item unauthorized payment situation under subsection (d), but the customer proves that the bank failed to exercise ordinary care in paying the item or items and that the failure substantially contributed to the loss, subsection (e) provides a comparative negligence test for allocating loss between the customer and the bank. Subsection (e) also states that, if the customer proves that the bank did not pay the item in good faith, the preclusion under subsection (d) does not apply.

Subsection (d)(2) changes former subsection (2)(b) by adopting a 30-day period in place of a 14-day period. Although the 14-day period may have been sufficient when the original version of Article 4 was drafted in the 1950s, given the much greater volume of checks at the time of the revision, a longer period was viewed as more appropriate. The rule of subsection (d)(2) follows pre-Code case law that payment of an additional item or items bearing an unauthorized signature or alteration by the same wrongdoer is a loss suffered by the bank traceable to the customer's failure to exercise reasonable care (See Comment 1) in examining the statement and notifying the bank of objections to it. One of the most serious consequences of failure of the customer to comply with the requirements of subsection (c) is the opportunity presented to the wrongdoer to repeat the misdeeds. Conversely, one of the best ways to keep down losses in this type of situation is for the customer to promptly examine the statement and notify the bank of an unauthorized signature or alteration so that the bank will be alerted to stop paying further items. Hence, the rule of subsection (d)(2) is prescribed, and to avoid dispute a specific time limit, 30 days, is designated for cases to which the subsection applies. These considerations are not present if there are no losses resulting from the payment of additional items. In these circumstances, a reasonable period for the customer to comply with its duties under subsection (c) would depend on the circumstances (Section 1–204(2)) [*unrevised Article 1; see Concordance, p. 12*] and the subsection (d)(2) time limit should not be imported by analogy into subsection (c).

3. Subsection (b) applies if the items are not returned to the customer. Check retention plans may include a simple payor bank check retention plan or the kind of check retention plan that would be authorized by a truncation agreement in which a collecting bank or the payee may retain the items. Even after agreeing to a check retention plan, a customer may need to see one or more checks for litigation or other purposes. The customer's request for the check may always be made to the payor bank. Under subsection (b) retaining banks may destroy items but must maintain the capacity to furnish legible copies for seven years. A legible copy may include an image of an item. This Act does not define the length of the reasonable period of time for a bank to provide the check or copy of the check. What is reasonable depends on the capacity of the bank and the needs of the customer. This Act does not specify sanctions for failure to retain or furnish the items or legible copies; this is left to other laws regulating banks. See Comment 3 to Section 4–101. Moreover, this Act does not regulate fees that banks charge their customers for furnishing items or copies or other services covered by the Act, but under principles of law such as unconscionability or good faith and fair dealing, courts have reviewed fees and the bank's exercise of a discretion to set fees. *Perdue v. Crocker National Bank*, 38 Cal.3d 913 (1985) (unconscionability); *Best v. United Bank of Oregon*, 739 P.2d 554, 562–566 (1987) (good faith and fair dealing). In addition, Section 1–203 [*unrevised Article 1; see Concordance, p. 12*] provides that every contract or duty within this Act imposes an obligation of good faith in its performance or enforcement.

4. Subsection (e) replaces former subsection (3) and poses a modified comparative negligence test for determining liability. See the discussion on this point in the Comments to Sections 3–404, 3–405, and 3–406. The term "good faith" is defined in Section 1–201(b)(20) as including "observance of reasonable commercial standards of fair dealing." The connotation of this standard is fairness and not absence of negligence.

The term "ordinary care" used in subsection (e) is defined in Section 3–103(a)(7), made applicable to Article 4 by Section 4–104(c), to provide that sight examination by a payor bank is not required if its procedure is reasonable and is commonly followed by other comparable banks in the area. The case law is divided on this issue. The definition of "ordinary care" in Section 3–103 rejects those authorities that hold, in effect, that failure to use sight examination is negligence as a matter of law. The effect of the definition of "ordinary care" on Section 4–406 is only to provide that in the small percentage of cases in which a customer's failure to examine its statement or returned items has led to loss under subsection (d) a bank should not have to share that loss solely because it has adopted an automated collection or payment procedure in order to deal with the great volume of items at a lower cost to all customers.

5. Several changes are made in former Section 4–406(5). First, former subsection (5) is deleted and its substance is made applicable only to the one-year notice preclusion in former subsection (4) (subsection (f)). Thus if a drawer has not notified the payor bank of an unauthorized check or material alteration within the one-year period, the payor bank may not choose to recredit the drawer's account and pass the loss to the collecting banks on the theory of breach of warranty. Second, the reference in former subsection (4) to unauthorized indorsements is deleted. Section 4–406 imposes no duties on the drawer to look for unauthorized indorsements. Section 4–111

sets out a statute of limitations allowing a customer a three-year period to seek a credit to an account improperly charged by payment of an item bearing an unauthorized indorsement. Third, subsection (c) is added to Section 4-208 to assure that if a depositary bank is sued for breach of a presentment warranty, it can defend by showing that the drawer is precluded by Section 3-406 or Section 4-406(c) and (d).

As amended in 1991 and 2002.

§ 4-407. Payor Bank's Right to Subrogation on Improper Payment.

If a payor bank has paid an item over the order of the drawer or maker to stop payment, or after an account has been closed, or otherwise under circumstances giving a basis for objection by the drawer or maker, to prevent unjust enrichment and only to the extent necessary to prevent loss to the bank by reason of its payment of the item, the payor bank is subrogated to the rights

(1) of any holder in due course on the item against the drawer or maker;

(2) of the payee or any other holder of the item against the drawer or maker either on the item or under the transaction out of which the item arose; and

(3) of the drawer or maker against the payee or any other holder of the item with respect to the transaction out of which the item arose.

As amended in 1990.

Official Comment

1. Section 4-403 states that a stop-payment order or an order to close an account is binding on a bank. If a bank pays an item over such an order it is prima facie liable, but under subsection (c) of Section 4-403 the burden of establishing the fact and amount of loss from such payment is on the customer. A defense frequently interposed by a bank in an action against it for wrongful payment over a stop-payment order is that the drawer or maker suffered no loss because it would have been liable to a holder in due course in any event. On this argument some cases have held that payment cannot be stopped against a holder in due course. Payment can be stopped, but if it is, the drawer or maker is liable and the sound rule is that the bank is subrogated to the rights of the holder in due course. The preamble and paragraph (1) of this section state this rule.

2. Paragraph (2) also subrogates the bank to the rights of the payee or other holder against the drawer or maker either on the item or under the transaction out of which it arose. It may well be that the payee is not a holder in due course but still has good rights against the drawer. These may be on the check but also may not be as, for example, where the drawer buys goods from the payee and the goods are partially defective so that the payee is not entitled to the full price, but the goods are still worth a portion of the contract price. If the drawer retains the goods it is obligated to pay a part of the agreed price. If the bank has paid the check it should be subrogated to this claim of the payee against the drawer.

3. Paragraph (3) subrogates the bank to the rights of the drawer or maker against the payee or other holder with respect to the transaction out of which the item arose. If, for example, the payee was a fraudulent salesman inducing the drawer to issue a check for defective securities, and the bank pays the check over a stop-payment order but reimburses the drawer for such payment, the bank should have a basis for getting the money back from the fraudulent salesman.

4. The limitations of the preamble prevent the bank itself from getting any double recovery or benefits out of its subrogation rights conferred by the section.

5. The spelling out of the affirmative rights of the bank in this section does not destroy other existing rights (Section 1-103). Among others these may include the defense of a payor bank that by conduct in recognizing the payment a customer has ratified the bank's action in paying in disregard of a stop-payment order or right to recover money paid under a mistake.

PART 5

COLLECTION OF DOCUMENTARY DRAFTS

§ 4–501. Handling of Documentary Drafts; Duty to Send for Presentment and to Notify Customer of Dishonor.

A bank that takes a documentary draft for collection shall present or send the draft and accompanying documents for presentment and, upon learning that the draft has not been paid or accepted in due course, shall seasonably notify its customer of the fact even though it may have discounted or bought the draft or extended credit available for withdrawal as of right.

As amended in 1990.

Official Comment

This section states the duty of a bank handling a documentary draft for a customer. "Documentary draft" is defined in Section 4–104. The duty stated exists even if the bank has bought the draft. This is because to the customer the draft normally represents an underlying commercial transaction, and if that is not going through as planned the customer should know it promptly. An electronic document of title may be presented through allowing access to the document or delivery of the document. Article 1, Section 1–201 (definition of "delivery").

As amended in 2003.

§ 4–502. Presentment of "On Arrival" Drafts.

If a draft or the relevant instructions require presentment "on arrival", "when goods arrive" or the like, the collecting bank need not present until in its judgment a reasonable time for arrival of the goods has expired. Refusal to pay or accept because the goods have not arrived is not dishonor; the bank must notify its transferor of the refusal but need not present the draft again until it is instructed to do so or learns of the arrival of the goods.

As amended in 1990.

Official Comment

The section is designed to establish a definite rule for "on arrival" drafts. The term includes not only drafts drawn payable "on arrival" but also drafts forwarded with instructions to present "on arrival." The term refers to the arrival of the relevant goods. Unless a bank has actual knowledge of the arrival of the goods, as for example, when it is the "notify" party on the bill of lading, the section only requires the exercise of such judgment in estimating time as a bank may be expected to have. Commonly the buyer-drawee will want the goods and will therefore call for the documents and take up the draft when they do arrive.

§ 4–503. Responsibility of Presenting Bank for Documents and Goods; Report of Reasons for Dishonor; Referee in Case of Need.

Unless otherwise instructed and except as provided in Article 5, a bank presenting a documentary draft:

(1) must deliver the documents to the drawee on acceptance of the draft if it is payable more than three days after presentment; otherwise, only on payment; and

(2) upon dishonor, either in the case of presentment for acceptance or presentment for payment, may seek and follow instructions from any referee in case of need designated in the draft or, if the presenting bank does not choose to utilize the referee's services, it must use diligence and good faith to ascertain the reason for dishonor, must notify its transferor of the dishonor and of the results of its effort to ascertain the reasons therefor, and must request instructions.

However the presenting bank is under no obligation with respect to goods represented by the documents except to follow any reasonable instructions seasonably received; it has a right to reimbursement for any expense incurred in following instructions and to prepayment of or indemnity for those expenses.

As amended in 1990.

Official Comment

1. This section states the rules governing, in the absence of instructions, the duty of the presenting bank in case either of honor or of dishonor of a documentary draft. The section should be read in connection with Section 2–514 on when documents are deliverable on acceptance, when on payment. In the case of a dishonor of the draft, the bank, subject to Section 4–504, must return possession or control of the documents to its principal.

2. If the draft is drawn under a letter of credit, Article 5 controls. See Sections 5–109 through 5–114 [*unrevised Article 5*]. As amended in 2003.

§ 4–504. Privilege of Presenting Bank to Deal With Goods; Security Interest for Expenses.

(a) A presenting bank that, following the dishonor of a documentary draft, has seasonably requested instructions but does not receive them within a reasonable time may store, sell, or otherwise deal with the goods in any reasonable manner.

(b) For its reasonable expenses incurred by action under subsection (a) the presenting bank has a lien upon the goods or their proceeds, which may be foreclosed in the same manner as an unpaid seller's lien.

As amended in 1990.

Official Comment

The section gives the presenting bank, after dishonor, a privilege to deal with the goods in any commercially reasonable manner pending instructions from its transferor and, if still unable to communicate with its principal after a reasonable time, a right to realize its expenditures as if foreclosing on an unpaid seller's lien (Section 2–706). The provision includes situations in which storage of goods or other action becomes commercially necessary pending receipt of any requested instructions, even if the requested instructions are later received.

The "reasonable manner" referred to means one reasonable in the light of business factors and the judgment of a business man.

UCC ARTICLE 4A (2019)

FUNDS TRANSFERS

Article 4A was promulgated in 1989.

PART 5. MISCELLANEOUS PROVISIONS

National Conference of Commissioners on Uniform State Laws

REPORTER

Robert L. Jordan, Los Angeles, California
William D. Warren, Los Angeles, California

DRAFTING COMMITTEE

CO-CHAIRMEN

Carlyle C. Ring, Jr., Alexandria, Virginia
Robert Haydock, Jr., Boston, Massachusetts

MEMBERS

Boris Auerbach, Cincinnati, Ohio
Richard F. Dole, Jr., Houston, Texas
William E. Hogan, New York, New York
Charles W. Joiner, Ann Arbor, Michigan
Frederick H. Miller, Norman, Oklahoma
Donald J. Rapson, Livingston, New Jersey, *The American Law Institute Representative*
Michael P. Sullivan, Minneapolis, Minnesota, *President, (Member Ex Officio)*
Neal Ossen, Hartford, Connecticut, *Chairman, Division C, (Member Ex Officio)*

REVIEW COMMITTEE

CHAIRMAN

Frank F. Jestrab, Chevy Chase, Maryland

MEMBERS

Rupert R. Bullivant, Portland, Oregon
Michael Franck, Lansing, Michigan

CONSULTANT

Fairfax Leary, Jr., Villanova, Pennsylvania

ADVISORS

Thomas C. Baxter, Jr., *Federal Reserve Bank of New York*
Roland E. Brandel, *American Bar Association*
Leon P. Ciferni, *National Westminster Bank, U.S.A.*
William B. Davenport, *American Bar Association, Section of Business Law, Ad Hoc Committee on Payment Systems*
Carl Felsenfeld, *Association of the Bar of the City of New York*
J. Kevin French, *Exxon Company, U.S.A.*
Thomas J. Greco, *American Bankers Association*
Arthur L. Herold, *National Corporate Cash Management Association*
John R. H. Kimball, *Federal Reserve Bank of Boston*

ARTICLE 4A (2019)

John F. Lee, *New York Clearing House Association*
W. Robert Moore, *American Bankers Association*
Ernest T. Patrikis, *Federal Reserve Bank of New York*
Richard B. Wagner, *General Motors Corporation*

ADDITIONAL PARTICIPANTS

Dean Bitner, *Sears, Roebuck & Company*
Henry N. Dyhouse, *U.S. Central Credit Union*
James Foorman, *First Chicago Corporation*
Richard M. Gottlieb, *Manufacturers Hanover Trust Company*
Shirley Holder, *Atlantic Richfield Company*
Paul E. Homrighausen, *Bankers Clearing House Association and National Automated Clearing House Association*
Gail M. Inaba, *Morgan Guaranty Trust Company of New York*
Oliver I. Ireland, *Board of Governors of Federal Reserve System*
Richard P. Kessler, Jr., *Credit Union National Association*
James W. Kopp, *Shell Oil Company*
Robert M. MacAllister, *Chase Manhattan Bank NA*
Thomas E. Montgomery, *California Bankers Association*
Norman R. Nelson, *New York Clearing House Association*
Samuel Newman, *Manufacturers Hanover Trust Company*
Nena Nodge, *National Corporate Cash Management Association*
Robert J. Pisapia, *Occidental Petroleum Corporation*
Deborah S. Prutzman, *Arnold & Porter*
Robert M. Rosenblith, *Manufacturers Hanover Trust Company*
Paul S. Turner, *Occidental Petroleum Corporation*
Irma Villarreal, *Aon Corporation*
Suzanne Weakley, *Atlantic Richfield Company*

PREFATORY NOTE

The National Conference of Commissioners on Uniform State laws and The American Law Institute have approved a new Article 4A to the Uniform Commercial Code. Comments that follow each of the sections of the statute are intended as official comments. They explain in detail the purpose and meaning of the various sections and the policy considerations on which they are based.

Description of transaction covered by Article 4A.

There are a number of mechanisms for making payments through the banking system. Most of these mechanisms are covered in whole or part by state or federal statutes. In terms of number of transactions, payments made by check or credit card are the most common payment methods. Payment by check is covered by Articles 3 and 4 of the UCC and some aspects of payment by credit card are covered by federal law. In recent years electronic funds transfers have been increasingly common in consumer transactions. For example, in some cases a retail customer can pay for purchases by use of an access or debit card inserted in a terminal at the retail store that allows the bank account of the customer to be instantly debited. Some aspects of these point-of-sale transactions and other consumer payments that are effected electronically are covered by a federal statute, the Electronic Fund Transfer Act (EFTA). If any part of a funds transfer is covered by EFTA, the entire funds transfer is excluded from Article 4A.

Another type of payment, commonly referred to as a wholesale wire transfer, is the primary focus of Article 4A. Payments that are covered by Article 4A are overwhelmingly between business or financial institutions. The dollar volume of payments made by wire transfer far exceeds the dollar volume of payments made by other means. The volume of payments by wire transfer over the two principal wire payment systems—the Federal Reserve wire transfer network (Fedwire) and the New York Clearing House Interbank Payments Systems (CHIPS)—exceeds one trillion dollars per day. Most payments carried out by use of automated clearing houses are consumer payments covered by EFTA and therefore not covered by Article

4A. There is, however, a significant volume of nonconsumer ACH payments that closely resemble wholesale wire transfers. These payments are also covered by Article 4A.

There is some resemblance between payments made by wire transfer and payments made by other means such as paper-based checks and credit cards or electronically-based consumer payments, but there are also many differences. Article 4A excludes from its coverage these other payment mechanisms. Article 4A follows a policy of treating the transaction that it covers—a "funds transfer"—as a unique method of payment that is governed by unique principles of law that address the operational and policy issues presented by this kind of payment.

The funds transfer that is covered by Article 4A is not a complex transaction and can be illustrated by the following example which is used throughout the Prefatory Note as a basis for discussion. X, a debtor, wants to pay an obligation owed to Y. Instead of delivering to Y a negotiable instrument such as a check or some other writing such as a credit card slip that enables Y to obtain payment from a bank, X transmits an instruction to X's bank to credit a sum of money to the bank account of Y. In most cases X's bank and Y's bank are different banks. X's bank may carry out X's instruction by instructing Y's bank to credit Y's account in the amount that X requested. The instruction that X issues to its bank is a "payment order." X is the "sender" of the payment order and X's bank is the "receiving bank" with respect to X's order. Y is the "beneficiary" of X's order. When X's bank issues an instruction to Y's bank to carry out X's payment order, X's bank "executes" X's order. The instruction of X's bank to Y's bank is also a payment order. With respect to that order, X's bank is the sender, Y's bank is the receiving bank, and Y is the beneficiary. The entire series of transactions by which X pays Y is known as the "funds transfer." With respect to the funds transfer, X is the "originator," X's bank is the "originator's bank," Y is the "beneficiary" and Y's bank is the "beneficiary's bank." In more complex transactions there are one or more additional banks known as "intermediary banks" between X's bank and Y's bank. In the funds transfer the instruction contained in the payment order of X to its bank is carried out by a series of payment orders by each bank in the transmission chain to the next bank in the chain until Y's bank receives a payment order to make the credit to Y's account. In most cases, the payment order of each bank to the next bank in the chain is transmitted electronically, and often the payment order of X to its bank is also transmitted electronically, but the means of transmission does not have any legal significance. A payment order may be transmitted by any means, and in some cases the payment order is transmitted by a slow means such as first class mail. To reflect this fact, the broader term "funds transfer" rather than the narrower term "wire transfer" is used in Article 4A to describe the overall payment transaction.

Funds transfers are divided into two categories determined by whether the instruction to pay is given by the person making payment or the person receiving payment. If the instruction is given by the person making the payment, the transfer is commonly referred to as a "credit transfer." If the instruction is given by the person receiving payment, the transfer is commonly referred to as a "debit transfer." Article 4A governs credit transfers and excludes debit transfers.

Why is Article 4A needed?

There is no comprehensive body of law that defines the rights and obligations that arise from wire transfers. Some aspects of wire transfers are governed by rules of the principal transfer systems. Transfers made by Fedwire are governed by Federal Reserve Regulation J and transfers over CHIPS are governed by the CHIPS rules. Transfers made by means of automated clearing houses are governed by uniform rules adopted by various associations of banks in various parts of the nation or by Federal Reserve rules or operating circulars. But the various funds transfer system rules apply to only limited aspects of wire transfer transactions. The resolution of the many issues that are not covered by funds transfer system rules depends on contracts of the parties, to the extent that they exist, or principles of law applicable to other payment mechanisms that might be applied by analogy. The result is a great deal of uncertainty. There is no consensus about the juridical nature of a wire transfer and consequently of the rights and obligations that are created. Article 4A is intended to provide the comprehensive body of law that we do not have today.

Characteristics of a funds transfer.

There are a number of characteristics of funds transfers covered by Article 4A that have influenced the drafting of the statute. The typical funds transfer involves a large amount of money. Multimillion dollar transactions are commonplace. The originator of the transfer and the beneficiary are typically sophisticated business or financial organizations. High speed is another predominant characteristic. Most funds transfers are completed on the same day, even in complex transactions in which there are several intermediary banks in the transmission chain. A funds transfer is a highly efficient substitute for payments made by the delivery of paper instruments. Another characteristic is extremely low cost. A transfer that involves many millions of dollars can be made for a price of a few dollars. Price does not normally vary very much or at all with the amount of the transfer. This system of pricing may not be feasible if the bank is exposed to very large liabilities in connection with the transaction. The pricing system assumes that the price reflects primarily the cost of the mechanical operation performed by the bank, but in fact, a bank may have more or less potential liability with respect to a funds transfer depending upon the amount of the transfer. Risk of loss to banks carrying out a funds transfer may arise from a variety of causes. In some funds transfers, there may be extensions of very large amounts of credit for short periods of time by the banks that carry out a funds transfer. If a payment order is issued to the beneficiary's bank, it is normal for the bank to release funds to the beneficiary immediately. Sometimes, payment to the beneficiary's bank by the bank that issued the order to the beneficiary's bank is delayed until the end of the day. If that payment is not received because of the insolvency of the bank that is obliged to pay, the beneficiary's bank may suffer a loss. There is also risk of loss if a bank fails to execute the payment order of a customer, or if the order is executed late. There also may be an error in the payment order issued by a bank that is executing the payment order of its customer. For example, the error might relate to the amount to be paid or to the identity of the person to be paid. Because the dollar amounts involved in funds transfers are so large, the risk of loss if something goes wrong in a transaction may also be very large. A major policy issue in the drafting of Article 4A is that of determining how risk of loss is to be allocated given the price structure in the industry.

Concept of acceptance and effect of acceptance by the beneficiary's bank.

Rights and obligations under Article 4A arise as the result of "acceptance" of a payment order by the bank to which the order is addressed. Section 4A–209. The effect of acceptance varies depending upon whether the payment order is issued to the beneficiary's bank or to a bank other than the beneficiary's bank. Acceptance by the beneficiary's bank is particularly important because it defines when the beneficiary's bank becomes obligated to the beneficiary to pay the amount of the payment order. Although Article 4A follows convention in using the term "funds transfer" to identify the payment from X to Y that is described above, no money or property right of X is actually transferred to Y. X pays Y by causing Y's bank to become indebted to Y in the amount of the payment. This debt arises when Y's bank accepts the payment order that X's bank issued to Y's bank to execute X's order. If the funds transfer was carried out by use of one or more intermediary banks between X's bank and Y's bank, Y's bank becomes indebted to Y when Y's bank accepts the payment order issued to it by an intermediary bank. The funds transfer is completed when this debt is incurred. Acceptance, the event that determines when the debt of Y's bank to Y arises, occurs (i) when Y's bank pays Y or notifies Y of receipt of the payment order, or (ii) when Y's bank receives payment from the bank that issued a payment order to Y's bank.

The only obligation of the beneficiary's bank that results from acceptance of a payment order is to pay the amount of the order to the beneficiary. No obligation is owed to either the sender of the payment order accepted by the beneficiary's bank or to the originator of the funds transfer. The obligation created by acceptance by the beneficiary's bank is for the benefit of the beneficiary. The purpose of the sender's payment order is to effect payment by the originator to the beneficiary and that purpose is achieved when the beneficiary's bank accepts the payment order. Section 4A–405 states rules for determining when the obligation of the beneficiary's bank to the beneficiary has been paid.

Acceptance by a bank other than the beneficiary's bank.

In the funds transfer described above, what is the obligation of X's bank when it receives X's payment order? Funds transfers by a bank on behalf of its customer are made pursuant to an agreement or arrangement that may or may not be reduced to a formal document signed by the parties. It is probably true that in most cases there is either no express agreement or the agreement addresses only some aspects of the transaction. Substantial risk is involved in funds transfers and a bank may not be willing to give this service to all customers, and may not be willing to offer it to any customer unless certain safeguards against loss such as security procedures are in effect. Funds transfers often involve the giving of credit by the receiving bank to the customer, and that also may involve an agreement. These considerations are reflected in Article 4A by the principle that, in the absence of a contrary agreement, a receiving bank does not incur liability with respect to a payment order until it accepts it. If X and X's bank in the hypothetical case had an agreement that obliged the bank to act on X's payment orders and the bank failed to comply with the agreement, the bank can be held liable for breach of the agreement. But apart from any obligation arising by agreement, the bank does not incur any liability with respect to X's payment order until the bank accepts the order. X's payment order is treated by Article 4A as a request by X to the bank to take action that will cause X's payment order to be carried out. That request can be accepted by X's bank by "executing" X's payment order. Execution occurs when X's bank sends a payment order to Y's bank intended by X's bank to carry out the payment order of X. X's bank could also execute X's payment order by issuing a payment order to an intermediary bank instructing the intermediary bank to instruct Y's bank to make the credit to Y's account. In that case execution and acceptance of X's order occur when the payment order of X's bank is sent to the intermediary bank. When X's bank executes X's payment order the bank is entitled to receive payment from X and may debit an authorized account of X. If X's bank does not execute X's order and the amount of the order is covered by a withdrawable credit balance in X's authorized account, the bank must pay X interest on the money represented by X's order unless X is given prompt notice of rejection of the order. Section 4A–210(b).

Bank error in funds transfers.

If a bank, other than the beneficiary's bank, accepts a payment order, the obligations and liabilities are owed to the originator of the funds transfer. Assume in the example stated above, that X's bank executes X's payment order by issuing a payment order to an intermediary bank that executes the order of X's bank by issuing a payment order to Y's bank. The obligations of X's bank with respect to execution are owed to X. The obligations of the intermediary bank with respect to execution are also owed to X. Section 4A–302 states standards with respect to the time and manner of execution of payment orders. Section 4A–305 states the measure of damages for improper execution. It also states that a receiving bank is liable for damages if it fails to execute a payment order that it was obliged by express agreement to execute. In each case consequential damages are not recoverable unless an express agreement of the receiving bank provides for them. The policy basis for this limitation is discussed in Comment 2 to Section 4A–305.

Error in the consummation of a funds transfer is not uncommon. There may be a discrepancy in the amount that the originator orders to be paid to the beneficiary and the amount that the beneficiary's bank is ordered to pay. For example, if the originator's payment order instructs payment of $100,000 and the payment order of the originator's bank instructs payment of $1,000,000, the originator's bank is entitled to receive only $100,000 from the originator and has the burden of recovering the additional $900,000 paid to the beneficiary by mistake. In some cases the originator's bank or an intermediary bank instructs payment to a beneficiary other than the beneficiary stated in the originator's payment order. If the wrong beneficiary is paid the bank that issued the erroneous payment order is not entitled to receive payment of the payment order that it executed and has the burden of recovering the mistaken payment. The originator is not obliged to pay its payment order. Section 4A–303 and Section 4A–207 state rules for determining the rights and obligations of the various parties to the funds transfer in these cases and in other typical cases in which error is made.

Pursuant to Section 4A–402(c) the originator is excused from the obligation to pay the originator's bank if the funds transfer is not completed, i.e. payment by the originator to the beneficiary is not made. Payment by the originator to the beneficiary occurs when the beneficiary's bank accepts a payment order for the benefit of the beneficiary of the originator's payment order. Section 4A–406. If for any reason that acceptance does not occur, the originator is not required to pay the payment order that it issued or, if it already paid, is entitled to refund of the payment with interest. This "money-back guarantee" is an important protection of the originator of a funds transfer. The same rule applies to any other sender in the funds transfer. Each sender's obligation to pay is excused if the beneficiary's bank does not accept a payment order for the benefit of the beneficiary of that sender's order. There is an important exception to this rule. It is common practice for the originator of a funds transfer to designate the intermediary bank or banks through which the funds transfer is to be routed. The originator's bank is required by Section 4A–302 to follow the instruction of the originator with respect to intermediary banks. If the originator's bank sends a payment order to the intermediary bank designated in the originator's order and the intermediary bank causes the funds transfer to miscarry by failing to execute the payment order or by instructing payment to the wrong beneficiary, the originator's bank is not required to pay its payment order and if it has already paid it is entitled to recover payment from the intermediary bank. This remedy is normally adequate, but if the originator's bank already paid its order and the intermediary bank has suspended payments or is not permitted by law to refund payment, the originator's bank will suffer a loss. Since the originator required the originator's bank to use the failed intermediary bank, Section 4A–402(e) provides that in this case the originator is obliged to pay its payment order and has a claim against the intermediary bank for the amount of the order. The same principle applies to any other sender that designates a subsequent intermediary bank.

Unauthorized payment orders.

An important issue addressed in Section 4A–202 and Section 4A–203 is how the risk of loss from unauthorized payment orders is to be allocated. In a large percentage of cases, the payment order of the originator of the funds transfer is transmitted electronically to the originator's bank. In these cases it may not be possible for the bank to know whether the electronic message has been authorized by its customer. To ensure that no unauthorized person is transmitting messages to the bank, the normal practice is to establish security procedures that usually involve the use of codes or identifying numbers or words. If the bank accepts a payment order that purports to be that of its customer after verifying its authenticity by complying with a security procedure agreed to by the customer and the bank, the customer is bound to pay the order even if it was not authorized. But there is an important limitation on this rule. The bank is entitled to payment in the case of an unauthorized order only if the court finds that the security procedure was a commercially reasonable method of providing security against unauthorized payment orders. The customer can also avoid liability if it can prove that the unauthorized order was not initiated by an employee or other agent of the customer having access to confidential security information or by a person who obtained that information from a source controlled by the customer. The policy issues are discussed in the comments following Section 4A–203. If the bank accepts an unauthorized payment order without verifying it in compliance with a security procedure, the loss falls on the bank.

Security procedures are also important in cases of error in the transmission of payment orders. There may be an error by the sender in the amount of the order, or a sender may transmit a payment order and then erroneously transmit a duplicate of the order. Normally, the sender is bound by the payment order even if it is issued by mistake. But in some cases an error of this kind can be detected by a security procedure. Although the receiving bank is not obliged to provide a security procedure for the detection of error, if such a procedure is agreed to by the bank Section 4A–205 provides that if the error is not detected because the receiving bank does not comply with the procedure, any resulting loss is borne by the bank failing to comply with the security procedure.

Insolvency losses.

Some payment orders do not involve the granting of credit to the sender by the receiving bank. In those cases, the receiving bank accepts the sender's order at the same time the bank receives payment of the order. This is true of a transfer of funds by Fedwire or of cases in which the receiving bank can debit a funded account of the sender. But in some cases the granting of credit is the norm. This is true of a payment order over CHIPS. In a CHIPS transaction the receiving bank usually will accept the order before receiving payment from the sending bank. Payment is delayed until the end of the day when settlement is made through the Federal Reserve System. If the receiving bank is an intermediary bank, it will accept by issuing a payment order to another bank and the intermediary bank is obliged to pay that payment order. If the receiving bank is the beneficiary's bank, the bank usually will accept by releasing funds to the beneficiary before the bank has received payment. If a sending bank suspends payments before settling its liabilities at the end of the day, the financial stability of banks that are net creditors of the insolvent bank may also be put into jeopardy, because the dollar volume of funds transfers between the banks may be extremely large. With respect to two banks that are dealing with each other in a series of transactions in which each bank is sometimes a receiving bank and sometimes a sender, the risk of insolvency can be managed if amounts payable as a sender and amounts receivable as a receiving bank are roughly equal. But if these amounts are significantly out of balance, a net creditor bank may have a very significant credit risk during the day before settlement occurs. The Federal Reserve System and the banking community are greatly concerned with this risk, and various measures have been instituted to reduce this credit exposure. Article 4A also addresses this problem. A receiving bank can always avoid this risk by delaying acceptance of a payment order until after the bank has received payment. For example, if the beneficiary's bank credits the beneficiary's account it can avoid acceptance by not notifying the beneficiary of the receipt of the order or by notifying the beneficiary that the credit may not be withdrawn until the beneficiary's bank receives payment. But if the beneficiary's bank releases funds to the beneficiary before receiving settlement, the result in a funds transfer other than a transfer by means of an automated clearing house or similar provisional settlement system is that the beneficiary's bank may not recover the funds if it fails to receive settlement. This rule encourages the banking system to impose credit limitations on banks that issue payment orders. These limitations are already in effect. CHIPS has also proposed a loss-sharing plan to be adopted for implementation in the second half of 1990 under which CHIPS participants will be required to provide funds necessary to complete settlement of the obligations of one or more participants that are unable to meet settlement obligations. Under this plan, it will be a virtual certainty that there will be settlement on CHIPS in the event of failure by a single bank. Section 4A-403(b) and (c) are also addressed to reducing risks of insolvency. Under these provisions the amount owed by a failed bank with respect to payment orders it issued is the net amount owing after setting off amounts owed to the failed bank with respect to payment orders it received. This rule allows credit exposure to be managed by limitations on the net debit position of a bank.

International transfers.

The major international legal document dealing with the subject of electronic funds transfers is the Model Law on International Credit Transfers adopted in 1992 by the United Nations Commission on International Trade Law. It covers basically the same type of transaction as does Article 4A, although it requires the funds transferred to have an international component. The Model Law and Article 4A basically live together in harmony, but to the extent there are differences they must be recognized and, to the extent possible, avoided or adjusted by agreement. See PEB Commentary No. 13, dated February 16, 1994.

PART 1
SUBJECT MATTER AND DEFINITIONS

§ 4A-101. Short Title.

This Article may be cited as Uniform Commercial Code—Funds Transfers.

§ 4A-102. Subject Matter.

Except as otherwise provided in Section 4A-108, this Article applies to funds transfers defined in Section 4A-104.

Official Comment

Article 4A governs a specialized method of payment referred to in the Article as a funds transfer but also commonly referred to in the commercial community as a wholesale wire transfer. A funds transfer is made by means of one or more payment orders. The scope of Article 4A is determined by the definitions of "payment order" and "funds transfer" found in Section 4A-103 and Section 4A-104.

The funds transfer governed by Article 4A is in large part a product of recent and developing technological changes. Before this Article was drafted there was no comprehensive body of law—statutory or judicial—that defined the juridical nature of a funds transfer or the rights and obligations flowing from payment orders. Judicial authority with respect to funds transfers is sparse, undeveloped and not uniform. Judges have had to resolve disputes by referring to general principles of common law or equity, or they have sought guidance in statutes such as Article 4 which are applicable to other payment methods. But attempts to define rights and obligations in funds transfers by general principles or by analogy to rights and obligations in negotiable instrument law or the law of check collection have not been satisfactory.

In the drafting of Article 4A, a deliberate decision was made to write on a clean slate and to treat a funds transfer as a unique method of payment to be governed by unique rules that address the particular issues raised by this method of payment. A deliberate decision was also made to use precise and detailed rules to assign responsibility, define behavioral norms, allocate risks and establish limits on liability, rather than to rely on broadly stated, flexible principles. In the drafting of these rules, a critical consideration was that the various parties to funds transfers need to be able to predict risk with certainty, to insure against risk, to adjust operational and security procedures, and to price funds transfer services appropriately. This consideration is particularly important given the very large amounts of money that are involved in funds transfers.

Funds transfers involve competing interests—those of the banks that provide funds transfer services and the commercial and financial organizations that use the services, as well as the public interest. These competing interests were represented in the drafting process and they were thoroughly considered. The rules that emerged represent a careful and delicate balancing of those interests and are intended to be the exclusive means of determining the rights, duties and liabilities of the affected parties in any situation covered by particular provisions of the Article. Consequently, resort to principles of law or equity outside of Article 4A is not appropriate to create rights, duties and liabilities inconsistent with those stated in this Article.

§ 4A–103. Payment Order—Definitions.

(a) In this Article:

(1) "Payment order" means an instruction of a sender to a receiving bank, transmitted orally, electronically, or in writing, to pay, or to cause another bank to pay, a fixed or determinable amount of money to a beneficiary if:

(i) the instruction does not state a condition to payment to the beneficiary other than time of payment,

(ii) the receiving bank is to be reimbursed by debiting an account of, or otherwise receiving payment from, the sender, and

(iii) the instruction is transmitted by the sender directly to the receiving bank or to an agent, funds-transfer system, or communication system for transmittal to the receiving bank.

(2) "Beneficiary" means the person to be paid by the beneficiary's bank.

(3) "Beneficiary's bank" means the bank identified in a payment order in which an account of the beneficiary is to be credited pursuant to the order or which otherwise is to make payment to the beneficiary if the order does not provide for payment to an account.

(4) "Receiving bank" means the bank to which the sender's instruction is addressed.

(5) "Sender" means the person giving the instruction to the receiving bank.

(b) If an instruction complying with subsection (a)(1) is to make more than one payment to a beneficiary, the instruction is a separate payment order with respect to each payment.

(c) A payment order is issued when it is sent to the receiving bank.

Official Comment

This section is discussed in the Comment following Section 4A–104.

§ 4A–104. Funds Transfer—Definitions.

In this Article:

(a) "Funds transfer" means the series of transactions, beginning with the originator's payment order, made for the purpose of making payment to the beneficiary of the order. The term includes any payment order issued by the originator's bank or an intermediary bank intended to carry out the originator's payment order. A funds transfer is completed by acceptance by the beneficiary's bank of a payment order for the benefit of the beneficiary of the originator's payment order.

(b) "Intermediary bank" means a receiving bank other than the originator's bank or the beneficiary's bank.

(c) "Originator" means the sender of the first payment order in a funds transfer.

(d) "Originator's bank" means (i) the receiving bank to which the payment order of the originator is issued if the originator is not a bank, or (ii) the originator if the originator is a bank.

Official Comment

1. Article 4A governs a method of payment in which the person making payment (the "originator") directly transmits an instruction to a bank either to make payment to the person receiving payment (the "beneficiary") or to instruct some other bank to make payment to the beneficiary. The payment from the originator to the

beneficiary occurs when the bank that is to pay the beneficiary becomes obligated to pay the beneficiary. There are two basic definitions: "Payment order" stated in Section 4A–103 and "Funds transfer" stated in Section 4A–104. These definitions, other related definitions, and the scope of Article 4A can best be understood in the context of specific fact situations. Consider the following cases:

Case # 1. X, which has an account in Bank A, instructs that bank to pay $1,000,000 to Y's account in Bank A. Bank A carries out X's instruction by making a credit of $1,000,000 to Y's account and notifying Y that the credit is available for immediate withdrawal. The instruction by X to Bank A is a "payment order" which was issued when it was sent to Bank A. Section 4A–103(a)(1) and (c). X is the "sender" of the payment order and Bank A is the "receiving bank." Section 4A–103(a)(5) and (a)(4). Y is the "beneficiary" of the payment order and Bank A is the "beneficiary's bank." Section 4A–103(a)(2) and (a)(3). When Bank A notified Y of receipt of the payment order, Bank A "accepted" the payment order. Section 4A–209(b)(1). When Bank A accepted the order it incurred an obligation to Y to pay the amount of the order. Section 4A–404(a). When Bank A accepted X's order, X incurred an obligation to pay Bank A the amount of the order. Section 4A–402(b). Payment from X to Bank A would normally be made by a debit to X's account in Bank A. Section 4A–403(a)(3). At the time Bank A incurred the obligation to pay Y, payment of $1,000,000 by X to Y was also made. Section 4A–406(a). Bank A paid Y when it gave notice to Y of a withdrawable credit of $1,000,000 to Y's account. Section 4A–405(a). The overall transaction, which comprises the acts of X and Bank A, in which the payment by X to Y is accomplished is referred to as the "funds transfer." Section 4A–104(a). In this case only one payment order was involved in the funds transfer. A one-payment-order funds transfer is usually referred to as a "book transfer" because the payment is accomplished by the receiving bank's debiting the account of the sender and crediting the account of the beneficiary in the same bank. X, in addition to being the sender of the payment order to Bank A, is the "originator" of the funds transfer. Section 4A–104(c). Bank A is the "originator's bank" in the funds transfer as well as the beneficiary's bank. Section 4A–104(d).

Case # 2. Assume the same facts as in Case # 1 except that X instructs Bank A to pay $1,000,000 to Y's account in Bank B. With respect to this payment order, X is the sender, Y is the beneficiary, and Bank A is the receiving bank. Bank A carries out X's order by instructing Bank B to pay $1,000,000 to Y's account. This instruction is a payment order in which Bank A is the sender, Bank B is the receiving bank, and Y is the beneficiary. When Bank A issued its payment order to Bank B, Bank A "executed" X's order. Section 4A–301(a). In the funds transfer, X is the originator, Bank A is the originator's bank, and Bank B is the beneficiary's bank. When Bank A executed X's order, X incurred an obligation to pay Bank A the amount of the order. Section 4A–402(c). When Bank B accepts the payment order issued to it by Bank A, Bank B incurs an obligation to Y to pay the amount of the order (Section 4A–404(a)) and Bank A incurs an obligation to pay Bank B. Section 4A–402(b). Acceptance by Bank B also results in payment of $1,000,000 by X to Y. Section 4A–406(a). In this case two payment orders are involved in the funds transfer.

Case # 3. Assume the same facts as in Case # 2 except that Bank A does not execute X's payment order by issuing a payment order to Bank B. One bank will not normally act to carry out a funds transfer for another bank unless there is a preexisting arrangement between the banks for transmittal of payment orders and settlement of accounts. For example, if Bank B is a foreign bank with which Bank A has no relationship, Bank A can utilize a bank that is a correspondent of both Bank A and Bank B. Assume Bank A issues a payment order to Bank C to pay $1,000,000 to Y's account in Bank B. With respect to this order, Bank A is the sender, Bank C is the receiving bank, and Y is the beneficiary. Bank C will execute the payment order of Bank A by issuing a payment order to Bank B to pay $1,000,000 to Y's account in Bank B. With respect to Bank C's payment order, Bank C is the sender, Bank B is the receiving bank, and Y is the beneficiary. Payment of $1,000,000 by X to Y occurs when Bank B accepts the payment order issued to it by Bank C. In this case the funds transfer involves three payment orders. In the funds transfer, X is the originator, Bank A is the originator's bank, Bank B is the beneficiary's bank, and Bank C is an "intermediary bank." Section 4A–104(b). In some cases there may be more than one intermediary bank, and in those cases each intermediary bank is treated like Bank C in Case # 3.

As the three cases demonstrate, a payment under Article 4A involves an overall transaction, the funds transfer, in which the originator, X, is making payment to the beneficiary, Y, but the funds transfer may encompass a series of payment orders that are issued in order to effect the payment initiated by the originator's payment order.

In some cases the originator and the beneficiary may be the same person. This will occur, for example, when a corporation orders a bank to transfer funds from an account of the corporation in that bank to another account of the corporation in that bank or in some other bank. In some funds transfers the first bank to issue a payment order is a bank that is executing a payment order of a customer that is not a bank. In this case the customer is the originator. In other cases, the first bank to issue a payment order is not acting for a customer, but is making a payment for its own account. In that event the first bank to issue a payment order is the originator as well as the originator's bank.

2. "Payment order" is defined in Section 4A–103(a)(1) as an instruction to a bank to pay, or to cause another bank to pay, a fixed or determinable amount of money. The bank to which the instruction is addressed is known as the "receiving bank." Section 4A–103(a)(4). "Bank" is defined in Section 4A–105(a)(2). The effect of this definition is to limit Article 4A to payments made through the banking system. A transfer of funds made by an entity outside the banking system is excluded. A transfer of funds through an entity other than a bank is usually a consumer transaction involving relatively small amounts of money and a single contract carried out by transfers of cash or a cash equivalent such as a check. Typically, the transferor delivers cash or a check to the company making the transfer, which agrees to pay a like amount to a person designated by the transferor. Transactions covered by Article 4A typically involve very large amounts of money in which several transactions involving several banks may be necessary to carry out the payment. Payments are normally made by debits or credits to bank accounts. Originators and beneficiaries are almost always business organizations and the transfers are usually made to pay obligations. Moreover, these transactions are frequently done on the basis of very short-term credit granted by the receiving bank to the sender of the payment order. Wholesale wire transfers involve policy questions that are distinct from those involved in consumer-based transactions by nonbanks.

3. Further limitations on the scope of Article 4A are found in the three requirements found in subparagraphs (i), (ii), and (iii) of Section 4A–103(a)(1). Subparagraph (i) states that the instruction to pay is a payment order only if it "does not state a condition to payment to the beneficiary other than time of payment." An instruction to pay a beneficiary sometimes is subject to a requirement that the beneficiary perform some act such as delivery of documents. For example, a New York bank may have issued a letter of credit in favor of X, a California seller of goods to be shipped to the New York bank's customer in New York. The terms of the letter of credit provide for payment to X if documents are presented to prove shipment of the goods. Instead of providing for presentment of the documents to the New York bank, the letter of credit states that they may be presented to a California bank that acts as an agent for payment. The New York bank sends an instruction to the California bank to pay X upon presentation of the required documents. The instruction is not covered by Article 4A because payment to the beneficiary is conditional upon receipt of shipping documents. The function of banks in a funds transfer under Article 4A is comparable to the role of banks in the collection and payment of checks in that it is essentially mechanical in nature. The low price and high speed that characterize funds transfers reflect this fact. Conditions to payment by the California bank other than time of payment impose responsibilities on that bank that go beyond those in Article 4A funds transfers. Although the payment by the New York bank to X under the letter of credit is not covered by Article 4A, if X is paid by the California bank, payment of the obligation of the New York bank to reimburse the California bank could be made by an Article 4A funds transfer. In such a case there is a distinction between the payment by the New York bank to X under the letter of credit and the payment by the New York bank to the California bank. For example, if the New York bank pays its reimbursement obligation to the California bank by a Fedwire naming the California bank as beneficiary (see Comment 1 to Section 4A–107), payment is made to the California bank rather than to X. That payment is governed by Article 4A and it could be made either before or after payment by the California bank to X. The payment by the New York bank to X under the letter of credit is not governed by Article 4A and it occurs when the California bank, as agent of the New York bank, pays X. No payment order was involved in that transaction. In this example, if the New York bank had erroneously sent an instruction to the California bank unconditionally instructing payment to X, the instruction would have been an Article 4A payment order. If the payment order was accepted (Section 4A–209(b)) by the California bank, a payment by the New York bank to X would have resulted (Section 4A–406(a)). But Article 4A would not prevent recovery of funds from X on the basis that X was not entitled to retain the funds under the law of mistake and restitution, letter of credit law or other applicable law.

4. Transfers of funds made through the banking system are commonly referred to as either "credit" transfers or "debit" transfers. In a credit transfer the instruction to pay is given by the person making payment. In a debit transfer the instruction to pay is given by the person receiving payment. The purpose of subparagraph (ii) of subsection (a)(1) of Section 4A–103 is to include credit transfers in Article 4A and to exclude debit transfers. All of the instructions to pay in the three cases described in Comment 1 fall within subparagraph (ii). Take Case # 2 as an example. With respect to X's instruction given to Bank A, Bank A will be reimbursed by debiting X's account or otherwise receiving payment from X. With respect to Bank A's instruction to Bank B, Bank B will be reimbursed by receiving payment from Bank A. In a debit transfer, a creditor, pursuant to authority from the debtor, is enabled to draw on the debtor's bank account by issuing an instruction to pay to the debtor's bank. If the debtor's bank pays, it will be reimbursed by the debtor rather than by the person giving the instruction. For example, the holder of an insurance policy may pay premiums by authorizing the insurance company to order the

policyholder's bank to pay the insurance company. The order to pay may be in the form of a draft covered by Article 3, or it might be an instruction to pay that is not an instrument under that Article. The bank receives reimbursement by debiting the policyholder's account. Or, a subsidiary corporation may make payments to its parent by authorizing the parent to order the subsidiary's bank to pay the parent from the subsidiary's account. These transactions are not covered by Article 4A because subparagraph (2) is not satisfied. Article 4A is limited to transactions in which the account to be debited by the receiving bank is that of the person in whose name the instruction is given.

If the beneficiary of a funds transfer is the originator of the transfer, the transfer is governed by Article 4A if it is a credit transfer in form. If it is in the form of a debit transfer it is not governed by Article 4A. For example, Corporation has accounts in Bank A and Bank B. Corporation instructs Bank A to pay to Corporation's account in Bank B. The funds transfer is governed by Article 4A. Sometimes, Corporation will authorize Bank B to draw on Corporation's account in Bank A for the purpose of transferring funds into Corporation's account in Bank B. If Corporation also makes an agreement with Bank A under which Bank A is authorized to follow instructions of Bank B, as agent of Corporation, to transfer funds from Customer's account in Bank A, the instruction of Bank B is a payment order of Customer and is governed by Article 4A. This kind of transaction is known in the wire-transfer business as a "drawdown transfer." If Corporation does not make such an agreement with Bank A and Bank B instructs Bank A to make the transfer, the order is in form a debit transfer and is not governed by Article 4A. These debit transfers are normally ACH transactions in which Bank A relies on Bank B's warranties pursuant to ACH rules, including the warranty that the transfer is authorized.

5. The principal effect of subparagraph (iii) of subsection (a) of Section 4A-103 is to exclude from Article 4A payments made by check or credit card. In those cases the instruction of the debtor to the bank on which the check is drawn or to which the credit card slip is to be presented is contained in the check or credit card slip signed by the debtor. The instruction is not transmitted by the debtor directly to the debtor's bank. Rather, the instruction is delivered or otherwise transmitted by the debtor to the creditor who then presents it to the bank either directly or through bank collection channels. These payments are governed by Articles 3 and 4 and federal law. There are, however, limited instances in which the paper on which a check is printed can be used as the means of transmitting a payment order that is covered by Article 4A. Assume that Originator instructs Originator's Bank to pay $10,000 to the account of Beneficiary in Beneficiary's Bank. Since the amount of Originator's payment order is small, if Originator's Bank and Beneficiary's Bank do not have an account relationship, Originator's Bank may execute Originator's order by issuing a teller's check payable to Beneficiary's Bank for $10,000 along with instructions to credit Beneficiary's account in that amount. The instruction to Beneficiary's Bank to credit Beneficiary's account is a payment order. The check is the means by which Originator's Bank pays its obligation as sender of the payment order. The instruction of Originator's Bank to Beneficiary's Bank might be given in a letter accompanying the check or it may be written on the check itself. In either case the instruction to Beneficiary's Bank is a payment order but the check itself (which is an order to pay addressed to the drawee rather than to Beneficiary's Bank) is an instrument under Article 3 and is not a payment order. The check can be both the means by which Originator's Bank pays its obligation under § 4A-402(b) to Beneficiary's Bank and the means by which the instruction to Beneficiary's Bank is transmitted.

6. Most payments covered by Article 4A are commonly referred to as wire transfers and usually involve some kind of electronic transmission, but the applicability of Article 4A does not depend upon the means used to transmit the instruction of the sender. Transmission may be by letter or other written communication, oral communication or electronic communication. An oral communication is normally given by telephone. Frequently the message is recorded by the receiving bank to provide evidence of the transaction, but apart from problems of proof there is no need to record the oral instruction. Transmission of an instruction may be a direct communication between the sender and the receiving bank or through an intermediary such as an agent of the sender, a communication system such as international cable, or a funds transfer system such as CHIPS, SWIFT or an automated clearing house.

§ 4A-105. Other Definitions.

(a) In this Article:

(1) "Authorized account" means a deposit account of a customer in a bank designated by the customer as a source of payment of payment orders issued by the customer to the bank. If a customer does not so designate an account, any account of the customer is an authorized account if payment of a payment order from that account is not inconsistent with a restriction on the use of that account.

(2) "Bank" means a person engaged in the business of banking and includes a savings bank, savings and loan association, credit union, and trust company. A branch or separate office of a bank is a separate bank for purposes of this Article.

(3) "Customer" means a person, including a bank, having an account with a bank or from whom a bank has agreed to receive payment orders.

(4) "Funds-transfer business day" of a receiving bank means the part of a day during which the receiving bank is open for the receipt, processing, and transmittal of payment orders and cancellations and amendments of payment orders.

(5) "Funds-transfer system" means a wire transfer network, automated clearing house, or other communication system of a clearing house or other association of banks through which a payment order by a bank may be transmitted to the bank to which the order is addressed.

(6) [reserved] ["Good faith" means honesty in fact and the observance of reasonable commercial standards of fair dealing.] [*Note from West Advisory Panel: This subsection will be deleted if the jurisdiction adopts the definition of good faith in revised Article 1.*]

(7) "Prove" with respect to a fact means to meet the burden of establishing the fact (Section 1–201(b)(8)).

(b) Other definitions applying to this Article and the sections in which they appear are:

"Acceptance" Section 4A–209
"Beneficiary" Section 4A–103
"Beneficiary's bank" Section 4A–103
"Executed" Section 4A–301
"Execution date" Section 4A–301
"Funds transfer" Section 4A–104
"Funds-transfer system rule" Section 4A–501
"Intermediary bank" Section 4A–104
"Originator" Section 4A–104
"Originator's bank" Section 4A–104
"Payment by beneficiary's bank to beneficiary" Section 4A–405
"Payment by originator to beneficiary" Section 4A–406
"Payment by sender to receiving bank" Section 4A–403
"Payment date" Section 4A–401
"Payment order" Section 4A–103
"Receiving bank" Section 4A–103
"Security procedure" Section 4A–201
"Sender" Section 4A–103

(c) The following definitions in Article 4 apply to this Article:

"Clearing house" Section 4–104
"Item" Section 4–104
"Suspends payments" Section 4–104

(d) In addition Article 1 contains general definitions and principles of construction and interpretation applicable throughout this Article.

As amended in 2001.

Official Comment

1. The definition of "bank" in subsection (a)(2) includes some institutions that are not commercial banks. The definition reflects the fact that many financial institutions now perform functions previously restricted to commercial banks, including acting on behalf of customers in funds transfers. Since many funds transfers involve payment orders to or from foreign countries the definition also covers foreign banks. The definition also includes Federal Reserve Banks. Funds transfers carried out by Federal Reserve Banks are described in Comments 1 and 2 to Section 4A–107.

2. Funds transfer business is frequently transacted by banks outside of general banking hours. Thus, the definition of banking day in Section 4-104(1)(c) cannot be used to describe when a bank is open for funds transfer business. Subsection (a)(4) defines a new term, "funds transfer business day," which is applicable to Article 4A. The definition states, "is open for the receipt, processing, and transmittal of payment orders and cancellations and amendments of payment orders." In some cases it is possible to electronically transmit payment orders and other communications to a receiving bank at any time. If the receiving bank is not open for the processing of an order when it is received, the communication is stored in the receiving bank's computer for retrieval when the receiving bank is open for processing. The use of the conjunctive makes clear that the defined term is limited to the period during which all functions of the receiving bank can be performed, i.e., receipt, processing, and transmittal of payment orders, cancellations and amendments.

3. Subsection (a)(5) defines "funds transfer system." The term includes a system such as CHIPS which provides for transmission of a payment order as well as settlement of the obligation of the sender to pay the order. It also includes automated clearing houses, operated by a clearing house or other association of banks, which process and transmit payment orders of banks to other banks. In addition the term includes organizations that provide only transmission services such as SWIFT. The definition also includes the wire transfer network and automated clearing houses of Federal Reserve Banks. Systems of the Federal Reserve Banks, however, are treated differently from systems of other associations of banks. Funds transfer systems other than systems of the Federal Reserve Banks are treated in Article 4A as a means of communication of payment orders between participating banks. Section 4A-206. The Comment to that section and the Comment to Section 4A-107 explain how Federal Reserve Banks function under Article 4A. Funds transfer systems are also able to promulgate rules binding on participating banks that, under Section 4A-501, may supplement or in some cases may even override provisions of Article 4A.

4. Subsection (d) incorporates definitions stated in Article 1 as well as principles of construction and interpretation stated in that Article. Included is Section 1-103. The last paragraph of the Comment to Section 4A-102 is addressed to the issue of the extent to which general principles of law and equity should apply to situations covered by provisions of Article 4A.

§ 4A-106. Time Payment Order Is Received.

(a) The time of receipt of a payment order or communication cancelling or amending a payment order is determined by the rules applicable to receipt of a notice stated in Section 1-202. A receiving bank may fix a cut-off time or times on a funds-transfer business day for the receipt and processing of payment orders and communications cancelling or amending payment orders. Different cut-off times may apply to payment orders, cancellations, or amendments, or to different categories of payment orders, cancellations, or amendments. A cut-off time may apply to senders generally or different cut-off times may apply to different senders or categories of payment orders. If a payment order or communication cancelling or amending a payment order is received after the close of a funds-transfer business day or after the appropriate cut-off time on a funds-transfer business day, the receiving bank may treat the payment order or communication as received at the opening of the next funds-transfer business day.

(b) If this Article refers to an execution date or payment date or states a day on which a receiving bank is required to take action, and the date or day does not fall on a funds-transfer business day, the next day that is a funds-transfer business day is treated as the date or day stated, unless the contrary is stated in this Article.

As amended in 2001.

Official Comment

The time that a payment order is received by a receiving bank usually defines the payment date or the execution date of a payment order. Section 4A-401 and Section 4A-301. The time of receipt of a payment order, or communication cancelling or amending a payment order is defined in subsection (a) by reference to the rules stated in Section 1-202. Thus, time of receipt is determined by the same rules that determine when a notice is received. Time of receipt, however, may be altered by a cut-off time.

As amended in 2001.

§ 4A–107. Federal Reserve Regulations and Operating Circulars.

Regulations of the Board of Governors of the Federal Reserve System and operating circulars of the Federal Reserve Banks supersede any inconsistent provision of this Article to the extent of the inconsistency.

Official Comment

1. Funds transfers under Article 4A may be made, in whole or in part, by payment orders through a Federal Reserve Bank in what is usually referred to as a transfer by Fedwire. If Bank A, which has an account in Federal Reserve Bank X, wants to pay $1,000,000 to Bank B, which has an account in Federal Reserve Bank Y, Bank A can issue an instruction to Reserve Bank X requesting a debit of $1,000,000 to Bank A's Reserve account and an equal credit to Bank B's Reserve account. Reserve Bank X will debit Bank A's account and will credit the account of Reserve Bank Y. Reserve Bank X will issue an instruction to Reserve Bank Y requesting a debit of $1,000,000 to the account of Reserve Bank X and an equal credit to Bank B's account in Reserve Bank Y. Reserve Bank Y will make the requested debit and credit and will give Bank B an advice of credit. The definition of "bank" in Section 4A–105(a)(2) includes both Reserve Bank X and Reserve Bank Y. Bank A's instruction to Reserve Bank X to pay money to Bank B is a payment order under Section 4A–103(a)(1). Bank A is the sender and Reserve Bank X is the receiving bank. Bank B is the beneficiary of Bank A's order and of the funds transfer. Bank A is the originator of the funds transfer and is also the originator's bank. Section 4A–104(c) and (d). Reserve Bank X, an intermediary bank under Section 4A–104(b), executes Bank A's order by sending a payment order to Reserve Bank Y instructing that bank to credit the Federal Reserve account of Bank B. Reserve Bank Y is the beneficiary's bank.

Suppose the transfer of funds from Bank A to Bank B is part of a larger transaction in which Originator, a customer of Bank A, wants to pay Beneficiary, a customer of Bank B. Originator issues a payment order to Bank A to pay $1,000,000 to the account of Beneficiary in Bank B. Bank A may execute Originator's order by means of Fedwire which simultaneously transfers $1,000,000 from Bank A to Bank B and carries a message instructing Bank B to pay $1,000,000 to the account of Y. The Fedwire transfer is carried out as described in the previous paragraph, except that the beneficiary of the funds transfer is Beneficiary rather than Bank B. Reserve Bank X and Reserve Bank Y are intermediary banks. When Reserve Bank Y advises Bank B of the credit to its Federal Reserve account it will also instruct Bank B to pay to the account of Beneficiary. The instruction is a payment order to Bank B which is the beneficiary's bank. When Reserve Bank Y advises Bank B of the credit to its Federal Reserve account Bank B receives payment of the payment order issued to it by Reserve Bank Y. Section 4A–403(a)(1). The payment order is automatically accepted by Bank B at the time it receives the payment order of Reserve Bank Y. Section 4A–209(b)(2). At the time of acceptance by Bank B payment by Originator to Beneficiary also occurs. Thus, in a Fedwire transfer, payment to the beneficiary's bank, acceptance by the beneficiary's bank and payment by the originator to the beneficiary all occur simultaneously by operation of law at the time the payment order to the beneficiary's bank is received.

If Originator orders payment to the account of Beneficiary in Bank C rather than Bank B, the analysis is somewhat modified. Bank A may not have any relationship with Bank C and may not be able to make payment directly to Bank C. In that case, Bank A could send a Fedwire instructing Bank B to instruct Bank C to pay Beneficiary. The analysis is the same as the previous case except that Bank B is an intermediary bank and Bank C is the beneficiary's bank.

2. A funds transfer can also be made through a Federal Reserve Bank in an automated clearing house transaction. In a typical case, Originator instructs Originator's Bank to pay to the account of Beneficiary in Beneficiary's Bank. Originator's instruction to pay a particular beneficiary is transmitted to Originator's Bank along with many other instructions for payment to other beneficiaries by many different beneficiary's banks. All of these instructions are contained in a magnetic tape or other electronic device. Transmission of instructions to the various beneficiary's banks requires that Originator's instructions be processed and repackaged with instructions of other originators so that all instructions to a particular beneficiary's bank are transmitted together to that bank. The repackaging is done in processing centers usually referred to as automated clearing houses. Automated clearing houses are operated either by Federal Reserve Banks or by other associations of banks. If Originator's Bank chooses to execute Originator's instructions by transmitting them to a Federal Reserve Bank for processing by the Federal Reserve Bank, the transmission to the Federal Reserve Bank results in the issuance of payment orders by Originator's Bank to the Federal Reserve Bank, which is an intermediary bank. Processing by the Federal Reserve Bank will result in the issuance of payment orders by the Federal Reserve Bank to Beneficiary's Bank as well as payment orders to other beneficiary's banks making payments to carry out Originator's instructions.

3. Although the terms of Article 4A apply to funds transfers involving Federal Reserve Banks, federal preemption would make ineffective any Article 4A provision that conflicts with federal law. The payments activities of the Federal Reserve Banks are governed by regulations of the Federal Reserve Board and by operating circulars issued by the Reserve Banks themselves. In some instances, the operating circulars are issued pursuant to a Federal Reserve Board regulation. In other cases, the Reserve Bank issues the operating circular under its own authority under the Federal Reserve Act, subject to review by the Federal Reserve Board. Section 4A–107 states that Federal Reserve Board regulations and operating circulars of the Federal Reserve Banks supersede any inconsistent provision of Article 4A to the extent of the inconsistency. Federal Reserve Board regulations, being valid exercises of regulatory authority pursuant to a federal statute, take precedence over state law if there is an inconsistency. *Childs v. Federal Reserve Bank of Dallas*, 719 F.2d 812 (5th Cir. 1983), reh. den. 724 F.2d 127 (5th Cir. 1984). Section 4A–107 treats operating circulars as having the same effect whether issued under the Reserve Bank's own authority or under a Federal Reserve Board regulation.

§ 4A–108. Relationship to Electronic Fund Transfer Act.

(a) Except as provided in subsection (b), this Article does not apply to a funds transfer any part of which is governed by the Electronic Fund Transfer Act of 1978 (Title XX, Public Law 95–630, 92 Stat. 3728, 15 U.S.C. sec. 1693 et. seq.) as amended from time to time.

(b) This Article applies to a funds transfer that is a remittance transfer as defined in the Electronic Fund Transfer Act (15 U.S.C. sec. 1693*o*–1) as amended from time to time, unless the remittance transfer is an electronic fund transfer as defined in the Electronic Fund Transfer Act (15 U.S.C. sec. 1693a) as amended from time to time.

(c) In a funds transfer to which this Article applies, in the event of an inconsistency between an applicable provision of this Article and an applicable provision of the Electronic Fund Transfer Act, the provision of the Electronic Fund Transfer Act governs to the extent of the inconsistency.

As amended in 2013.

Official Comment

1. The Electronic Fund Transfer Act (EFTA), implemented by Regulation E, 12 C.F.R. Part 1005, is a federal statute that covers aspects of electronic fund transfers involving consumers. EFTA also governs remittance transfers, defined in 15 U.S.C. sec. 1693*o*–1, which involve transfers of funds through electronic means by consumers to recipients in another country through persons or financial institutions that provide such transfers in the normal course of their business. Not all "remittance transfers" as defined in EFTA, however, qualify as "electronic fund transfers" as defined under the EFTA, 15 U.S.C. sec. 1693a(7). While Section 4A–108(a) broadly states that Article 4A does not apply to any funds transfer that is governed in any part by EFTA, subsection (b) provides an exception. The purpose of Section 4A–108(b) is to allow this Article to apply to a funds transfer as defined in Section 4A–104(a) (see Section 4A–102) that also is a remittance transfer as defined in EFTA, so long as that remittance transfer is not an electronic fund transfer as defined in EFTA. If the resulting application of this Article to an EFTA-defined "remittance transfer" that is not an EFTA-defined "electronic fund transfer" creates an inconsistency between an applicable provision of this Article and an applicable provision of EFTA, then, as a matter of federal supremacy, the provision of EFTA governs to the extent of the inconsistency. Section 4A–108(c). Of course, in the case of a funds transfer that also relates to another jurisdiction, the forum's conflict of laws principles determine whether it will apply the law in effect in this State (including this Article and EFTA) or the law of another jurisdiction to all or any part of the funds transfer. See Section 4A–507.

2. The following cases illustrate the relationship between EFTA and this Article pursuant to Section 4A–108.

Case # 1. A commercial customer of Bank A sends a payment order to Bank A, instructing Bank A to transfer funds from its account at Bank A to the account of a consumer at Bank B. The funds transfer is executed by a payment order from Bank A to an intermediary bank and is executed by the intermediary bank by means of an automated clearinghouse credit entry to the consumer's account at Bank B (the beneficiary's bank). The transfer into the consumer's account is an "electronic fund transfer" as defined in 15 U.S.C. sec. 1693a(7). Pursuant to Section 4A–108(a), Article 4A does not apply to any part of the funds transfer because EFTA governs part of the funds transfer. The transfer is not a "remittance transfer" as defined in 15 U.S.C. sec. 1693*o*–1 because the originator is not a consumer customer. Thus Section 4A–108(b) does not apply.

A court might, however, apply appropriate principles from Article 4A by analogy in analyzing any part of the funds transfer that is not subject to the provisions of EFTA or other law, such as the obligation of the intermediary bank to execute the payment order of the originator's bank (Section 4A–302), or whether the payment order of the commercial customer to Bank A is authorized or verified (Sections 4A–202 and 4A–203).

Case # 2. A consumer originates a payment order that is a remittance transfer as defined in 15 U.S.C. sec. 1693*o*–1 and provides the remittance transfer provider (Bank A) with cash in the amount of the transfer plus any relevant fees. The funds transfer is routed through an intermediary bank for final credit to the designated recipient's account at Bank B. Bank A's payment order identifies the designated recipient by both name and account number in Bank B, but the name and number provided identify different persons. This remittance transfer is not an "electronic fund transfer" as defined in 15 U.S.C. sec. 1693a(7) because it is not initiated by electronic means from a consumer's account, but does qualify as a "funds transfer" as defined in Section 4A–104. Both Article 4A and EFTA apply to the funds transfer. Sections 4A–102, 4A–108(a), (b). Article 4A's provision on mistakes in identifying the designated beneficiary, Section 4A–207, would apply as long as not inconsistent with the governing EFTA provisions. See 15 U.S.C. Sec. 1693*o*–1(d), Section 4A–108(c). See Comment 1 to this Section.

Case # 3. A consumer originates a payment order from the consumer's account at Bank A to the designated recipient's account at Bank B located outside the United States. Bank A uses the CHIPS system to execute that payment order. The funds transfer is a "remittance transfer" as defined in 15 U.S.C. sec. 1693*o*–1. This transfer is not an "electronic fund transfer" as defined in 15 U.S.C. Sec. 1693a(7) because of the exclusion for transfers through systems such as CHIPS in 15 U.S.C. Sec. 1693a(7)(B), but qualifies as a "funds transfer" as defined in Section 4A–104. Under Sections 4A–102 and 4A–108(b), both Article 4A and EFTA apply to the funds transfer. The EFTA will prevail to the extent of any inconsistency between EFTA and Article 4A. Section 4A–108(c). See Comment 1 to this Section. For example, if the consumer subsequently exercises a right under EFTA to cancel the remittance transfer and obtain a refund, Bank A would be required to comply with the EFTA rule even if Article 4A prevents Bank A from cancelling or reversing the payment order that Bank A sent to its receiving bank. Section 4A–211.

Case # 4. A person fraudulently originates an unauthorized payment order from a consumer's account through use of an online banking interface and the payment order is executed using a system that qualifies the transaction as an "electronic fund transfer" under EFTA. The funds transfer that results from execution of the unauthorized payment order is not governed by Article 4A. Section 4A–108(a). Whether the funds transfer also qualifies as a "remittance transfer" under EFTA has no bearing on the application of Article 4A.

Case # 5. A person fraudulently originates an unauthorized payment order from a consumer's account at Bank A through forging written documents that are provided in person to an employee of Bank A. This transaction is not an "electronic fund transfer" as defined in 15 U.S.C. Sec. 1693a(7) because it was not initiated by electronic means, but qualifies as a "funds transfer" as defined in Section 4A–104. Article 4A applies regardless of whether the funds transfer also qualifies as a "remittance transfer" under 15 U.S.C. sec. 1693*o*–1. If the funds transfer is not a remittance transfer, the provisions of Section 4A–108 are not implicated because the funds transfer does not fall under EFTA, and the general scope provision of Article 4A governs. Section 4A–102. If the funds transfer is a remittance transfer, and thus governed by EFTA, Section 4A–108(b) provides that Article 4A also applies. The provisions of Article 4A allocate the loss arising from the unauthorized payment order as long as those provisions are not inconsistent with the provisions of the EFTA applicable to remittance transfers. See 15 U.S.C. Sec. 1693*o*–1, Section 4A–108(c). See Comment 1 to this Section.

3. Regulation J, 12 C.F.R. Part 210, of the Federal Reserve Board addresses the application of that regulation and EFTA to fund transfers made through Fedwire. Fedwire transfers are further described in Official Comments 1 and 2 to Section 4A–107. In addition, funds transfer system rules may be applicable pursuant to Section 4A–501.

Legislative Note: The reference to EFTA "as amended from time to time" means that the operation of this section at any particular time after enactment may depend on federal legislative action occurring after enactment. In states in which such an arrangement may constitute improper delegation, the language "as amended from time to time" may be deleted. In that case, however, the legislature should consider other mechanisms to assure that this section continues to operate harmoniously with EFTA as it may be subsequently amended.

PART 2
ISSUE AND ACCEPTANCE OF PAYMENT ORDER

§ 4A-201. Security Procedure.

"Security procedure" means a procedure established by agreement of a customer and a receiving bank for the purpose of (i) verifying that a payment order or communication amending or cancelling a payment order is that of the customer, or (ii) detecting error in the transmission or the content of the payment order or communication. A security procedure may require the use of algorithms or other codes, identifying words or numbers, encryption, callback procedures, or similar security devices. Comparison of a signature on a payment order or communication with an authorized specimen signature of the customer is not by itself a security procedure.

Official Comment

A large percentage of payment orders and communications amending or cancelling payment orders are transmitted electronically and it is standard practice to use security procedures that are designed to assure the authenticity of the message. Security procedures can also be used to detect error in the content of messages or to detect payment orders that are transmitted by mistake as in the case of multiple transmission of the same payment order. Security procedures might also apply to communications that are transmitted by telephone or in writing. Section 4A-201 defines these security procedures. The definition of security procedure limits the term to a procedure "established by agreement of a customer and a receiving bank." The term does not apply to procedures that the receiving bank may follow unilaterally in processing payment orders. The question of whether loss that may result from the transmission of a spurious or erroneous payment order will be borne by the receiving bank or the sender or purported sender is affected by whether a security procedure was or was not in effect and whether there was or was not compliance with the procedure. Security procedures are referred to in Sections 4A-202 and 4A-203, which deal with authorized and verified payment orders, and Section 4A-205, which deals with erroneous payment orders.

§ 4A-202. Authorized and Verified Payment Orders.

(a) A payment order received by the receiving bank is the authorized order of the person identified as sender if that person authorized the order or is otherwise bound by it under the law of agency.

(b) If a bank and its customer have agreed that the authenticity of payment orders issued to the bank in the name of the customer as sender will be verified pursuant to a security procedure, a payment order received by the receiving bank is effective as the order of the customer, whether or not authorized, if (i) the security procedure is a commercially reasonable method of providing security against unauthorized payment orders, and (ii) the bank proves that it accepted the payment order in good faith and in compliance with the security procedure and any written agreement or instruction of the customer restricting acceptance of payment orders issued in the name of the customer. The bank is not required to follow an instruction that violates a written agreement with the customer or notice of which is not received at a time and in a manner affording the bank a reasonable opportunity to act on it before the payment order is accepted.

(c) Commercial reasonableness of a security procedure is a question of law to be determined by considering the wishes of the customer expressed to the bank, the circumstances of the customer known to the bank, including the size, type, and frequency of payment orders normally issued by the customer to the bank, alternative security procedures offered to the customer, and security procedures in general use by customers and receiving banks similarly situated. A security procedure is deemed to be commercially reasonable if (i) the security procedure was chosen by the customer after the bank offered, and the customer refused, a security procedure that was commercially reasonable for that customer, and (ii) the customer expressly agreed in writing to be bound by any payment order, whether or not authorized, issued in its name and accepted by the bank in compliance with the security procedure chosen by the customer.

(d) The term "sender" in this Article includes the customer in whose name a payment order is issued if the order is the authorized order of the customer under subsection (a), or it is effective as the order of the customer under subsection (b).

(e) This section applies to amendments and cancellations of payment orders to the same extent it applies to payment orders.

(f) Except as provided in this section and in Section 4A–203(a)(1), rights and obligations arising under this section or Section 4A–203 may not be varied by agreement.

Official Comment

This section is discussed in the Comment following Section 4A–203.

§ 4A–203. Unenforceability of Certain Verified Payment Orders.

(a) If an accepted payment order is not, under Section 4A–202(a), an authorized order of a customer identified as sender, but is effective as an order of the customer pursuant to Section 4A–202(b), the following rules apply:

(1) By express written agreement, the receiving bank may limit the extent to which it is entitled to enforce or retain payment of the payment order.

(2) The receiving bank is not entitled to enforce or retain payment of the payment order if the customer proves that the order was not caused, directly or indirectly, by a person (i) entrusted at any time with duties to act for the customer with respect to payment orders or the security procedure, or (ii) who obtained access to transmitting facilities of the customer or who obtained, from a source controlled by the customer and without authority of the receiving bank, information facilitating breach of the security procedure, regardless of how the information was obtained or whether the customer was at fault. Information includes any access device, computer software, or the like.

(b) This section applies to amendments of payment orders to the same extent it applies to payment orders.

Official Comment

1. Some person will always be identified as the sender of a payment order. Acceptance of the order by the receiving bank is based on a belief by the bank that the order was authorized by the person identified as the sender. If the receiving bank is the beneficiary's bank acceptance means that the receiving bank is obliged to pay the beneficiary. If the receiving bank is not the beneficiary's bank, acceptance means that the receiving bank has executed the sender's order and is obliged to pay the bank that accepted the order issued in execution of the sender's order. In either case the receiving bank may suffer a loss unless it is entitled to enforce payment of the payment order that it accepted. If the person identified as the sender of the order refuses to pay on the ground that the order was not authorized by that person, what are the rights of the receiving bank? In the absence of a statute or agreement that specifically addresses the issue, the question usually will be resolved by the law of agency. In some cases, the law of agency works well. For example, suppose the receiving bank executes a payment order given by means of a letter apparently written by a corporation that is a customer of the bank and apparently signed by an officer of the corporation. If the receiving bank acts solely on the basis of the letter, the corporation is not bound as the sender of the payment order unless the signature was that of the officer and the officer was authorized to act for the corporation in the issuance of payment orders, or some other agency doctrine such as apparent authority or estoppel causes the corporation to be bound. Estoppel can be illustrated by the following example. Suppose P is aware that A, who is unauthorized to act for P, has fraudulently misrepresented to T that A is authorized to act for P. T believes A and is about to rely on the misrepresentation. If P does not notify T of the true facts although P could easily do so, P may be estopped from denying A's lack of authority. A similar result could follow if the failure to notify T is the result of negligence rather than a deliberate decision. Restatement, Second, Agency § 8B. Other equitable principles such as subrogation or restitution might also allow a receiving bank to recover with respect to an unauthorized payment order that it accepted. In *Gatoil (U.S.A.), Inc. v. Forest Hill State Bank,* 1 U.C.C.Rep.Serv.2d 171 (D.Md. 1986), a joint venturer not authorized to order payments from the account of the joint venture, ordered a funds transfer from the account. The transfer paid a bona fide debt of the joint venture. Although the transfer was unauthorized the court refused to require recredit of the account because the joint venture suffered no loss. The result can be rationalized on the basis of subrogation of the receiving bank to the right of the beneficiary of the funds transfer to receive the payment from the joint venture.

But in most cases these legal principles give the receiving bank very little protection in the case of an authorized payment order. Cases like those just discussed are not typical of the way that most payment orders are transmitted and accepted, and such cases are likely to become even less common. Given the large amount of the typical payment order, a prudent receiving bank will be unwilling to accept a payment order unless it has assurance that the order is what it purports to be. This assurance is normally provided by security procedures described in Section 4A–201.

In a very large percentage of cases covered by Article 4A, transmission of the payment order is made electronically. The receiving bank may be required to act on the basis of a message that appears on a computer screen. Common law concepts of authority of agent to bind principal are not helpful. There is no way of determining the identity or the authority of the person who caused the message to be sent. The receiving bank is not relying on the authority of any particular person to act for the purported sender. The case is not comparable to payment of a check by the drawee bank on the basis of a signature that is forged. Rather, the receiving bank relies on a security procedure pursuant to which the authenticity of the message can be "tested" by various devices which are designed to provide certainty that the message is that of the sender identified in the payment order. In the wire transfer business the concept of "authorized" is different from that found in agency law. In that business a payment order is treated as the order of the person in whose name it is issued if it is properly tested pursuant to a security procedure and the order passes the test.

Section 4A–202 reflects the reality of the wire transfer business. A person in whose name a payment order is issued is considered to be the sender of the order if the order is "authorized" as stated in subsection (a) or if the order is "verified" pursuant to a security procedure in compliance with subsection (b). If subsection (b) does not apply, the question of whether the customer is responsible for the order is determined by the law of agency. The issue is one of actual or apparent authority of the person who caused the order to be issued in the name of the customer. In some cases the law of agency might allow the customer to be bound by an unauthorized order if conduct of the customer can be used to find an estoppel against the customer to deny that the order was unauthorized. If the customer is bound by the order under any of these agency doctrines, subsection (a) treats the order as authorized and thus the customer is deemed to be the sender of the order. In most cases, however, subsection (b) will apply. In that event there is no need to make an agency law analysis to determine authority. Under Section 4A–202, the issue of liability of the purported sender of the payment order will be determined by agency law only if the receiving bank did not comply with subsection (b).

2. The scope of Section 4A–202 can be illustrated by the following cases. *Case # 1.* A payment order purporting to be that of Customer is received by Receiving Bank but the order was fraudulently transmitted by a person who had no authority to act for Customer. *Case # 2.* An authentic payment order was sent by Customer, but before the order was received by Receiving Bank the order was fraudulently altered by an unauthorized person to change the beneficiary. *Case # 3.* An authentic payment order was received by Receiving Bank, but before the order was executed by Receiving Bank a person who had no authority to act for Customer fraudulently sent a communication purporting to amend the order by changing the beneficiary. In each case Receiving Bank acted on the fraudulent communication by accepting the payment order. These cases are all essentially similar and they are treated identically by Section 4A–202. In each case Receiving Bank acted on a communication that it thought was authorized by Customer when in fact the communication was fraudulent. No distinction is made between Case # 1 in which Customer took no part at all in the transaction and Case # 2 and Case # 3 in which an authentic order was fraudulently altered or amended by an unauthorized person. If subsection (b) does not apply, each case is governed by subsection (a). If there are no additional facts on which an estoppel might be found, Customer is not responsible in Case # 1 for the fraudulently issued payment order, in Case # 2 for the fraudulent alteration or in Case # 3 for the fraudulent amendment. Thus, in each case Customer is not liable to pay the order and Receiving Bank takes the loss. The only remedy of Receiving Bank is to seek recovery from the person who received payment as beneficiary of the fraudulent order. If there was verification in compliance with subsection (b), Customer will take the loss unless Section 4A–203 applies.

3. Subsection (b) of Section 4A–202 is based on the assumption that losses due to fraudulent payment orders can best be avoided by the use of commercially reasonable security procedures, and that the use of such procedures should be encouraged. The subsection is designed to protect both the customer and the receiving bank. A receiving bank needs to be able to rely on objective criteria to determine whether it can safely act on a payment order. Employees of the bank can be trained to "test" a payment order according to the various steps specified in the security procedure. The bank is responsible for the acts of these employees. Subsection (b)(ii) requires the bank to prove that it accepted the payment order in good faith and "in compliance with the security procedure." If the fraud was not detected because the bank's employee did not perform the acts required by the security procedure, the bank has not complied. Subsection (b)(ii) also requires the bank to prove that it complied with any agreement or instruction that restricts acceptance of payment orders issued in the name of the customer. A customer may want to protect itself by imposing limitations on acceptance of payment orders by the bank. For example, the customer may prohibit the bank from accepting a payment order that is not payable from an authorized account, that exceeds the credit balance in specified accounts of the customer, or that exceeds some other amount. Another

limitation may relate to the beneficiary. The customer may provide the bank with a list of authorized beneficiaries and prohibit acceptance of any payment order to a beneficiary not appearing on the list. Such limitations may be incorporated into the security procedure itself or they may be covered by a separate agreement or instruction. In either case, the bank must comply with the limitations if the conditions stated in subsection (b) are met. Normally limitations on acceptance would be incorporated into an agreement between the customer and the receiving bank, but in some cases the instruction might be unilaterally given by the customer. If standing instructions or an agreement state limitations on the ability of the receiving bank to act, provision must be made for later modification of the limitations. Normally this would be done by an agreement that specifies particular procedures to be followed. Thus, subsection (b) states that the receiving bank is not required to follow an instruction that violates a written agreement. The receiving bank is not bound by an instruction unless it has adequate notice of it. Subsections (25), (26) and (27) of Section 1–201 [*unrevised Article 1; see Concordance, p. 12*] apply.

Subsection (b)(i) assures that the interests of the customer will be protected by providing an incentive to a bank to make available to the customer a security procedure that is commercially reasonable. If a commercially reasonable security procedure is not made available to the customer, subsection (b) does not apply. The result is that subsection (a) applies and the bank acts at its peril in accepting a payment order that may be unauthorized. Prudent banking practice may require that security procedures be utilized in virtually all cases except for those in which personal contact between the customer and the bank eliminates the possibility of an unauthorized order. The burden of making available commercially reasonable security procedures is imposed on receiving banks because they generally determine what security procedures can be used and are in the best position to evaluate the efficacy of procedures offered to customers to combat fraud. The burden on the customer is to supervise its employees to assure compliance with the security procedure and to safeguard confidential security information and access to transmitting facilities so that the security procedure cannot be breached.

4. The principal issue that is likely to arise in litigation involving subsection (b) is whether the security procedure in effect when a fraudulent payment order was accepted was commercially reasonable. The concept of what is commercially reasonable in a given case is flexible. Verification entails labor and equipment costs that can vary greatly depending upon the degree of security that is sought. A customer that transmits very large numbers of payment orders in very large amounts may desire and may reasonably expect to be provided with state-of-the-art procedures that provide maximum security. But the expense involved may make use of a state-of-the-art procedure infeasible for a customer that normally transmits payment orders infrequently or in relatively low amounts. Another variable is the type of receiving bank. It is reasonable to require large money center banks to make available state of the art security procedures. On the other hand, the same requirement may not be reasonable for a small country bank. A receiving bank might have several security procedures that are designed to meet the varying needs of different customers. The type of payment order is another variable. For example, in a wholesale wire transfer, each payment order is normally transmitted electronically and individually. A testing procedure will be individually applied to each payment order. In funds transfers to be made by means of an automated clearing house many payment orders are incorporated into an electronic device such as a magnetic tape that is physically delivered. Testing of the individual payment orders is not feasible. Thus, a different kind of security procedure must be adopted to take into account the different mode of transmission.

The issue of whether a particular security procedure is commercially reasonable is a question of law. Whether the receiving bank complied with the procedure is a question of fact. It is appropriate to make the finding concerning commercial reasonability a matter of law because security procedures are likely to be standardized in the banking industry and a question of law standard leads to more predictability concerning the level of security that a bank must offer to its customers. The purpose of subsection (b) is to encourage banks to institute reasonable safeguards against fraud but not to make them insurers against fraud. A security procedure is not commercially unreasonable simply because another procedure might have been better or because the judge deciding the question would have opted for a more stringent procedure. The standard is not whether the security procedure is the best available. Rather it is whether the procedure is reasonable for the particular customer and the particular bank, which is a lower standard. On the other hand, a security procedure that fails to meet prevailing standards of good banking practice applicable to the particular bank should not be held to be commercially reasonable. Subsection (c) states factors to be considered by the judge in making the determination of commercial reasonableness. Sometimes an informed customer refuses a security procedure that is commercially reasonable and suitable for that customer and insists on using a higher-risk procedure because it is more convenient or cheaper. In that case, under the last sentence of subsection (c), the customer has voluntarily assumed the risk of failure of the procedure and cannot shift the loss to the bank. But this result follows only if the customer expressly agrees in writing to assume that risk. It is implicit in the last sentence of subsection (c) that a bank that accedes to the wishes of its customer in this regard is not acting in bad faith by so doing so long as the customer is made aware of the risk. In all cases, however, a receiving bank cannot get the benefit of subsection (b) unless it has made available to the customer a security procedure that is commercially reasonable and suitable for use by that customer. In most cases, the mutual interest of bank and customer to protect against fraud should lead to agreement to a security procedure which is commercially reasonable.

5. The effect of Section 4A–202(b) is to place the risk of loss on the customer if an unauthorized payment order is accepted by the receiving bank after verification by the bank in compliance with a commercially reasonable security procedure. An exception to this result is provided by Section 4A–203(a)(2). The customer may avoid the loss resulting from such a payment order if the customer can prove that the fraud was not committed by a person described in that subsection. Breach of a commercially reasonable security procedure requires that the person committing the fraud have knowledge of how the procedure works and knowledge of codes, identifying devices, and the like. That person may also need access to transmitting facilities through an access device or other software in order to breach the security procedure. This confidential information must be obtained either from a source controlled by the customer or from a source controlled by the receiving bank. If the customer can prove that the person committing the fraud did not obtain the confidential information from an agent or former agent of the customer or from a source controlled by the customer, the loss is shifted to the bank. "Prove" is defined in Section 4A–105(a)(7). Because of bank regulation requirements, in this kind of case there will always be a criminal investigation as well as an internal investigation of the bank to determine the probable explanation for the breach of security. Because a funds transfer fraud usually will involve a very large amount of money, both the criminal investigation and the internal investigation are likely to be thorough. In some cases there may be an investigation by bank examiners as well. Frequently, these investigations will develop evidence of who is at fault and the cause of the loss. The customer will have access to evidence developed in these investigations and that evidence can be used by the customer in meeting its burden of proof.

6. The effect of Section 4A–202(b) may also be changed by an agreement meeting the requirements of Section 4A–203(a)(1). Some customers may be unwilling to take all or part of the risk of loss with respect to unauthorized payment orders even if all of the requirements of Section 4A–202(b) are met. By virtue of Section 4A–203(a)(1), a receiving bank may assume all of the risk of loss with respect to unauthorized payment orders or the customer and bank may agree that losses from unauthorized payment orders are to be divided as provided in the agreement.

7. In a large majority of cases the sender of a payment order is a bank. In many cases in which there is a bank sender, both the sender and the receiving bank will be members of a funds transfer system over which the payment order is transmitted. Since Section 4A–202(f) does not prohibit a funds transfer system rule from varying rights and obligations under Section 4A–202, a rule of the funds transfer system can determine how loss due to an unauthorized payment order from a participating bank to another participating bank is to be allocated. A funds transfer system rule, however, cannot change the rights of a customer that is not a participating bank. § 4A–501(b). Section 4A–202(f) also prevents variation by agreement except to the extent stated.

§ 4A–204. Refund of Payment and Duty of Customer to Report With Respect to Unauthorized Payment Order.

(a) If a receiving bank accepts a payment order issued in the name of its customer as sender which is (i) not authorized and not effective as the order of the customer under Section 4A–202, or (ii) not enforceable, in whole or in part, against the customer under Section 4A–203, the bank shall refund any payment of the payment order received from the customer to the extent the bank is not entitled to enforce payment and shall pay interest on the refundable amount calculated from the date the bank received payment to the date of the refund. However, the customer is not entitled to interest from the bank on the amount to be refunded if the customer fails to exercise ordinary care to determine that the order was not authorized by the customer and to notify the bank of the relevant facts within a reasonable time not exceeding 90 days after the date the customer received notification from the bank that the order was accepted or that the customer's account was debited with respect to the order. The bank is not entitled to any recovery from the customer on account of a failure by the customer to give notification as stated in this section.

(b) Reasonable time under subsection (a) may be fixed by agreement as stated in Section 1–302(b), but the obligation of a receiving bank to refund payment as stated in subsection (a) may not otherwise be varied by agreement.

As amended in 2001.

Official Comment

1. With respect to unauthorized payment orders, in a very large percentage of cases a commercially reasonable security procedure will be in effect. Section 4A–204 applies only to cases in which (i) no commercially reasonable security procedure is in effect, (ii) the bank did not comply with a commercially reasonable security procedure that was in effect, (iii) the sender can prove, pursuant to Section 4A–203(a)(2), that the culprit did not obtain confidential security information controlled by the customer, or (iv) the bank, pursuant to Section 4A–203(a)(1) agreed to take all or part of the loss resulting from an unauthorized payment order. In each of these cases the bank takes the risk of loss with respect to an unauthorized payment order because the bank is not entitled to payment from the customer with respect to the order. The bank normally debits the customer's account or otherwise receives payment from the customer shortly after acceptance of the payment order. Subsection (a) of Section 4A–204 states that the bank must recredit the account or refund payment to the extent the bank is not entitled to enforce payment.

2. Section 4A–204 is designed to encourage a customer to promptly notify the receiving bank that it has accepted an unauthorized payment order. Since cases of unauthorized payment orders will almost always involve fraud, the bank's remedy is normally to recover from the beneficiary of the unauthorized order if the beneficiary was party to the fraud. This remedy may not be worth very much and it may not make any difference whether or not the bank promptly learns about the fraud. But in some cases prompt notification may make it easier for the bank to recover some part of its loss from the culprit. The customer will routinely be notified of the debit to its account with respect to an unauthorized order or will otherwise be notified of acceptance of the order. The customer has a duty to exercise ordinary care to determine that the order was unauthorized after it has received notification from the bank, and to advise the bank of the relevant facts within a reasonable time not exceeding 90 days after receipt of notification. Reasonable time is not defined and it may depend on the facts of the particular case. If a payment order for $1,000,000 is wholly unauthorized, the customer should normally discover it in far less than 90 days. If a $1,000,000 payment order was authorized but the name of the beneficiary was fraudulently changed, a much longer period may be necessary to discover the fraud. But in any event, if the customer delays more than 90 days the customer's duty has not been met. The only consequence of a failure of the customer to perform this duty is a loss of interest on the refund payable by the bank. A customer that acts promptly is entitled to interest from the time the customer's account was debited or the customer otherwise made payment. The rate of interest is stated in Section 4A–506. If the customer fails to perform the duty, no interest is recoverable for any part of the period before the bank learns that it accepted an unauthorized order. But the bank is not entitled to any recovery from the customer based on negligence for failure to inform the bank. Loss of interest is in the nature of a penalty on the customer designed to provide an incentive for the customer to police its account. There is no intention to impose a duty on the customer that might result in shifting loss from the unauthorized order to the customer.

§ 4A–205. Erroneous Payment Orders.

(a) If an accepted payment order was transmitted pursuant to a security procedure for the detection of error and the payment order (i) erroneously instructed payment to a beneficiary not intended by the sender, (ii) erroneously instructed payment in an amount greater than the amount intended by the sender, or (iii) was an erroneously transmitted duplicate of a payment order previously sent by the sender, the following rules apply:

(1) If the sender proves that the sender or a person acting on behalf of the sender pursuant to Section 4A–206 complied with the security procedure and that the error would have been detected if the receiving bank had also complied, the sender is not obliged to pay the order to the extent stated in paragraphs (2) and (3).

(2) If the funds transfer is completed on the basis of an erroneous payment order described in clause (i) or (iii) of subsection (a), the sender is not obliged to pay the order and the receiving bank is entitled to recover from the beneficiary any amount paid to the beneficiary to the extent allowed by the law governing mistake and restitution.

(3) If the funds transfer is completed on the basis of a payment order described in clause (ii) of subsection (a), the sender is not obliged to pay the order to the extent the amount received by the beneficiary is greater than the amount intended by the sender. In that case, the receiving bank is entitled to recover from the beneficiary the excess amount received to the extent allowed by the law governing mistake and restitution.

(b) If (i) the sender of an erroneous payment order described in subsection (a) is not obliged to pay all or part of the order, and (ii) the sender receives notification from the receiving bank that the order was accepted by the bank or that the sender's account was debited with respect to the order, the sender has a duty to exercise ordinary care, on the basis of information available to the sender, to discover the error with respect to the order and to advise the bank of the relevant facts within a reasonable time, not exceeding 90 days, after the bank's notification was received by the sender. If the bank proves that the sender failed to perform that duty, the sender is liable to the bank for the loss the bank proves it incurred as a result of the failure, but the liability of the sender may not exceed the amount of the sender's order.

(c) This section applies to amendments to payment orders to the same extent it applies to payment orders.

Official Comment

1. This section concerns error in the content or in the transmission of payment orders. It deals with three kinds of error. *Case # 1.* The order identifies a beneficiary not intended by the sender. For example, Sender intends to wire funds to a beneficiary identified only by an account number. The wrong account number is stated in the order. *Case # 2.* The error is in the amount of the order. For example, Sender intends to wire $1,000 to Beneficiary. Through error, the payment order instructs payment of $1,000,000. *Case # 3.* A payment order is sent to the receiving bank and then, by mistake, the same payment order is sent to the receiving bank again. In Case # 3, the receiving bank may have no way of knowing whether the second order is a duplicate of the first or is another order. Similarly, in Case # 1 and Case # 2, the receiving bank may have no way of knowing that the error exists. In each case, if this section does not apply and the funds transfer is completed, Sender is obliged to pay the order. Section 4A-402. Sender's remedy, based on payment by mistake, is to recover from the beneficiary that received payment.

Sometimes, however, transmission of payment orders of the sender to the receiving bank is made pursuant to a security procedure designed to detect one or more of the errors described above. Since "security procedure" is defined by Section 4A-201 as "a procedure established by agreement of a customer and a receiving bank for the purpose of . . . detecting error . . . ," Section 4A-205 does not apply if the receiving bank and the customer did not agree to the establishment of a procedure for detecting error. A security procedure may be designed to detect an account number that is not one to which Sender normally makes payment. In that case, the security procedure may require a special verification that payment to the stated account number was intended. In the case of dollar amounts, the security procedure may require different codes for different dollar amounts. If a $1,000,000 payment order contains a code that is inappropriate for that amount, the error in amount should be detected. In the case of duplicate orders, the security procedure may require that each payment order be identified by a number or code that applies to no other order. If the number or code of each payment order received is registered in a computer base, the receiving bank can quickly identify a duplicate order. The three cases covered by this section are essentially similar. In each, if the error is not detected, some beneficiary will receive funds that the beneficiary was not intended to receive. If this section applies, the risk of loss with respect to the error of the sender is shifted to the bank which has the burden of recovering the funds from the beneficiary. The risk of loss is shifted to the bank only if the sender proves that the error would have been detected if there had been compliance with the procedure and that the sender (or an agent under Section 4A-206) complied. In the case of a duplicate order or a wrong beneficiary, the sender doesn't have to pay the order. In the case of an overpayment, the sender does not have to pay the order to the extent of the overpayment. If subsection (a)(1) applies, the position of the receiving bank is comparable to that of a receiving bank that erroneously executes a payment order as stated in Section 4A-303. However, failure of the sender to timely report the error is covered by Section 4A-205(b) rather than by Section 4A-304 which applies only to erroneous execution under Section 4A-303. A receiving bank to which the risk of loss is shifted by subsection (a)(1) or (2) is entitled to recover the amount erroneously paid to the beneficiary to the extent allowed by the law of mistake and restitution. Rights of the receiving bank against the beneficiary are similar to those of a receiving bank that erroneously executes a payment order as stated in Section 4A-303. Those rights are discussed in Comment 2 to Section 4A-303.

2. A security procedure established for the purpose of detecting error is not effective unless both sender and receiving bank comply with the procedure. Thus, the bank undertakes a duty of complying with the procedure for the benefit of the sender. This duty is recognized in subsection (a)(1). The loss with respect to the sender's error is shifted to the bank if the bank fails to comply with the procedure and the sender (or an agent under Section 4A-206) does comply. Although the customer may have been negligent in transmitting the erroneous payment order, the loss is put on the bank on a last-clear-chance theory. A similar analysis applies to subsection (b). If the loss with respect to an error is shifted to the receiving bank and the sender is notified by the bank that the erroneous payment order was accepted, the sender has a duty to exercise ordinary care to discover the error and notify the bank of the relevant facts within a reasonable time not exceeding 90 days. If the bank can prove that the sender

failed in this duty it is entitled to compensation for the loss incurred as a result of the failure. Whether the bank is entitled to recover from the sender depends upon whether the failure to give timely notice would have made any difference. If the bank could not have recovered from the beneficiary that received payment under the erroneous payment order even if timely notice had been given, the sender's failure to notify did not cause any loss of the bank.

3. Section 4A–205 is subject to variation by agreement under Section 4A–501. Thus, if a receiving bank and its customer have agreed to a security procedure for detection of error, the liability of the receiving bank for failing to detect an error of the customer as provided in Section 4A–205 may be varied as provided in an agreement of the bank and the customer.

§ 4A–206. Transmission of Payment Order Through Funds-Transfer or Other Communication System.

(a) If a payment order addressed to a receiving bank is transmitted to a funds-transfer system or other third-party communication system for transmittal to the bank, the system is deemed to be an agent of the sender for the purpose of transmitting the payment order to the bank. If there is a discrepancy between the terms of the payment order transmitted to the system and the terms of the payment order transmitted by the system to the bank, the terms of the payment order of the sender are those transmitted by the system. This section does not apply to a funds-transfer system of the Federal Reserve Banks.

(b) This section applies to cancellations and amendments of payment orders to the same extent it applies to payment orders.

Official Comment

1. A payment order may be issued to a receiving bank directly by delivery of a writing or electronic device or by an oral or electronic communication. If an agent of the sender is employed to transmit orders on behalf of the sender, the sender is bound by the order transmitted by the agent on the basis of agency law. Section 4A–206 is an application of that principle to cases in which a funds transfer or communication system acts as an intermediary in transmitting the sender's order to the receiving bank. The intermediary is deemed to be an agent of the sender for the purpose of transmitting payment orders and related messages for the sender. Section 4A–206 deals with error by the intermediary.

2. Transmission by an automated clearing house of an association of banks other than the Federal Reserve Banks is an example of a transaction covered by Section 4A–206. Suppose Originator orders Originator's Bank to cause a large number of payments to be made to many accounts in banks in various parts of the country. These payment orders are electronically transmitted to Originator's Bank and stored in an electronic device that is held by Originator's Bank. Or, transmission of the various payment orders is made by delivery to Originator's Bank of an electronic device containing the instruction to the bank. In either case the terms of the various payment orders by Originator are determined by the information contained in the electronic device. In order to execute the various orders, the information in the electronic device must be processed. For example, if some of the orders are for payments to accounts in Bank X and some to accounts in Bank Y, Originator's Bank will execute these orders of Originator by issuing a series of payment orders to Bank X covering all payments to accounts in that bank, and by issuing a series of payment orders to Bank Y covering all payments to accounts in that bank. The orders to Bank X may be transmitted together by means of an electronic device, and those to Bank Y may be included in another electronic device. Typically, this processing is done by an automated clearing house acting for a group of banks including Originator's Bank. The automated clearing house is a funds transfer system. Section 4A–105(a)(5). Originator's Bank delivers Originator's electronic device or transmits the information contained in the device to the funds transfer system for processing into payment orders of Originator's Bank to the appropriate beneficiary's banks. The processing may result in an erroneous payment order. Originator's Bank, by use of Originator's electronic device, may have given information to the funds transfer system instructing payment of $100,000 to an account in Bank X, but because of human error or an equipment malfunction the processing may have converted that instruction into an instruction to Bank X to make a payment of $1,000,000. Under Section 4A–206, Originator's Bank issued a payment order for $1,000,000 to Bank X when the erroneous information was sent to Bank X. Originator's Bank is responsible for the error of the automated clearing house. The liability of the funds transfer system that made the error is not governed by Article 4A. It is left to the law of contract, a funds transfer system rule, or other applicable law.

In the hypothetical case just discussed, if the automated clearing house is operated by a Federal Reserve Bank, the analysis is different. Section 4A–206 does not apply. Originator's Bank will execute Originator's payment orders by delivery or transmission of the electronic information to the Federal Reserve Bank for processing. The result is that Originator's Bank has issued payment orders to the Federal Reserve Bank which, in this case, is acting as an intermediary bank. When the Federal Reserve Bank has processed the information given to it by Originator's Bank it will issue payment orders to the various beneficiary's banks. If the processing results in an erroneous payment order, the Federal Reserve Bank has erroneously executed the payment order of Originator's Bank and the case is governed by Section 4A–303.

§ 4A–207. Misdescription of Beneficiary.

(a) Subject to subsection (b), if, in a payment order received by the beneficiary's bank, the name, bank account number, or other identification of the beneficiary refers to a nonexistent or unidentifiable person or account, no person has rights as a beneficiary of the order and acceptance of the order cannot occur.

(b) If a payment order received by the beneficiary's bank identifies the beneficiary both by name and by an identifying or bank account number and the name and number identify different persons, the following rules apply:

(1) Except as otherwise provided in subsection (c), if the beneficiary's bank does not know that the name and number refer to different persons, it may rely on the number as the proper identification of the beneficiary of the order. The beneficiary's bank need not determine whether the name and number refer to the same person.

(2) If the beneficiary's bank pays the person identified by name or knows that the name and number identify different persons, no person has rights as beneficiary except the person paid by the beneficiary's bank if that person was entitled to receive payment from the originator of the funds transfer. If no person has rights as beneficiary, acceptance of the order cannot occur.

(c) If (i) a payment order described in subsection (b) is accepted, (ii) the originator's payment order described the beneficiary inconsistently by name and number, and (iii) the beneficiary's bank pays the person identified by number as permitted by subsection (b)(1), the following rules apply:

(1) If the originator is a bank, the originator is obliged to pay its order.

(2) If the originator is not a bank and proves that the person identified by number was not entitled to receive payment from the originator, the originator is not obliged to pay its order unless the originator's bank proves that the originator, before acceptance of the originator's order, had notice that payment of a payment order issued by the originator might be made by the beneficiary's bank on the basis of an identifying or bank account number even if it identifies a person different from the named beneficiary. Proof of notice may be made by any admissible evidence. The originator's bank satisfies the burden of proof if it proves that the originator, before the payment order was accepted, signed a writing stating the information to which the notice relates.

(d) In a case governed by subsection (b)(1), if the beneficiary's bank rightfully pays the person identified by number and that person was not entitled to receive payment from the originator, the amount paid may be recovered from that person to the extent allowed by the law governing mistake and restitution as follows:

(1) If the originator is obliged to pay its payment order as stated in subsection (c), the originator has the right to recover.

(2) If the originator is not a bank and is not obliged to pay its payment order, the originator's bank has the right to recover.

Official Comment

1. Subsection (a) deals with the problem of payment orders issued to the beneficiary's bank for payment to nonexistent or unidentifiable persons or accounts. Since it is not possible in that case for the funds transfer to be completed, subsection (a) states that the order cannot be accepted. Under Section 4A–402(c), a sender of a payment order is not obliged to pay its order unless the beneficiary's bank accepts a payment order instructing payment to the beneficiary of that sender's order. Thus, if the beneficiary of a funds transfer is nonexistent or unidentifiable, each sender in the funds transfer that has paid its payment order is entitled to get its money back.

2. Subsection (b), which takes precedence over subsection (a), deals with the problem of payment orders in which the description of the beneficiary does not allow identification of the beneficiary because the beneficiary is described by name and by an identifying number or an account number and the name and number refer to different persons. A very large percentage of payment orders issued to the beneficiary's bank by another bank are processed by automated means using machines capable of reading orders on standard formats that identify the beneficiary by an identifying number or the number of a bank account. The processing of the order by the beneficiary's bank and the crediting of the beneficiary's account are done by use of the identifying or bank account number without human reading of the payment order itself. The process is comparable to that used in automated payment of checks. The standard format, however, may also allow the inclusion of the name of the beneficiary and other information which can be useful to the beneficiary's bank and the beneficiary but which plays no part in the process of payment. If the beneficiary's bank has both the account number and name of the beneficiary supplied by the originator of the funds transfer, it is possible for the beneficiary's bank to determine whether the name and number refer to the same person, but if a duty to make that determination is imposed on the beneficiary's bank the benefits of automated payment are lost. Manual handling of payment orders is both expensive and subject to human error. If payment orders can be handled on an automated basis there are substantial economies of operation and the possibility of clerical error is reduced. Subsection (b) allows banks to utilize automated processing by allowing banks to act on the basis of the number without regard to the name if the bank does not know that the name and number refer to different persons. "Know" is defined in Section 1–201(25) [*unrevised Article 1; see Concordance, p. 12*] to mean actual knowledge, and Section 1–201(27) [*unrevised Article 1; see Concordance, p. 12*] states rules for determining when an organization has knowledge of information received by the organization. The time of payment is the pertinent time at which knowledge or lack of knowledge must be determined.

Although the clear trend is for beneficiary's banks to process payment orders by automated means, Section 4A–207 is not limited to cases in which processing is done by automated means. A bank that processes by semi-automated means or even manually may rely on number as stated in Section 4A–207.

In cases covered by subsection (b) the erroneous identification would in virtually all cases be the identifying or bank account number. In the typical case the error is made by the originator of the funds transfer. The originator should know the name of the person who is to receive payment and can further identify that person by an address that would normally be known to the originator. It is not unlikely, however, that the originator may not be sure whether the identifying or account number refers to the person the originator intends to pay. Subsection (b)(1) deals with the typical case in which the beneficiary's bank pays on the basis of the account number and is not aware at the time of payment that the named beneficiary is not the holder of the account which was paid. In some cases the false number will be the result of error by the originator. In other cases fraud is involved. For example, Doe is the holder of shares in Mutual Fund. Thief, impersonating Doe, requests redemption of the shares and directs Mutual Fund to wire the redemption proceeds to Doe's account # 12345 in Beneficiary's Bank. Mutual Fund originates a funds transfer by issuing a payment order to Originator's Bank to make the payment to Doe's account # 12345 in Beneficiary's Bank. Originator's Bank executes the order by issuing a conforming payment order to Beneficiary's Bank which makes payment to account # 12345. That account is the account of Roe rather than Doe. Roe might be a person acting in concert with Thief or Roe might be an innocent third party. Assume that Roe is a gem merchant that agreed to sell gems to Thief who agreed to wire the purchase price to Roe's account in Beneficiary's Bank. Roe believed that the credit to Roe's account was a transfer of funds from Thief and released the gems to Thief in good faith in reliance on the payment. The case law is unclear on the responsibility of a beneficiary's bank in carrying out a payment order in which the identification of the beneficiary by name and number is conflicting. See *Securities Fund Services, Inc. v. American National Bank*, 542 F.Supp. 323 (N.D.Ill. 1982) and *Bradford Trust Co. v. Texas American Bank*, 790 F.2d 407 (5th Cir. 1986). Section 4A–207 resolves the issue.

If Beneficiary's Bank did not know about the conflict between the name and number, subsection (b)(1) applies. Beneficiary's Bank has no duty to determine whether there is a conflict and it may rely on the number as the proper identification of the beneficiary of the order. When it accepts the order, it is entitled to payment from Originator's Bank. Section 4A–402(b). On the other hand, if Beneficiary's Bank knew about the conflict between the name and number and nevertheless paid Roe, subsection (b)(2) applies. Under that provision, acceptance of the payment order of Originator's Bank did not occur because there is no beneficiary of that order. Since acceptance did not occur Originator's Bank is not obliged to pay Beneficiary's Bank. Section 4A–402(b). Similarly, Mutual Fund is excused from its obligation to pay Originator's Bank. Section 4A–402(c). Thus, Beneficiary's Bank takes the loss. Its only cause of action is against Thief. Roe is not obliged to return the payment to the beneficiary's bank because Roe received the payment in good faith and for value. Article 4A makes irrelevant the issue of whether Mutual Fund was or was not negligent in issuing its payment order.

3. Normally, subsection (b)(1) will apply to the hypothetical case discussed in Comment 2. Beneficiary's Bank will pay on the basis of the number without knowledge of the conflict. In that case subsection (c) places the loss on either Mutual Fund or Originator's Bank. It is not unfair to assign the loss to Mutual Fund because it is the person who dealt with the imposter and it supplied the wrong account number. It could have avoided the loss if it had not used an account number that it was not sure was that of Doe. Mutual Fund, however, may not have been aware of the risk involved in giving both name and number. Subsection (c) is designed to protect the originator, Mutual Fund, in this case. Under that subsection, the originator is responsible for the inconsistent description of the beneficiary if it had notice that the order might be paid by the beneficiary's bank on the basis of the number. If the originator is a bank, the originator always has that responsibility. The rationale is that any bank should know how payment orders are processed and paid. If the originator is not a bank, the originator's bank must prove that its customer, the originator, had notice. Notice can be proved by any admissible evidence, but the bank can always prove notice by providing the customer with a written statement of the required information and obtaining the customer's signature to the statement. That statement will then apply to any payment order accepted by the bank thereafter. The information need not be supplied more than once.

In the hypothetical case if Originator's Bank made the disclosure stated in the last sentence of subsection (c)(2), Mutual Fund must pay Originator's Bank. Under subsection (d)(1), Mutual Fund has an action to recover from Roe if recovery from Roe is permitted by the law governing mistake and restitution. Under the assumed facts Roe should be entitled to keep the money as a person who took it in good faith and for value since it was taken as payment for the gems. In that case, Mutual Fund's only remedy is against Thief. If Roe was not acting in good faith, Roe has to return the money to Mutual Fund. If Originator's Bank does not prove that Mutual Fund had notice as stated in subsection (c)(2), Mutual Fund is not required to pay Originator's Bank. Thus, the risk of loss falls on Originator's Bank whose remedy is against Roe or Thief as stated above. Subsection (d)(2).

§ 4A-208. Misdescription of Intermediary Bank or Beneficiary's Bank.

(a) This subsection applies to a payment order identifying an intermediary bank or the beneficiary's bank only by an identifying number.

(1) The receiving bank may rely on the number as the proper identification of the intermediary or beneficiary's bank and need not determine whether the number identifies a bank.

(2) The sender is obliged to compensate the receiving bank for any loss and expenses incurred by the receiving bank as a result of its reliance on the number in executing or attempting to execute the order.

(b) This subsection applies to a payment order identifying an intermediary bank or the beneficiary's bank both by name and an identifying number if the name and number identify different persons.

(1) If the sender is a bank, the receiving bank may rely on the number as the proper identification of the intermediary or beneficiary's bank if the receiving bank, when it executes the sender's order, does not know that the name and number identify different persons. The receiving bank need not determine whether the name and number refer to the same person or whether the number refers to a bank. The sender is obliged to compensate the receiving bank for any loss and expenses incurred by the receiving bank as a result of its reliance on the number in executing or attempting to execute the order.

(2) If the sender is not a bank and the receiving bank proves that the sender, before the payment order was accepted, had notice that the receiving bank might rely on the number as the proper identification of the intermediary or beneficiary's bank even if it identifies a person different from the bank identified by name, the rights and obligations of the sender and the receiving bank are governed by subsection (b)(1), as though the sender were a bank. Proof of notice may be made by any admissible evidence. The receiving bank satisfies the burden of proof if it proves that the sender, before the payment order was accepted, signed a writing stating the information to which the notice relates.

(3) Regardless of whether the sender is a bank, the receiving bank may rely on the name as the proper identification of the intermediary or beneficiary's bank if the receiving bank, at the time it executes the sender's order, does not know that the name and number identify different persons. The receiving bank need not determine whether the name and number refer to the same person.

(4) If the receiving bank knows that the name and number identify different persons, reliance on either the name or the number in executing the sender's payment order is a breach of the obligation stated in Section 4A-302(a)(1).

Official Comment

1. This section addresses an issue similar to that addressed by Section 4A-207. Because of automation in the processing of payment orders, a payment order may identify the beneficiary's bank or an intermediary bank by an identifying number. The bank identified by number might or might not also be identified by name. The following two cases illustrate Section 4A-208(a) and (b):

Case # 1. Originator's payment order to Originator's Bank identifies the beneficiary's bank as Bank A and instructs payment to Account # 12345 in that bank. Originator's Bank executes Originator's order by issuing a payment order to Intermediary Bank. In the payment order of Originator's Bank the beneficiary's bank is identified as Bank A but is also identified by number, # 67890. The identifying number refers to Bank B rather than Bank A. If processing by Intermediary Bank of the payment order of Originator's Bank is done by automated means, Intermediary Bank, in executing the order, will rely on the identifying number and will issue a payment order to Bank B rather than Bank A. If there is an Account # 12345 in Bank B, the payment order of Intermediary Bank would normally be accepted and payment would be made to a person not intended by Originator. In this case, Section 4A-208(b)(1) puts the risk of loss on Originator's Bank. Intermediary Bank may rely on the number # 67890 as the proper identification of the beneficiary's bank. Intermediary Bank has properly executed the payment order of Originator's Bank. By using the wrong number to describe the beneficiary's bank, Originator's Bank has improperly executed Originator's payment order because the payment order of Originator's Bank provides for payment to the wrong beneficiary, the holder of Account # 12345 in Bank B rather than the holder of Account # 12345 in Bank A. Section 4A-302(a)(1) and Section 4A-303(c). Originator's Bank is not entitled to payment from Originator but is required to pay Intermediary Bank. Section 4A-303(c) and Section 4A-402(c). Intermediary Bank is also entitled to compensation for any loss and expenses resulting from the error by Originator's Bank.

If there is no Account # 12345 in Bank B, the result is that there is no beneficiary of the payment order issued by Originator's Bank and the funds transfer will not be completed. Originator's Bank is not entitled to payment from Originator and Intermediary Bank is not entitled to payment from Originator's Bank. Section 4A-402(c). Since Originator's Bank improperly executed Originator's payment order it may be liable for damages under Section 4A-305. As stated above, Intermediary Bank is entitled to compensation for loss and expenses resulting from the error by Originator's Bank.

Case # 2. Suppose the same payment order by Originator to Originator's Bank as in Case # 1. In executing the payment order Originator's Bank issues a payment order to Intermediary Bank in which the beneficiary's bank is identified only by number, # 67890. That number does not refer to Bank A. Rather, it identifies a person that is not a bank. If processing by Intermediary Bank of the payment order of Originator's Bank is done by automated means, Intermediary Bank will rely on the number # 67890 to identify the beneficiary's bank. Intermediary Bank has no duty to determine whether the number identifies a bank. The funds transfer cannot be completed in this case because no bank is identified as the beneficiary's bank. Subsection (a) puts the risk of loss on Originator's Bank. Originator's Bank is not entitled to payment from Originator. Section 4A-402(c). Originator's Bank has improperly executed Originator's payment order and may be liable for damages under Section 4A-305. Originator's Bank is obliged to compensate Intermediary Bank for loss and expenses resulting from the error by Originator's Bank.

Subsection (a) also applies if # 67890 identifies a bank, but the bank is not Bank A. Intermediary Bank may rely on the number as the proper identification of the beneficiary's bank. If the bank to which Intermediary Bank sends its payment order accepts the order, Intermediary Bank is entitled to payment from Originator's Bank, but Originator's Bank is not entitled to payment from Originator. The analysis is similar to that in Case # 1.

2. Subsection (b)(2) of Section 4A-208 addresses cases in which an erroneous identification of a beneficiary's bank or intermediary bank by name and number is made in a payment order of a sender that is not a bank. Suppose Originator issues a payment order to Originator's Bank that instructs that bank to use an intermediary bank identified as Bank A and by an identifying number, # 67890. The identifying number refers to Bank B. Originator intended to identify Bank A as intermediary bank. If Originator's Bank relied on the number and issued a payment order to Bank B the rights of Originator's Bank depend upon whether the proof of notice stated in subsection (b)(2) is made by Originator's Bank. If proof is made, Originator's Bank's rights are governed by subsection (b)(1) of Section 4A-208. Originator's Bank is not liable for breach of Section 4A-302(a)(1) and is

entitled to compensation from Originator for any loss and expenses resulting from Originator's error. If notice is not proved, Originator's Bank may not rely on the number in executing Originator's payment order. Since Originator's Bank does not get the benefit of subsection (b)(1) in that case, Originator's Bank improperly executed Originator's payment order and is in breach of the obligation stated in Section 4A–302(a)(1). If notice is not given, Originator's Bank can rely on the name if it is not aware of the conflict in name and number. Subsection (b)(3).

3. Although the principal purpose of Section 4A–208 is to accommodate automated processing of payment orders, Section 4A–208 applies regardless of whether processing is done by automation, semiautomated means or manually.

§ 4A–209. Acceptance of Payment Order.

(a) Subject to subsection (d), a receiving bank other than the beneficiary's bank accepts a payment order when it executes the order.

(b) Subject to subsections (c) and (d), a beneficiary's bank accepts a payment order at the earliest of the following times:

(1) when the bank (i) pays the beneficiary as stated in Section 4A–405(a) or 4A–405(b), or (ii) notifies the beneficiary of receipt of the order or that the account of the beneficiary has been credited with respect to the order unless the notice indicates that the bank is rejecting the order or that funds with respect to the order may not be withdrawn or used until receipt of payment from the sender of the order;

(2) when the bank receives payment of the entire amount of the sender's order pursuant to Section 4A–403(a)(1) or 4A–403(a)(2); or

(3) the opening of the next funds-transfer business day of the bank following the payment date of the order if, at that time, the amount of the sender's order is fully covered by a withdrawable credit balance in an authorized account of the sender or the bank has otherwise received full payment from the sender, unless the order was rejected before that time or is rejected within (i) one hour after that time, or (ii) one hour after the opening of the next business day of the sender following the payment date if that time is later. If notice of rejection is received by the sender after the payment date and the authorized account of the sender does not bear interest, the bank is obliged to pay interest to the sender on the amount of the order for the number of days elapsing after the payment date to the day the sender receives notice or learns that the order was not accepted, counting that day as an elapsed day. If the withdrawable credit balance during that period falls below the amount of the order, the amount of interest payable is reduced accordingly.

(c) Acceptance of a payment order cannot occur before the order is received by the receiving bank. Acceptance does not occur under subsection (b)(2) or (b)(3) if the beneficiary of the payment order does not have an account with the receiving bank, the account has been closed, or the receiving bank is not permitted by law to receive credits for the beneficiary's account.

(d) A payment order issued to the originator's bank cannot be accepted until the payment date if the bank is the beneficiary's bank, or the execution date if the bank is not the beneficiary's bank. If the originator's bank executes the originator's payment order before the execution date or pays the beneficiary of the originator's payment order before the payment date and the payment order is subsequently canceled pursuant to Section 4A–211(b), the bank may recover from the beneficiary any payment received to the extent allowed by the law governing mistake and restitution.

Official Comment

1. This section treats the sender's payment order as a request by the sender to the receiving bank to execute or pay the order and that request can be accepted or rejected by the receiving bank. Section 4A–209 defines when acceptance occurs. Section 4A–210 covers rejection. Acceptance of the payment order imposes an obligation on the receiving bank to the sender if the receiving bank is not the beneficiary's bank, or to the beneficiary if the receiving bank is the beneficiary's bank. These obligations are stated in Section 4A–302 and Section 4A–404.

2. Acceptance by a receiving bank other than the beneficiary's bank is defined in Section 4A–209(a). That subsection states the only way that a bank other than the beneficiary's bank can accept a payment order. A payment order to a bank other than the beneficiary's bank is, in effect, a request that the receiving bank execute the sender's order by issuing a payment order to the beneficiary's bank or to an intermediary bank. Normally,

acceptance occurs at the time of execution, but there is an exception stated in subsection (d) and discussed in Comment 9. Execution occurs when the receiving bank "issues a payment order intended to carry out" the sender's order. Section 4A–301(a). In some cases the payment order issued by the receiving bank may not conform to the sender's order. For example, the receiving bank might make a mistake in the amount of its order, or the order might be issued to the wrong beneficiary's bank or for the benefit of the wrong beneficiary. In all of these cases there is acceptance of the sender's order by the bank when the receiving bank issues its order intended to carry out the sender's order, even though the bank's payment order does not in fact carry out the instruction of the sender. Improper execution of the sender's order may lead to liability to the sender for damages or it may mean that the sender is not obliged to pay its payment order. These matters are covered in Section 4A–303, Section 4A–305, and Section 4A–402.

3. A receiving bank has no duty to accept a payment order unless the bank makes an agreement, either before or after issuance of the payment order, to accept it, or acceptance is required by a funds transfer system rule. If the bank makes such an agreement it incurs a contractual obligation based on the agreement and may be held liable for breach of contract if a failure to execute violates the agreement. In many cases a bank will enter into an agreement with its customer to govern the rights and obligations of the parties with respect to payment orders issued to the bank by the customer or, in cases in which the sender is also a bank, there may be a funds transfer system rule that governs the obligations of a receiving bank with respect to payment orders transmitted over the system. Such agreements or rules can specify the circumstances under which a receiving bank is obliged to execute a payment order and can define the extent of liability of the receiving bank for breach of the agreement or rule. Section 4A–305(d) states the liability for breach of an agreement to execute a payment order.

4. In the case of a payment order issued to the beneficiary's bank, acceptance is defined in Section 4A–209(b). The function of a beneficiary's bank that receives a payment order is different from that of a receiving bank that receives a payment order for execution. In the typical case, the beneficiary's bank simply receives payment from the sender of the order, credits the account of the beneficiary and notifies the beneficiary of the credit. Acceptance by the beneficiary's bank does not create any obligation to the sender. Acceptance by the beneficiary's bank means that the bank is liable to the beneficiary for the amount of the order. Section 4A–404(a). There are three ways in which the beneficiary's bank can accept a payment order which are described in the following comments.

5. Under Section 4A–209(b)(1), the beneficiary's bank can accept a payment order by paying the beneficiary. In the normal case of crediting an account of the beneficiary, payment occurs when the beneficiary is given notice of the right to withdraw the credit, the credit is applied to a debt of the beneficiary, or "funds with respect to the order" are otherwise made available to the beneficiary. Section 4A–405(a). The quoted phrase covers cases in which funds are made available to the beneficiary as a result of receipt of a payment order for the benefit of the beneficiary but the release of funds is not expressed as payment of the order. For example, the beneficiary's bank might express a release of funds equal to the amount of the order as a "loan" that will be automatically repaid when the beneficiary's bank receives payment by the sender of the order. If the release of funds is designated as a loan pursuant to a routine practice of the bank, the release is conditional payment of the order rather than a loan, particularly if normal incidents of a loan such as the signing of a loan agreement or note and the payment of interest are not present. Such a release of funds is payment to the beneficiary under Section 4A–405(a). Under Section 4A–405(c) the bank cannot recover the money from the beneficiary if the bank does not receive payment from the sender of the payment order that it accepted. Exceptions to this rule are stated in § 4A–405(d) and (e). The beneficiary's bank may also accept by notifying the beneficiary that the order has been received. "Notifies" is defined in Section 1–201(26) [*unrevised Article 1; see Concordance, p. 12*]. In some cases a beneficiary's bank will receive a payment order during the day but settlement of the sender's obligation to pay the order will not occur until the end of the day. If the beneficiary's bank wants to defer incurring liability to the beneficiary until the beneficiary's bank receives payment, it can do so. The beneficiary's bank incurs no liability to the beneficiary with respect to a payment order that it receives until it accepts the order. If the bank does not accept pursuant to subsection (b)(1), acceptance does not occur until the end of the day when the beneficiary's bank receives settlement. If the sender settles, the payment order will be accepted under subsection (b)(2) and the funds will be released to the beneficiary the next morning. If the sender doesn't settle, no acceptance occurs. In either case the beneficiary's bank suffers no loss.

6. In most cases the beneficiary's bank will receive a payment order from another bank. If the sender is a bank and the beneficiary's bank receives payment from the sender by final settlement through the Federal Reserve System or a funds transfer system (Section 4A–403(a)(1)) or, less commonly, through credit to an account of the beneficiary's bank with the sender or another bank (Section 4A–403(a)(2)), acceptance by the beneficiary's bank occurs at the time payment is made. Section 4A–209(b)(2). A minor exception to this rule is stated in Section 4A–209(c). Section 4A–209(b)(2) results in automatic acceptance of payment orders issued to a beneficiary's bank by

means of Fedwire because the Federal Reserve account of the beneficiary's bank is credited and final payment is made to that bank when the payment order is received.

Subsection (b)(2) would also apply to cases in which the beneficiary's bank mistakenly pays a person who is not the beneficiary of the payment order issued to the beneficiary's bank. For example, suppose the payment order provides for immediate payment to Account # 12345. The beneficiary's bank erroneously credits Account # 12346 and notifies the holder of that account of the credit. No acceptance occurs in this case under subsection (b)(1) because the beneficiary of the order has not been paid or notified. The holder of Account # 12345 is the beneficiary of the order issued to the beneficiary's bank. But acceptance will normally occur if the beneficiary's bank takes no other action, because the bank will normally receive settlement with respect to the payment order. At that time the bank has accepted because the sender paid its payment order. The bank is liable to pay the holder of Account # 12345. The bank has paid the holder of Account # 12346 by mistake, and has a right to recover the payment if the credit is withdrawn, to the extent provided in the law governing mistake and restitution.

7. Subsection (b)(3) covers cases of inaction by the beneficiary's bank. It applies whether or not the sender is a bank and covers a case in which the sender and the beneficiary both have accounts with the receiving bank and payment will be made by debiting the account of the sender and crediting the account of the beneficiary. Subsection (b)(3) is similar to subsection (b)(2) in that it bases acceptance by the beneficiary's bank on payment by the sender. Payment by the sender is effected by a debit to the sender's account if the account balance is sufficient to cover the amount of the order. On the payment date (Section 4A–401) of the order the beneficiary's bank will normally credit the beneficiary's account and notify the beneficiary of receipt of the order if it is satisfied that the sender's account balance covers the order or is willing to give credit to the sender. In some cases, however, the bank may not be willing to give credit to the sender and it may not be possible for the bank to determine until the end of the day on the payment date whether there are sufficient good funds in the sender's account. There may be various transactions during the day involving funds going into and out of the account. Some of these transactions may occur late in the day or after the close of the banking day. To accommodate this situation, subsection (b)(3) provides that the status of the account is determined at the opening of the next funds transfer business day of the beneficiary's bank after the payment date of the order. If the sender's account balance is sufficient to cover the order, the beneficiary's bank has a source of payment and the result in almost all cases is that the bank accepts the order at that time if it did not previously accept under subsection (b)(1). In rare cases, a bank may want to avoid acceptance under subsection (b)(3) by rejecting the order as discussed in Comment 8.

8. Section 4A–209 is based on a general principle that a receiving bank is not obliged to accept a payment order unless it has agreed or is bound by a funds transfer system rule to do so. Thus, provision is made to allow the receiving bank to prevent acceptance of the order. This principle is consistently followed if the receiving bank is not the beneficiary's bank. If the receiving bank is not the beneficiary's bank, acceptance is in the control of the receiving bank because it occurs only if the order is executed. But in the case of the beneficiary's bank acceptance can occur by passive receipt of payment under subsection (b)(2) or (3). In the case of a payment made by Fedwire acceptance cannot be prevented. In other cases the beneficiary's bank can prevent acceptance by giving notice of rejection to the sender before payment occurs under Section 4A–403(a)(1) or (2). A minor exception to the ability of the beneficiary's bank to reject is stated in Section 4A–502(c)(3).

Under subsection (b)(3) acceptance occurs at the opening of the next funds transfer business day of the beneficiary's bank following the payment date unless the bank rejected the order before that time or it rejects within one hour after that time. In some cases the sender and the beneficiary's bank may not be in the same time zone or the beginning of the business day of the sender and the funds transfer business day of the beneficiary's bank may not coincide. For example, the sender may be located in California and the beneficiary's bank in New York. Since in most cases notice of rejection would be communicated electronically or by telephone, it might not be feasible for the bank to give notice before one hour after the opening of the funds transfer business day in New York because at that hour, the sender's business day may not have started in California. For that reason, there are alternative deadlines stated in subsection (b)(3). In the case stated, the bank acts in time if it gives notice within one hour after the opening of the business day of the sender. But if the notice of rejection is received by the sender after the payment date, the bank is obliged to pay interest to the sender if the sender's account does not bear interest. In that case the bank had the use of funds of the sender that the sender could reasonably assume would be used to pay the beneficiary. The rate of interest is stated in Section 4A–506. If the sender receives notice on the day after the payment date the sender is entitled to one day's interest. If receipt of notice is delayed for more than one day, the sender is entitled to interest for each additional day of delay.

9. Subsection (d) applies only to a payment order by the originator of a funds transfer to the originator's bank and it refers to the following situation. On April 1, Originator instructs Bank A to make a payment on April 15 to the account of Beneficiary in Bank B. By mistake, on April 1, Bank A executes Originator's payment order

by issuing a payment order to Bank B instructing immediate payment to Beneficiary. Bank B credited Beneficiary's account and immediately released the funds to Beneficiary. Under subsection (d) no acceptance by Bank A occurred on April 1 when Originator's payment order was executed because acceptance cannot occur before the execution date which in this case would be April 15 or shortly before that date. Section 4A–301(b). Under Section 4A–402(c), Originator is not obliged to pay Bank A until the order is accepted and that can't occur until the execution date. But Bank A is required to pay Bank B when Bank B accepted Bank A's order on April 1. Unless Originator and Beneficiary are the same person, in almost all cases Originator is paying a debt owed to Beneficiary and early payment does not injure Originator because Originator does not have to pay Bank A until the execution date. Section 4A–402(c). Bank A takes the interest loss. But suppose that on April 3, Originator concludes that no debt was owed to Beneficiary or that the debt was less than the amount of the payment order. Under Section 4A–211(b) Originator can cancel its payment order if Bank A has not accepted. If early execution of Originator's payment order is acceptance, Originator can suffer a loss because cancellation after acceptance is not possible without the consent of Bank A and Bank B. Section 4A–211(c). If Originator has to pay Bank A, Originator would be required to seek recovery of the money from Beneficiary. Subsection (d) prevents this result and puts the risk of loss on Bank A by providing that the early execution does not result in acceptance until the execution date. Since on April 3 Originator's order was not yet accepted, Originator can cancel it under Section 4A–211(b). The result is that Bank A is not entitled to payment from Originator but is obliged to pay Bank B. Bank A has paid Beneficiary by mistake. If Originator's payment order is cancelled, Bank A becomes the originator of an erroneous funds transfer to Beneficiary. Bank A has the burden of recovering payment from Beneficiary on the basis of a payment by mistake. If Beneficiary received the money in good faith in payment of a debt owed to Beneficiary by Originator, the law of mistake and restitution may allow Beneficiary to keep all or part of the money received. If Originator owed money to Beneficiary, Bank A has paid Originator's debt and, under the law of restitution, which applies pursuant to Section 1–103, Bank A is subrogated to Beneficiary's rights against Originator on the debt.

If Bank A is the Beneficiary's bank and Bank A credited Beneficiary's account and released the funds to Beneficiary on April 1, the analysis is similar. If Originator's order is cancelled, Bank A has paid Beneficiary by mistake. The right of Bank A to recover the payment from Beneficiary is similar to Bank A's rights in the preceding paragraph.

§ 4A–210. Rejection of Payment Order.

(a) A payment order is rejected by the receiving bank by a notice of rejection transmitted to the sender orally, electronically, or in writing. A notice of rejection need not use any particular words and is sufficient if it indicates that the receiving bank is rejecting the order or will not execute or pay the order. Rejection is effective when the notice is given if transmission is by a means that is reasonable in the circumstances. If notice of rejection is given by a means that is not reasonable, rejection is effective when the notice is received. If an agreement of the sender and receiving bank establishes the means to be used to reject a payment order, (i) any means complying with the agreement is reasonable and (ii) any means not complying is not reasonable unless no significant delay in receipt of the notice resulted from the use of the noncomplying means.

(b) This subsection applies if a receiving bank other than the beneficiary's bank fails to execute a payment order despite the existence on the execution date of a withdrawable credit balance in an authorized account of the sender sufficient to cover the order. If the sender does not receive notice of rejection of the order on the execution date and the authorized account of the sender does not bear interest, the bank is obliged to pay interest to the sender on the amount of the order for the number of days elapsing after the execution date to the earlier of the day the order is canceled pursuant to Section 4A–211(d) or the day the sender receives notice or learns that the order was not executed, counting the final day of the period as an elapsed day. If the withdrawable credit balance during that period falls below the amount of the order, the amount of interest is reduced accordingly.

(c) If a receiving bank suspends payments, all unaccepted payment orders issued to it are deemed rejected at the time the bank suspends payments.

(d) Acceptance of a payment order precludes a later rejection of the order. Rejection of a payment order precludes a later acceptance of the order.

Official Comment

1. With respect to payment orders issued to a receiving bank other than the beneficiary's bank, notice of rejection is not necessary to prevent acceptance of the order. Acceptance can occur only if the receiving bank

executes the order. Section 4A–209(a). But notice of rejection will routinely be given by such a bank in cases in which the bank cannot or is not willing to execute the order for some reason. There are many reasons why a bank doesn't execute an order. The payment order may not clearly instruct the receiving bank because of some ambiguity in the order or an internal inconsistency. In some cases, the receiving bank may not be able to carry out the instruction because of equipment failure, credit limitations on the receiving bank, or some other factor which makes proper execution of the order infeasible. In those cases notice of rejection is a means of informing the sender of the facts so that a corrected payment order can be transmitted or the sender can seek alternate means of completing the funds transfer. The other major reason for not executing an order is that the sender's account is insufficient to cover the order and the receiving bank is not willing to give credit to the sender. If the sender's account is sufficient to cover the order and the receiving bank chooses not to execute the order, notice of rejection is necessary to prevent liability to pay interest to the sender if the case falls within Section 4A–210(b) which is discussed in Comment 3.

2. A payment order to the beneficiary's bank can be accepted by inaction of the bank. Section 4A–209(b)(2) and (3). To prevent acceptance under those provisions it is necessary for the receiving bank to send notice of rejection before acceptance occurs. Subsection (a) of Section 4A–210 states the rule that rejection is accomplished by giving notice of rejection. This incorporates the definitions in Section 1–201(26) [*unrevised Article 1; see Concordance, p. 12*]. Rejection is effective when notice is given if it is given by a means that is reasonable in the circumstances. Otherwise, it is effective when the notice is received. The question of when rejection is effective is important only in the relatively few cases under subsection (b)(2) and (3) in which a notice of rejection is necessary to prevent acceptance. The question of whether a particular means is reasonable depends on the facts in a particular case. In a very large percentage of cases the sender and the receiving bank will be in direct electronic contact with each other and in those cases a notice of rejection can be transmitted instantaneously. Since time is of the essence in a large proportion of funds transfers, some quick means of transmission would usually be required, but this is not always the case. The parties may specify by agreement the means by which communication between the parties is to be made.

3. Subsection (b) deals with cases in which a sender does not learn until after the execution date that the sender's order has not been executed. It applies only to cases in which the receiving bank was assured of payment because the sender's account was sufficient to cover the order. Normally, the receiving bank will accept the sender's order if it is assured of payment, but there may be some cases in which the bank chooses to reject. Unless the receiving bank had obligated itself by agreement to accept, the failure to accept is not wrongful. There is no duty of the receiving bank to accept the payment order unless it is obliged to accept by express agreement. Section 4A–212. But even if the bank has not acted wrongfully, the receiving bank had the use of the sender's money that the sender could reasonably assume was to be the source of payment of the funds transfer. Until the sender learns that the order was not accepted the sender is denied the use of that money. Subsection (b) obliges the receiving bank to pay interest to the sender as restitution unless the sender receives notice of rejection on the execution date. The time of receipt of notice is determined pursuant to § 1–201(27) [*unrevised Article 1; see Concordance, p. 12*]. The rate of interest is stated in Section 4A–506. If the sender receives notice on the day after the execution date, the sender is entitled to one day's interest. If receipt of notice is delayed for more than one day, the sender is entitled to interest for each additional day of delay.

4. Subsection (d) treats acceptance and rejection as mutually exclusive. If a payment order has been accepted, rejection of that order becomes impossible. If a payment order has been rejected it cannot be accepted later by the receiving bank. Once notice of rejection has been given, the sender may have acted on the notice by making the payment through other channels. If the receiving bank wants to act on a payment order that it has rejected it has to obtain the consent of the sender. In that case the consent of the sender would amount to the giving of a second payment order that substitutes for the rejected first order. If the receiving bank suspends payments (Section 4–104(1)(k)), subsection (c) provides that unaccepted payment orders are deemed rejected at the time suspension of payments occurs. This prevents acceptance by passage of time under Section 4A–209(b)(3).

§ 4A–211. Cancellation and Amendment of Payment Order.

(a) A communication of the sender of a payment order cancelling or amending the order may be transmitted to the receiving bank orally, electronically, or in writing. If a security procedure is in effect between the sender and the receiving bank, the communication is not effective to cancel or amend the order unless the communication is verified pursuant to the security procedure or the bank agrees to the cancellation or amendment.

(b) Subject to subsection (a), a communication by the sender cancelling or amending a payment order is effective to cancel or amend the order if notice of the communication is received at a time and in a manner affording the receiving bank a reasonable opportunity to act on the communication before the bank accepts the payment order.

(c) After a payment order has been accepted, cancellation or amendment of the order is not effective unless the receiving bank agrees or a funds-transfer system rule allows cancellation or amendment without agreement of the bank.

(1) With respect to a payment order accepted by a receiving bank other than the beneficiary's bank, cancellation or amendment is not effective unless a conforming cancellation or amendment of the payment order issued by the receiving bank is also made.

(2) With respect to a payment order accepted by the beneficiary's bank, cancellation or amendment is not effective unless the order was issued in execution of an unauthorized payment order, or because of a mistake by a sender in the funds transfer which resulted in the issuance of a payment order (i) that is a duplicate of a payment order previously issued by the sender, (ii) that orders payment to a beneficiary not entitled to receive payment from the originator, or (iii) that orders payment in an amount greater than the amount the beneficiary was entitled to receive from the originator. If the payment order is canceled or amended, the beneficiary's bank is entitled to recover from the beneficiary any amount paid to the beneficiary to the extent allowed by the law governing mistake and restitution.

(d) An unaccepted payment order is canceled by operation of law at the close of the fifth funds-transfer business day of the receiving bank after the execution date or payment date of the order.

(e) A canceled payment order cannot be accepted. If an accepted payment order is canceled, the acceptance is nullified and no person has any right or obligation based on the acceptance. Amendment of a payment order is deemed to be cancellation of the original order at the time of amendment and issue of a new payment order in the amended form at the same time.

(f) Unless otherwise provided in an agreement of the parties or in a funds-transfer system rule, if the receiving bank, after accepting a payment order, agrees to cancellation or amendment of the order by the sender or is bound by a funds-transfer system rule allowing cancellation or amendment without the bank's agreement, the sender, whether or not cancellation or amendment is effective, is liable to the bank for any loss and expenses, including reasonable attorney's fees, incurred by the bank as a result of the cancellation or amendment or attempted cancellation or amendment.

(g) A payment order is not revoked by the death or legal incapacity of the sender unless the receiving bank knows of the death or of an adjudication of incapacity by a court of competent jurisdiction and has reasonable opportunity to act before acceptance of the order.

(h) A funds-transfer system rule is not effective to the extent it conflicts with subsection (c)(2).

Official Comment

1. This section deals with cancellation and amendment of payment orders. It states the conditions under which cancellation or amendment is both effective and rightful. There is no concept of wrongful cancellation or amendment of a payment order. If the conditions stated in this section are not met the attempted cancellation or amendment is not effective. If the stated conditions are met the cancellation or amendment is effective and rightful. The sender of a payment order may want to withdraw or change the order because the sender has had a change of mind about the transaction or because the payment order was erroneously issued or for any other reason. One common situation is that of multiple transmission of the same order. The sender that mistakenly transmits the same order twice wants to correct the mistake by cancelling the duplicate order. Or, a sender may have intended to order a payment of $1,000,000 but mistakenly issued an order to pay $10,000,000. In this case the sender might try to correct the mistake by cancelling the order and issuing another order in the proper amount. Or, the mistake could be corrected by amending the order to change it to the proper amount. Whether the error is corrected by amendment or cancellation and reissue the net result is the same. This result is stated in the last sentence of subsection (e).

2. Subsection (a) allows a cancellation or amendment of a payment order to be communicated to the receiving bank "orally, electronically, or in writing." The quoted phrase is consistent with the language of Section 4A–103(a) applicable to payment orders. Cancellations and amendments are normally subject to verification pursuant to security procedures to the same extent as payment orders. Subsection (a) recognizes this fact by providing that in cases in which there is a security procedure in effect between the sender and the receiving bank

the bank is not bound by a communication cancelling or amending an order unless verification has been made. This is necessary to protect the bank because under subsection (b) a cancellation or amendment can be effective by unilateral action of the sender. Without verification the bank cannot be sure whether the communication was or was not effective to cancel or amend a previously verified payment order.

3. If the receiving bank has not yet accepted the order, there is no reason why the sender should not be able to cancel or amend the order unilaterally so long as the requirements of subsections (a) and (b) are met. If the receiving bank has accepted the order, it is possible to cancel or amend but only if the requirements of subsection (c) are met.

First consider the case of a receiving bank other than the beneficiary's bank. If the bank has not yet accepted the order, the sender can unilaterally cancel or amend. The communication amending or cancelling the payment order must be received in time to allow the bank to act on it before the bank issues its payment order in execution of the sender's order. The time that the sender's communication is received is governed by Section 4A-106. If a payment order does not specify a delayed payment date or execution date, the order will normally be executed shortly after receipt. Thus, as a practical matter, the sender will have very little time in which to instruct cancellation or amendment before acceptance. In addition, a receiving bank will normally have cut-off times for receipt of such communications, and the receiving bank is not obliged to act on communications received after the cut-off hour. Cancellation by the sender after execution of the order by the receiving bank requires the agreement of the bank unless a funds transfer rule otherwise provides. Subsection (c). Although execution of the sender's order by the receiving bank does not itself impose liability on the receiving bank (under Section 4A-402 no liability is incurred by the receiving bank to pay its order until it is accepted), it would commonly be the case that acceptance follows shortly after issuance. Thus, as a practical matter, a receiving bank that has executed a payment order will incur a liability to the next bank in the chain before it would be able to act on the cancellation request of its customer. It is unreasonable to impose on the receiving bank a risk of loss with respect to a cancellation request without the consent of the receiving bank.

The statute does not state how or when the agreement of the receiving bank must be obtained for cancellation after execution. The receiving bank's consent could be obtained at the time cancellation occurs or it could be based on a preexisting agreement. Or, a funds transfer system rule could provide that cancellation can be made unilaterally by the sender. By virtue of that rule any receiving bank covered by the rule is bound. Section 4A-501. If the receiving bank has already executed the sender's order, the bank would not consent to cancellation unless the bank to which the receiving bank has issued its payment order consents to cancellation of that order. It makes no sense to allow cancellation of a payment order unless all subsequent payment orders in the funds transfer that were issued because of the cancelled payment order are also cancelled. Under subsection (c)(1), if a receiving bank consents to cancellation of the payment order after it has executed, the cancellation is not effective unless the receiving bank also cancels the payment order issued by the bank.

4. With respect to a payment order issued to the beneficiary's bank, acceptance is particularly important because it creates liability to pay the beneficiary, it defines when the originator pays its obligation to the beneficiary, and it defines when any obligation for which the payment is made is discharged. Since acceptance affects the rights of the originator and the beneficiary it is not appropriate to allow the beneficiary's bank to agree to cancellation or amendment except in unusual cases. Except as provided in subsection (c)(2), cancellation or amendment after acceptance by the beneficiary's bank is not possible unless all parties affected by the order agree. Under subsection (c)(2), cancellation or amendment is possible only in the four cases stated. The following examples illustrate subsection (c)(2):

Case # 1. Originator's Bank executed a payment order issued in the name of its customer as sender. The order was not authorized by the customer and was fraudulently issued. Beneficiary's Bank accepted the payment order issued by Originator's Bank. Under subsection (c)(2) Originator's Bank can cancel the order if Beneficiary's Bank consents. It doesn't make any difference whether the payment order that Originator's Bank accepted was or was not enforceable against the customer under Section 4A-202(b). Verification under that provision is important in determining whether Originator's Bank or the customer has the risk of loss, but it has no relevance under Section 4A-211(c)(2). Whether or not verified, the payment order was not authorized by the customer. Cancellation of the payment order to Beneficiary's Bank causes the acceptance of Beneficiary's Bank to be nullified. Subsection (e). Beneficiary's Bank is entitled to recover payment from the beneficiary to the extent allowed by the law of mistake and restitution. In this kind of case the beneficiary is usually a party to the fraud who has no right to receive or retain payment of the order.

Case # 2. Originator owed Beneficiary $1,000,000 and ordered Bank A to pay that amount to the account of Beneficiary in Bank B. Bank A issued a complying order to Bank B, but by mistake issued a duplicate order as well. Bank B accepted both orders. Under subsection (c)(2)(i) cancellation of the duplicate order could be made by Bank A with the consent of Bank B. Beneficiary has no right to receive or retain payment of the duplicate payment order if only $1,000,000 was owed by Originator to Beneficiary. If Originator owed $2,000,000 to Beneficiary, the law of restitution might allow Beneficiary to retain the $1,000,000 paid by Bank B on the duplicate order. In that case Bank B is entitled to reimbursement from Bank A under subsection (f).

Case # 3. Originator owed $1,000,000 to X. Intending to pay X, Originator ordered Bank A to pay $1,000,000 to Y's account in Bank B. Bank A issued a complying payment order to Bank B which Bank B accepted by releasing the $1,000,000 to Y. Under subsection (c)(2)(ii) Bank A can cancel its payment order to Bank B with the consent of Bank B if Y was not entitled to receive payment from Originator. Originator can also cancel its order to Bank A with Bank A's consent. Subsection (c)(1). Bank B may recover the $1,000,000 from Y unless the law of mistake and restitution allows Y to retain some or all of the amount paid. If no debt was owed to Y, Bank B should have a right of recovery.

Case # 4. Originator owed Beneficiary $10,000. By mistake Originator ordered Bank A to pay $1,000,000 to the account of Beneficiary in Bank B. Bank A issued a complying order to Bank B which accepted by notifying Beneficiary of its right to withdraw $1,000,000. Cancellation is permitted in this case under subsection (c)(2)(iii). If Bank B paid Beneficiary it is entitled to recover the payment except to the extent the law of mistake and restitution allows Beneficiary to retain payment. In this case Beneficiary might be entitled to retain $10,000, the amount of the debt owed to Beneficiary. If Beneficiary may retain $10,000, Bank B would be entitled to $10,000 from Bank A pursuant to subsection (f). In this case Originator also cancelled its order. Thus Bank A would be entitled to $10,000 from Originator pursuant to subsection (f).

5. Unless constrained by a funds transfer system rule, a receiving bank may agree to cancellation or amendment of the payment order under subsection (c) but is not required to do so regardless of the circumstances. If the receiving bank has incurred liability as a result of its acceptance of the sender's order, there are substantial risks in agreeing to cancellation or amendment. This is particularly true for a beneficiary's bank. Cancellation or amendment after acceptance by the beneficiary's bank can be made only in the four cases stated and the beneficiary's bank may not have any way of knowing whether the requirements of subsection (c) have been met or whether it will be able to recover payment from the beneficiary that received payment. Even with indemnity the beneficiary's bank may be reluctant to alienate its customer, the beneficiary, by denying the customer the funds. Subsection (c) leaves the decision to the beneficiary's bank unless the consent of the beneficiary's bank is not required under a funds transfer system rule or other interbank agreement. If a receiving bank agrees to cancellation or amendment under subsection (c)(1) or (2), it is automatically entitled to indemnification from the sender under subsection (f). The indemnification provision recognizes that a sender has no right to cancel a payment order after it is accepted by the receiving bank. If the receiving bank agrees to cancellation, it is doing so as an accommodation to the sender and it should not incur a risk of loss in doing so.

6. Acceptance by the receiving bank of a payment order issued by the sender is comparable to acceptance of an offer under the law of contracts. Under that law the death or legal incapacity of an offeror terminates the offer even though the offeree has no notice of the death or incapacity. Restatement Second, Contracts § 48. Comment a. to that section states that the "rule seems to be a relic of the obsolete view that a contract requires a 'meeting of minds,' and it is out of harmony with the modern doctrine that a manifestation of assent is effective without regard to actual mental assent." Subsection (g), which reverses the Restatement rule in the case of a payment order, is similar to Section 4–405(1) which applies to checks. Subsection (g) does not address the effect of the bankruptcy of the sender of a payment order before the order is accepted, but the principle of subsection (g) has been recognized in *Bank of Marin v. England*, 385 U.S. 99 (1966). Although Bankruptcy Code Section 542(c) may not have been drafted with wire transfers in mind, its language can be read to allow the receiving bank to charge the sender's account for the amount of the payment order if the receiving bank executed it in ignorance of the bankruptcy.

7. Subsection (d) deals with stale payment orders. Payment orders normally are executed on the execution date or the day after. An order issued to the beneficiary's bank is normally accepted on the payment date or the day after. If a payment order is not accepted on its execution or payment date or shortly thereafter, it is probable that there was some problem with the terms of the order or the sender did not have sufficient funds or credit to cover the amount of the order. Delayed acceptance of such an order is normally not contemplated, but the order may not have been cancelled by the sender. Subsection (d) provides for cancellation by operation of law to prevent an unexpected delayed acceptance.

8. A funds transfer system rule can govern rights and obligations between banks that are parties to payment orders transmitted over the system even if the rule conflicts with Article 4A. In some cases, however, a rule governing a transaction between two banks can affect a third party in an unacceptable way. Subsection (h)

deals with such a case. A funds transfer system rule cannot allow cancellation of a payment order accepted by the beneficiary's bank if the rule conflicts with subsection (c)(2). Because rights of the beneficiary and the originator are directly affected by acceptance, subsection (c)(2) severely limits cancellation. These limitations cannot be altered by funds transfer system rule.

§ 4A–212. Liability and Duty of Receiving Bank Regarding Unaccepted Payment Order.

If a receiving bank fails to accept a payment order that it is obliged by express agreement to accept, the bank is liable for breach of the agreement to the extent provided in the agreement or in this Article, but does not otherwise have any duty to accept a payment order or, before acceptance, to take any action, or refrain from taking action, with respect to the order except as provided in this Article or by express agreement. Liability based on acceptance arises only when acceptance occurs as stated in Section 4A–209, and liability is limited to that provided in this Article. A receiving bank is not the agent of the sender or beneficiary of the payment order it accepts, or of any other party to the funds transfer, and the bank owes no duty to any party to the funds transfer except as provided in this Article or by express agreement.

Official Comment

With limited exceptions stated in this Article, the duties and obligations of receiving banks that carry out a funds transfer arise only as a result of acceptance of payment orders or of agreements made by receiving banks. Exceptions are stated in Section 4A–209(b)(3) and Section 4A–210(b). A receiving bank is not like a collecting bank under Article 4. No receiving bank, whether it be an originator's bank, an intermediary bank or a beneficiary's bank, is an agent for any other party in the funds transfer.

PART 3

EXECUTION OF SENDER'S PAYMENT ORDER BY RECEIVING BANK

§ 4A–301. Execution and Execution Date.

(a) A payment order is "executed" by the receiving bank when it issues a payment order intended to carry out the payment order received by the bank. A payment order received by the beneficiary's bank can be accepted but cannot be executed.

(b) "Execution date" of a payment order means the day on which the receiving bank may properly issue a payment order in execution of the sender's order. The execution date may be determined by instruction of the sender but cannot be earlier than the day the order is received and, unless otherwise determined, is the day the order is received. If the sender's instruction states a payment date, the execution date is the payment date or an earlier date on which execution is reasonably necessary to allow payment to the beneficiary on the payment date.

Official Comment

1. The terms "executed," "execution" and "execution date" are used only with respect to a payment order to a receiving bank other than the beneficiary's bank. The beneficiary's bank can accept the payment order that it receives, but it does not execute the order. Execution refers to the act of the receiving bank in issuing a payment order "intended to carry out" the payment order that the bank received. A receiving bank has executed an order even if the order issued by the bank does not carry out the order received by the bank. For example, the bank may have erroneously issued an order to the wrong beneficiary, or in the wrong amount or to the wrong beneficiary's bank. In each of these cases execution has occurred but the execution is erroneous. Erroneous execution is covered in Section 4A–303.

2. "Execution date" refers to the time a payment order should be executed rather than the day it is actually executed. Normally the sender will not specify an execution date, but most payment orders are meant to be executed immediately. Thus, the execution date is normally the day the order is received by the receiving bank. It is common for the sender to specify a "payment date" which is defined in Section 4A–401 as "the day on which the amount of the order is payable to the beneficiary by the beneficiary's bank." Except for automated clearing house transfers, if a funds transfer is entirely within the United States and the payment is to be carried out electronically, the execution date is the payment date unless the order is received after the payment date. If the payment is to be carried out through an automated clearing house, execution may occur before the payment date.

In an ACH transfer the beneficiary is usually paid one or two days after issue of the originator's payment order. The execution date is determined by the stated payment date and is a day before the payment date on which execution is reasonably necessary to allow payment on the payment date. A funds transfer system rule could also determine the execution date of orders received by the receiving bank if both the sender and the receiving bank are participants in the funds transfer system. The execution date can be determined by the payment order itself or by separate instructions of the sender or an agreement of the sender and the receiving bank. The second sentence of subsection (b) must be read in the light of Section 4A–106 which states that if a payment order is received after the cut-off time of the receiving bank it may be treated by the bank as received at the opening of the next funds transfer business day.

3. Execution on the execution date is timely, but the order can be executed before or after the execution date. Section 4A–209(d) and Section 4A–402(c) state the consequences of early execution and Section 4A–305(a) states the consequences of late execution.

§ 4A–302. Obligations of Receiving Bank in Execution of Payment Order.

(a) Except as provided in subsections (b) through (d), if the receiving bank accepts a payment order pursuant to Section 4A–209(a), the bank has the following obligations in executing the order:

(1) The receiving bank is obliged to issue, on the execution date, a payment order complying with the sender's order and to follow the sender's instructions concerning (i) any intermediary bank or funds-transfer system to be used in carrying out the funds transfer, or (ii) the means by which payment orders are to be transmitted in the funds transfer. If the originator's bank issues a payment order to an intermediary bank, the originator's bank is obliged to instruct the intermediary bank according to the instruction of the originator. An intermediary bank in the funds transfer is similarly bound by an instruction given to it by the sender of the payment order it accepts.

(2) If the sender's instruction states that the funds transfer is to be carried out telephonically or by wire transfer or otherwise indicates that the funds transfer is to be carried out by the most expeditious means, the receiving bank is obliged to transmit its payment order by the most expeditious available means, and to instruct any intermediary bank accordingly. If a sender's instruction states a payment date, the receiving bank is obliged to transmit its payment order at a time and by means reasonably necessary to allow payment to the beneficiary on the payment date or as soon thereafter as is feasible.

(b) Unless otherwise instructed, a receiving bank executing a payment order may (i) use any funds-transfer system if use of that system is reasonable in the circumstances, and (ii) issue a payment order to the beneficiary's bank or to an intermediary bank through which a payment order conforming to the sender's order can expeditiously be issued to the beneficiary's bank if the receiving bank exercises ordinary care in the selection of the intermediary bank. A receiving bank is not required to follow an instruction of the sender designating a funds-transfer system to be used in carrying out the funds transfer if the receiving bank, in good faith, determines that it is not feasible to follow the instruction or that following the instruction would unduly delay completion of the funds transfer.

(c) Unless subsection (a)(2) applies or the receiving bank is otherwise instructed, the bank may execute a payment order by transmitting its payment order by first class mail or by any means reasonable in the circumstances. If the receiving bank is instructed to execute the sender's order by transmitting its payment order by a particular means, the receiving bank may issue its payment order by the means stated or by any means as expeditious as the means stated.

(d) Unless instructed by the sender, (i) the receiving bank may not obtain payment of its charges for services and expenses in connection with the execution of the sender's order by issuing a payment order in an amount equal to the amount of the sender's order less the amount of the charges, and (ii) may not instruct a subsequent receiving bank to obtain payment of its charges in the same manner.

Official Comment

1. In the absence of agreement, the receiving bank is not obliged to execute an order of the sender. Section 4A–212. Section 4A–302 states the manner in which the receiving bank may execute the sender's order if execution occurs. Subsection (a)(1) states the residual rule. The payment order issued by the receiving bank must comply

with the sender's order and, unless some other rule is stated in the section, the receiving bank is obliged to follow any instruction of the sender concerning which funds transfer system is to be used, which intermediary banks are to be used, and what means of transmission is to be used. The instruction of the sender may be incorporated in the payment order itself or may be given separately. For example, there may be a master agreement between the sender and receiving bank containing instructions governing payment orders to be issued from time to time by the sender to the receiving bank. In most funds transfers, speed is a paramount consideration. A sender that wants assurance that the funds transfer will be expeditiously completed can specify the means to be used. The receiving bank can follow the instructions literally or it can use an equivalent means. For example, if the sender instructs the receiving bank to transmit by telex, the receiving bank could use telephone instead. Subsection (c). In most cases the sender will not specify a particular means but will use a general term such as "by wire" or "wire transfer" or "as soon as possible." These words signify that the sender wants a same-day transfer. In these cases the receiving bank is required to use a telephonic or electronic communication to transmit its order and is also required to instruct any intermediary bank to which it issues its order to transmit by similar means. Subsection (a)(2). In other cases, such as an automated clearing house transfer, a same-day transfer is not contemplated. Normally the sender's instruction or the context in which the payment order is received makes clear the type of funds transfer that is appropriate. If the sender states a payment date with respect to the payment order, the receiving bank is obliged to execute the order at a time and in a manner to meet the payment date if that is feasible. Subsection (a)(2). This provision would apply to many ACH transfers made to pay recurring debts of the sender. In other cases, involving relatively small amounts, time may not be an important factor and cost may be a more important element. Fast means, such as telephone or electronic transmission, are more expensive than slow means such as mailing. Subsection (c) states that in the absence of instructions the receiving bank is given discretion to decide. It may issue its payment order by first class mail or by any means reasonable in the circumstances. Section 4A-305 states the liability of a receiving bank for breach of the obligations stated in Section 4A-302.

2. Subsection (b) concerns the choice of intermediary banks to be used in completing the funds transfer, and the funds transfer system to be used. If the receiving bank is not instructed about the matter, it can issue an order directly to the beneficiary's bank or can issue an order to an intermediary bank. The receiving bank also has discretion concerning use of a funds transfer system. In some cases it may be reasonable to use either an automated clearing house system or a wire transfer system such as Fedwire or CHIPS. Normally, the receiving bank will follow the instruction of the sender in these matters, but in some cases it may be prudent for the bank not to follow instructions. The sender may have designated a funds transfer system to be used in carrying out the funds transfer, but it may not be feasible to use the designated system because of some impediment such as a computer breakdown which prevents prompt execution of the order. The receiving bank is permitted to use an alternate means of transmittal in a good faith effort to execute the order expeditiously. The same leeway is not given to the receiving bank if the sender designates an intermediary bank through which the funds transfer is to be routed. The sender's designation of that intermediary bank may mean that the beneficiary's bank is expecting to obtain a credit from that intermediary bank and may have relied on that anticipated credit. If the receiving bank uses another intermediary bank the expectations of the beneficiary's bank may not be realized. The receiving bank could choose to route the transfer to another intermediary bank and then to the designated intermediary bank if there were some reason such as a lack of a correspondent-bank relationship or a bilateral credit limitation, but the designated intermediary bank cannot be circumvented. To do so violates the sender's instructions.

3. The normal rule, under subsection (a)(1), is that the receiving bank, in executing a payment order, is required to issue a payment order that complies as to amount with that of the sender's order. In most cases the receiving bank issues an order equal to the amount of the sender's order and makes a separate charge for services and expenses in executing the sender's order. In some cases, particularly if it is an intermediary bank that is executing an order, charges are collected by deducting them from the amount of the payment order issued by the executing bank. If that is done, the amount of the payment order accepted by the beneficiary's bank will be slightly less than the amount of the originator's payment order. For example, Originator, in order to pay an obligation of $1,000,000 owed to Beneficiary, issues a payment order to Originator's Bank to pay $1,000,000 to the account of Beneficiary in Beneficiary's Bank. Originator's Bank issues a payment order to Intermediary Bank for $1,000,000 and debits Originator's account for $1,000,010. The extra $10 is the fee of Originator's Bank. Intermediary Bank executes the payment order of Originator's Bank by issuing a payment order to Beneficiary's Bank for $999,990, but under § 4A-402(c) is entitled to receive $1,000,000 from Originator's Bank. The $10 difference is the fee of Intermediary Bank. Beneficiary's Bank credits Beneficiary's account for $999,990. When Beneficiary's Bank accepts the payment order of Intermediary Bank the result is a payment of $999,990 from Originator to Beneficiary. Section 4A-406(a). If that payment discharges the $1,000,000 debt, the effect is that Beneficiary has paid the charges of Intermediary Bank and Originator has paid the charges of Originator's Bank. Subsection (d) of Section 4A-302 allows Intermediary Bank to collect its charges by deducting them from the amount of the payment order, but only if instructed to do so by Originator's Bank. Originator's Bank is not authorized to give

that instruction to Intermediary Bank unless Originator authorized the instruction. Thus, Originator can control how the charges of Originator's Bank and Intermediary Bank are to be paid. Subsection (d) does not apply to charges of Beneficiary's Bank to Beneficiary.

In the case discussed in the preceding paragraph the $10 charge is trivial in relation to the amount of the payment and it may not be important to Beneficiary how the charge is paid. But it may be very important if the $1,000,000 obligation represented the price of exercising a right such as an option favorable to Originator and unfavorable to Beneficiary. Beneficiary might well argue that it was entitled to receive $1,000,000. If the option was exercised shortly before its expiration date, the result could be loss of the option benefit because the required payment of $1,000,000 was not made before the option expired. Section 4A–406(c) allows Originator to preserve the option benefit. The amount received by Beneficiary is deemed to be $1,000,000 unless Beneficiary demands the $10 and Originator does not pay it.

§ 4A–303. Erroneous Execution of Payment Order.

(a) A receiving bank that (i) executes the payment order of the sender by issuing a payment order in an amount greater than the amount of the sender's order, or (ii) issues a payment order in execution of the sender's order and then issues a duplicate order, is entitled to payment of the amount of the sender's order under Section 4A–402(c) if that subsection is otherwise satisfied. The bank is entitled to recover from the beneficiary of the erroneous order the excess payment received to the extent allowed by the law governing mistake and restitution.

(b) A receiving bank that executes the payment order of the sender by issuing a payment order in an amount less than the amount of the sender's order is entitled to payment of the amount of the sender's order under Section 4A–402(c) if (i) that subsection is otherwise satisfied and (ii) the bank corrects its mistake by issuing an additional payment order for the benefit of the beneficiary of the sender's order. If the error is not corrected, the issuer of the erroneous order is entitled to receive or retain payment from the sender of the order it accepted only to the extent of the amount of the erroneous order. This subsection does not apply if the receiving bank executes the sender's payment order by issuing a payment order in an amount less than the amount of the sender's order for the purpose of obtaining payment of its charges for services and expenses pursuant to instruction of the sender.

(c) If a receiving bank executes the payment order of the sender by issuing a payment order to a beneficiary different from the beneficiary of the sender's order and the funds transfer is completed on the basis of that error, the sender of the payment order that was erroneously executed and all previous senders in the funds transfer are not obliged to pay the payment orders they issued. The issuer of the erroneous order is entitled to recover from the beneficiary of the order the payment received to the extent allowed by the law governing mistake and restitution.

Official Comment

1. Section 4A–303 states the effect of erroneous execution of a payment order by the receiving bank. Under Section 4A–402(c) the sender of a payment order is obliged to pay the amount of the order to the receiving bank if the bank executes the order, but the obligation to pay is excused if the beneficiary's bank does not accept a payment order instructing payment to the beneficiary of the sender's order. If erroneous execution of the sender's order causes the wrong beneficiary to be paid, the sender is not required to pay. If erroneous execution causes the wrong amount to be paid the sender is not obliged to pay the receiving bank an amount in excess of the amount of the sender's order. Section 4A–303 takes precedence over Section 4A–402(c) and states the liability of the sender and the rights of the receiving bank in various cases of erroneous execution.

2. Subsections (a) and (b) deal with cases in which the receiving bank executes by issuing a payment order in the wrong amount. If Originator ordered Originator's Bank to pay $1,000,000 to the account of Beneficiary in Beneficiary's Bank, but Originator's Bank erroneously instructed Beneficiary's Bank to pay $2,000,000 to Beneficiary's account, subsection (a) applies. If Beneficiary's Bank accepts the order of Originator's Bank, Beneficiary's Bank is entitled to receive $2,000,000 from Originator's Bank, but Originator's Bank is entitled to receive only $1,000,000 from Originator. Originator's Bank is entitled to recover the overpayment from Beneficiary to the extent allowed by the law governing mistake and restitution. Originator's Bank would normally have a right to recover the overpayment from Beneficiary, but in unusual cases the law of restitution might allow Beneficiary to keep all or part of the overpayment. For example, if Originator owed $2,000,000 to Beneficiary and Beneficiary received the extra $1,000,000 in good faith in discharge of the debt, Beneficiary may be allowed to keep it. In this case Originator's Bank has paid an obligation of Originator and under the law of restitution, which applies through

Section 1-103, Originator's Bank would be subrogated to Beneficiary's rights against Originator on the obligation paid by Originator's Bank.

If Originator's Bank erroneously executed Originator's order by instructing Beneficiary's Bank to pay less than $1,000,000, subsection (b) applies. If Originator's Bank corrects its error by issuing another payment order to Beneficiary's Bank that results in payment of $1,000,000 to Beneficiary, Originator's Bank is entitled to payment of $1,000,000 from Originator. If the mistake is not corrected, Originator's Bank is entitled to payment from Originator only in the amount of the order issued by Originator's Bank.

3. Subsection (a) also applies to duplicate payment orders. Assume Originator's Bank properly executes Originator's $1,000,000 payment order and then by mistake issues a second $1,000,000 payment order in execution of Originator's order. If Beneficiary's Bank accepts both orders issued by Originator's Bank, Beneficiary's Bank is entitled to receive $2,000,000 from Originator's Bank but Originator's Bank is entitled to receive only $1,000,000 from Originator. The remedy of Originator's Bank is the same as that of a receiving bank that executes by issuing an order in an amount greater than the sender's order. It may recover the overpayment from Beneficiary to the extent allowed by the law governing mistake and restitution and in a proper case as stated in Comment 2 may have subrogation rights if it is not entitled to recover from Beneficiary.

4. Suppose Originator instructs Originator's Bank to pay $1,000,000 to Account # 12345 in Beneficiary's Bank. Originator's Bank erroneously instructs Beneficiary's Bank to pay $1,000,000 to Account # 12346 and Beneficiary's Bank accepted. Subsection (c) covers this case. Originator is not obliged to pay its payment order, but Originator's Bank is required to pay $1,000,000 to Beneficiary's Bank. The remedy of Originator's Bank is to recover $1,000,000 from the holder of Account # 12346 that received payment by mistake. Recovery based on the law of mistake and restitution is described in Comment 2.

§ 4A-304. Duty of Sender to Report Erroneously Executed Payment Order.

If the sender of a payment order that is erroneously executed as stated in Section 4A-303 receives notification from the receiving bank that the order was executed or that the sender's account was debited with respect to the order, the sender has a duty to exercise ordinary care to determine, on the basis of information available to the sender, that the order was erroneously executed and to notify the bank of the relevant facts within a reasonable time not exceeding 90 days after the notification from the bank was received by the sender. If the sender fails to perform that duty, the bank is not obliged to pay interest on any amount refundable to the sender under Section 4A-402(d) for the period before the bank learns of the execution error. The bank is not entitled to any recovery from the sender on account of a failure by the sender to perform the duty stated in this section.

Official Comment

This section is identical in effect to Section 4A-204 which applies to unauthorized orders issued in the name of a customer of the receiving bank. The rationale is stated in Comment 2 to Section 4A-204.

§ 4A-305. Liability for Late or Improper Execution or Failure to Execute Payment Order.

(a) If a funds transfer is completed but execution of a payment order by the receiving bank in breach of Section 4A-302 results in delay in payment to the beneficiary, the bank is obliged to pay interest to either the originator or the beneficiary of the funds transfer for the period of delay caused by the improper execution. Except as provided in subsection (c), additional damages are not recoverable.

(b) If execution of a payment order by a receiving bank in breach of Section 4A-302 results in (i) noncompletion of the funds transfer, (ii) failure to use an intermediary bank designated by the originator, or (iii) issuance of a payment order that does not comply with the terms of the payment order of the originator, the bank is liable to the originator for its expenses in the funds transfer and for incidental expenses and interest losses, to the extent not covered by subsection (a), resulting from the improper execution. Except as provided in subsection (c), additional damages are not recoverable.

(c) In addition to the amounts payable under subsections (a) and (b), damages, including consequential damages, are recoverable to the extent provided in an express written agreement of the receiving bank.

(d) If a receiving bank fails to execute a payment order it was obliged by express agreement to execute, the receiving bank is liable to the sender for its expenses in the transaction and for incidental expenses and interest losses resulting from the failure to execute. Additional damages, including consequential damages, are recoverable to the extent provided in an express written agreement of the receiving bank, but are not otherwise recoverable.

(e) Reasonable attorney's fees are recoverable if demand for compensation under subsection (a) or (b) is made and refused before an action is brought on the claim. If a claim is made for breach of an agreement under subsection (d) and the agreement does not provide for damages, reasonable attorney's fees are recoverable if demand for compensation under subsection (d) is made and refused before an action is brought on the claim.

(f) Except as stated in this section, the liability of a receiving bank under subsections (a) and (b) may not be varied by agreement.

Official Comment

1. Subsection (a) covers cases of delay in completion of a funds transfer resulting from an execution by a receiving bank in breach of Section 4A–302(a). The receiving bank is obliged to pay interest on the amount of the order for the period of the delay. The rate of interest is stated in Section 4A–506. With respect to wire transfers (other than ACH transactions) within the United States, the expectation is that the funds transfer will be completed the same day. In those cases, the originator can reasonably expect that the originator's account will be debited on the same day as the beneficiary's account is credited. If the funds transfer is delayed, compensation can be paid either to the originator or to the beneficiary. The normal practice is to compensate the beneficiary's bank to allow that bank to compensate the beneficiary by back-valuing the payment by the number of days of delay. Thus, the beneficiary is in the same position that it would have been in if the funds transfer had been completed on the same day. Assume on Day 1, Originator's Bank issues its payment order to Intermediary Bank which is received on that day. Intermediary Bank does not execute that order until Day 2 when it issues an order to Beneficiary's Bank which is accepted on that day. Intermediary Bank complies with subsection (a) by paying one day's interest to Beneficiary's Bank for the account of Beneficiary.

2. Subsection (b) applies to cases of breach of Section 4A–302 involving more than mere delay. In those cases the bank is liable for damages for improper execution but they are limited to compensation for interest losses and incidental expenses of the sender resulting from the breach, the expenses of the sender in the funds transfer and attorney's fees. This subsection reflects the judgment that imposition of consequential damages on a bank for commission of an error is not justified.

The leading common law case on the subject of consequential damages is *Evra Corp. v. Swiss Bank Corp.*, 673 F.2d 951 (7th Cir. 1982), in which Swiss Bank, an intermediary bank, failed to execute a payment order. Because the beneficiary did not receive timely payment the originator lost a valuable ship charter. The lower court awarded the originator $2.1 million for lost profits even though the amount of the payment order was only $27,000. The Seventh Circuit reversed, in part on the basis of the common law rule of *Hadley v. Baxendale* that consequential damages may not be awarded unless the defendant is put on notice of the special circumstances giving rise to them. Swiss Bank may have known that the originator was paying the shipowner for the hire of a vessel but did not know that a favorable charter would be lost if the payment was delayed. "Electronic payments are not so unusual as to automatically place a bank on notice of extraordinary consequences if such a transfer goes awry. Swiss Bank did not have enough information to infer that if it lost a $27,000 payment order it would face liability in excess of $2 million." 673 F.2d at 956.

If *Evra* means that consequential damages can be imposed if the culpable bank has notice of particular circumstances giving rise to the damages, it does not provide an acceptable solution to the problem of bank liability for consequential damages. In the typical case transmission of the payment order is made electronically. Personnel of the receiving bank that process payment orders are not the appropriate people to evaluate the risk of liability for consequential damages in relation to the price charged for the wire transfer service. Even if notice is received by higher level management personnel who could make an appropriate decision whether the risk is justified by the price, liability based on notice would require evaluation of payment orders on an individual basis. This kind of evaluation is inconsistent with the high-speed, low-price, mechanical nature of the processing system that characterizes wire transfers. Moreover, in *Evra* the culpable bank was an intermediary bank with which the originator did not deal. Notice to the originator's bank would not bind the intermediary bank, and it seems impractical for the originator's bank to convey notice of this kind to intermediary banks in the funds transfer. The success of the wholesale wire transfer industry has largely been based on its ability to effect payment at low cost and great speed. Both of these essential aspects of the modern wire transfer system would be adversely affected by a rule that imposed on banks liability for consequential damages. A banking industry amicus brief in *Evra* stated: "Whether banks can continue to make EFT services available on a widespread basis, by charging reasonable rates, depends on whether they can do so without incurring unlimited consequential risks. Certainly, no bank would handle for $3.25 a transaction entailing potential liability in the millions of dollars."

As the court in *Evra* also noted, the originator of the funds transfer is in the best position to evaluate the risk that a funds transfer will not be made on time and to manage that risk by issuing a payment order in time to allow monitoring of the transaction. The originator, by asking the beneficiary, can quickly determine if the funds transfer has been completed. If the originator has sent the payment order at a time that allows a reasonable margin for correcting error, no loss is likely to result if the transaction is monitored. The other published cases on this issue reach the *Evra* result. *Central Coordinates, Inc. v. Morgan Guaranty Trust Co.*, 40 U.C.C.Rep.Serv. 1340 (N.Y.Sup.Ct. 1985), and *Gatoil (U.S.A.), Inc. v. Forest Hill State Bank*, 1 U.C.C.Rep.Serv.2d 171 (D.Md. 1986).

Subsection (c) allows the measure of damages in subsection (b) to be increased by an express written agreement of the receiving bank. An originator's bank might be willing to assume additional responsibilities and incur additional liability in exchange for a higher fee.

3. Subsection (d) governs cases in which a receiving bank has obligated itself by express agreement to accept payment orders of a sender. In the absence of such an agreement there is no obligation by a receiving bank to accept a payment order. Section 4A-212. The measure of damages for breach of an agreement to accept a payment order is the same as that stated in subsection (b). As in the case of subsection (b), additional damages, including consequential damages, may be recovered to the extent stated in an express written agreement of the receiving bank.

4. Reasonable attorney's fees are recoverable only in cases in which damages are limited to statutory damages stated in subsections (a), (b) and (d). If additional damages are recoverable because provided for by an express written agreement, attorney's fees are not recoverable. The rationale is that there is no need for statutory attorney's fees in the latter case, because the parties have agreed to a measure of damages which may or may not provide for attorney's fees.

5. The effect of subsection (f) is to prevent reduction of a receiving bank's liability under Section 4A-305.

PART 4
PAYMENT

§ 4A-401. Payment Date.

"Payment date" of a payment order means the day on which the amount of the order is payable to the beneficiary by the beneficiary's bank. The payment date may be determined by instruction of the sender but cannot be earlier than the day the order is received by the beneficiary's bank and, unless otherwise determined, is the day the order is received by the beneficiary's bank.

Official Comment

"Payment date" refers to the day the beneficiary's bank is to pay the beneficiary. The payment date may be expressed in various ways so long as it indicates the day the beneficiary is to receive payment. For example, in ACH transfers the payment date is the equivalent of "settlement date" or "effective date." Payment date applies to the payment order issued to the beneficiary's bank, but a payment order issued to a receiving bank other than the beneficiary's bank may also state a date for payment to the beneficiary. In the latter case, the statement of a payment date is to instruct the receiving bank concerning time of execution of the sender's order. Section 4A-301(b).

§ 4A-402. Obligation of Sender to Pay Receiving Bank.

(a) This section is subject to Sections 4A-205 and 4A-207.

(b) With respect to a payment order issued to the beneficiary's bank, acceptance of the order by the bank obliges the sender to pay the bank the amount of the order, but payment is not due until the payment date of the order.

(c) This subsection is subject to subsection (e) and to Section 4A-303. With respect to a payment order issued to a receiving bank other than the beneficiary's bank, acceptance of the order by the receiving bank obliges the sender to pay the bank the amount of the sender's order. Payment by the sender is not due until the execution date of the sender's order. The obligation of that sender to pay its payment order is excused if the funds transfer is not completed by acceptance by the beneficiary's bank of a payment order instructing payment to the beneficiary of that sender's payment order.

(d) If the sender of a payment order pays the order and was not obliged to pay all or part of the amount paid, the bank receiving payment is obliged to refund payment to the extent the sender was not obliged to pay. Except as provided in Sections 4A–204 and 4A–304, interest is payable on the refundable amount from the date of payment.

(e) If a funds transfer is not completed as stated in subsection (c) and an intermediary bank is obliged to refund payment as stated in subsection (d) but is unable to do so because not permitted by applicable law or because the bank suspends payments, a sender in the funds transfer that executed a payment order in compliance with an instruction, as stated in Section 4A–302(a)(1), to route the funds transfer through that intermediary bank is entitled to receive or retain payment from the sender of the payment order that it accepted. The first sender in the funds transfer that issued an instruction requiring routing through that intermediary bank is subrogated to the right of the bank that paid the intermediary bank to refund as stated in subsection (d).

(f) The right of the sender of a payment order to be excused from the obligation to pay the order as stated in subsection (c) or to receive refund under subsection (d) may not be varied by agreement.

Official Comment

1. Subsection (b) states that the sender of a payment order to the beneficiary's bank must pay the order when the beneficiary's bank accepts the order. At that point the beneficiary's bank is obliged to pay the beneficiary. Section 4A–404(a). The last clause of subsection (b) covers a case of premature acceptance by the beneficiary's bank. In some funds transfers, notably automated clearing house transfers, a beneficiary's bank may receive a payment order with a payment date after the day the order is received. The beneficiary's bank might accept the order before the payment date by notifying the beneficiary of receipt of the order. Although the acceptance obliges the beneficiary's bank to pay the beneficiary, payment is not due until the payment date. The last clause of subsection (b) is consistent with that result. The beneficiary's bank is also not entitled to payment from the sender until the payment date.

2. Assume that Originator instructs Bank A to order immediate payment to the account of Beneficiary in Bank B. Execution of Originator's payment ordered by Bank A is acceptance under Section 4A–209(a). Under the second sentence of Section 4A–402(c) the acceptance creates an obligation of Originator to pay Bank A the amount of the order. The last clause of that sentence deals with attempted funds transfers that are not completed. In that event the obligation of the sender to pay its payment order is excused. Originator makes payment to Beneficiary when Bank B, the beneficiary's bank, accepts a payment order for the benefit of Beneficiary. Section 4A–406(a). If that acceptance by Bank B does not occur, the funds transfer has miscarried because Originator has not paid Beneficiary. Originator doesn't have to pay its payment order, and if it has already paid it is entitled to refund of the payment with interest. The rate of interest is stated in Section 4A–506. This "money-back guarantee" is an important protection of Originator. Originator is assured that it will not lose its money if something goes wrong in the transfer. For example, risk of loss resulting from payment to the wrong beneficiary is borne by some bank, not by Originator. The most likely reason for noncompletion is a failure to execute or an erroneous execution of a payment order by Bank A or an intermediary bank. Bank A may have issued its payment order to the wrong bank or it may have identified the wrong beneficiary in its order. The money-back guarantee is particularly important to Originator if noncompletion of the funds transfer is due to the fault of an intermediary bank rather than Bank A. In that case Bank A must refund payment to Originator, and Bank A has the burden of obtaining refund from the intermediary bank that it paid.

Subsection (c) can result in loss if an intermediary bank suspends payments. Suppose Originator instructs Bank A to pay to Beneficiary's account in Bank B and to use Bank C as an intermediary bank. Bank A executes Originator's order by issuing a payment order to Bank C. Bank A pays Bank C. Bank C fails to execute the order of Bank A and suspends payments. Under subsections (c) and (d), Originator is not obliged to pay Bank A and is entitled to refund from Bank A of any payment that it may have made. Bank A is entitled to a refund from Bank C, but Bank C is insolvent. Subsection (e) deals with this case. Bank A was required to issue its payment order to Bank C because Bank C was designated as an intermediary bank by Originator. Section 4A–302(a)(1). In this case Originator takes the risk of insolvency of Bank C. Under subsection (e), Bank A is entitled to payment from

Originator and Originator is subrogated to the right of Bank A under subsection (d) to refund of payment from Bank C.

3. A payment order is not like a negotiable instrument on which the drawer or maker has liability. Acceptance of the order by the receiving bank creates an obligation of the sender to pay the receiving bank the amount of the order. That is the extent of the sender's liability to the receiving bank and no other person has any rights against the sender with respect to the sender's order.

§ 4A–403. Payment by Sender to Receiving Bank.

(a) Payment of the sender's obligation under Section 4A–402 to pay the receiving bank occurs as follows:

(1) If the sender is a bank, payment occurs when the receiving bank receives final settlement of the obligation through a Federal Reserve Bank or through a funds-transfer system.

(2) If the sender is a bank and the sender (i) credited an account of the receiving bank with the sender, or (ii) caused an account of the receiving bank in another bank to be credited, payment occurs when the credit is withdrawn or, if not withdrawn, at midnight of the day on which the credit is withdrawable and the receiving bank learns of that fact.

(3) If the receiving bank debits an account of the sender with the receiving bank, payment occurs when the debit is made to the extent the debit is covered by a withdrawable credit balance in the account.

(b) If the sender and receiving bank are members of a funds-transfer system that nets obligations multilaterally among participants, the receiving bank receives final settlement when settlement is complete in accordance with the rules of the system. The obligation of the sender to pay the amount of a payment order transmitted through the funds-transfer system may be satisfied, to the extent permitted by the rules of the system, by setting off and applying against the sender's obligation the right of the sender to receive payment from the receiving bank of the amount of any other payment order transmitted to the sender by the receiving bank through the funds-transfer system. The aggregate balance of obligations owed by each sender to each receiving bank in the funds-transfer system may be satisfied, to the extent permitted by the rules of the system, by setting off and applying against that balance the aggregate balance of obligations owed to the sender by other members of the system. The aggregate balance is determined after the right of setoff stated in the second sentence of this subsection has been exercised.

(c) If two banks transmit payment orders to each other under an agreement that settlement of the obligations of each bank to the other under Section 4A–402 will be made at the end of the day or other period, the total amount owed with respect to all orders transmitted by one bank shall be set off against the total amount owed with respect to all orders transmitted by the other bank. To the extent of the setoff, each bank has made payment to the other.

(d) In a case not covered by subsection (a), the time when payment of the sender's obligation under Section 4A–402(b) or 4A–402(c) occurs is governed by applicable principles of law that determine when an obligation is satisfied.

Official Comment

1. This section defines when a sender pays the obligation stated in Section 4A–402. If a group of two or more banks engage in funds transfers with each other, the participating banks will sometimes be senders and sometimes receiving banks. With respect to payment orders other than Fedwires, the amounts of the various payment orders may be credited and debited to accounts of one bank with another or to a clearing house account of each bank and amounts owed and amounts due are netted. Settlement is made through a Federal Reserve Bank by charges to the Federal Reserve accounts of the net debtor banks and credits to the Federal Reserve accounts of the net creditor banks. In the case of Fedwires the sender's obligation is settled by a debit to the Federal Reserve account of the sender and a credit to the Federal Reserve account of the receiving bank at the time the receiving bank receives the payment order. Both of these cases are covered by subsection (a)(1). When the Federal Reserve settlement becomes final the obligation of the sender under Section 4A–402 is paid.

2. In some cases a bank does not settle an obligation owed to another bank through a Federal Reserve Bank. This is the case if one of the banks is a foreign bank without access to the Federal Reserve payment system. In this kind of case, payment is usually made by credits or debits to accounts of the two banks with each other or

to accounts of the two banks in a third bank. Suppose Bank B has an account in Bank A. Bank A advises Bank B that its account in Bank A has been credited $1,000,000 and that the credit is immediately withdrawable. Bank A also instructs Bank B to pay $1,000,000 to the account of Beneficiary in Bank B. This case is covered by subsection (a)(2). Bank B may want to immediately withdraw this credit. For example, it might do so by instructing Bank A to debit the account and pay some third party. Payment by Bank A to Bank B of Bank A's payment order occurs when the withdrawal is made. Suppose Bank B does not withdraw the credit. Since Bank B is the beneficiary's bank, one of the effects of receipt of payment by Bank B is that acceptance of Bank A's payment order automatically occurs at the time of payment. Section 4A–209(b)(2). Acceptance means that Bank B is obliged to pay $1,000,000 to Beneficiary. Section 4A–404(a). Subsection (a)(2) of Section 4A–403 states that payment does not occur until midnight if the credit is not withdrawn. This allows Bank B an opportunity to reject the order if it does not have time to withdraw the credit to its account and it is not willing to incur the liability to Beneficiary before it has use of the funds represented by the credit.

3. Subsection (a)(3) applies to a case in which the sender (bank or nonbank) has a funded account in the receiving bank. If Sender has an account in Bank and issues a payment order to Bank, Bank can obtain payment from Sender by debiting the account of Sender, which pays its Section 4A–402 obligation to Bank when the debit is made.

4. Subsection (b) deals with multilateral settlements made through a funds transfer system and is based on the CHIPS settlement system. In a funds transfer system such as CHIPS, which allows the various banks that transmit payment orders over the system to settle obligations at the end of each day, settlement is not based on individual payment orders. Each bank using the system engages in funds transfers with many other banks using the system. Settlement for any participant is based on the net credit or debit position of that participant with all other banks using the system. Subsection (b) is designed to make clear that the obligations of any sender are paid when the net position of that sender is settled in accordance with the rules of the funds transfer system. This provision is intended to invalidate any argument, based on common-law principles, that multilateral netting is not valid because mutuality of obligation is not present. Subsection (b) dispenses with any mutuality of obligation requirements. Subsection (c) applies to cases in which two banks send payment orders to each other during the day and settle with each other at the end of the day or at the end of some other period. It is similar to subsection (b) in that it recognizes that a sender's obligation to pay a payment order is satisfied by a setoff. The obligations of each bank as sender to the other as receiving bank are obligations of the bank itself and not as representative of customers. These two sections are important in the case of insolvency of a bank. They make clear that liability under Section 4A–402 is based on the net position of the insolvent bank after setoff.

5. Subsection (d) relates to the uncommon case in which the sender doesn't have an account relationship with the receiving bank and doesn't settle through a Federal Reserve Bank. An example would be a customer that pays over the counter for a payment order that the customer issues to the receiving bank. Payment would normally be by cash, check or bank obligation. When payment occurs is determined by law outside Article 4A.

§ 4A–404. Obligation of Beneficiary's Bank to Pay and Give Notice to Beneficiary.

(a) Subject to Sections 4A–211(e), 4A–405(d), and 4A–405(e), if a beneficiary's bank accepts a payment order, the bank is obliged to pay the amount of the order to the beneficiary of the order. Payment is due on the payment date of the order, but if acceptance occurs on the payment date after the close of the funds-transfer business day of the bank, payment is due on the next funds-transfer business day. If the bank refuses to pay after demand by the beneficiary and receipt of notice of particular circumstances that will give rise to consequential damages as a result of nonpayment, the beneficiary may recover damages resulting from the refusal to pay to the extent the bank had notice of the damages, unless the bank proves that it did not pay because of a reasonable doubt concerning the right of the beneficiary to payment.

(b) If a payment order accepted by the beneficiary's bank instructs payment to an account of the beneficiary, the bank is obliged to notify the beneficiary of receipt of the order before midnight of the next funds-transfer business day following the payment date. If the payment order does not instruct payment to an account of the beneficiary, the bank is required to notify the beneficiary only if notice is required by the order. Notice may be given by first class mail or any other means reasonable in the circumstances. If the bank fails to give the required notice, the bank is obliged to pay interest to the beneficiary on the amount of the payment order from the day notice should have been given until the day the beneficiary learned of receipt of the payment order by the bank. No other damages are recoverable. Reasonable attorney's fees are also recoverable if demand for interest is made and refused before an action is brought on the claim.

(c) The right of a beneficiary to receive payment and damages as stated in subsection (a) may not be varied by agreement or a funds-transfer system rule. The right of a beneficiary to be notified as stated in subsection (b) may be varied by agreement of the beneficiary or by a funds-transfer system rule if the beneficiary is notified of the rule before initiation of the funds transfer.

Official Comment

1. The first sentence of subsection (a) states the time when the obligation of the beneficiary's bank arises. The second and third sentences state when the beneficiary's bank must make funds available to the beneficiary. They also state the measure of damages for failure, after demand, to comply. Since the Expedited Funds Availability Act, 12 U.S.C. 4001 et seq., also governs funds availability in a funds transfer, the second and third sentences of subsection (a) may be subject to preemption by that Act.

2. Subsection (a) provides that the beneficiary of an accepted payment order may recover consequential damages if the beneficiary's bank refuses to pay the order after demand by the beneficiary if the bank at that time had notice of the particular circumstances giving rise to the damages. Such damages are recoverable only to the extent the bank had "notice of the damages." The quoted phrase requires that the bank have notice of the general type or nature of the damages that will be suffered as a result of the refusal to pay and their general magnitude. There is no requirement that the bank have notice of the exact or even the approximate amount of the damages, but if the amount of damages is extraordinary the bank is entitled to notice of that fact. For example, in *Evra Corp. v. Swiss Bank Corp.*, 673 F.2d 951 (7th Cir. 1982), failure to complete a funds transfer of only $27,000 required to retain rights to a very favorable ship charter resulted in a claim for more than $2,000,000 of consequential damages. Since it is not reasonably foreseeable that a failure to make a relatively small payment will result in damages of this magnitude, notice is not sufficient if the beneficiary's bank has notice only that the $27,000 is necessary to retain rights on a ship charter. The bank is entitled to notice that an exceptional amount of damages will result as well. For example, there would be adequate notice if the bank had been made aware that damages of $1,000,000 or more might result.

3. Under the last clause of subsection (a) the beneficiary's bank is not liable for damages if its refusal to pay was "because of a reasonable doubt concerning the right of the beneficiary to payment." Normally there will not be any question about the right of the beneficiary to receive payment. Normally, the bank should be able to determine whether it has accepted the payment order and, if it has been accepted, the first sentence of subsection (a) states that the bank is obliged to pay. There may be uncommon cases, however, in which there is doubt whether acceptance occurred. For example, if acceptance is based on receipt of payment by the beneficiary's bank under Section 4A-403(a)(1) or (2), there may be cases in which the bank is not certain that payment has been received. There may also be cases in which there is doubt about whether the person demanding payment is the person identified in the payment order as beneficiary of the order.

The last clause of subsection (a) does not apply to cases in which a funds transfer is being used to pay an obligation and a dispute arises between the originator and the beneficiary concerning whether the obligation is in fact owed. For example, the originator may try to prevent payment to the beneficiary by the beneficiary's bank by alleging that the beneficiary is not entitled to payment because of fraud against the originator or a breach of contract relating to the obligation. The fraud or breach of contract claim of the originator may be grounds for recovery by the originator from the beneficiary after the beneficiary is paid, but it does not affect the obligation of the beneficiary's bank to pay the beneficiary. Unless the payment order has been cancelled pursuant to Section 4A-211(c), there is no excuse for refusing to pay the beneficiary and, in a proper case, the refusal may result in consequential damages. Except in the case of a book transfer, in which the beneficiary's bank is also the originator's bank, the originator of a funds transfer cannot cancel a payment order to the beneficiary's bank, with or without the consent of that bank, because the originator is not the sender of that order. Thus, the beneficiary's bank may safely ignore any instruction by the originator to withhold payment to the beneficiary.

4. Subsection (b) states the duty of the beneficiary's bank to notify the beneficiary of receipt of the order. If acceptance occurs under Section 4A-209(b)(1) the beneficiary is normally notified. Thus, subsection (b) applies primarily to cases in which acceptance occurs under Section 4A-209(b)(2) or (3). Notice under subsection (b) is not required if the person entitled to the notice agrees or a funds transfer system rule provides that notice is not required and the beneficiary is given notice of the rule. In ACH transactions the normal practice is not to give notice to the beneficiary unless notice is requested by the beneficiary. This practice can be continued by adoption of a funds transfer system rule. Subsection (a) is not subject to variation by agreement or by a funds transfer system rule.

§ 4A–405. Payment by Beneficiary's Bank to Beneficiary.

(a) If the beneficiary's bank credits an account of the beneficiary of a payment order, payment of the bank's obligation under Section 4A–404(a) occurs when and to the extent (i) the beneficiary is notified of the right to withdraw the credit, (ii) the bank lawfully applies the credit to a debt of the beneficiary, or (iii) funds with respect to the order are otherwise made available to the beneficiary by the bank.

(b) If the beneficiary's bank does not credit an account of the beneficiary of a payment order, the time when payment of the bank's obligation under Section 4A–404(a) occurs is governed by principles of law that determine when an obligation is satisfied.

(c) Except as stated in subsections (d) and (e), if the beneficiary's bank pays the beneficiary of a payment order under a condition to payment or agreement of the beneficiary giving the bank the right to recover payment from the beneficiary if the bank does not receive payment of the order, the condition to payment or agreement is not enforceable.

(d) A funds-transfer system rule may provide that payments made to beneficiaries of funds transfers made through the system are provisional until receipt of payment by the beneficiary's bank of the payment order it accepted. A beneficiary's bank that makes a payment that is provisional under the rule is entitled to refund from the beneficiary if (i) the rule requires that both the beneficiary and the originator be given notice of the provisional nature of the payment before the funds transfer is initiated, (ii) the beneficiary, the beneficiary's bank and the originator's bank agreed to be bound by the rule, and (iii) the beneficiary's bank did not receive payment of the payment order that it accepted. If the beneficiary is obliged to refund payment to the beneficiary's bank, acceptance of the payment order by the beneficiary's bank is nullified and no payment by the originator of the funds transfer to the beneficiary occurs under Section 4A–406.

(e) This subsection applies to a funds transfer that includes a payment order transmitted over a funds-transfer system that (i) nets obligations multilaterally among participants, and (ii) has in effect a loss-sharing agreement among participants for the purpose of providing funds necessary to complete settlement of the obligations of one or more participants that do not meet their settlement obligations. If the beneficiary's bank in the funds transfer accepts a payment order and the system fails to complete settlement pursuant to its rules with respect to any payment order in the funds transfer, (i) the acceptance by the beneficiary's bank is nullified and no person has any right or obligation based on the acceptance, (ii) the beneficiary's bank is entitled to recover payment from the beneficiary, (iii) no payment by the originator to the beneficiary occurs under Section 4A–406, and (iv) subject to Section 4A–402(e), each sender in the funds transfer is excused from its obligation to pay its payment order under Section 4A–402(c) because the funds transfer has not been completed.

Official Comment

1. This section defines when the beneficiary's bank pays the beneficiary and when the obligation of the beneficiary's bank under Section 4A–404 to pay the beneficiary is satisfied. In almost all cases the bank will credit an account of the beneficiary when it receives a payment order. In the typical case the beneficiary is paid when the beneficiary is given notice of the right to withdraw the credit. Subsection (a)(i). In some cases payment might be made to the beneficiary not by releasing funds to the beneficiary, but by applying the credit to a debt of the beneficiary. Subsection (a)(ii). In this case the beneficiary gets the benefit of the payment order because a debt of the beneficiary has been satisfied. The two principal cases in which payment will occur in this manner are setoff by the beneficiary's bank and payment of the proceeds of the payment order to a garnishing creditor of the beneficiary. These cases are discussed in Comment 2 to Section 4A–502.

2. If a beneficiary's bank releases funds to the beneficiary before it receives payment from the sender of the payment order, it assumes the risk that the sender may not pay the sender's order because of suspension of payments or other reason. Subsection (c). As stated in Comment 5 to Section 4A–209, the beneficiary's bank can protect itself against this risk by delaying acceptance. But if the bank accepts the order it is obliged to pay the beneficiary. If the beneficiary's bank has given the beneficiary notice of the right to withdraw a credit made to the beneficiary's account, the beneficiary has received payment from the bank. Once payment has been made to the beneficiary with respect to an obligation incurred by the bank under Section 4A–404(a), the payment cannot be recovered by the beneficiary's bank unless subsection (d) or (e) applies. Thus, a right to withdraw a credit cannot be revoked if the right to withdraw constituted payment of the bank's obligation. This principle applies even if funds were released as a "loan" (see Comment 5 to Section 4A–209), or were released subject to a condition that

they would be repaid in the event the bank does not receive payment from the sender of the payment order, or the beneficiary agreed to return the payment if the bank did not receive payment from the sender.

3. Subsection (c) is subject to an exception stated in subsection (d) which is intended to apply to automated clearing house transfers. ACH transfers are made in batches. A beneficiary's bank will normally accept, at the same time and as part of a single batch, payment orders with respect to many different originator's banks. Comment 2 to Section 4A–206. The custom in ACH transactions is to release funds to the beneficiary early on the payment date even though settlement to the beneficiary's bank does not occur until later in the day. The understanding is that payments to beneficiaries are provisional until the beneficiary's bank receives settlement. This practice is similar to what happens when a depositary bank releases funds with respect to a check forwarded for collection. If the check is dishonored the bank is entitled to recover the funds from the customer. ACH transfers are widely perceived as check substitutes. Section 4A–405(d) allows the funds transfer system to adopt a rule making payments to beneficiaries provisional. If such a rule is adopted, a beneficiary's bank that releases funds to the beneficiary will be able to recover the payment if it doesn't receive payment of the payment order that it accepted. There are two requirements with respect to the funds transfer system rule. The beneficiary, the beneficiary's bank and the originator's bank must all agree to be bound by the rule and the rule must require that both the beneficiary and the originator be given notice of the provisional nature of the payment before the funds transfer is initiated. There is no requirement that the notice be given with respect to a particular funds transfer. Once notice of the provisional nature of the payment has been given, the notice is effective for all subsequent payments to or from the person to whom the notice was given. Subsection (d) provides only that the funds transfer system rule must require notice to the beneficiary and the originator. The beneficiary's bank will know what the rule requires, but it has no way of knowing whether the originator's bank complied with the rule. Subsection (d) does not require proof that the originator received notice. If the originator's bank failed to give the required notice and the originator suffered as a result, the appropriate remedy is an action by the originator against the originator's bank based on that failure. But the beneficiary's bank will not be able to get the benefit of subsection (d) unless the beneficiary had notice of the provisional nature of the payment because subsection (d) requires an agreement by the beneficiary to be bound by the rule. Implicit in an agreement to be bound by a rule that makes a payment provisional is a requirement that notice be given of what the rule provides. The notice can be part of the agreement or separately given. For example, notice can be given by providing a copy of the system's operating rules.

With respect to ACH transfers made through a Federal Reserve Bank acting as an intermediary bank, the Federal Reserve Bank is obliged under Section 4A–402(b) to pay a beneficiary's bank that accepts the payment order. Unlike Fedwire transfers, under current ACH practice a Federal Reserve Bank that processes a payment order does not obligate itself to pay if the originator's bank fails to pay the Federal Reserve Bank. It is assumed that the Federal Reserve will use its right of preemption which is recognized in Section 4A–107 to disclaim the Section 4A–402(b) obligation in ACH transactions if it decides to retain the provisional payment rule.

4. Subsection (e) is another exception to subsection (c). It refers to funds transfer systems having loss-sharing rules described in the subsection. CHIPS has proposed a rule that fits the description. Under the CHIPS loss-sharing rule the CHIPS banks will have agreed to contribute funds to allow the system to settle for payment orders sent over the system during the day in the event that one or more banks are unable to meet their settlement obligations. Subsection (e) applies only if CHIPS fails to settle despite the loss-sharing rule. Since funds under the loss-sharing rule will be instantly available to CHIPS and will be in an amount sufficient to cover any failure that can be reasonably anticipated, it is extremely unlikely that CHIPS would ever fail to settle. Thus, subsection (e) addresses an event that should never occur. If that event were to occur, all payment orders made over the system would be cancelled under the CHIPS rule. Thus, no bank would receive settlement, whether or not a failed bank was involved in a particular funds transfer. Subsection (e) provides that each funds transfer in which there is a payment order with respect to which there is a settlement failure is unwound. Acceptance by the beneficiary's bank in each funds transfer is nullified. The consequences of nullification are that the beneficiary has no right to receive or retain payment by the beneficiary's bank, no payment is made by the originator to the beneficiary and each sender in the funds transfer is, subject to Section 4A–402(e), not obliged to pay its payment order and is entitled to refund under Section 4A–402(d) if it has already paid.

§ 4A–406. Payment by Originator to Beneficiary; Discharge of Underlying Obligation.

(a) Subject to Sections 4A–211(e), 4A–405(d), and 4A–405(e), the originator of a funds transfer pays the beneficiary of the originator's payment order (i) at the time a payment order for the benefit of the beneficiary is accepted by the beneficiary's bank in the funds transfer and (ii) in an amount equal to the amount of the order accepted by the beneficiary's bank, but not more than the amount of the originator's order.

(b) If payment under subsection (a) is made to satisfy an obligation, the obligation is discharged to the same extent discharge would result from payment to the beneficiary of the same amount in money, unless (i) the payment under subsection (a) was made by a means prohibited by the contract of the beneficiary with respect to the obligation, (ii) the beneficiary, within a reasonable time after receiving notice of receipt of the order by the beneficiary's bank, notified the originator of the beneficiary's refusal of the payment, (iii) funds with respect to the order were not withdrawn by the beneficiary or applied to a debt of the beneficiary, and (iv) the beneficiary would suffer a loss that could reasonably have been avoided if payment had been made by a means complying with the contract. If payment by the originator does not result in discharge under this section, the originator is subrogated to the rights of the beneficiary to receive payment from the beneficiary's bank under Section 4A–404(a).

(c) For the purpose of determining whether discharge of an obligation occurs under subsection (b), if the beneficiary's bank accepts a payment order in an amount equal to the amount of the originator's payment order less charges of one or more receiving banks in the funds transfer, payment to the beneficiary is deemed to be in the amount of the originator's order unless upon demand by the beneficiary the originator does not pay the beneficiary the amount of the deducted charges.

(d) Rights of the originator or of the beneficiary of a funds transfer under this section may be varied only by agreement of the originator and the beneficiary.

Official Comment

1. Subsection (a) states the fundamental rule of Article 4A that payment by the originator to the beneficiary is accomplished by providing to the beneficiary the obligation of the beneficiary's bank to pay. Since this obligation arises when the beneficiary's bank accepts a payment order, the originator pays the beneficiary at the time of acceptance and in the amount of the payment order accepted.

2. In a large percentage of funds transfers, the transfer is made to pay an obligation of the originator. Subsection (a) states that the beneficiary is paid by the originator when the beneficiary's bank accepts a payment order for the benefit of the beneficiary. When that happens the effect under subsection (b) is to substitute the obligation of the beneficiary's bank for the obligation of the originator. The effect is similar to that under Article 3 if a cashier's check payable to the beneficiary had been taken by the beneficiary. Normally, payment by funds transfer is sought by the beneficiary because it puts money into the hands of the beneficiary more quickly. As a practical matter the beneficiary and the originator will nearly always agree to the funds transfer in advance. Under subsection (b) acceptance by the beneficiary's bank will result in discharge of the obligation for which payment was made unless the beneficiary had made a contract with respect to the obligation which did not permit payment by the means used. Thus, if there is no contract of the beneficiary with respect to the means of payment of the obligation, acceptance by the beneficiary's bank of a payment order to the account of the beneficiary can result in discharge.

3. Suppose Beneficiary's contract stated that payment of an obligation owed by Originator was to be made by a cashier's check of Bank A. Instead, Originator paid by a funds transfer to Beneficiary's account in Bank B. Bank B accepted a payment order for the benefit of Beneficiary by immediately notifying Beneficiary that the funds were available for withdrawal. Before Beneficiary had a reasonable opportunity to withdraw the funds Bank B suspended payments. Under the unless clause of subsection (b) Beneficiary is not required to accept the payment as discharging the obligation owed by Originator to Beneficiary if Beneficiary's contract means that Beneficiary was not required to accept payment by wire transfer. Beneficiary could refuse the funds transfer as payment of the obligation and could resort to rights under the underlying contract to enforce the obligation. The rationale is that Originator cannot impose the risk of Bank B's insolvency on Beneficiary if Beneficiary had specified another means of payment that did not entail that risk. If Beneficiary is required to accept Originator's payment, Beneficiary would suffer a loss that would not have occurred if payment had been made by a cashier's check on Bank A, and Bank A has not suspended payments. In this case Originator will have to pay twice. It is obliged to pay the amount of its payment order to the bank that accepted it and has to pay the obligation it owes to Beneficiary which has not been discharged. Under the last sentence of subsection (b) Originator is subrogated to Beneficiary's right to receive payment from Bank B under Section 4A–404(a).

4. Suppose Beneficiary's contract called for payment by a Fedwire transfer to Bank B, but the payment order accepted by Bank B was not a Fedwire transfer. Before the funds were withdrawn by Beneficiary, Bank B suspended payments. The sender of the payment order to Bank B paid the amount of the order to Bank B. In this

case the payment by Originator did not comply with Beneficiary's contract, but the noncompliance did not result in a loss to Beneficiary as required by subsection (b)(iv). A Fedwire transfer avoids the risk of insolvency of the sender of the payment order to Bank B, but it does not affect the risk that Bank B will suspend payments before withdrawal of the funds by Beneficiary. Thus, the unless clause of subsection (b) is not applicable and the obligation owed to Beneficiary is discharged.

5. Charges of receiving banks in a funds transfer normally are nominal in relationship to the amount being paid by the originator to the beneficiary. Wire transfers are normally agreed to in advance and the parties may agree concerning how these charges are to be divided between the parties. Subsection (c) states a rule that applies in the absence of agreement. In some funds transfers charges of banks that execute payment orders are collected by deducting the charges from the amount of the payment order issued by the bank, i.e. the bank issues a payment order that is slightly less than the amount of the payment order that is being executed. The process is described in Comment 3 to Section 4A–302. The result in such a case is that the payment order accepted by the beneficiary's bank will be slightly less than the amount of the originator's order. Subsection (c) recognizes the principle that a beneficiary is entitled to full payment of a debt paid by wire transfer as a condition to discharge. On the other hand, subsection (c) prevents a beneficiary from denying the originator the benefit of the payment by asserting that discharge did not occur because deduction of bank charges resulted in less than full payment. The typical case is one in which the payment is made to exercise a valuable right such as an option which is unfavorable to the beneficiary. Subsection (c) allows discharge notwithstanding the deduction unless the originator fails to reimburse the beneficiary for the deducted charges after demand by the beneficiary.

PART 5

MISCELLANEOUS PROVISIONS

§ 4A–501. Variation by Agreement and Effect of Funds-Transfer System Rule.

(a) Except as otherwise provided in this Article, the rights and obligations of a party to a funds transfer may be varied by agreement of the affected party.

(b) "Funds-transfer system rule" means a rule of an association of banks (i) governing transmission of payment orders by means of a funds-transfer system of the association or rights and obligations with respect to those orders, or (ii) to the extent the rule governs rights and obligations between banks that are parties to a funds transfer in which a Federal Reserve Bank, acting as an intermediary bank, sends a payment order to the beneficiary's bank. Except as otherwise provided in this Article, a funds-transfer system rule governing rights and obligations between participating banks using the system may be effective even if the rule conflicts with this Article and indirectly affects another party to the funds transfer who does not consent to the rule. A funds-transfer system rule may also govern rights and obligations of parties other than participating banks using the system to the extent stated in Sections 4A–404(c), 4A–405(d), and 4A–507(c).

Official Comment

1. This section is designed to give some flexibility to Article 4A. Funds transfer system rules govern rights and obligations between banks that use the system. They may cover a wide variety of matters such as form and content of payment orders, security procedures, cancellation rights and procedures, indemnity rights, compensation rules for delays in completion of a funds transfer, time and method of settlement, credit restrictions with respect to senders of payment orders and risk allocation with respect to suspension of payments by a participating bank. Funds transfer system rules can be very effective in supplementing the provisions of Article 4A and in filling gaps that may be present in Article 4A. To the extent they do not conflict with Article 4A there is no problem with respect to their effectiveness. In that case they merely supplement Article 4A. Section 4A–501 goes further. It states that unless the contrary is stated, funds transfer system rules can override provisions of Article 4A. Thus, rights and obligations of a sender bank and a receiving bank with respect to each other can be different from that stated in Article 4A to the extent a funds transfer system rule applies. Since funds transfer system rules are defined as those governing the relationship between participating banks, a rule can have a direct effect only on participating banks. But a rule that affects the conduct of a participating bank may indirectly affect the rights of nonparticipants such as the originator or beneficiary of a funds transfer, and such a rule can be effective even though it may affect nonparticipants without their consent. For example, a rule might prevent execution of a payment order or might allow cancellation of a payment order with the result that a funds transfer is not completed or is delayed. But a rule purporting to define rights and obligations of nonparticipants in the

system would not be effective to alter Article 4A rights because the rule is not within the definition of funds transfer system rule. Rights and obligations arising under Article 4A may also be varied by agreement of the affected parties, except to the extent Article 4A otherwise provides. Rights and obligations arising under Article 4A can also be changed by Federal Reserve regulations and operating circulars of Federal Reserve Banks. Section 4A–107.

2. Subsection (b)(ii) refers to ACH transfers. Whether an ACH transfer is made through an automated clearing house of a Federal Reserve Bank or through an automated clearing house of another association of banks, the rights and obligations of the originator's bank and the beneficiary's bank are governed by uniform rules adopted by various associations of banks in various parts of the nation. With respect to transfers in which a Federal Reserve Bank acts as intermediary bank these rules may be incorporated, in whole or in part, in operating circulars of the Federal Reserve Bank. Even if not so incorporated these rules can still be binding on the association banks. If a transfer is made through a Federal Reserve Bank, the rules are effective under subsection (b)(ii). If the transfer is not made through a Federal Reserve Bank, the association rules are effective under subsection (b)(i).

§ 4A–502. Creditor Process Served on Receiving Bank; Setoff by Beneficiary's Bank.

(a) As used in this section, "creditor process" means levy, attachment, garnishment, notice of lien, sequestration, or similar process issued by or on behalf of a creditor or other claimant with respect to an account.

(b) This subsection applies to creditor process with respect to an authorized account of the sender of a payment order if the creditor process is served on the receiving bank. For the purpose of determining rights with respect to the creditor process, if the receiving bank accepts the payment order the balance in the authorized account is deemed to be reduced by the amount of the payment order to the extent the bank did not otherwise receive payment of the order, unless the creditor process is served at a time and in a manner affording the bank a reasonable opportunity to act on it before the bank accepts the payment order.

(c) If a beneficiary's bank has received a payment order for payment to the beneficiary's account in the bank, the following rules apply:

(1) The bank may credit the beneficiary's account. The amount credited may be set off against an obligation owed by the beneficiary to the bank or may be applied to satisfy creditor process served on the bank with respect to the account.

(2) The bank may credit the beneficiary's account and allow withdrawal of the amount credited unless creditor process with respect to the account is served at a time and in a manner affording the bank a reasonable opportunity to act to prevent withdrawal.

(3) If creditor process with respect to the beneficiary's account has been served and the bank has had a reasonable opportunity to act on it, the bank may not reject the payment order except for a reason unrelated to the service of process.

(d) Creditor process with respect to a payment by the originator to the beneficiary pursuant to a funds transfer may be served only on the beneficiary's bank with respect to the debt owed by that bank to the beneficiary. Any other bank served with the creditor process is not obliged to act with respect to the process.

Official Comment

1. When a receiving bank accepts a payment order, the bank normally receives payment from the sender by debiting an authorized account of the sender. In accepting the sender's order the bank may be relying on a credit balance in the account. If creditor process is served on the bank with respect to the account before the bank accepts the order but the bank employee responsible for the acceptance was not aware of the creditor process at the time the acceptance occurred, it is unjust to the bank to allow the creditor process to take the credit balance on which the bank may have relied. Subsection (b) allows the bank to obtain payment from the sender's account in this case. Under that provision, the balance in the sender's account to which the creditor process applies is deemed to be reduced by the amount of the payment order unless there was sufficient time for notice of the service of creditor process to be received by personnel of the bank responsible for the acceptance.

2. Subsection (c) deals with payment orders issued to the beneficiary's bank. The bank may credit the beneficiary's account when the order is received, but under Section 4A–404(a) the bank incurs no obligation to pay the beneficiary until the order is accepted pursuant to Section 4A–209(b). Thus, before acceptance, the credit to

the beneficiary's account is provisional. But under Section 4A–209(b) acceptance occurs if the beneficiary's bank pays the beneficiary pursuant to Section 4A–405(a). Under that provision, payment occurs if the credit to the beneficiary's account is applied to a debt of the beneficiary. Subsection (c)(1) allows the bank to credit the beneficiary's account with respect to a payment order and to accept the order by setting off the credit against an obligation owed to the bank or applying the credit to creditor process with respect to the account.

Suppose a beneficiary's bank receives a payment order for the benefit of a customer. Before the bank accepts the order, the bank learns that creditor process has been served on the bank with respect to the customer's account. Normally there is no reason for a beneficiary's bank to reject a payment order, but if the beneficiary's account is garnished, the bank may be faced with a difficult choice. If it rejects the order, the garnishing creditor's potential recovery of funds of the beneficiary is frustrated. It may be faced with a claim by the creditor that the rejection was a wrong to the creditor. If the bank accepts the order, the effect is to allow the creditor to seize funds of its customer, the beneficiary. Subsection (c)(3) gives the bank no choice in this case. It provides that it may not favor its customer over the creditor by rejecting the order. The beneficiary's bank may rightfully reject only if there is an independent basis for rejection.

3. Subsection (c)(2) is similar to subsection (b). Normally the beneficiary's bank will release funds to the beneficiary shortly after acceptance or it will accept by releasing funds. Since the bank is bound by a garnishment order served before funds are released to the beneficiary, the bank might suffer a loss if funds were released without knowledge that a garnishment order had been served. Subsection (c)(2) protects the bank if it did not have adequate notice of the garnishment when the funds were released.

4. A creditor may want to reach funds involved in a funds transfer. The creditor may try to do so by serving process on the originator's bank, an intermediary bank or the beneficiary's bank. The purpose of subsection (d) is to guide the creditor and the court as to the proper method of reaching the funds involved in a funds transfer. A creditor of the originator can levy on the account of the originator in the originator's bank before the funds transfer is initiated, but that levy is subject to the limitations stated in subsection (b). The creditor of the originator cannot reach any other funds because no property of the originator is being transferred. A creditor of the beneficiary cannot levy on property of the originator and until the funds transfer is completed by acceptance by the beneficiary's bank of a payment order for the benefit of the beneficiary, the beneficiary has no property interest in the funds transfer which the beneficiary's creditor can reach. A creditor of the beneficiary that wants to reach the funds to be received by the beneficiary must serve creditor process on the beneficiary's bank to reach the obligation of the beneficiary's bank to pay the beneficiary which arises upon acceptance by the beneficiary's bank under Section 4A–404(a).

5. "Creditor process" is defined in subsection (a) to cover a variety of devices by which a creditor of the holder of a bank account or a claimant to a bank account can seize the account. Procedure and nomenclature varies widely from state to state. The term used in Section 4A–502 is a generic term.

§ 4A–503. Injunction or Restraining Order With Respect to Funds Transfer.

For proper cause and in compliance with applicable law, a court may restrain (i) a person from issuing a payment order to initiate a funds transfer, (ii) an originator's bank from executing the payment order of the originator, or (iii) the beneficiary's bank from releasing funds to the beneficiary or the beneficiary from withdrawing the funds. A court may not otherwise restrain a person from issuing a payment order, paying or receiving payment of a payment order, or otherwise acting with respect to a funds transfer.

Official Comment

This section is related to Section 4A–502(d) and to Comment 4 to Section 4A–502. It is designed to prevent interruption of a funds transfer after it has been set in motion. The initiation of a funds transfer can be prevented by enjoining the originator or the originator's bank from issuing a payment order. After the funds transfer is completed by acceptance of a payment order by the beneficiary's bank, that bank can be enjoined from releasing funds to the beneficiary or the beneficiary can be enjoined from withdrawing the funds. No other injunction is permitted. In particular, intermediary banks are protected, and injunctions against the originator and the originator's bank are limited to issuance of a payment order. Except for the beneficiary's bank, nobody can be enjoined from paying a payment order, and no receiving bank can be enjoined from receiving payment from the sender of the order that it accepted.

§ 4A–504. Order in Which Items and Payment Orders May Be Charged to Account; Order of Withdrawals From Account.

(a) If a receiving bank has received more than one payment order of the sender or one or more payment orders and other items that are payable from the sender's account, the bank may charge the sender's account with respect to the various orders and items in any sequence.

(b) In determining whether a credit to an account has been withdrawn by the holder of the account or applied to a debt of the holder of the account, credits first made to the account are first withdrawn or applied.

Official Comment

1. Subsection (a) concerns priority among various obligations that are to be paid from the same account. A customer may have written checks on its account with the receiving bank and may have issued one or more payment orders payable from the same account. If the account balance is not sufficient to cover all of the checks and payment orders, some checks may be dishonored and some payment orders may not be accepted. Although there is no concept of wrongful dishonor of a payment order in Article 4A in the absence of an agreement to honor by the receiving bank, some rights and obligations may depend on the amount in the customer's account. Section 4A–209(b)(3) and Section 4A–210(b). Whether dishonor of a check is wrongful also may depend upon the balance in the customer's account. Under subsection (a), the bank is not required to consider the competing items and payment orders in any particular order. Rather it may charge the customer's account for the various items and orders in any order. Suppose there is $12,000 in the customer's account. If a check for $5,000 is presented for payment and the bank receives a $10,000 payment order from the customer, the bank could dishonor the check and accept the payment order. Dishonor of the check is not wrongful because the account balance was less than the amount of the check after the bank charged the account $10,000 on account of the payment order. Or, the bank could pay the check and not execute the payment order because the amount of the order is not covered by the balance in the account.

2. Subsection (b) follows Section 4–208(b) in using the first-in-first-out rule for determining the order in which credits to an account are withdrawn.

§ 4A–505. Preclusion of Objection to Debit of Customer's Account.

If a receiving bank has received payment from its customer with respect to a payment order issued in the name of the customer as sender and accepted by the bank, and the customer received notification reasonably identifying the order, the customer is precluded from asserting that the bank is not entitled to retain the payment unless the customer notifies the bank of the customer's objection to the payment within one year after the notification was received by the customer.

Official Comment

This section is in the nature of a statute of repose for objecting to debits made to the customer's account. A receiving bank that executes payment orders of a customer may have received payment from the customer by debiting the customer's account with respect to a payment order that the customer was not required to pay. For example, the payment order may not have been authorized or verified pursuant to Section 4A–202 or the funds transfer may not have been completed. In either case the receiving bank is obliged to refund the payment to the customer and this obligation to refund payment cannot be varied by agreement. Section 4A–204 and Section 4A–402. Refund may also be required if the receiving bank is not entitled to payment from the customer because the bank erroneously executed a payment order. Section 4A–303. A similar analysis applies to that case. Section 4A–402(d) and (f) require refund and the obligation to refund may not be varied by agreement. Under 4A–505, however, the obligation to refund may not be asserted by the customer if the customer has not objected to the debiting of the account within one year after the customer received notification of the debit.

§ 4A–506. Rate of Interest.

(a) If, under this Article, a receiving bank is obliged to pay interest with respect to a payment order issued to the bank, the amount payable may be determined (i) by agreement of the sender and receiving bank, or (ii) by a funds-transfer system rule if the payment order is transmitted through a funds-transfer system.

(b) If the amount of interest is not determined by an agreement or rule as stated in subsection (a), the amount is calculated by multiplying the applicable Federal Funds rate by the amount on which interest is payable, and then multiplying the product by the number of days for which interest is payable. The applicable Federal Funds rate is the average of the Federal Funds rates published by the Federal Reserve Bank of New York for each of the days for which interest is payable divided by 360. The Federal Funds rate for any day on which a published rate is not available is the same as the published rate for the next preceding day for which there is a published rate. If a receiving bank that accepted a payment order is required to refund payment to the sender of the order because the funds transfer was not completed, but the failure to complete was not due to any fault by the bank, the interest payable is reduced by a percentage equal to the reserve requirement on deposits of the receiving bank.

Official Comment

1. A receiving bank is required to pay interest on the amount of a payment order received by the bank in a number of situations. Sometimes the interest is payable to the sender and in other cases it is payable to either the originator or the beneficiary of the funds transfer. The relevant provisions are Section 4A–204(a), Section 4A–209(b)(3), Section 4A–210(b), Section 4A–305(a), Section 4A–402(d) and Section 4A–404(b). The rate of interest may be governed by a funds transfer system rule or by agreement as stated in subsection (a). If subsection (a) doesn't apply, the rate is determined under subsection (b). Subsection (b) is illustrated by the following example. A bank is obliged to pay interest on $1,000,000 for three days, July 3, July 4, and July 5. The published Fed Funds rate is .082 for July 3 and .081 for July 5. There is no published rate for July 4 because that day is not a banking day. The rate for July 3 applies to July 4. The applicable Fed Funds rate is .08167 (the average of .082, .082, and .081) divided by 360 which equals .0002268. The amount of interest payable is $1,000,000 × .0002268 × 3 = $680.40.

2. In some cases, interest is payable in spite of the fact that there is no fault by the receiving bank. The last sentence of subsection (b) applies to those cases. For example, a funds transfer might not be completed because the beneficiary's bank rejected the payment order issued to it by the originator's bank or an intermediary bank. Section 4A–402(c) provides that the originator is not obliged to pay its payment order and Section 4A–402(d) provides that the originator's bank must refund any payment received plus interest. The requirement to pay interest in this case is not based on fault by the originator's bank. Rather, it is based on restitution. Since the originator's bank had the use of the originator's money, it is required to pay the originator for the value of that use. The value of that use is not determined by multiplying the interest rate by the refundable amount because the originator's bank is required to deposit with the Federal Reserve a percentage of the bank's deposits as a reserve requirement. Since that deposit does not bear interest, the bank had use of the refundable amount reduced by a percentage equal to the reserve requirement. If the reserve requirement is 12%, the amount of interest payable by the bank under the formula stated in subsection (b) is reduced by 12%.

§ 4A–507. Choice of Law.

(a) The following rules apply unless the affected parties otherwise agree or subsection (c) applies:

(1) The rights and obligations between the sender of a payment order and the receiving bank are governed by the law of the jurisdiction in which the receiving bank is located.

(2) The rights and obligations between the beneficiary's bank and the beneficiary are governed by the law of the jurisdiction in which the beneficiary's bank is located.

(3) The issue of when payment is made pursuant to a funds transfer by the originator to the beneficiary is governed by the law of the jurisdiction in which the beneficiary's bank is located.

(b) If the parties described in each paragraph of subsection (a) have made an agreement selecting the law of a particular jurisdiction to govern rights and obligations between each other, the law of that jurisdiction governs those rights and obligations, whether or not the payment order or the funds transfer bears a reasonable relation to that jurisdiction.

(c) A funds-transfer system rule may select the law of a particular jurisdiction to govern (i) rights and obligations between participating banks with respect to payment orders transmitted or processed through the system, or (ii) the rights and obligations of some or all parties to a funds transfer any part of which is carried out by means of the system. A choice of law made pursuant to clause (i) is binding on participating banks. A choice of law made pursuant to clause (ii) is binding on the originator, other sender, or a receiving bank having notice that the funds-transfer system might be used in the funds transfer and of the choice of law by the system when the originator, other sender, or receiving bank issued or accepted a payment order. The beneficiary of a funds transfer is bound by the choice of law if, when the funds transfer is initiated, the beneficiary has notice that the funds-transfer system might be used in the funds transfer and of the choice of law by the system. The law of a jurisdiction selected pursuant to this subsection may govern, whether or not that law bears a reasonable relation to the matter in issue.

(d) In the event of inconsistency between an agreement under subsection (b) and a choice-of-law rule under subsection (c), the agreement under subsection (b) prevails.

(e) If a funds transfer is made by use of more than one funds-transfer system and there is inconsistency between choice-of-law rules of the systems, the matter in issue is governed by the law of the selected jurisdiction that has the most significant relationship to the matter in issue.

Official Comment

1. Funds transfers are typically interstate or international in character. If part of a funds transfer is governed by Article 4A and another part is governed by other law, the rights and obligations of parties to the funds transfer may be unclear because there is no clear consensus in various jurisdictions concerning the juridical nature of the transaction. Unless all of a funds transfer is governed by a single law it may be very difficult to predict the result if something goes wrong in the transfer. Section 4A–507 deals with this problem. Subsection (b) allows parties to a funds transfer to make a choice-of-law agreement. Subsection (c) allows a funds transfer system to select the law of a particular jurisdiction to govern funds transfers carried out by means of the system. Subsection (a) states residual rules if no choice of law has occurred under subsection (b) or subsection (c).

2. Subsection (a) deals with three sets of relationships. Rights and obligations between the sender of a payment order and the receiving bank are governed by the law of the jurisdiction in which the receiving bank is located. If the receiving bank is the beneficiary's bank the rights and obligations of the beneficiary are also governed by the law of the jurisdiction in which the receiving bank is located. Suppose Originator, located in Canada, sends a payment order to Originator's Bank located in a state in which Article 4A has been enacted. The order is for payment to an account of Beneficiary in a bank in England. Under subsection (a)(1), the rights and obligations of Originator and Originator's Bank toward each other are governed by Article 4A if an action is brought in a court in the Article 4A state. If an action is brought in a Canadian court, the conflict of laws issue will be determined by Canadian law which might or might not apply the law of the state in which Originator's Bank is located. If that law is applied, the execution of Originator's order will be governed by Article 4A, but with respect to the payment order of Originator's Bank to the English bank, Article 4A may or may not be applied with respect to the rights and obligations between the two banks. The result may depend upon whether action is brought in a court in the state in which Originator's Bank is located or in an English court. Article 4A is binding only on a court in a state that enacts it. It can have extraterritorial effect only to the extent courts of another jurisdiction are willing to apply it. Subsection (c) also bears on the issues discussed in this Comment.

Under Section 4A–406 payment by the originator to the beneficiary of the funds transfer occurs when the beneficiary's bank accepts a payment order for the benefit of the beneficiary. A jurisdiction in which Article 4A is not in effect may follow a different rule or it may not have a clear rule. Under Section 4A–507(a)(3) the issue is governed by the law of the jurisdiction in which the beneficiary's bank is located. Since the payment to the beneficiary is made through the beneficiary's bank it is reasonable that the issue of when payment occurs be governed by the law of the jurisdiction in which the bank is located. Since it is difficult in many cases to determine where a beneficiary is located, the location of the beneficiary's bank provides a more certain rule.

3. Subsection (b) deals with choice-of-law agreements and it gives maximum freedom of choice. Since the law of funds transfers is not highly developed in the case law there may be a strong incentive to choose the law of a jurisdiction in which Article 4A is in effect because it provides a greater degree of certainty with respect to the rights of various parties. With respect to commercial transactions, it is often said that "[u]niformity and predictability based upon commercial convenience are the prime considerations in making the choice of governing law . . . ." R. Leflar, *American Conflicts Law*, § 185 (1977). Subsection (b) is derived in part from recently enacted choice-of-law rules in the States of New York and California. N.Y.Gen. Obligations Law 5–1401 (McKinney's 1989 Supp.) and California Civil Code § 1646.5. This broad endorsement of freedom of contract is an enhancement of the approach taken by Restatement (Second) of Conflict of Laws § 187(b) (1971). The Restatement recognizes the basic right of freedom of contract, but the freedom granted the parties may be more limited than the freedom granted here. Under the formulation of the Restatement, if there is no substantial relationship to the jurisdiction whose law is selected and there is no "other" reasonable basis for the parties' choice, then the selection of the parties need not be honored by a court. Further, if the choice is violative of a fundamental policy of a state which has a materially greater interest than the chosen state, the selection could be disregarded by a court. Those limitations are not found in subsection (b).

4. Subsection (c) may be the most important provision in regard to creating uniformity of law in funds transfers. Most rights stated in Article 4A regard parties who are in privity of contract such as originator and beneficiary, sender and receiving bank, and beneficiary's bank and beneficiary. Since they are in privity they can make a choice of law by agreement. But that is not always the case. For example, an intermediary bank that improperly executes a payment order is not in privity with either the originator or the beneficiary. The ability of a funds transfer system to make a choice of law by rule is a convenient way of dispensing with individual agreements and to cover cases in which agreements are not feasible. It is probable that funds transfer systems will adopt a governing law to increase the certainty of commercial transactions that are effected over such systems. A system rule might adopt the law of an Article 4A state to govern transfers on the system in order to provide a consistent, unitary, law governing all transfers made on the system. To the extent such system rules develop, individual choice-of-law agreements become unnecessary.

Subsection (c) has broad application. A system choice of law applies not only to rights and obligations between banks that use the system, but may also apply to other parties to the funds transfer so long as some part of the transfer was carried out over the system. The originator and any other sender or receiving bank in the funds transfer is bound if at the time it issues or accepts a payment order it had notice that the funds transfer involved use of the system and that the system chose the law of a particular jurisdiction. Under Section 4A–107, the Federal Reserve by regulation could make a similar choice of law to govern funds transfers carried out by use of Federal Reserve Banks. Subsection (d) is a limitation on subsection (c). If parties have made a choice-of-law agreement that conflicts with a choice of law made under subsection (c), the agreement prevails.

5. Subsection (e) addresses the case in which a funds transfer involves more than one funds transfer system and the systems adopt conflicting choice-of-law rules. The rule that has the most significant relationship to the matter at issue prevails. For example, each system should be able to make a choice of law governing payment orders transmitted over that system with regard to a choice of law made by another system.

UCC ARTICLE 5 (2019)

LETTERS OF CREDIT

Article 5 was revised in 1995.

National Conference of Commissioners on Uniform State Laws

REPORTER

James J. White, Ann Arbor, Michigan

DRAFTING COMMITTEE

CHAIRMAN

Carlyle C. Ring, Jr., Vienna, Virginia

MEMBERS

Marion W. Benfield, Jr., Winston-Salem, North Carolina
John P. Burton, Santa Fe, New Mexico, *National Conference Representative and The American Law Institute Representative*
Bruce A. Coggeshall, Portland, Maine
William C. Hillman, Boston, Massachusetts
Edwin E. Huddleson, III, Washington, District of Columbia, *The American Law Institute Representative*
Jeremiah Marsh, Chicago, Illinois
Richard L. Morningstar, Washington, District of Columbia
Edwin E. Smith, Boston, Massachusetts
Sandra S. Stern, Scarsdale, New York
Richard C. Hite, Wichita, Kansas, *President (Member Ex Officio)*
Neal Ossen, Hartford, Connecticut, *Chairman, Division C (Member Ex Officio)*

UNIFORM COMMERCIAL CODE

REVIEW COMMITTEE

CHAIRMAN

William M. Burke, Los Angeles, California

MEMBERS

Boris Auerbach, Wyoming, Ohio
Robert J. Desiderio, Albuquerque, New Mexico

PREFATORY NOTE

Reason for Revision

When the original Article 5 was drafted 40 years ago, it was written for paper transactions and before many innovations in letters of credit. Now electronic and other media are used extensively. Since the 50's, standby letters of credit have developed and now nearly $500 billion standby letters of credit are issued annually worldwide, of which $250 billion are issued in the United States. The use of deferred payment letters of credit has also greatly increased. The customs and practices for letters of credit have evolved and are reflected in the Uniform Customs and Practice (UCP), usually incorporated into letters of credit, particularly international letters of credit, which have seen four revisions since the 1950's; the current version became effective in 1994 (UCP 500). Lastly, in a number of areas, court decisions have resulted in conflicting rules.

Prior to the appointment of a drafting committee, the ABA UCC Committee appointed a Task Force composed of knowledgeable practitioners and academics. The ABA Task Force studied the case law, evolving technologies and the changes in customs and practices. The Task Force identified a large number of issues which they discussed at some length, and made recommendations for revisions to Article 5. The Task Force stated in a foreword:

> "As a result of these increases and changes in usage, practice, players, and pressure, it comes as no surprise that there has been a sizable increase in litigation. Indeed, the approximately 62 cases reported in the United States in 1987 constituted double the cumulative reported cases up to 1965. . . .
>
> Moreover, almost forty years of hard use have revealed weaknesses, gaps and errors in the original statute which compromise its relevance. U.C.C. Article 5 was one of the few areas of the Uniform Commercial Code which did not benefit from prior codification and it should come as no surprise that it may require some revision. . . .
>
> Measured in terms of these areas which are vital to any system of commercial law, the current combination of statute and case law is found wanting in major respects both as to predictability and certainty. What is at issue here are not matters of sophistry but important issues of substance which have not been resolved by the current case law/code method and which admit of little likelihood of such resolution." (45 Bus. Lawyer 1521, at 1532, 1535–6)[1]

The Drafting Committee began its deliberations with the Task Force Report in hand. The final work of the Drafting Committee varies from many of the suggestions of the Task Force.

Need for Uniformity

Letters of Credit are a major instrument in international trade, as well as domestic transactions. To facilitate its usefulness and competitiveness, it is essential that U.S. law be in harmony with international rules and practices, as well as flexible enough to accommodate changes in technology and practices that have, and are, evolving. Not only should the rules be consistent within the United States, but they need to be substantively and procedurally consistent with international practices.

---

[1] The Task Force members were: Professor James E. Byrne (George Mason University School of Law) Chair; Professor Boris Kozolchyk (University of Arizona College of Law); Michael Evan Avidon (Moses & Singer); James G. Barnes (Baker & McKenzie); Arthur G. Lloyd (Citibank N.A.); Janis S. Penton (Rosen, Wachtell & Gilbert); Richard F. Purcell (Connell, Rice & Sugar Co.); Alan L. Bloodgood (Morgan Guaranty Trust Co.); Charles del Busto (Manufacturers Hanover Trust Co.); Vincent Maulella (Manufacturers Hanover Trust Co.).

Thus, the goals of the drafting effort were:

- conforming the Article 5 rules to current customs and practices;
- accommodating new forms of Letters of Credit, changes in customs and practices, and evolving technology, particularly the use of electronic media;
- maintaining Letters of Credit as an inexpensive and efficient instrument facilitating trade; and
- resolving conflicts among reported decisions.

Process of Achieving Uniformity

The essence of uniform law revision is to obtain a sufficient consensus and balance among the interests of the various participants so that universal and uniform enactment by the various States may be achieved.

In part this is accomplished by extensive consultation on and broad circulation of the drafts from 1990, when the project began, until approval of the final draft by the American law Institute (ALI) and the National Conference of Commissioners on Uniform State Laws (NCCUSL).

Hundreds of groups were invited to participate in the drafting process. Twenty Advisors were appointed, representing a cross-section of interested parties. In addition 20 Observers regularly attended drafting meetings and over 100 were on the mailing list to receive all drafts of the revision.

The Drafting Committee meetings were open and all those who attended were afforded full opportunity to express their views and participate in the dialogue. The Advisors and Observers were a balanced group with ten representatives of users (Beneficiaries and Applicants); five representatives of governmental agencies; five representatives of the U.S. Council on International Banking (USCIB); seven from major banks in letter of credit transactions; eight from regional banks; and seven law professors who teach and write on Letters of Credit.

Nine Drafting Committee meetings were held that began Friday morning and ended Sunday noon. In addition, the draft was twice debated in full by NCCUSL, once by the ALI Council, once considered by the ALI Consultative Group and once by an ad hoc Committee of the Council; and reviewed and discussed by the ABA Subcommittee on Letters of Credit semi-annually and by several state and city bar association committees.

The drafts were regularly reviewed and discussed in *The Business Lawyer, Letter of Credit Update*, and in other publications.

The consensus, balance and quality achieved in this lengthy deliberative process is a product of not only its Reporter and the Drafting Committee, but also the faithful and energetic participation of the following Advisors and active participants:

Advisors

Professor Gerald T. McLaughlin, *Loyola Law School, ABA, Section of Business Law*
James G. Barnes, *Baker & McKenzie/U.S. Council on International Banking, Inc.*
Harold S. Burman, *U.S. Department of State*
James E. Byrne, *George Mason University, Institute of International Banking Law and Practice Inc.*
Professor John Dolan, *original ABA Advisor*
Henry N. Dyhouse, *U.S. Central Credit Union*
David P. Goch, *Treasury Management Association*
Thomas J. Greco, *American Bankers Association*
Henry Harfield, *Shearman & Sterling*
Oliver I. Ireland, *Board of Governors of Federal Reserve Board*
James W. Kopp, *Shell Oil Company/Treasury Management Association*
Professor Boris Kozolchyk, *University of Arizona/National Law Center for Inter-American Free Trade, U.S. Council on International Banking, Inc.*
Vincent M. Maulella, *Manufacturers Hanover Trust Co./U.S. Council on International Banking, Inc.*
Robert M. Rosenblith, *National Westminster Bank*
Bradley K. Sabel, *Federal Reserve Bank of New York*
Joseph H. Sommer, *Federal Reserve Bank of New York*

UNIFORM COMMERCIAL CODE

Jamileh Soufan, *American General Corporation/Treasury Management Association*
Dan Taylor, *U.S. Council on International Banking, Inc.*
William H. Thornton, *Security Pacific National Bank/California Bankers Association*
Paul S. Turner, *Occidental Petroleum Corporation/Treasury Management Association*
Stanley M. Walker, *Exxon Company U.S.A./Treasury Management Association*

Active Participants

Michael E. Avidon, *Moses & Singer/N.Y. State Bar Association, Banking Law Committee, Subcommittee on Letters of Credit*
Walter B. Baker, *ABN AMRO Bank, N.V.*
Thomas C. Baxter, Jr., *Federal Reserve Bank of New York*
Professor Amelia H. Boss, *Pennsylvania Bar Association, Section of Corporation, Banking & Business Law, Commercial Law Committee*
Maria A. Chanco, *Bank of America, N.T. & S.A.*
Frank P. Curran, *Treasury Management Association*
Carol R. Dennis, *Office of Federal Procurement Policy, OFMB*
Albert J. Givray, *Oklahoma Bar Association, Section of Banking & Commercial Law*
Sidney S. Goldstein, *New York State Bar Association*
Professor Egon Guttman, *The American University*
George A. Hisert, *State Bar of California, Section of Business Law, Committee on UCC, Subcommittee on Letters of Credit*
Larry J. Jones, *Mobil Oil Credit Corporation*
Carter H. Klein, *Jenner & Block*
Arthur G. Lloyd, *ABA, Section of Business Law, Committee on UCC, Subcommittee on Letters of Credit, Working Group on UCC Article 5 Revision*
Rebecca S. McCulloch, *ABN AMRO Bank, N.V.*
Dennis L. Noah, *First National Bank of Maryland/U.S. Council on International Banking, Inc.*
James Purvis, *The Bank of California*
James E. Roselle, *First National Bank of Chicago*
R. David Whitaker, *ABA, Section of Business Law, Committee on UCC, Subcommittee on ECP, Working Group on EDC*
Brooke Wunnicke, *ABA, Section of Business Law, Committee on UCC, Subcommittee on Letters of Credit*

Balance of Benefits

Uniform laws can be enacted only if there is a consensus that the benefits achieved advance the public interest in a manner that can be embraced by all users of the law. It appears that as drafted, Revised Article 5 will enjoy substantial support by the participating interests in letter of credit transactions.

Benefits of Revised Article 5 in General

Independence Principle. Revised Article 5 clearly and forcefully states the independence of the letter of credit obligations from the underlying transactions that was unexpressed in, but was a fundamental predicate for, the original Article 5 (Sections 5–103(d) and 5–108(f)). Certainty of payment, independent of other claims, setoffs or other causes of action, is a core element of the commercial utility of letters of credit.

Clarifications. The revision authorizes the use of electronic technology (Sections 5–102(a)(14) and 5–104); expressly permits deferred payment letters of credit (Section 5–102(a)(8)) and two party letters of credit (Section 5–102(a)(10)); provides rules for unstated expiry dates (Section 5–106(c)), perpetual letters of credit (Section 5–106(d)), and non-documentary conditions (Section 5–108(g)); clarifies and establishes rules for successors by operation of law (Sections 5–102(a)(15) and 5–113); conforms to existing practice for assignment of proceeds (Section 5–114); and clarifies the rules where decisions have been in conflict (Section 5–106, Comment 1; Section 5–108, Comments 1, 3, 4, 7, and 9; Section 5–109, Comments 1 and 3; Section 5–113, Comment 1; and Section 5–117, Comment 1).

Harmonizes with International Practice

The UCP is used in most international letters of credit and in many domestic letters of credit. These international practices are well known and employed by the major issuers and users of letters of credit. Revisions have been made to Article 5 to coordinate the Article 5 rules with current international practice (e.g., deferred payment obligations, reasonable time to examine documents, preclusion, non-documentary conditions, return of documents, and irrevocable unless stated to be revocable).

Benefits of Revised Article 5 to Issuers

Consequential Damages. Section 5–111 precludes consequential and punitive damages. It, however, provides strong incentives for Issuers to honor, including provisions for attorneys fees and expenses of litigation, interest, and specific performance. If consequential and punitive damages were allowed, the cost of letters of credit could rise substantially.

Statute of Limitation. Section 5–115 establishes a one year statute of limitation from the expiration date or from accrual of the cause of action, whichever occurs later. Because it is usually obvious to all when there has been a breach, a short limitation period is fair to potential plaintiffs.

Choice of Law. Section 5–116 permits the issuer (or nominated party or adviser) to choose the law of the jurisdiction that will govern even if that law bears no relation to the transaction. Absent agreement, Section 5–116 states choice of law rules.

Assignment of Proceeds. Section 5–114 conforms more fully to existing practice and provides an orderly procedure for recording and accommodating assignments by consent of the issuer (or nominated party).

Subrogation. Section 5–117 clarifies the subrogation rights of an Issuer who has honored a letter of credit. These rights of subrogation also extend to an applicant who reimburses and a nominated party who pays or gives value.

Recognition of UCP. Section 5–116(c) expressly recognizes that if the UCP is incorporated by reference into the letter of credit, the agreement varies the provisions of Article 5 with which it may conflict except for the non-variable provisions of Article 5.

Benefits of Revised Article 5 to Applicants

Warranties. Section 5–110 specifies the warranties made by a beneficiary. It gives the applicant on a letter of credit which has been honored a direct cause of action if a drawing is fraudulent or forged or if a drawing violates any agreement augmented by a letter of credit.

Strict Compliance. Absent agreement to the contrary, the issuer must dishonor a presentation that does not strictly comply under standard practice with the terms and conditions of the letter of credit (Section 5–108).

Subrogation. New Section 5–117 clarifies the parties' rights of subrogation if the letter of credit is honored.

Limitations on General Disclaimers and Waivers. Section 5–103(c) limits the effect of general disclaimers and waivers in a letter of credit, or reimbursement or other agreement.

Benefits of Revised Article 5 to Beneficiaries

Irrevocable. A letter of credit is irrevocable unless the letter of credit expressly provides it is revocable (Section 5–106(a)).

Preclusion. Section 5–108(c) now provides that the Issuer is precluded from asserting any discrepancy not stated in its notice timely given, except for fraud, forgery or expiration.

Timely Examination. Section 5–108(b) requires examination and notice of any discrepancies within a reasonable time not to exceed the 7th business day after presentation of the documents.

Transfers by Operation of Law. New Section 5–113 allows a successor to a beneficiary by operation of law to make presentation and receive payment or acceptance.

Damages. The damages provided are expanded and clarified. They include attorneys fees and expenses of litigation and payment of the full amount of the wrongfully dishonored or repudiated demand, with interest, without an obligation of the beneficiary to mitigate damages (Section 5–111).

UNIFORM COMMERCIAL CODE

Revisions for Article 9 and Transition Provisions

The draft includes suggested revisions to conform Article 9 to the Article 5 changes. Article 9 itself is under revision and the interface with Revised Article 5 will be more fully examined by the Article 9 drafting committee, as well, in light of changes to Article 9. The Article 9 revisions will probably not be completed until 1998–9. Revised Article 8 (1994) also makes changes to Article 9 so care should be taken to coordinate the changes of both Revised Articles 5 and 8 within each State.

The draft also includes transition provisions and some cross reference changes in other Articles of the UCC.

Lastly, there follows a table showing the changes from the original Article 5 made by the revisions to Article 5.

Table of Disposition of Sections in Former Article 5

The reference to a section in revised Article 5 is to the section that refers to the issue addressed by the section in former Article 5. If there is no comparable section in Revised Article 5 to a section in former Article 5, that fact is indicated by the word "Omitted" and a reason is stated.

Former Article 5 Section	Revised Article 5 Section
5–101	5–101
5–102(1)	5–103(a)
5–102(2)	Omitted (inherent in 5–103(a) and definitions)
5–103(3)	(first sentence omitted) 5–103(b)
5–103(1)(a)	5–102(a)(10); 5–106(a); 5–102(a)(8)
5–103(1)(b)	5–102(a)(6)("Document"), and 5–102(a)(14)("Record"); "Documentary" draft or demand not used
5–103(1)(c)	5–102(a)(9)
5–103(1)(d)	5–102(a)(3)
5–103(1)(e)	5–102(a)(1)
5–103(1)(f)	5–102(a)(4)
5–103(1)(g)	("Applicant" rather than "Customer") 5–102(a)(2)
5–103(2)	Omitted as not applicable
5–103(3)	5–102(b)
5–103(4)	5–102(c)
5–104	5–104 and 5–102(6) and (14)
5–105	5–105
5–106(1)	5–106(a)
5–106(2)	5–106(b)
5–106(3)	5–106(b)
5–106(4)	5–106(b)
5–107(1)	5–107(c)
5–107(2)	5–107(a)
5–107(3)	5–107(c)
5–107(4)	Omitted as inadvisable default rule
5–108	Omitted (as outdated)
5–109(1)	5–108
5–109(2)	5–108
5–109(3)	Omitted (all issuers required to observe standard practices)
5–110(1)	Omitted (covered in definitions and comments)
5–110(2)	Omitted (covered in definitions and comments)
5–111(1)	5–110(a)
5–111(2)	5–110(b)

5-112(1)	5-108(b) and (c)
5-112(2)	5-108(h)
5-112(3)	5-102(a)(12)
5-113	Omitted (covered by other contract law)
5-114(1)	5-108(a)
5-114(2)(a)	5-109(a)(1)
5-114(2)(b)	5-109(a)(2)
5-114(3)	5-108(i)
5-114(4), (5)	Omitted; were optional
5-115(1)	5-111
5-115(2)	5-111
5-116(1)	5-112
5-116(2)	5-114
5-116(3)	5-114
5-117	Omitted (covered by other law)

Table of New Provisions

(Provisions which were not included in former Article 5 and subjects not addressed in former Article 5.)

Subject	Revised Article 5 Section
"Successor to a beneficiary"	5-102(15)
Non-variable terms	5-103(c)
Independence principle	5-103(d)
Unstated expiry date	5-106(c)
Perpetual letter of credit	5-106(d)
Preclusion of unstated deficiencies	5-108(c)
Standard practice	5-108(e)
Independence of obligation	5-108(f)
Non-documentary conditions	5-108(g)
Standards for issuing injunction	5-109(b)
Transfer by operation of law	5-113
Statute of Limitation	5-115
Choice of law	5-116
Subrogation	5-117

§ 5-101. Short Title.

This article may be cited as Uniform Commercial Code—Letters of Credit.

Official Comment

The Official Comment to the original Section 5-101 was a remarkably brief inaugural address. Noting that letters of credit had not been the subject of statutory enactment and that the law concerning them had been developed in the cases, the Comment stated that Article 5 was intended "within its limited scope" to set an independent theoretical frame for the further development of letters of credit. That statement addressed accurately conditions as they existed when the statement was made, nearly half a century ago. Since Article 5 was originally drafted, the use of letters of credit has expanded and developed, and the case law concerning these developments is, in some respects, discordant.

Revision of Article 5 therefore has required reappraisal both of the statutory goals and of the extent to which particular statutory provisions further or adversely affect achievement of those goals.

The statutory goal of Article 5 was originally stated to be: (1) to set a substantive theoretical frame that describes the function and legal nature of letters of credit; and (2) to preserve procedural flexibility in order to accommodate further development of the efficient use of letters of credit. A letter of credit is an idiosyncratic form of undertaking that supports performance of an obligation incurred in a separate financial, mercantile, or other transaction or arrangement. The objectives of the original and revised Article 5 are best achieved (1) by defining the peculiar characteristics of a letter of credit that distinguish it and the legal consequences of its use from other forms of assurance such as secondary guarantees, performance bonds, and insurance policies, and from ordinary contracts, fiduciary engagements, and escrow arrangements; and (2) by preserving flexibility through variation by agreement in order to respond to and accommodate developments in custom and usage that are not inconsistent with the essential definitions and substantive mandates of the statute. No statute can, however, prescribe the manner in which such substantive rights and duties are to be enforced or imposed without risking stultification of wholesome developments in the letter of credit mechanism. Letter of credit law should remain responsive to commercial reality and in particular to the customs and expectations of the international banking and mercantile community. Courts should read the terms of this article in a manner consistent with these customs and expectations.

The subject matter in Article 5, letters of credit, may also be governed by an international convention that is now being drafted by UNCITRAL, the draft Convention on Independent Guarantees and Standby Letters of Credit. The Uniform Customs and Practice is an international body of trade practice that is commonly adopted by international and domestic letters of credit and as such is the "law of the transaction" by agreement of the parties. Article 5 is consistent with and was influenced by the rules in the existing version of the UCP. In addition to the UCP and the international convention, other bodies of law apply to letters of credit. For example, the federal bankruptcy law applies to letters of credit with respect to applicants and beneficiaries that are in bankruptcy; regulations of the Federal Reserve Board and the Comptroller of the Currency lay out requirements for banks that issue letters of credit and describe how letters of credit are to be treated for calculating asset risk and for the purpose of loan limitations. In addition there is an array of anti-boycott and other similar laws that may affect the issuance and performance of letters of credit. All of these laws are beyond the scope of Article 5, but in certain circumstances they will override Article 5.

§ 5–102. Definitions.

(a) In this article:

(1) "Adviser" means a person who, at the request of the issuer, a confirmer, or another adviser, notifies or requests another adviser to notify the beneficiary that a letter of credit has been issued, confirmed, or amended.

(2) "Applicant" means a person at whose request or for whose account a letter of credit is issued. The term includes a person who requests an issuer to issue a letter of credit on behalf of another if the person making the request undertakes an obligation to reimburse the issuer.

(3) "Beneficiary" means a person who under the terms of a letter of credit is entitled to have its complying presentation honored. The term includes a person to whom drawing rights have been transferred under a transferable letter of credit.

(4) "Confirmer" means a nominated person who undertakes, at the request or with the consent of the issuer, to honor a presentation under a letter of credit issued by another.

(5) "Dishonor" of a letter of credit means failure timely to honor or to take an interim action, such as acceptance of a draft, that may be required by the letter of credit.

(6) "Document" means a draft or other demand, document of title, investment security, certificate, invoice, or other record, statement, or representation of fact, law, right, or opinion (i) which is presented in a written or other medium permitted by the letter of credit or, unless prohibited by the letter of credit, by the standard practice referred to in Section 5–108(e) and (ii) which is capable of being examined for compliance with the terms and conditions of the letter of credit. A document may not be oral.

(7) "Good faith" means honesty in fact in the conduct or transaction concerned.

(8) "Honor" of a letter of credit means performance of the issuer's undertaking in the letter of credit to pay or deliver an item of value. Unless the letter of credit otherwise provides, "honor" occurs

(i) upon payment,

(ii) if the letter of credit provides for acceptance, upon acceptance of a draft and, at maturity, its payment, or

(iii) if the letter of credit provides for incurring a deferred obligation, upon incurring the obligation and, at maturity, its performance.

(9) "Issuer" means a bank or other person that issues a letter of credit, but does not include an individual who makes an engagement for personal, family, or household purposes.

(10) "Letter of credit" means a definite undertaking that satisfies the requirements of Section 5–104 by an issuer to a beneficiary at the request or for the account of an applicant or, in the case of a financial institution, to itself or for its own account, to honor a documentary presentation by payment or delivery of an item of value.

(11) "Nominated person" means a person whom the issuer (i) designates or authorizes to pay, accept, negotiate, or otherwise give value under a letter of credit and (ii) undertakes by agreement or custom and practice to reimburse.

(12) "Presentation" means delivery of a document to an issuer or nominated person for honor or giving of value under a letter of credit.

(13) "Presenter" means a person making a presentation as or on behalf of a beneficiary or nominated person.

(14) "Record" means information that is inscribed on a tangible medium, or that is stored in an electronic or other medium and is retrievable in perceivable form.

(15) "Successor of a beneficiary" means a person who succeeds to substantially all of the rights of a beneficiary by operation of law, including a corporation with or into which the beneficiary has been merged or consolidated, an administrator, executor, personal representative, trustee in bankruptcy, debtor in possession, liquidator, and receiver.

(b) Definitions in other Articles applying to this article and the sections in which they appear are:

"Accept" or "Acceptance" Section 3–409
"Value" Sections 3–303, 4–211

(c) Article 1 contains certain additional general definitions and principles of construction and interpretation applicable throughout this article.

Official Comment

1. Since no one can be a confirmer unless that person is a nominated person as defined in Section 5–102(a)(11), those who agree to "confirm" without the designation or authorization of the issuer are not confirmers under Article 5. Nonetheless, the undertakings to the beneficiary of such persons may be enforceable by the beneficiary as letters of credit issued by the "confirmer" for its own account or as guarantees or contracts outside of Article 5.

2. The definition of "document" contemplates and facilitates the growing recognition of electronic and other nonpaper media as "documents," however, for the time being, data in those media constitute documents only in certain circumstances. For example, a facsimile received by an issuer would be a document only if the letter of credit explicitly permitted it, if the standard practice authorized it and the letter did not prohibit it, or the agreement of the issuer and beneficiary permitted it. The fact that data transmitted in a nonpaper (unwritten) medium can be recorded on paper by a recipient's computer printer, facsimile machine, or the like does not under current practice render the data so transmitted a "document." A facsimile or S.W.I.F.T. message received directly by the issuer is in an electronic medium when it crosses the boundary of the issuer's place of business. One wishing to make a presentation by facsimile (an electronic medium) will have to procure the explicit agreement of the issuer (assuming that the standard practice does not authorize it). Article 5 contemplates that electronic documents may be presented under a letter of credit and the provisions of this Article should be read to apply to electronic documents as well as tangible documents. An electronic document of title is delivered through the voluntary transfer of control. Article 1, Section 1–201 (definition of "delivery"). See Article 7, Section 7–106 on control of an electronic document. Where electronic transmissions are authorized neither by the letter of credit nor by the practice, the beneficiary may transmit the data electronically to its agent who may be able to put it in

written form and make a conforming presentation. Cf. Article 7, Section 7–105 on reissuing an electronic document in a tangible medium.

3. "Good faith" continues in revised Article 5 to be defined as "honesty in fact." "Observance of reasonable standards of fair dealing" has not been added to the definition. The narrower definition of "honesty in fact" reinforces the "independence principle" in the treatment of "fraud," "strict compliance," "preclusion," and other tests affecting the performance of obligations that are unique to letters of credit. This narrower definition—which does not include "fair dealing"—is appropriate to the decision to honor or dishonor a presentation of documents specified in a letter of credit. The narrower definition is also appropriate for other parts of revised Article 5 where greater certainty of obligations is necessary and is consistent with the goals of speed and low cost. It is important that U.S. letters of credit have continuing vitality and competitiveness in international transactions.

For example, it would be inconsistent with the "independence" principle if any of the following occurred: (i) the beneficiary's failure to adhere to the standard of "fair dealing" in the underlying transaction or otherwise in presenting documents were to provide applicants and issuers with an "unfairness" defense to dishonor even when the documents complied with the terms of the letter of credit; (ii) the issuer's obligation to honor in "strict compliance in accordance with standard practice" were changed to "reasonable compliance" by use of the "fair dealing" standard, or (iii) the preclusion against the issuer (Section 5–108(d)) were modified under the "fair dealing" standard to enable the issuer later to raise additional deficiencies in the presentation. The rights and obligations arising from presentation, honor, dishonor and reimbursement, are independent and strict, and thus "honesty in fact" is an appropriate standard.

The contract between the applicant and beneficiary is not governed by Article 5, but by applicable contract law, such as Article 2 or the general law of contracts. "Good faith" in that contract is defined by other law, such as Section 2–103(1)(b) [*The definition of good faith in 2–103(1)(b) will be deleted if the jurisdiction adopts the definition of good faith in revised Article 1*] or Restatement of Contracts 2d, § 205, which incorporate the principle of "fair dealing" in most cases, or a State's common law or other statutory provisions that may apply to that contract.

The contract between the applicant and the issuer (sometimes called the "reimbursement" agreement) is governed in part by this article (e.g., Sections 5–108(i), 5–111(b), and 5–103(c)) and partly by other law (e.g., the general law of contracts). The definition of good faith in Section 5–102(a)(7) applies only to the extent that the reimbursement contract is governed by provisions in this article; for other purposes good faith is defined by other law.

4. Payment and acceptance are familiar modes of honor. A third mode of honor, incurring an unconditional obligation, has legal effects similar to an acceptance of a time draft but does not technically constitute an acceptance. The practice of making letters of credit available by "deferred payment undertaking" as now provided in UCP 500 has grown up in other countries and spread to the United States. The definition of "honor" will accommodate that practice.

5. The exclusion of consumers from the definition of "issuer" is to keep creditors from using a letter of credit in consumer transactions in which the consumer might be made the issuer and the creditor would be the beneficiary. If that transaction were recognized under Article 5, the effect would be to leave the consumer without defenses against the creditor. That outcome would violate the policy behind the Federal Trade Commission Rule in 16 CFR Part 433. In a consumer transaction, an individual cannot be an issuer where that person would otherwise be either the principal debtor or a guarantor.

6. The label on a document is not conclusive; certain documents labelled "guarantees" in accordance with European (and occasionally, American) practice are letters of credit. On the other hand, even documents that are labelled "letter of credit" may not constitute letters of credit under the definition in Section 5–102(a). When a document labelled a letter of credit requires the issuer to pay not upon the presentation of documents, but upon the determination of an extrinsic fact such as applicant's failure to perform a construction contract, and where that condition appears on its face to be fundamental and would, if ignored, leave no obligation to the issuer under the document labelled letter of credit, the issuer's undertaking is not a letter of credit. It is probably some form of suretyship or other contractual arrangement and may be enforceable as such. See Sections 5–102(a)(10) and 5–103(d). Therefore, undertakings whose fundamental term requires an issuer to look beyond documents and beyond conventional reference to the clock, calendar, and practices concerning the form of various documents are not governed by Article 5. Although Section 5–108(g) recognizes that certain nondocumentary conditions can be included in a letter of credit without denying the undertaking the status of letter of credit, that section does not apply to cases where the nondocumentary condition is fundamental to the issuer's obligation. The rules in Sections

5–102(a)(10), 5–103(d), and 5–108(g) approve the conclusion in *Wichita Eagle & Beacon Publishing Co. v. Pacific Nat. Bank*, 493 F.2d 1285 (9th Cir. 1974).

The adjective "definite" is taken from the UCP. It approves cases that deny letter of credit status to documents that are unduly vague or incomplete. See, e.g., *Transparent Products Corp. v. Paysaver Credit Union*, 864 F.2d 60 (7th Cir. 1988). Note, however, that no particular phrase or label is necessary to establish a letter of credit. It is sufficient if the undertaking of the issuer shows that it is intended to be a letter of credit. In most cases the parties' intention will be indicated by a label on the undertaking itself indicating that it is a "letter of credit," but no such language is necessary.

A financial institution may be both the issuer and the applicant or the issuer and the beneficiary. Such letters are sometimes issued by a bank in support of the bank's own lease obligations or on behalf of one of its divisions as an applicant or to one of its divisions as beneficiary, such as an overseas branch. Because wide use of letters of credit in which the issuer and the applicant or the issuer and the beneficiary are the same would endanger the unique status of letters of credit, only financial institutions are authorized to issue them.

In almost all cases the ultimate performance of the issuer under a letter of credit is the payment of money. In rare cases the issuer's obligation is to deliver stock certificates or the like. The definition of letter of credit in Section 5–102(a)(10) contemplates those cases.

7. Under the UCP any bank is a nominated bank where the letter of credit is "freely negotiable." A letter of credit might also nominate by the following: "We hereby engage with the drawer, indorsers, and bona fide holders of drafts drawn under and in compliance with the terms of this credit that the same will be duly honored on due presentation" or "available with any bank by negotiation." A restricted negotiation credit might be "available with x bank by negotiation" or the like.

Several legal consequences may attach to the status of nominated person. First, when the issuer nominates a person, it is authorizing that person to pay or give value and is authorizing the beneficiary to make presentation to that person. Unless the letter of credit provides otherwise, the beneficiary need not present the documents to the issuer before the letter of credit expires; it need only present those documents to the nominated person. Secondly, a nominated person that gives value in good faith has a right to payment from the issuer despite fraud. Section 5–109(a)(1).

8. A "record" must be in or capable of being converted to a perceivable form. For example, an electronic message recorded in a computer memory that could be printed from that memory could constitute a record. Similarly, a tape recording of an oral conversation could be a record.

9. Absent a specific agreement to the contrary, documents of a beneficiary delivered to an issuer or nominated person are considered to be presented under the letter of credit to which they refer, and any payment or value given for them is considered to be made under that letter of credit. As the court held in *Alaska Textile Co. v. Chase Manhattan Bank, N.A.*, 982 F.2d 813, 820 (2d Cir. 1992), it takes a "significant showing" to make the presentation of a beneficiary's documents for "collection only" or otherwise outside letter of credit law and practice.

10. Although a successor of a beneficiary is one who succeeds "by operation of law," some of the successions contemplated by Section 5–102(a)(15) will have resulted from voluntary action of the beneficiary such as merger of a corporation. Any merger makes the successor corporation the "successor of a beneficiary" even though the transfer occurs partly by operation of law and partly by the voluntary action of the parties. The definition excludes certain transfers, where no part of the transfer is "by operation of law"—such as the sale of assets by one company to another.

11. "Draft" in Article 5 does not have the same meaning it has in Article 3. For example, a document may be a draft under Article 5 even though it would not be a negotiable instrument, and therefore would not qualify as a draft under Section 3–104(e).

As amended in 2003.

§ 5–103. Scope.

(a) This article applies to letters of credit and to certain rights and obligations arising out of transactions involving letters of credit.

(b) The statement of a rule in this article does not by itself require, imply, or negate application of the same or a different rule to a situation not provided for, or to a person not specified, in this article.

(c) With the exception of this subsection, subsections (a) and (d), Sections 5–102(a)(9) and (10), 5–106(d), and 5–114(d), and except to the extent prohibited in Sections 1–302 and 5–117(d), the effect of this article may be varied by agreement or by a provision stated or incorporated by reference in an undertaking. A term in an agreement or undertaking generally excusing liability or generally limiting remedies for failure to perform obligations is not sufficient to vary obligations prescribed by this article.

(d) Rights and obligations of an issuer to a beneficiary or a nominated person under a letter of credit are independent of the existence, performance, or nonperformance of a contract or arrangement out of which the letter of credit arises or which underlies it, including contracts or arrangements between the issuer and the applicant and between the applicant and the beneficiary.

As amended in 2001.

Official Comment

1. Sections 5–102(a)(10) and 5–103 are the principal limits on the scope of Article 5. Many undertakings in commerce and contract are similar, but not identical to the letter of credit. Principal among those are "secondary," "accessory," or "suretyship" guarantees. Although the word "guarantee" is sometimes used to describe an independent obligation like that of the issuer of a letter of credit (most often in the case of European bank undertakings but occasionally in the case of undertakings of American banks), in the United States the word "guarantee" is more typically used to describe a suretyship transaction in which the "guarantor" is only secondarily liable and has the right to assert the underlying debtor's defenses. This article does not apply to secondary or accessory guarantees and it is important to recognize the distinction between letters of credit and those guarantees. It is often a defense to a secondary or accessory guarantor's liability that the underlying debt has been discharged or that the debtor has other defenses to the underlying liability. In letter of credit law, on the other hand, the independence principle recognized throughout Article 5 states that the issuer's liability is independent of the underlying obligation. That the beneficiary may have breached the underlying contract and thus have given a good defense on that contract to the applicant against the beneficiary is no defense for the issuer's refusal to honor. Only staunch recognition of this principle by the issuers and the courts will give letters of credit the continuing vitality that arises from the certainty and speed of payment under letters of credit. To that end, it is important that the law not carry into letter of credit transactions rules that properly apply only to secondary guarantees or to other forms of engagement.

2. Like all of the provisions of the Uniform Commercial Code, Article 5 is supplemented by Section 1–103 and, through it, by many rules of statutory and common law. Because this article is quite short and has no rules on many issues that will affect liability with respect to a letter of credit transaction, law beyond Article 5 will often determine rights and liabilities in letter of credit transactions. Even within letter of credit law, the article is far from comprehensive; it deals only with "certain" rights of the parties. Particularly with respect to the standards of performance that are set out in Section 5–108, it is appropriate for the parties and the courts to turn to customs and practice such as the Uniform Customs and Practice for Documentary Credits, currently published by the International Chamber of Commerce as I.C.C. Pub. No. 500 (hereafter UCP). Many letters of credit specifically adopt the UCP as applicable to the particular transaction. Where the UCP are adopted but conflict with Article 5 and except where variation is prohibited, the UCP terms are permissible contractual modifications under Sections 1–302 and 5–103(c). See Section 5–116(c). Normally Article 5 should not be considered to conflict with practice except when a rule explicitly stated in the UCP or other practice is different from a rule explicitly stated in Article 5.

Except by choosing the law of a jurisdiction that has not adopted the Uniform Commercial Code, it is not possible entirely to escape the Uniform Commercial Code. Since incorporation of the UCP avoids only "conflicting" Article 5 rules, parties who do not wish to be governed by the nonconflicting provisions of Article 5 must normally either adopt the law of a jurisdiction other than a State of the United States or state explicitly the rule that is to govern. When rules of custom and practice are incorporated by reference, they are considered to be explicit terms of the agreement or undertaking.

Neither the obligation of an issuer under Section 5–108 nor that of an adviser under Section 5–107 is an obligation of the kind that is invariable under Section 1–102(3) [*unrevised Article 1; see Concordance, p. 12*]. Section 5–103(c) and Comment 1 to Section 5–108 make it clear that the applicant and the issuer may agree to almost any provision establishing the obligations of the issuer to the applicant. The last sentence of subsection (c) limits the power of the issuer to achieve that result by a nonnegotiated disclaimer or limitation of remedy.

What the issuer could achieve by an explicit agreement with its applicant or by a term that explicitly defines its duty, it cannot accomplish by a general disclaimer. The restriction on disclaimers in the last sentence of subsection (c) is based more on procedural than on substantive unfairness. Where, for example, the reimbursement agreement provides explicitly that the issuer need not examine any documents, the applicant understands the risk it has undertaken. A term in a reimbursement agreement which states generally that an issuer will not be liable unless it has acted in "bad faith" or committed "gross negligence" is ineffective under Section 5–103(c). On the other hand, less general terms such as terms that permit issuer reliance on an oral or electronic message believed in good faith to have been received from the applicant or terms that entitle an issuer to reimbursement when it honors a "substantially" though not "strictly" complying presentation, are effective. In each case the question is whether the disclaimer or limitation is sufficiently clear and explicit in reallocating a liability or risk that is allocated differently under a variable Article 5 provision.

Of course, no term in a letter of credit, whether incorporated by reference to practice rules or stated specifically, can free an issuer from a conflicting contractual obligation to its applicant. If, for example, an issuer promised its applicant that it would pay only against an inspection certificate of a particular company but failed to require such a certificate in its letter of credit or made the requirement only a nondocumentary condition that had to be disregarded, the issuer might be obliged to pay the beneficiary even though its payment might violate its contract with its applicant.

3. Parties should generally avoid modifying the definitions in Section 5–102. The effect of such an agreement is almost inevitably unclear. To say that something is a "guarantee" in the typical domestic transaction is to say that the parties intend that particular legal rules apply to it. By acknowledging that something is a guarantee, but asserting that it is to be treated as a "letter of credit," the parties leave a court uncertain about where the rules on guarantees stop and those concerning letters of credit begin.

4. Section 5–102(2) and (3) of Article 5 are omitted as unneeded; the omission does not change the law.

As amended in 2001.

§ 5–104. Formal Requirements.

A letter of credit, confirmation, advice, transfer, amendment, or cancellation may be issued in any form that is a record and is authenticated (i) by a signature or (ii) in accordance with the agreement of the parties or the standard practice referred to in Section 5–108(e).

Official Comment

1. Neither Section 5–104 nor the definition of letter of credit in Section 5–102(a)(10) requires inclusion of all the terms that are normally contained in a letter of credit in order for an undertaking to be recognized as a letter of credit under Article 5. For example, a letter of credit will typically specify the amount available, the expiration date, the place where presentation should be made, and the documents that must be presented to entitle a person to honor. Undertakings that have the formalities required by Section 5–104 and meet the conditions specified in Section 5–102(a)(10) will be recognized as letters of credit even though they omit one or more of the items usually contained in a letter of credit.

2. The authentication specified in this section is authentication only of the identity of the issuer, confirmer, or adviser.

An authentication agreement may be by system rule, by standard practice, or by direct agreement between the parties. The reference to practice is intended to incorporate future developments in the UCP and other practice rules as well as those that may arise spontaneously in commercial practice.

3. Many banking transactions, including the issuance of many letters of credit, are now conducted mostly by electronic means. For example, S.W.I.F.T. is currently used to transmit letters of credit from issuing to advising banks. The letter of credit text so transmitted may be printed at the advising bank, stamped "original" and provided to the beneficiary in that form. The printed document may then be used as a way of controlling and recording payments and of recording and authorizing assignments of proceeds or transfers of rights under the letter of credit. Nothing in this section should be construed to conflict with that practice.

To be a record sufficient to serve as a letter of credit or other undertaking under this section, data must have a durability consistent with that function. Because consideration is not required for a binding letter of credit or similar undertaking (Section 5–105) yet those undertakings are to be strictly construed (Section 5–108), parties to a letter of credit transaction are especially dependent on the continued availability of the terms and conditions of the letter of credit or other undertaking. By declining to specify any particular medium in which the letter of credit must be established or communicated, Section 5–104 leaves room for future developments.

§ 5–105. Consideration.

Consideration is not required to issue, amend, transfer, or cancel a letter of credit, advice, or confirmation.

Official Comment

It is not to be expected that any issuer will issue its letter of credit without some form of remuneration. But it is not expected that the beneficiary will know what the issuer's remuneration was or whether in fact there was any identifiable remuneration in a given case. And it might be difficult for the beneficiary to prove the issuer's remuneration. This section dispenses with this proof and is consistent with the position of Lord Mansfield in *Pillans v. Van Mierop,* 97 Eng.Rep. 1035 (K.B. 1765) in making consideration irrelevant.

§ 5–106. Issuance, Amendment, Cancellation, and Duration.

(a) A letter of credit is issued and becomes enforceable according to its terms against the issuer when the issuer sends or otherwise transmits it to the person requested to advise or to the beneficiary. A letter of credit is revocable only if it so provides.

(b) After a letter of credit is issued, rights and obligations of a beneficiary, applicant, confirmer, and issuer are not affected by an amendment or cancellation to which that person has not consented except to the extent the letter of credit provides that it is revocable or that the issuer may amend or cancel the letter of credit without that consent.

(c) If there is no stated expiration date or other provision that determines its duration, a letter of credit expires one year after its stated date of issuance or, if none is stated, after the date on which it is issued.

(d) A letter of credit that states that it is perpetual expires five years after its stated date of issuance, or if none is stated, after the date on which it is issued.

Official Comment

1. This section adopts the position taken by several courts, namely that letters of credit that are silent as to revocability are irrevocable. See, e.g., *Weyerhaeuser Co. v. First Nat. Bank,* 27 UCC Rep.Serv. 777 (S.D. Iowa 1979); *West Va. Hous. Dev. Fund v. Sroka,* 415 F.Supp. 1107 (W.D.Pa. 1976). This is the position of the current UCP (500). Given the usual commercial understanding and purpose of letters of credit, revocable letters of credit offer unhappy possibilities for misleading the parties who deal with them.

2. A person can consent to an amendment by implication. For example, a beneficiary that tenders documents for honor that conform to an amended letter of credit but not to the original letter of credit has probably consented to the amendment. By the same token an applicant that has procured the issuance of a transferable letter of credit has consented to its transfer and to performance under the letter of credit by a person to whom the beneficiary's rights are duly transferred. If some, but not all of the persons involved in a letter of credit transaction consent to performance that does not strictly conform to the original letter of credit, those persons assume the risk that other nonconsenting persons may insist on strict compliance with the original letter of credit. Under subsection (b) those not consenting are not bound. For example, an issuer might agree to amend its letter of credit or honor documents presented after the expiration date in the belief that the applicant has consented or will consent to the amendment or will waive presentation after the original expiration date. If that belief is mistaken, the issuer is bound to the beneficiary by the terms of the letter of credit as amended or waived, even though it may be unable to recover from the applicant.

In general, the rights of a recognized transferee beneficiary cannot be altered without the transferee's consent, but the same is not true of the rights of assignees of proceeds from the beneficiary. When the beneficiary makes a complete transfer of its interest that is effective under the terms for transfer established by the issuer, adviser, or other party controlling transfers, the beneficiary no longer has an interest in the letter of credit, and the transferee steps into the shoes of the beneficiary as the one with rights under the letter of credit. Section 5–102(a)(3). When there is a partial transfer, both the original beneficiary and the transferee beneficiary have an interest in performance of the letter of credit and each expects that its rights will not be altered by amendment unless it consents.

The assignee of proceeds under a letter of credit from the beneficiary enjoys no such expectation. Notwithstanding an assignee's notice to the issuer of the assignment of proceeds, the assignee is not a person protected by subsection (b). An assignee of proceeds should understand that its rights can be changed or completely extinguished by amendment or cancellation of the letter of credit. An assignee's claim is precarious, for it depends entirely upon the continued existence of the letter of credit and upon the beneficiary's preparation and presentation of documents that would entitle the beneficiary to honor under Section 5–108.

3. The issuer's right to cancel a revocable letter of credit does not free it from a duty to reimburse a nominated person who has honored, accepted, or undertaken a deferred obligation prior to receiving notice of the amendment or cancellation. Compare UCP Article 8.

4. Although all letters of credit should specify the date on which the issuer's engagement expires, the failure to specify an expiration date does not invalidate the letter of credit, or diminish or relieve the obligation of any party with respect to the letter of credit. A letter of credit that may be revoked or terminated at the discretion of the issuer by notice to the beneficiary is not "perpetual."

§ 5–107. Confirmer, Nominated Person, and Adviser.

(a) A confirmer is directly obligated on a letter of credit and has the rights and obligations of an issuer to the extent of its confirmation. The confirmer also has rights against and obligations to the issuer as if the issuer were an applicant and the confirmer had issued the letter of credit at the request and for the account of the issuer.

(b) A nominated person who is not a confirmer is not obligated to honor or otherwise give value for a presentation.

(c) A person requested to advise may decline to act as an adviser. An adviser that is not a confirmer is not obligated to honor or give value for a presentation. An adviser undertakes to the issuer and to the beneficiary accurately to advise the terms of the letter of credit, confirmation, amendment, or advice received by that person and undertakes to the beneficiary to check the apparent authenticity of the request to advise. Even if the advice is inaccurate, the letter of credit, confirmation, or amendment is enforceable as issued.

(d) A person who notifies a transferee beneficiary of the terms of a letter of credit, confirmation, amendment, or advice has the rights and obligations of an adviser under subsection (c). The terms in the notice to the transferee beneficiary may differ from the terms in any notice to the transferor beneficiary to the extent permitted by the letter of credit, confirmation, amendment, or advice received by the person who so notifies.

Official Comment

1. A confirmer has the rights and obligations identified in Section 5–108. Accordingly, unless the context otherwise requires, the terms "confirmer" and "confirmation" should be read into this article wherever the terms "issuer" and "letter of credit" appear.

A confirmer that has paid in accordance with the terms and conditions of the letter of credit is entitled to reimbursement by the issuer even if the beneficiary committed fraud (see Section 5–109(a)(1)(ii)) and, in that sense, has greater rights against the issuer than the beneficiary has. To be entitled to reimbursement from the issuer under the typical confirmed letter of credit, the confirmer must submit conforming documents, but the confirmer's presentation to the issuer need not be made before the expiration date of the letter of credit.

A letter of credit confirmation has been analogized to a guarantee of issuer performance, to a parallel letter of credit issued by the confirmer for the account of the issuer or the letter of credit applicant or both, and to a back-to-back letter of credit in which the confirmer is a kind of beneficiary of the original issuer's letter of credit. Like letter of credit undertakings, confirmations are both unique and flexible, so that no one of these analogies is perfect, but unless otherwise indicated in the letter of credit or confirmation, a confirmer should be viewed by the letter of credit issuer and the beneficiary as an issuer of a parallel letter of credit for the account of the original letter of credit issuer. Absent a direct agreement between the applicant and a confirmer, normally the obligations of a confirmer are to the issuer not the applicant, but the applicant might have a right to injunction against a confirmer under Section 5–109 or warranty claim under Section 5–110, and either might have claims against the other under Section 5–117.

2. No one has a duty to advise until that person agrees to be an adviser or undertakes to act in accordance with the instructions of the issuer. Except where there is a prior agreement to serve or where the silence of the adviser would be an acceptance of an offer to contract, a person's failure to respond to a request to advise a letter of credit does not in and of itself create any liability, nor does it establish a relationship of issuer and adviser

between the two. Since there is no duty to advise a letter of credit in the absence of a prior agreement, there can be no duty to advise it timely or at any particular time. When the adviser manifests its agreement to advise by actually doing so (as is normally the case), the adviser cannot have violated any duty to advise in a timely way. This analysis is consistent with the result of *Sound of Market Street v. Continental Bank International*, 819 F.2d 384 (3d Cir. 1987) which held that there is no such duty. This section takes no position on the reasoning of that case, but does not overrule the result. By advising or agreeing to advise a letter of credit, the adviser assumes a duty to the issuer and to the beneficiary accurately to report what it has received from the issuer, but, beyond determining the apparent authenticity of the letter, an adviser has no duty to investigate the accuracy of the message it has received from the issuer. "Checking" the apparent authenticity of the request to advise means only that the prospective adviser must attempt to authenticate the message (e.g., by "testing" the telex that comes from the purported issuer), and if it is unable to authenticate the message must report that fact to the issuer and, if it chooses to advise the message, to the beneficiary. By proper agreement, an adviser may disclaim its obligation under this section.

3. An issuer may issue a letter of credit which the adviser may advise with different terms. The issuer may then believe that it has undertaken a certain engagement, yet the text in the hands of the beneficiary will contain different terms, and the beneficiary would not be entitled to honor if the documents it submitted did not comply with the terms of the letter of credit as originally issued. On the other hand, if the adviser also confirmed the letter of credit, then as a confirmer it will be independently liable on the letter of credit as advised and confirmed. If in that situation the beneficiary's ultimate presentation entitled it to honor under the terms of the confirmation but not under those in the original letter of credit, the confirmer would have to honor but might not be entitled to reimbursement from the issuer.

4. When the issuer nominates another person to "pay," "negotiate," or otherwise to take up the documents and give value, there can be confusion about the legal status of the nominated person. In rare cases the person might actually be an agent of the issuer and its act might be the act of the issuer itself. In most cases the nominated person is not an agent of the issuer and has no authority to act on the issuer's behalf. Its "nomination" allows the beneficiary to present to it and earns it certain rights to payment under Section 5-109 that others do not enjoy. For example, when an issuer issues a "freely negotiable credit," it contemplates that banks or others might take up documents under that credit and advance value against them, and it is agreeing to pay those persons but only if the presentation to the issuer made by the nominated person complies with the credit. Usually there will be no agreement to pay, negotiate, or to serve in any other capacity by the nominated person, therefore the nominated person will have the right to decline to take the documents. It may return them or agree merely to act as a forwarding agent for the documents but without giving value against them or taking any responsibility for their conformity to the letter of credit.

§ 5-108. Issuer's Rights and Obligations.

(a) Except as otherwise provided in Section 5-109, an issuer shall honor a presentation that, as determined by the standard practice referred to in subsection (e), appears on its face strictly to comply with the terms and conditions of the letter of credit. Except as otherwise provided in Section 5-113 and unless otherwise agreed with the applicant, an issuer shall dishonor a presentation that does not appear so to comply.

(b) An issuer has a reasonable time after presentation, but not beyond the end of the seventh business day of the issuer after the day of its receipt of documents:

(1) to honor,

(2) if the letter of credit provides for honor to be completed more than seven business days after presentation, to accept a draft or incur a deferred obligation, or

(3) to give notice to the presenter of discrepancies in the presentation.

(c) Except as otherwise provided in subsection (d), an issuer is precluded from asserting as a basis for dishonor any discrepancy if timely notice is not given, or any discrepancy not stated in the notice if timely notice is given.

(d) Failure to give the notice specified in subsection (b) or to mention fraud, forgery, or expiration in the notice does not preclude the issuer from asserting as a basis for dishonor fraud or forgery as described in Section 5-109(a) or expiration of the letter of credit before presentation.

(e) An issuer shall observe standard practice of financial institutions that regularly issue letters of credit. Determination of the issuer's observance of the standard practice is a matter of interpretation for the court. The court shall offer the parties a reasonable opportunity to present evidence of the standard practice.

(f) An issuer is not responsible for:

(1) the performance or nonperformance of the underlying contract, arrangement, or transaction,

(2) an act or omission of others, or

(3) observance or knowledge of the usage of a particular trade other than the standard practice referred to in subsection (e).

(g) If an undertaking constituting a letter of credit under Section 5–102(a)(10) contains nondocumentary conditions, an issuer shall disregard the nondocumentary conditions and treat them as if they were not stated.

(h) An issuer that has dishonored a presentation shall return the documents or hold them at the disposal of, and send advice to that effect to, the presenter.

(i) An issuer that has honored a presentation as permitted or required by this article:

(1) is entitled to be reimbursed by the applicant in immediately available funds not later than the date of its payment of funds;

(2) takes the documents free of claims of the beneficiary or presenter;

(3) is precluded from asserting a right of recourse on a draft under Sections 3–414 and 3–415;

(4) except as otherwise provided in Sections 5–110 and 5–117, is precluded from restitution of money paid or other value given by mistake to the extent the mistake concerns discrepancies in the documents or tender which are apparent on the face of the presentation; and

(5) is discharged to the extent of its performance under the letter of credit unless the issuer honored a presentation in which a required signature of a beneficiary was forged.

Official Comment

1. This section combines some of the duties previously included in Sections 5–114 and 5–109. Because a confirmer has the rights and duties of an issuer, this section applies equally to a confirmer and an issuer. See Section 5–107(a).

The standard of strict compliance governs the issuer's obligation to the beneficiary and to the applicant. By requiring that a "presentation" appear strictly to comply, the section requires not only that the documents themselves appear on their face strictly to comply, but also that the other terms of the letter of credit such as those dealing with the time and place of presentation are strictly complied with. Typically, a letter of credit will provide that presentation is timely if made to the issuer, confirmer, or any other nominated person prior to expiration of the letter of credit. Accordingly, a nominated person that has honored a demand or otherwise given value before expiration will have a right to reimbursement from the issuer even though presentation to the issuer is made after the expiration of the letter of credit. Conversely, where the beneficiary negotiates documents to one who is not a nominated person, the beneficiary or that person acting on behalf of the beneficiary must make presentation to a nominated person, confirmer, or issuer prior to the expiration date.

This section does not impose a bifurcated standard under which an issuer's right to reimbursement might be broader than a beneficiary's right to honor. However, the explicit deference to standard practice in Section 5–108(a) and (e) and elsewhere expands issuers' rights of reimbursement where that practice so provides. Also, issuers can and often do contract with their applicants for expanded rights of reimbursement. Where that is done, the beneficiary will have to meet a more stringent standard of compliance as to the issuer than the issuer will have to meet as to the applicant. Similarly, a nominated person may have reimbursement and other rights against the issuer based on this article, the UCP, bank-to-bank reimbursement rules, or other agreement or undertaking of the issuer. These rights may allow the nominated person to recover from the issuer even when the nominated person would have no right to obtain honor under the letter of credit.

The section adopts strict compliance, rather than the standard that commentators have called "substantial compliance," the standard arguably applied in *Banco Español de Credito v. State Street Bank and Trust Company*, 385 F.2d 230 (1st Cir. 1967) and *Flagship Cruises Ltd. v. New England Merchants Nat. Bank*, 569 F.2d 699 (1st

Cir. 1978). Strict compliance does not mean slavish conformity to the terms of the letter of credit. For example, standard practice (what issuers do) may recognize certain presentations as complying that an unschooled layman would regard as discrepant. By adopting standard practice as a way of measuring strict compliance, this article indorses the conclusion of the court in *New Braunfels Nat. Bank v. Odiorne,* 780 S.W.2d 313 (Tex.Ct.App. 1989) (beneficiary could collect when draft requested payment on "Letter of Credit No. 86–122–5" and letter of credit specified "Letter of Credit No. 86–122–S" holding strict compliance does not demand oppressive perfectionism). The section also indorses the result in *Tosco Corp. v. Federal Deposit Insurance Corp.*, 723 F.2d 1242 (6th Cir. 1983). The letter of credit in that case called for "drafts Drawn under Bank of Clarksville Letter of Credit Number 105." The draft presented stated "drawn under Bank of Clarksville, Clarksville, Tennessee letter of Credit No. 105." The court correctly found that despite the change of upper case "L" to a lower case "l" and the use of the word "No." instead of "Number," and despite the addition of the words "Clarksville, Tennessee," the presentation conformed. Similarly a document addressed by a foreign person to General Motors as "Jeneral Motors" would strictly conform in the absence of other defects.

Identifying and determining compliance with standard practice are matters of interpretation for the court, not for the jury. As with similar rules in Sections 4A–202(c) and 2–302, it is hoped that there will be more consistency in the outcomes and speedier resolution of disputes if the responsibility for determining the nature and scope of standard practice is granted to the court, not to a jury. Granting the court authority to make these decisions will also encourage the salutary practice of courts' granting summary judgment in circumstances where there are no significant factual disputes. The statute encourages outcomes such as *American Coleman Co. v. Intrawest Bank,* 887 F.2d 1382 (10th Cir. 1989), where summary judgment was granted.

In some circumstances standards may be established between the issuer and the applicant by agreement or by custom that would free the issuer from liability that it might otherwise have. For example, an applicant might agree that the issuer would have no duty whatsoever to examine documents on certain presentations (e.g., those below a certain dollar amount). Where the transaction depended upon the issuer's payment in a very short time period (e.g., on the same day or within a few hours of presentation), the issuer and the applicant might agree to reduce the issuer's responsibility for failure to discover discrepancies. By the same token, an agreement between the applicant and the issuer might permit the issuer to examine documents exclusively by electronic or electro-optical means. Neither those agreements nor others like them explicitly made by issuers and applicants violate the terms of Section 5–108(a) or (b) or Section 5–103(c).

2. Section 5–108(a) balances the need of the issuer for time to examine the documents against the possibility that the examiner (at the urging of the applicant or for fear that it will not be reimbursed) will take excessive time to search for defects. What is a "reasonable time" is not extended to accommodate an issuer's procuring a waiver from the applicant. See Article 14c of the UCP.

Under both the UCC and the UCP the issuer has a reasonable time to honor or give notice. The outside limit of that time is measured in business days under the UCC and in banking days under the UCP, a difference that will rarely be significant. Neither business nor banking days are defined in Article 5, but a court may find useful analogies in Regulation CC, 12 CFR 229.2, in state law outside of the Uniform Commercial Code, and in Article 4.

Examiners must note that the seven-day period is not a safe harbor. The time within which the issuer must give notice is the lesser of a reasonable time or seven business days. Where there are few documents (as, for example, with the mine run standby letter of credit), the reasonable time would be less than seven days. If more than a reasonable time is consumed in examination, no timely notice is possible. What is a "reasonable time" is to be determined by examining the behavior of those in the business of examining documents, mostly banks. Absent prior agreement of the issuer, one could not expect a bank issuer to examine documents while the beneficiary waited in the lobby if the normal practice was to give the documents to a person who had the opportunity to examine those together with many others in an orderly process. That the applicant has not yet paid the issuer or that the applicant's account with the issuer is insufficient to cover the amount of the draft is not a basis for extension of the time period.

This section does not preclude the issuer from contacting the applicant during its examination; however, the decision to honor rests with the issuer, and it has no duty to seek a waiver from the applicant or to notify the applicant of receipt of the documents. If the issuer dishonors a conforming presentation, the beneficiary will be entitled to the remedies under Section 5–111, irrespective of the applicant's views.

Even though the person to whom presentation is made cannot conduct a reasonable examination of documents within the time after presentation and before the expiration date, presentation establishes the parties' rights. The beneficiary's right to honor or the issuer's right to dishonor arises upon presentation at the place provided in the letter of credit even though it might take the person to whom presentation has been made several days to determine whether honor or dishonor is the proper course. The issuer's time for honor or giving notice of dishonor may be extended or shortened by a term in the letter of credit. The time for the issuer's performance may be otherwise modified or waived in accordance with Section 5–106.

The issuer's time to inspect runs from the time of its "receipt of documents." Documents are considered to be received only when they are received at the place specified for presentation by the issuer or other party to whom presentation is made. "Receipt of documents" when documents of title are presented must be read in light of the definition of "delivery" in Article 1, Section 1–201 and the definition of "presentment" in Section 5–102(a)(12).

Failure of the issuer to act within the time permitted by subsection (b) constitutes dishonor. Because of the preclusion in subsection (c) and the liability that the issuer may incur under Section 5–111 for wrongful dishonor, the effect of such a silent dishonor may ultimately be the same as though the issuer had honored, i.e., it may owe damages in the amount drawn but unpaid under the letter of credit.

3. The requirement that the issuer send notice of the discrepancies or be precluded from asserting discrepancies is new to Article 5. It is taken from the similar provision in the UCP and is intended to promote certainty and finality.

The section thus substitutes a strict preclusion principle for the doctrines of waiver and estoppel that might otherwise apply under Section 1–103. It rejects the reasoning in *Flagship Cruises Ltd. v. New England Merchants' Nat. Bank*, 569 F.2d 699 (1st Cir. 1978) and *Wing On Bank Ltd. v. American Nat. Bank & Trust Co.*, 457 F.2d 328 (5th Cir. 1972) where the issuer was held to be estopped only if the beneficiary relied on the issuer's failure to give notice.

Assume, for example, that the beneficiary presented documents to the issuer shortly before the letter of credit expired, in circumstances in which the beneficiary could not have cured any discrepancy before expiration. Under the reasoning of *Flagship* and *Wing On*, the beneficiary's inability to cure, even if it had received notice, would absolve the issuer of its failure to give notice. The virtue of the preclusion obligation adopted in this section is that it forecloses litigation about reliance and detriment.

Even though issuers typically give notice of the discrepancy of tardy presentation when presentation is made after the expiration of a credit, they are not required to give that notice and the section permits them to raise late presentation as a defect despite their failure to give that notice.

4. To act within a reasonable time, the issuer must normally give notice without delay after the examining party makes its decision. If the examiner decides to dishonor on the first day, it would be obliged to notify the beneficiary shortly thereafter, perhaps on the same business day. This rule accepts the reasoning in cases such as *Datapoint Corp. v. M & I Bank*, 665 F.Supp. 722 (W.D.Wis. 1987) and *Esso Petroleum Canada, Div. of Imperial Oil, Ltd. v. Security Pacific Bank*, 710 F.Supp. 275 (D.Or. 1989).

The section deprives the examining party of the right simply to sit on a presentation that is made within seven days of expiration. The section requires the examiner to examine the documents and make a decision and, having made a decision to dishonor, to communicate promptly with the presenter. Nevertheless, a beneficiary who presents documents shortly before the expiration of a letter of credit runs the risk that it will never have the opportunity to cure any discrepancies.

5. Confirmers, other nominated persons, and collecting banks acting for beneficiaries can be presenters and, when so, are entitled to the notice provided in subsection (b). Even nominated persons who have honored or given value against an earlier presentation of the beneficiary and are themselves seeking reimbursement or honor need notice of discrepancies in the hope that they may be able to procure complying documents. The issuer has the obligations imposed by this section whether the issuer's performance is characterized as "reimbursement" of a nominated person or as "honor."

6. In many cases a letter of credit authorizes presentation by the beneficiary to someone other than the issuer. Sometimes that person is identified as a "payor" or "paying bank," or as an "acceptor" or "accepting bank," in other cases as a "negotiating bank," and in other cases there will be no specific designation. The section does not impose any duties on a person other than the issuer or confirmer, however a nominated person or other person may have liability under this article or at common law if it fails to perform an express or implied agreement with the beneficiary.

7. The issuer's obligation to honor runs not only to the beneficiary but also to the applicant. It is possible that an applicant who has made a favorable contract with the beneficiary will be injured by the issuer's wrongful dishonor. Except to the extent that the contract between the issuer and the applicant limits that liability, the issuer will have liability to the applicant for wrongful dishonor under Section 5–111 as a matter of contract law.

A good faith extension of the time in Section 5–108(b) by agreement between the issuer and beneficiary binds the applicant even if the applicant is not consulted or does not consent to the extension.

The issuer's obligation to dishonor when there is no apparent compliance with the letter of credit runs only to the applicant. No other party to the transaction can complain if the applicant waives compliance with terms or conditions of the letter of credit or agrees to a less stringent standard for compliance than that supplied by this article. Except as otherwise agreed with the applicant, an issuer may dishonor a noncomplying presentation despite an applicant's waiver.

Waiver of discrepancies by an issuer or an applicant in one or more presentations does not waive similar discrepancies in a future presentation. Neither the issuer nor the beneficiary can reasonably rely upon honor over past waivers as a basis for concluding that a future defective presentation will justify honor. The reasoning of *Courtaulds of North America Inc. v. North Carolina Nat. Bank,* 528 F.2d 802 (4th Cir. 1975) is accepted and that expressed in *Schweibish v. Pontchartrain State Bank,* 389 So.2d 731 (La.App. 1980) and *Titanium Metals Corp. v. Space Metals, Inc.,* 529 P.2d 431 (Utah 1974) is rejected.

8. The standard practice referred to in subsection (e) includes (i) international practice set forth in or referenced by the Uniform Customs and Practice, (ii) other practice rules published by associations of financial institutions, and (iii) local and regional practice. It is possible that standard practice will vary from one place to another. Where there are conflicting practices, the parties should indicate which practice governs their rights. A practice may be overridden by agreement or course of dealing. See Section 1–205(4) [*unrevised Article 1; see Concordance, p. 12*].

9. The responsibility of the issuer under a letter of credit is to examine documents and to make a prompt decision to honor or dishonor based upon that examination. Nondocumentary conditions have no place in this regime and are better accommodated under contract or suretyship law and practice. In requiring that nondocumentary conditions in letters of credit be ignored as surplusage, Article 5 remains aligned with the UCP (see UCP 500 Article 13c), approves cases like *Pringle-Associated Mortgage Corp. v. Southern National Bank,* 571 F.2d 871, 874 (5th Cir. 1978), and rejects the reasoning in cases such as *Sherwood & Roberts, Inc. v. First Security Bank,* 682 P.2d 149 (Mont. 1984).

Subsection (g) recognizes that letters of credit sometimes contain nondocumentary terms or conditions. Conditions such as a term prohibiting "shipment on vessels more than 15 years old," are to be disregarded and treated as surplusage. Similarly, a requirement that there be an award by a "duly appointed arbitrator" would not require the issuer to determine whether the arbitrator had been "duly appointed." Likewise a term in a standby letter of credit that provided for differing forms of certification depending upon the particular type of default does not oblige the issuer independently to determine which kind of default has occurred. These conditions must be disregarded by the issuer. Where the nondocumentary conditions are central and fundamental to the issuer's obligation (as for example a condition that would require the issuer to determine in fact whether the beneficiary had performed the underlying contract or whether the applicant had defaulted) their inclusion may remove the undertaking from the scope of Article 5 entirely. See Section 5–102(a)(10) and Comment 6 to Section 5–102.

Subsection (g) would not permit the beneficiary or the issuer to disregard terms in the letter of credit such as place, time, and mode of presentation. The rule in subsection (g) is intended to prevent an issuer from deciding or even investigating extrinsic facts, but not from consulting the clock, the calendar, the relevant law and practice, or its own general knowledge of documentation or transactions of the type underlying a particular letter of credit.

Even though nondocumentary conditions must be disregarded in determining compliance of a presentation (and thus in determining the issuer's duty to the beneficiary), an issuer that has promised its applicant that it will honor only on the occurrence of those nondocumentary conditions may have liability to its applicant for disregarding the conditions.

10. Subsection (f) condones an issuer's ignorance of "any usage of a particular trade"; that trade is the trade of the applicant, beneficiary, or others who may be involved in the underlying transaction. The issuer is expected to know usage that is commonly encountered in the course of document examination. For example, an issuer should know the common usage with respect to documents in the maritime shipping trade but would not be expected to understand synonyms used in a particular trade for product descriptions appearing in a letter of credit or an invoice.

11. Where the issuer's performance is the delivery of an item of value other than money, the applicant's reimbursement obligation would be to make the "item of value" available to the issuer.

12. An issuer is entitled to reimbursement from the applicant after honor of a forged or fraudulent drawing if honor was permitted under Section 5–109(a).

13. The last clause of Section 5–108(i)(5) deals with a special case in which the fraud is not committed by the beneficiary, but is committed by a stranger to the transaction who forges the beneficiary's signature. If the issuer pays against documents on which a required signature of the beneficiary is forged, it remains liable to the true beneficiary. This principle is applicable to both electronic and tangible documents.

As amended in 2003.

§ 5–109. Fraud and Forgery.

(a) If a presentation is made that appears on its face strictly to comply with the terms and conditions of the letter of credit, but a required document is forged or materially fraudulent, or honor of the presentation would facilitate a material fraud by the beneficiary on the issuer or applicant:

(1) the issuer shall honor the presentation, if honor is demanded by (i) a nominated person who has given value in good faith and without notice of forgery or material fraud, (ii) a confirmer who has honored its confirmation in good faith, (iii) a holder in due course of a draft drawn under the letter of credit which was taken after acceptance by the issuer or nominated person, or (iv) an assignee of the issuer's or nominated person's deferred obligation that was taken for value and without notice of forgery or material fraud after the obligation was incurred by the issuer or nominated person; and

(2) the issuer, acting in good faith, may honor or dishonor the presentation in any other case.

(b) If an applicant claims that a required document is forged or materially fraudulent or that honor of the presentation would facilitate a material fraud by the beneficiary on the issuer or applicant, a court of competent jurisdiction may temporarily or permanently enjoin the issuer from honoring a presentation or grant similar relief against the issuer or other persons only if the court finds that:

(1) the relief is not prohibited under the law applicable to an accepted draft or deferred obligation incurred by the issuer;

(2) a beneficiary, issuer, or nominated person who may be adversely affected is adequately protected against loss that it may suffer because the relief is granted;

(3) all of the conditions to entitle a person to the relief under the law of this State have been met; and

(4) on the basis of the information submitted to the court, the applicant is more likely than not to succeed under its claim of forgery or material fraud and the person demanding honor does not qualify for protection under subsection (a)(1).

Official Comment

1. This recodification makes clear that fraud must be found either in the documents or must have been committed by the beneficiary on the issuer or applicant. See *Cromwell v. Commerce & Energy Bank*, 464 So.2d 721 (La. 1985).

Secondly, it makes clear that fraud must be "material." Necessarily courts must decide the breadth and width of "materiality." The use of the word requires that the fraudulent aspect of a document be material to a purchaser of that document or that the fraudulent act be significant to the participants in the underlying transaction. Assume, for example, that the beneficiary has a contract to deliver 1,000 barrels of salad oil. Knowing that it has delivered only 998, the beneficiary nevertheless submits an invoice showing 1,000 barrels. If two barrels in a 1,000 barrel shipment would be an insubstantial and immaterial breach of the underlying contract, the beneficiary's act, though possibly fraudulent, is not materially so and would not justify an injunction. Conversely, the knowing submission of those invoices upon delivery of only five barrels would be materially fraudulent. The courts must examine the underlying transaction when there is an allegation of material fraud, for only by examining that transaction can one determine whether a document is fraudulent or the beneficiary has committed fraud and, if so, whether the fraud was material.

Material fraud by the beneficiary occurs only when the beneficiary has no colorable right to expect honor and where there is no basis in fact to support such a right to honor. The section indorses articulations such as those stated in *Intraworld Indus. v. Girard Trust Bank*, 336 A.2d 316 (Pa. 1975), *Roman Ceramics Corp. v. People's Nat. Bank*, 714 F.2d 1207 (3d Cir. 1983), and similar decisions and embraces certain decisions under Section 5–114 that relied upon the phrase "fraud in the transaction." Some of these decisions have been summarized as follows in *Ground Air Transfer v. Westate's Airlines,* 899 F.2d 1269, 1272–73 (1st Cir. 1990):

> We have said throughout that courts may not "*normally*" issue an injunction because of an important exception to the general "no injunction" rule. The exception, as we also explained in *Itek,* 730 F.2d at 24–25, concerns "fraud" so serious as to make it obviously pointless and unjust to permit the beneficiary to obtain the money. Where the circumstances "*plainly*" show that the underlying contract forbids the beneficiary to call a letter of credit, *Itek,* 730 F.2d at 24; where they show that the contract deprives the beneficiary of even a "*colorable*" right to do so, id., at 25; where the contract and circumstances reveal that the beneficiary's demand for payment has "absolutely no basis in fact," id.; see *Dynamics Corp. of America,* 356 F.Supp. at 999; where the beneficiary's conduct has "so vitiated the entire transaction that the legitimate purposes of the independence of the issuer's obligation would no longer be served," Itek, 730 F.2d at 25 (quoting *Roman Ceramics Corp. v. Peoples National Bank,* 714 F.2d 1207, 1212 n.12, 1215 (3d Cir. 1983)(quoting Intraworld Indus., 336 A.2d at 324–25)); *then* a court may enjoin payment.

2. Subsection (a)(2) makes clear that the issuer may honor in the face of the applicant's claim of fraud. The subsection also makes clear what was not stated in former Section 5–114, that the issuer may dishonor and defend that dishonor by showing fraud or forgery of the kind stated in subsection (a). Because issuers may be liable for wrongful dishonor if they are unable to prove forgery or material fraud, presumably most issuers will choose to honor despite applicant's claims of fraud or forgery unless the applicant procures an injunction. Merely because the issuer has a right to dishonor and to defend that dishonor by showing forgery or material fraud does not mean it has a duty to the applicant to dishonor. The applicant's normal recourse is to procure an injunction, if the applicant is unable to procure an injunction, it will have a claim against the issuer only in the rare case in which it can show that the issuer did not honor in good faith.

3. Whether a beneficiary can commit fraud by presenting a draft under a clean letter of credit (one calling only for a draft and no other documents) has been much debated. Under the current formulation it would be possible but difficult for there to be fraud in such a presentation. If the applicant were able to show that the beneficiary were committing material fraud on the applicant in the underlying transaction, then payment would facilitate a material fraud by the beneficiary on the applicant and honor could be enjoined. The courts should be skeptical of claims of fraud by one who has signed a "suicide" or clean credit and thus granted a beneficiary the right to draw by mere presentation of a draft.

4. The standard for injunctive relief is high, and the burden remains on the applicant to show, by evidence and not by mere allegation, that such relief is warranted. Some courts have enjoined payments on letters of credit on insufficient showing by the applicant. For example, in *Griffin Cos. v. First Nat. Bank,* 374 N.W.2d 768 (Minn.App. 1985), the court enjoined payment under a standby letter of credit, basing its decision on plaintiff's allegation, rather than competent evidence, of fraud.

There are at least two ways to prohibit injunctions against honor under this section after acceptance of a draft by the issuer. First is to define honor (see Section 5–102(a)(8)) in the particular letter of credit to occur upon acceptance and without regard to later payment of the acceptance. Second is explicitly to agree that the applicant has no right to an injunction after acceptance—whether or not the acceptance constitutes honor.

5. Although the statute deals principally with injunctions against honor, it also cautions against granting "similar relief" and the same principles apply when the applicant or issuer attempts to achieve the same legal outcome by injunction against presentation (see *Ground Air Transfer Inc. v. Westates Airlines, Inc.,* 899 F.2d 1269 (1st Cir. 1990)), interpleader, declaratory judgment, or attachment. These attempts should face the same obstacles that face efforts to enjoin the issuer from paying. Expanded use of any of these devices could threaten the independence principle just as much as injunctions against honor. For that reason courts should have the same hostility to them and place the same restrictions on their use as would be applied to injunctions against honor. Courts should not allow the "sacred cow of equity to trample the tender vines of letter of credit law."

6. Section 5–109(a)(1) also protects specified third parties against the risk of fraud. By issuing a letter of credit that nominates a person to negotiate or pay, the issuer (ultimately the applicant) induces that nominated person to give value and thereby assumes the risk that a draft drawn under the letter of credit will be transferred to one with a status like that of a holder in due course who deserves to be protected against a fraud defense.

7. The "loss" to be protected against—by bond or otherwise under subsection (b)(2)—includes incidental damages. Among those are legal fees that might be incurred by the beneficiary or issuer in defending against an injunction action.

§ 5–110. Warranties.

(a) If its presentation is honored, the beneficiary warrants:

(1) to the issuer, any other person to whom presentation is made, and the applicant that there is no fraud or forgery of the kind described in Section 5–109(a); and

(2) to the applicant that the drawing does not violate any agreement between the applicant and beneficiary or any other agreement intended by them to be augmented by the letter of credit.

(b) The warranties in subsection (a) are in addition to warranties arising under Article 3, 4, 7, and 8 because of the presentation or transfer of documents covered by any of those articles.

Official Comment

1. Since the warranties in subsection (a) are not given unless a letter of credit has been honored, no breach of warranty under this subsection can be a defense to dishonor by the issuer. Any defense must be based on Section 5–108 or 5–109 and not on this section. Also, breach of the warranties by the beneficiary in subsection (a) cannot excuse the applicant's duty to reimburse.

2. The warranty in Section 5–110(a)(2) assumes that payment under the letter of credit is final. It does not run to the issuer, only to the applicant. In most cases the applicant will have a direct cause of action for breach of the underlying contract. This warranty has primary application in standby letters of credit or other circumstances where the applicant is not a party to an underlying contract with the beneficiary. It is not a warranty that the statements made on the presentation of the documents presented are truthful nor is it a warranty that the documents strictly comply under Section 5–108(a). It is a warranty that the beneficiary has performed all the acts expressly and implicitly necessary under any underlying agreement to entitle the beneficiary to honor. If, for example, an underlying sales contract authorized the beneficiary to draw only upon "due performance" and the beneficiary drew even though it had breached the underlying contract by delivering defective goods, honor of its draw would break the warranty. By the same token, if the underlying contract authorized the beneficiary to draw only upon actual default or upon its or a third party's determination of default by the applicant and if the beneficiary drew in violation of its authorization, then upon honor of its draw the warranty would be breached. In many cases, therefore, the documents presented to the issuer will contain inaccurate statements (concerning the goods delivered or concerning default or other matters), but the breach of warranty arises not because the statements are untrue but because the beneficiary's drawing violated its express or implied obligations in the underlying transaction.

3. The damages for breach of warranty are not specified in Section 5–111. Courts may find damage analogies in Section 2–714 in Article 2 and in warranty decisions under Articles 3 and 4.

Unlike wrongful dishonor cases—where the damages usually equal the amount of the draw—the damages for breach of warranty will often be much less than the amount of the draw, sometimes zero. Assume a seller entitled to draw only on proper performance of its sales contract. Assume it breaches the sales contract in a way that gives the buyer a right to damages but no right to reject. The applicant's damages for breach of the warranty in subsection (a)(2) are limited to the damages it could recover for breach of the contract of sale. Alternatively assume an underlying agreement that authorizes a beneficiary to draw only the "amount in default." Assume a default of $200,000 and a draw of $500,000. The damages for breach of warranty would be no more than $300,000.

§ 5–111. Remedies.

(a) If an issuer wrongfully dishonors or repudiates its obligation to pay money under a letter of credit before presentation, the beneficiary, successor, or nominated person presenting on its own behalf may recover from the issuer the amount that is the subject of the dishonor or repudiation. If the issuer's obligation under the letter of credit is not for the payment of money, the claimant may obtain specific performance or, at the claimant's election, recover an amount equal to the value of performance from the issuer. In either case, the claimant may also recover incidental but not consequential damages. The claimant is not obligated to take action to avoid damages that might be due from the issuer under this subsection. If, although not obligated to do so, the claimant avoids damages, the claimant's recovery from the issuer must be reduced by the amount of damages avoided. The issuer has the burden of proving the amount of damages avoided. In the case of repudiation the claimant need not present any document.

(b) If an issuer wrongfully dishonors a draft or demand presented under a letter of credit or honors a draft or demand in breach of its obligation to the applicant, the applicant may recover damages resulting from the breach, including incidental but not consequential damages, less any amount saved as a result of the breach.

(c) If an adviser or nominated person other than a confirmer breaches an obligation under this article or an issuer breaches an obligation not covered in subsection (a) or (b), a person to whom the obligation is owed may recover damages resulting from the breach, including incidental but not consequential damages, less any amount saved as a result of the breach. To the extent of the confirmation, a confirmer has the liability of an issuer specified in this subsection and subsections (a) and (b).

(d) An issuer, nominated person, or adviser who is found liable under subsection (a), (b), or (c) shall pay interest on the amount owed thereunder from the date of wrongful dishonor or other appropriate date.

(e) Reasonable attorney's fees and other expenses of litigation must be awarded to the prevailing party in an action in which a remedy is sought under this article.

(f) Damages that would otherwise be payable by a party for breach of an obligation under this article may be liquidated by agreement or undertaking, but only in an amount or by a formula that is reasonable in light of the harm anticipated.

Official Comment

1. The right to specific performance is new. The express limitation on the duty of the beneficiary to mitigate damages adopts the position of certain courts and commentators. Because the letter of credit depends upon speed and certainty of payment, it is important that the issuer not be given an incentive to dishonor. The issuer might have an incentive to dishonor if it could rely on the burden of mitigation falling on the beneficiary, (to sell goods and sue only for the difference between the price of the goods sold and the amount due under the letter of credit). Under the scheme contemplated by Section 5-111(a), the beneficiary would present the documents to the issuer. If the issuer wrongfully dishonored, the beneficiary would have no further duty to the issuer with respect to the goods covered by documents that the issuer dishonored and returned. The issuer thus takes the risk that the beneficiary will let the goods rot or be destroyed. Of course the beneficiary may have a duty of mitigation to the applicant arising from the underlying agreement, but the issuer would not have the right to assert that duty by way of defense or setoff. See Section 5-117(d). If the beneficiary sells the goods covered by dishonored documents or if the beneficiary sells a draft after acceptance but before dishonor by the issuer, the net amount so gained should be subtracted from the amount of the beneficiary's damages—at least where the damage claim against the issuer equals or exceeds the damage suffered by the beneficiary. If, on the other hand, the beneficiary suffers damages in an underlying transaction in an amount that exceeds the amount of the wrongfully dishonored demand (e.g., where the letter of credit does not cover 100 percent of the underlying obligation), the damages avoided should not necessarily be deducted from the beneficiary's claim against the issuer. In such a case, the damages would be the lesser of (i) the amount recoverable in the absence of mitigation (that is, the amount that is subject to the dishonor or repudiation plus any incidental damages) and (ii) the damages remaining after deduction for the amount of damages actually avoided.

A beneficiary need not present documents as a condition of suit for anticipatory repudiation, but if a beneficiary could never have obtained documents necessary for a presentation conforming to the letter of credit, the beneficiary cannot recover for anticipatory repudiation of the letter of credit. *Doelger v. Battery Park Bank,* 201 A.D. 515, 194 N.Y.S. 582 (1922) and *Decor by Nikkei Int'l, Inc. v. Federal Republic of Nigeria,* 497 F.Supp. 893 (S.D.N.Y. 1980), *aff'd,* 647 F.2d 300 (2d Cir. 1981), *cert. denied,* 454 U.S. 1148 (1982). The last sentence of subsection (c) does not expand the liability of a confirmer to persons to whom the confirmer would not otherwise be liable under Section 5-107.

Almost all letters of credit, including those that call for an acceptance, are "obligations to pay money" as that term is used in Section 5-111(a).

2. What damages "result" from improper honor is for the courts to decide. Even though an issuer pays a beneficiary in violation of Section 5-108(a) or of its contract with the applicant, it may have no liability to an applicant. If the underlying contract has been fully performed, the applicant may not have been damaged by the issuer's breach. Such a case would occur when *A* contracts for goods at $100 per ton, but, upon delivery, the market value of conforming goods has decreased to $25 per ton. If the issuer pays over discrepancies, there should be no recovery by *A* for the price differential if the issuer's breach did not alter the applicant's obligation under the underlying contract, i.e., to pay $100 per ton for goods now worth $25 per ton. On the other hand, if the applicant intends to resell the goods and must itself satisfy the strict compliance requirements under a second letter of credit in connection with its sale, the applicant may be damaged by the issuer's payment despite discrepancies because the applicant itself may then be unable to procure honor on the letter of credit where it is the beneficiary, and may

be unable to mitigate its damages by enforcing its rights against others in the underlying transaction. Note that an issuer found liable to its applicant may have recourse under Section 5–117 by subrogation to the applicant's claim against the beneficiary or other persons.

One who inaccurately advises a letter of credit breaches its obligation to the beneficiary, but may cause no damage. If the beneficiary knows the terms of the letter of credit and understands the advice to be inaccurate, the beneficiary will have suffered no damage as a result of the adviser's breach.

3. Since the confirmer has the rights and duties of an issuer, in general it has an issuer's liability, see subsection (c). The confirmer is usually a confirming bank. A confirming bank often also plays the role of an adviser. If it breaks its obligation to the beneficiary, the confirming bank may have liability as an issuer or, depending upon the obligation that was broken, as an adviser. For example, a wrongful dishonor would give it liability as an issuer under Section 5–111(a). On the other hand a confirming bank that broke its obligation to advise the credit but did not commit wrongful dishonor would be treated under Section 5–111(c).

4. Consequential damages for breach of obligations under this article are excluded in the belief that these damages can best be avoided by the beneficiary or the applicant and out of the fear that imposing consequential damages on issuers would raise the cost of the letter of credit to a level that might render it uneconomic. *A fortiori* punitive and exemplary damages are excluded, however, this section does not bar recovery of consequential or even punitive damages for breach of statutory or common law duties arising outside of this article.

5. The section does not specify a rate of interest. It leaves the setting of the rate to the court. It would be appropriate for a court to use the rate that would normally apply in that court in other situations where interest is imposed by law.

6. The court must award attorney's fees to the prevailing party, whether that party is an applicant, a beneficiary, an issuer, a nominated person, or adviser. Since the issuer may be entitled to recover its legal fees and costs from the applicant under the reimbursement agreement, allowing the issuer to recover those fees from a losing beneficiary may also protect the applicant against undeserved losses. The party entitled to attorneys' fees has been described as the "prevailing party." Sometimes it will be unclear which party "prevailed," for example, where there are multiple issues and one party wins on some and the other party wins on others. Determining which is the prevailing party is in the discretion of the court. Subsection (e) authorizes attorney's fees in all actions where a remedy is sought "under this article." It applies even when the remedy might be an injunction under Section 5–109 or when the claimed remedy is otherwise outside of Section 5–111. Neither an issuer nor a confirmer should be treated as a "losing" party when an injunction is granted to the applicant over the objection of the issuer or confirmer; accordingly neither should be liable for fees and expenses in that case.

"Expenses of litigation" is intended to be broader than "costs." For example, expense of litigation would include travel expenses of witnesses, fees for expert witnesses, and expenses associated with taking depositions.

7. For the purposes of Section 5–111(f) "harm anticipated" must be anticipated at the time when the agreement that includes the liquidated damage clause is executed or at the time when the undertaking that includes the clause is issued. See Section 2A–504.

§ 5–112. Transfer of Letter of Credit.

(a) Except as otherwise provided in Section 5–113, unless a letter of credit provides that it is transferable, the right of a beneficiary to draw or otherwise demand performance under a letter of credit may not be transferred.

(b) Even if a letter of credit provides that it is transferable, the issuer may refuse to recognize or carry out a transfer if:

(1) the transfer would violate applicable law; or

(2) the transferor or transferee has failed to comply with any requirement stated in the letter of credit or any other requirement relating to transfer imposed by the issuer which is within the standard practice referred to in Section 5–108(e) or is otherwise reasonable under the circumstances.

Official Comment

1. In order to protect the applicant's reliance on the designated beneficiary, letter of credit law traditionally has forbidden the beneficiary to convey to third parties its right to draw or demand payment under the letter of credit. Subsection (a) codifies that rule. The term "transfer" refers to the beneficiary's conveyance of that right. Absent incorporation of the UCP (which make elaborate provision for partial transfer of a commercial

letter of credit) or similar trade practice and absent other express indication in the letter of credit that the term is used to mean something else, a term in the letter of credit indicating that the beneficiary has the right to transfer should be taken to mean that the beneficiary may convey to a third party its right to draw or demand payment. Even in that case, the issuer or other person controlling the transfer may make the beneficiary's right to transfer subject to conditions, such as timely notification, payment of a fee, delivery of the letter of credit to the issuer or other person controlling the transfer, or execution of appropriate forms to document the transfer. A nominated person who is not a confirmer has no obligation to recognize a transfer.

The power to establish "requirements" does not include the right absolutely to refuse to recognize transfers under a transferable letter of credit. An issuer who wishes to retain the right to deny all transfers should not issue transferable letters of credit or should incorporate the UCP. By stating its requirements in the letter of credit an issuer may impose any requirement without regard to its conformity to practice or reasonableness. Transfer requirements of issuers and nominated persons must be made known to potential transferors and transferees to enable those parties to comply with the requirements. A common method of making such requirements known is to use a form that indicates the information that must be provided and the instructions that must be given to enable the issuer or nominated person to comply with a request to transfer.

2. The issuance of a transferable letter of credit with the concurrence of the applicant is *ipso facto* an agreement by the issuer and applicant to permit a beneficiary to transfer its drawing right and permit a nominated person to recognize and carry out that transfer without further notice to them. In international commerce, transferable letters of credit are often issued under circumstances in which a nominated person or adviser is expected to facilitate the transfer from the original beneficiary to a transferee and to deal with that transferee. In those circumstances it is the responsibility of the nominated person or adviser to establish procedures satisfactory to protect itself against double presentation or dispute about the right to draw under the letter of credit. Commonly such a person will control the transfer by requiring that the original letter of credit be given to it or by causing a paper copy marked as an original to be issued where the original letter of credit was electronic. By keeping possession of the original letter of credit the nominated person or adviser can minimize or entirely exclude the possibility that the original beneficiary could properly procure payment from another bank. If the letter of credit requires presentation of the original letter of credit itself, no other payment could be procured. In addition to imposing whatever requirements it considers appropriate to protect itself against double payment the person that is facilitating the transfer has a right to charge an appropriate fee for its activity.

"Transfer" of a letter of credit should be distinguished from "assignment of proceeds." The former is analogous to a novation or a substitution of beneficiaries. It contemplates not merely payment to but also performance by the transferee. For example, under the typical terms of transfer for a commercial letter of credit, a transferee could comply with a letter of credit transferred to it by signing and presenting its own draft and invoice. An assignee of proceeds, on the other hand, is wholly dependent on the presentation of a draft and invoice signed by the beneficiary.

By agreeing to the issuance of a transferable letter of credit, which is not qualified or limited, the applicant may lose control over the identity of the person whose performance will earn payment under the letter of credit.

§ 5–113. Transfer by Operation of Law.

(a) A successor of a beneficiary may consent to amendments, sign and present documents, and receive payment or other items of value in the name of the beneficiary without disclosing its status as a successor.

(b) A successor of a beneficiary may consent to amendments, sign and present documents, and receive payment or other items of value in its own name as the disclosed successor of the beneficiary. Except as otherwise provided in subsection (e), an issuer shall recognize a disclosed successor of a beneficiary as beneficiary in full substitution for its predecessor upon compliance with the requirements for recognition by the issuer of a transfer of drawing rights by operation of law under the standard practice referred to in Section 5–108(e) or, in the absence of such a practice, compliance with other reasonable procedures sufficient to protect the issuer.

(c) An issuer is not obliged to determine whether a purported successor is a successor of a beneficiary or whether the signature of a purported successor is genuine or authorized.

(d) Honor of a purported successor's apparently complying presentation under subsection (a) or (b) has the consequences specified in Section 5–108(i) even if the purported successor is not the successor of a beneficiary. Documents signed in the name of the beneficiary or of a disclosed successor by a person who is neither the beneficiary nor the successor of the beneficiary are forged documents for the purposes of Section 5–109.

(e) An issuer whose rights of reimbursement are not covered by subsection (d) or substantially similar law and any confirmer or nominated person may decline to recognize a presentation under subsection (b).

(f) A beneficiary whose name is changed after the issuance of a letter of credit has the same rights and obligations as a successor of a beneficiary under this section.

Official Comment

This section affirms the result in *Pastor v. Nat. Republic Bank of Chicago,* 76 Ill.2d 139, 390 N.E.2d 894 (Ill. 1979) and *Federal Deposit Insurance Co. v. Bank of Boulder,* 911 F.2d 1466 (10th Cir. 1990). Both electronic and tangible documents may be signed.

An issuer's requirements for recognition of a successor's status might include presentation of a certificate of merger, a court order appointing a bankruptcy trustee or receiver, a certificate of appointment as bankruptcy trustee, or the like. The issuer is entitled to rely upon such documents which on their face demonstrate that presentation is made by a successor of a beneficiary. It is not obliged to make an independent investigation to determine the fact of succession.

As amended in 2003.

§ 5–114. Assignment of Proceeds.

(a) In this section, "proceeds of a letter of credit" means the cash, check, accepted draft, or other item of value paid or delivered upon honor or giving of value by the issuer or any nominated person under the letter of credit. The term does not include a beneficiary's drawing rights or documents presented by the beneficiary.

(b) A beneficiary may assign its right to part or all of the proceeds of a letter of credit. The beneficiary may do so before presentation as a present assignment of its right to receive proceeds contingent upon its compliance with the terms and conditions of the letter of credit.

(c) An issuer or nominated person need not recognize an assignment of proceeds of a letter of credit until it consents to the assignment.

(d) An issuer or nominated person has no obligation to give or withhold its consent to an assignment of proceeds of a letter of credit, but consent may not be unreasonably withheld if the assignee possesses and exhibits the letter of credit and presentation of the letter of credit is a condition to honor.

(e) Rights of a transferee beneficiary or nominated person are independent of the beneficiary's assignment of the proceeds of a letter of credit and are superior to the assignee's right to the proceeds.

(f) Neither the rights recognized by this section between an assignee and an issuer, transferee beneficiary, or nominated person nor the issuer's or nominated person's payment of proceeds to an assignee or a third person affect the rights between the assignee and any person other than the issuer, transferee beneficiary, or nominated person. The mode of creating and perfecting a security interest in or granting an assignment of a beneficiary's rights to proceeds is governed by Article 9 or other law. Against persons other than the issuer, transferee beneficiary, or nominated person, the rights and obligations arising upon the creation of a security interest or other assignment of a beneficiary's right to proceeds and its perfection are governed by Article 9 or other law.

Official Comment

1. Subsection (b) expressly validates the beneficiary's present assignment of letter of credit proceeds if made after the credit is established but before the proceeds are realized. This section adopts the prevailing usage—"assignment of proceeds"—to an assignee. That terminology carries with it no implication, however, that an assignee acquires no interest until the proceeds are paid by the issuer. For example, an "assignment of the right to proceeds" of a letter of credit for purposes of security that meets the requirements of Section 9–203(b) would constitute the present creation of a security interest in a "letter-of-credit right." This security interest can be perfected by control (Section 9–107). Although subsection (a) explains the meaning of " 'proceeds' of a letter of credit," it should be emphasized that those proceeds also may be Article 9 proceeds of other collateral. For example,

if a seller of inventory receives a letter of credit to support the account that arises upon the sale, payments made under the letter of credit are Article 9 proceeds of the inventory, account, and any document of title covering the inventory. Thus, the secured party who had a perfected security interest in that inventory, account, or document has a perfected security interest in the proceeds collected under the letter of credit, so long as they are identifiable cash proceeds (Section 9-315(a), (d)). This perfection is continuous, regardless of whether the secured party perfected a security interest in the right to letter of credit proceeds.

2. An assignee's rights to enforce an assignment of proceeds against an issuer and the priority of the assignee's rights against a nominated person or transferee beneficiary are governed by Article 5. Those rights and that priority are stated in subsections (c), (d), and (e). Note also that Section 4-210 gives first priority to a collecting bank that has given value for a documentary draft.

3. By requiring that an issuer or nominated person consent to the assignment of proceeds of a letter of credit, subsections (c) and (d) follow more closely recognized national and international letter of credit practices than did prior law. In most circumstances, it has always been advisable for the assignee to obtain the consent of the issuer in order better to safeguard its right to the proceeds. When notice of an assignment has been received, issuers normally have required signatures on a consent form. This practice is reflected in the revision. By unconditionally consenting to such an assignment, the issuer or nominated person becomes bound, subject to the rights of the superior parties specified in subsection (e), to pay to the assignee the assigned letter of credit proceeds that the issuer or nominated person would otherwise pay to the beneficiary or another assignee.

Where the letter of credit must be presented as a condition to honor and the assignee holds and exhibits the letter of credit to the issuer or nominated person, the risk to the issuer or nominated person of having to pay twice is minimized. In such a situation, subsection (d) provides that the issuer or nominated person may not unreasonably withhold its consent to the assignment.

§ 5-115. Statute of Limitations.

An action to enforce a right or obligation arising under this article must be commenced within one year after the expiration date of the relevant letter of credit or one year after the [claim for relief] [cause of action] accrues, whichever occurs later. A [claim for relief] [cause of action] accrues when the breach occurs, regardless of the aggrieved party's lack of knowledge of the breach.

Official Comment

1. This section is based upon Sections 4-111 and 2-725(2).

2. This section applies to all claims for which there are remedies under Section 5-111 and to other claims made under this article, such as claims for breach of warranty under Section 5-110. Because it covers all claims under Section 5-111, the statute of limitations applies not only to wrongful dishonor claims against the issuer but also to claims between the issuer and the applicant arising from the reimbursement agreement. These might be for reimbursement (issuer v. applicant) or for breach of the reimbursement contract by wrongful honor (applicant v. issuer).

3. The statute of limitations, like the rest of the statute, applies only to a letter of credit issued on or after the effective date and only to transactions, events, obligations, or duties arising out of or associated with such a letter. If a letter of credit was issued before the effective date and an obligation on that letter of credit was breached after the effective date, the complaining party could bring its suit within the time that would have been permitted prior to the adoption of Section 5-115 and would not be limited by the terms of Section 5-115.

§ 5-116. Choice of Law and Forum.

(a) The liability of an issuer, nominated person, or adviser for action or omission is governed by the law of the jurisdiction chosen by an agreement in the form of a record signed or otherwise authenticated by the affected parties in the manner provided in Section 5-104 or by a provision in the person's letter of credit, confirmation, or other undertaking. The jurisdiction whose law is chosen need not bear any relation to the transaction.

(b) Unless subsection (a) applies, the liability of an issuer, nominated person, or adviser for action or omission is governed by the law of the jurisdiction in which the person is located. The person is considered to be located at the address indicated in the person's undertaking. If more than one address is indicated, the person is considered to be located at the address from which the person's undertaking was issued. For the purpose of jurisdiction, choice of law, and recognition of interbranch letters of credit, but not enforcement of a judgment, all branches of a bank are considered separate juridical entities and a bank is considered to be located at the place where its relevant branch is considered to be located under this subsection.

(c) Except as otherwise provided in this subsection, the liability of an issuer, nominated person, or adviser is governed by any rules of custom or practice, such as the Uniform Customs and Practice for Documentary Credits, to which the letter of credit, confirmation, or other undertaking is expressly made subject. If (i) this article would govern the liability of an issuer, nominated person, or adviser under subsection (a) or (b), (ii) the relevant undertaking incorporates rules of custom or practice, and (iii) there is conflict between this article and those rules as applied to that undertaking, those rules govern except to the extent of any conflict with the nonvariable provisions specified in Section 5–103(c).

(d) If there is conflict between this article and Article 3, 4, 4A, or 9, this article governs.

(e) The forum for settling disputes arising out of an undertaking within this article may be chosen in the manner and with the binding effect that governing law may be chosen in accordance with subsection (a).

Official Comment

1. Although it would be possible for the parties to agree otherwise, the law normally chosen by agreement under subsection (a) and that provided in the absence of agreement under subsection (b) is the substantive law of a particular jurisdiction not including the choice of law principles of that jurisdiction. Thus, two parties, an issuer and an applicant, both located in Oklahoma might choose the law of New York. Unless they agree otherwise, the section anticipates that they wish the substantive law of New York to apply to their transaction and they do not intend that a New York choice of law principle might direct a court to Oklahoma law. By the same token, the liability of an issuer located in New York is governed by New York substantive law—in the absence of agreement—even in circumstances in which choice of law principles found in the common law of New York might direct one to the law of another State. Subsection (b) states the relevant choice of law principles and it should not be subordinated to some other choice of law rule. Within the States of the United States *renvoi* will not be a problem once every jurisdiction has enacted Section 5–116 because every jurisdiction will then have the same choice of law rule and in a particular case all choice of law rules will point to the same substantive law.

Subsection (b) does not state a choice of law rule for the "liability of an applicant." However, subsection (b) does state a choice of law rule for the liability of an issuer, nominated person, or adviser, and since some of the issues in suits by applicants against those persons involve the "liability of an issuer, nominated person, or adviser," subsection (b) states the choice of law rule for those issues. Because an issuer may have liability to a confirmer both as an issuer (Section 5–108(a), Comment 5 to Section 5–108) and as an applicant (Section 5–107(a), Comment 1 to Section 5–107, Section 5–108(i)), subsection (b) may state the choice of law rule for some but not all of the issuer's liability in a suit by a confirmer.

2. Because the confirmer or other nominated person may choose different law from that chosen by the issuer or may be located in a different jurisdiction and fail to choose law, it is possible that a confirmer or nominated person may be obligated to pay (under their law) but will not be entitled to payment from the issuer (under its law). Similarly, the rights of an unreimbursed issuer, confirmer, or nominated person against a beneficiary under Section 5–109, 5–110, or 5–117, will not necessarily be governed by the same law that applies to the issuer's or confirmer's obligation upon presentation. Because the UCP and other practice are incorporated in most international letters of credit, disputes arising from different legal obligations to honor have not been frequent. Since Section 5–108 incorporates standard practice, these problems should be further minimized—at least to the extent that the same practice is and continues to be widely followed.

3. This section does not permit what is now authorized by the nonuniform Section 5–102(4) in New York. Under the current law in New York a letter of credit that incorporates the UCP is not governed in any respect by Article 5. Under revised Section 5–116 letters of credit that incorporate the UCP or similar practice will still be subject to Article 5 in certain respects. First, incorporation of the UCP or other practice does not override the nonvariable terms of Article 5. Second, where there is no conflict between Article 5 and the relevant provision of the UCP or other practice, both apply. Third, practice provisions incorporated in a letter of credit will not be effective if they fail to comply with Section 5–103(c). Assume, for example, that a practice provision purported to free a party from any liability unless it were "grossly negligent" or that the practice generally limited the remedies that one party might have against another. Depending upon the circumstances, that disclaimer or limitation of liability might be ineffective because of Section 5–103(c).

Even though Article 5 is generally consistent with UCP 500, it is not necessarily consistent with other rules or with versions of the UCP that may be adopted after Article 5's revision, or with other practices that may develop.

Rules of practice incorporated in the letter of credit or other undertaking are those in effect when the letter of credit or other undertaking is issued. Except in the unusual cases discussed in the immediately preceding paragraph, practice adopted in a letter of credit will override the rules of Article 5 and the parties to letter of credit transactions must be familiar with practice (such as future versions of the UCP) that is explicitly adopted in letters of credit.

4. In several ways Article 5 conflicts with and overrides similar matters governed by Articles 3 and 4. For example, "draft" is more broadly defined in letter of credit practice than under Section 3–104. The time allowed for honor and the required notification of reasons for dishonor are different in letter of credit practice than in the handling of documentary and other drafts under Articles 3 and 4.

5. Subsection (e) must be read in conjunction with existing law governing subject matter jurisdiction. If the local law restricts a court to certain subject matter jurisdiction not including letter of credit disputes, subsection (e) does not authorize parties to choose that forum. For example, the parties' agreement under Section 5–116(e) would not confer jurisdiction on a probate court to decide a letter of credit case.

If the parties choose a forum under subsection (e) and if—because of other law—that forum will not take jurisdiction, the parties' agreement or undertaking should then be construed (for the purpose of forum selection) as though it did not contain a clause choosing a particular forum. That result is necessary to avoid sentencing the parties to eternal purgatory where neither the chosen State nor the State which would have jurisdiction but for the clause will take jurisdiction—the former in disregard of the clause and the latter in honor of the clause.

§ 5–117. Subrogation of Issuer, Applicant, and Nominated Person.

(a) An issuer that honors a beneficiary's presentation is subrogated to the rights of the beneficiary to the same extent as if the issuer were a secondary obligor of the underlying obligation owed to the beneficiary and of the applicant to the same extent as if the issuer were the secondary obligor of the underlying obligation owed to the applicant.

(b) An applicant that reimburses an issuer is subrogated to the rights of the issuer against any beneficiary, presenter, or nominated person to the same extent as if the applicant were the secondary obligor of the obligations owed to the issuer and has the rights of subrogation of the issuer to the rights of the beneficiary stated in subsection (a).

(c) A nominated person who pays or gives value against a draft or demand presented under a letter of credit is subrogated to the rights of:

(1) the issuer against the applicant to the same extent as if the nominated person were a secondary obligor of the obligation owed to the issuer by the applicant;

(2) the beneficiary to the same extent as if the nominated person were a secondary obligor of the underlying obligation owed to the beneficiary; and

(3) the applicant to same extent as if the nominated person were a secondary obligor of the underlying obligation owed to the applicant.

(d) Notwithstanding any agreement or term to the contrary, the rights of subrogation stated in subsections (a) and (b) do not arise until the issuer honors the letter of credit or otherwise pays and the rights in subsection (c) do not arise until the nominated person pays or otherwise gives value. Until then, the issuer, nominated person, and the applicant do not derive under this section present or prospective rights forming the basis of a claim, defense, or excuse.

Official Comment

1. By itself this section does not grant any right of subrogation. It grants only the right that would exist if the person seeking subrogation "were a secondary obligor." (The term "secondary obligor" refers to a surety, guarantor, or other person against whom or whose property an obligee has recourse with respect to the obligation of a third party. See Restatement of the Law Third, Suretyship and Guaranty § 1 (1996).) If the secondary obligor would not have a right to subrogation in the circumstances in which one is claimed under this section, none is granted by this section. In effect, the section does no more than to remove an impediment that some courts have found to subrogation because they conclude that the issuer's or other claimant's rights are "independent" of the underlying obligation. If, for example, a secondary obligor would not have a subrogation right because its payment did not fully satisfy the underlying obligation, none would be available under this section. The section indorses

the position of Judge Becker in *Tudor Development Group, Inc. v. United States Fidelity and Guaranty*, 968 F.2d 357 (3rd Cir. 1991).

2. To preserve the independence of the letter of credit obligation and to insure that subrogation not be used as an offensive weapon by an issuer or others, the admonition in subsection (d) must be carefully observed. Only one who has completed its performance in a letter of credit transaction can have a right to subrogation. For example, an issuer may not dishonor and then defend its dishonor or assert a setoff on the ground that it is subrogated to another person's rights. Nor may the issuer complain after honor that its subrogation rights have been impaired by any good faith dealings between the beneficiary and the applicant or any other person. Assume, for example, that the beneficiary under a standby letter of credit is a mortgagee. If the mortgagee were obliged to issue a release of the mortgage upon payment of the underlying debt (by the issuer under the letter of credit), that release might impair the issuer's rights of subrogation, but the beneficiary would have no liability to the issuer for having granted that release.

§ 5–118. Security Interest of Issuer or Nominated Person.

(a) An issuer or nominated person has a security interest in a document presented under a letter of credit to the extent that the issuer or nominated person honors or gives value for the presentation.

(b) So long as and to the extent that an issuer or nominated person has not been reimbursed or has not otherwise recovered the value given with respect to a security interest in a document under subsection (a), the security interest continues and is subject to Article 9, but:

(1) a security agreement is not necessary to make the security interest enforceable under Section 9–203(b)(3);

(2) if the document is presented in a medium other than a written or other tangible medium, the security interest is perfected; and

(3) if the document is presented in a written or other tangible medium and is not a certificated security, chattel paper, a document of title, an instrument, or a letter of credit, the security interest is perfected and has priority over a conflicting security interest in the document so long as the debtor does not have possession of the document.

As added in 1999.

Official Comment

1. This section gives the issuer of a letter of credit or a nominated person thereunder an automatic perfected security interest in a "document" (as that term is defined in Section 5–102(a)(6)). The security interest arises only if the document is presented to the issuer or nominated person under the letter of credit and only to the extent of the value that is given. This security interest is analogous to that awarded to a collecting bank under Section 4–210. Subsection (b) contains special rules governing the security interest arising under this section. In all other respects, a security interest arising under this section is subject to Article 9. See Section 9–109. Thus, for example, a security interest arising under this section may give rise to a security interest in proceeds under Section 9–315.

2. Subsection (b)(1) makes a security agreement unnecessary to the creation of a security interest under this section. Under subsection (b)(2), a security interest arising under this section is perfected if the document is presented in a medium other than a written or tangible medium. Documents that are written and that are not an otherwise-defined type of collateral under Article 9 (e.g., an invoice or inspection certificate) may be goods, in which an issuer or nominated person could perfect its security interest by possession. Because the definition of document in Section 5–102(a)(6) includes records (e.g., electronic records) that may not be goods, subsection (b)(2) provides for automatic perfection (i.e., without filing or possession).

Under subsection (b)(3), if the document (i) is in a written or tangible medium, (ii) is not a certificated security, chattel paper, a document of title, an instrument, or a letter of credit, and (iii) is not in the debtor's possession, the security interest is perfected and has priority over a conflicting security interest. If the document is a type of tangible collateral that subsection (b)(3) excludes from its perfection and priority rules, the issuer or nominated person must comply with the normal method of perfection (e.g., possession of an instrument) and is subject to the applicable Article 9 priority rules. Documents to which subsection (b)(3) applies may be important to an issuer or nominated person. For example, a confirmer who pays the beneficiary must be assured that its rights to all documents are not impaired. It will find it necessary to present all of the required documents to the issuer in order to be reimbursed. Moreover, when a nominated person sends documents to an issuer in connection with the nominated person's reimbursement, that activity is not a collection, enforcement, or disposition of collateral under Article 9.

One purpose of this section is to protect an issuer or nominated person from claims of a beneficiary's creditors. It is a fallback provision inasmuch as issuers and nominated persons frequently may obtain and perfect security interests under the usual Article 9 rules, and, in many cases, the documents will be owned by the issuer, nominated person, or applicant.

As added in 1999.

UCC ARTICLE 7 (2019)

DOCUMENTS OF TITLE

Article 7 was revised in 2003.

PART 1. GENERAL

PART 2. WAREHOUSE RECEIPTS: SPECIAL PROVISIONS

PART 3. BILLS OF LADING: SPECIAL PROVISIONS

PART 4. WAREHOUSE RECEIPTS AND BILLS OF LADING: GENERAL OBLIGATIONS

PART 5. WAREHOUSE RECEIPTS AND BILLS OF LADING: NEGOTIATION AND TRANSFER

PART 6. WAREHOUSE RECEIPTS AND BILLS OF LADING: MISCELLANEOUS PROVISIONS

PART 7. MISCELLANEOUS PROVISIONS

National Conference of Commissioners on Uniform State Laws

DRAFTING COMMITTEE

Henry Deeb Gabriel, Jr., New Orleans, Louisiana, *Chair*
Edward V. Cattell, Jr., Philadelphia, Pennsylvania, *The American Law Institute Representative*
Patricia Brumfield Fry, Columbia, Missouri
Sandra S. Stern, New York, New York
Neal Ossen, Hartford, Connecticut, *Enactment Plan Coordinator*
Drew Kershen, Norman, Oklahoma, *Co-Reporter*
Linda J. Rusch, St. Paul, Minnesota, *The American Law Institute Representative and Co-Reporter*

EX OFFICIO

K. King Burnett, Salisbury, Maryland, *President*
Joseph P. Mazurek, Helena, Montana, *Division Chair*

AMERICAN BAR ASSOCIATION ADVISOR

William H. Towle, Missoula, Montana

EXECUTIVE DIRECTOR

William H. Henning, Tuscaloosa, Alabama, *Executive Director*
William J. Pierce, Ann Arbor, Michigan, *Executive Director Emeritus*

PREFATORY NOTE

Article 7 is the last of the articles of the Uniform Commercial Code to be revised. The genesis of this project is twofold: to provide a framework for the further development of electronic documents of title and to update the article for modern times in light of state, federal and international developments. Each section has been reviewed to determine its suitability given modern practice, the need for medium and gender neutrality, and modern statutory drafting.

ARTICLE 7 (2019)

To provide for electronic documents of title, several definitions in Article 1 were revised including "bearer," "bill of lading," "delivery," "document of title," "holder," and "warehouse receipt." The concept of an electronic document of title allows for commercial practice to determine whether records issued by bailees are "in the regular course of business or financing" and are "treated as adequately evidencing that the person in possession or control of the record is entitled to receive, control, hold, and dispose of the record and the goods the record covers." Rev. Section 1–201(b)(16). Such records in electronic form are electronic documents of title and in tangible form are tangible documents of title. Conforming amendments to other Articles of the UCC are also necessary to fully integrate electronic documents of title into the UCC. Conforming amendments to other Articles of the UCC are contained in Appendix I. [*Note from West Advisory Panel: Article 7 conforming amendments are incorporated in the affected sections so the referenced appendix is not included in this volume.*]

Key to the integration of the electronic document of title scheme is the concept of "control" defined in Section 7–106. This definition is adapted from the Uniform Electronic Transactions Act § 16 on Transferrable Records and from Uniform Commercial Code § 9–105 concerning control of electronic chattel paper. Control of an electronic document of title is the conceptual equivalent to possession and indorsement of a tangible document of title. Of equal importance is the acknowledgment that parties may desire to substitute an electronic document of title for an already-issued paper document and vice versa. Section 7–105 sets forth the minimum requirements that need to be fulfilled in order to give effect to the substitute document issued in the alternate medium. To the extent possible, the rules for electronic documents of title are the same or as similar as possible to the rules for tangible documents of title. If a rule is meant to be limited to one medium or the other, that is clearly stated. Rules that reference documents of title, warehouse receipts, or bills of lading without a designation to "electronic" or "tangible" apply to documents of title in either medium. As with tangible negotiable documents of title, electronic negotiable documents of title may be negotiated and duly negotiated. Section 7–501.

Other changes that have been made are:

1. New definitions of "carrier," "good faith," "record", "sign" and "shipper" in Section 7–102.

2. Deletion of references to tariffs or filed classifications given the deregulation of the affected industries. See e.g. section 7–103 and 7–309.

3. Clarifying the rules regarding when a document is nonnegotiable. Section 7–104.

4. Making clear when rules apply just to warehouse receipts or bills of lading, thus eliminating the need for former section 7–105.

5. Clarifying that particular terms need not be included in order to have a valid warehouse receipt. Section 7–202.

6. Broadening the ability of the warehouse to make an effective limitation of liability in its warehouse receipt or storage agreement in accord with commercial practice. Section 7–204.

7. Allowing a warehouse to have a lien on goods covered by a storage agreement and clarifying the priority rules regarding the claim of a warehouse lien as against other interests. Section 7–209.

8. Conforming language usage to modern shipping practice. Sections 7–301 and 7–302.

9. Clarifying the extent of the carrier's lien. Section 7–307.

10. Adding references to Article 2A when appropriate. See e.g. Sections 7–503, 7–504, 7–509.

11. Clarifying that the warranty made by negotiation or delivery of a document of title should apply only in the case of a voluntary transfer of possession or control of the document. Section 7–507.

12. Providing greater flexibility to a court regarding adequate protection against loss when ordering delivery of the goods or issuance of a substitute document. Section 7–601.

13. Providing conforming amendments to the other Articles of the Uniform Commercial Code to accommodate electronic documents of title.

Legislative Note: All cross-references in this draft to Article 1 are to Revised Article 1 (2001). In the event a state has not enacted Revised Article 1, the cross-references should be changed to refer to the relevant sections in former Article 1.

PART 1
GENERAL

§ 7-101. Short Title.

This article may be cited as Uniform Commercial Code-Documents of Title.

Official Comment

Prior Uniform Statutory Provision: Former Section 7-101.

Changes: Revised for style only.

This Article is a revision of the 1962 Official Text with Comments as amended since 1962. The 1962 Official Text was a consolidation and revision of the Uniform Warehouse Receipts Act and the Uniform Bills of Lading Act, and embraced the provisions of the Uniform Sales Act relating to negotiation of documents of title.

This Article does not contain the substantive criminal provisions found in the Uniform Warehouse Receipts and Bills of Lading Acts. These criminal provisions are inappropriate to a Commercial Code, and for the most part duplicate portions of the ordinary criminal law relating to frauds. This revision deletes the former Section 7-105 that provided that courts could apply a rule from Parts 2 and 3 by analogy to a situation not explicitly covered in the provisions on warehouse receipts or bills of lading when it was appropriate. This is, of course, an unexceptional proposition and need not be stated explicitly in the statute. Thus former Section 7-105 has been deleted. Whether applying a rule by analogy to a situation is appropriate depends upon the facts of each case.

The Article does not attempt to define the tort liability of bailees, except to hold certain classes of bailees to a minimum standard of reasonable care. For important classes of bailees, liabilities in case of loss, damages or destruction, as well as other legal questions associated with particular documents of title, are governed by federal statutes, international treaties, and in some cases regulatory state laws, which supersede the provisions of this Article in case of inconsistency. See Section 7-103.

§ 7-102. Definitions and Index of Definitions.

(a) In this article, unless the context otherwise requires:

(1) "Bailee" means a person that by a warehouse receipt, bill of lading, or other document of title acknowledges possession of goods and contracts to deliver them.

(2) "Carrier" means a person that issues a bill of lading.

(3) "Consignee" means a person named in a bill of lading to which or to whose order the bill promises delivery.

(4) "Consignor" means a person named in a bill of lading as the person from which the goods have been received for shipment.

(5) "Delivery order" means a record that contains an order to deliver goods directed to a warehouse, carrier, or other person that in the ordinary course of business issues warehouse receipts or bills of lading.

(6) "Good faith" means honesty in fact and the observance of reasonable commercial standards of fair dealing.

(7) "Goods" means all things that are treated as movable for the purposes of a contract for storage or transportation.

(8) "Issuer" means a bailee that issues a document of title or, in the case of an unaccepted delivery order, the person that orders the possessor of goods to deliver. The term includes a person for

which an agent or employee purports to act in issuing a document if the agent or employee has real or apparent authority to issue documents, even if the issuer did not receive any goods, the goods were misdescribed, or in any other respect the agent or employee violated the issuer's instructions.

(9) "Person entitled under the document" means the holder, in the case of a negotiable document of title, or the person to which delivery of the goods is to be made by the terms of, or pursuant to instructions in a record under, a nonnegotiable document of title.

(10) "Record" means information that is inscribed on a tangible medium or that is stored in an electronic or other medium and is retrievable in perceivable form.

(11) "Sign" means, with present intent to authenticate or adopt a record:

(A) to execute or adopt a tangible symbol; or

(B) to attach to or logically associate with the record an electronic sound, symbol, or process.

(12) "Shipper" means a person that enters into a contract of transportation with a carrier.

(13) "Warehouse" means a person engaged in the business of storing goods for hire.

(b) Definitions in other articles applying to this article and the sections in which they appear are:

(1) "Contract for sale", Section 2–106.

(2) "Lessee in ordinary course", Section 2A–103.

(3) "Receipt" of goods, Section 2–103.

(c) In addition, Article 1 contains general definitions and principles of construction and interpretation applicable throughout this article.

Legislative Note: If the state has enacted Revised Article 1, the definitions of "good faith" in subsection (a)(6) and "record" in (a)(10) need not be enacted in this section as they are contained in Article 1, Section 1–201. These subsections should be marked as "reserved" in order to provide for uniform numbering of subsections.

Official Comment

Prior Uniform Statutory Provision: Former Section 7–102.

Changes: New definitions of "carrier," "good faith," "record," "sign," and "shipper." Other definitions revised to accommodate electronic mediums.

Purposes:

1. "Bailee" is used in this Article as a blanket term to designate carriers, warehousemen and others who normally issue documents of title on the basis of goods which they have received. The definition does not, however, require actual possession of the goods. If a bailee acknowledges possession when it does not have possession, the bailee is bound by sections of this Article which declare the "bailee's" obligations. (See definition of "Issuer" in this section and Sections 7–203 and 7–301 on liability in case of non-receipt.) A "carrier" is one type of bailee and is defined as a person that issues a bill of lading. A "shipper" is a person who enters into the contract of transportation with the carrier. The definitions of "bailee," "consignee," "consignor," "goods", and "issuer", are unchanged in substance from prior law. "Document of title" is defined in Article 1, and may be in either tangible or electronic form.

2. The definition of warehouse receipt contained in the general definitions section of this Act (Section 1–201) does not require that the issuing warehouse be "lawfully engaged" in business or for profit. The warehouse's compliance with applicable state regulations such as the filing of a bond has no bearing on the substantive issues dealt with in this Article. Certainly the issuer's violations of law should not diminish its responsibility on documents the issuer has put in commercial circulation. But it is still essential that the business be storing goods "for hire" (Section 1–201 and this section). A person does not become a warehouse by storing its own goods.

3. When a delivery order has been accepted by the bailee it is for practical purposes indistinguishable from a warehouse receipt. Prior to such acceptance there is no basis for imposing obligations on the bailee other than the ordinary obligation of contract which the bailee may have assumed to the depositor of the goods. Delivery orders may be either electronic or tangible documents of title. See definition of "document of title" in Section 1–201.

4. The obligation of good faith imposed by this Article and by Article 1, Section 1–304 includes the observance of reasonable commercial standards of fair dealing.

5. The definitions of "record" and "sign" are included to facilitate electronic mediums. See comment 9 to Section 9–102 discussing "record" and the comment to amended Section 2–103 discussing "sign" [*referring to 2003 amendments to Article 2, withdrawn in 2011*].

6. "Person entitled under the document" is moved from former Section 7–403.

7. These definitions apply in this Article unless the context otherwise requires. The "context" is intended to refer to the context in which the defined term is used in the Uniform Commercial Code. The definition applies whenever the defined term is used unless the context in which the defined term is used in the statute indicates that the term was not used in its defined sense. See comment to Section 1–201.

Cross References:

Point 1: Sections 1–201, 7–203 and 7–301.
Point 2: Sections 1–201 and 7–203.
Point 3: Section 1–201.
Point 4: Section 1–304.
Point 5: Section 9–102 and 2–103.
See general comment to document of title in Section 1–201.

Definitional Cross References:

"Bill of lading". Section 1–201.
"Contract". Section 1–201.
"Contract for sale". Section 2–106.
"Delivery". Section 1–201.
"Document of title". Section 1–201.
"Person". Section 1–201.
"Purchase". Section 1–201.
"Receipt of goods". Section 2–103.
"Right". Section 1–201.
"Warehouse receipt". Section 1–201.

§ 7–103. Relation of Article to Treaty or Statute.

(a) This article is subject to any treaty or statute of the United States or regulatory statute of this state to the extent the treaty, statute, or regulatory statute is applicable.

(b) This article does not modify or repeal any law prescribing the form or content of a document of title or the services or facilities to be afforded by a bailee, or otherwise regulating a bailee's business in respects not specifically treated in this article. However, violation of such a law does not affect the status of a document of title that otherwise is within the definition of a document of title.

(c) This [act] modifies, limits, and supersedes the federal Electronic Signatures in Global and National Commerce Act (15 U.S.C. Section 7001, et. seq.) but does not modify, limit, or supersede Section 101(c) of that act (15 U.S.C. Section 7001(c)) or authorize electronic delivery of any of the notices described in Section 103(b) of that act (15 U.S.C. Section 7003(b)).

(d) To the extent there is a conflict between [the Uniform Electronic Transactions Act] and this article, this article governs.

Legislative Note: In states that have not enacted the Uniform Electronic Transactions Act in some form, states should consider their own state laws to determine whether there is a conflict between the provisions of this article and those laws particularly as those other laws may affect electronic documents of title.

Official Comment

Prior Uniform Statutory Provision: Former Sections 7–103 and 10–104.

Changes: Deletion of references to tariffs and classifications; incorporation of former Section 10–104 into subsection (b), provide for intersection with federal and state law governing electronic transactions.

Purposes:

1. To make clear what would of course be true without the Section, that applicable Federal law is paramount.

2. To make clear also that regulatory state statutes (such as those fixing or authorizing a commission to fix rates and prescribe services, authorizing different charges for goods of different values, and limiting liability for loss to the declared value on which the charge was based) are not affected by the Article and are controlling on the matters which they cover unless preempted by federal law. The reference in former Section 7–103 to tariffs, classifications, and regulations filed or issued pursuant to regulatory state statutes has been deleted as inappropriate in the modern era of diminished regulation of carriers and warehouses. If a regulatory scheme requires a carrier or warehouse to issue a tariff or classification, that tariff or classification would be given effect via the state regulatory scheme that this Article recognizes as controlling. Permissive tariffs or classifications would not displace the provisions of this act, pursuant to this section, but may be given effect through the ability of parties to incorporate those terms by reference into their agreement.

3. The document of title provisions of this act supplement the federal law and regulatory state law governing bailees. This Article focuses on the commercial importance and usage of documents of title. *State ex. rel Public Service Commission v. Gunkelman & Sons, Inc.*, 219 N.W.2d 853 (N.D. 1974).

4. Subsection (c) is included to make clear the interrelationship between the federal Electronic Signatures in Global and National Commerce Act and this article and the conforming amendments to other articles of the Uniform Commercial Code promulgated as part of the revision of this article. Section 102 of the federal act allows a State statute to modify, limit, or supersede the provisions of Section 101 of the federal act. See the comments to Revised Article 1, Section 1–108.

5. Subsection (d) makes clear that once this article is in effect, its provisions regarding electronic commerce and regarding electronic documents of title control in the event there is a conflict with the provisions of the Uniform Electronic Transactions Act or other applicable state law governing electronic transactions.

Cross References:

Sections 1–108, 7–201, 7–202, 7–204, 7–206, 7–309, 7–401, 7–403.

Definitional Cross Reference:

"Bill of lading". Section 1–201.

§ 7–104. Negotiable and Nonnegotiable Document of Title.

(a) Except as otherwise provided in subsection (c), a document of title is negotiable if by its terms the goods are to be delivered to bearer or to the order of a named person.

(b) A document of title other than one described in subsection (a) is nonnegotiable. A bill of lading that states that the goods are consigned to a named person is not made negotiable by a provision that the goods are to be delivered only against an order in a record signed by the same or another named person.

(c) A document of title is nonnegotiable if, at the time it is issued, the document has a conspicuous legend, however expressed, that it is nonnegotiable.

Official Comment

Prior Uniform Statutory Provision: Former Section 7–104.

Changes: Subsection (a) is revised to reflect modern style and trade practice. Subsection (b) is revised for style and medium neutrality. Subsection (c) is new.

Purposes:

1. This Article deals with a class of commercial paper representing commodities in storage or transportation. This "commodity paper" is to be distinguished from what might be called "money paper" dealt with in the Article of this Act on Commercial Paper (Article 3) and "investment paper" dealt with in the Article of this Act on Investment Securities (Article 8). The class of "commodity paper" is designated "document of title" following the terminology of the Uniform Sales Act Section 76. Section 1–201. The distinctions between negotiable and nonnegotiable documents in this section makes the most important subclassification employed in the Article, in that the holder of negotiable documents may acquire more rights than its transferor had (See Section 7–502). The former Section 7–104, which provided that a document of title was negotiable if it runs to a named person or

assigns if such designation was recognized in overseas trade, has been deleted as not necessary in light of current commercial practice.

A document of title is negotiable only if it satisfies this section. "Deliverable on proper indorsement and surrender of this receipt" will not render a document negotiable. Bailees often include such provisions as a means of insuring return of nonnegotiable receipts for record purposes. Such language may be regarded as insistence by the bailee upon a particular kind of receipt in connection with delivery of the goods. Subsection (a) makes it clear that a document is not negotiable which provides for delivery to order or bearer only if written instructions to that effect are given by a named person. Either tangible or electronic documents of title may be negotiable if the document meets the requirement of this section.

2. Subsection (c) is derived from Section 3-104(d). Prior to issuance of the document of title, an issuer may stamp or otherwise provide by a notation on the document that it is nonnegotiable even if the document would otherwise comply with the requirement of subsection (a). Once issued as a negotiable document of title, the document cannot be changed from a negotiable document to a nonnegotiable document. A document of title that is nonnegotiable cannot be made negotiable by stamping or providing a notation that the document is negotiable. The only way to make a document of title negotiable is to comply with subsection (a). A negotiable document of title may fail to be duly negotiated if the negotiation does not comply with the requirements for "due negotiation" stated in Section 7-501.

Cross Reference:

Sections 7-501 and 7-502.

Definitional Cross References:

"Bearer". Section 1-201.
"Bill of lading". Section 1-201.
"Delivery". Section 1-201.
"Document of title". Section 1-201.
"Person". Section 1-201.
"Sign". Section 7-102
"Warehouse receipt". Section 1-201.

§ 7-105. Reissuance in Alternative Medium.

(a) Upon request of a person entitled under an electronic document of title, the issuer of the electronic document may issue a tangible document of title as a substitute for the electronic document if:

(1) the person entitled under the electronic document surrenders control of the document to the issuer; and

(2) the tangible document when issued contains a statement that it is issued in substitution for the electronic document.

(b) Upon issuance of a tangible document of title in substitution for an electronic document of title in accordance with subsection (a):

(1) the electronic document ceases to have any effect or validity; and

(2) the person that procured issuance of the tangible document warrants to all subsequent persons entitled under the tangible document that the warrantor was a person entitled under the electronic document when the warrantor surrendered control of the electronic document to the issuer.

(c) Upon request of a person entitled under a tangible document of title, the issuer of the tangible document may issue an electronic document of title as a substitute for the tangible document if:

(1) the person entitled under the tangible document surrenders possession of the document to the issuer; and

(2) the electronic document when issued contains a statement that it is issued in substitution for the tangible document.

(d) Upon issuance of an electronic document of title in substitution for a tangible document of title in accordance with subsection (c):

(1) the tangible document ceases to have any effect or validity; and

(2) the person that procured issuance of the electronic document warrants to all subsequent persons entitled under the electronic document that the warrantor was a person entitled under the tangible document when the warrantor surrendered possession of the tangible document to the issuer.

Official Comment

Prior Uniform Statutory Provisions: None.

Other relevant law: UNCITRAL Draft Instrument on the Carriage of Goods by Sea Transport Law.

Purpose:

1. This section allows for documents of title issued in one medium to be reissued in another medium. This section applies to both negotiable and nonnegotiable documents. This section sets forth minimum requirements for giving the reissued document effect and validity. The issuer is not required to issue a document in an alternative medium and if the issuer chooses to do so, it may impose additional requirements. Because a document of title imposes obligations on the issuer of the document, it is imperative for the issuer to be the one who issues the substitute document in order for the substitute document to be effective and valid.

2. The request must be made to the issuer by the person entitled to enforce the document of title (Section 7-102(a)(9)) and that person must surrender possession or control of the original document to the issuer. The reissued document must have a notation that it has been issued as a substitute for the original document. These minimum requirements must be met in order to give the substitute document effect and validity. If these minimum requirements are not met for issuance of a substitute document of title, the original document of title continues to be effective and valid. Section 7-402. However, if the minimum requirements imposed by this section are met, in addition to any other requirements that the issuer may impose, the substitute document will be the document that is effective and valid.

3. To protect parties who subsequently take the substitute document of title, the person who procured issuance of the substitute document warrants that it was a person entitled under the original document at the time it surrendered possession or control of the original document to the issuer. This warranty is modeled after the warranty found in Section 4-209.

Cross Reference:

Sections 7-106, 7-402 and 7-601.

Definitional Cross Reference:

"Person entitled to enforce". Section 7-102.

§ 7-106. Control of Electronic Document of Title.

(a) A person has control of an electronic document of title if a system employed for evidencing the transfer of interests in the electronic document reliably establishes that person as the person to which the electronic document was issued or transferred.

(b) A system satisfies subsection (a), and a person is deemed to have control of an electronic document of title, if the document is created, stored, and assigned in such a manner that:

(1) a single authoritative copy of the document exists which is unique, identifiable, and, except as otherwise provided in paragraphs (4), (5), and (6), unalterable;

(2) the authoritative copy identifies the person asserting control as:

(A) the person to which the document was issued; or

(B) if the authoritative copy indicates that the document has been transferred, the person to which the document was most recently transferred;

(3) the authoritative copy is communicated to and maintained by the person asserting control or its designated custodian;

(4) copies or amendments that add or change an identified assignee of the authoritative copy can be made only with the consent of the person asserting control;

(5) each copy of the authoritative copy and any copy of a copy is readily identifiable as a copy that is not the authoritative copy; and

(6) any amendment of the authoritative copy is readily identifiable as authorized or unauthorized.

Official Comment

Prior Uniform Statutory Provision: Uniform Electronic Transactions Act Section 16.

Purpose:

1. The section defines "control" for electronic documents of title and derives its rules from the Uniform Electronic Transactions Act § 16 on transferrable records. Unlike UETA § 16, however, a document of title may be reissued in an alternative medium pursuant to Section 7–105. At any point in time in which a document of title is in electronic form, the control concept of this section is relevant. As under UETA § 16, the control concept embodied in this section provides the legal framework for developing systems for electronic documents of title.

2. Control of an electronic document of title substitutes for the concept of indorsement and possession in the tangible document of title context. See Section 7–501. A person with a tangible document of title delivers the document by voluntarily transferring possession and a person with an electronic document of title delivers the document by voluntarily transferring control. (Delivery is defined in Section 1–201).

3. Subsection (a) sets forth the general rule that the "system employed for evidencing the transfer of interests in the electronic document reliably establishes that person as the person to which the electronic document was issued or transferred." The key to having a system that satisfies this test is that identity of *the* person to which the document was issued or transferred must be reliably established. Of great importance to the functioning of the control concept is to be able to demonstrate, at any point in time, *the person* entitled under the electronic document. For example, a carrier may issue an electronic bill of lading by having the required information in a database that is encrypted and accessible by virtue of a password. If the computer system in which the required information is maintained identifies the person as *the* person to which the electronic bill of lading was issued or transferred, that person has control of the electronic document of title. That identification may be by virtue of passwords or other encryption methods. Registry systems may satisfy this test. For example, see the electronic warehouse receipt system established pursuant to 7 C.F.R. Part 735. This Article leaves to the market place the development of sufficient technologies and business practices that will meet the test.

An electronic document of title is evidenced by a record consisting of information stored in an electronic medium. Section 1–201. For example, a record in a computer database could be an electronic document of title assuming that it otherwise meets the definition of document of title. To the extent that third parties wish to deal in paper mediums, Section 7–105 provides a mechanism for exiting the electronic environment by having the issuer reissue the document of title in a tangible medium. Thus if a person entitled to enforce an electronic document of title causes the information in the record to be printed onto paper without the issuer's involvement in issuing the document of title pursuant to Section 7–105, that paper is not a document of title.

4. Subsection (a) sets forth the general test for control. Subsection (b) sets forth a safe harbor test that if satisfied, results in control under the general test in subsection (a). The test in subsection (b) is also used in Section 9–105 although Section 9–105 does not include the general test of subsection (a) [*Article 9 version prior to the 2010 amendments*]. Under subsection (b), at any point in time, a party should be able to identify the single authoritative copy which is unique and identifiable as the authoritative copy. This does not mean that once created that the authoritative copy need be static and never moved or copied from its original location. To the extent that backup systems exist which result in multiple copies, the key to this idea is that at any point in time, the one authoritative copy needs to be unique and identifiable.

Parties may not by contract provide that control exists. The test for control is a factual test that depends upon whether the general test in subsection (a) or the safe harbor in subsection (b) is satisfied.

5. Article 7 has historically provided for rights under documents of title and rights of transferees of documents of title as those rights relate to the goods covered by the document. Third parties may possess or have control of documents of title. While misfeasance or negligence in failure to transfer or misdelivery of the document by those third parties may create serious issues, this Article has never dealt with those issues as it relates to tangible documents of title, preferring to leave those issues to the law of contracts, agency and tort law. In the electronic document of title regime, third party registry systems are just beginning to develop. It is very difficult to write rules regulating those third parties without some definitive sense of how the third party registry systems

will be structured. Systems that are evolving to date tend to be "closed" systems in which all participants must sign on to the master agreement which provides for rights as against the registry system as well as rights among the members. In those closed systems, the document of title never leaves the system so the parties rely upon the master agreement as to rights against the registry for its failures in dealing with the document. This article contemplates that those "closed" systems will continue to evolve and that the control mechanism in this statute provides a method for the participants in the closed system to achieve the benefits of obtaining control allowed by this article.

This article also contemplates that parties will evolve open systems where parties need not be subject to a master agreement. In an open system a party that is expecting to obtain rights through an electronic document may not be a party to the master agreement. To the extent that open systems evolve by use of the control concept contained in this section, the law of contracts, agency, and torts as it applies to the registry's misfeasance or negligence concerning the transfer of control of the electronic document will allocate the risks and liabilities of the parties as that other law now does so for third parties who hold tangible documents and fail to deliver the documents.

Cross Reference:

Sections 7–105 and 7–501.

Definitional Cross References:

"Delivery". Section 1–201.
"Document of title". Section 1–201.

PART 2

WAREHOUSE RECEIPTS: SPECIAL PROVISIONS

§ 7–201. Person That May Issue a Warehouse Receipt; Storage Under Bond.

(a) A warehouse receipt may be issued by any warehouse.

(b) If goods, including distilled spirits and agricultural commodities, are stored under a statute requiring a bond against withdrawal or a license for the issuance of receipts in the nature of warehouse receipts, a receipt issued for the goods is deemed to be a warehouse receipt even if issued by a person that is the owner of the goods and is not a warehouse.

Official Comment

Prior Uniform Statutory Provision: Former Section 7–201.

Changes: Update for style only.

Purposes:

It is not intended by re-enactment of subsection (a) to repeal any provisions of special licensing or other statutes regulating who may become a warehouse. Limitations on the transfer of the receipts and criminal sanctions for violation of such limitations are not impaired. Section 7–103. Compare Section 7–401(4) on the liability of the issuer in such cases. Subsection (b) covers receipts issued by the owner for whiskey or other goods stored in bonded warehouses under such statutes as 26 U.S.C. Chapter 51.

Cross References:

Sections 7–103, 7–401.

Definitional Cross References:

"Warehouse receipt". Section 1–201.
"Warehouse". Section 7–102.

§ 7-202. Form of Warehouse Receipt; Effect of Omission.

(a) A warehouse receipt need not be in any particular form.

(b) Unless a warehouse receipt provides for each of the following, the warehouse is liable for damages caused to a person injured by its omission:

(1) a statement of the location of the warehouse facility where the goods are stored;

(2) the date of issue of the receipt;

(3) the unique identification code of the receipt;

(4) a statement whether the goods received will be delivered to the bearer, to a named person, or to a named person or its order;

(5) the rate of storage and handling charges, unless goods are stored under a field warehousing arrangement, in which case a statement of that fact is sufficient on a nonnegotiable receipt;

(6) a description of the goods or the packages containing them;

(7) the signature of the warehouse or its agent;

(8) if the receipt is issued for goods that the warehouse owns, either solely, jointly, or in common with others, a statement of the fact of that ownership; and

(9) a statement of the amount of advances made and of liabilities incurred for which the warehouse claims a lien or security interest, unless the precise amount of advances made or liabilities incurred, at the time of the issue of the receipt, is unknown to the warehouse or to its agent that issued the receipt, in which case a statement of the fact that advances have been made or liabilities incurred and the purpose of the advances or liabilities is sufficient.

(c) A warehouse may insert in its receipt any terms that are not contrary to [the Uniform Commercial Code] and do not impair its obligation of delivery under Section 7-403 or its duty of care under Section 7-204. Any contrary provision is ineffective.

Official Comment

Prior Uniform Statutory Provision: Former Section 7-202.

Changes: Language is updated to accommodate electronic commerce and to reflect modern style.

Purposes:

1. This section does not displace any particular legislation that requires other terms in a warehouse receipt or that may require a particular form of a warehouse receipt. This section does not require that a warehouse receipt be issued. A warehouse receipt that is issued need not contain any of the terms listed in subsection (b) in order to qualify as a warehouse receipt as long as the receipt falls within the definition of "warehouse receipt" in Article 1. Thus the title has been changed to eliminate the phrase "essential terms" as provided in prior law. The only consequence of a warehouse receipt not containing any term listed in subsection (b) is that a person injured by a term's omission has a right as against the warehouse for harm caused by the omission. Cases, such as *In re Celotex Corp.*, 134 B. R. 993 (Bankr. M.D. Fla. 1991), that held that in order to have a valid warehouse receipt all of the terms listed in this section must be contained in the receipt, are disapproved.

2. The unique identification code referred to in subsection (b)(3) can include any combination of letters, number, signs, and/or symbols that provide a unique identification. Whether an electronic or tangible warehouse receipt contains a signature will be resolved with the definition of sign in Section 7-102.

Cross References:

Sections 7-103 and 7-401.

Definitional Cross References:

"Bearer". Section 1-201.
"Delivery". Section 1-201.
"Goods". Section 7-102.
"Person". Section 1-201.

"Security interest". Section 1-201.
"Sign". Section 7-102.
"Term". Section 1-201.
"Warehouse receipt". Section 1-201.
"Warehouse". Section 7-102.

§ 7-203. Liability for Nonreceipt or Misdescription.

A party to or purchaser for value in good faith of a document of title, other than a bill of lading, that relies upon the description of the goods in the document may recover from the issuer damages caused by the nonreceipt or misdescription of the goods, except to the extent that:

(1) the document conspicuously indicates that the issuer does not know whether all or part of the goods in fact were received or conform to the description, such as a case in which the description is in terms of marks or labels or kind, quantity, or condition, or the receipt or description is qualified by "contents, condition, and quality unknown", "said to contain", or words of similar import, if the indication is true; or

(2) the party or purchaser otherwise has notice of the nonreceipt or misdescription.

Official Comment

Prior Uniform Statutory Provision: Former Section 7-203.

Changes: Changes to this section are for style only.

Purpose:

This section is a simplified restatement of existing law as to the method by which a bailee may avoid responsibility for the accuracy of descriptions which are made by or in reliance upon information furnished by the depositor. The issuer is liable on documents issued by an agent, contrary to instructions of its principal, without receiving goods. No disclaimer of the latter liability is permitted.

Cross Reference:

Section 7-301.

Definitional Cross References:

"Conspicuous". Section 1-201.
"Document of title". Section 1-201.
"Goods". Section 7-102.
"Good Faith". Section 1-201. [7-102]
"Issuer". Section 7-102.
"Notice". Section 1-202.
"Party". Section 1-201.
"Purchaser". Section 1-201.
"Receipt of goods". Section 2-103.
"Value". Section 1-204.

§ 7-204. Duty of Care; Contractual Limitation of Warehouse's Liability.

(a) A warehouse is liable for damages for loss of or injury to the goods caused by its failure to exercise care with regard to the goods that a reasonably careful person would exercise under similar circumstances. Unless otherwise agreed, the warehouse is not liable for damages that could not have been avoided by the exercise of that care.

(b) Damages may be limited by a term in the warehouse receipt or storage agreement limiting the amount of liability in case of loss or damage beyond which the warehouse is not liable. Such a limitation is not effective with respect to the warehouse's liability for conversion to its own use. On request of the bailor in a record at the time of signing the storage agreement or within a reasonable time after receipt of the warehouse receipt, the warehouse's liability may be increased on part or all of the goods covered by the storage agreement or the warehouse receipt. In this event, increased rates may be charged based on an increased valuation of the goods.

(c) Reasonable provisions as to the time and manner of presenting claims and commencing actions based on the bailment may be included in the warehouse receipt or storage agreement.

[(d) This section does not modify or repeal [Insert reference to any statute that imposes a higher responsibility upon the warehouse or invalidates a contractual limitation that would be permissible under this Article].]

Legislative Note: Insert in subsection (d) a reference to any statute which imposes a higher responsibility upon the warehouse or invalidates a contractual limitation that would be permissible under this Article. If no such statutes exist, this section should be deleted.

Official Comment

Prior Uniform Statutory Provision: Former Section 7-204.

Changes: Updated to reflect modern, standard commercial practices.

Purposes of Changes:

1. Subsection (a) continues the rule without change from former Section 7-204 on the warehouse's obligation to exercise reasonable care.

2. Former Section 7-204(2) required that the term limiting damages do so by setting forth a specific liability per article or item or of a value per unit of weight. This requirement has been deleted as out of step with modern industry practice. Under subsection (b) a warehouse may limit its liability for damages for loss of or damage to the goods by a term in the warehouse receipt or storage agreement without the term constituting an impermissible disclaimer of the obligation of reasonable care. The parties cannot disclaim by contract the warehouse's obligation of care. Section 1-302. For example, limitations based upon per unit of weight, per package, per occurrence, or per receipt as well as limitations based upon a multiple of the storage rate may be commercially appropriate. As subsection (d) makes clear, the states or the federal government may supplement this section with more rigid standards of responsibility for some or all bailees.

3. Former Section 7-204(2) also provided that an increased rate can not be charged if contrary to a tariff. That language has been deleted. If a tariff is required under state or federal law, pursuant to Section 7-103(a), the tariff would control over the rule of this section allowing an increased rate. The provisions of a non-mandatory tariff may be incorporated by reference in the parties' agreement. See Comment 2 to Section 7-103. Subsection (c) deletes the reference to tariffs for the same reason that the reference has been omitted in subsection (b).

4. As under former Section 7-204(2), subsection (b) provides that a limitation of damages is ineffective if the warehouse has converted the goods to its own use. A mere failure to redeliver the goods is not conversion to the warehouse's own use. See *Adams v. Ryan & Christie Storage, Inc.*, 563 F. Supp. 409 (E.D. Pa. 1983) aff'd 725 F.2d 666 (3rd Cir. 1983). Cases such as *I.C.C. Metals Inc. v. Municipal Warehouse Co.*, 409 N.E.2d 849 (N.Y. Ct. App. 1980) holding that mere failure to redeliver results in a presumption of conversion to the warehouse's own use are disapproved. "Conversion to its own use" is narrower than the idea of conversion generally. Cases such as *Lipman v. Peterson*, 575 P.2d 19 (Kan. 1978) holding to the contrary are disapproved.

5. Storage agreements commonly establish the contractual relationship between warehouses and depositors who have an on-going relationship. The storage agreement may allow for the movement of goods into and out of a warehouse without the necessity of issuing or amending a warehouse receipt upon each entry or exit of goods from the warehouse.

Cross References:

Sections 1-302, 7-103, 7-309 and 7-403.

Definitional Cross References:

"Goods". Section 7-102.
"Reasonable time". Section 1-204.
"Sign". Section 7-102.
"Term". Section 1-201.
"Value". Section 1-204.
"Warehouse receipt". Section 1-201.
"Warehouse". Section 7-102.

§ 7–205. Title Under Warehouse Receipt Defeated in Certain Cases.

A buyer in ordinary course of business of fungible goods sold and delivered by a warehouse that is also in the business of buying and selling such goods takes the goods free of any claim under a warehouse receipt even if the receipt is negotiable and has been duly negotiated.

Official Comment

Prior Uniform Statutory Provision: Former Section 7–205.

Changes: Changes for style only.

Purposes:

1. The typical case covered by this section is that of the warehouse-dealer in grain, and the substantive question at issue is whether in case the warehouse becomes insolvent the receipt holders shall be able to trace and recover grain shipped to farmers and other purchasers from the elevator. This was possible under the old acts, although courts were eager to find estoppels to prevent it. The practical difficulty of tracing fungible grain means that the preservation of this theoretical right adds little to the commercial acceptability of negotiable grain receipts, which really circulate on the credit of the warehouse. Moreover, on default of the warehouse, the receipt holders at least share in what grain remains, whereas retaking the grain from a good faith cash purchaser reduces the purchaser completely to the status of general creditor in a situation where there was very little the purchaser could do to guard against the loss. Compare 15 U.S.C. Section 714p enacted in 1955.

2. This provision applies to both negotiable and nonnegotiable warehouse receipts. The concept of due negotiation is provided for in 7–501. The definition of "buyer in ordinary course" is in Article 1 and provides, among other things, that a buyer must either have possession or a right to obtain the goods under Article 2 in order to be a buyer in ordinary course. This section requires actual delivery of the fungible goods to the buyer in ordinary course. Delivery requires voluntary transfer of possession of the fungible goods to the buyer. See amended Section 2–103 [*2003 amendments to Article 2, withdrawn in 2011*] This section is not satisfied by the delivery of the document of title to the buyer in ordinary course.

Cross References:

Sections 2–403 and 9–320.

Definitional Cross References:

"Buyer in ordinary course of business". Section 1–201.
"Delivery". Section 1–201.
"Duly negotiate". Section 7–501.
"Fungible" goods. Section 1–201.
"Goods". Section 7–102.
"Value". Section 1–204.
"Warehouse receipt". Section 1–201.
"Warehouse". Section 7–102.

§ 7–206. Termination of Storage at Warehouse's Option.

(a) A warehouse, by giving notice to the person on whose account the goods are held and any other person known to claim an interest in the goods, may require payment of any charges and removal of the goods from the warehouse at the termination of the period of storage fixed by the document of title or, if a period is not fixed, within a stated period not less than 30 days after the warehouse gives notice. If the goods are not removed before the date specified in the notice, the warehouse may sell them pursuant to Section 7–210.

(b) If a warehouse in good faith believes that goods are about to deteriorate or decline in value to less than the amount of its lien within the time provided in subsection (a) and Section 7–210, the warehouse may specify in the notice given under subsection (a) any reasonable shorter time for removal of the goods and, if the goods are not removed, may sell them at public sale held not less than one week after a single advertisement or posting.

(c) If, as a result of a quality or condition of the goods of which the warehouse did not have notice at the time of deposit, the goods are a hazard to other property, the warehouse facilities, or other persons, the

warehouse may sell the goods at public or private sale without advertisement or posting on reasonable notification to all persons known to claim an interest in the goods. If the warehouse, after a reasonable effort, is unable to sell the goods, it may dispose of them in any lawful manner and does not incur liability by reason of that disposition.

(d) A warehouse shall deliver the goods to any person entitled to them under this article upon due demand made at any time before sale or other disposition under this section.

(e) A warehouse may satisfy its lien from the proceeds of any sale or disposition under this section but shall hold the balance for delivery on the demand of any person to which the warehouse would have been bound to deliver the goods.

Official Comment

Prior Uniform Statutory Provision: Former Section 7-206.

Changes: Changes for style.

Purposes:

1. This section provides for three situations in which the warehouse may terminate storage for reasons other then *[should be "than"]* enforcement of its lien as permitted by Section 7-210. Most warehousing is for an indefinite term, the bailor being entitled to delivery on reasonable demand. It is necessary to define the warehouse's power to terminate the bailment, since it would be commercially intolerable to allow warehouses to order removal of the goods on short notice. The thirty day period provided where the document does not carry its own period of termination corresponds to commercial practice of computing rates on a monthly basis. The right to terminate under subsection (a) includes a right to require payment of "any charges", but does not depend on the existence of unpaid charges.

2. In permitting expeditious disposition of perishable and hazardous goods the pre-Code Uniform Warehouse Receipts Act, Section 34, made no distinction between cases where the warehouse knowingly undertook to store such goods and cases where the goods were discovered to be of that character subsequent to storage. The former situation presents no such emergency as justifies the summary power of removal and sale. Subsections (b) and (c) distinguish between the two situations. The reason of this section should apply if the goods become hazardous during the course of storage. The process for selling the goods described in Section 7-210 governs the sale of goods under this section except as provided in subsections (b) and (c) for the situations described in those subsections respectively.

3. Protection of its lien is the only interest which the warehouse has to justify summary sale of perishable goods which are not hazardous. This same interest must be recognized when the stored goods, although not perishable, decline in market value to a point which threatens the warehouse's security.

4. The right to order removal of stored goods is subject to provisions of the public warehousing laws of some states forbidding warehouses from discriminating among customers. Nor does the section relieve the warehouse of any obligation under the state laws to secure the approval of a public official before disposing of deteriorating goods. Such regulatory statutes and the regulations under them remain in force and operative. Section 7-103.

Cross References:

Sections 7-103 and 7-403.

Definitional Cross References:

"Delivery". Section 1-201.
"Document of title". Section 1-102.
"Good faith". Section 1-201 [7-102].
"Goods". Section 7-102.
"Notice". Section 1-202.
"Notification". Section 1-202.
"Person". Section 1-201.
"Reasonable time". Section 1-205.
"Value". Section 1-204.
"Warehouse". Section 7-102.

§ 7–207. Goods Must Be Kept Separate; Fungible Goods.

(a) Unless the warehouse receipt provides otherwise, a warehouse shall keep separate the goods covered by each receipt so as to permit at all times identification and delivery of those goods. However, different lots of fungible goods may be commingled.

(b) If different lots of fungible goods are commingled, the goods are owned in common by the persons entitled thereto and the warehouse is severally liable to each owner for that owner's share. If, because of overissue, a mass of fungible goods is insufficient to meet all the receipts the warehouse has issued against it, the persons entitled include all holders to which overissued receipts have been duly negotiated.

Official Comment

Prior Uniform Statutory Provision: Former Section 7–207.

Changes: Changes for style only.

Purposes:

No change of substance is made from former Section 7–207. Holders to whom overissued receipts have been duly negotiated shall share in a mass of fungible goods. Where individual ownership interests are merged into claims on a common fund, as is necessarily the case with fungible goods, there is no policy reason for discriminating between successive purchasers of similar claims.

Definitional Cross References:

"Delivery". Section 1–201.
"Duly negotiate". Section 7–501.
"Fungible goods". Section 1–201.
"Goods". Section 7–102.
"Holder". Section 1–201.
"Person". Section 1–201.
"Warehouse receipt". Section 1–201.
"Warehouse". Section 7–102.

§ 7–208. Altered Warehouse Receipts.

If a blank in a negotiable tangible warehouse receipt has been filled in without authority, a good-faith purchaser for value and without notice of the lack of authority may treat the insertion as authorized. Any other unauthorized alteration leaves any tangible or electronic warehouse receipt enforceable against the issuer according to its original tenor.

Official Comment

Prior Uniform Statutory Provision: Former Section 7–208.

Changes: To accommodate electronic documents of title.

Purpose:

1. The execution of tangible warehouse receipts in blank is a dangerous practice. As between the issuer and an innocent purchaser the risks should clearly fall on the former. The purchaser must have purchased the tangible negotiable warehouse receipt in good faith and for value to be protected under the rule of the first sentence which is a limited exception to the general rule in the second sentence. Electronic document of title systems should have protection against unauthorized access and unauthorized changes. See 7–106. Thus the protection for good faith purchasers found in the first sentence is not necessary in the context of electronic documents.

2. Under the second sentence of this section, an unauthorized alteration whether made with or without fraudulent intent does not relieve the issuer of its liability on the warehouse receipt as originally executed. The unauthorized alteration itself is of course ineffective against the warehouse. The rule stated in the second sentence applies to both tangible and electronic warehouse receipts.

Definitional Cross References:

"Good faith". Section 1–201 [7–102].
"Issuer". Section 7–102.

"Notice". Section 1–202.
"Purchaser". Section 1–201.
"Value". Section 1–204.
"Warehouse receipt". Section 1–201.

§ 7–209. Lien of Warehouse.

(a) A warehouse has a lien against the bailor on the goods covered by a warehouse receipt or storage agreement or on the proceeds thereof in its possession for charges for storage or transportation, including demurrage and terminal charges, insurance, labor, or other charges, present or future, in relation to the goods, and for expenses necessary for preservation of the goods or reasonably incurred in their sale pursuant to law. If the person on whose account the goods are held is liable for similar charges or expenses in relation to other goods whenever deposited and it is stated in the warehouse receipt or storage agreement that a lien is claimed for charges and expenses in relation to other goods, the warehouse also has a lien against the goods covered by the warehouse receipt or storage agreement or on the proceeds thereof in its possession for those charges and expenses, whether or not the other goods have been delivered by the warehouse. However, as against a person to which a negotiable warehouse receipt is duly negotiated, a warehouse's lien is limited to charges in an amount or at a rate specified in the warehouse receipt or, if no charges are so specified, to a reasonable charge for storage of the specific goods covered by the receipt subsequent to the date of the receipt.

(b) A warehouse may also reserve a security interest against the bailor for the maximum amount specified on the receipt for charges other than those specified in subsection (a), such as for money advanced and interest. The security interest is governed by Article 9.

(c) A warehouse's lien for charges and expenses under subsection (a) or a security interest under subsection (b) is also effective against any person that so entrusted the bailor with possession of the goods that a pledge of them by the bailor to a good-faith purchaser for value would have been valid. However, the lien or security interest is not effective against a person that before issuance of a document of title had a legal interest or a perfected security interest in the goods and that did not:

(1) deliver or entrust the goods or any document of title covering the goods to the bailor or the bailor's nominee with:

(A) actual or apparent authority to ship, store, or sell;

(B) power to obtain delivery under Section 7–403; or

(C) power of disposition under Sections 2–403, 2A–304(2), 2A–305(2), 9–320, or 9–321(c) or other statute or rule of law; or

(2) acquiesce in the procurement by the bailor or its nominee of any document.

(d) A warehouse's lien on household goods for charges and expenses in relation to the goods under subsection (a) is also effective against all persons if the depositor was the legal possessor of the goods at the time of deposit. In this subsection, "household goods" means furniture, furnishings, or personal effects used by the depositor in a dwelling.

(e) A warehouse loses its lien on any goods that it voluntarily delivers or unjustifiably refuses to deliver.

Official Comment

Prior Uniform Statutory Provision: Former Sections 7–209 and 7–503.

Changes: Expanded to recognize warehouse lien when a warehouse receipt is not issued but goods are covered by a storage agreement.

Purposes:

1. Subsection (a) defines the warehouse's statutory lien. Other than allowing a warehouse to claim a lien under this section when there is a storage agreement and not a warehouse receipt, this section remains unchanged in substance from former Section 7–209(1). Under the first sentence, a specific lien attaches automatically without

express notation on the receipt or storage agreement with regard to goods stored under the receipt or the storage agreement. That lien is limited to the usual charges arising out of a storage transaction.

Example 1: Bailor stored goods with a warehouse and the warehouse issued a warehouse receipt. A lien against those goods arose as set forth in subsection (a), the first sentence, for the charges for storage and the other expenses of those goods. The warehouse may enforce its lien under Section 7–210 as against the bailor. Whether the warehouse receipt is negotiable or nonnegotiable is not important to the warehouse's rights as against the bailor.

Under the second sentence, by notation on the receipt or storage agreement, the lien can be made a general lien extending to like charges in relation to other goods. Both the specific lien and general lien are as to goods in the possession of the warehouse and extend to proceeds from the goods as long as the proceeds are in the possession of the warehouse. The same rules apply whether the receipt is negotiable or non-negotiable.

Example 2: Bailor stored goods (lot A) with a warehouse and the warehouse issued a warehouse receipt for those goods. In the warehouse receipt it is stated that the warehouse will also have a lien on goods covered by the warehouse receipt for storage charges and the other expenses for any other goods that are stored with the warehouse by the bailor. The statement about the lien on other goods does not specify an amount or a rate. Bailor then stored other goods (lot B) with the warehouse. Under subsection (a), first sentence, the warehouse has a lien on the specific goods (lot A) covered by the warehouse receipt. Under subsection (a), second sentence, the warehouse has a lien on the goods in lot A for the storage charges and the other expenses arising from the goods in lot B. That lien is enforceable as against the bailor regardless of whether the receipt is negotiable or nonnegotiable.

Under the third sentence, if the warehouse receipt is negotiable, the lien as against a holder of that receipt by due negotiation is limited to the amount or rate specified on the receipt for the specific lien or the general lien, or, if none is specified, to a reasonable charge for storage of the specific goods covered by the receipt for storage after the date of the receipt.

Example 3: Same facts as Example 1 except that the warehouse receipt is negotiable and has been duly negotiated (Section 7–501) to a person other than the bailor. Under the last sentence of subsection (a), the warehouse may enforce its lien against the bailor's goods stored in the warehouse as against the person to whom the negotiable warehouse receipt has been duly negotiated. Section 7–502. That lien is limited to the charges or rates specified in the receipt or a reasonable charge for storage as stated in the last sentence of subsection (a).

Example 4: Same facts as Example 2 except that the warehouse receipt is negotiable and has been duly negotiated (Section 7–501) to a person other than the bailor. Under the last sentence of subsection (a), the lien on lot A goods for the storage charges and the other expenses arising from storage of lot B goods is not enforceable as against the person to whom the receipt has been duly negotiated. Without a statement of a specified amount or rate for the general lien, the warehouse's general lien is not enforceable as against the person to whom the negotiable document has been duly negotiated. However, the warehouse lien for charges and expenses related to storage of lot A goods is still enforceable as against the person to whom the receipt was duly negotiated.

Example 5: Same facts as Examples 2 and 4 except the warehouse had stated on the negotiable warehouse receipt a specified amount or rate for the general lien on other goods (lot B). Under the last sentence of subsection (a), the general lien on lot A goods for the storage charges and the other expenses arising from storage of lot B goods is enforceable as against the person to whom the receipt has been duly negotiated.

2. Subsection (b) provides for a security interest based upon agreement. Such a security interest arises out of relations between the parties other than bailment for storage or transportation, as where the bailee assumes the role of financier or performs a manufacturing operation, extending credit in reliance upon the goods covered by the receipt. Such a security interest is not a statutory lien. Compare Sections 9–109 and 9–333. It is governed in all respects by Article 9, except that subsection (b) requires that the receipt specify a maximum amount and limits the security interest to the amount specified. A warehouse could also take a security interest to secure its charges for storage and the other expenses listed in subsection (a) to protect these claims upon the loss of the statutory possessory warehouse lien if the warehouse loses possession of the goods as provided in subsection (e).

Example 6: Bailor stores goods with a warehouse and the warehouse issues a warehouse receipt that states that the warehouse is taking a security interest in the bailed goods for charges of storage, expenses, for money advanced, for manufacturing services rendered, and all other obligations that the bailor may owe the warehouse. That is a security interest covered in all respects by Article 9. Subsection (b). As allowed by this section, a warehouse may rely upon its statutory possessory lien to protect its charges for storage and the other expenses related to storage. For those storage charges covered by the statutory possessory lien, the warehouse is not required to use a security interest under subsection (b).

3. Subsections (a) and (b) validate the lien and security interest "against the bailor." Under basic principles of derivative rights as provided in Section 7–504, the warehouse lien is also valid as against parties who obtain their rights from the bailor except as otherwise provided in subsection (a), third sentence, or subsection (c).

Example 7: Bailor stores goods with a warehouse and the warehouse issues a nonnegotiable warehouse receipt that also claims a general lien in other goods stored with the warehouse. A lien on the bailed goods for the charges for storage and the other expenses arises under subsection (a). Bailor notifies the warehouse that the goods have been sold to Buyer and the bailee acknowledges that fact to the Buyer. Section 2–503. The warehouse lien for storage of those goods is effective against Buyer for both the specific lien and the general lien. Section 7–504.

Example 8: Bailor stores goods with a warehouse and the warehouse issues a nonnegotiable warehouse receipt. A lien on the bailed goods for the charges for storage and the other expenses arises under subsection (a). Bailor grants a security interest in the goods while the goods are in the warehouse's possession to Secured Party (SP) who properly perfects a security interest in the goods. See Revised 9–312(d). The warehouse lien is superior in priority over SP's security interest. See Revised 9–203(b)(2) (debtor can grant a security interest to the extent of debtor's rights in the collateral).

Example 9: Bailor stores goods with a warehouse and the warehouse issues a negotiable warehouse receipt. A lien on the bailed goods for the charges for storage and the other expenses arises under subsection (a). Bailor grants a security interest in the negotiable document to SP. SP properly perfects its interest in the negotiable document by taking possession through a "due negotiation." Revised 9–312(c). SP's security interest is subordinate to the warehouse lien. Section 7–209(a), third sentence. Given that bailor's rights are subject to the warehouse lien, the bailor cannot grant to the SP greater rights than the bailor has under Section 9–203(b)(2), perfection of the security interest in the negotiable document and the goods covered by the document through SP's filing of a financing statement should not give a different result.

As against third parties who have interests in the goods prior to the storage with the warehouse, subsection (c) continues the rule under the prior uniform statutory provision that to validate the lien or security interest of the warehouse, the owner must have entrusted the goods to the depositor, and that the circumstances must be such that a pledge by the depositor to a good faith purchaser for value would have been valid. Thus the owner's interest will not be subjected to a lien or security interest arising out of a deposit of its goods by a thief. The warehouse may be protected because of the actual, implied or apparent authority of the depositor, because of a Factor's Act, or because of other circumstances which would protect a bona fide pledgee, unless those circumstances are denied effect under the second sentence of subsection (c). The language of Section 7–503 is brought into subsection (c) for purposes of clarity. The comments to Section 7–503 are helpful in interpreting delivery, entrustment or acquiescence.

Where the third party is the holder of a security interest, obtained prior to the issuance of a negotiable warehouse receipt, the rights of the warehouse depend on the priority given to a hypothetical bona fide pledgee by Article 9, particularly Section 9–322. Thus the special priority granted to statutory liens by Section 9–333 does not apply to liens under subsection (a) of this section, since subsection (c), second sentence, "expressly provides otherwise" within the meaning of Section 9–333.

As to household goods, however, subsection (d) makes the warehouse's lien "for charges and expenses in relation to the goods" effective against all persons if the depositor was the legal possessor. The purpose of the exception is to permit the warehouse to accept household goods for storage in sole reliance on the value of the goods themselves, especially in situations of family emergency.

Example 10: Bailor grants a perfected security interest in the goods to SP prior to storage of the goods with the warehouse. Bailor then stores goods with the warehouse and the warehouse issues a warehouse receipt for the goods. A warehouse lien on the bailed goods for the charges for storage or other expenses arises under subsection (a). The warehouse lien is not effective as against SP unless SP entrusted the goods to the bailor with actual or apparent authority to ship store, or sell the goods or with power of disposition under subsection (c)(1) or acquiesced in the bailor's procurement of a document of title under subsection (c)(2). This result obtains whether the receipt is negotiable or nonnegotiable.

Example 11: Sheriff who had lawfully repossessed household goods in an eviction action stored the goods with a warehouse. A lien on the bailed goods arises under subsection (a). The lien is effective as against the owner of the goods. Subsection (d).

4. As under previous law, this section creates a statutory possessory lien in favor of the warehouse on the goods stored with the warehouse or on the proceeds of the goods. The warehouse loses its lien if it loses possession of the goods or the proceeds. Subsection (e).

5. Where goods have been stored under a non-negotiable warehouse receipt and are sold by the person to whom the receipt has been issued, frequently the goods are not withdrawn by the new owner. The obligations of the seller of the goods in this situation are set forth in Section 2–503(4) on tender of delivery and include procurement of an acknowledgment by the bailee of the buyer's right to possession of the goods. If a new receipt is requested, such an acknowledgment can be withheld until storage charges have been paid or provided for. The statutory lien for charges on the goods sold, granted by the first sentence of subsection (a), continues valid unless the bailee gives it up. See Section 7–403. But once a new receipt is issued to the buyer, the buyer becomes "the person on whose account the goods are held" under the second sentence of subsection (a); unless the buyer undertakes liability for charges in relation to other goods stored by the seller, there is no general lien against the buyer for such charges. Of course, the bailee may preserve the general lien in such a case either by an arrangement by which the buyer "is liable for" such charges, or by reserving a security interest under subsection (b).

6. A possessory warehouse lien arises as provided under subsection (a) if the parties to the bailment have a storage agreement or a warehouse receipt is issued. In the modern warehouse, the bailor and the bailee may enter into a master contract governing the bailment with the bailee and bailor keeping track of the goods stored pursuant to the master contract by notation on their respective books and records and the parties send notification via electronic communication as to what goods are covered by the master contract. Warehouse receipts are not issued. See Comment 4 to Section 7–204. There is no particular form for a warehouse receipt and failure to contain any of the terms listed in Section 7–202 does not deprive the warehouse of its lien that arises under subsection (a). See the comment to Section 7–202.

Cross References:

Point 1: Sections 7–501 and 7–502.

Point 2: Sections 9–109 and 9–333.

Point 3: Sections 2–503, 7–503, 7–504, 9–203, 9–312, and 9–322.

Point 4: Sections 2–503, 7–501, 7–502, 7–504, 9–312, 9–331, 9–333, 9–401.

Point 5: Sections 2–503 and 7–403.

Point 6: Sections 7–202 and 7–204.

Definitional Cross References:

"Delivery". Section 1–201.
"Document of Title". Section 1–201
"Goods". Section 7–102.
"Money". Section 1–201.
"Person". Section 1–201.
"Purchaser". Section 1–201.
"Right". Section 1–201.
"Security interest". Section 1–201.
"Value". Section 1–204.
"Warehouse receipt". Section 1–201.
"Warehouse". Section 7–102.

§ 7–210. Enforcement of Warehouse's Lien.

(a) Except as otherwise provided in subsection (b), a warehouse's lien may be enforced by public or private sale of the goods, in bulk or in packages, at any time or place and on any terms that are commercially reasonable, after notifying all persons known to claim an interest in the goods. The notification must include a statement of the amount due, the nature of the proposed sale, and the time and place of any public sale. The fact that a better price could have been obtained by a sale at a different time or in a method different from that selected by the warehouse is not of itself sufficient to establish that the sale was not made in a commercially reasonable manner. The warehouse sells in a commercially reasonable manner if the

warehouse sells the goods in the usual manner in any recognized market therefor, sells at the price current in that market at the time of the sale, or otherwise sells in conformity with commercially reasonable practices among dealers in the type of goods sold. A sale of more goods than apparently necessary to be offered to ensure satisfaction of the obligation is not commercially reasonable, except in cases covered by the preceding sentence.

(b) A warehouse may enforce its lien on goods, other than goods stored by a merchant in the course of its business, only if the following requirements are satisfied:

(1) All persons known to claim an interest in the goods must be notified.

(2) The notification must include an itemized statement of the claim, a description of the goods subject to the lien, a demand for payment within a specified time not less than 10 days after receipt of the notification, and a conspicuous statement that unless the claim is paid within that time the goods will be advertised for sale and sold by auction at a specified time and place.

(3) The sale must conform to the terms of the notification.

(4) The sale must be held at the nearest suitable place to where the goods are held or stored.

(5) After the expiration of the time given in the notification, an advertisement of the sale must be published once a week for two weeks consecutively in a newspaper of general circulation where the sale is to be held. The advertisement must include a description of the goods, the name of the person on whose account the goods are being held, and the time and place of the sale. The sale must take place at least 15 days after the first publication. If there is no newspaper of general circulation where the sale is to be held, the advertisement must be posted at least 10 days before the sale in not fewer than six conspicuous places in the neighborhood of the proposed sale.

(c) Before any sale pursuant to this section, any person claiming a right in the goods may pay the amount necessary to satisfy the lien and the reasonable expenses incurred in complying with this section. In that event, the goods may not be sold but must be retained by the warehouse subject to the terms of the receipt and this article.

(d) A warehouse may buy at any public sale held pursuant to this section.

(e) A purchaser in good faith of goods sold to enforce a warehouse's lien takes the goods free of any rights of persons against which the lien was valid, despite the warehouse's noncompliance with this section.

(f) A warehouse may satisfy its lien from the proceeds of any sale pursuant to this section but shall hold the balance, if any, for delivery on demand to any person to which the warehouse would have been bound to deliver the goods.

(g) The rights provided by this section are in addition to all other rights allowed by law to a creditor against a debtor.

(h) If a lien is on goods stored by a merchant in the course of its business, the lien may be enforced in accordance with subsection (a) or (b).

(i) A warehouse is liable for damages caused by failure to comply with the requirements for sale under this section and, in case of willful violation, is liable for conversion.

Official Comment

Prior Uniform Statutory Provision: Former Section 7–210.

Changes: Update to accommodate electronic commerce and for style.

Purposes:

1. Subsection (a) makes "commercial reasonableness" the standard for foreclosure proceedings in all cases except non-commercial storage with a warehouse. The latter category embraces principally storage of household goods by private owners; and for such cases the detailed provisions as to notification, publication and public sale are retained in subsection (b) with one change. The requirement in former Section 7–210(2)(b) that the notification must be sent in person or by registered or certified mail has been deleted. Notification may be sent by any reasonable means as provided in Section 1–202. The swifter, more flexible procedure of subsection (a) is appropriate to commercial storage. Compare seller's power of resale on breach by buyer under the provisions of

the Article on Sales (Section 2–706). Commercial reasonableness is a flexible concept that allows for a wide variety of actions to satisfy the rule of this section, including electronic means of posting and sale.

2. The provisions of subsections (d) and (e) permitting the bailee to bid at public sales and confirming the title of purchasers at foreclosure sales are designed to secure more bidding and better prices and remain unchanged from former Section 7–210.

3. A warehouses may have recourse to an interpleader action in appropriate circumstances. See Section 7–603.

4. If a warehouse has both a warehouse lien and a security interest, the warehouse may enforce both the lien and the security interest simultaneously by using the procedures of Article 9. Section 7–210 adopts as its touchstone "commercial reasonableness" for the enforcement of a warehouse lien. Following the procedures of Article 9 satisfies "commercial reasonableness."

Cross Reference:

Sections 2–706, 7–403, 7–603 and Part 6 of Article 9.

Definitional Cross References:

"Bill of lading". Section 1–201.
"Conspicuous". Section 1–201.
"Creditor". Section 1–201.
"Delivery". Section 1–201.
"Document of title". Section 1–201.
"Good faith". Section 1–201 [7–102].
"Goods". Section 7–102.
"Notification". Section 1–202.
"Notifies". Section 1–202.
"Person". Section 1–201.
"Purchaser". Section 1–201.
"Rights". Section 1–201.
"Term". Section 1–201.
"Warehouse". Section 7–102.

PART 3

BILLS OF LADING: SPECIAL PROVISIONS

§ 7–301. Liability for Nonreceipt or Misdescription; "Said to Contain"; "Shipper's Weight, Load, and Count"; Improper Handling.

(a) A consignee of a nonnegotiable bill of lading which has given value in good faith, or a holder to which a negotiable bill has been duly negotiated, relying upon the description of the goods in the bill or upon the date shown in the bill, may recover from the issuer damages caused by the misdating of the bill or the nonreceipt or misdescription of the goods, except to the extent that the bill indicates that the issuer does not know whether any part or all of the goods in fact were received or conform to the description, such as in a case in which the description is in terms of marks or labels or kind, quantity, or condition or the receipt or description is qualified by "contents or condition of contents of packages unknown", "said to contain", "shipper's weight, load, and count," or words of similar import, if that indication is true.

(b) If goods are loaded by the issuer of a bill of lading;

(1) the issuer shall count the packages of goods if shipped in packages and ascertain the kind and quantity if shipped in bulk; and

(2) words such as "shipper's weight, load, and count," or words of similar import indicating that the description was made by the shipper are ineffective except as to goods concealed in packages.

(c) If bulk goods are loaded by a shipper that makes available to the issuer of a bill of lading adequate facilities for weighing those goods, the issuer shall ascertain the kind and quantity within a reasonable time

after receiving the shipper's request in a record to do so. In that case, "shipper's weight" or words of similar import are ineffective.

(d) The issuer of a bill of lading, by including in the bill the words "shipper's weight, load, and count," or words of similar import, may indicate that the goods were loaded by the shipper, and, if that statement is true, the issuer is not liable for damages caused by the improper loading. However, omission of such words does not imply liability for damages caused by improper loading.

(e) A shipper guarantees to an issuer the accuracy at the time of shipment of the description, marks, labels, number, kind, quantity, condition, and weight, as furnished by the shipper, and the shipper shall indemnify the issuer against damage caused by inaccuracies in those particulars. This right of indemnity does not limit the issuer's responsibility or liability under the contract of carriage to any person other than the shipper.

Official Comment

Prior Uniform Statutory Provision: Former Section 7–301.

Changes: Changes for clarity, style and to recognize deregulation in the transportation industry.

Purposes:

1. This section continues the rules from former Section 7–301 with one substantive change. The obligations of the issuer of the bill of lading under former subsections (2) and (3) were limited to issuers who were common carriers. Subsections (b) and (c) apply the same rules to all issuers not just common carriers. This section is compatible with the policies stated in the federal Bills of Lading Act, 49 U.S.C. § 80113 (2000).

2. The language of the pre-Code Uniform Bills of Lading Act suggested that a carrier is ordinarily liable for damage caused by improper loading, but may relieve itself of liability by disclosing on the bill that shipper actually loaded. A more accurate statement of the law is that the carrier is not liable for losses caused by act or default of the shipper, which would include improper loading. *D. H. Overmyer Co. v. Nelson Brantley Glass Co.*, 168 S.E.2d 176 (Ga. Ct. App. 1969). There was some question whether under pre-Code law a carrier was liable even to a good faith purchaser of a negotiable bill for such losses, if the shipper's faulty loading in fact caused the loss. Subsection (d) permits the carrier to bar, by disclosure of shipper's loading, liability to a good faith purchaser. There is no implication that decisions such as *Modern Tool Corp. v. Pennsylvania R. Co.*, 100 F.Supp. 595 (D.N.J. 1951), are disapproved.

3. This section is a restatement of existing law as to the method by which a bailee may avoid responsibility for the accuracy of descriptions which are made by or in reliance upon information furnished by the depositor or shipper. The wording in this section—"contents or condition of contents of packages unknown" or "shipper's weight, load and count"—to indicate that the shipper loaded the goods or that the carrier does not know the description, condition, or contents of the loaded packages continues to be appropriate as commonly understood in the transportation industry. The reasons for this wording are as important in 2002 as when the prior section initially was approved. The issuer is liable on documents issued by an agent, contrary to instructions of his principal, without receiving goods. No disclaimer of this liability is permitted since it is not a matter either of the care of the goods or their description.

4. The shipper's erroneous report to the carrier concerning the goods may cause damage to the carrier. Subsection (e) therefore provides appropriate indemnity.

5. The word "freight" in the former Section 7–301 has been changed to "goods" to conform to international and domestic land transport usage in which "freight" means the price paid for carriage of the goods and not the goods themselves. Hence, changing the word "freight" to the word "goods" is a clarifying change that fits both international and domestic practice.

Cross References:

Sections 7–203, 7–309 and 7–501.

Definitional Cross References:

"Bill of lading". Section 1–201.
"Consignee". Section 7–102.
"Document of title". Section 1–201.
"Duly negotiate". Section 7–501.

"Good faith". Section 1–201. [7–102].
"Goods". Section 7–102.
"Holder". Section 1–201.
"Issuer". Section 7–102.
"Notice". Section 1–202.
"Party". Section 1–201.
"Purchaser." Section 1–201.
"Receipt of goods". Section 2–103.
"Value". Section 1–204.

§ 7–302. Through Bills of Lading and Similar Documents of Title.

(a) The issuer of a through bill of lading, or other document of title embodying an undertaking to be performed in part by a person acting as its agent or by a performing carrier, is liable to any person entitled to recover on the bill or other document for any breach by the other person or the performing carrier of its obligation under the bill or other document. However, to the extent that the bill or other document covers an undertaking to be performed overseas or in territory not contiguous to the continental United States or an undertaking including matters other than transportation, this liability for breach by the other person or the performing carrier may be varied by agreement of the parties.

(b) If goods covered by a through bill of lading or other document of title embodying an undertaking to be performed in part by a person other than the issuer are received by that person, the person is subject, with respect to its own performance while the goods are in its possession, to the obligation of the issuer. The person's obligation is discharged by delivery of the goods to another person pursuant to the bill or other document and does not include liability for breach by any other person or by the issuer.

(c) The issuer of a through bill of lading or other document of title described in subsection (a) is entitled to recover from the performing carrier, or other person in possession of the goods when the breach of the obligation under the bill or other document occurred:

(1) the amount it may be required to pay to any person entitled to recover on the bill or other document for the breach, as may be evidenced by any receipt, judgment, or transcript of judgment; and

(2) the amount of any expense reasonably incurred by the issuer in defending any action commenced by any person entitled to recover on the bill or other document for the breach.

Official Comment

Prior Uniform Statutory Provision: Former Section 7–302.

Changes: To conform to current terminology and for style.

Purposes:

1. This section continues the rules from former Section 7–302 without substantive change. The term "performing carrier" is substituted for the term "connecting carrier" to conform the terminology of this section with terminology used in recent UNCITRAL and OAS proposals concerning transportation and through bills of lading. This change in terminology is not substantive. This section is compatible with liability on carriers under federal law. See 49 U.S.C. §§ 11706, 14706 and 15906.

The purpose of this section is to subject the initial carrier under a through bill to suit for breach of the contract of carriage by any performing carrier and to make it clear that any such performing carrier holds the goods on terms which are defined by the document of title even though such performing carrier did not issue the document. Since the performing carrier does hold the goods on the terms of the document, it must honor a proper demand for delivery or a diversion order just as the original bailee would have to. Similarly it has the benefits of the excuses for non-delivery and limitations of liability provided for the original bailee who issued the bill. Unlike the original bailee-issuer, the performing carrier's responsibility is limited to the period while the goods are in its possession. The section does not impose any obligation to issue through bills.

2. The reference to documents other than through bills looks to the possibility that multi-purpose documents may come into use, e.g., combination warehouse receipts and bills of lading. As electronic documents of title come into common usage, storage documents (e.g. warehouse receipts) and transportation documents (e.g.

bills of lading) may merge seamlessly into one electronic document that can serve both the storage and transportation segments of the movement of goods.

3. Under subsection (a) the issuer of a through bill of lading may become liable for the fault of another person. Subsection (c) gives the issuer appropriate rights of recourse.

4. Despite the broad language of subsection (a), Section 7-302 is subject to preemption by federal laws and treaties. Section 7-103. The precise scope of federal preemption in the transportation sector is a question determined under federal law.

Cross reference:

Section 7-103.

Definitional Cross References:

"Agreement". Section 1-201.
"Bailee". Section 7-102.
"Bill of lading". Section 1-201.
"Delivery". Section 1-201.
"Document of title". Section 1-201.
"Goods". Section 7-102.
"Issuer". Section 7-102.
"Party". Section 1-201.
"Person". Section 1-201.

§ 7-303. Diversion; Reconsignment; Change of Instructions.

(a) Unless the bill of lading otherwise provides, a carrier may deliver the goods to a person or destination other than that stated in the bill or may otherwise dispose of the goods, without liability for misdelivery, on instructions from:

(1) the holder of a negotiable bill;

(2) the consignor on a nonnegotiable bill, even if the consignee has given contrary instructions;

(3) the consignee on a nonnegotiable bill in the absence of contrary instructions from the consignor, if the goods have arrived at the billed destination or if the consignee is in possession of the tangible bill or in control of the electronic bill; or

(4) the consignee on a nonnegotiable bill, if the consignee is entitled as against the consignor to dispose of the goods.

(b) Unless instructions described in subsection (a) are included in a negotiable bill of lading, a person to which the bill is duly negotiated may hold the bailee according to the original terms.

Official Comment

Prior Uniform Statutory Provision: Former Section 7-303.

Changes: To accommodate electronic documents and for style.

Purposes:

1. Diversion is a very common commercial practice which defeats delivery to the consignee originally named in a bill of lading. This section continues former Section 7-303's safe harbor rules for carriers in situations involving diversion and adapts those rules to electronic documents of title. This section works compatibly with Section 2-705. Carriers may as a business matter be willing to accept instructions from consignees in which case the carrier will be liable for misdelivery if the consignee was not the owner or otherwise empowered to dispose of the goods under subsection (a)(4). The section imposes no duty on carriers to undertake diversion. The carrier is of course subject to the provisions of mandatory filed tariffs as provided in Section 7-103.

2. It should be noted that the section provides only an immunity for carriers against liability for "misdelivery." It does not, for example, defeat the title to the goods which the consignee-buyer may have acquired from the consignor-seller upon delivery of the goods to the carrier under a non-negotiable bill of lading. Thus if the carrier, upon instructions from the consignor, returns the goods to the consignor, the consignee may recover the

goods from the consignor or the consignor's insolvent estate. However, under certain circumstances, the consignee's title may be defeated by diversion of the goods in transit to a different consignee. The rights that arise between the consignor-seller and the consignee-buyer out of a contract for the sale of goods are governed by Article 2.

Cross References:

Point 1: Sections 2–705 and 7–103.
Point 2: Article 2, Sections 7–403 and 7–504(3).

Definitional Cross References:

"Bailee". Section 7–102.
"Bill of lading". Section 1–201.
"Carrier". Section 7–102
"Consignee". Section 7–102.
"Consignor". Section 7–102.
"Delivery". Section 1–201.
"Goods". Section 7–102.
"Holder". Section 1–201.
"Notice". Section 1–202.
"Person". Section 1–201.
"Purchaser". Section 1–201.
"Term". Section 1–201.

§ 7–304. Tangible Bills of Lading in a Set.

(a) Except as customary in international transportation, a tangible bill of lading may not be issued in a set of parts. The issuer is liable for damages caused by violation of this subsection.

(b) If a tangible bill of lading is lawfully issued in a set of parts, each of which contains an identification code and is expressed to be valid only if the goods have not been delivered against any other part, the whole of the parts constitutes one bill.

(c) If a tangible negotiable bill of lading is lawfully issued in a set of parts and different parts are negotiated to different persons, the title of the holder to which the first due negotiation is made prevails as to both the document of title and the goods even if any later holder may have received the goods from the carrier in good faith and discharged the carrier's obligation by surrendering its part.

(d) A person that negotiates or transfers a single part of a tangible bill of lading issued in a set is liable to holders of that part as if it were the whole set.

(e) The bailee shall deliver in accordance with Part 4 against the first presented part of a tangible bill of lading lawfully issued in a set. Delivery in this manner discharges the bailee's obligation on the whole bill.

Official Comment

Prior Uniform Statutory Provision: Former Section 7–304.

Changes: To limit bills in a set to tangible bills of lading and to use terminology more consistent with modern usage.

Purposes:

1. Tangible bills of lading in a set are still used in some nations in international trade. Consequently, a tangible bill of lading part of a set could be at issue in a lawsuit that might come within Article 7. The statement of the legal effect of a lawfully issued set is in accord with existing commercial law relating to maritime and other international tangible bills of lading. This law has been codified in the Hague and Warsaw Conventions and in the Carriage of Goods by Sea Act, the provisions of which would ordinarily govern in situations where bills in a set are recognized by this Article. Tangible bills of lading in a set are prohibited in domestic trade.

2. Electronic bills of lading in domestic or international trade will not be issued in a set given the requirements of control necessary to deliver the bill to another person. An electronic bill of lading will be a single,

authoritative copy. Section 7–106. Hence, this section differentiates between electronic bills of lading and tangible bills of lading. This section does not prohibit electronic data messages about goods in transit because these electronic data messages are not the issued bill of lading. Electronic data messages contain information for the carrier's management and handling of the cargo but this information for the carrier's use is not the issued bill of lading.

Cross Reference:

Section 7–103, 7–303 and 7–106.

Definitional Cross References:

"Bailee". Section 7–102.
"Bill of lading". Section 1–201.
"Delivery". Section 1–201.
"Document of title". Section 1–201.
"Duly negotiate". Section 7–501.
"Good faith". Section 1–201. [7–102].
"Goods". Section 7–102.
"Holder". Section 1–201.
"Issuer". Section 7–102.
"Person". Section 1–201.
"Receipt of goods". Section 2–103.

§ 7–305. Destination Bills.

(a) Instead of issuing a bill of lading to the consignor at the place of shipment, a carrier, at the request of the consignor, may procure the bill to be issued at destination or at any other place designated in the request.

(b) Upon request of any person entitled as against a carrier to control the goods while in transit and on surrender of possession or control of any outstanding bill of lading or other receipt covering the goods, the issuer, subject to Section 7–105, may procure a substitute bill to be issued at any place designated in the request.

Official Comment

Prior Uniform Statutory Provision: Former Section 7–305.

Changes: To accommodate electronic bills of lading and for style.

Purposes:

1. Subsection (a) continues the rules of former Section 7–305(1) without substantive change. This proposal is designed to facilitate the use of order bills in connection with fast shipments. Use of order bills on high speed shipments is impeded by the fact that the goods may arrive at destination before the documents, so that no one is ready to take delivery from the carrier. This is especially inconvenient for carriers by truck and air, who do not have terminal facilities where shipments can be held to await the consignee's appearance. Order bills would be useful to take advantage of bank collection. This may be preferable to C.O.D. shipment in which the carrier, e.g. a truck driver, is the collecting and remitting agent. Financing of shipments under this plan would be handled as follows: seller at San Francisco delivers the goods to an airline with instructions to issue a bill in New York to a named bank. Seller receives a receipt embodying this undertaking to issue a destination bill. Airline wires its New York freight agent to issue the bill as instructed by the seller. Seller wires the New York bank a draft on buyer. New York bank indorses the bill to buyer when the buyer honors the draft. Normally seller would act through its own bank in San Francisco, which would extend credit in reliance on the airline's contract to deliver a bill to the order of its New York correspondent. This section is entirely permissive; it imposes no duty to issue such bills. Whether a performing carrier will act as issuing agent is left to agreement between carriers.

2. Subsection (b) continues the rule from former Section 7–305(2) with accommodation for electronic bills of lading. If the substitute bill changes from an electronic to a tangible medium or vice versa, the issuance of the substitute bill must comply with Section 7–105 to give the substitute bill validity and effect.

Cross Reference:

Section 7–105.

Definitional Cross References:

"Bill of lading". Section 1–201.
"Consignor". Section 7–102.
"Goods". Section 7–102.
"Issuer". Section 7–102.
"Receipt of goods". Section 2–103.

§ 7–306. Altered Bills of Lading.

An unauthorized alteration or filling in of a blank in a bill of lading leaves the bill enforceable according to its original tenor.

Official Comment

Prior Uniform Statutory Provision: Former Section 7–306.

Changes: None

Purposes:

An unauthorized alteration or filling in of a blank, whether made with or without fraudulent intent, does not relieve the issuer of its liability on the document as originally executed. This section applies to both tangible and electronic bills of lading, applying the same rule to both types of bills of lading. The control concept of Section 7–106 requires that any changes to the electronic document of title be readily identifiable as authorized or unauthorized. Section 7–306 should be compared to Section 7–208 where a different rule applies to the unauthorized filling in of a blank for tangible warehouse receipts.

Cross Reference:

Sections 7–106 and 7–208.

Definitional Cross References:

"Bill of lading". Section 1–201.
"Issuer". Section 7–102.

§ 7–307. Lien of Carrier.

(a) A carrier has a lien on the goods covered by a bill of lading or on the proceeds thereof in its possession for charges after the date of the carrier's receipt of the goods for storage or transportation, including demurrage and terminal charges, and for expenses necessary for preservation of the goods incident to their transportation or reasonably incurred in their sale pursuant to law. However, against a purchaser for value of a negotiable bill of lading, a carrier's lien is limited to charges stated in the bill or the applicable tariffs or, if no charges are stated, a reasonable charge.

(b) A lien for charges and expenses under subsection (a) on goods that the carrier was required by law to receive for transportation is effective against the consignor or any person entitled to the goods unless the carrier had notice that the consignor lacked authority to subject the goods to those charges and expenses. Any other lien under subsection (a) is effective against the consignor and any person that permitted the bailor to have control or possession of the goods unless the carrier had notice that the bailor lacked authority.

(c) A carrier loses its lien on any goods that it voluntarily delivers or unjustifiably refuses to deliver.

Official Comment

Prior Uniform Statutory Provision: Former Section 7–307.

Changes: Expanded to cover proceeds of the goods transported.

Purposes:

1. The section is intended to give carriers a specific statutory lien for charges and expenses similar to that given to warehouses by the first sentence of Section 7–209(a) and extends that lien to the proceeds of the goods as

long as the carrier has possession of the proceeds. But because carriers do not commonly claim a lien for charges in relation to other goods or lend money on the security of goods in their hands, provisions for a general lien or a security interest similar to those in Section 7-209(a) and (b) are omitted. Carriers may utilize Article 9 to obtain a security interest and become a secured party or a carrier may agree to limit its lien rights in a transportation agreement with the shipper. As the lien given by this section is specific, and the storage or transportation often preserves or increases the value of the goods, subsection (b) validates the lien against anyone who permitted the bailor to have possession of the goods. Where the carrier is required to receive the goods for transportation, the owner's interest may be subjected to charges and expenses arising out of deposit of his goods by a thief. The crucial mental element is the carrier's knowledge or reason to know of the bailor's lack of authority. If the carrier does not know or have reason to know of the bailor's lack of authority, the carrier has a lien under this section against any person so long as the conditions of subsection (b) are satisfied. In light of the crucial mental element, Sections 7-307 and 9-333 combine to give priority to a carrier's lien over security interests in the goods. In this regard, the judicial decision in *In re Sharon Steel Corp.*, 25 U.C.C. Rep.2d 503, 176 B.R. 384 (W.D. Pa. 1995) is correct and is the controlling precedent.

2. The reference to charges in this section means charges relating to the bailment relationship for transportation. Charges does not mean that the bill of lading must state a specific rate or a specific amount. However, failure to state a specific amount has legal consequences under the second sentence of subsection (a).

3. The carrier's specific lien under this section is a possessory lien. See subsection (c). Part 3 of Article 7 does not require any particular form for a bill of lading. The carrier's lien arises when the carrier has issued a bill of lading.

Cross References:

Point 1: Sections 7-209, 9-109 and 9-333.
Point 3. Section 7-202 and 7-209.

Definitional Cross References:

"Bill of lading". Section 1-201.
"Carrier". Section 7-102.
"Consignor". Section 7-102.
"Delivery". Section 1-201.
"Goods". Section 7-102.
"Person". Section 1-201.
"Purchaser". Section 1-201.
"Value". Section 1-204.

§ 7-308. Enforcement of Carrier's Lien.

(a) A carrier's lien on goods may be enforced by public or private sale of the goods, in bulk or in packages, at any time or place and on any terms that are commercially reasonable, after notifying all persons known to claim an interest in the goods. The notification must include a statement of the amount due, the nature of the proposed sale, and the time and place of any public sale. The fact that a better price could have been obtained by a sale at a different time or in a method different from that selected by the carrier is not of itself sufficient to establish that the sale was not made in a commercially reasonable manner. The carrier sells goods in a commercially reasonable manner if the carrier sells the goods in the usual manner in any recognized market therefor, sells at the price current in that market at the time of the sale, or otherwise sells in conformity with commercially reasonable practices among dealers in the type of goods sold. A sale of more goods than apparently necessary to be offered to ensure satisfaction of the obligation is not commercially reasonable, except in cases covered by the preceding sentence.

(b) Before any sale pursuant to this section, any person claiming a right in the goods may pay the amount necessary to satisfy the lien and the reasonable expenses incurred in complying with this section. In that event, the goods may not be sold but must be retained by the carrier, subject to the terms of the bill of lading and this article.

(c) A carrier may buy at any public sale pursuant to this section.

(d) A purchaser in good faith of goods sold to enforce a carrier's lien takes the goods free of any rights of persons against which the lien was valid, despite the carrier's noncompliance with this section.

(e) A carrier may satisfy its lien from the proceeds of any sale pursuant to this section but shall hold the balance, if any, for delivery on demand to any person to which the carrier would have been bound to deliver the goods.

(f) The rights provided by this section are in addition to all other rights allowed by law to a creditor against a debtor.

(g) A carrier's lien may be enforced pursuant to either subsection (a) or the procedure set forth in Section 7–210(b).

(h) A carrier is liable for damages caused by failure to comply with the requirements for sale under this section and, in case of willful violation, is liable for conversion.

Official Comment

Prior Uniform Statutory Provision: Former Section 7–308.

Changes: To conform language to modern usage and for style.

Purposes:

This section is intended to give the carrier an enforcement procedure of its lien coextensive with that given the warehouse in cases other than those covering noncommercial storage by the warehouse. See Section 7–210 and comments.

Cross Reference:

Section 7–210.

Definitional Cross References:

"Bill of lading". Section 1–201.
"Carrier". Section 7–102.
"Creditor". Section 1–201.
"Delivery". Section 1–201.
"Good faith". Section 1–201. [7–102]
"Goods". Section 7–102.
"Notification". Section 1–202.
"Notifies". Section 1–202.
"Person". Section 1–201.
"Purchaser". Section 1–201.
"Rights". Section 1–201.
"Term". Section 1–201.

§ 7–309. Duty of Care; Contractual Limitation of Carrier's Liability.

(a) A carrier that issues a bill of lading, whether negotiable or nonnegotiable, shall exercise the degree of care in relation to the goods which a reasonably careful person would exercise under similar circumstances. This subsection does not affect any statute, regulation, or rule of law that imposes liability upon a common carrier for damages not caused by its negligence.

(b) Damages may be limited by a term in the bill of lading or in a transportation agreement that the carrier's liability may not exceed a value stated in the bill or transportation agreement if the carrier's rates are dependent upon value and the consignor is afforded an opportunity to declare a higher value and the consignor is advised of the opportunity. However, such a limitation is not effective with respect to the carrier's liability for conversion to its own use.

(c) Reasonable provisions as to the time and manner of presenting claims and commencing actions based on the shipment may be included in a bill of lading or a transportation agreement.

Official Comment

Prior Uniform Statutory Provision: Former Section 7–309.

Changes: References to tariffs eliminated because of deregulation, adding reference to transportation agreements, and for style.

Purposes:

1. A bill of lading may also serve as the contract between the carrier and the bailor. Parties in their contract should be able to limit the amount of damages for breach of that contract including breach of the duty to take reasonable care of the goods. The parties cannot disclaim by contract the carrier's obligation of care. Section 1–302.

Federal statutes and treaties for air, maritime and rail transport may alter the standard of care. These federal statutes and treaties preempt this section when applicable. Section 7–103. Subsection (a) does not impair any rule of law imposing the liability of an insurer on a common carrier in intrastate commerce. Subsection (b), however, applies to the common carrier's liability as an insurer as well as to liability based on negligence. Subsection (b) allows the term limiting damages to appear either in the bill of lading or in the parties' transportation agreement. Compare 7–204(b). Subsection (c) allows the parties to agree to provisions regarding time and manner of presenting claims or commencing actions if the provisions are either in the bill of lading or the transportation agreement. Compare 7–204(c). Transportation agreements are commonly used to establish agreed terms between carriers and shippers that have an on-going relationship.

2. References to public tariffs in former Section 7–309(2) and (3) have been deleted in light of the modern era of deregulation. See Comment 2 to Section 7–103. If a tariff is required under state or federal law, pursuant to Section 7–103(a), the tariff would control over the rule of this section. As governed by contract law, parties may incorporate by reference the limits on the amount of damages or the reasonable provisions as to the time and manner of presenting claims set forth in applicable tariffs, e.g. a maximum unit value beyond which goods are not taken or a disclaimer of responsibility for undeclared articles of extraordinary value.

3. As under former Section 7–309(2), subsection (b) provides that a limitation of damages is ineffective if the carrier has converted the goods to its own use. A mere failure to redeliver the goods is not conversion to the carrier's own use. "Conversion to its own use" is narrower than the idea of conversion generally. *Art Masters Associates, Ltd. v. United Parcel Service*, 77 N.Y.2d 200, 567 N.E.2d 226 (1990); *See, Kemper Ins. Co. v. Fed. Ex. Corp.*, 252 F.3d 509 (1st Cir.), *cert. denied* 534 U.S. 1020 (2001) (opinion interpreting federal law).

4. As used in this section, damages may include damages arising from delay in delivery. Delivery dates and times are often specified in the parties' contract. See Section 7–403.

Cross Reference:

Sections 1–302, 7–103, 7–204, 7–403.

Definitional Cross References:

"Action". Section 1–201.
"Bill of lading". Section 1–201.
"Carrier". Section 7–102.
"Consignor". Section 7–102.
"Document of title". Section 1–201.
"Goods". Section 7–102.
"Value". Section 1–204.

PART 4

WAREHOUSE RECEIPTS AND BILLS OF LADING: GENERAL OBLIGATIONS

§ 7–401. Irregularities in Issue of Receipt or Bill or Conduct of Issuer.

The obligations imposed by this article on an issuer apply to a document of title even if:

(1) the document does not comply with the requirements of this article or of any other statute, rule, or regulation regarding its issuance, form, or content;

(2) the issuer violated laws regulating the conduct of its business;

(3) the goods covered by the document were owned by the bailee when the document was issued; or

(4) the person issuing the document is not a warehouse but the document purports to be a warehouse receipt.

Official Comment

Prior Uniform Statutory Provision: Former Section 7–401.

Changes: Changes for style only.

Purposes:

The bailee's liability on its document despite non-receipt or misdescription of the goods is affirmed in Sections 7–203 and 7–301. The purpose of this section is to make it clear that regardless of irregularities a document which falls within the definition of document of title imposes on the issuer the obligations stated in this Article. For example, a bailee will not be permitted to avoid its obligation to deliver the goods (Section 7–403) or its obligation of due care with respect to them (Sections 7–204 and 7–309) by taking the position that no valid "document" was issued because it failed to file a statutory bond or did not pay stamp taxes or did not disclose the place of storage in the document. *Tate v. Action Moving & Storage, Inc.*, 383 S.E.2d 229 (N.C. App. 1989), rev. denied 389 S.E.2d 104 (N.C. 1990). Sanctions against violations of statutory or administrative duties with respect to documents should be limited to revocation of license or other measures prescribed by the regulation imposing the duty. See Section 7–103.

Cross References:

Sections 7–103, 7–203, 7–204, 7–301, 7–309.

Definitional Cross References:

"Bailee". Section 7–102.
"Document of title". Section 1–201.
"Goods". Section 7–102.
"Issuer". Section 7–102.
"Person". Section 1–201.
"Warehouse receipt". Section 1–201.
"Warehouse". Section 7–102.

§ 7–402. Duplicate Document of Title; Overissue.

A duplicate or any other document of title purporting to cover goods already represented by an outstanding document of the same issuer does not confer any right in the goods, except as provided in the case of tangible bills of lading in a set of parts, overissue of documents for fungible goods, substitutes for lost, stolen, or destroyed documents, or substitute documents issued pursuant to Section 7–105. The issuer is liable for damages caused by its overissue or failure to identify a duplicate document by a conspicuous notation.

Official Comment

Prior Uniform Statutory Provision: Former Section 7–402.

Changes: Changes to accommodate electronic documents.

Purposes:

1. This section treats a duplicate which is not properly identified as a duplicate like any other overissue of documents: a purchaser of such a document acquires no title but only a cause of action for damages against the person that made the deception possible, except in the cases noted in the section. But parts of a tangible bill lawfully issued in a set of parts are not "overissue" (Section 7–304). Of course, if the issuer has clearly indicated that a document is a duplicate so that no one can be deceived by it, and in fact the duplicate is a correct copy of the original, the issuer is not liable for preparing and delivering such a duplicate copy.

Section 7–105 allows documents of title to be reissued in another medium. Re-issuance of a document in an alternative medium under Section 7–105 requires that the original document be surrendered to the issuer in order to make the substitute document the effective document. If the substitute document is not issued in compliance with section 7–105, then the document should be treated as a duplicate under this section.

2. The section applies to nonnegotiable documents to the extent of providing an action for damages for one who acquires an unmarked duplicate from a transferor who knew the facts and would therefore have had no cause of action against the issuer of the duplicate. Ordinarily the transferee of a nonnegotiable document acquires only the rights of its transferor.

3. Overissue is defined so as to exclude the common situation where two valid documents of different issuers are outstanding for the same goods at the same time. Thus freight forwarders commonly issue bills of lading to their customers for small shipments to be combined into carload shipments for which the railroad will issue a bill of lading to the forwarder. So also a warehouse receipt may be outstanding against goods, and the holder of the receipt may issue delivery orders against the same goods. In these cases dealings with the subsequently issued documents may be effective to transfer title; e.g. negotiation of a delivery order will effectively transfer title in the ordinary case where no dishonesty has occurred and the goods are available to satisfy the orders. Section 7–503 provides for cases of conflict between documents of different issuers.

Cross References:

Point 1: Sections 7–105, 7–207, 7–304, and 7–601.
Point 3: Section 7–503.

Definitional Cross References:

"Bill of lading". Section 1–201.
"Conspicuous". Section 1–201.
"Document of title". Section 1–201.
"Fungible goods." Section 1–201.
"Goods". Section 7–102.
"Issuer". Section 7–102.
"Right". Section 1–201.

§ 7–403. Obligation of Bailee to Deliver; Excuse.

(a) A bailee shall deliver the goods to a person entitled under a document of title if the person complies with subsections (b) and (c), unless and to the extent that the bailee establishes any of the following:

(1) delivery of the goods to a person whose receipt was rightful as against the claimant;

(2) damage to or delay, loss, or destruction of the goods for which the bailee is not liable;

(3) previous sale or other disposition of the goods in lawful enforcement of a lien or on a warehouse's lawful termination of storage;

(4) the exercise by a seller of its right to stop delivery pursuant to Section 2–705 or by a lessor of its right to stop delivery pursuant to Section 2A–526;

(5) a diversion, reconsignment, or other disposition pursuant to Section 7–303;

(6) release, satisfaction, or any other personal defense against the claimant; or

(7) any other lawful excuse.

(b) A person claiming goods covered by a document of title shall satisfy the bailee's lien if the bailee so requests or if the bailee is prohibited by law from delivering the goods until the charges are paid.

(c) Unless a person claiming the goods is a person against which the document of title does not confer a right under Section 7–503(a):

(1) the person claiming under a document shall surrender possession or control of any outstanding negotiable document covering the goods for cancellation or indication of partial deliveries; and

(2) the bailee shall cancel the document or conspicuously indicate in the document the partial delivery or the bailee is liable to any person to which the document is duly negotiated.

Official Comment

Prior Uniform Statutory Provision: Former Section 7–403.

Changes: Definition in former Section 7–403(4) moved to Section 7–102; bracketed language in former Section 7–403(1)(b) deleted; added cross reference to Section 2A–526; changes for style.

Purposes:

1. The present section, following former Section 7–403, is constructed on the basis of stating what previous deliveries or other circumstances operate to excuse the bailee's normal obligation on the document. Accordingly, "justified" deliveries under the pre-Code uniform acts now find their place as "excuse" under subsection (a).

2. The principal case covered by subsection (a)(1) is delivery to a person whose title is paramount to the rights represented by the document. For example, if a thief deposits stolen goods in a warehouse facility and takes a negotiable receipt, the warehouse is not liable on the receipt if it has surrendered the goods to the true owner, even though the receipt is held by a good faith purchaser. See Section 7–503(a). However, if the owner entrusted the goods to a person with power of disposition, and that person deposited the goods and took a negotiable document, the owner receiving delivery would not be rightful as against a holder to whom the negotiable document was duly negotiated, and delivery to the owner would not give the bailee a defense against such a holder. See Sections 7–502(a)(2), 7–503(a)(1).

3. Subsection (a)(2) amounts to a cross reference to all the tort law that determines the varying responsibilities and standards of care applicable to commercial bailees. A restatement of this tort law would be beyond the scope of this Act. Much of the applicable law as to responsibility of bailees for the preservation of the goods and limitation of liability in case of loss has been codified for particular classes of bailees in interstate and foreign commerce by federal legislation and treaty and for intrastate carriers and other bailees by the regulatory state laws preserved by Section 7–103. In the absence of governing legislation the common law will prevail subject to the minimum standard of reasonable care prescribed by Sections 7–204 and 7–309 of this Article.

The bracketed language found in former Section 7–403(1)(b) has been deleted thereby leaving the allocations of the burden of going forward with the evidence and the burden of proof to the procedural law of the various states.

Subsection (a)(4) contains a cross reference to both the seller's and the lessor's rights to stop delivery under Article 2 and Article 2A respectively.

4. As under former Section 7–403, there is no requirement that a request for delivery must be accompanied by a formal tender of the amount of the charges due. Rather, the bailee must request payment of the amount of its lien when asked to deliver, and only in case this request is refused is it justified in declining to deliver because of nonpayment of charges. Where delivery without payment is forbidden by law, the request is treated as implicit. Such a prohibition reflects a policy of uniformity to prevent discrimination by failure to request payment in particular cases. Subsection (b) must be read in conjunction with the priorities given to the warehouse lien and the carrier lien under Section 7–209 and 7–307, respectively. If the parties are in dispute about whether the request for payment of the lien is legally proper, the bailee may have recourse to interpleader. See Section 7–603.

5. Subsection (c) states the obvious duty of a bailee to take up a negotiable document or note partial deliveries conspicuously thereon, and the result of failure in that duty. It is subject to only one exception, that stated in subsection (a)(1) of this section and in Section 7–503(a). Subsection (c) is limited to cases of delivery to a claimant; it has no application, for example, where goods held under a negotiable document are lawfully sold to enforce the bailee's lien.

6. When courts are considering subsection (a)(7), "any other lawful excuse," among others, refers to compliance with court orders under Sections 7–601, 7–602 and 7–603.

Cross References:

Point 2: Sections 7–502 and 7–503.
Point 3: Sections 2–705, 2A–526, 7–103, 7–204, and 7–309 and 10–103.
Point 4: Sections 7–209, 7–307 and 7–603.
Point 5: Section 7–503(1).
Point 6: Sections 7–601, 7–602, and 7–603.

Definitional Cross References:

"Bailee". Section 7-102.
"Conspicuous". Section 1-201.
"Delivery". Section 1-201.
"Document of title". Section 1-201.
"Duly negotiate". Section 7-501.
"Goods". Section 7-102.
"Lessor". Section 2A-103.
"Person". Section 1-201.
"Receipt of goods". Section 2-103.
"Right". Section 1-201.
"Terms". Section 1-201.
"Warehouse". Section 7-102.

§ 7-404. No Liability for Good-Faith Delivery Pursuant to Document of Title.

A bailee that in good faith has received goods and delivered or otherwise disposed of the goods according to the terms of a document of title or pursuant to this article is not liable for the goods even if:

(1) the person from which the bailee received the goods did not have authority to procure the document or to dispose of the goods; or

(2) the person to which the bailee delivered the goods did not have authority to receive the goods.

Official Comment

Prior Uniform Statutory Provision: Former Section 7-404.

Changes: Changes reflect the definition of good faith in Section 1-201 [7-102] and for style.

Purposes:

This section uses the test of good faith, as defined in Section 1-201 [7-102], to continue the policy of former Section 7-404. Good faith now means "honesty in fact and the observance of reasonable commercial standards of fair dealing." The section states explicitly that the common law rule of "innocent conversion" by unauthorized "intermeddling" with another's property is inapplicable to the operations of commercial carriers and warehousemen that in good faith perform obligations that they have assumed and that generally they are under a legal compulsion to assume. The section applies to delivery to a fraudulent holder of a valid document as well as to delivery to the holder of an invalid document. Of course, in appropriate circumstances, a bailee may use interpleader or other dispute resolution process. See Section 7-603.

Cross Reference:

Section 7-603.

Definitional Cross References:

"Bailee". Section 7-102.
"Delivery". Section 1-201.
"Document of title". Section 1-201.
"Good faith". Section 1-201. [7-102].
"Goods". Section 7-102.
"Person". Section 1-201.
"Receipt of goods". Section 2-103.
"Term". Section 1-201.

PART 5

WAREHOUSE RECEIPTS AND BILLS OF LADING: NEGOTIATION AND TRANSFER

§ 7–501. Form of Negotiation and Requirements of Due Negotiation.

(a) The following rules apply to a negotiable tangible document of title:

(1) If the document's original terms run to the order of a named person, the document is negotiated by the named person's indorsement and delivery. After the named person's indorsement in blank or to bearer, any person may negotiate the document by delivery alone.

(2) If the document's original terms run to bearer, it is negotiated by delivery alone.

(3) If the document's original terms run to the order of a named person and it is delivered to the named person, the effect is the same as if the document had been negotiated.

(4) Negotiation of the document after it has been indorsed to a named person requires indorsement by the named person and delivery.

(5) A document is duly negotiated if it is negotiated in the manner stated in this subsection to a holder that purchases it in good faith, without notice of any defense against or claim to it on the part of any person, and for value, unless it is established that the negotiation is not in the regular course of business or financing or involves receiving the document in settlement or payment of a monetary obligation.

(b) The following rules apply to a negotiable electronic document of title:

(1) If the document's original terms run to the order of a named person or to bearer, the document is negotiated by delivery of the document to another person. Indorsement by the named person is not required to negotiate the document.

(2) If the document's original terms run to the order of a named person and the named person has control of the document, the effect is the same as if the document had been negotiated.

(3) A document is duly negotiated if it is negotiated in the manner stated in this subsection to a holder that purchases it in good faith, without notice of any defense against or claim to it on the part of any person, and for value, unless it is established that the negotiation is not in the regular course of business or financing or involves taking delivery of the document in settlement or payment of a monetary obligation.

(c) Indorsement of a nonnegotiable document of title neither makes it negotiable nor adds to the transferee's rights.

(d) The naming in a negotiable bill of lading of a person to be notified of the arrival of the goods does not limit the negotiability of the bill or constitute notice to a purchaser of the bill of any interest of that person in the goods.

Official Comment

Prior Uniform Statutory Provision: Former Section 7–501.

Changes: To accommodate negotiable electronic documents of title.

Purpose:

1. Subsection (a) has been limited to tangible negotiable documents of title but otherwise remains unchanged in substance from the rules in former Section 7–501. Subsection (b) is new and applies to negotiable electronic documents of title. Delivery of a negotiable electronic document is through voluntary transfer of control. Section 1–201 definition of "delivery." The control concept as applied to negotiable electronic documents of title is the substitute for both possession and indorsement as applied to negotiable tangible documents of title. Section 7–106.

Article 7 does not separately define the term "duly negotiated." However, the elements of "duly negotiated" are set forth in subsection (a)(5) for tangible documents and (b)(3) for electronic documents. As under former Section 7–501, in order to effect a "due negotiation" the negotiation must be in the "regular course of business or financing" in order to transfer greater rights than those held by the person negotiating. The foundation of the mercantile doctrine of good faith purchase for value has always been, as shown by the case situations, the furtherance and protection of the regular course of trade. The reason for allowing a person, in bad faith or in error, to convey away rights which are not its own has from the beginning been to make possible the speedy handling of that great run of commercial transactions which are patently usual and normal.

There are two aspects to the usual and normal course of mercantile dealings, namely, the person making the transfer and the nature of the transaction itself. The first question which arises is: Is the transferor a person with whom it is reasonable to deal as having full powers? In regard to documents of title the only holder whose possession or control appears, commercially, to be in order is almost invariably a person in the trade. No commercial purpose is served by allowing a tramp or a professor to "duly negotiate" an order bill of lading for hides or cotton not their own, and since such a transfer is obviously not in the regular course of business, it is excluded from the scope of the protection of subsections (a)(5) or (b)(3).

The second question posed by the "regular course" qualification is: Is the transaction one which is normally proper to pass full rights without inquiry, even though the transferor itself may not have such rights to pass, and even though the transferor may be acting in breach of duty? In raising this question the "regular course" criterion has the further advantage of limiting, the effective wrongful disposition to transactions whose protection will really further trade. Obviously, the snapping up of goods for quick resale at a price suspiciously below the market deserves no protection as a matter of policy: it is also clearly outside the range of regular course.

Any notice on the document sufficient to put a merchant on inquiry as to the "regular course" quality of the transaction will frustrate a "due negotiation". Thus irregularity of the document or unexplained staleness of a bill of lading may appropriately be recognized as negating a negotiation in "regular" course.

A pre-existing claim constitutes value, and "due negotiation" does not require "new value." A usual and ordinary transaction in which documents are received as security for credit previously extended may be in "regular" course, even though there is a demand for additional collateral because the creditor "deems himself insecure." But the matter has moved out of the regular course of financing if the debtor is thought to be insolvent, the credit previously extended is in effect cancelled, and the creditor snatches a plank in the shipwreck under the guise of a demand for additional collateral. Where a money debt is "paid" in commodity paper, any question of "regular" course disappears, as the case is explicitly excepted from "due negotiation".

2. Negotiation under this section may be made by any holder no matter how the holder acquired possession or control of the document.

3. Subsections (a)(3) and (b)(2) make explicit a matter upon which the intent of the pre-Code law was clear but the language somewhat obscure: a negotiation results from a delivery to a banker or buyer to whose order the document has been taken by the person making the bailment. There is no presumption of irregularity in such a negotiation; it may very well be in "regular course."

4. This Article does not contain any provision creating a presumption of due negotiation to, and full rights in, a holder of a document of title akin to that created by Uniform Commercial Code Article 3. But the reason of the provisions of this Act (Section 1–307) on the prima facie authenticity and accuracy of third party documents, joins with the reason of the present section to work such a presumption in favor of any person who has power to make a due negotiation. It would not make sense for this Act to authorize a purchaser to indulge the presumption of regularity if the courts were not also called upon to do so. Allocations of the burden of going forward with the evidence and the burden of proof are left to the procedural law of the various states.

5. Subsections (c) and (d) are unchanged from prior law and apply to both tangible and electronic documents of title.

Cross References:

Sections 1–307, 7–502 and 7–503.

Definitional Cross References:

"Bearer". Section 1–201.

"Control". Section 7–106.

"Delivery". Section 1–201.

"Document of title". Section 1–201.

"Good faith". Section 1–201 [7–102].
"Holder". Section 1–201.
"Notice". Section 1–202.
"Person". Section 1–201.
"Purchase". Section 1–201.
"Rights". Section 1–201.
"Term". Section 1–201.
"Value". Section 1–204.

§ 7–502. Rights Acquired by Due Negotiation.

(a) Subject to Sections 7–205 and 7–503, a holder to which a negotiable document of title has been duly negotiated acquires thereby:

(1) title to the document;

(2) title to the goods;

(3) all rights accruing under the law of agency or estoppel, including rights to goods delivered to the bailee after the document was issued; and

(4) the direct obligation of the issuer to hold or deliver the goods according to the terms of the document free of any defense or claim by the issuer except those arising under the terms of the document or under this article, but in the case of a delivery order, the bailee's obligation accrues only upon the bailee's acceptance of the delivery order and the obligation acquired by the holder is that the issuer and any indorser will procure the acceptance of the bailee.

(b) Subject to Section 7–503, title and rights acquired by due negotiation are not defeated by any stoppage of the goods represented by the document of title or by surrender of the goods by the bailee and are not impaired even if:

(1) the due negotiation or any prior due negotiation constituted a breach of duty;

(2) any person has been deprived of possession of a negotiable tangible document or control of a negotiable electronic document by misrepresentation, fraud, accident, mistake, duress, loss, theft, or conversion; or

(3) a previous sale or other transfer of the goods or document has been made to a third person.

Official Comment

Prior Uniform Statutory Provision: Former Section 7–502.

Changes: To accommodate electronic documents of title and for style.

Purpose:

1. This section applies to both tangible and electronic documents of title. The elements of duly negotiated, which constitutes a due negotiation, are set forth in Section 7–501. The several necessary qualifications of the broad principle that the holder of a document acquired in a due negotiation is the owner of the document and the goods have been brought together in the next section (Section 7–503).

2. Subsection (a)(3) covers the case of "feeding" of a duly negotiated document by subsequent delivery to the bailee of such goods as the document falsely purported to cover; the bailee in such case is estopped as against the holder of the document.

3. The explicit statement in subsection (a)(4) of the bailee's direct obligation to the holder precludes the defense that the document in question was "spent" after the carrier had delivered the goods to a previous holder. But the holder is subject to such defenses as non-negligent destruction even though not apparent on the document. The sentence on delivery orders applies only to delivery orders in negotiable form which have been duly negotiated. On delivery orders, see also Section 7–503(b) and Comment.

4. Subsection (b) continues the law which gave full effect to the issuance or due negotiation of a negotiable document. The subsection adds nothing to the effect of the rules stated in subsection (a), but it has been included since such explicit reference was provided under former Section 7–502 to preserve the right of a purchaser by due

negotiation. The listing is not exhaustive. The language "any stoppage" is included lest an inference be drawn that a stoppage of the goods before or after transit might cut off or otherwise impair the purchaser's rights.

Cross References:

Sections 7–103, 7–205, 7–403, 7–501, and 7–503.

Definitional Cross References:

"Bailee". Section 7–102.
"Control". Section 7–106.
"Delivery". Section 1–201.
"Delivery order". Section 7–102.
"Document of title". Section 1–201.
"Duly negotiate". Section 7–501.
"Fungible". Section 1–201.
"Goods". Section 7–102.
"Holder". Section 1–201.
"Issuer". Section 7–102.
"Person". Section 1–201.
"Rights". Section 1–201.
"Term". Section 1–201.
"Warehouse receipt". Section 1–201.

§ 7–503. Document of Title to Goods Defeated in Certain Cases.

(a) A document of title confers no right in goods against a person who that before issuance of the document had a legal interest or a perfected security interest in the goods and that did not:

(1) deliver or entrust the goods or any document of title covering the goods to the bailor or the bailor's nominee with:

(A) actual or apparent authority to ship, store, or sell;

(B) power to obtain delivery under Section 7–403; or

(C) power of disposition under Section 2–403, 2A–304(2), 2A–305(2), 9–320, or 9–321(c) or other statute or rule of law; or

(2) acquiesce in the procurement by the bailor or its nominee of any document.

(b) Title to goods based upon an unaccepted delivery order is subject to the rights of any person to which a negotiable warehouse receipt or bill of lading covering the goods has been duly negotiated. That title may be defeated under Section 7–504 to the same extent as the rights of the issuer or a transferee from the issuer.

(c) Title to goods based upon a bill of lading issued to a freight forwarder is subject to the rights of any person to which a bill issued by the freight forwarder is duly negotiated. However, delivery by the carrier in accordance with Part 4 pursuant to its own bill of lading discharges the carrier's obligation to deliver.

Official Comment

Prior Uniform Statutory Provision: Former Section 7–503.

Changes: Changes to cross-reference to Article 2A and for style.

Purposes:

1. In general it may be said that the title of a purchaser by due negotiation prevails over almost any interest in the goods which existed prior to the procurement of the document of title if the possession of the goods by the person obtaining the document derived from any action by the prior claimant which introduced the goods into the stream of commerce or carried them along that stream. A thief of the goods cannot indeed by shipping or storing them to the thief's own order acquire power to transfer them to a good faith purchaser. Nor can a tenant or mortgagor defeat any rights of a landlord or mortgagee which have been perfected under the local law merely by wrongfully shipping or storing a portion of the crop or other goods. However, "acquiescence" by the landlord or

mortgagee does not require active consent under subsection (a)(2) and knowledge of the likelihood of storage or shipment with no objection or effort to control it is sufficient to defeat the landlord's or the mortgagee's rights as against one who takes by due negotiation of a negotiable document. *In re Sharon Steel*, 176 B.R. 384 (Bankr. W.D. Pa. 1995); *In re R.V. Segars Co*, 54 B.R. 170 (Bankr. S.C. 1985); *In re Jamestown Elevators, Inc.*, 49 B.R. 661 (Bankr. N.D. 1985).

On the other hand, where goods are delivered to a factor for sale, even though the factor has made no advances and is limited in its duty to sell for cash, the goods are "entrusted" to the factor "with actual . . . authority . . . to sell" under subsection (a)(1), and if the factor procures a negotiable document of title it can transfer the owner's interest to a purchaser by due negotiation. Further, where the factor is in the business of selling, goods entrusted to it simply for safekeeping or storage may be entrusted under circumstances which give the factor "apparent authority to ship, store or sell" under subsection (a)(1), or power of disposition under Section 2–403, 2A–304(2), 2A–305(2), 7–205, 9–320, or 9–321(c) or under a statute such as the earlier Factors Acts, or under a rule of law giving effect to apparent ownership. See Section 1–103.

Persons having an interest in goods also frequently deliver or entrust them to agents or servants other than factors for the purpose of shipping or warehousing or under circumstances reasonably contemplating such action. This Act is clear that such persons assume full risk that the agent to whom the goods are so delivered may ship or store in breach of duty, take a document to the agent's own order and then proceed to misappropriate the negotiable document of title that embodies the goods. This Act makes no distinction between possession or mere custody in such situations and finds no exception in the case of larceny by a bailee or the like. The safeguard in such situations lies in the requirement that a due negotiation can occur only "in the regular course of business or financing" and that the purchase be in good faith and without notice. See Section 7–501. Documents of title have no market among the commercially inexperienced and the commercially experienced do not take them without inquiry from persons known to be truck drivers or petty clerks even though such persons purport to be operating in their own names.

Again, where the seller allows a buyer to receive goods under a contract for sale, though as a "conditional delivery" or under "cash sale" terms and on explicit agreement for immediate payment, the buyer thereby acquires power to defeat the seller's interest by transfer of the goods to certain good faith purchasers. See Section 2–403. Both in policy and under the language of subsection (a)(1) that same power must be extended to accomplish the same result if the buyer procures a negotiable document of title to the goods and duly negotiates it.

This comment 1 should be considered in interpreting delivery, entrustment or acquiescence in application of Section 7–209.

2. Under subsection (a) a delivery order issued by a person having no right in or power over the goods is ineffective unless the owner acts as provided in subsection (a)(1) or (2). Thus the rights of a transferee of a non-negotiable warehouse receipt can be defeated by a delivery order subsequently issued by the transferor only if the transferee "delivers or entrusts" to the "person procuring" the delivery order or "acquiesces" in that person's procurement. Similarly, a second delivery order issued by the same issuer for the same goods will ordinarily be subject to the first, both under this section and under Section 7–402. After a delivery order is validly issued but before it is accepted, it may nevertheless be defeated under subsection (b) in much the same way that the rights of a transferee may be defeated under Section 7–504. For example, a buyer in ordinary course from the issuer may defeat the rights of the holder of a prior delivery order if the bailee receives notification of the buyer's rights before notification of the holder's rights. Section 7–504(b)(2). But an accepted delivery order has the same effect as a document issued by the bailee.

3. Under subsection (c) a bill of lading issued to a freight forwarder is subordinated to the freight forwarder's document of title, since the bill on its face gives notice of the fact that a freight forwarder is in the picture and the freight forwarder has in all probability issued a document of title. But the carrier is protected in following the terms of its own bill of lading.

Cross References:

Point 1: Sections 1–103, 2–403, 2A–304(2), 2A–305(2), 7–205, 7–209, 7–501, 9–320, 9–321(c), and 9–331.
Point 2: Sections 7–402 and 7–504.
Point 3: Sections 7–402, 7–403 and 7–404.

Definitional Cross References:

"Bill of lading". Section 1–201.
"Contract for sale". Section 2–106.

"Delivery". Section 1-201.
"Delivery order". Section 7-102.
"Document of title". Section 1-201.
"Duly negotiate". Section 7-501.
"Goods". Section 7-102.
"Person". Section 1-201.
"Right". Section 1-201.
"Warehouse receipt". Section 1-201.

§ 7-504. Rights Acquired in Absence of Due Negotiation; Effect of Diversion; Stoppage of Delivery.

(a) A transferee of a document of title, whether negotiable or nonnegotiable, to which the document has been delivered but not duly negotiated, acquires the title and rights that its transferor had or had actual authority to convey.

(b) In the case of a transfer of a nonnegotiable document of title, until but not after the bailee receives notice of the transfer, the rights of the transferee may be defeated:

(1) by those creditors of the transferor which could treat the transfer as void under Section 2-402 or 2A-308;

(2) by a buyer from the transferor in ordinary course of business if the bailee has delivered the goods to the buyer or received notification of the buyer's rights;

(3) by a lessee from the transferor in ordinary course of business if the bailee has delivered the goods to the lessee or received notification of the lessee's rights; or

(4) as against the bailee, by good-faith dealings of the bailee with the transferor.

(c) A diversion or other change of shipping instructions by the consignor in a nonnegotiable bill of lading which causes the bailee not to deliver the goods to the consignee defeats the consignee's title to the goods if the goods have been delivered to a buyer in ordinary course of business or a lessee in ordinary course of business and, in any event, defeats the consignee's rights against the bailee.

(d) Delivery of the goods pursuant to a nonnegotiable document of title may be stopped by a seller under Section 2-705 or a lessor under Section 2A-526, subject to the requirements of due notification in those sections. A bailee that honors the seller's or lessor's instructions is entitled to be indemnified by the seller or lessor against any resulting loss or expense.

Official Comment

Prior Uniform Statutory Provision: Former Section 7-504.

Changes: To include cross-references to Article 2A and for style.

Purposes:

1. Under the general principles controlling negotiable documents, it is clear that in the absence of due negotiation a transferor cannot convey greater rights than the transferor has, even when the negotiation is formally perfect. This section recognizes the transferor's power to transfer rights which the transferor has or has "actual authority to convey." Thus, where a negotiable document of title is being transferred the operation of the principle of estoppel is not recognized, as contrasted with situations involving the transfer of the goods themselves. (Compare Section 2-403 on good faith purchase of goods.) This section applies to both tangible and electronic documents of title.

A necessary part of the price for the protection of regular dealings with negotiable documents of title is an insistence that no dealing which is in any way irregular shall be recognized as a good faith purchase of the document or of any rights pertaining to it. So, where the transfer of a negotiable document fails as a negotiation because a requisite indorsement is forged or otherwise missing, the purchaser in good faith and for value may be in the anomalous position of having less rights, in part, than if the purchaser had purchased the goods themselves. True, the purchaser's rights are not subject to defeat by attachment of the goods or surrender of them to the purchaser's transferor (contrast subsection (b)); but on the other hand, the purchaser cannot acquire enforceable rights to control or receive the goods over the bailee's objection merely by giving notice to the bailee. Similarly, a consignee who makes payment to its consignor against a straight bill of lading can thereby acquire the position of a good faith purchaser of goods under provisions of the Article of this Act on Sales (Section 2–403), whereas the same payment made in good faith against an unendorsed order bill would not have such effect. The appropriate remedy of a purchaser in such a situation is to regularize its status by compelling indorsement of the document (see Section 7–506).

2. As in the case of transfer—as opposed to "due negotiation"—of negotiable documents, subsection (a) empowers the transferor of a nonnegotiable document to transfer only such rights as the transferor has or has "actual authority" to convey. In contrast to situations involving the goods themselves the operation of estoppel or agency principles is not here recognized to enable the transferor to convey greater rights than the transferor actually has. Subsection (b) makes it clear, however, that the transferee of a nonnegotiable document may acquire rights greater in some respects than those of his transferor by giving notice of the transfer to the bailee. New subsection (b)(3) provides for the rights of a lessee in the ordinary course.

Subsection (b)(2) & (3) require delivery of the goods. Delivery of the goods means the voluntary transfer of physical possession of the goods. See amended 2–103 [*2003 amendments to Article 2, withdrawn in 2011*].

3. Subsection (c) is in part a reiteration of the carrier's immunity from liability if it honors instructions of the consignor to divert, but there is added a provision protecting the title of the substituted consignee if the latter is a buyer in ordinary course of business. A typical situation would be where a manufacturer, having shipped a lot of standardized goods to A on nonnegotiable bill of lading, diverts the goods to customer B who pays for them. Under pre-Code passage-of-title-by-appropriation doctrine A might reclaim the goods from B. However, no consideration of commercial policy supports this involvement of an innocent third party in the default of the manufacturer on his contract to A; and the common commercial practice of diverting goods in transit suggests a trade understanding in accordance with this subsection. The same result should obtain if the substituted consignee is a lessee in ordinary course. The extent of the lessee's interest in the goods is less than a buyer's interest in the goods. However, as against the first consignee and the lessee in ordinary course as the substituted consignee, the lessee's rights in the goods as granted under the lease are superior to the first consignee's rights.

4. Subsection (d) gives the carrier an express right to indemnity where the carrier honors a seller's request to stop delivery.

5. Section 1–202 gives the bailee protection, if due diligence is exercised where the bailee's organization has not had time to act on a notification.

Cross References:

Point 1: Sections 2–403 and 7–506.
Point 2: Sections 2–403 and 2A–304.
Point 3: Sections 7–303, 7–403(a)(5) and 7–404.
Point 4: Sections 2–705 and 7–403(a)(4).
Point 5: Section 1–202.

Definitional Cross References:

"Bailee". Section 7–102.
"Bill of lading". Section 1–201.
"Buyer in ordinary course of business". Section 1–201.
"Consignee". Section 7–102.
"Consignor". Section 7–102.
"Creditor". Section 1–201.
"Delivery" Section 1–201.
"Document of title". Section 1–201.
"Duly negotiate". Section 7–501.
"Good faith". Section 1–201. [7–102].
"Goods". Section 7–102.
"Honor". Section 1–201.
"Lessee in ordinary course". Section 2A–103.
"Notification" Section 1–202.
"Purchaser". Section 1–201.
"Rights". Section 1–201.

§ 7-505. Indorser Not Guarantor for Other Parties.

The indorsement of a tangible document of title issued by a bailee does not make the indorser liable for any default by the bailee or previous indorsers.

Official Comment

Prior Uniform Statutory Provision: Former Section 7-505.

Changes: Limited to tangible documents of title.

Purposes:

This section is limited to tangible documents of title as the concept of indorsement is irrelevant to electronic documents of title. Electronic documents of title will be transferred by delivery of control. Section 7-106. The indorsement of a tangible document of title is generally understood to be directed towards perfecting the transferee's rights rather than towards assuming additional obligations. The language of the present section, however, does not preclude the one case in which an indorsement given for value guarantees future action, namely, that in which the bailee has not yet become liable upon the document at the time of the indorsement. Under such circumstances the indorser, of course, engages that appropriate honor of the document by the bailee will occur. See Section 7-502(a)(4) as to negotiable delivery orders. However, even in such a case, once the bailee attorns to the transferee, the indorser's obligation has been fulfilled and the policy of this section excludes any continuing obligation on the part of the indorser for the bailee's ultimate actual performance.

Cross Reference:

Sections 7-106 and 7-502.

Definitional Cross References:

"Bailee". Section 7-102.
"Document of title". Section 1-201.
"Party". Section 1-201.

§ 7-506. Delivery Without Indorsement: Right to Compel Indorsement.

The transferee of a negotiable tangible document of title has a specifically enforceable right to have its transferor supply any necessary indorsement, but the transfer becomes a negotiation only as of the time the indorsement is supplied.

Official Comment

Prior Uniform Statutory Provision: Former Section 7-506.

Changes: Limited to tangible documents of title.

Purposes:

1. This section is limited to tangible documents of title as the concept of indorsement is irrelevant to electronic documents of title. Electronic documents of title will be transferred by delivery of control. Section 7-106. From a commercial point of view the intention to transfer a tangible negotiable document of title which requires an indorsement for its transfer, is incompatible with an intention to withhold such indorsement and so defeat the effective use of the document. Further, the preceding section and the Comment thereto make it clear that an indorsement generally imposes no responsibility on the indorser.

2. Although this section provides that delivery of a tangible document of title without the necessary indorsement is effective as a transfer, the transferee, of course, has not regularized its position until such indorsement is supplied. Until this is done the transferee cannot claim rights under due negotiation within the requirements of this Article (Section 7-501(a)(5)) on "due negotiation". Similarly, despite the transfer to the transferee of the transferor's title, the transferee cannot demand the goods from the bailee until the negotiation has been completed and the document is in proper form for surrender. See Section 7-403(c).

Cross References:

Point 1: Sections 7-106 and 7-505.
Point 2: Sections 7-501(a)(5) and 7-403(c).

Definitional Cross References:

"Document of title". Section 1–201.
"Rights". Section 1–201.

§ 7–507. Warranties on Negotiation or Delivery of Document of Title.

If a person negotiates or delivers a document of title for value, otherwise than as a mere intermediary under Section 7–508, unless otherwise agreed, the transferor, in addition to any warranty made in selling or leasing the goods, warrants to its immediate purchaser only that:

(1) the document is genuine;

(2) the transferor does not have knowledge of any fact that would impair the document's validity or worth; and

(3) the negotiation or delivery is rightful and fully effective with respect to the title to the document and the goods it represents.

Official Comment

Prior Uniform Statutory Provision: Former Section 7–507.

Changes: Substitution of the word "delivery" for the word "transfer," reference leasing transactions and style.

Purposes:

1. Delivery of goods by use of a document of title does not limit or displace the ordinary obligations of a seller or lessor as to any warranties regarding the goods that arises under other law. If the transfer of documents attends or follows the making of a contract for the sale or lease of goods, the general obligations on warranties as to the goods (Sections 2–312 through 2–318 and Sections 2A–210 through 2A–316) are brought to bear as well as the special warranties under this section.

2. The limited warranties of a delivering or collecting intermediary, including a collecting bank, are stated in Section 7–508.

Cross References:

Point 1: Sections 2–312 through 2–318 and 2A–310 through 2A–316.
Point 2: Section 7–508.

Definitional Cross References:

"Delivery". Section 1–201.
"Document of title". Section 1–201.
"Genuine". Section 1–201.
"Goods". Section 7–102.
"Person". Section 1–201.
"Purchaser". Section 1–201.
"Value". Section 1–204.

§ 7–508. Warranties of Collecting Bank as to Documents of Title.

A collecting bank or other intermediary known to be entrusted with documents of title on behalf of another or with collection of a draft or other claim against delivery of documents warrants by the delivery of the documents only its own good faith and authority even if the collecting bank or other intermediary has purchased or made advances against the claim or draft to be collected.

Official Comment

Prior Uniform Statutory Provision: Former Section 7–508.

Changes: Changes for style only.

Purposes:

1. To state the limited warranties given with respect to the documents accompanying a documentary draft.

2. In warranting its authority a collecting bank or other intermediary only warrants its authority from its transferor. See Section 4–203. It does not warrant the genuineness or effectiveness of the document. Compare Section 7-507.

3. Other duties and rights of banks handling documentary drafts for collection are stated in Article 4, Part 5. On the meaning of draft, see Section 4–104 and Section 5–102, comment 11.

Cross References:

Sections 4–104, 4–203, 4–501 through 4–504, 5–102, and 7–507.

Definitional Cross References:

"Collecting bank". Section 4–105.
"Delivery". Section 1–201.
"Document of title". Section 1–102.
"Documentary draft". Section 4–104.
"Intermediary bank". Section 4–105.
"Good faith". Section 1–201 [7–102.]

§ 7–509. Adequate Compliance with Commercial Contract.

Whether a document of title is adequate to fulfill the obligations of a contract for sale, a contract for lease, or the conditions of a letter of credit is determined by Article 2, 2A, or 5.

Official Comment

Prior Uniform Statutory Provision: Former Section 7–509.

Changes: To reference Article 2A.

Purposes:

To cross-refer to the Articles of this Act which deal with the substantive issues of the type of document of title required under the contract entered into by the parties.

Cross References:

Articles 2, 2A and 5.

Definitional Cross References:

"Contract for sale". Section 2–106.
"Document of title". Section 1–201.
"Lease". Section 2A–103.

PART 6

WAREHOUSE RECEIPTS AND BILLS OF LADING: MISCELLANEOUS PROVISIONS

§ 7–601. Lost, Stolen, or Destroyed Documents of Title.

(a) If a document of title is lost, stolen, or destroyed, a court may order delivery of the goods or issuance of a substitute document and the bailee may without liability to any person comply with the order. If the document was negotiable, a court may not order delivery of the goods or issuance of a substitute document without the claimant's posting security unless it finds that any person that may suffer loss as a result of nonsurrender of possession or control of the document is adequately protected against the loss. If the document was nonnegotiable, the court may require security. The court may also order payment of the bailee's reasonable costs and attorney's fees in any action under this subsection.

(b) A bailee that, without a court order, delivers goods to a person claiming under a missing negotiable document of title is liable to any person injured thereby. If the delivery is not in good faith, the bailee is liable for conversion. Delivery in good faith is not conversion if the claimant posts security with the bailee in an amount at least double the value of the goods at the time of posting to indemnify any person injured by the delivery which files a notice of claim within one year after the delivery.

Official Comment

Prior Uniform Statutory Provision: Former Section 7–601.

Changes: To accommodate electronic documents; to provide flexibility to courts similar to the flexibility in Section 3–309; to update to the modern era of deregulation; and for style.

Purposes:

1. Subsection (a) authorizes courts to order compulsory delivery of the goods or compulsory issuance of a substitute document. Compare Section 7–402. Using language similar to that found in Section 3–309, courts are given discretion as to what is adequate protection when the lost, stolen or destroyed document was negotiable or whether security should be required when the lost, stolen or destroyed document was nonnegotiable. In determining whether a party is adequately protected against loss in the case of a negotiable document, the court should consider the likelihood that the party will suffer a loss. The court is also given discretion as to the bailee's costs and attorney fees. The rights and obligations of a bailee under this section depend upon whether the document of title is lost, stolen or destroyed and is in addition to the ability of the bailee to bring an action for interpleader. See Section 7–603.

2. Courts have the authority under this section to order a substitute document for either tangible or electronic documents. If the substitute document will be in a different medium than the original document, the court should fashion its order in light of the requirements of Section 7–105.

3. Subsection (b) follows prior Section 7–601 in recognizing the legality of the well established commercial practice of bailees making delivery in good faith when they are satisfied that the claimant is the person entitled under a missing (i.e. lost, stolen, or destroyed) negotiable document. Acting without a court order, the bailee remains liable on the original negotiable document and, to avoid conversion liability, the bailee may insist that the claimant provide an indemnity bond. Cf. Section 7–403.

4. Claimants on non-negotiable instruments are permitted to avail themselves of the subsection (a) procedure because straight (non-negotiable) bills of lading sometimes contain provisions that the goods shall not be delivered except upon production of the bill. If the carrier should choose to insist upon production of the bill, the consignee should have some means of compelling delivery on satisfactory proof of entitlement. Without a court order, a bailee may deliver, subject to Section 7–403, to a person claiming goods under a non-negotiable document that the same person claims is lost, stolen, or destroyed.

5. The bailee's lien should be protected when a court orders delivery of the goods pursuant to this section.

Cross References:

Point 1: Sections 3–309, 7–402 and 7–603.
Point 2: Section 7–105.
Point 3: Section 7–403.
Point 4: Section 7–403.
Point 5: Sections 7–209 and 7–307.

Definitional Cross References:

"Bailee". Section 7–102.
"Delivery". Section 1–201.
"Document of title". Section 1–201.
"Good faith". Section 1–201 [7–102].
"Goods". Section 7–102.
"Person". Section 1–201.

§ 7–602. Judicial Process Against Goods Covered by Negotiable Document of Title.

Unless a document of title was originally issued upon delivery of the goods by a person that did not have power to dispose of them, a lien does not attach by virtue of any judicial process to goods in the possession of a bailee for which a negotiable document of title is outstanding unless possession or control of the document is first surrendered to the bailee or the document's negotiation is enjoined. The bailee may not be compelled to deliver the goods pursuant to process until possession or control of the document is surrendered to the bailee or to the court. A purchaser of the document for value without notice of the process or injunction takes free of the lien imposed by judicial process.

Official Comment

Prior Uniform Statutory Provisions: Former Section 7-602.

Changes: Changes to accommodate electronic documents of title and for style.

Purposes:

1. The purpose of the section is to protect the bailee from conflicting claims of the document of title holder and the judgment creditors of the person who deposited the goods. The rights of the former prevail unless, in effect, the judgment creditors immobilize the negotiable document of title through the surrender of possession of a tangible document or control of an electronic document. However, if the document of title was issued upon deposit of the goods by a person who had no power to dispose of the goods so that the document is ineffective to pass title, judgment liens are valid to the extent of the debtor's interest in the goods.

2. The last sentence covers the possibility that the holder of a document who has been enjoined from negotiating it will violate the injunction by negotiating to an innocent purchaser for value. In such case the lien will be defeated.

Cross Reference:

Sections 7-106 and 7-501 through 7-503.

Definitional Cross References:

"Bailee". Section 7-102.
"Delivery". Section 1-201.
"Document of title". Section 1-201.
"Goods". Section 7-102.
"Notice". Section 1-202.
"Person". Section 1-201.
"Purchase". Section 1-201.
"Value". Section 1-204.

§ 7-603. Conflicting Claims; Interpleader.

If more than one person claims title to or possession of the goods, the bailee is excused from delivery until the bailee has a reasonable time to ascertain the validity of the adverse claims or to commence an action for interpleader. The bailee may assert an interpleader either in defending an action for nondelivery of the goods or by original action.

Official Comment

Prior Uniform Statutory Provisions: Former Section 7-603.

Changes: Changes for style only.

Purposes:

1. The section enables a bailee faced with conflicting claims to the goods to compel the claimants to litigate their claims with each other rather than with the bailee. The bailee is protected from legal liability when the bailee complies with court orders from the interpleader. *See e.g. Northwestern National Sales, Inc. v. Commercial Cold Storage, Inc.*, 162 Ga. App. 741, 293 S.E.2d. 30 (1982).

2. This section allows the bailee to bring an interpleader action but does not provide an exclusive basis for allowing interpleader. If either state or federal procedural rules allow an interpleader in other situations, the bailee may commence an interpleader under those rules. Even in an interpleader to which this section applies, the state or federal process of interpleader applies to the bailee's action for interpleader. For example, state or federal interpleader statutes or rules may permit a bailee to protect its lien or to seek attorney's fees and costs in the interpleader action.

Cross reference:

Point 1: Section 7–403.

Definitional Cross References:

"Action". Section 1–201.
"Bailee". Section 7–102.
"Delivery". Section 1–201.
"Goods". Section 7–102.
"Person". Section 1–201.
"Reasonable time". Section 1–205.

PART 7

MISCELLANEOUS PROVISIONS

Legislative Note: The following provisions should be used to apply to both the Article 7 provisions and the conforming amendments to other articles of the Uniform Commercial Code.

§ 7–701. Effective Date.

This [Act] takes effect on [ ].

§ 7–702. Repeals.

[Existing Article 7] and [Section 10–104 of the Uniform Commercial Code] are repealed.

Official Comment

A state should repeal its prior version of Uniform Commercial Code Article 7 on documents of title and Uniform Commercial Code section 10–204. The substance of Section 10–104 has been incorporated into Section 7–103(b).

§ 7–703. Applicability.

This [Act] applies to a document of title that is issued or a bailment that arises on or after the effective date of this [Act]. This [Act] does not apply to a document of title that is issued or a bailment that arises before the effective date of this [Act] even if the document of title or bailment would be subject to this [Act] if the document of title had been issued or bailment had arisen on or after the effective date of this [Act]. This [Act] does not apply to a right of action that has accrued before the effective date of this [Act].

Official Comment

This Act will apply prospectively only to documents of title issued or bailments that arise after the effective date of the Act.

§ 7–704. Savings Clause.

A document of title issued or a bailment that arises before the effective date of this [Act] and the rights, obligations, and interests flowing from that document or bailment are governed by any statute or other rule amended or repealed by this [Act] as if amendment or repeal had not occurred and may be terminated, completed, consummated, or enforced under that statute or other rule.

Official Comment

This Act will apply prospectively only to documents of title issued or bailments that arise after the effective date of the Act. To the extent that issues arise based upon documents of title or rights or obligations that arise prior to the effective date of this Act, prior law will apply to resolve those issues.

APPENDIX B

UCC ARTICLES 3 & 4 (PRE-1990 VERSION)

Set forth below are the text and Official Comments of Article 3 and the text of Article 4 as they existed prior to revision in 1990.

ARTICLE 3

COMMERCIAL PAPER

PART 1. SHORT TITLE, FORM AND INTERPRETATION

PART 2. TRANSFER AND NEGOTIATION

APPENDIX B

PART 3. RIGHTS OF A HOLDER

PART 4. LIABILITY OF PARTIES

PART 5. PRESENTMENT, NOTICE OF DISHONOR AND PROTEST

PART 6. DISCHARGE

PART 1

SHORT TITLE, FORM AND INTERPRETATION

§ 3–101. Short Title.

This Article shall be known and may be cited as Uniform Commercial Code—Commercial Paper.

Official Comment

This Article represents a complete revision and modernization of the Uniform Negotiable Instruments Law.

The Comments which follow will point out the respects in which this Article changes the Negotiable Instruments Law, which was promulgated by the National Conference of Commissioners on Uniform State Laws in 1896, and was subsequently enacted in every American jurisdiction. Needless to say, in the 50 odd years of the history of that statute, there have been vast changes in commercial practices relating to the handling of negotiable instruments. The need for revision of this important statute was felt for some years before the present project was undertaken.

It should be noted especially that this Article does not apply in any way to the handling of securities. Article 8 deals with that subject. See Sec. 3–103.

§ 3–102. Definitions and Index of Definitions.

(1) In this Article unless the context otherwise requires

(a) "Issue" means the first delivery of an instrument to a holder or a remitter.

(b) An "order" is a direction to pay and must be more than an authorization or request. It must identify the person to pay with reasonable certainty. It may be addressed to one or more such persons jointly or in the alternative but not in succession.

(c) A "promise" is an undertaking to pay and must be more than an acknowledgment of an obligation.

(d) "Secondary party" means a drawer or endorser.

(e) "Instrument" means a negotiable instrument.

(2) Other definitions applying to this Article and the sections in which they appear are:

"Acceptance". Section 3–410.
"Accommodation party". Section 3–415.
"Alteration". Section 3–407.
"Certificate of deposit". Section 3–104.
"Certification". Section 3–411.
"Check". Section 3–104.
"Definite time". Section 3–109.
"Dishonor". Section 3–507.
"Draft". Section 3–104.

"Holder in due course". Section 3–302.
"Negotiation". Section 3–202.
"Note". Section 3–104.
"Notice of dishonor". Section 3–508.
"On demand". Section 3–108.
"Presentment". Section 3–504.
"Protest". Section 3–509.
"Restrictive Indorsement". Section 3–205.
"Signature". Section 3–401.

(3) The following definitions in other Articles apply to this Article:

"Account". Section 4–104.
"Banking Day". Section 4–104.
"Clearing house". Section 4–104.
"Collecting bank". Section 4–105.
"Customer". Section 4–104.
"Depositary Bank". Section 4–105.
"Documentary Draft". Section 4–104.
"Intermediary Bank". Section 4–105.
"Item". Section 4–104.
"Midnight deadline". Section 4–104.
"Payor bank". Section 4–105.

(4) In addition Article 1 contains general definitions and principles of construction and interpretation applicable throughout this Article.

Official Comment

Prior Uniform Statutory Provision: Sections 1(5), 128 and 191, Uniform Negotiable Instruments Law.

Changes: See below.

Purposes of Changes:

1. The definition of "issue" in Section 191 of the original act has been clarified in two respects. The Section 191 definition required that the instrument delivered be "complete in form" inconsistently with the provisions of Sections 14 and 15 (relating to incomplete instruments) of the original act. The "complete in form" language has therefore been deleted. Furthermore the Section 191 definition required that the delivery be "to a person who takes as a holder", thus raising difficulties in the case of the remitter (see Comment 3 to Sec. 3–302) who may not be a party to the instrument and thus not a holder. The definition in subsection (1)(a) of this Section thus provides that the delivery may be to a holder or to a remitter.

2. The definitions of "order" [subsection (b)] and "promise" [subsection (c)] are new, but state principles clearly recognized by the courts. In the case of orders the dividing line between "a direction to pay" and "an authorization or request" may not be self-evident in the occasional unusual, and therefore non-commercial, case. The prefixing of words of courtesy to the direction—as "please pay" or "kindly pay"—should not lead to a holding that the direction has degenerated into a mere request. On the other hand informal language—such as "I wish you would pay"—would not qualify as an order and such an instrument would be non-negotiable. The definition of "promise" is intended to make it clear that a mere I.O.U. is not a negotiable instrument, and to change the result in occasional cases which have held that "Due Currier & Barker seventeen dollars and fourteen cents, value received," and "I borrowed from P. Shemonia the sum of five hundred dollars with four per cent interest; the borrowed money ought to be paid within four months from the above date" were promises sufficient to make the instruments into notes.

3. The last sentence of subsection (1)(b) ("order") permits the order to be addressed to one or more persons (as drawees) in the alternative, recognizing the practice of corporations issuing dividend checks and of other drawers who for commercial convenience name a number of drawees, usually in different parts of the country. The section on presentment provides that presentment may be made to any one of such drawees. Drawees in succession

are not permitted because the holder should not be required to make more than one presentment, and upon the first dishonor should have his recourse against the drawer and indorsers.

4. Comments on the definitions indexed follow the sections in which the definitions are contained.

Cross Reference:

Point 3: Section 3–504(3)(a).

Definitional Cross References:

"Bank". Section 1–201.
"Delivery". Section 1–201.
"Holder". Section 1–201.
"Money". Section 1–201.
"Person". Section 1–201.

§ 3–103. Limitations on Scope of Article.

(1) This Article does not apply to money, documents of title or investment securities.

(2) The provisions of this Article are subject to the provisions of the Article on Bank Deposits and Collections (Article 4) and Secured Transactions (Article 9).

Official Comment

Prior Uniform Statutory Provision: None.

Purposes:

1. This Article is restricted to commercial paper—that is to say, to drafts, checks, certificates of deposit and notes as defined in Section 3–104(2). Subsection (1) expressly excludes any money, as defined in this Act (Section 1–201), even though the money may be in the form of a bank note which meets all the requirements of Section 3–104(1). Money is of course negotiable at common law or under separate statutes, but no provision of this Article is applicable to it. Subsection (1) also expressly excludes documents of title and investment securities which fall within Articles 7 and 8, respectively. To this extent the section follows decisions which held that interim certificates calling for the delivery of securities were not negotiable instruments under the original statute. Such paper is now covered under Article 8, but is not within any section of this Article. Likewise, bills of lading, warehouse receipts and other documents of title which fall within Article 7 may be negotiable under the provision of that Article, but are not covered by any section of this Article.

2. Instruments which fall within the scope of this Article may also be subject to other Articles of the Code. Many items in course of bank collection will of course be negotiable instruments, and the same may be true of collateral pledged as security for a debt. In such cases this Article, which is general, is, in case of conflicting provisions, subject to the Articles which deal specifically with the type of transaction or instrument involved: Article 4 (Bank Deposits and Collections) and Article 9 (Secured Transactions). In the case of a negotiable instrument which is subject to Article 4 because it is in course of collection or to Article 9 because it is used as collateral, the provisions of this Article continue to be applicable except insofar as there may be conflicting provisions in the Bank Collection or Secured Transactions Article.

An instrument which qualifies as "negotiable" under this Article may also qualify as a "security" under Article 8. It will be noted that the formal requisites of negotiability (Section 3–104) go to matters of form exclusively; the definition of "security" on the other hand (Section 8–102) looks principally to the manner in which an instrument is used ("commonly dealt in upon securities exchanges . . . or commonly recognized . . . as a medium for investment"). If an instrument negotiable in form under Section 3–104 is, because of the manner of its use, a "security" under Section 8–102, Article 8 and not this Article applies. See subsection (1) of this Section and Section 8–102(1)(b).

Cross References:

Point 1: Articles 7 and 8; Sections 1–201, 3–104(1) and (2), 3–107.
Point 2: Articles 4 and 9; Sections 3–104 and 8–102.

Definitional Cross References:

"Document of title". Section 1–201.
"Money". Section 1–201.

§ 3–104. Form of Negotiable Instruments; "Draft"; "Check"; "Certificate of Deposit"; "Note".

(1) Any writing to be a negotiable instrument within this Article must

(a) be signed by the maker or drawer; and

(b) contain an unconditional promise or order to pay a sum certain in money and no other promise, order, obligation or power given by the maker or drawer except as authorized by this Article; and

(c) be payable on demand or at a definite time; and

(d) be payable to order or to bearer.

(2) A writing which complies with the requirements of this section is

(a) a "draft" ("bill of exchange") if it is an order;

(b) a "check" if it is a draft drawn on a bank and payable on demand;

(c) a "certificate of deposit" if it is an acknowledgment by a bank of receipt of money with an engagement to repay it;

(d) a "note" if it is a promise other than a certificate of deposit.

(3) As used in other Articles of this Act, and as the context may require, the terms "draft", "check", "certificate of deposit" and "note" may refer to instruments which are not negotiable within this Article as well as to instruments which are so negotiable.

Official Comment

Prior Uniform Statutory Provision: Sections 1, 5, 10, 126, 184 and 185, Uniform Negotiable Instruments Law.

Changes: Parts of original sections combined and reworded; new provisions; original Section 10 omitted.

Purposes of Changes and New Matter: The changes are intended to bring together in one section related provisions and definitions formerly widely separated.

1. Under subsection (1)(b) any writing, to be a negotiable instrument within this Article, must be payable in money. In a few states there are special statutes, enacted at an early date when currency was less sound and barter was prevalent, which make promises to pay in commodities negotiable. Even under these statutes commodity notes are now little used and have no general circulation. This Article makes no attempt to provide for such paper, as it is a matter of purely local concern. Even if retention of the old statutes is regarded in any state as important, amendment of this section may not be necessary, since "within this Article" in subsection (1) leaves open the possibility that some writings may be made negotiable by other statutes or by judicial decision. The same is true as to any new type of paper which commercial practice may develop in the future.

2. While a writing cannot be made a negotiable instrument within this Article by contract or by conduct, nothing in this section is intended to mean that in a particular case a court may not arrive at a result similar to that of negotiability by finding that the obligor is estopped by his conduct from asserting a defense against a bona fide purchaser. Such an estoppel rests upon ordinary principles of the law of simple contract; it does not depend upon negotiability, and it does not make the writing negotiable for any other purpose. But a contract to build a house or to employ a workman, or equally a security agreement does not become a negotiable instrument by the mere insertion of a clause agreeing that it shall be one.

3. The words "no other promise, order, obligation or power" in subsection (1)(b) are an expansion of the first sentence of the original Section 5. Section 3–112 permits an instrument to carry certain limited obligations or powers in addition to the simple promise or order to pay money. Subsection (1) of this Section is intended to say that it cannot carry others.

4. Any writing which meets the requirements of subsection (1) and is not excluded under Section 3–103 is a negotiable instrument, and all sections of this Article apply to it, even though it may contain additional language beyond that contemplated by this section. Such an instrument is a draft, a check, a certificate of deposit

or a note as defined in subsection (2). Traveler's checks in the usual form, for instance, are negotiable instruments under this Article when they have been completed by the identifying signature.

5. This Article omits the original Section 10, which provided that the instrument need not follow the language of the act if it "clearly indicates an intention to conform" to it. The provision has served no useful purpose, and it has been an encouragement to bad drafting and to liberality in holding questionable paper to be negotiable. The omission is not intended to mean that the instrument must follow the language of this section, or that one term may not be recognized as clearly the equivalent of another, as in the case of "I undertake" instead of "I promise," or "Pay to holder" instead of "Pay to bearer." It does mean that either the language of the section or a clear equivalent must be found, and that in doubtful cases the decision should be against negotiability.

6. Subsection (3) is intended to make clear the same policy expressed in Section 3-805.

Cross References:

Sections 3-105 through 3-112, 3-401, 3-402 and 3-403.

Point 1: Section 3-107.

Point 3: Section 3-112.

Point 4: Sections 3-103 and 3-805.

Point 6: Section 3-805.

Definitional Cross References:

"Bank". Section 1-201.

"Bearer". Section 1-201.

"Definite time". Section 3-109.

"Money". Section 1-201.

"On demand". Section 3-108.

"Order". Section 3-102.

"Promise". Section 3-102.

"Signed". Section 1-201.

"Term". Section 1-201.

"Writing". Section 1-201.

§ 3-105. When Promise or Order Unconditional.

(1) A promise or order otherwise unconditional is not made conditional by the fact that the instrument

(a) is subject to implied or constructive conditions; or

(b) states its consideration, whether performed or promised, or the transaction which gave rise to the instrument, or that the promise or order is made or the instrument matures in accordance with or "as per" such transaction; or

(c) refers to or states that it arises out of a separate agreement or refers to a separate agreement for rights as to prepayment or acceleration; or

(d) states that it is drawn under a letter of credit; or

(e) states that it is secured, whether by mortgage, reservation of title or otherwise; or

(f) indicates a particular account to be debited or any other fund or source from which reimbursement is expected; or

(g) is limited to payment out of a particular fund or the proceeds of a particular source, if the instrument is issued by a government or governmental agency or unit; or

(h) is limited to payment out of the entire assets of a partnership, unincorporated association, trust or estate by or on behalf of which the instrument is issued.

(2) A promise or order is not unconditional if the instrument

(a) states that it is subject to or governed by any other agreement; or

(b) states that it is to be paid only out of a particular fund or source except as provided in this section.

As amended in 1962.

Official Comment

Prior Uniform Statutory Provision: Section 3, Uniform Negotiable Instruments Law.

Changes: Completely revised.

Purposes of Changes: The section is intended to make it clear that, so far as negotiability is affected, the conditional or unconditional character of the promise or order is to be determined by what is expressed in the instrument itself; and to permit certain specific limitations upon the terms of payment.

1. Paragraph (a) of subsection (1) rejects the theory of decisions which have held that a recital in an instrument that it is given in return for an executory promise gives rise to an implied condition that the instrument is not to be paid if the promise is not performed, and that this condition destroys negotiability. Nothing in the section is intended to imply that language may not be fairly construed to mean what it says, but implications, whether of law or fact, are not to be considered in determining negotiability.

2. Paragraph (b) of subsection (1) is an amplification of Section 3(2) of the original act. The final clause is intended to resolve a conflict in the decisions over the effect of such language as "This note is given for payment as per contract for the purchase of goods of even date, maturity being in conformity with the terms of such contract." It adopts the general commercial understanding that such language is intended as a mere recital of the origin of the instrument and a reference to the transaction for information, but is not meant to condition payment according to the terms of any other agreement.

3. Paragraph (c) of subsection (1) likewise is intended to resolve a conflict, and to reject cases in which a reference to a separate agreement was held to mean that payment of the instrument must be limited in accordance with the terms of the agreement, and hence was conditioned by it. Such a reference normally is inserted for the purpose of making a record or giving information to anyone who may be interested, and in the absence of any express statement to that effect is not intended to limit the terms of payment. Inasmuch as rights as to prepayment or acceleration has to do with a "speed-up" in payment and since notes frequently refer to separate agreements for a statement of these rights, such reference does not destroy negotiability even though it has mild aspects of incorporation by reference. The general reasoning with respect to subparagraph (c) also applies to a draft which on its face states that it is drawn under a letter of credit (subparagraph (d)). Paragraphs (c) and (d) therefore adopt the position that negotiability is not affected. If the reference goes further and provides that payment must be made according to the terms of the agreement, it falls under paragraph (a) of subsection (2) [As amended 1962].

4. Paragraph (e) of subsection (1) is intended to settle another conflict in the decisions, over the effect of "title security notes" and other instruments which recite the security given. It rejects cases which have held that the mere statement that the instrument is secured, by reservation of title or otherwise, carries the implied condition that payment is to be made only if the security agreement is fully performed. Again such a recital normally is included only for the purpose of making a record or giving information, and is not intended to condition payment in any way. The provision adopts the position of the great majority of the courts.

5. Paragraph (f) of subsection (1) is a rewording of Section 3(1) of the original act.

6. Paragraph (g) of subsection (1) is new. It is intended to permit municipal corporations or other governments or governmental agencies to draw checks or to issue other short-term commercial paper in which payment is limited to a particular fund or to the proceeds of particular taxes or other sources of revenue. The provision will permit some municipal warrants to be negotiable if they are in proper form. Normally such warrants lack the words "order" or "bearer," or are marked "Not Negotiable," or are payable only in serial order, which makes them conditional.

7. Paragraph (h) of subsection (1) is new. It adopts the policy of decisions holding that an instrument issued by an unincorporated association is negotiable although its payment is expressly limited to the assets of the association, excluding the liability of individual members; and recognizing as negotiable an instrument issued by a trust estate without personal liability of the trustee. The policy is extended to a partnership and to any estate. The provision affects only the negotiability of the instrument, and is not intended to change the law of any state as to the liability of a partner, trustee, executor, administrator, or any other person on such an instrument.

8. Paragraph (a) of subsection (2) retains the generally accepted rule that where an instrument contains such language as "subject to terms of contract between maker and payee of this date," its payment is conditioned according to the terms of the agreement and the instrument is not negotiable. The distinction is between a mere

recital of the existence of the separate agreement or a reference to it for information, which under paragraph (c) of subsection (1) will not affect negotiability, and any language which, fairly construed, requires the holder to look to the other agreement for the terms of payment. The intent of the provision is that an instrument is not negotiable unless the holder can ascertain all of its essential terms from its face. In the specific instance of rights as to prepayment or acceleration, however, there may be a reference to a separate agreement without destroying negotiability [As amended 1962].

9. Paragraph (b) of subsection (2) restates the last sentence of Section 3 of the original act. As noted above, exceptions are made by paragraphs (g) and (h) of subsection (1) in favor of instruments issued by governments or governmental agencies, or by a partnership, unincorporated association, trust or estate.

Cross Reference:

Section 3-104.

Definitional Cross References:

"Account". Section 4-104.
"Agreement". Section 1-201.
"Instrument". Section 3-102.
"Issue". Section 3-102.
"Order". Section 3-102.
"Promise". Section 3-102.

§ 3-106. Sum Certain.

(1) The sum payable is a sum certain even though it is to be paid

(a) with stated interest or by stated installments; or

(b) with stated different rates of interest before and after default or a specified date; or

(c) with a stated discount or addition if paid before or after the date fixed for payment; or

(d) with exchange or less exchange, whether at a fixed rate or at the current rate; or

(e) with costs of collection or an attorney's fee or both upon default.

(2) Nothing in this section shall validate any term which is otherwise illegal.

Official Comment

Prior Uniform Statutory Provision: Sections 2 and 6(5), Uniform Negotiable Instruments Law.

Changes: Reworded.

Purposes of Changes: The new language is intended to clarify doubts arising under the original section as to interest, discounts or additions, exchange, costs and attorney's fees, and acceleration or extension.

1. The section rejects decisions which have denied negotiability to a note with a term providing for a discount for early payment on the ground that at the time of issue the amount payable was not certain. It is sufficient that at any time of payment the holder is able to determine the amount then payable from the instrument itself with any necessary computation. Thus a demand note bearing interest at six per cent is negotiable. A stated discount or addition for early or late payment does not affect the certainty of the sum so long as the computation can be made, nor do different rates of interest before and after default or a specified date. The computation must be one which can be made from the instrument itself without reference to any outside source, and this section does not make negotiable a note payable with interest "at the current rate."

2. Paragraph (d) recognizes the occasional practice of making the instrument payable with exchange deducted rather than added.

3. In paragraph (e) "upon default" is substituted for the language of the original Section 2(5) in order to include any default in payment of interest or installments.

4. The section contains no specific language relating to the effect of acceleration clauses on the certainty of the sum payable. Section 2(3) of the original act contained a saving clause for provisions accelerating principal on default in payment of an installment or of interest, which led to doubt as to the effect of other accelerating provisions. This Article (Section 3-109, Definite Time) broadly validates acceleration clauses; it is not necessary

to state the matter in this section as well. The disappearance of the language referred to in old Section 2(3) means merely that it was regarded as surplusage.

5. Most states have usury laws prohibiting excessive rates of interest. In some states there are statutes or rules of law invalidating a term providing for increased interest after maturity, or for costs and attorney's fees. Subsection (2) is intended to make it clear that this section is concerned only with the effect of such terms upon negotiability, and is not meant to change the law of any state as to the validity of the term itself.

Cross References:

Section 3–104.

Point 4: Section 3–109.

Definitional Cross Reference:

"Term". Section 1–201.

§ 3–107. Money.

(1) An instrument is payable in money if the medium of exchange in which it is payable is money at the time the instrument is made. An instrument payable in "currency" or "current funds" is payable in money.

(2) A promise or order to pay a sum stated in a foreign currency is for a sum certain in money and, unless a different medium of payment is specified in the instrument, may be satisfied by payment of that number of dollars which the stated foreign currency will purchase at the buying sight rate for that currency on the day on which the instrument is payable or, if payable on demand, on the day of demand. If such an instrument specifies a foreign currency as the medium of payment the instrument is payable in that currency.

Official Comment

Prior Uniform Statutory Provision: Section 6(5), Uniform Negotiable Instruments Law.

Changes: Completely rewritten.

Purposes of Changes and New Matter: To make clear when an instrument is payable in money and to state rules applicable to instruments drawn payable in a foreign currency.

1. The term "money" is defined in Section 1–201 as "a medium of exchange authorized or adopted by a domestic or foreign government as a part of its currency". That definition rejects the narrow view of some early cases that "money" is limited to legal tender. Legal tender acts do no more than designate a particular kind of money which the obligee will be required to accept in discharge of an obligation. It rejects also the contention sometimes advanced that "money" includes any medium of exchange current and accepted in the particular community whether it be gold dust, beaver pelts, or cigarettes in occupied Germany. Such unusual "currency" is necessarily of uncertain and fluctuating value, and an instrument intended to pass generally in commerce as negotiable may not be made payable therein.

The test adopted is that of the sanction of government, which recognizes the circulating medium as a part of the official currency of that government. In particular the provision adopts the position that an instrument expressing the amount to be paid in sterling, francs, lire or other recognized currency of a foreign government is negotiable even though payable in the United States.

2. The provision on "currency" or "current funds" accepts the view of the great majority of the decisions, that "currency" or "current funds" means that the instrument is payable in money.

3. Either the amount to be paid or the medium of payment may be expressed in terms of a particular kind of money. A draft passing between Toronto and Buffalo may, according to the desire and convenience of the parties, call for payment of 100 United States dollars or of 100 Canadian dollars; and it may require either sum to be paid in either currency. Under this section an instrument in any of these forms is negotiable, whether payable in Toronto or in Buffalo.

4. As stated in the preceding paragraph the intention of the parties in making an instrument payable in a foreign currency may be that the medium of payment shall be either dollars measured by the foreign currency or the foreign currency in which the instrument is drawn. Under subsection (2) the presumption is, unless the instrument otherwise specifies, that the obligation may be satisfied by payment in dollars in an amount

determined by the buying sight rate for the foreign currency on the day the instrument becomes payable. Inasmuch as the buying sight rate will fluctuate from day to day, it might be argued that an instrument expressed in a foreign currency but actually payable in dollars is not for a "sum certain". Subsection (2) makes it clear that for the purposes of negotiability under this Article such an instrument, despite exchange fluctuations, is for a sum certain.

Cross References:

Section 3–104.
Point 1: Section 1–201.
Point 4: Section 4–212(6).

Definitional Cross References:

"Instrument". Section 3–102.
"Money". Section 1–201.
"Order". Section 3–102.
"Promise". Section 3–102.
"Purchase". Section 1–201.

§ 3–108. Payable on Demand.

Instruments payable on demand include those payable at sight or on presentation and those in which no time for payment is stated.

Official Comment

Prior Uniform Statutory Provision: Section 7, Uniform Negotiable Instruments Law.

Changes: Reworded, final sentence of original section omitted.

Purposes of Changes: Except for the omission of the final sentence this section restates the substance of original Section 7. The final sentence dealt with the status of a person issuing, accepting or indorsing an instrument after maturity and provided that as to such a person the instrument was payable on demand. That language implied that the ordinary rules relating to demand instruments as to due course, holding, presentment, notice of dishonor and so on were applicable. This Article abandons that concept which served no special purpose except to trap the unwary. Under Section 3–302 (Holder in Due Course) and in view of the deletion from this section of the final sentence of original Section 7 there is no longer the possibility that one taking time paper after maturity may acquire due course rights against a post-maturity indorser. Section 3–501(4), however, provides that the indorser after maturity is not entitled to presentment, notice of dishonor or protest.

Cross References:

Sections 3–104, 3–302 and 3–501(4).

Definitional Cross Reference:

"Instrument". Section 3–102.

§ 3–109. Definite Time.

(1) An instrument is payable at a definite time if by its terms it is payable

(a) on or before a stated date or at a fixed period after a stated date; or

(b) at a fixed period after sight; or

(c) at a definite time subject to any acceleration; or

(d) at a definite time subject to extension at the option of the holder, or to extension to a further definite time at the option of the maker or acceptor or automatically upon or after a specified act or event.

(2) An instrument which by its terms is otherwise payable only upon an act or event uncertain as to time of occurrence is not payable at a definite time even though the act or event has occurred.

Official Comment

Prior Uniform Statutory Provision: Sections 4 and 17(3), Uniform Negotiable Instruments Law.

Changes: Reworded; new provisions; rule of original Section 4(3) reversed.

Purposes of Changes and New Matter: To remove uncertainties arising under the original section, and to eliminate commercially unacceptable instruments.

1. Subsection (2) reverses the rule of the original Section 4(3) as to instruments payable after events certain to happen but uncertain as to time. Almost the only use of such instruments has been in the anticipation of inheritance or future interests by borrowing on post-obituary notes. These have been much more common in England than in the United States. They are at best questionable paper, not acceptable in general commerce, with no good reason for according them free circulation as negotiable instruments. As in the case of the occasional note payable "one year after the war" or at a similar uncertain date, they are likely to be made under unusual circumstances suggesting good reason for preserving defenses of the maker. They are accordingly eliminated.

2. With this change "definite time" is substituted for "fixed or determinable future time." The time of payment is definite if it can be determined from the face of the instrument.

3. An undated instrument payable "thirty days after date" is not payable at a definite time, since the time of payment cannot be determined on its face. It is, however, an incomplete instrument within the provisions of Section 3–115 dealing with such instruments and may be completed by dating it. It is then payable at a definite time.

4. Paragraph (c) of subsection (1) resolves a conflict in the decisions on the negotiability of instruments containing acceleration clauses as to the meaning and effect of "on or before a fixed or determinable future time" in the original Section 4(2). (Instruments expressly stated to be payable "on or before" a given date are dealt with in subsection (1)(a)). So far as certainty of time of payment is concerned a note payable at a definite time but subject to acceleration is no less certain than a note payable on demand, whose negotiability never has been questioned. It is in fact more certain, since it at least states a definite time beyond which the instrument cannot run. Objections to the acceleration clause must be based rather on the possibility of abuse by the holder, which has nothing to do with negotiability and is not limited to negotiable instruments. That problem is now covered by Section 1–208.

Subsection (1)(c) is intended to mean that the certainty of time of payment or the negotiability of the instrument is not affected by any acceleration clause, whether acceleration be at the option of the maker or the holder, or automatic upon the occurrence of some event, and whether it be conditional or unrestricted. If the acceleration term itself is uncertain it may fail on ordinary contract principles, but the instrument then remains negotiable and is payable at the definite time.

The effect of acceleration clauses upon a holder in due course is covered by the new definition of the holder in due course (Section 3–302) and by the section on notice to purchaser (subsection (3) of Section 3–304). If the purchaser is not aware of any acceleration, his delay in making presentment may be excused under the section dealing with excused presentment (subsection (1) of Section 3–511).

5. Paragraph (d) of subsection (1) is new. It adopts the generally accepted rule that a clause providing for extension at the option of the holder, even without a time limit, does not affect negotiability since the holder is given only a right which he would have without the clause. If the extension is to be at the option of the maker or acceptor or is to be automatic, a definite time limit must be stated or the time of payment remains uncertain and the instrument is not negotiable. Where such a limit is stated, the effect upon certainty of time of payment is the same as if the instrument were made payable at the ultimate date with a term providing for acceleration.

The construction and effect of extension clauses is covered by paragraph (f) of Section 3–118 on ambiguous terms and rules of construction, to which reference should be made.

Cross References:

Section 3–104.
Point 3: Section 3–115.
Point 4: Sections 1–208, 3–118(f), 3–304(3), and 3–511(1).
Point 5: Section 3–118(f).

Definitional Cross References:

"Holder". Section 1-201.

"Instrument". Section 3-102.

"Term". Section 1-201.

§ 3-110. Payable to Order.

(1) An instrument is payable to order when by its terms it is payable to the order or assigns of any person therein specified with reasonable certainty, or to him or his order, or when it is conspicuously designated on its face as "exchange" or the like and names a payee. It may be payable to the order of

(a) the maker or drawer; or

(b) the drawee; or

(c) a payee who is not maker, drawer or drawee; or

(d) two or more payees together or in the alternative; or

(e) an estate, trust or fund, in which case it is payable to the order of the representative of such estate, trust or fund or his successors; or

(f) an office, or an officer by his title as such in which case it is payable to the principal but the incumbent of the office or his successors may act as if he or they were the holder; or

(g) a partnership or unincorporated association, in which case it is payable to the partnership or association and may be indorsed or transferred by any person thereto authorized.

(2) An instrument not payable to order is not made so payable by such words as "payable upon return of this instrument properly indorsed."

(3) An instrument made payable both to order and to bearer is payable to order unless the bearer words are handwritten or typewritten.

Official Comment

Prior Uniform Statutory Provision: Section 8, Uniform Negotiable Instruments Law.

Changes: Reworded, new provisions.

Purposes of Changes and New Matter: The changes are intended to remove uncertainties arising under the original section.

1. Paragraph (d) of subsection (1) replaces the original subsections (4) and (5). It eliminates the word "jointly," which has carried a possible implication of a right of survivorship. Normally an instrument payable to "A and B" is intended to be payable to the two parties as tenants in common, and there is no survivorship in the absence of express language to that effect. The instrument may be payable to "A or B," in which case it is payable to either A or B individually. It may even be made payable to "A and/or B," in which case it is payable either to A or to B singly, or to the two together. The negotiation, enforcement and discharge of the instrument in all such cases are covered by the section on instruments payable to two or more persons (Sec. 3-116).

2. Paragraph (e) of subsection (1) is intended to change the result of decisions which have held that an instrument payable to the order of the estate of a decedent was payable to bearer, on the ground that the name of the payee did not purport to be that of any person. The intent in such cases is obviously not to make the instrument payable to bearer, but to the order of the representative of the estate. The provision extends the same principle to an instrument payable to the order of "Tilden Trust," or "Community Fund". So long as the payee can be identified, it is not necessary that it be a legal entity; and in each case the instrument is treated as payable to the order of the appropriate representative or his successor.

3. Under paragraph (f) of subsection (1) an instrument may be made payable to the office itself ("Swedish Consulate") or to the officer by his title as such ("Treasurer of City Club"). In either case it runs to the incumbent of the office and his successors. The effect of instruments in such a form is covered by the section on instruments payable with words of description (Sec. 3-117).

4. Vestigial theories relating to the lack of "legal entity" of partnerships and various forms of unincorporated associations—such as labor unions and business trusts—make it the part of wisdom to specify that

instruments made payable to such groups are order paper payable as designated and not bearer paper (subsection (1)(g)). As in the case of incorporated associations, any person having authority from the partnership or association to whose order the instrument is payable may indorse or otherwise deal with the instrument.

5. Subsection (2) is intended to change the result of cases holding that "payable upon return of this certificate properly indorsed" indicated an intention to make the instrument payable to any indorsee and so must be construed as the equivalent of "Pay to order." Ordinarily the purpose of such language is only to insure return of the instrument with indorsement in lieu of a receipt, and the word "order" is omitted with the intention that the instrument shall not be negotiable.

6. Subsection (3) is directed at occasional instruments reading "Pay to the order of John Doe or bearer." Such language usually is found only where the drawer has filled in the name of the payee on a printed form, without intending the ambiguity or noticing the word "bearer." Under such circumstances the name of the specified payee indicates an intent that the order words shall control. If the word "bearer" is handwritten or typewritten, there is sufficient indication of an intent that the instrument shall be payable to bearer. Instruments payable to "order of bearer" are covered not by this section but by the following Section 3–111.

Cross References:

Sections 3–104 and 3–111.
Point 1: Section 3–116.
Points 2, 3 and 4: Section 3–117.

Definitional Cross References:

"Bearer". Section 1–201.
"Conspicuous". Section 1–201.
"Instrument". Section 3–102.
"Negotiation". Section 3–202.
"Person". Section 1–201.
"Term". Section 1–201.

§ 3–111. Payable to Bearer.

An instrument is payable to bearer when by its terms it is payable to

(a) bearer or the order of bearer; or

(b) a specified person or bearer; or

(c) "cash" or the order of "cash", or any other indication which does not purport to designate a specific payee.

Official Comment

Prior Uniform Statutory Provision: Section 9, Uniform Negotiable Instruments Law.

Changes: Reworded; original subsections (3) and (5) omitted here but covered by Sections on impostors and signature in name of payee (Section 3–405) and on special and blank indorsements (Section 3–204).

Purposes of Changes: The rewording is intended to remove uncertainties.

1. Language such as "order of bearer" usually results when a printed form is used and the word "bearer" is filled in. Subsection (a) rejects the view that the instrument is payable to order, and adopts the position that "bearer" is the unusual word and should control. Compare Comment 6 to Section 3–110.

2. Paragraph (c) is reworded to remove any possible implication that "Pay to the order of ______" makes the instrument payable to bearer. It is an incomplete order instrument, and falls under Section 3–115. Likewise "Pay Treasurer of X Corporation" does not mean pay bearer, even though there may be no such officer. Instruments payable to the order of an estate, trust, fund, partnership, unincorporated association or office are covered by the preceding section. This subsection applies only to such language as "Pay Cash," "Pay to the order of cash," "Pay bills payable," "Pay to the order of one keg of nails," or other words which do not purport to designate any specific payee.

3. Under Section 40 of the original Act an instrument payable to bearer on its face remained bearer paper negotiable by delivery although subsequently specially indorsed. It should be noted that Section 3–204 on special indorsement reverses this rule and allows the special indorsement to control.

Cross References:

Sections 3–104, 3–405 and 3–204.
Point 2: Sections 3–110(1)(a) and (f) and 3–115.
Point 3: Section 3–204.

Definitional Cross References:

"Bearer". Section 1–201.
"Instrument". Section 3–102.
"Person". Section 1–201.
"Term". Section 1–201.

§ 3–112. Terms and Omissions Not Affecting Negotiability.

(1) The negotiability of an instrument is not affected by

(a) the omission of a statement of any consideration or of the place where the instrument is drawn or payable; or

(b) a statement that collateral has been given to secure obligations either on the instrument or otherwise of an obligor on the instrument or that in case of default on those obligations the holder may realize on or dispose of the collateral; or

(c) a promise or power to maintain or protect collateral or to give additional collateral; or

(d) a term authorizing a confession of judgment on the instrument if it is not paid when due; or

(e) a term purporting to waive the benefit of any law intended for the advantage or protection of any obligor; or

(f) a term in a draft providing that the payee by indorsing or cashing it acknowledges full satisfaction of an obligation of the drawer; or

(g) A statement in a draft drawn in a set of parts (Section 3–801) to the effect that the order is effective only if no other part has been honored.

(2) Nothing in this section shall validate any term which is otherwise illegal.

As amended in 1962.

Official Comment

Prior Uniform Statutory Provision: Sections 5 and 6, Uniform Negotiable Instruments Law.

Changes: Reworded; new provisions; Subsection (4) of original Section 5 omitted. Subsection (4) of the original Section 6 is now covered by Section 3–113, and Subsection (5) by Section 3–107.

Purposes of Changes and New Matter: The changes are intended to remove uncertainties arising under the original sections. Subsection (4) of the original Section 5 is omitted because it has been important only in connection with bonds and other investment securities now covered by Article 8 of this Act. An option to require something to be done in lieu of payment of money is uncommon and not desirable in commercial paper.

This section permits the insertion of certain obligations and powers in addition to the simple promise or order to pay money. Under Section 3–104, dealing with form of negotiable instruments, the instrument may not contain any other promise, order, obligation or power.

1. Paragraph (b) of subsection (1) permits a clause authorizing the sale or disposition of collateral given to secure obligations either on the instrument or otherwise of an obligor on the instrument upon any default in those obligations, including a default in payment of an installment or of interest. It is not limited, as was the original Section 5(1), to default at maturity. The reference to obligations of an obligor on the instrument is intended to recognize so-called cross collateral provisions that appear in collateral note forms used by banks and others throughout the United States and to permit the use of these provisions without destroying negotiability.

Paragraph (c) is new. It permits a clause, apparently not within the original section, containing a promise or power to maintain or protect collateral or to give additional collateral, whether on demand or on some other condition. Such terms frequently are accompanied by a provision for acceleration if the collateral is not given, which is now permitted by the section on what constitutes a definite time. Section 1–208 should be consulted as to the construction to be given such clauses under this Act.

2. As under the original Section 5(2), paragraph (d) is intended to mean that a confession of judgment may be authorized only if the instrument is not paid when due, and that otherwise negotiability is affected. The use of judgment notes is confined to two or three states, and in others the judgment clauses are made illegal or ineffective either by special statutes or by decision. Subsection (2) is intended to say that any such local rule remains unchanged, and that the clause itself may be invalid, although the negotiability of the instrument is not affected.

3. As in the case of the original Section 5(3), paragraph (e) applies not only to any waiver of the benefits of this Article, such as presentment, notice of dishonor or protest, but also to a waiver of the benefits of any other law such as a homestead exemption. Again subsection (2) is intended to mean that any rule which invalidates the waiver itself is not changed, and that while negotiability is not affected, a waiver of the statute of limitations contained in an instrument may be invalid.

This paragraph is to be read together with subsection (1) of Section 3–104 on form of negotiable instruments. A waiver cannot make the instrument negotiable within this Article where it does not comply with the requirements of that section.

4. Paragraph (f) is new. The effect of a clause of acknowledgment of satisfaction upon negotiability has been uncertain under the original section.

5. Paragraph (g) is intended to insure that a condition arising from the statement in question will not adversely affect negotiability.

Cross References:

Sections 3–104 and 3–105.
Point 1: Sections 1–208 and 3–109(1)(c).
Point 3: Section 3–104.

Definitional Cross References:

"Draft". Section 3–104.
"Instrument". Section 3–102.
"On demand". Section 3–108.
"Promise". Section 3–102.
"Term". Section 1–201.

§ 3–113. Seal.

An instrument otherwise negotiable is within this Article even though it is under a seal.

Official Comment

Prior Uniform Statutory Provision: Section 6(4), Uniform Negotiable Instruments Law.

Changes: Reworded.

Purposes of Changes: The revised wording is intended to change the result of decisions holding that while a seal does not affect the negotiability of an instrument it may affect it in other respects falling within the statute, such as the conclusiveness of consideration. The section is intended to place sealed instruments on the same footing as any other instruments so far as all sections of this Article are concerned. It does not affect any other statutes or rules of law relating to sealed instruments except insofar as, in the case of negotiable instruments, they are inconsistent with this Article. Thus a sealed instrument which is within this Article may still be subject to a longer statute of limitations than negotiable instruments not under seal, or to such local rules of procedure as that it may be enforced by an action of special assumpsit.

Cross Reference:

Section 3–104.

Definitional Cross Reference:

"Instrument". Section 3–102.

§ 3–114. Date, Antedating, Postdating.

(1) The negotiability of an instrument is not affected by the fact that it is undated, antedated or postdated.

(2) Where an instrument is antedated or postdated the time when it is payable is determined by the stated date if the instrument is payable on demand or at a fixed period after date.

(3) Where the instrument or any signature thereon is dated, the date is presumed to be correct.

Official Comment

Prior Uniform Statutory Provision: Sections 6(1), 11, 12 and 17(3), Uniform Negotiable Instruments Law.

Changes: Reworded; new provision; parts of original section 12 omitted.

Purposes of Changes and New Matter: The rewording is intended to remove uncertainties arising under the original sections.

1. The reference to an "illegal or fraudulent purpose" in the original Section 12 is omitted as inaccurate and misleading. Any fraud or illegality connected with the date of an instrument does not affect its negotiability, but is merely a defense under Sections 3–306 and 3–307 to the same extent as any other fraud or illegality. The provision in the same section as to acquisition of title upon delivery is also omitted, as obvious and unnecessary.

2. Subsection (2) is new. An undated instrument payable "thirty days after date" is uncertain as to time of payment, and does not fall within Section 3–109(1)(a) on definite time. It is, however, an incomplete instrument, and the date may be inserted as provided in the section dealing with such instruments (Section 3–115). When the instrument has been dated, this subsection follows decisions under the original Act in providing that the time of payment is to be determined from the stated date, even though the instrument is antedated or postdated. An antedated instrument may thus be due before it is issued. As to the liability of indorsers in such a case, see Section 3–501(4), on indorsement after maturity.

3. Subsection (3) extends the original Section 11 to any signature on an instrument. As to the meaning of "presumed," see Section 1–201.

Cross References:

Point 1: Sections 3–306 and 3–307.
Point 2: Sections 3–109(1)(a), 3–115 and 3–501(4).
Point 3: Section 1–201.

Definitional Cross References:

"Instrument". Section 3–102.
"Issue". Section 3–102.
"On demand". Section 3–108.
"Presumed". Section 1–201.
"Signature". Section 3–401.

§ 3–115. Incomplete Instruments.

(1) When a paper whose contents at the time of signing show that it is intended to become an instrument is signed while still incomplete in any necessary respect it cannot be enforced until completed, but when it is completed in accordance with authority given it is effective as completed.

(2) If the completion is unauthorized the rules as to material alteration apply (Section 3–407), even though the paper was not delivered by the maker or drawer; but the burden of establishing that any completion is unauthorized is on the party so asserting.

Official Comment

Prior Uniform Statutory Provision: Sections 13, 14 and 15, Uniform Negotiable Instruments Law.

Changes: Condensed and reworded; original Section 13 and parts of Section 14 omitted; rule of Section 15 reversed.

Purposes of Changes:

1. The original sections were lengthy and confusing. Section 13 is eliminated because it has suggested some uncertain distinction between undated instruments and those incomplete in other respects, and has carried the inference that only a holder may fill in the date. An instrument lacking in an essential date is merely one kind of incomplete instrument, to be treated like any other. The third sentence of Section 14, providing that the instrument must be filled up strictly in accordance with the authority given and within a reasonable time, is eliminated as entirely superfluous, since any authority must always be exercised in accordance with its limitations, and expires within a reasonable time unless a time limit is fixed.

2. The language "signed while still incomplete in any necessary respect" in subsection (1) is substituted for "wanting in any material particular" in the original Section 14, in order to make it entirely clear that a complete writing which lacks an essential element of an instrument and contains no blanks or spaces or anything else to indicate that what is missing is to be supplied, does not fall within the section. "Necessary" means necessary to a complete instrument. It will always include the promise or order, the designation of the payee, and the amount payable. It may include the time of payment where a blank is left for that time to be filled in; but where it is clear that no time is intended to be stated the instrument is complete, and is payable on demand under Section 3–108. It does not include the date of issue, which under Section 3–114(1) is not essential, unless the instrument is made payable at a fixed period after that date.

3. This section omits the second sentence of the original Section 14, providing that "a signature on a blank paper delivered by the person making the signature in order that the paper may be converted into a negotiable instrument operates as a prima facie authority to fill it up as such for any amount." This had utility only in connection with the ancient practice of signing blank paper to be filled in later as an acceptance, at a time when communications were slow and difficult. The practice has been obsolete for nearly a century. It affords obvious opportunity for fraud, and should not be encouraged by express sanction in the statute. The omission is not intended, however, to mean that any person may not be authorized to write in an instrument over a signature either before or after delivery.

4. Subsection (2) states the rule generally recognized by the courts, that any unauthorized completion is an alteration of the instrument which stands on the same footing as any other alteration. Reference is therefore made to Section 3–407 where the effect of alteration is stated. Subsection (3) of that section provides that a subsequent holder in due course may in all cases enforce the instrument as completed, and replaces the final sentence of the original Section 14.

5. The language "even though the paper was not delivered" reverses the rule of the original Section 15, which provides that where an incomplete instrument has not been delivered it will not, if completed, be a valid contract in the hands of any holder as against any person whose signature was placed thereon before delivery. Since under this Article (Sections 3–305 and 3–407) neither non-delivery nor unauthorized completion is a defense against a holder in due course, it has always been illogical that the two together should invalidate the instrument in his hands. A holder in due course sees and takes the same paper, whether it was complete when stolen or completed afterward by the thief, and in each case he relies in good faith on the maker's signature. The loss should fall upon the party whose conduct in signing blank paper has made the fraud possible, rather than upon the innocent purchaser. The result is consistent with the theory of decisions holding the drawer of a check stolen and afterwards filled in to be estopped from setting up the non-delivery against an innocent party.

A similar provision protecting a depositary bank which pays an item in good faith is contained in Section 4–401. The policy of that Section should apply in favor of drawees other than banks.

6. The language on burden of establishing unauthorized completion is substituted for the "prima facie authority" of the original section 14. It follows the generally accepted rule that the full burden of proof by a preponderance of the evidence is upon the party attacking the completed instrument. "Burden of establishing" is defined in Section 1–201.

Cross References:

Point 2: Sections 3–108 and 3–114(1).

Point 4: Section 3–407.

Point 5: Sections 3–305(2), 3–407(3) and 4–401.
Point 6: Section 1–201.

Definitional Cross References:

"Alteration". Section 3–407.
"Burden of establishing". Section 1–201.
"Delivery". Section 1–201.
"Instrument". Section 3–102.
"Party". Section 1–201.
"Signed". Section 1–201.

§ 3–116. Instruments Payable to Two or More Persons.

An instrument payable to the order of two or more persons

(a) if in the alternative is payable to any one of them and may be negotiated, discharged or enforced by any of them who has possession of it;

(b) if not in the alternative is payable to all of them and may be negotiated, discharged or enforced only by all of them.

Official Comment

Prior Uniform Statutory Provision: Section 41, Uniform Negotiable Instruments Law.

Changes: Revised in wording and substance.

Purposes of Changes: The changes are intended to make clear the distinction between an instrument payable to "A or B" and one payable to "A and B." The first names either A or B as payee, so that either of them who is in possession becomes a holder as that term is defined in Section 1–201 and may negotiate, enforce or discharge the instrument. The second is payable only to A and B together, and as provided in the original section both must indorse in order to negotiate the instrument, although one may of course be authorized to sign for the other. Likewise both must join in any action to enforce the instrument, and the rights of one are not discharged without his consent by the act of the other.

If the instrument is payable to "A and/or B," it is payable in the alternative to A, or to B, or to A and B together, and it may be negotiated, enforced or discharged accordingly.

Cross Reference:

Section 1–201.

Definitional Cross References:

"Instrument". Section 3–102.
"Person". Section 1–201.

§ 3–117. Instruments Payable With Words of Description.

An instrument made payable to a named person with the addition of words describing him

(a) as agent or officer of a specified person is payable to his principal but the agent or officer may act as if he were the holder;

(b) as any other fiduciary for a specified person or purpose is payable to the payee and may be negotiated, discharged or enforced by him;

(c) in any other manner is payable to the payee unconditionally and the additional words are without effect on subsequent parties.

Official Comment

Prior Uniform Statutory Provision: Section 42, Uniform Negotiable Instruments Law.

Changes: Revised and extended.

Purposes of Changes:

1. Subsection (a) extends the policy of the original Section 42, which covered only cashiers and fiscal officers of banks and corporations, to any case where a payee is named with words describing him as agent or officer of another named person. The intent is to include all such descriptions as "John Doe, Treasurer of Town of Framingham," "John Doe, President Home Telephone Co.," "John Doe, Secretary of City Club," or "John Doe, agent of Richard Roe." In all such cases it is commercial understanding that the description is not added for mere identification but for the purpose of making the instrument payable to the principal, and that the agent or officer is named as payee only for convenience in enabling him to cash the check.

2. Subsection (b) covers such descriptions as "John Doe, Trustee of Smithers Trust," "John Doe, Administrator of the Estate of Richard Roe," or "John Doe, Executor under Will of Richard Roe." In such cases the instrument is payable to the individual named, and he may negotiate it, enforce it or discharge it, but he remains subject to any liability for breach of his obligation as a fiduciary. Any subsequent holder of the instrument is put on notice of the fiduciary position, and under the section on notice to purchaser (Section 3-304) is not a holder in due course if he takes with notice that John Doe has negotiated the instrument in payment of or as security for his own debt or in any transaction for his own benefit, or otherwise in breach of duty.

3. Any other words of description, such as "John Doe, 1121 Main Street," "John Doe, Attorney," or "Jane Doe, unremarried widow," are to be treated as mere identification, and not in any respect as a condition of payment. The same is true of any description of the payee as "Treasurer," "President," "Agent," "Trustee," "Executor," or "Administrator," which does not name the principal or beneficiary. In all such cases the person named may negotiate, enforce or discharge the instrument if he is otherwise identified, even though he does not meet the description. Any subsequent party dealing with the instrument may disregard the description and treat the paper as payable unconditionally to the individual, and is fully protected in the absence of independent notice of other facts sufficient to affect his position.

Cross Reference:

Point 2: Section 3-304(2).

Definitional Cross References:

"Holder". Section 1-201.
"Instrument". Section 3-102.
"Party". Section 1-201.
"Person". Section 1-201.

§ 3-118. Ambiguous Terms and Rules of Construction.

The following rules apply to every instrument:

(a) Where there is doubt whether the instrument is a draft or a note the holder may treat it as either. A draft drawn on the drawer is effective as a note.

(b) Handwritten terms control typewritten and printed terms, and typewritten control printed.

(c) Words control figures except that if the words are ambiguous figures control.

(d) Unless otherwise specified a provision for interest means interest at the judgment rate at the place of payment from the date of the instrument, or if it is undated from the date of issue.

(e) Unless the instrument otherwise specifies two or more persons who sign as maker, acceptor or drawer or indorser and as a part of the same transaction are jointly and severally liable even though the instrument contains such words as "I promise to pay."

(f) Unless otherwise specified consent to extension authorizes a single extension for not longer than the original period. A consent to extension, expressed in the instrument, is binding on secondary parties and accommodation makers. A holder may not exercise his option to extend an instrument over the objection of a maker or acceptor or other party who in accordance with Section 3-604 tenders full payment when the instrument is due.

Official Comment

Prior Uniform Statutory Provision: Sections 17 and 68, Uniform Negotiable Instruments Law.

Changes: Reworded; new provisions; original subsections (3) and (6) of Section 17 omitted. The original Section 17(3) is covered, so far as the question can arise, by Sections 3–109(1)(a) and 3–114 of this Article. The original Section 17(6) is now covered by Section 3–402.

Purposes of Changes and New Matter:

1. The purpose of this section is to protect holders and to encourage the free circulation of negotiable paper by stating rules of law which will preclude a resort to parol evidence for any purpose except reformation of the instrument. Except as to such reformation, these rules cannot be varied by any proof that any party intended the contrary.

2. Subsection (a): The language of the original Section 17(5) is changed to make it clear that the provision is not limited to ambiguities of phrasing, but extends to any case where the form of the instrument leaves its character as a draft or a note in doubt.

3. Subsection (b): The original Section 17(4) is revised to cover typewriting because of its frequent use in instruments, particularly in promissory notes.

4. Subsection (c): The rewording of the original Section 17(1) is intended to make it clear that figures control only where the words are ambiguous and the figures are not.

5. Subsection (d): The revision of the original Section 17(2) is intended to make it clear that where the instrument provides for payment "with interest" without specifying the rate, the judgment rate of interest of the place of payment is to be taken as intended.

6. Subsection (e): This subsection combines and revises the original Section 17(7) and the last sentence of the original Section 68. The rule applies to any two or more persons who sign in the same capacity, whether as makers, drawers, acceptors or indorsers. It applies only where such parties sign as a part of the same transaction; successive indorsers are, of course, liable severally but not jointly.

7. Subsection (f): This provision is new. It has reference to such clauses as "The makers and indorsers of this note consent that it may be extended without notice to them." Such terms usually are inserted to obtain the consent of the indorsers and any accommodation maker to extension which might otherwise discharge them under Section 3–606 dealing with impairment of recourse or collateral. An extension in accord with these terms binds secondary parties. The holder may not force an extension on a maker or acceptor who makes due tender; the holder is not free to refuse payment and keep interest running on a good note or other instrument by extending it over the objection of a maker or acceptor or other party who in accordance with Section 3–604 tenders full payment when the instrument is due. Where consent to extension has been given, the subsection provides that unless otherwise specified the consent is to be construed as authorizing only one extension for not longer than the original period of the note.

Cross References:

Sections 3–109, 3–114, 3–402 and 3–606.
Point 7: Sections 3–604 and 3–606.

Definitional Cross References:

"Draft". Section 3–104.
"Holder". Section 1–201.
"Instrument". Section 3–102.
"Issue". Section 3–102.
"Note". Section 3–104.
"Person". Section 1–201.
"Promise". Section 3–102.
"Signed". Section 1–201.
"Term". Section 1–201.

§ 3–119. Other Writings Affecting Instrument.

(1) As between the obligor and his immediate obligee or any transferee the terms of an instrument may be modified or affected by any other written agreement executed as a part of the same transaction, except that a holder in due course is not affected by any limitation of his rights arising out of the separate written agreement if he had no notice of the limitation when he took the instrument.

(2) A separate agreement does not affect the negotiability of an instrument.

Official Comment

Prior Uniform Statutory Provision: None.

Purposes: This section is new. It is intended to resolve conflicts as to the effect of a separate writing upon a negotiable instrument.

1. This Article does not attempt to state general rules as to when an instrument may be varied or affected by parol evidence, except to the extent indicated by the comment to the preceding section. This section is limited to the effect of a separate written agreement executed as a part of the same transaction. The separate writing is most commonly an agreement creating or providing for a security interest such as a mortgage, chattel mortgage, conditional sale or pledge. It may, however, be any type of contract, including an agreement that upon certain conditions the instrument shall be discharged or is not to be paid, or even an agreement that it is a sham and not to be enforced at all. Nothing in this section is intended to validate any such agreement which is fraudulent or void as against public policy, as in the case of a note given to deceive a bank examiner.

2. Other parties, such as an accommodation indorser, are not affected by the separate writing unless they were also parties to it as a part of the transaction by which they became bound on the instrument.

3. The section applies to negotiable instruments the ordinary rule that writings executed as a part of the same transaction are to be read together as a single agreement. As between the immediate parties a negotiable instrument is merely a contract, and is no exception to the principle that the courts will look to the entire contract in writing. Accordingly a note may be affected by an acceleration clause, a clause providing for discharge under certain conditions, or any other relevant term in the separate writing. "May be modified or affected" does not mean that the separate agreement must necessarily be given effect. There is still room for construction of the writing as not intended to affect the instrument at all, or as intended to affect it only for a limited purpose such as foreclosure or other realization of collateral. If there is outright contradiction between the two, as where the note is for $1,000 but the accompanying mortgage recites that it is for $2,000, the note may be held to stand on its own feet and not to be affected by the contradiction.

4. Under this Article a purchaser of the instrument may become a holder in due course although he takes it with knowledge that it was accompanied by a separate agreement, if he has no notice of any defense or claim arising from the terms of the agreement. If any limitation in the separate writing in itself amounts to a defense or claim, as in the case of an agreement that the note is a sham and cannot be enforced, a purchaser with notice of it cannot be a holder in due course. The section also covers limitations which do not in themselves give notice of any present defense or claim, such as conditions providing that under certain conditions the note shall be extended for one year. A purchaser with notice of such limitations may be a holder in due course, but he takes the instrument subject to the limitation. If he is without such notice, he is not affected by such a limiting clause in the separate writing.

5. Subsection (2) rejects decisions which have carried the rule that contemporaneous writings must be read together to the length of holding that a clause in a mortgage affecting a note destroyed the negotiability of the note. The negotiability of an instrument is always to be determined by what appears on the face of the instrument alone, and if it is negotiable in itself a purchaser without notice of a separate writing is in no way affected by it. If the instrument itself states that it is subject to or governed by any other agreement, it is not negotiable under this Article; but if it merely refers to a separate agreement or states that it arises out of such an agreement, it is negotiable.

Cross References:

Point 1: Section 3–119.
Point 4: Section 3–304(4)(b).
Point 5: Section 3–105(2)(a) and (1)(c).

Definitional Cross References:

"Agreement". Section 1–201.
"Holder in due course". Section 3–302.
"Instrument". Section 3–102.
"Notice". Section 1–201.
"Rights". Section 1–201.
"Term". Section 1–201.
"Written" and "writing". Section 1–201.

§ 3–120. Instruments "Payable Through" Bank.

An instrument which states that it is "payable through" a bank or the like designates that bank as a collecting bank to make presentment but does not of itself authorize the bank to pay the instrument.

Official Comment

Prior Uniform Statutory Provision: None.

Purposes: Insurance, dividend or payroll checks, and occasionally other types of instruments, are sometimes made payable "through" a particular bank. This section states the commercial understanding as to the effect of such language. The bank is not named as drawee, and it is not ordered or even authorized to pay the instrument out of the drawer's account or any other funds of the drawer in its hands. Neither is it required to take the instrument for collection in the absence of special agreement to that effect. It is merely designated as a collecting bank through which presentment is properly made to the drawee.

Definitional Cross References:

"Bank". Section 1–201.
"Collecting bank". Section 4–105.
"Instrument". Section 3–102.
"Presentment". Section 3–504.

§ 3–121. Instruments Payable at Bank.

Note: *If this Act is introduced in the Congress of the United States this section should be omitted.*

(States to select either alternative)

ALTERNATIVE A

A note or acceptance which states that it is payable at a bank is the equivalent of a draft drawn on the bank payable when it falls due out of any funds of the maker or acceptor in current account or otherwise available for such payment.

ALTERNATIVE B

A note or acceptance which states that it is payable at a bank is not of itself an order or authorization to the bank to pay it.

Official Comment

Prior Uniform Statutory Provision: Section 87, Uniform Negotiable Instruments Law.

Changes: Alternative sections offered.

Purposes of Changes: The original section 87 has been amended so extensively that no uniformity has been achieved; and in many parts of the country it has been consistently disregarded in practice.

The original section represents the commercial and banking practice of New York and the surrounding states, according to which a note or acceptance made payable at a bank is treated as the equivalent of a draft drawn on the bank. The bank is not only authorized but ordered to make payment out of the account of the maker or acceptor when the instrument falls due, and it is expected to do so without consulting him. In the western and southern states a contrary understanding prevails. The note or acceptance payable at a bank is treated as merely designating a place of payment, as if the instrument were made payable at the office of an attorney. The bank's only function is to notify the maker or acceptor that the instrument has been presented and to ask for his instructions; and in the absence of specific instructions it is not regarded as required or even authorized to pay. Notwithstanding the original section western and southern banks have consistently followed the practice of asking for instructions and treating a direction not to pay as a revocation, equivalent to a direction to stop payment.

Both practices are well established, and the division is along geographical lines. A change in either practice might lead to undesirable consequences for holders, banks or depositors. The instruments involved are chiefly promissory notes, which infrequently cross state lines. There is no great need for uniformity. This section therefore offers alternative provisions, the first of which states the New York commercial understanding, and the second that of the south and west.

Cross Reference:

Section 3–502.

Definitional Cross References:

"Acceptance". Section 3–410.
"Account". Section 4–104.
"Bank". Section 1–201.
"Draft". Section 3–104.
"Instrument". Section 3–102.
"Note". Section 3–104.
"Order". Section 3–102.

§ 3–122. Accrual of Cause of Action.

(1) A cause of action against a maker or an acceptor accrues

(a) in the case of a time instrument on the day after maturity;

(b) in the case of a demand instrument upon its date or, if no date is stated, on the date of issue.

(2) A cause of action against the obligor of a demand or time certificate of deposit accrues upon demand, but demand on a time certificate may not be made until on or after the date of maturity.

(3) A cause of action against a drawer of a draft or an indorser of any instrument accrues upon demand following dishonor of the instrument. Notice of dishonor is a demand.

(4) Unless an instrument provides otherwise, interest runs at the rate provided by law for a judgment

(a) in the case of a maker, acceptor or other primary obligor of a demand instrument, from the date of demand;

(b) in all other cases from the date of accrual of the cause of action.

As amended in 1962.

Official Comment

Prior Uniform Statutory Provision: None.

Purpose:

1. This section is new. It follows the generally accepted rule that action may be brought on a demand note immediately upon issue, without demand, since presentment is not required to charge the maker under the original Act or under this Article. An exception is made in the case of certificates of deposit for the reason that banking custom and expectation is that demand will be made before any liability is incurred by the bank, and the additional reason that such certificates are issued with the understanding that they will be held for a considerable length of time, which in many instances exceeds the period of the statute of limitations. As to makers and acceptors of time instruments generally, the cause of action accrues on the day after maturity. As to drawers of drafts (including checks) and all indorsers, the cause of action accrues, in conformity with their underlying contract on the instrument (Sections 3–413 and 3–414), only upon demand made, typically in the form of a notice of dishonor, after the instrument has been presented to and dishonored by the person designated on the instrument to pay it.

2. Closely related to the accrual of a cause of action is the question of when interest begins to run where the instrument is blank on the point. A term in the instrument providing for interest controls. (See Section 3–118(d) for the construction of a term which provides for interest but does not specify the rate or the time from

which it runs.) In the absence of such a term and except in the case of a maker, acceptor or other primary obligor of a demand instrument subsection (4) states the rule that interest at the judgment rate runs from the date the cause of action accrues. In the case of a primary obligor of a demand instrument, interest runs from the date of demand although the cause of action (subsection (1)(a)) accrues on the stated date of the instrument or on issue. There has been a conflict in the decisions as to when "legal" interest begins to run on a demand note. Some courts have taken the view that, since the note is due when issued without demand, it should follow that interest runs from the same date. On the other hand it is clear that there is no default until after demand by the holder and thus no reason for the imposition of the penalty on the maker. Subsection (4), therefore, adopts the position of the majority of the courts that on a demand note interest runs only from demand. This same rule is applied to acceptors and other primary obligors on a demand instrument.

Cross References:

Point 1: Sections 3-501, 3-413 and 3-414.
Point 2: Section 3-118(d).

Definitional Cross References:

"Action". Section 1-201.
"Certificate of deposit". Section 3-102.
"Dishonor". Section 3-507.
"Draft". Section 3-104.
"Instrument". Section 3-102.
"Note". Section 3-104.
"Notice of dishonor". Section 3-508.
"On demand". Section 3-108.

PART 2

TRANSFER AND NEGOTIATION

§ 3-201. Transfer: Right to Indorsement.

(1) Transfer of an instrument vests in the transferee such rights as the transferor has therein, except that a transferee who has himself been a party to any fraud or illegality affecting the instrument or who as a prior holder had notice of a defense or claim against it cannot improve his position by taking from a later holder in due course.

(2) A transfer of a security interest in an instrument vests the foregoing rights in the transferee to the extent of the interest transferred.

(3) Unless otherwise agreed any transfer for value of an instrument not then payable to bearer gives the transferee the specifically enforceable right to have the unqualified indorsement of the transferor. Negotiation takes effect only when the indorsement is made and until that time there is no presumption that the transferee is the owner.

Official Comment

Prior Uniform Statutory Provision: Sections 27, 49 and 58, Uniform Negotiable Instruments Law.

Changes: Combined and reworded; new provisions.

Purposes of Changes and New Matter: To make it clear that:

1. The section applies to any transfer, whether by a holder or not. Any person who transfers an instrument transfers whatever rights he has in it. The transferee acquires those rights even though they do not amount to "title."

2. The transfer of rights is not limited to transfers for value. An instrument may be transferred as a gift, and the donee acquires whatever rights the donor had.

3. A holder in due course may transfer his rights as such. The "shelter" provision of the last sentence of the original Section 58 is merely one illustration of the rule that anyone may transfer what he has. Its policy is to assure the holder in due course a free market for the paper, and that policy is continued in this section. The

provision is not intended and should not be used to permit any holder who has himself been a party to any fraud or illegality affecting the instrument, or who has received notice of any defense or claim against it, to wash the paper clean by passing it into the hands of a holder in due course and then repurchasing it. The operation of the provision is illustrated by the following examples:

(a) A induces M by fraud to make an instrument payable to A, A negotiates it to B, who takes as a holder in due course. After the instrument is overdue B gives it to C, who has notice of the fraud. C succeeds to B's rights as a holder in due course, cutting off the defense.

(b) A induces M by fraud to make an instrument payable to A, A negotiates it to B, who takes as a holder in due course. A then repurchases the instrument from B. A does not succeed to B's rights as a holder in due course, and remains subject to the defense of fraud.

(c) A induces M by fraud to make an instrument payable to A, A negotiates it to B, who takes with notice of the fraud. B negotiates it to C, a holder in due course, and then repurchases the instrument from C. B does not succeed to C's rights as a holder in due course, and remains subject to the defense of fraud.

(d) The same facts as (c), except that B had no notice of the fraud when he first acquired the instrument, but learned of it while he was a holder and with such knowledge negotiated to C. B does not succeed to C's rights as a holder in due course, and his position is not improved by the negotiation and repurchase.

4. The rights of a transferee with respect to collateral for the instrument are determined by Article 9 (Secured Transactions).

5. Subsection (2) restates original Section 27 and is intended to make it clear that a transfer of a limited interest in the instrument passes the rights of the transferor to the extent of the interest given. Thus a transferee for security acquires all such rights subject of course to the provisions of Article 9 (Secured Transactions).

6. Subsection (3) applies only to the transfer for value of an instrument payable to order or specially indorsed. It has no application to a gift, or to an instrument payable or indorsed to bearer or indorsed in blank. The transferee acquires, in the absence of any agreement to the contrary, the right to have the indorsement of the transferor. This right is now made enforceable by an action for specific performance. Unless otherwise agreed, it is a right to the general indorsement of the transferor with full liability as indorser, rather than to an indorsement without recourse. The question commonly arises where the purchaser has paid in advance and the indorsement is omitted fraudulently or through oversight; a transferor who is willing to indorse only without recourse or unwilling to indorse at all should make his intentions clear. The agreement for the transferee to take less than an unqualified indorsement need not be an express one, and the understanding may be implied from conduct, from past practice, or from the circumstances of the transaction.

7. Subsection (3) follows the second sentence of the original Section 49 in providing that there is no effective negotiation until the indorsement is made. Until that time the purchaser does not become a holder, and if he receives earlier notice of defense against or claim to the instrument he does not qualify as a holder in due course under Section 3–302(1)(c).

8. The final clause of subsection (3), which is new, is intended to make it clear that the transferee without indorsement of an order instrument is not a holder and so is not aided by the presumption that he is entitled to recover on the instrument provided in Section 3–307(2). The terms of the obligation do not run to him, and he must account for his possession of the unindorsed paper by proving the transaction through which he acquired it. Proof of a transfer to him by a holder is proof that he has acquired the rights of a holder and that he is entitled to the presumption.

Cross References:

Sections 3–202 and 3–416.
Point 5: Article 9.
Point 7: Section 3–302(1)(c).
Point 8: Section 3–307(2).

Definitional Cross References:

"Bearer". Section 1–201.
"Holder". Section 1–201.
"Holder in due course". Section 3–302.
"Instrument". Section 3–102.
"Negotiation". Section 3–202.

"Notice". Section 1–201.
"Party". Section 1–201.
"Presumption". Section 1–201.
"Rights". Section 1–201.
"Security interest". Section 1–201.

§ 3–202. Negotiation.

(1) Negotiation is the transfer of an instrument in such form that the transferee becomes a holder. If the instrument is payable to order it is negotiated by delivery with any necessary indorsement; if payable to bearer it is negotiated by delivery.

(2) An indorsement must be written by or on behalf of the holder and on the instrument or on a paper so firmly affixed thereto as to become a part thereof.

(3) An indorsement is effective for negotiation only when it conveys the entire instrument or any unpaid residue. If it purports to be of less it operates only as a partial assignment.

(4) Words of assignment, condition, waiver, guaranty, limitation or disclaimer of liability and the like accompanying an indorsement do not affect its character as an indorsement.

Official Comment

Prior Uniform Statutory Provision: Sections 30, 31 and 32, Uniform Negotiable Instruments Law.

Changes: Combined and reworded; new provisions.

Purposes of Changes and New Matter: To make it clear that:

1. Negotiation is merely a special form of transfer, the importance of which lies entirely in the fact that it makes the transferee a holder as defined in Section 1–201. Any negotiation carries a transfer of rights as provided in the section on transfer (subsections (1) and (2) of Section 3–201).

2. Any instrument which has been specially indorsed can be negotiated only with the indorsement of the special indorsee as provided in Section 3–204 on special indorsement. An instrument indorsed in blank may be negotiated by delivery alone, provided that it bears the indorsement of all prior special indorsees.

3. Subsection (2) follows decisions holding that a purported indorsement on a mortgage or other separate paper pinned or clipped to an instrument is not sufficient for negotiation. The indorsement must be on the instrument itself or on a paper intended for the purpose which is so firmly affixed to the instrument as to become an extension or part of it. Such a paper is called an allonge.

4. The cause of action on an instrument cannot be split. Any indorsement which purports to convey to any party less than the entire amount of the instrument is not effective for negotiation. This is true of either "Pay A one-half," or "Pay A two-thirds and B one-third," and neither A nor B becomes a holder. On the other hand an indorsement reading merely "Pay A and B" is effective, since it transfers the entire cause of action to A and B as tenants in common.

The partial indorsement does, however, operate as a partial assignment of the cause of action. The provision makes no attempt to state the legal effect of such an assignment, which is left to the local law. In a jurisdiction in which a partial assignee has any rights, either at law or in equity, the partial indorsee has such rights; and in any jurisdiction where a partial assignee has no rights the partial indorsee has none.

5. Subsection (4) is intended to reject decisions holding that the addition of such words as "I hereby assign all my right, title and interest in the within note" prevents the signature from operating as an indorsement. Such words usually are added by laymen out of an excess of caution and a desire to indicate formally that the instrument is conveyed, rather than with any intent to limit the effect of the signature.

6. Subsection (4) is also intended to reject decisions which have held that the addition of "I guarantee payment" indicates an intention not to indorse but merely to guarantee. Any signature with such added words is an indorsement, and if it is made by a holder is effective for negotiation; but the liability of the indorser may be affected by the words of guarantee as provided in the section on the contract of a guarantor. (Section 3–416.)

Cross References:

Section 3-417.
Point 1: Sections 1-201 and 3-201(1) and (2).
Point 2: Section 3-204.
Point 6: Section 3-416.

Definitional Cross References:

"Bearer". Section 1-201.
"Delivery". Section 1-201.
"Holder". Section 1-201.
"Instrument". Section 3-102.
"Written". Section 1-201.

§ 3-203. Wrong or Misspelled Name.

Where an instrument is made payable to a person under a misspelled name or one other than his own he may indorse in that name or his own or both; but signature in both names may be required by a person paying or giving value for the instrument.

Official Comment

Prior Uniform Statutory Provision: Section 43, Uniform Negotiable Instruments Law.

Changes: Reworded.

Purposes of Changes: To make it clear that:

1. The party whose name is wrongly designated or misspelled may make an indorsement effective for negotiation by signing in his true name only. This is not commercially satisfactory, since any subsequent purchaser may be left in doubt as to the state of the title; but whether it is done intentionally or through oversight, the party transfers his rights and is liable on his indorsement, and there is a negotiation if identity exists.

2. He may make an effective indorsement in the wrongly designated or misspelled name only. This again is not commercially satisfactory, since his liability as an indorser may require proof of identity.

3. He may indorse in both names. This is the proper and desirable form of indorsement, and any person called upon to pay an instrument or under contract to purchase it may protect his interest by demanding indorsement in both names, and is not in default if such demand is refused.

Cross Reference:

Section 3-401(2).

Definitional Cross References:

"Instrument". Section 3-102.
"Person". Section 1-201.
"Signature". Section 3-401.

§ 3-204. Special Indorsement; Blank Indorsement.

(1) A special indorsement specifies the person to whom or to whose order it makes the instrument payable. Any instrument specially indorsed becomes payable to the order of the special indorsee and may be further negotiated only by his indorsement.

(2) An indorsement in blank specifies no particular indorsee and may consist of a mere signature. An instrument payable to order and indorsed in blank becomes payable to bearer and may be negotiated by delivery alone until specially indorsed.

(3) The holder may convert a blank indorsement into a special indorsement by writing over the signature of the indorser in blank any contract consistent with the character of the indorsement.

Official Comment

Prior Uniform Statutory Provision: Sections 9(5), 33, 34, 35, 36, and 40, Uniform Negotiable Instruments Law.

Changes: Combined and reworded; rule of Section 40 reversed.

Purposes of Changes:

The last sentence of subsection (1) reverses the rule of the original Section 40, under which an instrument drawn payable to bearer and specially indorsed could be further negotiated by delivery alone. The principle here adopted is that the special indorser, as the owner even of a bearer instrument, has the right to direct the payment and to require the indorsement of his indorsee as evidence of the satisfaction of his own obligation. The special indorsee may of course make it payable to bearer again by himself indorsing in blank.

Cross Reference:

Section 3-202.

Definitional Cross References:

"Bearer". Section 1-201.
"Delivery". Section 1-201.
"Instrument". Section 3-102.
"Person". Section 1-201.
"Signature". Section 3-401.

§ 3-205. Restrictive Indorsements.

An indorsement is restrictive which either

(a) is conditional; or

(b) purports to prohibit further transfer of the instrument; or

(c) includes the words "for collection", "for deposit", "pay any bank", or like terms signifying a purpose of deposit or collection; or

(d) otherwise states that it is for the benefit or use of the indorser or of another person.

Official Comment

Prior Uniform Statutory Provision: Sections 36 and 39, Uniform Negotiable Instruments Law.

Changes: Combined and reworded; new provisions.

Purposes of Changes and New Matter:

1. This section is intended to provide a definition of restrictive indorsements which will include the varieties of indorsement described in original Sections 36 and 39. The separate mention of conditional indorsements, those prohibiting transfer, indorsements in the bank deposit or collection process, and other indorsements to a fiduciary, permits separate treatment in subsequent sections where policy so requires.

2. This is part of a series of changes of the prior uniform statutory provisions effected by Sections 3-102, 3-205, 3-206, 3-304, 3-419, 3-603, and in Article 4, Sections 4-203 and 4-205. The purpose of the changes is generally to require a taker or payor under restrictive indorsement to apply or pay value given consistently with the indorsement, but to provide certain exceptions applying to banks in the collection process (other than depositary banks), and to some other takers and payors.

Cross References:

Sections 3-102, 3-202(2), 3-205, 3-206, 3-304, 3-419, 3-603, 4-203 and 4-205.

Definitional Cross References:

"Instrument". Section 3-102.
"Person". Section 1-201.

§ 3-206. Effect of Restrictive Indorsement.

(1) No restrictive indorsement prevents further transfer or negotiation of the instrument.

(2) An intermediary bank, or a payor bank which is not the depositary bank, is neither given notice nor otherwise affected by a restrictive indorsement of any person except the bank's immediate transferor or the person presenting for payment.

(3) Except for an intermediary bank, any transferee under an indorsement which is conditional or includes the words "for collection", "for deposit", "pay any bank", or like terms (subparagraphs (a) and (c) of Section 3-205) must pay or apply any value given by him for or on the security of the instrument consistently with the indorsement and to the extent that he does so he becomes a holder for value. In addition such transferee is a holder in due course if he otherwise complies with the requirements of Section 3-302 on what constitutes a holder in due course.

(4) The first taker under an indorsement for the benefit of the indorser or another person (subparagraph (d) of Section 3-205) must pay or apply any value given by him for or on the security of the instrument consistently with the indorsement and to the extent that he does so he becomes a holder for value. In addition such taker is a holder in due course if he otherwise complies with the requirements of Section 3-302 on what constitutes a holder in due course. A later holder for value is neither given notice nor otherwise affected by such restrictive indorsement unless he has knowledge that a fiduciary or other person has negotiated the instrument in any transaction for his own benefit or otherwise in breach of duty (subsection (2) of Section 3-304).

Official Comment

Prior Uniform Statutory Provision: Sections 36, 37, 39 and 47, Uniform Negotiable Instruments Law.

Changes: Completely revised.

Purposes of Changes:

1. Subsections (1) and (2) apply to all four classes of restrictive indorsements defined in Section 3-205. Conditional indorsements and indorsements for deposit or collection, defined in paragraphs (a) and (c) of Section 3-205, are also subject to subsection (3); and trust indorsements as defined in paragraph (d) of Section 3-205 are subject to subsection (4). This section negates the implication which has sometimes been found in the original Sections 37 and 47, that under a restrictive indorsement neither the indorsee nor any subsequent taker from him could become a holder in due course. By omitting the original Section 47, this Article also avoids any implication that a discharge is effective against a holder in due course. See Section 3-602.

2. Under subsection (1) an indorsement reading "Pay A only," or any other indorsement purporting to prohibit further transfer, is without effect for that purpose. Such indorsements have rarely appeared in reported American cases. Ordinarily further negotiation will be contemplated by the indorser, if only for bank collection. The indorsee becomes a holder, and the indorsement does not of itself give notice to subsequent parties of any defense or claim of the indorser. Hence this section gives such an indorsement the same effect as an unrestricted indorsement.

3. Subsection (2) permits an intermediary bank (Sections 3-102(3) and 4-105) or a payor bank which is not a depositary bank (Sections 3-102(3) and 4-105) to disregard any restrictive indorsement except that of the bank's immediate transferor. Such banks ordinarily handle instruments, especially checks, in bulk and have no practicable opportunity to consider the effect of restrictive indorsements. Subsection (2) does not affect the rights of the restrictive indorser against parties outside the bank collection process or against the first bank in the collection process; such rights are governed by subsections (3) and (4) and Section 3-603.

4. Conditional indorsements are treated by this section like indorsements for deposit or collection. Under subsection (3) any transferee under such an indorsement except an intermediary bank becomes a holder for value to the extent that he acts consistently with the indorsement in paying or applying any value given by him for or on the security of the instrument. Contrary to the original Section 39, subsection (3) permits a transferee under a conditional indorsement to become a holder in due course free of the conditional indorser's claim.

5. Of the indorsements covered by this section those "for collection", "for deposit" and "pay any bank" are overwhelmingly the most frequent. Indorsements "for collection" or "for deposit" may be either special or blank; indorsements "pay any bank" are governed by Section 4-201(2). Instruments so indorsed are almost invariably destined to be lodged in a bank for collection. Subsection (3) requires any transferee other than an intermediary

bank to act consistently with the purpose of collection, and Section 3–603 lays down a similar rule for payors not covered by subsection (2).

6. Subsection (4), applying to trust indorsements other than those for deposit or collection (paragraph (d) of Section 3–205) is similar to subsection (3); but in subsection (4) the duty to act consistently with the indorsement is limited to the first taker under it. If an instrument is indorsed "Pay T in trust for B" or "Pay T for B" or "Pay T for account of B" or "Pay T as agent for B," whether B is the indorser or a third person, T is of course subject to liability for any breach of his obligation as fiduciary. But trustees commonly and legitimately sell trust assets in transactions entirely outside the bank collection process; the trustee therefore has power to negotiate the instrument and make his transferee a holder in due course. Whether transferees from T have notice of a breach of trust such as to deny them the status of holders in due course is governed by the section on notice to purchasers (Section 3–304); the trust indorsement does not of itself give such notice. Payors are immunized either by subsection (2) of this section or by Section 3–603: payment to the trustee or to a purchaser from the trustee is "consistent with the terms" of the trust indorsement under Section 3–603(1)(b).

7. Several sections of Article 3 and Article 4 are explicitly made subject to the rules stated in this section. See Sections 3–306, 3–419, 4–203 and 4–205.

Cross References:

Point 1: Sections 3–205 and 3–602.
Point 2: Section 3–205(b).
Point 3: Sections 3–102(3), 3–419(4), 3–603, 4–105, 4–205(2).
Point 4: Section 3–205(a).
Point 5: Sections 3–205, 3–603 and 4–201.
Point 6: Sections 3–205, 3–304 and 3–603.
Point 7: Sections 3–306, 3–419, 4–203 and 4–205.

Definitional Cross References:

"Bank". Section 1–201.
"Depositary bank". Sections 3–102(3) and 4–105.
"Holder in due course". Section 3–302.
"Intermediary bank". Sections 3–102(3) and 4–105.
"Negotiation". Sections 3–102(2) and 3–202.
"Payor bank". Sections 3–102(3) and 4–105.
"Restrictive indorsement". Section 3–205.
"Transfer". Section 3–201.

§ 3–207. Negotiation Effective Although It May Be Rescinded.

(1) Negotiation is effective to transfer the instrument although the negotiation is

(a) made by an infant, a corporation exceeding its powers, or any other person without capacity; or

(b) obtained by fraud, duress or mistake of any kind; or

(c) part of an illegal transaction; or

(d) made in breach of duty.

(2) Except as against a subsequent holder in due course such negotiation is in an appropriate case subject to rescission, the declaration of a constructive trust or any other remedy permitted by law.

Official Comment

Prior Uniform Statutory Provision: Sections 22, 58 and 59, Uniform Negotiable Instruments Law.

Changes: Completely revised.

Purposes of Changes: To make it clear that:

1. The original Section 22, which covered only negotiation by an infant or a corporation, is extended by this section to include other negotiations which may be rescinded. The provision applies even though the party's lack of capacity, or the illegality, is of a character which goes to the essence of the transaction and makes it entirely

void, and even though the party negotiating has incurred no liability and is entitled to recover the instrument and have his indorsement cancelled.

2. It is inherent in the character of negotiable paper that any person in possession of an instrument which by its terms runs to him is a holder, and that anyone may deal with him as a holder. The principle finds its most extreme application in the well settled rule that a holder in due course may take the paper even from a thief and be protected against the claim of the rightful owner. Where there is actual negotiation, even in an entirely void transaction, it is no less effective. The policy of this provision, as well as of the last sentence of the original Section 59, is that any person to whom an instrument is negotiated is a holder until the instrument has been recovered from his possession; and that any person who negotiates an instrument thereby parts with all his rights in it until such recovery. The remedy of any such claimant is to recover the paper by replevin or otherwise; to impound it or to enjoin its enforcement, collection or negotiation; to recover its proceeds from the holder; or to intervene in any action brought by the holder against the obligor. As provided in the section on the rights of one not a holder in due course (Section 3–306) his claim is not a defense to the obligor unless he himself defends the action.

3. Negotiation under this Article always includes delivery. (Section 3–202, and see Section 1–201(14)). Acquisition of possession by a thief can therefore never be negotiation under this section. But delivery by the thief to another person may be.

4. Nothing in this section is intended to impose any liability on the party negotiating. He may assert any defense available to him under Sections 3–305, 3–306 and 3–307.

5. A holder in due course takes the instrument free from all claims to it on the part of any person (Section 3–305(1)). Against him there can be no rescission or other remedy, even though the prior negotiation may have been fraudulent or illegal in its essence and entirely void. As against any other party the claimant may have any remedy permitted by law. This section is not intended to specify what that remedy may be, or to prevent any court from imposing conditions or limitations such as prompt action or return of the consideration received. All such questions are left to the law of the particular jurisdiction. Subsection (2) of Section 3–207 gives no right where it would not otherwise exist. The section is intended to mean that any remedies afforded by the local law are cut off only by a holder in due course, and that other parties, such as a bona fide purchaser with notice that the instrument is overdue, take it subject to the claim as provided in paragraph (a) of the section on the rights of one not a holder in due course (Section 3–306).

Cross References:

Point 2: Sections 1–201 and 3–306(d).
Point 3: Sections 1–201 and 3–202.
Point 4: Sections 3–305, 3–306 and 3–307.
Point 5: Sections 3–305(1) and 3–306(a).

Definitional Cross References:

"Holder in due course". Section 3–302.
"Instrument". Section 3–102.
"Negotiation". Section 3–202.
"Person". Section 1–201.
"Remedy". Section 1–201.

§ 3–208. Reacquisition.

Where an instrument is returned to or reacquired by a prior party he may cancel any indorsement which is not necessary to his title and reissue or further negotiate the instrument, but any intervening party is discharged as against the reacquiring party and subsequent holders not in due course and if his indorsement has been cancelled is discharged as against subsequent holders in due course as well.

Official Comment

Prior Uniform Statutory Provision: Sections 48, 50 and 121, Uniform Negotiable Instruments Law.

Changes: Parts of original sections combined and rephrased.

Purposes of Changes: No change in the substance of the law is intended. "Returned to or reacquired by" is substituted for "negotiated back to" in the original Section 50 in order to make it clear that the section applies to a return by an indorsee who does not himself indorse. "Discharged" is substituted for the original language to make it clear that the discharge of the intervening party is included within the rule of the section on effect of discharge against a holder in due course (Section 3–602) and is not effective against a subsequent holder in due course who takes without notice of it.

The reacquirer may keep the instrument himself or he may further negotiate it. On further negotiation he may or may not cancel intervening indorsements. In any case intervening indorsers are discharged as to the reacquirer, since if he attempted to enforce it against them they would have an action back against him. Where the reacquirer negotiates without cancelling the intervening indorsements, the section provides that such indorsers are discharged except against subsequent holders in due course. The intervening indorser whose indorsement is stricken is, in conformity with Section 3–605, discharged even as against subsequent holders in due course.

Cross References:

Sections 3–602, 3–603(2) and 3–605.

Definitional Cross References:

"Holder in due course". Section 3–302.

"Instrument". Section 3–102.

"Party". Section 1–201.

PART 3
RIGHTS OF A HOLDER

§ 3–301. Rights of a Holder.

The holder of an instrument whether or not he is the owner may transfer or negotiate it and, except as otherwise provided in Section 3–603 on payment or satisfaction, discharge it or enforce payment in his own name.

Official Comment

Prior Uniform Statutory Provision: Section 51, Uniform Negotiable Instruments Law.

Changes: Reworded. The provision in the original Section 51 as to discharge by payment is now covered by Section 3–603(1).

Purposes of Changes: The section is revised to state in one provision all the rights of a holder, and to make it clear that every holder has such rights. The only limitations are those found in Section 3–603 on payment or satisfaction. That section provides (with stated exceptions) that payment to a holder discharges the liability of the party paying even though made with knowledge of a claim of another person to the instrument, unless the adverse claimant posts indemnity or procures the issuance of appropriate legal process restraining the payment. Thus payment to a holder in an adverse claim situation would not give discharge if the adverse claimant had followed either of the procedures provided for in the "unless" clause of Section 3–603; nor would a discharge result from payment in two other specific situations described in Section 3–603.

Cross References:

Sections 1–201, 3–307 and 3–603(1).

Definitional Cross References:

"Holder". Section 1–201.

"Instrument". Section 3–102.

"Rights". Section 1–201.

§ 3–302. Holder in Due Course.

(1) A holder in due course is a holder who takes the instrument

(a) for value; and

(b) in good faith; and

(c) without notice that it is overdue or has been dishonored or of any defense against or claim to it on the part of any person.

(2) A payee may be a holder in due course.

(3) A holder does not become a holder in due course of an instrument:

(a) by purchase of it at judicial sale or by taking it under legal process; or

(b) by acquiring it in taking over an estate; or

(c) by purchasing it as part of a bulk transaction not in regular course of business of the transferor.

(4) A purchaser of a limited interest can be a holder in due course only to the extent of the interest purchased.

Official Comment

Prior Uniform Statutory Provision: Section 52, Uniform Negotiable Instruments Law.

Changes: Reworded; new provisions.

Purposes of Changes and New Matter: The changes are intended to remove uncertainties arising under the original section.

1. The language "without notice that it is overdue" is substituted for that of the original subsection (2) in order to make it clear that the purchaser of an instrument which is in fact overdue may be a holder in due course if he takes it without notice that it is overdue. Such notice is covered by the section on notice to purchaser (Section 3-304).

2. Subsection (2) is intended to settle the long continued conflict over the status of the payee as a holder in due course. This conflict has turned very largely upon the word "negotiated" in the original Section 52(4), which is now eliminated. The position here taken is that the payee may become a holder in due course to the same extent and under the same circumstances as any other holder. This is true whether he takes the instrument by purchase from a third person or directly from the obligor. All that is necessary is that the payee meet the requirements of this section. In the following cases, among others, the payee is a holder in due course:

a. A remitter, purchasing goods from P, obtains a bank draft payable to P and forwards it to P, who takes it for value, in good faith and without notice as required by this section.

b. The remitter buys the bank draft payable to P, but it is forwarded by the bank directly to P, who takes it in good faith and without notice in payment of the remitter's obligation to him.

c. A and B sign a note as comakers. A induces B to sign by fraud, and without authority from B delivers the note to P, who takes it for value, in good faith and without notice.

d. A defrauds the maker into signing an instrument payable to P. P pays A for it in good faith and without notice, and the maker delivers the instrument directly to P.

e. D draws a check payable to P and gives it to his agent to be delivered to P in payment of D's debt. The agent delivers it to P, who takes it in good faith and without notice in payment of the agent's debt to P. But as to this case see Section 3-304(2), which may apply.

f. D draws a check payable to P but blank as to the amount, and gives it to his agent to be delivered to P. The agent fills in the check with an excessive amount, and P takes it for value, in good faith and without notice.

g. D draws a check blank as to the name of the payee, and gives it to his agent to be filled in with the name of A and delivered to A. The agent fills in the name of P, and P takes the check in good faith, for value and without notice.

3. Subsection (3) is intended to state existing case law. It covers a few situations in which the purchaser takes the instrument under unusual circumstances which indicate that he is merely a successor in interest to the prior holder and can acquire no better rights. (If such prior holder was himself a holder in due course, the purchaser succeeds to that status under Section 3-201 on Transfer.) The provision applies to a purchaser at an execution sale, a sale in bankruptcy or a sale by a state bank commissioner of the assets of an insolvent bank. It applies equally to an attaching creditor or any other person who acquires the instrument by legal process, even under an antecedent claim; and equally to a representative, such as an executor, administrator, receiver or assignee for the

benefit of creditors, who takes over the instrument as part of an estate, even though he is representing antecedent creditors.

Subsection (3)(c) applies to bulk purchases lying outside of the ordinary course of business of the seller. It applies, for example, when a new partnership takes over for value all of the assets of an old one after a new member has entered the firm, or to a reorganized or consolidated corporation taking over in bulk the assets of a predecessor. It has particular application to the purchase by one bank of a substantial part of the paper held by another bank which is threatened with insolvency and seeking to liquidate its assets.

4. A purchaser of a limited interest—as a pledgee in a security transaction—may become a holder in due course, but he may enforce the instrument over defenses only to the extent of his interest, and defenses good against the pledgor remain available insofar as the pledgor retains an equity in the instrument. This is merely a special application of the general rule (Section 1-201) that a purchaser of a limited interest acquires rights only to the extent of the interest purchased. Section 27 of the original Act contained a similar provision.

Cross References:

Sections 1-201, 3-303, 3-305 and 3-306.
Point 1: Section 3-304(5).
Point 3: Section 3-201.
Point 4: Section 1-201.

Definitional Cross References:

"Good faith". Section 1-201.
"Holder". Section 1-201.
"Instrument". Section 3-102.
"Notice". Section 1-201.
"Notice of dishonor". Section 3-508.
"Person". Section 1-201.
"Purchase". Section 1-201.
"Purchaser". Section 1-201.
"Value". Section 3-303.

§ 3-303. Taking for Value.

A holder takes the instrument for value

(a) to the extent that the agreed consideration has been performed or that he acquires a security interest in or a lien on the instrument otherwise than by legal process; or

(b) when he takes the instrument in payment of or as security for an antecedent claim against any person whether or not the claim is due; or

(c) when he gives a negotiable instrument for it or makes an irrevocable commitment to a third person.

Official Comment

Prior Uniform Statutory Provision: Sections 25, 26, 27 and 54, Uniform Negotiable Instruments Law.

Changes: Combined and reworded; original Section 26 omitted.

Purposes of Changes: The changes are intended to remove uncertainties arising under the original Act.

1. The original Section 26 which had reference to the liability of accommodation parties is omitted as erroneous and misleading, since a holder who does not himself give value cannot qualify as a holder in due course in his own right merely because value has previously been given for the instrument.

2. In this Article value is divorced from consideration (Section 3-408). The latter is important only on the question of whether the obligation of a party can be enforced against him; while value is important only on the question of whether the holder who has acquired that obligation qualifies as a particular kind of holder.

3. Paragraph (a) resolves an apparent conflict between the original Section 54 and the first sentence of the original Section 25, by requiring that the agreed consideration shall actually have been given. An executory promise to give value is not itself value, except as provided in paragraph (c). The underlying reason of policy is

that when the purchaser learns of a defense against the instrument or of a defect in the title he is not required to enforce the instrument, but is free to rescind the transaction for breach of the transferor's warranty (Section 3–417). There is thus not the same necessity for giving him the status of a holder in due course, cutting off claims and defenses, as where he has actually paid value. A common illustration is the bank credit not drawn upon, which can be and is revoked when a claim or defense appears.

4. Paragraph (a) limits the language of the original Section 27, eliminating the attaching creditor or any other person who acquires a lien by legal process. Any such lienor has been uniformly held not to be a holder in due course.

5. Paragraph (b) restates the last sentence of the original Section 25. It adopts the generally accepted rule that the holder takes for value when he takes the instrument as security for an antecedent debt, even though there is no extension of time or other concession, and whether or not the debt is due. The provision extends the same rule to any claim against any person; there is no requirement that the claim arise out of contract. In particular the provision is intended to apply to an instrument given in payment of or as security for the debt of a third person, even though no concession is made in return.

6. Paragraph (c) is new, but states generally recognized exceptions to the rule that an executory promise is not value. A negotiable instrument is value because it carries the possibility of negotiation to a holder in due course, after which the party who gives it cannot refuse to pay. The same reasoning applies to any irrevocable commitment to a third person, such as a letter of credit issued when an instrument is taken.

Cross References:

Sections 3–302 and 3–415.
Point 1: Section 3–415.
Point 2: Section 3–408.
Point 3: Section 3–417.

Definitional Cross References:

"Holder". Section 1–201.
"Instrument". Section 3–102.
"Person". Section 1–201.
"Security interest". Section 1–201.

§ 3–304. Notice to Purchaser.

(1) The purchaser has notice of a claim or defense if

(a) the instrument is so incomplete, bears such visible evidence of forgery or alteration, or is otherwise so irregular as to call into question its validity, terms or ownership or to create an ambiguity as to the party to pay; or

(b) the purchaser has notice that the obligation of any party is voidable in whole or in part, or that all parties have been discharged.

(2) The purchaser has notice of a claim against the instrument when he has knowledge that a fiduciary has negotiated the instrument in payment of or as security for his own debt or in any transaction for his own benefit or otherwise in breach of duty.

(3) The purchaser has notice that an instrument is overdue if he has reason to know

(a) that any part of the principal amount is overdue or that there is an uncured default in payment of another instrument of the same series; or

(b) that acceleration of the instrument has been made; or

(c) that he is taking a demand instrument after demand has been made or more than a reasonable length of time after its issue. A reasonable time for a check drawn and payable within the states and territories of the United States and the District of Columbia is presumed to be thirty days.

(4) Knowledge of the following facts does not of itself give the purchaser notice of a defense or claim

(a) that the instrument is antedated or postdated;

(b) that it was issued or negotiated in return for an executory promise or accompanied by a separate agreement, unless the purchaser has notice that a defense or claim has arisen from the terms thereof;

(c) that any party has signed for accommodation;

(d) that an incomplete instrument has been completed, unless the purchaser has notice of any improper completion;

(e) that any person negotiating the instrument is or was a fiduciary;

(f) that there has been default in payment of interest on the instrument or in payment of any other instrument, except one of the same series.

(5) The filing or recording of a document does not of itself constitute notice within the provisions of this Article to a person who would otherwise be a holder in due course.

(6) To be effective notice must be received at such time and in such manner as to give a reasonable opportunity to act on it.

Official Comment

Prior Uniform Statutory Provision: Sections 45, 52, 53, 55 and 56, Uniform Negotiable Instruments Law.

Changes: Combined and reworded; new provisions.

Purposes of Changes and New Matter: The original sections are expanded, with the addition of specific provisions intended to remove uncertainties in the existing law.

1. "Notice" is defined in Section 1–201.

2. Paragraph (a) of subsection (1) replaces the provision in the original Section 52(1) requiring that the instrument be "complete and regular on its face." An instrument may be blank as to some unnecessary particular, may contain minor erasures, or even have an obvious change in the date, as where "January 2, 1948" is changed to "January 2, 1949", without even exciting suspicion. Irregularity is properly a question of notice to the purchaser of something wrong, and is so treated here.

3. "Voidable" obligation in paragraph (b) of subsection (1) is intended to limit the provision to notice of defense which will permit any party to avoid his original obligation on the instrument, as distinguished from a set-off or counterclaim.

4. Notice that one party has been discharged is not notice to the purchaser of an infirmity in the obligation of other parties who remain liable on the instrument. A purchaser with notice that an indorser is discharged takes subject to that discharge as provided in the section on effect of discharge against a holder in due course (Section 3–602) but is not prevented from taking the obligation of the maker in due course. If he has notice that all parties are discharged he cannot be a holder in due course.

5. Subsection (2) follows the policy of Section 6 of the Uniform Fiduciaries Act, and specifies the same elements as notice of improper conduct of a fiduciary. Under paragraph (e) of subsection (4) mere notice of the existence of the fiduciary relation is not enough in itself to prevent the holder from taking in due course, and he is free to take the instrument on the assumption that the fiduciary is acting properly. The purchaser may pay cash into the hands of the fiduciary without notice of any breach of the obligation. Section 3–206 should be consulted for the effect of a restrictive indorsement.

6. Subsection (3) removes an uncertainty in the original Act by providing that reason to know of an overdue installment or other part of the principal amount is notice that the instrument is overdue and thus prevents the purchaser from taking in due course. On the other hand subsection (4)(f) makes notice that interest is overdue insufficient, on the basis of banking and commercial practice, the decisions under the original Act, and the frequency with which interest payments are in fact delayed. Notice of default in payment of any other instrument, except an uncured default in another instrument of the same series, is likewise insufficient.

7. Subsection (3) departs from the original Section 52(2) by providing that the purchaser may take accelerated paper, or a demand instrument on which demand has in fact been made, as a holder in due course if he takes without notice of the acceleration or demand. With this change the original Section 45 is eliminated, as the presumption that any negotiation has taken place before the instrument was in fact overdue is of importance only in aid of a holder in due course. Under this section it is not conclusive that the instrument was in fact overdue when it was negotiated, if the holder takes without notice of that fact.

The "reasonable time after issue" is retained from the original Section 53, but paragraph (c) adds a presumption, as that term is defined in this Act (Section 1-201), that a domestic check is stale after thirty days.

8. Paragraph (a) of subsection (4) rejects decisions holding that an instrument known to be antedated or postdated is not "regular." Such knowledge does not prevent a holder from taking in due course.

9. Paragraph (b) of subsection (4) is to be read together with the provisions of this Article as to when a promise or order is unconditional and as to other writings affecting the instrument (Sections 3-105 and 3-119). Mere notice of the existence of an executory promise or a separate agreement does not prevent the holder from taking in due course, and such notice may even appear in the instrument itself. If the purchaser has notice of any default in the promise or agreement which gives rise to a defense or claim against the instrument, he is on notice to the same extent as in the case of any other information as to the existence of a defense or claim.

10. Paragraph (d) of subsection (4) follows the policy of the original Section 14, under which any person in possession of an instrument has prima facie authority to fill blanks. It is intended to mean that the holder may take in due course even though a blank is filled in his presence, if he is without notice that the filling is improper. Section 3-407 on alteration should be consulted as to the rights of subsequent holders following such an alteration.

11. Subsection (5) is new. It removes an uncertainty arising under the original Act as to the effect of "constructive notice" through public filing or recording.

12. Subsection (6) is new. It means that notice must be received with a sufficient margin of time to afford a reasonable opportunity to act on it, and that a notice received by the president of a bank one minute before the bank's teller cashes a check is not effective to prevent the bank from becoming a holder in due course. See in this connection the provision on notice to an organization, Sec. 1-201(27).

Cross References:

Sections 3-201 and 3-302.
Point 1: Section 1-201.
Point 4: Section 3-602.
Point 5: Section 3-206.
Point 7: Section 1-201.
Point 9: Sections 3-105(1)(b) and (c) and 3-119.
Point 10: Section 3-407.
Point 12: Section 1-201.

Definitional Cross References:

"Accommodation party". Section 3-415.
"Agreement". Section 1-201.
"Alteration". Section 3-407.
"Bank". Section 1-201.
"Check". Section 3-104.
"Holder in due course". Section 3-302.
"Instrument". Section 3-102.
"Issue". Section 3-102.
"Negotiation". Section 3-202.
"Notice". Section 1-201.
"Party". Section 1-201.
"Person". Section 1-201.
"Presumed". Section 1-201.
"Promise". Section 3-102.
"Purchaser". Section 1-201.
"Reasonable time". Section 1-204.
"Signed". Section 1-201.
"Term". Section 1-201.

§ 3-305. Rights of a Holder in Due Course.

To the extent that a holder is a holder in due course he takes the instrument free from

(1) all claims to it on the part of any person; and

(2) all defenses of any party to the instrument with whom the holder has not dealt except

(a) infancy, to the extent that it is a defense to a simple contract; and

(b) such other incapacity, or duress, or illegality of the transaction, as renders the obligation of the party a nullity; and

(c) such misrepresentation as has induced the party to sign the instrument with neither knowledge nor reasonable opportunity to obtain knowledge of its character or its essential terms; and

(d) discharge in insolvency proceedings; and

(e) any other discharge of which the holder has notice when he takes the instrument.

Official Comment

Prior Uniform Statutory Provision: Sections 15, 16 and 57, Uniform Negotiable Instruments Law.

Changes: Combined and reworded; new provisions; rule of original Section 15 reversed.

Purposes of Changes and New Matter:

1. The section applies to any person who is himself a holder in due course, and equally to any transferee who acquires the rights of one (Section 3-201). "Takes" is substituted for "holds" in the original Section 57 because a holder in due course may still be subject to any claims or defenses which arise against him after he has taken the instrument.

2. The language "all claims to it on the part of any person" is substituted for "any defect of title of prior parties" in the original Section 57 in order to make it clear that the holder in due course takes the instrument free not only from any claim of legal title but also from all liens, equities or claims of any other kind. This includes any claim for rescission of a prior negotiation, in accordance with the provisions of the section on reacquisition (Section 3-208).

3. "All defenses" includes nondelivery, conditional delivery or delivery for a special purpose. Under this Article such nondelivery or qualified delivery is a defense (Sections 3-306 and 3-307) and the defendant has the full burden of establishing it. Accordingly the "conclusive presumption" of the third sentence of the original Section 16 is abrogated in favor of a rule of law cutting off the defense.

The effect of this section, together with the sections dealing with incomplete instruments (Section 3-115) and alteration (Section 3-407) is to cut off the defense of nondelivery of an incomplete instrument against a holder in due course, and to change the rule of the original Section 15.

4. Paragraph (a) of subsection (2) is new. It follows the decisions under the original Act in providing that the defense of infancy may be asserted against a holder in due course, even though its effect is to render the instrument voidable but not void. The policy is one of protection of the infant against those who take advantage of him, even at the expense of occasional loss to an innocent purchaser. No attempt is made to state when infancy is available as a defense or the conditions under which it may be asserted. In some jurisdictions it is held that an infant cannot rescind the transaction or set up the defense unless he restores the holder to his former position, which in the case of a holder in due course is normally impossible. In other states an infant who has misrepresented his age may be estopped to assert his infancy. Such questions are left to the local law, as an integral part of the policy of each state as to the protection of infants.

5. Paragraph (b) of subsection (2) is new. It covers mental incompetence, guardianship, ultra vires acts or lack of corporate capacity to do business, any remaining incapacity of married women, or any other incapacity apart from infancy. Such incapacity is largely statutory. Its existence and effect is left to the law of each state. If under the local law the effect is to render the obligation of the instrument entirely null and void, the defense may be asserted against a holder in due course. If the effect is merely to render the obligation voidable at the election of the obligor, the defense is cut off.

6. Duress is a matter of degree. An instrument signed at the point of a gun is void, even in the hands of a holder in due course. One signed under threat to prosecute the son of the maker for theft may be merely voidable, so that the defense is cut off. Illegality is most frequently a matter of gambling or usury, but may arise in many

other forms under a great variety of statutes. The statutes differ greatly in their provisions and the interpretations given them. They are primarily a matter of local concern and local policy. All such matters are therefore left to the local law. If under that law the effect of the duress or the illegality is to make the obligation entirely null and void, the defense may be asserted against a holder in due course. Otherwise it is cut off.

7. Paragraph (c) of subsection (2) is new. It follows the great majority of the decisions under the original Act in recognizing the defense of "real" or "essential" fraud, sometimes called fraud in the essence or fraud in the factum, as effective against a holder in due course. The common illustration is that of the maker who is tricked into signing a note in the belief that it is merely a receipt or some other document. The theory of the defense is that his signature on the instrument is ineffective because he did not intend to sign such an instrument at all. Under this provision the defense extends to an instrument signed with knowledge that it is a negotiable instrument, but without knowledge of its essential terms.

The test of the defense here stated is that of excusable ignorance of the contents of the writing signed. The party must not only have been in ignorance, but must also have had no reasonable opportunity to obtain knowledge. In determining what is a reasonable opportunity all relevant factors are to be taken into account, including the age and sex of the party, his intelligence, education and business experience; his ability to read or to understand English, the representations made to him and his reason to rely on them or to have confidence in the person making them; the presence or absence of any third person who might read or explain the instrument to him, or any other possibility of obtaining independent information; and the apparent necessity, or lack of it, for acting without delay.

Unless the misrepresentation meets this test, the defense is cut off by a holder in due course.

8. Paragraph (d) is also new. It is inserted to make it clear that any discharge in bankruptcy or other insolvency proceedings, as defined in this Article, is not cut off when the instrument is purchased by a holder in due course.

9. Paragraph (e) of subsection (2) is also new. Under the notice to purchaser section of this Article (Section 3–304), notice of any discharge which leaves other parties liable on the instrument does not prevent the purchaser from becoming a holder in due course. The obvious case is that of the cancellation of an indorsement, which leaves the maker and prior indorsers liable. As to such parties the purchaser may be a holder in due course, but he takes the instrument subject to the discharge of which he has notice. If he is without such notice, the discharge is not effective against him (Section 3–602).

Cross References:

Point 1: Section 3–201(1).
Point 2: Section 3–208.
Point 3: Sections 3–115(2), 3–306(c), 3–307(2) and 3–407(3).
Point 9: Sections 3–304(1)(b) and 3–602.

Definitional Cross References:

"Contract". Section 1–201.
"Holder in due course". Section 3–302.
"Insolvency proceedings". Section 1–201.
"Instrument". Section 3–102.
"Notice". Section 1–201.
"Party". Section 1–201.
"Person". Section 1–201.
"Term". Section 1–201.

§ 3–306. Rights of One Not Holder in Due Course.

Unless he has the rights of a holder in due course any person takes the instrument subject to

(a) all valid claims to it on the part of any person; and

(b) all defenses of any party which would be available in an action on a simple contract; and

(c) the defenses of want or failure of consideration, non-performance of any condition precedent, non-delivery, or delivery for a special purpose (Section 3–408); and

(d) the defense that he or a person through whom he holds the instrument acquired it by theft, or that payment or satisfaction to such holder would be inconsistent with the terms of a restrictive indorsement. The claim of any third person to the instrument is not otherwise available as a defense to any party liable thereon unless the third person himself defends the action for such party.

Official Comment

Prior Uniform Statutory Provision: Sections 16, 28, 58 and 59, Uniform Negotiable Instruments Law.

Changes: Combined, condensed and reworded.

Purposes of Changes: The changes are intended to remove the following uncertainties arising under the original sections:

1. Any transferee who acquires the rights of a holder in due course under the transfer section of this Article (Section 3–201) is included within the provisions of the preceding Section 305. This section covers any person who neither qualifies in his own right as a holder in due course nor has acquired the rights of one by transfer. In particular the section applies to a bona fide purchaser with notice that the instrument is overdue.

2. "All valid claims to it on the part of any person" includes not only claims of legal title, but all liens, equities, or other claims of right against the instrument or its proceeds. It includes claims to rescind a prior negotiation and to recover the instrument or its proceeds.

3. Paragraph (b) restates the first sentence of the original Section 58.

4. Paragraph (c) condenses the original Sections 16 and 28. Want or failure of consideration is specifically mentioned, as in the original Section 28, in order to make it clear that either is a defense which the defendant has the burden of establishing under the following section of this Article. The language as to an "ascertained or liquidated amount or otherwise" in the original Section 28 is omitted because it is believed to be superfluous. The third sentence of Section 16 is now covered by the preceding section. The fourth sentence is omitted in favor of the rule stated in the following section, which places the full burden of establishing the defense of non-delivery, conditional delivery or delivery for a special purpose upon the defendant, and makes any presumption unnecessary.

5. Paragraph (d) is substituted for the last sentence of the original Section 59, as a more detailed and explicit statement of the same policy, which is also found in the original Section 22. The contract of the obligor is to pay the holder of the instrument, and the claims of other persons against the holder are generally not his concern. He is not required to set up such a claim as a defense, since he usually will have no satisfactory evidence of his own on the issue; and the provision that he may not do so is intended as much for his protection as for that of the holder. The claimant who has lost possession of an instrument so payable or indorsed that another may become a holder has lost his rights on the instrument, which by its terms no longer runs to him. The provision includes all claims for rescission of a negotiation, whether based in incapacity, fraud, duress, mistake, illegality, breach of trust or duty or any other reason. It includes claims based on conditional delivery or delivery for a special purpose. It includes claims of legal title, lien, constructive trust or other equity against the instrument or its proceeds. The exception made in the case of theft is based on the policy which refuses to aid a proved thief to recover, and refuses to aid him indirectly by permitting his transferee to recover unless the transferee is a holder in due course. The exception concerning restrictive indorsements is intended to achieve consistency with Section 3–603 and related sections.

Nothing in this section is intended to prevent the claimant from intervening in the holder's action against the obligor or defending the action for the latter, and asserting his claim in the course of such intervention or defense. Nothing here stated is intended to prevent any interpleader, deposit in court or other available procedure under which the defendant may bring the claimant into court or be discharged without himself litigating the claim as a defense. Compare Section 3–803 on vouching in other parties alleged to be liable.

Cross References:

Section 3–302.
Point 1: Sections 3–201(1) and 3–305.
Point 2: Section 3–207.
Point 3: Section 3–307(2).
Point 4: Sections 3–305 and 3–307(2).
Point 5: Section 3–803.

Definitional Cross References:

"Action". Section 1–201.
"Contract". Section 1–201.
"Delivery". Section 1–201.
"Holder in due course". Section 3–302.
"Instrument". Section 3–102.
"Party". Section 1–201.
"Person". Section 1–201.
"Rights". Section 1–201.

§ 3–307. Burden of Establishing Signatures, Defenses and Due Course.

(1) Unless specifically denied in the pleadings each signature on an instrument is admitted. When the effectiveness of a signature is put in issue

(a) the burden of establishing it is on the party claiming under the signature; but

(b) the signature is presumed to be genuine or authorized except where the action is to enforce the obligation of a purported signer who has died or become incompetent before proof is required.

(2) When signatures are admitted or established, production of the instrument entitles a holder to recover on it unless the defendant establishes a defense.

(3) After it is shown that a defense exists a person claiming the rights of a holder in due course has the burden of establishing that he or some person under whom he claims is in all respects a holder in due course.

Official Comment

Prior Uniform Statutory Provision: Section 59, Uniform Negotiable Instruments Law.

Changes: Reworded; new provisions.

Purposes of Changes and New Matter:

1. Subsection (1) is new, although similar provisions are found in a number of states. The purpose of the requirement of a specific denial in the pleadings is to give the plaintiff notice that he must meet a claim of forgery or lack of authority as to the particular signature, and to afford him an opportunity to investigate and obtain evidence. Where local rules of pleading permit, the denial may be on information and belief, or it may be a denial of knowledge or information sufficient to form a belief. It need not be under oath unless the local statutes or rules require verification. In the absence of such specific denial the signature stands admitted, and is not in issue. Nothing in this section is intended, however, to prevent amendment of the pleading in a proper case.

The question of the burden of establishing the signature arises only when it has been put in issue by specific denial. "Burden of establishing" is defined in the definitions section of this Act (Section 1–201). The burden is on the party claiming under the signature, but he is aided by the presumption that it is genuine or authorized [as] stated in paragraph (b). "Presumption" is also defined in this Act (Section 1–201). It means that until some evidence is introduced which would support a finding that the signature is forged or unauthorized the plaintiff is not required to prove that it is authentic. The presumption rests upon the fact that in ordinary experience forged or unauthorized signatures are very uncommon, and normally any evidence is within the control of the defendant or more accessible to him. He is therefore required to make some sufficient showing of the grounds for his denial before the plaintiff is put to his proof. His evidence need not be sufficient to require a directed verdict in his favor, but it must be enough to support his denial by permitting a finding in his favor. Until he introduces such evidence the presumption requires a finding for the plaintiff. Once such evidence is introduced the burden of establishing the signature by a preponderance of the total evidence is on the plaintiff.

Under paragraph (b) this presumption does not arise where the action is to enforce the obligation of a purported signer who has died or become incompetent before the evidence is required, and so is disabled from obtaining or introducing it. "Action" of course includes a claim asserted against the estate of a deceased or an incompetent.

2. Subsection (2) is substituted for the first clause of the original Section 59. Once signatures are proved or admitted, a holder makes out his case by mere production of the instrument, and is entitled to recover in the

absence of any further evidence. The defendant has the burden of establishing any and all defenses, not only in the first instance but by a preponderance of the total evidence. The provision applies only to a holder, as defined in this Act (Section 1–201). Any other person in possession of an instrument must prove his right to it and account for the absence of any necessary indorsement. If he establishes a transfer which gives him the rights of a holder (Section 3–201), this provision becomes applicable, and he is then entitled to recover unless the defendant establishes a defense.

3. Subsection (3) rephrases the last clause of the first sentence of the original Section 59. Until it is shown that a defense exists the issue as to whether the holder is a holder in due course does not arise. In the absence of a defense any holder is entitled to recover and there is no occasion to say that he is deemed prima facie to be a holder in due course. When it is shown that a defense exists the plaintiff may, if he so elects, seek to cut off the defense by establishing that he is himself a holder in due course, or that he has acquired the rights of a prior holder in due course (Section 3–201). On this issue he has the full burden of proof by a preponderance of the total evidence. "In all respects" means that he must sustain this burden by affirmative proof that the instrument was taken for value, that it was taken in good faith, and that it was taken without notice (Section 3–302).

Nothing in this section is intended to say that the plaintiff must necessarily prove that he is a holder in due course. He may elect to introduce no further evidence, in which case a verdict may be directed for the plaintiff or the defendant, or the issue of the defense may be left to the jury, according to the weight and sufficiency of the defendant's evidence. He may elect to rebut the defense itself by proof to the contrary, in which case again a verdict may be directed for either party or the issue may be for the jury. This subsection means only that if the plaintiff claims the rights of a holder in due course against the defense he has the burden of proof upon that issue.

Cross References:

Sections 3–305, 3–306, 3–401, 3–403 and 3–404.

Point 1: Section 1–201.

Point 2: Sections 1–201 and 3–201(1).

Point 3: Sections 3–201(1) and 3–302.

Definitional Cross References:

"Action". Section 1–201.
"Burden of establishing". Section 1–201.
"Defendant". Section 1–201.
"Genuine". Section 1–201.
"Holder". Section 1–201.
"Holder in due course". Section 3–302.
"Instrument". Section 3–102.
"Party". Section 1–201.
"Person". Section 1–201.
"Presumed". Section 1–201.
"Rights". Section 1–201.
"Signature". Section 3–401.

PART 4
LIABILITY OF PARTIES

§ 3-401. Signature.

(1) No person is liable on an instrument unless his signature appears thereon.

(2) A signature is made by use of any name, including any trade or assumed name, upon an instrument, or by any word or mark used in lieu of a written signature.

Official Comment

Prior Uniform Statutory Provision: Section 18, Uniform Negotiable Instruments Law.

Changes: Reworded.

Purposes of Changes: To make it clear that:

1. No one is liable on an instrument unless and until he has signed it. The chief application of the rule has been in cases holding that a principal whose name does not appear on an instrument signed by his agent is not liable on the instrument even though the payee knew when it was issued that it was intended to be the obligation of one who did not sign. The exceptions made as to collateral and virtual acceptances by the original Sections 134 and 135 are now abrogated by the definition of an acceptance and the rules governing its operation. An allonge is part of the instrument to which it is affixed. Section 3–202(2).

Nothing in this section is intended to prevent any liability arising apart from the instrument itself. The party who does not sign may still be liable on the original obligation for which the instrument was given, or for breach of any agreement to sign, or in tort for misrepresentation, or even on an oral guaranty of payment where the statute of frauds is satisfied. He may of course be liable under any separate writing. The provision is not intended to prevent an estoppel to deny that the party has signed, as where the instrument is purchased in good faith reliance upon his assurance that a forged signature is genuine.

2. A signature may be handwritten, typed, printed or made in any other manner. It need not be subscribed, and may appear in the body of the instrument, as in the case of "I, John Doe, promise to pay—" without any other signature. It may be made by mark, or even by thumbprint. It may be made in any name, including any trade name or assumed name, however false and fictitious, which is adopted for the purpose. Parol evidence is admissible to identify the signer, and when he is identified the signature is effective.

This section is not intended to affect any local statute or rule of law requiring a signature by mark to be witnessed, or any signature to be otherwise authenticated, or requiring any form of proof. It is to be read together with the provision under which a person paying or giving value for the instrument may require indorsement in both the right name and the wrong one; and with the provision that the absence of an indorsement in the right name may make an instrument so irregular as to call its ownership into question and put a purchaser upon notice which will prevent his taking as a holder in due course.

Cross References:

Sections 3–202(2), 3–402 through 3–406.
Point 1: Section 3–410.
Point 2: Section 3–203.

Definitional Cross References:

"Person". Section 1–201.
"Instrument". Section 3–102.
"Signed". Section 1–201.
"Written". Section 1–201.

§ 3–402. Signature in Ambiguous Capacity.

Unless the instrument clearly indicates that a signature is made in some other capacity it is an indorsement.

Official Comment

Prior Uniform Statutory Provision: Sections 17(6) and 63, Uniform Negotiable Instruments Law.

Changes: Combined and reworded.

Purposes of Changes: The revised language is intended to say that any ambiguity as to the capacity in which a signature is made must be resolved by a rule of law that it is an indorsement. Parol evidence is not admissible to show any other capacity, except for the purpose of reformation of the instrument as it may be permitted under the rules of the particular jurisdiction. The question is to be determined from the face of the instrument alone, and unless the instrument itself makes it clear that he has signed in some other capacity the signer must be treated as an indorser.

The indication that the signature is made in another capacity must be clear without reference to anything but the instrument. It may be found in the language used. Thus if John Doe signs after "I, John Doe, promise to pay," he is clearly a maker; and "John Doe, witness" is not liable at all. The capacity may be found in any clearly evidenced purpose of the signature, as where a drawee signing in an unusual place on the paper has no visible reason to sign at all unless he is an acceptor. It may be found in usage or custom. Thus by long established practice judicially noticed or otherwise established a signature in the lower right hand corner of an instrument indicates an intent to sign as the maker of a note or the drawer of a draft. Any similar clear indication of an intent to sign in some other capacity may be enough to remove the signature from the application of this section.

Cross Reference:

Section 3–401.

Definitional Cross References:

"Instrument". Section 3–102.

"Signature". Section 3–401.

§ 3–403. Signature by Authorized Representative.

(1) A signature may be made by an agent or other representative, and his authority to make it may be established as in other cases of representation. No particular form of appointment is necessary to establish such authority.

(2) An authorized representative who signs his own name to an instrument

(a) is personally obligated if the instrument neither names the person represented nor shows that the representative signed in a representative capacity;

(b) except as otherwise established between the immediate parties, is personally obligated if the instrument names the person represented but does not show that the representative signed in a representative capacity, or if the instrument does not name the person represented but does show that the representative signed in a representative capacity.

(3) Except as otherwise established the name of an organization preceded or followed by the name and office of an authorized individual is a signature made in a representative capacity.

Official Comment

Prior Uniform Statutory Provision: Sections 19, 20 and 21, Uniform Negotiable Instruments Law.

Changes: Combined and reworded; original Section 21 omitted.

Purposes of Changes:

1. The definition of "representative" in this Act (Section 1–201) includes an officer of a corporation or association, a trustee, an executor or administrator of an estate, or any person empowered to act for another. It is not intended to mean that a trust or an estate is necessarily a legal entity with the capacity to issue negotiable instruments, but merely that if it can issue them they may be signed by the representative.

The power to sign for another may be an express authority, or it may be implied in law or in fact, or it may rest merely upon apparent authority. It may be established as in other cases of representation, and when relevant parol evidence is admissible to prove or to deny it.

2. Subsection (2) applies only to the signature of a representative whose authority to sign for another is established. If he is not authorized his signature has the effect of an unauthorized signature (Section 3–404). Even though he is authorized the principal is not liable on the instrument, under the provisions (Section 3–401) relating to signatures, unless the instrument names him and clearly shows that the signature is made on his behalf.

3. Assuming that Peter Pringle is a principal and Arthur Adams is his agent, an instrument might, for example, bear the following signatures affixed by the agent—

(a) "Peter Pringle", or

(b) "Arthur Adams", or

(c) "Peter Pringle by Arthur Adams, Agent", or

(d) "Arthur Adams, Agent", or

(e) "Peter Pringle Arthur Adams".

A signature in form (a) does not bind Adams if authorized (Sections 3–401 and 3–404).

A signature as in (b) personally obligates the agent and parol evidence is inadmissible under subsection (2)(a) to disestablish his obligation.

The unambiguous way to make the representation clear is to sign as in (c). Any other definite indication is sufficient, as where the instrument reads "Peter Pringle promises to pay" and it is signed "Arthur Adams, Agent." Adams is not bound if he is authorized (Section 3–404).

Subsection 2(b) adopts the New York (minority) rule of Megowan v. Peterson, 173 N.Y. 1 (1902), in such a case as (d); and adopts the majority rule in such a case as (e). In both cases the section admits parol evidence in litigation between the immediate parties to prove signature by the agent in his representative capacity. [Paragraph 3 was amended in 1966].

4. The original Section 21, covering signatures by "procuration," is omitted. It was based on English practice under which the words "per procuration" added to any signature are understood to mean that the signer is acting under a power of attorney which the holder is free to examine. The holder is thus put on notice of the limited authority, and there can be no apparent authority extending beyond the power of attorney. This meaning of "per procuration" is almost unknown in the United States, and the words are understood by the ordinary banker or attorney to be merely the equivalent of "by." The omission is not intended to suggest that a signature "by procuration" can no longer have the effect which it had under the original Section 21, in any case where a party chooses to use the expression.

Cross References:

Point 1: Section 1–201.
Point 2: Sections 3–401(1), 3–404 and 3–405.

Definitional Cross References:

"Instrument". Section 3–102.
"Person". Section 1–201.
"Representative". Section 1–201.
"Signature". Section 3–401.

§ 3–404. Unauthorized Signatures.

(1) Any unauthorized signature is wholly inoperative as that of the person whose name is signed unless he ratifies it or is precluded from denying it; but it operates as the signature of the unauthorized signer in favor of any person who in good faith pays the instrument or takes it for value.

(2) Any unauthorized signature may be ratified for all purposes of this Article. Such ratification does not of itself affect any rights of the person ratifying against the actual signer.

Official Comment

Prior Uniform Statutory Provision: Section 23, Uniform Negotiable Instruments Law.

Changes: Reworded; new provisions.

Purpose of Changes and New Matter: The changes are intended to remove uncertainties arising under the original section:

1. "Unauthorized signature" is a defined term (Section 1–201). It includes both a forgery and a signature made by an agent exceeding his actual or apparent authority.

2. The final clause of subsection (1) is new. It states the generally accepted rule that the unauthorized signature, while it is wholly inoperative as that of the person whose name is signed, is effective to impose liability upon the actual signer or to transfer any rights that he may have in the instrument. His liability is not in damages for breach of a warranty of his authority, but is full liability on the instrument in the capacity in which he has signed. It is, however, limited to parties who take or pay the instrument in good faith; and one who knows that the signature is unauthorized cannot recover from the signer on the instrument.

3. Subsection (2) is new. It settles the conflict which has existed in the decisions as to whether a forgery may be ratified. A forged signature may at least be adopted; and the word "ratified" is used in order to make it clear that the adoption is retroactive, and that it may be found from conduct as well as from express statements. Thus it may be found from the retention of benefits received in the transaction with knowledge of the unauthorized

signature; and although the forger is not an agent, the ratification is governed by the same rules and principles as if he were.

This provision makes ratification effective only for the purposes of this Article. The unauthorized signature becomes valid so far as its effect as a signature is concerned. The ratification relieves the actual signer from liability on the signature. It does not of itself relieve him from liability to the person whose name is signed. It does not in any way affect the criminal law. No policy of the criminal law requires that the person whose name is forged shall not assume liability to others on the instrument; but he cannot affect the rights of the state. While the ratification may be taken into account with other relevant facts in determining punishment, it does not relieve the signer of criminal liability.

4. The words "or is precluded from denying it" are retained in subsection (1) to recognize the possibility of an estoppel against the person whose name is signed, as where he expressly or tacitly represents to an innocent purchaser that the signature is genuine; and to recognize the negligence which precludes a denial of the signature.

Cross References:

Sections 3–307, 3–401, 3–403 and 3–405.
Point 1: Section 1–201.
Point 4: Section 3–406.

Definitional Cross References:

"Good faith". Section 1–201.
"Instrument". Section 3–102.
"Person". Section 1–201.
"Rights". Section 1–201.
"Signature". Section 3–401.
"Signed". Section 1–201.
"Unauthorized signature". Section 1–201.
"Value". Section 3–303.

§ 3–405. Impostors; Signature in Name of Payee.

(1) An indorsement by any person in the name of a named payee is effective if

(a) an impostor by use of the mails or otherwise has induced the maker or drawer to issue the instrument to him or his confederate in the name of the payee; or

(b) a person signing as or on behalf of a maker or drawer intends the payee to have no interest in the instrument; or

(c) an agent or employee of the maker or drawer has supplied him with the name of the payee intending the latter to have no such interest.

(2) Nothing in this section shall affect the criminal or civil liability of the person so indorsing.

Official Comment

Prior Uniform Statutory Provision: Section 9(3), Uniform Negotiable Instruments Law.

Changes: Reworded; new provisions.

Purposes of Changes and New Matter:

1. This section enlarges the original subsection to include additional situations which it has not been held to cover. The words "fictitious or nonexisting person" have been eliminated as misleading, since the existence or nonexistence of the named payee is not decisive and is important only as it may bear on the intent that he shall have no interest in the instrument. The instrument is not made payable to bearer and indorsements are still necessary to negotiation. The section however recognizes as effective indorsement of the types of paper covered no matter by whom made. This solution is thought preferable to making such instruments bearer paper; on the face of things they are payable to order and a subsequent taker should require what purports to be a regular chain of indorsements. On the other hand it is thought to be unduly restrictive to require that the actual indorsement be made by the impostor or other fraudulent actor. In most cases the person whose fraud procured the instrument to be issued will himself indorse; when some other third person indorses it will most probably be a case of theft or a

second independent fraud superimposed upon the original fraud. In neither case does there seem to be sufficient reason to reverse the rule of the section. To recapitulate: the instrument does not become bearer paper, a purportedly regular chain in indorsements is required, but any person—first thief, second impostor or third murderer—can effectively indorse in the name of the payee.

2. Subsection (1)(a) is new. It rejects decisions which distinguish between face-to-face imposture and imposture by mail and hold that where the parties deal by mail the dominant intent of the drawer is to deal with the name rather than with the person so that the resulting instrument may be negotiated only by indorsement of the payee whose name has been taken in vain. The result of the distinction has been under some prior law, to throw the loss in the mail imposture forward to a subsequent holder or to the drawee. Since the maker or drawer believes the two to be one and the same, the two intentions cannot be separated, and the "dominant intent" is a fiction. The position here taken is that the loss, regardless of the type of fraud which the particular impostor has committed, should fall upon the maker or drawer.

"Impostor" refers to impersonation, and does not extend to a false representation that the party is the authorized agent of the payee. The maker or drawer who takes the precaution of making the instrument payable to the principal is entitled to have his indorsement.

3. Subsection (1)(b) restates the substance of the original subsection 9(3). The test stated is not whether the named payee is "fictitious," but whether the signer intends that he shall have no interest in the instrument. The following situations illustrate the application of the subsection.

a. The drawer of a check, for his own reasons, makes it payable to P knowing that P does not exist.

b. The drawer makes the check payable in the name of P. A person named P exists, but the drawer does not know it.

c. The drawer makes the check payable to P, an existing person whom he knows, intending to receive the money himself and that P shall have no interest in the check.

d. The treasurer of a corporation draws its check payable to P, who to the knowledge of the treasurer does not exist.

e. The treasurer of a corporation draws its check payable to P. P exists but the treasurer has fraudulently added his name to the payroll intending that he shall not receive the check.

f. The president and the treasurer of a corporation both sign its check payable to P. P does not exist. The treasurer knows it but the president does not.

g. The same facts as f, except that P exists and the treasurer knows it, but intends that P shall have no interest in the check.

In all the cases stated an indorsement by any person in the name of P is effective.

4. Paragraph (c) is new. It extends the rule of the original Subsection 9(3) to include the padded payroll cases, where the drawer's agent or employee prepares the check for signature or otherwise furnishes the signing officer with the name of the payee. The principle followed is that the loss should fall upon the employer as a risk of his business enterprise rather than upon the subsequent holder or drawee. The reasons are that the employer is normally in a better position to prevent such forgeries by reasonable care in the selection or supervision of his employees, or, if he is not, is at least in a better position to cover the loss by fidelity insurance; and that the cost of such insurance is properly an expense of his business rather than of the business of the holder or drawee.

The provision applies only to the agent or employee of the drawer, and only to the agent or employee who supplies him with the name of the payee. The following situations illustrate its application.

a. An employee of a corporation prepares a padded payroll for its treasurer, which includes the name of P. P does not exist, and the employee knows it, but the treasurer does not. The treasurer draws the corporation's check payable to P.

b. The same facts as a, except that P exists and the employee knows it but intends him to have no interest in the check. In both cases an indorsement by any person in the name of P is effective and the loss falls on the corporation.

5. The section is not intended to affect criminal liability for forgery or any other crime, or civil liability to the drawer or to any other person. It is to be read together with the section under which an unauthorized signer is personally liable on the signature to any person who takes the instrument in good faith (3–404(1)).

Cross References:

Sections 3–401, 3–403, 3–404 and 3–406.
Point 5: Section 3–404(1).

Definitional Cross References:

"Instrument". Section 3–102.
"Issue". Section 3–102.
"Person". Section 1–201.
"Signature". Section 3–401.

§ 3–406. Negligence Contributing to Alteration or Unauthorized Signature.

Any person who by his negligence substantially contributes to a material alteration of the instrument or to the making of an unauthorized signature is precluded from asserting the alteration or lack of authority against a holder in due course or against a drawee or other payor who pays the instrument in good faith and in accordance with the reasonable commercial standards of the drawee's or payor's business.

Official Comment

Prior Uniform Statutory Provision: None.

Purposes:

1. This section is new. It adopts the doctrine of Young v. Grote, 4 Bing. 253 (1827), which held that a drawer who so negligently draws an instrument as to facilitate its material alteration is liable to a drawee who pays the altered instrument in good faith. It should be noted that the rule as stated in the section requires that the negligence "substantially" contribute to the alteration.

2. The section extends the above principle to the protection of a holder in due course and of payors who may not technically be drawees. It rejects decisions which have held that the maker of a note owes no duty of care to the holder because at the time the instrument is drawn there is no contract between them. By drawing the instrument and "setting it afloat upon a sea of strangers" the maker or drawer voluntarily enters into a relation with later holders which justifies his responsibility. In this respect an instrument so negligently drawn as to facilitate alteration does not differ in principle from an instrument containing blanks which may be filled.

The holder in due course under the rules governing alteration (Section 3–407) may enforce the altered instrument according to its original tenor. Where negligence of the obligor has substantially contributed to the alteration, this section gives the holder the alternative right to enforce the instrument as altered.

3. No attempt is made to define negligence which will contribute to an alteration. The question is left to the court or the jury upon the circumstances of the particular cases. Negligence usually has been found where spaces are left in the body of the instrument in which words or figures may be inserted. No unusual precautions are required, and the section is not intended to change decisions holding that the drawer of a bill is under no duty to use sensitized paper, indelible ink or a protectograph; or that it is not negligence to leave spaces between the lines or at the end of the instrument in which a provision for interest or the like can be written.

4. The section applies only where the negligence contributes to the alteration. It must afford an opportunity of which advantage is in fact taken. The section approves decisions which have refused to hold the drawer responsible where he has left spaces in a check but the payee erased all the writing with chemicals and wrote in an entirely new check.

5. This section does not make the negligent party liable in tort for damages resulting from the alteration. Instead it estops him from asserting it against the holder in due course or drawee. The reason is that in the usual case the extent of the loss, which involves the possibility of ultimate recovery from the wrongdoer, cannot be determined at the time of litigation, and the decision would have to be made on the unsatisfactory basis of burden of proof. The holder or drawee is protected by an estoppel, and the task of pursuing the wrongdoer is left to the negligent party. Any amount in fact recovered from the wrongdoer must be held for the benefit of the negligent party under ordinary principles of equity.

6. The section protects parties who act not only in good faith, (Section 1–201) but also in observance of the reasonable standards of their business. Thus any bank which takes or pays an altered check which ordinary banking standards would require it to refuse cannot take advantage of the estoppel.

7. The section applies the same rule to negligence which contributes to a forgery or other unauthorized signature, as defined in this Act (Section 1–201). The most obvious case is that of the drawer who makes use of a signature stamp or other automatic signing device and is negligent in looking after it. The section extends, however, to cases where the party has notice that forgeries of his signature have occurred and is negligent in failing to prevent further forgeries by the same person. It extends to negligence which contributes to a forgery of the signature of another, as in the case where a check is negligently mailed to the wrong person having the same name as the payee. As in the case of alteration, no attempt is made to specify what is negligence, and the question is one for the court or the jury on the facts of the particular case.

Cross References:

Sections 3–401 and 3–404.
Point 2: Section 3–407(3).
Point 6: Section 1–201.
Point 7: Section 1–201.

Definitional Cross References:

"Alteration". Section 3–407.
"Good faith". Section 1–201.
"Holder in due course". Section 3–302.
"Instrument". Section 3–102.
"Person". Section 1–201.
"Unauthorized signature". Section 1–201.

§ 3–407. Alteration.

(1) Any alteration of an instrument is material which changes the contract of any party thereto in any respect, including any such change in

(a) the number or relations of the parties; or

(b) an incomplete instrument, by completing it otherwise than as authorized; or

(c) the writing as signed, by adding to it or by removing any part of it.

(2) As against any person other than a subsequent holder in due course,

(a) alteration by the holder which is both fraudulent and material discharges any party whose contract is thereby changed unless that party assents or is precluded from asserting the defense;

(b) no other alteration discharges any party and the instrument may be enforced according to its original tenor, or as to incomplete instruments according to the authority given.

(3) A subsequent holder in due course may in all cases enforce the instrument according to its original tenor, and when an incomplete instrument has been completed, he may enforce it as completed.

Official Comment

Prior Uniform Statutory Provision: Sections 14, 15, 124 and 125, Uniform Negotiable Instruments Law.

Changes: Combined and reworded; new provisions; rule of original Section 15 reversed.

Purposes of Changes and New Matter: The changes are intended to remove uncertainties arising under the original sections, and to modify the rules as to discharge:

1. Subsection (1) substitutes a general definition for the list of illustrations in the original Section 125. Any alteration is material only as it may change the contract of a party to the instrument; and the addition or deletion of words which do not in any way affect the contract of any previous signer is not material. But any change in the contract of a party, however slight, is a material alteration; and the addition of one cent to the amount payable, or an advance of one day in the date of payment, will operate as a discharge if it is fraudulent.

Specific mention is made of a change in the number or relations of the parties in order to make it clear that any such change is material only if it changes the contract of one who has signed. The addition of a co-maker or a surety does not change in most jurisdictions the contract of one who has already signed as maker and should not be held material as to him. The addition of the name of an alternative payee is material, since it changes his obligation. Paragraph (c) makes special mention of a change in the writing signed in order to cover occasional cases of addition of sticker clauses, scissoring or perforating instruments where the separation is not authorized.

2. Paragraph (b) of subsection (1) is to be read together with Section 3–115 on incomplete instruments. Where an instrument contains blanks or is otherwise incomplete, it may be completed in accordance with the authority given and is then valid and effective as completed. If the completion is unauthorized and has the effect of changing the contract of any previous signer, this provision follows the generally accepted rule in treating it as a material alteration which may operate as a discharge.

3. Subsection (2) modifies the very rigorous rule of the original Section 124. The changes made are as follows:

a. A material alteration does not discharge any party unless it is made by the holder. Spoliation by any meddling stranger does not affect the rights of the holder. It is of course intended that the acts of the holder's authorized agent or employee, or of his confederates, are to be attributed to him.

b. A material alteration does not discharge any party unless it is made for a fraudulent purpose. There is no discharge where a blank is filled in the honest belief that it is as authorized; or where a change is made with a benevolent motive such as a desire to give the obligor the benefit of a lower interest rate. Changes favorable to the obligor are unlikely to be made with any fraudulent intent; but if such an intent is found the alteration may operate as a discharge.

c. The discharge is a personal defense of the party whose contract is changed by the alteration, and anyone whose contract is not affected cannot assert it. The contract of any party is necessarily affected, however, by the discharge of any party against whom he has a right of recourse on the instrument. Assent to the alteration given before or after it is made will prevent the party from asserting the discharge. "Or is precluded from asserting the defense" is added in paragraph (a) to recognize the possibility of an estoppel or other ground barring the defense which does not rest on assent.

d. If the alteration is not material or if it is not made for a fraudulent purpose there is no discharge, and the instrument may be enforced according to its original tenor. Where blanks are filled or an incomplete instrument is otherwise completed there is no original tenor, but the instrument may be enforced according to the authority in fact given.

4. Subsection (3) combines the final sentences of the original Sections 14 and 124, and provides that a subsequent holder in due course takes free of the discharge in all cases. The provision is merely one form of the general rule governing the effect of discharge against a holder in due course (Section 3–602). The holder in due course may enforce the instrument according to its original tenor. In this connection reference should be made to the section giving the holder in due course the right, where the maker's or drawer's negligence has substantially contributed to the alteration, to enforce the instrument in its altered form (Section 3–406). Reference should also be made to Section 4–401 covering a bank's right to charge its customer's account in the case of altered instruments.

Where blanks are filled or an incomplete instrument is otherwise completed, this subsection follows the original Section 14 in placing the loss upon the party who left the instrument incomplete and permitting the holder to enforce it in its completed form. As indicated in the comment to Section 3–115 on incomplete instruments, this result is intended even though the instrument was stolen from the maker or drawer and completed after the theft; and the effect of this subsection, together with the section on incomplete instruments is to reverse the rule of the original Section 15.

There is no inconsistency between subsection (3) and paragraph (b) of subsection (2). The holder in due course may elect to enforce the instrument either as provided in that paragraph or as provided in subsection (3).

It should be noted that a purchaser who takes the instrument with notice of any material alteration, including the unauthorized completion of an incomplete instrument, takes with notice of a claim or defense and cannot be a holder in due course (Section 3–304).

Cross References:

Sections 3–305, 3–306 and 3–307.

Point 2: Section 3–115.

Point 4: Sections 3–115, 3–304(2), 3–602 and 4–401.

Definitional Cross References:

"Contract". Section 1-201.
"Holder". Section 1-201.
"Holder in due course". Section 3-302.
"Instrument". Section 3-102.
"Party". Section 1-201.
"Person". Section 1-201.
"Signed". Section 1-201.
"Writing". Section 1-201.

§ 3-408. Consideration.

Want or failure of consideration is a defense as against any person not having the rights of a holder in due course (Section 3-305), except that no consideration is necessary for an instrument or obligation thereon given in payment of or as security for an antecedent obligation of any kind. Nothing in this section shall be taken to displace any statute outside this Act under which a promise is enforceable notwithstanding lack or failure of consideration. Partial failure of consideration is a defense pro tanto whether or not the failure is in an ascertained or liquidated amount.

Official Comment

Prior Uniform Statutory Provision: Sections 24, 25 and 28, Uniform Negotiable Instruments Law.

Changes: Combined and reworded.

Purposes of Changes:

1. "Consideration" is distinguished from "value" throughout this Article. "Consideration" refers to what the obligor has received for his obligation, and is important only on the question of whether his obligation can be enforced against him.

2. The "except" clause is intended to remove the difficulties which have arisen where a note or a draft, or an indorsement of either, is given as payment or as security for a debt already owed by the party giving it, or by a third person. The provision is intended to change the result of decisions holding that where no extension of time or other concession is given by the creditor the new obligation fails for lack of legal consideration. It is intended also to mean that an instrument given for more or less than the amount of a liquidated obligation does not fail by reason of the common law rule that an obligation for a lesser liquidated amount cannot be consideration for the surrender of a greater.

3. With respect to the necessity or sufficiency of consideration other obligations on an instrument are subject to the ordinary rules of contract law relating to contracts not under seal. Promissory estoppel or any other equivalent or substitute for consideration is to be recognized as in other contract cases. The provision of the original Section 28 as to absence or failure of consideration is now covered by the section dealing with the rights of one not a holder in due course; and the "presumption" of consideration in the original Section 24 is replaced by the provision relating to the burden of establishing defenses.

Cross References:

Point 1: Section 3-303.
Point 3: Sections 3-306(c) and 3-307(2).

Definitional Cross References:

"Holder in due course". Section 3-302.
"Instrument". Section 3-102.
"Person". Section 1-201.
"Rights". Section 1-201.

§ 3-409. Draft Not an Assignment.

(1) A check or other draft does not of itself operate as an assignment of any funds in the hands of the drawee available for its payment, and the drawee is not liable on the instrument until he accepts it.

(2) Nothing in this section shall affect any liability in contract, tort or otherwise arising from any letter of credit or other obligation or representation which is not an acceptance.

Official Comment

Prior Uniform Statutory Provision: Sections 127 and 189, Uniform Negotiable Instruments Law.

Changes: Combined and reworded; new provisions.

Purposes of Changes and New Matter:

The two original sections are combined, brought forward to appear in connection with acceptance, and reworded to remove uncertainties.

1. As under the original sections, a check or other draft does not of itself operate as an assignment in law or equity. The assignment may, however, appear from other facts, and particularly from other agreements, express or implied; and when the intent to assign is clear the check may be the means by which the assignment is effected.

2. The language of the original Section 189, that the drawee is not liable "to the holder", is changed as inaccurate and not intended. The drawee is not liable on the instrument until he accepts; but he remains subject to any other liability to the holder. In this connection reference should be made to Section 4–302 on the payor bank's liability for late return. Such a bank if it does not either make prompt settlement or return on an item received by it will become liable to a holder of the item.

3. Subsection (2) is new. It is intended to make it clear that this section does not in any way affect any liability which may arise apart from the instrument itself. The drawee who fails to accept may be liable to the drawer or to the holder for breach of the terms of a letter of credit or any other agreement by which he is obligated to accept. He may be liable in tort or upon any other basis because of his representation that he has accepted, or that he intends to accept. The section leaves unaffected any liability of any kind apart from the instrument.

Cross References:

Sections 3–410, 3–411, 3–412 and 3–415.

Point 2: Section 4–302.

Definitional Cross References:

"Acceptance". Section 3–410.

"Check". Section 3–104.

"Contract". Section 1–201.

"Draft". Section 3–104.

"Instrument". Section 3–102.

"Letter of credit". Section 5–104.

§ 3–410. Definition and Operation of Acceptance.

(1) Acceptance is the drawee's signed engagement to honor the draft as presented. It must be written on the draft, and may consist of his signature alone. It becomes operative when completed by delivery or notification.

(2) A draft may be accepted although it has not been signed by the drawer or is otherwise incomplete or is overdue or has been dishonored.

(3) Where the draft is payable at a fixed period after sight and the acceptor fails to date his acceptance the holder may complete it by supplying a date in good faith.

Official Comment

Prior Uniform Statutory Provision: Sections 132, 133, 134, 135, 136, 137, 138, 161–170, and 191, Uniform Negotiable Instruments Law.

Changes: Combined, reworded; original Sections 134, 135, 137 and 161–170 eliminated.

Purposes of Changes:

1. The original Sections 161–170 providing for acceptance for honor are omitted from this Article. This ancient practice developed at a time when communications were slow, and particularly in overseas transactions there might be a delay of several months before the drawer could be notified of dishonor by nonacceptance and

take steps to protect his credit. The need for intervention by a third party has passed with the development of the cable transfer, the letter of credit, and numerous other devices by which a substitute arrangement is promptly made. The practice has been obsolete for many years, and the sections are therefore eliminated.

2. Under Section 3–417 a person obtaining acceptance gives a warranty against alteration of the instrument before acceptance.

3. Subsection (1) adopts the rule of Section 17 of the English Bills of Exchange Act that the acceptance must be written on the draft. It eliminates the original Sections 134 and 135, providing for "virtual" acceptance by a written promise to accept drafts to be drawn, and "collateral" acceptance by a separate writing. Both have been anomalous exceptions to the policy that no person is liable on an instrument unless his signature appears on it. Both are derived from a line of early American cases decided at a time when difficulties of communication, particularly overseas, might leave the holder in doubt for a long period whether the draft was accepted. Such conditions have long since ceased to exist, and the "virtual" or "collateral" acceptance is now almost entirely obsolete. Good commercial and banking practice does not sanction acceptance by any separate writing because of the dangers and uncertainties arising when it becomes separated from the draft. The instrument is now forwarded to the drawee for his acceptance upon it, or reliance is placed upon the obligation of the separate writing itself, as in the case of a letter of credit.

Nothing in this section is intended to eliminate any liability of the drawee in contract, tort or otherwise arising from the separate writing or any other obligation or representation, as provided in Section 3–409.

Subsection (1) likewise eliminates the original section 137, providing for acceptance by delay or refusal to return the instrument but the drawee may be liable for a conversion of the instrument under Section 3–419.

4. Subsection (1) states the generally recognized rule that the mere signature of the drawee on the instrument is a sufficient acceptance. Customarily the signature is written vertically across the face of the instrument; but since the drawee has no reason to sign for any other purpose his signature in any other place, even on the back of the instrument, is sufficient. It need not be accompanied by such words as "Accepted," "Certified," or "Good." It must not, however, bear any words indicating an intent to refuse to honor the bill; and nothing in this provision is intended to change such decisions as Norton v. Knapp, 64 Iowa 112, 19 N.W. 867 (1884), holding that the drawee's signature accompanied by the words "Kiss my foot" is not an acceptance.

5. The final sentence of subsection (1) expressly states the generally recognized rule, implied in the definition of acceptance in the original Section 191, that an acceptance written on the draft takes effect when the drawee notifies the holder or gives notice according to his instructions. Acceptance is thus an exception to the usual rule that no obligation on an instrument is effective until delivery.

6. Subsection (3) changes the last sentence of the original Section 138. The purpose of the provision is to provide a definite date of payment where none appears on the instrument. An undated acceptance of a draft payable "thirty days after sight" is incomplete; and unless the acceptor himself writes in a different date the holder is authorized to complete the acceptance according to the terms of the draft by supplying a date of presentment. Any date which the holder chooses to write in is effective providing his choice of date is made in good faith. Any different agreement not written on the draft is not effective, and parol evidence is not admissible to show it.

Cross References:

Sections 3–411, 3–412 and 3–418.
Point 2: Section 3–417.
Point 3: Sections 3–401(1), 3–409(2) and 3–419.
Point 6: Section 3–412.

Definitional Cross References:

"Delivery". Section 1–201.
"Dishonor". Section 3–507.
"Draft". Section 3–104.
"Good faith". Section 1–201.
"Holder". Section 1–201.
"Honor". Section 1–201.
"Notification". Section 1–201.
"Presentment". Section 3–504.
"Signature". Section 3–401.

"Signed". Section 1–201.
"Written". Section 1–201.

§ 3–411. Certification of a Check.

(1) Certification of a check is acceptance. Where a holder procures certification the drawer and all prior indorsers are discharged.

(2) Unless otherwise agreed a bank has no obligation to certify a check.

(3) A bank may certify a check before returning it for lack of proper indorsement. If it does so the drawer is discharged.

Official Comment

Prior Uniform Statutory Provision: Sections 187 and 188, Uniform Negotiable Instruments Law.

Changes: Combined and reworded; new provisions.

Purposes of Changes and New Matter:

1. The second sentence of subsection (1) continues the rule of original Section 188 that, while certification procured by a holder discharges the drawer and other prior parties, certification procured by the drawer leaves him liable. Under this provision any certification procured by a holder discharges the drawer and prior indorsers. Any indorsement made after a certification so procured remains effective; and where it is intended that any indorser shall remain liable notwithstanding certification, he may indorse with the words "after certification" to make his liability clear.

2. Subsection (2) is new. It states the generally recognized rule that in the absence of agreement a bank is under no obligation to certify a check, because it is a demand instrument calling for payment rather than acceptance. The bank may be liable for breach of any agreement with the drawer, the holder, or any other person by which it undertakes to certify. Its liability is not on the instrument, since the drawee is not so liable until acceptance (Section 3–409(1)). Any liability is for breach of the separate agreement.

3. Subsection (3) is new. It recognizes the banking practice of certifying a check which is returned for proper indorsement in order to protect the drawer against a longer contingent liability. It is consistent with the provision of Section 3–410(2) permitting certification although the check has not been signed or is otherwise incomplete.

Cross References:

Sections 3–412, 3–413, 3–417 and 3–418.
Point 2: Section 3–409(1).
Point 3: Section 3–410(2).

Definitional Cross References:

"Acceptance". Section 3–410.
"Bank". Section 1–201.
"Check". Section 3–104.
"Holder". Section 1–201.

§ 3–412. Acceptance Varying Draft.

(1) Where the drawee's proffered acceptance in any manner varies the draft as presented the holder may refuse the acceptance and treat the draft as dishonored in which case the drawee is entitled to have his acceptance cancelled.

(2) The terms of the draft are not varied by an acceptance to pay at any particular bank or place in the United States, unless the acceptance states that the draft is to be paid only at such bank or place.

(3) Where the holder assents to an acceptance varying the terms of the draft each drawer and indorser who does not affirmatively assent is discharged.

As amended in 1962.

Official Comment

Prior Uniform Statutory Provision: Sections 139, 140, 141 and 142, Uniform Negotiable Instruments Law.

Changes: Combined and reworded; law changed as to qualified acceptances.

Purposes of Changes:

1. The section applies to conditional acceptances, acceptances for part of the amount, acceptances to pay at a different time from that required by the draft, or to the acceptance of less than all of the drawees, all of which are covered by the original Section 141. It applies to any other engagement changing the essential terms of the draft.

2. Where the drawee offers such a varied engagement the holder has an election. He may reject the offer, insist on acceptance of the draft as presented, and treat the refusal to give it as a dishonor. In that event the drawee is not bound by his engagement, and is entitled to have it cancelled. After any necessary notice of dishonor and protest the holder may have his recourse against the drawer and indorsers.

If the holder elects to accept the offer, this section does not invalidate the drawee's varied engagement. It remains his effective obligation, which the holder may enforce against him. By his assent, however, the holder discharges any drawer or indorser who does not also assent. The rule of the original Section 142 is changed to require that the assent of the drawer or indorser be affirmatively expressed. Mere failure to object within a reasonable time is not assent which will prevent the discharge.

3. The rule of original Section 140 that an acceptance to pay at a particular place is an unqualified acceptance is modified by the provision of subsection (2) that the terms of the draft are not varied by an acceptance to pay at any particular bank or place in the United States unless the acceptance states that the draft is to be paid only at such bank or place. Section 3–504(4) provides that a draft accepted payable at a bank in the United States must be presented at the bank designated [As amended 1962].

Cross References:

Sections 3–410 and 3–413.
Point 3: Section 3–504(4).

Definitional Cross References:

"Acceptance". Section 3–410.
"Bank". Section 1–201.
"Dishonor". Section 3–507.
"Draft". Section 3–104.
"Holder". Section 1–201.
"Term". Section 1–201.
"Written". Section 1–201.

§ 3–413. Contract of Maker, Drawer and Acceptor.

(1) The maker or acceptor engages that he will pay the instrument according to its tenor at the time of his engagement or as completed pursuant to Section 3–115 on incomplete instruments.

(2) The drawer engages that upon dishonor of the draft and any necessary notice of dishonor or protest he will pay the amount of the draft to the holder or to any indorser who takes it up. The drawer may disclaim this liability by drawing without recourse.

(3) By making, drawing or accepting the party admits as against all subsequent parties including the drawee the existence of the payee and his then capacity to indorse.

Official Comment

Prior Uniform Statutory Provision: Sections 60, 61 and 62, Uniform Negotiable Instruments Law.

Changes: Combined and reworded.

Purposes of Changes:

The original sections are combined for convenience and condensed to avoid duplication of language. This section should be read in connection with the sections on incomplete instruments (3–115), negligence contributing to alteration or unauthorized signature (3-406), alteration (3-407), acceptances varying a draft (3-412) and finality of payment or acceptance (3-418). Thus a maker who signs an incomplete note engages under this section to pay it according to its tenor at the time he signs it, but by virtue of Sections 3-115 and 3-407 the note may thereafter be completed and enforced against him. In the same way, if the maker's negligence substantially contributes to alteration of the instrument, he will become liable on his note as altered under Section 3-406. When a holder assents to an acceptance varying a draft (Section 3-412) he can of course hold the acceptor only according to the form of acceptance to which the holder agreed. Section 3-418 applies the rule of Price v. Neal both to acceptance and payment; thus an acceptor may not, after acceptance, assert that the drawer's signature is unauthorized.

Subsection (1) applies to all drafts (including checks) the rule that the acceptance relates to the instrument as it was at the time of its acceptance and not (in case of alteration before acceptance) to its original tenor. The cases on this point under the original act (all of which involved checks) have been in conflict. It should be noted that under Section 3-417 a person who obtains acceptance warrants to the acceptor that the instrument has not been materially altered.

Except as indicated in the foregoing comment the section makes no change in substance from the provision of the original act.

Cross References:

Sections 3-115, 3-406, 3-407, 3-412, 3-417 and 3-418.

Definitional Cross References:

"Contract". Section 1-201.
"Dishonor". Section 3-507.
"Draft". Section 3-104.
"Holder". Section 1-201.
"Instrument". Section 3-102.
"Notice of dishonor". Section 3-508.
"Party". Section 1-201.
"Protest". Section 3-509.

§ 3-414. Contract of Indorser; Order of Liability.

(1) Unless the indorsement otherwise specifies (as by such words as "without recourse") every indorser engages that upon dishonor and any necessary notice of dishonor and protest he will pay the instrument according to its tenor at the time of his indorsement to the holder or to any subsequent indorser who takes it up, even though the indorser who takes it up was not obligated to do so.

(2) Unless they otherwise agree indorsers are liable to one another in the order in which they indorse, which is presumed to be the order in which their signatures appear on the instrument.

Official Comment

Prior Uniform Statutory Provision: Sections 38, 44, 66, 67 and 68, Uniform Negotiable Instruments Law.

Changes: Combined and reworded.

Purposes of Changes:

1. Subsection (1) states the contract of indorsement—that if the instrument is dishonored and any protest or notice of dishonor which may be necessary under Section 3-501 is given, the indorser will pay the instrument. The indorser's engagement runs to any holder (whether or not for value) and to any indorser subsequent to him who has taken the instrument up. An indorser may disclaim his liability on the contract of indorsement, but only if the indorsement itself so specifies. Since the disclaimer varies the written contract of indorsement, the disclaimer itself must be written on the instrument and cannot be proved by parol. The customary manner of disclaiming the indorser's liability under this section is to indorse "without recourse". Apart from such a disclaimer all indorsers incur this liability, without regard to whether or not the indorser transferred the instrument for value or received consideration for his indorsement.

Original Section 44, permitting a representative to indorse in such terms as to exclude personal liability, is omitted as unnecessary and included in the broader right to disclaim any liability. No change in the law is intended by this omission.

2. In addition to his liability on the contract of indorsement, an indorser, if a transferor, gives the warranties stated in Section 3–417.

3. As in the case of acceptor's liability (Section 3–413), this section conditions the indorser's liability on the tenor of the instrument at the time of his indorsement. Thus if a person indorses an altered instrument he assumes liability as indorser on the instrument as altered.

4. Subsection (2) is intended to clarify existing law under original Section 68.

The section states two presumptions: One is that the indorsers are liable to one another in the order in which they have in fact indorsed. The other is that they have in fact indorsed in the order in which their names appear. Parol evidence is admissible to show that they have indorsed in another order, or that they have otherwise agreed as to their liability to one another.

The last sentence of the original Section 68 is now covered by Section 3–118(e) (Ambiguous Terms and Rules of Construction).

Cross References:

Point 1: Section 3–501.
Point 2: Section 3–417.
Point 3: Section 3–413.
Point 4: Section 3–118(e).

Definitional Cross References:

"Contract". Section 1–201.
"Dishonor". Section 3–507.
"Holder". Section 1–201.
"Instrument". Section 3–102.
"Notice of dishonor". Section 3–508.
"Presumed". Section 1–201.
"Protest". Section 3–509.
"Signature". Section 3–401.

§ 3–415. Contract of Accommodation Party.

(1) An accommodation party is one who signs the instrument in any capacity for the purpose of lending his name to another party to it.

(2) When the instrument has been taken for value before it is due the accommodation party is liable in the capacity in which he has signed even though the taker knows of the accommodation.

(3) As against a holder in due course and without notice of the accommodation oral proof of the accommodation is not admissible to give the accommodation party the benefit of discharges dependent on his character as such. In other cases the accommodation character may be shown by oral proof.

(4) An indorsement which shows that it is not in the chain of title is notice of its accommodation character.

(5) An accommodation party is not liable to the party accommodated, and if he pays the instrument has a right of recourse on the instrument against such party.

Official Comment

Prior Uniform Statutory Provision: Sections 28, 29 and 64, Uniform Negotiable Instruments Law.

Changes: Combined and reworded; new provisions.

Purposes of Changes and New Matter: To make it clear that:

1. Subsection (1) recognizes that an accommodation party is always a surety (which includes a guarantor), and it is his only distinguishing feature. He differs from other sureties only in that his liability is on the instrument and he is a surety for another party to it. His obligation is therefore determined by the capacity in which he signs. An accommodation maker or acceptor is bound on the instrument without any resort to his principal, while an accommodation indorser may be liable only after presentment, notice of dishonor and protest. The subsection

recognizes the defenses of a surety in accordance with the provisions subjecting one not a holder in due course to all simple contract defenses, as well as his rights against his principal after payment. Under subsection (3) except as against a holder in due course without notice of the accommodation, parol evidence is admissible to prove that the party has signed for accommodation. In any case, however, under subsection (4) an indorsement which is not in the chain of title (the irregular or anomalous indorsement) is notice to all subsequent takers of the instrument of the accommodation character of the indorsement.

2. Subsection (1) eliminates the language of the old Section 29 requiring that the accommodation party sign the instrument "without receiving value therefor." The essential characteristic is that the accommodation party is a surety, and not that he has signed gratuitously. He may be a paid surety, or receive other compensation from the party accommodated. He may even receive it from the payee, as where A and B buy goods and it is understood that A is to pay for all of them and that B is to sign a note only as a surety for A.

3. The obligation of the accommodation party is supported by any consideration for which the instrument is taken before it is due. Subsection (2) is intended to change occasional decisions holding that there is no sufficient consideration where an accommodation party signs a note after it is in the hands of a holder who has given value. The party is liable to the holder in such a case even though there is no extension of time or other concession. This is consistent with the provision as to antecedent obligations as consideration (Section 3–408). The limitation to "before it is due" is one of suretyship law, by which the obligation of the surety is terminated at the time limit unless in the meantime the obligation of the principal has become effective.

4. As a surety the accommodation party is not liable to the party accommodated; but he is otherwise liable on the instrument in the capacity in which he has signed. This general statement of the rule makes unnecessary the detailed provisions of the original Section 64, which is therefore eliminated, without any change in substance.

5. Subsection (5) is intended to change the result of such decisions as Quimby v. Varnum, 190 Mass. 211, 76 N.E. 671 (1906), which held that an accommodation indorser who paid the instrument could not maintain an action on it against the accommodated party since he had no "former rights" to which he was remitted. Under ordinary principles of suretyship the accommodation party who pays is subrogated to the rights of the holder paid, and should have his recourse on the instrument.

Cross References:

Sections 3–305, 3–408, 3–603, 3–604 and 3–606.
Point 1: Section 3–306(b).
Point 3: Section 3–408.

Definitional Cross References:

"Holder in due course". Section 3–302.
"Instrument". Section 3–102.
"Notice". Section 1–201.
"Party". Section 1–201.
"Presentment". Section 3–504.
"Signed". Section 1–201.
"Writing". Section 1–201.

§ 3–416. Contract of Guarantor.

(1) "Payment guaranteed" or equivalent words added to a signature mean that the signer engages that if the instrument is not paid when due he will pay it according to its tenor without resort by the holder to any other party.

(2) "Collection guaranteed" or equivalent words added to a signature mean that the signer engages that if the instrument is not paid when due he will pay it according to its tenor, but only after the holder has reduced his claim against the maker or acceptor to judgment and execution has been returned unsatisfied, or after the maker or acceptor has become insolvent or it is otherwise apparent that it is useless to proceed against him.

(3) Words of guaranty which do not otherwise specify guarantee payment.

(4) No words of guaranty added to the signature of a sole maker or acceptor affect his liability on the instrument. Such words added to the signature of one of two or more makers or acceptors create a presumption that the signature is for the accommodation of the others.

(5) When words of guaranty are used presentment, notice of dishonor and protest are not necessary to charge the user.

(6) Any guaranty written on the instrument is enforceable notwithstanding any statute of frauds.

Official Comment

Prior Uniform Statutory Provision: None.

Purposes: The section is new. It states the commercial understanding as to the meaning and effect of words of guaranty added to a signature.

An indorser who guarantees payment waives not only presentment, notice of dishonor and protest, but also all demand upon the maker or drawee. Words of guaranty do not affect the character of the indorsement as an indorsement (Section 3–202(4)); but the liability of the indorser becomes indistinguishable from that of a co-maker. A guaranty of collection likewise waives formal presentment, notice of dishonor and protest, but requires that the holder first proceed against the maker or acceptor by suit and execution, or show that such proceeding would be useless.

Subsection (6) is concerned chiefly with the type of statute of frauds which provides that no promise to answer for the debt, default or miscarriage of another is enforceable unless it is evidenced by a writing which states the consideration for the promise. It is unusual to state any consideration when a guaranty is added to a signature on a negotiable instrument, which in itself sufficiently shows the nature of the transaction; and such statutes have commonly been held not to apply to such guaranties.

Cross References:

Sections 3–202(4) and 3–415.

Definitional Cross References:

"Holder". Section 1–201.
"Insolvent". Section 1–201.
"Instrument". Section 3–102.
"Notice of dishonor". Section 3–508.
"Party". Section 1–201.
"Presumption". Section 1–201.
"Protest". Section 3–509.
"Signature". Section 3–401.
"Written". Section 1–201.

§ 3–417. Warranties on Presentment and Transfer.

(1) Any person who obtains payment or acceptance and any prior transferor warrants to a person who in good faith pays or accepts that

(a) he has a good title to the instrument or is authorized to obtain payment or acceptance on behalf of one who has a good title; and

(b) he has no knowledge that the signature of the maker or drawer is unauthorized, except that this warranty is not given by a holder in due course acting in good faith

(i) to a maker with respect to the maker's own signature; or

(ii) to a drawer with respect to the drawer's own signature, whether or not the drawer is also the drawee; or

(iii) to an acceptor of a draft if the holder in due course took the draft after the acceptance or obtained the acceptance without knowledge that the drawer's signature was unauthorized; and

(c) the instrument has not been materially altered, except that this warranty is not given by a holder in due course acting in good faith

(i) to the maker of a note; or

(ii) to the drawer of a draft whether or not the drawer is also the drawee; or

(iii) to the acceptor of a draft with respect to an alteration made prior to the acceptance if the holder in due course took the draft after the acceptance, even though the acceptance provided "payable as originally drawn" or equivalent terms; or

(iv) to the acceptor of a draft with respect to an alteration made after the acceptance.

(2) Any person who transfers an instrument and receives consideration warrants to his transferee and if the transfer is by indorsement to any subsequent holder who takes the instrument in good faith that

(a) he has a good title to the instrument or is authorized to obtain payment or acceptance on behalf of one who has a good title and the transfer is otherwise rightful; and

(b) all signatures are genuine or authorized; and

(c) the instrument has not been materially altered; and

(d) no defense of any party is good against him; and

(e) he has no knowledge of any insolvency proceeding instituted with respect to the maker or acceptor or the drawer of an unaccepted instrument.

(3) By transferring "without recourse" the transferor limits the obligation stated in subsection (2)(d) to a warranty that he has no knowledge of such a defense.

(4) A selling agent or broker who does not disclose the fact that he is acting only as such gives the warranties provided in this section, but if he makes such disclosure warrants only his good faith and authority.

Official Comment

Prior Uniform Statutory Provision: Sections 65 and 69, Uniform Negotiable Instruments Law.

Changes: Combined and reworded; new provisions added.

Purposes of Changes and New Matter:

1. The obligations imposed by this section are stated in terms of warranty. Warranty terms, which are not limited to sale transactions, are used with the intention of bringing in all the usual rules of law applicable to warranties, and in particular the necessity of reliance in good faith and the availability of all remedies for breach of warranty, such as rescission of the transaction or an action for damages. Like other warranties, those stated in this section may be disclaimed by agreement between the immediate parties. In the case of an indorser, disclaimer of his liability as a transferor, to be effective, must appear in the form of the indorsement, and no parol proof of "agreement otherwise" is admissible. For corresponding warranties in the case of items in the bank collection process, Section 4–207 should be consulted.

2. Subsection (1) is new. It is intended to state the undertaking to a party who accepts or pays of one who obtains payment or acceptance or of any prior transferor. It is closely connected with the following section on the finality of acceptance or payment (Section 3–418), and should be read together with it.

3. Subsection (1)(a) retains the generally accepted rule that the party who accepts or pays does not "admit" the genuineness of indorsements, and may recover from the person presenting the instrument when they turn out to be forged. The justification for the distinction between forgery of the signature of the drawer and forgery of an indorsement is that the drawee is in a position to verify the drawer's signature by comparison with one in his hands, but has ordinarily no opportunity to verify an indorsement.

4. Subsection (1)(b) recognizes and deals with competing equities of parties accepting or paying instruments bearing unauthorized maker's or drawer's signatures and those obtaining acceptances or receiving payment. The warranties prescribed and exceptions thereto follow closely principles established at common law, particularly, those under Price v. Neal, 3 Burr. 1354 (1762).

The basic warranty that the person obtaining payment or acceptance and any prior transferor warrants that he has no knowledge that the signature of the maker or drawer is unauthorized stems from the general principle that one who presents an instrument knowing that the signature of the maker or drawer is forged or unauthorized commits an obvious fraud upon the party to whom presentment is made. However, few cases present this simple fact situation. If the signature of a maker or drawer has been forged, the parties include the dishonest forger himself and usually one or more innocent holders taking from him. Frequently, the state of knowledge of a holder is difficult to determine and sometimes a holder takes such a forged instrument in perfect good faith but subsequently learns of the forgery. Since in different fact situations holders have equities of varying strength, it is necessary to have some exceptions to the basic warranty.

The exceptions apply only in favor of a holder in due course and, within the provisions of Section 3–201, to all subsequent transferees from a holder in due course. Since a condition of the status of a holder in due course under Section 3–302(1)(a) is that the holder takes the instrument without notice of any defense against it, this condition presupposes that at the time of taking such a holder had no knowledge of the unauthorized signature. Consequently, the warranty of subsection (1)(b) is pertinent in the case of a holder in due course only in the relatively few cases where he acquires knowledge of the forgery after the taking but before the presentment. In this situation the holder in due course must continue to act in good faith to be exempted from the basic warranty.

The first exemption from the warranty by such a holder, made by subparagraph (i), is that the warranty does not run to a maker of a note with respect to the maker's own signature. This codifies the rule of Price v. Neal, and related cases. Since a maker of a note is presumed to know his own signature, if he fails to detect a forgery of his own signature and pays the note, under the Price v. Neal principle he should not be permitted to recover such payment from a holder in due course acting in good faith. Similarly, under subparagraph (ii) a drawer of a draft is presumed to know his own signature and if he fails to detect a forgery of his signature and pays a draft he may not recover that payment from a holder in due course acting in good faith. This rule applies if the drawer pays the instrument as drawer and also if he pays the instrument as drawee in a case where he is both drawer and drawee.

Under the principle of Price v. Neal a drawee of a draft is presumed to know the signature of his customer, the drawer. However, under subsection (1)(b) and subparagraph (iii) of this subsection this presumption is not strong enough to deprive such a drawee (either in accepting or paying an instrument) of the warranty of no knowledge of the unauthorized drawer's signature, unless the holder in due course took the instrument and became such a holder after the drawee's acceptance; or obtained the acceptance without knowledge that the drawer's signature was unauthorized. In the former case, the holder taking after and thereby presumably in reliance on the acceptance should be protected as against the drawee who accepted without detecting the unauthorized signature. In the latter case the holder, having no knowledge of the unauthorized signature at the time of the drawee's acceptance, would not be charged with this warranty and would be entitled to enforce such acceptance under Section 3–418, even if thereafter he acquired knowledge of the unauthorized signature prior to enforcement of the acceptance. Such right of the holder to enforce the acceptance would be valueless if immediately upon enforcing it and obtaining payment the holder became obligated to return the payment by reason of breach of the warranty of no knowledge at the time of payment.

5. Subsection (1)(c) retains the common law rule, followed by several decisions under the original Act, which has permitted a party paying a materially altered instrument in good faith to recover, and a party who accepts such an instrument to avoid such acceptance. As in the case of subsection (1)(b) this warranty is not imposed against a holder in due course acting in good faith in favor of a maker of a note or a drawer of a draft on the ground that such maker or drawer should know the form and amount of the note or draft which he has signed. The exception made by subparagraph (iii) in the case of a holder in due course of a draft accepted after the alteration follows the decisions in National City Bank of Chicago v. National Bank of Republic of Chicago, 300 Ill. 103, 132 N.E. 832, 22 A.L.R. 1153 (1921), and Wells Fargo Bank & Union Trust Company v. Bank of Italy, 214 Cal. 156, 4 P.2d 781 (1931), and is based on the principle that an acceptance is an undertaking relied upon in good faith by an innocent party. The attempt to avoid this result by certifying checks "payable as originally drawn" leaves the subsequent purchaser in uncertainty as to the amount for which the instrument is certified, and so defeats the entire purpose of certification, which is to obtain the definite obligation of the bank to honor a definite instrument. Subparagraph (iii) accordingly provides that such language is not sufficient to impose on the holder in due course the warranty of no material alteration where the holder took the draft after the acceptance and presumably in reliance on it.

Subparagraph (iv) of subsection (1)(c) exempts a holder in due course from the warranty of no material alteration to the acceptor of a draft with respect to an alteration made after the acceptance. A drawee accepting a draft has an opportunity of ascertaining the form and particularly the amount of the draft accepted. If, thereafter, the draft is materially altered and is thereupon presented for payment to the acceptor, the acceptor has the necessary information in its records to verify the form and particularly the amount of the draft. If in spite of this available information it pays the draft, there is as much reason to leave the responsibility for such payment upon the acceptor (as against a holder in due course acting in good faith) as there is in the case of a maker or drawer paying a materially altered note or draft.

6. Under Section 3–201 parties taking from or holding under a holder in due course, within the limits of that section, will have the same rights under Section 3–417(1) as a holder in due course. Of course such parties claiming under a holder in due course must act in good faith and be free from fraud, illegality and notice as provided in Section 3–201.

7. The liabilities imposed by subsection (2) in favor of the immediate transferee apply to all persons who transfer an instrument for consideration whether or not the transfer is accompanied by indorsement. Any consideration sufficient to support a simple contract will support those warranties.

8. Subsection (2) changes the original Section 65 to extend the warranties of any *indorser* beyond the immediate transferee in all cases. Where there is an indorsement the warranty runs with the instrument and the remote holder may sue the indorser-warrantor directly and thus avoid a multiplicity of suits which might be interrupted by the insolvency of an intermediate transferor. The language of subsections (2)(b) and (2)(c) is substituted for "genuine and what it purports to be" in the original Section 65(1). The language of subsection (2)(a) is substituted for that of Section 65(2) in order to cover the case of the agent who transfers for another.

9. Subsection (2)(d) resolves a conflict in the decisions as to whether the transferor warrants that there are no defenses to the instrument good against him. The position taken is that the buyer does not undertake to buy an instrument incapable of enforcement, and that in the absence of contrary understanding the warranty is implied. Even where the buyer takes as a holder in due course who will cut off the defense, he still does not undertake to buy a lawsuit with the necessity of proving his status. Subsection (3) however provides that an indorsement "without recourse" limits the (2)(d) warranty to one that the indorser has no knowledge of such defenses. With this exception the liabilities of a "without recourse" indorser under this section are the same as those of any other transferor. Under Section 3–414 "without recourse" in an indorsement is effective to disclaim the general contract of the indorser stated in that section.

10. Subsection (2)(e) is substituted for Section 65(4). The transferor does not warrant against difficulties of collection, apart from defenses, or against impairment of the credit of the obligor or even his insolvency in the commercial sense. The buyer is expected to determine such questions for himself before he takes the obligation. If insolvency proceedings as defined in this Act (Section 1–201) have been instituted against the party who is expected to pay and the transferor knows it, the concealment of that fact amounts to a fraud upon the buyer, and the warranty against knowledge of such proceedings is provided accordingly.

11. Subsection (4) is substituted for Section 69 of the original Act. It applies only to a selling agent, as distinguished from an agent for collection. It follows the rule generally accepted that an agent who makes the disclosure warrants his good faith and authority and may not by contract assume a lesser warranty.

Cross References:

Sections 3–404, 3–405, 3–406, 3–414 and 4–207.
Point 1: Section 4–207.
Point 2: Section 3–418.
Point 4: Sections 3–201, 3–302 and 3–418.
Point 9: Section 3–414.
Point 10: Section 1–201.

Definitional Cross References:

"Acceptance". Section 3–410.
"Alteration". Section 3–407.
"Bank". Section 1–201.
"Draft". Section 3–104.
"Genuine". Section 1–201.
"Good faith". Section 1–201.
"Holder in due course". Section 3–302.
"Instrument". Section 3–102.
"Note". Section 3–104.

"Party". Section 1–201.
"Person". Section 1–201.
"Signature". Section 3–401.
"Term". Section 1–201.

§ 3–418. Finality of Payment or Acceptance.

Except for recovery of bank payments as provided in the Article on Bank Deposits and Collections (Article 4) and except for liability for breach of warranty on presentment under the preceding section, payment or acceptance of any instrument is final in favor of a holder in due course, or a person who has in good faith changed his position in reliance on the payment.

Official Comment

Prior Uniform Statutory Provision: Section 62, Uniform Negotiable Instruments Law.

Changes: Completely restated.

Purposes of Changes:

The rewording is intended to remove a number of uncertainties arising under the original section.

1. The section follows the rule of Price v. Neal, 3 Burr. 1354 (1762), under which a drawee who accepts or pays an instrument on which the signature of the drawer is forged is bound on his acceptance and cannot recover back his payment. Although the original Act is silent as to payment, the common law rule has been applied to it by all but a very few jurisdictions. The traditional justification for the result is that the drawee is in a superior position to detect a forgery because he has the maker's signature and is expected to know and compare it; a less fictional rationalization is that it is highly desirable to end the transaction on an instrument when it is paid rather than reopen and upset a series of commercial transactions at a later date when the forgery is discovered.

The rule as stated in the section is not limited to drawees, but applies equally to the maker of a note or to any other party who pays an instrument.

2. The section follows the decisions under the original Act applying the rule of Price v. Neal to the payment of overdrafts, or any other payment made in error as to the state of the drawer's account. The same argument for finality applies, with the additional reason that the drawee is responsible for knowing the state of the account before he accepts or pays.

3. The section follows decisions under the original Act, in making payment or acceptance final only in favor of a holder in due course, or a transferee who has the rights of a holder in due course under the shelter principle. If no value has been given for the instrument the holder loses nothing by the recovery of the payment or the avoidance of the acceptance, and is not entitled to profit at the expense of the drawee; and if he has given only an executory promise or credit he is not compelled to perform it after the forgery or other reason for recovery is discovered. If he has taken the instrument in bad faith or with notice he has no equities as against the drawee.

4. The section rejects decisions under the original Act permitting recovery on the basis of mere negligence of the holder in taking the instrument. If such negligence amounts to a lack of good faith as defined in this Act (Section 1–201) or to notice under the rules (Section 3–304) relating to notice to a purchaser of an instrument, the holder is not a holder in due course and is not protected; but otherwise the holder's negligence does not affect the finality of the payment or acceptance.

5. This section is to be read together with the preceding section, which states the warranties given by the person obtaining acceptance or payment. It is also limited by the bank collection provision (Section 4–301) permitting a payor bank to recover a payment improperly paid if it returns the item or sends notice of dishonor within the limited time provided in that section. But notice that the latter right is sharply limited in time, and terminates in any case when the bank has made final payment, as defined in Section 4–213.

Cross References:

Sections 3–302, 3–303 and 3–417.
Point 2: Section 3–201(1).
Point 4: Sections 1–201, 3–302 and 3–304.
Point 5: Sections 3–417, 4–213 and 4–301.

Definitional Cross References:

"Acceptance". Section 3–410.
"Account". Section 4–104.
"Bank". Section 1–201.
"Holder in due course". Section 3–302.
"Instrument". Section 3–102.
"Presentment". Section 3–504.

§ 3-419. Conversion of Instrument; Innocent Representative.

(1) An instrument is converted when

(a) a drawee to whom it is delivered for acceptance refuses to return it on demand; or

(b) any person to whom it is delivered for payment refuses on demand either to pay or to return it; or

(c) it is paid on a forged indorsement.

(2) In an action against a drawee under subsection (1) the measure of the drawee's liability is the face amount of the instrument. In any other action under subsection (1) the measure of liability is presumed to be the face amount of the instrument.

(3) Subject to the provisions of this Act concerning restrictive indorsements a representative, including a depositary or collecting bank, who has in good faith and in accordance with the reasonable commercial standards applicable to the business of such representative dealt with an instrument or its proceeds on behalf of one who was not the true owner is not liable in conversion or otherwise to the true owner beyond the amount of any proceeds remaining in his hands.

(4) An intermediary bank or payor bank which is not a depositary bank is not liable in conversion solely by reason of the fact that proceeds of an item indorsed restrictively (Sections 3–205 and 3–206) are not paid or applied consistently with the restrictive indorsement of an indorser other than its immediate transferor.

Official Comment

Prior Uniform Statutory Provision: Section 137, Uniform Negotiable Instruments Law.

Changes: Rule changed; new provisions.

Purposes of Changes and New Matter: To remove difficulties arising under the original section, and to cover additional situations:

1. The provision of the original Section 137 that refusal to return a bill presented for acceptance is deemed to be acceptance has led to difficulties. If the bill is accepted it is not dishonored, and the holder is left without recourse against the drawer and indorsers when he has most need for immediate recourse. The drawee does not in fact accept and does everything he can to display an intention not to accept; and the "acceptance" is useless to the holder for any purpose other than an action against the drawee, since he has nothing that he can negotiate. The original rule has therefore been changed (see Section 3–410).

2. A negotiable instrument is the property of the holder. It is a mercantile specialty which embodies rights against other parties, and a thing of value. This section adopts the generally recognized rule that a refusal to return it on demand is a conversion. The provision is not limited to drafts presented for acceptance, but extends to any instrument presented for payment, including a note presented to the maker. The action is not on the instrument, but in tort for its conversion.

The detention of an instrument voluntarily delivered is not wrongful unless and until there is demand for its return. Demand for a return at a particular time may, however, be made at the time of delivery; or it may be implied under the circumstances or understood as a matter of custom. If the holder is to call for the instrument and fails to do so, he is to be regarded as extending the time. "Refuses" is meant to cover any intentional failure to return the instrument, including its intentional destruction. It does not cover a negligent loss or destruction, or any other unintentional failure to return. In such a case the party may be liable in tort for any damage sustained as a result of his negligence, but he is not liable as a converter under this section.

3. Subsection (1)(c) is new. It adopts the prevailing view of decisions holding that payment on a forged indorsement is not an acceptance, but that even though made in good faith it is an exercise of dominion and control over the instrument inconsistent with the rights of the owner, and results in liability for conversion.

4. Subsection (2) is new. It adopts the rule generally applied to the conversion of negotiable instruments, that the obligation of any party on the instrument is presumed, in the sense that the term is defined in this Act (Section 1–201), to be worth its face value. Evidence is admissible to show that for any reason such as insolvency or the existence of a defense the obligation is in fact worth less, or even that it is without value. In the case of the drawee, however, the presumption is replaced by a rule of absolute liability.

5. Subsection (3), which is new, is intended to adopt the rule of decisions which has held that a representative, such as a broker or depositary bank, who deals with a negotiable instrument for his principal in good faith is not liable to the true owner for conversion of the instrument or otherwise, except that he may be compelled to turn over to the true owner the instrument itself or any proceeds of the instrument remaining in his hands. The provisions of subsection (3) are, however, subject to the provisions of this Act concerning restrictive indorsements (Sections 3–205, 3–206 and related sections).

6. The provisions of this section are not intended to eliminate any liability on warranties of presentment and transfer (Section 3–417). Thus a collecting bank might be liable to a drawee bank which had been subject to liability under this section, even though the collecting bank might not be liable directly to the owner of the instrument.

Cross References:

Sections 3–409, 3–410, 3–411 and 3–603.
Point 4: Section 1–201.
Point 5: Sections 1–201, 3–205 and 3–206.
Point 6: Section 3–417.

Definitional Cross References:

"Acceptance". Section 3–410.
"Action". Section 1–201.
"Bank". Section 1–201.
"Collecting bank". Sections 3–102 and 4–105.
"Depositary bank". Sections 3–102 and 4–105.
"Good faith". Section 1–201.
"Instrument". Section 3–102.
"Intermediary bank". Sections 3–102 and 4–105.
"On demand". Section 3–108.
"Person". Section 1–201.
"Presumed". Section 1–201.
"Representative". Section 1–201.

PART 5

PRESENTMENT, NOTICE OF DISHONOR AND PROTEST

§ 3–501. When Presentment, Notice of Dishonor, and Protest Necessary or Permissible.

(1) Unless excused (Section 3–511) presentment is necessary to charge secondary parties as follows:

(a) presentment for acceptance is necessary to charge the drawer and indorsers of a draft where the draft so provides, or is payable elsewhere than at the residence or place of business of the drawee, or its date of payment depends upon such presentment. The holder may at his option present for acceptance any other draft payable at a stated date;

(b) presentment for payment is necessary to charge any indorser;

(c) in the case of any drawer, the acceptor of a draft payable at a bank or the maker of a note payable at a bank, presentment for payment is necessary, but failure to make presentment discharges such drawer, acceptor or maker only as stated in Section 3–502(1)(b).

(2) Unless excused (Section 3–511)

(a) notice of any dishonor is necessary to charge any indorser;

(b) in the case of any drawer, the acceptor of a draft payable at a bank or the maker of a note payable at a bank, notice of any dishonor is necessary, but failure to give such notice discharges such drawer, acceptor or maker only as stated in Section 3–502(1)(b).

(3) Unless excused (Section 3–511) protest of any dishonor is necessary to charge the drawer and indorsers of any draft which on its face appears to be drawn or payable outside of the states, territories, dependencies and possessions of the United States, the District of Columbia and the Commonwealth of Puerto Rico. The holder may at his option make protest of any dishonor of any other instrument and in the case of a foreign draft may on insolvency of the acceptor before maturity make protest for better security.

(4) Notwithstanding any provision of this section, neither presentment nor notice of dishonor nor protest is necessary to charge an indorser who has indorsed an instrument after maturity.

As amended in 1966.

Official Comment

Prior Uniform Statutory Provision: Sections 70, 89, 118, 129, 143, 144, 150, 151, 152, 157, 158 and 186, Uniform Negotiable Instruments Law.

Changes: Combined and simplified.

Purposes of Changes:

1. Part 5 simplifies the requirements of the original Act as to presentment for acceptance or payment, notice of dishonor and protest. This section assembles in one place all provisions as to when any such proceeding is necessary. It eliminates some of the requirements and simplifies others. The effect of unexcused delay in any such proceeding as a discharge is covered by the next section, and the sections following prescribe the details of the proceedings.

2. The words "Necessary to charge" are retained from the original Act. They mean that the necessary proceeding is a condition precedent to any right of action against the drawer or indorser. He is not liable and cannot be sued without the proceedings however long delayed. Under some circumstances delay is excused. If it is not excused it may operate as a discharge under the next section. Under some circumstances the proceeding may be entirely excused and the drawer or indorser is then liable as if the proceeding had been duly taken. Section 3–511 states the circumstances under which delay may be excused or the proceeding entirely excused.

3. Subsection (1)(a) retains the substance of the original Sections 143, 144 and 150. The last sentence of the subsection states the rule of the decisions both at common law and under the original Act, that the holder may at his option present any time draft for acceptance, and is not required to wait until the due date to know whether the drawee will accept it; but that if he does make presentment and acceptance is refused he must give notice of dishonor. There is no similar right to present for acceptance a draft payable on demand, since a demand draft entitles the holder to immediate payment but not to acceptance.

4. Subsections (1)(b) and (1)(c) on presentment for payment follow Section 70 of the original Act with one important change. Under the original Act and under this section ((1)(b)) presentment for payment is necessary (unless excused) to charge any drawer. Under the original Act drawers of drafts other than checks were wholly discharged by a failure to make due presentment but drawers of checks (Section 70 in conjunction with Section 186) were discharged only "to the extent of the loss caused by the delay"—that is to say, when insolvency of the drawee bank occurred after the time when presentment was due. The check rule of the original Act (somewhat modified—see Section 3–502(1)(b) and Comment thereto) is by subsection (1)(c) extended to all drawers, and also to the acceptors and makers of domiciled—"payable at a bank"—drafts and notes. Thus drawers of drafts other than checks are not, as they were under Section 70, wholly discharged by failure to make due presentment but, like drawers of checks, are discharged only as they may have suffered loss as provided in Section 3–502(1)(b). As to domiciled paper original Section 70 provided that ability and willingness to pay at the place named at maturity were "equivalent to a tender of payment"—that is to say would stop the running of interest, but had no other effect. Accordingly cases have held that makers and acceptors of domiciled paper were not discharged to any extent by the holder's failure to make presentment even when the obligor had funds available in the paying bank on the date for presentment and the bank subsequently failed. Subsection (1)(c) applies the check rule to such makers and acceptors; the "tender" language of Section 70 is eliminated; and the result in the cases referred to in the

preceding sentence is reversed. Under this section as under the original act presentment for payment is not necessary to charge primary parties (makers and acceptors of undomiciled paper).

5. Under subsection (2) the rules as to necessity of notice of dishonor run parallel with the rules as to necessity of presentment stated in subsection (1).

6. Under the original Sections 129 and 152 protest is required in the case of every "foreign draft", defined as a draft which on its face is not both drawn and payable "within this state." The result has been that upon dishonor in New York a check which appears on its face to be drawn in Jersey City must be protested in order to sue the drawer or any indorser. This has led to great inconvenience and expense of protest fees. The only function of protest is that of proof of dishonor, and it adds nothing to notice of dishonor as such.

Subsection (3) eliminates the requirement of protest except upon dishonor of a draft which on its face appears to be either drawn or payable outside of the states, territories, dependencies and possessions of the United States, the District of Columbia and the Commonwealth of Puerto Rico. The requirement is left as to such international drafts because it is generally required by foreign law, which this Article cannot affect. The formalities of protest are covered by Section 3–509 on protest, and substitutes for protest as proof of dishonor are provided for in Section 3–510 on evidence of dishonor and of notice. [This paragraph was amended in 1966].

This provision retains from the original Section 118 the rule permitting the holder at his option to make protest of any dishonor of any other instrument. Even where not required protest may have definite convenience where process does not run to another state and the taking of depositions is a slow and expensive matter. Even where the instrument is drawn and payable entirely within a state there may be convenience in saving the trip of a witness from Buffalo to New York to testify to dishonor, where the substitute evidence of dishonor and notice of dishonor cannot be relied on. Either required or optional protest is presumptive evidence of dishonor. (Section 3–510.)

7. The permissible "protest for better security" of original Section 158 is retained in the case of a foreign draft, as the practice is common in certain foreign countries.

8. Under the final sentence of Section 7 of the original Act an instrument indorsed when overdue became payable on demand as to the indorser. That language has been deleted from this Article—see Section 3–108 and Comment. It meant, among other things and in view of the provisions of the original Act as to demand paper, that such an indorser was discharged unless the instrument was presented for payment within a reasonable time after his indorsement. Presentment of overdue paper for the purpose of charging an indorser is unusual and not an expected commercial practice; the rule has been little more than a trap for those not familiar with the Act. Subsection (4), reversing the original Act, provides that as to indorsers after maturity neither presentment nor notice of dishonor nor protest is necessary; like primary parties therefore they will remain liable on the instrument for the period of the applicable statute of limitations.

Cross References:

Point 1: Sections 3–502 through 3–508.
Point 2: Sections 3–413, 3–414 and 3–511.
Point 3: Sections 3–413, 3–414 and 3–511.
Point 4: Section 3–502.
Point 6: Sections 3–413, 3–414, 3–509, 3–510 and 3–511.
Point 8: Section 3–108.

Definitional Cross References:

"Acceptance". Section 3–410.
"Bank". Section 1–201.
"Certificate of deposit". Section 3–104.
"Dishonor". Section 3–507.
"Draft". Section 3–104.
"Holder". Section 1–201.
"Instrument". Section 3–102.
"Note". Section 3–104.
"Notice of dishonor". Section 3–508.
"Party". Section 1–201.
"Presentment". Section 3–504.

"Protest". Section 3–509.
"Secondary party". Section 3–102.
"Signature". Section 3–401.

§ 3–502. Unexcused Delay; Discharge.

(1) Where without excuse any necessary presentment or notice of dishonor is delayed beyond the time when it is due

(a) any indorser is discharged; and

(b) any drawer or the acceptor of a draft payable at a bank or the maker of a note payable at a bank who because the drawee or payor bank becomes insolvent during the delay is deprived of funds maintained with the drawee or payor bank to cover the instrument may discharge his liability by written assignment to the holder of his rights against the drawee or payor bank in respect of such funds, but such drawer, acceptor or maker is not otherwise discharged.

(2) Where without excuse a necessary protest is delayed beyond the time when it is due any drawer or indorser is discharged.

Official Comment

Prior Uniform Statutory Provision: Sections 7, 70, 89, 144, 150, 152 and 186, Uniform Negotiable Instruments Law.

Changes: Combined and simplified.

This section is the complement of the preceding section. It covers in one section widely scattered provisions of the original Act:

1. The circumstances under which presentment or notice of dishonor or protest or delay therein are excused are stated in Section 3–511. When not excused delay operates as a discharge as provided in this section.

2. Subsection (1)(b) applies to any drawer, as well as to the makers and acceptors of drafts and notes payable at a bank, the rule of the original Section 186 providing for discharge only where the drawer of a check has sustained loss through the delay. This section expressly limits the rule to loss sustained through insolvency of the drawee or payor which was the only type of loss to which the Section 186 rule has ever been applied in the cases arising under it.

The purpose of the rule is to avoid hardship upon the holder through complete discharge, and unjust enrichment of the drawer or other party who normally has received goods or other consideration for the issue of the instrument. He is "deprived of funds" in any case where bank failure or other insolvency of the drawee or payor has prevented him from receiving the benefit of funds which would have paid the instrument if it had been duly presented.

The original language discharging the drawer "to the extent of the loss caused by the delay" has not worked out satisfactorily in the decided cases, since the amount of the loss caused by the failure of a bank is almost never ascertainable at the time of suit and may not be ascertained until some years later. The decisions have turned upon burden of proof, and the drawer has seldom succeeded in proving his discharge. Subsection (1)(b) therefore substitutes a right to discharge liability by written assignment to the holder of rights against the drawee or payor as to the funds which cover the particular instrument. The assignment is intended to give the holder an effective right to claim against the drawee or payor.

3. Subsection (2) retains the rule of the original Section 152, that any unexcused delay of a required protest is a complete discharge of all drawers and indorsers.

Cross References:

Point 1: Section 3–511(1).
Point 2: Section 3–501.
Point 3: Section 3–509.

Definitional Cross References:

"Bank". Section 1–201.
"Draft". Section 3–104.

"Holder". Section 1–201.
"Insolvent". Section 1–201.
"Instrument". Section 3–102.
"Note". Section 3–104.
"Notice of dishonor". Section 3–508.
"Payor bank". Section 4–105.
"Presentment". Section 3–504.
"Protest". Section 3–509.
"Rights". Section 1–201.
"Signature". Section 3–401.
"Written". Section 1–201.

§ 3–503. Time of Presentment.

(1) Unless a different time is expressed in the instrument the time for any presentment is determined as follows:

(a) where an instrument is payable at or a fixed period after a stated date any presentment for acceptance must be made on or before the date it is payable;

(b) where an instrument is payable after sight it must either be presented for acceptance or negotiated within a reasonable time after date or issue whichever is later;

(c) where an instrument shows the date on which it is payable presentment for payment is due on that date;

(d) where an instrument is accelerated presentment for payment is due within a reasonable time after the acceleration;

(e) with respect to the liability of any secondary party presentment for acceptance or payment of any other instrument is due within a reasonable time after such party becomes liable thereon.

(2) A reasonable time for presentment is determined by the nature of the instrument, any usage of banking or trade and the facts of the particular case. In the case of an uncertified check which is drawn and payable within the United States and which is not a draft drawn by a bank the following are presumed to be reasonable periods within which to present for payment or to initiate bank collection:

(a) with respect to the liability of the drawer, thirty days after date or issue whichever is later; and

(b) with respect to the liability of an indorser, seven days after his indorsement.

(3) Where any presentment is due on a day which is not a full business day for either the person making presentment or the party to pay or accept, presentment is due on the next following day which is a full business day for both parties.

(4) Presentment to be sufficient must be made at a reasonable hour, and if at a bank during its banking day.

Official Comment

Prior Uniform Statutory Provision: Sections 71, 72, 75, 85, 86, 144, 145, 146, 186 and 193, Uniform Negotiable Instruments Law.

Changes: Combined and simplified; new provisions.

Purposes of Changes and New Matter:

1. This section states in one place all of the rules applicable to the time of presentment. Excused delay is covered by Section 3–511 on waiver and excuse, and the effect of unexcused delay by Section 3–502 on discharge.

The original Section 86, as to the determination of the time of payment by calculation from the day the time is to run, is omitted as superfluous. It states a rule universally applied to all time calculations in the law of contracts, and has no special application to negotiable instruments. No change in the law is intended.

2. Subsection (1) contains new provisions stating the commercial understanding as to the presentment of instruments payable after sight, and of accelerated paper.

3. Subsection (2) retains the substance of the original Section 193 as to the determination of a reasonable time. It provides specific time limits which are presumed, as that term is defined in this Act (Section 1–201), to be reasonable for uncertified checks drawn and payable within the continental limits of the United States. The court-made time limit of one day after the receipt of the instrument found in decisions under the original Act has proved to be too short a time for some holders, such as the department store or other large business clearing many checks through its books shortly after the first of the month, as well as the farmer or other individual at a distance from a bank.

The time limit provided differs as to drawer and indorser. The drawer, who has himself issued the check and normally expects to have it paid and charged to his account is reasonably required to stand behind it for a longer period, especially in view of the protection now provided by Federal Deposit Insurance. The thirty days specified coincides with the time after which a purchaser has notice that a check has become stale (Section 3–304(3)(c)). The indorser, who has normally merely received the check and passed it on, and does not expect to have to pay it, is entitled to know more promptly whether it is to be dishonored, in order that he may have recourse against the person with whom he has dealt.

4. Subsection (3) replaces the original Sections 85 and 146. It is intended to make allowance for the increasing practice of closing banks or businesses on Saturday or other days of the week. It is not intended to mean that any drawee or obligor can avoid dishonor of instruments by extended closing.

5. Subsection (4) eliminates the provision of the original Section 75 permitting presentment "at any hour before the bank is closed" if the drawer has no funds in the bank. The change is made to avoid inconvenience to the bank.

"Banking day" is defined in Section 4–104.

Cross References:

Point 1: Sections 3–501, 3–502, 3–505, 3–506 and 3–511.
Point 3: Sections 1–201 and 3–304(3)(c).
Point 5: Section 4–104.

Definitional Cross References:

"Acceptance". Section 3–410.
"Bank". Section 1–201.
"Banking day". Section 4–104.
"Check". Section 3–104.
"Draft". Section 3–104.
"Instrument". Section 3–102.
"Issue". Section 3–102.
"Party". Section 1–201.
"Person". Section 1–201.
"Presentment". Section 3–504.
"Presumed". Section 1–201.
"Reasonable time". Section 1–204.
"Secondary party". Section 3–102.
"Usage of trade". Section 1–205.

§ 3–504. How Presentment Made.

(1) Presentment is a demand for acceptance or payment made upon the maker, acceptor, drawee or other payor by or on behalf of the holder.

(2) Presentment may be made

(a) by mail, in which event the time of presentment is determined by the time of receipt of the mail; or

(b) through a clearing house; or

(c) at the place of acceptance or payment specified in the instrument or if there be none at the place of business or residence of the party to accept or pay. If neither the party to accept or pay nor anyone authorized to act for him is present or accessible at such place presentment is excused.

(3) It may be made

(a) to any one of two or more makers, acceptors, drawees or other payors; or

(b) to any person who has authority to make or refuse the acceptance or payment.

(4) A draft accepted or a note made payable at a bank in the United States must be presented at such bank.

(5) In the cases described in Section 4–210 presentment may be made in the manner and with the result stated in that section.

As amended in 1962.

Official Comment

Prior Uniform Statutory Provision: Sections 72, 73, 77, 78 and 145, Uniform Negotiable Instruments Law.

Changes: Combined and simplified.

Purposes of Changes:

1. This section is intended to simplify the rules as to how presentment is made and to make it clear that any demand upon the party to pay is a presentment no matter where or how. Former technical requirements of exhibition of the instrument and the like are not required unless insisted upon by the party to pay (Section 3–505).

2. Paragraph (a) of subsection (2) authorizes presentment by mail directly to the obligor. The presentment is sufficient and the instrument is dishonored by non-acceptance or nonpayment even though the party making presentment may be liable for improper collection methods. "Through a clearing-house" means that presentment is not made when the demand reaches the clearing-house, but when it reaches the obligor. Section 4–210 should also be consulted for the methods of presenting which may properly be employed by a collecting bank. Subsection (5) of this section makes it clear that presentment made under Section 4–210 is proper presentment.

3. Paragraph (a) of subsection (3) eliminates the requirement of the original Sections 78 and 145(1) that presentment be made to each of two or more makers, acceptors or drawees unless they are partners or one has authority to act for the others. The holder is entitled to expect that any one of the named parties will pay or accept, and should not be required to go to the trouble and expense of making separate presentment to a number of them.

4. Section 3–412 provides that an acceptance made payable at a bank in the United States does not vary the draft. Subsection (4) of this section makes it clear that a draft so accepted must be presented at the bank so designated. The same rule is applied to notes made payable at a bank. The rule of the subsection is in conformity with the provisions of Section 3–501 on presentment and Section 3–502 on the effect of failure to make presentment with reference to domiciled paper [This paragraph was amended in 1962].

Cross References:

Point 1: Sections 3–501, 3–502, 3–505 and 3–511.
Point 2: Section 4–210.
Point 5: Sections 3–412, 3–501 and 3–502.

Definitional Cross References:

"Acceptance". Section 3–410.
"Bank". Section 1–201.
"Clearing house". Section 4–104.
"Draft". Section 3–104.
"Holder". Section 1–201.
"Instrument". Section 3–102.
"Note". Section 3–104.
"Party". Section 1–201.
"Person". Section 1–201.

§ 3–505. Rights of Party to Whom Presentment Is Made.

(1) The party to whom presentment is made may without dishonor require

(a) exhibition of the instrument; and

(b) reasonable identification of the person making presentment and evidence of his authority to make it if made for another; and

(c) that the instrument be produced for acceptance or payment at a place specified in it, or if there be none at any place reasonable in the circumstances; and

(d) a signed receipt on the instrument for any partial or full payment and its surrender upon full payment.

(2) Failure to comply with any such requirement invalidates the presentment but the person presenting has a reasonable time in which to comply and the time for acceptance or payment runs from the time of compliance.

Official Comment

Prior Uniform Statutory Provision: Section 74, Uniform Negotiable Instruments Law.

Changes: Expanded and modified.

Purposes of Changes: To supplement the provisions as to how presentment is made, by permitting the party to whom it is made to insist on additional requirements:

1. In the first instance a mere demand for acceptance or payment is sufficient presentment, and if the payment is unqualifiedly refused nothing more is required. The party to whom presentment is made may, however, require exhibition of the instrument, its production at the proper place, identification of the party making presentment, and a signed receipt on the instrument, or its surrender on full payment. Failure to comply with any such requirement invalidates the presentment and means that the instrument is not dishonored. The time for presentment is, however, extended to give the person presenting a reasonable opportunity to comply with the requirements.

2. "Reasonable identification" means identification reasonable under all the circumstances. If the party on whom demand is made knows the person making presentment, no requirement of identification is reasonable, while if the circumstances are suspicious a great deal may be required. The requirement applies whether the instrument presented is payable to order or to bearer.

Cross References:

Point 1: Sections 3–504 and 3–506.

Definitional Cross References:

"Acceptance". Section 3–410.
"Dishonor". Section 3–507.
"Instrument". Section 3–102.
"Party". Section 1–201.
"Person". Section 1–201.
"Presentment". Section 3–504.
"Reasonable time". Section 1–204.
"Signed". Section 1–201.

§ 3–506. Time Allowed for Acceptance or Payment.

(1) Acceptance may be deferred without dishonor until the close of the next business day following presentment. The holder may also in a good faith effort to obtain acceptance and without either dishonor of the instrument or discharge of secondary parties allow postponement of acceptance for an additional business day.

(2) Except as a longer time is allowed in the case of documentary drafts drawn under a letter of credit, and unless an earlier time is agreed to by the party to pay, payment of an instrument may be deferred

without dishonor pending reasonable examination to determine whether it is properly payable, but payment must be made in any event before the close of business on the day of presentment.

Official Comment

Prior Uniform Statutory Provision: Section 136, Uniform Negotiable Instruments Law.

Changes: Expanded.

Purposes of Changes: The original section covered only the time allowed to the drawee on presentment for acceptance. This section also covers the time allowed on presentment for payment.

Section 5–112 (Time Allowed for Honor) states the time, longer than here provided, during which a bank to which drafts are presented under a letter of credit may defer payment or acceptance without dishonor of the drafts. As to drafts drawn under a letter of credit Section 5–112 of course controls.

Section 4–301 on deferred posting should be consulted for the right of a payor bank to recover tentative settlements made by it on the day an item is received. That right does not survive final payment (Section 4–213).

Cross References:

Sections 4–301 and 5–112.

Definitional Cross References:

"Acceptance". Section 3–410.
"Dishonor". Section 3–507.
"Documentary draft". Sections 3–102 and 4–104.
"Instrument". Section 3–102.
"Letter of credit". Section 5–103.
"Party". Section 1–201.
"Presentment". Section 3–504.

§ 3–507. Dishonor; Holder's Right of Recourse; Term Allowing Re-presentment.

(1) An instrument is dishonored when

(a) a necessary or optional presentment is duly made and due acceptance or payment is refused or cannot be obtained within the prescribed time or in case of bank collections the instrument is seasonably returned by the midnight deadline (Section 4–301); or

(b) presentment is excused and the instrument is not duly accepted or paid.

(2) Subject to any necessary notice of dishonor and protest, the holder has upon dishonor an immediate right of recourse against the drawers and indorsers.

(3) Return of an instrument for lack of proper indorsement is not dishonor.

(4) A term in a draft or an indorsement thereof allowing a stated time for re-presentment in the event of any dishonor of the draft by nonacceptance if a time draft or by nonpayment if a sight draft gives the holder as against any secondary party bound by the term an option to waive the dishonor without affecting the liability of the secondary party and he may present again up to the end of the stated time.

Official Comment

Prior Uniform Statutory Provision: Sections 83 and 149, Uniform Negotiable Instruments Law.

Changes: Reworded.

Purposes of Changes:

1. The language of the section is changed in accordance with the provisions of the preceding section as to the time allowed for acceptance or payment.

2. Subsection (3) is new. It states general banking and commercial understanding. The time within which a payor bank must return items, and the methods of returning, are stated in Section 4–301. Under Section 3–411(3) a bank may certify an item so returned.

Cross References:

Point 1: Sections 3–503, 3–504, 3–505, 3–508 and 4–301.
Point 2: Sections 3–411(3), 4–301.

Definitional Cross References:

"Acceptance". Section 3–410.
"Bank". Section 1–201.
"Draft". Section 3–104.
"Holder". Section 1–201.
"Instrument". Section 3–102.
"Midnight deadline". Section 4–104.
"Notice of dishonor". Section 3–508.
"Presentment". Section 3–504.
"Protest". Section 3–509.
"Right". Section 1–201.
"Seasonably". Section 1–204.
"Secondary party". Section 3–102.
"Term". Section 1–201.

§ 3–508. Notice of Dishonor.

(1) Notice of dishonor may be given to any person who may be liable on the instrument by or on behalf of the holder or any party who has himself received notice, or any other party who can be compelled to pay the instrument. In addition an agent or bank in whose hands the instrument is dishonored may give notice to his principal or customer or to another agent or bank from which the instrument was received.

(2) Any necessary notice must be given by a bank before its midnight deadline and by any other person before midnight of the third business day after dishonor or receipt of notice of dishonor.

(3) Notice may be given in any reasonable manner. It may be oral or written and in any terms which identify the instrument and state that it has been dishonored. A misdescription which does not mislead the party notified does not vitiate the notice. Sending the instrument bearing a stamp, ticket or writing stating that acceptance or payment has been refused or sending a notice of debit with respect to the instrument is sufficient.

(4) Written notice is given when sent although it is not received.

(5) Notice to one partner is notice to each although the firm has been dissolved.

(6) When any party is in insolvency proceedings instituted after the issue of the instrument notice may be given either to the party or to the representative of his estate.

(7) When any party is dead or incompetent notice may be sent to his last known address or given to his personal representative.

(8) Notice operates for the benefit of all parties who have rights on the instrument against the party notified.

Official Comment

Prior Uniform Statutory Provision: Sections 90 through 108, Uniform Negotiable Instruments Law.

Changes: Combined and simplified.

Purposes of Changes: To simplify notice of dishonor and eliminate many of the detailed requirements of the original Act:

1. Notice is normally given by the holder or by an indorser who has himself received notice. Subsection (1) is intended to encourage and facilitate notice of dishonor by permitting any party who may be compelled to pay the instrument to notify any party who may be liable on it. Thus an indorser may notify another indorser who is not liable to the one who gives notice, even when the latter has not received notice from any other party to the instrument.

2. Except as to collecting banks, as to whom Section 4–212 controls, the time within which necessary notice must be given is extended to three days after dishonor or receipt of notice from another party. In the case of individuals the one-day time limit of the original Act has proved too short in many cases. It is extended to give the party a margin of time within which to ascertain what is required of him and get out an ordinary business letter. This time leeway eliminates the elaborate provisions as to the time of mailing in the original Sections 103 and 104.

3. Subsection (3) retains the substance of the original Sections 95 and 96. The provision approves the bank practice of returning the instrument bearing a stamp, ticket or other writing, or a notice of debit of the account, as sufficient notice. Subsection (4) retains the substance of the original Section 105.

4. Subsection (7) permits notice to be sent to the last known address of a party who is dead or incompetent rather than to his personal representative. The provision is intended to save time, as the name of the personal representative often cannot easily be ascertained, and mail addressed to the original party will reach the representative.

Cross References:

Sections 3–501, 3–507 and 3–511.
Point 2: Section 4–212.

Definitional Cross References:

"Acceptance". Section 3–410.
"Bank". Section 1–201.
"Customer". Section 4–104.
"Dishonor". Section 3–507.
"Holder". Section 1–201.
"Insolvency proceedings". Section 1–201.
"Instrument". Section 3–102.
"Issue". Section 3–102.
"Midnight deadline". Section 4–104.
"Notifies". Section 1–201.
"Party". Section 1–201.
"Person". Section 1–201.
"Representative". Section 1–201.
"Rights". Section 1–201.
"Send". Section 1–201.
"Written" and "writing". Section 1–201.

§ 3-509. Protest; Noting for Protest.

(1) A protest is a certificate of dishonor made under the hand and seal of a United States consul or vice consul or a notary public or other person authorized to certify dishonor by the law of the place where dishonor occurs. It may be made upon information satisfactory to such person.

(2) The protest must identify the instrument and certify either that due presentment has been made or the reason why it is excused and that the instrument has been dishonored by non-acceptance or nonpayment.

(3) The protest may also certify that notice of dishonor has been given to all parties or to specified parties.

(4) Subject to subsection (5) any necessary protest is due by the time that notice of dishonor is due.

(5) If, before protest is due, an instrument has been noted for protest by the officer to make protest, the protest may be made at any time thereafter as of the date of the noting.

Official Comment

Prior Uniform Statutory Provision: Sections 153, 154, 155, 156, 158 and 160, Uniform Negotiable Instruments Law.

Changes: Combined and simplified.

Purposes of Changes:

1. Protest is not necessary except on drafts drawn or payable outside of the United States. Section 3–501(3) which also permits the holder at his option to make protest on dishonor of any other instrument. This section is intended to simplify either necessary or optional protest when it is made.

2. "Protest" has been used to mean the act of making protest, and sometimes loosely to refer to the entire process of presentment, notice of dishonor and protest. In this Article it is given its original, technical meaning, that of the official certificate of dishonor.

3. Subsection (1) adds to the notary public the United States consul or vice consul, and any other person authorized to certify dishonor by the law of the place where dishonor occurs. It eliminates the requirement of the original Section 156 that protest must be made at the place of dishonor. It eliminates also the provision of the original Section 154 permitting protest by "any respectable resident of the place where the bill is dishonored, in the presence of two or more credible witnesses." This has at least left uncertainty as to the identity and credibility of the persons certifying, and has almost never been used. Any necessary delay in finding the proper officer to make protest is excused under Section 3–511.

4. "Information satisfactory to such person" does away with the requirement occasionally stated, that the person making protest must certify as of his own knowledge. The requirement has been more honored in the breach than in the observance, and in practice protest has been made upon hearsay which the officer regards as reliable, upon the admission of the person who has dishonored, or at most upon re-presentment, which is only indirect proof of the original dishonor. There is seldom any possible motive for false protest, and the basis on which it is made is never questioned. Subsection (1) leaves to the certifying officer the responsibility for determining whether he has satisfactory information. The provision is not intended to affect any personal liability of the officer for making a false certificate.

5. The protest need not be in any particular form, so long as it certifies the matters stated in Subsection (2). It need not be annexed to the instrument, and may be forwarded separately; but annexation may identify the instrument. If the instrument is lost, destroyed, or wrongfully withheld, protest is still sufficient if it identifies the instrument; but the owner must prove his rights as in any action under this Article on a lost, destroyed or stolen instrument (Section 3–804).

6. Subsection (3) recognizes the practice of including in the protest a certification that notice of dishonor has been given to all parties or to specified parties. The next section makes such a certification presumptive evidence that the notice has been given.

7. Protest is normally forwarded with notice of dishonor. Subsection (4) extends the time for making a necessary protest to coincide with the time for giving notice of dishonor. Any delay due to circumstances beyond the holder's control is excused under Section 3–511 on waiver or excuse. Any protest which is not necessary but merely optional with the holder may be made at any time before it is used as evidence.

8. Subsection (5) retains from the original Section 155 the provision permitting the officer to note the protest and extend it formally later.

Cross References:

Point 1: Sections 3–501(3) and 3–511.
Point 3: Section 3–511(1).
Point 5: Section 3–804.
Point 6: Section 3–510(a).
Point 7: Sections 3–508(2) and 3–511(1).

Definitional Cross References:

"Dishonor". Section 3–507.
"Instrument". Section 3–102.
"Notice of dishonor". Section 3–508.
"Party". Section 1–201.
"Person". Section 1–201.
"Presentment". Section 3–504.

§ 3-510. Evidence of Dishonor and Notice of Dishonor.

The following are admissible as evidence and create a presumption of dishonor and of any notice of dishonor therein shown:

(a) a document regular in form as provided in the preceding section which purports to be a protest;

(b) the purported stamp or writing of the drawee, payor bank or presenting bank on the instrument or accompanying it stating that acceptance or payment has been refused for reasons consistent with dishonor;

(c) any book or record of the drawee, payor bank, or any collecting bank kept in the usual course of business which shows dishonor, even though there is no evidence of who made the entry.

Official Comment

Prior Uniform Statutory Provision: None.

Purposes: This section is new. It states the effect of protest as evidence, and provides two substitutes for protest as proof of dishonor:

1. Paragraph (a) states the generally accepted rule that a protest is not only admissible as evidence, but creates a presumption, as that term is defined in this Act (Section 1–201), of the dishonor which it certifies. The rule is extended to include the giving of any notice of dishonor certified by the protest. The provision also relieves the holder of the necessity of proving that a document regular in form which purports to be a protest is authentic, or that the person making it was qualified. Nothing in the provision is intended to prevent the obligor from overthrowing the presumption by evidence that there was in fact no dishonor, that notice was not given, or that the protest is not authentic or not made by a proper officer.

2. Paragraph (b) recognizes as the full equivalent of protest the stamp, ticket or other writing of the drawee, payor or presenting bank. The drawee's statement that payment is refused on account of insufficient funds always has been commercially acceptable as full proof of dishonor. It should be satisfactory evidence in any court. It is therefore made admissible, and creates a presumption of dishonor. The provision applies only where the stamp or writing states reasons for refusal which are consistent with dishonor. Thus the following reasons for refusal are not evidence of dishonor, but of justifiable refusal to pay or accept:

Indorsement missing
Signature missing
Signature illegible
Forgery
Payee altered
Date altered
Post dated
Not on us

On the other hand the following reasons are satisfactory evidence of dishonor, consistent with due presentment, and are within this provision:

Not sufficient funds
Account garnisheed
No account
Payment stopped

3. Paragraph (c) recognizes as the full equivalent of protest any books or records of the drawee, payor bank or any collecting bank kept in its usual course of business, even though there is no evidence of who made the entries. The provision, as well as that of paragraph (b), rests upon the inherent improbability that bank records, or those of the drawee, will show any dishonor which has not in fact occurred, or that the holder will attempt to proceed on the basis of dishonor if he could in fact have obtained payment.

Cross References:

Sections 3–501 and 3–508.
Point 1: Section 1–201.

Definitional Cross References:

"Acceptance". Section 3–410.
"Collecting bank". Section 4–105.
"Dishonor". Section 3–507.
"Instrument". Section 3–102.
"Notice of dishonor". Section 3–508.
"Payor bank". Section 4–105.
"Presumption". Section 1–201.
"Protest." Section 3–509.
"Writing". Section 1–201.

§ 3–511. Waived or Excused Presentment, Protest or Notice of Dishonor or Delay Therein.

(1) Delay in presentment, protest or notice of dishonor is excused when the party is without notice that it is due or when the delay is caused by circumstances beyond his control and he exercises reasonable diligence after the cause of the delay ceases to operate.

(2) Presentment or notice or protest as the case may be is entirely excused when

(a) the party to be charged has waived it expressly or by implication either before or after it is due; or

(b) such party has himself dishonored the instrument or has countermanded payment or otherwise has no reason to expect or right to require that the instrument be accepted or paid; or

(c) by reasonable diligence the presentment or protest cannot be made or the notice given.

(3) Presentment is also entirely excused when

(a) the maker, acceptor or drawee of any instrument except a documentary draft is dead or in insolvency proceedings instituted after the issue of the instrument; or

(b) acceptance or payment is refused but not for want of proper presentment.

(4) Where a draft has been dishonored by nonacceptance a later presentment for payment and any notice of dishonor and protest for nonpayment are excused unless in the meantime the instrument has been accepted.

(5) A waiver of protest is also a waiver of presentment and of notice of dishonor even though protest is not required.

(6) Where a waiver of presentment or notice or protest is embodied in the instrument itself it is binding upon all parties; but where it is written above the signature of an indorser it binds him only.

Official Comment

Prior Uniform Statutory Provision: Sections 79, 80, 81, 82, 109, 111, 112, 113, 114, 115, 116, 130, 147, 148, 150, 151, 159, Uniform Negotiable Instruments Law.

Changes: Combined and simplified.

Purposes of Changes: This section combines widely scattered sections of the original act, and is intended to simplify the rules as to when presentment, notice or protest is excused:

1. The single term "excused" is substituted for "excused," "dispensed with," "not necessary," "not required," as used variously in the original act. No change in meaning is intended.

2. Subsection (1) combines provisions found in the original Sections 81, 113, 147 and 159. Delay in making presentment either for payment or for acceptance, in giving notice of dishonor or in making protest is excused when the party has acted with reasonable diligence and the delay is not his fault. This is true where an instrument has been accelerated without his knowledge, or demand has been made by a prior holder immediately before his purchase. It is true under any other circumstances where the delay is beyond his control. The words "not imputable to his default, misconduct or negligence" found in the original Sections 81, 113 and 159 are omitted as superfluous, but no change in substance is intended.

3. Any waived presentment, notice or protest is excused, as under the original Sections 82, 109, 110 and 111. The waiver may be express or implied, oral or written, and before or after the proceeding waived is due. It may be, and often is, a term of the instrument when it is issued. Subsection (5) retains as standard commercial usage the meaning attached by the original Section 111 to "protest waived."

4. Paragraph (b) of subsection (2) combines the substance of provisions found in the original Sections 79, 80, 114, 115 and 130. A party who has no right to require or reason to expect that the instrument will be honored is not entitled to presentment, notice or protest. This is of course true where he has himself dishonored the instrument or has countermanded payment. It is equally true, for example, where he is an accommodated party and has himself broken the accommodation agreement.

5. Paragraph (c) of subsection (2) combines provisions found in the original Sections 82(1), 112 and 159. The excuse is established only by proof that reasonable diligence has been exercised without success, or that reasonable diligence would in any case have been unsuccessful.

6. Paragraph (a) of subsection (3) is new. It excuses presentment in situations where immediate payment or acceptance is impossible or so unlikely that the holder cannot reasonably be expected to make presentment. He is permitted instead to have his immediate recourse upon the drawer or indorser, and let the latter file any necessary claim in probate or insolvency proceedings. The exception for the documentary draft is to preserve any profit on the resale of goods for the creditors of the drawee if his representative can find the funds to pay.

7. Paragraph (b) of subsection (3) extends the original Section 148(3) to include any case where payment or acceptance is definitely refused and the refusal is not on the ground that there has been no proper presentment. The purpose of presentment is to determine whether or not the maker, acceptor or drawee will pay or accept; and when that question is clearly determined the holder is not required to go through a useless ceremony. The provision applies to a definite refusal stating no reasons.

8. Subsection (4) retains the rule of the original Sections 116 and 151.

9. Subsection (6) retains the rule of original Section 110.

Cross References:

Sections 3–501, 3–502, 3–503, 3–507 and 3–509.

Definitional Cross References:

"Acceptance". Section 3–410.
"Dishonor". Section 3–507.
"Documentary draft". Section 4–104.
"Draft". Section 3–104.
"Insolvency proceedings". Section 1–201.
"Instrument". Section 3–102.
"Issue". Section 3–102.
"Notice of dishonor". Section 3–508.
"Party". Section 1–201.
"Presentment". Section 3–504.
"Protest". Section 3–509.
"Right". Section 1–201.

PART 6
DISCHARGE

§ 3–601. Discharge of Parties.

(1) The extent of the discharge of any party from liability on an instrument is governed by the sections on

(a) payment or satisfaction (Section 3–603); or

(b) tender of payment (Section 3–604); or

(c) cancellation or renunciation (Section 3–605); or

(d) impairment of right of recourse or of collateral (Section 3–606); or

(e) reacquisition of the instrument by a prior party (Section 3–208); or

(f) fraudulent and material alteration (Section 3–407); or

(g) certification of a check (Section 3–411); or

(h) acceptance varying a draft (Section 3–412); or

(i) unexcused delay in presentment or notice of dishonor or protest (Section 3–502).

(2) Any party is also discharged from his liability on an instrument to another party by any other act or agreement with such party which would discharge his simple contract for the payment of money.

(3) The liability of all parties is discharged when any party who has himself no right of action or recourse on the instrument

(a) reacquires the instrument in his own right; or

(b) is discharged under any provision of this Article, except as otherwise provided with respect to discharge for impairment of recourse or of collateral (Section 3–606).

Official Comment

Prior Uniform Statutory Provision: Sections 119, 120 and 121, Uniform Negotiable Instruments Law.

Changes: Portions of original sections combined and reworded; new provisions.

Purposes of Changes:

1. Subsection (1) contains an index referring to all of the sections of this Article which provide for the discharge of any party. The list is exclusive so far as the provisions of this Article are concerned, but it is not intended to prevent or affect any discharge arising apart from this statute, as for example a discharge in bankruptcy or a statutory provision for discharge if the instrument is negotiated in a gaming transaction.

2. A negotiable instrument is in itself merely a piece of paper bearing a writing, and strictly speaking is incapable of being discharged. The parties are rather discharged from liability on their contracts on the instrument. The language of the original Section 119 as to discharge of the instrument itself has left uncertainties as to the effect of the discharge upon the rights of a subsequent holder in due course. It is therefore eliminated, and this section now distinguishes instead between the discharge of a single party and the discharge of all parties.

So far as the discharge of any one party is concerned a negotiable instrument differs from any other contract only in the special rules arising out of its character to which paragraphs (a) to (i) of subsection (1) are an index, and in the effect of the discharge against a subsequent holder in due course (Section 3–602). Subsection (2) therefore retains from the original Section 119(4) the provision for discharge by "any other act which will discharge a simple contract for the payment of money," and specifically recognizes the possibility of a discharge by agreement.

The discharge of any party is a defense available to that party as provided in sections on rights of those who are and are not holders in due course (Sections 3–305 and 3–306). He has the burden of establishing the defense (Section 3–307).

3. Subsection (3) substitutes for the "discharge of the instrument" the discharge of all parties from liability on their contracts on the instrument. It covers a part of the substance of the original Section 119(1), (2) and (5), the original Section 120(1) and (3), and the original Section 121(1) and (2). It states a general principle in lieu of the original detailed provisions. The principle is that all parties to an instrument are discharged when no party is left with rights against any other party on the paper.

When any party reacquires the instrument in his own right his own liability is discharged; and any intervening party to whom he was liable is also discharged as provided in Section 3–208 on reacquisition. When he is left with no right of action against an intervening party and no right of recourse against any prior party, all parties are obviously discharged. The instrument itself is not necessarily extinct, since it may be reissued or renegotiated with a new and further liability; and if it subsequently reaches the hands of a holder in due course without notice of the discharge he may still enforce it as provided in Section 3–602 on effect of discharge against a holder in due course.

Under Section 3–606 on impairment of recourse or collateral, the discharge of any party discharges those who have a right of recourse against him, except in the case of a release with reservation of rights or a failure to give notice of dishonor. A discharge of one who has himself no right of action or recourse on the instrument may thus discharge all parties. Again the instrument itself is not necessarily extinct, and if it is negotiated to a subsequent holder in due course without notice of the discharge he may enforce it as provided in Section 3–602 on effect of discharge against a holder in due course.

4. The language "any party who has himself no right of action or recourse on the instrument" is substituted for "principal debtor," which is not defined by the original Act and has been misleading. This Article also omits the original Section 192, defining the "person primarily liable." Under Section 3–415 on accommodation parties an accommodation maker or acceptor, although he is primarily liable on the instrument in the sense that he is obligated to pay it without recourse upon another, has himself a right of recourse against the accommodated payee; and his reacquisition or discharge leaves the accommodated party liable to him. The accommodated payee, although he is not primarily liable to others, has no right of action or recourse against the accommodation maker, and his reacquisition or discharge may discharge all parties.

Cross References:

Sections 3–406, 3–411, 3–412, 3–509, 3–603, 3–604 and 3–605.
Point 2: Sections 3–305, 3–306, 3–307 and 3–602.
Point 3: Sections 3–208, 3–602 and 3–606.
Point 4: Section 3–415.

Definitional Cross References:

"Action". Section 1–201.
"Agreement". Section 1–201.
"Alteration". Section 3–407.
"Certification". Section 3–411.
"Check". Section 3–104.
"Contract". Section 1–201.
"Draft". Section 3–104.
"Instrument". Section 3–102.
"Money". Section 1–201.
"Notice of dishonor". Section 3–508.
"Party". Section 1–201.
"Presentment". Section 3–504.
"Rights". Section 1–201.

§ 3–602. Effect of Discharge Against Holder in Due Course.

No discharge of any party provided by this Article is effective against a subsequent holder in due course unless he has notice thereof when he takes the instrument.

Official Comment

Prior Uniform Statutory Provision: None.

Purposes:

The section is intended to remove an uncertainty as to which the original Act is silent. It rests on the principle that any discharge of a party provided under any section of this Article is a personal defense of the party, which is cut off when a subsequent holder in due course takes the instrument without notice of the defense. Thus where an instrument is paid without surrender such a subsequent purchase cuts off the defense. This section applies only to discharges arising under the provisions of this Article, and it has no application to any discharge arising apart from it, such as a discharge in bankruptcy.

Under Section 3–304(1)(b) on notice to purchaser it is possible for a holder to take the instrument in due course even though he has notice that one or more parties have been discharged, so long as any party remains undischarged. Thus he may take with notice that an indorser of a note has been released, and still be a holder in due course as to the liability of the maker. In that event, the holder in due course is subject to the defense of the discharge of which he had notice when he took the instrument.

Cross References:

Sections 3-302, 3-304, 3-305 and 3-601.

Definitional Cross References:

"Holder in due course". Section 3-302.
"Instrument". Section 3-102.
"Notice". Section 1-201.
"Party". Section 1-201.

§ 3-603. Payment or Satisfaction.

(1) The liability of any party is discharged to the extent of his payment or satisfaction to the holder even though it is made with knowledge of a claim of another person to the instrument unless prior to such payment or satisfaction the person making the claim either supplies indemnity deemed adequate by the party seeking the discharge or enjoins payment or satisfaction by order of a court of competent jurisdiction in an action in which the adverse claimant and the holder are parties. This subsection does not, however, result in the discharge of the liability

(a) of a party who in bad faith pays or satisfies a holder who acquired the instrument by theft or who (unless having the rights of a holder in due course) holds through one who so acquired it; or

(b) of a party (other than an intermediary bank or a payor bank which is not a depositary bank) who pays or satisfies the holder of an instrument which has been restrictively indorsed in a manner not consistent with the terms of such restrictive indorsement.

(2) Payment or satisfaction may be made with the consent of the holder by any person including a stranger to the instrument. Surrender of the instrument to such a person gives him the rights of a transferee (Section 3-201).

Official Comment

Prior Uniform Statutory Provision: Sections 51, 88, 119, 121 and 171-177, Uniform Negotiable Instruments Law.

Changes: Parts of original sections combined and reworded; law changed.

Purposes of Changes: This section changes the law as follows:

1. It eliminates the "payment in due course" found in the original Sections 51, 88 and 119. "Payment in due course" discharged all parties where it was made by one who has no right of recourse on the instrument; but this is true of any other discharge of such a party, and is now covered by Section 3-601(3) on discharge of parties. Such payment was effective as a discharge against a subsequent purchaser; but since it is made at or after maturity of the instrument a purchaser with notice of that fact cannot be a holder in due course, and one who takes without notice of the payment and the maturity should be protected against failure to take up the instrument. The matter is now covered by Section 3-602.

2. The original Sections 171-177 provide for payment of a draft "for honor" after protest. The practice originated at a time when communications were slow and difficult, and in overseas transactions there might be a delay of several months before the drawer could act upon any dishonor. It provided a method by which a third party might intervene to protect the credit of the drawer and at the same time preserve his own rights. Cable, telegraph and telephone have made the practice obsolete for nearly a century, and it is today almost entirely unknown. It has been replaced by the cable transfer, the letter of credit and numerous other devices by which a substitute arrangement is promptly made. "Payment for honor" is therefore eliminated; and subsection (2) now provides that any person may pay with the consent of the holder.

3. Payment to the holder discharges the party who makes it from his own liability on the instrument, and a part payment discharges him pro tanto. The same is true of any other satisfaction. Subsection (1) changes the law by eliminating the requirement of the original Section 88 that the payment be made in good faith and without notice that the title of the holder is defective. It adopts as a general principle the position that a payor is not required to obey an order to stop payment received from an indorser. However, this general principle is qualified by the provisions of subsection (1)(a) and (b) respecting persons who acquire an instrument by theft, or through a restrictive indorsement (Section 3-205). These provisions are thus consistent with Section 3-306 covering the rights of one not a holder in due course.

When the party to pay is notified of an adverse claim to the instrument he has normally no means of knowing whether the assertion is true. The "unless" clause of subsection (1) follows statutes which have been passed in many states on adverse claims to bank deposits. The paying party may pay despite notification of the adverse claim unless the adverse claimant supplies indemnity deemed adequate by the paying party or procures the issuance of process restraining payment in an action in which the adverse claimant and the holder of the instrument are both parties. If the paying party chooses to refuse payment and stand suit, even though not indemnified or enjoined, he is free to do so, although, under Section 3-306(d) on the rights of one not a holder in due course, except where theft or taking through a restrictive indorsement is alleged the payor must rely on the third party claimant to litigate the issue and may not himself defend on such a ground. His contract is to pay the holder of the instrument, and he performs it by making such payment. Except in cases of theft or restrictive indorsement there is no good reason to put him to inconvenience because of a dispute between two other parties unless he is indemnified or served with appropriate process.

4. With the elimination of "payment for honor", subsection (2) provides that with the consent of the holder payment may be made by anyone, including a stranger. The subsection omits the provision of the original Section 121 by which the payor is "remitted to his former rights". It rejects such decisions as Quimby v. Varnum, 190 Mass. 211, 76 N.E. 671 (1906), holding that an irregular indorser who makes payment cannot recover on the instrument. The same result is reached under Section 3-415(5) on accommodation parties. Upon payment and surrender of the paper the payor succeeds to the rights of the holder, subject to the limitation found in Section 3-201 on transfer that one who has himself been a party to any fraud or illegality affecting the instrument or who as a prior holder had notice of a defense or claim against it cannot improve his position by taking from a later holder in due course.

5. Payment discharges the liability of the person making it. It discharges the liability of other parties only as

a. The discharge of the payor discharges others who have a right of recourse against him under Section 3-606; or

b. Reacquisition of the instrument discharges intervening parties under Section 3-208 on reacquisition; or

c. The discharge of one who has himself no right of recourse on the instrument discharges all parties under Section 3-601 on discharge of parties.

Cross References:

Sections 3-604 and 3-606.
Point 1: Section 3-601(3).
Point 3: Sections 3-205 and 3-306(d).
Point 4: Sections 3-201 and 3-415(5).
Point 5: Sections 3-606, 3-208, 3-601.

Definitional Cross References:

"Action". Section 1-201.
"Holder". Section 1-201.
"Instrument". Section 3-102.
"Order". Section 3-102.
"Party". Section 1-201.
"Person". Section 1-201.
"Rights". Section 1-201.

§ 3-604. Tender of Payment.

(1) Any party making tender of full payment to a holder when or after it is due is discharged to the extent of all subsequent liability for interest, costs and attorney's fees.

(2) The holder's refusal of such tender wholly discharges any party who has a right of recourse against the party making the tender.

(3) Where the maker or acceptor of an instrument payable otherwise than on demand is able and ready to pay at every place of payment specified in the instrument when it is due, it is equivalent to tender.

Official Comment

Prior Uniform Statutory Provision: Sections 70 and 120, Uniform Negotiable Instruments Law.

Changes: Parts of original sections combined and reworded; new provisions.

Purposes of Changes and New Matter:

1. Subsection (1) is new. It states the generally accepted rule as to the effect of tender.

2. Subsection (2) rewords the original subsection 120(4). The party discharged is one who has a right of recourse against the party making tender, whether the latter be a prior party or a subsequent one who has been accommodated.

3. Subsection (3) rewords the final clause of the first sentence of the original Section 70. Where the instrument is payable at any one of two or more specified places, the maker or acceptor must be able and ready to pay at each of them. The language in original Section 70 was taken to mean that makers and acceptors of notes and drafts payable at a bank were not discharged by failure of a holder to make due presentment of such paper at the designated bank. This Article reverses that rule. See Sections 3–501 on necessity of presentment, 3–504 on how presentment is made, and 3–502 on effect of delay in presentment.

Cross References:

Section 3–601.
Point 3: Sections 3–501, 3–502 and 3–504.

Definitional Cross References:

"Holder". Section 1–201.
"Instrument". Section 3–102.
"On demand". Section 3–108.
"Party". Section 1–201.
"Right". Section 1–201.

§ 3-605. Cancellation and Renunciation.

(1) The holder of an instrument may even without consideration discharge any party

(a) in any manner apparent on the face of the instrument or the indorsement, as by intentionally cancelling the instrument or the party's signature by destruction or mutilation, or by striking out the party's signature; or

(b) by renouncing his rights by a writing signed and delivered or by surrender of the instrument to the party to be discharged.

(2) Neither cancellation nor renunciation without surrender of the instrument affects the title thereto.

Official Comment

Prior Uniform Statutory Provision: Sections 48, 119(3), 120(2), 122 and 123, Uniform Negotiable Instruments Law.

Changes: Combined and reworded.

Purposes of Changes:

1. The original Act does not state how cancellation is to be effected, except as to striking indorsements under the original Section 48. It must be done in such a manner as to be apparent on the face of the instrument, and the methods stated, which are supported by the decisions, are exclusive.

2. Subsection (1)(b) restates the original Section 122. The provision as to "discharge of the instrument" is now covered by discharge, Section 3–601(3); that as to subsequent holders in due course by Section 3–602 on effect of discharge against a holder in due course.

3. Subsection (2) is new. It is intended to make it clear that the striking of an indorsement, or any other cancellation or renunciation, does not affect the title.

Cross References:

Point 2: Sections 3-601 and 3-602.

Definitional Cross References:

"Holder". Section 1-201.
"Instrument". Section 3-102.
"Party". Section 1-201.
"Rights". Section 1-201.
"Signature". Section 3-401.
"Signed". Section 1-201.
"Writing". Section 1-201.

§ 3-606. Impairment of Recourse or of Collateral.

(1) The holder discharges any party to the instrument to the extent that without such party's consent the holder

(a) without express reservation of rights releases or agrees not to sue any person against whom the party has to the knowledge of the holder a right of recourse or agrees to suspend the right to enforce against such person the instrument or collateral or otherwise discharges such person, except that failure or delay in effecting any required presentment, protest or notice of dishonor with respect to any such person does not discharge any party as to whom presentment, protest or notice of dishonor is effective or unnecessary; or

(b) unjustifiably impairs any collateral for the instrument given by or on behalf of the party or any person against whom he has a right of recourse.

(2) By express reservation of rights against a party with a right of recourse the holder preserves

(a) all his rights against such party as of the time when the instrument was originally due; and

(b) the right of the party to pay the instrument as of that time; and

(c) all rights of such party to recourse against others.

Official Comment

Prior Uniform Statutory Provision: Section 120, Uniform Negotiable Instruments Law.

Changes: Reworded; new provisions.

Purposes of Changes and New Matter: To make it clear that:

1. The words "any party to the instrument" remove an uncertainty arising under the original section. The suretyship defenses here provided are not limited to parties who are "secondarily liable," but are available to any party who is in the position of a surety, having a right of recourse either on the instrument or dehors it, including an accommodation maker or acceptor known to the holder to be so.

2. Consent may be given in advance, and is commonly incorporated in the instrument; or it may be given afterward. It requires no consideration, and operates as a waiver of the consenting party's right to claim his own discharge.

3. The words "to the knowledge of the holder" exclude the latent surety, as for example the accommodation maker where there is nothing on the instrument to show that he has signed for accommodation and the holder is ignorant of that fact. In such a case the holder is entitled to proceed according to what is shown by the face of the paper or what he otherwise knows, and does not discharge the surety when he acts in ignorance of the relation.

4. This section retains the right of the holder to release one party, or to postpone his time of payment, while expressly reserving rights against others. Subsection (2), which is new, states the generally accepted rule as to the effect of such an express reservation of rights. [Comment 4 was amended in 1966].

5. Paragraph (b) of subsection (1) is new. The suretyship defense stated has been generally recognized as available to indorsers or accommodation parties. As to when a holder's actions in dealing with collateral may be "unjustifiable", the section on rights and duties with respect to collateral in the possession of a secured party (Section 9-207) should be consulted.

Cross Reference:

Point 5: Section 9–207.

Definitional Cross References:

"Agreement". Section 1–201.
"Holder". Section 1–201.
"Instrument". Section 3–102.
"Notice of dishonor". Section 3–508.
"Party". Section 1–201.
"Person". Section 1–201.
"Rights". Section 1–201.

PART 7

ADVICE OF INTERNATIONAL SIGHT DRAFT

§ 3–701. Letter of Advice of International Sight Draft.

(1) A "letter of advice" is a drawer's communication to the drawee that a described draft has been drawn.

(2) Unless otherwise agreed when a bank receives from another bank a letter of advice of an international sight draft the drawee bank may immediately debit the drawer's account and stop the running of interest pro tanto. Such a debit and any resulting credit to any account covering outstanding drafts leaves in the drawer full power to stop payment or otherwise dispose of the amount and creates no trust or interest in favor of the holder.

(3) Unless otherwise agreed and except where a draft is drawn under a credit issued by the drawee, the drawee of an international sight draft owes the drawer no duty to pay an unadvised draft but if it does so and the draft is genuine, may appropriately debit the drawer's account.

Official Comment

Prior Uniform Statutory Provision: None.

Purposes: To recognize and clarify, in law, certain established practices of international banking.

1. Checks drawn by one international bank on the account it carries (in a currency foreign to itself) in another international bank are still handled under practices which reflect older conditions, but which have a real, continuing reason in the typical, European rule that a bank paying a check in good faith and in ordinary course can charge its depositor's account notwithstanding forgery of a necessary indorsement. To decrease the risk that forgery will prove successful, the practice is to send a letter of advice that a draft has been drawn and will be forthcoming. Subsection 3 recognizes that a drawer who sends no such letter forfeits any rights for improper dishonor, while still permitting the drawee to protect his delinquent drawer's credit.

2. Subsection (2) clears up for American courts, the meaning of another international practice: that of charging the drawer's account on receipt of the letter of advice. This practice involves no conception of trust or the like and the rule of Section 3–409(1) (Draft not an assignment) still applies. The debit has to do with the payment of interest only. The section recognizes the fact.

Cross Reference:

Point 2: Section 3–409(1).

Definitional Cross References:

"Account". Section 4–104.
"Bank". Section 1–201.
"Credit". Section 5–103.
"Draft". Section 3–104.
"Genuine". Section 1–201.
"Holder". Section 1–201.

PART 8

MISCELLANEOUS

§ 3–801. Drafts in a Set.

(1) Where a draft is drawn in a set of parts, each of which is numbered and expressed to be an order only if no other part has been honored, the whole of the parts constitutes one draft but a taker of any part may become a holder in due course of the draft.

(2) Any person who negotiates, indorses or accepts a single part of a draft drawn in a set thereby becomes liable to any holder in due course of that part as if it were the whole set, but as between different holders in due course to whom different parts have been negotiated the holder whose title first accrues has all rights to the draft and its proceeds.

(3) As against the drawee the first presented part of a draft drawn in a set is the part entitled to payment, or if a time draft to acceptance and payment. Acceptance of any subsequently presented part renders the drawee liable thereon under subsection (2). With respect both to a holder and to the drawer payment of a subsequently presented part of a draft payable at sight has the same effect as payment of a check notwithstanding an effective stop order (Section 4–407).

(4) Except as otherwise provided in this section, where any part of a draft in a set is discharged by payment or otherwise the whole draft is discharged.

Official Comment

Prior Uniform Statutory Provision: Sections 178–183, Uniform Negotiable Instruments Law.

Changes: Combined and reworded.

Purposes of Changes:

The revised language makes no important change in substance, and is intended only as a clarification and supplementation of the original sections:

1. Drafts in a set customarily contain such language as "Pay _______ this first of exchange (second unpaid)," with equivalent language in the second part. Today a part also commonly bears conspicuous indication of its number. At least the first factor is necessary to notify the holder of his rights, and is therefore necessary in order to make this section apply. Subsection (1) so provides, thus stating in the statute a matter left previously to a commercial practice long uniform but expensive to establish in court.

2. The final sentence of subsection (3) is new. Payment of the part of the draft subsequently presented is improper and the drawee may not charge it to the account of the drawer, but some one has probably been unjustly enriched on the total transaction, at the expense of the drawee. So the drawee is like a bank which has paid a check over an effective stop payment order, and is subrogated as provided in that situation. Section 4–407.

3. A statement in a draft drawn in a set of parts to the effect that the order is effective only if no other part has been honored does not render the draft nonnegotiable as conditional. See Section 3–112(1)(g).

Cross References:

Point 2: Section 4–407.
Point 3: Section 3–112.

Definitional Cross References:

"Acceptance". Section 3–410.
"Check". Section 3–104.
"Draft". Section 3–104.
"Holder". Section 1–201.
"Holder in due course". Section 3–302.
"Honor". Section 1–201.
"Person". Section 1–201.
"Rights". Section 1–201.

§ 3-802. Effect of Instrument on Obligation for Which It Is Given.

(1) Unless otherwise agreed where an instrument is taken for an underlying obligation

(a) the obligation is pro tanto discharged if a bank is drawer, maker or acceptor of the instrument and there is no recourse on the instrument against the underlying obligor; and

(b) in any other case the obligation is suspended pro tanto until the instrument is due or if it is payable on demand until its presentment. If the instrument is dishonored action may be maintained on either the instrument or the obligation; discharge of the underlying obligor on the instrument also discharges him on the obligation.

(2) The taking in good faith of a check which is not post-dated does not of itself so extend the time on the original obligation as to discharge a surety.

Official Comment

Prior Uniform Statutory Provision: None.

Purposes:

1. The section is new. It is intended to settle conflicts as to the effect of an instrument as payment of the obligation for which it is given.

2. Where a holder procures certification of a check the drawer is discharged under Section 3-411 on check certification. Thereafter the original obligation is regarded as paid, and the holder must look to the certifying bank. The circumstances may indicate a similar intent in other transactions, and the question may be one of fact for the jury. Subsection (1)(a) states a rule discharging the obligation pro tanto when the instrument taken carries the obligation of a bank as drawer, maker or acceptor and there is no recourse on the instrument against the underlying obligor.

3. It is commonly said that a check or other negotiable instrument is "conditional payment." By this it is normally meant that taking the instrument is a surrender of the right to sue on the obligation until the instrument is due, but if the instrument is not paid on due presentment the right to sue on the obligation is "revived." Subsection (1)(b) states this result in terms of suspension of the obligation, which is intended to include suspension of the running of the statute of limitations. On dishonor of the instrument the holder is given his option to sue either on the instrument or on the underlying obligation. If, however, the original obligor has been discharged on the instrument (see Section 3-601) he is also discharged on the original obligation.

4. Subsection (2) is intended to remove any implication that a check given in payment of an obligation discharges a surety. The check is taken as a means of immediate payment; the thirty day period for presentment specified in Section 3-503 does not affect the surety's liability.

Cross References:

Point 2: Sections 1-201, 3-411 and 3-601.

Point 4: Section 3-503.

Definitional Cross References:

"Action". Section 1-201.
"Bank". Section 1-201.
"Check". Section 3-104.
"Dishonor". Section 3-507.
"Good faith". Section 1-201.
"Instrument". Section 3-102.
"On demand". Section 3-108.
"Presentment". Section 3-504.

§ 3-803. Notice to Third Party.

Where a defendant is sued for breach of an obligation for which a third person is answerable over under this Article he may give the third person written notice of the litigation, and the person notified may then give similar notice to any other person who is answerable over to him under this Article. If the notice states that the person notified may come in and defend and that if the person notified does not do so he will in any action against him by the person giving the notice be bound by any determination of fact common to the two litigations, then unless after seasonable receipt of the notice the person notified does come in and defend he is so bound.

Official Comment

Prior Uniform Statutory Provisions: None.

Purposes:

The section is new. It is intended to supplement, not to displace existing procedures for interpleader or joinder of parties.

The section conforms to the analogous provision in Section 2–607. It extends to such liabilities as those arising from forged indorsements even though not "on the instrument," and is intended to make it clear that the notification is not effective until received. In Hartford Accident & Indemnity Co. v. First Nat. Bank & Trust Co., 281 N.Y. 162, 22 N.E.2d 324, 123 A.L.R. 1149 (1939), the common-law doctrine of "vouching in" was held inapplicable where the party notified had no direct liability to the party giving the notice. In that case the drawer of a check, sued by the payee whose indorsement had been forged, gave notice to a collecting bank. In a second action the drawee was held liable to the drawer; but in an action by the drawee for judgment over against the collecting bank the determinations of fact in the first action were held not conclusive. This section does not disturb this result; the section is limited to cases where the person notified is "answerable over" to the person giving the notice.

Cross Reference:

Section 2–607.

Definitional Cross References:

"Action". Section 1–201.
"Defendant". Section 1–201.
"Instrument". Section 3–102.
"Notifies". Section 1–201.
"Person". Section 1–201.
"Right". Section 1–201.
"Seasonably". Section 1–204.
"Written". Section 1–201.

§ 3–804. Lost, Destroyed or Stolen Instruments.

The owner of an instrument which is lost, whether by destruction, theft or otherwise, may maintain an action in his own name and recover from any party liable thereon upon due proof of his ownership, the facts which prevent his production of the instrument and its terms. The court may require security indemnifying the defendant against loss by reason of further claims on the instrument.

Official Comment

Prior Uniform Statutory Provision: None.

Purposes:

This section is new. It is intended to provide a method of recovery on instruments which are lost, destroyed or stolen. The plaintiff who claims to be the owner of such an instrument is not a holder as that term is defined in this Act, since he is not in possession of the paper, and he does not have the holder's prima facie right to recover under the section on the burden of establishing signatures. He must prove his case. He must establish the terms of the instrument and his ownership, and must account for its absence.

If the claimant testifies falsely, or if the instrument subsequently turns up in the hands of a holder in due course, the obligor may be subjected to double liability. The court is therefore authorized to require security indemnifying the obligor against loss by reason of such possibilities. There may be cases in which so much time has elapsed, or there is so little possible doubt as to the destruction of the instrument and its ownership that there is no good reason to require the security. The requirement is therefore not an absolute one, and the matter is left to the discretion of the court.

Cross References:

Sections 1–201 and 3–307.

Definitional Cross References:

"Action". Section 1–201.
"Defendant". Section 1–201.
"Instrument". Section 3–102.
"Party". Section 1–201.
"Term". Section 1–201.

§ 3–805. Instruments Not Payable to Order or to Bearer.

This Article applies to any instrument whose terms do not preclude transfer and which is otherwise negotiable within this Article but which is not payable to order or to bearer, except that there can be no holder in due course of such an instrument.

Official Comment

Prior Uniform Statutory Provision: None.

Purposes:

This section covers the "non-negotiable instrument." As it has been used by most courts, this term has been a technical one of art. It does not refer to a writing, such as a note containing an express condition, which is not negotiable and is entirely outside of the scope of this Article and to be treated as a simple contract. It refers to a particular type of instrument which meets all requirements as to form of a negotiable instrument except that it is not payable to order or to bearer. The typical example is the check reading merely "Pay John Doe."

Such a check is not a negotiable instrument under this Article. At the same time it is still a check, a mercantile specialty which differs in many respects from a simple contract. Commercial and banking practice treats it as a check, and a long line of decisions before and after the original Act have made it clear that it is subject to the law merchant as distinguished from ordinary contract law. Although the Negotiable Instruments Law has been held by its terms not to apply to such "non-negotiable instruments" it has been recognized as a codification and restatement of the law merchant, and has in fact been applied to them by analogy.

Thus the holder of the check reading "Pay A" establishes his case by production of the instrument and proof of signatures; and the burden of proving want of consideration or any other defense is upon the obligor. Such a check passes by indorsement and delivery without words of assignment, and the indorser undertakes greater liabilities than those of an assignor. This section resolves a conflict in the decisions as to the extent of that undertaking by providing in effect that the indorser of such an instrument is not distinguished from any indorser of a negotiable instrument. The indorser is entitled to presentment, notice of dishonor and protest, and the procedure and liabilities in bank collection are the same. The rules as to alteration, the filling of blanks, accommodation parties, the liability of signing agents, discharge, and the like are those applied to negotiable instruments.

In short, the "non-negotiable instrument" is treated as a negotiable instrument, so far as its form permits. Since it lacks words of negotiability there can be no holder in due course of such an instrument, and any provision of any section of this Article peculiar to a holder in due course cannot apply to it. With this exception, such instruments are covered by all sections of this Article.

Cross Reference:

Section 3–104.

Definitional Cross References:

"Bearer". Section 1–201.
"Holder in due course". Section 3–302.
"Instrument". Section 3–102.
"Term". Section 1–201.

APPENDIX B

ARTICLE 4

BANK DEPOSITS AND COLLECTIONS

(Official Comments omitted)

PART 1
GENERAL PROVISIONS AND DEFINITIONS

§ 4-101. Short Title.

This Article shall be known and may be cited as Uniform Commercial Code—Bank Deposits and Collections.

§ 4-102. Applicability.

(1) To the extent that items within this Article are also within the scope of Articles 3 and 8, they are subject to the provisions of those Articles. In the event of conflict the provisions of this Article govern those of Article 3 but the provisions of Article 8 govern those of this Article.

(2) The liability of a bank for action or non-action with respect to any item handled by it for purposes of presentment, payment or collection is governed by the law of the place where the bank is located. In the case of action or non-action by or at a branch or separate office of a bank, its liability is governed by the law of the place where the branch or separate office is located.

§ 4-103. Variation by Agreement; Measure of Damages; Certain Action Constituting Ordinary Care.

(1) The effect of the provisions of this Article may be varied by agreement except that no agreement can disclaim a bank's responsibility for its own lack of good faith or failure to exercise ordinary care or can limit the measure of damages for such lack or failure; but the parties may by agreement determine the standards by which such responsibility is to be measured if such standards are not manifestly unreasonable.

(2) Federal Reserve regulations and operating letters, clearing house rules, and the like, have the effect of agreements under subsection (1), whether or not specifically assented to by all parties interested in items handled.

(3) Action or non-action approved by this Article or pursuant to Federal Reserve regulations or operating letters constitutes the exercise of ordinary care and, in the absence of special instructions, action or non-action consistent with clearing house rules and the like or with a general banking usage not disapproved by this Article, prima facie constitutes the exercise of ordinary care.

(4) The specification or approval of certain procedures by this Article does not constitute disapproval of other procedures which may be reasonable under the circumstances.

(5) The measure of damages for failure to exercise ordinary care in handling an item is the amount of the item reduced by an amount which could not have been realized by the use of ordinary care, and where there is bad faith it includes other damages, if any, suffered by the party as a proximate consequence.

§ 4–104. Definitions and Index of Definitions.

(1) In this Article unless the context otherwise requires

(a) "Account" means any account with a bank and includes a checking, time, interest or savings account;

(b) "Afternoon" means the period of a day between noon and midnight;

(c) "Banking day" means that part of any day on which a bank is open to the public for carrying on substantially all of its banking functions;

(d) "Clearing house" means any association of banks or other payors regularly clearing items;

(e) "Customer" means any person having an account with a bank or for whom a bank has agreed to collect items and includes a bank carrying an account with another bank;

(f) "Documentary draft" means any negotiable or non-negotiable draft with accompanying documents, securities or other papers to be delivered against honor of the draft;

(g) "Item" means any instrument for the payment of money even though it is not negotiable but does not include money;

(h) "Midnight deadline" with respect to a bank is midnight on its next banking day following the banking day on which it receives the relevant item or notice or from which the time for taking action commences to run, whichever is later;

(i) "Properly payable" includes the availability of funds for payment at the time of decision to pay or dishonor;

(j) "Settle" means to pay in cash, by clearing house settlement, in a charge or credit or by remittance, or otherwise as instructed. A settlement may be either provisional or final;

(k) "Suspends payments" with respect to a bank means that it has been closed by order of the supervisory authorities, that a public officer has been appointed to take it over or that it ceases or refuses to make payments in the ordinary course of business.

(2) Other definitions applying to this Article and the sections in which they appear are:

"Collecting bank"	Section 4–105.
"Depositary bank"	Section 4–105.
"Intermediary bank"	Section 4–105.
"Payor bank"	Section 4–105.
"Presenting bank"	Section 4–105.
"Remitting bank"	Section 4–105.

(3) The following definitions in other Articles apply to this Article:

"Acceptance"	Section 3–410.
"Certificate of deposit"	Section 3–104.
"Certification"	Section 3–411.
"Check"	Section 3–104.
"Draft"	Section 3–104.
"Holder in due course"	Section 3–302.
"Notice of dishonor"	Section 3–508.
"Presentment"	Section 3–504.
"Protest"	Section 3–509.
"Secondary party"	Section 3–102.

(4) In addition Article 1 contains general definitions and principles of construction and interpretation applicable throughout this Article.

§ 4-105. "Depositary Bank"; "Intermediary Bank"; "Collecting Bank"; "Payor Bank"; "Presenting Bank"; "Remitting Bank".

In this Article unless the context otherwise requires:

(a) "Depositary bank" means the first bank to which an item is transferred for collection even though it is also the payor bank;

(b) "Payor bank" means a bank by which an item is payable as drawn or accepted;

(c) "Intermediary bank" means any bank to which an item is transferred in course of collection except the depositary or payor bank;

(d) "Collecting bank" means any bank handling the item for collection except the payor bank;

(e) "Presenting bank" means any bank presenting an item except a payor bank;

(f) "Remitting bank" means any payor or intermediary bank remitting for an item.

§ 4-106. Separate Office of a Bank.

A branch or separate office of a bank [maintaining its own deposit ledgers] is a separate bank for the purpose of computing the time within which and determining the place at or to which action may be taken or notices or orders shall be given under this Article and under Article 3.

As amended in 1962.

Note: *The brackets are to make it optional with the several states whether to require a branch to maintain its own deposit ledgers in order to be considered to be a separate bank for certain purposes under Article 4. In some states "maintaining its own deposit ledgers" is a satisfactory test. In others branch banking practices are such that this test would not be suitable.*

§ 4-107. Time of Receipt of Items.

(1) For the purpose of allowing time to process items, prove balances and make the necessary entries on its books to determine its position for the day, a bank may fix an afternoon hour of 2 P.M. or later as a cut-off hour for the handling of money and items and the making of entries on its books.

(2) Any item or deposit of money received on any day after a cut-off hour so fixed or after the close of the banking day may be treated as being received at the opening of the next banking day.

§ 4-108. Delays.

(1) Unless otherwise instructed, a collecting bank in a good faith effort to secure payment may, in the case of specific items and with or without the approval of any person involved, waive, modify or extend time limits imposed or permitted by this Act for a period not in excess of an additional banking day without discharge of secondary parties and without liability to its transferor or any prior party.

(2) Delay by a collecting bank or payor bank beyond time limits prescribed or permitted by this Act or by instructions is excused if caused by interruption of communication facilities, suspension of payments by another bank, war, emergency conditions or other circumstances beyond the control of the bank provided it exercises such diligence as the circumstances require.

§ 4-109. Process of Posting.

The "process of posting" means the usual procedure followed by a payor bank in determining to pay an item and in recording the payment including one or more of the following or other steps as determined by the bank:

(a) verification of any signature;

(b) ascertaining that sufficient funds are available;

(c) affixing a "paid" or other stamp;

(d) entering a charge or entry to a customer's account;

(e) correcting or reversing an entry or erroneous action with respect to the item.

Added in 1962.

PART 2

COLLECTION OF ITEMS: DEPOSITARY AND COLLECTING BANKS

§ 4-201. Presumption and Duration of Agency Status of Collecting Banks and Provisional Status of Credits; Applicability of Article; Item Indorsed "Pay Any Bank".

(1) Unless a contrary intent clearly appears and prior to the time that a settlement given by a collecting bank for an item is or becomes final (subsection (3) of Section 4-211 and Sections 4-212 and 4-213) the bank is an agent or sub-agent of the owner of the item and any settlement given for the item is provisional. This provision applies regardless of the form of indorsement or lack of indorsement and even though credit given for the item is subject to immediate withdrawal as of right or is in fact withdrawn; but the continuance of ownership of an item by its owner and any rights of the owner to proceeds of the item are subject to rights of a collecting bank such as those resulting from outstanding advances on the item and valid rights of setoff. When an item is handled by banks for purposes of presentment, payment and collection, the relevant provisions of this Article apply even though action of parties clearly establishes that a particular bank has purchased the item and is the owner of it.

(2) After an item has been indorsed with the words "pay any bank" or the like, only a bank may acquire the rights of a holder

(a) until the item has been returned to the customer initiating collection; or

(b) until the item has been specially indorsed by a bank to a person who is not a bank.

§ 4-202. Responsibility for Collection; When Action Seasonable.

(1) A collecting bank must use ordinary care in

(a) presenting an item or sending it for presentment; and

(b) sending notice of dishonor or non-payment or returning an item other than a documentary draft to the bank's transferor [or directly to the depositary bank under subsection (2) of Section 4-212] (*see note to Section 4-212*) after learning that the item has not been paid or accepted, as the case may be; and

(c) settling for an item when the bank receives final settlement; and

(d) making or providing for any necessary protest; and

(e) notifying its transferor of any loss or delay in transit within a reasonable time after discovery thereof.

(2) A collecting bank taking proper action before its midnight deadline following receipt of an item, notice or payment acts seasonably; taking proper action within a reasonably longer time may be seasonable but the bank has the burden of so establishing.

(3) Subject to subsection (1)(a), a bank is not liable for the insolvency, neglect, misconduct, mistake or default of another bank or person or for loss or destruction of an item in transit or in the possession of others.

§ 4-203. Effect of Instructions.

Subject to the provisions of Article 3 concerning conversion of instruments (Section 3-419) and the provisions of both Article 3 and this Article concerning restrictive indorsements only a collecting bank's transferor can give instructions which affect the bank or constitute notice to it and a collecting bank is not liable to prior parties for any action taken pursuant to such instructions or in accordance with any agreement with its transferor.

§ 4–204. Methods of Sending and Presenting; Sending Direct to Payor Bank.

(1) A collecting bank must send items by reasonably prompt method taking into consideration any relevant instructions, the nature of the item, the number of such items on hand, and the cost of collection involved and the method generally used by it or others to present such items.

(2) A collecting bank may send

(a) any item direct to the payor bank;

(b) any item to any non-bank payor if authorized by its transferor; and

(c) any item other than documentary drafts to any non-bank payor, if authorized by Federal Reserve regulation or operating letter, clearing house rule or the like.

(3) Presentment may be made by a presenting bank at a place where the payor bank has requested that presentment be made.

As amended in 1962.

§ 4–205. Supplying Missing Indorsement; No Notice from Prior Indorsement.

(1) A depositary bank which has taken an item for collection may supply any indorsement of the customer which is necessary to title unless the item contains the words "payee's indorsement required" or the like. In the absence of such a requirement a statement placed on the item by the depositary bank to the effect that the item was deposited by a customer or credited to his account is effective as the customer's indorsement.

(2) An intermediary bank, or payor bank which is not a depositary bank, is neither given notice nor otherwise affected by a restrictive indorsement of any person except the bank's immediate transferor.

§ 4–206. Transfer Between Banks.

Any agreed method which identifies the transferor bank is sufficient for the item's further transfer to another bank.

§ 4–207. Warranties of Customer and Collecting Bank on Transfer or Presentment of Items; Time for Claims.

(1) Each customer or collecting bank who obtains payment or acceptance of an item and each prior customer and collecting bank warrants to the payor bank or other payor who in good faith pays or accepts the item that

(a) he has a good title to the item or is authorized to obtain payment or acceptance on behalf of one who has a good title; and

(b) he has no knowledge that the signature of the maker or drawer is unauthorized, except that this warranty is not given by any customer or collecting bank that is a holder in due course and acts in good faith

(i) to a maker with respect to the maker's own signature; or

(ii) to a drawer with respect to the drawer's own signature, whether or not the drawer is also the drawee; or

(iii) to an acceptor of an item if the holder in due course took the item after the acceptance or obtained the acceptance without knowledge that the drawer's signature was unauthorized; and

(c) the item has not been materially altered, except that this warranty is not given by any customer or collecting bank that is a holder in due course and acts in good faith

(i) to the maker of a note; or

(ii) to the drawer of a draft whether or not the drawer is also the drawee; or

(iii) to the acceptor of an item with respect to an alteration made prior to the acceptance if the holder in due course took the item after the acceptance, even though the acceptance provided "payable as originally drawn" or equivalent terms; or

(iv) to the acceptor of an item with respect to an alteration made after the acceptance.

(2) Each customer and collecting bank who transfers an item and receives a settlement or other consideration for it warrants to his transferee and to any subsequent collecting bank who takes the item in good faith that

(a) he has a good title to the item or is authorized to obtain payment or acceptance on behalf of one who has a good title and the transfer is otherwise rightful; and

(b) all signatures are genuine or authorized; and

(c) the item has not been materially altered; and

(d) no defense of any party is good against him; and

(e) he has no knowledge of any insolvency proceeding instituted with respect to the maker or acceptor or the drawer of an unaccepted item.

In addition each customer and collecting bank so transferring an item and receiving a settlement or other consideration engages that upon dishonor and any necessary notice of dishonor and protest he will take up the item.

(3) The warranties and the engagement to honor set forth in the two preceding subsections arise notwithstanding the absence of indorsement or words of guaranty or warranty in the transfer or presentment and a collecting bank remains liable for their breach despite remittance to its transferor. Damages for breach of such warranties or engagement to honor shall not exceed the consideration received by the customer or collecting bank responsible plus finance charges and expenses related to the item, if any.

(4) Unless a claim for breach of warranty under this section is made within a reasonable time after the person claiming learns of the breach, the person liable is discharged to the extent of any loss caused by the delay in making claim.

§ 4-208. Security Interest of Collecting Bank in Items, Accompanying Documents and Proceeds.

(1) A bank has a security interest in an item and any accompanying documents or the proceeds of either

(a) in case of an item deposited in an account to the extent to which credit given for the item has been withdrawn or applied;

(b) in case of an item for which it has given credit available for withdrawal as of right, to the extent of the credit given whether or not the credit is drawn upon and whether or not there is a right of charge-back; or

(c) if it makes an advance on or against the item.

(2) When credit which has been given for several items received at one time or pursuant to a single agreement is withdrawn or applied in part the security interest remains upon all the items, any accompanying documents or the proceeds of either. For the purpose of this section, credits first given are first withdrawn.

(3) Receipt by a collecting bank of a final settlement for an item is a realization on its security interest in the item, accompanying documents and proceeds. To the extent and so long as the bank does not receive final settlement for the item or give up possession of the item or accompanying documents for purposes other than collection, the security interest continues and is subject to the provisions of Article 9 except that

(a) no security agreement is necessary to make the security interest enforceable (subsection (1)(a) of Section 9–203); and

(b) no filing is required to perfect the security interest; and

(c) the security interest has priority over conflicting perfected security interests in the item, accompanying documents or proceeds.

§ 4–209. When Bank Gives Value for Purposes of Holder in Due Course.

For purposes of determining its status as a holder in due course, the bank has given value to the extent that it has a security interest in an item provided that the bank otherwise complies with the requirements of Section 3–302 on what constitutes a holder in due course.

§ 4–210. Presentment by Notice of Item Not Payable by, Through or at a Bank; Liability of Secondary Parties.

(1) Unless otherwise instructed, a collecting bank may present an item not payable by, through or at a bank by sending to the party to accept or pay a written notice that the bank holds the item for acceptance or payment. The notice must be sent in time to be received on or before the day when presentment is due and the bank must meet any requirement of the party to accept or pay under Section 3–505 by the close of the bank's next banking day after it knows of the requirement.

(2) Where presentment is made by notice and neither honor nor request for compliance with a requirement under Section 3–505 is received by the close of business on the day after maturity or in the case of demand items by the close of business on the third banking day after notice was sent, the presenting bank may treat the item as dishonored and charge any secondary party by sending him notice of the facts.

§ 4–211. Media of Remittance; Provisional and Final Settlement in Remittance Cases.

(1) A collecting bank may take in settlement of an item

(a) a check of the remitting bank or of another bank on any bank except the remitting bank; or

(b) a cashier's check or similar primary obligation of a remitting bank which is a member of or clears through a member of the same clearing house or group as the collecting bank; or

(c) appropriate authority to charge an account of the remitting bank or of another bank with the collecting bank; or

(d) if the item is drawn upon or payable by a person other than a bank, a cashier's check, certified check or other bank check or obligation.

(2) If before its midnight deadline the collecting bank properly dishonors a remittance check or authorization to charge on itself or presents or forwards for collection a remittance instrument of or on another bank which is of a kind approved by subsection (1) or has not been authorized by it, the collecting bank is not liable to prior parties in the event of the dishonor of such check, instrument or authorization.

(3) A settlement for an item by means of a remittance instrument or authorization to charge is or becomes a final settlement as to both the person making and the person receiving the settlement

(a) if the remittance instrument or authorization to charge is of a kind approved by subsection (1) or has not been authorized by the person receiving the settlement and in either case the person receiving the settlement acts seasonably before its midnight deadline in presenting, forwarding for collection or paying the instrument or authorization,—at the time the remittance instrument or authorization is finally paid by the payor by which it is payable;

(b) if the person receiving the settlement has authorized remittance by a non-bank check or obligation or by a cashier's check or similar primary obligation of or a check upon the payor or other remitting bank which is not of a kind approved by subsection (1)(b),—at the time of the receipt of such remittance check or obligation; or

(c) if in a case not covered by sub-paragraphs (a) or (b) the person receiving the settlement fails to seasonably present, forward for collection, pay or return a remittance instrument or authorization to it to charge before its midnight deadline,—at such midnight deadline.

§ 4–212. Right of Charge-Back or Refund.

(1) If a collecting bank has made provisional settlement with its customer for an item and itself fails by reason of dishonor, suspension of payments by a bank or otherwise to receive a settlement for the item which is or becomes final, the bank may revoke the settlement given by it, charge back the amount of any credit given for the item to its customer's account or obtain refund from its customer whether or not it is able to return the items if by its midnight deadline or within a longer reasonable time after it learns the facts it returns the item or sends notification of the facts. These rights to revoke, charge-back and obtain refund terminate if and when a settlement for the item received by the bank is or becomes final (subsection (3) of Section 4–211 and subsections (2) and (3) of Section 4–213).

[(2) Within the time and manner prescribed by this section and Section 4–301, an intermediary or payor bank, as the case may be, may return an unpaid item directly to the depositary bank and may send for collection a draft on the depositary bank and obtain reimbursement. In such case, if the depositary bank has received provisional settlement for the item, it must reimburse the bank drawing the draft and any provisional credits for the item between banks shall become and remain final.]

Note: *Direct returns is recognized as an innovation that is not yet established bank practice, and therefore, Paragraph 2 has been bracketed. Some lawyers have doubts whether it should be included in legislation or left to development by agreement.*

(3) A depositary bank which is also the payor may charge-back the amount of an item to its customer's account or obtain refund in accordance with the section governing return of an item received by a payor bank for credit on its books. (Section 4–301).

(4) The right to charge-back is not affected by

(a) prior use of the credit given for the item; or

(b) failure by any bank to exercise ordinary care with respect to the item but any bank so failing remains liable.

(5) A failure to charge-back or claim refund does not affect other rights of the bank against the customer or any other party.

(6) If credit is given in dollars as the equivalent of the value of an item payable in a foreign currency the dollar amount of any charge-back or refund shall be calculated on the basis of the buying sight rate for the foreign currency prevailing on the day when the person entitled to the charge-back or refund learns that it will not receive payment in ordinary course.

§ 4–213. Final Payment of Item by Payor Bank; When Provisional Debits and Credits Become Final; When Certain Credits Become Available for Withdrawal.

(1) An item is finally paid by a payor bank when the bank has done any of the following, whichever happens first:

(a) paid the item in cash; or

(b) settled for the item without reserving a right to revoke the settlement and without having such right under statute, clearing house rule or agreement; or

(c) completed the process of posting the item to the indicated account of the drawer, maker or other person to be charged therewith; or

(d) made a provisional settlement for the item and failed to revoke the settlement in the time and manner permitted by statute, clearing house rule or agreement.

Upon a final payment under subparagraphs (b), (c) or (d) the payor bank shall be accountable for the amount of the item.

(2) If provisional settlement for an item between the presenting and payor banks is made through a clearing house or by debits or credits in an account between them, then to the extent that provisional debits or credits for the item are entered in accounts between the presenting and payor banks or between the presenting and successive prior collecting banks seriatim, they become final upon final payment of the item by the payor bank.

(3) If a collecting bank receives a settlement for an item which is or becomes final (subsection (3) of Section 4-211, subsection (2) of Section 4-213) the bank is accountable to its customer for the amount of the item and any provisional credit given for the item in an account with its customer becomes final.

(4) Subject to any right of the bank to apply the credit to an obligation of the customer, credit given by a bank for an item in an account with its customer becomes available for withdrawal as of right

(a) in any case where the bank has received a provisional settlement for the item,—when such settlement becomes final and the bank has had a reasonable time to learn that the settlement is final;

(b) in any case where the bank is both a depositary bank and a payor bank and the item is finally paid,—at the opening of the bank's second banking day following receipt of the item.

(5) A deposit of money in a bank is final when made but, subject to any right of the bank to apply the deposit to an obligation of the customer, the deposit becomes available for withdrawal as of right at the opening of the bank's next banking day following receipt of the deposit.

§ 4-214. Insolvency and Preference.

(1) Any item in or coming into the possession of a payor or collecting bank which suspends payment and which item is not finally paid shall be returned by the receiver, trustee or agent in charge of the closed bank to the presenting bank or the closed bank's customer.

(2) If a payor bank finally pays an item and suspends payments without making a settlement for the item with its customer or the presenting bank which settlement is or becomes final, the owner of the item has a preferred claim against the payor bank.

(3) If a payor bank gives or a collecting bank gives or receives a provisional settlement for an item and thereafter suspends payments, the suspension does not prevent or interfere with the settlement becoming final if such finality occurs automatically upon the lapse of certain time or the happening of certain events (subsection (3) of Section 4-211, subsections (1)(d), (2) and (3) of Section 4-213).

(4) If a collecting bank receives from subsequent parties settlement for an item which settlement is or becomes final and suspends payments without making a settlement for the item with its customer which is or becomes final, the owner of the item has a preferred claim against such collecting bank.

PART 3

COLLECTION OF ITEMS: PAYOR BANKS

§ 4-301. Deferred Posting; Recovery of Payment by Return of Items; Time of Dishonor.

(1) Where an authorized settlement for a demand item (other than a documentary draft) received by a payor bank otherwise than for immediate payment over the counter has been made before midnight of the banking day of receipt the payor bank may revoke the settlement and recover any payment if before it has made final payment (subsection (1) of Section 4-213) and before its midnight deadline it

(a) returns the item; or

(b) sends written notice of dishonor or nonpayment if the item is held for protest or is otherwise unavailable for return.

(2) If a demand item is received by a payor bank for credit on its books it may return such item or send notice of dishonor and may revoke any credit given or recover the amount thereof withdrawn by its customer, if it acts within the time limit and in the manner specified in the preceding subsection.

(3) Unless previous notice of dishonor has been sent an item is dishonored at the time when for purposes of dishonor it is returned or notice sent in accordance with this section.

(4) An item is returned:

(a) as to an item received through a clearing house, when it is delivered to the presenting or last collecting bank or to the clearing house or is sent or delivered in accordance with its rules; or

(b) in all other cases, when it is sent or delivered to the bank's customer or transferor or pursuant to his instructions.

§ 4-302. Payor Bank's Responsibility for Late Return of Item.

In the absence of a valid defense such as breach of a presentment warranty (subsection (1) of Section 4-207), settlement effected or the like, if an item is presented on and received by a payor bank the bank is accountable for the amount of

(a) a demand item other than a documentary draft whether properly payable or not if the bank, in any case where it is not also the depositary bank, retains the item beyond midnight of the banking day of receipt without settling for it or, regardless of whether it is also the depositary bank, does not pay or return the item or send notice of dishonor until after its midnight deadline; or

(b) any other properly payable item unless within the time allowed for acceptance or payment of that item the bank either accepts or pays the item or returns it and accompanying documents.

§ 4-303. When Items Subject to Notice, Stop-Order, Legal Process or Setoff; Order in Which Items May Be Charged or Certified.

(1) Any knowledge, notice or stop-order received by, legal process served upon or setoff exercised by a payor bank, whether or not effective under other rules of law to terminate, suspend or modify the bank's right or duty to pay an item or to charge its customer's account for the item, comes too late to so terminate, suspend or modify such right or duty if the knowledge, notice, stop-order or legal process is received or served and a reasonable time for the bank to act thereon expires or the setoff is exercised after the bank has done any of the following:

(a) accepted or certified the item;

(b) paid the item in cash;

(c) settled for the item without reserving a right to revoke the settlement and without having such right under statute, clearing house rule or agreement;

(d) completed the process of posting the item to the indicated account of the drawer, maker or other person to be charged therewith or otherwise has evidenced by examination of such indicated account and by action its decision to pay the item; or

(e) become accountable for the amount of the item under subsection (1)(d) of Section 4-213 and Section 4-302 dealing with the payor bank's responsibility for late return of items.

(2) Subject to the provisions of subsection (1) items may be accepted, paid, certified or charged to the indicated account of its customer in any order convenient to the bank.

PART 4

RELATIONSHIP BETWEEN PAYOR BANK AND ITS CUSTOMER

§ 4-401. When Bank May Charge Customer's Account.

(1) As against its customer, a bank may charge against his account any item which is otherwise properly payable from that account even though the charge creates an overdraft.

(2) A bank which in good faith makes payment to a holder may charge the indicated account of its customer according to

(a) the original tenor of his altered item; or

(b) the tenor of his completed item, even though the bank knows the item has been completed unless the bank has notice that the completion was improper.

§ 4-402. Bank's Liability to Customer for Wrongful Dishonor.

A payor bank is liable to its customer for damages proximately caused by the wrongful dishonor of an item. When the dishonor occurs through mistake liability is limited to actual damages proved. If so proximately caused and proved damages may include damages for an arrest or prosecution of the customer or other consequential damages. Whether any consequential damages are proximately caused by the wrongful dishonor is a question of fact to be determined in each case.

§ 4-403. Customer's Right to Stop Payment; Burden of Proof of Loss.

(1) A customer may by order to his bank stop payment of any item payable for his account but the order must be received at such time and in such manner as to afford the bank a reasonable opportunity to act on it prior to any action by the bank with respect to the item described in Section 4-303.

(2) An oral order is binding upon the bank only for fourteen calendar days unless confirmed in writing within that period. A written order is effective for only six months unless renewed in writing.

(3) The burden of establishing the fact and amount of loss resulting from the payment of an item contrary to a binding stop payment order is on the customer.

§ 4-404. Bank Not Obligated to Pay Check More Than Six Months Old.

A bank is under no obligation to a customer having a checking account to pay a check, other than a certified check, which is presented more than six months after its date, but it may charge its customer's account for a payment made thereafter in good faith.

§ 4-405. Death or Incompetence of Customer.

(1) A payor or collecting bank's authority to accept, pay or collect an item or to account for proceeds of its collection if otherwise effective is not rendered ineffective by incompetence of a customer of either bank existing at the time the item is issued or its collection is undertaken if the bank does not know of an adjudication of incompetence. Neither death nor incompetence of a customer revokes such authority to accept, pay, collect or account until the bank knows of the fact of death or of an adjudication of incompetence and has reasonable opportunity to act on it.

(2) Even with knowledge a bank may for 10 days after the date of death pay or certify checks drawn on or prior to that date unless ordered to stop payment by a person claiming an interest in the account.

§ 4-406. Customer's Duty to Discover and Report Unauthorized Signature or Alteration.

(1) When a bank sends to its customer a statement of account accompanied by items paid in good faith in support of the debit entries or holds the statement and items pursuant to a request or instructions of its customer or otherwise in a reasonable manner makes the statement and items available to the customer, the customer must exercise reasonable care and promptness to examine the statement and items to discover his unauthorized signature or any alteration on an item and must notify the bank promptly after discovery thereof.

(2) If the bank establishes that the customer failed with respect to an item to comply with the duties imposed on the customer by subsection (1) the customer is precluded from asserting against the bank

(a) his unauthorized signature or any alteration on the item if the bank also establishes that it suffered a loss by reason of such failure; and

(b) an unauthorized signature or alteration by the same wrongdoer on any other item paid in good faith by the bank after the first item and statement was available to the customer for a reasonable period not exceeding fourteen calendar days and before the bank receives notification from the customer of any such unauthorized signature or alteration.

(3) The preclusion under subsection (2) does not apply if the customer establishes lack of ordinary care on the part of the bank in paying the item(s).

(4) Without regard to care or lack of care of either the customer or the bank a customer who does not within one year from the time the statement and items are made available to the customer (subsection (1)) discover and report his unauthorized signature or any alteration on the face or back of the item or does not within 3 years from that time discover and report any unauthorized indorsement is precluded from asserting against the bank such unauthorized signature or indorsement or such alteration.

(5) If under this section a payor bank has a valid defense against a claim of a customer upon or resulting from payment of an item and waives or fails upon request to assert the defense the bank may not assert against any collecting bank or other prior party presenting or transferring the item a claim based upon the unauthorized signature or alteration giving rise to the customer's claim.

§ 4-407. Payor Bank's Right to Subrogation on Improper Payment.

If a payor bank has paid an item over the stop payment order of the drawer or maker or otherwise under circumstances giving a basis for objection by the drawer or maker, to prevent unjust enrichment and only to the extent necessary to prevent loss to the bank by reason of its payment of the item, the payor bank shall be subrogated to the rights

(a) of any holder in due course on the item against the drawer or maker; and

(b) of the payee or any other holder of the item against the drawer or maker either on the item or under the transaction out of which the item arose; and

(c) of the drawer or maker against the payee or any other holder of the item with respect to the transaction out of which the item arose.

PART 5

COLLECTION OF DOCUMENTARY DRAFTS

§ 4-501. Handling of Documentary Drafts; Duty to Send for Presentment and to Notify Customer of Dishonor.

A bank which takes a documentary draft for collection must present or send the draft and accompanying documents for presentment and upon learning that the draft has not been paid or accepted in due course must seasonably notify its customer of such fact even though it may have discounted or bought the draft or extended credit available for withdrawal as of right.

§ 4-502. Presentment of "On Arrival" Drafts.

When a draft or the relevant instructions require presentment "on arrival", "when goods arrive" or the like, the collecting bank need not present until in its judgment a reasonable time for arrival of the goods has expired. Refusal to pay or accept because the goods have not arrived is not dishonor; the bank must notify its transferor of such refusal but need not present the draft again until it is instructed to do so or learns of the arrival of the goods.

§ 4-503. Responsibility of Presenting Bank for Documents and Goods; Report of Reasons for Dishonor; Referee in Case of Need.

Unless otherwise instructed and except as provided in Article 5 a bank presenting a documentary draft

(a) must deliver the documents to the drawee on acceptance of the draft if it is payable more than three days after presentment; otherwise, only on payment; and

(b) upon dishonor, either in the case of presentment for acceptance or presentment for payment, may seek and follow instructions from any referee in case of need designated in the draft or if the presenting bank does not choose to utilize his services it must use diligence and good faith to ascertain the reason for dishonor, must notify its transferor of the dishonor and of the results of its effort to ascertain the reasons therefor and must request instructions.

But the presenting bank is under no obligation with respect to goods represented by the documents except to follow any reasonable instructions seasonably received; it has a right to reimbursement for any expense incurred in following instructions and to prepayment of or indemnity for such expenses.

§ 4–504. Privilege of Presenting Bank to Deal With Goods; Security Interest for Expenses.

(1) A presenting bank which, following the dishonor of a documentary draft, has seasonably requested instructions but does not receive them within a reasonable time may store, sell, or otherwise deal with the goods in any reasonable manner.

(2) For its reasonable expenses incurred by action under subsection (1) the presenting bank has a lien upon the goods or their proceeds, which may be foreclosed in the same manner as an unpaid seller's lien.

APPENDIX C

2002 AMENDMENTS TO UCC ARTICLES 3 AND 4

In strikeout/underline format

DRAFTING COMMITTEE TO AMEND UNIFORM COMMERCIAL CODE ARTICLES 3 AND 4

Edwin E. Smith, Boston, Massachusetts, *Chair*
Michael M. Greenfield, St. Louis, Missouri, *The American Law Institute Representative*
Michael Houghton, Wilmington, Delaware, *Enactment Plan Coordinator*
H. Kathleen Patchel, Indianapolis, Indiana
Donald J. Rapson, Deal, New Jersey, *The American Law Institute Representative*
Carlyle C. Ring, Jr., Washington, DC
Paul M. Shupack, New York, New York, *The American Law Institute Representative*
Ronald Mann, Ann Arbor, Michigan, *Reporter*

EX OFFICIO

K. King Burnett, Salisbury, Maryland, *President*
Joseph P. Mazurek, Helena, Montana, *Division Chair*

AMERICAN BAR ASSOCIATION ADVISORS

Stephanie Heller, Brooklyn, New York, *ABA Advisor*
Michael A. Ferry, St. Louis, Missouri, *ABA Business Law Section Advisor*
Richard L. Field, Cliffside Park, New Jersey, *ABA Science and Technology Section Advisor*

EXECUTIVE DIRECTOR

William H. Henning, Columbia, Missouri, *Executive Director*
Fred H. Miller, Norman, Oklahoma, *Executive Director Emeritus*
William J. Pierce, Ann Arbor, Michigan, *Executive Director Emeritus*

PREFATORY NOTE

This project involves a small number of amendments to Articles 3 and 4 with respect to which there is a general consensus that the need for reform is plain and the opportunity for justifiable controversy small. The specific amendments cover the following topics.

1. Transferring Lost Instruments.—At least one case has held that the receiver of a failed bank cannot enforce an instrument transferred to it in the portfolio of a failed bank if the instrument was lost before the transfer. The result in that case poses a serious problem for the FDIC. An amendment to UCC § 3–309 calls for a contrary result, making it clear that the party seeking to enforce a lost instrument need not have been in possession of the instrument at the time that it was lost.

2. Payment and Discharge.—Amendments to UCC §§ 3–602 conform that provision to the rules for payment that appear in the *Restatement of Mortgages* and in the *Restatement of Contracts*.

3. Telephonically Generated Checks.—Several States have adopted non-uniform amendments dealing with the responsibility for unauthorized telephone-generated checks. The amendments include warranties that generally place the responsibility for such checks on depositary banks rather than payor

banks. The warranties are limited to items that are drawn on a consumer account and do not bear a manual signature.

4. Suretyship.—Amendments to UCC §§ 3–419 and 3–605 generally conform those provisions to the rules in the *Restatement of Suretyship and Guaranty*.

5. Electronic Communications.—Amendments to various provisions of Articles 3 and 4 implement the policy of the Uniform Electronic Transactions Act to remove unnecessary obstacles to electronic communications.

6. Consumer Notes.—A provision analogous to UCC § 9–404(d) indicates that a note for which the Federal Trade Commission requires a notice to be included will be treated is if the notice had been included.

7. United Nations Convention on International Bills of Exchange and International Promissory Notes.—The draft includes several comments indicating similarities and differences between Article 3 and the United Nations Convention, designed to facilitate implementation of the Convention if the United States ratifies that convention in the coming years.

AMENDMENTS TO ARTICLE 3

NEGOTIABLE INSTRUMENTS

§ 3–102. Subject Matter.

Official Comment

* * *

5. In 1989 the United Nations Commission on International Trade Law completed a Convention on International Bills of Exchange and International Promissory Notes. If the United States becomes a party to this Convention, the Convention will preempt state law with respect to international bills and notes governed by the Convention. Thus, an international bill of exchange or promissory note that meets the definition of instrument in Section 3–104 will not be governed by Article 3 if it is governed by the Convention. That Convention applies only to bills and notes that indicate on their face that they involve cross-border transactions. It does not apply at all to checks. Convention Articles 1(3), 2(1), 2(2). Moreover, because it applies only if the bill or note specifically calls for application of the Convention, Convention Article 1, there is little chance that the Convention will apply accidentally to a transaction that the parties intended to be governed by this Article. *Amendments approved by the Permanent Editorial Board for Uniform Commercial Code November 2, 2002.*

§ 3–103. Definitions.

(a) In this Article:

(1) "Acceptor" means a drawee who has accepted a draft.

(2) "Consumer account" means an account established by an individual primarily for personal, family, or household purposes.

(3) "Consumer transaction" means a transaction in which an individual incurs an obligation primarily for personal, family, or household purposes.

(4) "Drawee" means a person ordered in a draft to make payment.

~~(3)~~ (5) "Drawer" means a person who signs or is identified in a draft as a person ordering payment.

~~(4)~~ (6) ["Good faith" means honesty in fact and the observance of reasonable commercial standards of fair dealing.]

~~(5)~~ (7) "Maker" means a person who signs or is identified in a note as a person undertaking to pay.

~~(6)~~ (8) "Order" means a written instruction to pay money signed by the person giving the instruction. The instruction may be addressed to any person, including the person giving the instruction, or to one or more persons jointly or in the alternative but not in succession. An authorization to pay is not an order unless the person authorized to pay is also instructed to pay.

~~(7)~~ (9) "Ordinary care" in the case of a person engaged in business means observance of reasonable commercial standards, prevailing in the area in which the person is located, with respect to the business in which the person is engaged. In the case of a bank that takes an instrument for processing for collection or payment by automated means, reasonable commercial standards do not require the bank to examine the instrument if the failure to examine does not violate the bank's prescribed procedures and the bank's procedures do not vary unreasonably from general banking usage not disapproved by this Article or Article 4.

~~(8)~~ (10) "Party" means a party to an instrument.

(11) "Principal obligor," with respect to an instrument, means the accommodated party or any other party to the instrument against whom a secondary obligor has recourse under this article.

~~(9)~~ (12) "Promise" means a written undertaking to pay money signed by the person undertaking to pay. An acknowledgment of an obligation by the obligor is not a promise unless the obligor also undertakes to pay the obligation.

~~(10)~~ (13) "Prove" with respect to a fact means to meet the burden of establishing the fact (Section 1–201(8)).

(14) ["Record" means information that is inscribed on a tangible medium or that is stored in an electronic or other medium and is retrievable in perceivable form.]

~~(11)~~ (15) "Remitter" means a person who purchases an instrument from its issuer if the instrument is payable to an identified person other than the purchaser.

(16) "Remotely-created consumer item" means an item drawn on a consumer account, which is not created by the payor bank and does not bear a handwritten signature purporting to be the signature of the drawer.

(17) "Secondary obligor," with respect to an instrument, means (a) an indorser or an accommodation party, (b) a drawer having the obligation described in Section 3–414(d), or (c) any other party to the instrument that has recourse against another party to the instrument pursuant to Section 3–116(b).

(b) Other definitions applying to this Article and the sections in which they appear are:

"Acceptance" Section 3–409
"Accommodated party" Section 3–419
"Accommodation party" Section 3–419
"Account" Section 4–104
"Alteration" Section 3–407
"Anomalous indorsement" Section 3–205
"Blank indorsement" Section 3–205
"Cashier's check" Section 3–104
"Certificate of deposit" Section 3–104
"Certified check" Section 3–409
"Check" Section 3–104
"Consideration" Section 3–303
"Draft" Section 3–104
"Holder in due course" Section 3–302
"Incomplete instrument" Section 3–115
"Indorsement" Section 3–204
"Indorser" Section 3–204
"Instrument" Section 3–104
"Issue" Section 3–105
"Issuer" Section 3–105

"Negotiable instrument" Section 3–104
"Negotiation" Section 3–201
"Note" Section 3–104
"Payable at a definite time" Section 3–108
"Payable on demand" Section 3–108
"Payable to bearer" Section 3–109
"Payable to order" Section 3–109
"Payment" Section 3–602
"Person entitled to enforce" Section 3–301
"Presentment" Section 3–501
"Reacquisition" Section 3–207
"Special indorsement" Section 3–205
"Teller's check" Section 3–104
"Transfer of instrument" Section 3–203
"Traveler's check" Section 3–104
"Value" Section 3–303

(c) The following definitions in other Articles apply to this Article:

~~"Bank" Section 4–105~~
"Banking day" Section 4–104
"Clearing house" Section 4–104
"Collecting bank" Section 4–105
"Depositary bank" Section 4–105
"Documentary draft" Section 4–104
"Intermediary bank" Section 4–105
"Item" Section 4–104
"Payor bank" Section 4–105
"Suspends payments" Section 4–104

(d) In addition, Article 1 contains general definitions and principles of construction and interpretation applicable throughout this Article.

Legislative Note. A jurisdiction that enacts this statute that has not yet enacted the revised version of UCC Article 1 should add to Section 3–103 the definition of "good faith" that appears in the official version of Section 1–201(b)(20) and the definition of "record" that appears in the official version of Section 1–201(b)(31). Sections 3–103(a)(6) and (14) are reserved for that purpose. A jurisdiction that already has adopted or simultaneously adopts the revised Article 1 should not add those definitions, but should leave those numbers "reserved." If jurisdictions follow the numbering suggested here, the subsections will have the same numbering in all jurisdictions that have adopted these amendments (whether they have or have not adopted the revised version of UCC Article 1).

Official Comment

. . .

4. ~~Subsection (a)(4) introduces a definition of good faith to apply to Articles 3 and 4. Former Articles 3 and 4 used the definition in Section 1–201(19).~~ This Article now uses the broadened definition of good faith in revised Article 1. The definition requires not only honesty in fact but also "observance of reasonable commercial standards of fair dealing." Although fair dealing is a broad term that must be defined in context, it is clear that it is concerned with the fairness of conduct rather than the care with which an act is performed. Failure to exercise ordinary care in conducting a transaction is an entirely different concept than failure to deal fairly in conducting the transaction. Both fair dealing and ordinary care, which is defined in Section 3–103(a)(9), are to be judged in the light of reasonable commercial standards, but those standards in each case are directed to different aspects of commercial conduct.

5. Subsection (a)(9) is a definition of ordinary care which is applicable not only to Article 3 but to Article 4 as well. See Section 4–104(c). The general rule is stated in the first sentence of subsection (a)(9) and it applies both to banks and to persons engaged in businesses other than banking. Ordinary care means observance of reasonable commercial standards of the relevant businesses prevailing in the area in which the person is located. The second sentence of subsection (a)(9) is a particular rule limited to the duty of a bank to examine an instrument taken by a bank for processing for collection or payment by automated means. This particular rule applies

primarily to Section 4–406 and it is discussed in Comment 4 to that section. Nothing in Section 3–103(a)(9) is intended to prevent a customer from proving that the procedures followed by a bank are unreasonable, arbitrary, or unfair.

6. ~~In subsection (c) reference is made to a new definition of "bank" in amended Article 4.~~ The definition of consumer account includes a joint account established by more than one individual. See Section 1–106(1).

§ 3–104. Negotiable Instrument.

Official Comment

. . .

5. There are some differences between the requirements of Article 3 and the requirements included in Article 3 of the Convention on International Bills of Exchange and International Promissory Notes. Most obviously, the Convention does not include the limitation on extraneous undertakings set forth in Section 3–104(a)(3), and does not permit documents payable to bearer that would be permissible under Section 3–104(a)(1) and Section 3–109. See Convention Article 3. In most respects, however, the requirements of Section 3–104 and Article 3 of the Convention are quite similar. [Amendment approved by the Permanent Editorial Board for Uniform Commercial Code November 2, 2002.]

§ 3–106. Unconditional Promise or Order.

(a) Except as provided in this section, for the purposes of Section 3–104(a), a promise or order is unconditional unless it states (i) an express condition to payment, (ii) that the promise or order is subject to or governed by another ~~writing,~~ record, or (iii) that rights or obligations with respect to the promise or order are stated in another ~~writing.~~ record. A reference to another ~~writing~~ rccord does not of itself make the promise or order conditional.

(b) A promise or order is not made conditional (i) by a reference to another ~~writing~~ record for a statement of rights with respect to collateral, prepayment, or acceleration, or (ii) because payment is limited to resort to a particular fund or source.

. . .

§ 3–116. Joint and Several Liability; Contribution.

. . .

~~(c) Discharge of one party having joint and several liability by a person entitled to enforce the instrument does not affect the right under subsection (b) of a party having the same joint and several liability to receive contribution from the party discharged.~~

Official Comment

1. Subsection (a) replaces subsection (e) of former Section 3–118. Subsection (b) states contribution rights of parties with joint and several liability by referring to applicable law. But subsection (b) is subject to Section ~~3–419(e)~~ 3–419(f). If one of the parties with joint and several liability is an accommodation party and the other is the accommodated party, Section ~~3–419(e)~~ 3–419(f) applies. ~~Subsection (c) deals with discharge. The discharge of a jointly and severally liable obligor does not affect the right of other obligors to seek contribution from the discharged obligor.~~ Because one of the joint and several obligors may have recourse against the other joint and several obligor under subsection (b), each party that is jointly and severally liable under subsection (a) is a secondary obligor in part and a principal obligor in part, as those terms are defined in Section 3–103(a). Accordingly, Section 3–605 determines the effect of a release, an extension of time, or a modification of the obligation of one of the joint and several obligors, as well as the effect of an impairment of collateral provided by one of those obligors.

. . .

§ 3-118. Statute of Limitations.

Official Comment

. . .

7. One of the most significant differences between this Article and the Convention on International Bills of Exchange and International Promissory Notes is that the statute of limitation under the Convention generally is only four years, rather than the six years provided by this section. See Convention Article 84. [Amendments approved by the Permanent Editorial Board for Uniform Commercial Code November 2, 2002.]

§ 3-119. Notice of Right to Defend Action.

In an action for breach of an obligation for which a third person is answerable over pursuant to this article or article 4, the defendant may give the third person ~~written~~ notice of the litigation in a record, and the person notified may then give similar notice to any other person who is answerable over. if the notice states (i) that the person notified may come in and defend and (ii) that failure to do so will bind the person notified in an action later brought by the person giving the notice as to any determination of fact common to the two litigations, the person notified is so bound unless after seasonable receipt of the notice the person notified does come in and defend.

§ 3-203. Transfer of Instrument; Rights Acquired by Transfer.

Official Comment

. . .

6. The rules for transferring instruments set out in this section are similar to the rules in Article 13 of the Convention on International Bills of Exchange and International Promissory Notes. [Amendments approved by the Permanent Editorial Board for Uniform Commercial Code November 2, 2002.]

§ 3-205. Special Indorsement; Blank Indorsement; Anomalous Indorsement.

Official Comment

. . .

4. Articles 14 and 16 of the Convention on International Bills of Exchange and International Promissory Notes includes similar rules for blank and special indorsements. [Amendments approved by the Permanent Editorial Board for Uniform Commercial Code November 2, 2002.]

§ 3-301. Person Entitled to Enforce Instrument.

Official Comment

This section replaces former Section 3-301 that stated the rights of a holder. The rights stated in former Section 3-301 to transfer, negotiate, enforce, or discharge an instrument are stated in other sections of Article 3. In revised Article 3, Section 3-301 defines "person entitled to enforce" an instrument. The definition recognizes that enforcement is not limited to holders. The quoted phrase includes a person enforcing a lost or stolen instrument. Section 3-309. It also includes a person in possession of an instrument who is not a holder. A nonholder in possession of an instrument includes a person that acquired rights of a holder by subrogation or under Section 3-203(a). ~~It also includes any other person who under applicable law is a successor to the holder or otherwise acquires the holder's rights.~~ It also includes both a remitter that has received an instrument from the issuer but has not yet transferred or negotiated the instrument to another person and also any other person who under applicable law is a successor to the holder or otherwise acquires the holder's rights. [Amendments approved by the Permanent Editorial Board for Uniform Commercial Code November 2, 2002.]

§ 3-302. Holder in Due Course.

Official Comment

. . .

8. The status of holder in due course resembles the status of protected holder under Article 29 of the Convention on International Bills of Exchange and International Promissory Notes. The requirements for being a

protected holder under Article 29 generally track those of Section 3–302. [Amendment approved by the Permanent Editorial Board for Uniform Commercial Code November 2, 2002.]

§ 3–303. Value and Consideration.

Official Comment

. . .

6. The term "promise" in paragraph (a)(1) is used in the phrase "promise of performance" and for that reason does not have the specialized meaning given that term in Section 3–103(a)(12). See Section 1–201 ("Changes from Former Law"). No inference should be drawn from the decision to use the phrase "promise of performance," although the phrase does include the word "promise," which has the specialized definition set forth in Section 3–103. Indeed, that is true even though "undertaking" is used instead of "promise" in Section 3–104(a)(3). See Section 3–104 comment 1 (explaining the use of the term "undertaking" in Section 3–104 to avoid use of the defined term "promise"). [Amendment approved by the Permanent Editorial Board for Uniform Commercial Code November 2, 2002.]

§ 3–305. Defenses and Claims in Recoupment; Claims in Consumer Transactions.

(a) Except as ~~stated in subsection (b),~~ otherwise provided in this section, the right to enforce the obligation of a party to pay an instrument is subject to the following:

. . .

(e) In a consumer transaction, if law other than this article requires that an instrument include a statement to the effect that the rights of a holder or transferee are subject to a claim or defense that the issuer could assert against the original payee, and the instrument does not include such a statement:

(1) the instrument has the same effect as if the instrument included such a statement;

(2) the issuer may assert against the holder or transferee all claims and defenses that would have been available if the instrument included such a statement; and

(3) the extent to which claims may be asserted against the holder or transferee is determined as if the instrument included such a statement.

(f) This section is subject to law other than this article that establishes a different rule for consumer transactions.

Legislative Note: If a consumer protection law in this state addresses the same issue as subsection (g), it should be examined for consistency with subsection (g) and, if inconsistent, should be amended.

Official Comment

. . .

5. Subsection (d) applies to instruments signed for accommodation (Section 3–419) and this subsection equates the obligation of the accommodation party to that of the accommodated party. The accommodation party can assert whatever defense or claim the accommodated party had against the person enforcing the instrument. The only exceptions are discharge in bankruptcy, infancy and lack of capacity. The same rule does not apply to an indorsement by a holder of the instrument in negotiating the instrument. The indorser, as transferor, makes a warranty to the indorsee, as transferee, that no defense or claim in recoupment is good against the indorser. Section 3–416(a)(4). Thus, if the indorsee sues the indorser because of dishonor of the instrument, the indorser may not assert the defense or claim in recoupment of the maker or drawer against the indorsee.

Section 3–305(d) must be read in conjunction with Section 3–605, which provides rules (usually referred to as suretyship defenses) for determining when the obligation of an accommodation party is discharged, in whole or in part, because of some act or omission of a person entitled to enforce the instrument. To the extent a rule stated in Section 3–605 is inconsistent with Section 3–305(d), the Section 3–605 rule governs. For example, ~~under Section 3–605(b), discharge under Section 3–604 of the accommodated party does not discharge the accommodation party~~ Section 3–605(a) provides rules for determining when and to what extent a discharge of the accommodated party under Section 3–604 will discharge the accommodation party. As explained in Comment ~~3~~2 to Section 3–605, discharge of the accommodated party is normally part of a settlement under which the holder of a note accepts partial payment from an accommodated party who is financially unable to pay the entire amount of the note. If the holder then brings an action against the accommodation party to recover the remaining unpaid amount of the note, the accommodation party cannot use Section 3–305(d) to nullify Section 3–605(~~b~~a) by asserting the discharge of the accommodated party as a defense. On the other hand, suppose the accommodated party is a buyer of goods who issued the note to the seller who took the note for the buyer's obligation to pay for the goods. Suppose the buyer has a claim for breach of warranty with respect to the goods against the seller and the warranty claim may be asserted against the holder of the note. The warranty claim is a claim in recoupment. If the holder and the accommodated party reach a settlement under which the holder accepts payment less than the amount of the note in full satisfaction of the note and the warranty claim, the accommodation party could defend an action on the note by the holder by asserting the accord and satisfaction under Section 3–305(d). There is no conflict with Section 3–605(~~b~~a) because that provision is not intended to apply to settlement of disputed claims. ~~Another example of the use of Section 3–305(d) in cases in which Section 3–605 applies is stated in Comment 4 to Section 3–605. See PEB Commentary No. 11, dated February 10, 1994 [Appendix V, infra].~~

6. Subsection (e) is added to clarify the treatment of an instrument that omits the notice currently required by the Federal Trade Commission Rule related to certain consumer credit sales and consumer purchase money loans (16 C.F.R. Part 433). This subsection adopts the view that the instrument should be treated as if the language required by the FTC Rule were present. It is based on the language describing that rule in Section 3–106(d) and the analogous provision in Section 9–404(d).

7. Subsection (f) is modeled on Sections 9–403(e) and 9–404(c). It ensures that Section 3–305 is interpreted to accommodate relevant consumer-protection laws. The absence of such a provision from other sections in Article 3 should not justify any inference about the meaning of those sections.

8. Articles 28 and 30 of the Convention on International Bills of Exchange and International Promissory Notes includes a similar dichotomy, with a narrower group of defenses available against a protected holder under Articles 28(1) and 30 than are available under Article 28(2) against a holder that is not a protected holder.

§ 3–306. Claims to an Instrument.

Official Comment

This section expands on the reference to "claims to" the instrument mentioned in former Sections 3–305 and 3–306. Claims covered by the section include not only claims to ownership but also any other claim of a property or possessory right. It includes the claim to a lien or the claim of a person in rightful possession of an instrument who was wrongfully deprived of possession. Also included is a claim based on Section 3–202(b) for rescission of a negotiation of the instrument by the claimant. Claims to an instrument under Section 3–306 are different from claims in recoupment referred to in Section 3–305(a)(3). The rule of this section is similar to the rule of Article 30(2) of the Convention on International Bills of Exchange and International Promissory Notes. [Amendment approved by the Permanent Editorial Board for Uniform Commercial Code November 2, 2002.]

§ 3–309. Enforcement of Lost, Destroyed, or Stolen Instrument.

(a) A person not in possession of an instrument is entitled to enforce the instrument if:

(1) the person seeking to enforce the instrument:

~~(i) the person was in possession of the instrument and~~ (A) was entitled to enforce ~~it~~ the instrument when loss of possession occurred; or

(B) has directly or indirectly acquired ownership of the instrument from a person who was entitled to enforce the instrument when loss of possession occurred;

~~(ii)~~ (2) the loss of possession was not the result of a transfer by the person or a lawful seizure; and

~~seizure, and (iii)~~ (3) the person cannot reasonably obtain possession of the instrument because the instrument was destroyed, its whereabouts cannot be determined, or it is in the wrongful possession of an unknown person or a person that cannot be found or is not amenable to service of process.

(b) A person seeking enforcement of an instrument under subsection (a) must prove the terms of the instrument and the person's right to enforce the instrument. If that proof is made, Section 3–308 applies to the case as if the person seeking enforcement had produced the instrument. The court may not enter judgment in favor of the person seeking enforcement unless it finds that the person required to pay the instrument is adequately protected against loss that might occur by reason of a claim by another person to enforce the instrument. Adequate protection may be provided by any reasonable means.

Official Comment

1. Section 3–309 is a modification of former Section 3–804. The rights stated are those of "a person entitled to enforce the instrument" at the time of loss rather than those of an "owner" as in former Section 3–804. Under subsection (b), judgment to enforce the instrument cannot be given unless the court finds that the defendant will be adequately protected against a claim to the instrument by a holder that may appear at some later time. The court is given discretion in determining how adequate protection is to be assured. Former Section 3–804 allowed the court to "require security indemnifying the defendant against loss." Under Section 3–309 adequate protection is a flexible concept. For example, there is substantial risk that a holder in due course may make a demand for payment if the instrument was payable to bearer when it was lost or stolen. On the other hand if the instrument was payable to the person who lost the instrument and that person did not indorse the instrument, no other person could be a holder of the instrument. In some cases there is risk of loss only if there is doubt about whether the facts alleged by the person who lost the instrument are true. Thus, the type of adequate protection that is reasonable in the circumstances may depend on the degree of certainty about the facts in the case.

2. Subsection (a) is intended to reject the result in Dennis Joslin Co. v. Robinson Broadcasting Corp., 977 F. Supp. 491 (D.D.C. 1997). A transferee of a lost instrument need prove only that its transferor was entitled to enforce, not that the transferee was in possession at the time the instrument was lost. The protections of subsection (a) should also be available when instruments are lost during transit, because whatever the precise status of ownership at the point of loss, either the sender or the receiver ordinarily would have been entitled to enforce the instrument during the course of transit. The amendments to subsection (a) are not intended to alter in any way the rules that apply to the preservation of checks in connection with truncation or any other expedited method of check collection or processing.

3. A security interest may attach to the right of a person not in possession of an instrument to enforce the instrument. Although the secured party may not be the owner of the instrument, the secured party may nevertheless be entitled to exercise its debtor's right to enforce the instrument by resorting to its collection rights under the circumstances described in Section 9–607. This section does not address whether the person required to pay the instrument owes any duty to a secured party that is not itself the owner of the instrument.

§ 3–310. Effect of Instrument on Obligation for Which Taken.

Official Comment

. . .

3. Subsection (b) concerns cases in which an uncertified check or a note is taken for an obligation. The typical case is that in which a buyer pays for goods or services by giving the seller the buyer's personal check, or in which the buyer signs a note for the purchase price. Subsection (b) also applies to the uncommon cases in which a check or note of a third person is given in payment of the obligation. Subsection (b) preserves the rule under former Section 3–802(1)(b) that the buyer's obligation to pay the price is suspended, but subsection (b) spells out the effect more precisely. If the check or note is dishonored, the seller may sue on either the dishonored instrument or the contract of sale if the seller has possession of the instrument and is the person entitled to enforce it. If the right to enforce the instrument is held by somebody other than the seller, the seller can't enforce the right to payment of the price under the sales contract because that right is represented by the instrument which is enforceable by somebody else. Thus, if the seller sold the note or the check to a holder and has not reacquired it after dishonor, the only right that survives is the right to enforce the instrument. What that means is that even though the suspension of the obligation may end upon dishonor under paragraph (b)(1), the obligation is not revived in the circumstances described in paragraph (b)(4). [Amendment approved by the Permanent Editorial Board for Uniform Commercial Code November 2, 2002.]

. . .

§ 3–312. Lost, Destroyed, or Stolen Cashier's Check, Teller's Check, or Certified Check.

(a) In this section:

(1) "Check" means a cashier's check, teller's check, or certified check.

(2) "Claimant" means a person who claims the right to receive the amount of a cashier's check, teller's check, or certified check that was lost, destroyed, or stolen.

(3) "Declaration of loss" means a ~~written~~ statement, made in a record under penalty of perjury, to the effect that (i) the declarer lost possession of a check, (ii) the declarer is the drawer or payee of the check, in the case of a certified check, or the remitter or payee of the check, in the case of a cashier's check or teller's check, (iii) the loss of possession was not the result of a transfer by the declarer or a lawful seizure, and (iv) the declarer cannot reasonably obtain possession of the check because the check was destroyed, its whereabouts cannot be determined, or it is in the wrongful possession of an unknown person or a person that cannot be found or is not amenable to service of process.

§ 3-412. Obligation of Issuer of Note or Cashier's Check.

Official Comment

. . .

4. The rule of this section is similar to the rule of Article 39 of the Convention on International Bills of Exchange and International Promissory Notes. [Amendment approved by the Permanent Editorial Board for Uniform Commercial Code November 2, 2002.]

§ 3-413. Obligation of Acceptor.

Official Comment

Subsection (a) is consistent with former Section 3-413(1). Subsection (b) has primary importance with respect to certified checks. It protects the holder in due course of a certified check that was altered after certification and before negotiation to the holder in due course. A bank can avoid liability for the altered amount by stating on the check the amount the bank agrees to pay. The subsection applies to other accepted drafts as well. The rule of this section is similar to the rule of Articles 41 of the Convention on International Bills of Exchange and International Promissory Notes. Articles 42 and 43 of the Convention include more detailed rules that in many respects do not have parallels in this Article. [Amendment approved by the Permanent Editorial Board for Uniform Commercial Code November 2, 2002.]

§ 3-414. Obligation of Drawer.

Official Comment

. . .

7. The obligation of the drawer under this section is similar to the obligation of the drawer under Article 38 of the Convention on International Bills of Exchange and International Promissory Notes. [Amendments approved by the Permanent Editorial Board for Uniform Commercial Code November 2, 2002.]

§ 3-415. Obligation of Indorser.

Official Comment

. . .

6. The rule of this section is similar to the rule of Article 44 of the Convention on International Bills of Exchange and International Promissory Notes. [Amendment approved by the Permanent Editorial Board for Uniform Commercial Code November 2, 2002.]

§ 3-416. Transfer Warranties.

(a) A person who transfers an instrument for consideration warrants to the transferee and, if the transfer is by indorsement, to any subsequent transferee that:

(1) the warrantor is a person entitled to enforce the instrument;

(2) all signatures on the instrument are authentic and authorized;

(3) the instrument has not been altered;

(4) the instrument is not subject to a defense or claim in recoupment of any party which can be asserted against the warrantor; ~~and~~

(5) the warrantor has no knowledge of any insolvency proceeding commenced with respect to the maker or acceptor or, in the case of an unaccepted draft, the ~~drawer.~~ drawer; and

(6) with respect to a remotely-created consumer item, that the person on whose account the item is drawn authorized the issuance of the item in the amount for which the item is drawn.

Official Comment

. . .

8. Subsection (a)(6) is based on a number of nonuniform amendments designed to address concerns about certain kinds of check fraud. The provision implements a limited rejection of Price v. Neal, 97 Eng. Rep. 871 (K.B. 1762), so that in certain circumstances (those involving remotely-created consumer items) the payor bank can use a warranty claim to absolve itself of responsibility for honoring an unauthorized item. The provision rests on the premise that monitoring by depositary banks can control this type of fraud more effectively than any practices readily available to payor banks. The provision expressly includes both the case in which the consumer does not authorize the item at all and also the case in which the consumer authorizes the item but in an amount different from the amount in which the item is drawn. Similar provisions appear in Sections 3–417, 4–207, and 4–208.

The provision supplements applicable federal law, which requires telemarketers who submit instruments for payment to obtain the customer's "express verifiable authorization," which may be either in writing or tape recorded and must be made available upon request to the customer's bank. Federal Trade Commission's Telemarketing Sales Rule, 16 C.F.R. § 310.3(a)(3), implementing the Telemarketing and Consumer Fraud and Abuse Prevention Act, 15 U.S.C. §§ 6101–6108. Some states also have consumer-protection laws governing authorization of instruments in telemarketing transactions. *See, e.g.*, 9 Vt. Stat. Ann. § 2464.

9. Article 45 of the Convention on International Bills of Exchange and International Promissory Notes includes warranties that are similar (except for the warranty in subsection (a)(6)).

§ 3–417. Presentment Warranties.

(a) If an unaccepted draft is presented to the drawee for payment or acceptance and the drawee pays or accepts the draft, (i) the person obtaining payment or acceptance, at the time of presentment, and (ii) a previous transferor of the draft, at the time of transfer, warrant to the drawee making payment or accepting the draft in good faith that:

(1) the warrantor is, or was, at the time the warrantor transferred the draft, a person entitled to enforce the draft or authorized to obtain payment or acceptance of the draft on behalf of a person entitled to enforce the draft;

(2) the draft has not been altered; ~~and~~

(3) the warrantor has no knowledge that the signature of the drawer of the draft is ~~unauthorized.~~ unauthorized; and

(4) with respect to any remotely-created consumer item, that the person on whose account the item is drawn authorized the issuance of the item in the amount for which the item is drawn.

. . .

Official Comment

. . .

9. For discussion of subsection (a)(4), see Comment 8 to Section 3–416.

§ 3–419. Instruments Signed for Accommodation.

. . .

(e) If the signature of a party to an instrument is accompanied by words indicating that the party guarantees payment or the signer signs the instrument as an accommodation party in some other manner that does not unambiguously indicate an intention to guarantee collection rather than payment, the signer is obliged to pay the amount due on the instrument to a person entitled to enforce the instrument in the same circumstances as the accommodated party would be obliged, without prior resort to the accommodated party by the person entitled to enforce the instrument.

(f) An accommodation party who pays the instrument is entitled to reimbursement from the accommodated party and is entitled to enforce the instrument against the accommodated party. In proper circumstances, an accommodation party may obtain relief that requires the accommodated party to perform its obligations on the instrument. An accommodated party ~~who~~ that pays the instrument has no right of recourse against, and is not entitled to contribution from, an accommodation party.

Official Comment

. . .

3. As stated in Comment 1, whether a person is an accommodation party is a question of fact. But it is almost always the case that a co-maker who signs with words of guaranty after the signature is an accommodation party. The same is true of an anomalous indorser. In either case a person taking the instrument is put on notice of the accommodation status of the co-maker or indorser. This is relevant to Section 3-605(~~h~~e). But, under subsection (c), signing with words of guaranty or as an anomalous indorser also creates a presumption that the signer is an accommodation party. A party challenging accommodation party status would have to rebut this presumption by producing evidence that the signer was in fact a direct beneficiary of the value given for the instrument.

. . .

§ 3-502. Dishonor.

Official Comment

. . .

~~4. Subsection (b) applies to unaccepted drafts other than documentary drafts. Subsection (b)(1) applies to checks. Except for checks presented for immediate payment over the counter, which are covered by subsection (b)(2), dishonor occurs according to rules stated in Article 4. When a check is presented for payment through the check collection system, the drawee bank normally makes settlement for the amount of the check to the presenting bank. Under Section 4-301 the drawee bank may recover this settlement if it returns the check within its midnight deadline (Section 4-104). In that case the check is not paid and dishonor occurs under Section 3-502(b)(1). If the drawee bank does not return the check or give notice of dishonor or nonpayment within the midnight deadline, the settlement becomes final payment of the check. Section 4-215. Thus, no dishonor occurs regardless of whether the check is retained or is returned after the midnight deadline. In some cases the drawee bank might not settle for the check when it is received. Under Section 4-302 if the drawee bank is not also the depositary bank and retains the check without settling for it beyond midnight of the day it is presented for payment, the bank becomes "accountable" for the amount of the check, i.e. it is obliged to pay the amount of the check. If the drawee bank is also the depositary bank, the bank is accountable for the amount of the check if the bank does not pay the check or return it or send notice of dishonor within the midnight deadline. In all cases in which the drawee bank becomes accountable, the check has not been paid and, under Section 3-502(b)(1), the check is dishonored. The fact that the bank is obliged to pay the check does not mean that the check has been paid. When a check is presented for payment, the person presenting the check is entitled to payment not just the obligation of the drawee to pay. Until that payment is made, the check is dishonored. To say that the drawee bank is obliged to pay the check necessarily means that the check has not been paid. If the check is eventually paid, the drawee bank no longer is accountable.~~

4. Subsection (b) applies to unaccepted drafts other than documentary drafts. Subsection (b)(1) applies to checks. Except for checks presented for immediate payment over the counter, which are covered by subsection (b)(2), dishonor occurs according to rules stated in Article 4. Those rules contemplate four separate situations that warrant discussion. The first two situations arise in the normal course of affairs, in which the drawee bank makes settlement for the amount of the check to the presenting bank. In the first situation, the drawee bank under Section 4-301 recovers this settlement if it returns the check by its midnight deadline (Section 4-104). In that case the check is not paid and dishonor occurs under Section 3-502(b)(1). The second situation arises if the drawee bank has made such a settlement and does not return the check or give notice of dishonor or nonpayment within the midnight deadline. In that case, the settlement becomes final payment of the check under Section 4-215. Because the drawee bank already has paid such an item, it cannot be "accountable" for the item under the terms

of Section 4–302(a)(1). Thus, no dishonor occurs regardless of whether the drawee bank retains the check indefinitely or for some reason returns the check after its midnight deadline.

The third and fourth situations arise less commonly, in cases in which the drawee bank does not settle for the check when it is received. Under Section 4–302 if the drawee bank is not also the depositary bank and retains the check without settling for it beyond midnight of the day it is presented for payment, the bank at that point becomes "accountable" for the amount of the check, i.e., it is obliged to pay the amount of the check. If the drawee bank is also the depositary bank, the bank becomes accountable for the amount of the check if the bank does not pay the check or return it or send notice of dishonor by its midnight deadline. Hence, if the drawee bank is also the depositary bank and does not either settle for the check when it is received (a settlement that would ripen into final payment if the drawee bank failed to take action to recover the settlement by its midnight deadline) or return the check or an appropriate notice by its midnight deadline, the drawee bank will become accountable for the amount of the check under Section 4–302. Thus, in all cases in which the drawee bank becomes accountable under Section 4–302, the check has not been paid (either by a settlement that became unrecoverable or otherwise) and thus, under Section 3–502(b)(1), the check is dishonored.

The fact that a bank that is accountable for the amount of the check under Section 4–302 is obliged to pay the check does not mean that the check has been paid. Indeed, because each of the paragraphs of Section 4–302(b) is limited by its terms to situations in which a bank has not paid the item, a drawee bank will be accountable under Section 4–302 only in situations in which it has not previously paid the check. Section 3–502(b)(1) reflects the view that a person presenting a check is entitled to payment, not just the ability to hold the drawee accountable under Section 4–302. If that payment is not made in a timely manner, the check is dishonored.

Regulation CC Section 229.36(d) provides that settlement between banks for the forward collection of checks is final. The relationship of that section to Articles 3 and 4 is discussed in the Commentary to that section. [Amendment approved by the Permanent Editorial Board for Uniform Commercial Code November 2, 2002.]

. . .

§ 3-602. Payment.

(a) Subject to subsection ~~(b),~~ (e), an instrument is paid to the extent payment is made~~(i)~~ by or on behalf of a party obliged to pay the instrument, and~~(ii)~~ to a person entitled to enforce the instrument.

(b) Subject to subsection (e), a note is paid to the extent payment is made by or on behalf of a party obliged to pay the note to a person that formerly was entitled to enforce the note only if at the time of the payment the party obliged to pay has not received adequate notification that the note has been transferred and that payment is to be made to the transferee. A notification is adequate only if it is signed by the transferor or the transferee; reasonably identifies the transferred note; and provides an address at which payments subsequently are to be made. Upon request, a transferee shall seasonably furnish reasonable proof that the note has been transferred. Unless the transferee complies with the request, a payment to the person that formerly was entitled to enforce the note is effective for purposes of subsection (c) even if the party obliged to pay the note has received a notification under this paragraph.

(c) Subject to subsection (e), to the extent of ~~the payment,~~ a payment under subsections (a) and (b), the obligation of the party obliged to pay the instrument is discharged even though payment is made with knowledge of a claim to the instrument under Section 3–306 by another person.

(d) Subject to subsection (e), a transferee, or any party that has acquired rights in the instrument directly or indirectly from a transferee, including any such party that has rights as a holder in due course, is deemed to have notice of any payment that is made under subsection (b) after the date that the note is transferred to the transferee but before the party obliged to pay the note receives adequate notification of the transfer.

~~(b)~~ (e) The obligation of a party to pay the instrument is not discharged under ~~subsection (a)~~ subsections (a) through (d) if:

(1) a claim to the instrument under Section 3–306 is enforceable against the party receiving payment and (i) payment is made with knowledge by the payor that payment is prohibited by injunction or similar process of a court of competent jurisdiction, or (ii) in the case of an instrument other than a cashier's check, teller's check, or certified check, the party making payment accepted,

from the person having a claim to the instrument, indemnity against loss resulting from refusal to pay the person entitled to enforce the instrument; or

(2) the person making payment knows that the instrument is a stolen instrument and pays a person it knows is in wrongful possession of the instrument.

(f) As used in this section, "signed," with respect to a record that is not a writing, includes the attachment to or logical association with the record of an electronic symbol, sound, or process with the present intent to adopt or accept the record.

Official Comment

1. This section replaces former Section 3-603(1). The phrase "claim to the instrument" in subsection (a) means, by reference to Section 3-306, a claim of ownership or possession and not a claim in recoupment. Subsection (~~b~~e)(1)(ii) is added to conform to Section 3-411. Section 3-411 is intended to discourage an obligated bank from refusing payment of a cashier's check, certified check or dishonored teller's check at the request of a claimant to the check who provided the bank with indemnity against loss. See Comment 1 to Section 3-411. An obligated bank that refuses payment under those circumstances not only remains liable on the check but may also be liable to the holder of the check for consequential damages. Section 3-602(~~b~~e)(1)(ii) and Section 3-411, read together, change the rule of former Section 3-603(1) with respect to the obligation of the obligated bank on the check. Payment to the holder of a cashier's check, teller's check, or certified check discharges the obligation of the obligated bank on the check to both the holder and the claimant even though indemnity has been given by the person asserting the claim. If the obligated bank pays the check in violation of an agreement with the claimant in connection with the indemnity agreement, any liability that the bank may have for violation of the agreement is not governed by Article 3, but is left to other law. This section continues the rule that the obligor is not discharged on the instrument if payment is made in violation of an injunction against payment. See Section 3-411(c)(iv).

2. Subsection (a) covers payments made in a traditional manner, to the person entitled to enforce the instrument. Subsection (b), which provides an alternative method of payment, deals with the situation in which a person entitled to enforce the instrument transfers the instrument without giving notice to parties obligated to pay the instrument. If that happens and one of those parties subsequently makes a payment to the transferor, the payment is effective even though it is not made to the person entitled to enforce the instrument. Unlike the earlier version of Section 3-602, this rule is consistent with Section 9-406(a), Restatement of Mortgages § 5.5, and Restatement of Contracts § 338(1).

3. In determining the party to whom a payment is made for purposes of this section, courts should look to traditional rules of agency. Thus, if the original payee of a note transfers ownership of the note to a third party but continues to service the obligation, the law of agency might treat payments made to the original payee as payments made to the third party.

§ 3-604. Discharge by Cancellation or Renunciation.

(a) A person entitled to enforce an instrument, with or without consideration, may discharge the obligation of a party to pay the instrument (i) by an intentional voluntary act, such as surrender of the instrument to the party, destruction, mutilation, or cancellation of the instrument, cancellation or striking out of the party's signature, or the addition of words to the instrument indicating discharge, or (ii) by agreeing not to sue or otherwise renouncing rights against the party by a signed ~~writing.~~ record.

(b) Cancellation or striking out of an indorsement pursuant to subsection (a) does not affect the status and rights of a party derived from the indorsement.

(c) In this section, "signed," with respect to a record that is not a writing, includes the attachment to or logical association with the record of an electronic symbol, sound, or process with the present intent to adopt or accept the record.

§ 3-605. Discharge of Secondary Obligors. ~~Discharge of Indorsers and Accommodation Parties.~~

(a) If a person entitled to enforce an instrument releases the obligation of a principal obligor in whole or in part, and another party to the instrument is a secondary obligor with respect to the obligation of that principal obligor, the following rules apply:

(1) Any obligations of the principal obligor to the secondary obligor with respect to any previous payment by the secondary obligor are not affected. Unless the terms of the release preserve the secondary obligor's recourse, the principal obligor is discharged, to the extent of the release, from any other duties to the secondary obligor under this article.

(2) Unless the terms of the release provide that the person entitled to enforce the instrument retains the right to enforce the instrument against the secondary obligor, the secondary obligor is discharged to the same extent as the principal obligor from any unperformed portion of its obligation on the instrument. If the instrument is a check and the obligation of the secondary obligor is based on an indorsement of the check, the secondary obligor is discharged without regard to the language or circumstances of the discharge or other release.

(3) If the secondary obligor is not discharged under paragraph (2), the secondary obligor is discharged to the extent of the value of the consideration for the release, and to the extent that the release would otherwise cause the secondary obligor a loss.

(b) If a person entitled to enforce an instrument grants a principal obligor an extension of the time at which one or more payments are due on the instrument and another party to the instrument is a secondary obligor with respect to the obligation of that principal obligor, the following rules apply:

(1) Any obligations of the principal obligor to the secondary obligor with respect to any previous payment by the secondary obligor are not affected. Unless the terms of the extension preserve the secondary obligor's recourse, the extension correspondingly extends the time for performance of any other duties owed to the secondary obligor by the principal obligor under this article.

(2) The secondary obligor is discharged to the extent that the extension would otherwise cause the secondary obligor a loss.

(3) To the extent that the secondary obligor is not discharged under paragraph (2), the secondary obligor may perform its obligations to a person entitled to enforce the instrument as if the time for payment had not been extended or, unless the terms of the extension provide that the person entitled to enforce the instrument retains the right to enforce the instrument against the secondary obligor as if the time for payment had not been extended, treat the time for performance of its obligations as having been extended correspondingly.

(c) If a person entitled to enforce an instrument agrees, with or without consideration, to a modification of the obligation of a principal obligor other than a complete or partial release or an extension of the due date and another party to the instrument is a secondary obligor with respect to the obligation of that principal obligor, the following rules apply:

(1) Any obligations of the principal obligor to the secondary obligor with respect to any previous payment by the secondary obligor are not affected. The modification correspondingly modifies any other duties owed to the secondary obligor by the principal obligor under this article.

(2) The secondary obligor is discharged from any unperformed portion of its obligation to the extent that the modification would otherwise cause the secondary obligor a loss.

(3) To the extent that the secondary obligor is not discharged under paragraph (2), the secondary obligor may satisfy its obligation on the instrument as if the modification had not occurred, or treat its obligation on the instrument as having been modified correspondingly.

(d) If the obligation of a principal obligor is secured by an interest in collateral, another party to the instrument is a secondary obligor with respect to that obligation, and a person entitled to enforce the instrument impairs the value of the interest in collateral, the obligation of the secondary obligor is discharged to the extent of the impairment. The value of an interest in collateral is impaired to the extent the value of the interest is reduced to an amount less than the amount of the recourse of the secondary obligor, or the reduction in value of the interest causes an increase in the amount by which the amount of the recourse exceeds the value of the interest. For purposes of this subsection, impairing the value of an interest in collateral includes failure to obtain or maintain perfection or recordation of the interest in collateral, release of collateral without substitution of collateral of equal value or equivalent reduction of the underlying obligation, failure to perform a duty to preserve the value of collateral owed, under Article 9 or other law, to a debtor or other person secondarily liable, and failure to comply with applicable law in disposing of or otherwise enforcing the interest in collateral.

(e) A secondary obligor is not discharged under subsections (a)(3), (b), (c), or (d) unless the person entitled to enforce the instrument knows that the person is a secondary obligor or has notice under Section 3–419(c) that the instrument was signed for accommodation.

(f) A secondary obligor is not discharged under this section if the secondary obligor consents to the event or conduct that is the basis of the discharge, or the instrument or a separate agreement of the party provides for waiver of discharge under this section specifically or by general language indicating that parties waive defenses based on suretyship or impairment of collateral. Unless the circumstances indicate otherwise, consent by the principal obligor to an act that would lead to a discharge under this section constitutes consent to that act by the secondary obligor if the secondary obligor controls the principal obligor or deals with the person entitled to enforce the instrument on behalf of the principal obligor.

(g) A release or extension preserves a secondary obligor's recourse if the terms of the release or extension provide that:

(1) the person entitled to enforce the instrument retains the right to enforce the instrument against the secondary obligor; and

(2) the recourse of the secondary obligor continues as if the release or extension had not been granted.

(h) Except as otherwise provided in subsection (i), a secondary obligor asserting discharge under this section has the burden of persuasion both with respect to the occurrence of the acts alleged to harm the secondary obligor and loss or prejudice caused by those acts.

(i) If the secondary obligor demonstrates prejudice caused by an impairment of its recourse, and the circumstances of the case indicate that the amount of loss is not reasonably susceptible of calculation or requires proof of facts that are not ascertainable, it is presumed that the act impairing recourse caused a loss or impairment equal to the liability of the secondary obligor on the instrument. In that event, the burden of persuasion as to any lesser amount of the loss is on the person entitled to enforce the instrument.

~~(a) In this section, the term "indorser" includes a drawer having the obligation described in Section 3–414(d).~~

~~(b) Discharge, under Section 3–604, of the obligation of a party to pay an instrument does not discharge the obligation of an indorser or accommodation party having a right of recourse against the discharged party.~~

~~(c) If a person entitled to enforce an instrument agrees, with or without consideration, to an extension of the due date of the obligation of a party to pay the instrument, the extension discharges an indorser or accommodation party having a right of recourse against the party whose obligation is extended to the extent the indorser or accommodation party proves that the extension caused loss to the indorser or accommodation party with respect to the right of recourse.~~

~~(d) If a person entitled to enforce an instrument agrees, with or without consideration, to a material modification of the obligation of a party other than an extension of the due date, the modification discharges the obligation of an indorser or accommodation party having a right of recourse against the person whose obligation is modified to the extent the modification causes loss to the indorser or accommodation party with respect to the right of recourse. The loss suffered by the indorser or accommodation party as a result of the modification is equal to the amount of the right of recourse unless the person enforcing the instrument proves that no loss was caused by the modification or that the loss caused by the modification was an amount less than the amount of the right of recourse.~~

~~(e) If the obligation of a party to pay an instrument is secured by an interest in collateral and a person entitled to enforce the instrument impairs the value of the interest in collateral, the obligation of an indorser or accommodation party having a right of recourse against the obligor is discharged to the extent of the impairment. The value of an interest in collateral is impaired to the extent (i) the value of the interest is reduced to an amount less than the amount of the right of recourse of the party asserting discharge, or (ii) the reduction in value of the interest causes an increase in the amount by which the amount of the right~~

~~of recourse exceeds the value of the interest. The burden of proving impairment is on the party asserting discharge.~~

~~(f) If the obligation of a party is secured by an interest in collateral not provided by an accommodation party and a person entitled to enforce the instrument impairs the value of the interest in collateral, the obligation of any party who is jointly and severally liable with respect to the secured obligation is discharged to the extent the impairment causes the party asserting discharge to pay more than that party would have been obliged to pay, taking into account rights of contribution, if impairment had not occurred. If the party asserting discharge is an accommodation party not entitled to discharge under subsection (e), the party is deemed to have a right to contribution based on joint and several liability rather than a right to reimbursement. The burden of proving impairment is on the party asserting discharge.~~

~~(g) Under subsection (e) or (f), impairing value of an interest in collateral includes (i) failure to obtain or maintain perfection or recordation of the interest in collateral, (ii) release of collateral without substitution of collateral of equal value, (iii) failure to perform a duty to preserve the value of collateral owed, under Article 9 or other law, to a debtor or surety or other person secondarily liable, or (iv) failure to comply with applicable law in disposing of collateral.~~

~~(h) An accommodation party is not discharged under subsection (c), (d), or (e) unless the person entitled to enforce the instrument knows of the accommodation or has notice under Section 3-419(c) that the instrument was signed for accommodation.~~

~~(i) A party is not discharged under this section if (i) the party asserting discharge consents to the event or conduct that is the basis of the discharge, or (ii) the instrument or a separate agreement of the party provides for waiver of discharge under this section either specifically or by general language indicating that parties waive defenses based on suretyship or impairment of collateral.~~

Official Comment

~~1. Section 3-605, which replaces former Section 3-606, can be illustrated by an example. Bank lends $10,000 to Borrower who signs a note under which Borrower is obliged to pay $10,000 to Bank on a due date stated in the note. Bank insists, however, that Accommodation Party also become liable to pay the note. Accommodation Party can incur this liability by signing the note as a co-maker or by indorsing the note. In either case the note is signed for accommodation and Borrower is the accommodated party. Rights and obligations of Accommodation Party in this case are stated in Section 3-419. Suppose that after the note is signed, Bank agrees to a modification of the rights and obligations between Bank and Borrower. For example, Bank agrees that Borrower may pay the note at some date after the due date, or that Borrower may discharge Borrower's $10,000 obligation to pay the note by paying Bank $3,000, or that Bank releases collateral given by Borrower to secure the note. Under the law of suretyship Borrower is usually referred to as the principal debtor and Accommodation Party is referred to as the surety. Under that law, the surety can be discharged under certain circumstances if changes of this kind are made by Bank, the creditor, without the consent of Accommodation Party, the surety. Rights of the surety to discharge in such cases are commonly referred to as suretyship defenses. Section 3-605 is concerned with this kind of problem in the context of a negotiable instrument to which the principal debtor and the surety are parties. But Section 3-605 has a wider scope. It also applies to indorsers who are not accommodation parties. Unless an indorser signs without recourse, the indorser's liability under Section 3-415(a) is that of a guarantor of payment. If Bank in our hypothetical case indorsed the note and transferred it to Second Bank, Bank has rights given to an indorser under Section 3-605 if it is Second Bank that modifies rights and obligations of Borrower. Both accommodation parties and indorsers will be referred to in these Comments as sureties. The scope of Section 3-605 is also widened by subsection (e) which deals with rights of a non-accommodation party co-maker when collateral is impaired.~~

~~2. The importance of suretyship defenses is greatly diminished by the fact that they can be waived. The waiver is usually made by a provision in the note or other writing that represents the obligation of the principal debtor. It is standard practice to include a waiver of suretyship defenses in notes given to financial institutions or other commercial creditors. Section 3-605(i) allows waiver. Thus, Section 3-605 applies to the occasional case in which the creditor did not include a waiver clause in the instrument or in which the creditor did not obtain the permission of the surety to take the action that triggers the suretyship defense.~~

~~3. Subsection (b) addresses the effect of discharge under Section 3-604 of the principal debtor. In the hypothetical case stated in Comment 1, release of Borrower by Bank does not release Accommodation Party. As a practical matter, Bank will not gratuitously release Borrower. Discharge of Borrower normally would be part of a settlement with Borrower if Borrower is insolvent or in financial difficulty. If Borrower is unable to pay all~~

~~creditors, it may be prudent for Bank to take partial payment, but Borrower will normally insist on a release of the obligation. If Bank takes $3,000 and releases Borrower from the $10,000 debt, Accommodation Party is not injured. To the extent of the payment Accommodation Party's obligation to Bank is reduced. The release of Borrower by Bank does not affect the right of Accommodation Party to obtain reimbursement from Borrower or to enforce the note against Borrower if Accommodation Party pays Bank. Section 3-419(e). Subsection (b) is designed to allow a creditor to settle with the principal debtor without risk of losing rights against sureties. Settlement is in the interest of sureties as well as the creditor. Subsection (b), however, is not intended to apply to a settlement of a disputed claim which discharges the obligation.~~

~~Subsection (b) changes the law stated in former Section 3-606 but the change relates largely to formalities rather than substance. Under former Section 3-606, Bank in the hypothetical case stated in Comment 1 could settle with and release Borrower without releasing Accommodation Party, but to accomplish that result Bank had to either obtain the consent of Accommodation Party or make an express reservation of rights against Accommodation Party at the time it released Borrower. The reservation of rights was made in the agreement between Bank and Borrower by which the release of Borrower was made. There was no requirement in former Section 3-606 that any notice be given to Accommodation Party. Section 3-605 eliminates the necessity that Bank formally reserve rights against Accommodation Party in order to retain rights of recourse against Accommodation Party. See PEB Commentary No. 11, dated February 10, 1994 [Appendix V, infra].~~

~~4. Subsection (c) relates to extensions of the due date of the instrument. In most cases an extension of time to pay a note is a benefit to both the principal debtor and sureties having recourse against the principal debtor. In relatively few cases the extension may cause loss if deterioration of the financial condition of the principal debtor reduces the amount that the surety will be able to recover on its right of recourse when default occurs. Former Section 3-606(1)(a) did not take into account the presence or absence of loss to the surety. For example, suppose the instrument is an installment note and the principal debtor is temporarily short of funds to pay a monthly installment. The payee agrees to extend the due date of the installment for a month or two to allow the debtor to pay when funds are available. Under former Section 3-606 surety was discharged if consent was not given unless the payee expressly reserved rights against the surety. It did not matter that the extension of time was a trivial change in the guaranteed obligation and that there was no evidence that the surety suffered any loss because of the extension. Wilmington Trust Co. v. Gesullo, 29 U.C.C.Rep. 144 (Del.Super.Ct. 1980). Under subsection (c) an extension of time results in discharge only to the extent the surety proves that the extension caused loss. For example, if the extension is for a long period the surety might be able to prove that during the period of extension the principal debtor became insolvent, thus reducing the value of the right of recourse of the surety. By putting the burden on the surety to prove loss, subsection (c) more accurately reflects what the parties would have done by agreement, and it facilitates workouts.~~

~~Under other provisions of Article 3, what is the effect of an extension agreement between the holder of a note and the maker who is an accommodated party? The question is illustrated by the following case:~~

> ~~Case # 1. A borrows money from Lender and issues a note payable on April 1, 1992. B signs the note for accommodation at the request of Lender. B signed the note either as co-maker or as an anomalous indorser. In either case Lender subsequently makes an agreement with A extending the due date of A's obligation to pay the note to July 1, 1992. In either case B did not agree to the extension.~~

~~What is the effect of the extension agreement on B? Could Lender enforce the note against B if the note is not paid on April 1, 1992? A's obligation to Lender to pay the note on April 1, 1992 may be modified by the agreement of Lender. If B is an anomalous indorser Lender cannot enforce the note against B unless the note has been dishonored. Section 3-415(a). Under Section 3-502(a)(3) dishonor occurs if it is not paid on the day it becomes payable. Since the agreement between A and Lender extended the due date of A's obligation to July 1, 1992 there is no dishonor because A was not obligated to pay Lender on April 1, 1992. If B is a co-maker the analysis is somewhat different. Lender has no power to amend the terms of the note without the consent of both A and B. By an agreement with A, Lender can extend the due date of A's obligation to Lender to pay the note but B's obligation is to pay the note according to the terms of the note at the time of issue. Section 3-412. However, B's obligation to pay the note is subject to a defense because B is an accommodation party. B is not obliged to pay Lender if A is not obliged to pay Lender. Under Section 3-305(d), B as an accommodation party can assert against Lender any defense of A. A has a defense based on the extension agreement. Thus, the result is that Lender could not enforce the note against B until July 1, 1992. This result is consistent with the right of B if B is an anomalous indorser.~~

~~As a practical matter an extension of the due date will normally occur when the accommodated party is unable to pay on the due date. The interest of the accommodation party normally is to defer payment to the holder rather than to pay right away and rely on an action against the accommodated party that may have little or no value. But in unusual cases the accommodation party may prefer to pay the holder on the original due date. In~~

~~such cases, the accommodation party may do so. This is because the extension agreement between the accommodated party and the holder cannot bind the accommodation party to a change in its obligation without the accommodation party's consent. The effect on the recourse of the accommodation party against the accommodation party of performance by the accommodation party on the original due date is not addressed in § 3–419 and is left to the general law of suretyship.~~

~~Even though an accommodation party has the option of paying the instrument on the original due date, the accommodation party is not precluded from asserting its rights to discharge under Section 3–605(c) if it does not exercise that option. The critical issue is whether the extension caused the accommodation party a loss by increasing the difference between its cost of performing its obligation on the instrument and the amount recoverable from the accommodated party pursuant to Section 3–419(e). The decision by the accommodation party not to exercise its option to pay on the original due date may, under the circumstances, be a factor to be considered in the determination of that issue. See PEB Commentary No. 11, supra.~~

~~5. Former Section 3–606 applied to extensions of the due date of a note but not to other modifications of the obligation of the principal debtor. There was no apparent reason why former Section 3–606 did not follow general suretyship law in covering both. Under Section 3–605(d) a material modification of the obligation of the principal debtor, other than an extension of the due date, will result in discharge of the surety to the extent the modification caused loss to the surety with respect to the right of recourse. The loss caused by the modification is deemed to be the entire amount of the right of recourse unless the person seeking enforcement of the instrument proves that no loss occurred or that the loss was less than the full amount of the right of recourse. In the absence of that proof, the surety is completely discharged. The rationale for having different rules with respect to loss for extensions of the due date and other modifications is that extensions are likely to be beneficial to the surety and they are often made. Other modifications are less common and they may very well be detrimental to the surety. Modification of the obligation of the principal debtor without permission of the surety is unreasonable unless the modification is benign. Subsection (d) puts the burden on the person seeking enforcement of the instrument to prove the extent to which loss was not caused by the modification.~~

~~The following is an illustration of the kind of case to which Section 3–605(d) would apply:~~

~~Case # 2. Corporation borrows money from Lender and issues a note payable to Lender. X signs the note as an accommodation party for Corporation. The loan agreement under which the note was issued states various events of default which allow Lender to accelerate the due date of the note. Among the events of default are breach of covenants not to incur debt beyond specified limits and not to engage in any line of business substantially different from that currently carried on by Corporation. Without consent of X, Lender agrees to modify the covenants to allow Corporation to enter into a new line of business that X considers to be risky, and to incur debt beyond the limits specified in the loan agreement to finance the new venture. This modification releases X unless Lender proves that the modification did not cause loss to X or that the loss caused by the modification was less than X's right of recourse.~~

~~Sometimes there is both an extension of the due date and some other modification. In that case both subsections (c) and (d) apply. The following is an example:~~

~~Case # 3. Corporation was indebted to Lender on a note payable on April 1, 1992 and X signed the note as an accommodation party for Corporation. The interest rate on the note was 12 percent. Lender and Corporation agreed to a six-month extension of the due date of the note to October 1, 1992 and an increase in the interest rate to 14 percent after April 1, 1992. Corporation defaulted on October 1, 1992. Corporation paid no interest during the six-month extension period. Corporation is insolvent and has no assets from which unsecured creditors can be paid. Lender demanded payment from X.~~

~~Assume X is an anomalous indorser. First consider Section 3–605(c) alone. If there had been no change in the interest rate, the fact that Lender gave an extension of six months to Corporation would not result in discharge unless X could prove loss with respect to the right of recourse because of the extension. If the financial condition of Corporation on April 1, 1992 would not have allowed any recovery on the right of recourse, X can't show any loss as a result of the extension with respect to the amount due on the note on April 1, 1992. Since the note accrued interest during the six-month extension, is there a loss equal to the accrued interest? Since the interest rate was not raised, only Section 3–605(c) would apply and X probably could not prove any loss. The obligation of X includes interest on the note until the note is paid. To the extent payment was delayed X had the use of the money that X otherwise would have had to pay to Lender. X could have prevented the running of interest by paying the debt. Since X did not do so, X suffered no loss as the result of the extension.~~

~~If the interest rate was raised, Section 3–605(d) also must be considered. If X is an anomalous indorser, X's liability is to pay the note according to its terms at the time of indorsement. Section 3–415(a). Thus, X's obligation~~

~~to pay interest is measured by the terms of the note (12%) rather than by the increased amount of 14 percent. The same analysis applies if X had been a co-maker. Under Section 3–412 the liability of the issuer of a note is to pay the note according to its terms at the time it was issued. Either obligation could be changed by contract and that occurred with respect to Corporation when it agreed to the increase in the interest rate, but X did not join in that agreement and is not bound by it. Thus, the most that X can be required to pay is the amount due on the note plus interest at the rate of 12 percent.~~

~~Does the modification discharge X under Section 3–605(d)? Any modification that increases the monetary obligation of X is material. An increase of the interest rate from 12 percent to 14 percent is certainly a material modification. There is a presumption that X is discharged because Section 3–605(d) creates a presumption that the modification caused a loss to X equal to the amount of the right of recourse. Thus, Lender has the burden of proving absence of loss or a loss less than the amount of the right of recourse. Since Corporation paid no interest during the six-month period, the issue is like the issue presented under Section 3–605(c) which we have just discussed. The increase in the interest rate could not have affected the right of recourse because no interest was paid by Corporation. X is in the same position as X would have been in if there had been an extension without an increase in the interest rate.~~

~~The analysis with respect to Section 3–605(c) and (d) would have been different if we change the assumptions. Suppose Corporation was not insolvent on April 1, 1992, that Corporation paid interest at the higher rate during the six-month period, and that Corporation was insolvent at the end of the six-month period. In this case it is possible that the extension and the additional burden placed on Corporation by the increased interest rate may have been detrimental to X.~~

~~There are difficulties in properly allocating burden of proof when the agreement between Lender and Corporation involves both an extension under Section 3–605(c) and a modification under Section 3–605(d). The agreement may have caused loss to X but it may be difficult to identify the extent to which the loss was caused by the extension or the other modification. If neither Lender nor X introduces evidence on the issue, the result is full discharge because Section 3–605(d) applies. Thus, Lender has the burden of overcoming the presumption in Section 3–605(d). In doing so, Lender should be entitled to a presumption that the extension of time by itself caused no loss. Section 3–605(c) is based on such a presumption and X should be required to introduce evidence on the effect of the extension on the right of recourse. Lender would have to introduce evidence on the effect of the increased interest rate. Thus both sides will have to introduce evidence. On the basis of this evidence the court will have to make a determination of the overall effect of the agreement on X's right of recourse. See PEB Commentary No. 11, supra.~~

~~6. Subsection (e) deals with discharge of sureties by impairment of collateral. It generally conforms to former Section 3–606(1)(b). Subsection (g) states common examples of what is meant by impairment. By using the term "includes," it allows a court to find impairment in other cases as well. There is extensive case law on impairment of collateral. The surety is discharged to the extent the surety proves that impairment was caused by a person entitled to enforce the instrument. For example, suppose the payee of a secured note fails to perfect the security interest. The collateral is owned by the principal debtor who subsequently files in bankruptcy. As a result of the failure to perfect, the security interest is not enforceable in bankruptcy. If the payee obtains payment from the surety, the surety is subrogated to the payee's security interest in the collateral. In this case the value of the security interest is impaired completely because the security interest is unenforceable. If the value of the collateral is as much or more than the amount of the note there is a complete discharge.~~

~~In some states a real property grantee who assumes the obligation of the grantor as maker of a note secured by the real property becomes by operation of law a principal debtor and the grantor becomes a surety. The meager case authority was split on whether former Section 3–606 applied to release the grantor if the holder released or extended the obligation of the grantee. Revised Article 3 takes no position on the effect of the release of the grantee in this case. Section 3–605(b) does not apply because the holder has not discharged the obligation of a "party," a term defined in Section 3–103(a)(8) as "party to an instrument." The assuming grantee is not a party to the instrument. The resolution of this question is governed by general principles of law, including the law of suretyship. See PEB Commentary No. 11, supra.~~

~~7. Subsection (f) is illustrated by the following case. X and Y sign a note for $1,000 as co-makers. Neither is an accommodation party. X grants a security interest in X's property to secure the note. The collateral is worth more than $1,000. Payee fails to perfect the security interest in X's property before X files in bankruptcy. As a result the security interest is not enforceable in bankruptcy. Had Payee perfected the security interest, Y could have paid the note and gained rights to X's collateral by subrogation. If the security interest had been perfected, Y could have realized on the collateral to the extent of $500 to satisfy its right of contribution against X. Payee's failure to perfect deprived Y of the benefit of the collateral. Subsection (f) discharges Y to the extent of its loss. If~~

~~there are no assets in the bankruptcy for unsecured claims, the loss is $500, the amount of Y's contribution claim against X which now has a zero value. If some amount is payable on unsecured claims, the loss is reduced by the amount receivable by Y. The same result follows if Y is an accommodation party but Payee has no knowledge of the accommodation or notice under Section 3–419(c). In that event Y is not discharged under subsection (e), but subsection (f) applies because X and Y are jointly and severally liable on the note. Under subsection (f), Y is treated as a co-maker with a right of contribution rather than an accommodation party with a right of reimbursement. Y is discharged to the extent of $500. If Y is the principal debtor and X is the accommodation party subsection (f) doesn't apply. Y, as principal debtor, is not injured by the impairment of collateral because Y would have been obliged to reimburse X for the entire $1,000 even if Payee had obtained payment from sale of the collateral.~~

~~8. Subsection (i) is a continuation of former law which allowed suretyship defenses to be waived. As the subsection provides, a party is not discharged under this section if the instrument or a separate agreement of the party waives discharge either specifically or by general language indicating that defenses based on suretyship and impairment of collateral are waived. No particular language or form of agreement is required, and the standards for enforcing such a term are the same as the standards for enforcing any other term in an instrument or agreement.~~

~~Subsection (i), however, applies only to a "discharge under this section." The right of an accommodation party to be discharged under Section 3–605(e) because of an impairment of collateral can be waived. But with respect to a note secured by personal property collateral, Article 9 also applies. If an accommodation party is a "debtor" under Section 9–105(1)(d), the accommodation party has rights under Article 9. Under Section 9–501(3)(b) rights of an Article 9 debtor under Section 9–504(3) and Section 9–505(1), which deal with disposition of collateral, cannot be waived except as provided in Article 9. These Article 9 rights are independent of rights under Section 3–605. Since Section 3–605(i) is specifically limited to discharge under Section 3–605, a waiver of rights with respect to Section 3–605 has no effect on rights under Article 9. With respect to Article 9 rights, Section 9–501(3)(b) controls. See PEB Commentary No. 11, supra.~~

1. This section contains rules that are applicable when a secondary obligor (as defined in Section 3–103(a)(17)) is a party to an instrument. These rules essentially parallel modern interpretations of the law of suretyship and guaranty that apply when a secondary obligor is not a party to an instrument. See generally *Restatement of the Law, Third, Suretyship and Guaranty* (1996). Of course, the rules in this section do not resolve all possible issues concerning the rights and duties of the parties. In the event that a situation is presented that is not resolved by this section (or the other related sections of this Article), the resolution may be provided by the general law of suretyship because, pursuant to Section 1–103, that law is applicable unless displaced by provisions of this Act.

2. Like the law of suretyship and guaranty, Section 3–605 provides secondary obligors with defenses that are not available to other parties to instruments. The general operation of Section 3–605, and its relationship to the law of suretyship and guaranty, can be illustrated by an example. Bank agrees to lend $10,000 to Borrower, but only if Backer also is liable for repayment of the loan. The parties could consummate that transaction in three different ways. First, if Borrower and Backer incurred those obligations with contracts not governed by this Article (such as a note that is not an instrument for purposes of this Article), the general law of suretyship and guaranty would be applicable. Under modern nomenclature, Bank is the "obligee," Borrower is the "principal obligor," and Backer is the "secondary obligor." See *Restatement of Suretyship and Guaranty* § 1. Then assume that Bank and Borrower agree to a modification of their rights and obligations after the note is signed. For example, they might agree that Borrower may repay the loan at some date after the due date, or that Borrower may discharge its repayment obligation by paying Bank $3,000 rather than $10,000. Alternatively, suppose that Bank releases collateral that Borrower has given to secure the loan. Under the law of suretyship and guaranty, the secondary obligor may be discharged under certain circumstances if these modifications of the obligations between Bank (the obligee) and Borrower (the principal obligor) are made without the consent of Backer (the secondary obligor). The rights that the secondary obligor has to a discharge of its liability in such cases commonly are referred to as suretyship defenses. The extent of the discharge depends upon the particular circumstances. See *Restatement of Suretyship and Guaranty* §§ 37, 39–44.

A second possibility is that the parties might decide to evidence the loan by a negotiable instrument. In that scenario, Borrower signs a note under which Borrower is obliged to pay $10,000 to the order of Bank on a due date stated in the note. Backer becomes liable for the repayment obligation by signing the note as a co-maker or indorser. In either case the note is signed for accommodation, Backer is an accommodation party, and Borrower is the accommodated party. See Section 3–419 (describing the obligations of accommodation parties). For purposes of Section 3–605, Backer is also a "secondary obligor" and Borrower is a "principal obligor," as those terms are defined in Section 3–103. Because Backer is a party to the instrument, its rights to a discharge based on any modification of obligations between Bank and Borrower are governed by Section 3–605 rather than by the general law of suretyship and guaranty. Within Section 3–605, subsection (a) describes the consequences of a release of Borrower, subsection (b) describes the consequences of an extension of time, and subsection (c) describes the consequences of other modifications.

The third possibility is that Borrower would use an instrument governed by this Article to evidence its repayment obligation, but Backer's obligation would be created in some way other than by becoming party to that instrument. In that case, Backer's rights are determined by suretyship and guaranty law rather than by this Article. See Comment 3 to Section 3–419.

A person also can acquire secondary liability without having been a secondary obligor at the time that the principal obligation was created. For example, a transferee of real or personal property that assumes the obligation of the transferor as maker of a note secured by the property becomes by operation of law a principal obligor, with the transferor becoming a secondary obligor. *Restatement of Suretyship and Guaranty* § 2(e); *Restatement of Mortgages* § 5.1. Article 3 does not determine the effect of the release of the transferee in that case because the assuming transferee is not a "party" to the instrument as defined in Section 3–103(a)(10). Section 3–605(a) does not apply then because the holder has not discharged the obligation of a "principal obligor," a term defined in Section 3–103(a)(11). Thus, the resolution of that question is governed by the law of suretyship. See *Restatement of Suretyship and Guaranty* § 39.

3. Section 3–605 is not, however, limited to the conventional situation of the accommodation party discussed in Comment 2. It also applies in four other situations. First, it applies to indorsers of notes who are not accommodation parties. Unless an indorser signs without recourse, the indorser's liability under Section 3–415(a) is functionally similar to that of a guarantor of payment. For example, if Bank in the second hypothetical discussed in Comment 2 indorsed the note and transferred it to Second Bank, Bank is liable to Second Bank in the event of dishonor of the note by Borrower. Section 3–415(a). Because of that secondary liability as indorser, Bank qualifies as a "secondary obligor" under Section 3–103(a)(17) and has the same rights under Section 3–605 as an accommodation party.

Second, a similar analysis applies to the drawer of a draft that is accepted by a party that is not a bank. Under Section 3–414(d), that drawer has liability on the same terms as an indorser under Section 3–415(a). Thus, the drawer in that case is a "secondary obligor" under Section 3–103(a)(17) and has rights under Section 3–605 to that extent.

Third, a similar principle justifies application of Section 3–605 to persons who indorse a check. Assume that Drawer draws a check to the order of Payee. Payee then indorses the check and transfers it to Transferee. If Transferee presents the check and it is dishonored, Transferee may recover from Drawer under Section 3–414 or Payee under Section 3–415. Because of that secondary liability as an indorser, Payee is a secondary obligor under Section 3–103(a)(17). Drawer is a "principal obligor" under Section 3–103(a)(11). As noted in Comment 4, below, however, Section 3–605(a)(3) will discharge indorsers of checks in some cases in which other secondary obligors will not be discharged by this section.

Fourth, this section also deals with the rights of co-makers of instruments, even when those co-makers do not qualify as accommodation parties. The co-makers' rights of contribution under Section 3–116 make each co-maker a secondary obligor to the extent of that right of contribution.

4. Subsection (a) is based on *Restatement of Suretyship and Guaranty* § 39. It addresses the effects of a release of the principal obligor by the person entitled to enforce the instrument. Paragraph (a)(1) governs the effect of that release on the principal obligor's duties to the secondary obligor; paragraphs (a)(2) and (a)(3) govern the effect of that release on the secondary obligor's duties to the person entitled to enforce the instrument.

With respect to the duties of the principal obligor, the release of course cannot affect obligations of the principal obligor with respect to payments that the secondary obligor already has made. But with respect to future payments by the secondary obligor, paragraph (a)(1) (based on *Restatement of Suretyship and Guaranty* § 39(a)) provides that the principal obligor is discharged, to the extent of the release, from any other duties to the secondary obligor. That rule is appropriate because otherwise the discharge granted to the principal obligor would be illusory: it would have obtained a release from a person entitled to enforce that instrument, but it would be directly liable for the same sum to the secondary obligor if the secondary obligor later complied with its secondary obligation to pay the instrument. This discharge does not occur, though, if the terms of the release effect a "preservation of recourse" as described in subsection (g). See Comment 10, below.

The discharge under paragraph (a)(1) of the principal obligor's duties to the secondary obligor is broad, applying to all duties under this article. This includes not only the principal obligor's liability as a party to an instrument (as a maker, drawer or indorser under Sections 3–412 through 3–415) but also obligations under Sections 3–116 and 3–419.

Paragraph (a)(2) is based closely on *Restatement of Suretyship and Guaranty* § 39(b). It articulates a default rule that the release of a principal obligor also discharges the secondary obligor, to the extent of the release granted to the principal obligor, from any unperformed portion of its obligation on the instrument. The discharge of the secondary obligor under paragraph (a)(2) is phrased more narrowly than the discharge of the principal obligor is phrased under paragraph (a)(1) because, unlike principal obligors, the only obligations of secondary obligors in Article 3 are "on the instrument" as makers or indorsers.

The parties can opt out of that rule by including a contrary statement in the terms of the release. The provision does not contemplate that any "magic words" are necessary. Thus, discharge of the secondary obligor under paragraph (a)(2) is avoided not only if the terms of the release track the statutory language (e.g., the person entitled to enforce the instrument "retains the right to enforce the instrument" against the secondary obligor), or if the terms of the release effect a preservation of recourse under subsection (g), but also if the terms of the release include a simple statement that the parties intend to "release the principal obligor but not the secondary obligor" or that the person entitled to enforce the instrument "reserves its rights" against the secondary obligor. At the same time, because paragraph (a)(2) refers to the "terms of the release," extrinsic circumstances cannot be used to establish that the parties intended the secondary obligor to remain obligated. If a release of the principal obligor includes such a provision, the secondary obligor is, nonetheless, discharged to the extent of the consideration that is paid for the release; that consideration is treated as a payment in partial satisfaction of the instrument.

Notwithstanding language in the release that prevents discharge of the secondary obligor under paragraph (a)(2), paragraph (a)(3) discharges the secondary obligor from its obligation to a person entitled to enforce the instrument to the extent that the release otherwise would cause the secondary obligor a loss. The rationale for that provision is that a release of the principal obligor changes the economic risk for which the secondary obligor contracted. This risk may be increased in two ways. First, by releasing the principal obligor, the person entitled to enforce the instrument has eliminated the likelihood of future payments by the principal obligor that would lessen the obligation of the secondary obligor. Second, unless the release effects a preservation of the secondary obligor's recourse, the release eliminates the secondary obligor's claims against the principal obligor with respect to any future payment by the secondary obligor. The discharge provided by this paragraph prevents that increased risk from causing the secondary obligor a loss. Moreover, permitting releases to be negotiated between the principal obligor and the person entitled to enforce the instrument without regard to the consequences to the secondary obligor would create an undue risk of opportunistic behavior by the obligee and principal obligor. That concern is lessened, and the discharge is not provided by paragraph (a)(3), if the secondary obligor has consented to the release or is deemed to have consented to it under subsection (f) (which presumes consent by a secondary obligor to actions taken by a principal obligor if the secondary obligor controls the principal obligor or deals with the person entitled to enforce the instrument on behalf of the principal obligor). See Comment 9, below.

Subsection (a) (and Restatement Section 39(b), the concepts of which it follows quite closely) is designed to facilitate negotiated workouts between a creditor and a principal obligor, so long as they are not at the expense of a secondary obligor who has not consented to the arrangement (either specifically or by waiving its rights to discharge under this section). Thus, for example, the provision facilitates an arrangement in which the principal obligor pays some portion of a guaranteed obligation, the person entitled to enforce the instrument grants a release to the principal obligor in exchange for that payment, and the person entitled to enforce the instrument pursues the secondary obligor for the remainder of the obligation. Under paragraph (a)(2), the person entitled to enforce the instrument may pursue the secondary obligor despite the release of the principal obligor so long as the terms of the release provide for this result. Under paragraph (a)(3), though, the secondary obligor will be protected against any loss it might suffer by reason of that release (if the secondary obligor has not waived discharge under subsection (f)). It should be noted that the obligee may be able to minimize the risk of such loss (and, thus, of the secondary obligor's discharge) by giving the secondary obligor prompt notice of the release even though such notice is not required.

The foregoing principles are illustrated by the following cases:

Case 1. D borrows $1000 from C. The repayment obligation is evidenced by a note issued by D, payable to the order of C. S is an accommodation indorser of the note. As the due date of the note approaches, it becomes obvious that D cannot pay the full amount of the note and may soon be facing bankruptcy. C, in order to collect as much as possible from D and lessen the need to seek recovery from S, agrees to release D from its obligation under the note in exchange for $100 in cash. The agreement to release D is silent as to the effect of the release on S. Pursuant to Section 3–605(a)(2), the release of D discharges S from its obligations to C on the note.

Case 2. Same facts as Case 1, except that the terms of the release provide that C retains its rights to enforce the instrument against S. D is discharged from its obligations to S pursuant to Section 3–605(a)(1), but S is not discharged from its obligations to C pursuant to Section 3–605(a)(2). However, if S could have recovered from D any sum it paid to C (had D not been discharged from its obligation to S), S has been harmed by the release and is discharged pursuant to Section 3–605(a)(3) to the extent of that harm.

Case 3. Same facts as Case 1, except that the terms of the release provide that C retains its rights to enforce the instrument against S and that S retains its recourse against D. Under subsection (g), the release effects a preservation of recourse. Thus, S is not discharged from its obligations to C pursuant to Section 3–605(a)(2) and D is not discharged from its obligations to S pursuant to Section 3–605(a)(1). Because S's claims against D are preserved, S will not suffer the kind of loss described in Case 2. If no other loss is suffered by S as a result of the release, S is not discharged pursuant to this section.

Case 4. Same facts as Case 3, except that D had made arrangements to work at a second job in order to earn the money to fulfill its obligations on the note. When C released D, however, D canceled the plans for the second job. While S still retains its recourse against D, S may be discharged from its obligation under the instrument to the extent that D's decision to forgo the second job causes S a loss because forgoing the job renders D unable to fulfill its obligations to S under Section 3–419.

Subsection (a) reflects a change from former Section 3–605(b), which provided categorically that the release of a principal obligor by the person entitled to enforce the instrument did not discharge a secondary obligor's obligation on the instrument and assumed that the release also did not discharge the principal obligor's obligations to the secondary obligor under Section 3–419. The rule under subsection (a) is much closer to the policy of the *Restatement of Suretyship and Guaranty* than was former Section 3–605(b). The change, however, is likely to affect only a narrow category of cases. First, as discussed above, Section 3–605 applies only to transactions in which the payment obligation is represented by a negotiable instrument, and, within that set of transactions, only to those transactions in which the secondary obligation is incurred by indorsement or cosigning, not to transactions that involve a separate document of guaranty. See Comment 2, above. Second, as provided in subsection (f), secondary obligors cannot obtain a discharge under subsection (a) in any transaction in which they have consented to the challenged conduct. Thus, subsection (a) will not apply to any transaction that includes a provision waiving suretyship defenses (a provision that is almost universally included in commercial loan documentation) or to any transaction in which the creditor obtains the consent of the secondary obligor at the time of the release.

The principal way in which subsection (a) goes beyond the policy of *Restatement* § 39 is with respect to the liability of indorsers of checks. Specifically, the last sentence of paragraph (a)(2) provides that a release of a principal obligor grants a complete discharge to the indorser of a check, without requiring the indorser to prove harm. In that particular context, it seems likely that continuing responsibility for the indorser often would be so inconsistent with the expectations of the parties as to create a windfall for the creditor and an unfair surprise for the indorser. Thus, the statute implements a simple rule that grants a complete discharge. The creditor, of course, can avoid that rule by contracting with the secondary obligor for a different result at the time that the creditor grants the release to the principal obligor.

5. Subsection (b) is based on *Restatement of Suretyship and Guaranty* § 40 and relates to extensions of the due date of the instrument. An extension of time to pay a note is often beneficial to the secondary obligor because the additional time may enable the principal obligor to obtain the funds to pay the instrument. In some cases, however, the extension may cause loss to the secondary obligor, particularly if deterioration of the financial condition of the principal obligor reduces the amount that the secondary obligor is able to recover on its right of recourse when default occurs. For example, suppose that the instrument is an installment note and the principal debtor is temporarily short of funds to pay a monthly installment. The payee agrees to extend the due date of the installment for a month or two to allow the debtor to pay when funds are available. Paragraph (b)(2) provides that an extension of time results in a discharge of the secondary obligor, but only to the extent that the secondary obligor proves that the extension caused loss. See subsection (h) (discussing the burden of proof under Section 3–605). Thus, if the extension is for a long period, the secondary obligor might be able to prove that during the period of extension the principal obligor became insolvent, reducing the value of the right of recourse of the secondary obligor. In such a case, paragraph (b)(2) discharges the secondary obligor to the extent of that harm. Although not required to notify the secondary obligor of the extension, the payee can minimize the risk of loss by the secondary obligor by giving the secondary obligor prompt notice of the extension; prompt notice can enhance the likelihood that the secondary obligor's right of recourse can remain valuable, and thus can limit the likelihood that the secondary obligor will suffer a loss because of the extension. See *Restatement of Suretyship and Guaranty* Section 38 comment b.

If the secondary obligor is not discharged under paragraph (b)(2) (either because it would not suffer a loss by reason of the extension or because it has waived its right to discharge pursuant to subsection (f)), it is important to understand the effect of the extension on the rights and obligations of the secondary obligor. Consider the following cases:

Case 5. A borrows money from Lender and issues a note payable to the order of Lender that is due on April 1, 2002. B signs the note for accommodation at the request of Lender. B signed the note either as co-maker or as an anomalous indorser. In either case Lender subsequently makes an agreement with A extending the due date of A's obligation to pay the note to July 1, 2002. In either case B did not agree to the extension, and the extension did not address Lender's rights against B. Under paragraph (b)(1), A's obligations to B under this article are also extended to July 1, 2002. Under paragraph (b)(3), if B is not discharged, B may treat its obligations to Lender as also extended, or may pay the instrument on the original due date.

Case 6. Same facts as Case 5, except that the extension agreement includes a statement that the Lender retains its right to enforce the note against B on its original terms. Under paragraph (b)(3), B is liable on the original due date, but under paragraph (b)(1), A's obligations to B under Section 3–419 are not due until July 1, 2002.

Case 7. Same facts as Case 5, except that the extension agreement includes a statement that the Lender retains its right to enforce the note against B on its original terms and B retains its recourse against A as though no extension had been granted. Under paragraph (b)(3), B is liable on the original due date. Under paragraph (b)(1), A's obligations to B under Section 3–419 are not extended.

Under section 3–605(b), the results in Case 5 and Case 7 are identical to the results that follow from the law of suretyship and guaranty. See *Restatement of Suretyship and Guaranty* § 40. The situation in Case 6 is not specifically addressed in the Restatement, but the resolution in this Section is consistent with the concepts of suretyship and guaranty law as reflected in the Restatement. If the secondary obligor is called upon to pay on the due date, it may be difficult to quantify the extent to which the extension has impaired the right of recourse of the secondary obligor at that time. Still, the secondary obligor does have a right to make a claim against the obligee at that time. As a practical matter a suit making such a claim should establish the facts relevant to the extent of the impairment. *See Restatement of Suretyship and Guaranty* § 37(4).

As a practical matter, an extension of the due date will normally occur only when the principal obligor is unable to pay on the due date. The interest of the secondary obligor normally is to acquiesce in the willingness of the person entitled to enforce the instrument to wait for payment from the principal obligor rather than to pay right away and rely on an action against the principal obligor that may have little or no value. But in unusual cases the secondary obligor may prefer to pay the holder on the original due date so as to avoid continuing accrual of interest. In such cases, the secondary obligor may do so. See paragraph (b)(3). If the terms of the extension provide that the person entitled to enforce the instrument retains its right to enforce the instrument against the secondary obligor on the original due date, though, those terms are effective and the secondary obligor may not delay payment until the extended due date. Unless the extension agreement effects a preservation of recourse, however, the secondary obligor may not proceed against the principal obligor under Section 3–419 until the extended due date. See paragraph (b)(1). To the extent that delay causes loss to the secondary obligor it is discharged under paragraph (b)(2).

Even in those cases in which a secondary obligor does not have a duty to pay the instrument on the original due date, it always has the right to pay the instrument on that date, and perhaps minimize its loss by doing so. The secondary obligor is not precluded, however, from asserting its rights to discharge under Section 3–605(b)(2) if it does not exercise that option. The critical issue is whether the extension caused the secondary obligor a loss by increasing the difference between its cost of performing its obligation on the instrument and the amount recoverable from the principal obligor under this Article. The decision by the secondary obligor not to exercise its option to pay on the original due date may, under the circumstances, be a factor to be considered in the determination of that issue, especially if the secondary obligor has been given prompt notice of the extension (as discussed above).

6. Subsection (c) is based on *Restatement of Suretyship and Guaranty* § 41. It is a residual provision, which applies to modifications of the obligation of the principal obligor that are not covered by subsections (a) and (b). Under subsection (c)(1), a modification of the obligation of the principal obligor on the instrument (other than a release covered by subsection (a) or an extension of the due date covered by subsection (b)), will correspondingly modify the duties of the principal obligor to the secondary obligor. Under subsection (c)(2), such a modification also will result in discharge of the secondary obligor to the extent the modification causes loss to the secondary obligor. To the extent that the secondary obligor is not discharged and the obligation changes the amount of money

payable on the instrument, or the timing of such payment, subsection (c)(3) provides the secondary obligor with a choice: it may satisfy its obligation on the instrument as if the modification had not occurred, or it may treat its obligation to pay the instrument as having been modified in a manner corresponding to the modification of the principal obligor's obligation.

The following cases illustrate the application of subsection (c):

Case 8. Corporation borrows money from Lender and issues a note payable to Lender. X signs the note as an accommodation party for Corporation. The note refers to a loan agreement under which the note was issued, which states various events of default that allow Lender to accelerate the due date of the note. Among the events of default are breach of covenants not to incur debt beyond specified limits and not to engage in any line of business substantially different from that currently carried on by Corporation. Without consent of X, Lender agrees to modify the covenants to allow Corporation to enter into a new line of business that X considers to be risky, and to incur debt beyond the limits specified in the loan agreement to finance the new venture. This modification discharges X to the extent that the modification otherwise would cause X a loss.

Case 9. Corporation borrows money from Lender and issues a note payable to Lender in the amount of $100,000. X signs the note as an accommodation party for Corporation. The note calls for 60 equal monthly payments of interest and principal. Before the first payment is made, Corporation and Lender agree to modify the note by changing the repayment schedule to require four annual payments of interest only, followed by a fifth payment of interest and the entire $100,000 principal balance. To the extent that the modification does not discharge X, X has the option of fulfilling its obligation on the note in accordance with the original terms or the modified terms.

7. Subsection (d) is based on *Restatement of Suretyship and Guaranty* § 42 and deals with the discharge of secondary obligors by impairment of collateral. The last sentence of subsection (d) states four common examples of what is meant by impairment. Because it uses the term "includes," the provision allows a court to find impairment in other cases as well. There is extensive case law on impairment of collateral. The secondary obligor is discharged to the extent that the secondary obligor proves that impairment was caused by a person entitled to enforce the instrument. For example, assume that the payee of a secured note fails to perfect the security interest. The collateral is owned by the principal obligor who subsequently files in bankruptcy. As a result of the failure to perfect, the security interest is not enforceable in bankruptcy. If the payee were to obtain payment from the secondary obligor, the secondary obligor would be subrogated to the payee's security interest in the collateral under Section 3-419 and general principles of suretyship law. See *Restatement of Suretyship and Guaranty § 28(1)(c).* In this situation, though, the value of the security interest is impaired completely because the security interest is unenforceable. Thus, the secondary obligor is discharged from its obligation on the note to the extent of that impairment. If the value of the collateral impaired is as much or more than the amount of the note, and if there will be no recovery on the note as an unsecured claim, there is a complete discharge. Subsection (d) applies whether the collateral is personalty or realty, whenever the obligation in question is in the form of a negotiable instrument.

8. Subsection (e) is based on the former Section 3-605(h). The requirement of knowledge in the first clause is consistent with Section 9-628. The requirement of notice in the second clause is consistent with Section 3-419(c).

9. The importance of the suretyship defenses provided in Section 3-605 is greatly diminished by the fact that the right to discharge can be waived as provided in subsection (f). The waiver can be effectuated by a provision in the instrument or in a separate agreement. It is standard practice to include such a waiver of suretyship defenses in notes prepared by financial institutions or other commercial creditors. Thus, Section 3-605 will result in the discharge of an accommodation party on a note only in the occasional case in which the note does not include such a waiver clause and the person entitled to enforce the note nevertheless takes actions that would give rise to a discharge under this section without obtaining the consent of the secondary obligor.

Because subsection (f) by its terms applies only to a discharge "under this section," subsection (f) does not operate to waive a defense created by other law (such as the law governing enforcement of security interests under Article 9) that cannot be waived under that law. See, e.g., Section 9-602.

The last sentence of subsection (f) creates an inference of consent on the part of the secondary obligor whenever the secondary obligor controls the principal obligor or deals with the creditor on behalf of the principal obligor. That sentence is based on *Restatement of Suretyship and Guaranty* § 48(2).

10. Subsection (g) explains the criteria for determining whether the terms of a release or extension preserve the secondary obligor's recourse, a concept of importance in the application of subsections (a) and (b). First, the

terms of the release or extension must provide that the person entitled to enforce the instrument retains the right to enforce the instrument against the secondary obligor. Second, the terms of the release or extension must provide that the recourse of the secondary obligor against the principal obligor continues as though the release or extension had not been granted. Those requirements are drawn from *Restatement of Suretyship and Guaranty* § 38.

11. Subsections (h) and (i) articulate rules for the burden of persuasion under Section 3–605. Those rules are based on *Restatement of Suretyship and Guaranty* § 49.

AMENDMENTS TO ARTICLE 4

BANK DEPOSITS AND COLLECTIONS

§ 4–103. Variation by Agreement; Measure of Damages; Action Constituting Ordinary Care.

Official Comment

. . .

4. Under this Article banks come under the general obligations of the use of good faith and the exercise of ordinary care. "Good faith" is defined in ~~Section 3–103(a)(4)~~ Section 1–201(b)(20). The term "ordinary care" is defined in Section 3–103(a)(9). These definitions are made to apply to Article 4 by Section 4–104(c). Section 4–202 states respects in which collecting banks must use ordinary care. Subsection (c) of Section 4–103 provides that action or non-action approved by the Article or pursuant to Federal Reserve regulations or operating circulars constitutes the exercise of ordinary care. Federal Reserve regulations and operating circulars constitute an affirmative standard of ordinary care equally with the provisions of Article 4 itself.

. . .

§ 4–104. Definitions and Index of Definitions.

. . .

(b) Other definitions applying to this Article and the sections in which they appear are:

"Agreement for electronic presentment" Section 4–110.
~~"Bank" Section 4–105.~~
"Collecting bank" Section 4–105.
"Depositary bank" Section 4–105.
"Intermediary bank" Section 4–105.
"Payor bank" Section 4–105.
"Presenting bank" Section 4–105.
"Presentment notice" Section 4–110.

(c) The following definitions in other Articles apply to this Article:

"Acceptance" Section 3–409.
"Alteration" Section 3–407.
"Cashier's check" Section 3–104.
"Certificate of deposit" Section 3–104.
"Certified check" Section 3–409.
"Check" Section 3–104.
"Good faith" Section 3–103.
"Holder in due course" Section 3–302.
"Instrument" Section 3–104.
"Notice of dishonor" Section 3–503.
"Order" Section 3–103.
"Ordinary care" Section 3–103.

"Person entitled to enforce" Section 3–301.

"Presentment" Section 3–501.

"Promise" Section 3–103.

"Prove" Section 3–103.

"Record" Section 3–103.

"Remotely-Created Consumer item" Section 3–103.

"Teller's check" Section 3–104.

"Unauthorized signature" Section 3–403.

(d) In addition, Article 1 contains general definitions and principles of construction and interpretation applicable throughout this Article.

§ 4-105. Definitions of Types of Banks ~~"Bank"; "Depositary Bank"; "Payor Bank"; "Intermediary Bank"; "Collecting Bank"; "Presenting Bank".~~

In this Article:

(1) ["Bank" means a person engaged in the business of banking, including a savings bank, savings and loan association, credit union, or trust company;]

(2) "Depositary bank" means the first bank to take an item even though it is also the payor bank, unless the item is presented for immediate payment over the counter;

(3) "Payor bank" means a bank that is the drawee of a draft;

(4) "Intermediary bank" means a bank to which an item is transferred in course of collection except the depositary or payor bank;

(5) "Collecting bank" means a bank handling an item for collection except the payor bank;

(6) "Presenting bank" means a bank presenting an item except a payor bank.

Legislative Note: A jurisdiction that enacts this statute that has not yet enacted the revised version of UCC Article 1 should leave the definition of "Bank" in Section 4–105(1). Section 4–105(1) is reserved for that purpose. A jurisdiction that has adopted or simultaneously adopts the revised Article 1 should delete the definition of "Bank" from Section 4–105(1), but should leave those numbers "reserved." If jurisdictions follow the numbering suggested here, the subsections will have the same numbering in all jurisdictions that have adopted these amendments (whether they have or have not adopted the revised version of UCC Article 1). In either case, they should change the title of the section, as indicated in these revisions, so that all jurisdictions will have the same title for the section.

§ 4-207. Transfer Warranties.

(a) A customer or collecting bank that transfers an item and receives a settlement or other consideration warrants to the transferee and to any subsequent collecting bank that:

(1) the warrantor is a person entitled to enforce the item;

(2) all signatures on the item are authentic and authorized;

(3) the item has not been altered;

(4) the item is not subject to a defense or claim in recoupment (Section 3-305(a)) of any party that can be asserted against the warrantor; ~~and~~

(5) the warrantor has no knowledge of any insolvency proceeding commenced with respect to the maker or acceptor or, in the case of an unaccepted draft, the ~~drawer.~~ drawer; and

(6) with respect to any remotely-created consumer item, that the person on whose account the item is drawn authorized the issuance of the item in the amount for which the item is drawn.

. . .

Official Comment

1. Except for subsection (b), this section conforms to Section 3–416 and extends its coverage to items. The substance of this section is discussed in the Comment to Section 3–416. Subsection (b) provides that customers or collecting banks that transfer items, whether by indorsement or not, undertake to pay the item if the item is dishonored. This obligation cannot be disclaimed by a "without recourse" indorsement or otherwise. With respect to checks, Regulation CC Section 229.34 states the warranties made by paying and returning banks.

2. For an explanation of subsection (a)(6), see comment 8 to Section 3–416.

§ 4–208. Presentment Warranties.

(a) If an unaccepted draft is presented to the drawee for payment or acceptance and the drawee pays or accepts the draft, (i) the person obtaining payment or acceptance, at the time of presentment, and (ii) a previous transferor of the draft, at the time of transfer, warrant to the drawee that pays or accepts the draft in good faith that:

(1) the warrantor is, or was, at the time the warrantor transferred the draft, a person entitled to enforce the draft or authorized to obtain payment or acceptance of the draft on behalf of a person entitled to enforce the draft;

(2) the draft has not been altered; and

(3) the warrantor has no knowledge that the signature of the purported drawer of the draft is ~~unauthorized.~~ unauthorized; and

(4) with respect to any remotely-created consumer item, that the person on whose account the item is drawn authorized the issuance of the item in the amount for which the item is drawn.

. . .

Official Comment

1. This section conforms to Section 3–417 and extends its coverage to items. The substance of this section is discussed in the Comment to Section 3–417. "Draft" is defined in Section 4–104 as including an item that is an order to pay so as to make clear that the term "draft" in Article 4 may include items that are not instruments within Section 3–104.

2. For an explanation of subsection (a)(4), see comment 8 to Section 3–416.

§ 4–212. Presentment by Notice of Item Not Payable by, Through, or at Bank; Liability of Drawer or Indorser.

(a) Unless otherwise instructed, a collecting bank may present an item not payable by, through, or at a bank by sending to the party to accept or pay a ~~written~~ record providing notice that the bank holds the item for acceptance or payment. The notice must be sent in time to be received on or before the day when presentment is due and the bank must meet any requirement of the party to accept or pay under Section 3–501 by the close of the bank's next banking day after it knows of the requirement.

§ 4–301. Posting; Recovery of Payment by Return of Items; Time of Dishonor; Return of Items by Payor Bank.

(a) If a payor bank settles for a demand item other than a documentary draft presented otherwise than for immediate payment over the counter before midnight of the banking day of receipt, the payor bank may revoke the settlement and recover the settlement if, before it has made final payment and before its midnight deadline, it

~~(1) returns the item;~~ (1) returns the item;

(2) returns an image of the item, if the party to which the return is made has entered into an agreement to accept an image as a return of the item and the image is returned in accordance with that agreement; or

~~(2) sends written~~ (3) sends a record providing notice of dishonor or nonpayment if the item is unavailable for return.

. . .

Official Comment

. . .

8. Paragraph (a)(2) is designed to facilitate electronic check-processing by authorizing the payor bank to return an image of the item instead of the actual item. It applies only when the payor bank and the party to which the return has been made have agreed that the payor bank can make such a return and when the return complies with the agreement. The purpose of the paragraph is to prevent third parties (such as the depositor of the check) from contending that the payor bank missed its midnight deadline because it failed to return the actual item in a timely manner. If the payor bank missed its midnight deadline, payment would have become final under Section 4-215 and the depositary bank would have lost its right of chargeback under Section 4-214. Of course, the depositary bank might enter into an agreement with its depositor to resolve that problem, but it is not clear that agreements by banks with their customers can resolve all such issues. In any event, paragraph (a)(2) should eliminate the need for such agreements. The provision rests on the premise that it is inappropriate to penalize a payor bank simply because it returns the actual item a few business days after the midnight deadline of the payor bank sent notice before that deadline to a collecting bank that had agreed to accept such notices.

Nothing in paragraph (a)(2) authorizes the payor bank to destroy the check.

§ 4-302. Payor's Bank Responsibility for Late Return of Item.

Official Comment

. . .

2. If the settlement given by the payor bank does not become final, there has been no payment under Section 4-215(b), and the payor bank giving the failed settlement is accountable under subsection (a)(1) of Section 4-302. For instance, the payor bank makes provisional settlement by sending a teller's check that is dishonored. In such a case settlement is not final under Section 4-213(c) and no payment occurs under Section 4-215(b). Payor bank is accountable on the item. The general principle is that unless settlement provides the presenting bank with usable funds, settlement has failed and the payor bank is accountable for the amount of the item. On the other hand, if the payor bank makes a settlement for the item that becomes final under Section 4-215, the item has been paid and thus the payor bank is not accountable for the item under this Section. [Amendment approved by the Permanent Editorial Board for Uniform Commercial Code November 2, 2002.]

. . .

§ 4-403. Customer's Right to Stop Payment; Burden of Proof of Loss.

(b) A stop-payment order is effective for six months, but it lapses after 14 calendar days if the original order was oral and was not confirmed in ~~writing~~ a record within that period. A stop-payment order may be renewed for additional six-month periods by a ~~writing~~ record given to the bank within a period during which the stop-payment order is effective.

. . .

§ 4-406. Customer's Duty to Discover and Report Unauthorized Signature or Alteration.

Official Comment

. . .

4. Subsection (e) replaces former subsection (3) and poses a modified comparative negligence test for determining liability. See the discussion on this point in the Comments to Sections 3-404, 3-405, and 3-406. The

term "good faith" is defined in ~~Section 3–103(a)(4)~~ Section 1–201(b)(20) as including "observance of reasonable commercial standards of fair dealing." The connotation of this standard is fairness and not absence of negligence.

. . .

APPENDIX D

PEB COMMENTARIES AND REPORTS ON THE UNIFORM COMMERCIAL CODE

CONTENTS

PEB RESOLUTION ON PURPOSES, STANDARDS AND PROCEDURES FOR PEB COMMENTARY TO THE UCC

1. **The Permanent Editorial Board (PEB), in accordance with the standards and procedures set out in this resolution of March 14, 1987, and the authority given in the agreement between the American Law Institute and the National Conference of Commissioners on Uniform State Laws dated July 31, 1986, will issue supplemental commentary on the Uniform Commercial Code (UCC) from time to time.**

   a. The supplemental commentary of the PEB generally will be known as *PEB Commentary,* to distinguish it from the Official Comments to the UCC, and will be preserved separately from the Official Comments.

   b. The underlying purposes and policies of the *PEB Commentary* are those specified in UCC § 1–102(2). A *PEB Commentary* should come within one or more of the following specific purposes, which should be made apparent at the inception of the Commentary: (1) to resolve an ambiguity in the UCC by restating more clearly what the PEB considers to be the legal rule; (2) to state a preferred resolution of an issue on which judicial opinion or scholarly writing diverges; (3) to elaborate on the application of the UCC where the statute and/or the Official Comment leaves doubt as to inclusion or exclusion of, or application to, particular circumstances or transactions; (4) consistent with UCC § 1–102(2)(b), to apply the principles of the UCC to new or changed circumstances; (5) to clarify or elaborate upon the operation of the UCC as it relates to other statutes (such as the Bankruptcy Code and various federal and state consumer protection statutes) and general principles of law and equity pursuant to UCC § 1–103; or (6) to otherwise improve the operation of the UCC.

c. The format of the *PEB Commentary* normally will consist of an identification of the issue, a discussion concerning the possible resolutions of the issue to be addressed, and a statement of the view of the PEB as to how the issue should be resolved. On a carefully selected basis supplemental commentary may be issued as an identified supplement to the Official Comments, in which case it generally should take the form of a brief exposition modeled substantially on the form and style of the Official Comments.

d. Topics for *PEB Commentary* will be selected periodically by the PEB from suggestions, accompanied by supporting reasons, made by PEB members and by other persons. *PEB Commentary* may be issued whether or not a perceived issue has been litigated or is in litigation, and whether or not the position taken by the PEB accords with the weight of authority on the issue. The number of topics and topics that are chosen at any given time will be determined by the PEB weighing criteria appropriate under the circumstances, which may include the practical importance of the issue, the absence of other means of resolution, the time and effort to be involved in the preparation of the *PEB Commentary,* the extent to which the *PEB Commentary* is likely to be successful in addressing an issue, whether it is known to the PEB that the topic of the *PEB Commentary* is in specific litigation and, if so, the probable impact upon that litigation, and the availability of resources. However, normally no *PEB Commentary* should be begun with respect to a UCC Article that is undergoing amendment or initial promulgation except upon consultation with and concurrence of the study or drafting committee for such amendment or initial promulgation. Moreover, except in extraordinary cases and in the case of *PEB Commentary* identified as specific supplements to Official Comments, an Official Comment, as opposed to the text of the UCC, should not be the specific subject of *PEB Commentary.*

e. For a variety of reasons, topics initially identified by the PEB for *PEB Commentary* and advisors' drafts of *PEB Commentary* (discussed in paragraph 2 below) may not result in the final approval of *PEB Commentary.* Such reasons might include the failure of a consensus to emerge on the substance of an issue or a conclusion that the issue would better be treated by a change in the UCC Official Text. No inference should be drawn from, and no weight should be accorded to, any withdrawal of an advisor's draft or any failure to proceed with a *PEB Commentary* on any particular topic.

2. The process by which *PEB Commentary* is prepared and issued by the PEB should be flexible, but usually should include:

a. periodic publication of the topics under consideration by the PEB with a request for comment by interested persons by a stated date as to whether any listed topic should be deleted or a related topic added and as to the appropriate resolution of the issues presented by the topics under consideration;

b. selection of one or more appropriate advisers, who are not members of the PEB, to review any comments submitted by interested persons and other relevant materials and to prepare a tentative adviser's draft of the proposed *PEB Commentary;*

c. publication of the adviser's draft of the *PEB Commentary,* after supervisory review of the PEB, soliciting comments by interested persons by a stated date on the substance and style of the work;

d. approval by the PEB of the substance and style of the *PEB Commentary* as finally submitted by the adviser(s) and comments submitted by interested persons or, when warranted, the withdrawal of the proposal with the reasons for withdrawal stated; and

e. periodic publication of such *PEB Commentary* as is approved by the PEB on a regular schedule.

Approval by the PEB of *PEB Commentary* shall be by three quarters of the members of the PEB voting on the *Commentary.* The manner of publication of *PEB Commentary* by the PEB will be in accordance with procedures formulated under a resolution related to that subject generally.

PEB COMMENTARY NO. 10
SECTION 1–203*
(February 10, 1994)

ISSUE

Section 1–203 provides that "Every contract or duty within this Act imposes an obligation of good faith in its performance or enforcement."[1] While this concept applies generally to every contract, it finds particular expression throughout the Code. For example, out of over 400 Code provisions, more than 50 sections make specific reference to "good faith."[2]

The meaning of "good faith" varies with the context. Sometimes the context is as a standard of performance or enforcement; other times the context is that of good faith purchase.[3] This Commentary deals only with good faith performance or enforcement of a right or duty under a contract that is within the Code.

In the context in which the obligation of good faith functions as the standard of contract performance or enforcement, can the failure to meet this standard support a cause of action where no other basis for a cause of action exists? This Commentary examines this question in order to promote a uniform understanding of what it means to say that a general obligation of good faith is imposed on every contracting party. In so doing, several principles are discussed.

DISCUSSION

1. *Good Faith, Commercial Expectations, and the Concept of Agreement*

Section 1–201(19) defines good faith as "honesty in fact in the conduct or transaction concerned."[4] Commentators have said that this general requirement of good faith sets a "subjective" standard,[5] while the particularized definitions elsewhere also create an additional "objective" standard of the observance of reasonable commercial standards of fair dealing. This Commentary applies with equal force to both standards of good faith.

The principal author of the Code, Karl Llewellyn, recognized that parties develop expectations over time against the background of commercial practices and that if commercial law fails to account for those practices, it will cut against the parties' actual expectations. In an unpublished commentary on the Proposed Final Draft of the Uniform Revised Sales Act, Llewellyn had this to say about good faith:

> No inconsistency of language and background exists merely because the words used mean something different to an outsider than they do to the merchants who used that language in the light of the commercial background against which they contracted. This is the necessary result of applying commercial standards and principles of good faith to the agreement. . . . Moreover, where the commercial background normally gives to a term in question some breadth of meaning so that it

---

* *Note from West Advisory Panel: Referring to unrevised Article 1. See revised § 1–304.*

[1] This does not mean that the obligation of good faith as defined in the Code will necessarily apply to all aspects of the same transaction. As written, the scope of § 1–203 is co-extensive with the Code's coverage. For example, if a loan agreement that provides for an Article 9 security interest also contains financial covenants which are not governed by the Code, § 1–203 would apply to the former and the general law of contracts would apply to the latter. See, e.g., Restatement, Second, Contracts § 205 (1981).

[2] Farnsworth, *Good Faith Performance and Commercial Reasonableness Under the Uniform Commercial Code,* 30 U.Chi.L.Rev. 666, 667 (1963).

[3] See, e.g., UCC §§ 2–403 (good faith purchaser); 3–302 (holder in due course); 9–307 (buyer in the ordinary course of business). On the distinction between the doctrines of good faith performance and good faith purchase, see generally id.

[4] This sparse definition found in Article 1 is expanded elsewhere in the Code for purposes of particular Articles. See, e.g., §§ 2–103(1)(b); 2A–103(2); 3–103(a)(4); 4–104(c); 4A–105(a)(6). This expanded definition "is concerned with the fairness of conduct rather than the care with which an act is performed." UCC § 3–103, Comment 4.

[5] See Aronstein, *Good Faith Performance of Security Agreements: The Liability of Corporate Managers,* 120 U.Pa.L.Rev. 1, 31 (1971) ("Good faith [as] defined in § 1–201(19) . . . [has] been historically construed as applying only to the actor's subjective state of mind."); Braucher, *The Legislative History of the Uniform Commercial Code,* 58 Colum.L.Rev. 798, 812 (1958) (describing the test of good faith in § 1–201(19) as a "subjective" test, sometimes known as the rule of "the pure heart and empty head"); Lawrence, *The Prematurely Reported Demise of the Perfect Tender Rule,* 35 U.Kan.L.Rev. 557, 571 (1987) ("Good faith is a subjective term meaning 'honesty in fact in the contract or transaction concerned.' ").

describes a range of acceptable tolerances rather than a sharp-edged single line of action, any attempted narrowing of this meaning by one party is so unusual as not likely to be expected or perceived by the other. Therefore, attention must be called to a desire to contract at material variance from the accepted commercial pattern of contract or use of language. Thus, this Act rejects any "surprise" variation from the fair and normal meaning of the agreement.[6]

Explaining the doctrine of good faith in such terms is thus a recognition that, as expressed in the Code, it serves as a directive to protect the reasonable expectations of the contracting parties. The general imperative that the reasonable expectations of the parties are the measure of the good faith of each suggests that good faith is a concept with conceptual content related to that of agreement.

The Code definition of "Agreement" reads:

"Agreement" means the bargain of the parties in fact as found in their language or by implication from other circumstances including course of dealing or usage of trade or course of performance as provided in this Act (Sections 1–205 and 2–208).[7]

The agreement of the parties consists of more than their language alone. In elaborating on this theme, Comment 3 to § 1–201 emphasizes that "the word [agreement] is intended to include full recognition of usage of trade, course of dealing, *course of performance* and the surrounding circumstances as effective parts thereof. . . ." (emphasis added).[8]

"Course of dealing" is defined as follows:

A course of dealing is a sequence of previous conduct between the parties to a particular transaction which is fairly to be regarded as establishing a common basis of understanding for interpreting their expressions and other conduct.[9]

"Usage of trade" is defined as follows:

A usage of trade is any practice or method of dealing having such regularity of observance in a place, vocation or trade as to justify an expectation that it will be observed with respect to the transaction in question. The existence and scope of such a usage are to be proved as facts. If it is established that such a usage is embodied in a written trade code or similar writing the interpretation of the writing is for the court.[10]

---

[6] The Karl Llewellyn Papers, The University of Chicago Law Library, File J.X.2.K. 1, 9, *reprinted in* D. Patterson, *Good Faith and Lender Liability* 217 (1990).

[7] UCC § 1–201(3). Furthermore, Comment 1 to § 1–205 ("Course of Dealing and Usage of Trade") reinforces this definition by stating:

This Act rejects both the "lay-dictionary" and the "conveyancer's" reading of a commercial agreement. Instead the meaning of the agreement of the parties is to be determined by the language used by them and by their action, read and interpreted in the light of commercial practices and other surrounding circumstances. The measure and background for interpretation are set by the commercial context, which may explain and supplement even the language of a formal or final writing.

[8] This Commentary recognizes the fact that course of performance is defined in Articles 2 and 2A and was originally not a part of the general definition of "Agreement" in Article 1. The concept is included here as an element of the agreement of the parties because there exists no plausible justification for excluding it. This view is strongly supported by Comments 1 and 2 to § 2–208. Comment 2, in particular, emphasizes that "a course of performance is always relevant to determine the meaning of the agreement." See also Westinghouse Credit Corp. v. Shelton, 645 F.2d 869, 31 UCC Rep.Serv. (Callaghan) 410 (10th Cir. 1981) (course of performance may also be used for discerning the meaning of "Agreement" in Article 9).

The Restatement, Second, of Contracts does not reflect the Code's isolation of course of performance in Articles 2 and 2A. The Restatement provides that all four elements—express terms, course of dealing, course of performance, and usage of trade—are all elements of the meaning of "contract." See Restatement, Second, Contracts § 203. In fact, § 202(4) states that "any course of performance accepted or acquiesced in without objection is given great weight in the interpretation of the agreement."

[9] UCC § 1–205(1).

[10] UCC § 1–205(2).

"Course of performance" is defined as follows:

> Where the contract for sale involves repeated occasions for performance by either party with knowledge of the nature of the performance and opportunity for objection to it by the other, any course of performance accepted or acquiesced in without objection shall be relevant to determine the meaning of the agreement.[11]

In addition to two definitional sections, § 1–205 contains two additional methodological sections which direct how express terms, course of dealing, and usage of trade are to be synthesized:

> (3) A course of dealing between parties and any usage of trade in the vocation or trade in which they are engaged or of which they are or should be aware give particular meaning to and supplement or qualify terms of an agreement.
>
> (4) The express terms of an agreement and an applicable course of dealing or usage of trade shall be construed wherever reasonable as consistent with each other; but when such construction is unreasonable express terms control both course of dealing and usage of trade and course of dealing controls usage of trade.[12]

At this juncture it is important to recognize that one acts in good faith relative to the agreement of the parties. To decide the question whether a party has acted in good faith, a court must first ascertain the substance of the parties' agreement.

The performance and enforcement of agreements in a manner consistent with the reasonable expectations of the parties is in keeping with the broadest understanding of contract doctrine.[13] The Code is consistent with this tradition of thought. However, the Code's concept of agreement broadens the sources for determining the meaning of the parties' agreement. The concept of agreement is not limited to the terms of the parties' writing: it includes a variety of elements, all of which must be synthesized.

Under § 1–205(4), the initial interpretive effort is to read all the terms as consistent with one another. Only when this is impossible does the interpreter then move to a lexical ordering of the terms, with express terms at the head of the list. Cases which make no attempt to reconcile the various terms before according priority to express terms in the construction of the parties' agreement must be considered to have proceeded improperly.[14] The better application of § 1–205(4), and the issues of interpretation which are central to it, is illustrated in cases like *Nanakuli Paving & Rock Co. v. Shell Oil Co.*, 664 F.2d 772, 32 UCC Rep.Serv. (Callaghan) 1025 (9th Cir. 1981) (upholding a finding that the written price term in an asphalt supply

---

[11] UCC § 2–208(1). This definition is duplicated in § 2A–207(1).

[12] UCC § 1–205(3)–(4). The connection between § 1–205 and good faith is made explicit in the Comment to § 1–203, wherein it is stated that the obligation of good faith "is further implemented by Section 1–205 on course of dealing and usage of trade."

The interpretational priorities set forth in § 1–205 are, with the added inclusion of course of performance, duplicated in § 2–208(2). That section states as follows:

> The express terms of the agreement and any such course of performance, as well as any course of dealing and usage of trade, shall be construed whenever reasonable as consistent with each other; but when such construction is unreasonable, express terms shall control course of performance and course of performance shall control both course of dealing and usage of trade (Section 1–205).

See also UCC § 2A–207(2).

[13] See 3 A. Corbin, *Corbin on Contracts* § 570 (West Supp. 1993).

> If the purpose of contract law is to enforce the reasonable expectations of parties induced by promises, then at some point it becomes necessary for courts to look to the substance rather than to the form of the agreement, and to hold that substance controls over form. What courts are doing here, whether calling the process "implication" of promises, or interpreting the requirements of "good faith," as the current fashion may be, is but a recognition that the parties occasionally have understandings or expectations that were so fundamental that they did not need to negotiate about those expectations. When the court "implies a promise" or holds that "good faith" requires a party not to violate those expectations, it is recognizing that sometimes silence says more than words, and it is understanding its duty to the spirit of the bargain is higher than its duty to the technicalities of the language.

Id. Reiter & Swan, Contracts and the Protection of Reasonable Expectations, in *Studies in Contract Law* 1, 11 (B. Reiter & J. Swan eds. 1980) ("[T]hroughout the law of contract, a striving to protect reasonable expectations is visible. . . .").

[14] See, e.g., Southern Concrete Servs. v. Mableton Contractors, Inc., 407 F.Supp. 581, 19 UCC Rep.Serv. (Callaghan) 79 (N.D.Ga. 1975), *aff'd mem.*, 569 F.2d 1154 (5th Cir. 1978); Division of Triple T Serv. v. Mobil Oil Corp., 304 N.Y.S.2d 191, 6 UCC Rep.Serv. (Callaghan) 1011 (Sup.Ct. 1969).

contract was qualified by a trade practice requiring suppliers to delay price increases for jobs on which buyers have already bid). Accordingly, in order to answer the question, "Has a party performed or enforced a contractual right or duty in good faith?", the content of the parties' agreement must first be determined.[15]

2. *UCC § 1-203 Does Not Create an Independent Cause of Action*

The inherent flaw in the view that § 1–203 supports an independent cause of action is the belief that the obligation of good faith has an existence which is conceptually separate from the underlying agreement. As the above discussion demonstrates, however, this is an incorrect view of the duty. "A party cannot simply 'act in good faith.' One acts in good faith relative to the agreement of the parties. Thus the real question is 'What is the Agreement of the parties?' "[16] Put differently, good faith merely directs attention to the parties' reasonable expectations; it is not an independent source from which rights and duties evolve.[17] The language of § 1–203 itself makes this quite clear by providing that the obligation to perform or enforce in good faith extends only to the rights and duties resulting from the parties' contract. The term "contract" is, in turn, defined as "the total legal obligation which results from the parties' *agreement*. . . ."[18] Consequently, resort to principles of law or equity outside the Code are not appropriate to create rights, duties, and liabilities inconsistent with those stated in the Code.[19] For example, a breach of a contract or duty within the Code arising from a failure to act in good faith does not give rise to a claim for punitive damages unless specifically permitted.[20]

CONCLUSION

Section 1–203 does not support a cause of action where no other basis for a cause of action exists.

The concept of Agreement permeates the entirety of the Code. For example, § 9–105(1)(*l*) incorporates the Article 1 concept of Agreement directly into Article 9. The "agreement of the parties" cannot be read off the face of a document, but must be discerned against the background of actual commercial practice. Not only does the Code recognize "the reasonable practices and standards of the commercial community . . . [as] an appropriate source of legal obligation,"[21] but it also rejects the "premise that the language used [by the parties] has the meaning attributable to [it] by rules of construction existing in the law rather than the meaning which arises out of the commercial context in which it was used."[22] The correct perspective on the meaning of good faith performance and enforcement is the Agreement of the parties. The critical question is, "Has 'X' acted in good faith with respect to the performance or enforcement of some right or duty under the terms of the Agreement?" It is therefore wrong to conclude that as long as the agreement allows a party to do something, it is under all terms and conditions permissible. Such a conclusion overlooks completely the distinction between merely performing or enforcing a right or duty under an agreement on the one hand and, on the other hand, doing so in a way that recognizes that the agreement should be interpreted in a

[15] For a non-Code decision which is consistent with this approach, see Southwest Savings and Loan Association v. Sunamp Systems, Inc., 838 P.2d 1314 (Ariz.App. 1992) (holding that inquiry does not stop with recognition that lender had general authority in written loan agreement to take the particular action, but inquiry extends to whether lender exercised that authority "for a reason beyond the risks" assumed by borrower in loan agreement, or beyond borrower's "justified expectations," in the context of how a reasonable lender might act).

[16] Patterson, *supra,* at 143. Good faith is sometimes the basis of an implied term to fill a gap or deal with an omitted case, e.g., the duty of cooperation frequently imposed on a party whose cooperation is essential and not unreasonably burdensome; or, the duty to give notice within a reasonable time of some important fact of which the other party would otherwise be unaware. See § 2–309(3) and Comment 8; 2 Farnsworth on Contracts §§ 7.17, 7.17a (1990). A breach of such duties gives rise to a cause of action for breach of the contract of which the implied term becomes a part. Although such a cause of action arguably has the same practical content as a cause of action based upon a purported breach of § 1–203, there is an important methodological difference in that this Commentary requires, in the case of contracts within the Code, that the focus be upon the Agreement of the parties and their reasonable expectations.

[17] Cases reaching this conclusion include Management Assistance, Inc. v. Computer Dimensions, Inc., 546 F.Supp. 666 (N.D.Ga. 1982), *aff'd* 747 F.2d 708 (11th Cir. 1984), and Chandler v. Hunter, 340 So.2d 818, 21 UCC Rep.Serv. (Callaghan) 484 (Ala.Civ.App. 1976). A contrary conclusion was reached in Reid v. Key Bank of Southern Maine, Inc., 821 F.2d 9, 3 UCC Rep.Serv.2d (Callaghan) 1665 (1st Cir. 1987).

[18] UCC § 1–201(11) (emphasis supplied).

[19] See UCC § 1–103.

[20] See UCC § 1–106(1).

[21] Kastely, *Stock Equipment for the Bargain in Fact: Trade Usage, "Express Terms," and Consistency Under Section 1–205 of the Uniform Commercial Code,* 64 N.C.L.Rev. 777, 780 (1986).

[22] UCC § 2–202, Comment 1.

manner consistent with the reasonable expectations of the parties in the light of the commercial conditions existing in the context under scrutiny. The latter is the correct approach. Examples are: (1) Is it reasonable for a buyer in a particular locale or trade to expect that an express quantity term in a contract is "not really" a quantity term, but a mere projection to be adjusted according to market forces?;[23] (2) Does a party to a sales contract that permits discretionary termination have the right to expect that the decision whether to terminate will be made on the basis of sound business criteria?

The Official Comment to § 1–203 is amended by adding the following language at the end of the first paragraph:

This section does not support an independent cause of action for failure to perform or enforce in good faith. Rather, this section means that a failure to perform or enforce, in good faith, a specific duty or obligation under the contract, constitutes a breach of that contract or makes unavailable, under the particular circumstances, a remedial right or power. This distinction makes it clear that the doctrine of good faith merely directs a court towards interpreting contracts within the commercial context in which they are created, performed, and enforced, and does not create a separate duty of fairness and reasonableness which can be independently breached. See PEB Commentary No. 10, dated February 10, 1994.

PEB COMMENTARY NO. 11
SURETYSHIP ISSUES UNDER SECTIONS 3–116, 3–305, 3–415, 3–419, AND 3–605 (February 10, 1994, as amended to apply to Revised Article 9)*

INTRODUCTION

The promulgation of revised Article 3 of the Uniform Commercial Code has given rise to a number of questions concerning the provisions in that Article governing the rights and duties of accommodation parties. This heightened level of interest results from many factors. In particular, the provisions in revised Article 3 concerning accommodation parties differ significantly from those in former Article 3 in ways that are complex and not always obvious. Application of these rules often raises issues that were not pertinent under prior law. In addition, the promulgation in 1995 of the Restatement of Suretyship and Guaranty by The American Law Institute has generated greater interest in the rights and duties of sureties, including, of course, accommodation parties.

As a result of this heightened interest, the suretyship rules in Article 3 have been the subject of a great deal of scrutiny, which has resulted in a recognition that the treatment of some suretyship issues in revised Article 3 should be clarified. It is the purpose of this Commentary to answer several questions that have arisen concerning the rights and duties of accommodation parties. This Commentary concludes with a series of revisions and additions to the Comments to various sections in Article 3 that govern suretyship issues.

ISSUE 1

If another person agrees to be liable for the obligation of the maker of a note, are the rights and duties of that person determined by the provisions of Article 3 governing accommodation parties, by the general law of suretyship, or both?

DISCUSSION

A person who agrees to be liable for the debt of another is clearly a surety. See Restatement of Suretyship and Guaranty § 1. If the person effectuates the agreement by becoming a party (i.e., a co-maker or indorser) to the same instrument that creates the obligation, the surety is also an accommodation party. In such a case, the rules in §§ 3–116, 3–305, 3–415, 3–419, and 3–605 concerning accommodation parties

[23] See Columbia Nitrogen Corp. v. Royster Co., 451 F.2d 3, 9 UCC Rep.Serv. (Callaghan) 977 (4th Cir. 1971).

* PEB Commentary No. 11, which addresses suretyship issues that arise under Article 3 of the Uniform Commercial Code, was originally issued in 1994. Issue 11 in the original Commentary dealt with the power of an accommodation party on an instrument that is secured by a security interest governed by Uniform Commercial Code Article 9 to waive the rights of that party that were provided for in Part 5 of former Article 9. Since the issuance of the original Commentary, former Article 9 has been replaced with Revised Article 9 and the Restatement of Suretyship and Guaranty, which was in the process of being drafted in 1994, has been promulgated by the American Law Institute. This amended Commentary updates the discussion of Issue 11 to reflect Revised Article 9 and the promulgation of the Restatement of Suretyship and Guaranty.

are applicable. Of course, these sections will not resolve all possible issues concerning the rights and duties of the surety. In the event that a situation is presented that is not resolved by those sections, the resolution may be provided by the general law of suretyship because, pursuant to § 1–103, that law is applicable unless displaced by provisions of this Act. If the surety does not effectuate the obligation by becoming a party to the note, the surety is not an accommodation party. In that case, the surety's rights and duties are determined by the general law of suretyship.

In unusual cases, two parties to an instrument may have a surety relationship that is not governed by Article 3 because the requirements of § 3–419(a) are not fulfilled. For example, assume that the payee of an instrument would like to sell it, but the potential buyer will agree to buy the instrument only if, in the event that the instrument is dishonored, the buyer has recourse not only against the issuer and the payee but also against someone more creditworthy. Accordingly, the payee produces a creditworthy person who agrees to stand behind the payee's obligations with respect to the instrument. The transfer to the buyer is then made after both the payee and the creditworthy person indorse the instrument. The creditworthy person is a party to the instrument as an indorser and is an accommodation party for the issuer who is the accommodated party. The creditworthy person is also a surety with respect to the obligation of both the issuer and the payee as indorser. The creditworthy person, however, is not an accommodation party for the payee and the payee is not an accommodated party under § 3–419(a) inasmuch as the instrument was not issued for value given for the benefit of the payee. Therefore, the general law of suretyship, and not the provisions in Article 3 concerning accommodation parties, provides the rules that govern the suretyship relationship between the creditworthy person and the payee.[1]

ISSUE 2

What are the differences between the rights of an accommodation party with respect to the accommodated party under revised Article 3 and former Article 3?

DISCUSSION

Under the general law of suretyship, as between the principal obligor and the secondary obligor, it is the principal obligor who ought to bear the cost of performance. Restatement of Suretyship and Guaranty § 1. Suretyship law provides three mechanisms to effectuate that cost allocation. First, if the principal obligor is charged with notice of the secondary obligation, the principal obligor owes the secondary obligor a duty of performance; this duty of performance can be enforced by the secondary obligor through the mechanism commonly known as exoneration. Restatement of Suretyship and Guaranty § 21. Second, a secondary obligor who performs may be subrogated to the rights of the obligee against the principal obligor (regardless of whether the principal obligor was charged with notice of the secondary obligation). Restatement of Suretyship and Guaranty § 27. Third, if the principal obligor is charged with notice of the secondary obligation, the principal obligor must reimburse a secondary obligor who performs the obligation. Restatement of Suretyship and Guaranty § 22. If the principal obligor is not charged with notice of the secondary obligation, a secondary obligor who performs is nonetheless entitled to restitution from the principal obligor. Restatement of Suretyship and Guaranty § 26.

An accommodation party is always a surety. Former Article 3 explicitly provided in § 3–415(5) that an accommodation party who paid the instrument was entitled to enforce the instrument against the accommodated party. This right essentially codified the surety's right of subrogation. Other rights of the accommodation party against the accommodated party were left to the general law of suretyship through § 1–103. In § 3–419(e), revised Article 3 also in effect sets forth subrogation rights of accommodation parties by providing that such parties are "entitled to enforce the instrument against the accommodated party." That section also codifies the accommodation party's right to be reimbursed by the accommodated party. Unlike the general law of suretyship, however, that right is not limited to situations in which the accommodated party was charged with notice of the accommodation party's obligation. Thus, it need not be determined whether the accommodated party is charged with notice of the accommodation party's obligation, and the right of restitution that is present in the general law of suretyship is superfluous. Revised

---

[1] The revisions to Comment 3 to § 3–419 and Comment 6 to § 3–605 reflect this discussion. See Appendix, par. 3 and par. 10.

PEB COMMENTARY NO. 11

Article 3, like former Article 3, leaves the accommodated party's duty of performance and the accommodation party's concomitant right of exoneration to the general law of suretyship through § 1–103.[2]

ISSUE 3

Is an accommodation party entitled to reimbursement if the accommodated party had a defense to its obligation that could have been raised by the accommodation party against the person entitled to enforce the instrument?

DISCUSSION

The juxtaposition of the accommodated party's duty to reimburse the accommodation party (§ 3–419(e)) with the accommodated party's right to raise defenses (§ 3–305(b)) raises important policy issues. If a duty to reimburse exists even when the accommodated party had a defense, that duty could be said to obviate the value of the defense. On the other hand, if no duty to reimburse exists in such circumstances, the cost of performance will be borne ultimately by the accommodation party rather than the accommodated party.

There are a number of different contexts in which the situation may arise. Generally speaking, the accommodation party may raise as a defense to its obligation the defenses of the accommodated party to *its* obligation. See § 3–305(d). There are three exceptions. The accommodated party's defenses of discharge in insolvency proceedings, infancy, and lack of legal capacity are not available to the accommodation party. If the accommodation party pays the instrument when the accommodated party had one of these defenses, the accommodated party has no duty to reimburse the accommodation party. The accommodation party has, in a sense, assumed the risk that such defenses will exist.

Occasionally, an accommodation party will pay an instrument even though the accommodated party has a defense that is available to the accommodation party. In such cases, the existence of the duty to reimburse may depend on whether the accommodation party was aware of the defense at the time it paid the instrument. If the accommodation party was unaware of the defense, there is a duty to reimburse. Thus, there is an incentive for the accommodated party to make the accommodation party aware of any defenses it may have. If the accommodation party pays the instrument while aware of a defense of the accommodated party, however, reimbursement would ordinarily not be justified but might be justified in some circumstances. Resolution of this issue is left to the general law of suretyship through § 1–103.[3]

ISSUE 4

Section 3–415(a) provides that an indorser's obligation to pay the instrument upon dishonor is owed, *inter alia,* to a subsequent indorser who pays the instrument. What if both the prior indorser and subsequent indorser are anomalous indorsers?

DISCUSSION

In the general law of suretyship, when there are two secondary obligors for the same underlying obligation, the relationship between those two secondary obligors may be that of co-suretyship or sub-suretyship. In a co-suretyship situation, the two secondary obligors are jointly and severally liable and, as between themselves, have a right of contribution against each other. In a sub-suretyship situation, on the other hand, the second secondary obligor is, in a sense, a surety for the obligation of the first secondary obligor. Thus, as between the two secondary obligors, the first obligor occupies the position of a principal obligor while the later one occupies the position of a secondary obligor. It is often difficult to determine whether the two secondary obligors are co-sureties or sub-sureties, especially in the context of negotiable instruments when the obligations of those parties may be created by a signature alone, unaccompanied by words of explanation.

Article 3 treats successive anomalous indorsers as having joint and several liability on the instrument. See § 3–116(a). If one of the anomalous indorsers pays the instrument, that indorser has a right to receive contribution from the other indorser. See § 3–116(b). Accordingly, the general rule of § 3–415(a), that a subsequent indorser who pays the instrument may recover the full amount of the instrument from a prior indorser, does not apply in such cases. Section 3–116(b) does not recognize a distinction between a co-surety and a sub-surety, but in providing for a right to contribution, § 3–116(b) has the effect of treating anomalous

[2] The revision to Comment 5 to § 3–419 reflects this discussion. See Appendix, par. 5.

[3] The addition of Comments 6 and 7 to § 3–419 reflect this discussion. See Appendix, par. 6.

indorsers as though they were co-sureties. Section 3–116(b), however, is subject to "agreement of the affected parties." If the subsequent indorser can prove an agreement with the prior indorser giving the subsequent indorser rights as a sub-surety, that agreement changes the rule of § 3–116(b). If the subsequent indorser pays the instrument and has rights under the agreement as a sub-surety, the subsequent indorser has a right of recourse against the prior indorser for the amount of the payment rather than only a right to contribution; if the prior indorser pays the instrument, there is no right of recourse against the subsequent indorser.[4]

ISSUE 5

What effect do words of guaranty have on the obligation of an indorser to a person entitled to enforce an instrument?

DISCUSSION

Under former § 3–416, the obligation of an indorser who added the words "payment guaranteed" or "collection guaranteed" to the indorsement was different than that of an indorser who did not add those words. The addition of the words "payment guaranteed" (or their equivalent) meant that if the instrument was not paid when due the indorser would pay it without resort to any other party. Thus, an indorser who guaranteed payment could be said to have waived presentment, notice of dishonor, and protest, as well as all demand upon the maker or drawee. In contrast, the addition of the words "collection guaranteed" (or their equivalent) meant that the indorser was required to pay only after the holder reduced its claim against the maker or acceptor to judgment or it was shown that such a proceeding would be useless.

Section 3–419(d) preserves the concept of a guaranty of collection, but no provision is made for a guaranty of payment. Moreover, the preferred treatment given to a guarantor of collection is only applicable when the words accompanying the indorsement indicate "unambiguously that the party is guaranteeing collection rather than payment of the obligation of another party to the instrument." Thus, an indorser who adds the words "payment guaranteed," or the like, to the indorsement has the same liability as an indorser who added no special words to the indorsement. Such an indorser may be entitled, *inter alia*, to notice of dishonor pursuant to § 3–503.[5]

ISSUE 6

May a person entitled to enforce an instrument avoid discharge of an accommodation party pursuant to § 3–605 by "reserving rights" against that party in conjunction with a release, extension, or other modification of the duty of the accommodated party?

DISCUSSION

Under former UCC § 3–606(1)(a), a release, extension, or other modification of the accommodated party's duty accompanied by an express "reservation of rights" against the accommodation party would not discharge that party. This provision paralleled the general law of suretyship in many jurisdictions.

Article 3 rejects the reservation of rights doctrine. The effects of a release, extension, or other modification of the accommodated party's duty cannot be changed by the incantation of a "reservation of rights." Pursuant to § 3–605(b), a release of the accommodated party does not discharge the accommodation party, so there is no need for the person entitled to enforce the instrument to take any action, such as a reservation of rights, to preserve recourse against the accommodation party. Pursuant to § 3–605(c)–(d), an extension or modification of the accommodated party's duty discharges the accommodation party to the extent that the extension or modification would otherwise cause the accommodation party a loss. This discharge cannot be avoided by a "reservation of rights" by the person entitled to enforce the instrument.[6]

ISSUE 7

If a person entitled to enforce an instrument agrees to extend the due date of the accommodated party's performance and, pursuant to § 3–605(c), the extension does not discharge the accommodation party, what is the effect of the extension on the obligation of the accommodation party? In particular, is the due date for

---

[4] The addition of Comment 5 to § 3–415 reflects this discussion. See Appendix, par. 2.

[5] The revision to Comment 4 to § 3–419 reflects this discussion. See Appendix, par. 4.

[6] The revision to Comment 3 to § 3–605 reflects this discussion. See Appendix, par. 7.

the accommodation party's performance extended correspondingly? May the accommodation party perform on the original due date?

DISCUSSION

The person entitled to enforce the instrument will not be able to enforce the instrument against the accommodation party until the extended due date. If the accommodation party is an indorser, this is because an indorser is not liable until dishonor of the instrument, which, under these circumstances, cannot occur until it is unpaid on the extended due date. If the accommodation party is a co-maker, this is because, under § 3–305(d), until the extended due date the accommodation party will be able to assert the accommodated party's defense that, pursuant to the extension agreement, performance is not yet due.

The accommodation party may, however, perform on the original due date. The accommodation party is bound in accordance with the terms of its original engagement. The agreement between the accommodated party and the person entitled to enforce the instrument cannot bind the accommodation party to a change in its obligation without the accommodation party's consent. The effect on the recourse of the accommodation party against the accommodated party of performance by the accommodation party on the original due date is not addressed in § 3–419 and is left to the general law of suretyship.

Even though the accommodation party has the option of paying the instrument on the original due date, the accommodation party is not precluded from asserting its rights to discharge under § 3–605(c) if it does not exercise that option. The critical issue is whether the extension caused the accommodation party a loss by increasing the difference between the accommodation party's cost of performing its obligation on the instrument and the amount recoverable from the accommodated party pursuant to § 3–419(e). The decision by the accommodation party not to exercise its option to pay on the original due date may, under the circumstances, be a factor to be considered in the determination of that issue.[7]

ISSUE 8

What if the person entitled to enforce the instrument agrees, in one transaction, to both an extension of time for the accommodated party's performance and another modification of the accommodation party's obligation? What if there is a dispute as to whether, as a result of these changes, the accommodation party has suffered a loss?

DISCUSSION

This question highlights the difficulties in properly allocating the burden of persuasion when the agreement between the person entitled to enforce the instrument and the accommodated party involves both an extension governed by § 3–605(c) and a modification governed by § 3–605(d). The accommodation party has the burden of demonstrating loss from an extension, but the person entitled to enforce the instrument has the burden of overcoming a presumption of loss from other modifications.

If neither party introduces evidence as to loss causation, the result is full discharge of the accommodation party because § 3–605(d) applies. If the person entitled to enforce the instrument seeks to overcome the presumption of loss from the modification, it is entitled to a presumption that the extension alone caused no loss. Thus, the accommodation party will have to introduce evidence as to the effect of the extension, while the person entitled to enforce the instrument will have to introduce evidence as to the effect of the modification. On the basis of this evidence, the court will make an overall determination of the effect of the changes on the accommodation party's right of recourse against the accommodated party.[8]

ISSUE 9

How can § 3-305(d), which provides that the accommodation party can raise defenses of the accommodated party, be reconciled with § 3–605(b), which provides that a release of the accommodated party does not discharge the accommodation party?

DISCUSSION

While § 3–305(d) provides that an accommodation party can raise most defenses of the accommodated party, that section must be read in conjunction with § 3–605, which governs the effect on the obligation of

---

[7] The revision to Comment 4 to § 3–605 reflects this discussion. See Appendix, par. 8.

[8] The revision to Comment 5 to § 3–605 reflects this discussion. See Appendix, par. 9.

the accommodation party of an act or omission of the person entitled to enforce the instrument. Section 3–605(b) provides that a release of the accommodated party does not discharge the accommodation party. Thus, while examined in isolation, § 3–305(d) might seem to allow the accommodation party to raise, as a defense to *its* obligation, a release of the accommodated party granted by the person entitled to enforce the instrument, the applicability of that section to such a release must be considered in light of § 3–605(b). If the release of the accommodated party is part of a settlement pursuant to which the person entitled to enforce the instrument accepts partial payment from an accommodated party who is financially unable to pay the entire amount of the note, the transaction falls within the scope of § 3–605(b) and the accommodation party cannot escape liability by asserting § 3–305(d) essentially to nullify § 3–605(b). If, on the other hand, the release of the accommodated party is part of an accord and satisfaction settling a dispute as to the obligation of the accommodated party, the accommodation party may utilize § 3–305(d) to assert that release as a defense to its obligation because § 3–605(b) is not intended to apply to settlement of disputed claims.[9]

ISSUE 10

What sort of language is sufficient to waive discharge under § 3–605?

DISCUSSION

Section 3–605(i) provides that a party is not discharged under that section if the instrument or a separate agreement of the party waives such discharge "either specifically or by general language indicating that parties waive defenses based on suretyship or impairment of collateral." Thus, no particular language or form of agreement is required, and the standards for enforcing such a term are the same as the standards for enforcing any other term in an instrument or agreement. There is no requirement of particularity in referring to the four grounds for discharge established by § 3–605 so long as the language used indicates that suretyship defenses are waived. By allowing the use of general language, the rule recognizes that the use of lengthy provisions containing detailed waivers or even separate identification of each ground for discharge does not necessarily promote greater understanding of an instrument's terms. Yet, the requirement that the language indicate that defenses are being waived assures that a diligent indorser or accommodation party will, at the least, not be unjustly surprised when it is asserted that the terms of the instrument or agreement delete protections that would otherwise be available. In adopting this course, § 3–605 is consistent with the general law of suretyship. See Restatement of Suretyship and Guaranty § 48.[10]

ISSUE 11

As a result of § 3–605(i), may an accommodation party waive whatever protections it may have pursuant to Part 6 of Article 9?

DISCUSSION

Section 3–605(e) provides that impairment of an interest in collateral for the obligation of the accommodated party may discharge the accommodation party. Section 3–605(g) defines impairment of an interest in collateral as including, *inter alia,* failure to comply with applicable law in disposing of collateral. In the case of personal property or fixtures, applicable law includes, of course, Article 9. Thus, failure to comply with the rules in Part 6 of Article 9 concerning disposition of collateral for the accommodated party's obligation constitutes impairment of an interest in collateral. In addition, the accommodation party will qualify as an "obligor" and a "secondary obligor" with respect to that collateral. See § 9–102(a)(59), (71). Obligors and, to a much greater extent, secondary obligors, are provided with substantial protections in Part 6 of Article 9. Section 9–602 provides that, with few exceptions, obligors may not waive these protections. Section 3–605(i), on the other hand, provides that an accommodation party may waive discharge under this section (including discharge for impairment of an interest in collateral pursuant to § 3–605(e)). This does not mean that the accommodation party may waive *all* protections it may have concerning disposition of collateral; rather, it provides for the waiver of protections created by § 3–605. To the extent that Article 9 also provides the accommodation party similar protections, waiver of those protections is governed by Article 9 as interpreted in each jurisdiction.[11]

---

9 The revision to Comment 5 to § 3–305 reflects this discussion. See Appendix, par. 1.

10 The revision to Comment 8 to § 3–605 reflects this discussion. See Appendix, par. 11.

11 The revision to Comment 8 to § 3–605 reflects this discussion. See Appendix, par. 11.

PEB COMMENTARY NO. 11

APPENDIX

1. Comment 5 to § 3–305 is amended by adding an unnumbered paragraph as follows:

Section 3–305(d) must be read in conjunction with Section 3–605, which provides rules (usually referred to as suretyship defenses) for determining when the obligation of an accommodation party is discharged, in whole or in part, because of some act or omission of a person entitled to enforce the instrument. To the extent a rule stated in Section 3–605 is inconsistent with Section 3–305(d), the Section 3–605 rule governs. For example, under Section 3–605(b), discharge under Section 3–604 of the accommodated party does not discharge the accommodation party. As explained in Comment 3 to Section 3–605, discharge of the accommodated party is normally part of a settlement under which the holder of a note accepts partial payment from an accommodated party who is financially unable to pay the entire amount of the note. If the holder then brings an action against the accommodation party to recover the remaining unpaid amount of the note, the accommodation party cannot use Section 3–305(d) to nullify Section 3–605(b) by asserting the discharge of the accommodated party as a defense. On the other hand, suppose the accommodated party is a buyer of goods who issued the note to the seller who took the note for the buyer's obligation to pay for the goods. Suppose the buyer has a claim for breach of warranty with respect to the goods against the seller and the warranty claim may be asserted against the holder of the note. The warranty claim is a claim in recoupment. If the holder and the accommodated party reach a settlement under which the holder accepts payment less than the amount of the note in full satisfaction of the note and the warranty claim, the accommodation party could defend an action on the note by the holder by asserting the accord and satisfaction under Section 3–305(d). There is no conflict with Section 3–605(b) because that provision is not intended to apply to settlement of disputed claims. Other examples of the use of Section 3–305(d) in cases in which Section 3–605 applies are stated in Comment 4 to Section 3–605. See PEB Commentary No. 11, dated February 10, 1994.

2. A new Comment 5 to § 3–415 is added as follows:

5. As stated in subsection (a), the obligation of an indorser to pay the amount due on the instrument is generally owed not only to a person entitled to enforce the instrument but also to a subsequent indorser who paid the instrument. But if the prior indorser and the subsequent indorser are both anomalous indorsers, this rule does not apply. In that case, Section 3–116 applies. Under Section 3–116(a), the anomalous indorsers are jointly and severally liable and if either pays the instrument the indorser who pays has a right of contribution against the other. Section 3–116(b). The right to contribution in Section 3–116(b) is subject to "agreement of the affected parties." Suppose the subsequent indorser can prove an agreement with the prior indorser under which the prior indorser agreed to treat the subsequent indorser as a guarantor of the obligation of the prior indorser. Rights of the two indorsers between themselves would be governed by the agreement. Under suretyship law, the subsequent indorser under such an agreement is referred to as a sub-surety. Under the agreement, if the subsequent indorser pays the instrument there is a right to reimbursement from the prior indorser; if the prior indorser pays the instrument, there is no right of recourse against the subsequent indorser. See PEB Commentary No. 11, dated February 10, 1994.

3. Comment 3 to § 3–419 is amended by adding an unnumbered paragraph as follows:

An accommodation party is always a surety. A surety who is not a party to the instrument, however, is not an accommodation party. For example, if M issues a note payable to the order of P, and S signs a separate contract in which S agrees to pay P the amount of the instrument if it is dishonored, S is a surety but is not an accommodation party. In such a case, S's rights and duties are determined under the general law of suretyship. In unusual cases two parties to an instrument may have a surety relationship that is not governed by Article 3 because the requirements of Section 3–419(a) are not met. In those cases the general law of suretyship applies to the relationship. See PEB Commentary No. 11, dated February 10, 1994.

4. Comment 4 to § 3–419 is amended by adding the following two sentences:

Words added to an anomalous indorsement indicating that payment of the instrument is guaranteed by the indorser do not change the liability of the indorser as stated in Section 3–415. This is a change from former Section 3–416(5). See PEB Commentary No. 11, supra.

5. Comment 5 to § 3–419 is amended by deleting the struck-out words and adding the underlined words as follows:

5. Subsection (e) ~~restates subsection (5) of present Section 3–415~~ like former Section 3–415(5), provides that an accommodation party that pays the instrument is entitled to enforce the instrument against the accommodated party. Since the accommodation party that pays the instrument is entitled to enforce the instrument against the accommodated party, the accommodation party also obtains rights to any security interest or other collateral that secures payment of the instrument. Subsection (e) also provides that an accommodation party that pays the instrument is entitled to reimbursement from the accommodated party. See PEB Commentary No. 11, supra.

6. A new Comment 6 and a new Comment 7 to § 3–419 are added as follows:

6. In occasional cases, the accommodation party might pay the instrument even though the accommodated party had a defense to its obligation that was available to the accommodation party under Section 3–305(d). In such cases, the accommodation party's right to reimbursement may conflict with the accommodated party's right to raise its defense. For example, suppose the accommodation party pays the instrument without being aware of the defense. In that case the accommodation party should be entitled to reimbursement. Suppose the accommodation party paid the instrument with knowledge of the defense. In that case, to the extent of the defense, reimbursement ordinarily would not be justified, but under some circumstances reimbursement may be justified depending upon the facts of the case. The resolution of this conflict is left to the general law of suretyship. Section 1–103. See PEB Commentary No. 11, supra.

7. Section 3–419, along with Section 3–116(a) and (b), Section 3–305(d) and Section 3–605, provides rules governing the rights of accommodation parties. In addition, except to the extent that it is displaced by provisions of this Article, the general law of suretyship also applies to the rights of accommodation parties. Section 1–103. See PEB Commentary No. 11, supra.

7. Comment 3 to § 3–605 is amended by dividing it into two paragraphs, deleting the struck-out words, and adding the underlined words as follows:

3. Subsection (b) addresses the effect of discharge under Section 3–604 of the principal debtor. In the hypothetical case stated in Comment 1, release of Borrower by Bank does not release Accommodation Party. As a practical matter, Bank will not gratuitously release Borrower. Discharge of Borrower normally would be part of a settlement with Borrower if Borrower is insolvent or in financial difficulty. If Borrower is unable to pay all creditors, it may be prudent for Bank to take partial payment, but Borrower will normally insist on a release of the obligation. If Bank takes $3,000 and releases Borrower from the $10,000 debt, Accommodation Party is not injured. To the extent of the payment Accommodation Party's obligation to Bank is reduced. The release of Borrower by Bank does not affect the right of Accommodation Party to obtain reimbursement from Borrower or to enforce the note against Borrower if Accommodation Party pays Bank. Section 3–419(e). Subsection (b) is designed to allow a creditor to settle with the principal debtor without risk of losing rights against sureties. Settlement is in the interest of sureties as well as the creditor. Subsection (b), however, is not intended to apply to a settlement of a disputed claim which discharges the obligation.

Subsection (b) changes the law stated in former Section 3–606 but the change relates largely to formalities rather than substance. Under former Section 3–606, Bank in the hypothetical case stated in Comment 1 could settle with and release Borrower without releasing Accommodation Party, but to accomplish that result Bank had to either obtain the consent of Accommodation Party or make an express reservation of rights against Accommodation Party at the time it released Borrower. The reservation of rights was made in the agreement between Bank and Borrower by which the release of Borrower was made. There was no requirement in former Section 3–606 that any notice be given to Accommodation Party. ~~The reservation of rights doctrine is abolished in~~ Section 3–605 ~~with respect to rights on instruments~~ eliminates the necessity that Bank formally reserve rights against Accommodation Party in order to retain rights of recourse against Accommodation Party. See PEB Commentary No. 11, dated February 10, 1994.

8. Comment 4 to § 3–605 is amended by adding six unnumbered paragraphs as follows:

Under other provisions of Article 3, what is the effect of an extension agreement between the holder of a note and the maker who is an accommodated party? The question is illustrated by the following case:

Case # 1. A borrows money from Lender and issues a note payable on April 1, 1992. B signs the note for accommodation at the request of Lender. B signed the note either as co-maker or as an anomalous indorser. In either case Lender subsequently makes an agreement with A extending the due date of A's obligation to pay the note to July 1, 1992. In either case B did not agree to the extension.

What is the effect of the extension agreement on B? Could Lender enforce the note against B if the note is not paid on April 1, 1992? A's obligation to Lender to pay the note on April 1, 1992 may be modified by the agreement of Lender. If B is an anomalous indorser Lender cannot enforce the note against B unless the note has been dishonored. Section 3–415(a). Under Section 3–502(a)(3) dishonor occurs if it is not paid on the day it becomes payable. Since the agreement between A and Lender extended the due date of A's obligation to July 1, 1992 there is no dishonor because A was not obligated to pay Lender on April 1, 1992. If B is a co-maker the analysis is somewhat different. Lender has no power to amend the terms of the note without the consent of both A and B. By an agreement with A, Lender can extend the due date of A's obligation to Lender to pay the note but B's obligation is to pay the note according to the terms of the note at the time of issue. Section 3–412. However, B's obligation to pay the note is subject to a defense because B is an accommodation party. B is not obliged to pay Lender if A is not obliged to pay Lender. Under Section 3–305(d), B as an accommodation party can assert against Lender any defense of A. A has a defense based on the extension agreement. Thus, the result is that Lender could not enforce the note against B until July 1, 1992. This result is consistent with the right of B if B is an anomalous indorser.

As a practical matter an extension of the due date will normally occur when the accommodated party is unable to pay on the due date. The interest of the accommodation party normally is to defer payment to the holder rather than to pay right away and rely on an action against the accommodated party that may have little or no value. But in unusual cases the accommodation party may prefer to pay the holder on the original due date. In such cases, the accommodation party may do so. This is because the extension agreement between the accommodated party and the holder cannot bind the accommodation party to a change in its obligation without the accommodation party's consent. The effect on the recourse of the accommodation party against the accommodated party of performance by the accommodation party on the original due date is not addressed in § 3–419 and is left to the general law of suretyship.

Even though X has the option of paying the instrument on the original due date, X is not precluded from asserting its rights to discharge under Section 3–605(c) if it does not exercise that option. The critical issue is whether the extension caused X a loss by increasing the difference between X's cost of performing its obligation on the instrument and the amount recoverable from Corporation pursuant to Section 3–419(e). The decision by X not to exercise its option to pay on the original due date may, under the circumstances, be a factor to be considered in the determination of that issue. See PEB Commentary No. 11, supra.

9. Comment 5 to § 3–605 is amended by adding seven unnumbered paragraphs as follows:

The following is an illustration of the kind of case to which Section 3–605(d) would apply:

Case # 2. Corporation borrows money from Lender and issues a note payable to Lender. X signs the note as an accommodation party for Corporation. The loan agreement under which the note was issued states various events of default which allow Lender to accelerate the due date of the note. Among the events of default are breach of covenants not to incur debt beyond specified limits and not to engage in any line of business substantially different from that currently carried on by Corporation. Without consent of X, Lender agrees to modify the covenants to allow Corporation to enter into a new line of business that X considers to be risky, and to incur debt beyond the limits specified in the loan agreement to finance the new venture. This modification releases X unless Lender proves that the modification did not cause loss to X or that the loss caused by the modification was less than X's right of recourse.

Sometimes there is both an extension of the due date and some other modification. In that case both subsections (c) and (d) apply. The following is an example:

Case # 3. Corporation was indebted to Lender on a note payable on April 1, 1992 and X signed the note as an accommodation party for Corporation. The interest rate on the note was 12 percent. Lender and Corporation agreed to a six-month extension of the due date of the note to October 1, 1992 and an increase in the interest rate to 14 percent after April 1, 1992. Corporation defaulted on October 1, 1992. Corporation paid no interest during the six-month extension period. Corporation is insolvent and has no assets from which unsecured creditors can be paid. Lender demanded payment from X.

Assume X is an anomalous indorser. First consider Section 3–605(c) alone. If there had been no change in the interest rate, the fact that Lender gave an extension of six months to Corporation would not result in discharge unless X could prove loss with respect to the right of recourse because of the extension. If the financial condition of Corporation on April 1, 1992 would not have allowed any recovery on the right of recourse, X can't show any loss as a result of the extension with respect to the amount due on the note on April 1, 1992. Since the note accrued interest during the six-month extension, is there a loss equal to the accrued interest? Since the interest rate was not raised, only Section 3–605(c) would apply and X probably could not prove any loss. The obligation of X includes interest on the note until the note is paid. To the extent payment was delayed X had the use of the money that X otherwise would have had to pay to Lender. X could have prevented the running of interest by paying the debt. Since X did not do so, X suffered no loss as the result of the extension.

If the interest rate was raised, Section 3–605(d) also must be considered. If X is an anomalous indorser, X's liability is to pay the note according to its terms at the time of indorsement. Section 3–415(a). Thus, X's obligation to pay interest is measured by the terms of the note (12%) rather than by the increased amount of 14 percent. The same analysis applies if X had been a co-maker. Under Section 3–412 the liability of the issuer of a note is to pay the note according to its terms at the time it was issued. Either obligation could be changed by contract and that occurred with respect to Corporation when it agreed to the increase in the interest rate, but X did not join in that agreement and is not bound by it. Thus, the most that X can be required to pay is the amount due on the note plus interest at the rate of 12 percent.

Does the modification discharge X under Section 3–605(d)? Any modification that increases the monetary obligation of X is material. An increase of the interest rate from 12 percent to 14 percent is certainly a material modification. There is a presumption that X is discharged because Section 3–605(d) creates a presumption that the modification caused a loss to X equal to the amount of the right of recourse. Thus, Lender has the burden of proving absence of loss or a loss less than the amount of the right of recourse. Since Corporation paid no interest during the six-month period, the issue is like the issue presented under Section 3–605(c) which we have just discussed. The increase in the interest rate could not have affected the right of recourse because no interest was paid by Corporation. X is in the same position as X would have been in if there had been an extension without an increase in the interest rate.

The analysis with respect to Section 3–605(c) and (d) would have been different if we change the assumptions. Suppose Corporation was not insolvent on April 1, 1992, that Corporation paid interest at the higher rate during the six-month period, and that Corporation was insolvent at the end of the six-month period. In this case it is possible that the extension and the additional burden placed on Corporation by the increased interest rate may have been detrimental to X.

There are difficulties in properly allocating burden of proof when the agreement between Lender and Corporation involves both an extension under Section 3–605(c) and a modification under Section 3–605(d). The agreement may have caused loss to X but it may be difficult to identify the extent to which the loss was caused by the extension or the other modification. If neither Lender nor X introduces evidence on the issue, the result is full discharge because Section 3–605(d) applies. Thus, Lender has the burden of overcoming the presumption in Section 3–605(d). In doing so, Lender should be entitled to a presumption that the extension of time by itself caused no loss. Section 3–605(c) is based on such a presumption and X should be required to introduce evidence on the effect of the extension on the right of recourse. Lender would have to introduce evidence on the effect of the increased interest rate. Thus both sides will have to introduce evidence. On the basis of this evidence the court will have to make a determination of the overall effect of the agreement on X's right of recourse. See PEB Commentary No. 11, supra.

10. The second paragraph of Comment 6 to § 3–605 is amended to read as follows:

In some states a real property grantee who assumes the obligation of the grantor as maker of a note secured by the real property becomes by operation of law a principal debtor and the grantor becomes a surety. The meager case authority was split on whether former Section 3–606 applied to release the grantor if the holder released or extended the obligation of the grantee. Revised Article 3 takes no position on the effect of the release of the grantee in this case. Section 3–605(b) does not apply because the holder has not discharged the obligation of a "party," a term defined in Section 3–103(a)(8) as "party to an instrument." The assuming grantee is not a party to the instrument. The resolution of this question is governed by general principles of law, including the law of suretyship. See PEB Commentary No. 11, supra.

11. Comment 8 to § 3–605 is amended by adding the underlined words as follows:

8. Subsection (i) is a continuation of former law which allowed suretyship defenses to be waived. As the subsection provides, a party is not discharged under this section if the instrument or a separate agreement of the party waives discharge either specifically or by general language indicating that defenses based on suretyship and impairment of collateral are waived. No particular language or form of agreement is required, and the standards for enforcing such a term are the same as the standards for enforcing any other term in an instrument or agreement.

Subsection (i), however, applies only to a "discharge under this section." The right of an accommodation party to be discharged under Section 3–605(e) because of an impairment of collateral can be waived. But with respect to a note secured by personal property collateral, Article 9 also applies. If an accommodation party is a "debtor" under Section ~~9–105(1)(d)~~ 9–102(a)(28), an "obligor" under Section 9–102(a)(59), or a "secondary obligor" under Section 9–102(a)(71), the accommodation party has rights under Article 9. Under Section ~~9–501(3)(b)~~ 9–602, many rights of an Article 9 debtor or obligor under Part 6 of Article 9 ~~under Section 9–504(3) and Section 9–505(1), which deal with disposition of collateral,~~ cannot be waived except as provided in Article 9. These Article 9 rights are independent of rights under Section 3–605. Since Section 3–605(i) is specifically limited to discharge under Section 3–605, a waiver of rights with respect to Section 3–605 has no effect on rights under Article 9. With respect to Article 9 rights, Section ~~9–501(3)(b)~~ 9–602 controls. See PEB Commentary No. 11, supra.

PEB COMMENTARY NO. 13 THE PLACE OF ARTICLE 4A IN A WORLD OF ELECTRONIC FUNDS TRANSFERS (February 16, 1994)

ISSUE

Article 4A of the UCC deals primarily with electronic funds transfers made through the banking system.[1] Adopted by the ALI and the National Conference of Commissioners on Uniform State Laws in 1989, Article 4A has had a substantial measure of success. At this time it is law in all but a few states, has been incorporated into Regulation J of the Federal Reserve System[2] and, through their incorporation of New York State law, has been written into the Rules of CHIPS[3] and NACHA.[4]

---

[1] While Article 4A was clearly drafted with electronic funds transfers in mind and while its present effect will be upon such transfers, it is not limited to electronic transfers and applies by its terms to all transfers among banks outside the checking system. This concept is elaborated upon in Comment 6 to § 4A–104.

[2] 12 C.F.R. Part 210, Appendix B (1993).

[3] New York Clearing House Interbank Payments Systems, CHIPS Rule 3.

[4] National Automatic Clearing House Association, ACH Rule 1.7.

APPENDIX D

For a transfer of funds to be governed by Article 4A, an instruction must be given to a bank ("Bank I" in this scenario) either to make payment to the person who is the ultimate recipient of the funds or to instruct some other bank ("Bank II") to make the payment.[5] If the instruction is that Bank I make payment to the ultimate recipient, the bank is dealing with its own depositor or someone who has a direct customer relationship with the bank. That relationship, while occasionally dealt with by Article 4A, is largely outside the coverage of the statute.[6]

Article 4A concentrates principally upon the relationship of one bank with another bank. Assuming that the instruction given to Bank I is that Bank I instruct Bank II to make the payment,[7] Bank II can as easily be located abroad as in the United States. For this reason, it is desirable that Article 4A find compatibility with such international law as exists in this area.

The major international legal document dealing with the subject of electronic funds transfers is the Model Law on International Credit Transfers ("Model Law") adopted in 1992 by the United Nations Commission on International Trade Law ("UNCITRAL"). It covers basically the same type of transaction as does Article 4A, although it requires the funds transferred to have an international component.[8]

No foreign State has, to date, adopted the Model Law as its own local law. Nevertheless, in examining international payments, this Commentary assumes that the United States is subject to Article 4A and that the remainder of the world, because of the lack of development in the law otherwise, has adopted the Model Law now offered to it by the United Nations.[9]

DISCUSSION

We will hypothesize two funds transfers. One is sent by a New York bank to San Francisco ("NY-SF") and the other to London ("NY-L").[10]

We may correctly assume that a New York bank will have both business reason and technical capacity to send funds with equal ease to both San Francisco and London. Administratively, it will normally make little if any difference to the bank whether the transfer goes east or west. For the two transfers to be subject to different legal regimes can, however, create problems. For example, if New York imposes a different level of responsibility upon the bank for completion of the funds transfer depending upon where it goes, the bank's fee structure might vary between the two. Similarly, if there are different requirements, depending upon the location of the receiving bank, of persons who must receive notices or duties as to correcting a transfer made in error, different expectations will be created for the bank's systems. The banking system was clear in its reactions to Article 4A and the Model Law through its drafting that it would find it both difficult and expensive to administer electronic funds transfers subject to conflicting legal systems.

In its final form, the Model Law is close to Article 4A both in its overall structure and in its details, but is not the same.

A. Conflicts of Laws

The conflicts of law provisions of Article 4A and the Model Law tell us what law will apply to these transfers. In this respect, the two statutes are essentially harmonious: § 4A–507(a)(1) and an optional

---

[5] We need not deal with who gives the instruction to Bank I. It might be a company or an individual originating a funds transfer; it might be another bank which is moving along an instruction that had been given to it.

[6] Provisions of Article 4A that do deal with the relationship of beneficiary's bank and beneficiary are §§ 4A–404 and 4A–405.

[7] Bank II can, having received the instruction from Bank I, in turn instruct another bank to make the payment. In this way, a series of banks can be involved in one transfer of funds from the party originating the transfer (called the "Originator") to the party ultimately receiving it (called the "Beneficiary").

[8] Model Law, Article 1(1) requires that "any sending bank and its receiving bank (be) in different States." Henceforth, references to Article numbers will refer to the Model Law; references to sections beginning with "4A" will refer to the UCC.

[9] Full uniformity would of course occur if the United States adopted the Model Law. It is unlikely in the extreme that this will occur. See the Conclusion to this Commentary.

[10] We need not deal with funds transfers made to New York from different sending banks. The UCC and the Model Law generally base their choice of law provisions on the law of the receiving bank. Thus, all funds transfers received in New York would be dealt with by New York law and there would be no problem of inconsistencies. See the discussion, *infra*, under A. Conflicts of Laws.

Article Y[11] in the Model Law both prescribe that, for most issues, the law of the receiving bank will govern.[12] Thus, Article 4A will generally govern for NY-SF, and the Model Law for NY-L.[13]

B. Working of the Two Laws

Some examples will illustrate differences between Article 4A and the Model Law:

1. Consumer Transactions

Both Article 4A and the Model Law were written without a focus on consumer-related transactions and, therefore, without the particular protections that typically accompany laws written for the benefit of consumers. In Article 4A, this is evidenced by an exclusion through § 4A–108 of transactions covered by the federal Electronic Fund Transfer Act of 1978 ("EFTA"), which is tailored for the consumer funds transfer. In the Model Law, a footnote to Article 1 provides that the Law "does not deal with issues related to the protection of consumers."[14]

This surface harmony leads, however, to problems. For example, the EFTA does not deal with the number of issues treated by Article 4A. It does not, for example, define the time when the originator of a consumer funds transfer has made payment to the beneficiary, a question answered by both Article 4A and the Model Law. If the NY-L and the NY-SF funds transfers were consumer in nature and this question arose, it would be answered for NY-L and not for NY-SF (since the latter would be governed by the EFTA).[15]

2. Variation by Agreement

Both Article 4A[16] and the Model Law[17] generally permit the parties to vary their statutory obligations by agreement except as may be specifically prohibited. Areas of specific prohibition vary, however, between the two laws.

For example, the obligation of a receiving bank that is also the beneficiary's bank to pay the amount of an order that it has accepted to the beneficiary may not be varied by agreement under § 4A–404(c). It may be varied under Article 10 of the Model Law. If our New York bank were to enter into agreements with its receiving banks defining circumstances under which an accepted order should not thereupon be paid to the beneficiary, the agreements would be effective for the NY-L transfer and not for the NY-SF transfer.[18]

---

[11] UNCITRAL was unable to agree whether a conflicts of law article belonged in the Model Law and, consequently, created an optional provision.

[12] Details of both Article 4A and the Model Law introduce complexities. For example, both permit the parties to select the applicable law. In an Article 4A transaction, the relationship between a beneficiary (that is, the party who will ultimately receive the money being transferred) and its bank are governed pursuant to § 4A–507(a)(2) by the law of the jurisdiction where the bank is located. Article 4A also contains rules that will govern when the funds transfer is made through a funds-transfer system (see text *infra*, at Notes 22–24), and that system has its own choice of law rules. This Commentary does not deal with such variations.

[13] One cannot exhaust the potential conflicts problems that arise even within this simple structure. For example, when the originator of the funds transfer instructs its New York bank to send funds to San Francisco or to London, the relationship of originator and bank is governed by the law of the receiving bank—New York. A funds transfer may also pass through several jurisdictions and raise additional issues. For the NY-SF and the NY-L transfers, however, the rule is that the law of California and of England will, respectively, apply.

[14] The Model Law does not present the sharp distinction between consumer and business transactions represented by the positioning of Article 4A and EFTA. The quoted language reflects the philosophy behind the Model Law—that its design is really for large, commercially oriented funds transfers—and justifies the positions taken on various issues. The Model Law on its face governs both consumer and commercial funds transfers and it was left to individual states to decide how their consumers would be treated.

[15] Presumably a court would look to analogies in other laws to see how the question should be answered in the NY-SF context. Presumably, the closest law for this purpose would be Article 4A and the court would use the Article 4A solution.

A limited number of consumer transactions—those handled through the FedWire system and a few others such as unplanned telephone transfers—are excluded from the EFTA by Federal Reserve Regulation E and returned to coverage under Article 4A. See 12 C.F.R. § 205.3(b) (1992).

[16] Section 4A–501(a).

[17] Article 4.

[18] One might imagine a New York bank agreeing with certain of its correspondents that they would not pay money to certain named beneficiaries without checking first with New York. That such an agreement would be effective for foreign banks but not for American banks was not the subject of detailed discussion, but one might imagine that foreign

3. Use of a Funds-Transfer System

Most electronic funds transfers are executed through funds-transfer systems.[19] Section 4A–206(a) provides that a funds-transfer system is the agent of the sender. Errors made by a funds-transfer system are, therefore, the errors of the bank that sent the funds through the system. (For this purpose, however, the FedWire system is excluded, and the Federal Reserve bank operating FedWire is deemed to be just another bank.) The Model Law is silent on this subject.

Thus, if, in a NY-SF transfer, the New York bank gives a payment order of $100,000 to the CHIPS system and CHIPS mistakenly transmits $1,000,000, the error is that of the New York bank, which is considered to have sent $1,000,000.[20] In a NY-L transfer, one cannot be certain. It appears, however, that the error is that of CHIPS.[21]

Under Article 4A,[22] funds-transfer system rules are given legal effect and may bind even parties who are not members of the system. Under the Model Law, the effect of a systems rule upon nonparties is not prescribed and, therefore, will be determined according to the law of contracts.[23] Generally, under American contract law, those who are not parties to a contract are not bound by its terms. If a funds-transfer system with its own rules is part of the two described funds transfers, the law applicable to the NY-L and the NY-SF transfers can be different.

4. Authentication Procedures

For the protection of the banking system and bank customers, both Article 4A and the Model Law establish procedures for the authentication of messages. The two systems work in similar manners.[24] Both protect a receiving bank if it properly authenticates a message, even if the message was sent without the sender's proper authority.[25] Both also relieve the sender of responsibility if it can prove that the message was sent by someone outside the sender's influence.[26] The Model Law[27] reimposes responsibility on the sender if the receiver can prove that the sender was responsible. Article 4A does not contain the reimposition responsibility, although this is implicit since the receiving bank will attempt to disclaim its liability by proving that the sender was responsible.

The effect of agreements varying the terms of the law again varies between Article 4A and the Model Law. Article 4A holds that (subject to certain limited and restricted exceptions) the parties may not vary its statutory authentication rights and liabilities by agreement.[28] The Model Law has no such prescription and the parties may alter their legal authentication relationships by agreement.[29] Thus, if the New York bank

---

spokesmen could have wanted to support greater freedom for their banking system than the United States believes should be tolerated.

[19] A "funds-transfer system" is defined under § 4A–105(a)(5) as a "wire transfer network, automated clearing house, or other communication system of a clearing house or other association of banks through which a payment order by a bank may be transmitted to the bank to which the order is addressed." Well-known domestic funds-transfer systems include the FedWire system of the Federal Reserve Banks, the CHIPS system of the New York Clearing House Association, and the systems of the National Automated Clearing House Association. Foreign systems include the Society of Worldwide Interbank Financial Telecommunication ("SWIFT"), the United Kingdom Clearing House Automated Payments System ("CHAPS"), and the Japanese BOJ-NET system.

[20] See Comment 2 to § 4A–206.

[21] This sort of event and its consequences are typically covered in the rules of a funds-transfer system. As discussed above, both Article 4A, § 4A–501, and the Model Law, Article 4, authorize agreements varying their provisions. Rules of a funds-transfer system would probably be considered agreements under the Model Law and are agreements specifically under § 4A–501.

[22] Section 4A–501(b).

[23] *Report of UNCITRAL*, U.N. Doc. A/46/17 (1991), par. 98.

[24] The relevant sections are §§ 4A–201, 4A–202, and 4A–203 for Article 4A, and Article 5 for the Model Law.

[25] Section 4A–202(b); Article 5(2).

[26] Section 4A–203(a)(2); Article 5(4).

[27] Article 5(4).

[28] Section 4A–202(f).

[29] Article 5(3) does provide that for the parties to agree that a sending bank will be bound by an authenticated message, the authentication must be reasonable. Section 4A–202(b) has a similar requirement.

in our hypothetical agrees with its customers for a result other than as provided by the statutes, it will be effective for the NY-L transfer, but not for the NY-SF transfer.

5. Acceptance and Rejection

Under both Article 4A and the Model Law, a receiving bank is given the essentially unrestricted power to accept or reject an order sent to it. An order may be rejected by a notice sent to the sender.[30]

a. Receiving Banks Other Than the Beneficiary's Bank

If a bank (other than the beneficiary's bank) does not send a rejection notice, the legal consequences vary between the two laws; on the other hand, they resolve themselves, as the following discussion illustrates, without undue tension between them.

Under Article 4A, an order may be accepted by a bank other than the beneficiary's bank only by that bank executing a new order in favor of the next bank in line.[31] Failure to give a notice of rejection does not cause the bank to incur a penalty; neither does it result in acceptance. If the bank does not move, or "execute," the order, it is not deemed to have accepted the order, and the order is automatically canceled by operation of law in five days.[32] If the receiving bank has received actual funds covering the order, it must return the funds and pay interest to the sending bank until cancellation.[33]

Under the Model Law, a receiving bank that executes a new order is deemed to have accepted the order sent to it as under Article 4A.[34] An order that is neither executed nor rejected is deemed—unlike the Article 4A approach—to be accepted if funds covering the order have been paid to the receiving bank.[35] The receiving bank then is obligated to issue a new order in accordance with the responsibilities put by the Model Law upon the acceptor of an order. Similar to Article 4A, the payment order ceases to have effect after five days.[36] If the transfer is not completed, however, the bank must return any payment received by it plus interest to the date of payment[37] and does not suffer any further liability for its failure to execute the accepted order.

In the instant situation, still assuming that the San Francisco and the London banks are receiving banks that are not the beneficiary's bank, if an order is neither accepted nor rejected and if funds have been advanced to that bank (that is, if the order is "covered"), there would not be any duty upon the San Francisco bank to accept (that is, to execute the order in favor of the next bank in line) and the funds paid would bear interest for five days; for the NY-L transfer, the payment order would be accepted by the London bank, there would be a duty—albeit for a brief time—to move the funds, the acceptance would cease after five days, and the payment (the "cover") would bear interest until returned. The financial differences do not appear consequential since the receiving bank has the use of the funds until they are returned. Under the general structure of both laws not to impose more than interest penalties for failure to reject, the receiving bank in London would not incur other penalties for failing to honor its responsibility to move the funds.

b. The Beneficiary's Bank as a Receiving Bank

The ability of the beneficiary's bank to accept or reject payment orders is handled with essential comparability under the two laws. Under Article 4A, there are three events that trigger such a bank's acceptance, including rules based upon the relationship between the bank and the beneficiary, "cover" of the order to the bank, and the passage of time.[38] The Model Law contains eight events signifying acceptance by the beneficiary's bank.[39] One does not anticipate significant variations in practice between the two laws.

---

[30] Section 4A–210(a) and Model Law Articles 7 and 9.

[31] Section 4A–209(a).

[32] Section 4A–211(d).

[33] Section 4A–210(b) and §§ 4A–402(c) and 4A–402(d).

[34] Article 7(2)(c).

[35] While there is also a five-day cancellation provision, it is applicable only if the order is neither accepted nor rejected and we are dealing here with a deemed acceptance. Article 7(2), 7(3), and 7(4).

[36] Article 7(4).

[37] Article 14(1). This differs from Article 4A, which requires interest only for the five days.

[38] Section 4A–209(b).

[39] Article 9(1).

6. Time for Execution

Although their approaches to the question of when a receiving bank must take action upon an accepted payment order differ in the two laws, they have an essential similarity. For example, both Article 4A[40] and the Model Law[41] basically require that an order be executed on the day it is received. The Model Law, however, permits the order to be sent on the next day. In the event that occurs, however, the receiver must "execute for value as of' the prior day (that is, must give the next bank in line interest for the day that execution was delayed).

7. Cancellation

Both statutes provide the mechanism for a payment order to be canceled. Under Article 4A, if there is a security procedure between sender and receiver guarding the authenticity of the original order, "the" (that is, the same) procedure must be followed for cancellations.[42] If the original order was not subject to a security procedure, the cancellation order need not be authenticated. Under the Model Law, it is necessary that every cancellation be subject to some security procedure, not necessarily the same one originally used and even if no security procedure was originally used.[43] If the cancellation order is not authenticated, it is ineffective.

In addition, under the Model Law, it appears that every cancellation order must be authenticated. Under Article 4A, the cancellation must be authenticated only if there was an authentication procedure applicable to the original order.

The Article 4A approach is applicable in the NY-SF transfer; the Model Law governs the NY-L transfer.

8. The "Money-Back Guarantee"

As part of their underlying philosophy that the originator's funds will be transferred by the banking system, both Article 4A and the Model Law contain a so-called "money-back guarantee." This provides that, if the total transfer of money is not completed, the originator (who, under the model we have been following, either gave an order to the New York bank or was someone who gave an order at an earlier stage in the total funds transfer that was transmitted by another bank to the New York bank) will obtain a refund plus accumulated interest and certain other charges.[44] The provisions of the two laws are consistent in major respects. Neither permits variation by agreement. The Model Law, however, relieves receiving banks from the guarantee if they can demonstrate that they accepted the transfer despite what had been perceived as "a significant risk."[45]

9. Underpayments and the Recovery of Overpayments

Both laws contain essentially comparable provisions requiring sending banks who sent orders in amounts less than the amounts sent to them to send the differences and to permit banks who sent excessive payments to recover the excess.[46]

10. Consequential Damages

In general, the measure of damages provided by both laws for violations of their standards is the payment of interest for moneys held for the times beyond which the law allows. Occasionally, additional charges incident to the transfer will be included.[47]

Probably the single most controversial issue underlying the drafting of Article 4A was whether banks should have liability for consequential damages resulting from their negligence or failure to comply with the requirements of the statute. The banks argued that, given the traditionally low fees that they charged

---

40 Section 4A–301(b).

41 Article 11(1).

42 Section 4A–211(a).

43 Article 12(4).

44 Section 4A–402 and Model Law Article 14.

45 A "prudent" originator's bank may agree with the originator that the money-back guarantee will not apply to a funds transfer if the bank accepted the transfer despite what it perceived as a "significant risk" that the transfer might not be completed. The example frequently given for this situation is where the transfer is to pass through areas involved in armed conflict.

46 Section 4A–303(a) and § 4A–303(b), and Model Law Articles 15 and 16.

47 See §§ 4A–303(b) and 4A–305(b).

to transfer funds electronically, they could not at the same time subject themselves to the risk of immense and unquantifiable consequential damage recoveries. Business users of electronic funds-transfer systems asserted that consequential damages were an appropriate result of the banks' transfer responsibilities. Consequential damages were ultimately eliminated from Article 4A.[48]

Consequential damages may, however, be imposed against a bank under the Model Law. In view of the intense opposition of some national banking systems and their representatives in the United Nations to this concept, however, they were reduced in scope to where they will be imposed only where a bank has acted "(a) with the specific intent to cause loss, or (b) recklessly and with actual knowledge that loss would be likely to result."[49]

Thus, the NY-L transfer by a New York bank involves greater risk than does the NY-SF transfer.

11. Request for Assistance

Article 13 of the Model Law "requests" a bank that receives a payment order to assist the originator and each prior bank and to seek the assistance of the next receiving bank "in completing the banking procedures of the credit transfer." Article 4A has no equivalent. In the NY-L transfer, the New York bank is subject to the request; in the NY-SF transfer, it is not. There is no penalty for failing to abide by the request.[50]

The absence of penalty may suggest that a bank need have no concern about the requirement. On the other hand, the presence of a law does impose an obligation to comply. In addition, assuming that there are bank regulators enforcing compliance, the regulators in London could bring an action against the New York bank for specific performance of its obligation to assist under Article 13; United States regulators could not.

CONCLUSION

The Model Law was drafted for world-wide enactment. It is, however, unlikely in the extreme that it will be enacted in the United States in the foreseeable future.[51] It was generally accepted by the foreign states in UNCITRAL that there would be no movement to repeal Article 4A in the United States and adopt the Model Law in its stead. The two laws basically live together in harmony, but to the extent there are differences they must be recognized and, to the extent possible, avoided or adjusted by agreement.

The PREFATORY NOTE to Article 4A is amended by adding the following paragraph at the end of the PREFATORY NOTE:

International transfers.

The major international legal document dealing with the subject of electronic funds transfers is the Model Law on International Credit Transfers adopted in 1992 by the United Nations Commission on International Trade Law. It covers basically the same type of transaction as does Article 4A, although it requires the funds transferred to have an international component. The Model Law and Article 4A basically live together in harmony, but to the extent there are differences they must be recognized and, to the extent possible, avoided or adjusted by agreement. See PEB Commentary No. 13, dated February 16, 1994.

---

[48] This result was ultimately agreed to by the major business interests in exchange for the consent by the banks to the "money-back guarantee" discussed in paragraph 8 above. Consequential damages were, however, authorized in favor of an ultimate beneficiary of a funds transfer against its bank that refuses to pay it after being notified of the particular circumstances giving rise to such damages. Section 4A–404(a). Consequential damages may also be provided for by express written agreement with a receiving bank. Section 4A–305(c).

[49] Article 18. The terms used within the quotation marks have established meanings under United States tort law with the exception of "actual knowledge that loss would be likely to result."

[50] Banks normally engage in this type of assistance even without statutory direction.

[51] For further material on the subject of this Commentary, see Bhala, Rakesh K., *Paying for the Deal*, 42 Kan.L.Rev. No. 3 (1993), in which Professor Bhala uses micro-economic and banking concepts to evaluate the utility of both Article 4A and the UNCITRAL Model Law.

APPENDIX D

PEB COMMENTARY NO. 16
SECTIONS 4A–502(d) AND 4A–503
(July 1, 2009)

INTRODUCTION

A funds transfer is a series of payment orders starting with an originator's order to the originator's bank to cause a sum certain amount of money to be paid to a beneficiary. The series of payment orders culminates with a beneficiary bank crediting the account of a beneficiary for that sum certain. U.C.C. § 4A–104(a) (definition of funds transfer). The series of payment orders is a mechanism used to make a transfer of value through the debiting and crediting of bank accounts from the originator to the beneficiary. The funds transfer often involves one or more intermediary banks that receive a payment order from the originator's bank or another bank. The receiving intermediary bank then issues its own payment order to another intermediary bank or the beneficiary's bank. Several cases have raised the issue of whether a creditor of the beneficiary may serve creditor process on an intermediary bank and thus capture the value transfer while it is in process.

Article 4A provides that the creditor of the beneficiary may not serve creditor process on any bank other than the beneficiary's bank. U.C.C. § 4A–502(d). Official Comment 4 to § 4A–502 further explains the concept, and does so in relation to a creditor of either the beneficiary or the originator:

> A creditor of the originator can levy on the account of the originator in the originator's bank before the funds transfer is initiated . . . [but] cannot reach any other funds *because no property of the originator is being transferred*. A creditor of the beneficiary cannot levy on property of the originator and until the funds transfer is completed by acceptance by the beneficiary's bank of a payment order for the benefit of the beneficiary, *the beneficiary has no property interest in the funds transfer which the beneficiary's creditor can reach* (emphasis supplied).

Official Comment to § 4A–503 further explains both § 4A–502(d) and § 4A–503 are designed to prevent interruption of a funds transfer after it has been set in motion and that, in particular, intermediary banks are protected.

A funds transfer is a series of payment orders that create contractual obligations only as to the sender and receiver of each payment order. Those contractual obligations are not the property of either the originator or the beneficiary. In a simple funds transfer, the originator instructs its bank, the originator's bank, to debit the originator's account and order the beneficiary's bank to credit the beneficiary. Those instructions are payment orders. U.C.C. § 4A–103 (definition of payment order, "beneficiary," and "beneficiary's bank"); § 4A–104 (definition of "funds transfer," "originator," and "originator's bank"). See also Regulation J, 12 C.F.R. § 210.26 (governing payment orders issued to or by a federal reserve bank). The originator is the sender of the payment order and the originator's bank is the receiving bank. U.C.C. § 4A–103 (definitions of "sender" and "receiving bank"). If the originator's bank accepts the originator's payment order, the originator owes an obligation to the originator's bank to pay the amount of the payment order. U.C.C. § 4A–402(b). The originator's bank owes an obligation to the originator to execute the accepted payment order according to the instructions of the originator. U.C.C. § 4A–302.

In execution of the originator's payment order, the originator's bank may send its own payment order to the beneficiary's bank, but more commonly it will send its payment order to an intermediary bank. U.C.C. § 4A–104 (definition of "intermediary bank"). The originator's bank is the sender of its payment order and the intermediary bank is the receiving bank of that second payment order. Upon acceptance of that second payment order, the intermediary bank owes an obligation to the originator's bank, not the originator, to execute its own payment order that replicates *the originator's bank's payment order* (emphasis supplied). U.C.C. § 4A–302 (obligation in execution owed by receiving bank to its sender). The originator's bank, not the originator, owes payment of the originator bank's payment order to the intermediary bank. U.C.C. § 4A–402(b) (sender owes obligation to pay the amount of an accepted payment order to its receiving bank). In the event the originator is not able to pay the amount of its payment order to the originator's bank, but the originator's bank's payment order has been accepted by the intermediary bank, the originator's bank still owes a payment obligation to the intermediary bank. The intermediary bank has no right of recovery against the originator, but only has a right of recovery against the originator's bank (its sender) for payment of the payment order.

Further, the intermediary bank will then issue its own payment order to the beneficiary's bank for the beneficiary's bank to credit the account of the beneficiary when the beneficiary's bank accepts that payment order. Accordingly, the intermediary bank owes an obligation to pay for that order to the beneficiary bank, not the beneficiary. U.C.C. § 4A–402(b). Upon the beneficiary bank's acceptance of the payment order, it is the beneficiary's bank that owes an obligation to pay the beneficiary, usually by crediting an account of the beneficiary. U.C.C. § 4A–404. See also Regulation J §§ 210.28, 210.29, 210.30, 210.31, and 210.32.

In summation, under the Article 4A structure, the issuance and acceptance of payment orders create rights and obligations only as between the sender of the payment order and its receiving bank (e.g., between originator and originator's bank as to the originator's payment order), between the originator's bank and an intermediary bank as to the originator's bank's payment order, between the intermediary bank and the beneficiary bank as to the intermediary bank's payment order, and finally as between the beneficiary bank that has accepted a payment order and the beneficiary. Accepted and executed payment orders thus create contractual obligations that result in a series of credits and debits to bank accounts. They do not involve a transfer of property of the originator to the beneficiary. A receiving bank owes its contractual obligation to its sender to execute the payment order and the sender owes its contractual obligation to pay the amount of the payment order to its receiving bank. The intermediary bank has no contractual obligation to the originator or to the beneficiary, and neither the originator nor the beneficiary has any contractual obligation to or rights flowing from the intermediary bank. Thus, credits in an intermediary bank are credits in favor of the originator's bank, *and are not property of either the originator or the beneficiary* (emphasis supplied).

DISCUSSION

In a series of cases applying Admiralty Rule B regarding attachment, the federal courts in New York have held that the intermediary bank in a funds transfer is holding "property" of the originator or beneficiary and have thus allowed creditor process on an intermediary bank in an effort to collect a debt owed by either the originator or the beneficiary (as the case may be).[1] See, e.g., Winter Storm Shipping, Ltd. v. TPI, 310 F.3d 263 (2d Cir. 2002), cert. denied, 539 U.S. 927 (2003); Aqua Stoli Shipping Ltd. v. Gardner Smith Pty Ltd., 460 F.3d 434 (2d Cir. 2006); Con-sub Delaware LLC v. Schahin Engenharia Limitada and Standard Chartered Bank, 534 F.3d 104 (2d Cir. 2008); Navalmar (U.K.) Ltd. v. Welspun Gujarat Stahl Rohren, Ltd., 485 F. Supp. 2d 399 (S.D.N.Y. 2007); Compania Sudamericana de Vapores S.A. v. Sinochem Tianjin Co., 2007 WL 1002265 (S.D.N.Y. 2007); but see Seamar Shipping Corp. v. Kremikovtzi Trade Ltd., 461 F. Supp. 2d 222 (S.D.N.Y. 2006).

These decisions stem from the opinion of the court in *Winter Storm* that the value held by the intermediary bank is property of the originator. Under Article 4A, which is also adopted federal law in Regulation J for funds transfers through a federal reserve bank, the originator does not have any claim against the intermediary bank for return of the value in the event the funds transfer is not completed. Rather, the only party with a claim against the intermediary bank is the sender to that bank, which is typically the originator's bank. In an uncompleted funds transfer, it is the originator's bank that must refund the value to the originator. U.C.C. § 4A–402(d). The intermediary bank owes its refund obligation to its sender, the originator's bank, not to the originator. The originator's bank must refund to the originator even if it cannot recover from the intermediary bank.[2] The beneficiary likewise has no claim to any payment from the intermediary bank. The beneficiary's only claim to the funds is against its bank, the beneficiary bank, and then only when the beneficiary bank has accepted the payment order. U.C.C. § 4A–404. The intermediary bank thus holds no property of either the originator or the beneficiary. Since Admiralty Rule B does not define what is "property" of a party, normally courts look to other law on that issue.

---

[1] Federal Rules of Civil Procedure, Supplemental Rules for Certain Admiralty and Maritime Claims, Admiralty Rule B(1)(a) permits attachment of "the defendant's tangible or intangible personal property" in the hands of named garnishees and thus allows garnishment of such property held by a bank.

[2] A simple example illustrates how these courts conflated privity-based contract claims between two parties to create property rights in a third party. Assume A owes B an obligation, B owes C an obligation, and C owes D an obligation. Under garnishment law, D cannot garnish A to satisfy the obligation C owes D. A holds no property of C (A owes B). Now substitute the Article 4A terms to this simple example. A is the intermediary bank who has received payment of a payment order issued by B, the originator's bank, and C is the originator. D is the garnishing creditor. The court in *Winter Storm* and its progeny have in essence allowed D (the originator's creditor) to garnish A (the intermediary bank) to collect on the debt C (the originator) owes to D.

APPENDIX D

Other law is sufficient to define the parties' rights in a funds transfer. Article 4A is uniform law, enacted in every state in the United States, and Regulation J, which adopts in large part Article 4A's provisions, is uniform in applying to all funds transfers through the federal reserve system. Both define uniformly the rights of parties in a funds transfer. The *Consub* court reasoned that leaving the functional usefulness of Rule B attachments to the vagaries of the laws of 50 states would create a measure of anarchy, but did not take into account that Article 4A is uniform law in all U.S. jurisdictions and is adopted federal law.[3] Neither did the court explain how Rule B provides any basis for determining whether anyone had any property rights in the value held at the intermediary bank.[4]

Further, looking for a federal precedent concerning the "susceptibility of funds involved in an EFT to attachment under Admiralty Rule B," *Winter Storm* turned to *United States v. Daccarett*, 6 F.3d 37 (2d Cir. 1993), a forfeiture case involving the drug trafficking and money laundering activities of a Colombian drug cartel, 310 F.3d at 276–77 ("The case is instructive in the admiralty field because the attachments of funds in *Daccarett* were accomplished pursuant to the Admiralty Rules, incorporated by reference into the forfeiture statute.") Reasoning from *Daccarett's* holding that " 'an EFT while it takes the form of a bank credit at an intermediary bank is clearly a seizable *res* under the forfeiture statutes,' " id. at 276 (quoting *Daccarett*, 6 F.3d at 55), *Winter Storm* concluded that the "inclusive language of [Rule B] and the EFT analysis in *Daccarett* combine to fashion a rule in this Circuit that EFT funds in the hands of an intermediary bank may be attached pursuant to [Rule B]." 310 F.3d at 276. *Consub* endorsed *Winter Storm's* reliance on *Daccarett*, with minimal independent analysis. See 543 F.3d at 110–11. It should be noted that Rule B remains unchanged for all relevant intents and purposes since *Winter Storm* was decided in 2002 even though, effective December 1, 2006, the rules embodying the practice of maritime attachment in civil forfeiture actions and other in rem proceedings have been re-named the Supplemental Rules for Admiralty or Maritime Claims and Asset Forfeiture Actions (the "Supplemental Rules"). The revised Supplemental Rules added, inter alia, the reference to "Asset Forfeiture Actions," and Rule G, governing forfeiture actions in rem arising from a federal statute, "to bring together the central procedures that govern civil forfeiture actions." Supplemental Rule G, Advisory Committee's Note. The point is that *Daccarett* never decided whether either an originator or a beneficiary of the funds transfer had a *property interest* in the amount involved in a funds transfer received by an intermediary bank. It did not need to do so because in a forfeiture case funds can be seized even if they do not constitute property of the defendant. The *Daccarett* court, as appropriate in a forfeiture case, identified the amount of the funds as traceable to an illicit activity and therefore subject to attachment under 21 U.S.C. § 881(a). This is a critical difference.

Moreover, as a remedy quasi in rem, the validity of a Rule B attachment depends entirely on the determination that the res at issue is property of the judgment debtor at the moment it is attached. See J. Lauritzen A/S v. Dashwood Shipping, Ltd., 65 F.3d 139, 141 (9th Cir. 1995) (Rule B attachment characterized as quasi in rem jurisdiction because jurisdiction is derived solely from the attachment of the property of the defendant). Forfeiture, on the other hand, is a remedy in rem, based as it is on the legal fiction that " 'property used in violation of law [is] itself the wrongdoer that must be held to account for the harms it [has] caused.' " United States v. 92 Buena Vista Avenue, 507 U.S. 111, 125 (1993). This is a critical distinction between actions proceeding under Supplemental Rule C—now Rule G—and those brought under Rule B; it is not a "distinction without a difference," as *Winter Storm* found. 310 F.3d at 278.

---

[3] The courts following *Winter Storm* have not followed the applicable law directly on point regarding property rights, but have also not followed applicable precedent predating Article 4A. The court in Reibor International Limited v. Cargo Carriers (Kacz-Co.) Ltd., 759 F.2d 262 (2d Cir. 1985), considered whether the CHIPS credit involved was property subject to attachment under the Admiralty Rules. The court said that federal law generally governs questions as to the validity of Rule B attachments, but the Admiralty Rules themselves offered little guidance and so the court agreed with the district court that state law more directly in point should be turned to. This is entirely consistent with respect to other contexts where federal law relies on state law to determine whether property is involved, such as in bankruptcy. See, e.g., Butner v. United States, 440 U.S. 48 (1979). Also the Court in *Grain Traders, Inc. v. Citibank, N.A.*, 160 F.3d 97 (2d Cir. 1998), recognized the applicability of U.C.C. Article 4A when it held that law prevents an originator of a funds transfer from suing an intermediary bank. Id. at 102. *Grain Traders* remains good law in the Second Circuit and its logic applies to suits by beneficiaries as well.

[4] The *Consub* court believed that the *Winter Storm* rule was not shown to be unworkable. Note that U.C.C. Article 4A is substantially premised on the ability to net obligations because of the large sums involved. U.C.C. § 4A–403. If a particular creditor can seize funds and frustrate that plan, the resultant systemic risk may provide the demonstration that the *Winter Storm* approach and its progeny are unworkable.

Accordingly, unless there is superseding federal law, such as a drug forfeiture law or a regulation of the Treasury Department's Office of Foreign Assets Control ("OFAC"), Article 4A must be honored. Rule B is not such a superseding law.

Even absent that scenario, the Winter Storm approach is proving to be practically un-workable. The result of the *Winter Storm* approach has been a staggering number of maritime writs that New York banks are required to process on a daily basis. For example, from October 1, 2008 to January 31, 2009, maritime plaintiffs filed 962 lawsuits seeking to attach more than $1.35 billion. These lawsuits constituted 33 percent of all lawsuits filed in the Southern District of New York during that period, and the resulting maritime writs only add to the burden of 800 to 900 prior writs already served daily on the District's banks. The numbers have tapered off only slightly during the past months; from February 1, 2009 to April 30, 2009, maritime plaintiffs filed 498 lawsuits seeking to attach a total of $720 million. The explosion of maritime writs served on the banks has been logistically overwhelming.

Of even more significance, however, this explosion of writs creates an additional threat to the U.S. dollar as the world's primary reserve currency and New York's standing as a center of international banking and finance. Confronted with this situation, companies around the world may well consider restructuring their transactions to provide for payments in euros, sterling, yen, or some other currency to avoid using U.S. dollars cleared through intermediary banks in the United States, or clear transactions through one of the proliferating off-shore dollar clearing networks. Because the only contact with the United States in most of these transactions is the use of an intermediary bank in the United States to clear U.S. dollars, the U.S. litigation apparatus can be avoided entirely by the relatively simple expedient of using a different currency. As a result, *Winter Storm* and its progeny have had a far greater, and damaging, potential impact on U.S. and foreign banks located in New York than might have been anticipated.

An additional significant problem for banks is that the only practical way in which they can accommodate post-*Winter Storm* attachments is by frequent amendments to their software filters used to identify transactions involving entities and other persons whose financial transactions are blocked under OFAC regulations. OFAC administers U.S. economic sanctions pro-grams arising under the Trading with the Enemy Act, 50 U.S.C. app. § 5, the International Emergency Economic Powers Act, 50 U.S.C. §§ 1701–1706, and other statutes. OFAC regularly issues bulletins that add or delete entities or persons from its lists, and banks must update their screening software to reflect these changes. This year, OFAC has updated its lists 19 times through May 6, 2009 (83 business days). By contrast, new maritime attachment orders were filed nearly every business day. The process of constantly amending the software filters to deal with this flood of maritime attachments has greatly increased the burden on the banks, requiring them to take down their OFAC filters almost every day, vastly increasing the chance that the OFAC database will be corrupted by the manipulation, and substantially increasing the number of "hits," including numerous false positives that these filters now generate, creating real risks of inefficiency and error.

In addition, permitting a beneficiary's creditor to attach a funds-transfer credit, ordinarily held only momentarily in New York, would exacerbate the considerable due-process concerns inherent in restraining a funds transfer. The defendants in maritime cases invariably are foreign corporations with few or no contacts with the United States. In many of the cases the defendant does not appear to have significant contacts, if any, with New York. Indeed, for a maritime defendant's property to be prima facie subject to a Rule B attachment, the plaintiff is required to attest, pursuant to Rule B(1)(b), that the defendant could not be found within the District. See STX Panocean (UK) Co., Ltd. v. Glory Wealth Shipping Pte Ltd., 560 F.3d 127, 130–31 (2d Cir. 2009). Moreover, the funds transfers at issue are often meant to effect payment from a third party's non-U.S. account to the defendant's non-U.S. account, or vice versa. The New York garnishee banks in most cases are involved as intermediary banks only because the payment was denominated in U.S. dollars.

CONCLUSION

In uniform law under Article 4A and under Regulation J, neither the originator nor the beneficiary of a funds transfer has any property claim to the value held by an intermediary bank in a funds transfer. Thus, neither a creditor of an originator nor the creditor of a beneficiary may successfully issue creditor process[5]

[5] "Creditor process" means levy, attachment, garnishment, notice of lien, sequestration, or similar process issued by or on behalf of a creditor or other claimant with respect to an account. As to account, see authorized account defined in U.C.C. § 4A–105(a)(1).

to an intermediary bank as the intermediary bank is not holding property of either the originator or the beneficiary. To the extent that the cases cited earlier indicate to the contrary, that reasoning is disapproved and should not be followed.

PEB REPORT
APPLICATION OF THE UNIFORM COMMERCIAL CODE TO SELECTED ISSUES RELATING TO MORTGAGE NOTES
(November 14, 2011)

Preface

In 1961, the American Law Institute and the Uniform Law Commission, the organizations that jointly sponsor the Uniform Commercial Code, established the Permanent Editorial Board for the Uniform Commercial Code (PEB). One of the charges of the PEB is to issue commentaries "and other articulations as appropriate to reflect the correct interpretation of the [Uniform Commercial] Code and issuing the same in a manner and at times best calculated to advance the uniformity and orderly development of commercial law." Such commentaries and other articulations are issued directly by the PEB rather than by action of the American Law Institute and the Uniform Law Commission.

This Report of the Permanent Editorial Board is such an articulation, addressing the application of the Uniform Commercial Code to issues of legal, economic, and social importance arising from the issuance and transfer of mortgage notes. A draft of this Report was made available to the public for comment on March 29, 2011, and the comments that were received have been taken into account in preparing the final Report.

Introduction

Recent economic developments have brought to the forefront complex legal issues about the enforcement and collection of mortgage debt. Many of these issues are governed by local real property law and local rules of foreclosure procedure, but others are addressed in a uniform way throughout the United States by provisions of the Uniform Commercial Code (UCC).[1] Although the UCC provisions are settled law, it has become apparent that not all courts and attorneys are familiar with them. In addition, the complexity of some of the rules has proved daunting.

The Permanent Editorial Board for the Uniform Commercial Code[2] has prepared this Report in order to further the understanding of this statutory background by identifying and explaining several key rules in the UCC that govern the transfer and enforcement of notes secured by a mortgage[3] on real property. The UCC, of course, does not resolve all issues in this field. Most particularly, as to both substance and procedure, the enforcement of real estate mortgages by foreclosure is primarily the province of a state's real property law (although determinations made pursuant to the UCC are typically relevant under that law). Accordingly, this Report should be understood as providing guidance only as to the issues the Report addresses.[4]

---

[1] The UCC is a uniform law sponsored by the American Law Institute and the Uniform Law Commission. It has been enacted in every state (as well as the District of Columbia, Puerto Rico, and the United States Virgin Islands) in whole or significant part. This Report is based on the current Official Text of the UCC. Some states have enacted some non-uniform provisions that are generally not relevant to the issues discussed in this Report. Of course, the enacted text of the UCC in the state whose law is applicable governs. See note 6, *infra*, regarding the various different versions of Article 3 of the UCC in effect in the states.

[2] In 1961, the American Law Institute and the Uniform Law Commission, the organizations that jointly sponsor the UCC, established the Permanent Editorial Board for the Uniform Commercial Code (PEB). One of the charges of the PEB is to issue commentaries "and other articulations as appropriate to reflect the correct interpretation of the [Uniform Commercial] Code and issuing the same in a manner and at times best calculated to advance the uniformity and orderly development of commercial law."

[3] This Report, like Article 9 of the UCC, uses the term "mortgage" to include a consensual interest in real property to secure an obligation whether created by mortgage, trust deed, or the like. See UCC § 9–102(a)(55) and Official Comment 17 thereto and former UCC § 9–105(1)(j). This Report uses the term "mortgage note" to refer to a note secured by a mortgage, whether or not the note is a negotiable instrument under UCC Article 3.

[4] Of course, the application of the UCC rules to particular factual circumstances depends on the nature of those circumstances. Facts raising legal issues other than those addressed in this Report can result in different rights and obligations than would be the case in the absence of those facts. Accordingly, this Report should not be read as a statement

PEB REPORT

Background

Issues relating to the transfer, ownership, and enforcement of mortgage notes are primarily governed by two Articles of the UCC:

- In cases in which the mortgage note is a negotiable instrument,[5] Article 3 of the UCC[6] provides rules governing the obligations of parties on the note[7] and the enforcement of those obligations.
- In cases involving either negotiable or non-negotiable notes, Article 9 of the UCC[8] contains important rules governing how ownership of those notes may be transferred, the effect of the transfer of ownership of the notes on the ownership of the mortgages securing those notes, and the right of the transferee, under certain circumstances, to record its interest in the mortgage in the applicable real estate recording office.

This Report explains the application of the rules in both of those UCC Articles to provide guidance in:

- Identifying the person who is entitled to enforce the payment obligation of the maker[9] of a mortgage note, and to whom the maker owes that obligation; and
- Determining who owns the rights represented by the note and mortgage.

Together, the provisions in Articles 3 and 9 of the UCC (along with general principles that appear in Article 1 and that apply to all transactions governed by the UCC) provide legal rules that apply to these questions.[10] Moreover, these rules displace any inconsistent common law rules that might have otherwise previously governed the same questions.[11]

---

of the total legal implications of any factual scenario. Rather, the Report sets out the UCC rules that are common to the transactions discussed so as to provide a common basis for understanding the application of those rules. The impact of non-UCC law that applies to other aspects of such transactions is beyond the scope of this Report.

[5] The requirements that must be satisfied in order for a note to be a negotiable instrument are set out in UCC § 3–104.

[6] Except for New York, every state (as well as the District of Columbia, Puerto Rico, and the United States Virgin Islands) has enacted either the 1990 Official Text of Article 3 or the newer 2002 Official Text (the latter having been adopted in ten states as of the date of this Report). Unless indicated to the contrary all discussions of provisions in Article 3 apply equally to both versions. Much of the analysis of UCC Article 3 in this Report also applies under the older version of Article 3 in effect in New York, although many section numbers differ. The Report does not address those aspects of New York's Article 3 that are different from the 1990 or 2002 texts.

[7] In this Report, such notes are sometimes referred to as "negotiable notes."

[8] Unlike Article 3 (which has not been enacted in its modern form in New York), the current version of Article 9 has been enacted in all 50 states, the District of Columbia, and the United States Virgin Islands. Some states have enacted non-uniform provisions that are generally not relevant to the issues discussed in this Report (but see note 31 with respect to one relevant non-uniformity). A limited set of amendments to Article 9 was approved by the American Law Institute and the Uniform Law Commission in 2010. Except as noted in this Report, those amendments (which provide for a uniform effective date of July 1, 2013) are not germane to the matters addressed in this Report.

[9] A note can have more than one obligor. In some cases, this is because there is more than one maker (in which case they are jointly and severally liable; see UCC § 3–116(a)). In other cases, there may be an indorser. The obligation of an indorser is different from that of a maker in that the indorser's obligation is triggered by dishonor of the note (see UCC § 3–415) and, unless waived, indorsers have additional procedural protections (such as notice of dishonor; see UCC § 3–503)). These differences do not affect the issues addressed in this Report. For simplicity, this Report uses the term "maker" to refer to both makers and indorsers.

[10] Subject to limitations on the ability to affect the rights of third parties, the effect of these provisions may be varied by agreement. UCC § 1–302. Variation by agreement is not permitted when the variation would disclaim obligations of good faith, diligence, reasonableness, or care prescribed by the UCC or when the UCC otherwise so indicates (see, *e.g.*, UCC § 9–602). But the meaning of the statute itself cannot be varied by agreement. Thus, for example, private parties cannot make a note negotiable unless it complies with UCC § 3–104. See Official Comment 1 to UCC § 1–302. Similarly, parties may not avoid the application of UCC Article 9 to a transaction that falls within its scope. See *id.* and Official Comment 2 to UCC § 9–109.

[11] UCC § 1–103(b). As noted in Official Comment 2 to UCC § 1–103:

> The Uniform Commercial Code was drafted against the backdrop of existing bodies of law, including the common law and equity, and relies on those bodies of law to supplement its provisions in many important ways. At the same time, the Uniform Commercial Code is the primary source of commercial law rules in areas that it governs, and its rules represent choices made by its drafters and the enacting legislatures about the appropriate policies to be furthered in the transactions it covers. Therefore, while principles of common law and equity may *supplement* provisions of the

APPENDIX D

This Report does not, however, address all of the rules in the UCC relating to enforcement, transfer, and ownership of mortgage notes. Rather, it reviews the rules relating to four specific questions:

- Who is the person entitled to enforce a mortgage note and, correspondingly, to whom is the obligation to pay the note owed?
- How can the owner of a mortgage note effectively transfer ownership of that note to another person or effectively use that note as collateral for an obligation?
- What is the effect of transfer of an interest in a mortgage note on the mortgage securing it?
- May a person to whom an interest in a mortgage note has been transferred, but who has not taken a recordable assignment of the mortgage, take steps to become the assignee of record in the real estate recording system of the mortgage securing the note?[12]

Question One—To Whom is the Obligation to Pay a Mortgage Note Owed?

If the mortgage note is a negotiable instrument,[13] Article 3 of the UCC provides a largely complete set of rules governing the obligations of parties on the note, including how to determine who may enforce those obligations and, thus, to whom those obligations are owed. The following discussion analyzes the application of these rules to that determination in the context of mortgage notes that are negotiable instruments.[14]

In the context of mortgage notes that have been sold or used as collateral to secure an obligation, the central concept for making that determination is identification of the "person entitled to enforce" the note.[15] Several issues are resolved by that determination. Most particularly:

(i) the maker's obligation on the note is to pay the amount of the note to *the person entitled to enforce the note*,[16]

(ii) the maker's payment to *the person entitled to enforce the note* results in discharge of the maker's obligation,[17] and

(iii) the maker's failure to pay, when due, the amount of the note to *the person entitled to enforce the note* constitutes dishonor of the note.[18]

Uniform Commercial Code, they may not be used to *supplant* its provisions, or the purposes and policies those provisions reflect, unless a specific provision of the Uniform Commercial Code provides otherwise. In the absence of such a provision, the Uniform Commercial Code preempts principles of common law and equity that are inconsistent with either its provisions or its purposes and policies.

[12] The Report does not discuss the application of common law principles, such as the law of agency, that supplement the provisions of the UCC other than to note some situations in which the text or comments of the UCC identify such principles as being relevant. See UCC § 1–103(b).

[13] See UCC § 3–104 for the requirements that must be fulfilled in order for a payment obligation to qualify as a negotiable instrument. It should not be assumed that all mortgage notes are negotiable instruments. The issue of the negotiability of a particular mortgage note, which requires application of the standards in UCC § 3–104 to the words of the particular note, is beyond the scope of this Report.

[14] Law other than Article 3, including contract law, governs this determination for non-negotiable mortgage notes. That law is beyond the scope of this Report.

[15] The concept of "person entitled to enforce" a note is not synonymous with "owner" of the note. See Official Comment 1 to UCC § 3–203. A person need not be the owner of a note to be the person entitled to enforce it, and not all owners will qualify as persons entitled to enforce. Rules that address transfer of ownership of a note are addressed in the discussion of Question 2 below.

[16] UCC § 3–412. (If the note has been dishonored, and an indorser has paid the note to the person entitled to enforce it, the maker's obligation runs to the indorser.)

[17] UCC § 3–602. The law of agency is applicable in determining whether a payment has been made to a person entitled to enforce. See *id.*, Official Comment 3. Note that, in states that have enacted the 2002 Official Text of UCC Article 3, UCC § 3–602(b) provides that a maker is also discharged by paying a person formerly entitled to enforce the note if the maker has not received adequate notification that the note has been transferred and that payment is to be made to the transferee. This amendment aligns the protection afforded to makers of notes that have been assigned with comparable protection afforded to obligors on other payment rights that have been assigned. See, *e.g.*, UCC § 9–406(a); Restatement (Second), Contracts § 338(1).

[18] See UCC § 3–502. See also UCC § 3–602.

Thus, a person seeking to enforce rights based on the failure of the maker to pay a mortgage note must identify the person entitled to enforce the note and establish that that person has not been paid. This portion of this Report sets out the criteria for qualifying as a "person entitled to enforce" a mortgage note. The discussion of Question Two addresses how ownership of a mortgage note may be effectively transferred from an owner to another person.

UCC Section 3–301 provides only three ways in which a person may qualify as the person entitled to enforce a note, two of which require the person to be in possession of the note (which may include possession by a third party that possesses it for the person):[19]

- The first way that a person may qualify as the person entitled to enforce a note is to be its "holder." This familiar concept, set out in detail in UCC Section 1–201(b)(21)(A), requires that the person be in possession of the note and either (i) the note is payable to that person or (ii) the note is payable to bearer. Determining to whom a note is payable requires examination not only of the face of the note but also of any indorsements. This is because the party to whom a note is payable may be changed by indorsement[20] so that, for example, a note payable to the order of a named payee that is indorsed in blank by that payee becomes payable to bearer.[21]
- The second way that a person may be the person entitled to enforce a note is to be a "nonholder in possession of the [note] who has the rights of a holder."
    - How can a person who is not the holder of a note have the rights of a holder? This can occur by operation of law outside the UCC, such as the law of subrogation or estate administration, by which one person is the successor to or acquires another person's rights.[22] It can also occur if the delivery of the note to that person constitutes a "transfer" (as that term is defined in UCC Section 3–203, see below) because transfer of a note "vests in the transferee any right of the transferor to enforce the instrument."[23] Thus, if a holder (who, as seen above, is a person entitled to enforce a note) transfers the note to another person, that other person (the transferee) obtains from the holder the right to enforce the note even if the transferee does not become the holder (as in the example below). Similarly, a subsequent transfer will result in the subsequent transferee being a person entitled to enforce the note.
    - Under what circumstances does delivery of a note qualify as a transfer? As stated in UCC Section 3–203(a), a note is transferred "when it is delivered by a person other than its issuer for the purpose of giving to the person receiving delivery the right to enforce the instrument." For example, assume that the payee of a note sells it to an assignee, intending to transfer all of the payee's rights to the note, but delivers the note to the assignee without indorsing it. The assignee will not qualify as a holder (because the note is still payable to the payee) but, because the transaction between the payee and the assignee qualifies as a transfer, the assignee now has all of the payee's rights to enforce the note and thereby qualifies as the person entitled to enforce it. Thus, the failure to obtain the indorsement of the payee does not prevent a person in possession of the note from being the person entitled to enforce it,

[19] See UCC § 1–103(b) (unless displaced by particular provisions of the UCC, the law of, *inter alia*, principal and agent supplements the provisions of the UCC). See also UCC § 3–420, Comment 1 ("Delivery to an agent [of a payee] is delivery to the payee."). Note that "delivery" of a negotiable instrument is defined in UCC § 1–201(b)(15) as voluntary transfer of possession. This Report does not address the determination of whether a particular person is an agent of another person under the law of agency and the agency law implications of such a determination.

[20] "Indorsement," as defined in UCC § 3–204(a), requires the signature of the indorser. The law of agency determines whether a signature made by a person purporting to act as a representative binds the represented person. UCC § 3–402(a); see note 12, supra. An indorsement may appear either on the instrument or on a separate piece of paper (usually referred to as an *allonge*) affixed to the instrument. See UCC § 3–204(a) and Comment 1, par. 4.

[21] UCC Section 3–205 contains the rules concerning the effect of various types of indorsement on the party to whom a note is payable. Either a "special indorsement" (see UCC § 3–205(a)) or a "blank indorsement" (see UCC § 3–205(b)) can change the identity of the person to whom the note is payable. A special indorsement is an indorsement that identifies the person to whom it makes the note payable, while a blank indorsement is an indorsement that does not identify such a person and results in the instrument becoming payable to bearer. When an instrument is indorsed in blank (and, thus, is payable to bearer), it may be negotiated by transfer of possession alone until specially indorsed. UCC § 3–205(b).

[22] See Official Comment to UCC § 3–301.

[23] UCC § 3–203(b).

but demonstrating that status is more difficult. This is because the person in possession of the note must also demonstrate the purpose of the delivery of the note to it in order to qualify as the person entitled to enforce.[24]

- There is a third method of qualifying as a person entitled to enforce a note that, unlike the previous two methods, does not require possession of the note. This method is quite limited—it applies only in cases in which "the person cannot reasonably obtain possession of the instrument because the instrument was destroyed, its whereabouts cannot be determined, or it is in the wrongful possession of an unknown person or a person that cannot be found or is not amenable to service of process."[25] In such a case, a person qualifies as a person entitled to enforce the note if the person demonstrates not only that one of those circumstances is present but also demonstrates that the person was formerly in possession of the note and entitled to enforce it when the loss of possession occurred and that the loss of possession was not as a result of transfer (as defined above) or lawful seizure. If the person proves those facts, as well as the terms of the note, the person is a person entitled to enforce the note and may seek to enforce it even though it is not in possession of the note,[26] but the court may not enter judgment in favor of the person unless the court finds that the maker is adequately protected against loss that might occur if the note subsequently reappears.[27]

Illustrations:

1. Maker issued a negotiable mortgage note payable to the order of Payee. Payee is in possession of the note, which has not been indorsed. Payee is the holder of the note and, therefore, is the person entitled to enforce it. UCC §§ 1–201(b)(21)(A), 3–301(i).
2. Maker issued a negotiable mortgage note payable to the order of Payee. Payee indorsed the note in blank and gave possession of it to Transferee. Transferee is the holder of the note and, therefore, is the person entitled to enforce it. UCC §§ 1–201(b)(21)(A), 3–301(i).
3. Maker issued a negotiable mortgage note payable to the order of Payee. Payee sold the note to Transferee and gave possession of it to Transferee for the purpose of giving Transferee the right to enforce the note. Payee did not, however, indorse the note. Transferee is not the holder of the note because, while Transferee is in possession of the note, it is payable neither to bearer nor to Transferee. UCC § 1–201(b)(21)(A). Nonetheless, Transferee is a person entitled to enforce the note. This is because the note was transferred to Transferee and the transfer vested in Transferee Payee's right to enforce the note. UCC § 3-203(a)–(b). As a result, Transferee is a nonholder in possession of the note with the rights of a holder and, accordingly, a person entitled to enforce the note. UCC § 3-301(ii).
4. Same facts as Illustrations 2 and 3, except that (i) under the law of agency, Agent is the agent of Transferee for purposes of possessing the note and (ii) it is Agent, rather than Transferee, to whom actual physical possession of the note is given by Payee. In the facts of Illustration 2, Transferee is a holder of the note and a person entitled to enforce it. In the context of Illustration 3, Transferee is a person entitled to enforce the note. Whether Agent may enforce the note or mortgage on behalf of Transferee depends in part on the law of agency and, in the case of the mortgage, real property law.

[24] If the note was transferred for value and the transferee does not qualify as a holder because of the lack of indorsement by the transferor, "the transferee has a specifically enforceable right to the unqualified indorsement of the transferor." See UCC § 3-203(c).

[25] UCC § 3-309(a)(iii) (1990 text), 3-309(a)(3) (2002 text). The 2002 text goes on to provide that a transferee from the person who lost possession of a note may also qualify as a person entitled to enforce it. See UCC § 3-309(a)(1)(B) (2002). This point was thought to be implicit in the 1990 text, but was rejected in some cases in which the issue was raised. The reasoning of those cases was rejected in Official Comment 5 to UCC § 9-109 and the point was made explicit in the 2002 text of Article 3.

[26] To prevail the person must establish not only that the person is a person entitled to enforce the note but also the other elements of the maker's obligation to pay such a person. See generally UCC §§ 3-309(b), 3-412. Moreover, as is the case with respect to the enforcement of all rights under the UCC, the person enforcing the note must act in good faith in enforcing the note. UCC § 1-304.

[27] See *id.* UCC § 3-309(b) goes on to state that "Adequate protection may be provided by any reasonable means."

5. Same facts as Illustration 2, except that after obtaining possession of the note, Transferee lost the note and its whereabouts cannot be determined. Transferee is a person entitled to enforce the note even though Transferee does not have possession of it. UCC § 3–309(a). If Transferee brings an action on the note against Maker, Transferee must establish the terms of the note and the elements of Maker's obligation on it. The court may not enter judgment in favor of Transferee, however, unless the court finds that Maker is adequately protected against loss that might occur by reason of a claim of another person (such as the finder of the note) to enforce the note. UCC § 3–309(b).

Question Two—What Steps Must be Taken for the Owner of a Mortgage Note to Transfer Ownership of the Note to Another Person or Use the Note as Collateral for an Obligation?

In the discussion of Question One, this Report addresses identification of the person who is entitled to enforce a note. That discussion does not address who "owns" the note. While, in many cases, the person entitled to enforce a note is also its owner, this need not be the case. The rules that determine whether a person is a person entitled to enforce a note do not require that person to be the owner of the note,[28] and a change in ownership of a note does not necessarily bring about a concomitant change in the identity of the person entitled to enforce the note. This is because the rules that determine who is entitled to enforce a note and the rules that determine whether the note, or an interest in it, have been effectively transferred serve different functions:

- The rules that determine who is entitled to enforce a note are concerned primarily with the maker of the note, providing the maker with a relatively simple way of determining to whom his or her obligation is owed and, thus, whom to pay in order to be discharged.
- The rules concerning transfer of ownership and other interests in a note, on the other hand, primarily relate to who, among competing claimants, is entitled to the economic value of the note.

In a typical transaction, when a note is issued to a payee, the note is initially owned by that payee. If that payee seeks either to use the note as collateral or sell the note outright, Article 9 of the UCC governs that transaction and determines whether the creditor or buyer has obtained a property right in the note. As is generally known, Article 9 governs transactions in which property is used as collateral for an obligation.[29] In addition, however, Article 9 governs the sale of most payment rights, including the sale of both negotiable and non-negotiable notes.[30] With very few exceptions, the same Article 9 rules that apply to transactions in which a payment right is collateral for an obligation also apply to transactions in which a payment right is sold. Rather than contain two parallel sets of rules—one for transactions in which payment rights are collateral and the other for sales of payment rights—Article 9 uses nomenclature conventions to apply one set of rules to both types of transactions. This is accomplished primarily by defining the term "security interest" to include not only an interest in property that secures an obligation but also the right of a buyer of a payment right in a transaction governed by Article 9.[31] Similarly, definitional conventions denominate the seller of such a payment right as the "debtor," the buyer as the "secured party," and the sold payment right as the "collateral."[32] As a result, for purposes of Article 9, the buyer of a promissory note is a "secured party" that has acquired a "security interest" in the note from the "debtor," and the rules that apply to

[28] See UCC § 3–301, which provides, in relevant part, that "A person may be a person entitled to enforce the instrument even though the person is not the owner of the instrument. . . ."

[29] UCC § 9–109(a)(1).

[30] With certain limited exceptions not germane to this Report, Article 9 governs the sale of accounts, chattel paper, payment intangibles, and promissory notes. UCC § 9–109(a)(3). The term "promissory note" includes not only notes that fulfill the requirements of a negotiable instrument under UCC § 3–104 but also notes that do not fulfill those requirements but nonetheless are of a "type that in ordinary business is transferred by delivery with any necessary indorsement or assignment." See UCC §§ 9–102(a)(65) (definition of "promissory note") and 9–102(a)(47) (definition of "instrument" as the term is used in Article 9).

[31] See UCC § 1–201(b)(35) [UCC § 1–201(37) in states that have not yet enacted the 2001 revised text of UCC Article 1]. (For reasons that are not apparent, when South Carolina enacted the 1998 revised text of UCC Article 9, which included an amendment to UCC § 1–201 to expand the definition of "security interest" to include the right of a buyer of a promissory note, it did not enact the amendment to § 1–201. This Report does not address the effect of that omission.) The limitation to transactions governed by Article 9 refers to the exclusion, in cases not germane to this Report, of certain assignments of payment rights from the reach of Article 9.

[32] UCC §§ 9–102(a)(28)(B); 9–102(a)(72)(D); 9–102(a)(12)(B).

security interests that secure an obligation generally also apply to transactions in which a promissory note is sold.

Section 9–203(b) of the Uniform Commercial Code provides that three criteria must be fulfilled in order for the owner of a mortgage note effectively to create a "security interest" (either an interest in the note securing an obligation or the outright sale of the note to a buyer) in it.

- The first two criteria are straightforward—"value" must be given[33] and the debtor/seller must have rights in the note or the power to transfer rights in the note to a third party.[34]
- The third criterion may be fulfilled in either one of two ways. Either the debtor/seller must "authenticate"[35] a "security agreement"[36] that describes the note[37] or the secured party must take possession[38] of the note pursuant to the debtor's security agreement.[39]
    - Thus, if the secured party (including a buyer) takes possession of the mortgage note pursuant to the security agreement of the debtor (including a seller), this criterion is satisfied even if that agreement is oral or otherwise not evidenced by an authenticated record.
    - Alternatively, if the debtor authenticates a security agreement describing the note, this criterion is satisfied even if the secured party does *not* take possession of the note. (Note that in this situation, in which the seller of a note may retain possession of it, the owner of a note may be a different person than the person entitled to enforce the note.)[40]

---

[33] UCC § 9–203(b)(1). UCC § 1–204 provides that giving "value" for rights includes not only acquiring them for consideration but also acquiring them in return for a binding commitment to extend credit, as security for or in complete or partial satisfaction of a preexisting claim, or by accepting delivery of them under a preexisting contract for their purchase.

[34] UCC § 9–203(b)(2). Limited rights that are short of full ownership are sufficient for this purpose. See Official Comment 6 to UCC § 9–203.

[35] This term is defined to include signing and its electronic equivalent. See UCC § 9–102(a)(7).

[36] A "security agreement" is an agreement that creates or provides for a security interest (including the rights of a buyer arising upon the outright sale of a payment right). See UCC § 9–102(a)(73).

[37] Article 9's criteria for descriptions of property in a security agreement are quite flexible. Generally speaking, any description suffices, whether or not specific, if it reasonably identifies the property. See UCC § 9–108(a)–(b). A "supergeneric" description consisting solely of words such as "all of the debtor's assets" or "all of the debtor's personal property" is not sufficient, however. UCC § 9–108(c). A narrower description, limiting the property to a particular category or type, such as "all notes," is sufficient. For example, a description that refers to "all of the debtor's notes" is sufficient.

[38] See UCC § 9–313. As noted in Official Comment 3 to UCC § 9–313, "in determining whether a particular person has possession, the principles of agency apply." In addition, UCC § 9–313 also contains two special rules under which possession by a non-agent may constitute possession by the secured party. First, if a person who is not an agent is in possession of the collateral and the person authenticates a record acknowledging that the person holds the collateral for the secured party's benefit, possession by that person constitutes possession by the secured party. UCC § 9–313(c). Second, a secured party that has possession of collateral does not relinquish possession by delivering the collateral to another person (other than the debtor or a lessee of the collateral from the debtor in the ordinary course of the debtor's business) if the delivery is accompanied by instructions to that person to hold possession of the collateral for the benefit of the secured party or redeliver it to the secured party. UCC § 9–313(h). See also Official Comment 9 to UCC § 9–313 ("New subsections (h) and (i) address the practice of mortgage warehouse lenders.") Possession as contemplated by UCC § 9–313 is also possession for purposes of UCC § 9–203. See UCC § 9–203, Comment 4.

[39] UCC §§ 9–203(b)(3)(A)–(B).

[40] As noted in the discussion of Question One, payment by the maker of a negotiable note to the person entitled to enforce it discharges the maker's obligations on the note. UCC § 3–602. This is the case even if the person entitled to enforce the note is not its owner. As between the person entitled to enforce the note and the owner of the note, the right to the money paid by the maker is determined by the UCC and other applicable law, such as the law of contract and the law of restitution, as well as agency law. See, e.g., UCC §§ 3–306 and 9–315(a)(2). As noted in comment 3 to UCC § 3–602, "if the original payee of the note transfers ownership of the note to a third party but continues to service the obligation, the law of agency might treat payments made to the original payee as payments made to the third party."

Satisfaction of these three criteria of Section 9–203(b) results in the secured party (including a buyer of the note) obtaining a property right (whether outright ownership or a security interest to secure an obligation) in the note from the debtor (including a seller of the note).[41]

Illustrations:

6. Maker issued a mortgage note payable to the order of Payee.[42] Payee borrowed money from Funder and, to secure Payee's repayment obligation, Payee and Funder agreed that Funder would have a security interest in the note. Simultaneously with the funding of the loan, Payee gave possession of the note to Funder. Funder has an attached and enforceable security interest in the note. UCC § 9–203(b). This is the case even if Payee's agreement is oral or otherwise not evidenced by an authenticated record. Payee is no longer a person entitled to enforce the note (because Payee is no longer in possession of it and it has not been lost, stolen, or destroyed). UCC § 3–301. Funder is a person entitled to enforce the note if either (i) Payee indorsed the note by blank indorsement or by a special indorsement identifying Funder as the person to whom the indorsement makes the note payable (because, in such cases, Funder would be the holder of the note), or (ii) the delivery of the note from Payee to Funder constitutes a transfer of the note under UCC § 3–203 (because, in such case, Funder would be a nonholder in possession of the note with the rights of a holder). See also UCC §§ 1–201(b)(21)(A), 3–205(a)–(b), and 3–301(i)–(ii).

7. Maker issued a mortgage note payable to the order of Payee. Payee borrowed money from Funder and, in a signed writing that reasonably identified the note (whether specifically or as part of a category or a type of property defined in the UCC), granted Funder a security interest in the note to secure Payee's repayment obligation. Payee, however, retained possession of the note. Funder has an attached and enforceable security interest in the note. UCC § 9–203(b). If the note is negotiable, Payee remains the holder and the person entitled to enforce the note because Payee is in possession of it and it is payable to the order of Payee. UCC §§ 1–201(b)(21)(A), 3–301(i).

8. Maker issued a mortgage note payable to the order of Payee. Payee sold the note to Funder, giving possession of the note to Funder in exchange for the purchase price. The sale of the note is governed by Article 9 and the rights of Funder as buyer constitute a "security interest." UCC §§ 9–109(a)(3), 1–201(b)(35). The security interest is attached and is enforceable. UCC § 9–203(b). This is the case even if the sales agreement was oral or otherwise not evidenced by an authenticated record. If the note is negotiable, Funder is also a person entitled to enforce the note, whether or not Payee indorsed it, because either (i) Funder is a holder of the note (if Payee indorsed it by blank indorsement or by a special indorsement identifying Funder as the person to whom the indorsement makes the note payable) or (ii) Funder is a nonholder in possession of the note (if there is no such indorsement) who has obtained the rights of Payee by transfer of the note pursuant to UCC § 3–203. See also UCC §§ 1–201(b)(21)(A), 3–205(a)–(b), and 3–301(i)–(ii).

9. Maker issued a mortgage note payable to the order of Payee. Pursuant to a signed writing that reasonably identified the note (whether specifically or as part of a category or a type of property defined in the UCC), Payee sold the note to Funder. Payee, however, retained possession of the note. The sale of the note is governed by Article 9 and the rights of Funder as buyer constitute a "security interest." UCC § 1–201(b)(35). The security interest is attached and is enforceable. UCC § 9–203(b). If the note is negotiable, Payee remains the holder and the person entitled to enforce

---

[41] For cases in which another person claims an interest in the note (whether as a result of another voluntary transfer by the debtor or otherwise), reference to Article 9's rules governing perfection and priority of security interests may be required in order to rank order those claims (and, in some cases, determine whether a party has taken the note free of competing claims to the note). In the case of notes that are negotiable instruments, the Article 3 concept of "holder in due course" (see UCC § 3–302) should be considered as well, because a holder in due course takes its rights in an instrument free of competing property claims to it (as well as free of most defenses to obligations on it). See UCC §§ 3–305 and 3–306. With respect to determining whether the owner of a note has effectively transferred a property interest to a transferee, however, the perfection and priority rules are largely irrelevant. (The application of the perfection and priority rules can result in the rights of the transferee either being subordinate to the rights of a competing claimant or being extinguished by the rights of the competing claimant. See, *e.g.*, UCC §§ 9–317(b), 9–322(a), 9–330(d), and 9–331(a).)

[42] For this Illustration, as well as Illustrations 7–11, the analysis under UCC Article 9 is the same whether the mortgage note is negotiable or non-negotiable. This is because, in either case, the mortgage note will qualify as a "promissory note" and, therefore, an "instrument" under UCC Article 9. See UCC §§ 9–102(a)(47), (65).

the note (even though, as between Payee and Funder, Funder owns the note) because Payee is in possession of it and it is payable to the order of Payee. UCC §§ 1–201(b)(21)(A), 3–301(i).

Question Three—What is the Effect of Transfer of an Interest in a Mortgage Note on the Mortgage Securing It?

What if a note secured by a mortgage is sold (or the note is used as collateral to secure an obligation), but the parties do not take any additional actions to assign the mortgage that secures payment of the note, such as execution of a recordable assignment of the mortgage? UCC Section 9–203(g) explicitly provides that, in such cases, the assignment of the interest of the seller or other grantor of a security interest in the note automatically transfers a corresponding interest in the mortgage to the assignee: "The attachment of a security interest in a right to payment or performance secured by a security interest or other lien on personal or real property is also attachment of a security interest in the security interest, mortgage, or other lien." (As noted previously, a "security interest" in a note includes the right of a buyer of the note.)

While this question has provoked some uncertainty and has given rise to some judicial analysis that disregards the impact of Article 9,[43] the UCC is unambiguous: the sale of a mortgage note (or other grant of a security interest in the note) not accompanied by a separate conveyance of the mortgage securing the note does not result in the mortgage being severed from the note.[44]

It is important to note in this regard, however, that UCC Section 9–203(g) addresses only whether, as between the seller of a mortgage note (or a debtor who uses it as collateral) and the buyer or other secured party, the interest of the seller (or debtor) in the mortgage has been correspondingly transferred to the secured party. UCC Section 9–308(e) goes on to state that, if the secured party's security interest in the note is perfected, the secured party's security interest in the mortgage securing the note is also perfected,[45] with result that the right of the secured party is senior to the rights of a person who then or later becomes a lien creditor of the seller of (or other grantor of a security interest in) the note. Neither of these rules, however, determines the ranking of rights in the underlying real property itself, or the effect of recordation or non-recordation in the real property recording system on enforcement of the mortgage.[46]

Illustration:

10. Same facts as Illustration 9. The signed writing was silent with respect to the mortgage securing the note and the parties made no other agreement with respect to the mortgage. The attachment of Funder's interest in the rights of Payee in the note also constitutes attachment of an interest in the rights of Payee in the mortgage. UCC § 9–203(g).

[43] *See, e.g.*, the discussion of this issue in *U.S. Bank v. Ibanez*, 458 Mass. 637 at 652–53, 941 N.E.2d 40 at 53–54 (2011). In that discussion, the court cited Massachusetts common law precedents pre-dating the enactment of the current text of Article 9 to the effect that a mortgage does not follow a note in the absence of a separate assignment of the mortgage, but did not address the effect of Massachusetts's subsequent enactment of UCC § 9–203(g) on those precedents. Under the rule in UCC § 9–203(g), if the holder of the note in question demonstrated that it had an attached security interest (including the interest of a buyer) in the note, the holder of the note in question would also have a security interest in the mortgage securing the note even in the absence of a separate assignment of the mortgage. (This Report does not address whether, under the facts of the *Ibanez* case, the holder of the note had an attached security interest in the note and, thus, qualified for the application of UCC § 9–203(g). Moreover, even if the holder had an attached security interest in the note and, thus, had a security interest in the mortgage, this would not, of itself, mean that the holder could enforce the mortgage without a recordable assignment of the mortgage to the holder. Whatever steps are required in order to enforce a mortgage in the absence of a recordable assignment are the province of real property law. The matter is addressed, in part, in the discussion of Question 4 below.)

[44] Official Comment 9 to UCC § 9–203 confirms this point: "Subsection (g) codifies the common-law rule that a transfer of an obligation secured by a security interest or other lien on personal or real property also transfers the security interest or lien." Pursuant to UCC § 1–302(a), the parties to the transaction may agree that an interest in the mortgage securing the note does not accompany the note, but such an agreement is unlikely. See, *e.g.*, Restatement (3d), Property (Mortgages) § 5.4, comment *a* ("It is conceivable that on rare occasions a mortgagee will wish to disassociate the obligation and the mortgage, but that result should follow only upon evidence that the parties to the transfer so agreed.").

[45] See Official Comment 6 to UCC § 9–308, which also observes that "this result helps prevent the separation of the mortgage (or other lien) from the note." Note also that, as explained in Official Comment 7 to UCC § 9–109, "It also follows from [UCC § 9–109(b)] that an attempt to obtain or perfect a security interest in a secured obligation by complying with non-Article 9 law, as by an assignment of record of a real-property mortgage, would be ineffective."

[46] Similarly, Official Comment 6 to UCC § 9–308 states that "this Article does not determine who has the power to release a mortgage of record. That issue is determined by real-property law."

Question Four—What Actions May a Person to Whom an Interest in a Mortgage Note Has Been Transferred, but Who Has not Taken a Recordable Assignment of the Mortgage, Take in Order to Become the Assignee of Record of the Mortgage Securing the Note?

In some states, a party without a recorded interest in a mortgage may not enforce the mortgage non-judicially. In such states, even though the buyer of a mortgage note (or a creditor to whom a security interest in the note has been granted to secure an obligation) automatically obtains corresponding rights in the mortgage,[47] this may be insufficient as a matter of applicable real estate law to enable that buyer or secured creditor to enforce the mortgage upon default of the maker if the buyer or secured creditor does not have a recordable assignment. The buyer or other secured party may attempt to obtain such a recordable assignment from the seller or debtor at the time it seeks to enforce the mortgage, but such an attempt may be unsuccessful.[48]

Article 9 of the UCC provides such a buyer or secured creditor a mechanism by which it can record its interest in the realty records in order to conduct a non-judicial foreclosure. UCC Section 9–607(b) provides that "if necessary to enable a secured party [including the buyer of a mortgage note] to exercise . . . the right of [its transferor]to enforce a mortgage nonjudicially," the secured party may record in the office in which the mortgage is recorded (i) a copy of the security agreement transferring an interest in the note to the secured party and (ii) the secured party's sworn affidavit in recordable form stating that default has occurred[49] and that the secured party is entitled to enforce the mortgage non-judicially.[50]

Illustration:

11. Same facts as Illustration 10. Maker has defaulted on the note and mortgage and Funder would like to enforce the mortgage non-judicially. In the relevant state, however, only a party with a recorded interest in a mortgage may enforce it non-judicially. Funder may record in the relevant mortgage recording office a copy of the signed writing pursuant to which the note was sold to Funder and a sworn affidavit stating that Maker has defaulted and that Funder is entitled to enforce the mortgage non-judicially. UCC § 9–607(b).

Summary

The Uniform Commercial Code provides four sets of rules that determine matters that are important in the context of enforcement of mortgage notes and the mortgages that secure them:

- First, in the case of a mortgage note that is a negotiable instrument, Article 3 of the UCC determines the identity of the person who is entitled to enforce the note and to whom the maker owes its payment obligation; payment to the person entitled to enforce the note discharges the maker's obligation, but failure to pay that party when the note is due constitutes dishonor.
- Second, for both negotiable and non-negotiable mortgage notes, Article 9 of the UCC determines whether a transferee of the note from its owner has obtained an attached property right in the note.
- Third, Article 9 of the UCC provides that a transferee of a mortgage note whose property right in the note has attached also automatically has an attached property right in the mortgage that secures the note.
- Finally, Article 9 of the UCC provides a mechanism by which the owner of a note and the mortgage securing it may, upon default of the maker of the note, record its interest in the mortgage in the realty records in order to conduct a non-judicial foreclosure.

---

[47] See discussion of Question Three, *supra*.

[48] In some cases, the seller or debtor may no longer be in business. In other cases, it may simply be unresponsive to requests for execution of documents with respect to a transaction in which it no longer has an economic interest. Moreover, in cases in which mortgage note was collateral for an obligation owed to the secured party, the defaulting debtor may simply be unwilling to assist its secured party. See Official Comment 8 to UCC § 9–607.

[49] The 2010 amendments to Article 9 (see fn. 8, *supra*) add language to this provision to clarify that "default," in this context, means default with respect to the note or other obligation secured by the mortgage.

[50] UCC § 9–607(b) does not address other conditions that must be satisfied for judicial or non-judicial enforcement of a mortgage.

APPENDIX D

As noted previously, these UCC rules do not resolve all issues in this field. The enforcement of real estate mortgages by foreclosure is primarily the province of a state's real property law, but legal determinations made pursuant to the four sets of UCC rules described in this Report will, in many cases, be central to administration of that law. In such cases, proper application of real property law requires proper application of the UCC rules discussed in this Report.

UNIFORM ELECTRONIC TRANSACTIONS ACT (1999)*

PREFATORY NOTE

With the advent of electronic means of communication and information transfer, business models and methods for doing business have evolved to take advantage of the speed, efficiencies, and cost benefits of electronic technologies. These developments have occurred in the face of existing legal barriers to the legal efficacy of records and documents which exist solely in electronic media. Whether the legal requirement that information or an agreement or contract must be contained or set forth in a pen and paper writing derives from a statute of frauds affecting the enforceability of an agreement, or from a record retention statute that calls for keeping the paper record of a transaction, such legal requirements raise real barriers to the effective use of electronic media.

One striking example of electronic barriers involves so called check retention statutes in every State. A study conducted by the Federal Reserve Bank of Boston identified more than 2500 different state laws which require the retention of canceled checks by the issuers of those checks. These requirements not only impose burdens on the issuers, but also effectively restrain the ability of banks handling the checks to automate the process. Although check truncation is validated under the Uniform Commercial Code, if the bank's customer must store the canceled paper check, the bank will not be able to deal with the item through electronic transmission of the information. By establishing the equivalence of an electronic record of the information, the Uniform Electronic Transactions Act (UETA) removes these barriers without affecting the underlying legal rules and requirements.

It is important to understand that the purpose of the UETA is to remove barriers to electronic commerce by validating and effectuating electronic records and signatures. It is NOT a general contracting statute—the substantive rules of contracts remain unaffected by UETA. Nor is it a digital signature statute.

---

* Reproduced by permission of the Uniform Law Commission.

UNIFORM ELECTRONIC TRANSACTIONS ACT

To the extent that a State has a Digital Signature Law, the UETA is designed to support and compliment that statute.

A. Scope of the Act and Procedural Approach. The scope of this Act provides coverage which sets forth a clear framework for covered transactions, and also avoids unwarranted surprises for unsophisticated parties dealing in this relatively new media. The clarity and certainty of the scope of the Act have been obtained while still providing a solid legal framework that allows for the continued development of innovative technology to facilitate electronic transactions.

With regard to the general scope of the Act, the Act's coverage is inherently limited by the definition of "transaction." The Act does not apply to *all* writings and signatures, but only to electronic records and signatures relating to a transaction, defined as those interactions between people relating to business, commercial and governmental affairs. In general, there are few writing or signature requirements imposed by law on many of the "standard" transactions that had been considered for exclusion. A good example relates to trusts, where the general rule on creation of a trust imposes no formal writing requirement. Further, the writing requirements in other contexts derived from governmental filing issues. For example, real estate transactions were considered potentially troublesome because of the need to file a deed or other instrument for protection against third parties. Since the efficacy of a real estate purchase contract, or even a deed, between the parties is not affected by any sort of filing, the question was raised why these transactions should not be validated by this Act if done via an electronic medium. No sound reason was found. Filing requirements fall within Sections 17–19 on governmental records. An exclusion of all real estate transactions would be particularly unwarranted in the event that a State chose to convert to an electronic recording system, as many have for Article 9 financing statement filings under the Uniform Commercial Code.

The exclusion of specific Articles of the Uniform Commercial Code reflects the recognition that, particularly in the case of Articles 5, 8 and revised Article 9, electronic transactions were addressed in the specific contexts of those revision processes. In the context of Articles 2 and 2A the UETA provides the vehicle for assuring that such transactions may be accomplished and effected via an electronic medium. At such time as Articles 2 and 2A are revised the extent of coverage in those Articles/Acts may make application of this Act as a gap-filling law desirable. Similar considerations apply to the recently promulgated Uniform Computer Information Transactions Act ("UCITA").

The need for certainty as to the scope and applicability of this Act is critical, and makes any sort of a broad, general exception based on notions of inconsistency with existing writing and signature requirements unwise at best. The uncertainty inherent in leaving the applicability of the Act to judicial construction of this Act with other laws is unacceptable if electronic transactions are to be facilitated.

Finally, recognition that the paradigm for the Act involves two willing parties conducting a transaction electronically, makes it necessary to expressly provide that some form of acquiescence or intent on the part of a person to conduct transactions electronically is necessary before the Act can be invoked. Accordingly, Section 5 specifically provides that the Act only applies between parties that have agreed to conduct transactions electronically. In this context, the construction of the term agreement must be broad in order to assure that the Act applies whenever the circumstances show the parties intention to transact electronically, regardless of whether the intent rises to the level of a formal agreement.

B. Procedural Approach. Another fundamental premise of the Act is that it be minimalist and procedural. The general efficacy of existing law in an electronic context, so long as biases and barriers to the medium are removed, validates this approach. The Act defers to existing substantive law. Specific areas of deference to other law in this Act include: (1) the meaning and effect of "sign" under existing law, (2) the method and manner of displaying, transmitting and formatting information in Section 8, (3) rules of attribution in Section 9, and (4) the law of mistake in Section 10.

The Act's treatment of records and signatures demonstrates best the minimalist approach that has been adopted. Whether a record is attributed to a person is left to law outside this Act. Whether an electronic signature has any effect is left to the surrounding circumstances and other law. These provisions are salutary directives to assure that records and signatures will be treated in the same manner, under currently existing law, as written records and manual signatures.

The deference of the Act to other substantive law does not negate the necessity of setting forth rules and standards for using electronic media. The Act expressly validates electronic records, signatures and contracts. It provides for the use of electronic records and information for retention purposes, providing certainty in an area with great potential in cost savings and efficiency. The Act makes clear that the actions of machines ("electronic agents") programmed and used by people will bind the user of the machine, regardless of whether human review of a particular transaction has occurred. It specifies the standards for sending and receipt of electronic records, and it allows for innovation in financial services through the implementation of transferable records. In these ways the Act permits electronic transactions to be accomplished with certainty under existing substantive rules of law.

§ 1. Short Title.

This [Act] may be cited as the Uniform Electronic Transactions Act.

§ 2. Definitions.

In this [Act]:

(1) "Agreement" means the bargain of the parties in fact, as found in their language or inferred from other circumstances and from rules, regulations, and procedures given the effect of agreements under laws otherwise applicable to a particular transaction.

(2) "Automated transaction" means a transaction conducted or performed, in whole or in part, by electronic means or electronic records, in which the acts or records of one or both parties are not reviewed by an individual in the ordinary course in forming a contract, performing under an existing contract, or fulfilling an obligation required by the transaction.

(3) "Computer program" means a set of statements or instructions to be used directly or indirectly in an information processing system in order to bring about a certain result.

(4) "Contract" means the total legal obligation resulting from the parties' agreement as affected by this [Act] and other applicable law.

(5) "Electronic" means relating to technology having electrical, digital, magnetic, wireless, optical, electromagnetic, or similar capabilities.

(6) "Electronic agent" means a computer program or an electronic or other automated means used independently to initiate an action or respond to electronic records or performances in whole or in part, without review or action by an individual.

(7) "Electronic record" means a record created, generated, sent, communicated, received, or stored by electronic means.

(8) "Electronic signature" means an electronic sound, symbol, or process attached to or logically associated with a record and executed or adopted by a person with the intent to sign the record.

(9) "Governmental agency" means an executive, legislative, or judicial agency, department, board, commission, authority, institution, or instrumentality of the federal government or of a State or of a county, municipality, or other political subdivision of a State.

(10) "Information" means data, text, images, sounds, codes, computer programs, software, databases, or the like.

(11) "Information processing system" means an electronic system for creating, generating, sending, receiving, storing, displaying, or processing information.

(12) "Person" means an individual, corporation, business trust, estate, trust, partnership, limited liability company, association, joint venture, governmental agency, public corporation, or any other legal or commercial entity.

(13) "Record" means information that is inscribed on a tangible medium or that is stored in an electronic or other medium and is retrievable in perceivable form.

(14) "Security procedure" means a procedure employed for the purpose of verifying that an electronic signature, record, or performance is that of a specific person or for detecting changes or errors in the information in an electronic record. The term includes a procedure that requires the use of algorithms or other codes, identifying words or numbers, encryption, or callback or other acknowledgment procedures.

(15) "State" means a State of the United States, the District of Columbia, Puerto Rico, the United States Virgin Islands, or any territory or insular possession subject to the jurisdiction of the United States. The term includes an Indian tribe or band, or Alaskan native village, which is recognized by federal law or formally acknowledged by a State.

(16) "Transaction" means an action or set of actions occurring between two or more persons relating to the conduct of business, commercial, or governmental affairs.

Sources: UNCITRAL Model Law on Electronic Commerce; Uniform Commercial Code; Uniform Computer Information Transactions Act; Restatement 2d Contracts.

Comment

1. **"Agreement."** Whether the parties have reached an agreement is determined by their express language and all surrounding circumstances. The Restatement 2d Contracts § 3 provides that, "An agreement is a manifestation of mutual assent on the part of two or more persons." See also Restatement 2d Contracts, Section 2, Comment b. The Uniform Commercial Code specifically includes in the circumstances from which an agreement may be inferred "course of performance, course of dealing and usage of trade . . ." as defined in the UCC. Although the definition of agreement in this Act does not make specific reference to usage of trade and other party conduct, this definition is not intended to affect the construction of the parties' agreement under the substantive law applicable to a particular transaction. Where that law takes account of usage and conduct in informing the terms of the parties' agreement, the usage or conduct would be relevant as "other circumstances" included in the definition under this Act.

Where the law applicable to a given transaction provides that system rules and the like constitute part of the agreement of the parties, such rules will have the same effect in determining the parties agreement under this Act. For example, UCC Article 4 (Section 4–103(b)) provides that Federal Reserve regulations and operating circulars and clearinghouse rules have the effect of agreements. Such agreements by law properly would be included in the definition of agreement in this Act.

The parties' agreement is relevant in determining whether the provisions of this Act have been varied by agreement. In addition, the parties' agreement may establish the parameters of the parties' use of electronic records and signatures, security procedures and similar aspects of the transaction. See Model Trading Partner Agreement, 45 Business Lawyer Supp. Issue (June 1990). See Section 5(b) and Comments thereto.

2. **"Automated Transaction."** An automated transaction is a transaction performed or conducted by electronic means in which machines are used without human intervention to form contracts and perform obligations under existing contracts. Such broad coverage is necessary because of the diversity of transactions to which this Act may apply.

As with electronic agents, this definition addresses the circumstance where electronic records may result in action or performance by a party although no human review of the electronic records is anticipated. Section 14 provides specific rules to assure that where one or both parties do not review the electronic records, the resulting agreement will be effective.

The critical element in this definition is the lack of a human actor on one or both sides of a transaction. For example, if one orders books from Bookseller.com through Bookseller's website, the transaction would be an automated transaction because Bookseller took and confirmed the order via its machine. Similarly, if Automaker and supplier do business through Electronic Data Interchange, Automaker's computer, upon receiving information within certain pre-programmed parameters, will send an electronic order to supplier's computer. If Supplier's computer confirms the order and processes the shipment because the order falls within pre-programmed parameters in Supplier's computer, this would be a fully automated transaction. If, instead, the Supplier relies on a human employee to review, accept, and process the Buyer's order, then only the Automaker's side of the transaction would be automated. In either case, the entire transaction falls within this definition.

3. **"Computer program."** This definition refers to the functional and operating aspects of an electronic, digital system. It relates to operating instructions used in an electronic system such as an electronic agent. (See definition of "Electronic Agent.")

4. **"Electronic."** The basic nature of most current technologies and the need for a recognized, single term warrants the use of "electronic" as the defined term. The definition is intended to assure that the Act will be applied broadly as new technologies develop. The term must be construed broadly in light of developing technologies in order to fulfill the purpose of this Act to validate commercial transactions regardless of the medium used by the parties. Current legal requirements for "writings" can be satisfied by almost any tangible media, whether paper, other fibers, or even stone. The purpose and applicability of this Act covers intangible media which are technologically capable of storing, transmitting and reproducing information in human perceivable form, but which lack the tangible aspect of paper, papyrus or stone.

While not all technologies listed are technically "electronic" in nature (e.g., optical fiber technology), the term "electronic" is the most descriptive term available to describe the majority of current technologies. For example, the development of biological and chemical processes for communication and storage of data, while not specifically mentioned in the definition, are included within the technical definition because such processes operate on electromagnetic impulses. However, whether a particular technology may be characterized as technically "electronic," i.e., operates on electromagnetic impulses, should not be determinative of whether records and signatures created, used and stored by means of a particular technology are covered by this Act. This Act is intended to apply to all records and signatures created, used and stored by any medium which permits the information to be retrieved in perceivable form.

5. **"Electronic agent."** This definition establishes that an electronic agent is a machine. As the term "electronic agent" has come to be recognized, it is limited to a tool function. The effect on the party using the agent is addressed in the operative provisions of the Act (e.g., Section 14)

An electronic agent, such as a computer program or other automated means employed by a person, is a tool of that person. As a general rule, the employer of a tool is responsible for the results obtained by the use of that tool since the tool has no independent volition of its own. However, an electronic agent, by definition, is capable within the parameters of its programming, of initiating, responding or interacting with other parties or their electronic agents once it has been activated by a party, without further attention of that party.

While this Act proceeds on the paradigm that an electronic agent is capable of performing only within the technical strictures of its preset programming, it is conceivable that, within the useful life of this Act, electronic agents may be created with the ability to act autonomously, and not just automatically. That is, through developments in artificial intelligence, a computer may be able to "learn through experience, modify the instructions in their own programs, and even devise new instructions." Allen and Widdison, "Can Computers Make Contracts?" *9 Harv. J.L. & Tech 25* (Winter, 1996). If such developments occur, courts may construe the definition of electronic agent accordingly, in order to recognize such new capabilities.

The examples involving Bookseller.com and Automaker in the Comment to the definition of Automated Transaction are equally applicable here. Bookseller acts through an electronic agent in processing an order for books. Automaker and the supplier each act through electronic agents in facilitating and effectuating the just-in-time inventory process through EDI.

6. **"Electronic record."** An electronic record is a subset of the broader defined term "record." It is any record created, used or stored in a medium other than paper (see definition of electronic). The defined term is also used in this Act as a limiting definition in those provisions in which it is used.

Information processing systems, computer equipment and programs, electronic data interchange, electronic mail, voice mail, facsimile, telex, telecopying, scanning, and similar technologies all qualify as electronic under this Act. Accordingly information stored on a computer hard drive or floppy disc, facsimiles, voice mail messages, messages on a telephone answering machine, audio and video tape recordings, among other records, all would be electronic records under this Act.

7. **"Electronic signature."** The idea of a signature is broad and not specifically defined. Whether any particular record is "signed" is a question of fact. Proof of that fact must be made under other applicable law. This Act simply assures that the signature may be accomplished through electronic means. No specific technology need be used in order to create a valid signature. One's voice on an answering machine may suffice if the requisite intention is present. Similarly, including one's name as part of an electronic mail communication also may suffice, as may the firm name on a facsimile. It also may be shown that the requisite intent was not present and accordingly the symbol, sound or process did not amount to a signature. One may use a digital signature with the requisite intention, or one may use the private key solely as an access device with no intention to sign, or otherwise accomplish a legally binding act. In any case the critical element is the intention to execute or adopt the sound or symbol or process for the purpose of signing the related record.

The definition requires that the signer execute or adopt the sound, symbol, or process with the intent to sign the record. The act of applying a sound, symbol or process to an electronic record could have differing meanings and effects. The consequence of the act and the effect of the act as a signature are determined under other applicable law. However, the essential attribute of a signature involves applying a sound, symbol or process with an intent to do a legally significant act. It is that intention that is understood in the law as a part of the word "sign", without the need for a definition.

This Act establishes, to the greatest extent possible, the equivalency of electronic signatures and manual signatures. Therefore the term "signature" has been used to connote and convey that equivalency. The purpose is to overcome unwarranted biases against electronic methods of signing and authenticating records. The term "authentication," used in other laws, often has a narrower meaning and purpose than an electronic signature as used in this Act. However, an authentication under any of those other laws constitutes an electronic signature under this Act.

The precise effect of an electronic signature will be determined based on the surrounding circumstances under Section 9(b).

This definition includes as an electronic signature the standard webpage click through process. For example, when a person orders goods or services through a vendor's website, the person will be required to provide information as part of a process which will result in receipt of the goods or services. When the customer ultimately gets to the last step and clicks "I agree," the person has adopted the process and has done so with the intent to associate the person with the record of that process. The actual effect of the electronic signature will be determined from all the surrounding circumstances, however, the person adopted a process which the circumstances indicate s/he intended to have the effect of getting the goods/services and being bound to pay for them. The adoption of the process carried the intent to do a legally significant act, the hallmark of a signature.

Another important aspect of this definition lies in the necessity that the electronic signature be linked or logically associated with the record. In the paper world, it is assumed that the symbol adopted by a party is attached to or located somewhere in the same paper that is intended to be authenticated, e.g., an allonge firmly attached to a promissory note, or the classic signature at the end of a long contract. These tangible manifestations do not exist in the electronic environment, and accordingly, this definition expressly provides that the symbol must in some way be linked to, or connected with, the electronic record being signed. This linkage is consistent with the regulations promulgated by the Food and Drug Administration. 21 CFR Part 11 (March 20, 1997).

A digital signature using public key encryption technology would qualify as an electronic signature, as would the mere inclusion of one's name as a part of an e-mail message—so long as in each case the signer executed or adopted the symbol with the intent to sign.

8. **"Governmental agency."** This definition is important in the context of optional Sections 17–19.

9. **"Information processing system."** This definition is consistent with the UNCITRAL Model Law on Electronic Commerce. The term includes computers and other information systems. It is principally used in Section 15 in connection with the sending and receiving of information. In that context, the key aspect is that the information enter a system from which a person can access it.

10. **"Record."** This is a standard definition designed to embrace all means of communicating or storing information except human memory. It includes any method for storing or communicating information, including "writings." A record need not be indestructible or permanent, but the term does not include oral or other communications which are not stored or preserved by some means. Information that has not been retained other than through human memory does not qualify as a record. As in the case of the terms "writing" or "written," the term "record" does not establish the purposes, permitted uses or legal effect which a record may have under any particular provision of substantive law. ABA Report on Use of the Term "Record," October 1, 1996.

11. **"Security procedure."** A security procedure may be applied to verify an electronic signature, verify the identity of the sender, or assure the informational integrity of an electronic record. The definition does not identify any particular technology. This permits the use of procedures which the parties select or which are established by law. It permits the greatest flexibility among the parties and allows for future technological development.

The definition in this Act is broad and is used to illustrate one way of establishing attribution or content integrity of an electronic record or signature. The use of a security procedure is not accorded operative legal effect, through the use of presumptions or otherwise, by this Act. In this Act, the use of security procedures is simply one method for proving the source or content of an electronic record or signature.

A security procedure may be technologically very sophisticated, such as an asymmetric cryptographic system. At the other extreme the security procedure may be as simple as a telephone call to confirm the identity of the sender through another channel of communication. It may include the use of a mother's maiden name or a personal identification number (PIN). Each of these examples is a method for confirming the identity of a person or accuracy of a message.

12. **"Transaction."** The definition has been limited to actions between people taken in the context of business, commercial or governmental activities. The term includes all interactions between people for business, commercial, including specifically consumer, or governmental purposes. However, the term does not include unilateral or non-transactional actions. As such it provides a structural limitation on the scope of the Act as stated in the next section.

It is essential that the term commerce and business be understood and construed broadly to include commercial and business transactions involving individuals who may qualify as "consumers" under other applicable law. If Alice and Bob agree to the sale of Alice's car to Bob for $2000 using an internet auction site, that transaction is fully covered by this Act. Even if Alice and Bob each qualify as typical "consumers" under other applicable law, their interaction is a transaction in commerce. Accordingly their actions would be related to commercial affairs, and fully qualify as a transaction governed by this Act.

Other transaction types include:

1. A single purchase by an individual from a retail merchant, which may be accomplished by an order from a printed catalog sent by facsimile, or by exchange of electronic mail.

2. Recurring orders on a weekly or monthly basis between large companies which have entered into a master trading partner agreement to govern the methods and manner of their transaction parameters.

3. A purchase by an individual from an online internet retail vendor. Such an arrangement may develop into an ongoing series of individual purchases, with security procedures and the like, as a part of doing ongoing business.

4. The closing of a business purchase transaction via facsimile transmission of documents or even electronic mail. In such a transaction, all parties may participate through electronic conferencing technologies. At the appointed time all electronic records are executed electronically and transmitted to the other party. In such a case, the electronic records and electronic signatures are validated under this Act, obviating the need for "in person" closings.

A transaction must include interaction between two or more persons. Consequently, to the extent that the execution of a will, trust, or a health care power of attorney or similar health care designation does not involve another person and is a unilateral act, it would not be covered by this Act because not occurring as a part of a transaction as defined in this Act. However, this Act *does* apply to all electronic records and signatures *related* to a transaction, and so does cover, for example, internal auditing and accounting records related to a transaction.

§ 3. Scope.

(a) Except as otherwise provided in subsection (b), this [Act] applies to electronic records and electronic signatures relating to a transaction.

(b) This [Act] does not apply to a transaction to the extent it is governed by:

(1) a law governing the creation and execution of wills, codicils, or testamentary trusts;

(2) [The Uniform Commercial Code other than Sections 1–107 and 1–206, Article 2, and Article 2A];

(3) [the Uniform Computer Information Transactions Act]; and

(4) [other laws, if any, identified by State].

(c) This [Act] applies to an electronic record or electronic signature otherwise excluded from the application of this [Act] under subsection (b) to the extent it is governed by a law other than those specified in subsection (b).

(d) A transaction subject to this [Act] is also subject to other applicable substantive law.

See Legislative Note below, following Comment.

Comment

1. The scope of this Act is inherently limited by the fact that it only applies to transactions related to business, commercial (including consumer) and governmental matters. Consequently, transactions with no relation to business, commercial or governmental transactions would not be subject to this Act. Unilaterally generated electronic records and signatures which are not part of a transaction also are not covered by this Act. See Section 2, Comment 12.

2. This Act affects the medium in which information, records and signatures may be presented and retained under current legal requirements. While this Act covers all electronic records and signatures which are used in a business, commercial (including consumer) or governmental transaction, the operative provisions of the Act relate to requirements for writings and signatures under other laws. Accordingly, the exclusions in subsection (b) focus on those legal rules imposing certain writing and signature requirements which will ***not*** be affected by this Act.

3. The exclusions listed in subsection (b) provide clarity and certainty regarding the laws which are and are not affected by this Act. This section provides that transactions subject to specific laws are unaffected by this Act and leaves the balance subject to this Act.

4. Paragraph (1) excludes wills, codicils and testamentary trusts. This exclusion is largely salutary given the unilateral context in which such records are generally created and the unlikely use of such records in a transaction as defined in this Act (i.e., actions taken by two or more persons in the context of business, commercial or governmental affairs). Paragraph (2) excludes all of the Uniform Commercial Code other than UCC Sections 1–107 and 1–206, and Articles 2 and 2A. This Act does not apply to the excluded UCC articles, whether in "current" or "revised" form. The Act does apply to UCC Articles 2 and 2A and to UCC Sections 1–107 and 1–206.

5. Articles 3, 4 and 4A of the UCC impact payment systems and have specifically been removed from the coverage of this Act. The check collection and electronic fund transfer systems governed by Articles 3, 4 and 4A involve systems and relationships involving numerous parties beyond the parties to the underlying contract. The impact of validating electronic media in such systems involves considerations beyond the scope of this Act. Articles 5, 8 and 9 have been excluded because the revision process relating to those Articles included significant consideration of electronic practices. Paragraph 4 provides for exclusion from this Act of the Uniform Computer Information Transactions Act (UCITA) because the drafting process of that Act also included significant consideration of electronic contracting provisions.

6. The very limited application of this Act to Transferable Records in Section 16 does not affect payment systems, and the section is designed to apply to a transaction only through express agreement of the parties. The exclusion of Articles 3 and 4 will not affect the Act's coverage of Transferable Records. Section 16 is designed to allow for the development of systems which will provide "control" as defined in Section 16. Such control is necessary as a substitute for the idea of possession which undergirds negotiable instrument law. The technology has yet to be developed which will allow for the possession of a unique electronic token embodying the rights associated with a negotiable promissory note. Section 16's concept of control is intended as a substitute for possession.

The provisions in Section 16 operate as free standing rules, establishing the rights of parties using Transferable Records *under this Act*. The references in Section 16 to UCC Sections 3–302, 7–501, and 9–308 (R9–330(d)) are designed to incorporate the substance of those provisions into this Act for the limited purposes noted in Section 16(c). Accordingly, an electronic record which is also a Transferable Record, would not be used for purposes of a transaction governed by Articles 3, 4, or 9, but would be an electronic record used for purposes of a transaction governed by Section 16. However, it is important to remember that those UCC Articles will still apply to the transferable record in their own right. Accordingly any other substantive requirements, e.g., method and manner of perfection under Article 9, must be complied with under those other laws. See Comments to Section 16.

7. This Act does apply, *in toto*, to transactions under unrevised Articles 2 and 2A. There is every reason to validate electronic contracting in these situations. Sale and lease transactions do not implicate broad systems beyond the parties to the underlying transaction, such as are present in check collection and electronic funds transfers. Further sales and leases generally do not have as far reaching effect on the rights of third parties beyond the contracting parties, such as exists in the secured transactions system. Finally, it is in the area of sales, licenses and leases that electronic commerce is occurring to its greatest extent today. To exclude these transactions would largely gut the purpose of this Act.

In the event that Articles 2 and 2A are revised and adopted in the future, UETA will only apply to the extent provided in those Acts.

8. An electronic record/signature may be used for purposes of more than one legal requirement, or may be covered by more than one law. Consequently, it is important to make clear, despite any apparent redundancy, in subsection (c) that an electronic record used for purposes of a law which is ***not*** affected by this Act under subsection (b) may nonetheless be used and validated for purposes of other laws not excluded by subsection (b). For example, this Act does not apply to an electronic record of a check when used for purposes of a transaction governed by Article 4 of the Uniform Commercial Code, i.e., the Act does not validate so-called electronic checks. However, for purposes of check retention statutes, the same electronic record of the check is covered by this Act, so that retention of an electronic image/record of a check will satisfy such retention statutes, so long as the requirements of Section 12 are fulfilled.

In another context, subsection (c) would operate to allow this Act to apply to what would appear to be an excluded transaction under subsection (b). For example, Article 9 of the Uniform Commercial Code applies generally to any transaction that creates a security interest in personal property. However, Article 9 excludes landlord's liens. Accordingly, although this Act excludes from its application transactions subject to Article 9, this Act would apply to the creation of a landlord lien if the law otherwise applicable to landlord's liens did not provide otherwise, because the landlord's lien transaction is excluded from Article 9.

9. Additional exclusions under subparagraph (b)(4) should be limited to laws which govern electronic records and signatures which may be used in transactions as defined in Section 2(16). Records used unilaterally, or which do not relate to business, commercial (including consumer), or governmental affairs are not governed by this Act in any event, and exclusion of laws relating to such records may create unintended inferences about whether other records and signatures are covered by this Act.

It is also important that additional exclusions, if any, be incorporated under subsection (b)(4). As noted in Comment 8 above, an electronic record used in a transaction excluded under subsection (b), e.g., a check used to pay one's taxes, will nonetheless be validated for purposes of other, non-excluded laws under subsection (c), e.g., the check when used as proof of payment. It is critical that additional exclusions, if any, be incorporated into subsection (b) so that the salutary effect of subsection (c) apply to validate those records in other, non-excluded transactions. While a legislature may determine that a particular notice, such as a utility shutoff notice, be provided to a person in writing on paper, it is difficult to see why the utility should not be entitled to use electronic media for storage and evidentiary purposes.

Legislative Note Regarding Possible Additional Exclusions under Section 3(b)(4).

The following discussion is derived from the Report dated September 21, 1998 of The Task Force on State Law Exclusions (the "Task Force") presented to the Drafting Committee. After consideration of the Report, the Drafting Committee determined that exclusions other than those specified in the Act were not warranted. In addition, other inherent limitations on the applicability of the Act (the definition of transaction, the requirement that the parties acquiesce in the use of an electronic format) also militate against additional exclusions. Nonetheless, the Drafting Committee recognized that some legislatures may wish to exclude additional transactions from the Act, and determined that guidance in some major areas would be helpful to those legislatures considering additional areas for exclusion.

Because of the overwhelming number of references in state law to writings and signatures, the following list of possible transactions is not exhaustive. However, they do represent those areas most commonly raised during the course of the drafting process as areas that might be inappropriate for an electronic medium. It is important to keep in mind however, that the Drafting Committee determined that exclusion of these additional areas was not warranted.

1. **Trusts** (other than testamentary trusts). Trusts can be used for both business and personal purposes. By virtue of the definition of transaction, trusts used outside the area of business and commerce would not be governed by this Act. With respect to business or commercial trusts, the laws governing their formation contain few or no requirements for paper or signatures. Indeed, in most jurisdictions trusts of any kind may be created orally. Consequently, the Drafting Committee believed that the Act should apply to any transaction where the law leaves to the parties the decision of whether to use a writing. Thus, in the absence of legal requirements for writings, there is no sound reason to exclude laws governing trusts from the application of this Act.

2. **Powers of Attorney.** A power of attorney is simply a formalized type of agency agreement. In general, no formal requirements for paper or execution were found to be applicable to the validity of powers of attorney.

Special health powers of attorney have been established by statute in some States. These powers may have special requirements under state law regarding execution, acknowledgment and possibly notarization. In the normal case such powers will not arise in a transactional context and so would not be covered by this Act. However, even if such a record were to arise in a transactional context, this Act operates simply to remove the barrier to the use of an electronic medium, and preserves other requirements of applicable substantive law, avoiding any necessity to exclude such laws from the operation of this Act. Especially in light of the provisions of Sections 8 and 11, the substantive requirements under such laws will be preserved and may be satisfied in an electronic format.

3. **Real Estate Transactions.** It is important to distinguish between the efficacy of paper documents involving real estate between the parties, as opposed to their effect on third parties. As between the parties it is unnecessary to maintain existing barriers to electronic contracting. There are no unique characteristics to contracts relating to real property as opposed to other business and commercial (including consumer) contracts. Consequently, the decision whether to use an electronic medium for their agreements should be a matter for the parties to determine. Of course, to be effective against third parties state law generally requires filing with a governmental office. Pending adoption of electronic filing systems by States, the need for a piece of paper to file to perfect rights against third parties, will be a consideration for the parties. In the event notarization and acknowledgment are required under other laws, Section 11 provides a means for such actions to be accomplished electronically.

With respect to the requirements of government filing, those are left to the individual States in the decision of whether to adopt and implement electronic filing systems. (See optional Sections 17–19.) However, government recording systems currently require paper deeds including notarized, manual signatures. Although California and Illinois are experimenting with electronic filing systems, until such systems become widespread, the parties likely will choose to use, at the least, a paper deed for filing purposes. Nothing in this Act precludes the parties from selecting the medium best suited to the needs of the particular transaction. Parties may wish to consummate the transaction using electronic media in order to avoid expensive travel. Yet the actual deed may be in paper form to assure compliance with existing recording systems and requirements. The critical point is that nothing in this Act prevents the parties from selecting paper or electronic media for all or part of their transaction.

4. **Consumer Protection Statutes.** Consumer protection provisions in state law often require that information be disclosed or provided to a consumer in writing. Because this Act does apply to such transactions, the question of whether such laws should be specifically excluded was considered. Exclusion of consumer transactions would eliminate a huge group of commercial transactions which benefit consumers by enabling the efficiency of the electronic medium. Commerce over the internet is driven by consumer demands and concerns and must be included.

At the same time, it is important to recognize the protective effects of many consumer statutes. Consumer statutes often require that information be provided in writing, or may require that the consumer separately sign or initial a particular provision to evidence that the consumer's attention was brought to the provision. Subsection (1) requires electronic records to be retainable by a person whenever the law requires information to be delivered in writing. The section imposes a significant burden on the sender of information. The sender must assure that the information system of the recipient is compatible with, and capable of retaining the information sent by, the sender's system. Furthermore, nothing in this Act permits the avoidance of legal requirements of separate signatures or initialing. The Act simply permits the signature or initialing to be done electronically.

Other consumer protection statutes require (expressly or implicitly) that certain information be presented in a certain manner or format. Laws requiring information to be presented in particular fonts, formats or in similar fashion, as well as laws requiring conspicuous displays of information are preserved. Section 8(b)(3) specifically preserves the applicability of such requirements in an electronic environment. In the case of legal requirements that information be presented or appear conspicuous, the determination of what is conspicuous will be left to other law. Section 8 was included to specifically preserve the protective functions of such disclosure statutes, while at the same time allowing the use of electronic media if the substantive requirements of the other laws could be satisfied in the electronic medium.

Formatting and separate signing requirements serve a critical purpose in much consumer protection legislation, to assure that information is not slipped past the unsuspecting consumer. Not only does this Act not disturb those requirements, it preserves those requirements. In addition, other bodies of substantive law continue to operate to allow the courts to police any such bad conduct or overreaching, e.g., unconscionability, fraud, duress, mistake and the like. These bodies of law remain applicable regardless of the medium in which a record appears.

The requirement that both parties agree to conduct a transaction electronically also prevents the imposition of an electronic medium on unwilling parties See Section 5(b). In addition, where the law requires inclusion of specific terms or language, those requirements are preserved broadly by Section 5(e).

Requirements that information be sent to, or received by, someone have been preserved in Section 15. As in the paper world, obligations to send do not impose any duties on the sender to assure receipt, other than reasonable methods of dispatch. In those cases where receipt is required legally, Sections 5, 8, and 15 impose the burden on the sender to assure delivery to the recipient if satisfaction of the legal requirement is to be fulfilled.

The preservation of existing safeguards, together with the ability to opt out of the electronic medium entirely, demonstrate the lack of any need generally to exclude consumer protection laws from the operation of this Act. Legislatures may wish to focus any review on those statutes which provide for post-contract formation and post-breach notices to be in paper. However, any such consideration must also balance the needed protections against the potential burdens which may be imposed. Consumers and others will not be well served by restrictions which preclude the employment of electronic technologies sought and desired by consumers.

§ 4. Prospective Application.

This [Act] applies to any electronic record or electronic signature created, generated, sent, communicated, received, or stored on or after the effective date of this [Act].

Comment

This section makes clear that the Act only applies to validate electronic records and signatures which arise subsequent to the effective date of the Act. Whether electronic records and electronic signatures arising before the effective date of this Act are valid is left to other law.

§ 5. Use of Electronic Records and Electronic Signatures; Variation by Agreement.

(a) This [Act] does not require a record or signature to be created, generated, sent, communicated, received, stored, or otherwise processed or used by electronic means or in electronic form.

(b) This [Act] applies only to transactions between parties each of which has agreed to conduct transactions by electronic means. Whether the parties agree to conduct a transaction by electronic means is determined from the context and surrounding circumstances, including the parties' conduct.

(c) A party that agrees to conduct a transaction by electronic means may refuse to conduct other transactions by electronic means. The right granted by this subsection may not be waived by agreement.

(d) Except as otherwise provided in this [Act], the effect of any of its provisions may be varied by agreement. The presence in certain provisions of this [Act] of the words "unless otherwise agreed", or words of similar import, does not imply that the effect of other provisions may not be varied by agreement.

(e) Whether an electronic record or electronic signature has legal consequences is determined by this [Act] and other applicable law.

Comment

This section limits the applicability of this Act to transactions which parties have agreed to conduct electronically. Broad interpretation of the term agreement is necessary to assure that this Act has the widest possible application consistent with its purpose of removing barriers to electronic commerce.

1. This section makes clear that this Act is intended to facilitate the use of electronic means, but does not require the use of electronic records and signatures. This fundamental principle is set forth in subsection (a) and elaborated by subsections (b) and (c), which require an intention to conduct transactions electronically and preserve the right of a party to refuse to use electronics in any subsequent transaction.

2. The paradigm of this Act is two willing parties doing transactions electronically. It is therefore appropriate that the Act is voluntary and preserves the greatest possible party autonomy to refuse electronic transactions. The requirement that party agreement be found from all the surrounding circumstances is a limitation on the scope of this Act.

3. If this Act is to serve to facilitate electronic transactions, it must be applicable under circumstances not rising to a full fledged contract to use electronics. While absolute certainty can be accomplished by obtaining an explicit contract before relying on electronic transactions, such an explicit contract should not be necessary before one may feel safe in conducting transactions electronically. Indeed, such a requirement would itself be an unreasonable barrier to electronic commerce, at odds with the fundamental purpose of this Act. Accordingly, the requisite agreement, express or implied, must be determined from all available circumstances and evidence.

4. Subsection (b) provides that the Act applies to transactions in which the parties have agreed to conduct the transaction electronically. In this context it is essential that the parties' actions and words be broadly

construed in determining whether the requisite agreement exists. Accordingly, the Act expressly provides that the party's agreement is to be found from all circumstances, including the parties' conduct. The critical element is the intent of a party to conduct a transaction electronically. Once that intent is established, this Act applies. See Restatement 2d Contracts, Sections 2, 3, and 19.

Examples of circumstances from which it may be found that parties have reached an agreement to conduct transactions electronically include the following:

A. Automaker and supplier enter into a Trading Partner Agreement setting forth the terms, conditions and methods for the conduct of business between them electronically.

B. Joe gives out his business card with his business e-mail address. It may be reasonable, under the circumstances, for a recipient of the card to infer that Joe has agreed to communicate electronically for business purposes. However, in the absence of additional facts, it would not necessarily be reasonable to infer Joe's agreement to communicate electronically for purposes outside the scope of the business indicated by use of the business card.

C. Sally may have several e-mail addresses—home, main office, office of a non-profit organization on whose board Sally sits. In each case, it may be reasonable to infer that Sally is willing to communicate electronically with respect to business related to the business/purpose associated with the respective e-mail addresses. However, depending on the circumstances, it may not be reasonable to communicate with Sally for purposes other than those related to the purpose for which she maintained a particular e-mail account.

D. Among the circumstances to be considered in finding an agreement would be the time when the assent occurred relative to the timing of the use of electronic communications. If one orders books from an on-line vendor, such as Bookseller.com, the intention to conduct that transaction and to receive any correspondence related to the transaction electronically can be inferred from the conduct. Accordingly, as to information related to that transaction it is reasonable for Bookseller to deal with the individual electronically.

The examples noted above are intended to focus the inquiry on the party's agreement to conduct a transaction electronically. Similarly, if two people are at a meeting and one tells the other to send an e-mail to confirm a transaction—the requisite agreement under subsection (b) would exist. In each case, the use of a business card, statement at a meeting, or other evidence of willingness to conduct a transaction electronically must be viewed in light of all the surrounding circumstances with a view toward broad validation of electronic transactions.

5. Just as circumstances may indicate the existence of agreement, express or implied from surrounding circumstances, circumstances may also demonstrate the absence of true agreement. For example:

A. If Automaker, Inc. were to issue a recall of automobiles via its Internet website, it would not be able to rely on this Act to validate that notice in the case of a person who never logged on to the website, or indeed, had no ability to do so, notwithstanding a clause in a paper purchase contract by which the buyer agreed to receive such notices in such a manner.

B. Buyer executes a standard form contract in which an agreement to receive all notices electronically in set forth on page 3 in the midst of other fine print. Buyer has never communicated with Seller electronically, and has not provided any other information in the contract to suggest a willingness to deal electronically. Not only is it unlikely that any but the most formalistic of agreements may be found, but nothing in this Act prevents courts from policing such form contracts under common law doctrines relating to contract formation, unconscionability and the like.

6. Subsection (c) has been added to make clear the ability of a party to refuse to conduct a transaction electronically, even if the person has conducted transactions electronically in the past. The effectiveness of a party's refusal to conduct a transaction electronically will be determined under other applicable law in light of all surrounding circumstances. Such circumstances must include an assessment of the transaction involved.

A party's right to decline to act electronically under a specific contract, on the ground that each action under that contract amounts to a separate "transaction," must be considered in light of the purpose of the contract and the action to be taken electronically. For example, under a contract for the purchase of goods, the giving and receipt of notices electronically, as provided in the contract, should not be viewed as discreet transactions. Rather such notices amount to separate actions which are part of the "transaction" of purchase evidenced by the contract. Allowing one party to require a change of medium in the middle of the transaction evidenced by that contract is not the purpose of this subsection. Rather this subsection is intended to preserve the party's right to conduct the next purchase in a non-electronic medium.

7. Subsection (e) is an essential provision in the overall scheme of this Act. While this Act validates and effectuates electronic records and electronic signatures, the legal effect of such records and signatures is left to existing substantive law outside this Act except in very narrow circumstances. See, e.g., Section 16. Even when this Act operates to validate records and signatures in an electronic medium, it expressly preserves the substantive rules of other law applicable to such records. See, e.g., Section 11.

For example, beyond validation of records, signatures and contracts based on the medium used, Section 7 (a) and (b) should not be interpreted as establishing the legal effectiveness of any given record, signature or contract. Where a rule of law requires that the record contain minimum substantive content, the legal effect of such a record will depend on whether the record meets the substantive requirements of other applicable law.

Section 8 expressly preserves a number of legal requirements in currently existing law relating to the presentation of information in writing. Although this Act now would allow such information to be presented in an electronic record, Section 8 provides that the other substantive requirements of law must be satisfied in the electronic medium as well.

§ 6. Construction and Application.

This [Act] must be construed and applied:

(1) to facilitate electronic transactions consistent with other applicable law;

(2) to be consistent with reasonable practices concerning electronic transactions and with the continued expansion of those practices; and

(3) to effectuate its general purpose to make uniform the law with respect to the subject of this [Act] among States enacting it.

Comment

1. The purposes and policies of this Act are

(a) to facilitate and promote commerce and governmental transactions by validating and authorizing the use of electronic records and electronic signatures;

(b) to eliminate barriers to electronic commerce and governmental transactions resulting from uncertainties relating to writing and signature requirements;

(c) to simplify, clarify and modernize the law governing commerce and governmental transactions through the use of electronic means;

(d) to permit the continued expansion of commercial and governmental electronic practices through custom, usage and agreement of the parties;

(e) to promote uniformity of the law among the States (and worldwide) relating to the use of electronic and similar technological means of effecting and performing commercial and governmental transactions;

(f) to promote public confidence in the validity, integrity and reliability of electronic commerce and governmental transactions; and

(g) to promote the development of the legal and business infrastructure necessary to implement electronic commerce and governmental transactions.

2. This Act has been drafted to permit flexible application consistent with its purpose to validate electronic transactions. The provisions of this Act validating and effectuating the employ of electronic media allow the courts to apply them to new and unforeseen technologies and practices. As time progresses, it is anticipated that what is new and unforeseen today will be commonplace tomorrow. Accordingly, this legislation is intended to set a framework for the validation of media which may be developed in the future and which demonstrate the same qualities as the electronic media contemplated and validated under this Act.

§ 7. Legal Recognition of Electronic Records, Electronic Signatures, and Electronic Contracts.

(a) A record or signature may not be denied legal effect or enforceability solely because it is in electronic form.

(b) A contract may not be denied legal effect or enforceability solely because an electronic record was used in its formation.

(c) If a law requires a record to be in writing, an electronic record satisfies the law.

(d) If a law requires a signature, an electronic signature satisfies the law.

Source: UNCITRAL Model Law on Electronic Commerce, Articles 5, 6, and 7.

Comment

1. This section sets forth the fundamental premise of this Act: namely, that the medium in which a record, signature, or contract is created, presented or retained does not affect it's legal significance. Subsections (a) and (b) are designed to eliminate the single element of medium as a reason to deny effect or enforceability to a record, signature, or contract. The fact that the information is set forth in an electronic, as opposed to paper, record is irrelevant.

2. Under Restatement 2d Contracts Section 8, a contract may have legal effect and yet be unenforceable. Indeed, one circumstance where a record or contract may have effect but be unenforceable is in the context of the Statute of Frauds. Though a contract may be unenforceable, the records may have collateral effects, as in the case of a buyer that insures goods purchased under a contract unenforceable under the Statute of Frauds. The insurance company may not deny a claim on the ground that the buyer is not the owner, though the buyer may have no direct remedy against seller for failure to deliver. See Restatement 2d Contracts, Section 8, Illustration 4.

While this section would validate an electronic record for purposes of a statute of frauds, if an agreement to conduct the transaction electronically cannot reasonably be found (See Section 5(b)) then a necessary predicate to the applicability of this Act would be absent and this Act would not validate the electronic record. Whether the electronic record might be valid under other law is not addressed by this Act.

3. Subsections (c) and (d) provide the positive assertion that electronic records and signatures satisfy legal requirements for writings and signatures. The provisions are limited to requirements in laws that a record be in writing or be signed. This section does not address requirements imposed by other law in addition to requirements for writings and signatures See, e.g., Section 8.

Subsections (c) and (d) are particularized applications of subsection (a). The purpose is to validate and effectuate electronic records and signatures as the equivalent of writings, subject to all of the rules applicable to the efficacy of a writing, except as such other rules are modified by the more specific provisions of this Act.

> **Illustration 1:** A sends the following e-mail to B: "I hereby offer to buy widgets from you, delivery next Tuesday. /s/ A." B responds with the following e-mail: "I accept your offer to buy widgets for delivery next Tuesday. /s/ B." The e-mails may not be denied effect solely because they are electronic. In addition, the e-mails do qualify as records under the Statute of Frauds. However, because there is no quantity stated in either record, the parties' agreement would be unenforceable under existing UCC Section 2–201(1).

> **Illustration 2:** A sends the following e-mail to B: "I hereby offer to buy 100 widgets for $1000, delivery next Tuesday. /s/ A." B responds with the following e-mail: "I accept your offer to purchase 100 widgets for $1000, delivery next Tuesday. /s/ B." In this case the analysis is the same as in Illustration 1 except that here the records otherwise satisfy the requirements of UCC Section 2–201(1). The transaction may not be denied legal effect solely because there is not a pen and ink "writing" or "signature".

4. Section 8 addresses additional requirements imposed by other law which may affect the legal effect or enforceability of an electronic record in a particular case. For example, in Section 8(a) the legal requirement addressed is *the provision of information* in writing. The section then sets forth the standards to be applied in determining whether the provision of information by an electronic record is the equivalent of the provision of information in writing. The requirements in Section 8 are in addition to the bare validation that occurs under this section.

5. Under the substantive law applicable to a particular transaction within this Act, the legal effect of an electronic record may be separate from the issue of whether the record contains a signature. For example, where notice must be given as part of a contractual obligation, the effectiveness of the notice will turn on whether the party provided the notice regardless of whether the notice was signed (See Section 15). An electronic record attributed to a party under Section 9 and complying with the requirements of Section 15 would suffice in that case, notwithstanding that it may not contain an electronic signature.

§ 8. Provision of Information in Writing; Presentation of Records.

(a) If parties have agreed to conduct a transaction by electronic means and a law requires a person to provide, send, or deliver information in writing to another person, the requirement is satisfied if the information is provided, sent, or delivered, as the case may be, in an electronic record capable of retention by the recipient at the time of receipt. An electronic record is not capable of retention by the recipient if the sender or its information processing system inhibits the ability of the recipient to print or store the electronic record.

(b) If a law other than this [Act] requires a record (i) to be posted or displayed in a certain manner, (ii) to be sent, communicated, or transmitted by a specified method, or (iii) to contain information that is formatted in a certain manner, the following rules apply:

(1) The record must be posted or displayed in the manner specified in the other law.

(2) Except as otherwise provided in subsection (d)(2), the record must be sent, communicated, or transmitted by the method specified in the other law.

(3) The record must contain the information formatted in the manner specified in the other law.

(c) If a sender inhibits the ability of a recipient to store or print an electronic record, the electronic record is not enforceable against the recipient.

(d) The requirements of this section may not be varied by agreement, but:

(1) to the extent a law other than this [Act] requires information to be provided, sent, or delivered in writing but permits that requirement to be varied by agreement, the requirement under subsection (a) that the information be in the form of an electronic record capable of retention may also be varied by agreement; and

(2) a requirement under a law other than this [Act] to send, communicate, or transmit a record by [first-class mail, postage prepaid] [regular United States mail], may be varied by agreement to the extent permitted by the other law.

Source: Canadian-Uniform Electronic Commerce Act

Comment

1. This section is a savings provision, designed to assure, consistent with the fundamental purpose of this Act, that otherwise applicable substantive law will not be overridden by this Act. The section makes clear that while the pen and ink provisions of such other law may be satisfied electronically, nothing in this Act vitiates the other requirements of such laws. The section addresses a number of issues related to disclosures and notice provisions in other laws.

2. This section is independent of the prior section. Section 7 refers to legal requirements for a writing. This section refers to legal requirements for the provision of information in writing or relating to the method or manner of presentation or delivery of information. The section addresses more specific legal requirements of other laws, provides standards for satisfying the more particular legal requirements, and defers to other law for satisfaction of requirements under those laws.

3. Under subsection (a), to meet a requirement of other law that information be provided in writing, the recipient of an electronic record of the information must be able to get to the electronic record and read it, and must have the ability to get back to the information in some way at a later date. Accordingly, the section requires that the electronic record be capable of retention for later review.

The section specifically provides that any inhibition on retention imposed by the sender or the sender's system will preclude satisfaction of this section. Use of technological means now existing or later developed which prevents the recipient from retaining a copy the information would result in a determination that information has not been provided under subsection (a). The policies underlying laws requiring the provision of information in writing warrant the imposition of an additional burden on the sender to make the information available in a manner which will permit subsequent reference. A difficulty does exist for senders of information because of the disparate systems of their recipients and the capabilities of those systems. However, in order to satisfy the *legal requirement* of other law to make information available, the sender must assure that the recipient receives and can retain the information. However, it is left for the courts to determine whether the sender has complied with this subsection if evidence demonstrates that it is something peculiar the recipient's system which precludes subsequent reference to the information.

4. Subsection (b) is a savings provision for laws which provide for the means of delivering or displaying information and which are not affected by the Act. For example, if a law requires delivery of notice by first class US mail, that means of delivery would not be affected by this Act. The information to be delivered may be provided on a disc, i.e., in electronic form, but the particular means of delivery must still be via the US postal service. Display, delivery and formatting requirements will continue to be applicable to electronic records and signatures. If those legal requirements can be satisfied in an electronic medium, e.g., the information can be presented in the equivalent of 20 point bold type as required by other law, this Act will validate the use of the medium, leaving to the other applicable law the question of whether the particular electronic record meets the other legal requirements. If a law requires that particular records be delivered together, or attached to other records, this Act does not preclude the delivery of the records together in an electronic communication, so long as the records are connected or associated with each other in a way determined to satisfy the other law.

5. Subsection (c) provides incentives for senders of information to use systems which will not inhibit the other party from retaining the information. However, there are circumstances where a party providing certain information may wish to inhibit retention in order to protect intellectual property rights or prevent the other party from retaining confidential information about the sender. In such cases inhibition is understandable, but if the sender wishes to enforce the record in which the information is contained, the sender may not inhibit its retention by the recipient. Unlike subsection (a), subsection (c) applies in all transactions and simply provides for unenforceability against the recipient. Subsection (a) applies only where another law imposes the writing requirement, and subsection (a) imposes a broader responsibility on the sender to assure retention capability by the recipient.

6. The protective purposes of this section justify the non-waivability provided by subsection (d). However, since the requirements for sending and formatting and the like are imposed by other law, to the extent other law permits waiver of such protections, there is no justification for imposing a more severe burden in an electronic environment.

§ 9. Attribution and Effect of Electronic Record and Electronic Signature.

(a) An electronic record or electronic signature is attributable to a person if it was the act of the person. The act of the person may be shown in any manner, including a showing of the efficacy of any security procedure applied to determine the person to which the electronic record or electronic signature was attributable.

(b) The effect of an electronic record or electronic signature attributed to a person under subsection (a) is determined from the context and surrounding circumstances at the time of its creation, execution, or adoption, including the parties' agreement, if any, and otherwise as provided by law.

Comment

1. Under subsection (a), so long as the electronic record or electronic signature resulted from a person's action it will be attributed to that person—the legal effect of that attribution is addressed in subsection (b). This section does not alter existing rules of law regarding attribution. The section assures that such rules will be applied in the electronic environment. A person's actions include actions taken by human agents of the person, as well as actions taken by an electronic agent, i.e., the tool, of the person. Although the rule may appear to state the obvious, it assures that the record or signature is not ascribed to a machine, as opposed to the person operating or programing the machine.

In each of the following cases, both the electronic record and electronic signature would be attributable to a person under subsection (a):

A. The person types his/her name as part of an e-mail purchase order;

B. The person's employee, pursuant to authority, types the person's name as part of an e-mail purchase order;

C. The person's computer, programmed to order goods upon receipt of inventory information within particular parameters, issues a purchase order which includes the person's name, or other identifying information, as part of the order.

In each of the above cases, law other than this Act would ascribe both the signature and the action to the person if done in a paper medium. Subsection (a) expressly provides that the same result will occur when an electronic medium is used.

2. Nothing in this section affects the use of a signature as a device for attributing a record to a person. Indeed, a signature is often the primary method for attributing a record to a person. In the foregoing examples, once the electronic signature is attributed to the person, the electronic record would also be attributed to the person, unless the person established fraud, forgery, or other invalidating cause. However, a signature is not the only method for attribution.

3. The use of facsimile transmissions provides a number of examples of attribution using information other than a signature. A facsimile may be attributed to a person because of the information printed across the top of the page that indicates the machine from which it was sent. Similarly, the transmission may contain a letterhead which identifies the sender. Some cases have held that the letterhead actually constituted a signature because it was a symbol adopted by the sender with intent to authenticate the facsimile. However, the signature determination resulted from the necessary finding of intention in that case. Other cases have found facsimile letterheads NOT to be signatures because the requisite intention was not present. The critical point is that with or without a signature, information within the electronic record may well suffice to provide the facts resulting in attribution of an electronic record to a particular party.

In the context of attribution of records, normally the content of the record will provide the necessary information for a finding of attribution. It is also possible that an established course of dealing between parties may result in a finding of attribution Just as with a paper record, evidence of forgery or counterfeiting may be introduced to rebut the evidence of attribution.

4. Certain information may be present in an electronic environment that does not appear to attribute but which clearly links a person to a particular record. Numerical codes, personal identification numbers, public and private key combinations all serve to establish the party to whom an electronic record should be attributed. Of course security procedures will be another piece of evidence available to establish attribution.

The inclusion of a specific reference to security procedures as a means of proving attribution is salutary because of the unique importance of security procedures in the electronic environment. In certain processes, a technical and technological security procedure may be the best way to convince a trier of fact that a particular electronic record or signature was that of a particular person. In certain circumstances, the use of a security procedure to establish that the record and related signature came from the person's business might be necessary to overcome a claim that a hacker intervened. The reference to security procedures is not intended to suggest that other forms of proof of attribution should be accorded less persuasive effect. It is also important to recall that the particular strength of a given procedure does not affect the procedure's status as a security procedure, but only affects the weight to be accorded the evidence of the security procedure as tending to establish attribution.

5. This section does apply in determining the effect of a "click-through" transaction. A "click-through" transaction involves a process which, if executed with an intent to "sign," will be an electronic signature. See definition of Electronic Signature. In the context of an anonymous "click-through," issues of proof will be paramount. This section will be relevant to establish that the resulting electronic record is attributable to a particular person upon the requisite proof, including security procedures which may track the source of the click-through.

6. Once it is established that a record or signature is attributable to a particular party, the effect of a record or signature must be determined in light of the context and surrounding circumstances, including the parties' agreement, if any. Also informing the effect of any attribution will be other legal requirements considered in light of the context. Subsection (b) addresses the effect of the record or signature once attributed to a person.

§ 10. Effect of Change or Error.

If a change or error in an electronic record occurs in a transmission between parties to a transaction, the following rules apply:

(1) If the parties have agreed to use a security procedure to detect changes or errors and one party has conformed to the procedure, but the other party has not, and the nonconforming party would have detected the change or error had that party also conformed, the conforming party may avoid the effect of the changed or erroneous electronic record.

(2) In an automated transaction involving an individual, the individual may avoid the effect of an electronic record that resulted from an error made by the individual in dealing with the electronic agent of another person if the electronic agent did not provide an opportunity for the prevention or correction of the error and, at the time the individual learns of the error, the individual:

(A) promptly notifies the other person of the error and that the individual did not intend to be bound by the electronic record received by the other person;

(B) takes reasonable steps, including steps that conform to the other person's reasonable instructions, to return to the other person or, if instructed by the other person, to destroy the consideration received, if any, as a result of the erroneous electronic record; and

(C) has not used or received any benefit or value from the consideration, if any, received from the other person.

(3) If neither paragraph (1) nor paragraph (2) applies, the change or error has the effect provided by other law, including the law of mistake, and the parties' contract, if any.

(4) Paragraphs (2) and (3) may not be varied by agreement.

Source: Restatement 2d Contracts, Sections 152–155.

Comment

1. This section is limited to changes and errors occurring in transmissions between parties—whether person-person (paragraph 1) or in an automated transaction involving an individual and a machine (paragraphs 1 and 2). The section focuses on the effect of changes and errors occurring when records are exchanged between parties. In cases where changes and errors occur in contexts other than transmission, the law of mistake is expressly made applicable to resolve the conflict.

The section covers both changes and errors. For example, if Buyer sends a message to Seller ordering 100 widgets, but Buyer's information processing system changes the order to 1000 widgets, a "change" has occurred between what Buyer transmitted and what Seller received. If on the other hand, Buyer typed in 1000 intending to order only 100, but sent the message before noting the mistake, an error would have occurred which would also be covered by this section.

2. Paragraph (1) deals with any transmission where the parties have agreed to use a security procedure to detect changes and errors. It operates against the non-conforming party, i.e., the party in the best position to have avoided the change or error, regardless of whether that person is the sender or recipient. The source of the error/change is not indicated, and so both human and machine errors/changes would be covered. With respect to errors or changes that would not be detected by the security procedure even if applied, the parties are left to the general law of mistake to resolve the dispute.

3. Paragraph (1) applies only in the situation where a security procedure would detect the error/change but one party fails to use the procedure and does not detect the error/change. In such a case, consistent with the law of mistake generally, the record is made avoidable at the instance of the party who took all available steps to avoid the mistake. See Restatement 2d Contracts Sections 152–154.

Making the erroneous record avoidable by the conforming party is consistent with Sections 153 and 154 of the Restatement 2d Contracts because the non-conforming party was in the best position to avoid the problem, and would bear the risk of mistake. Such a case would constitute mistake by one party. The mistaken party (the conforming party) would be entitled to avoid any resulting contract under Section 153 because s/he does not have the risk of mistake and the non-conforming party had reason to know of the mistake.

4. As with paragraph (1), paragraph (2), when applicable, allows the mistaken party to avoid the effect of the erroneous electronic record. However, the subsection is limited to human error on the part of an individual when dealing with the electronic agent of the other party. In a transaction between individuals there is a greater ability to correct the error before parties have acted on it. However, when an individual makes an error while dealing with the electronic agent of the other party, it may not be possible to correct the error before the other party has shipped or taken other action in reliance on the erroneous record.

Paragraph (2) applies only to errors made by individuals. If the error results from the electronic agent, it would constitute a system error. In such a case the effect of that error would be resolved under paragraph (1) if applicable, otherwise under paragraph (3) and the general law of mistake.

5. The party acting through the electronic agent/machine is given incentives by this section to build in safeguards which enable the individual to prevent the sending of an erroneous record, or correct the error once sent. For example, the electronic agent may be programmed to provide a "confirmation screen" to the individual setting forth all the information the individual initially approved. This would provide the individual with the ability to prevent the erroneous record from ever being sent. Similarly, the electronic agent might receive the record sent by the individual and then send back a confirmation which the individual must again accept before the transaction is completed. This would allow for correction of an erroneous record. In either case, the electronic agent would "provide an opportunity for prevention or correction of the error," *and the subsection would not apply*. Rather, the affect of any error is governed by other law.

6. Paragraph (2) also places additional requirements on the mistaken individual before the paragraph may be invoked to avoid an erroneous electronic record. The individual must take prompt action to advise the other party of the error and the fact that the individual did not intend the electronic record. Whether the action is prompt must be determined from all the circumstances including the individual's ability to contact the other party. The individual should advise the other party both of the error and of the lack of intention to be bound (i.e., avoidance) by the electronic record received. Since this provision allows avoidance by the mistaken party, that party should also be required to expressly note that it is seeking to avoid the electronic record, i.e., lacked the intention to be bound.

Second, restitution is normally required in order to undo a mistaken transaction. Accordingly, the individual must also return or destroy any consideration received, adhering to instructions from the other party in any case. This is to assure that the other party retains control over the consideration sent in error.

Finally, and most importantly in regard to transactions involving intermediaries which may be harmed because transactions cannot be unwound, the individual cannot have received any benefit from the transaction. This section prevents a party from unwinding a transaction after the delivery of value and consideration which cannot be returned or destroyed. For example, if the consideration received is information, it may not be possible to avoid the benefit conferred. While the information itself could be returned, mere access to the information, or the ability to redistribute the information would constitute a benefit precluding the mistaken party from unwinding the transaction. It may also occur that the mistaken party receives consideration which changes in value between the time of receipt and the first opportunity to return. In such a case restitution cannot be made adequately, and the transaction would not be avoidable. In each of the foregoing cases, under subparagraph (2)(c), the individual would have received the benefit of the consideration and would NOT be able to avoid the erroneous electronic record under this section.

7. In all cases not covered by paragraphs (1) or (2), where error or change to a record occur, the parties contract, or other law, specifically including the law of mistake, applies to resolve any dispute. In the event that the parties' contract and other law would achieve different results, the construction of the parties' contract is left to the other law. If the error occurs in the context of record retention, Section 12 will apply. In that case the standard is one of accuracy and retrievability of the information.

8. Paragraph (4) makes the error correction provision in paragraph (2) and the application of the law of mistake in paragraph (3) non-variable. Paragraph (2) provides incentives for parties using electronic agents to establish safeguards for individuals dealing with them. It also avoids unjustified windfalls to the individual by erecting stringent requirements before the individual may exercise the right of avoidance under the paragraph. Therefore, there is no reason to permit parties to avoid the paragraph by agreement. Rather, parties should satisfy the paragraph's requirements.

§ 11. Notarization and Acknowledgment.

If a law requires a signature or record to be notarized, acknowledged, verified, or made under oath, the requirement is satisfied if the electronic signature of the person authorized to perform those acts, together with all other information required to be included by other applicable law, is attached to or logically associated with the signature or record.

Comment

This section permits a notary public and other authorized officers to act electronically, effectively removing the stamp/seal requirements. However, the section does not eliminate any of the other requirements of notarial laws, and consistent with the entire thrust of this Act, simply allows the signing and information to be accomplished in an electronic medium.

For example, Buyer wishes to send a notarized Real Estate Purchase Agreement to Seller via e-mail. The notary must appear in the room with the Buyer, satisfy him/herself as to the identity of the Buyer, and swear to that identification. All that activity must be reflected as part of the electronic Purchase Agreement and the notary's electronic signature must appear as a part of the electronic real estate purchase contract.

As another example, Buyer seeks to send Seller an affidavit averring defects in the products received. A court clerk, authorized under state law to administer oaths, is present with Buyer in a room. The Clerk administers the oath and includes the statement of the oath, together with any other requisite information, in the electronic record to be sent to the Seller. Upon administering the oath and witnessing the application of Buyer's electronic signature to the electronic record, the Clerk also applies his electronic signature to the electronic record. So long as all substantive requirements of other applicable law have been fulfilled and are reflected in the electronic record, the sworn electronic record of Buyer is as effective as if it had been transcribed on paper.

§ 12. Retention of Electronic Records; Originals.

(a) If a law requires that a record be retained, the requirement is satisfied by retaining an electronic record of the information in the record which:

(1) accurately reflects the information set forth in the record after it was first generated in its final form as an electronic record or otherwise; and

(2) remains accessible for later reference.

(b) A requirement to retain a record in accordance with subsection (a) does not apply to any information the sole purpose of which is to enable the record to be sent, communicated, or received.

(c) A person may satisfy subsection (a) by using the services of another person if the requirements of that subsection are satisfied.

(d) If a law requires a record to be presented or retained in its original form, or provides consequences if the record is not presented or retained in its original form, that law is satisfied by an electronic record retained in accordance with subsection (a).

(e) If a law requires retention of a check, that requirement is satisfied by retention of an electronic record of the information on the front and back of the check in accordance with subsection (a).

(f) A record retained as an electronic record in accordance with subsection (a) satisfies a law requiring a person to retain a record for evidentiary, audit, or like purposes, unless a law enacted after the effective date of this [Act] specifically prohibits the use of an electronic record for the specified purpose.

(g) This section does not preclude a governmental agency of this State from specifying additional requirements for the retention of a record subject to the agency's jurisdiction.

Source: UNCITRAL Model Law On Electronic Commerce Articles 8 and 10.

Comment

1. This section deals with the serviceability of electronic records as retained records and originals. So long as there exists reliable assurance that the electronic record accurately reproduces the information, this section continues the theme of establishing the functional equivalence of electronic and paper-based records. This is consistent with Fed.R.Evid. 1001(3) and Unif.R.Evid. 1001(3) (1974). This section assures that information stored electronically will remain effective for all audit, evidentiary, archival and similar purposes.

2. In an electronic medium, the concept of an original document is problematic. For example, as one drafts a document on a computer the "original" is either on a disc or the hard drive to which the document has been initially saved. If one periodically saves the draft, the fact is that at times a document may be first saved to disc then to hard drive, and at others vice versa. In such a case the "original" may change from the information on the disc to the information on the hard drive. Indeed, it may be argued that the "original" exists solely in RAM and, in a sense, the original is destroyed when a "copy" is saved to a disc or to the hard drive. In any event, in the context of record retention, the concern focuses on the integrity of the information, and not with its "originality."

3. Subsection (a) requires accuracy and the ability to access at a later time. The requirement of accuracy is derived from the Uniform and Federal Rules of Evidence. The requirement of continuing accessibility addresses the issue of technology obsolescence and the need to update and migrate information to developing systems. It is not unlikely that within the span of 5–10 years (a period during which retention of much information is required)

a corporation may evolve through one or more generations of technology. More to the point, this technology may be incompatible with each other necessitating the reconversion of information from one system to the other.

For example, certain operating systems from the early 1980's, e.g., memory typewriters, became obsolete with the development of personal computers. The information originally stored on the memory typewriter would need to be converted to the personal computer system in a way meeting the standards for accuracy contemplated by this section. It is also possible that the medium on which the information is stored is less stable. For example, information stored on floppy discs is generally less stable, and subject to a greater threat of disintegration, that information stored on a computer hard drive. In either case, the continuing accessibility issue must be satisfied to validate information stored by electronic means under this section.

This section permits parties to convert original written records to electronic records for retention so long as the requirements of subsection (a) are satisfied. Accordingly, in the absence of specific requirements to retain written records, written records may be destroyed once saved as electronic records satisfying the requirements of this section.

The subsection refers to the information contained in an electronic record, rather than relying on the term electronic record, as a matter of clarity that the critical aspect in retention is the information itself. What information must be retained is determined by the purpose for which the information is needed. If the addressing and pathway information regarding an e-mail is relevant, then that information should also be retained. However if it is the substance of the e-mail that is relevant, only that information need be retained. Of course, wise record retention would include all such information since what information will be relevant at a later time will not be known.

4. Subsections (b) and (c) simply make clear that certain ancillary information or the use of third parties, does not affect the serviceability of records and information retained electronically. Again, the relevance of particular information will not be known until that information is required at a subsequent time.

5. Subsection (d) continues the theme of the Act as validating electronic records as originals where the law requires retention of an original. The validation of electronic records and electronic information as originals is consistent with the Uniform Rules of Evidence. See Uniform Rules of Evidence 1001(3), 1002, 1003 and 1004.

6. Subsection (e) specifically addresses particular concerns regarding check retention statutes in many jurisdictions. A Report compiled by the Federal Reserve Bank of Boston identifies hundreds of state laws which require the retention or production of original canceled checks. Such requirements preclude banks and their customers from realizing the benefits and efficiencies related to truncation processes otherwise validated under current law. The benefits to banks and their customers from electronic check retention are effectuated by this provision.

7. Subsections (f) and (g) generally address other record retention statutes. As with check retention, all businesses and individuals may realize significant savings from electronic record retention. So long as the standards in Section 12 are satisfied, this section permits all parties to obtain those benefits. As always the government may require records in any medium, however, these subsections require a governmental agency to specifically identify the types of records and requirements that will be imposed.

§ 13. Admissibility in Evidence.

In a proceeding, evidence of a record or signature may not be excluded solely because it is in electronic form.

Source: UNCITRAL Model Law on Electronic Commerce Article 9.

Comment

Like Section 7, this section prevents the nonrecognition of electronic records and signatures solely on the ground of the media in which information is presented.

Nothing in this section relieves a party from establishing the necessary foundation for the admission of an electronic record. See Uniform Rules of Evidence 1001(3), 1002,1003 and 1004.

§ 14. Automated Transaction.

In an automated transaction, the following rules apply:

(1) A contract may be formed by the interaction of electronic agents of the parties, even if no individual was aware of or reviewed the electronic agents' actions or the resulting terms and agreements.

(2) A contract may be formed by the interaction of an electronic agent and an individual, acting on the individual's own behalf or for another person, including by an interaction in which the individual performs actions that the individual is free to refuse to perform and which the individual knows or has reason to know will cause the electronic agent to complete the transaction or performance.

(3) The terms of the contract are determined by the substantive law applicable to it.

Source: UNCITRAL Model Law on Electronic Commerce Article 11.

Comment

1. This section confirms that contracts can be formed by machines functioning as electronic agents for parties to a transaction. It negates any claim that lack of human intent, at the time of contract formation, prevents contract formation. When machines are involved, the requisite intention flows from the programing and use of the machine. As in other cases, these are salutary provisions consistent with the fundamental purpose of the Act to remove barriers to electronic transactions while leaving the substantive law, e.g., law of mistake, law of contract formation, unaffected to the greatest extent possible.

2. The process in paragraph (2) validates an anonymous click-through transaction. It is possible that an anonymous click-through process may simply result in no recognizable legal relationship, e.g., A goes to a person's website and acquires access without in any way identifying herself, or otherwise indicating agreement or assent to any limitation or obligation, and the owner's site grants A access. In such a case no legal relationship has been created.

On the other hand it may be possible that A's actions indicate agreement to a particular term. For example, A goes to a website and is confronted by an initial screen which advises her that the information at this site is proprietary, that A may use the information for her own personal purposes, but that, by clicking below, A agrees that any other use without the site owner's permission is prohibited. If A clicks "agree" and downloads the information and then uses the information for other, prohibited purposes, should not A be bound by the click? It seems the answer properly should be, and would be, yes.

If the owner can show that the only way A could have obtained the information was from his website, and that the process to access the subject information required that A must have clicked the "I agree" button after having the ability to see the conditions on use, A has performed actions which A was free to refuse, which A knew would cause the site to grant her access, i.e., "complete the transaction." The terms of the resulting contract will be determined under general contract principles, but will include the limitation on A's use of the information, as a condition precedent to granting her access to the information.

3. In the transaction set forth in Comment 2, the record of the transaction also will include an electronic signature. By clicking "I agree" A adopted a process with the intent to "sign," i.e., bind herself to a legal obligation, the resulting record of the transaction. If a "signed writing" were required under otherwise applicable law, this transaction would be enforceable. If a "signed writing" were not required, it may be sufficient to establish that the electronic record is attributable to A under Section 9. Attribution may be shown in any manner reasonable including showing that, of necessity, A could only have gotten the information through the process at the website.

§ 15. Time and Place of Sending and Receipt.

(a) Unless otherwise agreed between the sender and the recipient, an electronic record is sent when it:

(1) is addressed properly or otherwise directed properly to an information processing system that the recipient has designated or uses for the purpose of receiving electronic records or information of the type sent and from which the recipient is able to retrieve the electronic record;

(2) is in a form capable of being processed by that system; and

(3) enters an information processing system outside the control of the sender or of a person that sent the electronic record on behalf of the sender or enters a region of the information processing system designated or used by the recipient which is under the control of the recipient.

(b) Unless otherwise agreed between a sender and the recipient, an electronic record is received when:

(1) it enters an information processing system that the recipient has designated or uses for the purpose of receiving electronic records or information of the type sent and from which the recipient is able to retrieve the electronic record; and

(2) it is in a form capable of being processed by that system.

(c) Subsection (b) applies even if the place the information processing system is located is different from the place the electronic record is deemed to be received under subsection (d).

(d) Unless otherwise expressly provided in the electronic record or agreed between the sender and the recipient, an electronic record is deemed to be sent from the sender's place of business and to be received at the recipient's place of business. For purposes of this subsection, the following rules apply:

(1) If the sender or recipient has more than one place of business, the place of business of that person is the place having the closest relationship to the underlying transaction.

(2) If the sender or the recipient does not have a place of business, the place of business is the sender's or recipient's residence, as the case may be.

(e) An electronic record is received under subsection (b) even if no individual is aware of its receipt.

(f) Receipt of an electronic acknowledgment from an information processing system described in subsection (b) establishes that a record was received but, by itself, does not establish that the content sent corresponds to the content received.

(g) If a person is aware that an electronic record purportedly sent under subsection (a), or purportedly received under subsection (b), was not actually sent or received, the legal effect of the sending or receipt is determined by other applicable law. Except to the extent permitted by the other law, the requirements of this subsection may not be varied by agreement.

Source: UNCITRAL Model Law on Electronic Commerce Article 15.

Comment

1. This section provides default rules regarding when and from where an electronic record is sent and when and where an electronic record is received. This section does not address the efficacy of the record that is sent or received. That is, whether a record is unintelligible or unusable by a recipient is a separate issue from whether that record was sent or received. The effectiveness of an illegible record, whether it binds any party, are questions left to other law.

2. Subsection (a) furnishes rules for determining when an electronic record is sent. The effect of the sending and its import are determined by other law once it is determined that a sending has occurred.

In order to have a proper sending, the subsection requires that information be properly addressed or otherwise directed to the recipient. In order to send within the meaning of this section, there must be specific information which will direct the record to the intended recipient. Although mass electronic sending is not precluded, a general broadcast message, sent to systems rather than individuals, would not suffice as a sending.

The record will be considered sent once it leaves the control of the sender, or comes under the control of the recipient. Records sent through e-mail or the internet will pass through many different server systems. Accordingly, the critical element when more than one system is involved is the loss of control by the sender.

However, the structure of many message delivery systems is such that electronic records may actually never leave the control of the sender. For example, within a university or corporate setting, e-mail sent within the system to another faculty member is technically not out of the sender's control since it never leaves the organization's server. Accordingly, to qualify as a sending, the e-mail must arrive at a point where the recipient has control. This section does not address the effect of an electronic record that is thereafter "pulled back," e.g., removed from a mailbox. The analog in the paper world would be removing a letter from a person's mailbox. As in the case of providing information electronically under Section 8, the recipient's ability to receive a message should be judged from the perspective of whether the sender has done any action which would preclude retrieval. This is especially the case in regard to sending, since the sender must direct the record to a system designated or used by the recipient.

3. Subsection (b) provides simply that when a record enters the system which the recipient has designated or uses and to which it has access, in a form capable of being processed by that system, it is received. Keying receipt to a system accessible by the recipient removes the potential for a recipient leaving messages with a server or other service in order to avoid receipt. However, the section does not resolve the issue of how the sender proves the time of receipt.

To assure that the recipient retains control of the place of receipt, subsection (b) requires that the system be specified or used by the recipient, and that the system be used or designated for the type of record being sent. Many people have multiple e-mail addresses for different purposes. Subsection (b) assures that recipients can designate the e-mail address or system to be used in a particular transaction. For example, the recipient retains the ability to designate a home e-mail for personal matters, work e-mail for official business, or a separate organizational e-mail solely for the business purposes of that organization. If A sends B a notice at his home which relates to business, it may not be deemed received if B designated his business address as the sole address for business purposes. Whether actual knowledge upon seeing it at home would qualify as receipt is determined under the otherwise applicable substantive law.

4. Subsections (c) and (d) provide default rules for determining where a record will be considered to have been sent or received. The focus is on the place of business of the recipient and not the physical location of the information processing system, which may bear absolutely no relation to the transaction between the parties. It is not uncommon for users of electronic commerce to communicate from one State to another without knowing the location of information systems through which communication is operated. In addition, the location of certain communication systems may change without either of the parties being aware of the change. Accordingly, where the place of sending or receipt is an issue under other applicable law, e.g., conflict of laws issues, tax issues, the relevant location should be the location of the sender or recipient and not the location of the information processing system.

Subsection (d) assures individual flexibility in designating the place from which a record will be considered sent or at which a record will be considered received. Under subsection (d) a person may designate the place of sending or receipt unilaterally in an electronic record. This ability, as with the ability to designate by agreement, may be limited by otherwise applicable law to places having a reasonable relationship to the transaction.

5. Subsection (e) makes clear that receipt is not dependent on a person having notice that the record is in the person's system. Receipt occurs when the record reaches the designated system whether or not the recipient ever retrieves the record. The paper analog is the recipient who never reads a mail notice.

6. Subsection (f) provides legal certainty regarding the effect of an electronic acknowledgment. It only addresses the fact of receipt, not the quality of the content, nor whether the electronic record was read or "opened."

7. Subsection (g) limits the parties' ability to vary the method for sending and receipt provided in subsections (a) and (b), when there is a legal requirement for the sending or receipt. As in other circumstances where legal requirements derive from other substantive law, to the extent that the other law permits variation by agreement, this Act does not impose any additional requirements, and provisions of this Act may be varied to the extent provided in the other law.

§ 16. Transferable Records.

(a) In this section, "transferable record" means an electronic record that:

(1) would be a note under [Article 3 of the Uniform Commercial Code] or a document under [Article 7 of the Uniform Commercial Code] if the electronic record were in writing; and

(2) the issuer of the electronic record expressly has agreed is a transferable record.

(b) A person has control of a transferable record if a system employed for evidencing the transfer of interests in the transferable record reliably establishes that person as the person to which the transferable record was issued or transferred.

(c) A system satisfies subsection (b), and a person is deemed to have control of a transferable record, if the transferable record is created, stored, and assigned in such a manner that:

(1) a single authoritative copy of the transferable record exists which is unique, identifiable, and, except as otherwise provided in paragraphs (4), (5), and (6), unalterable;

(2) the authoritative copy identifies the person asserting control as:

(A) the person to which the transferable record was issued; or

(B) if the authoritative copy indicates that the transferable record has been transferred, the person to which the transferable record was most recently transferred;

(3) the authoritative copy is communicated to and maintained by the person asserting control or its designated custodian;

(4) copies or revisions that add or change an identified assignee of the authoritative copy can be made only with the consent of the person asserting control;

(5) each copy of the authoritative copy and any copy of a copy is readily identifiable as a copy that is not the authoritative copy; and

(6) any revision of the authoritative copy is readily identifiable as authorized or unauthorized.

(d) Except as otherwise agreed, a person having control of a transferable record is the holder, as defined in [Section 1–201(20) of the Uniform Commercial Code], of the transferable record and has the same rights and defenses as a holder of an equivalent record or writing under [the Uniform Commercial Code], including, if the applicable statutory requirements under [Section 3–302(a), 7–501, or 9–308 of the Uniform Commercial Code] are satisfied, the rights and defenses of a holder in due course, a holder to which a negotiable document of title has been duly negotiated, or a purchaser, respectively. Delivery, possession, and indorsement are not required to obtain or exercise any of the rights under this subsection.

(e) Except as otherwise agreed, an obligor under a transferable record has the same rights and defenses as an equivalent obligor under equivalent records or writings under [the Uniform Commercial Code].

(f) If requested by a person against which enforcement is sought, the person seeking to enforce the transferable record shall provide reasonable proof that the person is in control of the transferable record. Proof may include access to the authoritative copy of the transferable record and related business records sufficient to review the terms of the transferable record and to establish the identity of the person having control of the transferable record.

Source: Revised Article 9, Section 9–105.

Comment

1. Paper negotiable instruments and documents are unique in the fact that a tangible token—a piece of paper—actually embodies intangible rights and obligations. The extreme difficulty of creating a unique electronic token which embodies the singular attributes of a paper negotiable document or instrument dictates that the rules relating to negotiable documents and instruments not be simply amended to allow the use of an electronic record for the requisite paper writing. However, the desirability of establishing rules by which business parties might be able to acquire some of the benefits of negotiability in an electronic environment is recognized by the inclusion of this section on Transferable Records.

This section provides legal support for the creation, transferability and enforceability of electronic note and document equivalents, as against the issuer/obligor. The certainty created by the section provides the requisite incentive for industry to develop the systems and processes, which involve significant expenditures of time and resources, to enable the use of such electronic documents.

The importance of facilitating the development of systems which will permit electronic equivalents is a function of cost, efficiency and safety for the records. The storage cost and space needed for the billions of paper notes and documents is phenomenal. Further, natural disasters can wreak havoc on the ability to meet legal requirements for retaining, retrieving and delivering paper instruments. The development of electronic systems meeting the rigorous standards of this section will permit retention of copies which reflect the same integrity as the original. As a result storage, transmission and other costs will be reduced, while security and the ability to satisfy legal requirements governing such paper records will be enhanced.

Section 16 provides for the creation of an electronic record which may be controlled by the holder, who in turn may obtain the benefits of holder in due course and good faith purchaser status. If the benefits and efficiencies of electronic media are to be realized in this industry it is essential to establish a means by which transactions involving paper promissory notes may be accomplished completely electronically. Particularly as other aspects of such transactions are accomplished electronically, the drag on the transaction of requiring a paper note becomes evident. In addition to alleviating the logistical problems of generating, storing and retrieving paper, the mailing and transmission costs associated with such transactions will also be reduced.

2. The definition of transferable record is limited in two significant ways. First, only the equivalent of paper promissory notes and paper documents of title can be created as transferable records. Notes and Documents of Title do not impact the broad systems that relate to the broader payments mechanisms related, for example, to checks. Impacting the check collection system by allowing for "electronic checks" has ramifications well beyond the ability of this Act to address. Accordingly, this Act excludes from its scope transactions governed by UCC Articles 3 and 4. The limitation to promissory note equivalents in Section 16 is quite important in that regard because of the ability to deal with many enforcement issues by contract without affecting such systemic concerns.

Second, not only is Section 16 limited to electronic records which would qualify as negotiable promissory notes or documents if they were in writing, but the issuer of the electronic record must expressly agree that the electronic record is to be considered a transferable record. The definition of transferable record as "an electronic record that . . . the issuer of the electronic record expressly has agreed is a transferable record" indicates that the electronic record itself will likely set forth the issuer's agreement, though it may be argued that a contemporaneous electronic or written record might set forth the issuer's agreement. However, conversion of a paper note issued as such would not be possible because the issuer would not be the issuer, in such a case, of an electronic record. The purpose of such a restriction is to assure that transferable records can only be created at the time of issuance by the obligor. The possibility that a paper note might be converted to an electronic record and then intentionally destroyed, and the effect of such action, was not intended to be covered by Section 16.

The requirement that the obligor expressly agree in the electronic record to its treatment as a transferable record does not otherwise affect the characterization of a transferable record (i.e., does not affect what would be a paper note) because it is a statutory condition. Further, it does not obligate the issuer to undertake to do any other act than the payment of the obligation evidenced by the transferable record. Therefore, it does not make the transferable record "conditional" within the meaning of Section 3–104(a)(3) of the Uniform Commercial Code.

3. Under Section 16 acquisition of "control" over an electronic record serves as a substitute for "possession" in the paper analog. More precisely, "control" under Section 16 serves as the substitute for delivery, indorsement and possession of a negotiable promissory note or negotiable document of title. Section 16(b) allows control to be found so long as "a system employed for evidencing the transfer of interests in the transferable record reliably establishes [the person claiming control] as the person to which the transferable record was issued or transferred." The key point is that a system, whether involving third party registry or technological safeguards, must be shown to reliably establish the identity of *the* person entitled to payment. Section 16(c) then sets forth a safe harbor list of very strict requirements for such a system. The specific provisions listed in Section 16(c) are derived from Section 105 of Revised Article 9 of the Uniform Commercial Code. Generally, the transferable record must be unique, identifiable, and except as specifically permitted, unalterable. That "authoritative copy" must (i) identify the person claiming control as the person to whom the record was issued or most recently transferred, (ii) be maintained by the person claiming control or its designee, and (iii) be unalterable except with the permission of the person claiming control. In addition any copy of the authoritative copy must be readily identifiable as a copy and all revisions must be readily identifiable as authorized or unauthorized.

The control requirements may be satisfied through the use of a trusted third party registry system. Such systems are currently in place with regard to the transfer of securities entitlements under Article 8 of the Uniform Commercial Code, and in the transfer of cotton warehouse receipts under the program sponsored by the United States Department of Agriculture. This Act would recognize the use of such a system so long as the standards of subsection (c) were satisfied. In addition, a technological system which met such exacting standards would also be permitted under Section 16.

For example, a borrower signs an electronic record which would be a promissory note or document if it were paper. The borrower specifically agrees in the electronic record that it will qualify as a transferable record under this section. The lender implements a newly developed technological system which dates, encrypts, and stores all the electronic information in the transferable record in a manner which lender can demonstrate reliably establishes lender as the person to which the transferable record was issued. In the alternative, the lender may contract with a third party to act as a registry for all such transferable records, retaining records establishing the party to whom the record was issued and all subsequent transfers of the record. An example of this latter method for assuring control is the system established for the issuance and transfer of electronic cotton warehouse receipts under 7 C.F.R. section 735 et seq.

Of greatest importance in the system used is the ability to securely and demonstrably be able to transfer the record to others in a manner which assures that only one "holder" exists. The need for such certainty and security resulted in the very stringent standards for a system outlined in subsection (c). A system relying on a third party registry is likely the most effective way to satisfy the requirements of subsection (c) that the transferable record remain unique, identifiable and unalterable, while also providing the means to assure that the transferee is clearly noted and identified.

It must be remembered that Section 16 was drafted in order to provide sufficient legal certainty regarding the rights of those in control of such electronic records, that legal incentives would exist to warrant the development of systems which would establish the requisite control. During the drafting of Section 16, representatives from the Federal Reserve carefully scrutinized the impact of any electronicization of any aspect of the national payment system. Section 16 represents a compromise position which, as noted, serves as a bridge pending more detailed study and consideration of what legal changes, if any, are necessary or appropriate in the context of the payment systems impacted. Accordingly, Section 16 provides limited scope for the attainment of important rights derived from the concept of negotiability, in order to permit the development of systems which will satisfy its strict requirements for control.

4. It is important to note what the section does not provide. Issues related to enforceability against intermediate transferees and transferors (i.e., indorser liability under a paper note), warranty liability that would attach in a paper note, and issues of the effect of taking a transferable record on the underlying obligation, are NOT addressed by this section. Such matters must be addressed, if at all, by contract between and among the parties in the chain of transmission and transfer of the transferable record. In the event that such matters are not addressed by the contract, the issues would need to be resolved under otherwise applicable law. Other law may include general contract principles of assignment and assumption, or may include rules from Article 3 of the Uniform Commercial Code applied by analogy.

For example, Issuer agrees to pay a debt by means of a transferable record issued to A. Unless there is agreement between issuer and A that the transferable record "suspends" the underlying obligation (see Section 3–310 of the Uniform Commercial Code), A would not be prevented from enforcing the underlying obligation without the transferable record. Similarly, if A transfers the transferable record to B by means granting B control, B may obtain holder in due course rights against the obligor/issuer, but B's recourse against A would not be clear unless A agreed to remain liable under the transferable record. Although the rules of Article 3 may be applied by analogy in an appropriate context, in the absence of an express agreement in the transferable record or included by applicable system rules, the liability of the transferor would not be clear.

5. Current business models exist which rely for their efficacy on the benefits of negotiability. A principal example, and one which informed much of the development of Section 16, involves the mortgage backed securities industry. Aggregators of commercial paper acquire mortgage secured promissory notes following a chain of transfers beginning with the origination of the mortgage loan by a mortgage broker. In the course of the transfers of this paper, buyers of the notes and lenders/secured parties for these buyers will intervene. For the ultimate purchaser of the paper, the ability to rely on holder in due course and good faith purchaser status creates the legal security necessary to issue its own investment securities which are backed by the obligations evidenced by the notes purchased. Only through their HIDC status can these purchasers be assured that third party claims will be barred. Only through their HIDC status can the end purchaser avoid the incredible burden of requiring and assuring that each person in the chain of transfer has waived any and all defenses to performance which may be created during the chain of transfer.

6. This section is a stand-alone provision. Although references are made to specific provisions in Article 3, Article 7, and Article 9 of the Uniform Commercial Code, these provisions are incorporated into this Act and made the applicable rules for purposes of this Act. The rights of parties to transferable records are established under subsections (d) and (e). Subsection (d) provides rules for determining the rights of a party in control of a transferable record. The subsection makes clear that the rights are determined under this section, and not under other law, by incorporating the rules on the manner of acquisition into this statute. The last sentence of subsection (d) is intended to assure that requirements related to notions of possession, which are inherently inconsistent with the idea of an electronic record, are not incorporated into this statute.

If a person establishes control, Section 16(d) provides that that person is the "holder" of the transferable record which is equivalent to a holder of an analogous paper negotiable instrument. More importantly, if the person acquired control in a manner which would make it a holder in due course of an equivalent paper record, the person acquires the rights of a HIDC. The person in control would therefore be able to enforce the transferable record against the obligor regardless of intervening claims and defenses. However, by pulling these rights into Section 16, this Act does NOT validate the wholesale electrification of promissory notes under Article 3 of the Uniform Commercial Code.

Further, it is important to understand that a transferable record under Section 16, while having no counterpart under Article 3 of the Uniform Commercial Code, would be an "account," "general intangible," or "payment intangible" under Article 9 of the Uniform Commercial Code. Accordingly, two separate bodies of law would apply to that asset of the obligee. A taker of the transferable record under Section 16 may acquire purchaser rights under Article 9 of the Uniform Commercial Code, however, those rights may be defeated by a trustee in bankruptcy of a prior person in control unless perfection under Article 9 of the Uniform Commercial Code by filing is achieved. If the person in control also takes control in a manner granting it holder in due course status, of course that person would take free of any claim by a bankruptcy trustee or lien creditor.

7. Subsection (e) accords to the obligor of the transferable record rights equal to those of an obligor under an equivalent paper record. Accordingly, unless a waiver of defense clause is obtained in the electronic record, or the transferee obtains HDC rights under subsection (d), the obligor has all the rights and defenses available to it under a contract assignment. Additionally, the obligor has the right to have the payment noted or otherwise included as part of the electronic record.

8. Subsection (f) grants the obligor the right to have the transferable record and other information made available for purposes of assuring the correct person to pay. This will allow the obligor to protect its interest and obtain the defense of discharge by payment or performance. This is particularly important because a person receiving subsequent control under the appropriate circumstances may well qualify as a holder in course who can enforce payment of the transferable record.

9. Section 16 is a singular exception to the thrust of this Act to simply validate electronic media used in commercial transactions. Section 16 actually provides a means for expanding electronic commerce. It provides certainty to lenders and investors regarding the enforceability of a new class of financial services. It is hoped that the legal protections afforded by Section 16 will engender the development of technological and business models which will permit realization of the significant cost savings and efficiencies available through electronic transacting in the financial services industry. Although only a bridge to more detailed consideration of the broad issues related to negotiability in an electronic context, Section 16 provides the impetus for that broader consideration while allowing continuation of developing technological and business models.

§ 17. Creation and Retention of Electronic Records and Conversion of Written Records by Governmental Agencies.

[Each governmental agency] [The [designated state officer]] of this State shall determine whether, and the extent to which, [it] [a governmental agency] will create and retain electronic records and convert written records to electronic records.]

Comment

See Comments following Section 19.

§ 18. Acceptance and Distribution of Electronic Records by Governmental Agencies.

(a) Except as otherwise provided in Section 12(f), [each governmental agency] [the [designated state officer]] of this State shall determine whether, and the extent to which, [it] [a governmental agency] will send and accept electronic records and electronic signatures to and from other persons and otherwise create, generate, communicate, store, process, use, and rely upon electronic records and electronic signatures.

(b) To the extent that a governmental agency uses electronic records and electronic signatures under subsection (a), the [governmental agency] [designated state officer], giving due consideration to security, may specify:

(1) the manner and format in which the electronic records must be created, generated, sent, communicated, received, and stored and the systems established for those purposes;

(2) if electronic records must be signed by electronic means, the type of electronic signature required, the manner and format in which the electronic signature must be affixed to the electronic

record, and the identity of, or criteria that must be met by, any third party used by a person filing a document to facilitate the process;

(3) control processes and procedures as appropriate to ensure adequate preservation, disposition, integrity, security, confidentiality, and auditability of electronic records; and

(4) any other required attributes for electronic records which are specified for corresponding nonelectronic records or reasonably necessary under the circumstances.

(c) Except as otherwise provided in Section 12(f), this [Act] does not require a governmental agency of this State to use or permit the use of electronic records or electronic signatures.]

Source: Illinois Act Section 25–101; Florida Electronic Signature Act, Chapter 96–324, Section 7 (1996).

Comment

See Comments following Section 19.

§ 19. Interoperability.

The [governmental agency] [designated officer] of this State which adopts standards pursuant to Section 18 may encourage and promote consistency and interoperability with similar requirements adopted by other governmental agencies of this and other States and the federal government and nongovernmental persons interacting with governmental agencies of this State. If appropriate, those standards may specify differing levels of standards from which governmental agencies of this State may choose in implementing the most appropriate standard for a particular application.]

Source: Illinois Act Section 25–115.

See Legislative Note below, following Comment.

Comment

1. Sections 17–19 have been bracketed as optional provisions to be considered for adoption by each State. Among the barriers to electronic commerce are barriers which exist in the use of electronic media by state governmental agencies—whether among themselves or in external dealing with the private sector. In those circumstances where the government acts as a commercial party, e.g., in areas of procurement, the general validation provisions of this Act will apply. That is to say, the government must agree to conduct transactions electronically with vendors and customers of government services.

However, there are other circumstances when government ought to establish the ability to proceed in transactions electronically. Whether in regard to records and communications within and between governmental agencies, or with respect to information and filings which must be made with governmental agencies, these sections allow a State to establish the ground work for such electronicization.

2. The provisions in Sections 17–19 are broad and very general. In many States they will be unnecessary because enacted legislation designed to facilitate governmental use of electronic records and communications is in place. However, in many States broad validating rules are needed and desired. Accordingly, this Act provides these sections as a baseline.

Of paramount importance in all States however, is the need for States to assure that whatever systems and rules are adopted, the systems established are compatible with the systems of other governmental agencies and with common systems in the private sector. A very real risk exists that implementation of systems by myriad governmental agencies and offices may create barriers because of a failure to consider compatibility, than would be the case otherwise.

3. The provisions in Section 17–19 are broad and general to provide the greatest flexibility and adaptation to the specific needs of the individual States. The differences and variations in the organization and structure of governmental agencies mandates this approach. However, it is imperative that each State always keep in mind the need to prevent the erection of barriers through appropriate coordination of systems and rules within the parameters set by the State.

4. Section 17 authorizes state agencies to use electronic records and electronic signatures generally for intra-governmental purposes, and to convert written records and manual signatures to electronic records and electronic signatures. By its terms the section gives enacting legislatures the option to leave the decision to use

electronic records or convert written records and signatures to the governmental agency or assign that duty to a designated state officer. It also authorizes the destruction of written records after conversion to electronic form.

5. Section 18 broadly authorizes state agencies to send and receive electronic records and signatures in dealing with non-governmental persons. Again, the provision is permissive and not obligatory (see subsection (c)). However, it does provide specifically that with respect to electronic records used for evidentiary purposes, Section 12 will apply unless a particular agency expressly opts out.

6. Section 19 is the most important section of the three. It requires governmental agencies or state officers to take account of consistency in applications and interoperability to the extent practicable when promulgating standards. This section is critical in addressing the concern that inconsistent applications may promote barriers greater than currently exist. Without such direction the myriad systems that could develop independently would be new barriers to electronic commerce, not a removal of barriers. The key to interoperability is flexibility and adaptability. The requirement of a single system may be as big a barrier as the proliferation of many disparate systems.

Legislative Note Regarding Adoption of Sections 17–19

1. Sections 17–19 are optional sections for consideration by individual legislatures for adoption, and have been bracketed to make this clear. The inclusion or exclusion of Sections 17–19 will not have a detrimental impact on the uniformity of adoption of this Act, so long as Sections 1–16 are adopted uniformly as presented. In some States Sections 17–19 will be unnecessary because legislation is already in place to authorize and implement government use of electronic media. However, the general authorization provided by Sections 17–19 may be critical in some States which desire to move forward in this area.

2. In the event that a state legislature chooses to adopt Sections 17–19, a number of issues must be addressed:

A. Is the general authorization to adopt electronic media, provided by Sections 17–19 sufficient for the needs of the particular jurisdiction, or is more detailed and specific authorization necessary? This determination may be affected by the decision regarding the appropriate entity or person to oversee implementation of the use of electronic media (See next paragraph). Sections 17–19 are broad and general in the authorization granted. Certainly greater specificity can be added subsequent to adoption of these sections. The question for the legislature is whether greater direction and specificity is needed at this time. If so, the legislature should not enact Sections 17–19 at this time.

B. Assuming a legislature decides to enact Sections 17–19, what entity or person should oversee implementation of the government's use of electronic media? As noted in each of Sections 17–19, again by brackets, a choice must be made regarding the entity to make critical decisions regarding the systems and rules which will govern the use of electronic media by the State. Each State will need to consider its particular structure and administration in making this determination. However, legislatures are strongly encouraged to make compatibility and interoperability considerations paramount in making this determination.

C. Finally, a decision will have to be made regarding the process by which coordination of electronic systems will occur between the various branches of state government and among the various levels of government within the State. Again this will require consideration of the unique situation in each State.

3. If a State chooses not to enact Sections 17–19, UETA Sections 1–16 will still apply to governmental entities when acting as a "person" engaging in "transactions" within its scope. The definition of transaction includes "governmental affairs." Of course, like any other party, the circumstances surrounding a transaction must indicate that the governmental actor has agreed to act electronically (See Section 5(b)), but otherwise all the provisions of Sections 1–16 will apply to validate the use of electronic records and signatures in transactions involving governmental entities.

If a State does choose to enact Sections 17–19, Sections 1–16 will continue to apply as above. In addition, Sections 17–19 will provide authorization for intra-governmental uses of electronic media. Finally, Sections 17–19 provide a broader authorization for the State to develop systems and procedures for the use of electronic media in its relations with non-governmental entities and persons.

§ 20. Severability Clause.

If any provision of this [Act] or its application to any person or circumstance is held invalid, the invalidity does not affect other provisions or applications of this [Act] which can be given effect without the invalid provision or application, and to this end the provisions of this [Act] are severable.

§ 21. Effective Date.

This [Act] takes effect [ ].

ELECTRONIC SIGNATURES IN GLOBAL AND NATIONAL COMMERCE ACT (ESIGN)

15 U.S.C. §§ 7001–7031
Current through March 12, 2019; P.L. 116–9
For updates, see http://uscode.house.gov

SUBCHAPTER I—ELECTRONIC RECORDS AND SIGNATURES IN COMMERCE

§ 7001. General Rule of Validity [§ 101]

(a) In general

Notwithstanding any statute, regulation, or other rule of law (other than this subchapter and subchapter II of this chapter), with respect to any transaction in or affecting interstate or foreign commerce—

(1) a signature, contract, or other record relating to such transaction may not be denied legal effect, validity, or enforceability solely because it is in electronic form; and

(2) a contract relating to such transaction may not be denied legal effect, validity, or enforceability solely because an electronic signature or electronic record was used in its formation.

(b) Preservation of rights and obligations

This subchapter does not—

(1) limit, alter, or otherwise affect any requirement imposed by a statute, regulation, or rule of law relating to the rights and obligations of persons under such statute, regulation, or rule of law other than a requirement that contracts or other records be written, signed, or in nonelectronic form; or

(2) require any person to agree to use or accept electronic records or electronic signatures, other than a governmental agency with respect to a record other than a contract to which it is a party.

(c) Consumer disclosures

(1) Consent to electronic records

Notwithstanding subsection (a), if a statute, regulation, or other rule of law requires that information relating to a transaction or transactions in or affecting interstate or foreign commerce be provided or made available to a consumer in writing, the use of an electronic record to provide or make available (whichever is required) such information satisfies the requirement that such information be in writing if—

(A) the consumer has affirmatively consented to such use and has not withdrawn such consent;

(B) the consumer, prior to consenting, is provided with a clear and conspicuous statement—

(i) informing the consumer of (I) any right or option of the consumer to have the record provided or made available on paper or in nonelectronic form, and (II) the right of the consumer to withdraw the consent to have the record provided or made available in an electronic form and of any conditions, consequences (which may include termination of the parties' relationship), or fees in the event of such withdrawal;

(ii) informing the consumer of whether the consent applies (I) only to the particular transaction which gave rise to the obligation to provide the record, or (II) to identified categories of records that may be provided or made available during the course of the parties' relationship;

(iii) describing the procedures the consumer must use to withdraw consent as provided in clause (i) and to update information needed to contact the consumer electronically; and

(iv) informing the consumer (I) how, after the consent, the consumer may, upon request, obtain a paper copy of an electronic record, and (II) whether any fee will be charged for such copy;

(C) the consumer—

(i) prior to consenting, is provided with a statement of the hardware and software requirements for access to and retention of the electronic records; and

(ii) consents electronically, or confirms his or her consent electronically, in a manner that reasonably demonstrates that the consumer can access information in the electronic form that will be used to provide the information that is the subject of the consent; and

(D) after the consent of a consumer in accordance with subparagraph (A), if a change in the hardware or software requirements needed to access or retain electronic records creates a material risk that the consumer will not be able to access or retain a subsequent electronic record that was the subject of the consent, the person providing the electronic record—

(i) provides the consumer with a statement of (I) the revised hardware and software requirements for access to and retention of the electronic records, and (II) the right to withdraw consent without the imposition of any fees for such withdrawal and without the imposition of any condition or consequence that was not disclosed under subparagraph (B)(i); and

(ii) again complies with subparagraph (C).

(2) Other rights

(A) Preservation of consumer protections

Nothing in this subchapter affects the content or timing of any disclosure or other record required to be provided or made available to any consumer under any statute, regulation, or other rule of law.

(B) Verification or acknowledgment

If a law that was enacted prior to this chapter expressly requires a record to be provided or made available by a specified method that requires verification or acknowledgment of receipt, the record may be provided or made available electronically only if the method used provides verification or acknowledgment of receipt (whichever is required).

(3) Effect of failure to obtain electronic consent or confirmation of consent

The legal effectiveness, validity, or enforceability of any contract executed by a consumer shall not be denied solely because of the failure to obtain electronic consent or confirmation of consent by that consumer in accordance with paragraph (1)(C)(ii).

(4) Prospective effect

Withdrawal of consent by a consumer shall not affect the legal effectiveness, validity, or enforceability of electronic records provided or made available to that consumer in accordance with paragraph (1) prior to implementation of the consumer's withdrawal of consent. A consumer's withdrawal of consent shall be effective within a reasonable period of time after receipt of the withdrawal by the provider of the record. Failure to comply with paragraph (1)(D) may, at the election of the consumer, be treated as a withdrawal of consent for purposes of this paragraph.

(5) Prior consent

This subsection does not apply to any records that are provided or made available to a consumer who has consented prior to the effective date of this subchapter to receive such records in electronic form as permitted by any statute, regulation, or other rule of law.

(6) Oral communications

An oral communication or a recording of an oral communication shall not qualify as an electronic record for purposes of this subsection except as otherwise provided under applicable law.

(d) Retention of contracts and records

(1) Accuracy and accessibility

If a statute, regulation, or other rule of law requires that a contract or other record relating to a transaction in or affecting interstate or foreign commerce be retained, that requirement is met by retaining an electronic record of the information in the contract or other record that—

(A) accurately reflects the information set forth in the contract or other record; and

(B) remains accessible to all persons who are entitled to access by statute, regulation, or rule of law, for the period required by such statute, regulation, or rule of law, in a form that is capable of being accurately reproduced for later reference, whether by transmission, printing, or otherwise.

(2) Exception

A requirement to retain a contract or other record in accordance with paragraph (1) does not apply to any information whose sole purpose is to enable the contract or other record to be sent, communicated, or received.

(3) Originals

If a statute, regulation, or other rule of law requires a contract or other record relating to a transaction in or affecting interstate or foreign commerce to be provided, available, or retained in its original form, or provides consequences if the contract or other record is not provided, available, or retained in its original form, that statute, regulation, or rule of law is satisfied by an electronic record that complies with paragraph (1).

(4) Checks

If a statute, regulation, or other rule of law requires the retention of a check, that requirement is satisfied by retention of an electronic record of the information on the front and back of the check in accordance with paragraph (1).

(e) Accuracy and ability to retain contracts and other records

Notwithstanding subsection (a), if a statute, regulation, or other rule of law requires that a contract or other record relating to a transaction in or affecting interstate or foreign commerce be in writing, the legal effect, validity, or enforceability of an electronic record of such contract or other record may be denied if such electronic record is not in a form that is capable of being retained and accurately reproduced for later reference by all parties or persons who are entitled to retain the contract or other record.

(f) Proximity

Nothing in this subchapter affects the proximity required by any statute, regulation, or other rule of law with respect to any warning, notice, disclosure, or other record required to be posted, displayed, or publicly affixed.

(g) Notarization and acknowledgment

If a statute, regulation, or other rule of law requires a signature or record relating to a transaction in or affecting interstate or foreign commerce to be notarized, acknowledged, verified, or made under oath, that requirement is satisfied if the electronic signature of the person authorized to perform those acts, together with all other information required to be included by other applicable statute, regulation, or rule of law, is attached to or logically associated with the signature or record.

(h) Electronic agents

A contract or other record relating to a transaction in or affecting interstate or foreign commerce may not be denied legal effect, validity, or enforceability solely because its formation, creation, or delivery involved the action of one or more electronic agents so long as the action of any such electronic agent is legally attributable to the person to be bound.

(i) Insurance

It is the specific intent of the Congress that this subchapter and subchapter II of this chapter apply to the business of insurance.

(j) Insurance agents and brokers

An insurance agent or broker acting under the direction of a party that enters into a contract by means of an electronic record or electronic signature may not be held liable for any deficiency in the electronic procedures agreed to by the parties under that contract if—

(1) the agent or broker has not engaged in negligent, reckless, or intentional tortious conduct;

(2) the agent or broker was not involved in the development or establishment of such electronic procedures; and

(3) the agent or broker did not deviate from such procedures.

§ 7002. Exemption to Preemption [§ 102]

(a) In general

A State statute, regulation, or other rule of law may modify, limit, or supersede the provisions of section 7001 of this title with respect to State law only if such statute, regulation, or rule of law—

(1) constitutes an enactment or adoption of the Uniform Electronic Transactions Act as approved and recommended for enactment in all the States by the National Conference of Commissioners on Uniform State Laws in 1999, except that any exception to the scope of such Act enacted by a State under section 3(b)(4) of such Act shall be preempted to the extent such exception is inconsistent with this subchapter or subchapter II of this chapter, or would not be permitted under paragraph (2)(A)(ii) of this subsection; or

(2)(A) specifies the alternative procedures or requirements for the use or acceptance (or both) of electronic records or electronic signatures to establish the legal effect, validity, or enforceability of contracts or other records, if—

(i) such alternative procedures or requirements are consistent with this subchapter and subchapter II of this chapter; and

(ii) such alternative procedures or requirements do not require, or accord greater legal status or effect to, the implementation or application of a specific technology or technical specification for performing the functions of creating, storing, generating, receiving, communicating, or authenticating electronic records or electronic signatures; and

(B) if enacted or adopted after June 30, 2000, makes specific reference to this chapter.

(b) Exceptions for actions by States as market participants

Subsection (a)(2)(A)(ii) of this section shall not apply to the statutes, regulations, or other rules of law governing procurement by any State, or any agency or instrumentality thereof.

(c) Prevention of circumvention

Subsection (a) of this section does not permit a State to circumvent this subchapter or subchapter II of this chapter through the imposition of nonelectronic delivery methods under section 8(b)(2) of the Uniform Electronic Transactions Act.

§ 7003. Specific Exceptions [§ 103]

(a) Excepted requirements

The provisions of section 7001 of this title shall not apply to a contract or other record to the extent it is governed by—

(1) a statute, regulation, or other rule of law governing the creation and execution of wills, codicils, or testamentary trusts;

(2) a State statute, regulation, or other rule of law governing adoption, divorce, or other matters of family law; or

(3) the Uniform Commercial Code, as in effect in any State, other than sections 1–107 and 1–206 and Articles 2 and 2A.

(b) Additional exceptions

The provisions of section 7001 of this title shall not apply to—

(1) court orders or notices, or official court documents (including briefs, pleadings, and other writings) required to be executed in connection with court proceedings;

(2) any notice of—

(A) the cancellation or termination of utility services (including water, heat, and power);

(B) default, acceleration, repossession, foreclosure, or eviction, or the right to cure, under a credit agreement secured by, or a rental agreement for, a primary residence of an individual;

(C) the cancellation or termination of health insurance or benefits or life insurance benefits (excluding annuities); or

(D) recall of a product, or material failure of a product, that risks endangering health or safety; or

(3) any document required to accompany any transportation or handling of hazardous materials, pesticides, or other toxic or dangerous materials.

(c) Review of exceptions

(1) Evaluation required

The Secretary of Commerce, acting through the Assistant Secretary for Communications and Information, shall review the operation of the exceptions in subsections (a) and (b) of this section to evaluate, over a period of 3 years, whether such exceptions continue to be necessary for the protection of consumers. Within 3 years after June 30, 2000, the Assistant Secretary shall submit a report to the Congress on the results of such evaluation.

(2) Determinations

If a Federal regulatory agency, with respect to matter within its jurisdiction, determines after notice and an opportunity for public comment, and publishes a finding, that one or more such exceptions are no longer necessary for the protection of consumers and eliminating such exceptions will not increase the material risk of harm to consumers, such agency may extend the application of section 7001 of this title to the exceptions identified in such finding.

§ 7004. Applicability to Federal and State Governments [§ 104]

(a) Filing and access requirements

Subject to subsection (c)(2) of this section, nothing in this subchapter limits or supersedes any requirement by a Federal regulatory agency, self-regulatory organization, or State regulatory agency that records be filed with such agency or organization in accordance with specified standards or formats.

(b) Preservation of existing rulemaking authority

(1) Use of authority to interpret

Subject to paragraph (2) and subsection (c) of this section, a Federal regulatory agency or State regulatory agency that is responsible for rulemaking under any other statute may interpret section 7001 of this title with respect to such statute through—

(A) the issuance of regulations pursuant to a statute; or

(B) to the extent such agency is authorized by statute to issue orders or guidance, the issuance of orders or guidance of general applicability that are publicly available and published (in the Federal Register in the case of an order or guidance issued by a Federal regulatory agency).

This paragraph does not grant any Federal regulatory agency or State regulatory agency authority to issue regulations, orders, or guidance pursuant to any statute that does not authorize such issuance.

(2) Limitations on interpretation authority

Notwithstanding paragraph (1), a Federal regulatory agency shall not adopt any regulation, order, or guidance described in paragraph (1), and a State regulatory agency is preempted by section 7001 of this title from adopting any regulation, order, or guidance described in paragraph (1), unless—

(A) such regulation, order, or guidance is consistent with section 7001 of this title;

(B) such regulation, order, or guidance does not add to the requirements of such section; and

(C) such agency finds, in connection with the issuance of such regulation, order, or guidance, that—

(i) there is a substantial justification for the regulation, order, or guidance;

(ii) the methods selected to carry out that purpose—

(I) are substantially equivalent to the requirements imposed on records that are not electronic records; and

(II) will not impose unreasonable costs on the acceptance and use of electronic records; and

(iii) the methods selected to carry out that purpose do not require, or accord greater legal status or effect to, the implementation or application of a specific technology or technical specification for performing the functions of creating, storing, generating, receiving, communicating, or authenticating electronic records or electronic signatures.

(3) Performance standards

(A) Accuracy, record integrity, accessibility

Notwithstanding paragraph (2)(C)(iii), a Federal regulatory agency or State regulatory agency may interpret section 7001(d) of this title to specify performance standards to assure accuracy, record integrity, and accessibility of records that are required to be retained. Such performance standards may be specified in a manner that imposes a requirement in violation of paragraph (2)(C)(iii) if the requirement (i) serves an important governmental objective; and (ii) is substantially related to the achievement of that objective. Nothing in this paragraph shall be construed to grant any Federal regulatory agency or State regulatory agency authority to require use of a particular type of software or hardware in order to comply with section 7001(d) of this title.

(B) Paper or printed form

Notwithstanding subsection (c)(1) of this section, a Federal regulatory agency or State regulatory agency may interpret section 7001(d) of this title to require retention of a record in a tangible printed or paper form if—

(i) there is a compelling governmental interest relating to law enforcement or national security for imposing such requirement; and

(ii) imposing such requirement is essential to attaining such interest.

(4) Exceptions for actions by Government as market participant

Paragraph (2)(C)(iii) shall not apply to the statutes, regulations, or other rules of law governing procurement by the Federal or any State government, or any agency or instrumentality thereof.

(c) Additional limitations

(1) Reimposing paper prohibited

Nothing in subsection (b) of this section (other than paragraph (3)(B) thereof) shall be construed to grant any Federal regulatory agency or State regulatory agency authority to impose or reimpose any requirement that a record be in a tangible printed or paper form.

(2) Continuing obligation under Government Paperwork Elimination Act

Nothing in subsection (a) or (b) of this section relieves any Federal regulatory agency of its obligations under the Government Paperwork Elimination Act (title XVII of Public Law 105–277).

(d) Authority to exempt from consent provision

(1) In general

A Federal regulatory agency may, with respect to matter within its jurisdiction, by regulation or order issued after notice and an opportunity for public comment, exempt without condition a specified category or type of record from the requirements relating to consent in section 7001(c) of this title if such exemption is necessary to eliminate a substantial burden on electronic commerce and will not increase the material risk of harm to consumers.

(2) Prospectuses

Within 30 days after June 30, 2000, the Securities and Exchange Commission shall issue a regulation or order pursuant to paragraph (1) exempting from section 7001(c) of this title any records that are required to be provided in order to allow advertising, sales literature, or other information concerning a security issued by an investment company that is registered under the Investment Company Act of 1940 [15 U.S.C. § 80a–1 et seq.], or concerning the issuer thereof, to be excluded from the definition of a prospectus under section 77b(a)(10)(A) of this title.

(e) Electronic letters of agency

The Federal Communications Commission shall not hold any contract for telecommunications service or letter of agency for a preferred carrier change, that otherwise complies with the Commission's rules, to be legally ineffective, invalid, or unenforceable solely because an electronic record or electronic signature was used in its formation or authorization.

§ 7005. Studies [§ 105]

(a) Delivery

Within 12 months after June 30, 2000, the Secretary of Commerce shall conduct an inquiry regarding the effectiveness of the delivery of electronic records to consumers using electronic mail as compared with delivery of written records via the United States Postal Service and private express mail services. The Secretary shall submit a report to the Congress regarding the results of such inquiry by the conclusion of such 12-month period.

(b) Study of electronic consent

Within 12 months after June 30, 2000, the Secretary of Commerce and the Federal Trade Commission shall submit a report to the Congress evaluating any benefits provided to consumers by the procedure required by section 7001(c)(1)(C)(ii) of this title; any burdens imposed on electronic commerce by that provision; whether the benefits outweigh the burdens; whether the absence of the procedure required by section 7001(c)(1)(C)(ii) of this title would increase the incidence of fraud directed against consumers; and suggesting any revisions to the provision deemed appropriate by the Secretary and the Commission. In conducting this evaluation, the Secretary and the Commission shall solicit comment from the general public, consumer representatives, and electronic commerce businesses.

§ 7006. Definitions [§ 106]

For purposes of this subchapter:

(1) Consumer

The term "consumer" means an individual who obtains, through a transaction, products or services which are used primarily for personal, family, or household purposes, and also means the legal representative of such an individual.

(2) Electronic

The term "electronic" means relating to technology having electrical, digital, magnetic, wireless, optical, electromagnetic, or similar capabilities.

(3) Electronic agent

The term "electronic agent" means a computer program or an electronic or other automated means used independently to initiate an action or respond to electronic records or performances in whole or in part without review or action by an individual at the time of the action or response.

(4) Electronic record

The term "electronic record" means a contract or other record created, generated, sent, communicated, received, or stored by electronic means.

(5) Electronic signature

The term "electronic signature" means an electronic sound, symbol, or process, attached to or logically associated with a contract or other record and executed or adopted by a person with the intent to sign the record.

(6) Federal regulatory agency

The term "Federal regulatory agency" means an agency, as that term is defined in section 552(f) of Title 5.

(7) Information

The term "information" means data, text, images, sounds, codes, computer programs, software, databases, or the like.

(8) Person

The term "person" means an individual, corporation, business trust, estate, trust, partnership, limited liability company, association, joint venture, governmental agency, public corporation, or any other legal or commercial entity.

(9) Record

The term "record" means information that is inscribed on a tangible medium or that is stored in an electronic or other medium and is retrievable in perceivable form.

(10) Requirement

The term "requirement" includes a prohibition.

(11) Self-regulatory organization

The term "self-regulatory organization" means an organization or entity that is not a Federal regulatory agency or a State, but that is under the supervision of a Federal regulatory agency and is authorized under Federal law to adopt and administer rules applicable to its members that are enforced by such organization or entity, by a Federal regulatory agency, or by another self-regulatory organization.

(12) State

The term "State" includes the District of Columbia and the territories and possessions of the United States.

(13) Transaction

The term "transaction" means an action or set of actions relating to the conduct of business, consumer, or commercial affairs between two or more persons, including any of the following types of conduct—

(A) the sale, lease, exchange, licensing, or other disposition of (i) personal property, including goods and intangibles, (ii) services, and (iii) any combination thereof; and

(B) the sale, lease, exchange, or other disposition of any interest in real property, or any combination thereof.

SUBCHAPTER II—TRANSFERABLE RECORDS

§ 7021. Transferable Records [§ 201]

(a) Definitions

For purposes of this section:

(1) Transferable record

The term "transferable record" means an electronic record that—

(A) would be a note under Article 3 of the Uniform Commercial Code if the electronic record were in writing;

(B) the issuer of the electronic record expressly has agreed is a transferable record; and

(C) relates to a loan secured by real property.

A transferable record may be executed using an electronic signature.

(2) Other definitions

The terms "electronic record", "electronic signature", and "person" have the same meanings provided in section 7006 of this title.

(b) Control

A person has control of a transferable record if a system employed for evidencing the transfer of interests in the transferable record reliably establishes that person as the person to which the transferable record was issued or transferred.

(c) Conditions

A system satisfies subsection (b) of this section, and a person is deemed to have control of a transferable record, if the transferable record is created, stored, and assigned in such a manner that—

(1) a single authoritative copy of the transferable record exists which is unique, identifiable, and, except as otherwise provided in paragraphs (4), (5), and (6), unalterable;

(2) the authoritative copy identifies the person asserting control as—

(A) the person to which the transferable record was issued; or

(B) if the authoritative copy indicates that the transferable record has been transferred, the person to which the transferable record was most recently transferred;

(3) the authoritative copy is communicated to and maintained by the person asserting control or its designated custodian;

(4) copies or revisions that add or change an identified assignee of the authoritative copy can be made only with the consent of the person asserting control;

(5) each copy of the authoritative copy and any copy of a copy is readily identifiable as a copy that is not the authoritative copy; and

(6) any revision of the authoritative copy is readily identifiable as authorized or unauthorized.

(d) Status as holder

Except as otherwise agreed, a person having control of a transferable record is the holder, as defined in section 1–201(20) of the Uniform Commercial Code, of the transferable record and has the same rights and defenses as a holder of an equivalent record or writing under the Uniform Commercial Code, including, if the applicable statutory requirements under section 3–302(a), 9–308, or revised section 9–330 of the Uniform Commercial Code are satisfied, the rights and defenses of a holder in due course or a purchaser, respectively. Delivery, possession, and endorsement are not required to obtain or exercise any of the rights under this subsection.

(e) Obligor rights

Except as otherwise agreed, an obligor under a transferable record has the same rights and defenses as an equivalent obligor under equivalent records or writings under the Uniform Commercial Code.

(f) Proof of control

If requested by a person against which enforcement is sought, the person seeking to enforce the transferable record shall provide reasonable proof that the person is in control of the transferable record. Proof may include access to the authoritative copy of the transferable record and related business records sufficient to review the terms of the transferable record and to establish the identity of the person having control of the transferable record.

(g) UCC references

For purposes of this subsection, all references to the Uniform Commercial Code are to the Uniform Commercial Code as in effect in the jurisdiction the law of which governs the transferable record.

SUBCHAPTER III—PROMOTION OF INTERNATIONAL ELECTRONIC COMMERCE

§ 7031. Principles Governing the Use of Electronic Signatures in International Transactions [§ 301]

(a) Promotion of electronic signatures

(1) Required actions

The Secretary of Commerce shall promote the acceptance and use, on an international basis, of electronic signatures in accordance with the principles specified in paragraph (2) and in a manner consistent with section 7001 of this title. The Secretary of Commerce shall take all actions necessary in a manner consistent with such principles to eliminate or reduce, to the maximum extent possible, the impediments to commerce in electronic signatures, for the purpose of facilitating the development of interstate and foreign commerce.

(2) Principles

The principles specified in this paragraph are the following:

(A) Remove paper-based obstacles to electronic transactions by adopting relevant principles from the Model Law on Electronic Commerce adopted in 1996 by the United Nations Commission on International Trade Law.

(B) Permit parties to a transaction to determine the appropriate authentication technologies and implementation models for their transactions, with assurance that those technologies and implementation models will be recognized and enforced.

(C) Permit parties to a transaction to have the opportunity to prove in court or other proceedings that their authentication approaches and their transactions are valid.

(D) Take a nondiscriminatory approach to electronic signatures and authentication methods from other jurisdictions.

(b) Consultation

In conducting the activities required by this section, the Secretary shall consult with users and providers of electronic signature products and services and other interested persons.

(c) Definitions

As used in this section, the terms "electronic record" and "electronic signature" have the same meanings provided in section 7006 of this title.

(Pub.L. 106–229, Title I, § 101, June 30, 2000, 114 Stat. 464.)

CHECK CLEARING FOR THE 21ST CENTURY ACT (CHECK 21 ACT)

12 U.S.C. §§ 5001–5018

Current through March 12, 2019; P.L. 116–9

For updates, see http://uscode.house.gov

§ 5001. Findings; purposes

(a) Findings

The Congress finds as follows:

(1) In the Expedited Funds Availability Act, enacted on August 10, 1987 [12 U.S.C. § 4001 et seq.], the Congress directed the Board of Governors of the Federal Reserve System to consider establishing regulations requiring Federal reserve banks and depository institutions to provide for check truncation, in order to improve the check processing system.

(2) In that same Act, the Congress—

(A) provided the Board of Governors of the Federal Reserve System with full authority to regulate all aspects of the payment system, including the receipt, payment, collection, and clearing of checks, and related functions of the payment system pertaining to checks; and

(B) directed that the exercise of such authority by the Board superseded any State law, including the Uniform Commercial Code, as in effect in any State.

(3) Check truncation is no less desirable in 2003 for both financial service customers and the financial services industry, to reduce costs, improve efficiency in check collections, and expedite funds availability for customers than it was over 15 years ago when Congress first directed the Board to consider establishing such a process.

(b) Purposes

The purposes of this chapter are as follows:

(1) To facilitate check truncation by authorizing substitute checks.

(2) To foster innovation in the check collection system without mandating receipt of checks in electronic form.

(3) To improve the overall efficiency of the Nation's payments system.

§ 5002. Definitions

For purposes of this chapter, the following definitions shall apply:

(1) Account

The term "account" means a deposit account at a bank.

(2) Bank

The term "bank" means any person that is located in a State and engaged in the business of banking and includes—

(A) any depository institution (as defined in section 461 (b)(1)(A) of this title);

(B) any Federal reserve bank;

(C) any Federal home loan bank; or

(D) to the extent it acts as a payor—

(i) the Treasury of the United States;

(ii) the United States Postal Service;

(iii) a State government; or

(iv) a unit of general local government (as defined in section 4001(24) of this title).

(3) Banking terms

(A) Collecting bank

The term "collecting bank" means any bank handling a check for collection except the paying bank.

(B) Depositary bank

The term "depositary bank" means—

(i) the first bank to which a check is transferred, even if such bank is also the paying bank or the payee; or

(ii) a bank to which a check is transferred for deposit in an account at such bank, even if the check is physically received and indorsed first by another bank.

(C) Paying bank

The term "paying bank" means—

(i) the bank by which a check is payable, unless the check is payable at or through another bank and is sent to the other bank for payment or collection; or

(ii) the bank at or through which a check is payable and to which the check is sent for payment or collection.

(D) Returning bank

(i) In general

The term "returning bank" means a bank (other than the paying or depositary bank) handling a returned check or notice in lieu of return.

(ii) Treatment as collecting bank

No provision of this chapter shall be construed as affecting the treatment of a returning bank as a collecting bank for purposes of section 4–202(b) of the Uniform Commercial Code.

(4) Board

The term "Board" means the Board of Governors of the Federal Reserve System.

(5) Business day

The term "business day" has the same meaning as in section 4001(3) of this title.

(6) Check

The term "check"—

(A) means a draft, payable on demand and drawn on or payable through or at an office of a bank, whether or not negotiable, that is handled for forward collection or return, including a substitute check and a travelers check; and

(B) does not include a noncash item or an item payable in a medium other than United States dollars.

(7) Consumer

The term "consumer" means an individual who—

(A) with respect to a check handled for forward collection, draws the check on a consumer account; or

(B) with respect to a check handled for return, deposits the check into, or cashes the check against, a consumer account.

(8) Consumer account

The term "consumer account" has the same meaning as in section 4001(10) of this title.

(9) Customer

The term "customer" means a person having an account with a bank.

(10) Forward collection

The term "forward collection" means the transfer by a bank of a check to a collecting bank for settlement or the paying bank for payment.

(11) Indemnifying bank

The term "indemnifying bank" means a bank that is providing an indemnity under section 5005 of this title with respect to a substitute check.

(12) MICR line

The terms "MICR line" and "magnetic ink character recognition line" mean the numbers, which may include the bank routing number, account number, check number, check amount, and other information, that are printed near the bottom of a check in magnetic ink in accordance with generally applicable industry standards.

(13) Noncash item

The term "noncash item" has the same meaning as in section 4001(14) of this title.

(14) Person

The term "person" means a natural person, corporation, unincorporated company, partnership, government unit or instrumentality, trust, or any other entity or organization.

(15) Reconverting bank

The term "reconverting bank" means—

(A) the bank that creates a substitute check; or

(B) if a substitute check is created by a person other than a bank, the first bank that transfers or presents such substitute check.

(16) Substitute check

The term "substitute check" means a paper reproduction of the original check that—

(A) contains an image of the front and back of the original check;

(B) bears a MICR line containing all the information appearing on the MICR line of the original check, except as provided under generally applicable industry standards for substitute checks to facilitate the processing of substitute checks;

(C) conforms, in paper stock, dimension, and otherwise, with generally applicable industry standards for substitute checks; and

(D) is suitable for automated processing in the same manner as the original check.

(17) State

The term "State" has the same meaning as in 1813(a) of this title.

(18) Truncate

The term "truncate" means to remove an original paper check from the check collection or return process and send to a recipient, in lieu of such original paper check, a substitute check or, by agreement, information relating to the original check (including data taken from the MICR line of the original check or an electronic image of the original check), whether with or without subsequent delivery of the original paper check.

(19) Uniform Commercial Code

The term "Uniform Commercial Code" means the Uniform Commercial Code in effect in a State.

(20) Other terms

Unless the context requires otherwise, the terms not defined in this section shall have the same meanings as in the Uniform Commercial Code.

§ 5003. General provisions governing substitute checks

(a) No agreement required

A person may deposit, present, or send for collection or return a substitute check without an agreement with the recipient, so long as a bank has made the warranties in section 5004 of this title with respect to such substitute check.

(b) Legal equivalence

A substitute check shall be the legal equivalent of the original check for all purposes, including any provision of any Federal or State law, and for all persons if the substitute check—

(1) accurately represents all of the information on the front and back of the original check as of the time the original check was truncated; and

(2) bears the legend: "This is a legal copy of your check. You can use it the same way you would use the original check."

(c) Endorsements

A bank shall ensure that the substitute check for which the bank is the reconverting bank bears all endorsements applied by parties that previously handled the check (whether in electronic form or in the form of the original paper check or a substitute check) for forward collection or return.

(d) Identification of reconverting bank

A bank shall identify itself as a reconverting bank on any substitute check for which the bank is a reconverting bank so as to preserve any previous reconverting bank identifications in conformance with generally applicable industry standards.

(e) Applicable law

A substitute check that is the legal equivalent of the original check under subsection (b) of this section shall be subject to any provision, including any provision relating to the protection of customers, of part 229 of title 12 of the Code of Federal Regulations, the Uniform Commercial Code, and any other applicable Federal or State law as if such substitute check were the original check, to the extent such provision of law is not inconsistent with this chapter.

§ 5004. Substitute check warranties

A bank that transfers, presents, or returns a substitute check and receives consideration for the check warrants, as a matter of law, to the transferee, any subsequent collecting or returning bank, the depositary bank, the drawee, the drawer, the payee, the depositor, and any endorser (regardless of whether the warrantee receives the substitute check or another paper or electronic form of the substitute check or original check) that—

(1) the substitute check meets all the requirements for legal equivalence under section 5003(b) of this title; and

(2) no depositary bank, drawee, drawer, or endorser will receive presentment or return of the substitute check, the original check, or a copy or other paper or electronic version of the substitute check or original check such that the bank, drawee, drawer, or endorser will be asked to make a payment based on a check that the bank, drawee, drawer, or endorser has already paid.

§ 5005. Indemnity

(a) Indemnity

A reconverting bank and each bank that subsequently transfers, presents, or returns a substitute check in any electronic or paper form, and receives consideration for such transfer, presentment, or return shall indemnify the transferee, any subsequent collecting or returning bank, the depositary bank, the drawee, the drawer, the payee, the depositor, and any endorser, up to the amount described in subsections (b) and (c) of this section, as applicable, to the extent of any loss incurred by any recipient of a substitute check if that loss occurred due to the receipt of a substitute check instead of the original check.

(b) Indemnity amount

(1) Amount in event of breach of warranty

The amount of the indemnity under subsection (a) of this section shall be the amount of any loss (including costs and reasonable attorney's fees and other expenses of representation) proximately caused by a breach of a warranty provided under section 5004 of this title.

(2) Amount in absence of breach of warranty

In the absence of a breach of a warranty provided under section 5004 of this title, the amount of the indemnity under subsection (a) of this section shall be the sum of—

(A) the amount of any loss, up to the amount of the substitute check; and

(B) interest and expenses (including costs and reasonable attorney's fees and other expenses of representation).

(c) **Comparative negligence**

(1) **In general**

If a loss described in subsection (a) of this section results in whole or in part from the negligence or failure to act in good faith on the part of an indemnified party, then that party's indemnification under this section shall be reduced in proportion to the amount of negligence or bad faith attributable to that party.

(2) **Rule of construction**

Nothing in this subsection reduces the rights of a consumer or any other person under the Uniform Commercial Code or other applicable provision of Federal or State law.

(d) **Effect of producing original check or copy**

(1) **In general**

If the indemnifying bank produces the original check or a copy of the original check (including an image or a substitute check) that accurately represents all of the information on the front and back of the original check (as of the time the original check was truncated) or is otherwise sufficient to determine whether or not a claim is valid, the indemnifying bank shall—

(A) be liable under this section only for losses covered by the indemnity that are incurred up to the time that the original check or copy is provided to the indemnified party; and

(B) have a right to the return of any funds it has paid under the indemnity in excess of those losses.

(2) **Coordination of indemnity with implied warranty**

The production of the original check, a substitute check, or a copy under paragraph (1) by an indemnifying bank shall not absolve the bank from any liability on a warranty established under this chapter or any other provision of law.

(e) **Subrogation of rights**

(1) **In general**

Each indemnifying bank shall be subrogated to the rights of any indemnified party to the extent of the indemnity.

(2) **Recovery under warranty**

A bank that indemnifies a party under this section may attempt to recover from another party based on a warranty or other claim.

(3) **Duty of indemnified party**

Each indemnified party shall have a duty to comply with all reasonable requests for assistance from an indemnifying bank in connection with any claim the indemnifying bank brings against a warrantor or other party related to a check that forms the basis for the indemnification.

§ 5006. Expedited recredit for consumers

(a) **Recredit claims**

(1) **In general**

A consumer may make a claim for expedited recredit from the bank that holds the account of the consumer with respect to a substitute check, if the consumer asserts in good faith that—

(A) the bank charged the consumer's account for a substitute check that was provided to the consumer;

(B) either—

(i) the check was not properly charged to the consumer's account; or

(ii) the consumer has a warranty claim with respect to such substitute check;

(C) the consumer suffered a resulting loss; and

(D) the production of the original check or a better copy of the original check is necessary to determine the validity of any claim described in subparagraph (B).

(2) 40-day period

Any claim under paragraph (1) with respect to a consumer account may be submitted by a consumer before the end of the 40-day period beginning on the later of—

(A) the date on which the financial institution mails or delivers, by a means agreed to by the consumer, the periodic statement of account for such account which contains information concerning the transaction giving rise to the claim; or

(B) the date on which the substitute check is made available to the consumer.

(3) Extension under extenuating circumstances

If the ability of the consumer to submit the claim within the 40-day period under paragraph (2) is delayed due to extenuating circumstances, including extended travel or the illness of the consumer, the 40-day period shall be extended by a reasonable amount of time.

(b) Procedures for claims

(1) In general

To make a claim for an expedited recredit under subsection (a) of this section with respect to a substitute check, the consumer shall provide to the bank that holds the account of such consumer—

(A) a description of the claim, including an explanation of—

(i) why the substitute check was not properly charged to the consumer's account; or

(ii) the warranty claim with respect to such check;

(B) a statement that the consumer suffered a loss and an estimate of the amount of the loss;

(C) the reason why production of the original check or a better copy of the original check is necessary to determine the validity of the charge to the consumer's account or the warranty claim; and

(D) sufficient information to identify the substitute check and to investigate the claim.

(2) Claim in writing

(A) In general

The bank holding the consumer account that is the subject of a claim by the consumer under subsection (a) of this section may, in the discretion of the bank, require the consumer to submit the information required under paragraph (1) in writing.

(B) Means of submission

A bank that requires a submission of information under subparagraph (A) may permit the consumer to make the submission electronically, if the consumer has agreed to communicate with the bank in that manner.

(c) Recredit to consumer

(1) Conditions for recredit

The bank shall recredit a consumer account in accordance with paragraph (2) for the amount of a substitute check that was charged against the consumer account if—

(A) a consumer submits a claim to the bank with respect to that substitute check that meets the requirement of subsection (b) of this section; and

(B) the bank has not—

(i) provided to the consumer—

(I) the original check; or

(II) a copy of the original check (including an image or a substitute check) that accurately represents all of the information on the front and back of the original check, as of the time at which the original check was truncated; and

(ii) demonstrated to the consumer that the substitute check was properly charged to the consumer account.

(2) Timing of recredit

(A) In general

The bank shall recredit the consumer's account for the amount described in paragraph (1) no later than the end of the business day following the business day on which the bank determines the consumer's claim is valid.

(B) Recredit pending investigation

If the bank has not yet determined that the consumer's claim is valid before the end of the 10th business day after the business day on which the consumer submitted the claim, the bank shall recredit the consumer's account for—

(i) the lesser of the amount of the substitute check that was charged against the consumer account, or $2,500, together with interest if the account is an interest-bearing account, no later than the end of such 10th business day; and

(ii) the remaining amount of the substitute check that was charged against the consumer account, if any, together with interest if the account is an interest-bearing account, not later than the 45th calendar day following the business day on which the consumer submits the claim.

(d) Availability of recredit

(1) Next business day availability

Except as provided in paragraph (2), a bank that provides a recredit to a consumer account under subsection (c) of this section shall make the recredited funds available for withdrawal by the consumer by the start of the next business day after the business day on which the bank recredits the consumer's account under subsection (c) of this section.

(2) Safeguard exceptions

A bank may delay availability to a consumer of a recredit provided under subsection (c)(2)(B)(i) of this section until the start of either the business day following the business day on which the bank determines that the consumer's claim is valid or the 45th calendar day following the business day on which the consumer submits a claim for such recredit in accordance with subsection (b) of this section, whichever is earlier, in any of the following circumstances:

(A) New accounts

The claim is made during the 30-day period beginning on the business day the consumer account was established.

(B) Repeated overdrafts

Without regard to the charge that is the subject of the claim for which the recredit was made—

(i) on 6 or more business days during the 6-month period ending on the date on which the consumer submits the claim, the balance in the consumer account was negative or would have become negative if checks or other charges to the account had been paid; or

(ii) on 2 or more business days during such 6-month period, the balance in the consumer account was negative or would have become negative in the amount of $5,000 or more if checks or other charges to the account had been paid.

(C) Prevention of fraud losses

The bank has reasonable cause to believe that the claim is fraudulent, based on facts (other than the fact that the check in question or the consumer is of a particular class) that would cause a well-grounded belief in the mind of a reasonable person that the claim is fraudulent.

(3) Overdraft fees

No bank that, in accordance with paragraph (2), delays the availability of a recredit under subsection (c) of this section to any consumer account may impose any overdraft fees with respect to drafts drawn by the consumer on such recredited amount before the end of the 5-day period beginning on the date notice of the delay in the availability of such amount is sent by the bank to the consumer.

(e) Reversal of recredit

A bank may reverse a recredit to a consumer account if the bank—

(1) determines that a substitute check for which the bank recredited a consumer account under subsection (c) of this section was in fact properly charged to the consumer account; and

(2) notifies the consumer in accordance with subsection (f)(3) of this section.

(f) Notice to consumer

(1) Notice if consumer claim not valid

If a bank determines that a substitute check subject to the consumer's claim was in fact properly charged to the consumer's account, the bank shall send to the consumer, no later than the business day following the business day on which the bank makes a determination—

(A) the original check or a copy of the original check (including an image or a substitute check) that—

(i) accurately represents all of the information on the front and back of the original check (as of the time the original check was truncated); or

(ii) is otherwise sufficient to determine whether or not the consumer's claim is valid; and

(B) an explanation of the basis for the determination by the bank that the substitute check was properly charged, including a statement that the consumer may request copies of any information or documents on which the bank relied in making the determination.

(2) Notice of recredit

If a bank recredits a consumer account under subsection (c) of this section, the bank shall send to the consumer, no later than the business day following the business day on which the bank makes the recredit, a notice of—

(A) the amount of the recredit; and

(B) the date the recredited funds will be available for withdrawal.

(3) Notice of reversal of recredit

In addition to the notice required under paragraph (1), if a bank reverses a recredited amount under subsection (e) of this section, the bank shall send to the consumer, no later than the business day following the business day on which the bank reverses the recredit, a notice of—

(A) the amount of the reversal; and

(B) the date the recredit was reversed.

(4) **Mode of delivery**

A notice described in this subsection shall be delivered by United States mail or by any other means through which the consumer has agreed to receive account information.

(g) **Other claims not affected**

Providing a recredit in accordance with this section shall not absolve the bank from liability for a claim made under any other law, such as a claim for wrongful dishonor under the Uniform Commercial Code, or from liability for additional damages under section 5005 or 5009 of this title.

(h) **Clarification concerning consumer possession**

A consumer who was provided a substitute check may make a claim for an expedited recredit under this section with regard to a transaction involving the substitute check whether or not the consumer is in possession of the substitute check.

(i) **Scope of application**

This section shall only apply to customers who are consumers.

§ 5007. Expedited recredit procedures for banks

(a) **Recredit claims**

(1) **In general**

A bank may make a claim against an indemnifying bank for expedited recredit for which that bank is indemnified if—

(A) the claimant bank (or a bank that the claimant bank has indemnified) has received a claim for expedited recredit from a consumer under section 5006 of this title with respect to a substitute check or would have been subject to such a claim had the consumer's account been charged;

(B) the claimant bank has suffered a resulting loss or is obligated to recredit a consumer account under section 5006 of this title with respect to such substitute check; and

(C) production of the original check, another substitute check, or a better copy of the original check is necessary to determine the validity of the charge to the customer account or any warranty claim connected with such substitute check.

(2) **120-day period**

Any claim under paragraph (1) may be submitted by the claimant bank to an indemnifying bank before the end of the 120-day period beginning on the date of the transaction that gave rise to the claim.

(b) **Procedures for claims**

(1) **In general**

To make a claim under subsection (a) of this section for an expedited recredit relating to a substitute check, the claimant bank shall send to the indemnifying bank—

(A) a description of—

(i) the claim, including an explanation of why the substitute check cannot be properly charged to the consumer account; or

(ii) the warranty claim;

(B) a statement that the claimant bank has suffered a loss or is obligated to recredit the consumer's account under section 5006 of this title, together with an estimate of the amount of the loss or recredit;

(C) the reason why production of the original check, another substitute check, or a better copy of the original check is necessary to determine the validity of the charge to the consumer account or the warranty claim; and

(D) information sufficient for the indemnifying bank to identify the substitute check and to investigate the claim.

(2) Requirements relating to copies of substitute checks

If the information submitted by a claimant bank pursuant to paragraph (1) in connection with a claim for an expedited recredit includes a copy of any substitute check for which any such claim is made, the claimant bank shall take reasonable steps to ensure that any such copy cannot be—

(A) mistaken for the legal equivalent of the check under section 5003(b) of this title; or

(B) sent or handled by any bank, including the indemnifying bank, as a forward collection or returned check.

(3) Claim in writing

(A) In general

An indemnifying bank may, in the discretion of the bank, require the claimant bank to submit the information required by paragraph (1) in writing, including a copy of the written or electronically submitted claim, if any, that the consumer provided in accordance with section 5006(b) of this title.

(B) Means of submission

An indemnifying bank that requires a submission of information under subparagraph (A) may permit the claimant bank to make the submission electronically, if the claimant bank has agreed to communicate with the indemnifying bank in that manner.

(c) Recredit by indemnifying bank

(1) Prompt action required

No later than 10 business days after the business day on which an indemnifying bank receives a claim under subsection (a) of this section from a claimant bank with respect to a substitute check, the indemnifying bank shall—

(A) provide, to the claimant bank, the original check (with respect to such substitute check) or a copy of the original check (including an image or a substitute check) that—

(i) accurately represents all of the information on the front and back of the original check (as of the time the original check was truncated); or

(ii) is otherwise sufficient to determine the bank's claim is not valid; and

(B) recredit the claimant bank for the amount of the claim up to the amount of the substitute check, plus interest if applicable; or

(C) provide information to the claimant bank as to why the indemnifying bank is not obligated to comply with subparagraph (A) or (B).

(2) Recredit does not abrogate other liabilities

Providing a recredit under this subsection to a claimant bank with respect to a substitute check shall not absolve the indemnifying bank from liability for claims brought under any other law or from additional damages under section 5005 or 5009 of this title with respect to such check.

(3) Refund to indemnifying bank

If a claimant bank reverses, in accordance with section 5006(e) of this title, a recredit previously made to a consumer account under section 5006(c) of this title, or otherwise receives a credit or recredit with regard to such substitute check, the claimant bank shall promptly refund to any indemnifying bank any amount previously advanced by the indemnifying bank in connection with such substitute check.

(d) Production of original check or a sufficient copy governed by section 5005(d) of this title

If the indemnifying bank provides the claimant bank with the original check or a copy of the original check (including an image or a substitute check) under subsection (c)(1)(A) of this section, section 5005(d) of this title shall govern any right of the indemnifying bank to any repayment of any funds the indemnifying bank has recredited to the claimant bank pursuant to subsection (c) of this section.

§ 5008. Delays in an emergency

A delay by a bank beyond the time limits prescribed or permitted by this chapter shall be excused if the delay is caused by interruption of communication or computer facilities, suspension of payments by another bank, war, emergency conditions, failure of equipment, or other circumstances beyond the control of a bank and if the bank uses such diligence as the circumstances require.

§ 5009. Measure of damages

(a) Liability

(1) In general

Except as provided in section 5005 of this title, any person who, in connection with a substitute check, breaches any warranty under this chapter or fails to comply with any requirement imposed by, or regulation prescribed pursuant to, this chapter with respect to any other person shall be liable to such person in an amount equal to the sum of—

(A) the lesser of—

(i) the amount of the loss suffered by the other person as a result of the breach or failure; or

(ii) the amount of the substitute check; and

(B) interest and expenses (including costs and reasonable attorney's fees and other expenses of representation) related to the substitute check.

(2) Offset of recredits

The amount of damages any person receives under paragraph (1), if any, shall be reduced by the amount, if any, that the claimant receives and retains as a recredit under section 5006 or 5007 of this title.

(b) Comparative negligence

(1) In general

If a person incurs damages that resulted in whole or in part from the negligence or failure of that person to act in good faith, then the amount of any liability due to that person under subsection (a) of this section shall be reduced in proportion to the amount of negligence or bad faith attributable to that person.

(2) Rule of construction

Nothing in this subsection reduces the rights of a consumer or any other person under the Uniform Commercial Code or other applicable provision of Federal or State law.

§ 5010. Statute of limitations and notice of claim

(a) Actions under this chapter

(1) In general

An action to enforce a claim under this chapter may be brought in any United States district court, or in any other court of competent jurisdiction, before the end of the 1-year period beginning on the date the cause of action accrues.

(2) Accrual

A cause of action accrues as of the date the injured party first learns, or by which such person reasonably should have learned, of the facts and circumstances giving rise to the cause of action.

(b) Discharge of claims

Except as provided in subsection (c) of this section, unless a person gives notice of a claim to the indemnifying or warranting bank within 30 days after the person has reason to know of the claim and the identity of the indemnifying or warranting bank, the indemnifying or warranting bank is discharged from liability in an action to enforce a claim under this chapter to the extent of any loss caused by the delay in giving notice of the claim.

(c) Notice of claim by consumer

A timely claim by a consumer under section 5006 of this title for expedited recredit constitutes timely notice of a claim by the consumer for purposes of subsection (b) of this section.

§ 5011. Consumer awareness

(a) In general

Each bank shall provide, in accordance with subsection (b) of this section, a brief notice about substitute checks that describes—

(1) how a substitute check is the legal equivalent of an original check for all purposes, including any provision of any Federal or State law, and for all persons, if the substitute check—

(A) accurately represents all of the information on the front and back of the original check as of the time at which the original check was truncated; and

(B) bears the legend: "This is a legal copy of your check. You can use it in the same way you would use the original check."; and

(2) the consumer recredit rights established under section 5006 of this title when a consumer believes in good faith that a substitute check was not properly charged to the account of the consumer.

(b) Distribution

(1) Existing customers

With respect to consumers who are customers of a bank on the effective date of this chapter and who receive original checks or substitute checks, a bank shall provide the notice described in subsection (a) of this section to each such consumer no later than the first regularly scheduled communication with the consumer after the effective date of this chapter.

(2) New account holders

A bank shall provide the notice described in subsection (a) of this section to each consumer who will receive original checks or substitute checks, other than existing customers referred to in paragraph (1), at the time at which the customer relationship is initiated.

(3) Mode of delivery

A bank may send the notices required by this subsection by United States mail or by any other means through which the consumer has agreed to receive account information.

(4) Consumers who request copies of checks

Notice shall be provided to each consumer of the bank that requests a copy of a check and receives a substitute check, at the time of the request.

(c) Model language

(1) In general

Before the end of the 9-month period beginning on October 28, 2003, the Board shall publish model forms and clauses that a bank may use to describe each of the elements required by subsection (a) of this section.

(2) Safe harbor

(A) In general

A bank shall be treated as being in compliance with the requirements of subsection (a) of this section if the bank's substitute check notice uses a model form or clause published by the Board and such model form or clause accurately describes the bank's policies and practices.

(B) Deletion or rearrangement

A bank may delete any information in the model form or clause that is not required by this chapter or rearrange the format.

(3) Use of model language not required

This section shall not be construed as requiring any bank to use a model form or clause that the Board prepares under this subsection.

§ 5012. Effect on other law

This chapter shall supersede any provision of Federal or State law, including the Uniform Commercial Code, that is inconsistent with this chapter, but only to the extent of the inconsistency.

§ 5013. Variation by agreement

(a) Section 5007 of this title.

Any provision of section 5007 of this title may be varied by agreement of the banks involved.

(b) No other provisions may be varied

Except as provided in subsection (a) of this section, no provision of this chapter may be varied by agreement of any person or persons.

§ 5014. Regulations

The Board may prescribe such regulations as the Board determines to be necessary to implement, prevent circumvention or evasion of, or facilitate compliance with the provisions of this chapter.

§ 5015. Study and report on funds availability

(a) Study

In order to evaluate the implementation and the impact of this chapter, the Board shall conduct a study of—

(1) the percentage of total checks cleared in which the paper check is not returned to the paying bank;

(2) the extent to which banks make funds available to consumers for local and nonlocal checks prior to the expiration of maximum hold periods;

(3) the length of time within which depositary banks learn of the nonpayment of local and nonlocal checks;

(4) the increase or decrease in check-related losses over the study period; and

(5) the appropriateness of the time periods and amount limits applicable under sections 4002 and 4003 of this title, as in effect on October 28, 2003.

(b) Report to Congress

Before the end of the 30-month period beginning on the effective date of this chapter, the Board shall submit a report to the Congress containing the results of the study conducted under this section, together with recommendations for legislative action.

§ 5016. Statistical reporting of costs and revenues for transporting checks between reserve banks

In the annual report prepared by the Board for the first full calendar year after October 28, 2003 and in each of the 9 subsequent annual reports by the Board, the Board shall include the amount of operating costs attributable to, and an estimate of the Federal Reserve banks' imputed revenues derived from, the transportation of commercial checks between Federal Reserve bank check processing centers.

§ 5017. Evaluation and report by the comptroller general

(a) Study

During the 5-year period beginning on October 28, 2003, the Comptroller General of the United States shall evaluate the implementation and administration of this chapter, including—

(1) an estimate of the gains in economic efficiency made possible from check truncation;

(2) an evaluation of the benefits accruing to consumers and financial institutions from reduced transportation costs, longer hours for accepting deposits for credit within 1 business day, the impact of fraud losses, and an estimate of consumers' share of the total benefits derived from this chapter; and

(3) an assessment of consumer acceptance of the check truncation process resulting from this chapter, as well as any new costs incurred by consumers who had their original checks returned with their regular monthly statements prior to October 28, 2003.

(b) Report to Congress

Before the end of the 5-year period referred to in subsection (a) of this section, the Comptroller General shall submit a report to the Congress containing the findings and conclusions of the Comptroller General in connection with the evaluation conducted pursuant to subsection (a) of this section, together with such recommendations for legislative and administrative action as the Comptroller General may determine to be appropriate.

§ 5018. Depositary services efficiency and cost reduction

(a) Findings

The Congress finds as follows:

(1) The Secretary of the Treasury has long compensated financial institutions for various critical depositary and financial agency services provided for or on behalf of the United States by—

(A) placing large balances, commonly referred to as "compensating balances", on deposit at such institutions; and

(B) using imputed interest on such funds to offset charges for the various depositary and financial agency services provided to or on behalf of the Government.

(2) As a result of sharp declines in interest rates over the last few years to record low levels, or the public debt outstanding reaching the statutory debt limit, the Department of the Treasury often has had to dramatically increase or decrease the size of the compensating balances on deposit at these financial institutions.

(3) The fluctuation of the compensating balances, and the necessary pledging of collateral by financial institutions to secure the value of compensating balances placed with those institutions, have created unintended financial uncertainty for the Secretary of the Treasury and for the management by financial institutions of their cash and securities.

(4) It is imperative that the process for providing financial services to the Government be transparent, and provide the information necessary for the Congress to effectively exercise its appropriation and oversight responsibilities.

(5) The use of direct payment for services rendered would strengthen cash and debt management responsibilities of the Secretary of the Treasury because the Secretary would no longer need to dramatically increase or decrease the level of such balances when interest rates fluctuate sharply or when the public debt outstanding reaches the statutory debt limit.

(6) An alternative to the use of compensating balances, such as direct payments to financial institutions, would ensure that payments to financial institutions for the services they provide would be made in a more predictable manner and could result in cost savings.

(7) Limiting the use of compensating balances could result in a more direct and cost-efficient method of obtaining those services currently provided under compensating balance arrangements.

(8) A transition from the use of compensating balances to another compensation method must be carefully managed to prevent higher-than-necessary transitional costs and enable participating financial institutions to modify their planned investment of cash and securities.

(b) Authorization of appropriations for services rendered by depositaries and financial agencies of the United States

There are authorized to be appropriated for fiscal years beginning after fiscal year 2003 to the Secretary of the Treasury such sums as may be necessary for reimbursing financial institutions in their capacity as depositaries and financial agents of the United States for all services required or directed by the Secretary of the Treasury, or a designee of the Secretary, to be performed by such financial institutions on behalf of the Secretary of the Treasury or another Federal agency, including services rendered before fiscal year 2004.

(c) Orderly transition

(1) In general

As appropriations authorized in subsection (b) of this section become available, the Secretary of the Treasury shall promptly begin the process of phasing in the use of the appropriations to pay financial institutions serving as depositaries and financial agents of the United States, and transitioning from the use of compensating balances to fund these services.

(2) Post-transition use limited to extraordinary circumstances

(A) In general

Following the transition to the use of the appropriations authorized in subsection (b) of this section, the Secretary of the Treasury may use the compensating balances to pay financial institutions serving as depositaries and financial agents of the United States only in extraordinary situations where the Secretary determines that they are needed to ensure the fiscal operations of the Government continue to function in an efficient and effective manner.

(B) Report

Any use of compensating balances pursuant to subparagraph (A) shall promptly be reported by the Secretary of the Treasury to the Committee on Financial Services of the House of Representatives and the Committee on Banking, Housing, and Urban Affairs of the Senate.

(3) Requirements for orderly transition

In transitioning to the use of the appropriations authorized in subsection (b) of this section, the Secretary of the Treasury shall take such steps as may be appropriate to—

(A) prevent abrupt financial disruption to the functions of the Department of the Treasury or to the participating financial institutions; and

(B) maintain adequate accounting and management controls to ensure that payments to financial institutions for their banking services provided to the Government as depositaries and financial agents are accurate and that the arrangements last no longer than is necessary.

(4) Reports required

(A) Annual report

(i) In general

For each fiscal year, the Secretary of the Treasury shall submit a report to the Congress on the use of compensating balances and on the use of appropriations authorized in subsection (b) of this section during that fiscal year.

(ii) Inclusion in budget

The report required under clause (i) may be submitted as part of the budget submitted by the President under section 1105 of Title 31 for the following fiscal year and if so, the report shall be submitted concurrently to the Committee on Financial Services of the House of Representatives and the Committee on Banking, Housing, and Urban Affairs of the Senate.

(B) Final report following transition

(i) In general

Following completion of the transition from the use of compensating balances to the use of the appropriations authorized in subsection (b) of this section to pay financial institutions for their services as depositaries and financial agents of the United States, the Secretary of the Treasury shall submit a report on the transition to the Committee on Financial Services of the House of Representatives and the Committee on Banking, Housing, and Urban Affairs of the Senate.

(ii) Contents of report

The report submitted under clause (i) shall include a detailed analysis of—

(I) the cost of transition;

(II) the direct costs of the services being paid from the appropriations authorized in subsection (b) of this section; and

(III) the benefits realized from the use of direct payment for such services, rather than the use of compensating balance arrangements.

(d) Omitted

(e) Effective date

Notwithstanding section 20, this section shall take effect on October 28, 2003.

(Pub.L. 108–100, § 4, Oct. 28, 2003, 117 Stat. 1180.)

EXPEDITED FUNDS AVAILABILITY ACT

12 U.S.C. §§ 4001–4010

Current through March 12, 2019; P.L. 116–9

For updates, see http://uscode.house.gov

§ 4001. Definitions

For purposes of this chapter—

(1) Account

The term "account" means a demand deposit account or other similar transaction account at a depository institution.

(2) Board

The term "Board" means the Board of Governors of the Federal Reserve System.

(3) Business day

The term "business day" means any day other than a Saturday, Sunday, or legal holiday.

(4) Cash

The term "cash" means United States coins and currency, including Federal Reserve notes.

(5) Cashier's check

The term "cashier's check" means any check which—

(A) is drawn on a depository institution;

(B) is signed by an officer or employee of such depository institution; and

(C) is a direct obligation of such depository institution.

(6) Certified check

The term "certified check" means any check with respect to which a depository institution certifies that—

(A) the signature on the check is genuine; and

(B) such depository institution has set aside funds which—

(i) are equal to the amount of the check; and

(ii) will be used only to pay such check.

(7) Check

The term "check" means any negotiable demand draft drawn on or payable through an office of a depository institution located in the United States. Such term does not include noncash items.

(8) Check clearinghouse association

The term "check clearinghouse association" means any arrangement by which participant depository institutions exchange deposited checks on a local basis, including an entire metropolitan area, without using the check processing facilities of the Federal Reserve System.

(9) Check processing region

The term "check processing region" means the geographical area served by a Federal Reserve bank check processing center or such larger area as the Board may prescribe by regulations.

(10) Consumer account

The term "consumer account" means any account used primarily for personal, family, or household purposes.

(11) Depository check

The term "depository check" means any cashier's check, certified check, teller's check, and any other functionally equivalent instrument as determined by the Board.

(12) Depository institution

The term "depository institution" has the meaning given such term in clauses (i) through (vi) of section 461(b)(1)(A) of this title. Such term also includes an office, branch, or agency of a foreign bank located in the United States.

(13) Local originating depository institution

The term "local originating depository institution" means any originating depository institution which is located in the same check processing region as the receiving depository institution.

(14) Noncash item

The term "noncash item" means—

(A) a check or other demand item to which a passbook, certificate, or other document is attached;

(B) a check or other demand item which is accompanied by special instructions, such as a request for special advise of payment or dishonor; or

(C) any similar item which is otherwise classified as a noncash item in regulations of the Board.

(15) Nonlocal originating depository institution

The term "nonlocal originating depository institution" means any originating depository institution which is not a local depository institution.

(16) Proprietary ATM

The term "proprietary ATM" means an automated teller machine which is—

(A) located—

(i) at or adjacent to a branch of the receiving depository institution; or

(ii) in close proximity, as defined by the Board, to a branch of the receiving depository institution; or

(B) owned by, operated exclusively for, or operated by the receiving depository institution.

(17) Originating depository institution

The term "originating depository institution" means the branch of a depository institution on which a check is drawn.

(18) Nonproprietary ATM

The term "nonproprietary ATM" means an automated teller machine which is not a proprietary ATM.

(19) Participant

The term "participant" means a depository institution which—

(A) is located in the same geographic area as that served by a check clearinghouse association; and

(B) exchanges checks through the check clearinghouse association, either directly or through an intermediary.

(20) Receiving depository institution

The term "receiving depository institution" means the branch of a depository institution or the proprietary ATM, located in the United States, in which a check is first deposited.

(21) State

The term "State" means any State, the District of Columbia, the Commonwealth of Puerto Rico, American Samoa, the Commonwealth of the Northern Mariana Islands, Guam, or the Virgin Islands.

(22) Teller's check

The term "teller's check" means any check issued by a depository institution and drawn on another depository institution.

(23) United States

The term "United States" means the several States, the District of Columbia, the Commonwealth of Puerto Rico, American Samoa, the Commonwealth of the Northern Mariana Islands, Guam, and the Virgin Islands.

(24) Unit of general local government

The term "unit of general local government" means any city, county, town, township, parish, village, or other general purpose political subdivision of a State.

(25) Wire transfer

The term "wire transfer" has such meaning as the Board shall prescribe by regulations.

(Pub.L. 100–86, Title VI, § 602, Aug. 10, 1987, 101 Stat. 635; Pub.L. 115–174, Title II, § 208(a)(1), May 24, 2018, 132 Stat. 1312.)

§ 4002. Expedited funds availability schedules

(a) Next business day availability for certain deposits

(1) Cash deposits; wire transfers

Except as provided in subsection (e) of this section and in section 4003 of this title, in any case in which—

(A) any cash is deposited in an account at a receiving depository institution staffed by individuals employed by such institution, or

(B) funds are received by a depository institution by wire transfer for deposit in an account at such institution,

such cash or funds shall be available for withdrawal not later than the business day after the business day on which such cash is deposited or such funds are received for deposit.

(2) **Government checks; certain other checks**

Funds deposited in an account at a depository institution by check shall be available for withdrawal not later than the business day after the business day on which such funds are deposited in the case of—

(A) a check which—

(i) is drawn on the Treasury of the United States; and

(ii) is endorsed only by the person to whom it was issued;

(B) a check which—

(i) is drawn by a State;

(ii) is deposited in a receiving depository institution which is located in such State and is staffed by individuals employed by such institution;

(iii) is deposited with a special deposit slip which indicates it is a check drawn by a State; and

(iv) is endorsed only by the person to whom it was issued;

(C) a check which—

(i) is drawn by a unit of general local government;

(ii) is deposited in a receiving depository institution which is located in the same State as such unit of general local government and is staffed by individuals employed by such institution;

(iii) is deposited with a special deposit slip which indicates it is a check drawn by a unit of general local government; and

(iv) is endorsed only by the person to whom it was issued;

(D) the first $200 deposited by check or checks on any one business day;

(E) a check deposited in a branch of a depository institution and drawn on the same or another branch of the same depository institution if both such branches are located in the same State or the same check processing region;

(F) a cashier's check, certified check, teller's check, or depository check which—

(i) is deposited in a receiving depository institution which is staffed by individuals employed by such institution;

(ii) is deposited with a special deposit slip which indicates it is a cashier's check, certified check, teller's check, or depository check, as the case may be; and

(iii) is endorsed only by the person to whom it was issued.

(b) **Permanent schedule**

(1) **Availability of funds deposited by local checks**

Subject to paragraph (3) of this subsection, subsections (a)(2), (d), and (e) of this section, and section 4003 of this title, not more than 1 business day shall intervene between the business day on which funds are deposited in an account at a depository institution by a check drawn on a local originating depository institution and the business day on which the funds involved are available for withdrawal.

(2) **Availability of funds deposited by nonlocal checks**

Subject to paragraph (3) of this subsection, subsections (a)(2), (d), and (e) of this section, and section 4003 of this title, not more than 4 business days shall intervene between the business day on which funds are deposited in an account at a depository institution by a check drawn on a nonlocal originating depository institution and the business day on which such funds are available for withdrawal.

(3) Time period adjustments for cash withdrawal of certain checks

(A) In general

Except as provided in subparagraph (B), funds deposited in an account in a depository institution by check (other than a check described in subsection (a)(2) of this section) shall be available for cash withdrawal not later than the business day after the business day on which such funds otherwise are available under paragraph (1) or (2).

(B) 5 p.m. cash availability

Not more than $400 (or the maximum amount allowable in the case of a withdrawal from an automated teller machine but not more than $400) of funds deposited by one or more checks to which this paragraph applies shall be available for cash withdrawal not later than 5 o'clock post meridian of the business day on which such funds are available under paragraph (1) or (2). If funds deposited by checks described in both paragraph (1) and paragraph (2) become available for cash withdrawal under this paragraph on the same business day, the limitation contained in this subparagraph shall apply to the aggregate amount of such funds.

(C) $200 availability

Any amount available for withdrawal under this paragraph shall be in addition to the amount available under subsection (a)(2)(D) of this section.

(4) Applicability

This subsection shall apply with respect to funds deposited by check in an account at a depository institution on or after September 1, 1990, except that the Board may, by regulation, make this subsection or any part of this subsection applicable earlier than September 1, 1990.

(c) Temporary schedule

(1) Availability of local checks

(A) In general

Subject to subparagraph (B) of this paragraph, subsections (a)(2), (d), and (e) of this section, and section 4003 of this title, not more than 2 business days shall intervene between the business day on which funds are deposited in an account at a depository institution by a check drawn on a local originating depository institution and the business day on which such funds are available for withdrawal.

(B) Time period adjustment for cash withdrawal of certain checks

(i) In general

Except as provided in clause (ii), funds deposited in an account in a depository institution by check drawn on a local depository institution that is not a participant in the same check clearinghouse association as the receiving depository institution (other than a check described in subsection (a)(2) of this section) shall be available for cash withdrawal not later than the business day after the business day on which such funds otherwise are available under subparagraph (A).

(ii) 5 p.m. cash availability

Not more than $400 (or the maximum amount allowable in the case of a withdrawal from an automated teller machine but not more than $400) of funds deposited by one or more checks to which this subparagraph applies shall be available for cash withdrawal not later than 5 o'clock post meridian of the business day on which such funds are available under subparagraph (A).

(iii) $100 availability

Any amount available for withdrawal under this subparagraph shall be in addition to the amount available under subsection (a)(2)(D) of this section.

(2) Availability of nonlocal checks

Subject to subsections (a)(2), (d), and (e) of this section and section 4003 of this title, not more than 6 business days shall intervene between the business day on which funds are deposited in an account at a depository institution by a check drawn on a nonlocal originating depository institution and the business day on which such funds are available for withdrawal.

(3) Applicability

This subsection shall apply with respect to funds deposited by check in an account at a depository institution after August 31, 1988, and before September 1, 1990, except as may be otherwise provided under subsection (b)(4) of this section.

(d) Time period adjustments

(1) Reduction generally

Notwithstanding any other provision of law, the Board, jointly with the Director of the Bureau of Consumer Financial Protection, shall, by regulation, reduce the time periods established under subsections (b), (c), and (e) of this section to as short a time as possible and equal to the period of time achievable under the improved check clearing system for a receiving depository institution to reasonably expect to learn of the nonpayment of most items for each category of checks.

(2) Extension for certain deposits in noncontiguous States or territories

Notwithstanding any other provision of law, any time period established under subsection (b), (c), or (e) of this section shall be extended by 1 business day in the case of any deposit which is both—

(A) deposited in an account at a depository institution which is located in Alaska, Hawaii, Puerto Rico, American Samoa, the Commonwealth of the Northern Mariana Islands, Guam, or the Virgin Islands; and

(B) deposited by a check drawn on an originating depository institution which is not located in the same State, commonwealth, or territory as the receiving depository institution.

(e) Deposits at ATM

(1) Nonproprietary ATM

(A) In general

Not more than 4 business days shall intervene between the business day a deposit described in subparagraph (B) is made at a nonproprietary automated teller machine (for deposit in an account at a depository institution) and the business day on which funds from such deposit are available for withdrawal.

(B) Deposits described in this paragraph[1]

A deposit is described in this subparagraph if it is—

(i) a cash deposit;

(ii) a deposit made by a check described in subsection (a)(2) of this section;

(iii) a deposit made by a check drawn on a local originating depository institution (other than a check described in subsection (a)(2) of this section); or

(iv) a deposit made by a check drawn on a nonlocal originating depository institution (other than a check described in subsection (a)(2) of this section).

[1] So in original. Probably should be "subparagraph".

(2) Proprietary ATM—temporary and permanent schedules

The provisions of subsections (a), (b), and (c) of this section shall apply with respect to any funds deposited at a proprietary automated teller machine for deposit in an account at a depository institution.

(3) Study and report on ATM's

The Board shall, either directly or through the Consumer Advisory Council, establish and maintain a dialogue with depository institutions and their suppliers on the computer software and hardware available for use by automated teller machines, and shall, not later than September 1 of each of the first 3 calendar years beginning after August 10, 1987, report to the Congress regarding such software and hardware and regarding the potential for improving the processing of automated teller machine deposits.

(f) Check return; notice of nonpayment

No provision of this section shall be construed as requiring that, with respect to all checks deposited in a receiving depository institution—

(1) such checks be physically returned to such depository institution; or

(2) any notice of nonpayment of any such check be given to such depository institution within the times set forth in subsection (a), (b), (c), or (e) of this section or in the regulations issued under any such subsection.

(Pub.L. 100–86, Title VI, § 603, Aug. 10, 1987, 101 Stat. 637; Pub.L. 101–625, Title X, § 1001, Nov. 28, 1990, 104 Stat. 4424; Pub.L. 102–242, Title II, § 227(a), (b)(1), Dec. 19, 1991, 105 Stat. 2307, 2308; Pub.L. 111–203, Title X, § 1086, July 21, 2010, 124 Stat. 2085, 2086; Pub.L. 115–174, Title II, § 208(a)(2), May 24, 2018, 132 Stat. 1312.)

§ 4003. Safeguard exceptions

(a) New accounts

Notwithstanding section 4002 of this title, in the case of any account established at a depository institution by a new depositor, the following provisions shall apply with respect to any deposit in such account during the 30-day period (or such shorter period as the Board, jointly with the Director of the Bureau of Consumer Financial Protection, may establish) beginning on the date such account is established—

(1) Next business day availability of cash and certain items

Except as provided in paragraph (3), in the case of—

(A) any cash deposited in such account;

(B) any funds received by such depository institution by wire transfer for deposit in such account;

(C) any funds deposited in such account by cashier's check, certified check, teller's check, depository check, or traveler's check; and

(D) any funds deposited by a government check which is described in subparagraph (A), (B), or (C) of section 4002(a)(2) of this title,

such cash or funds shall be available for withdrawal on the business day after the business day on which such cash or funds are deposited or, in the case of a wire transfer, on the business day after the business day on which such funds are received for deposit.

(2) Availability of other items

In the case of any funds deposited in such account by a check (other than a check described in subparagraph (C) or (D) of paragraph (1)), the availability for withdrawal of such funds shall not be subject to the provisions of section 4002(b), 4002(c), or paragraphs[1] (1) of section 4002(e) of this title.

---

[1] So in original. Probably should be "paragraph".

(3) Limitation relating to certain checks in excess of $5,000

In the case of funds deposited in such account during such period by checks described in subparagraph (C) or (D) of paragraph (1) the aggregate amount of which exceeds $5,000—

(A) paragraph (1) shall apply only with respect to the first $5,000 of such aggregate amount; and

(B) not more than 8 business days shall intervene between the business day on which any such funds are deposited and the business day on which such excess amount shall be available for withdrawal.

(b) Large or redeposited checks; repeated overdrafts

The Board, jointly with the Director of the Bureau of Consumer Financial Protection, may, by regulation, establish reasonable exceptions to any time limitation established under subsection (a)(2), (b), (c), or (e) of section 4002 of this title for—

(1) the amount of deposits by one or more checks that exceeds the amount of $5,000 in any one day;

(2) checks that have been returned unpaid and redeposited; and

(3) deposit accounts which have been overdrawn repeatedly.

(c) Reasonable cause exception

(1) In general

In accordance with regulations which the Board, jointly with the Director of the Bureau of Consumer Financial Protection, shall prescribe, subsections (a)(2), (b), (c), and (e) of section 4002 of this title shall not apply with respect to any check deposited in an account at a depository institution if the receiving depository institution has reasonable cause to believe that the check is uncollectible from the originating depository institution. For purposes of the preceding sentence, reasonable cause to believe requires the existence of facts which would cause a well-grounded belief in the mind of a reasonable person. Such reasons shall be included in the notice required under subsection (f) of this section.

(2) Basis for determination

No determination under this subsection may be based on any class of checks or persons.

(3) Overdraft fees

If the receiving depository institution determines that a check deposited in an account is a check described in paragraph (1), the receiving depository institution shall not assess any fee for any subsequent overdraft with respect to such account, if—

(A) the depositor was not provided with the written notice required under subsection (f) of this section (with respect to such determination) at the time the deposit was made;

(B) the overdraft would not have occurred but for the fact that the funds so deposited are not available; and

(C) the amount of the check is collected from the originating depository institution.

(4) Compliance

Each agency referred to in section 4009(a) of this title shall monitor compliance with the requirements of this subsection in each regular examination of a depository institution and shall describe in each report to the Congress the extent to which this subsection is being complied with. For the purpose of this paragraph, each depository institution shall retain a record of each notice provided under subsection (f) of this section as a result of the application of this subsection.

(d) Emergency conditions

Subject to such regulations as the Board, jointly with the Director of the Bureau of Consumer Financial Protection, may prescribe, subsections (a)(2), (b), (c), and (e) of section 4002 of this title shall not apply to funds deposited by check in any receiving depository institution in the case of—

(1) any interruption of communication facilities;

(2) suspension of payments by another depository institution;

(3) any war; or

(4) any emergency condition beyond the control of the receiving depository institution,

if the receiving depository institution exercises such diligence as the circumstances require.

(e) Prevention of fraud losses

(1) In general

The Board, jointly with the Director of the Bureau of Consumer Financial Protection, may, by regulation or order, suspend the applicability of this chapter, or any portion thereof, to any classification of checks if the Board, jointly with the Director of the Bureau of Consumer Financial Protection, determines that—

(A) depository institutions are experiencing an unacceptable level of losses due to check-related fraud, and

(B) suspension of this chapter, or such portion of this chapter, with regard to the classification of checks involved in such fraud is necessary to diminish the volume of such fraud.

(2) Sunset provision

No regulation prescribed or order issued under paragraph (1) shall remain in effect for more than 45 days (excluding Saturdays, Sundays, legal holidays, or any day either House of Congress is not in session).

(3) Report to Congress

(A) Notice of each suspension

Within 10 days of prescribing any regulation or issuing any order under paragraph (1), the Board, jointly with the Director of the Bureau of Consumer Financial Protection, shall transmit a report of such action to the Committee on Banking, Finance and Urban Affairs of the House of Representatives and the Committee on Banking, Housing, and Urban Affairs of the Senate.

(B) Contents of report

Each report under subparagraph (A) shall contain—

(i) the specific reason for prescribing the regulation or issuing the order;

(ii) evidence considered by the Board in making the determination under paragraph (1) with respect to such regulation or order; and

(iii) specific examples of the check-related fraud giving rise to such regulation or order.

(f) Notice of exception; availability within reasonable time

(1) In general

If any exception contained in this section (other than subsection (a) of this section) applies with respect to funds deposited in an account at a depository institution—

(A) the depository institution shall provide notice in the manner provided in paragraph (2) of—

(i) the time period within which the funds shall be made available for withdrawal; and

(ii) the reason the exception was invoked; and

(B) except where other time periods are specifically provided in this chapter, the availability of the funds deposited shall be governed by the policy of the receiving depository institution, but shall not exceed a reasonable period of time as determined by the Board, jointly with the Director of the Bureau of Consumer Financial Protection.

(2) Time for notice

The notice required under paragraph (1)(A) with respect to a deposit to which an exception contained in this section applies shall be made by the time provided in the following subparagraphs:

(A) In the case of a deposit made in person by the depositor at the receiving depository institution, the depository institution shall immediately provide such notice in writing to the depositor.

(B) In the case of any other deposit (other than a deposit described in subparagraph (C)), the receiving depository institution shall mail the notice to the depositor not later than the close of the next business day following the business day on which the deposit is received.

(C) In the case of a deposit to which subsection (d) or (e) of this section applies, notice shall be provided by the depository institution in accordance with regulations of the Board, jointly with the Director of the Bureau of Consumer Financial Protection.

(D) In the case of a deposit to which subsection (b)(1) or (b)(2) of this section applies, the depository institution may, for nonconsumer accounts and other classes of accounts, as defined by the Board, that generally have a large number of such deposits, provide notice at or before the time it first determines that the subsection applies.

(E) In the case of a deposit to which subsection (b)(3) of this section applies, the depository institution may, subject to regulations of the Board, provide notice at the beginning of each time period it determines that the subsection applies. In addition to the requirements contained in paragraph (1)(A), the notice shall specify the time period for which the exception will apply.

(3) Subsequent determinations

If the facts upon which the determination of the applicability of an exception contained in subsection (b) or (c) of this section to any deposit only become known to the receiving depository institution after the time notice is required under paragraph (2) with respect to such deposit, the depository institution shall mail such notice to the depositor as soon as practicable, but not later than the first business day following the day such facts become known to the depository institution.

(Pub.L. 100–86, Title VI, § 604, Aug. 10, 1987, 101 Stat. 637; Pub.L. 102–242, Title II, § 225, 227(b)(2), Dec. 19, 1991, 105 Stat. 2307, 2308; Pub.L. 111–203, Title X, § 1086(b), July 21, 2010, 124 Stat. 2085.)

§ 4004. Disclosure of funds availability policies

(a) Notice for new accounts

Before an account is opened at a depository institution, the depository institution shall provide written notice to the potential customer of the specific policy of such depository institution with respect to when a customer may withdraw funds deposited into the customer's account.

(b) Preprinted deposit slips

All preprinted deposit slips that a depository institution furnishes to its customers shall contain a summary notice, as prescribed by the Board, jointly with the Director of the Bureau of Consumer Financial Protection, in regulations, that deposited items may not be available for immediate withdrawal.

(c) Mailing of notice

(1) First mailing after enactment

In the first regularly scheduled mailing to customers occurring after September 1, 1988, but not more than 60 days after September 1, 1988, each depository institution shall send a written notice containing the specific policy of such depository institution with respect to when a customer may withdraw funds deposited into such customer's account, unless the depository institution has provided a disclosure which meets the requirements of this section before September 1, 1988.

(2) Subsequent changes

A depository institution shall send a written notice to customers at least 30 days before implementing any change to the depository institution's policy with respect to when customers may withdraw funds deposited into consumer accounts, except that any change which expedites the availability of such funds shall be disclosed not later than 30 days after implementation.

(3) Upon request

Upon the request of any person, a depository institution shall provide or send such person a written notice containing the specific policy of such depository institution with respect to when a customer may withdraw funds deposited into a customer's account.

(d) Posting of notice

(1) Specific notice at manned teller stations

Each depository institution shall post, in a conspicuous place in each location where deposits are accepted by individuals employed by such depository institution, a specific notice which describes the time periods applicable to the availability of funds deposited in a consumer account.

(2) General notice at automated teller machines

In the case of any automated teller machine at which any funds are received for deposit in an account at any depository institution, the Board, jointly with the Director of the Bureau of Consumer Financial Protection, shall prescribe, by regulations, that the owner or operator of such automated teller machine shall post or provide a general notice that funds deposited in such machine may not be immediately available for withdrawal.

(e) Notice of interest payment policy

If a depository institution described in section 4005(b) of this title begins the accrual of interest or dividends at a later date than the date described in section 4005(a) of this title with respect to all funds, including cash, deposited in an interest-bearing account at such depository institution, any notice required to be provided under subsections (a) and (c) of this section shall contain a written description of the time at which such depository institution begins to accrue interest or dividends on such funds.

(f) Model disclosure forms

(1) Prepared by Board and Bureau

The Board, jointly with the Director of the Bureau of Consumer Financial Protection, shall publish model disclosure forms and clauses for common transactions to facilitate compliance with the disclosure requirements of this section and to aid customers by utilizing readily understandable language.

(2) Use of forms to achieve compliance

A depository institution shall be deemed to be in compliance with the requirements of this section if such institution—

(A) uses any appropriate model form or clause as published by the Board, jointly with the Director of the Bureau of Consumer Financial Protection,,[1] or

(B) uses any such model form or clause and changes such form or clause by—

(i) deleting any information which is not required by this chapter; or

(ii) rearranging the format.

[1] So in original.

(3) Voluntary use

Nothing in this chapter requires the use of any such model form or clause prescribed by the Board, jointly with the Director of the Bureau of Consumer Financial Protection, under this subsection.

(4) Notice and comment

Model disclosure forms and clauses shall be adopted by the Board, jointly with the Director of the Bureau of Consumer Financial Protection, only after notice duly given in the Federal Register and an opportunity for public comment in accordance with section 553 of Title 5.

(Pub.L. 100–86, Title VI, § 605, Aug. 10, 1987, 101 Stat. 644; Pub.L. 111–203, Title X, § 1086(c), July 21, 2010, 124 Stat. 2086.)

§ 4005. Payment of interest

(a) In general

Except as provided in subsection (b) or (c) of this section and notwithstanding any other provision of law, interest shall accrue on funds deposited in an interest-bearing account at a depository institution beginning not later than the business day on which the depository institution receives provisional credit for such funds.

(b) Special rule for credit unions

Subsection (a) of this section shall not apply to an account at a depository institution described in section 461(b)(1)(A)(iv) of this title if the depository institution—

(1) begins the accrual of interest or dividends at a later date than the date described in subsection (a) of this section with respect to all funds, including cash, deposited in such account; and

(2) provides notice of the interest payment policy in the manner required under section 4004(e) of this title.

(c) Exception for checks returned unpaid

No provision of this chapter shall be construed as requiring the payment of interest or dividends on funds deposited by a check which is returned unpaid.

(Pub.L. 100–86, Title VI, § 606, Aug. 10, 1987, 101 Stat. 646.)

§ 4006. Miscellaneous provisions

(a) After-hours deposits

For purposes of this chapter, any deposit which is made on a Saturday, Sunday, legal holiday, or after the close of business on any business day shall be deemed to have been made on the next business day.

(b) Availability at start of business day

Except as provided in subsections (b)(3) and (c)(1)(B) of section 4002 of this title, if any provision of this chapter requires that funds be available for withdrawal on any business day, such funds shall be available for withdrawal at the start of such business day.

(c) Effect on policies of depository institutions

No provision of this chapter shall be construed as—

(1) prohibiting a depository institution from making funds available for withdrawal in a shorter period of time than the period of time required by this chapter; or

(2) affecting a depository institution's right—

(A) to accept or reject a check for deposit;

(B) to revoke any provisional settlement made by the depository institution with respect to a check accepted by such institution for deposit;

(C) to charge back the depositor's account for the amount of such check; or

(D) to claim a refund of such provisional credit.

(d) Prohibition on freezing certain funds in an account

In any case in which a check is deposited in an account at a depository institution and the funds represented by such check are not yet available for withdrawal pursuant to this chapter, the depository institution may not freeze any other funds in such account (which are otherwise available for withdrawal pursuant to this chapter) solely because the funds so deposited are not yet available for withdrawal.

(e) Employee training on and compliance with requirements of this chapter

Each depository institution shall—

(1) take such actions as may be necessary fully to inform each employee (who performs duties subject to the requirements of this chapter) of the requirements of this chapter; and

(2) establish and maintain procedures reasonably designed to assure and monitor employee compliance with such requirements.

(f) Adjustments to dollar amounts for inflation

The dollar amounts under this title shall be adjusted every 5 years after December 31, 2011, by the annual percentage increase in the Consumer Price Index for Urban Wage Earners and Clerical Workers, as published by the Bureau of Labor Statistics, rounded to the nearest multiple of $25.

(Pub.L. 100–86, Title VI, § 607, Aug. 10, 1987, 101 Stat. 646; Pub.L. 111–203, Title X, § 1086(f), July 21, 2010, 124 Stat. 2086.)

§ 4007. Effect on State law

(a) In general

Any law or regulation of any State in effect on September 1, 1989, which requires that funds deposited or received for deposit in an account at a depository institution chartered by such State be made available for withdrawal in a shorter period of time than the period of time provided in this chapter or in regulations prescribed by the Board under this chapter (as in effect on September 1, 1989) shall—

(1) supersede the provisions of this chapter and any regulations by the Board to the extent such provisions relate to the time by which funds deposited or received for deposit in an account shall be available for withdrawal; and

(2) apply to all federally insured depository institutions located within such State.

(b) Override of certain State laws

Except as provided in subsection (a) of this section, this chapter and regulations prescribed under this chapter shall supersede any provision of the law of any State, including the Uniform Commercial Code as in effect in such State, which is inconsistent with this chapter or such regulations.

(Pub.L. 100–86, Title VI, § 608, Aug. 10, 1987, 101 Stat. 647.)

§ 4008. Regulations and reports by Board

(a) In general

After notice and opportunity to submit comment in accordance with section 553(c) of Title 5, the Board, jointly with the Director of the Bureau of Consumer Financial Protection, shall prescribe regulations—

(1) to carry out the provisions of this chapter;

(2) to prevent the circumvention or evasion of such provisions; and

(3) to facilitate compliance with such provisions.

(b) Regulations relating to improvement of check processing system

In order to improve the check processing system, the Board shall consider (among other proposals) requiring, by regulation, that—

(1) depository institutions be charged based upon notification that a check or similar instrument will be presented for payment;

(2) the Federal Reserve banks and depository institutions provide for check truncation;

(3) depository institutions be provided incentives to return items promptly to the depository institution of first deposit;

(4) the Federal Reserve banks and depository institutions take such actions as are necessary to automate the process of returning unpaid checks;

(5) each depository institution and Federal Reserve bank—

(A) place its endorsement, and other notations specified in regulations of the Board, on checks in the positions specified in such regulations; and

(B) take such actions as are necessary to—

(i) automate the process of reading endorsements; and

(ii) eliminate unnecessary endorsements;

(6) within one business day after an originating depository institution is presented a check (for more than such minimum amount as the Board may prescribe)—

(A) such originating depository institution determines whether it will pay such check; and

(B) if such originating depository institution determines that it will not pay such check, such originating depository institution directly notify the receiving depository institution of such determination;

(7) regardless of where a check is cleared initially, all returned checks be eligible to be returned through the Federal Reserve System;

(8) Federal Reserve banks and depository institutions participate in the development and implementation of an electronic clearinghouse process to the extent the Board determines, pursuant to the study under subsection (f) of this section, that such a process is feasible; and

(9) originating depository institutions be permitted to return unpaid checks directly to, and obtain reimbursement for such checks directly from, the receiving depository institution.

(c) Regulatory responsibility of Board for payment system

(1) Responsibility for payment system

In order to carry out the provisions of this chapter, the Board of Governors of the Federal Reserve System shall have the responsibility to regulate—

(A) any aspect of the payment system, including the receipt, payment, collection, or clearing of checks; and

(B) any related function of the payment system with respect to checks.

(2) Regulations

The Board shall prescribe such regulations as it may determine to be appropriate to carry out its responsibility under paragraph (1).

(d) Reports

(1) Implementation progress reports

(A) Required reports

The Board shall transmit a report to both Houses of the Congress not later than 18, 30, and 48 months after August 10, 1987.

(B) Contents of report

Each such report shall describe—

(i) the actions taken and progress made by the Board to implement the schedules established in section 4002 of this title, and

(ii) the impact of this chapter on consumers and depository institutions.

(2) Evaluation of temporary schedule report

(A) Report required

The Board shall transmit a report to both Houses of the Congress not later than 2 years after August 10, 1987, regarding the effects the temporary schedule established under section 4002(c) of this title have had on depository institutions and the public.

(B) Contents of report

Such report shall also assess the potential impact the implementation of the schedule established in section 4002(b) of this title will have on depository institutions and the public, including an estimate of the risks to and losses of depository institutions and the benefits to consumers. Such report shall also contain such recommendations for legislative or administrative action as the Board may determine to be necessary.

(3) Comptroller General evaluation report

Not later than 6 months after September 1, 1988, the Comptroller General of the United States shall transmit a report to the Congress evaluating the implementation and administration of this chapter.

(e) Consultations

In prescribing regulations under subsections (a) and (b), the Board and the Director of the Bureau of Consumer Financial Protection, in the case of subsection (a), and the Board, in the case of subsection (b), shall consult with the Comptroller of the Currency, the Board of Directors of the Federal Deposit Insurance Corporation, and the National Credit Union Administration Board.

(f) Electronic clearinghouse study

(1) Study required

The Board shall study the feasibility of modernizing and accelerating the check payment system through the development of an electronic clearinghouse process utilizing existing telecommunications technology to avoid the necessity of actual presentment of the paper instrument to a payor institution before such institution is charged for the item.

(2) Consultation; factors to be studied

In connection with the study required under paragraph (1), the Board shall—

(A) consult with appropriate experts in telecommunications technology; and

(B) consider all practical and legal impediments to the development of an electronic clearinghouse process.

(3) Report required

The Board shall report its conclusions to the Congress within 9 months of August 10, 1987.

(Pub.L. 100–86, Title VI, § 609, Aug. 10, 1987, 101 Stat. 647; Pub.L. 111–203, Title X, 108 6(d), July 21, 2010, 124 Stat. 2086.)

§ 4009. Administrative enforcement

(a) Administrative enforcement

Compliance with the requirements imposed under this chapter, including regulations prescribed by and orders issued by the Board of Governors of the Federal Reserve System under this chapter, shall be enforced under—

(1) section 8 of the Federal Deposit Insurance Act [12 U.S.C. § 1818] in the case of—

(A) national banks, and Federal branches and Federal agencies of foreign banks, by the Office of the Comptroller of the Currency;

(B) member banks of the Federal Reserve System (other than national banks), and offices, branches, and agencies of foreign banks located in the United States (other than Federal branches, Federal agencies, and insured State branches of foreign banks), by the Board of Governors of the Federal Reserve System; and

(C) banks insured by the Federal Deposit Insurance Corporation (other than members of the Federal Reserve System) and insured State branches of foreign banks, by the Board of Directors of the Federal Deposit Insurance Corporation;

(2) section 8 of the Federal Deposit Insurance Act [12 U.S.C. § 1818], by the Director of the Office of Thrift Supervision in the case of savings associations the deposits of which are insured by the Federal Deposit Insurance Corporation; and

(3) the Federal Credit Union Act [12 U.S.C. § 1751 et seq.], by the National Credit Union Administration Board with respect to any Federal credit union or insured credit union.

The terms used in paragraph (1) that are not defined in this chapter or otherwise defined in section 3(s) of the Federal Deposit Insurance Act (12 U.S.C. 1813(s)) shall have the meaning given to them in section 1(b) of the International Banking Act of 1978 (12 U.S.C. 3101).

(b) Additional powers

(1) Violation of this chapter treated as violation of other Acts

For purposes of the exercise by any agency referred to in subsection (a) of this section of its powers under any Act referred to in that subsection, a violation of any requirement imposed under this chapter shall be deemed to be a violation of a requirement imposed under that Act.

(2) Enforcement authority under other Acts

In addition to its powers under any provision of law specifically referred to in subsection (a) of this section, each of the agencies referred to in such subsection may exercise, for purposes of enforcing compliance with any requirement imposed under this chapter, any other authority conferred on it by law.

(c) Enforcement by Board

(1) In general

Except to the extent that enforcement of the requirements imposed under this chapter is specifically committed to some other Government agency under subsection (a) of this section, the Board of Governors of the Federal Reserve System shall enforce such requirements.

(2) Additional remedy

If the Board determines that—

(A) any depository institution which is not a depository institution described in subsection (a) of this section, or

(B) any other person subject to the authority of the Board under this chapter, including any person subject to the authority of the Board under section 4004(d)(2) or 4008(c) of this title, has failed to comply with any requirement imposed by this chapter or by the Board under this chapter, the Board may issue an order prohibiting any depository institution, any Federal Reserve bank, or any other person subject to the authority of the Board from engaging in any activity or transaction which directly or indirectly involves such noncomplying depository institution or person (including any activity or transaction involving the receipt, payment, collection, and clearing of checks and any related function of the payment system with respect to checks).

(d) Procedural rules

The authority of the Board to prescribe regulations under this chapter does not impair the authority of any other agency designated in this section to make rules regarding its own procedures in enforcing compliance with requirements imposed under this chapter.

(Pub.L. 100–86, Title VI, § 610, Aug. 10, 1987, 101 Stat. 649; Pub.L. 101–73, Title VII, § 744(d), Aug. 9, 1989, 103 Stat. 438; Pub.L. 102–242, Title II, § 212(h), Dec. 19, 1991, 105 Stat. 2303.)

§ 4010. Civil liability

(a) Civil liability

Except as otherwise provided in this section, any depository institution which fails to comply with any requirement imposed under this chapter or any regulation prescribed under this chapter with respect to any person other than another depository institution is liable to such person in an amount equal to the sum of—

(1) any actual damage sustained by such person as a result of the failure;

(2)(A) in the case of an individual action, such additional amount as the court may allow, except that the liability under this subparagraph shall not be less than $100 nor greater than $1,000; or

(B) in the case of a class action, such amount as the court may allow, except that—

(i) as to each member of the class, no minimum recovery shall be applicable; and

(ii) the total recovery under this subparagraph in any class action or series of class actions arising out of the same failure to comply by the same depository institution shall not be more than the lesser of $500,000 or 1 percent of the net worth of the depository institution involved; and

(3) in the case of any successful action to enforce the foregoing liability, the costs of the action, together with a reasonable attorney's fee as determined by the court.

(b) Class action awards

In determining the amount of any award in any class action, the court shall consider, among other relevant factors—

(1) the amount of any actual damages awarded;

(2) the frequency and persistence of failures of compliance;

(3) the resources of the depository institution;

(4) the number of persons adversely affected; and

(5) the extent to which the failure of compliance was intentional.

(c) Bona fide errors

(1) General rule

A depository institution may not be held liable in any action brought under this section for a violation of this chapter if the depository institution demonstrates by a preponderance of the evidence that the violation was not intentional and resulted from a bona fide error, notwithstanding the maintenance of procedures reasonably adapted to avoid any such error.

(2) Examples

Examples of a bona fide error include clerical, calculation, computer malfunction and programming, and printing errors, except that an error of legal judgment with respect to a depository institution's obligation under this chapter is not a bona fide error.

(d) Jurisdiction

Any action under this section may be brought in any United States district court, or in any other court of competent jurisdiction, within one year after the date of the occurrence of the violation involved.

(e) Reliance on Board rulings

No provision of this section imposing any liability shall apply to any act done or omitted in good faith in conformity with any rule, regulation, or interpretation thereof by the Board of Governors of the Federal Reserve System, notwithstanding the fact that after such act or omission has occurred, such rule, regulation, or interpretation is amended, rescinded, or determined by judicial or other authority to be invalid for any reason.

(f) Authority to establish rules regarding losses and liability among depository institutions

The Board is authorized to impose on or allocate among depository institutions the risks of loss and liability in connection with any aspect of the payment system, including the receipt, payment, collection, or clearing of checks, and any related function of the payment system with respect to checks. Liability under this subsection shall not exceed the amount of the check giving proximate consequence of any act or omission rise to the loss or liability, and, where there is bad faith, other damages, if any, suffered as a giving rise to the loss or liability.

(Pub.L. 100–86, Title VI, § 611, Aug. 10, 1987, 101 Stat. 650.)

CONSUMER CREDIT PROTECTION ACT (CCPA)

Selected Provisions: 15 U.S.C. §§ 1601–1667f, 1693–1693r

Current through March 12, 2019; P.L. 116-9

For updates, see http://uscode.house.gov

SUBCHAPTER I—CONSUMER CREDIT COST DISCLOSURE

PART A—GENERAL PROVISIONS

PART B—CREDIT TRANSACTIONS

PART C—CREDIT ADVERTISING AND LIMITS ON CREDIT CARD FEES

PART D—CREDIT BILLING

PART E—CONSUMER LEASES

SUBCHAPTER I—CONSUMER CREDIT COST DISCLOSURE

PART A—GENERAL PROVISIONS

§ 1601. Congressional findings and declaration of purpose [CCPA § 102]

(a) Informed use of credit

The Congress finds that economic stabilization would be enhanced and the competition among the various financial institutions and other firms engaged in the extension of consumer credit would be strengthened by the informed use of credit. The informed use of credit results from an awareness of the cost thereof by consumers. It is the purpose of this subchapter to assure a meaningful disclosure of credit terms so that the consumer will be able to compare more readily the various credit terms available to him and avoid the uninformed use of credit, and to protect the consumer against inaccurate and unfair credit billing and credit card practices.

(b) Terms of personal property leases

The Congress also finds that there has been a recent trend toward leasing automobiles and other durable goods for consumer use as an alternative to installment credit sales and that these leases have been offered without adequate cost disclosures. It is the purpose of this subchapter to assure a meaningful disclosure of the terms of leases of personal property for personal, family, or household purposes so as to enable the lessee to compare more readily the various lease terms available to him, limit balloon payments in consumer leasing, enable comparison of lease terms with credit terms where appropriate, and to assure meaningful and accurate disclosures of lease terms in advertisements.

(Pub.L. 90–321, Title I, § 102, May 29, 1968, 82 Stat. 146; Pub.L. 93–495, Title III, § 302, Oct. 28, 1974, 88 Stat. 1511; Pub.L. 94–240, § 2, Mar. 23, 1976, 90 Stat. 257.)

§ 1602. Definitions and rules of construction [CCPA § 103]

(a) The definitions and rules of construction set forth in this section are applicable for the purposes of this subchapter.

(b) The term "Bureau" means the Bureau of Consumer Financial Protection.*

(c) The term "Board" refers to the Board of Governors of the Federal Reserve System.

(d) The term "organization" means a corporation, government or governmental subdivision or agency, trust, estate, partnership, cooperative, or association.

(e) The term "person" means a natural person or an organization.

(f) The term "credit" means the right granted by a creditor to a debtor to defer payment of debt or to incur debt and defer its payment.

(g) The term "creditor" refers only to a person who both (1) regularly extends, whether in connection with loans, sales of property or services, or otherwise, consumer credit which is payable by agreement in more than four installments or for which the payment of a finance charge is or may be required, and (2) is the person to whom the debt arising from the consumer credit transaction is initially payable on the face of the evidence of indebtedness or, if there is no such evidence of indebtedness, by agreement. Notwithstanding the preceding sentence, in the case of an open-end credit plan involving a credit card, the card issuer and any person who honors the credit card and offers a discount which is a finance charge are creditors. For the purpose of the requirements imposed under part D of this subchapter and sections 1637(a)(5), 1637(a)(6), 1637(a)(7), 1637(b)(1), 1637(b)(2), 1637(b)(3), 1637(b)(8), and 1637(b)(10) of this title, the term "creditor" shall also include card issuers whether or not the amount due is payable by agreement in more than four installments or the payment of a finance charge is or may be required, and the Board shall, by regulation, apply these requirements to such card issuers, to the extent appropriate, even though the requirements are by their terms applicable only to creditors offering open-end credit plans. Any person who originates 2 or more mortgages referred to in subsection (aa) of this section in any 12-month period or any person who originates 1 or more such mortgages through a mortgage broker shall be considered to be a creditor for purposes of this subchapter. The term "creditor" includes a private educational lender (as that term is defined in section 1650 of this title) for purposes of this subchapter.

(h) The term "credit sale" refers to any sale in which the seller is a creditor. The term includes any contract in the form of a bailment or lease if the bailee or lessee contracts to pay as compensation for use a sum substantially equivalent to or in excess of the aggregate value of the property and services involved and it is agreed that the bailee or lessee will become, or for no other or a nominal consideration has the option to become, the owner of the property upon full compliance with his obligations under the contract.

(i) The adjective "consumer", used with reference to a credit transaction, characterizes the transaction as one in which the party to whom credit is offered or extended is a natural person, and the money, property, or services which are the subject of the transaction are primarily for personal, family, or household purposes.

(j) terms "open end credit plan" and "open end consumer credit plan" mean a plan under which the creditor reasonably contemplates repeated transactions, which prescribes the terms of such transactions, and which provides for a finance charge which may be computed from time to time on the outstanding unpaid balance. A credit plan or open end consumer credit plan which is an open end credit plan or open end consumer credit plan within the meaning of the preceding sentence is an open end credit plan even if credit information is verified from time to time.

(k) The term "adequate notice," as used in section 1643 of this title, means a printed notice to a cardholder which sets forth the pertinent facts clearly and conspicuously so that a person against whom it is to operate could reasonably be expected to have noticed it and understood its meaning. Such notice may be given to a cardholder by printing the notice on any credit card, or on each periodic statement of account, issued to the cardholder, or by any other means reasonably assuring the receipt thereof by the cardholder.

---

* *Note from West Advisory Panel: This definition was inserted as part of Pub.L. 111–203 (Dodd-Frank), changing the numbering of all subsequent definitions. Dodd-Frank appears to contain many clerical errors. Cross-references to definitions may not reflect the Dodd-Frank changes.*

(*l*) The term "credit card" means any card, plate, coupon book or other credit device existing for the purpose of obtaining money, property, labor, or services on credit.

(m) The term "accepted credit card" means any credit card which the cardholder has requested and received or has signed or has used, or authorized another to use, for the purpose of obtaining money, property, labor, or services on credit.

(n) The term "cardholder" means any person to whom a credit card is issued or any person who has agreed with the card issuer to pay obligations arising from the issuance of a credit card to another person.

(*o*) The term "card issuer" means any person who issues a credit card, or the agent of such person with respect to such card.

(p) The term "unauthorized use," as used in section 1643 of this title, means a use of a credit card by a person other than the cardholder who does not have actual, implied, or apparent authority for such use and from which the cardholder receives no benefit.

(q) The term "discount" as used in section 1666f of this title means a reduction made from the regular price. The term "discount" as used in section 1666f of this title shall not mean a surcharge.

(r) The term "surcharge" as used in this section and section 1666f of this title means any means of increasing the regular price to a cardholder which is not imposed upon customers paying by cash, check, or similar means.

(s) The term "State" refers to any State, the Commonwealth of Puerto Rico, the District of Columbia, and any territory or possession of the United States.

(t) The term "agricultural purposes" includes the production, harvest, exhibition, marketing, transportation, processing, or manufacture of agricultural products by a natural person who cultivates, plants, propagates, or nurtures those agricultural products, including but not limited to the acquisition of farmland, real property with a farm residence, and personal property and services used primarily in farming.

(u) The term "agricultural products" includes agricultural, horticultural, viticultural, and dairy products, livestock, wildlife, poultry, bees, forest products, fish and shellfish, and any products thereof, including processed and manufactured products, and any and all products raised or produced on farms and any processed or manufactured products thereof.

(v) The term "material disclosures" means the disclosure, as required by this subchapter, of the annual percentage rate, the method of determining the finance charge and the balance upon which a finance charge will be imposed, the amount of the finance charge, the amount to be financed, the total of payments, the number and amount of payments, the due dates or periods of payments scheduled to repay the indebtedness, and the disclosures required by section 1639(a) of this title.

(w) The term "dwelling" means a residential structure or mobile home which contains one to four family housing units, or individual units of condominiums or cooperatives.

(x) The term "residential mortgage transaction" means a transaction in which a mortgage, deed of trust, purchase money security interest arising under an installment sales contract, or equivalent consensual security interest is created or retained against the consumer's dwelling to finance the acquisition or initial construction of such dwelling.

(y) As used in this section and section 1666f of this title, the term "regular price" means the tag or posted price charged for the property or service if a single price is tagged or posted, or the price charged for the property or service when payment is made by use of an open-end credit plan or a credit card if either (1) no price is tagged or posted, or (2) two prices are tagged or posted, one of which is charged when payment is made by use of an open-end credit plan or a credit card and the other when payment is made by use of cash, check, or similar means. For purposes of this definition, payment by check, draft, or other negotiable instrument which may result in the debiting of an open-end credit plan or a credit cardholder's open-end account shall not be considered payment made by use of the plan or the account.

(z) Any reference to any requirement imposed under this subchapter or any provision thereof includes reference to the regulations of the Bureau under this subchapter or the provision thereof in question.

(aa) The disclosure of an amount or percentage which is greater than the amount or percentage required to be disclosed under this subchapter does not in itself constitute a violation of this subchapter.

(bb) High-cost mortgage

(1) Definition

(A) In general

The term "high-cost mortgage", and a mortgage referred to in this subsection, means a consumer credit transaction that is secured by the consumer's principal dwelling, other than a reverse mortgage transaction, if—

(i) in the case of a credit transaction secured—

(I) by a first mortgage on the consumer's principal dwelling, the annual percentage rate at consummation of the transaction will exceed by more than 6.5 percentage points (8.5 percentage points, if the dwelling is personal property and the transaction is for less than $50,000) the average prime offer rate, as defined in section 1639c(b)(2)(B) of this title, for a comparable transaction; or

(II) by a subordinate or junior mortgage on the consumer's principal dwelling, the annual percentage rate at consummation of the transaction will exceed by more than 8.5 percentage points the average prime offer rate, as defined in section 1639c(b)(2)(B) of this title, for a comparable transaction;

(ii) the total points and fees payable in connection with the transaction, other than bona fide third party charges not retained by the mortgage originator, creditor, or an affiliate of the creditor or mortgage originator, exceed—

(I) in the case of a transaction for $20,000 or more, 5 percent of the total transaction amount; or

(II) in the case of a transaction for less than $20,000, the lesser of 8 percent of the total transaction amount or $1,000 (or such other dollar amount as the Board shall prescribe by regulation); or

(iii) the credit transaction documents permit the creditor to charge or collect prepayment fees or penalties more than 36 months after the transaction closing or such fees or penalties exceed, in the aggregate, more than 2 percent of the amount prepaid.

(B) Introductory rates taken into account

For purposes of subparagraph (A)(i), the annual percentage rate of interest shall be determined based on the following interest rate:

(i) In the case of a fixed-rate transaction in which the annual percentage rate will not vary during the term of the loan, the interest rate in effect on the date of consummation of the transaction.

(ii) In the case of a transaction in which the rate of interest varies solely in accordance with an index, the interest rate determined by adding the index rate in effect on the date of consummation of the transaction to the maximum margin permitted at any time during the loan agreement.

(iii) In the case of any other transaction in which the rate may vary at any time during the term of the loan for any reason, the interest charged on the transaction at the maximum rate that may be charged during the term of the loan.

(C) Mortgage insurance

For the purposes of computing the total points and fees under paragraph (4), the total points and fees shall exclude—

(i) any premium provided by an agency of the Federal Government or an agency of a State;

(ii) any amount that is not in excess of the amount payable under policies in effect at the time of origination under section 203(c)(2)(A) of the National Housing Act (12 U.S.C. 1709(c)(2)(A)), provided that the premium, charge, or fee is required to be refundable on a pro-rated basis and the refund is automatically issued upon notification of the satisfaction of the underlying mortgage loan; and

(iii) any premium paid by the consumer after closing.

(2)(A) After the 2-year period beginning on the effective date of the regulations promulgated under section 155 of the Riegle Community Development and Regulatory Improvement Act of 1994, and no more frequently than biennially after the first increase or decrease under this subparagraph, the Board may by regulation increase or decrease the number of percentage points specified in paragraph (1)(A), if the Board determines that the increase or decrease is—

(i) consistent with the consumer protections against abusive lending provided by the amendments made by subtitle B of title I of the Riegle Community Development and Regulatory Improvement Act of 1994; and

(ii) warranted by the need for credit.

(B) An increase or decrease under subparagraph (A)—

(i) may not result in the number of percentage points referred to in paragraph (1)(A)(i)(I) being less than 6 percentage points or greater than 10 percentage points; and

(ii) may not result in the number of percentage points referred to in paragraph (1)(A)(i)(II) being less than 8 percentage points or greater than 12 percentage points.

(C) In determining whether to increase or decrease the number of percentage points referred to in subparagraph (A), the Board shall consult with representatives of consumers, including low-income consumers, and lenders.

(3) The amount specified in paragraph (1)(B)(ii) shall be adjusted annually on January 1 by the annual percentage change in the Consumer Price Index, as reported on June 1 of the year preceding such adjustment.

(4) For purposes of paragraph (1)(B), points and fees shall include—

(A) all items included in the finance charge, except interest or the time-price differential;

(B) all compensation paid directly or indirectly by a consumer or creditor to a mortgage originator from any source, including a mortgage originator that is also the creditor in a table-funded transaction;

(C) each of the charges listed in section 1605(e) of this title (except an escrow for future payment of taxes), unless—

(i) the charge is reasonable;

(ii) the creditor receives no direct or indirect compensation; and

(iii) the charge is paid to a third party unaffiliated with the creditor; and

(D) premiums or other charges payable at or before closing for any credit life, credit disability, credit unemployment, or credit property insurance, or any other accident, loss-of-income, life or health insurance, or any payments directly or indirectly for any debt cancellation or suspension agreement or contract, except that insurance premiums or debt cancellation or suspension fees calculated and paid in full on a monthly basis shall not be considered financed by the creditor;

(E) the maximum prepayment fees and penalties which may be charged or collected under the terms of the credit transaction;

(F) all prepayment fees or penalties that are incurred by the consumer if the loan refinances a previous loan made or currently held by the same creditor or an affiliate of the creditor; and

(G) such other charges as the Bureau determines to be appropriate.

(5) Calculation of points and fees for open-end consumer credit plans

In the case of open-end consumer credit plans, points and fees shall be calculated, for purposes of this section and section 1639 of this title, by adding the total points and fees known at or before closing, including the maximum prepayment penalties which may be charged or collected under the terms of the credit transaction, plus the minimum additional fees the consumer would be required to pay to draw down an amount equal to the total credit line.

(6) This subsection shall not be construed to limit the rate of interest or the finance charge that a person may charge a consumer for any extension of credit.

(cc) The term "reverse mortgage transaction" means a nonrecourse transaction in which a mortgage, deed of trust, or equivalent consensual security interest is created against the consumer's principal dwelling—

(1) securing one or more advances; and

(2) with respect to which the payment of any principal, interest, and shared appreciation or equity is due and payable (other than in the case of default) only after—

(A) the transfer of the dwelling;

(B) the consumer ceases to occupy the dwelling as a principal dwelling; or

(C) the death of the consumer.

(dd) Definitions relating to mortgage origination and residential mortgage loans

(1) Commission

Unless otherwise specified, the term "Commission" means the Federal Trade Commission.

(2) Mortgage originator

The term "mortgage originator"—

(A) means any person who, for direct or indirect compensation or gain, or in the expectation of direct or indirect compensation or gain—

(i) takes a residential mortgage loan application;

(ii) assists a consumer in obtaining or applying to obtain a residential mortgage loan; or

(iii) offers or negotiates terms of a residential mortgage loan;

(B) includes any person who represents to the public, through advertising or other means of communicating or providing information (including the use of business cards, stationery, brochures, signs, rate lists, or other promotional items), that such person can or will provide any of the services or perform any of the activities described in subparagraph (A);

(C) does not include any person who is—

(i) not otherwise described in subparagraph (A) or (B) and who performs purely administrative or clerical tasks on behalf of a person who is described in any such subparagraph; or

(ii) a retailer of manufactured or modular homes or an employee of the retailer if the retailer or employee, as applicable—

(I) does not receive compensation or gain for engaging in activities described in subparagraph (A) that is in excess of any compensation or gain received in a comparable cash transaction;

(II) discloses to the consumer—

(aa) in writing any corporate affiliation with any creditor; and

(bb) if the retailer has a corporate affiliation with any creditor, at least 1 unaffiliated creditor; and

(III) does not directly negotiate with the consumer or lender on loan terms (including rates, fees, and other costs).

(D) does not include a person or entity that only performs real estate brokerage activities and is licensed or registered in accordance with applicable State law, unless such person or entity is compensated by a lender, a mortgage broker, or other mortgage originator or by any agent of such lender, mortgage broker, or other mortgage originator;

(E) does not include, with respect to a residential mortgage loan, a person, estate, or trust that provides mortgage financing for the sale of 3 properties in any 12-month period to purchasers of such properties, each of which is owned by such person, estate, or trust and serves as security for the loan, provided that such loan—

(i) is not made by a person, estate, or trust that has constructed, or acted as a contractor for the construction of, a residence on the property in the ordinary course of business of such person, estate, or trust;

(ii) is fully amortizing;

(iii) is with respect to a sale for which the seller determines in good faith and documents that the buyer has a reasonable ability to repay the loan;

(iv) has a fixed rate or an adjustable rate that is adjustable after 5 or more years, subject to reasonable annual and lifetime limitations on interest rate increases; and

(v) meets any other criteria the Board may prescribe;

(F) does not include the creditor (except the creditor in a table-funded transaction) under paragraph (1), (2), or (4) of section 1639b(c) of this title; and

(G) does not include a servicer or servicer employees, agents and contractors, including but not limited to those who offer or negotiate terms of a residential mortgage loan for purposes of renegotiating, modifying, replacing and subordinating principal of existing mortgages where borrowers are behind in their payments, in default or have a reasonable likelihood of being in default or falling behind.

(3) Nationwide Mortgage Licensing System and Registry

The term "Nationwide Mortgage Licensing System and Registry" has the same meaning as in the Secure and Fair Enforcement for Mortgage Licensing Act of 2008.

(4) Other definitions relating to mortgage originator

For purposes of this subsection, a person "assists a consumer in obtaining or applying to obtain a residential mortgage loan" by, among other things, advising on residential mortgage loan terms (including rates, fees, and other costs), preparing residential mortgage loan packages, or collecting information on behalf of the consumer with regard to a residential mortgage loan.

(5) Residential mortgage loan

The term "residential mortgage loan" means any consumer credit transaction that is secured by a mortgage, deed of trust, or other equivalent consensual security interest on a dwelling or on residential real property that includes a dwelling, other than a consumer credit transaction under an open end credit plan or, for purposes of sections 1639b and 1639c of this title and section 1638(a)(16), (17), (18), and (19) of this title, and sections 1638(f) and 1640(k) of this title, and any regulations promulgated thereunder, an extension of credit relating to a plan described in section 101(53D) of Title 11.

(6) Secretary

The term "Secretary", when used in connection with any transaction or person involved with a residential mortgage loan, means the Secretary of Housing and Urban Development.

(7) Servicer

The term "servicer" has the same meaning as in section 2605(i)(2) of Title 12.

(ee) Bona fide discount points and prepayment penalties

For the purposes of determining the amount of points and fees for purposes of subsection (aa), either the amounts described in paragraph (1) or (2) of the following paragraphs, but not both, shall be excluded:

(1) Up to and including 2 bona fide discount points payable by the consumer in connection with the mortgage, but only if the interest rate from which the mortgage's interest rate will be discounted does not exceed by more than 1 percentage point—

(A) the average prime offer rate, as defined in section 1639c of this title; or

(B) if secured by a personal property loan, the average rate on a loan in connection with which insurance is provided under title I of the National Housing Act (12 U.S.C. 1702 et seq.).

(2) Unless 2 bona fide discount points have been excluded under paragraph (1), up to and including 1 bona fide discount point payable by the consumer in connection with the mortgage, but only if the interest rate from which the mortgage's interest rate will be discounted does not exceed by more than 2 percentage points—

(A) the average prime offer rate, as defined in section 1639c of this title; or

(B) if secured by a personal property loan, the average rate on a loan in connection with which insurance is provided under title I of the National Housing Act (12 U.S.C. 1702 et seq.).

(3) For purposes of paragraph (1), the term "bona fide discount points" means loan discount points which are knowingly paid by the consumer for the purpose of reducing, and which in fact result in a bona fide reduction of, the interest rate or time-price differential applicable to the mortgage.

(4) Paragraphs (1) and (2) shall not apply to discount points used to purchase an interest rate reduction unless the amount of the interest rate reduction purchased is reasonably consistent with established industry norms and practices for secondary mortgage market transactions.

(Pub.L. 90–321, Title I, § 103, May 29, 1968, 82 Stat. 147; Pub.L. 91–508, Title V, § 501, Oct. 26, 1970, 84 Stat. 1126; Pub.L. 93–495, Title III, § 303, Oct. 28, 1974, 88 Stat. 1511; Pub.L. 94–222, § 3(a), Feb. 27, 1976, 90 Stat. 197; Pub.L. 96–221, Title VI, §§ 602, 603(a), (b), 604, 612(a)(2), (b), Mar. 31, 1980, 94 Stat. 168, 169, 175, 176; Pub.L. 97–25, Title I, § 102, July 27, 1981, 95 Stat. 144; Pub.L. 97–320, Title VII, § 702(a), Oct. 15, 1982, 96 Stat. 1538; Pub.L. 103–325, Title I, §§ 152(a) to (c), 154(a), Sept. 23, 1994, 108 Stat. 2190, 2191, 2196; Pub.L. 110–315, Title X, § 1011(b), Aug. 14, 2008, 122 Stat. 3481; Pub.L. 111–24, Title I, § 108, May 22, 2009, 123 Stat. 1743; Pub.L. 111–203, Title X, §§ 1100A(2), 1100H, Title XIV, §§ 1400(c), 1401, 1431, 1432, 1433, July 21, 2010, 124 Stat. 2107, 2113, 2136, 2137, 2157, 2158, 2159; Pub.L. 115–174, Title I, § 107, May 24, 2018, 132 Stat. 1304.)

§ 1603. Exempted transactions [CCPA § 104]

This subchapter does not apply to the following:

(1) Credit transactions involving extensions of credit primarily for business, commercial, or agricultural purposes, or to government or governmental agencies or instrumentalities, or to organizations.

(2) Transactions in securities or commodities accounts by a broker-dealer registered with the Securities and Exchange Commission.

(3) Credit transactions, other than those in which a security interest is or will be acquired in real property, or in personal property used or expected to be used as the principal dwelling of the consumer and other than private education loans (as that term is defined in section 1650(a) of this title), in which the total amount financed exceeds $50,000.

(4) Transactions under public utility tariffs, if the Bureau determines that a State regulatory body regulates the charges for the public utility services involved, the charges for delayed payment, and any discount allowed for early payment.

(5) Transactions for which the Bureau, by rule, determines that coverage under this subchapter is not necessary to carry out the purposes of this subchapter.

(6) Repealed. Pub.L. 96–221, Title VI, § 603(c) (3), Mar. 31, 1980, 94 Stat. 169

(7) Loans made, insured, or guaranteed pursuant to a program authorized by Title IV of the Higher Education Act of 1965 (20 U.S.C. 1070 et seq.).

(Pub.L. 90–321, Title I, § 104, May 29, 1968, 82 Stat. 147; Pub.L. 93–495, Title IV, § 402, Oct. 28, 1974, 88 Stat. 1517; Pub.L. 96–221, Title VI, § 603(c), Mar. 31, 1980, 94 Stat. 169; Pub.L. 97–320, Title VII, § 701(a), Oct. 15, 1982, 96 Stat. 1538; Pub.L. 104–208, Div. A, Title II, § 2102(a), Sept. 30, 1996, 110 Stat. 3009–398; Pub.L. 110–315, Title X, § 1022, Aug. 14, 2008, 122 Stat. 3488; Pub.L. 111–203, Title X, §§ 1100A(2), 1100E(a)(1), 124 Stat. 2107, 2111.)

§ 1604. Disclosure guidelines [CCPA § 105]

(a) Promulgation, contents, etc., of regulations

The Bureau shall prescribe regulations to carry out the purposes of this subchapter. Except with respect to the provisions of section 1639 of this title that apply to a mortgage referred to in section 1602(aa)* of this title, such regulations may contain such additional requirements, classifications, differentiations, or other provisions, and may provide for such adjustments and exceptions for all or any class of transactions, as in the judgment of the Bureau are necessary or proper to effectuate the purposes of this subchapter, to prevent circumvention or evasion thereof, or to facilitate compliance therewith.

(b) Model disclosure forms and clauses; publication, criteria, compliance, etc.

The Bureau shall publish a single, integrated disclosure for mortgage loan transactions (including real estate settlement cost statements) which includes the disclosure requirements of this subchapter in conjunction with the disclosure requirements of the Real Estate Settlement Procedures Act of 1974 that, taken together, may apply to a transaction that is subject to both or either provisions of law. The purpose of such model disclosure shall be to facilitate compliance with the disclosure requirements of this subchapter and the Real Estate Settlement Procedures Act of 1974, and to aid the borrower or lessee in understanding the transaction by utilizing readily understandable language to simplify the technical nature of the disclosures. In devising such forms, the Bureau shall consider the use by creditors or lessors of data processing or similar automated equipment. Nothing in this subchapter may be construed to require a creditor or lessor to use any such model form or clause prescribed by the Bureau under this section. A creditor or lessor shall be deemed to be in compliance with the disclosure provisions of this subchapter with respect to other than numerical disclosures if the creditor or lessor (1) uses any appropriate model form or clause as published by the Bureau, or (2) uses any such model form or clause and changes it by (A) deleting any information which is not required by this subchapter, or (B) rearranging the format, if in making such deletion or rearranging the format, the creditor or lessor does not affect the substance, clarity, or meaningful sequence of the disclosure.

(c) Procedures applicable for adoption of model forms and clauses

Model disclosure forms and clauses shall be adopted by the Bureau after notice duly given in the Federal Register and an opportunity for public comment in accordance with section 553 of Title 5.

---

* *Note from West Advisory Panel: Pub.L. 111–203 (Dodd-Frank) appears to contain clerical errors. We believe this reference should be to § 1602(bb).*

(d) Effective dates of regulations containing new disclosure requirements

Any regulation of the Bureau, or any amendment or interpretation thereof, requiring any disclosure which differs from the disclosures previously required by this part, part D, or part E of this subchapter or by any regulation of the Bureau promulgated thereunder shall have an effective date of that October 1 which follows by at least six months the date of promulgation, except that the Bureau may at its discretion take interim action by regulation, amendment, or interpretation to lengthen the period of time permitted for creditors or lessors to adjust their forms to accommodate new requirements or shorten the length of time for creditors or lessors to make such adjustments when it makes a specific finding that such action is necessary to comply with the findings of a court or to prevent unfair or deceptive disclosure practices. Notwithstanding the previous sentence, any creditor or lessor may comply with any such newly promulgated disclosure requirements prior to the effective date of the requirements.

(e)[1] [Omitted.]

(f) Exemption authority

(1) In general

The Bureau may exempt, by regulation, from all or part of this subchapter all or any class of transactions, other than transactions involving any mortgage described in section 1602(aa) * of this title, for which, in the determination of the Bureau, coverage under all or part of this subchapter does not provide a meaningful benefit to consumers in the form of useful information or protection.

(2) Factors for consideration

In determining which classes of transactions to exempt in whole or in part under paragraph (1), the Bureau shall consider the following factors and publish its rationale at the time a proposed exemption is published for comment:

(A) The amount of the loan and whether the disclosures, right of rescission, and other provisions provide a benefit to the consumers who are parties to such transactions, as determined by the Bureau.

(B) The extent to which the requirements of this subchapter complicate, hinder, or make more expensive the credit process for the class of transactions.

(C) The status of the borrower, including—

(i) any related financial arrangements of the borrower, as determined by the Bureau;

(ii) the financial sophistication of the borrower relative to the type of transaction; and

(iii) the importance to the borrower of the credit, related supporting property, and coverage under this subchapter, as determined by the Bureau;

(D) whether the loan is secured by the principal residence of the consumer; and

(E) whether the goal of consumer protection would be undermined by such an exemption.

(g) Waiver for certain borrowers

(1) In general

The Bureau, by regulation, may exempt from the requirements of this subchapter certain credit transactions if—

(A) the transaction involves a consumer—

(i) with an annual earned income of more than $200,000; or

(ii) having net assets in excess of $1,000,000 at the time of the transaction; and

---

1 So in original. No subsec. (e) has been enacted.

* *Note from West Advisory Panel: This definition was inserted as part of Pub.L. 111–203 (Dodd-Frank), changing the numbering of all subsequent definitions. Dodd-Frank appears to contain many clerical errors. Cross-references to definitions may not reflect the Dodd-Frank changes.*

(B) a waiver that is handwritten, signed, and dated by the consumer is first obtained from the consumer.

(2) Adjustments by the Bureau

The Bureau, at its discretion, may adjust the annual earned income and net asset requirements of paragraph (1) for inflation.

(h) Deference

Notwithstanding any power granted to any Federal agency under this subchapter, the deference that a court affords to the Bureau with respect to a determination made by the Bureau relating to the meaning or interpretation of any provision of this subchapter, other than section 1639e or 1639h of this title, shall be applied as if the Bureau were the only agency authorized to apply, enforce, interpret, or administer the provisions of this subchapter.

(i) Authority of the Board to prescribe rules

Notwithstanding subsection (a), the Board shall have authority to prescribe rules under this subchapter with respect to a person described in section 5519(a) of Title 12. Regulations prescribed under this subsection may contain such classifications, differentiations, or other provisions, as in the judgment of the Board are necessary or proper to effectuate the purposes of this subchapter, to prevent circumvention or evasion thereof, or to facilitate compliance therewith.

(Pub.L. 90–321, Title I, § 105, May 29, 1968, 82 Stat. 148; Pub.L. 96–221, Title VI, § 605, Mar. 31, 1980, 94 Stat. 170; Pub.L. 103–325, Title I, § 152(e)(2)(A), Sept. 23, 1994, 108 Stat. 2194; Pub.L. 104–208, Div. A, Title II, §§ 2102(b), 2104, Sept. 30, 1996, 110 Stat. 3009–399, 3009–401; Pub.L. 111–203, Title X, §§ 1100A(2), 1100A(3), 1100A(5), 1100A(6), Title XIV, §§ 1400(c), 1472(c), July 21, 2010, 124 Stat. 2107, 2108, 2136, 2190.)

§ 1605. Determination of finance charge [CCPA § 106]

(a) "Finance charge" defined

Except as otherwise provided in this section, the amount of the finance charge in connection with any consumer credit transaction shall be determined as the sum of all charges, payable directly or indirectly by the person to whom the credit is extended, and imposed directly or indirectly by the creditor as an incident to the extension of credit. The finance charge does not include charges of a type payable in a comparable cash transaction. The finance charge shall not include fees and amounts imposed by third party closing agents (including settlement agents, attorneys, and escrow and title companies) if the creditor does not require the imposition of the charges or the services provided and does not retain the charges. Examples of charges which are included in the finance charge include any of the following types of charges which are applicable:

(1) Interest, time price differential, and any amount payable under a point, discount, or other system of additional charges.

(2) Service or carrying charge.

(3) Loan fee, finder's fee, or similar charge.

(4) Fee for an investigation or credit report.

(5) Premium or other charge for any guarantee or insurance protecting the creditor against the obligor's default or other credit loss.

(6) Borrower-paid mortgage broker fees, including fees paid directly to the broker or the lender (for delivery to the broker) whether such fees are paid in cash or financed.

(b) Life, accident, or health insurance premiums included in finance charge

Charges or premiums for credit life, accident, or health insurance written in connection with any consumer credit transaction shall be included in the finance charges unless

(1) the coverage of the debtor by the insurance is not a factor in the approval by the creditor of the extension of credit, and this fact is clearly disclosed in writing to the person applying for or obtaining the extension of credit; and

(2) in order to obtain the insurance in connection with the extension of credit, the person to whom the credit is extended must give specific affirmative written indication of his desire to do so after written disclosure to him of the cost thereof.

(c) Property damage and liability insurance premiums included in finance charge

Charges or premiums for insurance, written in connection with any consumer credit transaction, against loss of or damage to property or against liability arising out of the ownership or use of property, shall be included in the finance charge unless a clear and specific statement in writing is furnished by the creditor to the person to whom the credit is extended, setting forth the cost of the insurance if obtained from or through the creditor, and stating that the person to whom the credit is extended may choose the person through which the insurance is to be obtained.

(d) Items exempted from computation of finance charge in all credit transactions

If any of the following items is itemized and disclosed in accordance with the regulations of the Bureau in connection with any transaction, then the creditor need not include that item in the computation of the finance charge with respect to that transaction:

(1) Fees and charges prescribed by law which actually are or will be paid to public officials for determining the existence of or for perfecting or releasing or satisfying any security related to the credit transaction.

(2) The premium payable for any insurance in lieu of perfecting any security interest otherwise required by the creditor in connection with the transaction, if the premium does not exceed the fees and charges described in paragraph (1) which would otherwise be payable.

(3) Any tax levied on security instruments or on documents evidencing indebtedness if the payment of such taxes is a precondition for recording the instrument securing the evidence of indebtedness.

(e) Items exempted from computation of finance charge in extensions of credit secured by an interest in real property

The following items, when charged in connection with any extension of credit secured by an interest in real property, shall not be included in the computation of the finance charge with respect to that transaction:

(1) Fees or premiums for title examination, title insurance, or similar purposes.

(2) Fees for preparation of loan-related documents.

(3) Escrows for future payments of taxes and insurance.

(4) Fees for notarizing deeds and other documents.

(5) Appraisal fees, including fees related to any pest infestation or flood hazard inspections conducted prior to closing.

(6) Credit reports.

(f) Tolerances for accuracy

In connection with credit transactions not under an open end credit plan that are secured by real property or a dwelling, the disclosure of the finance charge and other disclosures affected by any finance charge—

(1) shall be treated as being accurate for purposes of this subchapter if the amount disclosed as the finance charge—

(A) does not vary from the actual finance charge by more than $100; or

(B) is greater than the amount required to be disclosed under this subchapter; and

(2) shall be treated as being accurate for purposes of section 1635 of this title if—

(A) except as provided in subparagraph (B), the amount disclosed as the finance charge does not vary from the actual finance charge by more than an amount equal to one-half of one percent of the total amount of credit extended; or

(B) in the case of a transaction, other than a mortgage referred to in section 1602(aa) of this title, which—

(i) is a refinancing of the principal balance then due and any accrued and unpaid finance charges of a residential mortgage transaction as defined in section 1602(w) of this title, or is any subsequent refinancing of such a transaction; and

(ii) does not provide any new consolidation or new advance;

if the amount disclosed as the finance charge does not vary from the actual finance charge by more than an amount equal to one percent of the total amount of credit extended.

(Pub.L. 90–321, Title I, § 106, May 29, 1968, 82 Stat. 148; Pub.L. 96–221, Title VI, § 606, Mar. 31, 1980, 94 Stat. 170; Pub.L. 104–29, §§ 2(a), (b)(1), (c) to (e), 3(a), Sept. 30, 1995, 109 Stat. 271, 272; Pub.L. 111–203, Title X, § 1100A(2), July 21, 2010, 124 Stat. 2107.)

§ 1606. Determination of annual percentage rate [CCPA § 107]

(a) "Annual percentage rate" defined

The annual percentage rate applicable to any extension of consumer credit shall be determined, in accordance with the regulations of the Bureau,

(1) in the case of any extension of credit other than under an open end credit plan, as

(A) that nominal annual percentage rate which will yield a sum equal to the amount of the finance charge when it is applied to the unpaid balances of the amount financed, calculated according to the actuarial method of allocating payments made on a debt between the amount financed and the amount of the finance charge, pursuant to which a payment is applied first to the accumulated finance charge and the balance is applied to the unpaid amount financed; or

(B) the rate determined by any method prescribed by the Bureau as a method which materially simplifies computation while retaining reasonable accuracy as compared with the rate determined under subparagraph (A).

(2) in the case of any extension of credit under an open end credit plan, as the quotient (expressed as a percentage) of the total finance charge for the period to which it relates divided by the amount upon which the finance charge for that period is based, multiplied by the number of such periods in a year.

(b) Computation of rate of finance charges for balances within a specified range

Where a creditor imposes the same finance charge for balances within a specified range, the annual percentage rate shall be computed on the median balance within the range, except that if the Bureau determines that a rate so computed would not be meaningful, or would be materially misleading, the annual percentage rate shall be computed on such other basis as the Bureau may by regulation require.

(c) Allowable tolerances for purposes of compliance with disclosure requirements

The disclosure of an annual percentage rate is accurate for the purpose of this subchapter if the rate disclosed is within a tolerance not greater than one-eighth of 1 per centum more or less than the actual rate or rounded to the nearest one-fourth of 1 per centum. The Bureau may allow a greater tolerance to simplify compliance where irregular payments are involved.

(d) Use of rate tables or charts having allowable variance from determined rates

The Bureau may authorize the use of rate tables or charts which may provide for the disclosure of annual percentage rates which vary from the rate determined in accordance with subsection (a)(1)(A) of this section by not more than such tolerances as the Bureau may allow. The Bureau may not allow a tolerance greater than 8 per centum of that rate except to simplify compliance where irregular payments are involved.

(e) Authorization of tolerances in determining annual percentage rates

In the case of creditors determining the annual percentage rate in a manner other than as described in subsection (d) of this section, the Bureau may authorize other reasonable tolerances.

(Pub.L. 90–321, Title I, § 107, May 29, 1968, 82 Stat. 149; Pub.L. 96–221, Title VI, § 607, Mar. 31, 1980, 94 Stat. 170; Pub.L. 111–203, Title X, § 1100A(2), July 21, 2010, 124 Stat. 2107.)

§ 1607. Administrative enforcement [CCPA § 108]

(a) Enforcing agencies

Subject to subtitle B of the Consumer Financial Protection Act of 2010 [12 U.S.C. §§ 5511–5519] compliance with the requirements imposed under this subchapter shall be enforced under—

(1) section 1818 of Title 12, by the appropriate Federal banking agency, as defined in section 1813(q) of Title 12, with respect to—

(A) national banks, Federal savings associations, and Federal branches and Federal agencies of foreign banks;

(B) member banks of the Federal Reserve System (other than national banks), branches and agencies of foreign banks (other than Federal branches, Federal agencies, and insured State branches of foreign banks), commercial lending companies owned or controlled by foreign banks, and organizations operating under section 25 or 25A of the Federal Reserve Act; and

(C) banks and State savings associations insured by the Federal Deposit Insurance Corporation (other than members of the Federal Reserve System), and insured State branches of foreign banks;

(2) the Federal Credit Union Act, by the Director of the National Credit Union Administration, with respect to any Federal credit union;

(3) part A of subtitle VII of Title 49, by the Secretary of Transportation, with respect to any air carrier or foreign air carrier subject to that part;

(4) the Packers and Stockyards Act, 1921 (except as provided in section 406 of that Act), by the Secretary of Agriculture, with respect to any activities subject to that Act;

(5) the Farm Credit Act of 1971, by the Farm Credit Administration with respect to any Federal land bank, Federal land bank association, Federal intermediate credit bank, or production credit association; and

(6) subtitle E of the Consumer Financial Protection Act of 2010 [12 U.S.C. §§ 5561–5567], by the Bureau, with respect to any person subject to this subchapter.

(7) sections 78u–2 and 78u–3 of this title, in the case of a broker or dealer, other than a depository institution, by the Securities and Exchange Commission.

(b) Violations of this subchapter deemed violations of pre-existing statutory requirements; additional agency powers

For the purpose of the exercise by any agency referred to in subsection (a) of this section of its powers under any Act referred to in that subsection, a violation of any requirement imposed under this subchapter shall be deemed to be a violation of a requirement imposed under that Act. In addition to its powers under any provision of law specifically referred to in subsection (a) of this section, each of the agencies referred to in that subsection may exercise, for the purpose of enforcing compliance with any requirement imposed under this subchapter, any other authority conferred on it by law.

(c) Overall enforcement authority of the Federal Trade Commission

Except to the extent that enforcement of the requirements imposed under this subchapter is specifically committed to some other Government agency under any of paragraphs (1) through (5) of subsection (a), and subject to subtitle B of the Consumer Financial Protection Act of 2010 [12 U.S.C. §§ 5511–5519], the Federal Trade Commission shall be authorized to enforce such requirements. For the purpose of the exercise by the Federal Trade Commission of its functions and powers under the Federal Trade Commission Act [15 U.S.C. § 41 et seq.], a violation of any requirement imposed under this subchapter shall be deemed a violation of a requirement imposed under that Act. All of the functions and powers of the Federal Trade Commission under the Federal Trade Commission Act are available to the Federal Trade Commission to enforce compliance by any person with the requirements under this subchapter, irrespective of whether that person is engaged in commerce or meets any other jurisdictional tests under the Federal Trade Commission Act.

(d) Rules and regulations

The authority of the Bureau to issue regulations under this subchapter does not impair the authority of any other agency designated in this section to make rules respecting its own procedures in enforcing compliance with requirements imposed under this subchapter.

(e) Adjustment of finance charges; procedures applicable, coverage, criteria, etc.

(1) In carrying out its enforcement activities under this section, each agency referred to in subsection (a) or (c) of this section, in cases where an annual percentage rate or finance charge was inaccurately disclosed, shall notify the creditor of such disclosure error and is authorized in accordance with the provisions of this subsection to require the creditor to make an adjustment to the account of the person to whom credit was extended, to assure that such person will not be required to pay a finance charge in excess of the finance charge actually disclosed or the dollar equivalent of the annual percentage rate actually disclosed, whichever is lower. For the purposes of this subsection, except where such disclosure error resulted from a willful violation which was intended to mislead the person to whom credit was extended, in determining whether a disclosure error has occurred and in calculating any adjustment, (A) each agency shall apply (i) with respect to the annual percentage rate, a tolerance of one-quarter of 1 percent more or less than the actual rate, determined without regard to section 1606(c) of this title, and (ii) with respect to the finance charge, a corresponding numerical tolerance as generated by the tolerance provided under this subsection for the annual percentage rate; except that (B) with respect to transactions consummated after two years following March 31, 1980, each agency shall apply (i) for transactions that have a scheduled amortization of ten years or less, with respect to the annual percentage rate, a tolerance not to exceed one-quarter of 1 percent more or less than the actual rate, determined without regard to section 1606(c) of this title, but in no event a tolerance of less than the tolerances allowed under section 1606(c) of this title, (ii) for transactions that have a scheduled amortization of more than ten years, with respect to the annual percentage rate, only such tolerances as are allowed under section 1606(c) of this title, and (iii) for all transactions, with respect to the finance charge, a corresponding numerical tolerance as generated by the tolerances provided under this subsection for the annual percentage rate.

(2) Each agency shall require such an adjustment when it determines that such disclosure error resulted from (A) a clear and consistent pattern or practice of violations, (B) gross negligence, or (C) a willful violation which was intended to mislead the person to whom the credit was extended. Notwithstanding the preceding sentence, except where such disclosure error resulted from a willful violation which was intended to mislead the person to whom credit was extended, an agency need not require such an adjustment if it determines that such disclosure error—

(A) resulted from an error involving the disclosure of a fee or charge that would otherwise be excludable in computing the finance charge, including but not limited to violations involving the disclosures described in sections 1605(b), (c) and (d) of this title, in which event the agency may require such remedial action as it determines to be equitable, except that for transactions consummated after two years after March 31, 1980, such an adjustment shall be ordered for violations of section 1605(b) of this title;

(B) involved a disclosed amount which was 10 per centum or less of the amount that should have been disclosed and (i) in cases where the error involved a disclosed finance charge, the annual percentage rate was disclosed correctly, and (ii) in cases where the error involved a disclosed annual percentage rate, the finance charge was disclosed correctly; in which event the agency may require such adjustment as it determines to be equitable;

(C) involved a total failure to disclose either the annual percentage rate or the finance charge, in which event the agency may require such adjustment as it determines to be equitable; or

(D) resulted from any other unique circumstance involving clearly technical and nonsubstantive disclosure violations that do not adversely affect information provided to the consumer and that have not misled or otherwise deceived the consumer.

In the case of other such disclosure errors, each agency may require such an adjustment.

(3) Notwithstanding paragraph (2), no adjustment shall be ordered—

(A) if it would have a significantly adverse impact upon the safety or soundness of the creditor, but in any such case, the agency may—

(i) require a partial adjustment in an amount which does not have such an impact; or

(ii) require the full adjustment, but permit the creditor to make the required adjustment in partial payments over an extended period of time which the agency considers to be reasonable, if (in the case of an agency referred to in paragraph (1), (2), or (3) of subsection (a) of this section), the agency determines that a partial adjustment or making partial payments over an extended period is necessary to avoid causing the creditor to become undercapitalized pursuant to section 38 of the Federal Deposit Insurance Act [12 U.S.C. § 1831*o*];

(B) the[1] amount of the adjustment would be less than $1, except that if more than one year has elapsed since the date of the violation, the agency may require that such amount be paid into the Treasury of the United States, or

(C) except where such disclosure error resulted from a willful violation which was intended to mislead the person to whom credit was extended, in the case of an open-end credit plan, more than two years after the violation, or in the case of any other extension of credit, as follows:

(i) with respect to creditors that are subject to examination by the agencies referred to in paragraphs (1) through (3) of subsection (a) of this section, except in connection with violations arising from practices identified in the current examination and only in connection with transactions that are consummated after the date of the immediately preceding examination, except that where practices giving rise to violations identified in earlier examinations have not been corrected, adjustments for those violations shall be required in connection with transactions consummated after the date of examination in which such practices were first identified;

(ii) with respect to creditors that are not subject to examination by such agencies, except in connection with transactions that are consummated after May 10, 1978; and

(iii) in no event after the later of (I) the expiration of the life of the credit extension, or (II) two years after the agreement to extend credit was consummated.

(4)(A) Notwithstanding any other provision of this section, an adjustment under this subsection may be required by an agency referred to in subsection (a) or (c) of this section only by an order issued in accordance with cease and desist procedures provided by the provision of law referred to in such subsections.

(B) In case of an agency which is not authorized to conduct cease and desist proceedings, such an order may be issued after an agency hearing on the record conducted at least thirty but not more than sixty days after notice of the alleged violation is served on the creditor. Such a hearing shall be deemed to be a hearing which is subject to the provisions of section 8(h) of the Federal Deposit Insurance Act [12 U.S.C. § 1818(h)] and shall be subject to judicial review as provided therein.

---

[1] So in original. Probably should be preceded by "if".

(5) Except as otherwise specifically provided in this subsection and notwithstanding any provision of law referred to in subsection (a) or (c) of this section, no agency referred to in subsection (a) or (c) of this section may require a creditor to make dollar adjustments for errors in any requirements under this subchapter, except with regard to the requirements of section 1666d of this title.

(6) A creditor shall not be subject to an order to make an adjustment, if within sixty days after discovering a disclosure error, whether pursuant to a final written examination report or through the creditor's own procedures, the creditor notifies the person concerned of the error and adjusts the account so as to assure that such person will not be required to pay a finance charge in excess of the finance charge actually disclosed or the dollar equivalent of the annual percentage rate actually disclosed, whichever is lower.

(7) Notwithstanding the second sentence of subsection (e)(1), subsection (e)(3)(C)(i), and subsection (e)(3)(C)(ii) of this section, each agency referred to in subsection (a) or (c) of this section shall require an adjustment for an annual percentage rate disclosure error that exceeds a tolerance of one quarter of one percent less than the actual rate, determined without regard to section 1606(c) of this title, with respect to any transaction consummated between January 1, 1977, and March 31, 1980.

(Pub.L. 90–321, Title I, § 108, May 29, 1968, 82 Stat. 150; Pub.L. 91–206, §§ 1, 3, Mar. 10, 1970, 84 Stat. 49; Pub.L. 93–495, Title IV, § 403, Oct. 28, 1974, 88 Stat. 1517; Pub.L. 95–630, Title V, § 501, Nov. 10, 1978, 92 Stat. 3680; Pub.L. 96–221, Title VI, § 608(a), (c), Mar. 21, 1980, 94 Stat. 171, 173; Pub.L. 98–443, § 9(n), Oct. 4, 1984, 98 Stat. 1708; Pub.L. 101–73, Title VII, § 744(k), Aug. 9, 1989, 103 Stat. 439; Pub.L. 102–242, Title II, § 212(b), Dec. 19, 1991, 105 Stat. 2299; Pub.L. 102–550, Title XVI, § 1604(a)(5), Oct. 28, 1992, 106 Stat. 4082; Pub.L. 104–208, Div. A, Title II, § 2106, Sept. 30, 1996, 110 Stat. 3009–402; Pub.L. 111–203, Title X, §§ 1100A(2), 1100A(8), Title XIV, §§ 1400(c), 1414(b), July 21, 2010, 124 Stat. 2107, 2108, 2109, 2136, 2152.)

§ 1608. Views of other agencies [CCPA § 109]

In the exercise of its functions under this subchapter, the Bureau may obtain upon requests the views of any other Federal agency which, in the judgment of the Bureau, exercises regulatory or supervisory functions with respect to any class of creditors subject to this subchapter.

(Pub.L. 90–321, Title I, § 109, May 29, 1968, 82 Stat. 150; Pub.L. 111–203, Title X, § 1100A(2), July 21, 2010, 124 Stat. 2107.)

§ 1609. Repealed. Pub.L. 94–239, § 3(b)(1), Mar. 23, 1976, 90 Stat. 253

§ 1610. Effect on other laws [CCPA § 111]

(a) Inconsistent provisions; procedures applicable for determination

(1) Except as provided in subsection (e) of this section, this part and parts B and C of this subchapter do not annul, alter, or affect the laws of any State relating to the disclosure of information in connection with credit transactions, except to the extent that those laws are inconsistent with the provisions of this subchapter and then only to the extent of the inconsistency. Upon its own motion or upon the request of any creditor, State or other interested party which is submitted in accordance with procedures prescribed in regulations of the Bureau, the Bureau shall determine whether any such inconsistency exists. If the Bureau determines that a State-required disclosure is inconsistent, creditors located in that State may not make disclosures using the inconsistent term or form, and shall incur no liability under the law of that State for failure to use such term or form, notwithstanding that such determination is subsequently amended, rescinded, or determined by judicial or other authority to be invalid for any reason.

(2) Upon its own motion or upon the request of any creditor, State, or other interested party which is submitted in accordance with procedures prescribed in regulations of the Bureau, the Bureau shall determine whether any disclosure required under the law of any State is substantially the same in meaning as a disclosure required under this subchapter. If the Bureau determines that a State-required disclosure is substantially the same in meaning as a disclosure required by this subchapter, then creditors located in that State may make such disclosure in compliance with such State law in lieu of the disclosure required by this subchapter, except that the annual percentage rate and finance charge shall be disclosed as required by section 1632 of this title, and such State-required disclosure may not be made in lieu of the disclosures applicable to certain mortgages under section 1639 of this title.

(b) State credit charge statutes

Except as provided in section 1639 of this title, this subchapter does not otherwise annul, alter or affect in any manner the meaning, scope or applicability of the laws of any State, including, but not limited to, laws relating to the types, amounts or rates of charges, or any element or elements of charges, permissible under such laws in connection with the extension or use of credit, nor does this subchapter extend the applicability of those laws to any class of persons or transactions to which they would not otherwise apply. The provisions of section 1639 of this title do not annul, alter, or affect the applicability of the laws of any State or exempt any person subject to the provisions of section 1639 of this title from complying with the laws of any State, with respect to the requirements for mortgages referred to in section 1602(aa) of this title, except to the extent that those State laws are inconsistent with any provisions of section 1639 of this title, and then only to the extent of the inconsistency.

(c) Disclosure as evidence

In any action or proceeding in any court involving a consumer credit sale, the disclosure of the annual percentage rate as required under this subchapter in connection with that sale may not be received as evidence that the sale was a loan or any type of transaction other than a credit sale.

(d) Contract or other obligations under State or Federal law

Except as specified in sections 1635, 1640, and 1666e of this title, this subchapter and the regulations issued thereunder do not affect the validity or enforceability of any contract or obligation under State or Federal law.

(e) Certain credit and charge card application and solicitation disclosure provisions

The provisions of subsection (c) of section 1632 of this title and subsections (c), (d), (e), and (f) of section 1637 of this title shall supersede any provision of the law of any State relating to the disclosure of information in any credit or charge card application or solicitation which is subject to the requirements of section 1637(c) of this title or any renewal notice which is subject to the requirements of section 1637(d) of this title, except that any State may employ or establish State laws for the purpose of enforcing the requirements of such sections.

(Pub.L. 90–321, Title I, § 111, May 29, 1968, 82 Stat. 151; Pub.L. 93–495, Title III, § 307(b), Oct. 28, 1974, 88 Stat. 1516; Pub.L. 96–221, Title VI, § 609, Mar. 31, 1980, 94 Stat. 173; Pub.L. 100–583, § 4, Nov. 3, 1988, 102 Stat. 2967; Pub.L. 103–325, Title I, § 152(e)(2)(B), (C), Sept. 23, 1994, 108 Stat. 2194; Pub.L. 111–203, Title X, § 1100A(2), July 21, 2010, 124 Stat. 2107.)

§ 1611. Criminal liability for willful and knowing violation [CCPA § 112]

Whoever willfully and knowingly

(1) gives false or inaccurate information or fails to provide information which he is required to disclose under the provisions of this subchapter or any regulation issued thereunder,

(2) uses any chart or table authorized by the Bureau under section 1606 of this title in such a manner as to consistently understate the annual percentage rate determined under section 1606(a)(1)(A) of this title, or

(3) otherwise fails to comply with any requirement imposed under this subchapter,

shall be fined not more than $5,000 or imprisoned not more than one year, or both.

(Pub.L. 90–321, Title I, § 112, May 29, 1968, 82 Stat. 151; Pub.L. 111–203, Title X, § 1100A(2), July 21, 2010, 124 Stat. 2107.)

§ 1612. Effect on government agencies [CCPA § 113]

(a) Consultation requirements respecting compliance of credit instruments issued to participating creditor

Any department or agency of the United States which administers a credit program in which it extends, insures, or guarantees consumer credit and in which it provides instruments to a creditor which contain any disclosures required by this subchapter shall, prior to the issuance or continued use of such instruments, consult with the Bureau to assure that such instruments comply with this subchapter.

(b) Inapplicability of Federal civil or criminal penalties to Federal, state, and local agencies

No civil or criminal penalty provided under this subchapter for any violation thereof may be imposed upon the United States or any department or agency thereof, or upon any State or political subdivision thereof, or any agency of any State or political subdivision.

(c) Inapplicability of Federal civil or criminal penalties to participating creditor where violating instrument issued by United States

A creditor participating in a credit program administered, insured, or guaranteed by any department or agency of the United States shall not be held liable for a civil or criminal penalty under this subchapter in any case in which the violation results from the use of an instrument required by any such department or agency.

(d) Applicability of State penalties to violations by participating creditor

A creditor participating in a credit program administered, insured, or guaranteed by any department or agency of the United States shall not be held liable for a civil or criminal penalty under the laws of any State (other than laws determined under section 1610 of this title to be inconsistent with this subchapter) for any technical or procedural failure, such as a failure to use a specific form, to make information available at a specific place on an instrument, or to use a specific typeface, as required by State law, which is caused by the use of an instrument required to be used by such department or agency.

(Pub.L. 90–321, Title I, § 113, May 29, 1968, 82 Stat. 151; Pub.L. 96–221, Title VI, § 622(a), Mar. 31, 1980, 94 Stat. 184; Pub.L. 111–203, Title X, § 1100A(2), July 21, 2010, 124 Stat. 2107.)

§ 1613. Annual reports to Congress by Bureau [CCPA § 114]

Each year the Bureau shall make a report to the Congress concerning the administration of its functions under this subchapter, including such recommendations as the Bureau deems necessary or appropriate. In addition, each report of the Bureau shall include its assessment of the extent to which compliance with the requirements imposed under this subchapter is being achieved.

(Pub.L. 90–321, Title I, § 114, May 29, 1968, 82 Stat. 151; Pub.L. 96–221, Title VI, § 610(a), Mar. 31, 1980, 94 Stat. 174; Pub.L. 97–375, Title II, § 209(b), Dec. 21, 1982, 96 Stat. 1825; Pub.L. 111–203, Title X, § 1100A(2), July 21, 2010, 124 Stat. 2107.)

§ 1614. Repealed. Pub.L. 96–221, Title VI, 616(b), Mar. 31, 1980, 94 Stat. 182

§ 1615. Prohibition on use of "Rule of 78's" in connection with mortgage refinancings and other consumer loans [CCPA § 116]

(a) Prompt refund of unearned interest required

(1) In general

If a consumer prepays in full the financed amount under any consumer credit transaction, the creditor shall promptly refund any unearned portion of the interest charge to the consumer.

(2) Exception for refund of de minimus[1] amount

No refund shall be required under paragraph (1) with respect to the prepayment of any consumer credit transaction if the total amount of the refund would be less than $1.

(3) Applicability to refinanced transactions and acceleration by the creditor

This subsection shall apply with respect to any prepayment of a consumer credit transaction described in paragraph (1) without regard to the manner or the reason for the prepayment, including—

(A) any prepayment made in connection with the refinancing, consolidation, or restructuring of the transaction; and

(B) any prepayment made as a result of the acceleration of the obligation to repay the amount due with respect to the transaction.

(b) Use of "Rule of 78's" prohibited

For the purpose of calculating any refund of interest required under subsection (a) of this section for any precomputed consumer credit transaction of a term exceeding 61 months which is consummated after September 30, 1993, the creditor shall compute the refund based on a method which is at least as favorable to the consumer as the actuarial method.

(c) Statement of prepayment amount

(1) In general

Before the end of the 5-day period beginning on the date an oral or written request is received by a creditor from a consumer for the disclosure of the amount due on any precomputed consumer credit account, the creditor or assignee shall provide the consumer with a statement of—

(A) the amount necessary to prepay the account in full; and

(B) if the amount disclosed pursuant to subparagraph (A) includes an amount which is required to be refunded under this section with respect to such prepayment, the amount of such refund.

(2) Written statement required if request is in writing

If the customer's request is in writing, the statement under paragraph (1) shall be in writing.

(3) 1 free annual statement

A consumer shall be entitled to obtain 1 statement under paragraph (1) each year without charge.

(4) Additional statements subject to reasonable fees

Any creditor may impose a reasonable fee to cover the cost of providing any statement under paragraph (1) to any consumer in addition to the 1 free annual statement required under paragraph (3) if the amount of the charge for such additional statement is disclosed to the consumer before furnishing such statement.

(d) Definitions

For the purpose of this section—

(1) Actuarial method

The term "actuarial method" means the method of allocating payments made on a debt between the amount financed and the finance charge pursuant to which a payment is applied first to the accumulated finance charge and any remainder is subtracted from, or any deficiency is added to, the unpaid balance of the amount financed.

[1] So in original. Probably should be "de minimis".

(2) Consumer, credit

The terms "consumer" and "creditor" have the meanings given to such terms in section 1602 of this title.

(3) Creditor

The term "creditor"—

(A) has the meaning given to such term in section 1602 of this title; and

(B) includes any assignee of any creditor with respect to credit extended in connection with any consumer credit transaction and any subsequent assignee with respect to such credit.

(Pub.L. 102–550, Title IX, § 933, Oct. 28, 1992, 106 Stat. 3891.)

§ 1616. Board review of consumer credit plans and regulations

(a) Required review

Not later than 2 years after the effective date of this Act and every 2 years thereafter, except as provided in subsection (c)(2), the Board shall conduct a review, within the limits of its existing resources available for reporting purposes, of the consumer credit card market, including—

(1) the terms of credit card agreements and the practices of credit card issuers;

(2) the effectiveness of disclosure of terms, fees, and other expenses of credit card plans;

(3) the adequacy of protections against unfair or deceptive acts or practices relating to credit card plans; and

(4) whether or not, and to what extent, the implementation of this Act and the amendments made by this Act has affected—

(A) cost and availability of credit, particularly with respect to non-prime borrowers;

(B) the safety and soundness of credit card issuers;

(C) the use of risk-based pricing; or

(D) credit card product innovation.

(b) Solicitation of public comment

In connection with conducting the review required by subsection (a), the Board shall solicit comment from consumers, credit card issuers, and other interested parties, such as through hearings or written comments.

(c) Regulations

(1) Notice

Following the review required by subsection (a), the Board shall publish a notice in the Federal Register that—

(A) summarizes the review, the comments received from the public solicitation, and other evidence gathered by the Board, such as through consumer testing or other research; and

(B) either—

(i) proposes new or revised regulations or interpretations to update or revise disclosures and protections for consumer credit cards, as appropriate; or

(ii) states the reason for the determination of the Board that new or revised regulations are not necessary.

(2) Revision of review period following material revision of regulations

In the event that the Board materially revises regulations on consumer credit card plans, a review need not be conducted until 2 years after the effective date of the revised regulations, which thereafter shall be treated as the new date for the biennial review required by subsection (a).

(d) Board report to the Congress

The Board shall report to Congress not less frequently than every 2 years, except as provided in subsection (c)(2), on the status of its most recent review, its efforts to address any issues identified from the review, and any recommendations for legislation.

(e) Additional reporting

The Federal banking agencies (as that term is defined in section 1813 of Title 12) and the Federal Trade Commission shall provide annually to the Board, and the Board shall include in its annual report to Congress under section 10 of the Federal Reserve Act, information about the supervisory and enforcement activities of the agencies with respect to compliance by credit card issuers with applicable Federal consumer protection statutes and regulations, including—

(1) this Act, the amendments made by this Act, and regulations prescribed under this Act and such amendments; and

(2) section 5 of the Federal Trade Commission Act, and regulations prescribed under the Federal Trade Commission Act, including part 227 of title 12 of the Code of Federal Regulations, as prescribed by the Board (referred to as "Regulation AA").

(Pub.L. 111–24, Title V, § 502, May 22, 2009, 123 Stat. 1755.)

PART B—CREDIT TRANSACTIONS

§ 1631. Disclosure requirements [CCPA § 121]

(a) Duty of creditor or lessor respecting one or more than one obligor

Subject to subsection (b) of this section, a creditor or lessor shall disclose to the person who is obligated on a consumer lease or a consumer credit transaction the information required under this subchapter. In a transaction involving more than one obligor, a creditor or lessor, except in a transaction under section 1635 of this title, need not disclose to more than one of such obligors if the obligor given disclosure is a primary obligor.

(b) Creditor or lessor required to make disclosure

If a transaction involves one creditor as defined in section 1602(f) of this title, or one lessor as defined in section 1667(3) of this title, such creditor or lessor shall make the disclosures. If a transaction involves more than one creditor or lessor, only one creditor or lessor shall be required to make the disclosures. The Bureau shall by regulation specify which creditor or lessor shall make the disclosures.

(c) Estimates as satisfying statutory requirements; basis of disclosure for per diem interest

The Bureau may provide by regulation that any portion of the information required to be disclosed by this subchapter may be given in the form of estimates where the provider of such information is not in a position to know exact information. In the case of any consumer credit transaction a portion of the interest on which is determined on a per diem basis and is to be collected upon the consummation of such transaction, any disclosure with respect to such portion of interest shall be deemed to be accurate for purposes of this subchapter if the disclosure is based on information actually known to the creditor at the time that the disclosure documents are being prepared for the consummation of the transaction.

(d) Tolerances for numerical disclosures

The Bureau shall determine whether tolerances for numerical disclosures other than the annual percentage rate are necessary to facilitate compliance with this subchapter, and if it determines that such tolerances are necessary to facilitate compliance, it shall by regulation permit disclosures within such tolerances. The Bureau shall exercise its authority to permit tolerances for numerical disclosures other than the annual percentage rate so that such tolerances are narrow enough to prevent such tolerances from resulting in misleading disclosures or disclosures that circumvent the purposes of this subchapter.

(Pub.L. 90–321, Title I, § 121, May 29, 1968, 82 Stat. 152; Pub.L. 93–495, Title III, § 307(c), (d), Title IV, § 409, Oct. 28, 1974, 88 Stat. 1516, 1519; Pub.L. 94–205, § 11, Jan. 2, 1976, 89 Stat. 1159; Pub.L. 96–221, Title VI, § 611, Mar. 31, 1980, 94 Stat. 174; Pub.L. 104–29, § 3(b), Sept. 30, 1995, 109 Stat. 273; Pub.L. 111–203, Title X, § 1100A(2), July 21, 2010, 124 Stat. 2107.)

§ 1632. Form of disclosure; additional information [CCPA § 122]

(a) Information clearly and conspicuously disclosed; "annual percentage rate" and "finance charge"; order of disclosures and use of different terminology

Information required by this subchapter shall be disclosed clearly and conspicuously, in accordance with regulations of the Bureau. The terms "annual percentage rate" and "finance charge" shall be disclosed more conspicuously than other terms, data, or information provided in connection with a transaction, except information relating to the identity of the creditor. Except as provided in subsection (c) of this section, regulations of the Bureau need not require that disclosures pursuant to this subchapter be made in the order set forth in this subchapter and, except as otherwise provided, may permit the use of terminology different from that employed in this subchapter if it conveys substantially the same meaning.

(b) Optional information by creditor or lessor

Any creditor or lessor may supply additional information or explanation with any disclosures required under parts D and E of this subchapter and, except as provided in sections 1637a(b)(3) and 1638(b)(1) of this title, under this part.

(c) Tabular format required for certain disclosures under section 1637(c)

(1) In general

The information described in paragraphs (1)(A), (3)(B)(i)(I), (4)(A), and (4)(C)(i)(I) of section 1637(c) of this title shall be—

(A) disclosed in the form and manner which the Bureau shall prescribe by regulations; and

(B) placed in a conspicuous and prominent location on or with any written application, solicitation, or other document or paper with respect to which such disclosure is required.

(2) Tabular format

(A) Form of table to be prescribed

In the regulations prescribed under paragraph (1)(A) of this subsection, the Bureau shall require that the disclosure of such information shall, to the extent the Bureau determines to be practicable and appropriate, be in the form of a table which—

(i) contains clear and concise headings for each item of such information; and

(ii) provides a clear and concise form for stating each item of information required to be disclosed under each such heading.

(B) Bureau discretion in prescribing order and wording of table

In prescribing the form of the table under subparagraph (A), the Bureau may—

(i) list the items required to be included in the table in a different order than the order in which such items are set forth in paragraph (1)(A) or (4)(A) of section 1637(c) of this title; and

(ii) subject to subparagraph (C), employ terminology which is different than the terminology which is employed in section 1637(c) of this title if such terminology conveys substantially the same meaning.

(C) Grace period

Either the heading or the statement under the heading which relates to the time period referred to in section 1637(c)(1)(A)(iii) of this title shall contain the term "grace period".

(d) Additional electronic disclosures

(1) Posting agreements

Each creditor shall establish and maintain an Internet site on which the creditor shall post the written agreement between the creditor and the consumer for each credit card account under an open-end consumer credit plan.

(2) Creditor to provide contracts to the Bureau

Each creditor shall provide to the Bureau, in electronic format, the consumer credit card agreements that it publishes on its Internet site.

(3) Record repository

The Bureau shall establish and maintain on its publicly available Internet site a central repository of the consumer credit card agreements received from creditors pursuant to this subsection, and such agreements shall be easily accessible and retrievable by the public.

(4) Exception

This subsection shall not apply to individually negotiated changes to contractual terms, such as individually modified workouts or renegotiations of amounts owed by a consumer under an open end consumer credit plan.

(5) Regulations

The Bureau, in consultation with the other Federal banking agencies (as that term is defined in section 603) and the Bureau,[1] may promulgate regulations to implement this subsection, including specifying the format for posting the agreements on the Internet sites of creditors and establishing exceptions to paragraphs (1) and (2), in any case in which the administrative burden outweighs the benefit of increased transparency, such as where a credit card plan has a de minimis number of consumer account holders.

(Pub.L. 90–321, Title I, § 122, May 29, 1968, 82 Stat. 152; Pub.L. 93–495, Title III, § 307(e), (f), Oct. 28, 1974, 88 Stat. 1516, 1517; Pub.L. 96–221, Title VI, § 611, Mar. 31, 1980, 94 Stat. 175; Pub.L. 100–583, § 2(b), Nov. 3, 1988, 102 Stat. 2966; Pub.L. 100–709, § 2(d), Nov. 23, 1988, 102 Stat. 4731; Pub.L. 111–24, Title II, § 204(a), May 22, 2009, 123 Stat. 1746; Pub.L. 111–203, Title X, § 1100A(2), (3), July 21, 2010, 124 Stat. 2107.)

§ 1633. Exemption for State-regulated transactions [CCPA § 123]

The Bureau shall by regulation exempt from the requirements of this part any class of credit transactions within any State if it determines that under the law of that State that class of transactions is subject to requirements substantially similar to those imposed under this part, and that there is adequate provision for enforcement.

(Pub.L. 90–321, Title I, § 123, May 29, 1968, 82 Stat. 152; Pub.L. 111–203, Title X, § 1100A(2), July 21, 2010, 124 Stat. 2107.)

§ 1634. Effect of subsequent occurrence [CCPA § 124]

If information disclosed in accordance with this part is subsequently rendered inaccurate as the result of any act, occurrence, or agreement subsequent to the delivery of the required disclosures, the inaccuracy resulting therefrom does not constitute a violation of this part.

(Pub.L. 90–321, Title I, § 124, May 29, 1968, 82 Stat. 152.)

---

[1] So in original.

§ 1635. Right of rescission as to certain transactions [CCPA § 125]

(a) Disclosure of obligor's right to rescind

Except as otherwise provided in this section, in the case of any consumer credit transaction (including opening or increasing the credit limit for an open end credit plan) in which a security interest, including any such interest arising by operation of law, is or will be retained or acquired in any property which is used as the principal dwelling of the person to whom credit is extended, the obligor shall have the right to rescind the transaction until midnight of the third business day following the consummation of the transaction or the delivery of the information and rescission forms required under this section together with a statement containing the material disclosures required under this subchapter, whichever is later, by notifying the creditor, in accordance with regulations of the Bureau, of his intention to do so. The creditor shall clearly and conspicuously disclose, in accordance with regulations of the Bureau, to any obligor in a transaction subject to this section the rights of the obligor under this section. The creditor shall also provide, in accordance with regulations of the Bureau, appropriate forms for the obligor to exercise his right to rescind any transaction subject to this section.

(b) Return of money or property following rescission

When an obligor exercises his right to rescind under subsection (a) of this section, he is not liable for any finance or other charge, and any security interest given by the obligor, including any such interest arising by operation of law, becomes void upon such a rescission. Within 20 days after receipt of a notice of rescission, the creditor shall return to the obligor any money or property given as earnest money, downpayment, or otherwise, and shall take any action necessary or appropriate to reflect the termination of any security interest created under the transaction. If the creditor has delivered any property to the obligor, the obligor may retain possession of it. Upon the performance of the creditor's obligations under this section, the obligor shall tender the property to the creditor, except that if return of the property in kind would be impracticable or inequitable, the obligor shall tender its reasonable value. Tender shall be made at the location of the property or at the residence of the obligor, at the option of the obligor. If the creditor does not take possession of the property within 20 days after tender by the obligor, ownership of the property vests in the obligor without obligation on his part to pay for it. The procedures prescribed by this subsection shall apply except when otherwise ordered by a court.

(c) Rebuttable presumption of delivery of required disclosures

Notwithstanding any rule of evidence, written acknowledgment of receipt of any disclosures required under this subchapter by a person to whom information, forms, and a statement is required to be given pursuant to this section does no more than create a rebuttable presumption of delivery thereof.

(d) Modification and waiver of rights

The Bureau may, if it finds that such action is necessary in order to permit homeowners to meet bona fide personal financial emergencies, prescribe regulations authorizing the modification or waiver of any rights created under this section to the extent and under the circumstances set forth in those regulations.

(e) Exempted transactions; reapplication of provisions

This section does not apply to—

(1) a residential mortgage transaction as defined in section 1602(w) of this title;

(2) a transaction which constitutes a refinancing or consolidation (with no new advances) of the principal balance then due and any accrued and unpaid finance charges of an existing extension of credit by the same creditor secured by an interest in the same property;

(3) a transaction in which an agency of a State is the creditor; or

(4) advances under a preexisting open end credit plan if a security interest has already been retained or acquired and such advances are in accordance with a previously established credit limit for such plan.

(f) Time limit for exercise of right

An obligor's right of rescission shall expire three years after the date of consummation of the transaction or upon the sale of the property, whichever occurs first, notwithstanding the fact that the information and forms required under this section or any other disclosures required under this part have not been delivered to the obligor, except that if (1) any agency empowered to enforce the provisions of this subchapter institutes a proceeding to enforce the provisions of this section within three years after the date of consummation of the transaction, (2) such agency finds a violation of this section, and (3) the obligor's right to rescind is based in whole or in part on any matter involved in such proceeding, then the obligor's right of rescission shall expire three years after the date of consummation of the transaction or upon the earlier sale of the property, or upon the expiration of one year following the conclusion of the proceeding, or any judicial review or period for judicial review thereof, whichever is later.

(g) Additional relief

In any action in which it is determined that a creditor has violated this section, in addition to rescission the court may award relief under section 1640 of this title for violations of this subchapter not relating to the right to rescind.

(h) Limitation on rescission

An obligor shall have no rescission rights arising solely from the form of written notice used by the creditor to inform the obligor of the rights of the obligor under this section, if the creditor provided the obligor the appropriate form of written notice published and adopted by the Bureau, or a comparable written notice of the rights of the obligor, that was properly completed by the creditor, and otherwise complied with all other requirements of this section regarding notice.

(i) Rescission rights in foreclosure

(1) In general

Notwithstanding section 1649 of this title, and subject to the time period provided in subsection (f) of this section, in addition to any other right of rescission available under this section for a transaction, after the initiation of any judicial or nonjudicial foreclosure process on the primary dwelling of an obligor securing an extension of credit, the obligor shall have a right to rescind the transaction equivalent to other rescission rights provided by this section, if—

(A) a mortgage broker fee is not included in the finance charge in accordance with the laws and regulations in effect at the time the consumer credit transaction was consummated; or

(B) the form of notice of rescission for the transaction is not the appropriate form of written notice published and adopted by the Bureau or a comparable written notice, and otherwise complied with all the requirements of this section regarding notice.

(2) Tolerance for disclosures

Notwithstanding section 1605(f) of this title, and subject to the time period provided in subsection (f) of this section, for the purposes of exercising any rescission rights after the initiation of any judicial or nonjudicial foreclosure process on the principal dwelling of the obligor securing an extension of credit, the disclosure of the finance charge and other disclosures affected by any finance charge shall be treated as being accurate for purposes of this section if the amount disclosed as the finance charge does not vary from the actual finance charge by more than $35 or is greater than the amount required to be disclosed under this subchapter.

(3) Right of recoupment under State law

Nothing in this subsection affects a consumer's right of rescission in recoupment under State law.

(4) Applicability

This subsection shall apply to all consumer credit transactions in existence or consummated on or after September 30, 1995.

(Pub.L. 90–321, Title I, § 125, May 29, 1968, 82 Stat. 153; Pub.L. 93–495, Title IV, §§ 404, 405, 412, Oct. 28, 1974, 88 Stat. 1517, 1519; Pub.L. 96–221, Title VI, § 612(a)(1), (3) to (6), Mar. 31, 1980, 94 Stat. 175,

176; Pub.L. 98–479, Title II, § 205, Oct. 17, 1984, 98 Stat. 2234; Pub.L. 104–29, §§ 5, 8, Sept. 30, 1995, 109 Stat. 274, 275; Pub.L. 111–203, Title X, § 1100A(2), July 21, 2010, 124 Stat. 2107.)

§ 1636. Repealed. Pub.L. 96–221, Title VI, § 614(e)(1), Mar. 31, 1980, 94 Stat. 180

§ 1637. Open end consumer credit plans [CCPA § 127]

(a) Required disclosures by creditor

Before opening any account under an open end consumer credit plan, the creditor shall disclose to the person to whom credit is to be extended each of the following items, to the extent applicable:

(1) The conditions under which a finance charge may be imposed, including the time period (if any) within which any credit extended may be repaid without incurring a finance charge, except that the creditor may, at his election and without disclosure, impose no such finance charge if payment is received after the termination of such time period. If no such time period is provided, the creditor shall disclose such fact.

(2) The method of determining the balance upon which a finance charge will be imposed.

(3) The method of determining the amount of the finance charge, including any minimum or fixed amount imposed as a finance charge.

(4) Where one or more periodic rates may be used to compute the finance charge, each such rate, the range of balances to which it is applicable, and the corresponding nominal annual percentage rate determined by multiplying the periodic rate by the number of periods in a year.

(5) Identification of other charges which may be imposed as part of the plan, and their method of computation, in accordance with regulations of the Bureau.

(6) In cases where the credit is or will be secured, a statement that a security interest has been or will be taken in (A) the property purchased as part of the credit transaction, or (B) property not purchased as part of the credit transaction identified by item or type.

(7) A statement, in a form prescribed by regulations of the Bureau of the protection provided by sections 1666 and 1666i of this title to an obligor and the creditor's responsibilities under sections 1666a and 1666i of this title. With respect to one billing cycle per calendar year, at intervals of not less than six months or more than eighteen months, the creditor shall transmit such statement to each obligor to whom the creditor is required to transmit a statement pursuant to subsection (b) of this section for such billing cycle.

(8) In the case of any account under an open end consumer credit plan which provides for any extension of credit which is secured by the consumer's principal dwelling, any information which—

(A) is required to be disclosed under section 1637a(a) of this title; and

(B) the Bureau determines is not described in any other paragraph of this subsection.

(b) Statement required with each billing cycle

The creditor of any account under an open end consumer credit plan shall transmit to the obligor, for each billing cycle at the end of which there is an outstanding balance in that account or with respect to which a finance charge is imposed, a statement setting forth each of the following items to the extent applicable:

(1) The outstanding balance in the account at the beginning of the statement period.

(2) The amount and date of each extension of credit during the period, and a brief identification, on or accompanying the statement of each extension of credit in a form prescribed by the Bureau sufficient to enable the obligor either to identify the transaction or to relate it to copies of sales vouchers or similar instruments previously furnished, except that a creditor's failure to disclose such information in accordance with this paragraph shall not be deemed a failure to comply with this part or this subchapter if (A) the creditor maintains procedures reasonably adapted to procure and provide such information, and (B) the creditor responds to and treats any inquiry for clarification or documentation as a billing error and an erroneously billed amount under section 1666 of this title. In lieu of complying with the requirements of the previous sentence, in the case of any transaction in which the creditor and seller are the same person, as defined by the Bureau, and such person's open end credit plan has fewer than 15,000 accounts, the creditor may elect to provide only the amount and date of each extension of credit during the period and the seller's name and location where the transaction took place if (A) a brief identification of the transaction has been previously furnished, and (B) the creditor responds to and treats any inquiry for clarification or documentation as a billing error and an erroneously billed amount under section 1666 of this title.

(3) The total amount credited to the account during the period.

(4) The amount of any finance charge added to the account during the period, itemized to show the amounts, if any, due to the application of percentage rates and the amount, if any, imposed as a minimum or fixed charge.

(5) Where one or more periodic rates may be used to compute the finance charge, each such rate, the range of balances to which it is applicable, and, unless the annual percentage rate (determined under section 1606(a)(2) of this title) is required to be disclosed pursuant to paragraph (6), the corresponding nominal annual percentage rate determined by multiplying the periodic rate by the number of periods in a year.

(6) Where the total finance charge exceeds 50 cents for a monthly or longer billing cycle, or the pro rata part of 50 cents for a billing cycle shorter than monthly, the total finance charge expressed as an annual percentage rate (determined under section 1606(a)(2) of this title), except that if the finance charge is the sum of two or more products of a rate times a portion of the balance, the creditor may, in lieu of disclosing a single rate for the total charge, disclose each such rate expressed as an annual percentage rate, and the part of the balance to which it is applicable.

(7) The balance on which the finance charge was computed and a statement of how the balance was determined. If the balance is determined without first deducting all credits during the period, that fact and the amount of such payments shall also be disclosed.

(8) The outstanding balance in the account at the end of the period.

(9) The date by which or the period (if any) within which, payment must be made to avoid additional finance charges, except that the creditor may, at his election and without disclosure, impose no such additional finance charge if payment is received after such date or the termination of such period.

(10) The address to be used by the creditor for the purpose of receiving billing inquiries from the obligor.

(11)(A) A written statement in the following form: "Minimum Payment Warning: Making only the minimum payment will increase the amount of interest you pay and the time it takes to repay your balance.", or such similar statement as is established by the Bureau pursuant to consumer testing.

(B) Repayment information that would apply to the outstanding balance of the consumer under the credit plan, including—

(i) the number of months (rounded to the nearest month) that it would take to pay the entire amount of that balance, if the consumer pays only the required minimum monthly payments and if no further advances are made;

(ii) the total cost to the consumer, including interest and principal payments, of paying that balance in full, if the consumer pays only the required minimum monthly payments and if no further advances are made;

(iii) the monthly payment amount that would be required for the consumer to eliminate the outstanding balance in 36 months, if no further advances are made, and the total cost to the consumer, including interest and principal payments, of paying that balance in full if the consumer pays the balance over 36 months; and

(iv) a toll-free telephone number at which the consumer may receive information about accessing credit counseling and debt management services.

(C)(i) Subject to clause (ii), in making the disclosures under subparagraph (B), the creditor shall apply the interest rate or rates in effect on the date on which the disclosure is made until the date on which the balance would be paid in full.

(ii) If the interest rate in effect on the date on which the disclosure is made is a temporary rate that will change under a contractual provision applying an index or formula for subsequent interest rate adjustment, the creditor shall apply the interest rate in effect on the date on which the disclosure is made for as long as that interest rate will apply under that contractual provision, and then apply an interest rate based on the index or formula in effect on the applicable billing date.

(D) All of the information described in subparagraph (B) shall—

(i) be disclosed in the form and manner which the Bureau shall prescribe, by regulation, and in a manner that avoids duplication; and

(ii) be placed in a conspicuous and prominent location on the billing statement.

(E) In the regulations prescribed under subparagraph (D), the Bureau shall require that the disclosure of such information shall be in the form of a table that—

(i) contains clear and concise headings for each item of such information; and

(ii) provides a clear and concise form stating each item of information required to be disclosed under each such heading.

(F) In prescribing the form of the table under subparagraph (E), the board shall require that—

(i) all of the information in the table, and not just a reference to the table, be placed on the billing statement, as required by this paragraph; and

(ii) the items required to be included in the table shall be listed in the order in which such items are set forth in subparagraph (B).

(G) In prescribing the form of the table under subparagraph (D), the Bureau shall employ terminology which is different than the terminology which is employed in subparagraph (B), if such terminology is more easily understood and conveys substantially the same meaning.

(12) Requirements relating to late payment deadlines and penalties

(A) Late payment deadline required to be disclosed

In the case of a credit card account under an open end consumer credit plan under which a late fee or charge may be imposed due to the failure of the obligor to make payment on or before the due date for such payment, the periodic statement required under subsection (b) with respect to the account shall include, in a conspicuous location on the billing statement, the date on which the payment is due or, if different, the date on which a late payment fee will be charged, together with the amount of the fee or charge to be imposed if payment is made after that date.

(B) Disclosure of increase in interest rates for late payments

If 1 or more late payments under an open end consumer credit plan may result in an increase in the annual percentage rate applicable to the account, the statement required under subsection (b) with respect to the account shall include conspicuous notice of such fact, together with the applicable penalty annual percentage rate, in close proximity to the disclosure required under subparagraph (A) of the date on which payment is due under the terms of the account.

(C) Payments at local branches

If the creditor, in the case of a credit card account referred to in subparagraph (A), is a financial institution which maintains branches or offices at which payments on any such account are accepted from the obligor in person, the date on which the obligor makes a payment on the account at such branch or office shall be considered to be the date on which the payment is made for purposes of determining whether a late fee or charge may be imposed due to the failure of the obligor to make payment on or before the due date for such payment.

(c) Disclosure in credit and charge card applications and solicitations

(1) Direct mail applications and solicitations

(A) Information in tabular format

Any application to open a credit card account for any person under an open end consumer credit plan, or a solicitation to open such an account without requiring an application, that is mailed to consumers shall disclose the following information, subject to subsection (e) of this section and section 1632(c) of this title:

(i) Annual percentage rates

(I) Each annual percentage rate applicable to extensions of credit under such credit plan.

(II) Where an extension of credit is subject to a variable rate, the fact that the rate is variable, the annual percentage rate in effect at the time of the mailing, and how the rate is determined.

(III) Where more than one rate applies, the range of balances to which each rate applies.

(ii) Annual and other fees

(I) Any annual fee, other periodic fee, or membership fee imposed for the issuance or availability of a credit card, including any account maintenance fee or other charge imposed based on activity or inactivity for the account during the billing cycle.

(II) Any minimum finance charge imposed for each period during which any extension of credit which is subject to a finance charge is outstanding.

(III) Any transaction charge imposed in connection with use of the card to purchase goods or services.

(iii) Grace period

(I) The date by which or the period within which any credit extended under such credit plan for purchases of goods or services must be repaid to avoid incurring a finance charge, and, if no such period is offered, such fact shall be clearly stated.

(II) If the length of such "grace period" varies, the card issuer may disclose the range of days in the grace period, the minimum number of days in the grace period, or the average number of days in the grace period, if the disclosure is identified as such.

(iv) Balance calculation method

(I) The name of the balance calculation method used in determining the balance on which the finance charge is computed if the method used has been defined by the Bureau, or a detailed explanation of the balance calculation method used if the method has not been so defined.

(II) In prescribing regulations to carry out this clause, the Bureau shall define and name not more than the 5 balance calculation methods determined by the Bureau to be the most commonly used methods.

(B) Other information

In addition to the information required to be disclosed under subparagraph (A), each application or solicitation to which such subparagraph applies shall disclose clearly and conspicuously the following information, subject to subsections (e) and (f) of this section:

(i) Cash advance fee

Any fee imposed for an extension of credit in the form of cash.

(ii) Late fee

Any fee imposed for a late payment.

(iii) Over-the-limit fee

Any fee imposed in connection with an extension of credit in excess of the amount of credit authorized to be extended with respect to such account.

(2) Telephone solicitations

(A) In general

In any telephone solicitation to open a credit card account for any person under an open end consumer credit plan, the person making the solicitation shall orally disclose the information described in paragraph (1)(A).

(B) Exception

Subparagraph (A) shall not apply to any telephone solicitation if—

(i) the credit card issuer—

(I) does not impose any fee described in paragraph (1)(A)(ii)(I); or

(II) does not impose any fee in connection with telephone solicitations unless the consumer signifies acceptance by using the card;

(ii) the card issuer discloses clearly and conspicuously in writing the information described in paragraph (1) within 30 days after the consumer requests the card, but in no event later than the date of delivery of the card; and

(iii) the card issuer discloses clearly and conspicuously that the consumer is not obligated to accept the card or account and the consumer will not be obligated to pay any of the fees or charges disclosed unless the consumer elects to accept the card or account by using the card.

(3) Applications and solicitations by other means

(A) In general

Any application to open a credit card account for any person under an open end consumer credit plan, and any solicitation to open such an account without requiring an application, that is made available to the public or contained in catalogs, magazines, or other publications shall meet the disclosure requirements of subparagraph (B), (C), or (D).

(B) Specific information

An application or solicitation described in subparagraph (A) meets the requirement of this subparagraph if such application or solicitation contains—

(i) the information—

(I) described in paragraph (1)(A) in the form required under section 1632(c) of this title, subject to subsection (e) of this section, and

(II) described in paragraph (1)(B) in a clear and conspicuous form, subject to subsections (e) and (f) of this section;

(ii) a statement, in a conspicuous and prominent location on the application or solicitation, that—

(I) the information is accurate as of the date the application or solicitation was printed;

(II) the information contained in the application or solicitation is subject to change after such date; and

(III) the applicant should contact the creditor for information on any change in the information contained in the application or solicitation since it was printed;

(iii) a clear and conspicuous disclosure of the date the application or solicitation was printed; and

(iv) a disclosure, in a conspicuous and prominent location on the application or solicitation, of a toll free telephone number or a mailing address at which the applicant may contact the creditor to obtain any change in the information provided in the application or solicitation since it was printed.

(C) General information without any specific term

An application or solicitation described in subparagraph (A) meets the requirement of this subparagraph if such application or solicitation—

(i) contains a statement, in a conspicuous and prominent location on the application or solicitation, that—

(I) there are costs associated with the use of credit cards; and

(II) the applicant may contact the creditor to request disclosure of specific information of such costs by calling a toll free telephone number or by writing to an address, specified in the application;

(ii) contains a disclosure, in a conspicuous and prominent location on the application or solicitation, of a toll free telephone number and a mailing address at which the applicant may contact the creditor to obtain such information; and

(iii) does not contain any of the items described in paragraph (1).

(D) Applications or solicitations containing subsection (a) disclosures

An application or solicitation meets the requirement of this subparagraph if it contains, or is accompanied by—

(i) the disclosures required by paragraphs (1) through (6) of subsection (a) of this section;

(ii) the disclosures required by subparagraphs (A) and (B) of paragraph (1) of this subsection included clearly and conspiciously[1] (except that the provisions of section 1632(c) of this title shall not apply); and

(iii) a toll free telephone number or a mailing address at which the applicant may contact the creditor to obtain any change in the information provided.

(E) Prompt response to information requests

Upon receipt of a request for any of the information referred to in subparagraph (B), (C), or (D), the card issuer or the agent of such issuer shall promptly disclose all of the information described in paragraph (1).

(4) Charge card applications and solicitations

(A) In general

Any application or solicitation to open a charge card account shall disclose clearly and conspicuously the following information in the form required by section 1632(c) of this title, subject to subsection (e) of this section:

(i) Any annual fee, other periodic fee, or membership fee imposed for the issuance or availability of the charge card, including any account maintenance fee or other charge imposed based on activity or inactivity for the account during the billing cycle.

---

1 So in original. Probably should be "conspicuously".

(ii) Any transaction charge imposed in connection with use of the card to purchase goods or services.

(iii) A statement that charges incurred by use of the charge card are due and payable upon receipt of a periodic statement rendered for such charge card account.

(B) Other information

In addition to the information required to be disclosed under subparagraph (A), each written application or solicitation to which such subparagraph applies shall disclose clearly and conspicuously the following information, subject to subsections (e) and (f) of this section:

(i) Cash advance fee

Any fee imposed for an extension of credit in the form of cash.

(ii) Late fee

Any fee imposed for a late payment.

(iii) Over-the-limit fee

Any fee imposed in connection with an extension of credit in excess of the amount of credit authorized to be extended with respect to such account.

(C) Applications and solicitations by other means

Any application to open a charge card account, and any solicitation to open such an account without requiring an application, that is made available to the public or contained in catalogs, magazines, or other publications shall contain—

(i) the information—

(I) described in subparagraph (A) in the form required under section 1632(c) of this title, subject to subsection (c) of this section, and

(II) described in subparagraph (B) in a clear and conspicuous form, subject to subsections (e) and (f) of this section;

(ii) a statement, in a conspicuous and prominent location on the application or solicitation, that—

(I) the information is accurate as of the date the application or solicitation was printed;

(II) the information contained in the application or solicitation is subject to change after such date; and

(III) the applicant should contact the creditor for information on any change in the information contained in the application or solicitation since it was printed;

(iii) a clear and conspicuous disclosure of the date the application or solicitation was printed; and

(iv) a disclosure, in a conspicuous and prominent location on the application or solicitation, of a toll free telephone number or a mailing address at which the applicant may contact the creditor to obtain any change in the information provided in the application or solicitation since it was printed.

(D) Issuers of charge cards which provide access to open end consumer credit plans

If a charge card permits the card holder to receive an extension of credit under an open end consumer credit plan, which is not maintained by the charge card issuer, the charge card issuer may provide the information described in subparagraphs (A) and (B) in the form required by such subparagraphs in lieu of the information required to be provided under paragraph (1), (2), or (3) with respect to any credit extended under such plan, if the charge card issuer discloses clearly and conspicuously to the consumer in the application or solicitation that—

(i) the charge card issuer will make an independent decision as to whether to issue the card;

(ii) the charge card may arrive before the decision is made with respect to an extension of credit under an open end consumer credit plan; and

(iii) approval by the charge card issuer does not constitute approval by the issuer of the extension of credit.

The information required to be disclosed under paragraph (1) shall be provided to the charge card holder by the creditor which maintains such open end consumer credit plan before the first extension of credit under such plan.

(E) Charge card defined

For the purposes of this subsection, the term "charge card" means a card, plate, or other single credit device that may be used from time to time to obtain credit which is not subject to a finance charge.

(5) Regulatory authority of the Bureau

The Bureau may, by regulation, require the disclosure of information in addition to that otherwise required by this subsection or subsection (d) of this section, and modify any disclosure of information required by this subsection or subsection (d) of this section, in any application to open a credit card account for any person under an open end consumer credit plan or any application to open a charge card account for any person, or a solicitation to open any such account without requiring an application, if the Bureau determines that such action is necessary to carry out the purposes of, or prevent evasions of, any paragraph of this subsection.

(6) Additional notice concerning "introductory rates"

(A) In general

Except as provided in subparagraph (B), an application or solicitation to open a credit card account and all promotional materials accompanying such application or solicitation for which a disclosure is required under paragraph (1), and that offers a temporary annual percentage rate of interest, shall—

(i) use the term "introductory" in immediate proximity to each listing of the temporary annual percentage rate applicable to such account, which term shall appear clearly and conspicuously;

(ii) if the annual percentage rate of interest that will apply after the end of the temporary rate period will be a fixed rate, state in a clear and conspicuous manner in a prominent location closely proximate to the first listing of the temporary annual percentage rate (other than a listing of the temporary annual percentage rate in the tabular format described in section 1632(c) of this title), the time period in which the introductory period will end and the annual percentage rate that will apply after the end of the introductory period; and

(iii) if the annual percentage rate that will apply after the end of the temporary rate period will vary in accordance with an index, state in a clear and conspicuous manner in a prominent location closely proximate to the first listing of the temporary annual percentage rate (other than a listing in the tabular format prescribed by section 1632(c) of this title), the time period in which the introductory period will end and the rate that will apply after that, based on an annual percentage rate that was in effect within 60 days before the date of mailing the application or solicitation.

(B) Exception

Clauses (ii) and (iii) of subparagraph (A) do not apply with respect to any listing of a temporary annual percentage rate on an envelope or other enclosure in which an application or solicitation to open a credit card account is mailed.

(C) Conditions for introductory rates

An application or solicitation to open a credit card account for which a disclosure is required under paragraph (1), and that offers a temporary annual percentage rate of interest shall, if that rate of interest is revocable under any circumstance or upon any event, clearly and conspicuously disclose, in a prominent manner on or with such application or solicitation—

(i) a general description of the circumstances that may result in the revocation of the temporary annual percentage rate; and

(ii) if the annual percentage rate that will apply upon the revocation of the temporary annual percentage rate—

(I) will be a fixed rate, the annual percentage rate that will apply upon the revocation of the temporary annual percentage rate; or

(II) will vary in accordance with an index, the rate that will apply after the temporary rate, based on an annual percentage rate that was in effect within 60 days before the date of mailing the application or solicitation.

(D) Definitions

In this paragraph—

(i) the terms "temporary annual percentage rate of interest" and "temporary annual percentage rate" mean any rate of interest applicable to a credit card account for an introductory period of less than 1 year, if that rate is less than an annual percentage rate that was in effect within 60 days before the date of mailing the application or solicitation; and

(ii) the term "introductory period" means the maximum time period for which the temporary annual percentage rate may be applicable.

(E) Relation to other disclosure requirements

Nothing in this paragraph may be construed to supersede subsection (a) of section 1632 of this title, or any disclosure required by paragraph (1) or any other provision of this subsection.

(7) Internet-based solicitations

(A) In general

In any solicitation to open a credit card account for any person under an open end consumer credit plan using the Internet or other interactive computer service, the person making the solicitation shall clearly and conspicuously disclose—

(i) the information described in subparagraphs (A) and (B) of paragraph (1); and

(ii) the information described in paragraph (6).

(B) Form of disclosure

The disclosures required by subparagraph (A) shall be—

(i) readily accessible to consumers in close proximity to the solicitation to open a credit card account; and

(ii) updated regularly to reflect the current policies, terms, and fee amounts applicable to the credit card account.

(C) Definitions

For purposes of this paragraph—

(i) the term "Internet" means the international computer network of both Federal and non-Federal interoperable packet switched data networks; and

(ii) the term "interactive computer service" means any information service, system, or access software provider that provides or enables computer access by multiple users to a computer server, including specifically a service or system that provides access to the Internet and such systems operated or services offered by libraries or educational institutions.

(8) Applications from underage consumers

(A) Prohibition on issuance

No credit card may be issued to, or open end consumer credit plan established by or on behalf of, a consumer who has not attained the age of 21, unless the consumer has submitted a written application to the card issuer that meets the requirements of subparagraph (B).

(B) Application requirements

An application to open a credit card account by a consumer who has not attained the age of 21 as of the date of submission of the application shall require—

(i) the signature of a cosigner, including the parent, legal guardian, spouse, or any other individual who has attained the age of 21 having a means to repay debts incurred by the consumer in connection with the account, indicating joint liability for debts incurred by the consumer in connection with the account before the consumer has attained the age of 21; or

(ii) submission by the consumer of financial information, including through an application, indicating an independent means of repaying any obligation arising from the proposed extension of credit in connection with the account.

(C) Safe harbor

The Bureau shall promulgate regulations providing standards that, if met, would satisfy the requirements of subparagraph (B)(ii).

(d) Disclosure prior to renewal

(1) In general

A card issuer that has changed or amended any term of the account since the last renewal that has not been previously disclosed or that imposes any fee described in subsection (c)(1)(A)(ii)(I) or (c)(4)(A)(i) of this section shall transmit to a consumer at least 30 days prior to the scheduled renewal date of the consumer's credit or charge card account a clear and conspicuous disclosure of—

(A) the date by which, the month by which, or the billing period at the close of which, the account will expire if not renewed;

(B) the information described in subsection (c)(1)(A) or (c)(4)(A) of this section that would apply if the account were renewed, subject to subsection (e) of this section; and

(C) the method by which the consumer may terminate continued credit availability under the account.

(2) Short-term renewals

The Bureau may by regulation provide for fewer disclosures than are required by paragraph (1) in the case of an account which is renewable for a period of less than 6 months.

(e) Other rules for disclosures under subsections (c) and (d)

(1) Fees determined on the basis of a percentage

If the amount of any fee required to be disclosed under subsection (c) or (d) of this section is determined on the basis of a percentage of another amount, the percentage used in making such determination and the identification of the amount against which such percentage is applied shall be disclosed in lieu of the amount of such fee.

(2) **Disclosure only of fees actually imposed**

If a credit or charge card issuer does not impose any fee required to be disclosed under any provision of subsection (c) or (d) of this section, such provision shall not apply with respect to such issuer.

(f) **Disclosure of range of certain fees which vary by State allowed**

If the amount of any fee required to be disclosed by a credit or charge card issuer under paragraph (1)(B), (3)(B)(i)(II), (4)(B), or (4)(C)(i)(II) of subsection (c) of this section varies from State to State, the card issuer may disclose the range of such fees for purposes of subsection (c) of this section in lieu of the amount for each applicable State, if such disclosure includes a statement that the amount of such fee varies from State to State.

(g) **Insurance in connection with certain open end credit card plans**

(1) **Change in insurance carrier**

Whenever a card issuer that offers any guarantee or insurance for repayment of all or part of the outstanding balance of an open end credit card plan proposes to change the person providing that guarantee or insurance, the card issuer shall send each insured consumer written notice of the proposed change not less than 30 days prior to the change, including notice of any increase in the rate or substantial decrease in coverage or service which will result from such change. Such notice may be included on or with the monthly statement provided to the consumer prior to the month in which the proposed change would take effect.

(2) **Notice of new insurance coverage**

In any case in which a proposed change described in paragraph (1) occurs, the insured consumer shall be given the name and address of the new guarantor or insurer and a copy of the policy or group certificate containing the basic terms and conditions, including the premium rate to be charged.

(3) **Right to discontinue guarantee or insurance**

The notices required under paragraphs (1) and (2) shall each include a statement that the consumer has the option to discontinue the insurance or guarantee.

(4) **No preemption of State law**

No provision of this subsection shall be construed as superseding any provision of State law which is applicable to the regulation of insurance.

(5) **Bureau definition of substantial decrease in coverage or service**

The Bureau shall define, in regulations, what constitutes a "substantial decrease in coverage or service" for purposes of paragraph (1).

(h) **Prohibition on certain actions for failure to incur finance charges**

A creditor of an account under an open end consumer credit plan may not terminate an account prior to its expiration date solely because the consumer has not incurred finance charges on the account. Nothing in this subsection shall prohibit a creditor from terminating an account for inactivity in 3 or more consecutive months.

(i) **Advance notice of rate increase and other changes required**

(1) **Advance notice of increase in interest rate required**

In the case of any credit card account under an open end consumer credit plan, a creditor shall provide a written notice of an increase in an annual percentage rate (except in the case of an increase described in paragraph (1), (2), or (3) of section 1666i–1(b) of this title) not later than 45 days prior to the effective date of the increase.

(2) **Advance notice of other significant changes required**

In the case of any credit card account under an open end consumer credit plan, a creditor shall provide a written notice of any significant change, as determined by rule of the Bureau, in the terms (including an increase in any fee or finance charge, other than as provided in paragraph (1)) of the cardholder agreement between the creditor and the obligor, not later than 45 days prior to the effective date of the change.

(3) Notice of right to cancel

Each notice required by paragraph (1) or (2) shall be made in a clear and conspicuous manner, and shall contain a brief statement of the right of the obligor to cancel the account pursuant to rules established by the Bureau before the effective date of the subject rate increase or other change.

(4) Rule of construction

Closure or cancellation of an account by the obligor shall not constitute a default under an existing cardholder agreement, and shall not trigger an obligation to immediately repay the obligation in full or through a method that is less beneficial to the obligor than one of the methods described in section 1666i–1(c)(2) of this title, or the imposition of any other penalty or fee.

(j) Prohibition on penalties for on-time payments

(1) Prohibition on double-cycle billing and penalties for on-time payments

Except as provided in paragraph (2), a creditor may not impose any finance charge on a credit card account under an open end consumer credit plan as a result of the loss of any time period provided by the creditor within which the obligor may repay any portion of the credit extended without incurring a finance charge, with respect to—

(A) any balances for days in billing cycles that precede the most recent billing cycle; or

(B) any balances or portions thereof in the current billing cycle that were repaid within such time period.

(2) Exceptions

Paragraph (1) does not apply to—

(A) any adjustment to a finance charge as a result of the resolution of a dispute; or

(B) any adjustment to a finance charge as a result of the return of a payment for insufficient funds.

(k) Opt-in required for over-the-limit transactions if fees are imposed

(1) In general

In the case of any credit card account under an open end consumer credit plan under which an over-the-limit fee may be imposed by the creditor for any extension of credit in excess of the amount of credit authorized to be extended under such account, no such fee shall be charged, unless the consumer has expressly elected to permit the creditor, with respect to such account, to complete transactions involving the extension of credit under such account in excess of the amount of credit authorized.

(2) Disclosure by creditor

No election by a consumer under paragraph (1) shall take effect unless the consumer, before making such election, received a notice from the creditor of any over-the-limit fee in the form and manner, and at the time, determined by the Bureau. If the consumer makes the election referred to in paragraph (1), the creditor shall provide notice to the consumer of the right to revoke the election, in the form prescribed by the Bureau, in any periodic statement that includes notice of the imposition of an over-the-limit fee during the period covered by the statement.

(3) Form of election

A consumer may make or revoke the election referred to in paragraph (1) orally, electronically, or in writing, pursuant to regulations prescribed by the Bureau. The Bureau shall prescribe regulations to ensure that the same options are available for both making and revoking such election.

(4) Time of election

A consumer may make the election referred to in paragraph (1) at any time, and such election shall be effective until the election is revoked in the manner prescribed under paragraph (3).

(5) Regulations

The Bureau shall prescribe regulations—

(A) governing disclosures under this subsection; and

(B) that prevent unfair or deceptive acts or practices in connection with the manipulation of credit limits designed to increase over-the-limit fees or other penalty fees.

(6) Rule of construction

Nothing in this subsection shall be construed to prohibit a creditor from completing an over-the-limit transaction, provided that a consumer who has not made a valid election under paragraph (1) is not charged an over-the-limit fee for such transaction.

(7) Restriction on fees charged for an over-the-limit transaction

With respect to a credit card account under an open end consumer credit plan, an over-the-limit fee may be imposed only once during a billing cycle if the credit limit on the account is exceeded, and an over-the-limit fee, with respect to such excess credit, may be imposed only once in each of the 2 subsequent billing cycles, unless the consumer has obtained an additional extension of credit in excess of such credit limit during any such subsequent cycle or the consumer reduces the outstanding balance below the credit limit as of the end of such billing cycle.

(*l*) Limit on fees related to method of payment

With respect to a credit card account under an open end consumer credit plan, the creditor may not impose a separate fee to allow the obligor to repay an extension of credit or finance charge, whether such repayment is made by mail, electronic transfer, telephone authorization, or other means, unless such payment involves an expedited service by a service representative of the creditor.

(m) Use of term "fixed rate"

With respect to the terms of any credit card account under an open end consumer credit plan, the term "fixed", when appearing in conjunction with a reference to the annual percentage rate or interest rate applicable with respect to such account, may only be used to refer to an annual percentage rate or interest rate that will not change or vary for any reason over the period specified clearly and conspicuously in the terms of the account.

(n) Standards applicable to initial issuance of subprime or "fee harvester" cards

(1) In general

If the terms of a credit card account under an open end consumer credit plan require the payment of any fees (other than any late fee, over-the-limit fee, or fee for a payment returned for insufficient funds) by the consumer in the first year during which the account is opened in an aggregate amount in excess of 25 percent of the total amount of credit authorized under the account when the account is opened, no payment of any fees (other than any late fee, over-the-limit fee, or fee for a payment returned for insufficient funds) may be made from the credit made available under the terms of the account.

(2) Rule of construction

No provision of this subsection may be construed as authorizing any imposition or payment of advance fees otherwise prohibited by any provision of law.

(*o*) Due dates for credit card accounts

(1) In general

The payment due date for a credit card account under an open end consumer credit plan shall be the same day each month.

(2) Weekend or holiday due dates

If the payment due date for a credit card account under an open end consumer credit plan is a day on which the creditor does not receive or accept payments by mail (including weekends and holidays), the creditor may not treat a payment received on the next business day as late for any purpose.

(p) Parental approval required to increase credit lines for accounts for which parent is jointly liable

No increase may be made in the amount of credit authorized to be extended under a credit card account for which a parent, legal guardian, or spouse of the consumer, or any other individual has assumed joint liability for debts incurred by the consumer in connection with the account before the consumer attains the age of 21, unless that parent, guardian, or spouse approves in writing, and assumes joint liability for, such increase.

(q) Omitted

(r) College card agreements

(1) Definitions

For purposes of this subsection, the following definitions shall apply:

(A) College affinity card

The term "college affinity card" means a credit card issued by a credit card issuer under an open end consumer credit plan in conjunction with an agreement between the issuer and an institution of higher education, or an alumni organization or foundation affiliated with or related to such institution, under which such cards are issued to college students who have an affinity with such institution, organization and—

(i) the creditor has agreed to donate a portion of the proceeds of the credit card to the institution, organization, or foundation (including a lump sum or 1-time payment of money for access);

(ii) the creditor has agreed to offer discounted terms to the consumer; or

(iii) the credit card bears the name, emblem, mascot, or logo of such institution, organization, or foundation, or other words, pictures, or symbols readily identified with such institution, organization, or foundation.

(B) College student credit card account

The term "college student credit card account" means a credit card account under an open end consumer credit plan established or maintained for or on behalf of any college student.

(C) College student

The term "college student" means an individual who is a full-time or a part-time student attending an institution of higher education.

(D) Institution of higher education

The term "institution of higher education" has the same meaning as in section[2] 1001 and 1002 of Title 20.

(2) Reports by creditors

(A) In general

Each creditor shall submit an annual report to the Bureau containing the terms and conditions of all business, marketing, and promotional agreements and college affinity card agreements with an institution of higher education, or an alumni organization or foundation

[2] So in original. Probably should be "sections".

affiliated with or related to such institution, with respect to any college student credit card issued to a college student at such institution.

(B) Details of report

The information required to be reported under subparagraph (A) includes—

(i) any memorandum of understanding between or among a creditor, an institution of higher education, an alumni association, or foundation that directly or indirectly relates to any aspect of any agreement referred to in such subparagraph or controls or directs any obligations or distribution of benefits between or among any such entities;

(ii) the amount of any payments from the creditor to the institution, organization, or foundation during the period covered by the report, and the precise terms of any agreement under which such amounts are determined; and

(iii) the number of credit card accounts covered by any such agreement that were opened during the period covered by the report, and the total number of credit card accounts covered by the agreement that were outstanding at the end of such period.

(C) Aggregation by institution

The information required to be reported under subparagraph (A) shall be aggregated with respect to each institution of higher education or alumni organization or foundation affiliated with or related to such institution.

(D) Initial report

The initial report required under subparagraph (A) shall be submitted to the Bureau before the end of the 9-month period beginning on May 22, 2009.

(3) Reports by Bureau

The Bureau shall submit to the Congress, and make available to the public, an annual report that lists the information concerning credit card agreements submitted to the Bureau under paragraph (2) by each institution of higher education, alumni organization, or foundation.

(Pub.L. 90–321, Title I, § 127, May 29, 1968, 82 Stat. 153; Pub.L. 93–495, Title III, §§ 304, 305, Title IV, §§ 411, 415, Oct. 28, 1974, 88 Stat. 1511, 1519, 1521; Pub.L. 96–221, Title VI, § 613(a) to (e), Mar. 31, 1980, 94 Stat. 176, 177; Pub.L. 100–583, §§ 2(a), 6, Nov. 3, 1988, 102 Stat. 2960, 2968; Pub.L. 100–709, § 2(b), Nov. 23, 1988, 102 Stat. 4729; Pub.L. 109–8, Title XIII, §§ 1301(a), 1303(a), 1304(a), 1305(a), 1306(a), Apr. 20, 2005, 119 Stat. 204, 209, 211, 212; Pub.L. 111–24, Title I, § 101(a)(1), 102(a), 103, 105, 106(a) Title II, 201(a), 202, 203, Title III, 301, 303, 305(a), May 22, 2009, 123 Stat. 1738, 1741, 1742, 1743, 1745, 1746, 1747, 1748, 1749; Pub.L. 111–203, Title X, § 1100A(2), July 21, 2010, 124 Stat. 2107.)

§ 1637a. Disclosure requirements for open end consumer credit plans secured by consumer's principal dwelling [CCPA § 127A]

(a) Application disclosures

In the case of any open end consumer credit plan which provides for any extension of credit which is secured by the consumer's principal dwelling, the creditor shall make the following disclosures in accordance with subsection (b) of this section:

(1) Fixed annual percentage rate

Each annual percentage rate imposed in connection with extensions of credit under the plan and a statement that such rate does not include costs other than interest.

(2) Variable percentage rate

In the case of a plan which provides for variable rates of interest on credit extended under the plan—

(A) a description of the manner in which such rate will be computed and a statement that such rate does not include costs other than interest;

(B) a description of the manner in which any changes in the annual percentage rate will be made, including—

(i) any negative amortization and interest rate carryover;

(ii) the timing of any such changes;

(iii) any index or margin to which such changes in the rate are related; and

(iv) a source of information about any such index;

(C) if an initial annual percentage rate is offered which is not based on an index—

(i) a statement of such rate and the period of time such initial rate will be in effect; and

(ii) a statement that such rate does not include costs other than interest;

(D) a statement that the consumer should ask about the current index value and interest rate;

(E) a statement of the maximum amount by which the annual percentage rate may change in any 1-year period or a statement that no such limit exists;

(F) a statement of the maximum annual percentage rate that may be imposed at any time under the plan;

(G) subject to subsection (b)(3) of this section, a table, based on a $10,000 extension of credit, showing how the annual percentage rate and the minimum periodic payment amount under each repayment option of the plan would have been affected during the preceding 15-year period by changes in any index used to compute such rate;

(H) a statement of—

(i) the maximum annual percentage rate which may be imposed under each repayment option of the plan;

(ii) the minimum amount of any periodic payment which may be required, based on a $10,000 outstanding balance, under each such option when such maximum annual percentage rate is in effect; and

(iii) the earliest date by which such maximum annual interest rate may be imposed; and

(I) a statement that interest rate information will be provided on or with each periodic statement.

(3) Other fees imposed by the creditor

An itemization of any fees imposed by the creditor in connection with the availability or use of credit under such plan, including annual fees, application fees, transaction fees, and closing costs (including costs commonly described as "points"), and the time when such fees are payable.

(4) Estimates of fees which may be imposed by third parties

(A) Aggregate amount

An estimate, based on the creditor's experience with such plans and stated as a single amount or as a reasonable range, of the aggregate amount of additional fees that may be imposed by third parties (such as governmental authorities, appraisers, and attorneys) in connection with opening an account under the plan.

(B) Statement of availability

A statement that the consumer may ask the creditor for a good faith estimate by the creditor of the fees that may be imposed by third parties.

(5) Statement of risk of loss of dwelling

A statement that—

(A) any extension of credit under the plan is secured by the consumer's dwelling; and

(B) in the event of any default, the consumer risks the loss of the dwelling.

(6) Conditions to which disclosed terms are subject

(A) Period during which such terms are available

A clear and conspicuous statement—

(i) of the time by which an application must be submitted to obtain the terms disclosed; or

(ii) if applicable, that the terms are subject to change.

(B) Right of refusal if certain terms change

A statement that—

(i) the consumer may elect not to enter into an agreement to open an account under the plan if any term changes (other than a change contemplated by a variable feature of the plan) before any such agreement is final; and

(ii) if the consumer makes an election described in clause (i), the consumer is entitled to a refund of all fees paid in connection with the application.

(C) Retention of information

A statement that the consumer should make or otherwise retain a copy of information disclosed under this subparagraph.

(7) Rights of creditor with respect to extensions of credit

A statement that—

(A) under certain conditions, the creditor may terminate any account under the plan and require immediate repayment of any outstanding balance, prohibit any additional extension of credit to the account, or reduce the credit limit applicable to the account; and

(B) the consumer may receive, upon request, more specific information about the conditions under which the creditor may take any action described in subparagraph (A).

(8) Repayment options and minimum periodic payments

The repayment options under the plan, including—

(A) if applicable, any differences in repayment options with regard to—

(i) any period during which additional extensions of credit may be obtained; and

(ii) any period during which repayment is required to be made and no additional extensions of credit may be obtained;

(B) the length of any repayment period, including any differences in the length of any repayment period with regard to the periods described in clauses (i) and (ii) of subparagraph (A); and

(C) an explanation of how the amount of any minimum monthly or periodic payment will be determined under each such option, including any differences in the determination of any such amount with regard to the periods described in clauses (i) and (ii) of subparagraph (A).

(9) Example of minimum payments and maximum repayment period

An example, based on a $10,000 outstanding balance and the interest rate (other than a rate not based on the index under the plan) which is, or was recently, in effect under such plan, showing the minimum monthly or periodic payment, and the time it would take to repay the entire $10,000 if the consumer paid only the minimum periodic payments and obtained no additional extensions of credit.

(10) Statement concerning balloon payments

If, under any repayment option of the plan, the payment of not more than the minimum periodic payments required under such option over the length of the repayment period—

(A) would not repay any of the principal balance; or

(B) would repay less than the outstanding balance by the end of such period,

as the case may be, a statement of such fact, including an explicit statement that at the end of such repayment period a balloon payment (as defined in section 1665b(f) of this title) would result which would be required to be paid in full at that time.

(11) Negative amortization

If applicable, a statement that—

(A) any limitation in the plan on the amount of any increase in the minimum payments may result in negative amortization;

(B) negative amortization increases the outstanding principal balance of the account; and

(C) negative amortization reduces the consumer's equity in the consumer's dwelling.

(12) Limitations and minimum amount requirements on extensions of credit

(A) Number and dollar amount limitations

Any limitation contained in the plan on the number of extensions of credit and the amount of credit which may be obtained during any month or other defined time period.

(B) Minimum balance and other transaction amount requirements

Any requirement which establishes a minimum amount for—

(i) the initial extension of credit to an account under the plan;

(ii) any subsequent extension of credit to an account under the plan; or

(iii) any outstanding balance of an account under the plan.

(13) Statement regarding tax deductibility

A statement that—

(A) the consumer should consult a tax advisor regarding the deductibility of interest and charges under the plan; and

(B) in any case in which the extension of credit exceeds the fair market value (as defined under Title 26) of the dwelling, the interest on the portion of the credit extension that is greater than the fair market value of the dwelling is not tax deductible for Federal income tax purposes.

(14) Disclosure requirements established by Bureau

Any other term which the Bureau requires, in regulations, to be disclosed.

(b) Time and form of disclosures

(1) Time of disclosure

(A) In general

The disclosures required under subsection (a) of this section with respect to any open end consumer credit plan which provides for any extension of credit which is secured by the consumer's principal dwelling and the pamphlet required under subsection (e) of this section shall be provided to any consumer at the time the creditor distributes an application to establish an account under such plan to such consumer.

(B) Telephone, publications, and third party applications

In the case of telephone applications, applications contained in magazines or other publications, or applications provided by a third party, the disclosures required under subsection (a) of this section and the pamphlet required under subsection (e) of this section shall be provided by the creditor before the end of the 3-day period beginning on the date the creditor receives a completed application from a consumer.

(2) Form

(A) In general

Except as provided in paragraph (1)(B), the disclosures required under subsection (a) of this section shall be provided on or with any application to establish an account under an open end consumer credit plan which provides for any extension of credit which is secured by the consumer's principal dwelling.

(B) Segregation of required disclosures from other information

The disclosures required under subsection (a) of this section shall be conspicuously segregated from all other terms, data, or additional information provided in connection with the application, either by grouping the disclosures separately on the application form or by providing the disclosures on a separate form, in accordance with regulations of the Bureau.

(C) Precedence of certain information

The disclosures required by paragraphs (5), (6), and (7) of subsection (a) of this section shall precede all of the other required disclosures.

(D) Special provision relating to variable interest rate information

Whether or not the disclosures required under subsection (a) of this section are provided on the application form, the variable rate information described in subsection (a)(2) of this section may be provided separately from the other information required to be disclosed.

(3) Requirement for historical table

In preparing the table required under subsection (a)(2)(G) of this section, the creditor shall consistently select one rate of interest for each year and the manner of selecting the rate from year to year shall be consistent with the plan.

(c) Third party applications

In the case of an application to open an account under any open end consumer credit plan described in subsection (a) of this section which is provided to a consumer by any person other than the creditor—

(1) such person shall provide such consumer with—

(A) the disclosures required under subsection (a) of this section with respect to such plan, in accordance with subsection (b) of this section; and

(B) the pamphlet required under subsection (e) of this section; or

(2) if such person cannot provide specific terms about the plan because specific information about the plan terms is not available, no nonrefundable fee may be imposed in connection with such application before the end of the 3-day period beginning on the date the consumer receives the disclosures required under subsection (a) of this section with respect to the application.

(d) "Principal dwelling" defined

For purposes of this section and sections 1647 and 1665b of this title, the term "principal dwelling" includes any second or vacation home of the consumer.

(e) Pamphlet

In addition to the disclosures required under subsection (a) of this section with respect to an application to open an account under any open end consumer credit plan described in such subsection, the creditor or other person providing such disclosures to the consumer shall provide—

(1) a pamphlet published by the Bureau pursuant to section 4 of the Home Equity Consumer Protection Act of 1988; or

(2) any pamphlet which provides substantially similar information to the information described in such section, as determined by the Bureau.

(Pub.L. 90–321, Title I, § 127A, as added Pub.L. 100–709, § 2(a), Nov. 23, 1988, 102 Stat. 4725, and amended Pub.L. 109–8, Title XIII, § 1302(a)(1), Apr. 20, 2005, 119 Stat. 208; Pub.L. 111–203, Title X, § 1100A(2), July 21, 2010, 124 Stat. 2107.)

§ 1638. Transactions other than under an open end credit plan [CCPA § 128]

(a) Required disclosures by creditor

For each consumer credit transaction other than under an open end credit plan, the creditor shall disclose each of the following items, to the extent applicable:

(1) The identity of the creditor required to make disclosure.

(2)(A) The "amount financed", using that term, which shall be the amount of credit of which the consumer has actual use. This amount shall be computed as follows, but the computations need not be disclosed and shall not be disclosed with the disclosures conspicuously segregated in accordance with subsection (b)(1) of this section:

(i) take the principal amount of the loan or the cash price less downpayment and trade-in;

(ii) add any charges which are not part of the finance charge or of the principal amount of the loan and which are financed by the consumer, including the cost of any items excluded from the finance charge pursuant to section 1605 of this title; and

(iii) subtract any charges which are part of the finance charge but which will be paid by the consumer before or at the time of the consummation of the transaction, or have been withheld from the proceeds of the credit.

(B) In conjunction with the disclosure of the amount financed, a creditor shall provide a statement of the consumer's right to obtain, upon a written request, a written itemization of the amount financed. The statement shall include spaces for a "yes" and "no" indication to be initialed by the consumer to indicate whether the consumer wants a written itemization of the amount financed. Upon receiving an affirmative indication, the creditor shall provide, at the time other disclosures are required to be furnished, a written itemization of the amount financed. For the purposes of this subparagraph, "itemization of the amount financed" means a disclosure of the following items, to the extent applicable:

(i) the amount that is or will be paid directly to the consumer;

(ii) the amount that is or will be credited to the consumer's account to discharge obligations owed to the creditor;

(iii) each amount that is or will be paid to third persons by the creditor on the consumer's behalf, together with an identification of or reference to the third person; and

(iv) the total amount of any charges described in the preceding subparagraph (A)(iii).

(3) The "finance charge", not itemized, using that term.

(4) The finance charge expressed as an "annual percentage rate", using that term. This shall not be required if the amount financed does not exceed $75 and the finance charge does not exceed $5, or if the amount financed exceeds $75 and the finance charge does not exceed $7.50.

(5) The sum of the amount financed and the finance charge, which shall be termed the "total of payments".

(6) The number, amount, and due dates or period of payments scheduled to repay the total of payments.

(7) In a sale of property or services in which the seller is the creditor required to disclose pursuant to section 1631(b) of this title, the "total sale price", using that term, which shall be the total of the cash price of the property or services, additional charges, and the finance charge.

(8) Descriptive explanations of the terms "amount financed", "finance charge", "annual percentage rate", "total of payments", and "total sale price" as specified by the Bureau. The descriptive explanation of "total sale price" shall include reference to the amount of the downpayment.

(9) Where the credit is secured, a statement that a security interest has been taken in (A) the property which is purchased as part of the credit transaction, or (B) property not purchased as part of the credit transaction identified by item or type.

(10) Any dollar charge or percentage amount which may be imposed by a creditor solely on account of a late payment, other than a deferral or extension charge.

(11) A statement indicating whether or not the consumer is entitled to a rebate of any finance charge upon refinancing or prepayment in full pursuant to acceleration or otherwise, if the obligation involves a precomputed finance charge. A statement indicating whether or not a penalty will be imposed in those same circumstances if the obligation involves a finance charge computed from time to time by application of a rate to the unpaid principal balance.

(12) A statement that the consumer should refer to the appropriate contract document for any information such document provides about nonpayment, default, the right to accelerate the maturity of the debt, and prepayment rebates and penalties.

(13) In any residential mortgage transaction, a statement indicating whether a subsequent purchaser or assignee of the consumer may assume the debt obligation on its original terms and conditions.

(14) In the case of any variable interest rate residential mortgage transaction, in disclosures provided at application as prescribed by the Bureau for a variable rate transaction secured by the consumer's principal dwelling, at the option of the creditor, a statement that the periodic payments may increase or decrease substantially, and the maximum interest rate and payment for a $10,000 loan originated at a recent interest rate, as determined by the Bureau, assuming the maximum periodic increases in rates and payments under the program, or a historical example illustrating the effects of interest rate changes implemented according to the loan program.

(15) In the case of a consumer credit transaction that is secured by the principal dwelling of the consumer, in which the extension of credit may exceed the fair market value of the dwelling, a clear and conspicuous statement that—

(A) the interest on the portion of the credit extension that is greater than the fair market value of the dwelling is not tax deductible for Federal income tax purposes; and

(B) the consumer should consult a tax adviser for further information regarding the deductibility of interest and charges.

(16) In the case of a variable rate residential mortgage loan for which an escrow or impound account will be established for the payment of all applicable taxes, insurance, and assessments—

(A) the amount of initial monthly payment due under the loan for the payment of principal and interest, and the amount of such initial monthly payment including the monthly payment deposited in the account for the payment of all applicable taxes, insurance, and assessments; and

(B) the amount of the fully indexed monthly payment due under the loan for the payment of principal and interest, and the amount of such fully indexed monthly payment including the monthly payment deposited in the account for the payment of all applicable taxes, insurance, and assessments.

(17) In the case of a residential mortgage loan, the aggregate amount of settlement charges for all settlement services provided in connection with the loan, the amount of charges that are included in the loan and the amount of such charges the borrower must pay at closing, the approximate amount of the wholesale rate of funds in connection with the loan, and the aggregate amount of other fees or required payments in connection with the loan.

(18) In the case of a residential mortgage loan, the aggregate amount of fees paid to the mortgage originator in connection with the loan, the amount of such fees paid directly by the consumer, and any additional amount received by the originator from the creditor.

(19) In the case of a residential mortgage loan, the total amount of interest that the consumer will pay over the life of the loan as a percentage of the principal of the loan. Such amount shall be computed assuming the consumer makes each monthly payment in full and on-time, and does not make any over-payments.

(b) Form and timing of disclosures; residential mortgage transaction requirements

(1) Except as otherwise provided in this part, the disclosures required under subsection (a) of this section shall be made before the credit is extended. Except for the disclosures required by subsection (a)(1) of this section, all disclosures required under subsection (a) of this section and any disclosure provided for in subsection (b), (c), or (d) of section 1605 of this title shall be conspicuously segregated from all other terms, data, or information provided in connection with a transaction, including any computations or itemization.

(2)(A) Except as provided in subparagraph (G), in the case of any extension of credit that is secured by the dwelling of a consumer, which is also subject to the Real Estate Settlement Procedures Act [12 U.S.C. 2601 et seq.], good faith estimates of the disclosures required under subsection (a) of this section shall be made in accordance with regulations of the Bureau under section 1631(c) of this title and shall be delivered or placed in the mail not later than three business days after the creditor receives the consumer's written application, which shall be at least 7 business days before consummation of the transaction.

(B) In the case of an extension of credit that is secured by the dwelling of a consumer, the disclosures provided under subparagraph (A),[1] shall be in addition to the other disclosures required by subsection (a), and shall—

(i) state in conspicuous type size and format, the following: "You are not required to complete this agreement merely because you have received these disclosures or signed a loan application."; and

(ii) be provided in the form of final disclosures at the time of consummation of the transaction, in the form and manner prescribed by this section.

(C) In the case of an extension of credit that is secured by the dwelling of a consumer, under which the annual rate of interest is variable, or with respect to which the regular payments may otherwise be variable, in addition to the other disclosures required by subsection (a), the disclosures provided under this subsection shall do the following:

(i) Label the payment schedule as follows: "Payment Schedule: Payments Will Vary Based on Interest Rate Changes".

(ii) State in conspicuous type size and format examples of adjustments to the regular required payment on the extension of credit based on the change in the interest rates specified by the contract for such extension of credit. Among the examples required to be provided under this clause is an example that reflects the maximum payment amount of the regular required payments on the extension of credit, based on the maximum interest rate allowed under the contract, in accordance with the rules of the Bureau. Prior to issuing any rules pursuant to this clause, the Bureau shall conduct consumer testing to determine the appropriate format for providing the disclosures required under this subparagraph to consumers so that such disclosures can be easily understood, including the fact that the initial regular payments are for a specific time period that will end on a certain date, that

1 So in original. The comma probably should not appear.

payments will adjust afterwards potentially to a higher amount, and that there is no guarantee that the borrower will be able to refinance to a lower amount.

(D) In any case in which the disclosure statement under subparagraph (A) contains an annual percentage rate of interest that is no longer accurate, as determined under section 1606(c) of this title, the creditor shall furnish an additional, corrected statement to the borrower, not later than 3 business days before the date of consummation of the transaction.

(E) The consumer shall receive the disclosures required under this paragraph before paying any fee to the creditor or other person in connection with the consumer's application for an extension of credit that is secured by the dwelling of a consumer. If the disclosures are mailed to the consumer, the consumer is considered to have received them 3 business days after they are mailed. A creditor or other person may impose a fee for obtaining the consumer's credit report before the consumer has received the disclosures under this paragraph, provided the fee is bona fide and reasonable in amount.

(F) Waiver of timeliness of disclosures

To expedite consummation of a transaction, if the consumer determines that the extension of credit is needed to meet a bona fide personal financial emergency, the consumer may waive or modify the timing requirements for disclosures under subparagraph (A), provided that—

(i) the term "bona fide personal emergency" may be further defined in regulations issued by the Bureau;

(ii) the consumer provides to the creditor a dated, written statement describing the emergency and specifically waiving or modifying those timing requirements, which statement shall bear the signature of all consumers entitled to receive the disclosures required by this paragraph; and

(iii) the creditor provides to the consumers at or before the time of such waiver or modification, the final disclosures required by paragraph (1).

(G)(i) In the case of an extension of credit relating to a plan described in section 101(53D) of Title 11—

(I) the requirements of subparagraphs (A) through (E) shall not apply; and

(II) a good faith estimate of the disclosures required under subsection (a) shall be made in accordance with regulations of the Bureau under section 1631(c) of this title before such credit is extended, or shall be delivered or placed in the mail not later than 3 business days after the date on which the creditor receives the written application of the consumer for such credit, whichever is earlier.

(ii) If a disclosure statement furnished within 3 business days of the written application (as provided under clause (i)(II)) contains an annual percentage rate which is subsequently rendered inaccurate, within the meaning of section 1606(c) of this title, the creditor shall furnish another disclosure statement at the time of settlement or consummation of the transaction.

(3) In the case of a credit transaction described in paragraph (15) of subsection (a) of this section, disclosures required by that paragraph shall be made to the consumer at the time of application for such extension of credit.

(4) Repayment analysis required to include escrow payments

(A) In general

In the case of any consumer credit transaction secured by a first mortgage or lien on the principal dwelling of the consumer, other than a consumer credit transaction under an open end credit plan or a reverse mortgage, for which an impound, trust, or other type of account has been or will be established in connection with the transaction for the payment of property taxes, hazard and flood (if any) insurance premiums, or other periodic payments or premiums with respect to the property, the information required to be provided under subsection (a) with respect to the number, amount, and due dates or period of payments scheduled to repay the total of payments shall take into account the amount of any monthly payment to such account for each such repayment in accordance with section 10(a)(2) of the Real Estate Settlement Procedures Act of 1974.

(B) Assessment value

The amount taken into account under subparagraph (A) for the payment of property taxes, hazard and flood (if any) insurance premiums, or other periodic payments or premiums with respect to the property shall reflect the taxable assessed value of the real property securing the transaction after the consummation of the transaction, including the value of any improvements on the property or to be constructed on the property (whether or not such construction will be financed from the proceeds of the transaction), if known, and the replacement costs of the property for hazard insurance, in the initial year after the transaction.

(c) Timing of disclosures on unsolicited mailed or telephone purchase orders or loan requests

(1) If a creditor receives a purchase order by mail or telephone without personal solicitation, and the cash price and the total sale price and the terms of financing, including the annual percentage rate, are set forth in the creditor's catalog or other printed material distributed to the public, then the disclosures required under subsection (a) of this section may be made at any time not later than the date the first payment is due.

(2) If a creditor receives a request for a loan by mail or telephone without personal solicitation and the terms of financing, including the annual percentage rate for representative amounts of credit, are set forth in the creditor's printed material distributed to the public, or in the contract of loan or other printed material delivered to the obligor, then the disclosures required under subsection (a) of this section may be made at any time not later than the date the first payment is due.

(d) Timing of disclosure in cases of an addition of a deferred payment price to an existing outstanding balance

If a consumer credit sale is one of a series of consumer credit sales transactions made pursuant to an agreement providing for the addition of the deferred payment price of that sale to an existing outstanding balance, and the person to whom the credit is extended has approved in writing both the annual percentage rate or rates and the method of computing the finance charge or charges, and the creditor retains no security interest in any property as to which he has received payments aggregating the amount of the sales price including any finance charges attributable thereto, then the disclosure required under subsection (a) of this section for the particular sale may be made at any time not later than the date the first payment for that sale is due. For the purposes of this subsection, in the case of items purchased on different dates, the first purchased shall be deemed first paid for, and in the case of items purchased on the same date, the lowest price shall be deemed first paid for.

(e) Terms and disclosure with respect to private education loans

(1) Disclosures required in private education loan applications and solicitations

In any application for a private education loan, or a solicitation for a private education loan without requiring an application, the private educational lender shall disclose to the borrower, clearly and conspicuously—

(A) the potential range of rates of interest applicable to the private education loan;

(B) whether the rate of interest applicable to the private education loan is fixed or variable;

(C) limitations on interest rate adjustments, both in terms of frequency and amount, or the lack thereof, if applicable;

(D) requirements for a co-borrower, including any changes in the applicable interest rates without a co-borrower;

(E) potential finance charges, late fees, penalties, and adjustments to principal, based on defaults or late payments of the borrower;

(F) fees or range of fees applicable to the private education loan;

(G) the term of the private education loan;

(H) whether interest will accrue while the student to whom the private education loan relates is enrolled at a covered educational institution;

(I) payment deferral options;

(J) general eligibility criteria for the private education loan;

(K) an example of the total cost of the private education loan over the life of the loan—

(i) which shall be calculated using the principal amount and the maximum rate of interest actually offered by the private educational lender; and

(ii) calculated both with and without capitalization of interest, if an option exists for postponing interest payments;

(L) that a covered educational institution may have school-specific education loan benefits and terms not detailed on the disclosure form;

(M) that the borrower may qualify for Federal student financial assistance through a program under title IV of the Higher Education Act of 1965 (20 U.S.C. 1070 et seq.), in lieu of, or in addition to, a loan from a non-Federal source;

(N) the interest rates available with respect to such Federal student financial assistance through a program under title IV of the Higher Education Act of 1965 (20 U.S.C. 1070 et seq.);

(O) that, as provided in paragraph (6)—

(i) the borrower shall have the right to accept the terms of the loan and consummate the transaction at any time within 30 calendar days (or such longer period as the private educational lender may provide) following the date on which the application for the private education loan is approved and the borrower receives the disclosure documents required under this subsection for the loan; and

(ii) except for changes based on adjustments to the index used for a loan, the rates and terms of the loan may not be changed by the private educational lender during the period described in clause (i);

(P) that, before a private education loan may be consummated, the borrower must obtain from the relevant institution of higher education the form required under paragraph (3), and complete, sign, and return such form to the private educational lender;

(Q) that the consumer may obtain additional information concerning such Federal student financial assistance from their institution of higher education, or at the website of the Department of Education; and

(R) such other information as the Bureau shall prescribe, by rule, as necessary or appropriate for consumers to make informed borrowing decisions.

(2) Disclosures at the time of private education loan approval

Contemporaneously with the approval of a private education loan application, and before the loan transaction is consummated, the private educational lender shall disclose to the borrower, clearly and conspicuously—

(A) the applicable rate of interest in effect on the date of approval;

(B) whether the rate of interest applicable to the private education loan is fixed or variable;

(C) limitations on interest rate adjustments, both in terms of frequency and amount, or the lack thereof, if applicable;

(D) the initial approved principal amount;

(E) applicable finance charges, late fees, penalties, and adjustments to principal, based on borrower defaults or late payments, including limitations on the discharge of a private education loan in bankruptcy;

(F) fees or range of fees applicable to the private education loan;

(G) the maximum term under the private education loan program;

(H) an estimate of the total amount for repayment, at both the interest rate in effect on the date of approval and at the maximum possible rate of interest offered by the private educational lender and applicable to the borrower, to the extent that such maximum rate may be determined, or if not, a good faith estimate thereof;

(I) any principal and interest payments required while the student for whom the private education loan is intended is enrolled at a covered educational institution and unpaid interest that will accrue during such enrollment;

(J) payment deferral options applicable to the borrower;

(K) whether monthly payments are graduated;

(L) that, as provided in paragraph (6)—

(i) the borrower shall have the right to accept the terms of the loan and consummate the transaction at any time within 30 calendar days (or such longer period as the private educational lender may provide) following the date on which the application for the private education loan is approved and the borrower receives the disclosure documents required under this subsection for the loan; and

(ii) except for changes based on adjustments to the index used for a loan, the rates and terms of the loan may not be changed by the private educational lender during the period described in clause (i);

(M) that the borrower—

(i) may qualify for Federal financial assistance through a program under title IV of the Higher Education Act of 1965 (20 U.S.C. 1070 et seq.), in lieu of, or in addition to, a loan from a non-Federal source; and

(ii) may obtain additional information concerning such assistance from their institution of higher education or the website of the Department of Education;

(N) the interest rates available with respect to such Federal financial assistance through a program under title IV of the Higher Education Act of 1965 (20 U.S.C. 1070 et seq.);

(O) the maximum monthly payment, calculated using the maximum rate of interest actually offered by the private educational lender and applicable to the borrower, to the extent that such maximum rate may be determined, or if not, a good faith estimate thereof; and

(P) such other information as the Bureau shall prescribe, by rule, as necessary or appropriate for consumers to make informed borrowing decisions.

(3) Self-certification of information

(A) In general

Before a private educational lender may consummate a private education loan with respect to a student attending an institution of higher education, the lender shall obtain from the applicant for the private education loan the form developed by the Secretary of Education under section 155 of the Higher Education Act of 1965, signed by the applicant, in written or electronic form.

(B) Rule of construction

No other provision of this subsection shall be construed to require a private educational lender to perform any additional duty under this paragraph, other than collecting the form required under subparagraph (A).

(4) Disclosures at the time of private education loan consummation

Contemporaneously with the consummation of a private education loan, a private educational lender shall make to the borrower each of the disclosures described in—

(A) paragraph (2)(A) (adjusted, as necessary, for the rate of interest in effect on the date of consummation, based on the index used for the loan);

(B) subparagraphs (B) through (K) and (M) through (P) of paragraph (2); and

(C) paragraph (7).

(5) Format of disclosures

(A) Model form

Not later than 2 years after August 14, 2008, the Bureau shall, based on consumer testing, and in consultation with the Secretary of Education, develop and issue model forms that may be used, at the option of the private educational lender, for the provision of disclosures required under this subsection.

(B) Format

Model forms developed under this paragraph shall—

(i) be comprehensible to borrowers, with a clear format and design;

(ii) provide for clear and conspicuous disclosures;

(iii) enable borrowers easily to identify material terms of the loan and to compare such terms among private education loans; and

(iv) be succinct, and use an easily readable type font.

(C) Safe harbor

Any private educational lender that elects to provide a model form developed under this subsection that accurately reflects the practices of the private educational lender shall be deemed to be in compliance with the disclosures required under this subsection.

(6) Effective period of approved rate of interest and loan terms

(A) In general

With respect to a private education loan, the borrower shall have the right to accept the terms of the loan and consummate the transaction at any time within 30 calendar days (or such longer period as the private educational lender may provide) following the date on which the application for the private education loan is approved and the borrower receives the disclosure documents required under this subsection for the loan, and the rates and terms of the loan may not be changed by the private educational lender during that period.

(B) Prohibition on changes

Except for changes based on adjustments to the index used for a loan, the rates and terms of the loan may not be changed by the private educational lender prior to the earlier of—

(i) the date of acceptance of the terms of the loan and consummation of the transaction by the borrower, as described in subparagraph (A); or

(ii) the expiration of the period described in subparagraph (A).

(7) Right to cancel

With respect to a private education loan, the borrower may cancel the loan, without penalty to the borrower, at any time within 3 business days of the date on which the loan is consummated, and the private educational lender shall disclose such right to the borrower in accordance with paragraph (4).

(8) Prohibition on disbursement

No funds may be disbursed with respect to a private education loan until the expiration of the 3-day period described in paragraph (7).

(9) Bureau regulations

In issuing regulations under this subsection, the Bureau shall prevent, to the extent possible, duplicative disclosure requirements for private educational lenders that are otherwise required to make disclosures under this subchapter, except that in any case in which the disclosure requirements of this subsection differ or conflict with the disclosure requirements of any other provision of this subchapter, the requirements of this subsection shall be controlling.

(10) Definitions

For purposes of this subsection, the terms "covered educational institution", "private educational lender", and "private education loan" have the same meanings as in section 1650 of Title 15.

(11) Duties of lenders participating in preferred lender arrangements

Each private educational lender that has a preferred lender arrangement with a covered educational institution shall annually, by a date determined by the Bureau, in consultation with the Secretary of Education, provide to the covered educational institution such information as the Bureau determines to include in the model form developed under paragraph (5) for each type of private education loan that the lender plans to offer to students attending the covered educational institution, or to the families of such students, for the next award year (as that term is defined in section 481 of the Higher Education Act of 1965).

(f) Periodic statements for residential mortgage loans

(1) In general

The creditor, assignee, or servicer with respect to any residential mortgage loan shall transmit to the obligor, for each billing cycle, a statement setting forth each of the following items, to the extent applicable, in a conspicuous and prominent manner:

(A) The amount of the principal obligation under the mortgage.

(B) The current interest rate in effect for the loan.

(C) The date on which the interest rate may next reset or adjust.

(D) The amount of any prepayment fee to be charged, if any.

(E) A description of any late payment fees.

(F) A telephone number and electronic mail address that may be used by the obligor to obtain information regarding the mortgage.

(G) The names, addresses, telephone numbers, and Internet addresses of counseling agencies or programs reasonably available to the consumer that have been certified or approved and made publicly available by the Secretary of Housing and Urban Development or a State housing finance authority (as defined in section 1441a–1 of Title 12).

(H) Such other information as the Board may prescribe in regulations.

(2) Development and use of standard form

The Board[2] shall develop and prescribe a standard form for the disclosure required under this subsection, taking into account that the statements required may be transmitted in writing or electronically.

[2] So in original. Probably should be "Bureau".

(3) Exception

Paragraph (1) shall not apply to any fixed rate residential mortgage loan where the creditor, assignee, or servicer provides the obligor with a coupon book that provides the obligor with substantially the same information as required in paragraph (1).

(Pub.L. 90–321, Title I, § 128, May 29, 1968, 82 Stat. 155; Pub.L. 96–221, Title VI, § 614(a) to (c), Mar. 31, 1980, 94 Stat. 178, 179; Pub.L. 104–208, Div. A, Title II, § 2105, Sept. 30, 1996, 110 Stat. 3009–402; Pub.L. 109–8, Title XIII, § 1302(b)(1), Apr. 20, 2005, 119 Stat. 209; Pub.L. 110–289, Div. B, Title V, § 2502(a), July 30, 2008, 122 Stat. 2855; Pub.L. 110–315, Title X, § 1021(a), Aug. 14, 2008, 122 Stat. 3483; Pub.L. 110–343, Div. A, Title I, § 130(a), Oct. 3, 2008, 122 Stat. 3797; Pub.L. 111–203, Title X, § 1100A(2), Title XIV, §§ 1400(c), 1419, 1420, 1465, July 21, 2010, 124 Stat. 2107, 2136, 2154, 2155, 2185.)

§ 1638a. Reset of hybrid adjustable rate mortgages [CCPA 128A]

(a) Hybrid adjustable rate mortgages defined

For purposes of this section, the term "hybrid adjustable rate mortgage" means a consumer credit transaction secured by the consumer's principal residence with a fixed interest rate for an introductory period that adjusts or resets to a variable interest rate after such period.

(b) Notice of reset and alternatives

During the 1-month period that ends 6 months before the date on which the interest rate in effect during the introductory period of a hybrid adjustable rate mortgage adjusts or resets to a variable interest rate or, in the case of such an adjustment or resetting that occurs within the first 6 months after consummation of such loan, at consummation, the creditor or servicer of such loan shall provide a written notice, separate and distinct from all other correspondence to the consumer, that includes the following:

(1) Any index or formula used in making adjustments to or resetting the interest rate and a source of information about the index or formula.

(2) An explanation of how the new interest rate and payment would be determined, including an explanation of how the index was adjusted, such as by the addition of a margin.

(3) A good faith estimate, based on accepted industry standards, of the creditor or servicer of the amount of the monthly payment that will apply after the date of the adjustment or reset, and the assumptions on which this estimate is based.

(4) A list of alternatives consumers may pursue before the date of adjustment or reset, and descriptions of the actions consumers must take to pursue these alternatives, including—

(A) refinancing;

(B) renegotiation of loan terms;

(C) payment forbearances; and

(D) pre-foreclosure sales.

(5) The names, addresses, telephone numbers, and Internet addresses of counseling agencies or programs reasonably available to the consumer that have been certified or approved and made publicly available by the Secretary of Housing and Urban Development or a State housing finance authority (as defined in section 1441a–1 of Title 12).

(6) The address, telephone number, and Internet address for the State housing finance authority (as so defined) for the State in which the consumer resides.

(c) Savings clause

The Board may require the notice in paragraph (b) or other notice consistent with this chapter for adjustable rate mortgage loans that are not hybrid adjustable rate mortgage loans.

(Pub.L. 90–321, Title I, § 128A, as added Pub.L. 111–203, Title XIV, § 1418(a), July 21, 2010, 124 Stat. 2153.)

§ 1639. Requirements for certain mortgages [CCPA § 129]

(a) Disclosures

(1) Specific disclosures

In addition to other disclosures required under this subchapter, for each mortgage referred to in section 1602(aa) of this title, the creditor shall provide the following disclosures in conspicuous type size:

(A) "You are not required to complete this agreement merely because you have received these disclosures or have signed a loan application.".

(B) "If you obtain this loan, the lender will have a mortgage on your home. You could lose your home, and any money you have put into it, if you do not meet your obligations under the loan.".

(2) Annual percentage rate

In addition to the disclosures required under paragraph (1), the creditor shall disclose—

(A) in the case of a credit transaction with a fixed rate of interest, the annual percentage rate and the amount of the regular monthly payment; or

(B) in the case of any other credit transaction, the annual percentage rate of the loan, the amount of the regular monthly payment, a statement that the interest rate and monthly payment may increase, and the amount of the maximum monthly payment, based on the maximum interest rate allowed pursuant to section 3806 of Title 12.

(b) Time of disclosures

(1) In general

The disclosures required by this section shall be given not less than 3 business days prior to consummation of the transaction.

(2) New disclosures required

(A) In general

After providing the disclosures required by this section, a creditor may not change the terms of the extension of credit if such changes make the disclosures inaccurate, unless new disclosures are provided that meet the requirements of this section.

(B) Telephone disclosure

A creditor may provide new disclosures pursuant to subparagraph (A) by telephone, if—

(i) the change is initiated by the consumer; and

(ii) at the consummation of the transaction under which the credit is extended—

(I) the creditor provides to the consumer the new disclosures, in writing; and

(II) the creditor and consumer certify in writing that the new disclosures were provided by telephone, by not later than 3 days prior to the date of consummation of the transaction.

(3) No wait for lower rate

If a creditor extends to a consumer a second offer of credit with a lower annual percentage rate, the transaction may be consummated without regard to the period specified in paragraph (1) with respect to the second offer.

(4) Modifications

The Bureau may, if it finds that such action is necessary to permit homeowners to meet bona fide personal financial emergencies, prescribe regulations authorizing the modification or waiver of rights created under this subsection, to the extent and under the circumstances set forth in those regulations.

(c) No prepayment penalty

(1) In general

(A) Limitation on terms

A mortgage referred to in section 1602(aa) of this title may not contain terms under which a consumer must pay a prepayment penalty for paying all or part of the principal before the date on which the principal is due.

(B) Construction

For purposes of this subsection, any method of computing a refund of unearned scheduled interest is a prepayment penalty if it is less favorable to the consumer than the actuarial method (as that term is defined in section 1615(d) of this title).

(2) Repealed. Pub.L. 111–203, Title XIV, § 1432(a), July 21, 2010, 124 Stat. 2160

(d) Limitations after default

A mortgage referred to in section 1602(aa) of this title may not provide for an interest rate applicable after default that is higher than the interest rate that applies before default. If the date of maturity of a mortgage referred to in subsection[1] 1602(aa) of this title is accelerated due to default and the consumer is entitled to a rebate of interest, that rebate shall be computed by any method that is not less favorable than the actuarial method (as that term is defined in section 1615(d) of this title).

(e) No balloon payments

No high-cost mortgage may contain a scheduled payment that is more than twice as large as the average of earlier scheduled payments. This subsection shall not apply when the payment schedule is adjusted to the seasonal or irregular income of the consumer.

(f) No negative amortization

A mortgage referred to in section 1602(aa) of this title may not include terms under which the outstanding principal balance will increase at any time over the course of the loan because the regular periodic payments do not cover the full amount of interest due.

(g) No prepaid payments

A mortgage referred to in section 1602(aa) of this title may not include terms under which more than 2 periodic payments required under the loan are consolidated and paid in advance from the loan proceeds provided to the consumer.

(h) Prohibition on extending credit without regard to payment ability of consumer

A creditor shall not engage in a pattern or practice of extending credit to consumers under mortgages referred to in section 1602(aa) of this title based on the consumers' collateral without regard to the consumers' repayment ability, including the consumers' current and expected income, current obligations, and employment.

(i) Requirements for payments under home improvement contracts

A creditor shall not make a payment to a contractor under a home improvement contract from amounts extended as credit under a mortgage referred to in section 1602(aa) of this title, other than—

(1) in the form of an instrument that is payable to the consumer or jointly to the consumer and the contractor; or

(2) at the election of the consumer, by a third party escrow agent in accordance with terms established in a written agreement signed by the consumer, the creditor, and the contractor before the date of payment.

---

[1] So in original. Probably should be "section".

(j) Recommended default

No creditor shall recommend or encourage default on an existing loan or other debt prior to and in connection with the closing or planned closing of a high-cost mortgage that refinances all or any portion of such existing loan or debt.

(k) Late fees

(1) In general

No creditor may impose a late payment charge or fee in connection with a high-cost mortgage—

(A) in an amount in excess of 4 percent of the amount of the payment past due;

(B) unless the loan documents specifically authorize the charge or fee;

(C) before the end of the 15-day period beginning on the date the payment is due, or in the case of a loan on which interest on each installment is paid in advance, before the end of the 30-day period beginning on the date the payment is due; or

(D) more than once with respect to a single late payment.

(2) Coordination with subsequent late fees

If a payment is otherwise a full payment for the applicable period and is paid on its due date or within an applicable grace period, and the only delinquency or insufficiency of payment is attributable to any late fee or delinquency charge assessed on any earlier payment, no late fee or delinquency charge may be imposed on such payment.

(3) Failure to make installment payment

If, in the case of a loan agreement the terms of which provide that any payment shall first be applied to any past due principal balance, the consumer fails to make an installment payment and the consumer subsequently resumes making installment payments but has not paid all past due installments, the creditor may impose a separate late payment charge or fee for any principal due (without deduction due to late fees or related fees) until the default is cured.

(*l*) Acceleration of debt

No high-cost mortgage may contain a provision which permits the creditor to accelerate the indebtedness, except when repayment of the loan has been accelerated by default in payment, or pursuant to a due-on-sale provision, or pursuant to a material violation of some other provision of the loan document unrelated to payment schedule.

(m) Restriction on financing points and fees

No creditor may directly or indirectly finance, in connection with any high-cost mortgage, any of the following.

(1) Any prepayment fee or penalty payable by the consumer in a refinancing transaction if the creditor or an affiliate of the creditor is the noteholder of the note being refinanced.

(2) Any points or fees.

(n) Consequence of failure to comply

Any mortgage that contains a provision prohibited by this section shall be deemed a failure to deliver the material disclosures required under this subchapter, for the purpose of section 1635 of this title.

(*o*) "Affiliate" defined

For purposes of this section, the term "affiliate" has the same meaning as in section 1841(k) of Title 12.

(p) Discretionary regulatory authority of Bureau

(1) Exemptions

The Bureau may, by regulation or order, exempt specific mortgage products or categories of mortgages from any or all of the prohibitions specified in subsections (c) through (i) of this section, if the Bureau finds that the exemption—

(A) is in the interest of the borrowing public; and

(B) will apply only to products that maintain and strengthen home ownership and equity protection.

(2) Prohibitions

The Bureau, by regulation or order, shall prohibit acts or practices in connection with—

(A) mortgage loans that the Bureau finds to be unfair, deceptive, or designed to evade the provisions of this section; and

(B) refinancing of mortgage loans that the Bureau finds to be associated with abusive lending practices, or that are otherwise not in the interest of the borrower.

(q) Civil penalties in Federal Trade Commission enforcement actions

For purposes of enforcement by the Federal Trade Commission, any violation of a regulation issued by the Bureau pursuant to subsection (*l*)(2) of this section shall be treated as a violation of a rule promulgated under section 57a of this title regarding unfair or deceptive acts or practices.

(r) Prohibitions on evasions, structuring of transactions, and reciprocal arrangements

A creditor may not take any action in connection with a high-cost mortgage—

(1) to structure a loan transaction as an open-end credit plan or another form of loan for the purpose and with the intent of evading the provisions of this subchapter; or

(2) to divide any loan transaction into separate parts for the purpose and with the intent of evading provisions of this subchapter.

(s) Modification and deferral fees prohibited

A creditor, successor in interest, assignee, or any agent of any of the above, may not charge a consumer any fee to modify, renew, extend, or amend a high-cost mortgage, or to defer any payment due under the terms of such mortgage.

(t) Payoff statement

(1) Fees

(A) In general

Except as provided in subparagraph (B), no creditor or servicer may charge a fee for informing or transmitting to any person the balance due to pay off the outstanding balance on a high-cost mortgage.

(B) Transaction fee

When payoff information referred to in subparagraph (A) is provided by facsimile transmission or by a courier service, a creditor or servicer may charge a processing fee to cover the cost of such transmission or service in an amount not to exceed an amount that is comparable to fees imposed for similar services provided in connection with consumer credit transactions that are secured by the consumer's principal dwelling and are not high-cost mortgages.

(C) Fee disclosure

Prior to charging a transaction fee as provided in subparagraph (B), a creditor or servicer shall disclose that payoff balances are available for free pursuant to subparagraph (A).

(D) Multiple requests

If a creditor or servicer has provided payoff information referred to in subparagraph (A) without charge, other than the transaction fee allowed by subparagraph (B), on 4 occasions during a calendar year, the creditor or servicer may thereafter charge a reasonable fee for providing such information during the remainder of the calendar year.

(2) Prompt delivery

Payoff balances shall be provided within 5 business days after receiving a request by a consumer or a person authorized by the consumer to obtain such information.

(u) Pre-loan counseling

(1) In general

A creditor may not extend credit to a consumer under a high-cost mortgage without first receiving certification from a counselor that is approved by the Secretary of Housing and Urban Development, or at the discretion of the Secretary, a State housing finance authority, that the consumer has received counseling on the advisability of the mortgage. Such counselor shall not be employed by the creditor or an affiliate of the creditor or be affiliated with the creditor.

(2) Disclosures required prior to counseling

No counselor may certify that a consumer has received counseling on the advisability of the high-cost mortgage unless the counselor can verify that the consumer has received each statement required (in connection with such loan) by this section or the Real Estate Settlement Procedures Act of 1974 with respect to the transaction.

(3) Regulations

The Board may prescribe such regulations as the Board determines to be appropriate to carry out the requirements of paragraph (1).

(v) Corrections and unintentional violations

A creditor or assignee in a high-cost mortgage who, when acting in good faith, fails to comply with any requirement under this section will not be deemed to have violated such requirement if the creditor or assignee establishes that either—

(1) within 30 days of the loan closing and prior to the institution of any action, the consumer is notified of or discovers the violation, appropriate restitution is made, and whatever adjustments are necessary are made to the loan to either, at the choice of the consumer—

(A) make the loan satisfy the requirements of this part; or

(B) in the case of a high-cost mortgage, change the terms of the loan in a manner beneficial to the consumer so that the loan will no longer be a high-cost mortgage; or

(2) within 60 days of the creditor's discovery or receipt of notification of an unintentional violation or bona fide error and prior to the institution of any action, the consumer is notified of the compliance failure, appropriate restitution is made, and whatever adjustments are necessary are made to the loan to either, at the choice of the consumer—

(A) make the loan satisfy the requirements of this part; or

(B) in the case of a high-cost mortgage, change the terms of the loan in a manner beneficial so that the loan will no longer be a high-cost mortgage.

(Pub.L. 90–321, Title I, § 129, as added Pub.L. 103–325, Title I, § 152(d), Sept. 23, 1994, 108 Stat. 2191, and amended Pub.L. 111–8, Div. D, Title VI, § 626(c), Mar. 11, 2009, 123 Stat. 679; Pub.L. 111–203, Title X, §§ 1100A(2), 1100A(9), 1100H, Title XIV, §§ 1400(c), 1433, July 21, 2010, 124 Stat. 2107, 2109, 2160; Pub.L. 115–174, Title I, § 109(a), May 24, 2018, 132 Stat. 1305.)

§ 1639a. Duty of servicers of residential mortgages [CCPA § 129A]

(a) In general

Notwithstanding any other provision of law, whenever a servicer of residential mortgages agrees to enter into a qualified loss mitigation plan with respect to 1 or more residential mortgages originated before May 20, 2009, including mortgages held in a securitization or other investment vehicle—

(1) to the extent that the servicer owes a duty to investors or other parties to maximize the net present value of such mortgages, the duty shall be construed to apply to all such investors and parties, and not to any individual party or group of parties; and

(2) the servicer shall be deemed to have satisfied the duty set forth in paragraph (1) if, before December 31, 2012, the servicer implements a qualified loss mitigation plan that meets the following criteria:

(A) Default on the payment of such mortgage has occurred, is imminent, or is reasonably foreseeable, as such terms are defined by guidelines issued by the Secretary of the Treasury or his designee under the Emergency Economic Stabilization Act of 2008.

(B) The mortgagor occupies the property securing the mortgage as his or her principal residence.

(C) The servicer reasonably determined, consistent with the guidelines issued by the Secretary of the Treasury or his designee, that the application of such qualified loss mitigation plan to a mortgage or class of mortgages will likely provide an anticipated recovery on the outstanding principal mortgage debt that will exceed the anticipated recovery through foreclosures.

(b) No liability

A servicer that is deemed to be acting in the best interests of all investors or other parties under this section shall not be liable to any party who is owed a duty under subsection (a)(1), and shall not be subject to any injunction, stay, or other equitable relief to such party, based solely upon the implementation by the servicer of a qualified loss mitigation plan.

(c) Standard industry practice

The qualified loss mitigation plan guidelines issued by the Secretary of the Treasury under the Emergency Economic Stabilization Act of 2008 shall constitute standard industry practice for purposes of all Federal and State laws.

(d) Scope of safe harbor

Any person, including a trustee, issuer, and loan originator, shall not be liable for monetary damages or be subject to an injunction, stay, or other equitable relief, based solely upon the cooperation of such person with a servicer when such cooperation is necessary for the servicer to implement a qualified loss mitigation plan that meets the requirements of subsection (a).

(e) Reporting

Each servicer that engages in qualified loss mitigation plans under this section shall regularly report to the Secretary of the Treasury the extent, scope, and results of the servicer's modification activities. The Secretary of the Treasury shall prescribe regulations or guidance specifying the form, content, and timing of such reports.

(f) Definitions

As used in this section—

(1) the term "qualified loss mitigation plan" means—

(A) a residential loan modification, workout, or other loss mitigation plan, including to the extent that the Secretary of the Treasury determines appropriate, a loan sale, real property disposition, trial modification, pre-foreclosure sale, and deed in lieu of foreclosure, that is described or authorized in guidelines issued by the Secretary of the Treasury or his designee under the Emergency Economic Stabilization Act of 2008; and

(B) a refinancing of a mortgage under the Hope for Homeowners program;

(2) the term "servicer" means the person responsible for the servicing for others of residential mortgage loans (including of a pool of residential mortgage loans); and

(3) the term "securitization vehicle" means a trust, special purpose entity, or other legal structure that is used to facilitate the issuing of securities, participation certificates, or similar instruments backed by or referring to a pool of assets that includes residential mortgages (or instruments that are related to residential mortgages such as credit-linked notes).

(g) Rule of construction

No provision of subsection (b) or (d) shall be construed as affecting the liability of any servicer or person as described in subsection (d) for actual fraud in the origination or servicing of a loan or in the implementation of a qualified loss mitigation plan, or for the violation of a State or Federal law, including laws regulating the origination of mortgage loans, commonly referred to as predatory lending laws.

(Pub.L. 90–321, Title I, § 129, formerly § 129A, as added Pub.L. 110–289, Div. A, Title IV, § 1403, July 30, 2008, 122 Stat. 2809; renumbered § 129, Pub.L. 111–22, Div. A, Title II, § 201(b), May 20, 2009, 123 Stat. 1638; renumbered § 129A, Pub.L. 111–203, Title XIV, §§ 1400(c), 1402(a)(1), July 21, 2010, 124 Stat. 2136, 2138.)

§ 1639b. Residential mortgage loan origination [CCPA 129B]

(a) Finding and purpose

(1) Finding

The Congress finds that economic stabilization would be enhanced by the protection, limitation, and regulation of the terms of residential mortgage credit and the practices related to such credit, while ensuring that responsible, affordable mortgage credit remains available to consumers.

(2) Purpose

It is the purpose of this section and section 1639c of this title to assure that consumers are offered and receive residential mortgage loans on terms that reasonably reflect their ability to repay the loans and that are understandable and not unfair, deceptive or abusive.

(b) Duty of care

(1) Standard

Subject to regulations prescribed under this subsection, each mortgage originator shall, in addition to the duties imposed by otherwise applicable provisions of State or Federal law—

(A) be qualified and, when required, registered and licensed as a mortgage originator in accordance with applicable State or Federal law, including the Secure and Fair Enforcement for Mortgage Licensing Act of 2008; and

(B) include on all loan documents any unique identifier of the mortgage originator provided by the Nationwide Mortgage Licensing System and Registry.

(2) Compliance procedures required

The Bureau shall prescribe regulations requiring depository institutions to establish and maintain procedures reasonably designed to assure and monitor the compliance of such depository institutions, the subsidiaries of such institutions, and the employees of such institutions or subsidiaries with the requirements of this section and the registration procedures established under section 1507 of the Secure and Fair Enforcement for Mortgage Licensing Act of 2008.

(c) Prohibition on steering incentives

(1) In general

For any residential mortgage loan, no mortgage originator shall receive from any person and no person shall pay to a mortgage originator, directly or indirectly, compensation that varies based on the terms of the loan (other than the amount of the principal).

(2) Restructuring of financing origination fee

(A) In general

For any mortgage loan, a mortgage originator may not receive from any person other than the consumer and no person, other than the consumer, who knows or has reason to know that a consumer has directly compensated or will directly compensate a mortgage originator may pay a mortgage originator any origination fee or charge except bona fide third party charges not retained by the creditor, mortgage originator, or an affiliate of the creditor or mortgage originator.

(B) Exception

Notwithstanding subparagraph (A), a mortgage originator may receive from a person other than the consumer an origination fee or charge, and a person other than the consumer may pay a mortgage originator an origination fee or charge, if—

(i) the mortgage originator does not receive any compensation directly from the consumer; and

(ii) the consumer does not make an upfront payment of discount points, origination points, or fees, however denominated (other than bona fide third party charges not retained by the mortgage originator, creditor, or an affiliate of the creditor or originator), except that the Bureau may, by rule, waive or provide exemptions to this clause if the Bureau determines that such waiver or exemption is in the interest of consumers and in the public interest.

(3) Regulations

The Bureau shall prescribe regulations to prohibit—

(A) mortgage originators from steering any consumer to a residential mortgage loan that—

(i) the consumer lacks a reasonable ability to repay (in accordance with regulations prescribed under section 1639c(a) of this title); or

(ii) has predatory characteristics or effects (such as equity stripping, excessive fees, or abusive terms);

(B) mortgage originators from steering any consumer from a residential mortgage loan for which the consumer is qualified that is a qualified mortgage (as defined in section 1639c(b)(2) of this title) to a residential mortgage loan that is not a qualified mortgage;

(C) abusive or unfair lending practices that promote disparities among consumers of equal credit worthiness but of different race, ethnicity, gender, or age; and

(D) mortgage originators from—

(i) mischaracterizing the credit history of a consumer or the residential mortgage loans available to a consumer;

(ii) mischaracterizing or suborning the mischaracterization of the appraised value of the property securing the extension of credit; or

(iii) if unable to suggest, offer, or recommend to a consumer a loan that is not more expensive than a loan for which the consumer qualifies, discouraging a consumer from seeking a residential mortgage loan secured by a consumer's principal dwelling from another mortgage originator.

(4) Rules of construction

No provision of this subsection shall be construed as—

(A) permitting any yield spread premium or other similar compensation that would, for any residential mortgage loan, permit the total amount of direct and indirect compensation from all sources permitted to a mortgage originator to vary based on the terms of the loan (other than the amount of the principal);

(B) limiting or affecting the amount of compensation received by a creditor upon the sale of a consummated loan to a subsequent purchaser;

(C) restricting a consumer's ability to finance, at the option of the consumer, including through principal or rate, any origination fees or costs permitted under this subsection, or the mortgage originator's right to receive such fees or costs (including compensation) from any person, subject to paragraph (2)(B), so long as such fees or costs do not vary based on the terms of the loan (other than the amount of the principal) or the consumer's decision about whether to finance such fees or costs; or

(D) prohibiting incentive payments to a mortgage originator based on the number of residential mortgage loans originated within a specified period of time.

(d) Liability for violations

(1) In general

For purposes of providing a cause of action for any failure by a mortgage originator, other than a creditor, to comply with any requirement imposed under this section and any regulation prescribed under this section, section 1640 of this title shall be applied with respect to any such failure by substituting "mortgage originator" for "creditor" each place such term appears in each such subsection.[1]

(2) Maximum

The maximum amount of any liability of a mortgage originator under paragraph (1) to a consumer for any violation of this section shall not exceed the greater of actual damages or an amount equal to 3 times the total amount of direct and indirect compensation or gain accruing to the mortgage originator in connection with the residential mortgage loan involved in the violation, plus the costs to the consumer of the action, including a reasonable attorney's fee.

(e) Discretionary regulatory authority

(1) In general

The Bureau shall, by regulations, prohibit or condition terms, acts or practices relating to residential mortgage loans that the Bureau finds to be abusive, unfair, deceptive, predatory, necessary or proper to ensure that responsible, affordable mortgage credit remains available to consumers in a manner consistent with the purposes of this section and section 1639c of this title, necessary or proper to effectuate the purposes of this section and section 1639c of this title, to prevent circumvention or evasion thereof, or to facilitate compliance with such sections, or are not in the interest of the borrower.

(2) Application

The regulations prescribed under paragraph (1) shall be applicable to all residential mortgage loans and shall be applied in the same manner as regulations prescribed under section 1604 of this title.

(f) Section 1639b of this title and any regulations promulgated thereunder do not apply to an extension of credit relating to a plan described in section 101(53D) of Title 11.

(Pub.L. 90–321, Title I, § 129B, as added and amended Pub.L. 111–203, Title X, § 1100A(2), Title XIV, §§ 1402(a)(2), 1403, 1404, 1405(a), July 21, 2010, 124 Stat. 2107, 2139, 2141.)

---

1 So in original. Probably should be "in such section."

§ 1639c. Minimum standards for residential mortgage loans [CCPA 129C]

(a) Ability to repay

(1) In general

In accordance with regulations prescribed by the Bureau, no creditor may make a residential mortgage loan unless the creditor makes a reasonable and good faith determination based on verified and documented information that, at the time the loan is consummated, the consumer has a reasonable ability to repay the loan, according to its terms, and all applicable taxes, insurance (including mortgage guarantee insurance), and assessments.

(2) Multiple loans

If the creditor knows, or has reason to know, that 1 or more residential mortgage loans secured by the same dwelling will be made to the same consumer, the creditor shall make a reasonable and good faith determination, based on verified and documented information, that the consumer has a reasonable ability to repay the combined payments of all loans on the same dwelling according to the terms of those loans and all applicable taxes, insurance (including mortgage guarantee insurance), and assessments.

(3) Basis for determination

A determination under this subsection of a consumer's ability to repay a residential mortgage loan shall include consideration of the consumer's credit history, current income, expected income the consumer is reasonably assured of receiving, current obligations, debt-to-income ratio or the residual income the consumer will have after paying non-mortgage debt and mortgage-related obligations, employment status, and other financial resources other than the consumer's equity in the dwelling or real property that secures repayment of the loan. A creditor shall determine the ability of the consumer to repay using a payment schedule that fully amortizes the loan over the term of the loan.

(4) Income verification

A creditor making a residential mortgage loan shall verify amounts of income or assets that such creditor relies on to determine repayment ability, including expected income or assets, by reviewing the consumer's Internal Revenue Service Form W-2, tax returns, payroll receipts, financial institution records, or other third-party documents that provide reasonably reliable evidence of the consumer's income or assets. In order to safeguard against fraudulent reporting, any consideration of a consumer's income history in making a determination under this subsection shall include the verification of such income by the use of—

(A) Internal Revenue Service transcripts of tax returns; or

(B) a method that quickly and effectively verifies income documentation by a third party subject to rules prescribed by the Bureau.

(5) Exemption

With respect to loans made, guaranteed, or insured by Federal departments or agencies identified in subsection (b)(3)(B)(ii), such departments or agencies may exempt refinancings under a streamlined refinancing from this income verification requirement as long as the following conditions are met:

(A) The consumer is not 30 days or more past due on the prior existing residential mortgage loan.

(B) The refinancing does not increase the principal balance outstanding on the prior existing residential mortgage loan, except to the extent of fees and charges allowed by the department or agency making, guaranteeing, or insuring the refinancing.

(C) Total points and fees (as defined in section 1602(aa)(4) of this title, other than bona fide third party charges not retained by the mortgage originator, creditor, or an affiliate of the creditor or mortgage originator) payable in connection with the refinancing do not exceed 3 percent of the total new loan amount.

(D) The interest rate on the refinanced loan is lower than the interest rate of the original loan, unless the borrower is refinancing from an adjustable rate to a fixed-rate loan, under guidelines that the department or agency shall establish for loans they make, guarantee, or issue.

(E) The refinancing is subject to a payment schedule that will fully amortize the refinancing in accordance with the regulations prescribed by the department or agency making, guaranteeing, or insuring the refinancing.

(F) The terms of the refinancing do not result in a balloon payment, as defined in subsection (b)(2)(A)(ii).

(G) Both the residential mortgage loan being refinanced and the refinancing satisfy all requirements of the department or agency making, guaranteeing, or insuring the refinancing.

(6) Nonstandard loans

(A) Variable rate loans that defer repayment of any principal or interest

For purposes of determining, under this subsection, a consumer's ability to repay a variable rate residential mortgage loan that allows or requires the consumer to defer the repayment of any principal or interest, the creditor shall use a fully amortizing repayment schedule.

(B) Interest-only loans

For purposes of determining, under this subsection, a consumer's ability to repay a residential mortgage loan that permits or requires the payment of interest only, the creditor shall use the payment amount required to amortize the loan by its final maturity.

(C) Calculation for negative amortization

In making any determination under this subsection, a creditor shall also take into consideration any balance increase that may accrue from any negative amortization provision.

(D) Calculation process

For purposes of making any determination under this subsection, a creditor shall calculate the monthly payment amount for principal and interest on any residential mortgage loan by assuming—

(i) the loan proceeds are fully disbursed on the date of the consummation of the loan;

(ii) the loan is to be repaid in substantially equal monthly amortizing payments for principal and interest over the entire term of the loan with no balloon payment, unless the loan contract requires more rapid repayment (including balloon payment), in which case the calculation shall be made (I) in accordance with regulations prescribed by the Bureau, with respect to any loan which has an annual percentage rate that does not exceed the average prime offer rate for a comparable transaction, as of the date the interest rate is set, by 1.5 or more percentage points for a first lien residential mortgage loan; and by 3.5 or more percentage points for a subordinate lien residential mortgage loan; or (II) using the contract's repayment schedule, with respect to a loan which has an annual percentage rate, as of the date the interest rate is set, that is at least 1.5 percentage points above the average prime offer rate for a first lien residential mortgage loan; and 3.5 percentage points above the average prime offer rate for a subordinate lien residential mortgage loan; and

(iii) the interest rate over the entire term of the loan is a fixed rate equal to the fully indexed rate at the time of the loan closing, without considering the introductory rate.

(E) Refinance of hybrid loans with current lender

In considering any application for refinancing an existing hybrid loan by the creditor into a standard loan to be made by the same creditor in any case in which there would be a reduction in monthly payment and the mortgagor has not been delinquent on any payment on the existing hybrid loan, the creditor may—

(i) consider the mortgagor's good standing on the existing mortgage;

(ii) consider if the extension of new credit would prevent a likely default should the original mortgage reset and give such concerns a higher priority as an acceptable underwriting practice; and

(iii) offer rate discounts and other favorable terms to such mortgagor that would be available to new customers with high credit ratings based on such underwriting practice.

(7) Fully-indexed rate defined

For purposes of this subsection, the term "fully indexed rate" means the index rate prevailing on a residential mortgage loan at the time the loan is made plus the margin that will apply after the expiration of any introductory interest rates.

(8) Reverse mortgages and bridge loans

This subsection shall not apply with respect to any reverse mortgage or temporary or bridge loan with a term of 12 months or less, including to any loan to purchase a new dwelling where the consumer plans to sell a different dwelling within 12 months.

(9) Seasonal income

If documented income, including income from a small business, is a repayment source for a residential mortgage loan, a creditor may consider the seasonality and irregularity of such income in the underwriting of and scheduling of payments for such credit.

(b) Presumption of ability to repay

(1) In general

Any creditor with respect to any residential mortgage loan, and any assignee of such loan subject to liability under this subchapter, may presume that the loan has met the requirements of subsection (a), if the loan is a qualified mortgage.

(2) Definitions

For purposes of this subsection, the following definitions shall apply:

(A) Qualified mortgage

The term "qualified mortgage" means any residential mortgage loan—

(i) for which the regular periodic payments for the loan may not—

(I) result in an increase of the principal balance; or

(II) except as provided in subparagraph (E), allow the consumer to defer repayment of principal;

(ii) except as provided in subparagraph (E), the terms of which do not result in a balloon payment, where a "balloon payment" is a scheduled payment that is more than twice as large as the average of earlier scheduled payments;

(iii) for which the income and financial resources relied upon to qualify the obligors on the loan are verified and documented;

(iv) in the case of a fixed rate loan, for which the underwriting process is based on a payment schedule that fully amortizes the loan over the loan term and takes into account all applicable taxes, insurance, and assessments;

(v) in the case of an adjustable rate loan, for which the underwriting is based on the maximum rate permitted under the loan during the first 5 years, and a payment schedule that fully amortizes the loan over the loan term and takes into account all applicable taxes, insurance, and assessments;

(vi) that complies with any guidelines or regulations established by the Bureau relating to ratios of total monthly debt to monthly income or alternative measures of ability to pay regular expenses after payment of total monthly debt, taking into account the income levels of the borrower and such other factors as the Bureau may determine relevant and consistent with the purposes described in paragraph (3)(B)(i);

(vii) for which the total points and fees (as defined in subparagraph (C)) payable in connection with the loan do not exceed 3 percent of the total loan amount;

(viii) for which the term of the loan does not exceed 30 years, except as such term may be extended under paragraph (3), such as in high-cost areas; and

(ix) in the case of a reverse mortgage (except for the purposes of subsection (a) of this section, to the extent that such mortgages are exempt altogether from those requirements), a reverse mortgage which meets the standards for a qualified mortgage, as set by the Bureau in rules that are consistent with the purposes of this subsection.

(B) Average prime offer rate

The term "average prime offer rate" means the average prime offer rate for a comparable transaction as of the date on which the interest rate for the transaction is set, as published by the Bureau.[1]

(C) Points and fees

(i) In general

For purposes of subparagraph (A), the term "points and fees" means points and fees as defined by section 1602(aa)(4) of this title (other than bona fide third party charges not retained by the mortgage originator, creditor, or an affiliate of the creditor or mortgage originator).

(ii) Computation

For purposes of computing the total points and fees under this subparagraph, the total points and fees shall exclude either of the amounts described in the following subclauses, but not both:

(I) Up to and including 2 bona fide discount points payable by the consumer in connection with the mortgage, but only if the interest rate from which the mortgage's interest rate will be discounted does not exceed by more than 1 percentage point the average prime offer rate.

(II) Unless 2 bona fide discount points have been excluded under subclause (I), up to and including 1 bona fide discount point payable by the consumer in connection with the mortgage, but only if the interest rate from which the mortgage's interest rate will be discounted does not exceed by more than 2 percentage points the average prime offer rate.

(iii) Bona fide discount points defined

For purposes of clause (ii), the term "bona fide discount points" means loan discount points which are knowingly paid by the consumer for the purpose of reducing, and which in fact result in a bona fide reduction of, the interest rate or time-price differential applicable to the mortgage.

(iv) Interest rate reduction

Subclauses (I) and (II) of clause (ii) shall not apply to discount points used to purchase an interest rate reduction unless the amount of the interest rate reduction purchased is reasonably consistent with established industry norms and practices for secondary mortgage market transactions.

(D) Smaller loans

The Bureau shall prescribe rules adjusting the criteria under subparagraph (A)(vii) in order to permit lenders that extend smaller loans to meet the requirements of the presumption of

[1] So in original. Second period probably should not appear.

compliance under paragraph (1). In prescribing such rules, the Bureau shall consider the potential impact of such rules on rural areas and other areas where home values are lower.

(E) Balloon loans

The Bureau may, by regulation, provide that the term "qualified mortgage" includes a balloon loan—

(i) that meets all of the criteria for a qualified mortgage under subparagraph (A) (except clauses (i)(II), (ii), (iv), and (v) of such subparagraph);

(ii) for which the creditor makes a determination that the consumer is able to make all scheduled payments, except the balloon payment, out of income or assets other than the collateral;

(iii) for which the underwriting is based on a payment schedule that fully amortizes the loan over a period of not more than 30 years and takes into account all applicable taxes, insurance, and assessments; and

(iv) that is extended by a creditor that—

(I) operates in rural or underserved areas;

(II) together with all affiliates, has total annual residential mortgage loan originations that do not exceed a limit set by the Bureau;

(III) retains the balloon loans in portfolio; and

(IV) meets any asset size threshold and any other criteria as the Bureau may establish, consistent with the purposes of this subtitle.

(F) Safe harbor

(i) Definitions

In this subparagraph—

(I) the term 'covered institution' means an insured depository institution or an insured credit union that, together with its affiliates, has less than $10,000,000,000 in total consolidated assets;

(II) the term 'insured credit union' has the meaning given the term in section 101 of the Federal Credit Union Act (12 U.S.C. 1752);

(III) the term 'insured depository institution' has the meaning given the term in section 3 of the Federal Deposit Insurance Act (12 U.S.C. 1813);

(IV) the term 'interest-only' means that, under the terms of the legal obligation, one or more of the periodic payments may be applied solely to accrued interest and not to loan principal; and

(V) the term 'negative amortization' means payment of periodic payments that will result in an increase in the principal balance under the terms of the legal obligation.

(ii) Safe harbor

In this section—

(I) the term 'qualified mortgage' includes any residential mortgage loan—

(aa) that is originated and retained in portfolio by a covered institution;

(bb) that is in compliance with the limitations with respect to prepayment penalties described in subsections (c)(1) and (c)(3);

(cc) that is in compliance with the requirements of clause (vii) of subparagraph (A);

(dd) that does not have negative amortization or interest-only features; and

(ee) for which the covered institution considers and documents the debt, income, and financial resources of the consumer in accordance with clause (iv); and

(II) a residential mortgage loan described in subclause (I) shall be deemed to meet the requirements of subsection (a).

(iii) Exception for certain transfers

A residential mortgage loan described in clause (ii)(I) shall not qualify for the safe harbor under clause (ii) if the legal title to the residential mortgage loan is sold, assigned, or otherwise transferred to another person unless the residential mortgage loan is sold, assigned, or otherwise transferred—

(I) to another person by reason of the bankruptcy or failure of a covered institution;

(II) to a covered institution so long as the loan is retained in portfolio by the covered institution to which the loan is sold, assigned, or otherwise transferred;

(III) pursuant to a merger of a covered institution with another person or the acquisition of a covered institution by another person or of another person by a covered institution, so long as the loan is retained in portfolio by the person to whom the loan is sold, assigned, or otherwise transferred; or

(IV) to a wholly owned subsidiary of a covered institution, provided that, after the sale, assignment, or transfer, the residential mortgage loan is considered to be an asset of the covered institution for regulatory accounting purposes.

(iv) Consideration and documentation requirements

The consideration and documentation requirements described in clause (ii)(I)(ee) shall—

(I) not be construed to require compliance with, or documentation in accordance with, appendix Q to part 1026 of title 12, Code of Federal Regulations, or any successor regulation; and

(II) be construed to permit multiple methods of documentation.

(3) Regulations

(A) In general

The Bureau shall prescribe regulations to carry out the purposes of this subsection.

(B) Revision of safe harbor criteria

(i) In general

The Bureau may prescribe regulations that revise, add to, or subtract from the criteria that define a qualified mortgage upon a finding that such regulations are necessary or proper to ensure that responsible, affordable mortgage credit remains available to consumers in a manner consistent with the purposes of this section, necessary and appropriate to effectuate the purposes of this section and section 1639b of this title, to prevent circumvention or evasion thereof, or to facilitate compliance with such sections.

(ii) Loan definition

The following agencies shall, in consultation with the Bureau, prescribe rules defining the types of loans they insure, guarantee, or administer, as the case may be, that are qualified mortgages for purposes of paragraph (2)(A), and such rules may revise, add to, or subtract from the criteria used to define a qualified mortgage under paragraph (2)(A), upon a finding that such rules are consistent with the purposes of this section and section 1639b of this title, to prevent circumvention or evasion thereof, or to facilitate compliance with such sections:

(I) The Department of Housing and Urban Development, with regard to mortgages insured under the National Housing Act (12 U.S.C. 1707 et seq.).

(II) The Department of Veterans Affairs, with regard to a loan made or guaranteed by the Secretary of Veterans Affairs.

(III) The Department of Agriculture, with regard[2] loans guaranteed by the Secretary of Agriculture pursuant to 42 U.S.C. 1472(h).

(IV) The Rural Housing Service, with regard to loans insured by the Rural Housing Service.

(C) Consideration of underwriting requirements for Property Assessed Clean Energy financing

(i) Definition

In this subparagraph, the term 'Property Assessed Clean Energy financing' means financing to cover the costs of home improvements that results in a tax assessment on the real property of the consumer.

(ii) Regulations

The Bureau shall prescribe regulations that carry out the purposes of subsection (a) and apply section 130 with respect to violations under subsection (a) of this section with respect to Property Assessed Clean Energy financing, which shall account for the unique nature of Property Assessed Clean Energy financing.

(iii) Collection of information and consultation

In prescribing the regulations under this subparagraph, the Bureau—

(I) may collect such information and data that the Bureau determines is necessary; and

(II) shall consult with State and local governments and bond-issuing authorities.

(c) Prohibition on certain prepayment penalties

(1) Prohibited on certain loans

(A) In general

A residential mortgage loan that is not a "qualified mortgage", as defined under subsection (b)(2), may not contain terms under which a consumer must pay a prepayment penalty for paying all or part of the principal after the loan is consummated.

(B) Exclusions

For purposes of this subsection, a "qualified mortgage" may not include a residential mortgage loan that—

(i) has an adjustable rate; or

(ii) has an annual percentage rate that exceeds the average prime offer rate for a comparable transaction, as of the date the interest rate is set—

(I) by 1.5 or more percentage points, in the case of a first lien residential mortgage loan having a original principal obligation amount that is equal to or less than the amount of the maximum limitation on the original principal obligation of mortgage in effect for a residence of the applicable size, as of the date of such interest rate set, pursuant to the 6th sentence of section 1454(a)(2) of Title 12;

[2] So in original. Probably should be followed by "to."

(II) by 2.5 or more percentage points, in the case of a first lien residential mortgage loan having a original principal obligation amount that is more than the amount of the maximum limitation on the original principal obligation of mortgage in effect for a residence of the applicable size, as of the date of such interest rate set, pursuant to the 6th sentence of section 1454(a)(2) of Title 12; and

(III) by 3.5 or more percentage points, in the case of a subordinate lien residential mortgage loan.

(2) Publication of average prime offer rate and APR thresholds

The Bureau—

(A) shall publish, and update at least weekly, average prime offer rates;

(B) may publish multiple rates based on varying types of mortgage transactions; and

(C) shall adjust the thresholds established under subclause (I), (II), and (III) of paragraph (1)(B)(ii) as necessary to reflect significant changes in market conditions and to effectuate the purposes of the Mortgage Reform and Anti-Predatory Lending Act.

(3) Phased-out penalties on qualified mortgages

A qualified mortgage (as defined in subsection (b)(2)) may not contain terms under which a consumer must pay a prepayment penalty for paying all or part of the principal after the loan is consummated in excess of the following limitations:

(A) During the 1-year period beginning on the date the loan is consummated, the prepayment penalty shall not exceed an amount equal to 3 percent of the outstanding balance on the loan.

(B) During the 1-year period beginning after the period described in subparagraph (A), the prepayment penalty shall not exceed an amount equal to 2 percent of the outstanding balance on the loan.

(C) During the 1-year period beginning after the 1-year period described in subparagraph (B), the prepayment penalty shall not exceed an amount equal to 1 percent of the outstanding balance on the loan.

(D) After the end of the 3-year period beginning on the date the loan is consummated, no prepayment penalty may be imposed on a qualified mortgage.

(4) Option for no prepayment penalty required

A creditor may not offer a consumer a residential mortgage loan product that has a prepayment penalty for paying all or part of the principal after the loan is consummated as a term of the loan without offering the consumer a residential mortgage loan product that does not have a prepayment penalty as a term of the loan.

(d) Single premium credit insurance prohibited

No creditor may finance, directly or indirectly, in connection with any residential mortgage loan or with any extension of credit under an open end consumer credit plan secured by the principal dwelling of the consumer, any credit life, credit disability, credit unemployment, or credit property insurance, or any other accident, loss-of-income, life, or health insurance, or any payments directly or indirectly for any debt cancellation or suspension agreement or contract, except that—

(1) insurance premiums or debt cancellation or suspension fees calculated and paid in full on a monthly basis shall not be considered financed by the creditor; and

(2) this subsection shall not apply to credit unemployment insurance for which the unemployment insurance premiums are reasonable, the creditor receives no direct or indirect compensation in connection with the unemployment insurance premiums, and the unemployment insurance premiums are paid pursuant to another insurance contract and not paid to an affiliate of the creditor.

(e) Arbitration

(1) In general

No residential mortgage loan and no extension of credit under an open end consumer credit plan secured by the principal dwelling of the consumer may include terms which require arbitration or any other nonjudicial procedure as the method for resolving any controversy or settling any claims arising out of the transaction.

(2) Post-controversy agreements

Subject to paragraph (3), paragraph (1) shall not be construed as limiting the right of the consumer and the creditor or any assignee to agree to arbitration or any other nonjudicial procedure as the method for resolving any controversy at any time after a dispute or claim under the transaction arises.

(3) No waiver of statutory cause of action

No provision of any residential mortgage loan or of any extension of credit under an open end consumer credit plan secured by the principal dwelling of the consumer, and no other agreement between the consumer and the creditor relating to the residential mortgage loan or extension of credit referred to in paragraph (1), shall be applied or interpreted so as to bar a consumer from bringing an action in an appropriate district court of the United States, or any other court of competent jurisdiction, pursuant to section 1640 of this title or any other provision of law, for damages or other relief in connection with any alleged violation of this section, any other provision of this subchapter, or any other Federal law.

(f) Mortgages with negative amortization

No creditor may extend credit to a borrower in connection with a consumer credit transaction under an open or closed end consumer credit plan secured by a dwelling or residential real property that includes a dwelling, other than a reverse mortgage, that provides or permits a payment plan that may, at any time over the term of the extension of credit, result in negative amortization unless, before such transaction is consummated—

(1) the creditor provides the consumer with a statement that—

(A) the pending transaction will or may, as the case may be, result in negative amortization;

(B) describes negative amortization in such manner as the Bureau shall prescribe;

(C) negative amortization increases the outstanding principal balance of the account; and

(D) negative amortization reduces the consumer's equity in the dwelling or real property; and

(2) in the case of a first-time borrower with respect to a residential mortgage loan that is not a qualified mortgage, the first-time borrower provides the creditor with sufficient documentation to demonstrate that the consumer received homeownership counseling from organizations or counselors certified by the Secretary of Housing and Urban Development as competent to provide such counseling.

(g) Protection against loss of anti-deficiency protection

(1) Definition

For purposes of this subsection, the term "anti-deficiency law" means the law of any State which provides that, in the event of foreclosure on the residential property of a consumer securing a mortgage, the consumer is not liable, in accordance with the terms and limitations of such State law, for any deficiency between the sale price obtained on such property through foreclosure and the outstanding balance of the mortgage.

(2) Notice at time of consummation

In the case of any residential mortgage loan that is, or upon consummation will be, subject to protection under an anti-deficiency law, the creditor or mortgage originator shall provide a written notice to the consumer describing the protection provided by the anti-deficiency law and the significance for the consumer of the loss of such protection before such loan is consummated.

(3) Notice before refinancing that would cause loss of protection

In the case of any residential mortgage loan that is subject to protection under an anti-deficiency law, if a creditor or mortgage originator provides an application to a consumer, or receives an application from a consumer, for any type of refinancing for such loan that would cause the loan to lose the protection of such anti-deficiency law, the creditor or mortgage originator shall provide a written notice to the consumer describing the protection provided by the anti-deficiency law and the significance for the consumer of the loss of such protection before any agreement for any such refinancing is consummated.

(h) Policy regarding acceptance of partial payment

In the case of any residential mortgage loan, a creditor shall disclose prior to settlement or, in the case of a person becoming a creditor with respect to an existing residential mortgage loan, at the time such person becomes a creditor—

(1) the creditor's policy regarding the acceptance of partial payments; and

(2) if partial payments are accepted, how such payments will be applied to such mortgage and if such payments will be placed in escrow.

(i) Timeshare plans

This section and any regulations promulgated under this section do not apply to an extension of credit relating to a plan described in section 101(53D) of Title 11.

(Pub.L. 90–321, Title I, § 129C; Pub.L. 111–203, Title X, § 1100A(2), Title XIV, §§ 1411(a)(2), 1412, 1414(a), (c), (d), July 21, 2010, 124 Stat. 2107, 2142, 2145, 2149, 2152; Pub.L. 114–94, Div. G, Title LXXXIX, § 89003, Dec. 4, 2015, 129 Stat. 1801; Pub.L. 115–174, Title I, § 101, Title III, § 307, May 24, 2018, 132 Stat. 1297, 1347.)

§ 1639d. Escrow or impound accounts relating to certain consumer credit transactions [CCPA 129D]

(a) In general

Except as provided in subsection (b), (c), (d), or (e), a creditor, in connection with the consummation of a consumer credit transaction secured by a first lien on the principal dwelling of the consumer, other than a consumer credit transaction under an open end credit plan or a reverse mortgage, shall establish, before the consummation of such transaction, an escrow or impound account for the payment of taxes and hazard insurance, and, if applicable, flood insurance, mortgage insurance, ground rents, and any other required periodic payments or premiums with respect to the property or the loan terms, as provided in, and in accordance with, this section.

(b) When required

No impound, trust, or other type of account for the payment of property taxes, insurance premiums, or other purposes relating to the property may be required as a condition of a real property sale contract or a loan secured by a first deed of trust or mortgage on the principal dwelling of the consumer, other than a consumer credit transaction under an open end credit plan or a reverse mortgage, except when—

(1) any such impound, trust, or other type of escrow or impound account for such purposes is required by Federal or State law;

(2) a loan is made, guaranteed, or insured by a State or Federal governmental lending or insuring agency;

(3) the transaction is secured by a first mortgage or lien on the consumer's principal dwelling having an original principal obligation amount that—

(A) does not exceed the amount of the maximum limitation on the original principal obligation of mortgage in effect for a residence of the applicable size, as of the date such interest rate set, pursuant to the sixth sentence of section 1454(a)(2) of Title 12, and the annual percentage rate will exceed the average prime offer rate as defined in section 1639c of this title by 1.5 or more percentage points; or

(B) exceeds the amount of the maximum limitation on the original principal obligation of mortgage in effect for a residence of the applicable size, as of the date such interest rate set, pursuant to the sixth sentence of section 1454(a)(2) of Title 12, and the annual percentage rate will exceed the average prime offer rate as defined in section 1639c of this title by 2.5 or more percentage points; or

(4) so required pursuant to regulation.

(c) Exemptions

(1) In general

The Bureau may, by regulation, exempt from the requirements of subsection (a) a creditor that—

(A) operates in rural or underserved areas;

(B) together with all affiliates, has total annual mortgage loan originations that do not exceed a limit set by the Bureau;

(C) retains its mortgage loan originations in portfolio; and

(D) meets any asset size threshold and any other criteria the Bureau may establish, consistent with the purposes of this subtitle.

(2) Treatment of loans held by smaller institutions

The Bureau shall, by regulation, exempt from the requirements of subsection (a) any loan made by an insured depository institution or an insured credit union secured by a first lien on the principal dwelling of a consumer if—

(A) the insured depository institution or insured credit union has assets of $10,000,000,000 or less;

(B) during the preceding calendar year, the insured depository institution or insured credit union and its affiliates originated 1,000 or fewer loans secured by a first lien on a principal dwelling; and

(C) the transaction satisfies the criteria in sections 1026.35(b)(2)(iii)(A), 1026.35(b)(2)(iii)(D), and 1026.35(b)(2)(v) of title 12, Code of Federal Regulations, or any successor regulation.

(d) Duration of mandatory escrow or impound account

An escrow or impound account established pursuant to subsection (b) shall remain in existence for a minimum period of 5 years, beginning with the date of the consummation of the loan, unless and until—

(1) such borrower has sufficient equity in the dwelling securing the consumer credit transaction so as to no longer be required to maintain private mortgage insurance;

(2) such borrower is delinquent;

(3) such borrower otherwise has not complied with the legal obligation, as established by rule; or

(4) the underlying mortgage establishing the account is terminated.

(e) Limited exemptions for loans secured by shares in a cooperative or in which an association must maintain a master insurance policy

Escrow accounts need not be established for loans secured by shares in a cooperative. Insurance premiums need not be included in escrow accounts for loans secured by dwellings or units, where the borrower must join an association as a condition of ownership, and that association has an obligation to the dwelling or unit owners to maintain a master policy insuring the dwellings or units.

(f) Clarification on escrow accounts for loans not meeting statutory test

For mortgages not covered by the requirements of subsection (b), no provision of this section shall be construed as precluding the establishment of an impound, trust, or other type of account for the payment of property taxes, insurance premiums, or other purposes relating to the property—

(1) on terms mutually agreeable to the parties to the loan;

(2) at the discretion of the lender or servicer, as provided by the contract between the lender or servicer and the borrower; or

(3) pursuant to the requirements for the escrowing of flood insurance payments for regulated lending institutions in section 102(d) of the Flood Disaster Protection Act of 1973.

(g) Administration of mandatory escrow or impound accounts

(1) In general

Except as may otherwise be provided for in this subchapter or in regulations prescribed by the Bureau, escrow or impound accounts established pursuant to subsection (b) shall be established in a federally insured depository institution or credit union.

(2) Administration

Except as provided in this section or regulations prescribed under this section, an escrow or impound account subject to this section shall be administered in accordance with—

(A) the Real Estate Settlement Procedures Act of 1974 and regulations prescribed under such Act;

(B) the Flood Disaster Protection Act of 1973 and regulations prescribed under such Act; and

(C) the law of the State, if applicable, where the real property securing the consumer credit transaction is located.

(3) Applicability of payment of interest

If prescribed by applicable State or Federal law, each creditor shall pay interest to the consumer on the amount held in any impound, trust, or escrow account that is subject to this section in the manner as prescribed by that applicable State or Federal law.

(4) Penalty coordination with RESPA

Any action or omission on the part of any person which constitutes a violation of the Real Estate Settlement Procedures Act of 1974 or any regulation prescribed under such Act for which the person has paid any fine, civil money penalty, or other damages shall not give rise to any additional fine, civil money penalty, or other damages under this section, unless the action or omission also constitutes a direct violation of this section.

(h) Disclosures relating to mandatory escrow or impound account

In the case of any impound, trust, or escrow account that is required under subsection (b), the creditor shall disclose by written notice to the consumer at least 3 business days before the consummation of the consumer credit transaction giving rise to such account or in accordance with timeframes established in prescribed regulations the following information:

(1) The fact that an escrow or impound account will be established at consummation of the transaction.

(2) The amount required at closing to initially fund the escrow or impound account.

(3) The amount, in the initial year after the consummation of the transaction, of the estimated taxes and hazard insurance, including flood insurance, if applicable, and any other required periodic payments or premiums that reflects, as appropriate, either the taxable assessed value of the real property securing the transaction, including the value of any improvements on the property or to be

constructed on the property (whether or not such construction will be financed from the proceeds of the transaction) or the replacement costs of the property.

(4) The estimated monthly amount payable to be escrowed for taxes, hazard insurance (including flood insurance, if applicable) and any other required periodic payments or premiums.

(5) The fact that, if the consumer chooses to terminate the account in the future, the consumer will become responsible for the payment of all taxes, hazard insurance, and flood insurance, if applicable, as well as any other required periodic payments or premiums on the property unless a new escrow or impound account is established.

(6) Such other information as the Bureau determines necessary for the protection of the consumer.

(i) Definitions

For purposes of this section, the following definitions shall apply:

(1) Flood insurance

The term "flood insurance" means flood insurance coverage provided under the national flood insurance program pursuant to the National Flood Insurance Act of 1968.

(2) Hazard insurance

The term "hazard insurance" shall have the same meaning as provided for "hazard insurance", "casualty insurance", "homeowner's insurance", or other similar term under the law of the State where the real property securing the consumer credit transaction is located.

(3) Insured credit union

The term 'insured credit union' has the meaning given the term in section 101 of the Federal Credit Union Act (12 U.S.C. 1752).

(4) Insured depository institution

The term 'insured depository institution' has the meaning given the term in section 3 of the Federal Deposit Insurance Act (12 U.S.C. 1813).

(j) Disclosure notice required for consumers who waive escrow services

(1) In general

If—

(A) an impound, trust, or other type of account for the payment of property taxes, insurance premiums, or other purposes relating to real property securing a consumer credit transaction is not established in connection with the transaction; or

(B) a consumer chooses, and provides written notice to the creditor or servicer of such choice, at any time after such an account is established in connection with any such transaction and in accordance with any statute, regulation, or contractual agreement, to close such account, the creditor or servicer shall provide a timely and clearly written disclosure to the consumer that advises the consumer of the responsibilities of the consumer and implications for the consumer in the absence of any such account.

(2) Disclosure requirements

Any disclosure provided to a consumer under paragraph (1) shall include the following:

(A) Information concerning any applicable fees or costs associated with either the non-establishment of any such account at the time of the transaction, or any subsequent closure of any such account.

(B) A clear and prominent statement that the consumer is responsible for personally and directly paying the non-escrowed items, in addition to paying the mortgage loan payment, in the absence of any such account, and the fact that the costs for taxes, insurance, and related fees can be substantial.

(C) A clear explanation of the consequences of any failure to pay non-escrowed items, including the possible requirement for the forced placement of insurance by the creditor or servicer and the potentially higher cost (including any potential commission payments to the servicer) or reduced coverage for the consumer in the event of any such creditor-placed insurance.

(D) Such other information as the Bureau determines necessary for the protection of the consumer.

(Pub.L. 90–321, Title I, § 129D; Pub.L. 111–203, Title X, § 1100A(2), Title XIV, §§ 1461(a), 1462, July 21, 2010, 124 Stat. 2107, 2178, 2181; Pub.L. 114–94, Div. G, Title LXXXIX, § 89003(1), Dec. 4, 2015, 129 Stat. 1801; Pub.L. 115–174, Title I, § 108, May 24, 2018, 132 Stat. 1304.)

§ 1639e. Appraisal independence requirements [CCPA 129E]

(a) In general

It shall be unlawful, in extending credit or in providing any services for a consumer credit transaction secured by the principal dwelling of the consumer, to engage in any act or practice that violates appraisal independence as described in or pursuant to regulations prescribed under this section.

(b) Appraisal independence

For purposes of subsection (a), acts or practices that violate appraisal independence shall include—

(1) any appraisal of a property offered as security for repayment of the consumer credit transaction that is conducted in connection with such transaction in which a person with an interest in the underlying transaction compensates, coerces, extorts, colludes, instructs, induces, bribes, or intimidates a person, appraisal management company, firm, or other entity conducting or involved in an appraisal, or attempts, to compensate, coerce, extort, collude, instruct, induce, bribe, or intimidate such a person, for the purpose of causing the appraised value assigned, under the appraisal, to the property to be based on any factor other than the independent judgment of the appraiser;

(2) mischaracterizing, or suborning any mischaracterization of, the appraised value of the property securing the extension of the credit;

(3) seeking to influence an appraiser or otherwise to encourage a targeted value in order to facilitate the making or pricing of the transaction; and

(4) withholding or threatening to withhold timely payment for an appraisal report or for appraisal services rendered when the appraisal report or services are provided for in accordance with the contract between the parties.

(c) Exceptions

The requirements of subsection (b) shall not be construed as prohibiting a mortgage lender, mortgage broker, mortgage banker, real estate broker, appraisal management company, employee of an appraisal management company, consumer, or any other person with an interest in a real estate transaction from asking an appraiser to undertake 1 or more of the following:

(1) Consider additional, appropriate property information, including the consideration of additional comparable properties to make or support an appraisal.

(2) Provide further detail, substantiation, or explanation for the appraiser's value conclusion.

(3) Correct errors in the appraisal report.

(d) Prohibitions on conflicts of interest

No certified or licensed appraiser conducting, and no appraisal management company procuring or facilitating, an appraisal in connection with a consumer credit transaction secured by the principal dwelling of a consumer may have a direct or indirect interest, financial or otherwise, in the property or transaction involving the appraisal.

(e) Mandatory reporting

Any mortgage lender, mortgage broker, mortgage banker, real estate broker, appraisal management company, employee of an appraisal management company, or any other person involved in a real estate transaction involving an appraisal in connection with a consumer credit transaction secured by the principal dwelling of a consumer who has a reasonable basis to believe an appraiser is failing to comply with the Uniform Standards of Professional Appraisal Practice, is violating applicable laws, or is otherwise engaging in unethical or unprofessional conduct, shall refer the matter to the applicable State appraiser certifying and licensing agency.

(f) No extension of credit

In connection with a consumer credit transaction secured by a consumer's principal dwelling, a creditor who knows, at or before loan consummation, of a violation of the appraisal independence standards established in subsections[1] (b) or (d) shall not extend credit based on such appraisal unless the creditor documents that the creditor has acted with reasonable diligence to determine that the appraisal does not materially misstate or misrepresent the value of such dwelling.

(g) Rules and interpretive guidelines

(1) In general

Except as provided under paragraph (2), the Board, the Comptroller of the Currency, the Federal Deposit Insurance Corporation, the National Credit Union Administration Board, the Federal Housing Finance Agency, and the Bureau may jointly issue rules, interpretive guidelines, and general statements of policy with respect to acts or practices that violate appraisal independence in the provision of mortgage lending services for a consumer credit transaction secured by the principal dwelling of the consumer and mortgage brokerage services for such a transaction, within the meaning of subsections (a), (b), (c), (d), (e), (f), (h), and (i).

(2) Interim final regulations

The Board shall, for purposes of this section, prescribe interim final regulations no later than 90 days after July 21, 2010, defining with specificity acts or practices that violate appraisal independence in the provision of mortgage lending services for a consumer credit transaction secured by the principal dwelling of the consumer or mortgage brokerage services for such a transaction and defining any terms in this section or such regulations. Rules prescribed by the Board under this paragraph shall be deemed to be rules prescribed by the agencies jointly under paragraph (1).

(h) Appraisal report portability

Consistent with the requirements of this section, the Board, the Comptroller of the Currency, the Federal Deposit Insurance Corporation, the National Credit Union Administration Board, the Federal Housing Finance Agency, and the Bureau may jointly issue regulations that address the issue of appraisal report portability, including regulations that ensure the portability of the appraisal report between lenders for a consumer credit transaction secured by a 1–4 unit single family residence that is the principal dwelling of the consumer, or mortgage brokerage services for such a transaction.

(i) Customary and reasonable fee

(1) In general

Lenders and their agents shall compensate fee appraisers at a rate that is customary and reasonable for appraisal services performed in the market area of the property being appraised. Evidence for such fees may be established by objective third-party information, such as government agency fee schedules, academic studies, and independent private sector surveys. Fee studies shall exclude assignments ordered by known appraisal management companies.

[1] So in original. Probably should be "subsection".

(2) Fee appraiser definition

(A) In general

For purposes of this section, the term "fee appraiser" means a person who is not an employee of the mortgage loan originator or appraisal management company engaging the appraiser and is—

(i) a State licensed or certified appraiser who receives a fee for performing an appraisal and certifies that the appraisal has been prepared in accordance with the Uniform Standards of Professional Appraisal Practice; or

(ii) a company not subject to the requirements of section 3353 of Title 12 that utilizes the services of State licensed or certified appraisers and receives a fee for performing appraisals in accordance with the Uniform Standards of Professional Appraisal Practice.

(B) Rule of construction related to appraisal donations

If a fee appraiser voluntarily donates appraisal services to an organization eligible to receive tax-deductible charitable contributions, such voluntary donation shall be considered customary and reasonable for the purposes of paragraph (1).

(3) Exception for complex assignments

In the case of an appraisal involving a complex assignment, the customary and reasonable fee may reflect the increased time, difficulty, and scope of the work required for such an appraisal and include an amount over and above the customary and reasonable fee for non-complex assignments.

(j) Sunset

Effective on the date the interim final regulations are promulgated pursuant to subsection (g), the Home Valuation Code of Conduct announced by the Federal Housing Finance Agency on December 23, 2008, shall have no force or effect.

(k) Penalties

(1) First violation

In addition to the enforcement provisions referred to in section 1640 of this title, each person who violates this section shall forfeit and pay a civil penalty of not more than $10,000 for each day any such violation continues.

(2) Subsequent violations

In the case of any person on whom a civil penalty has been imposed under paragraph (1), paragraph (1) shall be applied by substituting "$20,000" for "$10,000" with respect to all subsequent violations.

(3) Assessment

The agency referred to in subsection (a) or (c) of section 1607 of this title with respect to any person described in paragraph (1) shall assess any penalty under this subsection to which such person is subject.

(Pub.L. 90–321, Title I, § 129E, as added Pub.L. 111–203, Title XIV, § 1472, July 21, 2010, Stat. 2187; amended Pub.L. 115–174, Title I, § 102, May 24, 2018, 132 Stat. 1299.)

§ 1639f. Requirements for prompt crediting of home loan payments [CCPA 129F]

(a) In general

In connection with a consumer credit transaction secured by a consumer's principal dwelling, no servicer shall fail to credit a payment to the consumer's loan account as of the date of receipt, except when a delay in crediting does not result in any charge to the consumer or in the reporting of negative information to a consumer reporting agency, except as required in subsection (b).

(b) Exception

If a servicer specifies in writing requirements for the consumer to follow in making payments, but accepts a payment that does not conform to the requirements, the servicer shall credit the payment as of 5 days after receipt.

(Pub.L. 90–321, Title I, § 129F, as added Pub.L. 111–203, Title XIV, § 1464(a), July 21, 2010, 124 Stat. 2184.)

§ 1639g. Requests for payoff amounts of home loan [CCPA § 129G]

A creditor or servicer of a home loan shall send an accurate payoff balance within a reasonable time, but in no case more than 7 business days, after the receipt of a written request for such balance from or on behalf of the borrower.

(Pub.L. 90–321, Title I, § 129G, as added Pub.L. 111–203, Title XIV, § 1464(b), July 21, 2010, 124 Stat. 2184.)

§ 1639h. Property appraisal requirements [CCPA § 129H]

(a) In general

A creditor may not extend credit in the form of a higher-risk mortgage to any consumer without first obtaining a written appraisal of the property to be mortgaged prepared in accordance with the requirements of this section.

(b) Appraisal requirements

(1) Physical property visit

Subject to the rules prescribed under paragraph (4), an appraisal of property to be secured by a higher-risk mortgage does not meet the requirement of this section unless it is performed by a certified or licensed appraiser who conducts a physical property visit of the interior of the mortgaged property.

(2) Second appraisal under certain circumstances

(A) In general

If the purpose of a higher-risk mortgage is to finance the purchase or acquisition of the mortgaged property from a person within 180 days of the purchase or acquisition of such property by that person at a price that was lower than the current sale price of the property, the creditor shall obtain a second appraisal from a different certified or licensed appraiser. The second appraisal shall include an analysis of the difference in sale prices, changes in market conditions, and any improvements made to the property between the date of the previous sale and the current sale.

(B) No cost to applicant

The cost of any second appraisal required under subparagraph (A) may not be charged to the applicant.

(3) Certified or licensed appraiser defined

For purposes of this section, the term "certified or licensed appraiser" means a person who—

(A) is, at a minimum, certified or licensed by the State in which the property to be appraised is located; and

(B) performs each appraisal in conformity with the Uniform Standards of Professional Appraisal Practice and title XI of the Financial Institutions Reform, Recovery, and Enforcement Act of 1989, and the regulations prescribed under such title, as in effect on the date of the appraisal.

(4) Regulations

(A) In general

The Board, the Comptroller of the Currency, the Federal Deposit Insurance Corporation, the National Credit Union Administration Board, the Federal Housing Finance Agency, and the Bureau shall jointly prescribe regulations to implement this section.

(B) Exemption

The agencies listed in subparagraph (A) may jointly exempt, by rule, a class of loans from the requirements of this subsection or subsection (a) if the agencies determine that the exemption is in the public interest and promotes the safety and soundness of creditors.

(c) Free copy of appraisal

A creditor shall provide 1 copy of each appraisal conducted in accordance with this section in connection with a higher-risk mortgage to the applicant without charge, and at least 3 days prior to the transaction closing date.

(d) Consumer notification

At the time of the initial mortgage application, the applicant shall be provided with a statement by the creditor that any appraisal prepared for the mortgage is for the sole use of the creditor, and that the applicant may choose to have a separate appraisal conducted at the expense of the applicant.

(e) Violations

In addition to any other liability to any person under this subchapter, a creditor found to have willfully failed to obtain an appraisal as required in this section shall be liable to the applicant or borrower for the sum of $2,000.

(f) Higher-risk mortgage defined

For purposes of this section, the term "higher-risk mortgage" means a residential mortgage loan, other than a reverse mortgage loan that is a qualified mortgage, as defined in section 1639c of this title, secured by a principal dwelling—

(1) that is not a qualified mortgage, as defined in section 1639c of this title; and

(2) with an annual percentage rate that exceeds the average prime offer rate for a comparable transaction, as defined in section 1639c of this title, as of the date the interest rate is set—

(A) by 1.5 or more percentage points, in the case of a first lien residential mortgage loan having an original principal obligation amount that does not exceed the amount of the maximum limitation on the original principal obligation of mortgage in effect for a residence of the applicable size, as of the date of such interest rate set, pursuant to the sixth sentence of section 1454(a)(2) of Title 12;

(B) by 2.5 or more percentage points, in the case of a first lien residential mortgage loan having an original principal obligation amount that exceeds the amount of the maximum limitation on the original principal obligation of mortgage in effect for a residence of the applicable size, as of the date of such interest rate set, pursuant to the sixth sentence of section 1454(a)(2) of Title 12; and

(C) by 3.5 or more percentage points for a subordinate lien residential mortgage loan.

(Pub.L. 90–321, Title I, § 129H, as added Pub.L. 111–203, Title XIV, § 1471, July 21, 2010, Stat. 2185.)

§ 1640. Civil liability [CCPA § 130]

(a) Individual or class action for damages; amount of award; factors determining amount of award

Except as otherwise provided in this section, any creditor who fails to comply with any requirement imposed under this part, including any requirement under section 1635 of this title, subsection (f) or (g) of section 1641 of this title, or part D or E of this subchapter with respect to any person is liable to such person in an amount equal to the sum of—

(1) any actual damage sustained by such person as a result of the failure;

(2)(A) (i) in the case of an individual action twice the amount of any finance charge in connection with the transaction, (ii) in the case of an individual action relating to a consumer lease under part E of this subchapter, 25 per centum of the total amount of monthly payments under the lease, except that the liability under this subparagraph shall not be less than $200 nor greater than $2,000, (iii) in the case of an individual action relating to an open end consumer credit plan that is not secured by real property or a dwelling, twice the amount of any finance charge in connection with the transaction, with a minimum of $500 and a maximum of $5,000, or such higher amount as may be appropriate in the case of an established pattern or practice of such failures;[1] or (iv) in the case of an individual action relating to a credit transaction not under an open end credit plan that is secured by real property or a dwelling, not less than $400 or greater than $4,000; or

(B) in the case of a class action, such amount as the court may allow, except that as to each member of the class no minimum recovery shall be applicable, and the total recovery under this subparagraph in any class action or series of class actions arising out of the same failure to comply by the same creditor shall not be more than the lesser of $1,000,000 or 1 per centum of the net worth of the creditor;

(3) in the case of any successful action to enforce the foregoing liability or in any action in which a person is determined to have a right of rescission under section 1635 or 1638(e)(7) of this title, the costs of the action, together with a reasonable attorney's fee as determined by the court; and

(4) in the case of a failure to comply with any requirement under section 1639, paragraph (1) or (2) of section 1639b(c) of this title, or section 1639c(a) of this title, an amount equal to the sum of all finance charges and fees paid by the consumer, unless the creditor demonstrates that the failure to comply is not material.

In determining the amount of award in any class action, the court shall consider, among other relevant factors, the amount of any actual damages awarded, the frequency and persistence of failures of compliance by the creditor, the resources of the creditor, the number of persons adversely affected, and the extent to which the creditor's failure of compliance was intentional. In connection with the disclosures referred to in subsections (a) and (b) of section 1637 of this title, a creditor shall have a liability determined under paragraph (2) only for failing to comply with the requirements of section 1635, 1637(a)[2] of this title, or any of paragraphs (4) through (13) of section 1637(b) of this title, or for failing to comply with disclosure requirements under State law for any term or item that the Bureau has determined to be substantially the same in meaning under section 1610(a)(2) of this title as any of the terms or items referred to in section 1637(a) of this title, or any of paragraphs (4) through (13) of section 1637(b) of this title. In connection with the disclosures referred to in subsection (c) or (d) of section 1637 of this title, a card issuer shall have a liability under this section only to a cardholder who pays a fee described in section 1637(c)(1)(A)(ii)(I) or section 1637(c)(4)(A)(i) of this title or who uses the credit card or charge card. In connection with the disclosures referred to in section 1638 of this title, a creditor shall have a liability determined under paragraph (2) only for failing to comply with the requirements of section 1635 of this title, of paragraph (2) (insofar as it requires a disclosure of the "amount financed"), (3), (4), (5), (6), or (9) of section 1638(a) of this title, or section 1638(b)(2)(C)(ii) of this title, of subparagraphs (A), (B), (D), (F), or (J) of section 1638(e)(2) of this title (for purposes of paragraph (2) or (4) of section 1638(e) of this title), or paragraph (4)(C), (6), (7), or (8) of section 1638(e) of this title, or for failing to comply with disclosure requirements under State law for any term which the Bureau has determined to be substantially the same in meaning under section 1610(a)(2) of this title as any of the terms referred to in any of those paragraphs of section 1638(a) of this title or section 1638(b)(2)(C)(ii) of this title. With respect to any failure to make disclosures required under this part or part D or E of this subchapter, liability shall be imposed only upon the creditor required to make disclosure, except as provided in section 1641 of this title.

---

[1] So in original. The semicolon probably should be a comma.

[2] So in original. Probably should be preceded by "section".

(b) Correction of errors

A creditor or assignee has no liability under this section or section 1607 of this title or section 1611 of this title for any failure to comply with any requirement imposed under this part or part E of this subchapter, if within sixty days after discovering an error, whether pursuant to a final written examination report or notice issued under section 1607(e)(1) of this title or through the creditor's or assignee's own procedures, and prior to the institution of an action under this section or the receipt of written notice of the error from the obligor, the creditor or assignee notifies the person concerned of the error and makes whatever adjustments in the appropriate account are necessary to assure that the person will not be required to pay an amount in excess of the charge actually disclosed, or the dollar equivalent of the annual percentage rate actually disclosed, whichever is lower.

(c) Unintentional violations; bona fide errors

A creditor or assignee may not be held liable in any action brought under this section or section 1635 of this title for a violation of this subchapter if the creditor or assignee shows by a preponderance of evidence that the violation was not intentional and resulted from a bona fide error notwithstanding the maintenance of procedures reasonably adapted to avoid any such error. Examples of a bona fide error include, but are not limited to, clerical, calculation, computer malfunction and programing, and printing errors, except that an error of legal judgment with respect to a person's obligations under this subchapter is not a bona fide error.

(d) Liability in transaction or lease involving multiple obligors

When there are multiple obligors in a consumer credit transaction or consumer lease, there shall be no more than one recovery of damages under subsection (a)(2) of this section for a violation of this subchapter.

(e) Jurisdiction of courts; limitations on actions; State attorney general enforcement

Except as provided in the subsequent sentence, any action under this section may be brought in any United States district court, or in any other court of competent jurisdiction, within one year from the date of the occurrence of the violation or, in the case of a violation involving a private education loan (as that term is defined in section 1650(a) of this title), 1 year from the date on which the first regular payment of principal is due under the loan. Any action under this section with respect to any violation of section 1639, 1639b, or 1639c of this title may be brought in any United States district court, or in any other court of competent jurisdiction, before the end of the 3-year period beginning on the date of the occurrence of the violation. This subsection does not bar a person from asserting a violation of this subchapter in an action to collect the debt which was brought more than one year from the date of the occurrence of the violation as a matter of defense by recoupment or set-off in such action, except as otherwise provided by State law. An action to enforce a violation of section 1639, 1639b, 1639c, 1639d, 1639e, 1639f, 1639g, or 1639h of this title may also be brought by the appropriate State attorney general in any appropriate United States district court, or any other court of competent jurisdiction, not later than 3 years after the date on which the violation occurs. The State attorney general shall provide prior written notice of any such civil action to the Federal agency responsible for enforcement under section 1607 of this title and shall provide the agency with a copy of the complaint. If prior notice is not feasible, the State attorney general shall provide notice to such agency immediately upon instituting the action. The Federal agency may—

(1) intervene in the action;

(2) upon intervening—

(A) remove the action to the appropriate United States district court, if it was not originally brought there; and

(B) be heard on all matters arising in the action; and

(3) file a petition for appeal.

(f) Good faith compliance with rule, regulation, or interpretation of Board or with interpretation or approval of duly authorized official or employee of Federal Reserve System

No provision of this section, section 1607(b) of this title, section 1607(c) of this title, section 1607(e) of this title, or section 1611 of this title imposing any liability shall apply to any act done or omitted in good faith in conformity with any rule, regulation, or interpretation thereof by the Bureau or in conformity with any interpretation or approval by an official or employee of the Federal Reserve System duly authorized by the Bureau to issue such interpretations or approvals under such procedures as the Bureau may prescribe therefor, notwithstanding that after such act or omission has occurred, such rule, regulation, interpretation, or approval is amended, rescinded, or determined by judicial or other authority to be invalid for any reason.

(g) Recovery for multiple failures to disclose

The multiple failure to disclose to any person any information required under this part or part D or E of this subchapter to be disclosed in connection with a single account under an open end consumer credit plan, other single consumer credit sale, consumer loan, consumer lease, or other extension of consumer credit, shall entitle the person to a single recovery under this section but continued failure to disclose after a recovery has been granted shall give rise to rights to additional recoveries. This subsection does not bar any remedy permitted by section 1635 of this title.

(h) Offset from amount owed to creditor or assignee; rights of defaulting consumer

A person may not take any action to offset any amount for which a creditor or assignee is potentially liable to such person under subsection (a)(2) of this section against any amount owed by such person, unless the amount of the creditor's or assignee's liability under this subchapter has been determined by judgment of a court of competent jurisdiction in an action of which such person was a party. This subsection does not bar a consumer then in default on the obligation from asserting a violation of this subchapter as an original action, or as a defense or counterclaim to an action to collect amounts owed by the consumer brought by a person liable under this subchapter.

(i) Class action moratorium

(1) In general

During the period beginning on May 18, 1995, and ending on October 1, 1995, no court may enter any order certifying any class in any action under this subchapter—

(A) which is brought in connection with any credit transaction not under an open end credit plan which is secured by a first lien on real property or a dwelling and constitutes a refinancing or consolidation of an existing extension of credit; and

(B) which is based on the alleged failure of a creditor—

(i) to include a charge actually incurred (in connection with the transaction) in the finance charge disclosed pursuant to section 1638 of this title;

(ii) to properly make any other disclosure required under section 1638 of this title as a result of the failure described in clause (i); or

(iii) to provide proper notice of rescission rights under section 1635(a) of this title due to the selection by the creditor of the incorrect form from among the model forms prescribed by the Bureau or from among forms based on such model forms.

(2) Exceptions for certain alleged violations

Paragraph (1) shall not apply with respect to any action—

(A) described in clause (i) or (ii) of paragraph (1)(B), if the amount disclosed as the finance charge results in an annual percentage rate that exceeds the tolerance provided in section 1606(c) of this title; or

(B) described in paragraph (1)(B)(iii), if—

(i) no notice relating to rescission rights under section 1635(a) of this title was provided in any form; or

(ii) proper notice was not provided for any reason other than the reason described in such paragraph.

(j) Private educational lender

A private educational lender (as that term is defined in section 1650(a) of this title) has no liability under this section for failure to comply with section 1638(e)(3) of this title).[3]

(k) Defense to foreclosure

(1) In general

Notwithstanding any other provision of law, when a creditor, assignee, or other holder of a residential mortgage loan or anyone acting on behalf of such creditor, assignee, or holder, initiates a judicial or nonjudicial foreclosure of the residential mortgage loan, or any other action to collect the debt in connection with such loan, a consumer may assert a violation by a creditor of paragraph (1) or (2) of section 1639b(c) of this title, or of section 1639c(a) of this title, as a matter of defense by recoupment or set off without regard for the time limit on a private action for damages under subsection (e).

(2) Amount of recoupment or setoff

(A) In general

The amount of recoupment or set-off under paragraph (1) shall equal the amount to which the consumer would be entitled under subsection (a) for damages for a valid claim brought in an original action against the creditor, plus the costs to the consumer of the action, including a reasonable attorney's fee.

(B) Special rule

Where such judgment is rendered after the expiration of the applicable time limit on a private action for damages under subsection (e), the amount of recoupment or set-off under paragraph (1) derived from damages under subsection (a)(4) shall not exceed the amount to which the consumer would have been entitled under subsection (a)(4) for damages computed up to the day preceding the expiration of the applicable time limit.

(*l*) Exemption from liability and rescission in case of borrower fraud or deception

In addition to any other remedy available by law or contract, no creditor or assignee shall be liable to an obligor under this section, if such obligor, or co-obligor has been convicted of obtaining by actual fraud such residential mortgage loan.

(Pub.L. 90–321, Title I, § 130, May 29, 1968, 82 Stat. 157; Pub.L. 93–495, Title IV, §§ 406, 407, 408(a) to (d), Oct. 28, 1974, 88 Stat. 1518; Pub.L. 94–222, § 3(b), Feb. 27, 1976, 90 Stat. 197; Pub.L. 94–240, § 4, Mar. 23, 1976, 90 Stat. 260; Pub.L. 96–221, Title VI, § 615, Mar. 31, 1980, 94 Stat. 180; Pub.L. 100–583, § 3, Nov. 3, 1988, 102 Stat. 2966; Pub.L. 103–325, Title I, § 153(a), (b), Sept. 23, 1994, 108 Stat. 2195; Pub.L. 104–12, § 2, May 18, 1995, 109 Stat. 161; Pub.L. 104–29, § 6, Sept. 30, 1995, 109 Stat. 274; Pub.L. 110–289, Div. B, Title V, § 2502(b), July 30, 2008, 122 Stat. 2857; Pub.L. 110–315, Title X, § 1012(a), Aug. 14, 2008, 122 Stat. 3483; Pub.L. 111–22, Div. A, Title IV, § 404(b), May 20, 2009, 123 Stat. 1658; Pub.L. 111–24, Title I, § 107, Title II, § 201(b), May 22, 2009, 123 Stat. 1743, 1745; Pub.L. 111–203, Title X, § 1100A(2), Title XIV, §§ 1400(c), 1413, 1416, 1417, 1422, July 21, 2010, 124 Stat. 2107, 2148, 2153, 2157.)

§ 1641. Liability of assignees [CCPA § 131]

(a) Prerequisites

Except as otherwise specifically provided in this subchapter, any civil action for a violation of this subchapter or proceeding under section 1607 of this title which may be brought against a creditor may be maintained against any assignee of such creditor only if the violation for which such action or proceeding is brought is apparent on the face of the disclosure statement, except where the assignment was involuntary. For the purpose of this section, a violation apparent on the face of the disclosure statement includes, but is not limited to (1) a disclosure which can be determined to be incomplete or inaccurate from the face of the

[3] So in original. The closing parenthesis probably should not appear.

disclosure statement or other documents assigned, or (2) a disclosure which does not use the terms required to be used by this subchapter.

(b) Proof of compliance with statutory provisions

Except as provided in section 1635(c) of this title, in any action or proceeding by or against any subsequent assignee of the original creditor without knowledge to the contrary by the assignee when he acquires the obligation, written acknowledgement of receipt by a person to whom a statement is required to be given pursuant to this subchapter shall be conclusive proof of the delivery thereof and, except as provided in subsection (a) of this section, of compliance with this part. This section does not affect the rights of the obligor in any action against the original creditor.

(c) Right of rescission by consumer unaffected

Any consumer who has the right to rescind a transaction under section 1635 of this title may rescind the transaction as against any assignee of the obligation.

(d) Rights upon assignment of certain mortgages

(1) In general

Any person who purchases or is otherwise assigned a mortgage referred to in section 1602(aa)* of this title shall be subject to all claims and defenses with respect to that mortgage that the consumer could assert against the creditor of the mortgage, unless the purchaser or assignee demonstrates, by a preponderance of the evidence, that a reasonable person exercising ordinary due diligence, could not determine, based on the documentation required by this subchapter, the itemization of the amount financed, and other disclosure of disbursements that the mortgage was a mortgage referred to in section 1602(aa)* of this title. The preceding sentence does not affect rights of a consumer under subsection (a), (b), or (c) of this section or any other provision of this subchapter.

(2) Limitation on damages

Notwithstanding any other provision of law, relief provided as a result of any action made permissible by paragraph (1) may not exceed—

(A) with respect to actions based upon a violation of this subchapter, the amount specified in section 1640 of this title; and

(B) with respect to all other causes of action, the sum of—

(i) the amount of all remaining indebtedness; and

(ii) the total amount paid by the consumer in connection with the transaction.

(3) Offset

The amount of damages that may be awarded under paragraph (2)(B) shall be reduced by the amount of any damages awarded under paragraph (2)(A).

(4) Notice

Any person who sells or otherwise assigns a mortgage referred to in section 1602(aa)* of this title shall include a prominent notice of the potential liability under this subsection as determined by the Bureau.

(e) Liability of assignee for consumer credit transactions secured by real property

(1) In general

Except as otherwise specifically provided in this subchapter, any civil action against a creditor for a violation of this subchapter, and any proceeding under section 1607 of this title against a creditor, with respect to a consumer credit transaction secured by real property may be maintained against any assignee of such creditor only if—

* *Note from West Advisory Panel: Pub.L. 111–203 (Dodd-Frank) appears to contain clerical errors. We believe this reference should be to § 1602(bb).*

(A) the violation for which such action or proceeding is brought is apparent on the face of the disclosure statement provided in connection with such transaction pursuant to this subchapter; and

(B) the assignment to the assignee was voluntary.

(2) Violation apparent on the face of the disclosure described

For the purpose of this section, a violation is apparent on the face of the disclosure statement if—

(A) the disclosure can be determined to be incomplete or inaccurate by a comparison among the disclosure statement, any itemization of the amount financed, the note, or any other disclosure of disbursement; or

(B) the disclosure statement does not use the terms or format required to be used by this subchapter.

(f) Treatment of servicer

(1) In general

A servicer of a consumer obligation arising from a consumer credit transaction shall not be treated as an assignee of such obligation for purposes of this section unless the servicer is or was the owner of the obligation.

(2) Servicer not treated as owner on basis of assignment for administrative convenience

A servicer of a consumer obligation arising from a consumer credit transaction shall not be treated as the owner of the obligation for purposes of this section on the basis of an assignment of the obligation from the creditor or another assignee to the servicer solely for the administrative convenience of the servicer in servicing the obligation. Upon written request by the obligor, the servicer shall provide the obligor, to the best knowledge of the servicer, with the name, address, and telephone number of the owner of the obligation or the master servicer of the obligation.

(3) "Servicer" defined

For purposes of this subsection, the term "servicer" has the same meaning as in section 2605(i)(2) of Title 12.

(4) Applicability

This subsection shall apply to all consumer credit transactions in existence or consummated on or after September 30, 1995.

(g) Notice of new creditor

(1) In general

In addition to other disclosures required by this subchapter, not later than 30 days after the date on which a mortgage loan is sold or otherwise transferred or assigned to a third party, the creditor that is the new owner or assignee of the debt shall notify the borrower in writing of such transfer, including—

(A) the identity, address, telephone number of the new creditor;

(B) the date of transfer;

(C) how to reach an agent or party having authority to act on behalf of the new creditor;

(D) the location of the place where transfer of ownership of the debt is recorded; and

(E) any other relevant information regarding the new creditor.

(2) Definition

As used in this subsection, the term "mortgage loan" means any consumer credit transaction that is secured by the principal dwelling of a consumer.

(Pub.L. 90–321, Title I, § 131, May 29, 1968, 82 Stat. 157; Pub.L. 96–221, Title VI, § 616(a), Mar. 31, 1980, 94 Stat. 182; Pub.L. 103–325, Title I, § 153(c), Sept. 23, 1994, 108 Stat. 2195; Pub.L. 104–29, § 7, Sept. 30, 1995, 109 Stat. 274; Pub.L. 111–22, Title IV, § 404(a), May 20, 2009, 123 Stat. 1658; Pub.L. 111–203, Title X, § 1100A(2), July 21, 2010, 124 Stat. 2107.)

§ 1642. Issuance of credit cards [CCPA § 132]

No credit card shall be issued except in response to a request or application therefor. This prohibition does not apply to the issuance of a credit card in renewal of, or in substitution for, an accepted credit card.

(Pub.L. 90–321, Title I, § 132, as added Pub.L. 91–508, Title V, § 502(a), Oct. 26, 1970, 84 Stat. 1126.)

§ 1643. Liability of holder of credit card [CCPA § 133]

(a) Limits on liability

(1) A cardholder shall be liable for the unauthorized use of a credit card only if—

(A) the card is an accepted credit card;

(B) the liability is not in excess of $50;

(C) the card issuer gives adequate notice to the cardholder of the potential liability;

(D) the card issuer has provided the cardholder with a description of a means by which the card issuer may be notified of loss or theft of the card, which description may be provided on the face or reverse side of the statement required by section 1637(b) of this title or on a separate notice accompanying such statement;

(E) the unauthorized use occurs before the card issuer has been notified that an unauthorized use of the credit card has occurred or may occur as the result of loss, theft, or otherwise; and

(F) the card issuer has provided a method whereby the user of such card can be identified as the person authorized to use it.

(2) For purposes of this section, a card issuer has been notified when such steps as may be reasonably required in the ordinary course of business to provide the card issuer with the pertinent information have been taken, whether or not any particular officer, employee, or agent of the card issuer does in fact receive such information.

(b) Burden of proof

In any action by a card issuer to enforce liability for the use of a credit card, the burden of proof is upon the card issuer to show that the use was authorized or, if the use was unauthorized, then the burden of proof is upon the card issuer to show that the conditions of liability for the unauthorized use of a credit card, as set forth in subsection (a) of this section, have been met.

(c) Liability imposed by other laws or by agreement with issuer

Nothing in this section imposes liability upon a cardholder for the unauthorized use of a credit card in excess of his liability for such use under other applicable law or under any agreement with the card issuer.

(d) Exclusiveness of liability

Except as provided in this section, a cardholder incurs no liability from the unauthorized use of a credit card.

(Pub.L. 90–321, Title I, § 133, as added Pub.L. 91–508, Title V, § 502(a), Oct. 26, 1970, 84 Stat. 1126, and amended Pub.L. 96–221, Title VI, § 617, Mar. 31, 1980, 94 Stat. 182.)

§ 1644. Fraudulent use of credit cards; penalties [CCPA § 134]

(a) Use, attempt or conspiracy to use card in transaction affecting interstate or foreign commerce

Whoever knowingly in a transaction affecting interstate or foreign commerce, uses or attempts or conspires to use any counterfeit, fictitious, altered, forged, lost, stolen, or fraudulently obtained credit card to obtain money, goods, services, or anything else of value which within any one-year period has a value aggregating $1,000 or more; or

(b) Transporting, attempting or conspiring to transport card in interstate commerce

Whoever, with unlawful or fraudulent intent, transports or attempts or conspires to transport in interstate or foreign commerce a counterfeit, fictitious, altered, forged, lost, stolen, or fraudulently obtained credit card knowing the same to be counterfeit, fictitious, altered, forged, lost, stolen, or fraudulently obtained; or

(c) Use of interstate commerce to sell or transport card

Whoever, with unlawful or fraudulent intent, uses any instrumentality of interstate or foreign commerce to sell or transport a counterfeit, fictitious, altered, forged, lost, stolen, or fraudulently obtained credit card knowing the same to be counterfeit, fictitious, altered, forged, lost, stolen, or fraudulently obtained; or

(d) Receipt, concealment, etc., of goods obtained by use of card

Whoever knowingly receives, conceals, uses, or transports money, goods, services, or anything else of value (except tickets for interstate or foreign transportation) which (1) within any one-year period has a value aggregating $1,000 or more, (2) has moved in or is part of, or which constitutes interstate or foreign commerce, and (3) has been obtained with a counterfeit, fictitious, altered, forged, lost, stolen, or fraudulently obtained credit card; or

(e) Receipt, concealment, etc., of tickets for interstate or foreign transportation obtained by use of card

Whoever knowingly receives, conceals, uses, sells, or transports in interstate or foreign commerce one or more tickets for interstate or foreign transportation, which (1) within any one-year period have a value aggregating $500 or more, and (2) have been purchased or obtained with one or more counterfeit, fictitious, altered, forged, lost, stolen, or fraudulently obtained credit cards; or

(f) Furnishing of money, etc., through use of card

Whoever in a transaction affecting interstate or foreign commerce furnishes money, property, services, or anything else of value, which within any one-year period has a value aggregating $1,000 or more, through the use of any counterfeit, fictitious, altered, forged, lost, stolen, or fraudulently obtained credit card knowing the same to be counterfeit, fictitious, altered, forged, lost, stolen, or fraudulently obtained—

shall be fined not more than $10,000 or imprisoned not more than ten years, or both.

(Pub.L. 90–321, Title I, § 134, as added Pub.L. 91–508, Title V, § 502(a), Oct. 26, 1970, 84 Stat. 1127, and amended Pub.L. 93–495, Title IV, § 414, Oct. 28, 1974, 88 Stat. 1520.)

§ 1645. Business credit cards; limits on liability of employees [CCPA § 135]

The exemption provided by section 1603(1) of this title does not apply to the provisions of sections 1642, 1643, and 1644 of this title, except that a card issuer and a business or other organization which provides credit cards issued by the same card issuer to ten or more of its employees may by contract agree as to liability of the business or other organization with respect to unauthorized use of such credit cards without regard to the provisions of section 1643 of this title, but in no case may such business or other organization or card issuer impose liability upon any employee with respect to unauthorized use of such a credit card except in accordance with and subject to the limitations of section 1643 of this title.

(Pub.L. 90–321, Title I, § 135, as added Pub.L. 93–495, Title IV, § 410(a), Oct. 28, 1974, 88 Stat. 1519.)

§ 1646. Dissemination of annual percentage rates; implementation, etc. [CCPA § 136]

(a) Annual percentage rates

The Bureau shall collect, publish, and disseminate to the public, on a demonstration basis in a number of standard metropolitan statistical areas to be determined by the Bureau, the annual percentage rates charged for representative types of nonsale credit by creditors in such areas. For the purpose of this section, the Bureau is authorized to require creditors in such areas to furnish information necessary for the Bureau to collect, publish, and disseminate such information.

(b) Credit card price and availability information

(1) Collection required

The Bureau shall collect, on a semiannual basis, credit card price and availability information, including the information required to be disclosed under section 1637(c) of this title, from a broad sample of financial institutions which offer credit card services.

(2) Sample requirements

The broad sample of financial institutions required under paragraph (1) shall include—

(A) the 25 largest issuers of credit cards; and

(B) not less than 125 additional financial institutions selected by the Board in a manner that ensures—

(i) an equitable geographical distribution within the sample; and

(ii) the representation of a wide spectrum of institutions within the sample.

(3) Report of information from sample

Each financial institution in the broad sample established pursuant to paragraph (2) shall report the information to the Bureau in accordance with such regulations or orders as the Bureau may prescribe.

(4) Public availability of collected information; report to Congress

The Bureau shall—

(A) make the information collected pursuant to this subsection available to the public upon request; and

(B) report such information semiannually to Congress.

(c) Implementation

The Bureau is authorized to enter into contracts or other arrangements with appropriate persons, organizations, or State agencies to carry out its functions under subsections (a) and (b) of this section and to furnish financial assistance in support thereof.

(Pub.L. 90–321, Title I, § 136, as added Pub.L. 96–221, Title VI, § 618(a), Mar. 31, 1980, 94 Stat. 183, and amended Pub.L. 100–583, § 5, Nov. 3, 1988, 102 Stat. 2967; Pub.L. 111–203, Title X, § 1100A(2), July 21, 2010, 124 Stat. 2107.)

§ 1647. Home equity plans [CCPA § 137]

(a) Index requirement

In the case of extensions of credit under an open end consumer credit plan which are subject to a variable rate and are secured by a consumer's principal dwelling, the index or other rate of interest to which changes in the annual percentage rate are related shall be based on an index or rate of interest which is publicly available and is not under the control of the creditor.

(b) Grounds for acceleration of outstanding balance

A creditor may not unilaterally terminate any account under an open end consumer credit plan under which extensions of credit are secured by a consumer's principal dwelling and require the immediate repayment of any outstanding balance at such time, except in the case of—

(1) fraud or material misrepresentation on the part of the consumer in connection with the account;

(2) failure by the consumer to meet the repayment terms of the agreement for any outstanding balance; or

(3) any other action or failure to act by the consumer which adversely affects the creditor's security for the account or any right of the creditor in such security.

This subsection does not apply to reverse mortgage transactions.

(c) Change in terms

(1) In general

No open end consumer credit plan under which extensions of credit are secured by a consumer's principal dwelling may contain a provision which permits a creditor to change unilaterally any term required to be disclosed under section 1637a(a) of this title or any other term, except a change in insignificant terms such as the address of the creditor for billing purposes.

(2) Certain changes not precluded

Notwithstanding the provisions of subsection[1] (1), a creditor may make any of the following changes:

(A) Change the index and margin applicable to extensions of credit under such plan if the index used by the creditor is no longer available and the substitute index and margin would result in a substantially similar interest rate.

(B) Prohibit additional extensions of credit or reduce the credit limit applicable to an account under the plan during any period in which the value of the consumer's principal dwelling which secures any outstanding balance is significantly less than the original appraisal value of the dwelling.

(C) Prohibit additional extensions of credit or reduce the credit limit applicable to the account during any period in which the creditor has reason to believe that the consumer will be unable to comply with the repayment requirements of the account due to a material change in the consumer's financial circumstances.

(D) Prohibit additional extensions of credit or reduce the credit limit applicable to the account during any period in which the consumer is in default with respect to any material obligation of the consumer under the agreement.

(E) Prohibit additional extensions of credit or reduce the credit limit applicable to the account during any period in which—

(i) the creditor is precluded by government action from imposing the annual percentage rate provided for in the account agreement; or

(ii) any government action is in effect which adversely affects the priority of the creditor's security interest in the account to the extent that the value of the creditor's secured interest in the property is less than 120 percent of the amount of the credit limit applicable to the account.

(F) Any change that will benefit the consumer.

[1] So in original. Probably should be "paragraph".

(3) Material obligations

Upon the request of the consumer and at the time an agreement is entered into by a consumer to open an account under an open end consumer credit plan under which extensions of credit are secured by the consumer's principal dwelling, the consumer shall be given a list of the categories of contract obligations which are deemed by the creditor to be material obligations of the consumer under the agreement for purposes of paragraph (2)(D).

(4) Consumer benefit

(A) In general

For purposes of paragraph (2)(F), a change shall be deemed to benefit the consumer if the change is unequivocally beneficial to the borrower and the change is beneficial through the entire term of the agreement.

(B) Bureau categorization

The Bureau may, by regulation, determine categories of changes that benefit the consumer.

(d) Terms changed after application

If any term or condition described in section 1637a(a) of this title which is disclosed to a consumer in connection with an application to open an account under an open end consumer credit plan described in such section (other than a variable feature of the plan) changes before the account is opened, and if, as a result of such change, the consumer elects not to enter into the plan agreement, the creditor shall refund all fees paid by the consumer in connection with such application.

(e) Additional requirements relating to refunds and imposition of nonrefundable fees

(1) In general

No nonrefundable fee may be imposed by a creditor or any other person in connection with any application by a consumer to establish an account under any open end consumer credit plan which provides for extensions of credit which are secured by a consumer's principal dwelling before the end of the 3-day period beginning on the date such consumer receives the disclosure required under section 1637a(a) of this title and the pamphlet required under section 1637a(e) of this title with respect to such application.

(2) Constructive receipt

For purposes of determining when a nonrefundable fee may be imposed in accordance with this subsection if the disclosures and pamphlet referred to in paragraph (1) are mailed to the consumer, the date of the receipt of the disclosures by such consumer shall be deemed to be 3 business days after the date of mailing by the creditor.

(Pub.L. 100–709, § 3, Nov. 23, 1988, 102 Stat. 4731; Pub.L. 103–325, Title I, § 154(c), Sept. 23, 1994, 108 Stat. 2197; Pub.L. 111–203, Title X, § 1100A(2), July 21, 2010, 124 Stat. 2107.)

§ 1648. Reverse mortgages [CCPA § 138]

(a) In general

In addition to the disclosures required under this subchapter, for each reverse mortgage, the creditor shall, not less than 3 days prior to consummation of the transaction, disclose to the consumer in conspicuous type a good faith estimate of the projected total cost of the mortgage to the consumer expressed as a table of annual interest rates. Each annual interest rate shall be based on a projected total future credit extension balance under a projected appreciation rate for the dwelling and a term for the mortgage. The disclosure shall include—

(1) statements of the annual interest rates for not less than 3 projected appreciation rates and not less than 3 credit transaction periods, as determined by the Bureau, including—

(A) a short-term reverse mortgage;

(B) a term equaling the actuarial life expectancy of the consumer; and

(C) such longer term as the Bureau deems appropriate; and

(2) a statement that the consumer is not obligated to complete the reverse mortgage transaction merely because the consumer has received the disclosure required under this section or has signed an application for the reverse mortgage.

(b) Projected total cost

In determining the projected total cost of the mortgage to be disclosed to the consumer under subsection (a) of this section, the creditor shall take into account—

(1) any shared appreciation or equity that the lender will, by contract, be entitled to receive;

(2) all costs and charges to the consumer, including the costs of any associated annuity that the consumer elects or is required to purchase as part of the reverse mortgage transaction;

(3) all payments to and for the benefit of the consumer, including, in the case in which an associated annuity is purchased (whether or not required by the lender as a condition of making the reverse mortgage), the annuity payments received by the consumer and financed from the proceeds of the loan, instead of the proceeds used to finance the annuity; and

(4) any limitation on the liability of the consumer under reverse mortgage transactions (such as nonrecourse limits and equity conservation agreements).

(Pub.L. 90–321, Title I, § 138, as added Pub.L. 103–325, Title I, § 154(b), Sept. 23, 1994, 108 Stat. 2196; Pub.L. 111–203, Title X, § 1100A(2), July 21, 2010, 124 Stat. 2107.)

§ 1649. Certain limitations on liability [CCPA § 139]

(a) Limitations on liability

For any closed end consumer credit transaction that is secured by real property or a dwelling, that is subject to this subchapter, and that is consummated before September 30, 1995, a creditor or any assignee of a creditor shall have no civil, administrative, or criminal liability under this subchapter for, and a consumer shall have no extended rescission rights under section 1635(f) of this title with respect to—

(1) the creditor's treatment, for disclosure purposes, of—

(A) taxes described in section 1605(d)(3) of this title;

(B) fees described in section 1605(e)(2) and (5) of this title;

(C) fees and amounts referred to in the 3rd sentence of section 1605(a) of this title; or

(D) borrower-paid mortgage broker fees referred to in section 1605(a)(6) of this title;

(2) the form of written notice used by the creditor to inform the obligor of the rights of the obligor under section 1635 of this title if the creditor provided the obligor with a properly dated form of written notice published and adopted by the Bureau or a comparable written notice, and otherwise complied with all the requirements of this section regarding notice; or

(3) any disclosure relating to the finance charge imposed with respect to the transaction if the amount or percentage actually disclosed—

(A) may be treated as accurate for purposes of this subchapter if the amount disclosed as the finance charge does not vary from the actual finance charge by more than $200;

(B) may, under section 1605(f)(2) of this title, be treated as accurate for purposes of section 1635 of this title; or

(C) is greater than the amount or percentage required to be disclosed under this subchapter.

(b) Exceptions

Subsection (a) of this section shall not apply to—

(1) any individual action or counterclaim brought under this subchapter which was filed before June 1, 1995;

(2) any class action brought under this subchapter for which a final order certifying a class was entered before January 1, 1995;

(3) the named individual plaintiffs in any class action brought under this subchapter which was filed before June 1, 1995; or

(4) any consumer credit transaction with respect to which a timely notice of rescission was sent to the creditor before June 1, 1995.

(Pub.L. 90–321, Title I, § 139, as added Pub.L. 104–29, § 4(a), Sept. 30, 1995, 109 Stat. 273, and amended Pub.L. 104–208, Div. A, Title II, § 2107(a), Sept. 30, 1996, 110 Stat. 3009–402; Pub.L. 111–203, Title X, § 1100A(2), July 21, 2010, 124 Stat. 2107.)

§ 1650. Preventing unfair and deceptive private educational lending practices and eliminating conflicts of interest [CCPA § 140]

(a) Definitions

As used in this section—

(1) the term 'cosigner'—

(A) means any individual who is liable for the obligation of another without compensation, regardless of how designated in the contract or instrument with respect to that obligation, other than an obligation under a private education loan extended to consolidate a consumer's pre-existing private education loans;

(B) includes any person the signature of which is requested as condition to grant credit or to forbear on collection; and

(C) does not include a spouse of an individual described in subparagraph (A), the signature of whom is needed to perfect the security interest in a loan.

(2) the term "covered educational institution"—

(A) means any educational institution that offers a postsecondary educational degree, certificate, or program of study (including any institution of higher education); and

(B) includes an agent, officer, or employee of the educational institution;

(3) the term "gift"—

(A)(i) means any gratuity, favor, discount, entertainment, hospitality, loan, or other item having more than a de minimis monetary value, including services, transportation, lodging, or meals, whether provided in kind, by purchase of a ticket, payment in advance, or reimbursement after the expense has been incurred; and

(ii) includes an item described in clause (i) provided to a family member of an officer, employee, or agent of a covered educational institution, or to any other individual based on that individual's relationship with the officer, employee, or agent, if—

(I) the item is provided with the knowledge and acquiescence of the officer, employee, or agent; and

(II) the officer, employee, or agent has reason to believe the item was provided because of the official position of the officer, employee, or agent; and

(B) does not include—

(i) standard informational material related to a loan, default aversion, default prevention, or financial literacy;

(ii) food, refreshments, training, or informational material furnished to an officer, employee, or agent of a covered educational institution, as an integral part of a training session or through participation in an advisory council that is designed to improve the service of the private educational lender to the covered educational institution, if such training or participation contributes to the professional development of the officer, employee, or agent of the covered educational institution;

(iii) favorable terms, conditions, and borrower benefits on a private education loan provided to a student employed by the covered educational institution, if such terms, conditions, or benefits are not provided because of the student's employment with the covered educational institution;

(iv) the provision of financial literacy counseling or services, including counseling or services provided in coordination with a covered educational institution, to the extent that such counseling or services are not undertaken to secure—

(I) applications for private education loans or private education loan volume;

(II) applications or loan volume for any loan made, insured, or guaranteed under title IV of the Higher Education Act of 1965 (20 U.S.C. 1070 et seq.); or

(III) the purchase of a product or service of a specific private educational lender;

(v) philanthropic contributions to a covered educational institution from a private educational lender that are unrelated to private education loans and are not made in exchange for any advantage related to private education loans; or

(vi) State education grants, scholarships, or financial aid funds administered by or on behalf of a State;

(4) the term "institution of higher education" has the same meaning as in section 102 of the Higher Education Act of 1965 (20 U.S.C. 1002);

(5) the term "postsecondary educational expenses" means any of the expenses that are included as part of the cost of attendance of a student, as defined under section 472 of the Higher Education Act of 1965 (20 U.S.C. 1087*ll*);

(6) the term "preferred lender arrangement" has the same meaning as in section 151 of the Higher Education Act of 1965 [20 U.S.C. § 1019];

(7) the term "private educational lender" means—

(A) a financial institution, as defined in section 1813 of Title 12 that solicits, makes, or extends private education loans;

(B) a Federal credit union, as defined in section 1752 of Title 12 that solicits, makes, or extends private education loans; and

(C) any other person engaged in the business of soliciting, making, or extending private education loans;

(8) the term "private education loan"—

(A) means a loan provided by a private educational lender that—

(i) is not made, insured, or guaranteed under of[1] title IV of the Higher Education Act of 1965 (20 U.S.C. 1070 et seq.); and

(ii) is issued expressly for postsecondary educational expenses to a borrower, regardless of whether the loan is provided through the educational institution that the subject student attends or directly to the borrower from the private educational lender; and

(B) does not include an extension of credit under an open end consumer credit plan, a reverse mortgage transaction, a residential mortgage transaction, or any other loan that is secured by real property or a dwelling; and

[1] So in original. The word "of" probably should not appear.

(9) the term "revenue sharing" means an arrangement between a covered educational institution and a private educational lender under which—

(A) a private educational lender provides or issues private education loans with respect to students attending the covered educational institution;

(B) the covered educational institution recommends to students or others the private educational lender or the private education loans of the private educational lender; and

(C) the private educational lender pays a fee or provides other material benefits, including profit sharing, to the covered educational institution in connection with the private education loans provided to students attending the covered educational institution or a borrower acting on behalf of a student.

(b) Prohibition on certain gifts and arrangements

A private educational lender may not, directly or indirectly—

(1) offer or provide any gift to a covered educational institution in exchange for any advantage or consideration provided to such private educational lender related to its private education loan activities; or

(2) engage in revenue sharing with a covered educational institution.

(c) Prohibition on co-branding

A private educational lender may not use the name, emblem, mascot, or logo of the covered educational institution, or other words, pictures, or symbols readily identified with the covered educational institution, in the marketing of private education loans in any way that implies that the covered educational institution endorses the private education loans offered by the private educational lender.

(d) Advisory board compensation

Any person who is employed in the financial aid office of a covered educational institution, or who otherwise has responsibilities with respect to private education loans or other financial aid of the institution, and who serves on an advisory board, commission, or group established by a private educational lender or group of such lenders shall be prohibited from receiving anything of value from the private educational lender or group of lenders. Nothing in this subsection prohibits the reimbursement of reasonable expenses incurred by an employee of a covered educational institution as part of their service on an advisory board, commission, or group described in this subsection.

(e) Prohibition on prepayment or repayment fees or penalty

It shall be unlawful for any private educational lender to impose a fee or penalty on a borrower for early repayment or prepayment of any private education loan.

(f) Credit card protections for college students

(1) Disclosure required

An institution of higher education shall publicly disclose any contract or other agreement made with a card issuer or creditor for the purpose of marketing a credit card.

(2) Inducements prohibited

No card issuer or creditor may offer to a student at an institution of higher education any tangible item to induce such student to apply for or participate in an open end consumer credit plan offered by such card issuer or creditor, if such offer is made—

(A) on the campus of an institution of higher education;

(B) near the campus of an institution of higher education, as determined by rule of the Bureau; or

(C) at an event sponsored by or related to an institution of higher education.

(3) Sense of the Congress

It is the sense of the Congress that each institution of higher education should consider adopting the following policies relating to credit cards:

(A) That any card issuer that markets a credit card on the campus of such institution notify the institution of the location at which such marketing will take place.

(B) That the number of locations on the campus of such institution at which the marketing of credit cards takes place be limited.

(C) That credit card and debt education and counseling sessions be offered as a regular part of any orientation program for new students of such institution.

(g) Additional protections relating to borrower or cosigner of a private education loan

(1) Prohibition on automatic default in case of death or bankruptcy of non-student obligor

With respect to a private education loan involving a student obligor and 1 or more cosigners, the creditor shall not declare a default or accelerate the debt against the student obligor on the sole basis of a bankruptcy or death of a cosigner.

(2) Cosigner release in case of death of borrower

(A) Release of cosigner

The holder of a private education loan, when notified of the death of a student obligor, shall release within a reasonable timeframe any cosigner from the obligations of the cosigner under the private education loan.

(B) Notification of release

A holder or servicer of a private education loan, as applicable, shall within a reasonable time-frame notify any cosigners for the private education loan if a cosigner is released from the obligations of the cosigner for the private education loan under this paragraph.

(C) Designation of individual to act on behalf of the borrower

Any lender that extends a private education loan shall provide the student obligor an option to designate an individual to have the legal authority to act on behalf of the student obligor with respect to the private education loan in the event of the death of the student obligor.

(Pub.L. 90–321, Title I, § 140, as added Pub.L. 110–315, Title X, § 1011(a), Aug. 14, 2008, 122 Stat. 3479, and amended Pub.L. 111–24, Title III, § 304, May 22, 2009, 123 Stat. 1749; Pub.L. 111–203, Title X, § 1100A(2), July 21, 2010, 124 Stat. 2107; Pub.L. 115–174, Title VI, § 601(a), May 24, 2018, 132 Stat. 1365.)

§ 1651. Procedure for timely settlement of estates of decedent obligors [CCPA § 140A]

The Bureau,[1] in consultation with the Bureau[1] and each other agency referred to in section 1607(a) of this title, shall prescribe regulations to require any creditor, with respect to any credit card account under an open end consumer credit plan, to establish procedures to ensure that any administrator of an estate of any deceased obligor with respect to such account can resolve outstanding credit balances in a timely manner.

(Pub.L. 90–321, Title I, § 140A, as added Pub.L. 111–24, Title V, § 504(a), May 22, 2009, 123 Stat. 1756; Pub.L. 111–203, Title X, § 1100A(2), (3), July 21, 2010, 124 Stat. 2107.)

---

[1] So in original.

PART C—CREDIT ADVERTISING AND LIMITS ON CREDIT CARD FEES

§ 1661. Catalogs and multiple-page advertisements [CCPA § 141]

For the purposes of this part, a catalog or other multiple-page advertisement shall be considered a single advertisement if it clearly and conspicuously displays a credit terms table on which the information required to be stated under this part is clearly set forth.

(Pub.L. 90–321, Title I, § 141, May 29, 1968, 82 Stat. 158.)

§ 1662. Advertising of downpayments and installments [CCPA § 142]

No advertisement to aid, promote, or assist directly or indirectly any extension of consumer credit may state

(1) that a specific periodic consumer credit amount or installment amount can be arranged, unless the creditor usually and customarily arranges credit payments or installments for that period and in that amount.

(2) that a specified downpayment is required in connection with any extension of consumer credit, unless the creditor usually and customarily arranges downpayments in that amount.

(Pub.L. 90–321, Title I, § 142, May 29, 1968, 82 Stat. 158.)

§ 1663. Advertising of open end credit plans [CCPA § 143]

No advertisement to aid, promote, or assist directly or indirectly the extension of consumer credit under an open end credit plan may set forth any of the specific terms of that plan unless it also clearly and conspicuously sets forth all of the following items:

(1) Any minimum or fixed amount which could be imposed.

(2) In any case in which periodic rates may be used to compute the finance charge, the periodic rates expressed as annual percentage rates.

(3) Any other term that the Bureau may by regulation require to be disclosed.

(Pub.L. 90–321, Title I, §143, May 29, 1968, 82 Stat. 158; Pub.L. 96–221, Title VI, §§ 613(f), 619(a), Mar. 31, 1980, 94 Stat. 177, 183; Pub.L. 111–203, Title X, § 1100A(2), July 21, 2010, 124 Stat. 2107.)

§ 1664. Advertising of credit other than open end plans [CCPA § 144]

(a) Exclusion of open end credit plans

Except as provided in subsection (b) of this section, this section applies to any advertisement to aid, promote, or assist directly or indirectly any consumer credit sale, loan, or other extension of credit subject to the provisions of this subchapter, other than an open end credit plan.

(b) Advertisements of residential real estate

The provisions of this section do not apply to advertisements of residential real estate except to the extent that the Bureau may by regulation require.

(c) Rate of finance charge expressed as annual percentage rate

If any advertisement to which this section applies states the rate of a finance charge, the advertisement shall state the rate of that charge expressed as an annual percentage rate.

(d) Requisite disclosures in advertisement

If any advertisement to which this section applies states the amount of the downpayment, if any, the amount of any installment payment, the dollar amount of any finance charge, or the number of installments or the period of repayment, then the advertisement shall state all of the following items:

(1) The downpayment, if any.

(2) The terms of repayment.

(3) The rate of the finance charge expressed as an annual percentage rate.

(e) Credit transaction secured by principal dwelling of consumer

Each advertisement to which this section applies that relates to a consumer credit transaction that is secured by the principal dwelling of a consumer in which the extension of credit may exceed the fair market value of the dwelling, and which advertisement is disseminated in paper form to the public or through the internet, as opposed to by radio or television, shall clearly and conspicuously State that—

(1) the interest on the portion of the credit extension that is greater than the fair market value of the dwelling is not tax deductible for Federal income tax purposes; and

(2) the consumer should consult a tax adviser for further information regarding the deductibility of interest and charges.

(Pub.L. 90–321, Title I, § 144, May 29, 1968, 82 Stat. 158; Pub.L. 96–221, Title VI, § 619(b), Mar. 31, 1980, 94 Stat. 183; Pub.L. 109–8, Title XIII, § 1302(b)(2), Apr. 20, 2005, 119 Stat. 209; Pub.L. 111–203, Title X, § 1100A(2), July 21, 2010, 124 Stat. 2107.)

§ 1665. Nonliability of advertising media [CCPA § 145]

There is no liability under this part on the part of any owner or personnel, as such, of any medium in which an advertisement appears or through which it is disseminated.

(Pub.L. 90–321, Title I, § 145, May 29, 1968, 82 Stat. 159.)

§ 1665a. Use of annual percentage rate in oral disclosures; exceptions [CCPA § 146]

In responding orally to any inquiry about the cost of credit, a creditor, regardless of the method used to compute finance charges, shall state rates only in terms of the annual percentage rate, except that in the case of an open end credit plan, the periodic rate also may be stated and, in the case of an other than open end credit plan where a major component of the finance charge consists of interest computed at a simple annual rate, the simple annual rate also may be stated. The Bureau may, by regulation, modify the requirements of this section or provide an exception from this section for a transaction or class of transactions for which the creditor cannot determine in advance the applicable annual percentage rate.

(Pub.L. 90–321, Title I, § 146, as added Pub.L. 93–495, Title IV, § 401(a), Oct. 28, 1974, 88 Stat. 1517, and amended Pub.L. 96–221, Title VI, § 623(a), Mar. 31, 1980, 94 Stat. 185; Pub.L. 111–203, Title X, § 1100A(2), July 21, 2010, 124 Stat. 2107.)

§ 1665b. Advertising of open end consumer credit plans secured by consumer's principal dwelling [CCPA § 147]

(a) In general

If any advertisement to aid, promote, or assist, directly or indirectly, the extension of consumer credit through an open end consumer credit plan under which extensions of credit are secured by the consumer's principal dwelling states, affirmatively or negatively, any of the specific terms of the plan, including any periodic payment amount required under such plan, such advertisement shall also clearly and conspicuously set forth the following information, in such form and manner as the Bureau may require:

(1) Loan fees and opening cost estimates

Any loan fee the amount of which is determined as a percentage of the credit limit applicable to an account under the plan and an estimate of the aggregate amount of other fees for opening the account, based on the creditor's experience with the plan and stated as a single amount or as a reasonable range.

(2) Periodic rates

In any case in which periodic rates may be used to compute the finance charge, the periodic rates expressed as an annual percentage rate.

(3) Highest annual percentage rate

The highest annual percentage rate which may be imposed under the plan.

(4) Other information

Any other information the Bureau may by regulation require.

(b) Tax deductibility

(1) In general

If any advertisement described in subsection (a) of this section contains a statement that any interest expense incurred with respect to the plan is or may be tax deductible, the advertisement shall not be misleading with respect to such deductibility.

(2) Credit in excess of fair market value

Each advertisement described in subsection (a) of this section that relates to an extension of credit that may exceed the fair market value of the dwelling, and which advertisement is disseminated in paper form to the public or through the Internet, as opposed to by radio or television, shall include a clear and conspicuous statement that—

(A) the interest on the portion of the credit extension that is greater than the fair market value of the dwelling is not tax deductible for Federal income tax purposes; and

(B) the consumer should consult a tax adviser for further information regarding the deductibility of interest and charges.

(c) Certain terms prohibited

No advertisement described in subsection (a) of this section with respect to any home equity account may refer to such loan as "free money" or use other terms determined by the Bureau by regulation to be misleading.

(d) Discounted initial rate

(1) In general

If any advertisement described in subsection (a) of this section includes an initial annual percentage rate that is not determined by the index or formula used to make later interest rate adjustments, the advertisement shall also state with equal prominence the current annual percentage rate that would have been applied using the index or formula if such initial rate had not been offered.

(2) Quoted rate must be reasonably current

The annual percentage rate required to be disclosed under the paragraph (1) rate must be current as of a reasonable time given the media involved.

(3) Period during which initial rate is in effect

Any advertisement to which paragraph (1) applies shall also state the period of time during which the initial annual percentage rate referred to in such paragraph will be in effect.

(e) Balloon payment

If any advertisement described in subsection (a) of this section contains a statement regarding the minimum monthly payment under the plan, the advertisement shall also disclose, if applicable, the fact that the plan includes a balloon payment.

(f) "Balloon payment" defined

For purposes of this section and section 1637a of this title, the term "balloon payment" means, with respect to any open end consumer credit plan under which extensions of credit are secured by the consumer's principal dwelling, any repayment option under which—

(1) the account holder is required to repay the entire amount of any outstanding balance as of a specified date or at the end of a specified period of time, as determined in accordance with the terms of the agreement pursuant to which such credit is extended; and

(2) the aggregate amount of the minimum periodic payments required would not fully amortize such outstanding balance by such date or at the end of such period.

(Pub.L. 90–321, Title I, § 147, as added Pub.L. 100–709, § 2(c), Nov. 23, 1988, 102 Stat. 4730; Pub.L. 109–8, Title XIII, § 1302(a)(2), Apr. 20, 2005, 119 Stat. 208; Pub.L. 111–203, Title X, § 1100A(2), July 21, 2010, 124 Stat. 2107.)

§ 1665c. Interest rate reduction on open end consumer credit plans [CCPA § 148]

(a) In general

If a creditor increases the annual percentage rate applicable to a credit card account under an open end consumer credit plan, based on factors including the credit risk of the obligor, market conditions, or other factors, the creditor shall consider changes in such factors in subsequently determining whether to reduce the annual percentage rate for such obligor.

(b) Requirements

With respect to any credit card account under an open end consumer credit plan, the creditor shall—

(1) maintain reasonable methodologies for assessing the factors described in subsection (a);

(2) not less frequently than once every 6 months, review accounts as to which the annual percentage rate has been increased since January 1, 2009, to assess whether such factors have changed (including whether any risk has declined);

(3) reduce the annual percentage rate previously increased when a reduction is indicated by the review; and

(4) in the event of an increase in the annual percentage rate, provide in the written notice required under section 1637(i) of this title a statement of the reasons for the increase.

(c) Rule of construction

This section shall not be construed to require a reduction in any specific amount.

(d) Rulemaking

The Bureau[1] shall issue final rules not later than 9 months May 22, 2009 to implement the requirements of and evaluate compliance with this section, and subsections (a), (b), and (c) shall become effective 15 months after May 22, 2009.

(Pub.L. 90–321, Title I, § 148, as added Pub.L. 111–24, Title I, § 101(c), May 22, 2009, 123 Stat. 1737; Pub.L. 111–203, Title X, § 1100A(2), July 21, 2010, 124 Stat. 2107.)

§ 1665d. Reasonable penalty fees on open end consumer credit plans [CCPA § 149]

(a) In general

The amount of any penalty fee or charge that a card issuer may impose with respect to a credit card account under an open end consumer credit plan in connection with any omission with respect to, or violation of, the cardholder agreement, including any late payment fee, over-the-limit fee, or any other penalty fee or charge, shall be reasonable and proportional to such omission or violation.

(b) Rulemaking required

The Bureau, in consultation with the Comptroller of the Currency, the Board of Directors of the Federal Deposit Insurance Corporation, the Director of the Office of Thrift Supervision, and the National Credit Union Administration Board, shall issue final rules not later than 9 months after May 22, 2009, to establish standards for assessing whether the amount of any penalty fee or charge described under subsection (a) is reasonable and proportional to the omission or violation to which the fee or charge relates. Subsection (a) shall become effective 15 months after May 22, 2009.

[1] So in original. Probably should be "Board".

(c) Considerations

In issuing rules required by this section, the Bureau shall consider—

(1) the cost incurred by the creditor from such omission or violation;

(2) the deterrence of such omission or violation by the cardholder;

(3) the conduct of the cardholder; and

(4) such other factors as the Bureau may deem necessary or appropriate.

(d) Differentiation permitted

In issuing rules required by this subsection, the Bureau may establish different standards for different types of fees and charges, as appropriate.

(e) Safe harbor rule authorized

The Bureau, in consultation with the Comptroller of the Currency, the Board of Directors of the Federal Deposit Insurance Corporation, the Director of the Office of Thrift Supervision, and the National Credit Union Administration Board may issue rules to provide an amount for any penalty fee or charge described under subsection (a) that is presumed to be reasonable and proportional to the omission or violation to which the fee or charge relates.

(Pub.L. 90–321, Title I, § 149, as added Pub.L. 111–24, Title I, § 102(b)(1), May 22, 2009, 123 Stat. 1740; Pub.L. 111–203, Title X, § 1100A(2), July 21, 2010, 124 Stat. 2107.)

§ 1665e. Consideration of ability to repay [CCPA § 150]

A card issuer may not open any credit card account for any consumer under an open end consumer credit plan, or increase any credit limit applicable to such account, unless the card issuer considers the ability of the consumer to make the required payments under the terms of such account.

(Pub.L. 90–321, Title I, § 150, as added Pub.L. 111–24, Title I, § 109(a), May 22, 2009, 123 Stat. 1743.)

PART D—CREDIT BILLING

§ 1666. Correction of billing errors [CCPA § 161]

(a) Written notice by obligor to creditor; time for and contents of notice; procedure upon receipt of notice by creditor

If a creditor, within sixty days after having transmitted to an obligor a statement of the obligor's account in connection with an extension of consumer credit, receives at the address disclosed under section 1637(b)(10) of this title a written notice (other than notice on a payment stub or other payment medium supplied by the creditor if the creditor so stipulates with the disclosure required under section 1637(a)(7) of this title) from the obligor in which the obligor—

(1) sets forth or otherwise enables the creditor to identify the name and account number (if any) of the obligor,

(2) indicates the obligor's belief that the statement contains a billing error and the amount of such billing error, and

(3) sets forth the reasons for the obligor's belief (to the extent applicable) that the statement contains a billing error,

the creditor shall, unless the obligor has, after giving such written notice and before the expiration of the time limits herein specified, agreed that the statement was correct—

(A) not later than thirty days after the receipt of the notice, send a written acknowledgment thereof to the obligor, unless the action required in subparagraph (B) is taken within such thirty-day period, and

(B) not later than two complete billing cycles of the creditor (in no event later than ninety days) after the receipt of the notice and prior to taking any action to collect the amount, or any part thereof, indicated by the obligor under paragraph (2) either—

(i) make appropriate corrections in the account of the obligor, including the crediting of any finance charges on amounts erroneously billed, and transmit to the obligor a notification of such corrections and the creditor's explanation of any change in the amount indicated by the obligor under paragraph (2) and, if any such change is made and the obligor so requests, copies of documentary evidence of the obligor's indebtedness; or

(ii) send a written explanation or clarification to the obligor, after having conducted an investigation, setting forth to the extent applicable the reasons why the creditor believes the account of the obligor was correctly shown in the statement and, upon request of the obligor, provide copies of documentary evidence of the obligor's indebtedness. In the case of a billing error where the obligor alleges that the creditor's billing statement reflects goods not delivered to the obligor or his designee in accordance with the agreement made at the time of the transaction, a creditor may not construe such amount to be correctly shown unless he determines that such goods were actually delivered, mailed, or otherwise sent to the obligor and provides the obligor with a statement of such determination.

After complying with the provisions of this subsection with respect to an alleged billing error, a creditor has no further responsibility under this section if the obligor continues to make substantially the same allegation with respect to such error.

(b) Billing error

For the purpose of this section, a "billing error" consists of any of the following:

(1) A reflection on a statement of an extension of credit which was not made to the obligor or, if made, was not in the amount reflected on such statement.

(2) A reflection on a statement of an extension of credit for which the obligor requests additional clarification including documentary evidence thereof.

(3) A reflection on a statement of goods or services not accepted by the obligor or his designee or not delivered to the obligor or his designee in accordance with the agreement made at the time of a transaction.

(4) The creditor's failure to reflect properly on a statement a payment made by the obligor or a credit issued to the obligor.

(5) A computation error or similar error of an accounting nature of the creditor on a statement.

(6) Failure to transmit the statement required under section 1637(b) of this title to the last address of the obligor which has been disclosed to the creditor, unless that address was furnished less than twenty days before the end of the billing cycle for which the statement is required.

(7) Any other error described in regulations of the Bureau.

(c) Action by creditor to collect amount or any part thereof regarded by obligor to be a billing error

For the purposes of this section, "action to collect the amount, or any part thereof, indicated by an obligor under paragraph (2)" does not include the sending of statements of account, which may include finance charges on amounts in dispute, to the obligor following written notice from the obligor as specified under subsection (a) of this section, if—

(1) the obligor's account is not restricted or closed because of the failure of the obligor to pay the amount indicated under paragraph (2) of subsection (a) of this section, and

(2) the creditor indicates the payment of such amount is not required pending the creditor's compliance with this section.

Nothing in this section shall be construed to prohibit any action by a creditor to collect any amount which has not been indicated by the obligor to contain a billing error.

(d) Restricting or closing by creditor of account regarded by obligor to contain a billing error

Pursuant to regulations of the Bureau, a creditor operating an open end consumer credit plan may not, prior to the sending of the written explanation or clarification required under paragraph (B)(ii), restrict or close an account with respect to which the obligor has indicated pursuant to subsection (a) of this section that he believes such account to contain a billing error solely because of the obligor's failure to pay the amount indicated to be in error. Nothing in this subsection shall be deemed to prohibit a creditor from applying against the credit limit on the obligor's account the amount indicated to be in error.

(e) Effect of noncompliance with requirements by creditor

Any creditor who fails to comply with the requirements of this section or section 1666a of this title forfeits any right to collect from the obligor the amount indicated by the obligor under paragraph (2) of subsection (a) of this section, and any finance charges thereon, except that the amount required to be forfeited under this subsection may not exceed $50.

(Pub.L. 90–321, Title I, § 161, as added Pub.L. 93–495, Title III, § 306, Oct. 28, 1974, 88 Stat. 1512, and amended Pub.L. 96–221, Title VI, §§ 613(g), 620, Mar. 31, 1980, 94 Stat. 177, 184; Pub.L. 111–203, Title X, §§ 1087, 1100A(2), July 21, 2010, 124 Stat. 2086, 2107.)

§ 1666a. Regulation of credit reports [CCPA § 162]

(a) Reports by creditor on obligor's failure to pay amount regarded as billing error

After receiving a notice from an obligor as provided in section 1666(a) of this title, a creditor or his agent may not directly or indirectly threaten to report to any person adversely on the obligor's credit rating or credit standing because of the obligor's failure to pay the amount indicated by the obligor under section 1666(a)(2) of this title, and such amount may not be reported as delinquent to any third party until the creditor has met the requirements of section 1666 of this title and has allowed the obligor the same number of days (not less than ten) thereafter to make payment as is provided under the credit agreement with the obligor for the payment of undisputed amounts.

(b) Reports by creditor on delinquent amounts in dispute; notification of obligor of parties notified of delinquency

If a creditor receives a further written notice from an obligor that an amount is still in dispute within the time allowed for payment under subsection (a) of this section, a creditor may not report to any third party that the amount of the obligor is delinquent because the obligor has failed to pay an amount which he has indicated under section 1666(a)(2) of this title, unless the creditor also reports that the amount is in dispute and, at the same time, notifies the obligor of the name and address of each party to whom the creditor is reporting information concerning the delinquency.

(c) Reports by creditor of subsequent resolution of delinquent amounts

A creditor shall report any subsequent resolution of any delinquencies reported pursuant to subsection (b) of this section to the parties to whom such delinquencies were initially reported.

(Pub.L. 90–321, Title I, § 162, as added Pub.L. 93–495, Title III, § 306, Oct. 28, 1974, 88 Stat. 1513.)

§ 1666b. Timing of payments [CCPA § 163]

(a) Time to make payments

A creditor may not treat a payment on a credit card account under an open end consumer credit plan as late for any purpose, unless the creditor has adopted reasonable procedures designed to ensure that each periodic statement including the information required by section 1637(b) of this title is mailed or delivered to the consumer not later than 21 days before the payment due date.

(b) Grace period

If an open end consumer credit plan provides a time period within which an obligor may repay any portion of the credit extended without incurring an additional finance charge, such additional finance charge may not be imposed with respect to such portion of the credit extended for the billing cycle of which such period is a part, unless a statement which includes the amount upon which the finance charge for the period is based was mailed or delivered to the consumer not later than 21 days before the date specified in the statement by which payment must be made in order to avoid imposition of that finance charge.

(Pub.L. 90–321, Title I, § 163, as added Pub.L. 93–495, Title III, § 306, Oct. 28, 1974, 88 Stat. 1514, and amended Pub.L. 111–24, Title I, § 106(b)(1), May 22, 2009, 123 Stat. 1735; Pub.L. 111–93, § 2, Nov. 6, 2009, 123 Stat. 2998.)

§ 1666c. Prompt and fair crediting of payments [CCPA § 164]

(a) In general

Payments received from an obligor under an open end consumer credit plan by the creditor shall be posted promptly to the obligor's account as specified in regulations of the Bureau. Such regulations shall prevent a finance charge from being imposed on any obligor if the creditor has received the obligor's payment in readily identifiable form, by 5:00 p.m. on the date on which such payment is due, in the amount, manner, and location indicated by the creditor to avoid the imposition thereof.

(b) Application of payments

(1) In general

Upon receipt of a payment from a cardholder, the card issuer shall apply amounts in excess of the minimum payment amount first to the card balance bearing the highest rate of interest, and then to each successive balance bearing the next highest rate of interest, until the payment is exhausted.

(2) Clarification relating to certain deferred interest arrangements

A creditor shall allocate the entire amount paid by the consumer in excess of the minimum payment amount to a balance on which interest is deferred during the last 2 billing cycles immediately preceding the expiration of the period during which interest is deferred.

(c) Changes by card issuer

If a card issuer makes a material change in the mailing address, office, or procedures for handling cardholder payments, and such change causes a material delay in the crediting of a cardholder payment made during the 60-day period following the date on which such change took effect, the card issuer may not impose any late fee or finance charge for a late payment on the credit card account to which such payment was credited.

(Pub.L. 90–321, Title I, § 164, as added Pub.L. 93–495, Title III, § 306, Oct. 28, 1974, 88 Stat. 1514, and amended Pub.L. 111–24, Title I, § 104, May 22, 2009, 123 Stat. 1741; Pub.L. 111–203, Title X, § 1100A(2), July 21, 2010, 124 Stat. 2107.)

§ 1666d. Treatment of credit balances [CCPA § 165]

Whenever a credit balance in excess of $1 is created in connection with a consumer credit transaction through (1) transmittal of funds to a creditor in excess of the total balance due on an account, (2) rebates of unearned finance charges or insurance premiums, or (3) amounts otherwise owed to or held for the benefit of an obligor, the creditor shall—

(A) credit the amount of the credit balance to the consumer's account;

(B) refund any part of the amount of the remaining credit balance, upon request of the consumer; and

(C) make a good faith effort to refund to the consumer by cash, check, or money order any part of the amount of the credit balance remaining in the account for more than six months, except that no further action is required in any case in which the consumer's current location is not known by the creditor and cannot be traced through the consumer's last known address or telephone number.

(Pub.L. 90–321, Title I, § 165, as added Pub.L. 93–495, Title III, § 306, Oct. 28, 1974, 88 Stat. 1514, and amended Pub.L. 96–221, Title VI, § 621(a), Mar. 31, 1980, 94 Stat. 184.)

§ 1666e. Notification of credit card issuer by seller of return of goods, etc., by obligor; credit for account of obligor [CCPA § 166]

With respect to any sales transaction where a credit card has been used to obtain credit, where the seller is a person other than the card issuer, and where the seller accepts or allows a return of the goods or forgiveness of a debit for services which were the subject of such sale, the seller shall promptly transmit to the credit card issuer, a credit statement with respect thereto and the credit card issuer shall credit the account of the obligor for the amount of the transaction.

(Pub.L. 90–321, Title I, § 166, as added Pub.L. 93–495, Title III, § 306, Oct. 28, 1974, 88 Stat. 1514.)

§ 1666f. Inducements to cardholders by sellers of cash discounts for payments by cash, check or similar means; finance charge for sales transactions involving cash discounts [CCPA § 167]

(a) Cash discounts

With respect to credit card which may be used for extensions of credit in sales transactions in which the seller is a person other than the card issuer, the card issuer may not, by contract, or otherwise, prohibit any such seller from offering a discount to a cardholder to induce the cardholder to pay by cash, check, or similar means rather than use a credit card.

(b) Finance charge

With respect to any sales transaction, any discount from the regular price offered by the seller for the purpose of inducing payment by cash, checks, or other means not involving the use of an open-end credit plan or a credit card shall not constitute a finance charge as determined under section 1605 of this title if such discount is offered to all prospective buyers and its availability is disclosed clearly and conspicuously.

(Pub.L. 90–321, Title I, § 167, as added Pub.L. 93–495, Title III, § 306, Oct. 28, 1974, 88 Stat. 1515, and amended Pub.L. 94–222, § 3(c)(1), Feb. 27, 1976, 90 Stat. 197; Pub.L. 97–25, Title I, § 101, July 27, 1981, 95 Stat. 144.)

§ 1666g. Tie-in services prohibited for issuance of credit card [CCPA § 168]

Notwithstanding any agreement to the contrary, a card issuer may not require a seller, as a condition to participating in a credit card plan, to open an account with or procure any other service from the card issuer or its subsidiary or agent.

(Pub.L. 90–321, Title I, § 168, as added Pub.L. 93–495, Title III, § 306, Oct. 28, 1974, 88 Stat. 1515.)

§ 1666h. Offset of cardholder's indebtedness by issuer of credit card with funds deposited with issuer by cardholder; remedies of creditors under State law not affected [CCPA § 169]

(a) Offset against consumer's funds

A card issuer may not take any action to offset a cardholder's indebtedness arising in connection with a consumer credit transaction under the relevant credit card plan against funds of the cardholder held on deposit with the card issuer unless—

(1) such action was previously authorized in writing by the cardholder in accordance with a credit plan whereby the cardholder agrees periodically to pay debts incurred in his open end credit account by permitting the card issuer periodically to deduct all or a portion of such debt from the cardholder's deposit account, and

(2) such action with respect to any outstanding disputed amount not be taken by the card issuer upon request of the cardholder.

In the case of any credit card account in existence on the effective date of this section, the previous written authorization referred to in clause (1) shall not be required until the date (after such effective date) when such account is renewed, but in no case later than one year after such effective date. Such written authorization shall be deemed to exist if the card issuer has previously notified the cardholder that the use of his credit card account will subject any funds which the card issuer holds in deposit accounts of such cardholder to offset against any amounts due and payable on his credit card account which have not been paid in accordance with the terms of the agreement between the card issuer and the cardholder.

(b) Attachments and levies

This section does not alter or affect the right under State law of a card issuer to attach or otherwise levy upon funds of a cardholder held on deposit with the card issuer if that remedy is constitutionally available to creditors generally.

(Pub.L. 90–321, Title I, § 169, as added Pub.L. 93–495, Title III, § 306, Oct. 28, 1974, 88 Stat. 1515.)

§ 1666i. Assertion by cardholder against card issuer of claims and defenses arising out of credit card transaction; prerequisites; limitation on amount of claims or defenses [CCPA § 170]

(a) Claims and defenses assertible

Subject to the limitation contained in subsection (b) of this section, a card issuer who has issued a credit card to a cardholder pursuant to an open end consumer credit plan shall be subject to all claims (other than tort claims) and defenses arising out of any transaction in which the credit card is used as a method of payment or extension of credit if (1) the obligor has made a good faith attempt to obtain satisfactory resolution of a disagreement or problem relative to the transaction from the person honoring the credit card; (2) the amount of the initial transaction exceeds $50; and (3) the place where the initial transaction occurred was in the same State as the mailing address previously provided by the cardholder or was within 100 miles from such address, except that the limitations set forth in clauses (2) and (3) with respect to an obligor's right to assert claims and defenses against a card issuer shall not be applicable to any transaction in which the person honoring the credit card (A) is the same person as the card issuer, (B) is controlled by the card issuer, (C) is under direct or indirect common control with the card issuer, (D) is a franchised dealer in the card issuer's products or services, or (E) has obtained the order for such transaction through a mail solicitation made by or participated in by the card issuer in which the cardholder is solicited to enter into such transaction by using the credit card issued by the card issuer.

(b) Amount of claims and defenses assertible

The amount of claims or defenses asserted by the cardholder may not exceed the amount of credit outstanding with respect to such transaction at the time the cardholder first notifies the card issuer or the person honoring the credit card of such claim or defense. For the purpose of determining the amount of credit outstanding in the preceding sentence, payments and credits to the cardholder's account are deemed to have been applied, in the order indicated, to the payment of: (1) late charges in the order of their entry to the account; (2) finance charges in order of their entry to the account; and (3) debits to the account other than those set forth above, in the order in which each debit entry to the account was made.

(Pub.L. 90–321, Title I, § 170, as added Pub.L. 93–495, Title III, § 306, Oct. 28, 1974, 88 Stat. 1515.)

§ 1666i–1. Limits on interest rate, fee, and finance charge increases applicable to outstanding balances [CCPA § 171]

(a) In general

In the case of any credit card account under an open end consumer credit plan, no creditor may increase any annual percentage rate, fee, or finance charge applicable to any outstanding balance, except as permitted under subsection (b).

(b) Exceptions

The prohibition under subsection (a) shall not apply to—

(1) an increase in an annual percentage rate upon the expiration of a specified period of time, provided that—

(A) prior to commencement of that period, the creditor disclosed to the consumer, in a clear and conspicuous manner, the length of the period and the annual percentage rate that would apply after expiration of the period;

(B) the increased annual percentage rate does not exceed the rate disclosed pursuant to subparagraph (A); and

(C) the increased annual percentage rate is not applied to transactions that occurred prior to commencement of the period;

(2) an increase in a variable annual percentage rate in accordance with a credit card agreement that provides for changes in the rate according to operation of an index that is not under the control of the creditor and is available to the general public;

(3) an increase due to the completion of a workout or temporary hardship arrangement by the obligor or the failure of the obligor to comply with the terms of a workout or temporary hardship arrangement, provided that—

(A) the annual percentage rate, fee, or finance charge applicable to a category of transactions following any such increase does not exceed the rate, fee, or finance charge that applied to that category of transactions prior to commencement of the arrangement; and

(B) the creditor has provided the obligor, prior to the commencement of such arrangement, with clear and conspicuous disclosure of the terms of the arrangement (including any increases due to such completion or failure); or

(4) an increase due solely to the fact that a minimum payment by the obligor has not been received by the creditor within 60 days after the due date for such payment, provided that the creditor shall—

(A) include, together with the notice of such increase required under section 1637(i) of this title, a clear and conspicuous written statement of the reason for the increase and that the increase will terminate not later than 6 months after the date on which it is imposed, if the creditor receives the required minimum payments on time from the obligor during that period; and

(B) terminate such increase not later than 6 months after the date on which it is imposed, if the creditor receives the required minimum payments on time during that period.

(c) Repayment of outstanding balance

(1) In general

The creditor shall not change the terms governing the repayment of any outstanding balance, except that the creditor may provide the obligor with one of the methods described in paragraph (2) of repaying any outstanding balance, or a method that is no less beneficial to the obligor than one of those methods.

(2) Methods

The methods described in this paragraph are—

(A) an amortization period of not less than 5 years, beginning on the effective date of the increase set forth in the notice required under section 1637(i) of this title; or

(B) a required minimum periodic payment that includes a percentage of the outstanding balance that is equal to not more than twice the percentage required before the effective date of the increase set forth in the notice required under section 1637(i) of this title.

(d) Outstanding balance defined

For purposes of this section, the term "outstanding balance" means the amount owed on a credit card account under an open end consumer credit plan as of the end of the 14th day after the date on which the creditor provides notice of an increase in the annual percentage rate, fee, or finance charge in accordance with section 1637(i) of this title.

(Pub.L. 90–321, Title I, § 171, as added Pub.L. 111–24, Title I, § 101(b)(2), May 22, 2009, 123 Stat. 1736.)

§ 1666i–2. Additional limits on interest rate increases [CCPA § 172]

(a) Limitation on increases within first year

Except in the case of an increase described in paragraph (1), (2), (3), or (4) of section 1666i–1(b) of this title, no increase in any annual percentage rate, fee, or finance charge on any credit card account under an open end consumer credit plan shall be effective before the end of the 1-year period beginning on the date on which the account is opened.

(b) Promotional rate minimum term

No increase in any annual percentage rate applicable to a credit card account under an open end consumer credit plan that is a promotional rate (as that term is defined by the Bureau) shall be effective before the end of the 6-month period beginning on the date on which the promotional rate takes effect, subject to such reasonable exceptions as the Bureau may establish, by rule.

(Pub.L. 90–321, Title I, § 172, as added Pub.L. 111–24, Title I, § 101(d), May 22, 2009, 123 Stat. 1738; Pub.L. 111–203, Title X, § 1100A(2), July 21, 2010, 124 Stat. 2107.)

§ 1666j. Applicability of State laws [CCPA § 173]

(a) Consistency of provisions

This part does not annul, alter, or affect, or exempt any person subject to the provisions of this part from complying with, the laws of any State with respect to credit billing practices, except to the extent that those laws are inconsistent with any provision of this part, and then only to the extent of the inconsistency. The Bureau is authorized to determine whether such inconsistencies exist. The Bureau may not determine that any State law is inconsistent with any provision of this part if the Bureau determines that such law gives greater protection to the consumer.

(b) Exemptions by Bureau from credit billing requirements

The Bureau shall by regulation exempt from the requirements of this part any class of credit transactions within any State if it determines that under the law of that State that class of transactions is subject to requirements substantially similar to those imposed under this part or that such law gives greater protection to the consumer, and that there is adequate provision for enforcement.

(c) Finance charge or other charge for credit for sales transactions involving cash discounts

Notwithstanding any other provisions of this subchapter, any discount offered under section 1666f(b) of this title shall not be considered a finance charge or other charge for credit under the usury laws of any State or under the laws of any State relating to disclosure of information in connection with credit transactions, or relating to the types, amounts or rates of charges, or to any element or elements of charges permissible under such laws in connection with the extension or use of credit.

(Pub.L. 90–321, Title I, § 173, formerly § 171, as added Pub.L. 93–495, Title III, § 306, Oct. 28, 1974, 88 Stat. 1516, and amended Pub.L. 94–222, § 3(d), Feb. 27, 1976, 90 Stat. 198; renumbered § 173, P.L. 111–22, Title I, § 101(b)(1), May 20, 2009, 123 Stat. 1638; Pub.L. 111–203, Title X, §§ 1087, 1100A(2), July 21, 2010, 124 Stat. 2086, 2107.)

PART E—CONSUMER LEASES

§ 1667. Definitions [CCPA § 181]

For purposes of this part—

(1) The term "consumer lease" means a contract in the form of a lease or bailment for the use of personal property by a natural person for a period of time exceeding four months, and for a total contractual obligation not exceeding $50,000, primarily for personal, family, or household purposes, whether or not the lessee has the option to purchase or otherwise become the owner of the property at the expiration of the lease, except that such term shall not include any credit sale as defined in section 1602(g)* of this title. Such term does not include a lease for agricultural, business, or commercial purposes, or to a government or governmental agency or instrumentality, or to an organization.

(2) The term "lessee" means a natural person who leases or is offered a consumer lease.

(3) The term "lessor" means a person who is regularly engaged in leasing, offering to lease, or arranging to lease under a consumer lease.

(4) The term "personal property" means any property which is not real property under the laws of the State where situated at the time offered or otherwise made available for lease.

(5) The terms "security" and "security interest" mean any interest in property which secures payment or performance of an obligation.

(Pub.L. 90–321, Title I, § 181, as added Pub.L. 94–240, § 3, Mar. 23, 1976, 90 Stat. 257; Pub.L. 111–203, Title X, § 1100E(a)(2), July 21, 2010, 124 Stat. 2111.)

§ 1667a. Consumer lease disclosures [CCPA § 182]

Each lessor shall give a lessee prior to the consummation of the lease a dated written statement on which the lessor and lessee are identified setting out accurately and in a clear and conspicuous manner the following information with respect to that lease, as applicable:

(1) A brief description or identification of the leased property;

(2) The amount of any payment by the lessee required at the inception of the lease;

(3) The amount paid or payable by the lessee for official fees, registration, certificate of title, or license fees or taxes;

(4) The amount of other charges payable by the lessee not included in the periodic payments, a description of the charges and that the lessee shall be liable for the differential, if any, between the anticipated fair market value of the leased property and its appraised actual value at the termination of the lease, if the lessee has such liability;

(5) A statement of the amount or method of determining the amount of any liabilities the lease imposes upon the lessee at the end of the term and whether or not the lessee has the option to purchase the leased property and at what price and time;

(6) A statement identifying all express warranties and guarantees made by the manufacturer or lessor with respect to the leased property, and identifying the party responsible for maintaining or servicing the leased property together with a description of the responsibility;

(7) A brief description of insurance provided or paid for by the lessor or required of the lessee, including the types and amounts of the coverages and costs;

(8) A description of any security interest held or to be retained by the lessor in connection with the lease and a clear identification of the property to which the security interest relates;

(9) The number, amount, and due dates or periods of payments under the lease and the total amount of such periodic payments;

(10) Where the lease provides that the lessee shall be liable for the anticipated fair market value of the property on expiration of the lease, the fair market value of the property at the inception of the lease, the aggregate cost of the lease on expiration, and the differential between them; and

(11) A statement of the conditions under which the lessee or lessor may terminate the lease prior to the end of the term and the amount or method of determining any penalty or other charge for delinquency, default, late payments, or early termination.

---

* *Note from West Advisory Panel: This section was redesignated section 1602(h) of this title by Pub.L. 111–203, Title X, § 1100A(1)(A), July 21, 2010, 124 Stat. 2107.*

The disclosures required under this section may be made in the lease contract to be signed by the lessee. The Bureau may provide by regulation that any portion of the information required to be disclosed under this section may be given in the form of estimates where the lessor is not in a position to know exact information.

(Pub.L. 90–321, Title I, § 182, as added Pub.L. 94–240, § 3, Mar. 23, 1976, 90 Stat. 258; Pub.L. 111–203, Title X, §§ 1100A(2), 1100A(10)(B), July 21, 2010, 124 Stat. 2107, 2109.)

§ 1667b. Lessee's liability on expiration or termination of lease [CCPA § 183]

(a) Estimated residual value of property as basis; presumptions; action by lessor for excess liability; mutually agreeable final adjustment

Where the lessee's liability on expiration of a consumer lease is based on the estimated residual value of the property such estimated residual value shall be a reasonable approximation of the anticipated actual fair market value of the property on lease expiration. There shall be a rebuttable presumption that the estimated residual value is unreasonable to the extent that the estimated residual value exceeds the actual residual value by more than three times the average payment allocable to a monthly period under the lease. In addition, where the lessee has such liability on expiration of a consumer lease there shall be a rebuttable presumption that the lessor's estimated residual value is not in good faith to the extent that the estimated residual value exceeds the actual residual value by more than three times the average payment allocable to a monthly period under the lease and such lessor shall not collect from the lessee the amount of such excess liability on expiration of a consumer lease unless the lessor brings a successful action with respect to such excess liability. In all actions, the lessor shall pay the lessee's reasonable attorney's fees. The presumptions stated in this section shall not apply to the extent the excess of estimated over actual residual value is due to physical damage to the property beyond reasonable wear and use, or to excessive use, and the lease may set standards for such wear and use if such standards are not unreasonable. Nothing in this subsection shall preclude the right of a willing lessee to make any mutually agreeable final adjustment with respect to such excess residual liability, provided such an agreement is reached after termination of the lease.

(b) Penalties and charges for delinquency, default, or early termination

Penalties or other charges for delinquency, default, or early termination may be specified in the lease but only at an amount which is reasonable in the light of the anticipated or actual harm caused by the delinquency, default, or early termination, the difficulties of proof of loss, and the inconvenience or nonfeasibility of otherwise obtaining an adequate remedy.

(c) Independent professional appraisal of residual value of property at termination of lease; finality

If a lease has a residual value provision at the termination of the lease, the lessee may obtain at his expense, a professional appraisal of the leased property by an independent third party agreed to by both parties. Such appraisal shall be final and binding on the parties.

(Pub.L. 90–321, Title I, § 183, as added Pub.L. 94–240, § 3, Mar. 23, 1976, 90 Stat. 259.)

§ 1667c. Consumer lease advertising; liability of advertising media [CCPA § 184]

(a) In general

If an advertisement for a consumer lease includes a statement of the amount of any payment or a statement that any or no initial payment is required, the advertisement shall clearly and conspicuously state, as applicable—

(1) the transaction advertised is a lease;

(2) the total amount of any initial payments required on or before consummation of the lease or delivery of the property, whichever is later;

(3) that a security deposit is required;

(4) the number, amount, and timing of scheduled payments; and

(5) with respect to a lease in which the liability of the consumer at the end of the lease term is based on the anticipated residual value of the property, that an extra charge may be imposed at the end of the lease term.

(b) Advertising medium not liable

No owner or employee of any entity that serves as a medium in which an advertisement appears or through which an advertisement is disseminated, shall be liable under this section.

(c) Radio advertisements

(1) In general

An advertisement by radio broadcast to aid, promote, or assist, directly or indirectly, any consumer lease shall be deemed to be in compliance with the requirements of subsection (a) of this section if such advertisement clearly and conspicuously—

(A) states the information required by paragraphs (1) and (2) of subsection (a) of this section;

(B) states the number, amounts, due dates or periods of scheduled payments, and the total of such payments under the lease;

(C) includes—

(i) a referral to—

(I) a toll-free telephone number established in accordance with paragraph (2) that may be used by consumers to obtain the information required under subsection (a) of this section; or

(II) a written advertisement that—

(aa) appears in a publication in general circulation in the community served by the radio station on which such advertisement is broadcast during the period beginning 3 days before any such broadcast and ending 10 days after such broadcast; and

(bb) includes the information required to be disclosed under subsection (a) of this section; and

(ii) the name and dates of any publication referred to in clause (i)(II); and

(D) includes any other information which the Bureau determines necessary to carry out this part.

(2) Establishment of toll-free number

(A) In general

In the case of a radio broadcast advertisement described in paragraph (1) that includes a referral to a toll-free telephone number, the lessor who offers the consumer lease shall—

(i) establish such a toll-free telephone number not later than the date on which the advertisement including the referral is broadcast;

(ii) maintain such telephone number for a period of not less than 10 days, beginning on the date of any such broadcast; and

(iii) provide the information required under subsection (a) of this section with respect to the lease to any person who calls such number.

(B) Form of information

The information required to be provided under subparagraph (A)(iii) shall be provided verbally or, if requested by the consumer, in written form.

(3) No effect on other law

Nothing in this subsection shall affect the requirements of Federal law as such requirements apply to advertisement by any medium other than radio broadcast.

(Pub.L. 90–321, Title I, § 184, as added Pub.L. 94–240, § 3, Mar. 23, 1976, 90 Stat. 259, and amended Pub.L. 103–325, Title III, § 336(a), Sept. 23, 1994, 108 Stat. 2234; Pub.L. 104–208, Div. A, Title II, § 2605(c), Sept. 30, 1996, 110 Stat. 3009–473; Pub.L. 111–203, Title X, §§ 1100A(2), 1100A(10)(A), July 21, 2010, 124 Stat. 2107, 2109.)

§ 1667d. Civil liability of lessors [CCPA § 185]

(a) Grounds for maintenance of action

Any lessor who fails to comply with any requirement imposed under section 1667a or 1667b of this title with respect to any person is liable to such person as provided in section 1640 of this title.

(b) Additional grounds for maintenance of action; "creditor" defined

Any lessor who fails to comply with any requirement imposed under section 1667c of this title with respect to any person who suffers actual damage from the violation is liable to such person as provided in section 1640 of this title. For the purposes of this section, the term "creditor" as used in sections 1640 and 1641 of this title shall include a lessor as defined in this part.

(c) Jurisdiction of courts; time limitation

Notwithstanding section 1640(e) of this title, any action under this section may be brought in any United States district court or in any other court of competent jurisdiction. Such actions alleging a failure to disclose or otherwise comply with the requirements of this part shall be brought within one year of the termination of the lease agreement.

(Pub.L. 90–321, Title I, § 185, as added Pub.L. 94–240, § 3, Mar. 23, 1976, 90 Stat. 260, and amended Pub.L. 96–221, Title VI, § 624, Mar. 31, 1980, 94 Stat. 185.)

§ 1667e. Applicability of State laws; exemptions by Board from leasing requirements [CCPA § 186]

(a) This part does not annul, alter, or affect, or exempt any person subject to the provisions of this part from complying with, the laws of any State with respect to consumer leases, except to the extent that those laws are inconsistent with any provision of this part, and then only to the extent of the inconsistency. The Bureau is authorized to determine whether such inconsistencies exist. The Bureau may not determine that any State law is inconsistent with any provision of this part if the Bureau determines that such law gives greater protection and benefit to the consumer.

(b) The Bureau shall by regulation exempt from the requirements of this part any class of lease transactions within any State if it determines that under the law of that State that class of transactions is subject to requirements substantially similar to those imposed under this part or that such law gives greater protection and benefit to the consumer, and that there is adequate provision for enforcement.

(Pub.L. 90–321, Title I, § 186, as added Pub.L. 94–240, § 3, Mar. 23, 1976, 90 Stat. 260; Pub.L. 111–203, Title X, §§ 1100A(2), 1100A(10), July 21, 2010, 124 Stat. 2107, 2109.)

§ 1667f. Regulations [CCPA § 187]

(a) Regulations authorized

(1) In general

The Bureau shall prescribe regulations to update and clarify the requirements and definitions applicable to lease disclosures and contracts, and any other issues specifically related to consumer leasing, to the extent that the Bureau determines such action to be necessary—

(A) to carry out this part;

(B) to prevent any circumvention of this part; or

(C) to facilitate compliance with the requirements of the[1] part.

(2) Classifications, adjustments

Any regulations prescribed under paragraph (1) may contain classifications and differentiations, and may provide for adjustments and exceptions for any class of transactions, as the Bureau considers appropriate.

(b) Model disclosure

(1) Publication

The Bureau shall establish and publish model disclosure forms to facilitate compliance with the disclosure requirements of this part and to aid the consumer in understanding the transaction to which the subject disclosure form relates.

(2) Use of automated equipment

In establishing model forms under this subsection, the Bureau shall consider the use by lessors of data processing or similar automated equipment.

(3) Use optional

A lessor may utilize a model disclosure form established by the Bureau under this subsection for purposes of compliance with this part, at the discretion of the lessor.

(4) Effect of use

Any lessor who properly uses the material aspects of any model disclosure form established by the Bureau under this subsection shall be deemed to be in compliance with the disclosure requirements to which the form relates.

(Pub.L. 90–321, Title I, § 187, as added Pub.L. 104–208, Div. A, Title II, § 2605(b)(1), Sept. 30, 1996, 110 Stat. 3009–471; Pub.L. 111–203, Title X, §§ 1100A(2), 1100A(10), July 21, 2010, 124 Stat. 2107, 2109.)

SUBCHAPTER VI—ELECTRONIC FUND TRANSFERS

§ 1693. Congressional findings and declaration of purpose [CCPA § 902]

(a) Rights and liabilities undefined

The Congress finds that the use of electronic systems to transfer funds provides the potential for substantial benefits to consumers. However, due to the unique characteristics of such systems, the application of existing consumer protection legislation is unclear, leaving the rights and liabilities of consumers, financial institutions, and intermediaries in electronic fund transfers undefined.

(b) Purposes

It is the purpose of this subchapter to provide a basic framework establishing the rights, liabilities, and responsibilities of participants in electronic fund and remittance transfer systems. The primary objective of this subchapter, however, is the provision of individual consumer rights.

(Pub.L. 90–321, Title IX, § 902, as added Pub.L. 95–630, Title XX, § 2001, Nov. 10, 1978, 92 Stat. 3728, and amended Pub.L. 111–203, Title X, § 1073(a)(1), July 21, 2010, 124 Stat. 2060.)

§ 1693a. Definitions [CCPA § 903]

As used in this subchapter—

(1) the term "accepted card or other means of access" means a card, code, or other means of access to a consumer's account for the purpose of initiating electronic fund transfers when the person to whom such card or other means of access was issued has requested and received or has signed or

[1] So in original. Probably should be "this".

has used, or authorized another to use, such card or other means of access for the purpose of transferring money between accounts or obtaining money, property, labor, or services;

(2) the term "account" means a demand deposit, savings deposit, or other asset account (other than an occasional or incidental credit balance in an open end credit plan as defined in section 1602(i) of this title), as described in regulations of the Bureau, established primarily for personal, family, or household purposes, but such term does not include an account held by a financial institution pursuant to a bona fide trust agreement;

(4)[1] the term "Board" means the Board of Governors of the Federal Reserve System;

(4)[1] the term "Bureau" means the Bureau of Consumer Financial Protection;

(5) the term "business day" means any day on which the offices of the consumer's financial institution involved in an electronic fund transfer are open to the public for carrying on substantially all of its business functions;

(6) the term "consumer" means a natural person;

(7) the term "electronic fund transfer" means any transfer of funds, other than a transaction originated by check, draft, or similar paper instrument, which is initiated through an electronic terminal, telephonic instrument, or computer or magnetic tape so as to order, instruct, or authorize a financial institution to debit or credit an account. Such term includes, but is not limited to, point-of-sale transfers, automated teller machine transactions, direct deposits or withdrawals of funds, and transfers initiated by telephone. Such term does not include—

(A) any check guarantee or authorization service which does not directly result in a debit or credit to a consumer's account:[2]

(B) any transfer of funds, other than those processed by automated clearinghouse, made by a financial institution on behalf of a consumer by means of a service that transfers funds held at either Federal Reserve banks or other depository institutions and which is not designed primarily to transfer funds on behalf of a consumer;

(C) any transaction the primary purpose of which is the purchase or sale of securities or commodities through a broker-dealer registered with or regulated by the Securities and Exchange Commission;

(D) any automatic transfer from a savings account to a demand deposit account pursuant to an agreement between a consumer and a financial institution for the purpose of covering an overdraft or maintaining an agreed upon minimum balance in the consumer's demand deposit account; or

(E) any transfer of funds which is initiated by a telephone conversation between a consumer and an officer or employee of a financial institution which is not pursuant to a prearranged plan and under which periodic or recurring transfers are not contemplated;

as determined under regulations of the Bureau;

(8) the term "electronic terminal" means an electronic device, other than a telephone operated by a consumer, through which a consumer may initiate an electronic fund transfer. Such term includes, but is not limited to, point-of-sale terminals, automated teller machines, and cash dispensing machines;

(9) the term "financial institution" means a State or National bank, a State or Federal savings and loan association, a mutual savings bank, a State or Federal credit union, or any other person who, directly or indirectly, holds an account belonging to a consumer;

(10) the term "preauthorized electronic fund transfer" means an electronic fund transfer authorized in advance to recur at substantially regular intervals;

---

[1] So in original. There are two paragraphs designated "(4)" and no paragraph "(3)".

[2] So in original. The colon probably should be a semi colon.

(11) the term "State" means any State, territory, or possession of the United States, the District of Columbia, the Commonwealth of Puerto Rico, or any political subdivision of any of the foregoing; and

(12) the term "unauthorized electronic fund transfer" means an electronic fund transfer from a consumer's account initiated by a person other than the consumer without actual authority to initiate such transfer and from which the consumer receives no benefit, but the term does not include any electronic fund transfer (A) initiated by a person other than the consumer who was furnished with the card, code, or other means of access to such consumer's account by such consumer, unless the consumer has notified the financial institution involved that transfers by such other person are no longer authorized, (B) initiated with fraudulent intent by the consumer or any person acting in concert with the consumer, or (C) which constitutes an error committed by a financial institution.

(Pub.L. 90–321, Title IX, § 903, as added Pub.L. 95–630, Title XX, § 2001, Nov. 10, 1978, 92 Stat. 3728, and amended Pub.L. 111–203, Title X, §§ 1084(1), (2), July 21, 2010, 124 Stat. 2081.)

§ 1693b. Regulations [CCPA § 904]

(a) Prescription by the Bureau and the Board

(1) In General

Except as provided in paragraph (2), the Bureau shall prescribe rules to carry out the purposes of this title.

(2) Authority of the Board

The Board shall have sole authority to prescribe rules—

(A) to carry out the purposes of this title with respect to a person described section 5519(a) of Title 12; and

(B) to carry out the purposes of section 1693*o*–2 of this title.

In prescribing such regulations, the Board shall:

(1) consult with the other agencies referred to in section 1693*o* of this title and take into account, and allow for, the continuing evolution of electronic banking services and the technology utilized in such services,

(2) prepare an analysis of economic impact which considers the costs and benefits to financial institutions, consumers, and other users of electronic fund transfers, including the extent to which additional documentation, reports, records, or other paper work would be required, and the effects upon competition in the provision of electronic banking services among large and small financial institutions and the availability of such services to different classes of consumers, particularly low income consumers,

(3) to the extent practicable, the Board shall demonstrate that the consumer protections of the proposed regulations outweigh the compliance costs imposed upon consumers and financial institutions, and

(4) any proposed regulations and accompanying analyses shall be sent promptly to Congress by the Board.

(b) Issuance of model clauses

The Bureau shall issue model clauses for optional use by financial institutions to facilitate compliance with the disclosure requirements of section 1693c of this title and to aid consumers in understanding the rights and responsibilities of participants in electronic fund transfers by utilizing readily understandable language. Such model clauses shall be adopted after notice duly given in the Federal Register and opportunity for public comment in accordance with section 553 of Title 5. With respect to the disclosures required by section 1693c(a)(3) and (4) of this title, the Bureau shall take account of variations in the services and charges under different electronic fund transfer systems and, as appropriate, shall issue alternative model clauses for disclosure of these differing account terms.

(c) Criteria; modification of requirements

Regulations prescribed hereunder may contain such classifications, differentiations, or other provisions, and may provide for such adjustments and exceptions for any class of electronic fund transfers or remittance transfers, as in the judgment of the Bureau are necessary or proper to effectuate the purposes of this subchapter, to prevent circumvention or evasion thereof, or to facilitate compliance therewith. The Bureau shall by regulation modify the requirements imposed by this subchapter on small financial institutions if the Bureau determines that such modifications are necessary to alleviate any undue compliance burden on small financial institutions and such modifications are consistent with the purpose and objective of this subchapter.

(d) Applicability to service providers other than certain financial institutions

(1) In general

If electronic fund transfer services are made available to consumers by a person other than a financial institution holding a consumer's account, the Bureau shall by regulation assure that the disclosures, protections, responsibilities, and remedies created by this subchapter are made applicable to such persons and services.

(2) State and local government electronic benefit transfer systems

(A) "Electronic benefit transfer system" defined

In this paragraph, the term "electronic benefit transfer system"—

(i) means a system under which a government agency distributes needs-tested benefits by establishing accounts that may be accessed by recipients electronically, such as through automated teller machines or point-of-sale terminals; and

(ii) does not include employment-related payments, including salaries and pension, retirement, or unemployment benefits established by a Federal, State, or local government agency.

(B) Exemption generally

The disclosures, protections, responsibilities, and remedies established under this subchapter, and any regulation prescribed or order issued by the Bureau in accordance with this subchapter, shall not apply to any electronic benefit transfer system established under State or local law or administered by a State or local government.

(C) Exception for direct deposit into recipient's account

Subparagraph (B) shall not apply with respect to any electronic funds transfer under an electronic benefit transfer system for a deposit directly into a consumer account held by the recipient of the benefit.

(D) Rule of construction

No provision of this paragraph—

(i) affects or alters the protections otherwise applicable with respect to benefits established by any other provision[1] Federal, State, or local law; or

(ii) otherwise supersedes the application of any State or local law.

(3) Fee disclosures at automated teller machines

(A) In general

The regulations prescribed under paragraph (1) shall require any automated teller machine operator who imposes a fee on any consumer for providing host transfer services to such consumer to provide notice in accordance with subparagraph (B) to the consumer (at the time the service is provided) of—

[1] So in original. Probably should be followed by "of".

(i) the fact that a fee is imposed by such operator for providing the service; and

(ii) the amount of any such fee.

(B) Notice requirement

The notice required under clauses (i) and (ii) of subparagraph (A) with respect to any fee described in such subparagraph shall appear on the screen of the automated teller machine, or on a paper notice issued from such machine, after the transaction is initiated and before the consumer is irrevocably committed to completing the transaction.

(C) Prohibition on fees not properly disclosed and explicitly assumed by consumer

No fee may be imposed by any automated teller machine operator in connection with any electronic fund transfer initiated by a consumer for which a notice is required under subparagraph (A), unless—

(i) the consumer receives such notice in accordance with subparagraph (B); and

(ii) the consumer elects to continue in the manner necessary to effect the transaction after receiving such notice.

(D) Definitions

For purposes of this paragraph, the following definitions shall apply:

(i) Automated teller machine operator

The term "automated teller machine operator" means any person who—

(I) operates an automated teller machine at which consumers initiate electronic fund transfers; and

(II) is not the financial institution that holds the account of such consumer from which the transfer is made.

(ii) Electronic fund transfer

The term "electronic fund transfer" includes a transaction that involves a balance inquiry initiated by a consumer in the same manner as an electronic fund transfer, whether or not the consumer initiates a transfer of funds in the course of the transaction.

(iii) Host transfer services

The term "host transfer services" means any electronic fund transfer made by an automated teller machine operator in connection with a transaction initiated by a consumer at an automated teller machine operated by such operator.

(e) Deference

No provision of this subchapter may be construed as altering, limiting, or otherwise affecting the deference that a court affords to—

(1) the Bureau in making determinations regarding the meaning or interpretation of any provision of this subchapter for which the Bureau has authority to prescribe regulations; or

(2) the Board in making determinations regarding the meaning or interpretation of section 1693*o*–2 of this title.

(Pub.L. 90–321, Title IX, § 904, as added Pub.L. 95–630, Title XX, § 2001, Nov. 10, 1978, 92 Stat. 3730, and amended Pub.L. 104–193, Title VIII, § 891, Title IX, § 907, Aug. 22, 1996, 110 Stat. 2346, 2350; Pub.L. 106–102, Title VII, § 702, Nov. 12, 1999, 113 Stat. 1463; Pub.L. 111–203, Title X, §§ 1073(a)(2), 1084(1), (3), July 21, 2010, 124 Stat. 2060, 2081; Pub.L. 112–216, § 1, Dec. 20, 2012, 126 Stat. 1590.)

§ 1693c. Terms and conditions of transfers [CCPA § 905]

(a) Disclosures; time; form; contents

The terms and conditions of electronic fund transfers involving a consumer's account shall be disclosed at the time the consumer contracts for an electronic fund transfer service, in accordance with regulations of the Bureau. Such disclosures shall be in readily understandable language and shall include, to the extent applicable—

(1) the consumer's liability for unauthorized electronic fund transfers and, at the financial institution's option, notice of the advisability of prompt reporting of any loss, theft, or unauthorized use of a card, code, or other means of access;

(2) the telephone number and address of the person or office to be notified in the event the consumer believes than[1] an unauthorized electronic fund transfer has been or may be effected;

(3) the type and nature of electronic fund transfers which the consumer may initiate, including any limitations on the frequency or dollar amount of such transfers, except that the details of such limitations need not be disclosed if their confidentiality is necessary to maintain the security of an electronic fund transfer system, as determined by the Bureau;

(4) any charges for electronic fund transfers or for the right to make such transfers;

(5) the consumer's right to stop payment of a preauthorized electronic fund transfer and the procedure to initiate such a stop payment order;

(6) the consumer's right to receive documentation of electronic fund transfers under section 1693d of this title;

(7) a summary, in a form prescribed by regulations of the Bureau, of the error resolution provisions of section 1693f of this title and the consumer's rights thereunder. The financial institution shall thereafter transmit such summary at least once per calendar year;

(8) the financial institution's liability to the consumer under section 1693h of this title;

(9) under what circumstances the financial institution will in the ordinary course of business disclose information concerning the consumer's account to third persons; and

(10) a notice to the consumer that a fee may be imposed by—

(A) an automated teller machine operator (as defined in section 1693b(d)(3)(D)(i) of this title) if the consumer initiates a transfer from an automated teller machine that is not operated by the person issuing the card or other means of access; and

(B) any national, regional, or local network utilized to effect the transaction.

(b) Notification of changes to consumer

A financial institution shall notify a consumer in writing at least twenty-one days prior to the effective date of any change in any term or condition of the consumer's account required to be disclosed under subsection (a) of this section if such change would result in greater cost or liability for such consumer or decreased access to the consumer's account. A financial institution may, however, implement a change in the terms or conditions of an account without prior notice when such change is immediately necessary to maintain or restore the security of an electronic fund transfer system or a consumer's account. Subject to subsection (a)(3) of this section, the Bureau shall require subsequent notification if such a change is made permanent.

(c) Time for disclosures respecting accounts accessible prior to effective date of this subchapter

For any account of a consumer made accessible to electronic fund transfers prior to the effective date of this subchapter, the information required to be disclosed to the consumer under subsection (a) of this section shall be disclosed not later than the earlier of—

[1] So in original. Probably should be "that".

(1) the first periodic statement required by section 1693d(c) of this title after the effective date of this subchapter; or

(2) thirty days after the effective date of this subchapter.

(Pub.L. 90–321, Title IX, § 905, as added Pub.L. 95–630, Title XX, § 2001, Nov. 10, 1978, 92 Stat. 3730, and amended Pub.L. 106–102, Title VII, § 703, Nov. 12, 1999, 113 Stat. 1464; Pub.L. 111–203, Title X, § 1084(1), July 21, 2010, 124 Stat. 2081.)

§ 1693d. Documentation of transfers [CCPA § 906]

(a) Availability of written documentation to consumer; contents

For each electronic fund transfer initiated by a consumer from an electronic terminal, the financial institution holding such consumer's account shall, directly or indirectly, at the time the transfer is initiated, make available to the consumer written documentation of such transfer. The documentation shall clearly set forth to the extent applicable—

(1) the amount involved and date the transfer is initiated;

(2) the type of transfer;

(3) the identity of the consumer's account with the financial institution from which or to which funds are transferred;

(4) the identity of any third party to whom or from whom funds are transferred; and

(5) the location or identification of the electronic terminal involved.

(b) Notice of credit to consumer

For a consumer's account which is scheduled to be credited by a preauthorized electronic fund transfer from the same payor at least once in each successive sixty-day period, except where the payor provides positive notice of the transfer to the consumer, the financial institution shall elect to provide promptly either positive notice to the consumer when the credit is made as scheduled, or negative notice to the consumer when the credit is not made as scheduled, in accordance with regulations of the Bureau. The means of notice elected shall be disclosed to the consumer in accordance with section 1693c of this title.

(c) Periodic statement; contents

A financial institution shall provide each consumer with a periodic statement for each account of such consumer that may be accessed by means of an electronic fund transfer. Except as provided in subsections (d) and (e) of this section, such statement shall be provided at least monthly for each monthly or shorter cycle in which an electronic fund transfer affecting the account has occurred, or every three months, whichever is more frequent. The statement, which may include information regarding transactions other than electronic fund transfers, shall clearly set forth—

(1) with regard to each electronic fund transfer during the period, the information described in subsection (a) of this section, which may be provided on an accompanying document;

(2) the amount of any fee or charge assessed by the financial institution during the period for electronic fund transfers or for account maintenance;

(3) the balances in the consumer's account at the beginning of the period and at the close of the period; and

(4) the address and telephone number to be used by the financial institution for the purpose of receiving any statement inquiry or notice of account error from the consumer. Such address and telephone number shall be preceded by the caption "Direct Inquiries To:" or other similar language indicating that the address and number are to be used for such inquiries or notices.

(d) Consumer passbook accounts

In the case of a consumer's passbook account which may not be accessed by electronic fund transfers other than preauthorized electronic fund transfers crediting the account, a financial institution may, in lieu of complying with the requirements of subsection (c) of this section, upon presentation of the passbook provide the consumer in writing with the amount and date of each such transfer involving the account since the passbook was last presented.

(e) Accounts other than passbook accounts

In the case of a consumer's account, other than a passbook account, which may not be accessed by electronic fund transfers other than preauthorized electronic fund transfers crediting the account, the financial institution may provide a periodic statement on a quarterly basis which otherwise complies with the requirements of subsection (c) of this section.

(f) Documentation as evidence

In any action involving a consumer, any documentation required by this section to be given to the consumer which indicates that an electronic fund transfer was made to another person shall be admissible as evidence of such transfer and shall constitute prima facie proof that such transfer was made.

(Pub.L. 90–321, Title IX, § 906, as added Pub.L. 95–630, Title XX, § 2001, Nov. 10, 1978, 92 Stat. 3731; Pub.L. 111–203, Title X, § 1084(1), July 21, 2010, 124 Stat. 2081.)

§ 1693e. Preauthorized transfers [CCPA § 907]

(a) A preauthorized electronic fund transfer from a consumer's account may be authorized by the consumer only in writing, and a copy of such authorization shall be provided to the consumer when made. A consumer may stop payment of a preauthorized electronic fund transfer by notifying the financial institution orally or in writing at any time up to three business days preceding the scheduled date of such transfer. The financial institution may require written confirmation to be provided to it within fourteen days of an oral notification if, when the oral notification is made, the consumer is advised of such requirement and the address to which such confirmation should be sent.

(b) In the case of preauthorized transfers from a consumer's account to the same person which may vary in amount, the financial institution or designated payee shall, prior to each transfer, provide reasonable advance notice to the consumer, in accordance with regulations of the Bureau.

(Pub.L. 90–321, Title IX, § 907, as added Pub.L. 95–630, Title XX, § 2001, Nov. 10, 1978, 92 Stat. 3733; Pub.L. 111–203, Title X, § 1084(1), July 21, 2010, 124 Stat. 2081.)

§ 1693f. Error resolution [CCPA § 908]

(a) Notification to financial institution of error

If a financial institution, within sixty days after having transmitted to a consumer documentation pursuant to section 1693d(a), (c), or (d) of this title or notification pursuant to section 1693d(b) of this title, receives oral or written notice in which the consumer—

(1) sets forth or otherwise enables the financial institution to identify the name and account number of the consumer;

(2) indicates the consumer's belief that the documentation, or, in the case of notification pursuant to section 1693d(b) of this title, the consumer's account, contains an error and the amount of such error; and

(3) sets forth the reasons for the consumer's belief (where applicable) that an error has occurred,

the financial institution shall investigate the alleged error, determine whether an error has occurred, and report or mail the results of such investigation and determination to the consumer within ten business days. The financial institution may require written confirmation to be provided to it within ten business days of an oral notification of error if, when the oral notification is made, the consumer is advised of such requirement and the address to which such confirmation should be sent. A financial institution which requires written confirmation in accordance with the previous sentence need not provisionally recredit a consumer's account in accordance with subsection (c) of this section, nor shall the financial institution be liable under subsection (e) of this section if the written confirmation is not received within the ten-day period referred to in the previous sentence.

(b) Correction of error; interest

If the financial institution determines that an error did occur, it shall promptly, but in no event more than one business day after such determination, correct the error, subject to section 1693g of this title, including the crediting of interest where applicable.

(c) Provisional recredit of consumer's account

If a financial institution receives notice of an error in the manner and within the time period specified in subsection (a) of this section, it may, in lieu of the requirements of subsections (a) and (b) of this section, within ten business days after receiving such notice provisionally recredit the consumer's account for the amount alleged to be in error, subject to section 1693g of this title, including interest where applicable, pending the conclusion of its investigation and its determination of whether an error has occurred. Such investigation shall be concluded not later than forty-five days after receipt of notice of the error. During the pendency of the investigation, the consumer shall have full use of the funds provisionally recredited.

(d) Absence of error; finding; explanation

If the financial institution determines after its investigation pursuant to subsection (a) or (c) of this section that an error did not occur, it shall deliver or mail to the consumer an explanation of its findings within 3 business days after the conclusion of its investigation, and upon request of the consumer promptly deliver or mail to the consumer reproductions of all documents which the financial institution relied on to conclude that such error did not occur. The financial institution shall include notice of the right to request reproductions with the explanation of its findings.

(e) Treble damages

If in any action under section 1693m of this title, the court finds that—

(1) the financial institution did not provisionally recredit a consumer's account within the ten-day period specified in subsection (c) of this section, and the financial institution (A) did not make a good faith investigation of the alleged error, or (B) did not have a reasonable basis for believing that the consumer's account was not in error; or

(2) the financial institution knowingly and willfully concluded that the consumer's account was not in error when such conclusion could not reasonably have been drawn from the evidence available to the financial institution at the time of its investigation,

then the consumer shall be entitled to treble damages determined under section 1693m(a)(1) of this title.

(f) Acts constituting error

For the purpose of this section, an error consists of—

(1) an unauthorized electronic fund transfer;

(2) an incorrect electronic fund transfer from or to the consumer's account;

(3) the omission from a periodic statement of an electronic fund transfer affecting the consumer's account which should have been included;

(4) a computational error by the financial institution;

(5) the consumer's receipt of an incorrect amount of money from an electronic terminal;

(6) a consumer's request for additional information or clarification concerning an electronic fund transfer or any documentation required by this subchapter; or

(7) any other error described in regulations of the Bureau.

(Pub.L. 90–321, Title IX, § 908, as added Pub.L. 95–630, Title XX, § 2001, Nov. 10, 1978, 92 Stat. 3733; Pub.L. 111–203, Title X, § 1084(1), July 21, 2010, 124 Stat. 2081.)

§ 1693g. Consumer liability [CCPA § 909]

(a) Unauthorized electronic fund transfers; limit

A consumer shall be liable for any unauthorized electronic fund transfer involving the account of such consumer only if the card or other means of access utilized for such transfer was an accepted card or other meanas[1] of access and if the issuer of such card, code, or other means of access has provided a means whereby the user of such card, code, or other means of access can be identified as the person authorized to use it, such as by signature, photograph, or fingerprint or by electronic or mechanical confirmation. In no event, however, shall a consumer's liability for an unauthorized transfer exceed the lesser of—

(1) $50; or

(2) the amount of money or value of property or services obtained in such unauthorized electronic fund transfer prior to the time the financial institution is notified of, or otherwise becomes aware of, circumstances which lead to the reasonable belief that an unauthorized electronic fund transfer involving the consumer's account has been or may be effected. Notice under this paragraph is sufficient when such steps have been taken as may be reasonably required in the ordinary course of business to provide the financial institution with the pertinent information, whether or not any particular officer, employee, or agent of the financial institution does in fact receive such information.

Notwithstanding the foregoing, reimbursement need not be made to the consumer for losses the financial institution establishes would not have occurred but for the failure of the consumer to report within sixty days of transmittal of the statement (or in extenuating circumstances such as extended travel or hospitalization, within a reasonable time under the circumstances) any unauthorized electronic fund transfer or account error which appears on the periodic statement provided to the consumer under section 1693d of this title. In addition, reimbursement need not be made to the consumer for losses which the financial institution establishes would not have occurred but for the failure of the consumer to report any loss or theft of a card or other means of access within two business days after the consumer learns of the loss or theft (or in extenuating circumstances such as extended travel or hospitalization, within a longer period which is reasonable under the circumstances), but the consumer's liability under this subsection in any such case may not exceed a total of $500, or the amount of unauthorized electronic fund transfers which occur following the close of two business days (or such longer period) after the consumer learns of the loss or theft but prior to notice to the financial institution under this subsection, whichever is less.

(b) Burden of proof

In any action which involves a consumer's liability for an unauthorized electronic fund transfer, the burden of proof is upon the financial institution to show that the electronic fund transfer was authorized or, if the electronic fund transfer was unauthorized, then the burden of proof is upon the financial institution to establish that the conditions of liability set forth in subsection (a) of this section have been met, and, if the transfer was initiated after the effective date of section 1693c of this title, that the disclosures required to be made to the consumer under section 1693c(a)(1) and (2) of this title were in fact made in accordance with such section.

(c) Determination of limitation on liability

In the event of a transaction which involves both an unauthorized electronic fund transfer and an extension of credit as defined in section 1602(e) of this title pursuant to an agreement between the consumer and the financial institution to extend such credit to the consumer in the event the consumer's account is overdrawn, the limitation on the consumer's liability for such transaction shall be determined solely in accordance with this section.

(d) Restriction on liability

Nothing in this section imposes liability upon a consumer for an unauthorized electronic fund transfer in excess of his liability for such a transfer under other applicable law or under any agreement with the consumer's financial institution.

---

[1] So in original. Probably should be "means".

(e) Scope of liability

Except as provided in this section, a consumer incurs no liability from an unauthorized electronic fund transfer.

(Pub.L. 90–321, Title IX, § 909, as added Pub.L. 95–630, Title XX, § 2001, Nov. 10, 1978, 92 Stat. 3734.)

§ 1693h. Liability of financial institutions [CCPA § 910]

(a) Action or failure to act proximately causing damages

Subject to subsections (b) and (c) of this section, a financial institution shall be liable to a consumer for all damages proximately caused by—

(1) the financial institution's failure to make an electronic fund transfer, in accordance with the terms and conditions of an account, in the correct amount or in a timely manner when properly instructed to do so by the consumer, except where—

(A) the consumer's account has insufficient funds;

(B) the funds are subject to legal process or other encumbrance restricting such transfer;

(C) such transfer would exceed an established credit limit;

(D) an electronic terminal has insufficient cash to complete the transaction; or

(E) as otherwise provided in regulations of the Bureau;

(2) the financial institution's failure to make an electronic fund transfer due to insufficient funds when the financal[1] institution failed to credit, in accordance with the terms and conditions of an account, a deposit of funds to the consumer's account which would have provided sufficient funds to make the transfer, and

(3) the financial institution's failure to stop payment of a preauthorized transfer from a consumer's account when instructed to do so in accordance with the terms and conditions of the account.

(b) Acts of God and technical malfunctions

A financial institution shall not be liable under subsection (a)(1) or (2) of this section if the financial institution shows by a preponderance of the evidence that its action or failure to act resulted from—

(1) an act of God or other circumstance beyond its control, that it exercised reasonable care to prevent such an occurrence, and that it exercised such diligence as the circumstances required; or

(2) a technical malfunction which was known to the consumer at the time he attempted to initiate an electronic fund transfer or, in the case of a preauthorized transfer, at the time such transfer should have occurred.

(c) Intent

In the case of a failure described in subsection (a) of this section which was not intentional and which resulted from a bona fide error, notwithstanding the maintenance of procedures reasonably adapted to avoid any such error, the financial institution shall be liable for actual damages proved.

(d) Exception for damaged notices

If the notice required to be posted pursuant to section 1693b(d)(3)(B)(i) of this title by an automated teller machine operator has been posted by such operator in compliance with such section and the notice is subsequently removed, damaged, or altered by any person other than the operator of the automated teller machine, the operator shall have no liability under this section for failure to comply with section 1693b(d)(3)(B)(i) of this title.

---

[1] So in original. Probably should be "financial".

(Pub.L. 90–321, Title IX, § 910, as added Pub.L. 95–630, Title XX, § 2001, Nov. 10, 1978, 92 Stat. 3735, and amended Pub.L. 106–102, Title VII, § 705, Nov. 12, 1999, 113 Stat. 1465; Pub.L. 111–203, Title X, § 1084(1), July 21, 2010, 124 Stat. 2081.)

§ 1693i. Issuance of cards or other means of access [CCPA § 911]

(a) Prohibition; proper issuance

No person may issue to a consumer any card, code, or other means of access to such consumer's account for the purpose of initiating an electronic fund transfer other than—

(1) in response to a request or application therefor; or

(2) as a renewal of, or in substitution for, an accepted card, code, or other means of access, whether issued by the initial issuer or a successor.

(b) Exceptions

Notwithstanding the provisions of subsection (a) of this section, a person may distribute to a consumer on an unsolicited basis a card, code, or other means of access for use in initiating an electronic fund transfer from such consumer's account, if—

(1) such card, code, or other means of access is not validated;

(2) such distribution is accompanied by a complete disclosure, in accordance with section 1693c of this title, of the consumer's rights and liabilities which will apply if such card, code, or other means of access is validated;

(3) such distribution is accompanied by a clear explanation, in accordance with regulations of the Bureau, that such card, code, or other means of access is not validated and how the consumer may dispose of such code, card, or other means of access if validation is not desired; and

(4) such card, code, or other means of access is validated only in response to a request or application from the consumer, upon verification of the consumer's identity.

(c) Validation

For the purpose of subsection (b) of this section, a card, code, or other means of access is validated when it may be used to initiate an electronic fund transfer.

(Pub.L. 90–321, Title IX, § 911, as added Pub.L. 95–630, Title XX, § 2001, Nov. 10, 1978, 92 Stat. 3736; Pub.L. 111–203, Title X, § 1084(1), July 21, 2010, 124 Stat. 2081.)

§ 1693j. Suspension of obligations [CCPA § 912]

If a system malfunction prevents the effectuation of an electronic fund transfer initiated by a consumer to another person, and such other person has agreed to accept payment by such means, the consumer's obligation to the other person shall be suspended until the malfunction is corrected and the electronic fund transfer may be completed, unless such other person has subsequently, by written request, demanded payment by means other than an electronic fund transfer.

(Pub.L. 90–321, Title IX, § 912, as added Pub.L. 95–630, Title XX, § 2001, Nov. 10, 1978, 92 Stat. 3737.)

§ 1693k. Compulsory use of electronic fund transfers [CCPA § 913]

No person may—

(1) condition the extension of credit to a consumer on such consumer's repayment by means of preauthorized electronic fund transfers; or

(2) require a consumer to establish an account for receipt of electronic fund transfers with a particular financial institution as a condition of employment or receipt of a government benefit.

(Pub.L. 90–321, Title IX, § 913, as added Pub.L. 95–630, Title XX, § 2001, Nov. 10, 1978, 92 Stat. 3737.)

§ 1693*l*. Waiver of rights [CCPA § 914]

No writing or other agreement between a consumer and any other person may contain any provision which constitutes a waiver of any right conferred or cause of action created by this subchapter. Nothing in this section prohibits, however, any writing or other agreement which grants to a consumer a more extensive right or remedy or greater protection than contained in this subchapter or a waiver given in settlement of a dispute or action.

(Pub.L. 90–321, Title IX, § 914, as added Pub.L. 95–630, Title XX, § 2001, Nov. 10, 1978, 92 Stat. 3737.)

§ 1693*l*–1. General-use prepaid cards, gift certificates, and store gift cards [CCPA § 915]

(a) Definitions

In this section, the following definitions shall apply:

(1) Dormancy fee; inactivity charge or fee

The terms "dormancy fee" and "inactivity charge or fee" mean a fee, charge, or penalty for non-use or inactivity of a gift certificate, store gift card, or general-use prepaid card.

(2) General use prepaid card, gift certificate, and store gift card

(A) General use[1] prepaid card

The term "general-use prepaid card" means a card or other payment code or device issued by any person that is—

(i) redeemable at multiple, unaffiliated merchants or service providers, or automated teller machines;

(ii) issued in a requested amount, whether or not that amount may, at the option of the issuer, be increased in value or reloaded if requested by the holder;

(iii) purchased or loaded on a prepaid basis; and

(iv) honored, upon presentation, by merchants for goods or services, or at automated teller machines.

(B) Gift certificate

The term "gift certificate" means an electronic promise that is—

(i) redeemable at a single merchant or an affiliated group of merchants that share the same name, mark, or logo;

(ii) issued in a specified amount that may not be increased or reloaded;

(iii) purchased on a prepaid basis in exchange for payment; and

(iv) honored upon presentation by such single merchant or affiliated group of merchants for goods or services.

(C) Store gift card

The term "store gift card" means an electronic promise, plastic card, or other payment code or device that is—

(i) redeemable at a single merchant or an affiliated group of merchants that share the same name, mark, or logo;

(ii) issued in a specified amount, whether or not that amount may be increased in value or reloaded at the request of the holder;

(iii) purchased on a prepaid basis in exchange for payment; and

---

[1] So in original. Probably should be "General-use".

(iv) honored upon presentation by such single merchant or affiliated group of merchants for goods or services.

(D) Exclusions

The terms "general-use prepaid card", "gift certificate", and "store gift card" do not include an electronic promise, plastic card, or payment code or device that is—

(i) used solely for telephone services;

(ii) reloadable and not marketed or labeled as a gift card or gift certificate;

(iii) a loyalty, award, or promotional gift card, as defined by the Bureau;

(iv) not marketed to the general public;

(v) issued in paper form only (including for tickets and events); or

(vi) redeemable solely for admission to events or venues at a particular location or group of affiliated locations, which may also include services or goods obtainable—

(I) at the event or venue after admission; or

(II) in conjunction with admission to such events or venues, at specific locations affiliated with and in geographic proximity to the event or venue.

(3) Service fee

(A) In general

The term "service fee" means a periodic fee, charge, or penalty for holding or use of a gift certificate, store gift card, or general-use prepaid card.

(B) Exclusion

With respect to a general-use prepaid card, the term "service fee" does not include a one-time initial issuance fee.

(b) Prohibition on imposition of fees or charges

(1) In general

Except as provided under paragraphs (2) through (4), it shall be unlawful for any person to impose a dormancy fee, an inactivity charge or fee, or a service fee with respect to a gift certificate, store gift card, or general-use prepaid card.

(2) Exceptions

A dormancy fee, inactivity charge or fee, or service fee may be charged with respect to a gift certificate, store gift card, or general-use prepaid card, if—

(A) there has been no activity with respect to the certificate or card in the 12-month period ending on the date on which the charge or fee is imposed;

(B) the disclosure requirements of paragraph (3) have been met;

(C) not more than one fee may be charged in any given month; and

(D) any additional requirements that the Bureau may establish through rulemaking under subsection (d) have been met.

(3) Disclosure requirements

The disclosure requirements of this paragraph are met if—

(A) the gift certificate, store gift card, or general-use prepaid card clearly and conspicuously states—

(i) that a dormancy fee, inactivity charge or fee, or service fee may be charged;

(ii) the amount of such fee or charge;

(iii) how often such fee or charge may be assessed; and

(iv) that such fee or charge may be assessed for inactivity; and

(B) the issuer or vendor of such certificate or card informs the purchaser of such charge or fee before such certificate or card is purchased, regardless of whether the certificate or card is purchased in person, over the Internet, or by telephone.

(4) Exclusion

The prohibition under paragraph (1) shall not apply to any gift certificate—

(A) that is distributed pursuant to an award, loyalty, or promotional program, as defined by the Bureau; and

(B) with respect to which, there is no money or other value exchanged.

(c) Prohibition on sale of gift cards with expiration dates

(1) In general

Except as provided under paragraph (2), it shall be unlawful for any person to sell or issue a gift certificate, store gift card, or general-use prepaid card that is subject to an expiration date.

(2) Exceptions

A gift certificate, store gift card, or general-use prepaid card may contain an expiration date if—

(A) the expiration date is not earlier than 5 years after the date on which the gift certificate was issued, or the date on which card funds were last loaded to a store gift card or general-use prepaid card; and

(B) the terms of expiration are clearly and conspicuously stated.

(d) Additional rulemaking

(1) In general

The Bureau shall—

(A) prescribe regulations to carry out this section, in addition to any other rules or regulations required by this subchapter, including such additional requirements as appropriate relating to the amount of dormancy fees, inactivity charges or fees, or service fees that may be assessed and the amount of remaining value of a gift certificate, store gift card, or general-use prepaid card below which such charges or fees may be assessed; and

(B) shall[2] determine the extent to which the individual definitions and provisions of this subchapter or Regulation E should apply to general-use prepaid cards, gift certificates, and store gift cards.

(2) Consultation

In prescribing regulations under this subsection, the Bureau shall consult with the Federal Trade Commission.

(3) Timing; effective date

The regulations required by this subsection shall be issued in final form not later than 9 months after May 22, 2009.

(Pub.L. 90–321, Title IX, § 915, as added Pub.L. 111–24, Title IV, § 401(2), May 22, 2009, 123 Stat. 1751; Pub.L. 111–203, Title X, § 1084(1), July 21, 2010, 124 Stat. 2081.)

[2] So in original. The word "shall" probably should not appear.

§ 1693m. Civil liability [CCPA § 916]

(a) Individual or class action for damages; amount of award

Except as otherwise provided by this section and section 1693h of this title, any person who fails to comply with any provision of this subchapter with respect to any consumer, except for an error resolved in accordance with section 1693f of this title, is liable to such consumer in an amount equal to the sum of—

(1) any actual damage sustained by such consumer as a result of such failure;

(2)(A) in the case of an individual action, an amount not less than $100 nor greater than $1,000; or

(B) in the case of a class action, such amount as the court may allow, except that (i) as to each member of the class no minimum recovery shall be applicable, and (ii) the total recovery under this subparagraph in any class action or series of class actions arising out of the same failure to comply by the same person shall not be more than the lesser of $500,000 or 1 per centum of the net worth of the defendant; and

(3) in the case of any successful action to enforce the foregoing liability, the costs of the action, together with a reasonable attorney's fee as determined by the court.

(b) Factors determining amount of award

In determining the amount of liability in any action under subsection (a) of this section, the court shall consider, among other relevant factors—

(1) in any individual action under subsection (a)(2)(A) of this section, the frequency and persistence of noncompliance, the nature of such noncompliance, and the extent to which the noncompliance was intentional; or

(2) in any class action under subsection (a)(2)(B) of this section, the frequency and persistence of noncompliance, the nature of such noncompliance, the resources of the defendant, the number of persons adversely affected, and the extent to which the noncompliance was intentional.

(c) Unintentional violations; bona fide error

Except as provided in section 1693h of this title, a person may not be held liable in any action brought under this section for a violation of this subchapter if the person shows by a preponderance of evidence that the violation was not intentional and resulted from a bona fide error notwithstanding the maintenance of procedures reasonably adapted to avoid any such error.

(d) Good faith compliance with rule, regulation, or interpretation

No provision of this section or section 1693n of this title imposing any liability shall apply to—

(1) any act done or omitted in good faith in conformity with any rule, regulation, or interpretation thereof by the Bureau or the Board or in conformity with any interpretation or approval by an official or employee of the Bureau of Consumer Financial Protection or the Federal Reserve System duly authorized by the Bureau or the Board to issue such interpretations or approvals under such procedures as the Bureau or the Board may prescribe therefor; or

(2) any failure to make disclosure in proper form if a financial institution utilized an appropriate model clause issued by the Bureau or the Board,

notwithstanding that after such act, omission, or failure has occurred, such rule, regulation, approval, or model clause is amended, rescinded, or determined by judicial or other authority to be invalid for any reason.

(e) Notification to consumer prior to action; adjustment of consumer's account

A person has no liability under this section for any failure to comply with any requirement under this subchapter if, prior to the institution of an action under this section, the person notifies the consumer concerned of the failure, complies with the requirements of this subchapter, and makes an appropriate adjustment to the consumer's account and pays actual damages or, where applicable, damages in accordance with section 1693h of this title.

(f) Action in bad faith or for harassment; attorney's fees

On a finding by the court that an unsuccessful action under this section was brought in bad faith or for purposes of harassment, the court shall award to the defendant attorney's fees reasonable in relation to the work expended and costs.

(g) Jurisdiction of courts; time for maintenance of action

Without regard to the amount in controversy, any action under this section may be brought in any United States district court, or in any other court of competent jurisdiction, within one year from the date of the occurrence of the violation.

(Pub.L. 90–321, Title IX, § 916, formerly § 915, as added Pub.L. 95–630, Title XX, § 2001, Nov. 10, 1978, 92 Stat. 3737; renumbered § 916, Pub.L. 111–24, Title IV, § 401(1), May 22, 2009, 123 Stat. 1751; Pub.L. 111–203, Title X, §§ 1084(1), (4), July 21, 2010, 124 Stat. 2081, 2082.)

§ 1693n. Criminal liability [CCPA § 917]

(a) Violations respecting giving of false or inaccurate information, failure to provide information, and failure to comply with provisions of this subchapter

Whoever knowingly and willfully—

(1) gives false or inaccurate information or fails to provide information which he is required to disclose by this subchapter or any regulation issued thereunder; or

(2) otherwise fails to comply with any provision of this subchapter;

shall be fined not more than $5,000 or imprisoned not more than one year, or both.

(b) Violations affecting interstate or foreign commerce

Whoever—

(1) knowingly, in a transaction affecting interstate or foreign commerce, uses or attempts or conspires to use any counterfeit, fictitious, altered, forged, lost, stolen, or fraudulently obtained debit instrument to obtain money, goods, services, or anything else of value which within any one-year period has a value aggregating $1,000 or more; or

(2) with unlawful or fraudulent intent, transports or attempts or conspires to transport in interstate or foreign commerce a counterfeit, fictitious, altered, forged, lost, stolen, or fraudulently obtained debit instrument knowing the same to be counterfeit, fictitious, altered, forged, lost, stolen, or fraudulently obtained; or

(3) with unlawful or fraudulent intent, uses any instrumentality of interstate or foreign commerce to sell or transport a counterfeit, fictitious, altered, forged, lost, stolen, or fraudulently obtained debit instrument knowing the same to be counterfeit, fictitious, altered, forged, lost, stolen, or fraudulently obtained; or

(4) knowingly receives, conceals, uses, or transports money, goods, services, or anything else of value (except tickets for interstate or foreign transportation) which (A) within any one-year period has a value aggregating $1,000 or more, (B) has moved in or is part of, or which constitutes interstate or foreign commerce, and (C) has been obtained with a counterfeit, fictitious, altered, forged, lost, stolen, or fraudulently obtained debit instrument; or

(5) knowingly receives, conceals, uses, sells, or transports in interstate or foreign commerce one or more tickets for interstate or foreign transportation, which (A) within any one-year period have a value aggregating $500 or more, and (B) have been purchased or obtained with one or more counterfeit, fictitious, altered, forged, lost, stolen, or fraudulently obtained debit instrument; or

(6) in a transaction affecting interstate or foreign commerce, furnishes money, property, services, or anything else of value, which within any one-year period has a value aggregating $1,000 or more, through the use of any counterfeit, fictitious, altered, forged, lost, stolen, or fraudulently obtained debit instrument knowing the same to be counterfeit, fictitious, altered, forged, lost, stolen, or fraudulently obtained—

shall be fined not more than $10,000 or imprisoned not more than ten years, or both.

(c) "Debit instrument" defined

As used in this section, the term "debit instrument" means a card, code, or other device, other than a check, draft, or similar paper instrument, by the use of which a person may initiate an electronic fund transfer.

(Pub.L. 90–321, Title IX, § 917, formerly § 916, as added Pub.L. 95–630, Title XX, § 2001, Nov. 10, 1978, 92 Stat. 3738; renumbered § 917, Pub.L. 111–24, Title IV, § 401(1), May 22, 2009, 123 Stat. 1751.)

§ 1693*o*. Administrative enforcement [CCPA § 918]

(a) Enforcing agencies

Subject to subtitle B of the Consumer Protection Act of 2010 [12 U.S.C. §§ 5511–5519] compliance with the requirements imposed under this subchapter shall be enforced under—

(1) section 1818 of Title 12, by the appropriate Federal banking agency, as defined in section 1813(q) of Title 12, with respect to—

(A) national banks, Federal savings associations, and Federal branches and Federal agencies of foreign banks;

(B) member banks of the Federal Reserve System (other than national banks), branches and agencies of foreign banks (other than Federal branches, Federal agencies, and insured State branches of foreign banks), commercial lending companies owned or controlled by foreign banks, and organizations operating under section 25 or 25A of the Federal Reserve Act; and

(C) banks and State savings associations insured by the Federal Deposit Insurance Corporation (other than members of the Federal Reserve System), and insured State branches of foreign banks;

(2) the Federal Credit Union Act [12 U.S.C. § 1751 et seq.], by the Administrator of the National Credit Union Administration with respect to any Federal credit union;

(3) part A of subtitle VII of title 49, by the Secretary of Transportation, with respect to any air carrier or foreign air carrier subject to that part;

(4) the Securities Exchange Act of 1934 [15 U.S.C. § 78a et seq.], by the Securities and Exchange Commission, with respect to any broker or dealer subject to that Act and[1]

(5) subtitle E of the Consumer Financial Protection Act of 2010, by the Bureau, with respect to any person subject to this subchapter, except that the Bureau shall not have authority to enforce the requirements of section 1693*o*–2 of this title or any regulations prescribed by the Board under section 1693*o*–2 of this title.

The terms used in paragraph (1) that are not defined in this subchapter or otherwise defined in section 3(s) of the Federal Deposit Insurance Act (12 U.S.C. 1813(s)) shall have the meaning given to them in section 1(b) of the International Banking Act of 1978 (12 U.S.C. 3101).

(b) Violations of subchapter deemed violations of pre-existing statutory requirements; additional powers

For the purpose of the exercise by any agency referred to in any of paragraphs (1) through (4) subsection (a) of this section of its powers under any Act referred to in that subsection, a violation of any requirement imposed under this subchapter shall be deemed to be a violation of a requirement imposed under that Act. In addition to its powers under any provision of law specifically referred to in any of paragraphs (1) through (4) subsection (a) of this section, each of the agencies referred to in that subsection may exercise, for the

[1] So in original. Probably should be "; and".

purpose of enforcing compliance with any requirement imposed under this subchapter, any other authority conferred on it by law.

(c) Overall enforcement authority of the Federal Trade Commission

Except to the extent that enforcement of the requirements imposed under this subchapter is specifically committed to some other Government agency under any of paragraphs (1) through (4) of subsection (a), and subject to subtitle B of the Consumer Financial Protection Act of 2010, the Federal Trade Commission shall be authorized to enforce such requirements. For the purpose of the exercise by the Federal Trade Commission of its functions and powers under the Federal Trade Commission Act, a violation of any requirement imposed under this subchapter shall be deemed a violation of a requirement imposed under that Act. All of the functions and powers of the Federal Trade Commission under the Federal Trade Commission Act are available to the Federal Trade Commission to enforce compliance by any person subject to the jurisdiction of the Federal Trade Commission with the requirements imposed under this subchapter, irrespective of whether that person is engaged in commerce or meets any other jurisdictional tests under the Federal Trade Commission Act.

(Pub.L. 90–321, Title IX, § 918, formerly § 917, as added Pub.L. 95–630, Title XX, § 2001, Nov. 10, 1978, 92 Stat. 3739, and amended Pub.L. 101–73, Title VII, § 744(*o*), Aug. 9, 1989, 103 Stat. 440; Pub.L. 102–242, Title II, § 212(f), Dec. 19, 1991, 105 Stat. 2301; Pub.L. 104–287, § 6(h), Oct. 11, 1996, 110 Stat. 3399; renumbered § 918, Pub.L. 111–24, Title IV, § 401(1), May 22, 2009, 123 Stat. 1751; Pub.L. 111–203, Title X, § 1084(5), July 21, 2010, 124 Stat. 2082.)

§ 1693*o*–1. Remittance transfers [CCPA § 919]

(a) Disclosures required for remittance transfers

(1) In general

Each remittance transfer provider shall make disclosures as required under this section and in accordance with rules prescribed by the Bureau. Disclosures required under this section shall be in addition to any other disclosures applicable under this subchapter.

(2) Disclosures

Subject to rules prescribed by the Bureau, a remittance transfer provider shall provide, in writing and in a form that the sender may keep, to each sender requesting a remittance transfer, as applicable to the transaction—

(A) at the time at which the sender requests a remittance transfer to be initiated, and prior to the sender making any payment in connection with the remittance transfer, a disclosure describing—

(i) the amount of currency that will be received by the designated recipient, using the values of the currency into which the funds will be exchanged;

(ii) the amount of transfer and any other fees charged by the remittance transfer provider for the remittance transfer; and

(iii) any exchange rate to be used by the remittance transfer provider for the remittance transfer, to the nearest 1/100th of a point; and

(B) at the time at which the sender makes payment in connection with the remittance transfer—

(i) a receipt showing—

(I) the information described in subparagraph (A);

(II) the promised date of delivery to the designated recipient; and

(III) the name and either the telephone number or the address of the designated recipient, if either the telephone number or the address of the designated recipient is provided by the sender; and

(ii) a statement containing—

(I) information about the rights of the sender under this section regarding the resolution of errors; and

(II) appropriate contact information for—

(aa) the remittance transfer provider; and

(bb) the State agency that regulates the remittance transfer provider and the Bureau, including the toll-free telephone number established under section 5493 of Title 12.

(3) Requirements relating to disclosures

With respect to each disclosure required to be provided under paragraph (2) a remittance transfer provider shall—

(A) provide an initial notice and receipt, as required by subparagraphs (A) and (B) of paragraph (2), and an error resolution statement, as required by subsection (d), that clearly and conspicuously describe the information required to be disclosed therein; and

(B) with respect to any transaction that a sender conducts electronically, comply with the Electronic Signatures in Global and National Commerce Act (15 U.S.C. § 7001 et seq.).

(4) Exception for disclosures of amount received

(A) In general

Subject to the rules prescribed by the Bureau, and except as provided under subparagraph (B), the disclosures required regarding the amount of currency that will be received by the designated recipient shall be deemed to be accurate, so long as the disclosures provide a reasonably accurate estimate of the foreign currency to be received. This paragraph shall apply only to a remittance transfer provider who is an insured depository institution, (as defined in section 1813 of Title 12), or an insured credit union, as defined in section 1752 of Title 12, and if—

(i) a remittance transfer is conducted through a demand deposit, savings deposit, or other asset account that the sender holds with such remittance transfer provider; and

(ii) at the time at which the sender requests the transaction, the remittance transfer provider is unable to know, for reasons beyond its control, the amount of currency that will be made available to the designated recipient.

(B) Deadline

The application of subparagraph (A) shall terminate 5 years after July 21, 2010, unless the Bureau determines that termination of such provision would negatively affect the ability of remittance transfer providers described in subparagraph (A) to send remittances to locations in foreign countries, in which case, the Bureau may, by rule, extend the application of subparagraph (A) to not longer than 10 years after July 21, 2010.

(5) Exemption authority

The Bureau may, by rule, permit a remittance transfer provider to satisfy the requirements of—

(A) paragraph (2)(A) orally, if the transaction is conducted entirely by telephone;

(B) paragraph (2)(B), in the case of a transaction conducted entirely by telephone, by mailing the disclosures required under such subparagraph to the sender, not later than 1 business day after the date on which the transaction is conducted, or by including such documents in the next periodic statement, if the telephone transaction is conducted through a demand deposit, savings deposit, or other asset account that the sender holds with the remittance transfer provider;

(C) subparagraphs (A) and (B) of paragraph (2) together in one written disclosure, but only to the extent that the information provided in accordance with paragraph (3)(A) is accurate at the time at which payment is made in connection with the subject remittance transfer; and

(D) paragraph (2)(A), without compliance with section 101(c) of the Electronic Signatures in Global Commerce Act, if a sender initiates the transaction electronically and the information is displayed electronically in a manner that the sender can keep.

(6) Storefront and Internet notices

(A) In general

(i) Prominent posting

Subject to subparagraph (B), the Bureau may prescribe rules to require a remittance transfer provider to prominently post, and timely update, a notice describing a model remittance transfer for one or more amounts, as the Bureau may determine, which notice shall show the amount of currency that will be received by the designated recipient, using the values of the currency into which the funds will be exchanged.

(ii) Onsite displays

The Bureau may require the notice prescribed under this subparagraph to be displayed in every physical storefront location owned or controlled by the remittance transfer provider.

(iii) Internet notices

Subject to paragraph (3), the Bureau shall prescribe rules to require a remittance transfer provider that provides remittance transfers via the Internet to provide a notice, comparable to a storefront notice described in this subparagraph, located on the home page or landing page (with respect to such remittance transfer services) owned or controlled by the remittance transfer provider.

(iv) Rulemaking authority

In prescribing rules under this subparagraph, the Bureau may impose standards or requirements regarding the provision of the storefront and Internet notices required under this subparagraph and the provision of the disclosures required under paragraphs (2) and (3).

(B) Study and analysis

Prior to proposing rules under subparagraph (A), the Bureau shall undertake appropriate studies and analyses, which shall be consistent with section 1693b(a)(2) of this title, and may include an advanced notice of proposed rulemaking, to determine whether a storefront notice or Internet notice facilitates the ability of a consumer—

(i) to compare prices for remittance transfers; and

(ii) to understand the types and amounts of any fees or costs imposed on remittance transfers.

(b) Foreign language disclosures

The disclosures required under this section shall be made in English and in each of the foreign languages principally used by the remittance transfer provider, or any of its agents, to advertise, solicit, or market, either orally or in writing, at that office.

(c) Regulations regarding transfers to certain nations

If the Bureau determines that a recipient nation does not legally allow, or the method by which transactions are made in the recipient country do not allow, a remittance transfer provider to know the amount of currency that will be received by the designated recipient, the Bureau may prescribe rules (not later than 18 months after July 21, 2010) addressing the issue, which rules shall include standards for a remittance transfer provider to provide—

(1) a receipt that is consistent with subsections (a) and (b); and

(2) a reasonably accurate estimate of the foreign currency to be received, based on the rate provided to the sender by the remittance transfer provider at the time at which the transaction was initiated by the sender.

(d) Remittance transfer errors

(1) Error resolution

(A) In general

If a remittance transfer provider receives oral or written notice from the sender within 180 days of the promised date of delivery that an error occurred with respect to a remittance transfer, including the amount of currency designated in subsection (a)(3)(A) that was to be sent to the designated recipient of the remittance transfer, using the values of the currency into which the funds should have been exchanged, but was not made available to the designated recipient in the foreign country, the remittance transfer provider shall resolve the error pursuant to this subsection and investigate the reason for the error.

(B) Remedies

Not later than 90 days after the date of receipt of a notice from the sender pursuant to subparagraph (A), the remittance transfer provider shall, as applicable to the error and as designated by the sender—

(i) refund to the sender the total amount of funds tendered by the sender in connection with the remittance transfer which was not properly transmitted;

(ii) make available to the designated recipient, without additional cost to the designated recipient or to the sender, the amount appropriate to resolve the error;

(iii) provide such other remedy, as determined appropriate by rule of the Bureau for the protection of senders; or

(iv) provide written notice to the sender that there was no error with an explanation responding to the specific complaint of the sender.

(2) Rules

The Bureau shall establish, by rule issued not later than 18 months after July 21, 2010, clear and appropriate standards for remittance transfer providers with respect to error resolution relating to remittance transfers, to protect senders from such errors. Standards prescribed under this paragraph shall include appropriate standards regarding record keeping, as required, including documentation—

(A) of the complaint of the sender;

(B) that the sender provides the remittance transfer provider with respect to the alleged error; and

(C) of the findings of the remittance transfer provider regarding the investigation of the alleged error that the sender brought to their attention.

(3) Cancellation and refund policy rules

Not later than 18 months after July 21, 2010, the Bureau shall issue final rules regarding appropriate remittance transfer cancellation and refund policies for consumers.

(e) Applicability of this subchapter

(1) In general

A remittance transfer that is not an electronic fund transfer, as defined in section 1693a of this title, shall not be subject to any of the provisions of sections 1693c through 1693k of this title. A remittance transfer that is an electronic fund transfer, as defined in section 1693a of this title, shall be subject to all provisions of this subchapter, except for section 1693f of this title, that are otherwise applicable to electronic fund transfers under this subchapter.

(2) Rule of construction

Nothing in this section shall be construed—

(A) to affect the application to any transaction, to any remittance provider, or to any other person of any of the provisions of subchapter II of chapter 53 of Title 31, section 1829b of Title 12, or chapter 2 of title I of Public Law 91–508 (12 U.S.C. §§ 1951–1959), or any regulations promulgated thereunder; or

(B) to cause any fund transfer that would not otherwise be treated as such under paragraph (1) to be treated as an electronic fund transfer, or as otherwise subject to this subchapter, for the purposes of any of the provisions referred to in subparagraph (A) or any regulations promulgated thereunder.

(f) Acts of agents

(1) In general

A remittance transfer provider shall be liable for any violation of this section by any agent, authorized delegate, or person affiliated with such provider, when such agent, authorized delegate, or affiliate acts for that remittance transfer provider.

(2) Obligations of remittance transfer providers

The Bureau shall prescribe rules to implement appropriate standards or conditions of, liability of a remittance transfer provider, including a provider who acts through an agent or authorized delegate. An agency charged with enforcing the requirements of this section, or rules prescribed by the Bureau under this section, may consider, in any action or other proceeding against a remittance transfer provider, the extent to which the provider had established and maintained policies or procedures for compliance, including policies, procedures, or other appropriate oversight measures designed to assure compliance by an agent or authorized delegate acting for such provider.

(g) Definitions

As used in this section—

(1) the term "designated recipient" means any person located in a foreign country and identified by the sender as the authorized recipient of a remittance transfer to be made by a remittance transfer provider, except that a designated recipient shall not be deemed to be a consumer for purposes of this chapter;

(2) the term "remittance transfer"—

(A) means the electronic (as defined in section 106(2) of the Electronic Signatures in Global and National Commerce Act (15 U.S.C. § 7006(2))) transfer of funds requested by a sender located in any State to a designated recipient that is initiated by a remittance transfer provider, whether or not the sender holds an account with the remittance transfer provider or whether or not the remittance transfer is also an electronic fund transfer, as defined in section 1693a of this title; and

(B) does not include a transfer described in subparagraph (A) in an amount that is equal to or lesser than the amount of a small-value transaction determined, by rule, to be excluded from the requirements under section 1693d(a) of this title;

(3) the term "remittance transfer provider" means any person or financial institution that provides remittance transfers for a consumer in the normal course of its business, whether or not the consumer holds an account with such person or financial institution; and

(4) the term "sender" means a consumer who requests a remittance provider to send a remittance transfer for the consumer to a designated recipient.

(Pub.L. 90–321, Title IX, § 919, as added and amended Pub.L. 111–203, Title X, §§ 1073(a)(4), 1084(1), July 21, 2010, 124 Stat. 2060, 2081.)

§ 1693o–2. Reasonable fees and rules for payment card transactions [CCPA § 920]

(a) Reasonable interchange transaction fees for electronic debit transactions

(1) Regulatory authority over interchange transaction fees

The Board may prescribe regulations, pursuant to section 553 of Title 5, regarding any interchange transaction fee that an issuer may receive or charge with respect to an electronic debit transaction, to implement this subsection (including related definitions), and to prevent circumvention or evasion of this subsection.

(2) Reasonable interchange transaction fees

The amount of any interchange transaction fee that an issuer may receive or charge with respect to an electronic debit transaction shall be reasonable and proportional to the cost incurred by the issuer with respect to the transaction.

(3) Rulemaking required

(A) In general

The Board shall prescribe regulations in final form not later than 9 months after July 21, 2010, to establish standards for assessing whether the amount of any interchange transaction fee described in paragraph (2) is reasonable and proportional to the cost incurred by the issuer with respect to the transaction.

(B) Information collection

The Board may require any issuer (or agent of an issuer) or payment card network to provide the Board with such information as may be necessary to carry out the provisions of this subsection and the Board, in issuing rules under subparagraph (A) and on at least a bi-annual basis thereafter, shall disclose such aggregate or summary information concerning the costs incurred, and interchange transaction fees charged or received, by issuers or payment card networks in connection with the authorization, clearance or settlement of electronic debit transactions as the Board considers appropriate and in the public interest.

(4) Considerations; consultation

In prescribing regulations under paragraph (3)(A), the Board shall—

(A) consider the functional similarity between—

(i) electronic debit transactions; and

(ii) checking transactions that are required within the Federal Reserve bank system to clear at par;

(B) distinguish between—

(i) the incremental cost incurred by an issuer for the role of the issuer in the authorization, clearance, or settlement of a particular electronic debit transaction, which cost shall be considered under paragraph (2); and

(ii) other costs incurred by an issuer which are not specific to a particular electronic debit transaction, which costs shall not be considered under paragraph (2); and

(C) consult, as appropriate, with the Comptroller of the Currency, the Board of Directors of the Federal Deposit Insurance Corporation, the Director of the Office of Thrift Supervision, the National Credit Union Administration Board, the Administrator of the Small Business Administration, and the Director of the Bureau of Consumer Financial Protection.

(5) Adjustments to interchange transaction fees for fraud prevention costs

(A) Adjustments

The Board may allow for an adjustment to the fee amount received or charged by an issuer under paragraph (2), if—

(i) such adjustment is reasonably necessary to make allowance for costs incurred by the issuer in preventing fraud in relation to electronic debit transactions involving that issuer; and

(ii) the issuer complies with the fraud-related standards established by the Board under subparagraph (B), which standards shall—

(I) be designed to ensure that any fraud-related adjustment of the issuer is limited to the amount described in clause (i) and takes into account any fraud-related reimbursements (including amounts from charge-backs) received from consumers, merchants, or payment card networks in relation to electronic debit transactions involving the issuer; and

(II) require issuers to take effective steps to reduce the occurrence of, and costs from, fraud in relation to electronic debit transactions, including through the development and implementation of cost-effective fraud prevention technology.

(B) Rulemaking required

(i) In general

The Board shall prescribe regulations in final form not later than 9 months after July 21, 2010, to establish standards for making adjustments under this paragraph.

(ii) Factors for consideration

In issuing the standards and prescribing regulations under this paragraph, the Board shall consider—

(I) the nature, type, and occurrence of fraud in electronic debit transactions;

(II) the extent to which the occurrence of fraud depends on whether authorization in an electronic debit transaction is based on signature, PIN, or other means;

(III) the available and economical means by which fraud on electronic debit transactions may be reduced;

(IV) the fraud prevention and data security costs expended by each party involved in electronic debit transactions (including consumers, persons who accept debit cards as a form of payment, financial institutions, retailers and payment card networks);

(V) the costs of fraudulent transactions absorbed by each party involved in such transactions (including consumers, persons who accept debit cards as a form of payment, financial institutions, retailers and payment card networks);

(VI) the extent to which interchange transaction fees have in the past reduced or increased incentives for parties involved in electronic debit transactions to reduce fraud on such transactions; and

(VII) such other factors as the Board considers appropriate.

(6) Exemption for small issuers

(A) In general

This subsection shall not apply to any issuer that, together with its affiliates, has assets of less than $10,000,000,000, and the Board shall exempt such issuers from regulations prescribed under paragraph (3)(A).

(B) Definition

For purposes of this paragraph, the term "issuer" shall be limited to the person holding the asset account that is debited through an electronic debit transaction.

(7) Exemption for government-administered payment programs and reloadable prepaid cards

(A) In general

This subsection shall not apply to an interchange transaction fee charged or received with respect to an electronic debit transaction in which a person uses—

(i) a debit card or general-use prepaid card that has been provided to a person pursuant to a Federal, State or local government-administered payment program, in which the person may only use the debit card or general-use prepaid card to transfer or debit funds, monetary value, or other assets that have been provided pursuant to such program; or

(ii) a plastic card, payment code, or device that is—

(I) linked to funds, monetary value, or assets which are purchased or loaded on a prepaid basis;

(II) not issued or approved for use to access or debit any account held by or for the benefit of the card holder (other than a subaccount or other method of recording or tracking funds purchased or loaded on the card on a prepaid basis);

(III) redeemable at multiple, unaffiliated merchants or service providers, or automated teller machines;

(IV) used to transfer or debit funds, monetary value, or other assets; and

(V) reloadable and not marketed or labeled as a gift card or gift certificate.

(B) Exception

Notwithstanding subparagraph (A), after the end of the 1-year period beginning on the effective date provided in paragraph (9), this subsection shall apply to an interchange transaction fee charged or received with respect to an electronic debit transaction described in subparagraph (A)(i) in which a person uses a general-use prepaid card, or an electronic debit transaction described in subparagraph (A)(ii), if any of the following fees may be charged to a person with respect to the card:

(i) A fee for an overdraft, including a shortage of funds or a transaction processed for an amount exceeding the account balance.

(ii) A fee imposed by the issuer for the first withdrawal per month from an automated teller machine that is part of the issuer's designated automated teller machine network.

(C) Definition

For purposes of subparagraph (B), the term "designated automated teller machine network" means either—

(i) all automated teller machines identified in the name of the issuer; or

(ii) any network of automated teller machines identified by the issuer that provides reasonable and convenient access to the issuer's customers.

(D) Reporting

Beginning 12 months after July 21, 2010, the Board shall annually provide a report to the Congress regarding—

(i) the prevalence of the use of general-use prepaid cards in Federal, State or local government-administered payment programs; and

(ii) the interchange transaction fees and cardholder fees charged with respect to the use of such general-use prepaid cards.

(8) Regulatory authority over network fees

(A) In general

The Board may prescribe regulations, pursuant to section 553 of Title 5, regarding any network fee.

(B) Limitation

The authority under subparagraph (A) to prescribe regulations shall be limited to regulations to ensure that—

(i) a network fee is not used to directly or indirectly compensate an issuer with respect to an electronic debit transaction; and

(ii) a network fee is not used to circumvent or evade the restrictions of this subsection and regulations prescribed under such subsection.

(C) Rulemaking required

The Board shall prescribe regulations in final form before the end of the 9-month period beginning on July 21, 2010, to carry out the authorities provided under subparagraph (A).

(9) Effective date

This subsection shall take effect at the end of the 12-month period beginning on July 21, 2010.

(b) Limitation on payment card network restrictions

(1) Prohibitions against exclusivity arrangements

(A) No exclusive network

The Board shall, before the end of the 1-year period beginning on July 21, 2010, prescribe regulations providing that an issuer or payment card network shall not directly or through any agent, processor, or licensed member of a payment card network, by contract, requirement, condition, penalty, or otherwise, restrict the number of payment card networks on which an electronic debit transaction may be processed to—

(i) 1 such network; or

(ii) 2 or more such networks which are owned, controlled, or otherwise operated by—

(I) affiliated persons; or

(II) networks affiliated with such issuer.

(B) No routing restrictions

The Board shall, before the end of the 1-year period beginning on July 21, 2010, prescribe regulations providing that an issuer or payment card network shall not, directly or through any agent, processor, or licensed member of the network, by contract, requirement, condition, penalty, or otherwise, inhibit the ability of any person who accepts debit cards for payments to direct the routing of electronic debit transactions for processing over any payment card network that may process such transactions.

(2) Limitation on restrictions on offering discounts for use of a form of payment

(A) In general

A payment card network shall not, directly or through any agent, processor, or licensed member of the network, by contract, requirement, condition, penalty, or otherwise, inhibit the ability of any person to provide a discount or in-kind incentive for payment by the use of cash, checks, debit cards, or credit cards to the extent that—

(i) in the case of a discount or in-kind incentive for payment by the use of debit cards, the discount or in-kind incentive does not differentiate on the basis of the issuer or the payment card network;

(ii) in the case of a discount or in-kind incentive for payment by the use of credit cards, the discount or in-kind incentive does not differentiate on the basis of the issuer or the payment card network; and

(iii) to the extent required by Federal law and applicable State law, such discount or in-kind incentive is offered to all prospective buyers and disclosed clearly and conspicuously.

(B) Lawful discounts

For purposes of this paragraph, the network may not penalize any person for the providing of a discount that is in compliance with Federal law and applicable State law.

(3) Limitation on restrictions on setting transaction minimums or maximums

(A) In general

A payment card network shall not, directly or through any agent, processor, or licensed member of the network, by contract, requirement, condition, penalty, or otherwise, inhibit the ability—

(i) of any person to set a minimum dollar value for the acceptance by that person of credit cards, to the extent that—

(I) such minimum dollar value does not differentiate between issuers or between payment card networks; and

(II) such minimum dollar value does not exceed $10.00; or

(ii) of any Federal agency or institution of higher education to set a maximum dollar value for the acceptance by that Federal agency or institution of higher education of credit cards, to the extent that such maximum dollar value does not differentiate between issuers or between payment card networks.

(B) Increase in minimum dollar amount

The Board may, by regulation prescribed pursuant to section 553 of Title 5, increase the amount of the dollar value listed in subparagraph (A)(i)(II).

(4) Rule of construction

No provision of this subsection shall be construed to authorize any person—

(A) to discriminate between debit cards within a payment card network on the basis of the issuer that issued the debit card; or

(B) to discriminate between credit cards within a payment card network on the basis of the issuer that issued the credit card.

(c) Definitions

For purposes of this section, the following definitions shall apply:

(1) Affiliate

The term "affiliate" means any company that controls, is controlled by, or is under common control with another company.

(2) Debit card

The term "debit card"—

(A) means any card, or other payment code or device, issued or approved for use through a payment card network to debit an asset account (regardless of the purpose for which the account is established), whether authorization is based on signature, PIN, or other means;

(B) includes a general-use prepaid card, as that term is defined in section 1693*l*–1(a)(2)(A) of this title; and

(C) does not include paper checks.

(3) Credit card

The term "credit card" has the same meaning as in section 1602 of this title.

(4) Discount

The term "discount"—

(A) means a reduction made from the price that customers are informed is the regular price; and

(B) does not include any means of increasing the price that customers are informed is the regular price.

(5) Electronic debit transaction

The term "electronic debit transaction" means a transaction in which a person uses a debit card.

(6) Federal agency

The term "Federal agency" means—

(A) an agency (as defined in section 101 of Title 31); and

(B) a Government corporation (as defined in section 103 of Title 5).

(7) Institution of higher education

The term "institution of higher education" has the same meaning as in 1001[1] and 1002 of Title 20.

(8) Interchange transaction fee

The term "interchange transaction fee" means any fee established, charged or received by a payment card network for the purpose of compensating an issuer for its involvement in an electronic debit transaction.

(9) Issuer

The term "issuer" means any person who issues a debit card, or credit card, or the agent of such person with respect to such card.

(10) Network fee

The term "network fee" means any fee charged and received by a payment card network with respect to an electronic debit transaction, other than an interchange transaction fee.

(11) Payment card network

The term "payment card network" means an entity that directly, or through licensed members, processors, or agents, provides the proprietary services, infrastructure, and software that route information and data to conduct debit card or credit card transaction authorization, clearance, and settlement, and that a person uses in order to accept as a form of payment a brand of debit card, credit card or other device that may be used to carry out debit or credit transactions.

(d) Enforcement

(1) In general

Compliance with the requirements imposed under this section shall be enforced under section 1693*o* of this title.

(2) Exception

Sections 1693m and 1693n of this title shall not apply with respect to this section or the requirements imposed pursuant to this section.

(Pub.L. 90–321, Title IX, § 920, as added Pub.L. 111–203, Title X, § 1075(a)(2), July 21, 2010, 124 Stat. 2068.)

---

[1] So in original. Probably should be preceded by "sections".

§ 1693p. Reports to Congress [CCPA § 921]

(a) Not later than twelve months after the effective date of this subchapter and at one-year intervals thereafter, the Bureau shall make reports to the Congress concerning the administration of its functions under this subchapter, including such recommendations as the Bureau deems necessary and appropriate. In addition, each report of the Bureau shall include its assessment of the extent to which compliance with this subchapter is being achieved, and a summary of the enforcement actions taken under section 1693*o* of this title. In such report, the Bureau shall particularly address the effects of this subchapter on the costs and benefits to financial institutions and consumers, on competition, on the introduction of new technology, on the operations of financial institutions, and on the adequacy of consumer protection.

(b) In the exercise of its functions under this subchapter, the Bureau may obtain upon request the views of any other Federal agency which, in the judgment of the Bureau, exercises regulatory or supervisory functions with respect to any class of persons subject to this subchapter.

(Pub.L. 90–321, Title IX, § 921, formerly § 918, as added Pub.L. 95–630, Title XX, § 2001, Nov. 10, 1978, 92 Stat. 3740, and amended Pub.L. 97–375, Title II, § 209(a), Dec. 21, 1982, 96 Stat. 1825; renumbered § 919, Pub.L. 111–24, Title IV, § 401(1), May 22, 2009, 123 Stat. 1751; renumbered §§ 920, 921 and amended Pub.L. 111–203, Title X, §§ 1073(a)(3), 1075(a)(1), 1084(1), July 21, 2010, 124 Stat. 2060, 2068, 2081.)

§ 1693q. Relation to State laws [CCPA § 922]

This subchapter does not annul, alter, or affect the laws of any State relating to electronic fund transfers, dormancy fees, inactivity charges or fees, service fees, or expiration dates of gift certificates, store gift cards, or general-use prepaid cards, except to the extent that those laws are inconsistent with the provisions of this subchapter, and then only to the extent of the inconsistency. A State law is not inconsistent with this subchapter if the protection such law affords any consumer is greater than the protection afforded by this subchapter. The Bureau shall, upon its own motion or upon the request of any financial institution, State, or other interested party, submitted in accordance with procedures prescribed in regulations of the Bureau, determine whether a State requirement is inconsistent or affords greater protection. If the Bureau determines that a State requirement is inconsistent, financial institutions shall incur no liability under the law of that State for a good faith failure to comply with that law, notwithstanding that such determination is subsequently amended, rescinded, or determined by judicial or other authority to be invalid for any reason. This subchapter does not extend the applicability of any such law to any class of persons or transactions to which it would not otherwise apply.

(Pub.L. 90–321, Title IX, § 922, formerly § 919, as added Pub.L. 95–630, Title XX, § 2001, Nov. 10, 1978, 92 Stat. 3741, and renumbered § 920 and amended Pub.L. 111–24, Title IV, §§ 401(1), 402, May 22, 2009, 123 Stat. 1751, 1754; renumbered §§ 921, 922 and amended Pub.L. 111–203, Title X, §§ 1073(a)(3), 1075(a)(1), 1084(1), July 21, 2010, 124 Stat. 2060, 2068, 2081.)

§ 1693r. Exemption for State regulation [CCPA § 922]*

The Bureau shall by regulation exempt from the requirements of this subchapter any class of electronic fund transfers within any State if the Bureau determines that under the law of that State that class of electronic fund transfers is subject to requirements substantially similar to those imposed by this subchapter, and that there is adequate provision for enforcement.

(Pub.L. 90–321, Title IX, § 922, formerly § 920, as added Pub.L. 95–630, Title XX, § 2001, Nov. 10, 1978, 92 Stat. 3741; renumbered § 921, Pub.L. 111–24, Title IV, § 401(1), May 22, 2009, 123 Stat. 1638, renumbered § 922 and amended Pub.L. 111–203, Title X, §§ 1073(a)(3), 1084(1), July 21, 2010, 124 Stat. 2060, 2081.)

* *Note from West Advisory Panel: So in original. Probably should have been redesignated § 923.*

TRUTH IN LENDING (REGULATION Z)

12 C.F.R. Part 1026

Current through March 27, 2019; 84 F.R. 11636

For updates and appendices with Model Forms and Official Interpretations, see www.ecfr.gov

Note from West Advisory Board

This regulation is the Consumer Financial Protection Bureau's recodification of the Federal Reserve Board's Regulation Z (12 C.F.R. Part 226), as mandated by the Dodd-Frank Wall Street Reform and Consumer Protection Act of 2010. The Federal Reserve Board's regulation still has some applicability, primarily to auto dealers. The text of that regulation can be found at www.ecfr.gov.

SUBPART A. GENERAL

SUBPART B. OPEN-END CREDIT

SUBPART C. CLOSED-END CREDIT

SUBPART D. MISCELLANEOUS

SUBPART E. SPECIAL RULES FOR CERTAIN HOME MORTGAGE TRANSACTIONS

SUBPART F. SPECIAL RULES FOR PRIVATE EDUCATION LOANS

SUBPART G. SPECIAL RULES APPLICABLE TO CREDIT CARD ACCOUNTS AND OPEN-END CREDIT OFFERED TO COLLEGE STUDENTS

SUBPART A. GENERAL

§ 1026.1 Authority, purpose, coverage, organization, enforcement, and liability.

(a) Authority. This part, known as Regulation Z, is issued by the Bureau of Consumer Financial Protection to implement the Federal Truth in Lending Act, which is contained in title I of the Consumer Credit Protection Act, as amended (15 U.S.C. 1601 et seq.). This part also implements Title XII, section 1204 of the Competitive Equality Banking Act of 1987 (Pub.L. 100–86, 101 Stat. 552). Furthermore, this part implements certain provisions of the Real Estate Settlement Procedures Act of 1974, as amended (12 U.S.C. 2601 et seq.). In addition, this part implements certain provisions of the Financial Institutions Reform, Recovery, and Enforcement Act, as amended (12 U.S.C. 3331 et seq.). The Bureau's information-collection requirements contained in this part have been approved by the Office of Management and Budget under the provisions of 44 U.S.C. 3501 et seq. and have been assigned OMB No. 3170–0015 (Truth in Lending).

(b) Purpose. The purpose of this part is to promote the informed use of consumer credit by requiring disclosures about its terms and cost, to ensure that consumers are provided with greater and more timely information on the nature and costs of the residential real estate settlement process, and to effect certain changes in the settlement process for residential real estate that will result in more effective advance disclosure to home buyers and sellers of settlement costs. The regulation also includes substantive protections. It gives consumers the right to cancel certain credit transactions that involve a lien on a consumer's principal dwelling, regulates certain credit card practices, and provides a means for fair and timely resolution of credit billing disputes. The regulation does not generally govern charges for consumer credit, except that several provisions in subpart G set forth special rules addressing certain charges applicable to credit card accounts under an open-end (not home-secured) consumer credit plan. The regulation requires a maximum interest rate to be stated in variable-rate contracts secured by the consumer's dwelling. It also imposes limitations on home-equity plans that are subject to the requirements of § 1026.40 and mortgages that are subject to the requirements of § 1026.32. The regulation prohibits certain acts or practices in connection with credit secured by a dwelling in § 1026.36, and credit secured by a consumer's principal dwelling in § 1026.35. The regulation also regulates certain practices of creditors who extend private education loans as defined in § 1026.46(b)(5). In addition, it imposes certain limitations on increases in costs for mortgage transactions subject to § 1026.19(e) and (f).

(c) Coverage.

(1) In general, this part applies to each individual or business that offers or extends credit, other than a person excluded from coverage of this part by section 1029 of the Consumer Financial Protection Act of 2010, Title X of the Dodd-Frank Wall Street Reform and Consumer Protection Act, Public Law 111–203, 124 Stat. 1376, when four conditions are met:

(i) The credit is offered or extended to consumers;

(ii) The offering or extension of credit is done regularly;

(iii) The credit is subject to a finance charge or is payable by a written agreement in more than four installments; and

(iv) The credit is primarily for personal, family, or household purposes.

(2) If a credit card is involved, however, certain provisions apply even if the credit is not subject to a finance charge, or is not payable by a written agreement in more than four installments, or if the credit card is to be used for business purposes.

(3) In addition, certain requirements of § 1026.40 apply to persons who are not creditors but who provide applications for home-equity plans to consumers.

(4) Furthermore, certain requirements of § 1026.57 apply to institutions of higher education.

(5) Except in transactions subject to § 1026.19(e) and (f), no person is required to provide the disclosures required by sections 128(a)(16) through (19), 128(b)(4), 129C(f)(1), 129C(g)(2) and (3), 129D(h), or 129D(j)(1)(A) of the Truth in Lending Act, section 4(c) of the Real Estate Settlement Procedures Act, or the disclosure required prior to settlement by section 129C(h) of the Truth in Lending Act. Except in transactions subject to § 1026.20(e), no person is required to provide the disclosure required by section 129D(j)(1)(B) of the Truth in Lending Act. Except in transactions subject to § 1026.39(d)(5), no person becoming a creditor with respect to an existing residential mortgage loan is required to provide the disclosure required by section 129C(h) of the Truth in Lending Act.

(d) Organization. The regulation is divided into subparts and appendices as follows:

(1) Subpart A contains general information. It sets forth:

(i) The authority, purpose, coverage, and organization of the regulation;

(ii) The definitions of basic terms;

(iii) The transactions that are exempt from coverage; and

(iv) The method of determining the finance charge.

(2) Subpart B contains the rules for open-end credit. It requires that account-opening disclosures and periodic statements be provided, as well as additional disclosures for credit and charge card applications and solicitations and for home-equity plans subject to the requirements of § 1026.60 and § 1026.40, respectively. It also describes special rules that apply to credit card transactions, treatment of payments and credit balances, procedures for resolving credit billing errors, annual percentage rate calculations, rescission requirements, and advertising.

(3) Subpart C relates to closed-end credit. It contains rules on disclosures, treatment of credit balances, annual percentage rate calculations, rescission requirements, and advertising.

(4) Subpart D contains rules on oral disclosures, disclosures in languages other than English, record retention, effect on state laws, state exemptions, and rate limitations.

(5) Subpart E contains special rules for mortgage transactions. Section 1026.32 requires certain disclosures and provides limitations for closed-end credit transactions and open-end credit plans that have rates or fees above specified amounts or certain prepayment penalties. Section 1026.33 requires special disclosures, including the total annual loan cost rate, for reverse mortgage transactions. Section 1026.34 prohibits specific acts and practices in connection with high-cost mortgages, as defined in § 1026.32(a). Section 1026.35 prohibits specific acts and practices in connection with closed-end higher-priced mortgage loans, as defined in § 1026.35(a). Section 1026.36 prohibits specific acts and practices in connection with an extension of credit secured by a dwelling. Sections 1026.37 and 1026.38 set forth special disclosure requirements for certain closed-end transactions secured by real property or a cooperative unit, as required by § 1026.19(e) and (f).

(6) Subpart F relates to private education loans. It contains rules on disclosures, limitations on changes in terms after approval, the right to cancel the loan, and limitations on co-branding in the marketing of private education loans.

(7) Subpart G relates to credit card accounts under an open-end (not home-secured) consumer credit plan (except for § 1026.57(c), which applies to all open-end credit plans). Section 1026.51 contains rules on evaluation of a consumer's ability to make the required payments under the terms of an account. Section 1026.52 limits the fees that a consumer can be required to pay with respect to an open-end (not home-secured) consumer credit plan during the first year after account opening. Section 1026.53 contains rules on allocation of payments in excess of the minimum payment. Section 1026.54 sets forth certain limitations on the imposition of finance charges as the result of a loss of a grace period. Section 1026.55 contains limitations on increases in annual percentage rates, fees, and charges for credit card accounts. Section 1026.56 prohibits the assessment of fees or charges for over-the-limit transactions unless the consumer affirmatively consents to the creditor's payment of over-the-limit transactions. Section 1026.57 sets forth rules for reporting and marketing of college student open-end credit. Section 1026.58 sets forth requirements for the Internet posting of credit card accounts under an open-end (not home-secured) consumer credit plan.

(8) Several appendices contain information such as the procedures for determinations about state laws, state exemptions and issuance of official interpretations, special rules for certain kinds of credit plans, and the rules for computing annual percentage rates in closed-end credit transactions and total-annual-loan-cost rates for reverse mortgage transactions.

(e) Enforcement and liability. Section 108 of the Truth in Lending Act contains the administrative enforcement provisions for that Act. Sections 112, 113, 130, 131, and 134 contain provisions relating to liability for failure to comply with the requirements of the Truth in Lending Act and the regulation. Section 1204(c) of title XII of the Competitive Equality Banking Act of 1987, Public Law 100–86, 101 Stat. 552, incorporates by reference administrative enforcement and civil liability provisions of sections 108 and 130 of the Truth in Lending Act. Section 19 of the Real Estate Settlement Procedures Act contains the administrative enforcement provisions for that Act.

§ 1026.2 Definitions and rules of construction.

(a) Definitions. For purposes of this part, the following definitions apply:

(1) Act means the Truth in Lending Act (15 U.S.C. 1601 et seq.).

(2) Advertisement means a commercial message in any medium that promotes, directly or indirectly, a credit transaction.

(3)(i) Application means the submission of a consumer's financial information for the purposes of obtaining an extension of credit.

(ii) For transactions subject to § 1026.19(e), (f), or (g) of this part, an application consists of the submission of the consumer's name, the consumer's income, the consumer's social security number to obtain a credit report, the property address, an estimate of the value of the property, and the mortgage loan amount sought.

(4) Billing cycle or cycle means the interval between the days or dates of regular periodic statements. These intervals shall be equal and no longer than a quarter of a year. An interval will be considered equal if the number of days in the cycle does not vary more than four days from the regular day or date of the periodic statement.

(5) Bureau means the Bureau of Consumer Financial Protection.

(6) Business day means a day on which the creditor's offices are open to the public for carrying on substantially all of its business functions. However, for purposes of rescission under §§ 1026.15 and 1026.23, and for purposes of §§ 1026.19(a)(1)(ii), 1026.19(a)(2), 1026.19(e)(1)(iii)(B), 1026.19(e)(1)(iv), 1026.19(e)(2)(i)(A), 1026.19(e)(4)(ii), 1026.19(f)(1)(ii), 1026.19(f)(1)(iii), 1026.20(e)(5), 1026.31, and 1026.46(d)(4), the term means all calendar days except Sundays and the legal public holidays specified in 5 U.S.C. 6103(a), such as New Year's Day, the Birthday of Martin Luther King, Jr., Washington's Birthday, Memorial Day, Independence Day, Labor Day, Columbus Day, Veterans Day, Thanksgiving Day, and Christmas Day.

(7) Card issuer means a person that issues a credit card or that person's agent with respect to the card.

(8) Cardholder means a natural person to whom a credit card is issued for consumer credit purposes, or a natural person who has agreed with the card issuer to pay consumer credit obligations arising from the issuance of a credit card to another natural person. For purposes of § 1026.12(a) and (b), the term includes any person to whom a credit card is issued for any purpose, including business, commercial or agricultural use, or a person who has agreed with the card issuer to pay obligations arising from the issuance of such a credit card to another person.

(9) Cash price means the price at which a creditor, in the ordinary course of business, offers to sell for cash property or service that is the subject of the transaction. At the creditor's option, the term may include the price of accessories, services related to the sale, service contracts and taxes and fees for license, title, and registration. The term does not include any finance charge.

(10) Closed-end credit means consumer credit other than "open-end credit" as defined in this section.

(11) Consumer means a cardholder or natural person to whom consumer credit is offered or extended. However, for purposes of rescission under §§ 1026.15 and 1026.23, the term also includes a natural person in whose principal dwelling a security interest is or will be retained or acquired, if that person's ownership interest in the dwelling is or will be subject to the security interest.

(12) Consumer credit means credit offered or extended to a consumer primarily for personal, family, or household purposes.

(13) Consummation means the time that a consumer becomes contractually obligated on a credit transaction.

(14) Credit means the right to defer payment of debt or to incur debt and defer its payment.

(15)(i) The term credit card includes a hybrid prepaid-credit card as defined in § 1026.61.

(ii) Credit card account under an open-end (not home-secured) consumer credit plan means any open-end credit account that is accessed by a credit card, except:

(A) A home-equity plan subject to the requirements of § 1026.40 that is accessed by a credit card; or

(B) An overdraft line of credit that is accessed by a debit card; or

(C) An overdraft line of credit that is accessed by an account number, except if the account number is a hybrid prepaid-credit card that can access a covered separate credit feature as defined in § 1026.61.

(iii) Charge card means a credit card on an account for which no periodic rate is used to compute a finance charge.

(iv) Debit card means any card, plate, or other single device that may be used from time to time to access an asset account other than a prepaid account as defined in § 1026.61. The term debit card does not include a prepaid card as defined in § 1026.61.

(16) Credit sale means a sale in which the seller is a creditor. The term includes a bailment or lease (unless terminable without penalty at any time by the consumer) under which the consumer:

(i) Agrees to pay as compensation for use a sum substantially equivalent to, or in excess of, the total value of the property and service involved; and

(ii) Will become (or has the option to become), for no additional consideration or for nominal consideration, the owner of the property upon compliance with the agreement.

(17) Creditor means:

(i) A person who regularly extends consumer credit that is subject to a finance charge or is payable by written agreement in more than four installments (not including a down payment), and to whom the obligation is initially payable, either on the face of the note or contract, or by agreement when there is no note or contract.

(ii) For purposes of §§ 1026.4(c)(8) (Discounts), 1026.9(d) (Finance charge imposed at time of transaction), and 1026.12(e) (Prompt notification of returns and crediting of refunds), a person that honors a credit card.

(iii) For purposes of subpart B, any card issuer that extends either open-end credit or credit that is not subject to a finance charge and is not payable by written agreement in more than four installments.

(iv) For purposes of subpart B (except for the credit and charge card disclosures contained in §§ 1026.60 and 1026.9(e) and (f), the finance charge disclosures contained in § 1026.6(a)(1) and (b)(3)(i) and § 1026.7(a)(4) through (7) and (b)(4) through (6) and the right of rescission set forth in § 1026.15) and subpart C, any card issuer that extends closed-end credit that is subject to a finance charge or is payable by written agreement in more than four installments.

(v) A person regularly extends consumer credit only if it extended credit (other than credit subject to the requirements of § 1026.32) more than 25 times (or more than 5 times for transactions secured by a dwelling) in the preceding calendar year. If a person did not meet these numerical standards in the preceding calendar year, the numerical standards shall be applied to the current calendar year. A person regularly extends consumer credit if, in any 12-month period, the person originates more than one credit extension that is subject to the requirements of § 1026.32 or one or more such credit extensions through a mortgage broker.

(18) Downpayment means an amount, including the value of property used as a trade-in, paid to a seller to reduce the cash price of goods or services purchased in a credit sale transaction. A deferred portion of a downpayment may be treated as part of the downpayment if it is payable not later than the due date of the second otherwise regularly scheduled payment and is not subject to a finance charge.

(19) Dwelling means a residential structure that contains one to four units, whether or not that structure is attached to real property. The term includes an individual condominium unit, cooperative unit, mobile home, and trailer, if it is used as a residence.

(20) Open-end credit means consumer credit extended by a creditor under a plan in which:

(i) The creditor reasonably contemplates repeated transactions;

(ii) The creditor may impose a finance charge from time to time on an outstanding unpaid balance; and

(iii) The amount of credit that may be extended to the consumer during the term of the plan (up to any limit set by the creditor) is generally made available to the extent that any outstanding balance is repaid.

(21) Periodic rate means a rate of finance charge that is or may be imposed by a creditor on a balance for a day, week, month, or other subdivision of a year.

(22) Person means a natural person or an organization, including a corporation, partnership, proprietorship, association, cooperative, estate, trust, or government unit.

(23) Prepaid finance charge means any finance charge paid separately in cash or by check before or at consummation of a transaction, or withheld from the proceeds of the credit at any time.

(24) Residential mortgage transaction means a transaction in which a mortgage, deed of trust, purchase money security interest arising under an installment sales contract, or equivalent consensual security interest is created or retained in the consumer's principal dwelling to finance the acquisition or initial construction of that dwelling.

(25) Security interest means an interest in property that secures performance of a consumer credit obligation and that is recognized by state or Federal law. It does not include incidental interests such as interests in proceeds, accessions, additions, fixtures, insurance proceeds (whether or not the creditor is a loss payee or beneficiary), premium rebates, or interests in after-acquired property. For purposes of disclosures under §§ 1026.6, 1026.18, 1026.19(e) and (f), and 1026.38(*l*)(6). the term does not include an interest that arises solely by operation of law. However, for purposes of the right of rescission under §§ 1026.15 and 1026.23, the term does include interests that arise solely by operation of law.

(26) State means any state, the District of Columbia, the Commonwealth of Puerto Rico, and any territory or possession of the United States.

(27)(i) Successor in interest means a person to whom an ownership interest in a dwelling securing a closed-end consumer credit transaction is transferred from a consumer, provided that the transfer is:

(A) A transfer by devise, descent, or operation of law on the death of a joint tenant or tenant by the entirety;

(B) A transfer to a relative resulting from the death of the consumer;

(C) A transfer where the spouse or children of the consumer become an owner of the property;

(D) A transfer resulting from a decree of a dissolution of marriage, legal separation agreement, or from an incidental property settlement agreement, by which the spouse of the consumer becomes an owner of the property; or

(E) A transfer into an inter vivos trust in which the consumer is and remains a beneficiary and which does not relate to a transfer of rights of occupancy in the property.

(ii) Confirmed successor in interest means a successor in interest once a servicer has confirmed the successor in interest's identity and ownership interest in the dwelling.

(b) Rules of construction. For purposes of this part, the following rules of construction apply:

(1) Where appropriate, the singular form of a word includes the plural form and plural includes singular.

(2) Where the words obligation and transaction are used in the regulation, they refer to a consumer credit obligation or transaction, depending upon the context. Where the word credit is used in the regulation, it means consumer credit unless the context clearly indicates otherwise.

(3) Unless defined in this part, the words used have the meanings given to them by state law or contract.

(4) Where the word amount is used in this part to describe disclosure requirements, it refers to a numerical amount.

§ 1026.3 Exempt transactions.

The following transactions are not subject to this part or, if the exemption is limited to specified provisions of this part, are not subject to those provisions:

(a) Business, commercial, agricultural, or organizational credit.

(1) An extension of credit primarily for a business, commercial or agricultural purpose.

(2) An extension of credit to other than a natural person, including credit to government agencies or instrumentalities.

(b) Credit over applicable threshold amount.*

(1) Exemption.

(i) Requirements. An extension of credit in which the amount of credit extended exceeds the applicable threshold amount or in which there is an express written commitment to extend credit in excess of the applicable threshold amount, unless the extension of credit is:

(A) Secured by any real property, or by personal property used or expected to be used as the principal dwelling of the consumer; or

(B) A private education loan as defined in § 1026.46(b)(5).

(ii) Annual adjustments. The threshold amount in paragraph (b)(1)(i) of this section is adjusted annually to reflect increases in the Consumer Price Index for Urban Wage Earners and Clerical Workers, as applicable. See the official commentary to this paragraph (b) for the threshold amount applicable to a specific extension of credit or express written commitment to extend credit.

(2) Transition rule for open-end accounts exempt prior to July 21, 2011. An open-end account that is exempt on July 20, 2011 based on an express written commitment to extend credit in excess of $25,000 remains exempt until December 31, 2011 unless:

(i) The creditor takes a security interest in any real property, or in personal property used or expected to be used as the principal dwelling of the consumer; or

(ii) The creditor reduces the express written commitment to extend credit to $25,000 or less.

(c) Public utility credit. An extension of credit that involves public utility services provided through pipe, wire, other connected facilities, or radio or similar transmission (including extensions of such facilities), if the charges for service, delayed payment, or any discounts for prompt payment are filed with

* *Note from West Advisory Panel: From January 1, 2019 through December 31, 2019, the threshold amount is $57,200. See 83 Fed. Reg. 29276 (Nov. 23, 2018).*

or regulated by any government unit. The financing of durable goods or home improvements by a public utility is not exempt.

(d) Securities or commodities accounts. Transactions in securities or commodities accounts in which credit is extended by a broker-dealer registered with the Securities and Exchange Commission or the Commodity Futures Trading Commission.

(e) Home fuel budget plans. An installment agreement for the purchase of home fuels in which no finance charge is imposed.

(f) Student loan programs. Loans made, insured, or guaranteed pursuant to a program authorized by Title IV of the Higher Education Act of 1965 (20 U.S.C. 1070 et seq.).

(g) Employer-sponsored retirement plans. An extension of credit to a participant in an employer-sponsored retirement plan qualified under section 401(a) of the Internal Revenue Code, a tax-sheltered annuity under section 403(b) of the Internal Revenue Code, or an eligible governmental deferred compensation plan under section 457(b) of the Internal Revenue Code (26 U.S.C. 401(a); 26 U.S.C. 403(b); 26 U.S.C. 457(b)), provided that the extension of credit is comprised of fully vested funds from such participant's account and is made in compliance with the Internal Revenue Code (26 U.S.C. 1 et seq.).

(h) Partial exemption for certain mortgage loans. The special disclosure requirements in § 1026.19(g) and, unless the creditor chooses to provide the disclosures described in § 1026.19(e) and (f), in § 1026.19(e) and (f) do not apply to a transaction that satisfies all of the following criteria:

(1) The transaction is secured by a subordinate lien;

(2) The transaction is for the purpose of:

(i) Downpayment, closing costs, or other similar home buyer assistance, such as principal or interest subsidies;

(ii) Property rehabilitation assistance;

(iii) Energy efficiency assistance; or

(iv) Foreclosure avoidance or prevention;

(3) The credit contract does not require the payment of interest;

(4) The credit contract provides that repayment of the amount of credit extended is:

(i) Forgiven either incrementally or in whole, at a date certain, and subject only to specified ownership and occupancy conditions, such as a requirement that the consumer maintain the property as the consumer's principal dwelling for five years;

(ii) Deferred for a minimum of 20 years after consummation of the transaction;

(iii) Deferred until sale of the property securing the transaction; or

(iv) Deferred until the property securing the transaction is no longer the principal dwelling of the consumer;

(5)(i) The costs payable by the consumer in connection with the transaction at consummation are limited to:

(A) Recording fees;

(B) Transfer taxes;

(C) A bona fide and reasonable application fee; and

(D) A bona fide and reasonable fee for housing counseling services; and

(ii) The total of costs payable by the consumer under paragraph (h)(5)(i)(C) and (D) of this section is less than 1 percent of the amount of credit extended; and

(6) The following disclosures are provided:

(i) Disclosures described in § 1026.18 that comply with this part; or

(ii) Alternatively, disclosures described in § 1026.19(e) and (f) that comply with this part.

§ 1026.4 Finance charge.

(a) Definition. The finance charge is the cost of consumer credit as a dollar amount. It includes any charge payable directly or indirectly by the consumer and imposed directly or indirectly by the creditor as an incident to or a condition of the extension of credit. It does not include any charge of a type payable in a comparable cash transaction.

(1) Charges by third parties. The finance charge includes fees and amounts charged by someone other than the creditor, unless otherwise excluded under this section, if the creditor:

(2) Special rule; closing agent charges. Fees charged by a third party that conducts the loan closing (such as a settlement agent, attorney, or escrow or title company) are finance charges only if the creditor:

(i) Requires the particular services for which the consumer is charged;

(ii) Requires the imposition of the charge; or

(iii) Retains a portion of the third-party charge, to the extent of the portion retained.

(3) Special rule; mortgage broker fees. Fees charged by a mortgage broker (including fees paid by the consumer directly to the broker or to the creditor for delivery to the broker) are finance charges even if the creditor does not require the consumer to use a mortgage broker and even if the creditor does not retain any portion of the charge.

(b) Examples of finance charges. The finance charge includes the following types of charges, except for charges specifically excluded by paragraphs (c) through (e) of this section:

(1) Interest, time price differential, and any amount payable under an add-on or discount system of additional charges.

(2) Service, transaction, activity, and carrying charges, including any charge imposed on a checking or other transaction account (except a prepaid account as defined in § 1026.61) to the extent that the charge exceeds the charge for a similar account without a credit feature.

(3) Points, loan fees, assumption fees, finder's fees, and similar charges.

(4) Appraisal, investigation, and credit report fees.

(5) Premiums or other charges for any guarantee or insurance protecting the creditor against the consumer's default or other credit loss.

(6) Charges imposed on a creditor by another person for purchasing or accepting a consumer's obligation, if the consumer is required to pay the charges in cash, as an addition to the obligation, or as a deduction from the proceeds of the obligation.

(7) Premiums or other charges for credit life, accident, health, or loss-of-income insurance, written in connection with a credit transaction.

(8) Premiums or other charges for insurance against loss of or damage to property, or against liability arising out of the ownership or use of property, written in connection with a credit transaction.

(9) Discounts for the purpose of inducing payment by a means other than the use of credit.

(10) Charges or premiums paid for debt cancellation or debt suspension coverage written in connection with a credit transaction, whether or not the coverage is insurance under applicable law.

(11) With regard to a covered separate credit feature and an asset feature on a prepaid account that are both accessible by a hybrid prepaid-credit card as defined in § 1026.61:

(i) Any fee or charge described in paragraphs (b)(1) through (10) of this section imposed on the covered separate credit feature, whether it is structured as a credit subaccount of the prepaid account or a separate credit account.

(ii) Any fee or charge imposed on the asset feature of the prepaid account to the extent that the amount of the fee or charge exceeds comparable fees or charges imposed on prepaid accounts in the same prepaid account program that do not have a covered separate credit feature accessible by a hybrid prepaid-credit card.

(c) Charges excluded from the finance charge. The following charges are not finance charges:

(1) Application fees charged to all applicants for credit, whether or not credit is actually extended.

(2) Charges for actual unanticipated late payment, for exceeding a credit limit, or for delinquency, default, or a similar occurrence.

(3) Charges imposed by a financial institution for paying items that overdraw an account, unless the payment of such items and the imposition of the charge were previously agreed upon in writing. This paragraph does not apply to credit offered in connection with a prepaid account as defined in § 1026.61.

(4) Fees charged for participation in a credit plan, whether assessed on an annual or other periodic basis. This paragraph does not apply to a fee to participate in a covered separate credit feature accessible by a hybrid prepaid-credit card as defined in § 1026.61, regardless of whether this fee is imposed on the credit feature or on the asset feature of the prepaid account.

(5) Seller's points.

(6) Interest forfeited as a result of an interest reduction required by law on a time deposit used as security for an extension of credit.

(7) Real-estate related fees. The following fees in a transaction secured by real property or in a residential mortgage transaction, if the fees are bona fide and reasonable in amount:

(i) Fees for title examination, abstract of title, title insurance, property survey, and similar purposes.

(ii) Fees for preparing loan-related documents, such as deeds, mortgages, and reconveyance or settlement documents.

(iii) Notary and credit-report fees.

(iv) Property appraisal fees or fees for inspections to assess the value or condition of the property if the service is performed prior to closing, including fees related to pest-infestation or flood-hazard determinations.

(v) Amounts required to be paid into escrow or trustee accounts if the amounts would not otherwise be included in the finance charge.

(8) Discounts offered to induce payment for a purchase by cash, check, or other means, as provided in section 167(b) of the Act.

(d) Insurance and debt cancellation and debt suspension coverage.

(1) Voluntary credit insurance premiums. Premiums for credit life, accident, health, or loss-of-income insurance may be excluded from the finance charge if the following conditions are met:

(i) The insurance coverage is not required by the creditor, and this fact is disclosed in writing.

(ii) The premium for the initial term of insurance coverage is disclosed in writing. If the term of insurance is less than the term of the transaction, the term of insurance also shall be disclosed. The premium may be disclosed on a unit-cost basis only in open-end credit transactions, closed-end credit transactions by mail or telephone under § 1026.17(g), and certain closed-end credit transactions involving an insurance plan that limits the total amount of indebtedness subject to coverage.

(iii) The consumer signs or initials an affirmative written request for the insurance after receiving the disclosures specified in this paragraph, except as provided in paragraph (d)(4) of this section. Any consumer in the transaction may sign or initial the request.

(2) Property insurance premiums. Premiums for insurance against loss of or damage to property, or against liability arising out of the ownership or use of property, including single interest insurance if the insurer waives all right of subrogation against the consumer, may be excluded from the finance charge if the following conditions are met:

(i) The insurance coverage may be obtained from a person of the consumer's choice, and this fact is disclosed. (A creditor may reserve the right to refuse to accept, for reasonable cause, an insurer offered by the consumer.)

(ii) If the coverage is obtained from or through the creditor, the premium for the initial term of insurance coverage shall be disclosed. If the term of insurance is less than the term of the transaction, the term of insurance shall also be disclosed. The premium may be disclosed on a unit-cost basis only in open-end credit transactions, closed-end credit transactions by mail or telephone under § 1026.17(g), and certain closed-end credit transactions involving an insurance plan that limits the total amount of indebtedness subject to coverage.

(3) Voluntary debt cancellation or debt suspension fees. Charges or premiums paid for debt cancellation coverage for amounts exceeding the value of the collateral securing the obligation or for debt cancellation or debt suspension coverage in the event of the loss of life, health, or income or in case of accident may be excluded from the finance charge, whether or not the coverage is insurance, if the following conditions are met:

(i) The debt cancellation or debt suspension agreement or coverage is not required by the creditor, and this fact is disclosed in writing;

(ii) The fee or premium for the initial term of coverage is disclosed in writing. If the term of coverage is less than the term of the credit transaction, the term of coverage also shall be disclosed. The fee or premium may be disclosed on a unit-cost basis only in open-end credit transactions, closed-end credit transactions by mail or telephone under § 1026.17(g), and certain closed-end credit transactions involving a debt cancellation agreement that limits the total amount of indebtedness subject to coverage;

(iii) The following are disclosed, as applicable, for debt suspension coverage: That the obligation to pay loan principal and interest is only suspended, and that interest will continue to accrue during the period of suspension.

(iv) The consumer signs or initials an affirmative written request for coverage after receiving the disclosures specified in this paragraph, except as provided in paragraph (d)(4) of this section. Any consumer in the transaction may sign or initial the request.

(4) Telephone purchases. If a consumer purchases credit insurance or debt cancellation or debt suspension coverage for an open-end (not home-secured) plan by telephone, the creditor must make the disclosures under paragraphs (d)(1)(i) and (ii) or (d)(3)(i) through (iii) of this section, as applicable, orally. In such a case, the creditor shall:

(i) Maintain evidence that the consumer, after being provided the disclosures orally, affirmatively elected to purchase the insurance or coverage; and

(ii) Mail the disclosures under paragraphs (d)(1)(i) and (ii) or (d)(3)(i) through (iii) of this section, as applicable, within three business days after the telephone purchase.

(e) Certain security interest charges. If itemized and disclosed, the following charges may be excluded from the finance charge:

(1) Taxes and fees prescribed by law that actually are or will be paid to public officials for determining the existence of or for perfecting, releasing, or satisfying a security interest.

(2) The premium for insurance in lieu of perfecting a security interest to the extent that the premium does not exceed the fees described in paragraph (e)(1) of this section that otherwise would be payable.

(3) Taxes on security instruments. Any tax levied on security instruments or on documents evidencing indebtedness if the payment of such taxes is a requirement for recording the instrument securing the evidence of indebtedness.

(f) Prohibited offsets. Interest, dividends, or other income received or to be received by the consumer on deposits or investments shall not be deducted in computing the finance charge.

SUBPART B. OPEN-END CREDIT

§ 1026.5 General disclosure requirements.

(a) Form of disclosures.

(1) General.

(i) The creditor shall make the disclosures required by this subpart clearly and conspicuously.

(ii) The creditor shall make the disclosures required by this subpart in writing, in a form that the consumer may keep, except that:

(A) The following disclosures need not be written: Disclosures under § 1026.6(b)(3) of charges that are imposed as part of an open-end (not home-secured) plan that are not required to be disclosed under § 1026.6(b)(2) and related disclosures of charges under § 1026.9(c)(2)(iii)(B); disclosures under § 1026.9(c)(2)(vi); disclosures under § 1026.9(d) when a finance charge is imposed at the time of the transaction; and disclosures under § 1026.56(b)(1)(i).

(B) The following disclosures need not be in a retainable form: Disclosures that need not be written under paragraph (a)(1)(ii)(A) of this section; disclosures for credit and charge card applications and solicitations under § 1026.60; home-equity disclosures under § 1026.40(d); the alternative summary billing-rights statement under § 1026.9(a)(2); the credit and charge card renewal disclosures required under § 1026.9(e); and the payment requirements under § 1026.10(b), except as provided in § 1026.7(b)(13).

(iii) The disclosures required by this subpart may be provided to the consumer in electronic form, subject to compliance with the consumer consent and other applicable provisions of the Electronic Signatures in Global and National Commerce Act (E-Sign Act) (15 U.S.C. 7001 et seq.). The disclosures required by §§ 1026.60, 1026.40, and 1026.16 may be provided to the consumer in electronic form without regard to the consumer consent or other provisions of the E-Sign Act in the circumstances set forth in those sections.

(2) Terminology.

(i) Terminology used in providing the disclosures required by this subpart shall be consistent.

(ii) For home-equity plans subject to § 1026.40, the terms finance charge and annual percentage rate, when required to be disclosed with a corresponding amount or percentage rate, shall be more conspicuous than any other required disclosure. The terms need not be more conspicuous when used for periodic statement disclosures under § 1026.7(a)(4) and for advertisements under § 1026.16.

(iii) If disclosures are required to be presented in a tabular format pursuant to paragraph (a)(3) of this section, the term penalty APR shall be used, as applicable. The term penalty APR need not be used in reference to the annual percentage rate that applies with the loss of a promotional rate, assuming the annual percentage rate that applies is not greater than the annual percentage rate that would have applied at the end of the promotional period; or if the annual percentage rate that applies with the loss of a promotional rate is a variable rate, the annual percentage rate is calculated using the same index and margin as would have been used to calculate the annual percentage rate that would have applied at the end of the promotional period. If credit insurance or debt cancellation or debt suspension coverage is required as part of the plan, the term required shall be used and the program shall be identified by its name. If an annual percentage rate is required to be presented in a tabular format pursuant to paragraph (a)(3)(i) or (a)(3)(iii) of this section, the term fixed, or a similar term, may not be used to describe such rate unless the creditor also specifies a time period that the rate will be fixed and the rate will not increase during that period, or if no such time period is provided, the rate will not increase while the plan is open.

(3) Specific formats.

(i) Certain disclosures for credit and charge card applications and solicitations must be provided in a tabular format in accordance with the requirements of § 1026.60(a)(2).

(ii) Certain disclosures for home-equity plans must precede other disclosures and must be given in accordance with the requirements of § 1026.40(a).

(iii) Certain account-opening disclosures must be provided in a tabular format in accordance with the requirements of § 1026.6(b)(1).

(iv) Certain disclosures provided on periodic statements must be grouped together in accordance with the requirements of § 1026.7(b)(6) and (b)(13).

(v) Certain disclosures provided on periodic statements must be given in accordance with the requirements of § 1026.7(b)(12).

(vi) Certain disclosures accompanying checks that access a credit card account must be provided in a tabular format in accordance with the requirements of § 1026.9(b)(3).

(vii) Certain disclosures provided in a change-in-terms notice must be provided in a tabular format in accordance with the requirements of § 1026.9(c)(2)(iv)(D).

(viii) Certain disclosures provided when a rate is increased due to delinquency, default or as a penalty must be provided in a tabular format in accordance with the requirements of § 1026.9(g)(3)(ii).

(b) Time of disclosures.

(1) Account-opening disclosures.

(i) General rule. The creditor shall furnish account-opening disclosures required by § 1026.6 before the first transaction is made under the plan.

(ii) Charges imposed as part of an open-end (not home-secured) plan. Charges that are imposed as part of an open-end (not home-secured) plan and are not required to be disclosed under § 1026.6(b)(2) may be disclosed after account opening but before the consumer agrees to pay or becomes obligated to pay for the charge, provided they are disclosed at a time and in a manner that a consumer would be likely to notice them. This provision does not apply to charges imposed as part of a home-equity plan subject to the requirements of § 1026.40.

(iii) Telephone purchases. Disclosures required by § 1026.6 may be provided as soon as reasonably practicable after the first transaction if:

(A) The first transaction occurs when a consumer contacts a merchant by telephone to purchase goods and at the same time the consumer accepts an offer to finance the purchase by establishing an open-end plan with the merchant or third-party creditor;

(B) The merchant or third-party creditor permits consumers to return any goods financed under the plan and provides consumers with a sufficient time to reject the plan and return the goods free of cost after the merchant or third-party creditor has provided the written disclosures required by § 1026.6; and

(C) The consumer's right to reject the plan and return the goods is disclosed to the consumer as a part of the offer to finance the purchase.

(iv) Membership fees.

(A) General. In general, a creditor may not collect any fee before account-opening disclosures are provided. A creditor may collect, or obtain the consumer's agreement to pay, membership fees, including application fees excludable from the finance charge under § 1026.4(c)(1), before providing account-opening disclosures if, after receiving the disclosures, the consumer may reject the plan and have no obligation to pay these fees (including application fees) or any other fee or charge. A membership fee for purposes of this paragraph has the same meaning as a fee for the issuance or availability of credit described in § 1026.60(b)(2). If the consumer rejects the plan, the creditor must promptly refund the membership fee if it has been paid, or take other action necessary to ensure the consumer is not obligated to pay that fee or any other fee or charge.

(B) Home-equity plans. Creditors offering home-equity plans subject to the requirements of § 1026.40 are not subject to the requirements of paragraph (b)(1)(iv)(A) of this section.

(v) Application fees. A creditor may collect an application fee excludable from the finance charge under § 1026.4(c)(1) before providing account-opening disclosures. However, if a consumer rejects the plan after receiving account-opening disclosures, the consumer must have no obligation to pay such an application fee, or if the fee was paid, it must be refunded. See § 1026.5(b)(1)(iv)(A).

(2) Periodic statements.

(i) Statement required. The creditor shall mail or deliver a periodic statement as required by § 1026.7 for each billing cycle at the end of which an account has a debit or credit balance of more than $1 or on which a finance charge has been imposed. A periodic statement need not be sent for an account if the creditor deems it uncollectible, if delinquency collection proceedings have been instituted, if the creditor has charged off the account in accordance with loan-loss provisions and will not charge any additional fees or interest on the account, or if furnishing the statement would violate Federal law.

(ii) Timing requirements.

(A) Credit card accounts under an open-end (not home-secured) consumer credit plan. For credit card accounts under an open-end (not home-secured) consumer credit plan, a card issuer must adopt reasonable procedures designed to ensure that:

(1) Periodic statements are mailed or delivered at least 21 days prior to the payment due date disclosed on the statement pursuant to § 1026.7(b)(11)(i)(A); and

(2) The card issuer does not treat as late for any purpose a required minimum periodic payment received by the card issuer within 21 days after mailing or delivery of the periodic statement disclosing the due date for that payment.

(B) Open-end consumer credit plans. For accounts under an open-end consumer credit plan, a creditor must adopt reasonable procedures designed to ensure that:

(1) If a grace period applies to the account:

(i) Periodic statements are mailed or delivered at least 21 days prior to the date on which the grace period expires; and

(ii) The creditor does not impose finance charges as a result of the loss of the grace period if a payment that satisfies the terms of the grace period is received by the creditor within 21 days after mailing or delivery of the periodic statement.

(2) Regardless of whether a grace period applies to the account:

(i) Periodic statements are mailed or delivered at least 14 days prior to the date on which the required minimum periodic payment must be received in order to avoid being treated as late for any purpose; and

(ii) The creditor does not treat as late for any purpose a required minimum periodic payment received by the creditor within 14 days after mailing or delivery of the periodic statement.

(3) For purposes of paragraph (b)(2)(ii)(B) of this section, "grace period" means a period within which any credit extended may be repaid without incurring a finance charge due to a periodic interest rate.

(3) Credit and charge card application and solicitation disclosures. The card issuer shall furnish the disclosures for credit and charge card applications and solicitations in accordance with the timing requirements of § 1026.60.

(4) Home-equity plans. Disclosures for home-equity plans shall be made in accordance with the timing requirements of § 1026.40(b).

(c) Basis of disclosures and use of estimates. Disclosures shall reflect the terms of the legal obligation between the parties. If any information necessary for accurate disclosure is unknown to the creditor, it shall make the disclosure based on the best information reasonably available and shall state clearly that the disclosure is an estimate.

(d) Multiple creditors; multiple consumers. If the credit plan involves more than one creditor, only one set of disclosures shall be given, and the creditors shall agree among themselves which creditor must comply with the requirements that this part imposes on any or all of them. If there is more than one consumer, the disclosures may be made to any consumer who is primarily liable on the account. If the right of rescission under § 1026.15 is applicable, however, the disclosures required by §§ 1026.6 and 1026.15(b) shall be made to each consumer having the right to rescind.

(e) Effect of subsequent events. If a disclosure becomes inaccurate because of an event that occurs after the creditor mails or delivers the disclosures, the resulting inaccuracy is not a violation of this part, although new disclosures may be required under § 1026.9(c).

§ 1026.6 Account-opening disclosures.

(a) Rules affecting home-equity plans. The requirements of this paragraph (a) apply only to home-equity plans subject to the requirements of § 1026.40. A creditor shall disclose the items in this section, to the extent applicable:

(1) Finance charge. The circumstances under which a finance charge will be imposed and an explanation of how it will be determined, as follows:

(i) A statement of when finance charges begin to accrue, including an explanation of whether or not any time period exists within which any credit extended may be repaid without incurring a finance charge. If such a time period is provided, a creditor may, at its option and without disclosure, impose no finance charge when payment is received after the time period's expiration.

(ii) A disclosure of each periodic rate that may be used to compute the finance charge, the range of balances to which it is applicable, and the corresponding annual percentage rate. If a creditor offers a variable-rate plan, the creditor shall also disclose: The circumstances under which the rate(s) may increase; any limitations on the increase; and the effect(s) of an increase. When different periodic rates apply to different types of transactions, the types of transactions to which the periodic rates shall apply shall also be disclosed. A creditor is not required to adjust the range of balances disclosure to reflect the balance below which only a minimum charge applies.

(iii) An explanation of the method used to determine the balance on which the finance charge may be computed.

(iv) An explanation of how the amount of any finance charge will be determined, including a description of how any finance charge other than the periodic rate will be determined.

(2) Other charges. The amount of any charge other than a finance charge that may be imposed as part of the plan, or an explanation of how the charge will be determined.

(3) Home-equity plan information. The following disclosures described in § 1026.40(d), as applicable:

(i) A statement of the conditions under which the creditor may take certain action, as described in § 1026.40(d)(4)(i), such as terminating the plan or changing the terms.

(ii) The payment information described in § 1026.40(d)(5)(i) and (ii) for both the draw period and any repayment period.

(iii) A statement that negative amortization may occur as described in § 1026.40(d)(9).

(iv) A statement of any transaction requirements as described in § 1026.40(d)(10).

(v) A statement regarding the tax implications as described in § 1026.40(d)(11).

(vi) A statement that the annual percentage rate imposed under the plan does not include costs other than interest as described in § 1026.40(d)(6) and (d)(12)(ii).

(vii) The variable-rate disclosures described in § 1026.40(d)(12)(viii), (d)(12)(x), (d)(12)(xi), and (d)(12)(xii), as well as the disclosure described in § 1026.40(d)(5)(iii), unless the disclosures provided with the application were in a form the consumer could keep and included a representative payment example for the category of payment option chosen by the consumer.

(4) Security interests. The fact that the creditor has or will acquire a security interest in the property purchased under the plan, or in other property identified by item or type.

(5) Statement of billing rights. A statement that outlines the consumer's rights and the creditor's responsibilities under §§ 1026.12(c) and 1026.13 and that is substantially similar to the statement found in Model Form G-3 or, at the creditor's option, G-3(A), in Appendix G to this part.

(b) Rules affecting open-end (not home-secured) plans. The requirements of paragraph (b) of this section apply to plans other than home-equity plans subject to the requirements of § 1026.40.

(1) Form of disclosures; tabular format for open-end (not home-secured) plans. Creditors must provide the account-opening disclosures specified in paragraph (b)(2)(i) through (b)(2)(v) (except for (b)(2)(i)(D)(2)) and (b)(2)(vii) through (b)(2)(xiv) of this section in the form of a table with the headings, content, and format substantially similar to any of the applicable tables in G-17 in Appendix G.

(i) Highlighting. In the table, any annual percentage rate required to be disclosed pursuant to paragraph (b)(2)(i) of this section; any introductory rate permitted to be disclosed pursuant to paragraph (b)(2)(i)(B) or required to be disclosed under paragraph (b)(2)(i)(F) of this section, any rate that will apply after a premium initial rate expires permitted to be disclosed pursuant to paragraph (b)(2)(i)(C) or required to be disclosed pursuant to paragraph (b)(2)(i)(F), and any fee or percentage amounts or maximum limits on fee amounts disclosed pursuant to paragraphs (b)(2)(ii), (b)(2)(iv), (b)(2)(vii) through (b)(2)(xii) of this section must be disclosed in bold text. However, bold text shall not be used for: The amount of any periodic fee disclosed pursuant to paragraph (b)(2) of this section that is not an annualized amount; and other annual percentage rates or fee amounts disclosed in the table.

(ii) Location. Only the information required or permitted by paragraphs (b)(2)(i) through (v) (except for (b)(2)(i)(D)(2)) and (b)(2)(vii) through (xiv) of this section shall be in the table. Disclosures required by paragraphs (b)(2)(i)(D)(2), (b)(2)(i)(D)(3), (b)(2)(vi), and (b)(2)(xv) of this section shall be placed directly below the table. Disclosures required by paragraphs (b)(3) through (5) of this section that are not otherwise required to be in the table and other information may be presented with the account agreement or account-opening disclosure statement, provided such information appears outside the required table.

(iii) Fees that vary by state. Creditors that impose fees referred to in paragraphs (b)(2)(vii) through (b)(2)(xi) of this section that vary by state and that provide the disclosures required by paragraph (b) of this section in person at the time the open-end (not home-secured) plan is established in connection with financing the purchase of goods or services may, at the creditor's option, disclose in the account-opening table the specific fee applicable to the consumer's account, or the range of the fees, if the disclosure includes a statement that the amount of the fee varies by state and refers the consumer to the account agreement or other disclosure provided with the account-opening table where the amount of the fee applicable to the consumer's account is disclosed. A creditor may not list fees for multiple states in the account-opening summary table.

(iv) Fees based on a percentage. If the amount of any fee required to be disclosed under this section is determined on the basis of a percentage of another amount, the percentage used and the identification of the amount against which the percentage is applied may be disclosed instead of the amount of the fee.

(2) Required disclosures for account-opening table for open-end (not home-secured) plans. A creditor shall disclose the items in this section, to the extent applicable:

(i) Annual percentage rate. Each periodic rate that may be used to compute the finance charge on an outstanding balance for purchases, a cash advance, or a balance transfer, expressed as an annual percentage rate (as determined by § 1026.14(b)). When more than one rate applies for a category of transactions, the range of balances to which each rate is applicable shall also be disclosed. The annual percentage rate for purchases disclosed pursuant to this paragraph shall be in at least 16-point type, except for the following: A penalty rate that may apply upon the occurrence of one or more specific events.

(A) Variable-rate information. If a rate disclosed under paragraph (b)(2)(i) of this section is a variable rate, the creditor shall also disclose the fact that the rate may vary and how the rate is determined. In describing how the applicable rate will be determined, the creditor must identify the type of index or formula that is used in setting the rate. The value of the index and the amount of the margin that are used to calculate the variable rate shall not be disclosed in the table. A disclosure of any applicable limitations on rate increases or decreases shall not be included in the table.

(B) Discounted initial rates. If the initial rate is an introductory rate, as that term is defined in § 1026.16(g)(2)(ii), the creditor must disclose the rate that would otherwise apply to the account pursuant to paragraph (b)(2)(i) of this section. Where the rate is not tied to an index or formula, the creditor must disclose the rate that will apply after the introductory rate expires. In a variable-rate account, the creditor must disclose a rate based on the applicable index or formula in accordance with the accuracy requirements of paragraph (b)(4)(ii)(G) of this section. Except as provided in paragraph (b)(2)(i)(F) of this section, the creditor is not required to, but may disclose in the table the introductory rate along with the rate that would otherwise apply to the account if the creditor also discloses the time period during which the introductory rate will remain in effect, and uses the term "introductory" or "intro" in immediate proximity to the introductory rate.

(C) Premium initial rate. If the initial rate is temporary and is higher than the rate that will apply after the temporary rate expires, the creditor must disclose the premium initial rate pursuant to paragraph (b)(2)(i) of this section. Consistent with paragraph (b)(2)(i) of this section, the premium initial rate for purchases must be in at least 16-point type. Except as provided in paragraph (b)(2)(i)(F) of this section, the creditor is not required to, but may disclose in the table the rate that will apply after the premium initial rate expires if the creditor also discloses the time period during which the premium initial rate will remain in effect. If the creditor also discloses in the table the rate that will apply after the premium initial rate for purchases expires, that rate also must be in at least 16-point type.

(D) Penalty rates.

(1) In general. Except as provided in paragraph (b)(2)(i)(D)(2) and (b)(2)(i)(D)(3) of this section, if a rate may increase as a penalty for one or more events specified in the account agreement, such as a late payment or an extension of credit that exceeds the credit limit, the creditor must disclose pursuant to paragraph (b)(2)(i) of this section the increased rate that may apply, a brief description of the event or events that may result in the increased rate, and a brief description of how long the increased rate will remain in effect. If more than one penalty rate may apply, the creditor at its option may disclose the highest rate that could apply, instead of disclosing the specific rates or the range of rates that could apply.

(2) Introductory rates. If the creditor discloses in the table an introductory rate, as that term is defined in § 1026.16(g)(2)(ii), creditors must briefly disclose directly beneath the table the circumstances under which the introductory rate may be revoked, and the rate that will apply after the introductory rate is revoked.

(3) Employee preferential rates. If a creditor discloses in the table a preferential annual percentage rate for which only employees of the creditor, employees of a third party, or other individuals with similar affiliations with the creditor or third party, such as executive officers, directors, or principal shareholders are eligible, the creditor must briefly disclose directly beneath the table the circumstances under which such preferential rate may be revoked, and the rate that will apply after such preferential rate is revoked.

(E) Point of sale where APRs vary by state or based on creditworthiness. Creditors imposing annual percentage rates that vary by state or based on the consumer's creditworthiness and providing the disclosures required by paragraph (b) of this section in person at the time the open-end (not home-secured) plan is established in connection with financing the purchase of goods or services may, at the creditor's option, disclose pursuant to paragraph (b)(2)(i) of this section in the account-opening table:

(1) The specific annual percentage rate applicable to the consumer's account; or

(2) The range of the annual percentage rates, if the disclosure includes a statement that the annual percentage rate varies by state or will be determined based on the consumer's creditworthiness and refers the consumer to the account agreement or other disclosure provided with the account-opening table where the annual percentage rate applicable to the consumer's account is disclosed. A creditor may not list annual percentage rates for multiple states in the account-opening table.

(F) Credit card accounts under an open-end (not home-secured) consumer credit plan. Notwithstanding paragraphs (b)(2)(i)(B) and (b)(2)(i)(C) of this section, for credit card accounts under an open-end (not home-secured) plan, issuers must disclose in the table:

(1) Any introductory rate as that term is defined in § 1026.16(g)(2)(ii) that would apply to the account, consistent with the requirements of paragraph (b)(2)(i)(B) of this section, and

(2) Any rate that would apply upon the expiration of a premium initial rate, consistent with the requirements of paragraph (b)(2)(i)(C) of this section.

(ii) Fees for issuance or availability.

(A) Any annual or other periodic fee that may be imposed for the issuance or availability of an open-end plan, including any fee based on account activity or inactivity; how frequently it will be imposed; and the annualized amount of the fee.

(B) Any non-periodic fee that relates to opening the plan. A creditor must disclose that the fee is a one-time fee.

(iii) Fixed finance charge; minimum interest charge. Any fixed finance charge and a brief description of the charge. Any minimum interest charge if it exceeds $1.00 that could be imposed during a billing cycle, and a brief description of the charge. The $1.00 threshold amount shall be adjusted periodically by the Bureau to reflect changes in the Consumer Price Index. The Bureau shall calculate each year a price level adjusted minimum interest charge using the Consumer Price Index in effect on the June 1 of that year. When the cumulative change in the adjusted minimum value derived from applying the annual Consumer Price level to the current minimum interest charge threshold has risen by a whole dollar, the minimum interest charge will be increased by $1.00. The creditor may, at its option, disclose in the table minimum interest charges below this threshold.

(iv) Transaction charges. Any transaction charge imposed by the creditor for use of the open-end plan for purchases.

(v) Grace period. The date by which or the period within which any credit extended may be repaid without incurring a finance charge due to a periodic interest rate and any conditions on the availability of the grace period. If no grace period is provided, that fact must be disclosed. If the length of the grace period varies, the creditor may disclose the range of days, the minimum number of days, or the average number of the days in the grace period, if the disclosure is identified as a range, minimum, or average. In disclosing in the tabular format a grace period that applies to all features on the account, the phrase "How to Avoid Paying Interest" shall be used as the heading for the row describing the grace period. If a grace period is not offered on all features of the account, in disclosing this fact in the tabular format, the phrase "Paying Interest" shall be used as the heading for the row describing this fact.

(vi) Balance computation method. The name of the balance computation method listed in § 1026.60(g) that is used to determine the balance on which the finance charge is computed for each feature, or an explanation of the method used if it is not listed, along with a statement that an explanation of the method(s) required by paragraph (b)(4)(i)(D) of this section is provided with the account-opening disclosures. In determining which balance computation method to disclose, the creditor shall assume that credit extended will not be repaid within any grace period, if any.

(vii) Cash advance fee. Any fee imposed for an extension of credit in the form of cash or its equivalent.

(viii) Late payment fee. Any fee imposed for a late payment.

(ix) Over-the-limit fee. Any fee imposed for exceeding a credit limit.

(x) Balance transfer fee. Any fee imposed to transfer an outstanding balance.

(xi) Returned-payment fee. Any fee imposed by the creditor for a returned payment.

(xii) Required insurance, debt cancellation or debt suspension coverage.

(A) A fee for insurance described in § 1026.4(b)(7) or debt cancellation or suspension coverage described in § 1026.4(b)(10), if the insurance, or debt cancellation or suspension coverage is required as part of the plan; and

(B) A cross reference to any additional information provided about the insurance or coverage, as applicable.

(xiii) Available credit. If a creditor requires fees for the issuance or availability of credit described in paragraph (b)(2)(ii) of this section, or requires a security deposit for such credit, and the total amount of those required fees and/or security deposit that will be imposed and charged to the account when the account is opened is 15 percent or more of the minimum credit limit for the plan, a creditor must disclose the available credit remaining after these fees or security deposit are debited to the account. The determination whether the 15 percent threshold is met must be based on the minimum credit limit for the plan. However, the disclosure provided under this paragraph must be based on the actual initial credit limit provided on the account. In determining whether the 15 percent threshold test is met, the creditor must only consider fees for issuance or availability of credit, or a security deposit, that are required. If fees for issuance or availability are optional, these fees should not be considered in determining whether the disclosure must be given. Nonetheless, if the 15 percent threshold test is met, the creditor in providing the disclosure must disclose the amount of available credit calculated by excluding those optional fees, and the available credit including those optional fees. The creditor shall also disclose that the consumer has the right to reject the plan and not be obligated to pay those fees or any other fee or charges until the consumer has used the account or made a payment on the account after receiving a periodic statement. This paragraph does not apply with respect to fees or security deposits that are not debited to the account.

(xiv) Web site reference. For issuers of credit cards that are not charge cards, a reference to the Web site established by the Bureau and a statement that consumers may obtain on the Web site information about shopping for and using credit cards. Until January 1, 2013, issuers may substitute for this reference a reference to the Web site established by the Board of Governors of the Federal Reserve System.

(xv) Billing error rights reference. A statement that information about consumers' right to dispute transactions is included in the account-opening disclosures.

(3) Disclosure of charges imposed as part of open-end (not home-secured) plans. A creditor shall disclose, to the extent applicable:

(i) For charges imposed as part of an open-end (not home-secured) plan, the circumstances under which the charge may be imposed, including the amount of the charge or an explanation of how the charge is determined. For finance charges, a statement of when the charge begins to accrue and an explanation of whether or not any time period exists within which any credit that has been extended may be repaid without incurring the charge. If such a time period is provided, a creditor may, at its option and without disclosure, elect not to impose a finance charge when payment is received after the time period expires.

(ii) Charges imposed as part of the plan are:

(A) Finance charges identified under § 1026.4(a) and § 1026.4(b).

(B) Charges resulting from the consumer's failure to use the plan as agreed, except amounts payable for collection activity after default, attorney's fees whether or not automatically imposed, and post-judgment interest rates permitted by law.

(C) Taxes imposed on the credit transaction by a state or other governmental body, such as documentary stamp taxes on cash advances.

(D) Charges for which the payment, or nonpayment, affect the consumer's access to the plan, the duration of the plan, the amount of credit extended, the period for which credit is extended, or the timing or method of billing or payment.

(E) Charges imposed for terminating a plan.

(F) Charges for voluntary credit insurance, debt cancellation or debt suspension.

(iii) Charges that are not imposed as part of the plan include:

(A) Charges imposed on a cardholder by an institution other than the card issuer for the use of the other institution's ATM in a shared or interchange system.

(B) A charge for a package of services that includes an open-end credit feature, if the fee is required whether or not the open-end credit feature is included and the non-credit services are not merely incidental to the credit feature.

(C) Charges under § 1026.4(e) disclosed as specified.

(D) With regard to a covered separate credit feature and an asset feature on a prepaid account that are both accessible by a hybrid prepaid-credit card as defined in § 1026.61, any fee or charge imposed on the asset feature of the prepaid account to the extent that the amount of the fee or charge does not exceed comparable fees or charges imposed on prepaid accounts in the same prepaid account program that do not have a covered separate credit feature accessible by a hybrid prepaid-credit card.

(E) With regard to a non-covered separate credit feature accessible by a prepaid card as defined in § 1026.61, any fee or charge imposed on the asset feature of the prepaid account.

(4) Disclosure of rates for open-end (not home-secured) plans. A creditor shall disclose, to the extent applicable:

(i) For each periodic rate that may be used to calculate interest:

(A) Rates. The rate, expressed as a periodic rate and a corresponding annual percentage rate.

(B) Range of balances. The range of balances to which the rate is applicable; however, a creditor is not required to adjust the range of balances disclosure to reflect the balance below which only a minimum charge applies.

(C) Type of transaction. The type of transaction to which the rate applies, if different rates apply to different types of transactions.

(D) Balance computation method. An explanation of the method used to determine the balance to which the rate is applied.

(ii) Variable-rate accounts. For interest rate changes that are tied to increases in an index or formula (variable-rate accounts) specifically set forth in the account agreement:

(A) The fact that the annual percentage rate may increase.

(B) How the rate is determined, including the margin.

(C) The circumstances under which the rate may increase.

(D) The frequency with which the rate may increase.

(E) Any limitation on the amount the rate may change.

(F) The effect(s) of an increase.

(G) Except as specified in paragraph (b)(4)(ii)(H) of this section, a rate is accurate if it is a rate as of a specified date and this rate was in effect within the last 30 days before the disclosures are provided.

(H) Creditors imposing annual percentage rates that vary according to an index that is not under the creditor's control that provide the disclosures required by paragraph (b) of this section in person at the time the open-end (not home-secured) plan is established in connection with financing the purchase of goods or services may disclose in the table a rate, or range of rates to the extent permitted by § 1026.6(b)(2)(i)(E), that was in effect within the last 90 days before the disclosures are provided, along with a reference directing the consumer to the account agreement or other disclosure provided with the account-opening table where an annual percentage rate applicable to the consumer's account in effect within the last 30 days before the disclosures are provided is disclosed.

(iii) Rate changes not due to index or formula. For interest rate changes that are specifically set forth in the account agreement and not tied to increases in an index or formula:

(A) The initial rate (expressed as a periodic rate and a corresponding annual percentage rate) required under paragraph (b)(4)(i)(A) of this section.

(B) How long the initial rate will remain in effect and the specific events that cause the initial rate to change.

(C) The rate (expressed as a periodic rate and a corresponding annual percentage rate) that will apply when the initial rate is no longer in effect and any limitation on the time period the new rate will remain in effect.

(D) The balances to which the new rate will apply.

(E) The balances to which the current rate at the time of the change will apply.

(5) Additional disclosures for open-end (not home-secured) plans. A creditor shall disclose, to the extent applicable:

(i) Voluntary credit insurance, debt cancellation or debt suspension. The disclosures in §§ 1026.4(d)(1)(i) and (d)(1)(ii) and (d)(3)(i) through (d)(3)(iii) if the creditor offers optional credit insurance or debt cancellation or debt suspension coverage that is identified in § 1026.4(b)(7) or (b)(10).

(ii) Security interests. The fact that the creditor has or will acquire a security interest in the property purchased under the plan, or in other property identified by item or type.

(iii) Statement of billing rights. A statement that outlines the consumer's rights and the creditor's responsibilities under §§ 1026.12(c) and 1026.13 and that is substantially similar to the statement found in Model Form G-3(A) in Appendix G to this part.

§ 1026.7 Periodic statement.

The creditor shall furnish the consumer with a periodic statement that discloses the following items, to the extent applicable:

(a) Rules affecting home-equity plans. The requirements of paragraph (a) of this section apply only to home-equity plans subject to the requirements of § 1026.40. Alternatively, a creditor subject to this paragraph may, at its option, comply with any of the requirements of paragraph (b) of this section; however, any creditor that chooses not to provide a disclosure under paragraph (a)(7) of this section must comply with paragraph (b)(6) of this section.

(1) Previous balance. The account balance outstanding at the beginning of the billing cycle.

(2) Identification of transactions. An identification of each credit transaction in accordance with § 1026.8.

(3) Credits. Any credit to the account during the billing cycle, including the amount and the date of crediting. The date need not be provided if a delay in accounting does not result in any finance or other charge.

(4) Periodic rates.

(i) Except as provided in paragraph (a)(4)(ii) of this section, each periodic rate that may be used to compute the finance charge, the range of balances to which it is applicable, and the corresponding annual percentage rate. If no finance charge is imposed when the outstanding balance is less than a certain amount, the creditor is not required to disclose that fact, or the balance below which no finance charge will be imposed. If different periodic rates apply to different types of transactions, the types of transactions to which the periodic rates apply shall also be disclosed. For variable-rate plans, the fact that the periodic rate(s) may vary.

(ii) Exception. An annual percentage rate that differs from the rate that would otherwise apply and is offered only for a promotional period need not be disclosed except in periods in which the offered rate is actually applied.

(5) Balance on which finance charge computed. The amount of the balance to which a periodic rate was applied and an explanation of how that balance was determined. When a balance is determined without first deducting all credits and payments made during the billing cycle, the fact and the amount of the credits and payments shall be disclosed.

(6) Amount of finance charge and other charges. Creditors may comply with paragraphs (a)(6) of this section, or with paragraph (b)(6) of this section, at their option.

(i) Finance charges. The amount of any finance charge debited or added to the account during the billing cycle, using the term finance charge. The components of the finance charge shall be individually itemized and identified to show the amount(s) due to the application of any periodic rates and the amounts(s) of any other type of finance charge. If there is more than one periodic rate, the amount of the finance charge attributable to each rate need not be separately itemized and identified.

(ii) Other charges. The amounts, itemized and identified by type, of any charges other than finance charges debited to the account during the billing cycle.

(7) Annual percentage rate. At a creditor's option, when a finance charge is imposed during the billing cycle, the annual percentage rate(s) determined under § 1026.14(c) using the term annual percentage rate.

(8) Grace period. The date by which or the time period within which the new balance or any portion of the new balance must be paid to avoid additional finance charges. If such a time period is provided, a creditor may, at its option and without disclosure, impose no finance charge if payment is received after the time period's expiration.

(9) Address for notice of billing errors. The address to be used for notice of billing errors. Alternatively, the address may be provided on the billing rights statement permitted by § 1026.9(a)(2).

(10) Closing date of billing cycle; new balance. The closing date of the billing cycle and the account balance outstanding on that date.

(b) Rules affecting open-end (not home-secured) plans. The requirements of paragraph (b) of this section apply only to plans other than home-equity plans subject to the requirements of § 1026.40.

(1) Previous balance. The account balance outstanding at the beginning of the billing cycle.

(2) Identification of transactions. An identification of each credit transaction in accordance with § 1026.8.

(3) Credits. Any credit to the account during the billing cycle, including the amount and the date of crediting. The date need not be provided if a delay in crediting does not result in any finance or other charge.

(4) Periodic rates.

(i) Except as provided in paragraph (b)(4)(ii) of this section, each periodic rate that may be used to compute the interest charge expressed as an annual percentage rate and using the term Annual Percentage Rate, along with the range of balances to which it is applicable. If no interest charge is imposed when the outstanding balance is less than a certain amount, the creditor is not required to disclose that fact, or the balance below which no interest charge will be imposed. The types of transactions to which the periodic rates apply shall also be disclosed. For variable-rate plans, the fact that the annual percentage rate may vary.

(ii) Exception. A promotional rate, as that term is defined in § 1026.16(g)(2)(i), is required to be disclosed only in periods in which the offered rate is actually applied.

(5) Balance on which finance charge computed. The amount of the balance to which a periodic rate was applied and an explanation of how that balance was determined, using the term Balance Subject to Interest Rate. When a balance is determined without first deducting all credits and payments made during the billing cycle, the fact and the amount of the credits and payments shall be disclosed. As an alternative to providing an explanation of how the balance was determined, a creditor that uses a balance computation method identified in § 1026.60(g) may, at the creditor's option, identify the name of the balance computation method and provide a toll-free telephone number where consumers may obtain from the creditor more information about the balance computation method and how resulting interest charges were determined. If the method used is not identified in § 1026.60(g), the creditor shall provide a brief explanation of the method used.

(6) Charges imposed.

(i) The amounts of any charges imposed as part of a plan as stated in § 1026.6(b)(3), grouped together, in proximity to transactions identified under paragraph (b)(2) of this section, substantially similar to Sample G-18(A) in Appendix G to this part.

(ii) Interest. Finance charges attributable to periodic interest rates, using the term Interest Charge, must be grouped together under the heading Interest Charged, itemized and totaled by type of transaction, and a total of finance charges attributable to periodic interest rates, using the term Total Interest, must be disclosed for the statement period and calendar year to date, using a format substantially similar to Sample G-18(A) in Appendix G to this part.

(iii) Fees. Charges imposed as part of the plan other than charges attributable to periodic interest rates must be grouped together under the heading Fees, identified consistent with the feature or type, and itemized, and a total of charges, using the term Fees, must be disclosed for the statement period and calendar year to date, using a format substantially similar to Sample G-18(A) in Appendix G to this part.

(7) Change-in-terms and increased penalty rate summary for open-end (not home-secured) plans. Creditors that provide a change-in-terms notice required by § 1026.9(c), or a rate increase notice required by § 1026.9(g), on or with the periodic statement, must disclose the information in § 1026.9(c)(2)(iv)(A) and (c)(2)(iv)(B) (if applicable) or § 1026.9(g)(3)(i) on the periodic statement in accordance with the format requirements in § 1026.9(c)(2)(iv)(D), and § 1026.9(g)(3)(ii). See Forms G-18(F) and G-18(G) in Appendix G to this part.

(8) Grace period. The date by which or the time period within which the new balance or any portion of the new balance must be paid to avoid additional finance charges. If such a time period is provided, a creditor may, at its option and without disclosure, impose no finance charge if payment is received after the time period's expiration.

(9) Address for notice of billing errors. The address to be used for notice of billing errors. Alternatively, the address may be provided on the billing rights statement permitted by § 1026.9(a)(2).

(10) Closing date of billing cycle; new balance. The closing date of the billing cycle and the account balance outstanding on that date. The new balance must be disclosed in accordance with the format requirements of paragraph (b)(13) of this section.

(11) Due date; late payment costs.

(i) Except as provided in paragraph (b)(11)(ii) of this section and in accordance with the format requirements in paragraph (b)(13) of this section, for a credit card account under an open-end (not home-secured) consumer credit plan, a card issuer must provide on each periodic statement:

(A) The due date for a payment. The due date disclosed pursuant to this paragraph shall be the same day of the month for each billing cycle.

(B) The amount of any late payment fee and any increased periodic rate(s) (expressed as an annual percentage rate(s)) that may be imposed on the account as a result of a late payment. If a range of late payment fees may be assessed, the card issuer may state the range of fees, or the highest fee and an indication that the fee imposed could be lower. If the rate may be increased for more than one feature or balance, the card issuer may state the range of rates or the highest rate that could apply and at the issuer's option an indication that the rate imposed could be lower.

(ii) Exception. The requirements of paragraph (b)(11)(i) of this section do not apply to the following:

(A) Periodic statements provided solely for charge card accounts, other than covered separate credit features that are charge card accounts accessible by hybrid prepaid-credit cards as defined in § 1026.61; and

(B) Periodic statements provided for a charged-off account where payment of the entire account balance is due immediately.

(12) Repayment disclosures.

(i) In general. Except as provided in paragraphs (b)(12)(ii) and (b)(12)(v) of this section, for a credit card account under an open-end (not home-secured) consumer credit plan, a card issuer must provide the following disclosures on each periodic statement:

(A) The following statement with a bold heading: "Minimum Payment Warning: If you make only the minimum payment each period, you will pay more in interest and it will take you longer to pay off your balance;"

(B) The minimum payment repayment estimate, as described in Appendix M1 to this part. If the minimum payment repayment estimate is less than 2 years, the card issuer must disclose the estimate in months. Otherwise, the estimate must be disclosed in years and rounded to the nearest whole year;

(C) The minimum payment total cost estimate, as described in Appendix M1 to this part. The minimum payment total cost estimate must be rounded either to the nearest whole dollar or to the nearest cent, at the card issuer's option;

(D) A statement that the minimum payment repayment estimate and the minimum payment total cost estimate are based on the current outstanding balance shown on the periodic statement. A statement that the minimum payment repayment estimate and the minimum payment total cost estimate are based on the assumption that only minimum payments are made and no other amounts are added to the balance;

(E) A toll-free telephone number where the consumer may obtain from the card issuer information about credit counseling services consistent with paragraph (b)(12)(iv) of this section; and

(F)(1) Except as provided in paragraph (b)(12)(i)(F)(2) of this section, the following disclosures:

(i) The estimated monthly payment for repayment in 36 months, as described in Appendix M1 to this part. The estimated monthly payment for repayment in 36 months must be rounded either to the nearest whole dollar or to the nearest cent, at the card issuer's option;

(ii) A statement that the card issuer estimates that the consumer will repay the outstanding balance shown on the periodic statement in 3 years if the consumer pays the estimated monthly payment each month for 3 years;

(iii) The total cost estimate for repayment in 36 months, as described in Appendix M1 to this part. The total cost estimate for repayment in 36 months must be rounded either to the nearest whole dollar or to the nearest cent, at the card issuer's option; and

(iv) The savings estimate for repayment in 36 months, as described in Appendix M1 to this part. The savings estimate for repayment in 36 months must be rounded either to the nearest whole dollar or to the nearest cent, at the card issuer's option.

(2) The requirements of paragraph (b)(12)(i)(F)(1) of this section do not apply to a periodic statement in any of the following circumstances:

(i) The minimum payment repayment estimate that is disclosed on the periodic statement pursuant to paragraph (b)(12)(i)(B) of this section after rounding is three years or less;

(ii) The estimated monthly payment for repayment in 36 months, as described in Appendix M1 to this part, after rounding as set forth in paragraph (b)(12)(i)(F)(1)(i) of this section that is calculated for a particular billing cycle is less than the minimum payment required for the plan for that billing cycle; and

(iii) A billing cycle where an account has both a balance in a revolving feature where the required minimum payments for this feature will not amortize that balance in a fixed amount of time specified in the account agreement and a balance in a fixed repayment feature where the required minimum payment for this fixed repayment feature will amortize that balance in a fixed amount of time specified in the account agreement which is less than 36 months.

(ii) Negative or no amortization. If negative or no amortization occurs when calculating the minimum payment repayment estimate as described in Appendix M1 of this part, a card issuer must provide the following disclosures on the periodic statement instead of the disclosures set forth in paragraph (b)(12)(i) of this section:

(A) The following statement: "Minimum Payment Warning: Even if you make no more charges using this card, if you make only the minimum payment each month we estimate you will never pay off the balance shown on this statement because your payment will be less than the interest charged each month";

(B) The following statement: "If you make more than the minimum payment each period, you will pay less in interest and pay off your balance sooner";

(C) The estimated monthly payment for repayment in 36 months, as described in Appendix M1 to this part. The estimated monthly payment for repayment in 36 months must be rounded either to the nearest whole dollar or to the nearest cent, at the issuer's option;

(D) A statement that the card issuer estimates that the consumer will repay the outstanding balance shown on the periodic statement in 3 years if the consumer pays the estimated monthly payment each month for 3 years; and

(E) A toll-free telephone number where the consumer may obtain from the card issuer information about credit counseling services consistent with paragraph (b)(12)(iv) of this section.

(iii) Format requirements. A card issuer must provide the disclosures required by paragraph (b)(12)(i) or (b)(12)(ii) of this section in accordance with the format requirements of paragraph (b)(13) of this section, and in a format substantially similar to Samples G-18(C)(1), G-18(C)(2) and G-18(C)(3) in Appendix G to this part, as applicable.

(iv) Provision of information about credit counseling services.

(A) Required information. To the extent available from the United States Trustee or a bankruptcy administrator, a card issuer must provide through the toll-free telephone number disclosed pursuant to paragraphs (b)(12)(i) or (b)(12)(ii) of this section the name, street address, telephone number, and Web site address for at least three organizations that have been approved by the United States Trustee or a bankruptcy administrator pursuant to 11 U.S.C. 111(a)(1) to provide credit counseling services in, at the card issuer's option, either the state in which the billing address for the account is located or the state specified by the consumer.

(B) Updating required information. At least annually, a card issuer must update the information provided pursuant to paragraph (b)(12)(iv)(A) of this section for consistency with the information available from the United States Trustee or a bankruptcy administrator.

(v) Exemptions. Paragraph (b)(12) of this section does not apply to:

(A) Charge card accounts that require payment of outstanding balances in full at the end of each billing cycle;

(B) A billing cycle immediately following two consecutive billing cycles in which the consumer paid the entire balance in full, had a zero outstanding balance or had a credit balance; and

(C) A billing cycle where paying the minimum payment due for that billing cycle will pay the entire outstanding balance on the account for that billing cycle.

(13) Format requirements. The due date required by paragraph (b)(11) of this section shall be disclosed on the front of the first page of the periodic statement. The amount of the late payment fee and the annual percentage rate(s) required by paragraph (b)(11) of this section shall be stated in close proximity to the due date. The ending balance required by paragraph (b)(10) of this section and the disclosures required by paragraph (b)(12) of this section shall be disclosed closely proximate to the minimum payment due. The due date, late payment fee and annual percentage rate, ending balance, minimum payment due, and disclosures required by paragraph (b)(12) of this section shall be grouped together. Sample G-18(D) in Appendix G to this part sets forth an example of how these terms may be grouped.

(14) Deferred interest or similar transactions. For accounts with an outstanding balance subject to a deferred interest or similar program, the date by which that outstanding balance must be paid in full in order to avoid the obligation to pay finance charges on such balance must be disclosed on the front of any page of each periodic statement issued during the deferred interest period beginning with the first periodic statement issued during the deferred interest period that reflects the deferred interest or similar transaction. The disclosure provided pursuant to this paragraph must be substantially similar to Sample G-18(H) in Appendix G to this part.

§ 1026.8 Identifying transactions on periodic statements.

The creditor shall identify credit transactions on or with the first periodic statement that reflects the transaction by furnishing the following information, as applicable:

(a) Sale credit.

(1) Except as provided in paragraph (a)(2) of this section, for each credit transaction involving the sale of property or services, the creditor must disclose the amount and date of the transaction, and either:

(i) A brief identification of the property or services purchased, for creditors and sellers that are the same or related; or

(ii) The seller's name; and the city and state or foreign country where the transaction took place. The creditor may omit the address or provide any suitable designation that helps the consumer to identify the transaction when the transaction took place at a location that is not fixed; took place in the consumer's home; or was a mail, Internet, or telephone order.

(2) Creditors need not comply with paragraph (a)(1) of this section if an actual copy of the receipt or other credit document is provided with the first periodic statement reflecting the transaction, and the amount of the transaction and either the date of the transaction to the consumer's account or the date of debiting the transaction are disclosed on the copy or on the periodic statement.

(b) Nonsale credit. For each credit transaction not involving the sale of property or services, the creditor must disclose a brief identification of the transaction; the amount of the transaction; and at least one of the following dates: The date of the transaction, the date the transaction was debited to the consumer's account, or, if the consumer signed the credit document, the date appearing on the document. If an actual copy of the receipt or other credit document is provided and that copy shows the amount and at least one of the specified dates, the brief identification may be omitted.

(c) Alternative creditor procedures; consumer inquiries for clarification or documentation. The following procedures apply to creditors that treat an inquiry for clarification or documentation as a notice of a billing error, including correcting the account in accordance with § 1026.13(e):

(1) Failure to disclose the information required by paragraphs (a) and (b) of this section is not a failure to comply with the regulation, provided that the creditor also maintains procedures reasonably designed to obtain and provide the information. This applies to transactions that take place outside a state, as defined in § 1026.2(a)(26), whether or not the creditor maintains procedures reasonably adapted to obtain the required information.

(2) As an alternative to the brief identification for sale or nonsale credit, the creditor may disclose a number or symbol that also appears on the receipt or other credit document given to the consumer, if the number or symbol reasonably identifies that transaction with that creditor.

§ 1026.9 Subsequent disclosure requirements.

(a) Furnishing statement of billing rights.

(1) Annual statement. The creditor shall mail or deliver the billing rights statement required by § 1026.6(a)(5) and (b)(5)(iii) at least once per calendar year, at intervals of not less than 6 months nor more than 18 months, either to all consumers or to each consumer entitled to receive a periodic statement under § 1026.5(b)(2) for any one billing cycle.

(2) Alternative summary statement. As an alternative to paragraph (a)(1) of this section, the creditor may mail or deliver, on or with each periodic statement, a statement substantially similar to Model Form G-4 or Model Form G-4(A) in Appendix G to this part, as applicable. Creditors offering home-equity plans subject to the requirements of § 1026.40 may use either Model Form, at their option.

(b) Disclosures for supplemental credit access devices and additional features.

(1) If a creditor, within 30 days after mailing or delivering the account-opening disclosures under § 1026.6(a)(1) or (b)(3)(ii)(A), as applicable, adds a credit feature to the consumer's account or mails or delivers to the consumer a credit access device, including but not limited to checks that access a credit card account, for which the finance charge terms are the same as those previously disclosed, no additional disclosures are necessary. Except as provided in paragraph (b)(3) of this section, after 30 days, if the creditor adds a credit feature or furnishes a credit access device (other than as a renewal, resupply, or the original issuance of a credit card) on the same finance charge terms, the creditor shall disclose, before the consumer uses the feature or device for the first time, that it is for use in obtaining credit under the terms previously disclosed.

(2) Except as provided in paragraph (b)(3) of this section, whenever a credit feature is added or a credit access device is mailed or delivered to the consumer, and the finance charge terms for the feature or device differ from disclosures previously given, the disclosures required by § 1026.6(a)(1) or (b)(3)(ii)(A), as applicable, that are applicable to the added feature or device shall be given before the consumer uses the feature or device for the first time.

(3) Checks that access a credit card account.

(i) Disclosures. For open-end plans not subject to the requirements of § 1026.40, if checks that can be used to access a credit card account are provided more than 30 days after account-opening disclosures under § 1026.6(b) are mailed or delivered, or are provided within 30 days of the account-opening disclosures and the finance charge terms for the checks differ from the finance charge terms previously disclosed, the creditor shall disclose on the front of the page containing the checks the following terms in the form of a table with the headings, content, and form substantially similar to Sample G-19 in Appendix G to this part:

(A) If a promotional rate, as that term is defined in § 1026.16(g)(2)(i) applies to the checks:

(1) The promotional rate and the time period during which the promotional rate will remain in effect;

(2) The type of rate that will apply (such as whether the purchase or cash advance rate applies) after the promotional rate expires, and the annual percentage rate that will apply after the promotional rate expires. For a variable-rate account, a creditor must disclose an annual percentage rate based on the applicable index or formula in accordance with the accuracy requirements set forth in paragraph (b)(3)(ii) of this section; and

(3) The date, if any, by which the consumer must use the checks in order to qualify for the promotional rate. If the creditor will honor checks used after such date but will apply an annual percentage rate other than the promotional rate, the creditor must disclose this fact and the type of annual percentage rate that will apply if the consumer uses the checks after such date.

(B) If no promotional rate applies to the checks:

(1) The type of rate that will apply to the checks and the applicable annual percentage rate. For a variable-rate account, a creditor must disclose an annual percentage rate based on the applicable index or formula in accordance with the accuracy requirements set forth in paragraph (b)(3)(ii) of this section.

(2) [Reserved]

(C) Any transaction fees applicable to the checks disclosed under § 1026.6(b)(2)(iv); and

(D) Whether or not a grace period is given within which any credit extended by use of the checks may be repaid without incurring a finance charge due to a periodic interest rate. When disclosing whether there is a grace period, the phrase "How to Avoid Paying Interest on Check Transactions" shall be used as the row heading when a grace period applies to credit extended by the use of the checks. When disclosing the fact that no grace period exists for credit extended by use of the checks, the phrase "Paying Interest" shall be used as the row heading.

(ii) Accuracy. The disclosures in paragraph (b)(3)(i) of this section must be accurate as of the time the disclosures are mailed or delivered. A variable annual percentage rate is accurate if it was in effect within 60 days of when the disclosures are mailed or delivered.

(iii) Variable rates. If any annual percentage rate required to be disclosed pursuant to paragraph (b)(3)(i) of this section is a variable rate, the card issuer shall also disclose the fact that the rate may vary and how the rate is determined. In describing how the applicable rate will be determined, the card issuer must identify the type of index or formula that is used in setting the rate. The value of the index and the amount of the margin that are used to calculate the variable rate shall not be disclosed in the table. A disclosure of any applicable limitations on rate increases shall not be included in the table.

(c) Change in terms.

(1) Rules affecting home-equity plans.

(i) Written notice required. For home-equity plans subject to the requirements of § 1026.40, whenever any term required to be disclosed under § 1026.6(a) is changed or the required minimum periodic payment is increased, the creditor shall mail or deliver written notice of the change to each consumer who may be affected. The notice shall be mailed or delivered at least 15 days prior to the effective date of the change. The 15-day timing requirement does not apply if the change has been agreed to by the consumer; the notice shall be given, however, before the effective date of the change.

(ii) Notice not required. For home-equity plans subject to the requirements of § 1026.40, a creditor is not required to provide notice under this section when the change involves a reduction of any component of a finance or other charge or when the change results from an agreement involving a court proceeding.

(iii) Notice to restrict credit. For home-equity plans subject to the requirements of § 1026.40, if the creditor prohibits additional extensions of credit or reduces the credit limit pursuant to § 1026.40(f)(3)(i) or (f)(3)(vi), the creditor shall mail or deliver written notice of the action to each consumer who will be affected. The notice must be provided not later than three business days after the action is taken and shall contain specific reasons for the action. If the creditor requires the consumer to request reinstatement of credit privileges, the notice also shall state that fact.

(2) Rules affecting open-end (not home-secured) plans.

(i) Changes where written advance notice is required.

(A) General. For plans other than home-equity plans subject to the requirements of § 1026.40, except as provided in paragraphs (c)(2)(i)(B), (c)(2)(iii) and (c)(2)(v) of this section, when a significant change in account terms as described in paragraph (c)(2)(ii) of this section is made, a creditor must provide a written notice of the change at least 45 days prior to the effective date of the change to each consumer who may be affected. The 45-day timing requirement does not apply if the consumer has agreed to a particular change as described in paragraph (c)(2)(i)(B) of this section; for such changes, notice must be given in accordance with the timing requirements of paragraph (c)(2)(i)(B) of this section. Increases in the rate applicable to a consumer's account due to delinquency, default or as a penalty described in paragraph (g) of this section that are not due to a change in the contractual terms of the consumer's account must be disclosed pursuant to paragraph (g) of this section instead of paragraph (c)(2) of this section.

(B) Changes agreed to by the consumer. A notice of change in terms is required, but it may be mailed or delivered as late as the effective date of the change if the consumer agrees to the particular change. This paragraph (c)(2)(i)(B) applies only when a consumer substitutes collateral or when the creditor can advance additional credit only if a change relatively unique to that consumer is made, such as the consumer's providing additional security or paying an increased minimum payment amount. The following are not considered agreements between the consumer and the creditor for purposes of this paragraph (c)(2)(i)(B): The consumer's general acceptance of the creditor's contract reservation of the right to change terms; the consumer's use of the account (which might imply acceptance of its terms under state law); the consumer's acceptance of a unilateral term change that is not particular to that consumer, but rather is of general applicability to consumers with that type of account; and the consumer's request to reopen a closed account or to upgrade an existing account to another account offered by the creditor with different credit or other features.

(ii) Significant changes in account terms. For purposes of this section, a "significant change in account terms" means a change to a term required to be disclosed under § 1026.6(b)(1) and (b)(2), an increase in the required minimum periodic payment, a change to a term required to be disclosed under § 1026.6(b)(4), or the acquisition of a security interest.

(iii) Charges not covered by § 1026.6(b)(1) and (b)(2). Except as provided in paragraph (c)(2)(vi) of this section, if a creditor increases any component of a charge, or introduces a new charge, required to be disclosed under § 1026.6(b)(3) that is not a significant change in account terms as described in paragraph (c)(2)(ii) of this section, a creditor must either, at its option:

(A) Comply with the requirements of paragraph (c)(2)(i) of this section; or

(B) Provide notice of the amount of the charge before the consumer agrees to or becomes obligated to pay the charge, at a time and in a manner that a consumer would be likely to notice the disclosure of the charge. The notice may be provided orally or in writing.

(iv) Disclosure requirements.

(A) Significant changes in account terms. If a creditor makes a significant change in account terms as described in paragraph (c)(2)(ii) of this section, the notice provided pursuant to paragraph (c)(2)(i) of this section must provide the following information:

(1) A summary of the changes made to terms required by § 1026.6(b)(1) and (b)(2) or § 1026.6(b)(4), a description of any increase in the required minimum periodic payment, and a description of any security interest being acquired by the creditor;

(2) A statement that changes are being made to the account;

(3) For accounts other than credit card accounts under an open-end (not home-secured) consumer credit plan subject to § 1026.9(c)(2)(iv)(B), a statement indicating the consumer has the right to opt out of these changes, if applicable, and a reference to additional information describing the opt-out right provided in the notice, if applicable;

(4) The date the changes will become effective;

(5) If applicable, a statement that the consumer may find additional information about the summarized changes, and other changes to the account, in the notice;

(6) If the creditor is changing a rate on the account, other than a penalty rate, a statement that if a penalty rate currently applies to the consumer's account, the new rate described in the notice will not apply to the consumer's account until the consumer's account balances are no longer subject to the penalty rate;

(7) If the change in terms being disclosed is an increase in an annual percentage rate, the balances to which the increased rate will be applied. If applicable, a statement identifying the balances to which the current rate will continue to apply as of the effective date of the change in terms; and

(8) If the change in terms being disclosed is an increase in an annual percentage rate for a credit card account under an open-end (not home-secured) consumer credit plan, a statement of no more than four principal reasons for the rate increase, listed in their order of importance.

(B) Right to reject for credit card accounts under an open-end (not home-secured) consumer credit plan. In addition to the disclosures in paragraph (c)(2)(iv)(A) of this section, if a card issuer makes a significant change in account terms on a credit card account under an open-end (not home-secured) consumer credit plan, the creditor must generally provide the following information on the notice provided pursuant to paragraph (c)(2)(i) of this section. This information is not required to be provided in the case of an increase in the required minimum periodic payment, an increase in a fee as a result of a reevaluation of a determination made under § 1026.52(b)(1)(i) or an adjustment to the safe harbors in § 1026.52(b)(1)(ii) to reflect changes in the Consumer Price Index, a change in an annual percentage rate applicable to a consumer's account, an increase in a fee previously reduced consistent with 50 U.S.C. app. 527 or a similar Federal or state statute or regulation if the amount of the increased fee does not exceed the amount of that fee prior to the reduction, or when the change results from the creditor not receiving the consumer's required minimum periodic payment within 60 days after the due date for that payment:

(1) A statement that the consumer has the right to reject the change or changes prior to the effective date of the changes, unless the consumer fails to make a required minimum periodic payment within 60 days after the due date for that payment;

(2) Instructions for rejecting the change or changes, and a toll-free telephone number that the consumer may use to notify the creditor of the rejection; and

(3) If applicable, a statement that if the consumer rejects the change or changes, the consumer's ability to use the account for further advances will be terminated or suspended.

(C) Changes resulting from failure to make minimum periodic payment within 60 days from due date for credit card accounts under an open-end (not home-secured) consumer credit plan. For a credit card account under an open-end (not home-secured) consumer credit plan:

(1) If the significant change required to be disclosed pursuant to paragraph (c)(2)(i) of this section is an increase in an annual percentage rate or a fee or charge required to be disclosed under § 1026.6(b)(2)(ii), (b)(2)(iii), or (b)(2)(xii) based on the consumer's failure to make a minimum periodic payment within 60 days from the due date for that payment, the notice provided pursuant to paragraph (c)(2)(i) of this section must state that the increase will cease to apply to transactions that occurred prior to or within 14 days of provision of the notice, if the creditor receives six consecutive required minimum periodic payments on or before the payment due date, beginning with the first payment due following the effective date of the increase.

(2) If the significant change required to be disclosed pursuant to paragraph (c)(2)(i) of this section is an increase in a fee or charge required to be disclosed under § 1026.6(b)(2)(ii), (b)(2)(iii), or (b)(2)(xii) based on the consumer's failure to make a minimum periodic payment within 60 days from the due date for that payment, the notice provided pursuant to paragraph (c)(2)(i) of this section must also state the reason for the increase.

(D) Format requirements.

(1) Tabular format. The summary of changes described in paragraph (c)(2)(iv)(A)(1) of this section must be in a tabular format (except for a summary of any increase in the required minimum periodic payment, a summary of a term required to be disclosed under § 1026.6(b)(4) that is not required to be disclosed under § 1026.6(b)(1) and (b)(2), or a description of any security interest being acquired by the creditor), with headings and format substantially similar to any of the account-opening tables found in G-17 in Appendix G to this part. The table must disclose the changed term and information relevant to the change, if that relevant information is required by § 1026.6(b)(1) and (b)(2). The new terms shall be described in the same level of detail as required when disclosing the terms under § 1026.6(b)(2).

(2) Notice included with periodic statement. If a notice required by paragraph (c)(2)(i) of this section is included on or with a periodic statement, the information described in paragraph (c)(2)(iv)(A)(1) of this section must be disclosed on the front of any page of the statement. The summary of changes described in paragraph (c)(2)(iv)(A)(1) of this section must immediately follow the information described in paragraph (c)(2)(iv)(A)(2) through (c)(2)(iv)(A)(7) and, if applicable, paragraphs (c)(2)(iv)(A)(8), (c)(2)(iv)(B), and (c)(2)(iv)(C) of this section, and be substantially similar to the format shown in Sample G-20 or G-21 in Appendix G to this part.

(3) Notice provided separately from periodic statement. If a notice required by paragraph (c)(2)(i) of this section is not included on or with a periodic statement, the information described in paragraph (c)(2)(iv)(A)(1) of this section must, at the creditor's option, be disclosed on the front of the first page of the notice or segregated on a separate page from other information given with the notice. The summary of changes required to be in a table pursuant to paragraph (c)(2)(iv)(A)(1) of this section may be on more than one page, and may use both the front and reverse sides, so long as the table begins on the front of the first page of the notice and there is a reference on the first page indicating that the table continues on the following page. The summary of changes described in paragraph (c)(2)(iv)(A)(1) of this section must immediately follow the information described in paragraph (c)(2)(iv)(A)(2) through (c)(2)(iv)(A)(7) and, if applicable, paragraphs (c)(2)(iv)(A)(8), (c)(2)(iv)(B), and (c)(2)(iv)(C), of this section, substantially similar to the format shown in Sample G-20 or G-21 in Appendix G to this part.

(v) Notice not required. For open-end plans (other than home equity plans subject to the requirements of § 1026.40) a creditor is not required to provide notice under this section:

(A) When the change involves charges for documentary evidence; a reduction of any component of a finance or other charge; suspension of future credit privileges (except as provided in paragraph (c)(2)(vi) of this section) or termination of an account or plan; when the change results from an agreement involving a court proceeding; when the change is an extension of the grace period; or if the change is applicable only to checks that access a credit card account and the changed terms are disclosed on or with the checks in accordance with paragraph (b)(3) of this section;

(B) When the change is an increase in an annual percentage rate or fee upon the expiration of a specified period of time, provided that:

(1) Prior to commencement of that period, the creditor disclosed in writing to the consumer, in a clear and conspicuous manner, the length of the period and the annual percentage rate or fee that would apply after expiration of the period;

(2) The disclosure of the length of the period and the annual percentage rate or fee that would apply after expiration of the period are set forth in close proximity and in equal prominence to the first listing of the disclosure of the rate or fee that applies during the specified period of time; and

(3) The annual percentage rate or fee that applies after that period does not exceed the rate or fee disclosed pursuant to paragraph (c)(2)(v)(B)(1) of this paragraph or, if the rate disclosed pursuant to paragraph (c)(2)(v)(B)(1) of this section was a variable rate, the rate following any such increase is a variable rate determined by the same formula (index and margin) that was used to calculate the variable rate disclosed pursuant to paragraph (c)(2)(v)(B)(1);

(C) When the change is an increase in a variable annual percentage rate in accordance with a credit card or other account agreement that provides for changes in the rate according to operation of an index that is not under the control of the creditor and is available to the general public; or

(D) When the change is an increase in an annual percentage rate, a fee or charge required to be disclosed under § 1026.6(b)(2)(ii), (b)(2)(iii), (b)(2)(viii), (b)(2)(ix), or (b)(2)(xii), or the required minimum periodic payment due to the completion of a workout or temporary hardship arrangement by the consumer or the consumer's failure to comply with the terms of such an arrangement, provided that:

(1) The annual percentage rate or fee or charge applicable to a category of transactions or the required minimum periodic payment following any such increase does not exceed the rate or fee or charge or required minimum periodic payment that applied to that category of transactions prior to commencement of the arrangement or, if the rate that applied to a category of transactions prior to the commencement of the workout or temporary hardship arrangement was a variable rate, the rate following any such increase is a variable rate determined by the same formula (index and margin) that applied to the category of transactions prior to commencement of the workout or temporary hardship arrangement; and

(2) The creditor has provided the consumer, prior to the commencement of such arrangement, with a clear and conspicuous disclosure of the terms of the arrangement (including any increases due to such completion or failure). This disclosure must generally be provided in writing. However, a creditor may provide the disclosure of the terms of the arrangement orally by telephone, provided that the creditor mails or delivers a written disclosure of the terms of the arrangement to the consumer as soon as reasonably practicable after the oral disclosure is provided.

(vi) Reduction of the credit limit. For open-end plans that are not subject to the requirements of § 1026.40, if a creditor decreases the credit limit on an account, advance notice of the decrease must be provided before an over-the-limit fee or a penalty rate can be imposed solely as a result of the consumer exceeding the newly decreased credit limit. Notice shall be provided in writing or orally at least 45 days prior to imposing the over-the-limit fee or penalty rate and shall state that the credit limit on the account has been or will be decreased.

(d) Finance charge imposed at time of transaction.

(1) Any person, other than the card issuer, who imposes a finance charge at the time of honoring a consumer's credit card, shall disclose the amount of that finance charge prior to its imposition.

(2) The card issuer, other than the person honoring the consumer's credit card, shall have no responsibility for the disclosure required by paragraph (d)(1) of this section, and shall not consider any such charge for the purposes of §§ 1026.60, 1026.6 and 1026.7.

(e) Disclosures upon renewal of credit or charge card.

(1) Notice prior to renewal. A card issuer that imposes any annual or other periodic fee to renew a credit or charge card account of the type subject to § 1026.60, including any fee based on account activity or inactivity or any card issuer that has changed or amended any term of a cardholder's account required to be disclosed under § 1026.6(b)(1) and (b)(2) that has not previously been disclosed to the consumer, shall mail or deliver written notice of the renewal to the cardholder. If the card issuer imposes any annual or other periodic fee for renewal, the notice shall be provided at least 30 days or one billing cycle, whichever is less, before the mailing or the delivery of the periodic statement on which any renewal fee is initially charged to the account. If the card issuer has changed or amended any term required to be disclosed under § 1026.6(b)(1) and (b)(2) and such changed or amended term has not previously been disclosed to the consumer, the notice shall be provided at least 30 days prior to the scheduled renewal date of the consumer's credit or charge card. The notice shall contain the following information:

(i) The disclosures contained in § 1026.60(b)(1) through (b)(7) that would apply if the account were renewed; and

(ii) How and when the cardholder may terminate credit availability under the account to avoid paying the renewal fee, if applicable.

(2) Notification on periodic statements. The disclosures required by this paragraph may be made on or with a periodic statement. If any of the disclosures are provided on the back of a periodic statement, the card issuer shall include a reference to those disclosures on the front of the statement.

(f) Change in credit card account insurance provider.

(1) Notice prior to change. If a credit card issuer plans to change the provider of insurance for repayment of all or part of the outstanding balance of an open-end credit card account of the type subject to § 1026.60, the card issuer shall mail or deliver to the cardholder written notice of the change not less than 30 days before the change in provider occurs. The notice shall also include the following items, to the extent applicable:

(i) Any increase in the rate that will result from the change;

(ii) Any substantial decrease in coverage that will result from the change; and

(iii) A statement that the cardholder may discontinue the insurance.

(2) Notice when change in provider occurs. If a change described in paragraph (f)(1) of this section occurs, the card issuer shall provide the cardholder with a written notice no later than 30 days after the change, including the following items, to the extent applicable:

(i) The name and address of the new insurance provider;

(ii) A copy of the new policy or group certificate containing the basic terms of the insurance, including the rate to be charged; and

(iii) A statement that the cardholder may discontinue the insurance.

(3) Substantial decrease in coverage. For purposes of this paragraph, a substantial decrease in coverage is a decrease in a significant term of coverage that might reasonably be expected to affect the cardholder's decision to continue the insurance. Significant terms of coverage include, for example, the following:

(i) Type of coverage provided;

(ii) Age at which coverage terminates or becomes more restrictive;

(iii) Maximum insurable loan balance, maximum periodic benefit payment, maximum number of payments, or other term affecting the dollar amount of coverage or benefits provided;

(iv) Eligibility requirements and number and identity of persons covered;

(v) Definition of a key term of coverage such as disability;

(vi) Exclusions from or limitations on coverage; and

(vii) Waiting periods and whether coverage is retroactive.

(4) Combined notification. The notices required by paragraph (f)(1) and (2) of this section may be combined provided the timing requirement of paragraph (f)(1) of this section is met. The notices may be provided on or with a periodic statement.

(g) Increase in rates due to delinquency or default or as a penalty.

(1) Increases subject to this section. For plans other than home-equity plans subject to the requirements of § 1026.40, except as provided in paragraph (g)(4) of this section, a creditor must provide a written notice to each consumer who may be affected when:

(i) A rate is increased due to the consumer's delinquency or default; or

(ii) A rate is increased as a penalty for one or more events specified in the account agreement, such as making a late payment or obtaining an extension of credit that exceeds the credit limit.

(2) Timing of written notice. Whenever any notice is required to be given pursuant to paragraph (g)(1) of this section, the creditor shall provide written notice of the increase in rates at least 45 days prior to the effective date of the increase. The notice must be provided after the occurrence of the events described in paragraphs (g)(1)(i) and (g)(1)(ii) of this section that trigger the imposition of the rate increase.

(3)(i) Disclosure requirements for rate increases.

(A) General. If a creditor is increasing the rate due to delinquency or default or as a penalty, the creditor must provide the following information on the notice sent pursuant to paragraph (g)(1) of this section:

(1) A statement that the delinquency or default rate or penalty rate, as applicable, has been triggered;

(2) The date on which the delinquency or default rate or penalty rate will apply;

(3) The circumstances under which the delinquency or default rate or penalty rate, as applicable, will cease to apply to the consumer's account, or that the delinquency or default rate or penalty rate will remain in effect for a potentially indefinite time period;

(4) A statement indicating to which balances the delinquency or default rate or penalty rate will be applied;

(5) If applicable, a description of any balances to which the current rate will continue to apply as of the effective date of the rate increase, unless a consumer fails to make a minimum periodic payment within 60 days from the due date for that payment; and

(6) For a credit card account under an open-end (not home-secured) consumer credit plan, a statement of no more than four principal reasons for the rate increase, listed in their order of importance.

(B) Rate increases resulting from failure to make minimum periodic payment within 60 days from due date. For a credit card account under an open-end (not home-secured) consumer credit plan, if the rate increase required to be disclosed pursuant to paragraph (g)(1) of this section is an increase pursuant to § 1026.55(b)(4) based on the consumer's failure to make a minimum periodic payment within 60 days from the due date for that payment, the notice provided pursuant to paragraph (g)(1) of this section must also state that the increase will cease to apply to transactions that occurred prior to or within 14 days of provision of the notice, if the creditor receives six consecutive required minimum periodic payments on or before the payment due date, beginning with the first payment due following the effective date of the increase.

(ii) Format requirements.

(A) If a notice required by paragraph (g)(1) of this section is included on or with a periodic statement, the information described in paragraph (g)(3)(i) of this section must be in the form of a table and provided on the front of any page of the periodic statement, above the notice described in paragraph (c)(2)(iv) of this section if that notice is provided on the same statement.

(B) If a notice required by paragraph (g)(1) of this section is not included on or with a periodic statement, the information described in paragraph (g)(3)(i) of this section must be disclosed on the front of the first page of the notice. Only information related to the increase in the rate to a penalty rate may be included with the notice, except that this notice may be combined with a notice described in paragraph (c)(2)(iv) or (g)(4) of this section.

(4) Exception for decrease in credit limit. A creditor is not required to provide a notice pursuant to paragraph (g)(1) of this section prior to increasing the rate for obtaining an extension of credit that exceeds the credit limit, provided that:

(i) The creditor provides at least 45 days in advance of imposing the penalty rate a notice, in writing, that includes:

(A) A statement that the credit limit on the account has been or will be decreased.

(B) A statement indicating the date on which the penalty rate will apply, if the outstanding balance exceeds the credit limit as of that date;

(C) A statement that the penalty rate will not be imposed on the date specified in paragraph (g)(4)(i)(B) of this section, if the outstanding balance does not exceed the credit limit as of that date;

(D) The circumstances under which the penalty rate, if applied, will cease to apply to the account, or that the penalty rate, if applied, will remain in effect for a potentially indefinite time period;

(E) A statement indicating to which balances the penalty rate may be applied; and

(F) If applicable, a description of any balances to which the current rate will continue to apply as of the effective date of the rate increase, unless the consumer fails to make a minimum periodic payment within 60 days from the due date for that payment; and

(ii) The creditor does not increase the rate applicable to the consumer's account to the penalty rate if the outstanding balance does not exceed the credit limit on the date set forth in the notice and described in paragraph (g)(4)(i)(B) of this section.

(iii)(A) If a notice provided pursuant to paragraph (g)(4)(i) of this section is included on or with a periodic statement, the information described in paragraph (g)(4)(i) of this section must be in the form of a table and provided on the front of any page of the periodic statement; or

(B) If a notice required by paragraph (g)(4)(i) of this section is not included on or with a periodic statement, the information described in paragraph (g)(4)(i) of this section must be disclosed on the front of the first page of the notice. Only information related to the reduction in credit limit may be included with the notice, except that this notice may be combined with a notice described in paragraph (c)(2)(iv) or (g)(1) of this section.

(h) Consumer rejection of certain significant changes in terms.

(1) Right to reject. If paragraph (c)(2)(iv)(B) of this section requires disclosure of the consumer's right to reject a significant change to an account term, the consumer may reject that change by notifying the creditor of the rejection before the effective date of the change.

(2) Effect of rejection. If a creditor is notified of a rejection of a significant change to an account term as provided in paragraph (h)(1) of this section, the creditor must not:

(i) Apply the change to the account;

(ii) Impose a fee or charge or treat the account as in default solely as a result of the rejection; or

(iii) Require repayment of the balance on the account using a method that is less beneficial to the consumer than one of the methods listed in § 1026.55(c)(2).

(3) Exception. Section 1026.9(h) does not apply when the creditor has not received the consumer's required minimum periodic payment within 60 days after the due date for that payment.

§ 1026.10 Payments.

(a) General rule. A creditor shall credit a payment to the consumer's account as of the date of receipt, except when a delay in crediting does not result in a finance or other charge or except as provided in paragraph (b) of this section.

(b) Specific requirements for payments.

(1) General rule. A creditor may specify reasonable requirements for payments that enable most consumers to make conforming payments.

(2) Examples of reasonable requirements for payments. Reasonable requirements for making payment may include:

(i) Requiring that payments be accompanied by the account number or payment stub;

(ii) Setting reasonable cut-off times for payments to be received by mail, by electronic means, by telephone, and in person (except as provided in paragraph (b)(3) of this section), provided that such cut-off times shall be no earlier than 5 p.m. on the payment due date at the location specified by the creditor for the receipt of such payments;

(iii) Specifying that only checks or money orders should be sent by mail;

(iv) Specifying that payment is to be made in U.S. dollars; or

(v) Specifying one particular address for receiving payments, such as a post office box.

(3) In-person payments on credit card accounts.

(i) General. Notwithstanding § 1026.10(b), payments on a credit card account under an open-end (not home-secured) consumer credit plan made in person at a branch or office of a card issuer that is a financial institution prior to the close of business of that branch or office shall be considered received on the date on which the consumer makes the payment. A card issuer that is a financial institution shall not impose a cut-off time earlier than the close of business for any such payments made in person at any branch or office of the card issuer at which such payments are accepted. Notwithstanding § 1026.10(b)(2)(ii), a card issuer may impose a cut-off time earlier than 5 p.m. for such payments, if the close of business of the branch or office is earlier than 5 p.m.

(ii) Financial institution. For purposes of paragraph (b)(3) of this section, "financial institution" shall mean a bank, savings association, or credit union.

(4) Nonconforming payments.

(i) In general. Except as provided in paragraph (b)(4)(ii) of this section, if a creditor specifies, on or with the periodic statement, requirements for the consumer to follow in making payments as permitted under this § 1026.10, but accepts a payment that does not conform to the requirements, the creditor shall credit the payment within five days of receipt.

(ii) Payment methods promoted by creditor. If a creditor promotes a method for making payments, such payments shall be considered conforming payments in accordance with this paragraph (b) and shall be credited to the consumer's account as of the date of receipt, except when a delay in crediting does not result in a finance or other charge.

(c) Adjustment of account. If a creditor fails to credit a payment, as required by paragraphs (a) or (b) of this section, in time to avoid the imposition of finance or other charges, the creditor shall adjust the consumer's account so that the charges imposed are credited to the consumer's account during the next billing cycle.

(d) Crediting of payments when creditor does not receive or accept payments on due date.

(1) General. Except as provided in paragraph (d)(2) of this section, if a creditor does not receive or accept payments by mail on the due date for payments, the creditor may generally not treat a payment received the next business day as late for any purpose. For purposes of this paragraph (d), the "next business day" means the next day on which the creditor accepts or receives payments by mail.

(2) Payments accepted or received other than by mail. If a creditor accepts or receives payments made on the due date by a method other than mail, such as electronic or telephone payments, the creditor is not required to treat a payment made by that method on the next business day as timely, even if it does not accept mailed payments on the due date.

(e) Limitations on fees related to method of payment. For credit card accounts under an open-end (not home-secured) consumer credit plan, a creditor may not impose a separate fee to allow consumers to make a payment by any method, such as mail, electronic, or telephone payments, unless such payment method involves an expedited service by a customer service representative of the creditor. For purposes of paragraph (e) of this section, the term "creditor" includes a third party that collects, receives, or processes payments on behalf of a creditor.

(f) Changes by card issuer. If a card issuer makes a material change in the address for receiving payments or procedures for handling payments, and such change causes a material delay in the crediting of a payment to the consumer's account during the 60-day period following the date on which such change took effect, the card issuer may not impose any late fee or finance charge for a late payment on the credit card account during the 60-day period following the date on which the change took effect.

§ 1026.11 Treatment of credit balances; account termination.

(a) Credit balances. When a credit balance in excess of $1 is created on a credit account (through transmittal of funds to a creditor in excess of the total balance due on an account, through rebates of unearned finance charges or insurance premiums, or through amounts otherwise owed to or held for the benefit of the consumer), the creditor shall:

(1) Credit the amount of the credit balance to the consumer's account;

(2) Refund any part of the remaining credit balance within seven business days from receipt of a written request from the consumer;

(3) Make a good faith effort to refund to the consumer by cash, check, or money order, or credit to a deposit account of the consumer, any part of the credit balance remaining in the account for more than six months. No further action is required if the consumer's current location is not known to the creditor and cannot be traced through the consumer's last known address or telephone number.

(b) Account termination.

(1) A creditor shall not terminate an account prior to its expiration date solely because the consumer does not incur a finance charge.

(2) Nothing in paragraph (b)(1) of this section prohibits a creditor from terminating an account that is inactive for three or more consecutive months. An account is inactive for purposes of this paragraph if no credit has been extended (such as by purchase, cash advance or balance transfer) and if the account has no outstanding balance.

(c) Timely settlement of estate debts.

(1) General rule.

(i) Reasonable policies and procedures required. For credit card accounts under an open-end (not home-secured) consumer credit plan, card issuers must adopt reasonable written policies and procedures designed to ensure that an administrator of an estate of a deceased accountholder can determine the amount of and pay any balance on the account in a timely manner.

(ii) Application to joint accounts. Paragraph (c) of this section does not apply to the account of a deceased consumer if a joint accountholder remains on the account.

(2) Timely statement of balance.

(i) Requirement. Upon request by the administrator of an estate, a card issuer must provide the administrator with the amount of the balance on a deceased consumer's account in a timely manner.

(ii) Safe harbor. For purposes of paragraph (c)(2)(i) of this section, providing the amount of the balance on the account within 30 days of receiving the request is deemed to be timely.

(3) Limitations after receipt of request from administrator.

(i) Limitation on fees and increases in annual percentage rates. After receiving a request from the administrator of an estate for the amount of the balance on a deceased consumer's account, a card issuer must not impose any fees on the account (such as a late fee, annual fee, or over-the-limit fee) or increase any annual percentage rate, except as provided by § 1026.55(b)(2).

(ii) Limitation on trailing or residual interest. A card issuer must waive or rebate any additional finance charge due to a periodic interest rate if payment in full of the balance disclosed pursuant to paragraph (c)(2) of this section is received within 30 days after disclosure.

§ 1026.12 Special credit card provisions.

(a) Issuance of credit cards. Regardless of the purpose for which a credit card is to be used, including business, commercial, or agricultural use, no credit card shall be issued to any person except:

(1) In response to an oral or written request or application for the card; or

(2) As a renewal of, or substitute for, an accepted credit card.

(b) Liability of cardholder for unauthorized use.

(1)(i) Definition of unauthorized use. For purposes of this section, the term "unauthorized use" means the use of a credit card by a person, other than the cardholder, who does not have actual, implied, or apparent authority for such use, and from which the cardholder receives no benefit.

(ii) Limitation on amount. The liability of a cardholder for unauthorized use of a credit card shall not exceed the lesser of $50 or the amount of money, property, labor, or services obtained by the unauthorized use before notification to the card issuer under paragraph (b)(3) of this section.

(2) Conditions of liability. A cardholder shall be liable for unauthorized use of a credit card only if:

(i) The credit card is an accepted credit card;

(ii) The card issuer has provided adequate notice of the cardholder's maximum potential liability and of means by which the card issuer may be notified of loss or theft of the card. The notice shall state that the cardholder's liability shall not exceed $50 (or any lesser amount) and that the cardholder may give oral or written notification, and shall describe a means of notification (for example, a telephone number, an address, or both); and

(iii) The card issuer has provided a means to identify the cardholder on the account or the authorized user of the card.

(3) Notification to card issuer. Notification to a card issuer is given when steps have been taken as may be reasonably required in the ordinary course of business to provide the card issuer with the pertinent information about the loss, theft, or possible unauthorized use of a credit card, regardless of whether any particular officer, employee, or agent of the card issuer does, in fact, receive the information. Notification may be given, at the option of the person giving it, in person, by telephone, or in writing. Notification in writing is considered given at the time of receipt or, whether or not received, at the expiration of the time ordinarily required for transmission, whichever is earlier.

(4) Effect of other applicable law or agreement. If state law or an agreement between a cardholder and the card issuer imposes lesser liability than that provided in this paragraph, the lesser liability shall govern.

(5) Business use of credit cards. If 10 or more credit cards are issued by one card issuer for use by the employees of an organization, this section does not prohibit the card issuer and the organization from agreeing to liability for unauthorized use without regard to this section. However, liability for unauthorized use may be imposed on an employee of the organization, by either the card issuer or the organization, only in accordance with this section.

(c) Right of cardholder to assert claims or defenses against card issuer.

(1) General rule. When a person who honors a credit card fails to resolve satisfactorily a dispute as to property or services purchased with the credit card in a consumer credit transaction, the cardholder may assert against the card issuer all claims (other than tort claims) and defenses arising out of the transaction and relating to the failure to resolve the dispute. The cardholder may withhold payment up to the amount of credit outstanding for the property or services that gave rise to the dispute and any finance or other charges imposed on that amount.

(2) Adverse credit reports prohibited. If, in accordance with paragraph (c)(1) of this section, the cardholder withholds payment of the amount of credit outstanding for the disputed transaction, the card issuer shall not report that amount as delinquent until the dispute is settled or judgment is rendered.

(3) Limitations.

(i) General. The rights stated in paragraphs (c)(1) and (c)(2) of this section apply only if:

(A) The cardholder has made a good faith attempt to resolve the dispute with the person honoring the credit card; and

(B) The amount of credit extended to obtain the property or services that result in the assertion of the claim or defense by the cardholder exceeds $50, and the disputed transaction occurred in the same state as the cardholder's current designated address or, if not within the same state, within 100 miles from that address.

(ii) Exclusion. The limitations stated in paragraph (c)(3)(i)(B) of this section shall not apply when the person honoring the credit card:

(A) Is the same person as the card issuer;

(B) Is controlled by the card issuer directly or indirectly;

(C) Is under the direct or indirect control of a third person that also directly or indirectly controls the card issuer;

(D) Controls the card issuer directly or indirectly;

(E) Is a franchised dealer in the card issuer's products or services; or

(F) Has obtained the order for the disputed transaction through a mail solicitation made or participated in by the card issuer.

(d) Offsets by card issuer prohibited.

(1) General rule. A card issuer may not take any action, either before or after termination of credit card privileges, to offset a cardholder's indebtedness arising from a consumer credit transaction under the relevant credit card plan against funds of the cardholder held on deposit with the card issuer.

(2) Rights of the card issuer. This paragraph (d) does not alter or affect the right of a card issuer acting under state or Federal law to do any of the following with regard to funds of a cardholder held on deposit with the card issuer if the same procedure is constitutionally available to creditors generally: Obtain or enforce a consensual security interest in the funds; attach or otherwise levy upon the funds; or obtain or enforce a court order relating to the funds.

(3) Periodic deductions.

(i) This paragraph (d) does not prohibit a plan, if authorized in writing by the cardholder, under which the card issuer may periodically deduct all or part of the cardholder's credit card debt from a deposit account held with the card issuer (subject to the limitations in § 1026.13(d)(1)).

(ii) With respect to a covered separate credit feature accessible by a hybrid prepaid-credit card as defined in § 1026.61, for purposes of this paragraph (d)(3), "periodically" means no more frequently than once per calendar month, such as on a monthly due date disclosed on the applicable periodic statement in accordance with the requirements of § 1026.7(b)(11) (i)(A) or on an earlier date in each calendar month in accordance with a written authorization signed by the consumer.

(e) Prompt notification of returns and crediting of refunds.

(1) When a creditor other than the card issuer accepts the return of property or forgives a debt for services that is to be reflected as a credit to the consumer's credit card account, that creditor shall, within 7 business days from accepting the return or forgiving the debt, transmit a credit statement to the card issuer through the card issuer's normal channels for credit statements.

(2) The card issuer shall, within 3 business days from receipt of a credit statement, credit the consumer's account with the amount of the refund.

(3) If a creditor other than a card issuer routinely gives cash refunds to consumers paying in cash, the creditor shall also give credit or cash refunds to consumers using credit cards, unless it discloses at the time the transaction is consummated that credit or cash refunds for returns are not given. This section does not require refunds for returns nor does it prohibit refunds in kind.

(f) Discounts; tie-in arrangements. No card issuer may, by contract or otherwise:

(1) Prohibit any person who honors a credit card from offering a discount to a consumer to induce the consumer to pay by cash, check, or similar means rather than by use of a credit card or its underlying account for the purchase of property or services; or

(2) Require any person who honors the card issuer's credit card to open or maintain any account or obtain any other service not essential to the operation of the credit card plan from the card issuer or any other person, as a condition of participation in a credit card plan. If maintenance of an account for clearing purposes is determined to be essential to the operation of the credit card plan, it may be required only if no service charges or minimum balance requirements are imposed.

(g) Relation to Electronic Fund Transfer Act and Regulation E. For guidance on whether Regulation Z (12 CFR part 1026) or Regulation E (12 CFR part 1005) applies in instances involving both credit and electronic fund transfer aspects, refer to Regulation E, 12 CFR 1005.12(a) regarding issuance and liability for unauthorized use. On matters other than issuance and liability, this section applies to the credit aspects of combined credit/electronic fund transfer transactions, as applicable.

§ 1026.13 Billing error resolution.

(a) Definition of billing error. For purposes of this section, the term billing error means:

(1) A reflection on or with a periodic statement of an extension of credit that is not made to the consumer or to a person who has actual, implied, or apparent authority to use the consumer's credit card or open-end credit plan.

(2) A reflection on or with a periodic statement of an extension of credit that is not identified in accordance with the requirements of §§ 1026.7(a)(2) or (b)(2), as applicable, and 1026.8.

(3) A reflection on or with a periodic statement of an extension of credit for property or services not accepted by the consumer or the consumer's designee, or not delivered to the consumer or the consumer's designee as agreed.

(4) A reflection on a periodic statement of the creditor's failure to credit properly a payment or other credit issued to the consumer's account.

(5) A reflection on a periodic statement of a computational or similar error of an accounting nature that is made by the creditor.

(6) A reflection on a periodic statement of an extension of credit for which the consumer requests additional clarification, including documentary evidence.

(7) The creditor's failure to mail or deliver a periodic statement to the consumer's last known address if that address was received by the creditor, in writing, at least 20 days before the end of the billing cycle for which the statement was required.

(b) Billing error notice. A billing error notice is a written notice from a consumer that:

(1) Is received by a creditor at the address disclosed under § 1026.7(a)(9) or (b)(9), as applicable, no later than 60 days after the creditor transmitted the first periodic statement that reflects the alleged billing error;

(2) Enables the creditor to identify the consumer's name and account number; and

(3) To the extent possible, indicates the consumer's belief and the reasons for the belief that a billing error exists, and the type, date, and amount of the error.

(c) Time for resolution; general procedures.

(1) The creditor shall mail or deliver written acknowledgment to the consumer within 30 days of receiving a billing error notice, unless the creditor has complied with the appropriate resolution procedures of paragraphs (e) and (f) of this section, as applicable, within the 30-day period; and

(2) The creditor shall comply with the appropriate resolution procedures of paragraphs (e) and (f) of this section, as applicable, within 2 complete billing cycles (but in no event later than 90 days) after receiving a billing error notice.

(d) Rules pending resolution. Until a billing error is resolved under paragraph (e) or (f) of this section, the following rules apply:

(1) Consumer's right to withhold disputed amount; collection action prohibited. The consumer need not pay (and the creditor may not try to collect) any portion of any required payment that the consumer believes is related to the disputed amount (including related finance or other charges). If the cardholder has enrolled in an automatic payment plan offered by the card issuer and has agreed to pay the credit card indebtedness by periodic deductions from the cardholder's deposit account, the card issuer shall not deduct any part of the disputed amount or related finance or other charges if a billing error notice is received any time up to 3 business days before the scheduled payment date.

(2) Adverse credit reports prohibited. The creditor or its agent shall not (directly or indirectly) make or threaten to make an adverse report to any person about the consumer's credit standing, or report that an amount or account is delinquent, because the consumer failed to pay the disputed amount or related finance or other charges.

(3) Acceleration of debt and restriction of account prohibited. A creditor shall not accelerate any part of the consumer's indebtedness or restrict or close a consumer's account solely because the consumer has exercised in good faith rights provided by this section. A creditor may be subject to the forfeiture penalty under 15 U.S.C. 1666(e) for failure to comply with any of the requirements of this section.

(4) Permitted creditor actions. A creditor is not prohibited from taking action to collect any undisputed portion of the item or bill; from deducting any disputed amount and related finance or other charges from the consumer's credit limit on the account; or from reflecting a disputed amount and related finance or other charges on a periodic statement, provided that the creditor indicates on or with the periodic statement that payment of any disputed amount and related finance or other charges is not required pending the creditor's compliance with this section.

(e) Procedures if billing error occurred as asserted. If a creditor determines that a billing error occurred as asserted, it shall within the time limits in paragraph (c)(2) of this section:

(1) Correct the billing error and credit the consumer's account with any disputed amount and related finance or other charges, as applicable; and

(2) Mail or deliver a correction notice to the consumer.

(f) Procedures if different billing error or no billing error occurred. If, after conducting a reasonable investigation, a creditor determines that no billing error occurred or that a different billing error occurred from that asserted, the creditor shall within the time limits in paragraph (c)(2) of this section:

(1) Mail or deliver to the consumer an explanation that sets forth the reasons for the creditor's belief that the billing error alleged by the consumer is incorrect in whole or in part;

(2) Furnish copies of documentary evidence of the consumer's indebtedness, if the consumer so requests; and

(3) If a different billing error occurred, correct the billing error and credit the consumer's account with any disputed amount and related finance or other charges, as applicable.

(g) Creditor's rights and duties after resolution. If a creditor, after complying with all of the requirements of this section, determines that a consumer owes all or part of the disputed amount and related finance or other charges, the creditor:

(1) Shall promptly notify the consumer in writing of the time when payment is due and the portion of the disputed amount and related finance or other charges that the consumer still owes;

(2) Shall allow any time period disclosed under § 1026.6(a)(1) or (b)(2)(v), as applicable, and § 1026.7(a)(8) or (b)(8), as applicable, during which the consumer can pay the amount due under paragraph (g)(1) of this section without incurring additional finance or other charges;

(3) May report an account or amount as delinquent because the amount due under paragraph (g)(1) of this section remains unpaid after the creditor has allowed any time period disclosed under § 1026.6(a)(1) or (b)(2)(v), as applicable, and § 1026.7(a)(8) or (b)(8), as applicable or 10 days (whichever is longer) during which the consumer can pay the amount; but

(4) May not report that an amount or account is delinquent because the amount due under paragraph (g)(1) of the section remains unpaid, if the creditor receives (within the time allowed for payment in paragraph (g)(3) of this section) further written notice from the consumer that any portion of the billing error is still in dispute, unless the creditor also:

(i) Promptly reports that the amount or account is in dispute;

(ii) Mails or delivers to the consumer (at the same time the report is made) a written notice of the name and address of each person to whom the creditor makes a report; and

(iii) Promptly reports any subsequent resolution of the reported delinquency to all persons to whom the creditor has made a report.

(h) Reassertion of billing error. A creditor that has fully complied with the requirements of this section has no further responsibilities under this section (other than as provided in paragraph (g)(4) of this section) if a consumer reasserts substantially the same billing error.

(i) Relation to Electronic Fund Transfer Act and Regulation E. A creditor shall comply with the requirements of Regulation E, 12 CFR 1005.11, and 1005.18(e) as applicable, governing error resolution rather than those of paragraphs (a), (b), (c), (e), (f), and (h) of this section if:

(1) Except with respect to a prepaid account as defined in § 1026.61, an extension of credit that is incident to an electronic fund transfer occurs under an agreement between the consumer and a financial institution to extend credit when the consumer's account is overdrawn or to maintain a specified minimum balance in the consumer's account; or

(2) With regard to a covered separate credit feature and an asset feature of a prepaid account where both are accessible by a hybrid prepaid-credit card as defined in § 1026.61, an extension of credit that is incident to an electronic fund transfer occurs when the hybrid prepaid-credit card accesses both funds in the asset feature of the prepaid account and a credit extension from the credit feature with respect to a particular transaction.

§ 1026.14 Determination of annual percentage rate.

(a) General rule. The annual percentage rate is a measure of the cost of credit, expressed as a yearly rate. An annual percentage rate shall be considered accurate if it is not more than 1/8th of 1 percentage point above or below the annual percentage rate determined in accordance with this section. An error in disclosure of the annual percentage rate or finance charge shall not, in itself, be considered a violation of this part if:

(1) The error resulted from a corresponding error in a calculation tool used in good faith by the creditor; and

(2) Upon discovery of the error, the creditor promptly discontinues use of that calculation tool for disclosure purposes, and notifies the Bureau in writing of the error in the calculation tool.

(b) Annual percentage rate—in general. Where one or more periodic rates may be used to compute the finance charge, the annual percentage rate(s) to be disclosed for purposes of §§ 1026.60,

1026.40, 1026.6, 1026.7(a)(4) or (b)(4), 1026.9, 1026.15, 1026.16, 1026.26, 1026.55, and 1026.56 shall be computed by multiplying each periodic rate by the number of periods in a year.

(c) Optional effective annual percentage rate for periodic statements for creditors offering open-end credit plans secured by a consumer's dwelling. A creditor offering an open-end plan subject to the requirements of § 1026.40 need not disclose an effective annual percentage rate. Such a creditor may, at its option, disclose an effective annual percentage rate(s) pursuant to § 1026.7(a)(7) and compute the effective annual percentage rate as follows:

(1) Solely periodic rates imposed. If the finance charge is determined solely by applying one or more periodic rates, at the creditor's option, either:

(i) By multiplying each periodic rate by the number of periods in a year; or

(ii) By dividing the total finance charge for the billing cycle by the sum of the balances to which the periodic rates were applied and multiplying the quotient (expressed as a percentage) by the number of billing cycles in a year.

(2) Minimum or fixed charge, but not transaction charge, imposed. If the finance charge imposed during the billing cycle is or includes a minimum, fixed, or other charge not due to the application of a periodic rate, other than a charge with respect to any specific transaction during the billing cycle, by dividing the total finance charge for the billing cycle by the amount of the balance(s) to which it is applicable and multiplying the quotient (expressed as a percentage) by the number of billing cycles in a year. If there is no balance to which the finance charge is applicable, an annual percentage rate cannot be determined under this section. Where the finance charge imposed during the billing cycle is or includes a loan fee, points, or similar charge that relates to opening, renewing, or continuing an account, the amount of such charge shall not be included in the calculation of the annual percentage rate.

(3) Transaction charge imposed. If the finance charge imposed during the billing cycle is or includes a charge relating to a specific transaction during the billing cycle (even if the total finance charge also includes any other minimum, fixed, or other charge not due to the application of a periodic rate), by dividing the total finance charge imposed during the billing cycle by the total of all balances and other amounts on which a finance charge was imposed during the billing cycle without duplication, and multiplying the quotient (expressed as a percentage) by the number of billing cycles in a year, except that the annual percentage rate shall not be less than the largest rate determined by multiplying each periodic rate imposed during the billing cycle by the number of periods in a year. Where the finance charge imposed during the billing cycle is or includes a loan fee, points, or similar charge that relates to the opening, renewing, or continuing an account, the amount of such charge shall not be included in the calculation of the annual percentage rate. See Appendix F to this part regarding determination of the denominator of the fraction under this paragraph.

(4) If the finance charge imposed during the billing cycle is or includes a minimum, fixed, or other charge not due to the application of a periodic rate and the total finance charge imposed during the billing cycle does not exceed 50 cents for a monthly or longer billing cycle, or the pro rata part of 50 cents for a billing cycle shorter than monthly, at the creditor's option, by multiplying each applicable periodic rate by the number of periods in a year, notwithstanding the provisions of paragraphs (c)(2) and (c)(3) of this section.

(d) Calculations where daily periodic rate applied. If the provisions of paragraph (c)(1)(ii) or (c)(2) of this section apply and all or a portion of the finance charge is determined by the application of one or more daily periodic rates, the annual percentage rate may be determined either:

(1) By dividing the total finance charge by the average of the daily balances and multiplying the quotient by the number of billing cycles in a year; or

(2) By dividing the total finance charge by the sum of the daily balances and multiplying the quotient by 365.

§ 1026.15 Right of rescission.

(a) Consumer's right to rescind.

(1)(i) Except as provided in paragraph (a)(1)(ii) of this section, in a credit plan in which a security interest is or will be retained or acquired in a consumer's principal dwelling, each consumer whose ownership interest is or will be subject to the security interest shall have the right to rescind: each credit extension made under the plan; the plan when the plan is opened; a security interest when added or increased to secure an existing plan; and the increase when a credit limit on the plan is increased.

(ii) As provided in section 125(e) of the Act, the consumer does not have the right to rescind each credit extension made under the plan if such extension is made in accordance with a previously established credit limit for the plan.

(2) To exercise the right to rescind, the consumer shall notify the creditor of the rescission by mail, telegram, or other means of written communication. Notice is considered given when mailed, or when filed for telegraphic transmission, or, if sent by other means, when delivered to the creditor's designated place of business.

(3) The consumer may exercise the right to rescind until midnight of the third business day following the occurrence described in paragraph (a)(1) of this section that gave rise to the right of rescission, delivery of the notice required by paragraph (b) of this section, or delivery of all material disclosures, whichever occurs last. If the required notice and material disclosures are not delivered, the right to rescind shall expire 3 years after the occurrence giving rise to the right of rescission, or upon transfer of all of the consumer's interest in the property, or upon sale of the property, whichever occurs first. In the case of certain administrative proceedings, the rescission period shall be extended in accordance with section 125(f) of the Act. The term material disclosures means the information that must be provided to satisfy the requirements in § 1026.6 with regard to the method of determining the finance charge and the balance upon which a finance charge will be imposed, the annual percentage rate, the amount or method of determining the amount of any membership or participation fee that may be imposed as part of the plan, and the payment information described in § 1026.40(d)(5)(i) and (ii) that is required under § 1026.6(e)(2).

(4) When more than one consumer has the right to rescind, the exercise of the right by one consumer shall be effective as to all consumers.

(b) Notice of right to rescind. In any transaction or occurrence subject to rescission, a creditor shall deliver two copies of the notice of the right to rescind to each consumer entitled to rescind (one copy to each if the notice is delivered in electronic form in accordance with the consumer consent and other applicable provisions of the E-Sign Act). The notice shall identify the transaction or occurrence and clearly and conspicuously disclose the following:

(1) The retention or acquisition of a security interest in the consumer's principal dwelling.

(2) The consumer's right to rescind, as described in paragraph (a)(1) of this section.

(3) How to exercise the right to rescind, with a form for that purpose, designating the address of the creditor's place of business.

(4) The effects of rescission, as described in paragraph (d) of this section.

(5) The date the rescission period expires.

(c) Delay of creditor's performance. Unless a consumer waives the right to rescind under paragraph (e) of this section, no money shall be disbursed other than in escrow, no services shall be performed, and no materials delivered until after the rescission period has expired and the creditor is reasonably satisfied that the consumer has not rescinded. A creditor does not violate this section if a third party with no knowledge of the event activating the rescission right does not delay in providing materials or services, as long as the debt incurred for those materials or services is not secured by the property subject to rescission.

(d) Effects of rescission.

(1) When a consumer rescinds a transaction, the security interest giving rise to the right of rescission becomes void, and the consumer shall not be liable for any amount, including any finance charge.

(2) Within 20 calendar days after receipt of a notice of rescission, the creditor shall return any money or property that has been given to anyone in connection with the transaction and shall take any action necessary to reflect the termination of the security interest.

(3) If the creditor has delivered any money or property, the consumer may retain possession until the creditor has met its obligation under paragraph (d)(2) of this section. When the creditor has complied with that paragraph, the consumer shall tender the money or property to the creditor or, where the latter would be impracticable or inequitable, tender its reasonable value. At the consumer's option, tender of property may be made at the location of the property or at the consumer's residence. Tender of money must be made at the creditor's designated place of business. If the creditor does not take possession of the money or property within 20 calendar days after the consumer's tender, the consumer may keep it without further obligation.

(4) The procedures outlined in paragraphs (d)(2) and (3) of this section may be modified by court order.

(e) Consumer's waiver of right to rescind. The consumer may modify or waive the right to rescind if the consumer determines that the extension of credit is needed to meet a bona fide personal financial emergency. To modify or waive the right, the consumer shall give the creditor a dated written statement that describes the emergency, specifically modifies or waives the right to rescind, and bears the signature of all the consumers entitled to rescind. Printed forms for this purpose are prohibited.

(f) Exempt transactions. The right to rescind does not apply to the following:

(1) A residential mortgage transaction.

(2) A credit plan in which a state agency is a creditor.

§ 1026.16 Advertising.

(a) Actually available terms. If an advertisement for credit states specific credit terms, it shall state only those terms that actually are or will be arranged or offered by the creditor.

(b) Advertisement of terms that require additional disclosures.

(1) Any term required to be disclosed under § 1026.6(b)(3) set forth affirmatively or negatively in an advertisement for an open-end (not home-secured) credit plan triggers additional disclosures under this section. Any term required to be disclosed under §1026.6(a)(1) or (a)(2) set forth affirmatively or negatively in an advertisement for a home-equity plan subject to the requirements of § 1026.40 triggers additional disclosures under this section. If any of the terms that trigger additional disclosures under this paragraph is set forth in an advertisement, the advertisement shall also clearly and conspicuously set forth the following:

(i) Any minimum, fixed, transaction, activity or similar charge that is a finance charge under § 1026.4 that could be imposed.

(ii) Any periodic rate that may be applied expressed as an annual percentage rate as determined under § 1026.14(b). If the plan provides for a variable periodic rate, that fact shall be disclosed.

(iii) Any membership or participation fee that could be imposed.

(2) If an advertisement for credit to finance the purchase of goods or services specified in the advertisement states a periodic payment amount, the advertisement shall also state the total of payments and the time period to repay the obligation, assuming that the consumer pays only the periodic payment amount advertised. The disclosure of the total of payments and the time period to repay the obligation must be equally prominent to the statement of the periodic payment amount.

(c) Catalogs or other multiple-page advertisements; electronic advertisements.

(1) If a catalog or other multiple-page advertisement, or an electronic advertisement (such as an advertisement appearing on an Internet Web site), gives information in a table or schedule in sufficient detail to permit determination of the disclosures required by paragraph (b) of this section, it shall be considered a single advertisement if:

(i) The table or schedule is clearly and conspicuously set forth; and

(ii) Any statement of terms set forth in § 1026.6 appearing anywhere else in the catalog or advertisement clearly refers to the page or location where the table or schedule begins.

(2) A catalog or other multiple-page advertisement or an electronic advertisement (such as an advertisement appearing on an Internet Web site) complies with this paragraph if the table or schedule of terms includes all appropriate disclosures for a representative scale of amounts up to the level of the more commonly sold higher-priced property or services offered.

(d) Additional requirements for home-equity plans.

(1) Advertisement of terms that require additional disclosures. If any of the terms required to be disclosed under § 1026.6(a)(1) or (a)(2) or the payment terms of the plan are set forth, affirmatively or negatively, in an advertisement for a home-equity plan subject to the requirements of § 1026.40, the advertisement also shall clearly and conspicuously set forth the following:

(i) Any loan fee that is a percentage of the credit limit under the plan and an estimate of any other fees imposed for opening the plan, stated as a single dollar amount or a reasonable range.

(ii) Any periodic rate used to compute the finance charge, expressed as an annual percentage rate as determined under § 1026.14(b).

(iii) The maximum annual percentage rate that may be imposed in a variable-rate plan.

(2) Discounted and premium rates. If an advertisement states an initial annual percentage rate that is not based on the index and margin used to make later rate adjustments in a variable-rate plan, the advertisement also shall state with equal prominence and in close proximity to the initial rate:

(i) The period of time such initial rate will be in effect; and

(ii) A reasonably current annual percentage rate that would have been in effect using the index and margin.

(3) Balloon payment. If an advertisement contains a statement of any minimum periodic payment and a balloon payment may result if only the minimum periodic payments are made, even if such a payment is uncertain or unlikely, the advertisement also shall state with equal prominence and in close proximity to the minimum periodic payment statement that a balloon payment may result, if applicable. A balloon payment results if paying the minimum periodic payments does not fully amortize the outstanding balance by a specified date or time, and the consumer is required to repay the entire outstanding balance at such time. If a balloon payment will occur when the consumer makes only the minimum payments required under the plan, an advertisement for such a program which contains any statement of any minimum periodic payment shall also state with equal prominence and in close proximity to the minimum periodic payment statement:

(i) That a balloon payment will result; and

(ii) The amount and timing of the balloon payment that will result if the consumer makes only the minimum payments for the maximum period of time that the consumer is permitted to make such payments.

(4) Tax implications. An advertisement that states that any interest expense incurred under the home-equity plan is or may be tax deductible may not be misleading in this regard. If an advertisement distributed in paper form or through the Internet (rather than by radio or television) is for a home-equity plan secured by the consumer's principal dwelling, and the advertisement states that the advertised extension of credit may exceed the fair market value of the dwelling, the advertisement shall clearly and conspicuously state that:

(i) The interest on the portion of the credit extension that is greater than the fair market value of the dwelling is not tax deductible for Federal income tax purposes; and

(ii) The consumer should consult a tax adviser for further information regarding the deductibility of interest and charges.

(5) Misleading terms. An advertisement may not refer to a home-equity plan as "free money" or contain a similarly misleading term.

(6) Promotional rates and payments.

(i) Definitions. The following definitions apply for purposes of paragraph (d)(6) of this section:

(A) Promotional rate. The term "promotional rate" means, in a variable-rate plan, any annual percentage rate that is not based on the index and margin that will be used to make rate adjustments under the plan, if that rate is less than a reasonably current annual percentage rate that would be in effect under the index and margin that will be used to make rate adjustments under the plan.

(B) Promotional payment. The term "promotional payment" means:

(1) For a variable-rate plan, any minimum payment applicable for a promotional period that:

(i) Is not derived by applying the index and margin to the outstanding balance when such index and margin will be used to determine other minimum payments under the plan; and

(ii) Is less than other minimum payments under the plan derived by applying a reasonably current index and margin that will be used to determine the amount of such payments, given an assumed balance.

(2) For a plan other than a variable-rate plan, any minimum payment applicable for a promotional period if that payment is less than other payments required under the plan given an assumed balance.

(C) Promotional period. A "promotional period" means a period of time, less than the full term of the loan, that the promotional rate or promotional payment may be applicable.

(ii) Stating the promotional period and post-promotional rate or payments. If any annual percentage rate that may be applied to a plan is a promotional rate, or if any payment applicable to a plan is a promotional payment, the following must be disclosed in any advertisement, other than television or radio advertisements, in a clear and conspicuous manner with equal prominence and in close proximity to each listing of the promotional rate or payment:

(A) The period of time during which the promotional rate or promotional payment will apply;

(B) In the case of a promotional rate, any annual percentage rate that will apply under the plan. If such rate is variable, the annual percentage rate must be disclosed in accordance with the accuracy standards in §§ 1026.40 or 1026.16(b)(1)(ii) as applicable; and

(C) In the case of a promotional payment, the amounts and time periods of any payments that will apply under the plan. In variable-rate transactions, payments that will be determined based on application of an index and margin shall be disclosed based on a reasonably current index and margin.

(iii) Envelope excluded. The requirements in paragraph (d)(6)(ii) of this section do not apply to an envelope in which an application or solicitation is mailed, or to a banner advertisement or pop-up advertisement linked to an application or solicitation provided electronically.

(e) Alternative disclosures—television or radio advertisements. An advertisement made through television or radio stating any of the terms requiring additional disclosures under paragraphs (b)(1) or (d)(1) of this section may alternatively comply with paragraphs (b)(1) or (d)(1) of this section by stating the information required by paragraphs (b)(1)(ii) or (d)(1)(ii) of this section, as applicable, and listing a toll-free telephone number, or any telephone number that allows a consumer to reverse the phone charges when calling for information, along with a reference that such number may be used by consumers to obtain the additional cost information.

(f) Misleading terms. An advertisement may not refer to an annual percentage rate as "fixed," or use a similar term, unless the advertisement also specifies a time period that the rate will be fixed and the rate will not increase during that period, or if no such time period is provided, the rate will not increase while the plan is open.

(g) Promotional rates and fees.

(1) Scope. The requirements of this paragraph apply to any advertisement of an open-end (not home-secured) plan, including promotional materials accompanying applications or solicitations subject to § 1026.60(c) or accompanying applications or solicitations subject to § 1026.60(e).

(2) Definitions.

(i) Promotional rate means any annual percentage rate applicable to one or more balances or transactions on an open-end (not home-secured) plan for a specified period of time that is lower than the annual percentage rate that will be in effect at the end of that period on such balances or transactions.

(ii) Introductory rate means a promotional rate offered in connection with the opening of an account.

(iii) Promotional period means the maximum time period for which a promotional rate or promotional fee may be applicable.

(iv) Promotional fee means a fee required to be disclosed under § 1026.6(b)(1) and (2) applicable to an open-end (not home-secured) plan, or to one or more balances or transactions on an open-end (not home-secured) plan, for a specified period of time that is lower than the fee that will be in effect at the end of that period for such plan or types of balances or transactions.

(v) Introductory fee means a promotional fee offered in connection with the opening of an account.

(3) Stating the term "introductory". If any annual percentage rate or fee that may be applied to the account is an introductory rate or introductory fee, the term introductory or intro must be in immediate proximity to each listing of the introductory rate or introductory fee in a written or electronic advertisement.

(4) Stating the promotional period and post-promotional rate or fee. If any annual percentage rate that may be applied to the account is a promotional rate under paragraph (g)(2)(i) of this section or any fee that may be applied to the account is a promotional fee under paragraph (g)(2)(iv) of this section, the information in paragraphs (g)(4)(i) and, as applicable, (g)(4)(ii) or (iii) of this section must be stated in a clear and conspicuous manner in the advertisement. If the rate or fee is stated in a written or electronic advertisement, the information in paragraphs (g)(4)(i) and, as applicable, (g)(4)(ii) or (iii) of this section must also be stated in a prominent location closely proximate to the first listing of the promotional rate or promotional fee.

(i) When the promotional rate or promotional fee will end;

(ii) The annual percentage rate that will apply after the end of the promotional period. If such rate is variable, the annual percentage rate must comply with the accuracy standards in §§ 1026.60(c)(2), 1026.60(d)(3), 1026.60(e)(4), or 1026.16(b)(1)(ii), as applicable. If such rate cannot be determined at the time disclosures are given because the rate depends at least in part on a later determination of the consumer's creditworthiness, the advertisement must disclose the specific rates or the range of rates that might apply; and

(iii) The fee that will apply after the end of the promotional period.

(5) Envelope excluded. The requirements in paragraph (g)(4) of this section do not apply to an envelope or other enclosure in which an application or solicitation is mailed, or to a banner advertisement or pop-up advertisement, linked to an application or solicitation provided electronically.

(h) Deferred interest or similar offers.

(1) Scope. The requirements of this paragraph apply to any advertisement of an open-end credit plan not subject to § 1026.40, including promotional materials accompanying applications or solicitations subject to § 1026.60(c) or accompanying applications or solicitations subject to § 1026.60(e).

(2) Definitions. "Deferred interest" means finance charges, accrued on balances or transactions, that a consumer is not obligated to pay or that will be waived or refunded to a consumer if those balances or transactions are paid in full by a specified date. The maximum period from the date the consumer becomes obligated for the balance or transaction until the specified date by which the consumer must pay the balance or transaction in full in order to avoid finance charges, or receive a waiver or refund of finance charges, is the "deferred interest period." "Deferred interest" does not include any finance charges the consumer avoids paying in connection with any recurring grace period.

(3) Stating the deferred interest period. If a deferred interest offer is advertised, the deferred interest period must be stated in a clear and conspicuous manner in the advertisement. If the phrase "no interest" or similar term regarding the possible avoidance of interest obligations under the deferred interest program is stated, the term "if paid in full" must also be stated in a clear and conspicuous manner preceding the disclosure of the deferred interest period in the advertisement. If the deferred interest offer is included in a written or electronic advertisement, the deferred interest period and, if applicable, the term "if paid in full" must also be stated in immediate proximity to each statement of "no interest," "no payments," "deferred interest," "same as cash," or similar term regarding interest or payments during the deferred interest period.

(4) Stating the terms of the deferred interest or similar offer. If any deferred interest offer is advertised, the information in paragraphs (h)(4)(i) and (h)(4)(ii) of this section must be stated in the advertisement, in language similar to Sample G-24 in Appendix G to this part. If the deferred interest offer is included in a written or electronic advertisement, the information in paragraphs (h)(4)(i) and (h)(4)(ii) of this section must also be stated in a prominent location closely proximate to the first statement of "no interest," "no payments," "deferred interest," "same as cash," or similar term regarding interest or payments during the deferred interest period.

(i) A statement that interest will be charged from the date the consumer becomes obligated for the balance or transaction subject to the deferred interest offer if the balance or transaction is not paid in full within the deferred interest period; and

(ii) A statement, if applicable, that interest will be charged from the date the consumer incurs the balance or transaction subject to the deferred interest offer if the account is in default before the end of the deferred interest period.

(5) Envelope excluded. The requirements in paragraph (h)(4) of this section do not apply to an envelope or other enclosure in which an application or solicitation is mailed, or to a banner advertisement or pop-up advertisement linked to an application or solicitation provided electronically.

SUBPART C. CLOSED-END CREDIT

§ 1026.17 General disclosure requirements.

(a) Form of disclosures. Except for the disclosures required by § 1026.19(e), (f), and (g):

(1) The creditor shall make the disclosures required by this subpart clearly and conspicuously in writing, in a form that the consumer may keep. The disclosures required by this subpart may be provided to the consumer in electronic form, subject to compliance with the consumer consent and other applicable provisions of the Electronic Signatures in Global and National Commerce Act (E-Sign Act) (15 U.S.C. 7001 et seq.). The disclosures required by §§ 1026.17(g), 1026.19(b), and 1026.24 may be provided to the consumer in electronic form without regard to the consumer consent or other provisions of the E-Sign Act in the circumstances set forth in those sections. The disclosures shall be grouped together, shall be segregated from everything else, and shall not contain any information not directly related to the disclosures required under § 1026.18, § 1026.20(c) and (d), or § 1026.47. The disclosures required by § 1026.20(d) shall be provided as a separate document from all other written materials. The disclosures may include an acknowledgment of receipt, the date of the transaction, and the consumer's name, address, and account number. The following disclosures may be made together with or separately from other required disclosures: The creditor's identity under § 1026.18(a), the variable rate example under § 1026.18(f)(1)(iv), insurance or debt cancellation under § 1026.18(n), and certain security interest charges under § 1026.18(*o*). The itemization of the amount financed under § 1026.18(c)(1) must be separate from the other disclosures under § 1026.18, except for private education loan disclosures made in compliance with § 1026.47.

(2) Except for private education loan disclosures made in compliance with § 1026.47, the terms "finance charge" and "annual percentage rate," when required to be disclosed under § 1026.18(d) and (e) together with a corresponding amount or percentage rate, shall be more conspicuous than any other disclosure, except the creditor's identity under § 1026.18(a). For private education loan disclosures made in compliance with § 1026.47, the term "annual percentage rate," and the corresponding percentage rate must be less conspicuous than the term "finance charge" and corresponding amount under § 1026.18(d), the interest rate under §§ 1026.47(b)(1)(i) and (c)(1), and the notice of the right to cancel under § 1026.47(c)(4).

(b) Time of disclosures. The creditor shall make disclosures before consummation of the transaction. In certain residential mortgage transactions, special timing requirements are set forth in § 1026.19(a). In certain variable-rate transactions, special timing requirements for variable-rate disclosures are set forth in § 1026.19(b) and § 1026.20(c) and (d). For private education loan disclosures made in compliance with § 1026.47, special timing requirements are set forth in § 1026.46(d). In certain transactions involving mail or telephone orders or a series of sales, the timing of disclosures may be delayed in accordance with paragraphs (g) and (h) of this section. This paragraph (b) does not apply to the disclosures required by §§ 1026.19(e), (f), and (g) and 1026.20(e).

(c) Basis of disclosures and use of estimates.

(1) The disclosures shall reflect the terms of the legal obligation between the parties.

(2)(i) If any information necessary for an accurate disclosure is unknown to the creditor, the creditor shall make the disclosure based on the best information reasonably available at the time the disclosure is provided to the consumer, and shall state clearly that the disclosure is an estimate.

(ii) For a transaction in which a portion of the interest is determined on a per-diem basis and collected at consummation, any disclosure affected by the per-diem interest shall be considered accurate if the disclosure is based on the information known to the creditor at the time that the disclosure documents are prepared for consummation of the transaction.

(3) The creditor may disregard the effects of the following in making calculations and disclosures.

(i) That payments must be collected in whole cents.

(ii) That dates of scheduled payments and advances may be changed because the scheduled date is not a business day.

(iii) That months have different numbers of days.

(iv) The occurrence of leap year.

(4) In making calculations and disclosures, the creditor may disregard any irregularity in the first period that falls within the limits described below and any payment schedule irregularity that results from the irregular first period:

(i) For transactions in which the term is less than 1 year, a first period not more than 6 days shorter or 13 days longer than a regular period;

(ii) For transactions in which the term is at least 1 year and less than 10 years, a first period not more than 11 days shorter or 21 days longer than a regular period; and

(iii) For transactions in which the term is at least 10 years, a first period shorter than or not more than 32 days longer than a regular period.

(5) If an obligation is payable on demand, the creditor shall make the disclosures based on an assumed maturity of 1 year. If an alternate maturity date is stated in the legal obligation between the parties, the disclosures shall be based on that date.

(6)(i) A series of advances under an agreement to extend credit up to a certain amount may be considered as one transaction.

(ii) When a multiple-advance loan to finance the construction of a dwelling may be permanently financed by the same creditor, the construction phase and the permanent phase may be treated as either one transaction or more than one transaction.

(d) Multiple creditors; multiple consumers. If a transaction involves more than one creditor, only one set of disclosures shall be given and the creditors shall agree among themselves which creditor must comply with the requirements that this part imposes on any or all of them. If there is more than one consumer, the disclosures may be made to any consumer who is primarily liable on the obligation. If the transaction is rescindable under § 1026.23, however, the disclosures shall be made to each consumer who has the right to rescind.

(e) Effect of subsequent events. If a disclosure becomes inaccurate because of an event that occurs after the creditor delivers the required disclosures, the inaccuracy is not a violation of this part, although new disclosures may be required under paragraph (f) of this section, § 1026.19, § 1026.20, or § 1026.48(c)(4).

(f) Early disclosures. Except for private education loan disclosures made in compliance with § 1026.47, if disclosures required by this subpart are given before the date of consummation of a transaction and a subsequent event makes them inaccurate, the creditor shall disclose before consummation (subject to the provisions of § 1026.19(a)(2), (e), and (f):

(1) Any changed term unless the term was based on an estimate in accordance with § 1026.17(c)(2) and was labeled an estimate;

(2) All changed terms, if the annual percentage rate at the time of consummation varies from the annual percentage rate disclosed earlier by more than 1/8 of 1 percentage point in a regular transaction, or more than 1/4 of 1 percentage point in an irregular transaction, as defined in § 1026.22(a).

(g) Mail or telephone orders—delay in disclosures. Except for private education loan disclosures made in compliance with § 1026.47 and mortgage disclosures made in compliance with § 1026.19(a) or (e), (f), and (g), if a creditor receives a purchase order or a request for an extension of credit by mail, telephone, or facsimile machine without face-to-face or direct telephone solicitation, the creditor may delay the disclosures until the due date of the first payment, if the following information for representative amounts or ranges of credit is made available in written form or in electronic form to the consumer or to the public before the actual purchase order or request:

(1) The cash price or the principal loan amount.

(2) The total sale price.

(3) The finance charge.

(4) The annual percentage rate, and if the rate may increase after consummation, the following disclosures:

(i) The circumstances under which the rate may increase.

(ii) Any limitations on the increase.

(iii) The effect of an increase.

(5) The terms of repayment.

(h) Series of sales—delay in disclosures. Except for mortgage disclosures made in compliance with § 1026.19(a) or (e), (f), and (g), if a credit sale is one of a series made under an agreement providing that subsequent sales may be added to an outstanding balance, the creditor may delay the required disclosures until the due date of the first payment for the current sale, if the following two conditions are met:

(1) The consumer has approved in writing the annual percentage rate or rates, the range of balances to which they apply, and the method of treating any unearned finance charge on an existing balance.

(2) The creditor retains no security interest in any property after the creditor has received payments equal to the cash price and any finance charge attributable to the sale of that property. For purposes of this provision, in the case of items purchased on different dates, the first purchased is deemed the first item paid for; in the case of items purchased on the same date, the lowest priced is deemed the first item paid for.

(i) Interim student credit extensions. For transactions involving an interim credit extension under a student credit program for which an application is received prior to the mandatory compliance date of §§ 1026.46, 47, and 48, the creditor need not make the following disclosures: the finance charge under § 1026.18(d), the payment schedule under § 1026.18(g), the total of payments under § 1026.18(h), or the total sale price under § 1026.18(j) at the time the credit is actually extended. The creditor must make complete disclosures at the time the creditor and consumer agree upon the repayment schedule for the total obligation. At that time, a new set of disclosures must be made of all applicable items under § 1026.18.

§ 1026.18 Content of disclosures.

For each transaction other than a mortgage transaction subject to § 1026.19(e) and (f), the creditor shall disclose the following information as applicable:

(a) Creditor. The identity of the creditor making the disclosures.

(b) Amount financed. The amount financed, using that term, and a brief description such as the amount of credit provided to you or on your behalf. The amount financed is calculated by:

(1) Determining the principal loan amount or the cash price (subtracting any downpayment);

(2) Adding any other amounts that are financed by the creditor and are not part of the finance charge; and

(3) Subtracting any prepaid finance charge.

(c) Itemization of amount financed.

(1) Except as provided in paragraphs (c)(2) and (c)(3) of this section, a separate written itemization of the amount financed, including:

(i) The amount of any proceeds distributed directly to the consumer.

(ii) The amount credited to the consumer's account with the creditor.

(iii) Any amounts paid to other persons by the creditor on the consumer's behalf. The creditor shall identify those persons. The following payees may be described using generic or other general terms and need not be further identified: public officials or government agencies, credit reporting agencies, appraisers, and insurance companies.

(iv) The prepaid finance charge.

(2) The creditor need not comply with paragraph (c)(1) of this section if the creditor provides a statement that the consumer has the right to receive a written itemization of the amount financed, together with a space for the consumer to indicate whether it is desired, and the consumer does not request it.

(3) Good faith estimates of settlement costs provided for transactions subject to the Real Estate Settlement Procedures Act (12 U.S.C. 2601 et seq.) may be substituted for the disclosures required by paragraph (c)(1) of this section.

(d) Finance charge. The finance charge, using that term, and a brief description such as "the dollar amount the credit will cost you."

(1) Mortgage loans. In a transaction secured by real property or a dwelling, the disclosed finance charge and other disclosures affected by the disclosed finance charge (including the amount financed and the annual percentage rate) shall be treated as accurate if the amount disclosed as the finance charge:

(i) Is understated by no more than $100; or

(ii) Is greater than the amount required to be disclosed.

(2) Other credit. In any other transaction, the amount disclosed as the finance charge shall be treated as accurate if, in a transaction involving an amount financed of $1,000 or less, it is not more than $5 above or below the amount required to be disclosed; or, in a transaction involving an amount financed of more than $1,000, it is not more than $10 above or below the amount required to be disclosed.

(e) Annual percentage rate. The annual percentage rate, using that term, and a brief description such as "the cost of your credit as a yearly rate." For any transaction involving a finance charge of $5 or less on an amount financed of $75 or less, or a finance charge of $7.50 or less on an amount financed of more than $75, the creditor need not disclose the annual percentage rate.

(f) Variable rate.

(1) Except as provided in paragraph (f)(3) of this section, if the annual percentage rate may increase after consummation in a transaction not secured by the consumer's principal dwelling or in a transaction secured by the consumer's principal dwelling with a term of one year or less, the following disclosures:

(i) The circumstances under which the rate may increase.

(ii) Any limitations on the increase.

(iii) The effect of an increase.

(iv) An example of the payment terms that would result from an increase.

(2) If the annual percentage rate may increase after consummation in a transaction secured by the consumer's principal dwelling with a term greater than one year, the following disclosures:

(i) The fact that the transaction contains a variable-rate feature.

(ii) A statement that variable-rate disclosures have been provided earlier.

(3) Information provided in accordance with §§ 1026.18(f)(2) and 1026.19(b) may be substituted for the disclosures required by paragraph (f)(1) of this section.

(g) Payment schedule. Other than for a transaction that is subject to paragraph (s) of this section, the number, amounts, and timing of payments scheduled to repay the obligation.

(1) In a demand obligation with no alternate maturity date, the creditor may comply with this paragraph by disclosing the due dates or payment periods of any scheduled interest payments for the first year.

(2) In a transaction in which a series of payments varies because a finance charge is applied to the unpaid principal balance, the creditor may comply with this paragraph by disclosing the following information:

(i) The dollar amounts of the largest and smallest payments in the series.

(ii) A reference to the variations in the other payments in the series.

(h) Total of payments. The total of payments, using that term, and a descriptive explanation such as "the amount you will have paid when you have made all scheduled payments." In any transaction involving a single payment, the creditor need not disclose the total of payments.

(i) Demand feature. If the obligation has a demand feature, that fact shall be disclosed. When the disclosures are based on an assumed maturity of 1 year as provided in § 1026.17(c)(5), that fact shall also be disclosed.

(j) Total sale price. In a credit sale, the total sale price, using that term, and a descriptive explanation (including the amount of any downpayment) such as "the total price of your purchase on credit, including your downpayment of $__." The total sale price is the sum of the cash price, the items described in paragraph (b)(2), and the finance charge disclosed under paragraph (d) of this section.

(k) Prepayment.

(1) When an obligation includes a finance charge computed from time to time by application of a rate to the unpaid principal balance, a statement indicating whether or not a charge may be imposed for paying all or part of a loan's principal balance before the date on which the principal is due.

(2) When an obligation includes a finance charge other than the finance charge described in paragraph (k)(1) of this section, a statement indicating whether or not the consumer is entitled to a rebate of any finance charge if the obligation is prepaid in full or in part.

(*l*) Late payment. Any dollar or percentage charge that may be imposed before maturity due to a late payment, other than a deferral or extension charge.

(m) Security interest. The fact that the creditor has or will acquire a security interest in the property purchased as part of the transaction, or in other property identified by item or type.

(n) Insurance and debt cancellation. The items required by § 1026.4(d) in order to exclude certain insurance premiums and debt cancellation fees from the finance charge.

(*o*) Certain security interest charges. The disclosures required by § 1026.4(e) in order to exclude from the finance charge certain fees prescribed by law or certain premiums for insurance in lieu of perfecting a security interest.

(p) Contract reference. A statement that the consumer should refer to the appropriate contract document for information about nonpayment, default, the right to accelerate the maturity of the obligation, and prepayment rebates and penalties. At the creditor's option, the statement may also include a reference to the contract for further information about security interests and, in a residential mortgage transaction, about the creditor's policy regarding assumption of the obligation.

(q) Assumption policy. In a residential mortgage transaction, a statement whether or not a subsequent purchaser of the dwelling from the consumer may be permitted to assume the remaining obligation on its original terms.

(r) Required deposit. If the creditor requires the consumer to maintain a deposit as a condition of the specific transaction, a statement that the annual percentage rate does not reflect the effect of the required deposit. A required deposit need not include, for example:

(1) An escrow account for items such as taxes, insurance or repairs;

(2) A deposit that earns not less than 5 percent per year; or

(3) Payments under a Morris Plan.

(s) Interest rate and payment summary for mortgage transactions. For a closed-end transaction secured by real property or a dwelling, other than a transaction that is subject to § 1026.19(e) and (f), the creditor shall disclose the following information about the interest rate and payments:

(1) Form of disclosures. The information in paragraphs (s)(2)–(4) of this section shall be in the form of a table, with no more than five columns, with headings and format substantially similar to Model Clause H-4(E), H-4(F), H-4(G), or H-4(H) in Appendix H to this part. The table shall contain only the information required in paragraphs (s)(2)–(4) of this section, shall be placed in a prominent location, and shall be in a minimum 10-point font.

(2) Interest rates.

(i) Amortizing loans.

(A) For a fixed-rate mortgage, the interest rate at consummation.

(B) For an adjustable-rate or step-rate mortgage:

(1) The interest rate at consummation and the period of time until the first interest rate adjustment may occur, labeled as the "introductory rate and monthly payment";

(2) The maximum interest rate that may apply during the first five years after the date on which the first regular periodic payment will be due and the earliest date on which that rate may apply, labeled as "maximum during first five years"; and

(3) The maximum interest rate that may apply during the life of the loan and the earliest date on which that rate may apply, labeled as "maximum ever."

(C) If the loan provides for payment increases as described in paragraph (s)(3)(i)(B) of this section, the interest rate in effect at the time the first such payment increase is scheduled to occur and the date on which the increase will occur, labeled as "first adjustment" if the loan is an adjustable-rate mortgage or, otherwise, labeled as "first increase."

(ii) Negative amortization loans. For a negative amortization loan:

(A) The interest rate at consummation and, if it will adjust after consummation, the length of time until it will adjust, and the label "introductory" or "intro";

(B) The maximum interest rate that could apply when the consumer must begin making fully amortizing payments under the terms of the legal obligation;

(C) If the minimum required payment will increase before the consumer must begin making fully amortizing payments, the maximum interest rate that could apply at the time of the first payment increase and the date the increase is scheduled to occur; and

(D) If a second increase in the minimum required payment may occur before the consumer must begin making fully amortizing payments, the maximum interest rate that could apply at the time of the second payment increase and the date the increase is scheduled to occur.

(iii) Introductory rate disclosure for amortizing adjustable-rate mortgages. For an amortizing adjustable-rate mortgage, if the interest rate at consummation is less than the fully-indexed rate, placed in a box directly beneath the table required by paragraph (s)(1) of this section, in a format substantially similar to Model Clause H-4(I) in Appendix H to this part:

(A) The interest rate that applies at consummation and the period of time for which it applies;

(B) A statement that, even if market rates do not change, the interest rate will increase at the first adjustment and a designation of the place in sequence of the month or year, as applicable, of such rate adjustment; and

(C) The fully-indexed rate.

(3) Payments for amortizing loans.

(i) Principal and interest payments. If all periodic payments will be applied to accrued interest and principal, for each interest rate disclosed under paragraph (s)(2)(i) of this section:

(A) The corresponding periodic principal and interest payment, labeled as "principal and interest;"

(B) If the periodic payment may increase without regard to an interest rate adjustment, the payment that corresponds to the first such increase and the earliest date on which the increase could occur;

(C) If an escrow account will be established, an estimate of the amount of taxes and insurance, including any mortgage insurance or any functional equivalent, payable with each periodic payment; and

(D) The sum of the amounts disclosed under paragraphs (s)(3)(i)(A) and (C) of this section or (s)(3)(i)(B) and (C) of this section, as applicable, labeled as "total estimated monthly payment."

(ii) Interest-only payments. If the loan is an interest-only loan, for each interest rate disclosed under paragraph (s)(2)(i) of this section, the corresponding periodic payment and:

(A) If the payment will be applied to only accrued interest, the amount applied to interest, labeled as "interest payment," and a statement that none of the payment is being applied to principal;

(B) If the payment will be applied to accrued interest and principal, an itemization of the amount of the first such payment applied to accrued interest and to principal, labeled as "interest payment" and "principal payment," respectively;

(C) The escrow information described in paragraph (s)(3)(i)(C) of this section; and

(D) The sum of all amounts required to be disclosed under paragraphs (s)(3)(ii)(A) and (C) of this section or (s)(3)(ii)(B) and (C) of this section, as applicable, labeled as "total estimated monthly payment."

(4) Payments for negative amortization loans. For negative amortization loans:

(i)(A) The minimum periodic payment required until the first payment increase or interest rate increase, corresponding to the interest rate disclosed under paragraph (s)(2)(ii)(A) of this section;

(B) The minimum periodic payment that would be due at the first payment increase and the second, if any, corresponding to the interest rates described in paragraphs (s)(2)(ii)(C) and (D) of this section; and

(C) A statement that the minimum payment pays only some interest, does not repay any principal, and will cause the loan amount to increase;

(ii) The fully amortizing periodic payment amount at the earliest time when such a payment must be made, corresponding to the interest rate disclosed under paragraph (s)(2)(ii)(B) of this section; and

(iii) If applicable, in addition to the payments in paragraphs (s)(4)(i) and (ii) of this section, for each interest rate disclosed under paragraph (s)(2)(ii) of this section, the amount of the fully amortizing periodic payment, labeled as the "full payment option," and a statement that these payments pay all principal and all accrued interest.

(5) Balloon payments.

(i) Except as provided in paragraph (s)(5)(ii) of this section, if the transaction will require a balloon payment, defined as a payment that is more than two times a regular periodic payment, the balloon payment shall be disclosed separately from other periodic payments disclosed in the table under this paragraph (s), outside the table and in a manner substantially similar to Model Clause H-4(J) in Appendix H to this part.

(ii) If the balloon payment is scheduled to occur at the same time as another payment required to be disclosed in the table pursuant to paragraph (s)(3) or (s)(4) of this section, then the balloon payment must be disclosed in the table.

(6) Special disclosures for loans with negative amortization. For a negative amortization loan, the following information, in close proximity to the table required in paragraph (s)(1) of this section, with headings, content, and format substantially similar to Model Clause H-4(G) in Appendix H to this part:

(i) The maximum interest rate, the shortest period of time in which such interest rate could be reached, the amount of estimated taxes and insurance included in each payment disclosed, and a statement that the loan offers payment options, two of which are shown.

(ii) The dollar amount of the increase in the loan's principal balance if the consumer makes only the minimum required payments for the maximum possible time and the earliest date on which the consumer must begin making fully amortizing payments, assuming that the maximum interest rate is reached at the earliest possible time.

(7) Definitions. For purposes of this § 1026.18(s):

(i) The term "adjustable-rate mortgage" means a transaction secured by real property or a dwelling for which the annual percentage rate may increase after consummation.

(ii) The term "step-rate mortgage" means a transaction secured by real property or a dwelling for which the interest rate will change after consummation, and the rates that will apply and the periods for which they will apply are known at consummation.

(iii) The term "fixed-rate mortgage" means a transaction secured by real property or a dwelling that is not an adjustable-rate mortgage or a step-rate mortgage.

(iv) The term "interest-only" means that, under the terms of the legal obligation, one or more of the periodic payments may be applied solely to accrued interest and not to loan principal; an "interest-only loan" is a loan that permits interest-only payments.

(v) The term "amortizing loan" means a loan in which payment of the periodic payments does not result in an increase in the principal balance under the terms of the legal obligation; the term "negative amortization" means payment of periodic payments that will result in an increase in the principal balance under the terms of the legal obligation; the term "negative amortization loan" means a loan, other than a reverse mortgage subject to § 1026.33, that provides for a minimum periodic payment that covers only a portion of the accrued interest, resulting in negative amortization.

(vi) The term "fully-indexed rate" means the interest rate calculated using the index value and margin at the time of consummation.

(t) "No-guarantee-to-refinance" statement.

(1) Disclosure. For a closed-end transaction secured by real property or a dwelling, other than a transaction that is subject to § 1026.19(e) and (f), the creditor shall disclose a statement that there is no guarantee the consumer can refinance the transaction to lower the interest rate or periodic payments.

(2) Format. The statement required by paragraph (t)(1) of this section must be in a form substantially similar to Model Clause H-4(K) in Appendix H to this part.

§ 1026.19 Certain mortgage and variable-rate transactions.

(a) Mortgage transactions subject to RESPA.

(1)(i) Time of disclosures. In a reverse mortgage transaction subject to both § 1026.33 and the Real Estate Settlement Procedures Act (12 U.S.C. 2601 et seq.) that is secured by the consumer's dwelling, the creditor shall provide the consumer with good faith estimates of the disclosures required by § 1026.18 and shall deliver or place them in the mail not later than the third business day after the creditor receives the consumer's written application.

(ii) Imposition of fees. Except as provided in paragraph (a)(1)(iii) of this section, neither a creditor nor any other person may impose a fee on a consumer in connection with the consumer's application for a reverse mortgage transaction subject to paragraph (a)(1)(i) of this section before the consumer has received the disclosures required by paragraph (a)(1)(i) of this section. If the disclosures are mailed to the consumer, the consumer is considered to have received them three business days after they are mailed.

(iii) Exception to fee restriction. A creditor or other person may impose a fee for obtaining the consumer's credit history before the consumer has received the disclosures required by paragraph (a)(1)(i) of this section, provided the fee is bona fide and reasonable in amount.

(2) Waiting periods for early disclosures and corrected disclosures.

(i) The creditor shall deliver or place in the mail the good faith estimates required by paragraph (a)(1)(i) of this section not later than the seventh business day before consummation of the transaction.

(ii) If the annual percentage rate disclosed under paragraph (a)(1)(i) of this section becomes inaccurate, as defined in § 1026.22, the creditor shall provide corrected disclosures with all changed terms. The consumer must receive the corrected disclosures no later than three business days before consummation. If the corrected disclosures are mailed to the consumer or delivered to the consumer by means other than delivery in person, the consumer is deemed to have received the corrected disclosures three business days after they are mailed or delivered.

(3) Consumer's waiver of waiting period before consummation. If the consumer determines that the extension of credit is needed to meet a bona fide personal financial emergency, the consumer may modify or waive the seven-business-day waiting period or the three-business-day waiting period required by paragraph (a)(2) of this section, after receiving the disclosures required by § 1026.18. To modify or waive a waiting period, the consumer shall give the creditor a dated written statement that describes the emergency, specifically modifies or waives the waiting period, and bears the signature of all the consumers who are primarily liable on the legal obligation. Printed forms for this purpose are prohibited.

(4) Notice. Disclosures made pursuant to paragraph (a)(1) or paragraph (a)(2) of this section shall contain the following statement: "You are not required to complete this agreement merely because you have received these disclosures or signed a loan application." The disclosure required by this paragraph shall be grouped together with the disclosures required by paragraphs (a)(1) or (a)(2) of this section.

(5) Timeshare plans. In a mortgage transaction subject to the Real Estate Settlement Procedures Act (12 U.S.C. 2601 et seq.) that is secured by a consumer's interest in a timeshare plan described in 11 U.S.C. 101(53(D)):

(i) The requirements of paragraphs (a)(1) through (a)(4) of this section do not apply;

(ii) The creditor shall make good faith estimates of the disclosures required by § 1026.18 before consummation, or shall deliver or place them in the mail not later than three business days after the creditor receives the consumer's written application, whichever is earlier; and

(iii) If the annual percentage rate at the time of consummation varies from the annual percentage rate disclosed under paragraph (a)(5)(ii) of this section by more than 1/8 of 1 percentage point in a regular transaction or more than ¼ of 1 percentage point in an irregular transaction, as defined in § 1026.22, the creditor shall disclose all the changed terms no later than consummation or settlement.

(b) Certain variable-rate transactions. Except as provided in paragraph (d) of this section, if the annual percentage rate may increase after consummation in a transaction secured by the consumer's principal dwelling with a term greater than one year, the following disclosures must be provided at the time an application form is provided or before the consumer pays a non-refundable fee, whichever is earlier (except that the disclosures may be delivered or placed in the mail not later than three business days following receipt of a consumer's application when the application reaches the creditor by telephone, or through an intermediary agent or broker):

(1) The booklet titled Consumer Handbook on Adjustable Rate Mortgages, or a suitable substitute.

(2) A loan program disclosure for each variable-rate program in which the consumer expresses an interest. The following disclosures, as applicable, shall be provided:

(i) The fact that the interest rate, payment, or term of the loan can change.

(ii) The index or formula used in making adjustments, and a source of information about the index or formula.

(iii) An explanation of how the interest rate and payment will be determined, including an explanation of how the index is adjusted, such as by the addition of a margin.

(iv) A statement that the consumer should ask about the current margin value and current interest rate.

(v) The fact that the interest rate will be discounted, and a statement that the consumer should ask about the amount of the interest rate discount.

(vi) The frequency of interest rate and payment changes.

(vii) Any rules relating to changes in the index, interest rate, payment amount, and outstanding loan balance including, for example, an explanation of interest rate or payment limitations, negative amortization, and interest rate carryover.

(viii) At the option of the creditor, either of the following:

(A) A historical example, based on a $10,000 loan amount, illustrating how payments and the loan balance would have been affected by interest rate changes implemented according to the terms of the loan program disclosure. The example shall reflect the most recent 15 years of index values. The example shall reflect all significant loan program terms, such as negative amortization, interest rate carryover, interest rate discounts, and interest rate and payment limitations, that would have been affected by the index movement during the period.

(B) The maximum interest rate and payment for a $10,000 loan originated at the initial interest rate (index value plus margin, adjusted by the amount of any discount or premium) in effect as of an identified month and year for the loan program disclosure assuming the maximum periodic increases in rates and payments under the program; and the initial interest rate and payment for that loan and a statement that the periodic payment may increase or decrease substantially depending on changes in the rate.

(ix) An explanation of how the consumer may calculate the payments for the loan amount to be borrowed based on either:

(A) The most recent payment shown in the historical example in paragraph (b)(2)(viii)(A) of this section; or

(B) The initial interest rate used to calculate the maximum interest rate and payment in paragraph (b)(2)(viii)(B) of this section.

(x) The fact that the loan program contains a demand feature.

(xi) The type of information that will be provided in notices of adjustments and the timing of such notices.

(xii) A statement that disclosure forms are available for the creditor's other variable-rate loan programs.

(c) Electronic disclosures. For an application that is accessed by the consumer in electronic form, the disclosures required by paragraph (b) of this section may be provided to the consumer in electronic form on or with the application.

(d) Information provided in accordance with variable-rate regulations of other Federal agencies may be substituted for the disclosures required by paragraph (b) of this section.

(e) Mortgage loans—early disclosures.

(1) Provision of disclosures.

(i) Creditor. In a closed-end consumer credit transaction secured by real property or a cooperative unit, other than a reverse mortgage subject to § 1026.33, the creditor shall provide the consumer with good faith estimates of the disclosures in § 1026.37.

(ii) Mortgage broker.

(A) If a mortgage broker receives a consumer's application, either the creditor or the mortgage broker shall provide a consumer with the disclosures required under paragraph (e)(1)(i) of this section in accordance with paragraph (e)(1)(iii) of this section. If the mortgage broker provides the required disclosures, the mortgage broker shall comply with all relevant requirements of this paragraph (e). The creditor shall ensure that such disclosures are provided in accordance with all requirements of this paragraph (e). Disclosures provided by a mortgage broker in accordance with the requirements of this paragraph (e) satisfy the creditor's obligation under this paragraph (e).

(B) If a mortgage broker provides any disclosure under § 1026.19(e), the mortgage broker shall also comply with the requirements of § 1026.25(c).

(iii) Timing.

(A) The creditor shall deliver or place in the mail the disclosures required under paragraph (e)(1)(i) of this section not later than the third business day after the creditor receives the consumer's application, as defined in § 1026.2(a)(3).

(B) Except as set forth in paragraph (e)(1)(iii)(C) of this section, the creditor shall deliver or place in the mail the disclosures required under paragraph (e)(1)(i) of this section not later than the seventh business day before consummation of the transaction.

(C) For a transaction secured by a consumer's interest in a timeshare plan described in 11 U.S.C. 101(53D), paragraph (e)(1)(iii)(B) of this section does not apply.

(iv) Receipt of early disclosures. If any disclosures required under paragraph (e)(1)(i) of this section are not provided to the consumer in person, the consumer is considered to have received the disclosures three business days after they are delivered or placed in the mail.

(v) Consumer's waiver of waiting period before consummation. If the consumer determines that the extension of credit is needed to meet a bona fide personal financial emergency, the consumer may modify or waive the seven-business-day waiting period for early disclosures required under paragraph (e)(1)(iii)(B) of this section, after receiving the disclosures required under paragraph (e)(1)(i) of this section. To modify or waive the waiting period, the consumer shall give the creditor a dated written statement that describes the emergency, specifically modifies or waives the waiting period, and bears the signature of all the consumers who are primarily liable on the legal obligation. Printed forms for this purpose are prohibited.

(vi) Shopping for settlement service providers.

(A) Shopping permitted. A creditor permits a consumer to shop for a settlement service if the creditor permits the consumer to select the provider of that service, subject to reasonable requirements.

(B) Disclosure of services. The creditor shall identify the settlement services for which the consumer is permitted to shop in the disclosures required under paragraph (e)(1)(i) of this section.

(C) Written list of providers. If the consumer is permitted to shop for a settlement service, the creditor shall provide the consumer with a written list identifying available providers of that settlement service and stating that the consumer may choose a different provider for that service. The creditor must identify at least one available provider for each settlement service for which the consumer is permitted to shop. The creditor shall provide this written list of settlement service providers separately from the disclosures required by paragraph (e)(1)(i) of this section but in accordance with the timing requirements in paragraph (e)(1)(iii) of this section.

(2) Predisclosure activity.

(i) Imposition of fees on consumer.

(A) Fee restriction. Except as provided in paragraph (e)(2)(i)(B) of this section, neither a creditor nor any other person may impose a fee on a consumer in connection with the consumer's application for a mortgage transaction subject to paragraph (e)(1)(i) of this section before the consumer has received the disclosures required under paragraph (e)(1)(i) of this section and indicated to the creditor an intent to proceed with the transaction described by those disclosures. A consumer may indicate an intent to proceed with a transaction in any manner the consumer chooses, unless a particular manner of communication is required by the creditor. The creditor must document this communication to satisfy the requirements of § 1026.25.

(B) Exception to fee restriction. A creditor or other person may impose a bona fide and reasonable fee for obtaining the consumer's credit report before the consumer has received the disclosures required under paragraph (e)(1)(i) of this section.

(ii) Written information provided to consumer. If a creditor or other person provides a consumer with a written estimate of terms or costs specific to that consumer before the consumer receives the disclosures required under paragraph (e)(1)(i) of this section, the creditor or such person shall clearly and conspicuously state at the top of the front of the first page of the estimate in a font size that is no smaller than 12-point font: "Your actual rate, payment, and costs could be higher. Get an official Loan Estimate before choosing a loan." The written estimate of terms or costs may not be made with headings, content, and format substantially similar to form H-24 or H-25 of appendix H to this part.

(iii) Verification of information. The creditor or other person shall not require a consumer to submit documents verifying information related to the consumer's application before providing the disclosures required by paragraph (e)(1)(i) of this section.

(3) Good faith determination for estimates of closing costs.

(i) General rule. An estimated closing cost disclosed pursuant to paragraph (e) of this section is in good faith if the charge paid by or imposed on the consumer does not exceed the amount originally disclosed under paragraph (e)(1)(i) of this section, except as otherwise provided in paragraphs (e)(3)(ii) through (iv) of this section.

(ii) Limited increases permitted for certain charges. An estimate of a charge for a third-party service or a recording fee is in good faith if:

(A) The aggregate amount of charges for third-party services and recording fees paid by or imposed on the consumer does not exceed the aggregate amount of such charges disclosed under paragraph (e)(1)(i) of this section by more than 10 percent;

(B) The charge for the third-party service is not paid to the creditor or an affiliate of the creditor; and

(C) The creditor permits the consumer to shop for the third-party service, consistent with paragraph (e)(1)(vi) of this section.

(iii) Variations permitted for certain charges. An estimate of any of the charges specified in this paragraph (e)(3)(iii) is in good faith if it is consistent with the best information reasonably available to the creditor at the time it is disclosed, regardless of whether the amount paid by the consumer exceeds the amount disclosed under paragraph (e)(1)(i) of this section. For purposes of paragraph (e)(1)(i) of this section, good faith is determined under this paragraph (e)(3)(iii) even if such charges are paid to the creditor or affiliates of the creditor, so long as the charges are bona fide:

(A) Prepaid interest;

(B) Property insurance premiums;

(C) Amounts placed into an escrow, impound, reserve, or similar account;

(D) Charges paid to third-party service providers selected by the consumer consistent with paragraph (e)(1)(vi)(A) of this section that are not on the list provided under paragraph (e)(1)(vi)(C) of this section; and

(E) Property taxes and other charges paid for third-party services not required by the creditor.

(iv) Revised estimates. For the purpose of determining good faith under paragraph (e)(3)(i) and (ii) of this section, a creditor may use a revised estimate of a charge instead of the estimate of the charge originally disclosed under paragraph (e)(1)(i) of this section if the revision is due to any of the following reasons:

(A) Changed circumstance affecting settlement charges. Changed circumstances cause the estimated charges to increase or, in the case of estimated charges identified in paragraph (e)(3)(ii) of this section, cause the aggregate amount of such charges to increase by more than 10 percent. For purposes of this paragraph, "changed circumstance" means:

(1) An extraordinary event beyond the control of any interested party or other unexpected event specific to the consumer or transaction;

(2) Information specific to the consumer or transaction that the creditor relied upon when providing the disclosures required under paragraph (e)(1)(i) of this section and that was inaccurate or changed after the disclosures were provided; or

(3) New information specific to the consumer or transaction that the creditor did not rely on when providing the original disclosures required under paragraph (e)(1)(i) of this section.

(B) Changed circumstance affecting eligibility. The consumer is ineligible for an estimated charge previously disclosed because a changed circumstance, as defined under paragraph (e)(3)(iv)(A) of this section, affected the consumer's creditworthiness or the value of the security for the loan.

(C) Revisions requested by the consumer. The consumer requests revisions to the credit terms or the settlement that cause an estimated charge to increase.

(D) Interest rate dependent charges. The points or lender credits change because the interest rate was not locked when the disclosures required under paragraph (e)(1)(i) of this section were provided. No later than three business days after the date the interest rate is locked, the creditor shall provide a revised version of the disclosures required under paragraph (e)(1)(i) of this section to the consumer with the revised interest rate, the points disclosed pursuant to § 1026.37(f)(1), lender credits, and any other interest rate dependent charges and terms.

(E) Expiration. The consumer indicates an intent to proceed with the transaction more than 10 business days, or more than any additional number of days specified by the creditor before the offer expires, after the disclosures required under paragraph (e)(1)(i) of this section are provided pursuant to paragraph (e)(1)(iii) of this section.

(F) Delayed settlement date on a construction loan. In transactions involving new construction, where the creditor reasonably expects that settlement will occur more than 60 days after the disclosures required under paragraph (e)(1)(i) of this section are provided pursuant to paragraph (e)(1)(iii) of this section, the creditor may provide revised disclosures to the consumer if the original disclosures required under paragraph (e)(1)(i) of this section state clearly and conspicuously that at any time prior to 60 days before consummation, the creditor may issue revised disclosures. If no such statement is provided, the creditor may not issue revised disclosures, except as otherwise provided in paragraph (e)(3)(iv) of this section.

(4) **Provision and receipt of revised disclosures.**

(i) **General rule.** Subject to the requirements of paragraph (e)(4)(ii) of this section, if a creditor uses a revised estimate pursuant to paragraph (e)(3)(iv) of this section for the purpose of determining good faith under paragraphs (e)(3)(i) and (ii) of this section, the creditor shall provide a revised version of the disclosures required under paragraph (e)(1)(i) of this section or the disclosures required under paragraph (f)(1)(i) of this section (including any corrected disclosures provided under paragraph (f)(2)(i) or (ii) of this section) reflecting the revised estimate within three business days of receiving information sufficient to establish that one of the reasons for revision provided under paragraphs (e)(3)(iv)(A) through (F) of this section applies.

(ii) **Relationship between revised Loan Estimates and Closing Disclosures.** The creditor shall not provide a revised version of the disclosures required under paragraph (e)(1)(i) of this section on or after the date on which the creditor provides the disclosures required under paragraph (f)(1)(i) of this section. The consumer must receive any revised version of the disclosures required under paragraph (e)(1)(i) of this section not later than four business days prior to consummation. If the revised version of the disclosures required under paragraph (e)(1)(i) of this section is not provided to the consumer in person, the consumer is considered to have received such version three business days after the creditor delivers or places such version in the mail.

(f) **Mortgage loans secured by real property—final disclosures.**

(1) **Provision of disclosures.**

(i) **Scope.** In a transaction subject to paragraph (e)(1)(i) of this section, the creditor shall provide the consumer with the disclosures required under § 1026.38 reflecting the actual terms of the transaction.

(ii) **Timing.**

(A) **In general.** Except as provided in paragraphs (f)(1)(ii)(B), (f)(2)(i), (f)(2)(iii), (f)(2)(iv), and (f)(2)(v) of this section, the creditor shall ensure that the consumer receives the disclosures required under paragraph (f)(1)(i) of this section no later than three business days before consummation.

(B) **Timeshares.** For transactions secured by a consumer's interest in a timeshare plan described in 11 U.S.C. 101(53D), the creditor shall ensure that the consumer receives the disclosures required under paragraph (f)(1)(i) of this section no later than consummation.

(iii) **Receipt of disclosures.** If any disclosures required under paragraph (f)(1)(i) of this section are not provided to the consumer in person, the consumer is considered to have received the disclosures three business days after they are delivered or placed in the mail.

(iv) **Consumer's waiver of waiting period before consummation.** If the consumer determines that the extension of credit is needed to meet a bona fide personal financial emergency, the consumer may modify or waive the three-business-day waiting period under paragraph (f)(1)(ii)(A) or (f)(2)(ii) of this section, after receiving the disclosures required under paragraph (f)(1)(i) of this section. To modify or waive the waiting period, the consumer shall give the creditor a dated written statement that describes the emergency, specifically modifies or waives the waiting period, and bears the signature of all consumers who are primarily liable on the legal obligation. Printed forms for this purpose are prohibited.

(v) **Settlement agent.** A settlement agent may provide a consumer with the disclosures required under paragraph (f)(1)(i) of this section, provided the settlement agent complies with all relevant requirements of this paragraph (f). The creditor shall ensure that such disclosures are provided in accordance with all requirements of this paragraph (f). Disclosures provided by a settlement agent in accordance with the requirements of this paragraph (f) satisfy the creditor's obligation under this paragraph (f).

(2) Subsequent changes.

(i) Changes before consummation not requiring a new waiting period. Except as provided in paragraph (f)(2)(ii), if the disclosures provided under paragraph (f)(1)(i) of this section become inaccurate before consummation, the creditor shall provide corrected disclosures reflecting any changed terms to the consumer so that the consumer receives the corrected disclosures at or before consummation. Notwithstanding the requirement to provide corrected disclosures at or before consummation, the creditor shall permit the consumer to inspect the disclosures provided under this paragraph, completed to set forth those items that are known to the creditor at the time of inspection, during the business day immediately preceding consummation, but the creditor may omit from inspection items related only to the seller's transaction.

(ii) Changes before consummation requiring a new waiting period. If one of the following disclosures provided under paragraph (f)(1)(i) of this section becomes inaccurate in the following manner before consummation, the creditor shall ensure that the consumer receives corrected disclosures containing all changed terms in accordance with the requirements of paragraph (f)(1)(ii)(A) of this section:

(A) The annual percentage rate disclosed under § 1026.38(*o*)(4) becomes inaccurate, as defined in § 1026.22.

(B) The loan product is changed, causing the information disclosed under § 1026.38(a)(5)(iii) to become inaccurate.

(C) A prepayment penalty is added, causing the statement regarding a prepayment penalty required under § 1026.38(b) to become inaccurate.

(iii) Changes due to events occurring after consummation. If during the 30-day period following consummation, an event in connection with the settlement of the transaction occurs that causes the disclosures required under paragraph (f)(1)(i) of this section to become inaccurate, and such inaccuracy results in a change to an amount actually paid by the consumer from that amount disclosed under paragraph (f)(1)(i) of this section, the creditor shall deliver or place in the mail corrected disclosures not later than 30 days after receiving information sufficient to establish that such event has occurred.

(iv) Changes due to clerical errors. A creditor does not violate paragraph (f)(1)(i) of this section if the disclosures provided under paragraph (f)(1)(i) contain non-numeric clerical errors, provided the creditor delivers or places in the mail corrected disclosures no later than 60 days after consummation.

(v) Refunds related to the good faith analysis. If amounts paid by the consumer exceed the amounts specified under paragraph (e)(3)(i) or (ii) of this section, the creditor complies with paragraph (e)(1)(i) of this section if the creditor refunds the excess to the consumer no later than 60 days after consummation, and the creditor complies with paragraph (f)(1)(i) of this section if the creditor delivers or places in the mail corrected disclosures that reflect such refund no later than 60 days after consummation.

(3) Charges disclosed.

(i) Actual charge. The amount imposed upon the consumer for any settlement service shall not exceed the amount actually received by the settlement service provider for that service, except as otherwise provided in paragraph (f)(3)(ii) of this section.

(ii) Average charge. A creditor or settlement service provider may charge a consumer or seller the average charge for a settlement service if the following conditions are satisfied:

(A) The average charge is no more than the average amount paid for that service by or on behalf of all consumers and sellers for a class of transactions;

(B) The creditor or settlement service provider defines the class of transactions based on an appropriate period of time, geographic area, and type of loan;

(C) The creditor or settlement service provider uses the same average charge for every transaction within the defined class; and

(D) The creditor or settlement service provider does not use an average charge:

(1) For any type of insurance;

(2) For any charge based on the loan amount or property value; or by law.

(4) Transactions involving a seller.

(i) Provision to seller. In a transaction subject to paragraph (e)(1)(i) of this section that involves a seller, the settlement agent shall provide the seller with the disclosures required under § 1026.38 that relate to the seller's transaction reflecting the actual terms of the seller's transaction.

(ii) Timing. The settlement agent shall provide the disclosures required under paragraph (f)(4)(i) of this section no later than the day of consummation. If during the 30-day period following consummation, an event in connection with the settlement of the transaction occurs that causes disclosures required under paragraph (f)(4)(i) of this section to become inaccurate, and such inaccuracy results in a change to the amount actually paid by the seller from that amount disclosed under paragraph (f)(4)(i) of this section, the settlement agent shall deliver or place in the mail corrected disclosures not later than 30 days after receiving information sufficient to establish that such event has occurred.

(iii) Charges disclosed. The amount imposed on the seller for any settlement service shall not exceed the amount actually received by the service provider for that service, except as otherwise provided in paragraph (f)(3)(ii) of this section.

(iv) Creditor's copy. When the consumer's and seller's disclosures under this paragraph (f) are provided on separate documents, as permitted under § 1026.38(t)(5), the settlement agent shall provide to the creditor (if the creditor is not the settlement agent) a copy of the disclosures provided to the seller under paragraph (f)(4)(i) of this section.

(5) No fee. No fee may be imposed on any person, as a part of settlement costs or otherwise, by a creditor or by a servicer (as that term is defined under 12 U.S.C. 2605(i)(2)) for the preparation or delivery of the disclosures required under paragraph (f)(1)(i) of this section.

(g) Special information booklet at time of application.

(1) Creditor to provide special information booklet. Except as provided in paragraphs (g)(1)(ii) and (iii) of this section, the creditor shall provide a copy of the special information booklet (required pursuant to section 5 of the Real Estate Settlement Procedures Act (12 U.S.C. 2604) to help consumers applying for federally related mortgage loans understand the nature and cost of real estate settlement services) to a consumer who applies for a consumer credit transaction secured by real property or a cooperative unit.

(i) The creditor shall deliver or place in the mail the special information booklet not later than three business days after the consumer's application is received. However, if the creditor denies the consumer's application before the end of the three-business-day period, the creditor need not provide the booklet. If a consumer uses a mortgage broker, the mortgage broker shall provide the special information booklet and the creditor need not do so.

(ii) In the case of a home equity line of credit subject to § 1026.40, a creditor or mortgage broker that provides the consumer with a copy of the brochure entitled "When Your Home is On the Line: What You Should Know About Home Equity Lines of Credit," or any successor brochure issued by the Bureau, is deemed to be in compliance with this section.

(iii) The creditor or mortgage broker need not provide the booklet to the consumer for a consumer credit transaction secured by real property, the purpose of which is not the purchase of a one-to-four family residential property, including, but not limited to, the following:

(A) Refinancing transactions;

(B) Closed-end loans secured by a subordinate lien; and

(C) Reverse mortgages.

(2) Permissible changes. Creditors may not make changes to, deletions from, or additions to the special information booklet other than the changes specified in paragraphs (g)(2)(i) through (iv) of this section.

(i) In the "Complaints" section of the booklet, "the Bureau of Consumer Financial Protection" may be substituted for "HUD's Office of RESPA" and "the RESPA office."

(ii) In the "Avoiding Foreclosure" section of the booklet, it is permissible to inform homeowners that they may find information on and assistance in avoiding foreclosures at http://www.consumerfinance.gov. The reference to the HUD Web site, http://www.hud.gov/foreclosure/, in the "Avoiding Foreclosure" section of the booklet shall not be deleted.

(iii) In the "No Discrimination" section of the appendix to the booklet, "the Bureau of Consumer Financial Protection" may be substituted for the reference to the "Board of Governors of the Federal Reserve System." In the Contact Information section of the appendix to the booklet, the following contact information for the Bureau may be added: "Bureau of Consumer Financial Protection, 1700 G Street NW., Washington, DC 20552; www.consumerfinance.gov/learnmore." The contact information for HUD's Office of RESPA and Interstate Land Sales may be removed from the "Contact Information" section of the appendix to the booklet.

(iv) The cover of the booklet may be in any form and may contain any drawings, pictures or artwork, provided that the title appearing on the cover shall not be changed. Names, addresses, and telephone numbers of the creditor or others and similar information may appear on the cover, but no discussion of the matters covered in the booklet shall appear on the cover. References to HUD on the cover of the booklet may be changed to references to the Bureau.

§ 1026.20 Disclosure requirements regarding post-consummation events.

(a) Refinancings. A refinancing occurs when an existing obligation that was subject to this subpart is satisfied and replaced by a new obligation undertaken by the same consumer. A refinancing is a new transaction requiring new disclosures to the consumer. The new finance charge shall include any unearned portion of the old finance charge that is not credited to the existing obligation. The following shall not be treated as a refinancing:

(1) A renewal of a single payment obligation with no change in the original terms.

(2) A reduction in the annual percentage rate with a corresponding change in the payment schedule.

(3) An agreement involving a court proceeding.

(4) A change in the payment schedule or a change in collateral requirements as a result of the consumer's default or delinquency, unless the rate is increased, or the new amount financed exceeds the unpaid balance plus earned finance charge and premiums for continuation of insurance of the types described in § 1026.4(d).

(5) The renewal of optional insurance purchased by the consumer and added to an existing transaction, if disclosures relating to the initial purchase were provided as required by this subpart.

(b) Assumptions. An assumption occurs when a creditor expressly agrees in writing with a subsequent consumer to accept that consumer as a primary obligor on an existing residential mortgage transaction. Before the assumption occurs, the creditor shall make new disclosures to the subsequent consumer, based on the remaining obligation. If the finance charge originally imposed on the existing obligation was an add-on or discount finance charge, the creditor need only disclose:

(1) The unpaid balance of the obligation assumed.

(2) The total charges imposed by the creditor in connection with the assumption.

(3) The information required to be disclosed under § 1026.18(k), (*l*), (m), and (n).

(4) The annual percentage rate originally imposed on the obligation.

(5) The payment schedule under § 1026.18(g) and the total of payments under § 1026.18(h) based on the remaining obligation.

(c) Rate adjustments with a corresponding change in payment. The creditor, assignee, or servicer of an adjustable-rate mortgage shall provide consumers with disclosures, as described in this paragraph (c), in connection with the adjustment of interest rates pursuant to the loan contract that results in a corresponding adjustment to the payment. To the extent that other provisions of this subpart C govern the disclosures required by this paragraph (c), those provisions apply to assignees and servicers as well as to creditors. The disclosures required by this paragraph (c) also shall be provided for an interest rate adjustment resulting from the conversion of an adjustable-rate mortgage to a fixed-rate transaction, if that interest rate adjustment results in a corresponding payment change.

(1) Coverage.

(i) In general. For purposes of this paragraph (c), an adjustable-rate mortgage or "ARM" is a closed-end consumer credit transaction secured by the consumer's principal dwelling in which the annual percentage rate may increase after consummation.

(ii) Exemptions. The requirements of this paragraph (c) do not apply to:

(A) ARMs with terms of one year or less;

(B) The first interest rate adjustment to an ARM if the first payment at the adjusted level is due within 210 days after consummation and the new interest rate disclosed at consummation pursuant to § 1026.20(d) was not an estimate; or

(C) The creditor, assignee or servicer of an adjustable-rate mortgage when the servicer on the loan is subject to the Fair Debt Collections Practices Act (FDCPA) (15 U.S.C. 1692 et seq.) with regard to the loan and the consumer has sent a notification pursuant to FDCPA section 805(c) (15 U.S.C. 1692c(c)).

(2) Timing and content. Except as otherwise provided in paragraph (c)(2) of this section, the disclosures required by this paragraph (c) shall be provided to consumers at least 60, but no more than 120, days before the first payment at the adjusted level is due. The disclosures shall be provided to consumers at least 25, but no more than 120, days before the first payment at the adjusted level is due for ARMs with uniformly scheduled interest rate adjustments occurring every 60 days or more frequently and for ARMs originated prior to January 10, 2015 in which the loan contract requires the adjusted interest rate and payment to be calculated based on the index figure available as of a date that is less than 45 days prior to the adjustment date. The disclosures shall be provided to consumers as soon as practicable, but not less than 25 days before the first payment at the adjusted level is due, for the first adjustment to an ARM if it occurs within 60 days of consummation and the new interest rate disclosed at consummation pursuant to § 1026.20(d) was an estimate. The disclosures required by this paragraph (c) shall include:

(i) A statement providing:

(A) An explanation that under the terms of the consumer's adjustable-rate mortgage, the specific time period in which the current interest rate has been in effect is ending and the interest rate and mortgage payment will change;

(B) The effective date of the interest rate adjustment and when additional future interest rate adjustments are scheduled to occur; and

(C) Any other changes to loan terms, features, or options taking effect on the same date as the interest rate adjustment, such as the expiration of interest-only or payment-option features.

(ii) A table containing the following information:

(A) The current and new interest rates;

(B) The current and new payments and the date the first new payment is due; and

(C) For interest-only or negatively-amortizing payments, the amount of the current and new payment allocated to principal, interest, and taxes and insurance in escrow, as applicable. The current payment allocation disclosed shall be the payment allocation for the last payment prior to the date of the disclosure. The new payment allocation disclosed shall be the expected payment allocation for the first payment for which the new interest rate will apply.

(iii) An explanation of how the interest rate is determined, including:

(A) The specific index or formula used in making interest rate adjustments and a source of information about the index or formula; and

(B) The type and amount of any adjustment to the index, including any margin and an explanation that the margin is the addition of a certain number of percentage points to the index, and any application of previously foregone interest rate increases from past interest rate adjustments.

(iv) Any limits on the interest rate or payment increases at each interest rate adjustment and over the life of the loan, as applicable, including the extent to which such limits result in the creditor, assignee, or servicer foregoing any increase in the interest rate and the earliest date that such foregone interest rate increases may apply to future interest rate adjustments, subject to those limits.

(v) An explanation of how the new payment is determined, including:

(A) The index or formula used;

(B) Any adjustment to the index or formula, such as the addition of a margin or the application of any previously foregone interest rate increases from past interest rate adjustments;

(C) The loan balance expected on the date of the interest rate adjustment; and

(D) The length of the remaining loan term expected on the date of the interest rate adjustment and any change in the term of the loan caused by the adjustment.

(vi) If applicable, a statement that the new payment will not be allocated to pay loan principal and will not reduce the loan balance. If the new payment will result in negative amortization, a statement that the new payment will not be allocated to pay loan principal and will pay only part of the loan interest, thereby adding to the balance of the loan. If the new payment will result in negative amortization as a result of the interest rate adjustment, the statement shall set forth the payment required to amortize fully the remaining balance at the new interest rate over the remainder of the loan term.

(vii) The circumstances under which any prepayment penalty, as defined in § 1026.32(b)(6)(i), may be imposed, such as when paying the loan in full or selling or refinancing the principal dwelling; the time period during which such a penalty may be imposed; and a statement that the consumer may contact the servicer for additional information, including the maximum amount of the penalty.

(3) Format.

(i) The disclosures required by this paragraph (c) shall be provided in the form of a table and in the same order as, and with headings and format substantially similar to, forms H-4(D)(1) and (2) in appendix H to this part; and

(ii) The disclosures required by paragraph (c)(2)(ii) of this section shall be in the form of a table located within the table described in paragraph (c)(3)(i) of this section. These disclosures shall appear in the same order as, and with headings and format substantially similar to, the table inside the larger table in forms H-4(D)(1) and (2) in appendix H to this part.

(d) Initial rate adjustment. The creditor, assignee, or servicer of an adjustable-rate mortgage shall provide consumers with disclosures, as described in this paragraph (d), in connection with the initial interest rate adjustment pursuant to the loan contract. To the extent that other provisions of this subpart C govern the disclosures required by this paragraph (d), those provisions apply to assignees and servicers as well as to creditors. The disclosures required by this paragraph (d) shall be provided as a separate document from other documents provided by the creditor, assignee, or servicer. The disclosures shall be provided to consumers at least 210, but no more than 240, days before the first payment at the adjusted level is due. If the first payment at the adjusted level is due within the first 210 days after consummation, the disclosures shall be provided at consummation.

(1) Coverage.

(i) In general. For purposes of this paragraph (d), an adjustable-rate mortgage or "ARM" is a closed-end consumer credit transaction secured by the consumer's principal dwelling in which the annual percentage rate may increase after consummation.

(ii) Exemptions. The requirements of this paragraph (d) do not apply to ARMs with terms of one year or less.

(2) Content. If the new interest rate (or the new payment calculated from the new interest rate) is not known as of the date of the disclosure, an estimate shall be disclosed and labeled as such. This estimate shall be based on the calculation of the index reported in the source of information described in paragraph (d)(2)(iv)(A) of this section within fifteen business days prior to the date of the disclosure. The disclosures required by this paragraph (d) shall include:

(i) The date of the disclosure.

(ii) A statement providing:

(A) An explanation that under the terms of the consumer's adjustable-rate mortgage, the specific time period in which the current interest rate has been in effect is ending and that any change in the interest rate may result in a change in the mortgage payment;

(B) The effective date of the interest rate adjustment and when additional future interest rate adjustments are scheduled to occur; and

(C) Any other changes to loan terms, features, or options taking effect on the same date as the interest rate adjustment, such as the expiration of interest-only or payment-option features.

(iii) A table containing the following information:

(A) The current and new interest rates;

(B) The current and new payments and the date the first new payment is due; and

(C) For interest-only or negatively-amortizing payments, the amount of the current and new payment allocated to principal, interest, and taxes and insurance in escrow, as applicable. The current payment allocation disclosed shall be the payment allocation for the last payment prior to the date of the disclosure. The new payment allocation disclosed shall be the expected payment allocation for the first payment for which the new interest rate will apply.

(iv) An explanation of how the interest rate is determined, including:

(A) The specific index or formula used in making interest rate adjustments and a source of information about the index or formula; and

(B) The type and amount of any adjustment to the index, including any margin and an explanation that the margin is the addition of a certain number of percentage points to the index.

(v) Any limits on the interest rate or payment increases at each interest rate adjustment and over the life of the loan, as applicable, including the extent to which such limits result in the creditor, assignee, or servicer foregoing any increase in the interest rate and the earliest date that such foregone interest rate increases may apply to future interest rate adjustments, subject to those limits.

(vi) An explanation of how the new payment is determined, including:

(A) The index or formula used;

(B) Any adjustment to the index or formula, such as the addition of a margin;

(C) The loan balance expected on the date of the interest rate adjustment;

(D) The length of the remaining loan term expected on the date of the interest rate adjustment and any change in the term of the loan caused by the adjustment; and

(E) If the new interest rate or new payment provided is an estimate, a statement that another disclosure containing the actual new interest rate and new payment will be provided to the consumer between two and four months before the first payment at the adjusted level is due for interest rate adjustments that result in a corresponding payment change.

(vii) If applicable, a statement that the new payment will not be allocated to pay loan principal and will not reduce the loan balance. If the new payment will result in negative amortization, a statement that the new payment will not be allocated to pay loan principal and will pay only part of the loan interest, thereby adding to the balance of the loan. If the new payment will result in negative amortization as a result of the interest rate adjustment, the statement shall set forth the payment required to amortize fully the remaining balance at the new interest rate over the remainder of the loan term.

(viii) The circumstances under which any prepayment penalty, as defined in § 1026.32(b)(6)(i), may be imposed, such as when paying the loan in full or selling or refinancing the principal dwelling; the time period during which such a penalty may be imposed; and a statement that the consumer may contact the servicer for additional information, including the maximum amount of the penalty.

(ix) The telephone number of the creditor, assignee, or servicer for consumers to call if they anticipate not being able to make their new payments.

(x) The following alternatives to paying at the new rate that consumers may be able to pursue and a brief explanation of each alternative, expressed in simple and clear terms:

(A) Refinancing the loan with the current or another creditor or assignee;

(B) Selling the property and using the proceeds to pay the loan in full;

(C) Modifying the terms of the loan with the creditor, assignee, or servicer; and

(D) Arranging payment forbearance with the creditor, assignee, or servicer.

(xi) The Web site to access either the Bureau list or the HUD list of homeownership counselors and counseling organizations, the HUD toll-free telephone number to access the HUD list of homeownership counselors and counseling organizations, and the Bureau Web site to access contact information for State housing finance authorities (as defined in § 1301 of the Financial Institutions Reform, Recovery, and Enforcement Act of 1989).

(3) Format.

(i) Except for the disclosures required by paragraph (d)(2)(i) of this section, the disclosures required by this paragraph (d) shall be provided in the form of a table and in the same order as, and with headings and format substantially similar to, forms H-4(D)(3) and (4) in appendix H to this part;

(ii) The disclosures required by paragraph (d)(2)(i) of this section shall appear outside of and above the table required in paragraph (d)(3)(i) of this section; and

(iii) The disclosures required by paragraph (d)(2)(iii) of this section shall be in the form of a table located within the table described in paragraph (d)(3)(i) of this section. These disclosures shall appear in the same order as, and with headings and format substantially similar to, the table inside the larger table in forms H-4(D)(3) and (4) in appendix H to this part.

(e) Escrow account cancellation notice for certain mortgage transactions

(1) Scope. In a closed-end consumer credit transaction secured by a first lien on real property or a dwelling, other than a reverse mortgage subject to § 1026.33, for which an escrow account was established in connection with the transaction and will be cancelled, the creditor or servicer shall disclose the information specified in paragraph (e)(2) of this section in accordance with the form requirements in paragraph (e)(4) of this section, and the timing requirements in paragraph (e)(5) of this section. For purposes of this paragraph (e), the term "escrow account" has the same meaning as under 12 CFR 1024.17(b), and the term "servicer" has the same meaning as under 12 CFR 1024.2(b).

(2) Content requirements. If an escrow account was established in connection with a transaction subject to this paragraph (e) and the escrow account will be cancelled, the creditor or servicer shall clearly and conspicuously disclose, under the heading "Escrow Closing Notice," the following information:

(i) A statement informing the consumer of the date on which the consumer will no longer have an escrow account; a statement that an escrow account may also be called an impound or trust account; a statement of the reason why the escrow account will be closed; a statement that without an escrow account, the consumer must pay all property costs, such as taxes and homeowner's insurance, directly, possibly in one or two large payments a year; and a table, titled "Cost to you," that contains an itemization of the amount of any fee the creditor or servicer imposes on the consumer in connection with the closure of the consumer's escrow account, labeled "Escrow Closing Fee," and a statement that the fee is for closing the escrow account.

(ii) Under the reference "In the future":

(A) A statement of the consequences if the consumer fails to pay property costs, including the actions that a State or local government may take if property taxes are not paid and the actions the creditor or servicer may take if the consumer does not pay some or all property costs, such as adding amounts to the loan balance, adding an escrow account to the loan, or purchasing a property insurance policy on the consumer's behalf that may be more expensive and provide fewer benefits than a policy that the consumer could obtain directly;

(B) A statement with a telephone number that the consumer can use to request additional information about the cancellation of the escrow account;

(C) A statement of whether the creditor or servicer offers the option of keeping the escrow account open and, as applicable, a telephone number the consumer can use to request that the account be kept open; and

(D) A statement of whether there is a cut-off date by which the consumer can request that the account be kept open.

(3) Optional information. The creditor or servicer may, at its option, include its name or logo, the consumer's name, phone number, mailing address and property address, the issue date of the notice, the loan number, or the consumer's account number on the notice required by this paragraph (e). Except for the name and logo of the creditor or servicer, the information described in this paragraph may be placed between the heading required by paragraph (e)(2) of this section and the disclosures required by paragraphs (e)(2)(i) and (ii) of this section. The name and logo may be placed above the heading required by paragraph (e)(2) of this section.

(4) Form of disclosures. The disclosures required by paragraph (e)(2) of this section shall be provided in a minimum 10-point font, grouped together on the front side of a one-page document, separate from all other materials, with the headings, content, order, and format substantially similar to model form H-29 in appendix H to this part. The disclosure of the heading required by paragraph (e)(2) of this section shall be more conspicuous than, and shall precede, the other disclosures required by paragraph (e)(2) of this section.

(5) Timing.

(i) Cancellation upon consumer's request. If the creditor or servicer cancels the escrow account at the consumer's request, the creditor or servicer shall ensure that the consumer receives the disclosures required by paragraph (e)(2) of this section no later than three business days before the closure of the consumer's escrow account.

(ii) Cancellations other than upon the consumer's request. If the creditor or servicer cancels the escrow account and the cancellation is not at the consumer's request, the creditor or servicer shall ensure that the consumer receives the disclosures required by paragraph (e)(2) of this section no later than 30 business days before the closure of the consumer's escrow account.

(iii) Receipt of disclosure. If the disclosures required by paragraph (e)(2) of this section are not provided to the consumer in person, the consumer is considered to have received the disclosures three business days after they are delivered or placed in the mail.

(f) Successor in interest. If, upon confirmation, a servicer provides a confirmed successor in interest who is not liable on the mortgage loan obligation with a written notice and acknowledgment form in accordance with Regulation X, § 1024.32(c)(1) of this chapter, the servicer is not required to provide to the confirmed successor in interest any written disclosure required by paragraphs (c), (d), and (e) of this section unless and until the confirmed successor in interest either assumes the mortgage loan obligation under State law or has provided the servicer an executed acknowledgment in accordance with Regulation X, § 1024.32(c)(1)(iv) of this chapter, that the confirmed successor in interest has not revoked.

§ 1026.21 Treatment of credit balances.

When a credit balance in excess of $1 is created in connection with a transaction (through transmittal of funds to a creditor in excess of the total balance due on an account, through rebates of unearned finance charges or insurance premiums, or through amounts otherwise owed to or held for the benefit of a consumer), the creditor shall:

(a) Credit the amount of the credit balance to the consumer's account;

(b) Refund any part of the remaining credit balance, upon the written request of the consumer; and

(c) Make a good faith effort to refund to the consumer by cash, check, or money order, or credit to a deposit account of the consumer, any part of the credit balance remaining in the account for more than 6 months, except that no further action is required if the consumer's current location is not known to the creditor and cannot be traced through the consumer's last known address or telephone number.

§ 1026.22 Determination of annual percentage rate.

(a) Accuracy of annual percentage rate.

(1) The annual percentage rate is a measure of the cost of credit, expressed as a yearly rate, that relates the amount and timing of value received by the consumer to the amount and timing of payments made. The annual percentage rate shall be determined in accordance with either the actuarial method or the United States Rule method. Explanations, equations and instructions for determining the annual percentage rate in accordance with the actuarial method are set forth in Appendix J to this part. An error in disclosure of the annual percentage rate or finance charge shall not, in itself, be considered a violation of this part if:

(i) The error resulted from a corresponding error in a calculation tool used in good faith by the creditor; and

(ii) Upon discovery of the error, the creditor promptly discontinues use of that calculation tool for disclosure purposes and notifies the Bureau in writing of the error in the calculation tool.

(2) As a general rule, the annual percentage rate shall be considered accurate if it is not more than 1/8 of 1 percentage point above or below the annual percentage rate determined in accordance with paragraph (a)(1) of this section.

(3) In an irregular transaction, the annual percentage rate shall be considered accurate if it is not more than ¼ of 1 percentage point above or below the annual percentage rate determined in accordance with paragraph (a)(1) of this section. For purposes of this paragraph (a)(3), an irregular transaction is one that includes one or more of the following features: multiple advances, irregular payment periods, or irregular payment amounts (other than an irregular first period or an irregular first or final payment).

(4) Mortgage loans. If the annual percentage rate disclosed in a transaction secured by real property or a dwelling varies from the actual rate determined in accordance with paragraph (a)(1) of this section, in addition to the tolerances applicable under paragraphs (a)(2) and (3) of this section, the disclosed annual percentage rate shall also be considered accurate if:

(i) The rate results from the disclosed finance charge; and

(ii)(A) The disclosed finance charge would be considered accurate under § 1026.18(d)(1) or § 1026.38(*o*)(2), as applicable; or

(B) For purposes of rescission, if the disclosed finance charge would be considered accurate under § 1026.23(g) or (h), whichever applies.

(5) Additional tolerance for mortgage loans. In a transaction secured by real property or a dwelling, in addition to the tolerances applicable under paragraphs (a)(2) and (3) of this section, if the disclosed finance charge is calculated incorrectly but is considered accurate under § 1026.18(d)(1) or § 1026.38(*o*)(2), as applicable, or § 1026.23(g) or (h), the disclosed annual percentage rate shall be considered accurate:

(i) If the disclosed finance charge is understated, and the disclosed annual percentage rate is also understated but it is closer to the actual annual percentage rate than the rate that would be considered accurate under paragraph (a)(4) of this section;

(ii) If the disclosed finance charge is overstated, and the disclosed annual percentage rate is also overstated but it is closer to the actual annual percentage rate than the rate that would be considered accurate under paragraph (a)(4) of this section.

(b) Computation tools.

(1) The Regulation Z Annual Percentage Rate Tables produced by the Bureau may be used to determine the annual percentage rate, and any rate determined from those tables in accordance with the accompanying instructions complies with the requirements of this section. Volume I of the tables applies to single advance transactions involving up to 480 monthly payments or 104 weekly payments. It may be used for regular transactions and for transactions with any of the following irregularities: an irregular first period, an irregular first payment, and an irregular final payment. Volume II of the tables applies to transactions involving multiple advances and any type of payment or period irregularity.

(2) Creditors may use any other computation tool in determining the annual percentage rate if the rate so determined equals the rate determined in accordance with Appendix J to this part, within the degree of accuracy set forth in paragraph (a) of this section.

(c) Single add-on rate transactions. If a single add-on rate is applied to all transactions with maturities up to 60 months and if all payments are equal in amount and period, a single annual percentage rate may be disclosed for all those transactions, so long as it is the highest annual percentage rate for any such transaction.

(d) Certain transactions involving ranges of balances. For purposes of disclosing the annual percentage rate referred to in § 1026.17(g)(4) (Mail or telephone orders—delay in disclosures) and (h) (Series of sales—delay in disclosures), if the same finance charge is imposed on all balances within a specified range of balances, the annual percentage rate computed for the median balance may be disclosed for all the balances. However, if the annual percentage rate computed for the median balance understates the annual percentage rate computed for the lowest balance by more than 8 percent of the latter rate, the annual percentage rate shall be computed on whatever lower balance will produce an annual percentage rate that does not result in an understatement of more than 8 percent of the rate determined on the lowest balance.

§ 1026.23 Right of rescission.

(a) Consumer's right to rescind.

(1) In a credit transaction in which a security interest is or will be retained or acquired in a consumer's principal dwelling, each consumer whose ownership interest is or will be subject to the security interest shall have the right to rescind the transaction, except for transactions described in paragraph (f) of this section. For purposes of this section, the addition to an existing obligation of a security interest in a consumer's principal dwelling is a transaction. The right of rescission applies only to the addition of the security interest and not the existing obligation. The creditor shall deliver the notice required by paragraph (b) of this section but need not deliver new material disclosures. Delivery of the required notice shall begin the rescission period.

(2) To exercise the right to rescind, the consumer shall notify the creditor of the rescission by mail, telegram or other means of written communication. Notice is considered given when mailed, when filed for telegraphic transmission or, if sent by other means, when delivered to the creditor's designated place of business.

(3)(i) The consumer may exercise the right to rescind until midnight of the third business day following consummation, delivery of the notice required by paragraph (b) of this section, or delivery of all material disclosures, whichever occurs last. If the required notice or material disclosures are not delivered, the right to rescind shall expire 3 years after consummation, upon transfer of all of the consumer's interest in the property, or upon sale of the property, whichever occurs first. In the case of certain administrative proceedings, the rescission period shall be extended in accordance with section 125(f) of the Act.

(ii) For purposes of this paragraph (a)(3), the term "material disclosures" means the required disclosures of the annual percentage rate, the finance charge, the amount financed, the total of payments, the payment schedule, and the disclosures and limitations referred to in §§ 1026.32(c) and (d) and 1026.43(g).

(4) When more than one consumer in a transaction has the right to rescind, the exercise of the right by one consumer shall be effective as to all consumers.

(b)(1) Notice of right to rescind. In a transaction subject to rescission, a creditor shall deliver two copies of the notice of the right to rescind to each consumer entitled to rescind (one copy to each if the notice is delivered in electronic form in accordance with the consumer consent and other applicable provisions of the E-Sign Act). The notice shall be on a separate document that identifies the transaction and shall clearly and conspicuously disclose the following:

(i) The retention or acquisition of a security interest in the consumer's principal dwelling.

(ii) The consumer's right to rescind the transaction.

(iii) How to exercise the right to rescind, with a form for that purpose, designating the address of the creditor's place of business.

(iv) The effects of rescission, as described in paragraph (d) of this section.

(v) The date the rescission period expires.

(2) Proper form of notice. To satisfy the disclosure requirements of paragraph (b)(1) of this section, the creditor shall provide the appropriate model form in Appendix H of this part or a substantially similar notice.

(c) Delay of creditor's performance. Unless a consumer waives the right of rescission under paragraph (e) of this section, no money shall be disbursed other than in escrow, no services shall be performed and no materials delivered until the rescission period has expired and the creditor is reasonably satisfied that the consumer has not rescinded.

(d) Effects of rescission.

(1) When a consumer rescinds a transaction, the security interest giving rise to the right of rescission becomes void and the consumer shall not be liable for any amount, including any finance charge.

(2) Within 20 calendar days after receipt of a notice of rescission, the creditor shall return any money or property that has been given to anyone in connection with the transaction and shall take any action necessary to reflect the termination of the security interest.

(3) If the creditor has delivered any money or property, the consumer may retain possession until the creditor has met its obligation under paragraph (d)(2) of this section. When the creditor has complied with that paragraph, the consumer shall tender the money or property to the creditor or, where the latter would be impracticable or inequitable, tender its reasonable value. At the consumer's option, tender of property may be made at the location of the property or at the consumer's residence. Tender of money must be made at the creditor's designated place of business. If the creditor does not take possession of the money or property within 20 calendar days after the consumer's tender, the consumer may keep it without further obligation.

(4) The procedures outlined in paragraphs (d)(2) and (3) of this section may be modified by court order.

(e) Consumer's waiver of right to rescind. The consumer may modify or waive the right to rescind if the consumer determines that the extension of credit is needed to meet a bona fide personal financial emergency. To modify or waive the right, the consumer shall give the creditor a dated written statement that describes the emergency, specifically modifies or waives the right to rescind, and bears the signature of all the consumers entitled to rescind. Printed forms for this purpose are prohibited.

(f) Exempt transactions. The right to rescind does not apply to the following:

(1) A residential mortgage transaction.

(2) A refinancing or consolidation by the same creditor of an extension of credit already secured by the consumer's principal dwelling. The right of rescission shall apply, however, to the extent the new amount financed exceeds the unpaid principal balance, any earned unpaid finance charge on the existing debt, and amounts attributed solely to the costs of the refinancing or consolidation.

(3) A transaction in which a state agency is a creditor.

(4) An advance, other than an initial advance, in a series of advances or in a series of single-payment obligations that is treated as a single transaction under § 1026.17(c)(6), if the notice required by paragraph (b) of this section and all material disclosures have been given to the consumer.

(5) A renewal of optional insurance premiums that is not considered a refinancing under § 1026.20(a)(5).

(g) Tolerances for accuracy.

(1) One-half of 1 percent tolerance. Except as provided in paragraphs (g)(2) and (h)(2) of this section:

(i) The finance charge and other disclosures affected by the finance charge (such as the amount financed and the annual percentage rate) shall be considered accurate for purposes of this section if the disclosed finance charge:

(A) Is understated by no more than 1/2 of 1 percent of the face amount of the note or $100, whichever is greater; or

(B) Is greater than the amount required to be disclosed.

(ii) The total of payments for each transaction subject to § 1026.19(e) and (f) shall be considered accurate for purposes of this section if the disclosed total of payments:

(A) Is understated by no more than 1/2 of 1 percent of the face amount of the note or $100, whichever is greater; or

(B) Is greater than the amount required to be disclosed.

(2) One percent tolerance. In a refinancing of a residential mortgage transaction with a new creditor (other than a transaction covered by § 1026.32), if there is no new advance and no consolidation of existing loans:

(i) The finance charge and other disclosures affected by the finance charge (such as the amount financed and the annual percentage rate) shall be considered accurate for purposes of this section if the disclosed finance charge:

(A) Is understated by no more than 1 percent of the face amount of the note or $100, whichever is greater; or

(B) Is greater than the amount required to be disclosed.

(ii) The total of payments for each transaction subject to § 1026.19(e) and (f) shall be considered accurate for purposes of this section if the disclosed total of payments:

(A) Is understated by no more than 1 percent of the face amount of the note or $100, whichever is greater; or

(B) Is greater than the amount required to be disclosed.

(h) Special rules for foreclosures.

(1) Right to rescind. After the initiation of foreclosure on the consumer's principal dwelling that secures the credit obligation, the consumer shall have the right to rescind the transaction if:

(i) A mortgage broker fee that should have been included in the finance charge was not included; or

(ii) The creditor did not provide the properly completed appropriate model form in Appendix H of this part, or a substantially similar notice of rescission.

(2) Tolerance for disclosures. After the initiation of foreclosure on the consumer's principal dwelling that secures the credit obligation:

(i) The finance charge and other disclosures affected by the finance charge (such as the amount financed and the annual percentage rate) shall be considered accurate for purposes of this section if the disclosed finance charge:

(A) Is understated by no more than $35; or

(B) Is greater than the amount required to be disclosed.

(ii) The total of payments for each transaction subject to § 1026.19(e) and (f) shall be considered accurate for purposes of this section if the disclosed total of payments:

(A) Is understated by no more than $35; or

(B) Is greater than the amount required to be disclosed.

§ 1026.24 Advertising.

(a) Actually available terms. If an advertisement for credit states specific credit terms, it shall state only those terms that actually are or will be arranged or offered by the creditor.

(b) Clear and conspicuous standard. Disclosures required by this section shall be made clearly and conspicuously.

(c) Advertisement of rate of finance charge. If an advertisement states a rate of finance charge, it shall state the rate as an "annual percentage rate," using that term. If the annual percentage rate may be increased after consummation, the advertisement shall state that fact. If an advertisement is for credit not secured by a dwelling, the advertisement shall not state any other rate, except that a simple annual rate or periodic rate that is applied to an unpaid balance may be stated in conjunction with, but not more conspicuously than, the annual percentage rate. If an advertisement is for credit secured by a dwelling, the advertisement shall not state any other rate, except that a simple annual rate that is applied to an unpaid balance may be stated in conjunction with, but not more conspicuously than, the annual percentage rate.

(d) Advertisement of terms that require additional disclosures.

(1) Triggering terms. If any of the following terms is set forth in an advertisement, the advertisement shall meet the requirements of paragraph (d)(2) of this section:

(i) The amount or percentage of any downpayment.

(ii) The number of payments or period of repayment.

(iii) The amount of any payment.

(iv) The amount of any finance charge.

(2) Additional terms. An advertisement stating any of the terms in paragraph (d)(1) of this section shall state the following terms, as applicable (an example of one or more typical extensions of credit with a statement of all the terms applicable to each may be used):

(i) The amount or percentage of the downpayment.

(ii) The terms of repayment, which reflect the repayment obligations over the full term of the loan, including any balloon payment.

(iii) The "annual percentage rate," using that term, and, if the rate may be increased after consummation, that fact.

(e) Catalogs or other multiple-page advertisements; electronic advertisements.

(1) If a catalog or other multiple-page advertisement, or an electronic advertisement (such as an advertisement appearing on an Internet Web site), gives information in a table or schedule in sufficient detail to permit determination of the disclosures required by paragraph (d)(2) of this section, it shall be considered a single advertisement if:

(i) The table or schedule is clearly and conspicuously set forth; and

(ii) Any statement of the credit terms in paragraph (d)(1) of this section appearing anywhere else in the catalog or advertisement clearly refers to the page or location where the table or schedule begins.

(2) A catalog or other multiple-page advertisement or an electronic advertisement (such as an advertisement appearing on an Internet Web site) complies with paragraph (d)(2) of this section if the table or schedule of terms includes all appropriate disclosures for a representative scale of amounts up to the level of the more commonly sold higher-priced property or services offered.

(f) Disclosure of rates and payments in advertisements for credit secured by a dwelling.

(1) Scope. The requirements of this paragraph apply to any advertisement for credit secured by a dwelling, other than television or radio advertisements, including promotional materials accompanying applications.

(2) Disclosure of rates.

(i) In general. If an advertisement for credit secured by a dwelling states a simple annual rate of interest and more than one simple annual rate of interest will apply over the term of the advertised loan, the advertisement shall disclose in a clear and conspicuous manner:

(A) Each simple annual rate of interest that will apply. In variable-rate transactions, a rate determined by adding an index and margin shall be disclosed based on a reasonably current index and margin;

(B) The period of time during which each simple annual rate of interest will apply; and

(C) The annual percentage rate for the loan. If such rate is variable, the annual percentage rate shall comply with the accuracy standards in §§ 1026.17(c) and 1026.22.

(ii) Clear and conspicuous requirement. For purposes of paragraph (f)(2)(i) of this section, clearly and conspicuously disclosed means that the required information in paragraphs (f)(2)(i)(A) through (C) shall be disclosed with equal prominence and in close proximity to any advertised rate that triggered the required disclosures. The required information in paragraph (f)(2)(i)(C) may be disclosed with greater prominence than the other information.

(3) Disclosure of payments.

(i) In general. In addition to the requirements of paragraph (c) of this section, if an advertisement for credit secured by a dwelling states the amount of any payment, the advertisement shall disclose in a clear and conspicuous manner:

(A) The amount of each payment that will apply over the term of the loan, including any balloon payment. In variable-rate transactions, payments that will be determined based on the application of the sum of an index and margin shall be disclosed based on a reasonably current index and margin;

(B) The period of time during which each payment will apply; and

(C) In an advertisement for credit secured by a first lien on a dwelling, the fact that the payments do not include amounts for taxes and insurance premiums, if applicable, and that the actual payment obligation will be greater.

(ii) Clear and conspicuous requirement. For purposes of paragraph (f)(3)(i) of this section, a clear and conspicuous disclosure means that the required information in paragraphs (f)(3)(i)(A) and (B) shall be disclosed with equal prominence and in close proximity to any advertised payment that triggered the required disclosures, and that the required information in paragraph (f)(3)(i)(C) shall be disclosed with prominence and in close proximity to the advertised payments.

(4) Envelope excluded. The requirements in paragraphs (f)(2) and (f)(3) of this section do not apply to an envelope in which an application or solicitation is mailed, or to a banner advertisement or pop-up advertisement linked to an application or solicitation provided electronically.

(g) Alternative disclosures—television or radio advertisements. An advertisement made through television or radio stating any of the terms requiring additional disclosures under paragraph (d)(2) of this section may comply with paragraph (d)(2) of this section either by:

(1) Stating clearly and conspicuously each of the additional disclosures required under paragraph (d)(2) of this section; or

(2) Stating clearly and conspicuously the information required by paragraph (d)(2)(iii) of this section and listing a toll-free telephone number, or any telephone number that allows a consumer to reverse the phone charges when calling for information, along with a reference that such number may be used by consumers to obtain additional cost information.

(h) Tax implications. If an advertisement distributed in paper form or through the Internet (rather than by radio or television) is for a loan secured by the consumer's principal dwelling, and the advertisement states that the advertised extension of credit may exceed the fair market value of the dwelling, the advertisement shall clearly and conspicuously state that:

(1) The interest on the portion of the credit extension that is greater than the fair market value of the dwelling is not tax deductible for Federal income tax purposes; and

(2) The consumer should consult a tax adviser for further information regarding the deductibility of interest and charges.

(i) Prohibited acts or practices in advertisements for credit secured by a dwelling. The following acts or practices are prohibited in advertisements for credit secured by a dwelling:

(1) Misleading advertising of "fixed" rates and payments. Using the word "fixed" to refer to rates, payments, or the credit transaction in an advertisement for variable-rate transactions or other transactions where the payment will increase, unless:

(i) In the case of an advertisement solely for one or more variable-rate transactions,

(A) The phrase "Adjustable-Rate Mortgage," "Variable-Rate Mortgage," or "ARM" appears in the advertisement before the first use of the word "fixed" and is at least as conspicuous as any use of the word "fixed" in the advertisement; and

(B) Each use of the word "fixed" to refer to a rate or payment is accompanied by an equally prominent and closely proximate statement of the time period for which the rate or payment is fixed, and the fact that the rate may vary or the payment may increase after that period;

(ii) In the case of an advertisement solely for non-variable-rate transactions where the payment will increase (e.g., a stepped-rate mortgage transaction with an initial lower payment), each use of the word "fixed" to refer to the payment is accompanied by an equally prominent and closely proximate statement of the time period for which the payment is fixed, and the fact that the payment will increase after that period; or

(iii) In the case of an advertisement for both variable-rate transactions and non-variable-rate transactions,

(A) The phrase "Adjustable-Rate Mortgage," "Variable-Rate Mortgage," or "ARM" appears in the advertisement with equal prominence as any use of the term "fixed," "Fixed-Rate Mortgage," or similar terms; and

(B) Each use of the word "fixed" to refer to a rate, payment, or the credit transaction either refers solely to the transactions for which rates are fixed and complies with paragraph (i)(1)(ii) of this section, if applicable, or, if it refers to the variable-rate transactions, is accompanied by an equally prominent and closely proximate statement of the time period for which the rate or payment is fixed, and the fact that the rate may vary or the payment may increase after that period.

(2) Misleading comparisons in advertisements. Making any comparison in an advertisement between actual or hypothetical credit payments or rates and any payment or simple annual rate that will be available under the advertised product for a period less than the full term of the loan, unless:

(i) In general. The advertisement includes a clear and conspicuous comparison to the information required to be disclosed under § 1026.24(f)(2) and (3); and

(ii) Application to variable-rate transactions. If the advertisement is for a variable-rate transaction, and the advertised payment or simple annual rate is based on the index and margin that will be used to make subsequent rate or payment adjustments over the term of the loan, the advertisement includes an equally prominent statement in close proximity to the payment or rate that the payment or rate is subject to adjustment and the time period when the first adjustment will occur.

(3) Misrepresentations about government endorsement. Making any statement in an advertisement that the product offered is a "government loan program", "government-supported loan", or is otherwise endorsed or sponsored by any Federal, state, or local government entity, unless the advertisement is for an FHA loan, VA loan, or similar loan program that is, in fact, endorsed or sponsored by a Federal, state, or local government entity.

(4) Misleading use of the current lender's name. Using the name of the consumer's current lender in an advertisement that is not sent by or on behalf of the consumer's current lender, unless the advertisement:

(i) Discloses with equal prominence the name of the person or creditor making the advertisement; and

(ii) Includes a clear and conspicuous statement that the person making the advertisement is not associated with, or acting on behalf of, the consumer's current lender.

(5) Misleading claims of debt elimination. Making any misleading claim in an advertisement that the mortgage product offered will eliminate debt or result in a waiver or forgiveness of a consumer's existing loan terms with, or obligations to, another creditor.

(6) Misleading use of the term "counselor". Using the term "counselor" in an advertisement to refer to a for-profit mortgage broker or mortgage creditor, its employees, or persons working for the broker or creditor that are involved in offering, originating or selling mortgages.

(7) Misleading foreign-language advertisements. Providing information about some trigger terms or required disclosures, such as an initial rate or payment, only in a foreign language in an advertisement, but providing information about other trigger terms or required disclosures, such as information about the fully-indexed rate or fully amortizing payment, only in English in the same advertisement.

SUBPART D. MISCELLANEOUS

§ 1026.25 Record retention.

(a) General rule. A creditor shall retain evidence of compliance with this part (other than advertising requirements under §§ 1026.16 and 1026.24, and other than the requirements under § 1026.19(e) and (f)) for two years after the date disclosures are required to be made or action is required to be taken. The administrative agencies responsible for enforcing the regulation may require creditors under their jurisdictions to retain records for a longer period if necessary to carry out their enforcement responsibilities under section 108 of the Act.

(b) Inspection of records. A creditor shall permit the agency responsible for enforcing this part with respect to that creditor to inspect its relevant records for compliance.

(c) Records related to certain requirements for mortgage loans.

(1) Records related to requirements for loans secured by real property or a cooperative unit.

(i) General rule. Except as provided under paragraph (c)(1)(ii) of this section, a creditor shall retain evidence of compliance with the requirements of § 1026.19(e) and (f) for three years after the later of the date of consummation, the date disclosures are required to be made, or the date the action is required to be taken.

(ii) Closing disclosures. (A) A creditor shall retain each completed disclosure required under § 1026.19(f)(1)(i) or (f)(4)(i), and all documents related to such disclosures, for five years after consummation, notwithstanding paragraph (c)(1)(ii)(B) of this section.

(B) If a creditor sells, transfers, or otherwise disposes of its interest in a mortgage loan subject to § 1026.19(f) and does not service the mortgage loan, the creditor shall provide a copy of the disclosures required under § 1026.19(f)(1)(i) or (f)(4)(i) to the owner or servicer of the mortgage as a part of the transfer of the loan file. Such owner or servicer shall retain such disclosures for the remainder of the five-year period described under paragraph (c)(1)(ii)(A) of this section.

(C) The Bureau shall have the right to require provision of copies of records related to the disclosures required under § 1026.19(f)(1)(i) and (f)(4)(i).

(2) Records related to requirements for loan originator compensation. Notwithstanding paragraph (a) of this section, for transactions subject to § 1026.36:

(i) A creditor shall maintain records sufficient to evidence all compensation it pays to a loan originator, as defined in § 1026.36(a)(1), and the compensation agreement that governs those payments for three years after the date of payment.

(ii) A loan originator organization, as defined in § 1026.36(a)(1)(iii), shall maintain records sufficient to evidence all compensation it receives from a creditor, a consumer, or another person; all compensation it pays to any individual loan originator, as defined in § 1026.36(a)(1)(ii); and the compensation agreement that governs each such receipt or payment, for three years after the date of each such receipt or payment.

(3) Records related to minimum standards for transactions secured by a dwelling. Notwithstanding paragraph (a) of this section, a creditor shall retain evidence of compliance with § 1026.43 of this regulation for three years after consummation of a transaction covered by that section.

§ 1026.26 Use of annual percentage rate in oral disclosures.

(a) Open-end credit. In an oral response to a consumer's inquiry about the cost of open-end credit, only the annual percentage rate or rates shall be stated, except that the periodic rate or rates also may be stated. If the annual percentage rate cannot be determined in advance because there are finance charges other than a periodic rate, the corresponding annual percentage rate shall be stated, and other cost information may be given.

(b) Closed-end credit. In an oral response to a consumer's inquiry about the cost of closed-end credit, only the annual percentage rate shall be stated, except that a simple annual rate or periodic rate also may be stated if it is applied to an unpaid balance. If the annual percentage rate cannot be determined in advance, the annual percentage rate for a sample transaction shall be stated, and other cost information for the consumer's specific transaction may be given.

§ 1026.27 Language of disclosures.

Disclosures required by this part may be made in a language other than English, provided that the disclosures are made available in English upon the consumer's request. This requirement for providing English disclosures on request does not apply to advertisements subject to §§ 1026.16 and 1026.24.

§ 1026.28 Effect on state laws.

(a) Inconsistent disclosure requirements.

(1) Except as provided in paragraph (d) of this section, State law requirements that are inconsistent with the requirements contained in chapter 1 (General Provisions), chapter 2 (Credit Transactions), or chapter 3 (Credit Advertising) of the Act and the implementing provisions of this part are preempted to the extent of the inconsistency. A State law is inconsistent if it requires a creditor to make disclosures or take actions that contradict the requirements of the Federal law. A State law is contradictory if it requires the use of the same term to represent a different amount or a different meaning than the Federal law, or if it requires the use of a term different from that required in the Federal law to describe the same item. A creditor, State, or other interested party may request the Bureau to determine whether a State law requirement is inconsistent. After the Bureau determines that a state law is inconsistent, a creditor may not make disclosures using the inconsistent term or form. A determination as to whether a State law is inconsistent with the requirements of sections 4 and 5 of RESPA (other than the RESPA section 5(c) requirements regarding provision of a list of certified homeownership counselors) and §§ 1026.19(e) and (f), 1026.37, and 1026.38 shall be made in accordance with this section and not 12 CFR 1024.13.

(2)(i) State law requirements are inconsistent with the requirements contained in sections 161 (Correction of billing errors) or 162 (Regulation of credit reports) of the Act and the implementing provisions of this part and are preempted if they provide rights, responsibilities, or procedures for consumers or creditors that are different from those required by the Federal law. However, a state law that allows a consumer to inquire about an open-end credit account and imposes on the creditor an obligation to respond to such inquiry after the time allowed in the Federal law for the consumer to submit written notice of a billing error shall not be preempted in any situation where the time period for making written notice under this part has expired. If a creditor gives written notice of a consumer's rights under such state law, the notice shall state that reliance on the longer time period available under state law may result in the loss of important rights that could be preserved by acting more promptly under Federal law; it shall also explain that the state law provisions apply only after expiration of the time period for submitting a proper written notice of a billing error under the Federal law. If the state disclosures are made on the same side of a page as the required Federal disclosures, the state disclosures shall appear under a demarcation line below the Federal disclosures, and the Federal disclosures shall be identified by a heading indicating that they are made in compliance with Federal law.

(ii) State law requirements are inconsistent with the requirements contained in chapter 4 (Credit billing) of the Act (other than section 161 or 162) and the implementing provisions of this part and are preempted if the creditor cannot comply with state law without violating Federal law.

(iii) A state may request the Bureau to determine whether its law is inconsistent with chapter 4 of the Act and its implementing provisions.

(b) Equivalent disclosure requirements. If the Bureau determines that a disclosure required by state law (other than a requirement relating to the finance charge, annual percentage rate, or the disclosures required under § 1026.32) is substantially the same in meaning as a disclosure required under the Act or this part, creditors in that state may make the state disclosure in lieu of the Federal disclosure. A creditor, state, or other interested party may request the Bureau to determine whether a state disclosure is substantially the same in meaning as a Federal disclosure.

(c) Request for determination. The procedures under which a request for a determination may be made under this section are set forth in Appendix A.

(d) Special rule for credit and charge cards. State law requirements relating to the disclosure of credit information in any credit or charge card application or solicitation that is subject to the requirements of section 127(c) of chapter 2 of the Act (§ 1026.60 of the regulation) or in any renewal notice for a credit or charge card that is subject to the requirements of section 127(d) of chapter 2 of the Act (§ 1026.9(e) of the regulation) are preempted. State laws relating to the enforcement of section 127(c) and (d) of the Act are not preempted.

§ 1026.29 State exemptions.

(a) General rule. Any state may apply to the Bureau to exempt a class of transactions within the state from the requirements of chapter 2 (Credit transactions) or chapter 4 (Credit billing) of the Act and the corresponding provisions of this part. The Bureau shall grant an exemption if it determines that:

(1) The state law is substantially similar to the Federal law or, in the case of chapter 4, affords the consumer greater protection than the Federal law; and

(2) There is adequate provision for enforcement.

(b) Civil liability.

(1) No exemptions granted under this section shall extend to the civil liability provisions of sections 130 and 131 of the Act.

(2) If an exemption has been granted, the disclosures required by the applicable state law (except any additional requirements not imposed by Federal law) shall constitute the disclosures required by the Act.

(c) Applications. The procedures under which a state may apply for an exemption under this section are set forth in Appendix B to this part.

§ 1026.30 Limitation on rates.

A creditor shall include in any consumer credit contract secured by a dwelling and subject to the Act and this part the maximum interest rate that may be imposed during the term of the obligation when:

(a) In the case of closed-end credit, the annual percentage rate may increase after consummation, or

(b) In the case of open-end credit, the annual percentage rate may increase during the plan.

SUBPART E. SPECIAL RULES FOR CERTAIN HOME MORTGAGE TRANSACTIONS

§ 1026.31 General rules.

(a) Relation to other subparts in this part. The requirements and limitations of this subpart are in addition to and not in lieu of those contained in other subparts of this part.

(b) Form of disclosures. The creditor shall make the disclosures required by this subpart clearly and conspicuously in writing, in a form that the consumer may keep. The disclosures required by this subpart may be provided to the consumer in electronic form, subject to compliance with the consumer consent and other applicable provisions of the Electronic Signatures in Global and National Commerce Act (E-Sign Act) (15 U.S.C. 7001 et seq.).

(c) Timing of disclosure.

(1) Disclosures for high-cost mortgages. The creditor shall furnish the disclosures required by § 1026.32 at least three business days prior to consummation or account opening of a high-cost mortgage as defined in § 1026.32(a).

(i) Change in terms. After complying with this paragraph (c)(1) and prior to consummation or account opening, if the creditor changes any term that makes the disclosures inaccurate, new disclosures shall be provided in accordance with the requirements of this subpart.

(ii) Telephone disclosures. A creditor may provide new disclosures required by paragraph (c)(1)(i) of this section by telephone if the consumer initiates the change and if, prior to or at consummation or account opening:

(A) The creditor provides new written disclosures; and

(B) The consumer and creditor sign a statement that the new disclosures were provided by telephone at least three days prior to consummation or account opening, as applicable.

(iii) Consumer's waiver of waiting period before consummation or account opening. The consumer may, after receiving the disclosures required by this paragraph (c)(1), modify or waive the three-day waiting period between delivery of those disclosures and consummation or account opening if the consumer determines that the extension of credit is needed to meet a bona fide personal financial emergency. To modify or waive the right, the consumer shall give the creditor a dated written statement that describes the emergency, specifically modifies or waives the waiting period, and bears the signature of all the consumers entitled to the waiting period. Printed forms for this purpose are prohibited, except when creditors are permitted to use printed forms pursuant to § 1026.23(e)(2).

(2) Disclosures for reverse mortgages. The creditor shall furnish the disclosures required by § 1026.33 at least three business days prior to:

(i) Consummation of a closed-end credit transaction; or

(ii) The first transaction under an open-end credit plan.

(d) Basis of disclosures and use of estimates.

(1) Legal Obligation. Disclosures shall reflect the terms of the legal obligation between the parties.

(2) Estimates. If any information necessary for an accurate disclosure is unknown to the creditor, the creditor shall make the disclosure based on the best information reasonably available at the time the disclosure is provided, and shall state clearly that the disclosure is an estimate.

(3) Per-diem interest. For a transaction in which a portion of the interest is determined on a per-diem basis and collected at consummation, any disclosure affected by the per-diem interest shall be considered accurate if the disclosure is based on the information known to the creditor at the time that the disclosure documents are prepared.

(e) Multiple creditors; multiple consumers. If a transaction involves more than one creditor, only one set of disclosures shall be given and the creditors shall agree among themselves which creditor must comply with the requirements that this part imposes on any or all of them. If there is more than one consumer, the disclosures may be made to any consumer who is primarily liable on the obligation. If the transaction is rescindable under § 1026.15 or § 1026.23, however, the disclosures shall be made to each consumer who has the right to rescind.

(f) Effect of subsequent events. If a disclosure becomes inaccurate because of an event that occurs after the creditor delivers the required disclosures, the inaccuracy is not a violation of Regulation Z (12 CFR part 1026), although new disclosures may be required for mortgages covered by § 1026.32 under paragraph (c) of this section, § 1026.9(c), § 1026.19, or § 1026.20.

(g) Accuracy of annual percentage rate. For purposes of § 1026.32, the annual percentage rate shall be considered accurate, and may be used in determining whether a transaction is covered by § 1026.32, if it is accurate according to the requirements and within the tolerances under § 1026.22 for closed-end credit transactions or 1026.6(a) for open-end credit plans. The finance charge tolerances for rescission under § 1026.23(g) or (h) shall not apply for this purpose.

(h) Corrections and unintentional violations. A creditor or assignee in a high-cost mortgage, as defined in § 1026.32(a), who, when acting in good faith, failed to comply with any requirement under section 129 of the Act will not be deemed to have violated such requirement if the creditor or assignee satisfies either of the following sets of conditions:

(1)(i) Within 30 days of consummation or account opening and prior to the institution of any action, the consumer is notified of or discovers the violation;

(ii) Appropriate restitution is made within a reasonable time; and

(iii) Within a reasonable time, whatever adjustments are necessary are made to the loan or credit plan to either, at the choice of the consumer:

(A) Make the loan or credit plan satisfy the requirements of 15 U.S.C. 1631–1651; or

(B) Change the terms of the loan or credit plan in a manner beneficial to the consumer so that the loan or credit plan will no longer be a high-cost mortgage.

(2)(i) Within 60 days of the creditor's discovery or receipt of notification of an unintentional violation or bona fide error and prior to the institution of any action, the consumer is notified of the compliance failure;

(ii) Appropriate restitution is made within a reasonable time; and

(iii) Within a reasonable time, whatever adjustments are necessary are made to the loan or credit plan to either, at the choice of the consumer:

(A) Make the loan or credit plan satisfy the requirements of 15 U.S.C. 1631–1651; or

(B) Change the terms of the loan or credit plan in a manner beneficial to the consumer so that the loan or credit plan will no longer be a high-cost mortgage.

§ 1026.32 Requirements for high-cost home mortgages.

(a) Coverage. (1) The requirements of this section apply to a high-cost mortgage, which is any consumer credit transaction that is secured by the consumer's principal dwelling, other than as provided in paragraph (a)(2) of this section, and in which:

(i) The annual percentage rate applicable to the transaction, as determined in accordance with paragraph (a)(3) of this section, will exceed the average prime offer rate, as defined in § 1026.35(a)(2), for a comparable transaction by more than:

(A) 6.5 percentage points for a first-lien transaction, other than as described in paragraph (a)(1)(i)(B) of this section;

(B) 8.5 percentage points for a first-lien transaction if the dwelling is personal property and the loan amount is less than $50,000; or

(C) 8.5 percentage points for a subordinate-lien transaction; or

(ii) The transaction's total points and fees, as defined in paragraphs (b)(1) and (2) of this section, will exceed:

(A) 5 percent of the total loan amount for a transaction with a loan amount of $20,000 or more; the $20,000 figure shall be adjusted annually on January 1 by the annual percentage change in the Consumer Price Index that was reported on the preceding June 1; or

(B) The lesser of 8 percent of the total loan amount or $1,000 for a transaction with a loan amount of less than $20,000; the $1,000 and $20,000 figures shall be adjusted annually on January 1 by the annual percentage change in the Consumer Price Index that was reported on the preceding June 1; or

(iii) Under the terms of the loan contract or open-end credit agreement, the creditor can charge a prepayment penalty, as defined in paragraph (b)(6) of this section, more than 36 months after consummation or account opening, or prepayment penalties that can exceed, in total, more than 2 percent of the amount prepaid.

(2) Exemptions. This section does not apply to the following:

(i) A reverse mortgage transaction subject to § 1026.33;

(ii) A transaction to finance the initial construction of a dwelling;

(iii) A transaction originated by a Housing Finance Agency, where the Housing Finance Agency is the creditor for the transaction; or

(iv) A transaction originated pursuant to the United States Department of Agriculture's Rural Development Section 502 Direct Loan Program.

(3) Determination of annual percentage rate. For purposes of paragraph (a)(1)(i) of this section, a creditor shall determine the annual percentage rate for a closed-or open-end credit transaction based on the following:

(i) For a transaction in which the annual percentage rate will not vary during the term of the loan or credit plan, the interest rate in effect as of the date the interest rate for the transaction is set;

(ii) For a transaction in which the interest rate may vary during the term of the loan or credit plan in accordance with an index, the interest rate that results from adding the maximum margin permitted at any time during the term of the loan or credit plan to the value of the index rate in effect as of the date the interest rate for the transaction is set, or the introductory interest rate, whichever is greater; and

(iii) For a transaction in which the interest rate may or will vary during the term of the loan or credit plan, other than a transaction described in paragraph (a)(3)(ii) of this section, the maximum interest rate that may be imposed during the term of the loan or credit plan.

(b) Definitions. For purposes of this subpart, the following definitions apply:

(1) In connection with a closed-end credit transaction, points and fees means the following fees or charges that are known at or before consummation:

(i) All items included in the finance charge under § 1026.4(a) and (b), except that the following items are excluded:

(A) Interest or the time-price differential;

(B) Any premium or other charge imposed in connection with any Federal or State agency program for any guaranty or insurance that protects the creditor against the consumer's default or other credit loss;

(C) For any guaranty or insurance that protects the creditor against the consumer's default or other credit loss and that is not in connection with any Federal or State agency program:

(1) If the premium or other charge is payable after consummation, the entire amount of such premium or other charge; or

(2) If the premium or other charge is payable at or before consummation, the portion of any such premium or other charge that is not in excess of the amount payable under policies in effect at the time of origination under section 203(c)(2)(A) of the National Housing Act (12 U.S.C. 1709(c)(2)(A)), provided that the premium or charge is required to be refundable on a pro rata basis and the refund is automatically issued upon notification of the satisfaction of the underlying mortgage loan;

(D) Any bona fide third-party charge not retained by the creditor, loan originator, or an affiliate of either, unless the charge is required to be included in points and fees under paragraph (b)(1)(i)(C), (iii), or (iv) of this section;

(E) Up to two bona fide discount points paid by the consumer in connection with the transaction, if the interest rate without any discount does not exceed:

(1) The average prime offer rate, as defined in § 1026.35(a)(2), by more than one percentage point; or

(2) For purposes of paragraph (a)(1)(ii) of this section, for transactions that are secured by personal property, the average rate for a loan insured under Title I of the National Housing Act (12 U.S.C. 1702 et seq.) by more than one percentage point; and

(F) If no discount points have been excluded under paragraph (b)(1)(i)(E) of this section, then up to one bona fide discount point paid by the consumer in connection with the transaction, if the interest rate without any discount does not exceed:

(1) The average prime offer rate, as defined in § 1026.35(a)(2), by more than two percentage points; or

(2) For purposes of paragraph (a)(1)(ii) of this section, for transactions that are secured by personal property, the average rate for a loan insured under Title I of the National Housing Act (12 U.S.C. 1702 et seq.) by more than two percentage points;

(ii) All compensation paid directly or indirectly by a consumer or creditor to a loan originator, as defined in § 1026.36(a)(1), that can be attributed to that transaction at the time the interest rate is set unless:

(A) That compensation is paid by a consumer to a mortgage broker, as defined in § 1026.36(a)(2), and already has been included in points and fees under paragraph (b)(1)(i) of this section;

(B) That compensation is paid by a mortgage broker, as defined in § 1026.36(a)(2), to a loan originator that is an employee of the mortgage broker;

(C) That compensation is paid by a creditor to a loan originator that is an employee of the creditor; or

(D) That compensation is paid by a retailer of manufactured homes to its employee.

(iii) All items listed in § 1026.4(c)(7) (other than amounts held for future payment of taxes), unless:

(A) The charge is reasonable;

(B) The creditor receives no direct or indirect compensation in connection with the charge; and

(C) The charge is not paid to an affiliate of the creditor;

(iv) Premiums or other charges payable at or before consummation for any credit life, credit disability, credit unemployment, or credit property insurance, or any other life, accident, health, or loss-of-income insurance for which the creditor is a beneficiary, or any payments directly or indirectly for any debt cancellation or suspension agreement or contract;

(v) The maximum prepayment penalty, as defined in paragraph (b)(6)(i) of this section, that may be charged or collected under the terms of the mortgage loan; and

(vi) The total prepayment penalty, as defined in paragraph (b)(6)(i) or (ii) of this section, as applicable, incurred by the consumer if the consumer refinances the existing mortgage loan, or terminates an existing open-end credit plan in connection with obtaining a new mortgage loan, with the current holder of the existing loan or plan, a servicer acting on behalf of the current holder, or an affiliate of either.

(2) In connection with an open-end credit plan, points and fees means the following fees or charges that are known at or before account opening:

(i) All items included in the finance charge under § 1026.4(a) and (b), except that the following items are excluded:

(A) Interest or the time-price differential;

(B) Any premium or other charge imposed in connection with any Federal or State agency program for any guaranty or insurance that protects the creditor against the consumer's default or other credit loss;

(C) For any guaranty or insurance that protects the creditor against the consumer's default or other credit loss and that is not in connection with any Federal or State agency program:

(1) If the premium or other charge is payable after account opening, the entire amount of such premium or other charge; or

(2) If the premium or other charge is payable at or before account opening, the portion of any such premium or other charge that is not in excess of the amount payable under policies in effect at the time of account opening under section 203(c)(2)(A) of the National Housing Act (12 U.S.C. 1709(c)(2)(A)), provided that the premium or charge is required to be refundable on a pro rata basis and the refund is automatically issued upon notification of the satisfaction of the underlying mortgage transaction;

(D) Any bona fide third-party charge not retained by the creditor, loan originator, or an affiliate of either, unless the charge is required to be included in points and fees under paragraphs (b)(2)(i)(C), (b)(2)(iii) or (b)(2)(iv) of this section;

(E) Up to two bona fide discount points payable by the consumer in connection with the transaction, provided that the conditions specified in paragraph (b)(1)(i)(E) of this section are met; and

(F) Up to one bona fide discount point payable by the consumer in connection with the transaction, provided that no discount points have been excluded under paragraph (b)(2)(i)(E) of this section and the conditions specified in paragraph (b)(1)(i)(F) of this section are met;

(ii) All compensation paid directly or indirectly by a consumer or creditor to a loan originator, as defined in § 1026.36(a)(1), that can be attributed to that transaction at the time the interest rate is set unless:

(A) That compensation is paid by a consumer to a mortgage broker, as defined in § 1026.36(a)(2), and already has been included in points and fees under paragraph (b)(2)(i) of this section;

(B) That compensation is paid by a mortgage broker, as defined in § 1026.36(a)(2), to a loan originator that is an employee of the mortgage broker;

(C) That compensation is paid by a creditor to a loan originator that is an employee of the creditor; or

(D) That compensation is paid by a retailer of manufactured homes to its employee.

(iii) All items listed in § 1026.4(c)(7) (other than amounts held for future payment of taxes) unless:

(A) The charge is reasonable;

(B) The creditor receives no direct or indirect compensation in connection with the charge; and

(C) The charge is not paid to an affiliate of the creditor;

(iv) Premiums or other charges payable at or before account opening for any credit life, credit disability, credit unemployment, or credit property insurance, or any other life, accident, health, or loss-of-income insurance for which the creditor is a beneficiary, or any payments directly or indirectly for any debt cancellation or suspension agreement or contract;

(v) The maximum prepayment penalty, as defined in paragraph (b)(6)(ii) of this section, that may be charged or collected under the terms of the open-end credit plan;

(vi) The total prepayment penalty, as defined in paragraph (b)(6)(i) or (ii) of this section, as applicable, incurred by the consumer if the consumer refinances an existing closed-end credit transaction with an open-end credit plan, or terminates an existing open-end credit plan in connection with obtaining a new open-end credit plan, with the current holder of the existing transaction or plan, a servicer acting on behalf of the current holder, or an affiliate of either;

(vii) Any fees charged for participation in an open-end credit plan, payable at or before account opening, as described in § 1026.4(c)(4); and

(viii) Any transaction fee, including any minimum fee or per-transaction fee, that will be charged for a draw on the credit line, where the creditor must assume that the consumer will make at least one draw during the term of the plan.

(3) Bona fide discount point—

(i) Closed-end credit. The term bona fide discount point means an amount equal to 1 percent of the loan amount paid by the consumer that reduces the interest rate or time-price differential applicable to the transaction based on a calculation that is consistent with established industry practices for determining the amount of reduction in the interest rate or time-price differential appropriate for the amount of discount points paid by the consumer.

(ii) Open-end credit. The term bona fide discount point means an amount equal to 1 percent of the credit limit for the plan when the account is opened, paid by the consumer, and that reduces the interest rate or time-price differential applicable to the transaction based on a calculation that is consistent with established industry practices for determining the amount of reduction in the interest rate or time-price differential appropriate for the amount of discount points paid by the consumer. See comment 32(b)(3)(i)–1 for additional guidance in determining whether a discount point is bona fide.

(4) Total loan amount—

(i) Closed-end credit. The total loan amount for a closed-end credit transaction is calculated by taking the amount financed, as determined according to § 1026.18(b), and deducting any cost listed in § 1026.32(b)(1)(iii), (iv), or (vi) that is both included as points and fees under § 1026.32(b)(1) and financed by the creditor.

(ii) Open-end credit. The total loan amount for an open-end credit plan is the credit limit for the plan when the account is opened.

(5) Affiliate means any company that controls, is controlled by, or is under common control with another company, as set forth in the Bank Holding Company Act of 1956 (12 U.S.C. 1841 et seq.).

(6) Prepayment penalty—

(i) Closed-end credit transactions. For a closed-end credit transaction, prepayment penalty means a charge imposed for paying all or part of the transaction's principal before the date on which the principal is due, other than a waived, bona fide third-party charge that the creditor imposes if the consumer prepays all of the transaction's principal sooner than 36 months after consummation, provided, however, that interest charged consistent with the monthly interest accrual amortization method is not a prepayment penalty for extensions of credit insured by the Federal Housing Administration that are consummated before January 21, 2015.

(ii) Open-end credit. For an open-end credit plan, prepayment penalty means a charge imposed by the creditor if the consumer terminates the open-end credit plan prior to the end of its term, other than a waived, bona fide third-party charge that the creditor imposes if the consumer terminates the open-end credit plan sooner than 36 months after account opening.

(c) Disclosures. In addition to other disclosures required by this part, in a mortgage subject to this section, the creditor shall disclose the following in conspicuous type size:

(1) Notices. The following statement: "You are not required to complete this agreement merely because you have received these disclosures or have signed a loan application. If you obtain this loan, the lender will have a mortgage on your home. You could lose your home, and any money you have put into it, if you do not meet your obligations under the loan."

(2) Annual percentage rate. The annual percentage rate.

(3) Regular payment; minimum periodic payment example; balloon payment.

(i) For a closed-end credit transaction, the amount of the regular monthly (or other periodic) payment and the amount of any balloon payment provided in the credit contract, if permitted under paragraph (d)(1) of this section. The regular payment disclosed under this paragraph shall be treated as accurate if it is based on an amount borrowed that is deemed accurate and is disclosed under paragraph (c)(5) of this section.

(ii) For an open-end credit plan:

(A) An example showing the first minimum periodic payment for the draw period, the first minimum periodic payment for any repayment period, and the balance outstanding at the beginning of any repayment period. The example must be based on the following assumptions:

(1) The consumer borrows the full credit line, as disclosed in paragraph (c)(5) of this section, at account opening and does not obtain any additional extensions of credit;

(2) The consumer makes only minimum periodic payments during the draw period and any repayment period; and

(3) The annual percentage rate used to calculate the example payments remains the same during the draw period and any repayment period. The creditor must provide the minimum periodic payment example based on the annual percentage rate for the plan, as described in paragraph (c)(2) of this section, except that if an introductory annual percentage rate applies, the creditor must use the rate that will apply to the plan after the introductory rate expires.

(B) If the credit contract provides for a balloon payment under the plan as permitted under paragraph (d)(1) of this section, a disclosure of that fact and an example showing the amount of the balloon payment based on the assumptions described in paragraph (c)(3)(ii)(A) of this section.

(C) A statement that the example payments show the first minimum periodic payments at the current annual percentage rate if the consumer borrows the maximum credit available when the account is opened and does not obtain any additional extensions of credit, or a substantially similar statement.

(D) A statement that the example payments are not the consumer's actual payments and that the actual minimum periodic payments will depend on the amount the consumer borrows, the interest rate applicable to that period, and whether the consumer pays more than the required minimum periodic payment, or a substantially similar statement.

(4) Variable-rate. For variable-rate transactions, a statement that the interest rate and monthly payment may increase, and the amount of the single maximum monthly payment, based on the maximum interest rate required to be included in the contract by § 1026.30.

(5) Amount borrowed; credit limit.

(i) For a closed-end credit transaction, the total amount the consumer will borrow, as reflected by the face amount of the note. Where the amount borrowed includes financed charges that are not prohibited under § 1026.34(a)(10), that fact shall be stated, grouped together with the disclosure of the amount borrowed. The disclosure of the amount borrowed shall be treated as accurate if it is not more than $100 above or below the amount required to be disclosed.

(ii) For an open-end credit plan, the credit limit for the plan when the account is opened.

(d) Limitations. A high-cost mortgage shall not include the following terms:

(1)(i) Balloon payment. Except as provided by paragraphs (d)(1)(ii) and (iii) of this section, a payment schedule with a payment that is more than two times a regular periodic payment.

(ii) Exceptions. The limitations in paragraph (d)(1)(i) of this section do not apply to:

(A) A mortgage transaction with a payment schedule that is adjusted to the seasonal or irregular income of the consumer;

(B) A loan with maturity of 12 months or less, if the purpose of the loan is a "bridge" loan connected with the acquisition or construction of a dwelling intended to become the consumer's principal dwelling; or

(C) A loan that meets the criteria set forth in §§ 1026.43(f)(1)(i) through (vi) and 1026.43(f)(2), or the conditions set forth in § 1026.43(e)(6).

(iii) Open-end credit plans. If the terms of an open-end credit plan provide for a repayment period during which no further draws may be taken, the limitations in paragraph (d)(1)(i) of this section do not apply to any adjustment in the regular periodic payment that results solely from the credit plan's transition from the draw period to the repayment period. If the terms of an open-end credit plan do not provide for any repayment period, the limitations in paragraph (d)(1)(i) of this section apply to all periods of the credit plan.

(2) Negative amortization. A payment schedule with regular periodic payments that cause the principal balance to increase.

(3) Advance payments. A payment schedule that consolidates more than two periodic payments and pays them in advance from the proceeds.

(4) Increased interest rate. An increase in the interest rate after default.

(5) Rebates. A refund calculated by a method less favorable than the actuarial method (as defined by section 933(d) of the Housing and Community Development Act of 1992, 15 U.S.C. 1615(d)), for rebates of interest arising from a loan acceleration due to default.

(6) Prepayment penalties. A prepayment penalty, as defined in paragraph (b)(6) of this section.

(7) [Reserved.]

(8) Acceleration of debt. A demand feature that permits the creditor to accelerate the indebtedness by terminating the high-cost mortgage in advance of the original maturity date and to demand repayment of the entire outstanding balance, except in the following circumstances:

(i) There is fraud or material misrepresentation by the consumer in connection with the loan or open-end credit agreement;

(ii) The consumer fails to meet the repayment terms of the agreement for any outstanding balance that results in a default in payment under the loan; or

(iii) There is any action or inaction by the consumer that adversely affects the creditor's security for the loan, or any right of the creditor in such security.

§ 1026.33 Requirements for reverse mortgages.

(a) Definition. For purposes of this subpart, reverse mortgage transaction means a nonrecourse consumer credit obligation in which:

(1) A mortgage, deed of trust, or equivalent consensual security interest securing one or more advances is created in the consumer's principal dwelling; and

(2) Any principal, interest, or shared appreciation or equity is due and payable (other than in the case of default) only after:

(i) The consumer dies;

(ii) The dwelling is transferred; or

(iii) The consumer ceases to occupy the dwelling as a principal dwelling.

(b) Content of disclosures. In addition to other disclosures required by this part, in a reverse mortgage transaction the creditor shall provide the following disclosures in a form substantially similar to the model form found in paragraph (d) of Appendix K of this part:

(1) Notice. A statement that the consumer is not obligated to complete the reverse mortgage transaction merely because the consumer has received the disclosures required by this section or has signed an application for a reverse mortgage loan.

(2) Total annual loan cost rates. A good-faith projection of the total cost of the credit, determined in accordance with paragraph (c) of this section and expressed as a table of "total annual loan cost rates," using that term, in accordance with Appendix K of this part.

(3) Itemization of pertinent information. An itemization of loan terms, charges, the age of the youngest borrower and the appraised property value.

(4) Explanation of table. An explanation of the table of total annual loan cost rates as provided in the model form found in paragraph (d) of Appendix K of this part.

(c) Projected total cost of credit. The projected total cost of credit shall reflect the following factors, as applicable:

(1) Costs to consumer. All costs and charges to the consumer, including the costs of any annuity the consumer purchases as part of the reverse mortgage transaction.

(2) Payments to consumer. All advances to and for the benefit of the consumer, including annuity payments that the consumer will receive from an annuity that the consumer purchases as part of the reverse mortgage transaction.

(3) Additional creditor compensation. Any shared appreciation or equity in the dwelling that the creditor is entitled by contract to receive.

(4) Limitations on consumer liability. Any limitation on the consumer's liability (such as nonrecourse limits and equity conservation agreements).

(5) Assumed annual appreciation rates. Each of the following assumed annual appreciation rates for the dwelling:

(i) 0 percent.

(ii) 4 percent.

(iii) 8 percent.

(6) Assumed loan period.

(i) Each of the following assumed loan periods, as provided in Appendix L of this part:

(A) Two years.

(B) The actuarial life expectancy of the consumer to become obligated on the reverse mortgage transaction (as of that consumer's most recent birthday). In the case of multiple consumers, the period shall be the actuarial life expectancy of the youngest consumer (as of that consumer's most recent birthday).

(C) The actuarial life expectancy specified by paragraph (c)(6)(i)(B) of this section, multiplied by a factor of 1.4 and rounded to the nearest full year.

(ii) At the creditor's option, the actuarial life expectancy specified by paragraph (c)(6)(i)(B) of this section, multiplied by a factor of .5 and rounded to the nearest full year.

§ 1026.34 Prohibited acts or practices in connection with high-cost mortgages.

(a) Prohibited acts or practices for high-cost mortgages.

(1) Home improvement contracts. A creditor shall not pay a contractor under a home improvement contract from the proceeds of a high-cost mortgage, other than:

(i) By an instrument payable to the consumer or jointly to the consumer and the contractor; or

(ii) At the election of the consumer, through a third-party escrow agent in accordance with terms established in a written agreement signed by the consumer, the creditor, and the contractor prior to the disbursement.

(2) Notice to assignee. A creditor may not sell or otherwise assign a high-cost mortgage without furnishing the following statement to the purchaser or assignee: "Notice: This is a mortgage subject to special rules under the Federal Truth in Lending Act. Purchasers or assignees of this mortgage could be liable for all claims and defenses with respect to the mortgage that the consumer could assert against the creditor."

(3) Refinancings within one-year period. Within one year of having extended a high-cost mortgage, a creditor shall not refinance any high-cost mortgage to the same consumer into another high-cost mortgage, unless the refinancing is in the consumer's interest. An assignee holding or servicing a high-cost mortgage shall not, for the remainder of the one-year period following the date of origination of the credit, refinance any high-cost mortgage to the same consumer into another high-cost mortgage, unless the refinancing is in the consumer's interest. A creditor (or assignee) is prohibited from engaging in acts or practices to evade this provision, including a pattern or practice of arranging for the refinancing of its own loans by affiliated or unaffiliated creditors.

(4) Repayment ability for high-cost mortgages. In connection with an open-end, high-cost mortgage, a creditor shall not open a plan for a consumer where credit is or will be extended without regard to the consumer's repayment ability as of account opening, including the consumer's current and reasonably expected income, employment, assets other than the collateral, and current obligations including any mortgage-related obligations that are required by another credit obligation undertaken prior to or at account opening, and are secured by the same dwelling that secures the high-cost mortgage transaction. The requirements set forth in § 1026.34(a)(4)(i) through (iv) apply to open-end high-cost mortgages, but do not apply to closed-end high-cost mortgages. In connection with a closed-end, high-cost mortgage, a creditor must comply with the repayment ability requirements set forth in § 1026.43. Temporary or "bridge" loans with terms of twelve months or less, such as a loan to purchase a new dwelling where the consumer plans to sell a current dwelling within twelve months, are exempt from this repayment ability requirement.

(i) Mortgage-related obligations. For purposes of this paragraph (a)(4), mortgage-related obligations are expected property taxes, premiums for mortgage-related insurance required by the creditor as set forth in § 1026.35(b), and similar expenses.

(ii) Basis for determination of repayment ability. Under this paragraph (a)(4) a creditor must determine the consumer's repayment ability in connection with an open-end, high cost mortgage as follows:

(A) A creditor must verify amounts of income or assets that it relies on to determine repayment ability, including expected income or assets, by the consumer's Internal Revenue Service Form W-2, tax returns, payroll receipts, financial institution records, or other third-party documents that provide reasonably reliable evidence of the consumer's income or assets.

(B) A creditor must verify the consumer's current obligations, including any mortgage-related obligations that are required by another credit obligation undertaken prior to or at account opening, and are secured by the same dwelling that secures the high-cost mortgage transaction.

(iii) Presumption of compliance. For an open-end, high cost mortgage, a creditor is presumed to have complied with this paragraph (a)(4) with respect to a transaction if the creditor:

(A) Determines the consumer's repayment ability as provided in paragraph (a)(4)(ii);

(B) Determines the consumer's repayment ability taking into account current obligations and mortgage-related obligations as defined in paragraph (a)(4)(i) of this section, and using the largest required minimum periodic payment based on the following assumptions:

(1) The consumer borrows the full credit line at account opening with no additional extensions of credit;

(2) The consumer makes only required minimum periodic payments during the draw period and any repayment period;

(3) If the annual percentage rate may increase during the plan, the maximum annual percentage rate that is included in the contract, as required by § 1026.30, applies to the plan at account opening and will apply during the draw period and any repayment period.

(C) Assesses the consumer's repayment ability taking into account at least one of the following: The ratio of total current obligations, including any mortgage-related obligations that are required by another credit obligation undertaken prior to or at account opening, and are secured by the same dwelling that secures the high-cost mortgage transaction, to income, or the income the consumer will have after paying current obligations.

(iv) Exclusions from presumption of compliance. Notwithstanding the previous paragraph, no presumption of compliance is available for an open-end, high-cost mortgage transaction for which the regular periodic payments when aggregated do not fully amortize the outstanding principal balance except as otherwise provided by § 1026.32(d)(1)(ii).

(5) Pre-loan counseling.

(i) Certification of counseling required. A creditor shall not extend a high-cost mortgage to a consumer unless the creditor receives written certification that the consumer has obtained counseling on the advisability of the mortgage from a counselor that is approved to provide such counseling by the Secretary of the U.S. Department of Housing and Urban Development or, if permitted by the Secretary, by a State housing finance authority.

(ii) Timing of counseling. The counseling required under this paragraph (a)(5) must occur after:

(A) The consumer receives either the disclosure required by section 5(c) of the Real Estate Settlement Procedures Act of 1974 (12 U.S.C. 2604(c)) or the disclosures required by § 1026.40; or

(B) The consumer receives the disclosures required by § 1026.32(c), for transactions in which neither of the disclosures listed in paragraph (a)(5)(ii)(A) of this section are provided.

(iii) Affiliation prohibited. The counseling required under this paragraph (a)(5) shall not be provided by a counselor who is employed by or affiliated with the creditor.

(iv) Content of certification. The certification of counseling required under paragraph (a)(5)(i) must include:

(A) The name(s) of the consumer(s) who obtained counseling;

(B) The date(s) of counseling;

(C) The name and address of the counselor;

(D) A statement that the consumer(s) received counseling on the advisability of the high-cost mortgage based on the terms provided in either the disclosure required by section 5(c) of the Real Estate Settlement Procedures Act of 1974 (12 U.S.C. 2604(c)) or the disclosures required by § 1026.40.

(E) For transactions for which neither of the disclosures listed in paragraph (a)(5)(ii)(A) of this section are provided, a statement that the consumer(s) received counseling on the advisability of the high-cost mortgage based on the terms provided in the disclosures required by § 1026.32(c); and

(F) A statement that the counselor has verified that the consumer(s) received the disclosures required by either § 1026.32(c) or the Real Estate Settlement Procedures Act of 1974 (12 U.S.C. 2601 et seq.) with respect to the transaction.

(v) Counseling fees. A creditor may pay the fees of a counselor or counseling organization for providing counseling required under this paragraph (a)(5) but may not condition the payment of such fees on the consummation or account-opening of a mortgage transaction. If the consumer withdraws the application that would result in the extension of a high-cost mortgage, a creditor may not condition the payment of such fees on the receipt of certification from the counselor required by paragraph (a)(5)(i) of this section. A creditor may, however, confirm that a counselor has provided counseling to the consumer pursuant to this paragraph (a)(5) prior to paying the fee of a counselor or counseling organization.

(vi) Steering prohibited. A creditor that extends a high-cost mortgage shall not steer or otherwise direct a consumer to choose a particular counselor or counseling organization for the counseling required under this paragraph (a)(5).

(6) Recommended default. A creditor or mortgage broker, as defined in section 1026.36(a)(2), may not recommend or encourage default on an existing loan or other debt prior to and in connection with the consummation or account opening of a high-cost mortgage that refinances all or any portion of such existing loan or debt.

(7) Modification and deferral fees. A creditor, successor-in-interest, assignee, or any agent of such parties may not charge a consumer any fee to modify, renew, extend or amend a high-cost mortgage, or to defer any payment due under the terms of such mortgage.

(8) Late fees.

(i) General. Any late payment charge imposed in connection with a high-cost mortgage must be specifically permitted by the terms of the loan contract or open-end credit agreement and may not exceed 4 percent of the amount of the payment past due. No such charge may be imposed more than once for a single late payment.

(ii) Timing. A late payment charge may be imposed in connection with a high-cost mortgage only if the payment is not received by the end of the 15-day period beginning on the date the payment is due or, in the case of a high-cost mortgage on which interest on each installment is paid in advance, the end of the 30-day period beginning on the date the payment is due.

(iii) Multiple late charges assessed on payment subsequently paid. A late payment charge may not be imposed in connection with a high-cost mortgage payment if any delinquency is attributable only to a late payment charge imposed on an earlier payment, and the payment otherwise is a full payment for the applicable period and is paid by the due date or within any applicable grace period.

(iv) Failure to make required payment. The terms of a high-cost mortgage agreement may provide that any payment shall first be applied to any past due balance. If the consumer fails to make a timely payment by the due date and subsequently resumes making payments but has not paid all past due payments, the creditor may impose a separate late payment charge for any payment(s) outstanding (without deduction due to late fees or related fees) until the default is cured.

(9) Payoff statements.

(i) Fee prohibition. In general, a creditor or servicer (as defined in 12 CFR 1024.2(b)) may not charge a fee for providing to a consumer, or a person authorized by the consumer to obtain such information, a statement of the amount due to pay off the outstanding balance of a high-cost mortgage.

(ii) Processing fee. A creditor or servicer may charge a processing fee to cover the cost of providing a payoff statement, as described in paragraph (a)(9)(i) of this section, by fax or courier, provided that such fee may not exceed an amount that is comparable to fees imposed for similar services provided in connection with consumer credit transactions that are secured by the consumer's principal dwelling and are not high-cost mortgages. A creditor or servicer shall make a payoff statement available to a consumer, or a person authorized by the consumer to obtain such information, by a method other than by fax or courier and without charge pursuant to paragraph (a)(9)(i) of this section.

(iii) Processing fee disclosure. Prior to charging a processing fee for provision of a payoff statement by fax or courier, as permitted pursuant to paragraph (a)(9)(ii) of this section, a creditor or servicer shall disclose to a consumer or a person authorized by the consumer to obtain the consumer's payoff statement that payoff statements, as described in paragraph (a)(9)(i) of this section, are available by a method other than by fax or courier without charge.

(iv) Fees permitted after multiple requests. A creditor or servicer that has provided a payoff statement, as described in paragraph (a)(9)(i) of this section, to a consumer, or a person authorized by the consumer to obtain such information, without charge, other than the processing fee permitted under paragraph (a)(9)(ii) of this section, four times during a calendar year, may thereafter charge a reasonable fee for providing such statements during the remainder of the calendar year. Fees for payoff statements provided to a consumer, or a person authorized by the consumer to obtain such information, in a subsequent calendar year are subject to the requirements of this section.

(v) Timing of delivery of payoff statements. A payoff statement, as described in paragraph (a)(9)(i) of this section, for a high-cost mortgage shall be provided by a creditor or servicer within five business days after receiving a request for such statement by a consumer or a person authorized by the consumer to obtain such statement.

(10) Financing of points and fees. A creditor that extends credit under a high-cost mortgage may not finance charges that are required to be included in the calculation of points and fees, as that term is defined in § 1026.32(b)(1) and (2). Credit insurance premiums or debt cancellation or suspension fees that are required to be included in points and fees under § 1026.32(b)(1)(iv) or (2)(iv) shall not be considered financed by the creditor when they are calculated and paid in full on a monthly basis.

(b) Prohibited acts or practices for dwelling-secured loans; structuring loans to evade high-cost mortgage requirements. A creditor shall not structure any transaction that is otherwise a high-cost mortgage in a form, for the purpose, and with the intent to evade the requirements of a high-cost mortgage subject to this subpart, including by dividing any loan transaction into separate parts.

§ 1026.35 Requirements for higher-priced mortgage loans.

(a) Definitions. For purposes of this section:

(1) "Higher-priced mortgage loan" means a closed-end consumer credit transaction secured by the consumer's principal dwelling with an annual percentage rate that exceeds the average prime offer rate for a comparable transaction as of the date the interest rate is set:

(i) By 1.5 or more percentage points, for a loan secured by a first lien with a principal obligation at consummation that does not exceed the limit in effect as of the date the transaction's interest rate is set for the maximum principal obligation eligible for purchase by Freddie Mac;

(ii) By 2.5 or more percentage points, for a loan secured by a first lien with a principal obligation at consummation that exceeds the limit in effect as of the date the transaction's interest rate is set for the maximum principal obligation eligible for purchase by Freddie Mac; or

(iii) By 3.5 or more percentage points, for a loan secured by a subordinate lien.

(2) "Average prime offer rate" means an annual percentage rate that is derived from average interest rates, points, and other loan pricing terms currently offered to consumers by a representative sample of creditors for mortgage transactions that have low-risk pricing characteristics. The Bureau publishes average prime offer rates for a broad range of types of transactions in a table updated at least weekly as well as the methodology the Bureau uses to derive these rates.

(b) Escrow accounts—

(1) Requirement to escrow for property taxes and insurance. Except as provided in paragraph (b)(2) of this section, a creditor may not extend a higher-priced mortgage loan secured by a first lien on a consumer's principal dwelling unless an escrow account is established before consummation for payment of property taxes and premiums for mortgage-related insurance required by the creditor, such as insurance against loss of or damage to property, or against liability arising out of the ownership or use of the property, or insurance protecting the creditor against the consumer's default or other credit loss. For purposes of this paragraph (b), the term "escrow account" has the same meaning as under Regulation X (12 C.F.R. 1024.17(b)), as amended.

(2) Exemptions. Notwithstanding paragraph (b)(1) of this section:

(i) An escrow account need not be established for:

(A) A transaction secured by shares in a cooperative;

(B) A transaction to finance the initial construction of a dwelling;

(C) A temporary or "bridge" loan with a loan term of twelve months or less, such as a loan to purchase a new dwelling where the consumer plans to sell a current dwelling within twelve months; or

(D) A reverse mortgage transaction subject to § 1026.33.

(ii) Insurance premiums described in paragraph (b)(1) of this section need not be included in escrow accounts for loans secured by dwellings in condominiums, planned unit developments, or other common interest communities in which dwelling ownership requires participation in a governing association, where the governing association has an obligation to the dwelling owners to maintain a master policy insuring all dwellings.

(iii) Except as provided in paragraph (b)(2)(v) of this section, an escrow account need not be established for a transaction if, at the time of consummation:

(A) During the preceding calendar year, or, if the application for the transaction was received before April 1 of the current calendar year, during either of the two preceding calendar years, the creditor extended a covered transaction, as defined by § 1026.43(b)(1), secured by a first lien on a property that is located in an area that is either "rural" or "underserved," as set forth in paragraph (b)(2)(iv) of this section;

(B) During the preceding calendar year, or, if the application for the transaction was received before April 1 of the current calendar year, during either of the two preceding calendar years, the creditor and its affiliates together extended no more than 2,000 covered transactions, as defined by § 1026.43(b)(1), secured by first liens, that were sold, assigned, or otherwise transferred to another person, or that were subject at the time of consummation to a commitment to be acquired by another person;

(C) As of the preceding December 31st, or, if the application for the transaction was received before April 1 of the current calendar year, as of either of the two preceding December 31sts, the creditor and its affiliates that regularly extended covered transactions, as defined by § 1026.43(b)(1), secured by first liens, together, had total assets of less than $2,000,000,000; this asset threshold shall adjust automatically each year, based on the year-to-year change in the average of the Consumer Price Index for Urban Wage Earners and Clerical Workers, not seasonally adjusted, for each 12-month period ending in November, with rounding to the nearest million dollars (see comment 35(b)(2)(iii)–1.iii for the applicable threshold); and

(D) Neither the creditor nor its affiliate maintains an escrow account of the type described in paragraph (b)(1) of this section for any extension of consumer credit secured by real property or a dwelling that the creditor or its affiliate currently services, other than:

(1) Escrow accounts established for first-lien higher-priced mortgage loans for which applications were received on or after April 1, 2010, and before May 1, 2016; or

(2) Escrow accounts established after consummation as an accommodation to distressed consumers to assist such consumers in avoiding default or foreclosure.

(iv) For purposes of paragraph (b)(2)(iii)(A) of this section:

(A) An area is "rural" during a calendar year if it is:

(1) A county that is neither in a metropolitan statistical area nor in a micropolitan statistical area that is adjacent to a metropolitan statistical area, as those terms are defined by the U.S. Office of Management and Budget and as they are applied under currently applicable Urban Influence Codes (UICs), established by the United States Department of Agriculture's Economic Research Service (USDA-ERS);

(2) A census block that is not in an urban area, as defined by the U.S. Census Bureau using the latest decennial census of the United States; or

(3) A county or a census block that has been designated as rural by the Bureau pursuant to the application process established under section 89002 of the Helping Expand Lending Practices in Rural Communities Act, Public Law 114–94, title LXXXIX (2015). The provisions of this paragraph (b)(2)(iv)(A)(3) shall cease to have any force or effect on December 4, 2017.

(B) An area is "underserved" during a calendar year if, according to Home Mortgage Disclosure Act (HMDA) data for the preceding calendar year, it is a county in which no more than two creditors extended covered transactions, as defined in § 1026.43(b)(1), secured by first liens on properties in the county five or more times.

(C) A property shall be deemed to be in an area that is rural or underserved in a particular calendar year if the property is:

(1) Located in a county that appears on the lists published by the Bureau of counties that are rural or underserved, as defined by § 1026.35(b)(2)(iv)(A)(1) or § 1026.35(b)(2)(iv)(B), for that calendar year,

(2) Designated as rural or underserved for that calendar year by any automated tool that the Bureau provides on its public Web site, or

(3) Not designated as located in an urban area, as defined by the most recent delineation of urban areas announced by the Census Bureau, by any automated address search tool that the U.S. Census Bureau provides on its public Web site for that purpose and that specifically indicates the urban or rural designations of properties.

(v) Notwithstanding paragraph (b)(2)(iii) of this section, an escrow account must be established pursuant to paragraph (b)(1) of this section for any first-lien higher-priced mortgage loan that, at consummation, is subject to a commitment to be acquired by a person that does not satisfy the conditions in paragraph (b)(2)(iii) of this section, unless otherwise exempted by this paragraph (b)(2).

(3) Cancellation—

(i) General. Except as provided in paragraph (b)(3)(ii) of this section, a creditor or servicer may cancel an escrow account required in paragraph (b)(1) of this section only upon the earlier of:

(A) Termination of the underlying debt obligation; or

(B) Receipt no earlier than five years after consummation of a consumer's request to cancel the escrow account.

(ii) Delayed cancellation. Notwithstanding paragraph (b)(3)(i) of this section, a creditor or servicer shall not cancel an escrow account pursuant to a consumer's request described in paragraph (b)(3)(i)(B) of this section unless the following conditions are satisfied:

(A) The unpaid principal balance is less than 80 percent of the original value of the property securing the underlying debt obligation; and

(B) The consumer currently is not delinquent or in default on the underlying debt obligation.

(c) Appraisals—

(1) Definitions. For purposes of this section:

(i) Certified or licensed appraiser means a person who is certified or licensed by the State agency in the State in which the property that secures the transaction is located, and who performs the appraisal in conformity with the Uniform Standards of Professional Appraisal Practice and the requirements applicable to appraisers in title XI of the Financial Institutions Reform, Recovery, and Enforcement Act of 1989, as amended (12 U.S.C. 3331 et seq.), and any implementing regulations in effect at the time the appraiser signs the appraiser's certification.

(ii) Credit risk means the financial risk that a consumer will default on a loan.

(iii) Manufactured home has the same meaning as in 24 CFR 3280.2.

(iv) Manufacturer's invoice means a document issued by a manufacturer and provided with a manufactured home to a retail dealer that separately details the wholesale (base) prices at the factory for specific models or series of manufactured homes and itemized options (large appliances, built-in items and equipment), plus actual itemized charges for freight from the factory to the dealer's lot or the homesite (including any rental of wheels and axles) and for any sales taxes to be paid by the dealer. The invoice may recite such prices and charges on an itemized basis or by stating an aggregate price or charge, as appropriate, for each category.

(v) National Registry means the database of information about State certified and licensed appraisers maintained by the Appraisal Subcommittee of the Federal Financial Institutions Examination Council.

(vi) New manufactured home means a manufactured home that has not been previously occupied.

(vii) State agency means a "State appraiser certifying and licensing agency" recognized in accordance with section 1118(b) of the Financial Institutions Reform, Recovery, and Enforcement Act of 1989 (12 U.S.C. 3347(b)) and any implementing regulations.

(2) Exemptions. Unless otherwise specified, the requirements in paragraph (c)(3) through (6) of this section do not apply to the following types of transactions:

(i) A loan that satisfies the criteria of a qualified mortgage as defined pursuant to 15 U.S.C. 1639c;

(ii) An extension of credit for which the amount of credit extended is equal to or less than the applicable threshold amount, which is adjusted every year to reflect increases in the Consumer Price Index for Urban Wage Earners and Clerical Workers, as applicable, and published in the official staff commentary to this paragraph (c)(2)(ii);

(iii) A transaction secured by a mobile home, boat, or trailer.

(iv) A transaction to finance the initial construction of a dwelling.

(v) A loan with a maturity of 12 months or less, if the purpose of the loan is a "bridge" loan connected with the acquisition of a dwelling intended to become the consumer's principal dwelling.

(vi) A reverse-mortgage transaction subject to 12 CFR 1026.33(a).

(vii) An extension of credit that is a refinancing secured by a first lien, with refinancing defined as in § 1026.20(a) (except that the creditor need not be the original creditor or a holder or servicer of the original obligation), provided that the refinancing meets the following criteria:

(A) Either—

(1) The credit risk of the refinancing is retained by the person that held the credit risk of the existing obligation and there is no commitment, at consummation, to transfer the credit risk to another person; or

(2) The refinancing is insured or guaranteed by the same Federal government agency that insured or guaranteed the existing obligation;

(B) The regular periodic payments under the refinance loan do not—

(1) Cause the principal balance to increase;

(2) Allow the consumer to defer repayment of principal; or

(3) Result in a balloon payment, as defined in § 1026.18(s)(5)(i); and

(C) The proceeds from the refinancing are used solely to satisfy the existing obligation and amounts attributed solely to the costs of the refinancing; and

(viii) A transaction secured by:

(A) A new manufactured home and land, but the exemption shall only apply to the requirement in paragraph (c)(3)(i) of this section that the appraiser conduct a physical visit of the interior of the new manufactured home; or

(B) A manufactured home and not land, for which the creditor obtains one of the following and provides a copy to the consumer no later than three business days prior to consummation of the transaction—

(1) For a new manufactured home, the manufacturer's invoice for the manufactured home securing the transaction, provided that the date of manufacture is no earlier than 18 months prior to the creditor's receipt of the consumer's application for credit;

(2) A cost estimate of the value of the manufactured home securing the transaction obtained from an independent cost service provider; or

(3) A valuation, as defined in § 1026.42(b)(3), of the manufactured home performed by a person who has no direct or indirect interest, financial or otherwise, in the property or transaction for which the valuation is performed and has training in valuing manufactured homes.

(3) Appraisals required—

(i) In general. Except as provided in paragraph (c)(2) of this section, a creditor shall not extend a higher-priced mortgage loan to a consumer without obtaining, prior to consummation, a written appraisal of the property to be mortgaged. The appraisal must be performed by a certified or licensed appraiser who conducts a physical visit of the interior of the property that will secure the transaction.

(ii) Safe harbor. A creditor obtains a written appraisal that meets the requirements for an appraisal required under paragraph (c)(3)(i) of this section if the creditor:

(A) Orders that the appraiser perform the appraisal in conformity with the Uniform Standards of Professional Appraisal Practice and title XI of the Financial Institutions Reform, Recovery, and Enforcement Act of 1989, as amended (12 U.S.C. 3331 et seq.), and any implementing regulations in effect at the time the appraiser signs the appraiser's certification;

(B) Verifies through the National Registry that the appraiser who signed the appraiser's certification was a certified or licensed appraiser in the State in which the appraised property is located as of the date the appraiser signed the appraiser's certification;

(C) Confirms that the elements set forth in appendix N to this part are addressed in the written appraisal; and

(D) Has no actual knowledge contrary to the facts or certifications contained in the written appraisal.

(4) Additional appraisal for certain higher-priced mortgage loans—

(i) In general. Except as provided in paragraphs (c)(2) and (c)(4)(vii) of this section, a creditor shall not extend a higher-priced mortgage loan to a consumer to finance the acquisition of the consumer's principal dwelling without obtaining, prior to consummation, two written appraisals, if:

(A) The seller acquired the property 90 or fewer days prior to the date of the consumer's agreement to acquire the property and the price in the consumer's agreement to acquire the property exceeds the seller's acquisition price by more than 10 percent; or

(B) The seller acquired the property 91 to 180 days prior to the date of the consumer's agreement to acquire the property and the price in the consumer's agreement to acquire the property exceeds the seller's acquisition price by more than 20 percent.

(ii) Different certified or licensed appraisers. The two appraisals required under paragraph (c)(4)(i) of this section may not be performed by the same certified or licensed appraiser.

(iii) Relationship to general appraisal requirements. If two appraisals must be obtained under paragraph (c)(4)(i) of this section, each appraisal shall meet the requirements of paragraph (c)(3)(i) of this section.

(iv) Required analysis in the additional appraisal. One of the two required appraisals must include an analysis of:

(A) The difference between the price at which the seller acquired the property and the price that the consumer is obligated to pay to acquire the property, as specified in the consumer's agreement to acquire the property from the seller;

(B) Changes in market conditions between the date the seller acquired the property and the date of the consumer's agreement to acquire the property; and

(C) Any improvements made to the property between the date the seller acquired the property and the date of the consumer's agreement to acquire the property.

(v) No charge for the additional appraisal. If the creditor must obtain two appraisals under paragraph (c)(4)(i) of this section, the creditor may charge the consumer for only one of the appraisals.

(vi) Creditor's determination of prior sale date and price—

(A) Reasonable diligence. A creditor must obtain two written appraisals under paragraph (c)(4)(i) of this section unless the creditor can demonstrate by exercising reasonable diligence that the requirement to obtain two appraisals does not apply. A creditor acts with reasonable diligence if the creditor bases its determination on information contained in written source documents, such as the documents listed in Appendix O to this part.

(B) Inability to determine prior sale date or price—modified requirements for additional appraisal. If, after exercising reasonable diligence, a creditor cannot determine whether the conditions in paragraphs (c)(4)(i)(A) and (c)(4)(i)(B) are present and therefore must obtain two written appraisals in accordance with paragraphs (c)(4)(i) through (v) of this section, one of the two appraisals shall include an analysis of the factors in paragraph (c)(4)(iv) of this section only to the extent that the information necessary for the appraiser to perform the analysis can be determined.

(vii) Exemptions from the additional appraisal requirement. The additional appraisal required under paragraph (c)(4)(i) of this section shall not apply to extensions of credit that finance a consumer's acquisition of property:

(A) From a local, State or Federal government agency;

(B) From a person who acquired title to the property through foreclosure, deed-in-lieu of foreclosure, or other similar judicial or non-judicial procedure as a result of the person's exercise of rights as the holder of a defaulted mortgage loan;

(C) From a non-profit entity as part of a local, State, or Federal government program under which the non-profit entity is permitted to acquire title to single-family properties for resale from a seller who acquired title to the property through the process of foreclosure, deed-in-lieu of foreclosure, or other similar judicial or non-judicial procedure;

(D) From a person who acquired title to the property by inheritance or pursuant to a court order of dissolution of marriage, civil union, or domestic partnership, or of partition of joint or marital assets to which the seller was a party;

(E) From an employer or relocation agency in connection with the relocation of an employee;

(F) From a servicemember, as defined in 50 U.S.C. App. 511(1), who received a deployment or permanent change of station order after the servicemember purchased the property;

(G) Located in an area designated by the President as a federal disaster area, if and for as long as the Federal financial institutions regulatory agencies, as defined in 12 U.S.C. 3350(6), waive the requirements in title XI of the Financial Institutions Reform, Recovery, and Enforcement Act of 1989, as amended (12 U.S.C. 3331 et seq.), and any implementing regulations in that area; or

(H) Located in a rural county, as defined in 12 CFR 1026.35(b)(2)(iv)(A).

(5) Required disclosure—

(i) In general. Except as provided in paragraph (c)(2) of this section, a creditor shall disclose the following statement, in writing, to a consumer who applies for a higher-priced mortgage loan: "We may order an appraisal to determine the property's value and charge you for this appraisal. We will give you a copy of any appraisal, even if your loan does not close. You can pay for an additional appraisal for your own use at your own cost." Compliance with the disclosure requirement in Regulation B, 12 CFR 1002.14(a)(2), satisfies the requirements of this paragraph.

(ii) Timing of disclosure. The disclosure required by paragraph (c)(5)(i) of this section shall be delivered or placed in the mail no later than the third business day after the creditor receives the consumer's application for a higher-priced mortgage loan subject to paragraph (c) of this section. In the case of a loan that is not a higher-priced mortgage loan subject to paragraph (c) of this section at the time of application, but becomes a higher-priced mortgage loan subject to paragraph (c) of this section after application, the disclosure shall be delivered or placed in the mail not later than the third business day after the creditor determines that the loan is a higher-priced mortgage loan subject to paragraph (c) of this section.

(6) Copy of appraisals—

(i) In general. Except as provided in paragraph (c)(2) of this section, a creditor shall provide to the consumer a copy of any written appraisal performed in connection with a higher-priced mortgage loan pursuant to paragraphs (c)(3) and (c)(4) of this section.

(ii) Timing. A creditor shall provide to the consumer a copy of each written appraisal pursuant to paragraph (c)(6)(i) of this section:

(A) No later than three business days prior to consummation of the loan; or

(B) In the case of a loan that is not consummated, no later than 30 days after the creditor determines that the loan will not be consummated.

(iii) Form of copy. Any copy of a written appraisal required by paragraph (c)(6)(i) of this section may be provided to the applicant in electronic form, subject to compliance with the consumer consent and other applicable provisions of the Electronic Signatures in Global and National Commerce Act (E-Sign Act) (15 U.S.C. 7001 et seq.).

(iv) No charge for copy of appraisal. A creditor shall not charge the consumer for a copy of a written appraisal required to be provided to the consumer pursuant to paragraph (c)(6)(i) of this section.

(7) Relation to other rules. The rules in this paragraph (c) were adopted jointly by the Federal Reserve Board (Board), the Office of the Comptroller of the Currency (OCC), the Federal Deposit Insurance Corporation, the National Credit Union Administration, the Federal Housing Finance Agency, and the Bureau. These rules are substantively identical to the Board's and the OCC's higher-priced mortgage loan appraisal rules published separately in 12 CFR 226.43 (for the Board) and in 12 CFR part 34, subpart G and 12 CFR part 164, subpart B (for the OCC).

(d) Evasion; open-end credit. In connection with credit secured by a consumer's principal dwelling that does not meet the definition of open-end credit in § 1026.2(a)(20), a creditor shall not structure a home-secured loan as an open-end plan to evade the requirements of this section.

§ 1026.36 Prohibited acts or practices and certain requirements for credit secured by a dwelling.

(a) Definitions.

(1) Loan originator.

(i) For purposes of this section, the term "loan originator" means a person who, in expectation of direct or indirect compensation or other monetary gain or for direct or indirect compensation or other monetary gain, performs any of the following activities: takes an application, offers, arranges, assists a consumer in obtaining or applying to obtain, negotiates, or otherwise obtains or makes an extension of consumer credit for another person; or through advertising or other means of communication represents to the public that such person can or will perform any of these activities. The term "loan originator" includes an employee, agent, or contractor of the creditor or loan originator organization if the employee, agent, or contractor meets this definition. The term "loan originator" includes a creditor that engages in loan origination activities if the creditor does not finance the transaction at consummation out of the creditor's own resources, including by drawing on a bona fide warehouse line of credit or out of deposits held by the creditor. All creditors that engage in any of the foregoing loan origination activities are loan originators for purposes of paragraphs (f) and (g) of this section. The term does not include:

(A) A person who does not take a consumer credit application or offer or negotiate credit terms available from a creditor to that consumer selected based on the consumer's financial characteristics, but who performs purely administrative or clerical tasks on behalf of a person who does engage in such activities.

(B) An employee of a manufactured home retailer who does not take a consumer credit application, offer or negotiate credit terms, or advise a consumer on credit terms.

(C) A person that performs only real estate brokerage activities and is licensed or registered in accordance with applicable State law, unless such person is compensated by a creditor or loan originator or by any agent of such creditor or loan originator for a particular consumer credit transaction subject to this section.

(D) A seller financer that meets the criteria in paragraph (a)(4) or (a)(5) of this section, as applicable.

(E) A servicer or servicer's employees, agents, and contractors who offer or negotiate terms for purposes of renegotiating, modifying, replacing, or subordinating principal of existing mortgages where consumers are behind in their payments, in default, or have a reasonable likelihood of defaulting or falling behind. This exception does not apply, however, to a servicer or servicer's employees, agents, and contractors who offer or negotiate a transaction that constitutes a refinancing under § 1026.20(a) or obligates a different consumer on the existing debt.

(ii) An "**individual loan originator**" is a natural person who meets the definition of "loan originator" in paragraph (a)(1)(i) of this section.

(iii) A "**loan originator organization**" is any loan originator, as defined in paragraph (a)(1)(i) of this section, that is not an individual loan originator.

(2) Mortgage broker. For purposes of this section, a mortgage broker with respect to a particular transaction is any loan originator that is not an employee of the creditor.

(3) Compensation. The term "compensation" includes salaries, commissions, and any financial or similar incentive.

(4) Seller financers; three properties. A person (as defined in § 1026.2(a)(22)) that meets all of the following criteria is not a loan originator under paragraph (a)(1) of this section:

(i) The person provides seller financing for the sale of three or fewer properties in any 12-month period to purchasers of such properties, each of which is owned by the person and serves as security for the financing.

(ii) The person has not constructed, or acted as a contractor for the construction of, a residence on the property in the ordinary course of business of the person.

(iii) The person provides seller financing that meets the following requirements:

(A) The financing is fully amortizing.

(B) The financing is one that the person determines in good faith the consumer has a reasonable ability to repay.

(C) The financing has a fixed rate or an adjustable rate that is adjustable after five or more years, subject to reasonable annual and lifetime limitations on interest rate increases. If the financing agreement has an adjustable rate, the rate is determined by the addition of a margin to an index rate and is subject to reasonable rate adjustment limitations. The index the adjustable rate is based on is a widely available index such as indices for U.S. Treasury securities or LIBOR.

(5) Seller financers; one property. A natural person, estate, or trust that meets all of the following criteria is not a loan originator under paragraph (a)(1) of this section:

(i) The natural person, estate, or trust provides seller financing for the sale of only one property in any 12-month period to purchasers of such property, which is owned by the natural person, estate, or trust and serves as security for the financing.

(ii) The natural person, estate, or trust has not constructed, or acted as a contractor for the construction of, a residence on the property in the ordinary course of business of the person.

(iii) The natural person, estate, or trust provides seller financing that meets the following requirements:

(A) The financing has a repayment schedule that does not result in negative amortization.

(B) The financing has a fixed rate or an adjustable rate that is adjustable after five or more years, subject to reasonable annual and lifetime limitations on interest rate increases. If the financing agreement has an adjustable rate, the rate is determined by the addition of a margin to an index rate and is subject to reasonable rate adjustment limitations. The index the adjustable rate is based on is a widely available index such as indices for U.S. Treasury securities or LIBOR.

(6) Credit terms. For purposes of this section, the term "credit terms" includes rates, fees, and other costs. Credit terms are selected based on the consumer's financial characteristics when those terms are selected based on any factors that may influence a credit decision, such as debts, income, assets, or credit history.

(b) Scope. Paragraphs (c)(1) and (2) of this section apply to closed-end consumer credit transactions secured by a consumer's principal dwelling. Paragraph (c)(3) of this section applies to a consumer credit transaction secured by a dwelling. Paragraphs (d) through (i) of this section apply to closed-end consumer credit transactions secured by a dwelling. This section does not apply to a home equity line of credit subject to § 1026.40, except that paragraphs (h) and (i) of this section apply to such credit when secured by the consumer's principal dwelling and paragraph (c)(3) applies to such credit when secured by a dwelling. Paragraphs (d) through (i) of this section do not apply to a loan that is secured by a consumer's interest in a timeshare plan described in 11 U.S.C. 101(53D).

(c) Servicing practices. For purposes of this paragraph (c), the terms "servicer" and "servicing" have the same meanings as provided in 12 CFR 1024.2(b).

(1) Payment processing. In connection with a consumer credit transaction secured by a consumer's principal dwelling:

(i) Periodic payments. No servicer shall fail to credit a periodic payment to the consumer's loan account as of the date of receipt, except when a delay in crediting does not result in any charge to the consumer or in the reporting of negative information to a consumer reporting agency, or except as provided in paragraph (c)(1)(iii) of this section. A periodic payment, as used in this paragraph (c), is an amount sufficient to cover principal, interest, and escrow (if applicable) for a given billing cycle. A payment qualifies as a periodic payment even if it does not include amounts required to cover late fees, other fees, or non-escrow payments a servicer has advanced on a consumer's behalf.

(ii) Partial payments. Any servicer that retains a partial payment, meaning any payment less than a periodic payment, in a suspense or unapplied funds account shall:

(A) Disclose to the consumer the total amount of funds held in such suspense or unapplied funds account on the periodic statement as required by § 1026.41(d)(3), if a periodic statement is required; and

(B) On accumulation of sufficient funds to cover a periodic payment in any suspense or unapplied funds account, treat such funds as a periodic payment received in accordance with paragraph (c)(1)(i) of this section.

(iii) Non-conforming payments. If a servicer specifies in writing requirements for the consumer to follow in making payments, but accepts a payment that does not conform to the requirements, the servicer shall credit the payment as of five days after receipt.

(2) No pyramiding of late fees. In connection with a closed-end consumer credit transaction secured by a consumer's principal dwelling, a servicer shall not impose any late fee or delinquency charge for a payment if:

(i) Such a fee or charge is attributable solely to failure of the consumer to pay a late fee or delinquency charge on an earlier payment; and

(ii) The payment is otherwise a periodic payment received on the due date, or within any applicable courtesy period.

(3) Payoff statements. In connection with a consumer credit transaction secured by a consumer's dwelling, a creditor, assignee or servicer, as applicable, must provide an accurate statement of the total outstanding balance that would be required to pay the consumer's obligation in full as of a specified date. The statement shall be sent within a reasonable time, but in no case more than seven business days, after receiving a written request from the consumer or any person acting on behalf of the consumer. When a creditor, assignee, or servicer, as applicable, is not able to provide the statement within seven business days of such a request because a loan is in bankruptcy or foreclosure, because the loan is a reverse mortgage or shared appreciation mortgage, or because of natural disasters or other similar circumstances, the payoff statement must be provided within a reasonable time. A creditor or assignee that does not currently own the mortgage loan or the mortgage servicing rights is not subject to the requirement in this paragraph (c)(3) to provide a payoff statement.

(d) Prohibited payments to loan originators.

(1) Payments based on a term of a transaction.

(i) Except as provided in paragraph (d)(1)(iii) or (iv) of this section, in connection with a consumer credit transaction secured by a dwelling, no loan originator shall receive and no person shall pay to a loan originator, directly or indirectly, compensation in an amount that is based on a term of a transaction, the terms of multiple transactions by an individual loan originator, or the terms of multiple transactions by multiple individual loan originators. If a loan originator's compensation is based in whole or in part on a factor that is a proxy for a term of a transaction, the loan originator's compensation is based on a term of a transaction. A factor that is not itself a term of a transaction is a proxy for a term of the transaction if the factor consistently varies with that term over a significant number of transactions, and the loan originator has the ability, directly or indirectly, to add, drop, or change the factor in originating the transaction.

(ii) For purposes of this paragraph (d)(1) only, a "term of a transaction" is any right or obligation of the parties to a credit transaction. The amount of credit extended is not a term of a transaction or a proxy for a term of a transaction, provided that compensation received by or paid to a loan originator, directly or indirectly, is based on a fixed percentage of the amount of credit extended; however, such compensation may be subject to a minimum or maximum dollar amount.

(iii) An individual loan originator may receive, and a person may pay to an individual loan originator, compensation in the form of a contribution to a defined contribution plan that is a designated tax-advantaged plan or a benefit under a defined benefit plan that is a designated tax-advantaged plan. In the case of a contribution to a defined contribution plan, the contribution shall not be directly or indirectly based on the terms of that individual loan originator's transactions. As used in this paragraph (d)(1)(iii), "designated tax-advantaged plan" means any plan that meets the requirements of Internal Revenue Code section 401(a), 26 U.S.C. 401(a); employee annuity plan described in Internal Revenue Code section 403(a), 26 U.S.C. 403(a); simple retirement account, as defined in Internal Revenue Code section 408(p), 26 U.S.C. 408(p); simplified employee pension described in Internal Revenue Code section 408(k), 26 U.S.C. 408(k); annuity contract described in Internal Revenue Code section 403(b), 26 U.S.C. 403(b); or eligible deferred compensation plan, as defined in Internal Revenue Code section 457(b), 26 U.S.C. 457(b).

(iv) An individual loan originator may receive, and a person may pay to an individual loan originator, compensation under a non-deferred profits-based compensation plan (i.e., any arrangement for the payment of non-deferred compensation that is determined with reference to the profits of the person from mortgage-related business), provided that:

(A) The compensation paid to an individual loan originator pursuant to this paragraph (d)(1)(iv) is not directly or indirectly based on the terms of that individual loan originator's transactions that are subject to this paragraph (d); and

(B) At least one of the following conditions is satisfied:

(1) The compensation paid to an individual loan originator pursuant to this paragraph (d)(1)(iv) does not, in the aggregate, exceed 10 percent of the individual loan originator's total compensation corresponding to the time period for which the compensation under the non-deferred profits-based compensation plan is paid; or

(2) The individual loan originator was a loan originator for ten or fewer transactions subject to this paragraph (d) consummated during the 12-month period preceding the date of the compensation determination.

(2) Payments by persons other than consumer.

(i) Dual compensation.

(A) Except as provided in paragraph (d)(2)(i)(C) of this section, if any loan originator receives compensation directly from a consumer in a consumer credit transaction secured by a dwelling:

(1) No loan originator shall receive compensation, directly or indirectly, from any person other than the consumer in connection with the transaction; and

(2) No person who knows or has reason to know of the consumer-paid compensation to the loan originator (other than the consumer) shall pay any compensation to a loan originator, directly or indirectly, in connection with the transaction.

(B) Compensation received directly from a consumer includes payments to a loan originator made pursuant to an agreement between the consumer and a person other than the creditor or its affiliates, under which such other person agrees to provide funds toward the consumer's costs of the transaction (including loan originator compensation).

(C) If a loan originator organization receives compensation directly from a consumer in connection with a transaction, the loan originator organization may pay compensation to an individual loan originator, and the individual loan originator may receive compensation from the loan originator organization, subject to paragraph (d)(1) of this section.

(ii) Exemption. A payment to a loan originator that is otherwise prohibited by section 129B(c)(2)(A) of the Truth in Lending Act is nevertheless permitted pursuant to section 129B(c)(2)(B) of the Act, regardless of whether the consumer makes any upfront payment of discount points, origination points, or fees, as described in section 129B(c)(2)(B)(ii) of the Act, as long as the loan originator does not receive any compensation directly from the consumer as described in section 129B(c)(2)(B)(i) of the Act.

(3) Affiliates. For purposes of this paragraph (d), affiliates shall be treated as a single "person."

(e) Prohibition on steering.

(1) General. In connection with a consumer credit transaction secured by a dwelling, a loan originator shall not direct or "steer" a consumer to consummate a transaction based on the fact that the originator will receive greater compensation from the creditor in that transaction than in other transactions the originator offered or could have offered to the consumer, unless the consummated transaction is in the consumer's interest.

(2) Permissible transactions. A transaction does not violate paragraph (e)(1) of this section if the consumer is presented with loan options that meet the conditions in paragraph (e)(3) of this section for each type of transaction in which the consumer expressed an interest. For purposes of paragraph (e) of this section, the term "type of transaction" refers to whether:

(i) A loan has an annual percentage rate that cannot increase after consummation;

(ii) A loan has an annual percentage rate that may increase after consummation; or

(iii) A loan is a reverse mortgage.

(3) Loan options presented. A transaction satisfies paragraph (e)(2) of this section only if the loan originator presents the loan options required by that paragraph and all of the following conditions are met:

(i) The loan originator must obtain loan options from a significant number of the creditors with which the originator regularly does business and, for each type of transaction in which the consumer expressed an interest, must present the consumer with loan options that include:

(A) The loan with the lowest interest rate;

(B) The loan with the lowest interest rate without negative amortization, a prepayment penalty, interest-only payments, a balloon payment in the first 7 years of the life of the loan, a demand feature, shared equity, or shared appreciation; or, in the case of a reverse mortgage, a loan without a prepayment penalty, or shared equity or shared appreciation; and

(C) The loan with the lowest total dollar amount of discount points, origination points or origination fees (or, if two or more loans have the same total dollar amount of discount points, origination points or origination fees, the loan with the lowest interest rate that has the lowest total dollar amount of discount points, origination points or origination fees).

(ii) The loan originator must have a good faith belief that the options presented to the consumer pursuant to paragraph (e)(3)(i) of this section are loans for which the consumer likely qualifies.

(iii) For each type of transaction, if the originator presents to the consumer more than three loans, the originator must highlight the loans that satisfy the criteria specified in paragraph (e)(3)(i) of this section.

(4) Number of loan options presented. The loan originator can present fewer than three loans and satisfy paragraphs (e)(2) and (e)(3)(i) of this section if the loan(s) presented to the consumer satisfy the criteria of the options in paragraph (e)(3)(i) of this section and the provisions of paragraph (e)(3) of this section are otherwise met.

(f) Loan originator qualification requirements. A loan originator for a consumer credit transaction secured by a dwelling must, when required by applicable State or Federal law, be registered and licensed in accordance with those laws, including the Secure and Fair Enforcement for Mortgage Licensing Act of 2008 (SAFE Act, 12 U.S.C. 5102 et seq.), its implementing regulations (12 CFR part 1007 or part 1008), and State SAFE Act implementing law. To comply with this paragraph (f), a loan originator organization that is not a government agency or State housing finance agency must:

(1) Comply with all applicable State law requirements for legal existence and foreign qualification;

(2) Ensure that each individual loan originator who works for the loan originator organization is licensed or registered to the extent the individual is required to be licensed or registered under the SAFE Act, its implementing regulations, and State SAFE Act implementing law before the individual acts as a loan originator in a consumer credit transaction secured by a dwelling; and

(3) For each of its individual loan originator employees who is not required to be licensed and is not licensed as a loan originator pursuant to § 1008.103 of this chapter or State SAFE Act implementing law:

(i) Obtain for any individual whom the loan originator organization hired on or after January 1, 2014 (or whom the loan originator organization hired before this date but for whom there were no applicable statutory or regulatory background standards in effect at the time of hire or before January 1, 2014, used to screen the individual) and for any individual regardless of when hired who, based on reliable information known to the loan originator organization, likely does not meet the standards under § 1026.36(f)(3)(ii), before the individual acts as a loan originator in a consumer credit transaction secured by a dwelling:

(A) A criminal background check through the Nationwide Mortgage Licensing System and Registry (NMLSR) or, in the case of an individual loan originator who is not a registered loan originator under the NMLSR, a criminal background check from a law enforcement agency or commercial service;

(B) A credit report from a consumer reporting agency described in section 603(p) of the Fair Credit Reporting Act (15 U.S.C. 1681a(p)) secured, where applicable, in compliance with the requirements of section 604(b) of the Fair Credit Reporting Act, 15 U.S.C. 1681b(b); and

(C) Information from the NMLSR about any administrative, civil, or criminal findings by any government jurisdiction or, in the case of an individual loan originator who is not a registered loan originator under the NMLSR, such information from the individual loan originator;

(ii) Determine on the basis of the information obtained pursuant to paragraph (f)(3)(i) of this section and any other information reasonably available to the loan originator organization, for any individual whom the loan originator organization hired on or after January 1, 2014 (or whom the loan originator organization hired before this date but for whom there were no applicable statutory or regulatory background standards in effect at the time of hire or before January 1, 2014, used to screen the individual) and for any individual regardless of when hired who, based on reliable information known to the loan originator organization, likely does not meet the standards under this paragraph (f)(3)(ii), before the individual acts as a loan originator in a consumer credit transaction secured by a dwelling, that the individual loan originator:

(A)(1) Has not been convicted of, or pleaded guilty or nolo contendere to, a felony in a domestic or military court during the preceding seven-year period or, in the case of a felony involving an act of fraud, dishonesty, a breach of trust, or money laundering, at any time;

(2) For purposes of this paragraph (f)(3)(ii)(A):

(i) A crime is a felony only if at the time of conviction it was classified as a felony under the law of the jurisdiction under which the individual was convicted;

(ii) Expunged convictions and pardoned convictions do not render an individual unqualified; and

(iii) A conviction or plea of guilty or nolo contendere does not render an individual unqualified under this § 1026.36(f) if the loan originator organization has obtained consent to employ the individual from the Federal Deposit Insurance Corporation (or the Board of Governors of the Federal Reserve System, as applicable) pursuant to section 19 of the Federal Deposit Insurance Act (FDIA), 12 U.S.C. 1829, the National Credit Union Administration pursuant to section 205 of the Federal Credit Union Act (FCUA), 12 U.S.C. 1785(d), or the Farm Credit Administration pursuant to section 5.65(d) of the Farm Credit Act of 1971 (FCA), 12 U.S.C. 227a–14(d), notwithstanding the bars posed with respect to that conviction or plea by the FDIA, FCUA, and FCA, as applicable; and

(B) Has demonstrated financial responsibility, character, and general fitness such as to warrant a determination that the individual loan originator will operate honestly, fairly, and efficiently; and

(iii) Provide periodic training covering Federal and State law requirements that apply to the individual loan originator's loan origination activities.

(g) Name and NMLSR ID on loan documents. (1) For a consumer credit transaction secured by a dwelling, a loan originator organization must include on the loan documents described in paragraph (g)(2) of this section, whenever each such loan document is provided to a consumer or presented to a consumer for signature, as applicable:

(i) Its name and NMLSR ID, if the NMLSR has provided it an NMLSR ID; and

(ii) The name of the individual loan originator (as the name appears in the NMLSR) with primary responsibility for the origination and, if the NMLSR has provided such person an NMLSR ID, that NMLSR ID.

(2) The loan documents that must include the names and NMLSR IDs pursuant to paragraph (g)(1) of this section are:

(i) The credit application;

(ii) The disclosures required by § 1026.19(e) and (f);

(iii) The note or loan contract; and

(iv) The security instrument.

(3) For purposes of this section, NMLSR ID means a number assigned by the Nationwide Mortgage Licensing System and Registry to facilitate electronic tracking and uniform identification of loan originators and public access to the employment history of, and the publicly adjudicated disciplinary and enforcement actions against, loan originators.

(h) Prohibition on mandatory arbitration clauses and waivers of certain consumer rights.

(1) Arbitration. A contract or other agreement for a consumer credit transaction secured by a dwelling (including a home equity line of credit secured by the consumer's principal dwelling) may not include terms that require arbitration or any other non-judicial procedure to resolve any controversy or settle any claims arising out of the transaction. This prohibition does not limit a consumer and creditor or any assignee from agreeing, after a dispute or claim under the transaction arises, to settle or use arbitration or other non-judicial procedure to resolve that dispute or claim.

(2) No waivers of Federal statutory causes of action. A contract or other agreement relating to a consumer credit transaction secured by a dwelling (including a home equity line of credit secured by the consumer's principal dwelling) may not be applied or interpreted to bar a consumer from bringing a claim in court pursuant to any provision of law for damages or other relief in connection with any alleged violation of any Federal law. This prohibition does not limit a consumer and creditor or any assignee from agreeing, after a dispute or claim under the transaction arises, to settle or use arbitration or other non-judicial procedure to resolve that dispute or claim.

(i) Prohibition on financing credit insurance.

(1) A creditor may not finance, directly or indirectly, any premiums or fees for credit insurance in connection with a consumer credit transaction secured by a dwelling (including a home equity line of credit secured by the consumer's principal dwelling). This prohibition does not apply to credit insurance for which premiums or fees are calculated and paid in full on a monthly basis.

(2) For purposes of this paragraph (i):

(i) "Credit insurance":

(A) Means credit life, credit disability, credit unemployment, or credit property insurance, or any other accident, loss-of-income, life, or health insurance, or any payments directly or indirectly for any debt cancellation or suspension agreement or contract, but

(B) Excludes credit unemployment insurance for which the unemployment insurance premiums are reasonable, the creditor receives no direct or indirect compensation in connection with the unemployment insurance premiums, and the unemployment insurance premiums are paid pursuant to a separate insurance contract and are not paid to an affiliate of the creditor;

(ii) A creditor finances premiums or fees for credit insurance if it provides a consumer the right to defer payment of a credit insurance premium or fee owed by the consumer beyond the monthly period in which the premium or fee is due; and

(iii) Credit insurance premiums or fees are calculated on a monthly basis if they are determined mathematically by multiplying a rate by the actual monthly outstanding balance.

(j) Policies and procedures to ensure and monitor compliance.

(1) A depository institution must establish and maintain written policies and procedures reasonably designed to ensure and monitor the compliance of the depository institution, its employees, its subsidiaries, and its subsidiaries' employees with the requirements of paragraphs (d), (e), (f), and (g) of this section. These written policies and procedures must be appropriate to the nature, size, complexity, and scope of the mortgage lending activities of the depository institution and its subsidiaries.

(2) For purposes of this paragraph (j), "depository institution" has the meaning in section 1503(3) of the SAFE Act, 12 U.S.C. 5102(3). For purposes of this paragraph (j), "subsidiary" has the meaning in section 3 of the Federal Deposit Insurance Act, 12 U.S.C. 1813.

(k) Negative amortization counseling. (1) Counseling required. A creditor shall not extend credit to a first-time borrower in connection with a closed-end transaction secured by a dwelling, other than a reverse mortgage transaction subject to § 1026.33 or a transaction secured by a consumer's interest in a timeshare plan described in 11 U.S.C. 101(53D), that may result in negative amortization, unless the creditor receives documentation that the consumer has obtained homeownership counseling from a counseling organization or counselor certified or approved by the U.S. Department of Housing and Urban Development to provide such counseling.

(2) Definitions. For the purposes of this paragraph (k), the following definitions apply:

(i) A "first-time borrower" means a consumer who has not previously received a closed-end credit transaction or open-end credit plan secured by a dwelling.

(ii) "Negative amortization" means a payment schedule with regular periodic payments that cause the principal balance to increase.

(3) Steering prohibited. A creditor that extends credit to a first-time borrower in connection with a closed-end transaction secured by a dwelling, other than a reverse mortgage transaction subject to § 1026.33 or a transaction secured by a consumer's interest in a timeshare plan described in 11 U.S.C. 101(53D), that may result in negative amortization shall not steer or otherwise direct a consumer to choose a particular counselor or counseling organization for the counseling required under this paragraph (k).

§ 1026.37 Content of disclosures for certain mortgage transactions (Loan Estimate).

For each transaction subject to § 1026.19(e), the creditor shall disclose the information in this section:

(a) General information.

(1) Form title. The title of the form, "Loan Estimate," using that term.

(2) Form purpose. The statement, "Save this Loan Estimate to compare with your Closing Disclosure."

(3) Creditor. The name and address of the creditor making the disclosures.

(4) Date issued. The date the disclosures are mailed or delivered to the consumer by the creditor, labeled "Date Issued."

(5) Applicants. The name and mailing address of the consumer(s) applying for the credit, labeled "Applicants."

(6) Property. The address including the zip code of the property that secures or will secure the transaction, or if the address is unavailable, the location of such property including a zip code, labeled "Property."

(7) Sale price. (i) For transactions that involve a seller, the contract sale price of the property identified in paragraph (a)(6) of this section, labeled "Sale Price."

(ii) For transactions that do not involve a seller, the estimated value of the property identified in paragraph (a)(6), labeled "Prop. Value."

(8) Loan term. The term to maturity of the credit transaction, stated in years or months, or both, as applicable, labeled "Loan Term."

(9) Purpose. The consumer's intended use for the credit, labeled "Purpose," using one of the following terms:

(i) Purchase. If the credit is to finance the acquisition of the property identified in paragraph (a)(6) of this section, the creditor shall disclose that the loan is for a "Purchase."

(ii) Refinance. If the credit is not for the purpose described in paragraph (a)(9)(i) of this section, and if the credit will be used to refinance an existing obligation, as defined in § 1026.20(a) (but without regard to whether the creditor is the original creditor or a holder or servicer of the original obligation), that is secured by the property identified in paragraph (a)(6) of this section, the creditor shall disclose that the loan is for a "Refinance."

(iii) Construction. If the credit is not for one of the purposes described in paragraphs (a)(9)(i) or (ii) of this section and the credit will be used to finance the initial construction of a dwelling on the property identified in paragraph (a)(6) of this section, the creditor shall disclose that the loan is for "Construction."

(iv) Home equity loan. If the credit is not for one of the purposes described in paragraphs (a)(9)(i) through (iii) of this section, the creditor shall disclose that the loan is a "Home Equity Loan."

(10) Product. A description of the loan product, labeled "Product."

(i) The description of the loan product shall include one of the following terms:

(A) Adjustable rate. If the interest rate may increase after consummation, but the rates that will apply or the periods for which they will apply are not known at consummation, the creditor shall disclose the loan product as an "Adjustable Rate."

(B) Step rate. If the interest rate will change after consummation, and the rates that will apply and the periods for which they will apply are known at consummation, the creditor shall disclose the loan product as a "Step Rate."

(C) Fixed rate. If the loan product is not an Adjustable Rate or a Step Rate, as described in paragraphs (a)(10)(i)(A) and (B) of this section, respectively, the creditor shall disclose the loan product as a "Fixed Rate."

(ii) The description of the loan product shall include the features that may change the periodic payment using the following terms, subject to paragraph (a)(10)(iii) of this section, as applicable:

(A) Negative amortization. If the principal balance may increase due to the addition of accrued interest to the principal balance, the creditor shall disclose that the loan product has a "Negative Amortization" feature.

(B) Interest only. If one or more regular periodic payments may be applied only to interest accrued and not to the loan principal, the creditor shall disclose that the loan product has an "Interest Only" feature.

(C) Step payment. If scheduled variations in regular periodic payment amounts occur that are not caused by changes to the interest rate during the loan term, the creditor shall disclose that the loan product has a "Step Payment" feature.

(D) Balloon payment. If the terms of the legal obligation include a "balloon payment," as that term is defined in paragraph (b)(5) of this section, the creditor shall disclose that the loan has a "Balloon Payment" feature.

(E) Seasonal payment. If the terms of the legal obligation expressly provide that regular periodic payments are not scheduled between specified unit-periods on a regular basis, the creditor shall disclose that the loan product has a "Seasonal Payment" feature.

(iii) The disclosure of a loan feature under paragraph (a)(10)(ii) of this section shall precede the disclosure of the loan product under paragraph (a)(10)(i) of this section. If a transaction has more than one of the loan features described in paragraph (a)(10)(ii) of this section, the creditor shall disclose only the first applicable feature in the order the features are listed in paragraph (a)(10)(ii) of this section.

(iv) The disclosures required by paragraphs (a)(10)(i)(A) and (B), and (a)(10)(ii)(A) through (D) of this section must each be preceded by the duration of any introductory rate or payment period, and the first adjustment period, as applicable.

(11) Loan type. The type of loan, labeled "Loan Type," offered to the consumer using one of the following terms, as applicable:

(i) Conventional. If the loan is not guaranteed or insured by a Federal or State government agency, the creditor shall disclose that the loan is a "Conventional."

(ii) FHA. If the loan is insured by the Federal Housing Administration, the creditor shall disclose that the loan is an "FHA."

(iii) VA. If the loan is guaranteed by the U.S. Department of Veterans Affairs, the creditor shall disclose that the loan is a "VA."

(iv) Other. For federally-insured or guaranteed loans other than those described in paragraphs (a)(11)(ii) and (iii) of this section, and for loans insured or guaranteed by a State agency, the creditor shall disclose the loan type as "Other," and provide a brief description of the loan type.

(12) Loan identification number (Loan ID #). A number that may be used by the creditor, consumer, and other parties to identify the transaction, labeled "Loan ID # ."

(13) Rate lock. A statement of whether the interest rate disclosed pursuant to paragraph (b)(2) of this section is locked for a specific period of time, labeled "Rate Lock."

(i) For transactions in which the interest rate is locked for a specific period of time, the creditor must provide the date and time (including the applicable time zone) when that period ends.

(ii) The "Rate Lock" statement required by this paragraph (a)(13) shall be accompanied by a statement that the interest rate, any points, and any lender credits may change unless the interest rate has been locked, and the date and time (including the applicable time zone) at which estimated closing costs expire.

(b) Loan terms. A separate table under the heading "Loan Terms" that contains the following information and that satisfies the following requirements:

(1) Loan amount. The total amount the consumer will borrow, as reflected by the face amount of the note, labeled "Loan Amount."

(2) Interest rate. The interest rate that will be applicable to the transaction at consummation, labeled "Interest Rate." For an adjustable rate transaction, if the interest rate at consummation is not known, the rate disclosed shall be the fully-indexed rate, which, for purposes of this paragraph, means the interest rate calculated using the index value and margin at the time of consummation.

(3) Principal and interest payment. The initial periodic payment amount that will be due under the terms of the legal obligation, labeled "Principal & Interest," immediately preceded by the applicable unit-period, and a statement referring to the payment amount that includes any mortgage insurance and escrow payments that is required to be disclosed pursuant to paragraph (c) of this section. If the interest rate at consummation is not known, the amount disclosed shall be calculated using the fully-indexed rate disclosed under paragraph (b)(2) of this section.

(4) Prepayment penalty. A statement of whether the transaction includes a prepayment penalty, labeled "Prepayment Penalty." For purposes of this paragraph (b)(4), "prepayment penalty" means a charge imposed for paying all or part of a transaction's principal before the date on which the principal is due, other than a waived, bona fide third-party charge that the creditor imposes if the consumer prepays all of the transaction's principal sooner than 36 months after consummation.

(5) Balloon payment. A statement of whether the transaction includes a balloon payment, labeled "Balloon Payment." For purposes of this paragraph (b)(5), "balloon payment" means a payment that is more than two times a regular periodic payment. "Balloon payment" includes the payment or payments under a transaction that requires only one or two payments during the loan term.

(6) Adjustments after consummation. For each amount required to be disclosed by paragraphs (b)(1) through (3) of this section, a statement of whether the amount may increase after consummation as an affirmative or negative answer to the question, and under such question disclosed as a subheading, "Can this amount increase after closing?" and, in the case of an affirmative answer, the following additional information, as applicable:

(i) Adjustment in loan amount. The maximum principal balance for the transaction and the due date of the last payment that may cause the principal balance to increase. The disclosure further shall indicate whether the maximum principal balance is potential or is scheduled to occur under the terms of the legal obligation.

(ii) Adjustment in interest rate. The frequency of interest rate adjustments, the date when the interest rate may first adjust, the maximum interest rate, and the first date when the interest rate can reach the maximum interest rate, followed by a reference to the disclosure required by paragraph (j) of this section. If the loan term, as defined under paragraph (a)(8) of this section, may increase based on an interest rate adjustment, the disclosure required by this paragraph (b)(6)(ii) shall also state that fact and the maximum possible loan term determined in accordance with paragraph (a)(8) of this section.

(iii) Increase in periodic payment. The scheduled frequency of adjustments to the periodic principal and interest payment, the due date of the first adjusted principal and interest payment, the maximum possible periodic principal and interest payment, and the date when the periodic principal and interest payment may first equal the maximum principal and interest payment. If any adjustments to the principal and interest payment are not the result of a change to the interest rate, a reference to the disclosure required by paragraph (i) of this section. If there is a period during which only interest is required to be paid, the disclosure required by this paragraph (b)(6)(iii) shall also state that fact and the due date of the last periodic payment of such period.

(7) Details about prepayment penalty and balloon payment. The information required to be disclosed by paragraphs (b)(4) and (5) of this section shall be disclosed as an affirmative or negative answer to the question, and under such question disclosed as a subheading, "Does the loan have these features?" If an affirmative answer for a prepayment penalty or balloon payment is required to be disclosed, the following information shall be included, as applicable:

(i) The maximum amount of the prepayment penalty that may be imposed and the date when the period during which the penalty may be imposed terminates; and

(ii) The maximum amount of the balloon payment and the due date of such payment.

(8) Timing.

(i) The dates required to be disclosed by paragraph (b)(6)(ii) of this section shall be disclosed as the year in which the event occurs, counting from the date that interest for the first scheduled periodic payment begins to accrue after consummation.

(ii) The dates required to be disclosed by paragraphs (b)(6)(i), (b)(6)(iii) and (b)(7)(ii) of this section shall be disclosed as the year in which the event occurs, counting from the due date of the initial periodic payment.

(iii) The date required to be disclosed by paragraph (b)(7)(i) of this section shall be disclosed as the year in which the event occurs, counting from the date of consummation.

(c) Projected payments. In a separate table under the heading "Projected Payments," an itemization of each separate periodic payment or range of payments, together with an estimate of taxes, insurance, and assessments and the payments to be made with escrow account funds.

(1) Periodic payment or range of payments.

(i) The initial periodic payment or range of payments is a separate periodic payment or range of payments and, except as otherwise provided in paragraph (c)(1)(ii) and (iii) of this section, the following events require the disclosure of additional separate periodic payments or ranges of payments:

(A) The periodic principal and interest payment or range of such payments may change;

(B) A scheduled balloon payment, as defined in paragraph (b)(5) of this section;

(C) The creditor must automatically terminate mortgage insurance or any functional equivalent under applicable law; and

(D) The anniversary of the due date of the initial periodic payment or range of payments that immediately follows the occurrence of multiple events described in paragraph (c)(1)(i)(A) of this section during a single year.

(ii) The table required by this paragraph (c) shall not disclose more than four separate periodic payments or ranges of payments. For all events requiring disclosure of additional separate periodic payments or ranges of payments described in paragraph (c)(1)(i)(A) through (D) of this section occurring after the third separate periodic payment or range of payments disclosed, the separate periodic payments or ranges of payments shall be disclosed as a single range of payments, subject to the following exceptions:

(A) A balloon payment that is scheduled as a final payment under the terms of the legal obligation shall always be disclosed as a separate periodic payment or range of payments, in which case all events requiring disclosure of additional separate periodic payments or ranges of payments described in paragraph (c)(1)(i)(A) through (D) of this section occurring after the second separate periodic payment or range of payments disclosed, other than the balloon payment that is scheduled as a final payment, shall be disclosed as a single range of payments.

(B) The automatic termination of mortgage insurance or any functional equivalent under applicable law shall require disclosure of an additional separate periodic payment or range of payments only if the total number of separate periodic payments or ranges of payments otherwise disclosed pursuant to this paragraph (c)(1) does not exceed three.

(iii) When a range of payments is required to be disclosed under this paragraph (c)(1), the creditor must disclose the minimum and maximum amount for both the principal and interest payment under paragraph (c)(2)(i) of this section and the total periodic payment under paragraph (c)(2)(iv) of this section. A range of payments is required to be disclosed under this paragraph (c)(1) when:

(A) Multiple events described in paragraph (c)(1)(i) of this section are combined in a single range of payments pursuant to paragraph (c)(1)(ii) of this section;

(B) Multiple events described in paragraph (c)(1)(i)(A) of this section occur during a single year or an event described in paragraph (c)(1)(i)(A) of this section occurs during the same year as the initial periodic payment or range of payments, in which case the creditor discloses the range of payments that would apply during the year in which the events occur; or

(C) The periodic principal and interest payment may adjust based on index rates at the time an interest rate adjustment may occur.

(2) Itemization. Each separate periodic payment or range of payments disclosed on the table required by this paragraph (c) shall be itemized as follows:

(i) The amount payable for principal and interest, labeled "Principal & Interest," including the term "only interest" if the payment or range of payments includes any interest only payment:

(A) In the case of a loan that has an adjustable interest rate, the maximum principal and interest payment amounts are determined by assuming that the interest rate in effect throughout the loan term is the maximum possible interest rate, and the minimum amounts are determined by assuming that the interest rate in effect throughout the loan term is the minimum possible interest rate;

(B) In the case of a loan that has an adjustable interest rate and also contains a negative amortization feature, the maximum principal and interest payment amounts after the end of the period of the loan's term during which the loan's principal balance may increase due to the addition of accrued interest are determined by assuming the maximum principal amount permitted under the terms of the legal obligation at the end of such period, and the minimum amounts are determined pursuant to paragraph (c)(2)(i)(A) of this section;

(ii) The maximum amount payable for mortgage insurance premiums corresponding to the principal and interest payment disclosed pursuant to paragraph (c)(2)(i) of this section, labeled "Mortgage Insurance";

(iii) The amount payable into an escrow account to pay some or all of the charges described in paragraph (c)(4)(ii), as applicable, labeled "Escrow," together with a statement that the amount disclosed can increase over time; and

(iv) The total periodic payment, calculated as the sum of the amounts disclosed pursuant to paragraphs (c)(2)(i) through (iii) of this section, labeled "Total Monthly Payment."

(3) Subheadings. (i) The labels required pursuant to paragraph (c)(2) of this section must be listed under the subheading "Payment Calculation."

(ii) Except as provided in paragraph (c)(3)(iii) of this section, each separate periodic payment or range of payments to be disclosed under this paragraph (c) must be disclosed under a subheading that states the years of the loan during which that payment or range of payments will apply. The subheadings must be stated in a sequence of whole years from the due date of the initial periodic payment.

(iii) A balloon payment that is scheduled as a final payment under the terms of the legal obligation must be disclosed under the subheading "Final Payment."

(4) Taxes, insurance, and assessments. Under the information required by paragraphs (c)(1) through (3) of this section:

(i) The label "Taxes, Insurance & Assessments";

(ii) The sum of the charges identified in § 1026.43(b)(8), other than amounts identified in § 1026.4(b)(5), expressed as a monthly amount, even if no escrow account for the payment of some or any of such charges will be established;

(iii) A statement that the amount disclosed pursuant to paragraph (c)(4)(ii) of this section can increase over time;

(iv) A statement of whether the amount disclosed pursuant to paragraph (c)(4)(ii) of this section includes payments for property taxes, amounts identified in § 1026.4(b)(8), and other amounts described in paragraph (c)(4)(ii) of this section, along with a description of any such other amounts, and an indication of whether such amounts will be paid by the creditor using escrow account funds;

(v) A statement that the consumer must pay separately any amounts described in paragraph (c)(4)(ii) of this section that are not paid by the creditor using escrow account funds; and

(vi) A reference to the information disclosed pursuant to paragraph (g)(3) of this section.

(5) Calculation of taxes and insurance. For purposes of paragraphs (c)(2)(iii) and (c)(4)(ii) of this section, estimated property taxes and homeowner's insurance shall reflect:

(i) The taxable assessed value of the real property or cooperative unit securing the transaction after consummation, including the value of any improvements on the property or to be constructed on the property, if known, whether or not such construction will be financed from the proceeds of the transaction, for property taxes; and

(ii) The replacement costs of the property during the initial year after the transaction, for amounts identified in § 1026.4(b)(8).

(d) Costs at closing.

(1) Costs at closing table. In a separate table, under the heading "Costs at Closing":

(i) Labeled "Closing Costs," the dollar amount disclosed pursuant to paragraph (g)(6) of this section, together with:

(A) A statement that the amount disclosed pursuant to paragraph (d)(1)(i) of this section includes the amounts disclosed pursuant to paragraphs (f)(4), (g)(5), and (g)(6)(ii);

(B) The dollar amount disclosed pursuant to paragraph (f)(4) of this section, labeled "Loan Costs";

(C) The dollar amount disclosed pursuant to paragraph (g)(5) of this section, labeled "Other Costs";

(D) The dollar amount disclosed pursuant to paragraph (g)(6)(ii) of this section, labeled "Lender Credits"; and

(E) A statement referring the consumer to the tables disclosed pursuant to paragraphs (f) and (g) of this section for details.

(ii) Labeled "Cash to Close," the dollar amount calculated in accordance with paragraph (h)(1)(viii) of this section, together with:

(A) A statement that the amount includes the amount disclosed pursuant to paragraph (d)(1)(i) of this section, and

(B) A statement referring the consumer to the location of the table required pursuant to paragraph (h) of this section for details.

(2) Optional alternative table for transactions without a seller or for simultaneous subordinate financing. For transactions that do not involve a seller or for simultaneous subordinate financing, instead of the amount and statements described in paragraph (d)(1)(ii) of this section, the creditor may alternatively disclose, using the label "Cash to Close":

(i) The amount calculated in accordance with (h)(2)(iv) of this section;

(ii) A statement of whether the disclosed estimated amount is due from or to the consumer; and

(iii) A statement referring the consumer to the alternative table disclosed pursuant to paragraph (h)(2) of this section for details.

(e) Web site reference. A statement that the consumer may obtain general information and tools at the Web site of the Bureau, and the link or uniform resource locator address to the Web site: www.consumerfinance.gov/mortgage-estimate.

(f) Closing cost details; loan costs. Under the master heading "Closing Cost Details," in a table under the heading "Loan Costs," all loan costs associated with the transaction. The table shall contain the items and amounts listed under four subheadings, described in paragraphs (f)(1) through (4) of this section.

(1) Origination charges. Under the subheading "Origination Charges," an itemization of each amount, and a subtotal of all such amounts, that the consumer will pay to each creditor and loan originator for originating and extending the credit.

(i) The points paid to the creditor to reduce the interest rate shall be itemized separately, as both a percentage of the amount of credit extended and a dollar amount, and using the label "__% of Loan Amount (Points)." If points to reduce the interest rate are not paid, the disclosure required by this paragraph (f)(1)(i) must be blank.

(ii) The number of items disclosed under this paragraph (f)(1), including the points disclosed under paragraph (f)(1)(i) of this section, shall not exceed 13.

(2) Services you cannot shop for. Under the subheading "Services You Cannot Shop For," an itemization of each amount, and a subtotal of all such amounts, the consumer will pay for settlement services for which the consumer cannot shop in accordance with § 1026.19(e)(1)(vi)(A) and that are provided by persons other than the creditor or mortgage broker.

(i) For any item that is a component of title insurance or is for conducting the closing, the introductory description "Title __" shall appear at the beginning of the label for that item.

(ii) The number of items disclosed under this paragraph (f)(2) shall not exceed 13.

(3) Services you can shop for. Under the subheading "Services You Can Shop For," an itemization of each amount and a subtotal of all such amounts the consumer will pay for settlement services for which the consumer can shop in accordance with § 1026.19(e)(1)(vi)(A) and that are provided by persons other than the creditor or mortgage broker.

(i) For any item that is a component of title insurance or is for conducting the closing, the introductory description "Title __" shall appear at the beginning of the label for that item.

(ii) The number of items disclosed under this paragraph (f)(3) shall not exceed 14.

(4) Total loan costs. Under the subheading "Total Loan Costs," the sum of the subtotals disclosed under paragraphs (f)(1) through (3) of this section.

(5) Item descriptions and ordering. The items listed as loan costs pursuant to this paragraph (f) shall be labeled using terminology that describes each item, subject to the requirements of paragraphs (f)(1)(i), (f)(2)(i), and (f)(3)(i) of this section.

(i) The item prescribed in paragraph (f)(1)(i) of this section for points shall be the first item listed in the disclosure pursuant to paragraph (f)(1) of this section.

(ii) All other items must be listed in alphabetical order by their labels under the applicable subheading.

(6) Use of addenda.

(i) An addendum to a form of disclosures prescribed by this section may not be used for items described in paragraph (f)(1) or (2) of this section. If the creditor is not able to itemize every service and every corresponding charge required to be disclosed in the number of lines provided by paragraph (f)(1)(ii) or (f)(2)(ii) of this section, the remaining charges shall be disclosed as an aggregate amount in the last line permitted under paragraph (f)(1)(ii) or (f)(2)(ii), as applicable, labeled "Additional Charges."

(ii) An addendum to a form of disclosures prescribed by this section may be used for items described in paragraph (f)(3) of this section. If the creditor is not able to itemize all of the charges required to be disclosed in the number of lines provided by paragraph (f)(3)(ii), the remaining charges shall be disclosed as follows:

(A) Label the last line permitted under paragraph (f)(3)(ii) with an appropriate reference to an addendum and list the remaining items on the addendum in accordance with the requirements in paragraphs (f)(3) and (5) of this section; or

(B) Disclose the remaining charges as an aggregate amount in the last line permitted under paragraph (f)(3)(ii), labeled "Additional Charges."

(g) Closing cost details; other costs. Under the master heading "Closing Cost Details," in a table under the heading "Other Costs," all costs associated with the transaction that are in addition to the costs disclosed under paragraph (f) of this section. The table shall contain the items and amounts listed under six subheadings, described in paragraphs (g)(1) through (6) of this section.

(1) Taxes and other government fees. Under the subheading "Taxes and Other Government Fees," the amounts to be paid to State and local governments for taxes and other government fees, and the subtotal of all such amounts, as follows:

(i) On the first line, the sum of all recording fees and other government fees and taxes, except for transfer taxes paid by the consumer and disclosed pursuant to paragraph (g)(1)(ii) of this section, labeled "Recording Fees and Other Taxes."

(ii) On the second line, the sum of all transfer taxes paid by the consumer, labeled "Transfer Taxes."

(iii) If an amount required to be disclosed by this paragraph (g)(1) is not charged to the consumer, the amount disclosed on the applicable line required by this paragraph (g)(1) must be blank.

(2) Prepaids. Under the subheading "Prepaids," an itemization of the amounts to be paid by the consumer in advance of the first scheduled payment, and the subtotal of all such amounts, as follows:

(i) On the first line, the number of months for which homeowner's insurance premiums are to be paid by the consumer at consummation and the total dollar amount to be paid by the consumer at consummation for such premiums, labeled "Homeowner's Insurance Premium (__ months)."

(ii) On the second line, the number of months for which mortgage insurance premiums are to be paid by the consumer at consummation and the total dollar amount to be paid by the consumer at consummation for such premiums, labeled "Mortgage Insurance Premium (__ months)."

(iii) On the third line, the amount of prepaid interest to be paid per day, the number of days for which prepaid interest will be collected, the interest rate, and the total dollar amount to be paid by the consumer at consummation for such interest, labeled "Prepaid Interest (__ per day for __ days @__ %)."

(iv) On the fourth line, the number of months for which property taxes are to be paid by the consumer at consummation and the total dollar amount to be paid by the consumer at consummation for such taxes, labeled "Property Taxes (__ months)."

(v) If an amount is not charged to the consumer for any item for which this paragraph (g)(2) prescribes a label, each of the amounts required to be disclosed on that line must be blank.

(vi) A maximum of three additional items may be disclosed under this paragraph (g)(2), and each additional item must be identified and include the applicable time period covered by the amount to be paid by the consumer at consummation and the total amount to be paid.

(3) Initial escrow payment at closing. Under the subheading "Initial Escrow Payment at Closing," an itemization of the amounts that the consumer will be expected to place into a reserve or escrow account at consummation to be applied to recurring periodic charges, and the subtotal of all such amounts, as follows:

(i) On the first line, the amount escrowed per month, the number of months covered by an escrowed amount collected at consummation, and the total amount to be paid into the escrow account by the consumer at consummation for homeowner's insurance premiums, labeled "Homeowner's Insurance __ per month for __ mo."

(ii) On the second line, the amount escrowed per month, the number of months covered by an escrowed amount collected at consummation, and the total amount to be paid into the escrow account by the consumer at consummation for mortgage insurance premiums, labeled "Mortgage Insurance __ per month for __ mo."

(iii) On the third line, the amount escrowed per month, the number of months covered by an escrowed amount collected at consummation, and the total amount to be paid into the escrow account by the consumer at consummation for property taxes, labeled "Property Taxes __ per month for __ mo."

(iv) If an amount is not charged to the consumer for any item for which this paragraph (g)(3) prescribes a label, each of the amounts required to be disclosed on that line must be blank.

(v) A maximum of five items may be disclosed pursuant to this paragraph (g)(3) in addition to the items described in paragraph (g)(3)(i) through (iii) of this section, and each such additional item must be identified with a descriptive label and include the applicable amount per month, the number of months collected at consummation, and the total amount to be paid.

(4) Other. Under the subheading "Other," an itemization of any other amounts in connection with the transaction that the consumer is likely to pay or has contracted with a person other than the creditor or loan originator to pay at closing and of which the creditor is aware at the time of issuing the Loan Estimate, a descriptive label of each such amount, and the subtotal of all such amounts.

(i) For any item that is a component of title insurance, the introductory description "Title __" shall appear at the beginning of the label for that item.

(ii) The parenthetical description "(optional)" shall appear at the end of the label for items disclosing any premiums paid for separate insurance, warranty, guarantee, or event-coverage products.

(iii) The number of items disclosed under this paragraph (g)(4) shall not exceed five.

(5) Total other costs. Under the subheading "Total Other Costs," the sum of the subtotals disclosed pursuant to paragraphs (g)(1) through (4) of this section.

(6) Total closing costs. Under the subheading "Total Closing Costs," the component amounts and their sum, as follows:

(i) The sum of the amounts disclosed as loan costs and other costs under paragraphs (f)(4) and (g)(5) of this section, labeled "D + I"; and

(ii) The amount of any lender credits, disclosed as a negative number with the label "Lender Credits" provided that, if no such amount is disclosed, the amount must be blank.

(7) Item descriptions and ordering. The items listed as other costs pursuant to this paragraph (g) shall be labeled using terminology that describes each item.

(i) The items prescribed in paragraphs (g)(1)(i) and (ii), (g)(2)(i) through (iv), and (g)(3)(i) through (iii) of this section must be listed in the order prescribed as the initial items under the applicable subheading, with any additional items to follow.

(ii) All additional items must be listed in alphabetical order under the applicable subheading.

(8) Use of addenda. An addendum to a form of disclosures prescribed by this section may not be used for items required to be disclosed by this paragraph (g). If the creditor is not able to itemize all of the charges described in this paragraph (g) in the number of lines provided by paragraphs (g)(2)(vi), (3)(v), or (4)(iii) of this section, the remaining charges shall be disclosed as an aggregate amount in the last line permitted under paragraphs (g)(2)(vi), (g)(3)(v), or (g)(4)(iii), as applicable, using the label "Additional Charges."

(h) Calculating cash to close.

(1) For all transactions. Under the master heading "Closing Cost Details," under the heading "Calculating Cash to Close," the total amount of cash or other funds that must be provided by the consumer at consummation, with an itemization of that amount into the following component amounts:

(i) Total closing costs. The amount disclosed under paragraph (g)(6) of this section, labeled "Total Closing Costs";

(ii) Closing costs to be financed. The amount of any closing costs to be paid out of loan proceeds, disclosed as a negative number, labeled "Closing Costs Financed (Paid from your Loan Amount)";

(iii) Down payment and other funds from borrower. Labeled "Down Payment/Funds from Borrower":

(A)(1) In a purchase transaction as defined in paragraph (a)(9)(i) of this section, the amount determined by subtracting the sum of the loan amount disclosed under paragraph (b)(1) of this section and any amount of existing loans assumed or taken subject to that will be disclosed under § 1026.38(j)(2)(iv) from the sale price of the property disclosed under paragraph (a)(7)(i) of this section, except as required by paragraph (h)(1)(iii)(A)(2) of this section;

(2) In a purchase transaction as defined in paragraph (a)(9)(i) of this section that is a simultaneous subordinate financing transaction or that involves improvements to be made on the property, or when the sum of the loan amount disclosed under paragraph (b)(1) of this section and any amount of existing loans assumed or taken subject to that will be disclosed under § 1026.38(j)(2)(iv) exceeds the sale price of the property disclosed under paragraph (a)(7)(i) of this section, the amount of estimated funds from the consumer as determined in accordance with paragraph (h)(1)(v) of this section; or

(B) In all transactions not subject to paragraph (h)(1)(iii)(A) of this section, the amount of estimated funds from the consumer as determined in accordance with paragraph (h)(1)(v) of this section;

(iv) Deposit.

(A) In a purchase transaction as defined in paragraph (a)(9)(i) of this section, the amount that is paid to the seller or held in trust or escrow by an attorney or other party under the terms of the agreement for the sale of the property, disclosed as a negative number, labeled "Deposit";

(B) In all transactions other than purchase transactions as defined in paragraph (a)(9)(i) of this section, the amount of $0, labeled "Deposit";

(v) Funds for borrower. The amount of funds for the consumer, labeled "Funds for Borrower." The amount of the down payment and other funds from the consumer disclosed under paragraph (h)(1)(iii)(A)(2) or (h)(1)(iii)(B) of this section, as applicable, and of funds for the consumer disclosed under this paragraph (h)(1)(v), are determined by subtracting the sum of the loan amount disclosed under paragraph (b)(1) of this section and any amount of existing loans assumed or taken subject to that will be disclosed under § 1026.38(j)(2)(iv) (excluding any closing costs financed disclosed under paragraph (h)(1)(ii) of this section) from the total amount of all existing debt being satisfied in the transaction;

(A) If the calculation under this paragraph (h)(1)(v) yields an amount that is a positive number, such amount is disclosed under paragraph (h)(1)(iii)(A)(2) or (h)(1)(iii)(B) of this section, as applicable, and $0 is disclosed under this paragraph (h)(1)(v);

(B) If the calculation under this paragraph (h)(1)(v) yields an amount that is a negative number, such amount is disclosed under this paragraph (h)(1)(v) as a negative number, and $0 is disclosed under paragraph (h)(1)(iii)(A)(2) or (h)(1)(iii)(B) of this section, as applicable;

(C) If the calculation under this paragraph (h)(1)(v) yields $0, then $0 is disclosed under paragraph (h)(1)(iii)(A)(2) or (h)(1)(iii)(B) of this section, as applicable, and under this paragraph (h)(1)(v);

(vi) Seller credits. The total amount that the seller will pay for total loan costs as determined by paragraph (f)(4) of this section and total other costs as determined by paragraph (g)(5) of this section, to the extent known, disclosed as a negative number, labeled "Seller Credits";

(vii) Adjustments and other credits. The amount of all loan costs determined under paragraph (f) of this section and other costs determined under paragraph (g) of this section that are paid by persons other than the loan originator, creditor, consumer, or seller, together with any other amounts not otherwise disclosed under paragraph (f) or (g) of this section that are required to be paid by the consumer at closing in a transaction disclosed under paragraph (h)(1)(iii)(A)(1) of this section or pursuant to a purchase and sale contract, labeled "Adjustments and Other Credits"; and

(viii) Estimated Cash to Close. The sum of the amounts disclosed under paragraphs (h)(1)(i) through (vii) of this section labeled "Cash to Close."

(2) Optional alternative calculating cash to close table for transactions without a seller, or for simultaneous subordinate financing. For transactions that do not involve a seller or for simultaneous subordinate financing, instead of the table described in paragraph (h)(1) above, the creditor may alternatively provide, in a separate table, under the master heading "Closing Cost Details," under the heading "Calculating Cash to Close," the total amount of cash or other funds that must be provided by the consumer at consummation with an itemization of that amount into the following component amounts:

(i) Loan amount. The amount disclosed under paragraph (b)(1) of this section, labeled "Loan Amount";

(ii) Total closing costs. The amount disclosed under paragraph (g)(6) of this section, disclosed as a negative number, if the amount disclosed under paragraph (g)(6) of this section is a positive number and disclosed as a positive number if the amount disclosed under paragraph (g)(6) of this section is a negative number, labeled "Total Closing Costs";

(iii) Payoffs and payments. The total amount of payoffs and payments to be made to third parties not otherwise disclosed pursuant to paragraphs (f) and (g) of this section, labeled "Total Payoffs and Payments";

(iv) Cash to or from consumer. The amount of cash or other funds due from or to the consumer and a statement of whether the disclosed estimated amount is due from or to the consumer, calculated by the sum of the amounts disclosed under paragraphs (h)(2)(i) through (iii) of this section, labeled "Cash to Close"; and

(v) Closing costs financed. The sum of the amounts disclosed under paragraphs (h)(2)(i) and (iii) of this section, but only to the extent that the sum is greater than zero and less than or equal to the sum disclosed under paragraph (g)(6) of this section, labeled "Closing Costs Financed (Paid from your Loan Amount)."

(i) Adjustable payment table. If the periodic principal and interest payment may change after consummation but not based on an adjustment to the interest rate, or if the transaction is a seasonal payment product as described in paragraph (a)(10)(ii)(E) of this section, a separate table under the master heading "Closing Cost Details" required by paragraph (f) of this section and under the heading "Adjustable Payment (AP) Table" that contains the following information and satisfies the following requirements:

(1) Interest only payments. Whether the transaction is an interest only product pursuant to paragraph (a)(10)(ii)(B) of this section as an affirmative or negative answer to the question "Interest Only Payments?" and, if an affirmative answer is disclosed, the period during which interest only periodic payments are scheduled.

(2) Optional payments. Whether the terms of the legal obligation expressly provide that the consumer may elect to pay a specified periodic principal and interest payment in an amount other than the scheduled amount of the payment, as an affirmative or negative answer to the question "Optional Payments?" and, if an affirmative answer is disclosed, the period during which the consumer may elect to make such payments.

(3) Step payments. Whether the transaction is a step payment product pursuant to paragraph (a)(10)(ii)(C) of this section as an affirmative or negative answer to the question "Step Payments?" and, if an affirmative answer is disclosed, the period during which the regular periodic payments are scheduled to increase.

(4) Seasonal payments. Whether the transaction is a seasonal payment product pursuant to paragraph (a)(10)(ii)(E) of this section as an affirmative or negative answer to the question "Seasonal Payments?" and, if an affirmative answer is disclosed, the period during which periodic payments are not scheduled.

(5) Principal and interest payments. Under the subheading "Principal and Interest Payments," which subheading is immediately preceded by the applicable unit-period, the following information:

(i) The number of the payment of the first periodic principal and interest payment that may change under the terms of the legal obligation disclosed under this paragraph (i), counting from the first periodic payment due after consummation, and the amount or range of the periodic principal and interest payment for such payment, labeled "First Change/Amount";

(ii) The frequency of subsequent changes to the periodic principal and interest payment, labeled "Subsequent Changes"; and

(iii) The maximum periodic principal and interest payment that may occur during the term of the transaction, and the first periodic principal and interest payment that can reach such maximum, counting from the first periodic payment due after consummation, labeled "Maximum Payment."

(j) Adjustable interest rate table. If the interest rate may increase after consummation, a separate table under the master heading "Closing Cost Details" required by paragraph (f) of this section and under the heading "Adjustable Interest Rate (AIR) Table" that contains the following information and satisfies the following requirements:

(1) Index and margin. If the interest rate may adjust and the product type is not a "Step Rate" under paragraph (a)(10)(i)(B) of this section, the index upon which the adjustments to the interest rate are based and the margin that is added to the index to determine the interest rate, if any, labeled "Index + Margin."

(2) Increases in interest rate. If the product type is a "Step Rate" and not also an "Adjustable Rate" under paragraph (a)(10)(i)(A) of this section, the maximum amount of any adjustments to the interest rate that are scheduled and pre-determined, labeled "Interest Rate Adjustments."

(3) Initial interest rate. The interest rate at consummation of the loan transaction, labeled "Initial Interest Rate."

(4) Minimum and maximum interest rate. The minimum and maximum interest rates for the loan, after any introductory period expires, labeled "Minimum/Maximum Interest Rate."

(5) Frequency of adjustments. The following information, under the subheading "Change Frequency":

(i) The month when the interest rate after consummation may first change, calculated from the date interest for the first scheduled periodic payment begins to accrue, labeled "First Change"; and

(ii) The frequency of interest rate adjustments after the initial adjustment to the interest rate, labeled, "Subsequent Changes."

(6) Limits on interest rate changes. The following information, under the subheading "Limits on Interest Rate Changes":

(i) The maximum possible change for the first adjustment of the interest rate after consummation, labeled "First Change"; and

(ii) The maximum possible change for subsequent adjustments of the interest rate after consummation, labeled "Subsequent Changes."

(k) Contact information. Under the master heading, "Additional Information About This Loan," the following information:

(1) The name and Nationwide Mortgage Licensing System and Registry identification number (NMLSR ID)(labeled "NMLS ID/License ID") for the creditor (labeled "Lender") and the mortgage broker (labeled "Mortgage Broker"), if any. In the event the creditor or the mortgage broker has not been assigned an NMLSR ID, the license number or other unique identifier issued by the applicable jurisdiction or regulating body with which the creditor or mortgage broker is licensed and/or registered shall be disclosed, with the abbreviation for the State of the applicable jurisdiction or regulatory body stated before the word "License" in the label, if any;

(2) The name and NMLSR ID of the individual loan officer (labeled "Loan Officer" and "NMLS ID/License ID," respectively) of the creditor and the mortgage broker, if any, who is the primary contact for the consumer. In the event the individual loan officer has not been assigned an NMLSR ID, the license number or other unique identifier issued by the applicable jurisdiction or regulating body with which the loan officer is licensed and/or registered shall be disclosed with the abbreviation for the State of the applicable jurisdiction or regulatory body stated before the word "License" in the label, if any; and

(3) The email address and telephone number of the loan officer (labeled "Email" and "Phone," respectively).

(*l*) Comparisons. Under the master heading, "Additional Information About This Loan" required by paragraph (k) of this section, in a separate table under the heading "Comparisons" along with the statement "Use these measures to compare this loan with other loans":

(1) In five years. Using the label "In 5 Years":

(i) The total principal, interest, mortgage insurance, and loan costs scheduled to be paid through the end of the 60th month after the due date of the first periodic payment, expressed as a dollar amount, along with the statement "Total you will have paid in principal, interest, mortgage insurance, and loan costs"; and

(ii) The principal scheduled to be paid through the end of the 60th month after the due date of the first periodic payment, expressed as a dollar amount, along with the statement "Principal you will have paid off."

(2) Annual percentage rate. The "Annual Percentage Rate," using that term and the abbreviation "APR" and expressed as a percentage, and the following statement: "Your costs over the loan term expressed as a rate. This is not your interest rate."

(3) Total interest percentage. The total amount of interest that the consumer will pay over the life of the loan, expressed as a percentage of the amount of credit extended, using the term "Total Interest Percentage," the abbreviation "TIP," and the statement "The total amount of interest that you will pay over the loan term as a percentage of your loan amount."

(m) Other considerations. Under the master heading "Additional Information About This Loan" required by paragraph (k) of this section and under the heading "Other Considerations":

(1) Appraisal. For transactions subject to 15 U.S.C. 1639h or 1691(e), as implemented in this part or Regulation B, 12 CFR part 1002, respectively, a statement, labeled "Appraisal," that:

(i) The creditor may order an appraisal to determine the value of the property identified in paragraph (a)(6) of this section and may charge the consumer for that appraisal;

(ii) The creditor will promptly provide the consumer a copy of any appraisal, even if the transaction is not consummated; and

(iii) The consumer may choose to pay for an additional appraisal of the property for the consumer's use.

(2) Assumption. A statement of whether a subsequent purchaser of the property may be permitted to assume the remaining loan obligation on its original terms, labeled "Assumption."

(3) Homeowner's insurance. At the option of the creditor, a statement that homeowner's insurance is required on the property and that the consumer may choose the insurance provider, labeled "Homeowner's Insurance."

(4) Late payment. A statement detailing any charge that may be imposed for a late payment, stated as a dollar amount or percentage charge of the late payment amount, and the number of days that a payment must be late to trigger the late payment fee, labeled "Late Payment."

(5) Refinance. The following statement, labeled "Refinance": "Refinancing this loan will depend on your future financial situation, the property value, and market conditions. You may not be able to refinance this loan."

(6) Servicing. A statement of whether the creditor intends to service the loan or transfer the loan to another servicer, labeled "Servicing."

(7) Liability after foreclosure. If the purpose of the credit transaction is to refinance an extension of credit as described in paragraph (a)(9)(ii) of this section, a brief statement that certain State law protections against liability for any deficiency after foreclosure may be lost, the potential consequences of the loss of such protections, and a statement that the consumer should consult an attorney for additional information, labeled "Liability after Foreclosure."

(8) Construction loans. In transactions involving new construction, where the creditor reasonably expects that settlement will occur more than 60 days after the provision of the loan estimate, at the creditor's option, a clear and conspicuous statement that the creditor may issue a revised disclosure any time prior to 60 days before consummation, pursuant to § 1026.19(e)(3)(iv)(F).

(n) Signature statement.

(1) At the creditor's option, under the master heading required by paragraph (k) of this section and under the heading "Confirm Receipt," a line for the signatures of the consumers in the transaction. If the creditor includes a line for the consumer's signature, the creditor must disclose the following above the signature line: "By signing, you are only confirming that you have received this form. You do not have to accept this loan because you have signed or received this form."

(2) If the creditor does not include a line for the consumer's signature, the creditor must disclose the following statement under the heading "Other Considerations" required by paragraph (m) of this section, labeled "Loan Acceptance": "You do not have to accept this loan because you have received this form or signed a loan application."

(*o*) Form of disclosures.

(1) General requirements.

(i) The creditor shall make the disclosures required by this section clearly and conspicuously in writing, in a form that the consumer may keep. The disclosures also shall be grouped together and segregated from everything else.

(ii) Except as provided in paragraph (*o*)(5) of this section, the disclosures shall contain only the information required by paragraphs (a) through (n) of this section and shall be made in the same order, and positioned relative to the master headings, headings, subheadings, labels, and similar designations in the same manner, as shown in form H-24, set forth in appendix H to this part.

(2) Headings and labels. If a master heading, heading, subheading, label, or similar designation contains the word "estimated" or a capital letter designation in form H-24, set forth in appendix H to this part, that heading, label, or similar designation shall contain the word "estimated" and the applicable capital letter designation.

(3) Form. Except as provided in paragraph (*o*)(5) of this section:

(i) For a transaction subject to § 1026.19(e) that is a federally related mortgage loan, as defined in Regulation X, 12 CFR 1024.2, the disclosures must be made using form H-24, set forth in appendix H to this part.

(ii) For any other transaction subject to this section, the disclosures must be made with headings, content, and format substantially similar to form H-24, set forth in appendix H to this part.

(iii) The disclosures required by this section may be provided to the consumer in electronic form, subject to compliance with the consumer consent and other applicable provisions of the Electronic Signatures in Global and National Commerce Act (15 U.S.C. 7001 et seq.).

(4) Rounding.

(i) Nearest dollar.

(A) The dollar amounts required to be disclosed by paragraphs (b)(6) and (7), (c)(1)(iii), (c)(2)(ii) and (iii), (c)(4)(ii), (f), (g), (h), (i), and (*l*) of this section shall be rounded to the nearest whole dollar, except that the per-diem dollar amount required to be disclosed by paragraph (g)(2)(iii) of this section and the monthly dollar amounts required to be disclosed by paragraphs (g)(3)(i) through (iii) and (g)(3)(v) of this section shall not be rounded.

(B) The dollar amount required to be disclosed by paragraph (b)(1) of this section shall not be rounded, and if the amount is a whole number then the amount disclosed shall be truncated at the decimal point.

(C) The dollar amounts required to be disclosed by paragraph (c)(2)(iv) of this section shall be rounded to the nearest whole dollar, if any of the component amounts are required by paragraph (*o*)(4)(i)(A) of this section to be rounded to the nearest whole dollar.

(ii) Percentages. The percentage amounts required to be disclosed under paragraphs (b)(2) and (6), (f)(1)(i), (g)(2)(iii), (j), and (*l*)(2) and (3) of this section shall be disclosed by rounding the exact amounts to three decimal places and then dropping any trailing zeros that occur to the right of the decimal place.

(5) Exceptions.

(i) Unit-period. Wherever the form or this section uses "monthly" to describe the frequency of any payments or uses "month" to describe the applicable unit-period, the creditor shall substitute the appropriate term to reflect the fact that the transaction's terms provide for other than monthly periodic payments, such as bi-weekly or quarterly payments.

(ii) Translation. The form may be translated into languages other than English, and creditors may modify form H-24 of appendix H to this part to the extent that translation prevents the headings, labels, designations, and required disclosure items under this section from fitting in the space provided on form H-24.

(iii) Logo or slogan. The creditor providing the form may use a logo for, and include a slogan with, the information required by paragraph (a)(3) of this section in any font size or type, provided that such logo or slogan does not cause the information required by paragraph (a)(3) of this section to exceed the space provided for that information, as illustrated in form H-24 of appendix H to this part. If the creditor does not use a logo for the information required by paragraph (a)(3) of this section, the information shall be disclosed in a similar format as form H-24.

(iv) Business card. The creditor may physically attach a business card over the information required to be disclosed by paragraph (a)(3) of this section.

(v) Administrative information. The creditor may insert at the bottom of each page under the disclosures required by this section as illustrated by form H-24 of appendix H to this part, any administrative information, text, or codes that assist in identification of the form or the information disclosed on the form, provided that the space provided on form H-24 of appendix H to this part for any of the information required by this section is not altered.

§ 1026.38 Content of disclosures for certain mortgage transactions (Closing Disclosure).

For each transaction subject to § 1026.19(f), the creditor shall disclose the information in this section:

(a) General information.

(1) Form title. The title of the form, "Closing Disclosure," using that term.

(2) Form purpose. The following statement: "This form is a statement of final loan terms and closing costs. Compare this document with your Loan Estimate."

(3) Closing information. Under the heading "Closing Information":

(i) Date issued. The date the disclosures required by this section are delivered to the consumer, labeled "Date Issued."

(ii) Closing date. The date of consummation, labeled "Closing Date."

(iii) Disbursement date. The date the amount disclosed under paragraph (j)(3)(iii) (cash to close from or to borrower) or (k)(3)(iii) (cash from or to seller) of this section is expected to be paid in a purchase transaction under § 1026.37(a)(9)(i) to the consumer or seller, respectively, as applicable, except as provided in comment 38(a)(3)(iii)–1, or the date some or all of the loan amount disclosed under paragraph (b) of this section is expected to be paid to the consumer or a third party other than a settlement agent in a transaction that is not a purchase transaction under § 1026.37(a)(9)(i), labeled "Disbursement Date."

(iv) Settlement agent. The name of the settlement agent conducting the closing, labeled "Settlement Agent."

(v) File number. The number assigned to the transaction by the settlement agent for identification purposes, labeled "File # ."

(vi) Property. The address or location of the property required to be disclosed under § 1026.37(a)(6), labeled "Property."

(vii) Sale price. (A) In credit transactions where there is a seller, the contract sale price of the property identified in paragraph (a)(3)(vi) of this section, labeled "Sale Price."

(B) In credit transactions where there is no seller, the appraised value of the property identified in paragraph (a)(3)(vi) of this section, labeled "Appraised Prop. Value."

(4) Transaction information. Under the heading "Transaction Information":

(i) Borrower. The consumer's name and mailing address, labeled "Borrower."

(ii) Seller. Where applicable, the seller's name and mailing address, labeled "Seller."

(iii) Lender. The name of the creditor making the disclosure, labeled "Lender."

(5) Loan information. Under the heading "Loan Information":

(i) Loan term. The information required to be disclosed under § 1026.37(a)(8), labeled "Loan Term."

(ii) Purpose. The information required to be disclosed under § 1026.37(a)(9), labeled "Purpose."

(iii) Product. The information required to be disclosed under § 1026.37(a)(10), labeled "Product."

(iv) Loan type. The information required to be disclosed under § 1026.37(a)(11), labeled "Loan Type."

(v) Loan identification number. The information required to be disclosed under § 1026.37(a)(12), labeled "Loan ID # ."

(vi) Mortgage insurance case number. The case number for any mortgage insurance policy, if required by the creditor, labeled "MIC #."

(b) Loan terms. A separate table under the heading "Loan Terms" that includes the information required by § 1026.37(b).

(c) Projected payments. A separate table, under the heading "Projected Payments," that includes and satisfies the following information and requirements:

(1) Projected payments or range of payments. The information required to be disclosed pursuant to § 1026.37(c)(1) through (4), other than § 1026.37(c)(4)(vi). In disclosing estimated escrow payments as described in § 1026.37(c)(2)(iii) and (c)(4)(ii), the amount disclosed on the Closing Disclosure:

(i) For transactions subject to RESPA, is determined under the escrow account analysis described in Regulation X, 12 CFR 1024.17;

(ii) For transactions not subject to RESPA, may be determined under the escrow account analysis described in Regulation X, 12 CFR 1024.17 or in the manner set forth in § 1026.37(c)(5).

(2) Estimated taxes, insurance, and assessments. A reference to the disclosure required by paragraph (*l*)(7) of this section.

(d) Costs at closing.

(1) Costs at closing table. In a separate table, under the heading "Costs at Closing":

(i) Labeled "Closing Costs," the sum of the dollar amounts disclosed pursuant to paragraphs (f)(4), (g)(5), and (h)(3) of this section, together with:

(A) A statement that the amount disclosed pursuant to paragraph (d)(1)(i) of this section includes the amounts disclosed pursuant to paragraphs (f)(4), (g)(5), and (h)(3) of this section;

(B) The dollar amount disclosed pursuant to paragraph (f)(4) of this section, labeled "Loan Costs";

(C) The dollar amount disclosed pursuant to paragraph (g)(5) of this section, labeled "Other Costs";

(D) The dollar amount disclosed pursuant to paragraph (h)(3) of this section, labeled "Lender Credits"; and

(E) A statement referring the consumer to the tables disclosed pursuant to paragraphs (f) and (g) of this section for details.

(ii) Labeled "Cash to Close," the sum of the dollar amounts calculated in accordance with paragraph (i)(9)(ii) of this section, together with:

(A) A statement that the amount disclosed pursuant to paragraph (d)(1)(ii) of this section includes the amount disclosed pursuant to paragraph (d)(1)(i) of this section; and

(B) A statement referring the consumer to the table required pursuant to paragraph (i) of this section for details.

(2) Alternative table for transactions without a seller, or for simultaneous subordinate financing. For transactions that do not involve a seller, or for simultaneous subordinate financing, if the creditor disclosed the optional alternative table pursuant to § 1026.37(d)(2), the creditor shall disclose, with the label "Cash to Close," instead of the sum of the dollar amounts described in paragraph (d)(1)(ii) of this section:

(i) The amount calculated in accordance with paragraph (e)(5)(ii) of this section;

(ii) A statement of whether the disclosed amount is due from or to the consumer; and

(iii) A statement referring the consumer to the table required pursuant to paragraph (e) of this section for details.

(e) Alternative calculating cash to close table for transactions without a seller or for simultaneous subordinate financing. For transactions that do not involve a seller, or for simultaneous subordinate financing, if the creditor disclosed the optional alternative table pursuant to § 1026.37(h)(2), the creditor shall disclose, instead of the table described in paragraph (i) of this section, in a separate table, under the heading "Calculating Cash to Close," together with the statement "Use this table to see what has changed from your Loan Estimate":

(1) Loan amount. Labeled "Loan Amount:"

(i) Under the subheading "Loan Estimate," the loan amount disclosed on the Loan Estimate under § 1026.37(b)(1);

(ii) Under the subheading "Final," the loan amount disclosed under paragraph (b) of this section;

(iii) Disclosed more prominently than the other disclosures under paragraph (e)(1)(i) and (ii) of this section, under the subheading "Did this change?":

(A) If the amount disclosed under paragraph (e)(1)(ii) of this section is different than the amount disclosed under paragraph (e)(1)(i) of this section (unless the difference is due to rounding), a statement of that fact along with a statement of whether this amount increased or decreased; or

(B) If the amount disclosed under paragraph (e)(1)(i) of this section is equal to the amount disclosed under paragraph (e)(1)(ii) of this section a statement of that fact.

(2) Total closing costs. Labeled "Total Closing Costs":

(i) Under the subheading "Loan Estimate," the amount disclosed on the Loan Estimate under § 1026.37(h)(2)(ii);

(ii) Under the subheading "Final," the amount disclosed under paragraph (h)(1) of this section, disclosed as a negative number if the amount disclosed under paragraph (h)(1) of this section is a positive number and disclosed as a positive number if the amount disclosed under paragraph (h)(1) of this section is a negative number; and

(iii) Disclosed more prominently than the other disclosures under this paragraph (e)(2)(i) and (ii) of this section, under the subheading "Did this change?":

(A) If the amount disclosed under paragraph (e)(2)(ii) of this section is different than the amount disclosed under paragraph (e)(2)(i) of this section (unless the difference is due to rounding):

(1) A statement of that fact;

(2) If the difference in the amounts disclosed under paragraphs (e)(2)(i) and (e)(2)(ii) is attributable to differences in itemized charges that are included in either or both subtotals, a statement that the consumer should see the total loan costs and total other costs subtotals disclosed under paragraphs (f)(4) and (g)(5) of this section (together with references to such disclosures), as applicable; and

(3) If the increase exceeds the limitations on increases in closing costs under § 1026.19(e)(3), a statement that such increase exceeds the legal limits by the dollar amount of the excess and, if any refund is provided under § 1026.19(f)(2)(v), a statement directing the consumer to the disclosure required under paragraph (h)(3) of this section or, if applicable, a statement directing the consumer to the principal reduction disclosure under paragraph (t)(5)(vii)(B) of this section. Such dollar amount shall equal the sum total of all excesses of the limitations on increases in closing costs under § 1026.19(e)(3), taking into account the different methods of calculating excesses of the limitations on increases in closing costs under § 1026.19(e)(3)(i) and (ii).

(B) If the amount disclosed under paragraph (e)(2)(i) of this section is equal to the amount disclosed under paragraph (e)(2)(ii) of this section, a statement of that fact.

(3) Closing costs paid before closing. Labeled "Closing Costs Paid Before Closing:"

(i) Under the subheading "Loan Estimate," the amount of $0;

(ii) Under the subheading "Final," any amount designated as borrower-paid before closing under paragraph (h)(2) of this section, disclosed as a positive number; and

(iii) Disclosed more prominently than the other disclosures under this paragraph (e)(3)(i) and (ii) of this section, under the subheading "Did this change?":

(A) If the amount disclosed under paragraph (e)(3)(ii) of this section is different than the amount disclosed under paragraph (e)(3)(i) of this section (unless the difference is due to rounding), a statement of that fact, along with a statement that the consumer paid such amounts prior to consummation of the transaction; or

(B) If the amount disclosed under paragraph (e)(3)(ii) of this section is equal to the amount disclosed under paragraph (e)(3)(i) of this section, a statement of that fact.

(4) Payoffs and payments. Labeled "Total Payoffs and Payments,"

(i) Under the subheading "Loan Estimate," the total payoffs and payments disclosed on the Loan Estimate under § 1026.37(h)(2)(iii);

(ii) Under the subheading "Final," the total amount of payoffs and payments made to third parties disclosed pursuant to paragraph (t)(5)(vii)(B) of this section, to the extent known, disclosed as a negative number if the amount disclosed under paragraph (t)(5)(vii)(B) of this section is a positive number and disclosed as a positive number if the amount disclosed under paragraph (t)(5)(vii)(B) of this section is a negative number;

(iii) Disclosed more prominently than the other disclosures under this paragraph (e)(4)(i) and (ii), under the subheading "Did this change?":

(A) If the amount disclosed under paragraph (e)(4)(ii) of this section is different than the amount disclosed under paragraph (e)(4)(i) of this section (unless the difference is due to rounding), a statement of that fact along with a reference to the table disclosed under paragraph (t)(5)(vii)(B) of this section; or

(B) If the amount disclosed under paragraph (e)(4)(ii) of this section is equal to the amount disclosed under paragraph (e)(4)(i) of this section, a statement of that fact.

(5) Cash to or from consumer. Labeled "Cash to Close:"

(i) Under the subheading "Loan Estimate," the estimated cash to close on the Loan Estimate together with the statement of whether the estimated amount is due from or to the consumer as disclosed under § 1026.37(h)(2)(iv);

(ii) Under the subheading "Final," the amount due from or to the consumer, calculated by the sum of the amounts disclosed under paragraphs (e)(1)(ii), (e)(2)(ii), (e)(3)(ii), and (e)(4)(ii) of this section, disclosed as a positive number, together with a statement of whether the disclosed amount is due from or to the consumer.

(6) Closing costs financed. Labeled "Closing Costs Financed (Paid from your Loan Amount)," the sum of the amounts disclosed under paragraphs (e)(1)(ii) and (e)(4)(ii) of this section, but only to the extent that the sum is greater than zero and less than or equal to the sum disclosed under paragraph (h)(1) of this section minus the sum disclosed under paragraph (h)(2) of this section designated borrower-paid before closing.

(f) Closing cost details; loan costs. Under the master heading "Closing Cost Details" with columns stating whether the charge was borrower-paid at or before closing, seller-paid at or before closing, or paid by others, all loan costs associated with the transaction, listed in a table under the heading "Loan Costs." The table shall contain the items and amounts listed under four subheadings, described in paragraphs (f)(1) through (5) of this section.

(1) Origination charges. Under the subheading "Origination Charges," and in the applicable columns as described in paragraph (f) of this section, an itemization of each amount paid for charges described in § 1026.37(f)(1), the amount of compensation paid by the creditor to a third-party loan originator along with the name of the loan originator ultimately receiving the payment, and the total of all such itemized amounts that are designated borrower-paid at or before closing.

(2) Services borrower did not shop for. Under the subheading "Services Borrower Did Not Shop For" and in the applicable columns as described in paragraph (f) of this section, an itemization of the services and corresponding costs for each of the settlement services required by the creditor for which the consumer did not shop in accordance with § 1026.19(e)(1)(vi)(A) and that are provided by persons other than the creditor or mortgage broker, the name of the person ultimately receiving the payment for each such amount, and the total of all such itemized amounts that are designated borrower-paid at or before closing. Items that were disclosed pursuant to § 1026.37(f)(3) must be disclosed under this paragraph (f)(2) if the consumer was provided a written list of settlement service providers under § 1026.19(e)(1)(vi)(C) and the consumer selected a settlement service provider contained on that written list.

(3) Services borrower did shop for. Under the subheading "Services Borrower Did Shop For" and in the applicable column as described in paragraph (f) of this section, an itemization of the services and corresponding costs for each of the settlement services required by the creditor for which the consumer shopped in accordance with § 1026.19(e)(1)(vi)(A) and that are provided by persons other than the creditor or mortgage broker, the name of the person ultimately receiving the payment for each such amount, and the total of all such itemized costs that are designated borrower-paid at or before closing. Items that were disclosed pursuant to § 1026.37(f)(3) must be disclosed under this paragraph (f)(3) if the consumer was provided a written list of settlement service providers under § 1026.19(e)(1)(vi)(C) and the consumer did not select a settlement service provider contained on that written list.

(4) Total loan costs. Under the subheading "Total Loan Costs (Borrower-Paid)," the sum of the amounts disclosed as borrower-paid pursuant to paragraph (f)(5) of this section.

(5) Subtotal of loan costs. The sum of loan costs, calculated by totaling the amounts described in paragraphs (f)(1) through (3) of this section for costs designated borrower-paid at or before closing, labeled "Loan Costs Subtotals."

(g) Closing cost details; other costs. Under the master heading "Closing Cost Details" disclosed pursuant to paragraph (f) of this section, with columns stating whether the charge was borrower-paid at or before closing, seller-paid at or before closing, or paid by others, all costs in connection with the transaction, other than those disclosed under paragraph (f) of this section, listed in a table with a heading disclosed as "Other Costs." The table shall contain the items and amounts listed under five subheadings, described in paragraphs (g)(1) through (6) of this section.

(1) Taxes and other government fees. Under the subheading "Taxes and Other Government Fees," an itemization of each amount that is expected to be paid to State and local governments for taxes and government fees and the total of all such itemized amounts that are designated borrower-paid at or before closing, as follows:

(i) On the first line:

(A) Before the columns described in paragraph (g) of this section, the total amount of fees for recording deeds and, separately, the total amount of fees for recording security instruments; and

(B) In the applicable column as described in paragraph (g) of this section, the total amounts paid for recording fees (including, but not limited to, the amounts in paragraph (g)(1)(i)(A) of this section); and

(ii) On subsequent lines, in the applicable column as described in paragraph (g) of this section, an itemization of transfer taxes, with the name of the government entity assessing the transfer tax.

(2) Prepaids. Under the subheading "Prepaids" and in the applicable column as described in paragraph (g) of this section, an itemization of each amount for charges described in § 1026.37(g)(2), the name of the person ultimately receiving the payment or government entity assessing the property tax, provided that the person ultimately receiving the payment need not be disclosed for the disclosure required by § 1026.37(g)(2)(iii) when disclosed pursuant to this paragraph, and the total of all such itemized amounts that are designated borrower-paid at or before closing.

(3) Initial escrow payment at closing. Under the subheading "Initial escrow payment at closing" and in the applicable column as described in paragraph (g) of this section, an itemization of each amount for charges described in § 1026.37(g)(3), the applicable aggregate adjustment pursuant to 12 CFR 1024.17(d)(2) along with the label "aggregate adjustment," and the total of all such itemized amounts that are designated borrower-paid at or before closing.

(4) Other. Under the subheading "Other" and in the applicable column as described in paragraph (g) of this section, an itemization of each amount for charges in connection with the transaction that are in addition to the charges disclosed under paragraphs (f) and (g)(1) through (3) for services that are required or obtained in the real estate closing by the consumer, the seller, or other party, the name of the person ultimately receiving the payment, and the total of all such itemized amounts that are designated borrower-paid at or before closing.

(i) For any cost that is a component of title insurance services, the introductory description "Title __" shall appear at the beginning of the label for that actual cost.

(ii) The parenthetical description "(optional)" shall appear at the end of the label for costs designated borrower-paid at or before closing for any premiums paid for separate insurance, warranty, guarantee, or event-coverage products.

(5) Total other costs. Under the subheading "Total Other Costs (Borrower-Paid)," the sum of the amounts disclosed as borrower-paid pursuant to paragraph (g)(6) of this section.

(6) Subtotal of costs. The sum of other costs, calculated by totaling the costs disclosed in paragraphs (g)(1) through (4) of this section designated borrower-paid at or before closing, labeled "Other Costs Subtotals."

(h) Closing cost totals.

(1) The sum of the costs disclosed as borrower-paid pursuant to paragraph (h)(2) of this section and the amount disclosed in paragraph (h)(3) of this section, under the subheading "Total Closing Costs (Borrower-Paid)."

(2) The sum of the amounts disclosed in paragraphs (f)(5) and (g)(6) of this section, designated borrower-paid at or before closing, and the sum of the costs designated seller-paid at or before closing or paid by others disclosed pursuant to paragraphs (f) and (g) of this section, labeled "Closing Costs Subtotals."

(3) The amount of lender credits as a negative number, labeled "Lender Credits" and designated borrower-paid at closing, and if a refund is provided pursuant to § 1026.19(f)(2)(v), a statement that this amount includes a credit for an amount that exceeds the limitations on increases in closing costs under § 1026.19(e)(3), and the amount of such credit under § 1026.19(f)(2)(v).

(4) The services and costs disclosed pursuant to paragraphs (f) and (g) of this section on the Closing Disclosure shall be labeled using terminology that describes the item disclosed, in a manner that is consistent with the descriptions or prescribed labels, as applicable, used for such items on the Loan Estimate pursuant to § 1026.37. The creditor must also list the items on the Closing Disclosure in the same sequential order as on the Loan Estimate pursuant to § 1026.37.

(i) Calculating cash to close. In a separate table, under the heading "Calculating Cash to Close," together with the statement "Use this table to see what has changed from your Loan Estimate":

(1) Total closing costs.

(i) Under the subheading "Loan Estimate," the "Total Closing Costs" disclosed on the Loan Estimate under § 1026.37(h)(1)(i), labeled using that term.

(ii) Under the subheading "Final," the amount disclosed under paragraph (h)(1) of this section.

(iii) Under the subheading "Did this change?," disclosed more prominently than the other disclosures under this paragraph (i)(1):

(A) If the amount disclosed under paragraph (i)(1)(ii) of this section is different than the amount disclosed under paragraph (i)(1)(i) of this section (unless the difference is due to rounding):

(1) A statement of that fact;

(2) If the difference in the "Total Closing Costs" is attributable to differences in itemized charges that are included in either or both subtotals, a statement that the consumer should see the total loan costs and total other costs subtotals disclosed under paragraphs (f)(4) and (g)(5) of this section (together with references to such disclosures), as applicable; and

(3) If the increase exceeds the limitations on increases in closing costs under § 1026.19(e)(3), a statement that such increase exceeds the legal limits by the dollar amount of the excess, and if any refund is provided under § 1026.19(f)(2)(v), a statement directing the consumer to the disclosure required under paragraph (h)(3) of this section or, if a principal reduction is used to provide the refund, a statement directing the consumer to the principal reduction disclosure under paragraph (j)(1)(v) of this section. Such dollar amount shall equal the sum total of all excesses of the limitations on increases in closing costs under § 1026.19(e)(3), taking into account the different methods of calculating excesses of the limitations on increases in closing costs under § 1026.19(e)(3)(i) and (ii).

(B) If the amount disclosed under paragraph (i)(1)(ii) of this section is equal to the amount disclosed under paragraph (i)(1)(i) of this section, a statement of that fact.

(2) Closing costs paid before closing.

(i) Under the subheading "Loan Estimate," the dollar amount "$0," labeled "Closing Costs Paid Before Closing."

(ii) Under the subheading "Final," the amount of "Total Closing Costs" disclosed under paragraph (h)(2) of this section and designated as borrower-paid before closing, stated as a negative number.

(iii) Under the subheading "Did this change?," disclosed more prominently than the other disclosures under this paragraph (i)(2):

(A) If the amount disclosed under paragraph (i)(2)(ii) of this section is different than the amount disclosed under paragraph (i)(2)(i) of this section (unless the difference is due to rounding), a statement of that fact, along with a statement that the consumer paid such amounts prior to consummation of the transaction; or

(B) If the amount disclosed under paragraph (i)(2)(ii) of this section is equal to the amount disclosed under paragraph (i)(2)(i) of this section, a statement of that fact.

(3) Closing costs financed.

(i) Under the subheading "Loan Estimate," the amount disclosed under § 1026.37(h)(1)(ii), labeled "Closing Costs Financed (Paid from your Loan Amount)."

(ii) Under the subheading "Final," the actual amount of the closing costs that are to be paid out of loan proceeds, if any, stated as a negative number.

(iii) Under the subheading "Did this change?," disclosed more prominently than the other disclosures under this paragraph (i)(3):

(A) If the amount disclosed under paragraph (i)(3)(ii) of this section is different than the amount disclosed under paragraph (i)(3)(i) of this section (unless the difference is due to rounding), a statement of that fact, along with a statement that the consumer included the closing costs in the loan amount, which increased the loan amount; or

(B) If the amount disclosed under paragraph (i)(3)(ii) of this section is equal to the amount disclosed under paragraph (i)(3)(i) of this section, a statement of that fact.

(4) Down payment/funds from borrower.

(i) Under the subheading "Loan Estimate," the amount disclosed under § 1026.37(h)(1)(iii), labeled "Down Payment/Funds from Borrower."

(ii) Under the subheading "Final":

(A)(1) In a purchase transaction as defined in § 1026.37(a)(9)(i), the amount determined by subtracting the sum of the loan amount disclosed under paragraph (b) of this section and any amount of existing loans assumed or taken subject to that is disclosed under paragraph (j)(2)(iv) of this section from the sale price of the property disclosed under paragraph (a)(3)(vii)(A) of this section, labeled "Down Payment/Funds from Borrower," except as required by paragraph (i)(4)(ii)(A)(2) of this section;

(2) In a purchase transaction as defined in § 1026.37(a)(9)(i) that is a simultaneous subordinate financing transaction or that involves improvements to be made on the property, or when the sum of the loan amount disclosed under paragraph (b) of this section and any amount of existing loans assumed or taken subject to that is disclosed under paragraph (j)(2)(iv) of this section exceeds the sale price disclosed under paragraph (a)(3)(vii)(A) of this section, the amount of funds from the consumer as determined in accordance with paragraph (i)(6)(iv) of this section labeled "Down Payment/Funds from Borrower;" or

(B) In all transactions not subject to paragraph (i)(4)(ii)(A) of this section, the amount of funds from the consumer as determined in accordance with paragraph (i)(6)(iv) of this section, labeled "Down Payment/Funds from Borrower."

(iii) Under the subheading "Did this change?," disclosed more prominently than the other disclosures under this paragraph (i)(4):

(A) If the amount disclosed under paragraph (i)(4)(ii) of this section is different than the amount disclosed under paragraph (i)(4)(i) of this section (unless the difference is due to rounding), a statement of that fact, along with a statement that the consumer increased or decreased this payment and that the consumer should see the details disclosed under paragraph (j)(1) or (j)(2) of this section, as applicable; or

(B) If the amount disclosed under paragraph (i)(4)(ii) of this section is equal to the amount disclosed under paragraph (i)(4)(i) of this section, a statement of that fact.

(5) Deposit.

(i) Under the subheading "Loan Estimate," the amount disclosed under § 1026.37(h)(1)(iv), labeled "Deposit."

(ii) Under the subheading "Final," the amount disclosed under paragraph (j)(2)(ii) of this section, stated as a negative number.

(iii) Under the subheading "Did this change?," disclosed more prominently than the other disclosures under this paragraph (i)(5):

(A) If the amount disclosed under paragraph (i)(5)(ii) of this section is different than the amount disclosed under paragraph (i)(5)(i) of this section (unless the difference is due to rounding), a statement of that fact, along with a statement that the consumer increased or decreased this payment, as applicable, and that the consumer should see the details disclosed under paragraph (j)(2)(ii) of this section; or

(B) If the amount disclosed under paragraph (i)(5)(ii) of this section is equal to the amount disclosed under paragraph (i)(5)(i) of this section, a statement of that fact.

(6) Funds for borrower.

(i) Under the subheading "Loan Estimate," the amount disclosed under § 1026.37(h)(1)(v), labeled "Funds for Borrower."

(ii) Under the subheading "Final," the "Funds for Borrower," labeled using that term, as determined in accordance with paragraph (i)(6)(iv) of this section.

(iii) Under the subheading "Did this change?," disclosed more prominently than the other disclosures under this paragraph (i)(6):

(A) If the amount disclosed under paragraph (i)(6)(ii) of this section is different than the amount disclosed under paragraph (i)(6)(i) of this section (unless the difference is due to rounding), a statement of that fact, along with a statement that the consumer's available funds from the loan amount have increased or decreased, as applicable; or

(B) If the amount disclosed under paragraph (i)(6)(ii) of this section is equal to the amount disclosed under paragraph (i)(6)(i) of this section, a statement of that fact.

(iv) The "Down Payment/Funds from Borrower" to be disclosed under paragraph (i)(4)(ii)(A)(2) or (B) of this section, as applicable, and "Funds for Borrower" to be disclosed under paragraph (i)(6)(ii) of this section are determined by subtracting the sum of the loan amount disclosed under paragraph (b) of this section and any amount for existing loans assumed or taken subject to that is disclosed under paragraph (j)(2)(iv) of this section (excluding any closing costs financed disclosed under paragraph (i)(3)(ii) of this section) from the total amount of all existing debt being satisfied in the transaction disclosed under paragraphs (j)(1)(ii), (iii), and (v) of this section.

(A) If the calculation under this paragraph (i)(6)(iv) yields an amount that is a positive number, such amount shall be disclosed under paragraph (i)(4)(ii)(A)(2) or (B) of this section, as applicable, and $0 shall be disclosed under paragraph (i)(6)(ii) of this section.

(B) If the calculation under this paragraph (i)(6)(iv) yields an amount that is a negative number, such amount shall be disclosed under paragraph (i)(6)(ii) of this section, stated as a negative number, and $0 shall be disclosed under paragraph (i)(4)(ii)(A)(2) or (i)(4)(ii)(B) of this section, as applicable.

(C) If the calculation under this paragraph (i)(6)(iv) yields $0, $0 shall be disclosed under paragraph (i)(4)(ii)(A)(2) or (i)(4)(ii)(B) of this section, as applicable, and under paragraph (i)(6)(ii) of this section.

(7) Seller credits.

(i) Under the subheading "Loan Estimate," the amount disclosed under § 1026.37(h)(1)(vi), labeled "Seller Credits."

(ii) Under the subheading "Final," the amount disclosed under paragraph (j)(2)(v) of this section, stated as a negative number.

(iii) Under the subheading "Did this change?," disclosed more prominently than the other disclosures under this paragraph (i)(7):

(A) If the amount disclosed under paragraph (i)(7)(ii) of this section is different than the amount disclosed under paragraph (i)(7)(i) of this section (unless the difference is due to rounding), a statement of that fact, along with a statement that the consumer should see the details disclosed:

(1) Under paragraph (j)(2)(v) of this section and in the seller-paid column under paragraphs (f) and (g) of this section; or

(2) Under either paragraph (j)(2)(v) of this section or in the seller-paid column under paragraphs (f) or (g) of this section, if the details are only disclosed under paragraph (j)(2)(v) or paragraph (f) or (g); or

(B) If the amount disclosed under paragraph (i)(7)(ii) of this section is equal to the amount disclosed under paragraph (i)(7)(i) of this section, a statement of that fact.

(8) Adjustments and other credits.

(i) Under the subheading "Loan Estimate," the amount disclosed on the Loan Estimate under § 1026.37(h)(1)(vii), labeled "Adjustments and Other Credits."

(ii) Under the subheading "Final," the amount equal to the total of the amounts disclosed under paragraphs (j)(1)(iii) and (v) of this section, to the extent amounts in paragraphs (j)(1)(iii) and (v) were not included in the calculation required by paragraph (i)(4) or (6) of this section, and paragraphs (j)(1)(vi) through (x) of this section, reduced by the total of the amounts disclosed under paragraphs (j)(2)(vi) through (xi) of this section.

(iii) Under the subheading "Did this change?," disclosed more prominently than the other disclosures under this paragraph (i)(8):

(A) If the amount disclosed under paragraph (i)(8)(ii) of this section is different than the amount disclosed under paragraph (i)(8)(i) of this section (unless the difference is due to rounding), a statement of that fact, along with a statement that the consumer should see the details disclosed under paragraphs (j)(1)(iii) and (v) through (x) and (j)(2)(vi) through (xi) of this section, as applicable; or

(B) If the amount disclosed under paragraph (i)(8)(ii) of this section is equal to the amount disclosed under paragraph (i)(8)(i) of this section, a statement of that fact.

(9) Cash to close.

(i) Under the subheading "Loan Estimate," the amount disclosed on the Loan Estimate under § 1026.37(h)(1)(viii), labeled "Cash to Close" and disclosed more prominently than the other disclosures under this paragraph (i).

(ii) Under the subheading "Final," the sum of the amounts disclosed under paragraphs (i)(1) through (i)(8) of this section under the subheading "Final," and disclosed more prominently than the other disclosures under this paragraph (i).

(j) Summary of borrower's transaction. Under the heading "Summaries of Transactions," with a statement to "Use this table to see a summary of your transaction," two separate tables are disclosed. The first table shall include, under the subheading "Borrower's Transaction," the following information and shall satisfy the following requirements:

(1) Itemization of amounts due from borrower.

(i) The total amount due from the consumer at closing, calculated as the sum of items required to be disclosed by paragraph (j)(1)(ii) through (x) of this section, excluding items paid from funds other than closing funds as described in paragraph (j)(4)(i) of this section, labeled "Due from Borrower at Closing";

(ii) The amount of the contract sales price of the property being sold in a purchase real estate transaction, excluding the price of any tangible personal property if the consumer and seller have agreed to a separate price for such items, labeled "Sale Price of Property";

(iii) The amount of the sales price of any tangible personal property excluded from the contract sales price pursuant to paragraph (j)(1)(ii) of this section, labeled "Sale Price of Any Personal Property Included in Sale";

(iv) The total amount of closing costs disclosed that are designated borrower-paid at closing, as the sum of the amounts calculated pursuant to paragraphs (h)(2) and (3) of this section, labeled "Closing Costs Paid at Closing";

(v) A description and the amount of any additional items that the seller has paid prior to the real estate closing, but reimbursed by the consumer at the real estate closing, and a description and the amount of any other items owed by the consumer at the real estate closing not otherwise disclosed pursuant to paragraph (f), (g), or (j) of this section;

(vi) The description "Adjustments for Items Paid by Seller in Advance";

(vii) The prorated amount of any prepaid taxes due from the consumer to reimburse the seller at the real estate closing, and the time period corresponding to that amount, labeled "City/Town Taxes";

(viii) The prorated amount of any prepaid taxes due from the consumer to reimburse the seller at the real estate closing, and the time period corresponding to that amount, labeled "County Taxes";

(ix) The prorated amount of any prepaid assessments due from the consumer to reimburse the seller at the real estate closing, and the time period corresponding to that amount, labeled "Assessments"; and

(x) A description and the amount of any additional items paid by the seller prior to the real estate closing that are due from the consumer at the real estate closing.

(2) Itemization of amounts already paid by or on behalf of borrower.

(i) The sum of the amounts disclosed in this paragraphs (j)(2)(ii) through (xi) of this section, excluding items paid from funds other than closing funds as described in paragraph (j)(4)(i) of this section, labeled "Paid Already by or on Behalf of Borrower at Closing";

(ii) Any amount that is paid to the seller or held in trust or escrow by an attorney or other party under the terms of the agreement for the sale of the property, labeled "Deposit";

(iii) The amount of the consumer's new loan amount or first user loan as disclosed pursuant to paragraph (b) of this section, labeled "Loan Amount";

(iv) The amount of any existing loans that the consumer is assuming, or any loans subject to which the consumer is taking title to the property, labeled "Existing Loan(s) Assumed or Taken Subject to";

(v) The total amount of money that the seller will provide at the real estate closing as a lump sum not otherwise itemized to pay for loan costs as determined by paragraph (f) of this section and other costs as determined by paragraph (g) of this section and any other obligations of the seller to be paid directly to the consumer, labeled "Seller Credit";

(vi) Descriptions and amounts of other items paid by or on behalf of the consumer and not otherwise disclosed under paragraphs (f), (g), (h), and (j)(2) of this section, labeled "Other Credits," and descriptions and the amounts of any additional amounts owed the consumer but payable to the seller before the real estate closing, under the heading "Adjustments";

(vii) The description "Adjustments for Items Unpaid by Seller";

(viii) The prorated amount of any unpaid taxes due from the seller to reimburse the consumer at the real estate closing, and the time period corresponding to that amount, labeled "City/Town Taxes";

(ix) The prorated amount of any unpaid taxes due from the seller to reimburse the consumer at the real estate closing, and the time period corresponding to that amount, labeled "County Taxes";

(x) The prorated amount of any unpaid assessments due from the seller to reimburse the consumer at the real estate closing, and the time period corresponding to that amount, labeled "Assessments"; and

(xi) A description and the amount of any additional items which have not yet been paid and which the consumer is expected to pay after the real estate closing, but which are attributable in part to a period of time prior to the real estate closing.

(3) Calculation of borrower's transaction. Under the label "Calculation":

(i) The amount disclosed pursuant to paragraph (j)(1)(i) of this section, labeled "Total Due from Borrower at Closing";

(ii) The amount disclosed pursuant to paragraph (j)(2)(i) of this section, if any, disclosed as a negative number, labeled "Total Paid Already by or on Behalf of Borrower at Closing"; and

(iii) A statement that the disclosed amount is due from or to the consumer, and the amount due from or to the consumer at the real estate closing, calculated by the sum of the amounts disclosed under paragraphs (j)(3)(i) and (ii) of this section, labeled "Cash to Close."

(4) Items paid outside of closing funds.

(i) Costs that are not paid from closing funds but that would otherwise be disclosed in the table required pursuant to paragraph (j) of this section, should be marked with the phrase "Paid Outside of Closing" or the abbreviation "P.O.C." and include the name of the party making the payment.

(ii) For purposes of this paragraph (j), "closing funds" means funds collected and disbursed at real estate closing.

(k) Summary of seller's transaction. Under the heading "Summaries of Transactions" required by paragraph (j) of this section, a separate table under the subheading "Seller's Transaction," that includes the following information and satisfies the following requirements:

(1) Itemization of amounts due to seller.

(i) The total amount due to the seller at the real estate closing, calculated as the sum of items required to be disclosed pursuant to paragraphs (k)(1)(ii) through (ix) of this section, excluding items paid from funds other than closing funds as described in paragraph (k)(4)(i) of this section, labeled "Due to Seller at Closing";

(ii) The amount of the contract sales price of the property being sold, excluding the price of any tangible personal property if the consumer and seller have agreed to a separate price for such items, labeled "Sale Price of Property";

(iii) The amount of the sales price of any tangible personal property excluded from the contract sales price pursuant to paragraph (k)(1)(ii) of this section, labeled "Sale Price of Any Personal Property Included in Sale";

(iv) A description and the amount of other items paid to the seller by the consumer pursuant to the contract of sale or other agreement, such as charges that were not disclosed pursuant to § 1026.37 on the Loan Estimate or items paid by the seller prior to the real estate closing but reimbursed by the consumer at the real estate closing;

(v) The description "Adjustments for Items Paid by Seller in Advance";

(vi) The prorated amount of any prepaid taxes due from the consumer to reimburse the seller at the real estate closing, and the time period corresponding to that amount, labeled "City/Town Taxes";

(vii) The prorated amount of any prepaid taxes due from the consumer to reimburse the seller at the real estate closing, and the time period corresponding to that amount, labeled "County Taxes";

(viii) The prorated amount of any prepaid assessments due from the consumer to reimburse the seller at the real estate closing, and the time period corresponding to that amount, labeled "Assessments"; and

(ix) A description and the amount of additional items paid by the seller prior to the real estate closing that are reimbursed by the consumer at the real estate closing.

(2) Itemization of amounts due from seller.

(i) The total amount due from the seller at the real estate closing, calculated as the sum of items required to be disclosed pursuant to paragraphs (k)(2)(ii) through (xiii) of this section, excluding items paid from funds other than closing funds as described in paragraph (k)(4)(i) of this section, labeled "Due from Seller at Closing";

(ii) The amount of any excess deposit disbursed to the seller prior to the real estate closing, labeled "Excess Deposit";

(iii) The amount of closing costs designated seller-paid at closing disclosed pursuant to paragraph (h)(2) of this section, labeled "Closing Costs Paid at Closing";

(v) The amount of any loan secured by a first lien on the property that will be paid off as part of the real estate closing, labeled "Payoff of First Mortgage Loan";

(vi) The amount of any loan secured by a second lien on the property that will be paid off as part of the real estate closing, labeled "Payoff of Second Mortgage Loan";

(vii) The total amount of money that the seller will provide at the real estate closing as a lump sum not otherwise itemized to pay for loan costs as determined by paragraph (f) of this section and other costs as determined by paragraph (g) of this section and any other obligations of the seller to be paid directly to the consumer, labeled "Seller Credit";

(viii) A description and amount of any and all other obligations required to be paid by the seller at the real estate closing, including any lien-related payoffs, fees, or obligations;

(ix) The description "Adjustments for Items Unpaid by Seller";

(x) The prorated amount of any unpaid taxes due from the seller to reimburse the consumer at the real estate closing, and the time period corresponding to that amount, labeled "City/Town Taxes";

(xi) The prorated amount of any unpaid taxes due from the seller to the consumer at the real estate closing, and the time period corresponding to that amount, labeled "County Taxes";

(xii) The prorated amount of any unpaid assessments due from the seller to reimburse the consumer at the real estate closing, and the time period corresponding to that amount, labeled "Assessments"; and

(xiii) A description and the amount of any additional items which have not yet been paid and which the consumer is expected to pay after the real estate closing, but which are attributable in part to a period of time prior to the real estate closing.

(3) Calculation of seller's transaction. Under the label "Calculation":

(i) The amount described in paragraph (k)(1)(i) of this section, labeled "Total Due to Seller at Closing";

(ii) The amount described in paragraph (k)(2)(i) of this section, disclosed as a negative number, labeled "Total Due from Seller at Closing"; and

(iii) A statement that the disclosed amount is due from or to the seller, and the amount due from or to the seller at closing, calculated by the sum of the amounts disclosed pursuant to paragraphs (k)(3)(i) and (ii) of this section, labeled "Cash."

(4) Items paid outside of closing funds.

(i) Charges that are not paid from closing funds but that would otherwise be disclosed in the table described in paragraph (k) of this section, should be marked with the phrase "Paid Outside of Closing" or the acronym "P.O.C." and include a statement of the party making the payment.

(ii) For purposes of this paragraph (k), "closing funds" are defined as funds collected and disbursed at real estate closing.

(l) **Loan disclosures.** Under the master heading "Additional Information About This Loan" and under the heading "Loan Disclosures":

(1) Assumption. Under the subheading "Assumption," the information required by § 1026.37(m)(2).

(2) Demand feature. Under the subheading "Demand Feature," a statement of whether the legal obligation permits the creditor to demand early repayment of the loan and, if the statement is affirmative, a reference to the note or other loan contract for details.

(3) Late payment. Under the subheading "Late Payment," the information required by § 1026.37(m)(4).

(4) Negative amortization. Under the subheading "Negative Amortization (Increase in Loan Amount)," a statement of whether the regular periodic payments may cause the principal balance to increase.

(i) If the regular periodic payments do not cover all of the interest due, the creditor must provide a statement that the principal balance will increase, such balance will likely become larger than the original loan amount, and increases in such balance lower the consumer's equity in the property.

(ii) If the consumer may make regular periodic payments that do not cover all of the interest due, the creditor must provide a statement that, if the consumer chooses a monthly payment option that does not cover all of the interest due, the principal balance may become larger than the original loan amount and the increases in the principal balance lower the consumer's equity in the property.

(5) Partial payment policy. Under the subheading "Partial Payments":

(i) If periodic payments that are less than the full amount due are accepted, a statement that the creditor, using the term "lender," may accept partial payments and apply such payments to the consumer's loan;

(ii) If periodic payments that are less than the full amount due are accepted but not applied to a consumer's loan until the consumer pays the remainder of the full amount due, a statement that the creditor, using the term "lender," may hold partial payments in a separate account until the consumer pays the remainder of the payment and then apply the full periodic payment to the consumer's loan;

(iii) If periodic payments that are less than the full amount due are not accepted, a statement that the creditor, using the term "lender," does not accept any partial payments; and

(iv) A statement that, if the loan is sold, the new creditor, using the term "lender," may have a different policy.

(6) Security interest. Under the subheading "Security Interest," a statement that the consumer is granting a security interest in the property securing the transaction, the property address including a zip code, and a statement that the consumer may lose the property if the consumer does not make the required payments or satisfy other requirements under the legal obligation.

(7) Escrow account. Under the subheading "Escrow Account":

(i) Under the reference "For now," a statement that an escrow account may also be called an impound or trust account, a statement of whether the creditor has established or will establish (at or before consummation) an escrow account in connection with the transaction, and the information required under paragraphs (*l*)(7)(i)(A) and (B) of this section:

(A) A statement that the creditor may be liable for penalties and interest if it fails to make a payment for any cost for which the escrow account is established, a statement that the consumer would have to pay such costs directly in the absence of the escrow account, and a table, titled "Escrow," that contains, if an escrow account is or will be established, an itemization of the amounts listed in paragraphs (*l*)(7)(i)(A)(1) through (4) of this section;

(1) The total amount the consumer will be required to pay into an escrow account over the first year after consummation, labeled "Escrowed Property Costs over Year 1," together with a descriptive name of each charge to be paid (in whole or in part) from the escrow account, calculated as the amount disclosed under paragraph (*l*)(7)(i)(A)(4) of this section multiplied by the number of periodic payments scheduled to be made to the escrow account during the first year after consummation;

(2) The estimated amount the consumer is likely to pay during the first year after consummation for the mortgage-related obligations described in § 1026.43(b)(8) that are known to the creditor and that will not be paid using escrow account funds, labeled "Non-Escrowed Property Costs over Year 1," together with a descriptive name of each such charge and a statement that the consumer may have to pay other costs that are not listed;

(3) The total amount disclosed under paragraph (g)(3) of this section, a statement that the payment is a cushion for the escrow account, labeled "Initial Escrow Payment," and a reference to the information disclosed under paragraph (g)(3) of this section;

(4) The amount the consumer will be required to pay into the escrow account with each periodic payment during the first year after consummation, labeled "Monthly Escrow Payment."

(5) A creditor complies with the requirements of paragraphs (*l*)(7)(i)(A)(1) and (4) of this section if the creditor bases the numerical disclosures required by those paragraphs on amounts derived from the escrow account analysis required under Regulation X, 12 CFR 1024.17.

(B) A statement of whether the consumer will not have an escrow account, the reason why an escrow account will not be established, a statement that the consumer must pay all property costs, such as taxes and homeowner's insurance, directly, a statement that the consumer may contact the creditor to inquire about the availability of an escrow account, and a table, titled "No Escrow," that contains, if an escrow account will not be established, an itemization of the following:

(1) The estimated total amount the consumer will pay directly for the mortgage-related obligations described in § 1026.43(b)(8) during the first year after consummation that are known to the creditor and a statement that, without an escrow account, the consumer must pay the identified costs, possibly in one or two large payments, labeled "Property Costs over Year 1"; and

(2) The amount of any fee the creditor imposes on the consumer for not establishing an escrow account in connection with the transaction, labeled "Escrow Waiver Fee."

(ii) Under the reference "In the future":

(A) A statement that the consumer's property costs may change and that, as a result, the consumer's escrow payment may change;

(B) A statement that the consumer may be able to cancel any escrow account that has been established, but that the consumer is responsible for directly paying all property costs in the absence of an escrow account; and

(C) A description of the consequences if the consumer fails to pay property costs, including the actions that a State or local government may take if property taxes are not paid and the actions the creditor may take if the consumer does not pay some or all property costs, such as adding amounts to the loan balance, adding an escrow account to the loan, or purchasing a property insurance policy on the consumer's behalf that may be more expensive and provide fewer benefits than what the consumer could obtain directly.

(m) Adjustable payment table. Under the master heading "Additional Information About This Loan" required by paragraph (*l*) of this section, and under the heading "Adjustable Payment (AP) Table," the table required to be disclosed by § 1026.37(i).

(n) Adjustable interest rate table. Under the master heading "Additional Information About This Loan" required by paragraph (*l*) of this section, and under the heading "Adjustable Interest Rate (AIR) Table," the table required to be disclosed by § 1026.37(j).

(*o*) Loan calculations. In a separate table under the heading "Loan Calculations":

(1) Total of payments. The "Total of Payments," using that term and expressed as a dollar amount, and a statement that the disclosure is the total the consumer will have paid after making all payments of principal, interest, mortgage insurance, and loan costs, as scheduled. The disclosed total of payments shall be treated as accurate if the amount disclosed as the total of payments:

(i) Is understated by no more than $100; or

(ii) Is greater than the amount required to be disclosed.

(2) Finance charge. The "Finance Charge," using that term and expressed as a dollar amount, and the following statement: "The dollar amount the loan will cost you." The disclosed finance charge and other disclosures affected by the disclosed financed charge (including the amount financed and the annual percentage rate) shall be treated as accurate if the amount disclosed as the finance charge:

(i) Is understated by no more than $100; or

(ii) Is greater than the amount required to be disclosed.

(3) Amount financed. The "Amount Financed," using that term and expressed as a dollar amount, and the following statement: "The loan amount available after paying your upfront finance charge."

(4) Annual percentage rate. The "Annual Percentage Rate," using that term and the abbreviation "APR" and expressed as a percentage, and the following statement: "Your costs over the loan term expressed as a rate. This is not your interest rate."

(5) Total interest percentage. The "Total Interest Percentage," using that term and the abbreviation "TIP" and expressed as a percentage, and the following statement: "The total amount of interest that you will pay over the loan term as a percentage of your loan amount."

(p) Other disclosures. Under the heading "Other Disclosures":

(1) Appraisal. For transactions subject to 15 U.S.C. 1639h or 1691(e), as implemented in this part or Regulation B, 12 CFR part 1002, respectively, under the subheading "Appraisal," that:

(i) If there was an appraisal of the property in connection with the loan, the creditor is required to provide the consumer with a copy at no additional cost to the consumer at least three days prior to consummation; and

(ii) If the consumer has not yet received a copy of the appraisal, the consumer should contact the creditor using the information disclosed pursuant to paragraph (r) of this section.

(2) Contract details. A statement that the consumer should refer to the appropriate loan document and security instrument for information about nonpayment, what constitutes a default under the legal obligation, circumstances under which the creditor may accelerate the maturity of the obligation, and prepayment rebates and penalties, under the subheading "Contract Details."

(3) Liability after foreclosure. A brief statement of whether, and the conditions under which, the consumer may remain responsible for any deficiency after foreclosure under applicable State law, a brief statement that certain protections may be lost if the consumer refinances or incurs additional debt on the property, and a statement that the consumer should consult an attorney for additional information, under the subheading "Liability after Foreclosure."

(4) Refinance. Under the subheading "Refinance," the statement required by § 1026.37(m)(5).

(5) Tax deductions. Under the subheading "Tax Deductions," a statement that, if the extension of credit exceeds the fair market value of the property, the interest on the portion of the credit extension that is greater than the fair market value of the property is not tax deductible for

Federal income tax purposes and a statement that the consumer should consult a tax adviser for further information.

(q) Questions notice. In a separate notice labeled "Questions?":

(1) A statement directing the consumer to use the contact information disclosed under paragraph (r) of this section if the consumer has any questions about the disclosures required pursuant to § 1026.19(f);

(2) A reference to the Bureau's Web site to obtain more information or to submit a complaint; and the link or uniform resource locator address to the Web site: www.consumerfinance.gov/mortgage-closing; and

(3) A prominent question mark.

(r) Contact information. In a separate table, under the heading "Contact Information," the following information for each creditor (under the subheading "Lender"), mortgage broker (under the subheading "Mortgage Broker"), consumer's real estate broker (under the subheading "Real Estate Broker (B)"), seller's real estate broker (under the subheading "Real Estate Broker (S)"), and settlement agent (under the subheading "Settlement Agent") participating in the transaction:

(1) Name of the person, labeled "Name";

(2) Address, using that label;

(3) Nationwide Mortgage Licensing System & Registry (NMLSR ID) identification number, labeled "NMLS ID," or, if none, license number or other unique identifier issued by the applicable jurisdiction or regulating body with which the person is licensed and/or registered, labeled "License ID," with the abbreviation for the State of the applicable jurisdiction or regulatory body stated before the word "License" in the label, for the persons identified in paragraph (r)(1) of this section;

(4) Name of the natural person who is the primary contact for the consumer with the person identified in paragraph (r)(1) of this section, labeled "Contact";

(5) NMLSR ID, labeled "Contact NMLS ID," or, if none, license number or other unique identifier issued by the applicable jurisdiction or regulating body with which the person is licensed and/or registered, labeled "Contact License ID," with the abbreviation for the State of the applicable jurisdiction or regulatory body stated before the word "License" in the label, for the natural person identified in paragraph (r)(4) of this section,

(6) Email address for the person identified in paragraph (r)(4) of this section, labeled "Email"; and

(7) Telephone number for the person identified in paragraph (r)(4) of this section, labeled "Phone."

(s) Signature statement.

(1) At the creditor's option, under the heading "Confirm Receipt," a line for the signatures of the consumers in the transaction. If the creditor provides a line for the consumer's signature, the creditor must disclose above the signature line the statement required to be disclosed under § 1026.37(n)(1).

(2) If the creditor does not provide a line for the consumer's signature, the statement required to be disclosed under § 1026.37(n)(2) under the heading "Other Disclosures" required by paragraph (p) of this section.

(t) Form of disclosures.

(1) General requirements.

(i) The creditor shall make the disclosures required by this section clearly and conspicuously in writing, in a form that the consumer may keep. The disclosures also shall be grouped together and segregated from everything else.

(ii) Except as provided in paragraph (t)(5), the disclosures shall contain only the information required by paragraphs (a) through (s) of this section and shall be made in the same order, and positioned relative to the master headings, headings, subheadings, labels, and similar designations in the same manner, as shown in form H-25, set forth in appendix H to this part.

(2) Headings and labels. If a master heading, heading, subheading, label, or similar designation contains the word "estimated" or a capital letter designation in form H-25, set forth in appendix H to this part, that heading, label, or similar designation shall contain the word "estimated" and the applicable capital letter designation.

(3) Form. Except as provided in paragraph (t)(5) of this section:

(i) For a transaction subject to § 1026.19(f) that is a federally related mortgage loan, as defined in Regulation X, 12 CFR 1024.2, the disclosures must be made using form H-25, set forth in appendix H to this part.

(ii) For any other transaction subject to this section, the disclosures must be made with headings, content, and format substantially similar to form H-25, set forth in appendix H to this part.

(iii) The disclosures required by this section may be provided to the consumer in electronic form, subject to compliance with the consumer consent and other applicable provisions of the Electronic Signatures in Global and National Commerce Act (15 U.S.C. 7001 et seq.).

(4) Rounding.

(i) Nearest dollar. The following dollar amounts are required to be rounded to the nearest whole dollar:

(A) The dollar amounts required to be disclosed by paragraph (b) of this section that are required to be rounded by § 1026.37(*o*)(4)(i)(A) when disclosed under § 1026.37(b)(6) and (7);

(B) The dollar amounts required to be disclosed by paragraph (c) of this section that are required to be rounded by § 1026.37(*o*)(4)(i)(A) when disclosed under § 1026.37(c)(1)(iii);

(C) The dollar amounts required to be disclosed by paragraphs (e) and (i) of this section under the subheading "Loan Estimate";

(D) The dollar amounts required to be disclosed by paragraph (m) of this section; and

(E) The dollar amounts required to be disclosed by paragraph (c) of this section that are required to be rounded by § 1026.37(*o*)(4)(i)(C) when disclosed under § 1026.37(c)(2)(iv).

(ii) Percentages. The percentage amounts required to be disclosed under paragraphs (b), (f)(1), (n), and (*o*)(5) of this section shall be disclosed by rounding the exact amounts to three decimal places and then dropping any trailing zeros to the right of the decimal point.

(iii) Loan amount. The dollar amount required to be disclosed by paragraph (b) of this section as required by § 1026.37(b)(1) shall be disclosed as an unrounded number, except that if the amount is a whole number then the amount disclosed shall be truncated at the decimal point.

(5) Exceptions.

(i) Unit-period. Wherever the form or this section uses "monthly" to describe the frequency of any payments or uses "month" to describe the applicable unit-period, the creditor shall substitute the appropriate term to reflect the fact that the transaction's terms provide for other than monthly periodic payments, such as bi-weekly or quarterly payments.

(ii) Lender credits. The amount required to be disclosed by paragraph (d)(1)(i)(D) of this section may be omitted from the form if the amount is zero.

(iii) Administrative information. The creditor may insert at the bottom of each page under the disclosures required by this section as illustrated by form H-25 of appendix H to this part, any administrative information, text, or codes that assist in identification of the form or the information disclosed on the form, provided that the space provided on form H-25 for any of the information required by this section is not altered.

(iv) Closing cost details.

(A) Additional line numbers. Line numbers provided on form H-25 of appendix H to this part for the disclosure of the information required by paragraphs (f)(1) through (3) and (g)(1) through (4) of this section that are not used may be deleted and the deleted line numbers added to the space provided for any other of those paragraphs as necessary to accommodate the disclosure of additional items.

(B) Two pages. To the extent that adding or deleting line numbers provided on form H-25 of appendix H to this part, as permitted by paragraph (t)(5)(iv)(A) of this section, does not accommodate an itemization of all information required to be disclosed by paragraphs (f) through (h) on one page, the information required to be disclosed by paragraphs (f) through (h) of this section may be disclosed on two pages, provided that the information required by paragraph (f) is disclosed on a page separate from the information required by paragraph (g). The information required by paragraph (g), if disclosed on a page separate from paragraph (f), shall be disclosed on the same page as the information required by paragraph (h).

(v) Separation of consumer and seller information. The creditor or settlement agent preparing the form may use form H-25 of appendix H to this part for the disclosure provided to both the consumer and the seller, with the following modifications to separate the information of the consumer and seller, as necessary:

(A) The information required to be disclosed by paragraphs (j) and (k) of this section may be disclosed on separate pages to the consumer and the seller, respectively, with the information required by the other paragraph left blank. The information disclosed to the consumer pursuant to paragraph (j) of this section must be disclosed on the same page as the information required by paragraph (i) of this section.

(B) The information required to be disclosed by paragraphs (f) and (g) of this section with respect to costs paid by the consumer may be left blank on the disclosure provided to the seller.

(C) The information required by paragraphs (a)(2), (a)(4)(iii), (a)(5), (b) through (d), (i), (*l*) through (p), (r) with respect to the creditor and mortgage broker, and (s)(2) of this section may be left blank on the disclosure provided to the seller.

(vi) Modified version of the form for a seller or third-party. The information required by paragraphs (a)(2), (a)(4)(iii), (a)(5), (b) through (d), (f), and (g) with respect to costs paid by the consumer, (i), (j), (*l*) through (p), (q)(1), and (r) with respect to the creditor and mortgage broker, and (s) of this section may be deleted from the form provided to the seller or a third-party, as illustrated by form H-25(I) of appendix H to this part.

(vii) Transaction without a seller or simultaneous subordinate financing transaction. The following modifications to form H-25 of appendix H to this part may be made for a transaction that does not involve a seller or for simultaneous subordinate financing, and for which the alternative tables are disclosed pursuant to paragraphs (d)(2) and (e) of this section, as illustrated by form H-25(J) of appendix H to this part:

(A) The information required by paragraph (a)(4)(ii), and paragraphs (f), (g), and (h) of this section with respect to costs paid by the seller, may be deleted.

(B) A table under the master heading "Closing Cost Details" required by paragraph (f) of this section may be added with the heading "Payoffs and Payments" that itemizes the amounts of payments made at closing to other parties from the credit extended to the consumer or funds provided by the consumer in connection with the transaction, including designees of the consumer; the payees and a description of the purpose of such disbursements under the subheading "To"; and the total amount of such payments labeled "Total Payoffs and Payments."

(C) The tables required to be disclosed by paragraphs (j) and (k) of this section may be deleted.

(viii) Translation. The form may be translated into languages other than English, and creditors may modify form H-25 of appendix H to this part to the extent that translation prevents the headings, labels, designations, and required disclosure items under this section from fitting in the space provided on form H-25.

(ix) Customary recitals and information. An additional page may be attached to the form for the purpose of including customary recitals and information used locally in real estate settlements.

§ 1026.39 Mortgage transfer disclosures.

(a) Scope. The disclosure requirements of this section apply to any covered person except as otherwise provided in this section. For purposes of this section:

(1) A "covered person" means any person, as defined in § 1026.2(a)(22), that becomes the owner of an existing mortgage loan by acquiring legal title to the debt obligation, whether through a purchase, assignment or other transfer, and who acquires more than one mortgage loan in any twelve-month period. For purposes of this section, a servicer of a mortgage loan shall not be treated as the owner of the obligation if the servicer holds title to the loan, or title is assigned to the servicer, solely for the administrative convenience of the servicer in servicing the obligation.

(2) A "mortgage loan" means:

(i) An open-end consumer credit transaction that is secured by the principal dwelling of a consumer; and

(ii) A closed-end consumer credit transaction secured by a dwelling or real property.

(b) Disclosure required. Except as provided in paragraph (c) of this section, each covered person is subject to the requirements of this section and shall mail or deliver the disclosures required by this section to the consumer on or before the 30th calendar day following the date of transfer.

(1) Form of disclosures. The disclosures required by this section shall be provided clearly and conspicuously in writing, in a form that the consumer may keep. The disclosures required by this section may be provided to the consumer in electronic form, subject to compliance with the consumer consent and other applicable provisions of the Electronic Signatures in Global and National Commerce Act (E-Sign Act) (15 U.S.C. 7001 et seq.).

(2) The date of transfer. For purposes of this section, the date of transfer to the covered person may, at the covered person's option, be either the date of acquisition recognized in the books and records of the acquiring party, or the date of transfer recognized in the books and records of the transferring party.

(3) Multiple consumers. If more than one consumer is liable on the obligation, a covered person may mail or deliver the disclosures to any consumer who is primarily liable.

(4) Multiple transfers. If a mortgage loan is acquired by a covered person and subsequently sold, assigned, or otherwise transferred to another covered person, a single disclosure may be provided on behalf of both covered persons if the disclosure satisfies the timing and content requirements applicable to each covered person.

(5) Multiple covered persons. If an acquisition involves multiple covered persons who jointly acquire the loan, a single disclosure must be provided on behalf of all covered persons.

(c) Exceptions. Notwithstanding paragraph (b) of this section, a covered person is not subject to the requirements of this section with respect to a particular mortgage loan if:

(1) The covered person sells, or otherwise transfers or assigns legal title to the mortgage loan on or before the 30th calendar day following the date that the covered person acquired the mortgage loan which shall be the date of transfer recognized for purposes of paragraph (b)(2) of this section;

(2) The mortgage loan is transferred to the covered person in connection with a repurchase agreement that obligates the transferor to repurchase the loan. However, if the transferor does not repurchase the loan, the covered person must provide the disclosures required by this section within 30 days after the date that the transaction is recognized as an acquisition on its books and records; or

(3) The covered person acquires only a partial interest in the loan and the party authorized to receive the consumer's notice of the right to rescind and resolve issues concerning the consumer's payments on the loan does not change as a result of the transfer of the partial interest.

(d) Content of required disclosures. The disclosures required by this section shall identify the mortgage loan that was sold, assigned or otherwise transferred, and state the following, except that the information required by paragraph (d)(5) of this section shall be stated only for a mortgage loan that is a closed-end consumer credit transaction secured by a dwelling or real property other than a reverse mortgage transaction subject to § 1026.33 of this part:

(1) The name, address, and telephone number of the covered person.

(i) If a single disclosure is provided on behalf of more than one covered person, the information required by this paragraph shall be provided for each of them unless paragraph (d)(1)(ii) of this section applies.

(ii) If a single disclosure is provided on behalf of more than one covered person and one of them has been authorized in accordance with paragraph (d)(3) of this section to receive the consumer's notice of the right to rescind and resolve issues concerning the consumer's payments on the loan, the information required by paragraph (d)(1) of this section may be provided only for that covered person.

(2) The date of transfer.

(3) The name, address and telephone number of an agent or party authorized to receive notice of the right to rescind and resolve issues concerning the consumer's payments on the loan. However, no information is required to be provided under this paragraph if the consumer can use the information provided under paragraph (d)(1) of this section for these purposes.

(4) Where transfer of ownership of the debt to the covered person is or may be recorded in public records, or, alternatively, that the transfer of ownership has not been recorded in public records at the time the disclosure is provided.

(5) Partial payment policy. Under the subheading "Partial Payment":

(i) If periodic payments that are less than the full amount due are accepted, a statement that the covered person, using the term "lender," may accept partial payments and apply such payments to the consumer's loan;

(ii) If periodic payments that are less than the full amount due are accepted but not applied to a consumer's loan until the consumer pays the remainder of the full amount due, a statement that the covered person, using the term "lender," may hold partial payments in a separate account until the consumer pays the remainder of the payment and then apply the full periodic payment to the consumer's loan;

(iii) If periodic payments that are less than the full amount due are not accepted, a statement that the covered person, using the term "lender," does not accept any partial payments; and

(iv) A statement that, if the loan is sold, the new covered person, using the term "lender," may have a different policy.

(e) Optional disclosures. In addition to the information required to be disclosed under paragraph (d) of this section, a covered person may, at its option, provide any other information regarding the transaction.

(f) Successor in interest. If, upon confirmation, a servicer provides a confirmed successor in interest who is not liable on the mortgage loan obligation with a written notice and acknowledgment form in accordance with Regulation X, § 1024.32(c)(1) of this chapter, the servicer is not required to provide to the confirmed successor in interest any written disclosure required by paragraph (b) of this section unless and until the confirmed successor in interest either assumes the mortgage loan obligation under State law or has provided the servicer an executed acknowledgment in accordance with Regulation X, § 1024.32(c)(1)(iv) of this chapter, that the confirmed successor in interest has not revoked.

§ 1026.40 Requirements for home equity plans.

The requirements of this section apply to open-end credit plans secured by the consumer's dwelling. For purposes of this section, an annual percentage rate is the annual percentage rate corresponding to the periodic rate as determined under § 1026.14(b).

(a) Form of disclosures.

(1) General. The disclosures required by paragraph (d) of this section shall be made clearly and conspicuously and shall be grouped together and segregated from all unrelated information. The disclosures may be provided on the application form or on a separate form. The disclosure described in paragraph (d)(4)(iii), the itemization of third-party fees described in paragraph (d)(8), and the variable-rate information described in paragraph (d)(12) of this section may be provided separately from the other required disclosures.

(2) Precedence of certain disclosures. The disclosures described in paragraph (d)(1) through (4)(ii) of this section shall precede the other required disclosures.

(3) For an application that is accessed by the consumer in electronic form, the disclosures required under this section may be provided to the consumer in electronic form on or with the application.

(b) Time of disclosures. The disclosures and brochure required by paragraphs (d) and (e) of this section shall be provided at the time an application is provided to the consumer. The disclosures and the brochure may be delivered or placed in the mail not later than three business days following receipt of a consumer's application in the case of applications contained in magazines or other publications, or when the application is received by telephone or through an intermediary agent or broker.

(c) Duties of third parties. Persons other than the creditor who provide applications to consumers for home equity plans must provide the brochure required under paragraph (e) of this section at the time an application is provided. If such persons have the disclosures required under paragraph (d) of this section for a creditor's home equity plan, they also shall provide the disclosures at such time. The disclosures and the brochure may be delivered or placed in the mail not later than three business days following receipt of a consumer's application in the case of applications contained in magazines or other publications, or when the application is received by telephone or through an intermediary agent or broker.

(d) Content of disclosures. The creditor shall provide the following disclosures, as applicable:

(1) Retention of information. A statement that the consumer should make or otherwise retain a copy of the disclosures.

(2) Conditions for disclosed terms.

(i) A statement of the time by which the consumer must submit an application to obtain specific terms disclosed and an identification of any disclosed term that is subject to change prior to opening the plan.

(ii) A statement that, if a disclosed term changes (other than a change due to fluctuations in the index in a variable-rate plan) prior to opening the plan and the consumer therefore elects not to open the plan, the consumer may receive a refund of all fees paid in connection with the application.

(3) Security interest and risk to home. A statement that the creditor will acquire a security interest in the consumer's dwelling and that loss of the dwelling may occur in the event of default.

(4) Possible actions by creditor.

(i) A statement that, under certain conditions, the creditor may terminate the plan and require payment of the outstanding balance in full in a single payment and impose fees upon termination; prohibit additional extensions of credit or reduce the credit limit; and, as specified in the initial agreement, implement certain changes in the plan.

(ii) A statement that the consumer may receive, upon request, information about the conditions under which such actions may occur.

(iii) In lieu of the disclosure required under paragraph (d)(4)(ii) of this section, a statement of such conditions.

(5) Payment terms. The payment terms of the plan. If different payment terms may apply to the draw and any repayment period, or if different payment terms may apply within either period, the disclosures shall reflect the different payment terms. The payment terms of the plan include:

(i) The length of the draw period and any repayment period.

(ii) An explanation of how the minimum periodic payment will be determined and the timing of the payments. If paying only the minimum periodic payments may not repay any of the principal or may repay less than the outstanding balance, a statement of this fact, as well as a statement that a balloon payment may result. A balloon payment results if paying the minimum periodic payments does not fully amortize the outstanding balance by a specified date or time, and the consumer must repay the entire outstanding balance at such time.

(iii) An example, based on a $10,000 outstanding balance and a recent annual percentage rate, showing the minimum periodic payment, any balloon payment, and the time it would take to repay the $10,000 outstanding balance if the consumer made only those payments and obtained no additional extensions of credit. For fixed-rate plans, a recent annual percentage rate is a rate that has been in effect under the plan within the twelve months preceding the date the disclosures are provided to the consumer. For variable-rate plans, a recent annual percentage rate is the most recent rate provided in the historical example described in paragraph (d)(12)(xi) of this section or a rate that has been in effect under the plan since the date of the most recent rate in the table.

(6) Annual percentage rate. For fixed-rate plans, a recent annual percentage rate imposed under the plan and a statement that the rate does not include costs other than interest. A recent annual percentage rate is a rate that has been in effect under the plan within the twelve months preceding the date the disclosures are provided to the consumer.

(7) Fees imposed by creditor. An itemization of any fees imposed by the creditor to open, use, or maintain the plan, stated as a dollar amount or percentage, and when such fees are payable.

(8) Fees imposed by third parties to open a plan. A good faith estimate, stated as a single dollar amount or range, of any fees that may be imposed by persons other than the creditor to open the plan, as well as a statement that the consumer may receive, upon request, a good faith itemization of such fees. In lieu of the statement, the itemization of such fees may be provided.

(9) Negative amortization. A statement that negative amortization may occur and that negative amortization increases the principal balance and reduces the consumer's equity in the dwelling.

(10) Transaction requirements. Any limitations on the number of extensions of credit and the amount of credit that may be obtained during any time period, as well as any minimum outstanding balance and minimum draw requirements, stated as dollar amounts or percentages.

(11) Tax implications. A statement that the consumer should consult a tax advisor regarding the deductibility of interest and charges under the plan.

(12) Disclosures for variable-rate plans. For a plan in which the annual percentage rate is variable, the following disclosures, as applicable:

(i) The fact that the annual percentage rate, payment, or term may change due to the variable-rate feature.

(ii) A statement that the annual percentage rate does not include costs other than interest.

(iii) The index used in making rate adjustments and a source of information about the index.

(iv) An explanation of how the annual percentage rate will be determined, including an explanation of how the index is adjusted, such as by the addition of a margin.

(v) A statement that the consumer should ask about the current index value, margin, discount or premium, and annual percentage rate.

(vi) A statement that the initial annual percentage rate is not based on the index and margin used to make later rate adjustments, and the period of time such initial rate will be in effect.

(vii) The frequency of changes in the annual percentage rate.

(viii) Any rules relating to changes in the index value and the annual percentage rate and resulting changes in the payment amount, including, for example, an explanation of payment limitations and rate carryover.

(ix) A statement of any annual or more frequent periodic limitations on changes in the annual percentage rate (or a statement that no annual limitation exists), as well as a statement of the maximum annual percentage rate that may be imposed under each payment option.

(x) The minimum periodic payment required when the maximum annual percentage rate for each payment option is in effect for a $10,000 outstanding balance, and a statement of the earliest date or time the maximum rate may be imposed.

(xi) An historical example, based on a $10,000 extension of credit, illustrating how annual percentage rates and payments would have been affected by index value changes implemented according to the terms of the plan. The historical example shall be based on the most recent 15 years of index values (selected for the same time period each year) and shall reflect all significant plan terms, such as negative amortization, rate carryover, rate discounts, and rate and payment limitations, that would have been affected by the index movement during the period.

(xii) A statement that rate information will be provided on or with each periodic statement.

(e) Brochure. The home equity brochure entitled "What You Should Know About Home Equity Lines of Credit" or a suitable substitute shall be provided.

(f) Limitations on home equity plans. No creditor may, by contract or otherwise:

(1) Change the annual percentage rate unless:

(i) Such change is based on an index that is not under the creditor's control; and

(ii) Such index is available to the general public.

(2) Terminate a plan and demand repayment of the entire outstanding balance in advance of the original term (except for reverse mortgage transactions that are subject to paragraph (f)(4) of this section) unless:

(i) There is fraud or material misrepresentation by the consumer in connection with the plan;

(ii) The consumer fails to meet the repayment terms of the agreement for any outstanding balance;

(iii) Any action or inaction by the consumer adversely affects the creditor's security for the plan, or any right of the creditor in such security; or

(iv) Federal law dealing with credit extended by a depository institution to its executive officers specifically requires that as a condition of the plan the credit shall become due and payable on demand, provided that the creditor includes such a provision in the initial agreement.

(3) Change any term, except that a creditor may:

(i) Provide in the initial agreement that it may prohibit additional extensions of credit or reduce the credit limit during any period in which the maximum annual percentage rate is reached. A creditor also may provide in the initial agreement that specified changes will occur if a specified event takes place (for example, that the annual percentage rate will increase a specified amount if the consumer leaves the creditor's employment).

(ii) Change the index and margin used under the plan if the original index is no longer available, the new index has an historical movement substantially similar to that of the original index, and the new index and margin would have resulted in an annual percentage rate substantially similar to the rate in effect at the time the original index became unavailable.

(iii) Make a specified change if the consumer specifically agrees to it in writing at that time.

(iv) Make a change that will unequivocally benefit the consumer throughout the remainder of the plan.

(v) Make an insignificant change to terms.

(vi) Prohibit additional extensions of credit or reduce the credit limit applicable to an agreement during any period in which:

(A) The value of the dwelling that secures the plan declines significantly below the dwelling's appraised value for purposes of the plan;

(B) The creditor reasonably believes that the consumer will be unable to fulfill the repayment obligations under the plan because of a material change in the consumer's financial circumstances;

(C) The consumer is in default of any material obligation under the agreement;

(D) The creditor is precluded by government action from imposing the annual percentage rate provided for in the agreement;

(E) The priority of the creditor's security interest is adversely affected by government action to the extent that the value of the security interest is less than 120 percent of the credit line; or

(F) The creditor is notified by its regulatory agency that continued advances constitute an unsafe and unsound practice.

(4) For reverse mortgage transactions that are subject to § 1026.33, terminate a plan and demand repayment of the entire outstanding balance in advance of the original term except:

(i) In the case of default;

(ii) If the consumer transfers title to the property securing the note;

(iii) If the consumer ceases using the property securing the note as the primary dwelling; or

(iv) Upon the consumer's death.

(g) Refund of fees. A creditor shall refund all fees paid by the consumer to anyone in connection with an application if any term required to be disclosed under paragraph (d) of this section changes (other than a change due to fluctuations in the index in a variable-rate plan) before the plan is opened and, as a result, the consumer elects not to open the plan.

(h) Imposition of nonrefundable fees. Neither a creditor nor any other person may impose a nonrefundable fee in connection with an application until three business days after the consumer receives the disclosures and brochure required under this section. If the disclosures and brochure are mailed to the consumer, the consumer is considered to have received them three business days after they are mailed.

§ 1026.41 Periodic statements for residential mortgage loans.

(a) In general.

(1) Scope. This section applies to a closed-end consumer credit transaction secured by a dwelling, unless an exemption in paragraph (e) of this section applies. A closed-end consumer credit transaction secured by a dwelling is referred to as a mortgage loan for purposes of this section.

(2) Periodic statements. A servicer of a transaction subject to this section shall provide the consumer, for each billing cycle, a periodic statement meeting the requirements of paragraphs (b), (c), and (d) of this section. If a mortgage loan has a billing cycle shorter than a period of 31 days (for example, a bi-weekly billing cycle), a periodic statement covering an entire month may be used. For the purposes of this section, servicer includes the creditor, assignee, or servicer, as applicable. A creditor or assignee that does not currently own the mortgage loan or the mortgage servicing rights is not subject to the requirement in this section to provide a periodic statement.

(b) Timing of the periodic statement. The periodic statement must be delivered or placed in the mail within a reasonably prompt time after the payment due date or the end of any courtesy period provided for the previous billing cycle.

(c) Form of the periodic statement. The servicer must make the disclosures required by this section clearly and conspicuously in writing, or electronically if the consumer agrees, and in a form that the consumer may keep. Sample forms for periodic statements are provided in appendix H-30. Proper use of these forms complies with the requirements of this paragraph (c) and the layout requirements in paragraph (d) of this section.

(d) Content and layout of the periodic statement. The periodic statement required by this section shall include:

(1) Amount due. Grouped together in close proximity to each other and located at the top of the first page of the statement:

(i) The payment due date;

(ii) The amount of any late payment fee, and the date on which that fee will be imposed if payment has not been received; and

(iii) The amount due, shown more prominently than other disclosures on the page and, if the transaction has multiple payment options, the amount due under each of the payment options.

(2) Explanation of amount due. The following items, grouped together in close proximity to each other and located on the first page of the statement:

(i) The monthly payment amount, including a breakdown showing how much, if any, will be applied to principal, interest, and escrow and, if a mortgage loan has multiple payment options, a breakdown of each of the payment options along with information on whether the principal balance will increase, decrease, or stay the same for each option listed;

(ii) The total sum of any fees or charges imposed since the last statement; and

(iii) Any payment amount past due.

(3) Past Payment Breakdown. The following items, grouped together in close proximity to each other and located on the first page of the statement:

(i) The total of all payments received since the last statement, including a breakdown showing the amount, if any, that was applied to principal, interest, escrow, fees and charges, and the amount, if any, sent to any suspense or unapplied funds account; and

(ii) The total of all payments received since the beginning of the current calendar year, including a breakdown of that total showing the amount, if any, that was applied to principal, interest, escrow, fees and charges, and the amount, if any, currently held in any suspense or unapplied funds account.

(4) Transaction activity. A list of all the transaction activity that occurred since the last statement. For purposes of this paragraph (d)(4), transaction activity means any activity that causes a credit or debit to the amount currently due. This list must include the date of the transaction, a brief description of the transaction, and the amount of the transaction for each activity on the list.

(5) Partial payment information. If a statement reflects a partial payment that was placed in a suspense or unapplied funds account, information explaining what must be done for the funds to be applied. The information must be on the front page of the statement or, alternatively, may be included on a separate page enclosed with the periodic statement or in a separate letter.

(6) Contact information. A toll-free telephone number and, if applicable, an electronic mailing address that may be used by the consumer to obtain information about the consumer's account, located on the front page of the statement.

(7) Account information. The following information:

(i) The amount of the outstanding principal balance;

(ii) The current interest rate in effect for the mortgage loan;

(iii) The date after which the interest rate may next change;

(iv) The existence of any prepayment penalty, as defined in § 1026.32(b)(6)(i), that may be charged;

(v) The Web site to access either the Bureau list or the HUD list of homeownership counselors and counseling organizations and the HUD toll-free telephone number to access contact information for homeownership counselors or counseling organizations; and

(8) Delinquency information. If the consumer is more than 45 days delinquent, the following items, grouped together in close proximity to each other and located on the first page of the statement or, alternatively, on a separate page enclosed with the periodic statement or in a separate letter:

(i) The length of the consumer's delinquency;

(ii) A notification of possible risks, such as foreclosure, and expenses, that may be incurred if the delinquency is not cured;

(iii) An account history showing, for the previous six months or the period since the last time the account was current, whichever is shorter, the amount remaining past due from each billing cycle or, if any such payment was fully paid, the date on which it was credited as fully paid;

(iv) A notice indicating any loss mitigation program to which the consumer has agreed, if applicable;

(v) A notice of whether the servicer has made the first notice or filing required by applicable law for any judicial or non-judicial foreclosure process, if applicable;

(vi) The total payment amount needed to bring the account current; and

(vii) A reference to the homeownership counselor information disclosed pursuant to paragraph (d)(7)(v) of this section.

(e) Exemptions.

(1) Reverse mortgages. Reverse mortgage transactions, as defined by § 1026.33(a), are exempt from the requirements of this section.

(2) Timeshare plans. Transactions secured by consumers' interests in timeshare plans, as defined by 11 U.S.C. 101(53D), are exempt from the requirements of this section.

(3) Coupon books. The requirements of paragraph (a) of this section do not apply to fixed-rate loans if the servicer:

(i) Provides the consumer with a coupon book that includes on each coupon the information listed in paragraph (d)(1) of this section;

(ii) Provides the consumer with a coupon book that includes anywhere in the coupon book:

(A) The account information listed in paragraph (d)(7) of this section;

(B) The contact information for the servicer, listed in paragraph (d)(6) of this section; and

(C) Information on how the consumer can obtain the information listed in paragraph (e)(3)(iii) of this section;

(iii) Makes available upon request to the consumer by telephone, in writing, in person, or electronically, if the consumer consents, the information listed in paragraph (d)(2) through (5) of this section; and

(iv) Provides the consumer the information listed in paragraph (d)(8) of this section in writing, for any billing cycle during which the consumer is more than 45 days delinquent.

(4) Small servicers.

(i) Exemption. A creditor, assignee, or servicer is exempt from the requirements of this section for mortgage loans serviced by a small servicer.

(ii) Small servicer defined. A small servicer is a servicer that:

(A) Services, together with any affiliates, 5,000 or fewer mortgage loans, for all of which the servicer (or an affiliate) is the creditor or assignee;

(B) Is a Housing Finance Agency, as defined in 24 CFR 266.5; or

(C) Is a nonprofit entity that services 5,000 or fewer mortgage loans, including any mortgage loans serviced on behalf of associated nonprofit entities, for all of which the servicer or an associated nonprofit entity is the creditor. For purposes of this paragraph (e)(4)(ii)(C), the following definitions apply:

(1) The term "nonprofit entity" means an entity having a tax exemption ruling or determination letter from the Internal Revenue Service under section 501(c)(3) of the Internal Revenue Code of 1986 (26 U.S.C. 501(c)(3); 26 CFR 1.501(c)(3)–(1), and;

(2) The term "associated nonprofit entities" means nonprofit entities that by agreement operate using a common name, trademark, or servicemark to further and support a common charitable mission or purpose.

(iii) Small servicer determination. In determining whether a servicer satisfies paragraph (e)(4)(ii)(A) of this section, the servicer is evaluated based on the mortgage loans serviced by the servicer and any affiliates as of January 1 and for the remainder of the calendar year. In determining whether a servicer satisfies paragraph (e)(4)(ii)(C) of this section, the servicer is evaluated based on the mortgage loans serviced by the servicer as of January 1 and for the remainder of the calendar year. A servicer that ceases to qualify as a small servicer will have six months from the time it ceases to qualify or until the next January 1, whichever is later, to comply with any requirements from which the servicer is no longer exempt as a small servicer. The following mortgage loans are not considered in determining whether a servicer qualifies as a small servicer:

(A) Mortgage loans voluntarily serviced by the servicer for a non-affiliate of the servicer and for which the servicer does not receive any compensation or fees.

(B) Reverse mortgage transactions.

(C) Mortgage loans secured by consumers' interests in timeshare plans.

(D) Transactions serviced by the servicer for a seller financer that meets all of the criteria identified in § 1026.36(a)(5).

(5) Certain consumers in bankruptcy.

(i) Exemption. Except as provided in paragraph (e)(5)(ii) of this section, a servicer is exempt from the requirements of this section with regard to a mortgage loan if:

(A) Any consumer on the mortgage loan is a debtor in bankruptcy under title 11 of the United States Code or has discharged personal liability for the mortgage loan pursuant to 11 U.S.C. 727, 1141, 1228, or 1328; and

(B) With regard to any consumer on the mortgage loan:

(1) The consumer requests in writing that the servicer cease providing a periodic statement or coupon book;

(2) The consumer's bankruptcy plan provides that the consumer will surrender the dwelling securing the mortgage loan, provides for the avoidance of the lien securing the mortgage loan, or otherwise does not provide for, as applicable, the payment of pre-bankruptcy arrearage or the maintenance of payments due under the mortgage loan;

(3) A court enters an order in the bankruptcy case providing for the avoidance of the lien securing the mortgage loan, lifting the automatic stay pursuant to 11 U.S.C. 362 with regard to the dwelling securing the mortgage loan, or requiring the servicer to cease providing a periodic statement or coupon book; or

(4) The consumer files with the court overseeing the bankruptcy case a statement of intention pursuant to 11 U.S.C. 521(a) identifying an intent to surrender the dwelling securing the mortgage loan and a consumer has not made any partial or periodic payment on the mortgage loan after the commencement of the consumer's bankruptcy case.

(ii) Reaffirmation or consumer request to receive statement or coupon book. A servicer ceases to qualify for an exemption pursuant to paragraph (e)(5)(i) of this section with respect to a mortgage loan if the consumer reaffirms personal liability for the loan or any consumer on the loan requests in writing that the servicer provide a periodic statement or coupon book, unless a court enters an order in the bankruptcy case requiring the servicer to cease providing a periodic statement or coupon book.

(iii) Exclusive address. A servicer may establish an address that a consumer must use to submit a written request under paragraph (e)(5)(i)(B)(1) or (e)(5)(ii) of this section, provided that the servicer notifies the consumer of the address in a manner that is reasonably designed to inform the consumer of the address. If a servicer designates a specific address for requests under paragraph (e)(5)(i)(B)(1) or (e)(5)(ii) of this section, the servicer shall designate the same address for purposes of both paragraphs (e)(5)(i)(B)(1) and (e)(5)(ii) of this section.

(iv) Timing of compliance following transition.

(A) Triggering events for transitioning to modified and unmodified periodic statements. A servicer transitions to providing a periodic statement or coupon book with the modifications set forth in paragraph (f) of this section or to providing a periodic statement or coupon book without such modifications when one of the following three events occurs:

(1) A mortgage loan becomes subject to the requirements of paragraph (f) of this section;

(2) A mortgage loan ceases to be subject to the requirements of paragraph (f) of this section; or

(3) A servicer ceases to qualify for an exemption pursuant to paragraph (e)(5)(i) of this section with respect to a mortgage loan.

(B) Single-statement exemption. As of the date on which one of the events listed in paragraph (e)(5)(iv)(A) of this section occurs, a servicer is exempt from the requirements of this section with respect to the next periodic statement or coupon book that would otherwise be required but thereafter must provide modified or unmodified periodic statements or coupon books that comply with the requirements of this section.

(6) Charged-off loans.

(i) A servicer is exempt from the requirements of this section for a mortgage loan if the servicer:

(A) Has charged off the loan in accordance with loan-loss provisions and will not charge any additional fees or interest on the account; and

(B) Provides, within 30 days of charge-off or the most recent periodic statement, a periodic statement, clearly and conspicuously labeled "Suspension of Statements & Notice of Charge Off—Retain This Copy for Your Records." The periodic statement must clearly and conspicuously explain that, as applicable, the mortgage loan has been charged off and the servicer will not charge any additional fees or interest on the account; the servicer will no longer provide the consumer a periodic statement for each billing cycle; the lien on the property remains in place and the consumer remains liable for the mortgage loan obligation and any obligations arising from or related to the property, which may include property taxes; the consumer may be required to pay the balance on the account in the future, for example, upon sale of the property; the balance on the account is not being canceled or forgiven; and the loan may be purchased, assigned, or transferred.

(ii) Resuming compliance.

(A) If a servicer fails at any time to treat a mortgage loan that is exempt under paragraph (e)(6)(i) of this section as charged off or charges any additional fees or interest on the account, the obligation to provide a periodic statement pursuant to this section resumes.

(B) Prohibition on retroactive fees. A servicer may not retroactively assess fees or interest on the account for the period of time during which the exemption in paragraph (e)(6)(i) of this section applied.

(f) Modified periodic statements and coupon books for certain consumers in bankruptcy. While any consumer on a mortgage loan is a debtor in bankruptcy under title 11 of the United States Code, or if such consumer has discharged personal liability for the mortgage loan pursuant to 11 U.S.C. 727, 1141, 1228, or 1328, the requirements of this section are subject to the following modifications with regard to that mortgage loan:

(1) Requirements not applicable. The periodic statement may omit the information set forth in paragraphs (d)(1)(ii) and (d)(8)(i), (ii), and (v) of this section. The requirement in paragraph (d)(1)(iii) of this section that the amount due must be shown more prominently than other disclosures on the page shall not apply.

(2) Bankruptcy notices. The periodic statement must include the following:

(i) A statement identifying the consumer's status as a debtor in bankruptcy or the discharged status of the mortgage loan; and

(ii) A statement that the periodic statement is for informational purposes only.

(3) Chapter 12 and chapter 13 consumers. In addition to any other provisions of this paragraph (f) that may apply, with regard to a mortgage loan for which any consumer with primary liability is a debtor in a chapter 12 or chapter 13 bankruptcy case, the requirements of this section are subject to the following modifications:

(i) Requirements not applicable. In addition to omitting the information set forth in paragraph (f)(1) of this section, the periodic statement may also omit the information set forth in paragraphs (d)(8)(iii), (iv), (vi), and (vii) of this section.

(ii) Amount due. The amount due information set forth in paragraph (d)(1) of this section may be limited to the date and amount of the post-petition payments due and any post-petition fees and charges imposed by the servicer.

(iii) Explanation of amount due. The explanation of amount due information set forth in paragraph (d)(2) of this section may be limited to:

(A) The monthly post-petition payment amount, including a breakdown showing how much, if any, will be applied to principal, interest, and escrow;

(B) The total sum of any post-petition fees or charges imposed since the last statement; and

(C) Any post-petition payment amount past due.

(iv) Transaction activity. The transaction activity information set forth in paragraph (d)(4) of this section must include all payments the servicer has received since the last statement, including all post-petition and pre-petition payments and payments of post-petition fees and charges, and all post-petition fees and charges the servicer has imposed since the last statement. The brief description of the activity need not identify the source of any payments.

(v) Pre-petition arrearage. If applicable, a servicer must disclose, grouped in close proximity to each other and located on the first page of the statement or, alternatively, on a separate page enclosed with the periodic statement or in a separate letter:

(A) The total of all pre-petition payments received since the last statement;

(B) The total of all pre-petition payments received since the beginning of the consumer's bankruptcy case; and

(C) The current balance of the consumer's pre-petition arrearage.

(vi) Additional disclosures. The periodic statement must include, as applicable:

(A) A statement that the amount due includes only post-petition payments and does not include other payments that may be due under the terms of the consumer's bankruptcy plan;

(B) If the consumer's bankruptcy plan requires the consumer to make the post-petition mortgage payments directly to a bankruptcy trustee, a statement that the consumer should send the payment to the trustee and not to the servicer;

(C) A statement that the information disclosed on the periodic statement may not include payments the consumer has made to the trustee and may not be consistent with the trustee's records;

(D) A statement that encourages the consumer to contact the consumer's attorney or the trustee with questions regarding the application of payments; and

(E) If the consumer is more than 45 days delinquent on post-petition payments, a statement that the servicer has not received all the payments that became due since the consumer filed for bankruptcy.

(4) Multiple obligors. If this paragraph (f) applies in connection with a mortgage loan with more than one primary obligor, the servicer may provide the modified statement to any or all of the primary obligors, even if a primary obligor to whom the servicer provides the modified statement is not a debtor in bankruptcy.

(5) Coupon books. A servicer that provides a coupon book instead of a periodic statement under paragraph (e)(3) of this section must include in the coupon book the disclosures set forth in paragraphs (f)(2) and (f)(3)(vi) of this section, as applicable. The servicer may include these disclosures anywhere in the coupon book provided to the consumer or on a separate page enclosed with the coupon book. The servicer must make available upon request to the consumer by telephone, in writing, in person, or electronically, if the consumer consents, the information listed in paragraph (f)(3)(v) of this section, as applicable. The modifications set forth in paragraphs (f)(1) and (f)(3)(i) through (iv) and (vi) of this section apply to a coupon book and other information a servicer provides to the consumer under paragraph (e)(3) of this section.

(g) Successor in interest. If, upon confirmation, a servicer provides a confirmed successor in interest who is not liable on the mortgage loan obligation with a written notice and acknowledgment form in accordance with Regulation X, § 1024.32(c)(1) of this chapter, the servicer is not required to provide to the confirmed successor in interest any written disclosure required by this section unless and until the confirmed successor in interest either assumes the mortgage loan obligation under State law or has provided the servicer an executed acknowledgment in accordance with Regulation X, § 1024.32(c)(1)(iv) of this chapter, that the confirmed successor in interest has not revoked.

§ 1026.42 Valuation independence.

(a) Scope. This section applies to any consumer credit transaction secured by the consumer's principal dwelling.

(b) Definitions. For purposes of this section:

(1) "Covered person" means a creditor with respect to a covered transaction or a person that provides "settlement services," as defined in 12 U.S.C. 2602(3) and implementing regulations, in connection with a covered transaction.

(2) "Covered transaction" means an extension of consumer credit that is or will be secured by the consumer's principal dwelling, as defined in § 1026.2(a)(19).

(3) "Valuation" means an estimate of the value of the consumer's principal dwelling in written or electronic form, other than one produced solely by an automated model or system.

(4) "Valuation management functions" means:

(i) Recruiting, selecting, or retaining a person to prepare a valuation;

(ii) Contracting with or employing a person to prepare a valuation;

(iii) Managing or overseeing the process of preparing a valuation, including by providing administrative services such as receiving orders for and receiving a valuation, submitting a completed valuation to creditors and underwriters, collecting fees from creditors and underwriters for services provided in connection with a valuation, and compensating a person that prepares valuations; or

(iv) Reviewing or verifying the work of a person that prepares valuations.

(c) Valuation of consumer's principal dwelling.

(1) Coercion. In connection with a covered transaction, no covered person shall or shall attempt to directly or indirectly cause the value assigned to the consumer's principal dwelling to be based on any factor other than the independent judgment of a person that prepares valuations, through coercion, extortion, inducement, bribery, or intimidation of, compensation or instruction to, or collusion with a person that prepares valuations or performs valuation management functions.

(i) Examples of actions that violate paragraph (c)(1) include:

(A) Seeking to influence a person that prepares a valuation to report a minimum or maximum value for the consumer's principal dwelling;

(B) Withholding or threatening to withhold timely payment to a person that prepares a valuation or performs valuation management functions because the person does not value the consumer's principal dwelling at or above a certain amount;

(C) Implying to a person that prepares valuations that current or future retention of the person depends on the amount at which the person estimates the value of the consumer's principal dwelling;

(D) Excluding a person that prepares a valuation from consideration for future engagement because the person reports a value for the consumer's principal dwelling that does not meet or exceed a predetermined threshold; and

(E) Conditioning the compensation paid to a person that prepares a valuation on consummation of the covered transaction.

(2) Mischaracterization of value.

(i) Misrepresentation. In connection with a covered transaction, no person that prepares valuations shall materially misrepresent the value of the consumer's principal dwelling in a valuation. A misrepresentation is material for purposes of this paragraph (c)(2)(i) if it is likely to significantly affect the value assigned to the consumer's principal dwelling. A bona fide error shall not be a misrepresentation.

(ii) Falsification or alteration. In connection with a covered transaction, no covered person shall falsify and no covered person other than a person that prepares valuations shall materially alter a valuation. An alteration is material for purposes of this paragraph (c)(2)(ii) if it is likely to significantly affect the value assigned to the consumer's principal dwelling.

(iii) Inducement of mischaracterization. In connection with a covered transaction, no covered person shall induce a person to violate paragraph (c)(2)(i) or (ii) of this section.

(3) Permitted actions. Examples of actions that do not violate paragraph (c)(1) or (c)(2) include:

(i) Asking a person that prepares a valuation to consider additional, appropriate property information, including information about comparable properties, to make or support a valuation;

(ii) Requesting that a person that prepares a valuation provide further detail, substantiation, or explanation for the person's conclusion about the value of the consumer's principal dwelling;

(iii) Asking a person that prepares a valuation to correct errors in the valuation;

(iv) Obtaining multiple valuations for the consumer's principal dwelling to select the most reliable valuation;

(v) Withholding compensation due to breach of contract or substandard performance of services; and

(vi) Taking action permitted or required by applicable Federal or state statute, regulation, or agency guidance.

(d) Prohibition on conflicts of interest.

(1)(i) In general. No person preparing a valuation or performing valuation management functions for a covered transaction may have a direct or indirect interest, financial or otherwise, in the property or transaction for which the valuation is or will be performed.

(ii) Employees and affiliates of creditors; providers of multiple settlement services. In any covered transaction, no person violates paragraph (d)(1)(i) of this section based solely on the fact that the person:

(A) Is an employee or affiliate of the creditor; or

(B) Provides a settlement service in addition to preparing valuations or performing valuation management functions, or based solely on the fact that the person's affiliate performs another settlement service.

(2) Employees and affiliates of creditors with assets of more than $250 million for both of the past two calendar years. For any covered transaction in which the creditor had assets of more than $250 million as of December 31st for both of the past two calendar years, a person subject to paragraph (d)(1)(i) of this section who is employed by or affiliated with the creditor does not have a conflict of interest in violation of paragraph (d)(1)(i) of this section based on the person's employment or affiliate relationship with the creditor if:

(i) The compensation of the person preparing a valuation or performing valuation management functions is not based on the value arrived at in any valuation;

(ii) The person preparing a valuation or performing valuation management functions reports to a person who is not part of the creditor's loan production function, as defined in paragraph (d)(5)(i) of this section, and whose compensation is not based on the closing of the transaction to which the valuation relates; and

(iii) No employee, officer or director in the creditor's loan production function, as defined in paragraph (d)(5)(i) of this section, is directly or indirectly involved in selecting, retaining, recommending or influencing the selection of the person to prepare a valuation or perform valuation management functions, or to be included in or excluded from a list of approved persons who prepare valuations or perform valuation management functions.

(3) Employees and affiliates of creditors with assets of $250 million or less for either of the past two calendar years. For any covered transaction in which the creditor had assets of $250 million or less as of December 31st for either of the past two calendar years, a person subject to paragraph (d)(1)(i) of this section who is employed by or affiliated with the creditor does not have a conflict of interest in violation of paragraph (d)(1)(i) of this section based on the person's employment or affiliate relationship with the creditor if:

(i) The compensation of the person preparing a valuation or performing valuation management functions is not based on the value arrived at in any valuation; and

(ii) The creditor requires that any employee, officer or director of the creditor who orders, performs, or reviews a valuation for a covered transaction abstain from participating in any decision to approve, not approve, or set the terms of that transaction.

(4) Providers of multiple settlement services. For any covered transaction, a person who prepares a valuation or performs valuation management functions in addition to performing another settlement service for the transaction, or whose affiliate performs another settlement service for the transaction, does not have a conflict of interest in violation of paragraph (d)(1)(i) of this section as a result of the person or the person's affiliate performing another settlement service for the transaction if:

(i) The creditor had assets of more than $250 million as of December 31st for both of the past two calendar years and the conditions in paragraph (d)(2)(i)–(iii) are met; or

(ii) The creditor had assets of $250 million or less as of December 31st for either of the past two calendar years and the conditions in paragraph (d)(3)(i)–(ii) are met.

(5) Definitions. For purposes of this paragraph (d), the following definitions apply:

(i) Loan production function. The term "loan production function" means an employee, officer, director, department, division, or other unit of a creditor with responsibility for generating covered transactions, approving covered transactions, or both.

(ii) Settlement service. The term "settlement service" has the same meaning as in the Real Estate Settlement Procedures Act, 12 U.S.C. 2601 et seq.

(iii) Affiliate. The term "affiliate" has the same meaning as in Regulation Y of the Board of Governors of the Federal Reserve System, 12 CFR 225.2(a).

(e) When extension of credit prohibited. In connection with a covered transaction, a creditor that knows, at or before consummation, of a violation of paragraph (c) or (d) of this section in connection with a valuation shall not extend credit based on the valuation, unless the creditor documents that it has acted with reasonable diligence to determine that the valuation does not materially misstate or misrepresent the value of the consumer's principal dwelling. For purposes of this paragraph (e), a valuation materially misstates or misrepresents the value of the consumer's principal dwelling if the valuation contains a misstatement or misrepresentation that affects the credit decision or the terms on which credit is extended.

(f) Customary and reasonable compensation.

(1) Requirement to provide customary and reasonable compensation to fee appraisers. In any covered transaction, the creditor and its agents shall compensate a fee appraiser for performing appraisal services at a rate that is customary and reasonable for comparable appraisal services performed in the geographic market of the property being appraised. For purposes of paragraph (f) of this section, "agents" of the creditor do not include any fee appraiser as defined in paragraph (f)(4)(i) of this section.

(2) Presumption of compliance. A creditor and its agents shall be presumed to comply with paragraph (f)(1) of this section if:

(i) The creditor or its agents compensate the fee appraiser in an amount that is reasonably related to recent rates paid for comparable appraisal services performed in the geographic market of the property being appraised. In determining this amount, a creditor or its agents shall review the factors below and make any adjustments to recent rates paid in the relevant geographic market necessary to ensure that the amount of compensation is reasonable:

(A) The type of property,

(B) The scope of work,

(C) The time in which the appraisal services are required to be performed,

(D) Fee appraiser qualifications,

(E) Fee appraiser experience and professional record, and

(F) Fee appraiser work quality; and

(ii) The creditor and its agents do not engage in any anticompetitive acts in violation of state or Federal law that affect the compensation paid to fee appraisers, including:

(A) Entering into any contracts or engaging in any conspiracies to restrain trade through methods such as price fixing or market allocation, as prohibited under section 1 of the Sherman Antitrust Act, 15 U.S.C. 1, or any other relevant antitrust laws; or

(B) Engaging in any acts of monopolization such as restricting any person from entering the relevant geographic market or causing any person to leave the relevant geographic market, as prohibited under section 2 of the Sherman Antitrust Act, 15 U.S.C. 2, or any other relevant antitrust laws.

(3) Alternative presumption of compliance. A creditor and its agents shall be presumed to comply with paragraph (f)(1) of this section if the creditor or its agents determine the amount of compensation paid to the fee appraiser by relying on information about rates that:

(i) Is based on objective third-party information, including fee schedules, studies, and surveys prepared by independent third parties such as government agencies, academic institutions, and private research firms;

(ii) Is based on recent rates paid to a representative sample of providers of appraisal services in the geographic market of the property being appraised or the fee schedules of those providers; and

(iii) In the case of information based on fee schedules, studies, and surveys, such fee schedules, studies, or surveys, or the information derived therefrom, excludes compensation paid to fee appraisers for appraisals ordered by appraisal management companies, as defined in paragraph (f)(4)(iii) of this section.

(4) Definitions. For purposes of this paragraph (f), the following definitions apply:

(i) Fee appraiser. The term "fee appraiser" means:

(A) A natural person who is a state-licensed or state-certified appraiser and receives a fee for performing an appraisal, but who is not an employee of the person engaging the appraiser; or

(B) An organization that, in the ordinary course of business, employs state-licensed or state-certified appraisers to perform appraisals, receives a fee for performing appraisals, and is not subject to the requirements of section 1124 of the Financial Institutions Reform, Recovery, and Enforcement Act of 1989 (12 U.S.C. 3353).

(ii) Appraisal services. The term "appraisal services" means the services required to perform an appraisal, including defining the scope of work, inspecting the property, reviewing necessary and appropriate public and private data sources (for example, multiple listing services, tax assessment records and public land records), developing and rendering an opinion of value, and preparing and submitting the appraisal report.

(iii) Appraisal management company. The term "appraisal management company" means any person authorized to perform one or more of the following actions on behalf of the creditor:

(A) Recruit, select, and retain fee appraisers;

(B) Contract with fee appraisers to perform appraisal services;

(C) Manage the process of having an appraisal performed, including providing administrative services such as receiving appraisal orders and appraisal reports, submitting completed appraisal reports to creditors and underwriters, collecting fees from creditors and underwriters for services provided, and compensating fee appraisers for services performed; or

(D) Review and verify the work of fee appraisers.

(g) Mandatory reporting.

(1) Reporting required. Any covered person that reasonably believes an appraiser has not complied with the Uniform Standards of Professional Appraisal Practice or ethical or professional requirements for appraisers under applicable state or Federal statutes or regulations shall refer the matter to the appropriate state agency if the failure to comply is material. For purposes of this paragraph (g)(1), a failure to comply is material if it is likely to significantly affect the value assigned to the consumer's principal dwelling.

(2) Timing of reporting. A covered person shall notify the appropriate state agency within a reasonable period of time after the person determines that there is a reasonable basis to believe that a failure to comply required to be reported under paragraph (g)(1) of this section has occurred.

(3) Definition. For purposes of this paragraph (g), "state agency" means "state appraiser certifying and licensing agency" under 12 U.S.C. 3350(1) and any implementing regulations. The appropriate state agency to which a covered person must refer a matter under paragraph (g)(1) of this section is the agency for the state in which the consumer's principal dwelling is located.

(h) The Bureau issued a joint rule to implement the appraisal management company minimum requirements in the Financial Institutions Reform, Recovery, and Enforcement Act, as amended by section 1473 of the Dodd-Frank Wall Street Reform and Consumer Protection Act. See 12 CFR part 34.

§ 1026.43 Minimum standards for transactions secured by a dwelling.

(a) Scope. This section applies to any consumer credit transaction that is secured by a dwelling, as defined in § 1026.2(a)(19), including any real property attached to a dwelling, other than:

(1) A home equity line of credit subject to § 1026.40;

(2) A mortgage transaction secured by a consumer's interest in a timeshare plan, as defined in 11 U.S.C. 101(53(D); or

(3) For purposes of paragraphs (c) through (f) of this section:

(i) A reverse mortgage subject to § 1026.33;

(ii) A temporary or "bridge" loan with a term of 12 months or less, such as a loan to finance the purchase of a new dwelling where the consumer plans to sell a current dwelling within 12 months or a loan to finance the initial construction of a dwelling;

(iii) A construction phase of 12 months or less of a construction-to-permanent loan;

(iv) An extension of credit made pursuant to a program administered by a Housing Finance Agency, as defined under 24 CFR 266.5;

(v) An extension of credit made by:

(A) A creditor designated as a Community Development Financial Institution, as defined under 12 CFR 1805.104(h);

(B) A creditor designated as a Downpayment Assistance through Secondary Financing Provider, pursuant to 24 CFR 200.194(a), operating in accordance with regulations prescribed by the U.S. Department of Housing and Urban Development applicable to such persons;

(C) A creditor designated as a Community Housing Development Organization provided that the creditor has entered into a commitment with a participating jurisdiction and is undertaking a project under the HOME program, pursuant to the provisions of 24 CFR 92.300(a), and as the terms community housing development organization, commitment, participating jurisdiction, and project are defined under 24 CFR 92.2; or

(D) A creditor with a tax exemption ruling or determination letter from the Internal Revenue Service under section 501(c)(3) of the Internal Revenue Code of 1986 (26 U.S.C. 501(c)(3); 26 CFR 1.501(c)(3)–1), provided that:

(1) During the calendar year preceding receipt of the consumer's application, the creditor extended credit secured by a dwelling no more than 200 times, except as provided in paragraph (a)(3)(vii) of this section;

(2) During the calendar year preceding receipt of the consumer's application, the creditor extended credit secured by a dwelling only to consumers with income that did not exceed the low-and moderate-income household limit as established pursuant to section 102 of the Housing and Community Development Act of 1974 (42 U.S.C. 5302(a)(20)) and amended from time to time by the U.S. Department of Housing and Urban Development, pursuant to 24 CFR 570.3;

(3) The extension of credit is to a consumer with income that does not exceed the household limit specified in paragraph (a)(3)(v)(D)(2) of this section; and

(4) The creditor determines, in accordance with written procedures, that the consumer has a reasonable ability to repay the extension of credit.

(vi) An extension of credit made pursuant to a program authorized by sections 101 and 109 of the Emergency Economic Stabilization Act of 2008 (12 U.S.C. 5211; 5219);[1]

(vii) Consumer credit transactions that meet the following criteria are not considered in determining whether a creditor exceeds the credit extension limitation in paragraph (a)(3)(v)(D)(1) of this section:

(A) The transaction is secured by a subordinate lien;

(B) The transaction is for the purpose of:

(1) Downpayment, closing costs, or other similar home buyer assistance, such as principal or interest subsidies;

(2) Property rehabilitation assistance;

(3) Energy efficiency assistance; or

(4) Foreclosure avoidance or prevention;

(C) The credit contract does not require payment of interest;

(D) The credit contract provides that repayment of the amount of the credit extended is:

---

[1] So in original. Probably should be ".".

(1) Forgiven either incrementally or in whole, at a date certain, and subject only to specified ownership and occupancy conditions, such as a requirement that the consumer maintain the property as the consumer's principal dwelling for five years;

(2) Deferred for a minimum of 20 years after consummation of the transaction;

(3) Deferred until sale of the property securing the transaction; or

(4) Deferred until the property securing the transaction is no longer the principal dwelling of the consumer;

(E) The total of costs payable by the consumer in connection with the transaction at consummation is less than 1 percent of the amount of credit extended and includes no charges other than:

(1) Fees for recordation of security instruments, deeds, and similar documents;

(2) A bona fide and reasonable application fee; and

(3) A bona fide and reasonable fee for housing counseling services; and

(F) The creditor complies with all other applicable requirements of this part in connection with the transaction.

(b) Definitions. For purposes of this section:

(1) Covered transaction means a consumer credit transaction that is secured by a dwelling, as defined in § 1026.2(a)(19), including any real property attached to a dwelling, other than a transaction exempt from coverage under paragraph (a) of this section.

(2) Fully amortizing payment means a periodic payment of principal and interest that will fully repay the loan amount over the loan term.

(3) Fully indexed rate means the interest rate calculated using the index or formula that will apply after recast, as determined at the time of consummation, and the maximum margin that can apply at any time during the loan term.

(4) Higher-priced covered transaction means a covered transaction with an annual percentage rate that exceeds the average prime offer rate for a comparable transaction as of the date the interest rate is set by 1.5 or more percentage points for a first-lien covered transaction, other than a qualified mortgage under paragraph (e)(5), (e)(6), or (f) of this section; by 3.5 or more percentage points for a first-lien covered transaction that is a qualified mortgage under paragraph (e)(5), (e)(6), or (f) of this section; or by 3.5 or more percentage points for a subordinate-lien covered transaction.

(5) Loan amount means the principal amount the consumer will borrow as reflected in the promissory note or loan contract.

(6) Loan term means the period of time to repay the obligation in full.

(7) Maximum loan amount means the loan amount plus any increase in principal balance that results from negative amortization, as defined in § 1026.18(s)(7)(v), based on the terms of the legal obligation assuming:

(i) The consumer makes only the minimum periodic payments for the maximum possible time, until the consumer must begin making fully amortizing payments; and

(ii) The maximum interest rate is reached at the earliest possible time.

(8) Mortgage-related obligations mean property taxes; premiums and similar charges identified in § 1026.4(b)(5), (7), (8), and (10) that are required by the creditor; fees and special assessments imposed by a condominium, cooperative, or homeowners association; ground rent; and leasehold payments.

(9) Points and fees has the same meaning as in § 1026.32(b)(1).

(10) Prepayment penalty has the same meaning as in § 1026.32(b)(6).

(11) Recast means:

(i) For an adjustable-rate mortgage, as defined in § 1026.18(s)(7)(i), the expiration of the period during which payments based on the introductory fixed interest rate are permitted under the terms of the legal obligation;

(ii) For an interest-only loan, as defined in § 1026.18(s)(7)(iv), the expiration of the period during which interest-only payments are permitted under the terms of the legal obligation; and

(iii) For a negative amortization loan, as defined in § 1026.18(s)(7)(v), the expiration of the period during which negatively amortizing payments are permitted under the terms of the legal obligation.

(12) Simultaneous loan means another covered transaction or home equity line of credit subject to § 1026.40 that will be secured by the same dwelling and made to the same consumer at or before consummation of the covered transaction or, if to be made after consummation, will cover closing costs of the first covered transaction.

(13) Third-party record means:

(i) A document or other record prepared or reviewed by an appropriate person other than the consumer, the creditor, or the mortgage broker, as defined in § 1026.36(a)(2), or an agent of the creditor or mortgage broker;

(ii) A copy of a tax return filed with the Internal Revenue Service or a State taxing authority;

(iii) A record the creditor maintains for an account of the consumer held by the creditor; or

(iv) If the consumer is an employee of the creditor or the mortgage broker, a document or other record maintained by the creditor or mortgage broker regarding the consumer's employment status or employment income.

(c) Repayment ability—

(1) General requirement. A creditor shall not make a loan that is a covered transaction unless the creditor makes a reasonable and good faith determination at or before consummation that the consumer will have a reasonable ability to repay the loan according to its terms.

(2) Basis for determination. Except as provided otherwise in paragraphs (d), (e), and (f) of this section, in making the repayment ability determination required under paragraph (c)(1) of this section, a creditor must consider the following:

(i) The consumer's current or reasonably expected income or assets, other than the value of the dwelling, including any real property attached to the dwelling, that secures the loan;

(ii) If the creditor relies on income from the consumer's employment in determining repayment ability, the consumer's current employment status;

(iii) The consumer's monthly payment on the covered transaction, calculated in accordance with paragraph (c)(5) of this section;

(iv) The consumer's monthly payment on any simultaneous loan that the creditor knows or has reason to know will be made, calculated in accordance with paragraph (c)(6) of this section;

(v) The consumer's monthly payment for mortgage-related obligations;

(vi) The consumer's current debt obligations, alimony, and child support;

(vii) The consumer's monthly debt-to-income ratio or residual income in accordance with paragraph (c)(7) of this section; and

(viii) The consumer's credit history.

(3) Verification using third-party records. A creditor must verify the information that the creditor relies on in determining a consumer's repayment ability under § 1026.43(c)(2) using reasonably reliable third-party records, except that:

(i) For purposes of paragraph (c)(2)(i) of this section, a creditor must verify a consumer's income or assets that the creditor relies on in accordance with § 1026.43(c)(4);

(ii) For purposes of paragraph (c)(2)(ii) of this section, a creditor may verify a consumer's employment status orally if the creditor prepares a record of the information obtained orally; and

(iii) For purposes of paragraph (c)(2)(vi) of this section, if a creditor relies on a consumer's credit report to verify a consumer's current debt obligations and a consumer's application states a current debt obligation not shown in the consumer's credit report, the creditor need not independently verify such an obligation.

(4) Verification of income or assets. A creditor must verify the amounts of income or assets that the creditor relies on under § 1026.43(c)(2)(i) to determine a consumer's ability to repay a covered transaction using third-party records that provide reasonably reliable evidence of the consumer's income or assets. A creditor may verify the consumer's income using a tax-return transcript issued by the Internal Revenue Service (IRS). Examples of other records the creditor may use to verify the consumer's income or assets include:

(i) Copies of tax returns the consumer filed with the IRS or a State taxing authority;

(ii) IRS Form W-2s or similar IRS forms used for reporting wages or tax withholding;

(iii) Payroll statements, including military Leave and Earnings Statements;

(iv) Financial institution records;

(v) Records from the consumer's employer or a third party that obtained information from the employer;

(vi) Records from a Federal, State, or local government agency stating the consumer's income from benefits or entitlements;

(vii) Receipts from the consumer's use of check cashing services; and

(viii) Receipts from the consumer's use of a funds transfer service.

(5) Payment calculation—

(i) General rule. Except as provided in paragraph (c)(5)(ii) of this section, a creditor must make the consideration required under paragraph (c)(2)(iii) of this section using:

(A) The fully indexed rate or any introductory interest rate, whichever is greater; and

(B) Monthly, fully amortizing payments that are substantially equal.

(ii) Special rules for loans with a balloon payment, interest-only loans, and negative amortization loans. A creditor must make the consideration required under paragraph (c)(2)(iii) of this section for:

(A) A loan with a balloon payment, as defined in § 1026.18(s)(5)(i), using:

(1) The maximum payment scheduled during the first five years after the date on which the first regular periodic payment will be due for a loan that is not a higher-priced covered transaction; or

(2) The maximum payment in the payment schedule, including any balloon payment, for a higher-priced covered transaction;

(B) An interest-only loan, as defined in § 1026.18(s)(7)(iv), using:

(1) The fully indexed rate or any introductory interest rate, whichever is greater; and

(2) Substantially equal, monthly payments of principal and interest that will repay the loan amount over the term of the loan remaining as of the date the loan is recast.

(C) A negative amortization loan, as defined in § 1026.18(s)(7)(v), using:

(1) The fully indexed rate or any introductory interest rate, whichever is greater; and

(2) Substantially equal, monthly payments of principal and interest that will repay the maximum loan amount over the term of the loan remaining as of the date the loan is recast.

(6) Payment calculation for simultaneous loans. For purposes of making the evaluation required under paragraph (c)(2)(iv) of this section, a creditor must consider, taking into account any mortgage-related obligations, a consumer's payment on a simultaneous loan that is:

(i) A covered transaction, by following paragraph (c)(5) of this section; or

(ii) A home equity line of credit subject to § 1026.40, by using the periodic payment required under the terms of the plan and the amount of credit to be drawn at or before consummation of the covered transaction.

(7) Monthly debt-to-income ratio or residual income—

(i) Definitions. For purposes of this paragraph (c)(7), the following definitions apply:

(A) Total monthly debt obligations. The term total monthly debt obligations means the sum of: the payment on the covered transaction, as required to be calculated by paragraphs (c)(2)(iii) and (c)(5) of this section; simultaneous loans, as required by paragraphs (c)(2)(iv) and (c)(6) of this section; mortgage-related obligations, as required by paragraph (c)(2)(v) of this section; and current debt obligations, alimony, and child support, as required by paragraph (c)(2)(vi) of this section.

(B) Total monthly income. The term total monthly income means the sum of the consumer's current or reasonably expected income, including any income from assets, as required by paragraphs (c)(2)(i) and (c)(4) of this section.

(ii) Calculations—

(A) Monthly debt-to-income ratio. If a creditor considers the consumer's monthly debt-to-income ratio under paragraph (c)(2)(vii) of this section, the creditor must consider the ratio of the consumer's total monthly debt obligations to the consumer's total monthly income.

(B) Monthly residual income. If a creditor considers the consumer's monthly residual income under paragraph (c)(2)(vii) of this section, the creditor must consider the consumer's remaining income after subtracting the consumer's total monthly debt obligations from the consumer's total monthly income.

(d) Refinancing of non-standard mortgages—

(1) Definitions. For purposes of this paragraph (d), the following definitions apply:

(i) Non-standard mortgage. The term non-standard mortgage means a covered transaction that is:

(A) An adjustable-rate mortgage, as defined in § 1026.18(s)(7)(i), with an introductory fixed interest rate for a period of one year or longer;

(B) An interest-only loan, as defined in § 1026.18(s)(7)(iv); or

(C) A negative amortization loan, as defined in § 1026.18(s)(7)(v).

(ii) Standard mortgage. The term standard mortgage means a covered transaction:

(A) That provides for regular periodic payments that do not:

(1) Cause the principal balance to increase;

(2) Allow the consumer to defer repayment of principal; or

(3) Result in a balloon payment, as defined in § 1026.18(s)(5)(i);

(B) For which the total points and fees payable in connection with the transaction do not exceed the amounts specified in paragraph (e)(3) of this section;

(C) For which the term does not exceed 40 years;

(D) For which the interest rate is fixed for at least the first five years after consummation; and

(E) For which the proceeds from the loan are used solely for the following purposes:

(1) To pay off the outstanding principal balance on the non-standard mortgage; and

(2) To pay closing or settlement charges required to be disclosed under the Real Estate Settlement Procedures Act, 12 U.S.C. 2601 et seq.

(iii) Refinancing. The term refinancing has the same meaning as in § 1026.20(a).

(2) Scope. The provisions of this paragraph (d) apply to the refinancing of a non-standard mortgage into a standard mortgage when the following conditions are met:

(i) The creditor for the standard mortgage is the current holder of the existing non-standard mortgage or the servicer acting on behalf of the current holder;

(ii) The monthly payment for the standard mortgage is materially lower than the monthly payment for the non-standard mortgage, as calculated under paragraph (d)(5) of this section.

(iii) The creditor receives the consumer's written application for the standard mortgage no later than two months after the non-standard mortgage has recast.

(iv) The consumer has made no more than one payment more than 30 days late on the non-standard mortgage during the 12 months immediately preceding the creditor's receipt of the consumer's written application for the standard mortgage.

(v) The consumer has made no payments more than 30 days late during the six months immediately preceding the creditor's receipt of the consumer's written application for the standard mortgage; and

(vi) If the non-standard mortgage was consummated on or after January 10, 2014, the non-standard mortgage was made in accordance with paragraph (c) or (e) of this section, as applicable.

(3) Exemption from repayment ability requirements. A creditor is not required to comply with the requirements of paragraph (c) of this section if:

(i) The conditions in paragraph (d)(2) of this section are met; and

(ii) The creditor has considered whether the standard mortgage likely will prevent a default by the consumer on the non-standard mortgage once the loan is recast.

(4) Offer of rate discounts and other favorable terms. A creditor making a covered transaction under this paragraph (d) may offer to the consumer rate discounts and terms that are the same as, or better than, the rate discounts and terms that the creditor offers to new consumers, consistent with the creditor's documented underwriting practices and to the extent not prohibited by applicable State or Federal law.

(5) Payment calculations. For purposes of determining whether the consumer's monthly payment for a standard mortgage will be materially lower than the monthly payment for the non-standard mortgage, the following provisions shall be used:

(i) Non-standard mortgage. For purposes of the comparison conducted pursuant to paragraph (d)(2)(ii) of this section, the creditor must calculate the monthly payment for a non-standard mortgage based on substantially equal, monthly, fully amortizing payments of principal and interest using:

(A) The fully indexed rate as of a reasonable period of time before or after the date on which the creditor receives the consumer's written application for the standard mortgage;

(B) The term of the loan remaining as of the date on which the recast occurs, assuming all scheduled payments have been made up to the recast date and the payment due on the recast date is made and credited as of that date; and

(C) A remaining loan amount that is:

(1) For an adjustable-rate mortgage under paragraph (d)(1)(i)(A) of this section, the outstanding principal balance as of the date of the recast, assuming all scheduled payments have been made up to the recast date and the payment due on the recast date is made and credited as of that date;

(2) For an interest-only loan under paragraph (d)(1)(i)(B) of this section, the outstanding principal balance as of the date of the recast, assuming all scheduled payments have been made up to the recast date and the payment due on the recast date is made and credited as of that date; or

(3) For a negative amortization loan under paragraph (d)(1)(i)(C) of this section, the maximum loan amount, determined after adjusting for the outstanding principal balance.

(ii) Standard mortgage. For purposes of the comparison conducted pursuant to paragraph (d)(2)(ii) of this section, the monthly payment for a standard mortgage must be based on substantially equal, monthly, fully amortizing payments based on the maximum interest rate that may apply during the first five years after consummation.

(e) Qualified mortgages—

(1) Safe harbor and presumption of compliance—

(i) Safe harbor for loans that are not higher-priced covered transactions. A creditor or assignee of a qualified mortgage, as defined in paragraphs (e)(2), (e)(4), (e)(5), (e)(6), or (f) of this section, that is not a higher-priced covered transaction, as defined in paragraph (b)(4) of this section, complies with the repayment ability requirements of paragraph (c) of this section.

(ii) Presumption of compliance for higher-priced covered transactions.

(A) A creditor or assignee of a qualified mortgage, as defined in paragraph (e)(2), (e)(4), (e)(5), (e)(6), or (f) of this section, that is a higher-priced covered transaction, as defined in paragraph (b)(4) of this section, is presumed to comply with the repayment ability requirements of paragraph (c) of this section.

(B) To rebut the presumption of compliance described in paragraph (e)(1)(ii)(A) of this section, it must be proven that, despite meeting the prerequisites of paragraph (e)(2), (e)(4), (e)(5), (e)(6), or (f) of this section, the creditor did not make a reasonable and good faith determination of the consumer's repayment ability at the time of consummation, by showing that the consumer's income, debt obligations, alimony, child support, and the consumer's monthly payment (including mortgage-related obligations) on the covered transaction and on any simultaneous loans of which the creditor was aware at consummation would leave the consumer with insufficient residual income or assets other than the value of the dwelling (including any real property attached to the dwelling) that secures the loan with which to meet living expenses, including any recurring and material non-debt obligations of which the creditor was aware at the time of consummation.

(2) Qualified mortgage defined—general. Except as provided in paragraph (e)(4), (e)(5), (e)(6), or (f) of this section, a qualified mortgage is a covered transaction:

(i) That provides for regular periodic payments that are substantially equal, except for the effect that any interest rate change after consummation has on the payment in the case of an adjustable-rate or step-rate mortgage, that do not:

(A) Result in an increase of the principal balance;

(B) Allow the consumer to defer repayment of principal, except as provided in paragraph (f) of this section; or

(C) Result in a balloon payment, as defined in § 1026.18(s)(5)(i), except as provided in paragraph (f) of this section;

(ii) For which the loan term does not exceed 30 years;

(iii) For which the total points and fees payable in connection with the loan do not exceed the amounts specified in paragraph (e)(3) of this section;

(iv) For which the creditor underwrites the loan, taking into account the monthly payment for mortgage-related obligations, using:

(A) The maximum interest rate that may apply during the first five years after the date on which the first regular periodic payment will be due; and

(B) Periodic payments of principal and interest that will repay either:

(1) The outstanding principal balance over the remaining term of the loan as of the date the interest rate adjusts to the maximum interest rate set forth in paragraph (e)(2)(iv)(A) of this section, assuming the consumer will have made all required payments as due prior to that date; or

(2) The loan amount over the loan term;

(v) For which the creditor considers and verifies at or before consummation the following:

(A) The consumer's current or reasonably expected income or assets other than the value of the dwelling (including any real property attached to the dwelling) that secures the loan, in accordance with appendix Q and paragraphs (c)(2)(i) and (c)(4) of this section; and

(B) The consumer's current debt obligations, alimony, and child support in accordance with appendix Q and paragraphs (c)(2)(vi) and (c)(3) of this section; and

(vi) For which the ratio of the consumer's total monthly debt to total monthly income at the time of consummation does not exceed 43 percent. For purposes of this paragraph (e)(2)(vi), the ratio of the consumer's total monthly debt to total monthly income is determined:

(A) Except as provided in paragraph (e)(2)(vi)(B) of this section, in accordance with the standards in appendix Q;

(B) Using the consumer's monthly payment on:

(1) The covered transaction, including the monthly payment for mortgage-related obligations, in accordance with paragraph (e)(2)(iv) of this section; and

(2) Any simultaneous loan that the creditor knows or has reason to know will be made, in accordance with paragraphs (c)(2)(iv) and (c)(6) of this section.

(3) Limits on points and fees for qualified mortgages.

(i) Except as provided in paragraph (e)(3)(iii) of this section, a covered transaction is not a qualified mortgage unless the transaction's total points and fees, as defined in § 1026.32(b)(1), do not exceed:

(A) For a loan amount greater than or equal to $100,000 (indexed for inflation): 3 percent of the total loan amount;

(B) For a loan amount greater than or equal to $60,000 (indexed for inflation) but less than $100,000 (indexed for inflation): $3,000 (indexed for inflation);

(C) For a loan amount greater than or equal to $20,000 (indexed for inflation) but less than $60,000 (indexed for inflation): 5 percent of the total loan amount;

(D) For a loan amount greater than or equal to $12,500 (indexed for inflation) but less than $20,000 (indexed for inflation): $1,000 (indexed for inflation);

(E) For a loan amount less than $12,500 (indexed for inflation): 8 percent of the total loan amount.

(ii) The dollar amounts, including the loan amounts, in paragraph (e)(3)(i) of this section shall be adjusted annually on January 1 by the annual percentage change in the Consumer Price Index for All Urban Consumers (CPI-U) that was reported on the preceding June 1. See the official commentary to this paragraph (e)(3)(ii) for the current dollar amounts.

(iii) For covered transactions consummated on or before January 10, 2021, if the creditor or assignee determines after consummation that the transaction's total points and fees exceed the applicable limit under paragraph (e)(3)(i) of this section, the loan is not precluded from being a qualified mortgage, provided:

(A) The loan otherwise meets the requirements of paragraphs (e)(2), (e)(4), (e)(5), (e)(6), or (f) of this section, as applicable;

(B) The creditor or assignee pays to the consumer the amount described in paragraph (e)(3)(iv) of this section within 210 days after consummation and prior to the occurrence of any of the following events:

(1) The institution of any action by the consumer in connection with the loan;

(2) The receipt by the creditor, assignee, or servicer of written notice from the consumer that the transaction's total points and fees exceed the applicable limit under paragraph (e)(3)(i) of this section; or

(3) The consumer becoming 60 days past due on the legal obligation; and

(C) The creditor or assignee, as applicable, maintains and follows policies and procedures for post-consummation review of points and fees and for making payments to consumers in accordance with paragraphs (e)(3)(iii)(B) and (e)(3)(iv) of this section.

(iv) For purposes of paragraph (e)(3)(iii) of this section, the creditor or assignee must pay to the consumer an amount that is not less than the sum of the following:

(A) The dollar amount by which the transaction's total points and fees exceeds the applicable limit under paragraph (e)(3)(i) of this section; and

(B) Interest on the dollar amount described in paragraph (e)(3)(iv)(A) of this section, calculated using the contract interest rate applicable during the period from consummation until the payment described in this paragraph (e)(3)(iv) is made to the consumer.

(4) Qualified mortgage defined—special rules—

(i) General. Notwithstanding paragraph (e)(2) of this section, a qualified mortgage is a covered transaction that satisfies:

(A) The requirements of paragraphs (e)(2)(i) through (iii) of this section; and

(B) One or more of the criteria in paragraph (e)(4)(ii) of this section.

(ii) Eligible loans. A qualified mortgage under this paragraph (e)(4) must be one of the following at consummation:

(A) A loan that is eligible, except with regard to matters wholly unrelated to ability to repay:

(1) To be purchased or guaranteed by the Federal National Mortgage Association or the Federal Home Loan Mortgage Corporation operating under the conservatorship or receivership of the Federal Housing Finance Agency pursuant to section 1367(a) of the Federal Housing Enterprises Financial Safety and Soundness Act of 1992 (12 U.S.C. 4617(a)); or

(2) To be purchased or guaranteed by any limited-life regulatory entity succeeding the charter of either the Federal National Mortgage Association or the

Federal Home Loan Mortgage Corporation pursuant to section 1367(i) of the Federal Housing Enterprises Financial Safety and Soundness Act of 1992 (12 U.S.C. 4617(i));

(B) A loan that is eligible to be insured, except with regard to matters wholly unrelated to ability to repay, by the U.S. Department of Housing and Urban Development under the National Housing Act (12 U.S.C. 1707 et seq.);

(C) A loan that is eligible to be guaranteed, except with regard to matters wholly unrelated to ability to repay, by the U.S. Department of Veterans Affairs;

(D) A loan that is eligible to be guaranteed, except with regard to matters wholly unrelated to ability to repay, by the U.S. Department of Agriculture pursuant to 42 U.S.C. 1472(h); or

(E) A loan that is eligible to be insured, except with regard to matters wholly unrelated to ability to repay, by the Rural Housing Service.

(iii) Sunset of special rules. (A) Each respective special rule described in paragraph (e)(4)(ii)(B), (C), (D), or (E) of this section shall expire on the effective date of a rule issued by each respective agency pursuant to its authority under TILA section 129C(b)(3)(ii) to define a qualified mortgage.

(B) Unless otherwise expired under paragraph (e)(4)(iii)(A) of this section, the special rules in this paragraph (e)(4) are available only for covered transactions consummated on or before January 10, 2021.

(5) Qualified mortgage defined—small creditor portfolio loans.

(i) Notwithstanding paragraph (e)(2) of this section, a qualified mortgage is a covered transaction:

(A) That satisfies the requirements of paragraph (e)(2) of this section other than the requirements of paragraph (e)(2)(vi) and without regard to the standards in appendix Q to this part;

(B) For which the creditor considers at or before consummation the consumer's monthly debt-to-income ratio or residual income and verifies the debt obligations and income used to determine that ratio in accordance with paragraph (c)(7) of this section, except that the calculation of the payment on the covered transaction for purposes of determining the consumer's total monthly debt obligations in paragraph (c)(7)(i)(A) shall be determined in accordance with paragraph (e)(2)(iv) of this section instead of paragraph (c)(5) of this section;

(C) That is not subject, at consummation, to a commitment to be acquired by another person, other than a person that satisfies the requirements of paragraph (e)(5)(i)(D) of this section; and

(D) For which the creditor satisfies the requirements stated in § 1026.35(b)(2)(iii)(B) and (C).

(ii) A qualified mortgage extended pursuant to paragraph (e)(5)(i) of this section immediately loses its status as a qualified mortgage under paragraph (e)(5)(i) if legal title to the qualified mortgage is sold, assigned, or otherwise transferred to another person except when:

(A) The qualified mortgage is sold, assigned, or otherwise transferred to another person three years or more after consummation of the qualified mortgage;

(B) The qualified mortgage is sold, assigned, or otherwise transferred to a creditor that satisfies the requirements of paragraph (e)(5)(i)(D) of this section;

(C) The qualified mortgage is sold, assigned, or otherwise transferred to another person pursuant to a capital restoration plan or other action under 12 U.S.C. 1831*o*, actions or instructions of any person acting as conservator, receiver, or bankruptcy trustee, an order of a State or Federal government agency with jurisdiction to examine the creditor pursuant to State or Federal law, or an agreement between the creditor and such an agency; or

(D) The qualified mortgage is sold, assigned, or otherwise transferred pursuant to a merger of the creditor with another person or acquisition of the creditor by another person or of another person by the creditor.

(6) Qualified mortgage defined—temporary balloon-payment qualified mortgage rules.

(i) Notwithstanding paragraph (e)(2) of this section, a qualified mortgage is a covered transaction:

(A) That satisfies the requirements of paragraph (f) of this section other than the requirements of paragraph (f)(1)(vi); and

(B) For which the creditor satisfies the requirements stated in § 1026.35(b)(2)(iii)(B) and (C).

(ii) The provisions of this paragraph (e)(6) apply only to covered transactions for which the application was received before April 1, 2016.

(f) Balloon-payment qualified mortgages made by certain creditors—

(1) Exemption. Notwithstanding paragraph (e)(2) of this section, a qualified mortgage may provide for a balloon payment, provided:

(i) The loan satisfies the requirements for a qualified mortgage in paragraphs (e)(2)(i)(A), (e)(2)(ii), (e)(2)(iii), and (e)(2)(v) of this section, but without regard to the standards in appendix Q;

(ii) The creditor determines at or before consummation that the consumer can make all of the scheduled payments under the terms of the legal obligation, as described in paragraph (f)(1)(iv) of this section, together with the consumer's monthly payments for all mortgage-related obligations and excluding the balloon payment, from the consumer's current or reasonably expected income or assets other than the dwelling that secures the loan;

(iii) The creditor considers at or before consummation the consumer's monthly debt-to-income ratio or residual income and verifies the debt obligations and income used to determine that ratio in accordance with paragraph (c)(7) of this section, except that the calculation of the payment on the covered transaction for purposes of determining the consumer's total monthly debt obligations in (c)(7)(i)(A) shall be determined in accordance with paragraph (f)(iv)(A) of this section, together with the consumer's monthly payments for all mortgage-related obligations and excluding the balloon payment;

(iv) The legal obligation provides for:

(A) Scheduled payments that are substantially equal, calculated using an amortization period that does not exceed 30 years;

(B) An interest rate that does not increase over the term of the loan; and

(C) A loan term of five years or longer.

(v) The loan is not subject, at consummation, to a commitment to be acquired by another person, other than a person that satisfies the requirements of paragraph (f)(1)(vi) of this section; and

(vi) The creditor satisfies the requirements stated in § 1026.35(b)(2)(iii)(A), (B), and (C).

(2) Post-consummation transfer of balloon-payment qualified mortgage. A balloon-payment qualified mortgage, extended pursuant to paragraph (f)(1), immediately loses its status as a qualified mortgage under paragraph (f)(1) if legal title to the balloon-payment qualified mortgage is sold, assigned, or otherwise transferred to another person except when:

(i) The balloon-payment qualified mortgage is sold, assigned, or otherwise transferred to another person three years or more after consummation of the balloon-payment qualified mortgage;

(ii) The balloon-payment qualified mortgage is sold, assigned, or otherwise transferred to a creditor that satisfies the requirements of paragraph (f)(1)(vi) of this section;

(iii) The balloon-payment qualified mortgage is sold, assigned, or otherwise transferred to another person pursuant to a capital restoration plan or other action under 12 U.S.C. 1831*o*, actions or instructions of any person acting as conservator, receiver or bankruptcy trustee, an order of a State or Federal governmental agency with jurisdiction to examine the creditor pursuant to State or Federal law, or an agreement between the creditor and such an agency; or

(iv) The balloon-payment qualified mortgage is sold, assigned, or otherwise transferred pursuant to a merger of the creditor with another person or acquisition of the creditor by another person or of another person by the creditor.

(g) Prepayment penalties—

(1) When permitted. A covered transaction must not include a prepayment penalty unless:

(i) The prepayment penalty is otherwise permitted by law; and

(ii) The transaction:

(A) Has an annual percentage rate that cannot increase after consummation;

(B) Is a qualified mortgage under paragraph (e)(2), (e)(4), (e)(5), (e)(6), or (f) of this section; and

(C) Is not a higher-priced mortgage loan, as defined in § 1026.35(a).

(2) Limits on prepayment penalties. A prepayment penalty:

(i) Must not apply after the three-year period following consummation; and

(ii) Must not exceed the following percentages of the amount of the outstanding loan balance prepaid:

(A) 2 percent, if incurred during the first two years following consummation; and

(B) 1 percent, if incurred during the third year following consummation.

(3) Alternative offer required. A creditor must not offer a consumer a covered transaction with a prepayment penalty unless the creditor also offers the consumer an alternative covered transaction without a prepayment penalty and the alternative covered transaction:

(i) Has an annual percentage rate that cannot increase after consummation and has the same type of interest rate as the covered transaction with a prepayment penalty; for purposes of this paragraph (g), the term "type of interest rate" refers to whether a transaction:

(A) Is a fixed-rate mortgage, as defined in § 1026.18(s)(7)(iii); or

(B) Is a step-rate mortgage, as defined in § 1026.18(s)(7)(ii);

(ii) Has the same loan term as the loan term for the covered transaction with a prepayment penalty;

(iii) Satisfies the periodic payment conditions under paragraph (e)(2)(i) of this section;

(iv) Satisfies the points and fees conditions under paragraph (e)(2)(iii) of this section, based on the information known to the creditor at the time the transaction is offered; and

(v) Is a transaction for which the creditor has a good faith belief that the consumer likely qualifies, based on the information known to the creditor at the time the creditor offers the covered transaction without a prepayment penalty.

(4) Offer through a mortgage broker. If the creditor offers a covered transaction with a prepayment penalty to the consumer through a mortgage broker, as defined in § 1026.36(a)(2), the creditor must:

(i) Present the mortgage broker an alternative covered transaction without a prepayment penalty that satisfies the requirements of paragraph (g)(3) of this section; and

(ii) Establish by agreement that the mortgage broker must present the consumer an alternative covered transaction without a prepayment penalty that satisfies the requirements of paragraph (g)(3) of this section, offered by:

(A) The creditor; or

(B) Another creditor, if the transaction offered by the other creditor has a lower interest rate or a lower total dollar amount of discount points and origination points or fees.

(5) Creditor that is a loan originator. If the creditor is a loan originator, as defined in § 1026.36(a)(1), and the creditor presents the consumer a covered transaction offered by a person to which the creditor would assign the covered transaction after consummation, the creditor must present the consumer an alternative covered transaction without a prepayment penalty that satisfies the requirements of paragraph (g)(3) of this section, offered by:

(i) The assignee; or

(ii) Another person, if the transaction offered by the other person has a lower interest rate or a lower total dollar amount of origination discount points and points or fees.

(6) Applicability. This paragraph (g) applies only if a covered transaction is consummated with a prepayment penalty and is not violated if:

(i) A covered transaction is consummated without a prepayment penalty; or

(ii) The creditor and consumer do not consummate a covered transaction.

(h) Evasion; open-end credit. In connection with credit secured by a consumer's dwelling that does not meet the definition of open-end credit in § 1026.2(a)(20), a creditor shall not structure the loan as an open-end plan to evade the requirements of this section.

§§ 1026.44 to 1026.45 [Reserved].

SUBPART F. SPECIAL RULES FOR PRIVATE EDUCATION LOANS

§ 1026.46 Special disclosure requirements for private education loans.

(a) Coverage. The requirements of this subpart apply to private education loans as defined in § 1026.46(b)(5). A creditor may, at its option, comply with the requirements of this subpart for an extension of credit subject to §§ 1026.17 and 1026.18 that is extended to a consumer for expenses incurred after graduation from a law, medical, dental, veterinary, or other graduate school and related to relocation, study for a bar or other examination, participation in an internship or residency program, or similar purposes.

(1) Relation to other subparts in this part. Except as otherwise specifically provided, the requirements and limitations of this subpart are in addition to and not in lieu of those contained in other subparts of this Part.

(2) [Reserved]

(b) Definitions. For purposes of this subpart, the following definitions apply:

(1) Covered educational institution means:

(i) An educational institution that meets the definition of an institution of higher education, as defined in paragraph (b)(2) of this section, without regard to the institution's accreditation status; and

(ii) Includes an agent, officer, or employee of the institution of higher education. An agent means an institution-affiliated organization as defined by section 151 of the Higher Education Act of 1965 (20 U.S.C. 1019) or an officer or employee of an institution-affiliated organization.

(2) Institution of higher education has the same meaning as in sections 101 and 102 of the Higher Education Act of 1965 (20 U.S.C. 1001–1002) and the implementing regulations published by the U.S. Department of Education.

(3) Postsecondary educational expenses means any of the expenses that are listed as part of the cost of attendance, as defined under section 472 of the Higher Education Act of 1965 (20 U.S.C. 1087*ll*), of a student at a covered educational institution. These expenses include tuition and fees, books, supplies, miscellaneous personal expenses, room and board, and an allowance for any loan fee, origination fee, or insurance premium charged to a student or parent for a loan incurred to cover the cost of the student's attendance.

(4) Preferred lender arrangement has the same meaning as in section 151 of the Higher Education Act of 1965 (20 U.S.C. 1019).

(5) Private education loan means an extension of credit that:

(i) Is not made, insured, or guaranteed under Title IV of the Higher Education Act of 1965 (20 U.S.C 1070 et seq.);

(ii) Is extended to a consumer expressly, in whole or in part, for postsecondary educational expenses, regardless of whether the loan is provided by the educational institution that the student attends;

(iii) Does not include open-end credit or any loan that is secured by real property or a dwelling; and

(iv) Does not include an extension of credit in which the covered educational institution is the creditor if:

(A) The term of the extension of credit is 90 days or less; or

(B) an interest rate will not be applied to the credit balance and the term of the extension of credit is one year or less, even if the credit is payable in more than four installments.

(c) Form of disclosures.

(1) Clear and conspicuous. The disclosures required by this subpart shall be made clearly and conspicuously.

(2) Transaction disclosures.

(i) The disclosures required under §§ 1026.47(b) and (c) shall be made in writing, in a form that the consumer may keep. The disclosures shall be grouped together, shall be segregated from everything else, and shall not contain any information not directly related to the disclosures required under §§ 1026.47(b) and (c), which include the disclosures required under § 1026.18.

(ii) The disclosures may include an acknowledgement of receipt, the date of the transaction, and the consumer's name, address, and account number. The following disclosures may be made together with or separately from other required disclosures: the creditor's identity under § 1026.18(a), insurance or debt cancellation under § 1026.18(n), and certain security interest charges under § 1026.18(*o*).

(iii) The term "finance charge" and corresponding amount, when required to be disclosed under § 1026.18(d), and the interest rate required to be disclosed under §§ 1026.47(b)(1)(i) and (c)(1), shall be more conspicuous than any other disclosure, except the creditor's identity under § 1026.18(a).

(3) Electronic disclosures. The disclosures required under §§ 1026.47(b) and (c) may be provided to the consumer in electronic form, subject to compliance with the consumer consent and other applicable provisions of the Electronic Signatures in Global and National Commerce Act (E-Sign Act) (15 U.S.C. 7001 et seq.). The disclosures required by § 1026.47(a) may be provided to the consumer in electronic form on or with an application or solicitation that is accessed by the consumer in electronic form without regard to the consumer consent or other provisions of the E-Sign Act. The form required to be received under § 1026.48(e) may be accepted by the creditor in electronic form as provided for in that section.

(d) Timing of disclosures.

(1) Application or solicitation disclosures.

(i) The disclosures required by § 1026.47(a) shall be provided on or with any application or solicitation. For purposes of this subpart, the term solicitation means an offer of credit that does not require the consumer to complete an application. A "firm offer of credit" as defined in section 603(*l*) of the Fair Credit Reporting Act (15 U.S.C. 1681a(*l*)) is a solicitation for purposes of this section.

(ii) The creditor may, at its option, disclose orally the information in § 1026.47(a) in a telephone application or solicitation. Alternatively, if the creditor does not disclose orally the information in § 1026.47(a), the creditor must provide the disclosures or place them in the mail no later than three business days after the consumer has applied for the credit, except that, if the creditor either denies the consumer's application or provides or places in the mail the disclosures in § 1026.47(b) no later than three business days after the consumer requests the credit, the creditor need not also provide the § 1026.47(a) disclosures.

(iii) Notwithstanding paragraph (d)(1)(i) of this section, for a loan that the consumer may use for multiple purposes including, but not limited to, postsecondary educational expenses, the creditor need not provide the disclosures required by § 1026.47(a).

(2) Approval disclosures. The creditor shall provide the disclosures required by § 1026.47(b) before consummation on or with any notice of approval provided to the consumer. If the creditor mails notice of approval, the disclosures must be mailed with the notice. If the creditor communicates notice of approval by telephone, the creditor must mail the disclosures within three business days of providing the notice of approval. If the creditor communicates notice of approval electronically, the creditor may provide the disclosures in electronic form in accordance with § 1026.46(d)(3); otherwise the creditor must mail the disclosures within three business days of communicating the notice of approval. If the creditor communicates approval in person, the creditor must provide the disclosures to the consumer at that time.

(3) Final disclosures. The disclosures required by § 1026.47(c) shall be provided after the consumer accepts the loan in accordance with § 1026.48(c)(1).

(4) Receipt of mailed disclosures. If the disclosures under paragraphs (d)(1), (d)(2) or (d)(3) of this section are mailed to the consumer, the consumer is considered to have received them three business days after they are mailed.

(e) Basis of disclosures and use of estimates.

(1) Legal obligation. Disclosures shall reflect the terms of the legal obligation between the parties.

(2) Estimates. If any information necessary for an accurate disclosure is unknown to the creditor, the creditor shall make the disclosure based on the best information reasonably available at the time the disclosure is provided, and shall state clearly that the disclosure is an estimate.

(f) Multiple creditors; multiple consumers. If a transaction involves more than one creditor, only one set of disclosures shall be given and the creditors shall agree among themselves which creditor will comply with the requirements that this part imposes on any or all of them. If there is more than one consumer, the disclosures may be made to any consumer who is primarily liable on the obligation.

(g) Effect of subsequent events.

(1) Approval disclosures. If a disclosure under § 1026.47(b) becomes inaccurate because of an event that occurs after the creditor delivers the required disclosures, the inaccuracy is not a violation of Regulation Z (12 CFR part 1026), although new disclosures may be required under § 1026.48(c).

(2) Final disclosures. If a disclosure under § 1026.47(c) becomes inaccurate because of an event that occurs after the creditor delivers the required disclosures, the inaccuracy is not a violation of Regulation Z (12 CFR part 1026).

§ 1026.47 Content of disclosures.

(a) Application or solicitation disclosures. A creditor shall provide the disclosures required under paragraph (a) of this section on or with a solicitation or an application for a private education loan.

(1) Interest Rates.

(i) The interest rate or range of interest rates applicable to the loan and actually offered by the creditor at the time of application or solicitation. If the rate will depend, in part, on a later determination of the consumer's creditworthiness or other factors, a statement that the rate for which the consumer may qualify will depend on the consumer's creditworthiness and other factors, if applicable.

(ii) Whether the interest rates applicable to the loan are fixed or variable.

(iii) If the interest rate may increase after consummation of the transaction, any limitations on the interest rate adjustments, or lack thereof; a statement that the consumer's actual rate could be higher or lower than the rates disclosed under paragraph (a)(1)(i) of this section, if applicable; and, if the limitation is determined by applicable law, that fact.

(iv) Whether the applicable interest rates typically will be higher if the loan is not co-signed or guaranteed.

(2) Fees and default or late payment costs.

(i) An itemization of the fees or range of fees required to obtain the private education loan.

(ii) Any fees, changes to the interest rate, and adjustments to principal based on the consumer's defaults or late payments.

(3) Repayment terms.

(i) The term of the loan, which is the period during which regularly scheduled payments of principal and interest will be due.

(ii) A description of any payment deferral options, or, if the consumer does not have the option to defer payments, that fact.

(iii) For each payment deferral option applicable while the student is enrolled at a covered educational institution:

(A) Whether interest will accrue during the deferral period; and

(B) If interest accrues, whether payment of interest may be deferred and added to the principal balance.

(iv) A statement that if the consumer files for bankruptcy, the consumer may still be required to pay back the loan.

(4) Cost estimates. An example of the total cost of the loan calculated as the total of payments over the term of the loan:

(i) Using the highest rate of interest disclosed under paragraph (a)(1) of this section and including all finance charges applicable to loans at that rate;

(ii) Using an amount financed of $10,000, or $5000 if the creditor only offers loans of this type for less than $10,000; and

(iii) Calculated for each payment option.

(5) Eligibility. Any age or school enrollment eligibility requirements relating to the consumer or cosigner.

(6) Alternatives to private education loans.

(i) A statement that the consumer may qualify for Federal student financial assistance through a program under Title IV of the Higher Education Act of 1965 (20 U.S.C. 1070 et seq.).

(ii) The interest rates available under each program under Title IV of the Higher Education Act of 1965 (20 U.S.C. 1070 et seq.) and whether the rates are fixed or variable.

(iii) A statement that the consumer may obtain additional information concerning Federal student financial assistance from the institution of higher education that the student attends, or at the Web site of the U.S. Department of Education, including an appropriate Web site address.

(iv) A statement that a covered educational institution may have school-specific education loan benefits and terms not detailed on the disclosure form.

(7) Rights of the consumer. A statement that if the loan is approved, the terms of the loan will be available and will not change for 30 days except as a result of adjustments to the interest rate and other changes permitted by law.

(8) Self-certification information. A statement that, before the loan may be consummated, the consumer must complete the self-certification form and that the form may be obtained from the institution of higher education that the student attends.

(b) Approval disclosures. On or with any notice of approval provided to the consumer, the creditor shall disclose the information required under § 1026.18 and the following information:

(1) Interest rate.

(i) The interest rate applicable to the loan.

(ii) Whether the interest rate is fixed or variable.

(iii) If the interest rate may increase after consummation of the transaction, any limitations on the rate adjustments, or lack thereof.

(2) Fees and default or late payment costs.

(i) An itemization of the fees or range of fees required to obtain the private education loan.

(ii) Any fees, changes to the interest rate, and adjustments to principal based on the consumer's defaults or late payments.

(3) Repayment terms.

(i) The principal amount of the loan for which the consumer has been approved.

(ii) The term of the loan, which is the period during which regularly scheduled payments of principal and interest will be due.

(iii) A description of the payment deferral option chosen by the consumer, if applicable, and any other payment deferral options that the consumer may elect at a later time.

(iv) Any payments required while the student is enrolled at a covered educational institution, based on the deferral option chosen by the consumer.

(v) The amount of any unpaid interest that will accrue while the student is enrolled at a covered educational institution, based on the deferral option chosen by the consumer.

(vi) A statement that if the consumer files for bankruptcy, the consumer may still be required to pay back the loan.

(vii) An estimate of the total amount of payments calculated based on:

(A) The interest rate applicable to the loan. Compliance with § 1026.18(h) constitutes compliance with this requirement.

(B) The maximum possible rate of interest for the loan or, if a maximum rate cannot be determined, a rate of 25%.

(C) If a maximum rate cannot be determined, the estimate of the total amount for repayment must include a statement that there is no maximum rate and that the total amount for repayment disclosed under paragraph (b)(3)(vii)(B) of this section is an estimate and will be higher if the applicable interest rate increases.

(viii) The maximum monthly payment based on the maximum rate of interest for the loan or, if a maximum rate cannot be determined, a rate of 25%. If a maximum cannot be determined, a statement that there is no maximum rate and that the monthly payment amount disclosed is an estimate and will be higher if the applicable interest rate increases.

(4) Alternatives to private education loans.

(i) A statement that the consumer may qualify for Federal student financial assistance through a program under Title IV of the Higher Education Act of 1965 (20 U.S.C. 1070 et seq.).

(ii) The interest rates available under each program under Title IV of the Higher Education Act of 1965 (20 U.S.C. 1070 et seq.), and whether the rates are fixed or variable.

(iii) A statement that the consumer may obtain additional information concerning Federal student financial assistance from the institution of higher education that the student attends, or at the Web site of the U.S. Department of Education, including an appropriate Web site address.

(5) Rights of the consumer.

(i) A statement that the consumer may accept the terms of the loan until the acceptance period under § 1026.48(c)(1) has expired. The statement must include the specific date on which the acceptance period expires, based on the date upon which the consumer receives the disclosures required under this subsection for the loan. The disclosure must also specify the method or methods by which the consumer may communicate acceptance.

(ii) A statement that, except for changes to the interest rate and other changes permitted by law, the rates and terms of the loan may not be changed by the creditor during the period described in paragraph (b)(5)(i) of this section.

(c) Final disclosures. After the consumer has accepted the loan in accordance with § 1026.48(c)(1), the creditor shall disclose to the consumer the information required by § 1026.18 and the following information:

(1) Interest rate. Information required to be disclosed under § 1026.47(b)(1).

(2) Fees and default or late payment costs. Information required to be disclosed under § 1026.47(b)(2).

(3) Repayment terms. Information required to be disclosed under § 1026.47(b)(3).

(4) Cancellation right. A statement that:

(i) The consumer has the right to cancel the loan, without penalty, at any time before the cancellation period under § 1026.48(d) expires, and

(ii) Loan proceeds will not be disbursed until after the cancellation period under § 1026.48(d) expires. The statement must include the specific date on which the cancellation period expires and state that the consumer may cancel by that date. The statement must also specify the method or methods by which the consumer may cancel. If the creditor permits cancellation by mail, the statement must specify that the consumer's mailed request will be deemed timely if placed in the mail not later than the cancellation date specified on the disclosure. The disclosures required by this paragraph (c)(4) must be made more conspicuous than any other disclosure required under this section, except for the finance charge, the interest rate, and the creditor's identity, which must be disclosed in accordance with the requirements of § 1026.46(c)(2)(iii).

§ 1026.48 Limitations on private education loans.

(a) Co-branding prohibited.

(1) Except as provided in paragraph (b) of this section, a creditor, other than the covered educational institution itself, shall not use the name, emblem, mascot, or logo of a covered educational institution, or other words, pictures, or symbols identified with a covered educational institution, in the marketing of private education loans in a way that implies that the covered education institution endorses the creditor's loans.

(2) A creditor's marketing of private education loans does not imply that the covered education institution endorses the creditor's loans if the marketing includes a clear and conspicuous disclosure that is equally prominent and closely proximate to the reference to the covered educational institution that the covered educational institution does not endorse the creditor's loans and that the creditor is not affiliated with the covered educational institution.

(b) Endorsed lender arrangements. If a creditor and a covered educational institution have entered into an arrangement where the covered educational institution agrees to endorse the creditor's private education loans, and such arrangement is not prohibited by other applicable law or regulation, paragraph (a)(1) of this section does not apply if the private education loan marketing includes a clear and conspicuous disclosure that is equally prominent and closely proximate to the reference to the covered educational institution that the creditor's loans are not offered or made by the covered educational institution, but are made by the creditor.

(c) Consumer's right to accept.

(1) The consumer has the right to accept the terms of a private education loan at any time within 30 calendar days following the date on which the consumer receives the disclosures required under § 1026.47(b).

(2) Except for changes permitted under paragraphs (c)(3) and (c)(4), the rate and terms of the private education loan that are required to be disclosed under §§ 1026.47(b) and (c) may not be changed by the creditor prior to the earlier of:

(i) The date of disbursement of the loan; or

(ii) The expiration of the 30 calendar day period described in paragraph (c)(1) of this section if the consumer has not accepted the loan within that time.

(3) Exceptions not requiring re-disclosure.

(i) Notwithstanding paragraph (c)(2) of this section, nothing in this section prevents the creditor from:

(A) Withdrawing an offer before consummation of the transaction if the extension of credit would be prohibited by law or if the creditor has reason to believe that the consumer has committed fraud in connection with the loan application;

(B) Changing the interest rate based on adjustments to the index used for a loan;

(C) Changing the interest rate and terms if the change will unequivocally benefit the consumer; or

(D) Reducing the loan amount based upon a certification or other information received from the covered educational institution, or from the consumer, indicating that the student's cost of attendance has decreased or the consumer's other financial aid has increased. A creditor may make corresponding changes to the rate and other terms only to the extent that the consumer would have received the terms if the consumer had applied for the reduced loan amount.

(ii) If the creditor changes the rate or terms of the loan under this paragraph (c)(3), the creditor need not provide the disclosures required under § 1026.47(b) for the new loan terms, nor need the creditor provide an additional 30-day period to the consumer to accept the new terms of the loan under paragraph (c)(1) of this section.

(4) Exceptions requiring re-disclosure.

(i) Notwithstanding paragraphs (c)(2) or (c)(3) of this section, nothing in this section prevents the creditor, at its option, from changing the rate or terms of the loan to accommodate a specific request by the consumer. For example, if the consumer requests a different repayment option, the creditor may, but need not, offer to provide the requested repayment option and make any other changes to the rate and terms.

(ii) If the creditor changes the rate or terms of the loan under this paragraph (c)(4), the creditor shall provide the disclosures required under § 1026.47(b) and shall provide the consumer the 30-day period to accept the loan under paragraph (c)(1) of this section. The creditor shall not make further changes to the rates and terms of the loan, except as specified in paragraphs (c)(3) and (4) of this section. Except as permitted under § 1026.48(c)(3), unless the consumer accepts the loan offered by the creditor in response to the consumer's request, the creditor may not withdraw or change the rates or terms of the loan for which the consumer was approved prior to the consumer's request for a change in loan terms.

(d) Consumer's right to cancel. The consumer may cancel a private education loan, without penalty, until midnight of the third business day following the date on which the consumer receives the disclosures required by § 1026.47(c). No funds may be disbursed for a private education loan until the three-business day period has expired.

(e) Self-certification form. For a private education loan intended to be used for the postsecondary educational expenses of a student while the student is attending an institution of higher education, the creditor shall obtain from the consumer or the institution of higher education the form developed by the Secretary of Education under section 155 of the Higher Education Act of 1965, signed by the consumer, in written or electronic form, before consummating the private education loan.

(f) Provision of information by preferred lenders. A creditor that has a preferred lender arrangement with a covered educational institution shall provide to the covered educational institution the information required under §§ 1026.47(a)(1) through (5), for each type of private education loan that the lender plans to offer to consumers for students attending the covered educational institution for the period beginning July 1 of the current year and ending June 30 of the following year. The creditor shall provide the information annually by the later of the 1st day of April, or within 30 days after entering into, or learning the creditor is a party to, a preferred lender arrangement.

SUBPART G. SPECIAL RULES APPLICABLE TO CREDIT CARD ACCOUNTS AND OPEN-END CREDIT OFFERED TO COLLEGE STUDENTS

§ 1026.51 Ability to Pay.

(a) General rule.

(1)(i) Consideration of ability to pay. A card issuer must not open a credit card account for a consumer under an open-end (not home-secured) consumer credit plan, or increase any credit limit applicable to such account, unless the card issuer considers the consumer's ability to make the required minimum periodic payments under the terms of the account based on the consumer's income or assets and the consumer's current obligations.

(ii) Reasonable policies and procedures. Card issuers must establish and maintain reasonable written policies and procedures to consider the consumer's ability to make the required minimum payments under the terms of the account based on a consumer's income or assets and a consumer's current obligations. Reasonable policies and procedure include treating any income and assets to which the consumer has a reasonable expectation of access as the consumer's income or assets, or limiting consideration of the consumer's income or assets to the consumer's independent income and assets. Reasonable policies and procedures also include consideration of at least one of the following: The ratio of debt obligations to income; the ratio of debt obligations to assets; or the income the consumer will have after paying debt obligations. It would be unreasonable for a card issuer to not review any information about a consumer's income or assets and current obligations, or to issue a credit card to a consumer who does not have any income or assets.

(2) Minimum periodic payments.

(i) Reasonable method. For purposes of paragraph (a)(1) of this section, a card issuer must use a reasonable method for estimating the minimum periodic payments the consumer would be required to pay under the terms of the account.

(ii) Safe harbor. A card issuer complies with paragraph (a)(2)(i) of this section if it estimates required minimum periodic payments using the following method:

(A) The card issuer assumes utilization, from the first day of the billing cycle, of the full credit line that the issuer is considering offering to the consumer; and

(B) The card issuer uses a minimum payment formula employed by the issuer for the product the issuer is considering offering to the consumer or, in the case of an existing account, the minimum payment formula that currently applies to that account, provided that:

(1) If the applicable minimum payment formula includes interest charges, the card issuer estimates those charges using an interest rate that the issuer is considering offering to the consumer for purchases or, in the case of an existing account, the interest rate that currently applies to purchases; and

(2) If the applicable minimum payment formula includes mandatory fees, the card issuer must assume that such fees have been charged to the account.

(b) Rules affecting young consumers.

(1) Applications from young consumers. A card issuer may not open a credit card account under an open-end (not home-secured) consumer credit plan for a consumer less than 21 years old, unless the consumer has submitted a written application and the card issuer has:

(i) Financial information indicating the consumer has an independent ability to make the required minimum periodic payments on the proposed extension of credit in connection with the account; or

(ii)(A) A signed agreement of a cosigner, guarantor, or joint applicant who is at least 21 years old to be either secondarily liable for any debt on the account incurred by the consumer before the consumer has attained the age of 21 or jointly liable with the consumer for any debt on the account; and

(B) Financial information indicating such cosigner, guarantor, or joint applicant has the ability to make the required minimum periodic payments on such debts, consistent with paragraph (a) of this section.

(2) Credit line increases for young consumers.

(i) If a credit card account has been opened pursuant to paragraph (b)(1)(i) of this section, no increase in the credit limit may be made on such account before the consumer attains the age of 21 unless:

(A) At the time of the contemplated increase, the consumer has an independent ability to make the required minimum periodic payments on the increased limit consistent with paragraph (b)(1)(i) of this section; or

(B) A cosigner, guarantor, or joint applicant who is at least 21 years old agrees in writing to assume liability for any debt incurred on the account, consistent with paragraph (b)(1)(ii) of this section.

(ii) If a credit card account has been opened pursuant to paragraph (b)(1)(ii) of this section, no increase in the credit limit may be made on such account before the consumer attains the age of 21 unless the cosigner, guarantor, or joint accountholder who assumed liability at account opening agrees in writing to assume liability on the increase.

§ 1026.52 Limitations on fees.

(a) Limitations during first year after account opening.

(1) General rule. Except as provided in paragraph (a)(2) of this section, the total amount of fees a consumer is required to pay with respect to a credit card account under an open-end (not home-secured) consumer credit plan during the first year after account opening must not exceed 25 percent of the credit limit in effect when the account is opened. For purposes of this paragraph, an account is considered open no earlier than the date on which the account may first be used by the consumer to engage in transactions.

(2) Fees not subject to limitations. Paragraph (a) of this section does not apply to:

(i) Late payment fees, over-the-limit fees, and returned-payment fees; or

(ii) Fees that the consumer is not required to pay with respect to the account.

(3) Rule of construction. Paragraph (a) of this section does not authorize the imposition or payment of fees or charges otherwise prohibited by law.

(b) Limitations on penalty fees. A card issuer must not impose a fee for violating the terms or other requirements of a credit card account under an open-end (not home-secured) consumer credit plan unless the dollar amount of the fee is consistent with paragraphs (b)(1) and (b)(2) of this section.

(1) General rule. Except as provided in paragraph (b)(2) of this section, a card issuer may impose a fee for violating the terms or other requirements of a credit card account under an open-end (not home-secured) consumer credit plan if the dollar amount of the fee is consistent with either paragraph (b)(1)(i) or (b)(1)(ii) of this section.

(i) Fees based on costs. A card issuer may impose a fee for violating the terms or other requirements of an account if the card issuer has determined that the dollar amount of the fee represents a reasonable proportion of the total costs incurred by the card issuer as a result of that type of violation. A card issuer must reevaluate this determination at least once every twelve months. If as a result of the reevaluation the card issuer determines that a lower fee represents a reasonable proportion of the total costs incurred by the card issuer as a result of that type of violation, the card issuer must begin imposing the lower fee within 45 days after completing the reevaluation. If as a result of the reevaluation the card issuer determines that a higher fee represents a reasonable proportion of the total costs incurred by the card issuer as a result of that type of violation, the card issuer may begin imposing the higher fee after complying with the notice requirements in § 1026.9.

(ii) Safe harbors. A card issuer may impose a fee for violating the terms or other requirements of an account if the dollar amount of the fee does not exceed, as applicable:

(A) $28.00;

(B) $39.00 if the card issuer previously imposed a fee pursuant to paragraph (b)(1)(ii)(A) of this section for a violation of the same type that occurred during the same billing cycle or one of the next six billing cycles; or

(C) Three percent of the delinquent balance on a charge card account that requires payment of outstanding balances in full at the end of each billing cycle if the card issuer has not received the required payment for two or more consecutive billing cycles.

(D) The amounts in paragraphs (b)(1)(ii)(A) and (b)(1)(ii)(B) of this section will be adjusted annually by the Bureau to reflect changes in the Consumer Price Index.

(2) Prohibited fees.

(i) Fees that exceed dollar amount associated with violation.

(A) Generally. A card issuer must not impose a fee for violating the terms or other requirements of a credit card account under an open-end (not home-secured) consumer credit plan that exceeds the dollar amount associated with the violation.

(B) No dollar amount associated with violation. A card issuer must not impose a fee for violating the terms or other requirements of a credit card account under an open-end (not home-secured) consumer credit plan when there is no dollar amount associated with the violation. For purposes of paragraph (b)(2)(i) of this section, there is no dollar amount associated with the following violations:

(1) Transactions that the card issuer declines to authorize;

(2) Account inactivity; and

(3) The closure or termination of an account.

(ii) Multiple fees based on a single event or transaction. A card issuer must not impose more than one fee for violating the terms or other requirements of a credit card account under an open-end (not home-secured) consumer credit plan based on a single event or transaction. A card issuer may, at its option, comply with this prohibition by imposing no more than one fee for violating the terms or other requirements of an account during a billing cycle.

§ 1026.53 Allocation of payments.

(a) General rule. Except as provided in paragraph (b) of this section, when a consumer makes a payment in excess of the required minimum periodic payment for a credit card account under an open-end (not home-secured) consumer credit plan, the card issuer must allocate the excess amount first to the balance with the highest annual percentage rate and any remaining portion to the other balances in descending order based on the applicable annual percentage rate.

(b) Special rules.

(1) Accounts with balances subject to deferred interest or similar program. When a balance on a credit card account under an open-end (not home-secured) consumer credit plan is subject to a deferred interest or similar program that provides that a consumer will not be obligated to pay interest that accrues on the balance if the balance is paid in full prior to the expiration of a specified period of time:

(i) Last two billing cycles. The card issuer must allocate any amount paid by the consumer in excess of the required minimum periodic payment consistent with paragraph (a) of this section, except that, during the two billing cycles immediately preceding expiration of the specified period, the excess amount must be allocated first to the balance subject to the deferred interest or similar program and any remaining portion allocated to any other balances consistent with paragraph (a) of this section; or

(ii) Consumer request. The card issuer may at its option allocate any amount paid by the consumer in excess of the required minimum periodic payment among the balances on the account in the manner requested by the consumer.

(2) Accounts with secured balances. When a balance on a credit card account under an open-end (not home-secured) consumer credit plan is secured, the card issuer may at its option allocate any amount paid by the consumer in excess of the required minimum periodic payment to that balance if requested by the consumer.

§ 1026.54 Limitations on the imposition of finance charges.

(a) Limitations on imposing finance charges as a result of the loss of a grace period.

(1) General rule. Except as provided in paragraph (b) of this section, a card issuer must not impose finance charges as a result of the loss of a grace period on a credit card account under an open-end (not home-secured) consumer credit plan if those finance charges are based on:

(i) Balances for days in billing cycles that precede the most recent billing cycle; or

(ii) Any portion of a balance subject to a grace period that was repaid prior to the expiration of the grace period.

(2) Definition of grace period. For purposes of paragraph (a)(1) of this section, "grace period" has the same meaning as in § 1026.5(b)(2)(ii)(B)(3).

(b) Exceptions. Paragraph (a) of this section does not apply to:

(1) Adjustments to finance charges as a result of the resolution of a dispute under § 1026.12 or § 1026.13; or

(2) Adjustments to finance charges as a result of the return of a payment.

§ 1026.55 Limitations on increasing annual percentage rates, fees, and charges.

(a) General rule. Except as provided in paragraph (b) of this section, a card issuer must not increase an annual percentage rate or a fee or charge required to be disclosed under § 1026.6(b)(2)(ii), (b)(2)(iii), or (b)(2)(xii) on a credit card account under an open-end (not home-secured) consumer credit plan.

(b) Exceptions. A card issuer may increase an annual percentage rate or a fee or charge required to be disclosed under § 1026.6(b)(2)(ii), (b)(2)(iii), or (b)(2)(xii) pursuant to an exception set forth in this paragraph even if that increase would not be permitted under a different exception.

(1) Temporary rate, fee, or charge exception. A card issuer may increase an annual percentage rate or a fee or charge required to be disclosed under § 1026.6(b)(2)(ii), (b)(2)(iii), or (b)(2)(xii) upon the expiration of a specified period of six months or longer, provided that:

(i) Prior to the commencement of that period, the card issuer disclosed in writing to the consumer, in a clear and conspicuous manner, the length of the period and the annual percentage rate, fee, or charge that would apply after expiration of the period; and

(ii) Upon expiration of the specified period:

(A) The card issuer must not apply an annual percentage rate, fee, or charge to transactions that occurred prior to the period that exceeds the annual percentage rate, fee, or charge that applied to those transactions prior to the period;

(B) If the disclosures required by paragraph (b)(1)(i) of this section are provided pursuant to § 1026.9(c), the card issuer must not apply an annual percentage rate, fee, or charge to transactions that occurred within 14 days after provision of the notice that exceeds the annual percentage rate, fee, or charge that applied to that category of transactions prior to provision of the notice; and

(C) The card issuer must not apply an annual percentage rate, fee, or charge to transactions that occurred during the period that exceeds the increased annual percentage rate, fee, or charge disclosed pursuant to paragraph (b)(1)(i) of this section.

(2) Variable rate exception. A card issuer may increase an annual percentage rate when:

(i) The annual percentage rate varies according to an index that is not under the card issuer's control and is available to the general public; and

(ii) The increase in the annual percentage rate is due to an increase in the index.

(3) Advance notice exception. A card issuer may increase an annual percentage rate or a fee or charge required to be disclosed under § 1026.6(b)(2)(ii), (b)(2)(iii), or (b)(2)(xii) after complying with the applicable notice requirements in § 1026.9(b), (c), or (g), provided that:

(i) If a card issuer discloses an increased annual percentage rate, fee, or charge pursuant to § 1026.9(b), the card issuer must not apply that rate, fee, or charge to transactions that occurred prior to provision of the notice;

(ii) If a card issuer discloses an increased annual percentage rate, fee, or charge pursuant to § 1026.9(c) or (g), the card issuer must not apply that rate, fee, or charge to transactions that occurred prior to or within 14 days after provision of the notice; and

(iii) This exception does not permit a card issuer to increase an annual percentage rate or a fee or charge required to be disclosed under § 1026.6(b)(2)(ii), (iii), or (xii) during the first year after the account is opened, while the account is closed, or while the card issuer does not permit the consumer to use the account for new transactions. For purposes of this paragraph, an account is considered open no earlier than the date on which the account may first be used by the consumer to engage in transactions.

(4) Delinquency exception. A card issuer may increase an annual percentage rate or a fee or charge required to be disclosed under § 1026.6(b)(2)(ii), (b)(2)(iii), or (b)(2)(xii) due to the card issuer not receiving the consumer's required minimum periodic payment within 60 days after the due date for that payment, provided that:

(i) The card issuer must disclose in a clear and conspicuous manner in the notice of the increase pursuant to § 1026.9(c) or (g):

(A) A statement of the reason for the increase; and

(B) That the increased annual percentage rate, fee, or charge will cease to apply if the card issuer receives six consecutive required minimum periodic payments on or before the payment due date beginning with the first payment due following the effective date of the increase; and

(ii) If the card issuer receives six consecutive required minimum periodic payments on or before the payment due date beginning with the first payment due following the effective date of the increase, the card issuer must reduce any annual percentage rate, fee, or charge increased pursuant to this exception to the annual percentage rate, fee, or charge that applied prior to the increase with respect to transactions that occurred prior to or within 14 days after provision of the § 1026.9(c) or (g) notice.

(5) Workout and temporary hardship arrangement exception. A card issuer may increase an annual percentage rate or a fee or charge required to be disclosed under § 1026.6(b)(2)(ii), (b)(2)(iii), or (b)(2)(xii) due to the consumer's completion of a workout or temporary hardship arrangement or the consumer's failure to comply with the terms of such an arrangement, provided that:

(i) Prior to commencement of the arrangement (except as provided in § 1026.9(c)(2)(v)(D)), the card issuer has provided the consumer with a clear and conspicuous written disclosure of the terms of the arrangement (including any increases due to the completion or failure of the arrangement); and

(ii) Upon the completion or failure of the arrangement, the card issuer must not apply to any transactions that occurred prior to commencement of the arrangement an annual percentage rate, fee, or charge that exceeds the annual percentage rate, fee, or charge that applied to those transactions prior to commencement of the arrangement.

(6) Servicemembers Civil Relief Act exception. If an annual percentage rate or a fee or charge required to be disclosed under § 1026.6(b)(2)(ii), (iii), or (xii) has been decreased pursuant to 50 U.S.C. app. 527 or a similar Federal or state statute or regulation, a card issuer may increase that annual percentage rate, fee, or charge once 50 U.S.C. app. 527 or the similar statute or regulation no longer applies, provided that the card issuer must not apply to any transactions that occurred prior to the decrease an annual percentage rate, fee, or charge that exceeds the annual percentage rate, fee, or charge that applied to those transactions prior to the decrease.

(c) Treatment of protected balances.

(1) Definition of protected balance. For purposes of this paragraph, "protected balance" means the amount owed for a category of transactions to which an increased annual percentage rate or an increased fee or charge required to be disclosed under § 1026.6(b)(2)(ii), (b)(2)(iii), or (b)(2)(xii) cannot be applied after the annual percentage rate, fee, or charge for that category of transactions has been increased pursuant to paragraph (b)(3) of this section.

(2) Repayment of protected balance. The card issuer must not require repayment of the protected balance using a method that is less beneficial to the consumer than one of the following methods:

(i) The method of repayment for the account before the effective date of the increase;

(ii) An amortization period of not less than five years, beginning no earlier than the effective date of the increase; or

(iii) A required minimum periodic payment that includes a percentage of the balance that is equal to no more than twice the percentage required before the effective date of the increase.

(d) Continuing application. This section continues to apply to a balance on a credit card account under an open-end (not home-secured) consumer credit plan after:

(1) The account is closed or acquired by another creditor; or

(2) The balance is transferred from a credit card account under an open-end (not home-secured) consumer credit plan issued by a creditor to another credit account issued by the same creditor or its affiliate or subsidiary (unless the account to which the balance is transferred is subject to § 1026.40).

(e) Promotional waivers or rebates of interest, fees, and other charges. If a card issuer promotes the waiver or rebate of finance charges due to a periodic interest rate or fees or charges required to be disclosed under § 1026.6(b)(2)(ii), (iii), or (xii) and applies the waiver or rebate to a credit card account under an open-end (not home-secured) consumer credit plan, any cessation of the waiver or rebate on that account constitutes an increase in an annual percentage rate, fee, or charge for purposes of this section.

§ 1026.56 Requirements for over-the-limit transactions.

(a) Definition. For purposes of this section, the term "over-the-limit transaction" means any extension of credit by a card issuer to complete a transaction that causes a consumer's credit card account balance to exceed the credit limit.

(b) Opt-in requirement.

(1) General. A card issuer shall not assess a fee or charge on a consumer's credit card account under an open-end (not home-secured) consumer credit plan for an over-the-limit transaction unless the card issuer:

(i) Provides the consumer with an oral, written or electronic notice, segregated from all other information, describing the consumer's right to affirmatively consent, or opt in, to the card issuer's payment of an over-the-limit transaction;

(ii) Provides a reasonable opportunity for the consumer to affirmatively consent, or opt in, to the card issuer's payment of over-the-limit transactions;

(iii) Obtains the consumer's affirmative consent, or opt-in, to the card issuer's payment of such transactions;

(iv) Provides the consumer with confirmation of the consumer's consent in writing, or if the consumer agrees, electronically; and

(v) Provides the consumer notice in writing of the right to revoke that consent following the assessment of an over-the-limit fee or charge.

(2) Completion of over-the-limit transactions without consumer consent. Notwithstanding the absence of a consumer's affirmative consent under paragraph (b)(1)(iii) of this section, a card issuer may pay any over-the-limit transaction on a consumer's account provided that the card issuer does not impose any fee or charge on the account for paying that over-the-limit transaction.

(c) Method of election. A card issuer may permit a consumer to consent to the card issuer's payment of any over-the-limit transaction in writing, orally, or electronically, at the card issuer's option. The card issuer must also permit the consumer to revoke his or her consent using the same methods available to the consumer for providing consent.

(d) Timing and placement of notices.

(1) Initial notice.

(i) General. The notice required by paragraph (b)(1)(i) of this section shall be provided prior to the assessment of any over-the-limit fee or charge on a consumer's account.

(ii) Oral or electronic consent. If a consumer consents to the card issuer's payment of any over-the-limit transaction by oral or electronic means, the card issuer must provide the notice required by paragraph (b)(1)(i) of this section immediately prior to obtaining that consent.

(2) Confirmation of opt-in. The notice required by paragraph (b)(1)(iv) of this section may be provided no later than the first periodic statement sent after the consumer has consented to the card issuer's payment of over-the-limit transactions.

(3) Notice of right of revocation. The notice required by paragraph (b)(1)(v) of this section shall be provided on the front of any page of each periodic statement that reflects the assessment of an over-the-limit fee or charge on a consumer's account.

(e) Content.

(1) Initial notice. The notice required by paragraph (b)(1)(i) of this section shall include all applicable items in this paragraph (e)(1) and may not contain any information not specified in or otherwise permitted by this paragraph.

(i) Fees. The dollar amount of any fees or charges assessed by the card issuer on a consumer's account for an over-the-limit transaction;

(ii) APRs. Any increased periodic rate(s) (expressed as an annual percentage rate(s)) that may be imposed on the account as a result of an over-the-limit transaction; and

(iii) Disclosure of opt-in right. An explanation of the consumer's right to affirmatively consent to the card issuer's payment of over-the-limit transactions, including the method(s) by which the consumer may consent.

(2) Subsequent notice. The notice required by paragraph (b)(1)(v) of this section shall describe the consumer's right to revoke any consent provided under paragraph (b)(1)(iii) of this section, including the method(s) by which the consumer may revoke.

(3) Safe harbor. Use of Model Forms G-25(A) or G-25(B) of Appendix G to this part, or substantially similar notices, constitutes compliance with the notice content requirements of paragraph (e) of this section.

(f) Joint relationships. If two or more consumers are jointly liable on a credit card account under an open-end (not home-secured) consumer credit plan, the card issuer shall treat the affirmative consent of any of the joint consumers as affirmative consent for that account. Similarly, the card issuer shall treat a revocation of consent by any of the joint consumers as revocation of consent for that account.

(g) Continuing right to opt in or revoke opt-in. A consumer may affirmatively consent to the card issuer's payment of over-the-limit transactions at any time in the manner described in the notice required by paragraph (b)(1)(i) of this section. Similarly, the consumer may revoke the consent at any time in the manner described in the notice required by paragraph (b)(1)(v) of this section.

(h) Duration of opt-in. A consumer's affirmative consent to the card issuer's payment of over-the-limit transactions is effective until revoked by the consumer, or until the card issuer decides for any reason to cease paying over-the-limit transactions for the consumer.

(i) Time to comply with revocation request. A card issuer must comply with a consumer's revocation request as soon as reasonably practicable after the card issuer receives it.

(j) Prohibited practices. Notwithstanding a consumer's affirmative consent to a card issuer's payment of over-the-limit transactions, a card issuer is prohibited from engaging in the following practices:

(1) Fees or charges imposed per cycle.

(i) General rule. A card issuer may not impose more than one over-the-limit fee or charge on a consumer's credit card account per billing cycle, and, in any event, only if the credit limit was exceeded during the billing cycle. In addition, except as provided in paragraph (j)(1)(ii) of this section, a card issuer may not impose an over-the-limit fee or charge on the consumer's credit card account for more than three billing cycles for the same over-the-limit transaction where the consumer has not reduced the account balance below the credit limit by the payment due date for either of the last two billing cycles.

(ii) Exception. The prohibition in paragraph (j)(1)(i) of this section on imposing an over-the-limit fee or charge in more than three billing cycles for the same over-the-limit transaction(s) does not apply if another over-the-limit transaction occurs during either of the last two billing cycles.

(2) Failure to promptly replenish. A card issuer may not impose an over-the-limit fee or charge solely because of the card issuer's failure to promptly replenish the consumer's available credit following the crediting of the consumer's payment under § 1026.10.

(3) Conditioning. A card issuer may not condition the amount of a consumer's credit limit on the consumer affirmatively consenting to the card issuer's payment of over-the-limit transactions if the card issuer assesses a fee or charge for such service.

(4) Over-the-limit fees attributed to fees or interest. A card issuer may not impose an over-the-limit fee or charge for a billing cycle if a consumer exceeds a credit limit solely because of fees or interest charged by the card issuer to the consumer's account during that billing cycle. For purposes of this paragraph (j)(4), the relevant fees or interest charges are charges imposed as part of the plan under § 1026.6(b)(3).

§ 1026.57 Reporting and marketing rules for college student open-end credit.

(a) Definitions.

(1) College student credit card. The term "college student credit card" as used in this section means a credit card issued under a credit card account under an open-end (not home-secured) consumer credit plan to any college student.

(2) College student. The term "college student" as used in this section means a consumer who is a full-time or part-time student of an institution of higher education.

(3) Institution of higher education. The term "institution of higher education" as used in this section has the same meaning as in sections 101 and 102 of the Higher Education Act of 1965 (20 U.S.C. 1001 and 1002).

(4) Affiliated organization. The term "affiliated organization" as used in this section means an alumni organization or foundation affiliated with or related to an institution of higher education.

(5) College credit card agreement. The term "college credit card agreement" as used in this section means any business, marketing or promotional agreement between a card issuer and an institution of higher education or an affiliated organization in connection with which college student credit cards are issued to college students currently enrolled at that institution.

(b) Public disclosure of agreements. An institution of higher education shall publicly disclose any contract or other agreement made with a card issuer or creditor for the purpose of marketing a credit card.

(c) Prohibited inducements. No card issuer or creditor may offer a college student any tangible item to induce such student to apply for or open an open-end consumer credit plan offered by such card issuer or creditor, if such offer is made:

(1) On the campus of an institution of higher education;

(2) Near the campus of an institution of higher education; or

(3) At an event sponsored by or related to an institution of higher education.

(d) Annual report to the Bureau.

(1) Requirement to report. Any card issuer that was a party to one or more college credit card agreements in effect at any time during a calendar year must submit to the Bureau an annual report regarding those agreements in the form and manner prescribed by the Bureau.

(2) Contents of report. The annual report to the Bureau must include the following:

(i) Identifying information about the card issuer and the agreements submitted, including the issuer's name, address, and identifying number (such as an RSSD ID number or tax identification number);

(ii) A copy of any college credit card agreement to which the card issuer was a party that was in effect at any time during the period covered by the report;

(iii) A copy of any memorandum of understanding in effect at any time during the period covered by the report between the card issuer and an institution of higher education or affiliated organization that directly or indirectly relates to the college credit card agreement or that controls or directs any obligations or distribution of benefits between any such entities;

(iv) The total dollar amount of any payments pursuant to a college credit card agreement from the card issuer to an institution of higher education or affiliated organization during the period covered by the report, and the method or formula used to determine such amounts;

(v) The total number of credit card accounts opened pursuant to any college credit card agreement during the period covered by the report; and

(vi) The total number of credit card accounts opened pursuant to any such agreement that were open at the end of the period covered by the report.

(3) Timing of reports. Except for the initial report described in this paragraph (d)(3), a card issuer must submit its annual report for each calendar year to the Bureau by the first business day on or after March 31 of the following calendar year.

§ 1026.58 Internet posting of credit card agreements.

(a) Applicability. The requirements of this section apply to any card issuer that issues credit cards under a credit card account under an open-end (not home-secured) consumer credit plan.

(b) Definitions.

(1) Agreement. For purposes of this section, "agreement" or "credit card agreement" means the written document or documents evidencing the terms of the legal obligation, or the prospective legal obligation, between a card issuer and a consumer for a credit card account under an open-end (not home-secured) consumer credit plan. "Agreement" or "credit card agreement" also includes the pricing information, as defined in § 1026.58(b)(7).

(2) Amends. For purposes of this section, an issuer "amends" an agreement if it makes a substantive change (an "amendment") to the agreement. A change is substantive if it alters the rights or obligations of the card issuer or the consumer under the agreement. Any change in the pricing information, as defined in § 1026.58(b)(7), is deemed to be substantive.

(3) Business day. For purposes of this section, "business day" means a day on which the creditor's offices are open to the public for carrying on substantially all of its business functions.

(4) Card issuer. For purposes of this section, "card issuer" or "issuer" means the entity to which a consumer is legally obligated, or would be legally obligated, under the terms of a credit card agreement.

(5) Offers. For purposes of this section, an issuer "offers" or "offers to the public" an agreement if the issuer is soliciting or accepting applications for accounts that would be subject to that agreement.

(6) Open account. For purposes of this section, an account is an "open account" or "open credit card account" if it is a credit card account under an open-end (not home-secured) consumer credit plan and either:

(i) The cardholder can obtain extensions of credit on the account; or

(ii) There is an outstanding balance on the account that has not been charged off. An account that has been suspended temporarily (for example, due to a report by the cardholder of unauthorized use of the card) is considered an "open account" or "open credit card account."

(7) Pricing information. For purposes of this section, "pricing information" means the information listed in § 1026.6(b)(2)(i) through (b)(2)(xii). Pricing information does not include temporary or promotional rates and terms or rates and terms that apply only to protected balances.

(8) Private label credit card account and private label credit card plan. For purposes of this section:

(i) "private label credit card account" means a credit card account under an open-end (not home-secured) consumer credit plan with a credit card that can be used to make purchases only at a single merchant or an affiliated group of merchants; and

(ii) "private label credit card plan" means all of the private label credit card accounts issued by a particular issuer with credit cards usable at the same single merchant or affiliated group of merchants.

(c) Submission of agreements to Bureau.

(1) Quarterly submissions. A card issuer must make quarterly submissions to the Bureau, in the form and manner specified by the Bureau. Quarterly submissions must be sent to the Bureau no later than the first business day on or after January 31, April 30, July 31, and October 31 of each year. Each submission must contain:

(i) Identifying information about the card issuer and the agreements submitted, including the issuer's name, address, and identifying number (such as an RSSD ID number or tax identification number);

(ii) The credit card agreements that the card issuer offered to the public as of the last business day of the preceding calendar quarter that the card issuer has not previously submitted to the Bureau;

(iii) Any credit card agreement previously submitted to the Bureau that was amended during the preceding calendar quarter and that the card issuer offered to the public as of the last business day of the preceding calendar quarter, as described in § 1026.58(c)(3); and

(iv) Notification regarding any credit card agreement previously submitted to the Bureau that the issuer is withdrawing, as described in § 1026.58(c)(4), (c)(5), (c)(6), and (c)(7).

(2) [Reserved]

(3) Amended agreements. If a credit card agreement has been submitted to the Bureau, the agreement has not been amended and the card issuer continues to offer the agreement to the public, no additional submission regarding that agreement is required. If a credit card agreement that previously has been submitted to the Bureau is amended and the card issuer offered the amended agreement to the public as of the last business day of the calendar quarter in which the change became effective, the card issuer must submit the entire amended agreement to the Bureau, in the form and manner specified by the Bureau, by the first quarterly submission deadline after the last day of the calendar quarter in which the change became effective.

(4) Withdrawal of agreements. If a card issuer no longer offers to the public a credit card agreement that previously has been submitted to the Bureau, the card issuer must notify the Bureau, in the form and manner specified by the Bureau, by the first quarterly submission deadline after the last day of the calendar quarter in which the issuer ceased to offer the agreement.

(5) De minimis exception.

(i) A card issuer is not required to submit any credit card agreements to the Bureau if the card issuer had fewer than 10,000 open credit card accounts as of the last business day of the calendar quarter.

(ii) If an issuer that previously qualified for the de minimis exception ceases to qualify, the card issuer must begin making quarterly submissions to the Bureau no later than the first quarterly submission deadline after the date as of which the issuer ceased to qualify.

(iii) If a card issuer that did not previously qualify for the de minimis exception qualifies for the de minimis exception, the card issuer must continue to make quarterly submissions to the Bureau until the issuer notifies the Bureau that the card issuer is withdrawing all agreements it previously submitted to the Bureau.

(6) Private label credit card exception.

(i) A card issuer is not required to submit to the Bureau a credit card agreement if, as of the last business day of the calendar quarter, the agreement:

(A) Is offered for accounts under one or more private label credit card plans each of which has fewer than 10,000 open accounts; and

(B) Is not offered to the public other than for accounts under such a plan.

(ii) If an agreement that previously qualified for the private label credit card exception ceases to qualify, the card issuer must submit the agreement to the Bureau no later than the first quarterly submission deadline after the date as of which the agreement ceased to qualify.

(iii) If an agreement that did not previously qualify for the private label credit card exception qualifies for the exception, the card issuer must continue to make quarterly submissions to the Bureau with respect to that agreement until the issuer notifies the Bureau that the agreement is being withdrawn.

(7) Product testing exception.

(i) A card issuer is not required to submit to the Bureau a credit card agreement if, as of the last business day of the calendar quarter, the agreement:

(A) Is offered as part of a product test offered to only a limited group of consumers for a limited period of time;

(B) Is used for fewer than 10,000 open accounts; and

(C) Is not offered to the public other than in connection with such a product test.

(ii) If an agreement that previously qualified for the product testing exception ceases to qualify, the card issuer must submit the agreement to the Bureau no later than the first quarterly submission deadline after the date as of which the agreement ceased to qualify.

(iii) If an agreement that did not previously qualify for the product testing exception qualifies for the exception, the card issuer must continue to make quarterly submissions to the Bureau with respect to that agreement until the issuer notifies the Bureau that the agreement is being withdrawn.

(8) Form and content of agreements submitted to the Bureau.

(i) Form and content generally.

(A) Each agreement must contain the provisions of the agreement and the pricing information in effect as of the last business day of the preceding calendar quarter.

(B) Agreements must not include any personally identifiable information relating to any cardholder, such as name, address, telephone number, or account number.

(C) The following are not deemed to be part of the agreement for purposes of § 1026.58, and therefore are not required to be included in submissions to the Bureau:

(1) Disclosures required by state or Federal law, such as affiliate marketing notices, privacy policies, billing rights notices, or disclosures under the E-Sign Act;

(2) Solicitation materials;

(3) Periodic statements;

(4) Ancillary agreements between the issuer and the consumer, such as debt cancellation contracts or debt suspension agreements;

(5) Offers for credit insurance or other optional products and other similar advertisements; and

(6) Documents that may be sent to the consumer along with the credit card or credit card agreement such as a cover letter, a validation sticker on the card, or other information about card security.

(D) Agreements must be presented in a clear and legible font.

(ii) Pricing information.

(A) Pricing information must be set forth in a single addendum to the agreement. The addendum must contain all of the pricing information, as defined by § 1026.58(b)(7). The addendum may, but is not required to, contain any other information listed in § 1026.6(b), provided that information is complete and accurate as of the applicable date under § 1026.58. The addendum may not contain any other information.

(B) Pricing information that may vary from one cardholder to another depending on the cardholder's creditworthiness or state of residence or other factors must be disclosed either by setting forth all the possible variations (such as purchase APRs of 13 percent, 15 percent, 17 percent, and 19 percent) or by providing a range of possible variations (such as purchase APRs ranging from 13 percent to 19 percent).

(C) If a rate included in the pricing information is a variable rate, the issuer must identify the index or formula used in setting the rate and the margin. Rates that may vary from one cardholder to another must be disclosed by providing the index and the possible margins (such as the prime rate plus 5 percent, 8 percent, 10 percent, or 12 percent) or range of margins (such as the prime rate plus from 5 to 12 percent). The value of the rate and the value of the index are not required to be disclosed.

(iii) Optional variable terms addendum. Provisions of the agreement other than the pricing information that may vary from one cardholder to another depending on the cardholder's creditworthiness or state of residence or other factors may be set forth in a single addendum to the agreement separate from the pricing information addendum.

(iv) Integrated agreement. Issuers may not provide provisions of the agreement or pricing information in the form of change-in-terms notices or riders (other than the pricing information addendum and the optional variable terms addendum). Changes in provisions or pricing information must be integrated into the text of the agreement, the pricing information addendum or the optional variable terms addendum, as appropriate.

(d) Posting of agreements offered to the public.

(1) Except as provided below, a card issuer must post and maintain on its publicly available Web site the credit card agreements that the issuer is required to submit to the Bureau under § 1026.58(c). With respect to an agreement offered solely for accounts under one or more private label credit card plans, an issuer may fulfill this requirement by posting and maintaining the agreement in accordance with the requirements of this section on the publicly available Web site of at least one of the merchants at which credit cards issued under each private label credit card plan with 10,000 or more open accounts may be used.

(2) Except as provided in § 1026.58(d), agreements posted pursuant to § 1026.58(d) must conform to the form and content requirements for agreements submitted to the Bureau specified in § 1026.58(c)(8).

(3) Agreements posted pursuant to § 1026.58(d) may be posted in any electronic format that is readily usable by the general public. Agreements must be placed in a location that is prominent and readily accessible by the public and must be accessible without submission of personally identifiable information.

(4) The card issuer must update the agreements posted on its Web site pursuant to § 1026.58(d) at least as frequently as the quarterly schedule required for submission of agreements to the Bureau under § 1026.58(c). If the issuer chooses to update the agreements on its Web site more frequently, the agreements posted on the issuer's Web site may contain the provisions of the agreement and the pricing information in effect as of a date other than the last business day of the preceding calendar quarter.

(e) Agreements for all open accounts.

(1) Availability of individual cardholder's agreement. With respect to any open credit card account, a card issuer must either:

(i) Post and maintain the cardholder's agreement on its Web site; or

(ii) Promptly provide a copy of the cardholder's agreement to the cardholder upon the cardholder's request. If the card issuer makes an agreement available upon request, the issuer must provide the cardholder with the ability to request a copy of the agreement both by using the issuer's Web site (such as by clicking on a clearly identified box to make the request) and by calling a readily available telephone line the number for which is displayed on the issuer's Web site and clearly identified as to purpose. The card issuer must send to the cardholder or otherwise make available to the cardholder a copy of the cardholder's agreement in electronic or paper form no later than 30 days after the issuer receives the cardholder's request.

(2) Special rule for issuers without interactive Web sites. An issuer that does not maintain a Web site from which cardholders can access specific information about their individual accounts, instead of complying with § 1026.58(e)(1), may make agreements available upon request by providing the cardholder with the ability to request a copy of the agreement by calling a readily available telephone line, the number for which is displayed on the issuer's Web site and clearly identified as to purpose or included on each periodic statement sent to the cardholder and clearly identified as to purpose. The issuer must send to the cardholder or otherwise make available to the cardholder a copy of the cardholder's agreement in electronic or paper form no later than 30 days after the issuer receives the cardholder's request.

(3) Form and content of agreements.

(i) Except as provided in § 1026.58(e), agreements posted on the card issuer's Web site pursuant to § 1026.58(e)(1)(i) or made available upon the cardholder's request pursuant to § 1026.58(e)(1)(ii) or (e)(2) must conform to the form and content requirements for agreements submitted to the Bureau specified in § 1026.58(c)(8).

(ii) If the card issuer posts an agreement on its Web site or otherwise provides an agreement to a cardholder electronically under § 1026.58(e), the agreement may be posted or provided in any electronic format that is readily usable by the general public and must be placed in a location that is prominent and readily accessible to the cardholder.

(iii) Agreements posted or otherwise provided pursuant to § 1026.58(e) may contain personally identifiable information relating to the cardholder, such as name, address, telephone number, or account number, provided that the issuer takes appropriate measures to make the agreement accessible only to the cardholder or other authorized persons.

(iv) Agreements posted or otherwise provided pursuant to § 1026.58(e) must set forth the specific provisions and pricing information applicable to the particular cardholder. Provisions and pricing information must be complete and accurate as of a date no more than 60 days prior to:

(A) The date on which the agreement is posted on the card issuer's Web site under § 1026.58(e)(1)(i); or

(B) The date the cardholder's request is received under § 1026.58(e)(1)(ii) or (e)(2).

(v) Agreements provided upon cardholder request pursuant to § 1026.58(e)(1)(ii) or (e)(2) may be provided by the issuer in either electronic or paper form, regardless of the form of the cardholder's request.

(f) E-Sign Act requirements. Card issuers may provide credit card agreements in electronic form under § 1026.58(d) and (e) without regard to the consumer notice and consent requirements of section 101(c) of the Electronic Signatures in Global and National Commerce Act (E-Sign Act) (15 U.S.C. 7001 et seq.).

(g) Temporary suspension of agreement submission requirement.

(1) Quarterly submissions. The quarterly submission requirement in paragraph (c) of this section is suspended for the submissions that would otherwise be due to the Bureau by the first business day on or after April 30, 2015; July 31, 2015; October 31, 2015; and January 31, 2016.

(2) Posting of agreements offered to the public. Nothing in paragraph (g)(1) of this section shall affect the agreement posting requirements in paragraph (d) of this section.

§ 1026.59 Reevaluation of rate increases.

(a) General rule.

(1) Evaluation of increased rate. If a card issuer increases an annual percentage rate that applies to a credit card account under an open-end (not home-secured) consumer credit plan, based on the credit risk of the consumer, market conditions, or other factors, or increased such a rate on or after January 1, 2009, and 45 days' advance notice of the rate increase is required pursuant to § 1026.9(c)(2) or (g), the card issuer must:

(i) Evaluate the factors described in paragraph (d) of this section; and

(ii) Based on its review of such factors, reduce the annual percentage rate applicable to the consumer's account, as appropriate.

(2) Rate reductions.

(i) Timing. If a card issuer is required to reduce the rate applicable to an account pursuant to paragraph (a)(1) of this section, the card issuer must reduce the rate not later than 45 days after completion of the evaluation described in paragraph (a)(1).

(ii) Applicability of rate reduction. Any reduction in an annual percentage rate required pursuant to paragraph (a)(1) of this section shall apply to:

(A) Any outstanding balances to which the increased rate described in paragraph (a)(1) of this section has been applied; and

(B) New transactions that occur after the effective date of the rate reduction that would otherwise have been subject to the increased rate.

(b) Policies and procedures. A card issuer must have reasonable written policies and procedures in place to conduct the review described in paragraph (a) of this section.

(c) Timing. A card issuer that is subject to paragraph (a) of this section must conduct the review described in paragraph (a)(1) of this section not less frequently than once every six months after the rate increase.

(d) Factors.

(1) In general. Except as provided in paragraph (d)(2) of this section, a card issuer must review either:

(i) The factors on which the increase in an annual percentage rate was originally based; or

(ii) The factors that the card issuer currently considers when determining the annual percentage rates applicable to similar new credit card accounts under an open-end (not home-secured) consumer credit plan.

(2) Rate increases imposed between January 1, 2009 and February 21, 2010. For rate increases imposed between January 1, 2009 and February 21, 2010, an issuer must consider the factors described in paragraph (d)(1)(ii) when conducting the first two reviews required under paragraph (a) of this section, unless the rate increase subject to paragraph (a) of this section was based solely upon factors specific to the consumer, such as a decline in the consumer's credit risk, the consumer's delinquency or default, or a violation of the terms of the account.

(e) Rate increases due to delinquency. If an issuer increases a rate applicable to a consumer's account pursuant to § 1026.55(b)(4) based on the card issuer not receiving the consumer's required minimum periodic payment within 60 days after the due date, the issuer is not required to perform the review described in paragraph (a) of this section prior to the sixth payment due date after the effective date of the increase. However, if the annual percentage rate applicable to the consumer's account is not reduced pursuant to § 1026.55(b)(4)(ii), the card issuer must perform the review described in paragraph (a) of this section. The first such review must occur no later than six months after the sixth payment due following the effective date of the rate increase.

(f) Termination of obligation to review factors. The obligation to review factors described in paragraph (a) and (d) of this section ceases to apply:

(1) If the issuer reduces the annual percentage rate applicable to a credit card account under an open-end (not home-secured) consumer credit plan to the rate applicable immediately prior to the increase, or, if the rate applicable immediately prior to the increase was a variable rate, to a variable rate determined by the same formula (index and margin) that was used to calculate the rate applicable immediately prior to the increase; or

(2) If the issuer reduces the annual percentage rate to a rate that is lower than the rate described in paragraph (f)(1) of this section.

(g) Acquired accounts.

(1) General. Except as provided in paragraph (g)(2) of this section, this section applies to credit card accounts that have been acquired by the card issuer from another card issuer. A card issuer that complies with this section by reviewing the factors described in paragraph (d)(1)(i) must review the factors considered by the card issuer from which it acquired the accounts in connection with the rate increase.

(2) Review of acquired portfolio. If, not later than six months after the acquisition of such accounts, a card issuer reviews all of the credit card accounts it acquires in accordance with the factors that it currently considers in determining the rates applicable to its similar new credit card accounts:

(i) Except as provided in paragraph (g)(2)(iii), the card issuer is required to conduct reviews described in paragraph (a) of this section only for rate increases that are imposed as a result of its review under this paragraph. See §§ 1026.9 and 1026.55 for additional requirements regarding rate increases on acquired accounts.

(ii) Except as provided in paragraph (g)(2)(iii) of this section, the card issuer is not required to conduct reviews in accordance with paragraph (a) of this section for any rate increases made prior to the card issuer's acquisition of such accounts.

(iii) If as a result of the card issuer's review, an account is subject to, or continues to be subject to, an increased rate as a penalty, or due to the consumer's delinquency or default, the requirements of paragraph (a) of this section apply.

(h) Exceptions.

(1) Servicemembers Civil Relief Act exception. The requirements of this section do not apply to increases in an annual percentage rate that was previously decreased pursuant to 50 U.S.C. app. 527, provided that such a rate increase is made in accordance with § 1026.55(b)(6).

(2) Charged off accounts. The requirements of this section do not apply to accounts that the card issuer has charged off in accordance with loan-loss provisions.

§ 1026.60 Credit and charge card applications and solicitations.

(a) General rules. The card issuer shall provide the disclosures required under this section on or with a solicitation or an application to open a credit or charge card account.

(1) Definition of solicitation. For purposes of this section, the term solicitation means an offer by the card issuer to open a credit or charge card account that does not require the consumer to complete an application. A "firm offer of credit" as defined in section 603(*l*) of the Fair Credit Reporting Act (15 U.S.C. 1681a(*l*)) for a credit or charge card is a solicitation for purposes of this section.

(2) Form of disclosures; tabular format.

(i) The disclosures in paragraphs (b)(1) through (5) (except for (b)(1)(iv)(B)) and (b)(7) through (15) of this section made pursuant to paragraph (c), (d)(2), (e)(1) or (f) of this section generally shall be in the form of a table with headings, content, and format substantially similar to any of the applicable tables found in G-10 in Appendix G to this part.

(ii) The table described in paragraph (a)(2)(i) of this section shall contain only the information required or permitted by this section. Other information may be presented on or with an application or solicitation, provided such information appears outside the required table.

(iii) Disclosures required by paragraphs (b)(1)(iv)(B), (b)(1)(iv)(C) and (b)(6) of this section must be placed directly beneath the table.

(iv) When a tabular format is required, any annual percentage rate required to be disclosed pursuant to paragraph (b)(1) of this section, any introductory rate required to be disclosed pursuant to paragraph (b)(1)(ii) of this section, any rate that will apply after a premium initial rate expires required to be disclosed under paragraph (b)(1)(iii) of this section, and any fee or percentage amounts or maximum limits on fee amounts disclosed pursuant to paragraphs (b)(2), (b)(4), (b)(8) through (b)(13) of this section must be disclosed in bold text. However, bold text shall not be used for: The amount of any periodic fee disclosed pursuant to paragraph (b)(2) of this section that is not an annualized amount; and other annual percentage rates or fee amounts disclosed in the table.

(v) For an application or a solicitation that is accessed by the consumer in electronic form, the disclosures required under this section may be provided to the consumer in electronic form on or with the application or solicitation.

(vi)(A) Except as provided in paragraph (a)(2)(vi)(B) of this section, the table described in paragraph (a)(2)(i) of this section must be provided in a prominent location on or with an application or a solicitation.

(B) If the table described in paragraph (a)(2)(i) of this section is provided electronically, it must be provided in close proximity to the application or solicitation.

(3) Fees based on a percentage. If the amount of any fee required to be disclosed under this section is determined on the basis of a percentage of another amount, the percentage used and the identification of the amount against which the percentage is applied may be disclosed instead of the amount of the fee.

(4) Fees that vary by state. Card issuers that impose fees referred to in paragraphs (b)(8) through (12) of this section that vary by state may, at the issuer's option, disclose in the table required by paragraph (a)(2)(i) of this section: The specific fee applicable to the consumer's account; or the range of the fees, if the disclosure includes a statement that the amount of the fee varies by state and refers the consumer to a disclosure provided with the table where the amount of the fee applicable to the consumer's account is disclosed. A card issuer may not list fees for multiple states in the table.

(5) Exceptions. This section does not apply to:

(i) Home-equity plans accessible by a credit or charge card that are subject to the requirements of § 1026.40;

(ii) Overdraft lines of credit tied to asset accounts accessed by check-guarantee cards or by debit cards;

(iii) Lines of credit accessed by check-guarantee cards or by debit cards that can be used only at automated teller machines;

(iv) Lines of credit accessed solely by account numbers except for a covered separate credit feature solely accessible by an account number that is a hybrid prepaid-credit card as defined in § 1026.61;

(v) Additions of a credit or charge card to an existing open-end plan;

(vi) General purpose applications unless the application, or material accompanying it, indicates that it can be used to open a credit or charge card account; or

(vii) Consumer-initiated requests for applications.

(b) Required disclosures. The card issuer shall disclose the items in this paragraph on or with an application or a solicitation in accordance with the requirements of paragraphs (c), (d), (e)(1) or (f) of this section. A credit card issuer shall disclose all applicable items in this paragraph except for paragraph (b)(7) of this section. A charge card issuer shall disclose the applicable items in paragraphs (b)(2), (4), (7) through (12), and (15) of this section. With respect to a covered separate credit feature that is a charge card account accessible by a hybrid prepaid-credit card as defined in § 1026.61, a charge card issuer also shall disclose the applicable items in paragraphs (b)(3), (13), and (14) of this section.

(1) Annual percentage rate. Each periodic rate that may be used to compute the finance charge on an outstanding balance for purchases, a cash advance, or a balance transfer, expressed as an annual percentage rate (as determined by § 1026.14(b)). When more than one rate applies for a category of transactions, the range of balances to which each rate is applicable shall also be disclosed. The annual percentage rate for purchases disclosed pursuant to this paragraph shall be in at least 16-point type, except for the following: Oral disclosures of the annual percentage rate for purchases; or a penalty rate that may apply upon the occurrence of one or more specific events.

(i) Variable rate information. If a rate disclosed under paragraph (b)(1) of this section is a variable rate, the card issuer shall also disclose the fact that the rate may vary and how the rate is determined. In describing how the applicable rate will be determined, the card issuer must identify the type of index or formula that is used in setting the rate. The value of the index and the amount of the margin that are used to calculate the variable rate shall not be disclosed in the table. A disclosure of any applicable limitations on rate increases shall not be included in the table.

(ii) Discounted initial rate. If the initial rate is an introductory rate, as that term is defined in § 1026.16(g)(2)(ii), the card issuer must disclose in the table the introductory rate, the time period during which the introductory rate will remain in effect, and must use the term "introductory" or "intro" in immediate proximity to the introductory rate. The card issuer also must disclose the rate that would otherwise apply to the account pursuant to paragraph (b)(1) of this section. Where the rate is not tied to an index or formula, the card issuer must disclose the rate that will apply after the introductory rate expires. In a variable-rate account, the card issuer must disclose a rate based on the applicable index or formula in accordance with the accuracy requirements set forth in paragraphs (c)(2), (d)(3), or (e)(4) of this section, as applicable.

(iii) Premium initial rate. If the initial rate is temporary and is higher than the rate that will apply after the temporary rate expires, the card issuer must disclose the premium initial rate pursuant to paragraph (b)(1) of this section and the time period during which the premium initial rate will remain in effect. Consistent with paragraph (b)(1) of this section, the premium initial rate for purchases must be in at least 16-point type. The issuer must also disclose in the table the rate that will apply after the premium initial rate expires, in at least 16-point type.

(iv) Penalty rates.

(A) In general. Except as provided in paragraph (b)(1)(iv)(B) and (C) of this section, if a rate may increase as a penalty for one or more events specified in the account agreement, such as a late payment or an extension of credit that exceeds the credit limit, the card issuer must disclose pursuant to this paragraph (b)(1) the increased rate that may apply, a brief description of the event or events that may result in the increased rate, and a brief description of how long the increased rate will remain in effect.

(B) Introductory rates. If the issuer discloses an introductory rate, as that term is defined in § 1026.16(g)(2)(ii), in the table or in any written or electronic promotional materials accompanying applications or solicitations subject to paragraph (c) or (e) of this section, the issuer must briefly disclose directly beneath the table the circumstances, if any, under which the introductory rate may be revoked, and the type of rate that will apply after the introductory rate is revoked.

(C) Employee preferential rates. If a card issuer discloses in the table a preferential annual percentage rate for which only employees of the card issuer, employees of a third party, or other individuals with similar affiliations with the card issuer or third party, such as executive officers, directors, or principal shareholders are eligible, the card issuer must briefly disclose directly beneath the table the circumstances under which such preferential rate may be revoked, and the rate that will apply after such preferential rate is revoked.

(v) Rates that depend on consumer's creditworthiness. If a rate cannot be determined at the time disclosures are given because the rate depends, at least in part, on a later determination of the consumer's creditworthiness, the card issuer must disclose the specific rates or the range of rates that could apply and a statement that the rate for which the consumer may qualify at account opening will depend on the consumer's creditworthiness, and other factors if applicable. If the rate that depends, at least in part, on a later determination of the consumer's creditworthiness is a penalty rate, as described in paragraph (b)(1)(iv) of this section, the card issuer at its option may disclose the highest rate that could apply, instead of disclosing the specific rates or the range of rates that could apply.

(vi) APRs that vary by state. Issuers imposing annual percentage rates that vary by state may, at the issuer's option, disclose in the table: the specific annual percentage rate applicable to the consumer's account; or the range of the annual percentage rates, if the disclosure includes a statement that the annual percentage rate varies by state and refers the consumer to a disclosure provided with the table where the annual percentage rate applicable to the consumer's account is disclosed. A card issuer may not list annual percentage rates for multiple states in the table.

(2) Fees for issuance or availability.

(i) Any annual or other periodic fee that may be imposed for the issuance or availability of a credit or charge card, including any fee based on account activity or inactivity; how frequently it will be imposed; and the annualized amount of the fee.

(ii) Any non-periodic fee that relates to opening an account. A card issuer must disclose that the fee is a one-time fee.

(3) Fixed finance charge; minimum interest charge. Any fixed finance charge and a brief description of the charge. Any minimum interest charge if it exceeds $1.00 that could be imposed during a billing cycle, and a brief description of the charge. The $1.00 threshold amount shall be adjusted periodically by the Bureau to reflect changes in the Consumer Price Index. The Bureau shall calculate each year a price level adjusted minimum interest charge using the Consumer Price Index in effect on June 1 of that year. When the cumulative change in the adjusted minimum value derived from applying the annual Consumer Price level to the current minimum interest charge threshold has risen by a whole dollar, the minimum interest charge will be increased by $1.00. The issuer may, at its option, disclose in the table minimum interest charges below this threshold.

(4) Transaction charges. Any transaction charge imposed by the card issuer for the use of the card for purchases.

(5) Grace period. The date by which or the period within which any credit extended for purchases may be repaid without incurring a finance charge due to a periodic interest rate and any conditions on the availability of the grace period. If no grace period is provided, that fact must be disclosed. If the length of the grace period varies, the card issuer may disclose the range of days, the minimum number of days, or the average number of days in the grace period, if the disclosure is identified as a range, minimum, or average. In disclosing in the tabular format a grace period that applies to all types of purchases, the phrase "How to Avoid Paying Interest on Purchases" shall be used as the heading for the row describing the grace period. If a grace period is not offered on all types of purchases, in disclosing this fact in the tabular format, the phrase "Paying Interest" shall be used as the heading for the row describing this fact.

(6) Balance computation method. The name of the balance computation method listed in paragraph (g) of this section that is used to determine the balance for purchases on which the finance charge is computed, or an explanation of the method used if it is not listed. In determining which balance computation method to disclose, the card issuer shall assume that credit extended for purchases will not be repaid within the grace period, if any.

(7) Statement on charge card payments. A statement that charges incurred by use of the charge card are due when the periodic statement is received.

(8) Cash advance fee. Any fee imposed for an extension of credit in the form of cash or its equivalent.

(9) Late payment fee. Any fee imposed for a late payment.

(10) Over-the-limit fee. Any fee imposed for exceeding a credit limit.

(11) Balance transfer fee. Any fee imposed to transfer an outstanding balance.

(12) Returned-payment fee. Any fee imposed by the card issuer for a returned payment.

(13) Required insurance, debt cancellation or debt suspension coverage.

(i) A fee for insurance described in § 1026.4(b)(7) or debt cancellation or suspension coverage described in § 1026.4(b)(10), if the insurance or debt cancellation or suspension coverage is required as part of the plan; and

(ii) A cross reference to any additional information provided about the insurance or coverage accompanying the application or solicitation, as applicable.

(14) Available credit. If a card issuer requires fees for the issuance or availability of credit described in paragraph (b)(2) of this section, or requires a security deposit for such credit, and the total amount of those required fees and/or security deposit that will be imposed and charged to the account when the account is opened is 15 percent or more of the minimum credit limit for the card, a card issuer must disclose the available credit remaining after these fees or security deposit are debited to the account, assuming that the consumer receives the minimum credit limit. In determining whether the 15 percent threshold test is met, the issuer must only consider fees for issuance or availability of credit, or a security deposit, that are required. If fees for issuance or availability are optional, these fees should not be considered in determining whether the disclosure must be given. Nonetheless, if the 15 percent threshold test is met, the issuer in providing the disclosure must disclose the amount of available credit calculated by excluding those optional fees, and the available credit including those optional fees. This paragraph does not apply with respect to fees or security deposits that are not debited to the account.

(15) Web site reference. A reference to the Web site established by the Bureau and a statement that consumers may obtain on the Web site information about shopping for and using credit cards. Until January 1, 2013, issuers may substitute for this reference a reference to the Web site established by the Board of Governors of the Federal Reserve System.

(c) Direct mail and electronic applications and solicitations.

(1) General. The card issuer shall disclose the applicable items in paragraph (b) of this section on or with an application or solicitation that is mailed to consumers or provided to consumers in electronic form.

(2) Accuracy.

(i) Disclosures in direct mail applications and solicitations must be accurate as of the time the disclosures are mailed. An accurate variable annual percentage rate is one in effect within 60 days before mailing.

(ii) Disclosures provided in electronic form must be accurate as of the time they are sent, in the case of disclosures sent to a consumer's email address, or as of the time they are viewed by the public, in the case of disclosures made available at a location such as a card issuer's Web site. An accurate variable annual percentage rate provided in electronic form is one in effect within 30 days before it is sent to a consumer's email address, or viewed by the public, as applicable.

(d) Telephone applications and solicitations.

(1) Oral disclosure. The card issuer shall disclose orally the information in paragraphs (b)(1) through (7) and (b)(14) of this section, to the extent applicable, in a telephone application or solicitation initiated by the card issuer.

(2) Alternative disclosure. The oral disclosure under paragraph (d)(1) of this section need not be given if the card issuer either:

(i)(A) Does not impose a fee described in paragraph (b)(2) of this section; or

(B) Imposes such a fee but provides the consumer with a right to reject the plan consistent with § 1026.5(b)(1)(iv); and

(ii) The card issuer discloses in writing within 30 days after the consumer requests the card (but in no event later than the delivery of the card) the following:

(A) The applicable information in paragraph (b) of this section; and

(B) As applicable, the fact that the consumer has the right to reject the plan and not be obligated to pay fees described in paragraph (b)(2) or any other fees or charges until the consumer has used the account or made a payment on the account after receiving a billing statement.

(3) Accuracy.

(i) The oral disclosures under paragraph (d)(1) of this section must be accurate as of the time they are given.

(ii) The alternative disclosures under paragraph (d)(2) of this section generally must be accurate as of the time they are mailed or delivered. A variable annual percentage rate is one that is accurate if it was:

(A) In effect at the time the disclosures are mailed or delivered; or

(B) In effect as of a specified date (which rate is then updated from time to time, but no less frequently than each calendar month).

(e) Applications and solicitations made available to general public. The card issuer shall provide disclosures, to the extent applicable, on or with an application or solicitation that is made available to the general public, including one contained in a catalog, magazine, or other generally available publication. The disclosures shall be provided in accordance with paragraph (e)(1) or (e)(2) of this section.

(1) Disclosure of required credit information. The card issuer may disclose in a prominent location on the application or solicitation the following:

(i) The applicable information in paragraph (b) of this section;

(ii) The date the required information was printed, including a statement that the required information was accurate as of that date and is subject to change after that date; and

(iii) A statement that the consumer should contact the card issuer for any change in the required information since it was printed, and a toll-free telephone number or a mailing address for that purpose.

(2) No disclosure of credit information. If none of the items in paragraph (b) of this section is provided on or with the application or solicitation, the card issuer may state in a prominent location on the application or solicitation the following:

(i) There are costs associated with the use of the card; and

(ii) The consumer may contact the card issuer to request specific information about the costs, along with a toll-free telephone number and a mailing address for that purpose.

(3) Prompt response to requests for information. Upon receiving a request for any of the information referred to in this paragraph, the card issuer shall promptly and fully disclose the information requested.

(4) Accuracy. The disclosures given pursuant to paragraph (e)(1) of this section must be accurate as of the date of printing. A variable annual percentage rate is accurate if it was in effect within 30 days before printing.

(f) In-person applications and solicitations. A card issuer shall disclose the information in paragraph (b) of this section, to the extent applicable, on or with an application or solicitation that is initiated by the card issuer and given to the consumer in person. A card issuer complies with the requirements of this paragraph if the issuer provides disclosures in accordance with paragraph (c)(1) or (e)(1) of this section.

(g) Balance computation methods defined. The following methods may be described by name. Methods that differ due to variations such as the allocation of payments, whether the finance charge begins to accrue on the transaction date or the date of posting the transaction, the existence or length of a grace period, and whether the balance is adjusted by charges such as late payment fees, annual fees and unpaid finance charges do not constitute separate balance computation methods.

(1)(i) Average daily balance (including new purchases). This balance is figured by adding the outstanding balance (including new purchases and deducting payments and credits) for each day in the billing cycle, and then dividing by the number of days in the billing cycle.

(ii) Average daily balance (excluding new purchases). This balance is figured by adding the outstanding balance (excluding new purchases and deducting payments and credits) for each day in the billing cycle, and then dividing by the number of days in the billing cycle.

(2) Adjusted balance. This balance is figured by deducting payments and credits made during the billing cycle from the outstanding balance at the beginning of the billing cycle.

(3) Previous balance. This balance is the outstanding balance at the beginning of the billing cycle.

(4) Daily balance. For each day in the billing cycle, this balance is figured by taking the beginning balance each day, adding any new purchases, and subtracting any payment and credits.

§ 1026.61 Hybrid prepaid-credit cards.

(a) Hybrid prepaid-credit card.

(1) In general.

(i) Credit offered in connection with a prepaid account is subject to this section and this regulation as specified below.

(ii) For purposes of this regulation, except as provided in paragraph (a)(4) of this section, a prepaid card is a hybrid prepaid-credit card with respect to a separate credit feature as described in paragraph (a)(2)(i) of this section when it can access credit from that credit feature, or with respect to a credit feature structured as a negative balance on the asset feature of the prepaid account as described in paragraph (a)(3) of this section when it can access credit from that credit feature. A hybrid prepaid-credit card is a credit card for purposes of this regulation with respect to those credit features.

(iii) With respect to a credit feature structured as a negative balance on the asset feature of the prepaid account as described in paragraph (a)(3) of this section, a prepaid card is not a hybrid prepaid-credit card or a credit card for purposes of this regulation if the conditions set forth in paragraph (a)(4) of this section are met.

(2) Prepaid card can access credit from a covered separate credit feature.

(i) Covered separate credit feature.

(A) A separate credit feature that can be accessed by a hybrid prepaid-credit card as described in this paragraph (a)(2)(i) is defined as a covered separate credit feature. A prepaid card is a hybrid prepaid-credit card with respect to a separate credit feature when it is a single device that can be used from time to time to access the separate credit feature where the following two conditions are both satisfied:

(1) The card can be used to draw, transfer, or authorize the draw or transfer of credit from the separate credit feature in the course of authorizing, settling, or otherwise completing transactions conducted with the card to obtain goods or services, obtain cash, or conduct person-to-person transfers; and

(2) The separate credit feature is offered by the prepaid account issuer, its affiliate, or its business partner.

(B) A separate credit feature that meets the conditions set forth in paragraph (a)(2)(i)(A) of this section is a covered separate credit feature accessible by a hybrid prepaid-credit card even with respect to credit that is drawn or transferred, or authorized to be drawn or transferred, from the credit feature outside the course of a transaction conducted with the card to obtain goods or services, obtain cash, or conduct person-to-person transfers.

(ii) Non-covered separate credit feature. A separate credit feature that does not meet the two conditions set forth in paragraph (a)(2)(i) of this section is defined as a non-covered separate credit feature. A prepaid card is not a hybrid prepaid-credit card with respect to a non-covered separate credit feature, even if the prepaid card is a hybrid prepaid credit card with respect to a covered separate credit feature as described in paragraph (a)(2)(i) of this section. A noncovered separate credit feature is not subject to the rules applicable to hybrid prepaid-credit cards; however, it may be subject to this regulation depending on its own terms and conditions, independent of the connection to the prepaid account.

(3) Prepaid card can access credit extended through a negative balance on the asset feature of the prepaid account.

(i) In general. Except as provided in paragraph (a)(4) of this section, a prepaid card is a hybrid prepaid-credit card when it is a single device that can be used from time to time to access credit extended through a negative balance on the asset feature of the prepaid account.

(ii) Negative asset balances. Notwithstanding paragraph (a)(3)(i) of this section with regard to coverage under this regulation, structuring a hybrid prepaid-credit card to access credit through a negative balance on the asset feature violates paragraph (b) of this section. A prepaid account issuer can use a negative asset balance structure to extend credit on an asset feature of a prepaid account only if the prepaid card is not a hybrid prepaid-credit card with respect to that credit as described in paragraph (a)(4) of this section.

(4) Exception for credit extended through a negative balance. A prepaid card is not a hybrid prepaid-credit card with respect to credit extended through a negative balance on the asset feature of the prepaid account and is not a credit card for purposes of this regulation with respect to that credit where:

(i) The prepaid card cannot access credit from a covered separate credit feature as described in paragraph (a)(2)(i) of this section that is offered by a prepaid account issuer or its affiliate; and

(ii) The prepaid card only can access credit extended through a negative balance on the asset feature of the prepaid account where both paragraphs (a)(4)(ii)(A) and (B) of this section are satisfied.

(A) The prepaid account issuer has an established policy and practice of either declining to authorize any transaction for which it reasonably believes the consumer has insufficient or unavailable funds in the asset feature of the prepaid account at the time the transaction is authorized to cover the amount of the transaction, or declining to authorize any such transactions except in one or more of the following circumstances:

(1) The amount of the transaction will not cause the asset feature balance to become negative by more than $10 at the time of the authorization; or

(2) In cases where the prepaid account issuer has received an instruction or confirmation for an incoming electronic fund transfer originated from a separate asset account to load funds to the prepaid account or where the prepaid account issuer has received a request from the consumer to load funds to the prepaid account from a separate asset account but in either case the funds from the separate asset account have not yet settled, the amount of the transaction will not cause the asset feature balance to become negative at the time of the authorization by more than the incoming or requested load amount, as applicable.

(B) The following fees or charges are not imposed on the asset feature of the prepaid account:

(1) Any fees or charges for opening, issuing, or holding a negative balance on the asset feature, or for the availability of credit, whether imposed on a one-time or periodic basis. This paragraph does not include fees or charges to open, issue, or hold the prepaid account where the amount of the fee or charge imposed on the asset feature is not higher based on whether credit might be offered or has been accepted, whether or how much credit the consumer has accessed, or the amount of credit available;

(2) Any fees or charges that will be imposed only when credit is extended on the asset feature or when there is a negative balance on the asset feature, except that a prepaid account issuer may impose fees or charges for the actual costs of collecting the credit extended if otherwise permitted by law; or

(3) Any fees or charges where the amount of the fee or charge is higher when credit is extended on the asset feature or when there is a negative balance on the asset feature.

(C) A prepaid account issuer may still satisfy the exception in paragraph (a)(4) of this section even if it debits fees or charges from the asset feature when there are insufficient or unavailable funds in the asset feature to cover those fees or charges at the time they are imposed, so long as those fees or charges are not the type of fees or charges enumerated in paragraph (a)(4)(ii)(B) of this section.

(5) Definitions. For purposes of this section and other provisions in the regulation that relate to hybrid prepaid-credit cards:

(i) Affiliate means any company that controls, is controlled by, or is under common control with another company, as set forth in the Bank Holding Company Act of 1956 (12 U.S.C. 1841 et seq.).

(ii) Asset feature means an asset account that is a prepaid account, or an asset subaccount of a prepaid account.

(iii) Business partner means a person (other than the prepaid account issuer or its affiliates) that can extend credit through a separate credit feature where the person or its affiliate has an arrangement with a prepaid account issuer or its affiliate except as provided in paragraph (a)(5)(iii)(D) of this section.

(A) Arrangement defined. For purposes of paragraph (a)(5)(iii) of this section, a person that can extend credit through a separate credit feature or the person's affiliate has an arrangement with a prepaid account issuer or its affiliate if the circumstances in either paragraph (a)(5)(iii)(B) or (C) of this section are met.

(B) Arrangement by agreement. A person that can extend credit through a separate credit feature or its affiliate has an arrangement with a prepaid account issuer or its affiliate if the parties have an agreement that allows the prepaid card from time to time to draw, transfer, or authorize a draw or transfer of credit in the course of authorizing, settling, or otherwise completing transactions conducted with the card to obtain goods or services, obtain cash, or conduct person-to-person transfers.

(C) Marketing arrangement. A person that can extend credit through a separate credit feature or its affiliate has an arrangement with a prepaid account issuer or its affiliate if:

(1) The parties have a business, marketing, or promotional agreement or other arrangement which provides that prepaid accounts offered by the prepaid account issuer will be marketed to the customers of the person that can extend credit; or the separate credit feature offered by the person who can extend credit will be marketed to the holders of prepaid accounts offered by the prepaid account issuer (including any marketing to customers to encourage them to authorize the prepaid card to access the separate credit feature as described in paragraph (a)(5)(iii)(C)(2) of this section); and

(2) At the time of the marketing agreement or arrangement described in paragraph (a)(5)(iii)(C)(1) of this section, or at any time afterwards, the prepaid card from time to time can draw, transfer, or authorize the draw or transfer of credit from the separate credit feature offered by the person that can extend credit in the course of authorizing, settling, or otherwise completing transactions conducted with the card to obtain goods or services, obtain cash, or conduct person-to-person transfers. This requirement is satisfied even if there is no specific agreement between the parties that the card can access the credit feature, as described in paragraph (a)(5)(iii)(B) of this section.

(D) Exception for certain credit card account arrangements. For purposes of paragraph (a)(5)(iii) of this section, a person that can extend credit through a credit card account is not a business partner of a prepaid account issuer with which it has an arrangement as defined in paragraphs (a)(5)(iii)(A) through (C) of this section with regard to such credit card account if all of the following conditions are met:

(1) The credit card account is a credit card account under an open-end (not home-secured) consumer credit plan that a consumer can access through a traditional credit card.

(2) The prepaid account issuer and the card issuer do not allow the prepaid card to draw, transfer, or authorize the draw or transfer of credit from the credit card account from time to time in the course of authorizing, settling, or otherwise completing transactions conducted with the card to obtain goods or services, obtain cash, or conduct person-to-person transfers, except where the prepaid account issuer or the card issuer has received from the consumer a written request that is separately signed or initialized to authorize the prepaid card to access the credit card account as described above. If the credit card account is linked to the prepaid account prior to April 1, 2019, or prior to the arrangement between the prepaid account issuer and the card issuer as described in paragraphs (a)(5)(iii)(A) through (C) of this section, the prepaid account issuer and the card issuer will be deemed to have satisfied this condition even if they have not received from the consumer a written request that is separately signed or initialized to authorize the prepaid card to access the credit card account as described in this paragraph.

(3) The prepaid account issuer and the card issuer do not condition the acquisition or retention of the prepaid account or the credit card account on whether a consumer authorizes the prepaid card to access the credit card account as described in paragraph (a)(5)(iii)(D)(2) of this section. If the credit card account is linked to the prepaid account prior to April 1, 2019, this condition only applies to the retention of the prepaid account and the credit card account on or after April 1, 2019.

(4) The prepaid account issuer applies the same terms, conditions, or features to the prepaid account when a consumer authorizes linking the prepaid card to the credit card account as described in paragraph (a)(5)(iii)(D)(2) of this section as it applies to the consumer's prepaid account when the consumer does not authorize such a linkage. In addition, the prepaid account issuer applies the same fees to load funds from the credit card account that is linked to the prepaid account as described above as it charges for a comparable load on the consumer's prepaid account to access a credit feature offered by a person that is not the prepaid account issuer, its affiliate, or a person with which the prepaid account issuer has an arrangement as described in paragraphs (a)(5)(iii)(A) through (C) of this section.

(5) The card issuer applies the same specified terms and conditions to the credit card account when a consumer authorizes linking the prepaid card to the credit card account as described in paragraph (a)(5)(iii)(D)(2) of this section as it applies to the consumer's credit card account when the consumer does not authorize such a linkage. In addition, the card issuer applies the same specified terms and conditions to extensions of credit accessed by the prepaid card from the credit card account as it applies to extensions of credit accessed by the traditional credit card. For purposes of this paragraph, "specified terms and conditions" means the terms and conditions required to be disclosed under § 1026.6(b), any repayment terms and conditions, and the limits on liability for unauthorized credit transactions.

(iv) Credit feature means a separate credit account or a credit subaccount of a prepaid account through which credit can be extended in connection with a prepaid card, or a negative balance on an asset feature of a prepaid account through which credit can be extended in connection with a prepaid card.

(v) Prepaid account means a prepaid account as defined in Regulation E, 12 CFR 1005.2(b)(3).

(vi) Prepaid account issuer means a financial institution as defined in Regulation E, 12 CFR 1005.2(i), with respect to a prepaid account.

(vii) Prepaid card means any card, code, or other device that can be used to access a prepaid account.

(viii) Separate credit feature means a credit account or a credit subaccount of a prepaid account through which credit can be extended in connection with a prepaid card that is separate from the asset feature of the prepaid account. This term does not include a negative balance on an asset feature of a prepaid account.

(b) Structure of credit features accessible by hybrid prepaid-credit cards. With respect to a credit feature that is accessible by a hybrid prepaid-credit card, a card issuer shall not structure the credit feature as a negative balance on the asset feature of a prepaid account. A card issuer shall structure the credit feature as a separate credit feature, either as a separate credit account, or as a credit subaccount of a prepaid account that is separate from the asset feature of the prepaid account. The separate credit feature is a covered separate credit feature accessible by a hybrid prepaid-credit card under § 1026.61(a)(2)(i).

(c) Timing requirement for credit card solicitation or application with respect to hybrid prepaid-credit cards.

(1) With respect to a covered separate credit feature that could be accessible by a hybrid prepaid-credit card at any point, a card issuer must not do any of the following until 30 days after the prepaid account has been registered:

(i) Open a covered separate credit feature that could be accessible by the hybrid prepaid-credit card;

(ii) Make a solicitation or provide an application to open a covered separate credit feature that could be accessible by the hybrid prepaid-credit card; or

(iii) Allow an existing credit feature that was opened prior to the consumer obtaining the prepaid account to become a covered separate credit feature accessible by the hybrid prepaid-credit card.

(2) For purposes of paragraph (c) of this section, the term solicitation has the meaning set forth in § 1026.60(a)(1).

AVAILABILITY OF FUNDS AND COLLECTION OF CHECKS (REGULATION CC)

12 C.F.R. Part 229

Current through March 27, 2019; 84 F.R. 11636

For updates and appendices with Model Forms, Federal Reserve Commentary, and Official Board Interpretations, see www.ecfr.gov

SUBPART A—GENERAL

SUBPART B—AVAILABILITY OF FUNDS AND DISCLOSURE OF FUNDS AVAILABILITY POLICIES

SUBPART C—COLLECTION OF CHECKS

SUBPART D—SUBSTITUTE CHECKS

SUBPART A—GENERAL

§ 229.1 Authority and purpose; organization.

(a) Authority and purpose. This part is issued by the Board of Governors of the Federal Reserve System (Board) to implement the Expedited Funds Availability Act (12 U.S.C. 4001–4010) (the EFA Act) and the Check Clearing for the 21st Century Act (12 U.S.C. 5001–5018) (the Check 21 Act).

(b) Organization. This part is divided into subparts and appendices as follows—

(1) Subpart A contains general information. It sets forth—

(i) The authority, purpose, and organization;

(ii) Definition of terms; and

(iii) Authority for administrative enforcement of this part's provisions.

(2) Subpart B of this part contains rules regarding the duty of banks to make funds deposited into accounts available for withdrawal, including availability schedules. Subpart B of this part also contains rules regarding exceptions to the schedules, disclosure of funds availability policies, payment of interest, liability of banks for failure to comply with Subpart B of this part, and other matters.

(3) Subpart C of this part contains rules to expedite the collection and return of checks and electronic checks by banks. These rules cover the direct return of checks and electronic checks, the manner in which the paying bank and returning banks must return checks and electronic checks to the depositary bank, notification of nonpayment by the paying bank, indorsement and presentment of checks and electronic checks, same-day settlement for certain checks, the liability of banks for failure to comply with subpart C of this part, and other matters.

(4) Subpart D of this part contains rules relating to substitute checks. These rules address the creation and legal status of substitute checks; the substitute check warranties and indemnity; expedited recredit procedures for resolving improper charges and warranty claims associated with substitute checks provided to consumers; and the disclosure and notices that banks must provide.

(5) Appendix A of this part contains a routing number guide to next day availability checks. The guide lists the routing numbers of checks drawn on Federal Reserve Banks and Federal Home Loan Banks, and U.S. Treasury checks and Postal money orders that are subject to next-day availability.

(6) Appendix B of this part is reserved.

(7) Appendix C of this part contains model funds-availability policy disclosures, clauses, and notices and a model disclosure and notices related to substitute-check policies.

(8) Appendix D of this part is reserved.

(9) Appendix E of this part contains Board interpretations, which are labeled "Commentary," of the provisions of this part. The Commentary provides background material to explain the Board's intent in adopting a particular part of the regulation and provides examples to aid in understanding how a particular requirement is to work. The Commentary is an official Board interpretation under section 611(e) of the EFA Act (12 U.S.C. 4010(e)).

(10) Appendix F of this part contains the Board's determinations of the EFA Act and Regulation CC's preemption of state laws that were in effect on September 1, 1989.

§ 229.2 Definitions.

As used in this part, and unless the context requires otherwise, the following terms have the meanings set forth in this section, and the terms not defined in this section have the meanings set forth in the Uniform Commercial Code:

(a) Account.

(1) Except as provided in paragraphs (a)(2) and (a)(3) of this section, account means a deposit as defined in 12 CFR 204.2(a)(1)(i) that is a transaction account as described in 12 CFR 204.2(e). As defined in these sections, account generally includes accounts at a bank from which the account holder is permitted to make transfers or withdrawals by negotiable or transferable instrument, payment order of withdrawal, telephone transfer, electronic payment, or other similar means for the purpose of making payments or transfers to third persons or others. Account also includes accounts at a bank from which the account holder may make third party payments at an ATM, remote service unit, or other electronic device, including by debit card, but the term does not include savings deposits or accounts described in 12 CFR 204.2(d)(2) even though such accounts permit third party transfers. An account may be in the form of—

(i) A demand deposit account,

(ii) A negotiable order of withdrawal account,

(iii) A share draft account,

(iv) An automatic transfer account, or

(v) Any other transaction account described in 12 CFR 204.2(e).

(2) For purposes of subpart B of this part and, in connection therewith, this subpart A, account does not include an account where the account holder is a bank, where the account holder is an office of an institution described in paragraphs (e)(1) through (e)(6) of this section or an office of a "foreign bank" as defined in section 1(b) of the International Banking Act (12 U.S.C. 3101) that is located outside the United States, or where the direct or indirect account holder is the Treasury of the United States.

(3) For purposes of subpart D of this part and, in connection therewith, this subpart A, account means any deposit, as defined in 12 CFR 204.2(a)(1)(i), at a bank, including a demand deposit or other transaction account and a savings deposit or other time deposit, as those terms are defined in 12 CFR 204.2.

(b) Automated clearinghouse or **ACH** means a facility that processes debit and credit transfers under rules established by a Federal Reserve Bank operating circular on automated clearinghouse items or under rules of an automated clearinghouse association.

(c) Automated teller machine or **ATM** means an electronic device at which a natural person may make deposits to an account by cash or check and perform other account transactions.

(d) Available for withdrawal with respect to funds deposited means available for all uses generally permitted to the customer for actually and finally collected funds under the bank's account agreement or policies, such as for payment of checks drawn on the account, certification of checks drawn on the account, electronic payments, withdrawals by cash, and transfers between accounts.

(e) Bank means—

(1) An insured bank as defined in section 3 of the Federal Deposit Insurance Act (12 U.S.C. 18I3) or a bank that is eligible to apply to become an insured bank under section 5 of that Act (12 U.S.C. 1815);

(2) A mutual savings bank as defined in section 3 of the Federal Deposit Insurance Act (12 U.S.C. 1813);

(3) A savings bank as defined in section 3 of the Federal Deposit Insurance Act (12 U.S.C. 1813);

(4) An insured credit union as defined in section 101 of the Federal Credit Union Act (12 U.S.C. 1752) or a credit union that is eligible to make application to become an insured credit union under section 201 of that Act (12 U.S.C. 1781);

(5) A member as defined in section 2 of the Federal Home Loan Bank Act (12 U.S.C. 1422);

(6) A savings association as defined in section 3 of the Federal Deposit Insurance Act (12 U.S.C. 1813) that is an insured depository institution as defined in section 3 of that Act (12 U.S.C. 1813(c)(2)) or that is eligible to apply to become an insured depository institution under section 5 of that Act (12 U.S.C. 1815); or

(7) An agency or a branch of a foreign bank as defined in section l(b) of the International Banking Act (12 U.S.C. 3101).

For purposes of subparts C and D of this part and, in connection therewith, this subpart A, the term bank also includes any person engaged in the business of banking, as well as a Federal Reserve Bank, a Federal Home Loan Bank, and a state or unit of general local government to the extent that the state or unit of general local government acts as a paying bank. Unless otherwise specified, the term bank includes all of a bank's offices in the United States, but not offices located outside the United States. Note: For purposes of subpart D of this part and, in connection therewith, this subpart A, bank also includes the Treasury of the United States or the United States Postal Service to the extent that the Treasury or the Postal Service acts as a paying bank.

(f) Banking day means that part of any business day on which an office of a bank is open to the public for carrying on substantially all of its banking functions.

(g) Business day means a calendar day other than a Saturday or a Sunday, January 1, the third Monday in January, the third Monday in February, the last Monday in May, July 4, the first Monday in September, the second Monday in October, November 11, the fourth Thursday in November, or December 25. If January 1, July 4, November 11, or December 25 fall on a Sunday, the next Monday is not a business day.

(h) Cash means United States coins and currency.

(i) Cashier's check means a check that is—

(1) Drawn on a bank;

(2) Signed by an officer or employee of the bank on behalf of the bank as drawer;

(3) A direct obligation of the bank; and

(4) Provided to a customer of the bank or acquired from the bank for remittance purposes.

(j) Certified check means a check with respect to which the drawee bank certifies by signature on the check of an officer or other authorized employee of the bank that—

(1)(i) The signature of the drawer on the check is genuine; and

(ii) The bank has set aside funds that—

(A) Are equal to the amount of the check, and

(B) Will be used to pay the check; or

(2) The bank will pay the check upon presentment.

(k) **Check** means—

(1) A negotiable demand draft drawn on or payable through or at an office of a bank;

(2) A negotiable demand draft drawn on a Federal Reserve Bank or a Federal Home Loan Bank;

(3) A negotiable demand draft drawn on the Treasury of the United States;

(4) A demand draft drawn on a state government or unit of general local government that is not payable through or at a bank;

(5) A United States Postal Service money order; or

(6) A traveler's check drawn on or payable through or at a bank.

(7) The term check includes an original check and a substitute check. Note: The term check does not include a noncash item or an item payable in a medium other than United States money. A draft may be a check even though it is described on its face by another term, such as money order. For purposes of subparts C and D, and in connection therewith, subpart A, of this part, the term check also includes a demand draft of the type described above that is nonnegotiable.

(*l*) [Reserved]

(m) **Check processing region** means the geographical area served by an office of a Federal Reserve Bank for purposes of its check processing activities.

(n) **Consumer account** means any account used primarily for personal, family, or household purposes.

(*o*) **Depositary bank** means the first bank to which a check is transferred even though it is also the paying bank or the payee. A check deposited in an account is deemed to be transferred to the bank holding the account into which the check is deposited, even though the check is physically received and indorsed first by another bank.

(p) **Electronic payment** means a wire transfer or an ACH credit transfer.

(q) **Forward collection** means the process by which a bank sends a check on a cash basis to a collecting bank for settlement or to the paying bank for payment.

(r) **Local check** means a check payable by or at a local paying bank, or a check payable by a nonbank payor and payable through a local paying bank.

(s) **Local paying bank** means a paying bank that is located in the same check-processing region as the physical location of the branch, contractual branch, or proprietary ATM of the depositary bank in which that check was deposited.

(t) **Merger transaction** means—

(1) A merger or consolidation of two or more banks; or

(2) The transfer of substantially all of the assets of one or more banks or branches to another bank in consideration of the assumption by the acquiring bank of substantially all of the liabilities of the transferring banks, including the deposit liabilities.

(u) **Noncash item** means an item that would otherwise be a check, except that—

(1) A passbook, certificate, or other document is attached;

(2) It is accompanied by special instructions, such as a request for special advice of payment or dishonor;

(3) It consists of more than a single thickness of paper, except a check that qualifies for handling by automated check processing equipment; or

(4) It has not been preprinted or post-encoded in magnetic ink with the routing number of the paying bank.

(v) **Nonlocal check** means a check payable by, through, or at a nonlocal paying bank.

(w) Nonlocal paying bank means a paying bank that is not a local paying bank with respect to the depositary bank.

(x) Nonproprietary ATM means an ATM that is not a proprietary ATM.

(y) [Reserved]

(z) Paying bank means—

(1) The bank by which a check is payable, unless the check is payable at another bank and is sent to the other bank for payment or collection;

(2) The bank at which a check is payable and to which it is sent for payment or collection;

(3) The Federal Reserve Bank or Federal Home Loan Bank by which a check is payable;

(4) The bank through which a check is payable and to which it is sent for payment or collection, if the check is not payable by a bank; or

(5) The state or unit of general local government on which a check is drawn and to which it is sent for payment or collection.

For purposes of subparts C and D, and in connection therewith, subpart A, paying bank includes the bank through which a check is payable and to which the check is sent for payment or collection, regardless of whether the check is payable by another bank, and the bank whose routing number appears on a check in fractional or magnetic form and to which the check is sent for payment or collection. Note: For purposes of subpart D of this part and, in connection therewith, this subpart A, paying bank also includes the Treasury of the United States or the United States Postal Service for a check that is payable by that entity and that is sent to that entity for payment or collection.

(aa) Proprietary ATM means an ATM that is—

(1) Owned or operated by, or operated exclusively for, the depositary bank;

(2) Located on the premises (including the outside wall) of the depositary bank; or

(3) Located within 50 feet of the premises of the depositary bank, and not identified as being owned or operated by another entity.

If more than one bank meets the owned or operated criterion of paragraph (aa)(1) of this section, the ATM is considered proprietary to the bank that operates it.

(bb) Qualified returned check means a returned check that is prepared for automated return to the depositary bank by placing the check in a carrier envelope or placing a strip on the check and encoding the strip or envelope in magnetic ink. A qualified returned check need not contain other elements of a check drawn on the depositary bank, such as the name of the depositary bank.

(cc) Returning bank means a bank (other than the paying or depositary bank) handling a returned check or notice in lieu of return. A returning bank is also a collecting bank for purposes of UCC 4–202(b).

(dd) Routing number means—

(1) The number printed on the face of a check in fractional form on in nine-digit form; or

(2) The number in a bank's indorsement in fractional or nine-digit form; or

(3) For purposes of subpart C and subpart D, the bank-identification number contained in an electronic check or electronic returned check.

(ee) Similarly situated bank means a bank of similar size, located in the same community, and with similar check handling activities as the paying bank or returning bank.

(ff) State means a state, the District of Columbia, Puerto Rico, or the U.S. Virgin Islands. For purposes of subpart D of this part and, in connection therewith, this subpart A, state also means Guam, American Samoa, the Trust Territory of the Pacific Islands, the Northern Mariana Islands, and any other territory of the United States.

(gg) Teller's check means a check provided to a customer of a bank or acquired from a bank for remittance purposes, that is drawn by the bank, and drawn on another bank or payable through or at a bank.

(hh) Traveler's check means an instrument for the payment of money that—

(1) Is drawn on or payable through or at a bank;

(2) Is designated on its face by the term traveler's check or by any substantially similar term or is commonly known and marketed as a traveler's check by a corporation or bank that is an issuer of traveler's checks;

(3) Provides for a specimen signature of the purchaser to be completed at the time of purchase; and

(4) Provides for a countersignature of the purchaser to be completed at the time of negotiation.

(ii) Uniform Commercial Code, Code, or **U.C.C.** means the Uniform Commercial Code as adopted in a state.

(jj) United States means the states, including the District of Columbia, the U.S. Virgin Islands, and Puerto Rico.

(kk) Unit of general local government means any city, county, parish, town, township, village, or other general purpose political subdivision of a state. The term does not include special purpose units of government, such as school districts or water districts.

(*ll*) Wire transfer means an unconditional order to a bank to pay a fixed or determinable amount of money to a beneficiary upon receipt or on a day stated in the order, that is transmitted by electronic or other means through Fedwire, the Clearing House Interbank Payments System, other similar network, between banks, or on the books of a bank. Wire transfer does not include an electronic fund transfer as defined in section 903(6) of the Electronic Fund Transfer Act (15 U.S.C. 1693a(6)).

(mm) Fedwire has the same meaning as that set forth in § 210.26(e) of this chapter.

(nn) Good faith means honesty in fact and observance of reasonable commercial standards of fair dealing.

(*oo*) Interest compensation means an amount of money calculated at the average of the Federal Funds rates published by the Federal Reserve Bank of New York for each of the days for which interest compensation is payable, divided by 360. The Federal Funds rate for any day on which a published rate is not available is the same as the published rate for the last preceding day for which there is a published rate.

(pp) Contractual branch, with respect to a bank, means a branch of another bank that accepts a deposit on behalf of the first bank.

(qq) Claimant bank means a bank that submits a claim for a recredit for a substitute check to an indemnifying bank under § 229.55.

(rr) Collecting bank means any bank handling a check for forward collection, except the paying bank.

(ss) Consumer means a natural person who—

(1) With respect to a check handled for forward collection, draws the check on a consumer account; or

(2) With respect to a check handled for return, deposits the check into or cashes the check against a consumer account.

(tt) Customer means a person having an account with a bank.

(uu) Indemnifying bank. Indemnifying bank means—

(1) For the purposes of § 229.34, a bank that provides an indemnity under § 229.34 with respect to remote deposit capture or an electronically-created item, or

(2) For the purposes of § 229.53, a bank that provides an indemnity under § 229.53 with respect to a substitute check.

(vv) Magnetic ink character recognition line and MICR line mean the numbers, which may include the routing number, account number, check number, check amount, and other information, that are (unless the Board by rule or order determines that different standards apply)—

(1) Printed near the bottom of a check in magnetic ink in accordance with American National Standard Specifications for Placement and Location of MICR Printing, X9.13 (hereinafter ANS X9.13) for an original check and American National Standard Specifications for an Image Replacement Document—IRD, X9.100–140 (hereinafter ANS X9.100–140) for a substitute check, or

(2) For purposes of subpart C and subpart D, contained in a record specified for MICR line data in an electronic check or electronic returned check in accordance with American National Standard Specifications for Electronic Exchange of Check Image Data—Domestic, X9.100–187 (hereinafter ANS X9.100–187).

(ww) Original check means the first paper check issued with respect to a particular payment transaction.

(xx) Paper or electronic representation of a substitute check means any copy of or information related to a substitute check that a bank handles for forward collection or return, charges to a customer's account, or provides to a person as a record of a check payment made by the person.

(yy) Person means a natural person, corporation, unincorporated company, partnership, government unit or instrumentality, trust, or any other entity or organization.

(zz) Reconverting bank means—

(1) The bank that creates a substitute check; or

(2) With respect to a substitute check that was created by a person that is not a bank, the first bank that transfers, presents, or returns that substitute check or, in lieu thereof, the first paper or electronic representation of that substitute check.

(aaa) Substitute check means a paper reproduction of an original check that—

(1) Contains an image of the front and back of the original check;

(2) Bears a MICR line that, except as provided under ANS X9.100–140 (unless the Board by rule or order determines that a different standard applies), contains all the information appearing on the MICR line of the original check at the time that the original check was issued and any additional information that was encoded on the original check's MICR line before an image of the original check was captured;

(3) Conforms in paper stock, dimension, and otherwise with ANS X9.100–140 (unless the Board by rule or order determines that a different standard applies); and

(4) Is suitable for automated processing in the same manner as the original check.

(bbb) Copy and sufficient copy.

(1) A **copy of an original check** means—

(i) Any paper reproduction of an original check, including a paper printout of an electronic image of the check, a photocopy of the original check, or a substitute check; or

(ii) Any electronic reproduction of a check that a recipient has agreed to receive from the sender instead of a paper reproduction.

(2) A **sufficient copy** is a copy of an original check that accurately represents all of the information on the front and back of the original check as of the time the original check was truncated or is otherwise sufficient to determine whether or not a claim is valid.

(ccc) Transfer and consideration. The terms **transfer** and **consideration** have the meanings set forth in the Uniform Commercial Code and in addition, for purposes of subpart D—

(1) The term transfer with respect to a substitute check or a paper or electronic representation of a substitute check means delivery of the substitute check or other representation of the substitute check by a bank to a person other than a bank; and

(2) A bank that transfers a substitute check or a paper or electronic representation of a substitute check directly to a person other than a bank has received consideration for the substitute check or other paper or electronic representation of the substitute check if it has charged, or has the right to charge, the person's account or otherwise has received value for the original check, a substitute check, or a representation of the original check or substitute check.

(ddd) **Truncate** means to remove an original check from the forward collection or return process and send to a recipient, in lieu of such original check, a substitute check or, by agreement, information relating to the original check (including data taken from the MICR line of the original check or an electronic image of the original check), whether with or without the subsequent delivery of the original check.

(eee) **Truncating bank** means—

(1) The bank that truncates the original check; or

(2) If a person other than a bank truncates the original check, the first bank that transfers, presents, or returns, in lieu of such original check, a substitute check or, by agreement with the recipient, information relating to the original check (including data taken from the MICR line of the original check or an electronic image of the original check), whether with or without the subsequent delivery of the original check.

(fff) **Remotely created check** means a check that is not created by the paying bank and that does not bear a signature applied, or purported to be applied, by the person on whose account the check is drawn. For purposes of this definition, "account" means an account as defined in paragraph (a) of this section as well as a credit or other arrangement that allows a person to draw checks that are payable by, through, or at a bank.

(ggg) **Electronic check** and **electronic returned check** mean an electronic image of, and electronic information derived from, a paper check or paper returned check, respectively, that—

(1) Is sent to a receiving bank pursuant to an agreement between the sender and the receiving bank; and

(2) Conforms with ANS X9.100–187, unless the Board by rule or order determines that a different standard applies or the parties otherwise agree.

(hhh) **Electronically-created item** means an electronic image that has all the attributes of an electronic check or electronic returned check but was created electronically and not derived from a paper check.

§ 229.3 Administrative enforcement.

(a) **Enforcement agencies.** Compliance with this part is enforced under—

(1) Section 8 of the Federal Deposit Insurance Act (12 U.S.C. 1818 et seq.) in the case of—

(i) National banks, and Federal branches and Federal agencies of foreign banks, by the Office of the Comptroller of the Currency;

(ii) Member banks of the Federal Reserve System (other than national banks), and offices, branches, and agencies of foreign banks located in the United States (other than Federal branches, Federal agencies, and insured State branches of foreign banks), by the Board; and

(iii) Banks insured by the Federal Deposit Insurance Corporation (other than members of the Federal Reserve System) and insured State branches of foreign banks, by the Board of Directors of the Federal Deposit Insurance Corporation;

(2) Section 8 of the Federal Deposit Insurance Act, by the Director of the Office of Thrift Supervision in the case of savings associations the deposits of which are insured by the Federal Deposit Insurance Corporation; and

(3) The Federal Credit Union Act (12 U.S.C. 1751 et seq.) by the National Credit Union Administration Board with respect to any federal credit union or credit union insured by the National Credit Union Share Insurance Fund.

The terms used in paragraph (a)(1) of this section that are not defined in this part or otherwise defined in section 3(s) of the Federal Deposit Insurance Act (12 U.S.C. 1813(s)) shall have the meaning given to them in section 1(b) of the International Banking Act of 1978 (12 U.S.C. 3101).

(b) Additional powers.

(1) For the purposes of the exercise by any agency referred to in paragraph (a) of this section of its powers under any statute referred to in that paragraph, a violation of any requirement imposed under the EFA Act is deemed to be a violation of a requirement imposed under that statute.

(2) In addition to its powers under any provision of law specifically referred to in paragraph (a) of this section, each of the agencies referred to in that paragraph may exercise, for purposes of enforcing compliance with any requirement imposed under this part, any other authority conferred on it by law.

(c) Enforcement by the Board.

(1) Except to the extent that enforcement of the requirements imposed under this part is specifically committed to some other government agency, the Board shall enforce such requirements.

(2) If the Board determines that—

(i) Any bank that is not a bank described in paragraph (a) of this section; or

(ii) Any other person subject to the authority of the Board under the EFA Act and this part,

has failed to comply with any requirement imposed by this part, the Board may issue an order prohibiting any bank, any Federal Reserve Bank, or any other person subject to the authority of the Board from engaging in any activity or transaction that directly or indirectly involves such noncomplying bank or person (including any activity or transaction involving the receipt, payment, collection, and clearing of checks, and any related function of the payment system with respect to checks).

SUBPART B—AVAILABILITY OF FUNDS AND DISCLOSURE OF FUNDS AVAILABILITY POLICIES

§ 229.10 Next-day availability.

(a) Cash deposits.

(1) A bank shall make funds deposited in an account by cash available for withdrawal not later than the business day after the banking day on which the cash is deposited, if the deposit is made in person to an employee of the depositary bank.

(2) bank shall make funds deposited in an account by cash available for withdrawal not later than the second business day after the banking day on which the cash is deposited, if the deposit is not made in person to an employee of the depositary bank.

(b) Electronic payments—

(1) In general. A bank shall make funds received for deposit in an account by an electronic payment available for withdrawal not later than the business day after the banking day on which the bank received the electronic payment.

(2) When an electronic payment is received. An electronic payment is received when the bank receiving the payment has received both—

(i) Payment in actually and finally collected funds; and

(ii) Information on the account and amount to be credited.

A bank receives an electronic payment only to the extent that the bank has received payment in actually and finally collected funds.

(c) Certain check deposits—

(1) General rule. A depositary bank shall make funds deposited in an account by check available for withdrawal not later than the business day after the banking day on which the funds are deposited, in the case of—

(i) A check drawn on the Treasury of the United States and deposited in an account held by a payee of the check;

(ii) A U.S. Postal Service money order deposited—

(A) In an account held by a payee of the money order; and

(B) In person to an employee of the depositary bank.

(iii) A check drawn on a Federal Reserve Bank or Federal Home Loan Bank and deposited—

(A) In an account held by a payee of the check; and

(B) In person to an employee of the depositary bank;

(iv) A check drawn by a state or a unit of general local government and deposited—

(A) In an account held by a payee of the check;

(B) In a depositary bank located in the state that issued the check, or the same state as the unit of general local government that issued the check;

(C) In person to an employee of the depositary bank; and

(D) With a special deposit slip or deposit envelope, if such slip or envelope is required by the depositary bank under paragraph (c)(3) of this section.

(v) A cashier's, certified, or teller's check deposited—

(A) In an account held by a payee of the check;

(B) In person to an employee of the depositary bank; and

(C) With a special deposit slip or deposit envelope, if such slip or envelope is required by the depositary bank under paragraph (c)(3) of this section.

(vi) A check deposited in a branch of the depositary bank and drawn on the same or another branch of the same bank if both branches are located in the same state or the same check processing region; and,

(vii) The lesser of—

(A) $100,[1] or

(B) The aggregate amount deposited on any one banking day to all accounts of the customer by check or checks not subject to next-day availability under paragraphs (c)(1)(i) through (vi) of this section.

(2) Checks not deposited in person. A depositary bank shall make funds deposited in an account by check or checks available for withdrawal not later than the second business day after the banking day on which funds are deposited, in the case of a check deposit described in and that meets the requirements of paragraphs (c)(1)(ii), (iii), (iv), and (v), of this section, except that it is not deposited in person to an employee of the depositary bank.

(3) Special deposit slip.

(i) As a condition to making the funds available for withdrawal in accordance with this section, a depositary bank may require that a state or local government check or a cashier's, certified, or teller's check be deposited with a special deposit slip or deposit envelope that identifies the type of check.

1 *Note from West Advisory Panel: Should be $200. See 12 U.S.C. § 4002(a)(2)(D), included in this volume.*

(ii) If a depositary bank requires the use of a special deposit slip or deposit envelope, the bank must either provide the special deposit slip or deposit envelope to its customers or inform its customers how the slip or envelope may be prepared or obtained and make the slip or envelope reasonably available.

§ 229.11 [Reserved].

§ 229.12 Availability schedule.

(a) Effective date. The availability schedule contained in this section is effective September 1, 1990.

(b) Local checks and certain other checks. Except as provided in paragraphs (d), (e), and (f) of this section, a depository bank shall make funds deposited in an account by a check available for withdrawal not later than the second business day following the banking day on which funds are deposited, in the case of—

(1) A local check;

(2) A check drawn on the Treasury of the United States that is not governed by the availability requirements of § 229.10(c);

(3) A U.S. Postal Service money order that is not governed by the availability requirements of § 229.10(c); and

(4) A check drawn on a Federal Reserve Bank or Federal Home Loan Bank; a check drawn by a state or unit of general local government; or a cashier's, certified, or teller's check; if any check referred to in this paragraph (b)(4) is a local check that is not governed by the availability requirements of § 229.10(c).

(c) Nonlocal checks—

(1) In general. Except as provided in paragraphs (d), (e), and (f) of this section, a depositary bank shall make funds deposited in an account by a check available for withdrawal not later than the fifth business day following the banking day on which funds are deposited, in the case of—

(i) A nonlocal check; and

(ii) A check drawn on a Federal Reserve Bank or Federal Home Loan Bank; a check drawn by a state or unit of general local government; a cashier's, certified, or teller's check; or a check deposited in a branch of the depositary bank and drawn on the same or another branch of the same bank, if any check referred to in this paragraph (c)(1)(ii) is a nonlocal check that is not governed by the availability requirements of § 229.10(c).

(2) Nonlocal checks specified in Appendix B-2 to this part must be made available for withdrawal not later than the times prescribed in that Appendix.

(d) Time period adjustment for withdrawal by cash or similar means. A depositary bank may extend by one business day the time that funds deposited in an account by one or more checks subject to paragraphs (b), (c), or (f) of this section are available for withdrawal by cash or similar means. Similar means include electronic payment, issuance of a cashier's or teller's check, or certification of a check, or other irrevocable commitment to pay, but do not include the granting of credit to a bank, a Federal Reserve Bank, or a Federal Home Loan Bank that presents a check to the depositary bank for payment. A depositary bank shall, however, make $400 of these funds available for withdrawal by cash or similar means not later than 5:00 p.m. on the business day on which the funds are available under paragraphs (b), (c), or (f) of this section. This $400 is in addition to the $100[1] available under § 229.10(c)(1)(vii).

(e) Extension of schedule for certain deposits in Alaska, Hawaii, Puerto Rico, and the U.S. Virgin Islands. The depositary bank may extend the time periods set forth in this section by one business day in the case of any deposit, other than a deposit described in § 229.10, that is—

---

[1] *Note from West Advisory Panel: Should be $200. See 12 U.S.C. § 4002(a)(2)(D), included in this volume.*

(1) Deposited in an account at a branch of a depositary bank if the branch is located in Alaska, Hawaii, Puerto Rico, or the U.S. Virgin Islands; and

(2) Deposited by a check drawn on or payable at or through a paying bank not located in the same state as the depositary bank.

(f) Deposits at nonproprietary ATMs. A depositary bank shall make funds deposited in an account at a nonproprietary ATM by cash or check available for withdrawal not later than the fifth business day following the banking day on which the funds are deposited.

§ 229.13 Exceptions.

(a) New accounts. For purposes of this paragraph, checks subject to § 229.10(c)(1)(v) include traveler's checks.

(1) A deposit in a new account—

(i) Is subject to the requirements of § 229.10(a) and (b) to make funds from deposits by cash and electronic payments available for withdrawal on the business day following the banking day of deposit or receipt;

(ii) Is subject to the requirements of § 229.10(c)(1)(i) through (v) and § 229.10(c)(2) only with respect to the first $5,000 of funds deposited on any one banking day; but the amount of the deposit in excess of $5,000 shall be available for withdrawal not later than the ninth business day following the banking day on which funds are deposited; and

(iii) Is not subject to the availability requirements of §§ 229.10(c)(1)(vi) and (vii) and 229.12.

(2) An account is considered a new account during the first 30 calendar days after the account is established. An account is not considered a new account if each customer on the account has had, within 30 calendar days before the account is established, another account at the depositary bank for at least 30 calendar days.

(b) Large deposits. Sections 229.10(c) and 229.12 do not apply to the aggregate amount of deposits by one or more checks to the extent that the aggregate amount is in excess of $5,000 on any one banking day. For customers that have multiple accounts at a depositary bank, the bank may apply this exception to the aggregate deposits to all accounts held by the customer, even if the customer is not the sole holder of the accounts and not all of the holders of the accounts are the same.

(c) Redeposited checks. Sections 229.10(c) and 229.12 do not apply to a check that has been returned unpaid and redeposited by the customer or the depositary bank. This exception does not apply—

(1) To a check that has been returned due to a missing indorsement and redeposited after the missing indorsement has been obtained, if the reason for return indication on the check states that it was returned due to a missing indorsement; or

(2) To a check that has been returned because it was post dated, if the reason for return indicated on the check states that it was returned because it was post dated, and if the check is no longer postdated when redeposited.

(d) Repeated overdrafts. If any account or combination of accounts of a depositary bank's customer has been repeatedly overdrawn, then for a period of six months after the last such overdraft, §§ 229.10(c) and 229.12 do not apply to any of the accounts. A depositary bank may consider a customer's account to be repeatedly overdrawn if—

(1) On six or more banking days within the preceding six months, the account balance is negative, or the account balance would have become negative if checks or other charges to the account had been paid; or

(2) On two or more banking days within the preceding six months, the account balance is negative, or the account balance would have become negative, in the amount of $5,000 or more, if checks or other charges to the account had been paid.

(e) Reasonable cause to doubt collectibility—

(1) In general. Sections 229.10(c) and 229.12 do not apply to a check deposited in an account at a depositary bank if the depositary bank has reasonable cause to believe that the check is uncollectible from the paying bank. Reasonable cause to believe a check is uncollectible requires the existence of facts that would cause a well-grounded belief in the mind of a reasonable person. Such belief shall not be based on the fact that the check is of a particular class or is deposited by a particular class of persons. The reason for the bank's belief that the check is uncollectible shall be included in the notice required under paragraph (g) of this section.

(2) Overdraft and returned check fees. A depositary bank that extends the time when funds will be available for withdrawal as described in paragraph (e)(1) of this section, and does not furnish the depositor with written notice at the time of deposit shall not assess any fees for any subsequent overdrafts (including use of a line of credit) or return of checks of other debits to the account, if—

(i) The overdraft or return of the check would not have occurred except for the fact that the deposited funds were delayed under paragraph (e)(1) of this section; and

(ii) The deposited check was paid by the paying bank.

Notwithstanding the foregoing, the depositary bank may assess an overdraft or returned check fee if it includes a notice concerning overdraft and returned check fees with the notice of exception required in paragraph (g) of this section and, when required, refunds any such fees upon the request of the customer. The notice must state that the customer may be entitled to a refund of overdraft or returned check fees that are assessed if the check subject to the exception is paid and how to obtain a refund.

(f) Emergency conditions. Sections 229.10(c) and 229.12 do not apply to funds deposited by check in a depositary bank in the case of—

(1) An interruption of communications or computer or other equipment facilities;

(2) A suspension of payments by another bank;

(3) A war; or

(4) An emergency condition beyond the control of the depositary bank,

if the depositary bank exercises such diligence as the circumstances require.

(g) Notice of exception—

(1) In general. Subject to paragraphs (g)(2) and (g)(3) of this section, when a depositary bank extends the time when funds will be available for withdrawal based on the application of an exception contained in paragraphs (b) through (e) of this section, it must provide the depositor with a written notice.

(i) The notice shall include the following information—

(A) A number or code, which need not exceed four digits, that identifies the customer's account;

(B) The date of the deposit;

(C) The amount of the deposit that is being delayed;

(D) The reason the exception was invoked; and

(E) The time period within which the funds will be available for withdrawal.

(ii) **Timing of notice.** The notice shall be provided to the depositor at the time of the deposit, unless the deposit is not made in person to an employee of the depositary bank, or, if the facts upon which a determination to invoke one of the exceptions in paragraphs (b) through (e) of this section to delay a deposit only become known to the depositary bank after the time of the deposit. If the notice is not given at the time of the deposit, the depositary bank shall mail or deliver the notice to the customer as soon as practicable, but no later than the first business day following the day the facts become known to the depositary bank, or the deposit is made, whichever is later.

(2) One-time exception notice. In lieu of providing notice pursuant to paragraph (g)(1) of this section, a depositary bank that extends the time when the funds deposited in a nonconsumer account will be available for withdrawal based on an exception contained in paragraph (b) or (c) of this section may provide a single notice to the customer that includes the following information—

(i) The reason(s) the exception may be invoked; and

(ii) The time period within which deposits subject to the exception generally will be available for withdrawal.

This one-time notice shall be provided only if each type of exception cited in the notice will be invoked for most check deposits in the account to which the exception could apply. This notice shall be provided at or prior to the time notice must be provided under paragraph (g)(1)(ii) of this section.

(3) Notice of repeated overdrafts exception. In lieu of providing notice pursuant to paragraph (g)(1) of this section, a depositary bank that extends the time when funds deposited in an account will be available for withdrawal based on the exception contained in paragraph (d) of this section may provide a notice to the customer for each time period during which the exception will be in effect. The notice shall include the following information—

(i) The account number of the customer;

(ii) The fact that the availability of funds deposited in the customer's account will be delayed because the repeated overdrafts exception will be invoked;

(iii) The time period within which deposits subject to the exception generally will be available for withdrawal; and

(iv) The time period during which the exception will apply.

This notice shall be provided at or prior to the time notice must be provided under paragraph (g)(1)(ii) of this section and only if the exception cited in the notice will be invoked for most check deposits in the account.

(4) Emergency conditions exception notice. When a depositary bank extends the time when funds will be available for withdrawal based on the application of the emergency conditions exception contained in paragraph (f) of this section, it must provide the depositor with notice in a reasonable form and within a reasonable time given the circumstances. The notice shall include the reason the exception was invoked and the time period within which funds shall be made available for withdrawal, unless the depositary bank, in good faith, does not know at the time the notice is given the duration of the emergency and, consequently, when the funds must be made available. The depositary bank is not required to provide a notice if the funds subject to the exception become available before the notice must be sent.

(5) Record retention. A depositary bank shall retain a record, in accordance with § 229.21(g), of each notice provided pursuant to its application of the reasonable cause exception under paragraph (e) of this section, together with a brief statement of the facts giving rise to the bank's reason to doubt the collectibility of the check.

(h) Availability of deposits subject to exceptions.

(1) If an exception contained in paragraphs (b) through (f) of this section applies, the depositary bank may extend the time periods established under §§ 229.10(c) and 229.12 by a reasonable period of time.

(2) If a depositary bank invokes an exception contained in paragraphs (b) through (e) of this section with respect to a check described in § 229.10(c)(1)(i) through (v) or § 229.10(c)(2), it shall make the funds available for withdrawal not later than a reasonable period after the day the funds would have been required to be made available had the check been subject to 229.12.

(3) If a depositary bank invokes an exception under paragraph (f) of this section based on an emergency condition, the depositary bank shall make the funds available for withdrawal not later than a reasonable period after the emergency has ceased or the period established in §§ 229.10(c) and 229.12, whichever is later.

(4) For the purposes of this section, a "reasonable period" is an extension of up to one business day for checks described in § 229.10(c)(1)(vi), five business days for checks described in § 229.12(b)(1) through (4), and six business days for checks described in § 229.12(c)(1) and (2) or § 229.12(f). A longer extension may be reasonable, but the bank has the burden of so establishing.

§ 229.14 Payment of interest.

(a) In general. A depositary bank shall begin to accrue interest or dividends on funds deposited in an interest-bearing account not later than the business day on which the depositary bank receives credit for the funds. For the purposes of this section, the depositary bank may—

(1) Rely on the availability schedule of its Federal Reserve Bank, Federal Home Loan Bank, or correspondent bank to determine the time credit is actually received; and

(2) Accrue interest or dividends on funds deposited in interest-bearing accounts by checks that the depositary bank sends to paying banks or subsequent collecting banks for payment or collection based on the availability of funds the depositary bank receives from the paying or collecting banks.

(b) Special rule for credit unions. Paragraph (a) of this section does not apply to any account at a bank described in § 229.2(e)(4), if the bank—

(1) Begins the accrual of interest or dividends at a later date than the date described in paragraph (a) of this section with respect to all funds, including cash, deposited in the account; and

(2) Provides notice of its interest or dividend payment policy in the manner required under § 229.16(d).

(c) Exception for checks returned unpaid. This subpart does not require a bank to pay interest or dividends on funds deposited by a check that is returned unpaid.

§ 229.15 General disclosure requirements.

(a) Form of disclosures. A bank shall make the disclosures required by this subpart clearly and conspicuously in writing. Disclosures, other than those posted at locations where employees accept consumer deposits and ATMs and the notice on preprinted deposit slips, must be in a form that the customer may keep. The disclosures shall be grouped together and shall not contain any information not related to the disclosures required by this subpart. If contained in a document that sets forth other account terms, the disclosures shall be highlighted within the document by, for example, use of a separate heading.

(b) Uniform reference to day of availability. In its disclosure, a bank shall describe funds as being available for withdrawal on "the ______ business day after" the day of deposit. In this calculation, the first business day is the business day following the banking day the deposit was received, and the last business day is the day on which the funds are made available.

(c) Multiple accounts and multiple account holders. A bank need not give multiple disclosures to a customer that holds multiple accounts if the accounts are subject to the same availability policies. Similarly, a bank need not give separate disclosures to each customer on a jointly held account.

(d) Dormant or inactive accounts. A bank need not give availability disclosures to a customer that holds a dormant or inactive account.

§ 229.16 Specific availability policy disclosure.

(a) General. To meet the requirements of a specific availability policy disclosure under §§ 229.17 and 229.18(d), a bank shall provide a disclosure describing the bank's policy as to when funds deposited in an account are available for withdrawal. The disclosure must reflect the policy followed by the bank in most cases. A bank may impose longer delays on a case-by-case basis or by invoking one of the exceptions in § 229.13, provided this is reflected in the disclosure.

(b) Content of specific availability policy disclosure. The specific availability policy disclosure shall contain the following, as applicable—

(1) A summary of the bank's availability policy;

(2) A description of any categories of deposits or checks used by the bank when it delays availability (such as local or nonlocal checks); how to determine the category to which a particular deposit or check belongs; and when each category will be available for withdrawal (including a description of the bank's business days and when a deposit is considered received);[1]

(3) A description of any of the exceptions in § 229.13 that may be invoked by the bank, including the time following a deposit that funds generally will be available for withdrawal and a statement that the bank will notify the customer if the bank invokes one of the exceptions;

(4) A description, as specified in paragraph (c)(1) of this section, of any case-by-case policy of delaying availability that may result in deposited funds being available for withdrawal later than the time periods stated in the bank's availability policy; and

(5) A description of how the customer can differentiate between a proprietary and a nonproprietary ATM, if the bank makes funds from deposits at nonproprietary ATMs available for withdrawal later than funds from deposits at proprietary ATMs.

(c) Longer delays on a case-by-case basis—

(1) Notice in specific policy disclosure. A bank that has a policy of making deposited funds available for withdrawal sooner than required by this subpart may extend the time when funds are available up to the time periods allowed under this subpart on a case-by-case basis, provided the bank includes the following in its specific policy disclosure—

(i) A statement that the time when deposited funds are available for withdrawal may be extended in some cases, and the latest time following a deposit that funds will be available for withdrawal;

(ii) A statement that the bank will notify the customer if funds deposited in the customer's account will not be available for withdrawal until later than the time periods stated in the bank's availability policy; and

(iii) A statement that customers should ask if they need to be sure about when a particular deposit will be available for withdrawal.

(2) Notice at time of case-by-case delay—

(i) In general. When a depositary bank extends the time when funds will be available for withdrawal on a case-by-case basis, it must provide the depositor with a written notice. The notice shall include the following information—

(A) A number or code, which need not exceed four digits, that identifies the customer's account.

(B) The date of the deposit;

(C) The amount of the deposit that is being delayed; and

(D) The day the funds will be available for withdrawal.

(ii) Timing of notice. The notice shall be provided to the depositor at the time of the deposit, unless the deposit is not made in person to an employee of the depositary bank or the decision to extend the time when the deposited funds will be available is made after the time of the deposit. If notice is not given at the time of the deposit, the depositary bank shall mail or

---

[1] A bank that distinguishes in its disclosure between local and nonlocal checks based on the routing number on the check must disclose that certain checks, such as some credit union share drafts that are payable by one bank but payable through another bank, will be treated as local or nonlocal checks based upon the location of the bank by which they are payable and not on the basis of the location of the bank whose routing number appears on the check. A bank that makes funds from nonlocal checks available for withdrawal within the time periods required for local checks under §§ 229.12 and 229.13 is not required to provide this disclosure on payable-through checks to its customers. The statement concerning payable-through checks must describe how the customer can determine whether these checks will be treated as local or nonlocal, or state that special rules apply to such checks and that the customer may ask about the availability of these checks.

deliver the notice to the customer not later than the first business day following the banking day the deposit is made.

(3) Overdraft and returned check fees. A depositary bank that extends the time when funds will be available for withdrawal on a case-by-case basis and does not furnish the depositor with written notice at the time of deposit shall not assess any fees for any subsequent overdrafts (including use of a line of credit) or return of checks or other debits to the account, if—

(i) The overdraft or return of the check or other debit would not have occurred except for the fact that the deposited funds were delayed under paragraph (c)(1) of this section; and

(ii) The deposited check was paid by the paying bank.

Notwithstanding the foregoing, the depositary bank may assess an overdraft or returned check fee if it includes a notice concerning overdraft and returned check fees with the notice required in paragraph (c)(2) of this section and, when required, refunds any such fees upon the request of the customer. The notice must state that the customer may be entitled to a refund of overdraft or returned check fees that are assessed if the check subject to the delay is paid and how to obtain a refund.

(d) Credit union notice of interest payment policy. If a bank described in § 229.2(e)(4) begins to accrue interest or dividends on all deposits made in an interest-bearing account, including cash deposits, at a later time than the day specified in § 229.14(a), the bank's specific policy disclosures shall contain an explanation of when interest or dividends on deposited funds begin to accrue.

§ 229.17 Initial disclosures.

Before opening a new account, a bank shall provide a potential customer with the applicable specific availability policy disclosure described in § 229.16.

§ 229.18 Additional disclosure requirements.

(a) Deposit slips. A bank shall include on all preprinted deposit slips furnished to its customers a notice that deposits may not be available for immediate withdrawal.

(b) Locations where employees accept consumer deposits. A bank shall post in a conspicuous place in each location where its employees receive deposits to consumer accounts a notice that sets forth the time periods applicable to the availability of funds deposited in a consumer account.

(c) Automated teller machines.

(1) A depositary bank shall post or provide a notice at each ATM location that funds deposited in the ATM may not be available for immediate withdrawal.

(2) A depositary bank that operates an off-premises ATM from which deposits are removed not more than two times each week, as described in § 229.19(a)(4), shall disclose at or on the ATM the days on which deposits made at the ATM will be considered received.

(d) Upon request. A bank shall provide to any person, upon oral or written request, a notice containing the applicable specific availability policy disclosure described in § 229.16.

(e) Changes in policy. A bank shall send a notice to holders of consumer accounts at least 30 days before implementing a change to the bank's availability policy regarding such accounts, except that a change that expedites the availability of funds may be disclosed not later than 30 days after implementation.

§ 229.19 Miscellaneous.

(a) When funds are considered deposited. For the purposes of this subpart—

(1) Funds deposited at a staffed facility, ATM, or contractual branch are considered deposited when they are received at the staffed facility, ATM, or contractual branch;

(2) Funds mailed to the depositary bank are considered deposited on the day they are received by the depositary bank;

(3) Funds deposited to a night depository, lock box, or similar facility are considered deposited on the day on which the deposit is removed from such facility and is available for processing by the depositary bank;

(4) Funds deposited at an ATM that is not on, or within 50 feet of, the premises of the depositary bank are considered deposited on the day the funds are removed from the ATM, if funds normally are removed from the ATM not more than two times each week; and

(5) Funds may be considered deposited on the next banking day, in the case of funds that are deposited—

(i) On a day that is not a banking day for the depositary bank; or

(ii) After a cut-off hour set by the depositary bank for the receipt of deposits of 2:00 p.m. or later, or, for the receipt of deposits at ATMs, contractual branches, or off-premise facilities, of 12:00 noon or later. Different cut-off hours later than these times may be established for the receipt of different types of deposits, or receipt of deposits at different locations.

(b) Availability at start of business day. Except as otherwise provided in § 229.12(d), if any provision of this subpart requires that funds be made available for withdrawal on any business day, the funds shall be available for withdrawal by the later of:

(1) 9:00 a.m. (local time of the depositary bank); or

(2) The time the depositary bank's teller facilities (including ATMs) are available for customer account withdrawals.

(c) Effect on policies of depositary bank. This part does not—

(1) Prohibit a depositary bank from making funds available to a customer for withdrawal in a shorter period of time than the time required by this subpart;

(2) Affect a depositary bank's right—

(i) To accept or reject a check for deposit;

(ii) To revoke any settlement made by the depositary bank with respect to a check accepted by the bank for deposit, to charge back the customer's account for the amount of a check based on the return of the check or receipt of a notice of nonpayment of the check, or to claim a refund of such credit; and

(iii) To charge back funds made available to its customer for an electronic payment for which the bank has not received payment in actually and finally collected funds;

(3) Require a depositary bank to open or otherwise to make its facilities available for customer transactions on a given business day; or

(4) Supersede any policy of a depositary bank that limits the amount of cash a customer may withdraw from its account on any one day, if that policy—

(i) Is not dependent on the time the funds have been deposited in the account, as long as the funds have been on deposit for the time period specified in §§ 229.10, 229.12, or 229.13; and

(ii) In the case of withdrawals made in person to an employee of the depositary bank—

(A) Is applied without discrimination to all customers of the bank; and

(B) Is related to security, operating, or bonding requirements of the depositary bank.

(d) Use of calculated availability. A depositary bank may provide availability to its nonconsumer accounts based on a sample of checks that represents the average composition of the customer's deposits, if the terms for availability based on the sample are equivalent to or more prompt than the availability requirements of this subpart.

(e) Holds on other funds.

(1) A depositary bank that receives a check for deposit in an account may not place a hold on any funds of the customer at the bank, where—

(i) The amount of funds that are held exceeds the amount of the check; or

(ii) The funds are not made available for withdrawal within the times specified in §§ 229.10, 229.12, and 229.13.

(2) A depositary bank that cashes a check for a customer over the counter, other than a check drawn on the depositary bank, may not place a hold on funds in an account of the customer at the bank, if—

(i) The amount of funds that are held exceeds the amount of the check; or

(ii) The funds are not made available for withdrawal within the times specified in §§ 229.10, 229.12, and 229.13.

(f) Employee training and compliance. Each bank shall establish procedures to ensure that the bank complies with the requirements of this subpart, and shall provide each employee who performs duties subject to the requirements of this subpart with a statement of the procedures applicable to that employee.

(g) Effect of merger transaction—

(1) In general. For purposes of this subpart, except for the purposes of the new accounts exception of § 229.13(a), and when funds are considered deposited under § 229.19(a), two or more banks that have engaged in a merger transaction may be considered to be separate banks for a period of one year following the consummation of the merger transaction.

(2) Merger transactions on or after July 1, 1998, and before March 1, 2000. If banks have consummated a merger transaction on or after July 1, 1998, and before March 1, 2000, the merged banks may be considered separate banks until March 1, 2001.

§ 229.20 Relation to state law.

(a) In general. Any provision of a law or regulation of any state in effect on or before September 1, 1989, that requires funds deposited in an account at a bank chartered by the state to be made available for withdrawal in a shorter time than the time provided in subpart B, and, in connection therewith, subpart A, shall—

(1) Supersede the provisions of the EFA Act and subpart B, and, in connection therewith, subpart A, to the extent the provisions relate to the time by which funds deposited or received for deposit in an account are available for withdrawal; and

(2) Apply to all federally insured banks located within the state.

No amendment to a state law or regulation governing the availability of funds that becomes effective after September 1, 1989, shall supersede the EFA Act and subpart B, and, in connection therewith, subpart A, but unamended provisions of state law shall remain in effect.

(b) Preemption of inconsistent law. Except as provided in paragraph (a), the EFA Act and subpart B, and, in connection therewith, subpart A, supersede any provision of inconsistent state law.

(c) Standards for preemption. A provision of a state law in effect on or before September 2, 1989, is not inconsistent with the EFA Act, or subpart B, or in connection therewith, subpart A, if it requires that funds shall be available in a shorter period of time than the time provided in this subpart. Inconsistency with the EFA Act and subpart B, and in connection therewith, subpart A, may exist when state law—

(1) Permits a depositary bank to make funds deposited in an account by cash, electronic payment, or check available for withdrawal in a longer period of time than the maximum period of time permitted under subpart B, and, in connection therewith, subpart A; or

(2) Provides for disclosures or notices concerning funds availability relating to accounts.

(d) Preemption determinations. The Board may determine, upon the request of any state, bank, or other interested party, whether the EFA Act and subpart B, and, in connection therewith, subpart A, preempt provisions of state laws relating to the availability of funds.

(e) Procedures for preemption determinations. A request for a preemption determination shall include the following—

(1) A copy of the full text of the state law in question, including any implementing regulations or judicial interpretations of that law; and

(2) A comparison of the provisions of state law with the corresponding provisions in the EFA Act and subparts A and B of this part, together with a discussion of the reasons why specific provisions of state law are either consistent or inconsistent with corresponding sections of the EFA Act and subparts A and B of this part.

A request for a preemption determination shall be addressed to the Secretary, Board of Governors of the Federal Reserve System.

§ 229.21 Civil liability.

(a) Civil liability. A bank that fails to comply with any requirement imposed under subpart B, and in connection therewith, subpart A, of this part or any provision of state law that supersedes any provision of subpart B, and in connection therewith, subpart A, with respect to any person is liable to that person in an amount equal to the sum of—

(1) Any actual damage sustained by that person as a result of the failure;

(2) Such additional amount as the court may allow, except that—

(i) In the case of an individual action, liability under this paragraph shall not be less than $100 nor greater than $1,000; and

(ii) In the case of a class action—

(A) No minimum recovery shall be applicable to each member of the class; and

(B) The total recovery under this paragraph in any class action or series of class actions arising out of the same failure to comply by the same depositary bank shall not be more than the lesser of $500,000 or 1 percent of the net worth of the bank involved; and

(3) In the case of a successful action to enforce the foregoing liability, the costs of the action, together with a reasonable attorney's fee as determined by the court.

(b) Class action awards. In determining the amount of any award in any class action, the court shall consider, among other relevant factors—

(1) The amount of any damages awarded;

(2) The frequency and persistence of failures of compliance;

(3) The resources of the bank;

(4) The number of persons adversely affected; and

(5) The extent to which the failure of compliance was intentional.

(c) Bona fide errors—

(1) General rule. A bank is not liable in any action brought under this section for a violation of this subpart if the bank demonstrates by a preponderance of the evidence that the violation was not intentional and resulted from a bona fide error, notwithstanding the maintenance of procedures reasonably adapted to avoid any such error.

(2) Examples. Examples of a bona fide error include clerical, calculation, computer malfunction and programming, and printing errors, except that an error of legal judgment with respect to the bank's obligation under this subpart is not a bona fide error.

(d) Jurisdiction. Any action under this section may be brought in any United States district court or in any other court of competent jurisdiction, and shall be brought within one year after the date of the occurrence of the violation involved.

(e) Reliance on Board rulings. No provision of this subpart imposing any liability shall apply to any act done or omitted in good faith in conformity with any rule, regulation, or interpretation thereof by the Board, regardless of whether such rule, regulation, or interpretation is amended, rescinded, or determined by judicial or other authority to be invalid for any reason after the act or omission has occurred.

(f) Exclusions. This section does not apply to claims that arise under Subpart C of this part or to actions for wrongful dishonor.

(g) Record retention.

(1) A bank shall retain evidence of compliance with the requirements imposed by this subpart for not less than two years. Records may be stored by use of microfiche, microfilm, magnetic tape, or other methods capable of accurately retaining and reproducing information.

(2) If a bank has actual notice that it is being investigated, or is subject to an enforcement proceeding by an agency charged with monitoring that bank's compliance with the EFA Act and this subpart, or has been served with notice of an action filed under this section, it shall retain the records pertaining to the action or proceeding pending final disposition of the matter, unless an earlier time is allowed by order of the agency or court.

SUBPART C—COLLECTION OF CHECKS

§ 229.30 Electronic checks and electronic information.

(a) Checks under this subpart. Electronic checks and electronic returned checks are subject to this subpart as if they were checks or returned checks, except where "paper check" or "paper returned check" is specified. For the purposes of this subpart, the term "check" or "returned check" as used in Subpart A includes "electronic check" or "electronic returned check," except where "paper check" or "paper returned check" is specified.

(b) Writings. If a bank is required to provide information in writing under this subpart, the bank may satisfy that requirement by providing the information electronically if the receiving bank agrees to receive that information electronically.

§ 229.31 Paying bank's responsibility for return of checks and notices of nonpayment.

(a) Return of checks.

(1) Subject to the requirement of expeditious return under paragraph (b) of this section, a paying bank may send a returned check to the depositary bank, to any other bank agreeing to handle the returned check, or as provided in paragraph (a)(2) of this section.

(2) A paying bank that is unable to identify the depositary bank with respect to a check may send the returned check to any bank that handled the check for forward collection and must advise the bank to which the check is sent that the paying bank is unable to identify the depositary bank.

(3) A paying bank may convert a check to a qualified returned check. A qualified returned check shall be encoded in magnetic ink with the routing number of the depositary bank, the amount of the returned check, and a "2" in the case of an original check (or a "5" in the case of a substitute check) in position 44 of the qualified return MICR line as a return identifier. A qualified returned original check shall be encoded in accordance with ANS X9.13, and a qualified returned substitute check shall be encoded in accordance with ANS X9.100–140.

(4) Except as provided in paragraph (g) of this section, this section does not affect a paying bank's responsibility to return a check within the deadlines required by the UCC or Regulation J (12 CFR part 210).

(b) Expeditious return of checks.

(1) Except as provided in paragraph (d) of this section, if a paying bank determines not to pay a check, it shall return the check in an expeditious manner such that the check would normally be received by the depositary bank not later than 2 p.m. (local time of the depositary bank) on the second business day following the banking day on which the check was presented to the paying bank.

(2) If the second business day following the banking day on which the check was presented to the paying bank is not a banking day for the depositary bank, the paying bank satisfies the expeditious return requirement if it sends the returned check in a manner such that the depositary bank would normally receive the returned check not later than 2 p.m. (local time of the depositary bank) on the depositary bank's next banking day.

(c) Notice of nonpayment.

(1) If a paying bank determines not to pay a check in the amount of $5,000 or more, it shall provide notice of nonpayment such that the notice would normally be received by the depositary bank not later than 2 p.m. (local time of the depositary bank) on the second business day following the banking day on which the check was presented to the paying bank. If the day the paying bank is required to provide notice is not a banking day for the depositary bank, receipt of notice not later than 2 p.m. (local time of the depositary bank) on the depositary bank's next banking day constitutes timely notice. Notice may be provided by any reasonable means, including the returned check, a writing (including a copy of the check), or telephone.

(2)(i) To the extent available to the paying bank, notice must include the information contained in the check's MICR line when the check is received by the paying bank, as well as—

(A) Name of the payee(s);

(B) Amount;

(C) Date of the indorsement of the depositary bank;

(D) The bank name, routing number, and trace or sequence number associated with the indorsement of the depositary bank; and

(E) Reason for nonpayment.

(ii) If the paying bank is not sure of the accuracy of an item of information, it shall include the information required by this paragraph to the extent possible, and identify any item of information for which the bank is not sure of the accuracy.

(iii) The notice may include other information from the check that may be useful in identifying the check being returned and the customer.

(d) Exceptions to the expeditious return of checks and notice of nonpayment requirements. The expeditious return and notice of nonpayment requirements of paragraphs (b) and (c) of this section do not apply if—

(1) The check is deposited in a depositary bank that is not subject to subpart B of this part; or

(2) A paying bank is unable to identify the depositary bank with respect to the check.

(e) Identification of returned check. A paying bank returning a check shall clearly indicate on the front of the check that it is a returned check and the reason for return. If the paying bank is returning a substitute check or an electronic returned check, the paying bank shall include this information such that the information would be retained on any subsequent substitute check.

(f) Notice in Lieu of Return. If a check is unavailable for return, the paying bank may send in its place a copy of the front and back of the returned check, or, if no such copy is available, a written notice of nonpayment containing the information specified in paragraph (c)(2) of this section. The copy or written notice shall clearly state that it constitutes a notice in lieu of return. A notice in lieu of return is considered a returned check subject to the requirements of this subpart.

(g) Extension of deadline. The deadline for return or notice of dishonor or nonpayment under the UCC or Regulation J (12 CFR part 210), or § 229.36(d)(3) and (4) is extended to the time of dispatch of such return or notice if the depositary bank (or the receiving bank, if the depositary bank is unidentifiable) receives the returned check or notice—

(1) On or before the depositary bank's (or receiving bank's) next banking day following the otherwise applicable deadline by the earlier of the close of that banking day or a cutoff hour of 2 p.m. (local time of the depositary bank or receiving bank) or later set by the depositary bank (or receiving

bank) under UCC 4–108, for all deadlines other than those described in paragraph (g)(2) of this section; or

(2) Prior to the cut-off hour for the next processing cycle (if sent to a returning bank), or on the next banking day (if sent to the depositary bank), for a deadline falling on a Saturday that is a banking day (as defined in the UCC) for the paying bank.

(h) Payable-through and payable-at checks. A check payable at or through a paying bank is considered to be drawn on that bank for purposes of the expeditious return and notice of nonpayment requirements of this subpart.

(i) Reliance on routing number. A paying bank may return a returned check based on any routing number designating the depositary bank appearing on the returned check in the depositary bank's indorsement.

§ 229.32 Returning bank's responsibility for return of checks.

(a) Return of checks.

(1) Subject to the requirement of expeditious return under paragraph (b) of this section, a returning bank may send a returned check to the depositary bank, to any other bank agreeing to handle the returned check, or as provided in paragraph (a)(2) of this section.

(2) A returning bank that is unable to identify the depositary bank with respect to a check may send the returned check to any collecting bank that handled the returned check for forward collection if the returning bank was not a collecting bank with respect to the returned check, or to a prior collecting bank, if the returning bank was a collecting bank with respect to the returned check. A returning bank sending a returned check under this paragraph to a bank must advise the bank to which the returned check is sent that the returning bank is unable to identify the depositary bank.

(3) A returning bank may convert a check to a qualified returned check. A qualified returned check shall be encoded in magnetic ink with the routing number of the depositary bank, the amount of the returned check, and a "2" in the case of an original check (or a "5" in the case of a substitute check) in position 44 of the qualified return MICR line as a return identifier. A qualified returned original check shall be encoded in accordance with ANS X9.13, and a qualified returned substitute check shall be encoded in accordance with ANS X9.100–140.

(b) Expeditious return of checks.

(1) Except as provided in paragraph (c) of this section, a returning bank shall return a returned check in an expeditious manner such that the check would normally be received by the depositary bank not later than 2 p.m. (local time of the depositary bank) on the second business day following the banking day on which the check was presented to the paying bank.

(2) If the second business day following the banking day on which the check was presented to the paying bank is not a banking day for the depositary bank, the returning bank satisfies the expeditious return requirement if it sends the returned check in a manner such that the depositary bank would normally receive the returned check not later than 2 p.m. (local time of the depositary bank) on the depositary bank's next banking day.

(c) Exceptions to the expeditious return of checks. The expeditious return requirement of paragraph (b) of this section does not apply if—

(1) The check is deposited in a depositary bank that is not subject to subpart B of this part;

(2) A paying bank is unable to identify the depositary bank with respect to the check; or

(3) The bank handles a misrouted returned check pursuant to § 229.33(f).

(d) Notice in Lieu of Return. If a check is unavailable for return, the returning bank may send in its place a copy of the front and back of the returned check, or, if no such copy is available, a written notice of nonpayment containing the information specified in § 229.31(c). The copy or written notice shall clearly state that it constitutes a notice in lieu of return. A notice in lieu of return is considered a returned check subject to the requirements of this section and the other requirements of this subpart.

(e) Settlement. A returning bank shall settle with a bank sending a returned check to it for return by the same means that it settles or would settle with the sending bank for a check received for forward collection drawn on the depositary bank. This settlement is final when made.

(f) Charges. A returning bank may impose a charge on a bank sending a returned check for handling the returned check.

(g) Reliance on routing number. A returning bank may return a returned check based on any routing number designating the depositary bank appearing on the returned check in the depositary bank's indorsement or in magnetic ink on a qualified returned check.

§ 229.33 Depositary bank's responsibility for returned checks and notices of nonpayment.

(a) Right to assert claim.

(1) A paying bank or returning bank may be liable to a depositary bank under § 229.38 for failing to return a check in an expeditious manner only if the depositary bank has arrangements in place such that the paying bank or returning bank could return a returned check to the depositary bank electronically, directly or indirectly, by commercially reasonable means.

(2) For purposes of paragraph (a)(1) of this section, the depositary bank that has asserted a claim has the burden of proof for demonstrating that the depositary bank's arrangements meet the standard of paragraph (a)(1).

(b) Acceptance of electronic returned checks and electronic notices of nonpayment. A depositary bank's agreement with the transferor bank governs the terms under which the depositary bank will accept electronic returned checks and electronic written notices of nonpayment.

(c) Acceptance of paper returned checks and paper notices of nonpayment.

(1) A depositary bank shall accept paper returned checks and paper notices of nonpayment during its banking day—

(i) At a location, if any, at which presentment of paper checks for forward collection is requested by the depositary bank; and

(ii)(A) At a branch, head office, or other location consistent with the name and address of the bank in its indorsement on the check;

(B) If no address appears in the indorsement, at a branch or head office associated with the routing number of the bank in its indorsement on the check; or

(C) If no routing number or address appears in its indorsement on the check, at any branch or head office of the bank.

(2) A depositary bank may require that paper returned checks be separated from paper forward collection checks.

(d) Acceptance of oral notices of nonpayment. A depositary bank shall accept oral notices of nonpayment during its banking day—

(1) At the telephone number indicated in the indorsement; and

(2) At any other number held out by the bank for receipt of notice of nonpayment.

(e) Payment.

(1) A depositary bank shall pay the returning bank or paying bank returning the check to it for the amount of the check prior to the close of business on the depositary bank's banking day on which it received the check ("payment date") by—

(i) Debit to an account of the depositary bank on the books of the returning bank or paying bank;

(ii) Cash;

(iii) Wire transfer; or

(iv) Any other form of payment acceptable to the returning bank or paying bank.

(2) The proceeds of the payment must be available to the returning bank or paying bank in cash or by credit to an account of the returning bank or paying bank on or as of the payment date. If the payment date is not a banking day for the returning bank or paying bank or the depositary bank is unable to make the payment on the payment date, payment shall be made by the next day that is a banking day for the returning bank or paying bank. These payments are final when made.

(f) Misrouted returned checks and written notices of nonpayment. If a bank receives a returned check or written notice of nonpayment on the basis that it is the depositary bank, and the bank determines that it is not the depositary bank with respect to the check or notice, it shall either promptly send the returned check or notice to the depositary bank directly or by means of a returning bank agreeing to handle the returned check or notice, or send the check or notice back to the bank from which it was received.

(g) Charges. A depositary bank may not impose a charge for accepting and paying checks being returned to it.

(h) Notification to customer. If the depositary bank receives a returned check, notice of nonpayment, or notice of recovery under § 229.35(b), it shall send or give notice to its customer of the facts by midnight of the banking day following the banking day on which it received the returned check, notice of nonpayment, or notice of recovery, or within a longer reasonable time.

(i) Depositary bank without accounts. The requirements of this section with respect to notices of nonpayment do not apply to checks deposited in a depositary bank that does not maintain accounts.

§ 229.34 Warranties and indemnities.

(a) Warranties with respect to electronic checks and electronic returned checks.

(1) Each bank that transfers or presents an electronic check or electronic returned check and receives a settlement or other consideration for it warrants that—

(i) The electronic image accurately represents all of the information on the front and back of the original check as of the time that the original check was truncated and the electronic information includes an accurate record of all MICR line information required for a substitute check under § 229.2(aaa) and the amount of the check, and

(ii) No person will receive a transfer, presentment, or return of, or otherwise be charged for an electronic check or electronic returned check, the original check, a substitute check, or a paper or electronic representation of a substitute check such that the person will be asked to make payment based on a check it has already paid.

(2) Each bank that makes the warranties under paragraph (a)(1) of this section makes the warranties to—

(i) In the case of transfers for collection or presentment, the transferee bank, any subsequent collecting bank, the paying bank, and the drawer; and

(ii) In the case of transfers for return, the transferee returning bank, any subsequent returning bank, the depositary bank, and the owner.

(b) Transfer and presentment warranties with respect to a remotely created check. (1) A bank that transfers or presents a remotely created check and receives a settlement or other consideration warrants to the transferee bank, any subsequent collecting bank, and the paying bank that the person on whose account the remotely created check is drawn authorized the issuance of the check in the amount stated on the check and to the payee stated on the check. For purposes of this paragraph (b)(1), "account" includes an account as defined in § 229.2(a) as well as a credit or other arrangement that allows a person to draw checks that are payable by, through, or at a bank.

(2) If a paying bank asserts a claim for breach of warranty under paragraph (b)(1) of this section, the warranting bank may defend by proving that the customer of the paying bank is precluded under

UCC 4–406, as applicable, from asserting against the paying bank the unauthorized issuance of the check.

(c) Settlement amount, encoding, and offset warranties.

(1) Each bank that presents one or more checks to a paying bank and in return receives a settlement or other consideration warrants to the paying bank that the total amount of the checks presented is equal to the total amount of the settlement demanded by the presenting bank from the paying bank.

(2) Each bank that transfers one or more checks or returned checks to a collecting bank, returning bank, or depositary bank and in return receives a settlement or other consideration warrants to the transferee bank that the accompanying information, if any, accurately indicates the total amount of the checks or returned checks transferred.

(3) Each bank that presents or transfers a check or returned check warrants to any bank that subsequently handles it that, at the time of presentment or transfer, the information encoded after issue regarding the check or returned check is accurate. For purposes of this paragraph, the information encoded after issue regarding the check or returned check means any information that could be encoded in the MICR line of a paper check.

(4) If a bank settles with another bank for checks presented, or for returned checks for which it is the depositary bank, in an amount exceeding the total amount of the checks, the settling bank may set off the excess settlement amount against subsequent settlements for checks presented, or for returned checks for which it is the depositary bank, that it receives from the other bank.

(d) Returned check warranties.

(1) Each paying bank or returning bank that transfers a returned check and receives a settlement or other consideration for it warrants to the transferee returning bank, to any subsequent returning bank, to the depositary bank, and to the owner of the check, that—

(i) The paying bank, or in the case of a check payable by a bank and payable through another bank, the bank by which the check is payable, returned the check within its deadline under the UCC or § 229.31(g) of this part;

(ii) It is authorized to return the check;

(iii) The check has not been materially altered; and

(iv) In the case of a notice in lieu of return, the check has not and will not be returned.

(2) These warranties are not made with respect to checks drawn on the Treasury of the United States, U.S. Postal Service money orders, or checks drawn on a state or a unit of general local government that are not payable through or at a bank.

(e) Notice of nonpayment warranties.

(1) Each paying bank that gives a notice of nonpayment warrants to the transferee bank, to any subsequent transferee bank, to the depositary bank, and to the owner of the check that—

(i) The paying bank, or in the case of a check payable by a bank and payable through another bank, the bank by which the check is payable, returned or will return the check within its deadline under the UCC or § 229.31(g) of this part;

(ii) It is authorized to send the notice; and

(iii) The check has not been materially altered.

(2) These warranties are not made with respect to checks drawn on the Treasury of the United States, U.S. Postal Service money orders, or check drawn on a state or a unit of general local government that are not payable through or at a bank.

(f) Remote deposit capture indemnity.

(1) The indemnity described in paragraph (f)(2) of this section is provided by a depositary bank that—

(i) Is a truncating bank under § 229.2(eee)(2) because it accepts deposit of an electronic image or other electronic information related to an original check;

(ii) Does not receive the original check;

(iii) Receives settlement or other consideration for an electronic check or substitute check related to the original check; and

(iv) Does not receive a return of the check unpaid.

(2) A bank described in paragraph (f)(1) of this section shall indemnify, as set forth in § 229.34(i), a depositary bank that accepts the original check for deposit for losses incurred by that depositary bank if the loss is due to the check having already been paid.

(3) A depositary bank may not make an indemnity claim under paragraph (f)(2) of this section if the original check it accepted for deposit bore a restrictive indorsement inconsistent with the means of deposit.

(g) Indemnities with respect to electronically-created items. Each bank that transfers or presents an electronically-created item and receives a settlement or other consideration for it shall indemnify, as set forth in § 229.34(i), each transferee bank, any subsequent collecting bank, the paying bank, and any subsequent returning bank against losses that result from the fact that—

(1) The electronic image or electronic information is not derived from a paper check;

(2) The person on whose account the electronically-created item is drawn did not authorize the issuance of the item in the amount stated on the item or to the payee stated on the item (for purposes of this paragraph (g)(2), "account" includes an account as defined in section 229.2(a) as well as a credit or other arrangement that allows a person to draw checks that are payable by, through, or at a bank); or

(3) A person receives a transfer, presentment, or return of, or otherwise is charged for an electronically-created item such that the person is asked to make payment based on an item or check it has already paid.

(h) Damages. Damages for breach of the warranties in this section shall not exceed the consideration received by the bank that presents or transfers a check or returned check, plus interest compensation and expenses related to the check or returned check, if any.

(i) Indemnity amounts.

(1) The amount of the indemnity in paragraphs (f)(2) and (g) of this section shall not exceed the sum of—

(i) The amount of the loss of the indemnified bank, up to the amount of the settlement or other consideration received by the indemnifying bank; and

(ii) Interest and expenses of the indemnified bank (including costs and reasonable attorney's fees and other expenses of representation).

(2)(i) If a loss described in paragraph (f)(2) or (g) of this section results in whole or in part from the indemnified bank's negligence or failure to act in good faith, then the indemnity amount described in paragraph (i)(1) of this section shall be reduced in proportion to the amount of negligence or bad faith attributable to the indemnified bank.

(ii) Nothing in this paragraph (i)(2) affects the rights of a person under the UCC or other applicable provision of state or federal law.

(j) Tender of defense. If a bank is sued for breach of a warranty or for indemnity under this section, it may give a prior bank in the collection or return chain written notice of the litigation, and the bank notified may then give similar notice to any other prior bank. If the notice states that the bank notified may come in and defend and that failure to do so will bind the bank notified in an action later brought by the bank giving the notice as to any determination of fact common to the two litigations, the bank notified is so bound unless after seasonable receipt of the notice the bank notified does come in and defend.

(k) Notice of claim. Unless a claimant gives notice of a claim for breach of warranty or for indemnity under this section to the bank that made the warranty or indemnification within 30 days after the claimant has reason to know of the breach or facts and circumstances giving rise to the indemnity and the identity of the warranting or indemnifying bank, the warranting or indemnifying bank is discharged to the extent of any loss caused by the delay in giving notice of the claim.

§ 229.35 Indorsements.

(a) Indorsement standards. A bank (other than a paying bank) that handles a check during forward collection or a returned check shall indorse the check in a manner that permits a person to interpret the indorsement, in accordance with American National Standard (ANS) Specifications for Physical Check Endorsements, X9.100–111 (ANS X9.100–111), for a paper check other than a substitute check; ANS Specifications for an Image Replacement Document, X9.100–140 (ANS X9.100–140), for a substitute check; and ANS Specifications for Electronic Exchange of Check and Image Data-Domestic, X9.100–187 (ANS X9.100–187), for an electronic check; unless the Board by rule or order determines that different standards apply or the parties otherwise agree.

(b) Liability of bank handling check. A bank that handles a check for forward collection or return is liable to any bank that subsequently handles the check to the extent that the subsequent bank does not receive payment for the check because of suspension of payments by another bank or otherwise. This paragraph applies whether or not a bank has placed its indorsement on the check. This liability is not affected by the failure of any bank to exercise ordinary care, but any bank failing to do so remains liable. A bank seeking recovery against a prior bank shall send notice to that prior bank reasonably promptly after it learns the facts entitling it to recover. A bank may recover from the bank with which it settled for the check by revoking the settlement, charging back any credit given to an account, or obtaining a refund. A bank may have the rights of a holder with respect to each check it handles.

(c) Indorsement by a bank. After a check has been indorsed by a bank, only a bank may acquire the rights of a holder—

(1) Until the check has been returned to the person initiating collection; or

(2) Until the check has been specially indorsed by a bank to a person who is not a bank.

(d) Indorsement for depositary bank. A depositary bank may arrange with another bank to apply the other bank's indorsement as the depositary bank indorsement, provided that any indorsement of the depositary bank on the check avoids the area reserved for the depositary bank indorsement as specified in the indorsement standard applicable to the check under paragraph (a) of this section. The other bank indorsing as depositary bank is considered the depositary bank for purposes of Subpart C of this part.

§ 229.36 Presentment and issuance of checks.

(a) Receipt of electronic checks. The terms under which a paying bank will accept presentment of an electronic check is governed by the paying bank's agreement with the presenting bank.

(b) Receipt of paper checks.

(1) A paper check is considered received by the paying bank when it is received—

(i) At a location to which delivery is requested by the paying bank;

(ii) At an address of the bank associated with the routing number on the check, whether contained in the MICR line or in fractional form;

(iii) At a branch, head office, or other location consistent with the name and address of the bank on the check if the bank is identified on the check by name and address; or

(iv) At any branch or head office, if the bank is identified on the check by name without address.

(2) A bank may require that checks presented to it as a paying bank be separated from returned checks.

(c) Liability of bank during forward collection. Settlements between banks for the forward collection of a check are final when made; however, a collecting bank handling a check for forward collection may be liable to a prior collecting bank, including the depositary bank, and the depositary bank's customer.

(d) Same-day settlement.

(1) A paper check is considered presented, and a paying bank must settle for or return the check pursuant to paragraph (d)(2) of this section, if a presenting bank delivers the check in accordance with reasonable delivery requirements established by the paying bank and demands payment under this paragraph (d)—

(i) At a location designated by the paying bank for receipt of paper checks under this paragraph (d) at which the paying bank would be considered to have received the paper check under paragraph (b) of this section or, if no location is designated, at any location described in paragraph (b) of this section; and

(ii) By 8 a.m. on a business day (local time of the location described in paragraph (d)(1)(i) of this section).

(2) A paying bank may require that paper checks presented for settlement pursuant to paragraph (d)(1) of this section be separated from other forward collection checks or returned checks.

(3) If presentment of a paper check meets the requirements of paragraph (d)(1) of this section, the paying bank is accountable to the presenting bank for the amount of the check unless, by the close of Fedwire on the business day it receives the check, it either—

(i) Settles with the presenting bank for the amount of the check by credit to an account at a Federal Reserve Bank designated by the presenting bank; or

(ii) Returns the check.

(4) Notwithstanding paragraph (d)(3) of this section, if a paying bank closes on a business day and receives presentment of a paper check on that day in accordance with paragraph (d)(1) of this section—

(i) The paying bank is accountable to the presenting bank for the amount of the check unless, by the close of Fedwire on its next banking day, it either—

(A) Settles with the presenting bank for the amount of the check by credit to an account at a Federal Reserve Bank designated by the presenting bank; or

(B) Returns the check.

(ii) If the closing is voluntary, unless the paying bank settles for or returns the check in accordance with paragraph (d)(3) of this section, it shall pay interest compensation to the presenting bank for each day after the business day on which the check was presented until the paying bank settles for the check, including the day of settlement.

§ 229.37 Variation by agreement.

The effect of the provisions of Subpart C may be varied by agreement, except that no agreement can disclaim the responsibility of a bank for its own lack of good faith or failure to exercise ordinary care, or can limit the measure of damages for such lack or failure; but the parties may determine by agreement the standards by which such responsibility is to be measured if such standards are not manifestly unreasonable.

§ 229.38 Liability.

(a) Standard of care; liability; measure of damages. A bank shall exercise ordinary care and act in good faith in complying with the requirements of this subpart. A bank that fails to exercise ordinary care or act in good faith under this subpart may be liable to the depositary bank, the depositary bank's customer, the owner of a check, or another party to the check. The measure of damages for failure to exercise ordinary care is the amount of the loss incurred, up to the amount of the check, reduced by the amount of the loss that party would have incurred even if the bank had exercised ordinary care. A bank that fails to act in good faith under this subpart may be liable for other damages, if any, suffered by the party as a proximate consequence. Subject to a bank's duty to exercise ordinary care or act in good faith in choosing the means of return or notice of nonpayment, the bank is not liable for the insolvency, neglect, misconduct, mistake, or default of another bank or person, or for loss or destruction of a check or notice of nonpayment in transit or in the possession of others. This section does not affect a paying bank's liability to its customer under the U.C.C. or other law.

(b) Paying bank's failure to make timely return. If a paying bank fails both to comply with its expeditious return requirements under § 229.31(b) and with the deadline for return under the UCC, Regulation J (12 CFR part 210), or the extension of deadline under § 229.31(g) in connection with a single nonpayment of a check, the paying bank shall be liable under either § 229.31(b) or such other provision, but not both.

(c) Comparative negligence. If a person, including a bank, fails to exercise ordinary care or act in good faith under this subpart in indorsing a check (§ 229.35), accepting a returned check or notice of nonpayment (§ 229.33(b), (c), and (d)), or otherwise, the damages incurred by that person under § 229.38(a) shall be diminished in proportion to the amount of negligence or bad faith attributable to that person.

(d) Responsibility for certain aspects of checks.

(1) A paying bank, or in the case of a check payable through the paying bank and payable by another bank, the bank by which the check is payable, is responsible for damages under paragraph (a) of this section to the extent that the condition of the check when issued by it or its customer adversely affects the ability of a bank to indorse the check legibly in accordance with § 229.35. A depositary bank is responsible for damages under paragraph (a) of this section to the extent that the condition of the back of a check arising after the issuance of the check and prior to acceptance of the check by it adversely affects the ability of a bank to indorse the check legibly in accordance with § 229.35. A reconverting bank is responsible for damages under paragraph (a) of this section to the extent that the condition of the back of a substitute check transferred, presented, or returned by it—

(i) Adversely affects the ability of a subsequent bank to indorse the check legibly in accordance with § 229.35; or

(ii) Causes an indorsement that previously was applied in accordance with § 229.35 to become illegible.

(2) Responsibility under this paragraph (d) shall be treated as negligence of the paying bank, depositary bank, or reconverting bank for purposes of paragraph (c) of this section.

(e) Timeliness of action. If a bank is delayed in acting beyond the time limits set forth in this subpart because of interruption of communication or computer facilities, suspension of payments by a bank, war, emergency conditions, failure of equipment, or other circumstances beyond its control, its time for acting is extended for the time necessary to complete the action, if it exercises such diligence as the circumstances require.

(f) Exclusion. Section 229.21 of this part and section 611(a), (b), and (c) of the EFA Act (12 U.S.C. 4010(a), (b), and (c)) do not apply to this subpart.

(g) Jurisdiction. Any action under this subpart may be brought in any United States district court, or in any other court of competent jurisdiction, and shall be brought within one year after the date of the occurrence of the violation involved.

(h) Reliance on Board rulings. No provision of this subpart imposing any liability shall apply to any act done or omitted in good faith in conformity with any rule, regulation, or interpretation thereof by the Board, regardless of whether the rule, regulation, or interpretation is amended, rescinded, or determined by judicial or other authority to be invalid for any reason after the act or omission has occurred.

(i) Presumption of Alteration.

(1) Presumption. Subject to paragraphs (i)(2) and (3) of this section and in the absence of a Federal statute or regulation to the contrary, the presumption in this paragraph applies with respect to any dispute between banks arising under Federal or State law as to whether a substitute check or electronic check transferred between those banks contains an alteration or is derived from an original check that was issued with an unauthorized signature of the drawer. When such a dispute arises, there is a rebuttable presumption that the substitute check or electronic check contains an alteration.

(2) Rebuttal of presumption. The presumption of alteration may be overcome by proving by a preponderance of evidence that either the substitute check or electronic check does not contain an alteration, or that the substitute check or electronic check is derived from an original check that was issued with an unauthorized signature of the drawer.

(3) Effect of producing original check. If the original check is made available for examination by all banks involved in the dispute, the presumption in paragraph (i)(1) of this section shall no longer apply.

§ 229.39 Insolvency of bank.

(a) Duty of receiver to return unpaid checks. A check or returned check in, or coming into, the possession of a paying bank, collecting bank, depositary bank, or returning bank that suspends payment, and which is not paid, shall be returned by the receiver, trustee, or agent in charge of the closed bank to the bank or customer that transferred the check to the closed bank.

(b) Claims against banks for checks not returned by receiver. If a check or returned check is not returned by the receiver, trustee, or agent in charge of the closed bank under paragraph (a) of this section, a bank shall have claims with respect to the check or returned check as follows:

(1) If the paying bank has finally paid the check, or if a depositary bank is obligated to pay the returned check, and suspends payment without making a settlement for the check or returned check with the prior bank that is or becomes final, the prior bank has a claim against the paying bank or the depositary bank.

(2) If a collecting bank, paying bank, or returning bank receives settlement from a subsequent bank for a check or returned check, which settlement is or becomes final, and suspends payments without making a settlement for the check with the prior bank, which is or becomes final, the prior bank has a claim against the collecting bank or returning bank.

(c) Preferred claim against presenting bank for breach of warranty. If a paying bank settles with a presenting bank for one or more checks, and if the presenting bank breaches a warranty specified in § 229.34(c)(1) or (3) with respect to those checks and suspends payments before satisfying the paying bank's warranty claim, the paying bank has a preferred claim against the presenting bank for the amount of the warranty claim.

(d) Finality of settlement. If a paying bank or depositary bank gives, or a collecting bank, paying bank, or returning bank gives or receives, a settlement for a check or returned check and thereafter suspends payment, the suspension does not prevent or interfere with the settlement becoming final if such finality occurs automatically upon the lapse of a certain time or the happening of certain events.

§ 229.40 Effect of merger transaction.

For purposes of this subpart, two or more banks that have engaged in a merger transaction may be considered to be separate banks for a period of one year following the consummation of the merger transaction.

§ 229.41 Relation to state law.

The provisions of this subpart supersede any inconsistent provisions of the U.C.C. as adopted in any state, or of any other state law, but only to the extent of the inconsistency.

§ 229.42 Exclusions.

The expeditious-return (§§ 229.31(b) and 229.32(b)), notice-of-nonpayment (§ 229.31(c)), and same-day settlement (§ 229.36(d)) requirements of this subpart do not apply to a check drawn upon the United States Treasury, to a U.S. Postal Service money order, or to a check drawn on a state or a unit of general local government that is not payable through or at a bank.

§ 229.43 Checks payable in Guam, American Samoa, and the Northern Mariana Islands.

(a) Definitions. The definitions in § 229.2 apply to this section, unless otherwise noted. In addition, for the purposes of this section—

(1) Pacific island bank means an office of an institution that would be a bank as defined in § 229.2(e) but for the fact that the office is located in Guam, American Samoa, or the Northern Mariana Islands;

(2) Pacific island check means—

(i) A demand draft drawn on or payable through or at a Pacific island bank, which is not a check as defined in § 229.2(k); and

(ii) An electronic image of, and electronic information derived from, a demand draft or returned demand draft drawn on or payable through or at a Pacific island bank that—

(A) Is sent to a receiving bank pursuant to an agreement between the sender and the receiving bank; and

(B) Conforms with ANS X9.100–187, unless the Board by rule or order determines that a different standard applies or the parties otherwise agree.

(b) Rules applicable to Pacific island checks. To the extent a bank handles a Pacific island check as if it were a check defined in § 229.2(k) or an electronic check defined in § 229.2(ggg), the bank is subject to the following sections of this part (and the word "check" in each such section is construed to include a Pacific island check)—

(1) Section 229.30(a) (Checks under this subpart), and (b) (Writings);

(2) Section 229.32 (Returning bank's responsibilities for return of checks) except that the returning bank is not subject to the requirement to return a Pacific Island check in an expeditious manner;

(3) Section 229.33(b) (Acceptance of electronic returned checks and electronic notices of nonpayment), (c) (Acceptance of paper returned checks and paper notices of nonpayment), § 229.33(d) (Acceptances of oral notices of nonpayment), § 229.33(e) (Payment), § 229.33(f) (Misrouted returned checks and written notices of nonpayment), § 229.33(g) (Charges);

(4) Section 229.34(a) (Warranties with respect to electronic checks and electronic returned checks), § 229.34(b) (Transfer and presentment warranties with respect to a remotely-created check), § 229.34(c)(2) (Cash letter total warranty), § 229.34(c)(3) (Encoding warranty), § 229.34(f) (Remote deposit capture warranty), § 229.34(g) (Indemnities with respect to electronically-created items), § 229.34(h) (Damages), § 229.34(i) (Indemnity amounts), and § 229.34(j) (Tender of defense);

(5) Section 229.35 (Indorsements); for purposes of § 229.35(c) (Indorsement by a bank), the Pacific island bank is deemed to be a bank;

(6) Section 229.36(c) (Liability of bank during forward collection);

(7) Section 229.37 (Variation by agreement);

(8) Section 229.38 (Liability), except for § 229.38(b) (Paying bank's failure to make timely return);

(9) Section 229.39 (Insolvency of bank), except for § 229.39(c) (Preferred claim against presenting bank for breach of warranty); and

(10) Section 229.40 (Effect of merger transaction), § 229.41 (Relation to state law) and § 229.42 (Exclusions).

SUBPART D—SUBSTITUTE CHECKS

§ 229.51 General provisions governing substitute checks.

(a) Legal equivalence. A substitute check for which a bank has provided the warranties described in § 229.52 is the legal equivalent of an original check for all persons and all purposes, including any provision of federal or state law, if the substitute check—

(1) Accurately represents all of the information on the front and back of the original check as of the time the original check was truncated; and

(2) Bears the legend, "This is a legal copy of your check. You can use it the same way you would use the original check."

(b) Reconverting bank duties. A bank shall ensure that a substitute check for which it is the reconverting bank—

(1) Bears all indorsements applied by parties that previously handled the check in any form (including the original check, a substitute check, or another paper or electronic representation of such original check or substitute check) for forward collection or return;

(2) Identifies the reconverting bank in a manner that preserves any previous reconverting bank identifications, in accordance with ANS X9.100–140; and

(3) Identifies the bank that truncated the original check, in accordance with ANS X9.100–140.

(c) Applicable law. A substitute check that is the legal equivalent of an original check under paragraph (a) of this section shall be subject to any provision, including any provision relating to the protection of customers, of this part, the U.C.C., and any other applicable federal or state law as if such substitute check were the original check, to the extent such provision of law is not inconsistent with the Check 21 Act or this subpart.

§ 229.52 Substitute check warranties.

(a) Content and provision of substitute-check warranties.

(1) A bank that transfers, presents, or returns a substitute check (or a paper or electronic representation of a substitute check) for which it receives consideration warrants to the parties listed in paragraph (b) of this section that—

(i) The substitute check meets the requirements for legal equivalence described in § 229.51(a)(1) and (2); and

(ii) No depositary bank, drawee, drawer, or indorser will receive presentment or return of, or otherwise be charged for, the substitute check, the original check, or a paper or electronic representation of the substitute check or original check such that that person will be asked to make a payment based on a check that it already has paid.

(2) A bank that rejects a check submitted for deposit and returns to its customer a substitute check (or a paper or electronic representation of a substitute check) makes the warranties in paragraph (a)(1) of this section regardless of whether the bank received consideration.

(b) Warranty recipients. A bank makes the warranties described in paragraph (a) of this section to the person to which the bank transfers, presents, or returns the substitute check or a paper or electronic representation of such substitute check and to any subsequent recipient, which could include a collecting or returning bank, the depositary bank, the drawer, the drawee, the payee, the depositor, and any indorser. These parties receive the warranties regardless of whether they received the substitute check or a paper or electronic representation of a substitute check.

§ 229.53 Substitute check indemnity.

(a) Scope of indemnity.

(1) bank that transfers, presents, or returns a substitute check or a paper or electronic representation of a substitute check for which it receives consideration shall indemnify the recipient and any subsequent recipient (including a collecting or returning bank, the depositary bank, the drawer, the drawee, the payee, the depositor, and any indorser) for any loss incurred by any recipient of a substitute check if that loss occurred due to the receipt of a substitute check instead of the original check.

(2) A bank that rejects a check submitted for deposit and returns to its customer a substitute check (or a paper or electronic representation of a substitute check) shall indemnify the recipient as described in paragraph (a)(1) of this section regardless of whether the bank received consideration.

(b) Indemnity amount.

(1) In general. Unless otherwise indicated by paragraph (b)(2) or (b)(3) of this section, the amount of the indemnity under paragraph (a) of this section is as follows:

(i) If the loss resulted from a breach of a substitute check warranty provided under § 229.52, the amount of the indemnity shall be the amount of any loss (including interest, costs, reasonable attorney's fees, and other expenses of representation) proximately caused by the warranty breach.

(ii) If the loss did not result from a breach of a substitute check warranty provided under § 229.52, the amount of the indemnity shall be the sum of—

(A) The amount of the loss, up to the amount of the substitute check; and

(B) Interest and expenses (including costs and reasonable attorney's fees and other expenses of representation) related to the substitute check.

(2) Comparative negligence.

(i) If a loss described in paragraph (a) of this section results in whole or in part from the indemnified person's negligence or failure to act in good faith, then the indemnity amount described in paragraph (b)(1) of this section shall be reduced in proportion to the amount of negligence or bad faith attributable to the indemnified person.

(ii) Nothing in this paragraph (b)(2) reduces the rights of a consumer or any other person under the U.C.C. or other applicable provision of state or federal law.

(3) Effect of producing the original check or a sufficient copy—

(i) If an indemnifying bank produces the original check or a sufficient copy, the indemnifying bank shall—

(A) Be liable under this section only for losses that are incurred up to the time that the bank provides that original check or sufficient copy to the indemnified person; and

(B) Have a right to the return of any funds it has paid under this section in excess of those losses.

(ii) The production by the indemnifying bank of the original check or a sufficient copy under paragraph (b)(3)(i) of this section shall not absolve the indemnifying bank from any liability under any warranty that the bank has provided under § 229.52 or other applicable law.

(c) Subrogation of rights—

(1) In general. An indemnifying bank shall be subrogated to the rights of the person that it indemnifies to the extent of the indemnity it has provided and may attempt to recover from another person based on a warranty or other claim.

(2) Duty of indemnified person for subrogated claims. Each indemnified person shall have a duty to comply with all reasonable requests for assistance from an indemnifying bank in connection with any claim the indemnifying bank brings against a warrantor or other person related to a check that forms the basis for the indemnification.

§ 229.54 Expedited recredit for consumers.

(a) Circumstances giving rise to a claim. A consumer may make a claim under this section for a recredit with respect to a substitute check if the consumer asserts in good faith that—

(1) The bank holding the consumer's account charged that account for a substitute check that was provided to the consumer (although the consumer need not be in possession of that substitute check at the time he or she submits a claim);

(2) The substitute check was not properly charged to the consumer account or the consumer has a warranty claim with respect to the substitute check;

(3) The consumer suffered a resulting loss; and

(4) Production of the original check or a sufficient copy is necessary to determine whether or not the substitute check in fact was improperly charged or whether the consumer's warranty claim is valid.

(b) Procedures for making claims. A consumer shall make his or her claim for a recredit under this section with the bank that holds the consumer's account in accordance with the timing, content, and form requirements of this section.

(1) Timing of claim.

(i) The consumer shall submit his or her claim such that the bank receives the claim by the end of the 40th calendar day after the later of the calendar day on which the bank mailed or delivered, by a means agreed to by the consumer—

(A) The periodic account statement that contains information concerning the transaction giving rise to the claim; or

(B) The substitute check giving rise to the claim.

(ii) If the consumer cannot submit his or her claim by the time specified in paragraph (b)(1)(i) of this section because of extenuating circumstances, the bank shall extend the 40-calendar-day period by an additional reasonable amount of time.

(iii) If a consumer makes a claim orally and the bank requires the claim to be in writing, the consumer's claim is timely if the oral claim was received within the time described in paragraphs (b)(1)(i)–(ii) of this section and the written claim was received within the time described in paragraph (b)(3)(ii) of this section.

(2) Content of claim.

(i) The consumer's claim shall include the following information:

(A) A description of the consumer's claim, including the reason why the consumer believes his or her account was improperly charged for the substitute check or the nature of his or her warranty claim with respect to such check;

(B) A statement that the consumer suffered a loss and an estimate of the amount of that loss;

(C) The reason why production of the original check or a sufficient copy is necessary to determine whether or not the charge to the consumer's account was proper or the consumer's warranty claim is valid; and

(D) Sufficient information to allow the bank to identify the substitute check and investigate the claim.

(ii) If a consumer attempts to make a claim but fails to provide all the information in paragraph (b)(2)(i) of this section that is required to constitute a claim, the bank shall inform the consumer that the claim is not complete and identify the information that is missing.

(3) Form and submission of claim; computation of time for bank action. The bank holding the account that is the subject of the consumer's claim may, in its discretion, require the consumer to submit the information required by this section in writing. A bank that requires a written submission—

(i) May permit the consumer to submit the written claim electronically;

(ii) Shall inform a consumer who submits a claim orally of the written claim requirement at the time of the oral claim and may require such consumer to submit the written claim such that the bank receives the written claim by the 10th business day after the banking day on which the bank received the oral claim; and

(iii) Shall compute the time periods for acting on the consumer's claim described in paragraph (c) of this section from the date on which the bank received the written claim.

(c) Action on claims. A bank that receives a claim that meets the requirements of paragraph (b) of this section shall act as follows:

(1) Valid consumer claim. If the bank determines that the consumer's claim is valid, the bank shall—

(i) Recredit the consumer's account for the amount of the consumer's loss, up to the amount of the substitute check, plus interest if the account is an interest-bearing account, no later than the end of the business day after the banking day on which the bank makes that determination; and

(ii) Send to the consumer the notice required by paragraph (e)(1) of this section.

(2) Invalid consumer claim. If a bank determines that the consumer's claim is not valid, the bank shall send to the consumer the notice described in paragraph (e)(2) of this section.

(3) Recredit pending investigation. If the bank has not taken an action described in paragraph (c)(1) or (c)(2) of this section before the end of the 10th business day after the banking day on which the bank received the claim, the bank shall—

(i) By the end of that business day—

(A) Recredit the consumer's account for the amount of the consumer's loss, up to the lesser of the amount of the substitute check or $2,500, plus interest on that amount if the account is an interest-bearing account; and

(B) Send to the consumer the notice required by paragraph (e)(1) of this section; and

(ii) Recredit the consumer's account for the remaining amount of the consumer's loss, if any, up to the amount of the substitute check, plus interest if the account is an interest-bearing account, no later than the end of the 45th calendar day after the banking day on which the bank received the claim and send to the consumer the notice required by paragraph (e)(1) of this section, unless the bank prior to that time has determined that the consumer's claim is or is not valid in accordance with paragraph (c)(1) or (c)(2) of this section.

(4) Reversal of recredit. A bank may reverse a recredit that it has made to a consumer account under paragraph (c)(1) or (c)(3) of this section, plus interest that the bank has paid, if any, on that amount, if the bank—

(i) Determines that the consumer's claim was not valid; and

(ii) Notifies the consumer in accordance with paragraph (e)(3) of this section.

(d) Availability of recredit—

(1) Next-day availability. Except as provided in paragraph (d)(2) of this section, a bank shall make any amount that it recredits to a consumer account under this section available for withdrawal no later than the start of the business day after the banking day on which the bank provides the recredit.

(2) Safeguard exceptions. A bank may delay availability to a consumer of a recredit provided under paragraph (c)(3)(i) of this section until the start of the earlier of the business day after the banking day on which the bank determines the consumer's claim is valid or the 45th calendar day after the banking day on which the bank received the oral or written claim, as required by paragraph (b) of this section, if—

(i) The consumer submits the claim during the 30-calendar-day period beginning on the banking day on which the consumer account was established;

(ii) Without regard to the charge that gave rise to the recredit claim—

(A) On six or more business days during the six-month period ending on the calendar day on which the consumer submitted the claim, the balance in the consumer account was negative or would have become negative if checks or other charges to the account had been paid; or

(B) On two or more business days during such six-month period, the balance in the consumer account was negative or would have become negative in the amount of $5,000 or more if checks or other charges to the account had been paid; or

(iii) The bank has reasonable cause to believe that the claim is fraudulent, based on facts that would cause a well-grounded belief in the mind of a reasonable person that the claim is fraudulent. The fact that the check in question or the consumer is of a particular class may not be the basis for invoking this exception.

(3) Overdraft fees. A bank that delays availability as permitted in paragraph (d)(2) of this section may not impose an overdraft fee with respect to drafts drawn by the consumer on such recredited funds until the fifth calendar day after the calendar day on which the bank sent the notice required by paragraph (e)(1) of this section.

(e) Notices relating to consumer expedited recredit claims—

(1) Notice of recredit. A bank that recredits a consumer account under paragraph (c) of this section shall send notice to the consumer of the recredit no later than the business day after the banking day on which the bank recredits the consumer account. This notice shall describe—

(i) The amount of the recredit; and

(ii) The date on which the recredited funds will be available for withdrawal.

(2) Notice that the consumer's claim is not valid. If a bank determines that a substitute check for which a consumer made a claim under this section was in fact properly charged to the consumer account or that the consumer's warranty claim for that substitute check was not valid, the bank shall send notice to the consumer no later than the business day after the banking day on which the bank makes that determination. This notice shall—

(i) Include the original check or a sufficient copy, except as provided in § 229.58;

(ii) Demonstrate to the consumer that the substitute check was properly charged or the consumer's warranty claim is not valid; and

(iii) Include the information or documents (in addition to the original check or sufficient copy), if any, on which the bank relied in making its determination or a statement that the consumer may request copies of such information or documents.

(3) Notice of a reversal of recredit. A bank that reverses an amount it previously recredited to a consumer account shall send notice to the consumer no later than the business day after the banking day on which the bank made the reversal. This notice shall include the information listed in paragraph (e)(2) of this section and also describe—

(i) The amount of the reversal, including both the amount of the recredit (including the interest component, if any) and the amount of interest paid on the recredited amount, if any, being reversed; and

(ii) The date on which the bank made the reversal.

(f) Other claims not affected. Providing a recredit in accordance with this section shall not absolve the bank from liability for a claim made under any other provision of law, such as a claim for wrongful dishonor of a check under the U.C.C., or from liability for additional damages, such as damages under § 229.53 or § 229.56 of this subpart or U.C.C. 4–402.

§ 229.55 Expedited recredit for banks.

(a) Circumstances giving rise to a claim. A bank that has an indemnity claim under § 229.53 with respect to a substitute check may make an expedited recredit claim against an indemnifying bank if—

(1) The claimant bank or a bank that the claimant bank has indemnified—

(i) Has received a claim for expedited recredit from a consumer under § 229.54; or

(ii) Would have been subject to such a claim if the consumer account had been charged for the substitute check;

(2) The claimant bank is obligated to provide an expedited recredit with respect to such substitute check under § 229.54 or otherwise has suffered a resulting loss; and

(3) The production of the original check or a sufficient copy is necessary to determine the validity of the charge to the consumer account or the validity of any warranty claim connected with such substitute check.

(b) Procedures for making claims. A claimant bank shall send its claim to the indemnifying bank, subject to the timing, content, and form requirements of this section.

(1) Timing of claim. The claimant bank shall submit its claim such that the indemnifying bank receives the claim by the end of the 120th calendar day after the date of the transaction that gave rise to the claim.

(2) Content of claim. The claimant bank's claim shall include the following information—

(i) A description of the consumer's claim or the warranty claim related to the substitute check, including why the bank believes that the substitute check may not be properly charged to the consumer account;

(ii) A statement that the claimant bank is obligated to recredit a consumer account under § 229.54 or otherwise has suffered a loss and an estimate of the amount of that recredit or loss, including interest if applicable;

(iii) The reason why production of the original check or a sufficient copy is necessary to determine the validity of the charge to the consumer account or the warranty claim; and

(iv) Sufficient information to allow the indemnifying bank to identify the substitute check and investigate the claim.

(3) Requirements relating to copies of substitute checks. If the information submitted by a claimant bank under paragraph (b)(2) of this section includes a copy of any substitute check, the claimant bank shall take reasonable steps to ensure that the copy cannot be mistaken for the legal equivalent of the check under § 229.51(a) or sent or handled by any bank, including the indemnifying bank, for forward collection or return.

(4) Form and submission of claim; computation of time. The indemnifying bank may, in its discretion, require the claimant bank to submit the information required by this section in writing, including a copy of the paper or electronic claim submitted by the consumer, if any. An indemnifying bank that requires a written submission—

(i) May permit the claimant bank to submit the written claim electronically;

(ii) Shall inform a claimant bank that submits a claim orally of the written claim requirement at the time of the oral claim; and

(iii) Shall compute the 10-day time period for acting on the claim described in paragraph (c) of this section from the date on which the bank received the written claim.

(c) Action on claims. No later than the 10th business day after the banking day on which the indemnifying bank receives a claim that meets the requirements of paragraph (b) of this section, the indemnifying bank shall—

(1) Recredit the claimant bank for the amount of the claim, up to the amount of the substitute check, plus interest if applicable;

(2) Provide to the claimant bank the original check or a sufficient copy; or

(3) Provide information to the claimant bank regarding why the indemnifying bank is not obligated to comply with paragraph (c)(1) or (c)(2) of this section.

(d) Recredit does not abrogate other liabilities. Providing a recredit to a claimant bank under this section does not absolve the indemnifying bank from liability for claims brought under any other law or from additional damages under § 229.53 or § 229.56.

(e) Indemnifying bank's right to a refund.

(1) If a claimant bank reverses a recredit it previously made to a consumer account under § 229.54 or otherwise receives reimbursement for a substitute check that formed the basis of its claim under this section, the claimant bank shall provide a refund promptly to any indemnifying bank that previously advanced funds to the claimant bank. The amount of the refund to the indemnifying bank shall be the amount of the reversal or reimbursement obtained by the claimant bank, up to the amount previously advanced by the indemnifying bank.

(2) If the indemnifying bank provides the claimant bank with the original check or a sufficient copy under paragraph (c)(2) of this section, § 229.53(b)(3) governs the indemnifying bank's entitlement to repayment of any amount provided to the claimant bank that exceeds the amount of losses the claimant bank incurred up to that time.

§ 229.56 Liability.

(a) Measure of damages.

(1) In general. Except as provided in paragraph (a)(2) or (a)(3) of this section or § 229.53, any person that breaches a warranty described in § 229.52 or fails to comply with any requirement of this subpart with respect to any other person shall be liable to that person for an amount equal to the sum of—

(i) The amount of the loss suffered by the person as a result of the breach or failure, up to the amount of the substitute check; and

(ii) Interest and expenses (including costs and reasonable attorney's fees and other expenses of representation) related to the substitute check.

(2) Offset of recredits. The amount of damages a person receives under paragraph (a)(1) of this section shall be reduced by any amount that the person receives and retains as a recredit under § 229.54 or § 229.55.

(3) Comparative negligence.

(i) If a person incurs damages that resulted in whole or in part from that person's negligence or failure to act in good faith, then the amount of any damages due to that person under paragraph (a)(1) of this section shall be reduced in proportion to the amount of negligence or bad faith attributable to that person.

(ii) Nothing in this paragraph (a)(3) reduces the rights of a consumer or any other person under the U.C.C. or other applicable provision of federal or state law.

(b) Timeliness of action. Delay by a bank beyond any time limits prescribed or permitted by this subpart is excused if the delay is caused by interruption of communication or computer facilities, suspension of payments by another bank, war, emergency conditions, failure of equipment, or other circumstances beyond the control of the bank and if the bank uses such diligence as the circumstances require.

(c) Jurisdiction. A person may bring an action to enforce a claim under this subpart in any United States district court or in any other court of competent jurisdiction. Such claim shall be brought within one year of the date on which the person's cause of action accrues. For purposes of this paragraph, a cause of action accrues as of the date on which the injured person first learns, or by which such person reasonably should have learned, of the facts and circumstances giving rise to the cause of action, including the identity of the warranting or indemnifying bank against which the action is brought.

(d) Notice of claims. Except as otherwise provided in this paragraph (d), unless a person gives notice of a claim under this section to the warranting or indemnifying bank within 30 calendar days after the person has reason to know of both the claim and the identity of the warranting or indemnifying bank, the warranting or indemnifying bank is discharged from liability in an action to enforce a claim under this subpart to the extent of any loss caused by the delay in giving notice of the claim. A timely recredit claim by a consumer under § 229.54 constitutes timely notice under this paragraph.

§ 229.57 Consumer awareness.

(a) General disclosure requirement and content. Each bank shall provide, in accordance with paragraph (b) of this section, a brief disclosure to each of its consumer customers that describes—

(1) That a substitute check is the legal equivalent of an original check; and

(2) The consumer recredit rights that apply when a consumer in good faith believes that a substitute check was not properly charged to his or her account.

(b) Distribution—

(1) Disclosure to consumers who receive paid checks with periodic account statements. A bank shall provide the disclosure described in paragraph (a) of this section to a consumer customer who receives paid original checks or paid substitute checks with his or her periodic account statement—

(i) No later than the first regularly scheduled communication with the consumer after October 28, 2004, for each consumer who is a customer of the bank on that date; and

(ii) At the time the customer relationship is initiated, for each customer relationship established after October 28, 2004.

(2) Disclosure to consumers who receive substitute checks on an occasional basis—

(i) The bank shall provide the disclosure described in paragraph (a) of this section to a consumer customer of the bank who requests an original check or a copy of a check and receives a substitute check. If feasible, the bank shall provide this disclosure at the time of the consumer's request; otherwise, the bank shall provide this disclosure no later than the time at which the bank provides a substitute check in response to the consumer's request.

(ii) The bank shall provide the disclosure described in paragraph (a) of this section to a consumer customer of the bank who receives a returned substitute check, at the time the bank provides such substitute check.

(3) Multiple account holders. A bank need not give separate disclosures to each customer on a jointly held account.

§ 229.58 Mode of delivery of information.

A bank may deliver any notice or other information that it is required to provide under this subpart by United States mail or by any other means through which the recipient has agreed to receive account information. If a bank is required to provide an original check or a sufficient copy, the bank instead may provide an electronic image of the original check or sufficient copy if the recipient has agreed to receive that information electronically.

§ 229.59 Relation to other law.

The Check 21 Act and this subpart supersede any provision of federal or state law, including the Uniform Commercial Code, that is inconsistent with the Check 21 Act or this subpart, but only to the extent of the inconsistency.

§ 229.60 Variation by agreement.

Any provision of § 229.55 may be varied by agreement of the banks involved. No other provision of this subpart may be varied by agreement by any person or persons.

COLLECTION OF CHECKS AND OTHER ITEMS BY FEDERAL RESERVE BANKS AND FUNDS TRANSFERS THROUGH FEDWIRE (REGULATION J)

12 C.F.R. Part 210

Current through March 27, 2019; 84 F.R. 11636

For updates and Commentary, see www.ecfr.gov

SUBPART A—COLLECTION OF CHECKS AND OTHER ITEMS BY FEDERAL RESERVE BANKS

§ 210.1 Authority, purpose, and scope.

The Board of Governors of the Federal Reserve System (Board) has issued this subpart pursuant to the Federal Reserve Act, sections 11(i) and (j) (12 U.S.C. 248(i) and (j)), section 13 (12 U.S.C. 342), section

16 (12 U.S.C. 248(*o*) and 360), and section 19(f) (12 U.S.C. 464); the Expedited Funds Availability Act (12 U.S.C. 4001 et seq.); the Check Clearing for the 21st Century Act (12 U.S.C. 5001–5018) and other laws. This subpart governs the collection of checks and other cash and noncash items and the handling of returned checks by Federal Reserve Banks. Its purpose is to provide rules for collecting and returning items and settling balances.

§ 210.2 Definitions.

As used in this subpart, unless the context otherwise requires:

(a) Account means an account on the books of a Federal Reserve Bank. A subaccount is an informational record of a subset of transactions that affect an account and is not a separate account.

(b) Actually and finally collected funds means cash or any other form of payment that is, or has become, final and irrevocable.

(c) Administrative Reserve Bank with respect to an entity means the Reserve Bank in whose District the entity is located, as determined under the procedure described in § 204.3(g) of this chapter (Regulation D), even if the entity is not otherwise subject to that section.

(d) Bank means any person engaged in the business of banking. A branch or separate office of a bank is a separate bank to the extent provided in the Uniform Commercial Code.

(e) Bank draft means a check drawn by one bank on another bank.

(f) Banking day means the part of a day on which a bank is open to the public for carrying on substantially all of its banking functions.

(g) Cash item means—

(1) A check other than one classified as a noncash item under this section; or

(2) Any other item payable on demand and collectible at par that the Reserve Bank that receives the item is willing to accept as a cash item. Cash item does not include a returned check.

(h) Check means a check or an electronic check, as those terms are defined in § 229.2 of this chapter (Regulation CC).

(i) Item.

(1) Means—

(i) An instrument or a promise or order to pay money, whether negotiable or not, that is—

(A) Payable in a Federal Reserve District[1] (District);

(B) Sent by a sender to a Reserve Bank for handling under this subpart; and

(C) Collectible in funds acceptable to the Reserve Bank of the District in which the instrument is payable; or

(ii) A check.

(2) Unless otherwise indicated, *item* includes both a cash and a noncash item, and includes a returned check sent by a paying or returning bank. *Item* does not include a check that cannot be collected at par, or a *payment order* as defined in § 210.26(i) and handled under subpart B of this part. The term also does not include an electronically-created item as defined in § 229.2 of this chapter (Regulation CC).

(j) Nonbank payor means a payor of an item, other than a bank.

(k) Noncash item means an item that a receiving Reserve Bank classifies in its operating circulars as requiring special handling. The term also means an item normally received as a cash item if a Reserve Bank decides that special conditions require that it handle the item as a noncash item.

---

[1] For purposes of this subpart, the Virgin Islands and Puerto Rico are deemed to be in the Second District, and Guam, American Samoa, and the Northern Mariana Islands in the Twelfth District.

(*l*) Paying bank means—

(1) The bank by which an item is payable unless the item is payable or collectible at or through another bank and is sent to the other bank for payment or collection;

(2) The bank at or through which an item is payable or collectible and to which it sent for payment or collection; or

(3) The bank whose routing number appears on a check in the MICR line or in fractional form (or in the MICR-line information that accompanies an electronic item) and to which the check is sent for payment or collection.

(m) Returned check means a cash item returned by a paying bank, including an electronic returned check as defined in § 229.2 of this chapter (Regulation CC) and a notice of nonpayment in lieu of a returned check, whether or not a Reserve Bank handled the check for collection.

(n) Sender means any of the following entities that sends an item to a Reserve Bank for forward collection—

(1) A depository institution, as defined in section 19(b) of the Federal Reserve Act (12 U.S.C. 461(b));

(2) A member bank, as defined in section 1 of the Federal Reserve Act (12 U.S.C. 221);

(3) A clearing institution, defined as—

(i) An institution that is not a depository institution but that maintains with a Reserve Bank the balance referred to in the first paragraph of section 13 of the Federal Reserve Act (12 U.S.C. 342); or

(ii) A corporation that maintains an account with a Reserve Bank in conformity with § 211.4 of this chapter (Regulation K);

(4) Another Reserve Bank;

(5) An international organization for which a Reserve Bank is empowered to act as depositary or fiscal agent and maintains an account;

(6) A foreign correspondent, defined as any of the following entities for which a Reserve Bank maintains an account: A foreign bank or banker, a foreign state as defined in section 25(b) of the Federal Reserve Act (12 U.S.C. 632), or a foreign correspondent or agency referred to in section 14(e) of that act (12 U.S.C. 358); or

(7) A branch or agency of a foreign bank maintaining reserves under section 7 of the International Banking Act of 1978 (12 U.S.C. 347d, 3105).

(o) State means a State of the United States, the District of Columbia, Puerto Rico, or a territory, possession, or dependency of the United States.

(p) Clock hour and clock half-hour.

(1) Clock hour means a time that is on the hour, such as 1:00, 2:00, etc.

(2) Clock half-hour means a time that is on the half-hour, such as 1:30, 2:30, etc.

(q) Fedwire Funds Service and Fedwire have the same meaning as that set forth in § 210.26(e).

(r) Uniform Commercial Code and U.C.C. mean the Uniform Commercial Code as adopted in a state.

(s) Terms not defined in this section. Unless the context otherwise requires—

(1) The terms not defined herein have the meanings set forth in § 229.2 of this chapter applicable to subpart C or D of part 229 of this chapter (Regulation CC), as appropriate; and

(2) The terms not defined herein or in § 229.2 of this chapter have the meanings set forth in the Uniform Commercial Code.

§ 210.3 General provisions.

(a) General. Each Reserve Bank shall receive and handle items in accordance with this subpart, and shall issue operating circulars governing the details of its handling of items and other matters deemed appropriate by the Reserve Bank. The circulars may, among other things, classify cash items and noncash items, require separate sorts and letters, provide different closing times for the receipt of different classes or types of items, provide for instructions by an Administrative Reserve Bank to other Reserve Banks, set forth terms of services, and establish procedures for adjustments on a Reserve Bank's books, including amounts, waiver of expenses, and payment of compensation. As deemed appropriate by the Reserve Bank, the circulars may also require the sender to provide warranties and indemnities that only items and any noncash items the Reserve Banks have agreed to handle will be sent to the Reserve Banks. The Reserve Banks may provide to a subsequent collecting bank and to the paying bank any warranties and indemnities provided by the sender pursuant to this paragraph (a).

(b) Binding effect. This subpart, together with subparts C and D of Part 229 and the operating circulars of the Reserve Banks, are binding on all parties interested in an item handled by any Reserve Bank.

(c) Government items. As depositaries and fiscal agents of the United States, Reserve Banks handle certain items payable by the United States or certain Federal agencies as cash or noncash items. To the extent provided by regulations issued by, and arrangements made with, the United States Treasury Department and other Government departments and agencies, the handling of such items is governed by this subpart. The Reserve Banks shall include in their operating circulars such information regarding these regulations and arrangements as the Reserve Banks deem appropriate.

(d) Government senders. Except as otherwise provided by statutes of the United States, or regulations issued or arrangements made thereunder, this subpart and the operating circulars of the Reserve Banks apply to the following when acting as a sender: a department, agency, instrumentality, independent establishment, or office of the United States, or a wholly owned or controlled Government corporation, that maintains or uses an account with a Reserve Bank.

(e) Foreign items. A Reserve Bank also may receive and handle certain items payable outside a Federal Reserve District, as provided in its operating circulars. The handling of such items in a state is governed by this subpart, and the handling of such items outside a state is governed by the local law.

(f) Relation to other law. The provisions of this subpart supersede any inconsistent provisions of the Uniform Commercial Code, of any other state law, or of part 229 of this title, but only to the extent of the inconsistency.

§ 210.4 Sending items to Reserve Banks.

(a) Sending of items. A sender's Administrative Reserve Bank may direct a sender other than a Reserve Bank to send any item to a specified Reserve Bank, whether or not the item is payable in the Reserve Bank's district.

(b) Handling of items.

(1) The following parties, in the following order, are deemed to have handled an item that is sent to a Reserve Bank for collection:

(i) The initial sender;

(ii) The initial sender's Administrative Reserve Bank (which is deemed to have accepted deposit of the item from the initial sender);

(iii) The Reserve Bank that receives the item from the initial sender (if different from the initial sender's Administrative Reserve Bank); and

(iv) Another Reserve Bank, if any, that receives the item from a Reserve Bank.

(2) A Reserve Bank that is not described in paragraph (b)(1) of this section is not a person that handles an item and is not a collecting bank with respect to an item.

(3) The identity and order of the parties under paragraph (b)(1) of this section determine the relationships and the rights and liabilities of the parties under this subpart, part 229 of this chapter (Regulation CC), section 13(1) and section 16(13) of the Federal Reserve Act, and the Uniform Commercial Code. An initial sender's Administrative Reserve Bank that is deemed to accept an item for deposit or handle an item is also deemed to be a sender with respect to that item. The Reserve Banks that are deemed to handle an item are deemed to be agents or subagents of the owner of the item, as provided in § 210.6(a).

(c) **Checks received at par.** The Reserve Banks shall receive cash items and other checks at par.

§ 210.5 Sender's agreement; recovery by Reserve Bank.

(a) **Sender's agreement.** The warranties, indemnities, authorizations, and agreements made pursuant to this paragraph (a) may not be disclaimed and are made whether or not the item bears an indorsement of the sender. By sending an item to a Reserve Bank, the sender does all of the following.

(1) **Authorization to handle item.** The sender authorizes the sender's Administrative Reserve Bank and any other Reserve Bank or collecting bank to which the item is sent to handle the item (and authorizes any Reserve Bank that handles settlement for the item to make accounting entries), subject to this subpart and to the Reserve Banks' operating circulars, and warrants its authority to give this authorization.

(2) **Warranties for all items.** The sender warrants to each Reserve Bank handling the item that—

(i) The sender is a person entitled to enforce the item or authorized to obtain payment of the item on behalf of a person entitled to enforce the item;

(ii) The item has not been altered; and

(iii) The item bears all indorsements applied by parties that previously handled the item for forward collection or return.

(3) **Warranties and indemnities as set forth in Regulation CC and U.C.C.** As applicable and unless otherwise provided, the sender of an item makes to each Reserve Bank that handles the item all the warranties and indemnities set forth in and subject to the terms of subparts C and D of part 229 of this chapter (Regulation CC) and Article 4 of the U.C.C. The sender makes all the warranties set forth in and subject to the terms of 4–207 of the U.C.C. for an electronic check as if it were an item subject to the U.C.C.

(4) **Warranties and indemnities as set forth in Reserve Bank operating circulars.** The sender makes any warranties and indemnities regarding the sending of items as set forth in an operating circular issued in accordance with § 210.3(a).

(5) **Sender's liability to Reserve Bank.**

(i) Except as provided in paragraphs (a)(5)(ii) and (iii) of this section, the sender agrees to indemnify each Reserve Bank for any loss or expense sustained (including attorneys' fees and expenses of litigation) resulting from—

(A) The sender's lack of authority to make the warranty in paragraph (a)(1) of this section;

(B) Any action taken by the Reserve Bank within the scope of its authority in handling the item; or

(C) Any warranty or indemnity made by the Reserve Bank under § 210.6(b), part 229 of this chapter, the U.C.C., or, regarding the sending of items, an operating circular issued in accordance with § 210.3(a).

(ii) A sender's liability for warranties and indemnities that the Reserve Bank makes for a substitute check, a paper or electronic representation thereof, or for an electronic check is subject to the following conditions and limitations—

(A) A sender of an original check shall not be liable under paragraph (a)(5)(i) of this section for any amount that the Reserve Bank pays under subpart D of part 229 of this chapter, or under § 229.34 of this chapter with respect to an electronic check, absent the sender's agreement to the contrary; and

(B) Nothing in this subpart alters the liability of a sender of a substitute check or paper or electronic representation of a substitute check under subpart D of part 229 of this chapter, or a sender of an electronic check under § 229.34 of this chapter.

(iii) A sender shall not be liable for any amount that the Reserve Bank pays under this subpart or part 229 of this chapter that is attributable to the Reserve Bank's own lack of good faith or failure to exercise ordinary care.

(b) Sender's liability under other law. Nothing in paragraph (a) of this section limits any warranty or indemnity by a sender (or a person that handled an item prior to the sender) arising under state law or regulation (such as the U.C.C.), other federal law or regulation (such as part 229 of this chapter), or an agreement with a Reserve Bank.

(c) Recovery by Reserve Bank.

(1) A Reserve Bank that has handled an item may recover as provided in paragraph (c)(2) of this section if an action or proceeding is brought against (or if defense is tendered to) the Reserve Bank based on—

(i) The alleged failure of the sender to have the authority to make the warranty and agreement in paragraph (a)(1) of this section;

(ii) Any action by the Reserve Bank within the scope of its authority in handling the item; or

(iii) Any warranty or indemnity made by the Reserve Bank under § 210.6(b), part 229 of this chapter, or the U.C.C.

(2) Upon entry of a final judgment or decree in an action or proceeding described in paragraph (c)(1) of this section, a Reserve Bank may recover from the sender the amount of attorneys' fees and other expenses of litigation incurred, as well as any amount the Reserve Bank is required to pay because of the judgment or decree or the tender of defense, together with interest thereon.

(d) Methods of recovery.

(1) The Reserve Bank may recover the amount stated in paragraph (c) of this section by charging any account on its books that is maintained or used by the sender (or by charging a Reserve Bank sender), if—

(i) The Reserve Bank made seasonable written demand on the sender to assume defense of the action or proceeding; and

(ii) The sender has not made any other arrangement for payment that is acceptable to the Reserve Bank.

(2) The Reserve Bank is not responsible for defending the action or proceeding before using this method of recovery. A Reserve Bank that has been charged under this paragraph (d) may recover from its sender in the manner and under the circumstances set forth in this paragraph (d).

(3) A Reserve Bank's failure to avail itself of the remedy provided in this paragraph (d) does not prejudice its enforcement in any other manner of the indemnity agreement referred to in paragraph (a)(5) of this section.

(e) Security interest. When a sender sends an item to a Reserve Bank, the sender and any prior collecting bank grant to the sender's Administrative Reserve Bank a security interest in all of their respective assets in the possession of, or held for the account of, any Reserve Bank to secure their respective obligations due or to become due to the Administrative Reserve Bank under this subpart or subpart C or D of part 229 of this chapter (Regulation CC). The security interest attaches when a warranty is breached or any other obligation to the Reserve Bank is incurred. If the Reserve Bank, in its sole discretion, deems itself insecure and gives notice thereof to the sender or prior collecting bank, or if the sender or prior collecting bank suspends payments or is closed, the Reserve Bank may take any action authorized by law to recover the amount of an obligation, including, but not limited to, the exercise of rights of set off, the realization on any available collateral, and any other rights it may have as a creditor under applicable law.

§ 210.6 Status, warranties, and liability of Reserve Bank.

(a)(1) **Status.** A Reserve Bank that handles an item shall act as agent or subagent of the owner with respect to the item. This agency terminates when a Reserve Bank receives final payment for the item in actually and finally collected funds, a Reserve Bank makes the proceeds available for use by the sender, and the time for commencing all actions against the Reserve Bank has expired.

(2) **Limitations on Reserve Bank liability.** A Reserve Bank shall not have or assume any liability with respect to an item or its proceeds except—

(i) For the Reserve Bank's own lack of good faith or failure to exercise ordinary care;

(ii) As provided in paragraph (b) of this section;

(iii) As provided in an operating circular issued in accordance with § 210.3(a) regarding the sending of items; and

(iv) As provided in subparts C and D of part 229 of this chapter (Regulation CC).

(3) **Reliance on routing designation appearing on item.** A Reserve Bank may present or send an item based on the routing number or other designation of a paying bank or nonbank payor appearing in any form on the item when the Reserve Bank receives it. A Reserve Bank shall not be responsible for any delay resulting from its acting on any designation, whether inscribed by magnetic ink or by other means, and whether or not the designation acted on is consistent with any other designation appearing on the item.

(b) **Warranties and liability.** The following provisions apply when a Reserve Bank presents or sends an item.

(1) **Warranties for all items.** The Reserve Bank warrants to a subsequent collecting bank and to the paying bank and any other payor that—

(i) The Reserve Bank is a person entitled to enforce the item (or is authorized to obtain payment of the item on behalf of a person that is either entitled to enforce the item or authorized to obtain payment on behalf of a person entitled to enforce the item);

(ii) The item has not been altered; and

(iii) The item bears all indorsements applied by parties that previously handled the item for forward collection or return.

(2) **Warranties and indemnities as set forth in Reserve Bank operating circulars.** The Reserve Bank makes any warranties and indemnities regarding the sending of items as set forth in an operating circular issued in accordance with § 210.3(a).

(3) **Warranties and indemnities as set forth in Regulation CC and U.C.C.** As applicable and unless otherwise provided, the Reserve Bank makes all the warranties and indemnities set forth in and subject to the terms of subparts C and D of part 229 of this chapter (Regulation CC) and Article 4 of the U.C.C. The Reserve Bank makes all the warranties set forth in and subject to the terms of 4–207 of the U.C.C. for an electronic check as if it were an item subject to the U.C.C.

(4) **Indemnity for substitute check created from an electronic check.**

(i) Except as provided in paragraph (b)(4)(ii) of this section, the Reserve Bank shall indemnify the bank to which it transfers or presents an electronic check (the recipient bank) for the amount of any losses that the recipient bank incurs under subpart D of part 229 of this chapter (Regulation CC) for an indemnity that the recipient bank was required to make under subpart D of part 229 of this chapter in connection with a substitute check later created from the electronic check.

(ii) The Reserve Bank shall not be liable under paragraph (b)(4)(i) of this section for any amount that the recipient bank pays under subpart D of part 229 of this chapter that is attributable to the lack of good faith or failure to exercise ordinary care of the recipient bank or a person that handled the item, in any form, after the recipient bank.

(c) Time for commencing action against Reserve Bank.

(1) A claim against a Reserve Bank for lack of good faith or failure to exercise ordinary care shall be barred unless the action on the claim is commenced within two years after the claim accrues. Such a claim accrues on the date when a Reserve Bank's alleged failure to exercise ordinary care or to act in good faith first results in damages to the claimant.

(2) A claim that arises under paragraph (b)(3) of this section shall be barred unless the action on the claim is commenced within one year after the claim accrues. Such a claim accrues as of the date on which the claimant first learns, or by which the claimant reasonably should have learned, of the facts and circumstances giving rise to the claim.

(3) This paragraph (c) does not alter the time limit for claims under § 229.38(g) of this chapter (which include claims for breach of warranty under § 229.34 of this chapter) or subpart D of part 229 of this chapter.

§ 210.7 Presenting items for payment.

(a) Presenting or sending. As provided under State law or as otherwise permitted by this section:

(1) A Reserve Bank or a subsequent collecting bank may present an item for payment or send the item for presentment and payment; and

(2) A Reserve Bank may send an item to a subsequent collecting bank with authority to present it for payment or to send it for presentment and payment.

(b) Place of presentment. A Reserve Bank or subsequent collecting bank may present an item—

(1) At a place requested by the paying bank;

(2) In accordance with 12 CFR 229.36 of this chapter (Regulation CC);

(3) At a place requested by the nonbank payor, if the item is payable by a nonbank payor other than through or at a paying bank;

(4) Under a special collection agreement consistent with this subpart; or

(5) Through a clearinghouse and subject to its rules and practices.

(c) Presenting or sending direct. A Reserve Bank or subsequent collecting bank may, with respect to an item that may be sent to the paying bank or nonbank payor in the Reserve Bank's District—

(1) Present or send the item direct to the paying bank, or to a place requested by the paying bank; or

(2) If the item is payable by a nonbank payor other than through a paying bank, present it direct to the nonbank payor. Documents, securities, or other papers accompanying a noncash item shall not be delivered to the nonbank payor before the item is paid unless the sender specifically authorizes delivery.

(d) Item sent to another district. A Reserve Bank receiving an item that may be sent to a paying bank or nonbank payor in another District ordinarily sends the item to the Reserve Bank of the other District, but with the agreement of the other Reserve Bank, may present or send the item as if it were sent to a paying bank or nonbank payor in its own District.

§ 210.8 Presenting noncash items for acceptance.

(a) A Reserve Bank or a subsequent collecting bank may, if instructed by the sender, present a noncash item for acceptance in any manner authorized by law if—

(1) The item provides that it must be presented for acceptance;

(2) The item may be presented elsewhere than at the residence or place of business of the payor; or

(3) The date of payment of the item depends on presentment for acceptance.

(b) Documents accompanying a noncash item shall not be delivered to the payor upon acceptance of the item unless the sender specifically authorizes delivery. A Reserve Bank shall not have or assume any other obligation to present or to send for presentment for acceptance any noncash item.

§ 210.9 Settlement and payment.

(a) Settlement through Administrative Reserve Bank. A paying bank shall settle for an item under this subpart with its Administrative Reserve Bank, whether or not the paying bank received the item from that Reserve Bank. A paying bank's settlement with its Administrative Reserve Bank is deemed to be settlement with the Reserve Bank from which the paying bank received the item. A paying bank may settle for an item using any account on a Reserve Bank's books by agreement with its Administrative Reserve Bank, any other Reserve Bank holding the settlement account, and the account-holder. The paying bank remains responsible for settlement if the Reserve Bank holding the settlement account does not, for any reason, obtain settlement in that account.

(b) Cash items—

(1) Settlement obligation. On the day a paying bank receives[2] a cash item from a Reserve Bank, it shall settle for the item such that the proceeds of the settlement are available to its Administrative Reserve Bank by the close of Fedwire on that day, or it shall return the item by the later of the close of its banking day or the close of Fedwire. If the paying bank fails to settle for or return a cash item in accordance with this paragraph (b)(1), it is accountable for the amount of the item as of the close of its banking day or the close of Fedwire on the day it receives the item, whichever is earlier.

(2) Time of settlement.

(i) On the day a paying bank receives a cash item from a Reserve Bank, it shall settle for the item so that the proceeds of the settlement are available to its Administrative Reserve Bank, or return the item, by the latest of—

(A) The next clock hour or clock half-hour that is at least one half-hour after the paying bank receives the item;

(B) 8:30 a.m. eastern time; or

(C) Such later time as provided in the Reserve Banks' operating circulars.

(ii) If the paying bank fails to settle for or return a cash item in accordance with paragraph (b)(2)(i) of this section, it shall be subject to any applicable overdraft charges. Settlement under paragraph (b)(2)(i) of this section satisfies the settlement requirements of paragraph (b)(1) of this section.

(3) Paying bank closes voluntarily.

(i) If a paying bank closes voluntarily so that it does not receive a cash item on a day that is a banking day for a Reserve Bank, and the Reserve Bank makes a cash item available to the paying bank on that day, the paying bank shall either—

(A) On that day, settle for the item so that the proceeds of the settlement are available to its Administrative Reserve Bank, or return the item, by the latest of the next clock hour or clock half-hour that is at least one half-hour after it ordinarily would have received the item, 8:30 a.m. eastern time, or such later time as provided in the Reserve Banks' operating circulars; or

---

[2] A paying bank is deemed to receive a cash item on its next banking day if it receives the item—

(1) On a day other than a banking day for it; or

(2) On a banking day for it, but after a "cut-off hour" established by it in accordance with state law.

(B) On the next day that is a banking day for both the paying bank and the Reserve Bank, settle for the item so that the proceeds of the settlement are available to its Administrative Reserve Bank by 8:30 a.m. eastern time on that day or such later time as provided in the Reserve Banks' operating circulars; and compensate the Reserve Bank for the value of the float associated with the item in accordance with procedures provided in the Reserve Bank's operating circular.

(ii) If a paying bank closes voluntarily so that it does not receive a cash item on a day that is a banking day for a Reserve Bank, and the Reserve Bank makes a cash item available to the paying bank on that day, the paying bank is not considered to have received the item until its next banking day, but it shall be subject to any applicable overdraft charges if it fails to settle for or return the item in accordance with paragraph (b)(3)(i) of this section. The settlement requirements of paragraphs (b)(1) and (b)(2) of this section do not apply to a paying bank that settles in accordance with paragraph (b)(3)(i) of this section.

(4) Reserve Bank closed. If a paying bank receives a cash item from a Reserve Bank on a banking day that is not a banking day for the Reserve Bank, the paying bank shall—

(i) Settle for the item so that the proceeds of the settlement are available to its Administrative Reserve Bank by the close of the Fedwire Funds Service on the Reserve Bank's next banking day, or return the item by midnight of the day it receives the item (if the paying bank fails to settle for or return a cash item in accordance with this paragraph (b)(4)(i), it shall become accountable for the amount of the item as of the close of its banking day on the day it receives the item); and

(ii) Settle for the item so that the proceeds of the settlement are available to its Administrative Reserve Bank by 8:30 a.m. eastern time on the Reserve Bank's next banking day or such later time as provided in the Reserve Bank's operating circular, or return the item by midnight of the day it receives the item. If the paying bank fails to settle for or return a cash item in accordance with this paragraph (b)(4)(ii), it shall be subject to any applicable overdraft charges. Settlement under this paragraph (b)(4)(ii) satisfies the settlement requirements of paragraph (b)(4)(i) of this section.

(5) Manner of settlement. Settlement with a Reserve Bank under paragraphs (b)(1) through (4) of this section shall be made by debit to an account on the Reserve Bank's books or other form of settlement to which the Reserve Bank agrees, except that the Reserve Bank may, in its discretion, obtain settlement by charging the paying bank's account. A paying bank may not set off against the amount of a settlement under this section the amount of a claim with respect to another cash item, cash letter, or other claim under § 229.34 of this chapter (Regulation CC) or other law.

(6) Notice in lieu of return. If a cash item is unavailable for return, the paying bank may send a notice in lieu of return as provided in § 229.31(f) of this chapter (Regulation CC).

(c) Noncash items. A Reserve Bank may require the paying or collecting bank to which it has presented or sent a noncash item to pay for the item by a debit to an account maintained or used by the paying or collecting bank on the Reserve Bank's books or by any other form of settlement acceptable to the Reserve Bank.

(d) Nonbank payor. A Reserve Bank may require a nonbank payor to which it has presented an item to pay for it by debit to an account on the Reserve Bank's books or other form of settlement acceptable to the Reserve Bank.

(e) Liability of Reserve Bank. Except as set forth in § 229.35(b) of this chapter (Regulation CC), a Reserve Bank shall not be liable for the failure of a collecting bank, paying bank, or nonbank payor to pay for an item, or for any loss resulting from the Reserve Bank's acceptance of any form of payment other than cash authorized in paragraphs (b), (c), and (d) of this section. A Reserve Bank that acts in good faith and exercises ordinary care shall not be liable for the nonpayment of, or failure to realize upon, any noncash form of payment that it accepts under paragraphs (b), (c), and (d) of this section.

§ 210.10 Time schedule and availability of credits for cash items and returned checks.

(a) Each Reserve Bank shall publish a time schedule indicating when the amount of any cash item or returned check received by it is counted toward the balance maintained to satisfy a reserve balance requirement for purposes of part 204 of this chapter (Regulation D) and becomes available for use by the sender or paying or returning bank. The Reserve Bank that holds the settlement account shall give either immediate or deferred credit to a sender, a paying bank, or a returning bank (other than a foreign correspondent) in accordance with the time schedule of the receiving Reserve Bank. A Reserve Bank ordinarily gives credit to a foreign correspondent only when the Reserve Bank receives payment of the item in actually and finally collected funds, but, in its discretion, a Reserve Bank may give immediate or deferred credit in accordance with its time schedule.

(b) Notwithstanding its time schedule, a Reserve Bank may refuse at any time to permit the use of credit given by it for any cash item or returned check, and may defer availability after credit is received by the Reserve Bank for a period of time that is reasonable under the circumstances.

§ 210.11 Availability of proceeds of noncash items; time schedule.

(a) Availability of credit. A Reserve Bank shall give credit to the sender for the proceeds of a noncash item when it receives payment in actually and finally collected funds (or advice from another Reserve Bank of such payment to it). The amount of the item is counted toward the balance maintained to satisfy a reserve balance requirement for purposes of part 204 of this chapter (Regulation D) and becomes available for use by the sender when the Reserve Bank receives the payment or advice, except as provided in paragraph (b) of this section.

(b) Time schedule. A Reserve Bank may give credit for the proceeds of a noncash item subject to payment in actually and finally collected funds in accordance with a published time schedule. The time schedule shall indicate when the proceeds of the noncash item will be counted toward the balance maintained to satisfy a reserve balance requirement for purposes of part 204 of this chapter (Regulation D) and become available for use by the sender. A Reserve Bank may, however, refuse at any time to permit the use of credit given by it for a noncash item for which the Reserve Bank has not yet received payment in actually and finally collected funds.

§ 210.12 Return of cash items and handling of returned checks.

(a) Return of items.

(1) Return of cash items handled by Reserve Banks. A paying bank that receives a cash item from a Reserve Bank, other than for immediate payment over the counter, and that settles for the item as provided in § 210.9(b), may, before it has finally paid the item, return the item to any Reserve Bank (unless its Administrative Reserve Bank directs it to return the item to a specific Reserve Bank) in accordance with subpart C of part 229 of this chapter (Regulation CC), the Uniform Commercial Code, and the Reserve Banks' operating circulars. A paying bank that receives a cash item from a Reserve Bank also may return the item prior to settlement, in accordance with § 210.9(b) and the Reserve Banks' operating circulars. The rules or practices of a clearinghouse through which the item was presented, or a special collection agreement under which the item was presented, may not extend these return times, but may provide for a shorter return time.

(2) Return of checks not handled by Reserve Banks. A paying bank that receives a check, other than from a Reserve Bank, and that determines not to pay the check, may send the returned check to any Reserve Bank (unless its Administrative Reserve Bank directs it to send the returned check to a specific Reserve Bank) in accordance with subpart C of part 229 of this chapter (Regulation CC), the Uniform Commercial Code, and the Reserve Banks' operating circulars. A returning bank may send a returned check to any Reserve Bank (unless its Administrative Reserve Bank directs it to send the returned check to a specific Reserve Bank) in accordance with subpart C of part 229 of this chapter (Regulation CC), the Uniform Commercial Code, and the Reserve Banks' operating circulars.

(b) Handling of returned checks.

(1) The following parties, in the following order, are deemed to have handled a returned check sent to a Reserve Bank under paragraph (a) of this section—

(i) The paying or returning bank;

(ii) The paying bank's or returning bank's Administrative Reserve Bank;

(iii) The Reserve Bank that receives the returned check from the paying or returning bank (if different from the paying bank's or returning bank's Administrative Reserve Bank); and

(iv) Another Reserve Bank, if any, that receives the returned check from a Reserve Bank.

(2) A Reserve Bank that is not described in paragraph (b)(1) of this section is not a person that handles a returned check and is not a returning bank with respect to a returned check.

(3) The identity and order of the parties under paragraph (b)(1) of this section determine the relationships and the rights and liabilities of the parties under this subpart, part 229 of this chapter (Regulation CC), and the Uniform Commercial Code.

(c) Paying bank's and returning bank's agreement. The warranties, indemnities, authorizations, and agreements made pursuant to this paragraph (c) may not be disclaimed and are made whether or not the returned check bears an indorsement of the paying bank or returning bank. By sending a returned check to a Reserve Bank, the paying bank or returning bank does all of the following.

(1) Authorization to handle returned check. The paying bank or returning bank authorizes the paying bank's or returning bank's Administrative Reserve Bank, and any other Reserve Bank or returning bank to which the returned check is sent, to handle the returned check (and authorizes any Reserve Bank that handles settlement for the returned check to make accounting entries) subject to this subpart and to the Reserve Banks' operating circulars.

(2) Warranties for all returned checks. The paying bank or returning bank warrants to each Reserve Bank handling a returned check that the returned check bears all indorsements applied by parties that previously handled the returned check for forward collection or return.

(3) Warranties and indemnities as set forth in Regulation CC. As applicable and unless otherwise provided, a paying bank or returning bank makes to each Reserve Bank that handles the returned check all the warranties and indemnities set forth in and subject to the terms of subparts C and D of part 229 of this chapter (Regulation CC).

(4) Paying bank or returning bank's liability to Reserve Bank.

(i) Except as provided in paragraph (c)(4)(ii) and (iii) of this section, a paying bank or returning bank agrees to indemnify each Reserve Bank for any loss or expense (including attorneys' fees and expenses of litigation) resulting from—

(A) The paying or returning bank's lack of authority to give the authorization in paragraph (c)(1) of this section;

(B) Any action taken by a Reserve Bank within the scope of its authority in handling the returned check; or

(C) Any warranty or indemnity made by the Reserve Bank under paragraph (e) of this section or part 229 of this chapter.

(ii) A paying bank's or returning bank's liability for warranties and indemnities that a Reserve Bank makes for a returned check that is a substitute check, a paper or electronic representation thereof, or an electronic returned check is subject to the following conditions and limitations—

(A) A paying bank or returning bank that sent an original returned check shall not be liable for any amount that a Reserve Bank pays under subpart D of part 229 of this chapter, or under § 229.34 of this chapter with respect to an electronic returned check, absent the paying bank's or returning bank's agreement to the contrary; and

(B) Nothing in this subpart alters the liability under subpart D of part 229 of this chapter of a paying bank or returning bank that sent a substitute check or a paper or electronic representation of a substitute check or under § 229.34 of this chapter of a paying bank or returning bank that sent an electronic returned check; and

(iii) A paying bank or returning bank shall not be liable for any amount that the Reserve Bank pays under this subpart or part 229 of this chapter that is attributable to the Reserve Bank's own lack of good faith or failure to exercise ordinary care.

(d) Paying bank or returning bank's liability under other law. Nothing in paragraph (c) of this section limits any warranty or indemnity by a returning bank or paying bank (or a person that handled an item prior to that bank) arising under state law or regulation (such as the U.C.C.), other federal law or regulation (such as part 229 of this chapter), or an agreement with a Reserve Bank.

(e) Warranties by and liability of Reserve Bank.

(1) Warranties and indemnities. The following provisions apply when a Reserve Bank handles a returned check under this subpart.

(i) Warranties for all items. The Reserve Bank warrants to the bank to which it sends the returned check that the returned check bears all indorsements applied by parties that previously handled the returned check for forward collection or return.

(ii) Warranties and indemnities as set forth in Regulation CC. As applicable and unless otherwise provided, the Reserve Bank makes all the warranties and indemnities set forth in and subject to the terms of subparts C and D of part 229 of this chapter (Regulation CC).

(2) Indemnity for substitute check created from electronic returned check.

(i) Except as provided in paragraph (e)(2)(ii) of this section, the Reserve Bank shall indemnify the bank to which it transfers or presents an electronic returned check (the recipient bank) for the amount of any losses that the recipient bank incurs under subpart D of part 229 of this chapter (Regulation CC) for an indemnity that the recipient bank was required to make under subpart D of part 229 of this chapter in connection with a substitute check later created from the electronic returned check.

(ii) The Reserve Bank shall not be liable under paragraph (e)(2)(i) of this section for any amount that the recipient bank pays under subpart D of part 229 of this chapter that is attributable to the lack of good faith or failure to exercise ordinary care of the recipient bank or a person that handled the item, in any form, after the recipient bank.

(3) Liability of Reserve Bank. A Reserve Bank shall not have or assume any other liability to any person except—

(i) For the Reserve Bank's own lack of good faith or failure to exercise ordinary care;

(ii) As provided in this paragraph (e); and

(iii) As provided in subparts C and D of part 229 of this chapter (Regulation CC).

(f) Recovery by Reserve Bank.

(1) A Reserve Bank that has handled a returned check may recover as provided in paragraph (f)(2) of this section if an action or proceeding is brought against (or if defense is tendered to) the Reserve Bank based on—

(i) The alleged failure of the paying bank or returning bank to have the authority to give the authorization in paragraph (c)(1) of this section;

(ii) Any action by the Reserve Bank within the scope of its authority in handling the returned check; or

(iii) Any warranty or indemnity made by the Reserve Bank under paragraph (e) of this section or part 229 of this chapter; and

(2) Upon entry of a final judgment or decree in an action or proceeding described in paragraph (f)(1) of this section, a Reserve Bank may recover from the paying bank or returning bank the amount of attorneys' fees and other expenses of litigation incurred, as well as any amount the Reserve Bank is required to pay because of the judgment or decree or the tender of defense, together with interest thereon.

(g) Methods of recovery.

(1) The Reserve Bank may recover the amount stated in paragraph (f) of this section by charging any account on its books that is maintained or used by the paying bank or returning bank (or by charging another returning Reserve Bank), if—

(i) The Reserve Bank made seasonable written demand on the paying bank or returning bank to assume defense of the action or proceeding; and

(ii) The paying bank or returning bank has not made any other arrangement for payment that is acceptable to the Reserve Bank.

(2) The Reserve Bank is not responsible for defending the action or proceeding before using this method of recovery. A Reserve Bank that has been charged under this paragraph (g) may recover from the paying or returning bank in the manner and under the circumstances set forth in this paragraph (g).

(3) A Reserve Bank's failure to avail itself of the remedy provided in this paragraph (g) does not prejudice its enforcement in any other manner of the indemnity agreement referred to in paragraph (c)(4) of this section.

(h) Reserve Bank's responsibility. A Reserve Bank shall handle a returned check, or a notice of nonpayment, in accordance with Subpart C of Part 229 and its operating circular.

(i) Settlement. A subsequent returning bank or depositary bank shall settle with its Administrative Reserve Bank for returned checks in the same manner and by the same time as for cash items presented for payment under this subpart. Settlement with its Administrative Reserve Bank is deemed to be settlement with the Reserve Bank from which the returning bank or depositary bank received the item.

(j) Security interest. When a paying or returning bank sends a returned check to a Reserve Bank, the paying bank, returning bank, and any prior returning bank grant to the paying bank's or returning bank's Administrative Reserve Bank a security interest in all of their respective assets in the possession of, or held for the account of, any Reserve Bank, to secure their respective obligations due or to become due to the Administrative Reserve Bank under this subpart or subpart C of part 229 of this chapter (Regulation CC). The security interest attaches when a warranty is breached or any other obligation to the Reserve Bank is incurred. If the Reserve Bank, in its sole discretion, deems itself insecure and gives notice thereof to the paying bank, returning bank, or prior returning bank, or if the paying bank, returning bank, or prior returning bank suspends payments or is closed, the Reserve Bank may take any action authorized by law to recover the amount of an obligation, including, but not limited to, the exercise of rights of set off, the realization on any available collateral, and any other rights it may have as a creditor under applicable law.

§ 210.13 Unpaid items.

(a) Right of recovery. If a Reserve Bank does not receive payment in actually and finally collected funds for an item, the Reserve Bank shall recover by charge-back or otherwise the amount of the item from the sender, prior collecting bank, paying bank, or returning bank from or through which it was received, whether or not the item itself can be sent back. In the event of recovery from such a person, no person, including the owner or holder of the item, shall, for the purpose of obtaining payment of the amount of the item, have any interest in any reserve balance or other funds or property in the Reserve Bank's possession of the bank that failed to make payment in actually and finally collected funds.

(b) Suspension or closing of bank. A Reserve Bank shall not pay or act on a draft, authorization to charge (including a charge authorized by § 210.9(b)(5)), or other order on a reserve balance or other funds in its possession for the purpose of settling for items under § 210.9 or § 210.12 after it receives notice of suspension or closing of the bank making the settlement for that bank's own or another's account.

§ 210.14 Extension of time limits.

If a bank (including a Reserve Bank) or nonbank payor is delayed in acting on an item beyond applicable time limits because of interruption of communication or computer facilities, suspension of payments by a bank or nonbank payor, war, emergency conditions, failure of equipment, or other circumstances beyond its control, its time for acting is extended for the time necessary to complete the action, if it exercises such diligence as the circumstances require.

§ 210.15 Direct presentment of certain warrants.

If a Reserve Bank elects to present direct to the payor a bill, note, or warrant that is issued and payable by a State or a political subdivision and that is a cash item not payable or collectible through a bank: (a) Sections 210.9, 210.12, and 210.13 and the operating circulars of the Reserve Banks apply to the payor as if it were a paying bank; (b) § 210.14 applies to the payor as if it were a bank; and (c) under § 210.9 each day on which the payor is open for the regular conduct of its affairs or the accommodation of the public is considered a banking day.

SUBPART B—FUNDS TRANSFERS THROUGH FEDWIRE

§ 210.25 Authority, purpose, and scope.

(a) Authority and purpose. This subpart provides rules to govern funds transfers through the Fedwire Funds Service, and has been issued pursuant to the Federal Reserve Act—section 13 (12 U.S.C. 342), paragraph (f) of section 19 (12 U.S.C. 464), paragraph 14 of section 16 (12 U.S.C. 248(*o*)), and paragraphs (i) and (j) of section 11 (12 U.S.C. 248(i) and (j))—and other laws and has the force and effect of federal law. This Subpart is not a funds-transfer system rule as defined in Section 4A–501(b) of Article 4A.

(b) Scope.

(1) This subpart incorporates the provisions of article 4A set forth in appendix B to this subpart. In the event of an inconsistency between the provisions of the sections of this subpart and appendix B to this subpart, the provisions of the sections of this subpart shall prevail. In the event of an inconsistency between the provisions this subpart and section 919 of the Electronic Fund Transfer Act, section 919 of the Electronic Fund Transfer Act shall prevail.

(2) Except as otherwise provided in paragraphs (b)(3) and (4) of this section, including Article 4A as set forth in appendix B to this subpart, and operating circulars of the Reserve Banks issued in accordance with paragraph (c) of this section, this subpart governs the rights and obligations of:

(i) Federal Reserve Banks sending or receiving payment orders;

(ii) Senders that send payment orders directly to a Federal Reserve Bank;

(iii) Receiving banks that receive payment orders directly from a Federal Reserve Bank;

(iv) Beneficiaries that receive payment for payment orders sent to a Federal Reserve Bank by means of credit to an account maintained or used at a Federal Reserve Bank; and

(v) Other parties to a funds transfer any part of which is carried out through Fedwire to the same extent as if this subpart were considered a funds-transfer system rule under Article 4A.

(3) This subpart governs a funds transfer that is sent through the Fedwire Funds Service', as provided in paragraph (b)(2) of this section, even though a portion of the funds transfer is governed by the Electronic Fund Transfer Act, but the portion of such funds transfer that is governed by the Electronic Fund Transfer Act (other than section 919 governing remittance transfers) is not governed by this subpart.

(4) In the event that any portion of this Subpart establishes rights or obligations with respect to the availability of funds that are also governed by the Expedited Funds Availability Act or the Board's Regulation CC, Availability of Funds and Collection of Checks, those provisions of the Expedited Funds Availability Act or Regulation CC shall apply and the portion of this Subpart, including Article 4A as incorporated herein, shall not apply.

(c) Operating Circulars. Each Federal Reserve Bank shall issue an Operating Circular consistent with this Subpart that governs the details of its funds-transfer operations and other matters it deems appropriate. Among other things, the Operating Circular may: set cut-off hours and funds-transfer business days; address available security procedures; specify format and media requirements for payment orders; identify messages that are not payment orders; and impose charges for funds-transfer services.

(d) Government senders, receiving banks, and beneficiaries. Except as otherwise expressly provided by the statutes of the United States, the parties specified in paragraphs (b)(2)(ii) through (v) of this section include:

(1) A department, agency, instrumentality, independent establishment, or office of the United States, or a wholly-owned or controlled Government corporation;

(2) An international organization;

(3) A foreign central bank; and

(4) A department, agency, instrumentality, independent establishment, or office of a foreign government, or a wholly-owned or controlled corporation of a foreign government.

(e) Financial messaging standards. Financial messaging standards (*e.g.*, ISO 20022), including the financial messaging components, elements, technical documentation, tags, and terminology used to implement those standards, do not confer or connote legal status or responsibilities. This subpart, including Article 4A as set forth in appendix B to this subpart, and the operating circulars of the Reserve Banks issued in accordance with paragraph (c) of this section govern the rights and obligations of parties to funds transfers sent through the Fedwire Funds Service as provided in paragraph (b) of this section. To the extent there is any inconsistency between a financial messaging standard adopted by the Fedwire Funds Service and this subpart, this subpart shall prevail.

§ 210.26 Definitions.

As used in this subpart, the following definitions apply:

(a) Article 4A means article 4A of the Uniform Commercial Code as set forth in appendix B of this subpart.

(b) [Reserved]

(c) Automated clearing house transfer means any transfer designated as an automated clearing house transfer in a Federal Reserve Bank Operating Circular.

(d) Beneficiary's bank has the same meaning as in Article 4A, except that:

(1) A Federal Reserve Bank need not be identified in the payment order in order to be the beneficiary's bank; and

(2) The term includes a Federal Reserve Bank when that Federal Reserve Bank is the beneficiary of a payment order.

(e) Fedwire Funds Service and Fedwire means the funds-transfer system owned and operated by the Federal Reserve Banks that is used primarily for the transmission and settlement of payment orders governed by this subpart. Fedwire does not include the system for making automated clearing house transfers.

(f) Interdistrict transfer means a funds transfer involving entries to accounts maintained at two Federal Reserve Banks.

(g) Intradistrict transfer means a funds transfer involving entries to accounts maintained at one Federal Reserve Bank.

(h) Off-line bank means a bank that transmits payment orders to and receives payment orders from a Federal Reserve Bank by telephone orally or by other means other than electronic data transmission.

(i) Payment order has the same meaning as in Article 4A, except that the term does not include automated clearing house transfers or any communication designated in a Federal Reserve Bank Operating Circular issued under this Subpart as not being a payment order.

(j) Sender's account, receiving bank's account, and beneficiary's account mean the reserve, clearing, or other funds deposit account at a Federal Reserve Bank maintained or used by the sender, receiving bank, or beneficiary, respectively.

(k) Sender's Federal Reserve Bank and receiving bank's Federal Reserve Bank mean the Federal Reserve Bank at which the sender or receiving bank, respectively, maintains or uses an account.

§ 210.27 Reliance on identifying number.

(a) Reliance by a Federal Reserve Bank on number to identify an intermediary bank or beneficiary's bank. A Federal Reserve Bank may rely on the number in a payment order that identifies the intermediary bank or beneficiary's bank, even if it identifies a bank different from the bank identified by name in the payment order, if the Federal Reserve Bank does not know of such an inconsistency in identification. A Federal Reserve Bank has no duty to detect any such inconsistency in identification.

(b) Reliance by a Federal Reserve Bank on number to identify beneficiary. A Federal Reserve Bank, acting as a beneficiary's bank, may rely on the number in a payment order that identifies the beneficiary, even if it identifies a person different from the person identified by name in the payment order, if the Federal Reserve Bank does not know of such an inconsistency in identification. A Federal Reserve Bank has no duty to detect any such inconsistency in identification.

§ 210.28 Agreement of sender.

(a) Payment of sender's obligation to a Federal Reserve Bank. A sender (other than a Federal Reserve Bank), by maintaining or using an account with a Federal Reserve Bank, authorizes the sender's Federal Reserve Bank to obtain payment for the sender's payment orders by debiting the amount of the payment order from the sender's account.

(b) Overdrafts.

(1) A sender does not have the right to an overdraft in the sender's account. In the event an overdraft is created, the overdraft shall be due and payable immediately without the need for a demand by the Federal Reserve Bank, at the earliest of the following times:

(i) At the end of the funds-transfer business day;

(ii) At the time the Federal Reserve Bank, in its sole discretion, deems itself insecure and gives notice thereof to the sender; or

(iii) At the time the sender suspends payments or is closed.

(2) The sender shall have in its account, at the time the overdraft is due and payable, a balance of actually and finally collected funds sufficient to cover the aggregate amount of all its obligations to the Federal Reserve Bank, whether the obligations result from the execution of a payment order or otherwise.

(3) To secure any overdraft, as well as any other obligation due or to become due to its Federal Reserve Bank, each sender, by sending a payment order to a Federal Reserve Bank that is accepted by the Federal Reserve Bank, grants to the Federal Reserve Bank a security interest in all of the sender's assets in the possession of, or held for the account of, the Federal Reserve Bank. The security interest attaches when an overdraft, or any other obligation to the Federal Reserve Bank, becomes due and payable.

(4) A Federal Reserve Bank may take any action authorized by law to recover the amount of an overdraft that is due and payable, including, but not limited to, the exercise of rights of set off, the realization on any available collateral, and any other rights it may have as a creditor under applicable law.

(5) If a sender, other than a government sender described in § 210.25(d), incurs an overdraft in its account as a result of a debit to the account by a Federal Reserve Bank under paragraph (a) of this section, the account will be subject to any applicable overdraft charges, regardless of whether the overdraft has become due and payable. A Federal Reserve Bank may debit a sender's account under paragraph (a) of this section immediately on acceptance of the payment order.

(c) Review of payment orders. A sender, by sending a payment order to a Federal Reserve Bank, agrees that for the purposes of sections 4A–204(a) and 4A–304 of Article 4A, a reasonable time to notify a Federal Reserve Bank of the relevant facts concerning an unauthorized or erroneously executed payment order is within 30 calendar days after the sender receives notice that the payment order was accepted or executed, or that the sender's account was debited with respect to the payment order.

§ 210.29 Agreement of receiving bank.

(a) Payment. A receiving bank (other than a Federal Reserve Bank) that receives a payment order from its Federal Reserve Bank authorizes that Federal Reserve Bank to pay for the payment order by crediting the amount of the payment order to the receiving bank's account.

(b) Off-line banks. An off-line bank that does not expressly notify its Federal Reserve Bank in writing that it maintains an account for another bank warrants to that Federal Reserve Bank that the off-line bank does not act as an intermediary bank or a beneficiary's bank with respect to payment orders received through Fedwire for a beneficiary that is a bank.

§ 210.30 Payment orders.

(a) Rejection. A sender shall not send a payment order to a Federal Reserve Bank unless authorized to do so by the Federal Reserve Bank. A Federal Reserve Bank may reject, or impose conditions that must be satisfied before it will accept, a payment order for any reason.

(b) Selection of an intermediary bank. For an interdistrict transfer, a Federal Reserve Bank is authorized and directed to execute a payment order through another Federal Reserve Bank. A sender shall not send a payment order to a Federal Reserve Bank that requires the Federal Reserve Bank to issue a payment order to an intermediary bank (other than a Federal Reserve Bank) unless that intermediary bank is designated in the sender's payment order. A sender shall not send to a Federal Reserve Bank a payment order instructing use by a Federal Reserve Bank of a funds-transfer system or means of transmission other than the Fedwire Funds Service, unless the Federal Reserve Bank agrees with the sender in writing to follow such instructions.

(c) Same-day execution. A sender shall not issue a payment order that instructs a Federal Reserve Bank to execute the payment order on a funds-transfer business day that is later than the funds-transfer business day on which the order is received by the Federal Reserve Bank, unless the Federal Reserve Bank agrees with the sender in writing to follow such instructions.

§ 210.31 Payment by a Federal Reserve Bank to a receiving bank or beneficiary.

(a) Payment to a receiving bank. Payment of a Federal Reserve Bank's obligation to pay a receiving bank (other than a Federal Reserve Bank) occurs at the earlier of the time when the amount of the payment order is credited to the receiving bank's account or when the payment order is sent to the receiving bank.

(b) Payment to a beneficiary. Payment by a Federal Reserve Bank to a beneficiary of a payment order, where the Federal Reserve Bank is the beneficiary's bank, occurs at the earlier of the time when the amount of the payment order is credited to the beneficiary's account or when notice of the credit is sent to the beneficiary.

§ 210.32 Federal Reserve Bank liability; payment of interest.

(a) Damages. In connection with its handling of a payment order under this subpart, a Federal Reserve Bank shall not be liable to a sender, receiving bank, beneficiary, or other Federal Reserve Bank, governed by this subpart, for any damages other than those payable under Article 4A. A Federal Reserve

Bank shall not agree to be liable to a sender, receiving bank, beneficiary, or other Federal Reserve Bank for consequential damages under section 4A–305(d) of Article 4A.

(b) Payment of interest.

(1) A Federal Reserve Bank shall satisfy its obligation, or that of another Federal Reserve Bank, to pay compensation in the form of interest under article 4A by paying compensation in the form of interest to its sender, its receiving bank, its beneficiary, or another party to the funds transfer that is entitled to such payment, in an amount that is calculated in accordance with section 4A–506 of article 4A.

(2) If the sender or receiving bank that is the recipient of interest payment is not the party entitled to compensation under article 4A, the sender or receiving bank shall pass through the benefit of the interest payment by making an interest payment, as of the day the interest payment is effected, to the party entitled to compensation. The interest payment that is made to the party entitled to compensation shall not be less than the value of the interest payment that was provided by the Federal Reserve Bank to the sender or receiving bank. The party entitled to compensation may agree to accept compensation in a form other than a direct interest payment, provided that such an alternative form of compensation is not less than the value of the interest payment that otherwise would be made.

(c) Nonwaiver of right of recovery. Nothing in this subpart or any Operating Circular issued hereunder shall constitute, or be construed as constituting, a waiver by a Federal Reserve Bank of a cause of action for recovery under any applicable law of mistake and restitution.

ELECTRONIC FUND TRANSFERS (REGULATION E)

12 C.F.R. Part 1005

Current through March 27, 2019; 84 F.R. 11636

For updates and appendices with Model Forms and Official Interpretations, see www.ecfr.gov

Note from West Advisory Board

This regulation is the Consumer Financial Protection Bureau's recodification of the Federal Reserve Board's Regulation E (12 C.F.R. Part 205), as mandated by the Dodd-Frank Wall Street Reform and Consumer Protection Act of 2010. The Federal Reserve Board's regulation still has some applicability, primarily to auto dealers. The text of that regulation can be found at www.ecfr.gov.

SUBPART A—GENERAL

SUBPART B—REQUIREMENTS FOR REMITTANCE TRANSFERS

SUBPART A—GENERAL

§ 1005.1 Authority and purpose.

(a) Authority. The regulation in this part, known as Regulation E, is issued by the Bureau of Consumer Financial Protection (Bureau) pursuant to the Electronic Fund Transfer Act (15 U.S.C. 1693 et seq.). The information-collection requirements have been approved by the Office of Management and Budget under 44 U.S.C. 3501 et seq. and have been assigned OMB No. 3170–0014.

(b) Purpose. This part carries out the purposes of the Electronic Fund Transfer Act, which establishes the basic rights, liabilities, and responsibilities of consumers who use electronic fund transfer services and of financial institutions that offer these services. The primary objective of the Act and this part is the protection of individual consumers engaging in electronic fund transfers.

§ 1005.2 Definitions.

Except as otherwise provided in subpart B, for purposes of this part, the following definitions apply:

(a)(1) "Access device" means a card, code, or other means of access to a consumer's account, or any combination thereof, that may be used by the consumer to initiate electronic fund transfers.

(2) An access device becomes an "accepted access device" when the consumer:

(i) Requests and receives, or signs, or uses (or authorizes another to use) the access device to transfer money between accounts or to obtain money, property, or services;

(ii) Requests validation of an access device issued on an unsolicited basis; or

(iii) Receives an access device in renewal of, or in substitution for, an accepted access device from either the financial institution that initially issued the device or a successor.

(b)(1) "Account" means a demand deposit (checking), savings, or other consumer asset account (other than an occasional or incidental credit balance in a credit plan) held directly or indirectly by a financial institution and established primarily for personal, family, or household purposes.

(2) The term does not include an account held by a financial institution under a bona fide trust agreement.

(3) The term includes a prepaid account.

(i) "Prepaid account" means:

(A) A "payroll card account," which is an account that is directly or indirectly established through an employer and to which electronic fund transfers of the consumer's wages, salary, or other employee compensation (such as commissions) are made on a recurring basis, whether the account is operated or managed by the employer, a third-party payroll processor, a depository institution, or any other person; or

(B) A "government benefit account," as defined in § 1005.15(a)(2); or

(C) An account that is marketed or labeled as "prepaid" and that is redeemable upon presentation at multiple, unaffiliated merchants for goods or services or usable at automated teller machines; or

(D) An account:

(1) That is issued on a prepaid basis in a specified amount or not issued on a prepaid basis but capable of being loaded with funds thereafter,

(2) Whose primary function is to conduct transactions with multiple, unaffiliated merchants for goods or services, or at automated teller machines, or to conduct person-to-person transfers, and

(3) That is not a checking account, share draft account, or negotiable order of withdrawal account.

(ii) For purposes of paragraphs (b)(3)(i)(C) and (D) of this section, the term "prepaid account" does not include:

(A) An account that is loaded only with funds from a health savings account, flexible spending arrangement, medical savings account, health reimbursement arrangement, dependent care assistance program, or transit or parking reimbursement arrangement;

(B) An account that is directly or indirectly established through a third party and loaded only with qualified disaster relief payments;

(C) The person-to-person functionality of an account established by or through the United States government whose primary function is to conduct closed-loop transactions on U.S. military installations or vessels, or similar government facilities;

(D)(1) A gift certificate as defined in § 1005.20(a)(1) and (b);

(2) A store gift card as defined in § 1005.20(a)(2) and (b);

(3) A loyalty, award, or promotional gift card as defined in § 1005.20(a)(4), or that satisfies the criteria in § 1005.20(a)(4)(i) and (ii) and is excluded from § 1005.20 pursuant to § 1005.20(b)(4); or

(4) A general-use prepaid card as defined in § 1005.20(a)(3) and (b) that is both marketed and labeled as a gift card or gift certificate; or

(E) An account established for distributing needs-tested benefits in a program established under state or local law or administered by a state or local agency, as set forth in § 1005.15(a)(2).

(c) "Act" means the Electronic Fund Transfer Act (Title IX of the Consumer Credit Protection Act, 15 U.S.C. 1693 et seq.).

(d) "Business day" means any day on which the offices of the consumer's financial institution are open to the public for carrying on substantially all business functions.

(e) "Consumer" means a natural person.

(f) "Credit" means the right granted by a financial institution to a consumer to defer payment of debt, incur debt and defer its payment, or purchase property or services and defer payment therefor.

(g) "Electronic fund transfer" is defined in 1105.3.

(h) "Electronic terminal" means an electronic device, other than a telephone operated by a consumer, through which a consumer may initiate an electronic fund transfer. The term includes, but is not limited to, point-of-sale terminals, automated teller machines (ATMs), and cash dispensing machines.

(i) "Financial institution" means a bank, savings association, credit union, or any other person that directly or indirectly holds an account belonging to a consumer, or that issues an access device and agrees with a consumer to provide electronic fund transfer services, other than a person excluded from coverage of this part by section 1029 of the Consumer Financial Protection Act of 2010, Title X of the Dodd-Frank Wall Street Reform and Consumer Protection Act, Public Law 111–203, 124 Stat. 1376.

(j) "Person" means a natural person or an organization, including a corporation, government agency, estate, trust, partnership, proprietorship, cooperative, or association.

(k) "Preauthorized electronic fund transfer" means an electronic fund transfer authorized in advance to recur at substantially regular intervals.

(*l*) "State" means any state, territory, or possession of the United States; the District of Columbia; the Commonwealth of Puerto Rico; or any political subdivision of the thereof in this paragraph (*l*).

(m) "Unauthorized electronic fund transfer" means an electronic fund transfer from a consumer's account initiated by a person other than the consumer without actual authority to initiate the transfer and from which the consumer receives no benefit. The term does not include an electronic fund transfer initiated:

(1) By a person who was furnished the access device to the consumer's account by the consumer, unless the consumer has notified the financial institution that transfers by that person are no longer authorized;

(2) With fraudulent intent by the consumer or any person acting in concert with the consumer; or

(3) By the financial institution or its employee.

§ 1005.3 Coverage.

(a) General. This part applies to any electronic fund transfer that authorizes a financial institution to debit or credit a consumer's account. Generally, this part applies to financial institutions. For purposes of §§ 1005.3(b)(2) and (3), 1005.10(b), (d), and (e), 1005.13, and 1005.20 this part applies to any person, other than a person excluded from coverage of this part by section 1029 of the Consumer Financial Protection Act of 2010, Title X of the Dodd-Frank Wall Street Reform and Consumer Protection Act, Public Law 111–203, 124 Stat. 1376. The requirements of subpart B apply to remittance transfer providers.

(b) Electronic fund transfer.

(1) Definition. The term "electronic fund transfer" means any transfer of funds that is initiated through an electronic terminal, telephone, computer, or magnetic tape for the purpose of ordering, instructing, or authorizing a financial institution to debit or credit a consumer's account. The term includes, but is not limited to:

(i) Point-of-sale transfers;

(ii) Automated teller machine transfers;

(iii) Direct deposits or withdrawals of funds;

(iv) Transfers initiated by telephone; and

(v) Transfers resulting from debit card transactions, whether or not initiated through an electronic terminal.

(2) Electronic fund transfer using information from a check.

(i) This part applies where a check, draft, or similar paper instrument is used as a source of information to initiate a one-time electronic fund transfer from a consumer's account. The consumer must authorize the transfer.

(ii) The person initiating an electronic fund transfer using the consumer's check as a source of information for the transfer must provide a notice that the transaction will or may be processed as an electronic fund transfer, and obtain a consumer's authorization for each transfer. A consumer authorizes a one-time electronic fund transfer (in providing a check to a merchant or other payee for the MICR encoding, that is, the routing number of the financial institution, the consumer's account number and the serial number) when the consumer receives notice and goes forward with the underlying transaction. For point-of-sale transfers, the notice must be posted in a prominent and conspicuous location, and a copy thereof, or a substantially similar notice, must be provided to the consumer at the time of the transaction.

(iii) A person may provide notices that are substantially similar to those set forth in Appendix A-6 to comply with the requirements of this paragraph (b)(2).

(3) Collection of returned item fees via electronic fund transfer.

(i) General. The person initiating an electronic fund transfer to collect a fee for the return of an electronic fund transfer or a check that is unpaid, including due to insufficient or uncollected funds in the consumer's account, must obtain the consumer's authorization for each transfer. A consumer authorizes a one-time electronic fund transfer from his or her account to pay the fee for the returned item or transfer if the person collecting the fee provides notice to the consumer stating that the person may electronically collect the fee, and the consumer goes forward with the underlying transaction. The notice must state that the fee will be collected by means of an electronic fund transfer from the consumer's account if the payment is returned unpaid and must disclose the dollar amount of the fee. If the fee may vary due to the amount of the transaction or due to other factors, then, except as otherwise provided in paragraph (b)(3)(ii) of this section, the person collecting the fee may disclose, in place of the dollar amount of the fee, an explanation of how the fee will be determined.

(ii) Point-of-sale transactions. If a fee for an electronic fund transfer or check returned unpaid may be collected electronically in connection with a point-of-sale transaction, the person initiating an electronic fund transfer to collect the fee must post the notice described in paragraph (b)(3)(i) of this section in a prominent and conspicuous location. The person also must either provide the consumer with a copy of the posted notice (or a substantially similar notice) at the time of the transaction, or mail the copy (or a substantially similar notice) to the consumer's address as soon as reasonably practicable after the person initiates the electronic fund transfer to collect the fee. If the amount of the fee may vary due to the amount of the transaction or due to other factors, the posted notice may explain how the fee will be determined, but the notice provided to the consumer must state the dollar amount of the fee if the amount can be calculated at the time the notice is provided or mailed to the consumer.

(c) Exclusions from coverage. The term "electronic fund transfer" does not include:

(1) Checks. Any transfer of funds originated by check, draft, or similar paper instrument; or any payment made by check, draft, or similar paper instrument at an electronic terminal.

(2) Check guarantee or authorization. Any transfer of funds that guarantees payment or authorizes acceptance of a check, draft, or similar paper instrument but that does not directly result in a debit or credit to a consumer's account.

(3) Wire or other similar transfers. Any transfer of funds through Fedwire or through a similar wire transfer system that is used primarily for transfers between financial institutions or between businesses.

(4) Securities and commodities transfers. Any transfer of funds the primary purpose of which is the purchase or sale of a security or commodity, if the security or commodity is:

(i) Regulated by the Securities and Exchange Commission or the Commodity Futures Trading Commission;

(ii) Purchased or sold through a broker-dealer regulated by the Securities and Exchange Commission or through a futures commission merchant regulated by the Commodity Futures Trading Commission; or

(iii) Held in book-entry form by a Federal Reserve Bank or Federal agency.

(5) Automatic transfers by account-holding institution. Any transfer of funds under an agreement between a consumer and a financial institution which provides that the institution will initiate individual transfers without a specific request from the consumer:

(i) Between a consumer's accounts within the financial institution;

(ii) From a consumer's account to an account of a member of the consumer's family held in the same financial institution; or

(iii) Between a consumer's account and an account of the financial institution, except that these transfers remain subject to 1105.10(e) regarding compulsory use and sections 916 and 917 of the Act regarding civil and criminal liability.

(6) Telephone-initiated transfers. Any transfer of funds that:

(i) Is initiated by a telephone communication between a consumer and a financial institution making the transfer; and

(ii) Does not take place under a telephone bill-payment or other written plan in which periodic or recurring transfers are contemplated.

(7) Small institutions. Any preauthorized transfer to or from an account if the assets of the account-holding financial institution were $100 million or less on the preceding December 31. If assets of the account-holding institution subsequently exceed $100 million, the institution's exemption for preauthorized transfers terminates one year from the end of the calendar year in which the assets exceed $100 million. Preauthorized transfers exempt under this paragraph (c)(7) remain subject to 1105.10(e) regarding compulsory use and sections 916 and 917 of the Act regarding civil and criminal liability.

§ 1005.4 General disclosure requirements; jointly offered services.

(a)(1) Form of disclosures. Disclosures required under this part shall be clear and readily understandable, in writing, and in a form the consumer may keep, except as otherwise provided in this part. The disclosures required by this part may be provided to the consumer in electronic form, subject to compliance with the consumer-consent and other applicable provisions of the Electronic Signatures in Global and National Commerce Act (E-Sign Act) (15 U.S.C. 7001 et seq.). A financial institution may use commonly accepted or readily understandable abbreviations in complying with the disclosure requirements of this part.

(2) Foreign language disclosures. Disclosures required under this part may be made in a language other than English, provided that the disclosures are made available in English upon the consumer's request.

(b) Additional information; disclosures required by other laws. A financial institution may include additional information and may combine disclosures required by other laws (such as the Truth in Lending Act 15 U.S.C. 1601 et seq.) or the Truth in Savings Act (12 U.S.C. 4301 et seq.) with the disclosures required by this part.

(c) Multiple accounts and account holders.

(1) Multiple accounts. A financial institution may combine the required disclosures into a single statement for a consumer who holds more than one account at the institution.

(2) Multiple account holders. For joint accounts held by two or more consumers, a financial institution need provide only one set of the required disclosures and may provide them to any of the account holders.

(d) Services offered jointly. Financial institutions that provide electronic fund transfer services jointly may contract among themselves to comply with the requirements that this part imposes on any or all of them. An institution need make only the disclosures required by §§ 1005.7 and 1005.8 that are within its knowledge and within the purview of its relationship with the consumer for whom it holds an account.

§ 1005.5 Issuance of access devices.

(a) Solicited issuance. Except as provided in paragraph (b) of this section, a financial institution may issue an access device to a consumer only:

(1) In response to an oral or written request for the device; or

(2) As a renewal of, or in substitution for, an accepted access device whether issued by the institution or a successor.

(b) Unsolicited issuance. A financial institution may distribute an access device to a consumer on an unsolicited basis if the access device is:

(1) Not validated, meaning that the institution has not yet performed all the procedures that would enable a consumer to initiate an electronic fund transfer using the access device;

(2) Accompanied by a clear explanation that the access device is not validated and how the consumer may dispose of it if validation is not desired;

(3) Accompanied by the disclosures required by § 1005.7, of the consumer's rights and liabilities that will apply if the access device is validated; and

(4) Validated only in response to the consumer's oral or written request for validation, after the institution has verified the consumer's identity by a reasonable means.

§ 1005.6 Liability of consumer for unauthorized transfers.

(a) Conditions for liability. A consumer may be held liable, within the limitations described in paragraph (b) of this section, for an unauthorized electronic fund transfer involving the consumer's account only if the financial institution has provided the disclosures required by § 1005.7(b)(1), (2), and (3). If the unauthorized transfer involved an access device, it must be an accepted access device and the financial institution must have provided a means to identify the consumer to whom it was issued.

(b) Limitations on amount of liability. A consumer's liability for an unauthorized electronic fund transfer or a series of related unauthorized transfers shall be determined as follows:

(1) Timely notice given. If the consumer notifies the financial institution within two business days after learning of the loss or theft of the access device, the consumer's liability shall not exceed the lesser of $50 or the amount of unauthorized transfers that occur before notice to the financial institution.

(2) Timely notice not given. If the consumer fails to notify the financial institution within two business days after learning of the loss or theft of the access device, the consumer's liability shall not exceed the lesser of $500 or the sum of:

(i) $50 or the amount of unauthorized transfers that occur within the two business days, whichever is less; and

(ii) The amount of unauthorized transfers that occur after the close of two business days and before notice to the institution, provided the institution establishes that these transfers would not have occurred had the consumer notified the institution within that two-day period.

(3) Periodic statement; timely notice not given. A consumer must report an unauthorized electronic fund transfer that appears on a periodic statement within 60 days of the financial institution's transmittal of the statement to avoid liability for subsequent transfers. If the consumer fails to do so, the consumer's liability shall not exceed the amount of the unauthorized transfers that occur after the close of the 60 days and before notice to the institution, and that the institution establishes would not have occurred had the consumer notified the institution within the 60-day period. When an access device is involved in the unauthorized transfer, the consumer may be liable for other amounts set forth in paragraphs (b)(1) or (b)(2) of this section, as applicable.

(4) Extension of time limits. If the consumer's delay in notifying the financial institution was due to extenuating circumstances, the institution shall extend the times specified above to a reasonable period.

(5) Notice to financial institution.

(i) Notice to a financial institution is given when a consumer takes steps reasonably necessary to provide the institution with the pertinent information, whether or not a particular employee or agent of the institution actually receives the information.

(ii) The consumer may notify the institution in person, by telephone, or in writing.

(iii) Written notice is considered given at the time the consumer mails the notice or delivers it for transmission to the institution by any other usual means. Notice may be considered constructively given when the institution becomes aware of circumstances leading to the reasonable belief that an unauthorized transfer to or from the consumer's account has been or may be made.

(6) Liability under state law or agreement. If state law or an agreement between the consumer and the financial institution imposes less liability than is provided by this section, the consumer's liability shall not exceed the amount imposed under the state law or agreement.

§ 1005.7 Initial disclosures.

(a) Timing of disclosures. A financial institution shall make the disclosures required by this section at the time a consumer contracts for an electronic fund transfer service or before the first electronic fund transfer is made involving the consumer's account.

(b) Content of disclosures. A financial institution shall provide the following disclosures, as applicable:

(1) Liability of consumer. A summary of the consumer's liability, under 1005.6 or under state or other applicable law or agreement, for unauthorized electronic fund transfers.

(2) Telephone number and address. The telephone number and address of the person or office to be notified when the consumer believes that an unauthorized electronic fund transfer has been or may be made.

(3) Business days. The financial institution's business days.

(4) Types of transfers; limitations. The type of electronic fund transfers that the consumer may make and any limitations on the frequency and dollar amount of transfers. Details of the limitations need not be disclosed if confidentiality is essential to maintain the security of the electronic fund transfer system.

(5) Fees. Any fees imposed by the financial institution for electronic fund transfers or for the right to make transfers.

(6) Documentation. A summary of the consumer's right to receipts and periodic statements, as provided in §1005.9 of this part, and notices regarding preauthorized transfers as provided in § 1005.10(a) and (d).

(7) Stop payment. A summary of the consumer's right to stop payment of a preauthorized electronic fund transfer and the procedure for placing a stop-payment order, as provided in § 1005.10(c).

(8) Liability of institution. A summary of the financial institution's liability to the consumer under section 910 of the Act for failure to make or to stop certain transfers.

(9) Confidentiality. The circumstances under which, in the ordinary course of business, the financial institution may provide information concerning the consumer's account to third parties.

(10) Error resolution. A notice that is substantially similar to Model Form A-3 as set out in Appendix A of this part concerning error resolution.

(11) ATM fees. A notice that a fee may be imposed by an automated teller machine operator as defined in § 1005.16(a), when the consumer initiates an electronic fund transfer or makes a balance inquiry, and by any network used to complete the transaction.

(c) Addition of electronic fund transfer services. If an electronic fund transfer service is added to a consumer's account and is subject to terms and conditions different from those described in the initial disclosures, disclosures for the new service are required.

§ 1005.8 Change in terms notice; error resolution notice.

(a) Change in terms notice.

(1) Prior notice required. A financial institution shall mail or deliver a written notice to the consumer, at least 21 days before the effective date, of any change in a term or condition required to be disclosed under § 1005.7(b) of this part if the change would result in:

(i) Increased fees for the consumer;

(ii) Increased liability for the consumer;

(iii) Fewer types of available electronic fund transfers; or

(iv) Stricter limitations on the frequency or dollar amount of transfers.

(2) Prior notice exception. A financial institution need not give prior notice if an immediate change in terms or conditions is necessary to maintain or restore the security of an account or an electronic fund transfer system. If the institution makes such a change permanent and disclosure would not jeopardize the security of the account or system, the institution shall notify the consumer in writing on or with the next regularly scheduled periodic statement or within 30 days of making the change permanent.

(b) Error resolution notice. For accounts to or from which electronic fund transfers can be made, a financial institution shall mail or deliver to the consumer, at least once each calendar year, an error resolution notice substantially similar to the model form set forth in Appendix A of this part (Model Form A-3). Alternatively, an institution may include an abbreviated notice substantially similar to the model form error resolution notice set forth in Appendix A of this part (Model Form A-3), on or with each periodic statement required by § 1005.9(b).

§ 1005.9 Receipts at electronic terminals; periodic statements.

(a) Receipts at electronic terminals—General. Except as provided in paragraph (e) of this section, a financial institution shall make a receipt available to a consumer at the time the consumer initiates an electronic fund transfer at an electronic terminal. The receipt shall set forth the following information, as applicable:

(1) Amount. The amount of the transfer. A transaction fee may be included in this amount, provided the amount of the fee is disclosed on the receipt and displayed on or at the terminal.

(2) Date. The date the consumer initiates the transfer.

(3) Type. The type of transfer and the type of the consumer's account(s) to or from which funds are transferred. The type of account may be omitted if the access device used is able to access only one account at that terminal.

(4) Identification. A number or code that identifies the consumer's account or accounts, or the access device used to initiate the transfer. The number or code need not exceed four digits or letters to comply with the requirements of this paragraph (a)(4).

(5) Terminal location. The location of the terminal where the transfer is initiated, or an identification such as a code or terminal number. Except in limited circumstances where all terminals are located in the same city or state, if the location is disclosed, it shall include the city and state or foreign country and one of the following:

(i) The street address; or

(ii) A generally accepted name for the specific location; or

(iii) The name of the owner or operator of the terminal if other than the account-holding institution.

(6) Third party transfer. The name of any third party to or from whom funds are transferred.

(b) Periodic statements. For an account to or from which electronic fund transfers can be made, a financial institution shall send a periodic statement for each monthly cycle in which an electronic fund transfer has occurred; and shall send a periodic statement at least quarterly if no transfer has occurred. The statement shall set forth the following information, as applicable:

(1) Transaction information. For each electronic fund transfer occurring during the cycle:

(i) The amount of the transfer;

(ii) The date the transfer was credited or debited to the consumer's account;

(iii) The type of transfer and type of account to or from which funds were transferred;

(iv) For a transfer initiated by the consumer at an electronic terminal (except for a deposit of cash or a check, draft, or similar paper instrument), the terminal location described in paragraph (a)(5) of this section; and

(v) The name of any third party to or from whom funds were transferred.

(2) Account number. The number of the account.

(3) Fees. The amount of any fees assessed against the account during the statement period for electronic fund transfers, the right to make transfers, or account maintenance.

(4) Account balances. The balance in the account at the beginning and at the close of the statement period.

(5) Address and telephone number for inquiries. The address and telephone number to be used for inquiries or notice of errors, preceded by "Direct inquiries to" or similar language. The address and telephone number provided on an error resolution notice under § 1005.8(b) given on or with the statement satisfies this requirement.

(6) Telephone number for preauthorized transfers. A telephone number the consumer may call to ascertain whether preauthorized transfers to the consumer's account have occurred, if the financial institution uses the telephone-notice option under § 1005.10(a)(1)(iii).

(c) Exceptions to the periodic statement requirement for certain accounts.

(1) Preauthorized transfers to accounts. For accounts that may be accessed only by preauthorized transfers to the account the following rules apply:

(i) Passbook accounts. For passbook accounts, the financial institution need not provide a periodic statement if the institution updates the passbook upon presentation or enters on a separate document the amount and date of each electronic fund transfer since the passbook was last presented.

(ii) Other accounts. For accounts other than passbook accounts, the financial institution must send a periodic statement at least quarterly.

(2) Intra-institutional transfers. For an electronic fund transfer initiated by the consumer between two accounts of the consumer in the same institution, documenting the transfer on a periodic statement for one of the two accounts satisfies the periodic statement requirement.

(3) Relationship between paragraphs (c)(1) and (2) of this section. An account that is accessed by preauthorized transfers to the account described in paragraph (c)(1) of this section and by intra-institutional transfers described in paragraph (c)(2) of this section, but by no other type of electronic fund transfers, qualifies for the exceptions provided by paragraph (c)(1) of this section.

(d) Documentation for foreign-initiated transfers. The failure by a financial institution to provide a terminal receipt for an electronic fund transfer or to document the transfer on a periodic statement does not violate this part if:

(1) The transfer is not initiated within a state; and

(2) The financial institution treats an inquiry for clarification or documentation as a notice of error in accordance with § 1005.11.

(e) Exception for receipts in small-value transfers. A financial institution is not subject to the requirement to make available a receipt under paragraph (a) of this section if the amount of the transfer is $15 or less.

§ 1005.10 Preauthorized transfers.

(a) Preauthorized transfers to consumer's account.

(1) Notice by financial institution. When a person initiates preauthorized electronic fund transfers to a consumer's account at least once every 60 days, the account-holding financial institution shall provide notice to the consumer by:

(i) Positive notice. Providing oral or written notice of the transfer within two business days after the transfer occurs; or

(ii) Negative notice. Providing oral or written notice, within two business days after the date on which the transfer was scheduled to occur, that the transfer did not occur; or

(iii) Readily-available telephone line. Providing a readily available telephone line that the consumer may call to determine whether the transfer occurred and disclosing the telephone number on the initial disclosure of account terms and on each periodic statement.

(2) Notice by payor. A financial institution need not provide notice of a transfer if the payor gives the consumer positive notice that the transfer has been initiated.

(3) Crediting. A financial institution that receives a preauthorized transfer of the type described in paragraph (a)(1) of this section shall credit the amount of the transfer as of the date the funds for the transfer are received.

(b) Written authorization for preauthorized transfers from consumer's account. Preauthorized electronic fund transfers from a consumer's account may be authorized only by a writing signed or similarly authenticated by the consumer. The person that obtains the authorization shall provide a copy to the consumer.

(c) Consumer's right to stop payment.

(1) Notice. A consumer may stop payment of a preauthorized electronic fund transfer from the consumer's account by notifying the financial institution orally or in writing at least three business days before the scheduled date of the transfer.

(2) Written confirmation. The financial institution may require the consumer to give written confirmation of a stop-payment order within 14 days of an oral notification. An institution that requires written confirmation shall inform the consumer of the requirement and provide the address where confirmation must be sent when the consumer gives the oral notification. An oral stop-payment order ceases to be binding after 14 days if the consumer fails to provide the required written confirmation.

(d) Notice of transfers varying in amount.

(1) Notice. When a preauthorized electronic fund transfer from the consumer's account will vary in amount from the previous transfer under the same authorization or from the preauthorized amount, the designated payee or the financial institution shall send the consumer written notice of the amount and date of the transfer at least 10 days before the scheduled date of transfer.

(2) Range. The designated payee or the institution shall inform the consumer of the right to receive notice of all varying transfers, but may give the consumer the option of receiving notice only when a transfer falls outside a specified range of amounts or only when a transfer differs from the most recent transfer by more than an agreed-upon amount.

(e) Compulsory use.

(1) Credit. No financial institution or other person may condition an extension of credit to a consumer on the consumer's repayment by preauthorized electronic fund transfers, except for credit extended under an overdraft credit plan or extended to maintain a specified minimum balance in the consumer's account. This exception does not apply to a covered separate credit feature accessible by a hybrid prepaid-credit card as defined in Regulation Z, 12 CFR 1026.61.

(2) Employment or government benefit. No financial institution or other person may require a consumer to establish an account for receipt of electronic fund transfers with a particular institution as a condition of employment or receipt of a government benefit.

§ 1005.11 Procedures for resolving errors.

(a) Definition of error.

(1) Types of transfers or inquiries covered. The term "error" means:

(i) An unauthorized electronic fund transfer;

(ii) An incorrect electronic fund transfer to or from the consumer's account;

(iii) The omission of an electronic fund transfer from a periodic statement;

(iv) A computational or bookkeeping error made by the financial institution relating to an electronic fund transfer;

(v) The consumer's receipt of an incorrect amount of money from an electronic terminal;

(vi) An electronic fund transfer not identified in accordance with § 1005.9 or § 1005.10(a); or

(vii) The consumer's request for documentation required by § 1005.9 or § 1005.10(a) or for additional information or clarification concerning an electronic fund transfer, including a request the consumer makes to determine whether an error exists under paragraphs (a)(1)(i) through (vi) of this section.

(2) Types of inquiries not covered. The term "error" does not include:

(i) A routine inquiry about the consumer's account balance;

(ii) A request for information for tax or other recordkeeping purposes; or

(iii) A request for duplicate copies of documentation.

(b) Notice of error from consumer.

(1) Timing; contents. A financial institution shall comply with the requirements of this section with respect to any oral or written notice of error from the consumer that:

(i) Is received by the institution no later than 60 days after the institution sends the periodic statement or provides the passbook documentation, required by § 1005.9, on which the alleged error is first reflected;

(ii) Enables the institution to identify the consumer's name and account number; and

(iii) Indicates why the consumer believes an error exists and includes to the extent possible the type, date, and amount of the error, except for requests described in paragraph (a)(1)(vii) of this section.

(2) Written confirmation. A financial institution may require the consumer to give written confirmation of an error within 10 business days of an oral notice. An institution that requires written confirmation shall inform the consumer of the requirement and provide the address where confirmation must be sent when the consumer gives the oral notification.

(3) Request for documentation or clarifications. When a notice of error is based on documentation or clarification that the consumer requested under paragraph (a)(1)(vii) of this section, the consumer's notice of error is timely if received by the financial institution no later than 60 days after the institution sends the information requested.

(c) Time limits and extent of investigation.

(1) Ten-day period. A financial institution shall investigate promptly and, except as otherwise provided in this paragraph (c), shall determine whether an error occurred within 10 business days of receiving a notice of error. The institution shall report the results to the consumer within three business days after completing its investigation. The institution shall correct the error within one business day after determining that an error occurred.

(2) Forty-five day period. If the financial institution is unable to complete its investigation within 10 business days, the institution may take up to 45 days from receipt of a notice of error to investigate and determine whether an error occurred, provided the institution does the following:

(i) Provisionally credits the consumer's account in the amount of the alleged error (including interest where applicable) within 10 business days of receiving the error notice. If the financial institution has a reasonable basis for believing that an unauthorized electronic fund transfer has occurred and the institution has satisfied the requirements of § 1005.6(a), the institution may withhold a maximum of $50 from the amount credited. An institution need not provisionally credit the consumer's account if:

(A) The institution requires but does not receive written confirmation within 10 business days of an oral notice of error; or

(B) The alleged error involves an account that is subject to Regulation T of the Board of Governors of the Federal Reserve System (Securities Credit by Brokers and Dealers, 12 CFR part 220).

(ii) Informs the consumer, within two business days after the provisional crediting, of the amount and date of the provisional crediting and gives the consumer full use of the funds during the investigation;

(iii) Corrects the error, if any, within one business day after determining that an error occurred; and

(iv) Reports the results to the consumer within three business days after completing its investigation (including, if applicable, notice that a provisional credit has been made final).

(3) Extension of time periods. The time periods in paragraphs (c)(1) and (c)(2) of this section are extended as follows:

(i) The applicable time is 20 business days in place of 10 business days under paragraphs (c)(1) and (2) of this section if the notice of error involves an electronic fund transfer to or from the account within 30 days after the first deposit to the account was made.

(ii) The applicable time is 90 days in place of 45 days under paragraph (c)(2) of this section, for completing an investigation, if a notice of error involves an electronic fund transfer that:

(A) Was not initiated within a state;

(B) Resulted from a point-of-sale debit card transaction; or

(C) Occurred within 30 days after the first deposit to the account was made.

(4) Investigation. With the exception of transfers covered by § 1005.14 of this part, a financial institution's review of its own records regarding an alleged error satisfies the requirements of this section if:

(i) The alleged error concerns a transfer to or from a third party; and

(ii) There is no agreement between the institution and the third party for the type of electronic fund transfer involved.

(d) Procedures if financial institution determines no error or different error occurred. In addition to following the procedures specified in paragraph (c) of this section, the financial institution shall follow the procedures set forth in this paragraph (d) if it determines that no error occurred or that an error occurred in a manner or amount different from that described by the consumer:

(1) Written explanation. The institution's report of the results of its investigation shall include a written explanation of the institution's findings and shall note the consumer's right to request the documents that the institution relied on in making its determination. Upon request, the institution shall promptly provide copies of the documents.

(2) Debiting provisional credit. Upon debiting a provisionally credited amount, the financial institution shall:

(i) Notify the consumer of the date and amount of the debiting;

(ii) Notify the consumer that the institution will honor checks, drafts, or similar instruments payable to third parties and preauthorized transfers from the consumer's account (without charge to the consumer as a result of an overdraft) for five business days after the notification. The institution shall honor items as specified in the notice, but need honor only items that it would have paid if the provisionally credited funds had not been debited.

(e) Reassertion of error. A financial institution that has fully complied with the error resolution requirements has no further responsibilities under this section should the consumer later reassert the same error, except in the case of an error asserted by the consumer following receipt of information provided under paragraph (a)(1)(vii) of this section.

§ 1005.12 Relation to other laws.

(a) Relation to Truth in Lending.

(1) The Electronic Fund Transfer Act and this part govern:

(i) The addition to an accepted credit card, as defined in Regulation Z (12 CFR 1026.12, comment 12–2), of the capability to initiate electronic fund transfers;

(ii) The issuance of an access device (other than an access device for a prepaid account) that permits credit extensions (under a preexisting agreement between a consumer and a financial institution) only when the consumer's account is overdrawn or to maintain a specified minimum balance in the consumer's account, or under an overdraft service, as defined in § 1005.17(a) of this part;

(iii) The addition of an overdraft service, as defined in § 1005.17(a), to an accepted access device; and

(iv) A consumer's liability for an unauthorized electronic fund transfer and the investigation of errors involving:

(A) Except with respect to a prepaid account, an extension of credit that is incident to an electronic fund transfer that occurs under an agreement between the consumer and a financial institution to extend credit when the consumer's account is overdrawn or to maintain a specified minimum balance in the consumer's account, or under an overdraft service, as defined in § 1005.17(a);

(B) With respect to transactions that involve a covered separate credit feature and an asset feature on a prepaid account that are both accessible by a hybrid prepaid-credit card as those terms are defined in Regulation Z, 12 CFR 1026.61, an extension of credit that is incident to an electronic fund transfer that occurs when the hybrid prepaid-credit card accesses both funds in the asset feature of the prepaid account and a credit extension from the credit feature with respect to a particular transaction;

(C) Transactions that involves credit extended through a negative balance to the asset feature of a prepaid account that meets the conditions set forth in Regulation Z, 12 CFR 1026.61(a)(4); and

(D) With respect to transactions involving a prepaid account and a non-covered separate credit feature as defined in Regulation Z, 12 CFR 1026.61, transactions that access the prepaid account, as applicable.

(2) The Truth in Lending Act and Regulation Z (12 CFR part 1026), which prohibit the unsolicited issuance of credit cards, govern:

(i) The addition of a credit feature or plan to an accepted access device, including an access device for a prepaid account, that would make the access device into a credit card under Regulation Z (12 CFR part 1026);

(ii) Except as provided in paragraph (a)(1)(ii) of this section, the issuance of a credit card that is also an access device; and

(iii) With respect to transactions involving a prepaid account and a non-covered separate credit feature as defined in Regulation Z, 12 CFR 1026.61, a consumer's liability for unauthorized use and the investigation of errors involving transactions that access the non-covered separate credit feature, as applicable.

(b) Preemption of inconsistent state laws.

(1) Inconsistent requirements. The Bureau shall determine, upon its own motion or upon the request of a state, financial institution, or other interested party, whether the Act and this part preempt state law relating to electronic fund transfers, or dormancy, inactivity, or service fees, or expiration dates in the case of gift certificates, store gift cards, or general-use prepaid cards.

(2) Standards for determination. State law is inconsistent with the requirements of the Act and this part if state law:

(i) Requires or permits a practice or act prohibited by the Federal law;

(ii) Provides for consumer liability for unauthorized electronic fund transfers that exceeds the limits imposed by the Federal law;

(iii) Allows longer time periods than the Federal law for investigating and correcting alleged errors, or does not require the financial institution to credit the consumer's account during an error investigation in accordance with § 1005.11(c)(2)(i) of this part; or

(iv) Requires initial disclosures, periodic statements, or receipts that are different in content from those required by the Federal law except to the extent that the disclosures relate to consumer rights granted by the state law and not by the Federal law.

(c) State exemptions

(1) General rule. Any state may apply for an exemption from the requirements of the Act or this part for any class of electronic fund transfers within the state. The Bureau shall grant an exemption if it determines that:

(i) Under state law the class of electronic fund transfers is subject to requirements substantially similar to those imposed by the Federal law; and

(ii) There is adequate provision for state enforcement.

(2) Exception. To assure that the Federal and state courts continue to have concurrent jurisdiction, and to aid in implementing the Act:

(i) No exemption shall extend to the civil liability provisions of section 916 of the Act; and

(ii) When the Bureau grants an exemption, the state law requirements shall constitute the requirements of the Federal law for purposes of section 916 of the Act, except for state law requirements not imposed by the Federal law.

§ 1005.13 Administrative enforcement; record retention.

(a) Enforcement by Federal agencies. Compliance with this part is enforced in accordance with section 918 of the Act.

(b) Record retention.

(1) Any person subject to the Act and this part shall retain evidence of compliance with the requirements imposed by the Act and this part for a period of not less than two years from the date disclosures are required to be made or action is required to be taken.

(2) Any person subject to the Act and this part having actual notice that it is the subject of an investigation or an enforcement proceeding by its enforcement agency, or having been served with notice of an action filed under sections 910, 916, or 917(a) of the Act, shall retain the records that pertain to the investigation, action, or proceeding until final disposition of the matter unless an earlier time is allowed by court or agency order.

§ 1005.14 Electronic fund transfer service provider not holding consumer's account.

(a) Provider of electronic fund transfer service. A person that provides an electronic fund transfer service to a consumer but that does not hold the consumer's account is subject to all requirements of this part if the person:

(1) Issues a debit card (or other access device) that the consumer can use to access the consumer's account held by a financial institution; and

(2) Has no agreement with the account-holding institution regarding such access.

(b) Compliance by service provider. In addition to the requirements generally applicable under this part, the service provider shall comply with the following special rules:

(1) Disclosures and documentation. The service provider shall give the disclosures and documentation required by §§ 1105.7, 1105.8, and 1105.9 of this part that are within the purview of its relationship with the consumer. The service provider need not furnish the periodic statement required by § 1105.9(b) if the following conditions are met:

(i) The debit card (or other access device) issued to the consumer bears the service provider's name and an address or telephone number for making inquiries or giving notice of error;

(ii) The consumer receives a notice concerning use of the debit card that is substantially similar to the notice contained in Appendix A of this part;

(iii) The consumer receives, on or with the receipts required by § 1105.9(a), the address and telephone number to be used for an inquiry, to give notice of an error, or to report the loss or theft of the debit card;

(iv) The service provider transmits to the account-holding institution the information specified in § 1005.9(b)(1), in the format prescribed by the automated clearinghouse (ACH) system used to clear the fund transfers;

(v) The service provider extends the time period for notice of loss or theft of a debit card, set forth in § 1005.6(b)(1) and (2), from two business days to four business days after the consumer learns of the loss or theft; and extends the time periods for reporting unauthorized transfers or errors, set forth in §§ 1005.6(b)(3) and 1005.11(b)(1)(i), from 60 days to 90 days following the transmittal of a periodic statement by the account-holding institution.

(2) Error resolution.

(i) The service provider shall extend by a reasonable time the period in which notice of an error must be received, specified in § 1005.11(b)(1)(i), if a delay resulted from an initial attempt by the consumer to notify the account-holding institution.

(ii) The service provider shall disclose to the consumer the date on which it initiates a transfer to effect a provisional credit in accordance with § 1005.11(c)(2)(ii).

(iii) If the service provider determines an error occurred, it shall transfer funds to or from the consumer's account, in the appropriate amount and within the applicable time period, in accordance with § 1005.11(c)(2)(i).

(iv) If funds were provisionally credited and the service provider determines no error occurred, it may reverse the credit. The service provider shall notify the account-holding institution of the period during which the account-holding institution must honor debits to the account in accordance with § 1005.11(d)(2)(ii). If an overdraft results, the service provider shall promptly reimburse the account-holding institution in the amount of the overdraft.

(c) Compliance by account-holding institution. The account-holding institution need not comply with the requirements of the Act and this part with respect to electronic fund transfers initiated through the service provider except as follows:

(1) Documentation. The account-holding institution shall provide a periodic statement that describes each electronic fund transfer initiated by the consumer with the access device issued by the service provider. The account-holding institution has no liability for the failure to comply with this requirement if the service provider did not provide the necessary information; and

(2) Error resolution. Upon request, the account-holding institution shall provide information or copies of documents needed by the service provider to investigate errors or to furnish copies of documents to the consumer. The account-holding institution shall also honor debits to the account in accordance with § 1005.11(d)(2)(ii).

§ 1005.15 Electronic fund transfer of government benefits.

(a) Government agency subject to regulation.

(1) A government agency is deemed to be a financial institution for purposes of the Act and this part if directly or indirectly it issues an access device to a consumer for use in initiating an electronic fund transfer of government benefits from an account, other than needs-tested benefits in a program established under state or local law or administered by a state or local agency. The agency shall comply with all applicable requirements of the Act and this part except as modified by this section.

(2) For purposes of this section, the term "account" or "government benefit account" means an account established by a government agency for distributing government benefits to a consumer electronically, such as through automated teller machines or point-of-sale terminals, but does not include an account for distributing needs-tested benefits in a program established under state or local law or administered by a state or local agency.

(b) Issuance of access devices. For purposes of this section, a consumer is deemed to request an access device when the consumer applies for government benefits that the agency disburses or will disburse by means of an electronic fund transfer. The agency shall verify the identity of the consumer receiving the device by reasonable means before the device is activated.

(c) Pre-acquisition disclosure requirements.

(1) Before a consumer acquires a government benefit account, a government agency shall comply with the pre-acquisition disclosure requirements applicable to prepaid accounts as set forth in § 1005.18(b).

(2) Additional content for government benefit accounts.

(i) Statement regarding consumer's payment options. As part of its short form pre-acquisition disclosures, the agency must provide a statement that the consumer does not have to accept the government benefit account and directing the consumer to ask about other ways to receive their benefit payments from the agency instead of receiving them via the account, using the following clause or a substantially similar clause: "You do not have to accept this benefits card. Ask about other ways to receive your benefits." Alternatively, an agency may provide a statement that the consumer has several options to receive benefit payments, followed by a list of the options available to the consumer, and directing the consumer to indicate which option the consumer chooses using the following clause or a substantially similar clause: "You have several options to receive your payments: [list of options available to the consumer]; or this benefits card. Tell the benefits office which option you choose." This statement must be located above the information required by § 1005.18(b)(2)(i) through (iv). This statement must appear in a minimum type size of eight points (or 11 pixels) and appear in no larger a type size than what is used for the fee headings required by § 1005.18(b)(2)(i) through (iv).

(ii) Statement regarding state-required information or other fee discounts and waivers. An agency may, but is not required to, include a statement in one additional line of text in the short form disclosure directing the consumer to a particular location outside the short form disclosure for information on ways the consumer may access government benefit account funds and balance information for free or for a reduced fee. This statement must be located directly below any statements disclosed pursuant to § 1005.18(b)(3)(i) and (ii), or, if no such statements are disclosed, above the statement required by § 1005.18(b)(2)(x). This statement must appear in the same type size used to disclose variable fee information pursuant to § 1005.18(b)(3)(i) and (ii), or, if none, the same type size used for the information required by § 1005.18(b)(2)(x) through (xiii).

(3) Form of disclosures. When a short form disclosure required by paragraph (c) of this section is provided in writing or electronically, the information required by § 1005.18(b)(2)(i) through (ix) shall be provided in the form of a table. Except as provided in § 1005.18(b)(6)(iii)(B), the short form disclosure required by § 1005.18(b)(2) shall be provided in a form substantially similar to Model Form A-10(a) of appendix A of this part. Sample Form A-10(f) in appendix A of this part provides an example of the long form disclosure required by § 1005.18(b)(4) when the agency does not offer multiple service plans.

(d) Access to account information.

(1) Periodic statement alternative. A government agency need not furnish periodic statements required by § 1005.9(b) if the agency makes available to the consumer:

(i) The consumer's account balance, through a readily available telephone line and at a terminal (such as by providing balance information at a balance-inquiry terminal or providing it, routinely or upon request, on a terminal receipt at the time of an electronic fund transfer);

(ii) An electronic history of the consumer's account transactions, such as through a Web site, that covers at least 12 months preceding the date the consumer electronically accesses the account; and

(iii) A written history of the consumer's account transactions that is provided promptly in response to an oral or written request and that covers at least 24 months preceding the date the agency receives the consumer's request.

(2) Additional access to account information requirements. For government benefit accounts, a government agency shall comply with the account information requirements applicable to prepaid accounts as set forth in § 1005.18(c)(3) through (5).

(e) Modified disclosure, limitations on liability, and error resolution requirements. A government agency that provides information under paragraph (d)(1) of this section shall comply with the following:

(1) Initial disclosures. The agency shall modify the disclosures under § 1005.7(b) by disclosing:

(i) Access to account information. A telephone number that the consumer may call to obtain the account balance, the means by which the consumer can obtain an electronic account history, such as the address of a Web site, and a summary of the consumer's right to receive a written account history upon request (in place of the summary of the right to receive a periodic statement required by § 1005.7(b)(6)), including a telephone number to call to request a history. The disclosure required by this paragraph (e)(1)(i) may be made by providing a notice substantially similar to the notice contained in paragraph (a) of appendix A-5 of this part.

(ii) Error resolution. A notice concerning error resolution that is substantially similar to the notice contained in paragraph (b) of appendix A-5 of this part, in place of the notice required by § 1005.7(b)(10).

(2) Annual error resolution notice. The agency shall provide an annual notice concerning error resolution that is substantially similar to the notice contained in paragraph (b) of appendix A-5 of this part, in place of the notice required by § 1005.8(b). Alternatively, the agency may include on or with each electronic or written history provided in accordance with paragraph (d)(1) of this section, a notice substantially similar to the abbreviated notice for periodic statements contained in paragraph (b) in appendix A-3 of this part, modified as necessary to reflect the error resolution provisions set forth in this section.

(3) Modified limitations on liability requirements.

(i) For purposes of § 1005.6(b)(3), the 60-day period for reporting any unauthorized transfer shall begin on the earlier of:

(A) The date the consumer electronically accesses the consumer's account under paragraph (d)(1)(ii) of this section, provided that the electronic history made available to the consumer reflects the unauthorized transfer; or

(B) The date the agency sends a written history of the consumer's account transactions requested by the consumer under paragraph (d)(1)(iii) of this section in which the unauthorized transfer is first reflected.

(ii) An agency may comply with paragraph (e)(3)(i) of this section by limiting the consumer's liability for an unauthorized transfer as provided under § 1005.6(b)(3) for any transfer reported by the consumer within 120 days after the transfer was credited or debited to the consumer's account.

(4) Modified error resolution requirements.

(i) The agency shall comply with the requirements of § 1005.11 in response to an oral or written notice of an error from the consumer that is received by the earlier of:

(A) Sixty days after the date the consumer electronically accesses the consumer's account under paragraph (d)(1)(ii) of this section, provided that the electronic history made available to the consumer reflects the alleged error; or

(B) Sixty days after the date the agency sends a written history of the consumer's account transactions requested by the consumer under paragraph (d)(1)(iii) of this section in which the alleged error is first reflected.

(ii) In lieu of following the procedures in paragraph (e)(4)(i) of this section, an agency complies with the requirements for resolving errors in § 1005.11 if it investigates any oral or written notice of an error from the consumer that is received by the agency within 120 days after the transfer allegedly in error was credited or debited to the consumer's account.

(f) Disclosure of fees and other information. For government benefit accounts, a government agency shall comply with the disclosure and change-in-terms requirements applicable to prepaid accounts as set forth in § 1005.18(f).

(g) Government benefit accounts accessible by hybrid prepaid-credit cards. For government benefit accounts accessible by hybrid prepaid-credit cards as defined in Regulation Z, 12 CFR 1026.61, a government agency shall comply with prohibitions and requirements applicable to prepaid accounts as set forth in § 1005.18(g).

§ 1005.16 Disclosures at automated teller machines.

(a) Definition. "Automated teller machine operator" means any person that operates an automated teller machine at which a consumer initiates an electronic fund transfer or a balance inquiry and that does not hold the account to or from which the transfer is made, or about which an inquiry is made.

(b) General. An automated teller machine operator that imposes a fee on a consumer for initiating an electronic fund transfer or a balance inquiry must provide a notice that a fee will be imposed for providing electronic fund transfer services or a balance inquiry that discloses the amount of the fee.

(c) Notice requirement. An automated teller machine operator must provide the notice required by paragraph (b) of this section either by showing it on the screen of the automated teller machine or by providing it on paper, before the consumer is committed to paying a fee.

(d) Imposition of fee. An automated teller machine operator may impose a fee on a consumer for initiating an electronic fund transfer or a balance inquiry only if:

(1) The consumer is provided the notice required under paragraph (c) of this section, and

(2) The consumer elects to continue the transaction or inquiry after receiving such notice.

§ 1005.17 Requirements for overdraft services.

(a) Definition. For purposes of this section, the term "overdraft service" means a service under which a financial institution assesses a fee or charge on a consumer's account held by the institution for paying a transaction (including a check or other item) when the consumer has insufficient or unavailable funds in the account. The term "overdraft service" does not include any payment of overdrafts pursuant to:

(1) A line of credit subject to Regulation Z (12 CFR part 1026), including transfers from a credit card account, home equity line of credit, or overdraft line of credit;

(2) A service that transfers funds from another account held individually or jointly by a consumer, such as a savings account;

(3) A line of credit or other transaction exempt from Regulation Z (12 CFR part 1026) pursuant to 12 CFR 1026.3(d); or

(4) A covered separate credit feature accessible by a hybrid prepaid-credit card as defined in Regulation Z, 12 CFR 1026.61; or credit extended through a negative balance on the asset feature of the prepaid account that meets the conditions of 12 CFR 1026.61(a)(4).

(b) Opt-in requirement.

(1) General. Except as provided under paragraph (c) of this section, a financial institution holding a consumer's account shall not assess a fee or charge on a consumer's account for paying an ATM or one-time debit card transaction pursuant to the institution's overdraft service, unless the institution:

(i) Provides the consumer with a notice in writing, or if the consumer agrees, electronically, segregated from all other information, describing the institution's overdraft service;

(ii) Provides a reasonable opportunity for the consumer to affirmatively consent, or opt in, to the service for ATM and one-time debit card transactions;

(iii) Obtains the consumer's affirmative consent, or opt-in, to the institution's payment of ATM or one-time debit card transactions; and

(iv) Provides the consumer with confirmation of the consumer's consent in writing, or if the consumer agrees, electronically, which includes a statement informing the consumer of the right to revoke such consent.

(2) Conditioning payment of other overdrafts on consumer's affirmative consent. A financial institution shall not:

(i) Condition the payment of any overdrafts for checks, ACH transactions, and other types of transactions on the consumer affirmatively consenting to the institution's payment of ATM and one-time debit card transactions pursuant to the institution's overdraft service; or

(ii) Decline to pay checks, ACH transactions, and other types of transactions that overdraw the consumer's account because the consumer has not affirmatively consented to the institution's overdraft service for ATM and one-time debit card transactions.

(3) Same account terms, conditions, and features. A financial institution shall provide to consumers who do not affirmatively consent to the institution's overdraft service for ATM and one-time debit card transactions the same account terms, conditions, and features that it provides to consumers who affirmatively consent, except for the overdraft service for ATM and one-time debit card transactions.

(c) Timing.

(1) Existing account holders. For accounts opened prior to July 1, 2010, the financial institution must not assess any fees or charges on a consumer's account on or after August 15, 2010, for paying an ATM or one-time debit card transaction pursuant to the overdraft service, unless the institution has complied with § 1005.17(b)(1) and obtained the consumer's affirmative consent.

(2) New account holders. For accounts opened on or after July 1, 2010, the financial institution must comply with § 1005.17(b)(1) and obtain the consumer's affirmative consent before the institution assesses any fee or charge on the consumer's account for paying an ATM or one-time debit card transaction pursuant to the institution's overdraft service.

(d) Content and format. The notice required by paragraph (b)(1)(i) of this section shall be substantially similar to Model Form A-9 set forth in Appendix A of this part, include all applicable items in this paragraph, and may not contain any information not specified in or otherwise permitted by this paragraph.

(1) Overdraft service. A brief description of the financial institution's overdraft service and the types of transactions for which a fee or charge for paying an overdraft may be imposed, including ATM and one-time debit card transactions.

(2) Fees imposed. The dollar amount of any fees or charges assessed by the financial institution for paying an ATM or one-time debit card transaction pursuant to the institution's overdraft service, including any daily or other overdraft fees. If the amount of the fee is determined on the basis of the number of times the consumer has overdrawn the account, the amount of the overdraft, or other factors, the institution must disclose the maximum fee that may be imposed.

(3) Limits on fees charged. The maximum number of overdraft fees or charges that may be assessed per day, or, if applicable, that there is no limit.

(4) Disclosure of opt-in right. An explanation of the consumer's right to affirmatively consent to the financial institution's payment of overdrafts for ATM and one-time debit card transactions pursuant to the institution's overdraft service, including the methods by which the consumer may consent to the service; and

(5) Alternative plans for covering overdrafts. If the institution offers a line of credit subject to Regulation Z (12 CFR part 1026) or a service that transfers funds from another account of the consumer held at the institution to cover overdrafts, the institution must state that fact. An institution may, but is not required to, list additional alternatives for the payment of overdrafts.

(6) Permitted modifications and additional content. If applicable, the institution may modify the content required by § 1005.17(d) to indicate that the consumer has the right to opt into, or opt out of, the payment of overdrafts under the institution's overdraft service for other types of transactions, such as checks, ACH transactions, or automatic bill payments; to provide a means for the consumer to exercise this choice; and to disclose the associated returned item fee and that additional merchant fees may apply. The institution may also disclose the consumer's right to revoke consent. For notices provided to consumers who have opened accounts prior to July 1, 2010, the financial institution may describe the institution's overdraft service with respect to ATM and one-time debit card transactions with a statement such as "After August 15, 2010, we will not authorize and pay overdrafts for the following types of transactions unless you ask us to (see below)."

(e) Joint relationships. If two or more consumers jointly hold an account, the financial institution shall treat the affirmative consent of any of the joint consumers as affirmative consent for that account. Similarly, the financial institution shall treat a revocation of affirmative consent by any of the joint consumers as revocation of consent for that account.

(f) Continuing right to opt in or to revoke the opt-in. A consumer may affirmatively consent to the financial institution's overdraft service at any time in the manner described in the notice required by paragraph (b)(1)(i) of this section. A consumer may also revoke consent at any time in the manner made available to the consumer for providing consent. A financial institution must implement a consumer's revocation of consent as soon as reasonably practicable.

(g) Duration and revocation of opt-in. A consumer's affirmative consent to the institution's overdraft service is effective until revoked by the consumer, or unless the financial institution terminates the service.

§ 1005.18 Requirements for financial institutions offering prepaid accounts.

(a) Coverage. A financial institution shall comply with all applicable requirements of the Act and this part with respect to prepaid accounts except as modified by this section. For rules governing government benefit accounts, see § 1005.15.

(b) Pre-acquisition disclosure requirements.

(1) Timing of disclosures.

(i) General. Except as provided in paragraphs(b)(1)(ii) or (iii) of this section, a financial institution shall provide the disclosures required by paragraph (b) of this section before a consumer acquires a prepaid account. When a prepaid account is used for disbursing funds to a consumer, and the financial institution or third party making the disbursement does not offer any alternative means for the consumer to receive those funds in lieu of accepting the prepaid account, for purposes of this paragraph, the disclosures required by paragraph (b) of this section may be provided at the time the consumer receives the prepaid account.

(ii) Disclosures for prepaid accounts acquired in retail locations. A financial institution is not required to provide the long form disclosure required by paragraph (b)(4) of this section before a consumer acquires a prepaid account in person at a retail location if the following conditions are met:

(A) The prepaid account access device is contained inside the packaging material.

(B) The disclosure required by paragraph (b)(2) of this section is provided on or are visible through an outward-facing, external surface of a prepaid account access device's packaging material.

(C) The disclosure required by paragraph (b)(2) of this section includes the information set forth in paragraph (b)(2)(xiii) of this section that allows a consumer to access the information required to be disclosed by paragraph (b)(4) of this section by telephone and via a website.

(D) The long form disclosure required by paragraph (b)(4) of this section is provided after the consumer acquires the prepaid account. If a financial institution does not provide the long form disclosure inside the prepaid account packaging material, and it is not otherwise already mailing or delivering to the consumer written account-related communications within 30 days of obtaining the consumer's contact information, it may provide the long form disclosure pursuant to this paragraph in electronic form without regard to the consumer notice and consent requirements of section 101(c) of the Electronic Signature in Global and National Commerce Act (E-Sign Act) (15 U.S.C. 7001 et seq.).

(iii) Disclosures for prepaid accounts acquired orally by telephone. A financial institution is not required to provide the long form disclosures required by paragraph (b)(4) of this section before a consumer acquires a prepaid account orally by telephone if the following conditions are met:

(A) The financial institution communicates to the consumer orally, before the consumer acquires the prepaid account, that the information required to be disclosed by paragraph (b)(4) of this section is available both by telephone and on a Web site.

(B) The financial institution makes the information required to be disclosed by paragraph (b)(4) of this section available both by telephone and on a Web site.

(C) The long form disclosure required by paragraph (b)(4) of this section is provided after the consumer acquires the prepaid account.

(2) Short form disclosure content. In accordance with paragraph (b)(1) of this section, a financial institution shall provide a disclosure setting forth the following fees and information for a prepaid account, as applicable:

(i) Periodic fee. The periodic fee charged for holding the prepaid account, assessed on a monthly or other periodic basis, using the term "Monthly fee," "Annual fee," or a substantially similar term.

(ii) Per purchase fee. The fee for making a purchase using the prepaid account, using the term "Per purchase" or a substantially similar term.

(iii) ATM withdrawal fees. Two fees for using an automated teller machine to initiate a withdrawal of cash in the United States from the prepaid account, both within and outside of the financial institution's network or a network affiliated with the financial institution, using the term "ATM withdrawal" or a substantially similar term, and "in-network" or "out-of-network," respectively, or substantially similar terms.

(iv) Cash reload fee. The fee for reloading cash into the prepaid account using the term "Cash reload" or a substantially similar term. The fee disclosed must be the total of all charges from the financial institution and any third parties for a cash reload.

(v) ATM balance inquiry fees. Two fees for using an automated teller machine to check the balance of the prepaid account in the United States, both within and outside of the financial institution's network or a network affiliated with the financial institution, using the term "ATM balance inquiry" or a substantially similar term, and "in-network" or "out-of-network," respectively, or substantially similar terms.

(vi) Customer service fees. Two fees for calling the financial institution about the prepaid account, both for calling an interactive voice response system and a live customer service agent, using the term "Customer service" or a substantially similar term, and "automated" or "live agent," or substantially similar terms, respectively, and "per call" or a substantially similar term. When providing a short form disclosure for multiple service plans pursuant to paragraph (b)(6)(iii)(B)(2) of this section, disclose only the fee for calling the live agent customer service about the prepaid account, using the term "Live customer service" or a substantially similar term and "per call" or a substantially similar term.

(vii) Inactivity fee. The fee for non-use, dormancy, or inactivity of the prepaid account, using the term "Inactivity" or a substantially similar term, as well as the conditions that trigger the financial institution to impose that fee.

(viii) Statements regarding additional fee types.

(A) Statement regarding number of additional fee types charged. A statement disclosing the number of additional fee types the financial institution may charge consumers with respect to the prepaid account, using the following clause or a substantially similar clause: "We charge [x] other types of fees." The number of additional fee types disclosed must reflect the total number of fee types under which the financial institution may charge fees, excluding:

(1) Fees required to be disclosed pursuant to paragraphs (b)(2)(i) through (vii) and (b)(5) of this section; and

(2) Any finance charges as described in Regulation Z, 12 CFR 1026.4(b)(11), imposed in connection with a covered separate credit feature accessible by a hybrid prepaid-credit card as defined in 12 CFR 1026.61.

(B) Statement directing consumers to disclosure of additional fee types. If a financial institution makes a disclosure pursuant to paragraph (b)(2)(ix) of this section, a statement directing consumers to that disclosure, located after but on the same line of text as the statement regarding the number of additional fee types required by paragraph (b)(2)(viii)(A) of this section, using the following clause or a substantially similar clause: "Here are some of them:".

(ix) Disclosure of additional fee types.

(A) Determination of which additional fee types to disclose. The two fee types that generate the highest revenue from consumers for the prepaid account program or across prepaid account programs that share the same fee schedule during the time period provided in paragraphs (b)(2)(ix)(D) and (E) of this section, excluding:

(1) Fees required to be disclosed pursuant to paragraphs (b)(2)(i) through (vii) and (b)(5) of this section;

(2) Any fee types that generated less than 5 percent of the total revenue from consumers for the prepaid account program or across prepaid account programs that share the same fee schedule during the time period provided in paragraphs (b)(2)(ix)(D) and (E) of this section; and

(3) Any finance charges as described in Regulation Z, 12 CFR 1026.4(b)(11), imposed in connection with a covered separate credit feature accessible by a hybrid prepaid-credit card as defined in 12 CFR 1026.61.

(B) Disclosure of fewer than two additional fee types. A financial institution that has only one additional fee type that satisfies the criteria in paragraph (b)(2)(ix)(A) of this section must disclose that one additional fee type; it may, but is not required to, also disclose another additional fee type of its choice. A financial institution that has no additional fee types that satisfy the criteria in paragraph (b)(2)(ix)(A) of this section is not required to make a disclosure under this paragraph (b)(2)(ix); it may, but is not required to, disclose one or two fee types of its choice.

(C) Fee variations in additional fee types. If an additional fee type required to be disclosed pursuant to paragraph (b)(2)(ix)(A) of this section has more than two fee variations, or when providing a short form disclosure for multiple service plans pursuant to paragraph (b)(6)(iii)(B)(2) of this section, the financial institution must disclose the name of the additional fee type and the highest fee amount in accordance with paragraph (b)(3)(i) of this section; for disclosures other than for multiple service plans, it may, but is not required to, consolidate the fee variations into two categories and disclose the names of those two fee variation categories and the fee amounts in a format substantially similar to that used to disclose the two-tier fees required by paragraphs (b)(2)(v) and (vi) of this section and in accordance with paragraphs (b)(3)(i) and (b)(7)(ii)(B)(1) of this section. Except when providing a short form disclosure for multiple service plans pursuant to paragraph (b)(6)(iii)(B)(2) of this section, if an additional fee type has two fee variations, the financial institution must disclose the name of the additional fee type together with the names of the two fee variations and the fee amounts in a format substantially similar to that used to disclose the two-tier fees required by paragraphs (b)(2)(v) and (vi) of this section and in accordance with paragraph (b)(7)(ii)(B)(1) of this section. If a financial institution only charges one fee under a particular fee type, the financial institution must disclose the name of the additional fee type and the fee amount; it may, but is not required to, disclose also the name of the one fee variation for which the fee amount is charged, in a format substantially similar to that used to disclose the two-tier fees required by paragraphs (b)(2)(v) and (vi) of this section, except that the financial institution would disclose only the one fee variation name and fee amount instead of two.

(D) Timing of initial assessment of additional fee type disclosure.

(1) Existing prepaid account programs as of October 1, 2017. For a prepaid account program in effect as of October 1, 2017, the financial institution must disclose the additional fee types based on revenue for a 24-month period that begins no earlier than October 1, 2014.

(2) Existing prepaid account programs as of October 1, 2017 with unavailable data. If a financial institution does not have 24 months of fee revenue data for a particular prepaid account program from which to calculate the additional fee types disclosure in advance of October 1, 2017, the financial institution must disclose the additional fee types based on revenue it reasonably anticipates the prepaid account program will generate over the 24-month period that begins on October 1, 2017.

(3) New prepaid account programs created on or after October 1, 2017. For a prepaid account program created on or after October 1, 2017, the financial institution must disclose the additional fee types based on revenue it reasonably anticipates the prepaid account program will generate over the first 24 months of the program.

(E) Timing of periodic reassessment and update of additional fee types disclosure.

(1) General. A financial institution must reassess its additional fee types disclosure periodically as described in paragraph (b)(2)(ix)(E)(2) of this section and upon a fee schedule change as described in paragraph (b)(2)(ix)(E)(3) of this section. The financial institution must update its additional fee types disclosure if the previous disclosure no longer complies with the requirements of this paragraph (b)(2)(ix).

(2) Periodic reassessment. A financial institution must reassess whether its previously disclosed additional fee types continue to comply with the requirements of this paragraph (b)(2)(ix) every 24 months based on revenue for the previous 24-month period. The financial institution must complete this reassessment and update its disclosures, if applicable, within three months of the end of the 24-month period, except as provided in the update printing exception in paragraph (b)(2)(ix)(E)(4) of this section. A financial institution may, but is not required to, carry out this reassessment and update, if applicable, more frequently than every 24 months, at which time a new 24-month period commences.

(3) Fee schedule change. If a financial institution revises the fee schedule for a prepaid account program, it must determine whether it reasonably anticipates that the previously disclosed additional fee types will continue to comply with the requirements of this paragraph (b)(2)(ix) for the 24 months following implementation of the fee schedule change. If the financial institution reasonably anticipates that the previously disclosed additional fee types will not comply with the requirements of this paragraph (b)(2)(ix), it must update the disclosure based on its reasonable anticipation of what those additional fee types will be at the time the fee schedule change goes into effect, except as provided in the update printing exception in paragraph (b)(2)(ix)(E)(4) of this section. If an immediate change in terms and conditions is necessary to maintain or restore the security of an account or an electronic fund transfer system as described in § 1005.8(a)(2) and that change affects the prepaid account program's fee schedule, the financial institution must complete its reassessment and update its disclosures, if applicable, within three months of the date it makes the change permanent, except as provided in the update printing exception in paragraph (b)(2)(ix)(E)(4) of this section.

(4) Update printing exception. Notwithstanding the requirements to update additional fee types disclosures in paragraph (b)(2)(ix)(E) of this section, a financial institution is not required to update the listing of additional fee types that are provided on, in, or with prepaid account packaging materials that were manufactured, printed, or otherwise produced prior to a periodic reassessment and update pursuant to paragraph (b)(2)(ix)(E)(2) of this section or prior to a fee schedule change pursuant to paragraph (b)(2)(ix)(E)(3) of this section.

(x) Statement regarding overdraft credit features. If a covered separate credit feature accessible by a hybrid prepaid credit card as defined in Regulation Z, 12 CFR 1026.61, may be offered at any point to a consumer in connection with the prepaid account, a statement that overdraft/credit may be offered, the time period after which it may be offered, and that fees would apply, using the following clause or a substantially similar clause: "You may be offered overdraft/credit after [x] days. Fees would apply." If no such credit feature will be offered at any point to a consumer in connection with the prepaid account, a statement that no overdraft credit feature is offered, using the following clause or a substantially similar clause: "No overdraft/credit feature."

(xi) Statement regarding registration and FDIC or NCUA insurance. A statement regarding the prepaid account program's eligibility for FDIC deposit insurance or NCUA share insurance, as appropriate, and directing the consumer to register the prepaid account for insurance and other account protections, where applicable, as follows:

(A) Account is insurance eligible and does not have pre-acquisition customer identification/verification. If a prepaid account program is set up to be eligible for FDIC deposit or NCUA share insurance, and customer identification and verification does not occur before the account is opened, using the following clause or a substantially similar clause: "Register your card for [FDIC insurance eligibility] [NCUA insurance, if eligible,] and other protections."

(B) Account is not insurance eligible and does not have pre-acquisition customer identification/verification. If a prepaid account program is not set up to be eligible for FDIC deposit or NCUA share insurance, and customer identification and verification does not occur before the account is opened, using the following clause or a substantially similar clause: "Not [FDIC] [NCUA] insured. Register your card for other protections."

(C) Account is insurance eligible and has pre-acquisition customer identification/verification. If a prepaid account program is set up to be eligible for FDIC deposit or NCUA share insurance, and customer identification and verification occurs for all prepaid accounts within the prepaid program before the account is opened, using the following clause or a substantially similar clause: "Your funds are [eligible for FDIC insurance] [NCUA insured, if eligible]."

(D) Account is not insurance eligible and has pre-acquisition customer identification/verification. If a prepaid account program is not set up to be eligible for FDIC deposit or NCUA share insurance, and customer identification and verification occurs for all prepaid accounts within the prepaid account program before the account is opened, using the following clause or a substantially similar clause: "Your funds are not [FDIC] [NCUA] insured."

(E) No customer identification/verification. If a prepaid account program is set up such that there is no customer identification and verification process for any prepaid accounts within the prepaid account program, using the following clause or a substantially similar clause: "Treat this card like cash. Not [FDIC] [NCUA] insured."

(xii) Statement regarding CFPB Web site. A statement directing the consumer to a Web site URL of the Consumer Financial Protection Bureau (cfpb.gov/prepaid) for general information about prepaid accounts, using the following clause or a substantially similar clause: "For general information about prepaid accounts, visit cfpb.gov/prepaid."

(xiii) Statement regarding information on all fees and services. A statement directing the consumer to the location of the long form disclosure required by paragraph (b)(4) of this section to find details and conditions for all fees and services. For a financial institution offering prepaid accounts at a retail location pursuant to the retail location exception in paragraph (b)(1)(ii) of this section, this statement must also include a telephone number and a Web site URL that a consumer may use to directly access, respectively, an oral and an electronic version of the long form disclosure required under paragraph (b)(4) of this section. The disclosure required by this paragraph must be made using the following clause or a substantially similar clause: "Find details and conditions for all fees and services in [location]" or, for prepaid accounts offered at retail locations pursuant to paragraph (b)(1)(ii) of this section, made using the following clause or a substantially similar clause: "Find details and conditions for all fees and services inside the package, or call [telephone number] or visit [Web site]." The Web site URL may not exceed 22 characters and must be meaningfully named. A financial institution may, but is not required to, disclose an SMS code at the end of the statement disclosing the telephone number and Web site URL, if the SMS code can be accommodated on the same line of text as the statement required by this paragraph.

(xiv) Additional content for payroll card accounts.

(A) Statement regarding wage or salary payment options. For payroll card accounts, a statement that the consumer does not have to accept the payroll card account and directing the consumer to ask about other ways to receive wages or salary from the employer instead of receiving them via the payroll card account using the following clause or a substantially similar clause: "You do not have to accept this payroll card. Ask your employer about other ways to receive your wages." Alternatively, a financial institution may provide a statement that the consumer has several options to receive wages or salary, followed by a list of the options available to the consumer, and directing the consumer to tell the employer which option the consumer chooses using the following clause or a substantially similar clause: "You have several options to receive your wages: [list of options available to the consumer]; or this payroll card. Tell your employer which option you choose." This statement must be located above the information required by paragraphs (b)(2)(i) through (iv).

(B) Statement regarding state-required information or other fee discounts and waivers. For payroll card accounts, a financial institution may, but is not required to, include a statement in one additional line of text directing the consumer to a particular location outside the short form disclosure for information on ways the consumer may access payroll card account funds and balance information for free or for a reduced fee. This statement must be located directly below any statements disclosed pursuant to paragraphs (b)(3)(i) and (ii) of this section, or, if no such statements are disclosed, above the statement required by paragraph (b)(2)(x) of this section.

(3) Short form disclosure of variable fees and third-party fees and prohibition on disclosure of finance charges.

(i) General disclosure of variable fees. If the amount of any fee that is required to be disclosed in the short form disclosure pursuant to paragraphs (b)(2)(i) through (vii) and (ix) of this section could vary, a financial institution shall disclose the highest amount it may impose for that fee, followed by a symbol, such as an asterisk, linked to a statement explaining that the fee could be lower depending on how and where the prepaid account is used, using the following clause or a substantially similar clause: "This fee can be lower depending on how and where this card is used." Except as provided in paragraph (b)(3)(ii) of this section, a financial institution must use the same symbol and statement for all fees that could vary. The linked statement must be located above the statement required by paragraph (b)(2)(x) of this section.

(ii) Disclosure of variable periodic fee. If the amount of the periodic fee disclosed in the short form disclosure pursuant to paragraph (b)(2)(i) of this section could vary, as an alternative to the disclosure required by paragraph (b)(3)(i) of this section, the financial institution may disclose the highest amount it may impose for the periodic fee, followed by a symbol, such as a dagger, that is different from the symbol the financial institution uses pursuant to paragraph (b)(3)(i) of this section, to indicate that a waiver of the fee or a lower fee might apply, linked to a statement in one additional line of text disclosing the waiver or reduced fee amount and explaining the circumstances under which the fee waiver or reduction may occur. The linked statement must be located directly above or in place of the linked statement required by paragraph (b)(3)(i) of this section, as applicable.

(iii) Single disclosure for like fees. As an alternative to the two-tier fee disclosure required by paragraphs (b)(2)(iii), (v), and (vi) of this section and any two-tier fee required by paragraph (b)(2)(ix) of this section, a financial institution may disclose a single fee amount when the amount is the same for both fees.

(iv) Third-party fees in general. Except as provided in paragraph (b)(3)(v) of this section, a financial institution may not include any third-party fees in a disclosure made pursuant to paragraph (b)(2) of this section.

(v) Third-party cash reload fees. Any third-party fee included in the cash reload fee disclosed in the short form pursuant to paragraph (b)(2)(iv) of this section must be the highest fee known by the financial institution at the time it prints, or otherwise prepares, the short form disclosure required by paragraph (b)(2) of this section. A financial institution is not required to revise its short form disclosure to reflect a cash reload fee change by a third party until such time that the financial institution manufactures, prints, or otherwise produces new prepaid account packaging materials or otherwise updates the short form disclosure.

(vi) Prohibition on disclosure of finance charges. A financial institution may not include in a disclosure made pursuant to paragraphs (b)(2)(i) through (ix) of this section any finance charges as described in Regulation Z, 12 CFR 1026.4(b)(11), imposed in connection with a covered separate credit feature accessible by a hybrid prepaid-credit card as defined in 12 CFR 1026.61.

(4) Long form disclosure content. In accordance with paragraph (b)(1) of this section, a financial institution shall provide a disclosure setting forth the following fees and information for a prepaid account, as applicable:

(i) Title for long form disclosure. A heading stating the name of the prepaid account program and that the long form disclosure contains a list of all fees for that particular prepaid account program.

(ii) Fees. All fees that may be imposed in connection with a prepaid account. For each fee, the financial institution must disclose the amount of the fee and the conditions, if any, under which the fee may be imposed, waived, or reduced. A financial institution may not use any symbols, such as an asterisk, to explain conditions under which any fee may be imposed. A financial institution may, but is not required to, include in the long form disclosure any service or feature it provides or offers at no charge to the consumer. The financial institution must also disclose any third-party fee amounts known to the financial institution that may apply. For any such third-party fee disclosed, the financial institution may, but is not required to, include either or both a statement that the fee is accurate as of or through a specific date or that the third-party fee is subject to change. If a third-party fee may apply but the amount of that fee is not known by the financial institution, it must include a statement indicating that the third-party fee may apply without specifying the fee amount. A financial institution is not required to revise the long form disclosure required by paragraph (b)(4) of this section to reflect a fee change by a third party until such time that the financial institution manufactures, prints, or otherwise produces new prepaid account packaging materials or otherwise updates the long form disclosure.

(iii) Statement regarding registration and FDIC or NCUA insurance. The statement required by paragraph (b)(2)(xi) of this section, together with an explanation of FDIC or NCUA insurance coverage and the benefit of such coverage or the consequence of the lack of such coverage, as applicable.

(iv) Statement regarding overdraft credit features. The statement required by paragraph (b)(2)(x) of this section.

(v) Statement regarding financial institution contact information. A statement directing the consumer to a telephone number, mailing address, and Web site URL of the person or office that a consumer may contact to learn about the terms and conditions of the prepaid account, to obtain prepaid account balance information, to request a copy of transaction history pursuant to paragraph (c)(1)(iii) of this section if the financial institution does not provide periodic statements pursuant to § 1005.9(b), or to notify the financial institution when the consumer believes that an unauthorized electronic fund transfer occurred as required by § 1005.7(b)(2) and paragraph (d)(1)(ii) of this section.

(vi) Statement regarding CFPB Web site and telephone number. A statement directing the consumer to a Web site URL of the Consumer Financial Protection Bureau (cfpb.gov/prepaid) for general information about prepaid accounts, and a statement directing the consumer to a Consumer Financial Protection Bureau telephone number (1-855-411-2372) and Web site URL (cfpb.gov/complaint) to submit a complaint about a prepaid account, using the following clause or a substantially similar clause: "For general information about prepaid accounts, visit cfpb.gov/prepaid. If you have a complaint about a prepaid account, call the Consumer Financial Protection Bureau at 1-855-411-2372 or visit cfpb.gov/complaint."

(vii) Regulation Z disclosures for overdraft credit features. The disclosures described in Regulation Z, 12 CFR 1026.60(e) (1), in accordance with the requirements for such disclosures in 12 CFR 1026.60, if, at any point, a covered separate credit feature accessible by a hybrid prepaid-credit card as defined in 12 CFR 1026.61, may be offered in connection with the prepaid account. A financial institution may, but is not required to, include above the Regulation Z disclosures required by this paragraph a heading and other explanatory information introducing the overdraft credit feature. A financial institution is not required to revise the disclosure required by this paragraph to reflect a change in the fees or other terms disclosed therein until such time as the financial institution manufactures, prints, or otherwise produces new prepaid account packaging materials or otherwise updates the long form disclosure.

(5) Disclosure requirements outside the short form disclosure. At the time a financial institution provides the short form disclosure, it must also disclose the following information: the name of the financial institution; the name of the prepaid account program; the purchase price for the prepaid account, if any; and the fee for activating the prepaid account, if any. In a setting other than in a retail location, this information must be disclosed in close proximity to the short form. In a retail location, this information, other than the purchase price, must be disclosed on the exterior of the access device's packaging material. In a retail location, the purchase price must be disclosed either on the exterior of or in close proximity to the prepaid account access device's packaging material.

(6) Form of pre-acquisition disclosures.

(i) General.

(A) Written disclosures. Except as provided in paragraphs (b)(6)(i)(B) and (C) of this section, disclosures required by paragraph (b) of this section must be in writing.

(B) Electronic disclosures. Unless provided in written form prior to acquisition pursuant to paragraph (b)(1)(i) of this section, the disclosures required by paragraph (b) of this section must be provided in electronic form when a consumer acquires a prepaid account through electronic means, including via a website or mobile application, and must be viewable across all screen sizes. The long form disclosure must be provided electronically through a website when a financial institution is offering prepaid accounts at a retail location pursuant to the retail location exception in paragraph (b)(1)(ii) of this section. Electronic disclosures must be provided in a manner which is reasonably expected to be accessible in light of how a consumer is acquiring the prepaid account, in a responsive form, and using machine-readable text that is accessible via Web browsers or mobile applications, as applicable, and via screen readers. Electronic disclosures provided pursuant to paragraph (b) of this section need not meet the consumer consent and other applicable provisions of the Electronic Signatures in Global and National Commerce Act (E-Sign Act) (15 U.S.C. 7001 et seq.).

(C) Oral disclosures. Unless provided in written form prior to acquisition pursuant to paragraph (b)(1)(i) of this section, disclosures required by paragraphs (b)(2) and (5) of this section must be provided orally when a consumer acquires a prepaid account orally by telephone pursuant to the exception in paragraph (b)(1)(iii) of this section. For prepaid accounts acquired in retail locations or orally by telephone, the disclosure required by paragraph (b)(4) of this section provided by telephone pursuant to paragraph (b)(1)(ii)(C) or (b)(1)(iii)(B) of this section also must be made orally.

(ii) Retainable form. Pursuant to § 1005.4(a)(1), disclosures required by paragraph (b) of this section must be made in a form that a consumer may keep, except for disclosures provided orally pursuant to paragraphs (b)(1)(ii) or (iii) of this section, long form disclosures provided via SMS as permitted by paragraph (b)(2)(xiii) of this section for a prepaid account sold at retail locations pursuant to the retail location exception in paragraph (b)(1)(ii) of this section, and the disclosure of a purchase price pursuant to paragraph (b)(5) of this section that is not disclosed on the exterior of the packaging material for a prepaid account sold at a retail location pursuant to the retail location exception in paragraph (b)(1)(ii) of this section.

(iii) Tabular format.

(A) General. When a short form disclosure is provided in writing or electronically, the information required by paragraphs (b)(2)(i) through (ix) of this section shall be provided in the form of a table. Except as provided in paragraph (b)(6)(iii)(B) of this section, the short form disclosures required by paragraph (b)(2) of this section shall be provided in a form substantially similar to Model Forms A-10(a) through (d) in appendix A of this part, as applicable. When a long form disclosure is provided in writing or electronically, the information required by paragraph (b)(4)(ii) of this section shall be provided in the form of a table. Sample Form A-10(f) in appendix A of this part provides an example of the long form disclosure required by paragraph (b)(4) of this section when the financial institution does not offer multiple service plans.

(B) Multiple service plans.

(1) Short form disclosure for default service plan. When a financial institution offers multiple service plans within a particular prepaid account program and each plan has a different fee schedule, the information required by paragraphs (b)(2)(i) through (ix) of this section may be provided in the tabular format described in paragraph (b)(6)(iii)(A) of this section for the service plan in which a consumer is initially enrolled by default upon acquiring the prepaid account.

(2) Short form disclosure for multiple service plans. As an alternative to disclosing the default service plan pursuant to paragraph (b)(6)(iii)(B)(1) of this section, when a financial institution offers multiple service plans within a particular prepaid account program and each plan has a different fee schedule, fee disclosures required by paragraphs (b)(2)(i) through (vii) and (ix) of this section may be provided in the form of a table with separate columns for each service plan, in a form substantially similar to Model Form A-10(e) in appendix A of this part. Column headings must describe each service plan included in the table, using the terms "Pay-as-you-go plan," "Monthly plan," "Annual plan," or substantially similar terms; or, for multiple service plans offering preferred rates or fees for the prepaid accounts of consumers who also use another non-prepaid service, column headings must describe each service plan included in the table for the preferred- and non-preferred service plans, as applicable.

(3) Long form disclosure. The information in the long form disclosure required by paragraph (b)(4)(ii) of this section must be presented in the form of a table for all service plans.

(7) Specific formatting requirements for pre-acquisition disclosures.

(i) Grouping.

(A) Short form disclosure. The information required in the short form disclosure by paragraphs (b)(2)(i) through (iv) of this section must be grouped together and provided in that order. The information required by paragraphs (b)(2)(v) through (ix) of this section must be generally grouped together and provided in that order. The information required by paragraphs (b)(3)(i) and (ii) of this section, as applicable, must be generally grouped together and in the location described by paragraphs (b)(3)(i) and (ii) of this section. The information required by paragraphs (b)(2)(x) through (xiii) of this section must be generally grouped together and provided in that order. The statement regarding wage or salary payment options for payroll card accounts required by paragraph (b)(2)(xiv)(A) of this section must be located above the information required by paragraphs (b)(2)(i) through (iv) of this section, as described in paragraph (b)(2)(xiv)(A) of this section. The statement regarding state-required information or other fee discounts or waivers permitted by paragraph (b)(2)(xiv)(B) of this section, when applicable, must appear in the location described by paragraph (b)(2)(xiv)(B) of this section.

(B) Long form disclosure. The information required by paragraph (b)(4)(i) of this section must be located in the first line of the long form disclosure. The information required by paragraph (b)(4)(ii) of this section must be generally grouped together and organized under subheadings by the categories of function for which a financial institution may impose the fee. Text describing the conditions under which a fee may be imposed must appear in the table required by paragraph (b)(6)(iii)(A) of this section in close proximity to the fee amount. The statements in the long form disclosure required by paragraphs (b)(4)(iii) through (vi) of this section must be generally grouped together, provided in that order, and appear below the information required by paragraph (b)(4)(ii) of this section. If, pursuant to paragraph (b)(4)(vii) of this section, the financial institution includes the disclosures described in Regulation Z, 12 CFR 1026.60(e)(1), such disclosures must appear below the statements required by paragraph (b)(4)(vi) of this section.

(C) Multiple service plan disclosure. When providing a short form disclosure for multiple service plans pursuant to paragraph (b)(6)(iii)(B)(2) of this section, in lieu of the requirements in paragraph (b)(7)(i)(A) of this section for grouping of the disclosures required by paragraphs (b)(2)(i) through (iv) and (v) through (ix) of this section, the information required by paragraphs (b)(2)(i) through (ix) of this section must be grouped together and provided in that order.

(ii) Prominence and size.

(A) General. All text used to disclose information in the short form or in the long form disclosure pursuant to paragraphs (b)(2), (b)(3)(i) and (ii), and (b)(4) of this section must be in a single, easy-to-read type that is all black or one color and printed on a background that provides a clear contrast.

(B) Short form disclosure.

(1) Fees and other information. The information required in the short form disclosure by paragraphs (b)(2)(i) through (iv) of this section must appear as follows: Fee amounts in bold-faced type; single fee amounts in a minimum type size of 15 points (or 21 pixels); two-tier fee amounts for ATM withdrawal in a minimum type size of 11 points (or 16 pixels) and in no larger a type size than what is used for the single fee amounts; and fee headings in a minimum type size of eight points (or 11 pixels) and in no larger a type size than what is used for the single fee amounts. The information required by paragraphs (b)(2)(v) through (ix) of this section must appear in a minimum type size of eight points (or 11 pixels) and appear in the same or a smaller type size than what is used for the fee headings required by paragraphs (b)(2)(i) through (iv) of this section. The information required by paragraphs (b)(2)(x) through (xiii) of this section must appear in a minimum type size of seven points (or nine pixels) and appear in no larger a type size than what is used for the information required to be disclosed by paragraphs (b)(2)(v) through (ix) of this section. Additionally, the statements disclosed pursuant to paragraphs (b)(2)(viii)(A) and (b)(2)(x) of this section and the telephone number and URL disclosed pursuant to paragraph (b)(2)(xiii) of this section, where applicable, must appear in bold-faced type. The following information must appear in a minimum type size of six points (or eight pixels) and appear in no larger a type size that what is used for the information required by paragraphs (b)(2)(x) through (xiii) of this section: text used to distinguish each of the two-tier fees pursuant to paragraphs (b)(2)(iii), (v), (vi), and (ix) of this section; text used to explain that the fee required by paragraph (b)(2)(vi) of this section applies "per call," where applicable; and text used to explain the conditions that trigger an inactivity fee and that the fee applies monthly or for the applicable time period, pursuant to paragraph (b)(2)(vii) of this section.

(2) Variable fees. The symbols and corresponding statements regarding variable fees disclosed in the short form pursuant to paragraphs (b)(3)(i) and (ii) of this section, when applicable, must appear in a minimum type size of seven points (or nine pixels) and appear in no larger a type size than what is used for the information required by paragraphs (b)(2)(x) through (xiii) of this section. A symbol required next to the fee amount pursuant to paragraphs (b)(3)(i) and (ii) of this section must appear in the same type size or pixel size as what is used for the corresponding fee amount.

(3) Payroll card account additional content. The statement regarding wage or salary payment options for payroll card accounts required by paragraph (b)(2)(xiv)(A) of this section, when applicable, must appear in a minimum type size of eight points (or 11 pixels) and appear in no larger a type size than what is used for the fee headings required by paragraphs (b)(2)(i) through (iv) of this section. The statement regarding state-required information and other fee discounts or waivers permitted by paragraph (b)(2)(xiv)(B) of this section must appear in the same type size used to disclose variable fee information pursuant to paragraph (b)(3)(i) and (ii) of this section, or, if none, the same type size used for the information required by paragraphs (b)(2)(x) through (xiii) of this section.

(C) Long form disclosure. Long form disclosures required by paragraph (b)(4) of this section must appear in a minimum type size of eight points (or 11 pixels).

(D) Multiple service plan short form disclosure. When providing a short form disclosure for multiple service plans pursuant to paragraph (b)(6)(iii)(B)(2) of this section, the fee headings required by paragraphs (b)(2)(i) through (iv) of this section must appear in bold-faced type. The information required by paragraphs (b)(2)(i) through (xiii) of this section must appear in a minimum type size of seven points (or nine pixels), except the following must appear in a minimum type size of six points (or eight pixels) and appear in no larger a type size than what is used for the information required by paragraphs (b)(2)(i) through (xiii) of this section: Text used to distinguish each of the two-tier fees required by paragraphs (b)(2)(iii) and (v) of this section; text used to explain that the fee required by paragraph (b)(2)(vi) of this section applies "per call," where applicable; text used to explain the conditions that trigger an inactivity fee pursuant to paragraph (b)(2)(vii) of this section; and text used to distinguish that fees required by paragraphs (b)(2)(i) and (vii) of this section apply monthly or for the applicable time period.

(iii) Segregation. Short form and long form disclosures required by paragraphs (b)(2) and (4) of this section must be segregated from other information and must contain only information that is required or permitted for those disclosures by paragraph (b) of this section.

(8) Terminology of pre-acquisition disclosures. Fee names and other terms must be used consistently within and across the disclosures required by paragraph (b) of this section.

(9) Prepaid accounts acquired in foreign languages.

(i) General. A financial institution must provide the pre-acquisition disclosures required by paragraph (b) of this section in a foreign language, if the financial institution uses that same foreign language in connection with the acquisition of a prepaid account in the following circumstances:

(A) The financial institution principally uses a foreign language on the prepaid account packaging material;

(B) The financial institution principally uses a foreign language to advertise, solicit, or market a prepaid account and provides a means in the advertisement, solicitation, or marketing material that the consumer uses to acquire the prepaid account by telephone or electronically; or

(C) The financial institution provides a means for the consumer to acquire a prepaid account by telephone or electronically principally in a foreign language. However, foreign language pre-acquisition disclosures are not required for payroll card accounts and government benefit accounts where the foreign language is offered by telephone via a real-time language interpretation service provided by a third party or by the employer or government agency on an informal or ad hoc basis as an accommodation to prospective payroll card account or government benefit account holders.

(ii) Long form disclosures in English upon request. A financial institution required to provide pre-acquisition disclosures in a foreign language pursuant to paragraph (b)(9)(i) of this section must also provide the information required to be disclosed in its pre-acquisition long form disclosure pursuant to paragraph (b)(4) of this section in English upon a consumer's request and on any part of the Web site where it discloses this information in a foreign language.

(c) Access to prepaid account information.

(1) Periodic statement alternative. A financial institution need not furnish periodic statements required by § 1005.9(b) if the financial institution makes available to the consumer:

(i) The consumer's account balance, through a readily available telephone line;

(ii) An electronic history of the consumer's account transactions, such as through a Web site, that covers at least 12 months preceding the date the consumer electronically accesses the account; and

(iii) A written history of the consumer's account transactions that is provided promptly in response to an oral or written request and that covers at least 24 months preceding the date the financial institution receives the consumer's request.

(2) Periodic statement alternative for unverified prepaid accounts. For prepaid accounts that are not payroll card accounts or government benefit accounts, a financial institution is not required to provide a written history of the consumer's account transactions pursuant to paragraph (c)(1)(iii) of this section for any prepaid account for which the financial institution has not completed its consumer identification and verification process as described in paragraph (e)(3)(i)(A) through (C) of this section.

(3) Information included on electronic or written histories. The history of account transactions provided under paragraphs (c)(1)(ii) and (iii) of this section must include the information set forth in § 1005.9(b).

(4) Inclusion of all fees charged. A financial institution must disclose the amount of any fees assessed against the account, whether for electronic fund transfers or otherwise, on any periodic statement provided pursuant to § 1005.9(b) and on any history of account transactions provided or made available by the financial institution.

(5) Summary totals of fees. A financial institution must display a summary total of the amount of all fees assessed by the financial institution against the consumer's prepaid account for the prior calendar month and for the calendar year to date on any periodic statement provided pursuant to § 1005.9(b) and on any history of account transactions provided or made available by the financial institution.

(d) Modified disclosure requirements. A financial institution that provides information under paragraph (c)(1) of this section shall comply with the following:

(1) Initial disclosures. The financial institution shall modify the disclosures under § 1005.7(b) by disclosing:

(i) Access to account information. A telephone number that the consumer may call to obtain the account balance, the means by which the consumer can obtain an electronic account transaction history, such as the address of a Web site, and a summary of the consumer's right to receive a written account transaction history upon request (in place of the summary of the right to receive a periodic statement required by § 1005.7(b)(6)), including a telephone number to call to request a history. The disclosure required by this paragraph may be made by providing a notice substantially similar to the notice contained in paragraph (a) of appendix A-7 of this part.

(ii) Error resolution. A notice concerning error resolution that is substantially similar to the notice contained in paragraph (b) of appendix A-7 of this part, in place of the notice required by § 1005.7(b)(10). Alternatively, for prepaid account programs for which the financial institution does not have a consumer identification and verification process, the financial institution must describe its error resolution process and limitations on consumers' liability for unauthorized transfers or, if none, state that there are no such protections.

(2) Annual error resolution notice. The financial institution shall provide an annual notice concerning error resolution that is substantially similar to the notice contained in paragraph (b) of appendix A-7 of this part, in place of the notice required by § 1005.8(b). Alternatively, a financial institution may include on or with each electronic and written account transaction history provided in accordance with paragraph (c)(1) of this section, a notice substantially similar to the abbreviated notice for periodic statements contained in paragraph (b) of appendix A-3 of this part, modified as necessary to reflect the error resolution provisions set forth in paragraph (e) of this section.

(e) Modified limitations on liability and error resolution requirements.

(1) Modified limitations on liability requirements. A financial institution that provides information under paragraph (c)(1) of this section shall comply with the following:

(i) For purposes of § 1005.6(b)(3), the 60-day period for reporting any unauthorized transfer shall begin on the earlier of:

(A) The date the consumer electronically accesses the consumer's account under paragraph (c)(1)(ii) of this section, provided that the electronic account transaction history made available to the consumer reflects the unauthorized transfer; or

(B) The date the financial institution sends a written history of the consumer's account transactions requested by the consumer under paragraph (c)(1)(iii) of this section in which the unauthorized transfer is first reflected.

(ii) A financial institution may comply with paragraph (e)(1)(i) of this section by limiting the consumer's liability for an unauthorized transfer as provided under § 1005.6(b)(3) for any transfer reported by the consumer within 120 days after the transfer was credited or debited to the consumer's account.

(2) Modified error resolution requirements. A financial institution that provides information under paragraph (c)(1) of this section shall comply with the following:

(i) The financial institution shall comply with the requirements of § 1005.11 in response to an oral or written notice of an error from the consumer that is received by the earlier of:

(A) Sixty days after the date the consumer electronically accesses the consumer's account under paragraph (c)(1)(ii) of this section, provided that the electronic account transaction history made available to the consumer reflects the alleged error; or

(B) Sixty days after the date the financial institution sends a written history of the consumer's account transactions requested by the consumer under paragraph (c)(1)(iii) of this section in which the alleged error is first reflected.

(ii) In lieu of following the procedures in paragraph (e)(2)(i) of this section, a financial institution complies with the requirements for resolving errors in § 1005.11 if it investigates any oral or written notice of an error from the consumer that is received by the institution within 120 days after the transfer allegedly in error was credited or debited to the consumer's account.

(3) Limitations on liability and error resolution for unverified accounts.

(i) For prepaid accounts that are not payroll card accounts or government benefit accounts, a financial institution is not required to comply with the liability limits and error resolution requirements in §§ 1005.6 and 1005.11 for any prepaid account for which it has not successfully completed its consumer identification and verification process.

(ii) For purposes of paragraph (e)(3)(i) of this section, a financial institution has not successfully completed its consumer identification and verification process where:

(A) The financial institution has not concluded its consumer identification and verification process with respect to a particular prepaid account, provided that it has disclosed to the consumer the risks of not registering and verifying the account using a notice that is substantially similar to the model notice contained in paragraph (c) of appendix A-7 of this part.

(B) The financial institution has concluded its consumer identification and verification process with respect to a particular prepaid account, but could not verify the identity of the consumer, provided that it has disclosed to the consumer the risks of not registering and verifying the account using a notice that is substantially similar to the model notice contained in paragraph (c) of appendix A-7 of this part; or

(C) The financial institution does not have a consumer identification and verification process for the prepaid account program, provided that it has made the alternative disclosure described in paragraph (d)(1)(ii) of this section and complies with the process it has disclosed.

(iii) Resolution of errors following successful verification. Once a financial institution successfully completes its consumer identification and verification process with respect to a prepaid account, the financial institution must limit the consumer's liability for unauthorized transfers and resolve errors that occur following verification in accordance with § 1005.6 or § 1005.11, or the modified timing requirements in this paragraph (e), as applicable.

(A) Notwithstanding paragraph (e)(3)(iii) of this section, if, at the time the financial institution was required to provisionally credit the account (pursuant to § 1005.11(c)(2)(i) or (c)(3)(ii), as applicable), the financial institution has not yet completed its identification and verification process with respect to that account, the financial institution may take up to the maximum length of time permitted under § 1005.11(c)(2)(i) or (c)(3)(ii), as applicable, to investigate and determine whether an error occurred without provisionally crediting the account.

(f) Disclosure of fees and other information.

(1) Initial disclosure of fees and other information. A financial institution must include, as part of the initial disclosures given pursuant to § 1005.7, all of the information required to be disclosed in its pre-acquisition long form disclosure pursuant to paragraph (b)(4) of this section.

(2) Change-in-terms notice. The change-in-terms notice provisions in § 1005.8(a) apply to any change in a term or condition that is required to be disclosed under § 1005.7 or paragraph (f)(1) of this section. If a financial institution discloses the amount of a third-party fee in its pre-acquisition long form disclosure pursuant to paragraph (b)(4)(ii) of this section and initial disclosures pursuant to paragraph (f)(1) of this section, the financial institution is not required to provide a change-in-terms notice solely to reflect a change in that fee amount imposed by the third party. If a financial institution provides pursuant to paragraph (f)(1) of this section the Regulation Z disclosures required by paragraph (b)(4)(vii) of this section for an overdraft credit feature, the financial institution is not required to provide a change-in-terms notice solely to reflect a change in the fees or other terms disclosed therein.

(3) Disclosures on prepaid account access devices. The name of the financial institution and the Web site URL and a telephone number a consumer can use to contact the financial institution about the prepaid account must be disclosed on the prepaid account access device. If a financial institution does not provide a physical access device in connection with a prepaid account, the disclosure must appear on the Web site, mobile application, or other entry point a consumer must visit to access the prepaid account electronically.

(g) Prepaid accounts accessible by hybrid prepaid-credit cards.

(1) In general. Except as provided in paragraph (g)(2) of this section, with respect to a prepaid account program where consumers may be offered a covered separate credit feature accessible by a hybrid prepaid-credit card as defined by Regulation Z, 12 CFR 1026.61, a financial institution must provide to any prepaid account without a covered separate credit feature the same account terms, conditions, and features that it provides on prepaid accounts in the same prepaid account program that have such a credit feature.

(2) Exception for higher fees or charges. A financial institution is not prohibited under paragraph (g)(1) of this section from imposing a higher fee or charge on the asset feature of a prepaid account with a covered separate credit feature accessible by a hybrid prepaid-credit card than the amount of a comparable fee or charge that it imposes on any prepaid account in the same prepaid account program that does not have such a credit feature.

(h) Effective date and special transition rules for disclosure provisions.

(1) Effective date generally. Except as provided in paragraphs (h)(2) and (3) of this section, the requirements of this subpart, as modified by this section, apply to prepaid accounts as defined in § 1005.2(b)(3), including government benefit accounts subject to § 1005.15, beginning April 1, 2019.

(2) Early disclosures.

(i) Exception for disclosures on existing prepaid account access devices and prepaid account packaging materials. The disclosure requirements of this subpart, as modified by this section, shall not apply to any disclosures that are provided, or that would otherwise be required to be provided, on prepaid account access devices, or on, in, or with prepaid account packaging materials that were manufactured, printed, or otherwise produced in the normal course of business prior to April 1, 2019.

(ii) Disclosures for prepaid accounts acquired on or after April 1, 2019. This paragraph applies to prepaid accounts acquired by consumers on or after April 1, 2019, via packaging materials that were manufactured, printed, or otherwise produced prior to April 1, 2019.

(A) Notices of certain changes. If a financial institution has changed a prepaid account's terms and conditions as a result of paragraph (h)(1) of this section taking effect such that a change-in-terms notice would have been required under § 1005.8(a) or paragraph (f)(2) of this section for existing customers, the financial institution must provide to the consumer a notice of the change within 30 days of obtaining the consumer's contact information.

(B) Initial disclosures. The financial institution must mail or deliver to the consumer initial disclosures pursuant to § 1005.7 and paragraph (f)(1) of this section that have been updated as a result of paragraph (h)(1) of this section taking effect, within 30 days of obtaining the consumer's contact information.

(iii) Disclosures for prepaid accounts acquired before April 1, 2019. This paragraph applies to prepaid accounts acquired by consumers before April 1, 2019. If a financial institution has changed a prepaid account's terms and conditions as a result of paragraph (h)(1) of this section taking effect such that a change-in-terms notice would have been required under § 1005.8(a) or paragraph (f)(2) of this section for existing customers, the financial institution must provide to the consumer a notice of the change at least 21 days in advance of the change becoming effective, provided the financial institution has the consumer's contact information. If the financial institution obtains the consumer's contact information less than 30 days in advance of the change becoming effective or after it has become effective, the financial institution is permitted instead to notify the consumer of the change in accordance with the timing requirements set forth in paragraph (h)(2)(ii)(A) of this section.

(iv) Method of providing notice to consumers. With respect to prepaid accounts governed by paragraph (h)(2)(ii) or (iii) of this section, if a financial institution has not obtained a consumer's consent to provide disclosures in electronic form pursuant to the Electronic Signatures in Global and National Commerce Act (E-Sign Act) (15 U.S.C. 7001 et seq.), or is not otherwise already mailing or delivering to the consumer written account-related communications within the respective time periods specified in paragraphs (h)(2)(ii) or (iii) of this section, the financial institution may provide to the consumer a notice of a change in terms and conditions pursuant to paragraph (h)(2)(ii) or (iii) of this section or required or voluntary updated initial disclosures as a result of paragraph (h)(1) of this section taking effect in electronic form without regard to the consumer notice and consent requirements of section 101(c) of the E-Sign Act.

(3) Account information not available on April 1, 2019.

(i) Electronic and written account transaction history. If, on April 1, 2019, a financial institution does not have readily accessible the data necessary to make available 12 months of electronic account transaction history pursuant to paragraph (c)(1)(ii) of this section or to provide 24 months of written account transaction history upon request pursuant to paragraph (c)(1)(iii) of this section, the financial institution may make available or provide such histories using the data for the time period it has until the financial institution has accumulated the data necessary to comply in full with the requirements set forth in paragraphs (c)(1)(ii) and (iii) of this section.

(ii) Summary totals of fees. If, on April 1, 2019, the financial institution does not have readily accessible the data necessary to calculate the summary totals of the amount of all fees assessed by the financial institution on the consumer's prepaid account for the prior calendar month and for the calendar year to date pursuant to paragraph (c)(5) of this section, the financial institution may display the summary totals using the data it has until the financial institution has accumulated the data necessary to display the summary totals as required by paragraph (c)(5) of this section.

§ 1005.19 Internet posting of prepaid account agreements.

(a) Definitions.

(1) Agreement. For purposes of this section, "agreement" or "prepaid account agreement" means the written document or documents evidencing the terms of the legal obligation, or the prospective legal obligation, between a prepaid account issuer and a consumer for a prepaid account. "Agreement" or "prepaid account agreement" also includes fee information, as defined in paragraph (a)(3) of this section.

(2) Amends. For purposes of this section, an issuer "amends" an agreement if it makes a substantive change (an "amendment") to the agreement. A change is substantive if it alters the rights or obligations of the issuer or the consumer under the agreement. Any change in the fee information, as defined in paragraph (a)(3) of this section, is deemed to be substantive.

(3) Fee information. For purposes of this section, "fee information" means the short form disclosure for the prepaid account pursuant to § 1005.18(b)(2) and the fee information and statements required to be disclosed in the pre-acquisition long form disclosure for the prepaid account pursuant to § 1005.18(b)(4).

(4) Issuer. For purposes of this section, "issuer" or "prepaid account issuer" means the entity to which a consumer is legally obligated, or would be legally obligated, under the terms of a prepaid account agreement.

(5) Offers. For purposes of this section, an issuer "offers" an agreement if the issuer markets, solicits applications for, or otherwise makes available a prepaid account that would be subject to that agreement, regardless of whether the issuer offers the prepaid account to the general public.

(6) Offers to the general public. For purposes of this section, an issuer "offers to the general public" an agreement if the issuer markets, solicits applications for, or otherwise makes available to the general public a prepaid account that would be subject to that agreement.

(7) Open account. For purposes of this section, a prepaid account is an "open account" or "open prepaid account" if: There is an outstanding balance in the account; the consumer can load funds to the account even if the account does not currently hold a balance; or the consumer can access credit from a covered separate credit feature accessible by a hybrid prepaid-credit card as defined in Regulation Z, 12 CFR 1026.61, in connection with the account. A prepaid account that has been suspended temporarily (for example, due to a report by the consumer of unauthorized use of the card) is considered an "open account" or "open prepaid account."

(8) Prepaid account. For purposes of this section, "prepaid account" means a prepaid account as defined in § 1005.2(b)(3).

(b) Submission of agreements to the Bureau.

(1) Submissions on a rolling basis. An issuer must make submissions of prepaid account agreements to the Bureau on a rolling basis, in the form and manner specified by the Bureau. Rolling submissions must be sent to the Bureau no later than 30 days after an issuer offers, amends, or ceases to offer any prepaid account agreement as described in paragraphs (b)(1)(ii) through (iv) of this section. Each submission must contain:

(i) Identifying information about the issuer and the agreements submitted, including the issuer's name, address, and identifying number (such as an RSSD ID number or tax identification number), the effective date of the prepaid account agreement, the name of the program manager, if any, and the names of other relevant parties, if applicable (such as the employer for a payroll card program or the agency for a government benefit program);

(ii) Any prepaid account agreement offered by the issuer that has not been previously submitted to the Bureau;

(iii) Any prepaid account agreement previously submitted to the Bureau that has been amended, as described in paragraph (b)(2) of this section; and

(iv) Notification regarding any prepaid account agreement previously submitted to the Bureau that the issuer is withdrawing, as described in paragraphs (b)(3), (b)(4)(ii), and (b)(5)(ii) of this section.

(2) Amended agreements

(i) Submission of amended agreements generally. If a prepaid account agreement previously submitted to the Bureau is amended, the issuer must submit the entire amended agreement to the Bureau, in the form and manner specified by the Bureau, no later than 30 days after the change becomes effective. If other identifying information about the issuer and its submitted agreements pursuant to paragraph (b)(1)(i) of this section previously submitted to the Bureau is amended, the issuer must submit updated information to the Bureau, in the form and manner specified by the Bureau, no later than 30 days after the change becomes effective.

(ii) Submission of updated list of names of other relevant parties. Notwithstanding paragraph (b)(2)(i) of this section, an issuer may delay submitting a change to the list of names of other relevant parties to a particular agreement until the earlier of:

(A) Such time as the issuer is otherwise submitting an amended agreement or changes to other identifying information about the issuer and its submitted agreements pursuant to paragraph (b)(1)(i) of this section; or

(B) May 1 of each year, for any updates to the list of names of other relevant parties for that agreement that occurred between the issuer's last submission of relevant party information and April 1 of that year.

(3) Withdrawal of agreements no longer offered. If an issuer no longer offers a prepaid account agreement that was previously submitted to the Bureau, the issuer must notify the Bureau, in the form and manner specified by the Bureau, no later than 30 days after the issuer ceases to offer the agreement, that it is withdrawing the agreement.

(4) De minimis exception.

(i) An issuer is not required to submit any prepaid account agreements to the Bureau if the issuer has fewer than 3,000 open prepaid accounts. If the issuer has 3,000 or more open prepaid accounts as of the last day of the calendar quarter, the issuer must submit to the Bureau its prepaid account agreements no later than 30 days after the last day of that calendar quarter.

(ii) If an issuer that did not previously qualify for the de minimis exception newly qualifies for the de minimis exception, the issuer must continue to make submissions to the Bureau on a rolling basis until the issuer notifies the Bureau that the issuer is withdrawing all agreements it previously submitted to the Bureau.

(5) Product testing exception.

(i) An issuer is not required to submit a prepaid account agreement to the Bureau if the agreement meets the criteria set forth in paragraphs (b)(5)(i)(A) through (C) of this section. If the agreement fails to meet the criteria set forth in paragraphs (b)(5)(i)(A) through (C) of this section as of the last day of the calendar quarter, the issuer must submit to the Bureau that prepaid account agreement no later than 30 days after the last day of that calendar quarter. An agreement qualifies for the product testing exception if the agreement:

(A) Is offered as part of a product test offered to only a limited group of consumers for a limited period of time;

(B) Is used for fewer than 3,000 open prepaid accounts; and

(C) Is not offered other than in connection with such a product test.

(ii) If an agreement that did not previously qualify for the product testing exception newly qualifies for the exception, the issuer must continue to make submissions to the Bureau on a rolling basis with respect to that agreement until the issuer notifies the Bureau that the issuer is withdrawing the agreement.

(6) Form and content of agreements submitted to the Bureau.

(i) Form and content generally.

(A) Each agreement must contain the provisions of the agreement and the fee information currently in effect.

(B) Agreements must not include any personally identifiable information relating to any consumer, such as name, address, telephone number, or account number.

(C) The following are not deemed to be part of the agreement for purposes of this section, and therefore are not required to be included in submissions to the Bureau:

(1) Ancillary disclosures required by state or Federal law, such as affiliate marketing notices, privacy policies, or disclosures under the E-Sign Act;

(2) Solicitation or marketing materials;

(3) Periodic statements; and

(4) Documents that may be sent to the consumer along with the prepaid account or prepaid account agreement such as a cover letter, a validation sticker on the card, or other information about card security.

(D) Agreements must be presented in a clear and legible font.

(ii) Fee information. Fee information must be set forth either in the prepaid account agreement or in addenda to that agreement that attach either or both the short form disclosure for the prepaid account pursuant to § 1005.18(b)(2) and the fee information and statements required to be disclosed in the long form disclosure for the prepaid account pursuant to § 1005.18(b)(4). The agreement or addenda thereto must contain all of the fee information, as defined by paragraph (a)(3) of this section.

(iii) Integrated agreement. An issuer may not provide provisions of the agreement or fee information to the Bureau in the form of change-in-terms notices or riders (other than the optional fee information addenda described in paragraph (b)(6)(ii) of this section). Changes in provisions or fee information must be integrated into the text of the agreement, or the optional fee information addenda, as appropriate.

(c) Posting of agreements offered to the general public.

(1) An issuer must post and maintain on its publicly available Web site any prepaid account agreements offered to the general public that the issuer is required to submit to the Bureau under paragraph (b) of this section.

(2) Agreements posted pursuant to this paragraph (c) must conform to the form and content requirements for agreements submitted to the Bureau set forth in paragraph (b)(6) of this section.

(3) The issuer must post and update the agreements posted on its Web site pursuant to this paragraph (c) as frequently as the issuer is required to submit new or amended agreements to the Bureau pursuant to paragraph (b)(2) of this section.

(4) Agreements posted pursuant to this paragraph (c) may be posted in any electronic format that is readily usable by the general public. Agreements must be placed in a location that is prominent and readily accessible to the public and must be accessible without submission of personally identifiable information.

(d) Agreements for all open accounts.

(1) Availability of an individual consumer's prepaid account agreement. With respect to any open prepaid account, an issuer must either:

(i) Post and maintain the consumer's agreement on its Web site; or

(ii) Promptly provide a copy of the consumer's agreement to the consumer upon the consumer's request. If the issuer makes an agreement available upon request, the issuer must provide the consumer with the ability to request a copy of the agreement by telephone. The issuer must send to the consumer a copy of the consumer's prepaid account agreement no later than five business days after the issuer receives the consumer's request.

(2) Form and content of agreements.

(i) Except as provided in this paragraph (d), agreements posted on the issuer's Web site pursuant to paragraph (d)(1)(i) of this section or sent to the consumer upon the consumer's request pursuant to paragraph (d)(1)(ii) of this section must conform to the form and content requirements for agreements submitted to the Bureau as set forth in paragraph (b)(6) of this section.

(ii) If the issuer posts an agreement on its Web site under paragraph (d)(1)(i) of this section, the agreement may be posted in any electronic format that is readily usable by the general public and must be placed in a location that is prominent and readily accessible to the consumer.

(iii) Agreements posted or otherwise provided pursuant to this paragraph (d) may contain personally identifiable information relating to the consumer, such as name, address, telephone number, or account number, provided that the issuer takes appropriate measures to make the agreement accessible only to the consumer or other authorized persons.

(iv) Agreements posted or otherwise provided pursuant to this paragraph (d) must set forth the specific provisions and fee information applicable to the particular consumer.

(v) Agreements posted pursuant to paragraph (d)(1)(i) of this section must be updated as frequently as the issuer is required to submit amended agreements to the Bureau pursuant to paragraph (b)(2) of this section. Agreements provided upon consumer request pursuant to paragraph (d)(1)(ii) of this section must be accurate as of the date the agreement is sent to the consumer.

(vi) Agreements provided upon consumer request pursuant to paragraph (d)(1)(ii) of this section must be provided by the issuer in paper form, unless the consumer agrees to receive the agreement electronically.

(e) E-Sign Act requirements. Except as otherwise provided in this section, issuers may provide prepaid account agreements in electronic form under paragraphs (c) and (d) of this section without regard to the consumer notice and consent requirements of section 101(c) of the Electronic Signatures in Global and National Commerce Act (E-Sign Act) (15 U.S.C. 7001 et seq.).

(f) Initial submission date. The requirements of this section apply to prepaid accounts beginning on April 1, 2019. An issuer must submit to the Bureau no later than May 1, 2019 all prepaid account agreements it offers as of April 1, 2019.

§ 1005.20 Requirements for gift cards and gift certificates.

(a) Definitions. For purposes of this section, except as excluded under paragraph (b), the following definitions apply:

(1) "Gift certificate" means a card, code, or other device that is:

(i) Issued on a prepaid basis primarily for personal, family, or household purposes to a consumer in a specified amount that may not be increased or reloaded in exchange for payment; and

(ii) Redeemable upon presentation at a single merchant or an affiliated group of merchants for goods or services.

(2) "Store gift card" means a card, code, or other device that is:

(i) Issued on a prepaid basis primarily for personal, family, or household purposes to a consumer in a specified amount, whether or not that amount may be increased or reloaded, in exchange for payment; and

(ii) Redeemable upon presentation at a single merchant or an affiliated group of merchants for goods or services.

(3) "General-use prepaid card" means a card, code, or other device that is:

(i) Issued on a prepaid basis primarily for personal, family, or household purposes to a consumer in a specified amount, whether or not that amount may be increased or reloaded, in exchange for payment; and

(ii) Redeemable upon presentation at multiple, unaffiliated merchants for goods or services, or usable at automated teller machines.

(4) "Loyalty, award, or promotional gift card" means a card, code, or other device that:

(i) Is issued on a prepaid basis primarily for personal, family, or household purposes to a consumer in connection with a loyalty, award, or promotional program;

(ii) Is redeemable upon presentation at one or more merchants for goods or services, or usable at automated teller machines; and

(iii) Sets forth the following disclosures, as applicable:

(A) A statement indicating that the card, code, or other device is issued for loyalty, award, or promotional purposes, which must be included on the front of the card, code, or other device;

(B) The expiration date for the underlying funds, which must be included on the front of the card, code, or other device;

(C) The amount of any fees that may be imposed in connection with the card, code, or other device, and the conditions under which they may be imposed, which must be provided on or with the card, code, or other device; and

(D) A toll-free telephone number and, if one is maintained, a Web site, that a consumer may use to obtain fee information, which must be included on the card, code, or other device.

(5) **Dormancy or inactivity fee.** The terms "dormancy fee" and "inactivity fee" mean a fee for non-use of or inactivity on a gift certificate, store gift card, or general-use prepaid card.

(6) **Service fee.** The term "service fee" means a periodic fee for holding or use of a gift certificate, store gift card, or general-use prepaid card. A periodic fee includes any fee that may be imposed on a gift certificate, store gift card, or general-use prepaid card from time to time for holding or using the certificate or card.

(7) **Activity.** The term "activity" means any action that results in an increase or decrease of the funds underlying a certificate or card, other than the imposition of a fee, or an adjustment due to an error or a reversal of a prior transaction.

(b) **Exclusions.** The terms "gift certificate," "store gift card," and "general-use prepaid card", as defined in paragraph (a) of this section, do not include any card, code, or other device that is:

(1) Useable solely for telephone services;

(2) Reloadable and not marketed or labeled as a gift card or gift certificate. For purposes of this paragraph (b)(2), the term "reloadable" includes a temporary non-reloadable card issued solely in connection with a reloadable card, code, or other device;

(3) A loyalty, award, or promotional gift card;

(4) Not marketed to the general public;

(5) Issued in paper form only; or

(6) Redeemable solely for admission to events or venues at a particular location or group of affiliated locations, or to obtain goods or services in conjunction with admission to such events or venues, either at the event or venue or at specific locations affiliated with and in geographic proximity to the event or venue.

(c) Form of disclosures

(1) Clear and conspicuous. Disclosures made under this section must be clear and conspicuous. The disclosures may contain commonly accepted or readily understandable abbreviations or symbols.

(2) Format. Disclosures made under this section generally must be provided to the consumer in written or electronic form. Except for the disclosures in paragraphs (c)(3) and (h)(2) of this section, written and electronic disclosures made under this section must be in a retainable form. Only disclosures provided under paragraphs (c)(3) and (h)(2) may be given orally.

(3) Disclosures prior to purchase. Before a gift certificate, store gift card, or general-use prepaid card is purchased, a person that issues or sells such certificate or card must disclose to the consumer the information required by paragraphs (d)(2), (e)(3), and (f)(1) of this section. The fees and terms and conditions of expiration that are required to be disclosed prior to purchase may not be changed after purchase.

(4) Disclosures on the certificate or card. Disclosures required by paragraphs (a)(4)(iii), (d)(2), (e)(3), and (f)(2) of this section must be made on the certificate or card, or in the case of a loyalty, award, or promotional gift card, on the card, code, or other device. A disclosure made in an accompanying terms and conditions document, on packaging surrounding a certificate or card, or on a sticker or other label affixed to the certificate or card does not constitute a disclosure on the certificate or card. For an electronic certificate or card, disclosures must be provided electronically on the certificate or card provided to the consumer. An issuer that provides a code or confirmation to a consumer orally must provide to the consumer a written or electronic copy of the code or confirmation promptly, and the applicable disclosures must be provided on the written copy of the code or confirmation.

(d) Prohibition on imposition of fees or charges. No person may impose a dormancy, inactivity, or service fee with respect to a gift certificate, store gift card, or general-use prepaid card, unless:

(1) There has been no activity with respect to the certificate or card, in the one-year period ending on the date on which the fee is imposed;

(2) The following are stated, as applicable, clearly and conspicuously on the gift certificate, store gift card, or general-use prepaid card:

(i) The amount of any dormancy, inactivity, or service fee that may be charged;

(ii) How often such fee may be assessed; and

(iii) That such fee may be assessed for inactivity; and

(3) Not more than one dormancy, inactivity, or service fee is imposed in any given calendar month.

(e) Prohibition on sale of gift certificates or cards with expiration dates. No person may sell or issue a gift certificate, store gift card, or general-use prepaid card with an expiration date, unless:

(1) The person has established policies and procedures to provide consumers with a reasonable opportunity to purchase a certificate or card with at least five years remaining until the certificate or card expiration date;

(2) The expiration date for the underlying funds is at least the later of:

(i) Five years after the date the gift certificate was initially issued, or the date on which funds were last loaded to a store gift card or general-use prepaid card; or

(ii) The certificate or card expiration date, if any;

(3) The following disclosures are provided on the certificate or card, as applicable:

(i) The expiration date for the underlying funds or, if the underlying funds do not expire, that fact;

(ii) A toll-free telephone number and, if one is maintained, a Web site that a consumer may use to obtain a replacement certificate or card after the certificate or card expires if the underlying funds may be available; and

(iii) Except where a non-reloadable certificate or card bears an expiration date that is at least seven years from the date of manufacture, a statement, disclosed with equal prominence and in close proximity to the certificate or card expiration date, that:

(A) The certificate or card expires, but the underlying funds either do not expire or expire later than the certificate or card, and;

(B) The consumer may contact the issuer for a replacement card; and

(4) No fee or charge is imposed on the cardholder for replacing the gift certificate, store gift card, or general-use prepaid card or for providing the certificate or card holder with the remaining balance in some other manner prior to the funds expiration date, unless such certificate or card has been lost or stolen.

(f) Additional disclosure requirements for gift certificates or cards. The following disclosures must be provided in connection with a gift certificate, store gift card, or general-use prepaid card, as applicable:

(1) Fee disclosures. For each type of fee that may be imposed in connection with the certificate or card (other than a dormancy, inactivity, or service fee subject to the disclosure requirements under paragraph (d)(2) of this section), the following information must be provided on or with the certificate or card:

(i) The type of fee;

(ii) The amount of the fee (or an explanation of how the fee will be determined); and

(iii) The conditions under which the fee may be imposed.

(2) Telephone number for fee information. A toll-free telephone number and, if one is maintained, a Web site, that a consumer may use to obtain information about fees described in paragraphs (d)(2) and (f)(1) of this section must be disclosed on the certificate or card.

(g) Compliance dates.

(1) Effective date for gift certificates, store gift cards, and general-use prepaid cards. Except as provided in paragraph (h) of this section, the requirements of this section apply to any gift certificate, store gift card, or general-use prepaid card sold to a consumer on or after August 22, 2010, or provided to a consumer as a replacement for such certificate or card.

(2) Effective date for loyalty, award, or promotional gift cards. The requirements in paragraph (a)(4)(iii) of this section apply to any card, code, or other device provided to a consumer in connection with a loyalty, award, or promotional program if the period of eligibility for such program began on or after August 22, 2010.

(h) Temporary exemption.

(1) Delayed mandatory compliance date. For any gift certificate, store gift card, or general-use prepaid card produced prior to April 1, 2010, the mandatory compliance date of the requirements of paragraphs (c)(3), (d)(2), (e)(1), (e)(3), and (f) of this section is January 31, 2011, provided that an issuer of such certificate or card:

(i) Complies with all other provisions of this section;

(ii) Does not impose an expiration date with respect to the funds underlying such certificate or card;

(iii) At the consumer's request, replaces such certificate or card if it has funds remaining at no cost to the consumer; and

(iv) Satisfies the requirements of paragraph (h)(2) of this section.

(2) Additional disclosures. Issuers relying on the delayed effective date in § 1005.20(h)(1) must disclose through in-store signage, messages during customer service calls, Web sites, and general advertising, that:

(i) The underlying funds of such certificate or card do not expire;

(ii) Consumers holding such certificate or card have a right to a free replacement certificate or card, which must be accompanied by the packaging and materials typically associated with such certificate or card; and

(iii) Any dormancy, inactivity, or service fee for such certificate or card that might otherwise be charged will not be charged if such fees do not comply with section 916 of the Act.

(3) Expiration of additional disclosure requirements. The disclosures in paragraph (h)(2) of this section:

(i) Are not required to be provided on or after January 31, 2011, with respect to in-store signage and general advertising.

(ii) Are not required to be provided on or after January 31, 2013, with respect to messages during customer service calls and Web sites.

SUBPART B—REQUIREMENTS FOR REMITTANCE TRANSFERS

§ 1005.30 Remittance transfer definitions.

Except as otherwise provided, for purposes of the subpart, the following definitions apply:

(a) "Agent" means an agent, authorized delegate, or person affiliated with a remittance transfer provider, as defined under State or other applicable law, when such agent, authorized delegate, or affiliate acts for that remittance transfer provider.

(b) "Business day" means any day on which the offices of a remittance transfer provider are open to the public for carrying on substantially all business functions.

(c) "Designated recipient" means any person specified by the sender as the authorized recipient of a remittance transfer to be received at a location in a foreign country.

(d) "Preauthorized remittance transfer" means a remittance transfer authorized in advance to recur at substantially regular intervals.

(e) Remittance transfer.

(1) General definition. A "remittance transfer" means the electronic transfer of funds requested by a sender to a designated recipient that is sent by a remittance transfer provider. The term applies regardless of whether the sender holds an account with the remittance transfer provider, and regardless of whether the transaction is also an electronic fund transfer, as defined in § 1005.3(b).

(2) Exclusions from coverage. The term "remittance transfer" does not include:

(i) Small value transactions. Transfer amounts, as described in § 1005.31(b)(1)(i), of $15 or less.

(ii) Securities and commodities transfers. Any transfer that is excluded from the definition of electronic fund transfer under § 1005.3(c)(4).

(f) Remittance transfer provider.

(1) General definition. "Remittance transfer provider" or "provider" means any person that provides remittance transfers for a consumer in the normal course of its business, regardless of whether the consumer holds an account with such person.

(2) Normal course of business.

(i) Safe harbor. For purposes of paragraph (f)(1) of this section, a person is deemed not to be providing remittance transfers for a consumer in the normal course of its business if the person:

(A) Provided 100 or fewer remittance transfers in the previous calendar year; and

(B) Provides 100 or fewer remittance transfers in the current calendar year.

(ii) Transition period. If a person that provided 100 or fewer remittance transfers in the previous calendar year provides more than 100 remittance transfers in the current calendar year, and if that person is then providing remittance transfers for a consumer in the normal course of its business pursuant to paragraph (f)(1) of this section, the person has a reasonable period of time, not to exceed six months, to begin complying with this subpart. Compliance with this subpart will not be required for any remittance transfers for which payment is made during that reasonable period of time.

(g) "Sender" means a consumer in a State who primarily for personal, family, or household purposes requests a remittance transfer provider to send a remittance transfer to a designated recipient.

(h) Third-party fees. (1) "Covered third-party fees." The term "covered third-party fees" means any fees imposed on the remittance transfer by a person other than the remittance transfer provider except for fees described in paragraph (h)(2) of this section.

(2) "Non-covered third-party fees." The term "non-covered third-party fees" means any fees imposed by the designated recipient's institution for receiving a remittance transfer into an account except if the institution acts as an agent of the remittance transfer provider.

§ 1005.31 Disclosures.

(a) General form of disclosures.

(1) Clear and conspicuous. Disclosures required by this subpart or permitted by paragraph (b)(1)(viii) of this section or § 1005.33(h)(3) must be clear and conspicuous. Disclosures required by this subpart or permitted by paragraph (b)(1)(viii) of this section or § 1005.33(h)(3) may contain commonly accepted or readily understandable abbreviations or symbols.

(2) Written and electronic disclosures. Disclosures required by this subpart generally must be provided to the sender in writing. Disclosures required by paragraph (b)(1) of this section may be provided electronically, if the sender electronically requests the remittance transfer provider to send the remittance transfer. Written and electronic disclosures required by this subpart generally must be made in a retainable form. Disclosures provided via mobile application or text message, to the extent permitted by paragraph (a)(5) of this section, need not be retainable.

(3) Disclosures for oral telephone transactions. The information required by paragraph (b)(1) of this section may be disclosed orally if:

(i) The transaction is conducted orally and entirely by telephone;

(ii) The remittance transfer provider complies with the requirements of paragraph (g)(2) of this section;

(iii) The provider discloses orally a statement about the rights of the sender regarding cancellation required by paragraph (b)(2)(iv) of this section pursuant to the timing requirements in paragraph (e)(1) of this section; and

(iv) The provider discloses orally, as each is applicable, the information required by paragraph (b)(2)(vii) of this section and the information required by § 1005.36(d)(1)(i)(A), with respect to transfers subject to § 1005.36(d)(2)(ii), pursuant to the timing requirements in paragraph (e)(1) of this section.

(4) Oral disclosures for certain error resolution notices. The information required by § 1005.33(c)(1) may be disclosed orally if:

(i) The remittance transfer provider determines that an error occurred as described by the sender; and

(ii) The remittance transfer provider complies with the requirements of paragraph (g)(2) of this section.

(5) Disclosures for mobile application or text message transactions. The information required by paragraph (b)(1) of this section may be disclosed orally or via mobile application or text message if:

(i) The transaction is conducted entirely by telephone via mobile application or text message;

(ii) The remittance transfer provider complies with the requirements of paragraph (g)(2) of this section; and

(iii) The provider discloses orally or via mobile application or text message a statement about the rights of the sender regarding cancellation required by paragraph (b)(2)(iv) of this section pursuant to the timing requirements in paragraph (e)(1) of this section; and

(iv) The provider discloses orally or via mobile application or text message, as each is applicable, the information required by paragraph (b)(2)(vii) of this section and the information required by § 1005.36(d)(1)(i)(A), with respect to transfers subject to § 1005.36(d)(2)(ii), pursuant to the timing requirements in paragraph (e)(1) of this section.

(b) Disclosure requirements.

(1) Pre-payment disclosure. A remittance transfer provider must disclose to a sender, as applicable:

(i) The amount that will be transferred to the designated recipient, in the currency in which the remittance transfer is funded, using the term "Transfer Amount" or a substantially similar term;

(ii) Any fees and any taxes collected on the remittance transfer by the provider, in the currency in which the remittance transfer is funded, using the terms "Transfer Fees" for fees and "Transfer Taxes" for taxes, or substantially similar terms;

(iii) The total amount of the transaction, which is the sum of paragraphs (b)(1)(i) and (ii) of this section, in the currency in which the remittance transfer is funded, using the term "Total" or a substantially similar term;

(iv) The exchange rate used by the provider for the remittance transfer, rounded consistently for each currency to no fewer than two decimal places and no more than four decimal places, using the term "Exchange Rate" or a substantially similar term;

(v) The amount in paragraph (b)(1)(i) of this section, in the currency in which the funds will be received by the designated recipient, but only if covered third-party fees are imposed under paragraph (b)(1)(vi) of this section, using the term "Transfer Amount" or a substantially similar term. The exchange rate used to calculate this amount is the exchange rate in paragraph (b)(1)(iv) of this section, including an estimated exchange rate to the extent permitted by § 1005.32, prior to any rounding of the exchange rate;

(vi) Any covered third-party fees, in the currency in which the funds will be received by the designated recipient, using the term "Other Fees," or a substantially similar term. The exchange rate used to calculate any covered third-party fees is the exchange rate in paragraph (b)(1)(iv) of this section, including an estimated exchange rate to the extent permitted by § 1005.32, prior to any rounding of the exchange rate;

(vii) The amount that will be received by the designated recipient, in the currency in which the funds will be received, using the term "Total to Recipient" or a substantially similar term except that this amount shall not include non-covered third party fees or taxes collected on the remittance transfer by a person other than the provider regardless of whether such fees or taxes are disclosed pursuant to paragraph (b)(1)(viii) of this section. The exchange rate used to calculate this amount is the exchange rate in paragraph (b)(1)(iv) of this section, including an estimated exchange rate to the extent permitted by § 1005.32, prior to any rounding of the exchange rate.

(viii) A statement indicating that non-covered third-party fees or taxes collected on the remittance transfer by a person other than the provider may apply to the remittance transfer and result in the designated recipient receiving less than the amount disclosed pursuant to paragraph (b)(1)(vii) of this section. A provider may only include this statement to the extent that such fees or taxes do or may apply to the transfer, using the language set forth in Model Forms A-30(a) through (c) of Appendix A to this part, as appropriate, or substantially similar language. In this statement, a provider also may, but is not required, to disclose any applicable non-covered third-party fees or taxes collected by a person other than the provider. Any such figure must be disclosed in the currency in which the funds will be received, using the language set forth in Model Forms A-30(b) through (d) of Appendix A to this part, as appropriate, or substantially similar language. The exchange rate used to calculate any disclosed non-covered third-party fees or taxes collected on the remittance transfer by a person other than the provider is the exchange rate in paragraph (b)(1)(iv) of this section, including an estimated exchange rate to the extent permitted by § 1005.32, prior to any rounding of the exchange rate;

(2) Receipt. A remittance transfer provider must disclose to a sender, as applicable:

(i) The disclosures described in paragraphs (b)(1)(i) through (viii) of this section;

(ii) The date in the foreign country on which funds will be available to the designated recipient, using the term "Date Available" or a substantially similar term. A provider may provide a statement that funds may be available to the designated recipient earlier than the date disclosed, using the term "may be available sooner" or a substantially similar term;

(iii) The name and, if provided by the sender, the telephone number and/or address of the designated recipient, using the term "Recipient" or a substantially similar term;

(iv) A statement about the rights of the sender regarding the resolution of errors and cancellation, using language set forth in Model Form A-37 of Appendix A to this part or substantially similar language. For any remittance transfer scheduled by the sender at least three business days before the date of the transfer, the statement about the rights of the sender regarding cancellation must instead reflect the requirements of § 1005.36(c);

(v) The name, telephone number(s), and Web site of the remittance transfer provider;

(vi) A statement that the sender can contact the State agency that licenses or charters the remittance transfer provider with respect to the remittance transfer and the Consumer Financial Protection Bureau for questions or complaints about the remittance transfer provider, using language set forth in Model Form A-37 of Appendix A to this part or substantially similar language. The disclosure must provide the name, telephone number(s), and Web site of the State agency that licenses or charters the remittance transfer provider with respect to the remittance transfer and the name, toll-free telephone number(s), and Web site of the Consumer Financial Protection Bureau; and

(vii) For any remittance transfer scheduled by the sender at least three business days before the date of the transfer, or the first transfer in a series of preauthorized remittance transfers, the date the remittance transfer provider will make or made the remittance transfer, using the term "Transfer Date," or a substantially similar term.

(3) Combined disclosure—(i) In general. As an alternative to providing the disclosures described in paragraph (b)(1) and (2) of this section, a remittance transfer provider may provide the disclosures described in paragraph (b)(2) of this section, as applicable, in a single disclosure pursuant to the timing requirements in paragraph (e)(1) of this section. Except as provided in paragraph (b)(3)(ii) of this section, if the remittance transfer provider provides the combined disclosure and the sender completes the transfer, the remittance transfer provider must provide the sender with proof of payment when payment is made for the remittance transfer. The proof of payment must be clear and conspicuous, provided in writing or electronically, and provided in a retainable form.

(ii) Transfers scheduled before the date of transfer. If the disclosure described in paragraph (b)(3)(i) of this section is provided in accordance with § 1005.36(a)(1)(i) and payment is not processed by the remittance transfer provider at the time the remittance transfer is scheduled, a remittance transfer provider may provide confirmation that the transaction has been scheduled in lieu of the proof of payment otherwise required by paragraph (b)(3)(i) of this section. The confirmation of scheduling must be clear and conspicuous, provided in writing or electronically, and provided in a retainable form.

(4) Long form error resolution and cancellation notice. Upon the sender's request, a remittance transfer provider must promptly provide to the sender a notice describing the sender's error resolution and cancellation rights, using language set forth in Model Form A-36 of Appendix A to this part or substantially similar language. For any remittance transfer scheduled by the sender at least three business days before the date of the transfer, the description of the rights of the sender regarding cancellation must instead reflect the requirements of § 1005.36(c).

(c) Specific format requirements.

(1) Grouping. The information required by paragraphs (b)(1)(i), (ii), and (iii) of this section generally must be grouped together. The information required by paragraphs (b)(1)(v), (vi), (vii), and (viii) of this section generally must be grouped together. Disclosures provided via mobile application or text message, to the extent permitted by paragraph (a)(5) of this section, generally need not comply with the grouping requirements of this paragraph, however information required or permitted by paragraph (b)(1)(viii) of this section must be grouped with information required by paragraph (b)(1)(vii) of this section.

(2) Proximity. The information required by paragraph (b)(1)(iv) of this section generally must be disclosed in close proximity to the other information required by paragraph (b)(1) of this section. The information required by paragraph (b)(2)(iv) of this section generally must be disclosed in close proximity to the other information required by paragraph (b)(2) of this section. The information required or permitted by paragraph (b)(1)(viii) must be in close proximity to the information required by paragraph (b)(1)(vii) of this section. Disclosures provided via mobile application or text message, to the extent permitted by paragraph (a)(5) of this section, generally need not comply with the proximity requirements of this paragraph, however information required or permitted by paragraph (b)(1)(viii) of this section must follow the information required by paragraph (b)(1)(vii) of this section.

(3) Prominence and size. Written disclosures required by this subpart or permitted by paragraph (b)(1)(viii) of this section must be provided on the front of the page on which the disclosure is printed. Disclosures required by this subpart or permitted by paragraph (b)(1)(viii) of this section that are provided in writing or electronically must be in a minimum eight-point font, except for disclosures provided via mobile application or text message, to the extent permitted by paragraph (a)(5) of this section. Disclosures required by paragraph (b) of this section or permitted by paragraph (b)(1)(viii) of this section that are provided in writing or electronically must be in equal prominence to each other.

(4) Segregation. Except for disclosures provided via mobile application or text message, to the extent permitted by paragraph (a)(5) of this section, disclosures required by this subpart that are provided in writing or electronically must be segregated from everything else and must contain only information that is directly related to the disclosures required under this subpart.

(d) Estimates. Estimated disclosures may be provided to the extent permitted by § 1005.32. Estimated disclosures must be described using the term "Estimated" or a substantially similar term in close proximity to the estimated term or terms.

(e) Timing.

(1) Except as provided in § 1005.36(a), a pre-payment disclosure required by paragraph (b)(1) of this section or a combined disclosure required by paragraph (b)(3) of this section must be provided to the sender when the sender requests the remittance transfer, but prior to payment for the transfer.

(2) Except as provided in § 1005.36(a), a receipt required by paragraph (b)(2) of this section generally must be provided to the sender when payment is made for the remittance transfer. If a transaction is conducted entirely by telephone, a receipt required by paragraph (b)(2) of this section may be mailed or delivered to the sender no later than one business day after the date on which payment is made for the remittance transfer. If a transaction is conducted entirely by telephone and involves the transfer of funds from the sender's account held by the provider, the receipt required by paragraph (b)(2) of this section may be provided on or with the next regularly scheduled periodic statement for that account or within 30 days after payment is made for the remittance transfer if a periodic statement is not provided. The statement about the rights of the sender regarding cancellation required by paragraph (b)(2)(iv) of this section may, but need not, be disclosed pursuant to the timing requirements of this paragraph if a provider discloses this information pursuant to paragraphs (a)(3)(iii) or (a)(5)(iii) of this section.

(f) Accurate when payment is made. Except as provided in § 1005.36(b), disclosures required by this section or permitted by paragraph (b)(1)(viii) of this section must be accurate when a sender makes payment for the remittance transfer, except to the extent estimates are permitted by § 1005.32.

(g) Foreign language disclosures.

(1) General. Except as provided in paragraph (g)(2) of this section, disclosures required by this subpart or permitted by paragraph (b)(1)(viii) of this section or § 1005.33(h)(3) must be made in English and, if applicable, either in:

(i) Each of the foreign languages principally used by the remittance transfer provider to advertise, solicit, or market remittance transfer services, either orally, in writing, or electronically, at the office in which a sender conducts a transaction or asserts an error; or

(ii) The foreign language primarily used by the sender with the remittance transfer provider to conduct the transaction (or for written or electronic disclosures made pursuant to § 1005.33, in the foreign language primarily used by the sender with the remittance transfer provider to assert the error), provided that such foreign language is principally used by the remittance transfer provider to advertise, solicit, or market remittance transfer services, either orally, in writing, or electronically, at the office in which a sender conducts a transaction or asserts an error, respectively.

(2) Oral, mobile application, or text message disclosures. Disclosures provided orally for transactions conducted orally and entirely by telephone under paragraph (a)(3) of this section or orally or via mobile application or text message for transactions conducted via mobile application or text message under paragraph (a)(5) of this section shall be made in the language primarily used by the sender with the remittance transfer provider to conduct the transaction. Disclosures provided orally under paragraph (a)(4) of this section for error resolution purposes shall be made in the language primarily used by the sender with the remittance transfer provider to assert the error.

§ 1005.32 Estimates.

(a) Temporary exception for insured institutions.

(1) General. For disclosures described in §§ 1005.31(b)(1) through (3) and 1005.36(a)(1) and (2), estimates may be provided in accordance with paragraph (c) of this section for the amounts required to be disclosed under § 1005.31(b)(1)(iv) through (vii), if:

(i) A remittance transfer provider cannot determine the exact amounts for reasons beyond its control;

(ii) A remittance transfer provider is an insured institution; and

(iii) The remittance transfer is sent from the sender's account with the institution; provided however, for the purposes of this paragraph, a sender's account does not include a prepaid account, unless the prepaid account is a payroll card account or a government benefit account.

(2) Sunset date. Paragraph (a)(1) of this section expires on July 21, 2020.

(3) Insured institution. For purposes of this section, the term "insured institution" means insured depository institutions (which includes uninsured U.S. branches and agencies of foreign depository institutions) as defined in section 3 of the Federal Deposit Insurance Act (12 U.S.C. 1813), and insured credit unions as defined in section 101 of the Federal Credit Union Act (12 U.S.C. 1752).

(b) Permanent exceptions.

(1) Permanent exception for transfers to certain countries.

(i) General. For disclosures described in §§ 1005.31(b)(1) through (b)(3) and 1005.36(a)(1) and (a)(2), estimates may be provided for transfers to certain countries in accordance with paragraph (c) of this section for the amounts required to be disclosed under § 1005.31(b)(1)(iv) through (b)(1)(vii), if a remittance transfer provider cannot determine the exact amounts when the disclosure is required because:

(A) The laws of the recipient country do not permit such a determination, or

(B) The method by which transactions are made in the recipient country does not permit such determination.

(ii) Safe harbor. A remittance transfer provider may rely on the list of countries published by the Bureau to determine whether estimates may be provided under paragraph (b)(1) of this section, unless the provider has information that a country's laws or the method by which transactions are conducted in that country permits a determination of the exact disclosure amount.

(2) Permanent exception for transfers scheduled before the date of transfer.

(i) Except as provided in paragraph (b)(2)(ii) of this section, for disclosures described in §§ 1005.36(a)(1)(i) and (a)(2)(i), estimates may be provided in accordance with paragraph (d) of this section for the amounts to be disclosed under §§ 1005.31(b)(1)(iv) through (vii) if the remittance transfer is scheduled by a sender five or more business days before the date of the transfer. In addition, if, at the time the sender schedules such a transfer, the provider agrees to a sender's request to fix the amount to be transferred in the currency in which the remittance transfer will be received and not the currency in which it is funded, estimates may also be provided for the amounts to be disclosed under §§ 1005.31(b)(1)(i) through (iii), except as provided in paragraph (b)(2)(iii) of this section.

(ii) Fees and taxes described in § 1005.31(b)(1)(vi) may be estimated under paragraph (b)(2)(i) of this section only if the exchange rate is also estimated under paragraph (b)(2)(i) and the estimated exchange rate affects the amount of such fees and taxes.

(iii) Covered third-party fees described in § 1005.31(b)(1)(ii) may be estimated under paragraph (b)(2)(i) of this section only if the amount that will be transferred in the currency in which it is funded is also estimated under paragraph (b)(2)(i) of this section, and the estimated amount affects the amount of such fees.

(3) Permanent exception for optional disclosure of non-covered third-party fees and taxes collected by a person other than the provider. For disclosures described in §§ 1005.31(b)(1) through (3) and 1005.36(a)(1) and (2), estimates may be provided for applicable non-covered third-party fees and taxes collected on the remittance transfer by a person other than the provider, which are permitted to be disclosed under § 1005.31(b)(1)(viii), provided such estimates are based on reasonable sources of information.

(c) Bases for estimates generally. Estimates provided pursuant to the exceptions in paragraph (a) or (b)(1) of this section must be based on the below-listed approach or approaches, except as otherwise permitted by this paragraph. If a remittance transfer provider bases an estimate on an approach that is not listed in this paragraph, the provider is deemed to be in compliance with this paragraph so long as the designated recipient receives the same, or greater, amount of funds than the remittance transfer provider disclosed under § 1005.31(b)(1)(vii).

(1) Exchange rate. In disclosing the exchange rate as required under 1005.31(b)(1)(iv), an estimate must be based on one of the following:

(i) For remittance transfers sent via international ACH that qualify for the exception in paragraph (b)(1)(ii) of this section, the most recent exchange rate set by the recipient country's central bank or other governmental authority and reported by a Federal Reserve Bank;

(ii) The most recent publicly available wholesale exchange rate and, if applicable, any spread that the remittance transfer provider or its correspondent typically applies to such a wholesale rate for remittance transfers for that currency; or

(iii) The most recent exchange rate offered or used by the person making funds available directly to the designated recipient or by the person setting the exchange rate.

(2) Transfer amount in the currency in which the funds will be received by the designated recipient. In disclosing the transfer amount in the currency in which the funds will be received by the designated recipient, as required under § 1005.31(b)(1)(v), an estimate must be based on the estimated exchange rate provided in accordance with paragraph (c)(1) of this section, prior to any rounding of the estimated exchange rate.

(3) Other fees. (i) Imposed as percentage of amount transferred. In disclosing covered third-party fees as required under § 1005.31(b)(1)(vi) that are a percentage of the amount transferred to the designated recipient, an estimated exchange rate must be based on the estimated exchange rate provided in accordance with paragraph (c)(1) of this section, prior to any rounding of the estimated exchange rate.

(ii) Imposed by intermediary or final institution. In disclosing covered third-party fees pursuant to § 1005.31(b)(1)(vi), an estimate must be based on one of the following:

(A) The remittance transfer provider's most recent remittance transfer to the designated recipient's institution, or

(B) A representative transmittal route identified by the remittance transfer provider.

(4) Other taxes imposed in the recipient country. In disclosing taxes imposed in the recipient country as required under § 1005.31(b)(1)(vi) that are a percentage of the amount transferred to the designated recipient, an estimate must be based on the estimated exchange rate provided in accordance with paragraph (c)(1) of this section, prior to any rounding of the estimated exchange rate, and the estimated fees provided in accordance with paragraph (c)(3) of this section.

(5) Amount of currency that will be received by the designated recipient. In disclosing the amount of currency that will be received by the designated recipient as required under § 1005.31(b)(1)(vii), an estimate must be based on the information provided in accordance with paragraphs (c)(1) through (3) of this section, as applicable.

(d) Bases for estimates for transfers scheduled before the date of transfer. Estimates provided pursuant to paragraph (b)(2) of this section must be based on the exchange rate or, where applicable, the estimated exchange rate based on an estimation methodology permitted under paragraph (c) of this section that the provider would have used or did use that day in providing disclosures to a sender requesting such a remittance transfer to be made on the same day. If, in accordance with this paragraph, a remittance transfer provider uses a basis described in paragraph (c) of this section but not listed in paragraph (c)(1) of this section, the provider is deemed to be in compliance with this paragraph regardless of the amount received by the designated recipient, so long as the estimation methodology is the same that the provider would have used or did use in providing disclosures to a sender requesting such a remittance transfer to be made on the same day.

§ 1005.33 Procedures for resolving errors.

(a) Definition of error.

(1) Types of transfers or inquiries covered. For purposes of this section, the term error means:

(i) An incorrect amount paid by a sender in connection with a remittance transfer unless the disclosure stated an estimate of the amount paid by a sender in accordance with § 1005.32(b)(2) and the difference results from application of the actual exchange rate, fees, and taxes, rather than any estimated amount;

(ii) A computational or bookkeeping error made by the remittance transfer provider relating to a remittance transfer;

(iii) The failure to make available to a designated recipient the amount of currency disclosed pursuant to § 1005.31(b)(2) or (3) for the remittance transfer, unless:

(A) The disclosure stated an estimate of the amount to be received in accordance with § 1005.32(a), (b)(1), or (b)(2) and the difference results from application of the actual exchange rate, fees, and taxes, rather than any estimated amounts; or

(B) The failure resulted from extraordinary circumstances outside the remittance transfer provider's control that could not have been reasonably anticipated; or

(C) The difference results from the application of non-covered third-party fees or taxes collected on the remittance transfer by a person other than the provider and the provider provided the disclosure required by § 1005.31(b)(1)(viii).

(iv) The failure to make funds available to a designated recipient by the date of availability stated in the disclosure provided to the sender under § 1005.31(b)(2) or (3) for the remittance transfer, unless the failure to make the funds available resulted from:

(A) Extraordinary circumstances outside the remittance transfer provider's control that could not have been reasonably anticipated;

(B) Delays related to a necessary investigation or other special action by the remittance transfer provider or a third party as required by the provider's fraud screening procedures or in accordance with the Bank Secrecy Act, 31 U.S.C. 5311 et seq., Office of Foreign Assets Control requirements, or similar laws or requirements;

(C) The remittance transfer being made with fraudulent intent by the sender or any person acting in concert with the sender; or

(D) The sender having provided the remittance transfer provider an incorrect account number or recipient institution identifier for the designated recipient's account or institution, provided that the remittance transfer provider meets the conditions set forth in paragraph (h) of this section;

(v) The sender's request for documentation required by § 1005.31 or for additional information or clarification concerning a remittance transfer, including a request a sender makes to determine whether an error exists under paragraphs (a)(1)(i) through (iv) of this section.

(2) Types of transfers or inquiries not covered. The term error does not include:

(i) An inquiry about the status of a remittance transfer, except where the funds from the transfer were not made available to a designated recipient by the disclosed date of availability as described in paragraph (a)(1)(iv) of this section;

(ii) A request for information for tax or other recordkeeping purposes;

(iii) A change requested by the designated recipient; or

(iv) A change in the amount or type of currency received by the designated recipient from the amount or type of currency stated in the disclosure provided to the sender under § 1005.31(b)(2) or (3) if the remittance transfer provider relied on information provided by the sender as permitted under § 1005.31 in making such disclosure.

(b) Notice of error from sender.

(1) Timing; contents. A remittance transfer provider shall comply with the requirements of this section with respect to any oral or written notice of error from a sender that:

(i) Is received by the remittance transfer provider no later than 180 days after the disclosed date of availability of the remittance transfer;

(ii) Enables the provider to identify:

(A) The sender's name and telephone number or address;

(B) The recipient's name, and if known, the telephone number or address of the recipient; and

(C) The remittance transfer to which the notice of error applies; and

(iii) Indicates why the sender believes an error exists and includes to the extent possible the type, date, and amount of the error, except for requests for documentation, additional information, or clarification described in paragraph (a)(1)(v) of this section.

(2) Request for documentation or clarification. When a notice of error is based on documentation, additional information, or clarification that the sender previously requested under paragraph (a)(1)(v) of this section, the sender's notice of error is timely if received by the remittance transfer provider the later of 180 days after the disclosed date of availability of the remittance transfer or 60 days after the provider sent the documentation, information, or clarification that had been requested.

(c) Time limits and extent of investigation.

(1) Time limits for investigation and report to consumer of error. A remittance transfer provider shall investigate promptly and determine whether an error occurred within 90 days of receiving a notice of error. The remittance transfer provider shall report the results to the sender, including notice of any remedies available for correcting any error that the provider determines has occurred, within three business days after completing its investigation.

(2) Remedies. Except as provided in paragraph (c)(2)(iii) of this section, if, following an assertion of an error by a sender, the remittance transfer provider determines an error occurred, the provider shall, within one business day of, or as soon as reasonably practicable after, receiving the sender's instructions regarding the appropriate remedy, correct the error as designated by the sender by:

(i) In the case of any error under paragraphs (a)(1)(i) through (iii) of this section, as applicable, either:

(A) Refunding to the sender the amount of funds provided by the sender in connection with a remittance transfer which was not properly transmitted, or the amount appropriate to resolve the error; or

(B) Making available to the designated recipient, without additional cost to the sender or to the designated recipient, the amount appropriate to resolve the error;

(ii) Except as provided in paragraph (c)(2)(iii), in the case of an error under paragraph (a)(1)(iv) of this section:

(A) As applicable, either:

(1) Refunding to the sender the amount of funds provided by the sender in connection with a remittance transfer which was not properly transmitted, or the amount appropriate to resolve the error; or

(2) Making available to the designated recipient the amount appropriate to resolve the error. Such amount must be made available to the designated recipient without additional cost to the sender or to the designated recipient; and

(B) Refunding to the sender any fees imposed and, to the extent not prohibited by law, taxes collected on the remittance transfer;

(iii) In the case of an error under paragraph (a)(1)(iv) of this section that occurred because the sender provided incorrect or insufficient information in connection with the remittance transfer, the remittance transfer provider shall provide the remedies required by paragraphs (c)(2)(ii)(A)(1) and (c)(2)(ii)(B) of this section within three business days of providing the report required by paragraph (c)(1) or (d)(1) of this section except that the provider may agree to the sender's request, upon receiving the results of the error investigation, that the funds be applied towards a new remittance transfer, rather than be refunded, if the provider has not yet processed a refund. The provider may deduct from the amount refunded or applied towards a new transfer any fees actually imposed on or, to the extent not prohibited by law, taxes actually collected on the remittance transfer as part of the first unsuccessful remittance transfer attempt, except that the provider shall not deduct its own fee.

(d) Procedures if remittance transfer provider determines no error or different error occurred. In addition to following the procedures specified in paragraph (c) of this section, the remittance transfer provider shall follow the procedures set forth in this paragraph (d) if it determines that no error occurred or that an error occurred in a manner or amount different from that described by the sender.

(1) Explanation of results of investigation. The remittance transfer provider's report of the results of the investigation shall include a written explanation of the provider's findings and shall note the sender's right to request the documents on which the provider relied in making its determination. The explanation shall also address the specific complaint of the sender.

(2) Copies of documentation. Upon the sender's request, the remittance transfer provider shall promptly provide copies of the documents on which the provider relied in making its error determination.

(e) Reassertion of error. A remittance transfer provider that has fully complied with the error resolution requirements of this section has no further responsibilities under this section should the sender later reassert the same error, except in the case of an error asserted by the sender following receipt of information provided under paragraph (a)(1)(v) of this section.

(f) Relation to other laws—(1) Relation to Regulation E § 1005.11 for incorrect EFTs from a sender's account. If an alleged error involves an incorrect electronic fund transfer from a sender's account in connection with a remittance transfer, and the sender provides a notice of error to the account-holding institution, the account-holding institution shall comply with the requirements of § 1005.11 governing error resolution rather than the requirements of this section, provided that the account-holding institution is not also the remittance transfer provider. If the remittance transfer provider is also the financial institution that holds the consumer's account, then the error-resolution provisions of this section apply when the sender provides such notice of error.

(2) Relation to Truth in Lending Act and Regulation Z. If an alleged error involves an incorrect extension of credit in connection with a remittance transfer, an incorrect amount received by the designated recipient under paragraph (a)(1)(iii) of this section that is an extension of credit for property or services not delivered as agreed, or the failure to make funds available by the disclosed date of availability under paragraph (a)(1)(iv) of this section that is an extension of credit for property or services not delivered as agreed, and the sender provides a notice of error to the creditor extending the credit, the provisions of Regulation Z, 12 CFR 1026.13, governing error resolution apply to the creditor, rather than the requirements of this section, even if the creditor is the remittance transfer provider. However, if the creditor is the remittance transfer provider, paragraph (b) of this section will apply instead of 12 CFR 1026.13(b). If the sender instead provides a notice of error to the remittance transfer provider that is not also the creditor, then the error-resolution provisions of this section apply to the remittance transfer provider.

(3) Unauthorized remittance transfers. If an alleged error involves an unauthorized electronic fund transfer for payment in connection with a remittance transfer, §§ 1005.6 and 1005.11 apply with respect to the account-holding institution. If an alleged error involves an unauthorized use of a credit account for payment in connection with a remittance transfer, the provisions of Regulation Z, 12 CFR 1026.12(b), if applicable, and § 1026.13, apply with respect to the creditor.

(g) Error resolution standards and recordkeeping requirements.

(1) Compliance program. A remittance transfer provider shall develop and maintain written policies and procedures that are designed to ensure compliance with the error resolution requirements applicable to remittance transfers under this section.

(2) Retention of error-related documentation. The remittance transfer provider's policies and procedures required under paragraph (g)(1) of this section shall include policies and procedures regarding the retention of documentation related to error investigations. Such policies and procedures must ensure, at a minimum, the retention of any notices of error submitted by a sender, documentation provided by the sender to the provider with respect to the alleged error, and the findings of the remittance transfer provider regarding the investigation of the alleged error. Remittance transfer providers are subject to the record retention requirements under § 1005.13.

(h) Incorrect account number or recipient institution identifier provided by the sender. The exception in paragraph (a)(1)(iv)(D) of this section applies if:

(1) The remittance transfer provider can demonstrate that the sender provided an incorrect account number or recipient institution identifier to the provider in connection with the remittance transfer;

(2) For any instance in which the sender provided the incorrect recipient institution identifier, prior to or when sending the transfer, the provider used reasonably available means to verify that the recipient institution identifier provided by the sender corresponded to the recipient institution name provided by the sender;

(3) The provider provided notice to the sender before the sender made payment for the remittance transfer that, in the event the sender provided an incorrect account number or recipient institution identifier, the sender could lose the transfer amount. For purposes of providing this disclosure, § 1005.31(a)(2) applies to this notice unless the notice is given at the same time as other disclosures required by this subpart for which information is permitted to be disclosed orally or via mobile application or text message, in which case this disclosure may be given in the same medium as those other disclosures;

(4) The incorrect account number or recipient institution identifier resulted in the deposit of the remittance transfer into a customer's account that is not the designated recipient's account; and

(5) The provider promptly used reasonable efforts to recover the amount that was to be received by the designated recipient.

§ 1005.34 Procedures for cancellation and refund of remittance transfers.

(a) Sender right of cancellation and refund. Except as provided in 1005.36(c), a remittance transfer provider shall comply with the requirements of this section with respect to any oral or written request to cancel a remittance transfer from the sender that is received by the provider no later than 30 minutes after the sender makes payment in connection with the remittance transfer if:

(1) The request to cancel enables the provider to identify the sender's name and address or telephone number and the particular transfer to be cancelled; and

(2) The transferred funds have not been picked up by the designated recipient or deposited into an account of the designated recipient.

(b) Time limits and refund requirements. A remittance transfer provider shall refund, at no additional cost to the sender, the total amount of funds provided by the sender in connection with a remittance transfer, including any fees and, to the extent not prohibited by law, taxes imposed in connection with the remittance transfer, within three business days of receiving a sender's request to cancel the remittance transfer.

§ 1005.35 Acts of agents.

A remittance transfer provider is liable for any violation of this subpart by an agent when such agent acts for the provider.

§ 1005.36 Transfers scheduled before the date of transfer.

(a) Timing.

(1) For a one-time transfer scheduled five or more business days before the date of transfer or for the first in a series of preauthorized remittance transfers, the remittance transfer provider must:

(i) Provide either the pre-payment disclosure described in § 1005.31(b)(1) and the receipt described in § 1005.31(b)(2) or the combined disclosure described in § 1005.31(b)(3), in accordance with the timing requirements set forth in § 1005.31(e); and

(ii) If any of the disclosures provided pursuant to paragraph (a)(1)(i) of this section contain estimates as permitted by § 1005.32(b)(2), mail or deliver to the sender an additional receipt meeting the requirements described in § 1005.31(b)(2) no later than one business day after the date of the transfer. If the transfer involves the transfer of funds from the sender's account held by the provider, the receipt required by this paragraph may be provided on or with the next periodic statement for that account, or within 30 days after the date of the transfer if a periodic statement is not provided.

(2) For each subsequent preauthorized remittance transfer:

(i) If any of the information on the most recent receipt provided pursuant to paragraph (a)(1)(i) of this section, or by this paragraph (a)(2)(i), other than the temporal disclosures required by § 1005.31(b)(2)(ii) and (b)(2)(vii), is no longer accurate with respect to a subsequent preauthorized remittance transfer for reasons other than as permitted by § 1005.32, then the remittance transfer provider must provide an updated receipt meeting the requirements described in § 1005.31(b)(2) to the sender. The provider must mail or deliver this receipt to the sender within a reasonable time prior to the scheduled date of the next subsequent preauthorized remittance transfer. Such receipt must clearly and conspicuously indicate that it contains updated disclosures.

(ii) Unless a receipt was provided in accordance with paragraph (a)(2)(i) of this section that contained no estimates pursuant to § 1005.32, the remittance transfer provider must mail or deliver to the sender a receipt meeting the requirements described in § 1005.31(b)(2) no later than one business day after the date of the transfer. If the remittance transfer involves the transfer of funds from the sender's account held by the provider, the receipt required by this paragraph may be provided on or with the next periodic statement for that account, or within 30 days after the date of the transfer if a periodic statement is not provided.

(iii) A remittance transfer provider must provide the disclosures required by paragraph (d) of this section in accordance with the timing requirements of that section.

(b) Accuracy.

(1) For a one-time transfer scheduled five or more business days in advance or for the first in a series of preauthorized remittance transfers, disclosures provided pursuant to paragraph (a)(1)(i) of this section must comply with § 1005.31(f) by being accurate when a sender makes payment except to the extent estimates are permitted by § 1005.32.

(2) For each subsequent preauthorized remittance transfer, the most recent receipt provided pursuant to paragraph (a)(1)(i) or (a)(2)(i) of this section must be accurate as of when such transfer is made, except:

(i) The temporal elements required by § 1005.31(b)(2)(ii) and (b)(2)(vii) must be accurate only if the transfer is the first transfer to occur after the disclosure was provided; and

(ii) To the extent estimates are permitted by § 1005.32.

(3) Disclosures provided pursuant to paragraph (a)(1)(ii) or (a)(2)(ii) of this section must be accurate as of when the remittance transfer to which it pertains is made, except to the extent estimates are permitted by § 1005.32(a) or (b)(1).

(c) Cancellation. For any remittance transfer scheduled by the sender at least three business days before the date of the transfer, a remittance transfer provider shall comply with any oral or written request to cancel the remittance transfer from the sender if the request to cancel:

(1) Enables the provider to identify the sender's name and address or telephone number and the particular transfer to be cancelled; and

(2) Is received by the provider at least three business days before the scheduled date of the remittance transfer.

(d) Additional requirements for subsequent preauthorized remittance transfers.

(1) Disclosure requirement.

(i) For any subsequent transfer in a series of preauthorized remittance transfers, the remittance transfer provider must disclose to the sender:

(A) The date the provider will make the subsequent transfer, using the term "Future Transfer Date," or a substantially similar term;

(B) A statement about the rights of the sender regarding cancellation as described in § 1005.31(b)(2)(iv); and

(C) The name, telephone number(s), and Web site of the remittance transfer provider.

(ii) If the future date or dates of transfer are described as occurring in regular periodic intervals, e.g., the 15th of every month, rather than as a specific calendar date or dates, the remittance transfer provider must disclose any future date or dates of transfer that do not conform to the described interval.

(2) Notice requirements.

(i) Except as described in paragraph (d)(2)(ii) of this section, the disclosures required by paragraph (d)(1) of this section must be received by the sender no more than 12 months, and no less than five business days prior to the date of any subsequent transfer to which it pertains. The disclosures required by paragraph (d)(1) of this section may be provided in a separate disclosure or may be provided on one or more disclosures required by this subpart related to the same series of preauthorized transfers, so long as the consumer receives the required information for each subsequent preauthorized remittance transfer in accordance with the timing requirements of this paragraph (d)(2)(i).

(ii) For any subsequent preauthorized remittance transfer for which the date of transfer is four or fewer business days after the date payment is made for that transfer, the information required by paragraph (d)(1) of this section must be provided on or with the receipt described in § 1005.31(b)(2), or disclosed as permitted by § 1005.31(a)(3) or (a)(5), for the initial transfer in that series in accordance with paragraph (a)(1)(i) of this section.

(3) Specific format requirement. The information required by paragraph (d)(1)(i)(A) of this section generally must be disclosed in close proximity to the other information required by paragraph (d)(1)(i)(B) of this section.

(4) Accuracy. Any disclosure required by paragraph (d)(1) of this section must be accurate as of the date the preauthorized remittance transfer to which it pertains is made.

FEDERAL TRADE COMMISSION HOLDER-IN-DUE-COURSE REGULATIONS

16 C.F.R. Part 433

Current through March 27, 2019; 84 F.R. 11636

For updates, see www.ecfr.gov

§ 433.1 Definitions.

(a) Person. An individual, corporation, or any other business organization.

(b) Consumer. A natural person who seeks or acquires goods or services for personal, family, or household use.

(c) Creditor. A person who, in the ordinary course of business, lends purchase money or finances the sale of goods or services to consumers on a deferred payment basis; Provided, such person is not acting, for the purposes of a particular transaction, in the capacity of a credit card issuer.

(d) Purchase money loan. A cash advance which is received by a consumer in return for a "Finance Charge" within the meaning of the Truth in Lending Act and Regulation Z, which is applied, in whole or substantial part, to a purchase of goods or services from a seller who (1) refers consumers to the creditor or (2) is affiliated with the creditor by common control, contract, or business arrangement.

(e) Financing a sale. Extending credit to a consumer in connection with a "Credit Sale" within the meaning of the Truth in Lending Act and Regulation Z.

(f) Contract. Any oral or written agreement, formal or informal, between a creditor and a seller, which contemplates or provides for cooperative or concerted activity in connection with the sale of goods or services to consumers or the financing thereof.

(g) Business arrangement. Any understanding, procedure, course of dealing, or arrangement, formal or informal, between a creditor and a seller, in connection with the sale of goods or services to consumers or the financing thereof.

(h) Credit card issuer. A person who extends to cardholders the right to use a credit card in connection with purchases of goods or services.

(i) Consumer credit contract. Any instrument which evidences or embodies a debt arising from a "Purchase Money Loan" transaction or a "financed sale" as defined in paragraphs (d) and (e) of this section.

(j) Seller. A person who, in the ordinary course of business, sells or leases goods or services to consumers.

§ 433.2 Preservation of consumers' claims and defenses, unfair or deceptive acts or practices.

In connection with any sale or lease of goods or services to consumers, in or affecting commerce as "commerce" is defined in the Federal Trade Commission Act, it is an unfair or deceptive act or practice within the meaning of Section 5 of that Act for a seller, directly or indirectly, to:

(a) Take or receive a consumer credit contract which fails to contain the following provision in at least ten point, bold face, type:

NOTICE

ANY HOLDER OF THIS CONSUMER CREDIT CONTRACT IS SUBJECT TO ALL CLAIMS AND DEFENSES WHICH THE DEBTOR COULD ASSERT AGAINST THE SELLER OF GOODS OR SERVICES OBTAINED PURSUANT HERETO OR WITH THE PROCEEDS HEREOF. RECOVERY HEREUNDER BY THE DEBTOR SHALL NOT EXCEED AMOUNTS PAID BY THE DEBTOR HEREUNDER.

or,

(b) Accept, as full or partial payment for such sale or lease, the proceeds of any purchase money loan (as purchase money loan is defined herein), unless any consumer credit contract made in connection with such purchase money loan contains the following provision in at least ten point, bold face, type:

NOTICE

ANY HOLDER OF THIS CONSUMER CREDIT CONTRACT IS SUBJECT TO ALL CLAIMS AND DEFENSES WHICH THE DEBTOR COULD ASSERT AGAINST THE SELLER OF GOODS OR SERVICES OBTAINED WITH THE PROCEEDS HEREOF. RECOVERY HEREUNDER BY THE DEBTOR SHALL NOT EXCEED AMOUNTS PAID BY THE DEBTOR HEREUNDER.

§ 433.3 Exemption of sellers taking or receiving open end consumer credit contracts before November 1, 1977 from requirements of § 433.2(a).

(a) Any seller who has taken or received an open end consumer credit contract before November 1, 1977, shall be exempt from the requirements of 16 CFR part 433 with respect to such contract provided the contract does not cut off consumers' claims and defenses.

(b) Definitions. The following definitions apply to this exemption:

(1) All pertinent definitions contained in 16 CFR 433.1.

(2) Open end consumer credit contract: a consumer credit contract pursuant to which "open end credit" is extended.

(3) "Open end credit": consumer credit extended on an account pursuant to a plan under which a creditor may permit an applicant to make purchases or make loans, from time to time, directly from the creditor or indirectly by use of a credit card, check, or other device, as the plan may provide. The term does not include negotiated advances under an open-end real estate mortgage or a letter of credit.

(4) Contract which does not cut off consumers' claims and defenses: A consumer credit contract which does not constitute or contain a negotiable instrument, or contain any waiver, limitation, term, or condition which has the effect of limiting a consumer's right to assert against any holder of the contract all legally sufficient claims and defenses which the consumer could assert against the seller of goods or services purchased pursuant to the contract.

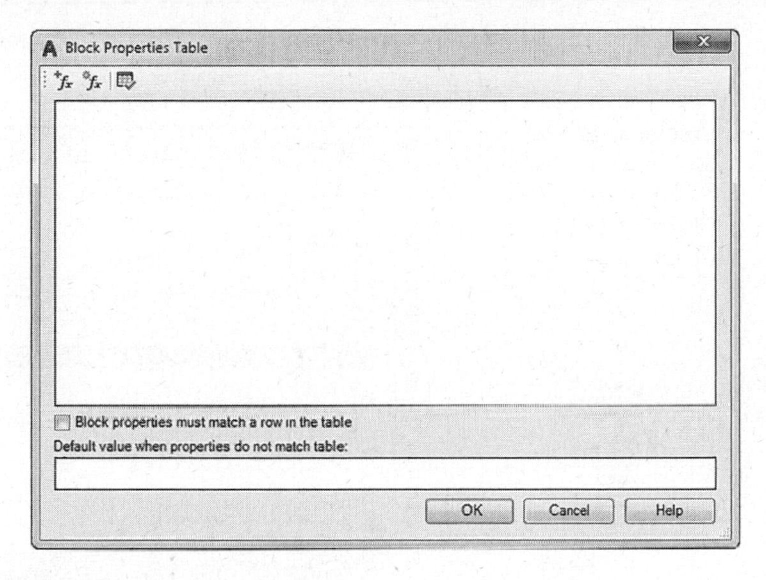

FIGURE 17.17
The Block Properties Table dialog box

5. Click the Add Properties tool in the upper-left corner of the Block Properties Table dialog box. The Add Parameter Properties dialog box appears (see Figure 17.18).

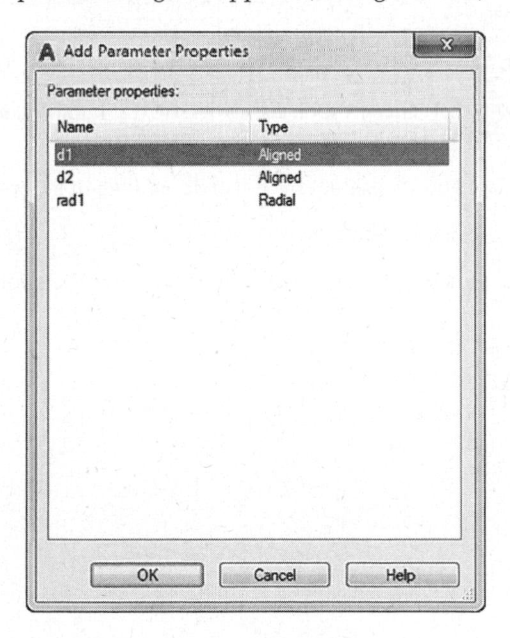

FIGURE 17.18
The Add Parameter Properties dialog box

6. Click the d1 listing at the top of the Add Parameter Properties dialog box and click OK. The Block Properties Table returns with a d1 heading in the list box.
7. Click just below the d1 listing; then type **12**↵. You see 1′-0″ added to the list.
8. Type **18**↵; 1′-6″ is added to the list.

9. Type **24↵30↵36↵**. The values that you enter are added to the list in feet and inches format (see Figure 17.19).

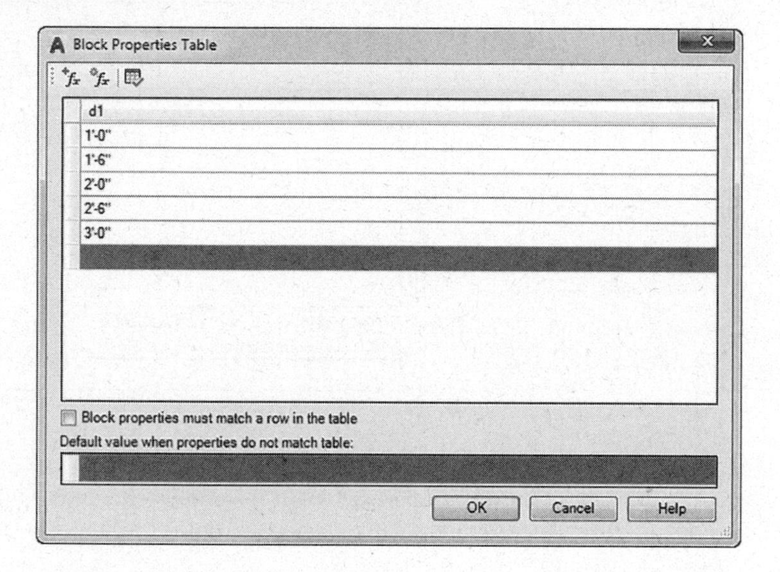

FIGURE 17.19
The Block Properties Table dialog box with the values added

10. Click OK to exit the Block Properties Table dialog box.
11. Click Close Block Editor in the Close panel, and save the changes to return to your drawing.

Now you can select from the door sizes in a pop-up list:

1. Click the door to select it.
2. Click the down-pointing grip below the door, as shown at the left side of Figure 17.20.

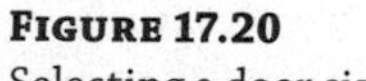

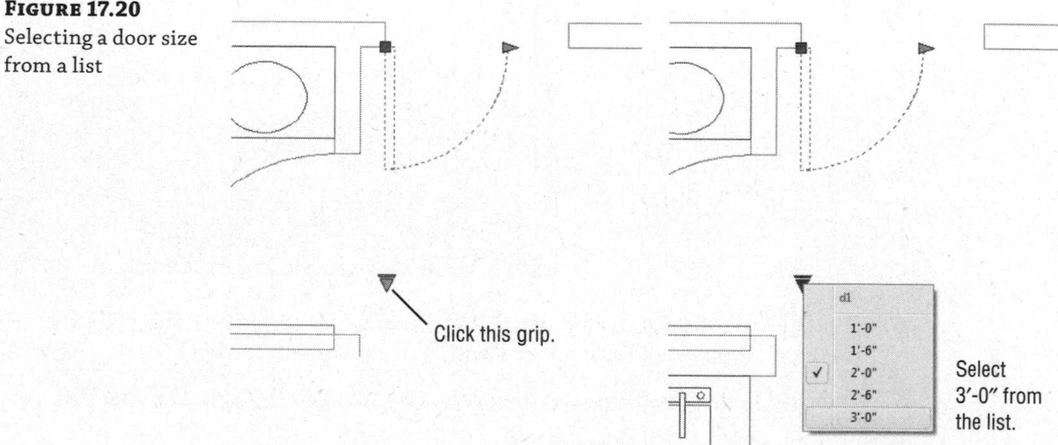

FIGURE 17.20
Selecting a door size from a list

3. Select the 3′-0″ door from the list that appears. (See the view to the right in Figure 17.20.) The door changes to a 36″-wide door.

If at a later time you need to make changes to the list or add more dimensions, you can open the block in the Block Editor and then click the Block Table tool. The Block Properties Table dialog box will appear with the data you entered earlier. You can then make changes to the table.

In this example, you saw that you can easily add predefined sizes to the dimensional constraint that appear in a selectable list. You can also give the list a more meaningful name. Right now, when you click the grip that opens the list, you see d1 as the name. Try the following to change the name from d1 to Width:

1. Double-click the door, and in the Edit Block Definition dialog box, click OK.
2. Select the d1 dimensional constraint, and then right-click and select Properties.
3. In the Properties palette, select the Name option under the Constraint group and then type **Width**↵. Notice that all the dimensional constraints that reference the dimension will change to show the name Width instead of d1.
4. Close the Properties palette, click the Close Block Editor tool in the Close panel, and then click to save the changes in the dialog box.
5. To see the change, click the down-pointing grip below the door as you did in the previous exercise. Now you see the word *Width* as the heading in the list of door widths (see Figure 17.21).

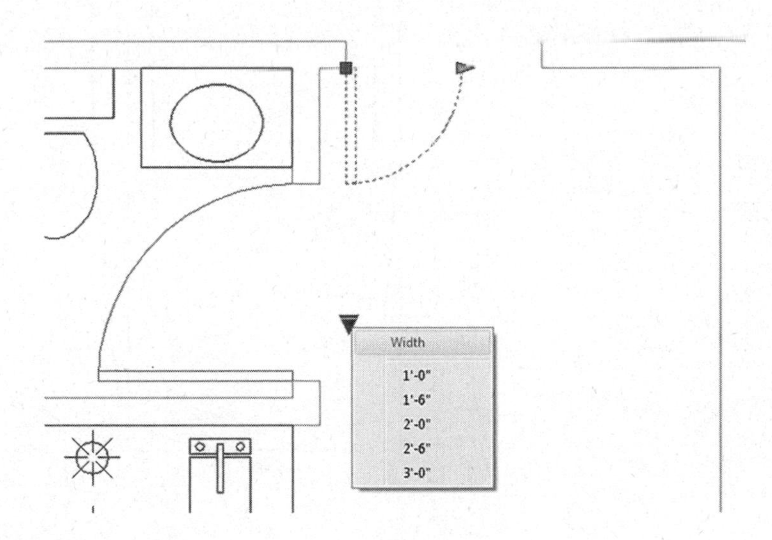

FIGURE 17.21 The list with the word *Width* appearing as the column title

6. Save and close the file.

As you can see, you have a lot of control over the behavior of various components of the dynamic block. In the next section, you'll learn how you can control the visibility of different parts of your block.

Creating Multiple Shapes in One Block

Depending on circumstances, you may need a block to display a completely different form. For example, you might want a single generic bath that can morph into a standard bath, a corner bath, or a large spa-style bath with jets.

Using dynamic blocks, you can hide or display elements of a block by selecting a *visibility state* from a list. For example, you can draw the three different bath sizes and then set up a visibility state for each size. Each visibility state displays only one bath size. You can then select a visibility state depending on the bath size that you want.

Try the following exercise to see how this works firsthand:

1. Open the `visibilitysample.dwg` file, and then click the Block Editor tool on the Home tab's Block panel.
2. In the Edit Block Definition dialog box, select Bathtub from the list and click OK.

You see the contents of the Bathtub block (see Figure 17.22). It's just the three existing blocks—Standard, Jetted, and Corner—inserted at the same origin.

Figure 17.22
The Bathtub block

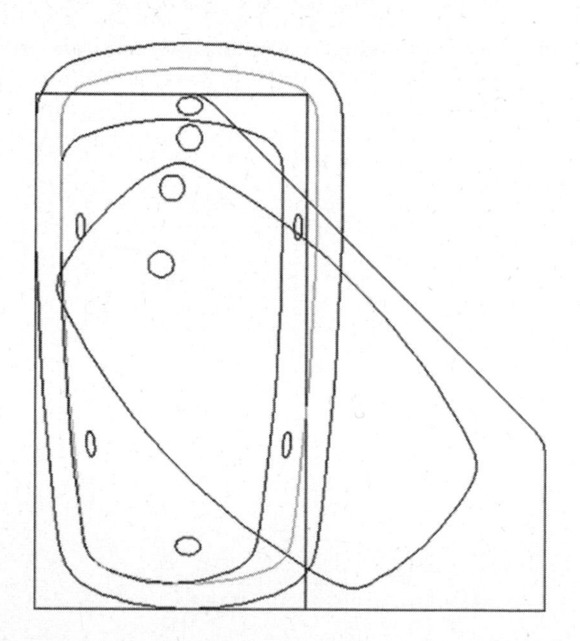

If you were to insert this block in a drawing, it would appear just as you currently see it, with each bathtub type overlaid on another. Next you'll see how you can add control over the visibility of each bathtub type so that only one is displayed at a time.

The first thing you need to do is to add a Visibility parameter:

1. On the Parameters tab of the Block Authoring palettes, click Visibility.
2. Click below the blocks to place the Visibility parameter, as shown in Figure 17.23.

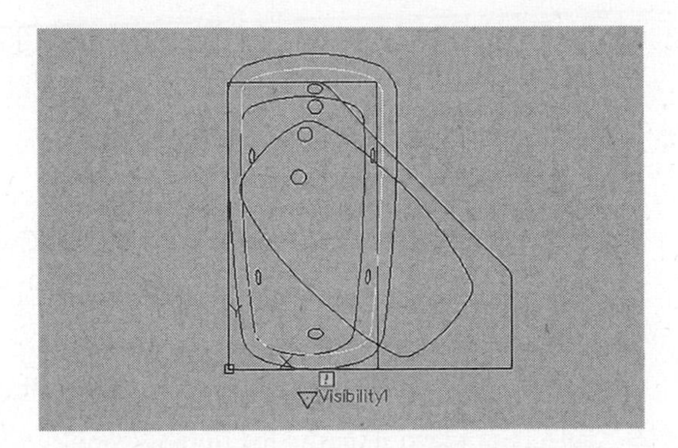

FIGURE 17.23
Adding the Visibility parameter

3. Double-click the Visibility parameter that you just added to open the Visibility States dialog box (see Figure 17.24). One visibility state, VisibilityState0, is already provided.

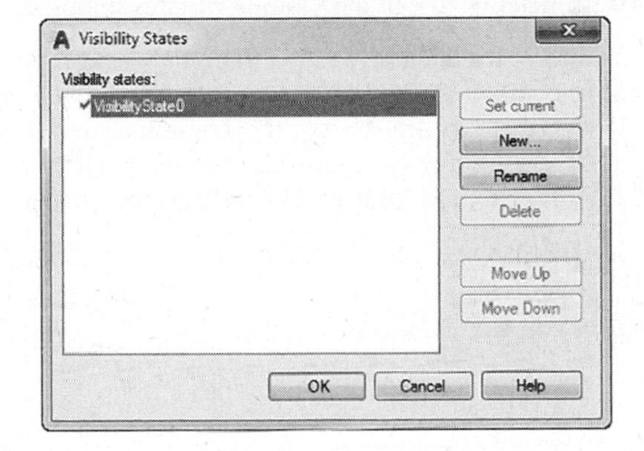

FIGURE 17.24
The Visibility States dialog box

You'll need three visibility states, one for each type of bathtub whose visibility you want to control. You've already got one, but you want a name that is more appropriate to the application:

1. Click the Rename button. The existing visibility state in the list to the left becomes editable.
2. Enter **Standard**↵. This is the visibility state for your standard bathtub.
3. Click the New button to open the New Visibility State dialog box (see Figure 17.25).

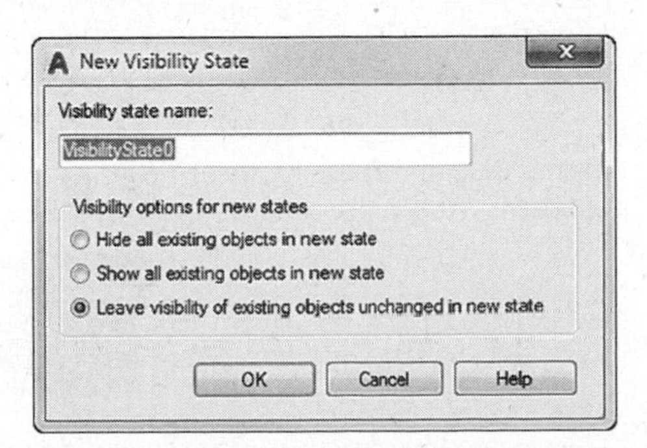

FIGURE 17.25
Adding a visibility state

4. Enter **Jetted** in the Visibility State Name box.
5. Make sure that the Leave Visibility Of Existing Objects Unchanged In New State radio button is selected, and then click OK.
6. Click the New button again.
7. In the New Visibility State dialog box, enter **Corner** in the Visibility State Name box.
8. Make sure that Leave Visibility Of Existing Objects Unchanged In New State is selected, and click OK.

   You've just created all of the visibility states that you need.
9. Select Standard from the list in the Visibility States dialog box, and click the Set Current button. (You can also double-click the Standard item.) A check mark appears to the left of Standard, showing you that it's now the current state.
10. Click OK to exit the Visibility States dialog box.

You have the visibility states that you need, and you have the objects whose visibility you want to control. Now you need to determine which block is visible for each state.

Remember that in step 9 of the previous exercise, you made Standard the current visibility state. You'll want only the standard Bathtub block visible for this state. Do the following to turn off the other two Bathtub blocks for the current state:

1. Select the Jetted and Corner blocks (see Figure 17.26).

FIGURE 17.26
Locating the blocks

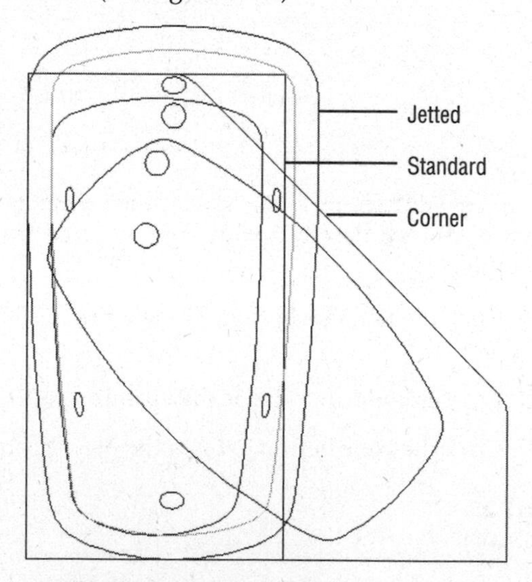

2. Right-click, and choose Object Visibility ➢ Hide For Current State. You can also click the Make Invisible tool on the right side of the Block Editor tab's Visibility panel.

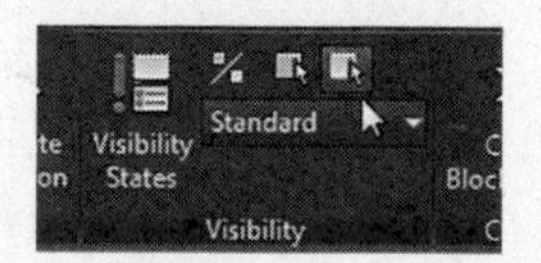

The selected blocks disappear. They didn't go anywhere; they are just made invisible.

3. Click the drop-down list on the Block Editor tab's Visibility panel, and select Jetted. The hidden blocks appear.

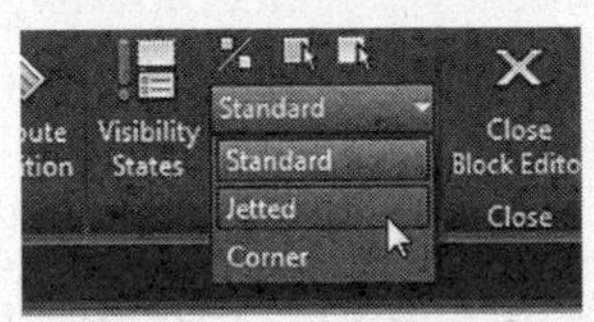

The current visibility state is now Jetted, so you want only the Jetted block to be visible. Select the Standard and Corner blocks, and then right-click and choose Object Visibility ➤ Hide For Current State. You can also click the Make Invisible tool from the Visibility panel. Now only the Jetted block is visible.

1. On the Block Editor tab's Visibility panel, click the drop-down list again and select Corner. All of the blocks appear.
2. Select the Standard and Jetted blocks, and click the Make Invisible tool. Now only the Corner block is visible.

You've created visibility states and set up the blocks so that they appear only when the appropriate visibility state is current. Next you'll test the blocks:

1. Click Close Block Editor, and save the changes that you've made.

2. Click the Insert tool on the Home tab's Block panel, click More Options, and then select Bathtub from the Name drop-down list in the Insert dialog box.
3. Make sure that Specify On-Screen is checked for the Insertion Point group and unchecked for the Scale and Rotation groups.
4. Click OK, and then place the block to the right of the other three blocks.
5. Click the Bathtub block that you just inserted, and then click the Visibility grip (see the left image in Figure 17.27).

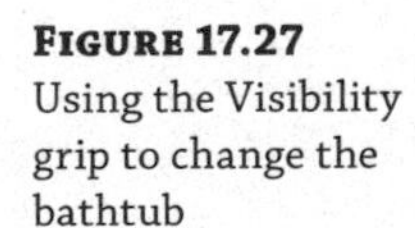
FIGURE 17.27 Using the Visibility grip to change the bathtub

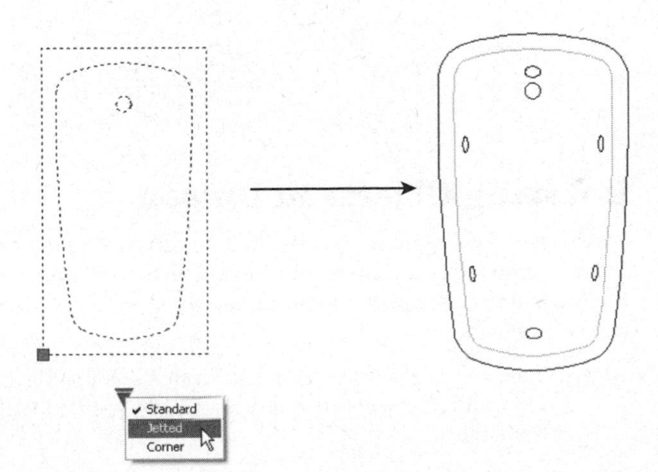

6. Select Jetted from the list. The jetted bathtub appears (see the right image in Figure 17.27).
7. Click the Bathtub block again, click the Visibility grip, and select Corner. The Corner tub appears.
8. Save and close the drawing.

CONTROLLING THE VISIBILITY OF INVISIBLE OBJECTS

While you're editing in the Block Editor, you can set up AutoCAD to display objects whose visibility has been turned off. If you set the `bvmode` system variable to 1, objects appear gray when their visibility has been turned off. You can also click the Visibility Mode tool in the Block Editor tab's Visibility panel.

In this example, you used a set of bathtubs, but you can use the Visibility parameter for anything that requires a different appearance. As mentioned at the beginning of this chapter, another use might be a block that contains a double, a queen-sized, and a king-sized bed. Going back to the door example, you can create a left- and right-hand door in the same block and then use the Visibility parameter to display a left- or right-hand door in the drawing. Figure 17.28 shows such a door block. The Visibility parameter has been renamed Hand in the block. When the door is inserted in the drawing, you see a list that allows you to select Left or Right.

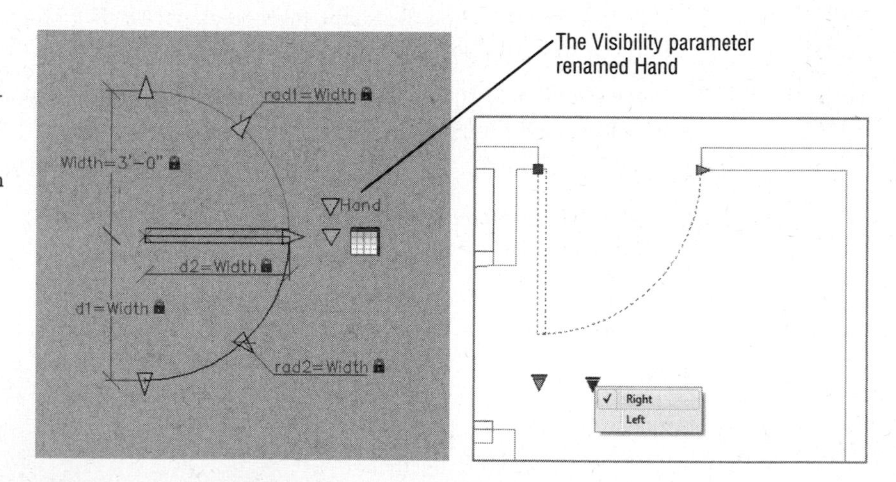

FIGURE 17.28 The Door dynamic block showing a left- and right-hand door (left), and the Door block as it appears in the drawing (right)

Rotating Objects in Unison

You've seen how actions and parameters can control the behavior of a single object in a block. You can also apply actions to multiple objects so that they move or change in unison. The following example shows how you can apply more than one Angular Constraint parameter to control two objects:

1. Open the `gatesample.dwg` file. In this sample file, the part that will move consists of the two non-red objects. The red lines have been added to help facilitate the rotation feature of the block.

2. Double-click the object in the drawing to open the Edit Block Definition dialog box, and then click OK. The Gate block opens for editing.

3. Click the Show All Geometric Constraints tool in the Block Editor tab's Geometric panel to reveal some of the existing constraints.

You can see how this drawing has been prepared for this exercise. The non-red parts of the drawing, which we'll call *gates*, are blocks that are constrained to the red lines with coincident constraints. The endpoints of the lines are constrained to the center of the arcs. The horizontal red lines are constrained to the vertical ones, also with Coincident constraints, and the vertical lines are constrained at both ends with a fixed constraint (see Figure 17.29).

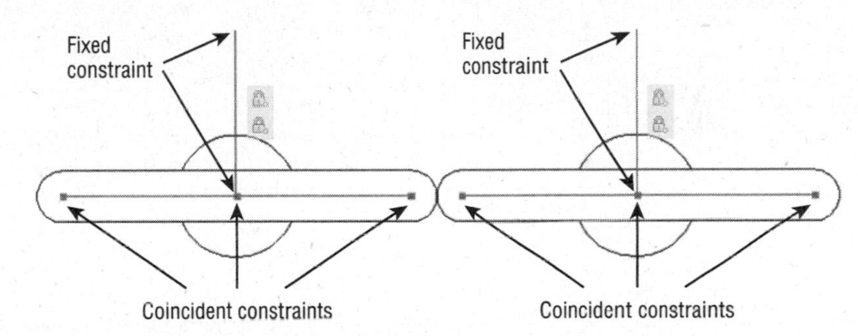

FIGURE 17.29
How the parts of the block are constrained

You'll use the red lines to define the rotation angle of the parts. The vertical line is fixed in place, whereas the rest of the parts are constrained in such a way as to allow a rotational motion.

Now add some angular constraints to define the rotation:

1. In the Dimensional panel, click the Angular tool.

2. Click the left vertical line toward the top, as shown in Figure 17.30.

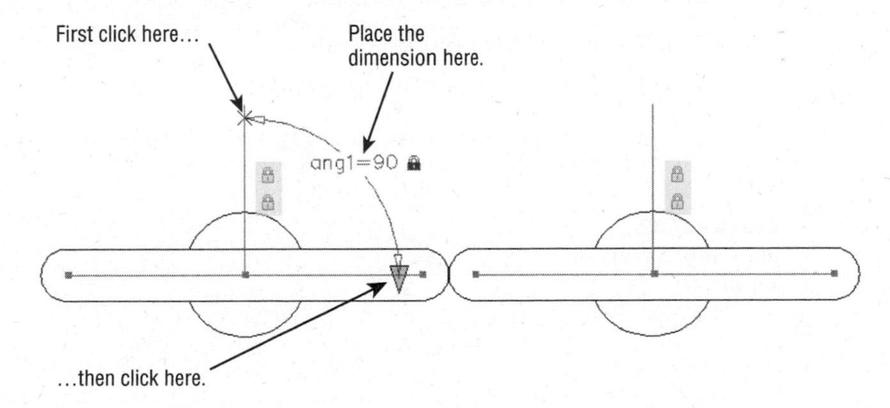

FIGURE 17.30
Adding the angular constraint to the `gatesample.dwg` drawing

3. Next, click the left horizontal line toward the right end of the line, as shown in Figure 17.30.

4. Place the dimension as shown in Figure 17.30.

5. The dimension text is highlighted. You want to keep the current value, so press ↵ to accept the default.

You have the first angular dimensional constraint in place. Next add a second one to the gate on the right, but this time you'll use the name of the first angular constraint as the dimension for the second one:

1. In the Dimensional panel, click the Angular tool.
2. Click the right vertical line near its top, as shown in Figure 17.31.

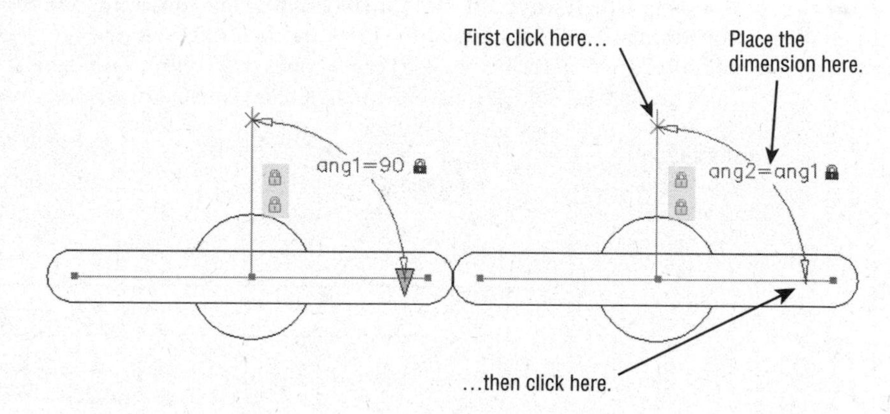

FIGURE 17.31 Adding the angular constraint to the second gate

3. Click the right horizontal line near its right end (see Figure 17.31).
4. Place the dimension as shown in Figure 17.31.
5. At the highlighted text, type **ang1**↵. This will cause this constraint to follow the first one that you added.

Now you're ready to save the block and try it out:

1. Click Close Block Editor on the Block Editor tab's Close panel, and save the block.
2. Click the block to expose its grips.
3. Click the arrow grip on the horizontal line.
4. Type **45**↵. Both sides of the block rotate about their own centers to a 45-degree angle (see Figure 17.32).

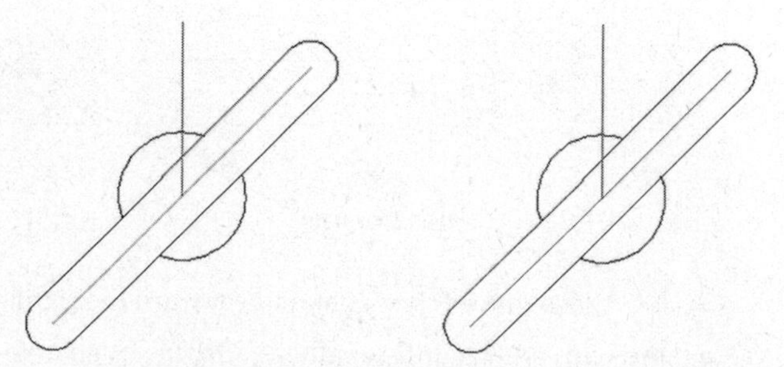

FIGURE 17.32 The two parts rotate in unison.

5. Click the arrow grip again, and type **90**↵ to set the gate back to its original position.

You've got the basic function of the gate working, but you don't want the red lines to appear in the drawing since they are there to facilitate the action of the gate and are not really part of the drawing. Do the following to hide the red lines:

1. Double-click the Gate block to open the Edit Block Definition dialog box, and then click OK. The Gate block opens for editing.
2. Click the Construction Geometry tool in the Manage panel.
3. Select the four red lines and press ↵↵. Notice that the lines change from solid to dashed, indicating that they are now construction geometry.
4. Click the Close Block Editor tool, and save the block. The block now appears without the red lines. If you click the block, the rotation grip still appears, and you can alter the block as before.

Now suppose that you want to have the gates rotate in opposite directions instead of in the same direction. You can add a user-defined formula to modify the behavior of the angular constraints:

1. Double-click the Gate block to open the Edit Block Definition dialog box, and then click OK. The Gate block opens for editing.

2. Click the Parameters Manager tool to open the Parameters Manager palette. You may recall that in Chapter 16, you used this palette to control the size of a concentric circle.
3. Double-click in the Expression column of the ang2 option, and type **ang1 * -1**↵.
4. Close the Parameters Manager palette, and then save and close the block.
5. Click the gate to select it, and then click the arrow grip.
6. Type 22↵. Now the two parts rotate in opposite directions (see Figure 17.33).

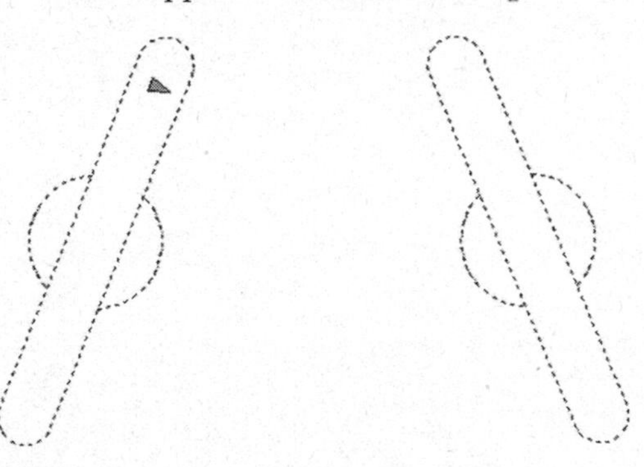

FIGURE 17.33
The gates moving in opposite directions

7. Press Esc to clear the selection, and then save and close the file.

You can go on to add a block table using the Block Table tool to create a predefined set of angles, just as you did for the Door block earlier in this chapter. You can also add incremental values by using the Properties palette to change the angle constraint in a way similar to how you changed constraints in the sink exercise in the first part of this chapter.

Next let's take a look at a way to array objects automatically with dynamic blocks.

Filling in a Space Automatically with Objects

Perhaps one of the more tedious tasks that you'll face is drawing the vertical bars of a hand railing for an elevation view. You can draw a single bar and then use the Array command to repeat the bar as many times as needed, but when you have to edit the railing, you may find that you're spending more time adding and erasing bars.

In the next example, you'll see how you can create a block that automatically fills in vertical bars as the width of the railing changes. You'll start with an existing drawing of a single vertical bar and an outline of the railing opening around the bar:

1. Open the `railsample.dwg` file.
2. Double-click the object in the drawing to open the Edit Block Definition dialog box, and then click OK. This opens the Railvertical block for editing.

   When the Block Editor opens, notice that the block already has a Linear parameter and a Stretch action added. Recall from the sink example at the beginning of this chapter that the Linear parameter and Stretch action let you vary the width of an object. In this case, the outermost rectangle is being stretched.

3. On the Actions tab of the Block Authoring palettes, click the Array action.
4. At the `Select parameter:` prompt, click the blue Linear parameter (labeled as Distance), as shown in Figure 17.34.

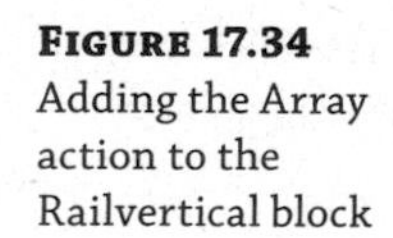

FIGURE 17.34
Adding the Array action to the Railvertical block

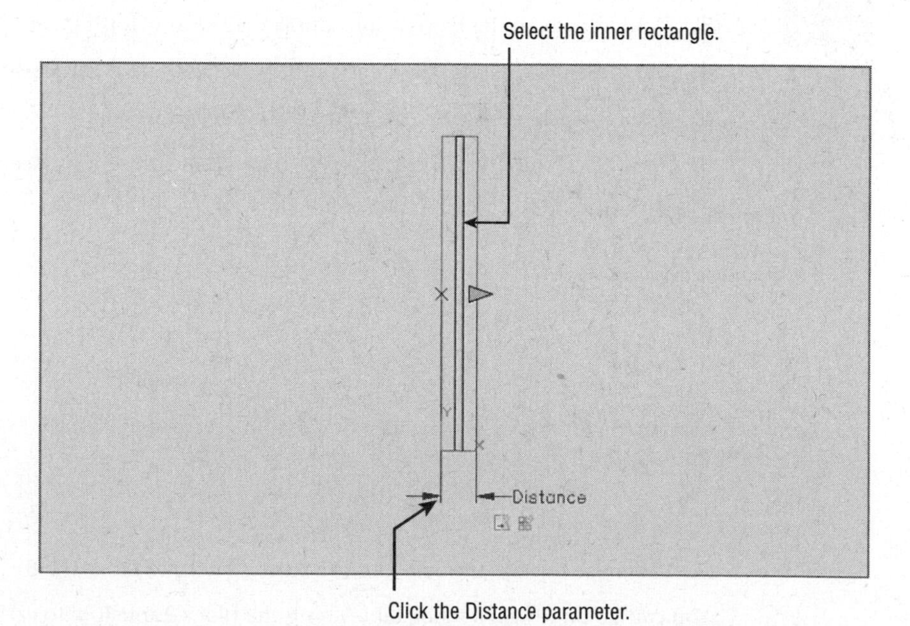

5. At the `Select objects:` prompt, select the dark vertical rectangle representing the vertical bar of the railing, as shown in Figure 17.34, and then press ↵.

6. At the `Enter the distance between columns (|||):` prompt, enter **4↵**.
7. Click Close Block Editor on the Block Editor tab's Close panel and save the changes.
8. Click the block to expose its grips.
9. Click and drag the blue arrow grip to the right. As the rail expands, additional vertical bars are added at 4″ intervals (see Figure 17.35).

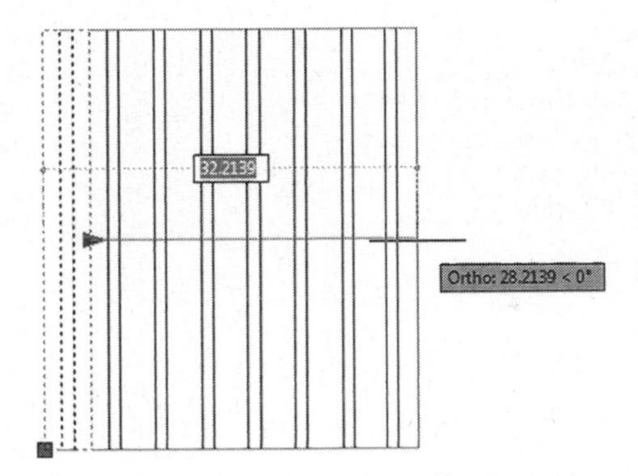

FIGURE 17.35
The Railvertical block adds vertical bars as its width expands.

10. Exit and save the file.

You can now use this block wherever you need to draw a simple railing with vertical bars. Another example of how the Array action might be used is in a side view of a bolt. You could show the threads of the bolt and use the Array action to increase the number of threads as the bolt is lengthened.

USING PARAMETER SETS

You probably noticed the Parameter Sets tab in the Block Authoring palettes. The options in this tab are predefined combinations of parameters and actions that are commonly used together. For example, the Polar Array set inserts a Polar parameter with an Array action. You only need to supply the object. The Polar Array set causes the associated object to rotate about a center point with a grip. You can also array the object by stretching the grip away from the rotation center.

To associate an object with a parameter set, right-click the action icon associated with a parameter (usually appearing below the parameter), and then select Action Selection Set ➤ New Selection Set. At the `Select objects:` prompt, select an object. If a stretch is employed, select a stretch frame and an object to stretch.

Including Block Information with Data Extraction

In Chapter 12, "Using Attributes," you learned how you could attach data to blocks through attributes and then extract that data to spreadsheets or AutoCAD tables. You can also include dynamic block information that has been included in a property lookup table. This can be extremely useful for generating data for a bill of materials or in other situations if you need to track the numbers and types of items in your drawing.

To see how this works, you'll return to a version of the Door block that has some additions. This enhanced version of the Door block includes a left- and right-hand version of the door that is controlled with the Visibility parameter. Figure 17.36 shows the door inserted into a drawing using different door sizes and left and right variations.

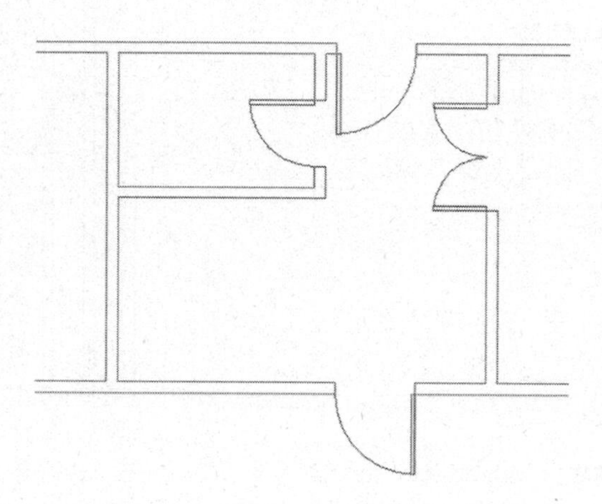

FIGURE 17.36 The door block inserted several times into a drawing with various widths and handedness

You'll use the Attribute Extraction command to see how the dynamic block data appears as an exported table or a spreadsheet:

1. Open the `17-extractsample.dwg` file. This file contains a dynamic door block that is similar to the one that you created earlier with the addition of a left and a right Visibility parameter.

2. From the Annotate tab's Tables panel, click the Extract Data tool to start the Data Extraction Wizard.
3. On the Begin screen, click Next.
4. In the Save Data Extraction As dialog box, enter **Test** for the name and click Save. Note that the `Test` file will be saved in the `My Documents` folder. If you want to place it somewhere else, make sure that you browse to the location that you prefer.
5. On the Define Data Source screen, click Next.
6. On the Select Objects screen, remove the check mark from the Display All Object Types option so that only the Door block appears in the list and then click Next.
7. On the Select Properties screen, remove the check mark from all but the Dynamic Block option in the right column, and make sure the Hand and Width options in the left column are the only ones selected (see Figure 17.37).

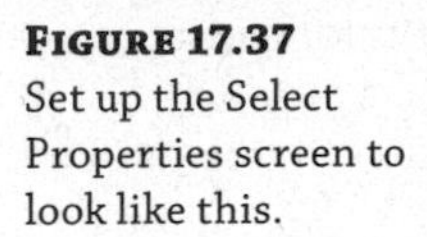

FIGURE 17.37
Set up the Select Properties screen to look like this.

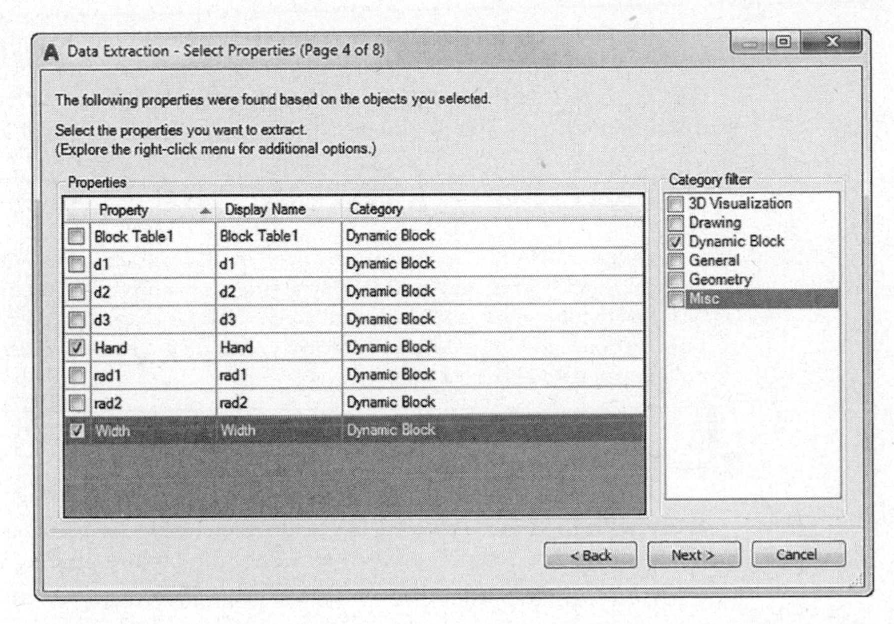

8. Click Next. On the Refine Data page, you see the data that will be exported to a spreadsheet file or a table (see Figure 17.38).

FIGURE 17.38
The resulting table to be extracted, as shown on the Refine Data screen of the Data Extraction Wizard

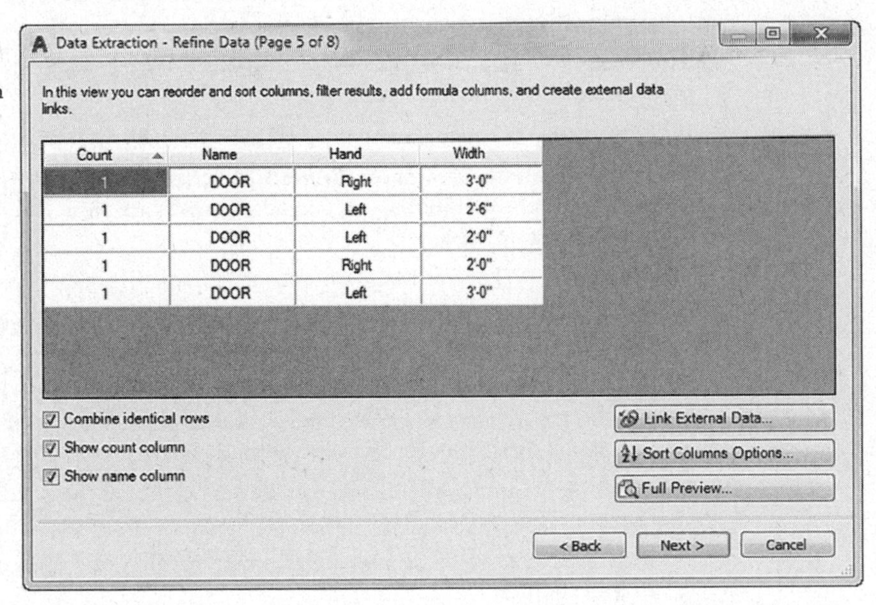

9. You don't really want to extract this data, so once you've taken a good look at this screen, click Cancel and then Yes in the Quit Wizard dialog box.

This is the end of the door example, so you can exit this file. Save it for future reference if you like.

As you can see in Figure 17.38, a list is generated that shows each door in the drawing with its size and handedness. You could use this data as part of a door schedule.

TAKE CARE USING THE MIRROR TOOL

If you use the Mirror command to mirror a block that contains a Visibility parameter to control left- and right-hand doors, the Attribute Extraction command will report erroneous results. Therefore, be sure that if you set up a block with a visibility parameter to control mirrored states, you use those actions to edit the door and don't rely on standard editing tools. That way, you'll ensure the accuracy of your extracted data.

The Bottom Line

Work with the Block Editor. To create dynamic blocks, you need to become familiar with the Block Editor. You can use the Block Editor to modify existing blocks in your drawing.

Master It What does the Edit Block Definition dialog box allow you to do?

Create a dynamic block. A dynamic block is one to which you add grips so that you can modify the block in a number of ways.

Master It Name some of the features of the Block Editor that let you add additional grip-editing functions to a block.

Add Scale and Stretch actions to a parameter. You can set up a dynamic block to perform multiple operations with a single grip.

Master It What do you need to do to have one grip perform two functions?

Add more than one parameter for multiple grip functions. In addition to having one grip perform multiple operations, you can add as many grips as you need to make your block even more customizable.

Master It What feature do you use to set up a list of options for a block?

Create multiple shapes in one block. Many of the dynamic block functions let you adjust the shape of the original block. Another feature lets you choose completely different shapes for the block.

Master It When a block uses the Visibility parameter to set up different shapes, how do you select a different block shape in the drawing?

Rotate objects in unison. Blocks can be set up so that the action of one set of objects affects another set. This chapter gives the example of rotating objects in unison.

Master It Name the dimensional constraint that was used in the object rotation example in this chapter.

Fill in a space automatically with objects. A dynamic block can help you automate the addition of repetitive elements to your drawing.

Master It What is the name of the action used to produce copies of a block object at regular intervals in both the x- and y-axes when the block is stretched?

Chapter 18

Drawing Curves

So far in this book, you've been using basic lines, arcs, and circles to create your drawings in the Autodesk® AutoCAD® software. Now it's time to add polylines and spline curves to your repertoire. Polylines offer many options for creating forms, including solid fills and free-form curved lines. Spline curves are perfect for drawing accurate and smooth nonlinear objects.

In this chapter, you will learn to

- Create and edit polylines
- Create a polyline spline curve
- Create and edit true spline curves
- Mark divisions on curves

Introducing Polylines

Polylines are like composite line segments and arcs. A polyline may look like a series of line segments, but it acts like a single object. This characteristic makes polylines useful for a variety of applications, as you'll see in the upcoming exercises.

Drawing a Polyline

First, to learn about the polyline, you'll begin a drawing of the top view of the joint shown in Figure 18.1.

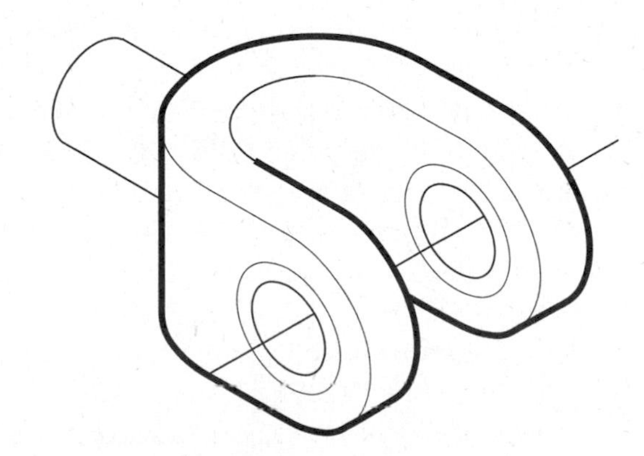

Figure 18.1
A sketch of a metal joint

Follow these steps to draw the joint:

1. Open a new file using the `acad.dwt` template, switch off the grid, and save it as **Joint2d.dwg**. Don't bother to make special setting changes because you'll create this drawing with the default settings.
2. From the Navigation bar, choose Zoom All from the flyout or type **Z↵A↵**.

3. Click the Polyline tool on the Draw panel, or type **PL↵**.
4. At the `Specify start point:` prompt, enter a point at coordinate 3,3 to start your polyline.
5. At the `Specify next point or [Arc/Halfwidth/Length/Undo/Width]:` prompt, enter **@3<0↵** to draw a horizontal line of the joint.
6. At the `Specify next point or [Arc/Close/Halfwidth/Length/Undo/Width]:` prompt, click the Arc option in the prompt or enter **A↵** to continue your polyline with an arc.

Using the Arc Option in the Polyline Tool

The Arc option lets you draw an arc that starts from the last polyline point that you selected. While in the Polyline tool, select the Arc option; as you move your cursor, an arc follows it in a tangential direction from the previous line segment of the polyline. You can return to drawing straight line segments by entering **L↵**. If you want the arc to be drawn in the opposite direction from the last point instead of a tangent direction, hold down the Ctrl key.

7. At the prompt

```
Specify endpoint of arc (hold Ctrl to switch direction) or
[Angle/CEnter/CLose/Direction/Halfwidth/Line/Radius/Second pt/Undo/Width]:
```

enter **@4<90↵** to draw a 180° arc from the last point you entered. Your drawing should now look similar to Figure 18.2.

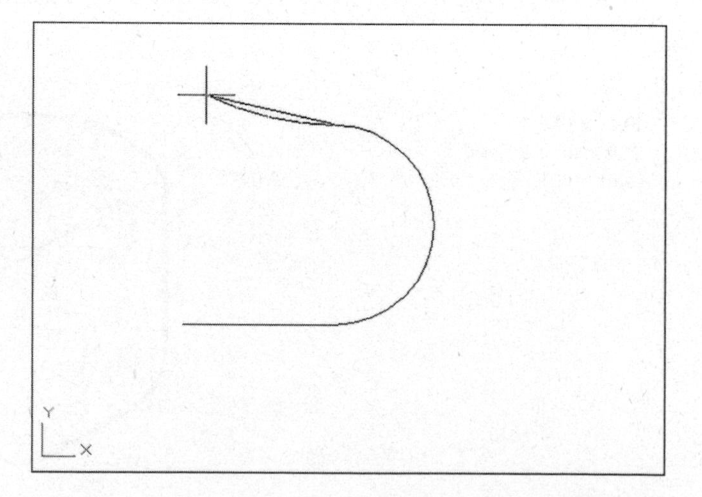

FIGURE 18.2
A polyline consisting of a line segment and an arc

8. To continue the polyline with another line segment, click the Line option in the prompt or enter **L**↵.

9. At the `Specify next point or [Arc/Close/Halfwidth/Length/Undo/Width]:` prompt, enter **@3<180**↵. Another line segment continues from the end of the arc.

10. Press ↵ to exit the Polyline tool.

You now have a sideways, U-shaped polyline that you'll use in the next exercise to complete the top view of your joint.

Setting Polyline Options

Let's take a break from the exercise to look at some of the options that you didn't use in the Polyline prompt:

Close Draws a line segment from the last endpoint of a sequence of line segments to the first point picked in that sequence. This works exactly like the Close option for the Line command.

Length Enables you to specify the length of a line that will be drawn at the same angle as the last line entered.

Halfwidth Creates a tapered line segment or an arc by specifying half of its beginning and ending widths (see Figure 18.3).

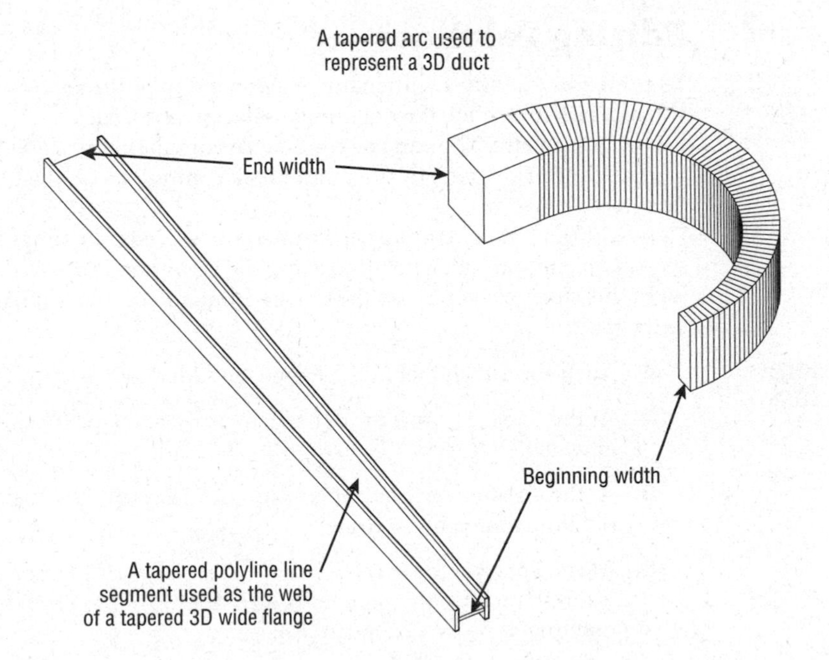

FIGURE 18.3 A tapered line segment and an arc created with Halfwidth

Width Creates a tapered line segment or an arc by specifying the full width of the segment's beginning and ending points.

Undo Deletes the last polyline segment drawn.

Radius/Second Pt The Radius and Second Pt options appear when you use the arc option to draw polyline segments. Radius lets you specify a radius for the arc, and Second Pt lets you specify a second point in a three-point arc.

If you want to break a polyline into simple lines and arcs, you can use the Explode option on the Modify panel, just as you would with blocks. After a polyline is exploded, it becomes a set of individual lines or arcs.

To turn off the filling of solid polylines, open the Options dialog box and click the Display tab. Clear the Apply Solid Fill check box in the Display Performance group.

FILLETING A POLYLINE

You can use the Fillet tool on the Modify panel to fillet all the vertices of a polyline at once. Click the Fillet tool, set your fillet radius by typing **R**↵ and entering a radius value, type **P**↵ to select the Polyline option, and then pick the polyline you want to fillet. If you want to fillet only two line segments of a polyline, use the Fillet tool as you normally would to fillet simple lines.

You can also close a polyline with a radius by using the Fillet command on the polyline's endpoints.

Editing Polylines

You can edit polylines with many of the standard editing commands. To change the properties of a polyline, click the polyline to select it, right-click, and select Properties to open the Properties palette. You can use the Stretch command on the Modify panel to move vertices of a polyline. The Trim, Extend, and Break commands on the Modify panel also work with polylines.

In addition, many editing capabilities are offered only for polylines. For instance, later you'll see how to smooth out a polyline using the Fit option in the Pedit command.

In this exercise, you'll use the Offset command on the Modify panel to add the inside portion of the joint:

1. Click the Offset tool in the Home tab's Modify panel, or type **O**↵.
2. At the Specify offset distance or [Through/Erase/Layer] <Through>: prompt, enter **1**↵ .
3. At the Select object to offset or [Exit/Undo]<Exit>: prompt, pick the U-shaped polyline that you just drew.
4. At the Specify point on side to offset or [Exit/Multiple/Undo] <Exit>: prompt, pick a point on the inside of the U shape. You'll see a concentric copy of the polyline appear (see Figure 18.4).
5. Press ↵ to exit the Offset command.

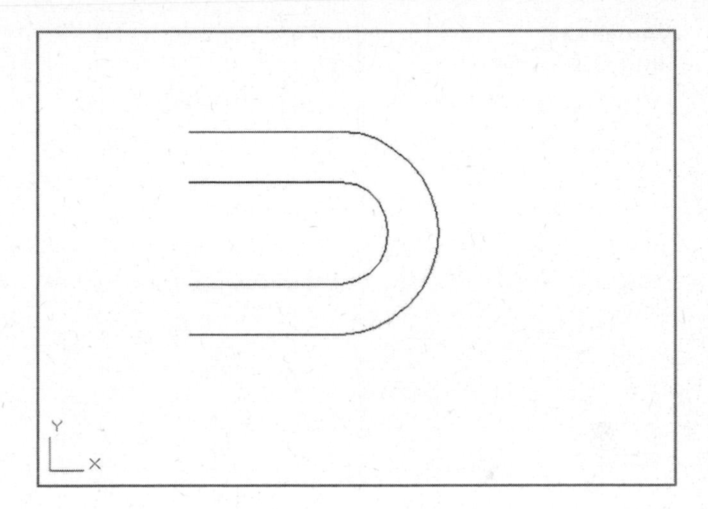

FIGURE 18.4
The offset polyline

The concentric copy of a polyline made by choosing the Offset tool can be useful when you need to draw complex parallel curves like the ones shown in Figure 18.5.

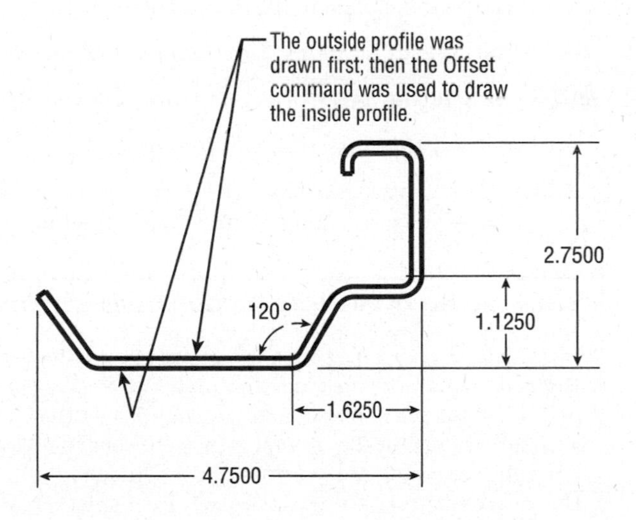

FIGURE 18.5
Sample complex curves drawn by using offset polylines

Next, complete the top view of the joint. To do this, you'll use the Edit Polyline tool, otherwise known as the Pedit command:

1. Connect the ends of the polylines with two short line segments (see Figure 18.6).
2. Choose Edit Polyline from the expanded Modify panel or type **PE**↵.
3. At the `Select polyline or [Multiple]:` prompt, pick the outermost polyline.

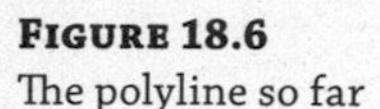

FIGURE 18.6
The polyline so far

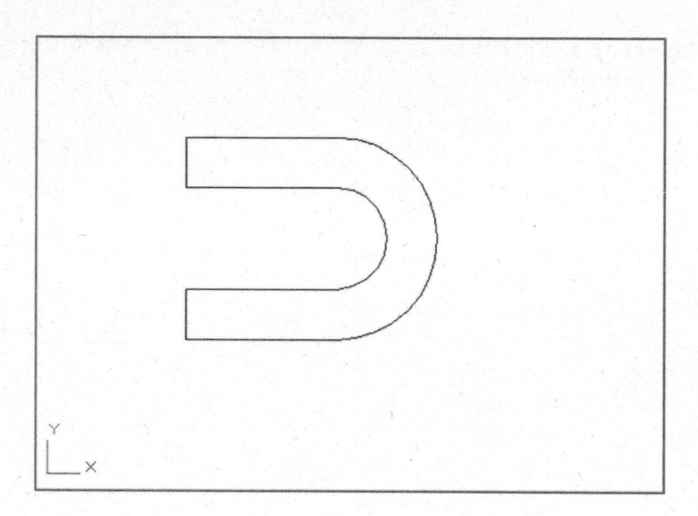

4. At the prompt

```
Enter an option
[Close/Join/Width/Edit vertex/Fit/Spline/Decurve/Ltype gen/Reverse/Undo]:
```

   click the Join option in the prompt or enter **J**↵.
5. At the `Select objects:` prompt, select all the objects you've drawn so far.
6. Press ↵ to join all the objects into one polyline. It appears that nothing has happened.
7. Press ↵ again to exit the Pedit command.
8. Click the drawing to expose its grips. The entire object is highlighted, indicating that all the lines have been joined into a single polyline.

WHAT TO DO IF THE JOIN OPTION DOESN'T WORK

If the objects to be joined don't touch, you can use the *fuzz* join feature. Type **PE**↵**M**↵ to start the Pedit command with the Multiple option, and then select all the objects that you want to join and press ↵. If you see a convert message, enter **Y**↵. At the `Enter an option [Close/Open/Join/Width/Fit/Spline/Decurve/Ltype gen/Reverse/Undo]:` prompt, click the Join option in the prompt or enter **J**↵. At the `Enter fuzz distance or [Jointype]:` prompt, enter a distance that approximates the size of the gap between objects. By default, AutoCAD extends the lines so that they join end to end. You can use the Jointype option if you want Pedit to join segments with an additional segment.

By using the Width option under Edit Polyline, you can change the width of a polyline. Let's change the width of your polyline to give some width to the outline of the joint. To do this, you'll use the Edit Polyline tool again, but this time you'll use a shortcut:

1. Double-click the polyline.

2. At the `Enter an option [Open/Join/Width/Edit vertex/Fit/Spline/Decurve/Ltype gen/Reverse/Undo]:` prompt, enter **W**↵ for the Width option.

3. At the `Specify new width for all segments:` prompt, enter **.03**↵ for the new width of the polyline. The line changes to the new width (see Figure 18.7), and you now have a top view of your joint.

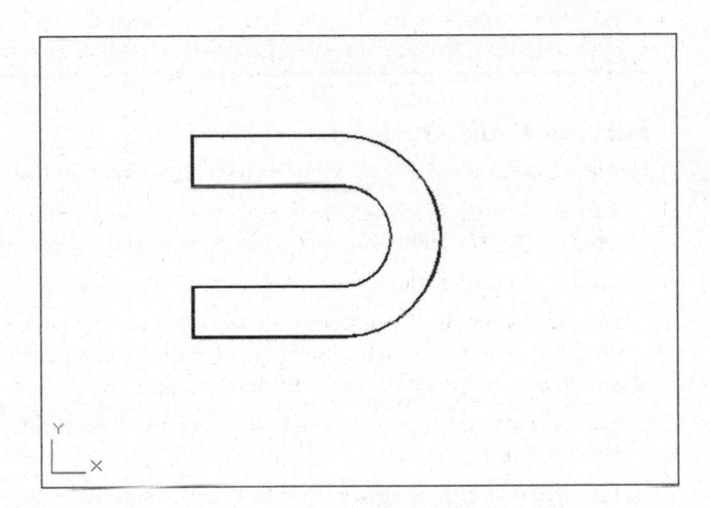

FIGURE 18.7
The polyline with a new thickness

4. Press ↵ to exit the Pedit command.

5. Save this file.

In most cases, you can simply double-click a polyline to start the Pedit command. But if you want to edit multiple polylines or if you want to convert an object or set of objects into a polyline, use the Edit Polyline tool from the expanded Modify panel to start Pedit.

In addition, you can select the Edit Polyline options from a menu that appears at the cursor (see Figure 18.8) if the Dynamic Input feature is on or by selecting the polyline and then right-clicking anywhere in the drawing to access the Polyline options from the context menu.

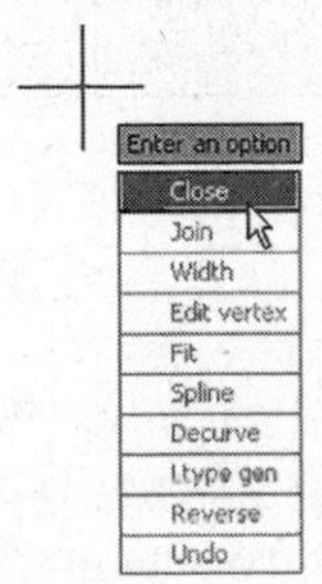

FIGURE 18.8
The Edit Polyline options that appear at the cursor

Find the Geometric Center of a Closed Polyline or Spline

You can use object snaps (osnaps) to snap to the geometric center of a closed polyline or spline. When you are in a command that asks you to select a point, Shift+right-click and select Geometric Center from the Osnap menu. You can also type **Gcen**↵. Place the cursor on the closed polyline or spline, and the Geometric Center osnap marker appears at its geometric center. There may be a momentary delay as AutoCAD locates the center. You can also move the cursor inside the closed polyline or spline to find the center. The Geometric Center osnap marker looks like an asterisk to differentiate it from the Center osnap marker used for arcs and circles.

Setting Pedit Options

Here's a brief look at a few of the Pedit options that you didn't try:

Close Connects the two endpoints of a polyline with a line segment. If the polyline that you selected to be edited is already closed, this option changes to Open.

Open Removes the last segment added to a closed polyline.

Spline/Decurve Smooths a polyline into a spline curve (discussed in detail later in this chapter). The Decurve option changes a spline or fit curve polyline back into its original shape before the Spline or Fit option was applied.

Edit Vertex Lets you edit each vertex of a polyline individually (discussed in detail later in this chapter).

Fit Turns polyline segments into a series of arcs.

Ltype Gen Controls the way noncontinuous linetypes pass through the vertices of a polyline. If you have a fitted or spline curve with a noncontinuous linetype, turn on this option.

Reverse Reverses the orientation of a polyline. The orientation is based on the order in which points are selected to create the polyline. The first point picked is the beginning (or point 1), the next point is point 2, and so on. In some cases, you may want to reverse this order using the Reverse option.

Undo Removes the last polyline line segment.

Using Polylines to Set Lineweights

Typically, you would use the Lineweight feature of AutoCAD to set lineweights in your drawing. In cases where the Lineweight feature will not work, you can change the thickness of regular lines and arcs using Pedit to change them into polylines and then use the Width option to change their width.

Smoothing Polylines

You can create a curve in AutoCAD in many ways. If you don't need the representation of a curve to be accurate, you can use a polyline curve. In the following exercise, you'll draw a polyline curve to represent a contour on a topographical map:

1. Open the `topo.dwg` file. The top image in Figure 18.9 contains the drawing of survey data. Some of the contours have already been drawn in between the data points.

2. Zoom in to the upper-right corner of the drawing so that your screen displays the area shown in the bottom image in Figure 18.9.

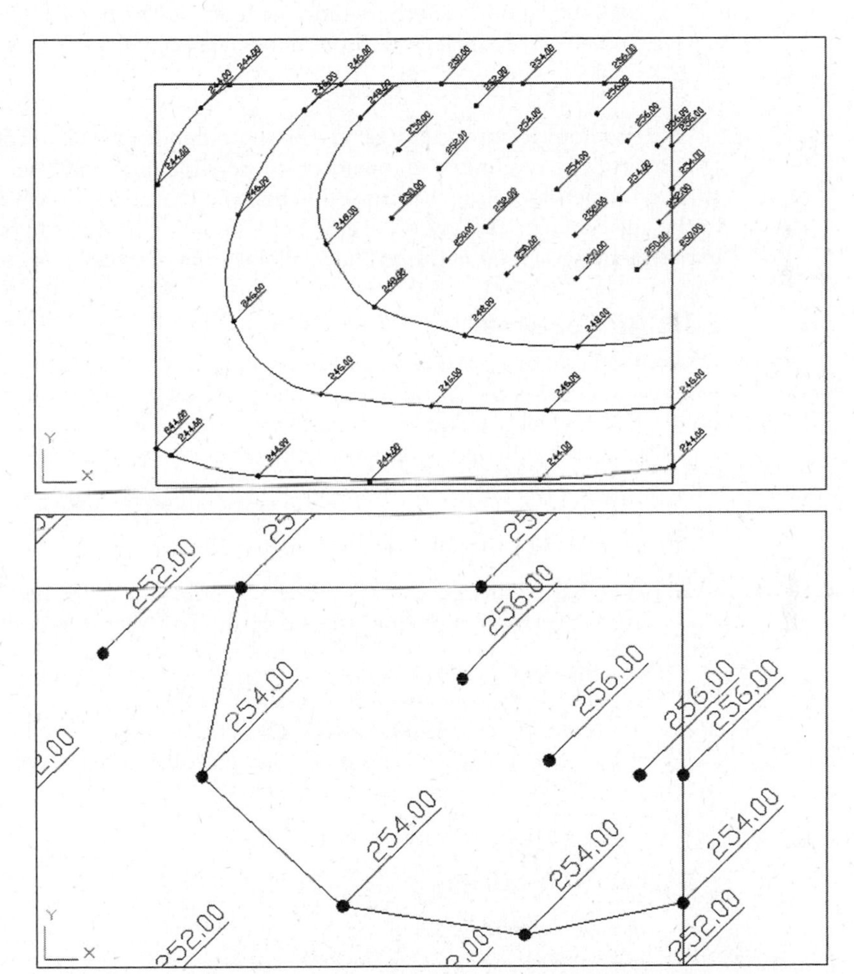

FIGURE 18.9
The `topo.dwg` file shows survey data portrayed in an AutoCAD drawing. Notice the dots indicating where elevations were taken. The actual elevation value is shown with a diagonal line from the point.

3. Click the Polyline tool on the Draw panel. Using the Center osnap, draw a polyline that connects the points labeled 254.00. Your drawing should look like the bottom image in Figure 18.9.
4. Press ↵.
5. Next you'll convert the polyline that you just drew into a smooth contour line. Double-click the contour polyline line that you just drew.

6. At the prompt

```
Enter an option
[Close/Join/Width/Edit vertex/Fit/Spline/Decurve/Ltype gen/Reverse/Undo]:
```

click the Fit option in the prompt or type **F**↵. The polyline smooths out into a series of connected arcs that pass through the data points.

7. Press ↵ to end the command.

Your contour is now complete. The Fit option under the Pedit command causes AutoCAD to convert the straight-line segments of the polyline into arcs. The endpoints of the arcs pass through the endpoints of the line segments, and the curve of each arc depends on the direction of the adjacent arc. This gives the effect of a smooth curve. Next you'll use this polyline curve to experiment with some of the editing options unique to the Pedit command.

Editing Vertices

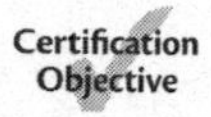

One of the Pedit options that we haven't yet discussed, Edit Vertex, is like a command within a command. Edit Vertex has numerous suboptions that enable you to fine-tune your polyline by giving you control over individual vertices.

To access the Edit Vertex options, follow these steps:

1. Turn off the DATA and BORDER layers to hide the data points and border.
2. Double-click the polyline that you just drew.
3. Type **E**↵ to enter Edit Vertex mode. An X appears at the beginning of the polyline indicating the vertex that will be affected by the Edit Vertex options.

When using Edit Vertex, you must be careful about selecting the correct vertex to be edited. Edit Vertex has 10 options. You often have to exit the Edit Vertex operation and use Pedit's Fit option to see the effect of several Edit Vertex options on a curved polyline.

After you enter the Edit Vertex mode of the Pedit command, you can perform the following functions:

- Break the polyline between two vertices.
- Insert a new vertex.
- Move an existing vertex.
- Regenerate (type **RE**↵) the drawing to view the current shape of the polyline.
- Straighten a polyline between two vertices.
- Change the tangential direction of a vertex.
- Change the width of the polyline at a vertex.

These functions are presented in the form of the following prompt:

```
[Next/Previous/Break/Insert/Move/Regen/Straighten/Tangent/Width/eXit] :
```

The following sections examine each of the options in this prompt, starting with Next and Previous.

The Next and Previous Options

The Next and Previous options let you select a vertex for editing. When you start the Edit Vertex option, an X appears on the selected polyline to designate its beginning. As you select Next or Previous, the X moves from vertex to vertex to show which one is being edited. Let's try it:

1. Press ↵ a few times to move the X along the polyline. (Because Next is the default option, you only need to press ↵ to move the X.)
2. Type **P**↵ for Previous. The X moves in the opposite direction. The default option becomes P.

Why Reverse a Polyline?

One of the more frequently asked questions that we receive from readers is "How can I reverse the direction of a polyline?" It may seem like an odd question to someone new to AutoCAD, but reversing a polyline has quite a few uses. Perhaps the most common use is to turn a polyline that uses a complex linetype, one that includes text, right side up so that the text can be read more easily. (See Chapter 24, "Customizing Toolbars, Menus, Linetypes, and Hatch Patterns," for an example of a linetype that includes text.) If for some reason you need to reverse the direction of a polyline or spline, you can do so by using the Reverse option in the Pedit command.

Turning Objects into Polylines and Polylines into Splines

At times, you'll want to convert regular lines, arcs, or even circles into polylines. You might want to change the width of lines or join lines to form a single object such as a boundary. Here are the steps to convert lines, arcs, and circles into polylines:

1. Click the Edit Polyline tool from the Home tab's expanded Modify panel, or type **PE**↵ at the Command prompt.
2. At the `Select polyline or [Multiple]:` prompt, pick the object that you want to convert. If you want to convert a circle to a polyline, first break the circle (using the Break tool on the expanded Modify panel) so that it becomes an arc of approximately 359.
3. At the prompt

   `Object selected is not a polyline. Do you want to turn it into one? :`

   press ↵. The object is converted into a polyline.

   If you want to convert several objects to polylines, type **M**↵ at the `Select polyline or [Multiple]:` prompt; then select the objects that you want to convert and press ↵. You will see the `Convert Lines, Arcs and Splines to polylines [Yes/No]? <Y>:` prompt. Type **Y**↵, and all the selected objects are converted to polylines. You can then go on to use other Pedit options on the selected objects.

To turn a polyline into a true spline curve, do the following:

1. Click the Edit Polyline tool from the Home tab's expanded Modify panel, or type **PE**↵. Select the polyline that you want to convert.

continues

continued

2. Type **S**↵ to turn it into a polyline spline, and then press ↵ to exit the Pedit command.
3. Click the Spline Fit tool on the Home tab's expanded Draw panel or type **SPL**↵.
4. At the `Specify first point or [Method/Knots/Object]:` prompt, click the Object option in the prompt or type **O**↵.
5. At the `Select spline-fit polyline:` prompt, click the polyline spline and press ↵. Although it may not be apparent at first, the polyline is converted into a true spline.

You can also use the Edit Spline tool on the Home tab's expanded Modify panel (or enter **SPE**↵) to edit a polyline spline. If you do, the polyline spline is automatically converted into a true spline.

If you know you'll always want to convert an object into a polyline when using Pedit, you can turn on the `Peditaccept` system variable. Enter **peditaccept**↵ at the Command prompt, and then enter **1**↵.

THE BREAK OPTION

The Break option breaks the polyline between two vertices:

1. Position the X on one end of the segment that you want to break.
2. Enter **B**↵ at the Command prompt.
3. At the `Enter an option [Next/Previous/Go/eXit] <N>:` prompt, use Next or Previous to move the X to the other end of the segment to be broken.
4. When the X is in the proper position, enter **G**↵ to break the polyline (see Figure 18.10).

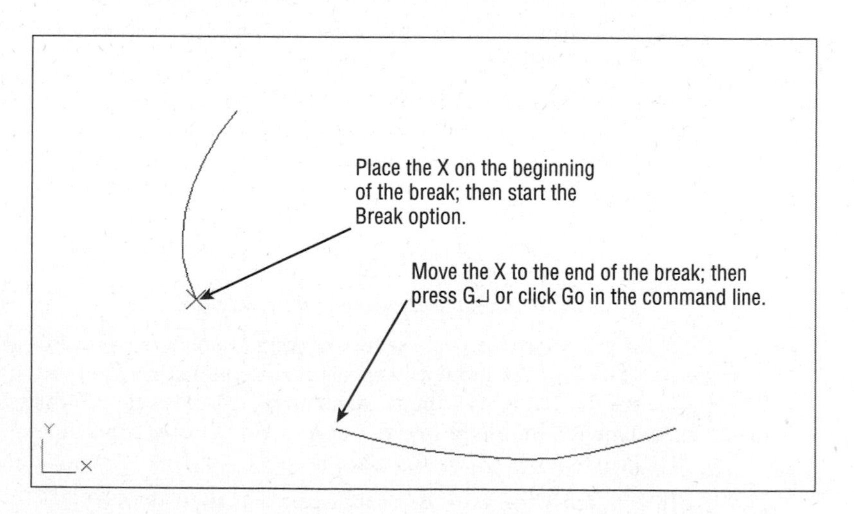

FIGURE 18.10
How the Break option works

You can also use the Trim options on the Modify panel or the Break option on the expanded Modify panel to break a polyline anywhere, as you did when you drew the toilet seat in Chapter 3, "Setting Up and Using the Drafting Tools."

THE INSERT OPTION

Next try the Insert option, which inserts a new vertex:

1. Type **X**↵ to exit the Edit Vertex option temporarily. Then type **U**↵ to undo the break.
2. Type **E**↵ to return to the Edit Vertex option.
3. Press ↵ to advance the X marker to the next point.
4. Enter **I**↵ to select the Insert option.
5. When the prompt `Specify location for new vertex:` appears, along with a rubber-banding line originating from the current X position (see Figure 18.11), pick a point indicating the new vertex location. The polyline is redrawn with the new vertex.

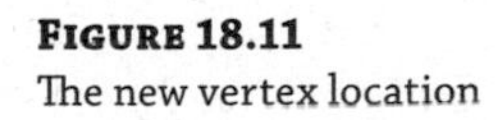

FIGURE 18.11
The new vertex location

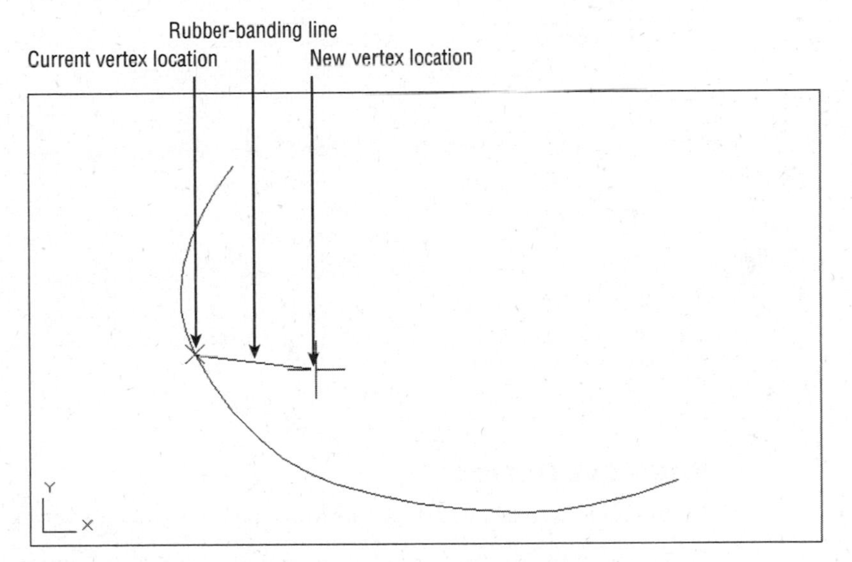

Notice that the inserted vertex appears between the currently marked vertex and the *next* vertex; this demonstrates that the Insert option is sensitive to the direction of the polyline. If the polyline is curved, the new vertex won't immediately be shown as curved. (See the first image in Figure 18.12.) You must smooth it out by exiting the Edit Vertex option and then using the Fit option, as you did to edit the site plan. (See the second image in Figure 18.12.) You can also use the Stretch command (on the Modify panel) to move a polyline vertex.

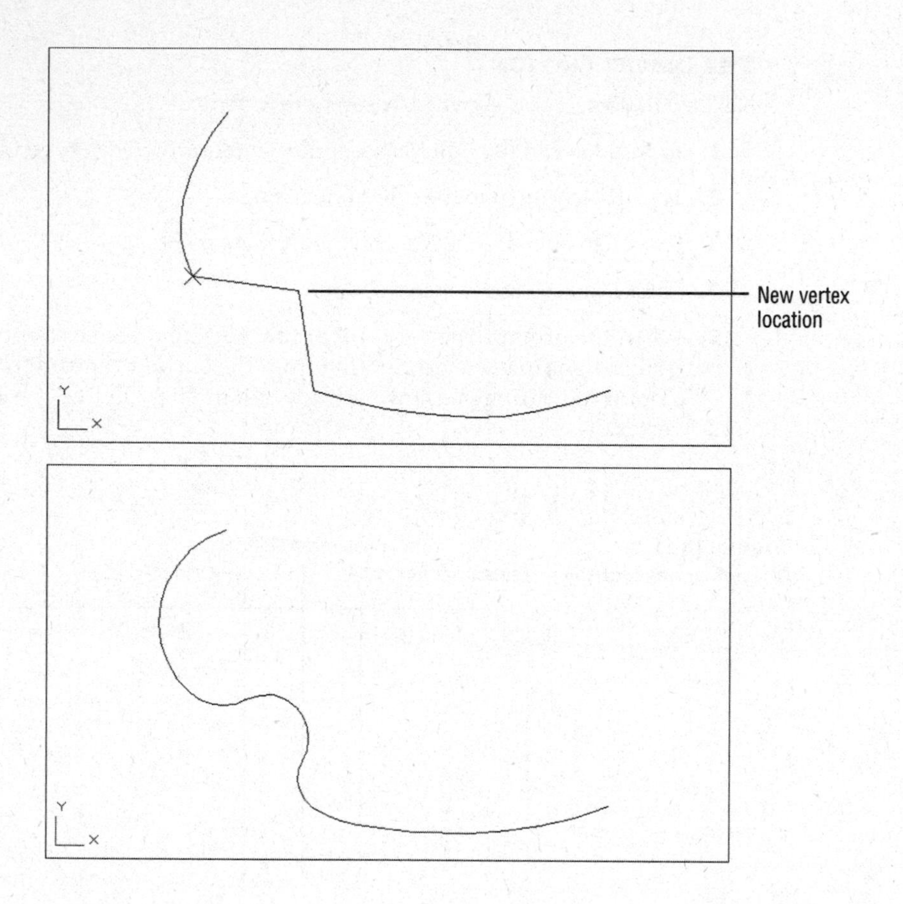

FIGURE 18.12 The polyline before and after the curve is fitted

THE MOVE OPTION

In this brief exercise, you'll use the Move option to move a vertex:

1. Undo the inserted vertex by exiting the Edit Vertex option (enter **X**↵) and typing **U**↵.
2. Restart the Edit Vertex option, and use the Next or Previous option to place the X on the vertex that you want to move.
3. Enter **M**↵ for the Move option.
4. When the `Specify new location for marked vertex:` prompt appears, along with a rubber-banding line originating from the X (see the first image in Figure 18.13), pick the new vertex. The polyline is redrawn (see the second image in Figure 18.13). Again, if the line is curved, the new vertex appears as a sharp angle until you use the Fit option (see the final image in Figure 18.13).

You can also move a polyline vertex by using its grip.

FIGURE 18.13
Picking a new location for a vertex with the polyline before and after the curve is fitted

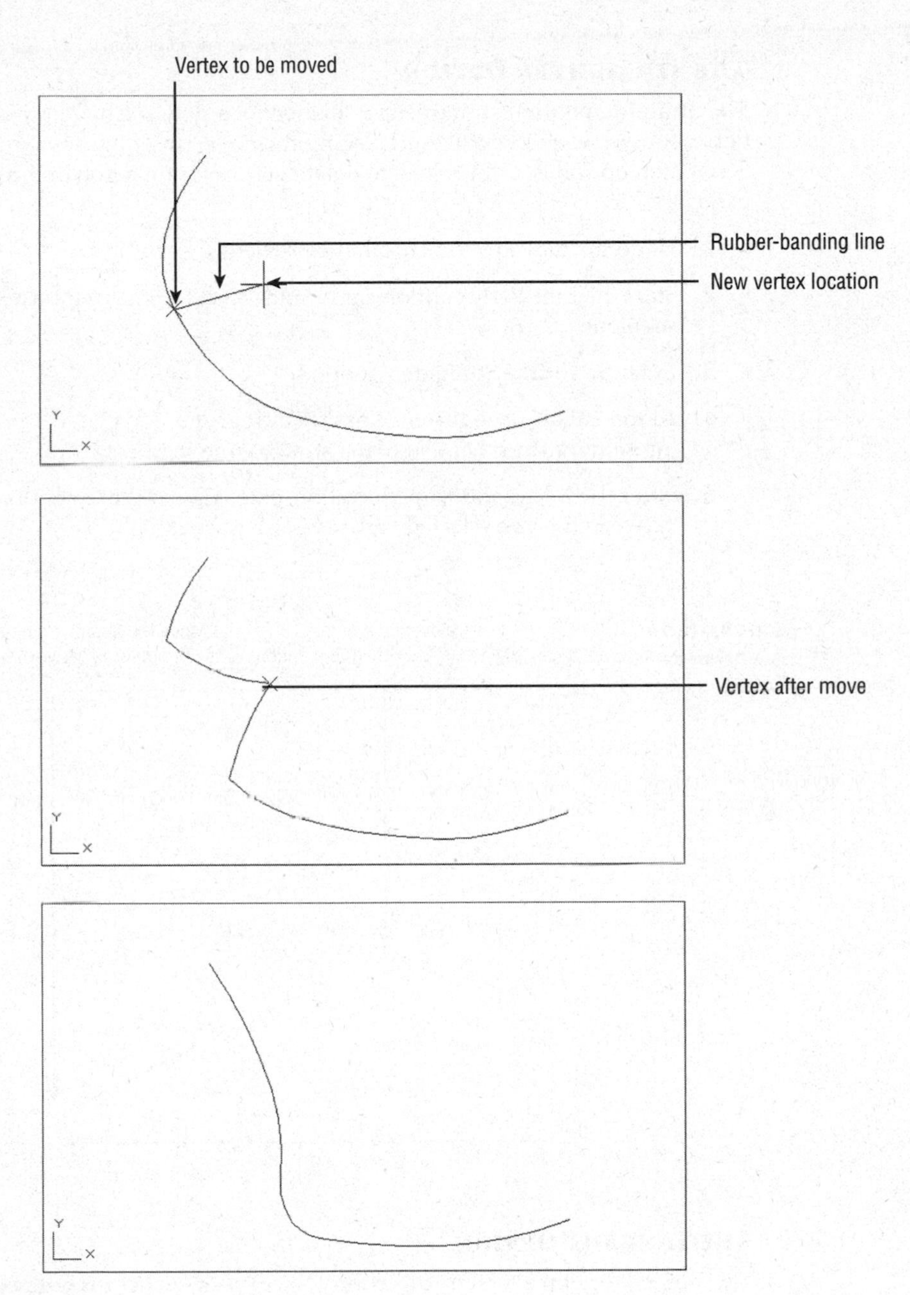

THE REGEN OPTION

In some cases, the effect of an option does not appear in the drawing immediately. You can use the Regen option to update the display of the polyline and see any changes that you've made up to that point.

The Straighten Option

The Straighten option straightens a segment of a polyline by removing all the vertices between two selected vertices, replacing them with a straight-line segment. Using the Straighten option is a quick way to delete vertices from a polyline, as shown in the following exercise:

1. Undo the moved vertex (from the previous exercise).
2. Start the Edit Vertex option again, and select the starting vertex for the straight-line segment.
3. Enter **S↵** for the Straighten option.
4. At the `Enter an option [Next/Previous/Go/eXit] <N>:` prompt, move the X to the location for the other end of the straight-line segment.
5. After the X is in the proper position, enter **G↵** for the Go option. The polyline straightens between the two selected vertices (see Figure 18.14).

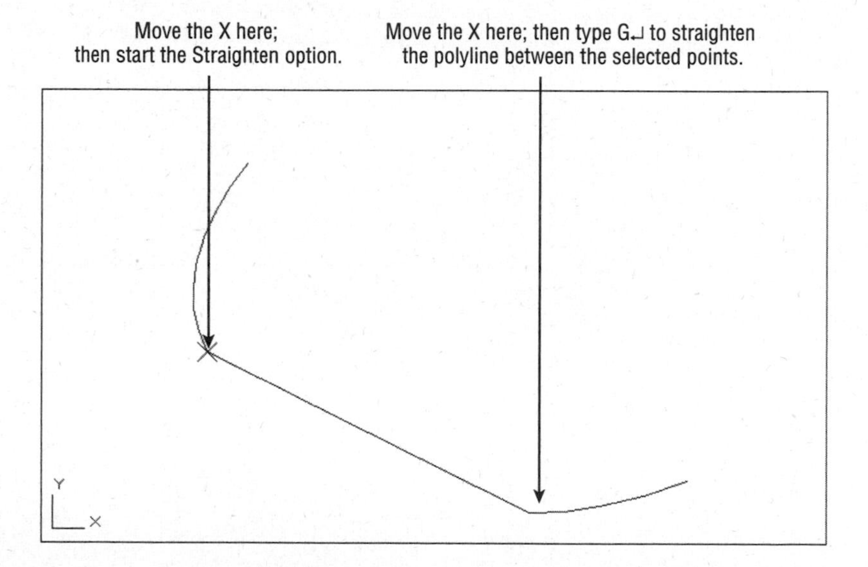

Figure 18.14 A polyline after straightening

The Tangent Option

The Tangent option alters the direction of a curve on a curve-fitted polyline:

1. Undo the straightened segment from the previous exercise.
2. Restart the Edit Vertex option, and position the X on the vertex that you want to alter.
3. Enter **T↵** for the Tangent option. A rubber-banding line appears (see the top image in Figure 18.15).

4. Point the rubber-banding line in the direction of the new tangent, and click. An arrow appears, indicating the new tangent direction (see the second image in Figure 18.15).

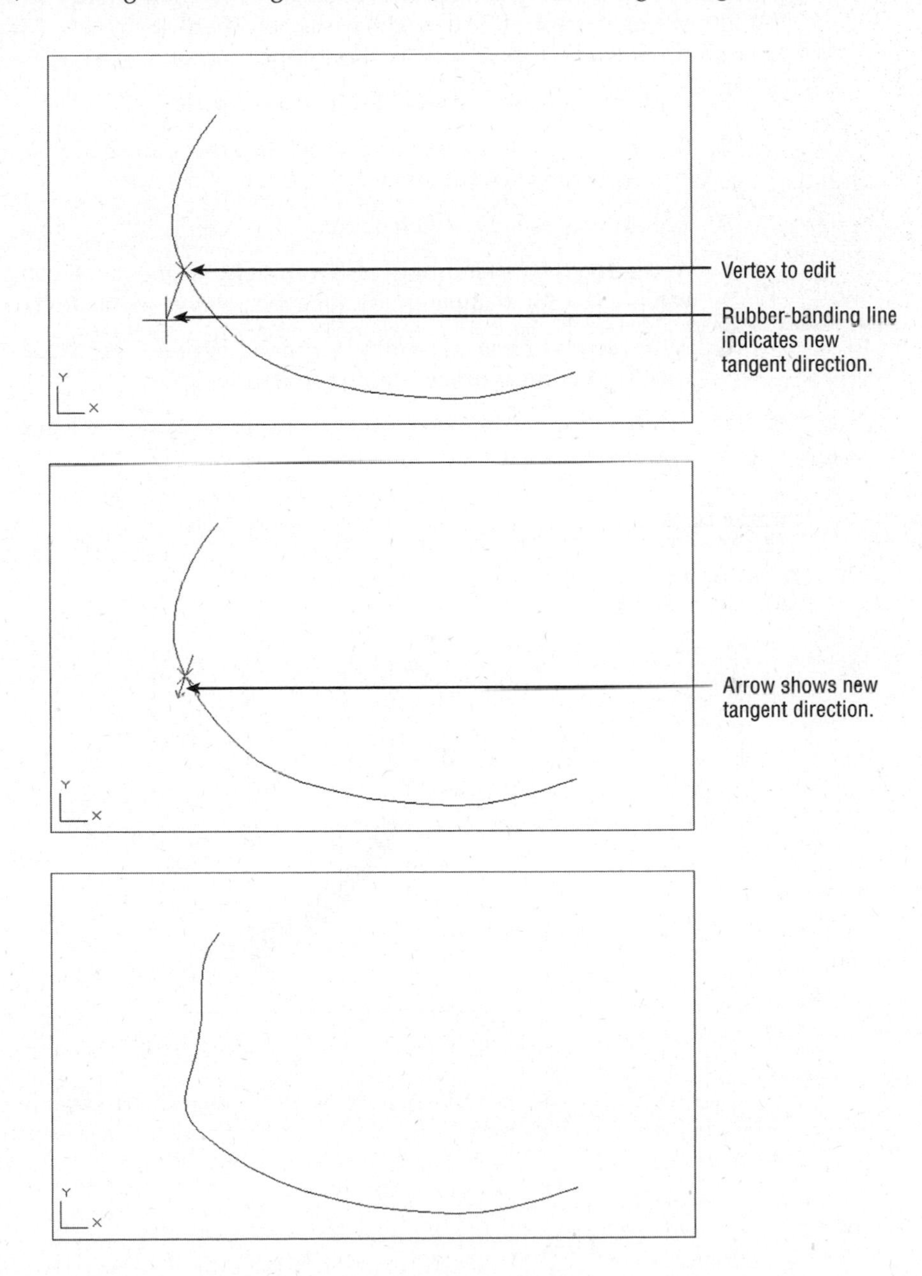

FIGURE 18.15 Picking a new tangent direction

Don't worry if the polyline shape doesn't change right away. If this happens, use the Fit option to see the effect of the Tangent (see the final image in Figure 18.15).

The Width Option

Finally, you'll try the Width option. Unlike the Pedit command's Width option, the Edit Vertex/Width option lets you alter the width of the polyline at any vertex. Thus, you can taper or otherwise vary polyline thicknesses. Try these steps:

1. Undo the tangent arc from the previous exercise.
2. Return to the Edit Vertex option, and place the X at the beginning vertex of a polyline segment that you want to change.
3. Type **W↵** to issue the Width option.
4. At the `Specify starting width for next segment <0.0000>:` prompt, enter a value—**12↵**, for example—indicating the polyline width desired at this vertex.
5. At the `Specify ending width for next segment <12.0000>:` prompt, enter the width—**24↵**, for example—for the next vertex.

The width of the polyline changes to your specifications (see Figure 18.16).

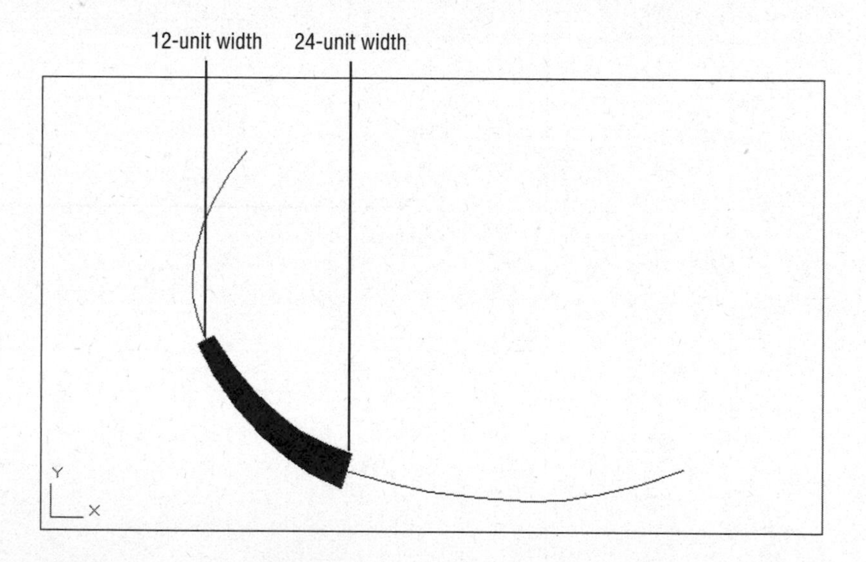

Figure 18.16
A polyline with the width of one segment increased

The Width option is useful when you want to create an irregular or curved area in your drawing that is to be filled in solid. This is another option that is sensitive to the polyline direction.

As you've seen throughout these exercises, you can use the Undo option to reverse the last Edit Vertex option used. You can also use the Exit option to leave Edit Vertex at any time. Enter **X↵** to display the Pedit prompt:

```
Enter an option
 [Close/Join/Width/Edit vertex/Fit/Spline/Decurve/Ltype gen/Reverse/Undo]:
```

FILLING IN SOLID AREAS

You've learned how to create a solid area by increasing the width of a polyline segment. But suppose that you want to create a solid shape or a thick line. AutoCAD provides the Solid and Donut commands to help you draw simple filled areas. Solid lets you create solid filled areas with straight sides, and Donut draws circles with a solid width.

You can create free-form, solid-filled areas by using the Solid hatch pattern. Create an enclosed area by using any set of objects, and then use the Hatch tool to apply a solid hatch pattern to the area. See Chapter 7, "Mastering Viewing Tools, Hatches, and External References," for details on using the Hatch tool.

Creating a Polyline Spline Curve

The Pedit command's Spline option offers you a way to draw smoother and more controllable curves than those produced by the Fit option. A polyline spline doesn't pass through the vertex points as does a fitted curve. Instead, the vertex points act as weights pulling the curve in their direction. These "weighted" vertex points are called *control vertices*. The polyline spline touches only its beginning and end vertices. Figure 18.17 illustrates this concept.

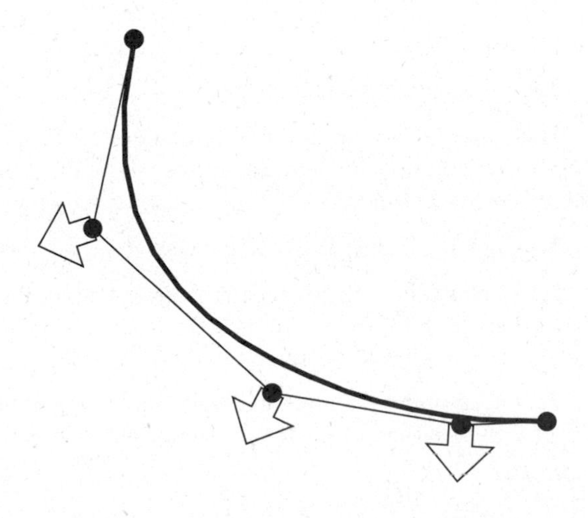

FIGURE 18.17
The polyline spline curve pulled toward its control vertices

A polyline spline curve doesn't represent a mathematically true curve. See the next section, "Using True Spline Curves," to learn how to draw a more accurate spline curve.

Let's see how using a polyline spline curve may influence the way you edit a curve:

1. Undo the width changes you made in the previous exercise. If you're still in the polyline edit mode, you can do this by pressing the Esc key.
2. To change the contour into a polyline spline curve, double-click the polyline to be curved.
3. At the `Enter an option [Close/Join/Width/Edit vertex/Fit/Spline/Decurve/Ltype gen/Reverse/Undo]:` prompt, type **S**↵. Your curve changes to look like Figure 18.18.

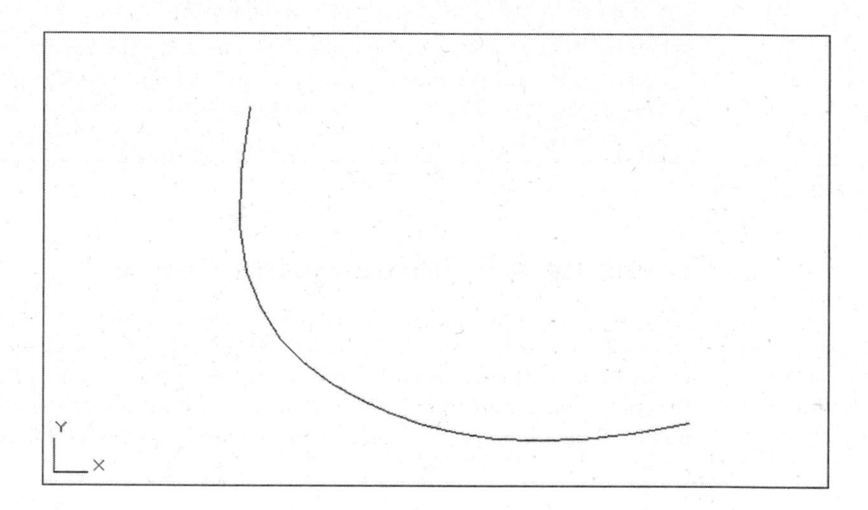

FIGURE 18.18
A spline curve

4. Press ↵ to exit Edit Polyline.

The curve takes on a smoother, more graceful appearance. It no longer passes through the points that you used to define it. To see where the points went and to find out how spline curves act, follow these steps:

1. Click the curve. The original vertices appear as grips (see the first image in Figure 18.19).
2. Click the grip that is second from the top of the curve, as shown in the first image in Figure 18.19, and move the grip around. The curve follows your moves, giving you immediate feedback on how it will look.
3. Pick a point as shown in the second image in Figure 18.19. The curve is now fixed in its new position, as shown in the bottom image of Figure 18.19.

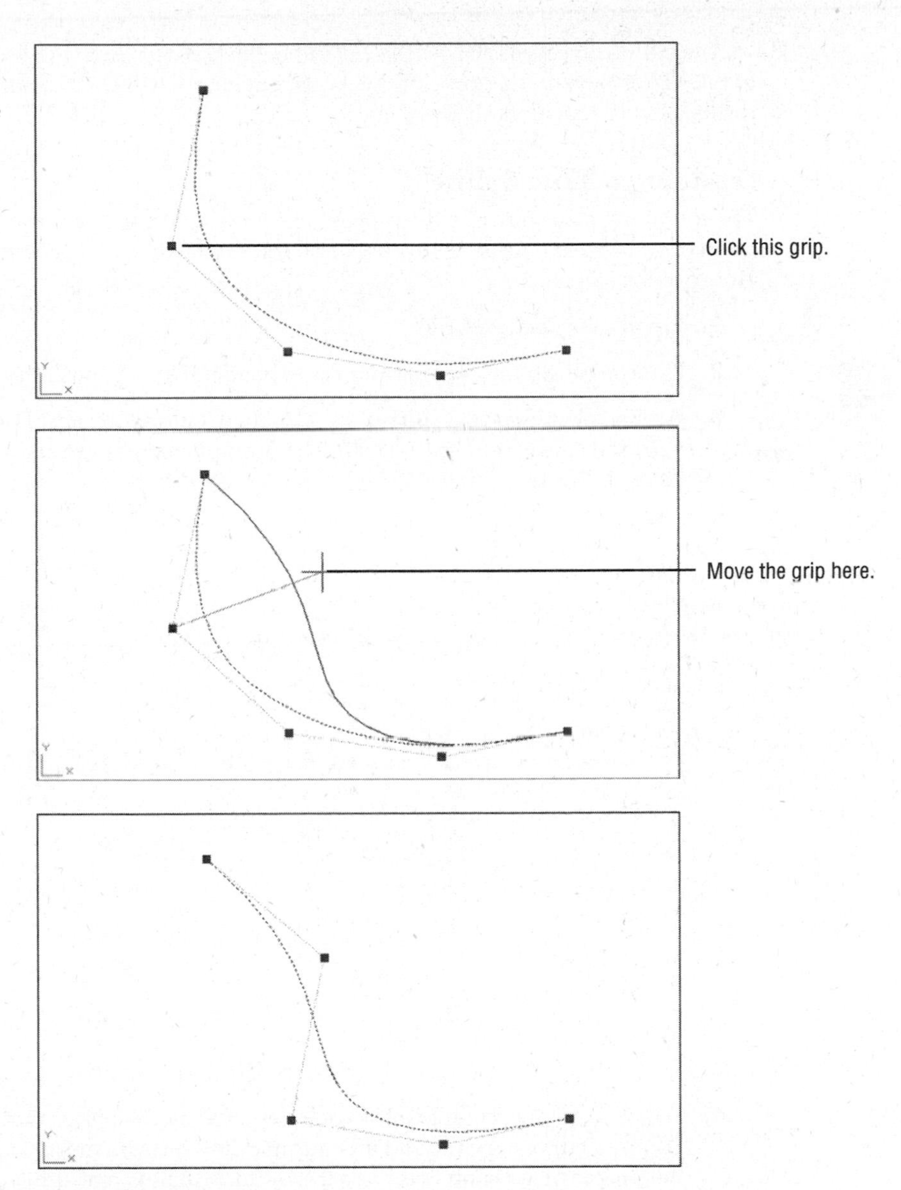

FIGURE 18.19
The fitted curve changed to a spline curve, with the location of the second vertex and the new curve

Using True Spline Curves

So far, you've been working with polylines to generate spline curves. The advantage of using polylines for curves is that they can be enhanced in many ways. You can modify their width, for instance, or join several curves. But at times, you'll need a more exact representation of a curve.

The spline object, created by choosing the Spline Fit or Spline CV tool in the Home tab's expanded Draw panel, produces a more accurate model of a spline curve in addition to giving you more control over its shape.

The spline objects are true *Non-Uniform Rational B-Spline (NURBS)* curves. A full description of NURBS is beyond the scope of this book, but basically NURBS are standard mathematical forms used to represent shapes.

Drawing a True Spline

The following steps describe the process used to create a spline curve. You don't have to create them now. Make a note of this section, and refer to it when you need to draw and edit a spline. Here are the steps:

1. Open the `topo2.dwg` file.

2. Choose the Spline Fit tool from the expanded Draw panel, or type **SPL↵**.
3. At the `Specify first point or [Method/Knots/Object]:` prompt, select a point to start the curve (see Figure 18.20). The prompt changes to `Enter next point or [start Tangency/toLerance]:`.

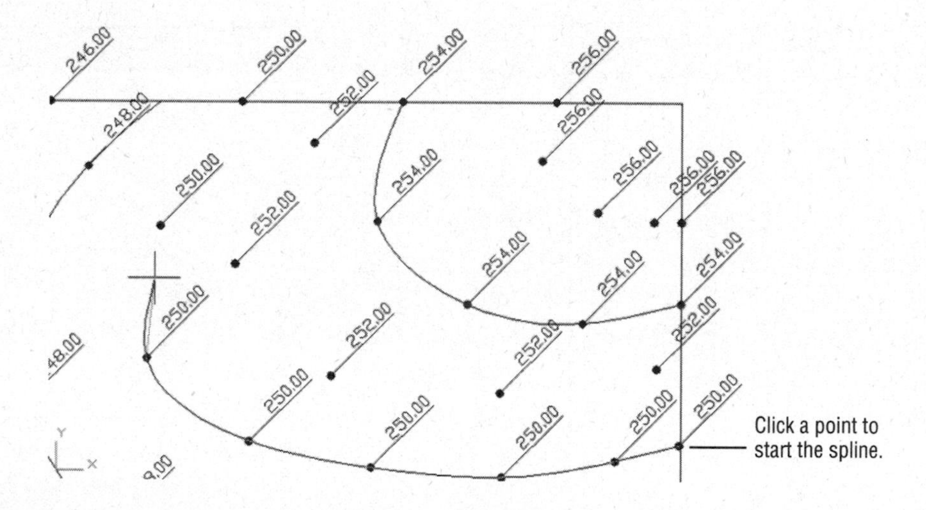

FIGURE 18.20 Start the spline curve at the first data point, and then continue to select points.

4. Continue to select points until you've entered all the points that you need. As you pick points, a curve appears, and it bends and flows as you move your cursor. In Figure 18.20, the Center object snap was used to select the donuts that appear as dots in the survey plan.
5. After you've selected the last point, press ↵ to exit the Spline command.

If you prefer, you can also control the tangency of the spline at its first and last points. The following steps describe how you can use the start Tangency option:

1. Start the spline just as before, and select the start point. At the `Enter next point or [start Tangency/toLerance]:` prompt, type **T↵**. A rubber-banding line appears from the first point of the curve.

2. The prompt changes to `Specify start tangent:`. Select a point indicating the tangency of the first point.

3. Continue to select the other points of your spline. After you've selected the last point, type T↵.

4. Use the cursor to indicate the tangency of the spline at the last point.

You now have a smooth curve that passes through the points that you selected. These points are called the *fit points*. If you click the curve, you'll see the grips appear at the location of these fit points, and you can adjust the curve by clicking the grip points and moving them. You'll also see an arrowhead grip that appears at the beginning of the spline. If you click this arrowhead grip, you see two options: Fit and Control Vertices (see Figure 18.21).

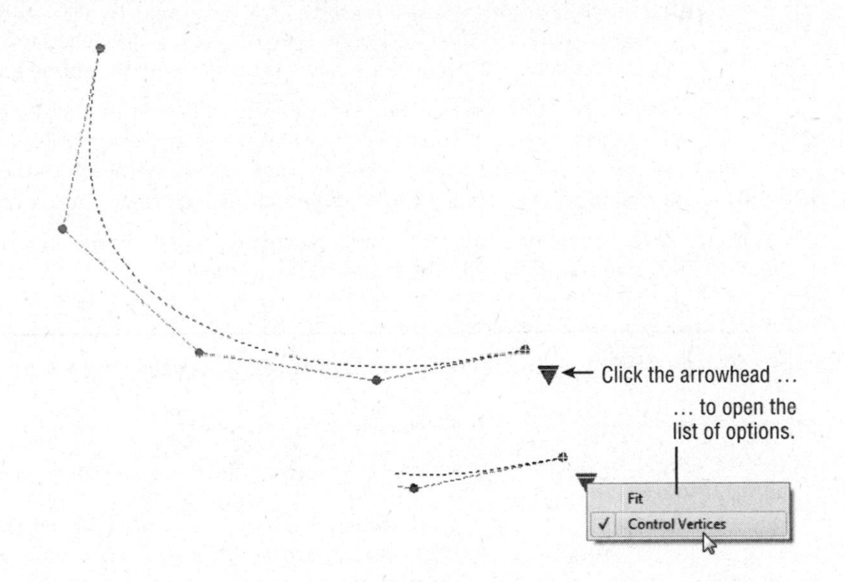

FIGURE 18.21
The Fit and Control Vertices options

The Show Fit Points option will display the grips at the fit points, which are the points that you used to draw the spline in the previous example. By default, these fit points lie on the spline, though you can adjust how closely the spline follows the fit points. You can also view the control vertices (CVs), which are points that control the curvature of the spline and do not lie on the spline itself (see Figure 18.17 earlier). Along with the CVs, you see a set of vectors called the *control polyline*. The control polyline helps you to visualize the relationship between the CVs and the spline.

Understanding the Spline Options

You may have noticed a few other options in the first Spline command prompt. When you start the Spline command, you see the Method, Knots, Degree, and Object options:

Method Method lets you choose between Fit and CV. The Fit option causes the spline to be drawn through the lines that you select. The CV, or Control Vertices, option causes the spline to use your selected points as control vertices (see Figure 18.17 earlier). After you've drawn a spline, you can switch between fit and CV views of your polyline (see Figure 18.21 earlier).

Knots This option is available only if Fit is chosen in the Method option discussed previously. This option offers three additional options: Chord, Square Root, and Uniform. These options affect the shape of the spline as it passes through the fit point.

Chord The Chord option numbers the knots with decimal values.

Square Root The Square Root option numbers the knots based on the square root of the chord length between consecutive knots.

Uniform The Uniform option numbers the knots in consecutive integers.

Degree This option is available only if CV is chosen in the Method option discussed previously. The Degree option gives you control over the number of control vectors required to create a bend in the spline. You can use the values 1 through 10. The value 1 will cause the spline to produce straight lines, 2 will generate sharp curves, 3 will generate less sharp curves, and so on. In simple terms, the Degree value controls how closely the spline follows its control polyline.

Object Object lets you convert a polyline into a spline. If the Fit option is selected under the Method option, you can convert only a spline-fitted polyline. If the CV option is selected under the Method option, you can select any polyline. With the CV Method option, the polyline will change shape so that the polyline vectors become control vectors.

After you start to select points for the spline, you see the end Tangency, toLerance, Undo, and Close options. Table 18.1 describes these options.

TABLE 18.1: The Spline command options for selecting points

OPTION	FUNCTION
end Tangency	Gives you control over the tangency at the beginning and end points of the spline.
toLerance	Lets you control how the curve passes through the fit points. The default value 0 causes the curve to pass through the fit points. Any value greater than 0 causes the curve to pass close to, but not through, the points.
Undo	Lets you undo a point selection in case you select the wrong point.
Close	Lets you close the curve into a loop. If you choose this option, you're prompted to indicate a tangent direction for the closing point. This option does not appear until at least three points have been chosen.

JOINING SPLINES TO OTHER OBJECTS

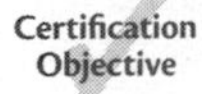

While editing drawings, you may encounter a situation where a spline has been broken into two splines and you need the broken spline to behave as a single spline. The Join command will "mend" a broken spline, or any set of splines for that matter, as long as the splines are contiguous (touching

end to end). To use the Join command, click the Join tool from the Home tab's expanded Modify panel or type **Join**↵. Select the splines that you want to join.

Join can be used with other objects as well. You can join lines, polylines, 3D polylines, arcs, elliptical arcs, and helixes with the following restrictions:

- Any of these objects can be joined to a spline, polyline, 3D polyline, or helix.
- Lines cannot be joined to arcs or elliptical arcs.
- Arcs cannot be joined to elliptical arcs.
- Arcs must have the same center point and radius but can have a gap between the segments that you wish to join. The same is true for elliptical arcs.
- Lines must be collinear, but there can be gaps between the lines to be joined.
- Unless you are joining to a polyline or 3D polyline, objects must be on the same plane.

Fine-Tuning Spline Curves

Spline curves are different from other types of objects, and many of the standard editing commands won't work on splines. For making changes to splines, AutoCAD offers the Edit Spline tool, otherwise known as the Splinedit command, in the Home tab's expanded Modify panel.

Controlling the Fit Data of a Spline

The Fit Data option of the Splinedit command lets you adjust the tangency of the beginning and endpoints, add new control points, and adjust spline tolerance settings. To get to these options, follow these steps:

1. Choose Edit Spline from the expanded Modify panel, or type **SPE**↵ at the Command prompt.
2. At the `Select spline:` prompt, select the last spline that you drew in the previous exercise.
3. At the `Enter an option [Close/Join/Fit data/Edit vertex/convert to Polyline/Reverse/Undo/eXit]:` prompt, type **F**↵ to select the Fit Data option.
4. At the `Add/Close/Delete/Kink/Move/Purge/Tangents/toLerance/eXit] <eXit>:` prompt, enter the option that you want to use. For example, to change the tangency of the first and last points of your spline, type **T**↵. You're prompted to select the tangent point of the first and last points. Table 18.2 lists the Splinedit Fit Data options and their purposes.

If you prefer, you can double-click a spline to start the Splinedit command instead of selecting the Edit Spline tool in the Modify panel. If you have the Dynamic Input feature turned on, you can select Splinedit options from a menu that appears at the cursor (see Figure 18.22) instead of typing in the option keyboard shortcuts. If you double-click the polyline to select it and then right-click anywhere in the drawing, a context menu will appear that also shows the options.

FIGURE 18.22
The Splinedit options

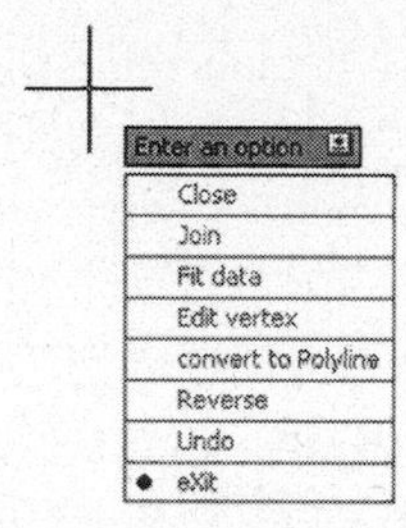

TABLE 18.2: The Fit Data options of the Splinedit command

OPTION	FUNCTION
Add	Lets you add more control points
Close	Lets you close the spline into a loop
Delete	Removes a control point from the spline
Kink	Lets you add a control point, which does not maintain curvature
Move	Lets you move a control point
Purge	Deletes the fit data of the spline, thereby eliminating the Fit Data option for the purged spline
Tangents	Lets you change the tangency of the first and last points
toLerance	Controls the distance between the spline and a control point
eXit	Exits the Splinedit command

USING GRIP OPTIONS

The Splinedit command gives you a lot of control when you want to edit a spline. But if you want to make some minor changes, you can use the pop-up menu that appears when you hover over a grip on the spline. First, click the spline to expose its grips, and then hover over a fit point or CV. The list of options appears.

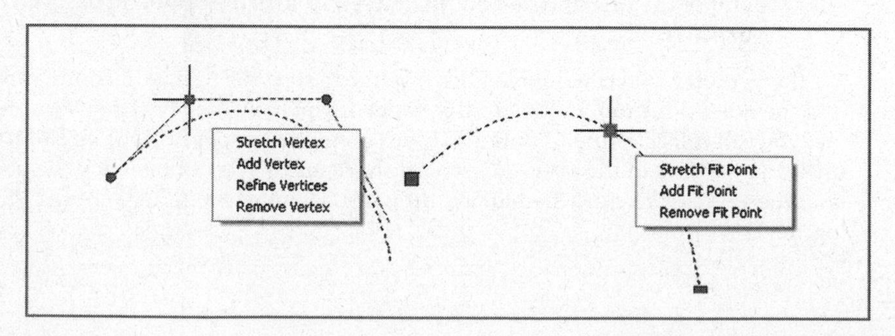

The options are slightly different depending on whether you have the fit points or CVs displayed. The options enable you to add or remove a fit point or CV quickly, and in the case of CVs, you also have the Refine Vertices option. The Refine option lets you control the pull exerted on a spline by a CV.

WHEN CAN'T YOU USE FIT DATA?

The Fit Data option of the Splinedit command offers many ways to edit a spline. However, this option isn't available to all spline curves. When you invoke certain other Splinedit options, a spline curve loses its fit data, thereby disabling the Fit Data option. These operations are as follows:

- Fitting a spline to a tolerance (Spline toLerance) and moving its control vertices.
- Fitting a spline to a tolerance and opening or closing it.
- Refining the spline.
- Purging the spline of its fit data by using the Purge option of the Splinedit command. (Choose Edit Spline from the expanded Modify panel, or enter **SPE↵**; then select the spline and enter **F↵P↵**.)

Also note that the Fit Data option isn't available when you edit spline curves that were created from polyline splines. See the sidebar "Turning Objects into Polylines and Polylines into Splines" earlier in this chapter.

If you'd like to learn more about the Splinedit options, check the AutoCAD Exchange website. It offers a detailed description of how these options work.

Marking Divisions on Curves

Perhaps one of the most difficult things to do in manual drafting is to mark regular intervals on a curve. AutoCAD offers the Divide and Measure commands to help you perform this task with speed and accuracy.

You can find the Divide and Measure tools on the expanded Draw Ribbon panel, as shown in Figure 18.23. Click the title bar of the Draw panel to find the Divide and Measure tools.

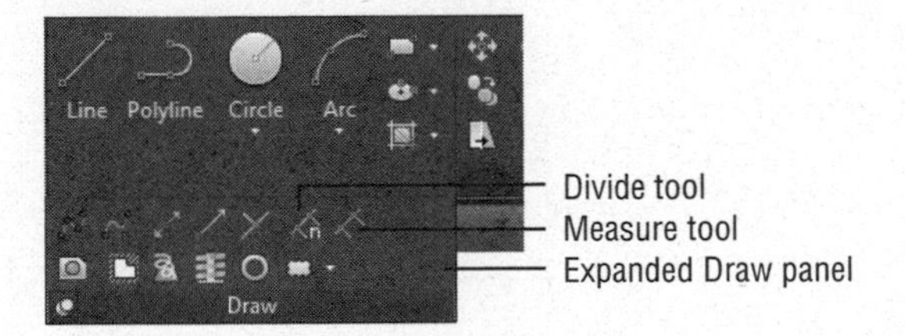

FIGURE 18.23
The Divide and Measure tools are in the expanded Draw Ribbon panel.

CONVERTING A SPLINE INTO A POLYLINE

AutoCAD allows you to convert a spline object into a polyline. This can be very useful when you want to edit a spline using the polyline edit tools instead of the spline editing tools. You will lose some precision in the conversion, but more often than not this is not an issue.

continues

continued

To convert a spline to a polyline, double-click the spline and then, at the `Enter an option` prompt, type **P**↵. At the `Specify a precision <10>:` prompt, enter a value from 0 to 99. Note that a higher precision value may reduce the performance of AutoCAD, so use a reasonable value. You may want to experiment with different values and pick the lowest value that will still give you the results you want.

The Divide and Measure commands are discussed here in conjunction with polylines, but you can use these commands on any object except blocks and text.

Dividing Objects into Segments of Equal Length

Use the Divide command to divide an object into a specific number of equal segments. For example, suppose that you need to mark off the contour on which you've been working in this chapter into nine equal segments. One way to do this is first to find the length of the contour by using the List command and then sit down with a pencil and paper to figure out the exact distances between the marks. There is another, easier way, however.

The Divide command places a set of point objects on a line, an arc, a circle, or a polyline, marking off exact divisions. The following exercise shows how it works:

1. Open the `18a-divd.dwg` file. This file is similar to the one with which you've been working in the previous exercises.
2. Click the Divide tool in the expanded Draw panel, or type **DIV**↵.
3. At the `Select object to divide:` prompt, pick the spline contour line that shows Xs in Figure 18.24.

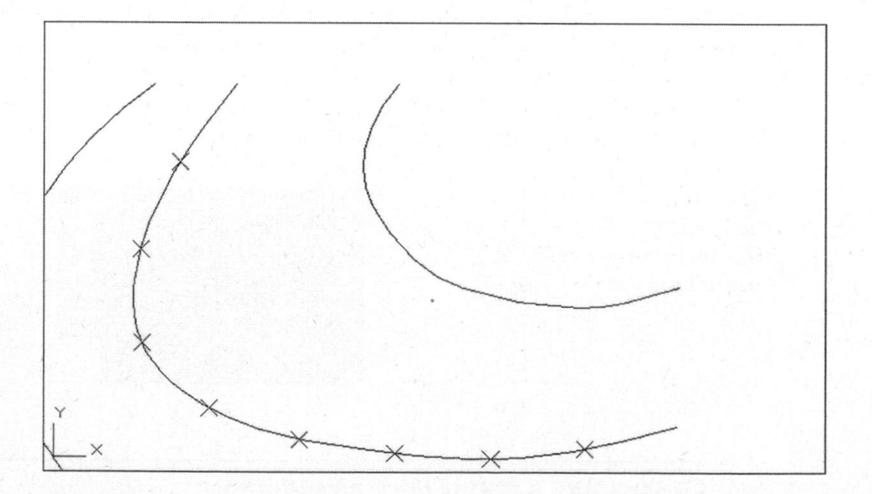

FIGURE 18.24 Using the Divide command on a polyline

4. The `Enter the number of segments or [Block]:` prompt that appears next is asking for the number of divisions that you want on the selected object. Enter **9**↵. The Command

prompt returns, and it appears that nothing has happened. But AutoCAD has placed several point objects on the contour that indicate the locations of the nine divisions you that requested. To see these points more clearly, continue with the exercise.

5. Choose Point Style from the Home tab's expanded Utilities panel or type **DDPTYPE**↵ to open the Point Style dialog box (see Figure 18.25).

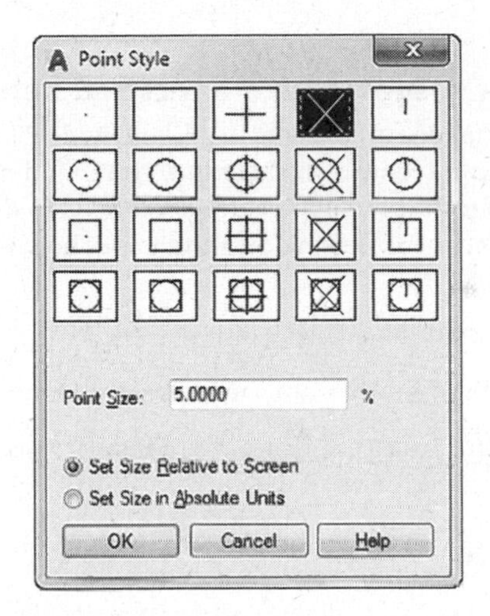

FIGURE 18.25
The Point Style dialog box

6. Click the X point style in the top row of the dialog box, click the Set Size Relative To Screen radio button, and then click OK.

7. If the Xs don't appear, enter **RE**↵. A set of Xs appears showing the nine divisions (shown earlier in Figure 18.24).

You can also change the point style by changing the `Pdmode` system variable. When `Pdmode` is set to 3, the point appears as an X.

The Divide command uses *point* objects to indicate the division points. You create point objects by using the Point command. They usually appear as dots. Unfortunately, such points are nearly invisible when placed on top of other objects. But, as you've seen, you can alter their shape by using the Point Style dialog box. You can use these X points to place objects or references to break the object being divided. (The Divide command doesn't cut the object into smaller divisions.)

SKETCHING WITH AUTOCAD

AutoCAD offers the Sketch command, which lets you do freehand drawing. The Sketch command can be set to draw polylines. If you'd like to know more about Sketch, the AutoCAD Help window offers several excellent descriptions of how it works. Click the Help tool (the question mark icon) in the InfoCenter, and then at the AutoCAD 2018 Help website, enter **Sketch** in the search box.

Finding Hidden Node Points

If you're in a hurry and you don't want to bother changing the shape of the point objects, you can do the following: Set Running Osnaps to Node. Then, when you're in Point Selection mode, move the cursor over the divided curve. When the cursor gets close to a point object, the Node osnap marker appears.

Dividing Objects into Specified Lengths

The Measure command acts just like Divide. However, instead of dividing an object into segments of equal length, the Measure command marks intervals of a specified distance along an object. For example, suppose that you need to mark some segments exactly 60″ apart along the contour. Try the following exercise to see how the Measure command is used to accomplish this task:

1. Erase the X-shaped point objects.
2. Click Measure from the expanded Draw panel, or type **ME↵**.
3. At the Select object to measure: prompt, pick the contour at a point closest to its lower endpoint. We'll explain shortly why this is important.
4. At the Specify length of segment or [Block]: prompt, enter **60↵**. The X points appear at the specified distance.
5. Exit without saving this file.

Bear in mind that the point you pick on the object to be measured determines where the Measure command begins measuring. In the previous exercise, for example, you picked the contour near its bottom endpoint. If you picked the top of the contour, the results would be different because the measurement would start at the top, not the bottom. If the object's length is not equally divisible by the measured segment length, the last segment will be shorter than 60 units.

Marking Off Intervals by Using Blocks Instead of Points

You can also use the Block option under the Divide and Measure commands to place blocks at regular intervals along a line, a polyline, or an arc. Here's how to use blocks as markers:

1. Be sure that the block that you want to use is part of the current drawing file.
2. Start either the Divide or Measure command, and then select an object.
3. At the Specify length of segment or [Block]: prompt, enter **B↵**.
4. At the Enter name of block to insert: prompt, enter the name of a block.
5. At the Align Block with Object? [Yes/No] <Y>: prompt, press ↵ if you want the blocks to follow the alignment of the selected object. (Entering **N↵** inserts each block at a 0-degree angle.)

6. At the `Enter the number of segments:` prompt or the `Specify length of segment:` prompt, enter the number or length of the segments. The blocks appear at regular intervals on the selected object.

One example of using the Block option of Divide or Measure is to place a row of sinks equally spaced along a wall. Alternatively, you might use this technique to make multiple copies of an object along an irregular path defined by a polyline. In civil engineering projects, you can indicate a fence line by using Divide or Measure to place Xs along a polyline. You can also use the Array command to have blocks appear at regular intervals along a spline or polyline. See Chapter 6, "Editing and Reusing Data to Work Efficiently," for more on the Array command.

The Bottom Line

Create and edit polylines. Polylines are extremely versatile. You can use them in just about any situation where you need to draw line work that is continuous. For this reason, you'll want to master polylines early in your AutoCAD training.

Master It Draw the part shown here.

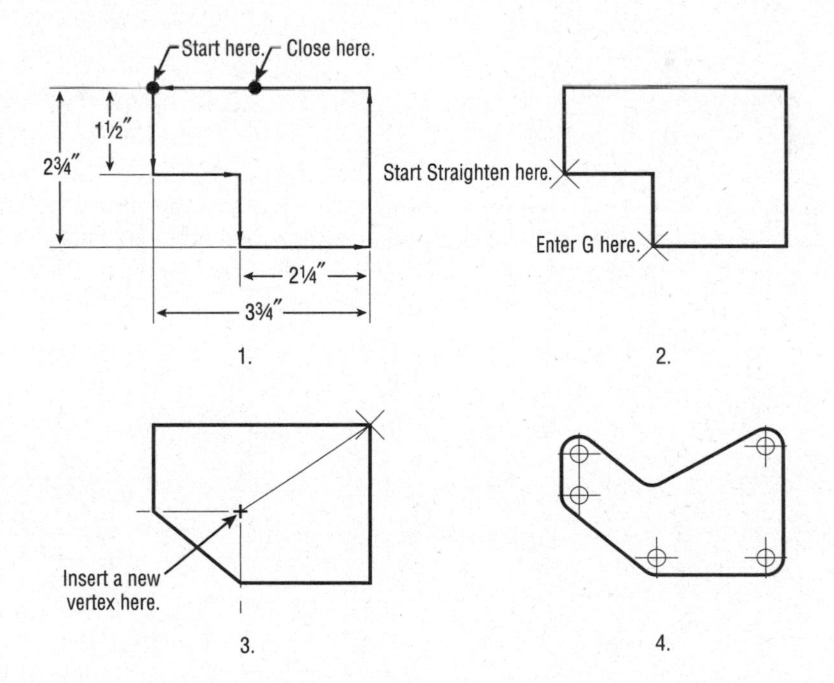

Create a polyline spline curve. Polylines can be used to draw fairly accurate renditions of spline curves. This feature of polylines makes them very useful AutoCAD objects.

Master It Try drawing the outline of an object that contains no or few straight lines, as shown in the file `lowerfairing.jpg`, which is included in the Chapter 18 sample files. You can use the methods described in Chapter 13 to import a raster image of your object and then trace over the image using polyline splines.

Create and edit true spline curves. If you need an accurate spline curve, you'll want to use the Spline tool. Spline objects offer many fine-tuning options that you won't find with polylines.

Master It Try tracing over the same image from the earlier "Master It" section, but this time use the Spline tool.

Mark divisions on curves. The Divide and Measure tools offer a quick way to mark off distances on a curved object. This can be a powerful resource in AutoCAD that you may use often.

Master It Mark off 12 equal divisions of the spline curve that you drew in the previous "Master It" exercise.

Chapter 19

Getting and Exchanging Data from Drawings

Autodesk® AutoCAD® drawings contain a wealth of data—graphic information such as distances and angles between objects as well as precise areas and the properties of objects. However, as you become more experienced with AutoCAD, you'll also need data of a different nature. For example, as you begin to work in groups, the various settings in a drawing become important. You'll need statistics on the amount of time that you spend on a drawing when you're billing computer time. As your projects become more complex, file maintenance requires a greater degree of attention. To take full advantage of AutoCAD, you'll want to exchange information about your drawing with other people and other programs.

In this chapter, you'll explore the ways in which all types of data can be extracted from AutoCAD and made available to you, to your co-workers, and to other programs. First, you'll learn how to obtain specific data about your drawings. Then, you'll look at ways to exchange data with other programs, such as word processors, desktop publishing software, and even other CAD programs.

In this chapter, you will learn to

- Find the area of closed boundaries
- Get general information
- Use the DXF file format to exchange CAD data with other programs
- Use AutoCAD drawings in page layout programs
- Use OLE to import data

Finding the Area of Closed Boundaries

One of the most frequently sought pieces of data that you can extract from an AutoCAD drawing is the area of a closed boundary. In architecture, you often need to find the area of a room or the footprint of a building. In civil engineering, you may want to determine the area covered by the boundary of a property line or the area of cut for a roadway. In the following sections, you'll learn how to use AutoCAD to obtain exact area information from your drawings.

Finding the Area of an Object

Architects, engineers, and facilities planners often need to know the square footage of a room or a section of a building. A structural engineer might want to find the cross-sectional area of a beam. In this section, you'll practice determining the areas of regular objects.

First, you'll determine the square-footage area of the living room and entry of your studio unit plan:

1. Start AutoCAD. Open the `Unit.dwg` file that you created in a previous chapter, or use the `19a-unit.dwg` file.
2. Zoom into the living room and entry area so that you have a view similar to Figure 19.1.

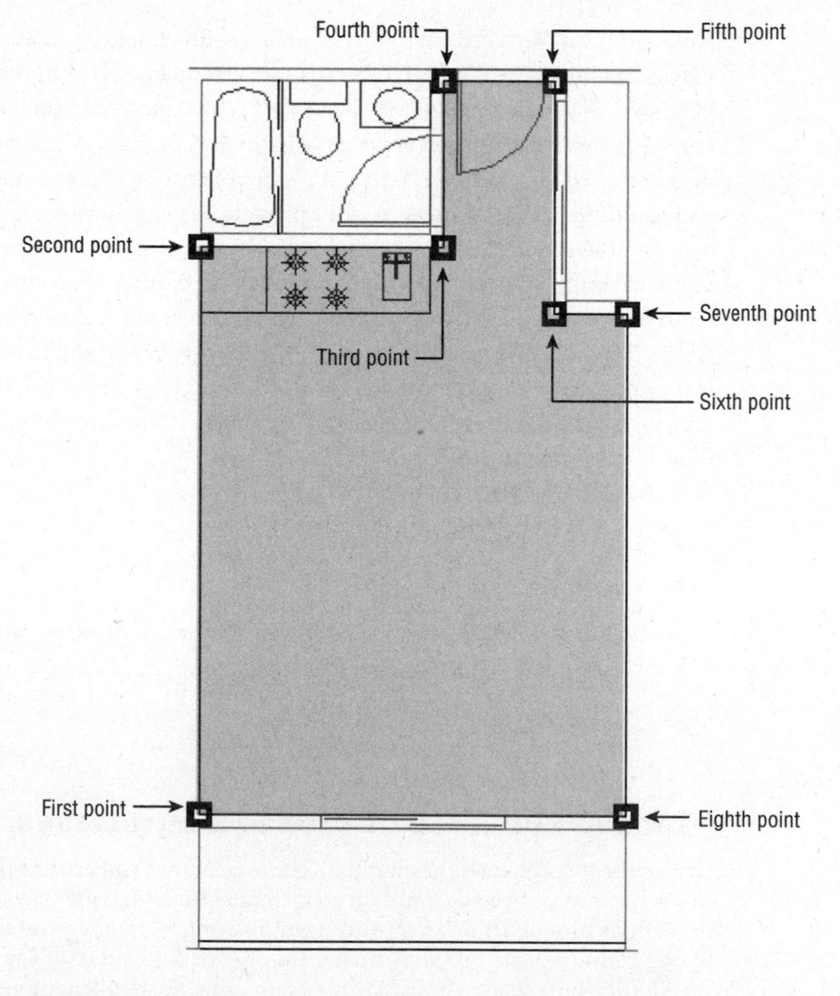

FIGURE 19.1 Selecting the points to determine the area of the living room and entry

3. On the Home tab's Utilities panel, click the Area tool on the Measure flyout, or type **MEA↵AR↵** at the Command prompt. This starts the Measuregeom command with the Area option.

4. Using the Endpoint osnap, start with the lower-left corner of the living room and select the points shown in Figure 19.1. You're indicating the boundary. Notice that as you click points, the area being calculated is indicated in green.

5. When you've come to the eighth point shown in Figure 19.1, press ↵. You'll see the following message:

   ```
   Area = 39570.00 square in. (274.7917 square ft), Perimeter = 76'-0"
   ```

6. Type **X**↵ to exit the Measuregeom command.

The number of points that you can pick to define an area is limitless, which means that you can obtain the areas of complex shapes.

FIND THE COORDINATE OF A POINT OR A DISTANCE IN A DRAWING

To find absolute coordinates in a drawing, use the ID command. Click the ID Point tool on the Home tab's expanded Utilities panel, or type **ID**↵. At the `Specify point:` prompt, use the osnap overrides to pick a point; its x-, y-, and z-coordinates are displayed on the command line.

To find the distance between two points, choose Distance from the Measure flyout on the Home tab's Utilities panel or type **Dist**↵ and then click two points. AutoCAD will display the distance in the drawing as Delta X, Delta Y, and Delta Z coordinates and as a direct distance between the selected points. Angle information is also provided. The distance is also displayed in the command line.

Using Hatch Patterns to Find Areas

Hatch patterns are used primarily to add graphics to your drawing, but they can also serve as a means for finding areas. You can use any hatch pattern that you want to because you're interested only in the area that it reports back to you. You can also set up a special layer devoted to area calculations and then add to this layer the hatch patterns that you use to find areas. That way, you can turn off the hatch patterns so that they don't plot, or you can turn off the Plot setting for that layer to ensure that it doesn't appear in your final output.

To practice using hatch patterns to find an area, do the following:

1. Set the current layer to FLOOR.

2. Turn off the DOOR and FIXTURE layers. Also make sure that the CEILING layer is turned on. You want the hatch pattern to follow the interior wall outline, so you will need to turn off any objects that will affect the outline, such as the door and kitchen.

3. Click Hatch on the Home tab's Draw panel or type **H**↵ to open the Hatch Creation tab.

MEASURING BOUNDARIES THAT HAVE GAPS

If the area that you're trying to measure has gaps, set the Gap Tolerance setting in the Hatch Creation tab's expanded Options panel to a value higher than the size of the gaps.

4. At the `Pick internal point or [Select objects/Undo/seTtings]:` prompt, click in the interior of the unit plan. The outline of the interior is highlighted, and the pattern is placed in the plan (see Figure 19.2). You might also notice that before you click in the unit plan, you get a preview of the hatch.

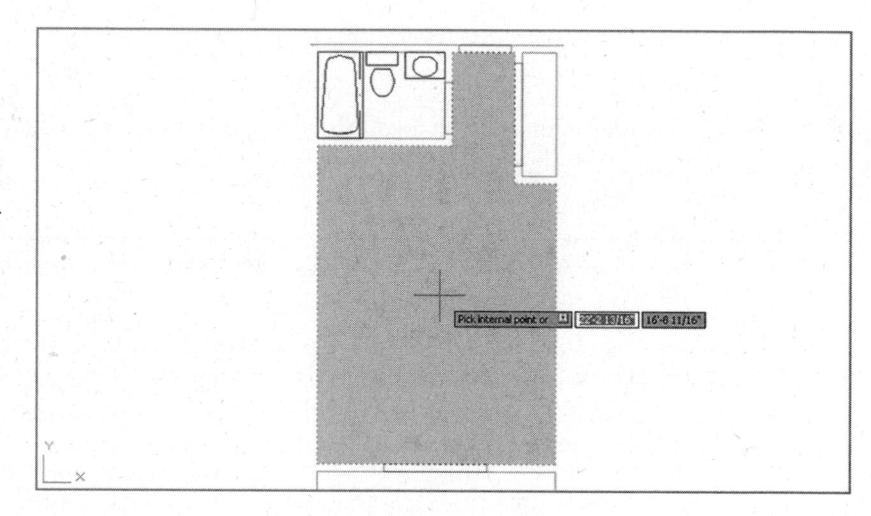

FIGURE 19.2
After you click a point on the interior of the plan to place a hatch pattern, an outline of the area is highlighted and the hatch appears.

5. Press ↵ to complete the hatch.

6. On the Home tab's Utilities panel, click the Area tool on the Measure flyout and then type **O**↵, or type **MEA**↵**AR**↵**O**↵ at the Command prompt.
7. Click the hatch pattern that you just created. Again, you get the following message:

```
Area = 39570.00 square in. (274.7917 square ft), Perimeter = 76'-0"
```

8. Press **X**↵ to exit the command.

If you need to recall the last area calculation value that you received, enter **'Setvar**↵**Area**↵. The area is displayed in the prompt. Enter **'Perimeter**↵ to get the last perimeter calculated.

The Hatch command creates a hatch pattern that conforms to the boundary of an area. This feature, combined with the ability of the Measuregeom command to find the area of a hatch pattern, makes short work of area calculations. Another advantage of using hatch patterns is that, by default, hatch patterns avoid islands within the boundary of the area that you're trying to find.

The Properties palette also reports the area of a hatch pattern. Select the hatch pattern whose area you want to find, and then right-click and select Properties. Scroll down to the bottom of the Geometry group and you'll see the Area listing for the hatch pattern that you selected. You can select more than one hatch pattern and find the cumulative area of the selected hatch patterns in the Properties palette.

Adding and Subtracting Areas with the Area Command

Hatch patterns work extremely well for finding areas, but if you find that you can't use hatch patterns for some reason, you have an alternative. You can still use a command called Boundary to generate a polyline outline of an enclosed boundary and then obtain the area of the outline using the Measuregeom command (Measure on the Home tab's Utilities panel). If islands are present within the boundary, you have to use the Subtract feature of the Measuregeom command to remove their area from the overall boundary area. In this section, you'll use the example of the flange part, which contains two islands in the form of the two circles, at the lower end (see Figure 19.3).

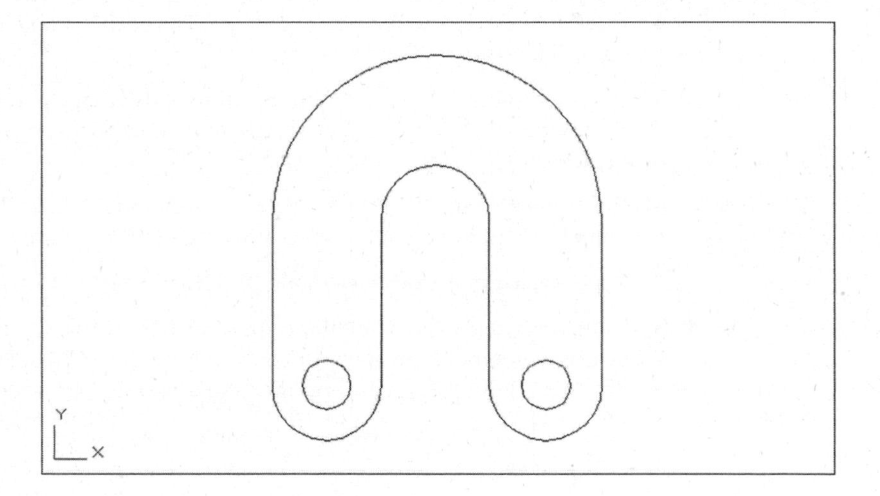

FIGURE 19.3
A flange to a mechanical device

By using the Add and Subtract options of the Measuregeom command, you can maintain a running total of several separate areas being calculated, a capability that gives you flexibility in finding areas of complex shapes. This section guides you through the use of these options.

For the following exercise, you'll use a flange shape that contains circles. This shape is composed of simple arcs, lines, and circles. Use these steps to see how you can keep a running tally of areas:

1. Exit the `Unit.dwg` file, and open the file `Flange.dwg` (see Figure 19.3). Don't bother to save changes in the `Unit.dwg` file.

2. Select Boundary from the Hatch flyout on the Home tab's Draw panel or type **BO**↵ to open the Boundary Creation dialog box (see Figure 19.4).
3. Click the Pick Points icon.

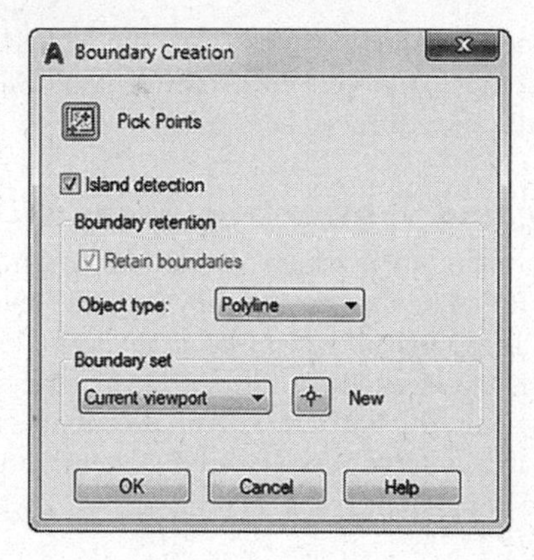

FIGURE 19.4
The Boundary Creation dialog box

4. Click in the interior of the flange shape. The entire shape is highlighted, including the circle islands.

5. Press ↵. You now have a polyline outline of the shape and the circles, although it won't be obvious that polylines have been created because they're drawn over the boundary objects.

6. Continue by using the Measuregeom command's Add and Subtract options. Select Area from the Measure flyout on the Home tab's Utilities panel.

7. Type **A**↵ to enter Add Area mode, and then type **O**↵ to select an object.

8. Click a vertical edge of the flange outline. If Selection Cycling is on, you will see a pop-up asking you what type of object you want to select. Choose Polyline. You see the selected area highlighted in green, and the following message appears in the Command window:

```
Area = 27.7080, Perimeter = 30.8496
Total area = 27.7080
```

9. Press ↵ to exit Add Area mode.

10. Type **S**↵ to enter Subtract Area mode, and then type **O**↵ to select an object.

11. Click one of the circles. If Selection Cycling is on, select Polyline from the pop-up menu. You see the following message:

```
Total area = 0.6070, Circumference = 2.7618
Total area = 27.1010
```

This shows you the area and perimeter of the selected object and a running count of the total area of the flange outline minus the circle. You also see the area of the subtracted circle change to a different color so that you can distinguish between the calculated area and the subtracted area.

12. Click the other circle. If Selection Cycling is on, select Polyline from the pop-up menu. You see the following message:

```
Total area = 0.6070, Circumference = 2.7618
Total area = 26.4940
```

Again, you see a listing of the area and circumference of the selected object along with a running count of the total area, which now shows a value of 26.4940. This last value is the true area of the flange.

13. Press ↵ and type **X↵X↵** to exit the Measuregeom command. You can also press the Esc key to exit the command.

In this exercise, you first selected the main object outline and then subtracted the island objects. You don't have to follow this order; you can start by subtracting areas to get negative area values and then add other areas to come up with a total. You can also alternate between Add and Subtract modes, in case you forget to add or subtract areas.

You may have noticed that the Measuregeom Command prompt offered `Specify first corner point or [Object/Add area/Subtract area/eXit]:` as the default option for both the Add Area and Subtract Area modes. Instead of using the Object option to pick the circles, you can start selecting points to indicate a rectangular area as you did in the first exercise in this chapter.

Whenever you press ↵ while selecting points for an area calculation, AutoCAD automatically connects the first and last points and returns the calculated area. If you're in Add or Subtract mode, you can then continue to select points, but the additional areas are calculated from the *next* point that you pick.

As you can see from these exercises, it's simpler to outline an area first with a polyline wherever possible and then use the Object option to add and subtract area values of polylines.

In this example, you obtained the area of a mechanical object. However, the same process works for any type of area that you want to calculate. It can be the area of a piece of property on a topographical map or the area of a floor plan. For example, you can use the Object option to find the area of an irregular shape, such as the one shown in Figure 19.5, as long as it's a closed polyline.

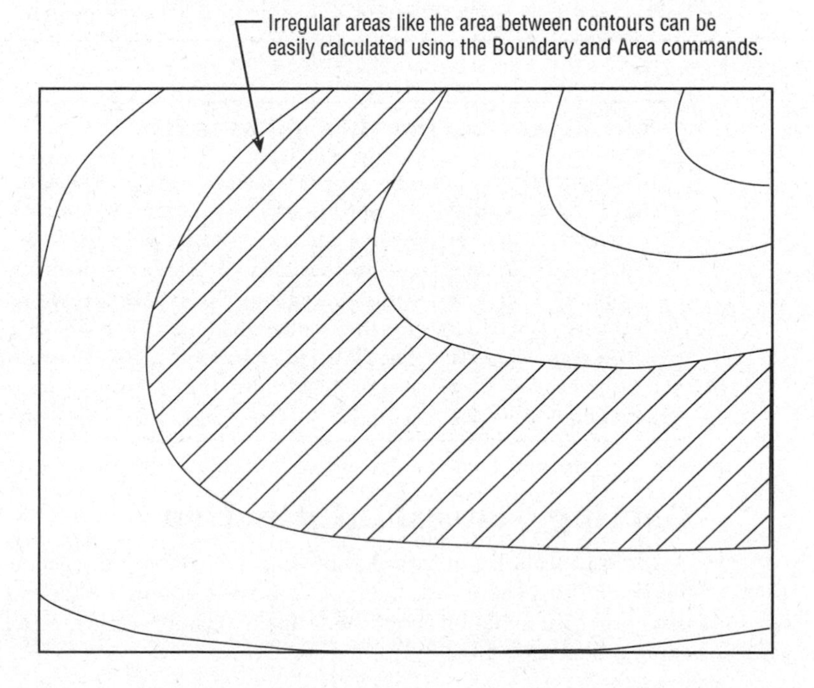

FIGURE 19.5
The site plan with an area to be calculated

When issued through the keyboard as **MEA**↵, the Measuregeom command offers a number of other options for measuring your drawing. The options appear in the Command window as `[Distance/Radius/Angle/ARea/Volume]<Distance>` or at the cursor as a Dynamic Input option. These options are automatically selected when you click the related tool from the Measure flyout on the Utilities panel. Remember that to use an option, you must type the capitalized letter or letters of the option shown in the list. Table 19.1 gives you descriptions of the options and how they are used.

TABLE 19.1: The Measuregeom command options

OPTION	USE
Distance	Returns the distance between two points. Type **D**↵ and select two points. You can also measure cumulative distances by typing **M**↵ after selecting the first point.
Radius	Returns the radius of an arc or circle. Type **R**↵ and select an arc or circle.
Angle	Returns the angle of an arc or the angle between two lines. Type **A**↵ and select the arc or two nonparallel lines.
ARea	Returns the area of a set of points or boundary. Type **AR**↵ to use this option. See previous exercises for instruction on the use of this option.
Volume	Returns the 3D volume based on an area times height.
eXit	Exits the current option. This option appears only if a Measuregeom option is carried out. Otherwise, you can press the Esc key to exit the command.

RECORDING AREA DATA IN A DRAWING FILE

In just about every project we've worked on, area calculations were an important part of the drawing process. As an aid in recording area calculations, we created a block that contains attributes for the room number, the room area, and the date when the room area was last measured. The area and date attributes were made invisible so that only the room number appears. The block with the attribute is then inserted into every room. Once the area of the room is discovered, it can be added to the block attribute with the Ddatte command. Such a block can be used with any drawing in which area data needs to be gathered and stored. See Chapter 12, "Using Attributes," for more on attributes. You can also use the Field object type to display the area of a polyline automatically as a text object. See Chapter 10, "Using Fields and Tables," for more on fields.

Getting General Information

So far in this book, you've seen how to get data about the geometry of your drawings. AutoCAD also includes a set of tools that you can use to access the general state of your drawings. You can gather information about the status of current settings in a file or the time a drawing was created and last edited.

In the following sections, you'll practice extracting this type of information from your drawing.

Determining the Drawing's Status

When you work with a group of people on a large project, keeping track of a drawing's setup becomes crucial. You can use the Status command to obtain general information about the drawing on which you're working, such as the base point, current mode settings, and workspace or computer memory use. The Status command is especially helpful when you're editing a drawing on which someone else has worked, because you may want to identify and change settings for your own style of working. Select Application ➤ Drawing Utilities ➤ Status to display a list like the one shown in Figure 19.6. Note that you may see the `Press ENTER to continue:` prompt to display all of the data from the Status command.

FIGURE 19.6 The Status screen of the AutoCAD command-line interface

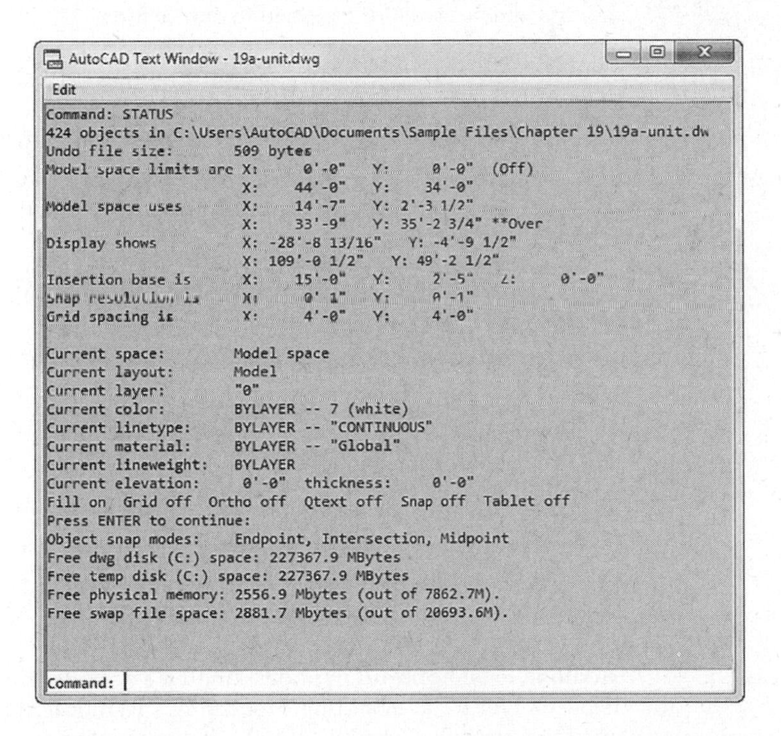

Here is a brief description of each item on the Status command's display in the expanded command line. Note that some of the items that you see on the screen will vary somewhat from what we've shown here, but the information applies to virtually all situations except where noted:

Number Objects In Drive:\Folder\Subfolder\Name.dwg The number of entities or objects in the drawing.

Undo File Size The size of the Undo file located in the user temp folder.

Model Space Limits Are The coordinates of the model space limits. It also indicates whether limits are turned off or on. (See Chapter 3, "Setting Up and Using the Drafting Tools," for more details on limits.)

Model Space Uses The area the drawing occupies; equivalent to the extents of the drawing.

****Over** If present, this means that part of the drawing is outside the limit boundary.

Display Shows The area covered by the current view.

Insertion Base Is, Snap Resolution Is, and Grid Spacing Is The current default values for these mode settings.

Current Space Model space or paper space.

Current Layout The current tab.

Current Layer The current layer.

Current Color The color assigned to new objects.

Current Linetype The linetype assigned to new objects.

Current Material The material assigned to new objects.

Current Lineweight The current default lineweight setting.

Current Elevation/Thickness The current default z-coordinate for new objects plus the default thickness of objects. These are both 3D-related settings. (See Chapter 20, "Creating 3D Drawings," for details.)

Fill, Grid, Ortho, Qtext, Snap, and Tablet The status of these options.

Object Snap Modes The current active osnap setting.

Free Dwg Disk (Drive:) Space The amount of space available to store drawing-specific temporary files.

Free Temp Disk (Drive:) Space The amount of space left on your hard drive for the AutoCAD resource temporary files.

Free Physical Memory The amount of free RAM available.

Free Swap File Space The amount of Windows swap-file space available.

When you're in paper space, the Status command displays information regarding the paper space limits. See Chapter 15, "Laying Out Your Printer Output," for more on model space and paper space.

In addition to being useful in understanding a drawing file, the Status command is an invaluable tool for troubleshooting. Frequently, a technical support person can isolate problems by using the information provided by the Status command.

Keeping Track of Time

The Time command enables you to keep track of the time spent on a drawing for billing or analysis purposes. You can also use the Time command to check the current time and find out when the drawing was created and most recently edited. Because the AutoCAD timer uses your computer's time, be sure the time is set correctly in Windows.

To access the Time command, enter **Time**↵ at the Command prompt. You get a message like the one shown in Figure 19.7.

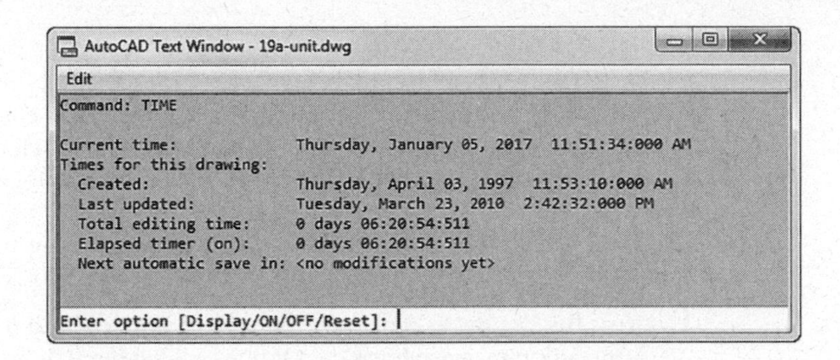

FIGURE 19.7
The Time screen in the AutoCAD command-line interface

The first four lines of this message tell you the current date and time, the date and time the drawing was created, and the last time the drawing was saved.

The fifth line shows the total time spent on the drawing from the point at which the file was opened. This elapsed timer lets you time a particular activity, such as changing the width of all of the walls in a floor plan or redesigning a piece of machinery. The last line tells you the timing of the next automatic save.

You can turn the elapsed timer on or off or reset it by entering ON, OFF, or Reset at the prompt shown at the bottom of the message, or you can press ↵ to exit the Time command.

Getting Information from System Variables

If you've been working through this book's ongoing studio apartment building exercise, you'll have noticed that we've occasionally mentioned a *system variable* in conjunction with a command. You can check the status or change the setting of any system variable while you're in the middle of another command. To do this, you type an apostrophe (') followed by the name of the system variable at the Command prompt.

For example, if you start to draw a line and suddenly decide that you need to restrict your cursor movement to 45°, you can do the following:

1. At the Specify next point or [Undo]: prompt, enter **'snapang**.
2. At the >>Enter new value for SNAPANG <0>: prompt, enter a new cursor angle. You're returned to the Line command with the cursor in its new orientation.

You can also recall information such as the last area or distance calculated by AutoCAD. Type **'Setvar↵Area↵** to read the last area calculation. The Setvar command also lets you list all of the system variables and their status as well as access each system variable individually by entering **'Setvar↵?↵**. You can then indicate which variables to list using wildcard characters such as the asterisk or question mark. For example, you can enter **g*↵** to list all the system variables that start with the letter *G*.

Many system variables give you direct access to detailed information about your drawing. They also let you fine-tune your drawing and editing activities. In Bonus Chapter 4, "System Variables and Dimension Styles," available at www.omura.com/chapters, you'll find all the information that you need to familiarize yourself with the system variables. Don't feel that you have to memorize them all at once; just be aware that they're available.

Keeping a Log of Your Activity

At times, you may find it helpful to keep a log of your activity in an AutoCAD session. A *log* is a text file containing a record of your activities. It can also contain notes to yourself or others about how a drawing is set up. Such a log can help you determine how frequently you use a particular command, or it can help you construct a macro for a commonly used sequence of commands.

The following exercise demonstrates how to save and view a detailed record of an AutoCAD session by using the Log feature:

1. Press the Esc key to cancel any current commands and then choose Options from the Application menu to open the Options dialog box. Click the Open And Save tab. A new set of options appears.
2. In the File Safety Precautions group, click the Maintain A Log File check box and then click OK.
3. Type **Status**↵ at the Command prompt.
4. Return to the Open And Save tab of the Options dialog box, and deselect the Maintain A Log File option.
5. Click OK to exit the dialog box.
6. Switch to Windows, and start the Notepad application or any text editor.
7. With the text editor, open the log file whose name starts with `Flange` in the folder listed here:

   `C:\Users\User Name\AppData\Local\Autodesk\AutoCAD 2018\R22.0\enu\`

This file stores the text data from the command line whenever the Log File option is turned on. You must turn off the Log File option before you can view this file. When you're attempting to view the log file using Windows Notepad, make sure that you set Files Of Type in the Notepad Open dialog box to All Files. Note that this location is usually a hidden one. See the section "Finding Folders That Contain AutoCAD Files" in Appendix B, "Installing and Setting Up AutoCAD," for more information.

You can quickly turn the Maintain A Log File feature on and off by typing **Logfileon**↵ and **Logfileoff**↵, respectively, at the Command prompt. As you can see in step 7, the log file is given the name of the drawing file from which the log is derived, with some additional numeric values. Because the `Flange.dwg` log file is a standard text file, you can easily send it to other members of your workgroup or print it for a permanent record.

Finding the Log File

If you can't find the log file for the current drawing, you can enter **logfilename**↵ at the Command prompt and AutoCAD will display the filename, including the full path. If you want to change the default location for the log file, open the Options dialog box and click the Files tab. Click the plus sign to the left of the Log File Location option in the list box. A listing appears showing you where the drawing log file is stored. You can then modify this setting to indicate a new location. Users of the AutoCAD LT® software should enter **Modemacro**↵ and then **$(getvar, logfilepath)**.

Capturing and Saving Text Data from the AutoCAD Text Window

If you're working in groups, it's often helpful to have a record of the status, editing time, and system variables for particular files readily available to other group members. It's also convenient to keep records of block and layer information so that you can see whether a specific block is included in a drawing or what layers are normally on or off.

You can use the Windows Clipboard to capture and save such data from the AutoCAD Text Window. The following steps show you how it's done:

1. Move the arrow cursor to the Command prompt at the bottom of the AutoCAD Text Window. If the Text Window isn't open, enter **TEXTSCR**↵.
2. Right-click and choose Copy History from the context menu to copy the contents of the AutoCAD Text Window to the Clipboard.
3. Open Notepad or another text-editing application and paste the information.

Enabling the Function Keys

On some keyboards, the function keys, F1 through F12, serve a dual function. For example, on most laptops, you can use the Fn key to select an alternate function for the function keys, like toggling Wi-Fi on or off or switching to an external monitor. If you find that the F2 key on your PC is not expanding the AutoCAD command-line interface, make sure that you have disabled the special features of the function keys. There may be an F Lock or F Mode key near the row of function keys that performs this function.

If you want to copy only a portion of the command-line data to the Clipboard, perform the following steps:

1. Press the F2 function key to expand the command-line interface.
2. Using the I-beam text cursor, highlight the text that you want to copy to the Clipboard.
3. Right-click and choose Copy from the context menu, or you can press Ctrl+C. The highlighted text is copied to the Clipboard.
4. Open Notepad or another text-editing application and paste the information.

The context menu that appears in step 3 also appears when you right-click in the Command window. Items copied to the Clipboard from the command-line interface or the AutoCAD Text Window can be pasted into dialog box text boxes. This can be a quick way to transfer layers, linetypes, or other named items into dialog boxes. You can even paste text into the drawing area.

Understanding the Command Window Context Menu

You may notice other options on the Command window or text window context menu: Recent Commands, Input Settings, Copy History, Paste, Paste To CmdLine, and Options. Choosing

Recent Commands displays a list of the most recent commands. For most activities, you'll use a handful of commands repeatedly; the Recent Commands option can save you time by giving you a shortcut to those commands that you use the most. The Input Settings option offers a flyout menu with additional options (see Table 19.2). These options can be switched on or off. Options that show a check mark are "on." You can also find these option settings in the Input Search Options dialog box, which you can open by typing **Inputsearchoptions**↵.

TABLE 19.2: The Input Settings options

OPTION	USE
AutoComplete	Suggests command names as you type. A list of suggested commands appears as you type.
AutoCorrect	Automatically corrects common command names as you type.
Search System Variables	Includes system variables in the AutoComplete list.
Search Content at command line	Includes named objects in the AutoComplete list. A checklist lets you choose the type of objects allowed in the list.
Mid-String Search	Suggests commands that not only start with but also contain the letters that you type.
Delay Time	Sets the time in milliseconds before suggestions are displayed after typing.

The Paste to CmdLine options paste the first line of the contents of the Clipboard into the command line or text box of a dialog box. This can be useful for entering repetitive text or for storing and retrieving a frequently used command. Choosing Options opens the Display tab of the Options dialog box. (See Appendix B for more on the Options dialog box.)

Storing Searchable Information in AutoCAD Files

As you start to build a library of AutoCAD files, you'll have to decide how to manage them. Keeping track of AutoCAD files can be a daunting task. Most AutoCAD users start to name files by their job number to keep things organized. But even the best organization schemes don't help if you need to find that one special file among thousands of files in your library. In this section, you'll learn how to include information in an AutoCAD file that you can use later to locate the file with the Windows Search utility.

AutoCAD includes the DesignCenter™, which can help you locate a file more easily based on a keyword or description. Chapter 25, "Managing and Sharing Your Drawings," provides a complete discussion of DesignCenter.

To add general, searchable information about your drawing file, use the drawing's Properties dialog box (see Figure 19.8). Choose Drawing Utilities ➤ Drawing Properties from the Application menu.

FIGURE 19.8
A drawing's properties

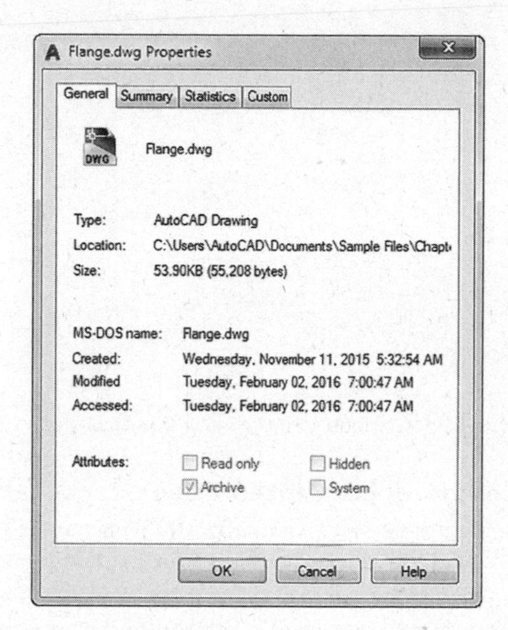

Here are descriptions of the four tabs in this dialog box:

General The General tab gives you general information about the file. This information is similar to what you see if you use the Properties options in Windows File Explorer to view the properties of a file.

Summary In the Summary tab, enter any text in the Title, Subject, Author, and Keywords fields that is appropriate to the drawing. The information you enter here is stored with the drawing, and it can be used to locate the file through the AutoCAD DesignCenter or the Windows Search utility. In addition, you can enter a base location for hyperlinks that are applied to objects in your drawing. This base location can be a folder on your computer or network or an Internet web address. See Chapter 25 for more information on hyperlinks.

Statistics The Statistics tab contains the Windows username of the person who last saved the drawing as well as the time spent on the file. The username is the name used to log in at the beginning of the Windows session.

Custom The Custom tab contains two columns of text boxes. This tab lets you store additional custom data with the drawing that is also searchable. For example, you might enter Job Number in the Name column and then enter 9901 in the Value column. You might also include information such as project manager names, consultants, or revision numbers. You can then locate the file by using the AutoCAD DesignCenter or the Windows Search utility to search for those keywords from the Name and Value columns.

Searching for AutoCAD Files

After you've included information in a file's Properties palette, you can use the AutoCAD DesignCenter, the Content Explorer, the File dialog box, or the Windows Search function to locate your file.

A Find option is also located in the Tools menu in the upper-right corner of the AutoCAD Select File dialog box. To access it, click the Open tool from the Quick Access toolbar; then, in the Select File dialog box, choose Tools ➢ Find.

This option opens a Find dialog box that works just like the Windows Search Results window.

Recovering Corrupted Files

No system is perfect. Eventually, you'll encounter a file that is corrupted in some way. Two AutoCAD tools can frequently salvage a corrupted file:

Audit Enables you to check a file that you can open but suspect has a problem. Audit checks the currently opened file for errors and displays the results in the command-line interface.

Recover/Recover With Xrefs Enables you to open a file that is so badly corrupted that AutoCAD is unable to open it in a normal way. A Select File dialog box appears in which you select a file for recovery. After you select a file, it's opened and checked for errors. The Recover With Xrefs option will attempt to recover the file and any attached Xrefs.

You can access these tools from the Drawing Utilities option on the Application menu. More often than not, these tools will do the job, although they aren't a panacea for all file corruption problems. In the event that you can't recover a file even with these tools, make sure that your computer is running smoothly and that other systems aren't faulty.

If for some reason your computer shuts down while you're in the middle of editing a file, you'll see the Drawing Recovery Manager the next time you start AutoCAD. The Drawing Recovery Manager lets you recover the file on which you were working when AutoCAD unexpectedly shut down. This feature works just like the file recovery feature in Microsoft Office: A panel appears to the left of the AutoCAD Text Window showing you a list of recoverable files. You can then select the filename from the panel to open the file. You can open the Drawing Recovery Manager by choosing Application ➢ Drawing Utilities ➢ Open The Drawing Recovery Manager.

Using the DXF File Format to Exchange CAD Data with Other Programs

AutoCAD offers many ways to share data with other programs. Perhaps the most common type of data exchange is to share drawing data with other CAD programs. In the following sections, you'll see how to export and import CAD drawings using the DXF file format.

A *Drawing Interchange Format (DXF)* file is a plain-text file that contains all the information needed to reconstruct a drawing. It's often used to exchange drawings created with other programs. Many

CAD and technical drawing programs, including some 3D programs, can generate or read files in DXF format. You might want to use a 3D program to view your drawing in a perspective view, or you might have a consultant who uses a different CAD program that accepts DXF files.

Be aware that not all programs that read DXF files accept all the data stored therein. Many programs that claim to read DXF files throw away much of the DXF files' information. Attributes are perhaps the most commonly ignored objects, followed by many of the 3D objects, such as meshes and 3D faces.

Exporting DXF Files

To export your current drawing as a DXF file, follow these steps:

1. Choose Save As from the Application menu or from the Quick Access toolbar to open the Save Drawing As dialog box.
2. Click the Files Of Type drop-down list. You can export your drawing under a number of formats, including six DXF formats.

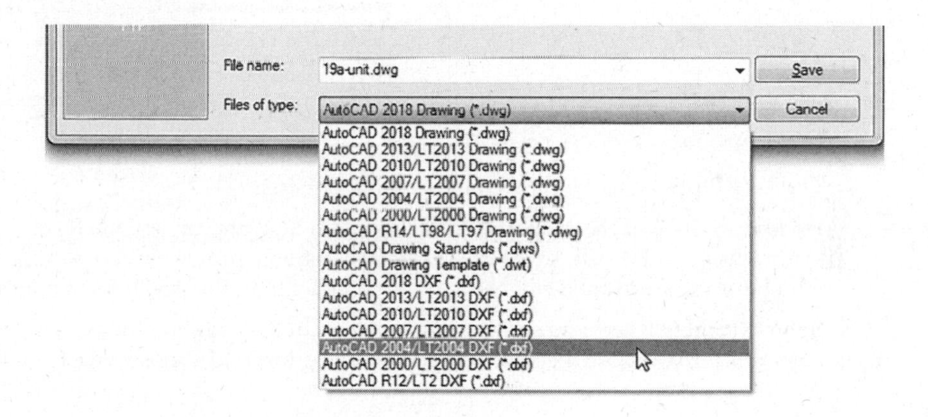

3. Select the appropriate DXF format, and then enter a name for your file. You don't have to include the `.dxf` filename extension.
4. Select a folder for the file and click Save.

In step 3, you can select from the following DXF file formats:

- AutoCAD 2018 DXF
- AutoCAD 2013 DXF (AutoCAD 2013, 2014, 2015, 2016, and 2017 share file formats.)
- AutoCAD 2010/LT 2010 DXF (AutoCAD 2010, 2011, and 2012 share file formats.)
- AutoCAD 2007/LT 2007 DXF (AutoCAD 2007, 2008, and 2009 share file formats.)
- AutoCAD 2004/LT 2004 DXF
- AutoCAD 2000/LT 2000 DXF
- AutoCAD R12/LT2 DXF

Choose the appropriate format for the program to which you're exporting. In most cases, the safest choice is AutoCAD R12/LT2 DXF if you're exporting to another CAD program, although AutoCAD won't maintain the complete functionality of AutoCAD 2018 for such files.

After you've selected a DXF format from the Files Of Type drop-down list, you can set more detailed specifications by choosing Tools ➤ Options in the upper-right corner of the Save Drawing As dialog box. Doing so opens the Saveas Options dialog box. For DXF files, select the DXF Options tab (see Figure 19.9).

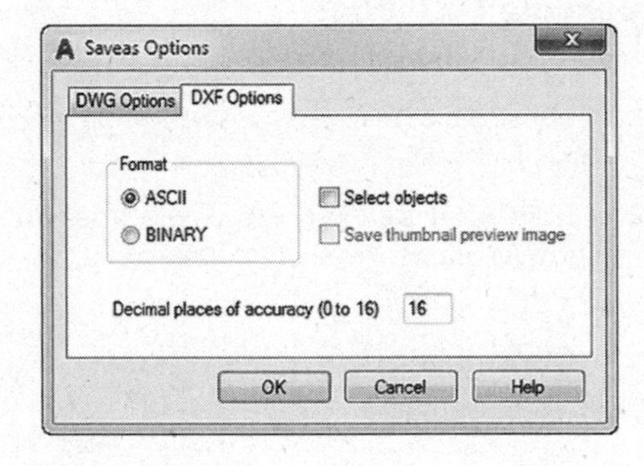

FIGURE 19.9
The Saveas Options dialog box open to the DXF Options tab

The DXF Options tab contains the following options:

Format Lets you choose between ASCII (plain-text) and binary file formats. Most other programs accept ASCII, so it's the safest choice. Some programs accept binary DXF files, which have the advantage of being more compact than the ASCII format files.

Select Objects Lets you select specific objects in the drawing for export. You can select objects after you close the Saveas Options dialog box and choose Save from the Save Drawing As dialog box.

Decimal Places Of Accuracy (0 To 16) Enables you to determine the accuracy of the exported file. Keeping this value low helps to reduce the size of the exported file, particularly if it's to be in ASCII format. Some CAD programs don't support the high accuracy of AutoCAD, so using a high value here may have no significance.

In addition to using the Save Drawing As tool, you can type **Dxfout**↵ at the Command prompt to open the Save Drawing As dialog box. This is a standard Windows file dialog box that includes the Options button described in the next section.

Opening or Importing DXF Files

Some offices have made the DXF file format their standard for CAD drawings. This is most commonly seen in offices that use a variety of CAD software besides AutoCAD.

AutoCAD can be set up to read and write DXF files instead of the standard DWG file format by default. Here's how it's done:

1. Choose Options from the Application menu to open the Options dialog box.
2. Select the Open And Save tab.

3. In the File Save group, select any of the DXF formats from the Save As drop-down list.
4. Click OK.

After you do this, all your drawings are automatically saved in the DXF format of your choice.

You can also set the default AutoCAD file type by clicking the Tools button in the Save Drawing As dialog box and clicking Options. As you saw in the preceding section, the Saveas Options dialog box includes the DWG Options tab (see Figure 19.10). You can select a default file type from the Save All Drawings As drop-down list.

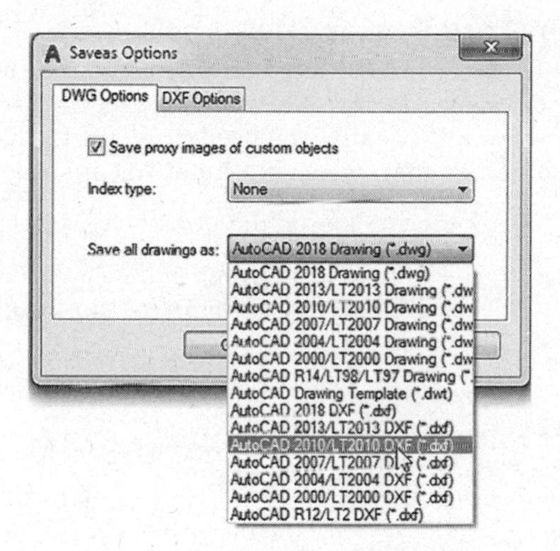

FIGURE 19.10
The Saveas Options dialog box open to the DWG Options tab

If you need to open a DXF file only once in a while, you can do so by selecting DXF from the Files Of Type drop-down list in the Select File dialog box. This is the dialog box that you see when you click Open on the Quick Access toolbar. You can also use the Dxfin command:

1. Type **Dxfin**↵ at the Command prompt to open the Select File dialog box.
2. Locate and select the DXF file that you want to import.
3. Double-click the filename. If the drawing is large, the imported file may take several minutes to open.

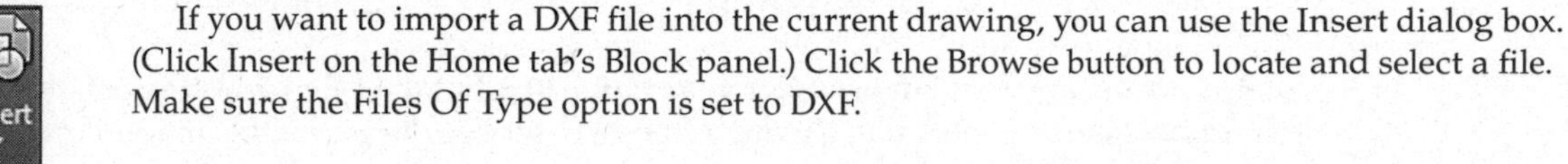

If you want to import a DXF file into the current drawing, you can use the Insert dialog box. (Click Insert on the Home tab's Block panel.) Click the Browse button to locate and select a file. Make sure the Files Of Type option is set to DXF.

Using AutoCAD Drawings in Page Layout Programs

As you probably know, AutoCAD is a natural for creating line art, and because of its popularity, most page layout programs are designed to import AutoCAD drawings in one form or another. Those of you who employ page layout software to generate user manuals or other technical documents will probably want to use AutoCAD drawings in your work. In this section, you'll examine ways to output AutoCAD drawings to formats that most page layout programs can accept.

You can export AutoCAD files to page layout software formats in two ways: by using raster export and by using vector file export.

Exporting Raster Files

In some cases, you may need only a rough image of your AutoCAD drawing. You can export your drawing as a raster file that can be read in virtually any page layout or word processing program. To do this, you need to use the PublishToWebJPG.pc3 or PublishToWebPNG.pc3 printer option that comes with AutoCAD, as shown in these steps:

1. Click the Plot tool on the Quick Access toolbar.
2. In the Printer/Plotter group of the Plot dialog box, select PublishToWebJPG.pc3 or PublishToWebPNG.pc3 from the Name drop-down list.
3. The first time that you use this printer option, you'll see the Plot – Paper Size Not Found dialog box. Select from the options presented in the dialog box.
4. Back in the Plot dialog box, you can select a size in pixels for your image file from the Paper Size drop-down list.
5. Click OK to create the image file.
6. In the Browse For Plot File dialog box, select a location for your file and click Save.

If you don't see a "paper size" that you want to use, you can create a custom size using the Properties button in the Plot dialog box:

1. Follow the steps in the previous exercise, but at step 5, instead of clicking OK, click the Properties button to the right of the Printer/Plotter group's Name drop-down list. The Plotter Configuration Editor dialog box appears (see Figure 19.11).
2. Click Custom Paper Sizes in the large list box at the top of the dialog box. The options change in the lower half of the dialog box.
3. Click the Add button to start the Custom Paper Size Wizard.
4. Click the Start From Scratch radio button, and then click Next to open the Media Bounds screen.
5. Enter a height and width in pixels for your image file, and then click Next to open the Paper Size Name screen. Enter a name that best describes the size of the image file, and click Next to open the File Name screen.
6. On the Finish screen, click Finish. The Plotter Configuration Editor dialog box reappears. Click OK.

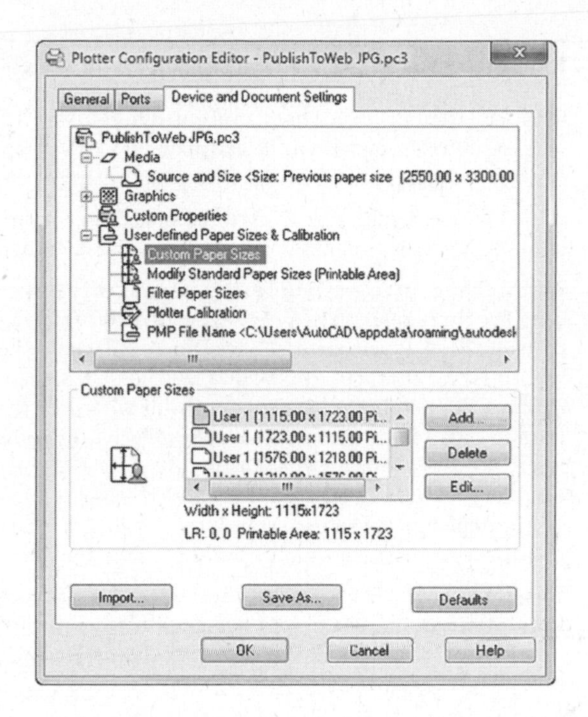

FIGURE 19.11
Editing the plotter configuration

You can edit these settings at any time by opening the PC3 file in the `AppData\Roaming\Autodesk\AutoCAD 2018\R22.0\enu\Plotters` subfolder of your profile folder. You can access this file through Windows File Explorer or from AutoCAD by clicking Plotter Manager in the Output tab's Plot panel.

FINDING THE *APPDATA* OR *APPLICATION DATA* FOLDER

The `AppData` or `Application Data` folder is typically a hidden folder. To get to it, you have to turn off the "hide hidden folders" feature of Windows File Explorer. See "Finding Folders That Contain AutoCAD Files" in Appendix B for more information.

To create a raster file version of your drawing, click Plot on the Quick Access toolbar. Then, in the Plot dialog box, select your raster file plotter configuration from the Name drop-down list of the Printer/Plotter group. You can then proceed to plot your drawing, but instead of paper output, you'll get a raster file. You can specify the filename and location when you click OK to plot the file.

If you need to make changes to your raster file configuration, click Plotter Manager in the Output tab's Plot panel. Then, in the Plotters window, double-click your raster file configuration file. You'll see the same Plotter Configuration Editor that you used to set up the raster plotter configuration.

You can set up a different plotter configuration for each type of raster file that you use. You can also set up plotter configurations for different resolutions if you choose. To learn more about plotting in general, see Chapter 8, "Introducing Printing, Plotting, and Layouts." Bonus Chapter 3, "Hardware and Software Tips," available at `www.omura.com/chapters`, provides detailed information on the Plotter Configuration Editor.

Exchanging Files with Earlier Releases

One persistent dilemma that has plagued AutoCAD users is how to exchange files between earlier versions of the program. In the early days of CAD, if you upgraded AutoCAD, you were locked out from exchanging your drawings with people using earlier versions.

With Release 13, the file structure was changed radically from the file structure used in earlier versions of AutoCAD. Then, AutoCAD 14 made it possible to exchange files freely between Releases 13 and 14.

With a change in release numbering, starting with AutoCAD 2000, file formats have typically been used for three releases in a row. AutoCAD 2000 through 2002 files are compatible, as are 2004 through 2006. If you open the Save Drawing As dialog box and check the Files Of Type drop-down list, you'll see that R14, 2000, 2004, 2007, 2010, and 2013 are listed as options. Release numbers that are skipped in the list are compatible with only the next higher release. For example, if you want to save a file in a format that your colleague using AutoCAD 2005 can open, you would choose AutoCAD 2004 from the Files Of Type drop-down list. AutoCAD 2004 is a format compatible with AutoCAD releases 2004, 2005, and 2006. If compatibility with earlier releases is important, you can set the default behavior to save as AutoCAD 2010 format or earlier. Or, if you're willing to work with DXF files, you can set up AutoCAD 2018 to save drawings automatically as AutoCAD 2013 DXF files.

To set up AutoCAD to save drawings in the format used by an earlier version automatically, use the Options dialog box to set the default file type as described earlier in the section "Opening or Importing DXF Files." However, rather than selecting a DXF file type, select the DWG file type that you want to use.

If you want to batch-convert multiple files to an earlier version, AutoCAD offers the DWG Convert dialog box. You can open this dialog box by typing **DWGCONVERT**↵ at the Command prompt. The DWG Convert dialog box enables you to create and save a list of files to convert in case you have a set of files that you need to down-convert often.

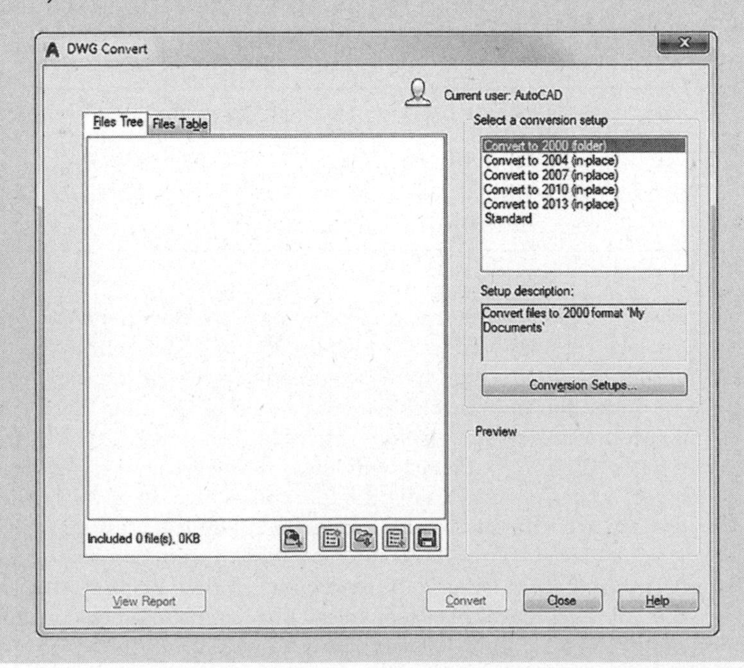

Select the Conversion Setups option in the dialog box to open the Conversion Setups dialog box. This dialog box lets you create or modify conversion setup presets to customize your most frequently used conversion methods.

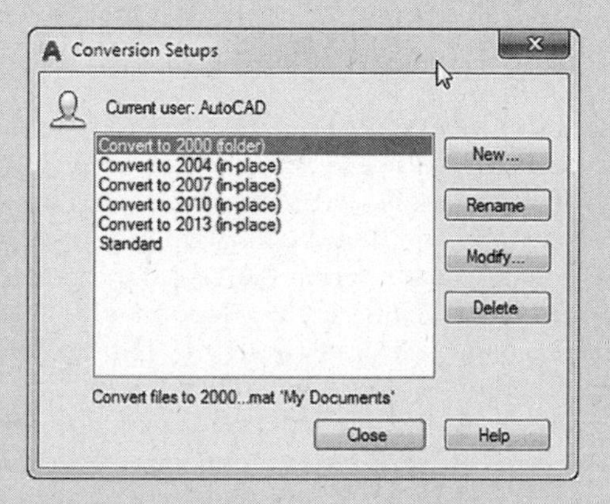

Click New or Modify to create a new conversion preset option or to modify an existing one. You will see the New Conversion Setup or Modify Conversion Setup dialog box, either of which lets you set the parameters for your conversion setup.

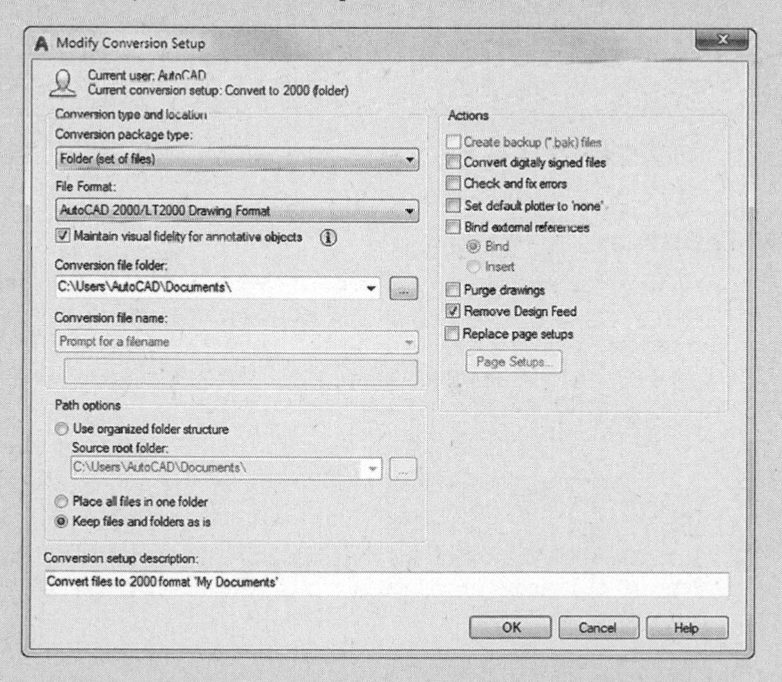

Another option is to use a separate program to "downgrade" drawings to earlier versions. Autodesk offers its DWG TrueView™ software as a free download. DWG TrueView will batch-convert 2018 files to earlier versions, and it works in a way that is similar to the DWG Convert dialog box. The advantage to DWG TrueView is that it is a stand-alone application, so you don't need to have AutoCAD open to use it.

Exporting Vector Files

If you need to preserve the accuracy of your drawing or if you want to take advantage of TrueType or PostScript fonts, you can use the DXF, Windows Metafile (WMF), or PostScript vector format. You can also export to DGN and SAT file formats. Intergraph's DGN format is popular in civil engineering, mapping, and other CAD applications. SAT is a 3D modeling format associated with ACIS.

For vector format files, DXF is the easiest to work with, and with TrueType support, DXF can preserve font information between AutoCAD and page layout programs that support the DXF format. The WMF format is also a commonly accepted file format for vector information, and it preserves TrueType fonts and lineweights used in your drawings.

PostScript is a raster/vector hybrid file format that AutoCAD supports. Unfortunately, AutoCAD dropped direct PostScript font support with Release 14. However, you can still use substitute fonts to stand in for PostScript fonts. These substitute fonts are converted to true PostScript fonts when AutoCAD exports the drawing. You don't see the true results of your PostScript output until you print your drawing on a PostScript printer.

The DXF file export was covered in a previous section of this chapter, so the following sections will concentrate on the WMF and PostScript file formats.

Exchanging 3D Data with FBX

AutoCAD can export to the FBX file format, which is a platform-independent 3D authoring/ interchange format. FBX can be exported through the Application menu's Export option. To import FBX files, choose Import from the Insert tab's Import panel or type **Import↵**. Select FBX (*.fbx) from the Files Of Type drop-down menu.

WMF Output

The WMF file type is one of the most popular vector file formats in Windows. It can be opened and edited by most illustration programs, including CorelDRAW and Adobe Illustrator. Most word processing, database, and worksheet programs can also import WMF files. It's a great option for AutoCAD file export because it preserves TrueType fonts and lineweight settings. You can export WMF files that preserve lineweights as well.

To export WMF files, do the following:

1. Select Export ➤ Other Formats from the Application menu to open the Export Data dialog box.
2. Enter a name and location for your WMF file, select Metafile (*.wmf) from the Files Of Type drop-down list, and then click Save. The dialog box closes, and you're prompted to select objects.
3. Select the objects that you want to export to the WMF file and press ↵. The objects are saved to your WMF file.

PostScript Output

AutoCAD can export to the Encapsulated PostScript (EPS) file format. If you're using AutoCAD 2018, you can obtain PostScript output in two ways: You can choose Export ➤ Other Formats from the Application menu, or you can enter **Psout**↵ at the Command prompt. If you choose Export ➤ Other Formats, you can use the Files Of Type drop-down list in the Export Data dialog box to select Encapsulated PS. Another method is to install a PostScript printer driver and plot your drawing to an EPS file. If you're an AutoCAD LT user, you can't export to EPS by clicking Export; you must set up a PostScript plotter and use it to plot to a file.

To set up AutoCAD to plot your drawing to an EPS file, follow these steps:

1. Click Plotter Manager in the Output tab's Plot panel, and then, in the Plotters dialog box, double-click the Add-A-Plotter Wizard.
2. Choose Next on the Introduction Page screen.
3. On the Begin screen of the Add-A-Plotter Wizard, choose My Computer.
4. On the Plotter Model screen, select Adobe from the Manufacturers list and then select the appropriate PostScript level from the Models list.
5. Skip the Import PCP Or PC2 screen and the Ports screen.
6. Enter a name for your EPS output settings on the Plotter Name screen.
7. On the Finish screen, click the Finish button.

AutoCAD doesn't preserve font information when creating EPS files from the printer option. It also produces larger files, especially if your drawing contains a lot of area fills and filled fonts. As an alternative to EPS, you can "plot" to an Adobe PDF file. EPS files can often be replaced by PDF files. When you get to the Plotter Model screen, select the Autodesk ePlot (PDF) option from the Manufacturers list. You can also use the full version of Adobe Acrobat or Acrobat Professional to produce PDF files from AutoCAD.

The HPGL plot-file format is another vector format that you can use to export your AutoCAD drawings. Use the method described earlier in the section "Exporting Raster Files" to add the HPGL plotter driver to your printer/plotter configuration.

Using AutoCAD DWF Files

The Autodesk DWF file format is another format that you can use to exchange drawing data with others. It offers features that are geared toward AutoCAD users. You can import DWF files as external references and, using a free DWF viewer, you can gather information about a drawing such as block information, attribute data, and distance measurements. See Chapter 25 for more on DWF.

Using OLE to Import Data

To import data from other applications, you use the Cut and Paste features found in virtually all Windows programs. You cut the data from the source document and then paste it into AutoCAD. Typically, you'll want to paste data into AutoCAD in its native object format, but if you prefer, you can use a Windows feature called Object Linking and Embedding (OLE) to import files.

Finding the Copy and Paste Tools

There are several variations of the Copy and Paste tools in AutoCAD, so they have been combined into tools and flyouts on the Home tab's Clipboard panel. The Paste flyout is in the large icon to the left, and the Copy Clip tool is to the right of the Paste flyout.

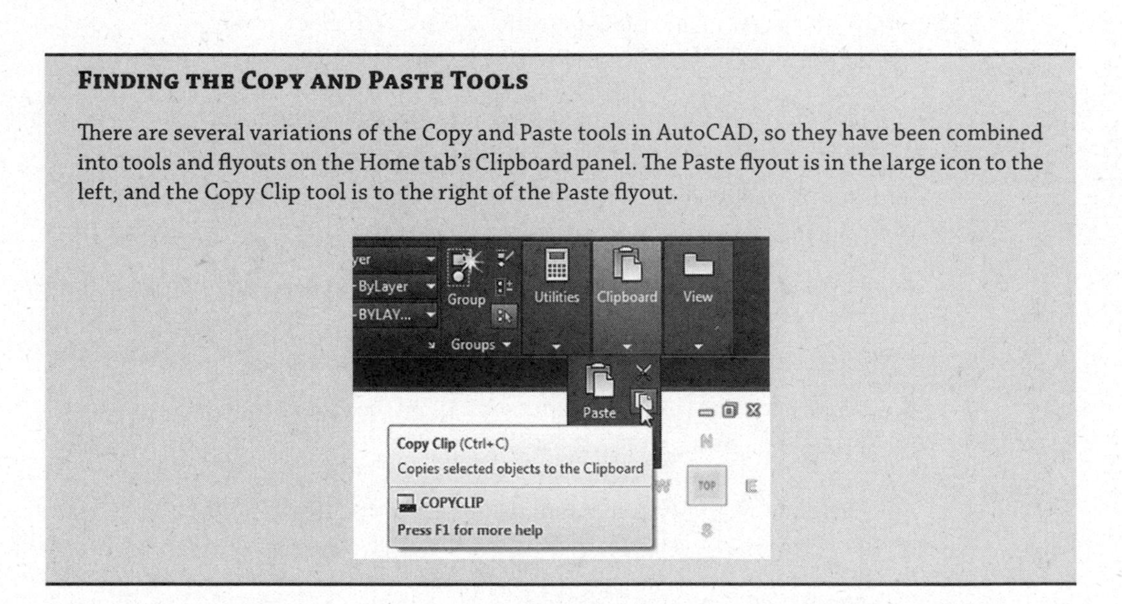

When you paste data into your AutoCAD file using OLE, you can link it to the source file or you can embed it. If you *link* it to the source file, the pasted data is updated whenever the source file is modified. This is similar to an AutoCAD Xref file. (See Chapter 14, "Advanced Editing and Organizing," for more on Xref files.) If you *embed* data, you're pasting it into AutoCAD without linking it. You can still open the application associated with the data by double-clicking it, but the data is no longer associated with the source file. Importing files using OLE is similar to other cut-and-paste operations. First, cut the data from the source application. This could be Microsoft Excel or Microsoft Word. In AutoCAD, click Paste Special from the Paste flyout on the Home tab's Clipboard panel to open the Paste Special dialog box (see Figure 19.12).

Click the Paste Link radio button to tell AutoCAD that you want this paste to be a link. The list of source types will depend on the source document. Click OK. You're prompted to select an insertion point. Place the cursor in the location for the paste, and click. The imported data appears within the drawing. Depending on the type of data, it may appear in a bounding box. You can adjust the size of the bounding box to fit the scale of the drawing.

OLE Object

In addition to using the Paste Special tool, you can import an OLE object by clicking OLE Object in the Insert tab's Data panel to open the Insert Object dialog box (see Figure 19.13).

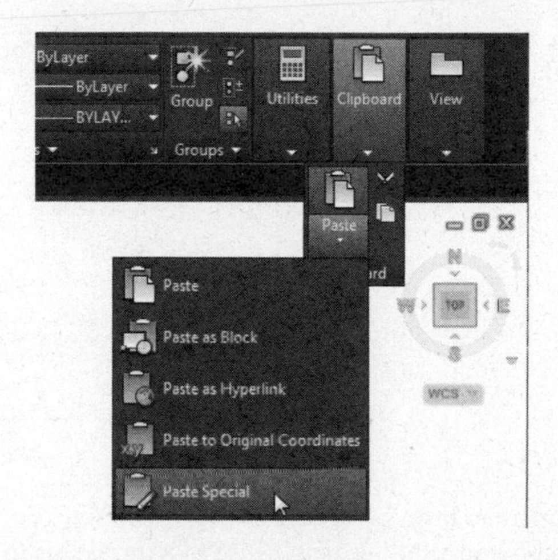

FIGURE 19.12
Use Paste Special to link your data.

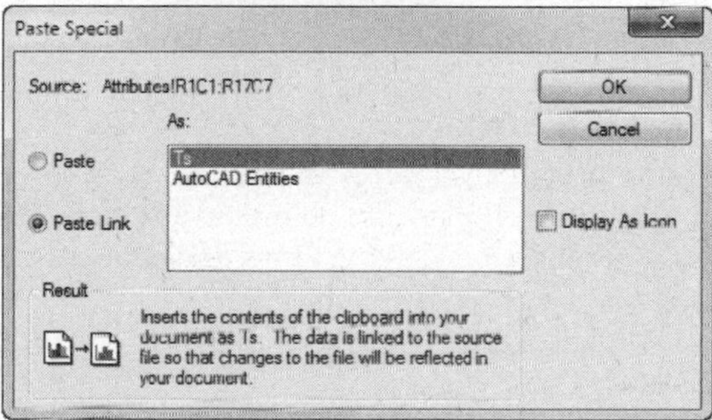

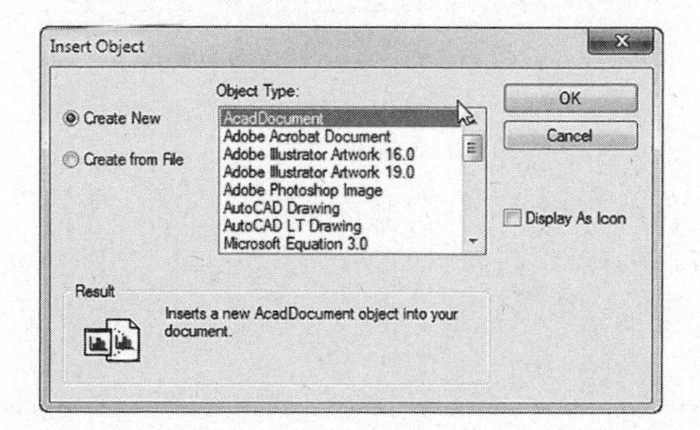

FIGURE 19.13
Inserting a new object

You can then select the type of object that you want to import from the Object Type list box. Two radio buttons to the left of the list box let you import an existing object or create a new object of the type listed in the list box. If you choose the Create New radio button, the application associated with the object type will start and open a new file. If you select the Create From File radio button (see Figure 19.14), the dialog box changes to show a filename and a Browse button.

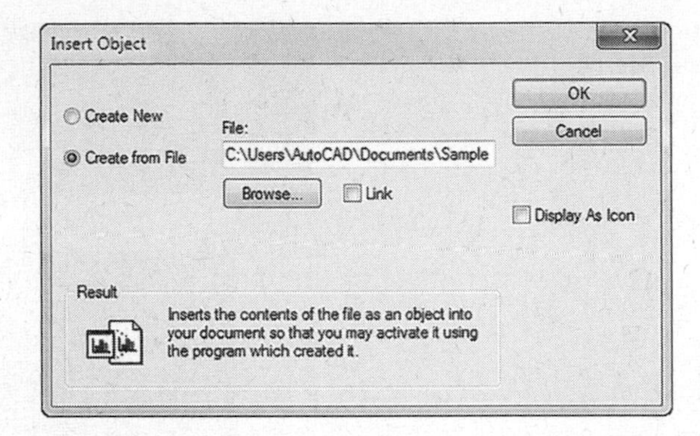

FIGURE 19.14 Inserting an existing object

You can then browse for an existing file to import. The Link check box lets you specify whether the imported file is to be linked and needs to be selected in order to use the Olelinks command described in the next section.

Editing OLE Links

After you've pasted an object with links, you can control the links by typing **Olelinks**↵ at the Command prompt. If there are no linked objects in the drawing, the Olelinks command does nothing; otherwise, it opens the Links dialog box (see Figure 19.15).

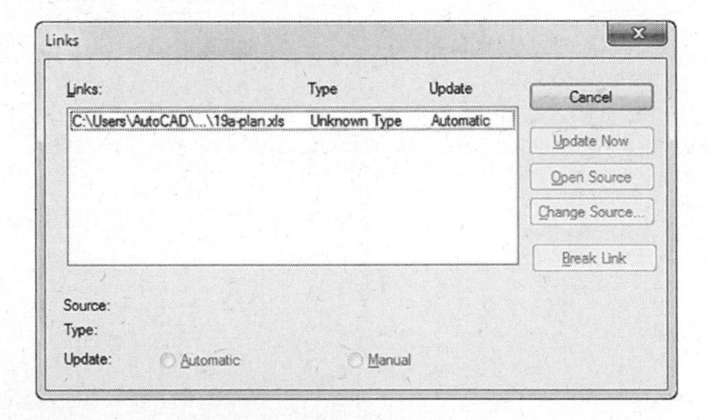

FIGURE 19.15 Editing links

The options available in the Links dialog box are as follows:

Cancel/Close Cancels the link between a pasted object and its source file. After you use this option, changes in the source file have no effect on the pasted object. This is similar to using the Bind option in the Xref command. This option changes to Close once any of the other options listed here are used.

Update Now Updates an object's link when the Manual option is selected.

Open Source Opens the linked file in the application associated with the object and lets you edit it.

Change Source Lets you change the object's link to a different file. When you select this option, AutoCAD opens the Change Source dialog box, where you can select another file of the same type. For example, if you're editing the link to a sound file, the Change Source dialog box displays files with the `.wav` filename extension.

Break Link Disconnects the link between the inserted data and the source document. The inserted data then becomes embedded rather than linked.

Automatic and Manual Radio buttons that control whether linked objects are updated automatically or manually.

Importing Worksheets as AutoCAD Tables

Although it can be beneficial to import worksheets as linked OLE objects, you may prefer to import worksheets as AutoCAD entities. You may not need the direct link to the source material that OLE linking offers. The ability to edit the imported worksheet directly in AutoCAD may have a higher priority for you.

In Chapter 10, you saw how you can create tables in AutoCAD by using the Table tool. You can import an Excel worksheet as an AutoCAD table by using the AutoCAD Entities option in the Paste Special dialog box. By importing worksheets as tables, you have more control over the layout and appearance of the worksheet data.

Try the following exercise to see how you can create a table from a worksheet:

1. Open the Excel worksheet called `19a-plan.xls` and highlight the door data, as shown in Figure 19.16.

FIGURE 19.16 The Excel worksheet

	A	B	C	D	E	F	G	H
1	D-TYPE	D-SIZE	D-NUMBER	D-THICK	D-RATE	D-MATRL	D-CONST	
2	B	3'-0"	116	1 3/4"	20 min.	Wood	Solid Core	
3	B	3'-0"	114	1 3/4"	20 min.	Wood	Solid Core	
4	B	3'-0"	112	1 3/4"	20 min.	Wood	Solid Core	
5	B	3'-0"	110	1 3/4"	20 min.	Wood	Solid Core	
6	B	3'-0"	106	1 3/4"	20 min.	Wood	Solid Core	
7	B	3'-0"	108	1 3/4"	20 min.	Wood	Solid Core	
8	B	3'-0"	102	1 3/4"	20 min.	Wood	Solid Core	
9	B	3'-0"	104	1 3/4"	20 min.	Wood	Solid Core	
10	B	3'-0"	115	1 3/4"	20 min.	Wood	Solid Core	
11	B	3'-0"	111	1 3/4"	20 min	Wood	Solid Core	
12	B	3'-0"	107	1 3/4"	20 min.	Wood	Solid Core	
13	B	3'-0"	103	1 3/4"	20 min.	Wood	Solid Core	
14	B	3'-0"	101	1 3/4"	20 min.	Wood	Solid Core	
15	B	3'-0"	105	1 3/4"	20 min.	Wood	Solid Core	
16	B	3'-0"	109	1 3/4"	20 min.	Wood	Solid Core	
17	B	3'-0"	113	1 3/4"	20 min.	Wood	Solid Core	
18	116							
19	114							
20	112							

2. Press Ctrl+C to place a copy of the selected data into the Windows Clipboard, and then switch back to AutoCAD.
3. Click Paste Special from the Paste flyout on the Home tab's Clipboard panel (see Figure 19.17) to open the Paste Special dialog box.
4. With the Paste radio button selected, select AutoCAD Entities from the list and click OK.
5. At the `Specify insertion point or [paste as Text]:` prompt, click a point in the lower-right area of the drawing. The worksheet data appears in the drawing as a table object (see Chapter 10 for more on tables).

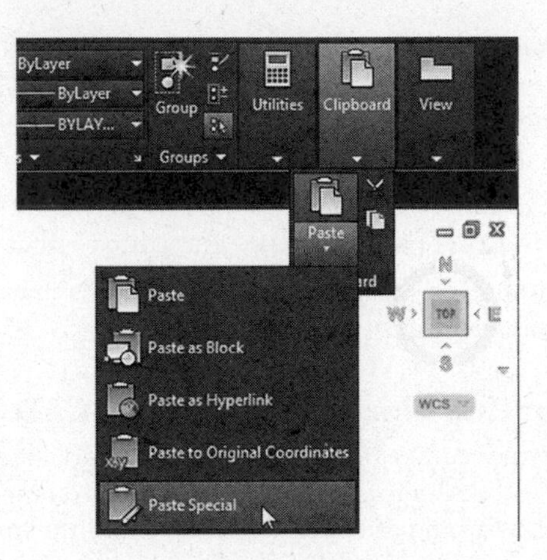

FIGURE 19.17
The Paste Special tool

6. Use the Scale tool to enlarge the table to a readable size (see Figure 19.18), and use the corner grips to adjust the width.

FIGURE 19.18
Scale and size the table

D-TYPE	D-SIZE	D-NUMBER	D-THICK	D-RATE	D-MATRL	D-CONST
B	3'-0"	116	1 3/4"	no rating	Wood	Solid Core
B	3'-0"	114	1 3/4"	20 min.	Wood	Solid Core
B	3'-0"	112	1 3/4"	20 min.	Wood	Solid Core
B	3'-0"	110	1 3/4"	20 min.	Wood	Solid Core
B	3'-0"	106	1 3/4"	20 min.	Wood	Solid Core
B	3'-0"	108	1 3/4"	20 min.	Wood	Solid Core
B	3'-0"	102	1 3/4"	20 min.	Wood	Solid Core
B	3'-0"	104	1 3/4"	20 min.	Wood	Solid Core
B	3'-0"	115	1 3/4"	20 min	Wood	Solid Core
B	3'-0"	111	1 3/4"	20 min	Wood	Solid Core
B	3'-0"	107	1 3/4"	20 min.	Wood	Solid Core
B	3'-0"	103	1 3/4"	20 min.	Wood	Solid Core
B	3'-0"	101	1 3/4"	20 min.	Wood	Solid Core
B	3'-0"	105	1 3/4"	20 min.	Wood	Solid Core
B	3'-0"	109	1 3/4"	20 min.	Wood	Solid Core
B	3'-0"	113	1 3/4"	20 min.	Wood	Solid Core

7. Close the Excel file.

You can edit this imported worksheet using the editing methods for AutoCAD tables described in Chapter 10. In that chapter, you learned that you could edit the text format, the border lineweight and color, and the background of cells. You can add rows and columns and rotate text so that it fits more uniformly in a vertical column.

In this exercise, the worksheet was imported using the default standard table style. This gives you a simple-looking table using the TrueType Arial font. You can set up a custom table style with the fonts and borders that you want and then import the table for a more custom appearance. Make sure that your custom table style is the current style before you import the worksheet.

USE AUTOCAD SHX FONTS FOR ADDITIONAL PDF FEATURES

If you frequently export your drawings to the PDF format, you'll want to be aware that text formatted in an AutoCAD SHX font can be highlighted, copied, and searched as comments in a PDF viewer. SHX fonts can be recognized by their SHX filename extension when selecting fonts in the Text Style dialog box or by the "Caliper-A" icon in the Text Editor ribbon tab's Formatting panel. See Chapter 9, "Adding Text to Drawings," for more on text styles and fonts.

Understanding Options for Embedding Data

The Paste Special dialog box offers several other options that may better suit your needs. Here is a brief description of each format that is available:

Microsoft Document Imports data from Microsoft Office documents. This option may show Word or Excel in the title, depending on the source. The pasted object will inherit the appearance of the source document. When using this option, you may receive a security warning message. Always make sure that your files are from a trusted source.

Picture (Metafile) Imports the data as a vector or bitmap image, whichever is appropriate. If applicable, text is also maintained as text, although you can't edit it in AutoCAD.

Bitmap Imports the data as a bitmap image, closely reflecting the appearance of the data as it appears on your computer screen in the source application.

Picture (Enhanced Metafile) Similar to the Picture (Metafile) option, with support for more features.

AutoCAD Entities Converts the data into AutoCAD objects such as lines, arcs, and circles. Text is converted into AutoCAD single-line text objects. Worksheets are converted into AutoCAD tables.

Image Entity Converts the data into an AutoCAD raster image. You can then edit it by using the raster image-related tools such as Adobe Photoshop or the Microsoft Windows Paint program. See Chapter 13, "Copying Existing Drawings from Other Sources," for more on how to use raster images.

Unicode Text Imports text data in the Unicode format. Unicode is an international standard for encoding text. If the Text option doesn't work, try Unicode Text.

Text Converts the data into AutoCAD multiline text objects. Formatting isn't imported with text.

The options you see in the Paste Special dialog box depend on the type of data being imported. You saw how the Microsoft Excel Worksheet option maintains the imported data as an Excel worksheet. If the contents of the Clipboard come from another program, you're offered that program as a choice in place of Excel.

Using the Clipboard to Export AutoCAD Drawings

Just as you can cut and paste data into AutoCAD from applications that support OLE, you can cut entities from AutoCAD and paste them as images to other applications. This can be useful as a way of including AutoCAD illustrations in word processing documents, worksheets, or page layout program documents. It can also be useful in creating background images for visualization programs such as Autodesk® 3ds Max® and 3ds Max® Design and for paint programs such as Corel Painter.

If you cut and paste an AutoCAD drawing to another file by using OLE and then send the file to someone using another computer, they must also have AutoCAD installed before they can edit the pasted AutoCAD drawing.

The receiving application doesn't need to support OLE, but if it does, the exported drawing can be edited with AutoCAD and will maintain its accuracy as a CAD drawing. Otherwise, the AutoCAD image will be converted to a bitmap graphic.

To use the Clipboard to export an object or a set of objects from an AutoCAD drawing, click Copy Clip from the Home tab's Clipboard panel. You're then prompted to select the objects that you want to export. If you want to export and erase objects simultaneously from AutoCAD, click Cut from the Home tab's Clipboard panel.

In the receiving application, choose Edit ➤ Paste Special. You'll see a dialog box similar to the Paste Special dialog box in AutoCAD. Select the method for pasting your AutoCAD image, and then click OK. If the receiving application doesn't have a Paste Special option, choose Edit ➤ Paste. The receiving application converts the image into a format that it can accept.

The Bottom Line

Find the area of closed boundaries. There are a number of ways to find the area of a closed boundary. The easiest way is also perhaps the least obvious.

Master It Which AutoCAD feature would you use to find the area of an irregular shape, such as a pond or lake, quickly?

Get general information. A lot of information that is stored in AutoCAD drawings can tell you about the files. You can find out how much memory a file uses as well as the amount of time that has been spent editing the file.

Master It What feature lets you store your own searchable information about a drawing file, and how do you get to this feature?

Use the DXF file format to exchange CAD data with other programs. Autodesk created the DXF file format as a means of sharing vector drawings with other programs.

Master It Name some of the versions of AutoCAD that you can export to using the Save As option.

Use AutoCAD drawings in page layout programs. AutoCAD drawings find their way into all types of documents, including brochures and technical manuals. Users are often asked to convert their CAD drawings into formats that can be read by page layout software.

Master It Name some file formats, by filename extension or type, that page layout programs can accept.

Use OLE to import data. You can import data into AutoCAD from a variety of sources. Most sources, such as bitmap images and text, can be imported as native AutoCAD objects. Other sources may need to be imported as OLE objects.

Master It To link imported data to a source program through OLE, what dialog box would you use?

Part 4

3D Modeling and Imaging

- Chapter 20: Creating 3D Drawings
- Chapter 21: Using Advanced 3D Features
- Chapter 22: Editing and Visualizing 3D Solids
- Chapter 23: Exploring 3D Mesh and Surface Modeling

Chapter 20

Creating 3D Drawings

Viewing an object in three dimensions gives you a sense of its true shape and form. It also helps you conceptualize your design, which results in better design decisions. In addition, using three-dimensional objects helps you communicate your ideas to those who may not be familiar with the plans, sections, and side views of your design.

A further advantage to drawing in three dimensions is that you can derive 2D drawings from your 3D models, which may take considerably less time than creating them with standard 2D drawing methods. For example, you can model a mechanical part in 3D and then quickly derive its 2D top, front, and right-side views by using the techniques discussed in this chapter.

The AutoCAD LT® software does not support any of the 3D-related features described in this chapter.

In this chapter, you will learn to

- Know the 3D Modeling workspace
- Draw in 3D using solids
- Create 3D forms from 2D shapes
- Isolate coordinates with point filters
- Move around your model
- Get a visual effect
- Turn a 3D view into a 2D AutoCAD drawing

Getting to Know the 3D Modeling Workspace

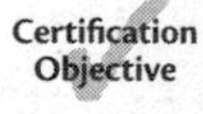

Most of this book is devoted to showing you how to work in the Drafting & Annotation workspace. This workspace is basically a 2D drawing environment, although you can certainly work in 3D as well.

The AutoCAD® 2018 program offers the *3D Modeling* and *3D Basics* workspaces, which give you a set of tools to help ease your way into 3D modeling. The 3D Modeling workspace gives AutoCAD a different set of Ribbon panels, but don't worry: AutoCAD behaves in the same basic way, and the AutoCAD files produced are the same regardless of whether they're 2D or 3D drawings. The 3D Basics workspace contains the minimum 3D tools needed to perform 3D functions.

To get to the 3D Modeling workspace, you first open a new drawing and then click the Workspace Switching tool in the status bar. Then select 3D Modeling (see Figure 20.1).

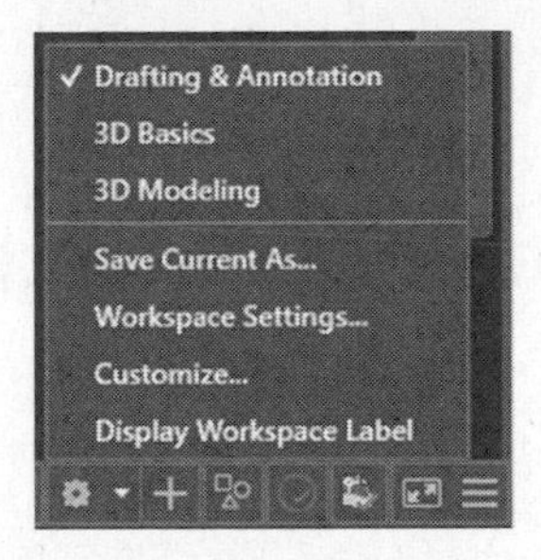

FIGURE 20.1
The Workspace Switching tool

If you're starting a new 3D model, you'll also want to create a new file using a 3D template. Try the following exercise to get started with 3D modeling:

1. Start AutoCAD. To create a new 3D modeling file, click New in the Quick Access toolbar to open the Select Template dialog box. Select `acad3D.dwt` and click Open.
2. Click the Workspace Switching tool in the status bar at the bottom of the screen, and select 3D Modeling. You'll see a new set of panels appear. Your screen will look similar to Figure 20.2.

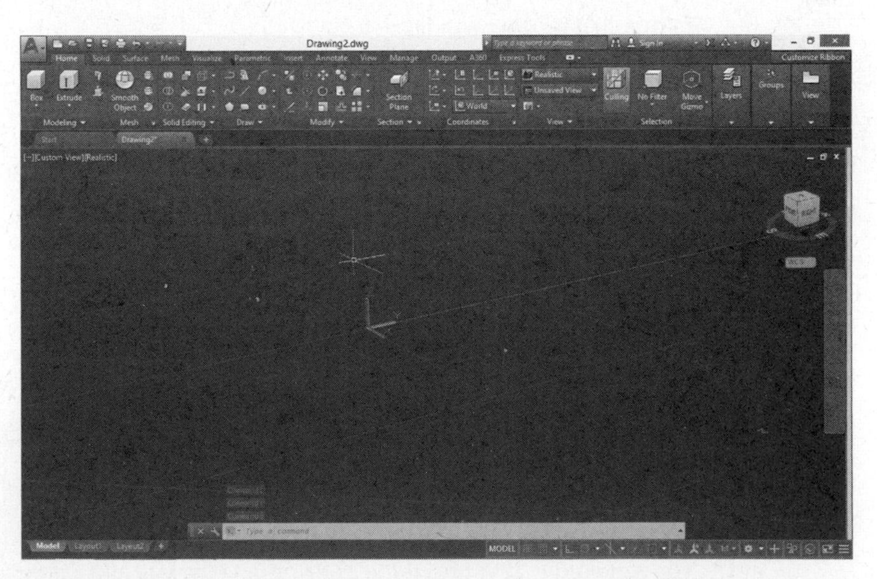

FIGURE 20.2
The AutoCAD 3D Modeling workspace

The drawing area displays the workspace as a perspective view with a dark gray background and a grid. This is just a typical AutoCAD drawing file with a couple of setting changes. The view has been set up to be a perspective view by default, and a feature called *Visual Styles* has been set to Realistic, which will show 3D objects as solid objects. You'll learn more about the tools that you can use to adjust the appearance of your workspace later in this chapter. For now, let's look at the tool palette and Ribbon that appear in the AutoCAD window.

To the far right is the AutoCAD Materials Browser palette. It shows a graphical list of surface materials that you can easily assign to 3D objects in your model. If the Materials Browser does not open by default, you'll see how to open it and learn more about materials in Chapter 22, "Editing and Visualizing 3D Solids."

The Ribbon along the top of the AutoCAD window offers all the tools that you'll need to create 3D models. The 3D Modeling workspace Ribbon offers a few of the tabs and panels with which you're already familiar, but many of the tabs will be new to you (see Figure 20.3). You see the familiar Draw and Modify panels in the Home tab, as well as several other panels devoted to 3D modeling: Modeling, Mesh, Solid Editing, Section, Coordinates, View, and Selection.

FIGURE 20.3 The Home Ribbon tab and panels of the 3D Modeling workspace

In addition, other Ribbon tabs offer more sets of tools designed for 3D modeling. For example, the Visualize tab contains tools that control the way the model looks. You can set up lighting and shadows and apply materials to objects such as brick or glass by using the Lights, Sun, and Location, and Materials panels. In the next sections, you'll gain firsthand experience creating and editing some 3D shapes using the Home tab's Modeling and View panels and the View tab's Visual Styles panel. This way, you'll get a feel for how things work in the 3D Modeling workspace.

Drawing in 3D Using Solids

You can work with three types of 3D objects in AutoCAD: solids, surfaces, and mesh objects. You can treat solid objects as if they're solid material. For example, you can create a box and then remove shapes from the box as if you're carving it, as shown in Figure 20.4.

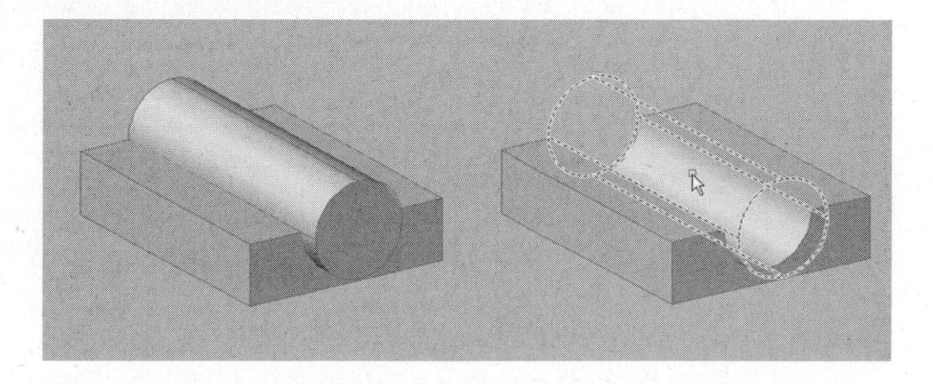

FIGURE 20.4 Solid modeling lets you remove or add shapes.

With surfaces, you create complex surface shapes by building on lines, arcs, or polylines. For example, you can quickly turn a series of curved polylines, arcs, or lines into a warped surface, as shown in Figure 20.5.

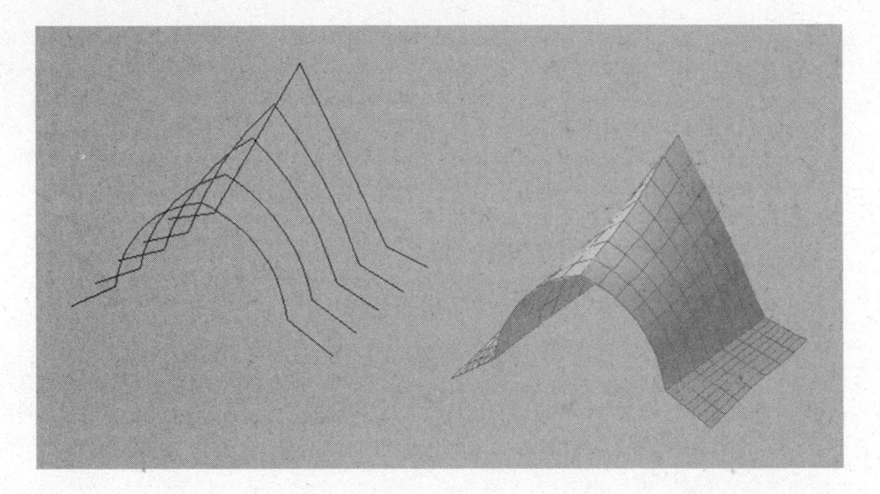

FIGURE 20.5
Using the Loft tool, you can use a set of 2D objects (left) to define a complex surface (right).

A mesh object is made up of edges, faces, and vertices. These basic parts create a series of square or triangular areas to define a three-dimensional form. You can create mesh objects with primitives in the same way as you create solid primitives. Their behavior is different, though. Mesh objects do not have mass properties like solids, but they can be altered through free-form modeling techniques. You can add creases as well as splits to the forms. You can alter the level of smoothness, which means that you can add more edges, faces, and vertices for a more rounded and organic-looking object.

Next, you'll learn how to create a solid box and then make simple changes to it as an introduction to 3D modeling.

CONVERTING OLD-STYLE SURFACE OBJECTS

If you have some experience with AutoCAD 3D prior to AutoCAD® 2011, note that the current surface-modeling features aren't the same as the surface objects you may have created in the older version of AutoCAD. The current surface objects can interact with solid primitive objects and can be converted into 3D solids. You can convert the old-style surfaces into the new 3D surfaces using the Convtosurface command described in the sidebar "Converting Objects with Thickness into 3D Solids" later in this chapter.

Adjusting Appearances

Before you start to work on the exercises, you'll want to change to a visual style that will make your work a little easier to visualize in the creation phase. Visual styles let you see your model in different modes, from sketch-like to realistic. You'll learn more about visual styles in the section "Getting a Visual Effect" later in this chapter. For now, you'll get a brief introduction by changing the style for the exercises that follow:

1. In the upper-left corner of the drawing area, click the Visual Style Control drop-down list to view the options.
2. Select the Shades Of Gray option. This will give the solid objects in your model a uniform gray color and will also "highlight" the edges of the solids with a dark line so that you can see them clearly.

Creating a 3D Box

Start by creating a box using the Box tool in the Home tab's Modeling panel:

1. Close the Materials Browser, if it is visible, by clicking the X on the title bar. You won't need it for this chapter. If you need it later, you can go to the Materials panel in the Visualize tab and click the Materials Browser tool.
2. Select the Box tool from the Solids flyout on the Home tab's Modeling panel.

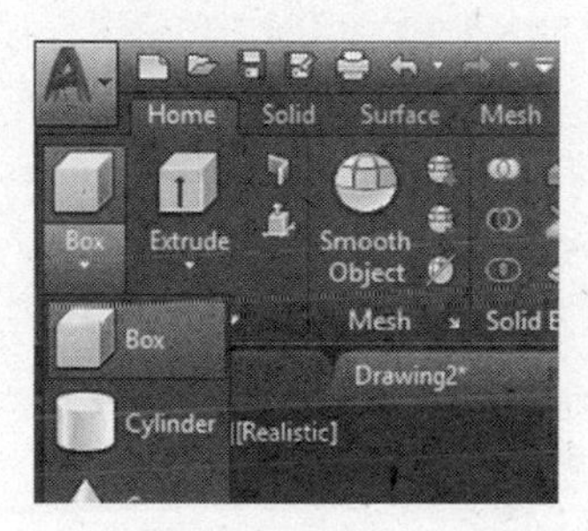

3. Click a point near the origin of the drawing shown in Figure 20.6. You can use the coordinate readout to select a point near 0,0. After you click, you'll see a rectangle follow the cursor.
4. Click another point near coordinate 20,15, as shown in Figure 20.6. As you move the cursor, the rectangle is fixed and the height of the 3D box appears.
5. Enter 4↵ for a height of 4 units for the box. You can also click to fix the height of the box.

FIGURE 20.6
Drawing a 3D solid box

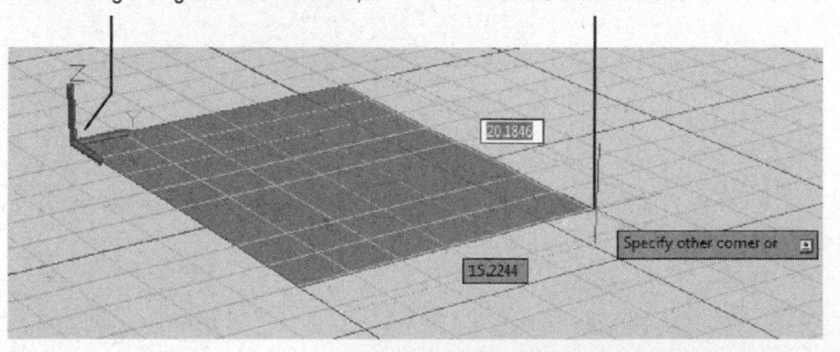

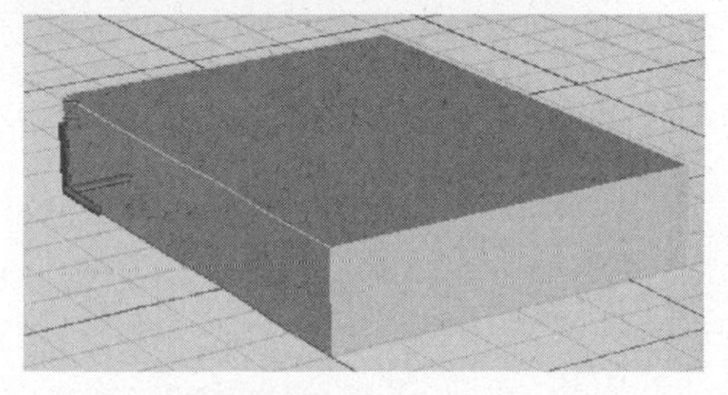

You used three basic steps in creating the box. First, you clicked one corner to establish a location for the box. Then, you clicked another corner to establish the base size. Finally, you selected a height. You use a similar set of steps to create any of the other 3D solid primitives found in the Solids flyout of the Home tab's Modeling panel. For example, for a cylinder you select the center, then the radius, and finally the height. For a wedge, you select two corners as you did with the box, and then you select the height.

WHY THE SCREEN LOOKS DIFFERENT

The display shown in this book is set up with a lighter background than the default background in AutoCAD so that you can see the various parts of the display more easily on the printed page.

In addition, when you start a 3D model using the `acad3D.dwt` template, the default layer 0 is set to a color that is a light blue instead of the white or black that is used in the standard `acad.dwt` template. The blue color is used so that you can see the 3D shapes clearly when the model is displayed using a shaded visual style. If you happen to start a 3D model using the `acad.dwt` template, you may want to change the default layer color to something other than white or black.

Editing 3D Solids with Grips

After you've created a solid, you can fine-tune its shape by using grips:

1. Adjust your view so that it looks similar to Figure 20.7, and then click the solid to select it. Grips appear on the 3D solid as shown in the figure.

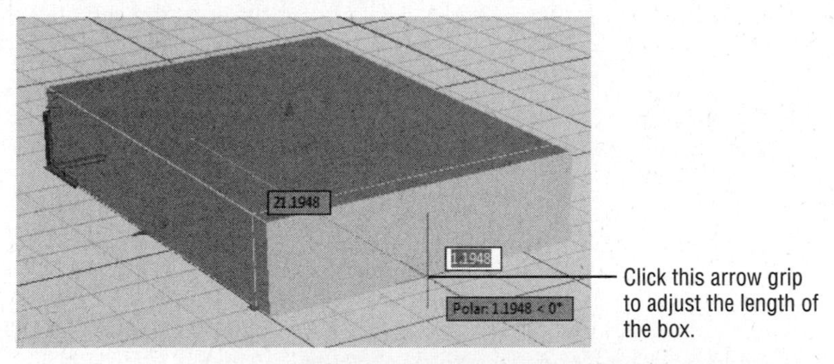

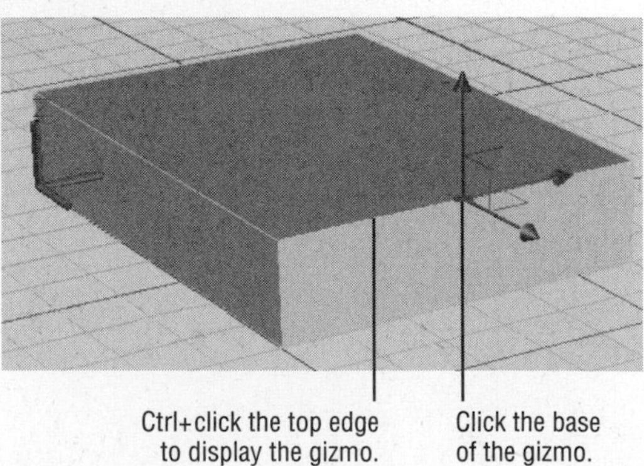

FIGURE 20.7
Grips appear on the 3D solid.

You can adjust the location of the square grips at the base of the solid in a way that is similar to adjusting the grips on 2D objects. The arrow grips let you adjust the length of the site to which the arrows are attached. If you click an arrow grip and you have Dynamic Input turned on, a dimension appears at the cursor, as shown in Figure 20.7. You can enter a new dimension for the length associated with the selected grip, or you can drag and click the arrow to adjust the length. Remember that you can press the Tab key to shift between dimensions shown in the Dynamic Input display.

2. Click the arrow grip toward the front of the box, as shown at the upper left in Figure 20.7. Now, as you move the cursor, the box changes in length.
3. Press Esc twice to clear the grip selection and the box selection.

Constraining Motion with the Gizmo

You can move individual edges by using a Ctrl+click. This will activate the gizmo. The gizmo is an icon that looks like the UCS icon and appears whenever you select a 3D solid or any part of a 3D solid. Try the next exercise to see how it works:

1. Hold down the Ctrl key and move the cursor over different surfaces and edges of the box. They will be highlighted as you do this. Ctrl+click the top-front edge of the box to expose the edge's grip. The gizmo will appear.
2. The gizmo has three legs pointing in the x-, y-, and z-axes. It also has a grip at the base of the three legs. If your Ctrl+click doesn't work as described, you may need to change the setting for the `Legacyctrlpick` system variable. At the `Type a Command` prompt, enter **legacyctrlpick**↵, and then enter **0**↵. Place the cursor on the blue z-axis of the gizmo, but don't click. A blue line appears that extends across the drawing area, and the z-axis of the gizmo changes color, as shown in Figure 20.8.

FIGURE 20.8
Using the gizmo to constrain motion

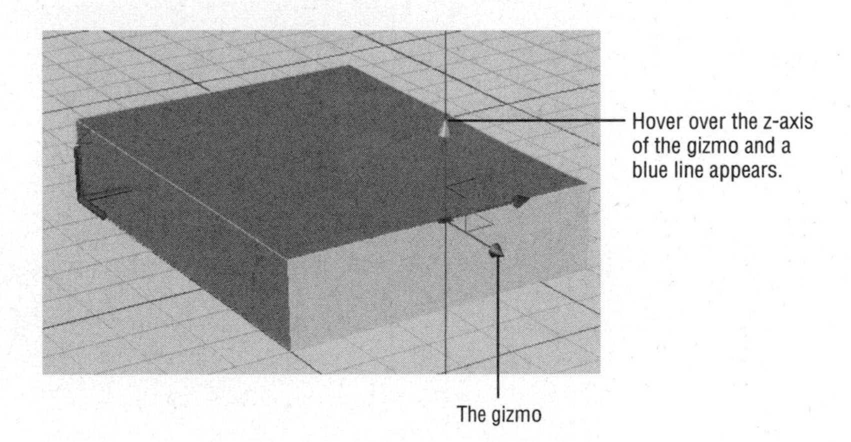

3. Click the z-axis. Now, as you move the cursor, the grip motion is constrained in the z-axis.
4. Click again to fix the location of the grip.

5. Press the Esc key to clear your grip selection.
6. Click the Undo tool to undo the grip edit.

Here you used the gizmo to change the Z location of a grip easily. You can use the gizmo to modify the location of a single grip or the entire object.

Rotating Objects in 3D Using Dynamic UCS

Typically, you work in what is known as the *World Coordinate System (WCS)*. This is the default coordinate system that AutoCAD uses in new drawings, but you can also create your own coordinate systems that are subsets of the WCS. A coordinate system that you create is known as a *User Coordinate System (UCS)*.

UCSs are significant in 3D modeling because they can help you orient your work in 3D space. For example, you could set up a UCS on a vertical face of the 3D box that you created earlier. You could then draw on that vertical face just as you would on the drawing's WCS. Figure 20.9 shows a cylinder drawn on the side of a box. If you click the Cylinder tool, for example, and place the cursor on the side of the box, the side will be highlighted to indicate the surface to which the cylinder will be applied. In addition, if you could see the cursor in color, you would see that the blue z-axis is pointing sideways to the left and is perpendicular to the side of the box.

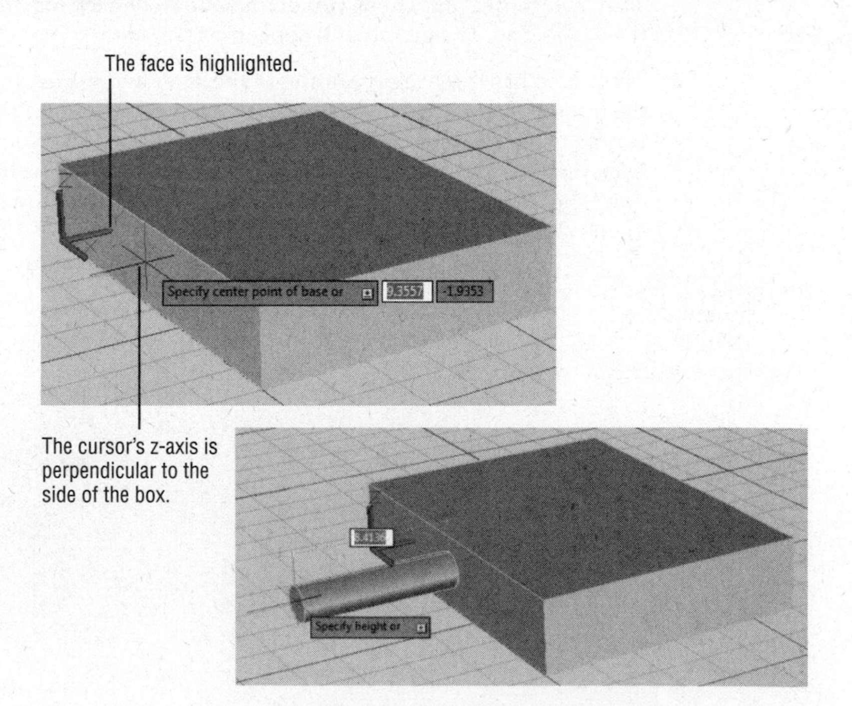

FIGURE 20.9
Drawing on the side of a box

The UCS has always been an important tool for 3D modeling in AutoCAD. The example just described demonstrates the Dynamic UCS, which automatically changes the orientation of the x-, y-, and z-axes to conform to the flat surface of a 3D object.

You may have noticed that when you created the new 3D file using the `acad3D.dwt` template, the cursor looked different. Instead of the usual cross, you saw three intersecting lines. If you look carefully, you'll see that each line of the cursor is a different color. In its default configuration, AutoCAD shows a red line for the x-axis, a green line for the y-axis, and a blue line for the z-axis. This mimics the color scheme of the UCS icon, as shown in Figure 20.10.

FIGURE 20.10
The UCS icon at the left and the cursor in 3D to the right are color matched.

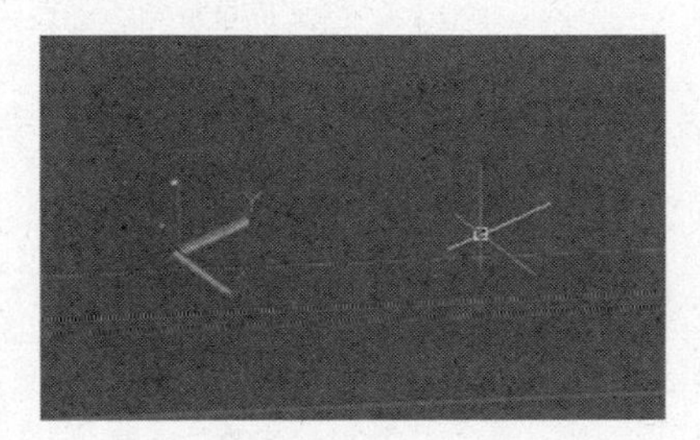

As you work with the Dynamic UCS, you'll see that the orientation of these lines changes when you point at a surface on a 3D object. The following exercise shows you how to use the Dynamic UCS to help you rotate the box about the x-axis:

1. Be sure that the Object Snap and Allow/Disallow Dynamic UCS features are turned on. If a specific icon is not in the status bar, click the Customization button on the far right and turn on whichever icon is missing by clicking it on the list.

2. Click Rotate in the Home tab's Modify panel or enter **RO**↵.
3. At the `Select objects:` prompt, click the box and then press ↵ to finish your selection.
4. At the `Specify base point:` prompt, don't click anything, but move the cursor from one surface of the box to a side of the box. As you do this, notice that the surface you point to becomes highlighted. The orientation of the cursor also changes depending on which surface you're pointing to.

5. Place the cursor on the left side as shown in the top image of Figure 20.11; then Shift+right-click and select Endpoint from the Osnap context menu.
6. While keeping the side highlighted, place the osnap marker on the lower-front corner of the box, as shown in the top image in Figure 20.11. Click this corner. As you move the cursor, the box rotates about the y-axis.
7. Enter **-30** for the rotation angle. Your box should look like the image at the bottom in Figure 20.11.

Here you saw that you could hover over a surface to indicate the plane about which the rotation is to occur. Now suppose that you want to add an object to one of the sides of the rotated box. The next section will show you another essential tool—one you can use to do just that.

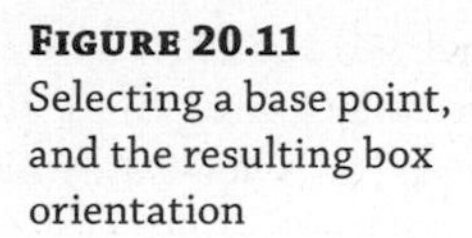

FIGURE 20.11
Selecting a base point, and the resulting box orientation

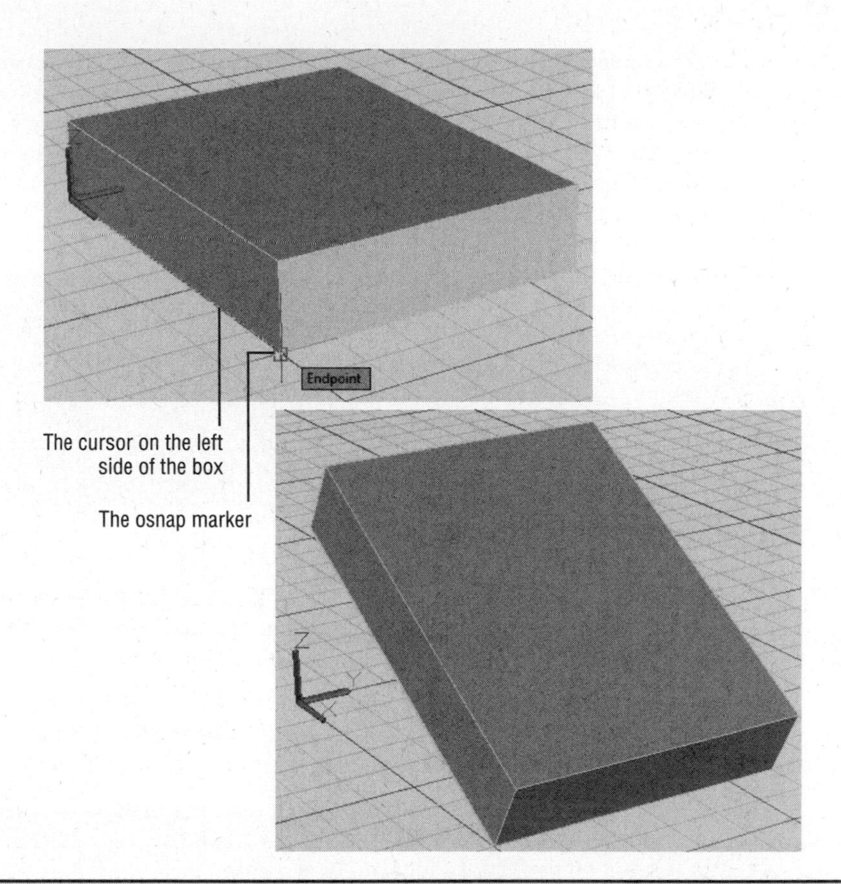

> **USING OBJECT SNAPS AND OSNAP TRACKING IN 3D SPACE**
>
> If you need to place objects in precise locations in 3D, such as at endpoints or midpoints of other objects, you can do so using object snaps, just as you would in 2D. But you must take care when using osnaps where the Dynamic UCS is concerned.
>
> In the exercise in the section "Rotating Objects in 3D Using Dynamic UCS," you were asked to make sure that you placed the cursor on the side of the box that coincided with the rotational plane before you selected the Endpoint osnap. This ensures that the Dynamic UCS feature has selected the proper rotational plane; otherwise, the box may rotate in the wrong direction.

Drawing on a 3D Object's Surface

In the rotation exercise, you saw that you could hover over a surface to indicate the plane of rotation. You can use the same method to indicate the plane on which you want to place an object. Try the following exercise to see how it's done:

1. Select Center, Radius from the Circle flyout on the Home tab's Draw panel or enter **C**↵.
2. Place the cursor on the top surface of the box, as indicated in the top image of Figure 20.12, and hold it there for a moment. The surface is highlighted, and the cursor aligns with the angle of the top surface.

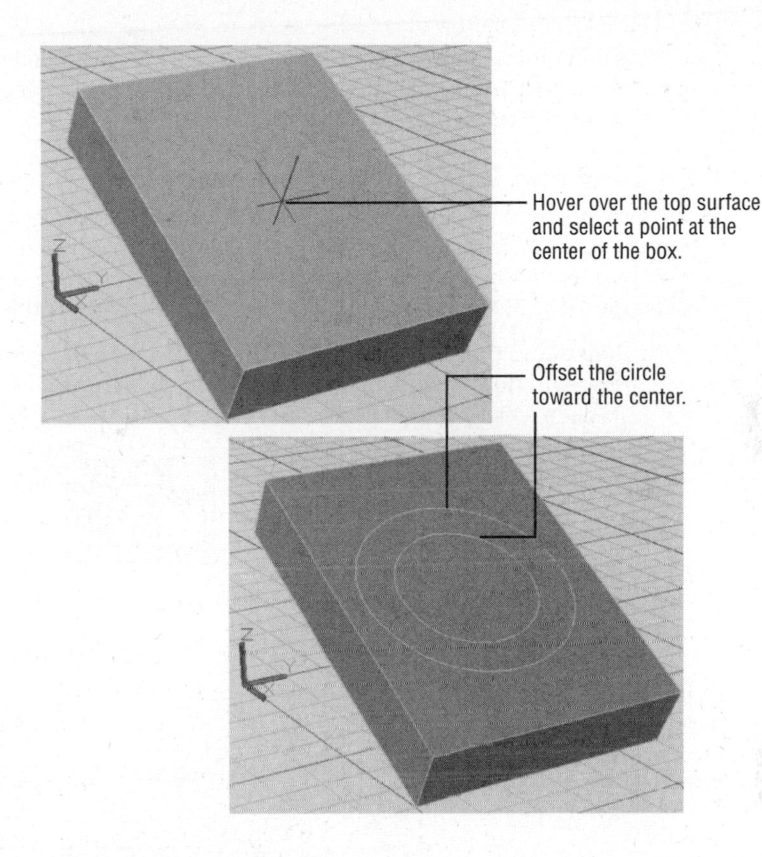

FIGURE 20.12
Drawing circles on the surface of a 3D solid

3. Click a point roughly at the center of the box. The circle appears on the surface and, as you move the cursor, the circle's radius follows.

4. Adjust the circle so that it's roughly the same 6-unit radius as the one shown on the lower image in Figure 20.12, and then click to set the radius. You can also enter **6**↵.

5. Select Offset from the Home tab's Modify panel, and offset the circle 2 units inward, as shown in the lower image of Figure 20.12. You can use the Center osnap to indicate a direction toward the center of the circle.

USING A FIXED UCS

If you're working in a crowded area of a drawing or if you know you need to do a lot of work on one particular surface of an object, you can create a UCS that remains in a fixed orientation until you change it instead of relying on the Dynamic UCS feature. Select Face from the View flyout on the Home tab's Coordinates panel, and then click the surface that defines the plane on which you want to work. The UCS aligns with the selected surface. Press ↵ to accept the face that the Face option has found, or you can use one of the options `[Next/Xflip/Yflip]` to move to another surface or flip the UCS. Once you've set the UCS, you won't have to worry about accidentally drawing in the wrong orientation. To return to the WCS, click UCS, World in the View tab's Coordinates panel. You'll learn more about the UCS in Chapter 21, "Using Advanced 3D Features."

This demonstrates that you can use Dynamic UCS to align objects with the surface of an object. Note that Dynamic UCS works only on flat surfaces. For example, you can't use it to place an object on the curved side of a cylinder.

Pushing and Pulling Shapes from a Solid

You've just added two 2D circles to the top surface of the 3D box. AutoCAD offers a tool that lets you use those 2D circles, or any closed 2D shapes, to modify the shape of your 3D object. The Presspull tool in the Home tab's Modeling panel lets you "press" or "pull" a 3D shape to or from the surface of a 3D object. The following exercise shows how this works:

1. Make sure that the Polar Tracking tool in the status bar is turned on, and then click the Presspull tool in the Home tab's Modeling panel. You can also enter **Presspull**↵ at the `Type a Command` prompt.

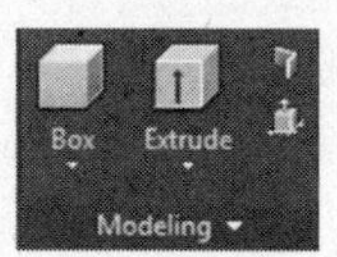

2. Move the cursor to the top surface of the box between both circles. (See the lower-right panel of Figure 20.13.)

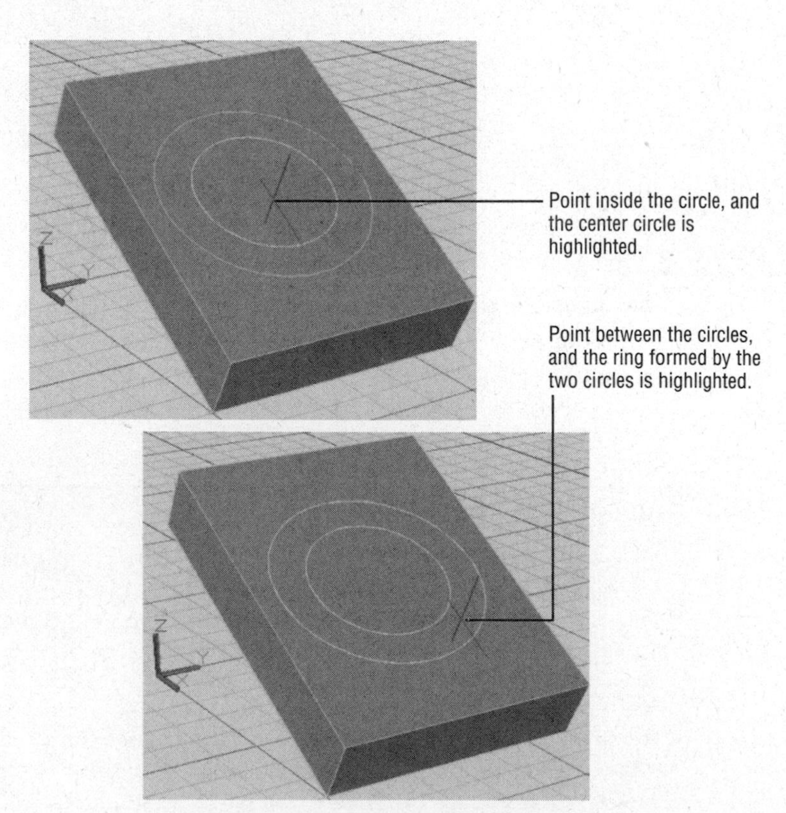

FIGURE 20.13
Move the cursor over different areas of the box and notice how the areas are highlighted.

3. With the cursor between the two circles, click. As you move the mouse, the circular area defined by the two circles moves.
4. Adjust the cursor location so that the cursor is positioned below the center of the circle, as shown in the top-left panel of Figure 20.13. Enter **3**↵ to create a 3-unit indentation, as shown in Figure 20.14.

FIGURE 20.14
Creating an indentation in the box using Presspull

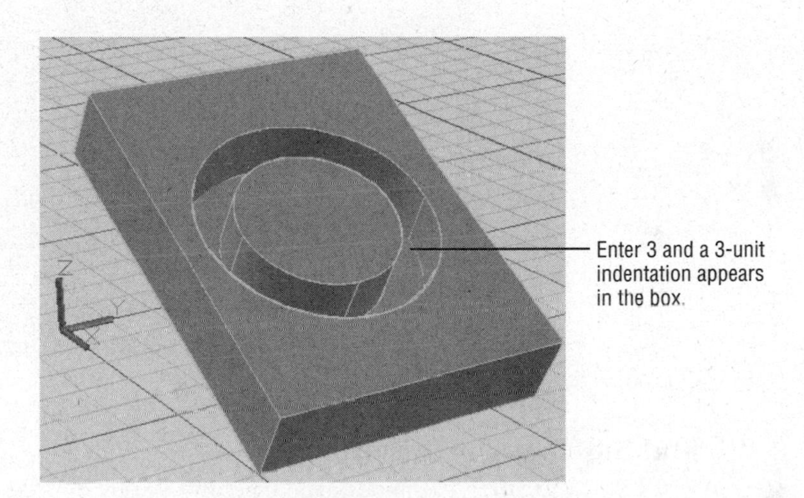

You've created a circular indentation in the box by pressing the circular area defined by the two circles. You could have pulled the area upward to form a circular ridge on the box. Pressing the circle into the solid is essentially the same as subtracting one solid from another. When you press the shape into the solid, AutoCAD assumes that you want to subtract the shape.

Presspull works with any closed 2D shape, such as a circle, closed polyline, or other completely enclosed area. An existing 3D solid isn't needed. For example, you can draw two concentric circles without the 3D box and then use Presspull to convert the circles into a 3D solid ring. In the previous exercise, the solid box showed that you can use Presspull to subtract a shape from an existing solid.

As you saw in this exercise, the Presspull tool can help you quickly subtract a shape from an existing 3D solid. Figure 20.15 shows some other examples of how you can use Presspull. For example, you can draw a line from one edge to another and then use Presspull to extrude the resulting triangular shape. You can also draw concentric shapes and extrude them; you can even use offset spline curves to add a trough to a solid.

DRAWING OUTSIDE THE SURFACE

If you use an open 2D object such as a curved spline or line on a 3D surface, the endpoints must touch exactly on the edge of the surface before Presspull will work.

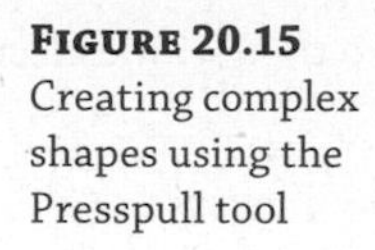

FIGURE 20.15
Creating complex shapes using the Presspull tool

Making Changes to Your Solid

When you're creating a 3D model, you'll hardly ever get the shape right the first time. Suppose you decide that you need to modify the shape you've created so far by moving the hole from the center of the box to a corner. The next exercise will show you how to access the individual components of a 3D solid to make changes.

Your working model is composed of two objects: a box and a cylinder formed from two circles. These two components of the solid are referred to as *subobjects* of the main solid object. Faces and edges of 3D solids are also considered subobjects. When you use the Union, Subtract, and Intersect tools later in this book, you'll see that objects merge into a single solid—or at least that is how it seems at first. You can use Ctrl+click to access and modify the shapes of the subobjects. Try the following:

1. Press Esc to cancel the previous command. Place the cursor on the components of the solid that you've made so far. They are highlighted as if they were one object. If you were to click it (don't do it yet), the entire object would be selected.
2. Hold down the Ctrl key, and move the cursor over the circular indentation. As you do this, the indentation is highlighted (see the top-left image in Figure 20.16).
3. While still holding down the Ctrl key, click both of the indentation sides. The grip for the indentation appears, as shown in the lower-right image in Figure 20.16. As you may guess, you can use these grips to change the shape and location of a feature of the selected solid. Release the Ctrl key when finished.
4. Click the center square grip of the indentation, and move your cursor around. If you find it a bit uncontrollable, turn off Polar Tracking mode and osnaps. As you move the cursor, the indentation moves with it.

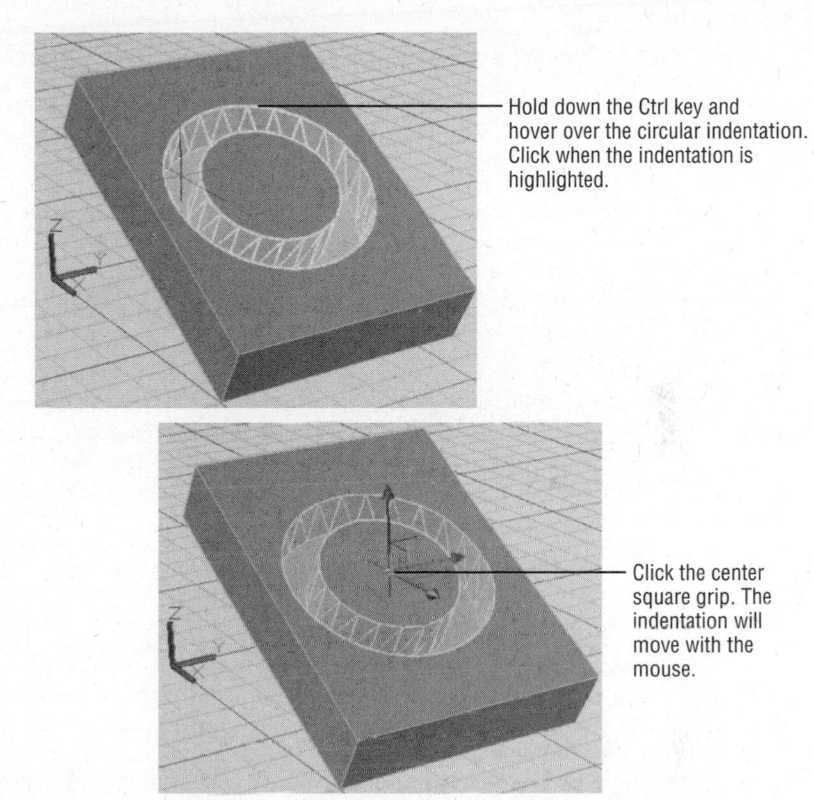

FIGURE 20.16
You can select subobjects of a 3D solid when you hold down the Ctrl key.

5. Place the indentation in the location shown in Figure 20.17 and click. You've just moved the indentation from the center to the edge of the cylinder.

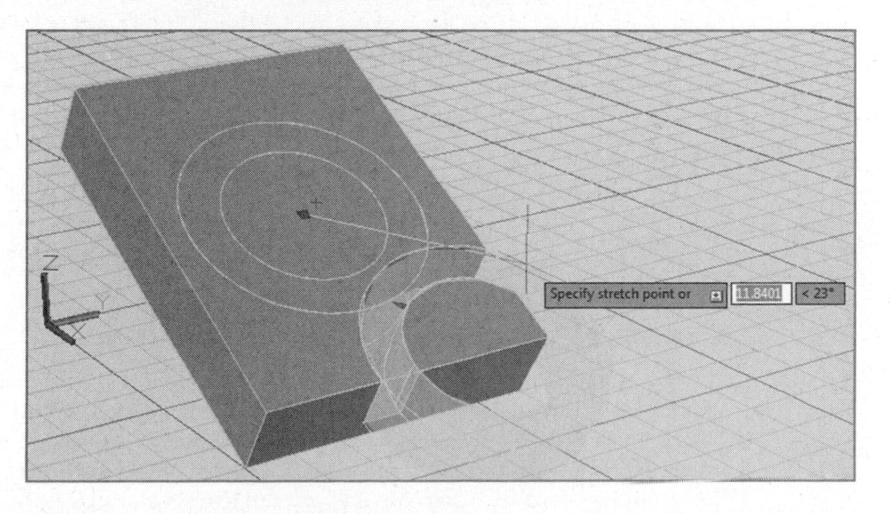

FIGURE 20.17
You can move the indentation to a new location using its grip.

6. Press the Esc key to clear the selection. Exit the file and save it.

Things to Watch Out for When Editing 3D Objects

You can use the Move and Stretch commands on 3D objects to modify their z-coordinate values—but you have to be careful with these commands when editing in 3D. Here are a few tips that we've picked up while working on various 3D projects:

- If you want to move a 3D solid using grips, you need to select the square grip at the bottom center of the solid. The other grips move only the feature associated with the grip, like a corner or an edge. When that bottom grip is selected, you can switch to another grip as the base point for the move by doing the following: After selecting the base grip, right-click, select Base Point from the context menu, and click the grip that you want to use.
- The Scale command will scale an object's z-coordinate value as well as the standard x-coordinate and y-coordinate. Suppose that you have an object with an elevation of 2 units. If you use the Scale command to enlarge that object by a factor of 4, the object will have a new elevation of 2 units times 4, or 8 units. If, on the other hand, that object has an elevation of 0, its elevation won't change because 0 times 4 is still 0. You can use the 3dscale command to restrict the scaling of an object to a single plane.
- You can also use Mirror and Rotate (on the Modify panel) on 3D solid objects, but these commands don't affect their z-coordinate values. You can specify z-coordinates for base and insertion points, so take care when using these commands with 3D models.
- Using the Move, Stretch, and Copy commands (on the Modify panel) with osnaps can produce unpredictable and unwanted results. As a rule, it's best to use coordinate filters when selecting points with osnap overrides. For example, to move an object from the endpoint of one object to the endpoint of another on the same z-coordinate, invoke the .XY point filter at the `Specify base point:` and `Specify second point:` prompts before you issue the Endpoint override. Proceed to pick the endpoint of the object you want, and then enter the z-coordinate or pick any point to use the current default z-coordinate.
- When you create a block, it uses the currently active UCS to determine its own local coordinate system. When that block is later inserted, it orients its own coordinate system with the current UCS. (The UCS is discussed in more detail in Chapter 21.)

This example showed that the Ctrl key can be an extremely useful tool when you have to edit a solid; it allows you to select the subobjects that form your model. Once the subobjects are selected, you can move them, or you can use the arrow grips to change their size.

Creating 3D Forms from 2D Shapes

You've seen that 3D solid primitives are great for creating basic shapes, but in many situations, you'll want to create a 3D form from a more complex shape. Fortunately, you can extrude 2D objects into a variety of shapes using the additional tools found in the Home tab's Modeling panel. For example, you can draw a shape like a star and then extrude it along the z-axis, as shown in Figure 20.18. Alternatively, you can use several strategically placed 2D objects to form a flowing surface like the wing of an airplane.

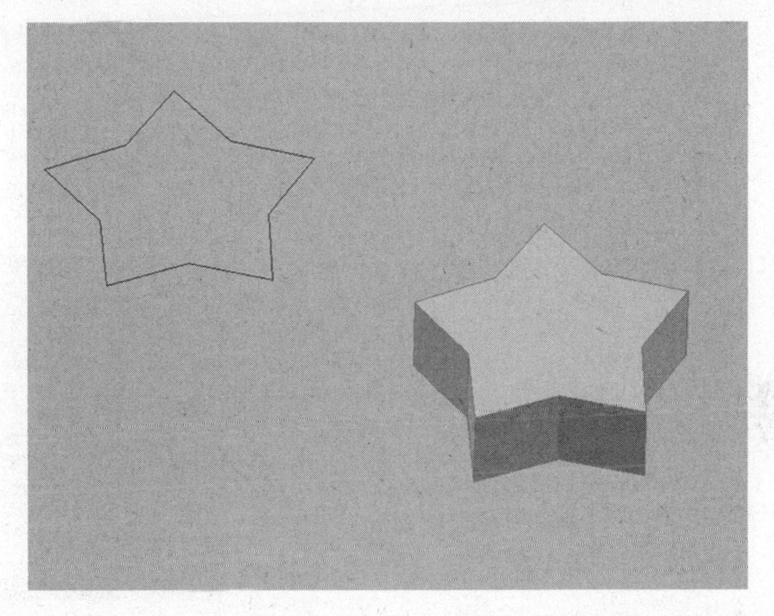

FIGURE 20.18
The closed polyline on the left can be used to construct the 3D shape on the right.

You can create a 3D solid by extruding a 2D closed polyline. This is a flexible way to create shapes because you can create a polyline of any shape and extrude it to a fairly complex form.

In the following set of exercises, you'll turn the apartment room from previous chapters into a 3D model. We've created a version of the apartment floor plan that has a few additions to make things a little easier for you. Figure 20.19 shows the file that you'll use in the exercise. It's the same floor plan from earlier chapters but with the addition of closed polylines outlining the walls.

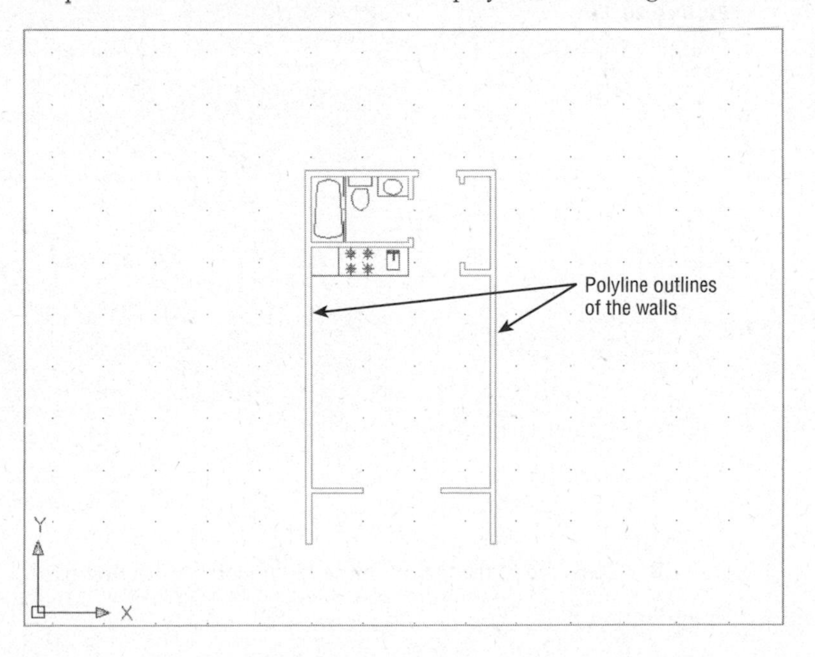

FIGURE 20.19
The unit plan with closed polylines outlining the walls

The plan isn't shaded as in the previous examples in this chapter. You can work in 3D in this display mode just as easily as in a shaded mode:

1. Open the `20-unit.dwg` file. Metric users should open `20-unit-metric.dwg`.
2. Choose SW Isometric from the 3D Navigation drop-down list in the Home tab's View panel (see Figure 20.20). You can also type **-View↵Swiso↵**.

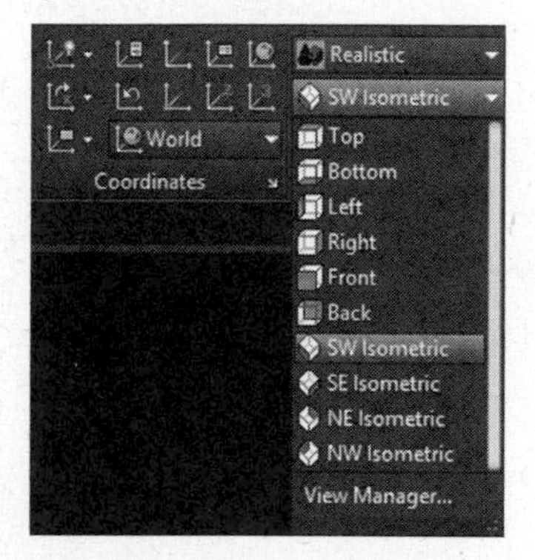

FIGURE 20.20
Selecting a view from the 3D Navigation drop-down list

Your view now looks as if you're standing above and to the left of your drawing rather than directly above it (see Figure 20.21). The UCS icon helps you to get a sense of your new orientation.

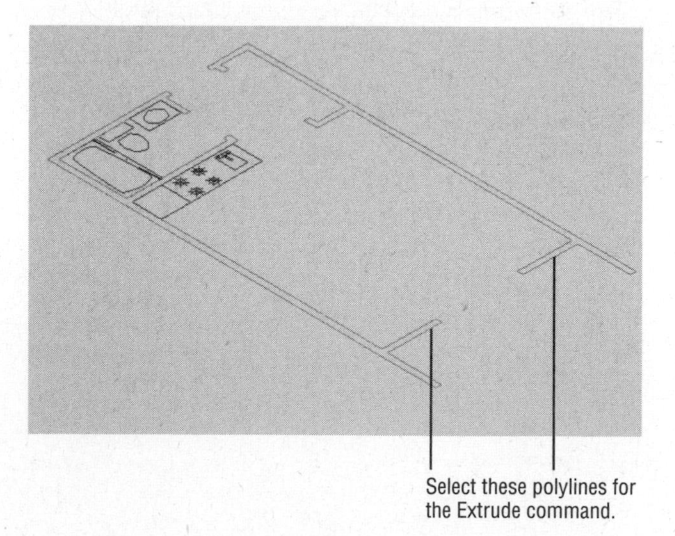

FIGURE 20.21
A 3D view of the unit plan

3. Click the Extrude tool in the Home tab's Modeling panel (see Figure 20.22).

FIGURE 20.22
Selecting the Extrude tool from the Modeling panel

You can also enter **Extrude**↵ at the command-line interface. You see the message `Current wire frame density: ISOLINES=4, Closed profiles creation mode = Solid Select objects to extrude or [Mode:_MO Closed profiles creation mode [Solid/Surface] <Solid>:_SO` in the Command window followed by the `Select objects to extrude or [MOde]:` prompt.

4. Select the wall outlines shown in Figure 20.21, and then press ↵.
5. At the `Specify height of extrusion or [Direction/Path/Taper angle/ Expression] <-0'-3">:` prompt, place the cursor near the top of the drawing area and enter **8'**↵. Metric users should enter **224**↵. The walls extrude to the height you entered, as shown in Figure 20.23.

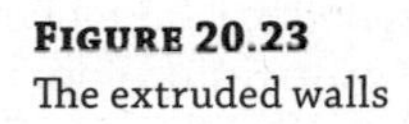

FIGURE 20.23
The extruded walls

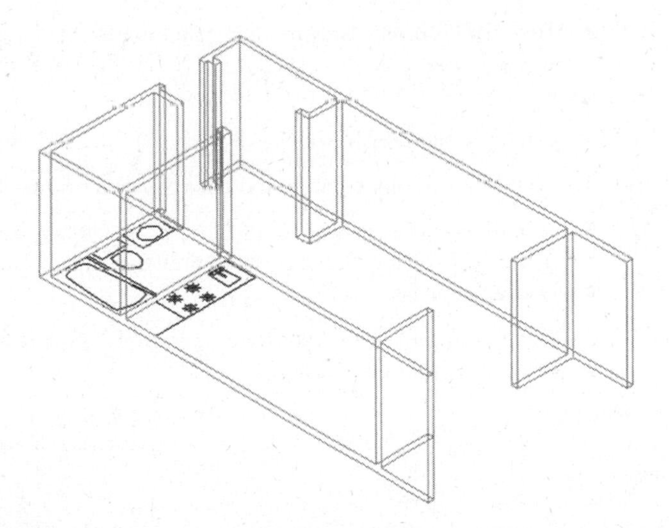

Unlike in the earlier exercise with the box, you can see through the walls because this is a Wireframe view. A *Wireframe view* shows the volume of a 3D object by displaying the lines representing the edges of surfaces. Later in this chapter, we'll discuss how to make an object's surfaces appear opaque as they do on the box earlier in this chapter.

Next you'll add door headers to define the wall openings:

1. Adjust your view so that you get a close look at the doorway shown in Figure 20.24. You can use the Pan and Zoom tools in this 3D view as you would in a 2D view.

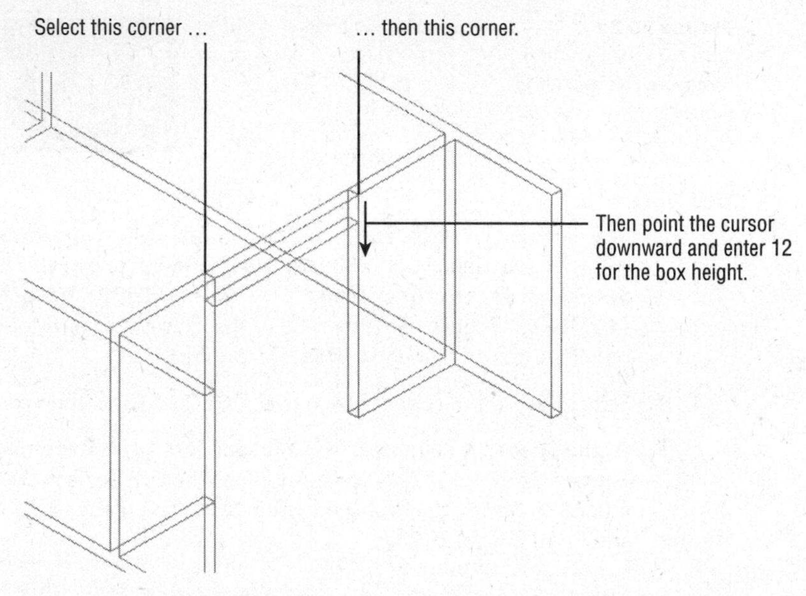

FIGURE 20.24
Adding the door header to the opening at the balcony of the unit plan

2. Turn off Dynamic UCS mode by clicking the Allow/Disallow Dynamic UCS tool in the status bar so that it's grayed out. This helps you avoid accidentally orienting your cursor to the wall behind the door header.

3. Click the Box tool in the Solids flyout of the Modeling panel.
4. Use the Endpoint osnaps, and click the two points shown in Figure 20.24.
5. At the `Specify height or [2Point] <8'-0">:` prompt, point the cursor downward from the points you just selected and enter **12**↵. Metric users should enter **30**↵. The door header appears.
6. Zoom and pan so that your view resembles Figure 20.25, and then repeat steps 4 and 5 to draw the other door headers.

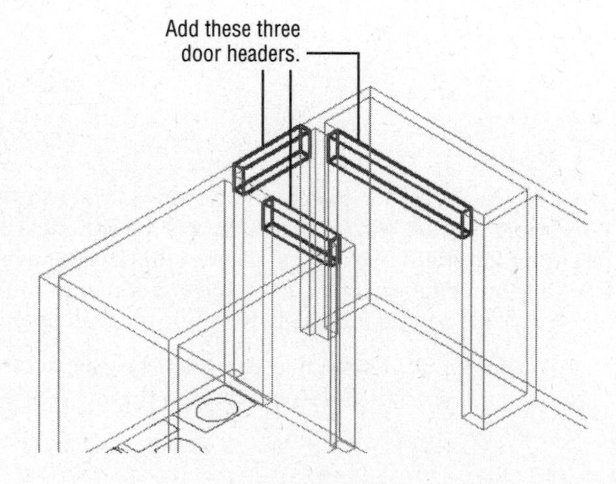

FIGURE 20.25
Adding the remaining door headers

The walls and door headers give you a better sense of the space in the unit plan. To enhance the appearance of the 3D model further, you can join the walls and door headers so that they appear as seamless walls and openings:

1. Zoom out so that you can see the entire unit. Click the Union tool in the Solid tab's Boolean panel (see Figure 20.26). You can also enter **UNI**↵.

FIGURE 20.26
Select the Union tool.

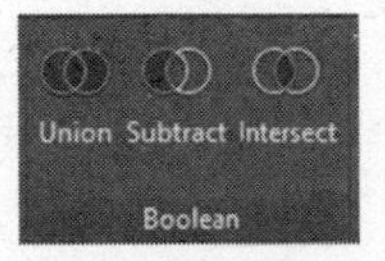

2. At the `Select objects:` prompt, select all the walls and headers, and then press ↵.

Now the walls and headers appear as one seamless surface without any distracting joint lines. You can get a sense of the space of the unit plan. You'll want to explore ways of viewing the unit in 3D, but before you do that, you need to know about one more 3D modeling feature: *point filters*.

Isolating Coordinates with Point Filters

AutoCAD offers a method for 3D point selection that can help you isolate the x-, y-, or z-coordinate of a location in 3D. Using *point filters* (described in the help files as "coordinate filters"), you can enter an X, Y, or Z value by picking a point on the screen and telling AutoCAD to use only the X, Y, or Z value of that point or any combination of those values. For example, suppose that you want to start the corner of a 3D box at the x- and y-coordinates of the corner of the unit plan but you want the Z location at 3′ instead of at ground level. You can use point or coordinate filters to select only the x- and y-coordinates of a point and then specify the z-coordinate as a separate value. The following exercise demonstrates how this works:

1. Zoom into the balcony door, and turn on the F-RAIL layer. Turn off Dynamic Input.
2. Choose the Box tool from the Solids flyout on the Modeling panel.
3. At the `Specify first corner or [Center]:` prompt, Shift+right-click to display the Object Snap menu and then choose Point Filters ➤ .XY. As an alternative, you can enter **.xy**↵. By doing this, you are telling AutoCAD that first you're going to specify the x- and y-coordinates for this beginning point and then later indicate the z-coordinate.

   You may have noticed the .X, .Y, and .Z options on the Object Snap menu (Shift+right-click). These are the 3D point filters. By choosing one of these options as you select points in a 3D command, you can filter an X, Y, or Z value, or any combination of values, from that selected point. You can also enter filters through the keyboard.

4. At the `Specify first corner or [Center]: .XY of:` prompt, pick the corner of the unit plan, as shown in Figure 20.27.

FIGURE 20.27
Constructing the rail using point filters

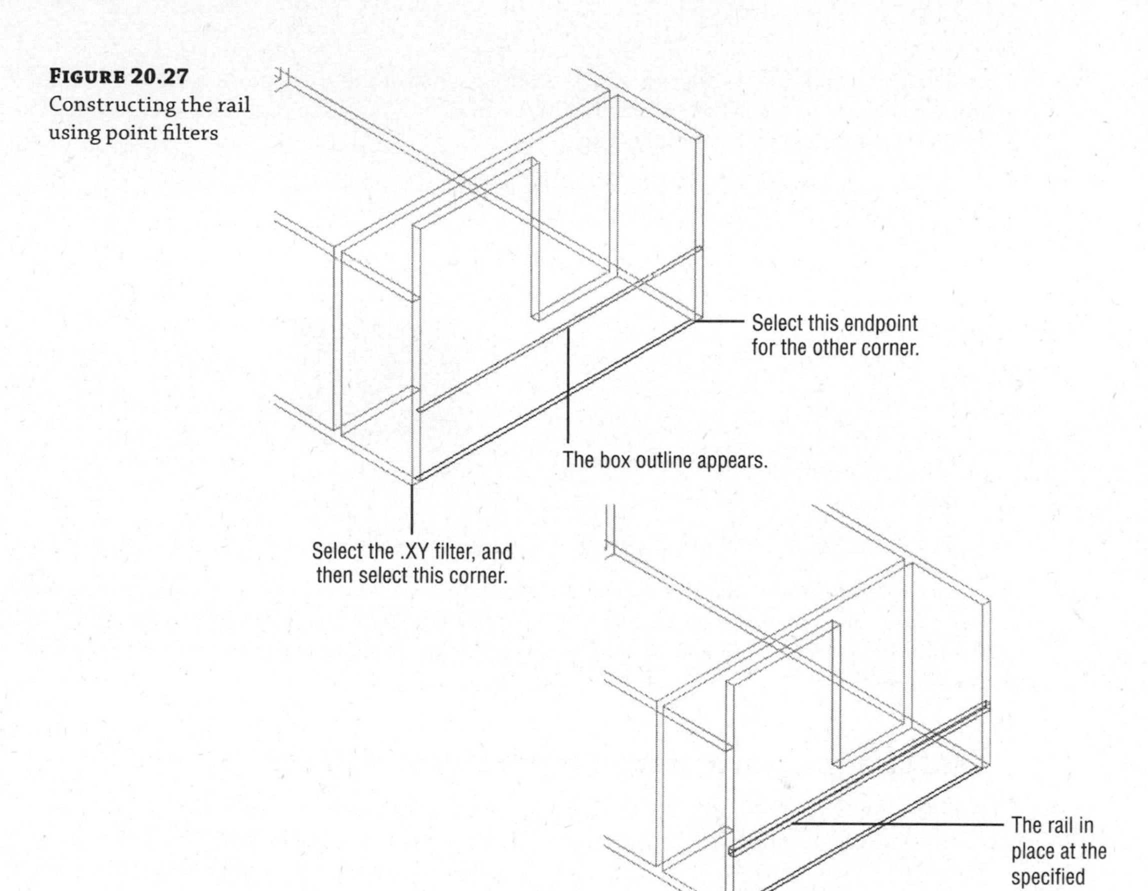

5. At the `(need Z):` prompt, enter **36↵** (the z-coordinate). Metric users enter **92↵**. The outline of the box appears at the 36″ (or 92 cm) elevation and at the corner you selected in step 4.
6. At the `Specify other corner or [Cube/Length]:` prompt, Shift+right-click to display the Osnap menu again and choose Point Filters ➤ XY. Select the other endpoint indicated in Figure 20.27.
7. At the `(need Z):` prompt, a temporary outline of the box appears at the 36″ height.

   Enter **40↵** (**101↵** for metric users) for the height of the box. The box appears as the balcony rail, as shown in the bottom image in Figure 20.27.

In step 4, you selected the corner of the unit, but the box didn't appear right away. You had to enter a Z value in step 5 before the outline of the box appeared. Then, in step 6, you saw the box begin at the 36″ elevation. Using point filters allowed you to place the box accurately in the drawing even though there were no features that you could snap to directly.

Converting Objects with Thickness into 3D Solids

If you've worked with 3D in AutoCAD before, you probably know that you can give an object a thickness property greater than 0 to make it a 3D object. For example, a line with a thickness property greater than 0 looks like a vertical surface.

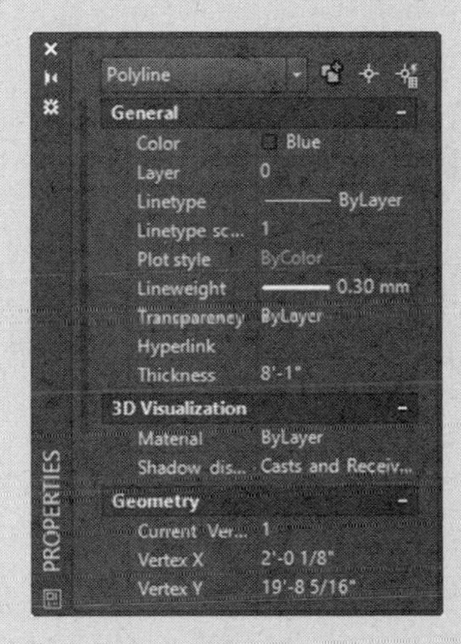

In the unit plan exercise, you can do the same for the polylines used to draw the walls. Click the wall polylines, and then right-click and choose Properties. In the Properties palette, change the Thickness value to 8′ or 224 cm.

The walls appear in three dimensions. But be aware that these walls aren't 3D solids. If you zoom in to a detail of the walls, they appear hollow.

Fortunately, AutoCAD supplies a tool that converts a closed polyline with thickness into a solid. Expand the Home tab's Solid Editing panel, and then click the Convert To Solid tool. You can also enter **convtosolid↵**.

Select the polyline walls; press ↵ when you've finished your selection. After you do this, the walls become 3D solids. This operation works with any closed polyline, providing an alternate way of creating a 3D solid. If you have existing 3D models that have been produced using the Thickness property, you can use the Convert To Solid tool to bring your 3D models up-to-date. The Convert To Solid tool can also convert open polylines that have a width and thickness greater than 0. (See Chapter 18, "Drawing Curves," for more on polylines.)

Another tool, called Convert To Surface, converts objects with thickness into 3D surface objects. You can use 3D surfaces to slice or thicken 3D solids into full 3D solids. You'll learn more about 3D surfaces in Chapter 23, "Exploring 3D Mesh and Surface Modeling."

Now that you've gotten most of the unit modeled in 3D, you'll want to be able to look at it from different angles. Next, you'll see some of the tools available to control your views in 3D.

Get to Know Coordinate Filters

In our own work in 3D, coordinate filters are a real lifesaver. They can help you locate a position in 3D when the drawing becomes crowded with objects. And because a lot of architectural models start from floor plans, you can easily "project" locations into 3D using coordinate filters. Understanding this tool will greatly improve your ability to work in 3D.

Moving Around Your Model

AutoCAD offers a number of tools to help you view your 3D model. You've already used one to get the current 3D view. Choosing Southwest Isometric from the View panel's drop-down list displays an isometric view from a southwest direction. You may have noticed several other isometric view options in that list. The following sections introduce you to some of the ways that you can move around in your 3D model.

Finding Isometric and Orthogonal Views

Figure 20.28 illustrates the isometric view options that you saw earlier in the Home tab's View panel drop-down list: Southeast Isometric, Southwest Isometric, Northeast Isometric, and Northwest Isometric. The cameras represent the different viewpoint locations. You can get an idea of their location in reference to the grid and UCS icon.

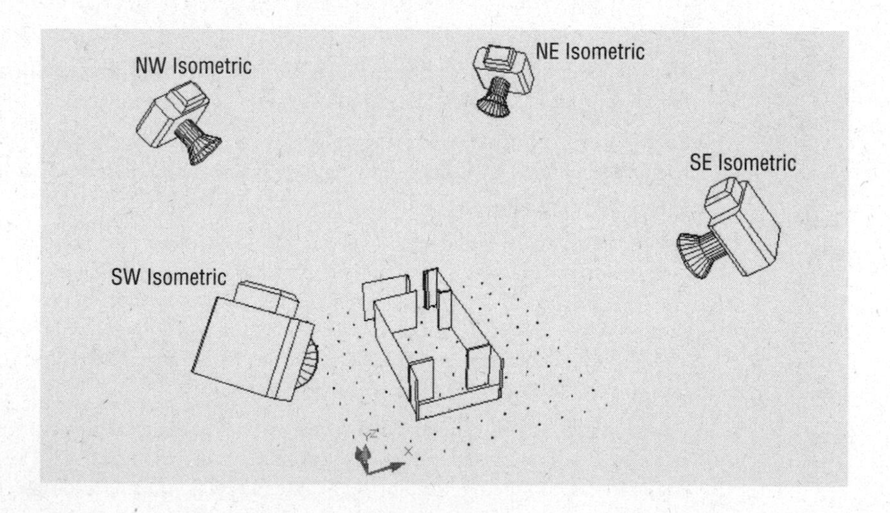

Figure 20.28 The isometric viewpoints for the four isometric views available from the Home tab's View panel drop-down list

The Home tab's View panel's 3D Navigation drop-down list also offers another set of options: Top, Bottom, Left, Right, Front, and Back. These are orthogonal views that show the sides, top, and bottom of the model, as illustrated in Figure 20.29. In this figure, the cameras once again show the points of view.

When you use any of the view options described here, AutoCAD attempts to display the extents of the drawing. You can then use the Pan and Zoom tools to adjust your view.

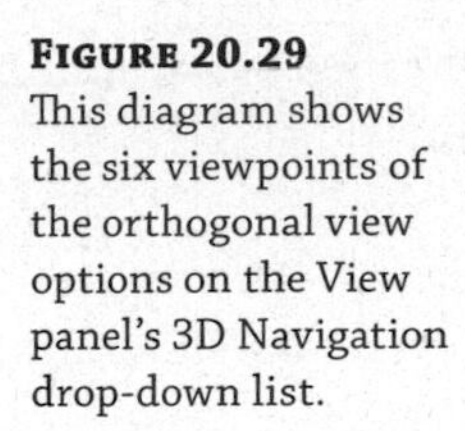

FIGURE 20.29
This diagram shows the six viewpoints of the orthogonal view options on the View panel's 3D Navigation drop-down list.

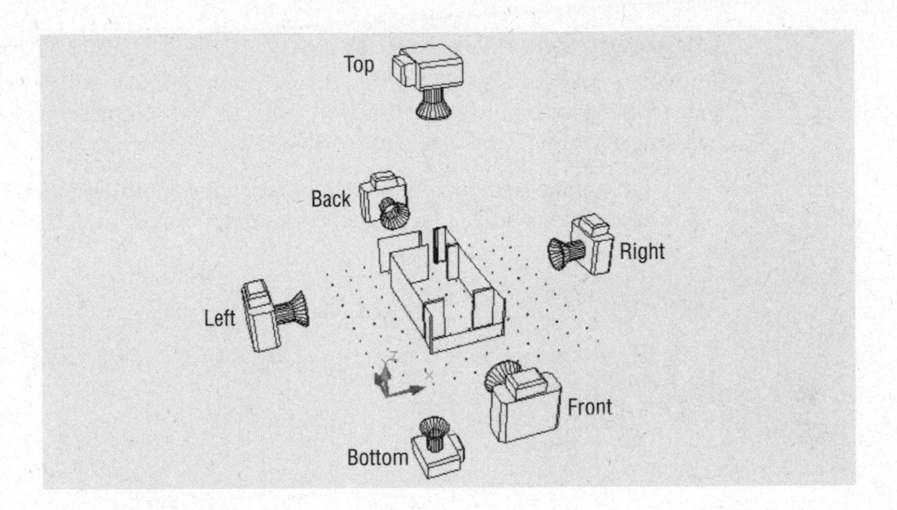

Rotating Freely Around Your Model

You may find the isometric and orthogonal views a bit restrictive. The Orbit tool lets you move around your model in real time. You can fine-tune your view by clicking and dragging the mouse using this tool. Try the following to see how it works:

1. Zoom out so that you see an overall view of your model.
2. Click the Orbit tool in the Orbit flyout on the View tab's Navigate panel. If the Navigate panel is not there, right-click the Ribbon, click Show Panels, and then click Navigate. This will display the Navigate panel.

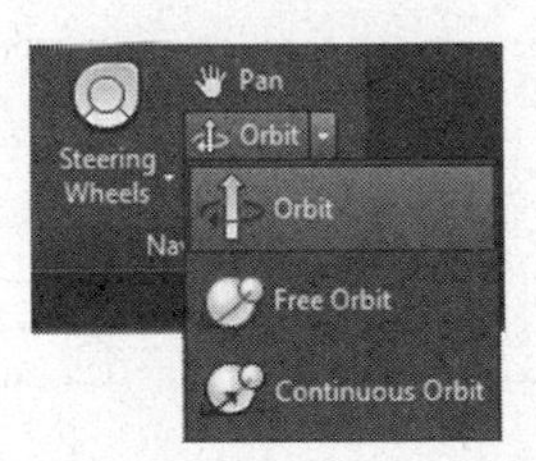

You can also enter **3dorbit**↵ and then right-click and select Other Navigation Modes ➤ Constrained Orbit.

3. Click and drag in the drawing area. As you drag the mouse, the view revolves around your model. The cursor changes to an orbit icon to let you know that you're in the middle of using the Constrained Orbit tool.

If you have several objects in your model, you can select an object that you want to revolve around and then click the Orbit tool. It also helps to pan your view so that the object you select is in the center of the view.

When you've reached the view that you want, right-click and choose Exit. You're then ready to make more changes or use another tool.

Changing Your View Direction

One of the first tasks you'll want to do with a model is to look at it from all angles. The ViewCube® tool is perfect for this purpose. The ViewCube is a device that lets you select a view by using a sample cube. If it is not visible in your drawing, follow these steps:

1. First make sure that Visual Styles is set to something other than 2D Wireframe by selecting an option from the Visual Styles drop-down list.

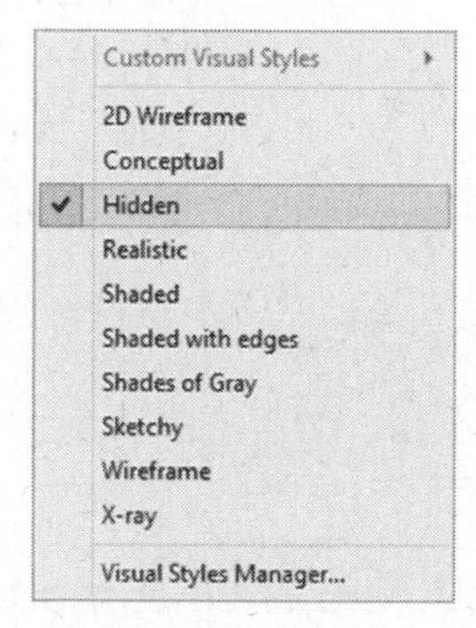

2. If you don't already see the ViewCube in the upper-right corner of the drawing area, go to the View tab's Viewport Tools panel and turn on the ViewCube option by clicking the View Cube button.

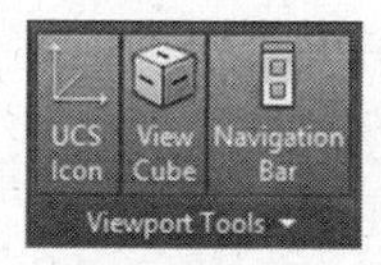

Constrained Orbit Shortcut

If you have a mouse with a scroll wheel, you can hold down the Shift key while clicking and dragging the wheel to get the same effect as using the Constrained Orbit tool. If this doesn't work for you, try installing the manufacturer's software and drivers.

The following list explains what you can do with the ViewCube (see Figure 20.30):

- Click the Home icon to bring your view to the "home" position. This is helpful if you lose sight of your model.
- You can get a top, front, right-side, or other orthogonal view just by clicking the word *Top, Front*, or *Right* on the ViewCube.
- Click a corner of the cube to get an isometric-style view, or click an edge to get an "edge-on" view.
- Click and drag the N, S, E, or W label to rotate the model in the XY plane.
- To rotate your view of the object in 3D freely, click and drag the cube.
- From the icon at the bottom, select an existing UCS or create a new one from the UCS list.

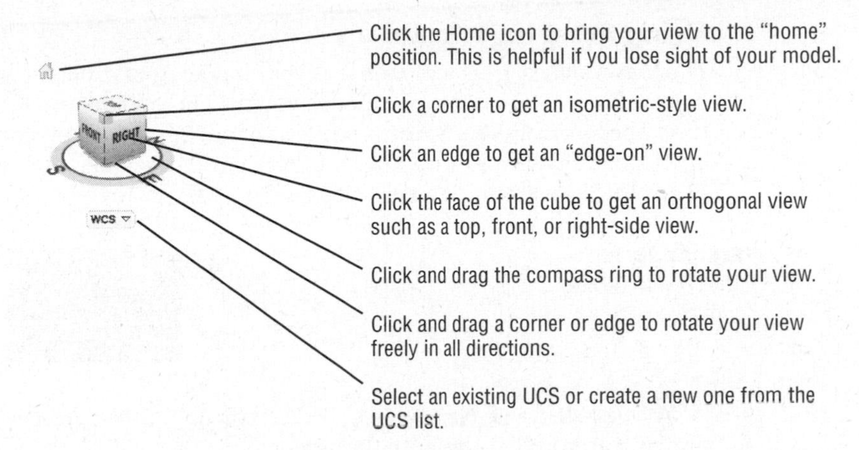

FIGURE 20.30
The ViewCube and its options

You can also change from a perspective view to a parallel projection view by right-clicking the cube and selecting Parallel Projection. To go from parallel projection to perspective, right-click and select Perspective or Perspective With Ortho Faces. The Perspective With Ortho Faces option works like the Perspective option, except that it will force a parallel projection view when you use the ViewCube to select a top, bottom, or side orthographic view.

When you are in a plan or top view, the ViewCube will look like a square, and when you hover your cursor over the cube, you'll see two curved arrows to the upper right of the cube (see Figure 20.31).

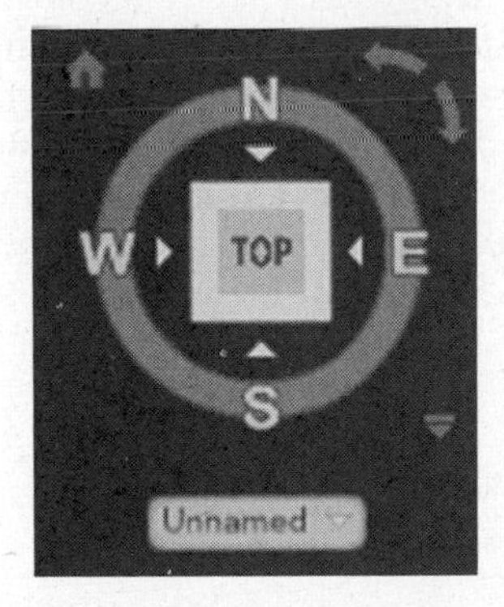

FIGURE 20.31
The ViewCube top view

You can click on any of the visible corners to go to an isometric view or click the double-curved arrows to rotate the view 90 degrees. The four arrowheads that you see pointing toward the cube allow you to change to an orthographic view of any of the four sides.

SETTING THE HOME VIEW

In a new file, the ViewCube's home view is similar to the SW Isometric view. To set your own home view, right-click the ViewCube and select Set Current View As Home.

Using SteeringWheels

The ViewCube is great for looking at your model from different angles. But if your application requires you to be inside your model, you'll want to know how to use the *SteeringWheels®* feature. The SteeringWheels feature collects a number of viewing tools in one interface. You can open SteeringWheels by clicking the SteeringWheels tool in the View tab's Navigate panel (see Figure 20.32) or from the Navigation bar.

FIGURE 20.32
The SteeringWheels tool

You can also type **Navswheel↵**. When you do this, the SteeringWheels tool appears in the drawing area and moves with the cursor.

The SteeringWheels options are fairly self-explanatory. Just be aware that you need to use a click-and-drag motion to use them:

Pan To pan your view, click and drag the Pan option.

Zoom To zoom, click and drag the Zoom option.

Orbit The Orbit option lets you revolve your view about your model.

Look The Look option swivels your point of view around your model as if you were standing still and moving your "camera" around.

Center The Center option is a bit less obvious, but it is an important tool for the SteeringWheels feature. Click and hold the Center option and then drag the circular cursor that appears onto a 3D object. In any visual style other than 2D Wireframe, you will see a green sphere that indicates the center of your view for the Orbit option. Place this green sphere on the object at the desired center of your orbit. For example, if you want to use the Orbit option to look at all sides of a cube, click and drag the Center option so that the green sphere is at the center of the cube. Release the mouse button when you've placed the sphere where you want it (see Figure 20.33).

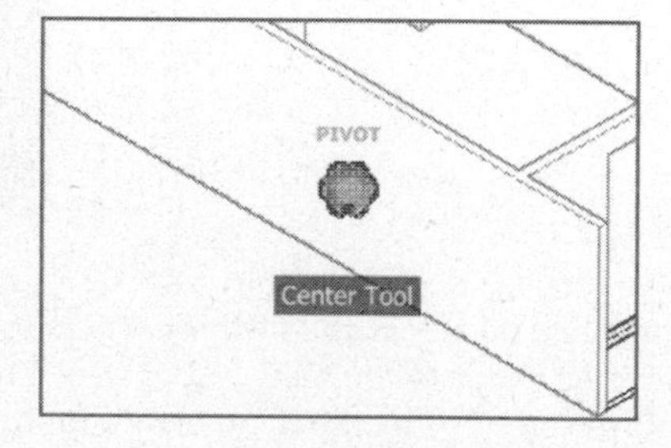

FIGURE 20.33
Placing the green sphere of the Center option

If you are in a 2D Wireframe view, you will have to place the cursor on the edge of the object before you'll see the green sphere.

Walk The Walk option is similar to the Walk tool in the Render tab's Animations panel. (See "Changing Where You Are Looking" later in this chapter for more on the Walk tool.)

Click and drag the Walk option, and you'll see a blue circle and a cursor arrow that points in a direction away from the circle (see Figure 20.34). Your view moves smoothly in the direction of the arrow as if to follow it.

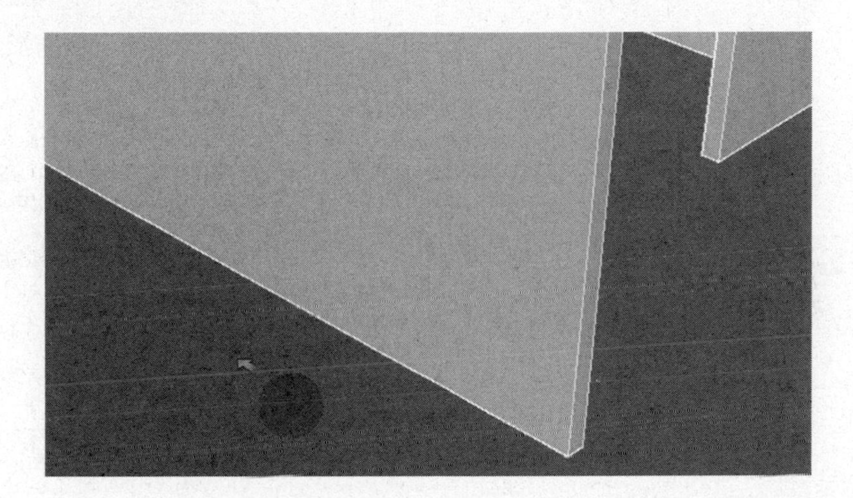

FIGURE 20.34
Using the Walk option

Rewind The Rewind option rewinds the views that you've seen while using the SteeringWheels feature. Click and drag the Rewind option, and you see a series of panels like movie frames in a video-editing program (see Figure 20.35).

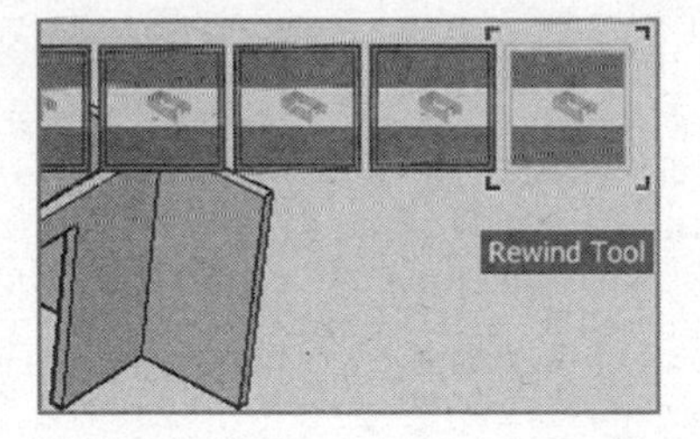

FIGURE 20.35
The frames of the Rewind tool

As you move the mouse from right to left, the views in the AutoCAD drawing area are played back smoothly in reverse order. Move left to right to move forward in time through the views. This is especially helpful if your model has accidentally shifted out of view. You can roll back your views to one before the model flew out of view.

Up/Down The Up/Down option will move your view up or down respectively along the z-axis using a slider control.

You can right-click SteeringWheels for a number of options in the context menu. You can also open this menu by clicking the arrowhead in the lower-right corner of the wheel. Most of these context menu options are self-explanatory, but a few of them are worth a brief description.

If you click the Basic Wheels option in the SteeringWheels context menu, you'll see Tour Building and View Object. Select the Tour Building Wheel option. Figure 20.36 shows these variations on the basic SteeringWheels wheel, and they offer a pared-down set of options for the two types of viewing options indicated by the name of the wheels.

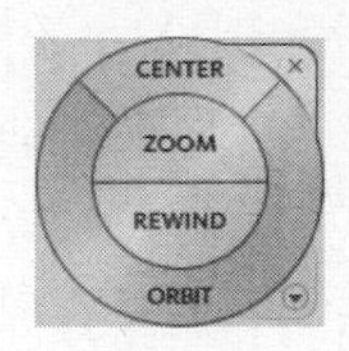

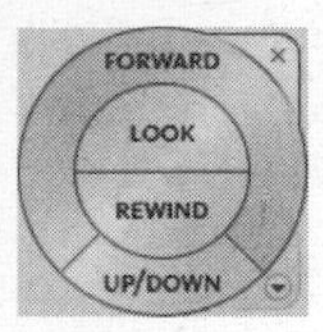

FIGURE 20.36
Variations of the SteeringWheels wheel

You'll also see mini versions available for the wheels from the SteeringWheels menu. The mini versions are much smaller, and they do not have labels indicating the options. Instead you see segmented circles, like a pie. Each segment of the circle is an option. Tool tips appear when you point at a segment, telling you what option that segment represents. Other than that, the mini versions work the same as the full-sized wheels.

The SteeringWheels feature takes a little practice, but when you've become familiar with it, you may find that you use it frequently when studying a 3D model. Just remember that a click-and-drag motion is required to use the tools effectively.

Changing Where You Are Looking

AutoCAD uses a camera analogy to help you set up views in your 3D model. With a camera, you have a camera location and a target, and you can fine-tune both in AutoCAD. AutoCAD also offers the Swivel tool to let you adjust your view orientation. Using the Swivel tool is like keeping the camera stationary while pointing in a different direction. While viewing your drawing in perspective mode, click Pan on the View tab's Navigation bar, right-click in the drawing area, and select Other Navigation Modes ➤ Swivel. (Remember that you need to right-click the ViewCube and select Perspective for the perspective mode.)

At first, the Swivel tool might seem just like the Pan tool. But in the 3D world, Pan actually moves both the camera and the target in unison. Using Pan is a bit like pointing a camera out the side of a moving car. If you don't keep the view in the camera fixed on an object, you are panning across the scenery. Using the Swivel tool is like standing on the side of the road and turning the camera to take in a panoramic view.

To use the Swivel tool, follow these steps:

1. While in a perspective view, click Pan on the View tab's Navigate panel or on the Navigation bar.
2. Right-click in the drawing area, and choose Other Navigation Modes ➤ Swivel. You can also type **3dswivel**↵ at the `Type a Command` prompt.
3. Click and drag in the drawing to swivel your point of view.
4. When you have the view you want, right-click and select Exit.

If you happen to lose your view entirely, you can use the Undo tool in the Quick Access toolbar to return to your previous view and start over.

Flying through Your View

Another way to get around in your model is to use the Walk or Fly view options. If you're familiar with computer games, this tool is for you. To get to these options, start the Pan tool as you did in the last exercise, and then right-click and select Other Navigation Modes ➤ Fly. If you don't see the Other Navigation Modes menu option, make sure that you are in a perspective view.

WHERE TO FIND WALK

The Walk tool is part of a flyout on the Animations panel. Typically, the Animations panel is not displayed. To display it, select the Visualize tab, right-click in a Ribbon panel, and select Show Panels ➤ Animations. The Walk tool is in the upper-right corner of the panel. The Fly tool is in the flyout of the Walk tool.

If you right-click while in this mode and click Display Instruction Window, a window will appear on the Communications Center. The message in the window tells you all you need to know about the Walk and Fly tools. You can use the arrow keys to move through your model. Click and drag the mouse to change the direction where you're looking.

If you press the F key, Walk changes to Fly mode. The main difference between Walk and Fly is that in Walk, both your position in the model and the point where you're looking move with the Up and Down arrow keys. Walk is a bit like Pan. When you're in Fly mode, the arrow keys move you toward the center of your view, which is indicated by a crosshair.

In addition to the crosshair, you'll see a palette that shows your position in the model from a top-down view (see Figure 20.37).

FIGURE 20.37
The Position Locator palette uses a top-down view.

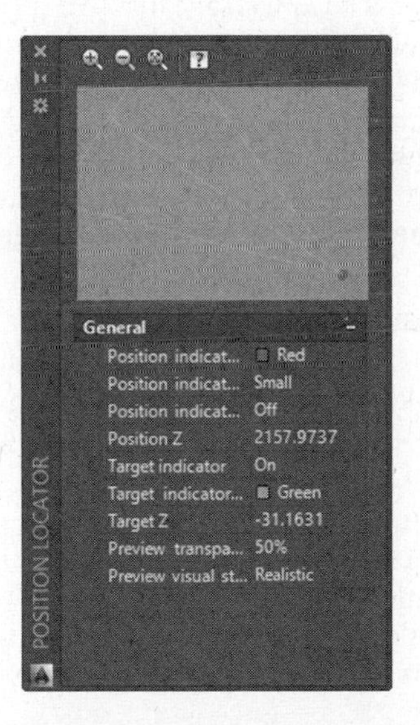

You can use the palette to control your view by clicking and dragging the camera or the view target graphic. If you prefer, you can close the palette and continue to "walk" through your model. When you're finished using Walk, right-click and choose Exit.

Changing from Perspective to Parallel Projection

When you create a new drawing using the `acad3D.dwt` template, you're automatically given a perspective view of the file. If you need a more schematic parallel projection style of view, you can get one from the ViewCube's right-click menu (see Figure 20.38). You can return to a perspective view by using the same context menu shown in the figure.

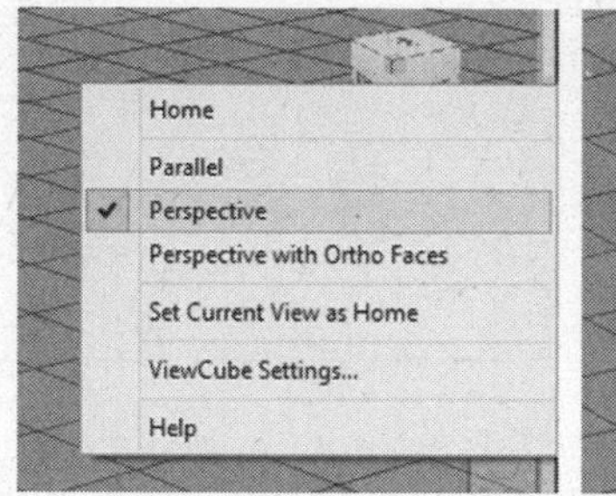

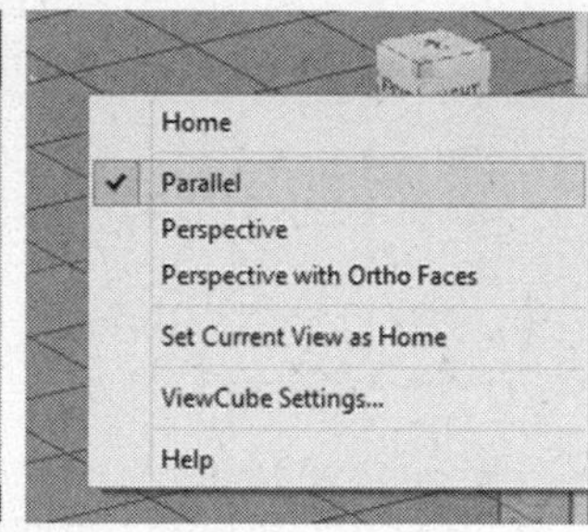

Figure 20.38
The Perspective projection and Parallel projection tools

Getting a Visual Effect

Although 3D models are extremely useful in communicating your ideas to others, sometimes you find that the default appearance of your model isn't exactly what you want. If you're only in a schematic design stage, you may want your model to look more like a sketch instead of a finished product. Conversely, if you're trying to sell someone on a concept, you may want a realistic look that includes materials and even special lighting.

AutoCAD provides a variety of tools to help you get a visual style, from a simple wireframe to a fully rendered image complete with chrome and wood. In the following sections, you'll get a preview of what is available to control the appearance of your model. Later, in Chapter 22, you'll get an in-depth look at rendering and camera tools that allow you to produce views from hand-sketched "napkin" designs to finished renderings.

Using Visual Styles

In the earlier exercises in this chapter, you drew a box that appeared to be solid. When you then opened an existing file to extrude the unit plan into the third dimension, you worked in a Wireframe view. These views are known as *visual styles* in AutoCAD. You used the Shades Of Gray visual style when you drew the box. The unit plan used the default 2D Wireframe view that is used in the AutoCAD Classic style of drawing.

Sometimes, it helps to use a different visual style, depending on your task. For example, the 2D Wireframe view in your unit plan model can help you visualize and select things that are behind a solid. AutoCAD includes several shaded view options that can bring out various features of your model. Try the following exercises to explore some of the other visual styles:

1. Click the Visual Styles drop-down list in the Home tab's View panel. You can also find the list in the View tab's Visual Styles panel, which will display the Visual Styles Manager palette. A set of graphic images appears that gives you an idea of what each visual style shows you (see Figure 20.39). You can also access the visual styles from the Visual Styles drop-down list located at the upper-left side of the drawing screen, but you will not get the graphical images.

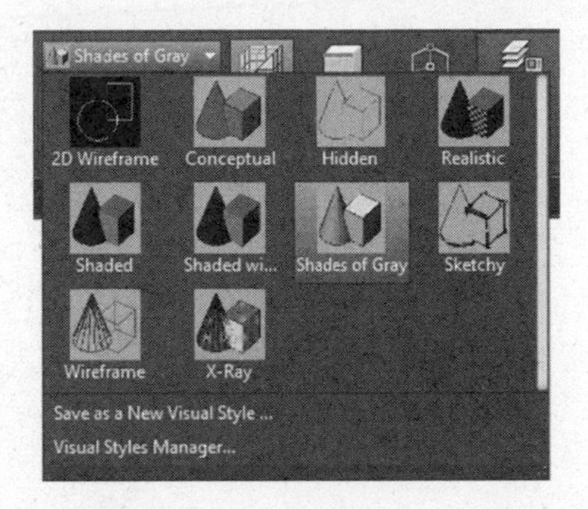

FIGURE 20.39
The Visual Styles drop-down

2. Select Wireframe. You can also enter **Vscurrent↵ Wireframe↵**. Your model appears as a transparent wireframe object with a gray background.
3. To get to the shaded view of your model, choose Realistic from the Visual Styles drop-down list or enter **Vscurrent↵Realistic↵**.

You may have noticed a few other visual styles options. Figure 20.40 shows a few of those options as they're applied to a sphere. 2D Wireframe and Wireframe may appear the same, but Wireframe uses a perspective view and a background color, whereas 2D Wireframe uses a parallel projection view and no background color.

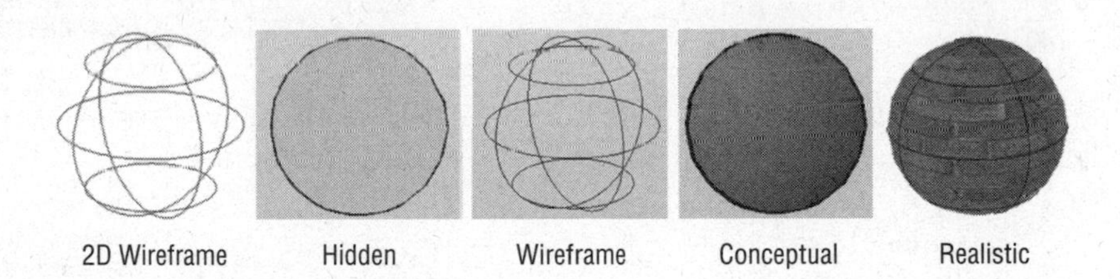

FIGURE 20.40
Visual styles applied to a sphere

Creating a Sketched Look with Visual Styles

You may notice blanks in the visual styles options in the View tab's Visual Styles drop-down list. These spaces allow you to create custom visual styles. For practice, you'll create a visual style similar to the existing Sketchy style so that you can learn how the rough look of that style was created. The following exercise will step you through the process:

1. Click the Visual Styles Manager from the Visual Styles drop-down. The Visual Styles Manager appears (see Figure 20.41). You can also enter **Visualstyles↵**. This palette looks similar to the Properties palette with the addition of thumbnail examples of the visual styles at the top of the palette.

FIGURE 20.41
The Visual Styles Manager

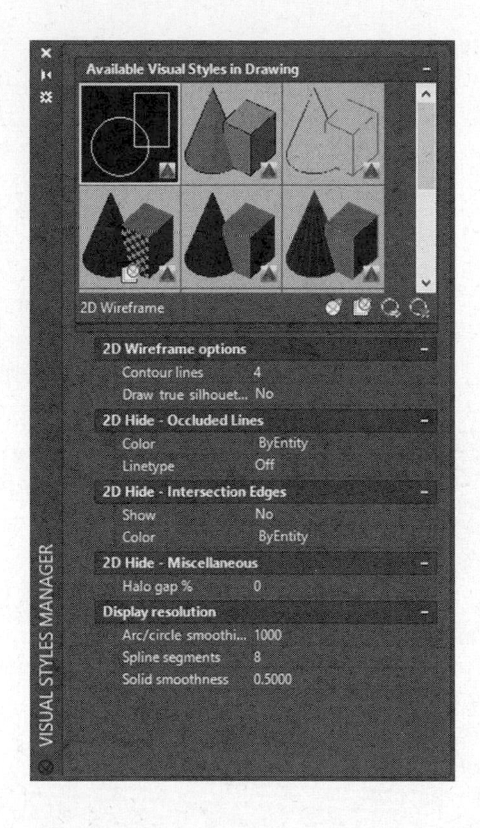

2. Click the Create New Visual Style tool in the Visual Styles Manager toolbar. The Create New Visual Style dialog box opens (see Figure 20.42).

FIGURE 20.42
The Create New Visual Style dialog box

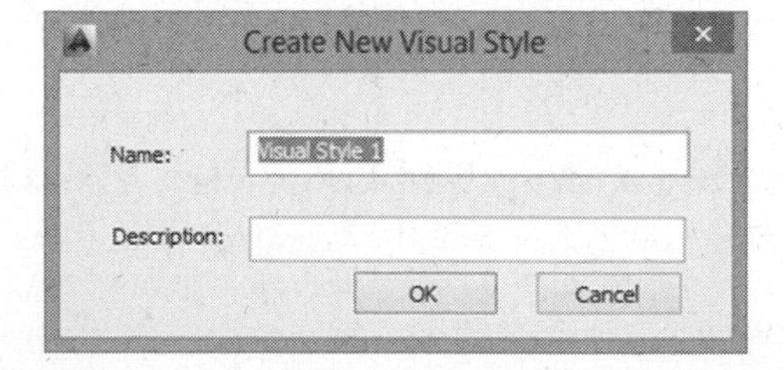

3. Enter **Sketch** in the Name box.
4. Enter **Hand Drawn Appearance** in the Description box, and then click OK. You see a new thumbnail in the bottom-left corner of the samples at the top of the palette.

You've just created a new visual style. This new style uses the default settings that are similar to the Realistic visual style but without the Material Display option turned on. The material setting causes objects in your drawing to display any material assignments that have been given to objects. You'll learn more about materials in Chapter 22.

Now that you have a new visual style, you can begin to customize it. But before you start your customization, make your new visual style the current one so that you can see the effects of your changes as you make them:

1. Click the Apply Selected Visual Style To Current Viewport tool in the Visual Styles Manager toolbar.

   The display changes slightly, and you see the name Sketch appear in the Visual Styles drop-down list as well as the upper-left corner of the drawing area.

   Next, you'll turn on the two features that will give your new visual style a sketch-like appearance.

2. Use the scroll bar to the left of the Visual Styles Manager to scroll down to the bottom of the list of options.
3. Locate the Edge Modifiers option group, and click the Line Extensions Edges tool in the Edge Modifiers title bar.

   Edges of your model now appear to be drawn with lines extending beyond the corners.

4. Click the Jitter Edges tool in the Edge Modifiers title bar. The edges take on a sketched look, as shown in Figure 20.43.

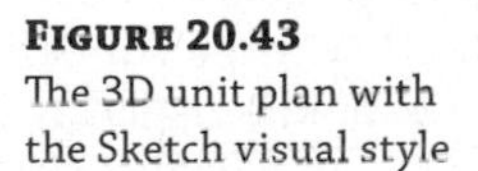

FIGURE 20.43
The 3D unit plan with the Sketch visual style

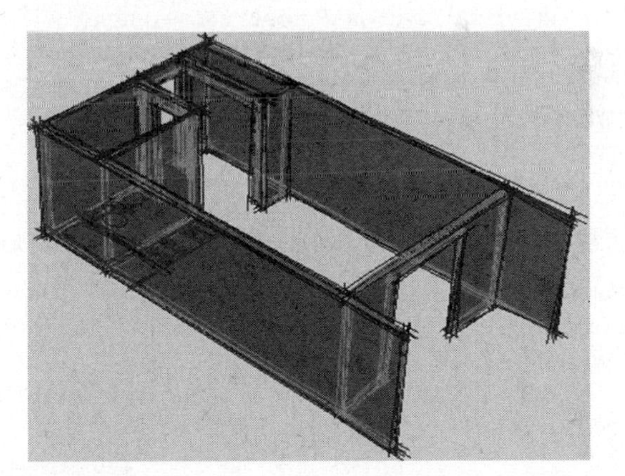

5. Save the unit plan file.

The 3D view has taken on a hand-drawn appearance. Notice that the lines overhang the corners in a typical architectural sketch style. This is the effect of the Line Extensions Edges option that you used in step 3. The lines are made rough and broken by the Jitter Edges setting. You can control the amount of overhang and jitter in the Edge Modifiers group of the Visual Styles Manager to exaggerate or soften these effects.

With your newly created Sketch visual style, the model looks like it's transparent. You can make it appear opaque by turning off the Show option under the Occluded Edges group in the Visual Styles Manager (see Figure 20.44).

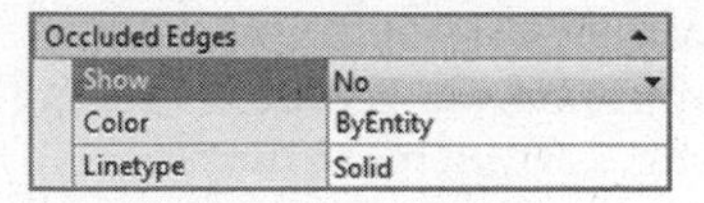

FIGURE 20.44
The Show option in the Occluded Edges group in the Visual Styles Manager

Finally, you can control some of the commonly used visual style properties using options in the Visualize tab's Visual Styles panel. This panel offers control over isolines, color, face style, shadows, and textures for the current visual style (see Figure 20.45).

FIGURE 20.45
Options in the Visual Styles panel

In-Canvas Viewport Controls

Since AutoCAD® 2012, controls have been built into each viewport that allow you to change between visual styles and model views quickly without starting either command. You'll find these controls in the upper-left portion of the viewport. Clicking the view name will bring up a list of the available views from which you may choose. Likewise, clicking the visual style will bring up a list of available visual styles. Clicking either of them will instantly make the selected style or view current in that viewport.

Turning a 3D View into a 2D AutoCAD Drawing

Many architectural firms use AutoCAD 3D models to study their designs. After a specific part of a design is modeled and approved, they convert the model into 2D elevations, ready to plug into their elevation drawing.

If you need to convert your 3D models into 2D line drawings, you can use the Flatshot tool in the Home tab's expanded Section panel.

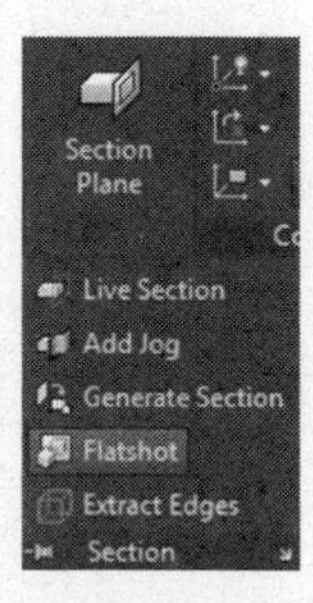

Set up your drawing view, and then click the Flatshot tool or enter **Flatshot↵** at the command-line interface to open the Flatshot dialog box (see Figure 20.46).

Figure 20.46
The Flatshot dialog box

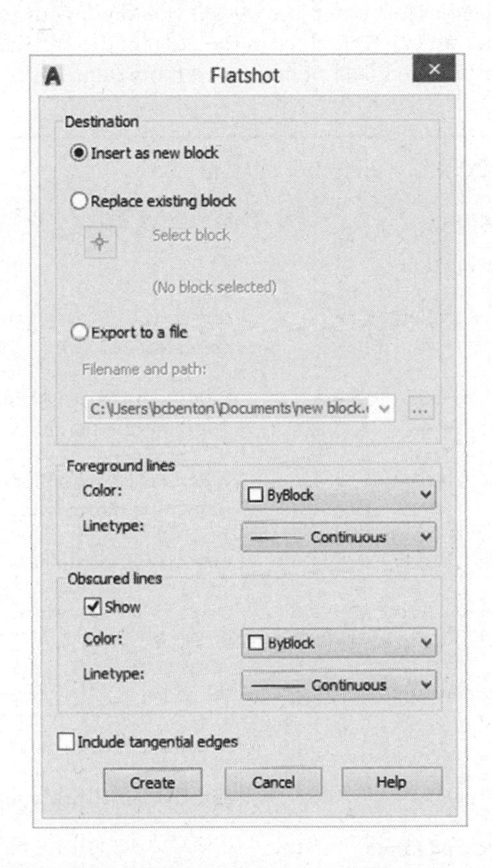

Printing Your Model Using Visual Styles

You can print a drawing that uses visual styles either from the Model tab or from a Layout tab. If you're printing from the model view, click Plot from the Quick Access toolbar. Then, in the Plot dialog box, select the visual style from the Shade Plot drop-down list in the Shaded Viewport Options group. If you're plotting from a Layout tab, select the layout viewport border, right-click, and choose Shade Plot from the context menu. You can select from a list of visual styles on a cascading menu. Once you've done this, plot your layout as you normally would.

Select the options that you want to use for the 2D line drawing, and then click Create. Depending on the options you select, you'll be prompted to select an insertion point or indicate a location for an exported drawing file. The 2D line drawing will be placed on the plane of the current UCS, so if you are viewing your model in a 3D view but you are in the World UCS, the 2D line drawing will appear to be projected onto the XY plane.

Flatshot lets you place the 2D version of your model in the current drawing as a block, replace an existing block in the current drawing, or save the 2D version as a DWG file. Table 20.1 describes the Flatshot options in more detail.

TABLE 20.1: Flatshot options

OPTION	WHAT IT DOES
Destination	
Insert As New Block	Inserts the 2D view in the current drawing as a block. You're prompted for an insertion point, a scale, and a rotation.
Replace Existing Block	Replaces an existing block with a block of the 2D view. You're prompted to select an existing block.
Select Block	If Replace Existing Block is selected, lets you select a block to be replaced. A warning is shown if no block is selected.
Export To A File	Exports the 2D view as a drawing file.
Filename And Path	Displays the location for the export file. Click the Browse button to specify a location.
Foreground Lines	
Color	Sets the overall color for the 2D view.
Linetype	Sets the overall linetype for the 2D view.
Obscured Lines	
Show	Displays hidden lines.
Color	If Show is turned on, sets the color for hidden lines.
Linetype	If Show is turned on, sets the linetype for hidden lines. The Current Linetype Scale setting is used for linetypes other than continuous.
Include Tangential Edges	Displays edges for curved surfaces.

One useful feature of Flatshot is that it can create a 2D drawing that displays the hidden lines of a 3D mechanical drawing. Turn on the Show option, and then select a linetype such as Hidden for obscured lines to produce a 2D drawing like the one shown in Figure 20.47.

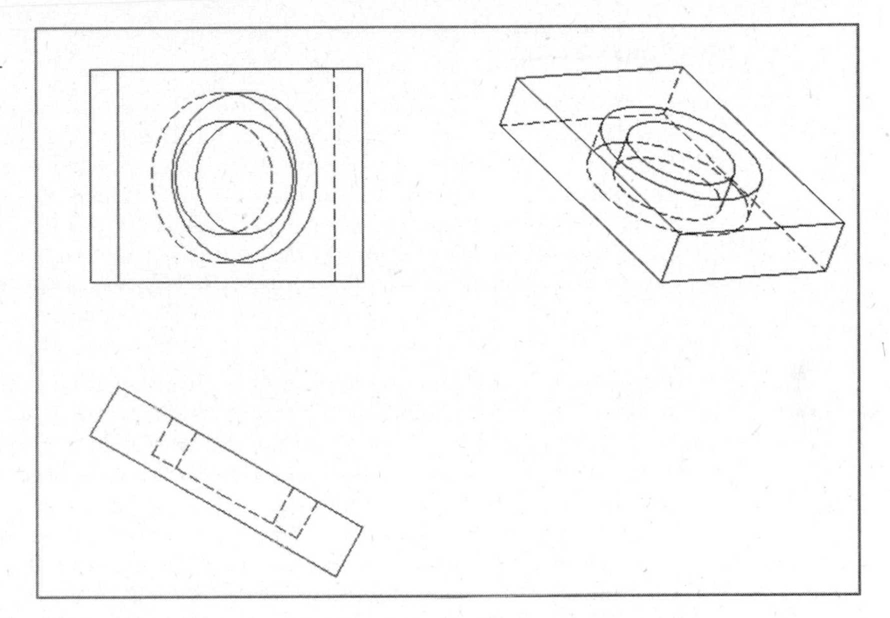

FIGURE 20.47
A sample of a 2D drawing generated from a 3D model using Flatshot. Note the dashed lines showing the hidden lines of the view.

Using the Point Cloud Feature

As you might guess from the name, a *point cloud* is a set of data points in a 3D coordinate system. They are often the product of 3D scanners, which are devices that can analyze and record the shape of real-world objects or environments. With point cloud data, you can reproduce an object or environment as a digital model that can then be used for a video game, movie production, 3D model, or even as-built drawings.

AutoCAD lets you import raw point cloud data through a set of tools that can be found in the Insert tab's Point Cloud panel (see Figure 20.48).

FIGURE 20.48
The Point Cloud panel in the Insert tab

AutoCAD can import point cloud data in the form of RCP (Recap Project) or RCS (RecapScan) files. These file types can be produced with the Autodesk® ReCap™ program, a separate application that comes with AutoCAD (see the sidebar "Autodesk ReCap").

AUTODESK RECAP

Autodesk ReCap is an application that runs outside AutoCAD. This additional program lets you take raw data from 3D scans and package it in a way that AutoCAD can use. ReCap can handle the massive amounts of data collected from 3D scanners so that you can aggregate the scans. It features tools that enable you to clean up the data, sort it, compress it, and visualize it. Once this is accomplished, ReCap will put the data into a file format that AutoCAD can easily digest and use. ReCap requires users to have and log into their Autodesk® 360 account.

After you import the point cloud data, AutoCAD displays it in your file. To import the data, use the Attach tool in the Point Cloud panel on the Insert tab. If you have raw point cloud data that hasn't been processed yet, click the Autodesk ReCap button to launch ReCap. Use the resulting dialog box to load the raw data and prepare it to be used in AutoCAD.

Selecting an attached point cloud displays a bounding box around the data and activates the contextual Cloud Edit Ribbon tab. This tab provides a set of tools that you can use to manipulate your point cloud by clipping it (similar to the Clip tool), changing the point density, adjusting the color display of the point cloud, or running analysis tools.

Because point clouds can consume a great deal of memory, you can use the Level Of Detail slider in the Display panel to control the density of the point. The lower the density, the less impact the point cloud will have on performance. When you have the point cloud attached to a drawing, you can use the points to help guide you in building a 3D model. You can use the Node osnap to snap to the individual points in the point cloud. The referenced point cloud is selectable. When you do select it, a contextual Ribbon tab has several tools that will help you display your point cloud. It includes slider bars to increase or decrease the density of the points (how many are currently being displayed). You can change the color of the points or use any color data your scanning device may have gathered. Cropping tools are also available to help speed up the performance of your computer by reducing the number of points to process. This cropping feature can also help you control what is being displayed in your file.

The Bottom Line

Know the 3D Modeling workspace. When you work in 3D, you need a different set of tools from those for 2D drafting. AutoCAD offers the 3D Modeling workspace, which provides the tools that you need to create 3D models.

Master It Name some of the Ribbon panels that are unique to the 3D Modeling workspace.

Draw in 3D using solids. AutoCAD offers a type of object called a 3D solid that lets you quickly create and edit shapes.

Master It What does the Presspull command do?

Create 3D forms from 2D shapes. The Modeling panel offers a set of basic 3D shapes, but other tools enable you to create virtually any shape you want from 2D drawings.

Master It Name the command that lets you change a closed 2D polyline into a 3D solid.

Isolate coordinates with point filters. When you're working in 3D, selecting points can be a complicated task. AutoCAD offers point filters or coordinates to let you specify the individual x-, y-, and z-coordinates of a location in space.

Master It What does the .XY point filter do?

Move around your model. Getting the view you want in a 3D model can be tricky.

Master It Where is the drop-down list that lets you select a view from a list of predefined 3D views?

Get a visual effect. At certain points in your model making, you'll want to view your 3D model with surface colors and even material assignments. AutoCAD offers several ways to do this.

Master It What are the steps to take to change the view from Wireframe to Conceptual?

Turn a 3D view into a 2D AutoCAD drawing. Sometimes, it's helpful to convert a 3D model view into a 2D AutoCAD drawing. AutoCAD offers the Flatshot tool, which quickly converts a 3D view into a 2D line drawing.

Master It What type of object does Flatshot create?

Chapter 21

Using Advanced 3D Features

The Autodesk® AutoCAD® 2018 software has an extended set of tools for working with 3D drawings that lets you create 3D objects with few limitations on shape and orientation. This chapter focuses on the use of these tools, which help you easily generate 3D forms and view them in both perspective and orthogonal modes.

The AutoCAD LT® software doesn't support any of the features described in this chapter.

In this chapter, you will learn to

- Master the User Coordinate System
- Understand the UCS options
- Use viewports to aid in 3D drawing
- Use the array tools
- Create complex 3D surfaces
- Create spiral forms
- Create surface models
- Move objects in 3D space

Setting Up AutoCAD for This Chapter

Before you start, we'd like you to set up AutoCAD in a way that will make your work a little easier. You'll use the 3D Modeling workspace to which you were introduced in Chapter 20, "Creating 3D Drawings." To do so, start AutoCAD. In Chapter 20, you started a new 3D model using a template set up for 3D modeling. Here you'll start to work with the default 2D drawing, `acad.dwt`.

Now click the Workspace Switching button in the status bar and select 3D Modeling, as shown in Figure 21.1. You'll see a new set of panels appear, as shown in Figure 21.2. The Home panel is different in that it now contains many of the 3D tools that we will be using. Additional panels include Solid, Surface, Mesh, and Visualize, which contain the 3D modeling and editing tools available in AutoCAD.

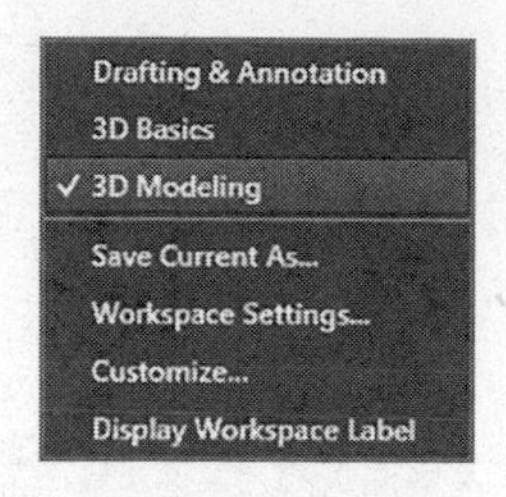

FIGURE 21.1
Select 3D Modeling from the Workspace drop-down.

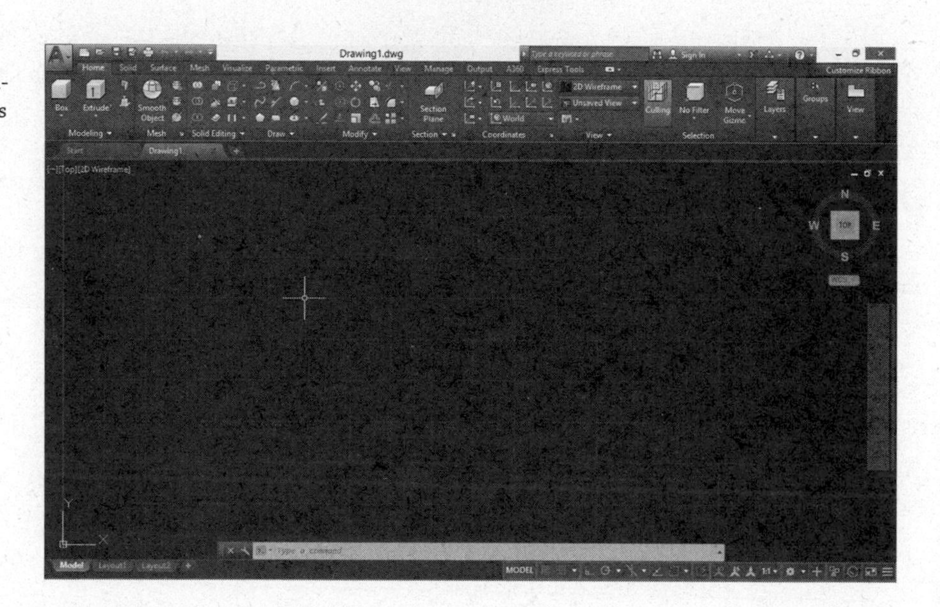

FIGURE 21.2
The AutoCAD window set up for this chapter

Mastering the User Coordinate System

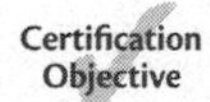

The User Coordinate System (UCS) enables you to define a custom coordinate system in 2D and 3D space. You've been using the default coordinate system called the *World Coordinate System (WCS)* all along. By now, you're familiar with the L-shaped icon in the lower-left corner of the AutoCAD screen, containing a small square and the letters *X* and *Y*. The square indicates that you're currently in the WCS; the *X* and *Y* indicate the positive directions of the x- and y-axes. The WCS is a global system of reference from which you can define other UCSs.

It may help to think of these AutoCAD UCSs as different drawing surfaces or two-dimensional planes. You can have several UCSs at any given time. By setting up these different UCSs, you can draw as you would in the WCS in 2D and still create a 3D image.

Suppose that you want to draw a house in 3D with doors and windows on each of its sides. You can set up a UCS for each of the sides, and then you can move from UCS to UCS to add your doors and windows (see Figure 21.3). In each UCS, you draw your doors and windows as you would in a typical 2D drawing. You can even insert elevation views of doors and windows that you created in other drawings.

In this chapter, you'll experiment with several views and UCSs. All of the commands that you'll use are available both at the command line and via the Visualize tab's Coordinates panel.

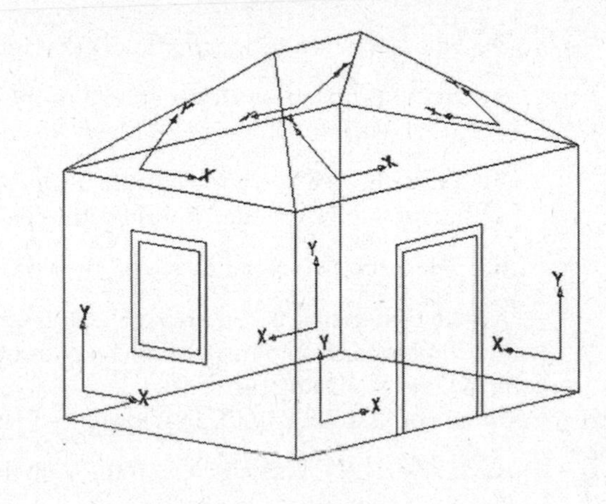

FIGURE 21.3
Different UCSs in a 3D drawing

Defining a UCS

In the first set of exercises, you'll draw a chair that you can later add to your 3D unit drawing. In drawing this chair, you'll be exposed to the UCS as well as to some of the other 3D capabilities available in AutoCAD:

1. Open the `barcelona1.dwg` file. Metric users should open `barcelona1_metric.dwg`. This file contains two rectangles that you'll use to create a chair.
2. Select SW Isometric from the 3D Navigation drop-down list on the Home tab's View panel. You can also type **-V↵SWISO↵**. This gives you a 3D view from the lower-left corner of the rectangles, as shown in Figure 21.4. Zoom out a bit to give yourself some room to work.

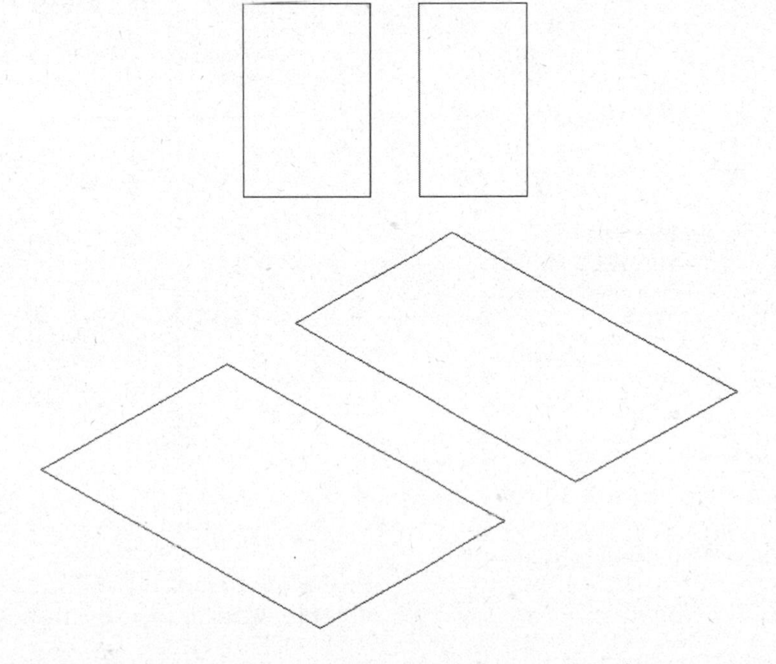

FIGURE 21.4
The chair seat and back in the Plan (top) and Isometric (bottom) views

3. Select the two rectangles, and then right-click and select Properties.
4. In the Properties palette, enter **3** in the Thickness setting and press ↵. This gives the seat and back a thickness of 3″. Metric users should make the thickness 7.6 cm.

5. Press the Esc key, and close the Properties palette. Click the Convert To Solid tool in the Home tab's expanded Solid Editing panel.
6. Select the two rectangles, and then press ↵.

Notice that the UCS icon appears in the same plane as the current coordinate system. The icon will help you keep track of which coordinate system you're in. Now you can see the chair components as 3D objects.

Next, you'll define a UCS that is aligned with one side of the seat:

1. Click UCS ➤ Named UCS in the Visualize tab's Coordinates panel or type **Ucsman**↵ to open the UCS dialog box.
2. Select the Orthographic UCSs tab to view a set of predefined UCSs.
3. Select Front in the list box, shown in Figure 21.5. Figure 21.6 shows the orientation of the Front UCS.

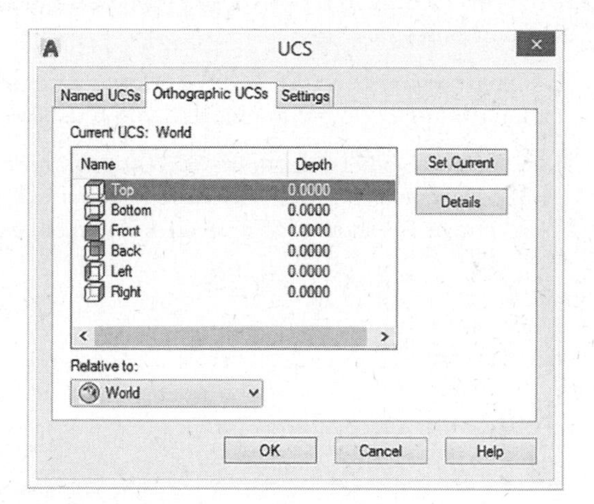

FIGURE 21.5
The UCS dialog box

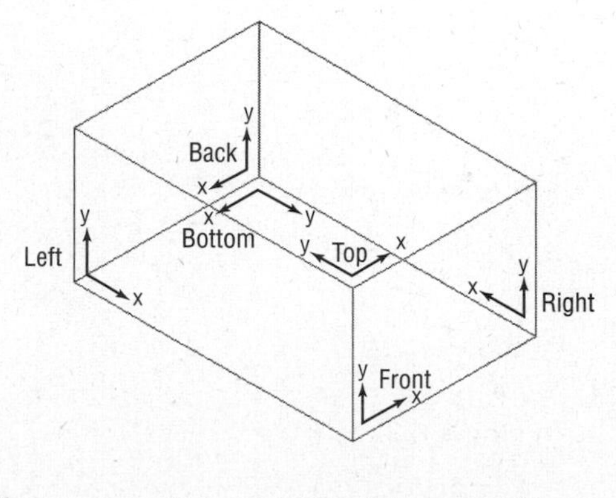

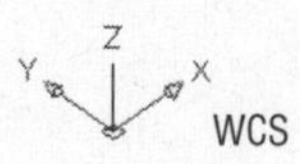

FIGURE 21.6
The six predefined UCS orientations

4. Click the Set Current button to make the Front UCS current.
5. Click OK to close the dialog box.

The Orthographic UCSs tab offers a set of predefined UCSs for each of the six standard orthographic projection planes. Figure 21.6 shows these UCSs in relation to the WCS.

Because a good part of 3D work involves drawing in these orthographic planes, AutoCAD supplies the ready-made UCS orientations for quick access. But you aren't limited to these six orientations. If you're familiar with mechanical drafting, you'll see that the orthographic UCSs correspond to the typical orthographic projections used in mechanical drafting. If you're an architect, you'll see that the Front, Left, Back, and Right UCSs correspond to the south, west, north, and east elevations of a building.

Before you continue building the chair model, you'll move the UCS to the surface on which you'll be working. Right now, the UCS has its origin located in the same place as the WCS origin.

You can move a UCS so that its origin is anywhere in the drawing:

1. Click the Origin tool in the Visualize tab's Coordinates panel, or type **UCS↵O↵**.
2. At the `Specify new origin point <0,0,0>:` prompt, use the Endpoint osnap and click the bottom-front corner of the chair seat, as shown in Figure 21.7. The UCS icon moves to indicate its new origin's location. If you typed in the command, press Enter to accept the other default values.

FIGURE 21.7
Setting up a UCS

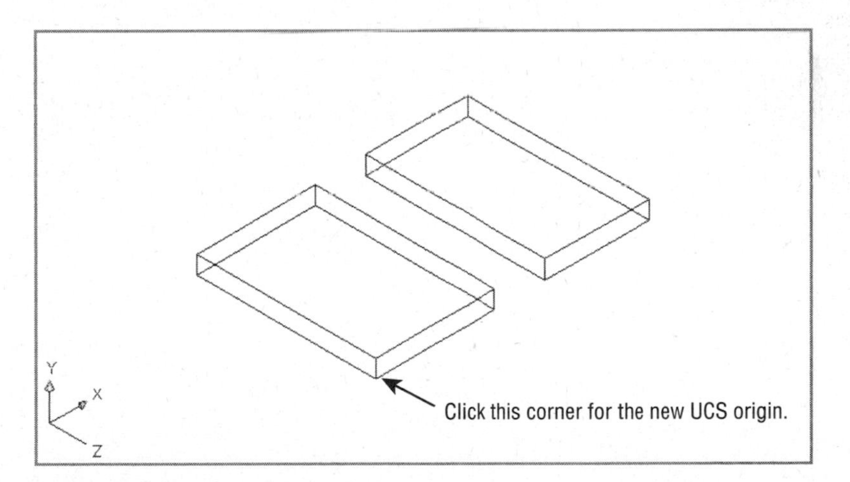

You just created a new UCS based on the Front UCS that you selected from the UCS dialog box. Now, as you move your cursor, the origin of the UCS icon corresponds to a 0,0 coordinate. Although you have a new UCS, the WCS still exists; you can always return to it when you need to.

Saving a UCS

After you've gone through the work of creating a UCS, you may want to save it—especially if you think that you'll come back to it later. Here's how to save a UCS:

1. Choose Named from the Coordinates panel or type **Ucsman↵** to open the UCS dialog box.

2. Make sure that the Named UCSs tab is selected, and then highlight the Unnamed option in the Current UCS list box.
3. Click the word *Unnamed*. The item changes to allow editing.
4. Type **3DSW**↵ for the name of your new UCS.
5. Click OK to exit the dialog box.

Your UCS is now saved with the name 3DSW. You can recall it from the UCS dialog box or by using other methods that you'll learn about later in this chapter.

Working in a UCS

Next, you'll arrange the seat and back and draw the legs of the chair. Your UCS is oriented so that you can easily adjust the orientation of the chair components. As you work through the next exercise, notice that, although you're manipulating 3D objects, you're really using the same tools that you've used to edit 2D objects.

Follow these steps to adjust the seat and back and to draw legs:

1. Click the seat back to expose its grips. The seat back is the box to the right.
2. Click the bottom grip, as shown in the first image in Figure 21.8.

FIGURE 21.8
Moving the components of the chair into place

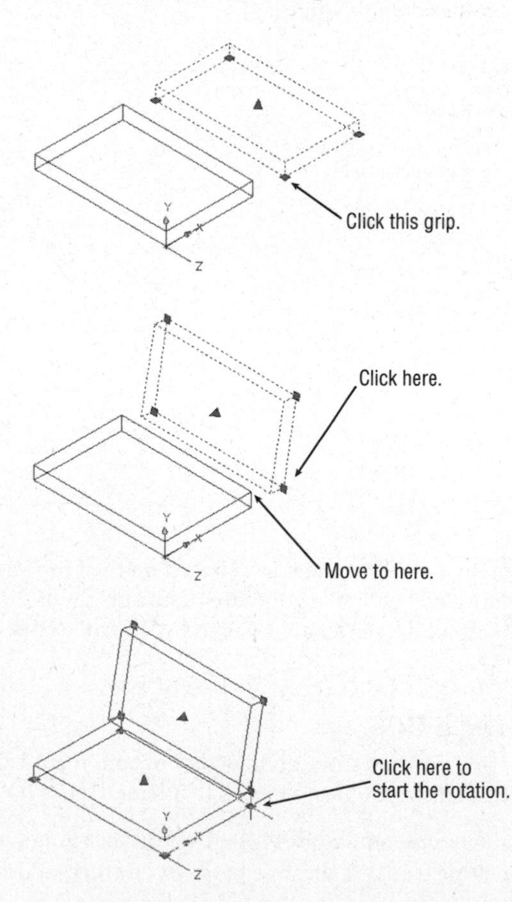

3. Right-click to open the Grip Edit context menu.
4. Choose Rotate from the menu. The seat back now rotates with the movement of the cursor. It rotates in the plane of the new UCS you created earlier.
5. Type **80**↵ to rotate the seat back 80 degrees. Your view looks like the second image in Figure 21.8.
6. Click the bottom grip, as shown in the second image in Figure 21.8.
7. Right-click again and choose Move.
8. Using the Endpoint osnap, click the bottom-rear corner of the chair seat to join the chair back to the seat, as shown in the second image in Figure 21.8.
9. Click the chair seat, making sure that the chair back is also selected; then click the bottom-corner grip of the seat, as shown in the third image in Figure 21.8.
10. Right-click and choose Rotate from the Grip Edit context menu.
11. Enter **-10**↵ to rotate both the seat and back negative 10 degrees. Press the Esc key to clear the grips. Your chair looks like Figure 21.9.

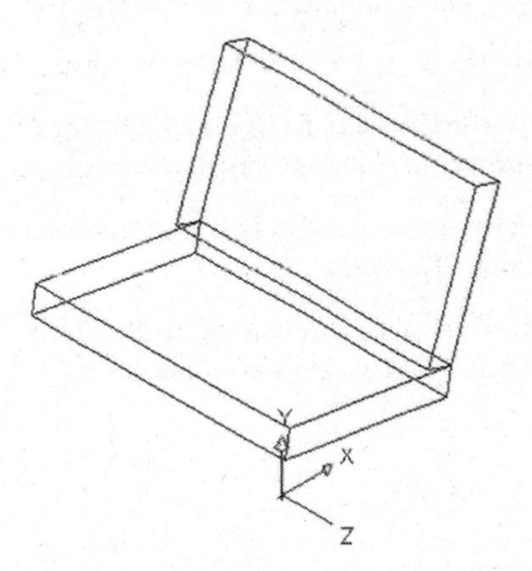

FIGURE 21.9
The chair after rotating and moving the components

The new UCS orientation enabled you to use the grips to adjust the chair seat and back. All of the grip rotation in the previous exercise was confined to the plane of the new UCS. Mirroring and scaling will also occur in relation to the current UCS.

Building 3D Parts in Separate Files

As you work in 3D, your models will become fairly complex. When your model becomes too crowded for you to see things clearly, it helps to build parts of the model and then import them instead of building everything in one file. In the next set of exercises, you'll draw the legs of the chair and then import them to the main chair file to give you some practice in the procedure.

We've prepared a drawing called `legs.dwg`, which consists of two polylines that describe the shape of the legs. We did this to save you some tedious work that isn't related to 3D modeling.

You'll use this file as a starting point for the legs, and then you'll import the legs into the `barcelona1.dwg` file:

1. Open the `legs.dwg` file. Metric users should open the `legs_metric.dwg` file. The file consists of two polyline splines that are in the shape of one set of legs. You'll turn these simple lines into 3D solids.

2. Click the Edit Polyline tool in the Home tab's expanded Modify panel.
3. At the `Select polyline or [Multiple]:` prompt, enter **M**↵ to select multiple polylines. Then select the two polylines and press ↵.
4. At the `Enter an option [Close/Open/Join/Width/Fit/Spline/Decurve/Ltype gen/Reverse/Undo]:` prompt, enter **W**↵.
5. At the `Specify new width for all segments:` prompt, enter **0.5**↵ to give the polylines a width of 0.5″. Metric users should enter **1.27**↵.
6. Press ↵ to exit the Pedit command.

Next you need to change the Thickness property of the two polylines to make them 2″, or 5 cm, wide:

1. With the two polylines selected, open the Properties palette and set their thickness to **2**. Metric users should set their thickness to **5**.
2. Close the Properties palette, or you can leave it open for the next exercise.
3. Click the Convert To Solid tool in the Home tab's expanded Solid Editing panel, or enter **convtosolid**↵ at the Command prompt.
4. Select the two polylines if they're not already selected, and then press ↵. The lines become 3D solids.
5. Click the Solid, Union tool in the Home tab's Solid Editing panel, select the two legs, and press ↵. The two legs are now a single 3D solid, as shown in Figure 21.10.

FIGURE 21.10
The polylines converted to 3D solids

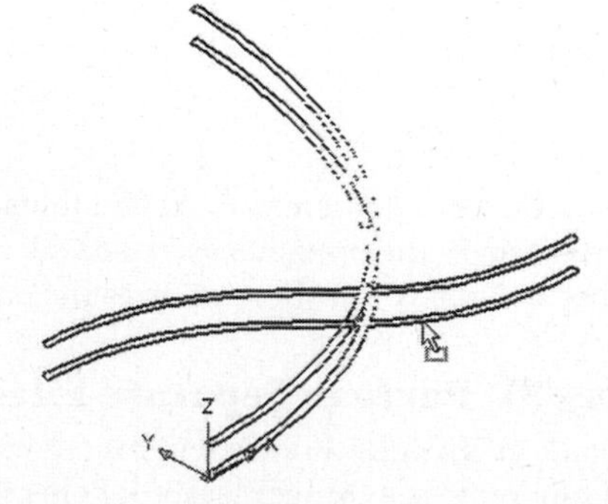

As you've just seen, you can convert polylines that have both a width and a thickness into 3D solids. Now you're ready to add the legs to the rest of the chair:

1. Click the Tile Vertically tool in the View tab's User Interface panel. You see the legs drawing on the left and the rest of the chair on the right.
2. Adjust the views so that your screen looks similar to Figure 21.11. If you see a third `Drawing1.dwg` panel, or if you see the Start Tab, minimize it and click the Tile Vertically tool again.

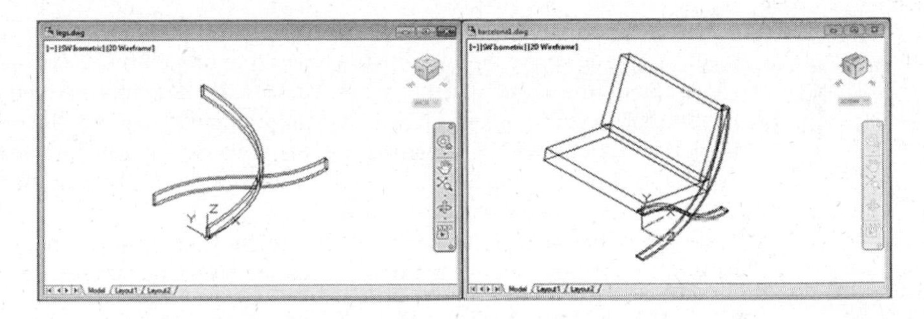

FIGURE 21.11
Click and drag the leg from the left window to the right window, and align the leg with the chair seat and back.

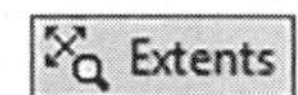

3. Click in the `barcelona1` drawing, and select Extents from the Zoom flyout Navigation bar to get an overall view of the chair so far.
4. Click in the legs drawing, and then click the legs 3D solid to select it.
5. Click and hold the cursor on the legs until you see the arrow cursor with a small rectangle.
6. When you see the rectangle, drag the mouse into the `barcelona1` drawing. The legs appear in the proper orientation.
7. Release the mouse button to place the legs in the `barcelona1` drawing. You don't need to be precise about placing the legs; you can move them into position next.
8. Use the Move tool to move the legs so that the endpoint of the horizontal leg joins the chair seat, as shown in the image in the right panel of Figure 21.11.
9. Save and close the `legs.dwg` file, and expand the `barcelona1.dwg` file to fill the AutoCAD window.

USE COPY AND PASTE

You can also use Copy and Paste to copy the legs to the `barcelona1` drawing. In step 4, right-click and select Copy from the context menu. Skip steps 5 through 7 and instead click in the `barcelona1` drawing, right-click, and select Paste.

In these last few exercises, you worked on the legs of the chair in a separate file and then imported them into the main chair file with a click-and-drag motion. By working on parts in separate files, you can keep your model organized and more manageable. You may have also noticed that although the legs were drawn in the WCS, they were inserted in the 3DSW UCS that you created earlier. This shows you that imported objects are placed in the current UCS. The same would have happened if you inserted an Xref or another file.

Understanding the UCS Options

You've seen how to select a UCS from a set of predefined UCSs. You can frequently use these preset UCSs and make minor adjustments to them to get the exact UCS you want.

You can define a UCS in other ways. You can, for example, use the surface of your chair seat to define the orientation of a UCS. In the following sections, you'll be shown the various ways that you can set up a UCS. Learning how to move effortlessly between UCSs is crucial to mastering the creation of 3D models, so you'll want to pay special attention to the command options shown in these examples.

Note that these examples are for your reference. You can try them out on your own model. These options are accessible from the Visualize tab's Coordinates panel.

UCS Based on Object Orientation

You can define a UCS based on the orientation of an object. This is helpful when you want to work on a predefined object to fill in details on its surface plane. The following steps are for information only and aren't part of the tutorial. You can try this at another time when you aren't working through an exercise.

Follow these steps to define a UCS this way:

1. Type **UCS↵OB↵**.
2. At the `Select object to align UCS:` prompt, pick the object that you want to use to define the UCS. For example, you could click a 3D solid that you want to edit. The UCS icon shifts to reflect the new coordinate system's orientation. Figure 21.12 shows an example of using the OB option to select the edge of the chair back.

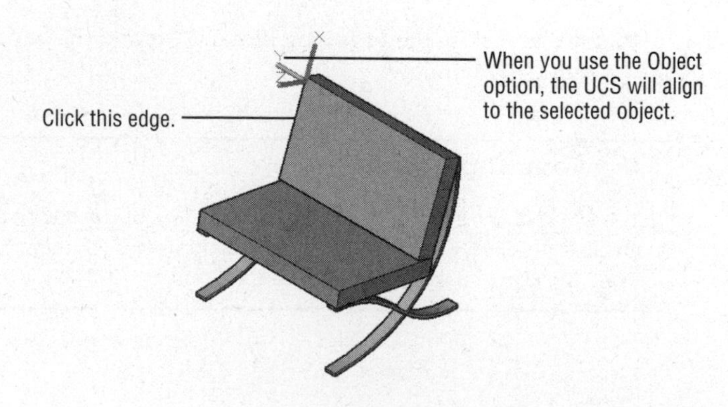

FIGURE 21.12 Using the Object option of the UCS command to locate a UCS

Controlling the UCS Icon

If the UCS icon isn't behaving as described in this chapter's exercises, chances are that its settings have been altered. You can control the behavior of the UCS icon through the UCS dialog box. To open the UCS dialog box, click Named in the Visualize tab's Coordinates panel or type **Ucsman↵**; then click the Settings tab.

The settings in the UCS Icon Settings group affect the way the UCS icon behaves. Normally, the On and Display At UCS Origin Point check boxes are selected. If On isn't selected, you won't see the UCS icon. If the Display At UCS Origin Point check box isn't selected, the UCS icon remains in the lower-left corner of the drawing window no matter where its origin is placed in the drawing.

If you have multiple viewports set up in a drawing, you can set these two options independently for each viewport. The third option, Apply To All Active Viewports, forces the first two settings to apply in all viewports. We will discuss the fourth option, Allow Selecting UCS icon, later in this chapter.

Two more options appear in the UCS Settings group. If you have multiple viewports open, the Save UCS With Viewport option enables AutoCAD to maintain a separate UCS for each viewport. The Update View To Plan When UCS Is Changed option forces the display to show a plan view of the current UCS. This means that if you change a UCS orientation, AutoCAD automatically shows a plan view of the new UCS orientation. This option also forces viewport views to show the extents of plan views. If you find that your views are automatically zooming to extents when you don't want them to, turn off this setting.

Another tool for controlling the UCS icon is the UCS Icon dialog box. To open it, right-click the UCS Icon, click UCS Icon Settings, click Properties, or enter **Ucsicon↵P↵**.

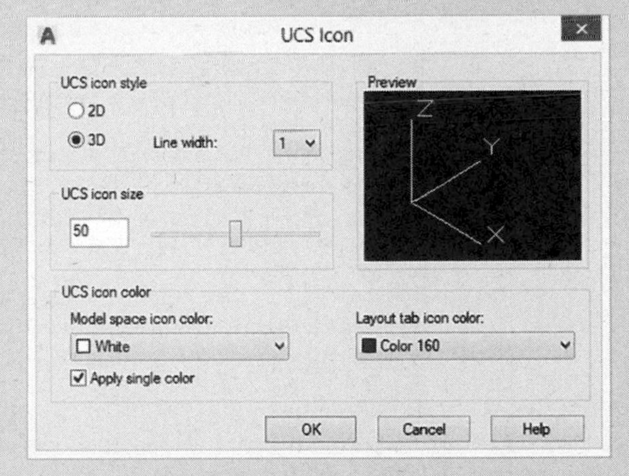

Using this dialog box, you can fine-tune the appearance of the UCS icon, including its size and color. The 2D radio button in the UCS Icon Style group changes the UCS icon to the old-style UCS icon used in earlier versions of AutoCAD.

When you create a UCS using the Object option, the location of the UCS origin and its orientation depend on how the selected object was created. Table 21.1 describes how an object can determine the orientation of a UCS.

TABLE 21.1: Effects of objects on the orientation of a UCS

OBJECT TYPE	UCS ORIENTATION
Arc	The center of the arc establishes the UCS origin. The x-axis of the UCS passes through the pick point on the arc.
Circle	The center of the circle establishes the UCS origin. The x-axis of the UCS passes through the pick point on the circle.
Dimension	The midpoint of the dimension text establishes the UCS origin. The x-axis of the UCS is parallel to the x-axis that was active when the dimension was drawn.
Face (of a 3D solid)	The origin of the UCS is placed on a quadrant of a circular surface or on the corner of a polygonal surface.
Line	The endpoint nearest the pick point establishes the origin of the UCS, and the XZ plane of the UCS contains the line.
Point	The point location establishes the UCS origin. The UCS orientation is arbitrary.
2D polyline	The starting point of the polyline establishes the UCS origin. The x-axis is determined by the direction from the first point to the next vertex.
3D polyline	Returns the message `This object does not define a coordinate system.`
Spline	The UCS is created with its XY plane parallel to the XY plane of the UCS that was current when the spline was created.
Solid	The first point of the solid establishes the origin of the UCS. The second point of the solid establishes the x-axis.
Trace	The direction of the trace establishes the x-axis of the UCS, and the beginning point sets the origin.
3D face	The first point of the 3D face establishes the origin. The first and second points establish the x-axis. The plane defined by the 3D face determines the orientation of the UCS.
Shapes, text, blocks, attributes, and attribute definitions	The insertion point establishes the origin of the UCS. The object's rotation angle establishes the x-axis.

UCS Based on Offset Orientation

At times, you may want to work in a UCS that has the same orientation as the current UCS but is offset. For example, you might be drawing a building that has several parallel walls offset with a sawtooth effect (see Figure 21.13).

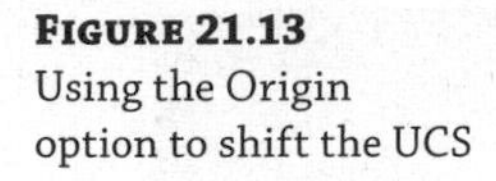
FIGURE 21.13
Using the Origin option to shift the UCS

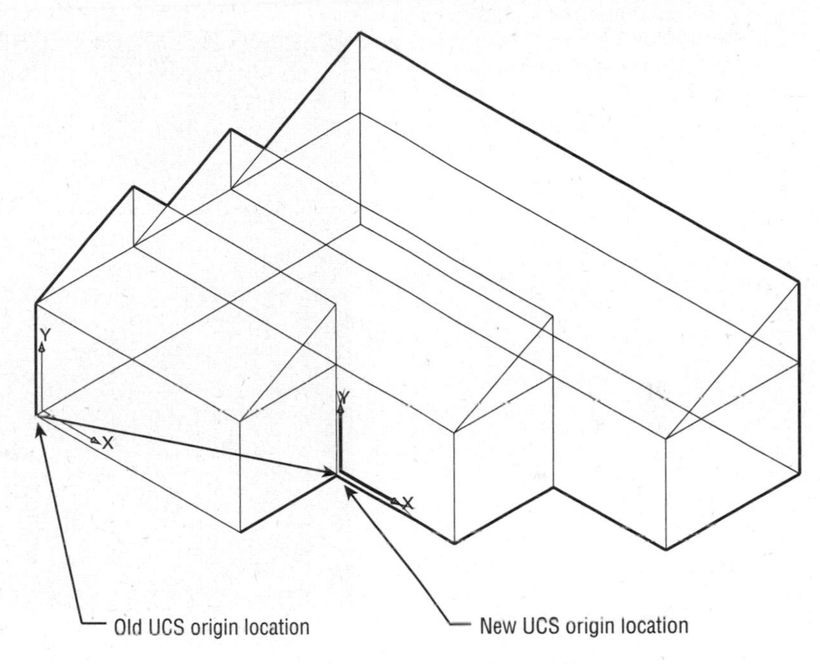

You can easily hop from one UCS to a new, parallel UCS by using the Origin option. Click the Origin tool in the Coordinates panel, or type **UCS↵O↵**. At the `Specify new origin point <0,0,0>:` prompt, pick the new origin for your UCS.

Another UCS option, called Move, will move an existing, named UCS to a new location and keep its original orientation. You won't find the UCS Move option on any panel or toolbar, but you can use it by entering **UCS↵M↵** at the Command prompt.

The steps in the following section are for information only and aren't part of the exercise. Again, you can try this at another time when you aren't working through an exercise.

UCS Rotated Around an Axis

Suppose that you want to change the orientation of the x-, y-, or z-axis of a UCS. You can do so by using the X, Y, or Z flyout on the Visualize tab's Coordinates panel. These are perhaps among the most frequently used UCS options:

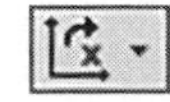

1. Click the X tool flyout arrowhead in the Visualize tab's Coordinates panel, and select Z from the flyout. You can also type **UCS↵Z↵**. This enables you to rotate the current UCS around the z-axis.
2. At the `Specify rotation angle about Z axis <90>:` prompt, press ↵ to accept the default of 90. The UCS icon rotates about the z-axis to reflect the new orientation of the current UCS (see Figure 21.14).

FIGURE 21.14
Rotating the UCS about the z-axis

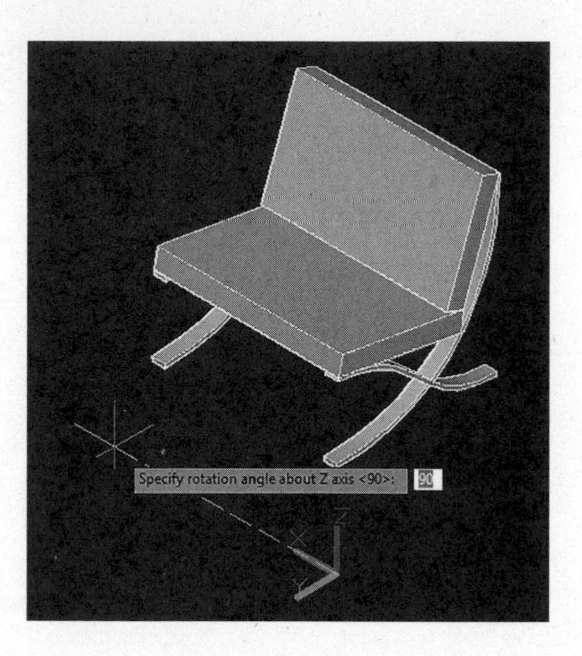

Similarly, the X and Y options let you rotate the UCS about the current x- and y-axis, respectively, just as you did for the z-axis earlier. The X and Y tools are helpful in orienting a UCS to an inclined plane. For example, if you want to work on the plane of a sloped roof of a building, you can first use the Origin UCS tool to align the UCS to the edge of a roof and then use the X tool to rotate the UCS to the angle of the roof slope, as shown in Figure 21.15. Note that the default is 90°, so you only have to press ↵ to rotate the UCS 90°, but you can also enter a rotation angle.

FIGURE 21.15
Moving a UCS to the plane of a sloping roof

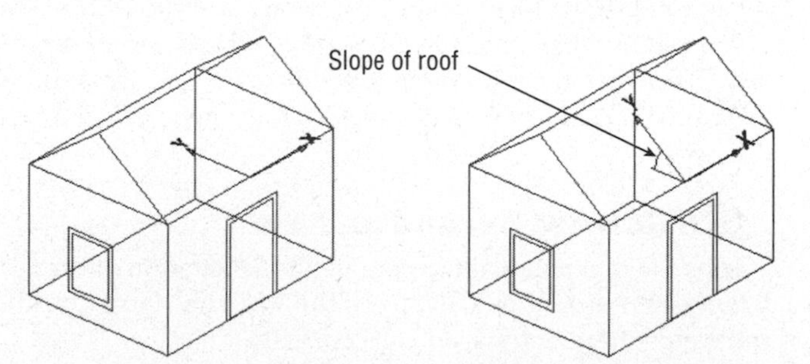

Finally, you align the z-axis between two points using the Z-Axis Vector option. This is useful when you have objects in the drawing that you can use to align the z-axis. Here are the steps:

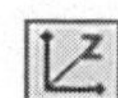

1. Click the Z-Axis Vector tool in the Coordinates panel, or type **UCS↵ZA↵**.
2. At the `Specify new origin point or [Object]<0,0,0>:` prompt, press ↵ to accept the default, which is the current UCS origin, or you can select a new origin.

3. At the prompt

```
Specify point on positive portion of Z-axis
<0'-0", 0'-0", 0'-1">:
```

select another point to indicate the z-axis orientation. Figure 21.16 shows the resulting UCS if you use the bottom of the `barcelona1` chair leg to define the z-axis.

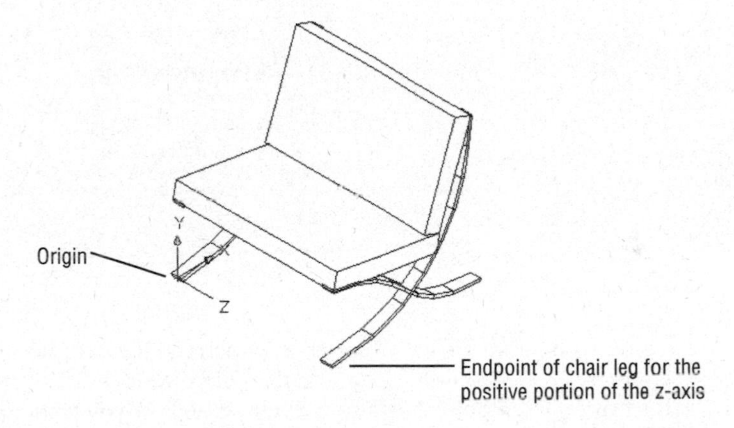

FIGURE 21.16
Picking points for the Z-Axis Vector tool

Because your cursor location is in the plane of the current UCS, it's best to pick a point on an object by using either the Osnap overrides or the coordinate filters.

Orienting a UCS in the View Plane

Finally, you can define a UCS in the current view plane. This points the z-axis toward the user. This approach is useful if you want to switch quickly to the current view plane for editing or for adding text to a 3D view.

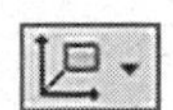

Click the View tool in the Coordinates panel, or type **UCS↵V↵**. Note that the View tool also has a flyout arrowhead that contains the Object and Face tools. If you accidentally click the fly-out arrowhead, make sure to click the View tool in the flyout. The UCS icon changes to show that the UCS is aligned with the current view.

AutoCAD uses the current UCS origin point for the origin of the new UCS. By defining a view as a UCS, you can enter text to label your drawing, just as you would in a technical illustration. Text entered in a plane created this way appears normal.

You've finished your tour of the UCS command. Set the UCS back to the WCS by clicking the UCS World tool in the Visualize tab's Coordinates panel, and save the `barcelona1.dwg` file.

You've explored nearly every option in creating a UCS except one. Later in this chapter, you'll learn about the 3-Point option for creating a UCS. This is the most versatile method for creating a UCS, but it's more involved than some of the other UCS options.

Manipulating the UCS Icon

The UCS icon displays the direction of the axes in your drawing file. You can also directly manipulate it by selecting and right-clicking it or by using its multifunction grips. If your UCS icon is not selectable, or to turn off this selectable feature, open the UCS dialog box (click Named in the Visualize tab's Coordinates panel), click the Settings tab, and see if the Allow Selecting UCS Icon option is checked (see Figure 21.17).

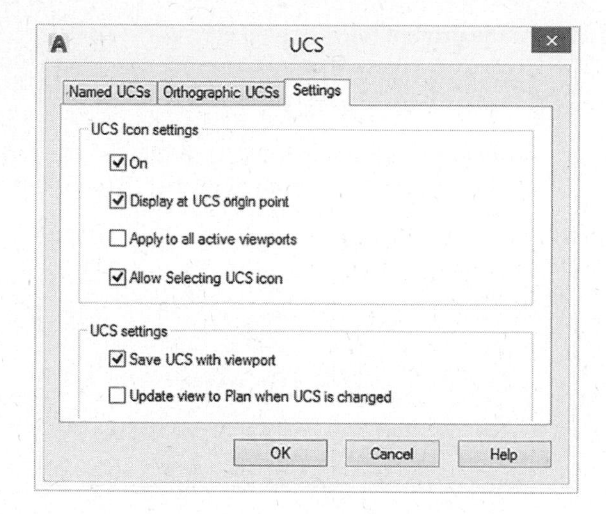

FIGURE 21.17
Making the UCS icon selectable

There are essentially two selection options on the icon: the origin and the end of an axis. In either case, select the UCS icon, and then place your cursor over the appropriate grip and click the origin or endpoint (see Figure 21.18). Select how you want to change the UCS (move and align) and move the cursor. The UCS icon will relocate, showing you where your new coordinate system will be. You can move the origin to a new location or align it to another object or surface using this method. This makes working in a 3D environment a bit easier. Selecting the origin also lets you return the current UCS to the World Coordinate System (it resets the UCS). The x-, y-, and z-axes all work the same way. Pick the endpoint of the axis (the grip) to rotate the selected axis around the other axis (for example, if the x-axis is selected, it can rotate around either the y- or z-axis).

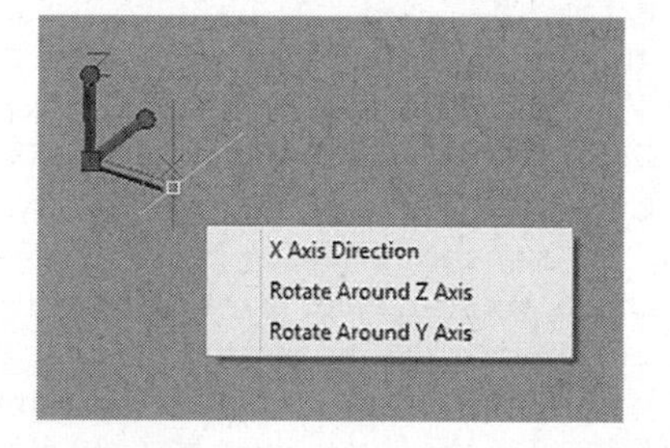

FIGURE 21.18
Selecting and moving the UCS icon will alter your UCS.

When you right-click the UCS icon, you will see a context menu containing a list of the UCS commands that you can choose without having to leave the drawing area. Pick the UCS command that you want to access.

Saving a UCS with a View

In AutoCAD, you can save a UCS with a view. Either click the View Manager option in the in-canvas View Controls (top-left corner of the drawing area) or click the View Manager option at the bottom of the 3D Navigation drop-down list in the Home tab's View panel (see Figure 21.19). In the View Manager dialog box, click the New button. This opens the New View/Shot Properties dialog box. Enter a name for your new view in the View Name box, and then choose a UCS to save with a new view by using the UCS drop-down list in the Settings group of the dialog box. Click OK to complete.

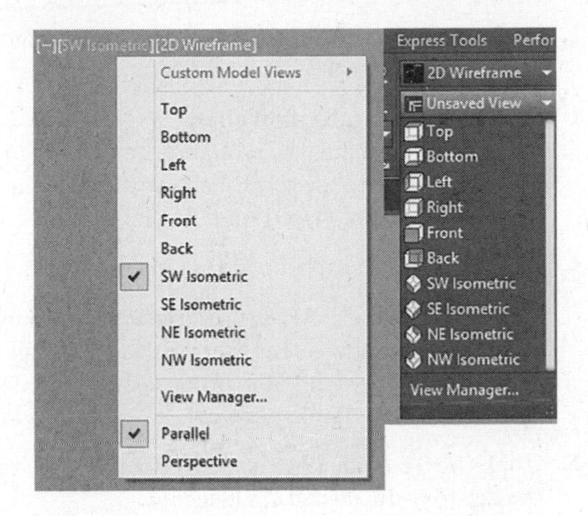

FIGURE 21.19 Select the View Manager option in either the in-canvas View Controls or the 3D Navigation drop-down list.

Using Viewports to Aid in 3D Drawing

In Chapter 15, "Laying Out Your Printer Output," you worked extensively with floating viewports in paper space. In this section, you'll use *tiled* viewports to see your 3D model from several sides at the same time. This is helpful in both creating and editing 3D drawings because it enables you to refer to different portions of the drawing without having to change views.

Tiled viewports are created directly in model space, as you'll see in the following exercise:

1. Click the Named tool in the Visualize tab's Model Viewports panel to open the Viewports dialog box (see Figure 21.20).

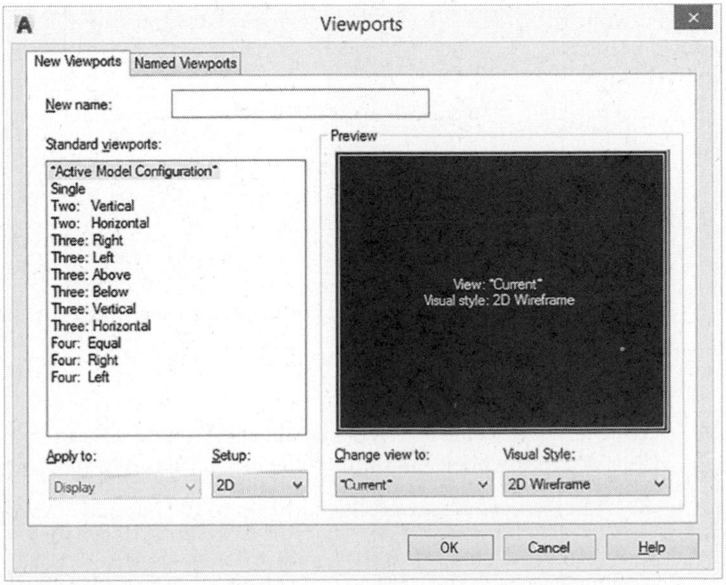

FIGURE 21.20 The Viewports dialog box

2. Make sure that the New Viewports tab is selected, and then select Three: Right from the Standard Viewports list on the left.

   The window on the right changes to display a sample of the viewport configuration. It shows three rectangles, which represent the viewports, arranged with two on the left and one larger one to the right. Each rectangle is labeled as Current; this tells you that the current view will be placed in each viewport.

3. Open the Setup drop-down list at the bottom of the dialog box and select 3D.

   The labels in the viewport sample change to indicate Top, Front, and SE Isometric. This is close to the arrangement that you want, but you need to make one more adjustment. The viewport to the right, SE Isometric, will show the back side of the chair. You want an SW Isometric view in this window.

4. Click the SE Isometric viewport sample. The sample viewport border changes to a double border to indicate that it's selected.

5. Open the Change View To drop-down list just below the sample viewports, and select SW Isometric. The label in the selected viewport changes to let you know that the view will now contain the SW Isometric view. If your viewport samples do not match Figure 21.21, repeat step 4 and this step with the two viewports on the left to change them.

   The Change View To list contains the standard four isometric views and the six orthogonal views. By clicking a sample viewport and selecting an option from the Change View To drop-down list, you can arrange your viewport views nearly any way that you want.

6. To name this viewport arrangement, enter My Viewport Setup in the New Name box.

7. Click OK. Your display changes to show three viewports arranged as they were indicated in the Viewports dialog box (see Figure 21.21).

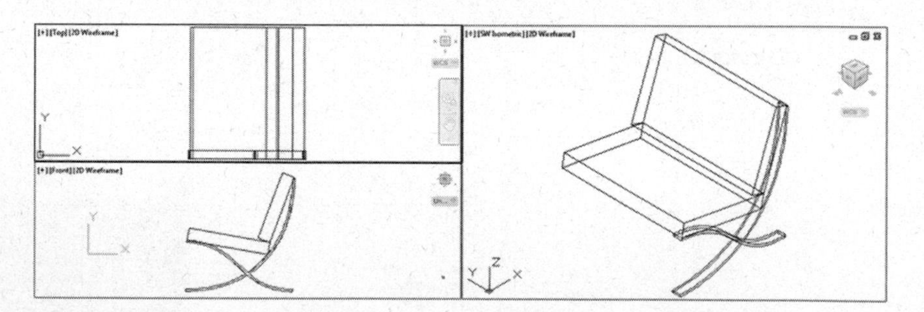

FIGURE 21.21
Three viewports, each displaying a different view

You've set up your viewports. Let's check to see that your viewport arrangement was saved:

1. Click the Named tool in the Visualize tab's Model Viewports panel to open the Viewports dialog box again.

2. Click the Named Viewports tab. My Viewport Setup is listed in the Named Viewports list box. If you click it, a sample view of your viewport arrangement appears on the right.

3. After you've reviewed the addition to the Named Viewports list, close the dialog box.

Now take a close look at your viewport setup. The UCS icon in the orthogonal views in the two left viewports is oriented to the plane of the view. AutoCAD lets you set up a different UCS for each viewport. The top view uses the WCS because it's in the same plane as the WCS. The side view has its own UCS, which is parallel to its view. The isometric view to the right retains the current UCS.

A Viewports dialog box option that you haven't tried yet is the Apply To drop-down list in the New Viewports tab (see Figure 21.22).

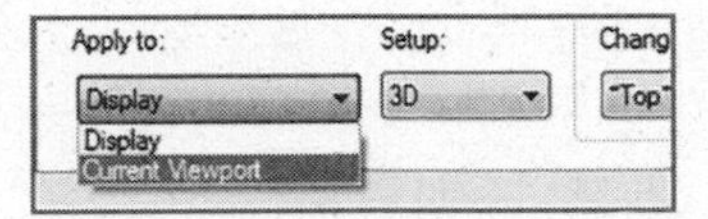

FIGURE 21.22
The Apply To drop-down list

This list shows two options: Display and Current Viewport. When Display is selected, the option you choose from the Standard Viewports list applies to the overall display. When Current Viewport is selected, the option you select applies to the selected viewport in the sample view in the right side of the dialog box. You can use the Current Viewport option to build multiple viewports in custom arrangements.

You have the legs for one side. The next step is to mirror those legs for the other side:

1. Click the top view of the chair in the upper-left viewport.

2. Turn on Polar Tracking in the status bar, and then click the Mirror tool in the Home tab's expanded Modify panel.
3. In the upper-left viewport, click the 3D solid representing the chair legs and then press ↵.
4. At the `Specify first point of mirror line:` prompt, use the Midpoint osnap and select the midpoint of the chair seat, as shown in Figure 21.23.

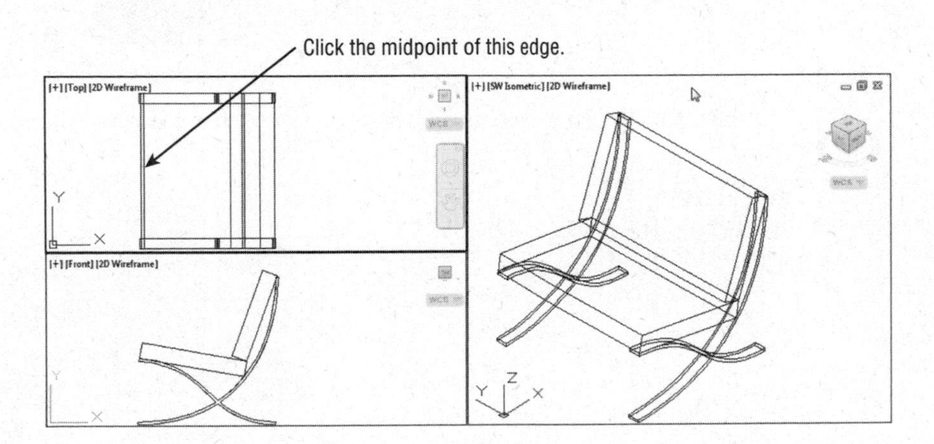

FIGURE 21.23
Mirroring the legs from one side to another

5. At the `Specify second point of mirror line:` prompt, pick any location to the right of the point that you selected so that the rubber-banding line is exactly horizontal.

6. Press ↵ at the `Erase source objects? [Yes/No] <N>:` prompt. The legs are mirrored to the opposite side of the chair. Your screen should look similar to Figure 21.23.

Your chair is complete. Let's finish by getting a better look at it:

1. Click the viewport to the right showing the isometric view.
2. Choose Single from the Viewport Configurations List drop-down list in the Visualize tab's Model Viewports panel (see Figure 21.24), or enter **-Vports**↵**Si**↵.

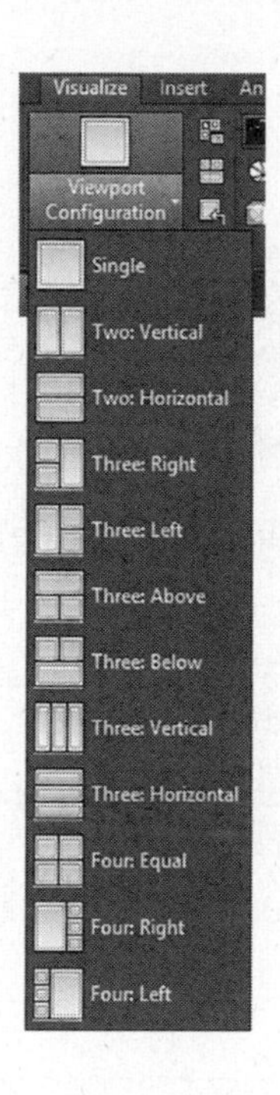

FIGURE 21.24
Click Single in the Viewport Configurations List drop-down list.

3. Use the Zoom tool to adjust your view so that it looks similar to Figure 21.25.

FIGURE 21.25
The chair in 3D with hidden lines removed

4. Click the Visual Styles drop-down list, and select Shades Of Gray. Note that your background may appear much darker.

5. Exit the file. You can save if you like or close without saving in case you want to do the exercise again.

Using the Array Tools

In Chapter 6, "Editing and Reusing Data to Work Efficiently," you were introduced to the Array command. Let's take a look at how this works in the 3D world. In AutoCAD 2018, you can create a 3D array from any type of array, whether it is rectangular, polar, or path. Let's do an example using the path array:

1. Open the file `3Dseating.dwg`. Make sure that Selection Cycling is turned off for these exercises.

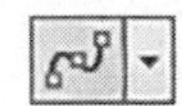

2. Click the Path Array tool in the Array flyout on the Modify panel of the Home tab, or type **ARRAYPATH**↵.

3. At the `Select objects:` prompt, click the chair at the left end of the arc in the drawing and then press ↵.

4. At the `Select path curve:` prompt, select the magenta arc toward the left end.

5. At the `Select grip to edit array or [Associative/Method/Base point/Tangent direction/Items/Rows/Levels/Align items/Z direction/eXit] <eXit>:` prompt, enter **I**↵.

6. At the `Specify the distance between items along path or [Expression] <35.7596>:` prompt, press ↵.

7. At the `Specify number of items or [Fill entire path / Expression] <6>:` prompt, enter **5**↵.

8. At the `Select grip to edit array or [ASsociative/Method/Base point Tangent direction/Items/Rows/Levels/Align items/Z direction ] <eXit>:` prompt, enter **R**↵.

9. At the `Enter the number of rows or [Expression] <1>:` prompt, enter **3**↵.

10. At the `Specify the distance between rows or [Total / Expression] <40.7253>:` prompt, enter **48**↵.

11. At the `Specify the incrementing elevation between rows or [Expression] <0.0000>:` prompt, enter **12**↵.

12. At the `Select grip to edit array or [ASsociative/Method/Base point Tangent direction/Items/Rows/Levels/Align items/Z direction ] <eXit>:` prompt, enter **AS**↵.

13. At the `Create associative array [Yes/No] <no>:` prompt, enter **Yes**↵.

14. Press ↵ to exit the command.

In this exercise, you made an array of a chair that follows the path of an arc. The distance between chairs is 48″ (1219.2 mm), and the vertical riser between each section is 12″ (304.8 mm).

Now suppose that you want to adjust the curvature of your array. This is a simple matter of adjusting the shape of the arc, as described here:

1. Click the arc to expose its grips.
2. Click the middle grip, and then drag it upward. Notice that all the chairs adjust as you drag the arc.

Here you see how the associative feature of the Arraypath command lets you control the array by adjusting the object that you used for the path. Arrays can be edited through a variety of methods, as you'll see in the next section.

Making Changes to an Associative Array

Now let's take a look at how you can make changes to an array. You may have noticed the Associative option in the Array command's prompt. By default, the Associative option is turned on, which enables you to edit array objects as a group. You'll see how this works in the following exercises.

You'll start by editing the array that you created using the Path Array tool. You'll see that the chairs are now skewed and are no longer pointing to the center of the arc. You can realign them by making a simple change to the original chair.

The following steps show you how this is done:

1. Click the array of chairs. Notice that the contextual Array ribbon tab appears (see Figure 21.26).

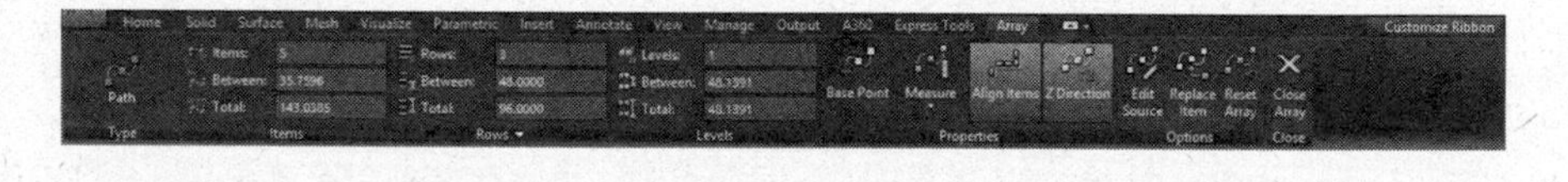

FIGURE 21.26 The Array ribbon tab appears, and a new set of panels and options is displayed.

   We'll change the number of chairs to allow for more seating.

2. In the contextual Array ribbon tab in the Properties panel, change from Measure Method to Divide Method by clicking the flyout arrow below the Measure button. Select the Divide Method button. The chairs will automatically space themselves along the curve. In the Items panel, change the item count from 5 to 10 and press the Tab key.

   The number of chairs dynamically changes to the new value.

3. Save the file.

Experiment with other values in the Array ribbon tab to see what effects they have.

As you can see from this exercises, you can easily make changes to an array through the Array Contextual ribbon tab options in the Ribbon. Many of these options are also available through the multifunction grip menus when you have Dynamic Input turned on.

Creating Complex 3D Surfaces

In one of the previous exercises, you drew a chair composed of objects that were mostly straight lines or curves with a thickness. All of the forms in that chair were defined in planes perpendicular to one another. For a 3D model such as this, you can get by using the orthographic UCSs.

At times, however, you'll want to draw objects that don't fit so easily into perpendicular or parallel planes. In the following sections, you'll create more complex forms by using some of the other 3D commands in AutoCAD.

Laying Out a 3D Form

In this next group of exercises, you'll draw a butterfly chair. This chair has no perpendicular or parallel planes with which to work, so you'll start by setting up some points that you'll use for reference only. This is similar in concept to laying out a 2D drawing. As you progress through the drawing construction, notice how the reference points are established to help create the chair. You'll also construct some temporary 3D lines to use for reference. These temporary lines will be your layout. These points will define the major UCSs needed to construct the drawing. The main point is to show you some of the options for creating and saving UCSs.

To save time, we've created the 2D drawing that you'll use to build your 3D layout. This drawing consists of two rectangles that are offset by 4″ (10 cm). To make it more interesting, they're also off-center from each other (see Figure 21.27).

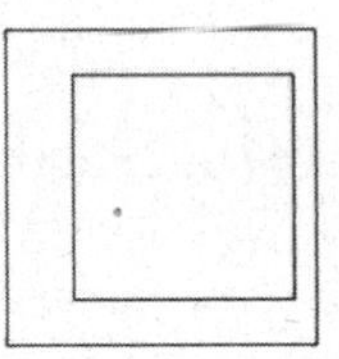

FIGURE 21.27
Setting up a layout for a butterfly chair

The first thing that you'll need to do is to set up the drawing for the layout:

1. Open the `butterfly1.dwg` file. Metric users should open `butterfly1-metric.dwg`.

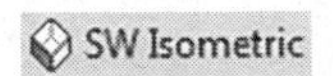

2. Click SW Isometric in the 3D Navigation drop-down list, or type **–V↵SWISO↵**. This gives you a view from the lower-left side of the rectangles.
3. Zoom out so that the rectangles occupy about a third of the drawing area window.

Now you need to move the outer rectangle in the z-axis so that its elevation is 30″ (76 cm):

1. Click the outer rectangle, and then click one of its grips.
2. Right-click to open the Grip Edit context menu.
3. Choose Move, and then enter **@0,0,30↵**; metric users should enter **@0,0,76↵**. This tells AutoCAD to move the rectangle a 0 distance in both the x- and y-axes and 30″ (or 76 cm) in the z-axis.
4. Pan your view downward so that it looks similar to Figure 21.28.

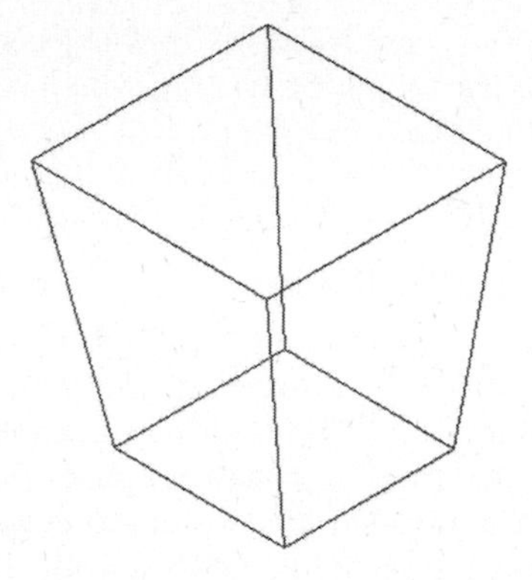

FIGURE 21.28
The finished chair layout

5. Use the Line tool to draw lines from the corners of the outer square to the corners of the inner square. Use the Endpoint osnap to select the exact corners of the squares. This is the layout for your chair—not the finished product.

As an alternate method in step 3, after choosing Move from the Grip Edit context menu, you can turn on Ortho mode and point the cursor vertically so that it shows –Z in the coordinate readout. Then enter **30↵** (**76↵** for metric users).

Spherical and Cylindrical Coordinate Formats

In the previous exercise, you used relative Cartesian coordinates to locate the second point for the Move command. For commands that accept 3D input, you can also specify displacements by using the Spherical and Cylindrical Coordinate formats.

The *Spherical Coordinate format* lets you specify a distance in 3D space while specifying the angle in terms of degrees from the x-axis of the current UCS and degrees from the XY plane of the current UCS (see the top image in Figure 21.29). For example, to specify a distance of 4.5″ (11.43 cm) at a 30° angle from the x-axis and 45° from the XY plane, enter **@4.5<30<45** (or **@11.43<30<45** for metric users). This refers to the direct distance followed by a < symbol, then the angle from the x-axis of the current UCS followed by another < symbol, and then the angle from the XY plane of the current UCS. To use the Spherical Coordinate format to move the rectangle in the exercise, enter **@30<0<90** (or **@76<0<90** for metric users) at the `Second point:` prompt.

The *Cylindrical Coordinate format,* on the other hand, lets you specify a location in terms of a distance in the plane of the current UCS and a distance in the z-axis. You also specify an angle from the x-axis of the current UCS (see the bottom image in Figure 21.29). For example, to locate a point that is a distance of 4.5″ (11.43 cm) in the plane of the current UCS at an angle of 30° from the x-axis and a distance of 3.3″ (8.38 cm) in the z-axis, enter **@4.5<30,3.3** (or **@11.43<30,8.38** for metric users). This refers to the distance of the displacement from the plane of the current UCS followed by the < symbol, then the angle from the x-axis followed by a comma, and then the distance in the z-axis. Using the Cylindrical Coordinate format to move the rectangle, you enter **@0<0,30** (or **@0<0,76** for metric users) at the `Second point:` prompt.

FIGURE 21.29
The Spherical and Cylindrical Coordinate formats

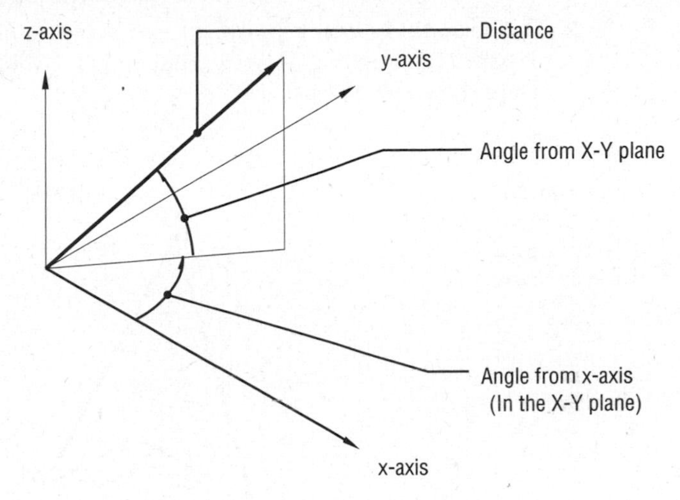

[Distance] < [Angle from x-axis] < [Angle from X-Y plane]

The Spherical Coordinate Format

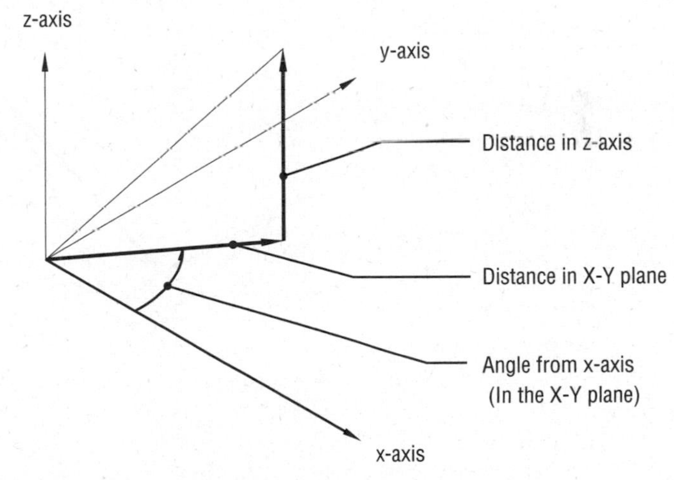

[Distance in X-Y plane] < [Angle from x-axis] , [Distance in z-axis]

The Cylindrical Coordinate Format

Using a 3D Polyline

Now you'll draw the legs for the butterfly chair by using a 3D polyline. This is a polyline that can be drawn in 3D space. Here are the steps:

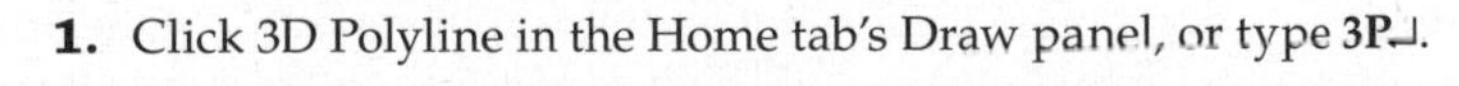

1. Click 3D Polyline in the Home tab's Draw panel, or type **3P**↵.

2. At the `Specify start point of polyline:` prompt, pick a series of points, as shown in Figure 21.30 (top), by using the Endpoint and Midpoint osnaps. Use the Close option to close the series of lines.

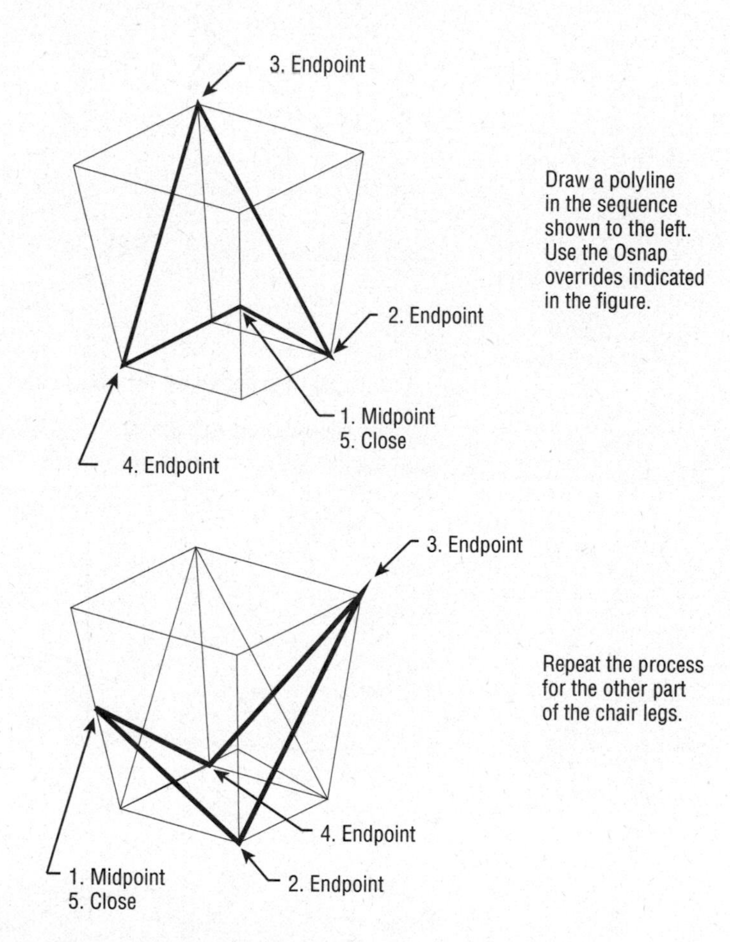

FIGURE 21.30
Using 3D polylines to draw the legs of the butterfly chair

3. Draw another 3D polyline in the mirror image of the first (see the lower image in Figure 21.30).
4. Erase the connecting vertical lines that make up the frame, but keep the rectangles. You'll use them later.

All objects, with the exception of lines and 3D polylines, are restricted to the plane of your current UCS. Two other legacy 3D objects, 3D faces and 3D meshes, are also restricted. You can use the Pline command to draw polylines in only one plane, but you can use the 3DPoly command to create a polyline in three dimensions. 3DPoly objects cannot, however, be given thickness or width.

Creating a Curved 3D Surface

Next, you'll draw the seat of the chair. The seat of a butterfly chair is usually made of canvas, and it drapes from the four corners of the chair legs. You'll first define the perimeter of the seat by using arcs, and then you'll use the Edge Surface tool in the Home tab's Modeling panel to form the shape of the draped canvas. The Edge Surface tool creates a surface based on four objects defining the edges of that surface. In this example, you'll use arcs to define the edges of the seat.

To draw the arcs defining the seat edges, you must first establish the UCSs in the planes of those edges. In the previous example, you created a UCS for the side of the chair before you could draw the legs. In the same way, you must create a UCS defining the planes that contain the edges of the seat.

Because the UCS that you want to define isn't orthogonal, you'll need to use the 3-point method. This lets you define the plane of the UCS based on three points:

1. Click the 3-Point tool on the Visualize tab's Coordinates panel, or type **UCS↵3↵**. With this option, you can define a UCS based on three points that you select. Remember, it helps to think of a UCS as a drawing surface situated on the surface of the object that you want to draw or edit.
2. At the `Specify new origin point <0,0,0>:` prompt, use the Endpoint osnap to pick the bottom of the chair leg to the far left, as shown in the left image of Figure 21.31. This is the origin point of your new UCS.
3. At the `Specify point on positive portion of X-axis:` prompt, use the Endpoint osnap to pick the bottom of the next leg to the right of the first one, as shown in the left image in Figure 21.31.

FIGURE 21.31
Defining and saving three UCSs

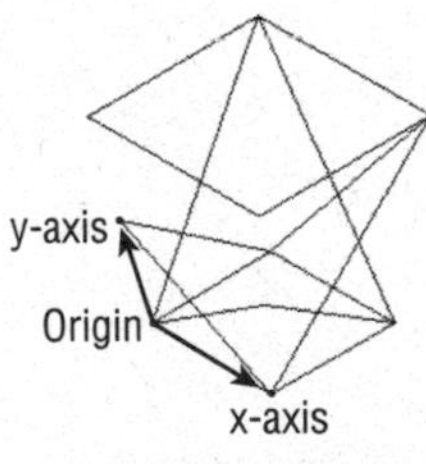

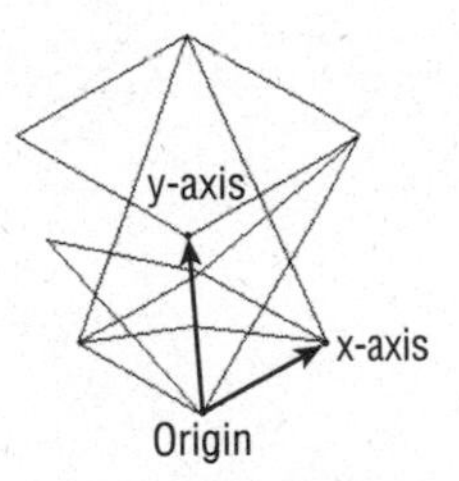

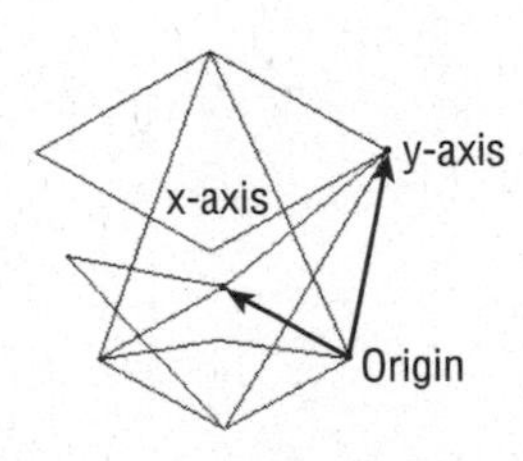

4. At the `Specify point on positive-Y portion of the UCS XY plane:` prompt, pick the top corner of the butterfly chair seat, as shown in the left image in Figure 21.31. The UCS icon changes to indicate your new UCS.

5. Now that you've defined a UCS, you need to save it so that you can return to it later. Click UCS ➤ Named UCS in the Visualize tab's Coordinates panel or type **UC↵** to open the UCS dialog box.
6. With the Named UCSs tab selected, right-click the Unnamed item in the list box and choose Rename from the context menu.

7. Enter **Front↵**.
8. Click OK to exit the UCS dialog box.

You've defined and saved a UCS for the front side of the chair. As you can see from the UCS icon, this UCS is at a nonorthogonal angle to the WCS. Continue by creating UCSs for two more sides of the butterfly chair.

1. Define a UCS for the side of the chair, as shown in the middle image in Figure 21.31. Use the UCS dialog box to rename this **UCS Side**, just as you did for Front in steps 5 through 8 in the previous exercise. Remember that you renamed the unnamed UCS.
2. Repeat these steps for a UCS for the back of the chair, named Back. Use the right image in Figure 21.31 for reference.
3. Open the UCS dialog box again. In the Named UCSs tab, highlight Front.
4. Click the Set Current button, and then click OK. This activates Front as the current UCS.

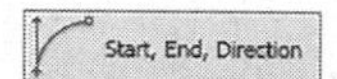

5. Click the Start, End, Direction tool from the Arc flyout in the Home tab's Draw panel.
6. Draw the arc defining the front edge of the chair (see Figure 21.32). Use the Endpoint osnap override to pick the top endpoints of the chair legs as the endpoints of the arc.

FIGURE 21.32
Drawing the front and back seat edge using arcs and a polyline spline

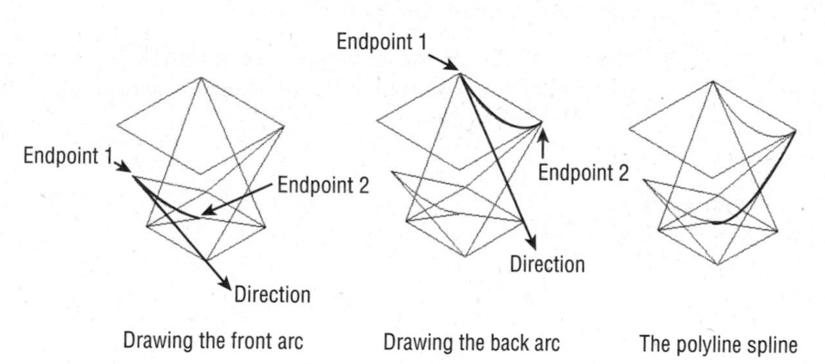

7. Repeat steps 3 through 6 for the UCS named Back, each time using the top endpoints of the legs for the endpoints of the arc.
8. Restore the UCS for the side, but instead of drawing an arc, use the Polyline tool and draw a polyline spline similar to the one in Figure 21.32. If you need help with polyline splines, see Chapter 18, "Drawing Curves."

Next, you'll mirror the side-edge spline to the opposite side. This will save you from having to define a UCS for that side:

1. Click the World UCS tool on the Visualize tab's Coordinates panel to restore the WCS. You do this because you want to mirror the arc along an axis that is parallel to the plane of the WCS. Remember that you must use the coordinate system that defines the plane in which you want to work.

2. Click the polyline you drew for the side of the chair (the one drawn on the Side UCS).
3. Start the 3DMirror command on the Home tab's Modify panel. At the `Specify first point of mirror plane (3 points)or [Object/ Last/ Zaxis/View/XY/ YZ/ ZX/ 3points] <3points>:` prompt, use the Midpoint override to pick the midpoint of the first side of the rectangle at the bottom of the model, then the opposite midpoint, and finally the midpoint of the top rectangle on the same side as the second point. Refer to Figure 21.33 for help. The polyline should mirror to the opposite side, and your chair should look like Figure 21.34.
4. Press the Esc key twice to clear the grips.

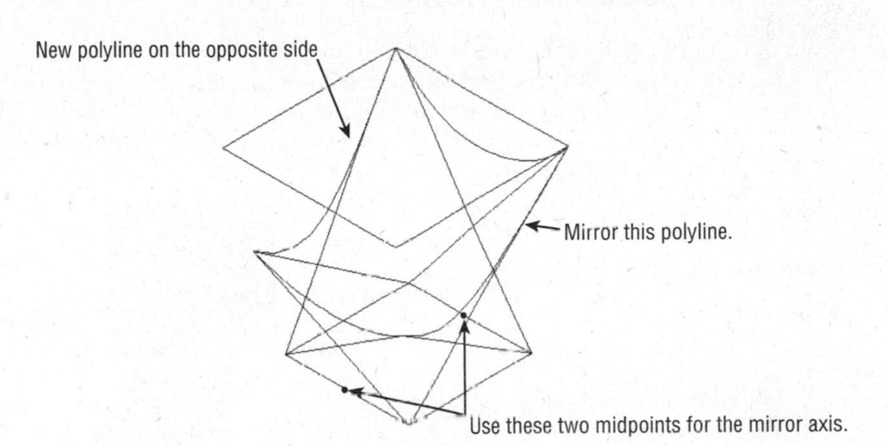

FIGURE 21.33 Set your UCS to World, and then mirror the arc that defines the side of the chair seat.

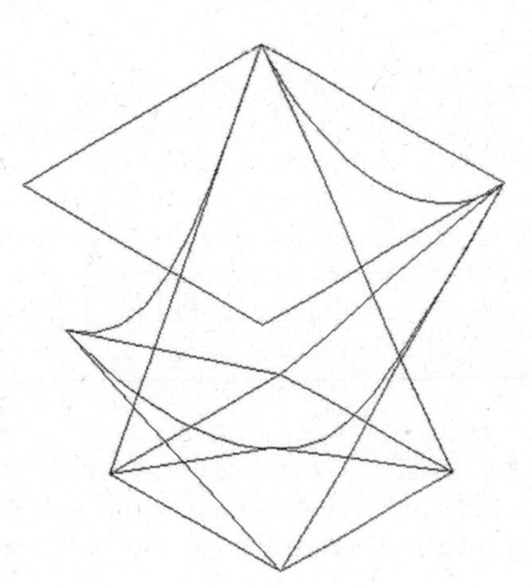

FIGURE 21.34 Your butterfly chair so far

Finally, let's finish this chair by adding the mesh representing the chair seat:

1. Click the Loft tool from the Extrude flyout in the Home tab's Modeling panel, or enter **Loft**↵ at the command line.

2. At the Select cross-sections in lofting order or [POint/Join multiple edges/MOde]: prompt, click the arc at the front of the layout.
3. At the Select cross-sections in lofting order or [POint/Join multiple edges/MOde]: prompt, click the arc at the back of the layout and then press ↵ to finish your selection of cross sections.
4. At the Enter an option [Guides/Path/Cross sections only/settings] <Cross sections only>: prompt, enter **G**↵ for the Guides option. You'll use the two polylines as guides.

Quick Hops to Your UCSs

If you find that you're jumping from one saved UCS to another, you'll want to know about the Named UCS Combo Control drop-down list. This list is located in the Visualize tab's Coordinates panel, and it contains the World and other standard UCS options as well as all the saved UCSs in a drawing. You can use this list as a quick way to move between UCSs that you've set up or between the predefined orthogonal UCSs.

Another great way to jump quickly between UCSs is to use the UCS Face option. The Face option requires a 3D solid, but once you have one in place, you can choose Face from the View flyout on the Visualize tab's Coordinates panel and then click on the face of the solid to which you want to align your UCS. For example, you can use the Loft command (see the section "Shaping the Solid" later in this chapter) to create a solid similar to the solid shown later in Figure 21.37 that connects the top and bottom rectangles of the butterfly chair. You can then use the UCS Face option to align to the sides of that solid to draw the arcs and polylines for the seat outline. This way, you're using the 3D solid as a layout tool.

5. At the Select guide profiles or [Join multiple edges]: prompt, select the two polylines on the sides of the layout, and then press ↵ to complete your selection. Your chair begins to take form, as shown in Figure 21.35.

6. Select Save from the Quick Access toolbar to save the chair so far.

You've got the beginnings of a butterfly chair with the legs drawn in schematically and the seat as a 3D surface. You can add some detail by using a few other tools, as you'll see in the next set of exercises.

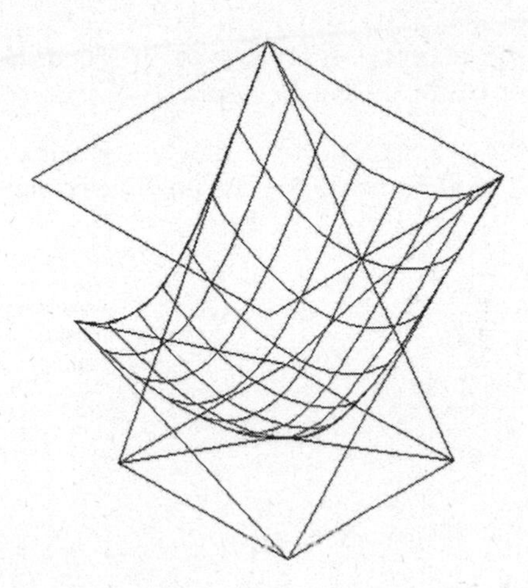

FIGURE 21.35
The butterfly chair with a mesh seat

Converting the Surface into a Solid

In the previous example, you used the Loft tool to create a 3D surface. After you have a surface, you can convert it to a solid to perform other modifications.

You'll want to round the corners of the seat surface to simulate the way a butterfly chair hangs off its frame. You'll also round the corners of the frame and turn the frame into a tubular form. Start by rounding the seat surface. This will involve turning the surface into a solid so that you can use solid-editing tools to get the shape that you want:

1. Click the Thicken tool in the Home tab's Solid Editing panel.

   You can also enter **Thicken↵** at the Command prompt.

2. Select the seat surface, and press ↵ to finish your selection.
3. At the `Specify thickness <0'-0">:` prompt, enter **0.01↵** (**0.025↵** for metric users).

The seat surface appears to lose its webbing, but it has just been converted to a very thin 3D solid.

Shaping the Solid

The butterfly chair is in a fairly schematic state. The corners of the chair are sharply pointed, whereas a real butterfly chair would have rounded corners. In this section, you'll round the corners of the seat with a little help from the original rectangles that you used to form the layout frame.

First you'll use the Fillet command to round the corners of the rectangles. Then you'll use the rounded rectangles to create a solid from which you'll form a new seat:

1. Choose the Fillet tool from the Home tab's Modify panel, or enter **F↵** at the command line.
2. At the `Select first object or [Undo/Polyline/Radius/Trim/Multiple]:` prompt, enter **R↵**.
3. At the `Specify fillet radius <0'-0">:` prompt, enter **3↵**. Metric users enter **7.5↵**.

4. At the `Select first object or [Undo/Polyline/Radius/Trim/Multiple]:` prompt, enter **P**↵ for the Polyline option.
5. At the `Select 2D polyline or [Radius]:` prompt, select the top rectangle, as shown at the top of Figure 21.36. The polyline corners become rounded.

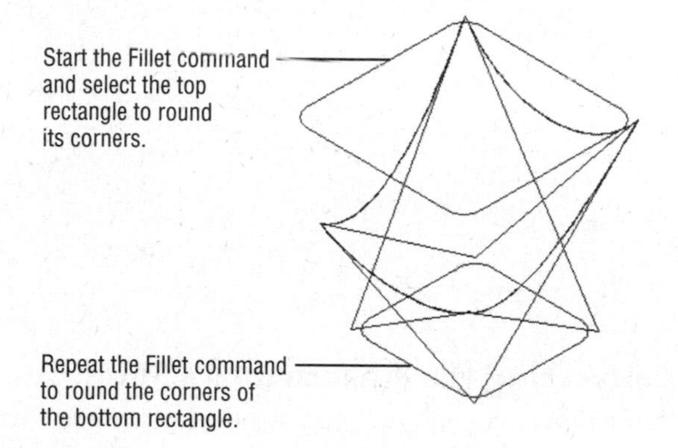

FIGURE 21.36
Round the corners of the rectangles with the Fillet command.

6. Press ↵ to repeat the Fillet command.
7. Enter **P**↵ to use the Polyline option, and then click the bottom rectangle, as shown at the bottom of Figure 21.36. Now both polylines have rounded corners.

Next create a 3D solid from the two rectangles using the Loft tool:

1. Click the Loft tool in the Home tab's Modeling panel, or enter **Loft**↵.
2. At the `Select crosssections in lofting order or [POint/Join multiple edges/MOde]:` prompt, select the two rectangles and press ↵ to finish your selection. Click the multifunction grip, and choose the Ruled option.
3. At the `Enter an option [Guides/Path/Cross sections only/Settings] <Cross sections only>:` prompt, press ↵. The rectangles join to form a 3D solid (see Figure 21.37).

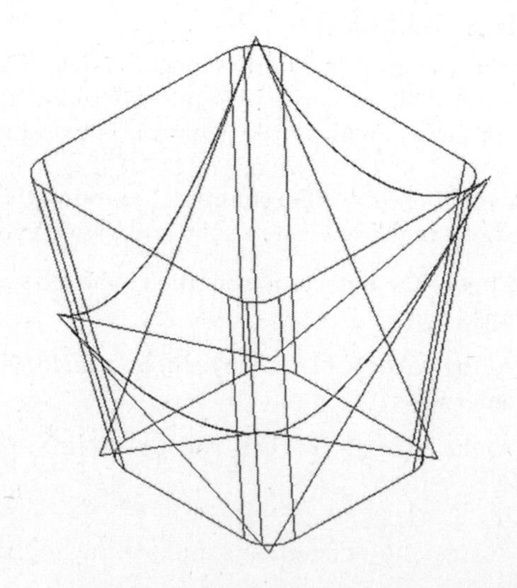

FIGURE 21.37
The lofted rectangles form a 3D solid.

Finding the Interference between Two Solids

In the next exercise, you'll use a tool that is intended to find the interference between two solids. This is useful if you're working with crowded 3D models and you need to check whether objects may be interfering with each other. For example, a mechanical designer might want to check that duct locations aren't passing through a structural beam.

You'll use Interfere as a modeling tool to obtain a shape that is a combination of two solids: the seat and the rectangular solid that you just created. Here are the steps:

1. Click the Interfere tool in the Home tab's Solid Editing panel.

   You can also enter **Interfere**↵ at the Command prompt.

2. At the Select first set of objects or [Nested selection/Settings]: prompt, select the chair seat solid and then press ↵.

3. At the Select second set of objects or [Nested selection/checK first set] <checK>: prompt, click the rectangular solid that you created in the previous exercise and press ↵. The Interference Checking dialog box appears (see Figure 21.38), and the drawing temporarily changes to a view similar to the Realistic visual style.

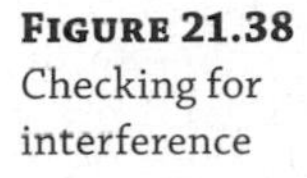

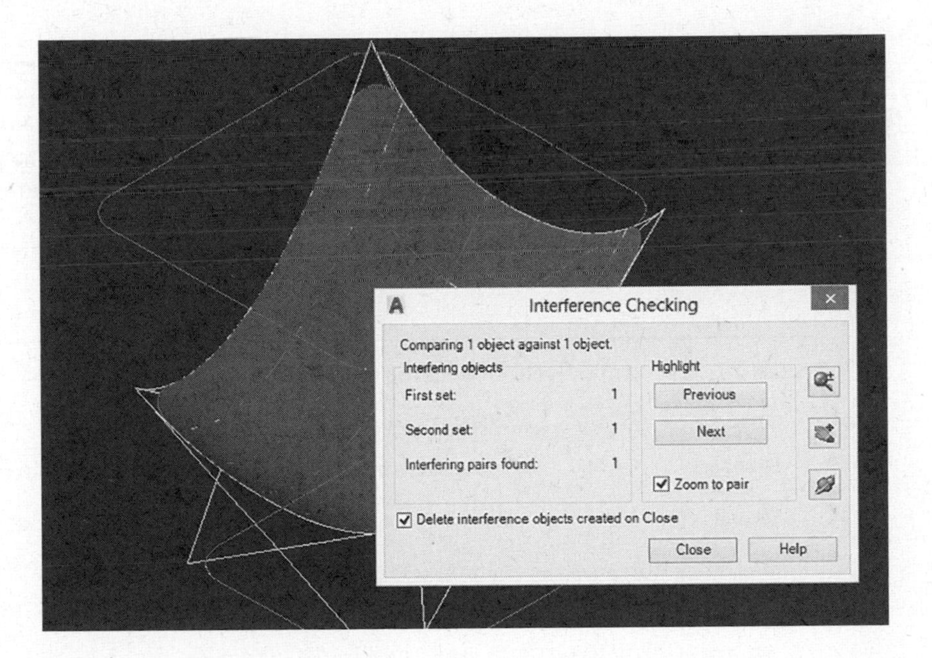

FIGURE 21.38 Checking for interference

The view shows the interference of the two solids in red. Notice that the corners are rounded on the red interference.

4. In the Interference Checking dialog box, deselect the Delete Interference Objects Created On Close check box and click Close. The display returns to the Wireframe view. If you look carefully at the seat corners, you see a new solid overlaid on the seat (see Figure 21.39).

5. Delete the rectangular solid and the original seat, as shown in Figure 21.39.

FIGURE 21.39
The interference solid appears on top of the original seat.

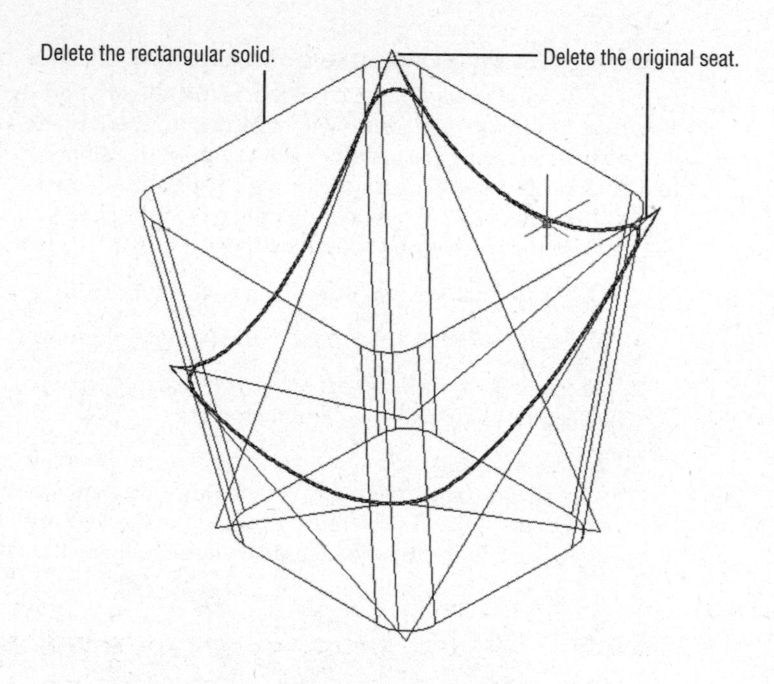

As mentioned earlier, the Interference Checking tool is intended to help you find out whether objects are colliding in a 3D model; as you've just seen, though, it can be an excellent modeling tool for deriving a form that you could not create otherwise.

A number of other options are available when you're using the Interference Checking tool. Table 21.2 lists the options in the Interference Checking dialog box.

TABLE 21.2: Interference Checking dialog box options

OPTION	WHAT IT DOES
First Set	Specifies the number of objects in the first set of selected objects
Second Set	Specifies the number of objects in the second set of selected objects
Interfering Pairs Found	Indicates the number of interferences found
Previous	Highlights the previous interference object
Next	Highlights the next interference object if multiple objects are present
Zoom To Pair	Zooms to the interference object while you're using the Previous and Next options
Zoom Realtime	Closes the dialog box to allow you to use Zoom Realtime
Pan Realtime	Closes the dialog box to allow you to use Pan

TABLE 21.2: Interference Checking dialog box options *(CONTINUED)*

OPTION	WHAT IT DOES
3D Orbit	Closes the dialog box to allow you to use 3D Orbit
Delete Interference Objects Created On Close	Deletes the interference object after the dialog box is closed

The prompt for the Interference Checking command also showed some options. The prompt in step 2 shows `Nested selection/Settings`. The `Nested selection` option lets you select objects that are nested in a block or an Xref. The `Settings` option opens the Interference Settings dialog box (see Figure 21.40).

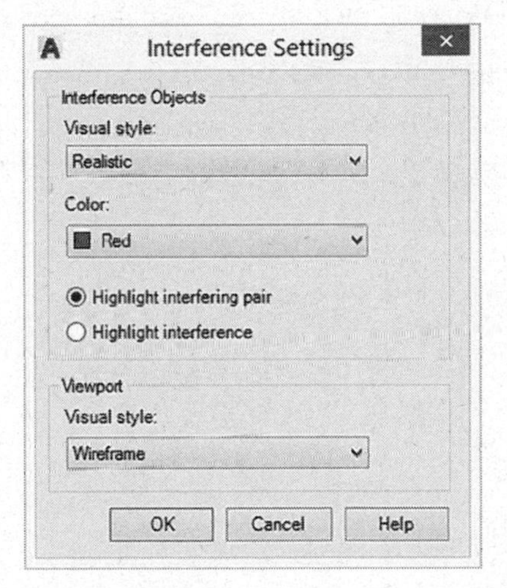

FIGURE 21.40 Settings for interference

This dialog box offers settings for the temporary display of interference objects while you're using the Interference command. Table 21.3 lists the options for this dialog box.

TABLE 21.3: Interference Settings dialog box options

OPTION	WHAT IT DOES
Visual Style	Controls the visual style for interference objects
Color	Controls the color for interference objects
Highlight Interfering Pair	Highlights the interfering objects
Highlight Interference	Highlights the resulting interference objects
Visual Style	Controls the visual style for the drawing while displaying the interference objects

Creating Tubes with the Sweep Tool

You need to take care of one more element before your chair is complete. The legs are currently simple lines with sharp corners. In this section, you'll learn how to convert lines into 3D tubes. To make it more interesting, you'll add rounded corners to the legs.

Start by rounding the corners on the lines that you've created for the legs:

1. Use the Explode tool to explode the 3D polyline legs into simple lines.
2. Choose the Fillet tool from the Home tab's Modify panel, or enter **F↵** at the command line.
3. At the `Select first object or [Undo/Polyline/Radius/Trim/Multiple]:` prompt, enter **R↵**.
4. At the `Specify fillet radius <0'-0">:` prompt, enter **2↵**. Metric users should enter **5↵**.
5. At the `Select first object or [Undo/Polyline/Radius/Trim/Multiple]:` prompt, enter **M↵** and then select pairs of lines to fillet their corners.
6. When all the corners are rounded, press ↵ to exit the Fillet command.
7. Delete the two polyline splines that you used to form the sides of the seat, along with the curves used for the front and back. Your drawing should look like Figure 21.41.

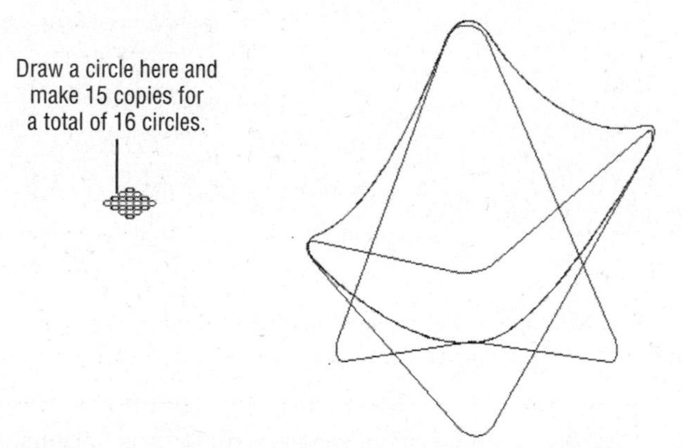

FIGURE 21.41
Drawing the circles for the tubes

The chair is almost complete, but the legs are just wireframes. Next you'll give them some thickness by turning them into tubes. Start by creating a set of circles. You'll use the circles to define the diameter of the tubes:

1. Draw a 3/8" (0.95 cm) radius circle in the location shown in Figure 21.41. Don't worry if your location is a little off; the placement of the circle isn't important.

2. Use the Rectangular Array command to make 15 copies of the circle. In Figure 21.41, a 4×4 array is used with the default 1″ spacing. Metric users should use a spacing of about 30 cm. Use the Explode command in the Home Tab's Modify panel to convert the circles from an associative array to regular circles. Start the Explode command, and select the circles ↵.

Now you're ready to form the tubes:

1. Select the Sweep tool from the Extrude flyout in the Home tab's Modeling panel. You can also enter **sweep**↵ at the command line.
2. At the `Select objects to sweep or [MOde]:` prompt, click one of the circles that you just created. It doesn't matter which circle you use because they're identical. Press ↵ when you're finished.
3. At the `Select sweep path or [Alignment/Base point/Scale/Twist]:` prompt, select one of the lines or fillet arcs that make up the legs.
4. Press ↵ to repeat the Sweep command, and then repeat steps 2 and 3 for each part of the leg segments, including the fillet arcs.
5. Continue with step 4 until all the lines in the legs have been converted into tubes.
6. Change the color of the solid representing the seat to cyan, and then select the Realistic visual style from the Visual Style viewport control. Your drawing will look similar to the image on the left of Figure 21.42, which shows a perspective view. The image on the right is the chair with some materials assigned to its parts and a slight adjustment to the seat location.

FIGURE 21.42
A perspective view of the butterfly chair with tubes for legs

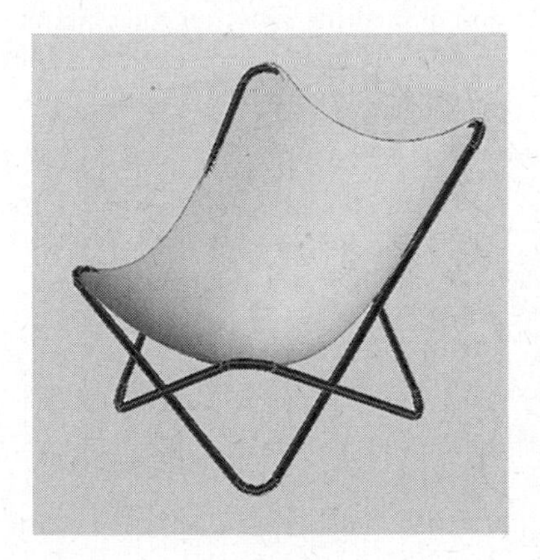

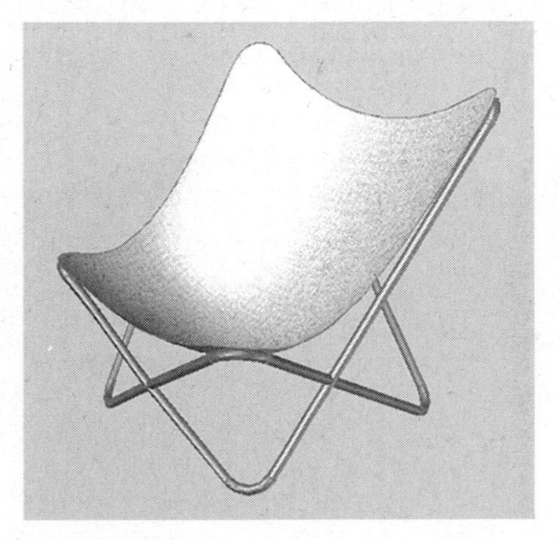

7. Close the file. You can save it or, if you intend to repeat the exercise, close and do not save.

Using Sweep to Create Complex Forms

Although you used circles with the Sweep command to create tubes, you can use any closed polyline shape. Figure 21.43 gives some examples of other shapes that you can use with the Sweep command.

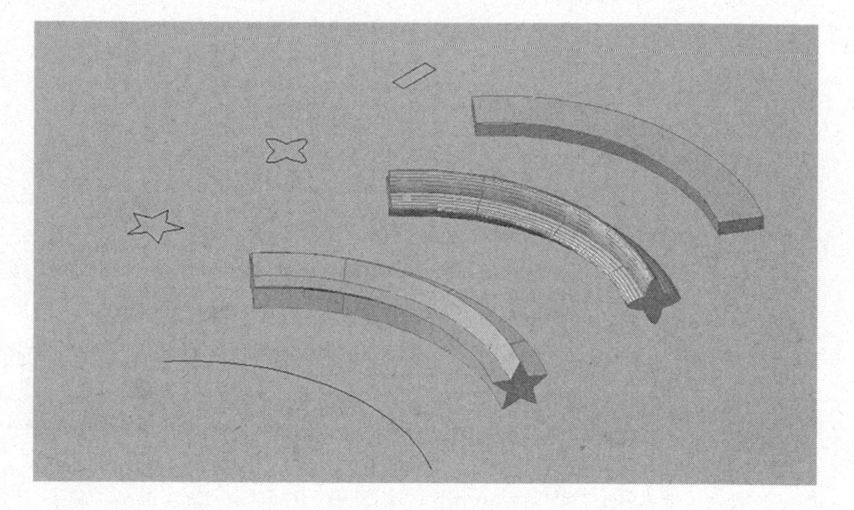

FIGURE 21.43
You can use any closed shape with the Sweep command.

In step 3 of the previous exercise, you may have noticed some command-line options. These options offer additional control over the way Sweep works. Here is a rundown on how they work:

Alignment This option lets you determine whether the object to sweep is automatically set perpendicular to the sweep path. By default, this option is set to Yes. If set to No, Sweep assumes the current angle of the object, as shown in Figure 21.44.

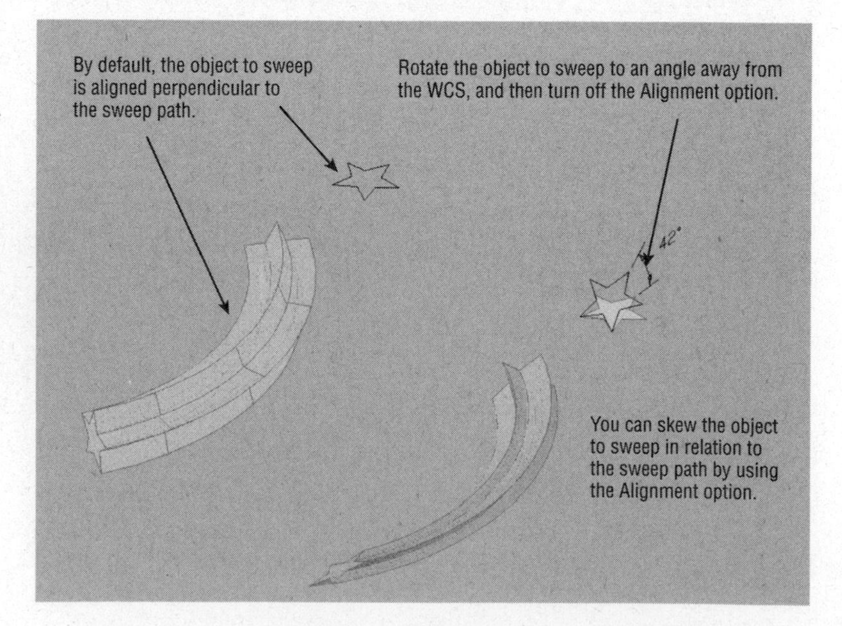

FIGURE 21.44
Alignment lets you set the angle between the object to sweep and the sweep path.

Base Point By default, Sweep uses the center of the object to sweep as the location to align with the path, as shown in Figure 21.45. Base Point lets you set a specific location on the object.

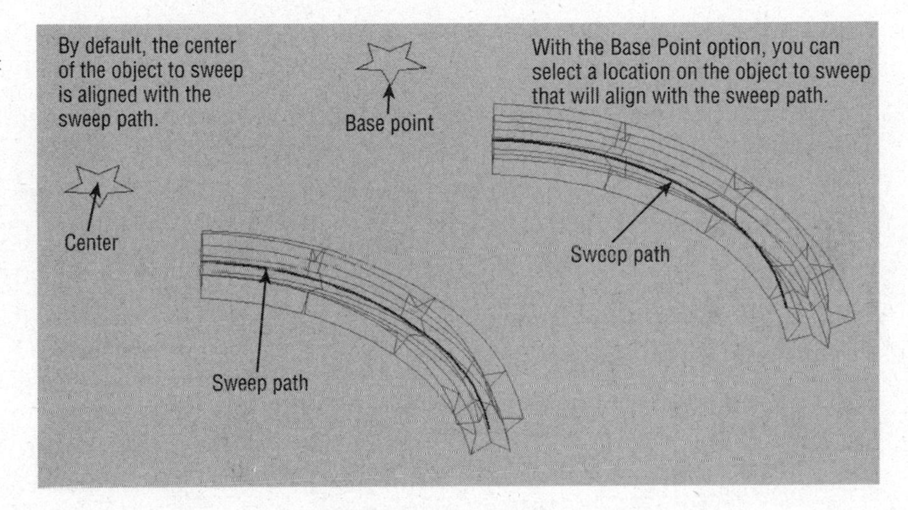

FIGURE 21.45
Using the Base Point option

Scale You can have Sweep scale the sweep object from one end of the path to the other to create a tapered shape, as shown in Figure 21.46. This option requires a numeric scale value.

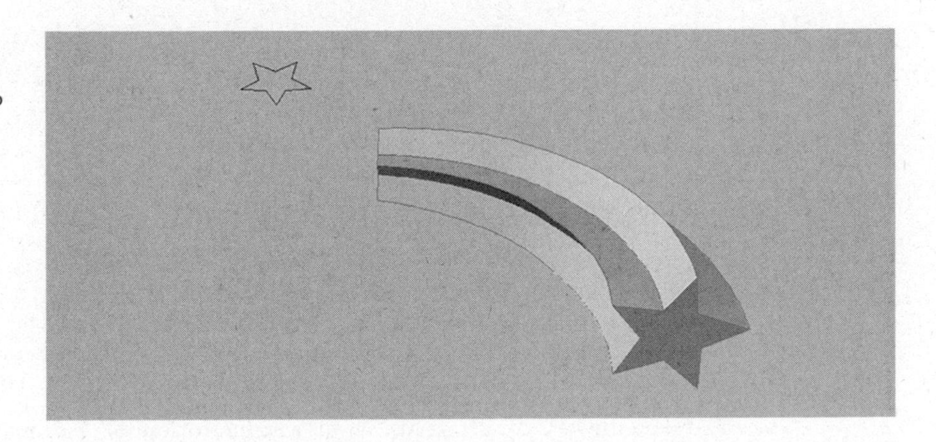

FIGURE 21.46
Scale lets you scale the object to sweep as it's swept along the path.

Twist You can have the object sweep twist along the path to form a spiral shape, as shown in Figure 21.47. This option requires a numeric value in the form of degrees of rotation.

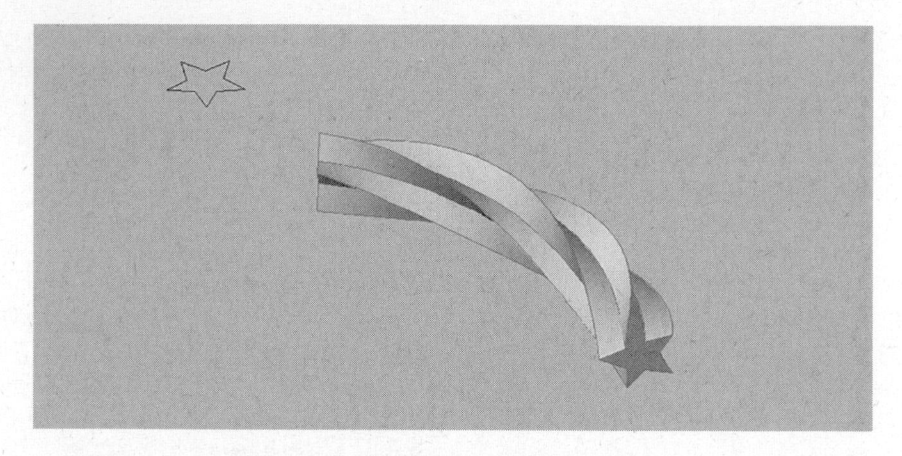

FIGURE 21.47
You can have the object sweep twist along the path to create a spiral effect.

These options are available as soon as you select the sweep object and before you select the path object. You can use any combination of options that you need. For example, you can apply the Twist and Scale options together, as shown in Figure 21.48.

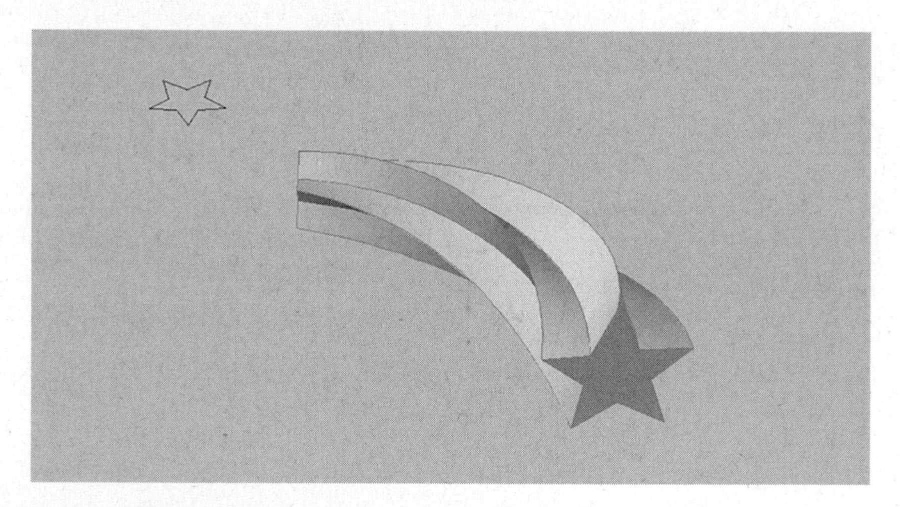

FIGURE 21.48
The Scale and Twist options applied together

Creating Spiral Forms

You can use the Sweep tool in conjunction with the Helix tool to create a spiral form, such as a spring or the threads of a screw. You've already seen how the Sweep tool works. Try the following exercise to learn how the Helix tool works firsthand.

In this exercise, you'll draw a helicoil thread insert. This is a device used to repair stripped threads; it's basically a coiled steel strip that forms internal and external threads. Here are the steps:

1. Open the `Helicoil.dwg` file. This is a standard AutoCAD drawing containing a closed polyline in a stretched octagon shape. This is the cross section of the helicoil thread, and you'll use it as an object to sweep after you've created a helix.

2. Click the Helix tool in the Home tab's expanded Draw panel, or type **Helix**↵.

You see the following prompt:

```
Number of turns = 3.0000 Twist=CCW
Specify center point of base:
```

3. Pick a point roughly in the center of the view. A rubber-banding line appears along with a circle.
4. At the Specify base radius or [Diameter] <1.0000>: prompt, enter **0.375**↵.
5. At the Specify top radius or [Diameter] <0.3750>: prompt, press ↵ to accept the default, which is the same as the value that you entered in step 4.
6. At the Specify helix height or [Axis endpoint/Turns/turn Height/tWist] <1.0000>: prompt, enter **T**↵ to use the Turns option.
7. At the Enter number of turns <3.0000>: prompt, enter **15**↵ to create a helix with 15 turns total.
8. At the Specify helix height or [Axis endpoint/Turns/turn Height/tWist] <1.0000>: prompt, press ↵ to accept the default height of 1. The helix appears as a spiral drawn to the dimensions that you've just specified for diameter, turns, and height (see Figure 21.49).

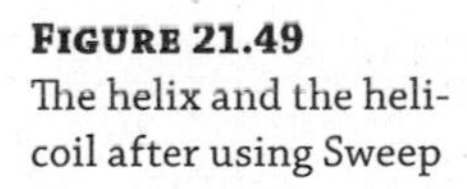

FIGURE 21.49
The helix and the heli-coil after using Sweep

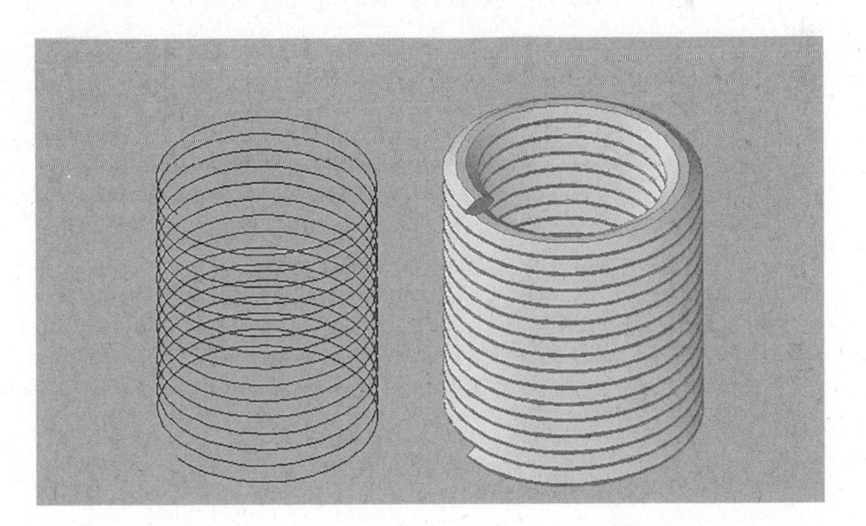

In step 6, you used the Turns option to specify the total number of turns in the helix. You also have other options that give you control over the shape of the helix. Figure 21.50 shows you the effects of the Helix command options. You may want to experiment with them on your own to become familiar with Helix.

FIGURE 21.50
The Helix command options

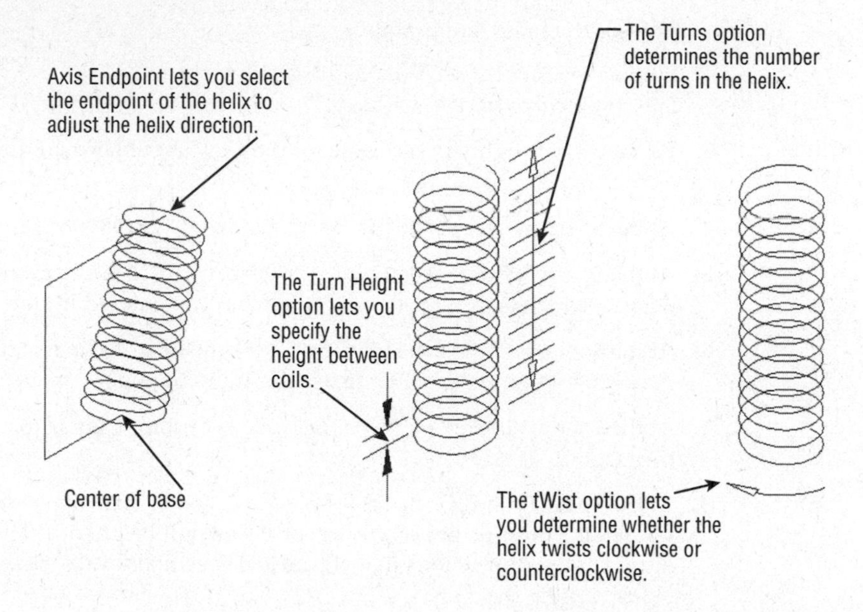

EDITING A HELIX WITH THE PROPERTIES PALETTE

If you find that you've created a helix with the wrong settings, you don't have to erase and re-create it. You can use the Properties palette to make adjustments to any of the helix options presented in Figure 21.50, even after a helix has been created. Select the helix, right-click, and choose Properties. Look in the Geometry section of the Properties palette for the helix settings.

Now use the Sweep tool to complete the helicoil:

1. Click the Sweep tool from the Extrude flyout in the Home tab's Modeling panel, or enter **Sweep** at the command line.
2. At the `Select objects to sweep or [MOde]:` prompt, select the thread cross section in the lower-left corner of the drawing and then press ↵.
3. At the `Select sweep path or [Alignment/Base point/Scale/Twist]:` prompt, select the helix. After a moment, the helicoil appears.
4. To see the helicoil more clearly, choose the Realistic option from the Visual Styles drop-down list, and then change the helicoil to the Helicoil layer.
5. Close and save the file. If you intend to repeat this exercise, close but don't save.

If the space between the coils is too small for the cross section, you may get an error message. If you get an error message at step 3, make sure that you created the helix exactly as specified in the previous exercise. You may also try increasing the helix height.

In step 3, instead of selecting the sweep path, you can select an option to apply to the object to sweep. For example, by default, Sweep aligns the object to sweep at an angle that is perpendicular to the path and centers it. See "Using Sweep to Create Complex Forms" earlier in this chapter.

Creating Surface Models

In an earlier exercise, you used the Loft command to create the seat of a butterfly chair. In this section, you'll return to the Loft command to explore some of its other uses. This time, you'll use it to create a 3D model of a hillside based on a set of site-contour lines. You'll also see how you can use a surface created from the Loft command to slice a solid into two pieces, imprinting the solid with the surface shape.

Real World Scenario

Architectural Applications for the Helix Tool

In the exercises for the Helix tool, we used a device often used to repair spark plug threads that have been stripped, but the helix can be used in other applications besides mechanical modeling. For example, we've used a helix to draw a circular ramp for a parking garage. To do this, instead of multiple turns, you would use a single rotation or a half rotation. The radius of the helix would need to be much larger to accommodate the width of a car.

Real World Scenario

Old vs. New Surfaces

If you've used earlier (pre-2007) versions of AutoCAD to create 3D models, you've probably used surface modeling to create some of your 3D objects. If you open an old drawing file that contains those 3D surfaces, you'll see that they are called polygon meshes. You can convert those older mesh objects into new surface objects using the Convert To Surface tool, which is next to the Convert To Solid tool in the Home tab's expanded Solid Editing panel. If you prefer to use the older 3D surface modeling tools like Revsurf and Rulesurf, they are still available, though they now create mesh surfaces. You will learn more about mesh modeling in Chapter 23, "Exploring 3D Mesh and Surface Modeling."

Start by creating a 3D surface using the Loft command:

1. Open the `contour.dwg` file.
2. Select the Loft tool from the Extrude flyout on the Home tab's Modeling panel.
3. Select each brown contour in consecutive order from right to left or left to right. It doesn't matter whether you start at the left end or the right end, but you must select the contours in order.

4. When you're finished selecting all the contours, press ↵. You see the surface applied over the contour lines (see Figure 21.51).

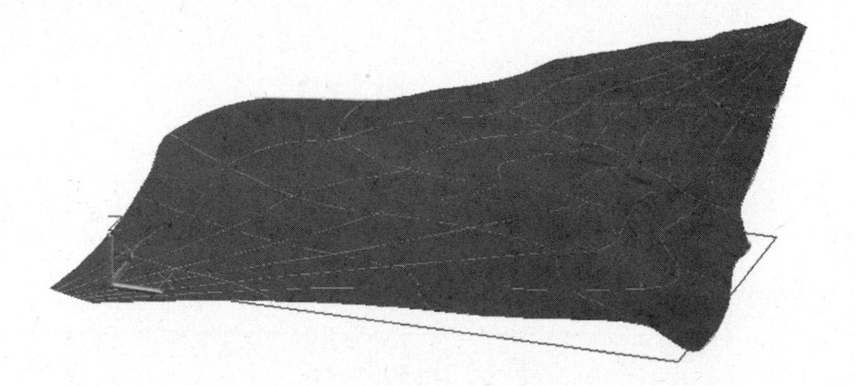

FIGURE 21.51
Creating a 3D surface from contour lines

5. At the Enter an option [Guides/Path/Cross sections only/Settings] <Cross sections only>: prompt, press ↵ to exit the Loft command.

Once the loft surface has been placed, you can make adjustments to the way the loft is generated by using the arrow grip that appears when you select the surface:

1. Click the surface to select it.
2. Click the arrowhead that appears by the surface. This is known as a multifunction grip.
3. Select the Ruled option from the menu. The surface changes slightly to conform to the new Ruled surface option (see Figure 21.52). Press Esc to make sure that you don't have any objects selected.

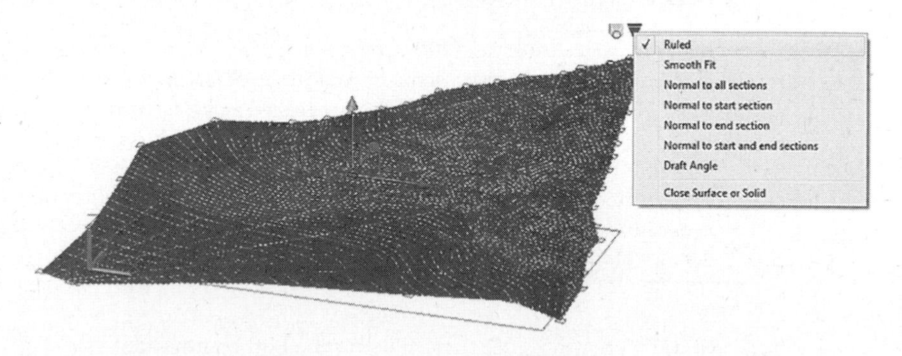

FIGURE 21.52
The surface showing the multifunction grip menu with the Ruled option selected

In the butterfly chair exercise, you used the Guides option in the Loft Command prompt. This allowed you to use the polyline curves to guide the loft shape from the front arc to the back arc. In this exercise, you didn't use the command options and went straight to the multifunction grip menu. The Ruled setting from step 3 generates a surface that connects the cross sections in a straight line.

Slicing a Solid with a Surface

In the barcelona1.dwg chair example, you converted a surface into a solid using the Thicken command. Next, you'll use a surface to create a solid in a slightly different way. This time, you'll use the surface to slice a solid into two pieces. This will give you a form that is more easily read and understood as a terrain model:

1. Select the Extrude tool from the Extrude flyout in the Home tab's Modeling panel.
2. At the `Select objects to extrude or [MOde]:` prompt, select the large rectangle below the contours and press ↵. The rectangle turns into a box whose height follows your cursor.
3. At the `Specify height of extrusion or [Direction/Path/Taper angle/ Expression]:` prompt, move the cursor upward so that the box looks similar to the one shown in Figure 21.53. Then click the mouse to fix the box's height.

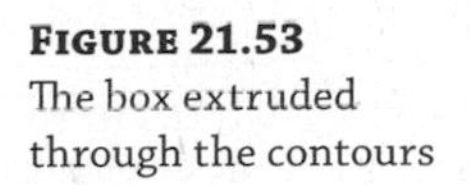

FIGURE 21.53 The box extruded through the contours

You may have noticed that as you raised the box height, you could see how it intersected the contour surface. Next you'll slice the box into two pieces:

1. Click the Slice tool in the Home tab's Solid Editing panel.
2. At the `Select objects to slice:` prompt, select the box and press ↵.
3. At the `Specify start point of slicing plane or [planar Object/Surface/ Zaxis/View/XY/YZ/ZX/3points] <3points>:` prompt, enter **S**↵ to use the Surface option.
4. At the `Select a surface:` prompt, select the contour surface.
5. At the `Select sliced object to keep or [keep Both sides] <Both>:` prompt, click the part of the box that is below the surface. The top part of the box disappears, and you see the surface once again.

6. Delete the contour surface and the contour lines. The box remains with an imprint of the surface, as shown in Figure 21.54.

FIGURE 21.54
The box with the contour surface imprinted

In step 3, you saw a prompt that offered a variety of methods for slicing the box. The Surface option allowed you to slice the box using an irregular shape, but most of the other options let you slice a solid by defining a plane or a series of planar objects.

Finding the Volume of a Cut

Civil engineers frequently ask us how they can find the volume of earth from an excavated area. This is often referred to as a *cut* from a *cut and fill* operation. To do this, you first have to create the cut shape. Next you use the Interfere command to find the intersection between the cut shape and the contour surface. You can then find the volume of the cut shape using one of the inquiry commands in AutoCAD. The following exercise demonstrates how this is done.

Suppose that the contour model you've just created represents a site where you'll excavate a rectangular area for a structure. You want to find the amount of earth involved in the excavation. A rectangle has been placed in the contour drawing representing such an area:

1. Select Wireframe from the Visual Styles flyout on the Home tab's View panel (see Figure 21.55). This allows you to see the excavation rectangle more clearly.

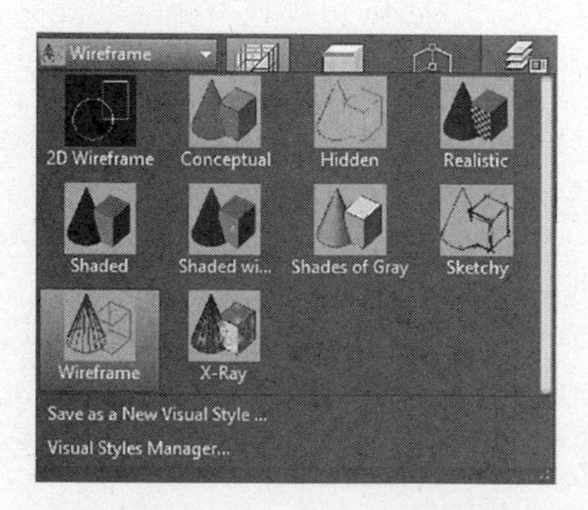

FIGURE 21.55
Select Wireframe from the Visual Styles flyout.

2. Turn on the Selection Cycling tool in the status bar. This will help you select the rectangle in step 4 if you have issues. Otherwise, it can be turned off. If the Selection Cycling tool is not in the status bar, click the Customization icon on the far right side of the status bar. In the window that pops up, click the Selection Cycling option to make it available in the status bar.
3. Click the Extrude tool in the Home tab's Modeling panel.
4. Select the rectangle shown in Figure 21.56.

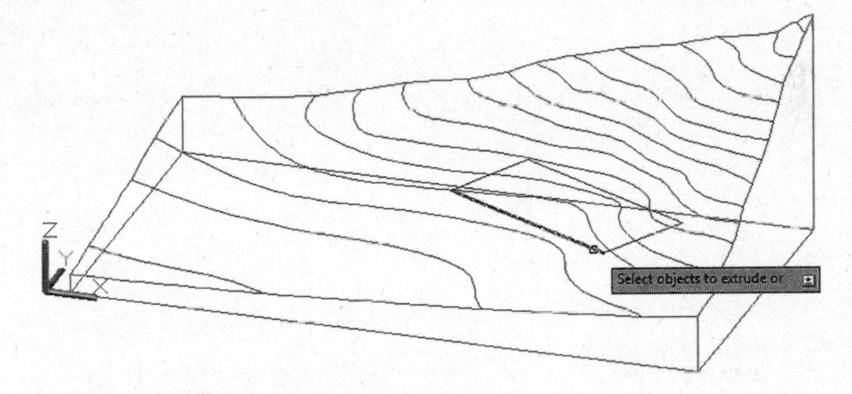

FIGURE 21.56
Selecting the rectangle representing the excavation area

5. In the Selection dialog box, select Polyline and then press ↵. Make sure to move your cursor away from the objects in the drawing before you proceed.
6. Extrude the rectangle to the height of 10′ (3 meters).

Here you used the Selection Cycling tool to help you select the rectangle, which is overlapped by the contour solid. The Selection Cycling tool presents the Selection dialog box, which lets you determine the type of object that you want to select, thereby filtering out other objects nearby that might be selected accidentally.

With the excavation rectangle in place, you can use the Interfere command to find the volume of the excavation:

1. Click the Interfere tool in the Home tab's Solid Editing panel.
2. At the `Select first set of objects or [Nested selection/Settings]:` prompt, click the contour and press ↵.
3. At the `Select second set of objects or [Nested selection/checK first set] <checK>:` prompt, select the box and press ↵. The Interference Checking dialog box appears.
4. In the Interference Checking dialog box, deselect the Delete Interference Objects Created On Close check box and click Close.
5. Delete the box that you used to represent the excavation area. The remaining shape contains the volume of the excavation.

6. Start the Region/Mass Properties tool by typing **Massprop**↵.
7. At the `Select objects:` prompt, select the excavation solid as shown in Figure 21.57 and then press ↵. The properties of the excavation area display in the command-line interface. At the top, you see the volume of the selected solid (see Figure 21.58).

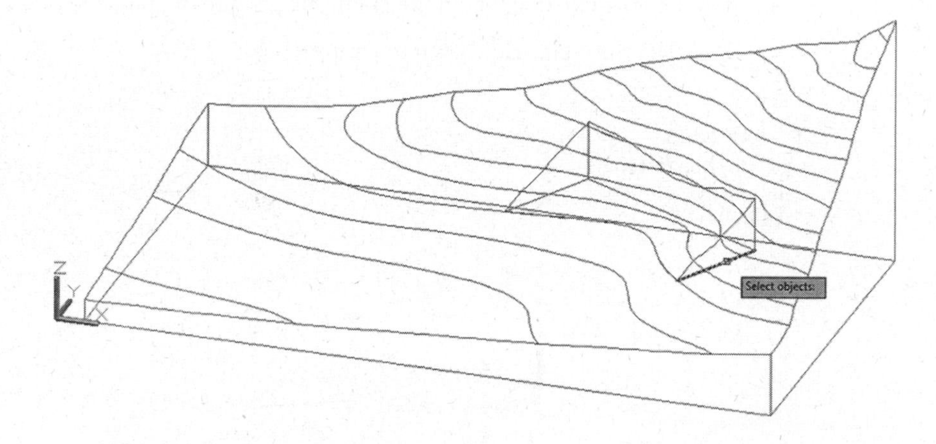

FIGURE 21.57
The 3D solid representing the excavation

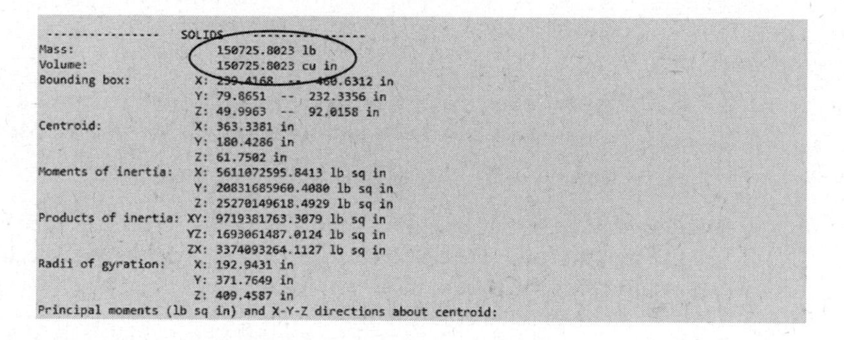

FIGURE 21.58
The mass and volume information from the Region/Mass Properties tool

8. Press ↵ and then at the `Write analysis to a file? [Yes/No] <N>:` prompt, press ↵ to exit the command or enter **Y**↵ to save the information to a text file.

Understanding the Loft Command

As you've seen from the exercises in this chapter, the Loft command lets you create just about any shape that you can imagine, from a simple sling to the complex curves of a contour map. If your loft cross sections are a set of closed objects like circles or closed polygons, the resulting object is a 3D solid instead of a surface.

The order in which you select the cross sections is important because Loft will follow your selection order to create the surface or solid. For example, Figure 21.59 shows a series of circles used for a lofted solid. The circles on each side are identical in size and placement, but the order of selection is different. The solid on the left was created by selecting the circles in consecutive order from bottom to top, creating an hourglass shape. The solid on the right was created by selecting the two larger circles first from bottom to top; the smaller, intermediate circle was selected last. This selection order created a hollowed-out shape with more vertical sides.

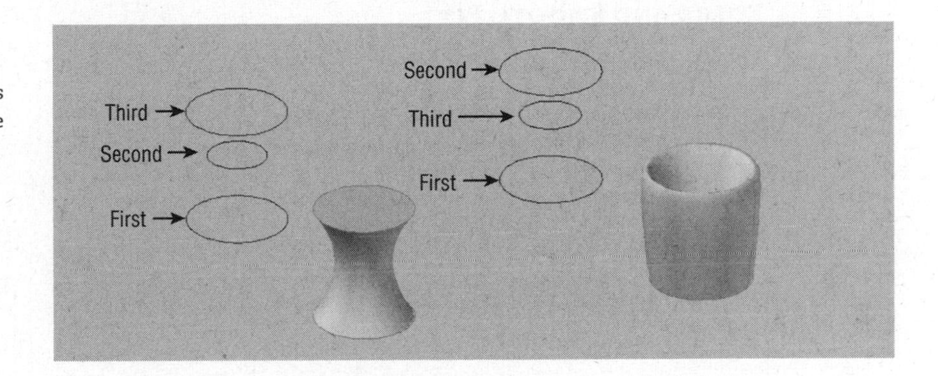

FIGURE 21.59 The order in which you select the cross sections affects the result of the Loft command.

In addition to the selection order, several other settings affect the shape of a solid created by the Loft command. In the contour-map example, you selected the Ruled setting from a multifunction grip after you had completed the Loft command. You can also set Loft command options through the Loft Settings dialog box (see Figure 21.60). This dialog box appears during the Loft command when you select the Settings option after you've selected a set of cross sections.

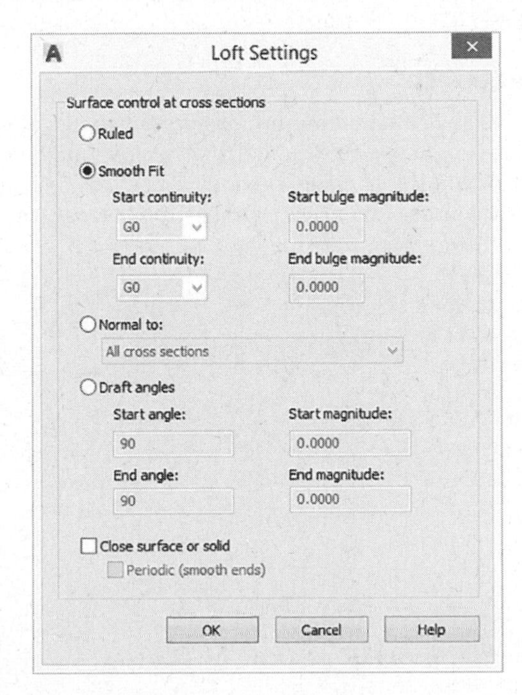

FIGURE 21.60 Loft Settings dialog box

You can radically affect the way the Loft command forms a surface or a solid through the options in this dialog box, so it pays to understand what those settings do. Take a moment to study the following sections that describe the Loft Settings dialog box options.

Ruled and Smooth Fit

The Ruled option connects the cross sections with straight surfaces, as shown in the sample to the left in Figure 21.61.

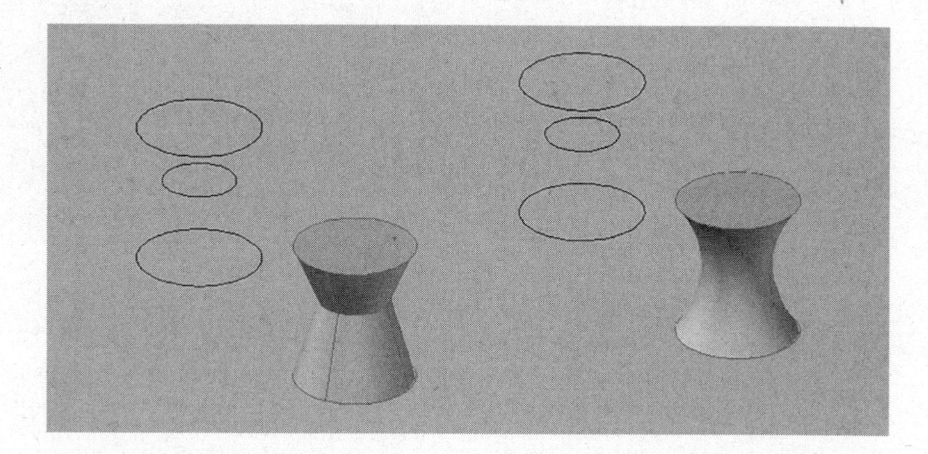

Figure 21.61
Samples of a Ruled loft at left and a Smooth Fit loft on the right

The Smooth Fit option connects the cross sections with a smooth surface. It attempts to make the best smooth transitions between the cross sections, as shown in the right image in Figure 21.61.

Normal To

Normal To is a set of four options presented in a drop-down list. To understand what this setting does, you need to know that *normal* is a mathematical term referring to a direction that is perpendicular to a plane, as shown in Figure 21.62. In these options, *normal* refers to the direction the surface takes as it emerges from a cross section.

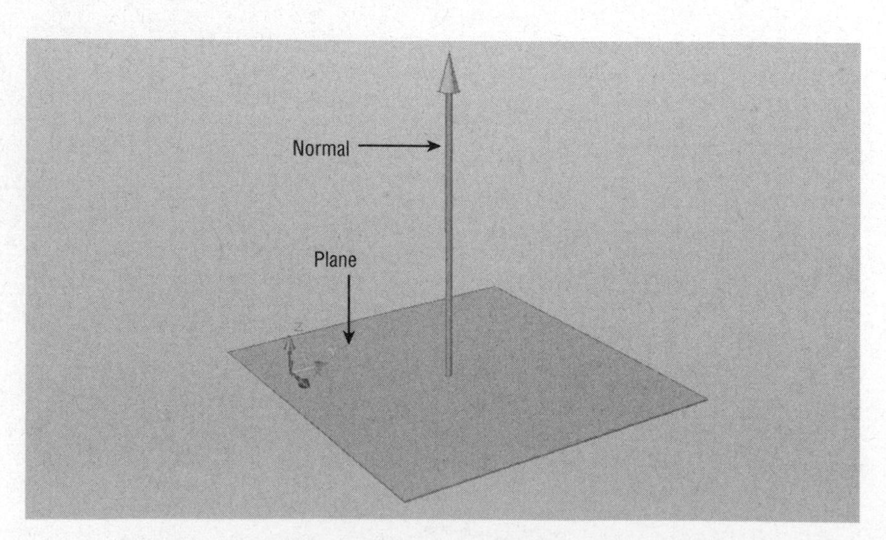

Figure 21.62
A normal is a direction perpendicular to a plane.

If you use the All Cross Sections option, the surfaces emerge in a perpendicular direction from all of the cross sections, as shown in the first image in Figure 21.63. If you use the End Cross Section option, the surface emerges in a direction that is perpendicular to just the end cross section, as shown in the second image in Figure 21.63. The Start Cross Section option causes the surface to emerge in a direction perpendicular to the start cross section. The Start And End Cross Sections option combines the effect of the Start Cross Section and End Cross Section options.

FIGURE 21.63
Samples of the Normal To options applied to the same set of cross sections

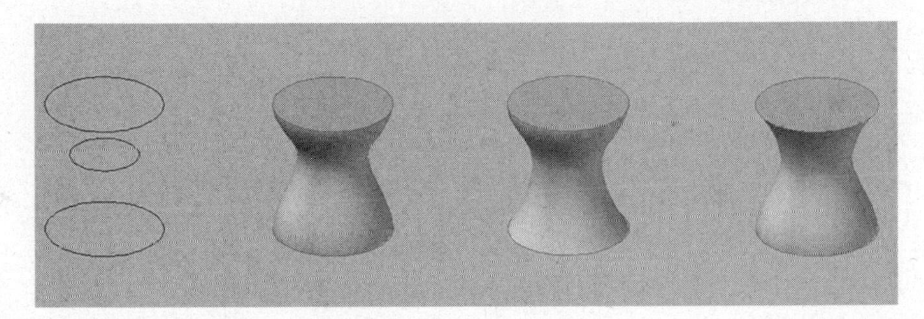

DRAFT ANGLES

The Draft Angles option affects only the first and last cross sections. This option generates a smooth surface with added control over the start and end angles. Unlike the Normal To option, which forces a perpendicular direction to the cross sections, Draft Angles allows you to set an angle for the surface direction. For example, if you set Start Angle to a value of 0, the surface will bulge outward from the start cross section, as shown in the first image of Figure 21.64.

FIGURE 21.64
The Draft Angles options

Likewise, an End Angle setting of 0 will cause the surface to bulge at the end cross section (see the second image in Figure 21.64).

The Start and End Magnitude settings let you determine a relative strength of the bulge. The right image in Figure 21.64 shows a draft angle of 0 and magnitude of 50 for the last cross section.

Close Surface or Solid

The Close Surface Or Solid option is available only when the Smooth Fit option is selected. It causes the first and last cross section objects to be connected, so the surface or solid loops back from the last to the first cross section. Figure 21.65 shows the cross sections at the left, a smooth version in the middle, and a smooth version with the Close Surface Or Solid option turned on. The Close Surface Or Solid option causes the solid to become a tube.

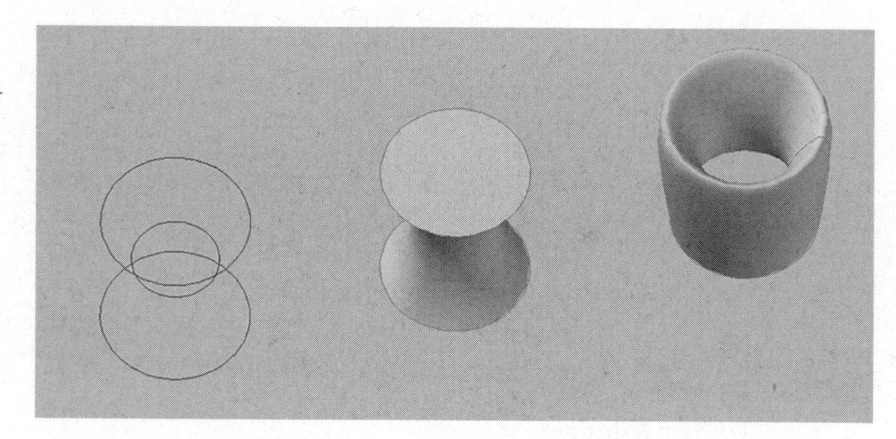

Figure 21.65
The Close Surface Or Solid option connects the end and the beginning cross sections.

Moving Objects in 3D Space

AutoCAD provides three tools specifically designed for moving objects in 3D space: 3D Align, 3D Move, and 3D Rotate. You can find all three commands in the Home tab's Modify panel. These tools help you perform common moves associated with 3D editing.

Aligning Objects in 3D Space

In mechanical drawing, you often create the parts in 3D and then show an assembly of the parts. The 3D Align command can greatly simplify the assembly process. The following steps show how to use 3D Align to line up two objects at specific points:

1. Open the `align.dwg` file.

2. Click the 3D Align tool on the Home tab's Modify panel, or type **3dalign**↵.
3. At the `Select objects:` prompt, select the 3D wedge-shaped object and press ↵. (The *source object* is the object that you want to move.)
4. At the `Specify base point or [Copy]:` prompt, pick a point on the source object that is the first point of an alignment axis, such as the center of a hole or the corner of a surface. For the align drawing, use the upper-left corner of the wedge.
5. At the `Specify second point or [Continue] <C>:` prompt, pick a point on the source object that is the second point of an alignment axis, such as another center point or other corner of a surface. For this example, select the other top corner of the wedge.

6. At the Specify third point or [Continue] <C>: prompt, if two points are adequate to describe the alignment, press ↵. Otherwise, pick a third point on the source object that, along with the first two points, best describes the surface plane that you want aligned with the destination object. Pick the lower-right corner of the wedge shown in Figure 21.66.

FIGURE 21.66
Aligning two 3D objects

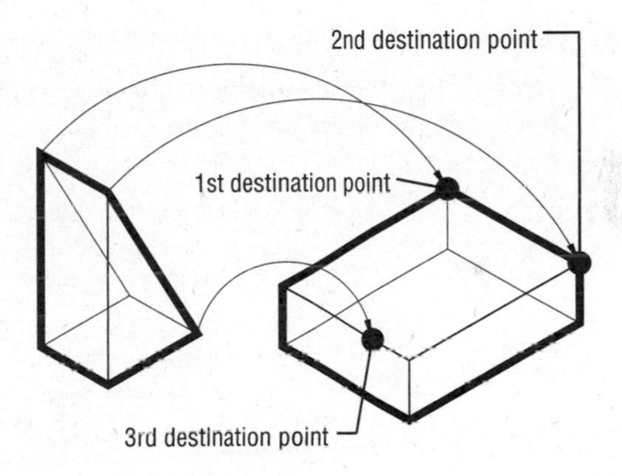

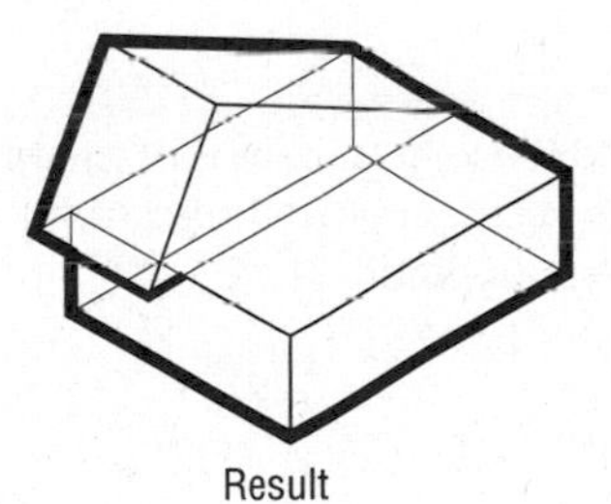

7. At the Specify first destination point: prompt, pick a point on the destination object to which you want the first source point to move. (The *destination object* is the object with which you want the source object to align.) This is the top corner of the rectangular shape. (See the first destination point in Figure 21.66.)

8. At the Specify second destination point or [eXit] <X>: prompt, pick a point on the destination object indicating how the first and second source points are to align in relation to the destination object. (See the second destination point in Figure 21.66.)

9. You're prompted for a third destination point. Pick a point on the destination object that, along with the previous two destination points, describes the plane with which you want the source object to be aligned. (See the third destination point in Figure 21.66.) The source object will move into alignment with the destination object.

Moving an Object in 3D

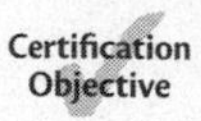

In Chapter 20, you saw how you can use the Move gizmo tool to help restrain the motion of an object in the x-, y-, or z-axis. AutoCAD offers a Move command specifically designed for 3D editing that includes a move gizmo tool to restrain motion.

You don't need to perform these steps as an exercise. You can try the command on your own when you need to use it.

Here's how it works:

1. Click the 3D Move tool in the Home tab's Modify panel. You can also enter **3dmove↵**.
2. Select the object or set of objects that you want to move and press ↵. The Move gizmo appears on the object (see Figure 21.67).

FIGURE 21.67
The Move gizmo

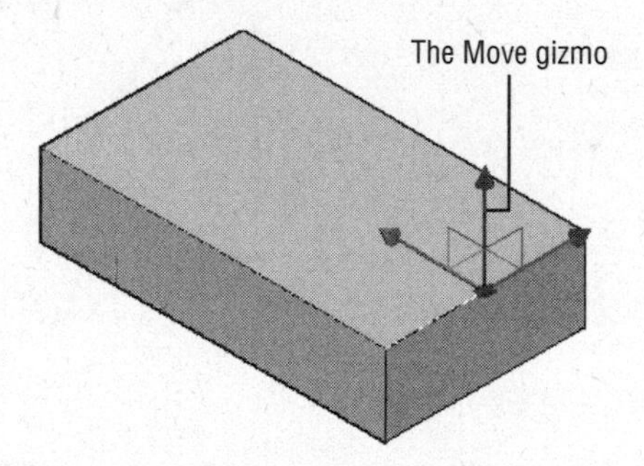

3. Point to the x-, y-, or z-axis of the Move gizmo but don't click it. As you hover over an axis, an axis vector appears indicating the direction your object will move if you click the axis, as shown in Figure 21.68.

FIGURE 21.68
An axis vector appears when you hover over an axis of the gizmo.

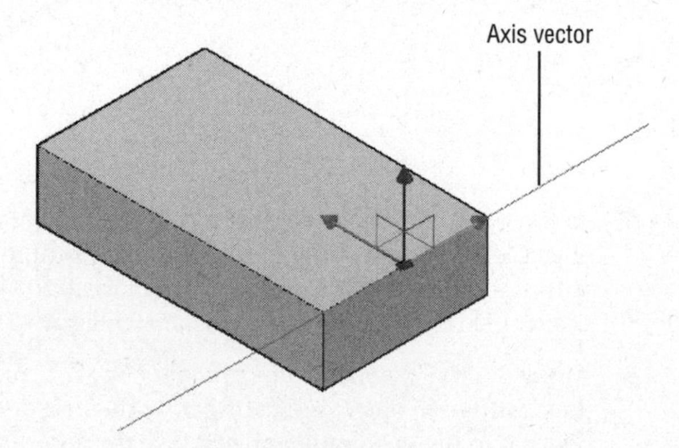

4. Click an axis while the vector appears, and then enter a distance along the axis or click a point to complete the move.

Alternately, in step 3, you can hover over and click a plane indicator on the gizmo to restrain the motion along one of the planes defined by two of the axes (see Figure 21.69).

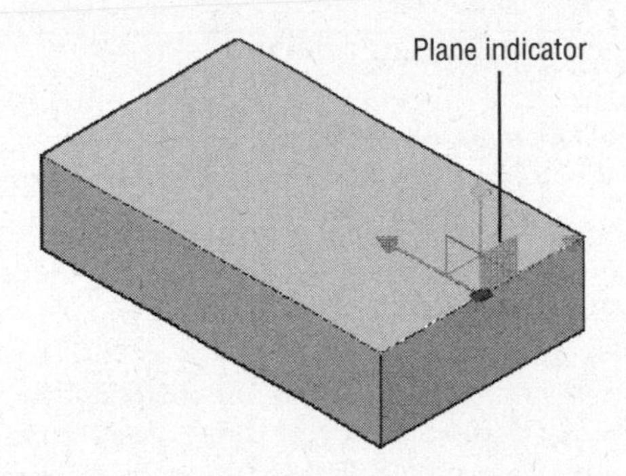

FIGURE 21.69
Hover over the plane indicator to restrain the motion along a plane.

Rotating an Object in 3D

The 3D Rotate command is another command that is like an extension of its 2D counterpart. With 3D Rotate, a Rotate gizmo appears that restrains the rotation about the x-, y-, or z-axis.

Again, you don't need to perform these steps as an exercise. You can try the command on your own when you need to use it.

Here's how it works:

1. Click the 3D Move tool in the Home tab's Modify panel. You can also enter **3drotate**↵.
2. Select the object or objects that you want to rotate and then press ↵. The Rotate gizmo appears on the object (see Figure 21.70).

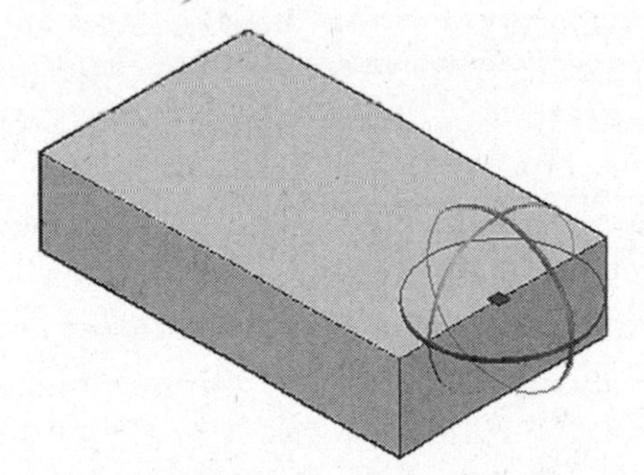

FIGURE 21.70
The Rotate gizmo

3. At the `Specify a base point:` prompt, you can select a point about which the selected objects are to be rotated. The gizmo will move to the point you select.
4. Point to the colored circle that represents the axis of rotation for your objects. A vector appears, representing the axis of rotation. When you're happy with the selected axis, click.
5. At the `Specify angle start point or type an angle:` prompt, you can enter an angle value or click a point. You can use the Shift key or Ortho mode to restrain the direction to 90°.
6. If you click a point in step 5, you will see the `Specify angle end point:` prompt. Enter an angle value or click another point for the rotation angle.

You can also just select one of the circles in step 3 instead of selecting a base point. If you do this, then the selected object begins to rotate. You don't have to select a start and end angle.

Using 3D Mirror

Two other tools, 3D Mirror and 3D Array, are available in the Home tab's Modify panel. They work in a way that's similar to how the standard Mirror and Array tools work, with a slight difference.

3D Mirror begins by asking you to select objects. Then you're asked to specify a mirror plane instead of a mirror axis. You can define a plane using the default three points, or you can use one of the seven other options: `Object/Last/Zaxis/View/XY/YZ/ZX`. By using a plane instead of an axis, you can mirror an object or set of objects anywhere in 3D space. One way to visualize this is to imagine holding a mirror up to your 3D model. The mirror is your 3D plane, and the reflected image is the mirrored version of the object. Imagine tilting the mirror to various angles to get a different mirror image. In the same way, you can tilt the plane in the 3D Mirror tool to mirror an object in any number of ways.

The Bottom Line

Master the User Coordinate System. The User Coordinate System (UCS) is a vital key to editing in 3D space. If you want to master 3D modeling, you should become familiar with this tool.

Master It Name some of the predefined UCS planes.

Understand the UCS options. You can set up the UCS orientation for any situation. It isn't limited to the predefined settings.

Master It Briefly describe some of the ways that you can set up a UCS.

Use viewports to aid in 3D drawing. In some 3D modeling operations, it helps to have several different views of the model through the Viewports feature.

Master It Name some of the predefined standard viewports offered in the Viewports dialog box.

Use the array tools. The array tools—Rectangular, Path, and Polar Array—allow you to create 3D arrays dynamically.

Master It What prompt in the Array command will allow you to have a 3D array?

Create complex 3D surfaces. You aren't limited to straight, flat surfaces in AutoCAD. You can create just about any shape that you want, including curved surfaces.

Master It What tool did you use in this chapter's butterfly chair exercise to convert a surface into a solid?

Create spiral forms. Spiral forms frequently occur in nature, so it's no wonder that we often use spirals in our own designs. Spirals are seen in screws, stairs, and ramps as well as in other man-made forms.

Master It Name the tools used in the example in the section "Creating Spiral Forms," and name two elements that are needed to create a spiral.

Create surface models. You can create a 3D surface by connecting a series of lines that define a surface contour. You can create anything from a 3D landscape to a car fender using this method.

Master It What is the tool used to convert a series of lines into a 3D surface?

Move objects in 3D space. You can move objects in 3D space using tools that are similar to those for 2D drafting. But when it comes to editing objects, 3D modeling is much more complex than 2D drafting.

Master It What does the Rotate gizmo do?

Chapter 22

Editing and Visualizing 3D Solids

In the previous 3D chapters, you spent some time becoming familiar with the AutoCAD® software's 3D modeling features. In this chapter, we'll focus on 3D solids and how they're created and edited. You'll learn how you can use some special visualization tools to show your 3D solid in a variety of ways.

You'll create a fictitious mechanical part to explore ways that you can shape 3D solids. This will also give you a chance to see how you can turn your 3D model into a standard 2D mechanical drawing. In addition, you'll learn about the 3D solid-editing tools that are available through the Solid Editing Ribbon panel.

In this chapter, you will learn to

- Understand solid modeling
- Create solid forms
- Create complex solids
- Edit solids
- Streamline the 2D drawing process
- Visualize solids

Understanding Solid Modeling

Solid modeling is a way of defining 3D objects as solid forms. When you create a 3D model by using solid modeling, you start with the basic forms of your model—boxes, cones, and cylinders, for example. These basic solids are called *primitives*. Then, using more of these primitives, you begin to add to or subtract from your basic forms.

3D Solids Are Not Available in AutoCAD LT

Autodesk® AutoCAD LT® users don't have solid-modeling capabilities. However, you can take advantage of the region objects and their related editing commands described in the sidebar "Using 3D Solid Operations on 2D Drawings" later in this chapter.

For example, to create a model of a tube, you first create two solid cylinders, one smaller in diameter than the other. You then align the two cylinders so that they're concentric and tell

AutoCAD to subtract the smaller cylinder from the larger one. The larger of the two cylinders becomes a tube whose inside diameter is that of the smaller cylinder, as shown in Figure 22.1. Several primitives are available for modeling solids in AutoCAD (see Figure 22.2).

FIGURE 22.1
Creating a tube by using solid modeling

Create two cylinder primitives, one for the outside diameter and one for the inside diameter.

Cylinder for inside diameter

Cylinder for outside diameter

Superimpose the cylinder for the inside diameter onto the cylinder for the outside diameter.

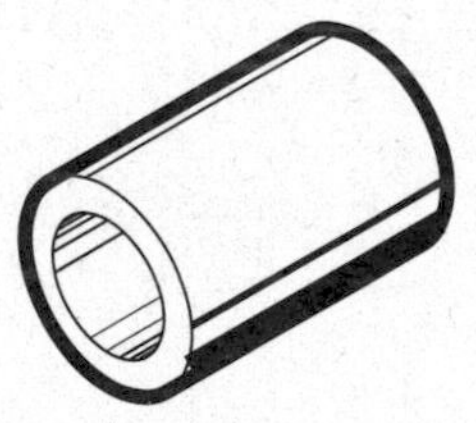

Use the Subtract command to subtract the inside diameter cylinder from the outside diameter cylinder.

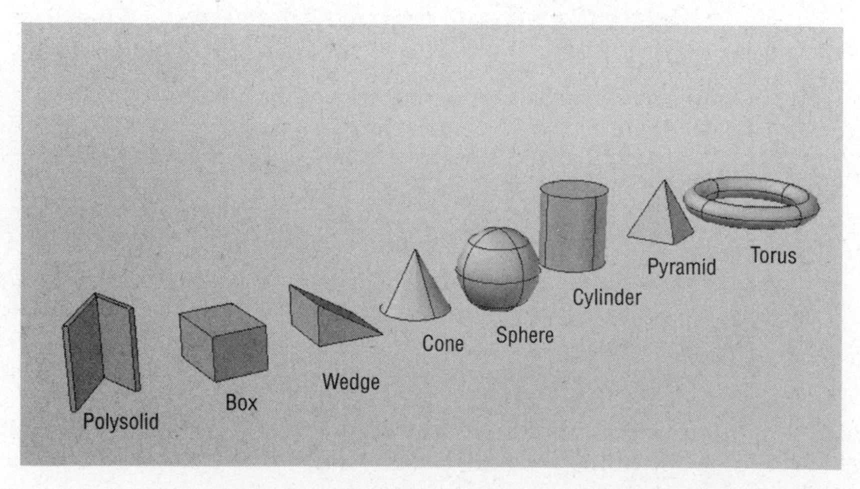

FIGURE 22.2
The solid primitives

You can join these shapes—polysolid, box, wedge, cone, sphere, cylinder, pyramid, and donut (or *torus*)—in one of four ways to produce secondary shapes. The first three, demonstrated in Figure 22.3 using a cube and a cylinder as examples, are called *Boolean operations*. (The name comes from the nineteenth-century mathematician George Boole.)

FIGURE 22.3
The intersection, subtraction, and union of a cube and a cylinder

A solid box and a solid cylinder are superimposed.

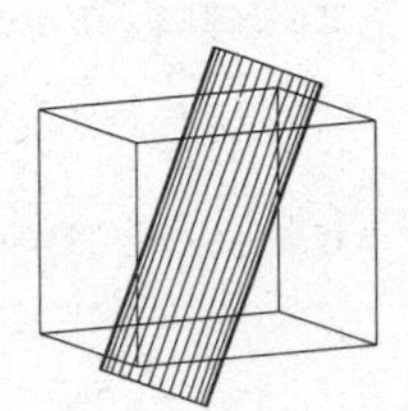

The intersection of the primitives creates a solid cylinder with the ends skewed.

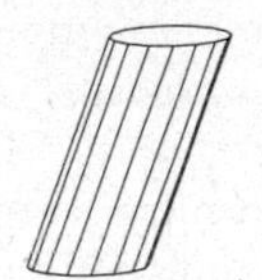

The cylinder subtracted from thc box creates a hole in the box.

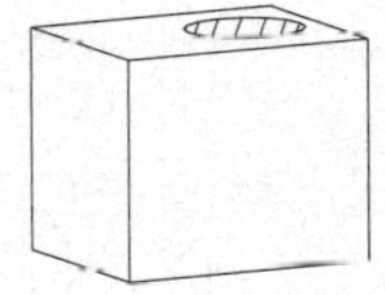

The union of the two primitives creates a box with two round pegs.

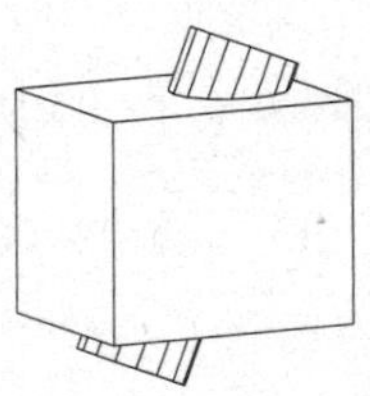

The three Boolean operations are as follows:

Intersection Uses only the intersecting volume of two objects to define a solid shape

Subtraction Uses one object to cut out a shape in another

Union Joins two primitives so that they act as one object

The fourth option, Interfere, lets you find exactly where two or more solids coincide in space—similar to the results of a union. The main difference between interference and union is that interference enables you to keep the original solid shapes, whereas Union discards the original solids, leaving only their combined form. Interfere creates a temporary 3D solid of the coincident space. You can close the command or have AutoCAD create a solid based on the shape created. The selected objects will remain unchanged.

Joined primitives are called *composite solids*. You can join primitives to primitives, composite solids to primitives, and composite solids to other composite solids.

Now let's look at how you can use these concepts to create models in AutoCAD.

> **EXERCISE EXAMPLES ARE "UNITLESS"**
>
> To simplify the exercises in this chapter, the instructions don't specify inches or centimeters. This way, users of both the metric and Imperial measurement systems can use the exercises without having to read through duplicate information.

Creating Solid Forms

In the following sections, you'll begin to draw the object shown later in the chapter in Figure 22.18. In the process, you'll explore the creation of solid models by creating primitives and then setting up special relationships between them.

Primitives are the basic building blocks of solid modeling. At first, it may seem limiting to have only eight primitives with which to work, but consider the varied forms that you can create with just a few 2D objects. Let's begin by creating the basic mass of your steel bracket.

First, prepare your drawing for the exercise:

1. Open the file called bracket.dwg. This file contains some objects that you'll use in the first half of this chapter to build a 3D solid shape.

2. If you aren't already in the 3D Modeling workspace, select 3D Modeling from the Workspace Switching tool or the Workspace drop-down list in the Quick Access toolbar.
3. Close the Materials Browser if it opens with the 3D Modeling workspace.

Joining Primitives

In this section, you'll merge the two box objects. First, you'll move the new box into place. Then, you'll join the two boxes to form a single solid:

1. Start the Move command, pick the smaller of the two boxes, and then press ↵.
2. At the Specify base point or [Displacement] <Displacement>: prompt, use the Midpoint osnap override and pick the middle of the front edge of the smaller box, as shown in the top image in Figure 22.4.
3. At the Specify second point or <use first point as displacement>: prompt, use the Midpoint osnap to pick the middle of the bottom edge of the larger box, as shown in the bottom image in Figure 22.4.

4. Click the Solid, Union tool in the Home tab's Solid Editing panel, or type **UNI**↵.
5. At the Select objects: prompt, pick both boxes and press ↵. Your drawing now looks like Figure 22.5.

As you can see in Figure 22.5, the form has joined to appear as one object. It also acts like one object when you select it. You now have a composite solid made up of two box primitives.

FIGURE 22.4
Moving the smaller box

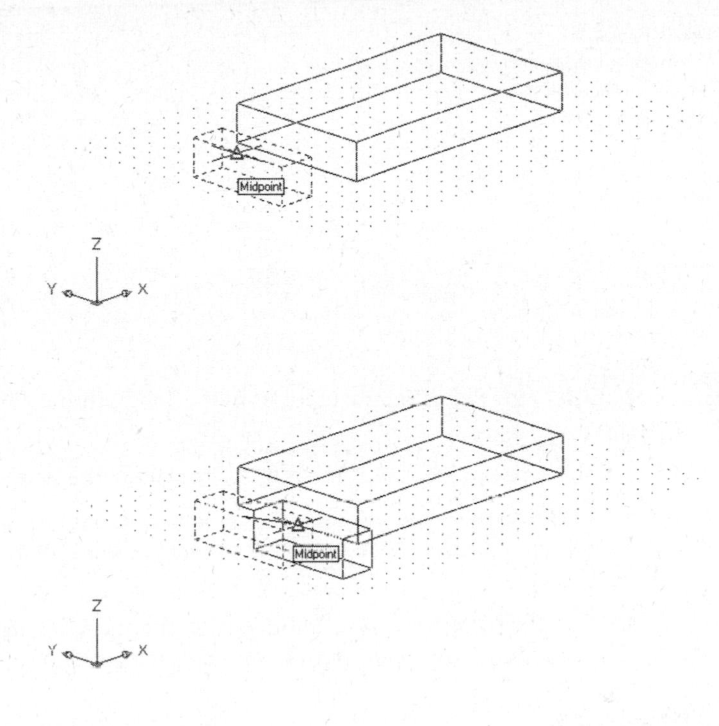

FIGURE 22.5
The two boxes joined

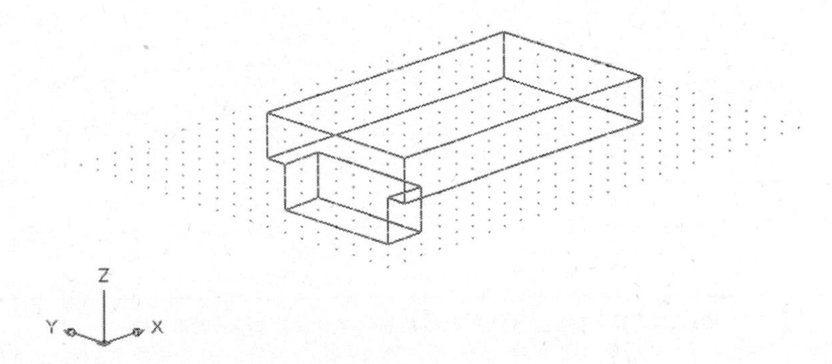

Cutting Portions Out of a Solid

Now let's place some holes in the bracket. In this next exercise, you'll discover how to create negative forms to cut portions out of a solid:

1. Turn on the layer called Cylinder. Two cylinder solids appear in the model, as shown in Figure 22.6. These cylinders are 1.5 units tall.

FIGURE 22.6
The cylinders appear when the Cylinder layer is turned on.

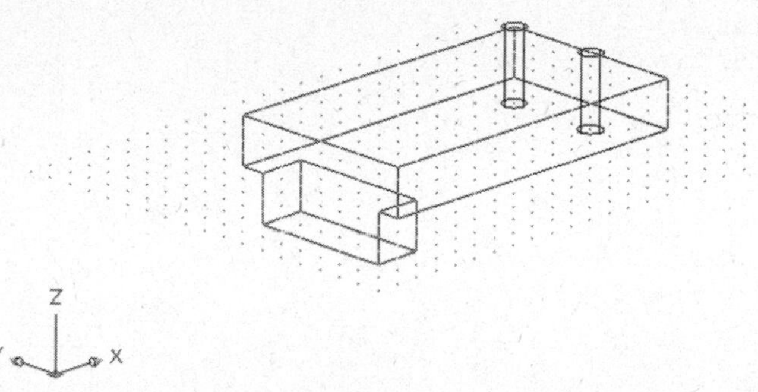

2. Select the Solid, Subtract tool from the Solid Editing panel, or type **SU**↵.
3. At the `Select solids, surfaces and regions to subtract from… Select objects:` prompt, pick the composite solid of the two boxes and press ↵.
4. At the `Select solids, surfaces and regions to subtract... Select objects:` prompt, pick the two cylinders and press ↵. The cylinders are subtracted from the bracket.
5. To view the solid, choose Hidden from the Visual Styles Control in the drawing area. You see a hidden-line view of the solid, as shown in Figure 22.7.

FIGURE 22.7
The bracket so far, with hidden lines removed

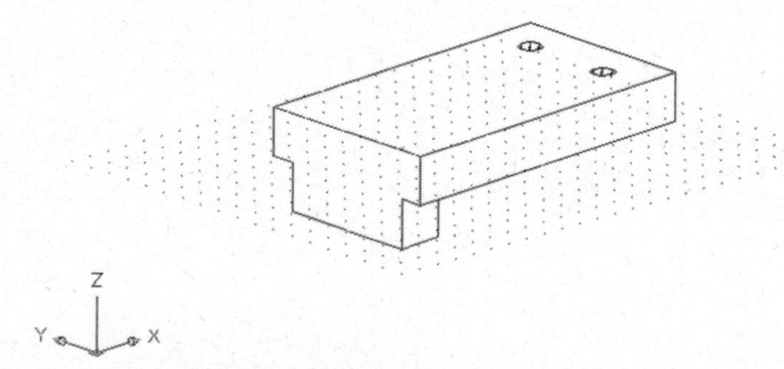

USING 3D SOLID OPERATIONS ON 2D DRAWINGS

You can apply some of the features described in this chapter to 2D drafting by taking advantage of the AutoCAD region object. *Regions* are two-dimensional objects to which you can apply Boolean operations.

The following illustration shows how you can use regions to turn a set of closed polyline shapes quickly into a drawing of a wrench. First, you convert the shapes at the top of the figure into regions using the Region tool on the Draw panel. Next, you align the shapes, as shown in the middle of the image. Finally, you join the circles and rectangle with the Union command (type **UNI**↵); then the hexagonal shapes are subtracted from the combined shape (type **SU**↵). You can use the `Region.dwg` sample file if you'd like to experiment.

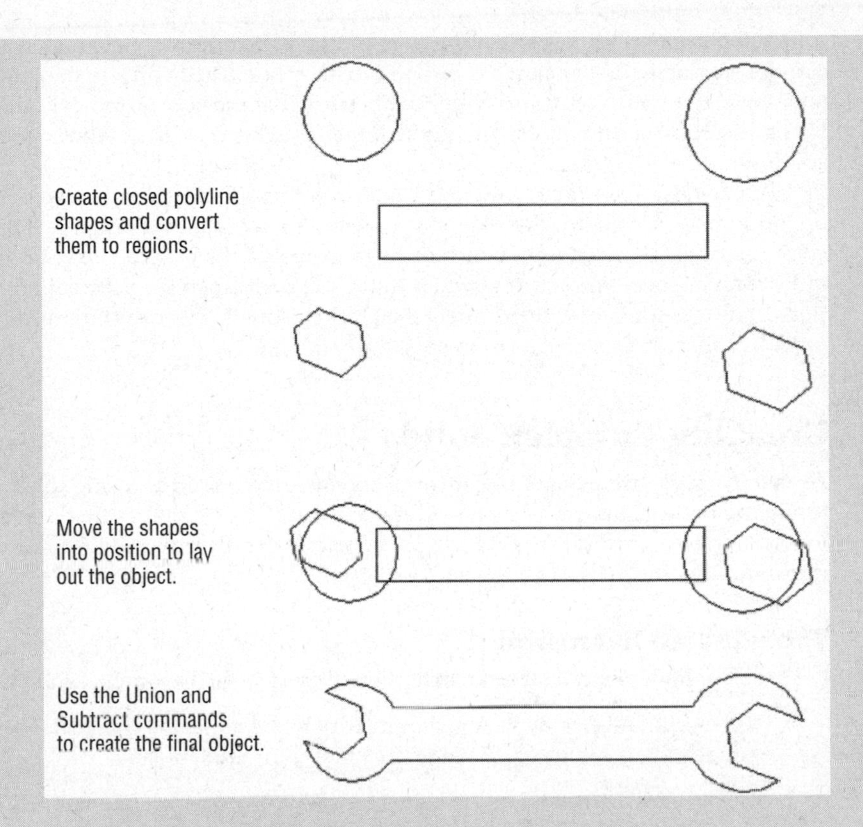

You can use regions to generate complex surfaces that may include holes or unusual bends as in the next image. Keep in mind the following:

- Regions act like surfaces; when you remove hidden lines, objects behind the regions are hidden.
- You can explode regions to edit them. However, exploding a region causes the region to lose its surface-like quality and objects no longer hide behind its surface(s).
- You can Ctrl+click the edge of a region to edit the region's shape.
- You can use the regional model to create complex 2D surfaces for use in 3D surface modeling, as in this image:

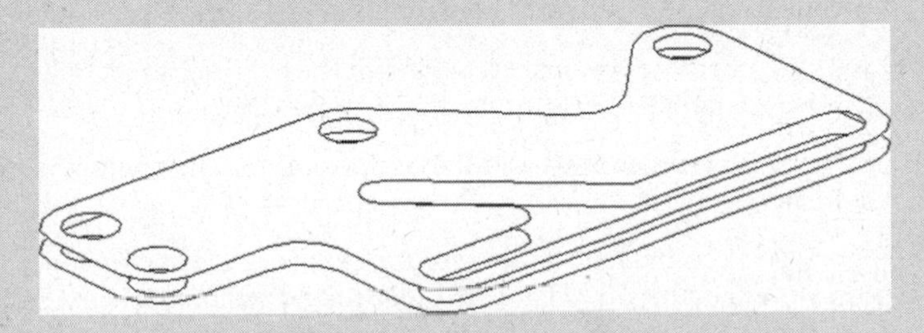

As you learned in the earlier chapters in Part 4, Wireframe views, such as the one in the previous exercise, are somewhat difficult to decipher. Until you use the Hidden visual style (step 5) or the Hide command, you can't be sure that the subtracted cylinders are in fact holes. Using the Hide command frequently will help you keep track of what's going on with your solid model.

You may also have noticed in step 4 that, even though the cylinders were taller than the opening they created, they worked fine to remove part of the rectangular solid. The cylinders were 1.5 units tall, not 1 unit, which is the thickness of the bracket. Having drawn the cylinders taller than needed, you saw that when AutoCAD performed the subtraction, it ignored the portion of the cylinders that didn't affect the bracket. AutoCAD always discards the portion of a primitive that isn't used in a subtract operation.

Creating Complex Solids

As you learned earlier, you can convert a polyline into a solid by using the Extrude tool in the Modeling panel. This process lets you create more complex shapes than the built-in primitives. In addition to the simple straight extrusion that you've already tried, you can extrude shapes into curved paths or you can taper an extrusion.

Tapering an Extrusion

Let's look at how you can taper an extrusion to create a fairly complex solid with little effort:

1. Turn on the Taper layer. A rectangular polyline appears. This rectangle has its corners rounded to a radius of 0.5 using the Fillet command.

2. Click the Extrude tool in the Home tab's Modeling panel, or enter **EXT↵** at the Command prompt.
3. At the `Select objects to extrude or [MOde]:` prompt, pick the polyline that you just turned on from the Taper layer and press ↵. If you have Selection Cycling on, pick the polyline option from the list that appears.
4. At the `Specify height of extrusion or [Direction/Path/Taper angle/Expression]:` prompt, enter **T↵**.
5. At the `Specify angle of taper for extrusion or [Expression] <0>:` prompt, enter **4↵**.
6. At the `Specify height of extrusion or [Direction/Path/Taper angle/Expression]:` prompt, enter **3↵**. The extruded polyline looks like Figure 22.8.
7. Join the part that you just created with the original solid. Select the Solid, Union tool from the Home tab's Solid Editing panel or type **UNI↵**.
8. Select the extruded part and the composite solid just below it. Press ↵ to complete your selection.

In step 5, you can indicate a taper for the extrusion. Specify a taper in terms of degrees from the z-axis, or enter a negative value to taper the extrusion outward. You can also press ↵ to accept the default of 0 to extrude the polyline without a taper.

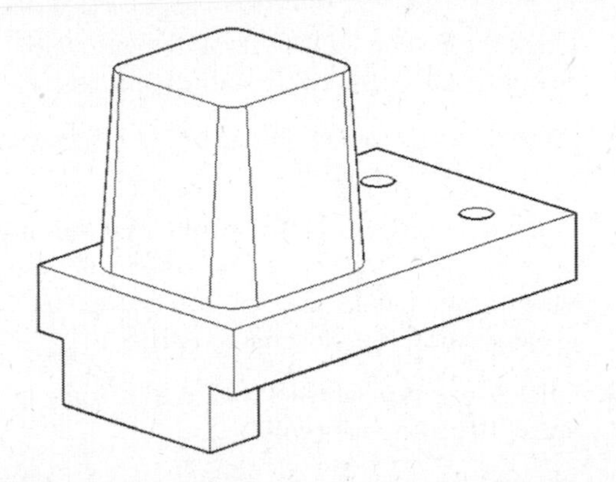

FIGURE 22.8
The extruded polyline

THE *ISOLINES* SYSTEM VARIABLE

You may have noticed the message that reads as follows:

Current wire frame density: ISOLINES=4

This message tells you the current setting for the `Isolines` system variable. This variable controls the way that curved objects, such as cylinders and holes, are displayed. A setting of 4 causes a cylinder to be represented by four lines with a circle at each end. You can see this in the holes that you created for the Bracket model in the previous exercise. You can change the `Isolines` setting by entering **Isolines**↵ at the Command prompt. You then enter a value for the number of lines to use to represent surfaces. This setting is also controlled by the Contour Lines Per Surface option in the Display tab of the Options dialog box.

Sweeping a Shape on a Curved Path

As you'll see in the following exercise, the Sweep command lets you extrude virtually any polyline shape along a path defined by a polyline, an arc, or a 3D polyline. At this point, you've created the components needed to do the extrusion. Next, you'll finish the extruded shape:

1. Turn on the Path layer. This layer contains the circle that you'll extrude and the polyline path, which looks like an *S*, as shown in Figure 22.9.

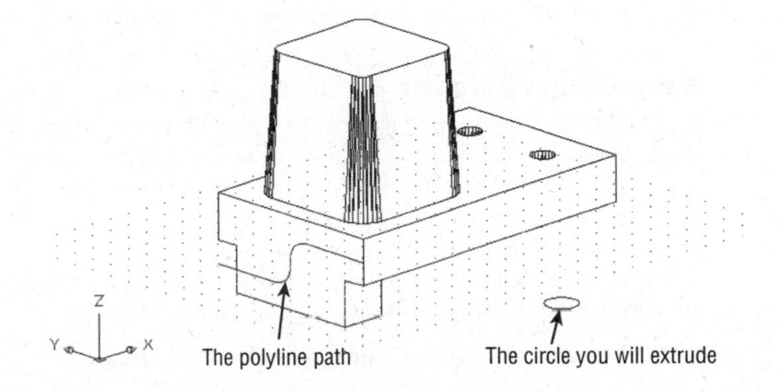

FIGURE 22.9
Hidden-line view showing parts of the drawing that you'll use to create a curved extrusion

2. Click the Sweep tool from the Extrude flyout in the Home tab's Modeling panel, or type **Sweep**↵. Click the circle, and then press ↵.
3. At the `Select sweep path or [Alignment/Base point/Scale/Twist]:` prompt, click the polyline curve.
4. AutoCAD generates a solid tube that follows the path. The tube may not look like a tube because AutoCAD draws extruded solids such as this with four lines while using the wireframe visual style. You can change the number of lines shown with the `Isolines` system variable as discussed earlier.

5. Click the Solid, Subtract tool in the Home tab's Solid Editing panel or type **SU**↵ and then select the composite solid.
6. Press ↵. At the `Select objects:` prompt, click the curved solid and press ↵. The curved solid is subtracted from the square solid, and your drawing looks like Figure 22.10.

FIGURE 22.10
The solid after subtracting the curve

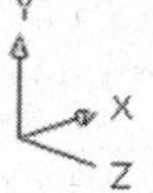

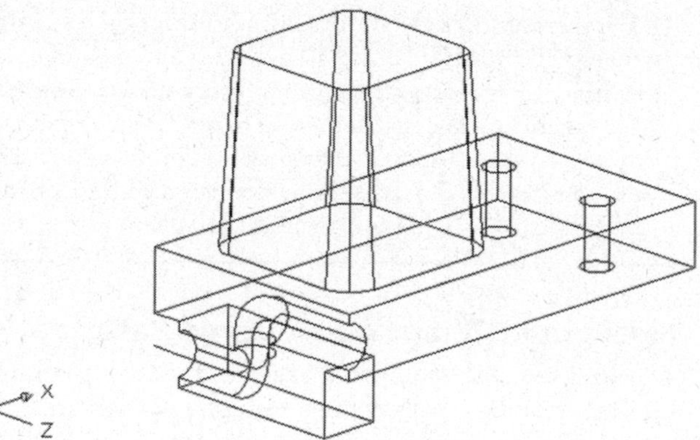

In this exercise, you used a curved polyline for the extrusion path, but you can use any type of 2D or 3D polyline, as well as a line or arc, for an extrusion path.

Revolving a Polyline

When your goal is to draw a circular object, you can use the Revolve command on the Modeling panel to create a solid that is *revolved*, or swept in a circular path. Think of Revolve's action as being similar to a lathe that lets you carve a shape from an object on a spinning shaft. In this case, the object is a polyline and, rather than carve it, you define the profile and then revolve the profile around an axis.

In the following exercise, you'll draw a solid that will form a slot in the tapered solid. We've already created a 2D polyline that is the profile of the slot.

1. In the Visual Styles Control, select 2D Wireframe.
2. Zoom in to the top of the tapered box so that you have a view similar to Figure 22.11.

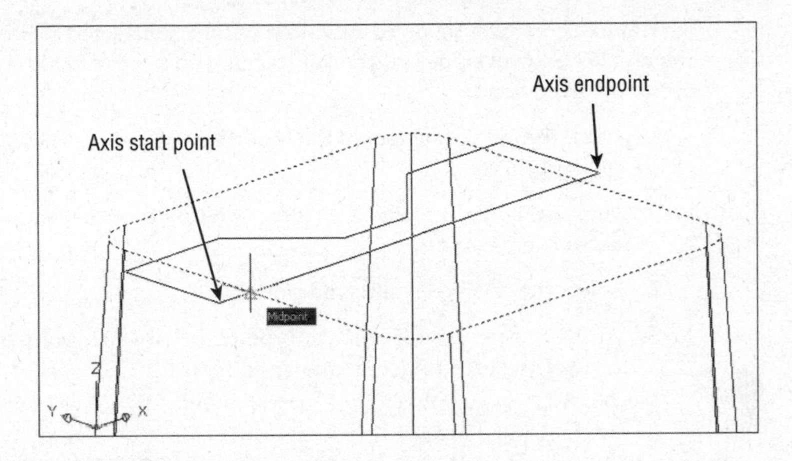

FIGURE 22.11
An enlarged view of the top of the tapered box and pasted polyline

3. Turn on the Revolve layer. This layer contains a closed polyline that you'll use to create a cylindrical shape.

4. Select the Revolve tool from the Extrude flyout in the Home tab's Modeling panel, or type **REV**↵ at the Command prompt.
5. At the `Select objects to revolve or [MOde]:` prompt, pick the polyline on the top of the tapered surface and press ↵.
6. When you see the prompt

   `Specify axis start point or define axis by [Object/X/Y/Z] <Object>:`

   use the Endpoint osnap override and pick the beginning corner endpoint of the polyline that you just added, as shown in Figure 22.11.
7. At the `Specify axis endpoint:` prompt, pick the axis endpoint indicated in Figure 22.11.
8. At the `Specify angle of revolution or [STart angle/Reverse/EXpression] <360>:` prompt, press ↵ to sweep the polyline a full 360°. The revolved form appears as shown in Figure 22.12.

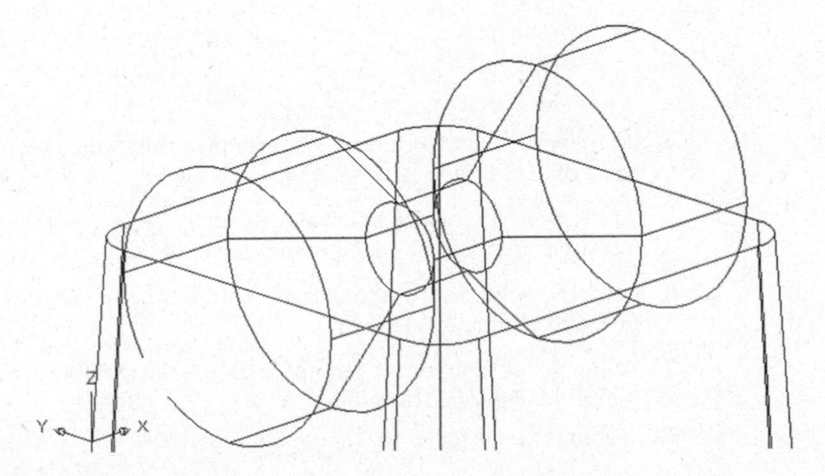

FIGURE 22.12
The revolved polyline

You just created a revolved solid that will be subtracted from the tapered box to form a slot in the bracket. However, before you subtract it, you need to make a slight change in the orientation of the revolved solid:

1. Click the 3D Rotate tool in the Modify panel, or type **3drotate**↵. You see the following prompt:

```
Current positive angle in UCS: ANGDIR=counterclockwise ANGBASE=0
Select objects:
```

2. Select the revolved solid, and press ↵.
3. At the `Specify base point:` prompt, use the Midpoint osnap and click the right side edge of the top surface, as shown in Figure 22.13.

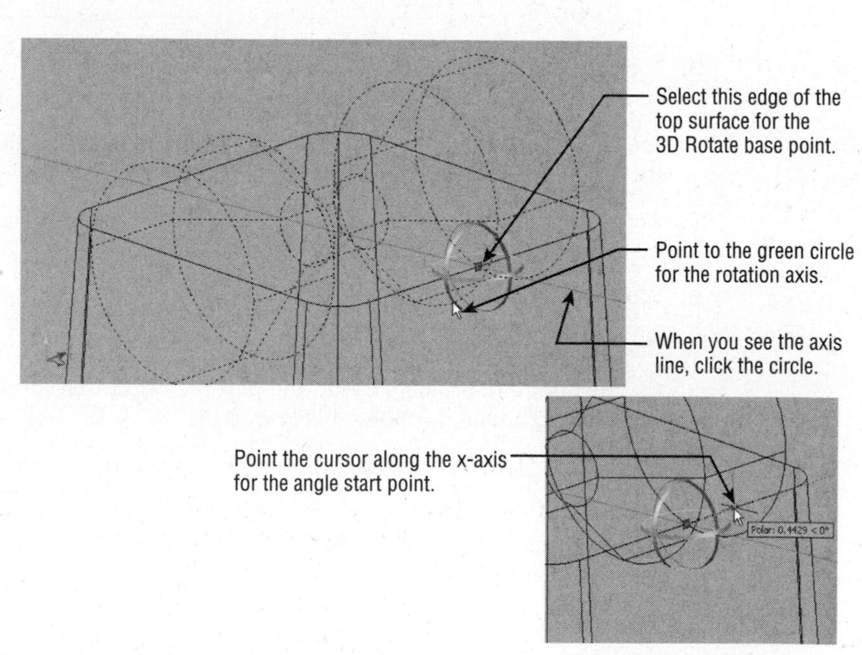

FIGURE 22.13 Selecting the points to rotate the revolved solid in 3D space

4. At the `Pick a rotation axis:` prompt, point to the green rotation grip tool. When you see a green line appear along the y-axis, click.
5. At the `Specify angle start point or type an angle:` prompt, enter **−5**↵ for a minus 5 degrees rotation. The solid rotates 5° about the y-axis.

6. Click the Solid, Subtract tool in the Solid Editing panel, or type **SU**↵. Click the tapered box, and then press ↵.
7. At the `Select objects:` prompt, click the revolved solid and press ↵. Your drawing looks like Figure 22.14.

FIGURE 22.14
The composite solid

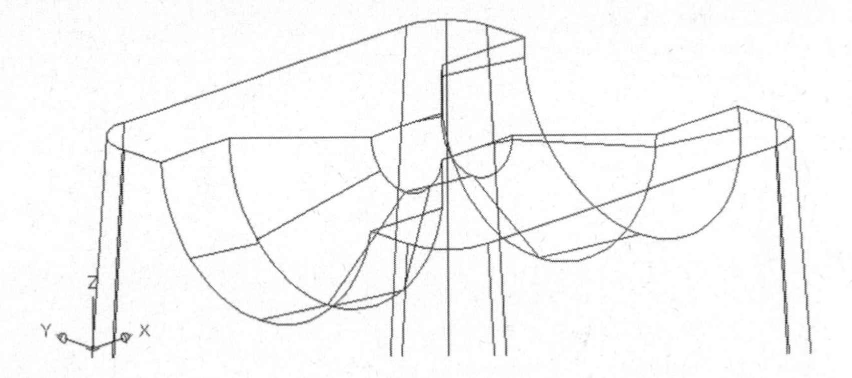

Editing Solids

Basic solid forms are fairly easy to create. Refining those forms requires some special tools. In the following sections, you'll learn how to use familiar 2D editing tools, as well as some new tools, to edit a solid. But first you'll be shown the Slice tool, which lets you cut a solid into two pieces.

Splitting a Solid into Two Pieces

One of the more common solid-editing tools that you'll use is the Slice tool. As you may guess from its name, Slice enables you to cut a solid into two pieces. The following exercise demonstrates how it works:

1. Click the Zoom All option to get an overall view of your work so far.

2. Click the Slice tool in the Home tab's Solid Editing panel, or type **Slice**↵.
3. At the `Select objects to slice:` prompt, click the part on which you've been working and press ↵.

   Alternatively, you could select more than one solid. The Slice command would then slice all of the solids through the plane that you'll indicate in steps 4 and 5.
4. At the prompt

   ```
   Specify start point of slicing plane or
   [planar Object/Surface/Zaxis/View/XY/YZ/ZX/
   3points] :
   ```

   type **XY**↵. This lets you indicate a slice plane parallel to the XY plane.
5. At the `Specify a point on the XY-plane <0,0,0>:` prompt, type **0,0,0.5**↵. This places the slice plane at the z-coordinate of 0.5 units. You can also use the Midpoint osnap and pick any vertical edge of the rectangular base of the solid. If you want to delete one side of the sliced solid, you can indicate the side that you want to keep by clicking it in step 6 instead of entering **B**↵.
6. At the `Specify a point on desired side or [keep Both sides]<Both>:` prompt, type **B**↵ to keep both sides of the solid. AutoCAD divides the solid horizontally, one-half unit above the base of the part, as shown in Figure 22.15.

FIGURE 22.15
The solid sliced through the base

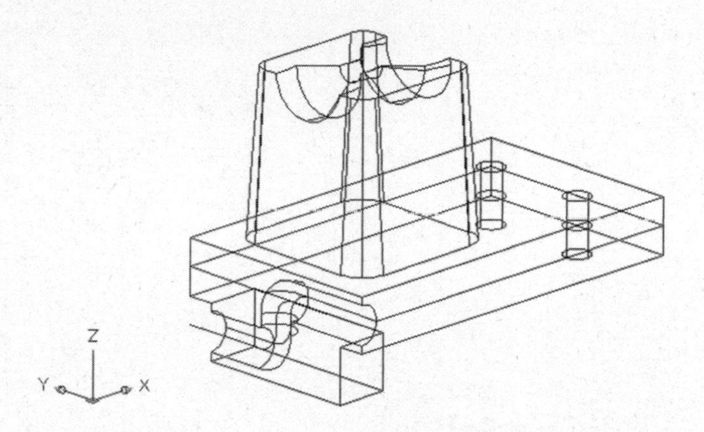

In step 4, you saw a number of options for the Slice command. You may want to take note of those options for future reference. Table 22.1 provides a list of the options and their purposes.

TABLE 22.1: Slice command options

OPTION	PURPOSE
`planar Object`	Lets you select an object to define the slice plane.
`Surface`	Lets you select a surface object to define the shape of a slice.
`Zaxis`	Lets you select two points defining the z-axis of the slice plane. The two points that you pick are perpendicular to the slice plane.
`View`	Generates a slice plane that is perpendicular to your current view. You're prompted for the coordinate through which the slice plane must pass—usually a point on the object.
`XY/YZ/ZX`	Pick one of these to determine the slice plane based on the x-, y-, or z-axis. You're prompted to pick a point through which the slice plane must pass.
`3points`	The default setting; lets you select three points defining the slice plane. Normally, you pick points on the solid.

Rounding Corners with the Fillet Tool

Your bracket has a few sharp corners that you may want to round in order to give it a more realistic appearance. You can use the Modify panel's Fillet and Chamfer tools to add these rounded corners to your solid model:

1. Click the Fillet tool in the Home tab's Modify panel or type **F**↵.
2. At the `Select first object or [Undo/Polyline/Radius/Trim/Multiple]:` prompt, pick the edge indicated in the first image in Figure 22.16.

3. At the `Enter fillet radius or [Expression] <0.5000>:` prompt, type **0.2**↵.
4. At the `Select an edge or [Chain/Loop/Radius]:` prompt, type **C**↵ for the Chain option. Chain lets you select a series of solid edges to be filleted.
5. Select one of the other seven edges at the base of the tapered form and press ↵.
6. Type **Hide**↵ to get a quick look at your model in a hidden line view, as shown in the second image in Figure 22.16.

FIGURE 22.16
Filleting solids

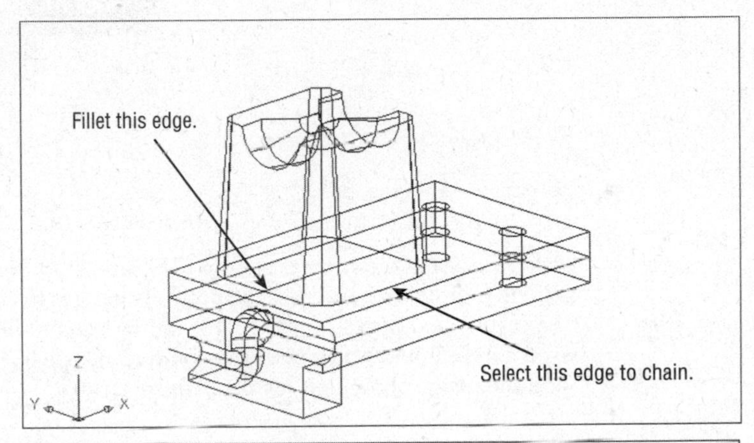

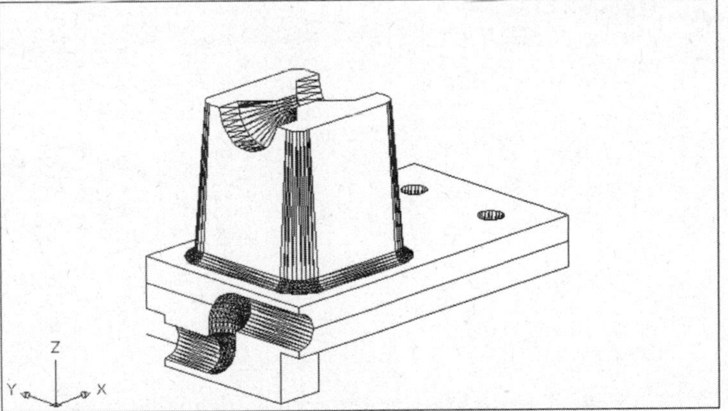

As you saw in step 4, Fillet acts a bit differently when you use it on solids. The Chain option lets you select a set of edges instead of just two adjoining objects.

Chamfering Corners with the Chamfer Tool

Now let's try chamfering a corner. To practice using Chamfer, you'll add a countersink to the cylindrical holes that you created in the first solid:

1. Type **Regen**↵ to return to a Wireframe view of your model.

2. Click the Chamfer tool on the Modify panel (click the Fillet flyout if you don't see Chamfer; see Figure 22.17) or type **CHA**↵.

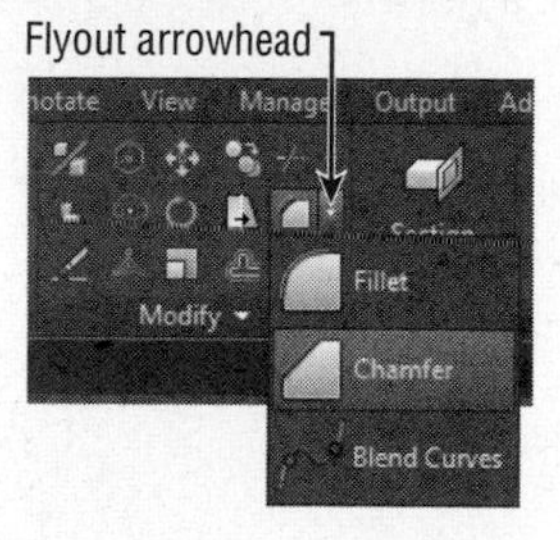

FIGURE 22.17
Click the Chamfer tool.

3. At the prompt

   `Select first line or`
   `[Undo/Polyline/Distance/Angle/Trim/mEthod/Multiple]:`

   pick the edge of the hole, as shown in Figure 22.18. Notice that the top surface of the solid is highlighted and that the prompt changes to `Enter surface selection option [Next/OK (current)] <OK>:`. The highlighting indicates the base surface, which will be used as a reference in step 5. (You could also type **N**↵ to choose the other adjoining surface, the inside of the hole, as the base surface.)

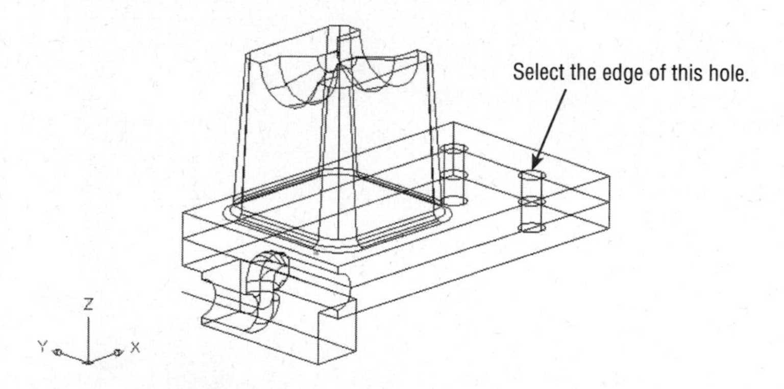

FIGURE 22.18
Picking the edge to chamfer

4. Press ↵ to accept the current highlighted face.
5. At the `Specify base surface chamfer distance or [Expression] <0.1250>:` prompt, type **0.125**↵. This indicates that you want the chamfer to have a width of 0.125 across the highlighted surface.
6. At the `Specify other surface chamfer distance or [Expression] <0.2000>:` prompt, type **0.2**↵.
7. At the `Select an edge or [Loop]:` prompt, click the top edges of both holes and then press ↵. When the Chamfer command has completed its work, your drawing looks like Figure 22.19.

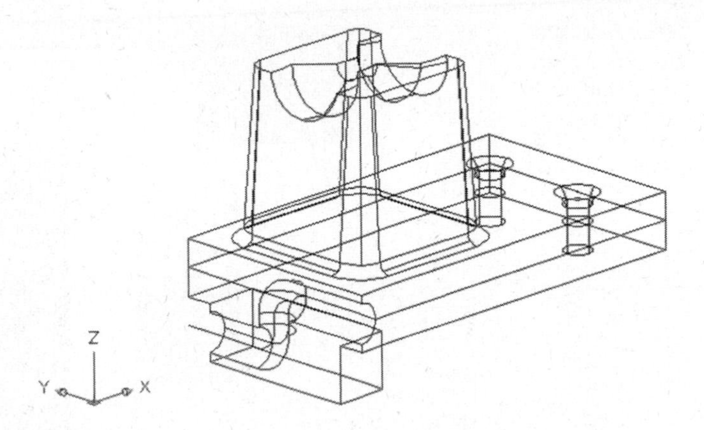

FIGURE 22.19
The chamfered edges

8. After reviewing the work you've done here, save the `bracket.dwg` file.

The Loop option in step 7 lets you chamfer the entire circumference of an object. You don't need to use it here because the edge forms a circle. The Loop option is used when you have a rectangular or other polygonal edge that you want to chamfer.

Using the Solid-Editing Tools

You've added some refinements to the Bracket model by using standard AutoCAD editing tools. There is a set of tools that is specifically geared toward editing solids. You already used the Union and Subtract tools found in the Solid Editing panel. In the following sections, you'll explore some of the other tools in that panel.

You don't have to perform the following exercises, but reviewing them will show you what's available. When you're more comfortable working in 3D, you may want to come back and experiment with the file called `solidedit.dwg`, which is shown in the figures in the following sections.

PARALLEL PROJECTION NEEDED FOR SOME FEATURES

Many of the features discussed in these sections work only in a parallel-projection view. You can switch to a parallel-projection view by choosing the 2D Wireframe visual style or, if you have the ViewCube® turned on, right-click it and select Parallel.

FINDING TOOLS IN THE SOLID EDITING PANEL

Many of the tools in the Solid Editing panel are in flyouts. This makes it a bit difficult to describe their location because the default tool changes depending on the last flyout tool that was selected. To help you easily find the tools described in these sections, Figure 22.20 shows the flyouts in their open position with each tool labeled. You can use this figure for reference when you are ready to use a tool.

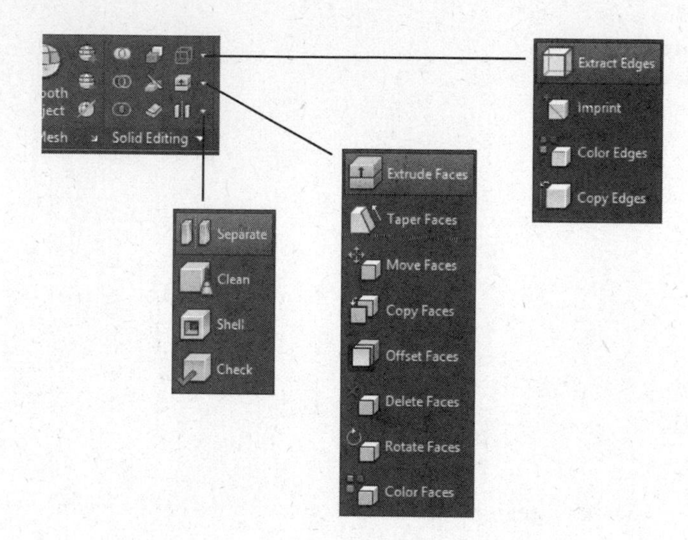

FIGURE 22.20
The flyouts in the Home tab's Solid Editing panel

MOVING A SURFACE

You can move any flat surface of a 3D solid using the Move Faces tool from the Faces flyout on the Solid Editing panel. When you click this tool, you're prompted to select faces. Because you can select only the edge of two joining faces, you must select an edge and then use the Remove option to remove one of the two selected faces from the selection set (see Figure 22.21). After you've made your selection, press ↵. You can then specify a distance for the move.

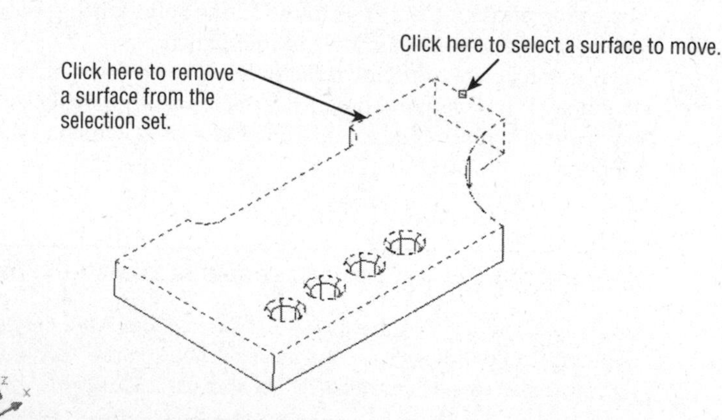

FIGURE 22.21
To select the vertical surface to the far right of the model, click the edge and then use the Remove option to remove the top surface from the selection.

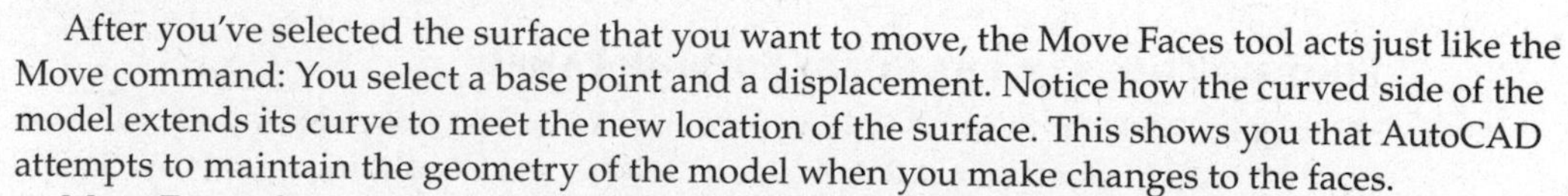

After you've selected the surface that you want to move, the Move Faces tool acts just like the Move command: You select a base point and a displacement. Notice how the curved side of the model extends its curve to meet the new location of the surface. This shows you that AutoCAD attempts to maintain the geometry of the model when you make changes to the faces.

Move Faces also lets you move entire features, such as the hole in the model. In Figure 22.22, one of the holes has been moved so that it's no longer in line with the other three. This was done by selecting the countersink and the hole while using the Move Faces tool.

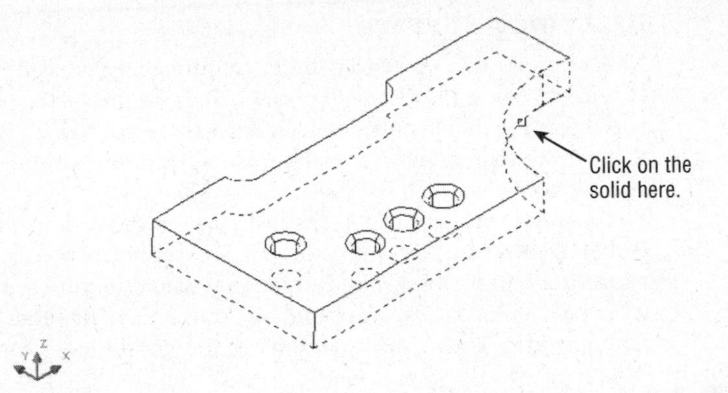

FIGURE 22.22
Selecting a surface to offset

If a solid's History setting is set to record, you can Ctrl+click its surface to expose the surface's grip. (Recording the history of a solid is turned on by selecting the solid, then in the Properties palette, go to the Solid History section at the bottom, and set the History option to Record.) You can then use the grip at the center of the surface to move the surface.

OFFSETTING A SURFACE

Suppose that you want to decrease the radius of the arc in the right corner of the model, and you also want to thicken the model by the same amount as the decrease in the arc radius. To do this, you can use the Offset Faces tool. The Offset Faces tool and the Offset command you used earlier in this book perform similar functions. The difference is that the Offset Faces tool in the Faces flyout on the Solid Editing panel affects 3D solids.

When you select the Offset Faces tool from the Faces flyout on the Solid Editing panel, you're prompted to select faces. As with the Move tool, you must select an edge that will select two faces. If you want to offset only one face, you must use the Remove option to remove one of the faces. In Figure 22.22 earlier, an edge is selected. Figure 22.23 shows the effect of the Offset Faces tool when both faces are offset.

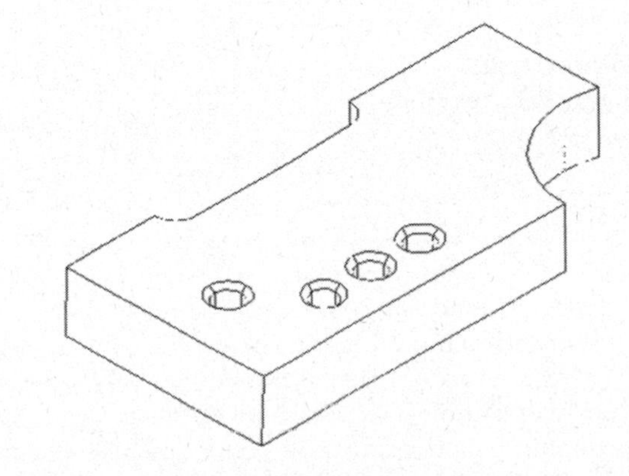

FIGURE 22.23
The model after offsetting the curved and bottom surfaces

Deleting a Surface

Now suppose that you've decided to eliminate the curved part of the model. You can delete a surface by using the Delete Faces tool. Once again, you're prompted to select faces. Typically, you'll want to delete only one face, such as the curved surface in the example model. If you select more than one face to delete, use the remove option in the command to remove faces from your selection set.

When you attempt to delete surfaces, keep in mind that the surface you delete must be recoverable by other surfaces in the model. For example, you can't remove the top surface of a cube, expecting it to turn into a pyramid. That would require the sides to change their orientation, which isn't allowed in this operation. You can, on the other hand, remove the top of a box with tapered sides. Then, when you remove the top, the sides converge to form a pyramid.

Rotating a Surface

All of the surfaces of the model are parallel or perpendicular to each other. Imagine that your design requires two sides to be at an angle. You can change the angle of a surface by using the Rotate Faces tool.

As with the prior solid-editing tools, you're prompted to select faces. You must then specify an axis of rotation. You can either select a point or use the default of selecting two points to define an axis of rotation, as shown in Figure 22.24. Once the axis is determined, you can specify a rotation angle. Figure 22.25 shows the result of rotating the two front-facing surfaces 4°.

Figure 22.24
Defining the axis of rotation

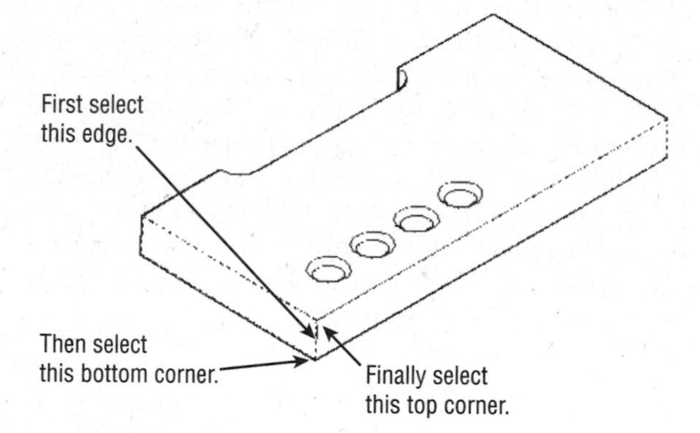

Figure 22.25
The model after rotating two surfaces

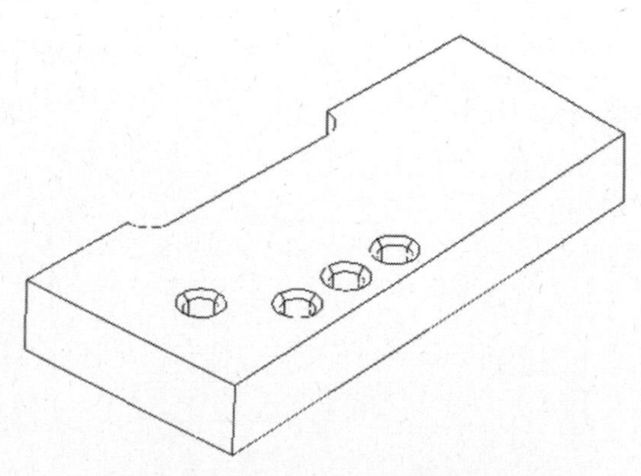

Tapering a Surface

In an earlier exercise, you saw how to create a new tapered solid by using the Extrude command. But what if you want to taper an existing solid? Here's what you can do.

The Taper Faces tool from the Faces flyout on the Solid Editing panel prompts you to select faces. You can select faces, as described for the previously discussed solid-editing tools, using the Remove or Add option (see Figure 22.26). Make sure the top face has been removed from the selection set. Press ↵ when you finish your selection, and then indicate the axis from which the taper is to occur. In the model example in Figure 22.26, select two corners defining a vertical axis. Finally, enter the taper angle. Figure 22.27 shows the model tapered at a 4° angle.

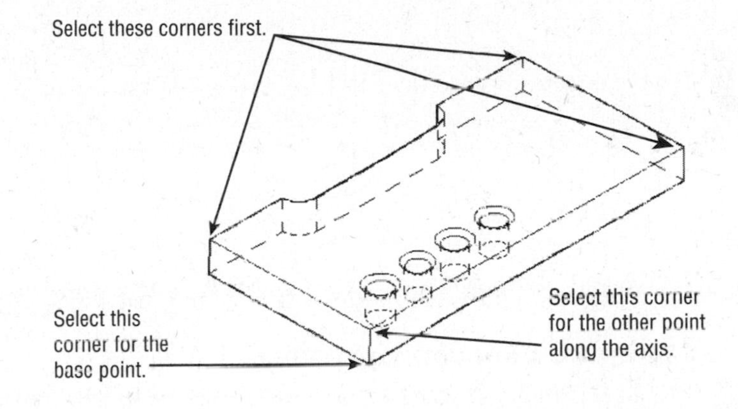

Figure 22.26
Selecting the surfaces to taper and indicating the direction of the taper

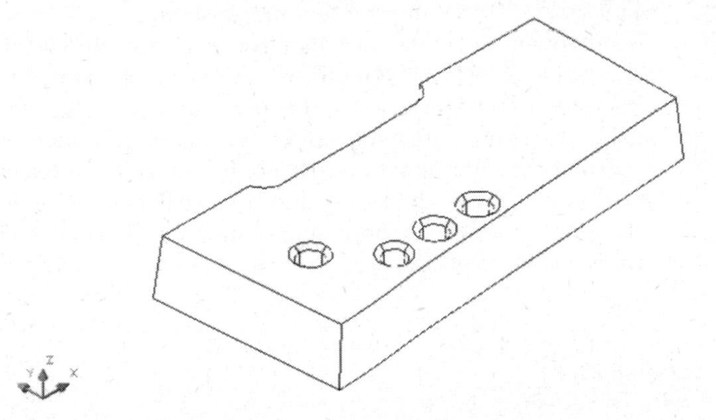

Figure 22.27
The model after tapering the sides

Extruding a Surface

You've used the Extrude tool to create two of the solids in the Bracket model. The Extrude tool requires a closed polyline as a basis for the extrusion. As an alternative, the Solid Editing panel offers the Extrude Faces tool, which extrudes a surface of an existing solid.

When you select the Extrude Faces tool from the Faces flyout on the Solid Editing panel or type **Solidedit↵F↵E↵**, you see the `Select faces or [Undo/Remove]:` prompt. Select an edge or a set of edges or use the Remove or Add option to select the faces that you want to extrude. Press ↵ when you've finished your selection, and then specify a height and taper angle. Figure 22.28 shows the sample model with the front surface extruded and tapered at a 45° angle. You can extrude multiple surfaces simultaneously if you need to by selecting them.

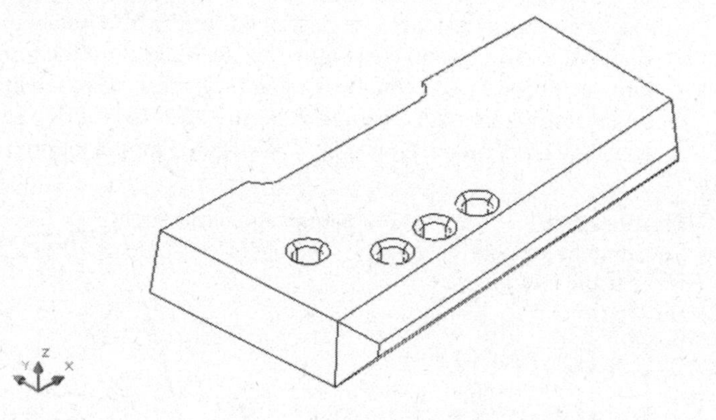

FIGURE 22.28
The model with a surface extruded and tapered

Aside from those features, the Extrude Faces tool works just like the Extrude command.

TURNING A SOLID INTO A SHELL

In many situations, you'll want your 3D model to be a hollow mass rather than a solid mass. The Shell tool lets you convert a solid into a shell.

When you select the Shell tool from the Separate/Clean/Shell/Check flyout on the Solid Editing panel or type **Solidedit↵B↵S↵**, you're prompted to select a 3D solid. You're then prompted to remove faces. At this point, you can select an edge of the solid to indicate the surface that you want removed. The surface you select is completely removed from the model, exposing the interior of the shell. For example, if you select the front edge of the sample model shown in Figure 22.29, the top and front surfaces are removed from the model, revealing the interior of the solid, as shown in Figure 22.30. After selecting the surfaces to remove, you must enter a shell offset distance.

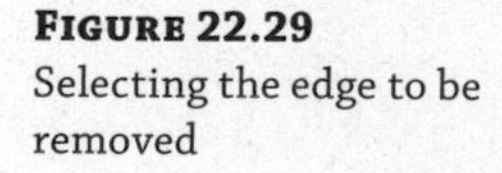

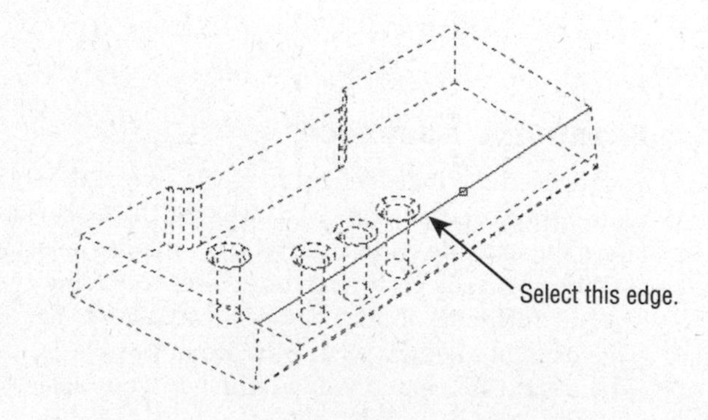

FIGURE 22.29
Selecting the edge to be removed

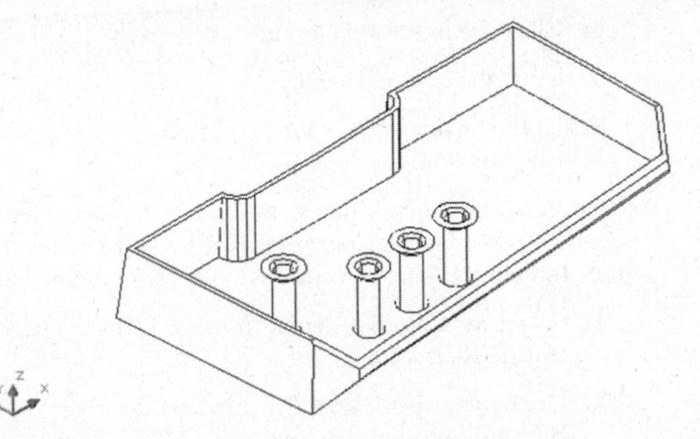

FIGURE 22.30
The solid model after using the Shell tool

The shell thickness is added to the outside surface of the solid. When you're constructing your solid with the intention of creating a shell, you need to take this into account.

COPYING FACES AND EDGES

At times, you may want to create a copy of a surface of a solid to analyze its area or to produce another part that mates to that surface. The Copy Faces tool (found in the Extrude Faces flyout) creates a copy of any surface on your model. The copy it produces is a type of object called a *region*.

The copies of the surfaces are opaque and can hide objects behind them when you perform a hidden-line removal (type **Hide**↵).

Another tool that is similar to Copy Faces is Copy Edges (found in the Extract Edges flyout). Instead of selecting surfaces as in the Copy Faces tool, you select all the edges that you want to copy. The result is a series of simple lines representing the edges of your model. This tool can be useful if you want to convert a solid into a set of 3D faces. The Copy Edges tool creates a framework onto which you can add 3D faces.

ADDING SURFACE FEATURES

If you need to add a feature to a flat surface, you can do so with the Imprint tool. An added surface feature can then be colored using the Color Faces tool or extruded using the Presspull tool. This feature is a little more complicated than some of the other solid-editing tools, so you may want to try the following exercise to see firsthand how it works.

You'll start by inserting an object that will be the source of the imprint. You'll then imprint the main solid model with the object's profile:

1. Back in the saved `bracket.dwg`, click the Insert tool in the Insert tab's Block panel; then click More Options to open the Insert dialog box, or type **I**↵.
2. Click Browse, and then locate the `imprint.dwg` sample file and select it.
3. In the Insert dialog box, make sure that the Explode check box is selected and remove the check mark from the Specify On-Screen check box in the Insertion Point group.
4. Click OK. The block appears in the middle of the solid.

5. Select the Imprint tool from the Edges flyout on the Home tab's Solid Editing panel or type **Imprint**↵.

6. Click the main solid model.
7. Click the inserted solid.
8. At the `Delete the source object [Yes/No]<N>:` prompt, enter **Y↵↵**. Press Esc to clear the selection.

You now have an outline of the intersection between the two solids imprinted on the top surface of your model. The imprint is really a set of edges that have been added to the surface of the solid. To help the imprint stand out, try the following steps to change its color:

1. Select the Color Faces tool from the Faces flyout on the Solid Editing panel, or type **Solidedit↵F↵L↵**.
2. Click the imprint from the previous exercise. The imprint and the entire top surface are highlighted.
3. At the `Select faces or [Undo/Remove/ALL]:` prompt, type **R↵**; then click the outer edge of the top surface to remove it from the selection set.
4. Press ↵ to open the Select Color dialog box.
5. Click the red color sample in the dialog box, and then click OK. The imprint is now red.
6. Press ↵ twice to exit the command.
7. To see the full effect of the Color Faces tool, choose the Conceptual or Realistic visual style from the Visual Styles Control in the drawing screen.

If you want to remove an imprint from a surface, Ctrl+click each imprint face and line and press the Delete key. Repeat the process until all imprint items are removed.

Separating a Divided Solid

While editing solids, you can end up with two separate solid forms that were created from one solid, as shown in Figure 22.31. Even though the two solids appear separated, they act like a single object. In these situations, AutoCAD offers the Separate tool from the Separate/Clean/Shell/Check flyout on the Solid Editing panel. To use it, click the Separate tool or type **Solidedit↵B↵P↵** and select the solid that has been separated into two forms.

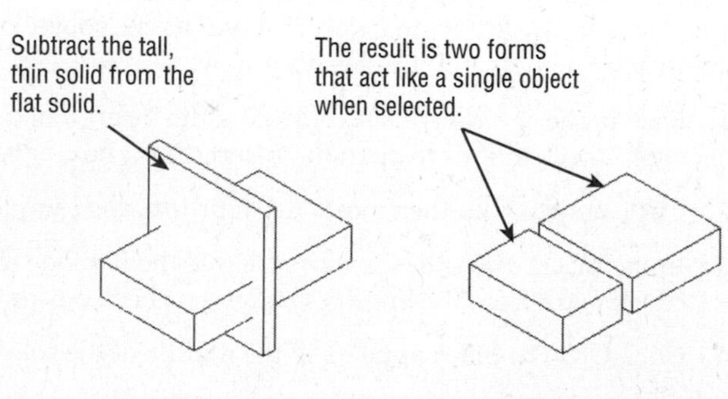

FIGURE 22.31
When the tall, thin solid is subtracted from the larger solid, the result is two separate forms, yet they still behave as a single object.

Figure 22.31 is included in the sample files under the name `Separate example.dwg`. You can try the Separate tool in this file on your own.

Through some simple examples, you've seen how each of the solid-editing tools works. You aren't limited to using these tools in the way that they were demonstrated in this chapter, and this book can't anticipate every situation that you might encounter as you create solid models. These examples are intended as an introduction to these tools, so feel free to experiment with them. You can always use the Undo option to backtrack in case you don't get the results that you expect.

This concludes your tour of the Solid Editing panel. Next, you'll learn how to use 3D solid models to generate 2D working drawings quickly.

Finding the Properties of a Solid

All this effort to create a solid model isn't designed just to create a pretty picture. After your model is drawn and built, you can obtain information about its physical properties.

You can find the volume, the moment of inertia, and other physical properties of your model by using the Massprop command. These properties can also be recorded as a file on disk, so you can modify your model without worrying about losing track of its original properties.

To find the mass properties of a solid, enter **Massprop↵**, and then follow the prompts. AutoCAD LT users can use the Massprop command described here to find the properties of solids that are part of an existing drawing.

Using the Command Line for Solid Editing

The solid-editing tools are options of a single AutoCAD command called Solidedit. If you prefer to use the keyboard, here are some tips on using the Solidedit command. When you first enter **Solidedit↵** at the Command prompt, you see the following prompt:

```
Enter a solids editing option [Face/Edge/Body/Undo/eXit] :
```

You can select the `Face`, `Edge`, or `Body` option to edit the various parts of a solid. If you select `Face`, you see the following prompt:

```
[Extrude/Move/Rotate/Offset/Taper/Delete/Copy/coLor/mAterial/Undo/eXit] :
```

The options from this prompt produce the same results as their counterparts on the Solid Editing panel.

If you select `Edge` at the first prompt, you see the following prompt:

```
Enter an edge editing option [Copy/coLor/Undo/eXit] :
```

The `Copy` option lets you copy a surface, and the `coLor` option lets you add color to a surface.

If you select `Body` from the first prompt, you see the following prompt:

```
[Imprint/seParate solids/Shell/cLean/Check/Undo/eXit] :
```

These options also perform the same functions as their counterparts on the Solid Editing panel. As you work with this command, you can use the `Undo` option to undo the last Solidedit option that you used without exiting the command.

Streamlining the 2D Drawing Process

Using solids to model a part—such as with the bracket and Solidedit examples in this chapter—may seem a bit exotic, but there are definite advantages to modeling in 3D, even if you only want to show the part in 2D as a page in a set of manufacturing specs.

The exercises in the following sections show you how to generate a typical mechanical drawing from your 3D model quickly by using paper space and the Solid Editing panel. You'll also examine techniques for dimensioning and including hidden lines.

Architectural Elevations from 3D Solids

If your application is architectural and you've created a 3D model of a building by using solids, you can use the tools described in the following sections to generate 2D elevation drawings from your 3D solid model.

We've used solid models in the past to generate 2D line drawings of elevations. Such line drawings can be "rendered" in a 2D drawing program like Adobe Photoshop or Illustrator. Be aware that such drawings will not be as accurate as those drawn from scratch, but they are fine for the early stages of a design project.

Drawing Standard Top, Front, and Right-Side Views

One of the more common types of mechanical drawings is the *orthogonal projection*. This style of drawing shows separate top, front, and right-side views of an object. Sometimes, a 3D image is added for clarity. You can derive such a drawing in a few minutes using the Flatshot tool described in Chapter 20, "Creating 3D Drawings" (see "Turning a 3D View into a 2D AutoCAD Drawing" in that chapter).

With Flatshot, you can generate the standard top, front, and right-side orthogonal projection views, which you can further enhance with dimensions, hatch patterns, and other 2D drawing features. Follow these steps:

1. In the `bracket.dwg` file, open the 3D Navigation drop-down list in the in-canvas View Controls, and then click an orthogonal projection view from the list, such as Top, Left, or Right (see Figure 22.32). You can also use the 3D Navigation flyout in the Visualize tab's Views panel or use the ViewCube to select an orthogonal view. See Chapter 20 for more on the ViewCube.

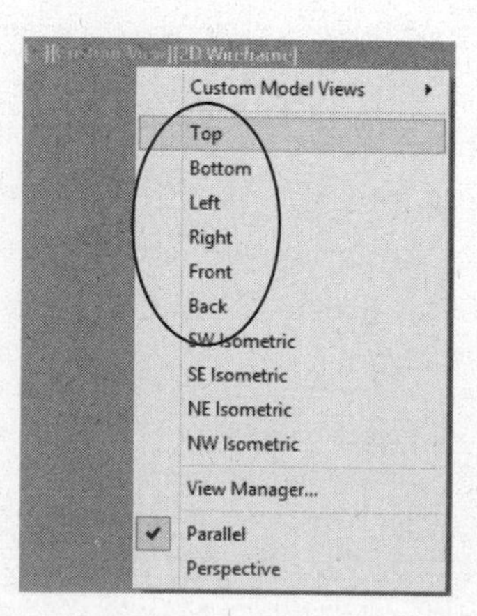

FIGURE 22.32
The 3D Navigation drop-down list

2. Click the Flatshot tool on the Home tab's expanded Section panel, or type **Flatshot**↵.
3. In the Flatshot dialog box, select the options that you want and click Create (see Figure 22.33). See Table 20.1 in Chapter 20 for the Flatshot options.

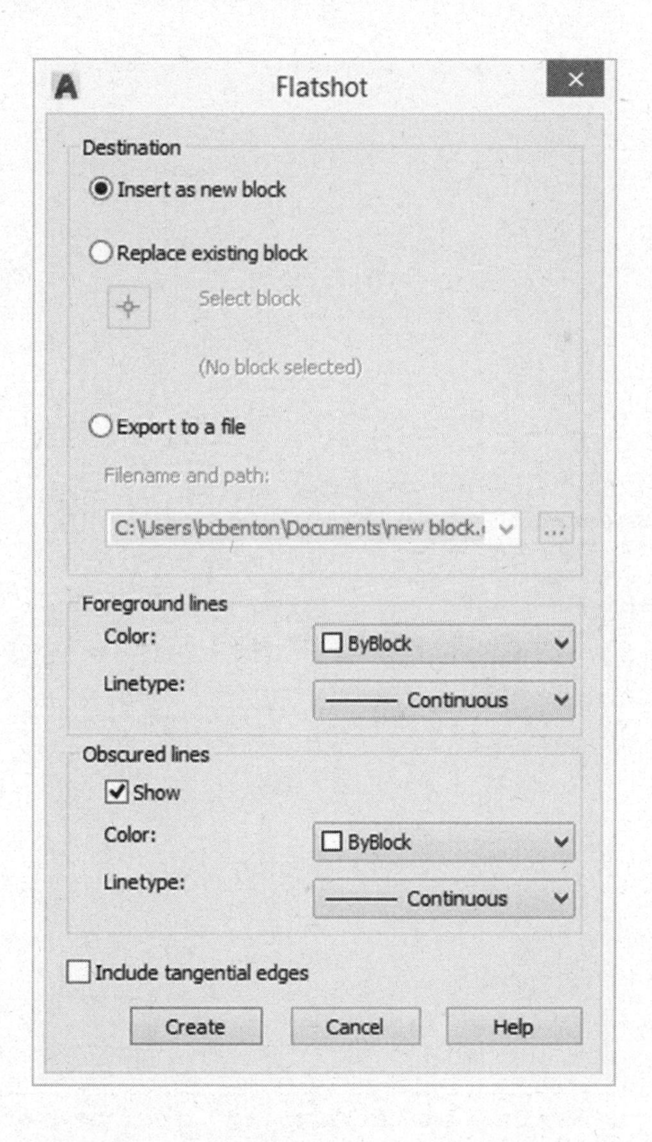

FIGURE 22.33
The Flatshot dialog box

If you select Insert As New Block in the Flatshot dialog box, you're prompted to select an insertion point to insert the block that is the 2D orthogonal view of your model. By default, the view is placed in the same plane as your current view, as shown in Figure 22.34. After you've created all your views, you can move them to a different location in your drawing so that you can create a set of layout views to your 2D orthogonal views, as shown in Figure 22.35. You can also place the orthogonal view blocks on a separate layer and then, for each layout viewport, freeze the layer of the 3D model so that only the 2D views are displayed.

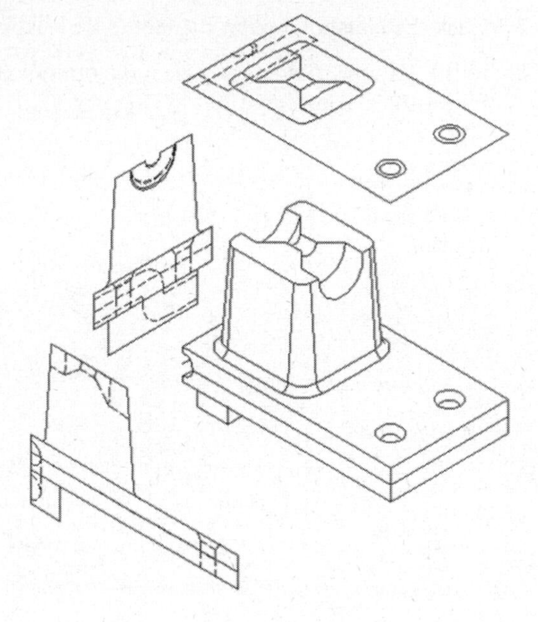

FIGURE 22.34
The 2D orthogonal views shown in relation to the 3D model

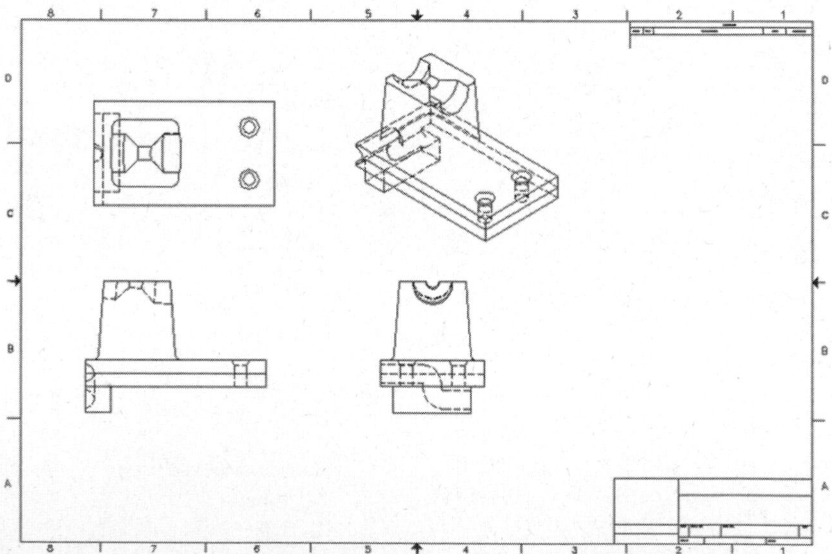

FIGURE 22.35
You can use a layout to arrange a set of views created by Flatshot. Dimensions, notes, and a title block can be added to complete the layout.

SET UP STANDARD VIEWS IN A LAYOUT VIEWPORT

To set up a layout viewport to display a view, like a top or right-side view of a 3D model, select a view from the 3D Navigation drop-down list in the Home tab's View panel and then click on the viewport border. To set the scale of a viewport, click the viewport border and then select a scale from the VP Scale drop-down list on the status bar. If you'd like to refresh your memory on layouts in general, refer to Chapter 15, "Laying Out Your Printer Output."

If your model changes and you need to update the orthogonal views, you can repeat the steps listed here. However, instead of selecting Insert As New Block in the Flatshot dialog box, select Replace Existing Block to update the original orthogonal view blocks. If you want, you can include an isometric view to help communicate your design more clearly.

Creating 2D Drawings with the Base View Command

You saw how 2D views of a 3D model can be made using the Flatshot command. The Base View command also creates 2D views, but in a different way. Follow these steps for a demonstration:

1. In the `bracket.dwg` file, go to paper space and activate the Layout tab in the Ribbon (see Figure 22.36). The Create View panel contains the Viewbase command (the command's full name is Viewbase, but the Ribbon simply shows Base).

FIGURE 22.36
The Viewbase command in the Layout tab of the Ribbon

2. Start the Viewbase command, and choose the From Model Space option.

   You can also import an Autodesk® Inventor® file if you have one available.

3. A preview of your model will be shown. Pick a place in your drawing to insert your first view.

   If you aren't happy with the location, you can always move the view later with the Move command or by using the move grip edit. Views are objects that can be moved, deleted, and so on, just like any other object.

4. When the view is placed, you have several options (see Figure 22.37). You can control the orientation and set the visibility of hidden lines and the scale of the view. The visibility setting provides further control of how your model's edges will be displayed. When all is set, click Exit. Setting up your view can be tricky because the changes that you make won't be applied until you exit the command. Once the views are set, you can alter them, or you can erase them and start over.

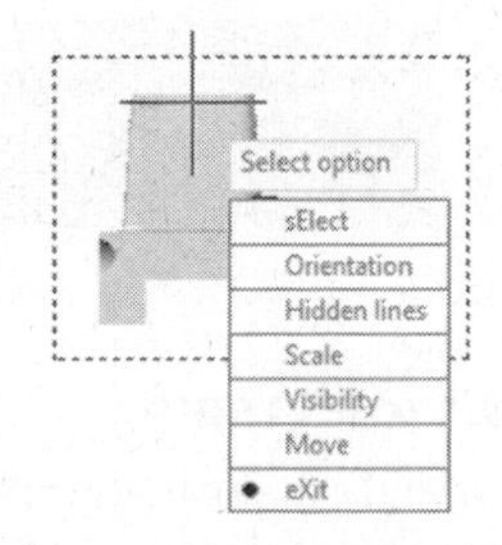

FIGURE 22.37
After you place the parent base view, this menu displays the options that you can set.

   The Viewbase command is still running, and it is ready for you to insert additional views.

5. Move the cursor around the first view that you inserted. The appropriate views—left, right, and isometric—will be previewed, as shown in Figure 22.38. When you have inserted all the views you want, press Enter.

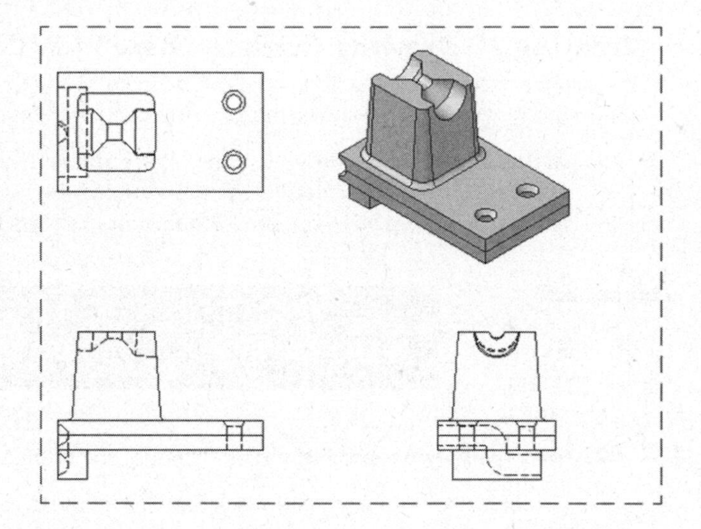

FIGURE 22.38
The Viewbase command can quickly create projection views of your 3D model.

You can now perform basic manipulations on the inserted views. Specifically, you can add or remove views at any time. Any view can be selected. The grip control lets you quickly change to a view's scale. Each child view inherits the Scale setting, as well as all other settings, from the parent (or first) view. You can change each view's settings independently of each other or leave them the way that they are. Orthogonal views cannot move except for in relation to the parent view (up/down or left/right). Isometric views can be moved in any direction.

To change the settings on your views, select one. This will activate a contextual Ribbon tab called Drawing View (see Figure 22.39), bringing up the tools that you need to edit your selected view. Use the Projected command to create new projections from the selected view. The Section command will create a cross-section view. Detail will create a detail view. Edit View allows you to make changes to the hidden lines, scale, and visibility settings.

FIGURE 22.39
Selecting a view will activate the contextual Drawing View Ribbon tab.

CREATING SECTION VIEWS

The Section command can create several types of cross sections, but they all work in a similar way. You can create full, half, offset, or aligned sections. You can also create a section based on an object. The Section button in the Ribbon has a flyout that will display these commands, but you can always just click the Section command itself (see Figure 22.40). This will start the Aligned Section command, which should fill most of your needs.

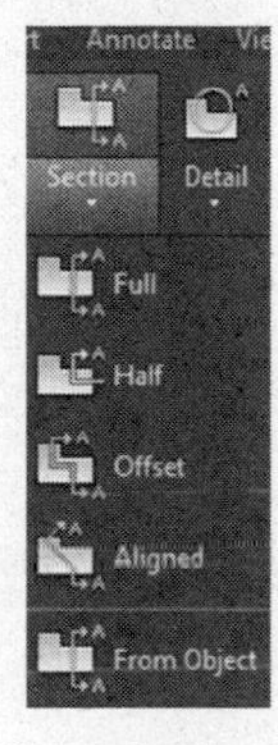

FIGURE 22.40
Select the Section command or choose a specific type of section to create.

1. Click the Section command and select a view. In drafting, a cross section is defined by the section callout arrows. Cross sections in the Section command work the same way.
2. Pick a place for your first section arrow, and then pick the second. This creates the section plane. These arrows can always be changed, and the section will then automatically update itself to reflect the new section arrow placement.
3. Continue to add more points in your section plane if you want.
4. After you have picked all the points needed, press Enter and pick a direction for the arrows to point by moving the cursor to either side of the section arrows. You will also see a preview of what the section will look like.

A section has display settings similar to those for the base views but with a few more elements that you have to define. Double-click the section view to activate the Section View Editor contextual ribbon tab. Two of the more obvious additional items are the label and the hatching. The Annotation setting controls the label and callouts. The first section of a drawing is typically labeled as A-A. As you insert new sections, AutoCAD will continue down the alphabet automatically for you. The second section created will be labeled B, then C, and so on. Of course, you can change any of these at any time.

As illustrated in Figure 22.41, the section will be labeled. It will be called Section and will display the scale. These items are text fields and can be changed too, or you can turn them off. The label is an Mtext object, and it can be manipulated just as any other text object. Double-click the label to open the text editor. The hatching in the section is a hatch object, and it can be edited with the hatch editor. It, too, can be turned off.

To change the display features of the section, you can click the Edit View command in the Ribbon and select the section view. (In fact, you can use the Edit View command to make changes to any type of view that you have created.) A contextual Ribbon tab appears (also shown in Figure 22.41). You can change how the section is displayed in the Appearance panel, change the method by which the section is generated in the Method panel, alter the label in the Annotation panel, and toggle the hatch on or off in the Hatch panel.

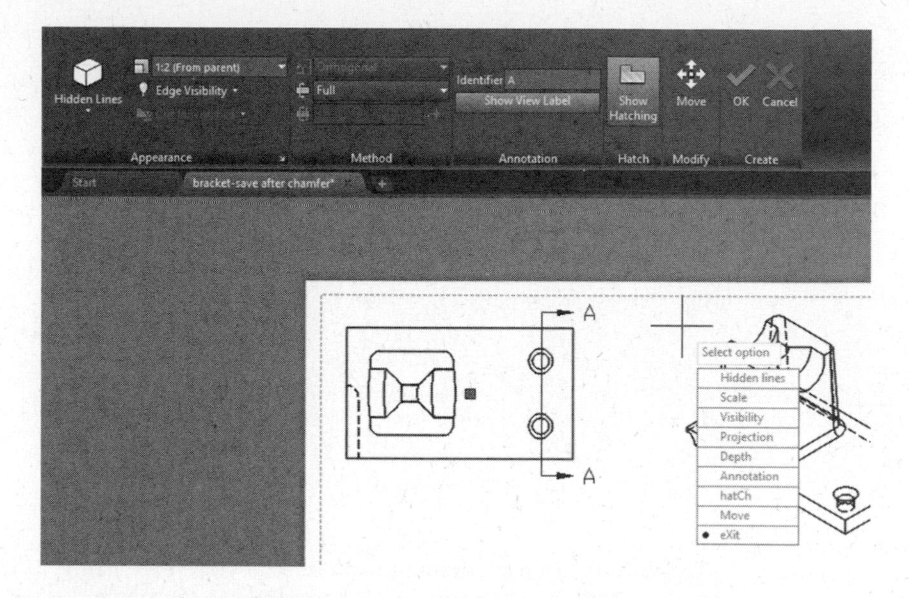

FIGURE 22.41 Section views are edited in the same way as all other view types. They also contain hatch objects and annotation labels.

You can create section styles, similar to dimension styles, by typing **viewsectionstyle** at the command line. If you have worked with dimension styles, discussed in Chapter 11, "Using Dimensions," the following process will be second nature:

1. In the Section View Style Manager dialog box, click the New button.
2. Name your new style, and then click Continue to open the New Section View Style dialog box.
3. The first tab, Identifiers And Arrows, lets you specify the appearance and placement of the section identifiers and arrowheads. Select the text style, color, and size of your identifiers.

   You can make similar adjustments to the arrowheads. Change the type of symbol, its size, color, and so on.
4. In the Arrangement area, specify how the identifiers are positioned and aligned.

The remaining tabs allow you to define the section cutting plane lines and end lines (linetype, color), the view label content and appearance, and the hatch settings. You can create styles that have different labels, use different arrowheads, or have different hatch patterns.

CREATING DETAIL VIEWS

The Detail command, located in the Create View panel in the Layout tab in the Ribbon, creates an enlarged detail view, either circular or rectangular, of a specific area of your model. Follow these steps:

1. To choose which type of detail view you want to create, use the Detail command's pull-down menu. If you click the Detail button, the command will default to the detail type last used.
2. Select the view that you want to display, and then define the area that you want detailed.
3. Pick a center point for the detail, and then pick an outer edge.

4. A preview of the detail appears and prompts you to select a location. Click where you want the detail placed.

Detail views have settings similar to the settings for the other views, with a few that are unique. Figure 22.42 illustrates the detail view contextual Ribbon tab (double-click a detail view to activate). The Boundary setting controls whether the detail is a rectangle or circle. The Model Edge setting controls the boundary around the detail; it can be jagged, smooth, smooth with a border, or smooth with a connection line. The remaining settings are the same as for other view types. Views typically inherit the scale from the parent view. Detail views will be "zoomed in" so that you can see the details more clearly.

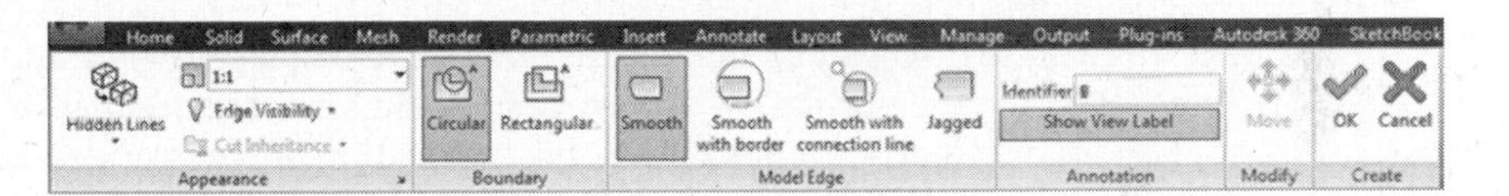

FIGURE 22.42 While you're creating a detail view, a contextual Ribbon tab appears that will provide access to the detail view settings.

When you have created your views (see Figure 22.43 for a finished set of views), you can always remove them or add more. If the model changes, you can update the views by using the Update View command in the Update panel of the Layout tab. Toggle on the Auto Update setting (also in the Update panel), and whenever the model is changed, the views will automatically update.

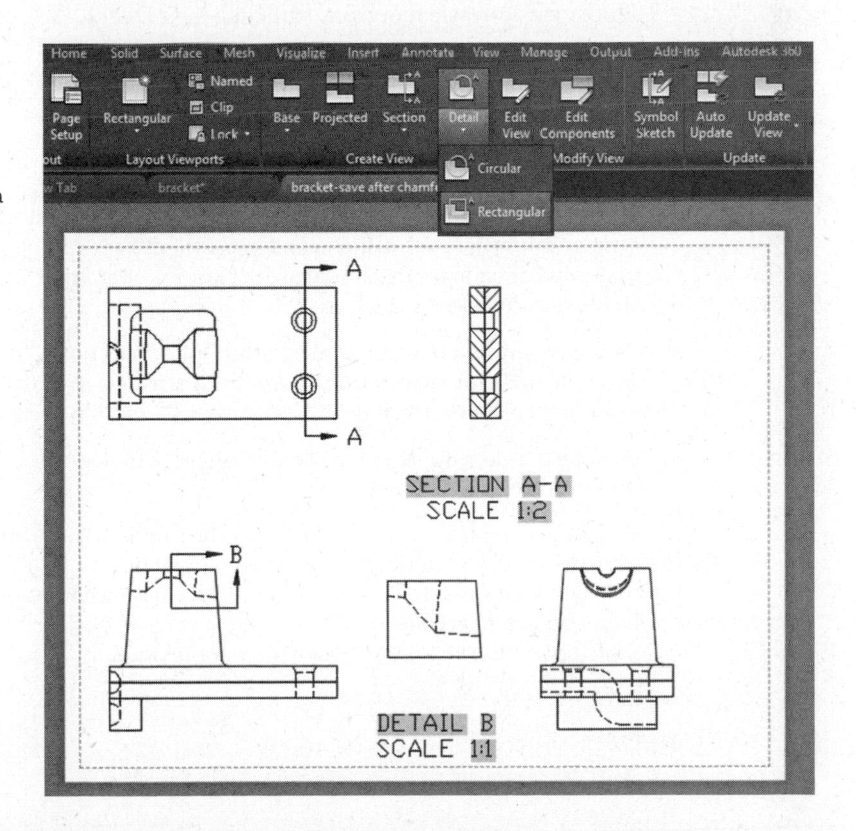

FIGURE 22.43 The Viewbase command along with the section and detail views can make creating 2D drawings from a 3D model a simple and quick process.

Adding Dimensions and Notes in a Layout

Although we don't recommend adding dimensions in paper space for architectural drawings, doing so may be a good idea for mechanical drawings such as the one in this chapter. By maintaining the dimensions and notes separate from the actual model, you keep these elements from getting in the way of your work on the solid model. You also avoid the confusion of having to scale the text and dimension features properly to ensure that they will plot at the correct size. See Chapter 9, "Adding Text to Drawings," and Chapter 11 for a more detailed discussion of notes and dimensions.

As long as you set up your paper space work area to be equivalent to the final plot size, you can set the dimension and text to the sizes that you want at plot time. If you want text 1/4" high, you set your text styles to be 1/4" high.

To include dimensions, make sure that you're in a layout view and then use the dimension commands in the normal way. However, you must make sure that full associative dimensioning is turned on. Choose Options from the Application menu to open the Options dialog box, and then click the User Preferences tab. In the Associative Dimensioning group, make sure that the Make New Dimensions Associative check box is selected. With associative dimensioning turned on, dimensions in a layout view display the true dimension of the object being dimensioned regardless of the scale setting of the viewport.

If you don't have associative dimensioning turned on and your viewports are set to a scale other than 1 to 1, you have another option: You can set the Annotation Units option in the Dimension Style dialog box to a proper value. The following steps show you how:

1. Back in the `bracket.dwg` drawing, select the Model tool in the status bar and then select the Dimension Style tool from Annotate tab's Dimension's panel to open the Dimension Style Manager.
2. Make sure that you've selected the style you want to use, and then click Modify to open the Modify Dimension Style dialog box.
3. Click the Primary Units tab.
4. In the Scale Factor box in the Measurement Scale group, enter the value by which you want your paper space dimensions multiplied. For example, if your paper space views are scaled at one-half the actual size of your model, enter **2** in this box to multiply your dimensions' values by 2.
5. Click the Apply To Layout Dimensions Only check box. This ensures that your dimension is scaled only while you're adding dimensions in paper space. Dimensions added in model space aren't affected.
6. Click OK to close the Modify Dimension Style dialog box, and then click Close in the Dimension Style Manager.

You've had to complete a lot of steps to get the final drawing, but compared with drawing these views by hand, you undoubtedly saved a great deal of time. In addition, as you'll see later in this chapter, what you have is more than just a 2D drafted image. With what you created, further refinements are now easy.

Using Visual Styles with a Viewport

In Chapter 20, you saw how you could view your 3D model using visual styles. A visual style can give you a more realistic representation of your 3D model, and it can show off more of the details, especially on rounded surfaces. You can also view and plot a visual style in a layout view. To do so, you make a viewport active and then turn on the visual style that you want to use for that viewport. The following exercise gives you a look at how this is done:

1. Continuing in the `bracket.dwg` drawing, create a new Paper Space tab by clicking the plus icon in the status bar (next to the far-right Paper Space tab) at the bottom of the screen.
2. Double-click inside the viewport with the isometric view of the model to switch to Floating Model Space.
3. Select Conceptual from the Visual Styles drop-down list in the Visualize tab's Visual Styles panel or the Home tab's View panel (see Figure 22.44).

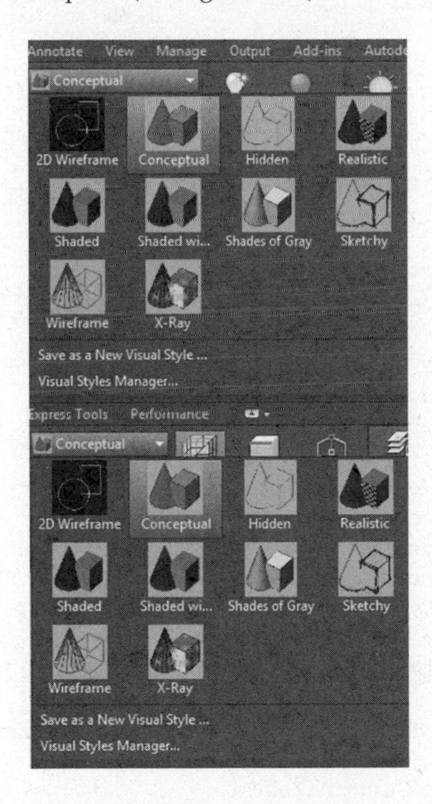

FIGURE 22.44
The Visual Styles panel and the View panel

The view may appear a bit dark because of the black color setting for the object. You can change the color to a lighter one, such as cyan or blue, to get a better look.

4. Double-click outside the isometric viewport to return to paper space.

If you have multiple viewports in a layout, you can change the visual style of one viewport without affecting the other viewports. This can help others visualize your 3D model more clearly.

You'll also want to know how to control the hard-copy output of a shaded view. For this you use the context menu:

1. Click the isometric view's viewport border to select it.
2. Right-click to open the context menu, and select the Shade Plot option to display a set of Shade Plot options (see Figure 22.45).

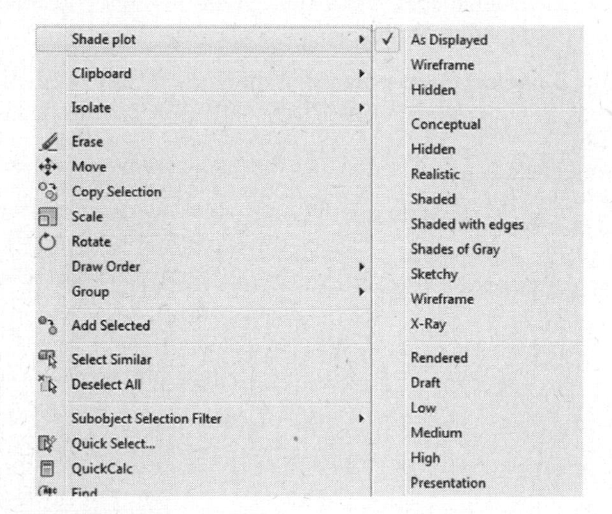

FIGURE 22.45
The Shade Plot options

3. Take a moment to study the menu, and then click As Displayed.

The As Displayed option plots the viewport as it appears in the AutoCAD window. You use this option to plot the currently displayed visual style. Wireframe plots the viewport as a Wireframe view. Hidden plots the viewport as a hidden-line view similar to the view you see when you use the Hide command. Below the Hidden option in the context menu is a list of the available visual styles. At the bottom of the menu is the Rendered option, which plots the view by using the Render feature, described in Bonus Chapter 6, "Rendering 3D Drawings," available at `www.omura.com/chapters`. You can use the Rendered option to plot raytraced renderings of your 3D models.

Remember these options on the context menu as you work on your drawings and when you plot. They can be helpful in communicating your ideas, but they can also get lost in the array of tools that AutoCAD offers.

Visualizing Solids

If you're designing a complex object, sometimes it helps to be able to see it in ways that you couldn't in the real world. AutoCAD offers two visualization tools that can help others understand your design ideas.

If you want to show off the internal workings of a part or an assembly, you can use X-Ray Effect, which you can find in the Visualize tab's Visual Styles panel.

Figure 22.46 shows an isometric view of the bracket using the Realistic visual style and with X-Ray Effect turned on. The color of the bracket has also been changed to a light gray to help visibility. You can see the internal elements as if the object were semitransparent. X-Ray Effect works with any visual style, although it works best with a style that shows some of the surface features (such as the Conceptual or Realistic visual style).

FIGURE 22.46
The bracket displayed using a Realistic visual style and X-Ray Effect

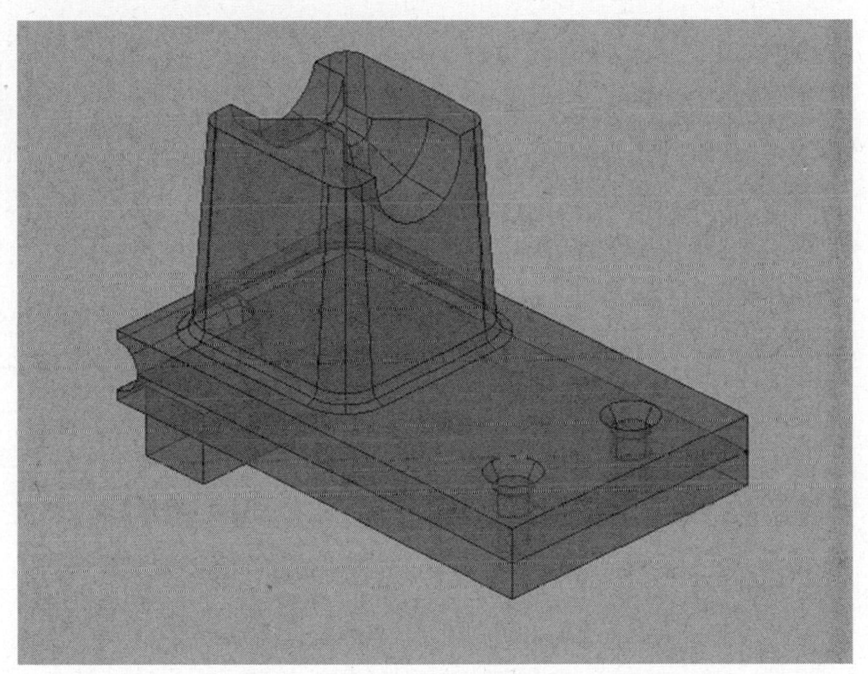

Another tool to help you visualize the internal workings of a design is the Section Plane command. This command creates a plane that defines the location of a cross section. A section plane can also do more than just show a cross section. Try the following exercise to see how it works:

1. In the `bracket.dwg` file, click the Model tab at the bottom of the drawing area and then change the color of layer 0 to a light gray so that you can see the bracket more clearly when using the Realistic visual style. If you changed the color of the object in a previous step, you will have to change the object's color back to ByLayer using the Properties palette.
2. Select Realistic from the Visual Styles Control drop-down list in the drawing screen.
3. Make sure that the Object Snap and Object Snap Tracking tools are turned off in the status bar. This will allow you to point to surfaces on the model while using the Sectionplane command.
4. Adjust your view so that it looks similar to Figure 22.47.

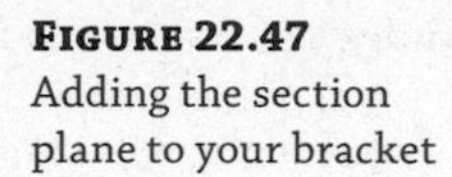

FIGURE 22.47
Adding the section plane to your bracket

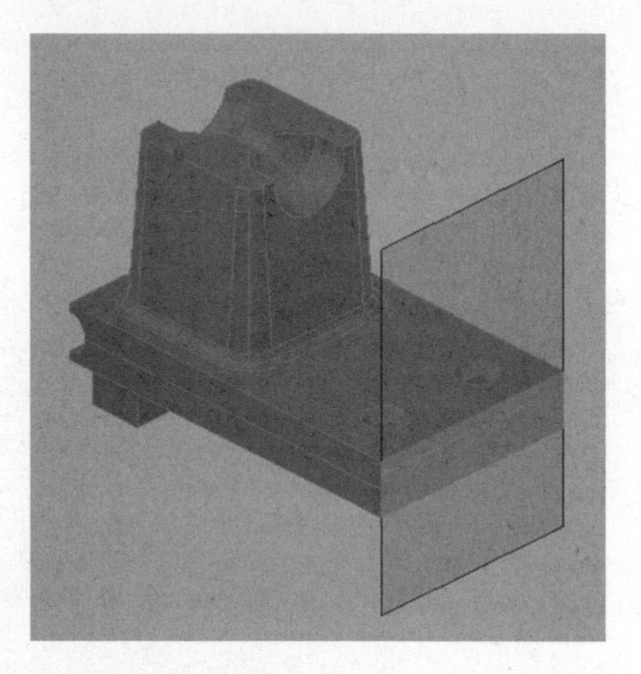

5. In the Home tab's Section panel, click the Section Plane tool. You can also enter **sectionplane**↵ at the Command prompt. You'll see the following prompt:

```
Select face or any point to locate
section line or [Draw section/Orthographic/ Type]:
```

6. Select the front face of the bracket to place the section plane as shown in Figure 22.47. A plane appears on that surface.

You can move the section plane object along the solid to get a real-time view of the section it traverses. To do this, you need to turn on the Live Section feature. To check whether Live Section is turned on, follow these steps:

1. Click the section plane, and then right-click. If you see a check mark by the Activate Live Sectioning option, then you know it's on. If you don't see a check mark, then choose Activate Live Sectioning to turn it on.
2. Click the red axis on the gizmo, as shown in Figure 22.48. The axis turns yellow to indicate that it is active and you see a red vector appear.

FIGURE 22.48
Moving the surface plane across the bracket

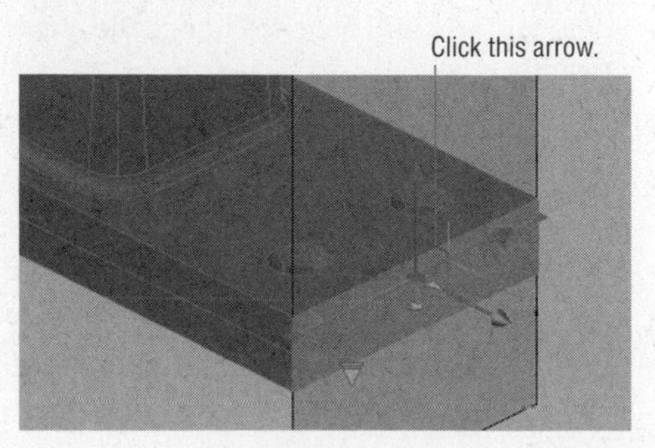

3. Move the cursor slowly toward the back of the bracket. As you do this, the bracket becomes lighter in the foreground.
4. When the section plane is roughly in the middle of the tapered portion of the bracket, click to fix the plane in place. You should have a view similar to Figure 22.49.

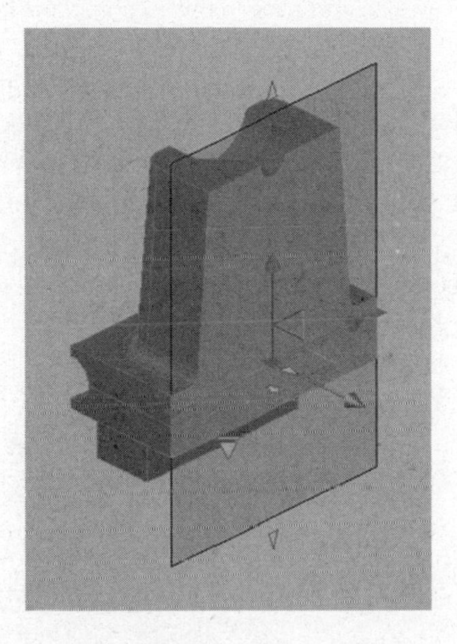

FIGURE 22.49
The surface plane fixed at a location

Now you see only a portion of the bracket behind the section plane plus the cross section of the plane, as shown in Figure 22.49. You can have the section plane display the front portion as a ghosted image by following these steps:

1. With the section plane selected (you should still see its Move gizmo), right-click and choose Show Cut-Away Geometry. The front portion of the bracket appears (see Figure 22.50).

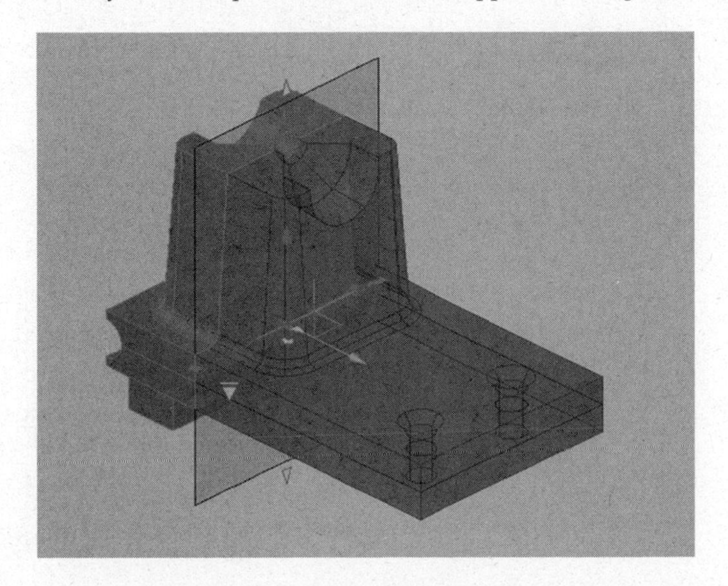

FIGURE 22.50
The front portion of the bracket is displayed with the Show Cut-Away Geometry option turned on.

2. Press the Esc key to end the command. The section plane and the cut-away geometry remain in view.

You can double-click the section plane to toggle between a solid view and a cut-away view of the geometry. This toggles the Active Live Sectioning option.

You can also add a jog in the section plane to create a more complex section cut. Here's how it's done:

1. Select the section plane, right-click, and select Show Cut-Away Geometry to turn this feature off. There should be no check mark by this feature name in the menu. This is necessary in order to gain access to the section plane Jog features.
2. Right-click, and choose Add Jog To Section.
3. At the `Specify a point on the section line to add jog:` prompt, use the Nearest object snap to select a point on the section plane line (see Figure 22.51).

FIGURE 22.51
Moving the jog in the section plane

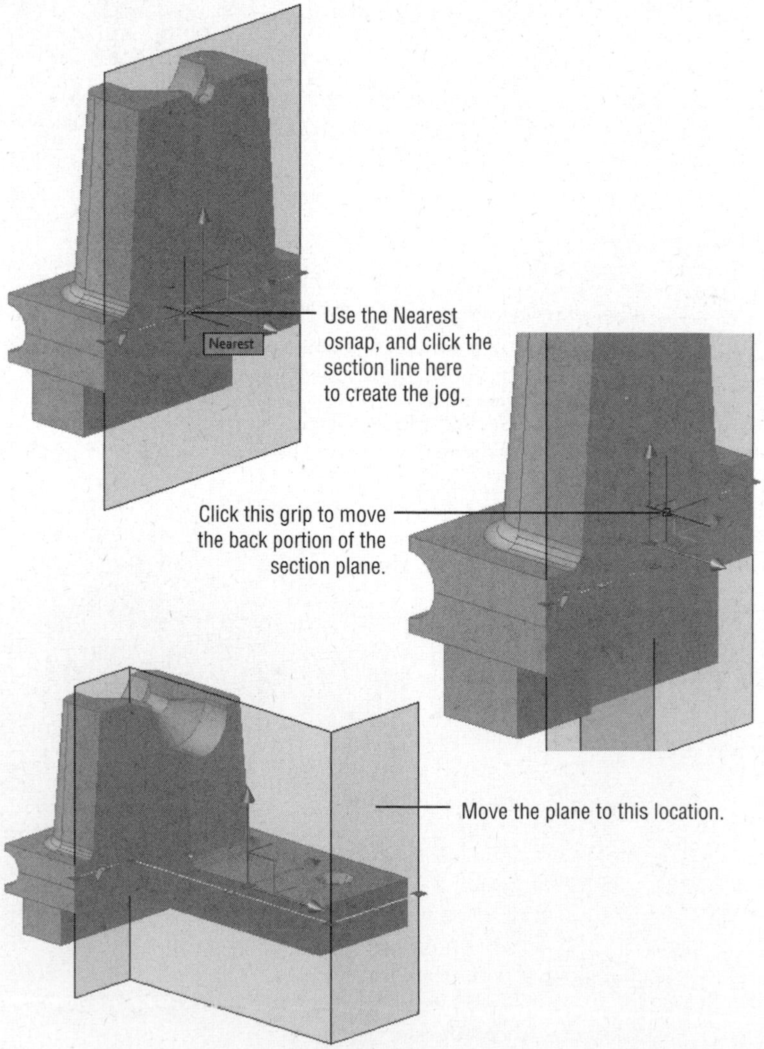

4. Click the grip on the back portion of the section plane, as shown in the center image of Figure 22.51, and drag it toward the right so that the jog looks similar to the third panel in the figure.

5. Press the Esc key to end the command.

As you can see from this example, you can adjust the section using the grips on the section plane line. (A contextual ribbon is also available to make most of the adjustments that we will discuss here.) You can use the Nearest osnap to select a point anywhere along the section line to a jog. Click and drag the endpoint grips to rotate the section plane to an angle.

You may have also noticed another arrow in the section plane (see Figure 22.52).

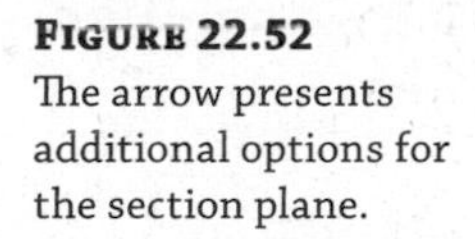

FIGURE 22.52
The arrow presents additional options for the section plane.

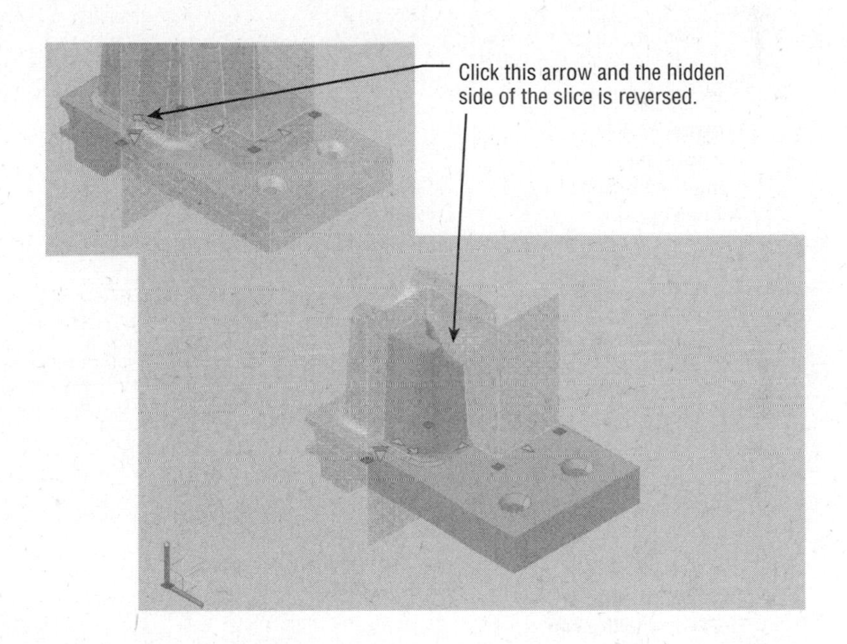

When you click the down-pointing arrow, you see four options for visualizing the section boundary: Plane, Slice, Boundary, and Volume.

By using these other settings, you can start to include sections through the sides, back, top, or bottom of the solid. For example, if you click the Boundary option, another boundary line appears with grips (see Figure 22.53). To see it clearly, you may have to press Esc and then select the section plane again. You can then manipulate these grips to show section cuts along those boundaries.

The Volume option displays the boundary of a volume along with grips at the top and bottom of the volume (see Figure 22.54). These grips allow you to create a cut plane from the top or bottom of the solid.

The Slice option is used to generate thin cuts through your model that will consist of parallel lines using front and back section planes. A slice's thickness can be adjusted, but the slice cannot contain jogs. If you previously created jogs with other options, they will be removed. There are grips that allow you to control the length, width, and height of the solid and a grip to flip the solid to the other side (see Figure 22.55).

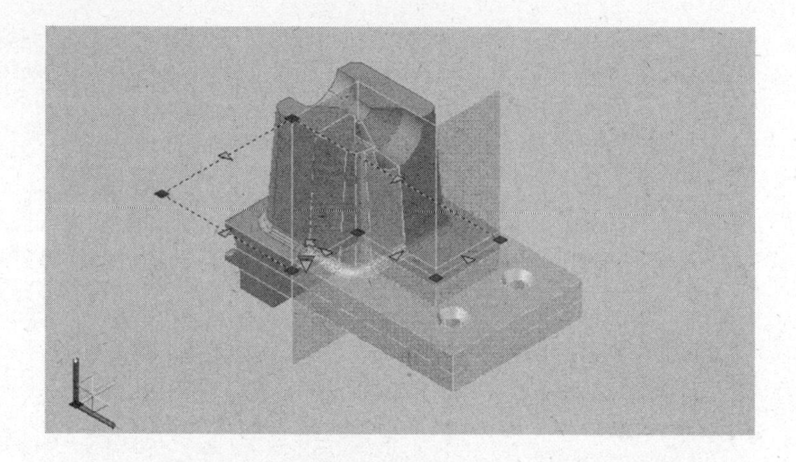

FIGURE 22.53
Another boundary line appears with grips when you click the Section Boundary option.

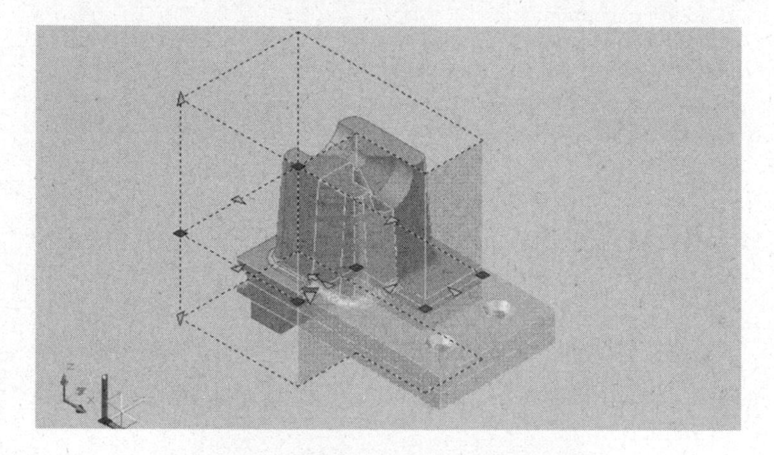

FIGURE 22.54
The boundaries shown using the Section Volume option

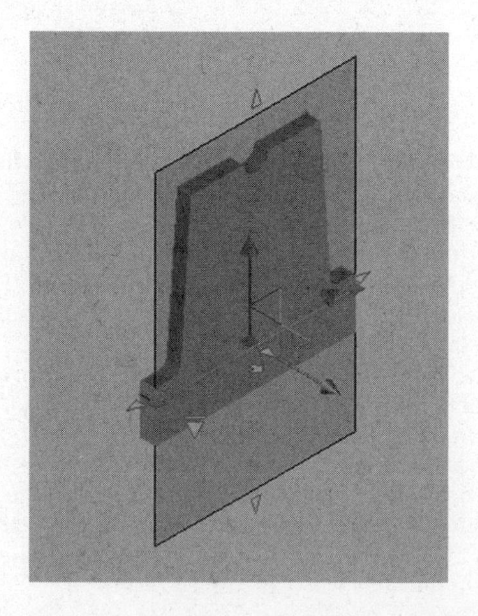

FIGURE 22.55
The Section Slice can be manipulated similarly to other section options.

Finally, you can get a copy of the solid that is behind or in front of the section plane. Right-click the section plane, and choose Generate Section; then select the 2D/3D Block option to open the Generate Section/Elevation dialog box. Click the Show Details button to expand the dialog box and display more options (see Figure 22.56).

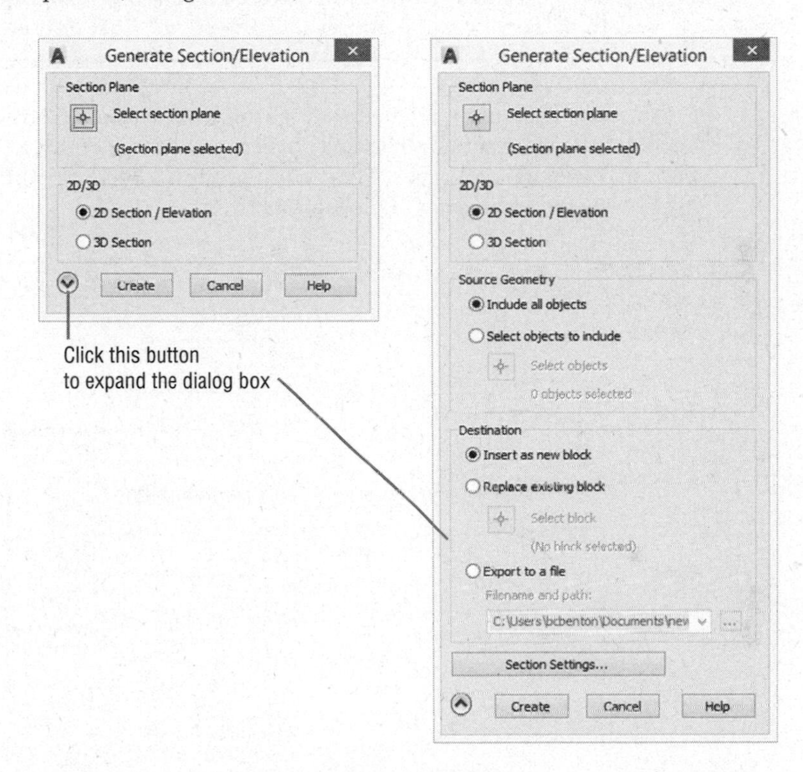

FIGURE 22.56
The Generate Section/Elevation dialog box

If you select 2D Section/Elevation, a 2D image of the section plane is inserted in the drawing in a manner similar to the insertion of a block. You're asked for an insertion point, an X and Y scale, and a rotation angle.

The 3D Section option creates a copy of the portion of the solid that is bounded by the section plane or planes, as shown in Figure 22.57.

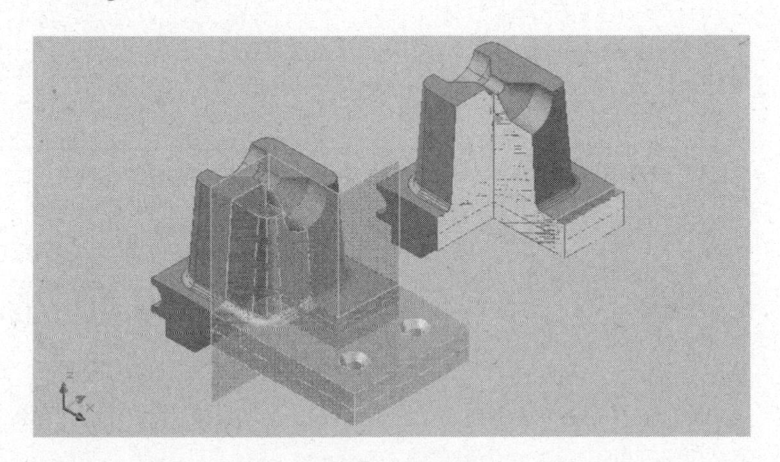

FIGURE 22.57
A copy of the solid minus the section area is created using the 3D Section option of the Generate Section/Elevation dialog box.

Using a Section Plane in an Architectural Model

If your application is architectural, you can use a section plane and the 2D Section/Elevation option to get an accurate elevation drawing. Instead of placing the section plane inside the solid, move it away from the solid model and use the 2D Section/Elevation context menu option.

You can access more detailed settings for the 2D Section/Elevation, 3D Section, and Live Section Settings options by clicking the Section Settings button at the bottom of the Generate Section/Elevation dialog box. This button opens the Section Settings dialog box (see Figure 22.58), which lists the settings for the section feature.

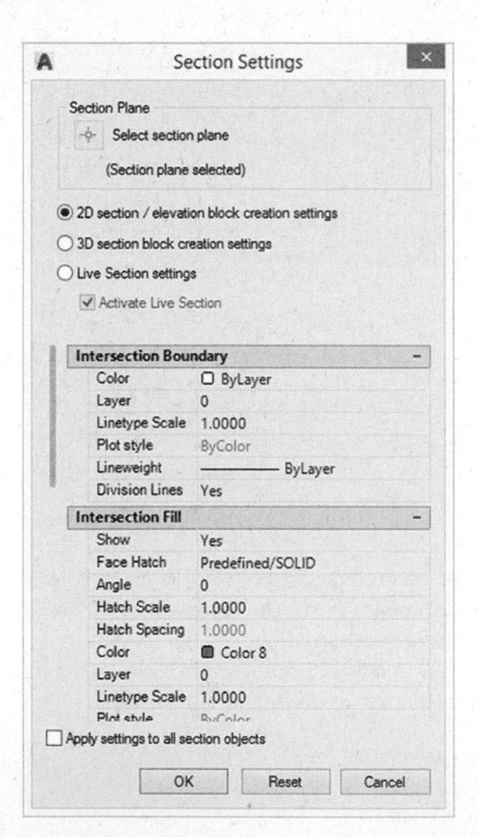

Figure 22.58
The Section Settings dialog box

Taking Advantage of Stereolithography

A discussion of solid modeling wouldn't be complete without mentioning stereolithography. This is one of the most interesting technological wonders that has appeared as a by-product of 3D computer modeling. *Stereolithography* is a process that generates physical reproductions of 3D computer solid models. Special equipment converts your AutoCAD-generated files into a physical model.

This process offers the mechanical designer a method for rapidly prototyping designs directly from AutoCAD drawings, though applications don't have to be limited to mechanical design. Architects can take advantage of this process too. One of the authors' interest in Tibetan art led him to create a 3D AutoCAD model of a type of statue called a Zola, shown here. He sent this model to a service to have it reproduced in resin.

AutoCAD supports stereolithography through the 3dprint and Stlout commands. These commands generate an STL file, which can be used with a *Stereolithography Apparatus (SLA)* to generate a model. You must first create a 3D solid model in AutoCAD. Then you can use the Export Data dialog box to export your drawing in the STL format. Choose Export To Another File Format from the Application menu, and make sure that the Files Of Type drop-down list shows Lithography (*.stl) before you click the Save button. You can also choose Send To 3D Print Service from the Output tab's 3D Print panel.

The AutoCAD 3D solids are translated into a set of triangular-faceted meshes in the STL file. You can use the Rendered Object Smoothness setting in the Display tab of the Options dialog box to control the fineness of these meshes.

When you use Send To 3D Print Service, which can also be found in the Application menu's Publish options, you will see a message box asking if you want to learn more about preparing a 3D model for printing. If you are unfamiliar with stereolithography and 3D printing, it is a good idea to select the Learn About Preparing A 3D Model For Printing option so that you don't make some of the common mistakes.

The price of 3D printers has dropped dramatically recently, and there are more desktop models than ever before. If you have access to a 3D printer, then you can make a physical copy of your model rather easily.

If you create a set of orthogonal views in a layout, the work you do to find a section is also reflected in the layout views (see Figure 22.59).

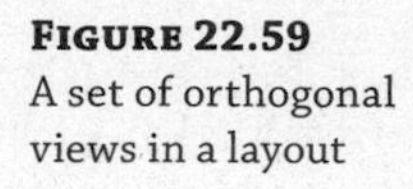

FIGURE 22.59
A set of orthogonal views in a layout

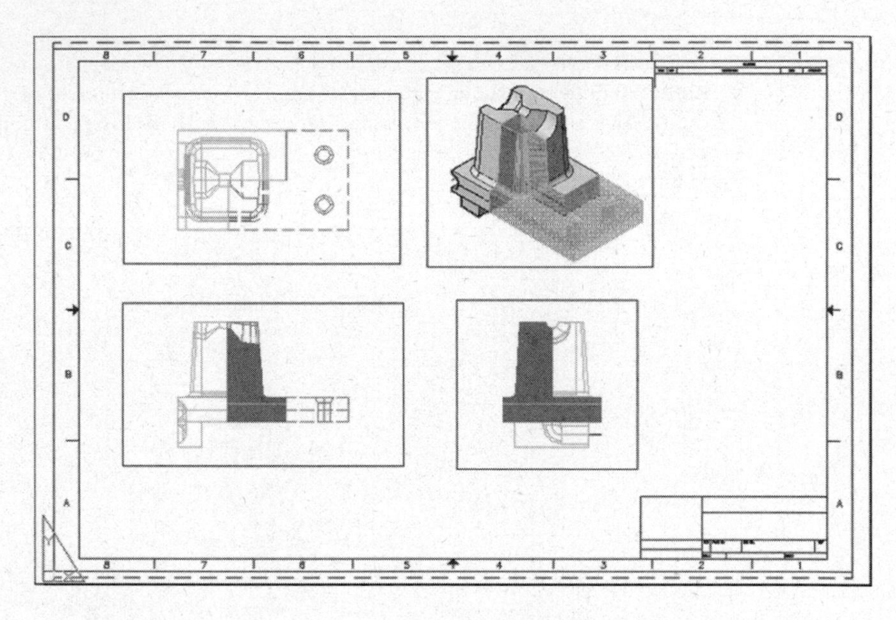

The Bottom Line

Understand solid modeling. Solid modeling lets you build 3D models by creating and joining 3D shapes called solids. There are several built-in solid shapes called primitives, and you can create others using the Extrude tool.

Master It Name some of the built-in solid primitives available in AutoCAD.

Create solid forms. You can use Boolean operations to sculpt 3D solids into the shape you want. Two solids can be joined to form a more complex one, or you can remove one solid from another.

Master It Name the three Boolean operations that you can use on solids.

Create complex solids. Besides the primitives, you can create your own shapes based on 2D polylines.

Master It Name three tools that let you convert closed polylines and circles into 3D solids.

Edit solids. After you've created a solid, you can make changes to it using the solid-editing tools offered on the Solid Editing panel.

Master It Name at least four of the tools found on the Solid Editing panel.

Streamline the 2D drawing process. You can create 3D orthogonal views of your 3D model to create standard 2D mechanical drawings.

Master It What is the name of the tool in the expanded Section panel that lets you create a 2D drawing of a 3D model?

Visualize solids. In addition to viewing your 3D model in a number of different orientations, you can view it as if it were transparent or cut in half.

Master It What is the name of the command that lets you create a cut view of your 3D model?

Chapter 23

Exploring 3D Mesh and Surface Modeling

Autodesk® AutoCAD® software has always offered tools that allow users to construct fairly complex 3D models. With the introduction of the latest solid modeling tools, you can even model some very organic forms. But some forms require a type of modeling known as *mesh modeling*. Mesh modeling lets you create smooth, curved volumes by manipulating faces that make up an object's surface.

With mesh modeling, you can quickly create curved shapes that are difficult or even impossible to create by other means. With AutoCAD you can also convert a mesh model into a 3D solid so that you can perform Boolean operations. In addition, AutoCAD has a set of 3D surface modeling tools that extend its ability to produce and edit curved, organic forms.

In this chapter, you'll get a chance to explore many of the current features of mesh modeling through a series of exercises, and you'll be introduced to the surface modeling tools. You'll also learn how you can convert a mesh or 3D surface into a solid. You'll start by creating a simple shape as an introduction, and then you'll move on to a more complex form.

In this chapter, you will learn to

- Create a simple 3D mesh
- Edit faces and edges
- Create mesh surfaces
- Convert meshes to solids
- Understand 3D surfaces
- Edit 3D surfaces

Creating a Simple 3D Mesh

As an introduction to the mesh modeling features in AutoCAD, you'll draw a simple box and then smooth the box. This first exercise will show you some of the basic mesh modeling tools and what types of control you can exert on a model.

First, you'll make sure that you are in the 3D Modeling workspace and that you have a blank drawing set up for the mesh. Follow these steps:

1. Click the New tool on the Quick Access toolbar.

2. In the Select Template dialog box, select the `acad3D.dwt` template and then click Open.
3. Click the Workspace pop-up list in the status bar and select 3D Modeling, as shown in Figure 23.1.

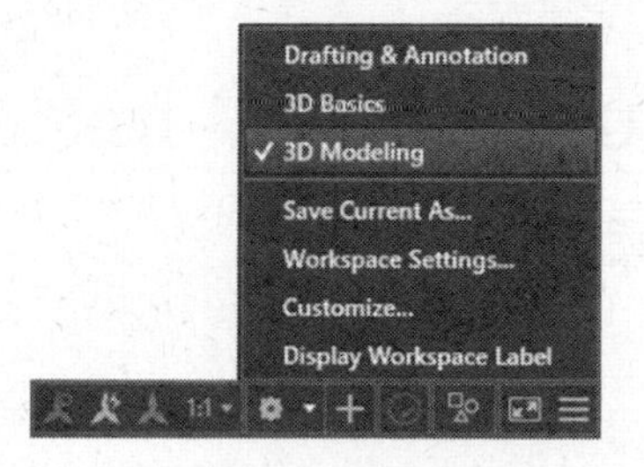

FIGURE 23.1
Selecting the 3D Modeling workspace

4. Choose the Shaded With Edges visual style from the Visual Styles drop-down list on the drawing screen. This will give you a close approximation of the appearance of the meshes that you'll see in the illustrations in this book.

Creating a Mesh Primitive

Meshes are similar to solids in that they start from a *primitive*. You may recall that 3D solid primitives are predetermined shapes from which you can form more complex shapes. The mesh primitives are similar to the 3D solid primitives that you learned about in Chapter 20, "Creating 3D Drawings," and Chapter 22, "Editing and Visualizing 3D Solids." You can see the different mesh primitives that are available by clicking the Mesh flyout in the Mesh tab's Primitives panel (see Figure 23.2).

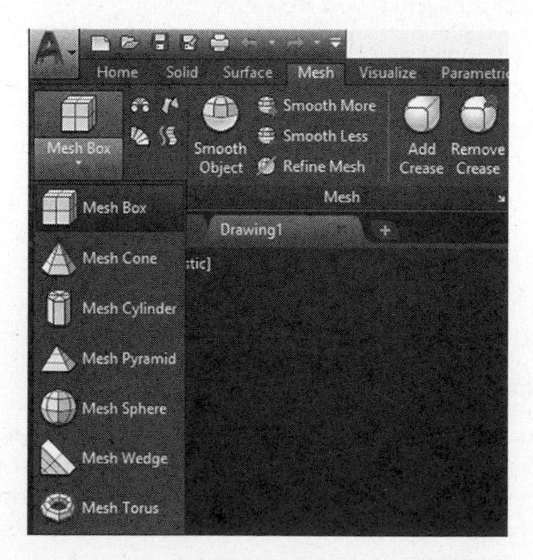

FIGURE 23.2
The primitives in the Mesh flyout of the Primitives panel

In the next exercise, you'll use the Mesh Box primitive to start your cushion:

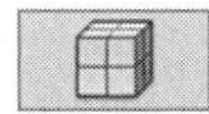

1. In the Mesh tab's Primitives panel, click the Mesh Box tool or type **Mesh↵B↵**.
2. At the `Specify first corner or [Center]:` prompt, enter **0,0↵** to start the mesh at the drawing origin.
3. You'll want a mesh that is 21 units in the x-axis by 32 units in the y-axis, so at the `Specify other corner or [Cube/Length]:` prompt, enter **21,32↵**.
4. At the `Specify height or [2Point]:` prompt, place your cursor anywhere above the base of the mesh and enter **4↵** for a 4 unit height. You now have a basic shape for your mesh (see Figure 23.3).

FIGURE 23.3
The Mesh Box primitive

You've just created a mesh box, but you have several other mesh primitives at your disposal. If you click the Mesh flyout on the Primitives panel, you'll see the cone, cylinder, pyramid, sphere, wedge, and torus primitives. When creating your model, consider which of these primitives will best suit your needs.

Understanding the Parts of a Mesh

Before you go any further, you'll want to understand the structure of a mesh. Notice that each side is divided into nine panels, or *faces*, as they are called in AutoCAD. You can edit these faces to change the shape and contour of your mesh. You can control the number of faces of a mesh through an options dialog box that you'll learn about later in this chapter.

Figure 23.4 shows the names of the different parts of a simple mesh: the vertex, the edge, and the face. These three parts are called *subobjects* of the mesh, and you can move their position in the mesh to modify a mesh's shape.

To help you select different subobjects on a mesh, the Selection panel offers the Filter flyout, which shows the No Filter tool by default. You'll use this flyout in many of the exercises in this chapter.

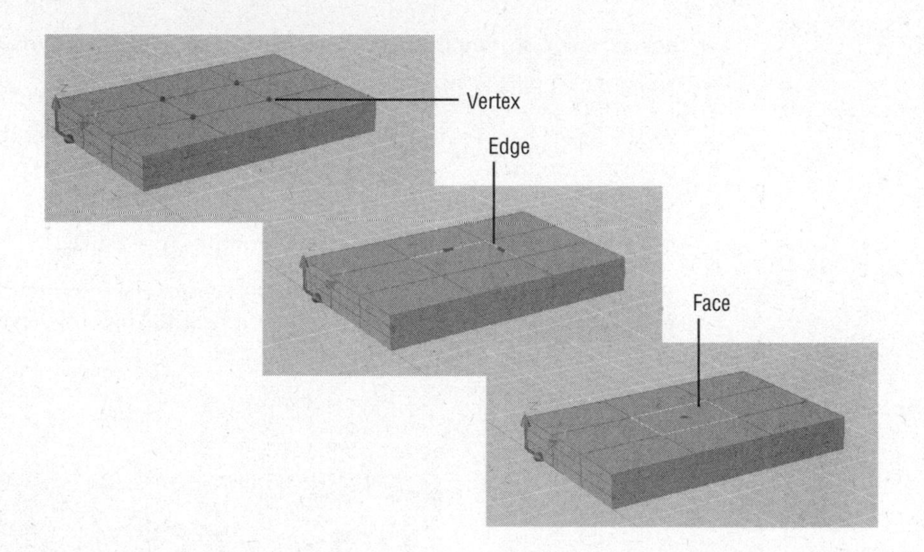

FIGURE 23.4
The subobjects of a mesh

Smoothing a Mesh

One of the main features of a mesh is its ability to become a smooth, curved object. Right now your cushion has sharp edges, but you can round the corners using the Smooth tools.

Try modifying the mesh to smooth its corners:

1. Click the rectangular mesh to select it.
2. Click the Smooth More tool in the Mesh panel or the Smooth panel, or type **Meshsmoothmore**↵. The edges of the mesh become faceted and smoother in appearance.
3. Click Smooth More again. The mesh becomes smoother still (see Figure 23.5).

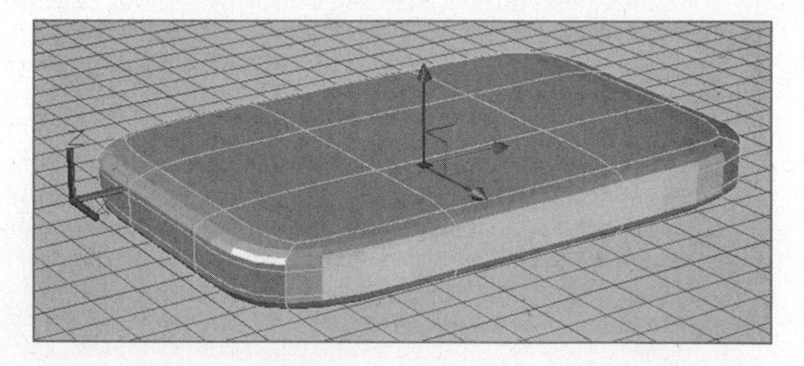

FIGURE 23.5
The mesh after applying the Smooth More tool twice

4. Now click Smooth Less, or type **Meshsmoothless**↵. The mesh becomes less smooth.
5. Press Esc to clear the selection.

As you can see from this exercise, you can smooth a mesh using the Smooth More tool. The more times you apply it to a mesh, the smoother your mesh becomes. The number of faces of the mesh determines how the Smooth More tool affects the mesh. The fewer the number of faces, the broader the application of smoothness.

When you apply the Smooth More tool to a mesh, the faces of the mesh become faceted. This simulates the smooth appearance. If you look closely at a mesh that has only one or two levels of smoothing applied, you can see the facets.

Editing Faces and Edges

The shape that you created earlier demonstrates one of the main features of meshes. In this section, you'll create a model of a surfboard to see how you can push and pull the subobjects of a mesh to create a form.

> **KNOW THE VIEWCUBE**
>
> Throughout the following exercise, you'll make heavy use of the ViewCube®. Be sure that you are familiar with how it works. If you need a refresher, go to Chapter 20.

You'll start with the same form, a box shape, but this time you'll modify some of the parameters that define the box's structure. You can control the number of faces that a mesh primitive will have before it is created. The following exercise introduces you to the tools and methods used to edit meshes.

Start by creating a new drawing and setting up the parameters for the mesh:

1. Click the New tool in the Quick Access toolbar, select `acad3D.dwt`, and then click Open.
2. In the Mesh tab, click the Mesh Primitives Options tool in the Primitives panel title bar. The Mesh Primitive Options dialog box appears (see Figure 23.6).

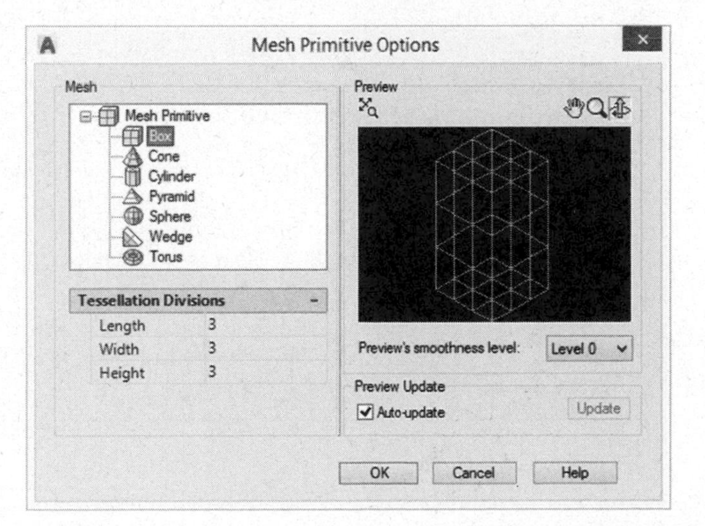

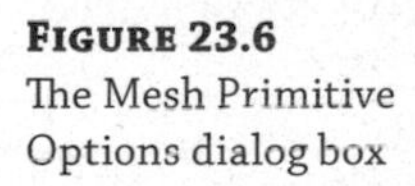

FIGURE 23.6
The Mesh Primitive Options dialog box

3. In the Tessellation Divisions rollout in the Mesh group, change the Length and Width values to **4** and the Height value to **1**. Click OK when you've finished making the changes.
4. In the Home tab's View panel, choose the Shaded With Edges visual style from the Visual Styles drop-down list.

The parameters you change alter the number of faces on mesh primitives that you create, including the box primitive that you will create in the next exercise. You'll see the results after following the next set of steps:

1. Click the Mesh Box tool found on the Mesh tab in the Primitives panel.
2. At the `Specify first corner or [Center]:` prompt, type **0,0**↵ to start the corner at the origin of the drawing.
3. At the `Specify other corner or [Cube/Length]:` prompt, enter **50,30**↵ to create a 50'30 unit base for the box.
4. At the `Specify height or [2Point]` prompt, point the cursor in the positive Z direction and then enter **3.5**↵ for a 3.5 unit thickness.
5. Center the box in your view. Your model should look similar to Figure 23.7.

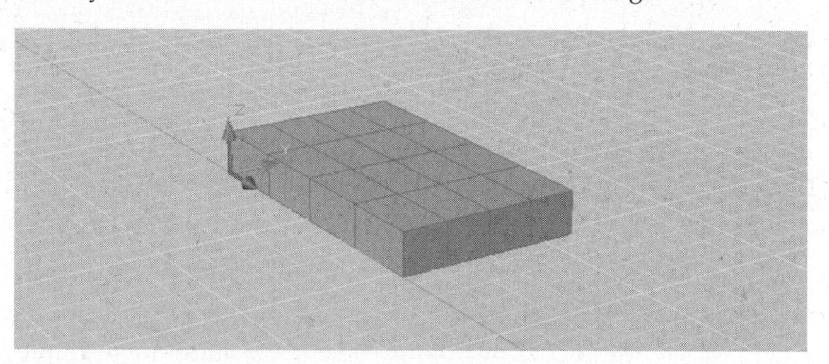

FIGURE 23.7
The mesh box

6. Click the box to select it. Then, in the Mesh panel, click the Smooth More tool twice. The edges of the mesh become more rounded.

WHAT DOES THE SMOOTH OBJECT TOOL DO?

It's hard not to notice the very large Smooth Object tool in the Mesh panel. Your first reaction might be to try to use this tool on a mesh, but it is not intended to work on meshes. Instead, it converts 3D objects other than meshes into mesh objects. You can convert a solid into a mesh, for example, using this tool. 3D surfaces can also be converted, and it even works on region objects that are technically not 3D objects.

You might be tempted to convert a mesh to a solid, edit it, and then turn it back into a mesh. Although this can be done, we don't recommend it. You'll find that your model becomes too unwieldy to work with.

Stretching Faces

You now have the basis for the surfboard, though it might seem like an odd shape for a surfboard. Next you'll start to form the surfboard by manipulating the faces and edges of the mesh. Start by pulling two sides of the mesh to give it a shape more like a surfboard:

1. Use the ViewCube and Pan tools to adjust your view so that it looks similar to Figure 23.8. This view will allow you to easily select and "pull" some of the faces that will become the front and back of the surfboard.

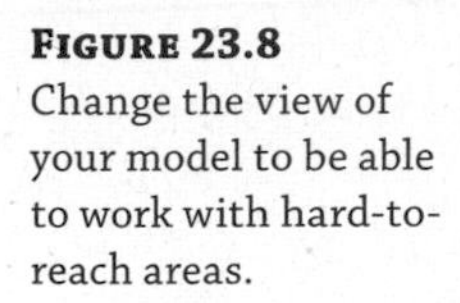

FIGURE 23.8
Change the view of your model to be able to work with hard-to-reach areas.

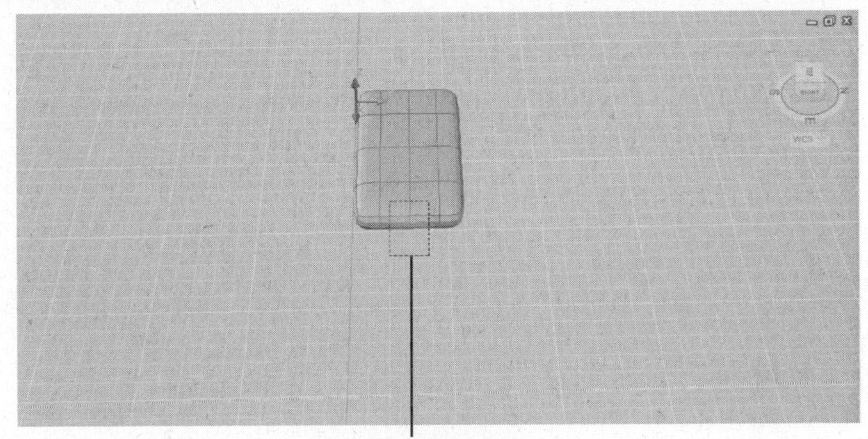

2. In the Selection panel, select Face from the Filter flyout (see Figure 23.9).

FIGURE 23.9
Select the Face filter.

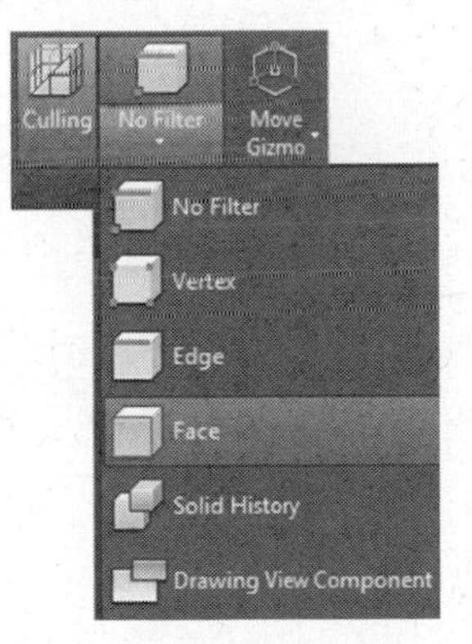

3. Hold down the Ctrl key, and then click and drag a crossing selection window over the middle faces at the front edge of the box, as shown previously in Figure 23.8. The faces are highlighted, and you see the XYZ gizmo.
4. Place your cursor on the red x-axis of the gizmo.
5. When the red axis vector line appears, click the gizmo and move your mouse downward in a positive X direction. The mesh begins to elongate.
6. When your mesh looks similar to Figure 23.10, click your mouse button to release the mesh.
7. Press Esc to remove the faces from the current selection.

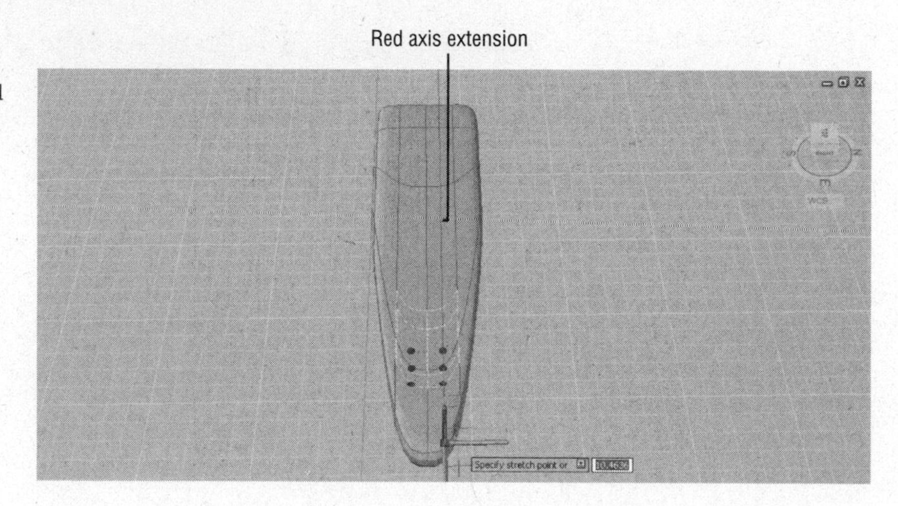

FIGURE 23.10
Use the gizmo, and when you see the red axis vector, drag the cursor to pull the object.

The portion of the mesh you "pull" out will become the front. Next, you'll do the same for the back of the surfboard:

1. Use the Pan tool to adjust your view so that it looks similar to Figure 23.11. This view lets you easily select and "pull" some of the faces that will become the back of the surfboard.

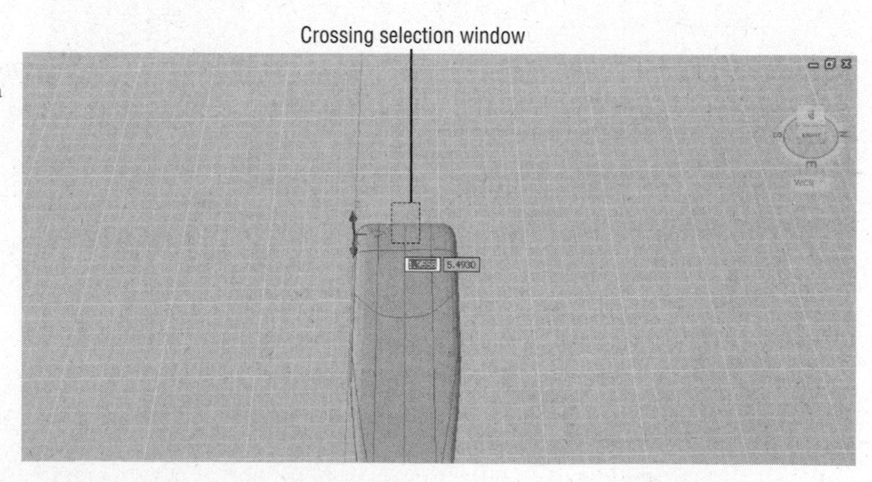

FIGURE 23.11
Place a crossing selection window as shown here. Be sure to press and hold the Ctrl key in order to make the proper selection.

2. Click the box mesh to expose its mesh lines again.
3. Hold down the Ctrl key, and then place a crossing selection window over the middle faces at the back edge of the box, as shown in Figure 23.11. The faces are highlighted, and you see the XYZ gizmo.
4. Place your cursor on the red x-axis of the gizmo, and when the red axis vector line appears, click once and move the gizmo upward in a negative X direction.

5. When your mesh looks similar to Figure 23.12, click your mouse button.

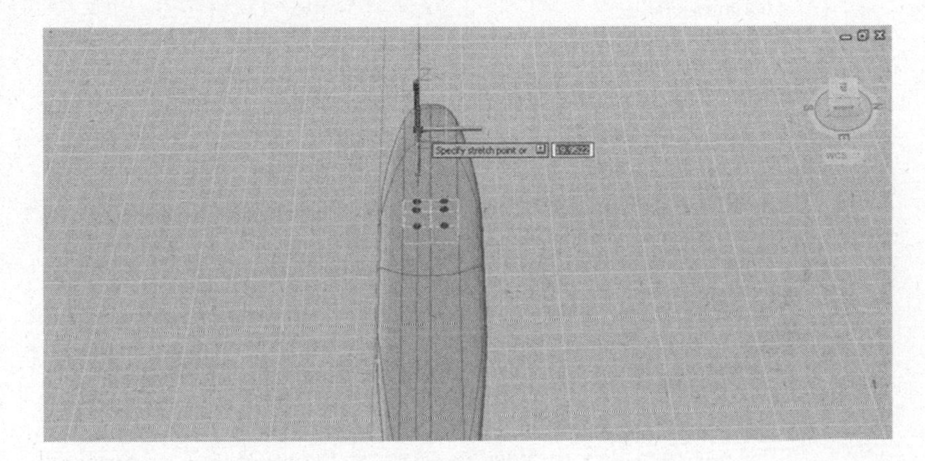

FIGURE 23.12
Adjust the mesh to look similar to this one.

6. Press Esc to remove the faces from the current selection.

7. Click the Home tool on the ViewCube to get a better view of your mesh at this point (see Figure 23.13).

FIGURE 23.13
The mesh so far

Moving an Edge

The surfboard needs a sharper point at the front. Instead of moving the faces as you've already done, you can move an edge to give the front a more pointed shape. The next set of steps will show you how to do this:

1. Using the ViewCube, adjust your view so that you have a close-up of the front tip of the surfboard, as shown in Figure 23.14.

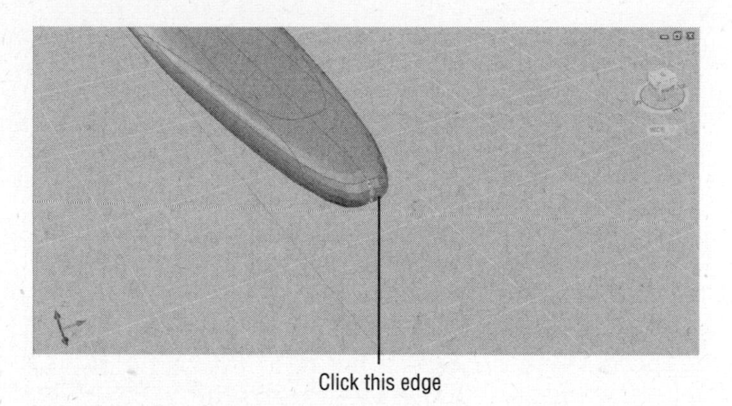

FIGURE 23.14
Click the front-center edge shown here.

2. In the Selection panel, select Edge from the Filter flyout.
3. Hold down the Ctrl key and hover over the front edge until you see the edge line, and then click the edge, as shown in Figure 23.14. The Move gizmo appears.
4. Hover over the x-axis of the gizmo, and when the red vector line appears, click once and move the x-axis downward along the positive X direction.
5. When it looks similar to Figure 23.15, click the mouse button.

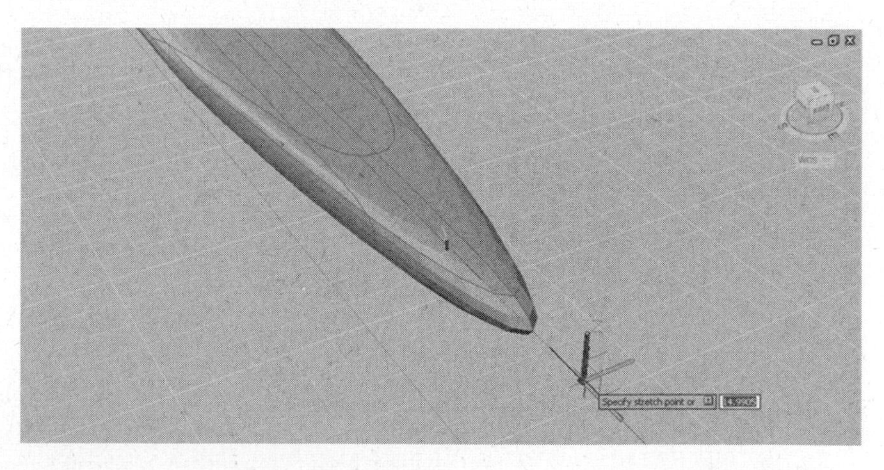

FIGURE 23.15
Pull the front edge so that the mesh looks similar to this image.

Next, give the front of the mesh a slight curve by adjusting the z-axis of the front edge:

1. Hover over the z-axis of the gizmo, and when the blue axis vector line appears, click once and move the z-axis downward in the negative Z direction.
2. When it looks similar to Figure 23.16, click the mouse button.
3. Press the Esc key twice to clear your edge selection.
4. Click the Home tool in the ViewCube to return to the home view.

We asked you to adjust the edge downward because you'll want to have a bottom view of your surfboard. This will enable you to add fins to the board without having to flip the mesh over.

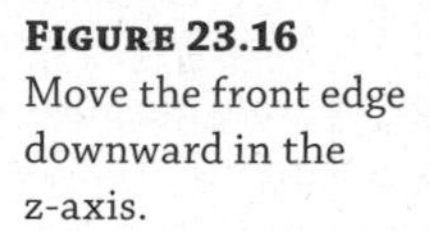

FIGURE 23.16
Move the front edge downward in the z-axis.

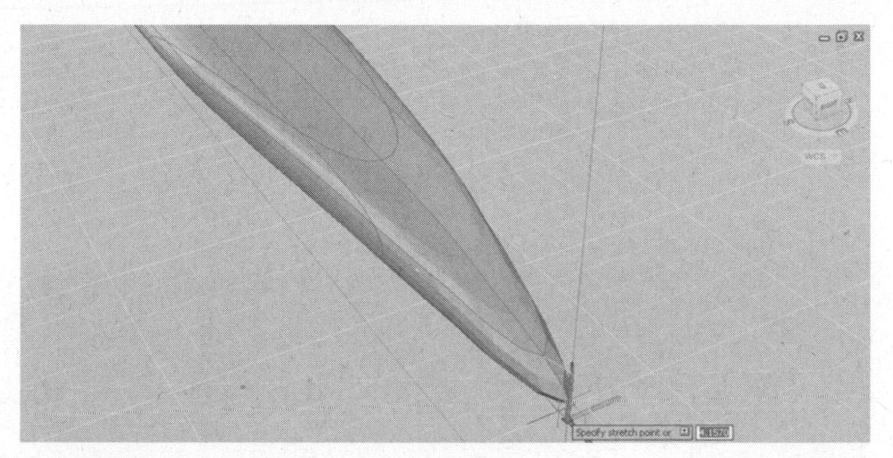

FINE-TUNING THE MESH

You might notice that the surfboard has a slight trough down the middle after you move the front edge downward. You can remove that trough and add some additional curvature to the board by moving the two edges on the side of the mesh toward the front.

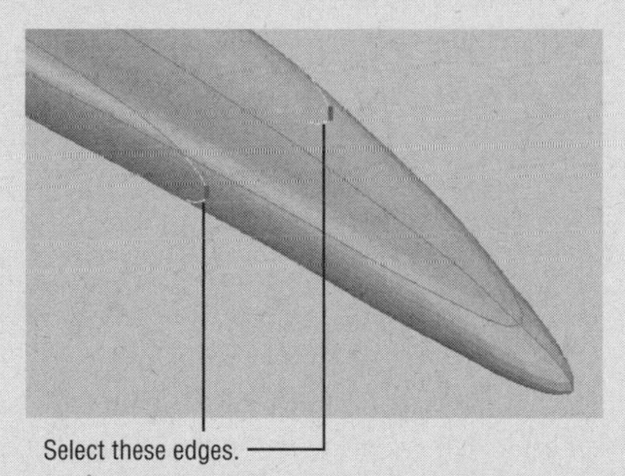

You can click these edges with the Edge subobject filter selected. After you have these edges selected, use the z-axis on the gizmo to move them down to eliminate the trough.

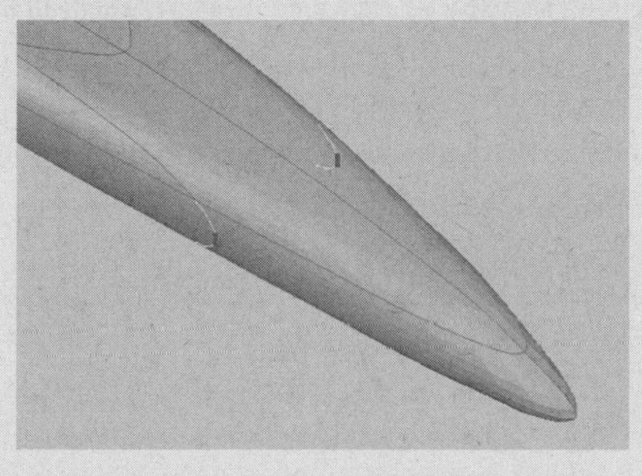

Adding More Faces

The surfboard is still missing some fins. You could model some fins as separate meshes and then later join them to the surfboard. You can also use the Refine Mesh tool to add more edges and then use those edges as the basis for your fins. The following exercise will show how this is done:

1. Adjust your view so that it looks similar to the top image in Figure 23.17.

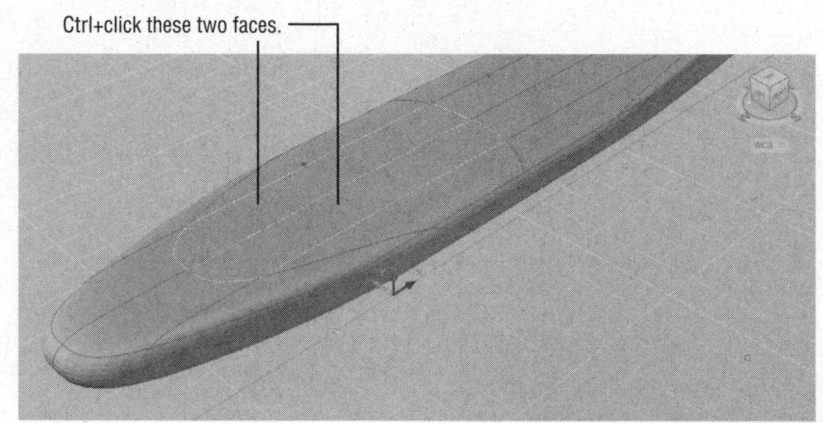

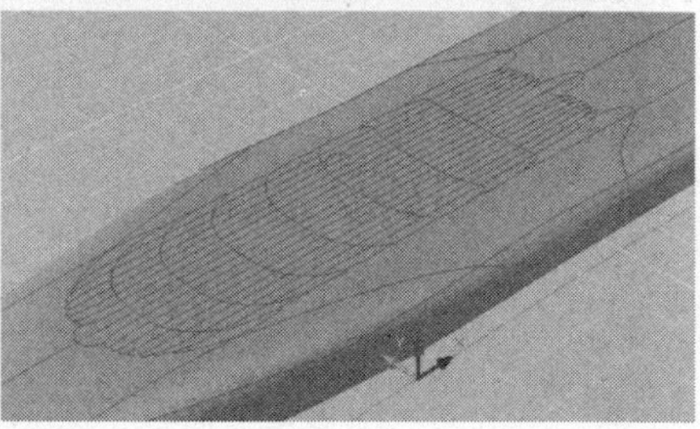

FIGURE 23.17
Select the faces to refine.

2. From the View tab's Visual Styles panel, open the Visual Styles drop-down list and select Shaded With Edges if it isn't already activated. This will allow you to see the edge lines of the mesh as you work through the following steps.
3. Click No Filter from the Selection panel's Filter flyout; then click the mesh, and, from the Mesh tab's Mesh panel, click Smooth More. This will increase the number of edges that are generated in the next step.

4. Press the Esc key to clear your selection.
5. On the Selection panel, select Face from the Filter flyout.
6. Hold the Ctrl key and click the two faces shown in the top image of Figure 23.17.

7. Click the Refine Mesh tool on the Mesh panel, or type **Meshrefine**↵. The selected faces will be subdivided into smaller faces and edges, as shown in the bottom image of Figure 23.17.

UNDERSTANDING HOW REFINE MESH WORKS

You have some control over the number of faces that Refine Mesh creates, through the level of smoothness applied to a mesh. If you reduce the smoothness of a mesh, the Refine Mesh tool will produce fewer faces. If you increase the smoothness, Refine Mesh will produce more faces—four more per facet, to be precise.

To understand how this works, you have to take a closer look at how the Smooth More tool works. Each time you apply the Smooth More tool to a mesh, every face of the mesh is divided into four facets. These facets aren't actually faces, but they divide a face in such a way as to simulate a rounded surface. The Refine Mesh tool further divides each of these facets into four faces. You can see this division clearly if you apply Refine Mesh to a face in a mesh that has only one level of smoothness applied.

The next step in creating the fins is to edit some of the newly created edges:

1. Zoom into the surfboard so that your view looks similar to Figure 23.18.

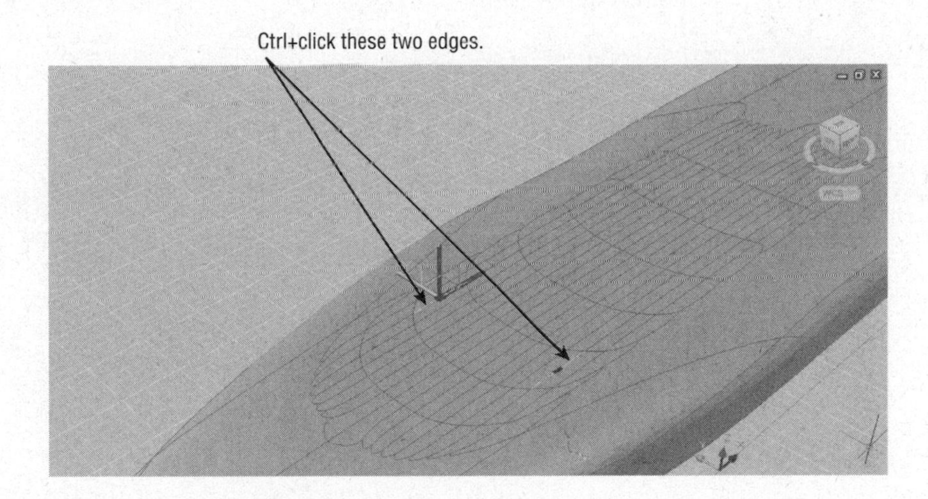

FIGURE 23.18 Select the edges for the fins.

2. On the Selection panel, select Edge from the Filter flyout.
3. Hold the Ctrl key and click the edges shown in Figure 23.18.
4. Hover over the z-axis on the gizmo so that the axis vector appears, and then click once and move the z-axis upward in the positive Z direction. If you run out of room at the top of the window, you can move the z-axis as far as you can with one click and drag and then repeat the move.
5. Adjust the edges so that they look similar to those in Figure 23.19, and then click the mouse button.

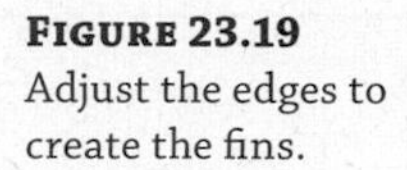

FIGURE 23.19
Adjust the edges to create the fins.

6. Adjust the x-axis of the gizmo toward the back of the surfboard so that the fins look similar to Figure 23.20.

FIGURE 23.20
Adjust the fins toward the back of the surfboard.

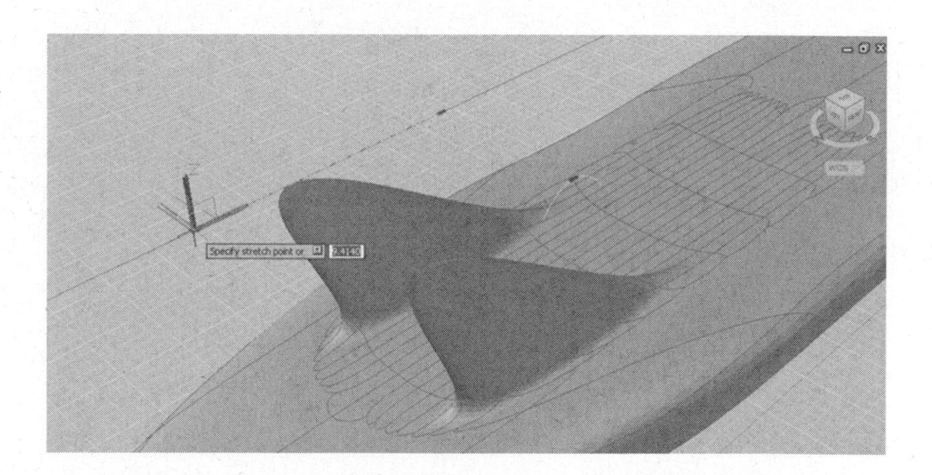

7. Press the Esc key to clear your selection of mesh edges.

Rotating an Edge

The fins aren't quite the right shape. They are a bit too broad at the base. The next exercise shows you how to rotate an edge to adjust the shape of the fins further:

1. With the Edge subobject filter still selected, click the back edge of the fins, as shown in Figure 23.21.

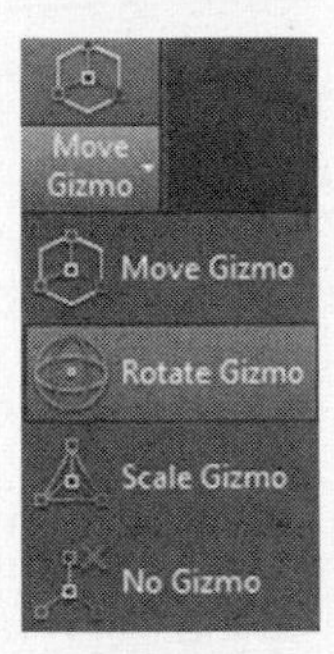

FIGURE 23.21
Select the Rotate Gizmo tool.

2. In the Selection panel, select the Rotate Gizmo tool from the Gizmo flyout (see Figure 23.22).

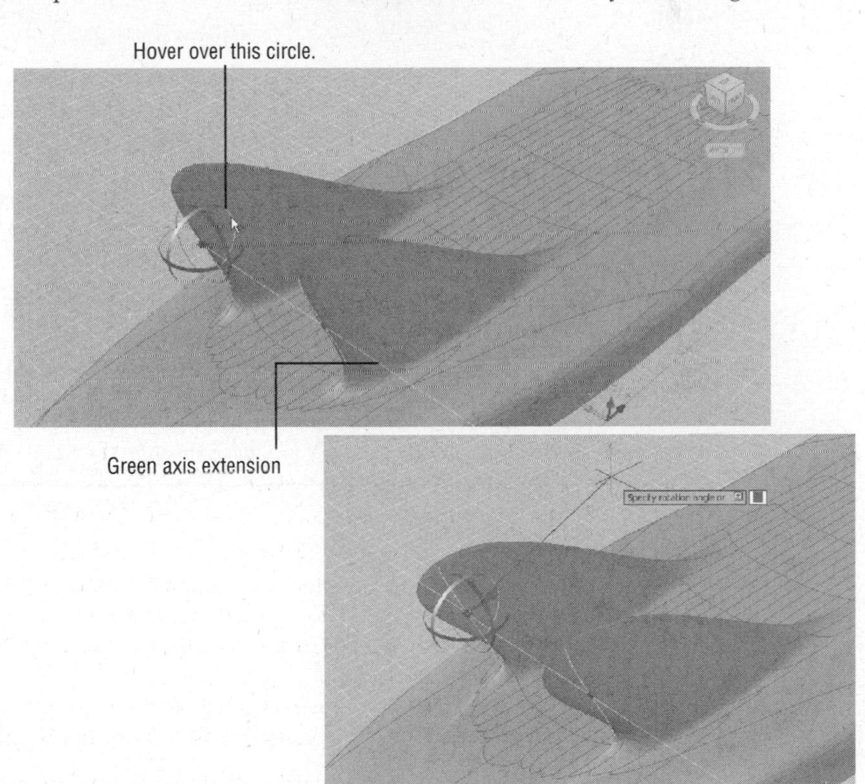

FIGURE 23.22
Click and drag the green circle on the Rotate gizmo.

3. Hover over the green circle of the Rotate gizmo in the location shown in the top panel of Figure 23.21 until you see the green axis vector, and then click once and move the mouse to rotate the edge. Adjust the rotation of the edge so that the fins look similar to those in the lower panel of Figure 23.21, and then click the mouse button.

4. Press the Esc key to clear your selection.
5. Use the Home tool on the ViewCube to get an overall view of the surfboard (see Figure 23.23).

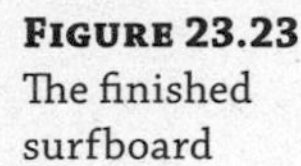
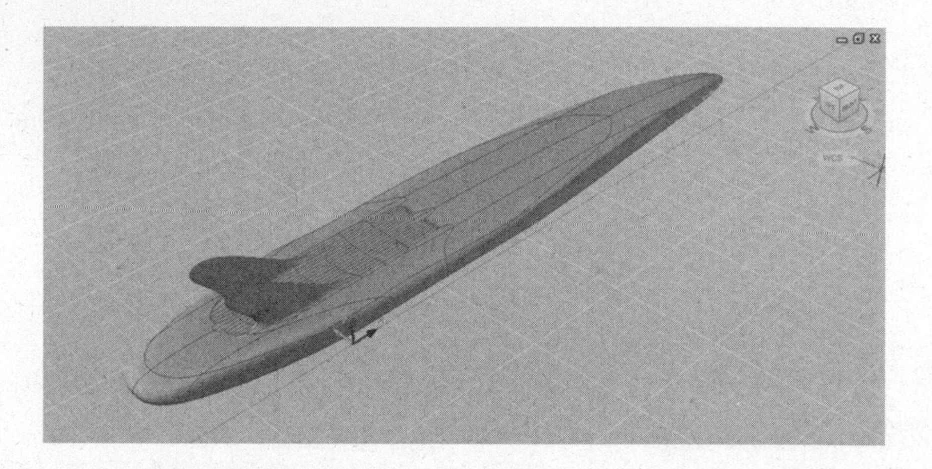

FIGURE 23.23
The finished surfboard

In this exercise, you switched from the Move gizmo to the Rotate gizmo. You can also use the Scale gizmo to scale a face or edge.

This may not be the most accurate rendition of a surfboard (our apologies if you are a surfer), but the general shape of the surfboard has given you a chance to explore many of the features of the Mesh toolset.

> **CHANGING THE GIZMO ON THE FLY**
>
> Instead of using the Gizmo flyout on the Selection panel, you can right-click the gizmo to change it. You can also set the orientation of the gizmo through the context menu, which will allow you to move subobjects in directions other than perpendicular to the face or edge. You can orient the gizmo to the WCS, the current UCS, or a face on a mesh through the Align Gizmo With right-click option.

Adding a Crease

You'll want to know about one more tool that can help you fine-tune your mesh shapes. The Add Crease tool on the Mesh panel does exactly what it says. It can introduce a crease in your otherwise smooth mesh shape. Add Crease does this in two ways: It can flatten a face or remove the smoothing around an edge.

In the following exercises, you'll use the surfboard one more time to experiment with the Add Crease tool. First you'll see how you can add a sharp point to the surfboard:

1. Adjust your view of the surfboard so that you can see the front point, as shown in Figure 23.24. Turn off the grid so that you can see the shape clearly.

2. From the Mesh tab's Selection panel, select the Move Gizmo tool from the Gizmo flyout.

3. Click the Add Crease tool in the Mesh panel.
4. At the `Select Mesh Subobjects to Crease:` prompt, click the front edge of the surfboard, as shown in Figure 23.24.
5. Press ↵. At the `Specify Crease Value [Always] <Always>:` prompt, press ↵.
6. The point of the surfboard becomes much sharper.

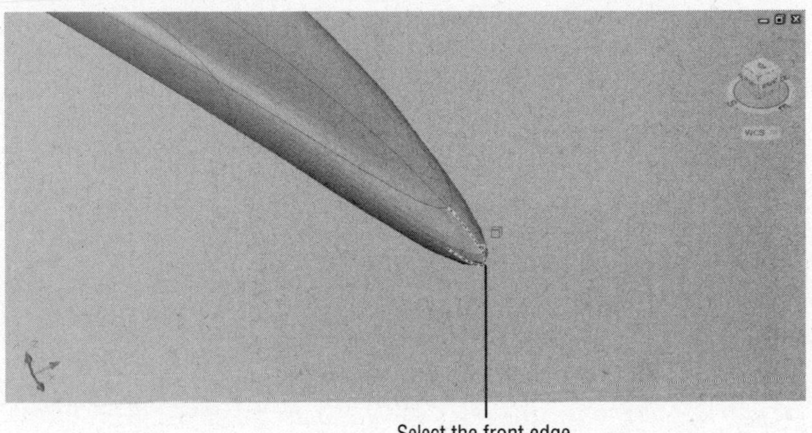

FIGURE 23.24
Set up your view. Select the front edge of the surfboard.

You can see from this exercise that the front edge of the surfboard is now quite sharp since it no longer has any smoothness.

Now try applying the Add Crease tool to a face:

1. From the Selection panel, select Face from the Filter flyout.
2. Click the Add Crease tool and, at the `Select Mesh Subobjects to Crease:` prompt, click the two faces on either side of the front edge, as shown in Figure 23.25, and press ↵.

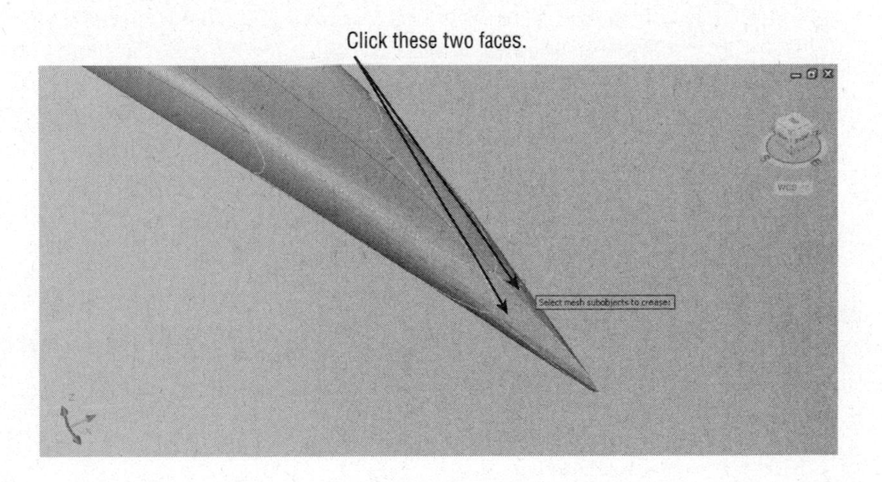

FIGURE 23.25
Click these faces to flatten them.

3. At the `Specify Crease Value [Always] <Always>:` prompt, press ↵.

   The faces are flattened, and the point of the surfboard becomes even sharper, as shown in Figure 23.26.

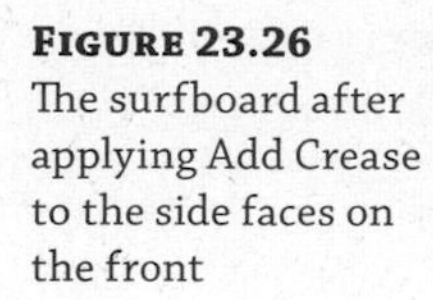

FIGURE 23.26
The surfboard after applying Add Crease to the side faces on the front

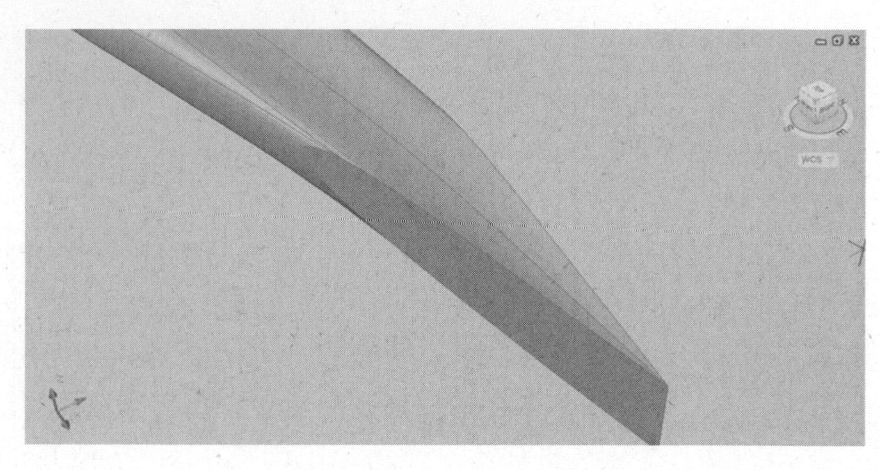

4. Save your drawing.

The surfboard is grossly deformed, but you can see how the side faces have now become flat and the edges of the face form a crease. You could use the Add Crease tool to sharpen the edge of the fins. This would also have the effect of making the fins thinner. We didn't use that example for this exercise because the effects would have been too subtle to see clearly.

Splitting and Extruding a Mesh Face

Before we move on to the next topic, let's discuss two more tools that can be a great aid in editing your meshes. The Split Face tool does just what its name says. It will split a face into two faces. The Extrude Face tool behaves like the Extrude Face tool you have seen for 3D solids. Both of these tools are a bit tricky to use, so they bear a closer look.

To use the Split Face tool, you first select a mesh face and then select two points, one on each side of the face. The following exercise shows how it works:

1. Open the `SplitMesh.dwg` sample file from the Chapter 23 folder at this book's web page (`www.sybex.com/go/masteringautocad2018`). This file contains a simple mesh box that has been smoothed.

2. In the Mesh tab's Mesh Edit panel, click the Split Mesh Face tool, or type **Meshsplit↵**.
3. Make sure the Face filter tool is selected in the Selection panel.

4. Click the face shown in the top panel of Figure 23.27.
5. Move the cursor to the left edge of the face until you see a knife icon appear next to the cursor.
6. Click roughly in the middle of the edge.
7. Move the cursor along the right edge of the face. You'll see some temporary lines, giving you a preview of the location of the split (see Figure 23.27).
8. Move the cursor roughly in the middle of the right edge. The face changes temporarily to show you how it will look when it is divided into two faces.

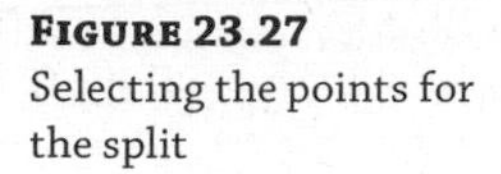

FIGURE 23.27
Selecting the points for the split

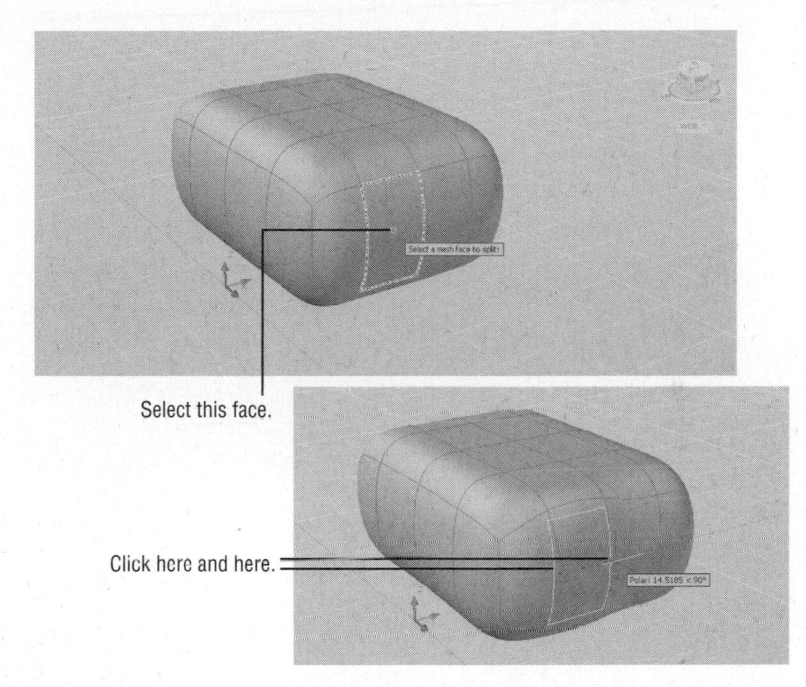

9. Click. The shape of the mesh changes to accommodate the new face.

As you can see, Split Face is not a precision tool, but if you don't like the location of the split, you can move the newly created edge using one of the gizmos.

Next let's look at the Extrude Face tool. At first, you might think that the Extrude Face tool is redundant since you can use the Move gizmo to move a face in a direction away from the mesh, as you saw in an earlier exercise. Using the Extrude Face tool is different from moving a face because it isolates the movement to the selected face as much as possible. To see how this works, try the following:

1. With the Face filter selected in the Selection panel, hold the Ctrl key and click the face indicated in Figure 23.28.

FIGURE 23.28
Select this face.

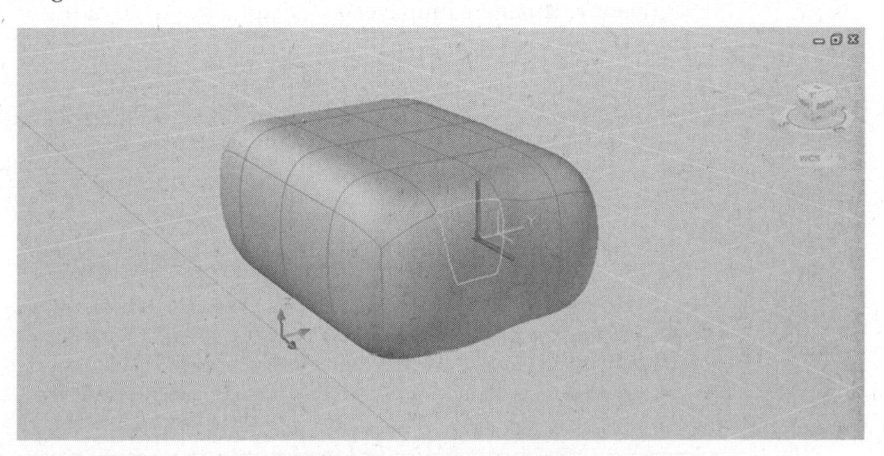

2. Click and drag the x-axis in the positive direction. When the mesh looks similar to the upper panel of Figure 23.29, click to finish the move. The smoothness of the side is maintained as you pull the face.

FIGURE 23.29
A moved face and an extruded face

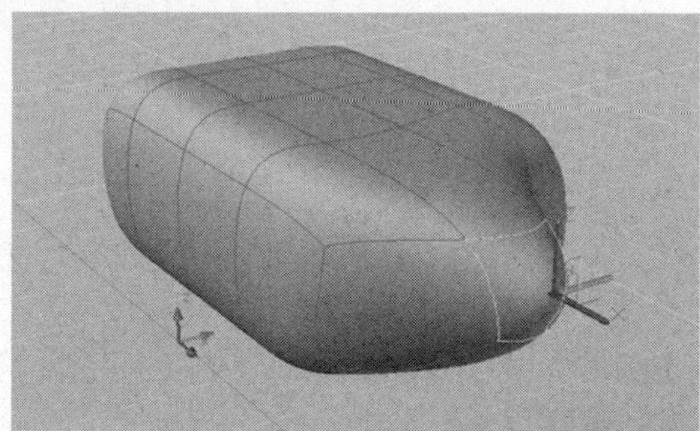

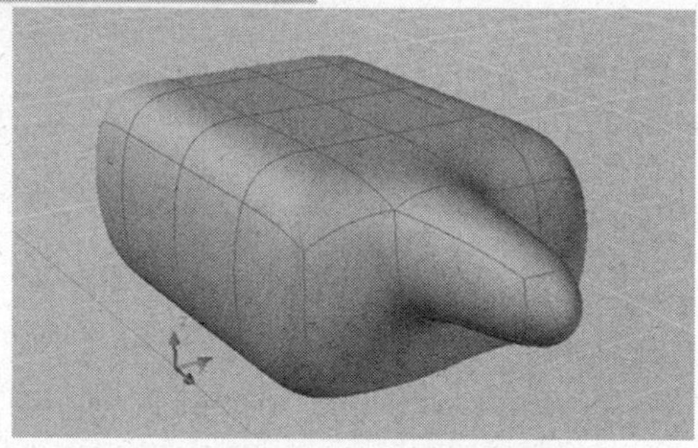

3. Press the Esc key and click Undo to revert to the mesh as it was before you moved the face.
4. Click the Extrude Face tool in the Mesh Edit panel.
5. Click the same face that you selected before, and then press ↵.
6. Move the cursor along the z-axis in the positive direction. The face is extruded, leaving the faces around it unmoved except for a slight curvature at the base (see the lower panel of Figure 23.29).

You can see from this example that the Extrude Face tool confines the deformation of the mesh to only the face that you select. Note that you can select multiple faces for the extrusion.

 **Real World Scenario**

USING SPLIT MESH FACE AND ADD CREASE TOGETHER

In a usability study conducted by Autodesk, the product designers gave an example of how to add a crease to the top surface of a computer mouse model. In the example, the Split Face and Add Crease tools were used together. First a new edge was created using the Split Face tool, and then the Add Crease tool was applied to the newly created edge to form the crease. Using these two tools together in this way, you can add a crease just about anywhere on a mesh.

Creating Mesh Surfaces

So far, you've been working with mesh volumes, but the Primitives panel of the Mesh tab offers four tools that let you create a variety of surface meshes. These are the *revolved, edge, ruled,* and *tabulated surfaces*. If you're an old hand at working with 3D in AutoCAD software, these tools should be familiar. They are the latest incarnation of some of the earliest 3D tools offered by AutoCAD, and they work exactly like the old features they replace. But just like the mesh volumes with which you've been working, the mesh surfaces can be quickly smoothed and their subobjects can be edited using the gizmos that you learned about in this and earlier chapters. The following sections give a little more detail about these tools and how they are used. The figures used in these sections are taken directly from the cue cards for each tool.

> **TRY OUT THESE TOOLS ON A SAMPLE FILE**
>
> The following instructions are for your reference only, and you are not required to do them as exercises. But if you like, you can try them out on the `SurfaceMeshSamples.dwg` file provided with the sample drawings for this chapter.

Revolved Surface

To create a revolved surface, you need a profile to revolve and a line that acts as an axis of revolution (see Figure 23.30). The profile can be any object, but a polyline or spline is usually used.

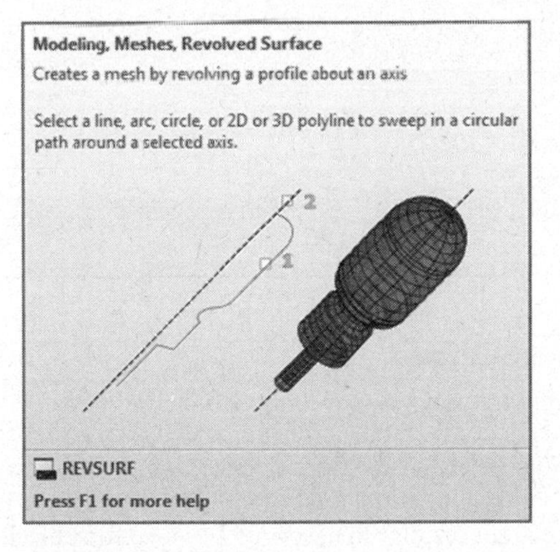

FIGURE 23.30
The Revolved Surface tool's cue card

To create a revolved surface, follow these steps:

1. Click the Modeling, Meshes, Revolved Surface tool in the Primitives panel, or type **Revsurf**↵.
2. Select the profile object, and then select the axis object.
3. At the `Specify start angle <0>:` prompt, enter a start angle, or just press ↵ to accept the default angle of 0.

4. At the `Specify included angle (+=ccw, -=cw) <360>:` prompt, enter the angle of rotation for the surface, or just press ↵ to accept the default angle of 360 degrees. As you might infer from the prompt, you can create a revolved surface that is not completely closed.

GETTING SMOOTHER SURFACES

The mesh surfaces will appear faceted when you first create them. Typically, the revolved, ruled, and tabulated surfaces will have six faces. The edge surface will have an array of 36 faces. You can increase the number of faces that are generated by these tools by changing the Surftab1 and Surftab2 settings. Surftab1 will increase the faces generated by the revolved, ruled, and tabulated surface tools. Surftab1 and Surftab2 can be used to increase the faces of an edge surface.

To use the Surftab settings, type **Surftab1↵** or **Surftab2↵** and enter a numeric value. The value you enter will be the number of faces generated by these surface mesh tools. Don't get carried away, because an increase in the number of faces will also increase the size of your file. Besides, you can always use the Smooth More tool to smooth out the appearance of these surface objects up to the maximum smoothness level allowed.

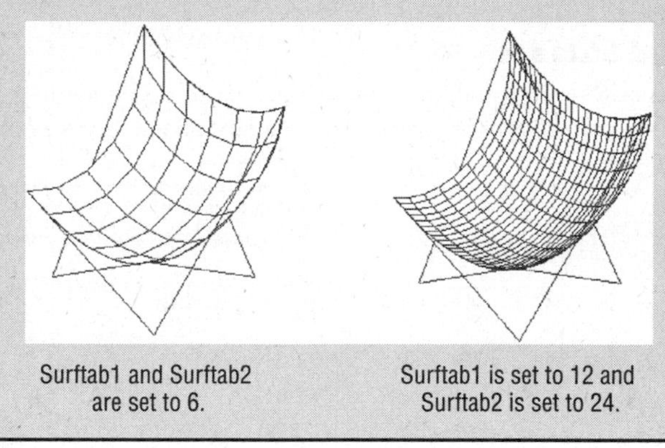

Surftab1 and Surftab2 are set to 6.

Surftab1 is set to 12 and Surftab2 is set to 24.

Edge Surface

In Chapter 21, "Using Advanced 3D Features," you learned how to use the Loft tool to draw a butterfly chair that has the shape of a draped fabric seat. Other 3D modeling tools that you could use to create the seat have been introduced in recent AutoCAD releases.

One tool to use in the butterfly chair example is the Edge Surface tool (see Figure 23.31). This tool is a bit trickier to use, only because the objects defining the surface must be selected in sequential order. In other words, you can't randomly select the objects.

Here's how it works:

1. On the Mesh tab's Primitives panel, click the Modeling, Meshes, Edge Surface tool, or type **Edgesurf↵**.
2. Select the four objects that are the edges of the surface that you want to create. Make sure that you select the objects in clockwise or counterclockwise order. Don't select them "crosswise."

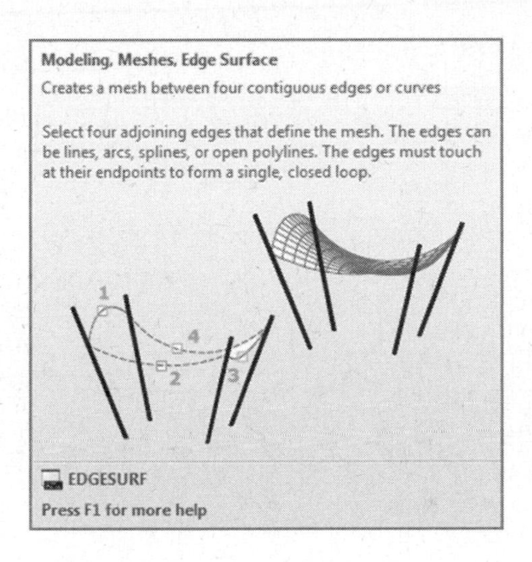

FIGURE 23.31
The Edge Surface cue card

Ruled Surface

The Ruled Mesh tool creates a surface mesh from two 2D objects such as lines, arcs, polylines, or splines. This is perhaps the simplest mesh tool to use since you have to click only two objects to form a mesh (see Figure 23.32). But like Edge Mesh, it has a tricky side. The location where you click will affect the way the mesh is generated. You'll want to click the same side of each object unless you want the surface to twist, as shown in Figure 23.33.

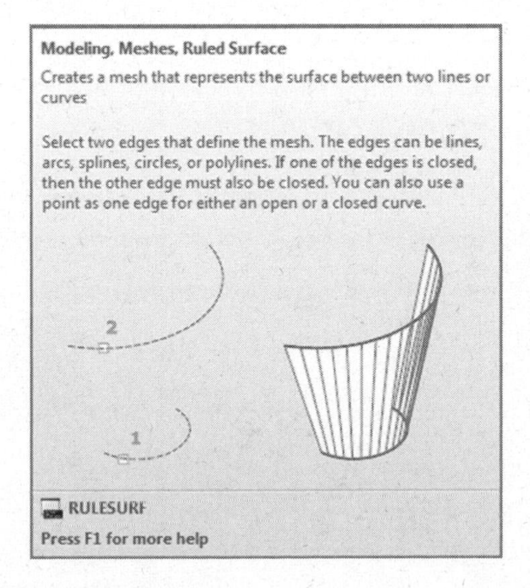

FIGURE 23.32
The Ruled Surface cue card

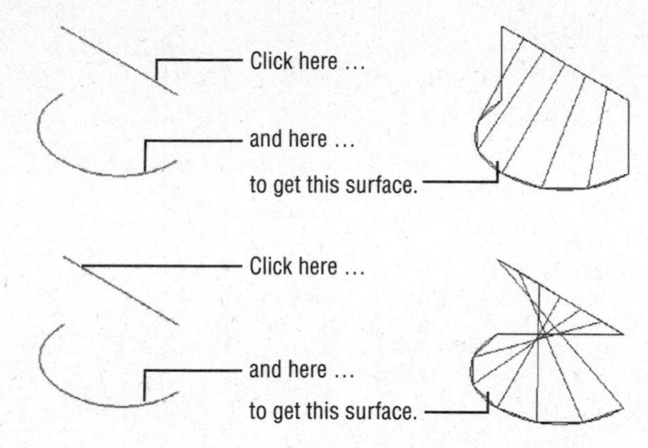

FIGURE 23.33
Where you click an object affects the outcome.

To create a ruled mesh, follow these steps:

1. On the Mesh tab's Primitives panel, click the Modeling, Meshes, Ruled Surface tool, or type **Rulesurf↵**.
2. Click two objects that are not on the same XY plane. The mesh is created between the objects.

Tabulated Surface

The Tabulated Mesh tool is like an extrude tool for surfaces (see Figure 23.34). Chapter 20 showed you how you can use the Extrude tool to create a 3D solid from a closed polygon. The Extrude tool will also work on open polygons, lines, and arcs, but it will extrude the object in only a perpendicular direction. The Tabulated Surface tool lets you "extrude" an object in a direction you control with a line. The line can point in any direction in space.

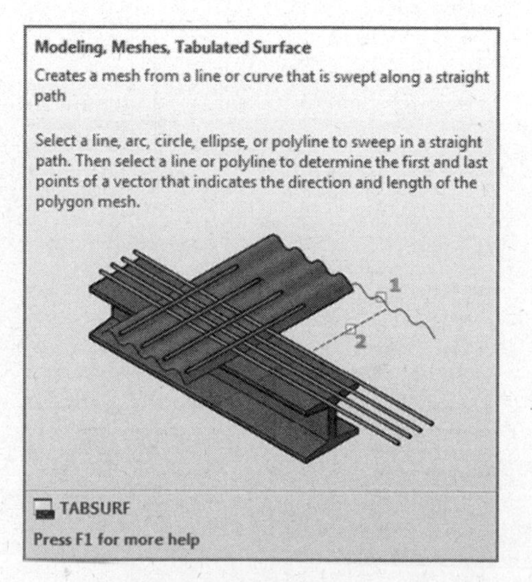

FIGURE 23.34
The Tabulated Surface cue card

Here's how to use it:

1. On the Mesh tab's Primitives panel, click the Modeling, Meshes, Tabulated Surface tool in the Primitives panel, or enter **Tabsurf**↵.
2. Select the object that defines the profile of your mesh.
3. Click the object that defines the direction for the surface.

As with the other surface mesh tools, the point at which you select objects will affect the way the object is generated. For the tabulated mesh, the direction of the mesh depends on where you click the line that defines the surface direction.

Converting Meshes to Solids

We mentioned earlier that you could convert a mesh to a solid. In doing so, you can take advantage of the many solid-editing tools available in AutoCAD. The Boolean tools can be especially useful in editing meshes that have been turned into solids.

Conversion is a fairly simple process using the tools in the Convert Mesh panel of the Mesh tab. Just click the Convert To Solid tool, or type **Convtosolid**↵, and then select the mesh or meshes that you want to convert. Press ↵ to complete the process. The Convert To Surface tool (**Convtosurface**↵) works in much the same way, but it creates a surface object instead of a solid.

When you convert a mesh to a solid, you have the option to apply more or less smoothing to the conversion process. The Smoothed, Optimized flyout in the Convert Mesh panel gives you four options. You can select one of these options before you use the Convert To Solid or Convert To Surface tool to get a different smoothing effect during the conversion. Table 23.1 describes these options and how they affect the conversion of meshes.

TABLE 23.1: Options on the Convert Mesh panel's flyout

OPTION	EFFECT ON MESH
Smoothed, Optimized	The mesh is smoothed, and the faces are merged.
Smoothed, Not Optimized	The mesh is smoothed but maintains the same number of faces as the original.
Faceted, Optimized	The facets are maintained, the smoothing remains the same, but planar faces are merged.
Faceted, Not Optimized	The facets are maintained, the smoothing remains the same, and the number of faces also remains the same.

WHY CONTROL FACES IN THE CONVERSION?

The mesh-to-solid conversion options shown in Table 23.1 may seem like overkill, but there is a good reason for offering these settings. Many of the solid-editing tools in the Home tab's Solid Editing panel are designed to work on solid faces. You can apply many of these tools to the faces of a converted mesh. Having control over the way faces are converted from a mesh to a solid will give you some control over how you are able to edit the solid later. See Chapter 22 for more on the solid-editing tools.

Understanding 3D Surfaces

So far in this book you've worked with 3D solids and meshes. A third type of 3D object called a *surface* completes the AutoCAD set of 3D modeling tools to make it a complete 3D modeling application in its own right.

Click the Surface tab, and you'll see the Surface panels that offer the tools that you'll need to work with surface modeling (see Figure 23.35).

FIGURE 23.35
The Surface tab and Ribbon panels

In the Create panel, you see a different set of tools from the Mesh and Solid tabs, but a handful should look familiar. The Loft, Sweep, Extrude, and Revolve tools at the far left of the Create panel are tools that you've seen in previous chapters. These surface creation tools work in the same way as the tools of the same name in the Solid tab. In fact, they are essentially the same tools. They just use a different command option to create a surface instead of a solid. The big difference is that to create a solid, you need to start with a closed polyline. With the surface version of the Loft, Sweep, Extrude, and Revolve tools, you can start with an open spline, polyline, or other object. And even if you do use a closed object such as a circle or closed polyline, you will still get a 3D surface instead of a solid (see Figure 23.36).

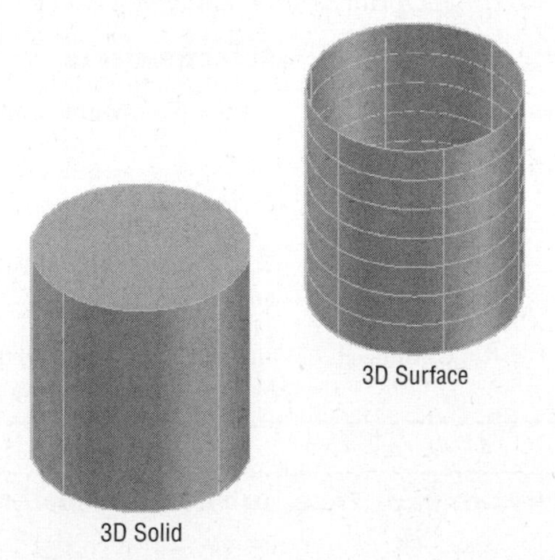

FIGURE 23.36
A circle extruded using the solid Extrude and the surface Extrude

Drawing 2D Curves with the Curves Panel

Since 3D surfaces are derived from 2D objects, the Surface tab has the convenient Curves panel that offers most of the 2D drawing tools that you'll need to build your surfaces from scratch. The Spline flyout even features the Spline Freehand tool, which will let you draw a curve "freehand" with a click and drag of your mouse. Experienced users will recognize this Spline Freehand tool as an updated version of the Sketch command.

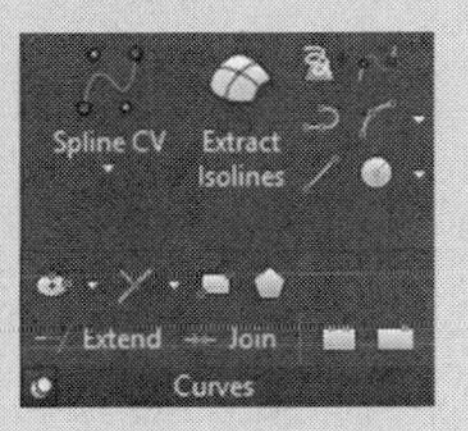

Two other surface-creation tools that are unique to the Surface tab of the Ribbon are the Network Surface and Planar Surface tools. Here's a brief description of each:

Network Surface Tool The Network Surface tool lets you create a surface from several curves. The cue card for the Network Surface tool gives you a good idea of how this tool works (see Figure 23.37).

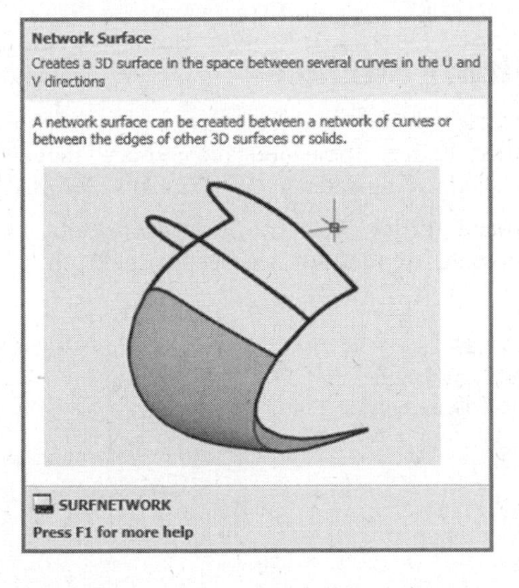

Figure 23.37
The cue card description of the Network Surface tool

Planar Surface Tool The Planar Surface tool creates a flat surface either by selecting two points to indicate a rectangular surface or by selecting a closed 2D object to create a flat surface with an irregular boundary (see Figure 23.38).

FIGURE 23.38
Creating a planar surface

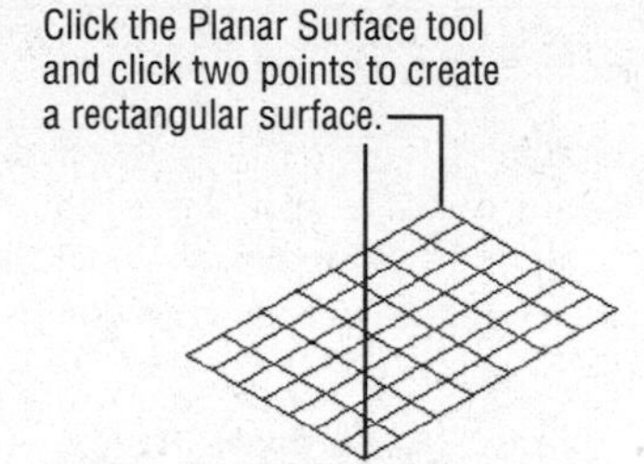

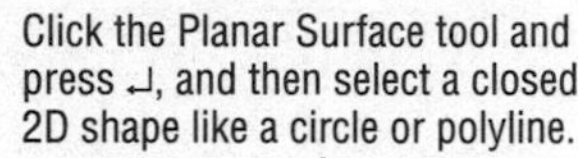

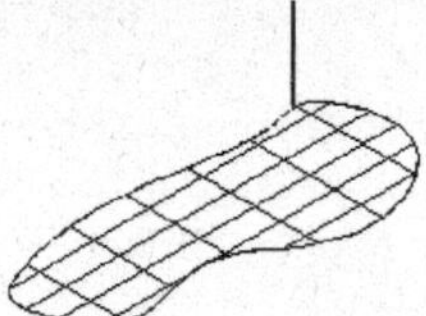

LEARNING FROM ANIMATED CUE CARDS

Animated cue cards show you how many of the tools on the Surface Ribbon tab work. These animated cue cards can help get you up and running with surface modeling. Just hover over a tool for a moment after the tool tip appears. For tools that have animated cue cards, you will see the message "Video is loading" in the lower-right corner of the tool tip.

Editing Surfaces

Once created, surface objects have a unique set of editing tools that allow you to create fairly detailed models. Some tools, like Surface Fillet and Surface Trim, offer the same function as their 2D drawing counterparts. The following list includes a description of each tool:

Surface Fillet With the Surface Fillet tool, you can join one surface to another with an intermediate rounded surface (see Figure 23.39).

FIGURE 23.39
Using the Surface Fillet and Surface Trim tools

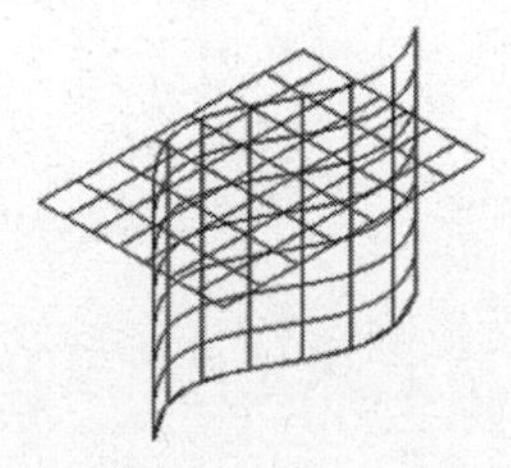

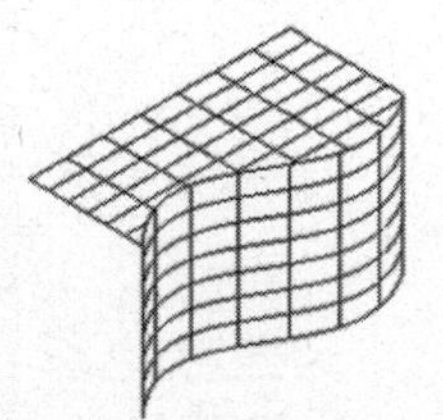

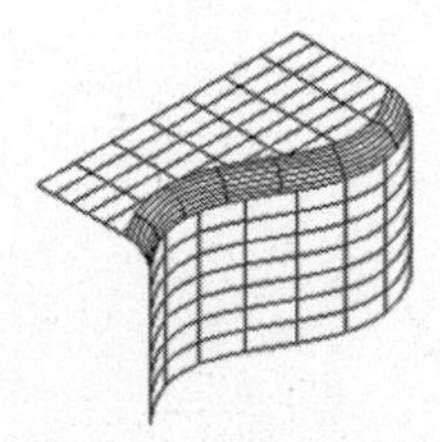

Surface Trim The Surface Trim tool lets you trim one or several surfaces to other surfaces.

Surface Untrim Surface Untrim does exactly what it says—it reverses a trim operation.

Surface Extend The Surface Extend tool enables you to extend the edge of a surface beyond its current location. Unlike its 2D equivalent, it does not extend a surface to another surface object, though you could extend beyond a surface and then use the Trim tool.

Surface Sculpt The Surface Sculpt tool is like a super trim. You can align several surfaces to enclose a volume completely (the left image in Figure 23.40) and then use the Sculpt tool to trim all the surfaces at once into a completely closed 3D shape (the right image in Figure 23.40). By default, the new object is a solid.

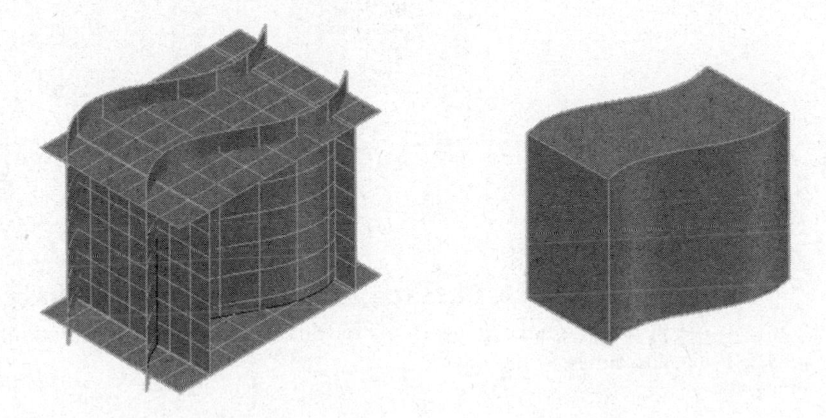

FIGURE 23.40
The Surface Sculpt tool creates a container-like shape from several surfaces.

The Create panel also offers three other tools that could be considered editing tools. Blend, Patch, and Offset need existing surfaces to do their job, so they may seem a bit like editing tools. Here's a description of each:

Surface Blend Surface Blend will connect two surfaces with an intermediate surface.

Surface Patch The Surface Patch tool will close an open surface like the end of a tube. Surface Patch also lets you control whether the closing "patch" is flat or curved, as shown in Figure 23.41.

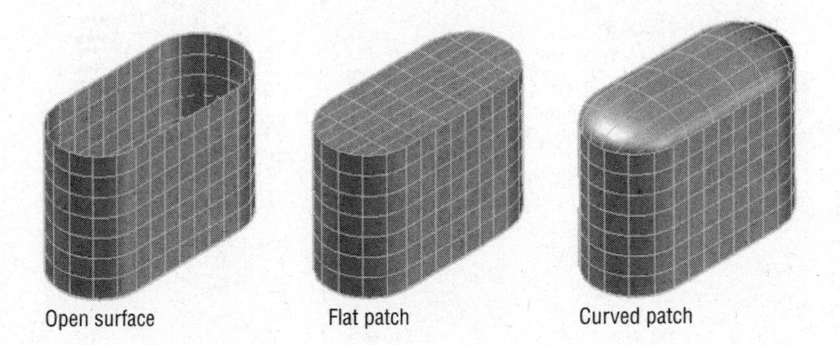

FIGURE 23.41
The Surface Patch tool can create a flat or rounded patch over an open surface.

Surface Offset Surface Offset, like the Surface Trim tool, mimics its 2D counterpart. It will create a new surface that is parallel to the original. When you start the Surface Offset tool from the Create panel and select a surface, you'll see arrows indicating the direction of the offset. You can type **F**↵ to flip the direction of the offset. Enter a distance for the offset, and press ↵ to create the offset surface (see Figure 23.42).

Figure 23.42
Using the Create panel's Surface Offset tool

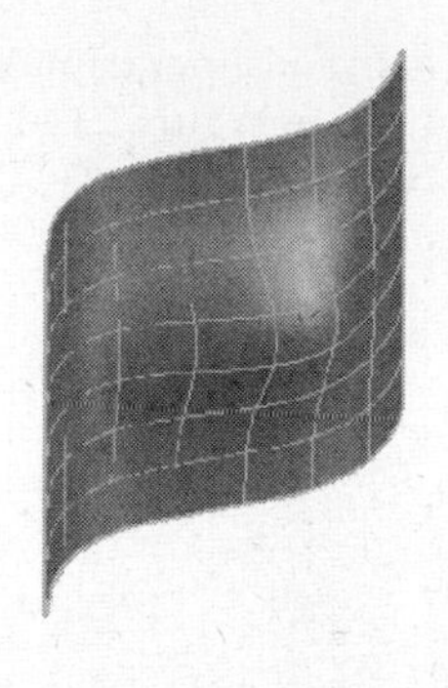
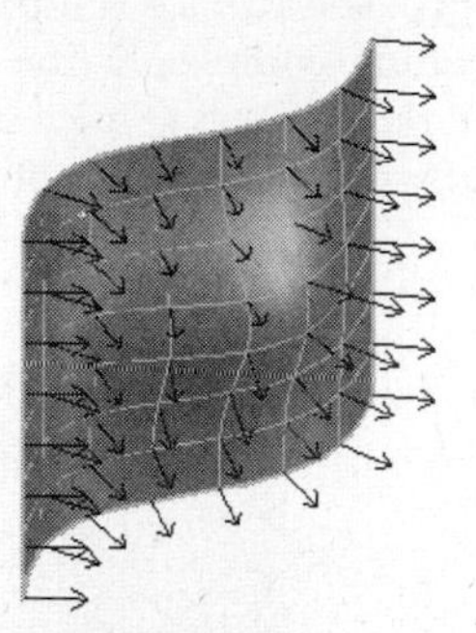
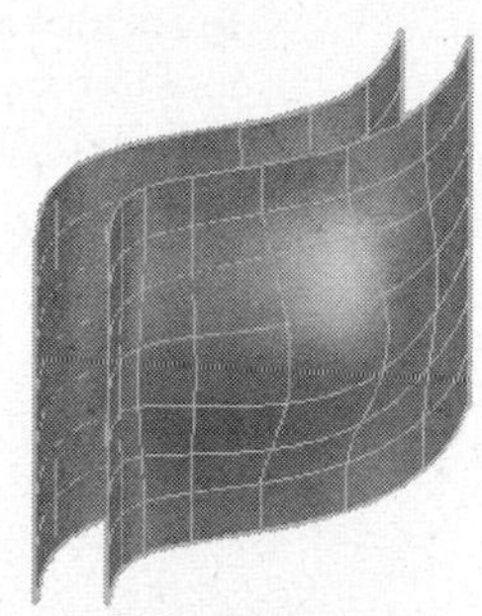
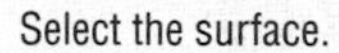

Determine the direction of the offset.

Enter a distance for the offset.

Using Extrude, Surface Trim, and Surface Fillet

Now that you have an overview of the basic surface modeling tools, try the following set of exercises to see how they work.

Using the Extrude Tool

Start with the Extrude tool on two basic shapes:

1. Open the `Surfaces1.dwg` file from the sample folder.

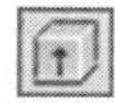

2. Choose Extrude from the Surface tab's Create panel.
3. Click the circle in the drawing, and then press ↵. A surface appears and its length changes as you move the cursor.
4. Adjust the surface height to 5 units so that it looks similar to Figure 23.43 on the right.

Figure 23.43
Extrude the circle and arc (left image) 5 units to look like the image on the right.

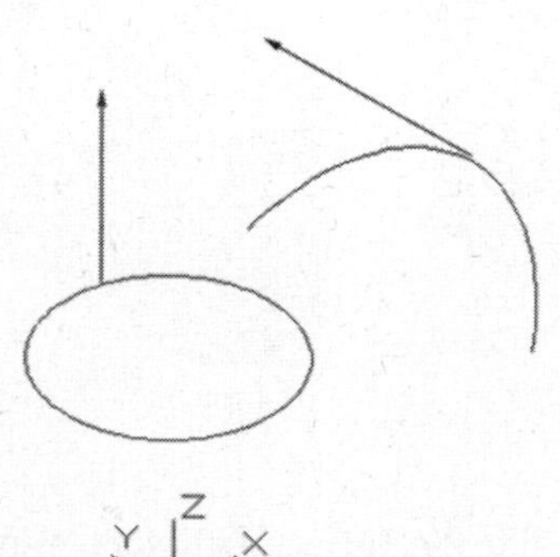
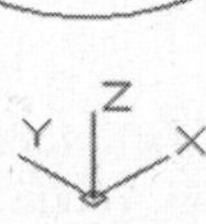

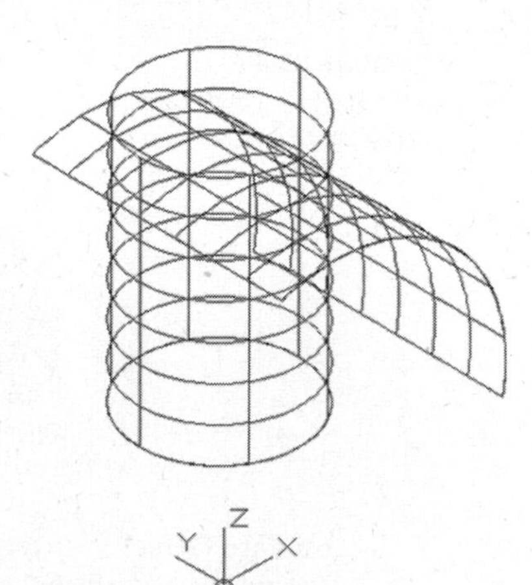

5. Repeat the Extrude command to extrude the arc in the drawing 5 units in the direction shown on the right side of Figure 23.43.

As you can see, the Extrude tool is similar to the Extrude tool in the Solid tab in how it works, but the objects created are surfaces.

Using the Surface Trim Tool

The Surface Trim tool is similar to the 2D Trim tool, except that there is an additional step at the beginning where you select the object that you intend to trim. At first this step seems redundant, but after you use the tool for a while, it begins to make more sense. Also notice that the original arc that you used to extrude the arc surface is still there. You'll use that a little later in this chapter.

Next try out the Surface Trim tool:

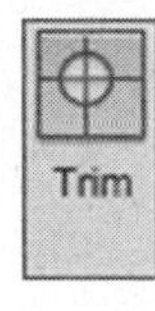

1. Click Surface Trim in the Surface tab's Edit panel.
2. Click both the cylinder and the extruded arc surface, and then press ↵. This first step selects the objects to trim.
3. Click both objects again, and then press ↵. This time you're selecting the objects to trim to. You want to trim the top of the cylinder to the arc and the arc to the cylinder.
4. Finally, click the cylinder near the top edge to indicate what part you want to trim. The cursor will not display a pickbox during this process, and selection windows are disabled. Also click the extruded arc surface anywhere outside the cylinder. Press ↵ to end the command. Your surfaces should look like the right-side image in Figure 23.44.

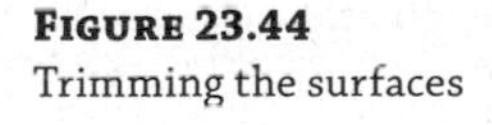

Figure 23.44
Trimming the surfaces

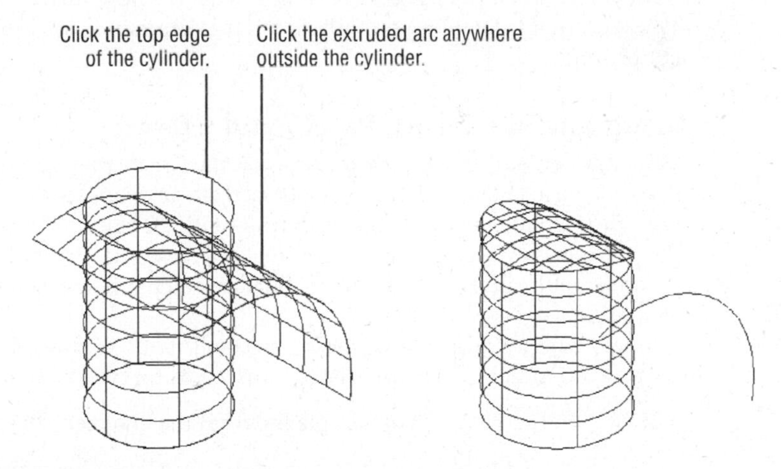

Using the Surface Fillet Tool

Now try out the Surface Fillet tool:

1. Click the Surface Fillet tool in the Surface tab's Edit panel.
2. Click the top surface, and then click the cylinder. The two surfaces are "filleted," as shown in Figure 23.45.

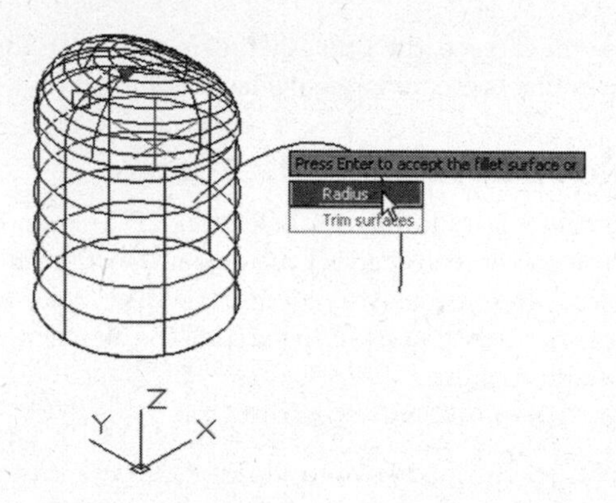

FIGURE 23.45
Using the Surface Fillet tool

3. The following prompt appears: `Press Enter to accept the fillet surface or [Radius/Trim surfaces]`. Type **R**↵ to enter a different radius.
4. Type **0.5**↵. The radius changes. You still have the opportunity to change the radius again.
5. Type **R**↵, and then type **0.2**↵. The radius changes again.
6. Press ↵ to finish the fillet.

In this case, we created a fillet all the way around the top of the cylinder. While you're creating surface fillets, you'll see a preview of what the new surface will look like. You don't have to stick with that fillet until you fully finish the command; you are free to make changes to the fillet until then.

Using Surface Blend, Patch, and Offset

As mentioned earlier, a few of the tools on the Create panel are a bit like editing tools. Surface Blend, Surface Patch, and Surface Offset create new surfaces that use existing surfaces as their basis. Surface Blend is a bit like the Surface Fillet tool in that it will join two surfaces with an intermediate surface. Surface Offset creates a new surface that is parallel to an existing one and is similar to the 2D offset command. Surface Patch will create a surface that closes an open-ended surface.

To get a better idea of how these three tools work, try the following set of exercises. Start by creating a parallel copy of an existing surface using the Offset tool:

1. Open the `Patch1.dwg` sample file from the `Chapter 23` sample folder.

2. Click the Surface Offset tool in the Surface tab's Create panel.
3. Click the surface in the drawing, and then press ↵. You see a set of arrows appear, as shown in the left image of Figure 23.46.
4. Type **F**↵. The arrows now point in the opposite direction.
5. Type **F**↵ again to return the arrows to their previous direction facing outward.
6. Enter **0.5**↵ for the offset distance. The offset surface appears around the original surface, as shown on the right in Figure 23.46.

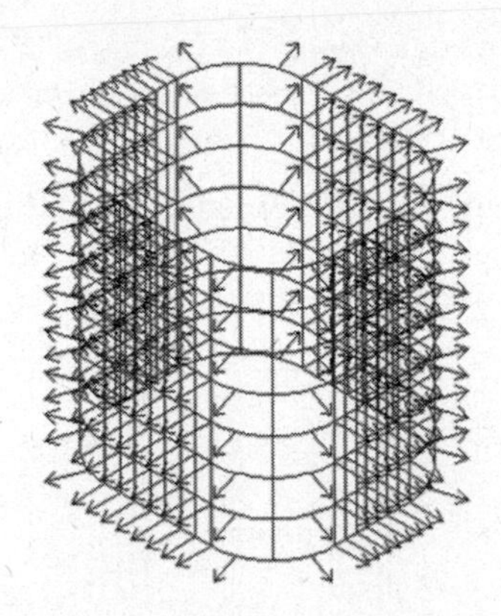
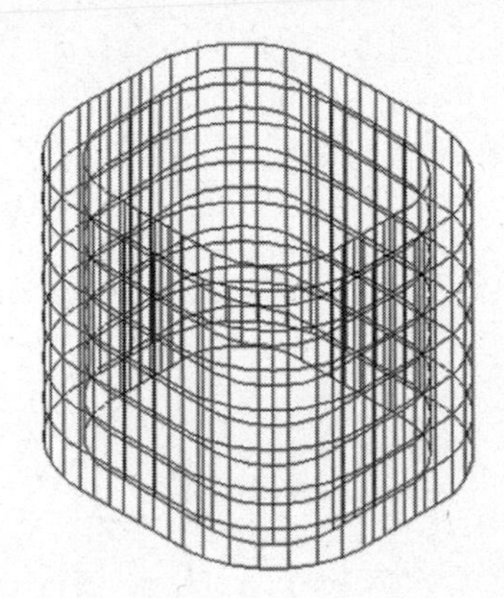

FIGURE 23.46
Using the Surface Offset tool

Here you see how the Surface Offset tool differs from the 2D Offset tool that you've seen in Chapter 18, "Drawing Curves." The arrows play an important role in helping you visualize the result of your offset, so instead of picking a direction, you adjust the direction of the arrows.

USING THE SURFACE BLEND TOOL

Now try the Surface Blend tool:

1. Use the Move command to move the outer surface vertically in the z-axis roughly 5 units. Remember that you can hold down the Shift key to restrain the cursor to the z-axis. If you see the Surface Associativity message, click Continue. You'll learn more about associativity later in this chapter.

2. Adjust your view so that you can see both surfaces, and then click the Surface Blend tool in the Surface tab's Create panel.

3. Hold Ctrl and click to select the eight edges along the top of the lower surface, as shown in Figure 23.47. When you're sure that you've selected all the edges, press ↵. You can also select the Chain option, which will find all edges that are connected.

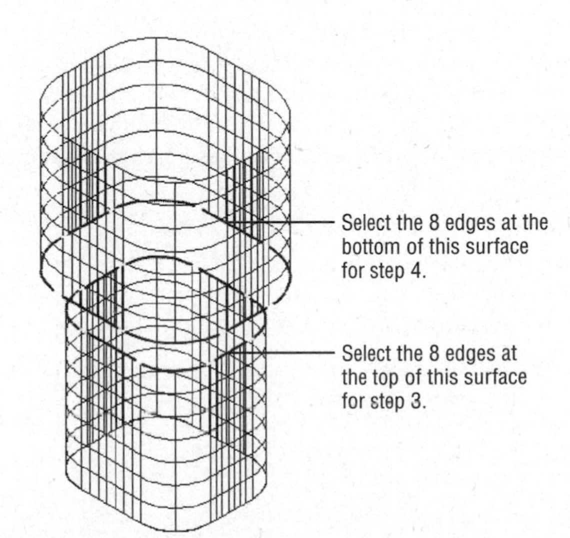

FIGURE 23.47
Selecting the edges for the Surface Blend tool

4. Hold Ctrl and select the eight edges along the bottom of the upper surface, as shown in Figure 23.47. When you're sure that you've selected all the edges, press ↵. A new preview surface appears that joins the upper and lower surfaces.
5. You might notice a couple of grip arrowheads that appear along the top and bottom edges of the new blend surface. Click one of them and a menu appears offering three options: Position, Tangent, and Curvature (see Figure 23.48).

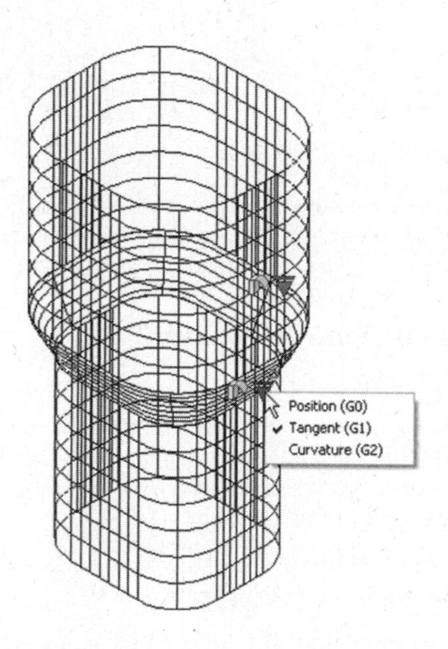

FIGURE 23.48
Using the grip arrowhead to adjust the blend surface

6. Click Curvature, and then press ↵ to place the blend surface.

The Surface Blend tool offers a number of options that control the shape of the blend surface. You saw three options available from the grip arrowhead. The options are available even after you have placed the surface. You can click the surface to expose the grip arrowheads.

In addition, the Surface Blend tool offers two command options: CONtinuity and Bulge Magnitude. Table 23.2 describes these features and their functions.

USING THE SURFACE PATCH TOOL

Now let's take a look at the Surface Patch tool. This tool lets you close the end of a surface with another surface. You can add a flat or curved surface, as you'll see in the next exercise.

Try adding a patch surface to the top of the upper surface in the `Patch1.dwg` model:

1. Pan your view so that you can clearly see the top of the surface model, as shown in the left image in Figure 23.49.

FIGURE 23.49 Adding the patch surface to the end of the model

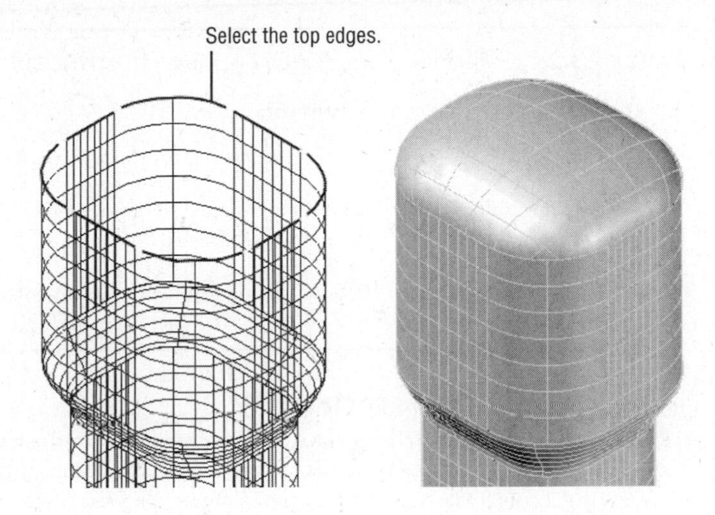

2. Click the Surface Patch tool in the Surface tab's Create panel.
3. Select the edges of the surface, as shown in Figure 23.49.
4. Press ↵ when you are sure that you've selected all the edges. The patch surface appears.
5. Click the grip arrowhead that appears along the edge of the patch and select Tangent. The surface is now curved.
6. Press ↵ to finish the patch surface.
7. To get a better view of the surface, select the Shaded With Edges option from the Visual Styles drop-down list in the Visualize tab's Visual Styles panel. Your model should resemble the right side of Figure 23.49.

You may have noticed that the grip arrowhead options in step 5 were similar to the grip options that you saw for the Surface Blend tool. The Surface Patch tool offers an additional command option called Guides. Table 23.2 describes these options.

TABLE 23.2: The Blend and Patch options

FEATURE OPTION	FUNCTION
Position (G0)	Causes the surface to connect without any blending curvature.
Tangent (G1)	Causes the surface to blend with direction.
Curvature (G2)	Causes the surface to blend with direction and similar curvature or similar rate of change in the surface direction.

TABLE 23.2: The Blend and Patch options *(CONTINUED)*

COMMAND OPTION	FUNCTION
CONtinuity	Controls how smoothly the surfaces flow into each other.
Bulge Magnitude	Allows you to adjust the amount of bulge or curvature in the blend surface. Values can be between 0 and 1.
Guides (Surfpatch command)	Offers additional guide curves to control the patch surface.

Understanding Associativity

You may have noticed the Surface Associativity icon in the Create panel. This feature is on by default, and its function is similar to the Associative feature of hatches (see Chapter 7, "Mastering Viewing Tools, Hatches, and External References," for more on hatches). You may recall that when you create a 2D hatch pattern with the hatch associative feature turned on, the hatch's shape will conform to any changes made to the boundary used to enclose the hatch pattern.

The Associativity feature in surface modeling works in a similar way, only instead of a hatch pattern conforming to changes in a boundary, the surface conforms to changes in the shapes that are used to create them. For example, if you were to make changes to the arc that you used to extrude the arc surface, the arc surface and the trimmed cylinder would also follow the changes.

USING ASSOCIATIVITY TO EDIT A SURFACE MODEL

This concept is a bit tricky to explain. Try the following exercise to see how associativity works:

1. Return to the `Surfaces1.dwg` file, and click the arc to expose its grips.
2. Click the square grip at the arc's left endpoint and drag it downward along the z-axis. When it is roughly in the position shown in Figure 23.50, click again to fix the grip's location. The shape of the surface model changes to conform to the new shape of the arc.

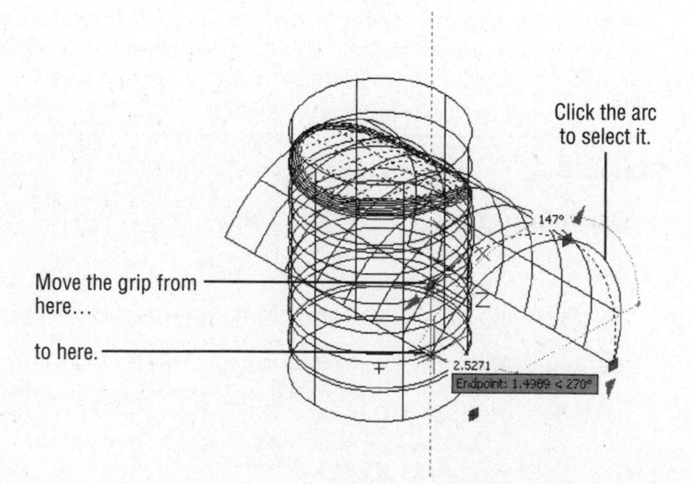

FIGURE 23.50
Adjusting the shape of the arc

3. Zoom into the top of the surface model so that you have a view similar to Figure 23.51.

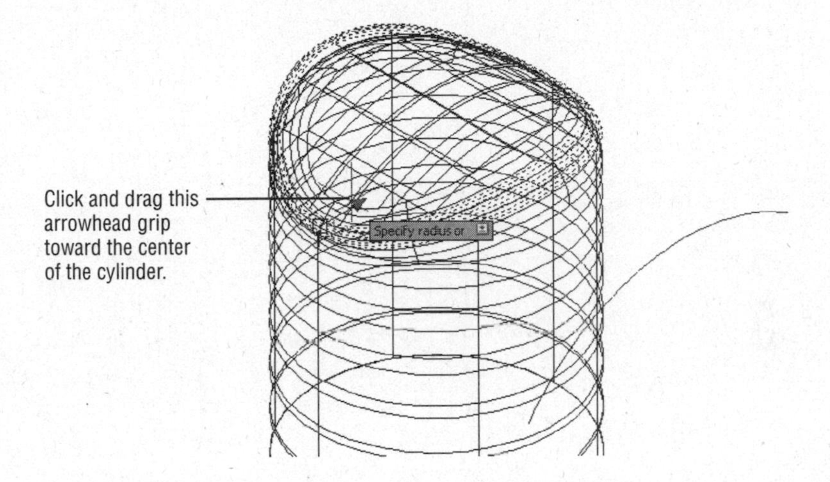

FIGURE 23.51
Adjusting the fillet radius

4. Click the filleted portion of the surface. An arrowhead grip appears.
5. Click the arrowhead grip. Another arrowhead grip appears.
6. Click this arrowhead grip, and slowly drag it toward the center of the cylinder. Notice that the radius of the fillet changes as you move the grip.
7. Click to fix the fillet radius to its new size.
8. Press the Esc key to clear your selection.

USING ARROWHEAD GRIPS TO EDIT A SURFACE

You've just seen the Associativity feature in action. You can also change the shape of the circle used to extrude the cylinder to modify the surface model's diameter. Additional hidden grips are available that allow you to adjust the shape of the surfaces directly. For example, you can modify the taper of the cylinder using an arrowhead grip that you can turn on using the Properties palette, as shown in these steps:

1. Make sure that Dynamic Input is on in the status bar. Click the cylindrical part of the surface model.
2. Right-click and select Properties.
3. Scroll down to the bottom of the Properties palette to the Surface Associativity panel.
4. Click the Show Associativity option, and select Yes.
5. Close the Properties palette.
6. At the top of the cylinder, click the right-pointing arrowhead grip and drag it to the right. As you do this, you see the dynamic display showing you an angle (see the image on the left in Figure 23.52).

FIGURE 23.52
Changing the taper of the cylinder

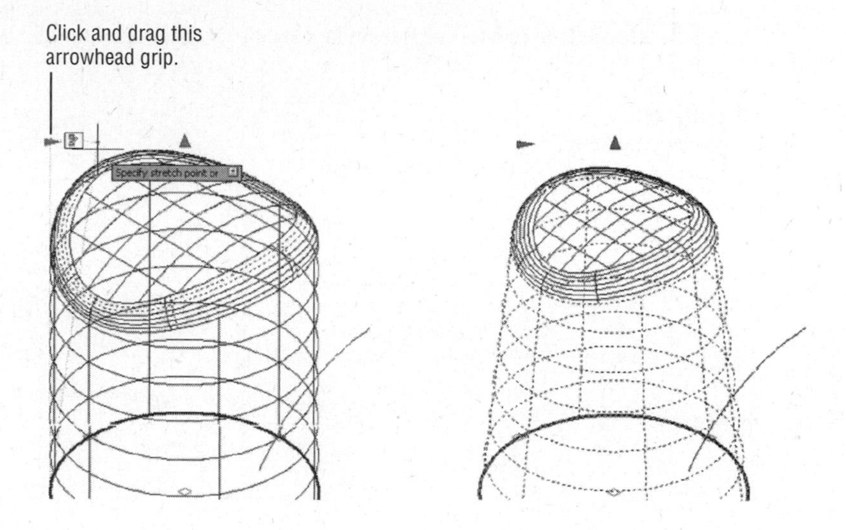

7. Position the arrowhead grip so that the angle shows 6, and then click to fix the grip in place. The cylinder is now tapered, and the top surface conforms to the new shape, as shown in the image on the right in Figure 23.52.

Surface Associativity can be very useful, but in order to take full advantage of this feature, you will want to plan your model construction carefully. In addition, the Associativity feature can limit some editing and creation functions. For example, the Surface Fillet tool may not work on a complex surface model with associativity turned on but will work when the associativity is turned off for the objects involved.

TURNING OFF OR REMOVING ASSOCIATIVITY

You can turn off or remove associativity for an object through the Properties palette. Select the object, and then right-click and select Properties. In the Properties palette, scroll down the palette to the Surface Associativity group (see Figure 23.53). This group offers two options: Maintain Associativity and Show Associativity. The Maintain Associativity option offers Yes, Remove, and None.

FIGURE 23.53
The Surface Associativity group in the Properties palette

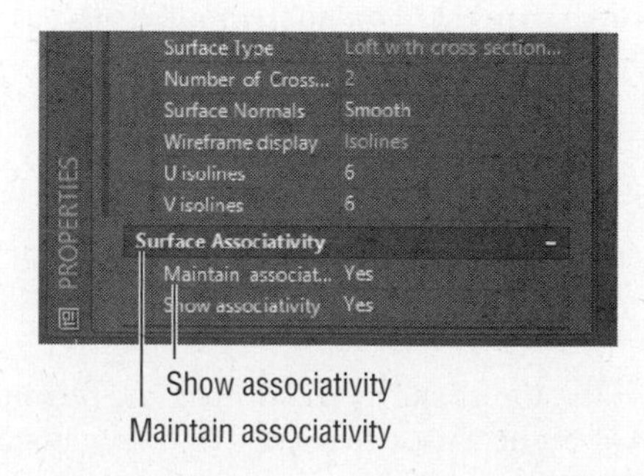

You can select Remove to remove associativity altogether or None to limit the associativity to the set of objects currently associated with the surface model. After you change this setting, you can't return to a previous setting except with the Undo command.

Constraints, Surfaces, and Associativity

In Chapter 16, "Making 'Smart' Drawings with Parametric Tools," you learned that you can add constraints to objects to control their behavior. With Surface Associativity turned on, you can extrude constrained objects and the resulting surface will also follow the constraints of the source 2D objects. But remember that if you use constraints with 3D surfaces in this way, you need to plan the way you build your model carefully to make efficient use of the constraints.

Editing with Control Vertices

So far, you've been creating what are called *procedural surfaces*, which are surfaces that allow you to take advantage of associativity. AutoCAD also allows you to create NURBS surfaces. You may recall that splines are also NURBS, so you might think of a NURBS surface as a kind of 3D surface spline. Splines allow you to move, add, or subtract control vertices (CVs), and you can control the way the CVs "pull" on the curve of the spline. Likewise, NURBS surfaces allow you to add or remove CVs and adjust the direction and force of the CVs.

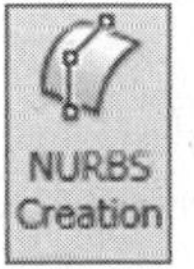

There are two ways to create a NURBS surface. You can turn on the NURBS Creation option in the Surface tab's Create panel and then go about creating your 3D surfaces. Any 3D surface you create with this option turned on will be a NURBS surface. Or you can convert an existing surface to a NURBS surface.

Converting a Surface to a NURBS Surface

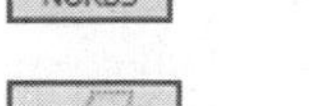

You can convert an existing surface to a NURBS surface by using the Convert To NURBS tool on the Surface tab's Control Vertices panel. This tool also converts 3D solids and meshes. To use it, follow these steps:

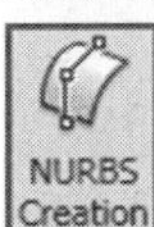

1. Open the `CVedit1.dwg` sample file.
2. Turn on Surface Associativity in the Surface tab's Create panel.
3. Turn off NURBS Creation in the Surface tab's Create panel.
4. Click the Extrude tool in the Surface tab's Create panel.
5. Click the spline and press ↵.
6. Point the cursor upward, and type **6**↵ to make the extruded surface 6 units in the z-axis.
7. Click the Convert To NURBS tool in the Surface tab's Control Vertices panel.
8. Select the surface that you extruded in step 4 and press ↵. The surface is now a NURBS surface.

If you want to create NURBS objects, be sure to turn on NURBS Creation. It's easier to create objects as NURBS than to have to go through the extra step of converting them later.

Exposing CVs to Edit a NURBS Surface

You've just created a NURBS surface. You can expose the CVs for the surface using the Show CV tool. Follow these steps to view and edit the CVs:

1. Click the Surface CV – Show tool in the Control Vertices panel.
2. Click the surface that you just created and press ↵. The CVs appear for the surface.
3. Click the surface to select it, and then click the CV, as shown in Figure 23.54.

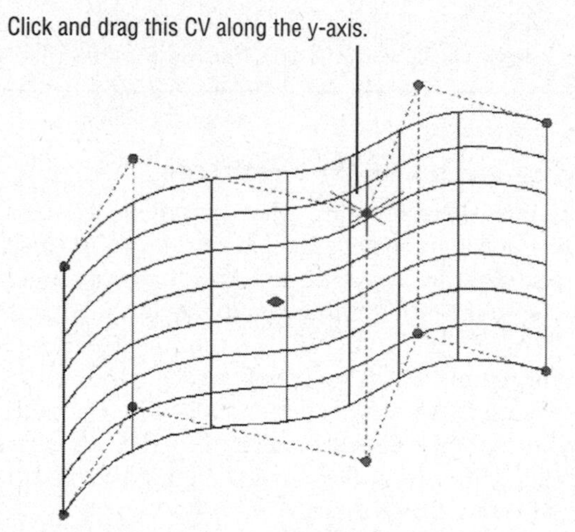

Figure 23.54
Exposing the CVs

4. Move the CV in the y-axis, and note how the surface deforms. The top edge moves with the CV, whereas the bottom edge maintains its shape.
5. Press the Esc key twice to clear your selection.

In this exercise, you saw how you can gain access to the CVs of a NURBS surface to make changes to the shape. Right now, the CVs are located only at the top and bottom of the surface, but you can add more CVs to give you more control over the shape of the surface.

Adding CVs to a NURBS Surface

The next exercise shows you how you can add additional CVs through the Rebuild option:

1. Click the Surface – Rebuild tool in the Control Vertices panel, and then click the surface. Or you can click the surface to select it and then right-click and select NURBS Editing ➢ Rebuild. The Rebuild Surface dialog box appears (see Figure 23.55).
2. In the Control Vertices Count group of the Rebuild Surface dialog box, make sure that the In U Direction option is set to 8 and the In V Direction option is set to 7. You'll see what these settings do in a moment.
3. Click OK. Now you see that many more CVs are available.

FIGURE 23.55
The Rebuild Surface dialog box

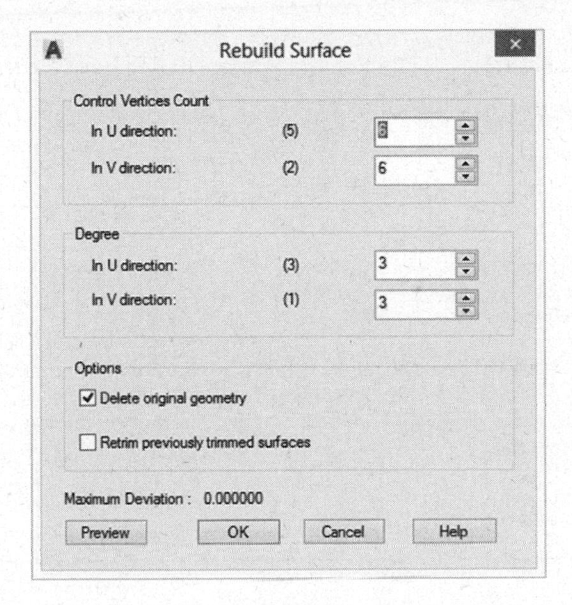

In step 2, you specified the number of CVs that you want in the U and V directions. The U direction is along the horizontal curve, and the V direction is along the straight, vertical direction. If you count the CVs in each row or column, you'll see that they match the values that you entered in step 2.

Now if you were to move a CV, the surface is able to deform along the z-axis, whereas it remained a straight line before.

WHAT ARE THE U AND V DIRECTIONS?

While working in 3D, you'll see references to the U and V directions. You can think of these as the x- and y-axes of a 3D surface. There is also a W direction, which corresponds to the z-axis, or the normal direction of a surface.

The Rebuild Surface dialog box offers a number of other options that you'll want to know about. Table 23.3 gives you a rundown.

TABLE 23.3: The Rebuild Surface dialog box

SECTION/OPTION	EFFECT
Control Vertices Count	
In U Direction	Sets the number of CVs in the U direction
In V Direction	Sets the number of CVs in the V direction

TABLE 23.3: The Rebuild Surface dialog box *(CONTINUED)*

SECTION/OPTION	EFFECT
Degree	
In U Direction	Sets the number of CVs available per span in the U direction
In V Direction	Sets the number of CVs available per span in the V direction
Options	
Delete Original Geometry	Determines whether the original geometry is retained
Retrim Previously Trimmed Surfaces	Determines whether trimmed surfaces are retained from the original surface
Maximum Deviation	Displays the maximum deviation between the original and rebuilt surface

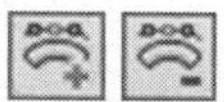

Two other tools just below the Surface Rebuild tool allow you either to add or remove a set of CVs. The Surface CV – Add tool lets you place a row of CVs. The Surface CV – Remove tool will remove a row of CVs. Both options allow you to toggle between the U and V directions for the row addition or removal by typing **D**↵.

The Surface CV Add and Remove tools can be useful when you want to fine-tune the curvature of a surface. Where you want a "tighter" curve, you can add more CVs to an area of the surface. You can then move the CVs in the selected area to increase the curvature. To smooth out the curvature of an area, remove the CVs.

Editing with the CV Edit Bar

You've seen how a NURBS surface can be set up to add additional CVs, which in turn allow you to adjust the shape of the surface. But the CVs by themselves allow you to adjust their pull on the surface only by moving them closer to or farther away from the surface.

The CV Edit bar gives you more control over the behavior of individual CVs. With the CV Edit bar, you can change the strength and direction of the "pull" exerted by a CV.

Try the following exercise to see how the CV Edit bar works:

1. Click the Surface CV Edit Bar tool in the Control Vertices panel.
2. Select the surface. Now as you move the cursor across the surface, you see two red lines that follow the U and V directions of the surface (see Figure 23.56).
3. Click the point shown in Figure 23.56. A Move gizmo appears along with two other features called the magnitude handle and the expansion grip (see Figure 23.57).

The Move gizmo gives you a bit more control over the location of the CV since it allows you to isolate movement in the X, Y, or Z direction. The expansion grip lets you change the tangency of the CV, whereas the magnitude grip lets you control the strength of the CV.

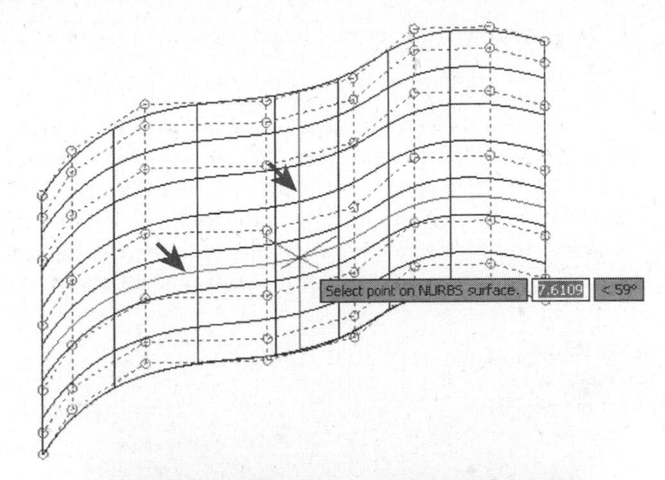

FIGURE 23.56
The CV Edit bar's U and V directions are shown by two red lines.

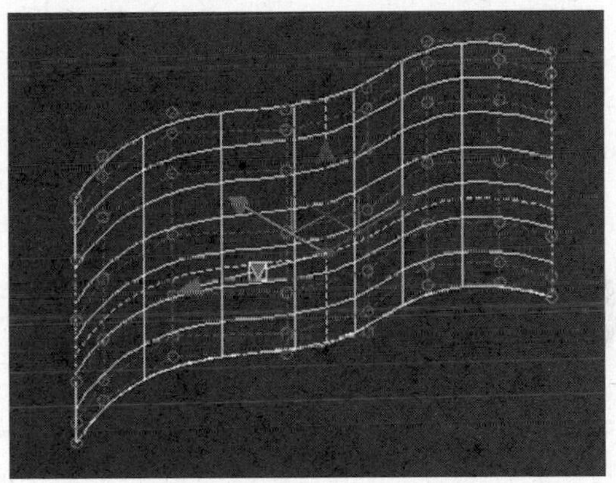

FIGURE 23.57
The magnitude handle and expansion grips

Perform these steps to see how these two features work:

1. Click the expansion grip, and select the Tangent Direction option. Notice that the Move gizmo switches to the location of the expansion grip.
2. Hover over the green y-axis of the gizmo, and when you see the green y-axis vector, click and drag the mouse. Notice how the surface warps as you move the mouse. If you look carefully at the CV Edit bar, you see that it pivots around the new location of the expansion grip—the CV location.
3. Press the Esc key to release the y-axis, and then click the expansion grip and choose the Move Point option. The Move gizmo returns to its original location at the CV.
4. Now click the magnitude handle, and move it horizontally. You see that the surface is "pulled" in both directions of the U direction of the surface.
5. Press the Esc key to release the magnitude handle.
6. Right-click the CV Edit bar, and select V Tangent Direction. Notice that the magnitude handle changes its orientation so that it is aligned to the V direction of the surface.

7. Click and drag the magnitude handle to see how it affects the surface.
8. Press the Esc key twice to exit the CV Edit bar.

As you can see from this exercise, the CV Edit bar gives you much more control over a CV than you would have otherwise. You also saw the context menu for the CV Edit bar in step 6 (see Figure 23.58). The context menu allows you to change the direction of the magnitude grip, but it also lets you switch the position of the Move gizmo and the expansion grip with the Move Point Location and Move Tangent Direction options. The Relocate option lets you move to a different CV location. Table 23.4 includes descriptions of these options.

FIGURE 23.58
The CV Edit bar's context menu

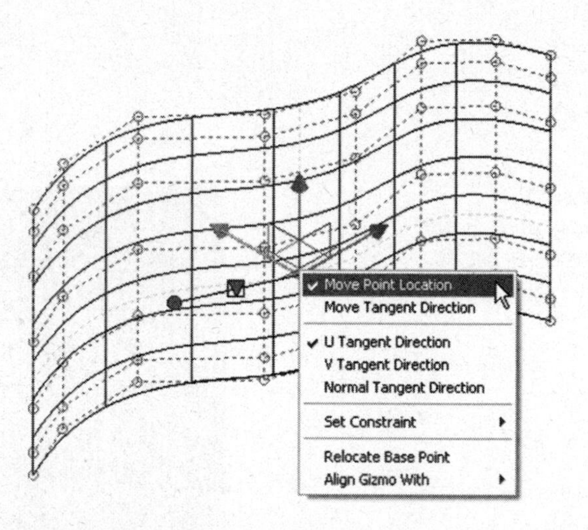

TABLE 23.4: The CV Edit bar's right-click options

OPTION	PURPOSE
Move Point Location	Places the Move gizmo at the CV location
Move Tangent Direction	Places the Move gizmo at the expansion grip location to allow adjustment to the tangent direction of the CV
U Tangent Direction	Aligns the magnitude grip to the surface's U direction
V Tangent Direction	Aligns the magnitude grip to the surface's V direction
Normal Tangent Direction	Aligns the magnitude grip to a direction that is normal (perpendicular) to the surface
Set Constraint	Constrains changes to the tangency in a specific direction, such as X, Y, or Z or in a plane defined by a pair of axes
Relocate Base Point	Moves the CV Edit bar to a different location on the surface
Align Gizmo With	Aligns the gizmo with the world or current UCS, or with an object

Making Holes in a Surface with the Project Geometry Panel

Eventually, you'll need to place an opening in a surface, so AutoCAD offers the Project Geometry panel. This panel contains several tools that allow you to project a closed 2D object's shape onto a 3D surface. For example, if you want to place a circular hole in the surface that you edited in the previous exercise, you would draw a circle parallel to that surface and then use the Surface Projection UCS tool.

The following exercise shows you how the Project Geometry feature works:

1. Select Hide CV on the Control Vertices panel of the Surface tab, and then select the Layer Properties tool from the Layers panel of the Home tab.
2. Turn on the Circle layer. A circle appears in the drawing. Close the Layer Properties Manager if you find it gets in the way.
3. Type **UCS**↵, and then type **OB**↵. This lets you align the UCS to an object.
4. Click the circle to align the UCS to it.

5. In the Surface tab's Project Geometry panel, click the Surface Auto Trim tool to turn it on.
6. Click the Surface Projection UCS tool in the Project Geometry panel.
7. Click the circle and press ↵.
8. Click the surface. The circle is projected onto the surface, and the area inside the projected circle is trimmed (see Figure 23.59).

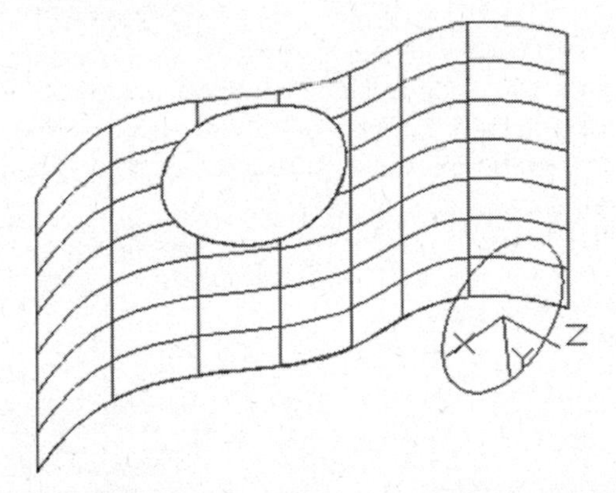

Figure 23.59
The circle projected onto the surface

In this exercise, you aligned the UCS to the circle. The Surface Projection UCS tool that you used in step 6 projected the circle in the z-axis of this new UCS that is aligned with the circle.

The other two Project Geometry tools use different criteria to project geometry. The Surface Projection View projects geometry along the line of sight. If you had used this tool in the previous exercise, the projected circle and opening would appear directly behind the circle in your current view. The Surface Projection Vector projects geometry along a vector that you indicate with two points. You can use the 3D object snaps to select points on the geometry and the surface.

Visualizing Curvature: Understanding the Analysis Panel

In addition to the surface editing tools, AutoCAD offers several surface analysis options. These options offer some visual aids to help you see the curvature of your surface models more clearly.

They can be found in the Analysis panel of the Surface tab and are called Analysis Zebra, Analysis Curvature, and Analysis Draft.

Analysis Zebra displays stripes that let you better visualize how the curvatures of surfaces blend (see Figure 23.60). The smoother the stripes, the better the transition between surfaces.

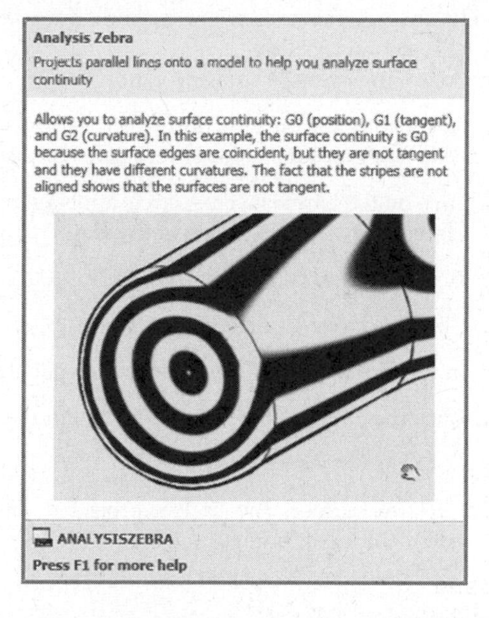

FIGURE 23.60
The cue card description for Analysis Zebra

Analysis Curvature displays colors to indicate the direction and amount of curvature in a surface (see Figure 23.61). As the cue card describes, a negative curvature is a saddle shape and displays a blue color. A positive curvature, or bowl shape, displays in red.

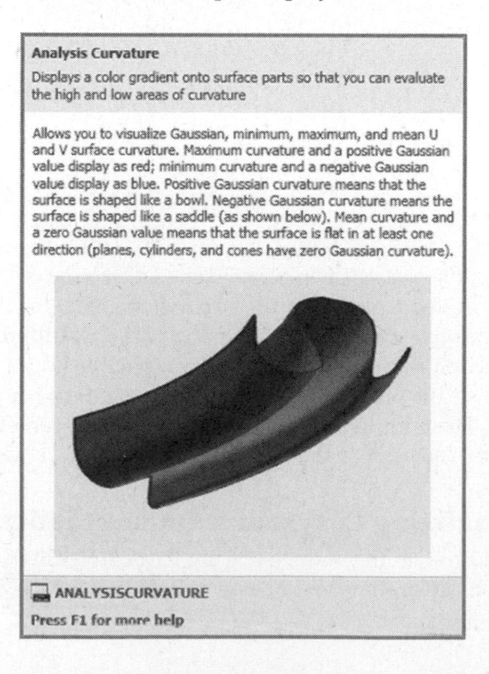

FIGURE 23.61
The cue card description for Analysis Curvature

Analysis Draft displays colors to help you determine draft angles (see Figure 23.62). Draft angles are often used in the design of objects that are to be cast from a mold, and they are important in allowing the cast object to be removed easily from the mold.

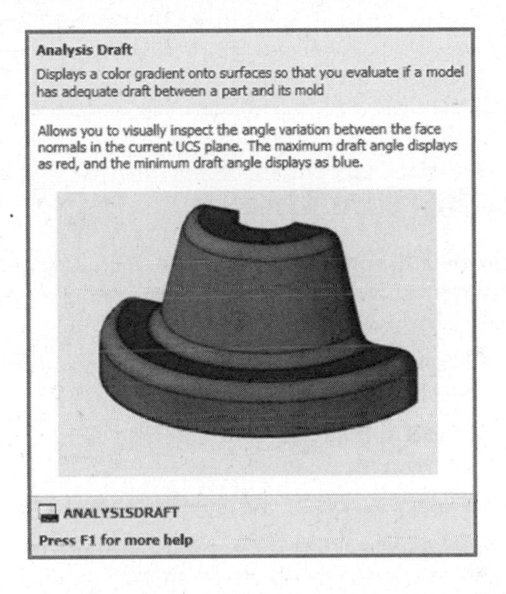

FIGURE 23.62
The cue card description for Analysis Draft

The Analysis Options tool opens the Analysis Options dialog box, where you can control the way the different analysis tools are displayed. Note that graphics hardware acceleration must be turned on before you can use these tools. You must also use a visual style other than Wireframe.

To turn on graphics hardware acceleration, right-click the Hardware Acceleration tool in the right portion of the status bar and select Hardware Acceleration.

USING THE 3D OBJECT SNAPS

You may have noticed the 3D Object Snap tool in the status bar:

It might not be turned on. Click the Customization button on the far right of the status bar to bring up a list of possible status bar icons. Click the 3D Object Snap option to turn it on. This tool works in a way similar to the Object Snap tool that you've used in earlier chapters. When the 3D Object Snap tool is on, you can snap to geometry on 3D objects. If you right-click this tool, you'll see the list of locations to which you can snap:

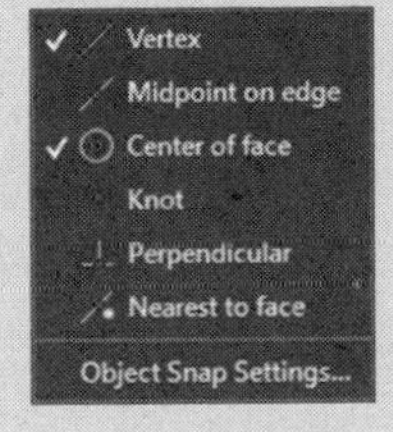

continues

continued

You can think of the 3D Object Snap tool as an extension of the standard set of object snaps that allow you to pick locations on 3D solids, meshes, and surfaces. Right-click the 3D Object Snap tool, and select Settings. You will see the Drafting Settings dialog box open to the 3D Object Snap tab. There you can choose which 3D object snap you want to appear as the default when this tool is turned on.

The Bottom Line

Create a simple 3D mesh. Mesh modeling allows you to create more organic 3D forms by giving you unique smoothing and editing tools. You can start your mesh model by creating a basic shape using the mesh primitives.

Master It Name the seven mesh primitives available on the Primitives panel of the Mesh Modeling tab.

Edit faces and edges. The ability to edit faces and edges is essential to creating complex shapes with mesh objects.

Master It Name the tool that is used to divide a face into multiple faces.

Create mesh surfaces. The Mesh primitives let you create shapes that enclose a volume. If you just want to model a smooth, curved surface in 3D, you might find the surface mesh tools helpful.

Master It How many objects are needed to use the Edge Surface tool?

Convert meshes to solids. You can convert a mesh into a 3D solid to take advantage of many of the solid-editing tools available.

Master It Name at least two tools that you can use on a solid that you cannot use on a mesh.

Understand 3D surfaces. 3D surfaces can be created using some of the same tools you use to create 3D solids.

Master It Name at least two tools that you can use to create both 3D solids and 3D surfaces.

Edit 3D surfaces. AutoCAD offers a wide range of tools that are unique to 3D surfaces.

Master It Name at least four tools devoted to CV editing.

Part 5

Customization and Integration

Chapter 24

Customizing Toolbars, Menus, Linetypes, and Hatch Patterns

AutoCAD® 2018 software offers a high degree of flexibility and customization, enabling you to tailor the software's look and feel to your requirements. In this chapter, you'll see how to customize AutoCAD so that it integrates more smoothly into your workgroup and office environment.

The first part of the chapter shows you how to adapt AutoCAD to fit your particular needs. You'll learn how to customize AutoCAD by modifying its menus, and you'll learn how to create custom macros for commands that your workgroup uses frequently.

In this chapter, you will learn to

- Use workspaces
- Customize the user interface
- Create macros in tools and menus
- Edit keyboard shortcuts
- Save, load, and unload your customizations
- Understand the DIESEL macro language
- Create custom linetypes
- Create hatch patterns

Using Workspaces

When you're comfortable with AutoCAD, you may find that you like a certain arrangement of Ribbon panels, toolbars, and palettes or that you have several sets of panels and toolbars that you like to use, depending on your type of work. You've already worked with two of the workspaces AutoCAD offers out of the box: Drafting & Annotation and 3D Modeling. You can also set up your own custom panel and toolbar arrangements and then save those arrangements for later retrieval using the Workspace feature. Let's take a closer look at how you can create a custom workspace.

The Workspace Switching tool and its menu are shown in Figure 24.1. In the section "Getting to Know the 3D Modeling Workspace" in Chapter 20, "Creating 3D Drawings," you saw how you can use this tool to switch to a 3D modeling workspace. You can save several arrangements of panels, toolbars, and palettes and then recall them easily by selecting them from the Workspace Switching tool in the status bar or the Workspace drop-down list in the Quick Access toolbar.

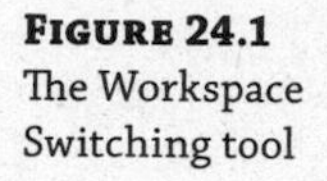

FIGURE 24.1
The Workspace Switching tool

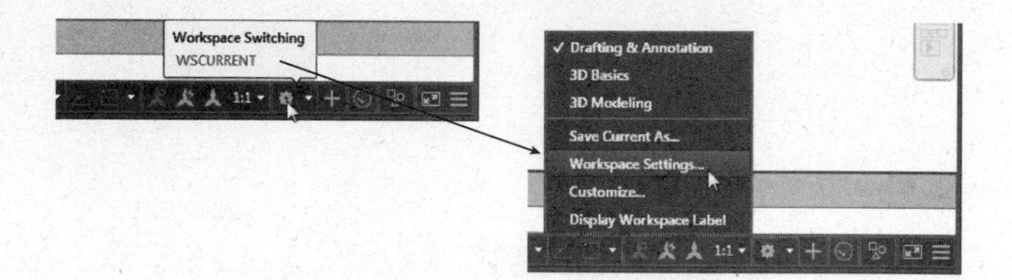

Click the Workspace Switching tool on the status bar, and select Workspace Settings to open the Workspace Settings dialog box, as shown in Figure 24.2. You can also select Workspace Settings from the Workspace drop-down list in the Quick Access toolbar or type **Wssettings**↵.

FIGURE 24.2
The Workspace Settings dialog box

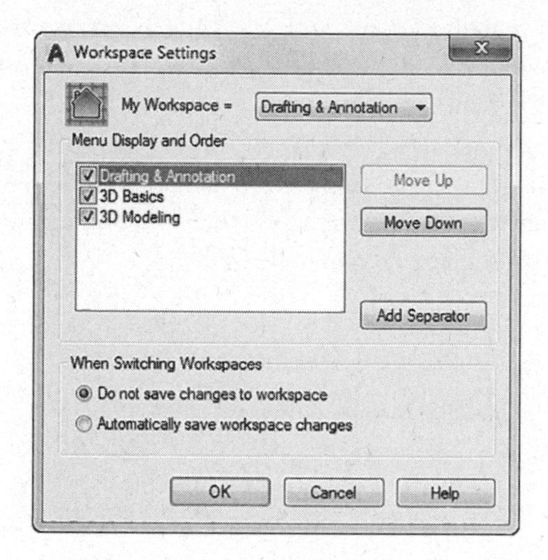

With the Workspace Settings dialog box open, you can see the Drafting & Annotation, 3D Basics, and 3D Modeling options. If you've used the Initial Setup Wizard to create an industry-specific workspace, you'll see the Initial Setup Workspace option here as well. From here, you can control the behavior of the settings.

The check box next to each setting lets you control whether the item appears in the Workspace Switching tool menu. For example, if you remove the check mark from the 3D Basics setting, you'll see only Drafting & Annotation and 3D Modeling in the Workspace Switching tool menu.

The My Workspace drop-down list lets you select which workspace setting is activated when you click the My Workspace tool on the Workspace toolbar. You can use this option for your most frequently used workspace settings.

The options in the When Switching Workspaces group at the bottom of the Workspace Settings dialog box let you determine whether workspace changes are saved automatically. For example, if you select Automatically Save Workspace Changes, then the next time you switch to a different workspace setting, AutoCAD will save any changes that you've made to the current workspace.

The Workspace Switching tool is the easiest customization feature that you'll find in AutoCAD, and it can go a long way toward helping you stay organized. But workspaces are just the tip of the iceberg when it comes to customizing AutoCAD. Next, you'll delve into the Customize User Interface (CUI) feature to see how you can customize the AutoCAD menus, panels, and toolbars directly.

Are You in the Right Workspace?

The exercises in this chapter assume that you are in the Drafting & Annotation workspace.

Customizing the User Interface

Out of the box, AutoCAD offers a generic arrangement of Ribbon panels, tools, and palettes that works fine for most applications. But the more you use AutoCAD, the more you may find that you tend to use tools that are scattered over several Ribbon panels. You'll probably feel that your work would go more easily if you could create a custom set of panels and menus to consolidate those tools. If you're at the point of creating custom macros, you may want a way to have easy access to them.

The *Customize User Interface (CUI)* dialog box is a one-stop location that gives you nearly total control over the menus, panels, and toolbars in AutoCAD. With the CUI feature, you can mold the AutoCAD interface to your liking. The main entry point to the CUI is the Customize User Interface dialog box.

The following section introduces you to the CUI by showing you how to add a tool to the Draw Ribbon panel. You'll also get a chance to see how to create an entirely new panel and custom tools.

Taking a Quick Customization Tour

The most direct way to adapt AutoCAD to your way of working is to customize the Ribbon. AutoCAD offers new users an easy route to customization through the Customize User Interface dialog box. With this dialog box, you can create new Ribbon panels and toolbars, customize tools, and even create new icons. You can also create keyboard shortcuts.

To get your feet wet, try adding a tool to the Draw panel:

1. If it's still open, close the Workspace Settings dialog box.
2. Click the User Interface tool in the Manage tab's Customization panel to open the Customize User Interface dialog box, shown in Figure 24.3. You can also type **CUI↵**. You see three groups in this dialog box: Customizations In All Files, Command List, and Properties.
3. In the Customizations In All Files group, expand the Ribbon option and then expand the Panels option that appears just below. Scroll down the list and expand the Home 2D – Draw option. You see a set of options labeled Row 1, Row 2, and so on.
4. Click the Home 2D – Draw option. A view of the Draw Ribbon panel appears in the Panel Preview area (see Figure 24.4).

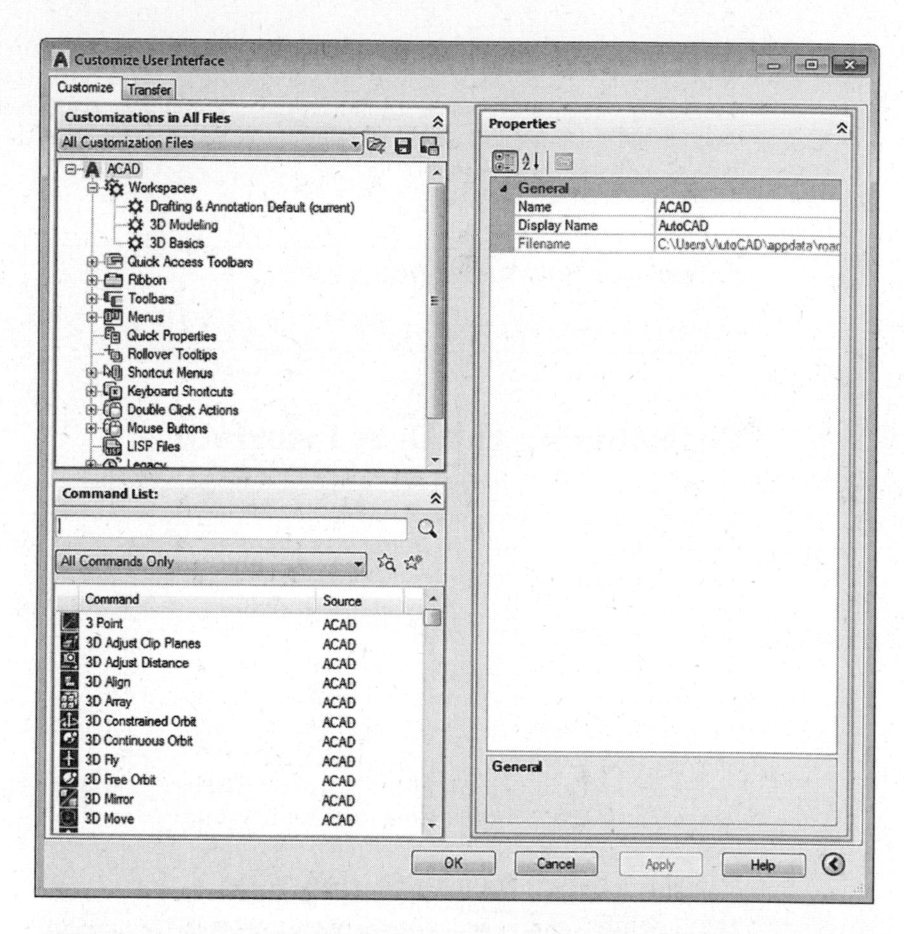

FIGURE 24.3
The Customize User Interface dialog box

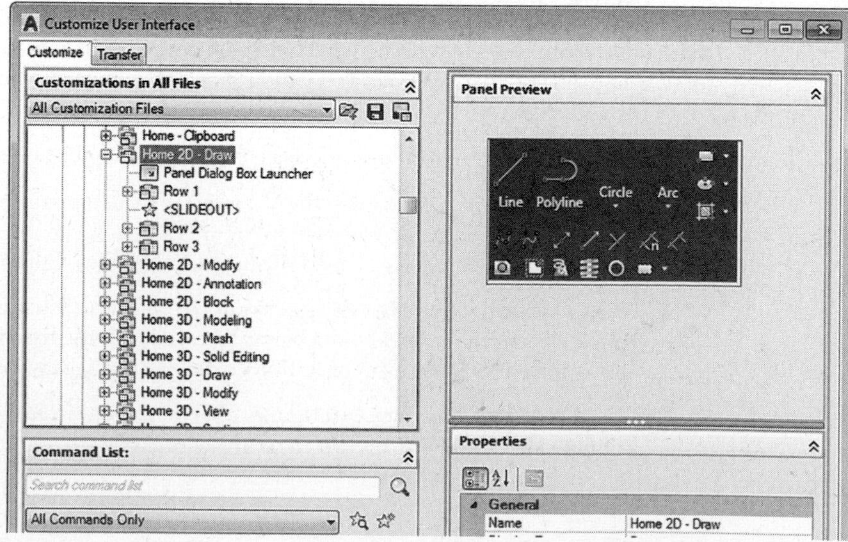

FIGURE 24.4
The Draw Ribbon panel appears.

5. Expand the Row 3 item under the Home 2D – Draw option. You'll see the names of the several tools that appear at the very bottom of the Draw panel. These tools are Region, Wipeout, 3D Polyline, Helix, Donut, and Revision Cloud.

6. In the Command List group, select Dimension from the Filter The Command List By Category drop-down list (see Figure 24.5).

FIGURE 24.5
Choose the Dimension category.

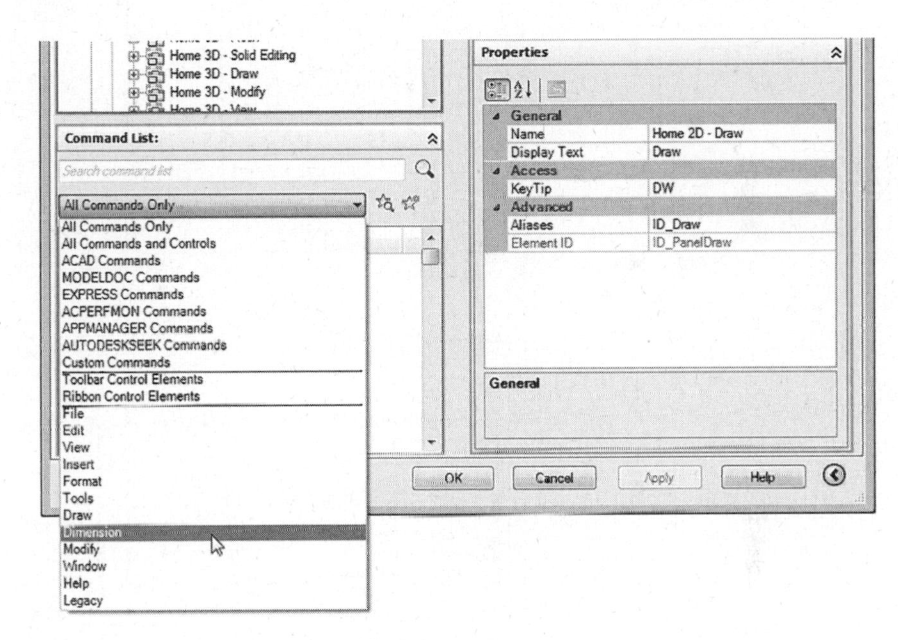

7. In the bottom panel of the Command List group, scroll down the list and then locate and select Dimension, Linear. This is the Linear Dimension command. When you select Linear, the Properties group displays the properties of the Linear command. The Panel Preview area changes to show the Button Image group, and you see the Linear Dimension icon, as shown in Figure 24.6.

8. Carefully click and drag the Dimension, Linear item from the Command List group into the Customizations In All Files group, but don't release the mouse button yet. As you drag the item over the tool names in the Customizations In All Files group, a bar tells you where your dragged item will appear (see Figure 24.6). If you pause over a folder option that contains a list of commands, you'll see an arrowhead appear next to the option. The arrowhead also indicates where the dragged command will be placed. The list may automatically scroll up or down depending on where you place the bar. This is to allow you to place the bar in an area of the list that isn't currently displayed.

9. Place the bar just above 3D Polyline, and release the mouse button. Dimension, Linear appears above 3D Polyline in the list (see Figure 24.7), and though it may be difficult to see, the Dimension Linear icon appears in the Panel Preview area.

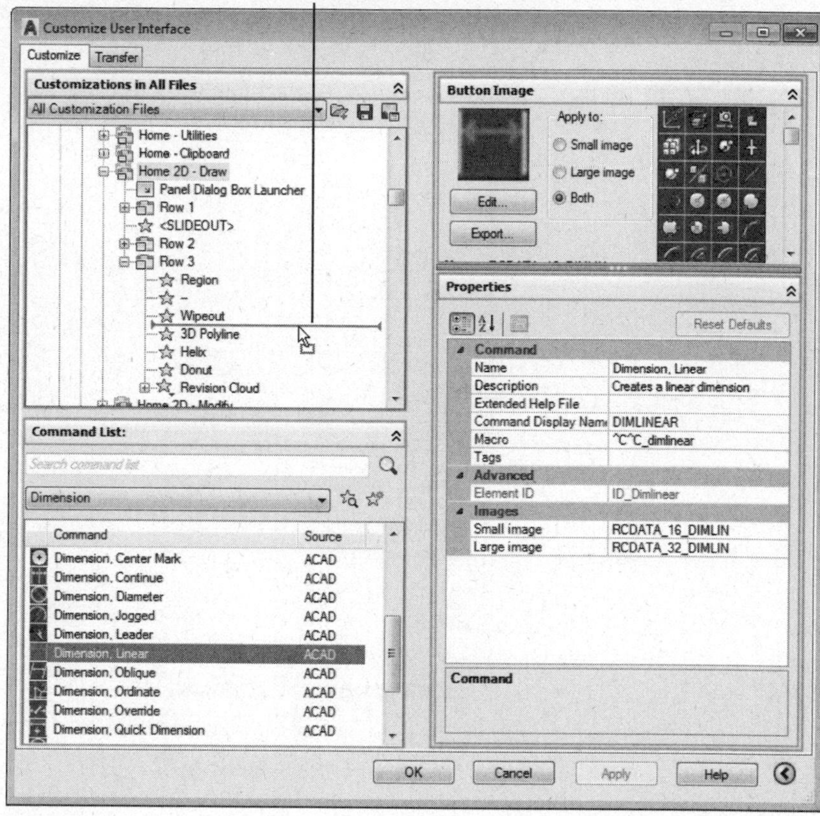

FIGURE 24.6
The Panel Preview area changes when you select an element from the Command List group or the Customizations In All Files group.

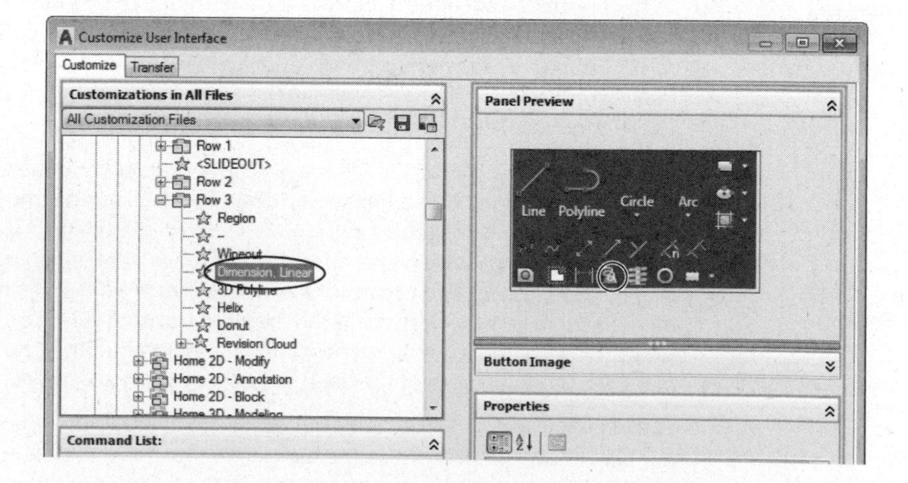

FIGURE 24.7
After positioning the Dimension icon

10. Click OK. The next time you check, you'll see the Dimension, Linear tool appear in the expanded Draw panel just to the left of the 3D Polyline tool (see Figure 24.8).

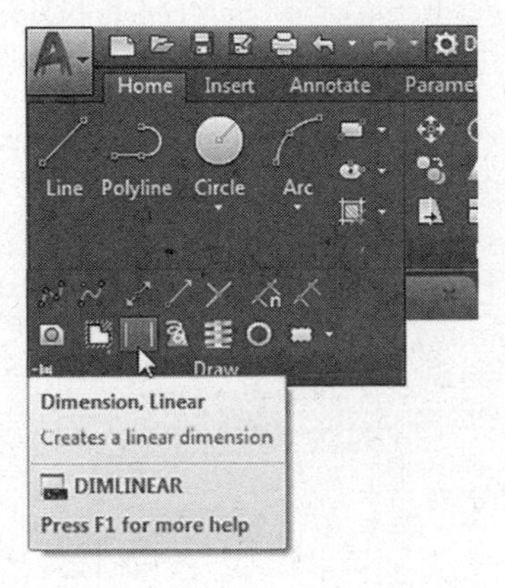

FIGURE 24.8
The tool is in place.

You've just added a command to the Draw panel. You can follow the previous steps to add any command to any Ribbon panel, toolbar, or menu bar menu. Now suppose that you change your mind and you decide to remove Dimension, Linear from the Draw panel. Here's how it's done:

1. Click User Interface in the Manage tab's Customization panel, or type **CUI**↵.
2. In the Customizations In All Files group of the Customize User Interface dialog box, expand the Ribbon option and Panels option and then continue to expand options as you did before to get to the Dimension, Linear command that you added earlier.
3. Click Dimension, Linear, and then right-click and choose Remove from the context menu. You'll see a warning message asking if you "really want to delete this element."
4. Click Yes. The Dimension, Linear command is removed.
5. Click OK to close the dialog box.

Dimension, Linear has been removed from the Draw panel. As you've just seen, adding tools to a panel is a matter of clicking and dragging the appropriate item from one list to another. To remove tools, right-click the tool and select Remove.

Before you go too much further, you may want to know a little more about the Customize User Interface dialog box and how it works. You saw briefly how each group displayed different elements of the AutoCAD interface, from a listing of panel tools to an individual tool's icon. Let's look at each group independently to see how it's organized.

Understanding the Customizations In All Files Panel

In the previous exercise, where you placed the Dimension, Linear command in the Draw panel, you saw an arrowhead appear when you hovered over a folder option. The arrowhead indicates where the command will be placed when you release the mouse button. If you see a horizontal bar appear between a list of commands, the new command will be placed at the location indicated by the bar. If the item is a folder icon, the new command will be placed inside that folder.

You may see items called *Sub-Panel* options. These allow you to mix single tools and rows like the Line tool and the three rows that you see to the right of the Line tool at the top of the Draw panel. Finally, the <SLIDEOUT> item that you see in the list indicates the division between the main part of the panel and the expanded panel. Figure 24.9 shows how the list in the Customizations In All Files group relates to the Ribbon panel components.

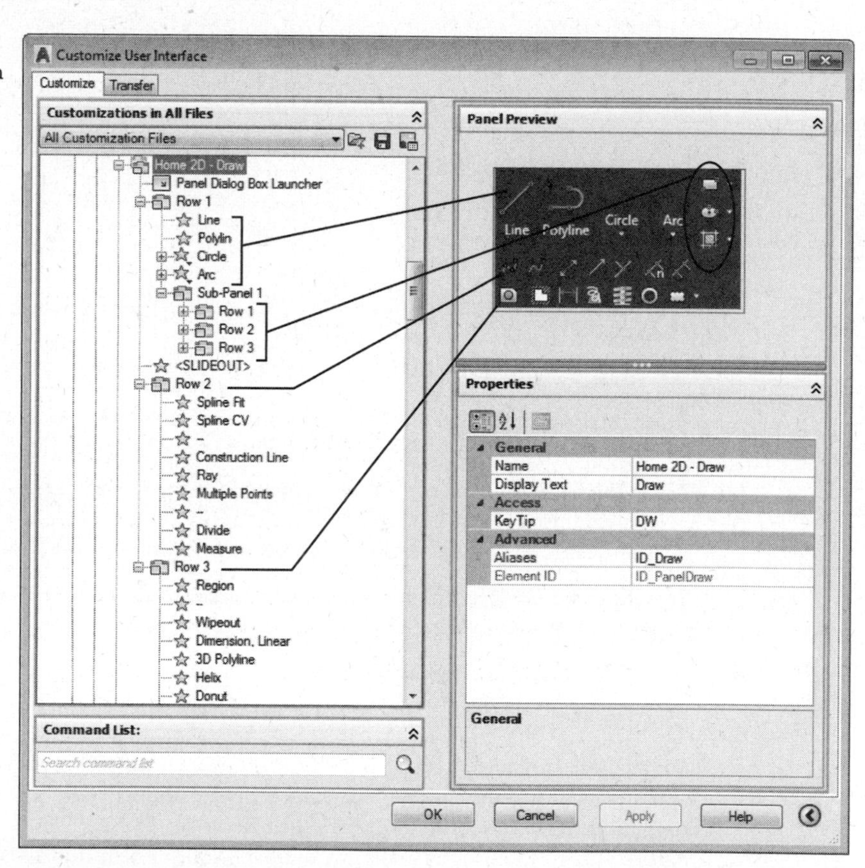

FIGURE 24.9 The Customizations In All Files list compared to the Ribbon panel preview

Notice that the Line, Polyline, Circle, and Arc tools straddle the two rows in the expanded Draw panel and are at the same level as the Sub-Panel 1 options of Rectangle, Ellipse, and Hatch. Placing the Line, Polyline, Circle, and Arc commands at the same level as the Sub-Panel 1 option does this. The Sub-Panel 1 option is further divided into rows. Figure 24.10 shows how the rows appear when they are expanded. Flyouts on the Ribbon panel appear as "Drop-down" options in the Customizations In All Files group.

If you expand a Drop-down option, you'll see the tools that appear in the flyouts of the tool in the panel (see Figure 24.11).

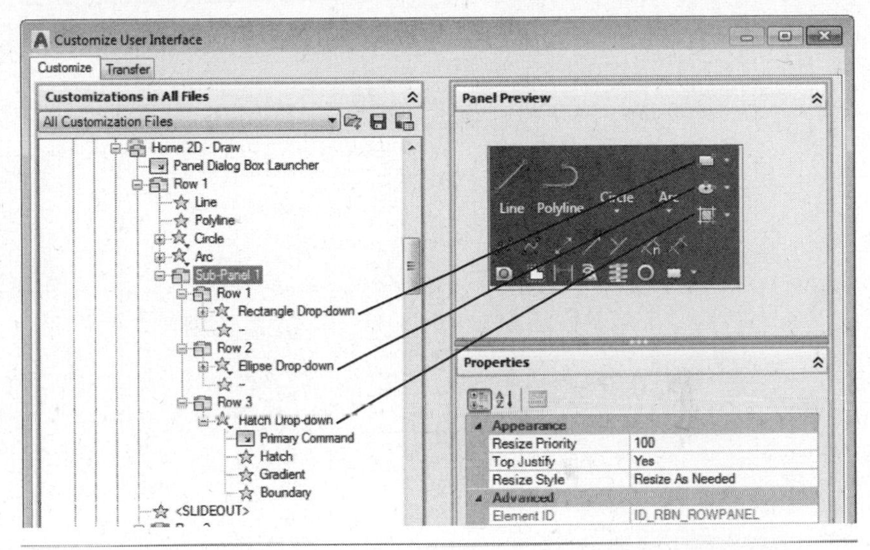

FIGURE 24.10
The Sub-Panel 1 option contains the rows that in turn contain flyouts labeled as Drop-down options.

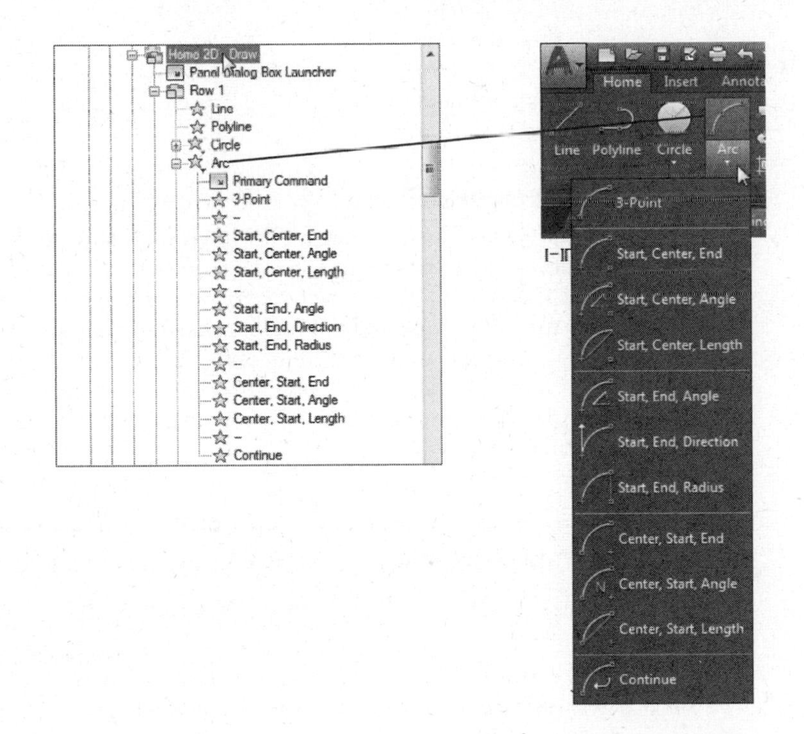

FIGURE 24.11
The tools in the Customizations In All Files panel's Drop-down list appear in the appropriate flyout.

You can add new panels, rows, subpanels, and drop-downs (flyouts) by right-clicking an item in the list and selecting the appropriate option from the context menu (see Figure 24.12). These types of interface elements are called *containers* in the Customize User Interface dialog box.

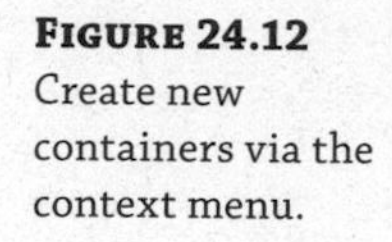

FIGURE 24.12
Create new containers via the context menu.

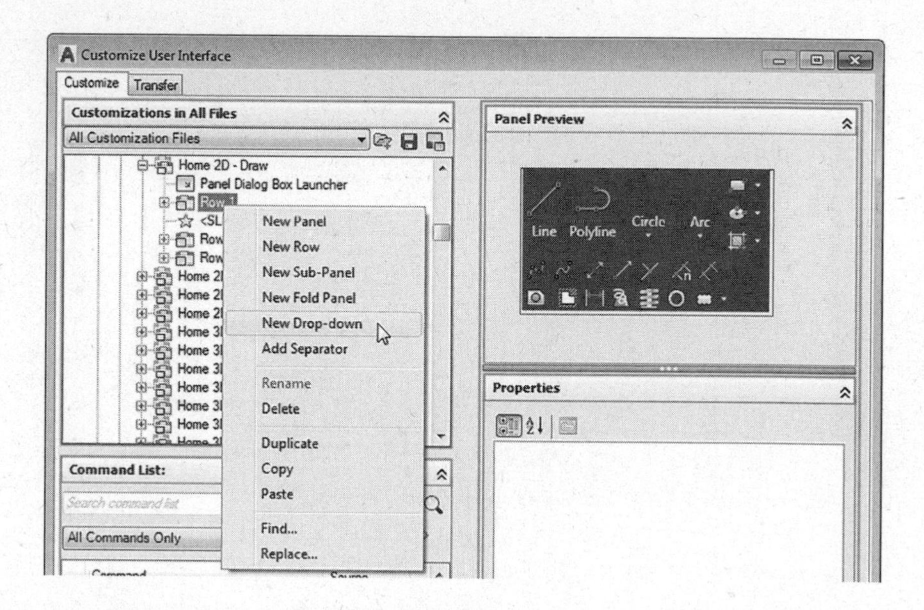

If you understand the structure of these lists, you'll find that it is quite easy to customize the Ribbon panels to your liking.

Getting the Overall View

When you first opened the Customize User Interface dialog box, you saw a listing of the AutoCAD interface elements in the Customizations In All Files group. Just as you saw with the Ribbon panels, each of the other interface elements in the list can be expanded to get to its individual commands. If you expand the Toolbars list, for example, all of the AutoCAD toolbars are available. Expand a toolbar and the commands contained in the toolbar are displayed. As you saw earlier, you can expand the Ribbon Panels list to gain access to the Ribbon panels. Table 24.1 lists all of the interface elements in the Customizations In All Files group with a brief explanation of their contents.

TABLE 24.1: Main headings in the Customizations in All Files group

ITEM	WHAT IT CONTAINS
Workspaces	Workspaces that are currently available
Quick Access Toolbars	Quick Access toolbars
Ribbon	The Ribbon tabs, panels, and contextual tab states
Toolbars	Toolbars

TABLE 24.1: Main headings in the Customizations in All Files group *(CONTINUED)*

ITEM	WHAT IT CONTAINS
Menus	Menu bar menus
Quick Properties	Options on the Quick Properties palette
Rollover Tooltips	Rollover tool tip settings
Shortcut Menus	Menus shown with right-clicks
Keyboard Shortcuts	Current keyboard shortcuts, such as Ctrl+C and Ctrl+V
Double-Click Actions	Object-dependent double-click actions
Mouse Buttons	Mouse button options, such as Shift+click and Ctrl+click
LISP Files	Any custom LISP files that are used with your CUI
Legacy	Any legacy custom items you use, such as tablet or screen menus
Partial Customization Files	Custom CUI files that have been included in the main CUI file

You can customize any of the interface elements. For example, if you want to create new keyboard shortcuts, you can expand the Keyboard Shortcuts listing and add new shortcuts or edit existing ones. Right-click any item to add or delete options. If you click an item, its properties appear in the Properties group, where you can modify the item's function. Just as you added the Dimension, Linear command to the Draw panel, you can click and drag a command into one of the menus under the Menus listing to add a command there.

You also see some options in the Customizations In All Files title bar. These options give you control over what is displayed in this group. You can also load and save CUI files from here.

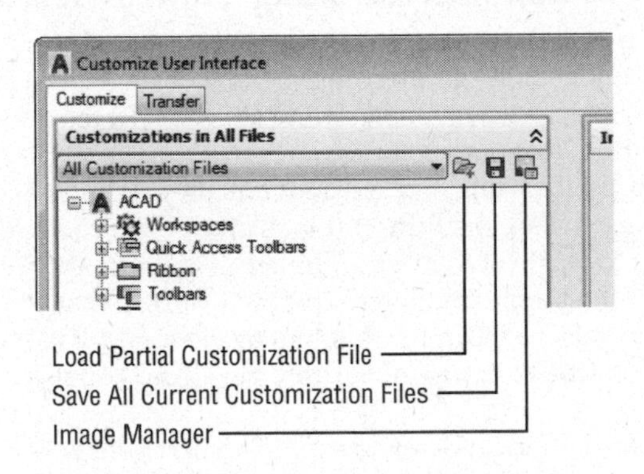

You'll learn more about these options later in this chapter.

Adding a Panel Title Bar Command with the Panel Dialog Box Launcher

You may have noticed the Panel Dialog Box Launcher item that appears just below a panel name (when expanded) in the Customize User Interface dialog box. With this placeholder, you can add a command that will launch when you click an arrow icon in the right side of the panel title bar. You can see an example of such an icon in the Insert tab's Reference panel or the Annotate tab's Text and Dimensions panels. These arrow icons typically open dialog boxes that control the main features presented in the panel. For example, the one in the Annotate tab's Text panel opens the Text Style dialog box.

To add a command to the Panel Dialog Box Launcher item, click and drag a command from the Command List area to the Panel Dialog Box Launcher item. To remove a command, right-click the Panel Dialog Box Launcher item and select Remove Command. Click Yes to confirm the removal.

The Panel Dialog Box Launcher item is included automatically whenever you create a new panel.

Finding Commands in the Command List

You've already seen how the Command List group contains all of the commands in AutoCAD. You also saw that you can click and drag these items into options in the Customizations In All Files group. This list also contains predefined macros, icons used for tools, and control elements (called combo boxes in the Ribbon panels), which are the drop-down lists that you see in panels and toolbars. The layer drop-down lists in the Layers panel and the lists in the Home tab's Properties panel are examples of control elements. When you select an item in the Command List group, you see its properties in the Properties group or its icon in the Button Image group, or both. The control elements are the exception to this because they have no editable features.

Opening Preview, Button Image, and Shortcuts

You've already seen how you can get a preview of a Ribbon panel by selecting the panel from the Customizations In All Files group. If you click a Ribbon panel from the list, you'll see the Panel Preview group, which shows you how the selected panel will appear. Previews aren't editable and are there for your reference.

If you click a tool listing—or element in AutoCAD nomenclature—in the Customizations In All Files group, you see the Button Image group. You can open this group by clicking the double arrowhead to the right of the Button Image group title bar. You may also need to adjust the bottom border of the Button Image group downward so that you can see more of the group. This group lets you select an icon for that tool by clicking a list of icons (see Figure 24.13), or you can edit an existing icon or create an entirely new icon. You'll get a chance to see this firsthand later in this chapter.

The Keyboard Shortcuts area in the Customizations In All Files group shows the Shortcuts group, which lists the existing keyboard shortcuts.

FIGURE 24.13
The Button Image group

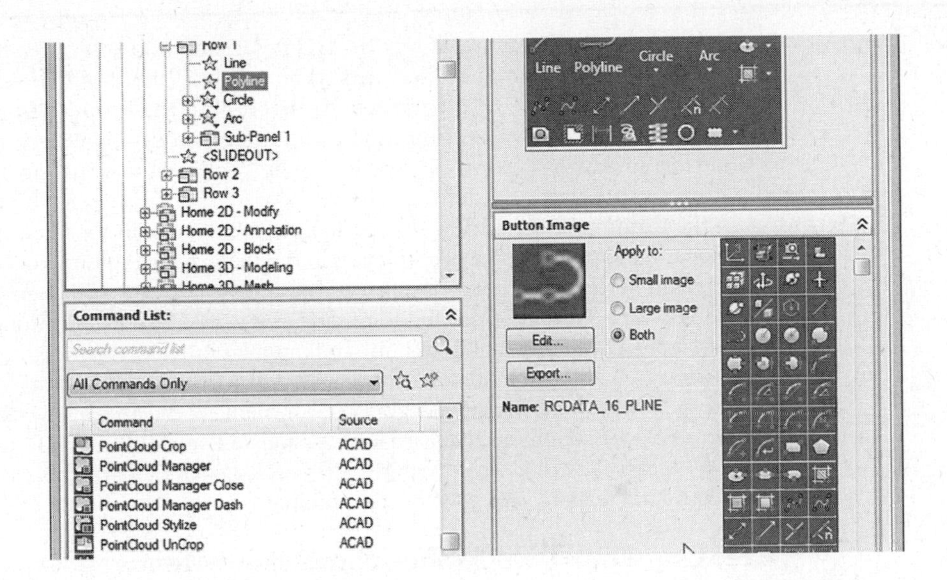

Getting to the Core of Customization in the Properties Group

Finally, when you're ready to do some serious customizing, you'll work with the Properties group. You see the Properties group in the lower half of the right side of the Customize User Interface dialog box when you select a command from the left side of the dialog box.

The Properties group is set up just like the Properties palette, and it works the same way. On the left side, you see a listing of options. To the right of each option is a description or a text box where you can make changes (see Figure 24.14).

FIGURE 24.14
The Properties group showing the properties for the Line tool

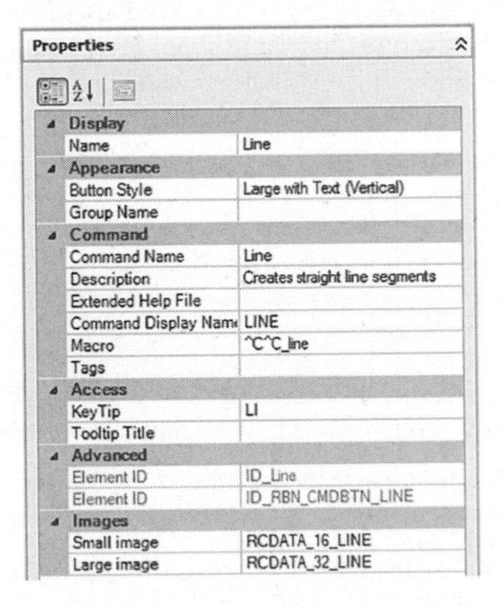

If you go to the Customizations In All Files group and select the Line tool under the Home 2D – Draw option that you worked on earlier (Ribbon ➤ Panels ➤ Home 2D – Draw ➤ Row 1 ➤ Line), you see the properties for that tool in the Properties group, as shown in Figure 24.14. You'll have to close the Button Image group to get a complete view of the Properties group. You can close any group by clicking the double arrow on the right side of the group's title bar.

In the Command category, you see the Line tool's name in the Command Name listing. You also see the description that is displayed in the tool tip for the Line tool. You can change this description here in the Properties group, and the description will change in the status bar.

In the Macro listing, you see the command as it would be entered through the keyboard. The `^C^C` that precedes the actual line command input is equivalent to pressing the Esc key twice. If you scroll down, you'll see the Advanced category, which offers information regarding the ID of this particular tool. Finally, the Images category lists the name of the image files used for the Line tool icon. Two icons are listed: one for the large icon version and one for the small icon version of the tool.

You'll get a chance to work with the Properties group later in this chapter. Next you'll try your hand at creating your own custom toolbar.

Creating Your Own Ribbon Panels and Menus

Earlier, we mentioned that you can collect your most frequently used tools into a custom Ribbon panel or toolbar. Now that you've familiarized yourself with the Customize User Interface dialog box, you can try the following exercise to create your own Ribbon panel:

1. If the Customize User Interface dialog box isn't open, click User Interface in the Manage tab's Customization panel.
2. In the Customizations In All Files group, expand the Ribbon option and then right-click Panels and choose New Panel. The list expands and you see a new panel called Panel1 at the bottom of the Panels list. The name Panel1 is highlighted and ready to be edited.
3. Replace Panel1 by typing **My Panel** to give your panel a distinct name (see Figure 24.15). As you type, the name changes. If you decide to change a panel name later, right-click a panel listing and then choose Rename.

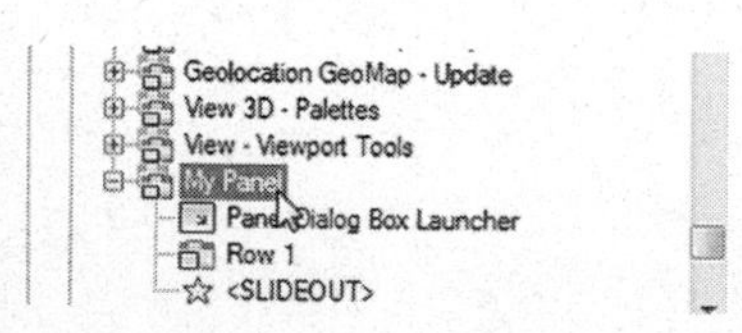

FIGURE 24.15
The new Panel1 name changed to My Panel

You now have a custom Ribbon panel. You'll want to start to populate your panel with some commands. You've already seen how this works, but to review, try adding a few commands:

1. Select Draw from the Filter The Command List By Category drop-down list. It's the list that is below the Search box under Command List.
2. In the Command List group, locate the command that you want to add. In this instance, locate the Line tool.

3. Click and drag the Line command to your new panel so that you see an arrowhead pointing to the Row 1 option (see Figure 24.16).

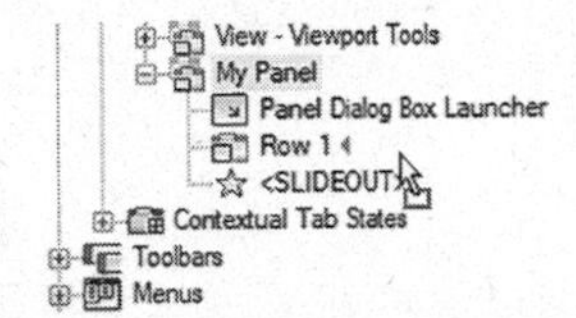

FIGURE 24.16
Point to the Row 1 option, and you'll see the arrowhead appear.

4. Release the mouse button. The Line tool appears below Row 1.
5. Repeat steps 2, 3, and 4 to add more commands to your panel.
6. To add another row, right-click My Panel and select New Row. You can add more tools to your second row.

You can add several more rows to your panel, but after the first row, additional rows will be placed below <SLIDEOUT> in the expanded portion of the panel. You'll see how the panel is placed in the Ribbon after the next exercise.

> **DELETING A CUSTOM TOOL OR PANEL**
>
> You can delete any tool from your custom panel by right-clicking the tool and choosing Remove while in the Customizations In All Files group of the Customize User Interface dialog box. You can also delete your entire panel using this method. Take care not to delete any of the panels that you want to keep.

Customizing Ribbon Panel Tools

Let's move on to more serious customization. Suppose that you want to create an entirely new button with its own functions. For example, you might want to create a set of buttons that insert your favorite symbols. Or you might want to create a Ribbon panel containing a set of tools that open some of the other toolbars that are normally put away.

CREATING A CUSTOM TOOL

Follow these steps to create a custom tool:

1. Open the Customize User Interface dialog box, expand the Ribbon Panels list, and then expand the My Panel list.

2. In the Command List panel title bar, click the Create A New Command tool. A new command called Command1 appears in the list of commands (see Figure 24.17).
3. Right-click the Command1 item, select Rename from the context menu, and change the name to Door.

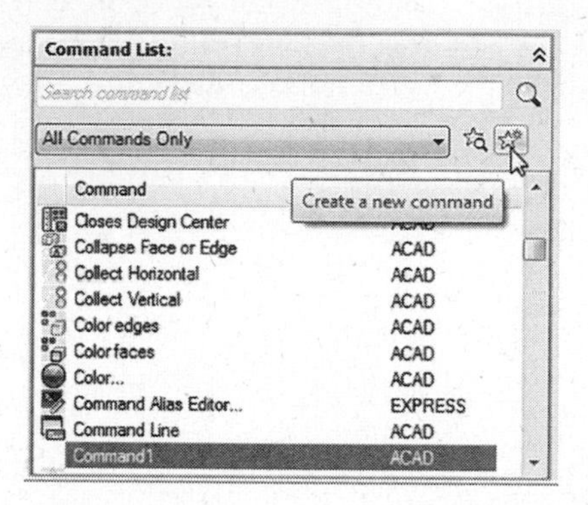

FIGURE 24.17
Click the Create A New Command tool and a new command appears in the list.

4. In the Properties group to the right, change Description to **Insert a 36″ door**.
5. Change the Macro option to the following:

```
^C^C-insert door;\36;;
```

6. Click and drag the Door element from the Command List panel into Row 1 of your My Panel item in the Customizations In All Files group. If you look at the Panel Preview group, you see that the Door tool that you just added appears as a blank tool. This happens when no icon has been assigned to the tool.

The series of keystrokes that you entered for the macro in step 5 are the same as those you would use to insert the door with the addition of a few special characters. The semicolons are equivalent to ↵, and the backward slash (\) is a special macro code that tells AutoCAD to pause the macro for user input. In this case, the pause allows you to select the insertion point for the door. The Properties group should look similar to Figure 24.18.

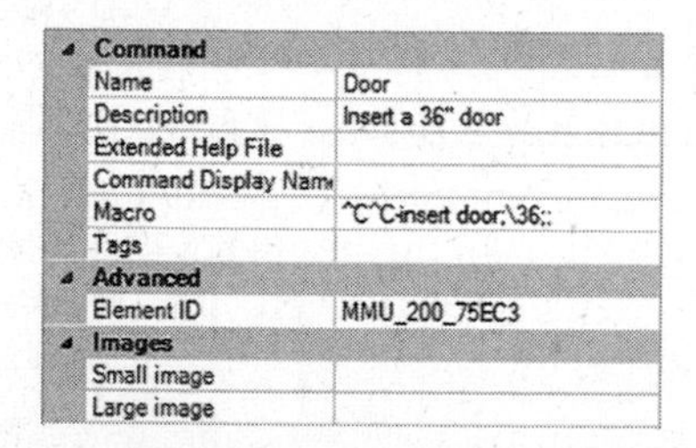

FIGURE 24.18
The Properties group for your new custom tool that inserts a door block

LOCATING FILES SO AUTOCAD CAN FIND THEM

A misplaced file is a common problem that you have to troubleshoot when you're supporting an office full of AutoCAD users. AutoCAD tends to put files in a lot of different places. When it can't find a file that it needs, it will give you an error message, or worse, it just won't work. It helps to know where AutoCAD looks for files so that you can put the resources for your custom tools in the right places.

In the Door example, the door drawing used in your macro must be in the default folder, `My Documents`, or in the `acad` search path before the door will be inserted. For easy access, copy the `Door.dwg` file from the `Chapter 4` project folder to the `My Documents` folder.

You've created your panel, but it will not appear anywhere in the AutoCAD interface until you add it to a Ribbon tab group. Here's how this is done:

1. Under your My Panel listing in the Customizations In All Files group, click the My Panel panel option that you just created and then right-click and select Copy.
2. In the Customizations In All Files group, scroll up to the top of the list and expand the Tabs option.
3. Right-click Home – 2D just below Ribbon ➤ Tabs, and then select Paste from the context menu. Your My Panel panel appears at the bottom of the Home – 2D list.
4. Click OK in the Customize User Interface dialog box to close it. Your panel appears in the Home tab of the Ribbon.

Next try the custom tool to make sure that it works:

1. Put a copy of the `Door.dwg` file in your `My Documents` folder.
2. Point to the Door tool in your My Panel panel in the Home tab. You see the Door tool tip.

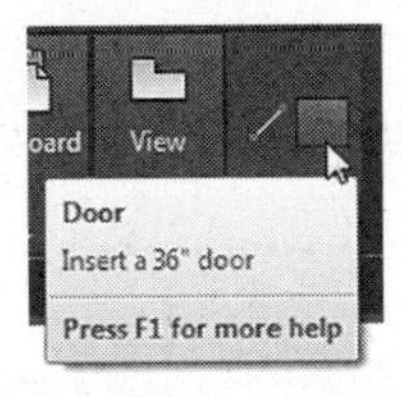

3. Click the Door tool. The door appears in the drawing area at the cursor. It may appear very small because initially it's being inserted at its default size of 1 unit.
4. Click a location to place the door, and then click a point to set the door rotation. The door appears in the drawing.

In this example, you created a custom tool that inserts the door block. Later in this chapter, you'll learn more about creating macros for menus and tools. Next you'll learn how to add a custom icon for your custom tool.

Creating a Custom Icon

You have all the essential parts of the button defined. Now you just need to create a custom icon to go with your Door button:

1. Open the Customize User Interface dialog box.
2. Expand the Customizations In All Files Ribbon list to your My Panel option (Ribbon ➤ Panels ➤ My Panel).
3. Expand the Row1 list, and select Door.
4. Open the Button Image group, and click any icon image. The icon appears in the Panel Preview group, replacing the blank image for your Door tool.
5. In the Button Image group, click the Edit button to open the Button Editor. The Button Editor is like a simple drawing program. Across the top are the tools for drawing lines, circles, and points as well as an eraser. Along the left side is a color toolbar from which you can choose colors for your icon. At the upper right, you see a preview of your button.

> **You Can Use the Existing Icons**
>
> If you prefer, you can use any of the predefined icons in the scroll box to the right of the Button Image group in the Customize User Interface dialog box. Click the icon that you want to use, and then click Apply.

6. Before you do anything else, click the Clear button. This clears the current image.
7. Draw the door icon shown in Figure 24.19. Don't worry if it's not perfect; you can always go back and fix it.

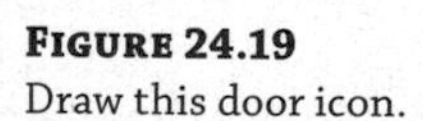

Figure 24.19
Draw this door icon.

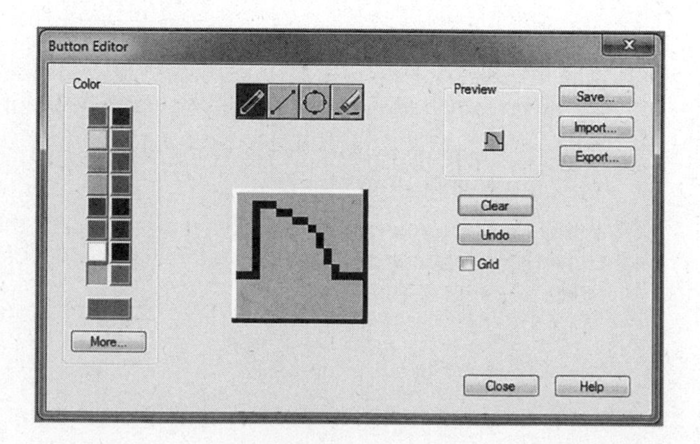

8. Click Save, and then at the Save Image dialog box, enter **Door36** for the name. The door icon is saved in the AutoCAD CUI file that stores all of the interface data.
9. Click OK, and then click Close at the Button Editor dialog box.
10. Click OK to close the Customize User Interface dialog box. You see your custom icon for the Door tool.

The Button Editor behaves like a simplified image editing tool, and it is fairly straightforward to use. The only part that may be confusing is that you have to clear the image and save any new image under a new name.

You can continue to add more buttons to build a panel of symbols. Of course, you're not limited to a symbols library. You can also incorporate your favorite macros or even AutoLISP® routines that you accumulate as you work with AutoCAD. The possibilities are endless.

Creating Macros in Tools and Menus

Combining existing commands into new panels or toolbars can be useful, but you'll get even more benefit from the CUI by creating your own macros. Macros are predefined sets of responses to commands that can help automate your most frequently used processes.

Early on, you saw how a macro was included in a tool to insert a door. You added a special set of instructions in the Macro option of the Properties group to perform the door insertion and scale. You also saw how the Line command was formatted as part of a tool.

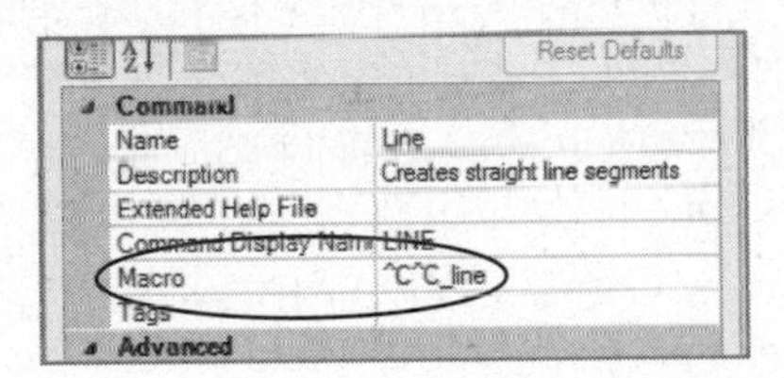

Let's take a closer look at how macros are built. Start by looking at the existing Line tool and how it's formatted.

The Macro option for the Line tool starts with two `^C` elements, which are equivalent to pressing the Esc key twice. This cancels any command that is currently operative. The Line command follows, written just as it would be entered through the keyboard. Two Cancels are issued in case you're in a command that has two levels, such as the Edit Vertex option of the Pedit command.

The underscore character (_) that precedes the Line command tells AutoCAD that you're using the English-language version of this command. This feature lets you program non-English versions of AutoCAD by using the English-language command names.

What Is the Hyphen For?

In the previous door macro example, you used a hyphen in front of the Insert command. The hyphen causes the Insert command to run in the command line instead of using a dialog box, where the macro keyboard input will not work. Many commands will run in the command line when preceded with a hyphen.

You may also notice that there is no space between the second ^C and the Line command. A space in the line would be the same as ↵. If there were a space between these two elements, ↵ would be entered between the last ^C and the Line command, causing the command sequence to misstep. Another way to indicate ↵ is by using the semicolon, as in the following example:

```
^C^C_Line;;
```

Help Make Your Macro Readable

If a menu macro contains multiple instances of ↵, using semicolons instead of spaces can help make your macro more readable.

In this sample menu option, the Line command is issued and then an additional ↵ is added. The effect of choosing this option is a line that continues from the last line entered into your drawing. The two semicolons following Line tell AutoCAD to start the Line command and then issue ↵ twice; the first ↵ starts the Line command, and then the second ↵ tells AutoCAD to begin a line from the endpoint of the last line entered. (AutoCAD automatically issues a single ↵ at the end of a menu line. In this case, however, you want two instances of ↵, so they must be represented as semicolons.)

Pausing for User Input

Another symbol used in the Macro option is the backslash (\); it's used when a pause is required for user input. For example, the following sample macro starts the Arc command and then pauses for your input:

```
^C^C_arc \_e \_d
```

The space between ^C^C_arc and the backslash (\) represents pressing the spacebar. The backslash indicates a pause to enable you to select the starting endpoint for the arc. The _e represents the selection of the Endpoint option under the Arc command after you've picked a point. A second backslash allows another point selection. Finally, the _d represents the selection of the Direction option. Figure 24.20 illustrates this. If you want the last character in a menu item to be a backslash, you must follow the backslash with a semicolon.

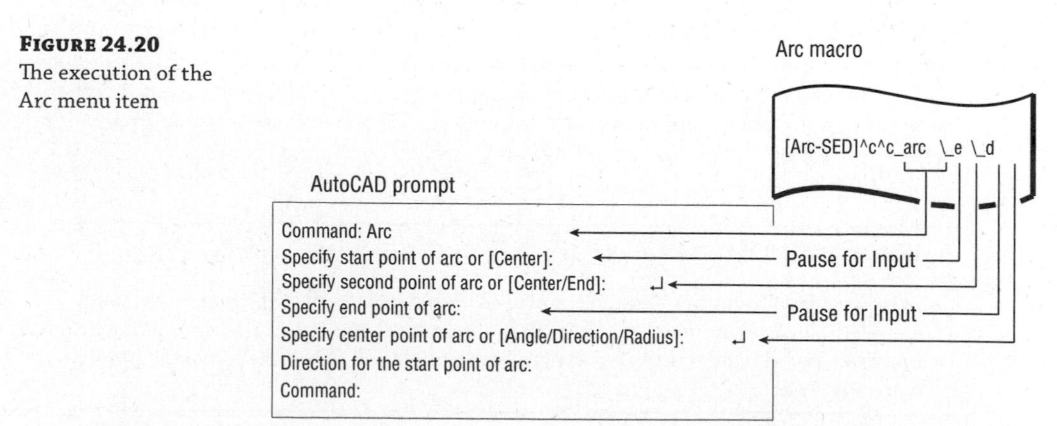

Figure 24.20
The execution of the Arc menu item

Opening an Expanded Text Box for the Macro Option

As you become more expert at creating macros, you may find the line provided in the Macro option too small for your needs. Fortunately, you can open an expanded text box in which to write longer macros. For example, suppose that you want to include the following macro in a tool:

```
(defun c:breakat ()
(command "break" pause "f" pause "@")
)
breakat
```

This example shows the `Breakat` AutoLISP macro. Everything in this segment is entered just as it would be from the keyboard at the Command prompt. You may find it a bit cumbersome to try to enter this macro in the text box provided by the Macro option in the Properties group of the Customize User Interface dialog box, but if you click the Macro text box, a Browse button appears to the right (see Figure 24.21).

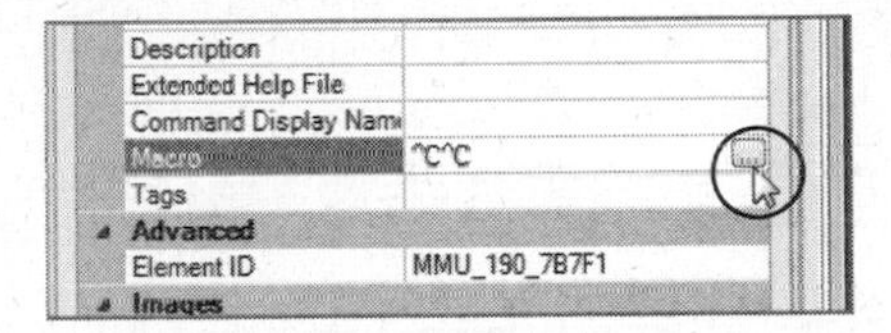

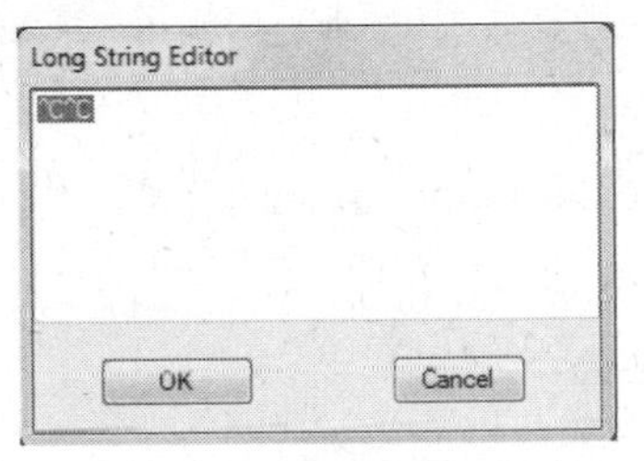

FIGURE 24.21
The Browse button in the Macro option

Click the Browse button to open the Long String Editor. You can then enter the macro and see it clearly. The following shows how it would be entered:

```
^C^C(defun c:breakat ()+
(command "break" pause "f" pause "@")+
);breakat
```

It starts with the usual `^C^C` to clear any current commands. The plus sign at the end of lines 1 and 2 tells AutoCAD that the macro continues in the next line without actually breaking it. The break is there to help make the macro easier to read as you enter it. It's okay to break an AutoLISP macro into smaller lines. Doing so can help you read and understand the program more easily.

LOADING AUTOLISP MACROS

As you become a more advanced AutoCAD user, you may want many of your own AutoLISP macros to load with your custom interface. You can make them do that by combining all your AutoLISP macros into a single file. Give this file the same name as your menu file but with the `.mnl` filename extension. Such a file automatically loads with its menu counterpart. For example, say that you have a file called `Mymenu.mnl` containing the `Breakat` AutoLISP macro. Whenever you load `Mymenu.cui`, `Mymenu.mnl` is automatically loaded along with it, giving you access to the `Breakat` macro. This is a good way to manage and organize any AutoLISP program code that you want to include with a menu.

To learn more about the AutoLISP language, see Bonus Chapter 2, "Exploring AutoLISP," available at `www.omura.com/chapters`.

Editing Keyboard Shortcuts

Another area of customization that can be useful is the keyboard shortcut. You probably already know about the standard Ctrl+C and Ctrl+V, which are shortcuts for the Windows Copy and Paste functions. In AutoCAD, Shift+Ctrl+A toggles groups on and off, and Ctrl+1 opens the Properties palette.

You can edit existing keyboard shortcuts or create new ones by opening the Keyboard Shortcuts list in the Customizations In All Files group of the Customize User Interface dialog box. If you expand this list, you see Shortcut Keys and Temporary Override Keys. These can be expanded to reveal their elements. Select an element to display its properties in the Properties group.

You can click and drag a command from the Command List group into the Shortcut Keys group and then edit its properties to set the shortcut keys that you want to use for the command. For example, if you click and drag the 3D Free Orbit command from the Command List group into the Shortcut Keys list and then select it from that list, you see its properties in the Properties group (see Figure 24.22).

FIGURE 24.22
The Properties group

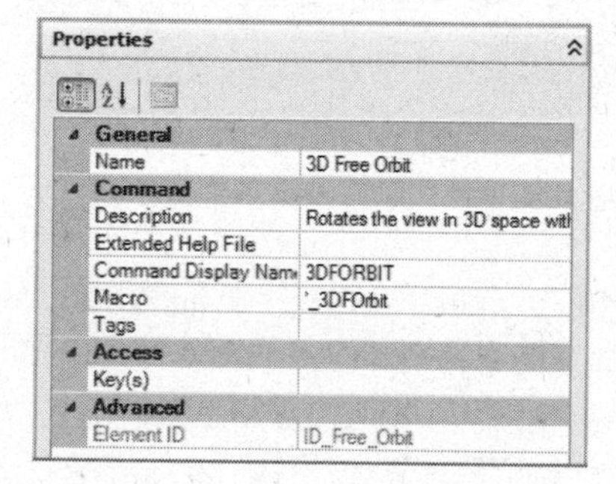

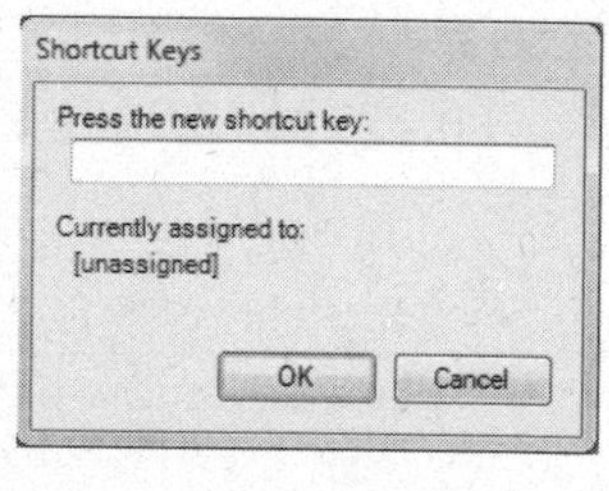

RECORD AND PLAY BACK ACTIONS

If AutoLISP seems a bit too intimidating but you still need a way to automate certain tasks, the Action Recorder is a feature that you'll want to explore. The Action Recorder enables you to record a series of actions in AutoCAD and store them as action macros. You can play back your action macros at any time. This is a great time-saver when you are performing repetitive tasks, something that you may find yourself doing frequently in AutoCAD.

An entire panel is devoted to the Action Recorder in the Manage tab:

To use the Action Recorder, click the Record button. The Record button changes to a Stop button, and a red dot appears next to the cursor to remind you that you are recording your activity. You'll also see the Action Tree appear just below the recorder.

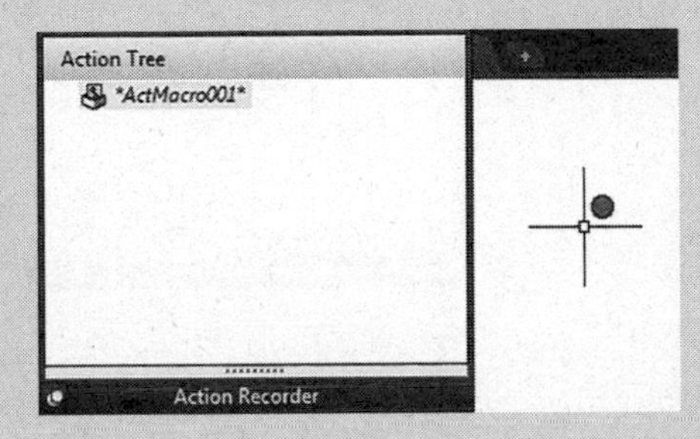

Continue working as you normally would in AutoCAD. As you work, your activity is displayed in the Action Tree. When you've completed the activity that you want to record, click the Stop button. The Action Macro dialog box appears, where you can give the recorded activity a name and description.

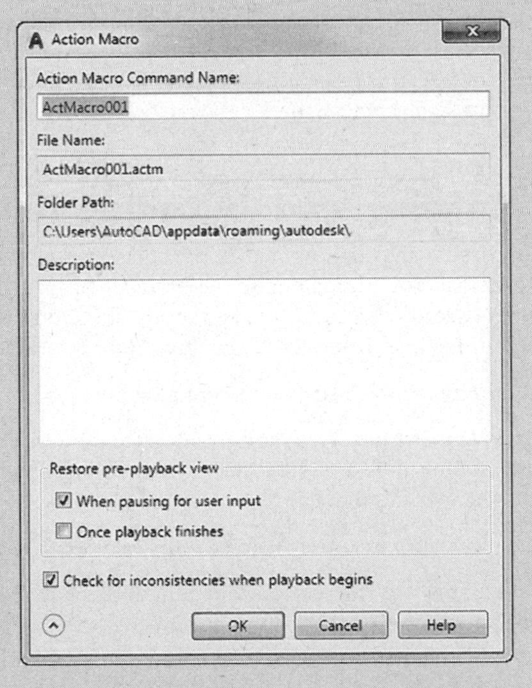

After you've closed the Action Macro dialog box, you can play back your recorded action macro at any time. From the Action Recorder panel, select the macro name from the Available Action Macro drop-down list and then click Play.

The Action Tree lets you include some interactivity in your macro. You can right-click an individual action in the Action Tree to modify its behavior to allow user input. Perhaps the most common modification that you'll want to make is to allow different selections or to change coordinate input and point selections. To do this, right-click an action and select Pause For User Input.

continues

continued

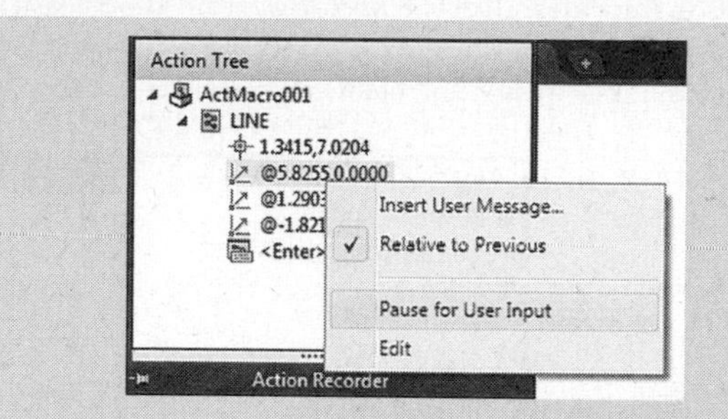

Upon selecting this option, you will be prompted for input when this particular action comes up in the macro. You can also use the Insert User Message option to have a message display while the macro is running. Messages can be helpful for users who are unfamiliar with your macro.

Click the Key(s) option in the Properties group, and then click the Browse button that appears to the far right of the Keys option to open the Shortcut Keys dialog box.

Click in the Press The New Shortcut Key text box, and then press the shortcut key that you want to use for this command. For example, if you press Shift+Ctrl+Z, that sequence appears in the text box. If the shortcut that you selected is already assigned to another command, you see a message that says so just below the text box. Click OK when you're done.

Saving, Loading, and Unloading Your Customizations

You may want to save the custom menus, panels, and toolbars that you create with the Customize User Interface dialog box so that you can carry them with you to other computers and load them for ready access. To save your customization work, you need to use the Transfer tab of the Customize User Interface dialog box. Here's how it works:

1. Open the Customize User Interface dialog box.
2. Click the Transfer tab. This tab contains two panels: The left panel shows the Customizations In Main File group, and the right panel shows a similar group called Customizations In New File.
3. In the left panel, locate your custom component, such as a menu, a Ribbon panel, or a toolbar.
4. Click and drag it to the appropriate item in the right panel. For example, click and drag a custom panel from the Ribbon panel list of the left group to the Ribbon panel section in the right group.
5. Repeat step 4 for each custom component that you've created.
6. When you've copied everything from the left group to the right, click the drop-down list in the Customizations In New File title bar and select Save As.
7. In the Save As dialog box, enter a name for your customization file and select a location.
8. Click Save to complete the process.

Synchronize Your Custom Settings with A360 Drive

When you use A360 Drive® and the Sync My Settings Through The Cloud option, you can always have your custom settings available no matter where you are. To use this option, log into A360 Drive (see the section "Getting Started with A360 Drive" in Chapter 25, "Managing and Sharing Your Drawings"). Then make sure that the Sync My Settings Through The Cloud option is checked in the InfoCenter's A360 drop-down menu. AutoCAD will automatically store your custom settings in the A360 Drive cloud service. If you start an AutoCAD 2018 session at another location and log into A360 Drive, your custom settings will be synchronized with the settings stored in the cloud.

You can control which settings are synced by using the Online tab of the Options dialog box. Click the A360 drop-down list from the InfoCenter (if you are logged into your account, this will be displaying your name), and then select Online Options. Doing so opens the Online tab of the Options dialog box. Click the Choose Which Settings Are Synced button to open a dialog box that lets you select which settings to sync.

Your customization is saved with the `.cuix` filename extension. After it's saved as a file, you can load it into another copy of AutoCAD by doing the following:

1. Open the Customize User Interface dialog box.
2. Click the Load Partial Customization File tool in the Customizations In All Files group toolbar.

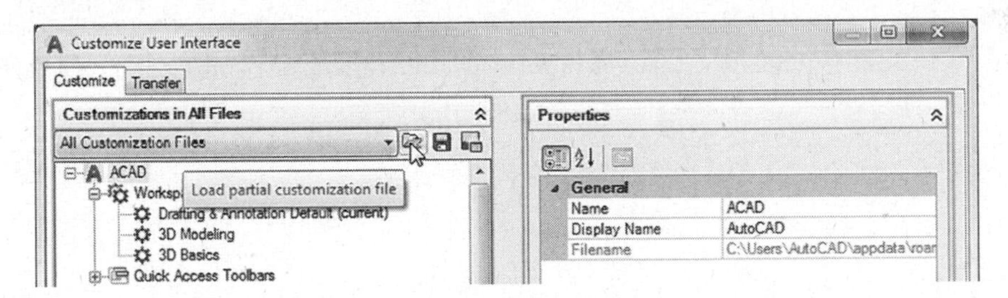

3. In the Open dialog box, locate and select your CUI file and then click Open.
4. Back in the Customize User Interface dialog box, click OK.
5. If your CUI file contains menus, enter **Workspace** ↵↵ at the Command prompt, or select a workspace from the Workspace Switching tool in the status bar. If it contains toolbars, right-click in a blank area next to an existing docked toolbar, and then select the name of your CUI file and the toolbar.

As an alternative to using the Customize User Interface dialog box, you can use the CUIload command. Enter **Cuiload**↵ at the Command prompt to open the Load/Unload Customizations dialog box.

Click the Browse button to locate and select your CUI file. After you've done this, the name of your file appears in the File Name text box. You can then click the Load button to import it into your AutoCAD session.

Finally, if you want to unload a CUI file, do the following:

1. Open the Customize User Interface dialog box.
2. Scroll down to the bottom of the list in the Customizations In All Files group, and expand the Partial Customization Files item.
3. Right-click the partial CUI file that you want to unload, and select Unload *name*.cuix.
4. Close the dialog box by clicking OK.

Customizing the AutoComplete Command Entry Feature

AutoComplete provides a way to speed up your keyboard entry by offering command and system variable name suggestions as you type. For example, if you want to start the polygon command but you're not sure of the command name, you can type **poly** and AutoComplete will fill in the rest of the name for you.

AutoComplete offers a few options in the way it presents command and system variable name suggestions. To get to these options, right-click in the command-line interface and then select Input Settings. You will see a list of options that you can toggle on or off. These options are AutoComplete, AutoCorrect, Search System Variables, Search Content, Mid-string Search, and Delay Time.

The AutoComplete option lets you enable or disable the AutoComplete feature. The AutoCorrect option will correct for misspelled entries. Search System Variables will include system variables when looking for AutoComplete suggestions. Search Content will search for names of objects in the drawing. Mid-string Search will suggest names that start with or contain the letters you type. Delay Time lets you control the delay between the time you start to type and when AutoComplete offers a suggestion.

Besides these selections, you can also make more detailed setting modifications through the Input Search Options dialog box.

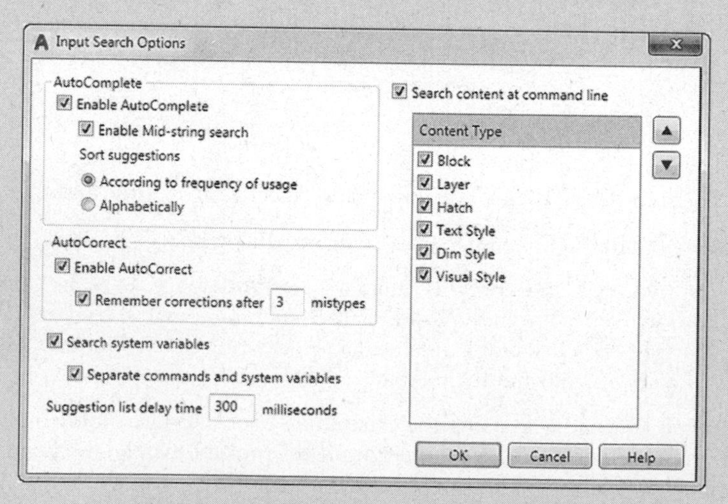

This dialog box offers some additional control over how the AutoComplete feature works. To open this dialog box, right-click in the Command window and select Input Search Options in the context menu.

Understanding the DIESEL Macro Language

DIESEL is one of many macro languages that AutoCAD supports, and you can use it to perform simple operations and add some automation to menus. As with AutoLISP, parentheses are used to enclose program code.

In the following sections, you'll look at the various ways to use the DIESEL macro language. You'll start by using DIESEL directly from the command line. This section will show you how a DIESEL macro is formatted, and it will give you a chance to see DIESEL in action. Then you'll go on to see how DIESEL can be used as part of a menu option to test the current state of AutoCAD. In the third section, you'll see how DIESEL can be used as part of the menu label to control what is shown in the menu. Finally, you'll learn how to use DIESEL with field objects to control text in your drawing.

Using DIESEL at the Command Line

You can use DIESEL at the AutoCAD command line by using a command called Modemacro. The Modemacro command sends information to the status bar. DIESEL can be used with Modemacro to perform simple tasks.

Try the following exercise to experiment with DIESEL:

1. Open a drawing, and then at the Command prompt, type **Modemacro**↵.
2. At the `Enter new value for MODEMACRO, or. for none <" ">:` prompt, enter **$(/,25,2)**↵. The answer to the equation appears at the left end of the status bar icons.

3. To clear the status bar, enter **Modemacro**↵.
4. At the `Enter new value for MODEMACRO, or . for none <" ">:` prompt, enter . (a period). The status will then clear.

The equation you entered in step 2 is referred to as an *expression*. The structure of DIESEL expressions is similar to that of AutoLISP expressions. The dollar sign tells AutoCAD that the information that follows is a DIESEL expression.

A DIESEL expression must include an operator of some sort, followed by the items to be operated on. An *operator* is an instruction to take a specific action, such as adding two numbers or dividing one number by another. Examples of mathematical operators include the plus sign (+) for addition and the forward slash (/) for division.

The operator is often referred to as a *function* and the items to be operated on are referred to as the *arguments* to the function, or simply the arguments. In the expression `(/,25,2)`, the / is the function and 25 and 2 are the arguments. All DIESEL expressions, no matter what size, follow this structure and are enclosed by parentheses.

Parentheses are important elements of an expression. All parentheses must be balanced—that is, for each left parenthesis, there must be a right parenthesis.

You can do other things with DIESEL besides performing calculations. The `getvar` function is an AutoLISP function that you can use to obtain the drawing prefix and name. Try the following to see how DIESEL uses `getvar`:

1. Type **Modemacro**↵ again.
2. Type **$(getvar,dwgprefix)**↵. The location of the current drawing appears in the status bar.
3. Press ↵ to reissue the Modemacro command; then type **$(getvar,dwgname)**↵. The name of the drawing appears in the status bar.

In this example, the `getvar` function extracts the drawing prefix and name and displays it in the status bar. You can use `getvar` to extract any system variable that you want. If you've been working through the exercises in this book, you've seen that virtually all AutoCAD settings are also controlled through system variables. (The Help section of the Autodesk Exchange window contains a list of all the system variables. See Chapter 2, "Creating Your First Drawing," for more on Autodesk Exchange.) This can be a great tool when you're creating custom menus because with `getvar`, you can poll AutoCAD to determine the state of a given system variable. For example, you can find out what command is currently being used. Try the following exercise to see how this works:

1. Make sure that Dynamic Input is turned off, and click the Line tool on the Draw panel.
2. Type **'Modemacro**↵. The apostrophe at the beginning of Modemacro lets you use the command while in another command.
3. Type **$(getvar,cmdnames)**↵. The word *LINE* appears in the status bar, indicating that the current command is the Line command.

This information can be useful in building a menu when you want an option to perform a specific task depending on which command is currently active.

AutoCAD LT Users Can Use DIESEL

Users of AutoCAD LT® software can't use AutoLISP to find the location of AutoCAD resource files. However, they can use the DIESEL macro language. For example, to find the log file path, enter **Modemacro**↵ and then **$(getvar,logfilepath)**. The path is displayed in the status bar. To get the status bar tools back, enter **Modemacro**↵ and then enter a period.

Using DIESEL in a Custom Menu Macro

So far, you've been experimenting with DIESEL through the Modemacro command. Next, you'll see how DIESEL can be used in a menu macro. A menu macro is a piece of code that changes a menu option depending on some condition. For example, you could have a menu option that says, "Turn on the grid." But if the grid is already on, you would want the menu option to say, "Turn off the grid." DIESEL could help you accomplish this. You'll start by examining a DIESEL expression, and then you'll set up a menu option that turns a feature called Blipmode on and off.

Using DIESEL in a menu macro requires a slightly different format from what you've seen so far. You still use the same DIESEL format of a dollar sign followed by the expression, but you don't use the Modemacro command to access DIESEL. Instead, you use `$M=`. You can think of `$M=` as an abbreviation for Modemacro.

For the purpose of completing the following sections, you will need to activate a system variable called `Blipmode`. To do this, type **Redefine**↵, and at the `Enter command name:` prompt, type **Blipmode**↵.

Here's a DIESEL expression that you can use in a menu macro:

```
^C^C_Blipmode;$M=$(-,1,$(getvar,Blipmode))
```

This menu option turns the Blipmode display on or off depending on its current state. Blipmode displays point selections in the drawing area as tiny crosses. These tiny crosses, or *blips*, don't print and can be cleared from the screen with a redraw. They can be helpful when you need to track your point selections.

In this example, the Blipmode command is invoked, and then the `$M=` tells AutoCAD that a DIESEL expression follows. The expression

```
$(-,1,$(getvar,Blipmode))
```

returns either 1 or a 0, which is applied to the Blipmode command to turn it either on or off. This expression shows that you can nest expressions. The most deeply nested expression is evaluated first, so AutoCAD begins by evaluating

```
$(getvar,Blipmode)
```

This returns either 1 or a 0, depending on whether Blipmode is on or off. AutoCAD then evaluates the next level in the expression

```
$(-,1,getvar_result)
```

in which `getvar_result` is either 1 or a 0. If `getvar_result` is 1, the expression looks like

```
$(-,1,1)
```

which returns 0. If `getvar_result` is 0, the expression looks like

```
$(-,1,0)
```

which returns 1. In either case, the end result is that the Blipmode command is assigned a value that is the opposite of the current Blipmode setting.

Using DIESEL as a Menu Bar Option Label

In the previous example, you saw how to use DIESEL in a menu macro to read the status of a command and then return a numeric value to alter that status. You can also use DIESEL as part of the menu bar option name so that the text it displays depends on certain conditions.

WHERE IS THE MENU BAR?

The menu bar is turned off by default, but you can turn it on by selecting Show Menu Bar from the Customize Quick Access Toolbar tool. See Chapter 1, "Exploring the Interface," for more on this tool.

The following expression shows how to write a menu option name to display the current setting for Blipmode. It includes DIESEL code as the menu option label:

```
$(eval,Blipmode = $(getvar,blipmode))
```

Normally, you would just have a menu name, but here you see some DIESEL instructions. These instructions tell AutoCAD to display the message `Blipmode = 1` or `Blipmode = 0` in the menu, depending on the current `Blipmode` setting. You would place this code in the Properties group for the Blipmode custom command in the Customize User Interface dialog box. It goes in the Display/Name text box.

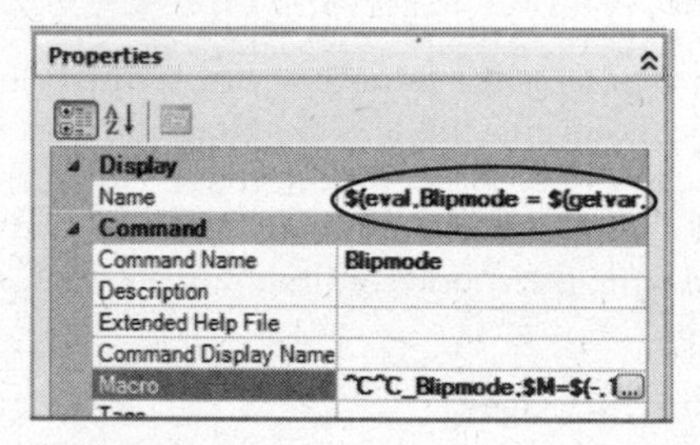

Here's how it works. You see the familiar `$(getvar,blipmode)` expression, this time embedded in a different expression. You know that `$(getvar,blipmode)` returns either 1 or a 0, depending on whether `Blipmode` is on or off. The outer expression

```
$(eval,Blipmode = getvar_result)
```

displays `Blipmode` = and then combines this with `getvar_result`, which, as you've learned, will be either 1 or 0. The `eval` function evaluates any text that follows it and returns its contents. The end result is the appearance of Blipmode = 1 or Blipmode = 0 in the menu. Here's how the properties look as a menu bar option under the Tools list of the Menus option in the Customizations In All Files panel:

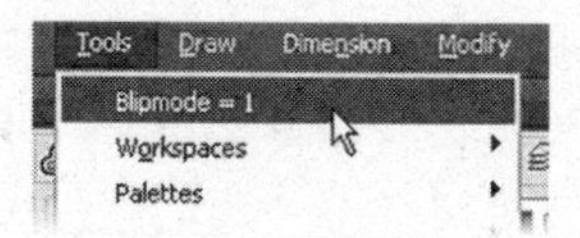

You can get even fancier and set up the menu option label to read Blipmode On or Blipmode Off by using the `if` DIESEL function. Here's that same menu listing with additional DIESEL code to accomplish this:

```
$(eval,Blipmode = $(if,$(getvar,blipmode),On,Off))
```

In this example, the simple `$(getvar,blipmode)` expression is expanded to include the `if` function. The `if` function reads the result of `$(getvar,blipmode)` and then returns the Off or On value depending on whether `$(getvar,blipmode)` returns 0 or 1. Here's a simpler look at the expression:

```
$(if, getvar_result, Off, On)
```

If `getvar_result` returns 1, the `if` function returns the first of the two options listed after `getvar_result`, which is Off. If `getvar_result` returns 0, the `if` function returns On. The second of the two options is optional. Here's how the fancier Blipmode option appears in a menu:

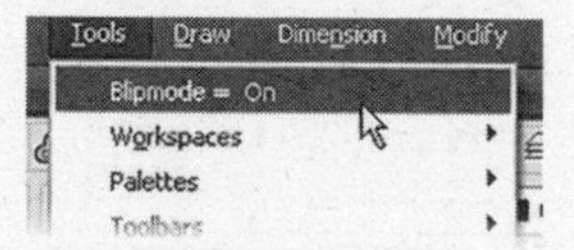

We've just skimmed the surface of what DIESEL can do. To get a more detailed description of how DIESEL works, press the F1 function key to open the Autodesk Help Homepage. Enter **DIESEL↵** in the search box at the top of the left column of the Help Homepage, and then select the Customization Guide entry that appears below the search box. Scroll down the right side panel to locate the DIESEL heading.

Table 24.2 shows some of the commonly used DIESEL functions. Check the AutoCAD Help dialog box for a more detailed list.

TABLE 24.2: Sample of DIESEL functions

CODE	FUNCTION	EXAMPLE	RESULT	COMMENTS
`+`	`Add`	`$(+,202,144)`	346	
`-`	`Subtract`	`$(-,202,144)`	58	
`****`	`Multiply`	`$(*,202,144)`	29,088	
`/`	`Divide`	`$(/,202,144)`	1.4028	
`=`	`Equal to`	`$(=,202,144)`	0	If numbers are equal, 1 is returned.
`<`	`Less than`	`$(<,202,144)`	0	If the first number is less than the second, 1 is returned.
`>`	`Greater than`	`$(>,202,144)`	1	If the first number is greater than the second, 1 is returned; otherwise, 0 is returned.
`!`	`Not equal to`	`$(!=,202,144`	1	If the numbers are equal, 0 is returned.
`<=`	`Less than or equal to`	`$(<=,202,144)`	0	If the first number is less than or equal to the second, 1 is returned.
`>=`	`Greater than or equal to`	`$(>=,202,144)`	1	If the first number is greater than or equal to the second, 1 is returned; otherwise, 0 is returned.
`eq`	`Equal string`	`$(eq,Yes, No)`	0	If both text strings are the same, 1 is returned.
`eval`	`Evaluate text`	`$(eval,Here I Am)`	Here I Am	Returns the text that follows.
`getvar`	`Get system variable value`	`$(getvar,ltscale)`	Current line-type scale	Returns the value of the system variable.
`if`	`If/Then`	`$(if,1,Yes,No)`	Yes	The second argument is returned if the first argument evaluates to 1. Otherwise, the third argument is returned. The third argument is optional.

Note: To indicate true or false, DIESEL uses 1 or 0.

Using DIESEL and Fields to Generate Text

Using DIESEL expressions in the status bar or in a menu can be helpful to gather information or to create a more interactive interface, but what if you want the results of a DIESEL expression to become part of the drawing? You can employ field objects to do just that.

For example, suppose that you want to create a note that shows the scale of a drawing based on the dimension scale. Further, you want the scale in the note to be updated automatically whenever the dimension scale changes. You can add a field object and associate it with a DIESEL expression that displays the dimension scale as it relates to the drawing scale. Try the following steps to see how it's done:

1. In the Annotate tab, click the Multiline Text tool and select two points to indicate the text location. The Text Editor Ribbon tab and text editor appear.
2. Right-click in the text editor, and select Insert Field to open the Field dialog box.
3. In the Field Category drop-down list, select Other; then, in the Field Names list box, select DIESELExpression.
4. Add the following text in the DIESEL Expression box to the right. If you need to expand the width of the dialog box, click and drag its right edge:

```
$(eval,Dimension Scale: 1/)$(/,$(getvar, dimscale),12)
$(eval, inch = 1 foot)
```

5. Click OK in the Field dialog box, and then click Close Text Editor in the Text Editor Ribbon tab. The following text is displayed in the drawing:

```
Dimension Scale: 1/0.08333333 inch = 1 foot
```

Zoom into the text if needed. The resulting text may not make sense until you change the dimension scale to a value that represents a scale other than 1-to-1. Here's how to do that:

1. Enter **Dimscale**↵ at the Command prompt.
2. At the `Enter new value for DIMSCALE <1.0000>:` prompt, enter 96↵. This is the value for a 1/8″ scale drawing.
3. Type **RE**↵. The text changes to read

```
Dimension Scale: 1/8 inch = 1 foot
```

In this example, several DIESEL operations were used. The beginning of the expression uses the `eval` operation to tell AutoCAD to display a string of text:

```
$(eval Dimension Scale: 1/)
```

The next part tells AutoCAD to get the current value of the `Dimscale` system variable and divide it by 12:

```
$(/,$(getvar, dimscale),12)
```

Notice that this is a nested expression: `$(getvar,dimscale)` obtains the value of the `Dimscale` system variable, which is then divided by 12. The end of the expression adds the final part to the text:

```
$(eval, inch = 1 foot)
```

When it's all put together, you get the text that shows the dimension scale as an architectural scale. Because it's an AutoCAD text object, this text is part of the drawing.

Creating Custom Linetypes

As your drawing needs expand, the standard linetypes may not be adequate for your application. Fortunately, you can create your own. The following sections explain how to do so.

You'll get an in-depth view of the process of creating linetypes. You'll also learn how to create complex linetypes that can't be created by using the Make Linetype Express tool.

Viewing Available Linetypes

Although AutoCAD provides the linetypes most commonly used in drafting (see Figure 24.23), the dashes and dots may not be spaced the way you would like, or you may want an entirely new linetype.

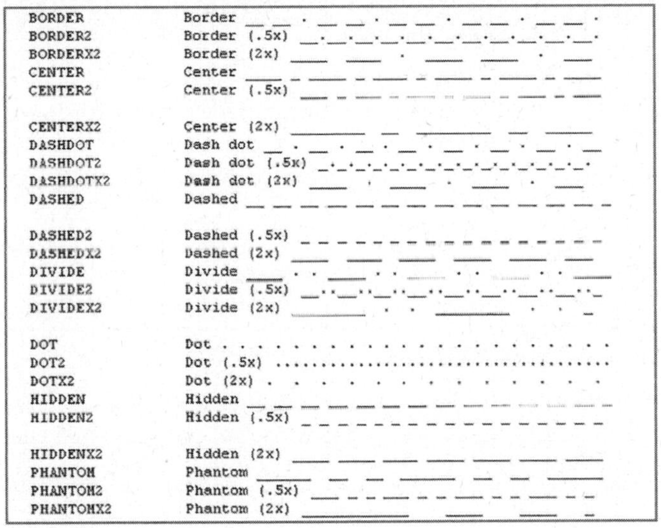

FIGURE 24.23
The lines in this partial list of standard linetypes were generated with the underscore key (_), the period (.), and other symbols and are only rough representations of the actual lines.

```
BORDER       Border
BORDER2      Border (.5x)
BORDERX2     Border (2x)
CENTER       Center
CENTER2      Center (.5x)

CENTERX2     Center (2x)
DASHDOT      Dash dot
DASHDOT2     Dash dot (.5x)
DASHDOTX2    Dash dot (2x)
DASHED       Dashed

DASHED2      Dashed (.5x)
DASHEDX2     Dashed (2x)
DIVIDE       Divide
DIVIDE2      Divide (.5x)
DIVIDEX2     Divide (2x)

DOT          Dot
DOT2         Dot (.5x)
DOTX2        Dot (2x)
HIDDEN       Hidden
HIDDEN2      Hidden (.5x)

HIDDENX2     Hidden (2x)
PHANTOM      Phantom
PHANTOM2     Phantom (.5x)
PHANTOMX2    Phantom (2x)
```

WHERE ARE THE LINETYPES STORED?

AutoCAD stores the linetypes in a file called `acad.lin`, which is in ASCII format. When you create a new linetype, you add information to this file. Or, if you create a new file containing your own linetype definitions, it too will have the extension `.lin` at the end of its name. You can edit linetypes as described here, or you can edit them directly in these files.

To create a custom linetype, use the -Linetype command. Let's see how this handy command works by first listing the available linetypes:

1. Open a new AutoCAD file.
2. At the Command prompt, enter **-Linetype**↵. (Don't forget the hyphen at the beginning.)
3. At the `Enter an option [?/Create/Load/Set]:` prompt, enter **?**↵.

4. In the dialog box, locate and double-click `acad.lin` in the listing of available linetype files. You get a list that shows the linetypes available in the `acad.lin` file along with a simple description of each line. You will also notice an identical LIN file in this folder for the metric version of the linetypes if you use the metric system.
5. A message at the bottom says `Press ENTER to continue:`. Press ↵ twice to return to the Command prompt. If the file was opened in a separate floating command window, close it.

Creating a New Linetype

Next, let's try creating a new linetype:

1. Enter **-Linetype↵** again.
2. At the `[?/Create/Load/Set]:` prompt, enter **C↵**.
3. At the `Enter name of linetype to create:` prompt, enter **Custom↵** as the name of your new linetype.
4. The dialog box that you see next is named Create Or Append Linetype File. You need to enter the name of the linetype file that you want to create or add to. If you select the default linetype file, `acad`, your new linetype is added to the `acad.lin` (`acadios.lin` for metric users) file. If you choose to create a new linetype file, AutoCAD opens a file containing the linetype that you create and adds `.lin` to the filename that you supply.
5. Let's assume that you want to start a new linetype file. Clear any text in the File Name text box, and then enter **Newline↵**.

New or Existing Linetype File

If you accept the default linetype file, `acad`, the prompt in step 4 is `Wait, checking if linetype already defined`. This protects you from inadvertently overwriting an existing linetype that you want to keep.

6. At the `Descriptive text:` prompt, enter a text description of your linetype. You can use any keyboard character as part of your description, but the actual linetype can be composed of only a series of lines, points, and blank spaces. For this exercise, enter the following, using the underscore key (_) to simulate, as closely as possible, the appearance of your line:

```
Custom - My own center line _
```

7. Press ↵ when complete, and at the `Enter linetype pattern (on next line):` prompt, enter the following numbers, known as the *linetype code* (after the `A`, which appears automatically):

```
A,1.0,-.125,.25,-.125
```

You Can Set the Default Linetype

If you use the Set option of the -Linetype command to set a new default linetype, you'll get that linetype no matter what layer you're on.

8. Press ↵ again, and at the `New linetype definition saved to file. Enter an option [?/Create/Load/Set]:` prompt, press ↵ to exit the -Linetype command.

Remember, after you've created a linetype, you must load it in order to use it, as discussed in Chapter 5, "Keeping Track of Layers and Blocks."

ADD LINETYPES DIRECTLY TO THE *ACAD.LIN* FILE

You can also open the `acad.lin` or other LIN file in Windows Notepad and add the descriptive text and linetype code directly to the end of the file.

Understanding the Linetype Code

In step 7 of the previous exercise, you entered a series of numbers separated by commas. This is the linetype code, representing the lengths of the components that make up the linetype. The separate elements of the linetype code are as follows:

- The `1.0` following the `A` is the length of the first part of the line. (The `A` that begins the linetype definition is a code that is applied to all linetypes.)
- The first `-.125` is the blank or broken part of the line. The minus sign tells AutoCAD that the line is *not* to be drawn for the specified length, which is 0.125 units in this example.
- Next comes the positive value `0.25`. This tells AutoCAD to draw a line segment 0.25 units long after the blank part of the line.
- The last negative value, `-.125`, again tells AutoCAD to skip drawing the line for the distance of 0.125 units.

This series of numbers represents the one segment that is repeated to form the line (see Figure 24.24). You can also create a complex linetype that looks like a random broken line, as shown in Figure 24.25.

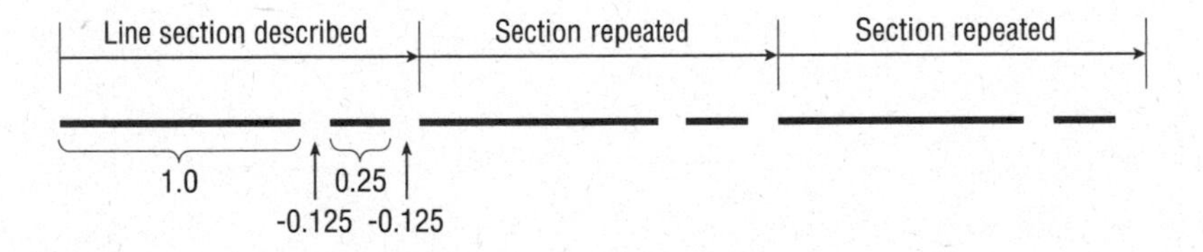

FIGURE 24.24
Linetype description with plotted line

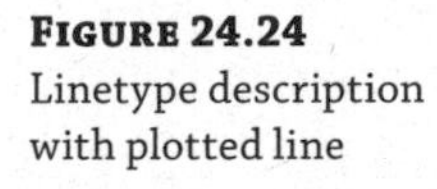

FIGURE 24.25
Random broken line

You may be wondering what purpose the `A` serves at the beginning of the linetype code. A linetype is composed of a series of line segments and points. The `A`, which is supplied by AutoCAD automatically, is a code that forces the linetype to start and end on a line segment rather than on a blank space in the series of lines. At times, AutoCAD stretches the last line segment to force this condition, as shown in Figure 24.26.

FIGURE 24.26
AutoCAD stretches the beginning and the end of the line as necessary.

LINE SEGMENT LENGTHS AND SCALE

The values that you enter for the line segment lengths are multiplied by the Ltscale factor, so be sure to enter values for the plotted lengths.

As mentioned earlier, you can also create linetypes outside AutoCAD by using a word processor or text editor such as Windows Notepad. The standard `acad.lin` file looks like Figure 24.23 with the addition of the code used by AutoCAD to determine the line segment lengths.

Normally, to use a linetype that you've created, you have to load it through either the Layer Properties Manager or the Linetype Manager dialog box (choose Other from the Linetype drop-down list in the Home tab's Properties panel). If you use one of your own linetypes frequently, you may want to create a button macro so that it will be available as an option on a menu.

Creating Complex Linetypes

A *complex linetype* is one that incorporates text or special graphics. For example, if you want to show an underground gas line in a site plan, you normally show a line with the intermittent word *GAS*, as in Figure 24.27. Fences are often shown with an intermittent circle, square, or X.

FIGURE 24.27
Samples of complex linetypes

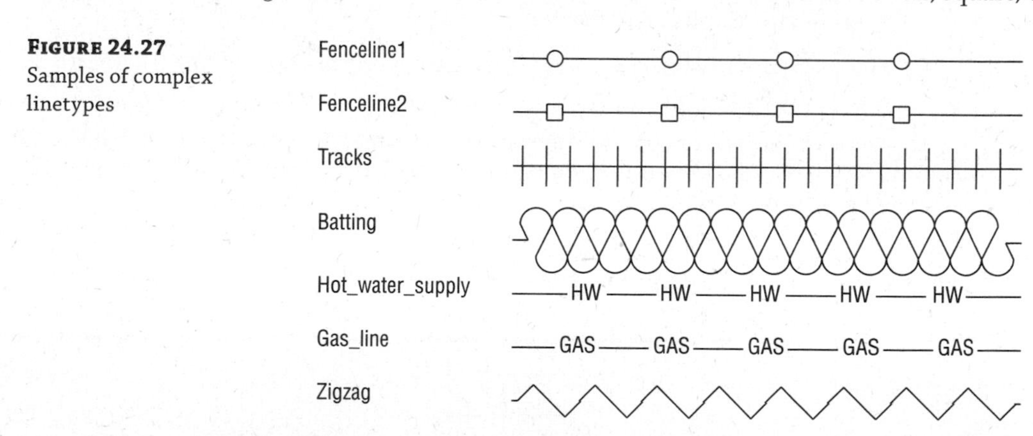

For the graphics needed to compose complex linetypes, use any of the symbols in the AutoCAD font files discussed in Chapter 9, "Adding Text to Drawings." Create a text style by using these symbol fonts, and then specify the appropriate symbol by using its corresponding letter in the linetype description.

To create a linetype that includes text, use the same linetype code described earlier but add the necessary font file information in brackets. For example, say that you want to create the linetype for the underground gas line mentioned previously by using just the letter *G*. You add the following to your `acad.lin` file:

```
*Gas_line, -G-G-G-
A,1.0,-0.25,["G",STANDARD,S=.2,R=0,X=-.1,Y=-.1],-0.25
```

The first line serves as a description for anyone looking at this linetype code. The next line is the code itself. Note that the code should not contain spaces.

The information in the square brackets describes the characteristics of the text. The actual text that you want to appear in the line is surrounded by quotation marks. Next are the text style, scale, rotation angle, X displacement, and Y displacement.

EDIT THE *ACAD.LIN* FILE TO CREATE COMPLEX LINETYPES

You can't use the -Linetype command to define complex linetypes. Instead, you must open the `acad.lin` file by using a text editor, such as Notepad, and add the linetype information to the end of the file. Be sure that you don't duplicate the name of an existing linetype.

You can substitute `A` for the rotation angle (the `R` value), as in the following example:

```
A,1.0,-0.25,["G",standard,S=.2,A=0,X=-.1,Y=-.1],-0.25
```

This has the effect of keeping the text at the same angle regardless of the line's direction. Notice that in this sample, the X and Y values are `-.1`; this will center the Gs on the line. The scale value of `.2` will cause the text to be 0.2 units high, so .1 is half the height.

In addition to fonts, you can specify shapes for linetype definitions. Instead of letters, shapes display symbols. Shapes are stored not as drawings but as definition files, similar to text font files. Shape files have the same `.shx` filename extension as font files and are also defined similarly. Figure 24.28 shows some symbols from sample shape files. The names of the files are shown at the top of each column.

FIGURE 24.28
Samples of shapes

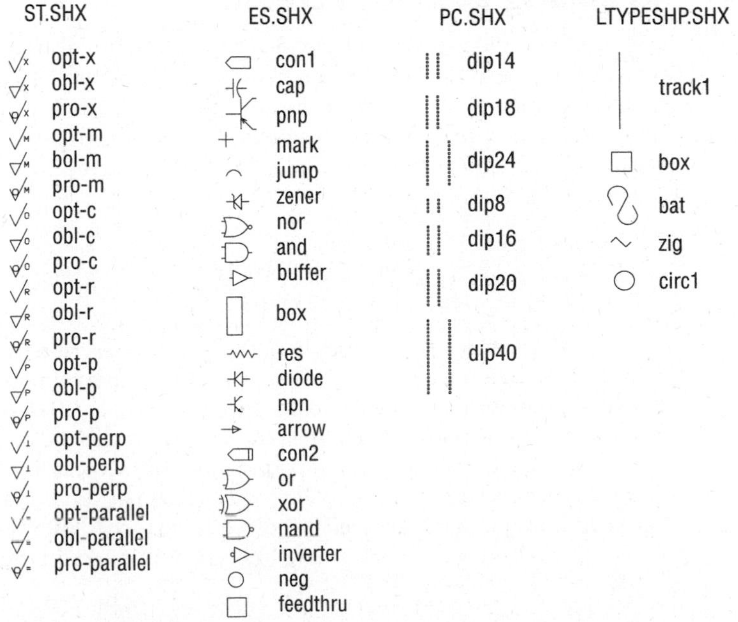

To use a shape in a linetype code, you use the same format as shown previously for text. However, instead of using a letter and style name, you use the shape name and the shape filename as in the following example:

```
*Capline, ====
a,1.0,-0.25,[CAP,ES.SHX,S=.5,R=0,X=-.1,Y=-.1],-0.25
```

This example uses the CAP symbol from the `Es.shx` shape file. The symbol is scaled to 0.5 units with 0 rotation and an X and Y displacement of –0.1.

Here is another example, this one using the arrow shape:

```
*Arrowline, -|-|-|-
a,1.0,-0.25,[ARROW,ES.SHX,S=.5,R=90,X=-.1,Y=-.1],-0.25
```

Just as with the Capline example, the ARROW symbol in this example is scaled to 0.5 units with 90 rotation and an X and Y displacement of –0.1. Figure 24.29 shows what the Arrowline linetype looks like when used with a spline.

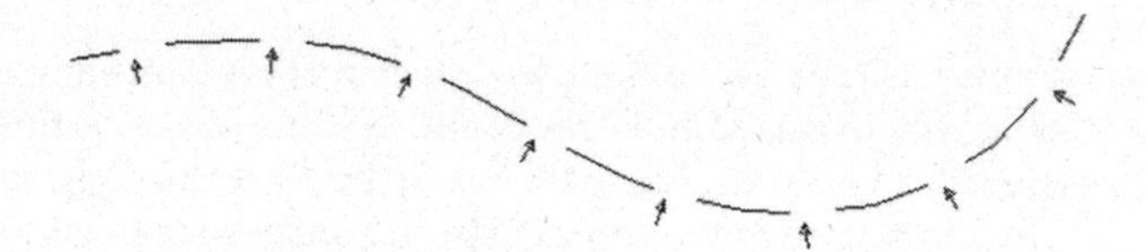

FIGURE 24.29
The Arrowline linetype used with a spline

In this example, the Ltype generation option is turned on for the polyline. Note that the arrow from the `Es.shx` sample shape file is used for the arrow in this linetype.

Creating Hatch Patterns

AutoCAD provides several predefined hatch patterns from which you can choose, but you can also create your own. This section demonstrates the basic elements of pattern definition.

Unlike linetypes, hatch patterns can't be created while you're in an AutoCAD file. The pattern definitions are contained in an external file named `acad.pat`. You can open and edit this file with a text editor that can handle ASCII files, such as Notepad. Here is one hatch pattern definition from that file:

```
*SQUARE,Small aligned squares
0, 0,0, 0,.125, .125,-.125
90, 0,0, 0,.125, .125,-.125
```

You can see some similarities between pattern descriptions and linetype descriptions. They both start with a line of descriptive text and then give numeric values defining the pattern. However, the numbers in pattern descriptions have a different meaning. This example shows two lines of information. Each line represents a line in the pattern. The first line determines the horizontal line component of the pattern, and the second line represents the vertical component (see the image to the far right in Figure 24.30). A pattern is made up of line groups. A *line group* is like a linetype that is arrayed a specified distance to fill the area to be hatched. A line group is defined by a line of code, much as a linetype is defined. In the square pattern, for instance, two lines—one horizontal and one vertical—are used. Each of these lines is duplicated in a fashion that makes the lines appear as boxes when they're combined. Figure 24.30 illustrates this point.

FIGURE 24.30
The individual and combined line groups

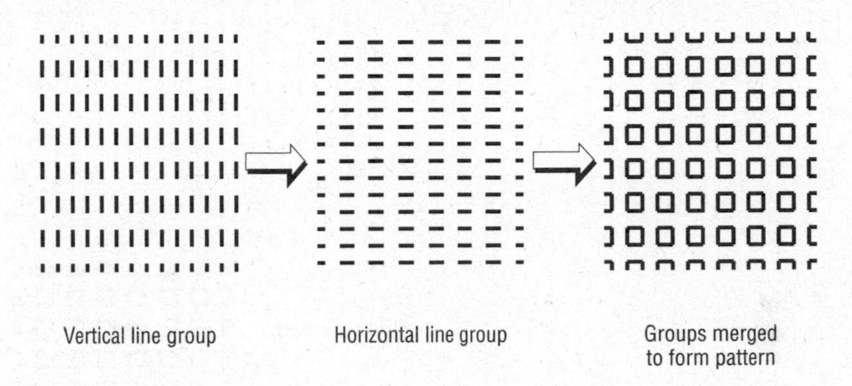

Look at the first line in the definition:

```
0, 0,0, 0,.125, .125,-.125
```

This example shows a series of numbers separated by commas. It represents one line group. It contains four sets of information separated by blank spaces:

- The first component is the `0` at the beginning. This value indicates the angle of the line group, as determined by the line's orientation. In this case, it's 0 for a horizontal line that runs from left to right.
- The next component is the origin of the line group, `0,0`. This is the hatch pattern origin, not the drawing origin. (See "Positioning Hatch Patterns Accurately" in Chapter 7, "Mastering Viewing Tools, Hatches, and External References," for more on the hatch pattern origin.) It gives you a reference point to determine the location of other line groups involved in generating the pattern.
- The next component is `0,.125`. This determines the distance and direction for arraying the line, as illustrated in Figure 24.31. This value is like a relative coordinate indicating X and Y distances for a rectangular array. It isn't based on the drawing coordinates, but on a coordinate system relative to the orientation of the line. For a line oriented at a 0° angle, the code `0,.125` indicates a precisely vertical direction. For a line oriented at a 45° angle, the code `0,.125` represents a 135° direction. Remember that the very first number in the line definition determines the angle of the line. In this example, the duplication occurs 90° in relation to the line group, because the X value is 0. Figure 24.32 illustrates this point.
- The last component is the description of the line pattern. This value is equivalent to the value given when you create a linetype. Positive values are line segments, and negative values are blank segments. This part of the line group definition works exactly as in the linetype definitions that you studied in the previous section.

This system of defining hatch patterns may seem somewhat limiting, but you can do a lot with it. Autodesk managed to come up with 69 patterns—and that was only scratching the surface.

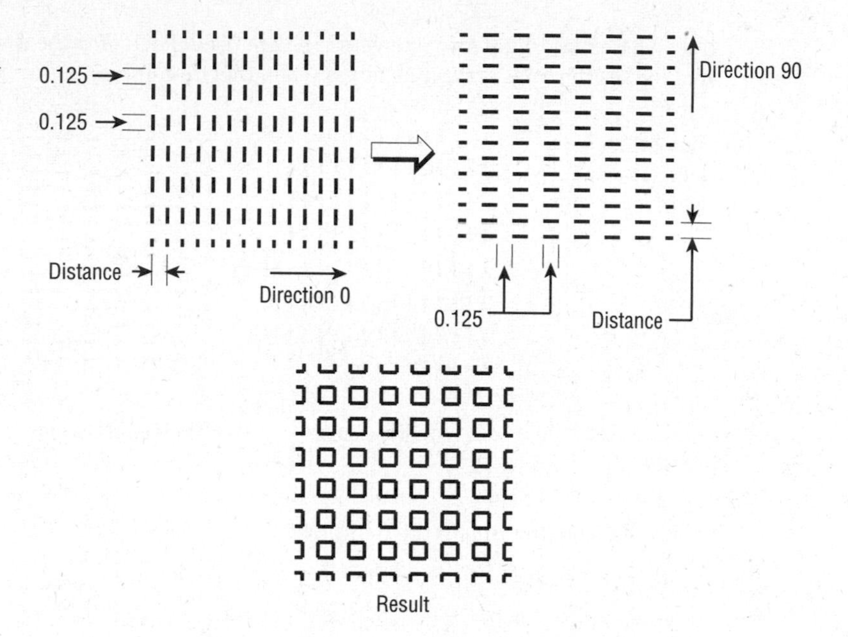

FIGURE 24.31
The distance and direction of duplication

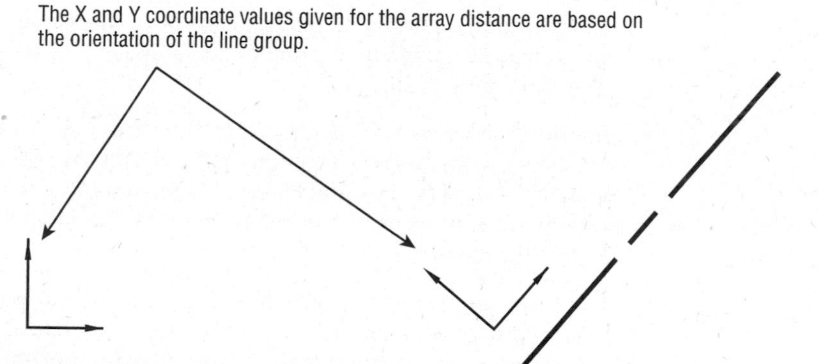

FIGURE 24.32
How the direction of the line group copy is determined

> **ADDING THICK LINES TO HATCH PATTERN LINETYPES**
>
> If you want to include thick lines in your hatch patterns, you have to build up line widths with multiple linetype definitions.

The Bottom Line

Use workspaces. Often with AutoCAD, you find that you have different sets of panels or toolbars open to perform specific tasks. You might have one set of Ribbon panels for editing text and dimensions, whereas another set is more useful for design. Using workspaces is a great way to organize your different editing modes.

Master It Where do you find the Customize option for workspaces?

Customize the user interface. In addition to using workspaces to organize tools and Ribbon panels, you can customize the AutoCAD interface to make it fit the way you like to work. You can add tools to Ribbon panels, or you can even create your own tools for operations you perform frequently.

Master It What does the Customizations In All Files group display?

Create macros in tools and menus. A macro is a set of instructions that performs more complex operations than single commands. Macros are often built on commands with additional predefined responses to help speed data input.

Master It What does the `^C` do in a macro?

Edit keyboard shortcuts. Keyboard shortcuts can help improve your speed when drawing in AutoCAD. They can reduce several clicks of the mouse to a simple keystroke. AutoCAD lets you create custom shortcuts for your favorite commands.

Master It What is the name of the feature that lets you record and play back actions?

Save, load, and unload your customizations. To keep your customizations organized, you can save new toolbars, menus, and Ribbons as files that you can load on demand. When you save your custom elements as a file, you can move them to other computers. In addition, you can use the cloud to synchronize your custom settings with other computers.

Master It Name the feature that lets you synchronize your custom settings from a cloud source.

Understand the DIESEL macro language. If you're adventurous, you may want to try your hand at creating more complex macros. The DIESEL macro language is an easy introduction to AutoCAD macro customization, and it is most useful in controlling the behavior in menu options.

Master It What does the expression `$(getvar, Blipmode)` do?

Create custom linetypes. AutoCAD offers a number of noncontinuous linetypes, and you may find them adequate for most of your work. But every now and then, you may need a specific linetype that isn't available. Creating custom linetypes is easy when you understand the process.

Master It What is the purpose of a negative value in the linetype code?

Create hatch patterns. Like linetypes, the hatch patterns provided by AutoCAD will probably fill most of your needs. But every now and then you may need to produce a specific pattern.

Master It How are a hatch pattern code and a linetype code similar?

Chapter 25

Managing and Sharing Your Drawings

Whether you're a one-person operation working out of your home or one of several hundred Autodesk® AutoCAD® software users in a large company, file sharing and file maintenance can become the focus of much of your time. In our interconnected world, the volume of messages and files crossing our paths seems to be increasing exponentially. In addition, the Internet has enabled us to be more mobile, adding yet more complexity to file management and data sharing tasks.

In this chapter, you'll learn about some of the tools AutoCAD offers to help you manage your files and the files you share with others. You'll also examine some general issues that arise while using AutoCAD in a workgroup environment. You may find help with problems you've encountered when using AutoCAD.

In this chapter, you will learn to

- Share drawings online
- Publish your drawings
- Get started with A360 Drive®
- Manage your drawings with DesignCenter™ and the tool palettes
- Establish office standards
- Convert multiple layer settings

Sharing Drawings Online

Through AutoCAD, you can use tools to post drawings on the Internet that others can view and download. In the architecture, engineering, and construction (AEC) industry in particular, this can mean easier access to documents needed by contractors, engineers, cost estimators, and others involved in the design, bidding, and construction of building projects. Suppliers of products can post symbol libraries of their products or even 3D solid models.

In the following sections, you'll learn about the tools that AutoCAD provides for publishing and accessing drawings over the Internet (and on any local or wide area network). You'll start by looking at one of the most common uses of the Internet: file transmission.

Sharing Project Files with eTransmit

Whether you're a one-person office or a member of a 50-person firm, you'll eventually have to share your work with others outside your building. Before eTransmit existed as a feature in AutoCAD, you had to examine carefully what you were sending to make sure that you included all of the ancillary files needed to view or work on your drawings. Xref, font, and custom linetype files all had to be included with the drawings that you sent to consultants or partners in a project, and often one of these items was omitted from the transmission.

By using eTransmit, you can quickly collect all your project drawings into a single archive file, or you can store the files in a separate folder for later processing. This collection of files is included with a report file as a transmittal. Try the following to see how eTransmit works:

1. In AutoCAD, open `15-xref1.dwg` from the Chapter 15 sample files and then choose Publish ➤ eTransmit from the Application menu to open the Create Transmittal dialog box (see Figure 25.1). If you've edited the file before choosing eTransmit, you will see a message telling you that you must save the drawing before continuing.

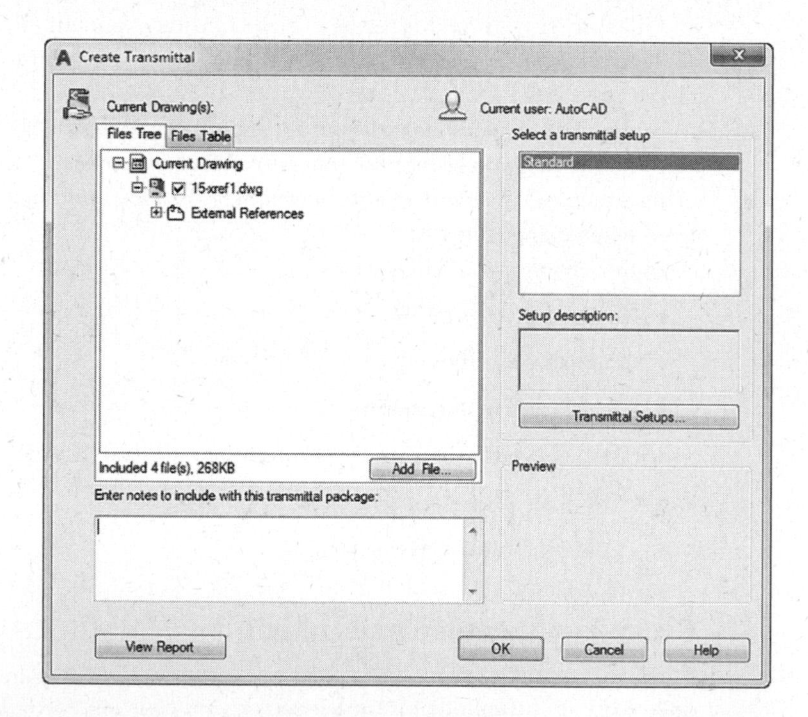

FIGURE 25.1
Creating a transmittal

2. In the dialog box, a tree structure lists the files that are included in the transmittal. If you need to add more files to the transmittal than are shown in the list, you can click the Add File button to open the Add File To Transmittal dialog box. To remove files, expand the listed item and remove the check mark that appears next to the file that you want to exclude. You can also use the Files Table tab to view the files as a simple list.

3. Click in the Enter Notes To Include With This Transmittal Package box, and enter a description or other note.

4. In the Select A Transmittal Setup group, click the Transmittal Setups button to open the Transmittal Setups dialog box (see Figure 25.2). Here you can create a new transmittal or rename or modify an existing one.

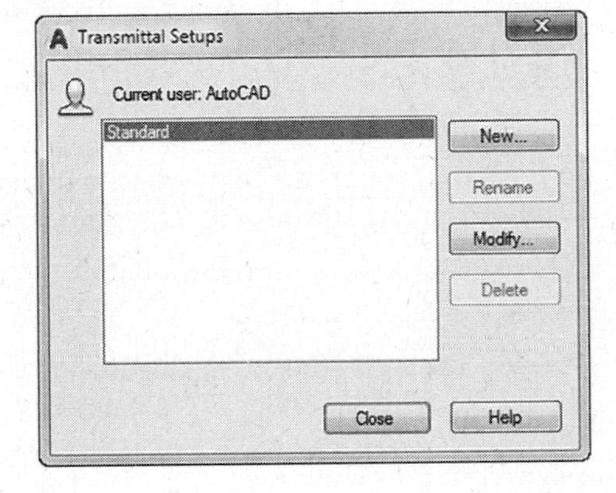

FIGURE 25.2
Choose whether to create from scratch or edit an existing transmittal.

5. Click the Modify button to open the Modify Transmittal Setup dialog box (see Figure 25.3).

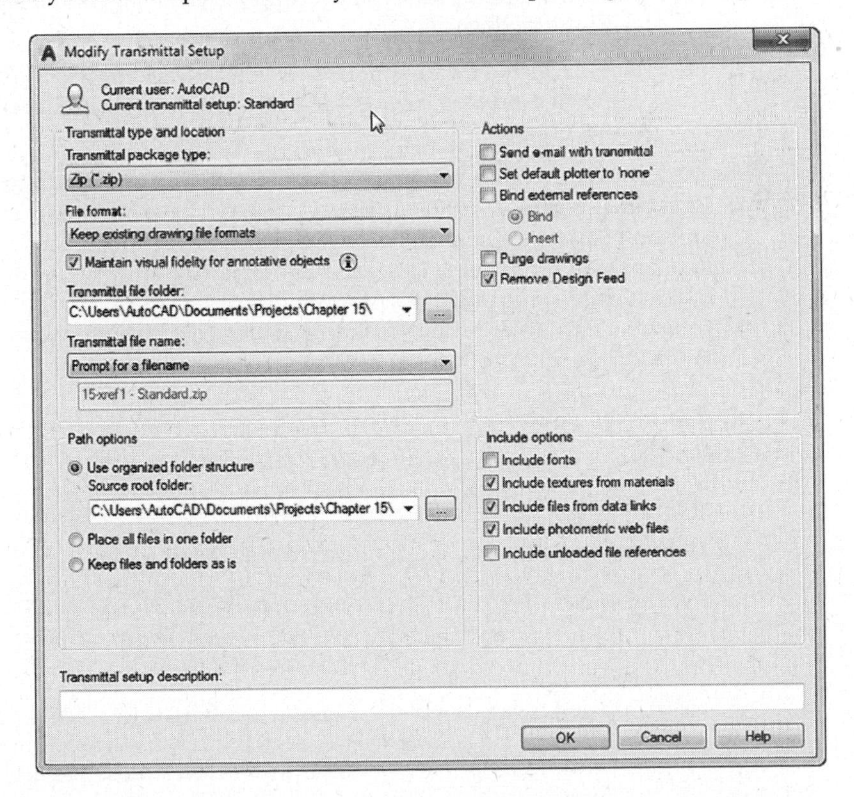

FIGURE 25.3
Set your transmittal options.

6. In the Transmittal Package Type drop-down list, select the format for your collection of files. You can create a Zip archive or you can save the files in a folder.

You can tell AutoCAD where to place the files by using the Browse button to the right of the Transmittal File Folder drop-down list. For this exercise, choose the Folder option in the Transmittal Package Type list.

7. Click the Browse button next to the Transmittal File Folder drop-down list to open the Specify Location Folder dialog box. This is a typical AutoCAD file open dialog box that you can use to select a location for your files.

   You can use the Create New Folder tool to create a new folder for your files. You'll want to keep your transmittal files separate from other files. After you select a location, click Open to return to the Modify Transmittal Setup dialog box.

8. After you've set up your transmittal, click OK. Then click Close in the Transmittal Setups dialog box.

9. Preview the report file by clicking the View Report button in the Create Transmittal dialog box. This report gives you a detailed description of the types of files included in the transmittal. It also alerts you to files that AutoCAD was unable to find but that are required for the drawing.

10. Close the report. After you've set up the eTransmit options, click OK in the Create Transmittal dialog box.

11. If you selected the Zip option in step 6, you see the Specify Zip File dialog box. You can then send the files over the Internet or put them on a removable disk for manual transport.

You probably noticed that you can create additional transmittal setup options in the Transmittal Setups dialog box. That way, you can have multiple transmittal options on hand that you don't have to set up each time a different situation arises. For example, you might have the Standard setup configured to create a Zip file and another setup configured to copy the files into a folder. A third setup might be created with a password.

Several options are available for configuring the transmittal setup. Table 25.1 gives a rundown of those options.

TABLE 25.1: Modify Transmittal Setup dialog box options

OPTION	PURPOSE
Transmittal Package Type	Lets you select Folder or Zip.
File Format	Lets you select 2018, 2013, 2010, 2007, 2004, or 2000 file formats in case your recipient requires an earlier version. The default option is to keep the current format.
Maintain Visual Fidelity For Annotative Objects	Maintains visual fidelity for annotative objects when drawings are viewed in AutoCAD 2007 and earlier. This option also has an Information/Help icon that, when clicked, opens the AutoCAD online help site.
Transmittal File Folder	Lets you determine the location for your transmittal package.

TABLE 25.1: Modify Transmittal Setup dialog box options *(CONTINUED)*

OPTION	PURPOSE
Transmittal File Name	Not available if you select Folder as the transmittal package type. Options are Prompt For A Filename, Overwrite If Necessary, and Increment File Name If Necessary.
Use Organized Folder Structure	Preserves the folder structure for the files in the transmittal. This can be important when Xref and other files are located across several folder locations.
Place All Files In One Folder	Self-explanatory.
Keep Files And Folders As Is	Preserves the entire folder structure for the files in the transmittal.
Include Fonts	Tells AutoCAD to include the font files in the transmittal.
Include Textures From Materials	Lets you include bitmap files that are part of a file's material settings.
Include Files From Data Links	Lets you include external data-link files for tables.
Include Photometric Web Files	Lets you include photometric web files for 3D lighting models.
Include Unloaded File References	Lets you include references for unloaded Xref files.
Send E-Mail With Transmittal	Lets you send an email with the files included as an attachment. This requires a default email application.
Set Default Plotter To 'None'	Removes any reference to printers or plotters that you've set up for the drawing. (The type of printer you've set up for your files is stored with the drawing file.)
Bind External References	Lets you bind external references to the drawings that contain them if it isn't important for the recipient to maintain the external references as separate drawings.
Purge Drawings	Purges drawings of unused elements.
Remove Design Feed	Removes association to design feed data.
Transmittal Setup Description	Lets you add a description to the transmittal file.

eTransmit gives you a quick way to package a set of files to be sent to others working on the same project. However, you may need to offer a wider distribution of your files. You may want to let others view and plot your drawings from a website without exposing your drawing database to anyone who might visit your site. If you need this approach, you'll want to know about the AutoCAD DWF file format, which lets anyone view AutoCAD files whether or not they own the program. You'll learn more about the DWF file format in the section "Publishing Your Drawings" later in this chapter.

AutoCAD and Mobile Devices

If you've been hoping to work with AutoCAD files on mobile devices, such as smartphones or tablets using the Apple iOS and Android operating systems, you're in luck. Autodesk® A360 Drive® (formerly known as Autodesk 360 Sync) lets you view and perform basic editing on AutoCAD files that have been uploaded to the A360 Drive website. In addition, any PC can be used to view and edit drawings on the A360 Drive website, whether or not you have AutoCAD installed.

The site is account based, but it's free, and even if you're not using a mobile device, you might consider using the A360 Drive website to share files with others. If you have AutoCAD installed on your PC, an AutoCAD plug-in lets you seamlessly open, edit, and upload drawings to your AutoCAD® 360 account. If you're on a PC that doesn't have AutoCAD, you can upload, download, and edit a drawing using the basic editor that runs in your browser. To start an account, just go to `https://360.autodesk.com` or `www.autocad360.com` and sign up.

Protecting AutoCAD Drawing Files

Because AutoCAD drawings specify the methods and materials used to produce an object or a building, they are frequently treated like legal documents. After an AutoCAD drawing is issued, it's often archived and guarded as a legal record of a design. For this reason, many AutoCAD users are concerned about possible tampering with drawings that are sent to third parties. Even minor unauthorized changes to a drawing can have major repercussions on the integrity of a design.

AutoCAD offers a digital signature feature that helps protect both the author of a drawing and the recipient in the event of file tampering. In addition, there are methods outside AutoCAD that you can use to protect your drawings.

Legacy Password Protection in AutoCAD

Earlier versions of AutoCAD offered a password protection scheme that allowed you to add a password to your DWG files. Once a password is added, you are asked to enter a password when you attempt to open the file. After you give the password and open a password-protected file, you can open and close the file repeatedly during that AutoCAD session without having to reenter the password. If you close and reopen AutoCAD, however, the program will prompt you for a password the next time you attempt to open the password-protected file. This feature is no longer offered.

Using a Digital Signature

You can use a digital signature to authenticate files. A digital signature can't prevent someone from tampering with a file, but it offers a way to validate whether a file has been modified after it has been saved. This protects you in the event that your file is unofficially altered. It also protects the recipient of your file by verifying the file's authenticity and by verifying that it was not altered from the time it left your computer.

The first time you attempt to use the digital signature feature, you see a message telling you that you need a digital certificate. AutoCAD uses a digital certificate issued by a certificate authority, and there are many to choose from. You will have to do a little research to find the certificate authority and pricing scheme with which you are most comfortable. `Identrust.com` is one example of a certificate authority that can provide a low-cost ID for email and encryption.

After you've obtained a digital ID, the signature resides in the Registry on your computer. You can then access the digital ID from AutoCAD by using the Digital Signature tab of the Security Options dialog box. Here are the steps:

1. Open the drawing to which you want to attach the digital signature, and then open the Digital Signatures dialog box by entering **Digitalsign**↵ at the Command prompt. The Digital Signatures dialog box appears (see Figure 25.4).

FIGURE 25.4
Attach a signature.

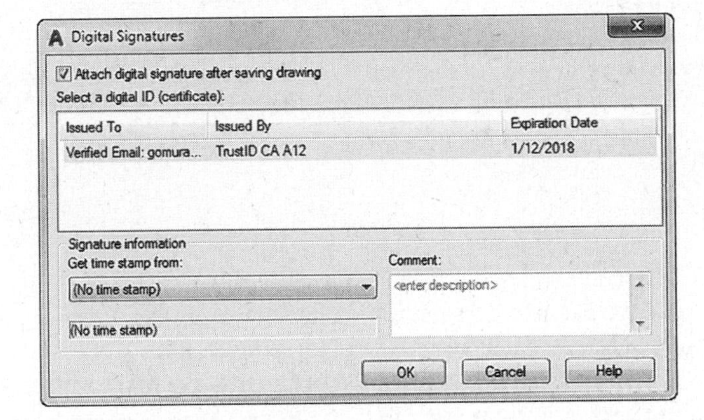

2. Select the Attach Digital Signature After Saving Drawing option. The Signature Information options become available. You can add a date stamp and a brief description.

3. Click OK to exit the dialog box.

The next time you save the file, depending on the level of security you chose during the digital ID setup, you may be prompted for a password. After you enter the password, the file is saved.

The next time the file is opened, you'll see the Digital Signature Contents dialog box (see Figure 25.5), which verifies that no one has tampered with the drawing.

FIGURE 25.5
The signature is verified when the file opens.

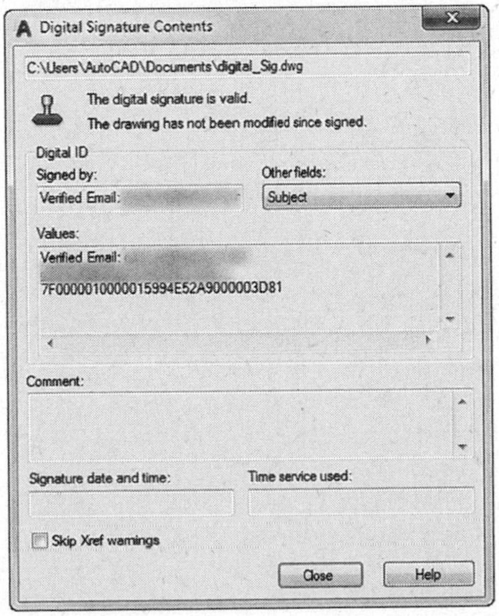

You'll also see a stamp icon in the lower-right corner of the AutoCAD window. You can click this icon at any time to view the file's digital signature status. You can also issue the SigValidate command to view the status.

A file containing a digital signature displays a warning when the user attempts to save the file after making modifications (see Figure 25.6). If the user continues to save the file, the signature is detached and the file no longer displays the Digital Signature Contents dialog box when opened.

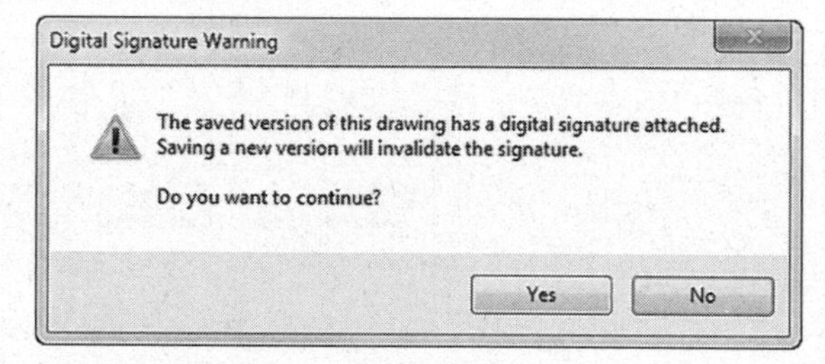

FIGURE 25.6
Checking signature status

If you need to update a drawing that contains your digital signature, you can do so and then use the Security Options dialog box to reissue the digital signature.

ADDING YOUR DIGITAL SIGNATURE TO MULTIPLE FILES

If you have multiple files to which you'd like to attach your digital signature, you should use the Attach Digital Signatures utility. This program runs outside AutoCAD, and it provides a convenient way to attach your digital signature to a set of drawings. Here's how it works:

1. From the Windows Taskbar, choose Start ➤ All Programs ➤ Autodesk ➤ AutoCAD 2018 ➤ Attach Digital Signatures to open the Attach Digital Signatures dialog box (see Figure 25.7).

FIGURE 25.7
Signing multiple files

2. Click the Add Files button to locate and select files. You can also search for files in a particular folder by clicking the Search Folders button. The files you add appear in the Files To Be Signed list box.
3. If you decide to remove a file from the list box, highlight it and then click Remove. You can also remove all the files from the list by clicking Clear List.

A Digital ID Is Required

If you haven't obtained a digital ID, you see a message telling you that no valid digital ID is available on your system. To proceed, you'll have to obtain a digital ID from a certificate authority.

4. You can enter the date and time and a comment for the files that you've selected in the Signature information panel of the dialog box.
5. Click Sign Files when you're sure that you've selected the correct files and entered an appropriate comment.

If you exchange AutoCAD drawings regularly with clients and consultants, you'll want to obtain a digital ID and use the digital signature feature. Be aware, however, that because this feature was new in AutoCAD 2004, it works only if you exchange files with others using AutoCAD 2004 or later. In fact, a quick way to remove a digital signature from a file is to save the file in the AutoCAD 2000 or Release 14 file format.

Using Other Security Options

Digital signatures allow you to detect whether a file has been tampered with, but they don't lock out unauthorized users. Many third-party options are available to help you protect your sensitive files from unauthorized users. For example, you can save your drawing as a PDF and add a password to the PDF. Such a password will prevent others from opening the file, and since it is a PDF, it is not easily edited. Zip files can also be password protected. When placed on a server, make sure that proper network permissions are in place to access drawing files. Finally, you can use password-protected cloud services, such as Autodesk A360, to share files with trusted users.

Digital IDs and PDFs

In today's offices, PDFs are often being used for submittals, which are common documents used during the construction phase of a project. In the past, an architect stamped paper submittals to validate their review. PDF submittals can be "stamped" using digital IDs that are unique to the individual who is reviewing the submittal. If you've obtained a digital ID from a certificate authority and you have the full version of Adobe Acrobat, you can use the Acrobat Advanced Security and stamp features to apply an ID to any PDF document. Acrobat will also generate its own digital ID. Unfortunately, the "self-signed" ID from Acrobat cannot be used with AutoCAD.

Publishing Your Drawings

The features discussed so far are intended mostly for exchanging files with others who need to work directly with your AutoCAD files. However, there are always associates and clients who only need to see your final drawings and don't care whether they get AutoCAD files. Alternatively, you might be working with people who don't have AutoCAD but still need to view and print your drawings. For those non-AutoCAD end users, AutoCAD offers a way to produce a set of drawings in the PDF format.

Exchanging Drawing Sets

Imagine that you're working on a skylight addition to a house and you need to send your drawings to your client for review. In addition to the skylight plans, you want to include some alternate floor plans that your client has asked you to generate. In this exercise, you'll put together a set of drawings that will become a single PDF file that you'll send as an email attachment to your client:

1. Open the `Sample house.dwg` file, which can be found in the Chapter 25 sample files. The file has several layout views, each representing a separate drawing sheet.
2. Click the Save tool in the Quick Access toolbar. If you don't do this, the Publish tool that you'll use later will ask you to do it.
3. Choose Publish from the Application menu to open the Publish dialog box (see Figure 25.8). You can also type **Publish**↵. The dialog box lists all the layouts in its main list box, including the Model layout, which is equivalent to the Model Space tab. (See Chapter 8, "Introducing Printing, Plotting, and Layouts," for more on layouts.)

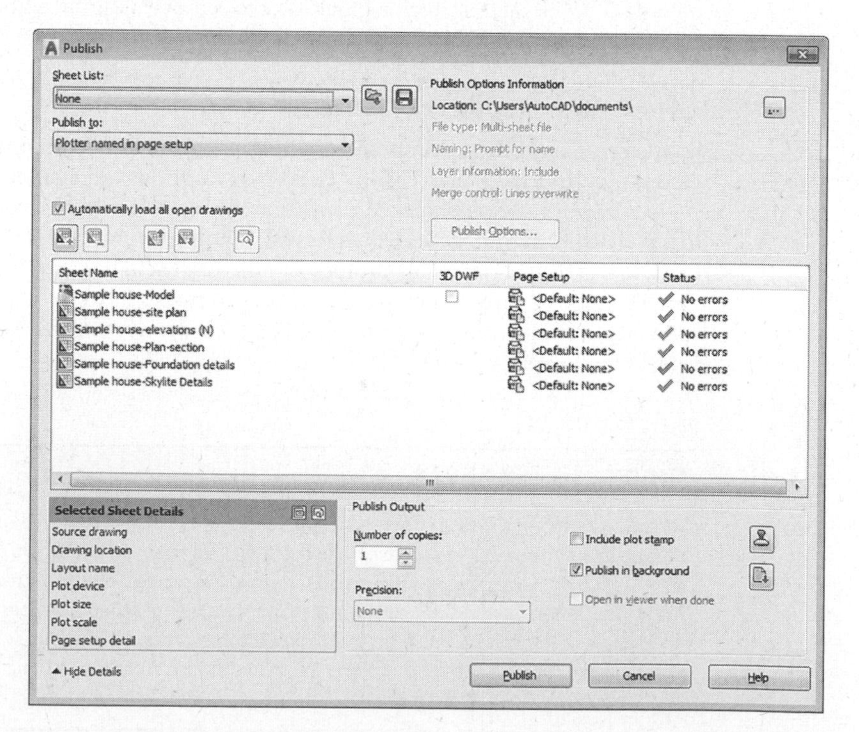

FIGURE 25.8 Choosing the layouts to publish

4. In the list box, Ctrl+click Sample House-Model, Sample House-Foundation Details, and Sample House-Skylite Details to select them. You don't want to include these layouts in your PDF file.

5. Right-click any of the selected files and choose Remove, or click the Remove Sheets button just above the list of sheets. The items that you have selected are removed from the list.

At this point, you could go ahead and create a PDF file. However, suppose that you want to include layouts from a file that isn't currently open? The following steps show you how to accomplish this:

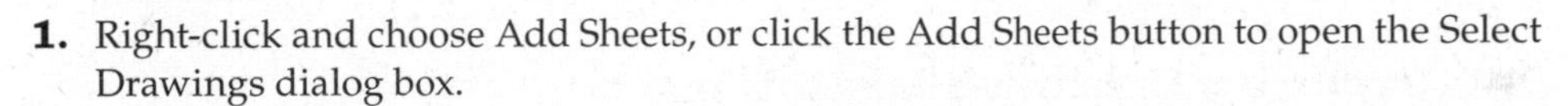

1. Right-click and choose Add Sheets, or click the Add Sheets button to open the Select Drawings dialog box.

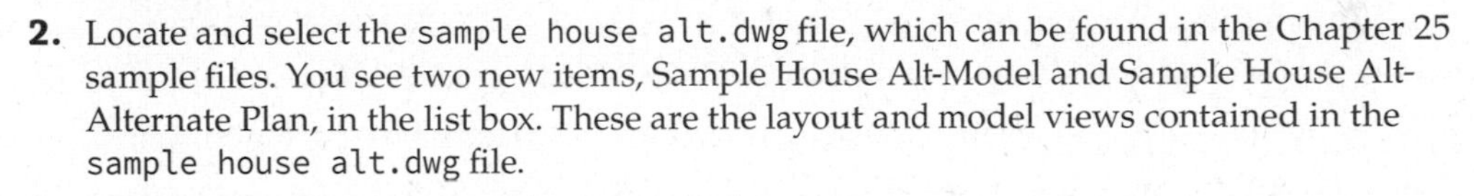

2. Locate and select the `sample house alt.dwg` file, which can be found in the Chapter 25 sample files. You see two new items, Sample House Alt-Model and Sample House Alt-Alternate Plan, in the list box. These are the layout and model views contained in the `sample house alt.dwg` file.

Automatically Excluding Layouts

In step 2 of the previous exercise, the Model tab was imported. You can prevent Model tabs from being included in the sheets list by turning off the Include Model When Adding Sheets option. This option is located in the context menu when you right-click in the Sheets list.

All of the sheets that your client needs appear in the list box. You're ready to create the PDF file:

1. Save the current list in case you want to reproduce it later. Click the Save Sheet List button. The Save List As dialog box, which is a standard file dialog box, appears.
2. Select a location and name for the sheet list and click Save.
3. Back in the Publish dialog box, in the Publish To drop-down list near the top of the dialog box, make sure that the PDF option is selected. Notice that you can also select Plotter Named In Page Setup, DWF, and DWFx.
4. Turn off the Publish In Background option. By turning off this feature, you'll get your results faster.
5. Click the Publish button. The Specify PDF File dialog box appears. This is a standard file dialog box in which you can find a location for your PDF file and also name it. Select a name and location for the PDF file. By default, AutoCAD uses the same name as the current file and the folder location of the current file. You can also set up a default location in the Publish Setup dialog box.
6. When AutoCAD is finished publishing your drawings, you may see a message stating that you do not have a PDF viewing application installed. You can view the PDF file using the free Acrobat Reader from the Adobe website.

7. Go back to AutoCAD, and click the Plot And Publish Details Report icon in the right side of the status bar. The Plot And Publish Details dialog box appears, offering detailed information about the sheets that you published. You can then click the Copy To Clipboard button to export the list to a file as a record. If you want to recall this dialog box later, you can do so by choosing Print ➢ View Plot And Publish Details from the Application menu.

You may notice that when you click the Publish button in the previous exercise, AutoCAD behaves as if it's printing the layouts in your list—and that is exactly what it's doing. AutoCAD uses its own PDF printer driver to "print" your drawings to a PDF file. AutoCAD uses the layout settings from the Plot dialog box for each layout to produce the PDF pages.

Exploring Other Publish Options

A few more options are available when you use the Publish feature. Let's take a moment to review some of the options in the Publish dialog box toolbar:

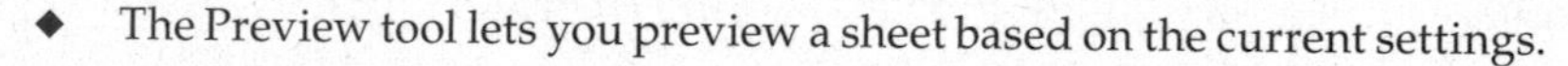

- The Preview tool lets you preview a sheet based on the current settings.

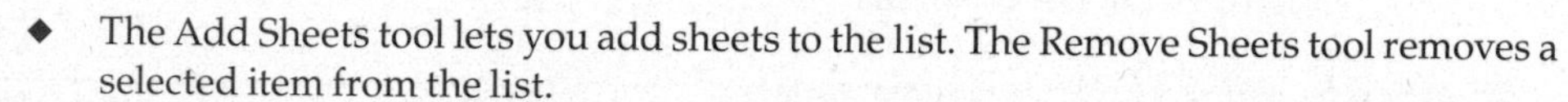

- The Add Sheets tool lets you add sheets to the list. The Remove Sheets tool removes a selected item from the list.

- The Move Sheet Up and Move Sheet Down tools let you move an item in the list up and down. These are important options because the order of drawings in the list determines the order in which the drawings will appear in the Acrobat Reader. The item at the top of the list appears first; the next one on the list is second, and so on.

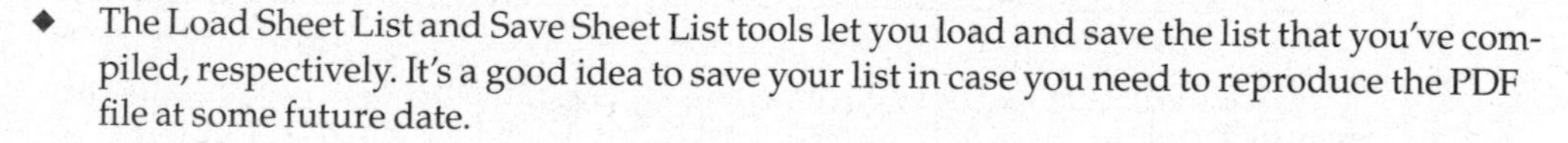

- The Load Sheet List and Save Sheet List tools let you load and save the list that you've compiled, respectively. It's a good idea to save your list in case you need to reproduce the PDF file at some future date.

- You can use the Plot Stamp Settings tool to specify the data you want to include in the plot stamp. This tool opens the Plot Stamp dialog box. (See Bonus Chapter 3, "Hardware and Software Tips," available at `www.omura.com/chapters`, for more on the Plot Stamp dialog box.)

Context Menu Options

If you right-click an item or a set of items in the Publish dialog box list box, you see a menu with the standard options mentioned earlier plus some additional options. You'll want to know about a few of these options.

Viewing and Annotating DWG, PDF, and DWF Files

If you prefer, you can publish your drawings using the Autodesk DWF file format. Autodesk offers the free Design Review program, which provides a fast and simple way to view and annotate PDF and DWF files. In addition to viewing files, the Autodesk® Design Review program enables users to annotate and mark up drawings, take measurements, and track changes. When used in conjunction with Autodesk's free DWG TrueView program, Design Review also lets you perform these functions on DWG files. You can download a copy of Autodesk Design Review and TrueView from the Autodesk website. The last version of Design Review is 2013.

By default, AutoCAD applies the existing layout settings for each layout when it produces the PDF file. These are the settings found in the Plot Or Page Setup dialog box and include the sheet size, scale, and page orientation. The Change Page Setup option lets you use a different set of layout settings for a selected layout in the list. To use this option, you must have saved a page setup in the file's Page Setup or Plot dialog box. (See Chapter 8 for more on the Page Setup dialog box and its options.) You can import a page setup from a different AutoCAD file, or you can assign a page setup to a sheet. Do this by clicking the sheet name and selecting a page setup from the list box that appears in the Page Setup column.

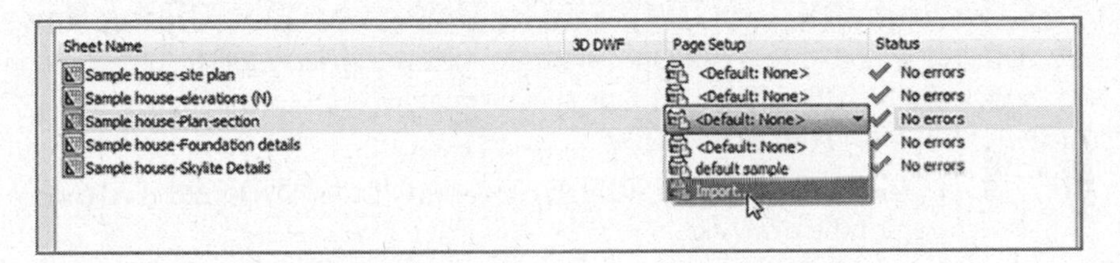

To change the page setup for multiple sheets, select all of the sheets from the list first and then select the page setup from the list box of the first file in the list.

If you happen to have two layouts with the same name, right-click a layout name, and then select the Rename Sheet option on the context menu to rename a layout. The Copy Selected Sheets option adds copies of selected layouts to the list. The copies have the word *copy* appended to their names. The last two items in the context menu let you control what is displayed in the list box. Include Layouts When Adding Sheets controls whether layouts are automatically imported from a drawing into the list box. Include Model When Adding Sheets controls whether Model Space views are automatically imported from a drawing into the list box.

The Publish Options Dialog Box

You can set up additional options by clicking the Publish Options button in the Publish dialog box. You'll then see the PDF Publish Options dialog box (see Figure 25.9).

FIGURE 25.9
PDF Publish Options dialog box

This dialog box offers options for the location and type of output. If you select DWF in the Publish To drop-down list, you'll see a different set of options.

The Location option lets you select the location for PDF files. The Prompt For Name option will ask you for a PDF filename before it begins to publish your drawing. The Multi-Sheet File option will produce a single PDF file containing all of the sheets of your published drawing set. Other options let you set the drawing quality and specify whether or not you include layer information, hyperlinks, or bookmarks.

Creating a PDF or DWF File by Using the Plot Dialog Box

Another way to create PDF and DWF files is through the Plot dialog box. If you need to create a PDF or DWF file of only a single sheet, you may want to use the Plot dialog box because it's a simple and familiar procedure.

1. Open the file that you want to convert to PDF or DWF, and then proceed as if you're going to plot the drawing.
2. In the Plot dialog box, select DWFx ePlot (XPS Compatible) .pc3 or DWF6 ePlot.pc3 from the Name drop-down list in the Printer/Plotter area. The DWFx ePlot (XPS Compatible) .pc3 option creates a file that is readable in Windows 10, Windows 8, or Windows 7 without the need for any special viewing program. Although you may see an incorrect paper size message, you can continue.
3. For PDF output, select the DWG To PDF.pc3 option from the Name drop-down list in the Printer/Plotter area. Or, if you have Adobe Acrobat Pro installed, you can select the Adobe PDF option.
4. Proceed with the plot the normal way. When AutoCAD would normally send the drawing to the printer, you'll see a dialog box asking you to enter a name for your plot file and finish with the rest of the plot. You can control the PDF or DWF plot as you would any plot.

You can save your plotter settings in the Page Setup panel at the top of the Plot dialog box by clicking the Add button. You are asked for a name for your page setup. Later, you can use the page setup in the Publish dialog box by selecting it from the Page Setup column (see "Context Menu Options" earlier in this chapter). Page setups are saved with the DWG file, and you can import them from any drawing file in the Publishing dialog box using the Import option in the Page setup column's drop-down list.

In addition to using the settings available in the Plot dialog box, you can make some special configuration adjustments to the PDF or DWF plotter configuration file. Here is where to find those configuration settings:

1. Select a layout tab to make it current, and then right-click the tab and select Page Setup Manager to open the Page Setup Manager dialog box. Select a setup from the Page Setups list, and then click Modify to open the Page Setup dialog box.
2. Make sure that the PDF or DWF configuration file is listed in the Name list box of the Printer/Plotter group. Although you may see an incorrect paper size message, you can continue.
3. Click the Properties button to the right of the Name drop-down list to open the Plotter Configuration Editor dialog box.

4. Make sure that the Device And Document Settings tab is selected, and then click Custom Properties in the list box (see Figure 25.10).

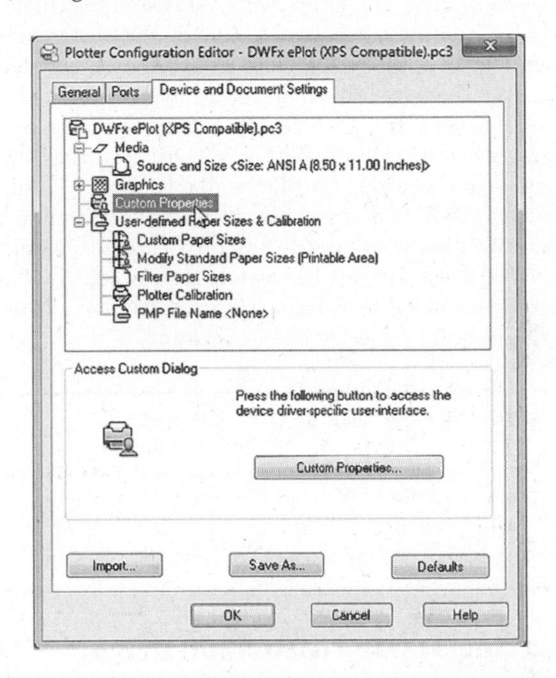

FIGURE 25.10
Controlling the plotter configuration file

5. Click the Custom Properties button that appears in the lower half of the dialog box to open the PC3 Properties dialog box. Here you can make a variety of setting changes to fine-tune your output.

6. Click OK after selecting your settings. The Plotter Configuration Editor dialog box reappears. After you've set the custom properties, you can save any new settings in the PC3 file, or you can create a new PC3 plot-configuration file. To save any setting changes, click the Save As button and select the PC3 file in which you want to save the settings. For more information about PC3 plot configuration files, see "Fine-Tuning the Appearance of Output" in Bonus Chapter 3.

7. Click OK in the Plotter Configuration Editor dialog box to return to the Page Setup dialog box.

8. Click OK to exit the Page Setup dialog box, and then close the Page Setup Manager.

After you select your custom configuration settings in step 5, you needn't open the Plotter Configuration Editor dialog box again the next time you plot a PDF or DWF file. If you save your new settings as a new PC3 file, you can select it from the File drop-down list in the Plotter Configuration group. You don't have to reenter the custom settings.

If you plot a drawing using the DWFx ePlot plotter, you can use the Microsoft XPS viewer to view the plotted DWFx file. To start the XPS viewer in Windows 7, click the Start button and type **xpsrchvw.exe**↵. In Windows 8 and 10, press and hold the Start button and select Run from the menu. Enter **xpsrchvw**↵ in the text box.

Sharing Files with A360 Drive

Whether you share native AutoCAD DWG files or share files using the DWF or PDF formats, you have a number of ways to convey the files to those who need them. Downloading from websites, transferring via FTP, and exchanging through email are all common methods for sharing files, but they are limited and can leave a user wanting more flexibility.

Autodesk offers the free A360 Drive service, where you can share files in a much more open and organized fashion. With A360 Drive, you can make files available to others in a way similar to how you would make files available on an FTP site or a website, with the addition of more easily controlled access. You can track the shared history of a document or set of documents and organize files to suit nearly any project requirement.

A360 Drive also enables you to have access to your files from anywhere you have an Internet connection. You can upload a file to A360 Drive from your office and open it while on the road by logging into your Autodesk account.

UPGRADE TO THE LATEST BROWSER

The A360 Drive website works best when viewed using Internet Explorer 11, Apple Safari v5.1, Mozilla Firefox v19, Google Chrome v33, or later versions. If you are not using one of these versions of your browser, you may want to upgrade before proceeding with the exercises. Some features may not work or appear properly under earlier versions.

Getting Started with A360 Drive

To appreciate what A360 Drive can do for you, you'll want to try out some of its features. The entry point to the cloud service is the A360 Drive Sign In option in the InfoCenter. Try the following to get started:

1. If you are not signed in already, sign into your Autodesk account by selecting the Sign In To Autodesk Account option in the InfoCenter drop-down menu (see Figure 25.11).

FIGURE 25.11
The Sign In To Autodesk Account menu option

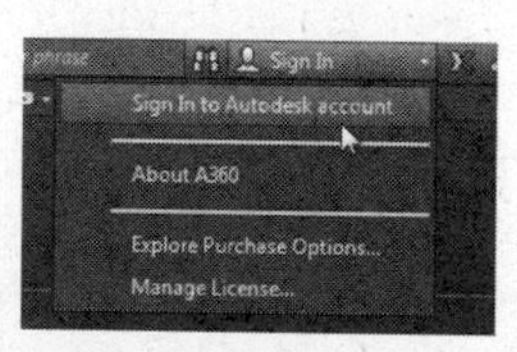

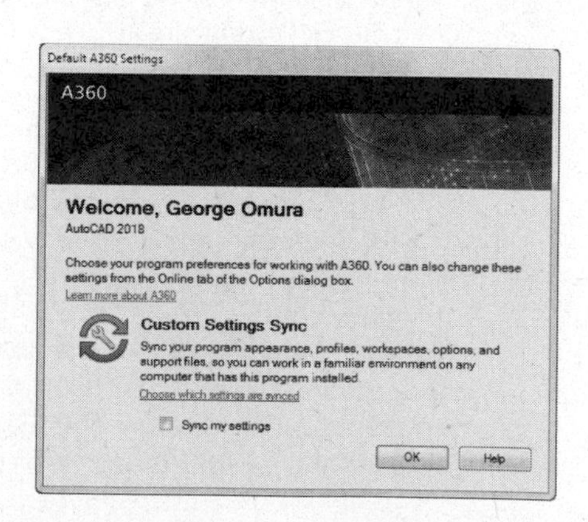

Once you are signed in, the InfoCenter Sign In drop-down list offers a new set of options (Figure 25.12).

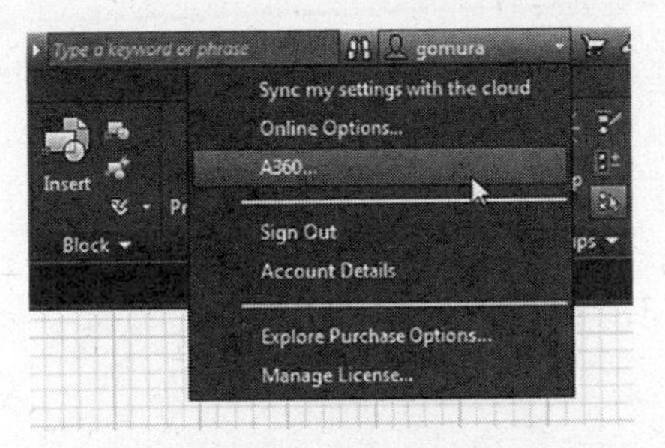

FIGURE 25.12
The InfoCenter Sign In drop-down list with new options

2. Open a file and then click the Sign In drop-down list and select A360. Your default browser opens, and the A360 Drive site appears (see Figure 25.13).

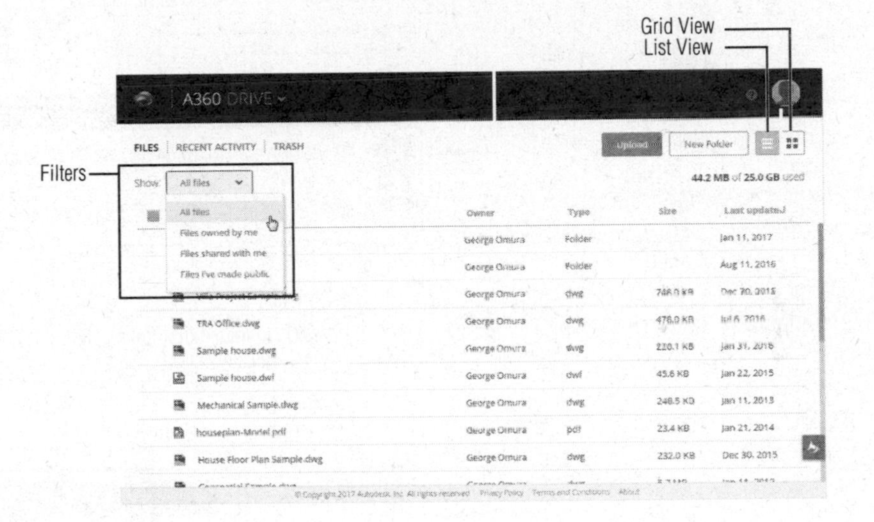

FIGURE 25.13
The A360 Drive page showing several documents

You can switch between a thumbnail grid view and a list view by using the icons in the upper-right corner of the page just left of the New Folder option (see Figure 25.13). You can filter the display of files using the drop-down menu to the left of the window. Upload files to A360 Drive using the Upload button, and create new folders using the New Folder button.

If you hover over a file, you will see a set of icons to the right of the name (see Figure 25.14). These icons let you perform actions such as share or download a file. The arrow icon to the far right opens a menu that offers additional file related tasks (see Figure 25.15). To the left of the file name, a check box appears enabling you to select multiple files for file operations.

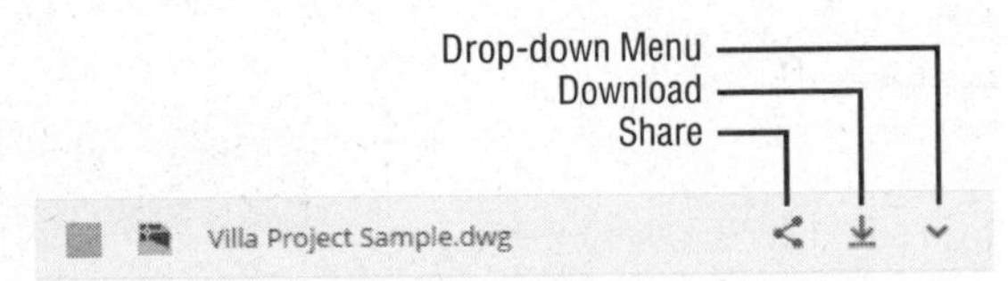

FIGURE 25.14
Hover over a file name to show additional options

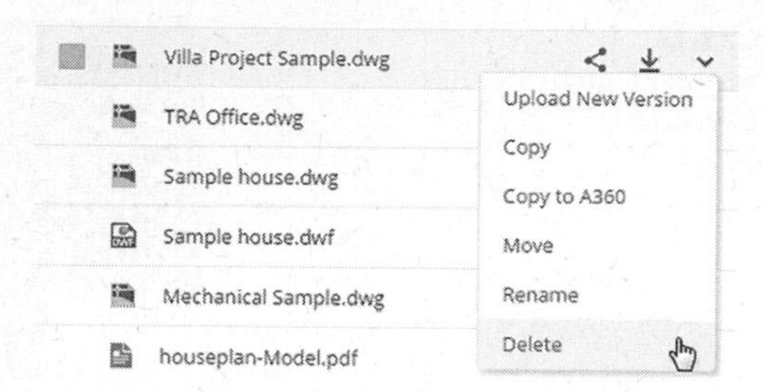

FIGURE 25.15 Options in the drop-down menu when hovering over a file name

Viewing Files and Adding Comments

To view a file, just click the file name, or if you are in the grid view, click the Overview button on the file icon. The file opens with a set of tools that allows you to view and make comments about your file (see Figure 25.16).

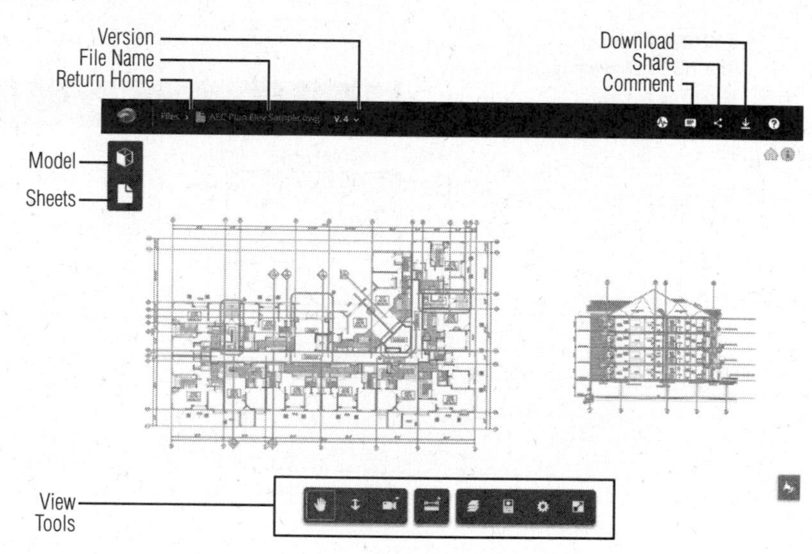

FIGURE 25.16 Viewing a file in A360 Drive

In the upper-right, you see options that allow you to add comments to the file as well as share or download the file. Toward the top left, the Files option takes you back to the list or grid view, while the "V" option opens to allow you to select a different version of the file.

Just below the A360 icon are the Model and Sheets icons. These are the equivalent of the Model and Layout tabs in AutoCAD. At the very bottom, you see the view tools, which include the Measure, Properties, and Settings tools (see Figure 25.17).

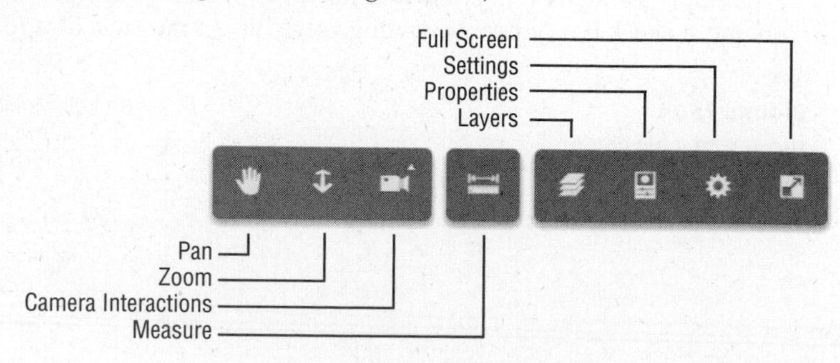

FIGURE 25.17 The View, Measure, Properties, and Settings tools

Sharing Files

As you've already seen, A360 Drive allows you to share files. You can share files publicly or restrict your sharing to a select few recipients. When you click the Share icon, then the word *Share* that appears in the tool tip, you will see a pop-up with two options: Get Link and Invite People (see Figure 25.18). The Get Link option displays a switch that lets you turn on the shared link feature. Click the Invite People option and the pop-up changes to show an input box that allows you to enter email addresses of people with whom you'd like to share your file.

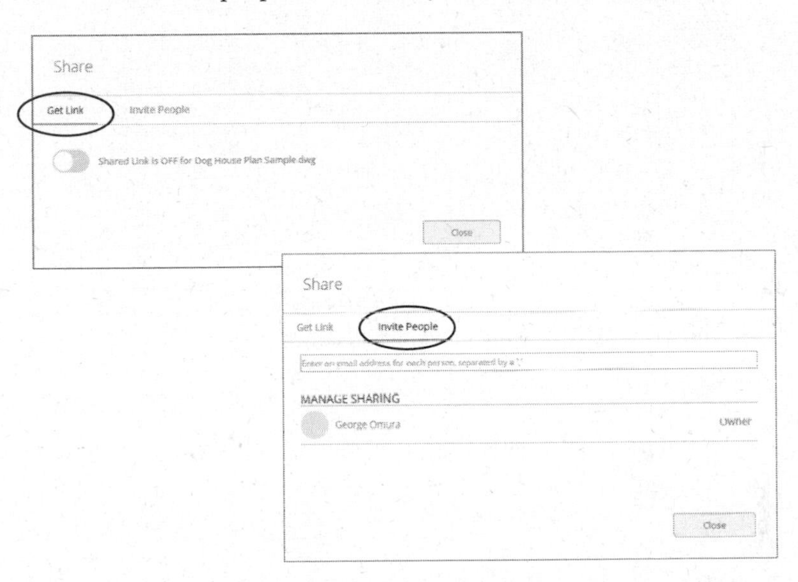

FIGURE 25.18
The Share pop-up options

Share
Get Link
Invite People
Shared Link is OFF for Dog House Plan Sample.dwg
Close
Share
Get Link
Invite People
MANAGE SHARING
George Omura
Owner
Close

If you click the Share Link switch in the Get Link view of the Share pop-up, a new set of options appears enabling you to copy a link to your file and to allow viewers to download the file (see Figure 25.19). You can copy and share the link with anyone through email or through a web post.

FIGURE 25.19
The Share Get Link options

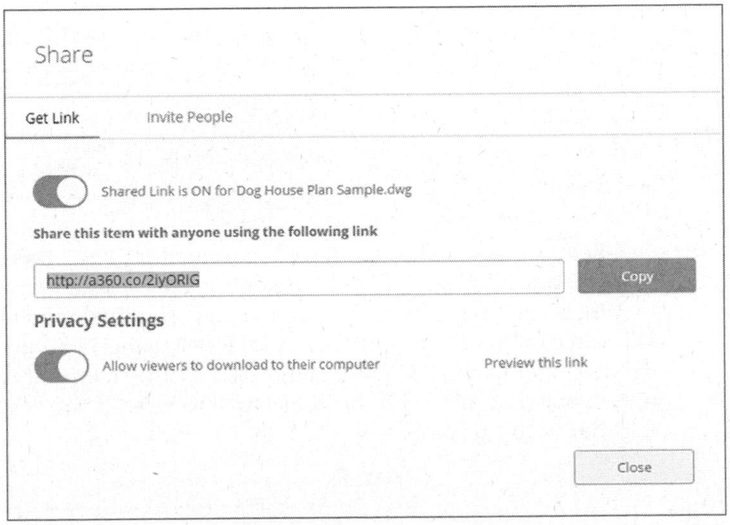

Share
Get Link
Invite People
Shared Link is ON for Dog House Plan Sample.dwg
Share this item with anyone using the following link
http://a360.co/2iyORIG
Copy
Privacy Settings
Allow viewers to download to their computer
Preview this link
Close

If you are in the Invite People view, you can click in the "Enter an email address for each person" text box to display some additional options (see Figure 25.20). As stated in the text box, you can enter an email address for each person you wish to invite to view the file. An email will be sent to those addresses with a link to the file view. You can also control the permission level for the share and enter a message for the emailed link.

FIGURE 25.20
The Share Invite People options

Share
Get Link
Invite People
Enter an email address for each person, separated by a ','
Permission: View
Cancel
Invite
MANAGE SHARING
George Omura
Owner
Close

Opening and Saving Files Directly to A360 Drive

If you want to have access to your files while traveling, you can use the AutoCAD file dialog box to save files to or open files from the A360 Drive. Typically, when you save a file for the first time or when you use the Save As tool, you are presented with a file dialog box. At the top of the left column, you will see the A360 icon.

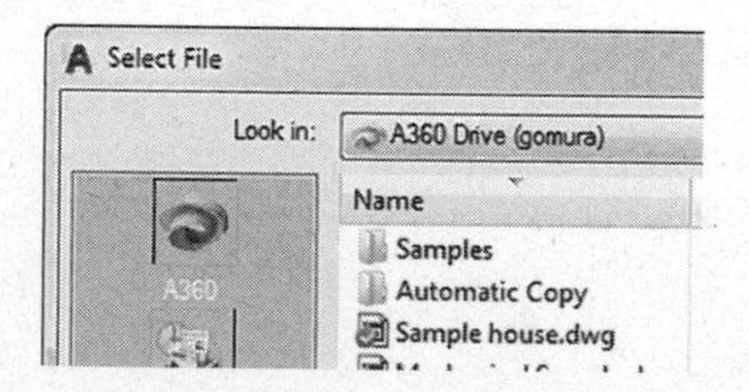

Click this icon and you will see the contents of A360 Drive. You can then save your drawing there. In addition, you can use the same icon to open files from A360 Drive.

When you save a file to A360 Drive, you are actually saving the file locally in a folder on your PC. You can browse to your local A360 Drive using Windows Explorer. It's located in the list of drives under Computer. Once you've saved a file to this location, the A360 Desktop app synchronizes your local files with the A360 Drive website. If you've ever used Dropbox, you're probably familiar with this process.

INSERTED DRAWINGS NOT TO SCALE?

If you're sharing files that have the potential for being inserted as blocks or Xrefs, you'll want to know about a little setting that can have a big effect on your work. The Insertion Scale setting in the Units dialog box controls how DWG files are scaled when they are inserted into a drawing. To get to the Insertion Scale setting, open the Application menu and select Drawing Utilities ➢ Units or type **Units**↵. The Insertion Scale drop-down list is in the middle of the dialog box, as shown here:

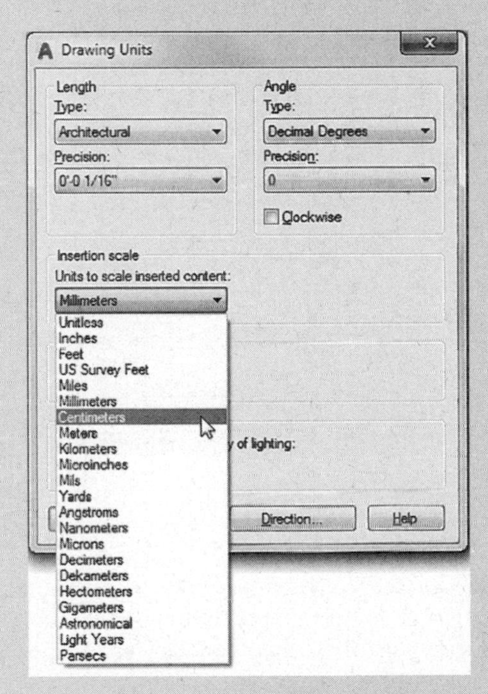

Suppose that your drawing is in centimeters and you anticipate that someone will be inserting your drawing into another one that is using millimeters. You would set Insertion Scale in your drawing to Centimeters. When the person receiving your drawing inserts it in their millimeter drawing, your drawing will be automatically scaled to the appropriate size. Likewise, if you receive a drawing that does not scale properly when inserted in your drawing, check the Insertion Scale value of both your drawing and the inserted drawing and adjust the settings so that the inserted drawing appears at the appropriate scale. Drawings that use the Architectural unit type should always be set to Inches, but drawings set to the Decimal unit type can have any Insertion Scale setting.

Collaborating with Others Using Design Feed

Besides sharing and editing files, you can add comments and images to files shared on A360 Drive through the Design Feed feature. Design Feed gives you a way to communicate ideas through your drawings by letting you post messages and images directly onto your AutoCAD files. You can open Design Feed by typing **designfeedopen** at the command prompt. The Design Feed panel opens (see Figure 25.21).

FIGURE 25.21
Design Feed panel

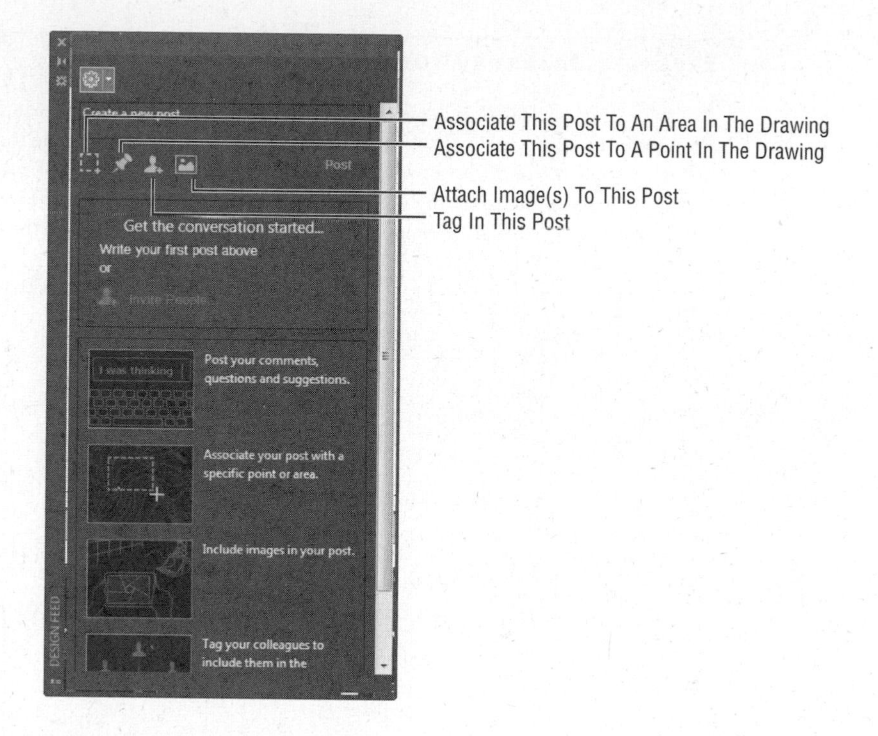

If the drawing has not been saved to the A360 Drive site, you will see a message at the top of the Design Feed panel asking you to save to A360 Drive. When this is done, you can start to add comments to the drawing that others can view and respond to. The comments will appear in the middle portion of the panel.

There are four tools just below the Create A New Post box:

- Associate This Post To An Area In The Drawing
- Associate This Post To A Point In The Drawing
- Tag In This Post
- Attach Image(s) To This Post

To use the area or point tool, click the tool icon and then click in the drawing to indicate the post's location (see Figure 25.22). Next, enter a message in the Create A New Post box. Click the Create Post button when you're done. With the Tag tool, you can alert the recipient to your post via an email. The Attach Image tool will open a file dialog box where you can locate an image file to include with your post.

When recipients of your post view the drawing in A360 Drive, they will see a post as a numbered icon. They can click the icon, and the post associated with it will be highlighted in the Design Feed panel. They can then add their comments and replies to the post. Close the Design Feed panel by clicking the X in the top corner or by typing **DESIGNFEEDCLOSE**.

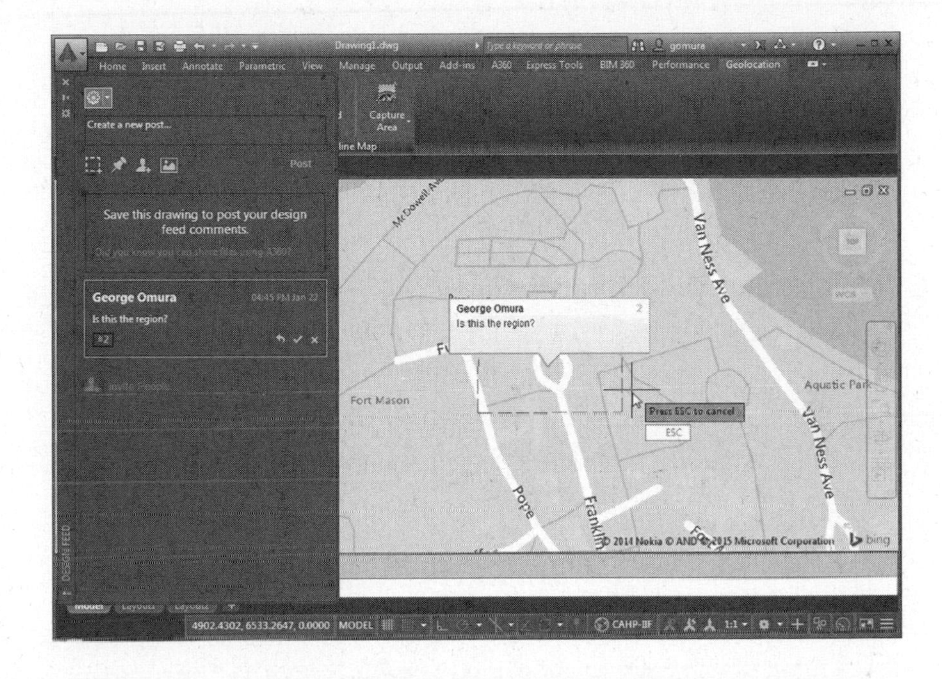

FIGURE 25.22
A drawing with a post attached to an area

WHAT IS A360?

You may have noticed references to A360 while examining the A360 Drive website. A360 is another collaboration feature that you can use with A360 Drive to share your drawings and exchange ideas with other members of a design team. While it may share many features with A360 Drive, it offers a much richer environment for sharing of design ideas. To learn more about A360, click the A360 Drive drop-down menu in the upper left of the A360 Drive page and select A360.

This will take you to the A360 website. Click the Help icon in the upper right to view the tutorial videos that will help you get started with A360.

Adding Hyperlinks to Drawings

AutoCAD offers the Hyperlink tool, which enables you to link any document to an AutoCAD object. Then, with a few clicks of your mouse, you can follow the links to view other drawings, text files, spreadsheets, or web pages. Hyperlinks persist even after you've exported your drawing to a PDF file. You can then post that PDF file on a web page where others can gain access to those links.

Creating Hyperlinks

The following steps show you how to add links to a sample floor plan:

1. In AutoCAD, open the file `houseplan.dwg`.

2. In the Insert tab's Data panel, click the Hyperlink tool.
3. At the `Select objects:` prompt, click the hexagonal door symbol, as shown in Figure 25.23.

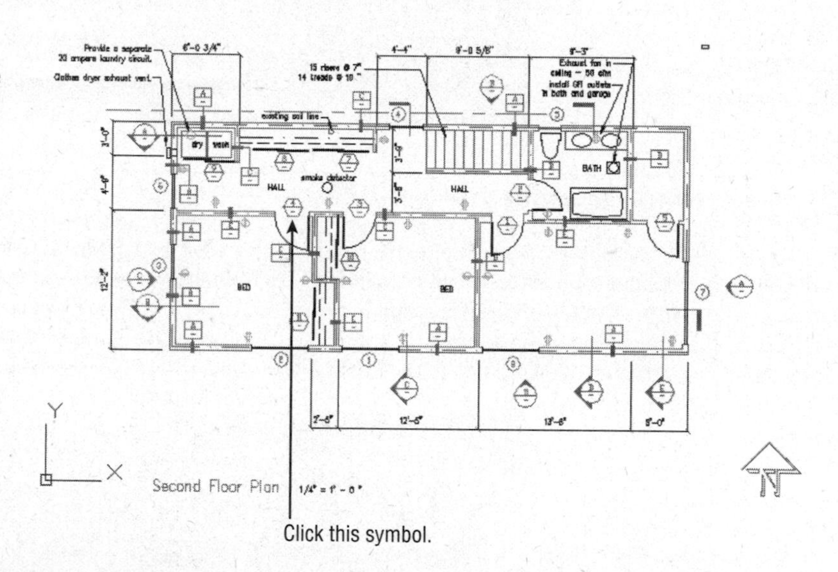

FIGURE 25.23
The door symbol in the `houseplan.dwg` file

4. When you're done, press ↵. The Insert Hyperlink dialog box opens (see Figure 25.24).
5. Click the File button on the right side of the dialog box to open the Browse The Web – Select Hyperlink dialog box. It's a typical file dialog box.
6. Locate the `doorsch.pdf` file and select it.
7. Click Open. The Insert Hyperlink dialog box reappears. Notice that `doorsch.pdf` appears in the list box at the top of the dialog box in the Type The File Or Web Page Name box.
8. Make sure that the Use Relative Path For Hyperlink option isn't selected, and then click OK.

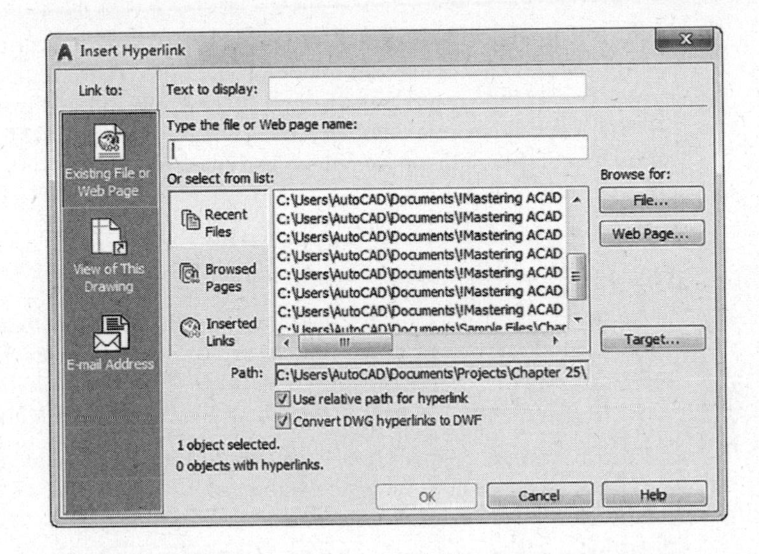

FIGURE 25.24 The Insert Hyperlink dialog box

The link you just created is stored with the drawing file. You can create a PDF file from this drawing, and the link will be preserved in the PDF file.

Now let's see how you can use the link from within the AutoCAD file:

1. Move your cursor over the hexagonal door symbol. Notice that the cursor changes to the hyperlink icon when it's placed on the symbol. It also shows the name of the file to which the object is linked. This tells you that the object is linked to another document somewhere on your system, on your network, or on the Internet (see Figure 25.25).

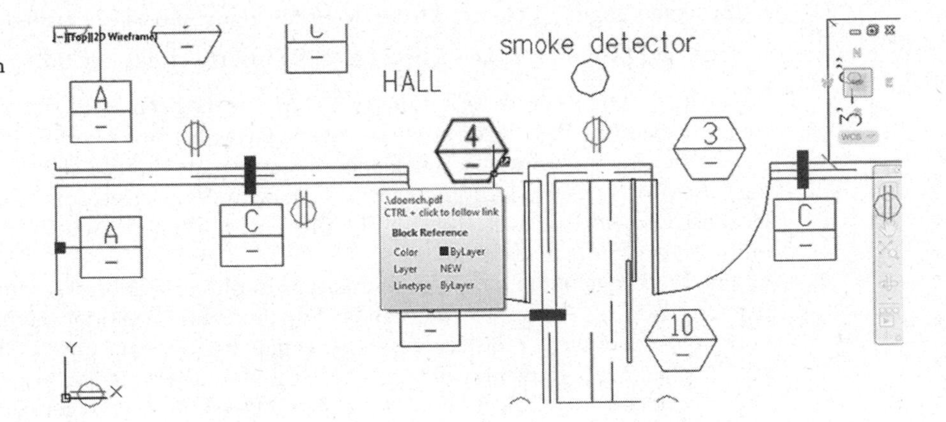

FIGURE 25.25 The hyperlink icon and tool tip

2. Click the hexagonal door symbol to select it.
3. Right-click in a blank area of the drawing. In the context menu, choose Hyperlink ➢ Open ".\doorsch.pdf" to choose the link to the `doorsch.dwf` file. You can also Ctrl+click the door symbol.

Your PDF viewer program opens and displays the file `doorsch.pdf`. If you installed the sample figures on another drive or folder location, the Hyperlink option will reflect that location.

You've used the `doorsch.pdf` file as an example in these exercises, but this could have been a text file, a spreadsheet, a database, or even another AutoCAD file. AutoCAD will start the application associated with the linked file and open the file.

Editing and Deleting Hyperlinks

You can edit or delete a hyperlink by doing the following:

1. Select and right-click the object whose link you want to edit, and then choose Hyperlink ➤ Edit Hyperlink from the context menu. Doing so opens the Edit Hyperlink dialog box, which offers the same options as the Insert Hyperlink dialog box (see Figure 25.24, earlier in this chapter), with the addition of the Remove Link button.
2. You can now either change the link or click the Remove Link button in the lower-left corner of the dialog box to delete the link.

Taking a Closer Look at the Hyperlink Options

You were introduced to the Insert Hyperlink dialog box, shown in Figure 25.24, in the previous exercises. Let's take a moment to study this dialog box in a little more detail.

To specify a file or a website to link to, you can enter either a filename or a website URL in the Type The File Or Web Page Name box or use the Or Select From List area, which offers a list box and three button options. When you select one of the buttons, the list box changes to offer additional related options:

Recent Files Displays a list of recently edited AutoCAD files, as illustrated in Figure 25.24. You can then link the object to a file in the list by clicking the filename.

Browsed Pages Displays a list of websites that you recently visited using your web browser.

Inserted Links Displays a list of recently inserted links, including files or websites.

You can also use the three buttons to the right of the list box to locate specific files (the File button), websites (the Web Page button), or saved views (the Target button) in the current drawing.

As you saw in the exercise, the File button opens the Browse The Web – Select Hyperlink dialog box, which lets you locate and select a file from A360 Drive, from your computer, from your local area network, or even from an FTP site. This is a typical AutoCAD open file dialog box with some additional features.

The Web Page button on the right opens a simplified web browser that lets you locate a web page for linking. You can use the standard methods for accessing web pages, such as using the Look In drop-down list to select recently visited pages or entering a URL in the Name Or URL box. The page is then displayed in the main window of the dialog box.

If the selected hyperlink file is an AutoCAD DWG file, the Target button in the Insert Hyperlink dialog box opens the Select Place In Document dialog box, which lists the saved views in the drawing.

Views are subdivided by layout tabs. At the top is the Model Space tab listing, and below that are other layout tab listings. If the current drawing contains saved views, you see a plus sign next to the layout tab name. Click the plus sign to display a listing of the views in that layout.

At the top of the Insert Hyperlink and Edit Hyperlink dialog boxes is a box labeled Text To Display. When a hyperlink is added to an object in AutoCAD, AutoCAD will display a hyperlink icon whenever the cursor passes over the object. You can also include descriptive text that will display along with the icon by entering the description in the Text To Display box.

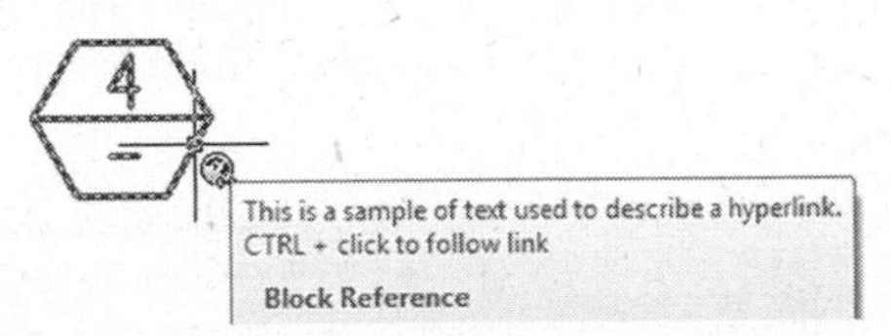

By default, the text is the name of the hyperlinked item that you select. You can change the text to provide a better description of the link.

The Insert Hyperlink dialog box contains a column of options at the far left labeled Link To. The top button, Existing File Or Web Page, displays the options discussed so far in this section. The other two buttons change the appearance of the Insert Hyperlink dialog box to offer different but familiar options:

View Of This Drawing This button changes the display to show just the views that are available in the current drawing. This option performs the same function as the Target button described earlier.

E-Mail Address This button changes the Insert Hyperlink dialog box to enable you to link an email address to an object. Clicking the object will then open your default email application, letting you send a message to the address.

Managing Your Drawings with DesignCenter and the Tool Palettes

As you start to build a library of drawings, you'll find that you reuse many components of existing drawing files. Most of the time, you'll probably be producing similar types of drawings with some variation, so you'll reuse drawing components such as layer settings, dimension styles, and layouts. It can be a major task to keep track of all the projects on which you've worked. It's especially frustrating when you remember setting up a past drawing in a way that you know would be useful in a current project but you can't remember that file's name or location.

AutoCAD offers DesignCenter™ to help you keep track of the documents that you use in your projects. You can think of DesignCenter as a kind of super Windows File Explorer that is focused on AutoCAD files. DesignCenter lets you keep track of your favorite files and helps you locate files, blocks, and other drawing components. In addition, you can import blocks and other drawing components from one drawing to another by using a simple click and drag. If you've been diligent about setting a unit format for each of your drawings, you can use DesignCenter to import symbols and drawings of different unit formats into a drawing and the symbols will maintain their proper size. For example, a 90 cm door symbol from a metric drawing can be imported into a drawing in Imperial units and DesignCenter will translate the 90 cm metric door size to a 35.43″ door.

Getting Familiar with DesignCenter

At first glance, DesignCenter looks a bit mysterious. But it takes only a few mouse clicks to reveal a tool that looks much like Windows File Explorer. Try the following steps to become familiar with DesignCenter:

1. Open AutoCAD to a new file, and then click the DesignCenter tool in the View tab's Palettes panel. Design Center opens as a floating palette (see Figure 25.26).

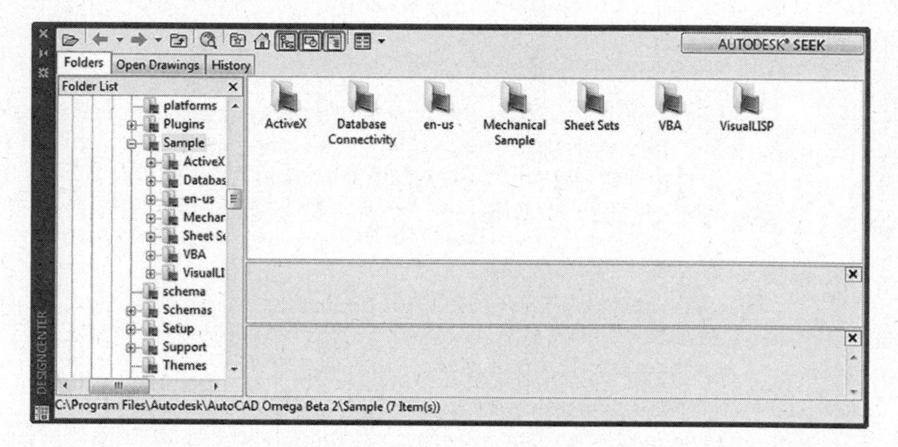

FIGURE 25.26 DesignCenter opens as a floating palette.

OPENING THE TREE VIEW

If your DesignCenter view doesn't look like Figure 25.26, with the DesignCenter window divided into two parts, click the Tree View Toggle tool on the DesignCenter toolbar. The Tree view opens on the left side of the DesignCenter window. Click the Home tool to display the contents of the `C:\Program Files\Autodesk\AutoCAD 2018\Sample\DesignCenter` folder.

2. Click the Favorites tool on the DesignCenter toolbar.
3. DesignCenter displays a listing of the `Favorites` folder. You're actually looking at a view of the `C:\Users\`*`User Name`*`\Favorites\Autodesk` folder, where *`User Name`* is your login name. Unless you've already added items to the `\Favorites\Autodesk` folder, you see a blank view in the right panel. You can add shortcuts to this folder as you work with DesignCenter. You may also see a view showing the tree structure of the files that you have open in AutoCAD.
4. Place your cursor in the lower-right corner of the DesignCenter window so that a double-headed diagonal arrow shows. Then click and drag the corner out so that you have an enlarged DesignCenter window that looks similar to Figure 25.27. The view on the right, containing the `Favorites` folder, is called the Palette view. The view on the left is called the Tree view.

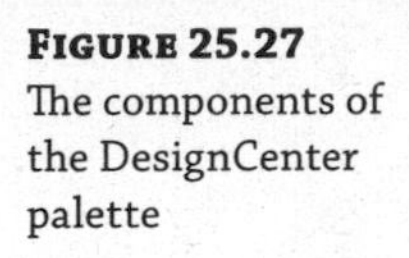

FIGURE 25.27
The components of the DesignCenter palette

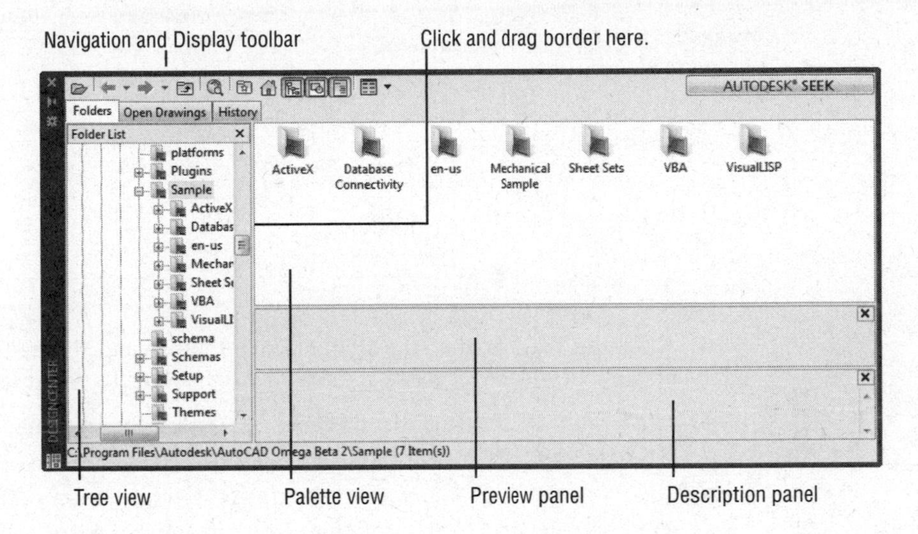

5. Place your cursor on the border between the Tree view and the Palette view until you see a double-headed cursor. Then click and drag the border to the right to enlarge the Tree view until it covers about one-third of the window.

6. Use the scroll bar at the bottom to adjust your view of the Tree view so that you can easily read its contents.

AUTO-HIDE DESIGNCENTER

Like the tool palettes and the Properties palette, DesignCenter has an Auto-Hide feature. To use it, click the double-headed arrow icon near the top of the DesignCenter title bar, under the Close DesignCenter icon. DesignCenter will disappear except for the title bar. You can quickly open DesignCenter by placing the cursor on the title bar.

After you have it set up like this, you can see the similarities between DesignCenter and Windows File Explorer. You can navigate your computer or network by using the Tree view, just as you would in Windows File Explorer. There are a few differences, however, as you'll see in the following exercise:

1. Click the Home tool on the DesignCenter toolbar. The Palette view changes to display the contents of the `Sample` folder under the `Program Files\Autodesk\AutoCAD 2018\` folder.

2. Double-click en-us, under Sample, to open the `en-us` folder, and then double-click the `DesignCenter` folder.

   Instead of the usual list of files, you see a sample image of each file. These are called *preview icons* (see Figure 25.28).

FIGURE 25.28
The DesignCenter display

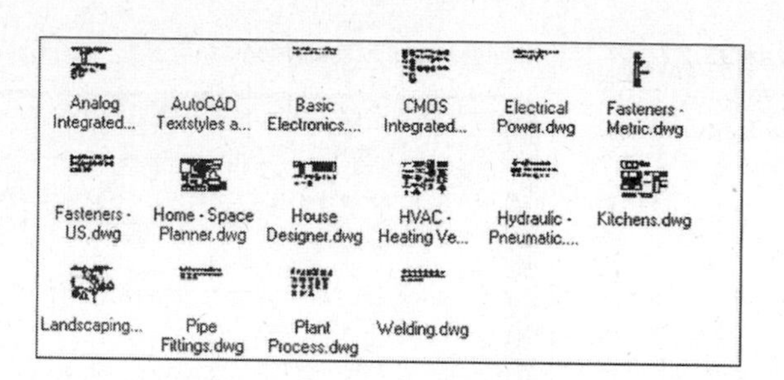

3. Click the Views tool on the DesignCenter toolbar, and choose Details from the menu. The Palette view changes to show a detailed list of the files in the `DesignCenter` folder.
4. Click the Views tool again, and choose Large Icons to return to the previous view. The Views tool is similar to the various View options in Windows File Explorer.
5. Click the `Basic Electronics.dwg` file to select it. You see a preview of the selected file in the Preview panel of DesignCenter. You can adjust the vertical size of the Preview panel by clicking and dragging its top or bottom border.

You can also open and close the Preview panel by clicking the Preview tool in the DesignCenter toolbar. The preview can be helpful if you prefer viewing files and drawing components as a list in the main part of the Palette view.

Below the Preview panel is the Description panel. This panel displays any text information included with the drawing or drawing element selected in the Palette view. To add a description to a drawing that will be visible here, choose Drawing Utilities ➢ Drawing Properties from the Application menu; to add a description to a block, use the Summary tab in the Block Definition dialog box.

You can open and close this panel by clicking the Description tool on the DesignCenter toolbar. Because the `Basic Electronics.dwg` file doesn't have a description attached, the Description panel shows the message `Last saved by: Autodesk`.

Both the Preview and Description panels can offer help in identifying files for which you may be looking. After you find a file, you can click and drag it into a folder in the Tree view to organize your files into separate folders.

You can also add files to the `Favorites` folder by right-clicking and then choosing Add To Favorites. The file itself isn't moved to the `Favorites` folder; instead, a shortcut to the file is created in the `Favorites` folder. If you want to work on organizing your `Favorites` folder, you can open a window to the `Favorites` folder by right-clicking a file in the Palette view and choosing Organize Favorites. A window to the `Favorites` folder appears.

Because you'll be working with the sample drawings, go ahead and add your `Samples` folder to the `Favorites` folder:

1. In the left panel Tree view, locate the `Samples` folder you created when you installed the sample files, and right-click it.
2. Choose Add To Favorites from the context menu.

3. To go directly to the `Favorites` folder, click the Favorites tool on the DesignCenter toolbar. Your `Samples` folder appears in the right panel in the Palette view.
4. Double-click the shortcut in the Palette view. You see the contents of your `Samples` folder.

You can go beyond just looking at file listings. You can also look inside files to view their components:

1. In the Palette view, locate the file named `15-unit.dwg` in the `Chapter 15` folder and double-click it. You see a listing of its components in the Palette view. The Tree view also shows the file highlighted.
2. Double-click the Blocks listing in the Palette view. Now you see a listing of all the blocks in `15-unit.dwg`.

WHAT IS AUTODESK SEEK?

You might notice the Autodesk® Seek banner in the upper-right corner of the DesignCenter palette. If you click this banner, your web browser opens to the BIMObjects home page, where you will find a rich resource for drawings and models from manufacturers and users. There are 2D and 3D files available in a number of formats, including DWG, DWF, and PDF.

If you prefer to use your web browser to explore the Autodesk Seek site without opening AutoCAD, the website address is `https://bimobjects.com`.

Here, you can import any of the drawing components from the DesignCenter palette into an open drawing in AutoCAD. But before you try that, let's look at a few other features of DesignCenter.

Opening and Inserting Files with DesignCenter

By using DesignCenter, you can more easily locate the files you're seeking because you can view thumbnail preview icons. But often that isn't enough. For example, you might want to locate all the files that contain the name of a particular manufacturer in an attribute of a drawing. This can be accomplished using the search feature of DesignCenter, which you'll learn about later in the chapter.

After you've found the file you're seeking, you can load it into AutoCAD by right-clicking the filename in the Palette view and then choosing Open In Window. Try it with the following exercise:

1. Click the Up tool in the DesignCenter toolbar three times. This takes you up two levels in the Palette view, from the view of the drawing blocks to the list of filenames.
2. In the Tree view, select the `Chapter 11` folder. Then, in the Palette view of DesignCenter, locate the `11c-unit.dwg` sample.
3. Right-click the `11c-unit.dwg` file, and select Open In Application Window. The drawing appears in the AutoCAD window.

If you want to insert a file into another drawing as a block, you can do so by clicking and dragging the file from the DesignCenter Palette view into an open drawing window. You're then prompted for the insertion point, scale, and rotation angle. If you prefer to use the Insert dialog box to insert a drawing from DesignCenter, right-click the filename in the Palette view and then choose Insert As Block. The Insert dialog box opens, offering you the full set of Insert options, as described in Chapter 4, "Organizing Objects with Blocks and Groups."

Finally, you can attach a drawing as an Xref by right-clicking a file in the Palette view of DesignCenter and choosing Attach As Xref. The Attach External Reference dialog box opens, offering the insertion point, scale, and rotation options similar to the options in the Insert dialog box. This is the same dialog box described in Chapter 7, "Mastering Viewing Tools, Hatches, and External References."

Finding and Extracting the Contents of a Drawing

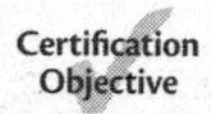

Aside from the convenience of being able to see thumbnail views of your drawing, DesignCenter may not seem like much of an improvement over Windows File Explorer. But DesignCenter goes beyond Windows File Explorer in many ways. One of the main features of DesignCenter is that it enables you to locate and extract components of a drawing.

Imagine that you want to find a specific block in a drawing. You remember the name of the block, but you don't remember the drawing into which you put it. You can search the contents of drawings by using DesignCenter's Search dialog box. In the following exercise, you'll search for a block named Kitchen2-metric among a set of files:

1. In the DesignCenter toolbar, click the Search tool to open the Search dialog box. It looks similar to the Search tool that comes with Windows.
2. Select the drive and folder that contains your `Samples` files from the In drop-down list. Make sure that the Search Subfolders option is checked.
3. Select Blocks from the Look For drop-down list. As you can see from the list, you can look for a variety of drawing component types (see Figure 25.29).

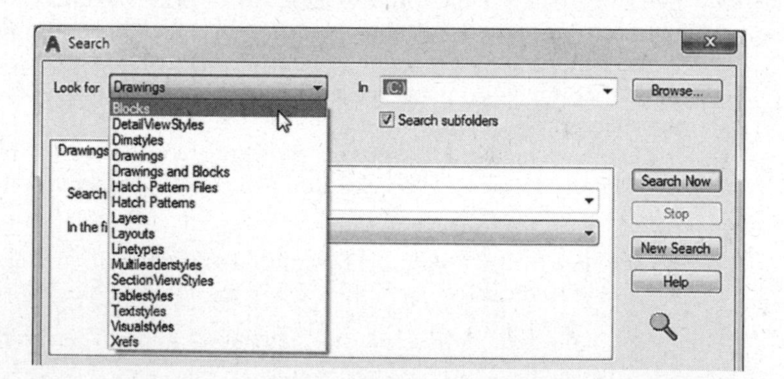

FIGURE 25.29
Select Blocks from the Look For drop-down list.

4. Enter **Kitchen2-metric** in the Search For The Name box, and then click the Search Now button to start the search. The magnifying glass icon in the lower-right corner moves in a circular pattern, telling you that the Search function is working. After a minute or two, the name of the block appears in the window at the bottom of the dialog box.
5. Double-click the block name. DesignCenter displays the block in the Palette view and the file that contains the block in the Tree view.

Exploring the Search Options

As you saw from the previous example, the Search dialog box can be helpful in finding items that are buried in a set of drawings. In the exercise, you searched for a block, but you can search for any named drawing component, including attribute data and text. For example, if you want to find all attributes that contain the name *ABC Manufacturing Company* in your drawings, you can do so with the DesignCenter Search dialog box. Table 25.2 shows a summary of its features. When you select Drawings from the Look For drop-down list, you see a set of additional tabs in the Search dialog box, as described in Table 25.3.

Table 25.2: DesignCenter Search dialog box options

Option	Purpose
Look For options	Lets you select the type of item to search for. The options are Blocks, Detail View Styles, Dimstyles, Drawings, Drawings And Blocks, Hatch Pattern Files, Hatch Patterns, Layers, Layouts, Linetypes, Multileaderstyles, Section View Styles, Tablestyles, Textstyles, Visual Styles, and Xrefs.
In	Lets you select the drive that you want to search.
Browse	Lets you locate a specific folder to search.
Search Subfolders	Lets you determine whether Search searches subfolders in the drive and folder that you specify.
Search Now	Starts the search process.
Stop	Cancels the current search.
New Search	Clears all the settings for the current search so that you can start fresh on a new search.
Help	Opens the AutoCAD help system to the Search topic.

Table 25.3: DesignCenter Search dialog box tab options when Drawings is selected from the Look For drop-down list

Tab Option	Purpose
Drawings tab	
Search For The Word(s)	Lets you specify the text to search for in the Drawing Properties fields.
In The Field(s)	Lets you specify the field of the Drawing Properties dialog box to search through, including Filename, Title, Subject, Author, and Keywords. These are the fields that you see in the Summary tab of the Drawing Properties dialog box, which can be opened by choosing Drawing Utilities ➢ Drawing Properties from the Application menu.

Table 25.3: DesignCenter Search dialog box tab options when Drawings is selected from the Look For drop-down list *(continued)*

Tab Option	Purpose
Date Modified tab	
Radio buttons	Let you limit search criteria based on dates.
Advanced tab	
Containing	Lets you select from a list of data to search for, including block name, block and drawing description, attribute tag, and attribute value.
Containing Text	Lets you specify the text to search for in the types of data that you select from the Containing option.
Size Is	Lets you restrict the search to files larger than or smaller than the size that you specify.

Automatically Scaling Blocks at Insertion

After you've found a block by using DesignCenter, you can click and drag the block into your open drawing. In the following exercise, you'll do that but with a slight twist. The block you've found is drawn in centimeters, but you'll insert the Kitchen2-metric block into a drawing named `11c-unit.dwg`, which was created in the Imperial measurement system. If you were to insert the Kitchen2-metric block into `11c-unit.dwg`, the kitchen would be exactly 2.54 times as large as it should be for `11c-unit.dwg`. But as you'll see, DesignCenter takes care of scaling for you. Follow these steps:

1. If you haven't done so already, open the `11c-unit.dwg` sample drawing in AutoCAD. You can temporarily close DesignCenter to do this.
2. Back in DesignCenter, click and drag the Kitchen2-metric block from the Palette view into the `11c-unit.dwg` window in AutoCAD. The kitchen appears at the appropriate scale.
3. To confirm that DesignCenter did indeed adjust the scale, select the Kitchen2-metric block, right-click, and select Properties.
4. Check the Unit factor value under the Misc category. Notice the value shows 3/8″. This is the value at which the Kitchen2-metric block has been scaled. If no scaling is applied, this value would be 1.
5. After reviewing the Properties palette, close it.

You may recall from Chapter 3, "Setting Up and Using the Drafting Tools," that you can specify the type of units for which the drawing is set up in the Drawing Units dialog box under the Insertion Scale group. DesignCenter uses this information when you drag and drop blocks from DesignCenter into an open drawing. This is how DesignCenter is able to scale a block drawn in metric correctly to a drawing that is drawn in the Imperial format. The same option is offered in the Block Definition dialog box.

Blocks aren't the only type of drawing component that you can click and drag from the Palette view. Linetypes, layouts, dimension styles, and text styles can all be imported from files on your computer or network through DesignCenter's Palette view.

Exchanging Data between Open Files

You've seen how you can extract a block from a file stored on your hard disk and place it into an open drawing, but what if you want to copy a block from one open drawing to another open drawing? You change the way the Tree view displays data so that it shows only the files that are loaded in AutoCAD. The following exercise demonstrates how this works:

1. In AutoCAD, make sure that `11c-unit.dwg` is still open, and then open the `11b-unit-metric.dwg` file.
2. In DesignCenter, click the Open Drawings tab above the Tree view. The Tree view changes to display only the drawings that are open.
3. Click the plus sign (+) to the left of the `11c-unit.dwg` filename in the Tree view. The list expands to show the components in `11c-unit.dwg`.
4. Click Blocks in the Tree view. The Palette view changes to show a list of blocks available in `11c-unit.dwg`.
5. Locate the Kitchen block in the Palette view.
6. Click and drag Kitchen from the Palette view into the open `11b-unit-metric.dwg` drawing in AutoCAD. The block moves with the cursor. Once again, DesignCenter has automatically scaled the block to the appropriate size, this time from Imperial to metric.
7. Release anywhere in the drawing to place the Kitchen block.

In this example, you inserted a block from one open drawing into another drawing. If you prefer to use the Insert dialog box, you can right-click the block name in step 6 and choose Insert Block. The Insert dialog box opens, enabling you to set the Insertion Point, Scale, and Rotation options.

Just as with drawings, you can see a preview and descriptive text for blocks below the Palette view. In Chapter 4, you had the option to save a preview image with the block when you first created a block. This is where that preview icon can be really helpful. The preview icon gives you a chance to see what the block looks like when you use DesignCenter to browse through your drawing files. If you don't save a preview icon, you'll see the same block icon that was displayed in the previous Palette view.

You can also add the text description at the time you create the block. Before saving the block, enter a description in the Description box of the Block Definition dialog box.

If you're updating older drawing files to be used with DesignCenter, you can add text descriptions to blocks by using the Create tool in the Home tab's Block panel or the Create Block tool in the Insert tab's Block Definition panel. Click the Create tool and then, in the Block Definition dialog box, select the name of a block from the Name drop-down list. Enter the description that you want for this block in the Description box toward the bottom of the Block Definition dialog box. When you're finished, click OK.

Loading Specific Files into DesignCenter

You've seen how you can locate files through the Tree view and Palette view. If you already know the name and location of the file with which you want to work, you can use a file dialog box to open files in DesignCenter. Instead of choosing the Open tool on the Quick Access toolbar, you use the Load tool on the DesignCenter toolbar to open the Load dialog box. This is a standard file dialog box that lets you search for files on your computer or network.

If you want to open a file in DesignCenter that you've recently opened, you can use the History tab just above the Tree view. The Tree view closes, and you see a list of the files that you've worked on most recently.

Customizing the Tool Palettes with DesignCenter

Many AutoCAD users have built their own custom library of symbols. In Chapter 1, "Exploring the Interface," you saw how easy it is to drag and drop a symbol, known as a tool, from the tool palettes. At first glance, there is no obvious way to add your own tools to the palettes, but adding tools and additional palettes to the tool palettes is fairly simple once you're familiar with DesignCenter. The following exercise shows you how it's done:

1. If tool palettes aren't open already, click the Tool Palettes tool in the View tab's Palettes panel.
2. Right-click in the tool palettes title bar, and then choose New Palette from the context menu.
3. Enter **My Tool Palette**↵. A new, blank tab is added to the tool palettes.

4. Go back to DesignCenter, make sure the Folders tab is selected, click the Home tool, and select en-us ➤ DesignCenter.
5. In the Palette view to the right, double-click the `Landscaping.dwg` file and then double-click the Blocks icon that appears in the Palette view.
6. Make sure the tool palettes are visible behind DesignCenter, and then Ctrl+click Clump Of Trees Or Bushes – Plan and North Arrow.
7. Click and drag the selection to the tool palettes.

> **BE CAREFUL CLICKING IN THE TOOL PALETTE**
>
> If you click a tool in a tool palette, it's inserted in the current drawing, so take care when clicking around in the tool palettes.

You've just created a tool palette and added two symbols. You can continue to add symbols from other drawings to your custom tool palette. Or, if you have a drawing that contains all the blocks that you need for a tool palette, you can quickly create a tool palette directly from a file. Here's how that's done:

1. In DesignCenter, go up two folder levels so that you can select the `Landscaping.dwg` file.
2. Right-click `Landscaping.dwg`, and then choose Create Tool Palette. After a few moments, a new tool palette called Landscaping appears in the tool palettes. This new palette contains all the blocks found in the `Landscaping.dwg` file.

This exercise showed that you can quickly create a palette of all the blocks from a file. You can do the same thing with entire folders of drawings, although you may want to make sure that such folders don't contain too many files.

But what if you don't want some of the items in your custom palette? You can remove items easily by using the context menu:

1. In the Landscaping palette, select the top three symbols by right-clicking the tool that is third from the top and then Shift+clicking the top tool. This is a little different from the typical Windows method for selecting items from a list.
2. Right-click and choose Delete from the context menu. Click OK to confirm the deletion.

You may have noticed the Cut and Copy options in the context menu in step 2. You can use these options to move symbols from one palette to another. For example, instead of deleting the three symbols in step 2, you can choose Cut from the context menu, open another palette, right-click, and choose Paste. The symbols move to the new palette location. In the next section, you'll see how you can use the Copy and Paste context menu options to make a copy of a tool in the same palette.

Customizing a Tool

Other context menu options let you delete entire palettes or rename tools or palettes. You can also edit the properties of symbols in a palette. The following exercise shows how to use the context menu options to create two scale versions of the same tool:

1. In the Landscaping tab of the tool palettes, right-click the North Arrow tool and choose Copy from the context menu.
2. Right-click in a blank area of the palette (you may need to expand the tool palettes to create some space) and choose Paste. A copy of the North Arrow tool appears at the bottom of the palette.
3. Right-click the copy of the North Arrow tool, choose Rename from the context menu, and then enter **North Arrow Copy**↵.
4. Right-click the North Arrow Copy tool and choose Properties to open the Tool Properties dialog box (see Figure 25.30).

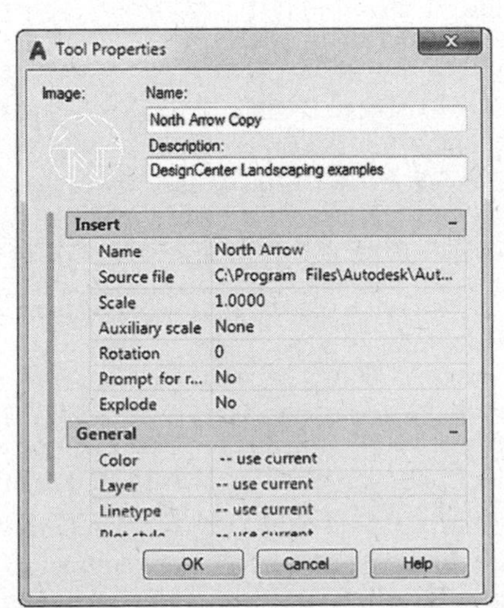

Figure 25.30
The Tool Properties dialog box

5. Click 1 to the right of the Scale listing, and change the value to 4.
6. Click OK, and then click and drag the North Arrow Copy tool into the drawing.
7. Click and drag the original North Arrow tool into the drawing. Notice that the original North Arrow is smaller than the North Arrow Copy, whose scale you changed to 4.

This exercise demonstrated that you can have multiple versions of a tool at different scales. You can then use the tool that's appropriate to the scale of your drawing. As you can see from the Tool Properties dialog box, you can also modify other tool properties, such as color and layer assignments. You can use this feature to create sets of tools for different scale drawings. For example, you can create a palette of architectural reference symbols for 1/4″-scale drawings, and you can create another palette for 1/8″-scale drawings.

Adding Hatch Patterns and Solid Fills

You've seen how you can turn blocks into tool palette tools, but what about solid fills? In Chapter 1, you learned that sample hatch patterns and solid fills are available in the tool palettes. Here's how you can add your own:

1. In DesignCenter, use the Tree view to locate the `AutoCAD 2018 Support` folder. In Windows 10, Windows 8, or Windows 7, it's typically in `C:\Users\`*`User Name`*`\AppData\Roaming\Autodesk\AutoCAD 2018\R22.0\enu\Support` (*`User Name`* is your Windows login name).
2. Double-click the `acad.pat` file shown in the Palette view. AutoCAD builds a list of the patterns and displays the list in the Palette view.
3. You can now click and drag a pattern into any tool palette. You can also click and drag an entire PAT file into the tool palette to create a palette of all the patterns in a hatch pattern file.

Locating Support and Hidden Files

To find out exactly where support files are located, choose Options from the Application menu to open the Options dialog box. Click the Files tab. Expand the Support File Search Path item at the top of the list, and then place the cursor on the item just below Support File Search Path. You see the path to the `Support` folder. You can also enter **(findfile "acad.pat")** at the Command prompt as a shortcut to find the support file search path. If you use this shortcut, note that the directory names are separated with double hash marks (\\). This is an artifact of AutoLISP®. User support files are in a hidden folder. See "Finding Folders That Contain AutoCAD Files" in Appendix B, "Installing and Setting Up AutoCAD," for information on how to unhide hidden folders.

In this exercise, you used the standard hatch patterns that come with AutoCAD. You can also create your own custom hatch patterns and import them to the tool palettes by using the method described here. See Chapter 24, "Customizing Toolbars, Menus, Linetypes, and Hatch Patterns," for more information on creating custom hatch patterns.

If you want to set up a set of solid fill colors, you can do the following:

1. Click and drag the SOLID pattern from the `acad.pat` file into the tool palette.
2. Click the new solid fill tool, choose Properties from the context menu, and select a color from the Color drop-down list in the Tool Properties dialog box.

You can select any color, including colors from the True Color or Color Books tab in the Select Color dialog box that you learned about in Chapter 5, "Keeping Track of Layers and Blocks." You can also cut and paste an existing solid fill tool to make copies. You can then modify the color property for each copy to get a set of custom solid fill colors.

Managing the Tool Palettes

You can perform other types of tool palette maintenance operations by using the Customize dialog box. For example, you can change the order of the tool palette tabs, or you can group tabs into categories that can be turned on or off. The following steps offer a glimpse of what you can do by showing you how to group palettes:

1. To open the Customize dialog box (see Figure 25.31), right-click the tool palettes title bar and choose Customize Palettes from the context menu.

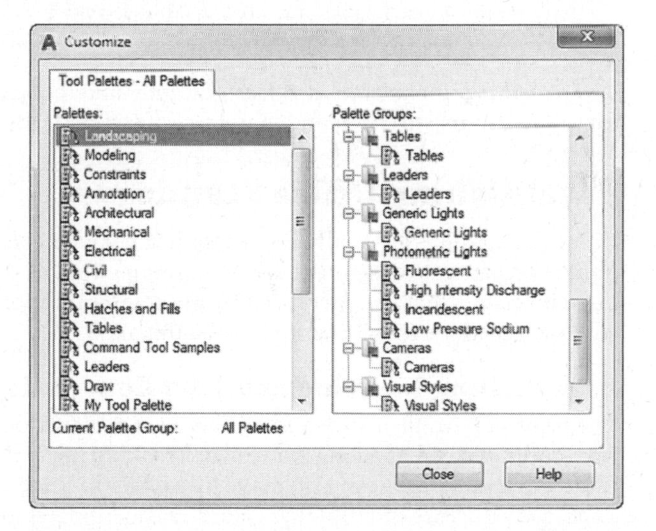

Figure 25.31
Customize dialog box for tool palettes

2. Right-click in a blank area of the Palette Groups panel, and choose New Group.
3. Enter **My Group** for the new group name.
4. Click and drag My Group to a position just above another group; that way, My Group is its own group instead of a subgroup.
5. Click and drag Landscaping from the left panel to the right panel just below My Group. A black bar appears below My Group. Release the mouse button.
6. Click and drag My Tool Palette from the left panel to the right, just below Landscaping.

You've just created a new palette group and moved the two new palettes. You can view the palettes separately or all together:

1. Click Close to close the Customize dialog box. The tool palette still displays all the tabs.
2. To display only the new tabs, click the Properties button at the top of the palette title bar.
3. Select My Group. Now the tool palette shows only the two tabs that you just created.

You may have noticed that in the Properties menu, you also have the option to show just the new groups or all the palettes. This feature lets you keep the tabs in the tool palettes organized.

The list on the left side of the Customize dialog box also lets you change the order of the tabs by clicking and dragging the tab names up or down in the left panel. If you select a palette in the left panel and right-click, you can rename, delete, import, or export a palette.

DesignCenter and tool palettes offer great features that will prove invaluable to AutoCAD users. Although these examples show you how to use DesignCenter on a stand-alone computer, you can just as easily perform the same functions across a network or even across the Internet.

DON'T FORGET THE SOURCE FILES WHEN EXPORTING

If you use the Export or Import option to move a palette from one computer to another, be aware that you must also import or export the drawings that are the source files for the palette tools.

This ends our exploration of DesignCenter and tool palettes. In the next section, you'll look at tools you can use to set up and maintain office standards for your drawing files.

Establishing Office Standards

Communication is especially important when you're one of many people working on the same project on separate computers. A well-developed set of standards and procedures helps to minimize problems that may be caused by miscommunication. In the following sections, you'll find some suggestions for setting up these standards.

Establishing Layering and Text Conventions

The issue of CAD standards has always been difficult to resolve. Standardizing layers, dimensions, and text can go a long way toward making file exchange more seamless between different trades, and standards can also make files easier to understand. When everyone follows a standard, the structure of a drawing is more easily understood, and those who have to edit or interpret your work can do so without having to ask a lot of questions.

You've seen how layers can be a useful tool. But they can easily get out of hand when you have free rein over their creation and naming. Users may become confused while attempting to isolate or identify objects and layers in a drawing with which they're not familiar. Inconsistent layer naming can also inhibit the use of timesaving tools like the Layer Translator (covered later in this chapter), AutoLISP routines, and script files that might otherwise be able to automate many repetitive tasks. With an appropriate layer-naming convention, you can minimize this type of problem (although you may not eliminate it entirely). A too-rigid naming convention can cause as many problems as no convention at all, so it's best to give general guidelines rather than force everyone to stay within narrow limits. As mentioned in Chapter 5, you can create layer names in a way that enables you to group them by using wildcards. AutoCAD allows up to 255 characters in a layer name, so you can use descriptive names.

Lineweights should be standardized along with colors. If you intend to use a reprographics service for your plotting, check with them first; they may require that you conform to their color and lineweight standards.

KNOW THE STANDARDS

If you're an architect or an engineer or you are in the construction business, check out some of the CAD layering standards set forth by the American Institute of Architects (AIA) and the Construction Specifications Institute (CSI). The AIA's website is located at `www.aia.org`, and the CSI's website can be found at `http://www.csiresources.org`. The most popular framework for drawing standards remains the National CAD Standard (NCS) from the National Institute of Building Sciences, and it includes the AIA layering guidelines. See `www.nationalcadstandard.org` for more information. For European standards, take a look at `www.iso.org`.

Checking Office Standards

AutoCAD offers an open-ended environment that lends itself to easy customization, but this also leaves the door wide open for on-the-fly creation of layer names, dimension styles, and other drawing format options. It's easy to stray from standards, especially when you're under pressure to get a project out on a deadline. To help you and your office maintain a level of conformity to office or industry standards, AutoCAD includes the Standards command.

The Standards command lets you quickly compare a drawing against a set of standard layer names, dimension style settings, linetypes, and text styles. A dialog box displays any item that doesn't conform to the standards you selected. You can then adjust the file to make it conform to your standards.

You can create several sets of standards for different types of files, and you can assign the standards directly to a file so that anyone editing that file can make periodic checks against your office standards while the drawing is being edited.

The Standards command discussed here isn't available in the Autodesk® AutoCAD LT® software.

SETTING UP STANDARDS FILES

The first step in using the Standards command is to set up a file to which other drawing files can be compared. This *standards file* will be an AutoCAD drawing file with a `.dws` filename extension. Here are the steps to create a new DWS standards file:

1. Open AutoCAD, and click New on the Quick Access toolbar to create a new file.
2. Set up the file with the layers, linetypes, dimension styles, and text styles that you want as your standards.
3. Choose Save As from the Application menu.
4. In the Save Drawing As dialog box, choose AutoCAD Drawing Standards (*.dws) from the Files Of Type drop-down list.
5. Choose a convenient folder for the location of your standards file and click Save.

As an alternative to creating a new file, you can open an existing file that contains the typical settings you'll want to use on your projects. You can then delete all the graphics in the file and purge all its blocks and shapes. After you've done this, you can begin at step 3 of the previous exercise to save the file as a DWS standards file.

You can set up as many DWS files as you need for your office. Often, a single set of standards is too limiting if your office is involved in a diverse range of projects, so you may want to set up DWS files on a project basis, drawing on a core of generic DWS files.

Using the Standards Command to Associate Standards

After you've created your DWS standards files, you can begin to check other files for conformity. The next task is to assign your DWS file to the drawing file that you want to check:

1. In AutoCAD, open the file that you want to check for standards conformity.
2. Click Configure on the Manage tab's CAD Standards panel to open the Configure Standards dialog box. The Standards tab of this dialog box contains a list box and a description area. A row of buttons appears vertically between the list box and description.

3. Click the Add Standards File (F3) button in the middle column of the dialog box.
4. The Select Standards File dialog box opens. This is a typical AutoCAD file dialog box. Notice that the Files Of Type drop-down list shows the Standards (*.dws) file type.
5. Locate and select the standards file that you want to use to check the current file and click Open. After a moment, the name of the file that you select appears in the list box (see Figure 25.32). On the right side of the dialog box you see a description of the standards file.

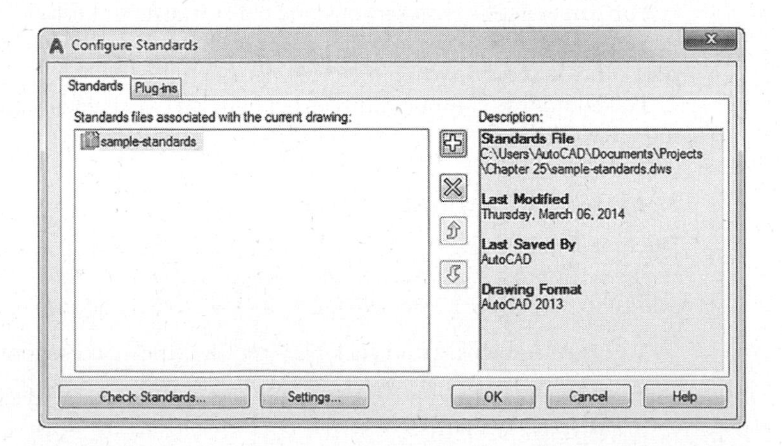

Figure 25.32
Associating a set of standards with a file

6. Check the current file against the DWS standards file. Click the Check Standards button in the lower-left corner of the Configure Standards dialog box. AutoCAD pauses while it checks the current file, and then you see the Check Standards dialog box.

If AutoCAD finds a discrepancy between the standards file and the current file, a description of the problem appears at the top of the dialog box. For example, if the name of a dimension style that isn't in the standards file appears in the current file, a message appears indicating that a nonstandard dimension style exists in the current drawing. If this happens, take the following steps:

1. Below the problem statement is the Replace With list box, which contains options related to the nonstandard item. You can replace the nonstandard item in your file with an option in the Replace With list box by selecting the option and clicking the Fix button in the lower half of the dialog box. Or you can leave the problem alone for now.
2. Click the Next button in the lower-right corner of the Check Standards dialog box to move to the next problem.
3. Repeat steps 1 and 2 until you see the statement `Checking is complete` in the Problem list box and the Checking Complete dialog box opens to display a summary of the checking results.

You can check Mark This Problem As Ignored if you want the Check Standards dialog box to ignore the problem in future standards-checking sessions.

In this example, you entered the Check Standards dialog box directly from the Configure Standards dialog box. After you've used the Check Standards dialog box on a file, the DWS standards file is associated with the checked file. You can go directly to the Check Standards dialog box by choosing Manage ➤ CAD Standards ➤ Check during any subsequent editing session.

DON'T LOSE THE DWS

After you've assigned a DWS standards file to a drawing, you'll need to save the drawing or its association with the DWS file will be lost.

CHECKING STANDARDS FOR MULTIPLE DRAWINGS

The Standards and Check Standards commands are great for checking individual files, but eventually you'll want a method to batch-check a set of files. AutoCAD 2018 provides a utility that does just that. The Batch Standards Checker is a stand-alone utility that audits a set of drawing files and checks them against their associated DWS files. The Batch Standards Checker can also check a set of drawings against a single DWS file of your choice. It then generates an audit report showing any problems it encounters.

Here's how it works:

1. From the Windows Desktop, choose Start ➤ All Programs ➤ Autodesk ➤ AutoCAD 2018 ➤ Batch Standards Checker to open the Batch Standards Checker dialog box (see Figure 25.33).

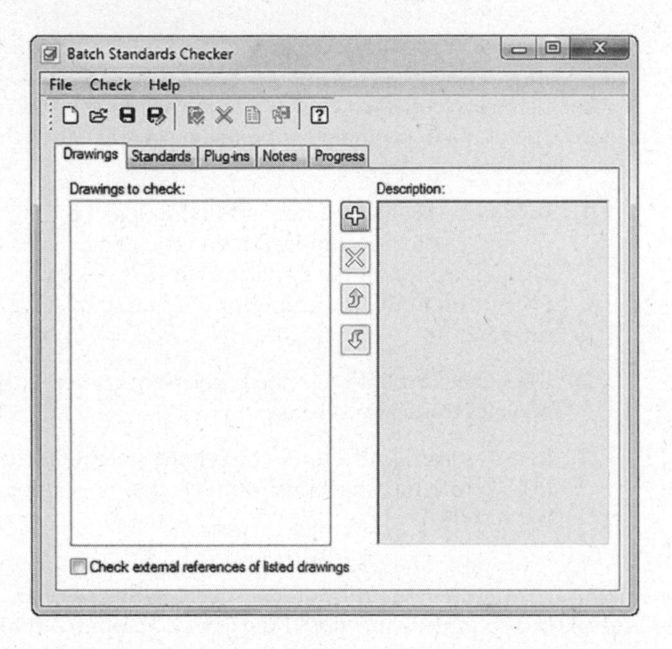

Figure 25.33
The Batch Standards Checker dialog box

2. Click the plus button in the middle of the dialog box to open the Batch Standards Checker – File Open dialog box. This is a typical AutoCAD file dialog box.
3. Locate and select the drawings that you want to check. You return to the Batch Standards Checker dialog box and, after a moment, a list of the drawings that you selected appears in the Drawings To Check list box.
4. Click the Standards tab (see Figure 25.34). This is where you can select the standards file against which your selection will be checked.

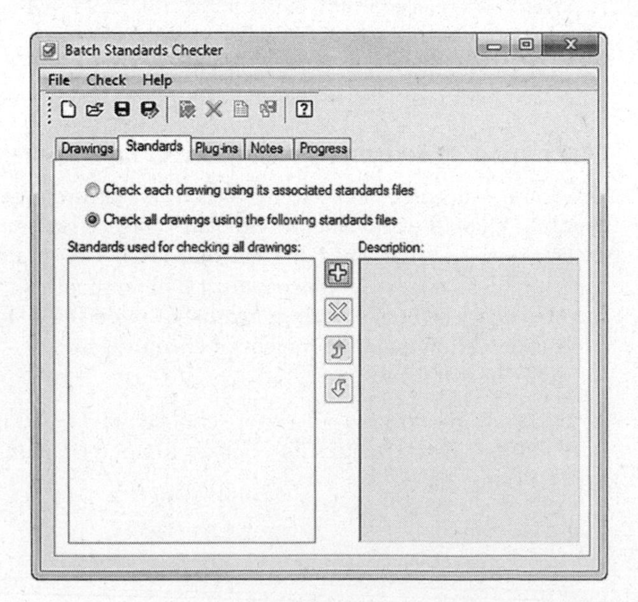

Figure 25.34
Choose the files that you want to check and then select the Standards tab.

If the drawings you selected in step 3 already have a standards file associated with them, you can use the Check Each Drawing Using Its Associated Standards Files option to check each file. You can then skip to step 7.

5. If you select the Check All Drawings Using The Following Standards Files option, click the plus sign in the middle of the dialog box to open the file dialog box.
6. Locate and select a DWS standards file. The file then appears in the Standards Used For Checking All Drawings list box on the left of the Standards tab in the Batch Standards Checker dialog box.
7. Click the Save button at the top of the Batch Standards Checker dialog box.

   The Batch Standards Checker's file save dialog box opens to enable you to specify a standards check filename and location. This file has a `.chx` filename extension.

8. After you've specified the location and name of a check file, click the Start Check button.

WHAT IS A CHX FILE?

The Batch Standards Checker file is an audit file that stores the drawing list and the list of standards files in the current session. It also stores the results of the audit. The CHX file is an XML-based file.

AutoCAD proceeds to check each file listed in the Drawings tab list box. The progress is shown in the Progress tab of the Batch Standards Checker dialog box. If you decide to cancel the audit, you can click the Stop Check button, which cancels the audit currently in progress. When files are being checked, the Stop Check button turns red.

When all the files have been checked, the data from the audit is automatically saved in the check file that you created in step 7. Then the audit file is opened in your web browser and you see the results of the audit. If your browser is blocking Active X, the options described next will be unavailable.

The audit report file displays a number of options in a set of radio buttons:

Overview Displays a simplified view of the problems encountered by the audit. It lists the drawings audited and the number of problems encountered.

Plug-Ins Shows the standard plug-ins used to audit the drawings. Autodesk supplies these standard plug-ins, which test for layers, dimension styles, linetypes, and text styles. Third-party developers can create other plug-ins to check for additional problems.

Standards Lists the DWS standards files used for the audit.

Problems Displays a detailed description of the problems encountered in the audit. It gives the drawing name and the name of the specific item that is a problem. For example, if the audit discovers a nonstandard layer name, the layer name is listed under the drawing name as a nonstandard layer name.

Ignored Problems Displays problems that have previously been flagged as problems to ignore. You can flag problems to be ignored by using the Check Standards command in AutoCAD. (See the section "Using the Standards Command to Associate Standards" earlier in this chapter.)

All Displays all the audit information.

Reviewing Previously Saved Standards Audits

After you've created a check file and completed a standards audit, you can always return to the audit by opening the Batch Standards Checker utility and clicking the Open tool in the toolbar.

This opens the Batch Standards Checker file open dialog box, where you can locate and open a previously saved standards check file with the `.chx` filename extension. In this file, you see a list of the files that were checked in the Drawings tab and the DWS standards file used in the Standards tab.

You can then view the results of the audit by clicking the View Report tool in the toolbar. This opens a web browser and displays the audit results contained in the standards check file.

Converting Multiple Layer Settings

As AutoCAD files flow in and out of your office, you're likely to find yourself working with layering standards from another system. You might, for example, receive files from an architect who uses the CSI standard for layer names, whereas your office prefers the AIA standard. If your job involves extensive reworking of such files, you'll want to change the layering system to one with which you're most familiar. But converting layer settings is a painstaking and time-consuming process, especially if several files need conversion.

Fortunately, AutoCAD offers a tool that can make layer conversion from one standard to another much easier. The Layer Translator lets you map nonstandard layers (that is, those using a system different from your own) to your own set of standards. It can then convert those layers to match your office standards. After you've mapped a set of layers between two files, you can save the map settings in a drawing file. Then any other files you receive that contain the same nonstandard layer settings can be converted to your own layer standards quickly. Let's take a closer look at how the Layer Translator works.

When using the Layer Translator, you must initially match the layers of your incoming file with those of a file whose layers are set up in the way that you want. Here are the steps to do this:

1. Open the file whose layers you want to convert in AutoCAD. Select the Layer Translator tool from the Manage tab's CAD Standards panel to open the Layer Translator dialog box, which lists the layers from the current file in the Translate From list box.
2. Click the Load button in the Translate To group to open the Select Drawing File dialog box. Locate and select a file that contains the layer settings that you want to use for this project. The file can be a standard DWG file, or it can be a DWS standards file or a DWT template file. After you've opened a file, its layer names appear in the Translate To list box.
3. Select a layer name in the Translate From list, and then select the layer with the settings that you want to use from the Translate To list box. After you've made your two selections, click the Map button in the middle of the dialog box. An item in the Layer Translation Mappings group shows you the old and new layer names and the layer settings for the conversion (see Figure 25.35).

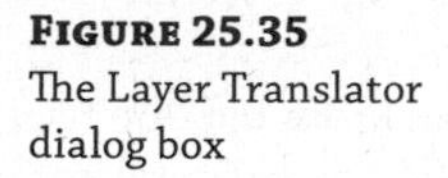

FIGURE 25.35
The Layer Translator dialog box

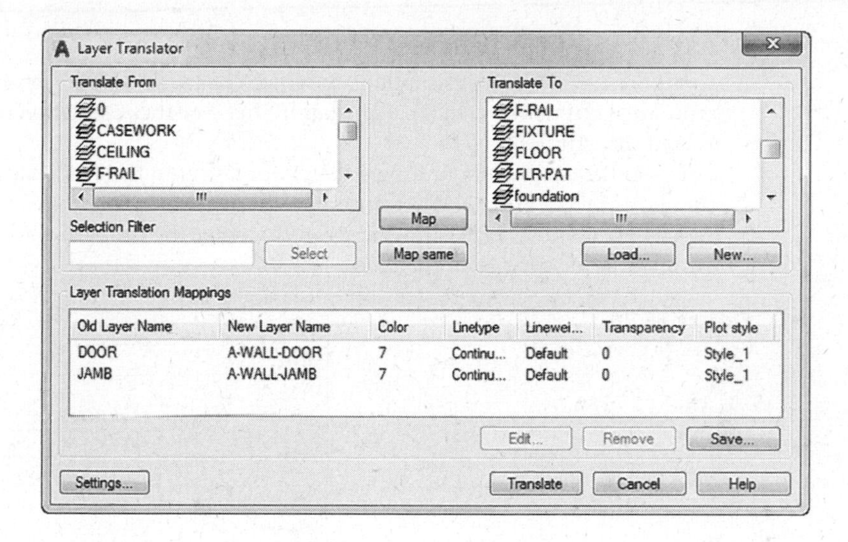

4. Repeat step 3 for all the layers that you want to convert. You can map several layers from the Translate From list to a single layer in the Translate To list if you need to do so.
5. If there are matching layers in the Translate From and Translate To list boxes, the Map Same button in the middle of the dialog box becomes active. You can then click this button to automatically map layers that have the same names in both the Translate From and the Translate To lists.

After you've completed your layer mapping, you can save the mapping for future use:

1. While still in the Layer Translator dialog box, click the Save button in the Layer Translation Mappings group to open the Save Layer Mappings dialog box. This is a typical AutoCAD file dialog box.
2. Enter a name for your saved settings and click Save. You can save the layer map settings as either a DWS standards file or a DWG file.
3. Click the Translate button and AutoCAD will proceed to translate the mapped layers. You may see a warning message saying that a standards violation has occurred. The message can be ignored as they will have been translated.

After you've saved the layer mapping in step 2, you can load the saved layer map settings into the Layer Translator dialog box in future layer translations. This saves you the effort of mapping each layer individually each time you want to perform a translation. This will work for incoming files that use the same layer settings, but you'll have to create another layer map settings file for each different layer system you encounter.

To use a saved layer map, click the Load button in the Translate To group of the Layer Translator dialog box and then select the layer map file you saved in step 2. You can have several layer map files for each project involving files with nonstandard layer settings.

Exploring Other Layer Translator Options

You'll often come across situations in which the layers in the Translate From list don't correspond directly to those in the Translate To list. For these situations, the Layer Translator offers a few additional options.

If you have difficulty finding a match for layers in the Translate From list, you can create a new layer by clicking the New button in the Translate To group. This opens the New Layer dialog box (see Figure 25.36), in which you can enter the properties for your new layer. Note that the layer name cannot be changed.

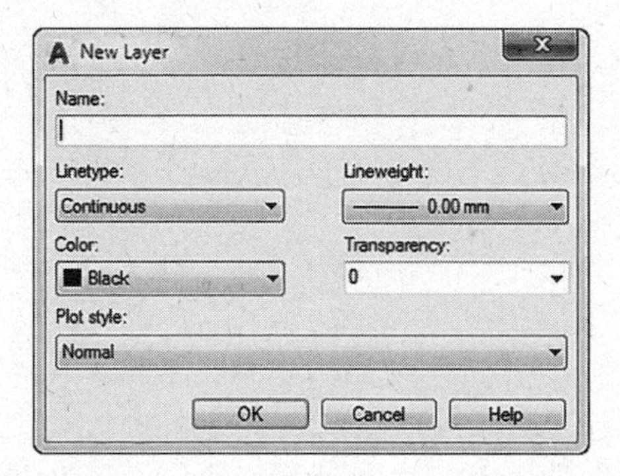

FIGURE 25.36
Creating a new layer

After you create a new layer with this dialog box, it appears in the Translate To list box, enabling you to map Translate From layers to your new layer.

Another option that you'll find to be useful is the Edit button in the Layer Translation Mappings group. You may find that after you've mapped a Translate From layer to a Translate To layer, the Translate To layer isn't exactly what you want. You can highlight the mapped layer in the Layer Translation Mappings group list box and then click Edit to open the Edit Layer dialog box (see Figure 25.37). From here, you can modify the new layer's settings from their original values.

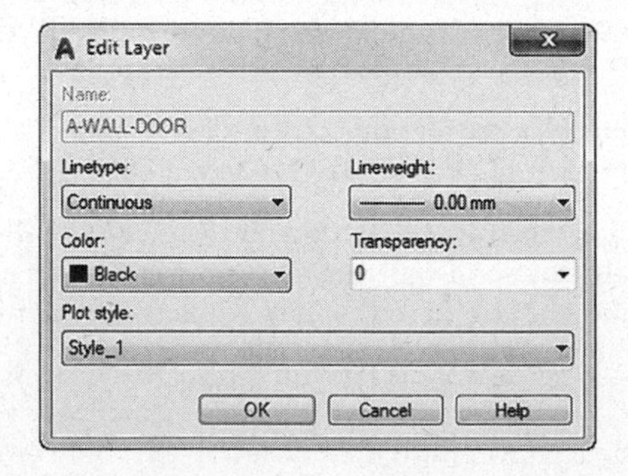

FIGURE 25.37
Changing a layer's properties

Finally, the Layer Translator offers a set of options that give you some control over the way translations are performed. For example, you can control whether layer colors and linetypes are forced to the ByLayer setting or whether layer assignments for objects in blocks are translated. You can access these options by clicking the Settings button in the lower-left corner of the Layer Translator dialog box. Figure 25.38 shows the Settings dialog box. The options are self-explanatory.

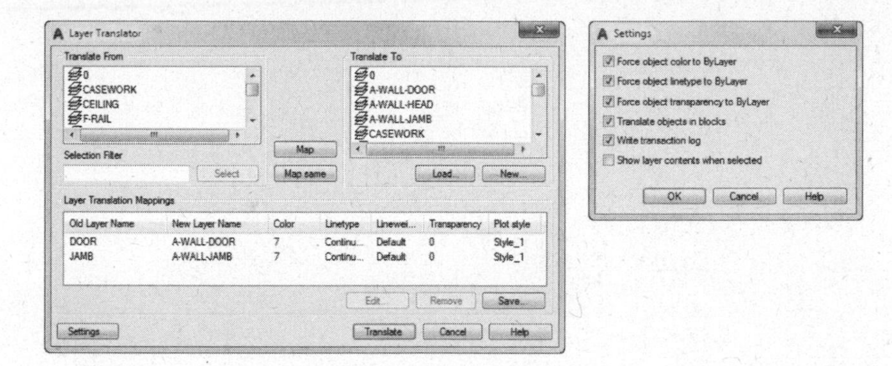

FIGURE 25.38
The Layer Translator and its Settings dialog box

The Bottom Line

Share drawings online. As a drafter or designer, you'll likely be involved in collaborative efforts, which means that you'll have to share your work with others. The Internet has made it much easier to do this.

Master It Why is eTransmit important for sending AutoCAD drawings over the Internet?

Publish your drawings. Autodesk offers the PDF drawing format, which lets non-CAD users view and add comments to simplified versions of your drawings. You can use the Publish feature to create a single PDF file from several drawings.

Master It True or false: The Publish feature can be used to plot multiple drawings in the background.

Get started with A360 Drive. A360 Drive makes sharing files and exchanging design ideas much easier.

Master It Name the feature that lets you revert a revised drawing to its prior state.

Manage your drawings with DesignCenter and the tool palettes. DesignCenter is a great tool for managing your drawings' resources, like blocks, custom linetypes, and other elements.

Master It True or false: DesignCenter has the capacity to scale a block automatically to the correct size when moving from metric to Imperial drawings.

Establish office standards. AutoCAD allows for a wide range of settings in a drawing. For this reason, it's a good idea to create standards for the way drawings are set up.

Master It Name the filename extension for an AutoCAD drawing standards file.

Convert multiple layer settings. If you exchange files with another office, you may find that their layer scheme is different than yours. AutoCAD offers the Layer Translator to help you translate layer names from an unfamiliar drawing to names with which you're more comfortable.

Master It Name the filename extensions of the types of files that you can use as a template for layer name translations.

Appendixes

In this section you will find:

- **Appendix A: The Bottom Line**
- **Appendix B: Installing and Setting Up AutoCAD**
- **Appendix C: The Autodesk AutoCAD 2018 Certification**

Appendix A

The Bottom Line

Each of "The Bottom Line" sections in the chapters suggests exercises to deepen skills and understanding. Sometimes there is only one possible solution, but often you are encouraged to use your skills and creativity to create something that builds on what you know and lets you explore one of many possibilities.

Chapter 1: Exploring the Interface

Use the AutoCAD® window. AutoCAD® is a typical Windows graphics program that makes use of menus, toolbars, Ribbon panels, and palettes. If you've used other graphics programs, you'll see at least a few familiar tools.

Master It Name the components of the AutoCAD window that you can use to select a function.

Solution AutoCAD offers the Quick Access toolbar, the Application menu, Ribbon panels, the Navigation bar, and the status bar to give you access to the most common functions.

Get a closer look with the Zoom command. One of the first things that you'll want to learn is how to manipulate your views. The Zoom command is a common tool in graphics programs.

Master It Name at least two ways of zooming into a view.

Solution Choose options from the Zoom flyout in the View tab's Navigate panel. You can also right-click and select Zoom from the shortcut menu and select Zoom options from the Navigation bar's Zoom flyout.

Save a file as you work. Nothing is more frustrating than having a power failure that causes you to lose hours of work. It's a good idea to save your work frequently. AutoCAD offers an Automatic Save feature that can be a lifesaver if you happen to forget to save your files.

Master It How often does the AutoCAD Automatic Save feature save your drawing?

Solution Automatic Save saves a copy of a drawing every 10 minutes by default. The user can modify this interval.

Make changes and open multiple files. As with other Windows programs, you can have multiple files open and exchange data between them.

Master It With two drawings open, how can you copy parts of one drawing into the other?

Solution Use Windows Copy and Paste. Select the parts you want to copy, right-click, and select Clipboard and then Copy. Go to the other drawing, right-click in the drawing area, and select Clipboard and then Paste.

Chapter 2: Creating Your First Drawing

Specify distances with coordinates. One of the most basic skills that you need to learn is how to indicate exact distances through the keyboard. AutoCAD uses a simple annotation system to indicate distance and direction.

Master It What would you type to indicate a relative distance of 14 units at a 45° angle?

Solution **@14<45**

Interpret the cursor modes and understand prompts. The AutoCAD cursor changes its shape depending on the command that is currently active. These different cursor modes can give you a clue regarding what you should be doing.

Master It Describe the Point Selection cursor and the Pickbox cursor.

Solution The Point Selection cursor is a simple crosshair. The Pickbox cursor is a small square, or pickbox.

Select objects and edit with grips. Grips are small squares or arrowheads that appear at key points on the object when they're selected. They offer a powerful way to edit objects.

Master It How do you select multiple grips?

Solution Hold down the Shift key while clicking the grips.

Use Dynamic Input. Besides grips, objects display their dimensional properties when selected. These dimensional properties can be edited to change an object's shape.

Master It How do you turn on the Dynamic Input display? And once it's on, what key lets you shift between the different dimensions of an object?

Solution The Dynamic Input button on the AutoCAD status bar turns Dynamic Input on and off. When an object is selected, you can move between the dimensional properties by pressing the Tab key.

Display data in a text window. AutoCAD offers the AutoCAD Text Window, which keeps a running account of the commands that you use. This can be helpful in retrieving input that you've entered when constructing your drawing.

Master It Name a command that displays its results in the AutoCAD Text Window.

Solution The List command.

Display the properties of an object. The Properties palette is one of the most useful sources for drawing information. Not only does it list the properties of an object, it also lets you change the shape, color, and other properties of objects.

Master It How do you open the Properties palette for a particular object?

Solution You select the object whose properties you want to view, right-click the object, and select Properties.

Get help. The AutoCAD Autodesk Exchange website is thorough in its coverage of AutoCAD features. New and experienced users alike can often find answers to their questions through the Help window, so it pays to become familiar with it.

Master It What keyboard key do you press for context-sensitive help?

Solution For help, you press the F1 key.

Chapter 3: Setting Up and Using the Drafting Tools

Set up a work area. A blank AutoCAD drawing offers few clues about the size of the area with which you're working, but you can get a rough idea of the area shown in the AutoCAD window.

Master It Name two ways to set up the area of your work.

Solution You can use the Limits command to define the work area, otherwise known as the limits of the drawing. You can also draw a rectangle that is the size of your work area.

Explore the drawing process. To use AutoCAD effectively, you'll want to know how the different tools work together to achieve an effect. The drawing process often involves many cycles of adding objects and then editing them.

Master It Name the tool that causes the cursor to point in an exact horizontal or vertical direction.

Solution Polar Tracking. Ortho mode can also perform this function.

Plan and lay out a drawing. If you've ever had to draw a precise sketch with just a pencil and pad, you've probably used a set of lightly drawn guidelines to lay out your drawing first. You do the same thing in AutoCAD, but instead of lightly drawn guidelines, you can use any object you want. In AutoCAD, objects are easily modified or deleted, so you don't have to be as careful when adding guidelines.

Master It What is the name of the feature that lets you select exact locations on objects?

Solution Object Snap, or Osnap.

Use the AutoCAD modes as drafting tools. The main reason for using AutoCAD is to produce precision technical drawings. AutoCAD offers many tools to help you produce a drawing with the precision you need.

Master It What dialog box lets you set both the grid and snap spacing?

Solution The Drafting Settings dialog box.

Chapter 4: Organizing Objects with Blocks and Groups

Create and insert a symbol. If you have a symbol that you use often in a drawing, you can draw it once and then turn it into an AutoCAD block. A block can be placed in a drawing multiple times in any location, like a rubber stamp. A block is stored in a drawing as a block definition, which can be called up at any time.

Master It Name the dialog box used to create a block from objects in a drawing, and also name the tool used to open this dialog box.

Solution The Block Definition dialog box can be opened using the Create tool.

Modify a block. Once you've created a block, it isn't set in stone. One of the features of a block is that you can change the block definition and all of the copies of the block are updated to the new definition.

Master It What is the name of the tool used to "unblock" a block?

Solution You can use the Explode tool to break a block down to its component objects. Once this is done, you can modify the objects and then redefine the block.

Understand the annotation scale. In some cases, you'll want to create a block that is dependent on the drawing scale. You can create a block that adjusts itself to the scale of your drawing through the annotation scale feature. When the annotation scale feature is turned on for a block, the block can be set to appear at the correct size depending on the scale of your drawing.

Master It What setting in the Block Definition dialog box turns on the annotation scale feature, and how do you set the annotation scale of a block?

Solution The Annotative option in the Block Definition dialog box turns on the annotation scale feature. You can set the scales for a block by selecting the block, right-clicking, and selecting Object Scale ➤ Add/Delete Scales.

Group objects. Blocks can be used as a tool to group objects together, but blocks can be too rigid for some grouping applications. AutoCAD offers groups, which are collections of objects that are similar to blocks but aren't as rigidly defined.

Master It How are groups different from blocks?

Solution You can easily edit objects in a group by turning groups off with a Shift+Ctrl+A keystroke. Also, unlike blocks, groups don't have a single definition that's stored in the drawing and that defines the group's appearance. You can copy a group, but each copy is independent of the other groups.

Chapter 5: Keeping Track of Layers and Blocks

Organize information with layers. Layers are perhaps the most powerful feature in AutoCAD. They help to keep drawings well organized, and they give you control over the visibility of objects. They also let you control the appearance of your drawing by setting colors, lineweights, and linetypes.

Master It Describe the process of creating a layer.

Solution First, click the Layer Properties Manager tool in the Home tab's Layers panel. Second, click the New Layer button at the top of the palette. Finally, type the name for your new layer.

Control layer visibility. When a drawing becomes dense with information, it can be difficult to edit. If you've organized your drawing using layers, you can reduce its complexity by turning off layers that aren't important to your current session.

Master It Describe at least two methods for hiding a layer.

Solution Open the Layer Properties Manager, select a layer, and click the Freeze icon for the layer. You can also open the layer drop-down list in the Home tab's Layers panel and click the Freeze icon for the layer you want to hide. You can also use the On/Off (lightbulb) icon in the Layer Properties Manager or the layer drop-down list to change a layer's visibility.

Keep track of blocks and layers. At times, you may want a record of the layers or blocks in your drawing. You can create a list of layers using the log-file feature in AutoCAD.

Master It Where do you go to turn on the log-file feature?

Solution You can use the `Logfilemode` system variable.

Chapter 6: Editing and Reusing Data to Work Efficiently

Create and use templates. If you find that you're using the same settings when you create a new drawing file, you can set up an existing file the way you like and save it as a template. You can then use your saved template for any new drawings you create.

Master It Describe the method for saving a file as a template.

Solution After setting up a blank drawing with the settings you use most frequently, choose Save As from the Application menu. In the Save Drawing As dialog box, choose AutoCAD Drawing Template (*.dwt) from the Files Of Type drop-down list, give the file a name, and click Save. In the Template Options dialog box, enter a description and click OK to save the template.

Copy an object multiple times. Many tools in AutoCAD allow you to create multiple copies. The Array command offers a way to create circular copies, row and column copies, and copies that follow a path.

Master It What names are given to the three types of arrays offered in the Modify panel?

Solution Rectangular, polar, and path.

Develop your drawing. When laying down simple line work, you'll use a few tools frequently. The exercises in the early part of this book showed you some of these commonly used tools.

Master It What tool can you use to join two lines end to end?

Solution Fillet.

Find an exact distance along a curve. AutoCAD offers some tools that allow you to find an exact distance along a curve.

Master It Name the two tools that you can use to mark off exact distances along a curve.

Solution Measure and Divide.

Change the length of objects. You can accurately adjust the length of a line or arc in AutoCAD using a single command.

Master It What is the keyboard alias for the command that changes the length of objects?

Solution The command is Lengthen. You can also use len.

Create a new drawing by using parts from another drawing. You can save a lot of time by reusing parts of drawings. The Export command can help.

Master It True or false: The Export command saves only blocks as drawing files.

Solution False. You can use Export on any type of object or set of objects in a drawing.

Chapter 7: Mastering Viewing Tools, Hatches, and External References

Assemble the parts. Technical drawings are often made up of repetitive parts that are drawn over and over. AutoCAD makes quick work of repetitive elements in a drawing, as shown in the first part of this chapter.

Master It What is the object used as the basic building block for the floor plan drawing in the beginning of this chapter?

Solution Blocks of a typical unit plan are used to build a floor plan of an apartment building.

Take control of the AutoCAD display. Understanding the way the AutoCAD display works can save you time, especially in a complex drawing.

Master It Name the dialog box used to save views in AutoCAD. Describe how to recall a saved view.

Solution The View Manager dialog box allows you to save views. You can recall views by selecting them from the Views flyout on the View tab's Views panel.

Use hatch patterns in your drawings. Patterns can convey a lot of information at a glance. You can show the material of an object or you can indicate a type of view, like a cross section, by applying hatch patterns.

Master It How do you open the Hatch And Gradient dialog box?

Solution Choose Hatch from the Home tab's Draw panel, and then click the Hatch Settings tool in the Hatch Creation tab's Options panel title bar.

Understand the boundary hatch options. The hatch options give you control over the way that hatch patterns fill an enclosed area.

Master It Describe an island as it relates to boundary hatch patterns.

Solution An island is an enclosed object that is found in an area to be hatched.

Use external references. External references are drawing files that you've attached to the current drawing to include as part of the drawing. Because external references aren't part of the current file, they can be worked on at the same time as the referencing file.

Master It Describe how drawing files are attached as external references.

Solution Open the External References palette, click the Attach DWG tool at the upper left, and then locate and select the file you want to attach.

Chapter 8: Introducing Printing, Plotting, and Layouts

Understand the plotter settings. Unlike other types of documents, AutoCAD drawings can end up on nearly any size sheet of paper. To accommodate the range of paper sizes, the AutoCAD plotter settings are fairly extensive and give you a high level of control over your output.

Master It Name at least two of the settings available in the Plot Scale panel of the Plot dialog box.

Solution Fit To paper, Scale, Inches, mm, Scale Lineweights.

Use layout views to control how your plots look. The Layout tabs in AutoCAD offer a way to let you set up how a drawing will be plotted. You can think of the layout views as paste-up areas for your drawings.

Master It Name some of the items that you see in a layout view.

Solution Layout views show the paper orientation, plotter margins, and the location of your drawing on the final plotted output.

Add an output device. Typically, AutoCAD will use the Windows system printer as an output device, but often you will find that the printer you use is a dedicated plotter that is not connected to Windows in the usual way. AutoCAD lets you add custom plotters and printers through the Add-A-Plotter Wizard.

Master It How do you start the Add-A-Plotter Wizard?

Solution Click the Plotter Manager tool on the Output tab's Plot panel, and double-click the Add-A-Plotter Wizard application in the Plotters window.

Store a page setup. Most of the time, you will use the same plotter settings for your drawings. You can save plotter settings using the Page Setup feature.

Master It Describe a way to create a page setup. Describe how to retrieve a setup.

Solution Click the Page Setup Manager tool in the Output tab's Plot panel; then click New in the Page Setup Manager dialog box. Enter a name for your page setup in the New Page Setup dialog box and then click OK. When you plot your drawing, you can retrieve a page setup by selecting it from the Page Setup drop-down list in the Plot dialog box.

Chapter 9: Adding Text to Drawings

Prepare a drawing for text. AutoCAD offers an extensive set of features for adding text to a drawing, but you need to do a little prep work before you dive in.

Master It Name two things that you need to do to prepare a drawing for text.

Solution Set up a layer for your text. Create a text style for your drawing.

Set the annotation scale and add text. Before you start to add text, you should set the annotation scale for your drawing. Once this is done, you can begin to add text.

Master It In a sentence or two, briefly describe the purpose of the annotation scale feature. Name the tool that you use to add text to a drawing.

Solution The annotation scale feature converts your text size to the proper height for the scale of your drawing. To add text to a drawing, use the Mtext tool.

Explore text formatting in AutoCAD. Because text styles contain font and text-size settings, you can usually set up a text style and then begin to add text to your drawing. For those special cases where you need to vary the text height and font or other text features, you can use the Formatting panel of the Text Editor tab.

Master It What text formatting tool can you use to change text to boldface type?

Solution The Bold button.

Add simple single-line text objects. In many situations, you need only a single word or a short string of text. AutoCAD offers the single-line text object for these instances.

Master It Describe the methods for starting the single-line text command.

Solution Click the Single Line tool in the Annotate tab's Text panel or the Home tab's Annotation panel. Enter DT↵ at the Command prompt.

Use the Check Spelling feature. It isn't uncommon for a drawing to contain the equivalent of several pages of text, and the likelihood of having misspelled words can be high. AutoCAD offers the Check Spelling feature to help you keep your spelling under control.

Master It What option do you select in the Check Spelling dialog box when it finds a misspelled word and you want to accept the suggestion it offers?

Solution Change.

Find and replace text. A common activity when editing technical drawings is finding and replacing a word throughout a drawing.

Master It True or false: The Find And Replace feature in AutoCAD works very differently from the find-and-replace feature in other programs.

Solution False.

Chapter 10: Using Fields and Tables

Use fields to associate text with drawing properties. Fields are a special type of text object that can be linked to object properties. They can help to automate certain text-related tasks.

Master It Name two uses for fields that you learned about in the first part of this chapter.

Solution Fields can be used to update text that labels a block. They can also be used to update text and report the area enclosed by a polyline.

Add tables to your drawing. The Tables feature can help you make quick work of schedules and other tabular data that you want to include in a drawing.

Master It What is the name of the dialog box that appears when you click the Table tool in the Annotate tab's Tables panel?

Solution Insert Table.

Edit the table line work. Because tables include line work to delineate their different cells, AutoCAD gives you control over table borders and lines.

Master It How do you get to the Cell Border Properties dialog box?

Solution Select the cell or cells in the table, right-click, and choose Borders.

Add formulas to cells. Tables can also function like a spreadsheet by allowing you to add formulas to cells.

Master It What type of text object lets you add formulas to cells?

Solution Field.

Import and export tables. The Table feature allows you to import Microsoft Excel spreadsheets into AutoCAD.

Master It Describe how to import a spreadsheet from Excel into AutoCAD.

Solution Open the spreadsheet, and select the cells you want to import. Right-click and select Copy to copy the spreadsheet data into the Clipboard. In AutoCAD, choose Paste Special from the Paste flyout of the Home tab's Clipboard panel. In the Paste Special dialog box, select AutoCAD Entities and click OK.

Create table styles. Table styles can save time by enabling you to set up preformatted tables with a title, column headings, and other data.

Master It Name the four groups in the New Table Style dialog box.

Solution Starting Table, General, Cell Styles, and Cell Style Preview.

Chapter 11: Using Dimensions

Understand the components of a dimension. Before you start to dimension with AutoCAD, become familiar with the different parts of a dimension. Doing so will help you set up your dimensions to fit the style you need.

Master It Name a few of the dimension components.

Solution Dimension line, dimension text, extension line, and arrow.

Create a dimension style. As you become more familiar with technical drawing and drafting, you'll learn that there are standard formats for drawing dimensions. Arrows, text size, and even the way dimension lines are drawn are all subject to a standard format. Fortunately, AutoCAD offers dimension styles that let you set up your dimension format once and then call up that format whenever you need it.

Master It What is the name of the dialog box that lets you manage dimension styles and how do you open it?

Solution The Dimension Style Manager is the name of the dialog box. You can open it by clicking the Dimension Style tool in the Annotate tab's Dimensions panel title bar.

Draw linear dimensions. The most common dimension that you'll use is the linear dimension. Knowing how to place a linear dimension is a big first step in learning how to dimension in AutoCAD.

Master It Name the three locations for which you are prompted when placing a linear dimension.

Solution First extension line origin, second extension line origin, and dimension line location.

Edit dimensions. Dimensions often change in the course of a project, so you should know how to make changes to dimension text or other parts of a dimension.

Master It How do you start the command to edit dimension text?

Solution Enter **ED**↵ at the Command prompt.

Dimension nonorthogonal objects. Not everything you dimension will use linear dimensions. AutoCAD offers a set of dimension tools for dimensioning objects that aren't made up of straight lines.

Master It Name some of the types of objects for which a linear dimension isn't appropriate.

Solution Arc and angle between two lines. Linear dimensions can be used for circles in certain situations.

Add a note with a leader arrow. In addition to dimensions, you'll probably add lots of notes with arrows pointing to features in a design. AutoCAD offers the multileader for this purpose.

Master It What two types of objects does the multileader combine?

Solution Leader lines (arrowhead and line) and text.

Apply ordinate dimensions. When accuracy counts, ordinate dimensions are often used because they measure distances that are similar to coordinates from a single feature.

Master It What AutoCAD feature do you use for ordinate dimensions that aren't strictly associated with dimensions?

Solution UCS.

Add tolerance notation. Mechanical drafting often requires the use of special notation to describe tolerances. AutoCAD offers some predefined symbols that address the need to include tolerance notation in a drawing.

Master It How do you open the Geometric Tolerance dialog box?

Solution Click the Tolerance tool in the Dimensions panel or type **TOL**↵.

Chapter 12: Using Attributes

Create attributes. Attributes are a great tool for storing data with drawn objects. You can include as little or as much data as you like in an AutoCAD block.

Master It What is the name of the object that you must include in a block to store data?

Solution Attribute definition.

Edit attributes. The data that you include in a block is easily changed. You may have several copies of a block, each of which must contain its own unique set of data.

Master It What is the simplest way to gain access to a block's attribute data?

Solution Double-click the block to open the Enhanced Attribute Editor.

Extract and export attribute information. Attribute data can be extracted in a number of ways so that you can keep track of the data in a drawing.

Master It How do you start the data-extraction process?

Solution Click the Extract Data tool in the Insert tab's Linking & Extraction panel to open the Data Extraction Wizard.

Chapter 13: Copying Existing Drawings from Other Sources

Convert paper drawings into AutoCAD files. AutoCAD gives you some great tools that let you convert your paper drawings into AutoCAD files. Several options are available. Depending on your needs, you'll find at least one solution that will allow you to convert your drawings quickly.

Master It Describe the different methods available in AutoCAD for converting paper drawings into CAD files.

Solution The methods are scaling directly from a drawing, scanning and converting with a third-party program, and scanning to a raster file that can then be imported into AutoCAD to be traced over.

Import a raster image. You can use bitmap raster images as backgrounds for your CAD drawings or as underlay drawings that you can trace over.

Master It Import a raster image of your choice, and use the AutoCAD drawing tools to trace over your image.

Solution Click Attach from the Insert tab's Reference panel, or type **Attach↵** to open the Select Reference File dialog box. Locate and select the raster image file that you want to import. Click Open to open the Attach Image dialog box and then click OK. Specify an insertion point and scale factor.

Work with a raster image. Once imported, raster images can be adjusted for size, brightness, contrast, and transparency.

Master It Import a raster image of your choice, and fade the image so that it appears to blend into the background with less contrast.

Solution Click a raster image's border to expose the Image tab. Click and drag the Fade slider to the right so that it's near the middle of the slider scale, or enter 50 in the Fade box to the right of the slider. Click OK. The raster image appears faded.

Work with PDF files. AutoCAD allows you to import and control the display of PDF files. This is significant since the PDF file format is so prevalent in the business world.

Master It In a PDF that includes layers, how do you gain access to the layer settings?

Solution Click the imported PDF drawing, and then click the Edit Layers tool that appears in the PDF Underlay tab. You can then control layer visibility through the Underlay Layers dialog box.

Use a geolocation map. You can include a correctly scaled background aerial view or road map of a site in your drawing to help you better coordinate your design with site conditions.

Master It Name three types of information that you can use to find a site in the Geographic Location dialog box.

Solution You can enter latitude/longitude, street addresses, or name of a site.

Chapter 14: Advanced Editing and Organizing

Use external references (Xrefs). You've seen how you can use Xrefs to quickly build variations of a floor plan that contain repetitive elements. This isn't necessarily the only way to use Xrefs, but the basic idea of how to use Xrefs is presented in the early exercises.

Master It Try putting together another floor plan that contains nothing but the Unit2 plan.

Solution Replace the eight studio units in the `Common.dwg` file with four of the Unit2 plans.

Manage layers. Once you start to edit complex drawings, you'll find that you'll want to save the On/Off or Freeze/Thaw layer states so that you can access parts of a drawing more easily. The Layer States Manager lets you save as many layer conditions as you may need in the course of a project.

Master It What part of the Layer States Manager dialog box lets you control the layer properties that are affected by a saved layer state?

Solution The Layer Properties To Restore group in the expanded view of the Layer States Manager.

Use advanced tools: Filter and Quick Select. The Filter and Quick Select tools are great for isolating objects in a crowded drawing. You can select objects by their color or layer assignment. You can select all instances of a specific block.

Master It True or false: The Quick Select tool lets you select a set of objects to limit your selections.

Solution True.

Use the QuickCalc calculator. The QuickCalc calculator offers many standard calculator tools plus a few that you may not see in other calculators.

Master It Name a few of the more unusual features offered by the QuickCalc calculator.

Solution Add feet and inch lengths; find percentages of lengths; and obtain coordinates, lengths, and angles graphically from a drawing.

Chapter 15: Laying Out Your Printer Output

Understand model space and paper space. AutoCAD offers two viewing modes for viewing and printing your drawings. Model space is where you do most of your work; it's the view that you see when you create a new file. Layouts, also called paper space, are views that let you arrange the layout of your drawing, similar to the way that you would in a page-layout program.

Master It What are three ways of moving from model space to paper space?

Solution You can hover over the drawing tab above the drawing area to display the Model and Layout preview panels, or you can use the Model and Layout tabs in the lower-left corner of the drawing area. Finally, you can use the keyboard shortcuts Ctrl+PgUp and Ctrl+PgDn.

Work with paper space viewports. While in paper space, you can create views in your drawing using viewports. You can have several viewports, each showing a different part of your drawing.

Master It Name some of the ways that you can enlarge a view in a viewport.

Solution You can double-click inside a viewport and then use the Zoom tools to enlarge the view. You can also use the Viewport Scale tool in the status bar to set the scale of the view.

Create odd-shaped viewports. Most of the time, you'll probably use rectangular viewports, but you have the option to create a viewport of any shape.

Master It Describe the process for creating a circular viewport.

Solution In paper space, draw a circle. Next, click Object from the Viewport flyout in the Layout tab's Layout Viewports panel, and then follow the prompts.

Understand lineweights, linetypes, and dimensions in paper space. You can get an accurate view of how your drawing will look on paper by making a few adjustments to AutoCAD. Your layout view will reflect how your drawing will look when plotted.

Master It Name the two dialog boxes that you must use to display lineweights in a layout view.

Solution You use the Layer Properties Manager (to set up lineweights) and the Lineweight Settings dialog box.

Chapter 16: Making "Smart" Drawings with Parametric Tools

Use parametric drawing tools. Parametric drawing tools enable you to create an assembly of objects that are linked to each other based on geometric or dimensional properties. With the parametric drawing tools, you can create a drawing that automatically adjusts the size of all its components when you change a single dimension.

Master It Name two examples given in the beginning of the chapter of a mechanical assembly that can be shown using parametric drawing tools.

Solution The examples are a crankshaft and piston and a Luxo lamp.

Connect objects with geometric constraints. You can link objects together so that they maintain a particular orientation to each other.

Master It Name at least six of the geometric constraints available in AutoCAD.

Solution The constraints are Coincident, Collinear, Concentric, Fix, Parallel, Perpendicular, Horizontal, Vertical, Tangent, Smooth, Symmetric, and Equal.

Control sizes with dimensional constraints. Dimensional constraints, in conjunction with geometric constraints, let you apply dimensions to an assembly of objects to control the size of the assembly.

Master It Name at least four dimensional constraints.

Solution The dimensional constraints are Linear, Horizontal, Vertical, Aligned, Radius, Diameter, and Angular. In addition, a tool allows you to convert a normal dimension into a dimensional constraint.

Use formulas to control dimensions. Dimensional constraints allow you to link dimensions of objects so that if one dimension changes, another dimension follows.

Master It What example was used to show how formulas could be used with dimensional constraints?

Solution A circle's diameter was linked to the width dimension of a drawing of a simple part.

Put constraints to use. Constraints can be used in a variety of ways to simulate the behavior of real objects.

Master It Name at least three geometric or dimensional constraints used in the `piston.dwg` sample file to help simulate the motion of a piston and crankshaft.

Solution The geometric constraints used were Horizontal, Parallel, Fix, and Coincident. The dimensional constraints used were Horizontal, Vertical, Aligned, and Diameter.

Chapter 17: Using Dynamic Blocks

Work with the Block Editor. To create dynamic blocks, you need to become familiar with the Block Editor. You can use the Block Editor to modify existing blocks in your drawing.

Master It What does the Edit Block Definition dialog box allow you to do?

Solution The Edit Block Definition dialog box lets you select the block that you want to edit from a list of blocks in the drawing.

Create a dynamic block. A dynamic block is one to which you add grips so that you can modify the block in a number of ways.

Master It Name some of the features of the Block Editor that let you add additional grip-editing functions to a block.

Solution Geometric constraints, dimensional constraints, parameters, and actions.

Add Scale and Stretch actions to a parameter. You can set up a dynamic block to perform multiple operations with a single grip.

Master It What do you need to do to have one grip perform two functions?

Solution Use a single parameter to control two actions.

Add more than one parameter for multiple grip functions. In addition to having one grip perform multiple operations, you can add as many grips as you need to make your block even more customizable.

Master It What feature do you use to set up a list of options for a block?

Solution The Block Table.

Create multiple shapes in one block. Many of the dynamic block functions let you adjust the shape of the original block. Another feature lets you choose completely different shapes for the block.

Master It When a block uses the Visibility parameter to set up different shapes, how do you select a different block shape in the drawing?

Solution Click the block, and then click the Visibility grip. A list appears showing the different shapes that are available.

Rotate objects in unison. Blocks can be set up so that the action of one set of objects affects another set. This chapter gives the example of rotating objects in unison.

Master It Name the dimensional constraint that was used in the object rotation example in this chapter.

Solution Angular.

Fill in a space automatically with objects. A dynamic block can help you automate the addition of repetitive elements to your drawing.

Master It What is the name of the action used to produce copies of a block object at regular intervals in both the x- and y-axes when the block is stretched?

Solution The Array action.

Chapter 18: Drawing Curves

Create and edit polylines. Polylines are extremely versatile. You can use them in just about any situation where you need to draw line work that is continuous. For this reason, you'll want to master polylines early in your AutoCAD training.

Master It Draw the part shown here.

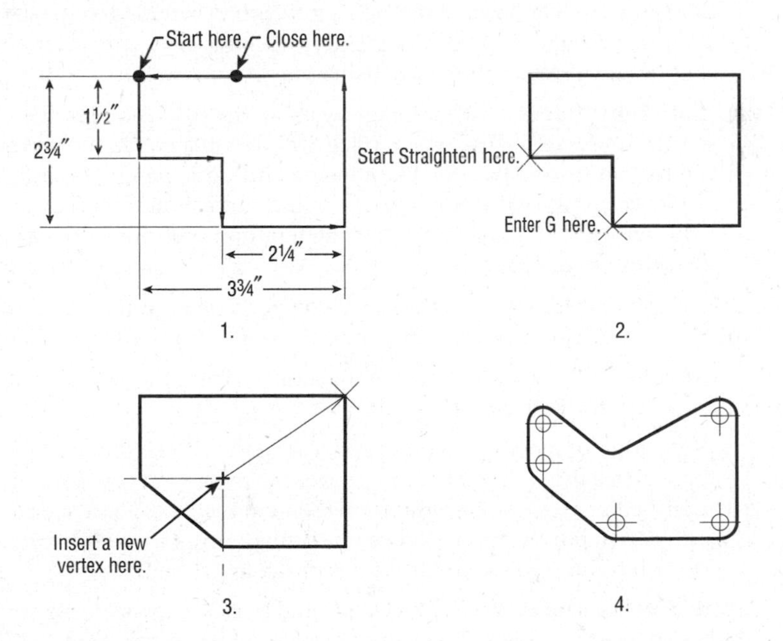

Solution There are many ways to create this drawing, including using the following instructions:

1. Open a new file called PART14 using the acad.dwt template. Set the Snap spacing to 0.25, and be sure that Snap mode is on. Use the Pline command to draw the object shown just before this step. Also, use the Units dialog box to change the units to Architectural. Start at the upper-left corner and draw in the direction indicated by the arrows. Use the Close option to add the last line segment.

2. Start the Edit Polyline tool, select the polyline, and then type **E**↵ to issue the Edit Vertex option. Press ↵ until the X mark moves to the corner labeled "Start Straighten here." Enter **S**↵ for the Straighten option.
3. At the `Enter an option` prompt, press ↵ twice to move the X to the other corner labeled "Enter G here" in step 2 of the drawing. Press **G**↵ for Go to straighten the polyline between the two selected corners.
4. Press ↵ three times to move the X to the upper-right corner, and then enter **I**↵ for Insert. Pick a point as shown in step 3 of the drawing. The polyline changes to reflect the new vertex. Enter **X**↵ to exit the Edit Vertex option, and then press ↵ to exit the Pedit command.
5. Start the Fillet command, use the Radius option to set the fillet radius to 0.30, and then use the Polyline option and pick the polyline that you just edited. All of the corners become rounded to the 0.30 radius. Add the 0.15 radius circles, as shown in step 4 of the drawing, and exit and save the file.

Create a polyline spline curve. Polylines can be used to draw fairly accurate renditions of spline curves. This feature of polylines makes them very useful AutoCAD objects.

Master It Try drawing the outline of an object that contains no or few straight lines, as shown in the file `lowerfairing.jpg`, which is included in the Chapter 18 sample files. You can use the methods described in Chapter 13 to import a raster image of your object and then trace over the image using polyline splines.

Solution Import a raster image by using the Attach tool in the Insert tab's Reference panel. Use the Polyline tool to trace over the image. Use short, straight polyline segments while you trace. After you place the polyline, double-click it and select the Spline option. After you change the polyline to a spline curve, it may shift away from the original line over which you traced. Click the polyline, and then adjust the grips so that the line fits over the raster image.

Create and edit true spline curves. If you need an accurate spline curve, you'll want to use the Spline tool. Spline objects offer many fine-tuning options that you won't find with polylines.

Master It Try tracing over the same image from the earlier "Master It" section, but this time use the Spline tool.

Solution Import a raster image by using the Attach tool in the Insert tab's Reference panel. Use the Spline tool to trace over the image. As you draw the spline, select control points that are close together for tighter curves. The closer the control points, the tighter you can make the curve. Notice that, unlike using a polyline spline, with this method you don't have to readjust the curve after it's been placed.

Mark divisions on curves. The Divide and Measure tools offer a quick way to mark off distances on a curved object. This can be a powerful resource in AutoCAD that you may use often.

Master It Mark off 12 equal divisions of the spline curve that you drew in the previous "Master It" exercise.

Solution Choose Divide from the expanded Draw panel, click the spline, and then enter **12**↵. If you don't see the points that mark off the divisions, type **DDPTYPE**↵, select the X point style, and click OK.

Chapter 19: Getting and Exchanging Data from Drawings

Find the area of closed boundaries. There are a number of ways to find the area of a closed boundary. The easiest way is also perhaps the least obvious.

Master It Which AutoCAD feature would you use to find the area of an irregular shape, such as a pond or lake, quickly?

Solution Hatch.

Get general information. A lot of information that is stored in AutoCAD drawings can tell you about the files. You can find out how much memory a file uses as well as the amount of time that has been spent editing the file.

Master It What feature lets you store your own searchable information about a drawing file, and how do you get to this feature?

Solution The Drawing Properties dialog box. You can open it by choosing Drawing Utilities ➤ Drawing Properties from the Application menu.

Use the DXF file format to exchange CAD data with other programs. Autodesk created the DXF file format as a means of sharing vector drawings with other programs.

Master It Name some of the versions of AutoCAD that you can export to using the Save As option.

Solution 2013, 2010, 2007, 2004, 2000, and R12.

Use AutoCAD drawings in page layout programs. AutoCAD drawings find their way into all types of documents, including brochures and technical manuals. Users are often asked to convert their CAD drawings into formats that can be read by page layout software.

Master It Name some file formats, by filename extension or type, that page layout programs can accept.

Solution PDF (`.pdf`), WMF (`.wmf`), EPS (`.eps.`), and a wide variety of bitmap image files.

Use OLE to import data. You can import data into AutoCAD from a variety of sources. Most sources, such as bitmap images and text, can be imported as native AutoCAD objects. Other sources may need to be imported as OLE objects.

Master It To link imported data to a source program through OLE, what dialog box would you use?

Solution Paste Special.

Chapter 20: Creating 3D Drawings

Know the 3D Modeling workspace When you work in 3D, you need a different set of tools from those for 2D drafting. AutoCAD offers the 3D Modeling workspace, which provides the tools that you need to create 3D models.

Master It Name some of the Ribbon panels that are unique to the 3D Modeling workspace.

Solution Modeling, Mesh, Solid Editing, Primitive, Boolean, Section, Selection, Create, Edit, Control Vertices, Curves, Project Geometry, Analysis, Mesh Edit, Convert Mesh, Lights, Materials, Camera, and Render.

Draw in 3D using solids. AutoCAD offers a type of object called a 3D solid that lets you quickly create and edit shapes.

Master It What does the Presspull command do?

Solution The command dynamically modifies objects by extrusion and offset. It can add to or subtract from a shape by extruding a defined area.

Create 3D forms from 2D shapes. The Modeling panel offers a set of basic 3D shapes, but other tools enable you to create virtually any shape you want from 2D drawings.

Master It Name the command that lets you change a closed 2D polyline into a 3D solid.

Solution Extrude.

Isolate coordinates with point filters. When you're working in 3D, selecting points can be a complicated task. AutoCAD offers point filters or coordinates to let you specify the individual x-, y-, and z-coordinates of a location in space.

Master It What does the .XY point filter do?

Solution The .XY point filter uses the X and Y coordinates of a selected object, allowing the user to enter an alternate Z value. It enables the user to use certain coordinates from existing objects without having to determine what those values are as well as negating the need for construction lines.

Move around your model. Getting the view you want in a 3D model can be tricky.

Master It Where is the drop-down list that lets you select a view from a list of predefined 3D views?

Solution Use the View command to select a predefined view. It appears in several places: in the top-left corner of the drawing area, in the View panel on the Home tab, and in the Views panel on the Visualization tab.

Get a visual effect. At certain points in your model making, you'll want to view your 3D model with surface colors and even material assignments. AutoCAD offers several ways to do this.

Master It What are the steps to take to change the view from Wireframe to Conceptual?

Solution Use the Visual Styles drop-down list. It can be found in the upper-left corner of the drawing area, in the View panel on the Home tab, or in the Visual Styles panel on the Visualization tab. Click the Visual Styles drop-down, and select the Conceptual option.

Turn a 3D view into a 2D AutoCAD drawing. Sometimes, it's helpful to convert a 3D model view into a 2D AutoCAD drawing. AutoCAD offers the Flatshot tool, which quickly converts a 3D view into a 2D line drawing.

Master It What type of object does Flatshot create?

Solution This tool creates a 2D representation of all 3D objects based on the current view in the form of a 2D block.

Chapter 21: Using Advanced 3D Features

Master the User Coordinate System. The User Coordinate System (UCS) is a vital key to editing in 3D space. If you want to master 3D modeling, you should become familiar with this tool.

Master It Name some of the predefined UCS planes.

Solution Top, Bottom, Front, Back, Left, Right.

Understand the UCS options. You can set up the UCS orientation for any situation. It isn't limited to the predefined settings.

Master It Briefly describe some of the ways that you can set up a UCS.

Solution There are several ways to establish a UCS. You can orient the UCS by object. You can align the UCS with the face of an object, by a view, or about an axis. Whenever a UCS is created, it can be saved by giving it a name, and it can be recalled at any time. You can also choose the previous UCS used or return to World Coordinates. All of these can be set up with the UCS command.

Use viewports to aid in 3D drawing. In some 3D modeling operations, it helps to have several different views of the model through the Viewports feature.

Master It Name some of the predefined standard viewports offered in the Viewports dialog box.

Solution A single viewport, two viewports, three viewports, or four viewports are offered. Each has combinations of vertical and horizontal arrangements as well as a large viewport at the right, left, top, or bottom, along with smaller viewports on the opposite sides. The four viewport options can have four equal rectangles or one large viewport with three equal viewports at the top, bottom, left, or right.

Use the array tools. The array tools—Rectangular, Path, and Polar Array—allow you to create 3D arrays dynamically.

Master It What prompt in the Array command will allow you to have a 3D array?

Solution The Levels prompt will create a 3D array.

Create complex 3D surfaces. You aren't limited to straight, flat surfaces in AutoCAD. You can create just about any shape that you want, including curved surfaces.

Master It What tool did you use in this chapter's butterfly chair exercise to convert a surface into a solid?

Solution We used the Thicken tool to convert the surface into a solid.

Create spiral forms. Spiral forms frequently occur in nature, so it's no wonder that we often use spirals in our own designs. Spirals are seen in screws, stairs, and ramps as well as in other man-made forms.

Master It Name the tools used in the example in the section "Creating Spiral Forms," and name two elements that are needed to create a spiral.

Solution The Helix tool and the Sweep tool. To make a helix, you need the following elements: number of turns, base radius, top radius, helix height, turn height, and the twist direction.

Create surface models. You can create a 3D surface by connecting a series of lines that define a surface contour. You can create anything from a 3D landscape to a car fender using this method.

Master It What is the tool used to convert a series of lines into a 3D surface?

Solution The Loft tool will link a series of objects into a 3D surface.

Move objects in 3D space. You can move objects in 3D space using tools that are similar to those for 2D drafting. But when it comes to editing objects, 3D modeling is much more complex than 2D drafting.

Master It What does the Rotate gizmo do?

Solution The Rotate gizmo restrains an object's rotation about the x-, y-, or z-axis to assist in properly rotating objects. It will allow you to rotate a 3D object in one axis at a time.

Chapter 22: Editing and Visualizing 3D Solids

Understand solid modeling. Solid modeling lets you build 3D models by creating and joining 3D shapes called solids. There are several built-in solid shapes called primitives, and you can create others using the Extrude tool.

Master It Name some of the built-in solid primitives available in AutoCAD.

Solution Box, Cylinder, Cone, Sphere, Pyramid, Wedge, Torus.

Create solid forms. You can use Boolean operations to sculpt 3D solids into the shape you want. Two solids can be joined to form a more complex one, or you can remove one solid from another.

Master It Name the three Boolean operations that you can use on solids.

Solution Union, Subtract, Intersect.

Create complex solids. Besides the primitives, you can create your own shapes based on 2D polylines.

Master It Name three tools that let you convert closed polylines and circles into 3D solids.

Solution Extrude, Sweep, Revolve.

Edit solids. After you've created a solid, you can make changes to it using the solid-editing tools offered on the Solid Editing panel.

Master It Name at least four of the tools found on the Solid Editing panel.

Solution Union, Subtract, Intersect, Interfere, Slice, Thicken, Extract Edges, Imprint, Color Edges, Copy Edges, Extrude Faces, Taper Faces, Move Faces, Copy Faces, Offset Faces, Delete Faces, Rotate Faces, Color Faces, Separate, Clean, Shell, Check.

Streamline the 2D drawing process. You can create 3D orthogonal views of your 3D model to create standard 2D mechanical drawings.

Master It What is the name of the tool in the expanded Section panel that lets you create a 2D drawing of a 3D model?

Solution Flatshot.

Visualize solids. In addition to viewing your 3D model in a number of different orientations, you can view it as if it were transparent or cut in half.

Master It What is the name of the command that lets you create a cut view of your 3D model?

Solution Section Plane.

Chapter 23: Exploring 3D Mesh and Surface Modeling

Create a simple 3D mesh. Mesh modeling allows you to create more organic 3D forms by giving you unique smoothing and editing tools. You can start your mesh model by creating a basic shape using the mesh primitives.

Master It Name the seven mesh primitives available on the Primitives panel of the Mesh Modeling tab.

Solution Mesh Box, Mesh Cone, Mesh Cylinder, Mesh Pyramid, Mesh Sphere, Mesh Wedge, Mesh Torus.

Edit faces and edges. The ability to edit faces and edges is essential to creating complex shapes with mesh objects.

Master It Name the tool that is used to divide a face into multiple faces.

Solution Split Face.

Create mesh surfaces. The Mesh primitives let you create shapes that enclose a volume. If you just want to model a smooth, curved surface in 3D, you might find the surface mesh tools helpful.

Master It How many objects are needed to use the Edge Surface tool?

Solution Four.

Convert meshes to solids. You can convert a mesh into a 3D solid to take advantage of many of the solid-editing tools available.

Master It Name at least two tools that you can use on a solid that you cannot use on a mesh.

Solution Union, Subtract, Intersect, Slice, Thicken, Imprint, Interfere, Offset Edge, Solidedit.

Understand 3D surfaces. 3D surfaces can be created using some of the same tools you use to create 3D solids.

Master It Name at least two tools that you can use to create both 3D solids and 3D surfaces.

Solution Loft, Sweep, Extrude, Revolve.

Edit 3D surfaces. AutoCAD offers a wide range of tools that are unique to 3D surfaces.

Master It Name at least four tools devoted to CV editing.

Solution Surface CV Show, Surface CV Hide, Surface Rebuild, Surface CV Add, Surface CV Remove, CV Edit Bar, Convert to NURBS.

Chapter 24: Customizing Toolbars, Menus, Linetypes, and Hatch Patterns

Use workspaces. Often with AutoCAD, you find that you have different sets of panels or toolbars open to perform specific tasks. You might have one set of Ribbon panels for editing text and dimensions, whereas another set is more useful for design. Using workspaces is a great way to organize your different editing modes.

Master It Where do you find the Customize option for workspaces?

Solution The Workspace drop-down menu or the Workspace Switching tool.

Customize the user interface. In addition to using workspaces to organize tools and Ribbon panels, you can customize the AutoCAD interface to make it fit the way you like to work. You can add tools to Ribbon panels, or you can even create your own tools for operations you perform frequently.

Master It What does the Customizations In All Files group display?

Solution Interface elements like toolbars, menus, Ribbon panels, and so on.

Create macros in tools and menus. A macro is a set of instructions that performs more complex operations than single commands. Macros are often built on commands with additional predefined responses to help speed data input.

Master It What does the `^C` do in a macro?

Solution The `^C` is equivalent to pressing the Esc key.

Edit keyboard shortcuts. Keyboard shortcuts can help improve your speed when drawing in AutoCAD. They can reduce several clicks of the mouse to a simple keystroke. AutoCAD lets you create custom shortcuts for your favorite commands.

Master It What is the name of the feature that lets you record and play back actions?

Solution Action Recorder.

Save, load, and unload your customizations. To keep your customizations organized, you can save new toolbars, menus, and Ribbons as files that you can load on demand. When you save your custom elements as a file, you can move them to other computers. In addition, you can use the cloud to synchronize your custom settings with other computers.

Master It Name the feature that lets you synchronize your custom settings from a cloud source.

Solution Autodesk® 360.

Understand the DIESEL macro language. If you're adventurous, you may want to try your hand at creating more complex macros. The DIESEL macro language is an easy introduction to AutoCAD macro customization, and it is most useful in controlling the behavior in menu options.

Master It What does the expression `$(getvar, Blipmode)` do?

Solution It returns 1 or 0 depending on the current state of the `Blipmode` system variable.

Create custom linetypes. AutoCAD offers a number of noncontinuous linetypes, and you may find them adequate for most of your work. But every now and then, you may need a specific linetype that isn't available. Creating custom linetypes is easy when you understand the process.

Master It What is the purpose of a negative value in the linetype code?

Solution A blank or break in the line.

Create hatch patterns. Like linetypes, the hatch patterns provided by AutoCAD will probably fill most of your needs. But every now and then you may need to produce a specific pattern.

Master It How are a hatch pattern code and a linetype code similar?

Solution They both use numeric values to describe lines.

Chapter 25: Managing and Sharing Your Drawings

Share drawings online. As a drafter or designer, you'll likely be involved in collaborative efforts, which means that you'll have to share your work with others. The Internet has made it much easier to do this.

Master It Why is eTransmit important for sending AutoCAD drawings over the Internet?

Solution An AutoCAD drawing can have many different external files associated with it, such as fonts, Xrefs, and image files. eTransmit offers a quick way to gather these files into one place or into a single archive file.

Publish your drawings. Autodesk offers the PDF drawing format, which lets non-CAD users view and add comments to simplified versions of your drawings. You can use the Publish feature to create a single PDF file from several drawings.

Master It True or false: The Publish feature can be used to plot multiple drawings in the background.

Solution True.

Get started with A360 Drive. A360 Drive makes sharing files and exchanging design ideas much easier.

Master It Name the feature that lets you revert a revised drawing to its prior state.

Solution Versions.

Manage your drawings with DesignCenter and the tool palettes. DesignCenter is a great tool for managing your drawings' resources, like blocks, custom linetypes, and other elements.

Master It True or false: DesignCenter has the capacity to scale a block automatically to the correct size when moving from metric to Imperial drawings.

Solution True.

Establish office standards. AutoCAD allows for a wide range of settings in a drawing. For this reason, it's a good idea to create standards for the way drawings are set up.

Master It Name the filename extension for an AutoCAD drawing standards file.

Solution `.dws`.

Convert multiple layer settings. If you exchange files with another office, you may find that their layer scheme is different than yours. AutoCAD offers the Layer Translator to help you translate layer names from an unfamiliar drawing to names with which you're more comfortable.

Master It Name the filename extensions of the types of files that you can use as a template for layer name translations.

Solution `.dwg`, `.dws`, and `.dwt`.

Appendix B

Installing and Setting Up AutoCAD

This appendix gives you information about installing Autodesk® AutoCAD® 2018 software on your system and describes the system parameters that you should set to configure AutoCAD to meet the needs of your operating environment. Throughout this appendix, the system variable associated with a setting, when available, is included at the end of an option description, enclosed in brackets. System variables are settings that enable you to control the behavior of AutoCAD when you're using commands and features. You'll find a detailed description of the AutoCAD system variables on the AutoCAD 2018 Help website.

Before Installing AutoCAD

Before you begin the installation process, be sure that you have at least 6 GB of free disk space. You should also have at least an additional 100 MB of free disk space for AutoCAD temporary files and swap files, plus another 20 MB for the tutorial files that you'll create. AutoCAD will work with Microsoft Windows 7, 8, or 10. AutoCAD also works with Internet Explorer 11, Google Chrome v33, Mozilla Firefox v19, and Apple Safari v5.1.

For 2D work, you'll also need a dual-core processor with at least 2 GB of RAM and a video card that supports at least 1366 by 768 resolution and True Color.

For serious 3D work, Autodesk recommends at least 8 GB of RAM, 6 GB of free disk space (not including the AutoCAD installation), and a 128 MB or greater Direct3D-capable workstation-class graphics card. Autodesk has a list of certified graphics cards for 3D modeling. This list is always being updated, so check the Autodesk website for the latest information.

Single-user systems have a 30-day grace period, so you can install and use AutoCAD without entering an authorization code right away. You can authorize your installation over the Internet at any time within the 30-day grace period as indicated when you first start AutoCAD. The trial software available on the Autodesk website can't be authorized unless you purchase a license, so be sure to have a good block of free time to study AutoCAD before you install it.

Proceeding with the Installation

AutoCAD 2018 installs like most other Windows programs, but you should know a few things before you start.

Installing AutoCAD is straightforward. AutoCAD uses an installation wizard like most other Windows programs. Here are some guidelines to follow during the installation process:

- Before you start, make sure you have enough disk space, and also make sure no other programs are running. If you purchased a license, you'll need your AutoCAD serial number and product key. If you're installing the trial version from the Autodesk website, select the "I want to try this product for 30 days" option on the Product Information page of the installation wizard.
- Typically, the AutoCAD installation program starts automatically when you double-click on the installation file. After the program launches, follow the directions in the installation wizard.

If you have an earlier release of AutoCAD installed on your PC, you will see the Migrate Custom Settings dialog box when you first start AutoCAD 2018. This dialog box enables you to import custom settings selectively from your prior AutoCAD release. If you do not want to import settings, you can click the Cancel button in the dialog box.

Configuring AutoCAD

In the following sections, you'll learn how to configure AutoCAD to work in the way you that want it to function. You can configure AutoCAD at any time during an AutoCAD session by using the Options dialog box.

The exercises in this book assume that you're using the default Options settings. As you become more familiar with the workings of AutoCAD, you may want to adjust the way that AutoCAD works by using the Options dialog box. You can also set many of the options in the Options dialog box through system variables. You can only access the Options dialog box, however, when a new or existing drawing is open.

Open a new or existing drawing and then choose Options from the Application menu, or type **options**↵ at the Command prompt to open the Options dialog box, which has the tabs and settings described in the following sections.

Many of the options in the Options dialog box show an AutoCAD file icon. This icon indicates that the option's setting is saved with individual files instead of being saved as part of the default AutoCAD settings. Other options, such as the User Profiles and command alias settings, can be exported or imported using the Migrate Custom Settings feature. This feature can be found in the Windows Start menu under All Programs ➢ Autodesk ➢ AutoCAD 2018 ➢ Migrate Custom Settings.

The Files Tab

You use the options on the Files tab (see Figure B.1) to tell AutoCAD where to place or find the files that it needs to operate. It uses a hierarchical list, similar to the one presented by Windows File Explorer. You first see the general topics in the Search Paths, File Names, and File Locations list box. You can expand any item in the list by clicking its plus sign.

The following are descriptions of each item in the list box. Chances are that you won't have to use most of them, but you may change others occasionally.

FIGURE B.1
The Files tab

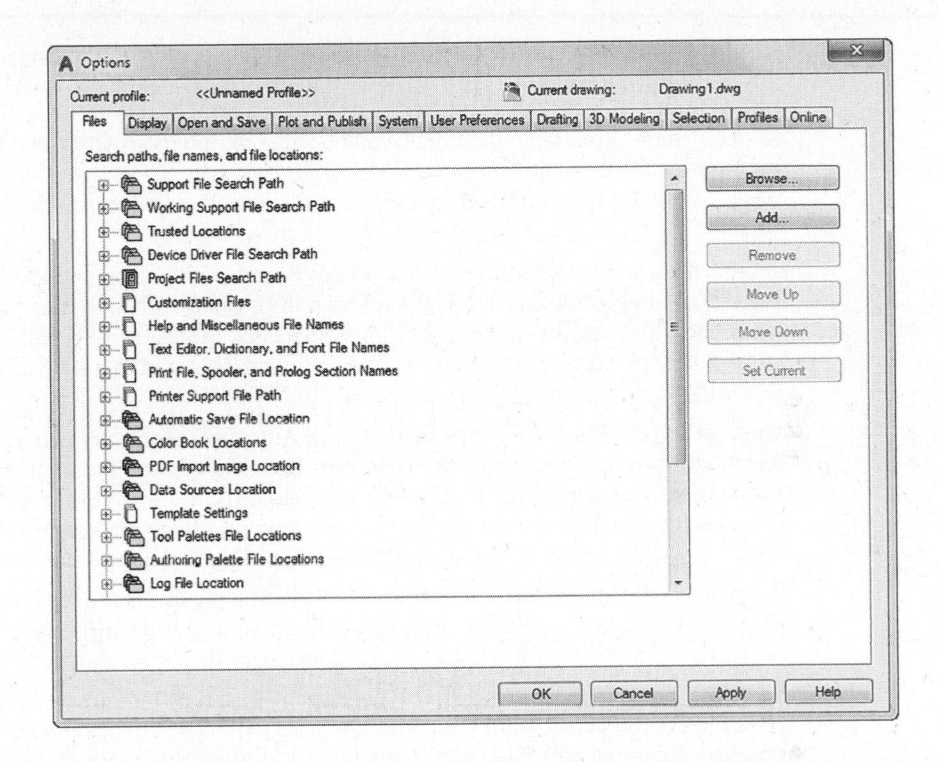

When available, the related system variable is shown in brackets at the end of the description.

Support File Search Path AutoCAD relies on external files for many of its functions. Menus, text fonts, linetypes, and hatch patterns are a few examples of features that rely on external files. The Support File Search Path item tells AutoCAD where to look for these files. You can add folder paths to this listing by selecting it, clicking the Add button, and entering a new path, or you can select it and use the Browse button. It's probably not a good idea to delete any of the existing items under this heading unless you really know what you're doing.

If you're familiar with using environment variables, you can include them in the search paths.

Working Support File Search Path The Working Support File Search Path item contains a read-only list of the support file search paths for the current session, together with any special settings that may be included with command switches and environment settings.

Trusted Locations Data security has become an increasingly important feature for Autodesk software. The Trusted Locations option lets you set a location on your system where you keep files that contain trusted executable code. See the Security group under the System tab for related information.

Device Driver File Search Path The Device Driver File Search Path item locates the device drivers for AutoCAD. Device drivers are applications that enable AutoCAD to communicate directly with printers, plotters, and input devices. In most cases, you don't have to do anything with this setting.

Project Files Search Path Eventually, a consultant or other AutoCAD user will provide you with files that rely on Xrefs or raster images. Often, such files expect the Xref or raster image to be in a particular folder. When they are moved to another location with a different folder system, Xref-dependent files won't be able to find their Xrefs. The Project Files Search Path item enables you to specify a folder where Xrefs or other dependent files are stored. If AutoCAD is unable to find an Xref or other file, it will look in the folder that you specify in this listing.

To specify this folder, highlight Project Files Search Path and then click the Add button. AutoCAD suggests `Project1` as the folder name. You can change the name if you prefer. Click the plus sign next to `Project1`, and then click Browse to select a location for your project file search path. The project file search path is stored in a system variable called `Projectname`.

Customization Files If you're customizing AutoCAD with your own menu files and icons, you can use this setting to locate your files. This option makes it convenient to keep your customization files in a place that is separate from the built-in AutoCAD files. You can specify a location for the main customization files like your CUI menu files, enterprise customization files for files you want to share, and your custom icons.

Help And Miscellaneous File Names This item lets you set the location of a variety of support files, including menu, help, automatic save, log, and configuration files. If you have a network installation, you can also set the License Manager location on your network.

Text Editor, Dictionary, And Font File Names Use this item to set the location of the text editor [`Mtexted`], custom and main dictionaries [`Dctmain`, `Dctcust`], and the alternate font and font-mapping files [`Fontalt`]. Chapter 9, "Adding Text to Drawings," describes these tools in more detail.

Print File, Spooler, And Prolog Section Names You can specify a print filename other than the default that is supplied by AutoCAD whenever you plot to a file. The Spooler option lets you specify an application intended to read and plot a plot file. The Prolog option is intended for PostScript export. It lets you specify the Prolog section from the `acad.psf` file that you want AutoCAD to include with exported Encapsulated PostScript (EPS) files [`Psprolog`].

Printer Support File Path Several support files are associated with the AutoCAD printing and plotting system. This item enables you to indicate where you want AutoCAD to look for these files.

Automatic Save File Location You can indicate the location for the Automatic Save file in AutoCAD by using this item [`Savefilepath`].

Color Book Locations This item lets you specify the locations for the PANTONE color books. This is an optional installation item, so if the PANTONE color books aren't installed, you can install them through your AutoCAD 2018 Installation DVD.

PDF Import Image Location This item lets you specify the location where you want to store image files from imported PDFs.

Data Sources Location This item lets you specify the location for Open Database Connectivity (ODBC) data-link files for linking AutoCAD drawings to database files.

Template Settings When you select the Use A Template option in the Create New Drawing dialog box, AutoCAD looks at this setting for the location of template files. You can modify this setting, but chances are you won't need to.

Tool Palettes File Locations This item lets you specify a location for the resource files for your custom tool palettes. When you create custom palettes, AutoCAD stores its data regarding those palettes in this location.

Authoring Palette File Locations If you're creating custom dynamic blocks, you can designate a folder location where you keep your custom block settings and files.

Log File Location With this item, you can indicate where log files are to be placed [`Logfilepath`].

Action Recorder Settings The Action Recorder saves action macros as files on your computer. You can specify the location of those saved macros in this option.

Plot And Publish Log File Location With this item, you can indicate where plot and publish log files are to be placed [`Logfilepath`].

Temporary Drawing File Location AutoCAD creates temporary files to store portions of your drawings as you work on them. You usually don't have to think about these temporary files unless they start crowding your hard disk or unless you're working on a particular large file on a system with little memory. This item lets you set the location for temporary files. The default location is the `C:\Users\`*`User Name`*`\appdata\local\temp\` folder (*`User Name`* is your login name). If you have a hard disk that has lots of room and is very fast, you may want to change this setting to a location on that drive to improve performance [`Tempprefix`, read-only].

Temporary External Reference File Location If you're on a network and you foresee a situation where another user will want to open an Xref of a file on which you're working, you can set the Demand Load Xrefs setting in the Open And Save tab to Enabled With Copy. This causes AutoCAD to make and use a copy of any Xref that is currently loaded. This way, others can open the original file. The Temporary External Reference File Location item lets you specify the folder where AutoCAD stores this copy of an Xref [`Xloadpath`].

Texture Maps Search Path This item specifies the location for AutoCAD Render texture maps. In most cases, you won't have to change this setting. You can, however, add a folder name to this item for your own texture maps as you acquire or create them.

Web File Search Path Although you may think this is for Internet files, it's really for photometric web files that are used to control the way lights behave in 3D models. These files have an `.ies` filename extension. See Bonus Chapter 6, "Rendering 3D Drawings," available at `www.omura.com/chapters`, for more about using these files.

DGN Mapping Setup Locations You can specify the location for the `DGNsetup.ini` file, which is a file used for DGN commands. Using these commands, you can import or export DGN files. You can also control the translation of layers, linetypes, lineweights, and color between the AutoCAD DWG file format and the DGN file format.

While in AutoCAD, you may want to find the location of a resource file quickly, such as a log file or the Automatic Save file. You can do so by using the system variable associated with the resource. For example, to find the location of the log file path quickly, enter **logfilepath**↵ at the Command prompt. For the Automatic Save file, enter **savefilepath**↵. Autodesk® AutoCAD LT® users can employ the Modemacro command as in **Modemacro**↵**$(getvar,logfilepath)**↵ or **Mode macro**↵**$(getvar,savefilepath)**↵. See Chapter 24, "Customizing Toolbars, Menus, Linetypes, and Hatch Patterns," for more on Modemacro.

The Display Tab

The settings on this tab (see Figure B.2) let you control the appearance of AutoCAD. You can make AutoCAD look completely different with these settings if you choose. Scroll bars, fonts, and colors are all up for grabs.

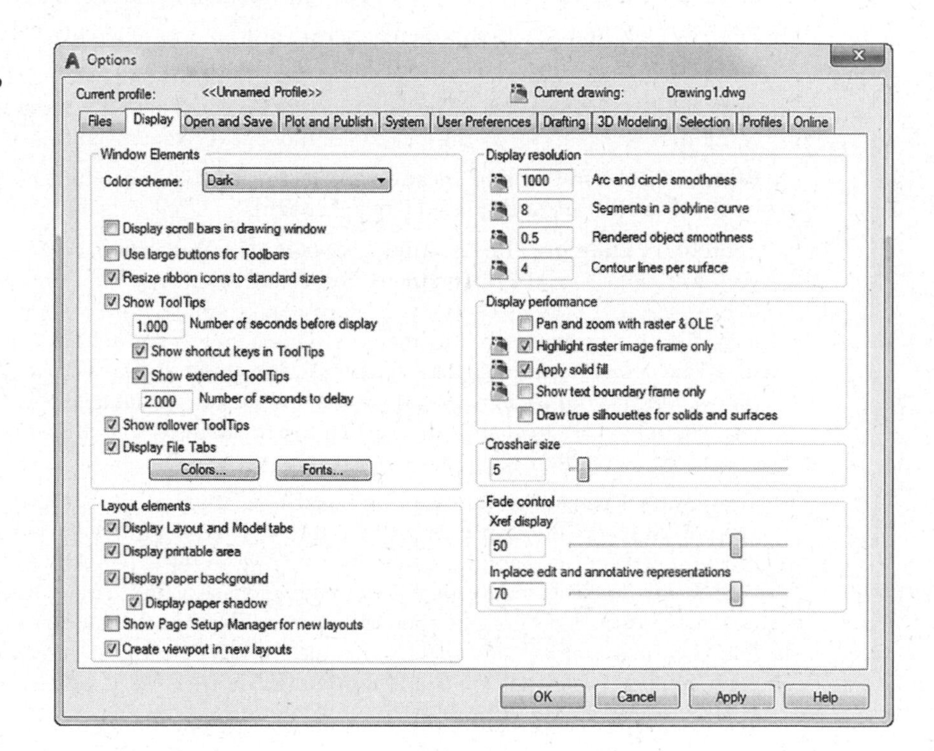

FIGURE B.2
The Display tab

THE WINDOW ELEMENTS GROUP

These options control the general settings for AutoCAD windows:

Color Scheme Lets you select between a dark or light color scheme for the AutoCAD interface, including toolbars, Ribbon panels, and dialog boxes.

Display Scroll Bars In Drawing Window Lets you turn the scroll bars on and off. If you have a small monitor with low resolution, you may want to disable the scroll bars for a larger drawing area.

Use Large Buttons For Toolbars Controls whether large icon buttons are used in toolbars.

Resize Ribbon Icons To Standard Sizes When Ribbon icons do not match the standard sizes, they can be scaled to match the small (16x16) or large (32x32) default pixel size.

Show ToolTips Controls whether tool tips are shown when you hover the mouse over tools [`Tooltips`].

Show Shortcut Keys In ToolTips Controls whether shortcut keys are displayed in tool tips.

Show Extended ToolTips Controls whether extended tool tips are displayed. Also allows users to specify the duration of time before the extended tool tip is displayed in the Number Of Seconds To Delay text box.

Show Rollover ToolTips Controls whether rollover tool tips are displayed [Rollovertips].

Display File Tabs Displays (or hides when unchecked) the drawing file tabs at the top of the drawing.

Colors Opens a dialog box that lets you set the color for the various components of the AutoCAD window. This is where you can change the background color of the drawing area if you find that black doesn't work for you.

Fonts Opens a dialog box that lets you set the fonts of the AutoCAD window. You can select from the standard set of Windows fonts available in your system.

The Display Resolution Group

These options control the way objects are displayed in AutoCAD. You can choose between display accuracy and speed:

Arc And Circle Smoothness Controls the appearance of arcs and circles, particularly when you zoom in on them. In some instances, arcs and circles appear to be octagons even though they plot as smooth arcs and circles. If you want arcs and circles to appear smoother, you can increase this setting. An increase also increases memory use [Viewres].

Segments In A Polyline Curve Controls the smoothness of polyline curves. Increase the value to make curved polylines appear smoother and less segmented. Decrease the value for improved display performance [Splinesegs].

Rendered Object Smoothness Controls the smoothness of curved solids when they're rendered or shaded. Values can range from 0.01 to 10 [Facetres].

Contour Lines Per Surface Lets you set the number of contour lines used to represent solid, curved surfaces. Values can range from 0 to 2047 [Isolines].

The Layout Elements Group

These options control the display of elements in the Paper Space Layout tabs. See Chapter 8, "Introducing Printing, Plotting, and Layouts," and Chapter 15, "Laying Out Your Printer Output," for more information. Most of these options are self-explanatory. The Show Page Setup Manager For New Layouts option opens the Page Setup Manager dialog box whenever a layout is first opened. The Create Viewport In New Layouts option automatically creates a viewport in a layout when it's first opened.

The Display Performance Group

You can adjust a variety of display-related settings in this group:

Pan And Zoom With Raster & OLE Controls the way raster images react to real-time pans and zooms. If this option is selected, raster images move with the cursor. Deselect this option for better performance [Rtdisplay].

Highlight Raster Image Frame Only Determines how raster images appear when selected. Select this option for better performance [Imagehlt].

Apply Solid Fill Controls the display of filled objects such as wide polylines and areas filled with the solid hatch pattern. This option is also controlled by the `Fillmode` system variable. Deselect this option for better performance.

Show Text Boundary Frame Only Controls the way text is displayed. Select this option to display text as rectangular boundaries [`Qtextmode`].

Draw True Silhouettes For Solids And Surfaces Controls whether surface meshes for solid models are displayed. Deselect this option for better performance [`Dispsilh`].

THE CROSSHAIR SIZE GROUP

This slider controls the size of the crosshair cursor. You can set it to 100 percent to simulate the full-screen crosshair cursor of earlier versions of AutoCAD [`Cursorsize`].

THE FADE CONTROL GROUP

These two sliders control the fade effect on external references. The Xref Display option sets the overall fade effect [`Xdwgfadectl`]. The In-Place Edit And Annotative Representations option controls the display of nonselected objects during in-place reference editing. See Chapter 7, "Mastering Viewing Tools, Hatches, and External References," for more information on in-place reference editing [`Xfadectl`].

The Open And Save Tab

The Open And Save tab (see Figure B.3) offers general file-related options such as the frequency of the automatic save and the default file version for the Save and Save As options.

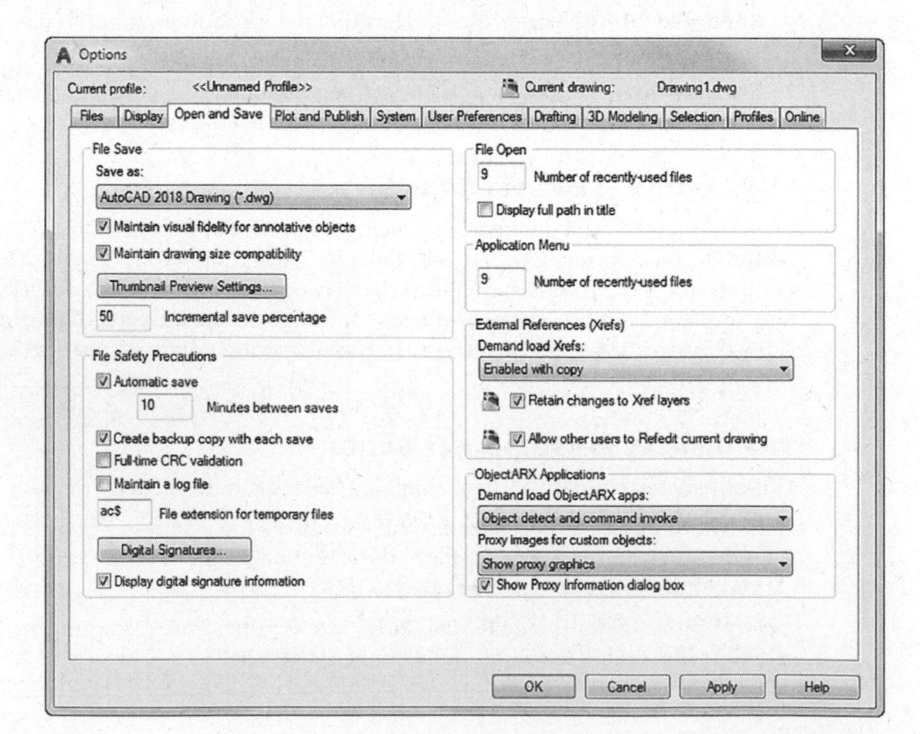

FIGURE B.3 The Open And Save tab

The File Save Group

You can control how AutoCAD saves files by using the options in this group:

Save As Lets you set the default file type for the Save and the Save As Application menu options. If you're working in an environment that requires Release 14 files as the standard file type, for example, you can use this option to select Release 14 as the default file type. You can also set up AutoCAD to save DXF files by default.

Maintain Visual Fidelity For Annotative Objects Ensures that annotative scale is preserved in layouts when you save drawings to earlier versions of AutoCAD. If you work primarily in model space, leave this setting off [`Savefidelity`].

Maintain Drawing Size Compatibility AutoCAD 2018 has no restrictions on object size. This option ensures that restrictions are applied in case you want to save your file to an earlier version [`Largeobjectsupport`].

Thumbnail Preview Settings Lets you determine whether a preview image is saved with a drawing. Preview images are used in the AutoCAD file dialog box and in DesignCenter™ to let you preview a file before opening it [`Rasterpreview`]. You can also control the display of the sheet set preview [`Updatethumbnail`].

Incremental Save Percentage Controls the degree to which the Incremental Save feature is applied when a file is saved. An incremental save improves the time required to save a file to disk, but it also makes the file size larger. If you have limited disk space, you can set this value to 25. A value of 0 turns off Incremental Save altogether but reduces AutoCAD performance [`Isavepercent`].

The File Safety Precautions Group

These options control the automatic backup features in AutoCAD:

Automatic Save Offers control over the Automatic Save features. You can turn it on or off by using the check box or set the frequency at which files are saved by using the Minutes Between Saves box. You can set the location for the Automatic Save files by using the Automatic Save File Location item in the Files tab of the Options dialog box. You can also set the frequency of automatic saves through the `Savetime` system variable [`Savefilepath`, `Savefile`].

Create Backup Copy With Each Save Lets you determine whether a BAK file is saved along with every save you perform. You can deselect this option to conserve disk space [`Isavebak`, `Tempprefix`].

Full-Time CRC Validation Controls the cyclic redundancy check feature, which checks for file errors whenever AutoCAD reads a file. This feature is helpful in troubleshooting hardware problems in your system.

Maintain A Log File Lets you record the data in the AutoCAD Text Window. See Chapter 19, "Getting and Exchanging Data from Drawings," for more on this feature. You can set the location for log files in the Files tab of the Options dialog box [`Logfilemode`, `Logfilename`].

File Extension For Temporary Files Lets you set the filename extension for AutoCAD temporary files. These are files AutoCAD uses to store drawing data temporarily as you work on a file. If you're working on a network where temporary files from multiple users may be stored in the same folder, you may want to change this setting to identify your temporary files.

Digital Signatures Opens the Digital Signatures dialog box, in which you can add a digital signature. See Chapter 25, "Managing and Sharing Your Drawings," for more on this feature [`Digitalsign`].

Display Digital Signature Information When a file containing a digital signature is opened, this option will display a warning message alerting you to the presence of the signature [`Sigwarn`]. See Chapter 25 for more on the digital signature feature.

The File Open Group

You can control how AutoCAD displays filenames in the File menu or the drawing title bar:

Number Of Recently-Used Files Lets you specify the number of files listed in the File menu history list. The default is 9, but you can enter a value from 0 to 50.

Display Full Path In Title Controls whether the full path is included in the title bar with a drawing's name.

The Application Menu Group

This option controls the number of recently used files that are displayed in the Application menu.

The External References (Xrefs) Group

These options let you control memory and layer features of Xrefs:

Demand Load Xrefs Lets you turn on the Demand Load feature of Xrefs. Demand Load helps to improve the performance of files that use Xrefs by loading only those portions of an Xref drawing that are required for the current open drawing. This option has a drop-down list with three choices: Disabled turns off demand loading, Enabled turns on demand loading, and Enabled With Copy turns on demand loading by using a copy of the Xref source file. This last option enables others on a network to edit the Xref source file while you're working on a file that also uses it [`Xloadctl`].

Retain Changes To Xref Layers Lets you save layer settings of Xref files in the current drawing. This doesn't affect the source Xref file. With this setting turned off, the current file imports the layer settings of the Xref file when it loads that file [`Visretain`].

Allow Other Users To Refedit Current Drawing Lets you specify whether others can simultaneously edit a file that you're editing. This option is intended to enable others to use the Xref And Block Editing option (the `Refedit` command or the Edit Reference tool found on the Insert tab's expanded Reference panel) on files that you currently have loaded in AutoCAD [`Xedit`].

The ObjectARX Applications Group

AutoCAD allows users and third-party developers to create a custom object that usually requires the presence of a custom ObjectARX® application to support it. These options control the way AutoCAD treats custom objects and their related ObjectARX applications:

Demand Load ObjectARX Apps This option controls when a supporting third-party application is loaded if a custom object is present in a file. This option offers several settings that you can select from a drop-down list. The available settings are Disable Load On Demand, Custom Object Detect, Command Invoke, and Object Detect And Command Invoke. Disable Load On Demand prevents AutoCAD from loading third-party applications when a custom object is present. Some standard AutoCAD commands won't work if you select Disable Load On Demand because AutoCAD itself uses ObjectARX applications. Custom Object Detect causes AutoCAD to load an ARX application automatically if a custom object is present. Command Invoke loads a custom application when you invoke a command from that application. The Object Detect And Command Invoke option loads an ARX application either when a custom object is present or if you invoke a command from that application [`Demandload`].

Proxy Images For Custom Objects Offers a drop-down list with three settings that control the display of custom objects when the objects supporting ARX applications aren't present on your system. Do Not Show Proxy Graphics turns off the display of custom objects. Show Proxy Graphics displays the custom objects. Show Proxy Bounding Box shows a bounding box in place of a custom object [`Proxyshow`].

Show Proxy Information Dialog Box Lets you determine whether the Show Proxy Information warning dialog box is used. When this option is selected, the Show Proxy Information warning appears when a drawing with custom objects is opened but AutoCAD can't find the objects' associated ARX application [`Proxynotice`].

The Plot and Publish Tab

The Plot And Publish tab in the Options dialog box offers settings related to printing and plotting. See Chapter 8 for a description of these options.

The System Tab

The options in the System tab (see Figure B.4) offer control over some of the general AutoCAD interface settings, such as settings for display drivers and pointing devices.

FIGURE B.4
The System tab

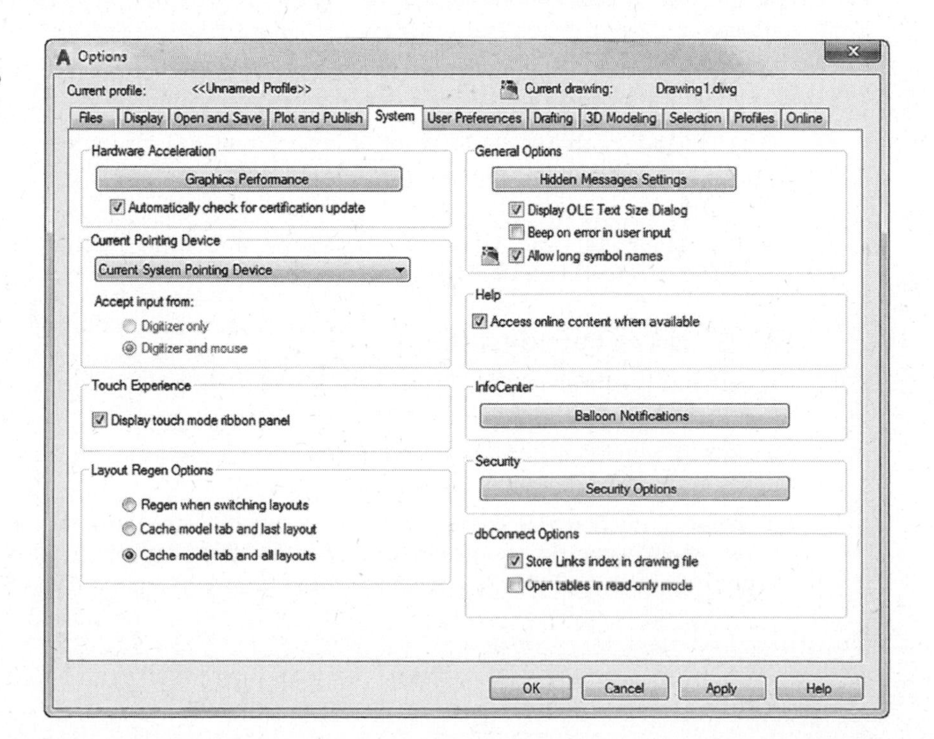

The Hardware Acceleration Group

Clicking the Graphics Performance button in this group displays a variety of settings to help you fine-tune the performance of your 3D graphics. When you click this option, the Graphics Performance dialog box opens. See the section "Adjusting the AutoCAD 3D Graphics System" later in this appendix.

The Current Pointing Device Group

You can choose the type of pointing device you want to use with AutoCAD through the options in this group. The drop-down list offers Current System Pointing Device and Wintab Compatible Digitizer ADI 4.2 – By Autodesk. If you want to use the default Windows pointing device, choose Current System Pointing Device. If you have a digitizer that uses the Wintab driver, you can select Wintab Compatible Digitizer.

You can further limit AutoCAD to use only the Wintab Compatible Digitizer by selecting the Digitizer Only radio button. If you select the Digitizer And Mouse radio button, AutoCAD will accept input from both devices.

The Touch Experience Group

If you are using a touch-enabled PC such as a Windows 8 or Windows 10 tablet, the Display touch mode Ribbon panel option will display the Touch Ribbon panel. This panel offers the Select Mode tool, which enables you to cancel the current command.

The Layout Regen Options Group

With this set of radio buttons you can specify how regens are applied when you are working with layout tabs:

Regen When Switching Layouts Causes AutoCAD to force a regen when you select a layout tab or the Model tab. Use this option when your computer is limited in RAM.

Cache Model Tab And Last Layout Causes AutoCAD to suppress regens when you switch to the Model tab or the most recently opened layout tab. Other layouts will regen when selected.

Cache Model Tab And All Layouts Causes AutoCAD to suppress regens when you select any layout tab or the Model tab.

The General Options Group

This set of check boxes lets you set options related to the general operation of AutoCAD:

Hidden Messages Settings A number of dialog boxes offer the "Do not show me again" option. If you select it and later find that you would like to see the dialog box again, you can use this button to view the message.

Display OLE Text Size Dialog Lets you control the display of the OLE Text Size dialog box, which normally appears when you insert OLE text objects into an AutoCAD drawing by choosing Paste from the Paste flyout in the Home tab's Clipboard panel.

Beep On Error In User Input Turns on an alarm beep that sounds whenever there is an input error.

Allow Long Symbol Names Enables you to use long names for items such as layers, blocks, linetypes, and text styles. With this option turned on, you can enter as many as 255 characters for names [Extnames].

The Help Group

AutoCAD uses a web-based help system. If for some reason you do not have web access, you can install help files using the AutoCAD 2018 installation tools. The Access Online Content When Available option should be deselected after help files have been installed.

The InfoCenter Group

This group contains just one button: Balloon Notifications. This button opens the InfoCenter Settings dialog box, which gives you control over the behavior of the InfoCenter feature, including balloon notifications, the Product Support information channel, and the Did You Know messages.

The Security Group

The Security Options button in this group opens the Security Options dialog box, where you can set restrictions on how executable files are loaded [Securityoptions].

The dbConnect Options Group

The check boxes in this group offer controls over the dbConnect feature:

Store Links Index In Drawing File Lets you specify where database link data is stored. If this check box is selected, link data is stored in the drawing that is linked to a database. This increases file size and file-loading time.

Open Tables In Read-Only Mode Lets you limit access to database files.

The User Preferences Tab

The options in the User Preferences tab (see Figure B.5) enable you to adjust the way AutoCAD reacts to user input.

The Windows Standard Behavior Group

These settings let you control how AutoCAD reacts to keyboard accelerators and mouse right-clicks:

Double Click Editing Controls whether a double-click on an object automatically starts an editing command for the object. If this option is turned off, double-clicking objects has no effect [Dblclkedit].

Shortcut Menus In Drawing Area Lets you see the context menu when you right-click. When this check box isn't selected, AutoCAD responds to a right-click with a ↵ [Shortcutmenu].

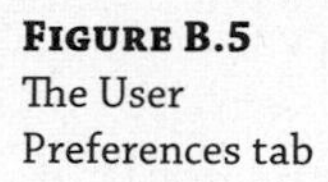

FIGURE B.5
The User Preferences tab

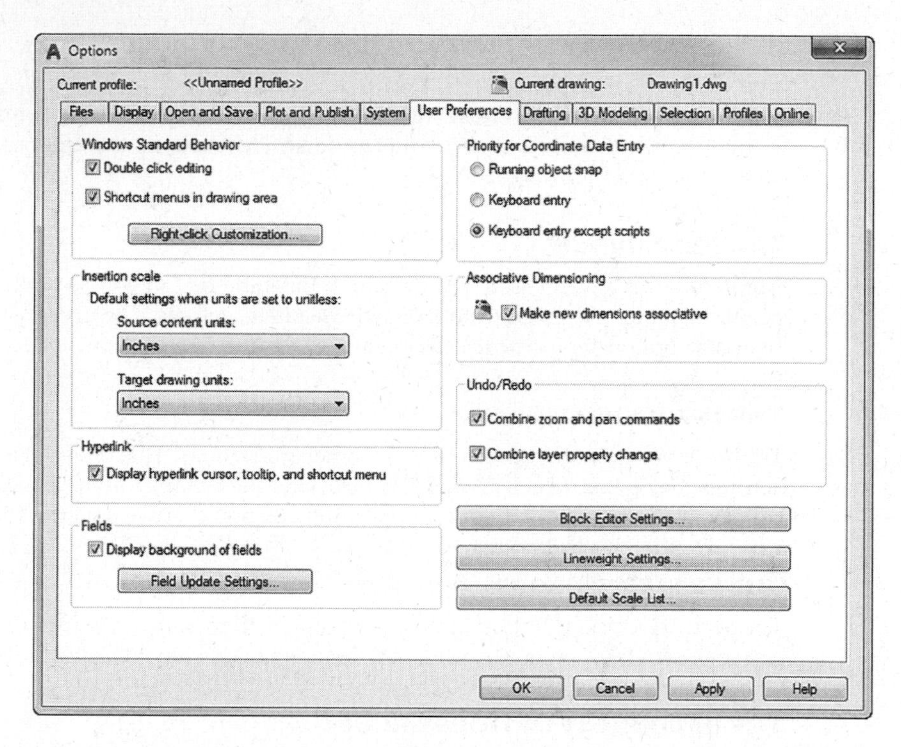

Right-Click Customization Opens the Right-Click Customization dialog box (see Figure B.6), which offers further options for the behavior of the right-click in AutoCAD. The Turn On Time-Sensitive Right-Click option causes AutoCAD to respond differently depending on whether you right-click quickly or hold the right mouse button down momentarily. With this option, a rapid right-click issues an ↵—as if you pressed the Enter key. If you hold down the right mouse button, the context menu appears. You can further adjust the time required to hold down the mouse button by modifying this setting.

FIGURE B.6
The Right-Click Customization dialog box

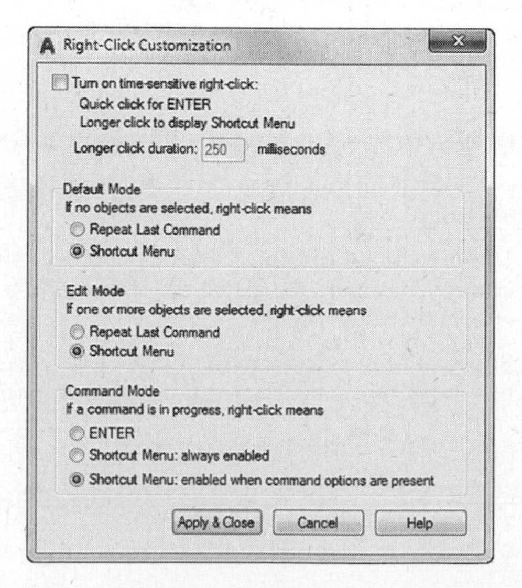

The Insertion Scale Group

These settings control how DesignCenter determines the scale of blocks when blocks are given a unitless setting for their DesignCenter unit type. Each drop-down list offers the standard set of unit types that are available in the Block Definition dialog box under the Insert Units drop-down list. See Chapter 4, "Organizing Objects with Blocks and Groups," for more information on blocks and Chapter 25 for information on DesignCenter [`Insunits`, `Insunitsdefsource`, `Insunitsdeftarget`].

The Hyperlink Group

The one option in this group turns on or off the display of the hyperlink cursor, tool tip, and context menu [`Hyperlinkoptions`].

The Fields Group

These settings offer control over the display of fields and how they refresh. Display Background Of Fields lets you control the display of the gray background on fields. This background lets you see at a glance which text object in a drawing is a field. The background doesn't print. Clicking the Field Update Settings button opens a dialog box that lets you select the action that updates fields [`Fielddisplay`, `Fieldeval`].

The Priority for Coordinate Data Entry Group

These options control the way AutoCAD responds to coordinate input:

Running Object Snap Forces AutoCAD to use running osnaps at all times [`Osnapcoord`]

Keyboard Entry Lets you use keyboard entry for coordinate input [`Osnapcoord`]

Keyboard Entry Except Scripts Lets you use keyboard entry for coordinate input for everything but scripts [`Osnapcoord`]

The Associative Dimensioning Group

This area has one option, Make New Dimensions Associative, which you can toggle on or off. This option lets you control whether AutoCAD uses the Associative Dimensioning feature. With true associative dimensioning, a dimension follows changes to an object whenever the object is edited. In the old method, you have to include a dimension definition point during the editing process to have the dimension follow changes in an object [`Dimassoc`].

The Undo/Redo Group

These options control how Undo and Redo react with the Zoom, Pan, and Layer Properties Manager commands.

Block Editor Settings

Click the Block Editor Settings button to open the Block Editor Settings dialog box. This dialog box allows you to control the appearance of objects and features in the Block Editor.

Lineweight Settings

Click the Lineweight Settings button to open the Lineweight Settings dialog box. See Chapter 15 in this book as well as Bonus Chapter 5, "Understanding Plot Styles," available at `www.omura.com/chapters`, for more information about the Lineweight Settings dialog box.

DEFAULT SCALE LIST

Click the Default Scale List button to open the Default Scale List dialog box. You can add your own custom scales for use with viewports and layouts and while plotting.

The Drafting Tab

The Drafting tab (see Figure B.7) offers settings that relate to the drawing cursor, including the AutoSnap and AutoTrack features.

FIGURE B.7
The Drafting tab

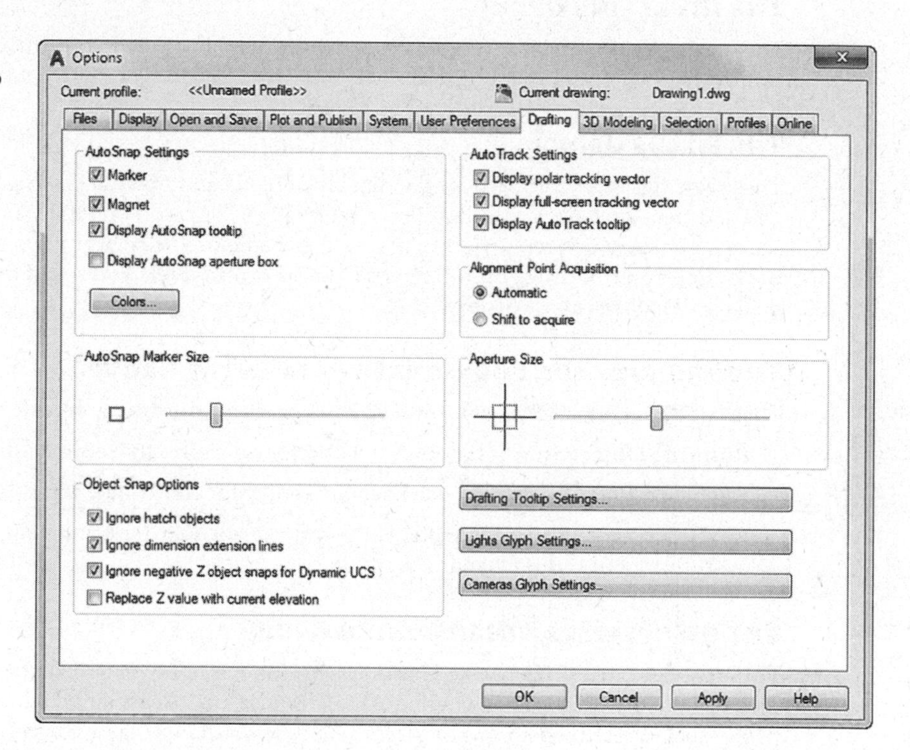

THE AUTOSNAP SETTINGS GROUP

The options in this group control the AutoSnap features that are engaged when you use osnaps:

Marker Turns on the small, square graphic that appears on the osnap location. If you prefer not to see this marker, clear this check box [`Autosnap`].

Magnet Causes the Osnap cursor to jump to an osnap location as it moves close to that location [`Autosnap`].

Display AutoSnap Tooltip Controls the display of the osnap tool tip [`Autosnap`].

Display AutoSnap Aperture Box Displays a square over the cursor whenever osnaps are active. If you're familiar with earlier versions of AutoCAD, you'll recognize the aperture box as the graphic used to indicate osnaps before the AutoSnap feature was introduced [`Apbox`].

Colors Opens the Drawing Window Colors dialog box. Lets you determine the color for the AutoSnap marker and other interface elements.

The AutoSnap Marker Size Group

Move the slider to control the size of the AutoSnap marker.

The Object Snap Options Group

This group offers four settings. When Ignore Hatch Objects is deselected, osnaps attempt to snap to geometry in hatch patterns. When Ignore Dimension Extension Lines is selected, osnaps will ignore dimension extension lines. Ignore Negative Z Object Snaps For Dynamic UCS causes osnaps to ignore locations with negative Z values while you're using the Dynamic UCS feature [`Osoptions`]. When selected, Replace Z Value With Current Elevation causes AutoCAD to use the current UCS default Z value instead of the Z value of the selected point.

The AutoTrack Settings Group

These options offer control over the tracking vector used for Polar Tracking and Osnap Tracking:

Display Polar Tracking Vector Turns the Polar Tracking vector on or off [`Trackpath`]

Display Full-Screen Tracking Vector Lets you control whether the tracking vector appears across the full width of the drawing window or stops at the cursor location or the intersection of two tracking vectors [`Trackpath`]

Display AutoTrack Tooltip Turns the Osnap Tracking tool tip on or off [`Autosnap`]

The Alignment Point Acquisition Group

These options let you determine the method for acquiring Osnap Tracking alignment points.

The Aperture Size Group

Move the slider to set the size of the osnap aperture pickbox [`Aperture`].

Drafting Tooltip Settings

Click the Drafting Tooltip Settings button to control the color, size, and transparency of tool tips.

Lights Glyph Settings

Click the Lights Glyph Settings button to control the color and size of the spot and point light glyphs.

Cameras Glyph Settings

Click the Cameras Glyph Settings button to control the color and size of the cameras glyph.

The 3D Modeling Tab

The options on this tab (see Figure B.8) control the behavior and display of your drawing when you're working in 3D modes. You can adjust the appearance of the crosshair and the UCS icon. You can specify the default method for displaying 3D objects, and you can specify the default settings for Walk And Fly and Animation features.

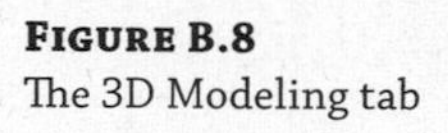

FIGURE B.8
The 3D Modeling tab

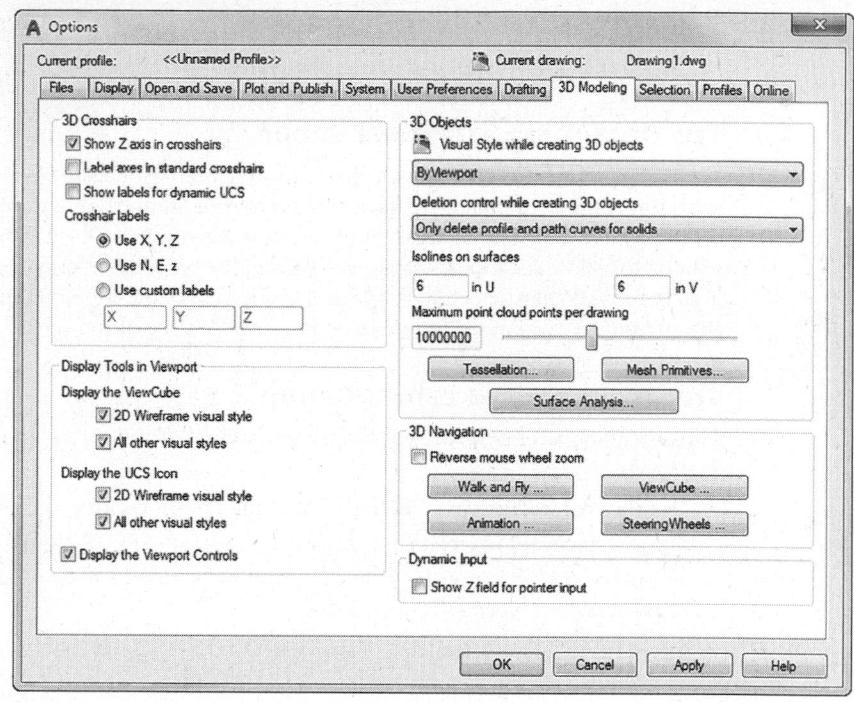

The 3D Crosshairs Group

These settings control the behavior and appearance of the crosshair cursor when you're viewing your drawing in 3D:

Show ZAxis In Crosshairs Displays the z-axis in the crosshair.

Label Axes In Standard Crosshairs Displays the x-, y-, and z-axes' labels on the crosshair.

Show Labels For Dynamic UCS Displays axis labels during the use of Dynamic UCS regardless of the Label Axes In Standard Crosshairs setting.

Crosshair Labels Lets you select from three label styles: Use X, Y, Z; Use N, E, Z; or Use Custom Labels. If you select Use Custom Labels, you can enter the labels that you want to display for the x-, y-, and z-axes in the boxes provided.

The Display Tools in Viewport Group

These three options pretty much explain themselves. The options determine when the ViewCube®, UCS icon, and Viewport controls are displayed. By default, they're all turned on and are always displayed.

The 3D Objects Group

These settings affect the display of 3D objects. Visual Style While Creating 3D Objects is self-explanatory. Deletion Control While Creating 3D Objects lets you determine whether the objects that AutoCAD uses to create 3D objects are saved or deleted.

The U and V isoline settings let you set the number of isolines on 3D solids and surface meshes. Isolines are the lines that you see on a mesh or solid, which help you visualize their shape. You see them in wireframe and realistic visual styles [Surfu, Surfv].

The Maximum Point Cloud Points Per Drawing control lets you set a limit to the number of point cloud points so they don't overwhelm your computer.

The Tessellation button opens the Mesh Tessellation Options dialog box where you can set how the Meshsmooth command affects objects. The Mesh Primitives button opens the Mesh Primitive Options dialog box where you adjust the default mesh primitive settings. The Surface Analysis button lets you make adjustments to the way the surface analysis tools behave.

The 3D Navigation Group

If you want to adjust the way AutoCAD behaves when you're navigating a 3D view, these settings will help. Reverse Mouse Wheel Zoom is self-explanatory [Zoomwheel]. The remaining four buttons give you control over the behavior of the Walk And Fly feature, the Animation settings, the ViewCube display and behavior, and the SteeringWheels® display and behavior:

Walk And Fly Click this button to open the Walk And Fly Settings dialog box (see Figure B.9). When you first start the 3DWalk or 3DFly feature, you see an instructional window that tells you how to use it. You use the options in the Settings group of the Walk And Fly Settings dialog box to specify when that instructional window appears. After using these features a few times, you may find the instructional window annoying and turn it off. You can turn it back on in this dialog box. You can also set the Position Locator window to appear or not appear automatically.

Figure B.9
The Walk And Fly Settings dialog box

The Current Drawing Settings group lets you set the step size and steps per second when you're "walking" or "flying" through your model. These are the same settings that you see in the Navigate control panel for Step Size and Steps Per Second [Stepsize, Stepspersec].

ViewCube Click this button to open the ViewCube Settings dialog box (see Figure B.10). These settings allow you to control the behavior and appearance of the ViewCube [Navvcubelocation, Navvcubeopacity, Navvcubeorient, Northdirection].

FIGURE B.10
The ViewCube Settings dialog box

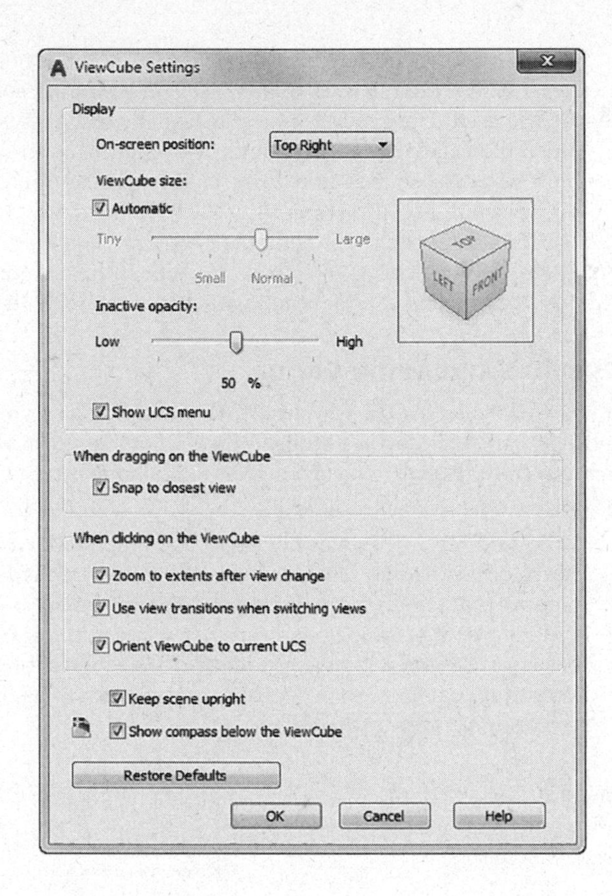

Animation Click this button to open the Animation Settings dialog box (see Figure B.11). Here you can control the default visual style, resolution, frame rate, and animation file format when using the Motion Path Animation (`Anipath`) feature. You can find more information on Motion Path Animation in the bonus chapters available at `www.omura.com/chapters`.

FIGURE B.11
The Animation Settings dialog box

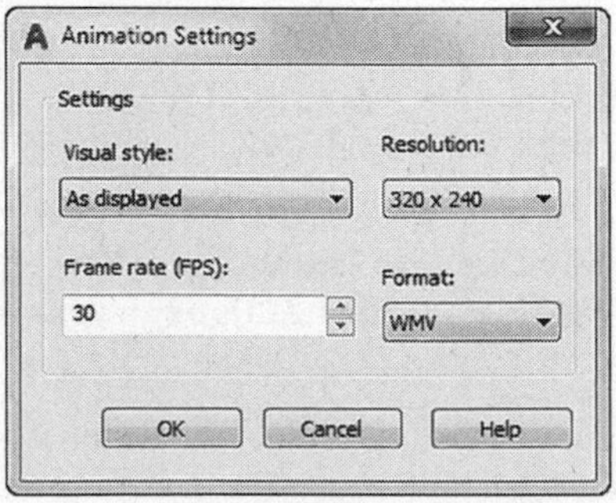

SteeringWheels Click this button to open the SteeringWheels Settings dialog box (see Figure B.12). Here you can set the appearance and behavior of the SteeringWheels feature [`Navswheelsizemini`, `Navswheelsizebig`, `Navswheelopacitymini`, `Navswheelopacitybig`].

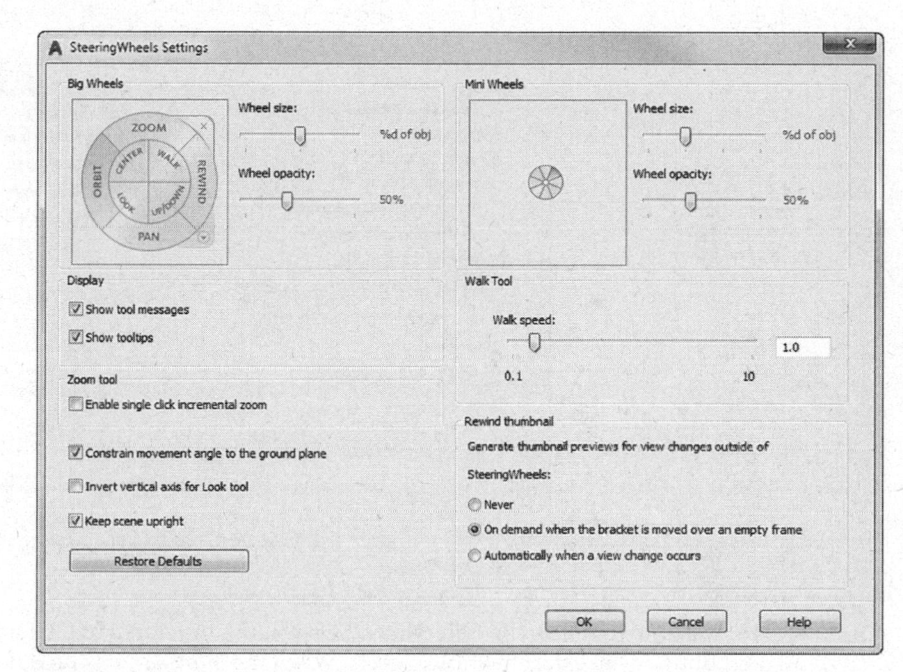

FIGURE B.12
The SteeringWheels Settings dialog box

THE DYNAMIC INPUT GROUP

When selected, the Show Z Field For Pointer Input option offers a z-coordinate for input when Dynamic Input mode is used.

The Selection Tab

The options in the Selection tab of the Options dialog box (see Figure B.13) control the way you select objects in AutoCAD. You can also make adjustments to the Grips feature.

THE PICKBOX SIZE GROUP

This slider control lets you adjust the size of the pickbox [`Pickbox`].

THE SELECTION MODES GROUP

These options let you control the degree to which AutoCAD conforms to standard graphical user interface (GUI) methods of operation:

Noun/Verb Selection Makes AutoCAD work more like other Windows programs by letting you select objects before you choose an action or command [`Pickfirst`].

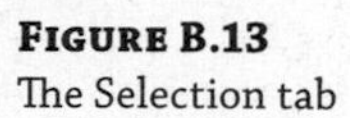

FIGURE B.13
The Selection tab

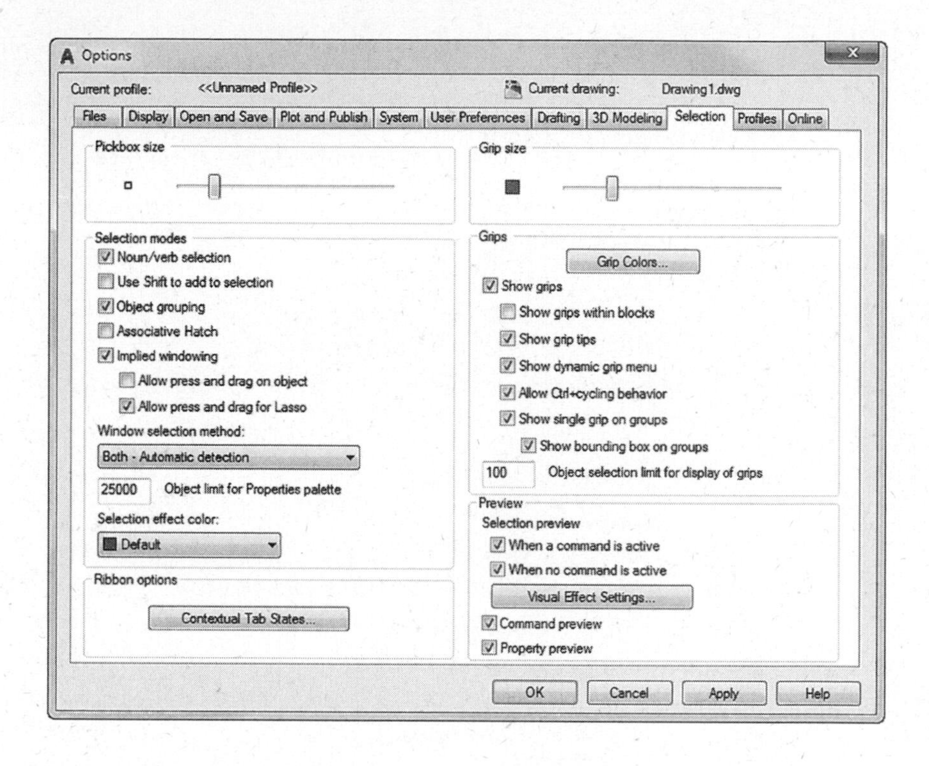

Use Shift To Add To Selection Lets you use the standard GUI method of holding down the Shift key to select multiple objects. When the Shift key isn't held down, only the single object picked or the group of objects indicated with a window will be selected. Previously selected objects are deselected unless the Shift key is held down during selection. To turn on this feature by using system variables, set `Pickadd` to 0.

Object Grouping Lets you select groups as single objects [`Pickstyle`].

Associative Hatch Lets you select both a hatch pattern and its associated boundary by using a single pick [`Pickstyle`].

Implied Windowing Causes a window or crossing window to start automatically if no object is picked at the `Select objects:` prompt. This setting has no effect on the Noun/Verb setting. In the system variables, set `Pickauto` to 1 for this option.

Allow Press And Drag On Object Lets you use the standard GUI method for placing window selections. When this option is selected, you click and hold down the Pick button on the first corner of the window. Then, while holding down the Pick button, drag the other corner of the window into position. When the other corner is in place, you let go of the Pick button to finish the window. This setting applies to both Verb/Noun and Noun/Verb operations. In the system variables, set `Pickdrag` to 1 for this option.

Allow Press And Drag For Lasso Enables the Lasso selection feature that lets you create a free-form selection area. When this option is selected, you click and hold the left mouse button while drawing a "free-hand" selection area. A counterclockwise direction creates a "crossing" lasso selection area, and a clockwise direction creates a standard lasso selection area.

Window Selection Method Lets you determine how window selections work. There are three options offered in a drop-down list: Click And Click, Press And Drag, and Both – Automatic Detection. Click And Click places a window by clicking the first corner and then the second. Press And Drag places a window with a press and drag motion of the mouse. Both – Automatic Detection lets you use both Click And Click and Press And Drag depending on whether you click and hold your mouse on the first click [`Pickdrag`].

Object Limit For Properties Palette Lets you set the limit for the number of objects that can be edited using the Properties palette at one time. The Value range is 0 to 32,767 [`Propobjlimit`].

Selection Effect Color Lets you set the color for the selection highlight effect [`Selectioneffectcolor`].

The Ribbon Options Group

The Contextual Tab States button in the Ribbon Options group opens the Ribbon Contextual Tab State Options dialog box. This dialog box lets you set the conditions under which the Ribbon contextual tabs are displayed. Contextual tabs are Ribbon tabs that offer tools to edit certain types of objects, such as Xrefs or 3D meshes [`Ribbonselectmode`, `Ribboncontextsellim`].

The Grip Size Group

This slider control lets you adjust the size of grips [`Gripsize`].

The Grips Group

These options control the Grips feature:

Grip Colors Lets you select a color for grips in their various states, such as unselected, selected, hovered, and contour [`Gripcolor`].

Show Grips Controls the display of grips [`Grips`].

Show Grips Within Blocks Turns on the display of grips in blocks. Although you can't edit grips in blocks, you can use grips in blocks as selection points [`Gripblock`].

Show Grip Tips Controls the display of grip tool tips [`Griptips`].

Show Dynamic Grip Menu Displays a dynamic menu when you're hovering over a multifunction grip [`Gripmultifunctional`].

Allow Ctrl+Cycling Behavior Turns on Ctrl+cycling behavior for multifunction grips [`Gripmultifunctional`].

Show Single Grip On Groups Displays a single grip on groups. When this option is not selected, all the grips in the set of objects in a group are displayed [`Groupdisplaymode`].

Show Bounding Box On Groups Displays a bounding box around a selected group [`Groupdisplaymode`].

Object Selection Limit For Display Of Grips Controls the display of grips based on the number of objects selected. If this is set to 1, grips aren't displayed if more than one object is selected. You can select a range from 1 to 32,767. The default is 100 [`Gripobjlimit`].

The Preview Group

These options let you control the behavior of the selection preview when you hover over objects or when you are using a command. Click the Visual Effect Settings button to fine-tune the visual effects of the object selection, including the color and pattern of Autoselect windows and which entities to exclude [Selectionpreview]. The Command Preview toggle determines whether the result of a command is displayed before you commit to the command. The Property Preview toggle determines whether you see a live view of property changes when rolling over drop-down lists and galleries.

The Profiles Tab

In Windows, a user profile is saved for each login name. Depending on the login name you use, you can have a different Windows setup. The Profiles tab (see Figure B.14) offers a similar function for AutoCAD users. You can store different settings from the Options dialog box in a profile and recall them at any time. You can also save them to a file with the .arg filename extension and then take that file to another system. It's a bit like being able to take your Options settings with you wherever you go.

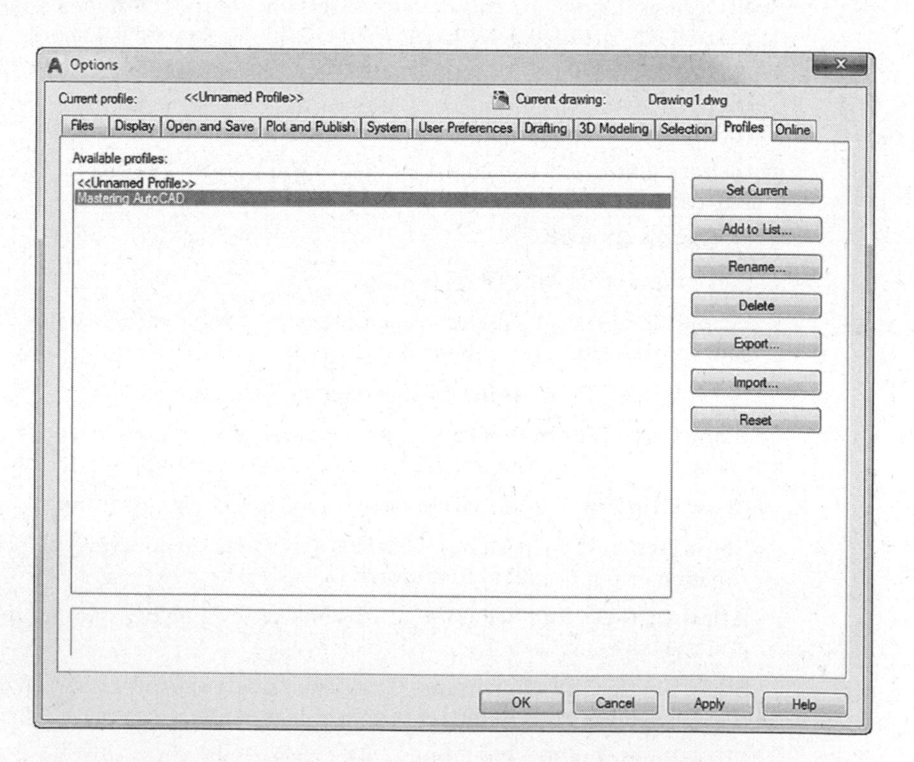

Figure B.14
The Profiles tab

The main part of the Profiles tab displays a list of available profiles. The default profile is shown as <<Unnamed Profile>>. As you add more profiles, they appear in the list.

To create a new profile, highlight a profile name from the list that will be the template for the new profile, and then click Add To List. The Add Profile dialog box opens, where you can enter a profile name and a description of the profile. The description appears in the box below the list on the Profiles tab whenever that profile is selected.

After you've created a new profile, you can modify the settings on the other tabs of the Options dialog box and the new settings will be associated with the new profile. Profiles store the way menus are set up, so you can use them as an aid to managing both your own custom schemes and third-party software. Here is a brief description of the options on the Profiles tab:

Set Current Installs the settings from the selected profile

Add To List Creates a new profile

Rename Lets you rename a profile and change its description

Delete Removes the selected profile from the list

Export Lets you save a profile to a file

Import Imports a profile that has been saved to a file

Reset Resets the values for a selected profile to its default settings

The Online Tab

Autodesk A360® is a feature that allows you to store drawings and AutoCAD settings in a secure, online location known as A360 Drive®. The Online tab enables you to determine the level to which you intend to use A360 Drive. This tab doesn't show any options until you sign in to your A360 Drive account using the Sign In option in the AutoCAD InfoCenter. Once signed in, you will see the options in the Online tab, shown in Figure B.15.

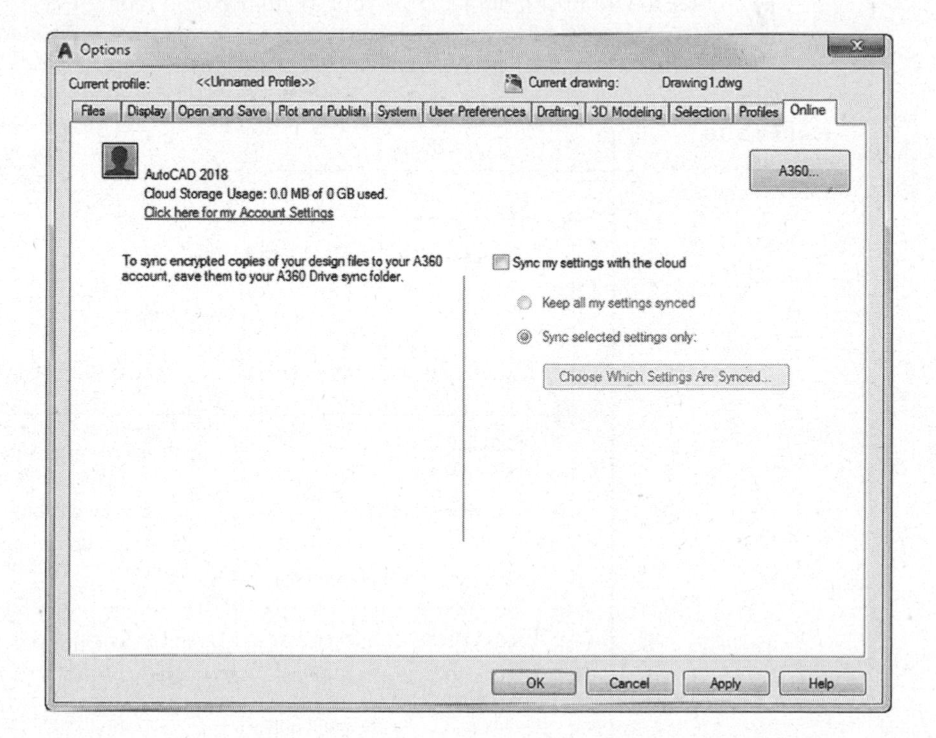

FIGURE B.15
The Online tab

There is one main setting on the Online tab: Sync My Settings With The Cloud. With the Sync My Settings With The Cloud option turned on, you can have all of your AutoCAD settings saved to the cloud, or you can select a set of options to be saved.

If you'd like to learn more about Autodesk 360, see "Sharing Files with A360 Drive" in Chapter 25.

Configuring the Tablet Menu Area

If you own a digitizing tablet and would like to use it with a Tablet menu template, you must configure your Tablet menu. Install your Tablet menu into AutoCAD using the Menuload command, and then do the following:

1. Securely fasten your Tablet menu template to the tablet. Be sure that the area covered by the template is completely within the tablet's active drawing area.
2. Type **Options**, and then select the System tab.
3. In the Current Pointing Device group, select Wintab Compatible Digitizer ADI 4.2 – By Autodesk, Inc. from the drop-down menu and then make sure that the Digitizer And Mouse radio button is selected.
4. Click Apply and then click OK to close the dialog box.
5. Type **Tablet↵Cfg↵**. The following prompt appears:

```
Enter number of tablet menus desired (0-4) <0>:
```

Enter the number of tablet areas your menu uses and then press ↵. For the next series of prompts, you'll be locating the Tablet menu areas, starting with Menu Area 1. Figure B.16 shows an example of how to locate the Tablet menu areas for the legacy AutoCAD Tablet menu.

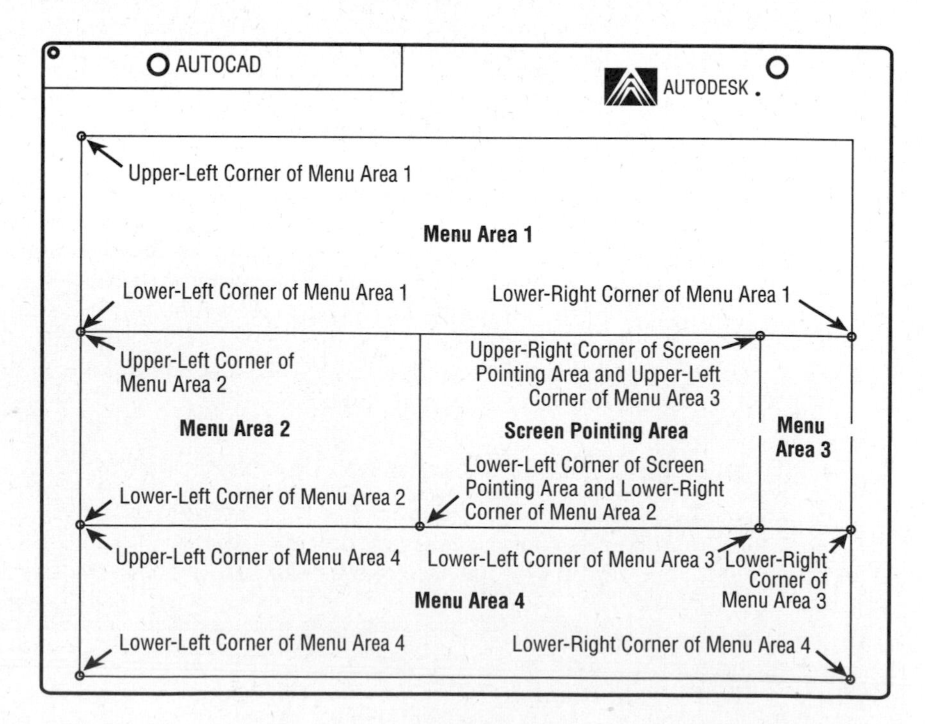

FIGURE B.16 How to locate the Tablet menu areas

6. Follow the instructions provided by the command-line interface.
7. When you're asked if you want to respecify the fixed screen pointing area, enter **Y↵** and then select the corners of the pointing area as indicated by the prompts.

Turning On the Noun/Verb Selection Method

If for some reason the Noun/Verb Selection method isn't available, follow these steps to turn it on:

1. Choose Options from the Application menu. Then, in the Options dialog box, click the Selection tab.
2. In the Selection Modes group, click the Noun/Verb Selection check box.
3. Click OK.

You should now see a small square at the intersection of the crosshair cursor. This square is an object selection cursor superimposed on the point selection cursor. It tells you that you can select objects, even while the Command prompt appears at the bottom of the screen and no command is currently active. As you saw earlier, the square momentarily disappears when you're in a command that asks you to select points.

You can also turn on the Noun/Verb Selection method by entering **'Pickfirst↵** at the `Type a command:` prompt. At the `Enter new value for PICKFIRST <0>:` prompt, enter **1↵**. (Entering **0** turns off the Pickfirst function.) The `Pickfirst` system variable is stored in the AutoCAD configuration file.

Turning on the Grips Feature

If for some reason the Grips feature isn't available, follow these steps to turn it on:

1. Choose Options from the Application menu. Then, in the Options dialog box, click the Selection tab.
2. In the Grips group, click the Show Grips check box.
3. Click OK, and you're ready to proceed.

The Selection tab of the Options dialog box also lets you specify whether grips appear on objects that compose a block (see Chapter 4 for more on blocks) as well as set the grip color and size. You can also set these options by using the system variables.

You can also turn the Grips feature on and off by entering **'Grips↵**. At the `Enter new value for GRIPS <0>:` prompt, enter **1** or **2** to turn grips on or **0** to turn grips off. Option 2 turns on grips and displays additional midpoint grips on polyline line segments. The `Grips` system variable is stored in the AutoCAD configuration file.

Setting Up the Tracking Vector Feature

If AutoCAD doesn't display a tracking vector as described in the early chapters of this book, or if the tracking vector doesn't behave as described, chances are this feature has been turned off or altered. Take the following steps to configure the tracking vector so that it behaves as described in this book:

1. Open the Options dialog box by choosing Options from the Application menu.
2. Click the Drafting tab.

3. Click all three options in the AutoTrack Settings group.
4. Make sure that the Marker, Magnet, and Display AutoSnap Tooltip check boxes are selected in the AutoSnap Settings group.
5. Make sure that the Automatic radio button in the Alignment Point Acquisition group is selected.
6. Click OK to exit the dialog box.

Adjusting the AutoCAD 3D Graphics System

You can adjust the performance of the 2D and 3D graphics system in AutoCAD using the Graphics Performance dialog box (see Figure B.17). To open this dialog box, click the System tab in the Options dialog box and then click the Graphics Performance button in the Hardware Acceleration group.

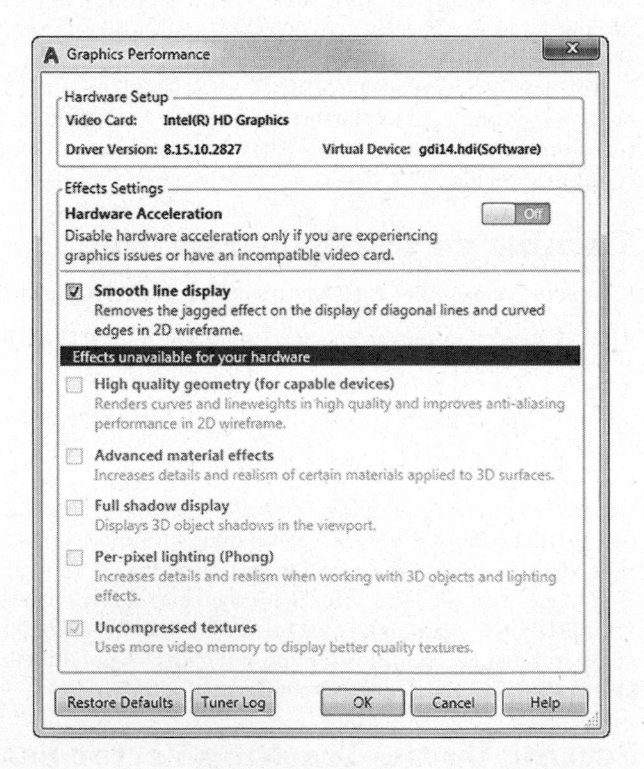

FIGURE B.17 Tuning graphics performance

This dialog box lets you turn on hardware acceleration for your graphic display. If you find that the AutoCAD display is not working properly, you can turn off hardware acceleration. This dialog box also offers control over the way AutoCAD displays 3D modeling features. Note that some PCs may not be equipped with the hardware required for hardware acceleration.

Finding Folders That Contain AutoCAD Files

Many AutoCAD features rely on external files to store settings and other resources. Many of these files reside in folders that are difficult to find. These folders are as follows:

```
C:\Users\User Name\AppData\Local\Autodesk\AutoCAD 2018\R22.0\enu
C:\Users\User Name\AppData\Roaming\Autodesk\AutoCAD 2018\R22.0\enu
```

When you've located these folders, you may want to create a shortcut to them (right-click the folder, and choose Create Shortcut). Place the shortcut on your desktop or other convenient location. That way, you can get to them without having to navigate through several layers of folders.

The AppData folder is a hidden folder so you'll need to make it visible to get to the rest of the folders below it. Do the following to unhide the AppData folder:

1. Open Windows Explorer, select Organize ➤ Folder and search options.
2. In the Folder Options dialog box, select the View tab.
3. Select "Show hidden files, folders, and drives" in the Advanced settings list.
4. Click OK to exit the dialog box.

Setting Up AutoCAD with a White Background

As mentioned in the beginning of Chapter 2, "Creating Your First Drawing," the 2D screen shots in this book are shown with a white background instead of the default dark gray. This is intended to help keep the figures legible in the printed version of this book. You can easily set up your AutoCAD to display the 2D drawing area in the same way by taking the following steps:

1. Open the Application menu, and select Options near the bottom of the menu. You can also type **Options↵** in the Command window.
2. Select the Display tab in the Options dialog box.
3. Click the Colors button in the Windows Elements group.
4. In the Drawing Window Colors dialog box, make sure that 3D Parallel Projection is selected in the Context settings and that Uniform Background is selected in the Interface Elements settings.
5. From the Color drop-down list, select white.
6. Select Grid Major Lines in the Interface Element list.
7. In the Color drop-down list, click the Select Color option. In the Select Color dialog box, click the Index Color tab and enter **253** in the Color box. Click OK.
8. Select Grid Minor Lines in the Interface Element list.
9. In the Color drop-down list, click the Select Color option. In the Select Color dialog box, click the Index Color tab and enter **254** in the Color box. Click OK.
10. Click Apply & Close in the Drawing Window Colors dialog box, and then click OK in the Options dialog box.

Appendix C

The Autodesk AutoCAD 2018 Certification

Autodesk certifications are industry-recognized credentials that can help you succeed in your design career, providing benefits to both you and your employer. Getting certified is a reliable validation of skills and knowledge, and it can lead to accelerated professional development, improved productivity, and enhanced credibility.

This Autodesk® Official Press guide can be an effective component of your exam preparation. Autodesk highly recommends (and we agree!) that you schedule regular time to prepare, review the most current exam preparation road map, use the Autodesk Official Press guide, take a class at an Authorized Training Center, and use a variety of resources to prepare for your certification—including plenty of actual hands-on experience.

The exam preparation road map is available here:

`www.autodesk.com/training-and-certification/certification`

You can find ATCs near you here:

`www.autodesk.com/training-and-certification/authorized-training-centers/locate-an-atc`

Certification Objective

To help you focus your studies on the skills that you'll need for these exams, Table C.1 shows objectives that could potentially appear on an exam and the chapters in which you can find information on the corresponding topic. Next to the relevant topics in each chapter, you'll find certification icons like the one in the margin here.

The exam objectives listed in the table are from the Autodesk Certification Exam Guide. These Autodesk exam objectives were accurate at press time. Please refer to `www.autodesk.com/certification` for the most current exam road map and objectives.

Good luck preparing for your certification!

TABLE C.1: Certified objectives

OBJECTIVE	USER	PROFESSIONAL	CHAPTER
DRAW OBJECTS			
Draw lines and rectangles	✓	✓	Chapters 1 and 2
Draw Circles, Arcs, and Polygons	✓	✓	Chapters 1, 2, and 18

TABLE C.1: Certified objectives *(CONTINUED)*

OBJECTIVE	USER	PROFESSIONAL	CHAPTER
DRAW WITH ACCURACY			
Use object-snap tracking		✓	Chapter 3
Use Coordinate Systems	✓	✓	Chapters 2, 3, and 21
Make isometric drawings		✓	Chapters 20 and 22 Chapter 3 for isometric snap
MODIFY OBJECTS			
Move and copy objects		✓	Chapter 2
Rotate and scale objects		✓	Chapter 2
Create and use arrays		✓	Chapters 6 and 21
Trim and extend objects	✓	✓	Chapters 3 and 6
Offset and mirror objects	✓	✓	Chapters 3 and 9
Use grip editing	✓	✓	Chapter 2
Fillet and chamfer objects	✓	✓	Chapters 3 and 6
USE ADDITIONAL DRAWING TECHNIQUES			
Draw and edit polylines	✓	✓	Chapter 18
Blend between objects with splines		✓	Chapters 6 and 18
Apply hatches and gradients	✓	✓	Chapter 7
ORGANIZE OBJECTS			
Change object properties	✓	✓	Chapters 2, 5, 7, and 12
Alter layer assignments for objects	✓	✓	Chapter 5
Control layer visibility	✓	✓	Chapter 5
Assign properties by object or layer		✓	Chapters 2, 5, and 7
Manage layer properties		✓	Chapter 5

TABLE C.1: Certified objectives *(CONTINUED)*

OBJECTIVE	USER	PROFESSIONAL	CHAPTER
REUSE EXISTING CONTENT			
Work with blocks	✓	✓	Chapters 4, 12, and 17
Manage block attributes		✓	Chapter 12
Reference external drawings and images		✓	Chapters 7, 13, and 14
ANNOTATE DRAWINGS			
Add and modify text	✓	✓	Chapter 9
Use dimensions	✓	✓	Chapter 11
Add and modify multileaders		✓	Chapter 11
Create and assign annotative styles		✓	Chapters 4, 9, and 11
Use tables		✓	Chapter 10
LAYOUTS AND PRINTING			
Create layouts		✓	Chapters 8 and 15
Use viewports	✓	✓	Chapters 8 and 15
Set printing and plotting options	✓	✓	Chapters 8, 25, and Bonus Chapter 5, "Understanding Plot Styles"

Index

Note to the Reader: Throughout this index **boldfaced** page numbers indicate primary discussions of a topic. *Italicized* page numbers indicate illustrations.

Symbols

Numbers

B

E

F

G

H

J

K

L

M

N

O

Q

R

S

T